$ 19.95

D0131073

HUXFORD'S OLD BOOK VALUE GUIDE

Seventh Edition

COLLECTOR BOOKS
A Division of Schroeder Publishing Co., Inc.

The current values in this book should be used only as a guide. They are not intended to set prices, which vary from one section of the country to another. Auction prices as well as dealer prices vary greatly and are affected by condition as well as demand. Neither the Author nor the Publisher assumes responsibility for any losses that might be incurred as a result of consulting this guide.

Searching For A Publisher?

We are always looking for knowledgeable people considered to be experts within their fields. If you feel that there is a real need for a book on your collectible subject and have a large comprehensive collection contact Collector Books.

On the Cover:

Anon. *The Art Annuals.* London J. S. Virtue & Co Ltd. 4to. full calf. G. $500.00

Wright, Walter P. *Beautiful Gardens.* 1911. London. Cassell & Co. 1st ed. G/VG. $28.00

Dopp, Katherine E. *The Tree Dwellers.* Rand McNally & Co. 1st ed. F. $15.00

Wilson, Sloan. *The Man in the Gray Flannel Suit.* 1955. Simon & Schuster. BC. G/dj. $14.00

Tryon, Thomas. *Harvest Home.* 1973. Alfred A. Knopf. 1st ed. VG/dj. $12.00

Miles, Alfred H. *The Universal Natural History.* 1895. Dodd, Mead & Co. VG. $50.00

Isham, Frederic S. *Under the Rose.* The Bobbs-Merrill Co. 1st ed. NF. $27.00

Books featured on cover courtesy of:

Natalya Haden & Jack Cody
Creatures of Habit
403 Jefferson
Paducah, KY 42001
(502)442-2923

Cover Design: Beth Summers
Book Design: Beth Ray

Introduction

This book was compiled to help the owner of old books evaluate his holdings and find a buyer for them. Most of us have a box, trunk, stack, or bookcase of old books. Chances are they are not rare books, but they may have value. Two questions that we are asked most frequently are 'Can you tell me the value of my old books?' and 'Where can I sell them?' *Huxford's Old Book Value Guide* will help answer both of these questions. Not only does this book place retail values on nearly 25,000 old books, it also lists scores of buyers along with the type of material each is interested in purchasing. Note that we list retail values (values that an interested party would be willing to pay to obtain possession of the book). These prices are taken from dealers' selling lists that have been issued within the past year. All of the listings are coded (A1, S7, etc.) before the price. This coding refers to a specific dealer's listing for that book. When two or more dealers have listed the same book, their codes will be listed alphabetically in the description line. Please refer to the section titled 'Book Sellers' for codes.

If you were to sell your books to a dealer, you should expect to receive no more than 50% of the values listed in this book, unless the dealer has a specific buyer in mind for some of your material. In many cases, a dealer will pay less than 50% of retail for a book to stock.

Do not ask a dealer to evaluate your old books unless you intend to sell them to him. Most antiquarian book dealers in the larger cities will appraise your books and ephemera for a fee that ranges from a low of $10.00 per hour to $50.00 per hour (or more). If you have an extensive library of rare books, the $50.00-an-hour figure would be money well spent (assuming, of course, the appraiser to be qualified and honest).

Huxford's Old Book Value Guide places values on the more common holdings that many seem to accumulate. You will notice that the majority of the books listed are in the $10.00 to $40.00 range. Many such guides list only the rare, almost non-existent books that the average person will never see. The format is very simple: listings are alphabetized first by the name of the author, translator, editor, or illustrator; if more than one book is listed for a particular author, each title is listed alphabetically under his or her name. When pseudonyms are known, names have been cross-referenced. (Please also see the section titled 'Pseudonyms' for additional information.) Dust jackets or wrappers are noted when present, and sizes (when given) are approximate. Condition is usually noted as well.

Fine condition refers to books that are perfect, in as-issued condition with no defects. Books in near-fine condition are perfect, but not as crisp as those graded fine. Near-fine condition books show only a little wear from reading (such as very small marks on binding); they are not as crisp as those graded fine, but they still have no major defects. Books rated very good may show wear but must have no tears on pages, binding, or dust jacket (if issued). A rating of good applies to an average used book that has all of its pages and yet may have small tears and other defects. The term reading copy (some dealers also use 'poor') describes a book having major defects; however, its text must be complete. Ex-library books are always indicated as such; they may be found in any condition. This rule also applies to any Book Club edition. Some of our booksellers indicate intermediate grades with a + or ++, or VG-EX. We have endeavored to use the grade that best corresponded to the description of condition as given in each dealer's listing. If you want to check further on the condition of a specific book, please consult the bookseller indicated. Please note that the condition stated in the description is for the book and then the dust jacket. (Dust jackets on many modern first editions may account for up to 80% of their value.)

In the back of the book we have listed buyers of books and book-related material. When you correspond with these dealers, be sure to enclose a self-addressed, stamped envelope if you want a reply. Please do not send lists of books for an appraisal. If you wish to sell your books, quote the price that you want or negotiate price only on the items the buyer is interested in purchasing. When you list your books, do so by author, full title, publisher and place, date, and edition. Indicate condition, noting any defects on cover or contents.

When shipping your books, first wrap each book in paper such as brown kraft or a similar type of material. Never use newspaper for the inner wrap, since newsprint tends to rub off. (It may, however be used as a cushioning material within the outer carton.) Place your books in a sturdy corrugated box and use a good shipping tape to seal it. Tape reinforced with nylon string is preferable, as it will not tear. Books shipped by parcel post may be sent at a special fourth class book rate, which may be lower than regular parcel post zone rates.

Listing of Standard Abbreviations

/ ....and, also, with, or indicates dual-title book
ACS ....advance copy slip
aeg ....all edge gilt
AJA.......American Jewish Archives
AJC ......American Jewish Congress
AJHS...American Jewish Historical Society
Am......................................American
AP ..proof, advance proof, advance uncorrected proof, or galley
ARC .....advance reading or review copy
bdg..........................binding, bound
decor............decoration, decorated
bl..blue
blk..black
BC ....any book club edition
brd................................boards
c......................................copyright
ca ....circa
cbdg..................comb binding
clip ....clipped price
CMG..Coward McCann Geoghegan
dk ....dark
dj............................dust jacket
DSP ....Duell Sloan Pearce
dtd..dated
E.....................................east, eastern
edit..editor
ed ....edition
emb...........embossed or embossing
Eng....................England, English
ep..end pages
ES......................................errata slip
ERB ....Edgar Rice Burroughs Inc.
F..fine
fld..............................folding, folder
FSC...........Farrar, Straus & Cudahy
FSG ....Farrar, Straus & Giroux
fwd..forward
G..good
GPO...Government Printing Office

gr ....green
HBJ .....Harcourt Brace Jovanovich, Inc.
HBW............Harcourt Brace World
hist ....history
hc ....hard cover
HRW ....Holt Rinehart Winston
ils ....illustrated
imp..................impression, imprint
intl................................initialed
inscr ....inscribed
Inst..Institute
Internat........................International
intro......................introduction
LEC................Limited Edition Club
lg....................................large
Lib ....library
ltd..limited
MIT.....MA Institute of Technology
MOMA.....Museum of Modern Art
MPA ....Museum of Primitive Art
mtd..................................mounted
Mus....................................museum
N..................................north, northern
NAL ....New American Library
Nat..national
NEL...............New English Library
nd ....no date
ne ....no edition given
NF..near fine
np................................no place given
orig................................original
p................................page, pages
pb..................................paperback
pict..................................pictorial
pl..plate
Pr..press
pref ....preface
pres........................presentation
promo........................promotion
prt................................print, printing
pub ....publisher, publishing
rem mk..................remainder mark

repro ....reproduction
rpr ....repair
RS.............................review slip
S ....south, southern
s/wrp ....shrink wrap
sans ....none issued
sbdg..................spiral binding
sc ....softcover
SF..........................science fiction
sgn..................signature, signed
sm ....small
sq ....square
stp........................stamp or stamped
supp ....supplement
TB..textbook
teg ....top edge gilt
trans ....translated
U ....University
unp ....unpaged
UP......................uncorrected proof
VG..................................very good
W..........................west, western
w/..with, indicates laid in material
wht ....white
wrp..wrappers
xl..ex-library
yel..yellow
#d..numbered
12mo ....about 7" tall
16mo ....6" to 7" tall
24mo ....5" to 6" tall
32mo ....4" to 5" tall
48mo..................less than 4" tall
64mo..........................about 3" tall
sm 8vo ....7½" to 8" tall
8vo..............................8" to 9" tall
sm 4to ....about 10" tall, quarto
4to................between 11" to 13" tall
folio ....13" or larger
elephant folio ....23" or larger
atlas folio ....25"
double elephant folio ....larger than

A.E.G.; see Gallatin, A.E.

ABBEY, Edward. *Abbey's Road.* 1979. NY. simultaneous wrp issue. sgn. F. A11. $175.00

ABBEY, Edward. *Beyond the Wall.* (1984). HRW. AP. NF/F. B4. $350.00

ABBEY, Edward. *Blk Sun.* (1971). Simon Schuster. 1st ed. F/F. B4. $300.00

ABBEY, Edward. *Brave Cowboy.* (1993). Dream Garden. 1/26 lettered. sgn Kirk Douglas/pub. w/photo. F/F box. B3. $250.00

ABBEY, Edward. *Brave Cowboy.* (1993). Dream Garden. 1/500. sgn Kirk Douglas. F/F. A18/B3. $95.00

ABBEY, Edward. *Cactus Country.* (1973). Time Life. 1st ed. NF/sans. B3. $40.00

ABBEY, Edward. *Fool's Progress.* (1988). Holt. 1st ed. F/F. C4. $40.00

ABBEY, Edward. *Fool's Progress.* (1988). Holt. 1st ed. inscr/sgn. F/F. B2. $125.00

ABBEY, Edward. *Fool's Progress.* (1989). London. Bodley Head. 1st ed. F/F. B3. $40.00

ABBEY, Edward. *Hayduke Lives.* (1990). Little Brn. 1st ed. M/dj. A18. $25.00

ABBEY, Edward. *Jonathan Troy.* 1954. Dodd Mead. 1st ed. author's 1st book. F/NF. Q1. $950.00

ABBEY, Edward. *Monkey Wrench Gang.* 1985. Dream Garden. ltd/10th-Anniversary ed. 1/250. sgn. M/pict slipcase. A18. $650.00

ABBEY, Edward. *Monkey Wrench Gang.* 1990. Dream Garden. revised ed. ils R Crumb. F/dj. A17. $40.00

ABBEY, Edward. *One Life at a Time, Please.* (1988). Holt. 1st ed. last book of essays. F/F. B3. $40.00

ABBEY, Edward. *Voice Crying in the Wilderness.* (1990). St Martin. 1st ed. F/F. B3. $35.00

ABBEY, Edward. *Vox Clamantis in Deserto.* 1989. Santa Fe. Rydal Pr. posthumous ed. 1/225. F/slipcase. L3. $125.00

ABBEY, Edwin Austin. *Selections From Poetry of Robert Herrick.* 1882. Harper. 188 p. aeg. gilt bdg. VG. D2. $150.00

ABBEY & ASPRIN. *Catwoman.* 1992. Warner. 1st hc ed. F/F. F4. $20.00

ABBEY & HYDE. *Slickrock.* (1971). Sierra Club. 1st ed. folio. F/F clip. B4. $250.00

ABBEY & NICHOLS. *In Praise of Mtn Lions.* 1984. Albuquerque Sierra Club. 1/600. sgns. F/wrp. L3. $175.00

ABBEY & OVERTON. *Eng Church in the 18th Century.* 1878. London. Longman Gr. xl. 2 vols. H10. $47.50

ABBEY & RUSSELL. *Mtns of Am.* (1975). Abrams. 1st ed. NF/VG. B3. $55.00

ABBOT, Anthony. *Shudders.* 1943. Farrar Rinehart. 1st ed. VG/dj. M15. $135.00

ABBOTT, Elizabeth. *Chagall, My Life.* 1960. Orion. 1st ed. VG/G+. A1. $20.00

ABBOTT, G.F. *Macedonian Folklore.* 1903. Cambridge. 1st ed. 8vo. cloth/leather label. scarce. O2. $85.00

ABBOTT, G.F. *Macedonian Folklore.* 1969. Chicago. 372 p. cloth. O2. $30.00

ABBOTT, G.F. *Turkey in Transition.* 1909. London. 8vo. presentation. 370 p. cloth. F. O2. $75.00

ABBOTT, J.S.C. *Lives of the Presidents of the US.* 1867. Boston. xl. royal 8vo. 480 p. brn cloth. G. T3. $29.00

ABBOTT, J.S.C. *Peter Stuyvesant, Last Dutch Governor of New Amsterdam.* 1873. Dodd Mead. 1st ed. 12mo. 362 p. brn cloth. B11. $30.00

ABBOTT, Keene. *Tree of Life.* 1927. Doubleday Page. 1st ed. VG. V2. $5.00

ABBOTT, Lee K. *Love Is the Crooked Thing.* (1986). Chapel Hill. Algonquin. 1st ed. F/NF. B3. $20.00

ABBOTT, Lyman. *Impressions of a Careless Traveler.* 1907. NY. 1st ed. 16mo. 210 p. VG/gr wrp. H3. $15.00

ABBOTT, Willis J. *Nations at War.* 1914. Syndicate Pub. 4to. G. A8. $7.00

ABBOTT, Willis J. *Panama & the Canal in Picture & Prose.* 1913. NY. 1st ed. pls/fld map frontis. 412 p. VG. H3. $35.00

ABDILL, George B. *Civil War Railroads.* 1961. Bonanza. G/dj. A16. $25.00

ABDUL-HAK. *Treasures of the Nat Mus of Damascus.* ca 1950. Damascus. 2nd ed. 69 pls. pict wrp. O2. $30.00

ABDULLAH, King. *Memoirs of King Abdullah of Transjordan.* 1950. London. Cape. 1st ed. 280 p. teg. gilt red cloth. VG+/VG+. M7. $75.00

ABDULLAH & PAKENHAM. *Dreamers of Empire.* 1968. NY. reprint of 1929 ed. 368 p. F3. $20.00

ABEL, Clarke. *Narrative of Voyage in Interior of China...1816-17.* 1818. London. Longman Hurst Rees Orne Brn. 420 p. modern buckram. B14. $250.00

ABEL, Robert. *Progress of a Fire.* (1985). Simon Schuster. 1st ed. 509 p. F/F. A7. $30.00

ABEL, Suzanne. *Between Continents/Between Seas.* 1981. Abrams. 1st ed. 4to. 240 p. wrp. F3. $60.00

ABER. *Art of Judaic Needlework.* 1979. np. pb. G2. $12.50

ABERCROMBIE & MAWE. *Universal Gardener & Botanist...* 1797. London. 2nd ed. 12 full-p pls. full leather. B28. $375.00

ABERNATHY, Glenn. *Right of Assembly & Assn.* 1961. SC U. M11. $35.00

ABERNETHY, Arthur T. *Jew & a Negro: Being a Study of Jewish Ancestry...* 1910. Dixie Pub. sgn. 110 p. G. S3. $60.00

ABERNETHY, John. *Surgical & Physiological Works of...* 1830. London. Longman. 4 vols. xl. sheep/new cloth backs. G7. $250.00

ABISH, Walter. *Eclipse Fever.* 1993. Knopf. AP. F/wrp. B4. $35.00

ABRAHAM, J. Johnston. *Surgeon's Log. Impressions of the Far E.* 1926. NY. Dutton. new ed. 8vo. 31 p. 261 p. VG. W1. $16.00

ABRAHAMS, Israel. *By-Paths in Hebraic Bookland.* 1920. Phil. 8vo. 371 p. cloth. O2. $30.00

ABRAHAMS, Peter. *Lights Out.* (1994). London. Warner. UP. F/red wrp. B3. $20.00

ABRAMS, Robert D. *New Tavern Tales.* 1930. Walter Neall. 1st ed. sgn. VG. V2. $8.00

ABRANSON, Erik. *Ships of the High Seas.* 1976. Crescent. 4to. 124 p. NF/VG. P4. $15.00

ABRESTIA. *Abramo Lincoln.* 1909. Roma. 16 p. VG. A6. $10.00

ABSE, Dannie. *Wht Coat Purple Coat.* 1990. NY. 1st ed. sgn. F/F. V1. $20.00

ACHEBE, Chinua. *Anthills of the Savannah.* 1988. Anchor/Doubleday. 1st Am ed of 1987 1st ed. NF/NF. A14. $30.00

ACIER, Marcel. *From Spanish Trenches: Recent Letters From Spain.* ca 1937. Modern Age. 1st ed. VG/G. V4. $25.00

ACKER, Kathy. *In Memoriam To Identity.* (1990). NY. Grove Wiedenfeld. ARC. RS. w/photo. F/F. B3. $25.00

ACKER, Kathy. *Literal Madness.* (1987). Grove. 1st thus ed. F/F. B3. $15.00

ACKER, Susan. *Bag Book.* 1985. Feathered Serpent. 1/50. ils Dianne Weiss. tan leather. w/extra suite pls. B24. $225.00

ACKERKNECHT, Erwin H. *Medicine at the Paris Hospital, 1794-1848.* 1967. Johns Hopkins. VG. N2. $20.00

ACKERLEY, J.R. *EM Forster: A Portrait.* 1970. London. 1st unexpurgated book ed. F/plain wht wrp/gr dj. A11. $40.00

ACKERLEY, J.R. *My Father & Myself.* 1969. NY. 1st Am ed. F/NF. A11. $35.00

ACKLEY, Edith F. *Doll Shop of Your Own.* 1941. Lippincott. ils Telka Ackley. 114 p. VG. S10. $18.00

ACKROYD, Peter. *Eng Music.* (1992). Knopf. 1st ed. F/NF. B3. $20.00

ACKROYD, Peter. *First Light.* (1989). Grove Weidenfeld. 1st ed. F/F. B3. $25.00

ACZEL, Tamas. *Hunt.* (1990). London. Faber. 1st ed. NF/F. B3. $15.00

ADAIR, Douglas. *Fame & the Founding Fathers.* 1974. Williamsburg, VA. Instit of Early Am Hist. 8vo. 2 pls. 315 p. F/VG. B11. $25.00

ADAIR, Gilbert. *Vietnam on Film.* (1981). NY. Proteus. 1st Am ed. VG+/dj. A7. $50.00

ADAIR, Robert. *Physics of Baseball.* 1990. Harper Row. 1st ed. F/F. P8. $10.00

ADAM, Colin Forbes. *Life of Lord Lloyd.* 1948. London. Macmillan. 1st UK ed. 318 p. gilt bl cloth. G. M7. $22.00

ADAM, Paul. *Exceptional Corpse.* 1993. Harper Collins. 1st ed. F/F. S5. $25.00

ADAM, Paul. *Les Eches de TE Lawrence.* 1962. private prt. 1st French ed. 199 p. gray cloth. M7. $90.00

ADAMIC, Louis. *Nation of Nations.* 1945. Harper. 1st ed. G/G. V2. $5.00

ADAMS, Alexander B. *Sunlight & Storm: Great Am Plains.* (1977). NY. ils. 479 p. NF/dj. A17. $22.50

ADAMS, Alice. *After You're Gone.* (1989). Knopf. 1st ed. F/F. B3. $25.00

ADAMS, Alice. *Rich Rewards.* (1980). Knopf. 1st ed. F/F. B3. $35.00

ADAMS, Ansel. *Making a Photograph: Intro to Photography.* 1935. NY/London. The Studio. 1st ed. 4to. 96 p. NF/dj. B20. $250.00

ADAMS, Arthur. *Quimby.* (1988). St Martin. stated 1st ed. F/F. A7. $17.00

ADAMS, Cindy. *Sukarno. An Autobiography As Told to Cindy Adams.* 1962. Bobbs Merrill. 1st prt. sgn. 16 pls. 324 p. VG/dj. W1. $20.00

ADAMS, Clinton. *Fritz Scholder: Lithos.* 1975. Boston. NY Graphic Soc. w/sgn bookplate & note. F/NF. L3. $150.00

ADAMS, Douglas. *Dirk Gently's Holistic Detective Agency.* 1987. Simon Schuster. 1st ed. NF/NF. M20. $15.00

ADAMS, Douglas. *Hitchhiker's Guide to the Galaxy.* (1979). Harmony. 1st ed. author's 1st book. F/F. B3. $60.00

ADAMS, Douglas. *Life, the Universe & Everything.* (1982). Harmony 1st ed. F/VG. B3. $25.00

ADAMS, Douglas. *Long Dark Tea-Time of the Soul.* (1988). Simon Schuster. 1st ed. sgn. F/F. B3. $30.00

ADAMS, Douglas. *So Long & Thanks for All the Fish.* (1985). Harmony. 1st ed. F/F. B3. $25.00

ADAMS, E.C.L. *Potee's Gal: Drama of Negro Life Near Big Congaree Swamps.* 1929. Columbia, SC. ltd ed. sgn. 12mo. 49 p. maroon cloth. B11. $95.00

ADAMS, Eustace L. *Flying Windmill.* 1930. Grosset. 1st ed. F/dj. M2. $20.00

ADAMS, Frank. *Mother Goose.* nd. NY. Dodge. 8 color pls. brds w/color pl. M5. $95.00

ADAMS, Frederick U. *Conquest of the Tropics.* 1914. NY. 1st ed. ils. 368 p. gilt gr cloth. F. H3. $20.00

ADAMS, George Worthington. *Doctors in Bl: Medical Hist of Union Army in Civil War.* 1952. NY. Schuman. 1st ed. inscr/sgn. VG. M8. $45.00

ADAMS, George Worthington. *Doctors in Bl: Medical Hist of Union Army in Civil War.* 1985. Dayton, OH. 12mo. ils. 237 p. VG. T3. $19.00

ADAMS, H.G. *Favorite Song Birds.* ca 1857. London. Groombridge. 3rd ed. 5 full-p color pls. 192 p. G+. S9. $65.00

ADAMS, H.G. *Language & Poetry of Flowers.* 1866 (1853). Phil. 6 color pls. 272 p. cloth. VG. B26. $74.00

ADAMS, Harold. *Barbed Wire Noose.* (1987). Mysterious. 1st ed. F/F. B9. $10.00

ADAMS, Harold. *Man Who Met the Train.* (1988). Mysterious. 1st ed. F/F. B9. $10.00

ADAMS, Harold. *Missing Moon.* 1983. NY. Charter. 1st ed/PBO. F/wrp. M15. $25.00

ADAMS, Harry. *Beyond the Barrier w/Byrd.* ca 1932. Donohue. 8vo. ils/photos. 253 p. gr cloth. VG. P4. $35.00

ADAMS, Henry. *Letters to a Niece & Prayer to the Virgin of Chartes.* 1920. Houghton Mifflin. 1st ed. VG. N2. $15.00

ADAMS, Joey. *Here's to the Friars: Heart of Show Business.* 1976. Crown. dj. N2. $7.50

ADAMS, Joey. *On the Road for Uncle Sam.* (1963). Bernard Geis. 1st ed. 311 p. VG/torn dj. A7. $30.00

ADAMS, John F. *Beekeeping, the Gentle Craft.* 1972. Doubleday. 1st ed. 182 p. H10. $10.00

ADAMS, Julia Davis. *Stonewall.* ca 1931. Dutton. 1st ed. 255 p. VG. B10. $45.00

ADAMS, O.R. *Lameness in Horses.* nd. np. 2nd ed. G+. O3. $25.00

ADAMS, Percy G. *Travelers & Travel Liars 1660-1800.* 1962. Berkeley. presentation. 292 p. cloth. O2. $40.00

ADAMS, Ramon F. *Rampaging Herd.* 1959. OK U. 1st ed. 463 p. rebound gr buckram. VG. B19. $45.00

ADAMS, Ramon F. *Six-Guns & Saddle Leather: Biblio of Books & Pamphlets...* (1954). OK U. 1st ed. F/dj. A18. $100.00

ADAMS, Randolph. *British Headquarters Maps & Sketches.* 1928. Ann Arbor. xl. NF. O6. $85.00

ADAMS, Richard. *Ceramics of Altar de Sacrificios.* 1971. Peabody Mus. 4to. 308 p. wrp. F3. $45.00

ADAMS, Richard. *Traveller.* 1988. Knopf. AP. pub promo stapled to ep. F/prt wrp. Q1. $40.00

ADAMS, Robert. *Evolution of Urban Soc.* (1966). Chicago. Aldine. 1st ed. 191 p. VG/dj. F3. $20.00

ADAMS, Samuel Hopkins. *Grandafather Stories.* 1954. Random. G/dj. A16. $10.00

ADAMS, W.H. *Witch, Warlock & Magician: Hist Sketches of Magic...* 1889. Chatto Windus. 1st ed. recased. G. L3. $75.00

ADAMS, Willis Seaver. *Willis Seaver Adams: Retrospection.* 1966. Deerfield Academy, MA. ils/photos/checklist. 64 p. D2. $35.00

ADAMS & CARWARDINE. *Last Chance To See.* (1991). Harmony. 1st ed. F/F. B3. $20.00

ADAMS & COLEMAN. *Atlas of Am Hist.* 1943. Scribner. lg 8vo. 147 maps. 350 p. gr buckram. H9. $40.00

ADAMS & CORRELL. *Orchids of Guatemal & Belize.* 1985. NY. Dover. reprint of 1952/1965 ed. 3 vols in 1. 779 p. wrp. F3. $20.00

ADAMS & LLOYD. *Deeper Meaning of Life.* (1990). London. Pan Books. 1st ed. ils Bert Kitchen. NF/F. B3. $30.00

ADAMS & LUNGWITZ. *TB of Horseshoeing...* 1966. Corvallis. G+. O3. $25.00

ADANCOURT, Francis. *Am Farrier or NY Horse Doctor...* 1826. Troy. self pub. 10 pls. leather. H10. $225.00

ADDAMS, Charles. *Charles Addams' Mother Goose.* 1967. NY. 1st ed. author's 1st children's book. 4to. NF/NF. A11. $30.00

ADDAMS, Charles. *Drawn & Quartered.* 1946. Bantam. 1st pb ed. lists 1st 40 Bantam books. NF. A11. $25.00

ADDIS, William E. *Catholic Dictionary.* 1884. NY. Catholic Pub Soc. 1st ed. 889 p. VG. C5. $35.00

ADDISON, Charles G. *Damascus & Palmyra.* 1838. London. 2 vols. 9 (of 10) pls. quarter leather. O2. $450.00

ADDISON, Julia De Wolf. *Arts & Crafts of the Middle Ages.* 1908. London. Bell. 1st ed. 8vo. 378 p. F. A2. $50.00

ADDISON, William. *Eng Fairs & Markets.* 1953. London. Batsford. 1st ed. ils. 199 p. dj. H10. $17.50

ADEGOKE, Oluwafayisola S. *Stratigraphy & Paleontology of Marine Neogene Formations...* 1969. CA U. 1st ed. maps. 267 p. NF/wrp. B19. $25.00

ADELMAN, Bob. *Down Home.* (1972). McGraw Hill. lg 4to. dj. A7. $30.00

ADELMAN, Melvin. *Sporting Time.* 1986. IL U. 1st ed. photos. M/M. P8. $25.00

ADELMAN & HALL. *Out of Left Field: Willie Stargell & Pittsburgh Pirates.* (1976). NY. 2 Continents. 1st ed. 224 p. F/F. A2. $25.00

ADORATSKY, V. *Hist of the Communist Manifesto of Marx & Engels.* (1938). NY. Internat. 31 p. wrp. A7. $22.00

ADRIEL, Jean. *Avatar: Life Story of Meher Baba.* 1947. Santa Barbara, CA. Rowny. author's ed. 8vo. 284 p. F/VG. A2. $25.00

ADVIES, Nigel. *Toltecs Until the Fall of Tula.* (1977). OK U. 1st ed. 533 p. F/dj. A17. $19.50

AESOP. *Aesop's Fables.* 1912. Heinemann. 1st ltd ed. ils/sgn Rackham. NF/slipcase. D1. $1,450.00

AESOP. *Fables of...* nd. (1909). Hodder Stoughton. ils Detmold/23 mtd pls. pict gr cloth. G. scarce. F1. $200.00

AESOP. *Fables.* 1793. London. Stockdale. 2 vols. contemporary calf. B14. $125.00

AGARWALA & SINGH. *Economics of Underdevelopment.* (1958). London. Oxford. 2nd prt. 510 p. A7. $20.00

AGASSIZ, Alexander. *Letters & Recollections...* 1913. Houghton Mifflin. pocket maps. 454 p. cloth. B14. $35.00

AGASSIZ, Alexander. *Three Cruises on the US Coast & Geodetic Survey Steamer...* 1888. Boston. Riverside. 2 vols. worn brds. H9. $125.00

AGASSIZ & AGASSIZ. *Journey in Brazil.* 1868. Ticknor Fields. 8vo. woodcuts. 540 p. cloth. VG. P4. $115.00

AGASSIZ & GOULD. *Principles of Zoology...* 1848. Boston. Gould Kendall Lincoln. 1st ed. 216 p. B14. $55.00

AGEE, Alva. *Crops & Methods for Soil Improvement.* 1912. Macmillan. 1st ed. 246 p. VG. H1. $7.50

AGEE, Helene Barret. *Facets of Goochland (VA) County's Hist.* 1962(1830s). Richmond, VA. Dietz. 1st ed. 8vo. ils. 227 p. bl cloth. F/VG. B11. $18.00

AGEE, James. *On Film.* 1958 & 1960. NY. 1st ed. 2 vols. VG/VG. B5. $50.00

AGEE, James. *Permit Me Voyage.* 1934. New Haven. Yale. Younger Poets series. VG/mylar dj. A11. $125.00

AGEE & WALKER. *Let Us Now Praise Famous Men.* (1960). Boston. Houghton Mifflin. 2nd prt. 471 p. cloth. NF/dj. B14. $65.00

AGEL, Jerome. *Making of Kubrick's 2001.* 1970. Signet. pb. NF. C8. $30.00

AGNEW, Daniel. *Early Memories of Methodism in Beaver & Vicinity.* 1896. np. G/wrp. D7. $12.50

AGNON, S.J. *Bridal Canopy.* 1937. Literary Guild of Am. trans IM Lask. 373 p. G. S3. $22.00

AGNON, Shmuel Yosef. *In the Heart of the Seas. Story of Journey to...Israel.* 1947. NY. Schocken. 1/300. F/torn unprt dj/F slipcase. B2. $45.00

AGRICOLA, Georgius. *De Re Metallica. Trans From 1st Latin Ed of 1556...* 1912. London. Mining Magazine. trans/presentation Herbert Hoover. full vellum. NF. R3. $1,500.00

AGUS, Jacob B. *Jewish Identity in Age of Idealogies...* 1978. Frederick Ungar. 463 p. VG+/VG-. S3. $22.00

AHMAD, Feroz. *Turkish Experiment in Democracy 1950-75.* 1977. London. 8vo. 474 p. cloth. dj. O2. $60.00

AICKMAN, Robert. *Cold Hand in Mine: Strange Stories.* 1977. Scribner. 1st Am ed. F/F Gorey dj. N3. $15.00

AIKEN, Conrad. *Letter From Li Po & Other Poems.* 1955. Oxford. 1st ed. F/NF. C4. $35.00

AIKEN, Conrad. *Morning Song of Lord Zero.* 1963. NY. Oxford. 1st ed. F/F. C4. $35.00

AIKEN, Conrad. *Mr Arcularis.* 1957. Cambridge. 1st ed. VG/G. B5. $45.00

AIKEN, Conrad. *Preludes for Memnon.* 1931. Scribner. 1st ed. gilt brn brds. VG+. C4. $40.00

AIKEN, Conrad. *Thee.* 1967. NY. Braziller. 1st ed. F/NF. C4. $30.00

AIKEN, George D. *Pioneering w/Wild Flowers.* 1933. Putney. 1st ed/1st prt (before NY pub). 122 p. VG. B28. $25.00

AIKEN, Joan. *Midnight Is a Place.* (1974). Viking. 2nd prt. 8vo. 287 p. gr cloth. VG/G. T5. $15.00

AIKEN, Joan. *Nightbirds on Nantucket.* 1966. Doubleday. 1st ed. 8vo. 215 p. VG. T5. $35.00

AIKEN, Joan. *Stoken Lake.* 1981. np. 1st ed. F/F. C1. $15.00

AIKEN, Joan. *Winterthing: Play for Children.* 1972. HRW. 1st ed. F/F. N3. $35.00

AIKEN, John. *Biographical Memoirs of Medicine in Great Britain...* 1780. London. Johnson. 338 p. rebound contemporary full calf. G7. $495.00

AIKEN, P.F. *Comparative View of the Constitutions of Great Britain...* 1842. London. Longman. emb bl-gr cloth. M11. $175.00

AIKEN, S.C. *Charter of the Town of Aiken, w/By-Laws & Ordinances...1860.* 1860. Charleston. Burke. 1st ed. 24 p. orig prt wrp. M8. $85.00

AIKEN & AIKEN. *Dictionary of Chemistry & Mineralogy...* 1807 & 1814. London. Arch. 1st ed. 2 vols. new buckram. F. H10. $100.00

AINSLIE, G.M. *Hand Grenades: Handbook on Rifle & Hand Grenades.* 1917. NY. 1st ed. 59 p. VG. B18. $65.00

AINSLIE, Kathleen. *Catharine Susan & Me Goes Abroad.* ca 1909. London. Casteel. 1st ed. VG/wrp/silk ribbon ties. D1. $125.00

AINSLIE, Kathleen. *Oh! Poor Amelia Jane!* ca 1900. London. Castell. VG/stiff pict wrp/silk ribbon. D1. $125.00

AINSWORTH, William Harrison. *Tower of London.* nd. London. Bentley. 1st ed. 8vo. 439 p. Riviere bdg. F1. $400.00

AKERMAN & BUISSERET. *Monarchs, Ministers & Maps.* 1885. Chicago. Newberry Lib. 10 pls. F/wrp. O6. $20.00

AKHMATOVA, Anna. *Requiem & Poem Without a Hero.* 1976. OH U. 1st ed. F/NF. V1. $25.00

AKURGAL, Ekrem. *Ancient Civilization & Ruins of Turkey.* 1978. Istanbul. 8vo. ils/maps. pict cloth/cloth spine. dj. O2. $25.00

ALAIN. *Magic Stones.* 1957. NY. 1st ed. 32 p. pict bl cloth. F/G. H3. $12.00

ALAMAN, Mohammed. *Arabia Unified.* 1932 (1930). London. Hutchinson Benin. revised ed. 323 p. F/F. M7. $25.00

ALARCON, Francisco. *Body in Flames/ Cuerpo en Llamas.* (1990). Chronicle Books. 1st ed. 4to. 162 p. F3. $10.00

ALAUX, Jean-Paul. *L'Historie Merveilleuse de Christophe Columb.* 1924. Paris. Devambez. ils Gustave Alaux. 243 p. VG/pict wrp. M20. $75.00

ALBA, Victor. *Politics & the Labor Movement in Latin Am.* 1968. Stanford. 404 p. F/F clip. A7. $23.00

ALBEE, Edward. *Ballad of the Sad Cafe: The Play.* 1963. Boston. sgn. F/wrp. A11. $45.00

ALBEE, Edward. *Tiny Alice.* 1965. NY. correct 1st ed. F/clip. A15. $30.00

ALBEE, Edward. *Zoo Story & the Sandbox: 2 Short Plays.* 1960. NY. 1st ed. VG+/prt gr wrp. A11. $75.00

ALBERS, Anni. *On Weaving.* 1965. np. ils. cloth. G2. $25.99

ALBERS, Anni. *Pre-Columbian Mexican Miniatures.* (1970). Praeger. 1st ed. ils. 128 p. VG. F3. $45.00

ALBERT, Marvin. *Hood Came Calling.* 1958. Gold Medal. PBO. inscr as Albert/Quarry. F/wrp ils B Phillips. A11. $75.00

ALBERT, Marvin. *Road's End.* 1952. Gold Medal. PBO. 1st book under any of his noms de plume. F/unread. A11. $115.00

ALBERT & ALPERT. *60s Papers: Documents of a Rebellious Decade.* 1984. Praeger. 1st ed. inscr/sgns. 550 p. F. B2. $75.00

ALBERTS, Robert C. *Benjamin W: A Biography.* 1978. Houghton Mifflin. 525 p. cloth. dj. D2. $40.00

ALBIN & LISTER-KAYE. *Welsh Corgi.* 1986. London. Popular Dogs. 10th ed. ils. F/F. O3. $15.00

ALBION, Robert G. *Naval & Maritime Hist.* 1966. Marine Hist Assn. 62 p. VG/wrp. B19. $15.00

ALBRIGHT, Raymond W. *Hist of Protestant Episcopal Church.* 1964. NY. Macmillan. 1st ed. 317 p. H10. $25.00

ALBRIGHT, William F. *Archaeology & the Religion of Israel.* 1953. Baltimore. index. 246 p. F/torn. B14. $45.00

ALBRIGHT & TAYLOR. *Oh, Ranger!* 1929. Stanford. 2nd ed. 178 p. pict cloth. VG. D3. $12.50

ALCOCK, Frederick. *Trade & Travel in S Am.* 1907. London. Philip. 2nd ed. 8vo. ils/maps. G. B11. $65.00

ALCOTT, Louisa M. *Good Wives: Story for Girls.* 1913. London. 1st thus ed. ils Harold Copping. gilt wht cloth. VG. M5. $40.00

ALCOTT, Louisa M. *Jo's Boys.* 1886. Roberts Bros. 1st ed. 365 p. brn cloth. G+. M20. $35.00

ALCOTT, Louisa M. *Little Button Rose.* 1901 (1887). Little Brn. 8vo. 61 p. VG/worn. T5. $45.00

ALCOTT, Louisa M. *Little Men.* 1871. Boston. 1st ed. VG. B5. $100.00

ALCOTT, Louisa M. *Little Men.* 1928. Winston. 1st thus ed. ils Clara Burd. 349 p. G. P2. $25.00

ALCOTT, Louisa M. *Little Men.* 1930. Little Brn. G. A16. $10.00

ALCOTT, Louisa M. *Little Women.* 1929. Little Brn. G. A16. $10.00

ALCOTT, Louisa M. *Spinning-Wheel Stories.* 1884. Boston. Roberts Bros. 1st ed. 12mo. 276 p. gr cloth. F. M1. $350.00

ALDEN, John Richard. *Robert Dinwiddie: Servant of the Crown.* 1973. VA U. ils/maps. 126 p. VG/G. B10. $25.00

ALDERSON & OPIE. *Treasures of Childhood: Books, Toys & Games of Opie...* 1989. 4to. 190 p. F/F. A4. $85.00

ALDIN, Cecil. *Artist's Models.* 1930. Scribner. 1st Am ed. 80 p. NF/NF. B20. $50.00

ALDIN & HUNLOKE. *Riding.* 1913. Eyre Spottiswoode McCann. 1st ed. VG/VG. O3. $35.00

ALDINGTON, Richard. *AE Housman & WB Yeats.* 1955. Hurst, Berkshire. Peacocks Pr. 1st ed. 1/10 on Chatham. NF/slipcase. H5. $350.00

ALDINGTON, Richard. *Decameron of Giovanni Boccaccio.* 1930. Garden City. G/dj. A16. $60.00

ALDINGTON, Richard. *Der Fall TE Lawrence. Ein Kritische Biographie.* nd. Germany. Hermann Rinn. 1st German ed. 349 p. brn oatmeal cloth. NF. M7. $125.00

ALDINGTON, Richard. *DH Lawrence.* 1935. London. correct 1st ed. w/2-p checklist of Lawrence's works. VG+/wrp. A11. $15.00

ALDINGTON, Richard. *Lawrence l'Imposteur.* 1954. Paris. Amoit-Dumont. 1st French ed. 332 p. VG. M7. $85.00

ALDINGTON, Richard. *Lawrence of Arabia.* 1954. London. Collins. AP of 1st ed. 447 p. VG/brn wrp/bl-gr label. M7. $500.00

ALDINGTON, Richard. *Lawrence of Arabia.* 1955. London. Collins. 1st ed. 448 p. ES. VG+/fair clip. M7. $45.00

ALDINGTON, Richard. *Lawrence of Arabia.* 1971. Eng/Australia. Penguin. 1st thus ed. 504 p. pict bdg. M7. $30.00

ALDINGTON & DURRELL. *Literary Lifelines.* 1981. Viking. 1st ed. 236 p. gilt red cloth. F/NF. M7. $24.50

ALDISS, Brian. *Enemies of the System.* 1978. Harper Row. 1st Am ed. F/F. N3. $15.00

ALDISS, Brian. *Forgotten Life.* (1988). Atheneum. 1st ed. F/F. B3. $20.00

ALDISS, Brian. *Hand-Reared Boy.* 1970. McCall. 1st Am ed. F/dj. M2. $25.00

ALDISS, Brian. *Helliconia Spring.* (1982). London. Cape. 1st ed. F/F. B3. $30.00

ALDISS, Brian. *Life in the W.* (1980). Weidenfeld Nicolson. 1st ed. NF/VG. B3. $45.00

ALDISS, Brian. *Pile: Petals From St Klaed's Computer.* 1979. HRW. 1st Am ed. ils Mike Wilks. pict brds. F/sans. N3. $20.00

ALDISS, Brian. *Romance of the Equater: Best Fantasy Stories.* (1989). Atheneum. 1st ed. F/F. B3. $20.00

ALDISS, Brian. *Ruins.* (1987). London. Hutchinson. 1st ed. ils Patell. F/F. B3. $25.00

ALDISS, Brian. *Seasons in Flight.* (1984). London. Jonathan Cape. 1st ed. F/NF. B3. $25.00

ALDISS, Brian. *SF As SF.* (1978). London. Bran's Head. 1st ed. VG/prt bl wrp. B3. $30.00

ALDISS, Brian. *This World & Nearer Ones...* (1979). Weidenfeld Nicolson. 1st ed. NF/VG. B3. $25.00

ALDISS & HARRISON. *Decade: The 1940s.* 1978. St Martin. 1st Am ed. F/F. N3. $15.00

ALDRICH, Ann; see Meaker, Marijane.

ALDRICH, Chilson D. *Real Log Cabin.* 1930s. Macmillan. 8vo. 278 p. VG. B11/H10. $35.00

ALDRIDGE, James. *Heroes of the Empty View.* 1954. Knopf. 1st ed. 432 p. maroon cloth. F/VG. M7. $55.00

ALEKSEYEV, A. *Basic Economic Law of Modern Capitalism.* 1955. Moscow. Foreign Languages Pub. 68 p. wrp. A7. $12.00

ALEXANDER, Charles. *John McGraw.* 1988. Viking. 1st ed. F/F. P8. $22.50

ALEXANDER, Charles. *Ku Klux Klan in the SW.* (1965). KY U. 288 p. VG. A17. $15.00

ALEXANDER, Edwin P. *Am Locomotives.* 1950. Bonanza. VG/dj. A16. $15.00

ALEXANDER, Edwin P. *Iron Horses.* (1941). NY. orig ed. 4to. 239 p. pict ep. VG/dj. D3. $35.00

ALEXANDER, Gabriel. *Fair Maid of WY: Tale of War of Independence.* 1846. London. 1st ed. oblong folio. calf/cloth sides. VG. M1. $150.00

ALEXANDER, Gary. *Deadly Drought.* 1991. St Martin. 1st ed. 5th Bamsan Kiet mystery. M/M. T2. $12.50

ALEXANDER, Gary. *Unfunny Money.* 1992. St Martin. 1st ed. M/M. T2. $13.00

ALEXANDER, Hartley. *Manito Masks.* (1925). NY. 1st ed. 209 p. VG. D3. $12.50

ALEXANDER, Hartley. *Pueblo Indian Painting.* 1979. Santa Fe. Bell. 1/750. reissue of 1932 portfolio. sgn Jamake Highwater. L3. $500.00

ALEXANDER, Lloyd. *First Two Lives of Lukas-Kasha.* 1978. Dutton. 1st ed. 8vo. 213 p. NF/NF. T5. $45.00

ALEXANDER, Paul J. *Byzantine Apocalyptic Tradition.* ca 1985. Berkeley. 1st ed. 239 p. M. H10. $35.00

ALEXANDER, Peter. *Roy Campbell: A Critical Biography.* 1932. Oxford. 1st ed. 8vo. 277 p. F/NF. M7. $40.00

ALEXANDER, W.D. *Brief Hist of the HI People.* ca 1891. NY/Cincinnati/Chicago. 8vo. ils/maps. 341 p. cloth. H9. $95.00

ALEXANDER, William. *Costume of the Russian Empire...* 1803. London. 1st ed. French/Eng text. lg quarto. 73 pls. rstr bdg. H5. $1,650.00

ALEXANDER & SELESNICK. *Hist of Psychiatry: An Evaluation of Psychiatric Thought...* 1966. Harper Row. 1st ed. blk cloth. VG/dj. G1. $30.00

ALEXANDRI & ROSELLI. *Theologica Dogmatica et Moralis.* 1787. Rome. Barbiellini. vol I only. calf. C5. $10.00

ALEXIE, Sherman. *Lone Ranger & Tonto Fistfight in Heaven.* (1993). Atlantic Monthly. 1st ed. sgn. F/F. B3. $40.00

ALGER, Horatio. *Erie Train Boy.* nd. Hurst. G. A16. $15.00

ALGER & JUNE. *Shadow's Holiday.* 1931. NY. 1st prt. 42 p. gilt bl cloth. F/G. H3. $12.00

ALGER & NASH. *Cricket of Carador.* 1925. Doubleday Page. 1st ed. author's 1st book. ils Chrisopher Rule. F/dj. B24. $750.00

ALGREN, Nelson. *Galena Guide.* 1937. Federal Writers Project. VG+/bl & gold wrp. A11. $175.00

ALGREN, Nelson. *Walk on the Wild Side.* (1956). FSC. 1st ed. NF/VG. B3. $35.00

ALGREN, Nelson. *Who Lost an Am?* 1963. Macmillan. 1st ed. F/NF. B2. $40.00

ALGUE, P. Jose. *Atlas of the Philippine Islands.* 1900. GPO. 30 color maps. VG+. O6. $125.00

ALIBRANDI, Tom. *Privileged Information.* 1984. Dodd Mead. M11. $25.00

ALINSKY, Saul. *John L Lewis: An Unauthorized Biography.* ca 1949. NY. Putnam. 1st ed. F/G. V4. $25.00

ALLAIN & SOUVESTRE. *Fantomas.* (1986). Morrow. NF/dj. B9. $12.50

ALLAIN & SOUVESTRE. *Silent Executioner.* (1987). Morrow. 1st ed. 2nd of Fantomas Adventures series. F/dj. B9. $10.00

ALLAN, Doug. *Lightning Strikes Once.* (1944). McBride. reprint. 8vo. 285 p. VG+/VG. A2. $10.00

ALLAN, Ivan. *Atlanta From the Ashes.* 1928. Atlanta. Ruralist. ltd ed. sgn. 144 p. NF. B28. $55.00

ALLAN, John B.; see Westlake, Donald E.

ALLAN, R.H. *Part-Time Farming in the SW.* 1937. GPO. 1st ed. xl. 317 p. wrp. H10. $22.50

ALLARD, R.W. *Principles of Plant Breeding.* ca 1960. NY. Wiley. 1st ed. 485 p. F/dj. H10. $15.00

ALLARD, William A. *Vanishing Breed. Photographs of Cowboys of the W.* 1983. NY Graphic Soc/Little Brn. 8vo. VG/VG. B11. $20.00

ALLBAUGH, Leland G. *Crete: Case Study of an Underdeveloped Area.* 1953. Princeton. 1st ed. ils/fld maps/tables. cloth. dj. O2. $75.00

ALLBEURY, Ted. *Children of Tender Yrs.* 1985. NY. 1st ed. dj. T9. $10.00

ALLBEURY, Ted. *Seeds of Treason.* 1986. London. NEL. 1st ed. F/F. S5. $30.00

ALLBEURY, Ted. *Wilderness of Mirrors.* 1988. London. ARC of 1st ed. w/promo material. F/F. S5. $27.50

ALLBUTT, T. Clifford. *Hist Relations of Medicine & Surgery to End of 16th Century.* 1905. London. Macmillan. xl. H9. $65.00

ALLEGRETTO, Michael. *Blood Stone.* 1989. London. Macmillan. ARC of 1st British ed. RS. NF/NF. S5. $22.50

ALLEGRETTO, Michael. *Dead of Winter.* (1990). London. Macmillan. 1st ed. F/F. B3. $20.00

ALLEGRETTO, Michael. *Death on the Rocks.* 1987. Scribner. 1st ed. F/F. M15. $35.00

ALLEGRETTO, Michael. *Night of Reunion.* (1990). Scribner. 1st ed. F/NF. B3. $30.00

ALLEGRETTO, Michael. *Watchmen.* (1991). Simon Schuster. 1st ed. VG/NF. B3. $25.00

ALLEN, A.J. *Ten Yrs in OR: Travels & Adventures of Dr E Wht...* 1848. Ithaca. Mack Andrus. 430 p. full leather. G. H7. $125.00

ALLEN, Benedict. *Who Goes Out in the Midday Sun?* (1986). Viking. 1st Am ed. 249 p. dj. F3. $15.00

ALLEN, Betsy. *Brn Satchel Mystery.* 1954. Grosset Dunlap. lists to Silver Secret. 177 p. VG+/dj. M20. $40.00

ALLEN, Betsy. *Ghost Wore Wht.* 1950. Grosset Dunlap. lists to Silver Secret. 204 p. cloth. VG/dj. M20. $22.00

ALLEN, Betsy. *Silver Secret.* 1956. Grosset Dunlap. 1st ed. 174 p. cloth. VG/dj. M20. $65.00

ALLEN, Betsy. *Yel Warning.* 1951. Grosset Dunlap. lists to Brn Satchel (dj lists to this title). VG/dj. M20. $25.00

ALLEN, Charles F. *David Crockett, Scout...* (1911). Phil. 8th prt. 5 pls. 308 p. cloth. VG. D3. $12.50

ALLEN, CLARK, MCCORD & ROWE. *NE Engineer's Strikes of 1871: 9 Hours' League.* ca 1971. Gateshead. Northumbeland. VG/G. V4. $12.50

ALLEN, Dick. *SF: The Future.* 1971. Harcourt. 1st ed. VG/lg wrp. M2. $10.00

ALLEN, Durward. *MI Fox Squirrel Management.* 1943. Lansing. 1st ed. 404 p. VG. A17. $35.00

ALLEN, Ethan. *Major League Baseball.* 1945. Macmillan. later prt. VG/G. P8. $11.50

ALLEN, Francis H. *Men of Concord & Some Others...Journal of Henry D Thoreau.* 1936. Houghton Mifflin. 1st ed. ils NC Wyeth. 8vo. gr brds. VG. B11. $120.00

ALLEN, Frank W. *Apple Growing in CA.* 1951. Berkeley. ils/photos. self wrp. B26. $15.00

ALLEN, Frederick Lewis. *Paul Revere Reynolds.* 1944. private prt. 105 p. N2. $20.00

ALLEN, Gay Wilson. *William James: A Biography.* 1967. Viking. 1st ed. 566 p. VG/dj. G1. $25.00

ALLEN, Henry T. *Report of an Expedition to the Copper, Tanana & Koyukuk...* 1887. GPO. xl. 5 fld maps. fair. A16. $200.00

ALLEN, Hervey. *Anthony Adverse.* 1934. NY. 1st ils ed. 2 vols. VG. A11. $35.00

ALLEN, Hugh. *House of Goodyear.* 1936. Akron. 2nd ed. photos. 46 p. dj. A17. $20.00

ALLEN, Leslie. *Liberty: The Statue & the Am Dream.* 1985. Ellis Island Found. sq 8vo. ils. 304 p. VG/VG. B11. $25.00

ALLEN, Lewis F. *Am Cattle: Their Hist, Breeding & Management.* ca 1868. NY. Judd. 528 p. H10. $45.00

ALLEN, Malcolm. *Medievalism of Lawrence of Arabia.* 1991. PA State. 1st ed. 1st ed. 224 p. bl-gr cloth. F/NF. M7. $28.50

ALLEN, Maury. *Damn Yankee.* 1980. Times. 1st ed. F/VG+. P8. $20.00

ALLEN, Maury. *Where Have You Gone Joe DiMaggio?* 1975. Dutton. 1st ed. F/F. P8. $45.00

ALLEN, Paula Gunn. *Spider Woman's Granddaughters.* 1989. Boston. Beacon. 1st ed. F/F. L3. $45.00

ALLEN, Paula Gunn. *Studies in Am Indian Literature.* 1983. NY. Modern Language Assn. 1st ed. F/sans. L3. $35.00

ALLEN, Paula Gunn. *Woman who Owned the Shadows.* (1983). San Francisco. Spinsters Ink. 1st ed. F/wrp. L3. $65.00

ALLEN, Richard Sanders. *Covered Bridges of the Middle Atlantic States.* 1959. Brattleboro. Stephen Greene. 1st ed. VG/VG. B28. $35.00

ALLEN, Samuel. *Ivory Tusks & Other Poems.* 1968. Millbrook, NY. 1st ed. 1/200. F/ils beige wrp. A11. $45.00

ALLEN, Samuel. *Paul Vesey's Ledger.* 1975. London. 1st ed. F/photo-ils gray wrp. A11. $20.00

ALLEN, Steve. *Murder in Vegas.* 1991. NY. Zebra. 1st ed. sgn. F/F. S5. $35.00

ALLEN, Thomas. *Lancashire Ils.* 1832. London. 4to. 108 pls. 112 p. dk gr cloth. H3. $325.00

ALLEN, W.B. *Works of Fisher Ames.* (1983). Indianapolis. Liberty Classics. 1st ed. 2 vols. F. A17. $25.00

ALLEN, W.E.D. *Problems of Turkish Power in the 16th Century.* 1963. London. 8vo. fld map. 92 p. O2. $15.00

ALLEN, Walter C. *Hendersonia: Music of Fletcher Henderson...* 1973. Highland Park. Allen. 1st ed. NF. B2. $100.00

ALLEN, William. *Life of...w/Selections From His Correspondence.* 1847. Phil. Longstreth. 8vo. 2 vols. fair. V3. $40.00

ALLEN, William C. *Son of the Morning: Incidents in Life of Richard Davies.* 1894. Porter Coates. 24mo. 94 p. VG. V3. $10.00

ALLEN, Willis Boyd. *Red Mtn of AK.* (1889). Boston. ils. 348 p. gilt pict cloth. VG. A17. $17.50

ALLEN, Willis Boyd. *Story of Isles of Shoals.* 1888. D Lothrop. 1st ed. 242 p. decor gr cloth. VG. S10. $18.00

ALLEN & MCCLURE. *200 Yrs: Hist of Soc for Promoting Christian Knowledge...* 1970. NY. Burt Franklin. 551 p. H10. $27.50

ALLEN & MEANY. *Kings of the Diamond.* 1965. Putnam. 1st ed. VG/G. P8. $17.50

ALLEN & RUST. *King Joe Oliver.* 1955. Belleville. Allen. #d ed. mimeo. wrp. B2. $125.00

ALLENDE, Isabel. *House of the Spirits.* 1985. Knopf. 1st Am ed. author's 1st book. NF/NF. A14. $150.00

ALLENDE, Isabel. *House of the Spirits.* 1985. NY. Knopf. 1st Am ed. sgn. F/NF. L3. $250.00

ALLENDE, Isabel. *Infinite Plan.* 1991. Harper Collins. 1st ed. inscr. F/F. B2. $60.00

ALLENDE, Isabel. *Of Love & Shadows.* 1987. London. Cape. 1st ed. trans from Spanish. NF/NF. A14. $40.00

ALLENTUCK, Marcia. *Achievement of Isaac Bashevis Singer.* 1969. IL U. xl. VG+/VG. S3. $24.00

ALLHOFF, Fred. *Lightning in the Night.* 1979. Prentice Hall. 1st ed. ils. F/F. N3. $35.00

ALLINGHAM, Margery. *Fashion in Shrouds.* 1938. Doubleday Doran. 1st Am ed. inscr. VG/NF. B4. $225.00

ALLINGHAM, Margery. *Gyrth Chalice Mystery.* 1931. Doubleday Crime Club. 1st Am ed. VG/dj. M15. $65.00

ALLINGHAM, Margery. *Mind Readers.* 1965. Morrow. 1st ed. F/NF. M15. $45.00

ALLIONI, Charles. *Materia, Medica Animalium Tradita, a Clar Doctore...* 1767. Taurini Anno. sm 4to. 170 p. mottled calf. G7. $695.00

ALLISON, Clyde; see Knowles, William.

ALLMAN, C.B. *Life & Times of Lewis Wetzel.* 1939. Nappanee. gilt pict bdg. VG. E5. $65.00

ALLOWAY, Clifford C. *US Constitutional Law.* 1958. Coral Gables, FL. xl. worn. M11. $25.00

ALLSON, Kenneth. *Hard Travelin': Hobo & His Hist.* (1967). NAL. 1st Am ed. 8vo. 448 p. F/F. A2. $30.00

ALLSTROM, Oliver. *Old Rocky: World's 1st Billionaire Centenary 1839-1939.* 1939. Chicago. Donohue. 1st ed. 12mo. 186 p. VG+/VG. A2. $25.00

ALLTON & SELVIDGE. *Blacksmithing: A Manual...* 1925. Peoria. Manual Arts Pr. O3. $35.00

ALMAGIA, Roberto. *Monvementa Cartographica Vaticana...Volvmen I...* 1944. Citta del Vaticano. lg folio. 56 maps. Samuel E Morison's copy. NF. O6. $475.00

ALOUF, Michel M. *Hist of Baalbek by One of Its Inhabitants.* 1890. Beyrouth. 1st ed. 136 p. VG/prt wrp. M8. $85.00

ALOUF, Michel M. *Hist of Baalbek.* 1949. Beirut. 8th Eng ed/revised & completed. 8vo. 122 p. O2. $35.00

ALSBERG, Henry G. *Am Guide.* ca 1949. NY. Hastings. thick 8vo. 1348 p. cloth. H9. $20.00

ALTGELD, John P. *Oratory: Its Reguirements & Its Rewards.* nd. Chicago. private prt. 1/500. NF. B2. $35.00

ALTHER, Lisa. *Bedrock.* (1990). London. Viking. 1st ed. NF/NF. B3. $20.00

ALTHER, Lisa. *Other Women.* (1984). Knopf. 1st ed. VG/VG. B3. $20.00

ALTHERR. *Overture & Finale to Linen Embroidery.* 1987. np. wrp. G2. $8.00

ALTMAN & RUDOLPH. *Buffalo Bill & the Indians.* 1976. NY. 1st ed of PBO. NF/wrp. A11. $25.00

ALTMANN, Alexander. *Studies in the 19th-Century Jewish Intellectual Hist.* 1964. Harvard. 7 essays. 215 p. VG+. S3. $24.00

ALTOMARE, Donato Antonio. *Omnia, Quae Hucusque in Lucem Prodiervnt, Opera...* 1574. Venetiis. Svmptibvs Iacobi Anieli De Maria. 379 p. calf. G7. $295.00

ALTOUNYAN, E.H.R. *Ornament of Honour.* 1937. Cambridge. 1st ed. 131 p. red cloth. VG. M7. $95.00

ALTROCCHI, Julia Cooley. *Old CA Trail: Traces in Folklore & Furrow.* 1945. Caldwell. Caxton. 1st ed. ils/index. VG/dj. A18/D3. $25.00

ALTROCCHI, Julia Cooley. *Snow-Covered Wagons: A Pioneer Epic, Donner Party.* 1936. Macmillan. 1st ed. F. A18. $35.00

ALTSCHULE, Mark D. *Development of Traditional Psychopathology.* 1976. Hemisphere Pub Corp. 1st ed. 330 p. VG/dj. G1. $45.00

ALTSHELER, Joseph A. *Border Watch.* 1912. Appleton. 18th prt. Young Trail Keepers series. 371 p. VG+/dj. M20. $30.00

ALTSHELER, Joseph A. *Hunters of the Hills.* 1916. Appleton. 11th prt. French & Indian series. 360 p. VG. M20. $22.50

ALTSHELER, Joseph A. *Recovery.* 1908. Lovell. 1st ed. 353 p. VG. M20. $30.00

ALURIDSEN, Peter. *Vitus Bering: Discoverer of Bering Strait.* 1889. Chicago. Griggs. revised ed. trans Julius Olson. 223 p. P4. $125.00

ALVAREZ, A. *Biggest Game in Town.* 1983. Houghton Mifflin. 1st ed. F/NF. Q1. $30.00

ALVEREZ, Walter C. *Minds That Came Back.* 1961. Lippincott. 2nd prt. 384 p. bl-gr cloth. VG/dj. G1. $40.00

ALVEY, Edward Jr. *Hist of Mary WA College, 1908-72.* (ca 1974). VA U. 1st ed. sgn. 682 p. VG. B10. $25.00

AMADO, Jorge. *Home Is the Sailor.* (1964). Knopf. 1st ed. trans Harriet de Onis. VG/VG. B3. $40.00

AMADO, Jorge. *Show Down.* (1988). Bantam. 1st ed. trans Rabassa. F/F. B3. $30.00

AMADO, Jorge. *Tieta.* 1979. Knopf. 1st Am ed. trans Barbara S Merello. NF/NF. A14. $25.00

AMADO, Jorge. *Violent Land.* 1965. Knopf. reissue of 1945 ed. trans from Portuguese. NF/NF clip. A14. $30.00

AMBLER, Eric. *Ability To Kill.* (1987). Mysterious. 1/250. sgn. F/slipcase. B9. $50.00

AMBLER, Eric. *Ability To Kill.* (1987). Mysterious. 1st ed. F/dj. B9. $10.00

AMBLER, Eric. *Levanter.* 1972. Atheneum. 1st ed. VG+/dj. B9. $15.00

AMBLER, Eric. *October Man.* 1947. London. only book version. VG+/wrp. A11. $25.00

AMBLER, Eric. *Passage of Arms.* (1959). Heinemann. 1st ed. NF/clip. B9. $30.00

AMBUTER, Carolyn. *Carolyn Ambuter's Needlepoint Celebration.* 1976. Workman. ils. cloth. G2. $30.00

AMBUTER, Carolyn. *Open Canvas. Complete Guide to All Facets of Openwork.* 1982. np. pb. NF. G2. $17.00

AMEREL. *Winter Holidays.* 1850. Appleton. 1st ed. 117 p. VG-. S10. $45.00

AMERICAN AMBULANCE. *Friends of France.* 1916. Houghton Mifflin. 1st ed. 12mo. G. A8. $7.50

AMERICAN HERITAGE. *Hist of WWI.* 1964. Am Heritage. 1st ed. 4to. VG. A8. $15.00

AMERICAN QUILTERS SOCIETY. *Award Winning Quilts & Their Makers, Vol I.* 1991. Paducah, KY. color photos. wrp. G2. $25.00

AMERICAN QUILTERS SOCIETY. *Gallery of Am Quilts, 1849-1988.* 1988. Paducah, KY. 500 photos w/values. wrp. G2. $20.00

AMERICAN QUILTERS SOCIETY. *Gallery of Am Quilts, 1860-1989: Book II.* 1990. Paducah, KY. photos. wrp. G2. $20.00

AMERICAN QUILTERS SOCIETY. *OK Heritage Quilts.* 1990. Paducah, KY. ils. wrp. G2. $20.00

AMERICAN QUILTERS SOCIETY. *Protecting Your Quilts.* 1990. Paducah, KY. wrp. G2. $6.00

AMERICAN QUILTERS SOCIETY. *Quilts: Museum of AQS Permanent Collection.* nd. Paducah, KY. ils. wrp. G2. $10.00

AMERICAN TOBACCO COMPANY. *Sold Am: 1st 50 Yrs.* 1954. 1st/only ed. lg quarto. 144 p. NF. E5. $45.00

AMES, Azel. *May-Flower & Her Log. July 15, 1620-May 6, 1621.* 1901. Houghton Mifflin/Riverside. sm folio. orig buckram. H9. $75.00

AMES, Clyde; see Knowles, William.

AMES, Susie M. *County Court Records of Accomack-Northampton, VA 1640-45.* ca 1973. VA U. 494 p. VG. B10. $45.00

AMICHAI, Yehuda. *Selected Poetry.* 1987. London. 1st ed. F/F. V1. $20.00

AMIS, Kingsley. *Colonel Sun: A James Bond Adventure.* 1968. Harper. 1st Am ed. F/F. S5. $30.00

AMIS, Kingsley. *Folks That Live on the Hill.* 1990. NY. 1st ed. dj. T9. $12.00

AMIS, Kingsley. *Look Round the Estate: Poems 1957-67.* 1968. NY. 1st ed. VG+/VG+. V1. $15.00

AMIS, Kingsley. *Old Devils.* (1986). London. Century Hutchinson. 1st ed. F/F. B3. $30.00

AMIS, Kingsley. *Russian Girl.* 1994. Viking. AP/1st Am ed. F/wrp. B2. $30.00

AMIS, Kingsley. *Stanley & the Women.* (1984). London. Hutchinson. 1st ed. F/F. B3. $40.00

AMIS, Martin. *Dead Babies.* 1975. London. Cape. 1st ed. sgn. author's 2nd book. F/NF clip. L3. $400.00

AMIS, Martin. *Einstein's Monsters.* 1987. Harmony. 1st Am ed. sgn. F/F. B2. $75.00

AMIS, Martin. *Einstein's Monsters.* 1987. Harmony. 1st ed. F/NF. B3. $30.00

AMIS, Martin. *London Fields.* 1989. Harmony. 1st ed. F/F. B3. $35.00

AMIS, Martin. *London Fields.* 1989. NY. Harmony. 1st Am ed. inscr. F/F. B2. $50.00

AMIS, Martin. *Moronic Inferno.* 1986. London. sgn. F/F. A11. $55.00

AMIS, Martin. *Success.* (1987). Harmony. 1st ed. NF/NF. B3. $25.00

AMIS, Martin. *Time's Arrow.* 1991. Harmony. 1st ed. F/F. B3. $25.00

AMIS, Martin. *Time's Arrow.* 1991. NY. Harmony. 1st ed. inscr. F/F. B2. $45.00

AMMONS, A.R. *Collected Poems 1951-71.* 1972. Norton. 1st ed. F/NF. C4. $25.00

AMORY, C. *Trouble w/Nowadays: Curmudgeon Strikes Back.* 1979. Arbor House. ARC. presentation/sgn. 215 p. NF/NF. A7. $15.00

AMORY, John H. *Alnomuc; or, The Golden Rule, Tale of the Sea.* 1837. Boston. Weeks Jorday. xl. 24 full-p engravings. 144 p. G. B14. $100.00

AMOS, James. *Memorial: Novel of Vietnam War.* (1989). Crown. 1st ed. 261 p. F/NF. A7. $20.00

AMOSOFF, Nikolai. *Open Heart: Journal of 2 Days & Nights...Russian Surgeon.* 1966. Simon Schuster. 1st Eng-language ed. 248 p. VG+/G+. S9. $18.00

AMSDEN, Georgianna. *Family Facts.* 1956. Webster City. Hahne. 1st ed. O3. $65.00

AN ANGLER. *Salmonia: Days of Fly Fishing...Account of Habits...* 1970. NY. Freshet. facsimile of 1828 ed. 16mo. M/slipcase. A17. $25.00

ANAGNOSTOU, Manos D. *Samos: Post Hist & Stamps 1800-1915.* 1992. Nicosia. ils/maps. 220 p. pict brds. O2, $60.00

ANASTASI, Anne. *Visual Perception: The 19th Century.* 1964. NY. Wiley. trade pb. 222 p. G1. $22.50

ANATOLE, Ray; see Weiss, Joe.

ANBUREY, Thomas. *Travels Through the Interior Parts of Am.* 1789. London. Wm Lane. 1st ed. 2 vols. octavo. pls/fld map. H9. $900.00

ANCKARSVARD, Karin. *Mysterious Schoolmaster.* 1959. Harcourt Brace. 1st Am ed. 8vo. 190 p. red cloth. G+/torn. T5. $25.00

ANDERSEN, Hans Christian. *Ausgewahlte Marchen.* ca 1906. Wein Leipzig. ils H Steiner-Prag. 142 p. pict cloth. VG. D1. $100.00

ANDERSEN, Hans Christian. *Fairy Tales by Hans Andersen.* nd. David McKay. 1st Am ed. ils Rackham. teg. rose-red cloth. NF/dj. D1. $285.00

ANDERSEN, Hans Christian. *Fairy Tales.* 1932. London. 1/525. ils/sgn Rackham. orig vellum brds. F/pub slipcase. H5. $2,250.00

ANDERSEN, Hans Christian. *Fairytales.* 1924. Doran. 1st Am ed. ils Nielsen. ils ep. 280 p. bl cloth. VG. D1. $650.00

ANDERSEN, Hans Christian. *Fairytales.* 1924. Hodder Stoughton. 1st ed. ils Nielsen. 197 p. bl cloth. VG. D1. $650.00

ANDERSEN, Hans Christian. *Hans Andersen's Fairy Tales.* (1913). Eng. Boots the Chemist. ils W Heath Robinson. 320 p. VG. D1. $250.00

ANDERSEN, Hans Christian. *Little Mermaid.* 1939. Macmillan. 1st thus ed. ils Lathrop. VG/dj. D1. $295.00

ANDERSEN, Hans Christian. *Marchen.* 1955. Stuttgart. German text. 8vo. 8 color pls. F/G. H3. $25.00

ANDERSEN, Hans Christian. *Mermaid & Other Stories.* 1923. NY. ils DS Walker. F. B14. $75.00

ANDERSEN, Hans Christian. *Red Shoes.* 1928. Bristol. Douglas Cleverdon. 1/460. octavo. 31 p. NF. B24. $150.00

ANDERSEN, Hans Christian. *Snow Queen.* 1982. Dial. 1st ed. ils Susan Jeffers. 40 p. gray brds. F/VG. D1. $45.00

ANDERSEN, Hans Christian. *Stories From Hans Andersen.* 1911. London. Hodder Stoughton. 1/750. ils/sgn Edmund Dulac. 28 mtd pls. Zaehnsdorf bdg. H5. $2,250.00

ANDERSEN, Hans Christian. *Thumbelina.* ca 1971. MO. Hallmark Cards. probable 1st prt. oversize 8vo. 8 popups. VG. T5. $45.00

ANDERSEN, Hans Christian. *Wild Swan.* 1981. Dial. 1st ed. ils Susan Jeffers. 40 p. bl brds. F/VG. D1. $45.00

ANDERSEN-ROSENDAL, Jorgen. *Happy Lagoons: Adventures of a S Sea Wanderer.* (1961). HRW. 1st Am ed. 8vo. 272 p. F/VG+. A2. $15.00

ANDERSON, B.G. *Topsy Turvy & the Easter Bunny.* 1939. Rand McNally #269. VG-/pict brds. A3. $40.00

ANDERSON, Barry C. *Lifeline to the Yukon: Hist of Yukon River Navigation.* (1983). Seattle. Superior. 1st ed. 4to. 152 p. F/dj. A17. $25.00

ANDERSON, C.W. *Blaze & Thunderbolt.* 1956. Macmillan. 2nd prt. 4to. 46 p. VG/VG. A3. $25.00

ANDERSON, C.W. *Blaze Finds Forgotten Roads.* 1970. NY. Macmillan. 3rd prt. xl. VG. O3. $12.00

ANDERSON, C.W. *Blaze Finds the Trail.* 1962. NY. Macmillan. 8th prt. VG. O3. $25.00

ANDERSON, C.W. *Blk, Bay & Chestnut.* 1939. NY. Macmillan. 2nd prt. oblong 4to. VG. O3. $38.00

ANDERSON, C.W. *Crooked Colt.* 1956. Macmillan. 3rd prt. 4to. VG/VG. A3. $17.50

ANDERSON, C.W. *CW Anderson's Favorite Horse Stories...* 1967. Dutton. 1st ed. VG/G. O3. $30.00

ANDERSON, C.W. *Deep Through the Heat. Profiles of 20 Valiant Horses.* 1940. Macmillan. 1st ed. oblong 4to. VG/G. A3. $22.50

ANDERSON, C.W. *High Courage.* 1941. NY. Macmillan. 1st ed. VG/G. O3. $48.00

ANDERSON, C.W. *Horse Show.* 1951. Harper. later prt. VG/VG. O3. $40.00

ANDERSON, C.W. *Smashers.* 1954. NY. Macmillan. later prt. oblong 4to. VG/G. O3. $58.00

ANDERSON, C.W. *Tomorrow's Champion.* 1946. NY. Macmillan. later prt. oblong 4to. VG/G. O3. $40.00

ANDERSON, C.W. *Touch of Greatness.* 1945. Macmillan. 1st ed. VG. M5. $15.00

ANDERSON, C.W. *Touch of Greatness.* 1945. Macmillan. 1st ed. 12mo. 96 p. gr cloth. VG/dj. D1. $47.50

ANDERSON, Duncan. *Hist of the Abbey & Palace of Holyrood.* 1857. Edinburgh. 2nd ed. 16mo. 192 p. VG/prt wrp. H3. $35.00

ANDERSON, F. *Applique Designs My Mother Taught Me To Sew.* 1990. np. wrp. G2. $13.00

ANDERSON, Frank J. *Ils Hist of the Herbals.* 1977. NY. 100 woodcuts. 270 p. F/dj. B26. $44.00

ANDERSON, Frederick Irving. *Farmer of Tomorrow.* 1913. Macmillan. 1st ed. F. H10. $10.00

ANDERSON, Gary Clayton. *Little Crow: Spokesman for the Sioux.* 1986. NM Hist Soc. 4th prt. 259 p. M/wrp. A17. $11.50

ANDERSON, Gary. *Atlantic Salmon: Fact & Fantasy.* (1990). Montreal. 1st ed. 175 p. M/dj. A17. $22.50

ANDERSON, Isabel. *From Corsair to Riffian.* 1927. Houghton Mifflin. 1st ed. 8vo. 209 p. VG+/G. A2. $35.00

ANDERSON, Isabel. *Spell of Belgium.* 1915. Boston. 8vo. ils. 442 p. teg. gilt bl cloth. VG. H3. $20.00

ANDERSON, J.R.L. *Vinland Voyage: Guardian Expedition to Vinland 1966.* (1967). London. Eyre Spottiswoode. 1st ed. 8vo. 278 p. F/VG. A2. $17.50

ANDERSON, James. *Assault & Matrimony.* 1980. London. Muller. 1st ed. NF/dj. S5. $22.50

ANDERSON, James. *Making the Am Thoroughbred.* 1916. Norwood. 1st ed. VG. O3. $95.00

ANDERSON, James. *Murder She Wrote.* 1986. Nelson Doubleday. 1st ed. F/F. F4. $14.00

ANDERSON, John Henry. *Am Civil War: Operations in the E Theatre...1863...* 1910. London. Hugh Rees. 1st ed. fld pocket maps. 120 p. cloth. NF. M8. $350.00

ANDERSON, Kent. *Sympathy for the Devil.* 1987. Doubleday. 1st ed. F/F. A7. $35.00

ANDERSON, Lauri. *Hunting Hemingway's Trout.* (1990). Atheneum. 1st ed. F/F. B3. $15.00

ANDERSON, Lloyd. *Writing System of La Mojarra & Associated Monuments.* 1993. WA, DC. 2nd ed. 2 vols. sbdg. M. F3. $40.00

ANDERSON, Margaret. *My 30 Yrs War.* 1930. Covici Friede. VG. B2. $45.00

ANDERSON, Marta. *Dho Tsu Hwi/Gifts of the Tsetseka Season.* 1974. Madison, WI. Crepuscular. 1/40. oblong octavo. M/Japanese-style wrp. B24. $350.00

ANDERSON, Maxwell. *Night Over Taos. A Play in 3 Acts.* 1935. NY. later ed. xl. 12mo. 200 p. D3. $15.00

ANDERSON, Maxwell. *Notes on a Dream.* 1971. TX. Humanities Research Center. 1/750. 48 p. VG. N2. $7.50

ANDERSON, Nancy K. *Albert Bierstadt: Cho-Looke, the Yosemite Fall.* 1986. San Diego. Timken Art Gallery. 34 p. D2. $15.00

ANDERSON, Poul. *Broken Sword.* 1954. Abelard Schuman. 1st ed. author's 2nd book. VG/VG+. Q1. $150.00

ANDERSON, Poul. *Queen of Air & Darkness.* 1978. Gregg. 1st hc ed. VG/dj. M2. $17.00

ANDERSON, Poul. *Shield of Time.* 1990. Tor. 1st ed. sgn. F/F. F4. $30.00

ANDERSON, Poul. *Star Fox.* 1965. Doubleday. 1st ed. F/NF. N3. $65.00

ANDERSON, Poul. *Vault of the Ages.* 1952. Winston. 1st ed. inscr. VG/Canon dj. M2. $40.00

ANDERSON, Raymond. *Baby Sweet's.* 1983. NY. ARC. RS. RS. F/NF. A11. $25.00

ANDERSON, Rhea. *Sullivan Co, Blountville, Citizens, Homes & Reminiscences...* 1934. Abingdon, VA. WA Co Hist Soc. removed from bdg vol. VG/prt wrp. M8. $37.50

ANDERSON, Robert A. *Service for the Dead.* (1986). Arbor. 1st ed. F/F. A7. $30.00

ANDERSON, Rufus. *Hist of Sandwich Islands Mission.* 1870. Boston. Congregational Pub Soc. ils. NF. O6. $325.00

ANDERSON, S. *Collector's Guide to Quilts.* 1991. np. ils. cloth. G2. $25.00

ANDERSON, Sherwood. *Memoirs.* 1942. Harcourt Brace. 1st ed. 507 p. VG/VG. B5. $50.00

ANDERSON, Sherwood. *Modern Writer.* 1925. Lantern Pr. 1/1000. A1. $60.00

ANDERSON, Sherwood. *Plays, Winesburg & Others.* 1947. NY. 1st ed. 242 p. VG. B18. $15.00

ANDERSON, Sherwood. *Return to Winesburg.* 1967. NC U. 1st ed. 223 p. VG+/dj. M20. $25.00

ANDERSON, Sherwood. *Tar: A Midwest Childhood.* 1926. Boni Liveright. 1st ed. 346 p. VG+/dj. M20. $75.00

ANDERSON, Sherwood. *Triumph of the Egg.* 1957 & 1959. Tokyo. 1st prt. 2 vols. VG+/gilt bl wrp. A11. $30.00

ANDERSON, Sherwood. *Winesburg, OH.* (1979). Franklin Lib. 1st ed. ils John Berkey. full leather. F. B3. $65.00

ANDERSON, Verily. *Friends & Relations: 3 Centuries of Quaker Families.* 1980. London. Hodder Stoughton. 1st ed. 320 p. VG/VG. V3. $16.00

ANDERSON, Wayne Jr. *Harmon Killebrew: Baseball's Superstar.* 1971. Deseret. 1st ed. VG+/VG. P8. $45.00

ANDERSON, William Ashley. *Angel of Hudson Bay: True Story of Maud Watt.* (1961). Clarke Irwin. 1st ed. 217 p. dj. A17. $15.00

ANDERSON, William Ashley. *Angel of Hudson Bay: True Story of Maud Watt.* 1961. Dutton. 1st ed. 8vo. 217 p. F/VG. A2. $12.00

ANDERSON, William. *Strawberry: World Bibliography, 1920-1966.* 1969. Metuchen. Scarecrow. 1st ed. 731 p. M. H10. $25.00

ANDERSON & ANDERSON. *Quicksilver: Hundred Yrs of Coaching.* 1973. Newton Abbott. 1st ed. VG/VG. O3. $58.00

ANDERSON & ANDERSON. *Roma Mater.* 1986. NY. Baen. AP of 1st ed. F/prt wrp. N3. $20.00

ANDERSON & ANDERSON. *Sailing Ship: 6 Thousand Yrs of Hist.* 1963. Bonanza. N2. $7.50

ANDERSON & BUECHEL. *Crying for a Vision: Rosebut Sioux Trilogy 1886-1976.* 1976. Morgan. 1st ed. oblong quarto. VG/wrp. L3. $25.00

ANDERSON & DAVIS. *True Story of Ramona: Its Facts & Fictions...* (1914). Dodge. 1st ed. photos. pict bdg. F. A18. $50.00

ANDERSON & DICKSON. *Earthman's Burden.* 1957. Gnome. 1st ed. F/F. M2. $100.00

ANDERSON & EKLUND. *Inheritors of Earth.* 1974. Chilton. 1st ed. F/F. N3. $20.00

ANDERSON & KORG. *Westwart to OR: Selected Source Materials...* 1958. Boston. DC Heath. thin 8vo. 112 p. wrp. T8. $7.50

ANDERSON & ONOPA. *Triquarterly 45: War Stories.* 1979. Spring. 311 p. wrp. A7. $30.00

ANDERSON & PRONZINI. *Cambodia File.* 1981. Doubleday. 1st ed. 431 p. NF/VG. A7. $35.00

ANDERSON & ROBINSON. *Frank (Robinson): The 1st Yr.* 1976. Holt. 1st ed. xl. rem m. G/G. P8. $6.00

ANDERTON, D.A. *B-29 Superfortress at War.* (1978). NY. 1st ed. ils. 176 p. VG+/dj. B18. $15.00

ANDES. *Practical Macrame.* 1971. np. ils. wrp. G2. $5.00

ANDORN, PIERCY & PIERCY. *Selected Papers.* 1957. Cleveland. Shaker Hist Soc. 1st ed. 111 p. G. D7. $40.00

ANDREANO, Ralph. *No Joy in Mudville.* 1965. Schenckman. 1st ed. F/VG. P8. $25.00

ANDREW, Felicia; see Grant, Charles L.

ANDREW, John. *Hist of the War w/Am, France, Spain & Holland.* (1785). London. Fielding/Jarvis. 3 vols of 4. xl. old calf. H9. $65.00

ANDREW. *Smocking.* 1990. np. ils. cloth. G2. $19.00

ANDREWS, Byron. *Facts About the Candidate.* 1904. Chicago. Sam Stone. miniature. 224 p. pict gray wrp. H10. $85.00

ANDREWS, C.L. *Story of Sitka: Hist Outpost of NW Coast.* ca 1922. Seattle. Lowman Hanford. 1st ed. 108 p. VG. P4. $85.00

ANDREWS, J.N. *Hist of the Sabbath & 1st Day of the Week.* 1873. Battle Creek. 7th-Day Adventist Pub. 2nd ed. 528 p. cloth. H10. $65.00

ANDREWS, J.R.H. *S Ark: Zoological Discovery in New Zealand 1769-1900.* (1986). HI U. ils/pls. 237 p. dj. A17. $25.00

ANDREWS, James DeWitt. *Treatise on Jurisprudence, Constitutions & Laws of the US.* 1900. Chicago. full sheep. M11. $50.00

ANDREWS, Jane. *Seven Little Sisters Who Live on the Round Ball...* 1861. Ticknor Fields. 1st ed. 12mo. ils SS Kilburn. 127 p. gilt brn cloth. B24. $250.00

ANDREWS, Kenneth R. *Drake's Voyages: Re-Assessment of Their Place...Expansion.* 1967. Scribner. 7 maps. M/dj. O6. $25.00

ANDREWS, Kenneth R. *Eng Privateering Voyages to the W Indies 1588-95.* 1959. London. Cambridge. 8vo. pls/maps. gilt bl cloth. B11. $120.00

ANDREWS, Peter. *Classic Country Inns of Am.* (1978). Knapp. 1st ed. 3 vols. F/slipcase. A17. $30.00

ANDREWS, Ralph W. *Redwood Classic.* 1958. Seattle. 239 photos. 174 p. VG. B26. $27.50

ANDREWS, Roy Chapman. *Nature's Ways: How Nature Takes Care of Its Own.* (1951). NY. 4to. ils/photos. 206 p. VG. A17. $15.00

ANDREWS, Stephen Pearl. *Primary Synopisis of Universology & Alwato.* 1871. NY. Dion Thomas. 1st ed. VG. N2. $150.00

ANDRIC, Ivo. *Bridge on the Drina (Na Drina Cuprija).* (1959). London. Allen Unwin. 1st ed. trans LF Edwards. VG/VG. B3. $60.00

ANDRIC, Ivo. *Devil's Yard.* 1962. NY. 1st ed. 8vo. 137 p. cloth. dj. O2. $35.00

ANET, Claude. *End of a World.* 1927. Knopf. 1st ed. trans Jeffery E Jeffery. NF/VG. A14. $40.00

ANGEL, Marie. *Beasts in Heraldry.* 1974. Stephen Greene. 1st ed. 12mo. VG+/box. D1. $85.00

ANGELL, Roger. *Five Seasons.* 1977. Simon Schuster. 1st ed. inscr to sportswriter Ritter Collett. F/VG. P8. $75.00

ANGELL, Roger. *Summer Game.* 1972. Viking. later prt. sgn. F/VG+. P8. $45.00

ANGELO, Valenti. *Rooster Club.* 1944. Viking. 1st ed. VG/VG. Q1. $75.00

ANGELO, Valenti. *Song of Songs Which Is Solomon's.* 1935. Heritage. VG/box. A16. $12.00

ANGELO, Valenti. *Valenti Angelo: Author, Ils, Printer.* 1976. San Francisco. BC of CA. 1/400. sgn. w/hand-colored drawing & prospectus. F. H5. $1,250.00

ANGELO. *L'Ecole des Armes, Avec l'Explication...Principales...* 1763. Londres. R & J Dodsley. 1st ed. French text. oblong folio. half morocco/bl brds. R3. $3,750.00

ANGELOU, Maya. *All God's Children Need Traveling Shoes.* 1986. Random. 1st ed. NF/NF. A14. $25.00

ANGELOU, Maya. *I Know Why the Caged Bird Sings.* 1969. Random. 1st ed/2nd issue (no red stain at top edge). NF/NF. A13. $60.00

ANGELOU, Maya. *I Shall Not Be Moved.* 1990. Random. 1st ed. rem mk. F/F. A14. $20.00

ANGELOU, Maya. *Shaker, Why Don't You Sing.* 1983. Random. 1st ed. F/F. B3. $55.00

ANGELOU, Maya. *Singin' & Swingin' & Getting Merry Like Christmas.* 1976. Random. 1st ed. VG+/NF clip. A14. $35.00

ANGELOU, Maya. *Wouldn't Take Nothing for My Journey Now.* 1993. Random. ltd ed. 1/500. sgn. F/box. B3. $125.00

ANGELOU, Maya. *Wouldn't Take Nothing for My Journey Now.* 1993. Random. 1st ed. w/inscr bookplate. M/M. E3. $45.00

ANGERS, Marie-Louise-Felicite. *Angeline de Montbrun: Psychological Romance of Quebec.* 1974. Toronto U. 1st ed. F/F. A14. $30.00

ANGIER & COLBY. *Art & Science of Taking to the Woods.* (1970). Stackpole. 288 p. F/dj. A17. $17.50

ANGLE, Paul M. *Bloody Williamson: Chapter in Am Lawlessness.* 1952. Knopf. 1st ed. N2. $20.00

ANGLE, Paul M. *Foundations of Lincoln's Fame.* June 1939. Carleton College. A6. $10.00

ANGLUND, Joan Walsh. *Childhood Is a Time of Innocence.* 1964. Harcourt. stated 1st ed. cloth. VG/G. M5. $22.00

ANGLUND, Joan Walsh. *Morning Is a Little Child.* 1969. Harcourt Brace. 1st ed. sm 4to. VG+/VG. T5. $40.00

ANGLUND, Joan Walsh. *What Color Is Love?* 1966. Harcourt. 1st ed. cloth. VG/G. M5. $22.00

ANGLUND, John Walsh. *Christmas Book.* 1983. Random. 1st prt. 44 p. pict brds. VG. S10. $25.00

ANGOLD, Michael. *Byzantine Government in Exile.* 1975. Oxford. 8vo. maps. 332 p. dj. O2. $35.00

ANGUS, Douglas. *Death on Jerusalem Road.* (1963). Random. 1st ed. F/dj. B9. $6.50

ANGUS, Irving. *Heroic Age of Franco-German Jewry...* 1969. NY. Yeshiva U. 380 p. VG+. S3. $28.00

ANLEY, Gwendolyn. *Alpine House Culture for Amateurs.* 1938. London. Country Life. ils/index. 188 p. H10. $20.00

ANOBILE, Richard J. *Frankenstein.* 1974. Flare/Avon. NF/wrp. C8. $40.00

ANOBILE, Richard J. *Stagecoach.* 1975. Flare/Avon. NF/wrp. C8. $35.00

ANON. *Abstract of Infantry Tactics...* 1830. Boston. 1st ed. 138 p. orig leather. G. D7. $125.00

ANON. *All About Story Book.* 1929. NY. 8vo. ils Gruelle/Gooch/others. reddish-orange cloth. VG. H3. $25.00

ANON. *All-Am Book.* 1938. Lacona, NY. Holstein-Friesian World. ils. VG. O3. $45.00

ANON. *Alphabet in Rhyme.* nd. (1830s). NY. Kiggins Kellogg. 48mo. 16 ils alphabet p. VG/wht pict wrp. H3. $50.00

ANON. *Animal & Train ABC.* ca 1908. London. Dean & Sons. gilt gr cloth. NF. D1. $250.00

ANON. *Arabs & What They Can Do.* 1950s. LA. IAHA. 30 p. wrp. O3. $12.00

ANON. *Army Horseshoer: A Manual...* 1909. Ft Riley. 2nd/revised ed. 12mo. 48 p. VG. O3. $65.00

ANON. *Autobiography Ex-Colored Man.* 1912. Boston. 1st ed. G. B5. $225.00

ANON. *Big Top Circus Book.* ca 1940s-50s. np. panorama w/6 3-D scenes. cloth w/string ties. NF. D1. $120.00

ANON. *Blackburd's Nest.* 1912. Phil. Johnson Warner. 1st known ed. 12mo. 36 p. prt wrp. B24. $185.00

ANON. *Brief Account of Lewis & Clark Expedition...* 1954. GPO. 12 p. F/prt wrp. T8. $6.00

ANON. *Champions of the Nation.* 1941. NY. AHSA. 4to. O3. $45.00

ANON. *Children in the Woods.* nd. (1830s). Bath, NY. Underhill. 48mo. 16 p. VG/wht wrp. H3. $50.00

ANON. *Devil & Tom Walker: Together w/Deacon Grubb & Old Nick.* 1830. Woodstock. Colton. 32mo. 32 p. G/plain gr wrp. H3. $35.00

ANON. *Die Schonen Ferien von Bibiche.* 1948. Lyon. 1st trade ed. ils Blanchard. VG. D1. $95.00

ANON. *Dolly in Town.* ca 1900. London/Paris. Raphael Tuck. chromos. VG/stiff chromo wrp. D1. $95.00

ANON. *Dr Dick.* 1897. Dutton. 18mo. 2 chromolithos. VG. S10. $40.00

ANON. *Easy Art of Flower Crochet.* 1972. Graphic Enterprises. ils. wrp. G2. $4.00

ANON. *Equality; or, Hist of Lithconia.* 1947. Prime Pr. 1/500. F/dj. M2. $65.00

ANON. *Farmhouse.* 1847. NY. SM Crane. 32mo. 16 p. NF/prt wrp. B24. $85.00

ANON. *Father's Legacy to His Daughter.* (1840). NY. miniature. aeg. gilt full blk leather. F. H3. $350.00

ANON. *Four Little People; or, Bob, Trot, Jamie & Lina.* (1874). Am Sunday School Union. 24mo. 138 p. G+. S10. $25.00

ANON. *Friends in the ABC Field.* 1911. NY. 4to. 12 p. F/pict wrp. scarce. H3. $25.00

ANON. *Funny Little Darkies.* ca 1900. McLoughlin. 6 chromos. VG/stiff pict wrp. D1. $350.00

ANON. *Garfield Album.* 1884. NY. 12mo. G. D7. $35.00

ANON. *Gay Mother Goose.* 1938. Scribner. 1st ed. ils Francoise. 63 p. F. D1. $200.00

ANON. *Gems for Boys & Girls.* 1850. Rufus Merrill. 48mo. woodcuts. NM/prt wrp. H3. $50.00

ANON. *General Jack.* 1897. Dutton. 2 chromolithos. 12 p. VG. S10. $40.00

ANON. *Guide to Phil.* 1866. Phil. Dainty. 12mo. 164 p. G. D7. $50.00

ANON. *Handwoven Design Collection 1.* nd. Interweave Pr. pb. ils/instructions. G2. $3.59

ANON. *Higher Life.* nd. Phil Yearly Meeting. 12mo. 74 p. VG+. V3. $8.50

ANON. *Hist of Animals for the Use of Children.* 1843. Concord. Rufus Merrill. 64mo. 6 color woodcuts. 8 p. M/tan prt wrp. H3. $100.00

ANON. *Hist of Little Silver Fish.* 1822. Woodstock. Watson. 48mo. woodcuts. 30 p. VG/pict wrp. H3. $45.00

ANON. *Hist of Portage Co, OH.* 1885. Chicago. Warner Beers. 1st ed. 927 p. orig leather. G. D7. $135.00

ANON. *How To Play Baseball.* 1913. Crowell. reprint of 1912 ed. VG+/clip. P8. $125.00

ANON. *Human Rights in Turkey's Transition to Democracy.* 1983. NY. 8vo. 117 p. O2. $10.00

ANON. *Ils Alphabet of Animals.* ca 1851. Boston. Crosby Nichols. Young People's Lib. G. S10. $35.00

ANON. *Inner Light: Devotional Anthology.* 1934. Allen Unwin. 3rd ed/5th prt. 12mo. 377 p. G. V3. $8.50

ANON. *Interesting Story of Children in the Wood.* ca 1820s. Banbury. JG Rusher. 32 p. 9 woodcuts. 15 p. F/self wrp. B24. $75.00

ANON. *John Whopper the Newsboy.* 1871. Boston. 1st ed. 16mo. 128 p. gilt red cloth. VG. H3. $150.00

ANON. *Jolly Jump-Ups See the Circus.* 1944. Springfield. oblong 8vo. 6 pop-ups. VG. D1. $185.00

ANON. *Juvenile Poems.* 1841. Northampton. 48mo. woodcuts. 18 p. F/wht pict wrp. H3. $50.00

ANON. *La Verite sur la Grece Monarcho-Fasciste.* 1947. Belgrade. 8vo. disbound as issued. O2. $30.00

ANON. *Ladies' Hand-Book of Baby Linen...* 1844. NY. Redfield. 1st ed. 24mo. ils. 60 p. flexible cloth. M1. $400.00

ANON. *Ladies' Indispensable Assistant. Being a Companion...* 1851. NY. 1st ed. 8vo. 138 p. cloth. M1. $275.00

ANON. *Life of Col Fremont.* 1856. NY. 32 p. G/wrp. D7. $50.00

ANON. *Life of Major-General Wm Henry Harrison...* 1840. Phil. 96 p. lacks 1 pl/1 leaf. D7. $30.00

ANON. *Little Brook & Other Stories.* (1878). Dodd Mead. sm 24mo. 40 p. VG. S10. $30.00

ANON. *Little Folks' Picture Book.* ca 1880. Am Tract Soc. 18mo. 48 p. bl cloth. VG. S10. $25.00

ANON. *Little Lucy; or, The Careless Child Reformed.* 1820. Cambridge. Hilliard Metcalf. 1st ed. 24mo. 33 p. M1. $150.00

ANON. *Little Lucy; or, The Pleasant Day.* ca 1840s. New Haven. Babcock. Chapbook. woodcuts. 16 p. VG/wrp. D1. $50.00

ANON. *Little Present.* 1840. Northampton. Metcalf. 64mo. woodcuts. 8 p. VG/brn pict wrp. H3. $35.00

ANON. *Little Primer. Book for Children.* 1847. Pittsfield, MA. Werden. 64mo. woodcuts. 8 p. G/pict wrp. H3. $30.00

ANON. *Lives of Grant & Colfax.* 1868. Cincinnati. campaign ed. 104 p. G/wrp. D7. $100.00

ANON. *Mac & His Do-Ings.* (1879). Lothrop. 16mo. ils. 46 p. G+. S10. $25.00

ANON. *Manners & Customs of the Jews & Other Nations in Bible.* 1831. London. 12mo. woodcuts. 176 p. cloth/leather label. O2. $65.00

ANON. *Mother Bird Stories.* (1909). Altemus. ils. 128 p. decor tan cloth. VG. S10. $45.00

ANON. *Mother Goose Playhouse.* ca 1940s. np. 3-D pop-ups. NF/box. D1. $250.00

ANON. *Mother Goose's Rhymes, Chimes & Jingles.* 1898. McLoughlin. 128 p. VG/pict wrp. D1. $110.00

ANON. *Mother Goose.* 1934. Donohue. full-p ils. VG. L1. $42.50

ANON. *Mtn & Moorland Ponies of Great Britain.* nd. London. Nat Pony Soc. cloth. G+/G+. O3. $22.00

ANON. *My Father. A Poem.* (1836). NY. Mahlon Day. 64mo. woodcuts. 8 p. VG/wht pict wrp. H3. $45.00

ANON. *My Honey's ABC.* nd. London/Paris/NY. Raphael Tuck. rare. D1. $285.00

ANON. *Ned Valentine; or, The Honest Fisher Boy.* ca 1880. Am Baptist Pub. 24mo. ils. 91 p. VG-. S10. $25.00

ANON. *Needlepoint.* 1972. Sunset Books. pb. ils. G2. $6.00

ANON. *New Cries of London.* 1837. NY. Mahlon Day. 18mo. 24 p. prt wrp. M1. $200.00

ANON. *New Yorker Book of Dog Cartoons.* 1992. Knopf. 1st ed. VG+/VG+. O3. $12.00

ANON. *Nouvelle Methode D'Operations de Chirurgie...* 1693. Paris. Laurnet d'Houry. 12mo. 324 p. new full calf/raised bands. G7. $295.00

ANON. *Old Mother Hubbard.* (1905). Altemus. sm 12mo. 46 p. VG+/VG. S10. $55.00

ANON. *Orig Mother Goose Melodies.* 1880. Lee Shepard. ils Goodridge/50 silhouettes. VG. D1. $95.00

ANON. *Pebbles From the Sea-Shore; or, Lizzie's 1st Gleanings.* 1860. NY. 24mo. 4 pls. 26 p. gilt red cloth. VG. H3. $25.00

ANON. *Peter Rabbit & Jimmy Chipmunk.* (1918). Saalfield. ils Virginia Albert. 54 p. VG. S10. $25.00

ANON. *Pets & Toys.* (1918). Saalfield Muslin #242G. 16mo. 6 p. VG+/yel pict self wrp. D1. $42.00

ANON. *Picture of Life.* nd. (1830s). Williams Maynard. 48mo. ils. F/orange wrp. H3. $75.00

ANON. *Pictures of Animals.* nd. (1830s). Northampton. Metcalf. 48mo. woodcuts. 18 p. G/wht wrp. H3. $35.00

ANON. *Pioneer Life in the W.* 1859. Phil. later prt. 332 p. rebound half leather. D7. $100.00

ANON. *Ploughed Under: Story of an Indian Chief. Told by Himself.* 1881. NY. Fords Howard Hulbert. 1st ed. VG. L3. $450.00

ANON. *Poetic Present.* 1842. Northampton. Merrifield. 32mo. 24 p. F/wht pict wrp. H3. $50.00

ANON. *Prayers for Every Day.* (1860). London. miniature. 128 p. aeg. gilt full brn leather/metal clasp. H3. $225.00

ANON. *Pride of Peter Prim; or, Proverbs, That Suit Young & Old.* 1829. Cooperstown. Phinney. 18mo. 32 p. wrp. M1. $250.00

ANON. *Proceedings of City Council of Boston...Death of Lincoln.* 1865. Boston. royal 8vo. 35 p. aeg. gray cloth. G. T3. $29.00

ANON. *Railway Rag Book.* ca 1900. London. Dean Rag Book 150. 16mo. VG. D1. $200.00

ANON. *Red Squirrel.* 1830. Northampton. 64mo. woodcuts. 8 p. F/pict wrp. H3. $50.00

ANON. *Riddle Book.* 1824. New Haven. Babcock. 48mo. woodcuts. 23 p. G/pict wrp. H3. $35.00

ANON. *Rome: As Seen by a New-Yorker in 1843-44.* 1845. NY. 8vo. fld map. 216 p. O2. $50.00

ANON. *Rules for Government of Prison of Allegheny Co.* 1892. Pittsburgh. 12mo. orig cloth. G. D7. $40.00

ANON. *Shepherd Boy.* 1837. Northampton. Metcalf. 48mo. woodcuts. 18 p. VG/double wrp. H3. $45.00

ANON. *Slave's Friend. No 1.* nd. (1850s). NY. 48mo. 12 p. F/gr wrp. H3. $75.00

ANON. *Slave's Friend. No 2.* nd. (1850s). NY. 48mo. 16 p. F/wht wrp. H3. $100.00

ANON. *Snow Storm: A Scottish Tale.* 1823. NY. 1st ed? 12mo. prt wrp. M1. $125.00

ANON. *Something for a Wet Day.* 1897. Dutton. 18mo. ils. 12 p. color pict brds. VG. S10. $40.00

ANON. *Spin Top Spin & Rosemarie & Thyme.* 1930. Macmillan. 2nd prt. ils Elsa Eisgruber. 30 p. G+. S10. $75.00

ANON. *Stories & Pictures for Children.* 1847. Pittsfield, MA. Werden. 64mo. woodcuts. 8 p. NF/pict wrp. H3. $50.00

ANON. *Stories About Dogs.* 1850. Concord, NH. Rufus Merrill. 48mo. 16 p. F/prt wrp. H3. $50.00

ANON. *Stories for Children About Whales.* 1843. Concord, NH. Rufus Merrill. 48mo. woodcuts. 16 p. F/tan wrp. H3. $100.00

ANON. *Story of State (OH) Columbus Centennial.* 1912. Columbus. 1st ed. 32 p. G/wrp. D7. $35.00

ANON. *Sun Flower or Poetical Blossoms.* nd. (1830s). New Haven. S Babcock. 48mo. woodcuts. 16 p. VG/bl wrp. H3. $35.00

ANON. *Sweets for Leisure Hours; or, Flowers of Instruction.* nd. (1830s). New Haven. S Babcock. 48mo. woodcuts. 16 p. VG/pict wrp. H3. $35.00

ANON. *Swiss Family Robinson.* nd. Doran. 12 color ils. G. L1. $30.00

ANON. *Thoughts on Importance of Manners of Great to Gen Soc.* 1788. Phil. Dobson. 4th ed. 12mo. 81 p. calf/rebacked. H9. $150.00

ANON. *Three Bears.* (1905). Altemus. 12mo. 45 p. VG+/VG. S10. $55.00

ANON. *Tiny Story Book.* nd. (1830s). Charlestown. GW Hobbs. 64mo. 17 color ils. gr brds. VG. H3. $75.00

ANON. *TN Walking Horse.* ca 1950. Lewisburg. TN Walking Horse Breeders' Assn. ils. VG/wrp. O3. $18.00

ANON. *Tommy Tinker's Stories. Cross-Patch.* nd. (1850s). Phil. Davis Porter. 24mo. 10 p. F. H3. $100.00

ANON. *Visit to the Circus.* 1986. London. Bracken Books. ils. VG/VG. L1. $15.00

ANON. *Voices From an Earlier Am.* 1980. np. 1st ed. tall 8vo. pumpkin cloth. teg. F/tan slipcase. A11. $35.00

ANON. *Wanderings Over Bible Lands & Seas.* 1866. London. 8vo. 301 p. gilt cloth. O2. $135.00

ANON. *Who's Who in Arabian Horses.* 1988. Agoura Hills. ltd ed. 1st ed. VG. O3. $25.00

ANON. *Woman's Handiwork in Modern Homes.* 1881. np. ils/pls. cloth. G2. $50.00

ANON. *Yel Dwarf.* ca 1880. McLoughlin. ils Howard. 16 p. VG/ils wrp. D1. $120.00

ANON. *Young Lady's Equestrian Manual.* 1839. New Orleans. 18mo. 102 p. cloth. M1. $275.00

ANON. *10 Little Colored Boys.* 1942. Howell Soskin Pub. oblong 4to. ils Emery I Gondor. sbdg. VG. D1. $200.00

ANON. *10 Little Nigger Boys.* 1940s. London. Juvenile Productions Ltd. VG/pict wrp. D1. $250.00

ANSON, Adrian C. *Ball Player's Career.* 1900. Era Pub. 1st ed. photos. G+/sans. P8. $500.00

ANSON, George. *Voyage Round the World...* 1748. London. Anson/Knapton. 1st ed. thick quarto. fold pls/maps. contemporary calf. H9. $5,750.00

ANSON, George. *Voyage Round the World...* 1748. London. Knapton. 3rd ed. 3 fld charts. contemporary calf/rebacked. H9. $750.00

ANSON, Jay. *Amityville Horror.* 1977. Prentice Hall. 1st ed. author's 1st book. NF/NF. N3. $45.00

ANSTED, D.T. *Ionian Islands in the Yr 1863.* 1863. London. ils/maps. new half brn calf/raised bands. O2. $550.00

ANTHOLOGY. *Best Am Essays 1989.* 1989. Tichnor Fields. AP. sgn Robert Stone. F/prt gray wrp. C4. $65.00

ANTHOLOGY. *Best Am Short Stories 1959.* 1959. Houghton Mifflin. 1st ed. NF/NF. B4. $125.00

ANTHOLOGY. *Children's Hour.* 1889. LP Miller. ils Palmer Cox/EH Garrett/L Wain/others. 159 p. G. S10. $35.00

ANTHOLOGY. *Children's Story Garden.* 1920. Lippincott. 1st ed. ils Wireman. 247 p. VG. S10. $30.00

ANTHOLOGY. *Chit Chat: Bright Stories & Pictures for Little Folks.* ca 1880. Grand Union Tea Co. sm 4to. pict brds. G. S10. $55.00

ANTHOLOGY. *Contact Collection of Contemporary Writers.* 1925. Paris. 3 Mtns Pr. 1st ed. sq octavo. 338 p. prt gray wrp. H5. $1,250.00

ANTHOLOGY. *Fantasy Reader. 7th World Fantasy Convention Book.* 1981. Pendragon. 1st ed. 1/1000. F/F. N3. $125.00

ANTHOLOGY. *Four & 20 Fairy Tales.* (1921). Whitman. ils Florence M Pettee. gr cloth/pict label. VG. S10. $25.00

ANTHOLOGY. *Free Fire Zone. Short Stories by Vietnam Veterans.* 1973. Coventry. 1st Casualty. true 1st ed. NF/wrp. L3. $100.00

ANTHOLOGY. *Granta 11.* (1984). London. Granta. 1st ed. F/pict wrp. B3. $20.00

ANTHOLOGY. *Hist of Game Strains.* ca 1955. Gaffney, SC. De Camp. sm 4to. 241 p. VG. E5. $85.00

ANTHOLOGY. *Little Bright Eyes.* 1890. Juvenile Pub. sm 4to. ils Palmer Cox/others. G. S10. $45.00

ANTHOLOGY. *Little Lads.* 1906 (1904). Saalfield. ils. bl/tan decor gr cloth. VG. S10. $25.00

ANTHOLOGY. *Murder CA Style.* 1987. St Martin. ARC. 10 contributors sgn. RS. F/F. S5. $40.00

ANTHOLOGY. *New Crimes 2.* 1991. NY. Carroll Graf. 1st Am ed. sgn Melville/Pronzini/Vachss. F/F. S5. $35.00

ANTHOLOGY. *Photographic Hist of the Civil War.* 1911. NY. Review of Reviews. 10 vols. teg. orig bl cloth. VG. H5. $600.00

ANTHOLOGY. *Rose of the Valley.* 1839. Cincinnati. Moore. 24 p. orig paper wrp. D7. $50.00

ANTHOLOGY. *Sapatqayn. 20th-Century Nez Perce Artists.* 1991. Seattle/Lewiston. NW Interpretive Assn/Confluence Pr. hc. sgns. F/F. L3. $200.00

ANTHOLOGY. *Soldiers & Civilians: Am at War & at Home.* 1986. Bantam. 1st ed. F/F. C4. $50.00

ANTHOLOGY. *Standard Fairy Tales.* ca 1890. Porter Coates. ils Dore/Cruikshang. 525 p. decor rust cloth. VG. S10. $50.00

ANTHOLOGY. *World of Modern Fiction.* (1966). Simon Schuster. 1st ed. 2 vols. NF/box. B3. $75.00

ANTHOLOGY. *World Unsuspected.* (1987). Chapel Hill. 1st ed. F/F. B3. $25.00

ANTHONY, David. *Long Hard Cure.* (1979). London. Crime Club. 1st ed. F/F. B9. $15.00

ANTHONY, David. *Midnight Lady & the Mourning Man.* (1970). London. Crime Club. 1st ed. F/dj. B9. $25.00

ANTHONY, David. *Organization.* (1971). London. Crime Club. 1st ed. F/dj. B9. $20.00

ANTHONY, Florence. *Cruelty.* 1973. Boston. 1st ed. presentation inscr. F/NF clip. A11. $75.00

ANTHONY, Irvin. *Paddlewheels & Pistols.* nd. Grosset Dunlap. reprint of 1929 ed. royal 8vo. 329 p. VG. D3. $25.00

ANTHONY, Katharine. *Susan B Anthony: Her Personal Hist & Her Era.* 1954. Doubleday. 1st ed. 8vo. 521 p. VG. V3. $15.00

ANTHONY, Piers. *Hard Sell.* 1990. Tafford. 1st ed. F/F. F4. $18.00

ANTHONY, Piers. *On a Pale Horse.* 1983. Ballantine. 1st ed. F/F clip. N3. $15.00

ANTHONY, Piers. *Phaze Doubt.* 1990. Putnam. 1st ed. 7th of Apprentice Adept series. F/F. N3. $15.00

ANTHONY, Piers. *Question Quest.* 1991. Morrow. 1st ed. RS. 14th Xanth novel. F/F. N3. $15.00

ANTHONY, Piers. *Wielding a Red Sword.* 1986. Ballantine. AP of 1st ed. F/wrp. N3. $20.00

ANTHONY & LEHMAN. *Quiltmakers' Big Book of Pattern Grids.* 1980. np. wrp. G2. $15.00

ANTHONY & MARGROFF. *Chimaera's Copper.* 1990. NY. Tor. 1st ed. F/F/wrp-around band. N3. $20.00

ANTIEAU, Chester J. *Rights of Our Fathers.* 1968. Vienna. Coiner. M11. $35.00

ANTON, Ferdinand. *Art of Ancient Peru.* (1972). Putnam. 1st Am ed. sm folio. 368 p. F3. $150.00

ANTON & DOCKSTADER. *Pre-Columbian Art & Later Indian Tribal Arts.* (1968). Abrams. sq royal 8vo. 264 p. cloth. NF/pict dj. D3. $60.00

ANTONIUS, Brother; see Everson, William.

ANTONIUS, George. *Arab Awakening: Story of Arab National Movement.* 1945. Hamish Hamilton. 2nd prt. 472 p. gilt bl cloth. G. M7. $35.00

ANTUNES, Antonio Lobo. *Explanation of the Birds.* 1991. Grove Weidenfeld. 1st ed. trans Richard Zenith. F/F. A14. $30.00

APIANUS, Petrus. *La Cosmographie...* 1553. Paris. quarto. quarter sheep/marbled brds. VG. H5. $3,750.00

APIANUS, Petrus. *Quadrans Apiani Astronomicus...* 1532. Ingolstadt. 1st ed. folio. ils/woodcuts. NF. H5. $7,500.00

APICIUS. *Cooking & Dining in Imperial Rome.* 1936. Chicago. Walter Hill. 1st Eng ed. 1/500. 4to. 310 p. NF. E5. $465.00

APOLLONIO, Umbro. *Campigli.* 1958. Italy. ltd ed. VG/VG. A1. $50.00

APPERLEY, Charles James. *Life of a Sportsman. By Nimrod.* 1914. London. Kegan Paul. lg octavo. 400 p. Riviere red morocco. NF. H5. $1,500.00

APPERLEY, Charles James. *Life of John Mytton, Esq... By Nimrod.* 1877. London. Routledge. 4th ed. octavo. Bayntum morocco. VG. H5. $850.00

APPIAH, Peggy. *Children of Ananse.* 1968. London. Evans. 1st ed. NF/wrp. B2. $35.00

APPLE, Max. *Free Agents.* (1984). Harper Row. 1st ed. VG/VG clip. B3. $25.00

APPLE, Max. *Oranging of Am.* 1986. London. Faber. PBO. F/wrp ils Brian Grimwood. A11. $15.00

APPLE, Max. *3 Stories.* 1983. Dallas. 1/226. sgn. gr cloth w/prt labels. F/acetate. A11. $45.00

APPLEBY, John. *Arms of Venus.* (1951). Coward McCann. VG+/dj. B9. $6.00

APPLETON, Victor II. *Tom Swift Jr & His Jetmarine.* 1954. Grosset. VG/dj. M2. $15.00

APPLETON, Victor II. *Tom Swift Jr in the Race for the Moon.* 1958. Grosset. 1st ed. F/dj. M2. $15.00

APPLETON, Victor. *Don Sturdy on the Ocean Bottom.* 1931. Grosset. VG. M2. $15.00

APPLETON, Victor. *Tom Swift & His Magnetic Silencer.* 1941. Whitman. Big Little Book. 434 p. G. scarce. M20. $55.00

APPLETON, Victor. *Tom Swift & His Motorcycle.* 1910. Grosset. VG. M2. $15.00

APPLETON, Victor. *Tom Swift & His Ocean Airport.* 1934. Whitman. 12mo. VG+/G. A8. $5.00

APPLETON, Victor. *Tom Swift & His Talking Pictures.* 1928. Grosset Dunlap. 216 p. VG/dj. M20. $50.00

APPLETON. *Appleton's Dictionary of Machines, Mechanics, Engine Work...* 1851. NY/Phil. 2 vols. brn cloth/leather spine. B30. $125.00

APPLETON. *Appleton's General Guide to the US & Canada.* 1890. NY. Appleton. sm 8vo. maps/charts/ils. 554 p. bl cloth. H9. $85.00

APPLETON. *Appleton's Hand-Book of Am Travel.* 1871. Appleton. sm quarto. fld maps. 284 p. H9. $75.00

APPLETON. *Appleton's Hand-Book of Am Travel. S Tour.* 1876. NY/London. Appleton/Sampson Low. revised ed. 8vo. 269 p. H9. $225.00

APPLETON. *Appleton's Hand-Book of Am Travel. W Tour.* 1873. NY. Appleton. revised ed. sm 4to. 321 p. rose cloth. lacks 2 maps. H9. $135.00

APPLETON. *Appleton's Ils Hand-Book of Am Travel.* 1857. NY/London. Appleton/Trubner. 8vo. maps. rose cloth. H9. $250.00

APPLETON. *Appleton's New & Complete US Guide Book for Travellers.* 1854. NY. Appleton. 2 vols in 1. 12mo. 12 fld map sheets. gilt red cloth. H9. $350.00

APPLETON. *Appleton's Railroad & Steamboat Companion.* 1848. NY. Appleton. 1st ed. 12mo. 30 maps on 19 fld sheets. red cloth. H9. $325.00

APPLETON. *Appleton's Railway & Steam Navigation Guide.* August 1864. Appleton. 12mo. 75 railway maps. VG/prt paper wrp. H9. $165.00

APSLEY, Lady. *Bridleways Through Hist.* 1948. London. Hutchinson. 2nd/revised ed. G+/G+. O3. $30.00

APTHEKER, Bettina. *Academic Rebellion in the US.* (1972). Citadel. stated 1st. 218 p. F/NF. A7. $20.00

APTHEKER, Herbert. *Am Civil War.* (1961). NY. Internat. 22 p. wrp. A7. $12.00

APTHEKER, Herbert. *Czechoslovakia & Counter-Revolution.* 1969. New Outlook. 30 p. wrp. A7. $10.00

APTHEKER, Herbert. *Heavenly Days in Dixie.* 1974. NY. Political Affairs. 31 p. wrp. A7. $10.00

APTHEKER, Herbert. *Mission to Hanoi.* (1966). Internat Pub. 1st ed. 128 p. F/dj. A7. $35.00

APTHEKER, Herbert. *One Continual Cry.* 1965. Humanities. sgn. 150 p. dj. A7. $40.00

APULEIUS. *Cupid & Psyche.* 1903. London. ils Jessie Mothersol. full vellum. G+. A1. $125.00

ARAGO, Francois. *Biographies of Distinguished Scientific Men.* 1859. Boston. Ticknor Fields. 2 vols. F. B14. $50.00

ARAGON, Louis. *Red Front.* (1933). Chapel Hill. 1st ed. 1/200. trans EE Cummings. F/prt red wrp. B24. $325.00

ARAMATA, H. *Birds of the World.* 1987. np. lg 4to. ils/index. 239 p. dj. O7. $23.50

ARBEED, Lucille. *Baalbek. Hist & Description.* 1941. Beyrouth (Lebanon). 16mo. 10 pls. 64 p. prt pink wrp. VG. H3. $40.00

ARBUCKLE, John Twobirds. *Singing Words.* 1978. Lincoln. Word Services. 1st ed. sgn. ils brds. F. L3. $65.00

ARCEO, Francisco. *De Recta Curandorum Vulnerum Ratione...* 1658. Amsterdam. Petrus Vanden Berge. 3rd ed. w/engraved title leaf. G7. $750.00

ARCHER, Jeffrey. *As the Crow Flies.* 1991. Harper Collins. Lg Prt BC. VG. A16. $12.50

ARCHER, Jeffrey. *Matter of Honor.* (1986). NY. Linden. 1st ed. VG/VG. B3. $20.00

ARCHER, Jeffrey. *Prodigal Daughter.* (1982). NY. Linden. 1st ed. VG/VG. B3. $15.00

ARCHER, Jeffrey. *Shall We Tell the President?* 1977. Viking. 1st ed. author's 2nd novel. F/F. T2. $9.00

ARCINIEGAS, German. *Knight of El Dorado.* 1942. Viking. 1st ed. 301 p. map ep. F3. $20.00

ARD, William. *Blonde & Johnny Malloy.* 1958. NY. Popular Lib. PBO. NF/wrp. A11. $35.00

ARD, William. *Perfect Frame.* 1951. Morrow. 1st ed. author's 1st mystery. F/VG. M15. $50.00

ARD, William. *Sins of Billy Serene.* 1960. Derby, CT. NF/wrp ils & sgn Robert Maquire. A11. $45.00

ARDIZZONE, Edward. *Book for Eleanor Farjeon: Tribute to Her Life & Work...* 1966. NY. Walck. 1st Am ed. 184 p. VG/G+. A3. $25.00

ARDIZZONE, Edward. *Tim & Ginger.* 1965. Walck. ils. VG+/dj. M20. $30.00

ARDIZZONE, Edward. *Young Ardizzone: Autobiographical Fragment.* 1970. Macmillan. 1st Am ed. 144 p. olive brds. F/VG. T5. $55.00

ARDIZZONE, Tony. *Evening News.* 1986. Athens, GA. 1st ed. sgn. F/F. A11. $30.00

ARENAS, Reinaldo. *Farewell to the Sea.* 1986. Viking/Penguin. 1st ed. trans from Spanish. rem mk. NF/NF. A14. $25.00

ARENS, W. *Man-Eating Myth: Anthropology & Anthropophagy.* 1979. NY. Oxford. 1st ed. 8vo. 206 p. F/VG+. A2. $15.00

ARENSBERG, Ann. *Group Sex.* 1986. NY. Knopf. AP. VG/prt yel wrp. Q1. $30.00

ARGENTI, Philip P. *Expedition of Col Fabvier to Chios.* 1933. London. presentation slip. Blackmer's copy. 383 p. uncut. O2. $200.00

ARGENTI, Philip P. *Occupation of Chios by the Genoese & Their Administration...* 1958. Cambridge. 3 vols thick 8vo. cloth. dj. O2. $475.00

ARGHEZI, Tudor. *Selected Poems.* 1976. Princeton. 1st ed. F/F. V1. $20.00

ARGYLL, Duke of. *Primeval Man: Examination of Some Recent Speculations.* 1871. NY. Rutledge. 200 p. purple cloth. NF. S9. $10.00

ARIES, Philippe. *Hour of Our Death.* 1981. Knopf. 1st Am ed. thick 8vo. blk cloth. VG/dj. G1. $27.50

ARISTOPHANES. *Lysistrata.* (1926). London. Fanfrolico. 1/725. ils Norman Lindsay. teg. gilt bl calf. K1. $350.00

ARKANSAS QUILTERS GUILD INC. *AR Quilts: AR Warmth.* 1988. np. ils. cloth. G2. $25.00

ARLEN, Michael. *Hell! Said the Duchess.* (1934). London. Heinemann. 1st ed. VG. B4. $100.00

ARLOW, Jacob A. *Legacy of Sigmund Freud.* 1956. IUP. 1st ed. 12mo. 96 p. cloth. G1. $20.00

ARLT, Roberto. *Seven Madmen.* 1984. Boston. Godine. 1st Am ed. trans from Spanish. NF/NF. A14. $25.00

ARMER, Laura Adams. *Dk Circle of Branches.* 1933. Longman Gr. 1st ed. 212 p. VG. P2. $20.00

ARMES, Jay J. *Jay J Armes, Investigator.* 1976. Macmillan. 1st ed. VG/dj. A16. $20.00

ARMES & NOLAN. *Jay J Armes, Investigator.* (1976). Macmillan. 2nd prt. presentation/sgn. dj. A7. $12.00

ARMITAGE, Angus. *Copernicus: Founder of Modern Astronomy.* 1957. NY. Yoseloff. G+/fair. N2. $6.00

ARMITAGE, Flora. *Desert & the Stars.* 1955. Holt. 2nd prt. photos. 318 p. gilt brn brds. NF/NF. M7. $18.00

ARMITAGE, Merle. *Art of Edward Weston.* 1932. NY. E Weyhe. 1st ed. 1/500. sm folio. sgn Weston. D3. $600.00

ARMITAGE, Merle. *Pagans, Conquistadores, Heroes & Martyrs.* 1960. Fresno. Academy Guild. 1/1500. ils. M/dj. O6. $75.00

ARMOR, William C. *Lives of the Governors of PA...Incidental Hist...1609-1872.* 1872. Phil. 528 p. orig cloth. VG-. A17. $25.00

ARMROYD, George. *Connected View of Whole Internal Navigation of the US...* 1971. Burt Franklin. facsimile reprint. 617 p. F/sans. B19. $25.00

ARMSTRONG, Campbell. *Mambo.* 1990. Harper. ARC. sgn. w/promo & publicity photo. F/NF. S5. $35.00

ARMSTRONG, Joe C.W. *From Sea to Sea: Art & Discovery Maps of Canada.* 1982. Scarborough. Fleet. 38 full-p maps. half leather. M. O6. $75.00

ARMSTRONG, Louis. *Satchmo.* (1955). Signet. 1st pb prt. VG. A7. $8.00

ARMSTRONG, R. Warwick. *Atlas of HI.* 1973. Honolulu. 222 p. NF/wrp. O6. $20.00

ARMSTRONG, Virginia Winmill. *Gone Away w/the Winmills.* 1977. Leamington. 1st ed. VG/VG. O3. $35.00

ARMSTRONG, W.H. *Barefoot in the Grass: Story of Grandma Moses.* 1970. Doubleday. 1st ed. 96 p. VG/G. A3. $15.00

ARMSTRONG, William Clinton. *Patriotic Poems of NJ.* 1906. NJ Soc Sons of Am Revolution. 8vo. pls. 248 p. VG. B11. $60.00

ARMSTRONG, William. *Tale of Tawny & Dingo.* 1979. Harper Row. 1st ed. 44 p. F/G+. P2. $15.00

ARNDT, Karl. *Treaty of Amity & Commerce of 1785...Prussia & the USA.* 1977. Munchen. Heinz Moos. 1st German trans/facsimile French & Am texts. M/dj. O6. $45.00

ARNESON, Ben Albert. *Elements of Constitutional Law.* 1928. Harper. worn. M11. $35.00

ARNESON, D.J. *Strange UFO Stories.* 1979. Watermill. 1st ed. VG/wrp. M2. $12.00

ARNO, Peter. *Whoops, Dearie!* (1927). Simon Schuster. 1st ed. 8vo. NF/VG+. B20. $100.00

ARNOLD, Edwin. *Japonica.* 1891. NY. 1st ed. 128 p. teg. pict gr cloth. VG. H3. $60.00

ARNOLD, Edwin. *Voyage of Ithobal.* 1901. NY. Dilligham. 1st ed. ils A Lumley. gilt navy cloth. NF. V1. $25.00

ARNOLD, Eve. *In China.* 1983. Knopf. folio. 201 p. NF/dj. W1. $45.00

ARNOLD, H.J.P. *Herbert Ponting: Another World.* (1975). London. Sidgwick Jackson. 1st ed. 4to. 128 p. F/F. A2. $25.00

ARNOLD, Isaac Newton. *Life of Abraham Lincoln.* 1887. Chicago. McClurg. 4th ed. 471 p. cloth. VG. M8. $45.00

ARNOLD, Julian B. *Giants in Dressing Gowns.* 1942. Chicago. Argus. 1st ed. 242 p. gilt dk bl cloth. NF. M7. $45.00

ARNOLD, Matthew. *Civilization in the US.* 1888. Boston. 12mo. 192 p. VG/coarse paper wrp. T3. $26.00

ARNOLD, Oren. *Wildlife in the SW.* (1936). Dallas. 2nd prt. 274 p. pict leatherette. F. scarce. A17. $25.00

ARNOLD, R. Ross. *Indian Wars of ID.* 1932. Caldwell. Caxton. 1st ed. ils. 268 p. VG+. B20. $75.00

ARNOLD, Ralph. *First Big Oil Hunt: Venezuela 1911-16.* 1960. NY. 1st ed. 353 p. gilt gr cloth. F/dj. H3. $40.00

ARNOLD, William. *Shadowland.* 1978. McGraw Hill. 1st ed. dj. N2. $7.50

ARNOT, R. Page. *There Are No Aryans.* ca 1943. London. Labour Monthly. 32 p. wrp. A7. $10.00

ARORA, David. *Mushrooms Demystified.* 1986 (1979). Berkeley. 2nd ed. 959 p. M. B26. $19.00

ARP, Jean. *Arp on Arp.* 1972. Viking. 1st ed. w/promo photo. F/F. B2. $65.00

ARRILAGA, Francisco. *Cardiacos Negros.* 1912. Buenos Aires. orig thesis w/6 additional reprints. half calf. G7. $295.00

ARRIOLA, Jorge Luis. *Galvez en la Encrucijada.* 1961. Mexico. 1st ed. 1/1000. inscr. 467 p. wrp. F3. $25.00

ARSANES. *Orations of Arsanes Agaynst Philip the Trecherous Kyng...* (1560). London. John Day. sm 8vo in fours. rebound full calf. O2. $1,250.00

ARTHUR, David Stuart. *Oasis Project.* 1981. Sword & Stone Pr. 1st ed. F/dj. N3. $10.00

ARTHUR, George. *Life of Lord Kitchener.* 1920. London. Macmillan. 1st ed. 8vo. 3 vols. VG. A2. $60.00

ARTHUR & CARPENTER. *Hist of GA.* 1852. Phil. Lippincott/Grambo. 1st ed. 331 p. cloth. VG. D3. $35.00

ARTMAN & HALL. *Beauties & Achievements of the Blind.* 1859. Auburn. not 1st ed. VG. N2. $20.00

ARTZYBASHEFF, Boris. *Fairy Shoemaker & Other Fairy Poems.* 1928. Macmillan. 1st ed. 115 p. VG/poor. P2. $70.00

ARTZYBASHEFF, Boris. *Seven Simeons.* 1938. Viking. 1st ed. 4to. gr cloth. VG/dj. D1. $70.00

ASBJORNSEN, Peter Christen. *E of the Sun & W of the Moon.* nd. (1914). NY. 1st Am trade ed. presentation. 25 mtd color pls. Sutcliffe bdg. F. H5. $2,000.00

ASBJORNSEN, Peter Christen. *E of the Sun & W of the Moon.* 1914. London. Hodder Stoughton. 1st trade ed. ils Nielsen/25 color pls. VG/slipcase. H5. $1,800.00

ASCH, Brian. *Who's Who in Science Fiction.* 1976. NY. 1st ed. VG/VG. B5. $30.00

ASCH, Sholem. *Apostle: Novel Based on Life of St Paul.* 1943. Putnam. 1st ed. inscr presentation. trans Maurice Samuel. VG/dj. E3. $40.00

ASCH, Sholem. *Nazarene: Novel Based on Life of Christ.* 1939. Putnam. 1st/special gift ed. 1/500. sgn. NF/dj. E3. $40.00

ASCH, Sholem. *Salvation.* 1951. Putnam. revised enlarged ed. 343 p. VG. S3. $19.00

ASCHAM, Roger. *Schoolemaster; or, Playne & Perfite Way of Teaching...* 1589. London. Abell Jeffes. 5th ed. mottled calf-backed marbled brds. B24. $2,500.00

ASCHERSON, Neal. *Polish August: Self-Limiting Revolution.* (1982). Viking. 1st ed. NF/VG. A7. $15.00

ASH & MURRAY. *Serial Publications Containing Medical Classics.* 1979. Bethany, CT. Antiquarium. 2nd ed. 169 p. gr cloth. F. S9. $20.00

ASHBERY, John. *April Galleons.* 1987. NY. 1st ed. sgn. F/NF. V1. $25.00

ASHBERY, John. *Rivers & Mtns.* 1966. Holt. 1/1000. F/F. B2. $75.00

ASHBERY, John. *Shadow Train.* 1981. NY. 1st ed. sgn. F/ils wrp. A11. $20.00

ASHBY, N.B. *Riddle of the Sphinx.* 1890. Des Moines. Industrial Pub. 474 p. maroon brds. NF. B2. $150.00

ASHBY, Professor. *Viola: The Redeemed.* 1845. Boston. Gleason's Pub Hall. 1st ed. 8vo. 66 p. M1. $150.00

ASHE, Geoffrey. *King Arthur's Avalon: Story of Glastonbury.* 1958. np. 1st Am ed. VG+/dj. rare in this form. C1. $19.50

ASHE, Geoffrey. *King Arthur's Avalon: Story of Glastonbury.* 1992 (1958). np. new intro. F/dj. C1. $9.50

ASHE, Gordon; see Creasey, John.

ASHE, Mike. *Pendragon Chronicles.* nd. np. trade pb. VG+. C1. $9.00

ASHE & RAMPERSAND. *Days of Grace.* (1993). Knopf. 1st ed. F/NF. B3. $25.00

ASHEIM & GOLD. *Episcopacy in the Lutheran Church?* ca 1970. Phil. Fortress. xl. 261 p. H10. $15.00

ASHER, G.M. *Bibliographical & Hist Essay on Dutch Books & Phamplets...* 1854-67. NY. Norton. 5 parts in 1 vol. brds. O6. $150.00

ASHFORD, Jeffrey. *Crime Remembered.* (1988). St Martin. 1st Am ed. F/dj. B9. $10.00

ASHFORD, Jeffrey. *Forget What You Saw.* (1967). Walker. 1st ed. VG+/dj. B9. $6.50

ASHLEY, Clifford W. *Ashley Book of Knots.* 1944. Doubleday. G/dj. A16. $75.00

ASHMAN, Charles R. *Finest Judges Money Can Buy...* 1973. LA. Nash. M11. $15.00

ASHTON, Francis. *Alas, That Great City.* 1947. London. 1st ed. F/F. M2. $35.00

ASHTON, T.S. *Industrial Revolution 1760-1830.* (1960). London. Oxford. reprint of 1948 ed. 16mo. 167 p. A7. $10.00

ASHTOR, Eliyahu. *Jews of Moslem Spain.* 1973-84. JPS. 3 vols. notes/maps. VG+/VG. S3. $70.00

ASHWAL, Stephen. *Founders of Child Neurology.* 1990. San Francisco. Norman. 935 p. G7. $105.00

ASIMOV, Isaac. *Asimov Chronicles.* 1989. Dark Harvest. ltd ed. 1/500. sgn. as new/slipcase. M2. $100.00

ASIMOV, Isaac. *Asimov's Biographical Encyclopedia of Science & Technology.* nd. np. xl. ils. 662 p. VG. S9. $5.00

ASIMOV, Isaac. *Asimov's Galaxy: Reflections on SF.* 1989. Doubleday. 1st ed. M/M. T2. $14.50

ASIMOV, Isaac. *Currents of Space.* 1952. Doubleday. 1st ed. 3rd Trantorian Empire series. NF/NF. Q1. $125.00

ASIMOV, Isaac. *Foundations's Edge.* (1982). Doubleday. UP. NF/prt wrp. B3. $110.00

ASIMOV, Isaac. *In Memory Yet Gr.* 1979. Doubleday. 1st ed. F/F. M2. $35.00

ASIMOV, Isaac. *Inside the Atom.* 1961. Abelard Schuman. 2nd revised ed/1st prt. F/dj. N3. $15.00

ASIMOV, Isaac. *Lucky Starr & the Rings of Saturn.* 1958. Doubleday. 1st ed. VG/worn. M2. $125.00

ASIMOV, Isaac. *Nemesis.* (1989). Doubleday. 1st ed. VG/VG. B3. $10.00

ASIMOV, Isaac. *Puzzles of the Blk Widowers.* 1990. London. Doubleday. 1st ed. F/F. T2. $16.00

ASIMOV, Isaac. *Robot Dreams.* 1986. Berkley. 1st ed. F/wrp. M2. $10.00

ASIMOV, Isaac. *Robots & Empire.* 1985. Doubleday. 1st ed. sgn. F/F. F4. $45.00

ASIMOV, Isaac. *Robots of Dawn.* 1983. Doubleday. 1st trade ed. F/F. N3. $15.00

ASIMOV, Isaac. *Shaping of N Am.* 1973. Houghton Mifflin. 1st ed. F/F. F4. $20.00

ASIMOV, Isaac. *Stars, Like Dust.* 1951. Doubleday. 1st ed. 2nd Trantorian Empire series. NF/NF. Q1. $150.00

ASIMOV, Isaac. *Tomorrow's Voices.* 1984. Dial. 1st ed. 15 stories. F/F. N3. $20.00

ASIMOV & DOLE. *Planets for Man.* 1964. Random. 1st ed. fld chart. F/VG+. S9. $8.00

ASIMOV & GREENBERG. *Visions of Fantasy: Tales From the Masters.* 1989. Doubleday. 1st ed. F/F. T2. $16.00

ASIMOV & JEPPSON. *Laughing Space-Funny SF.* 1982. Houghton Mifflin. galleys mk Author's Set in pencil. B4. $200.00

ASIMOV & SILVERBERG. *Positronic Man.* (1993). Doubleday. AP. F/wrp. B4. $35.00

ASKINS, Charles. *Am Shotgun.* 1910. NY. Outing Pub. 1st ed. 321 p. tan cloth. H9. $55.00

ASPIRIN, Robert. *Another Fine Myth...* (1978). Norfolk. Donning Co. 1st book in series. F/wrp. B4. $50.00

ASPIRIN, Robert. *Myth Inc Link.* (1986). Norfolk. Donning Co. 1/1200. sgn. ils/sgn Foglio. 7th in series. M/slipcase. B4. $45.00

ASPIRIN, Robert. *Myth-Nomers & Im-per-vections.* (1987). Norfolk. Donning Co. 1/1200. sgn. ils/sgn Foglio. 8th in series. M/slipcase. B4. $50.00

ASPIRIN, Robert. *Mything Persons.* (1984). Norfolk. Donning Co. 1st ed. 1/1200. sgn. ils/sgn Foglio. M/slipcase. B4. $45.00

ASPLER & PAPE. *Chain Reaction.* 1978. Viking. 1st ed. F/F. F4. $16.00

ASPRIN, Robert. *Cold Cash War.* 1977. London. NEL. 1st ed. author's 1st book. F/F. N3. $15.00

ASQUITH, Cynthia. *This Mortal Coil.* 1947. Arkham. 1st ed. F/F. M2. $80.00

ASQUITH, Cynthia. *Treasure Ship.* 1926. Scribner. 1st thus ed. VG. M18. $40.00

ASQUITH, Cynthia. *Treasure Ship: Book of Prose & Verse.* nd. London. Partridge. sm 4to. decor red cloth. VG. S10. $35.00

ASSN FOR CHILDHOOD EDUCATION. *Sung Under the Silver Umbrella.* 1939 (1935). Macmillan. ils Dorothy Lathrop. rose cloth. VG-. T5. $25.00

ASTOR, John Jacob. *Journey in Other Worlds: Romance of the Future.* 1894. NY. Appleton. 1st ed. octavo. 476 p. bl cloth. NF. B24. $165.00

ATALIE, Princess. *Earth Speaks.* 1940. NY. Revell. 1st ed. inscr. gilt brds. VG. L3. $100.00

ATATURK, Mustapha Kemal. *Speech Delivered by Ghazi...Oct 1927.* 1929. Leipzig. thick 8vo. Harry Howard's copy. lacks map. O2. $60.00

ATHEARN, Robert G. *Mythic W in 20th-Century Am.* (1986). KS U. 1st ed. F/F. A18. $25.00

ATHERTON, Gertrude. *Adventures of a Novelist.* (1932). London. 1st Eng ed. 575 p. cloth. VG. D3. $25.00

ATHERTON, Gertrude. *CA: An Intimate Hist.* 1914. NY. 1st ed. 329 p. VG. D3. $25.00

ATHERTON, Gertrude. *Golden Gate Country.* (1945). Golden Gate Country. 1st ed. 256 p. cloth. D3. $15.00

ATHERTON, Gertrude. *Rezanov.* 1906. NY. 1st ed. 320 p. VG. D3. $25.00

ATHERTON, Gertude. *Blk Oxen.* nd. Grosset. photoplay ed. VG/worn. M2. $12.00

ATIYA, Aziz. *Crusates: Historiography & Bibliography.* 1962. IN U. as new. C1. $8.50

ATKIN, Ronald. *Maintain the Right: Hist of NW Mounted Police, 1873-1900.* (1973). John Day. 1st ed. 8vo. 400 p. F/VG. A2. $20.00

ATKINS, Elizabeth Howard. *Treasures of the Medranos.* 1957. Parnassus. 112 p. F/NF clip. B19. $10.00

ATKINS, John Black. *War in Cuba. Experiences of Englishman w/US Army.* 1899. London. Smith Elder. 1st ed. 12mo. 291 p. red cloth. scarce. B11. $75.00

ATKINS, Meg Elizabeth. *Palimpsest.* (1981). London. Quartet. 1st ed. F/F. B9. $7.50

ATKINSON, Barry. *New Angles for the Angler.* (1966). NY. 191 p. dj. A17. $9.50

ATKINSON, George Francis. *Studies of Am Fungi...* 1903. Holt. 2nd ed. 322 p. H10. $22.50

ATKINSON, Herbert. *Cockfighting & Game Fowl...* 1986. Liss. Nimrod. 10 color pls. 253 p. M. H10. $45.00

ATKINSON, Linda. *Mother Jones: Most Dangerous Woman in Am.* ca 1978. Crown. ils/photos. G. V4. $8.00

ATKINSON, Robert E. *Spot Gardens: A Guide...* ca 1973. NY. McKay. 1st ed. 277 p. dj. H10. $9.50

ATKINSON, Samuel C. *Atkinson's Casket or Gems of Literature, Wit & Sentiment.* 1836. Phil. Atkinson. thick octavo. pls/fld map/woodcuts. new morocco. H9. $1,200.00

ATKINSON, Thomas Witlam. *Oriental & W Siberia.* ca 1880. Phil. Potter. xl. 12mo. ils. 483 p. VG. W1. $45.00

ATLEE, Philip; see Philips, James Atlee.

ATTROPS, Gosta. *De Tre Musketorerna och Andra Essayer.* 1938. Stockholm. 1st Swedish ed. 159 p. uncut. VG/tan wrp. M7. $45.00

ATTWATER, Donald. *Avenel Dictionary of the Saints.* 1965. NY. Avenel. 377 p. H10. $12.50

ATTWATER, Donald. *Catholic Dictionary...* 1958. Macmillan. 3rd ed. 552 p. H10. $17.50

ATTWATER, Donald. *Christian Churches of the E...* 1962. Milwaukee. revised ed. ils. 260 p. cloth. dj. O2. $20.00

ATWATER, Caleb. *Hist of State of OH, Natural & Civil.* 1838. Cincinnati. stated 2nd ed. 407 p. leather. G. D7. $145.00

ATWATER, Caleb. *Indians of the NW: Their Manners, Customs...* (1831). Columbus. 296 p. rebound leather. B18. $125.00

ATWATER, Caleb. *Remarks Made on Tour to Prairie du Chien...in 1829.* 1831. Columbus, OH. 1st ed. 12mo. 296 p. contemporary calf. M1. $425.00

ATWOOD, Margaret. *Bluebeard's Egg.* (1983). Toronto. McClelland Stewart. 1st ed. sgn. F/F. B3. $65.00

ATWOOD, Margaret. *Cat's Eye.* (1989). Doubleday. 1st ed. NF/NF. B3. $30.00

ATWOOD, Margaret. *Good Bones.* (1992). London. Bloomsbury. 1st ed (not pub in US). NF/F. B3. $45.00

ATWOOD, Margaret. *Handmaid's Tale.* 1986. Houghton Mifflin. ARC. F/wrp. B2. $35.00

ATWOOD, Margaret. *Second Words: Selected Critical Prose.* 1982. Toronto. Anansi. 1st Canadian ed. F/dj. C4. $40.00

ATWOOD, Margaret. *You Are Happy.* 1974. Harper. 1st Am ed. F/F. B2. $60.00

AUBERT, BELLEMARE & BILODEAU. *Saumon Atlantique.* (1988). Montreal. French-language ed. sgns. 206 p. A17. $22.50

AUCHINCLOSS, Louis. *Edith Wharton: Woman in Her Time.* 1971. NY. 1st ed. sgn. F/VG+ clip. A11. $40.00

AUCHINCLOSS, Louis. *False Gods.* (1992). Houghton Mifflin. 1st ed. F/F. B3. $15.00

AUCHINCLOSS, Louis. *Lady of Situations.* (1990). Houghton Mifflin. 1st ed. F/F. B3. $15.00

AUCHINCLOSS, Louis. *Quotations From Henry James.* 1984. Charlottesville. 1st ed. sgn. F/F. A11. $45.00

AUCHINCLOSS, Louis. *Reflections of a Jacobite.* 1961. London. Gollancz. 1st ed. F/NF. C4. $40.00

AUCHINCLOSS, Louis. *Watchfires: Novel of the Civil War.* (1982). Houghton Mifflin. 1st ed. F/NF clip. B3. $25.00

AUCHTER & KNAPP. *Orchard & Sm Fruit Culture.* 1945 (1929). NY. 3rd ed. ils/figures. 627 p. B26. $19.00

AUDEMARS, Pierre. *Bitter Path of Death.* (1982). Walker. 1st ed. F/dj. B9. $6.50

AUDEN, W.H. *Collected Longer Poems.* 1968. London. 1st ed. F/NF. T9. $28.00

AUDEN, W.H. *Collected Poems.* 1976. NY. 1st ed. F/F. V1. $25.00

AUDEN, W.H. *Collected Shorter Poems. 1930-1944.* 1950. London. Faber. 1st ed. F/NF. C4. $50.00

AUDEN, W.H. *Mtns.* 1954. London. 8 p. NF/8vo wrp/peach mailing envelope. A11. $25.00

AUDEN, W.H. *Nones.* 1952. London. 1st ed. F/dj. T9. $75.00

AUDEN, W.H. *On This Island.* 1937. NY. 1st ed. NF. V1. $15.00

AUDEN, W.H. *Paul Bunyan.* 1976. London. Faber Music Ltd. 1st ed. F/12mo gr wrp. A11. $20.00

AUDEN & ISHERWOOD. *Tragedy in 2 Acts: Ascent of F6.* 1936. London. Faber. 1st ed. 123 p. gilt bl cloth. VG. M7. $45.00

AUDOUIN-DUBREUIL & HAARDT. *La Raid Citroen. La Premiere Traversee du Sahara...* 1924. Paris. Librairie Plon. 4to. inscr/sgns. 245 p. maroon leather. NF/slipcase. F1. $700.00

AUDUBON, John James. *Birds of Am.* 1957 (1937). Macmillan. 2nd prt. 435 color pls. dj. D2. $45.00

AUDUBON, John James. *Orig Water-Colour Paintings by...for Birds of Am.* 1966. London. Michael Joseph. 2 vols. tan cloth. rpr slipcase. D2. $225.00

AUEL, Jean M. *Mammoth Hunters.* 1985. Crown. 1st ed. F/dj. M2. $25.00

AUEL, Jean M. *Plains of Passage.* 1990. Crown. 1st ed. 4th Earth's Children series. NF/F. Q1. $25.00

AUEL, Jean M. *Valley of Horses.* (1982). NY. Crown. 1st ed. NF/NF clip. B3. $25.00

AUGUR, Helen. *Zapotec.* 1954. Doubleday. 1st ed. 279 p. F3. $20.00

AUGUSTINOS, Olga. *French Odysseys. Greece in French Travel Literature...* 1994. Baltimore. 345 p. dj. O2. $36.00

AUGUSTUS, Albert Jr.; see Nuetzel, Charles.

AULT, Phil. *Whistles 'Round the Bend.* 1982. Dodd Mead. VG/dj. A16. $10.00

AUNT LAURA. *Faithful Sheep.* 1863. Buffalo. Breed Butler. miniature. 62 p. red cloth. H10. $135.00

AUNT LAURA. *Grandma's Story of the Vain Little Girl.* 1863. Buffalo. Breed Butler. miniature. 61 p. gr cloth. H10. $75.00

AUNT LAURA. *New Testament Stories.* 1862. Buffalo. Breed Butler. miniature. 64 p. gr cloth. H10. $200.00

AUNT LAURA. *Talk w/the Little Folks.* 1863. Buffalo. Breed Butler. miniature. aeg. gilt gr cloth. H10. $150.00

AUPHAN & MORDAL. *Marine Francaise Pendant la Seconde Guerre Mondiale.* 1958. Paris. Hachette. 17 maps. NF/wrp. O6. $75.00

AUSTEN, Jane. *Emma.* 1964. LEC. 1/1500. ils/sgn Fritz Kredel. F/slipcase. B24. $85.00

AUSTEN, Jane. *Northanger Abbey.* 1965. NY. 1st Signet Classic pb ed. afterword/sgn Hardwick. F. A11. $40.00

AUSTEN, Jane. *Northanger Abbey: Persuasion...* 1818. London. 1st ed. 12mo. 4 vols. rebacked/facsimle labels. slipcase. H5. $12,500.00

AUSTEN, Jane. *Pride & Prejudice.* 1904. Century. ils. spine label torn. E3. $20.00

AUSTEN & PEPPER. *Myra Breckinridge Cookbook.* (1970). Little Brn. 1st ed. 8vo. 344 p. F/pict wrp. B20. $35.00

AUSTER, Paul. *Auggie Wren's Christmas Story.* 1992. NY. Drentel. 1/100. sgn. buckram/marbled paper. F. C4. $130.00

AUSTER, Paul. *City of Glass.* 1985. LA. Sun Moon. 1st ed. 1st of NY Trilogy. NF/NF. L3. $150.00

AUSTER, Paul. *Invention of Solitude.* 1982. NY. 1st ed/1st issue (orig $6 price). F/wrp. A11. $30.00

AUSTER, Paul. *Invention of Solitude.* 1982. NY. 1st ed. sgn. F/8vo wrp. A11. $55.00

AUSTER, Paul. *Moon Palace.* (1989). London. Faber. 1st ed. VG/NF clip. B3. $35.00

AUSTER, Paul. *Moon Palace.* 1989. Viking. 1st ed. inscr. F/F. B2. $75.00

AUSTER, Paul. *Mr Vertigo.* (1994). London. Faber. 1st ed. F/F. B3. $20.00

AUSTER, Paul. *Music of Chance.* 1990. Viking. AP. F/wrp. L3. $60.00

AUSTER, Paul. *Squeeze Play.* 1991. London. 1st ed. F/unread glossy ils wrp. A11. $35.00

AUSTER, Paul. *Unearth.* 1974. Weston, CT. 1st ed. sgn. F/pale bl wrp. A11. $195.00

AUSTIN, L.G. *Ils Hist & Business Review of WA Co, OH...* 1891. Coschocton, OH. 1st ed. 283 p. G+. scarce. D7. $50.00

AUSTIN, Margot. *Churchmouse Stories.* 1960 (1956). Dutton/Weekly Reader. BC. 4to. 63 p. yel brds. G+. T5. $15.00

AUSTIN, Margot. *Lutie.* 1944. Dutton. 1st ed. ils. G/G. P2. $17.50

AUSTIN, Margot. *Manuel's Kite String & Other Stories.* 1943. Scribner. 112 p. VG/G. P2. $15.00

AUSTIN, Mary. *Earth Horizon.* 1932. Boston. 1st ed. 381 p. orig buckram. VG. F3. $35.00

AUSTIN, Mary. *Flock.* 1906. Boston. 1st ed. 266 p. teg. pict cloth. D3. $60.00

AUSTIN, Mary. *Isidro.* 1905. Boston. 1st ed. 424 p. gilt pict cloth. VG. D3. $50.00

AUSTIN, Richard L. *Yearbook of Landscape Architecture.* 1983. NY. Hist Preservation. ils. 192 p. M/dj. B26. $29.00

AUSTIN, Sarah. *Story Without an End.* 1913. Duffield. ils FC Pape/8 color pls. gilt cloth. VG-. M5. $65.00

AUTERBACH, Leo. *Babylonian Talmud.* 1944. Philosophical Lib. 2nd ed. VG/fair. S3. $10.00

AVADENKA, Lynne. *An Only Kid.* 1990. Huntington Woods. Land Marks Pr. 1/75. sgn. M/wrp/prt label. B24. $225.00

AVALLONE, Michael. *Shock Corridor.* 1963. NY. 1st ed. sgn. F. A11. $45.00

AVALLONE, Michael. *Tall Dolores.* 1953. NY. Noon. 1st ed. sgn. NF/VG. A11. $85.00

AVARY, Myrta Lockett. *Dixie After the War...* 1906. NY. 1st ed. royal 8vo. 435 p. cloth. VG. D3. $35.00

AVERIL, Naomi. *Whitling Two Teeth & the 49 Buffalos.* 1949. NY. pict brds. VG. M5. $25.00

AVERY, Lillian Drake. *Genealogy of Ingersoll Family in Am 1629-1925.* 1926. NY. 585 p. VG. B28. $35.00

AVERY, Thomas. *Slow Me Down, Oh Lord!* 1972. Avery Color Studios. sgn. color photos. 72 p. wrp. A17. $8.50

AVERY. *Quilts To Wear.* 1982. np. ils. cloth. G2. $23.00

AVERY. *Wonderful Wearables: A Celebration of Creative Clothing.* 1991. np. wrp. G2. $25.00

AVI. *Man From the Sky.* 1992. Morrow Jr Books. 1st ed. 8vo. 12o p. F/F. A3. $13.00

AVI-YONAH, M. *Jews of Palestine: Political Hist...Bar Kokhba War...* 1976. Basil Blackwell. orig ed. 386 p. VG/VG. S3. $21.00

AVICENNA. *Canon Medicinae.* 1490. Venice. Bonetus Locatellus. 438 (of 442 p). Gothic type. G7. $6,500.00

AWIAKTA, Marilou. *Abiding Appalachia.* 1986. Memphis. St Luke. 6th prt. inscr. VG/wrp. L3. $35.00

AXELROD, Emmens. *Exotic Tropical Fish.* (1981). TFH. 8vo. photos/index. 650 p. A17. $16.50

AXELROD, George. *Where Am I Now — When I Need Me?* 1971. Viking. 1st ed. F/F. F4. $15.00

AXFORD, H. William. *Gilpin County Gold: Peter McFarlane, Mining Entrepreneur...* 1976. Swallow Pr. 1st ed. ils/index. 210 p. F/F clip. B19. $17.50

AXTON, David; see Koontz, Dean R.

AYERS & WILLIS. *Edge of the S: Life in 19th-Century VA.* ca 1911. VA U. ils/map. 256 p. VG. B10. $8.00

AYMAR, Gordon. *Bird Flight.* (1938). NY. deluxe ed. 4to. 234 p. VG/dj. A17. $17.50

AYMAR, Gordon. *Yacht Racing Rules & Tactics.* 1962. NY. Van Nostrand. VG/dj. A16. $9.00

AYRES, Paul; see Aarons, Edward S.

B

B., J.H. *Poetical Fortuneteller.* 1861. Buffalo. Breed Butler. miniature. 95 p. gilt cloth. H10. $85.00

BABBITT, Bruce E. *Color & Light.* 1988. Northland. ils. 76 p. F/wrp. B19. $12.50

BABCOCK, Mary Kent Davey. *Christ Church, Salem Street, Boston...1723-75.* ca 1947. np. ils. 271 p. H10. $17.50

BABSON, Marian. *Death Warmed Up.* 1982. NY. Walker. 1st Am ed. sgn. F/F. S5. $35.00

BABSON, Marian. *There Must Be Some Mistake.* (1987). St Martin. 1st ed. F/dj. B9. $10.00

BABSON, Marian. *Untimely Guest.* 1976. London. Collins Crime Club. 1st ed. F/F. M15. $40.00

BABSON, R.W. *Our Campaign for the Presidency in 1940: Am & Churches.* 1941. Chicago. Nat Prohibitionist. 1st ed. 12mo. 254 p. F/VG. A2. $25.00

BACH, Marcus. *Chiropractic Story.* 1968. LA. De Vorss. 250 p. dj. N2. $12.50

BACHE, Richard Mead. *Am Wonderland.* 1871. Phil. Claxton Remsen. 1st ed. 258 p. gilt gr cloth. G. M20. $45.00

BACHE & WOOD. *Dispensatory of US of A.* 1845. Phil. 6ht ed. 1346 p. full leather. fair. B18. $65.00

BACHELDER, John B. *Bachelder's Ils Tourist's Guide of the US...* 1873. Boston. Bachelder. 1st ed. inscr to wife. 8vo. aeg. F. M1. $500.00

BACHMAN, Richard; see King, Stephen.

BACKES, C. *Growing Up W: Recollections.* 1990. Knopf. 1st ed. fwd Larry McMurtry. F/F. L3. $45.00

BACKES, C. *Growing Up W: Recollections.* 1990. Knopf. 1st ed. sgn Stegner. M/M. A18. $80.00

BACKES, C. *Mormon Country.* (1942). DSP. 1st ed. F. A18. $40.00

BACKES, C. *On the Teaching of Creative Writing.* (1988). New Eng U. 1st ed. sgn. M/sans. A18. $100.00

BACKES, C. *One Nation.* 1945. Houghton Mifflin. 1st ed. photos. VG+/rpr dj. A18. $40.00

BACKHOUSE, James. *Memoir...* 1877. York. Wm Sessions. 2nd ed. 16mo. 191 p. cloth. worn. V3. $22.00

BACON, Edgar Mayhew. *Hudson River: From Ocean to Source.* 1902. Putnam. G. A16. $65.00

BACON, Leonard. *Biographical Notes Mostly in Verse.* 1938. NY. 1st ed. F/sans. V1. $10.00

BACON, Margaret Hope. *Rebellion at Christiana.* 1975. Crown. 2nd prt. 8vo. 216 p. G/dj. V3. $12.00

BACON, Walter. *Highway to Wilderness: Sojourn Beyond Arctic Circle.* (1961). Vanguard. 1st ed. 8vo. 189 p. F/F. A2. $15.00

BACON & IMBACH. *Adventures in Patchwork.* 1985. np. 25 full-size patterns. wrp. G2. $10.00

BACON & IMBACH. *Miniature Magic.* nd. np. 150+ patterns. wrp. G2. $15.00

BACQUEVILLE DE LA POTHERIE, C. *Historie de l'Amerique Septentroinale.* 1722. Paris. Jean-Luc Nion et F Didot. 1st ed. 4 vols. calf. H9. $4,500.00

BADCOCK, G. *Hist of Transport Services of Egyptian Expeditonary Force...* 1925. London. Hugh Rees Ltd. 1st ed. 333 p. gilt bl cloth. VG. M7. $65.00

BADDELEY, John F. *Russian Conquest of the Caucasus.* 1908. London. thick 4to. ils/maps/plans. 518 p. O2. $275.00

BADER, Barbara. *Am Picturebooks From Noah's Ark to Beast Within.* 1976. Macmillan. 4to. ils. 615 p. gilt brn cloth. F/VG+. F1. $75.00

BADLAM, Alexander. *Wonders of AK.* 1890. San Francisco. Bancroft. 2nd ed. 8vo. ils/maps. VG. P4. $75.00

BAECK, Leo. *Judaism & Christianity.* 1958. JPS. 1st ed. 292 p. VG+/VG-. S3. $22.00

BAEDEKER. *Austria.* 1920. Leipzig. 12th ed. F. O2. $40.00

BAEDEKER. *Belgien und Holland.* 1878. Leipzig. 14th ed. O2. $65.00

BAEDEKER. *Central Italy & Rome.* 1909. Leipzig. 19 maps/55 plans/views. red cloth. F/dj. B14. $55.00

BAEDEKER. *Die Rheinlande.* 1862. Coblenz. 12th ed. front cover loose. O2. $225.00

BAEDEKER. *Hannover und die Deutsche Nordseekuste.* 1921. Leipsig. rebound in imitation Baedeker bdg. O2. $150.00

BAEDEKER. *Holland.* 1927. Leipzig. 26th ed. F. O2. $50.00

BAEDEKER. *S Germany & Austria, Including the E Alps.* 1873. Coblenz. 3rd ed. O2. $95.00

BAEDEKER. *S Italy.* 1874. Leipsic. 3rd ed. O2. $100.00

BAEDEKER. *Switzerland & the Adjacent Portions of Italy.* 1869. Coblenz. 4th ed. O2. $150.00

BAEDEKER. *US w/Excursion Into Mexico.* 1904. Leipzig/London/NY. 3rd revised ed. 25 maps/35 plans. rose cloth. H9. $120.00

BAER, Carlyle S. *Year Book 1954-55. Am Soc of Bookplate Collectors...* 1956. Sewanee, TN. ltd ed. 1/250. NF. D2. $55.00

BAGLEY, Desmond. *Enemy.* 1977. London. Collins. 1st ed. NF/NF. S5. $30.00

BAGLEY, Desmond. *Spoilers.* 1969. London. Collins. 1st ed. F/NF. M15. $45.00

BAGNOLD, Enid. *National Velvet.* 1954 (1935). Morrow. 5th prt. 8vo. 307 p. gray cloth. G+. T5. $15.00

BAGROW, Leo. *Hist of Cartography of Russia...* 1975. Wolfe Island, Ontario. Walker. 2 vols. 152 maps/17 tables. decor brds. O6. $100.00

BAGUST, Harold. *Miniature Geraniums.* 1968. London. photos. 99 p. F/dj. B26. $14.00

BAHR, Fritz. *Fritz Bahr's Commercial Floriculture...* 1927. NY. De La Mare. revised ed. xl. 615 p. NF. H10. $10.00

BAIGENT. *Holy Blood, Holy Grail.* 1982. np. 1st ed. F/VG. C1. $12.00

BAILEY, Alice Cooper. *Footprints in the Dust.* 1936. Longman Gr. 1st ed. sgn. 255 p. NF/VG. P2. $25.00

BAILEY, Alice Cooper. *Kimo: The Whistling Boy. Story of HI.* (1928). Wise Parslow. ils Lucille Holling. 96 p. G+. A3. $12.50

BAILEY, Alice Cooper. *Tale of the Muley Cow.* 1921. Grosset Dunlap. 114 p. VG. P2. $10.00

BAILEY, Alice Ward. *Flower Fancies.* 1889. Boston. Prang. 1st ed. quarto. aeg. patterned cloth. H5. $350.00

BAILEY, BUCHANAN & BUCY. *Intracranial Tumors of Infancy & Childhood.* 1939. Chicago. xl. 23 pls. 598 p. G7. $85.00

BAILEY, Carolyn Sherwin. *Wonderful Window.* 1926. np. ils Katherine Wireman/4 color pls. VG. M5. $35.00

BAILEY, George. *Germans: Biography of an Obsession.* 1991. NY. 1st ed. F/dj. T9. $12.00

BAILEY, H.C. *Mr Chunk's Text.* 1939. Crime Club. 1st ed. F/NF. F4. $45.00

BAILEY, H.J. *Reminiscences of a Christian Life.* 1885. Portland, ME. Hoyt Fogg Donham. 3rd ed. 12mo. 419 p. V3. $12.00

BAILEY, J.H. *Pictures of the Past: Petersburg Seen by Simpsons...1819-95.* ca 1989. Ft Henry Branch, APVA. ils. 55 p. VG. B10. $10.00

BAILEY, J.O. *Pilgrims Through Time & Space.* 1947. Argus. 1st ed. VG/tape rpr. M2. $30.00

BAILEY, John M. *Book of Ensilage...* 1881. NY. Judd. ils/ads. 140 p. H10. $20.00

BAILEY, L.H. *Cultivated Evergreens...* 1923. NY. 1st ed. 48 pls. 434 p. gr/wht cloth. VG. B28. $40.00

BAILEY, L.H. *Cyclopedia of Am Horiticulture.* 1906. Doubleday. 5th ed. 4 vols. H10. $125.00

BAILEY, L.H. *Garden of Bellflowers in N Am.* 1953. Macmillan. 1st ed. ils/index. 155 p. dj. H10. $45.00

BAILEY, L.H. *Garden of Gourds.* 1937. NY. 1st ed. 41 pls. 134 p. VG-. B26. $27.50

BAILEY, L.H. *Garden-Making: Suggestions for Utilizing of Home Grounds.* ca 1898. Grosset Dunlap. ils. 417 p. H10. $10.00

BAILEY, L.H. *Gardener's Handbook.* 1934. NY. Macmillan. 1st ed. 292 p. VG. H10. $10.00

BAILEY, L.H. *Gardener's Handbook.* 1947 (1934). NY. ils. 292 p. VG+/dj. B26. $20.00

BAILEY, L.H. *Plant Breeding.* 1912. NY. Macmillan. ils. 365 p. H10. $12.50

BAILEY, L.H. *Principles of Agriculture...* ca 1909. Macmillan. ils. 336 p. H10. $10.00

BAILEY, L.H. *Principles of Fruit-Growing.* 1915 (1897). NY. revised ed/later prt. ils. 432 p. B26. $19.00

BAILEY, L.H. *Standard Cyclopedia of Horticulture.* 1935. Macmillan. 3 vols. VG. H10. $145.00

BAILEY, Pearl. *Raw Pearl.* (1968). HBW. 1st ed. clip dj. A7. $10.00

BAILEY, Robert G. *Hell's Canyon.* (1943). Lewiston. RG Bailey. 1/1500. sgn. 575 p. A7. $125.00

BAILEY & FELTS. *Naturescapes...Field Guide to Woods, Forests...* 1988. 4 pop-up scenes. F. A4. $35.00

BAILLIE, Matthew. *Account of Particular Change of Structure of Human Ovarium.* 1789. London Medical Journal. 8vo. brds/rebacked. G7. $135.00

BAILYN & DE WOLFE. *Voyagers to the W: Passage in Peopling of Am...* 1986. NY. 1st ed. ils/maps/charts. VG+/dj. B18. $17.50

BAIN, Kenneth. *Friendly Islanders: Story of Queen Salote & Her People.* (1967). London. Hodder Stoughton. 1st ed. 8vo. 207 p. F/F clip. A2. $20.00

BAIRD, Spencer Fullerton. *US & Mexican Boundary Survey...* 1859. WA, DC. 1st ed. quarto. 2 vols. 25 pls. brn morcco/brds. H5. $2,250.00

BAITY, Elizabeth. *Americans Before Columbus.* 1951. Viking. 1st ed. 256 p. dj. F3. $20.00

BAKAN, David. *Sigmund Freud & the Jewish Mystical Tradition.* 1975 (1958). Beacon. trade pb. G1. $25.00

BAKE & KILPATRICK. *Am South: 4 Seasons of the Land.* ca 1980. Oxmore House. 1st ed. 187 p. VG/VG. B10. $25.00

BAKELESS, John. *Eyes of Discovery: Pageant of N Am As Seen by 1st Explorers.* 1950. Lippincott. 1st ed. 8vo. 439 p. NF. T8. $25.00

BAKELESS, John. *Lewis & Clark: Partners in Discovery.* 1947. Morrow. 1st ed/2nd prt. 8vo. 498 p. T8. $20.00

BAKENHUS, R.E. *Panama Canal...Hist & Construction...Law & Commerce.* 1915. NY. Wiley. 1st ed. 8vo. 257 p. VG. A2. $40.00

BAKER, Betty. *Great Ghost Stories of the W.* 1968. 4 Winds. 8vo. VG/VG. A8. $6.00

BAKER, Carlos. *40 Yrs of Pulitzer Prizes.* 1956. NY. 1st separate ed. NF/gr wrp. A11. $30.00

BAKER, Charles H. *Gentleman's Companion.* 1946. Crown. 1st trade ed. 2 vols. VG. C1. $11.50

BAKER, Denys Val. *Face in the Mirror.* 1971. Arkham. 1st ed. F/dj. M2. $40.00

BAKER, Elizabeth W. *Sonny-Boy Sim.* 1948. Rand McNally. 1st ed. 8vo. 31 p. red brds. VG/torn. T5. $18.00

BAKER, Elliot. *Unhealthful Air.* (1988). NY. Viking. 1st ed. rem mk. VG/NF. B3. $15.00

BAKER, Frank. *Miss Hargreaves.* 1941. Coward McCann. 1st ed. G+. M2. $15.00

BAKER, George. *Opuscula Medica, Iterrum Edita.* 177. London. Hughs. 2 engraved pls. 228 p. full polished calf. G7. $145.00

BAKER, George. *Sad Sack.* 1944. NY. 2nd prt. 238 p. pict gray cloth. VG. H3. $12.00

BAKER, Ira O. *Treatise on Masonry Construction.* 1905. NY. Wiley. 9th ed. ils/6 fld pls. 556 p. H10. $25.00

BAKER, J.N.L. *Hist of Geography: Papers.* 1963. Oxford. Blackwell. Samuel Eliot Morison's copy. M/dj. O6. $65.00

BAKER, James Robert. *Fuel-Injected Dreams.* 1986. Dutton. 1st ed. author's 1st hc book. NF/VG+ clip. A14. $25.00

BAKER, Kevin. *Sometimes You See It Coming.* (1993). NY. Crown. ARC. author's 1st novel. RS. F/F. B3. $30.00

BAKER, Nicholson. *Mezzanine.* 1988. NY. 1st ed. author's 1st novel. sgn. F/F. A11. $125.00

BAKER, Nicholson. *Room Temperature.* 1990. Grove Weidenfeld. 1st ed. sgn. F/F. B2. $100.00

BAKER, Nicholson. *U & I.* 1991. Random. 1st ed. sgn. author's 3rd book. F/F. B3. $50.00

BAKER, Nicholson. *U & I.* 1991. Random. 1st ed. M/M. T2. $18.00

BAKER, Nicholson. *Vox.* 1992. London. 1st Eng ed. sgn. F/gilt stp wrp. A11. $50.00

BAKER, Nicholson. *Vox.* 1992. Random. 1st ed. inscr. F/NF. B2. $75.00

BAKER, Pearl. *Handbook of Hist of McDuffie Co, GA, 1870-1970.* ca 1970. np. Progress-News Pub. 1st ed. 238 p. NF. M8. $37.50

BAKER, Robert A. *They Call It Hypnosis.* 1990. Prometheus. 1st ed. 313 p. blk fabrikoid. VG/dj. G1. $18.50

BAKER, Samuel W. *Eight Yr's Wanderings in Celon.* 1883. Phil. Lippincott. 8vo. ils. 323 p. pict red cloth. F. B14. $95.00

BAKER, Samuel W. *Exploration of Nile Tributaries of Abyssinia.* 1868. Hartford. Case. 1st Am ed. 8vo. 608 p. NF. F1. $225.00

BAKER, Scott. *Night Child.* 1979. Berkley. 1st ed. author's 2nd novel. F/NF. N3. $15.00

BAKER, Stanley L. *Collector's Book of Railroadiana.* 1981. Castle Books. G/dj. A16. $20.00

BAKER, Walter. *Cocoa & Chocolate: Short Hist of Their Production & Use.* 1886. Dorchester, MA. Walter Baker Co. sm 8vo. 165 p. gilt brn cloth. VG. F1. $250.00

BAKER, William King. *Quaker Warrior: Life of Wm Hobson.* nd. London. Headley Bros. 12mo. 178 p. VG. V3. $16.00

BAKER & MEHALKO. *Story Book Quilting.* nd. np. ils. wrp. G2. $16.00

BAKER & YOUNG. *Simply Serge Any Fabric: How-To-Handbook...* 1990. np. pb. G2. $15.00

BAKER. *Handbook of Am Crewel Embroidery.* 1966. np. cloth. G2. $11.00

BAKEWELL, Robert. *Intro to Geology.* 1839. New Haven. Noyes. lg 8vo. 596 p. orig legal calf. H9. $125.00

BAKKER, Elna S. *Island Called CA: Ecological Intro to Natural Communitities.* 1984. CA U. 2nd ed. ils/index. 484 p. F/F. B19. $30.00

BALABAN, John. *Coming Down Again.* (1985). HBJ. 1st ed. rem mk. NF/dj. A7. $30.00

BALABAN, John. *Remembering Heaven's Face.* (1991). Poseidon. 334 p. F/F. A7. $15.00

BALCH, Glenn. *Keeping Horse.* 1966. NY. Crowell. 1st ed. VG/VG. O3. $18.00

BALCHIN, Nigel. *Sort of Traitors.* 1949. London. 1st ed. NF/dj. M2. $10.00

BALD, F. Clever. *MI in 4 Centuries.* 1954. Harper. 1st ed. G+. N2. $7.50

BALDWIN, Charles W. *Geog of the HI Islands.* 1920. Am Book Co. 7 maps. VG. O6. $25.00

BALDWIN, Hanson W. *Sea Fights & Shipwrecks: True Tales of the 7 Seas.* ca 1955. Hanover. 8vo. maps. 315 p. VG/VG. P4. $30.00

BALDWIN, Hanson. *Navy at War: Paintings & Drawings by Combat Artists.* (1943). NY. Morrow. 1st ed. 4to. 160 p. F/VG. A2. $25.00

BALDWIN, J.D. *Ancient Am: In Notes on Am Archeology.* 1871. NY. Harper. 299 p. VG+. H7. $35.00

BALDWIN, James. *Another Country.* 1962. Dial Pr. galley proof. sbdg. Q1. $500.00

BALDWIN, James. *Devil Finds Work.* 1976. NY. 1st ed. F/F. A11. $40.00

BALDWIN, James. *Evidence of Things Not Seen.* 1985. HRW. 1st ed. NF/NF. A14. $25.00

BALDWIN, James. *Fire Next Time.* 1963. NY. coarse wht linen. NF/NF clip. A11. $25.00

BALDWIN, James. *Gypsy & Other Poems.* 1989. Gehenna. 1/275. ils/sgn/#d Leonard Baskin. w/sgn/#d etching. F. Q1. $375.00

BALDWIN, James. *Jimmy's Blues: Selected Poems.* 1985. St Martin. 1st ed. NF/NF. E3. $20.00

BALDWIN, James. *Just Above My Head.* 1979. Dial. 1st ed. F/F clip. A14. $40.00

BALDWIN, James. *One Day, When I Was Lost.* 1972. London. correct 1st ed. F/F. A11. $65.00

BALDWIN, James. *Price of the Ticket.* 1985. St Martin. 1/150. sgn/#d. stp tan cloth brds/ribbon marker. NF/slipcase. Q1. $250.00

BALDWIN, James. *Tell Me How Long the Train's Been Gone.* 1968. Dial. 1st ed. NF/NF clip. A14. $50.00

BALDWIN, James. *Tell Me How Long the Train's Been Gone.* 1968. Dial. 1st ed. sgn. VG/VG. B3. $200.00

BALDWIN, Joseph G. *Flush Times of AL & MS.* 1891. San Francisco. 12mo. 330 p. cloth. H9. $20.00

BALDWIN, Joseph G. *Party Leaders.* 1855. NY. gr bdg. B30. $30.00

BALDWIN, William Wright. *Chicago, Burlington & Quincy RR Co.* 1928-29. Chicago. 1st ed. 2 vols. VG. D3. $150.00

BALDWIN & MEAD. *Rap on Race.* 1971. Lippincott. 1st ed. 256 p. NF/NF. A7/E3. $30.00

BALDWIN. *Quilted Clothing Collection.* 1984. np. wrp. G2. $11.00

BALES, W.A. *Tiger in the Streets.* 1962. Dodd Mead. 1st ed. 8vo. 212 p. F/VG clip. A2. $12.50

BALET, Jan. *Ned & Ed & the Lion.* 1949. Oxford. 1st ed. VG/VG-. P2. $23.00

BALL, Eustace Hale. *Gaucho.* nd. Grosset Dunlap. photoplay ed. VG/color Canon dj. M2. $35.00

BALL, John Jr. *Phonograph Record Industry.* 1947. Boston. Am Industries Monograph 13. NF/bl-prt gray wrp. A11. $125.00

BALL, John. *Arctic Showdown.* (1966). DSP. F/dj. B9. $25.00

BALL, John. *Chief Tallon & the SOR.* (1984). Dodd Mead. 1st ed. F/dj. B9. $12.50

BALL, John. *Dragon Hotel.* (1969). NY. Walker. 1st ed. F/dj. B9. $20.00

BALL, John. *Eyes of Buddha.* (1976). Little Brn. 1st ed. F/dj. B9. $20.00

BALL, John. *Eyes of Buddha.* 1976. Little Brn. 1st ed. inscr/sgn. F/F. S5. $37.50

BALL, John. *Five Pieces of Jade.* (1972). Little Brn. F/dj. B9. $10.00

BALL, John. *Five Pieces of Jade.* (1972). London. Michael Joseph. 1st ed. F/dj. B9. $20.00

BALL, John. *Five Pieces of Jade.* 1972. London. Michael Joseph. 1st ed. presentation/sgn. F/F. S5. $37.50

BALL, John. *Murder Children.* (1979). Dodd Mead. 1st ed. F/dj. B9. $20.00

BALL, John. *Then Came Violence.* (1981). London. Michael Joseph. 1st ed. F/dj. B9. $15.00

BALL, John. *Trouble for Tallon.* 1981. Doubleday. 1st ed. F/dj. B9. $15.00

BALL, John. *1st Team.* (1971). Little Brn. 1st ed. F/dj. B9. $15.00

BALL, John. *14th Point.* (1975. London. Michael Joseph. 1st ed. F/dj. B9. $20.00

BALL, Robert Stawell. *Star-Land: Being Talks w/Young People...* 1892. Boston. Ginn. ils/index. 376 p. bl cloth. G+. S9. $15.00

BALLANTINE, Ian. *W Art of James Bama.* 1975. Bantam. ils. 91 p. VG/wrp. B19. $15.00

BALLARD, Colin Robert. *Military Genius of Abraham Lincoln.* 1952. Cleveland/NY. World. 1st Am ed. 246 p. cloth. NF/NF. M8. $45.00

BALLARD, G.A. *Rulers of the Indian Ocean.* 1928. Houghton Mifflin. ils/maps. VG+. O6. $75.00

BALLARD, J.G. *Concrete Island.* 1974. NY. 1st Am ed. F/F. A11. $30.00

BALLARD, J.G. *Day of Creation.* 1988. Farrar. 1st Am ed. sgn. F/F. F4. $25.00

BALLARD, J.G. *Hello Am.* 1981. London. 1st ed. F/NF clip. A11. $40.00

BALLARD, J.G. *High-Rise.* 1977. Holt. 1st ed. inscr. F/NF. B2. $50.00

BALLARD, J.G. *Kindness of Women.* 1991. NY. 1st ed. F/dj. T9. $15.00

BALLARD, J.G. *Love & Napalm Export USA.* 1972. Grove. 1st Am ed. F/NF. N3. $45.00

BALLARD, J.G. *Vermilion Sands.* 1971. NY. Berkeley. PBO. F/unread. A11. $30.00

BALLARD, J.G. *Wind From Nowhere.* 1962. Berkeley. PBO. NF/ils wrp. A11. $35.00

BALLARD, J.G. *Wind From Nowhere.* 1967. London. 1st Eng ed/PBO. sgn. VG+/wrp ils Alan Aldridge. A11. $145.00

BALLENTYNE, Robert M. *Young Fur-Traders; or, Snowflakes & Sunbeams From Far N.* 1897. London. new ed. xl. 12mo. 402 p. VG. D3. $15.00

BALLIET, Whitney. *NY Notes: Journal of Jazz, 1972-1975* 1976. Houghton Mifflin. 1st ed. NF/NF. A7. $35.00

BALLIET, Whitney. *Such Sweet Thunder: 49 Pieces on Jazz.* (1966). Bobbs Merrill. 1st ed. VG+/dj. A7. $40.00

BALLOU, Adin. *True Spiritual Doctrine of 2nd Advent...* 1843. Hopedale. Community Pr. 1st ed. 8vo. 32 p. prt wrp. M1. $250.00

BALLOU, Aldin. *Christian Non-Resistance in All Its Important Bearings.* 1910. Universal Peace Union. 12mo. 278 p. VG. V3. $18.00

BALLOU, M.M. *Under the S Cross. Travels in Australia, Tasmania...* 1888. Boston. 1st ed. 12mo. 405 p. gilt red cloth. G. H3. $35.00

BALLOU, Marturin. *Aztec Land.* 1890. Houghton Mifflin. 1st ed. 355 p. pict cloth. F3. $45.00

BALMFORTH, Henry. *Intro to Pastoral Theology.* 1937. Macmillan. 306 p. H10. $15.00

BALOGH, Penelope. *Freud: Biographical Intro.* 1971. Scribner. 1st ed/pb issue. 144 p. G1. $17.50

BALTIMORE YEARLY MEETING. *Rules of Discipline of Yearly Meeting of Friends...* 1844. Baltimore. Wm Wooddy. 16mo. 115 p. worn. V3. $15.00

BALTZELL, E. Digby. *Puritan Boston & Quaker Phil.* 1979. NY. Free Pr. 1st ed. 8vo. 585 p. VG/VG. V3. $15.00

BAMBERGER, Bernard J. *Bible: Modern Jewish Approach.* 1960. N'nai B'rith Hillel. 3rd imp. 12mo. 96 p. G+. S3. $14.00

BANCROFT, A.L. *Bancroft's Tourist Guide to the Geysers.* 1871. San Francisco. Bancroft. 16mo. 227 p. gr cloth. H9. $125.00

BANCROFT, Edith. *Jane Allen, Center.* 1920. Cupples Leon. 1st ed. 310 p. cloth/pict label. VG+/dj. M20. $25.00

BANCROFT, Edith. *Jane Allen of the Sub Team.* 1917. Cupples Leon. lists 5 titles. 338 p. VG/dj. M20. $20.00

BANCROFT, George. *Abraham Lincoln: A Tribute.* 1908. NY. Wessels. 1st thus ed. 76 p. cloth. M8. $25.00

BANCROFT, Hubert Howe. *CA Inter Pocula (1848-56): Works of..., Vol XXXV.* 1888. Hist Co. 828 p. brn cloth. B19. $50.00

BANCROFT, Hubert Howe. *CA Pastoral, 1769-1848: Works of..., Vol XXXIII.* 1888. Hist Co. 808 p. w/newspaper ephemera. B19. $65.00

BANCROFT, Hubert Howe. *Hist of AK, 1730-1885: Works of..., Vol XXXIV.* 1886. AL Bancroft. 1st ed. maps/index. 775 p. F. B19. $75.00

BANCROFT, Hubert Howe. *Hist of Mexico, 1516-1887.* 1883-88. San Francisco. AL Bancroft. 6 vols. full leather. G+. P4. $200.00

BANCROFT, Hubert Howe. *Native Races of the Pacific States of N Am.* 1876. Appleton. 2 fld maps. 796 p. half morocco. H9. $45.00

BANCROFT, Hubert Howe. *Resources & Development of Mexico.* 1893. San Francisco. 1st ed. xl. 8vo. photos/2 fld maps. red silk. H9. $50.00

BANCROFT, Sidney. *Report...Case of Oliver Earle & Others...* 1855. Little Brn. 8vo. 260 p. G+. V3. $35.00

BANDELIER, Adolf F. *Delight Makers.* (1890). NY. 1st ed. xl. 490 p. cloth. VG. D3. $35.00

BANDINI, Angelo Maria. *Vita e Lettere Amerigo Vespvcci...* 1745. Florence. quarto. fld genealogical chart. modern vellum. H9. $350.00

BANFIELD, E.J. *My Tropic Isle.* (1913). NY. 3rd imp. ils/index, 315 p. G. A17. $15.00

BANGS, John K. *Pursuit of the House-Boat.* 1900. Harper. ils. orig brds. E3. $10.00

BANGS, John K. *Pursuit of the House-Boat.* 1903. London. emb gilt bdg. VG. E5. $25.00

BANKS, Charles Edward. *Planters of the Commonwealth.* 1930. Houghton Mifflin. 1/787. NF. O6. $225.00

BANKS, Ian. *Wasp Factory.* 1984. Houghton Mifflin. 1st Am ed. author's 1st book. F/F. N3. $20.00

BANKS, Lynne Reid. *Secret of the Indian.* 1989. Doubleday. 1st ed. 3rd of Indian series. F/F. N3. $15.00

BANKS, Russell. *Affliction.* (1989). Harper Row. 1st ed. F/NF. B3. $20.00

BANKS, Russell. *Family Life.* 1975. NY. Avon Equinox. PBO. sgn. F/8vo wrp. A11. $60.00

BANKS, Russell. *New World.* 1978. Urbana, IL. 1st ed. F/unread wrp. A11. $20.00

BANKS, Russell. *Relations of My Imprisonment: A Fiction.* 1983. WA, DC. Sun & Moon. 1st ed. 1/100. sgn/#d. F/F. Q1. $75.00

BANKS, Russell. *Snow. Meditations of a Cautious Man in Winter.* 1974. Hanover, NH. 1st ed. 24 p. VG+/8vo wrp. A11. $50.00

BANKS, Russell. *Success Stories.* (1986). Harper Row. 1st ed. F/F. B3. $25.00

BANKS, Russell. *Success Stories.* (1986). Harper Row. 1st ed. sgn. F/F. A7. $37.00

BANKS, Russell. *Sweet Hereafter.* (1992). London. Picador. 1st ed. F/F. B3. $20.00

BANKS & BANKS. *Feminism & Family Planning in Victorian Eng.* 1964. Schocken. 142 p. dj. A7. $12.00

BANKS & ENRIGHT. *Mr Cub.* 1971. Follet. 1st ed. photos. F/VG. P8. $40.00

BANKS & READ. *Complete Hist of San Francisco Disaster & Mt Vesuvius...* 1906. CE Thomas. ils. 464 p. pict red cloth. VG. M20. $15.00

BANKS & SWIFT. *Jokes on Us: Women in Comedy From Music Hall to Present Day.* 1987. London. Pandora. 294 p. prt stiff wrp. G1. $17.50

BANNERMAN, Helen. *Little Blk Sambo.* 1932. Platt Munk #3100-B. ils Eulalie. VG/pict wrp. A3. $25.00

BANNERMAN, Helen. *Little Blk Sambo.* 1943 (1931). Am Crayon Co/Mary Perks. ils FB Peat. G+. A3. $50.00

BANNERMAN, Helen. *Little Blk Sambo.* 1950. Whitman Tell-a-Tale. ils Suzanne. 28 p. VG. A3. $15.00

BANNERMAN, Helen. *Little Blk Sambo/Red Hen/Peter Rabbit.* 1942. Saalfield. ils Ethel Hays. sbdg. VG. D1. $185.00

BANNERMAN, Helen. *Little Blk Sambo: A New Story.* 1926. Whitman. 1st ed. G. L1. $135.00

BANNERMAN, Helen. *Story of Little Blk Mingo.* (1902). London. Nisbet. ils Bannerman. red cloth. VG/VG. D1. $225.00

BANNERMAN, Helen. *Story of Little Blk Quash.* (1908). London. Nisbet. ils Bannerman. VG/VG. D1. $225.00

BANNERMAN, Helen. *Story of Little Blk Sambo.* (1919). Chicago. Donohue. sm 8vo. red cloth brds/pict label. G. D1. $200.00

BANNERMAN, Helen. *Story of Little Blk Sambo.* 1941. Chatto Windus. 12mo. 113 p. NF/rare dj. D1. $250.00

BANNING & BANNING. *Six Horses.* 1930. NY. Century. VG. O3. $65.00

BANNION, Della; see Sellers, Con.

BANNISTER, P. *Intro to Physiological Plant Ecology.* 1976. NY. 273 p. F/dj. B26. $22.50

BANNISTER & FORD. *US Patchwork Pattern Book.* 1976. np. ils. wrp. G2. $4.00

BANNON, Laura. *Best House in the World.* 1952. Houghton Mifflin. 1st ed. ils. G. P2. $12.50

BANNON, Laura. *Katy Comes Next.* (1959). Chicago. Whitman. xl. pict bl cloth. VG. T5. $20.00

BANTEL & BOYLE. *William Rush: Am Sculptor.* 1982. PA Academy Fine Arts. 8 color pls. 212 p. brds. D2. $30.00

BANTOCK, Nick. *Wings.* (1990). London. Bodley Head. 1st ed. pop-up. brds. F/plastic wrp. B3. $25.00

BANVILLE, John. *Birchwood.* (1973). Norton. 1st Am ed. author's 2nd book. F/NF. B4. $200.00

BANVILLE, John. *Book of Evidence.* (1989). London. Secker Warburg. 1st ed. F/F. B4. $65.00

BANVILLE, John. *Dr Copernicus.* (1976). Norton. ARC/1st Am ed. RS. NF/F clip. B4. $200.00

BANVILLE, John. *Ghosts.* 1993. Knopf. ARC. F/wrp. B2. $25.00

BANVILLE, John. *Kepler: A Novel.* (1983). Boston. Godine. 1st Am ed. F/NF. B4. $85.00

BANVILLE, John. *Mefisto.* 1989. Boston. Godine. 1st Am ed. F/F. L3. $35.00

BANVILLE, John. *Newton Letter.* (1987). Godine. 1st Am ed. F/F. B4. $65.00

BANVILLE, John. *Nightspawn.* 1971. Norton. 1st Am ed. author's 2nd book. NF/VG. B2. $45.00

BARAKA, Amiri. *Dead Lecturer. Poems.* 1964. NY. 1st ed. sgn. correct 1st state bdg/2 sets marron ep. F/wrp. A11. $65.00

BARATZ, Joseph. *Village by the Jordan. Story of Degania.* 1960. Tel Aviv. 8vo. inscr. 174 p. dj. o2. $20.00

BARBA, Simone Della. *Nuova Spositone del Sonetto...* 1554. Florence. Torrentino. sm 8vo. 44 p. modern navy calf. K1. $300.00

BARBER, Noel. *War of the Running Dogs.* 1972. NY. 1st Am ed. 284 p. VG/dj. A18. $22.50

BARBER, Noel. *7 Days of Freedom: Hungarian Uprising 1956.* 1975. Newton Abbott. BC. 268 p. dj. A7. $12.00

BARBER, Richard. *Figure of Arthur.* 1990 (1972). np. F/dj. C1. $12.50

BARBER, Richard. *King Arthur, Hero & Legend.* 1990. Boydell Pr. trade pb. VG+. C1. $9.00

BARBER, Theodore X. *LSD, Marihuana, Yoga & Hypnosis.* 1971. Chicago. Aldine. 2nd prt. NF/F. B2. $25.00

BARBER & HOWE. *All the W States & Territories...* 1867. Cincinnati. 1st ed. 733 p. orig brds rebacked. VG. D7. $125.00

BARBER & HOWE. *Our Whole Country...* 1861. NY/Cincinnati. subscription ed. 2 vols. brn cloth. H9. $55.00

BARBER & SCHABELITZ. *Drawback to Murder.* 1947. Scribner. 1st ed. NF/NF. M15. $40.00

BARBER. *Somewhere in Between Quilts & Quilters of IL.* 1986. np. wrp. G2. $15.00

BARBOUR, Hugh. *Quakers in Puritan Eng.* 1965. New Haven. Yale. 2nd ed. 8vo. 272 p. VG/torn. V3. $30.00

BARCLAY, Bill; see Moorcock, Michael.

BARCLAY, John. *Argenis.* 1724. Nuremberg. Wolfgang. 12mo. 36 pls. contemporary calf. K1. $200.00

BARCLAY, Robert. *Apology for True Christian Divinity.* 1843. Providence. Knowles Vose. 8vo. 587 p. full leather. V3. $45.00

BARCLAY, Robert. *Catechism & Confession of Faith...* 1821. Wilmington, DE. Wilson. 1st Am ed. 16mo. 163 p. marbled brds. V3. $28.00

BARCLAY, Robert. *Truth Triumphant Through Spiritual Warfare...* 1831. Phil. Benjamin Stanton. 3 vols. 8vo. leather. VG. V3. $150.00

BARCUS, Frank. *Fresh-Water Fury.* 1960. MI. Wayne State U. 1st ed. VG/dj. A16. $50.00

BARDIN, John Franklin. *Devil Take the Blue-Tail Fly.* 1948. London. 1st/only hc ed. 12mo. bl cloth. VG. A11. $55.00

BARDOL, A. *L'Hysterie Simulatrice des Maladies Organique...Infants.* 1893. Paris. Battaille. 130 p. new quarter cloth/marbled brds. G7. $135.00

BARDSWELL, Frances A. *Herb Garden.* 1930 (1911). London. 2nd ed. 173 p. VG. B26. $39.00

BARGER & LANDSBERG. *Am Agriculture 1899-1939.* 1942. Nat Bureau Economy. 1st ed. 440 p. F. H10. $22.50

BARICH, Bill. *Hard To Be Good.* 1987. NY. 1st ed. sgn. F/F. A11. $25.00

BARICH, Bill. *Laughing in the Hills.* (1980). NY. Viking. 1st ed. author's 1st book. NF/NF. B4. $45.00

BARING-GOULD, W.S. *Book of Ghosts.* 1904. Putnam. 1st ed/Am issue. 383 p. red cloth. NF. H5. $300.00

BARING-GOULD, W.S. *Book of Werewolves, Being Account of Terrible Superstition.* (1973). NY. Causeway. 1st thus ed. 8vo. 266 p. VG/VG+. A2. $12.50

BARING-GOULD, W.S. *Silver Store.* 1898. London. 4th ed. VG. C1. $12.50

BARITZ, Loren. *Backfire: Hist of How Am Culture Led Us Into Vietnam...* (1985). Morrow. stated 1st ed. 393 p. dj. A7. $25.00

BARK, Conrad Voss. *On Flyfishing.* (1989). London. 166 p. M/dj. A17. $20.00

BARKATAKI, S. *Tribes of Assam.* 1969. New Delhi. Nat Book Trust. 8vo. 12 pls. 167 p. VG. W1. $18.00

BARKER, Clive. *Damnation Game.* 1987. Ace/Putnam. 1st Am ed. sgn. F/dj. M2. $50.00

BARKER, Clive. *Great & Secret Show.* (1989). Harper Row. 1st ed. VG/VG. B3. $20.00

BARKER, Clive. *In the Flesh.* (1986). Poseidon. 1st Am ed. sgn. F/dj. B4. $75.00

BARKER, Clive. *Thief of Always.* (1992). London. Harper Collins. 1st ed. F/F. B3. $45.00

BARKER, Clive. *Weaveworld.* 1987. NY. Poseidon. 1st ed. ES. VG/VG. B3. $35.00

BARKER, Clive. *Weaveworld.* 1987. Poseidon. AP of 1st ed. F/wrp. M7. $70.00

BARKER, F. *Oliviers.* 1953. Phil. 1st ed. VG/VG. B5. $40.00

BARKER, H.M. *Droving Days.* (1966). Melbourne. Pitman. 1st ed. 8vo. 147 p. F/VG+. A2. $15.00

BARKER, H.R. *Hist of 43rd Division Artillery, WWII 1941-45.* ca 1960. np. ils/fld map. 251 p. VG/torn. B18. $55.00

BARKER, Riginald C. *Hair-Trigger Brand.* 1929. Boston. Page. 1st ed. inscr/dtd 1931. VG/dj. B9. $125.00

BARKER, Rodney. *Hiroshima Maidens.* 1985. NY. Viking. 1st ed. 8vo. 240 p. VG/dj. V3. $14.00

BARKER & BIRD. *Fine Art of Quilting.* 1988. np. ils. cloth. G2. $30.00

BARKLEY, H.C. *Studies in the Art of Rat-Catching.* 1896. London. Murray. later prt. VG. O3. $65.00

BARKMAN, Carl. *Ambassador in Athens.* 1989. London. 8vo. 297 p. cloth. dj. O2. $30.00

BARLAEUS, Caspar. *Rerum...in Brasilia... Gestarum...Historia.* 1647. Amsterdam. J Blaeu. lg folio. 6 engraved pls/56 maps. full vellum/rebacked. H9. $18,000.00

BARLOW, Joel. *Hasty Pudding.* 1969. Boston. 1/700. octavo. ils Godine. F/wrp. B24. $125.00

BARLOWE, Wayne D. *Star Wars: A Pop-Up Book.* 1978. Random. 1st ed. NF. M2. $25.00

BARLY, Joseph. *Judging Saddle Horses & Roadsters.* 1945. Milwaukee. 1st ed. VG. O3. $40.00

BARNARD, Henry. *School Architecture.* 1849. NY/Cincinnati. 8vo. 387 p. brn pebbled cloth. VG. H9. $75.00

BARNARD, Robert. *City of Strangers.* (1990). London. Bantam. 1st ed. sgn. F/F. B3. $40.00

BARNARD, Robert. *Death in Purple Prose.* 1987. London. Collins. ARC. RS. F/dj. S5. $30.00

BARNARD, Robert. *Death of a Salesperson.* (1989). Scribner. 1st ed. F/F. B3. $25.00

BARNARD, Robert. *Death of a Salesperson.* 1989. London. Collins Crime Club. 1st ed. F/F. M15. $45.00

BARNARD, Robert. *Death of an Old Goat.* (1977). Walker. 1st Am ed. sgn. F/F. B4. $150.00

BARNARD, Robert. *Political Suicide.* 1986. London. Collins. 1st ed. sgn. F/F. S5. $40.00

BARNARD, Robert. *Talent to Deceive: Appreciation of Agatha Christie.* 1980. London. Collins. 1st ed. sgn. F/dj. S5. $40.00

BARNARD, Robert. *To Die Like a Gentleman.* 1993. London. Macmillan. 1st ed. F/F. S5. $27.50

BARNARD, Seymour. *Child's Garden of Relatives.* 1950. NY. 8vo. 84 p. gilt gr cloth. F/VG. H3. $20.00

BARNERS, R.M. *Military Uniforms of Britain & the Empire.* (1960). London. Seeley. 1st ed. 8vo. 347 p. F/VG+. A2. $35.00

BARNERS, R.M. *Soldiers of London.* (1963). London. Seeley. 8vo. 376 p. VG+/VG+. A2. $35.00

BARNES, Al. *Vinegar Pie & Other Tales of the Grand Traverse Region.* 1959. Detroit. 1st ed. 184 p. F/dj. A17. $25.00

BARNES, Arthur K. *Interplanetary Hunter.* 1956. Gnome. 1st ed. F/F. M2. $27.00

BARNES, Djuna. *Book.* 1923. Boni Liveright. 1st ed. G. M18. $100.00

BARNES, Djuna. *Ladies Almanak.* 1928. Paris. Barnes/Titus. 1st ed. 1/1050. sq octavo. 84 p. VG/wht wrp. H5. $350.00

BARNES, Harry Elmer. *In Quest of Truth & Justice.* 1928. Chicago. Nat Hist Soc. N2. $27.50

BARNES, Jim. *Am Book of the Dead.* 1982. Urbana. IL U. hc ed. F/NF. L3. $35.00

BARNES, Julian; see Kavanagh, Dan.

BARNES, Linda. *Snake Tattoo.* 1989. St Martin. ARC. sgn. w/promo material & photo. F/dj. S5. $40.00

BARNES, Linda. *Snake Tattoo.* 1989. St Martin. 1st ed. F/F. M15. $35.00

BARNES, Linda. *Snapshot.* 1993. Delacorte. 1st ed. F/F. T2. $19.95

BARNES, Linda. *Trouble of Fools.* 1987. St Martin. 1st ed. 1st Carlotta Carlyle. F/F. M15. $65.00

BARNES, Warner. *Bibliography of Elizabeth Barrett Browning.* 1967. Austin, TX. 8vo. 178 p. silvered bl cloth. F/NF. F1. $35.00

BARNES, Will C. *AZ Place Names.* (1970). AZ U/Granger. revised/enlarged prt (3rd ed). 519 p. cloth. NF. D3. $45.00

BARNES, Will C. *AZ Place Names.* (1977). Tucson, AZ. 6th prt. 4to. 519 p. yel cloth. B20. $40.00

BARNES & BLAKE. *Needlepoint Design Projects.* 1974. np. ils. wrp. G2. $7.00

BARNETT, A. Doak. *Cadres, Bureaucracy & Political Power in Communist China.* 1967. Columbia. 563 p. A7. $19.00

BARNETT, Donald L. *Mau Mau From Within.* (1966). MacGibbon Kee. 512 p. F/NF. A7. $35.00

BARNHOLTH, W.I. *Before Akron Was.* 1964. np. xl. 1/44. 36 p. G. B18. $25.00

BARNUM, P.T. *Struggles & Triumphs.* 1869. Hartford. 1st ed. 780 p. gilt half leather. VG. B28. $55.00

BAROJA, Pio. *Restlessness of Shanti Andia & Other Writings.* (1959). Ann Arbor. 2nd prt. 415 p. dj. A7. $14.00

BARON, Alexander. *Lowlife.* 1964. Thomas Yoseloff. 1st ed. F/NF. F4. $20.00

BARON, Walter. *Devil-Brother.* 1934. Minton Balch. 1st ed. 268 p. VG. F3. $20.00

BARON & CARVER. *Bud Stewart: MI's Legendary Lure Maker.* 1990. Marceline, MO. 1st ed. 4to. 227 p. M. A17. $75.00

BARON & FELTNER. *Shipwrecks of the Straits of Mackinac.* 1991. Dearborn. Seajay. 1st ed. sgn. 337 p. cloth. M/dj. A17. $30.00

BARR, A.H. *Matisse.* 1951. NY. VG/G+. A1. $105.00

BARR, Donald. *Space Relations.* 1973. Charterhouse. 1st ed. F/dj. M2. $15.00

BARRANCO, Manuel. *Mexico: Its Educational Problems...* 1914. NY. Columbia U. 4to. 79 p. wrp. F3. $10.00

BARRETT, Marvin. *Meet Thomas Jefferson.* ca 1967. Random. ils. 86 p. VG/G. B10. $12.00

BARRETT, Monte. *Smoke Up the Valley.* 1949. Bobbs Merrill. 1st ed. F/clip. B9. $30.00

BARRETT, Timothy. *Japanese Papermaking.* (1983). Weatherhill. 1st ed. F/NF. A7. $23.00

BARRETTO & SAYE. *Hong Kong Orchids.* 1980. Hong Kong. ils/photos. VG. B26. $22.50

BARRIE, J.M. *Courage.* 1922. London. Hodder Stoughton. wrp. A1. $25.00

BARRIE, J.M. *Greenwood Hat.* 1937. London. 1st ed. F/NF. T9. $15.00

BARRIE, J.M. *Margaret Ogilvy.* 1896. London. Hodder Stoughton. G. A1. $30.00

BARRIE, J.M. *Peter & Wendy.* 1911. Scribner. 1st Am ed. 8vo. 267 p. gr cloth. VG. F1. $85.00

BARRIE, J.M. *Peter Pan & Wendy.* 1953 (1940). Scribner. ils Edmund Blampied. 216 p. VG+/G. S10. $50.00

BARRIE, J.M. *Peter Pan in Kensington Gardens.* 1906. London. Hodder Stoughton. 1st trade ed. quarto. 125 p. Bayntun bdg. VG. H5. $850.00

BARRIE, J.M. *Peter Pan in Kensington Gardens.* 1906. London. 1/500. ils/sgn Rackham. 50 mtd color pls. vellum/silk ties. NF. H5. $5,000.00

BARRIE, J.M. *Peter Pan in Kensington Gardens.* 1910. Hodder Stoughton. 7th ed. ils Rackham/50 mtd pls. 125 p. VG. D1. $450.00

BARRIE, J.M. *Peter Pan in Kensington Gardens.* 1925 (1906). Scribner. ils Rackham/16 color pls. 126 p. VG+/dj. M20. $100.00

BARRIE, J.M. *Peter Pan.* 1911. Grosset Dunlap. photoplay ed. 220 p. VG/torn. M20. $25.00

BARRIE, J.M. *Peter Pan.* 1940. Scribner. later ed. ils Edmund Blampied. G. L1. $30.00

BARRIE, J.M. *Peter Pan.* 1950. NY. 1st ed. ils Nora S Unwin. NF. T9. $20.00

BARRIE, J.M. *Sentimental Tommy.* 1896. Scribner. 1st ed. 478 p. G+. S10. $25.00

BARRIE, J.M. *Tommy & Grizel.* 1900. Scribner. 1st ed. ils Bernard Partridge. VG. S10. $30.00

BARRIE, J.M. *Window in Thrums.* 1911. Scribner. 1st thus ed. ils AC·Michael. VG. M18. $60.00

BARRIE, J.M. *Works of...* 1929. Scribner. Peter Pan ed. 1/1030. 14 vols. lg 8vo. F/slipcases. B20. $225.00

BARRINGER, GARNETT & PAGE. *U of VA: Its Hist, Influence, Equipment & Characteristics...* 1904. Lewis. 2 vols. aeg. half leather. G. B10. $100.00

BARRINGER, Leslie. *Gerfalcon.* 1927. Doubleday. 1st ed. VG. M2. $30.00

BARRON, L. *Lawns & How To Make Them...Proper Keeping of Putting Greens.* 1914. NY. ils/index. 174 p. A17. $12.50

BARRON, Neil. *Anatomy of Wonder.* 1976. Bowker. 1st ed. VG/wrp. M2. $12.00

BARRON, Neil. *Anatomy of Wonder: SF.* 1981. NY. Bowker. 2nd ed. inscr/sgn. F/sans. N3. $15.00

BARROW, Fanny. *Fairy Nightcaps.* 1861. NY. 1st ed. 16mo. pls. 215 p. gilt bl cloth. VG. H3. $30.00

BARROW, George. *Fire of Life.* 1940s. London. Hutchinson. 2nd prt. 256 p. red cloth. VG. M7. $60.00

BARROW, John. *Life of Richard Earl Howe...* 1838. London. 1st ed. 432 p. rebound leather. VG. D7. $35.00

BARROWS, William. *OR: Struggle for Possession.* 1901. Boston. xl. 11th imp. 12mo. 383 p. VG. D3. $12.50

BARRUEL, Augustin. *Memoirs, Ils the Hist of Jacobinism.* 1797-98. London. prt for author. 4 vols. old calf/rebacked gilt red calf spine labels. K1. $175.00

BARRY, James. *Ships of the Great Lakes: 300 Yrs of Navigation.* 1974. Howell N Books. 2nd ed. VG/dj. A16. $40.00

BARRY, James. *Wrecks & Rescues of the Great Lakes.* 1981. Howell N Books. VG/dj. A16. $40.00

BARRY, Patrick. *Fruit Garden...* 1863. Rochester. 398 p. H10. $35.00

BARRY, Patrick. *Fruit Garden: A Treatise...* 1853 (1851). Auburn, NY. ils 398 p. B26. $49.00

BARRY, Philip. *Phil Story.* 1941. Pocket Book #102. 1st pb ed. VG+/K Hepburn on wrp. A11. $25.00

BARRY, Philip. *Wht Wings: A Play.* 1927. NY. Boni. 1st ed. presentation to Alexander Woolcott. VG+. B20. $100.00

BART, Barry. *It's Story Time.* ca 1940. no pub. 24 p. VG+. A3. $12.50

BARTH, John. *Chimera.* 1972. Random. 1st ed. F/NF. N3. $20.00

BARTH, John. *End of the Road.* 1958. Doubleday. 1st ed. author's 2nd book. F/prt dj. B24. $225.00

BARTH, John. *Giles, the Goat-Boy.* 1966. NY. correct 1st ed w/code. F/clip. A15. $50.00

BARTH, John. *Last Voyage of Somebody the Sailor.* 1991. Little Brn. ARC. NF/wrp. B2. $35.00

BARTH, John. *Lost in the Funhouse.* 1968. Garden City. 1st ed. w/sgn label. NF/NF. E3. $55.00

BARTH, John. *Once Upon a Time. A Floating Opera.* 1994. Little Brn. AP. 400 p. NF/wrp. B2. $40.00

BARTH, John. *Sot-Weed Factor.* 1961. Secker Warburg. 1st ed. F/F. C4. $100.00

BARTH, John. *Tidewater Tales.* 1987. NY. 1st ed. F/NF. A11. $40.00

BARTH, Richard. *Rag Bag Clan.* 1983. London. Gollancz. 1st ed. author's 1st book. F/F. S5. $20.00

BARTHA, Reinhold. *Fodder Plants in Sahal Zone of Africa.* 1970. Munchen/NY. 118 pls. 306 p. B26. $26.00

BARTHEL, Thomas S. *8th Land: Polynesian Discovery & Settlement Easter Island.* 1978. Honolulu. 1st Eng ed. 8vo. 372 p. NF/dj. S10. $30.00

BARTHELME, Donald. *Amateurs.* (1977). Kegan Paul. 1st ed. F/F. B3. $25.00

BARTHELME, Donald. *Come Back, Dr Caligari.* 1964. Little Brn. 1st ed. sgn. author's 1st book. NF/NF. L3. $300.00

BARTHELME, Donald. *Guilty Pleasures.* 1974. FSG. 1st ed. NF/NF. E3. $25.00

BARTHELME, Donald. *Guilty Pleasures.* 1974. NY. 1st ed. sgn. F/F. A11. $35.00

BARTHELME, Donald. *Here in the Village.* 1978. Lord John. 1st ed. 1/275. sgn. gilt linen/brds. F. F1. $80.00

BARTHELME, Donald. *King.* (1990). Harper Row. 1st ed. ils Barry Moser. F/F. B3. $25.00

BARTHELME, Donald. *Presents.* 1980. Dallas. Pressworks. 1st ed. 1/376. sgn. F. F1. $95.00

BARTHELME, Donald. *Slightly Irregular Fire Engine.* 1971. FSG. 1st ed. F/VG+. scarce. P2. $100.00

BARTHELME, Donald. *Unspeakable Practices, Unnatural Acts.* 1968. FSG. 1st ed. F/NF. C4. $35.00

BARTHELME, Donald. *40 Stories.* (1987). Putnam. 1st ed. F/NF. B3. $30.00

BARTHELME, Frederick. *Brothers.* (1993). Viking. AP. NF/prt cream wrp. B3. $15.00

BARTHES, Roland. *Barthes Reader.* nd. Hill Wang. AP. edit Susan Sontag. NF/tall wrp. L3. $35.00

BARTHOLOMAEI, De Moor. *Instauratione Medicnae, ad Sanitatis Tutelam...* 1695. Amsterdam. Borstius. 440 p. contemporary full polished vellum. G7. $165.00

BARTHOLOW, Roberts. *Cholera: Its Causes, Symptoms, Pathology & Treatment.* 1893. Phil. Lea Bros. pub file copy. G7. $75.00

BARTLETT, Charles H. *Tales of Kankakee Land.* (1977). Berrien Springs. facsimile of 1907 ed. 232 p. F/dj. A17. $9.50

BARTLETT, Francis H. *Sigmund Freud: Marxian Essay.* 1938. London. Gollancz. 12mo. 141 p. bl cloth. G1. $30.00

BARTLETT, John Russell. *Personal Narrative of Explorations & Incidents...* 1854. NY. Appleton. 2 vols (mismatched bdg). cloth. H9. $425.00

BARTLETT, Percy W. *Barrow Caldbury: A Memoir.* 1960. London. Bannisdale. 1st ed. 8vo. 159 p. M/NF. V3. $14.00

BARTLETT, Rachel. *Off the Wall: Collection of Feminist Graffiti.* 1982. London. Proteus. wrp. N2. $7.50

BARTLETT, Richard A. *Great Surveys of the Am W.* ca 1962. Norman, OK. 8vo. 410 p. pict wrp. H9. $30.00

BARTLEY. *Joy of Machine Embroidery.* 1976. np. pb. G2. $6.00

BARTON, Clara. *Red Cross in Peace & War.* 1899. WA, DC. 1st ed. pls. 703 p. gilt cloth. VG. S9. $28.00

BARTON, Clara. *Red Cross: Hist of This Remarkable Internat Movement...* (1898). WA, DC. Red Cross. pls. 684 p. VG. S9. $18.00

BARTON, Frank Townend. *Ponies & All About Them.* 1911. London. 1st ed. 506 p. VG. O3. $58.00

BARTON, Frank. *Hounds: Their Points & Management.* 1913. London. Long. 1st ed. VG. O3. $65.00

BARTON, George. *World's Greatest Military Spies.* 1947. np. xl. ils. 322 p. O7. $9.50

BARTON, J.G. *Wild Flowers.* 1992. Spring Books. VG/dj. A16. $15.00

BARTON, William E. *Abraham Lincoln & Walt Whitman.* nd. Bobbs Merrill. VG. V2. $9.00

BARTON, William E. *Paternity of Abraham Lincoln.* 1920. np. 1st ed. index. 416 p. O7. $14.50

BARTOSZEWSKI & LEWIN. *Righteous Among Nations: How Poles Helped the Jews.* 1969. London. Earlscourt. 834 p. VG/fair. S3. $35.00

BARTRAM, W. *Travels Through N & SC.* 1791. Phil. 1st ed. pls/map. sheepskin. VG. C6. $7,000.00

BARTUSEK, Libushka. *Happy Times in Finland.* 1941. Knopf. 1st ed. ils Warren Chappell. 146 p. VG/G+. T5. $30.00

BARUCH, Bernard M. *Baruch, My Own Story.* 1957. Holt. 337 p. VG/poor. S3. $20.00

BARUCH, Bernard M. *Public Yrs.* 1960. Holt. 1st ed. G+. V2. $5.00

BARZUN, Jacques. *Birthday Tribute to Rex Stout: Dec 1, 1965.* 1965. Viking. 1st ed. 15-p stapled pamphlet. F/wrp. M15. $50.00

BASHLINE & SAULTS. *Am's Great Outdoors: Ils Anthology of 200 Yrs Writing.* (1976). NY. ils/pls. 367 p. dj. A17. $17.50

BASHORE, H.B. *Sanitation of Recreation Camps & Parks.* 1908. Wiley. 1st ed. xl. G. A2. $12.50

BASKIN, John. *New Burlington: Life & Death of an Am Village.* 1976. Norton. 1st ed. 8vo. 260 p. VG/dj. V3. $12.00

BASKIN, Leonard. *Ars Anatomica: Medical Fantasia.* 1972. NY. Medicina Rara. 1/2800. ils/sgn Baskin. F/slipcase. F1. $200.00

BASKIN, Leonard. *Ars Anatomica: Medical Fantasia.* 1972. Phil. Lippincott. 2nd ed. 352 p. orig cloth. H9. $150.00

BASKIN, Leonard. *Hosie's Zoo.* 1981. Viking. 1st ed. 4to. F/VG. D1. $40.00

BASKIN, Leonard. *Imps, Demons, Hobgoblins, Witches, Fairies & Elves.* 1984. Pantheon. 1st ed. F/dj. M2. $10.00

BASKIN, Leonard. *Leonard Baskin: Bowdoin College Mus of Art.* 1962. Brunswick, ME. lg octavo. 84 photos. 110 p. w/orig prt. F. B24. $100.00

BASLER, Roy P. *Collected Works of Abraham Lincoln.* 1953-55. Rutgers. 1st ed. 9 vols. cloth. VG. M8. $150.00

BASS, Jack. *Unlikely Heroes.* (1981). Simon Schuster. 1st ed. 352 p. NF/NF. A7. $18.00

BASS, Rick. *Deer Pasture.* (1985). TX A&M. 1st ed. sgn. ils/sgn Elizabeth Hughes. F/F. B3. $90.00

BASS, Rick. *Nine Mile Wolves.* 1992. Livingston. Clark City. 1/125. sgn/#d. F/slipcase. C4. $125.00

BASS, Rick. *Oil Notes.* 1989. London. Collins. 1st ed. F/F. L3. $35.00

BASS, Rick. *Watch.* 1989. Norton. 1st ed. author's 1st book of fiction. F/F. L3. $45.00

BASS, Rick. *Wild to the Heart.* (1987). Stackpole. 1st ed. sgn. ils/sgn Elizabeth Hughes. F/F. B3. $65.00

BASS, Rick. *Winter Notes From MT.* 1991. Houghton Mifflin/Lawrence. AP. inscr. F/bl wrp. C4. $50.00

BASSANI, Georgio. *Smell of Hay.* (1975). HBJ. ARC/1st Am ed. sgn. RS. w/pub party invitation. F/F. B4. $200.00

BASSHAM, Ben L. *John Taylor Arms: Am Etcher.* 1975. Elvehjem Art Center. essay/exhibition catalog. 76 p. D2. $25.00

BASTABLE, Bernard; see Barnard, Robert.

BATAILLE, Georges. *Death & Sensuality.* 1962. NY. Walker. 1st Eng-language ed. F/NF. B2. $100.00

BATES, Daisy. *Long Shadow of Little Rock.* 1962. McKay. 234 p. clip dj. A7. $35.00

BATES, Daisy. *Passing of the Aborigines.* 1938. London. 1st ed. ils. 258 p. gilt red cloth. F. H3. $75.00

BATES, Elisha. *Doctrines of Friends.* 1825. Mt Pleasant, OH. 2nd ed. 320 p. leather. G. D7. $85.00

BATES, H.E. *Down the River.* 1937. Holt. ARC. ils Anges Miller Parker. RS. VG+/dj. M20. $150.00

BATES, Joseph D. Jr. *Atlantic Salmon Flies & Fishing.* (1970). Stackpole. 1st ed. 362 p. F/dj. A17. $50.00

BATES, Mrs. D.B. *Incidents on Land & Later; or, 4 Yrs on Pacific Coast.* 1857. Boston. James French. 1st ed. 336 p. orig gilt blk cloth. VG+. K1. $150.00

BATES, Mrs. D.B. *Incidents on Land & Water; or, 4 Yrs on Pacific Coast.* 1857. Boston. James French. 2nd ed. 336 p. gilt bdg. G. H7. $40.00

BATES, Mrs. D.B. *Incidents on Land & Water; or, 4 Yrs on Pacific Coast.* 1860. Boston. thick 12mo. 336 p. gilt blk cloth. H9. $35.00

BATH. *Needlework in Am.* 1979. np. cloth. G2. $40.00

BATMAN, Richard. *James Pattie's W: The Dream & Reality.* 1986. OK U. ils/maps/index. 378 p. F/wrp. B19. $9.50

BATTEN, Auriol. *Flowers of S Africa.* 1986. Sandton. 1/4000. sgn. 100 full-p pls. 401 p. NF/dj. B26. $139.00

BATTEN, John Mullin. *Random Thoughts.* 1896. private prt. 1st thus ed. 320 p. NF. M8. $125.00

BATTEY, Thomas C. *Life & Adventures of a Quaker Among the Indians.* 1875. Lee Shepard. 1st ed. ils. 339 p. VG. H7. $125.00

BAUDELAIRE, Charles. *Little Poems in Prose.* ca 1927. Paris. Titus. 1st thus ed. 1/800. ils Bosschere/12 pls. NF. B24. $165.00

BAUDELAIRE, Charles. *Paris Spleen.* 1947. New Directions. 1st ed. trans Varese. F. B2. $35.00

BAUER, Eddy. *Ils WWII Encyclopedia.* 1978. Stuttman. 1st ed. 8vo. F. A8. $50.00

BAUER, Elisabeth. *Armenie. Son Histoire et Son Present.* 1977. Paris. 4to. photos. 180 p. cloth. O2. $30.00

BAUER, Erwin. *Bear in Their World.* (1990). Outdoor Life. 2nd prt. 4to. 254 p. F/dj. A17. $17.50

BAUER, Marion Dane. *Ghost Eye.* 1992. Scholastic. 1st ed. 8vo. 82 p. F/F. A3. $12.95

BAUER, Steven. *Satyrday.* 1980. Berkley. 1st ed. author's 1st book. F/F. N3. $15.00

BAUER & ROBINSON. *Putting It All Together.* 1971. Hawthorn. 1st ed. F/VG. P8. $55.00

BAUM, L. Frank. *Cowardly Lion of Oz.* pre 1935. Reilly Lee. ils Neill/12 color pls. 266 p. VG/dj. D1. $400.00

BAUM, L. Frank. *Dorothy & the Wizard in Oz.* 1908. Reilly Britton. 1st ed/2nd state. 16 color pls. VG. M18. $200.00

BAUM, L. Frank. *Dorothy & the Wizard of Oz.* nd. Reilly Lee. blk & wht Neill ils. gray bdg. G. L1. $75.00

BAUM, L. Frank. *Dorothy & the Wizard of Oz.* nd. Reilly Lee. ils Neill/12 color pls. bl stp gr cloth. G. L1. $125.00

BAUM, L. Frank. *Dorothy & the Wizard of Oz.* 1980. Toronto. Coles. 1st thus ed. ils Neill. VG/sans. L1. $26.50

BAUM, L. Frank. *Emerald City of Oz.* nd. Reilly Lee. blk & wht Neill ils. G/G. L1. $100.00

BAUM, L. Frank. *Emerald City of Oz.* 1920. Reilly Lee. ils Neill/12 pls. 295 p. tan cloth. G. A3. $100.00

BAUM, L. Frank. *Father Goose, His Book.* ca 1910. Donahue. 6th ed. ils Denslow. VG/dj. D1. $385.00

BAUM, L. Frank. *Father Goose's Yearbook.* 1907. Reilly Britton. ils Walter J Enright. pict cloth. G. M20. $100.00

BAUM, L. Frank. *Father Goose's Yr Book: Quaint Quacks & Feathered Shafts...* 1907. Reilly Britton. 1st/only ed. narrow octavo. gr cloth/pict label. NF. B24. $275.00

BAUM, L. Frank. *Glinda of Oz.* nd. Reilly Lee. blk & wht Neill ils. olive cloth/color label. VG. L1. $150.00

BAUM, L. Frank. *Glinda of Oz.* 1920. Reilly Lee. 1st ed. 4to. tan cloth. lists to Glinda of Oz. G. A3. $250.00

BAUM, L. Frank. *Land of Oz.* nd. Reilly Lee. popular ed. VG-. M2. $40.00

BAUM, L. Frank. *Land of Oz.* nd. Reilly Lee. wht cloth. G/sans. L1. $17.50

BAUM, L. Frank. *Land of Oz.* 1925. Reilly Lee. ils Neill. popular ed. 4to. 286 p. gr cloth w/pict label. G. A3/L1. $75.00

BAUM, L. Frank. *Land of Oz.* 1939. Reilly Lee. ils Neill. yel cloth w/pict label. G. A3. $40.00

BAUM, L. Frank. *Little Wizard Stories of Oz.* 1985. NY. Schocken. 1st thus ed. ils Neill. rem mk. VG/VG. L1. $13.50

BAUM, L. Frank. *Lost Princess of Oz.* ca 1940s-50s. 4to. 312 p. gr cloth. VG/Roy Craft ils dj. A3. $25.00

BAUM, L. Frank. *Lost Princess of Oz.* ca 1930. Reilly Lee. early reprint. bl cloth. lists to Glinda of Oz. G. A3. $95.00

BAUM, L. Frank. *Lost Princess of Oz.* nd. Reilly Lee. blk & wht John Neill ils. G/G. L1. $100.00

BAUM, L. Frank. *Lost Princess of Oz.* 1917. Reilly Lee. ils Neill/12 color pls. G. L1. $175.00

BAUM, L. Frank. *Lucky Bucky in Oz.* 1942. Reilly Lee. ils Neill. bright gr bdg/pict label. G. L1. $250.00

BAUM, L. Frank. *Magic of Oz.* nd. Reilly Lee. blk & wht John R Neill ils. burgandy bdg/pict label. VG. L1. $120.00

BAUM, L. Frank. *Magic of Oz.* 1920. Reilly Lee. 1st ed/3rd state. gr cloth. lists to Glinda of Oz. G. A3. $150.00

BAUM, L. Frank. *Marvelous Land of Oz.* 1989. Easton Pr. gilt bl leatherette. VG. L1. $50.00

BAUM, L. Frank. *Master Key, an Electrical Fairy Tale.* 1901. Bowen Merrill. 1st ed/1st state. ils Cory/12 color pls. VG. F1. $295.00

BAUM, L. Frank. *Mother Goose in Prose.* nd. Bounty Books. 1st thus ed. ils Maxfield Parrish. VG/VG. L1. $25.00

BAUM, L. Frank. *New Wizard of Oz.* (1939). Bobbs Merrill. ils Denslow/8 pls. 208 p. gilt gr cloth. VG/dj. D1. $275.00

BAUM, L. Frank. *New Wizard of Oz.* 1903. Bobbs Merrill. ils Denslow/7 color ils. gr bdg. G. L1. $85.00

BAUM, L. Frank. *Ozma of Oz.* 1911. Reilly Britton. 1st ed/2nd state. G. M18. $175.00

BAUM, L. Frank. *Ozma of Oz.* 1989. Easton Pr. 1st thus ed. red leatherette. VG. L1. $50.00

BAUM, L. Frank. *Patchwork Girl of Oz.* 1913. Reilly Lee. color ils. fair/poor. L1. $75.00

BAUM, L. Frank. *Purple Dragon.* 1976. Fictioneer Books. 1st ed. VG/dj. M2. $35.00

BAUM, L. Frank. *Rinkitink in Oz.* nd. Reilly Lee. ils Neill. gr bdg. G. L1. $45.00

BAUM, L. Frank. *Rinkitink in Oz.* pre 1935. Reilly Lee. ils Neill/12 color pls. 314 p. NF/dj. D1. $400.00

BAUM, L. Frank. *Road to Oz.* ca 1965. Reilly Lee. 4to. 268 p. wht cloth w/pict label. VG. A3. $17.50

BAUM, L. Frank. *Road to Oz.* 1909. Reilly Britton. 1st ed/1st state. ils JR Neill. pict gr cloth. NF. B24. $850.00

BAUM, L. Frank. *Road to Oz.* 1939. Rand McNally. abridged ed. ils Neill. VG. L1. $30.00

BAUM, L. Frank. *Road to Oz.* 1939. Reilly Lee. Jr ed. color pls. VG. M18. $25.00

BAUM, L. Frank. *Royal Book of Oz.* nd. Reilly Lee. ils Neill. VG. scarce. L1. $150.00

BAUM, L. Frank. *Scalawagons of Oz.* nd. Reilly Lee. blk & wht Neill ils. rose bdg/pict label. VG. L1. $300.00

BAUM, L. Frank. *Scarecrow & the Tin Woodman.* ca 1932. Reilly Lee. Little Wizard Series/Jell-O. 29 p. VG+/wrp. A3. $50.00

BAUM, L. Frank. *Scarecrow of Oz.* ca 1940s. Reilly Lee. ils JR Neill. 288 p. VG/dj lists to Magic Mimic. D1. $150.00

BAUM, L. Frank. *Scarecrow of Oz.* nd. Reilly Lee. gold bdg/pict label. VG. L1. $120.00

BAUM, L. Frank. *Scarecrow of Oz.* 1940. Reilly Lee. ils Neill. 4to. 288 p. red cloth w/pict label. G. A3. $30.00

BAUM, L. Frank. *See Fairies.* 1911. Reilly Lee. bl bdg/pict label. VG. L1. $85.00

BAUM, L. Frank. *Sky Island.* ca 1927. Reilly Lee. ils JR Neill. red cloth/pict label. F/NF. F1. $275.00

BAUM, L. Frank. *Sky Island.* 1912. Reilly Lee. ils Neill. orange bdg. VG/VG. L1. $55.00

BAUM, L. Frank. *Surprising Adventures of Magical Monarch of Mo.* 1903. Bobbs Merrill. 1st ed/2nd state. 12 color pls. G. M18. $175.00

BAUM, L. Frank. *Tik-Tok of Oz.* nd. Reilly Lee. blk & wht Neill ils. olive bdg/pict label. G+. L1. $125.00

BAUM, L. Frank. *Tik-Tok of Oz.* 1920. Reilly Lee. 4to. 271 p. bl cloth w/pict label. G. A3. $85.00

BAUM, L. Frank. *Tik-Tok of Oz.* 1932. Reilly Lee. ils Neill/12 color pls. olive bdg. L1. $225.00

BAUM, L. Frank. *Tin Woodman of Oz.* ca 1940s. Reilly Lee. 8vo. 287 p. beige cloth. VG/dj. D1. $150.00

BAUM, L. Frank. *Tin Woodman of Oz.* nd. Reilly Lee. blk & wht Neill ils. olive bdg/pict label. VG. L1. $135.00

BAUM, L. Frank. *Tin Woodman of Oz.* 1918. Reilly Lee. 1st ed/1st state. ils Neill/12 color pls. 288 p. VG. D1. $1,000.00

BAUM, L. Frank. *Tin Woodman of Oz.* 1930. Reilly Lee. VG. M18. $60.00

BAUM, L. Frank. *Tin Woodman of Oz...Orig Oz Story.* ca 1955. Reilly Lee. ils Dale Ulrey. 262 p. cloth. VG/G+. A3. $20.00

BAUM, L. Frank. *Visitors From Oz.* 1960. Reilly Lee. ils Dick Martin. G. L1. $35.00

BAUM, L. Frank. *Wizard of Oz.* 1903? Bobbs Merrill. ils Denslow/8 color pls. gr cloth. VG. L1. $125.00

BAUM, L. Frank. *Wizard of Oz.* (1944). Saalfield. ils Julian Wehr/6 movable color pls. VG. D1. $200.00

BAUM, L. Frank. *Wizard of Oz.* 1944. Bobbs Merrill. ils Evelyn Copelman/8 color pls. VG/G. L1. $30.00

BAUM, L. Frank. *Wizard of Oz.* 1956. Reilly Lee. ils WW Denslow. wht bdg. fair. L1. $25.00

BAUM, L. Frank. *Wizard of Oz.* 1983. Weekly Reader BC. G. L1. $17.50

BAUM, L. Frank. *Wizard of Oz.* 1986. Western Pub. 1st thus ed. ils Kathy Mitchell. VG. L1. $15.00

BAUM, L. Frank. *Wonder City of Oz.* 1940. Reilly Lee. blk & wht Neill ils. bl bdg/pict label. G. L1. $300.00

BAUM, L. Frank. *Wonderful Wizard of Oz.* 1982. Lemon Tree. 1st thus ed. VG/VG. L1. $12.50

BAUMAN, Richard. *For the Reputation of Truth...PA Quakers, 1750-1800.* 1991. New Haven. Yale. 1st ed. 8vo. 378 p. VG/VG. V3. $16.00

BAUMBACH, Jonathan. *Landscape of Nightmare.* nd. np. 1st ed. author's 1st book. sgn. NF/VG+. A11. $50.00

BAUMEL, Rachel Bail. *Alec Templeton's Music Boxes.* 1958. NY. Wilfred Funk. dj. N2. $10.00

BAUMGARTEL, Walter H. *Other Side of the Chinese Question...* (1971). San Francisco. facsimile of 1886 ed. xl. 76 p. cloth. NF. D3. $25.00

BAUMGARTNER & LIEB. *Phil Phillies.* 1953. Putnam. 1st ed. VG/G+. P8. $175.00

BAUR, John I. *Joseph Stella.* 1971. Praeger. 10 color pls. 154 p. cloth. dj. D2. $80.00

BAUSCH, Richard. *Rebel Powers.* 1993. Houghton Mifflin. ARC. F/wrp. B2/B3. $35.00

BAXT, George. *Talking Pictures Murder Case.* 1990. St Martin. NF/dj. C8. $30.00

BAXT, George. *Tallulah Bankhead Murder Case.* 1987. St Martin. 1st ed. inscr. F/F. M15. $35.00

BAXTER, Charles. *First Light.* 1987. Viking. 1st ed. inscr. author's 1st book. F/F. B2. $75.00

BAXTER, Charles. *Relative Stranger.* 1990. Norton. 1st ed. F/NF. B3. $35.00

BAXTER, Charles. *Relative Stranger.* 1990. Norton. AP. w/edit letter. F/bl wrp. C4. $40.00

BAXTER, Charles. *Shadow Play.* (1993). Norton. 1st ed/1st prt. F/F. B3. $75.00

BAXTER, Charles. *Through the Safety Net.* 1985. Viking. 1st ed. sgn. F/NF. B2. $75.00

BAXTER, George Owen. *Brother of the Cheyennes.* 1935. NY. Macaulay. 1st ed. VG/dj. B9. $35.00

BAXTER, George Owen. *Call of the Blood.* 1934. Macauley. 1st ed. VG+/dj. B9. $75.00

BAXTER, Glen. *Impending Gleam.* 1981. NY. NF/sans. A11. $25.00

BAXTER, John. *New & Impartial Hist of Eng.* ca 1800. London. Symonds. sm folio. 45 pls. 830 p. contemporary calf. K1. $350.00

BAXTER, Richard. *Gildas Salvianus: Reformed Pastor.* 1950. London. Epworth. 191 p. H10. $15.00

BAXTER, W.E. *Winter in India.* 1883. NY. 1st Am ed. 154 p. pict tan wrp. scarce. H3. $30.00

BAXTER, W.T. *House of Hancock.* 1945. Cambridge, MA. 1st ed. 8vo. 321 p. VG/G. A2. $15.00

BAYARD, James. *Brief Exposition of Constitution of US.* 1850. Phil. Hogan Thompson. contemporary leather. M11. $150.00

BAYARD, Thomas F. *Am Rights in Samoa.* 1988 (1848). GPO. w/sgn p. 300+ p. quarter leather. VG. O6. $95.00

BAYER, William. *Blind Side.* 1989. Villard. 1st ed. F/dj. B9. $10.00

BAYER, William. *Punish Me w/Kisses.* (1980). Congdon Lattes. 1st ed. F/dj. B9. $12.50

BAYLE, A.L.J. *Variae Organorum Degenerations ab una Eadem Causa Pendent?* 1826. Paris. 4to. 18 p. wrp. H9. $175.00

BAYLES, William D. *Caesars in Goose Step.* (1940). Harper. 1st ed. 8vo. 262 p. F/NF. B20. $25.00

BAYLEY, Barrington J. *Soul of the Robot.* 1974. Doubleday. 1st ed. F/VG. N3. $10.00

BAYLEY & MAYNE. *Mouldy.* 1982. Knopf. 1st Am ed. ils Nicola Bayley. M/M. D1. $50.00

BAYLIES, Francis. *Hist Memoir of Colony of New Plymouth 1620-1641.* 1830. Boston. 1st ed. 4 parts in 2 vols. VG. B28. $95.00

BAYNTON-WILLIAMS,, Ashley. *Town & City Maps of the British Isles, 1800-55.* 1992. London. Studio. 56 plans. M/M. O6. $50.00

BAZIN, Andre. *French Cinema of the Occupation & Resistance.* (1982). Ungar Film Lib series. 166 p. clip dj. A7. $15.00

BAZIN, Andre. *Jean Renoir.* (1973). Simon Schuster. 1st ed. 320 p. clip dj. A7. $15.00

BEACH, Belle. *Riding & Driving for Women.* 1978. Northland. facsimile. M/M. O3. $35.00

BEACH, Rex. *Silver Horde.* 1909. NY. 1st ed. 389 p. cloth. VG. D3. $12.50

BEACH, Rex. *Spoilers.* ca 1942. Grosset Dunlap. photoplay ed. VG/dj. B4. $75.00

BEACH, S.A. *Apples of NY.* 1905. Albany. Lyon. 2 vols. H10. $150.00

BEACH, Sylvia. *Shakespeare & Co.* 1959. NY. 1st ed. VG/VG. B5. $30.00

BEADLE, J.H. *W Wilds & the Men Who Redeem Them.* 1879. Cincinnati. Jones Bros. subscriber ed. thick 8vo. 628 p. gilt half morocco. H9. $110.00

BEAGLE, Peter S. *Folk of the Air.* 1986. Del Rey. 1st ed. F/dj. M2. $20.00

BEAGLE, Peter S. *Folk of the Air.* 1986. NY. Del Rey/Ballantine. 1st ed. inscr. F/F. B20. $35.00

BEAGLE, Peter S. *Lila the Werewolf.* 1974. Santa Barbara. Capra. 2nd prt. F/wrp. N3. $10.00

BEAGLEHOLE, J.C. *Life of Capt James Cook.* 1974. Stanford. 760 p. NF/dj. O6. $75.00

BEAHM, George. *Stephen King Story.* 1991. Andrews McMeel. 1st ed. M/M. T2. $16.95

BEALS, Carleton. *Brimstone & Chili.* 1927. Knopf. 1st ed. ils. cloth. F3. $15.00

BEALS, Ralph L. *Cheran: Sierra Tarascan Village.* 1946. Smithsonian. 1st ed. ils/notes/glossary. 234 p. NF/wrp. B19. $20.00

BEALS, Ralph L. *Ethnology of the W Mix.* 1945. Berkeley. 1st ed. ils. 175 p. prt gray wrp. H3. $15.00

BEALS, Ralph. *Ethnology of the W Mix.* 1973. Cooper Sq. reprint of 1945 UCPAAE Vol 42, No 1 ed. 175 p. F3. $15.00

BEAMES, John. *Treatise on Laws & Customs of Kingdom of Eng.* 1812. London. Valpy. rebacked/orig label. M11. $450.00

BEAMONT, William. *Diary of Journey From Warrington to the E...1854.* 1855. Warrington. 1st ed. 8vo. 268 p. new quarter calf. O2. $175.00

BEANEY. *Art of the Needle, Designing in Fabric Thread.* 1988. np. cloth. G2. $28.00

BEAR, Greg. *Heads.* 1991. St Martin. 1st Am ed. M/M. T2. $12.00

BEARD, Dan. *Am Boys Handy Book.* 1882. Scribner. 1st ed. octavo. 391 p. olive gr cloth. VG/slipcase. H5. $225.00

BEARD, Dan. *Moonblight & 6 Feet of Romance.* 1892. NY. Webster. 1st ed. presentation inscr. 222 p. gr cloth. K1. $200.00

BEARD, Gordon. *Birds on the Wing.* 1967. Doubleday. later prt. F/VG+. P8. $65.00

BEARDSLEY, Aubrey. *Uncollected Work of Aubrey Beardsley.* 1925. Bodley Head. 1st ed. 4to. 155 pls. bl cloth. F/VG+. F1. $200.00

BEARDSLEY, Harry M. *Joseph Smith & His Mormon Empire.* 1931. Boston. 1st ed. ils. 421 p. cloth. VG. D3. $35.00

BEATIE, R.H. Jr. *Road to Manassas. Growth of Union Command in E Theatre...* 1961. Cooper Sq. G/dj. A16. $25.00

BEATON, Cecil. *Yrs Between: Diaries, 1939-44.* (1965). HRW. stated 1st ed. photos. NF/NF. A7. $30.00

BEATTIE, Ann. *Jacklightning.* 1981. Worcester. ltd ed. 1/250. sgn. F/sewn wrp. E3. $60.00

BEATTIE, Ann. *Where You'll Find Me.* 1986. Linden/Simon Schuster. ARC/1st ed. RS. w/promo material. F/NF. A7. $30.00

BEATTY & SARGENT. *Basic Rug Hooking.* 1977. np. ils. wrp. G2. $15.00

BEAUCHAMP, Loren; see Silverberg, Robert.

BEAUDRY, Evien G. *Puppy Stories.* (1934). Saalfield. ils Diana Thorne. 92 p. VG/G. T5. $45.00

BEAUMONT, Charles. *Intruder.* 1959. NY. 1st/only novel. F/VG+. A11. $75.00

BEAUMONT, Charles. *Magic Man.* 1965. Fawcett/Gold Medal. PBO. VG/wrp. L3. $35.00

BEAUMONT, Charles. *Night Ride & Other Journeys.* 1960. Bantam. PBO. F/unread. A11. $30.00

BEAUMONT, Charles. *Run From the Hunter.* 1957. Greenwich, CT. PBO. VG+/ils wrp. A11. $25.00

BEAUMONT, Cyril W. *Design for the Ballet.* 1937. London. Studio. 4to. bl cloth. NF/dj. F1. $125.00

BEAUMONT, William. *Experiments & Observations on the Gastric Juice...* 1838. Edinburgh. Maclachlan Steward. 1st British ed. VG. G7. $775.00

BEAUMONT, William. *Physiology of Digestion w/Experiments on Gastric Juice...* 1848. Burlington. C Goodrich. 2nd/corrected ed. 303 p. orig brds/rebacked. G7. $475.00

BEAVER, L.J. *Hist Memories From Monuments & Plaques of W WA.* (ca 1964). self pub. ltd ed. 4to. 272 p. F/wrp. A2. $20.00

BEAVER, Paul. *Attack Helicopters.* 1987. Arms & Armour Pr. VG/dj. A16. $18.00

BECK, Henry Houghton. *Cuba's Fight for Freedom & War w/Spain.* 1898. Phil. Globe Bible Pub. 2 vols in 1. 569 p. bl brds. B11. $25.00

BECK, Horace. *Folklore & the Sea.* (1973). Middletown, CT. Mystic Seaport/Wesleyan U. 1st trade ed. F/VG. A2. $30.00

BECK, Horace. *Folklore & the Sea.* (1973). Middletown, CT. 1st ed. ils/index. 464 p. M/M. B14. $55.00

BECK, James M. *Vanishing Rights of the States...* 1926. NY. Doran. M11. $35.00

BECK, Thomasina. *Embroidered Gardens.* 1979. NY. 1st Am ed. 144 p. VG/dj. B26. $26.00

BECK, William. *Friends: Who They Are, What They Have Done.* 1893. London. Hicks. 16mo. 277 p. VG. V3. $12.00

BECKER, Carl L. *Freedom & Responsibility in the Am Way of Life.* 1953. Knopf. M11. $50.00

BECKER, Peter. *Dingane, King of the Zulu 1828-1840.* 1965. Crowell. 1st ed. 271 p. VG/dj. M20. $8.50

BECKER, Robert H. *Designs on the Land. Disenos of CA Ranchos & Their Makers.* 1969. San Francisco. Grabhorn. BC of CA. 1/500. lg oblong folio. suede over cloth. K1. $200.00

BECKER, Robert H. *Disenos of CA Ranchos: Maps of 37 Land Grants 1822-46.* 1964. BC of CA. folio. M. O6. $825.00

BECKER-DONNER, Etta. *Ancient Am Painting.* 1963. Crown. 1st Am ed. 24 color pls. 64 p. F3. $15.00

BECKETT, Samuel. *All That Fall.* 1957. Grove. 1st Eng-language ed. F/NF. B2. $100.00

BECKETT, Samuel. *Beginning to End. A Selection From Works...* 1988. Gotham. 1st ed. 1/300. sgn Beckett/Gorey. pict brds. F. B24. $400.00

BECKETT, Samuel. *Endgame. A Play in 1 Act.* 1958. Evergreen. 1st Am trade ed/wrp issue/correct 1st prt. NF. A11. $65.00

BECKETT, Samuel. *Krapp's Last Tape & Other Dramatic Pieces.* 1960. Evergreen. PBO. NF/8vo wrp. A11. $55.00

BECKETT, Samuel. *Play.* 1968. London. Faber. 1st pb ed. F/12mo wrp. A11. $15.00

BECKFORD, Peter. *Thoughts on Hunting.* 1810. London. Albion. octavo. 8 pls/fld plan. gilt contemporary calf. VG. H5. $200.00

BECKHAM, S.D. *Requiem for a People.* (1971). Norman, OK. ils. 214 p. VG+/dj. B18. $22.50

BECKING, Rudolf W. *Pocket Flora of the Redwood Forest.* 1983. Covelo, CA. 29 color photos. 237 p. VG. B26. $15.00

BECKWITH, Osmond. *Vernon.* 1981. Breaking Point. 1st ed. VG/dj. A16. $6.50

BECLARD, P.A. *Elements of General Anatomy: Trans From Last Ed in French...* 1830. Edinburgh. presentation/trans George Sinclair. 399 p. brds. G7. $195.00

BEDDIE, M.K. *Bibliography of Capt James Cook.* 1970. Sydney. 2nd ed. 8vo. 894 p. NF/NF. P4. $75.00

BEDFORD, Sybille. *Aldous Huxley: A Biography.* 1974. Harper Row. 1st Am ed. sm 4to. 769+ p. NF/NF. S8. $20.00

BEDFORD-JONES, H. *Cross & the Hammer: Tale of Days of the Vikings.* 1912. Elgin, IL. 8vo. 95 double-column p. gilt bdg. F. scarce. H3. $40.00

BEDFORD-JONES, J. *New Adventures of D'Artagnan.* 1933. Doubleday. 1st ed. F. F4. $40.00

BEDINI, Silvio A. *Thomas Jefferson & His Copying Machines.* ca 1984. VA U. 1st ed. 239 p. as new. B10. $20.00

BEE, Clair. *Backboard Fever.* 1953. Grosset Dunlap. lists to Pay-Off Pitch. 210 p. cloth. VG/dj. M20. $22.00

BEE, Clair. *Championship Ball.* 1948. Grosset Dunlap. later ed. Chip Hilton series. 210 p. VG/dj. M20. $16.00

BEEBE, Lucius. *Hear the Train Blow.* 1952. Dutton. G. A16. $35.00

BEEBE, Lucius. *Trains in Transition.* nd. Bonanza. reprint. VG/dj. A16. $25.00

BEEBE, Lucius. *20th Century.* 1962. Howell N. VG/dj. A16. $30.00

BEEBE & CLEGG. *Am W: Pictorial Epic of a Continent.* 1955. NY. Dutton. 4to. 511 p. cloth. H9. $35.00

BEEBE & CLEGG. *Legends of the Comstock Lode.* 1952. Carson City, NV. 4th prt. sgns. cloth. D3. $45.00

BEEBE & CLEGG. *Story of VA City & Comstock Times.* 1949. Grahame Hardy. 4th ed. ils. 70 p. NF/VG clip. B19. $20.00

BEEBE & CLEGG. *US W: Saga of Wells Fargo.* 1949. NY. Dutton. 1st ed. sgns. w/promo leaflet. VG/G+. O3. $125.00

BEECHER, Edward. *Narrative of Riots at Alton: In Connection w/Death of...* 1838. Alton, IL. George Holton. 1st ed. 12mo. 159 p. cloth. M1. $300.00

BEECHER, Henry Ward. *Plain & Pleasant Talk About Fruits...* 1859. NY. Derby. 1st ed. 420 p. H10. $35.00

BEECHEY, Frederick William. *Narrative of a Voyage to the Pacific...* 1831. London. Colburn Bentley. 1st ed. quarto. 2 vols. VG. H5. $4,500.00

BEEDING, Francis. *Hidden Kingdom.* 1927. Little Brn. 1st ed. VG. M2. $13.00

BEER, M. *General Hist of Socialism & Social Struggles.* ca 1957. NY. Russell. 2 vols. VG/VG. V4. $40.00

BEER, Morris Abel. *Street Lamps.* 1927. NY. Harold Vinal. 1st ed. VG. E3. $15.00

BEER, Thomas. *Mrs Egg & Other Barbarians.* 1933. NY. NF/VG. A11. $30.00

BEERBOHM, Julius. *Among the Ostrich Hunters.* nd. NY. Burt. 12mo. 293 p. pict cloth. F3. $25.00

BEERBOHM, Max. *And Even Now.* 1920. London. 1st ed. G. A1. $45.00

BEERBOHM, Max. *And Even Now.* 1920. London. Heinemann. 1st ed. 8vo. yel cloth. VG. M7. $65.00

BEERBOHM, Max. *Caricatures of 25 Gentlemen.* 1896. London. Smithers. 1st ed. pub ils cloth. E3. $125.00

BEERBOHM, Max. *7 Men.* 1919. London. 1st issue. cloth. G. A1. $60.00

BEERISFORD, Judith. *Wild Garden.* 1973 (1966). Newton Abbot. BC. 16 full-p photos. dj. B26. $12.50

BEERS, F.W. *County Atlas of Berkshire, MA.* 1876. NY. RT Wht. rebound. VG. O6. $600.00

BEERS, Henry Putney. *Bibliographies in Am Hist: Guide to Materials for Research.* 1938. NY. Wilson. 1st ed. xl. VG+. O6. $55.00

BEERS, Henry Putney. *Confederacy: Guide to the Archives...Confederate States...* (1986). Nat Archives & Records. 2nd ed. 536 p. cloth. NF. M8. $35.00

BEESON, Emma Burbank. *Early Life & Letters of Luther Burbank.* 1927. San Francisco. xl. 155 p. scarce. B26. $34.00

BEETON, Isabella. *Book of Household Management...* 1861. London. 1st ed. sm octavo. 14 color pls. contemporary calf. VG. H5. $1,500.00

BEGBIE, Harold. *Political Struwwelpeter.* 1899. London. Grant Richards. 2nd ed. ils VG. D1. $275.00

BEGBIE, Harold. *William Booth: Founder of the Salvation Army.* nd. London. Macmillan. 2 vols. VG. C5. $27.50

BEGEMAN, Myron L. *Manufacturing Processes.* 1946. NY. Wiley. ils/index. 579 p. F. B14. $45.00

BEHAN, Leslie; see Mark, Ted.

BEHRMAN, S.N. *Worcester Account.* 1954. NY. 1st ed. inscr. F/NF. A11. $35.00

BEIDLER, Philip D. *Am Literature & the Experience of Vietnam.* 1982. GA U. 1st ed. sgn Robert Stone. F/F. C4. $50.00

BEILHARZ & LOPEZ. *We are 49ers: Chilean Accounts of CA Gold Rush.* 1976. Ward Ritchie. 1st ed. ils. 230 p. F/F clip. B19. $20.00

BEIM & BEIM. *Little Igloo.* (1941). Harcourt Brace. 1st ed. ils Howard Simon. NF/NF. B4. $45.00

BEIM & BEIM. *Two Is a Team.* (1945). HBW. ils Crichlow. 9th prt. cloth. VG-/dj. A3. $15.00

BEINHART, Larry. *You Get What You Pay For.* 1988. NY. Morrow. 1st ed. F/dj. M15. $25.00

BELASCO, David. *Return of Peter Grimm.* 1912. Dodd Mead. 1st ed. ils John Rae. 344 p. rust cloth/pict label. NF. S10. $25.00

BELDEN, George. *Belden, the Wht Chief: 12 Yrs Among the Indians.* 1870. OH U. 513 p. dj. F. E5. $25.00

BELIN, Jean. *Secrets of the Surete.* (1950). Putnam. 1st Am ed. 8vo. 277 p. VG+/VG. A2. $15.00

BELL, Alexander Melville. *Science of Speech.* 1897. WA. Volta Bureau. 56 p. cloth/brds. B14. $50.00

BELL, Charles. *Letters Concerning Diseases of the Urethra.* 1811. Boston. 1st Am ed. 6 pls after Bell. modern polished calf. G7. $250.00

BELL, Charles. *Manuscript of Drawings of the Arteries.* 1970. Eds Medicina Rare. 1/2500. pls. w/prospectus & bio. F/slipcase. G7. $65.00

BELL, Gertrude. *Poems From the Divan of Hafiz.* 1897. London. rare. O2. $150.00

BELL, Horace. *On the Old W Coast...Reminiscences of a Ranger.* 1930. NY. Morrow. 1st ed. VG. H7. $30.00

BELL, Isaac. *Huntsman's Log Book.* 1947. NY. 1st ed. 249 p. F/dj. A17. $20.00

BELL, J. Boyer. *Time of Terror.* (1987). Basic Books. 292 p. NF/VG. A7. $13.00

BELL, Madison Smartt. *Barking Man & Other Stories.* (1990). Ticknor Fields. 1st ed. F/F. B3. $20.00

BELL, Madison Smartt. *Dr Sleep.* (1992). London. Bloomsbury. 1st ed. F/F. B3. $20.00

BELL, Madison Smartt. *Soldier's Joy.* (1989). Ticknor Fields. 1st ed. F/F. B3. $25.00

BELL, Madison Smartt. *Soldier's Joy.* 1989. Ticknor Fields. AP. NF/prt gray wrp. Q1. $75.00

BELL, Madison Smartt. *Straight Cut.* (1987). London. Chatto Windus. 1st ed. NF/NF. B3. $25.00

BELL, Madison Smartt. *WA Square Ensemble.* 1983. London. Deutsch. 1st ed. author's 1st book. F/F. C4. $50.00

BELL, Madison Smartt. *WA Square Ensemble.* 1983. London. Deutsch. 1st ed. mk Andre Deutsch File Copy. VG/NF. B3. $40.00

BELL, Madison Smartt. *Waiting for the End of the World.* 1985. NY. 1st ed. author's 2nd novel. sgn. F/F. A11. $45.00

BELL, Madison Smartt. *Year of Silence.* (1987). Ticknor Fields. 1st ed. F/VG. B3. $25.00

BELL, Madison Smartt. *Zero DB & Other Stories.* (1987). Ticknor Fields. 1st ed. NF/VG. B3. $20.00

BELL, Mrs. N.S. *Pathways of the Puritans.* (1930). Framingham, MA. 1st ed. 212 p. VG. A17. $17.50

BELL, Pauline. *Feast Into Mourning.* 1991. London. Macmillan. 1st ed. F/F. S5. $25.00

BELL, Rudolph M. *Holy Anorexia.* 1985. Chicago. 1st ed. 248 p. blk cloth. VG/dj. G1. $30.00

BELL, Whitfield J. Jr. *Early Am Science Needs & Opportunities for Study.* 1955. Williamsburg, VA. 8vo. 85 p. bl/gray cloth. VG. B11. $75.00

BELL & BELL. *Anatomy & Physiology of the Human Body.* 1829. London. Longman. 7th ed. 3 vols. ils/woodcuts. orig brds. G7. $225.00

BELL & ELLIOT. *Hardball.* 1990. Key Porter. 1st ed. F/F. P8. $25.00

BELL & WHITFIELD. *Cabinet of Curiosities: 5 Episodes in Evolution Am Mus.* 1967. Charlottesville. VA U. 1st ed. 8vo. 166 p. cream cloth. VG. B11. $45.00

BELLAMY, Edward. *Equality.* 1897. Appleton. 1st ed. VG. E3. $40.00

BELLAMY, Joseph. *4 Sermons on Wisdom of God...* 1804. Morristown. Russell. 1st ed. 130 p. plain wrp. H10. $125.00

BELLARMINO, Robert. *Institutiones Linguae Hebraicae.* 1596. Antwerp. Ex Offinican Pla Ex Officina Plantiniana. 8vo. 197 p. 19th-Century calf. K1. $450.00

BELLASIS, Margaret. *Honorable Company.* (1952). London. Hollis Carter. 1st ed. 8vo. 285 p. VG/G+. A2. $15.00

BELLI, Melvin M. *Ready for the Plaintiff.* 1956. Holt. G/worn. M11. $35.00

BELLOC, Hilaire. *Avril: Essays on Poetry of French Renaissance.* 1910. London. Duckworth. 238 p. H10. $22.50

BELLOC, Hilaire. *Book of the Bayeux Tapestry.* 1913. Chatto Windus. 1st ed. VG. E3. $50.00

BELLOC, Hilaire. *Campaign of 1812 & the Retreat From Moscow.* 1925. London. Nelson. map. 270 p. H10. $17.50

BELLOC, Hilaire. *Complete Verse...* 1970. London. Duckworth. 296 p. F/dj. H10. $25.00

BELLOC, Hilaire. *Crisis of Civilization.* 1937. Fordham U. 1st ed. VG/dj. N2. $10.00

BELLOC, Hilaire. *Cromwell.* 1934. Lippincott. 1st Am ed. ils/index. 356 p. H10. $17.50

BELLOC, Hilaire. *Cruise of the Nona...* 1925. Houghton Mifflin. 1st Am ed. 329 p. H3/H10. $20.00

BELLOC, Hilaire. *Great Heresies.* nd. London. Catholic BC. 277 p. H10. $10.00

BELLOC, Hilaire. *How the Reformation Happened.* 1938. London. Cape. 293 p. H10. $17.50

BELLOC, Hilaire. *Old Road.* 1904. London. Constable. 1st ed. xl. 172 p. lib buckram. H10. $85.00

BELLOC, Hilaire. *Pyrenees.* 1910. London. Methuen. 340 p. H10. $27.50

BELLOC, Hilaire. *Romance of Tristan & Iseult.* 1913. London. Allen. 184 p. H10. $35.00

BELLOC, Hilaire. *Short Talks w/the Dead & Others.* 1926. Harper. 1st ed. VG. E3. $25.00

BELLOC, Hilaire. *Stane Street: A Monograph.* 1913. London. Constable. 1st ed. xl. 304 p. H10. $27.50

BELLOSTE, Augustin. *Chirurgien d'Hopital...Avec Moyen d'Eviter l'Exfoliation...* 1714. Paris. Laurent d'Houry. 2nd ed. 12mo. contemporary sheep. G7. $295.00

BELLOSTE, Augustin. *Hospital Surgeon; or, New Gentle Easie Way To Cure...* 1713. London. Sprint. 12mo. contemporary full calf. G7. $450.00

BELLOW, Saul. *Bellarosa Connection.* (1989). Penguin. ARC. F/burnt-orange wrp. C4. $50.00

BELLOW, Saul. *Dean's December.* (1982). Harper Row. 1st ed. VG/F. B3. $25.00

BELLOW, Saul. *Herzog.* 1964. Viking. 1st ed. NF/F. B2. $35.00

BELLOW, Saul. *Him w/His Foot in His Mouth & Other Stories.* 1984. Harper Row. 1st ed. inscr. F/NF. Q1. $60.00

BELLOW, Saul. *It All Adds Up.* 1994. Viking. ARC. F/wrp. B2. $100.00

BELLOW, Saul. *Last Analysis: A Play.* 1965. Viking. 1st ed. sgn/dtd 1980. NF/NF/slip-case/fld box. Q1. $125.00

BELLOW, Saul. *More Die of Heartbreak.* (1987). Morrow. 1st ed. F/F. B3. $25.00

BELLOW, Saul. *Mosby's Memoirs & Other Stories.* 1969. Weidenfeld Nicolson. 1st ed. NF/NF. C4. $55.00

BELLOW, Saul. *Mr Sammler's Planet.* (1970). Viking. Taiwanee Piracy. 1st ed. F/F. C4. $35.00

BELLOW, Saul. *Theft.* (1989). Penguin. ARC of Penguin PBO. F/pict wrp. C4. $35.00

BELLOW, Saul. *Theft.* 1989. NY. ARC of Penguin PBO. sgn. RS. F/glossy wrp. A11. $50.00

BELLOW, Saul. *Victim.* 1947. NY. 1st ed. author's 2nd book. VG+/rpr. A15. $90.00

BELLOW, Saul. *Victim.* 1947. Vanguard. 1st ed. F/NF. Q1. $475.00

BELLOW, Saul. *Writer At Work.* 1967. Viking. 1st ed. F/F. C4. $35.00

BELLOW, Saul. *Writer's Dilemma.* 1961. London. Oxford. 1st ed. F/F. C4. $35.00

BELMONT, Bob; see Reynolds, Mack.

BELTING, Natalia. *Summer's Coming In.* 1970. HRW. 1st ed. ils Adrienne Adams. NF/NF. T5. $30.00

BELTRAMI, Giacomo Constantino. *Pilgrimage in Europe & Am, Leading to...MS...* 1828. London. Hunt Clarke. 1st ed. 2 vols. octavo. H9. $875.00

BEMELMANS, Ludwig. *Are You Hungry, Are You Cold.* (1960). Cleveland. 1st ed. 245 p. VG/dj. B18. $15.00

BEMELMANS, Ludwig. *Aunt Brn's Birthday.* (1930). Harper. ils Elsa Beskow/12 color lithos. VG. D1. $65.00

BEMELMANS, Ludwig. *Golden Basket.* 1936. Viking. 1st ed. 8vo. 96 p. orange cloth. VG. D1. $85.00

BEMELMANS, Ludwig. *Madeline & the Bad Hat.* (1956). Viking. 1st trade ed. VG/VG. D1. $275.00

BEMELMANS, Ludwig. *Madeline & the Gypsies.* 1959. Viking. 1st ed. tall 4to. 56 p. gr cloth. VG/dj. D1. $225.00

BEMELMANS, Ludwig. *Madeline's Rescue.* 1959. Viking. 1st ed. tall 4to. 56 p. VG/dj. D1. $250.00

BEMENT, C.N. *Am Poulterer's Companion...* ca 1856. NY. Harper. ils. 304 p. H10. $35.00

BEMIS, George. *Report of Case of John W Webster...* 1850. Boston. 1st ed. quarter calf/marbled brds. M11. $175.00

BEMMANN, Hans. *Stone & the Flute.* 1986. Viking. 1st Eng-language ed. F/F. N3. $20.00

BEMROSE, William. *Manual of Wood Carving.* 1880s. London. Bemrose. 15 full-p pls. 51 p. cloth. F. B14. $60.00

BEN & GRUNBERG. *Who's Who in Israel & in the Work for Israel Abroad.* 1976. Tel-Aviv. Bronfman Cohen. 17th prt. 560 p. VG. S3. $30.00

BEN-GURION, David. *Israel: A Personal Hist.* 1971. Funk Wagnall/Sabra. 862 p. VG+. S3. $35.00

BENBERRY. *Always There: African-Am Presence in Am Quilts.* 1991. KY Heritage Quilt Project. G2. $25.00

BENCH, Johnny. *From Behind the Pl.* 1972. Rutledge. later prt. VG+/VG. P8. $20.00

BENCHLEY, Nathaniel. *Robert Benchley: A Biography.* 1955. McGraw Hill. G/dj. A16. $25.00

BENCHLEY, Robert. *Benchley Roundup.* (1954). Harper. 1st ed. ils Gluyas Williams. F/NF. B4. $50.00

BENCHLEY, Robert. *No Poems; or, Around the World Backwards & Sideways.* 1932. NY. Harper. 1st ed. ils Gluyas Williams. w/sgn letter. NF/dj. B24. $300.00

BENDAZZI, G. *Films of Woody Allen.* 1987. Ravette Ltd. photos. VG+. C8. $40.00

BENDER. *Plain & Simple: Woman's Journey to the Amish.* 1989. np. cloth. G2. $17.00

BENDIRE, Charles. *Life Histories of N Am Birds.* 1892-95. Smithsonian. 2 vols. lt 4to. later bdg. K1. $200.00

BENEDICT, Dorothy. *Fabulous.* 1961. NY. Pantheon. 1st ed. juvenile. VG/VG. O3. $25.00

BENEDICT, Elizabeth. *Beginners Book of Dreams.* (1988). Knopf. 1st ed. F/NF. B3. $20.00

BENEDICT, Emma L. *Happy Time Fancies in Rhyme.* 1893. Lee Shepard. 1st ed. pict yel brds. G+. S10. $20.00

BENEDICT, Murray R. *Farm Policies of the US 1790-1950...* 1975. Millwood. Kraus. 548 p. H10. $25.00

BENEDICT, Pinckney. *Town Smokes.* 1987. Princeton. Ontario Review. 1st ed. author's 1st book. F/wrp. L3. $85.00

BENEDICT, Ruth. *Chrysanthemum & the Sword.* 1946. Houghton Mifflin. 1st ed. 324 p. VG. W1. $16.00

BENEDICTUS, David. *4th of June.* 1962. London. 1st ed. inscr. NF/VG+ clip. A11. $45.00

BENET, Stephen Vincent. *Devil & Daniel Webster.* (1937). Farrar Rinehart. 1st trade ed. VG/VG. B4. $60.00

BENET, Stephen Vincent. *John Brn's Body.* 1928. Doubleday Doran. 1st trade ed. cloth. NF/dj. M8. $85.00

BENET, Stephen Vincent. *John Brn's Body.* 1928. NY. 1st ed. NF/VG. V1. $35.00

BENET, Stephen Vincent. *Nightmare at Noon.* 1940. NY. 1st ed. F. V1. $10.00

BENGTSSON, F.G. *Folk Son Sjong.* 1955. Stockholm. Norstedt. 1st Swedish ed. 320 p. uncut. VG+/tan wrp. M7. $45.00

BENITEZ, Fernando. *In the Magic Land of Peyote.* 1975. Austin, TX. 1st ed. 198 p. dj. F3. $25.00

BENITEZ, Sandra. *Place Where the Sea Remembers.* (1993). Coffee House. 1st ed. author's 1st book. F/F. B3. $30.00

BENJAMIN, Asher. *Architect; or, Practical House Carpenter.* 1839. Boston. Mussey. 64 pls. 119 p. contemporary sheepskin. B14. $425.00

BENJAMIN, Earl W. *Marketing Poultry Products.* 1925. NY. Wiley. 2nd ed. ils. 332 p. H10. $9.50

BENKARD, E. *Undying Faces: Collection of Death Masks.* 1929. London. Hogarth. VG. B5. $75.00

BENNER & PELLMAN. *Country Lily Quilt.* 1990. np. patterns/instructions. wrp. G2. $12.95

BENNER & PELLMAN. *Country Paradise Quilt.* 1991. np. ils. wrp. G2. $12.95

BENNET, Robert Ames. *Crossed Trails.* 1937. Ives Washburn. 12mo. G. A8. $5.00

BENNETT, Alan. *Beyond the Fringe.* 1963. London. 1st ed. intro Michael Frayn. NF/NF. T9. $65.00

BENNETT, Alan. *Horsewoman.* 1979. Dorset. 1st Uk ed. 207 p. gilt bl cloth. VG/VG. M7. $26.50

BENNETT, C.H. *Bennett's Fables: From Aesop & Others.* 1978. Viking. 1st thus ed. 54 p. VG/VG. A3. $10.00

BENNETT, Edmund H. *Farm Law: Treatise on Legal Rights & Liabilities...* ca 1880. Portland. Hoyt. 1st ed. 120 p. H10. $15.00

BENNETT, Edna Mae. *Turquoise & the Indian.* 1970. Swallow. ils. 152 p. F/F clip. B19. $12.50

BENNETT, Edward T. *Soc for Psychical Research: Its Rise & Progress...* 1903. London. RB Johnson. thin 8vo. 58 p. prt gr cloth. G1. $45.00

BENNETT, Estelline. *Old Deadwood Days.* 1928. NY. JH Sears. 1st ed. 12mo. 300 p. orange brds. VG. B11. $25.00

BENNETT, Hal. *Wilderness of Vines.* 1966. Doubleday. 1st ed. author's scarce 1st book. F/F. B4. $250.00

BENNETT, J.H. *Big Game Angling.* (1958). London. Faber. 220 p. clip dj. A17. $17.50

BENNETT, Patrick. *Talking w/TX Writers.* (1980). TX A&M. 1st ed. F/F. A18. $30.00

BENNETT, Wendell. *Ancient Arts of the Andes.* (1954). MOMA. 1st ed. 187 p. dj. F3. $30.00

BENNETT, William P. *Sky-Sifter.* (1892). np. self pub. 1st ed. 12mo. 302 p. cloth. NF. D3. $75.00

BENNETT & MONTAPERTO. *Red Guard.* 1971. Doubleday. 1st ed. 267 p. NF/dj. A7. $15.00

BENNETTS, Pamela. *Death of the Red King.* 1976. St Martin. ARC of 1st Am ed. RS. F/F. F4. $25.00

BENSHEA, Noah. *Jacob the Baker.* (1989). NY. Villard. 1st ed. F/F. B3. $15.00

BENSMAN, David. *Practice of Solidarity: Am Hat Finishers in 19th Century.* ca 1985. Urbana. M/VG. V4. $12.50

BENSON, Allan L. *Inviting War to Am.* 1916. Girard. Appeal to Reason. 190 p. wrp. A7. $25.00

BENSON, Ben. *Frightened Ladies.* 1960. Morrow. 1st ed. F/F. F4. $25.00

BENSON, E.F. *More Spook Stories.* 1934. London. 1st ed. VG. M2. $50.00

BENSON, E.F. *Spook Stories.* 1976. Arno. reprint of 1928 ed. VG. M2. $30.00

BENSON, Larry D. *Art & Tradition in Sir Gawain & the Gr Knight.* ca 1965. np. 2nd prt. VG+/dj. C1. $9.50

BENSON, R.M. *Steamships & Motorships of W Coast.* (1968). Seattle. Superior. 1st ed. inscr to pub. 4to. 175 p. F/F. A2. $40.00

BENSON, R.M. *Virgin Birth of Our Lord & Saviour Jesus Christ...* ca 1904. Norwich. Goose. 2nd ed. 40 p. wrp. H10. $15.00

BENSON, Raymond. *James Bond Companion: All About the World According to 007.* 1984. NY. Dodd Mead. 1st ed/oversize trade pb. F/wrp. S5. $22.50

BENSON & CHARWOOD. *Abraham Lincoln.* 1917. Garden City. 1st ed. 482 p. cloth. VG. M8. $35.00

BENSON & WEAVER. *Book of the Queen's Dolls' House.* 1924. London. Methuen. miniature. 1st ed. 1/1500. 2 vols. H10. $385.00

BENSON. *Applique.* 1991. np. 32 orig designs/56-full size patterns. slipcase. G2. $40.00

BENT, Arthur C. *Life Histories of N Am Gulls & Terns.* 1947. NY. Dodd Mead. 1st NY ed. 333 p. gray cloth. VG. B14. $30.00

BENTLEY, E.C. *Elephant's Work.* 1950. London. Hodder Stoughton. 1st ed. VG/dj. M15. $45.00

BENTON, Frank. *Cowboy Life on the Sidetrack...* (1903). Denver. 1st ed. 207 p. pict cloth. VG. D3. $90.00

BERCOVICI, Konrad. *For a Song.* 1931. Dodd Mead. ARC of 1st ed. RS. F/VG. F4. $45.00

BERENBERG, David P. *Am at the Crossroads.* 1934. NY. Rand School. 1st ed. NF/wrp. B2. $35.00

BERENDZEN, Richard. *Life Beyond Earth & the Mind of Man.* 1973. NASA. 1st ed. VG/wrp. M2. $5.00

BERENT, Mark. *Rolling Thunder.* (1989). NY. 1st ed. F/F. A7. $20.00

BERGDORF, R.S. *Life Along the Canal.* 1990. Peninsula, OH. 39 p. VG/sbdg. B18. $6.50

BERGE, Dennis. *Mexican Republic 1847.* 1975. El Paso, TX. Monograph 45. 1st ed. 62 p. wrp. F3. $10.00

BERGE & WYSHAM. *Pearl Diver. Adventuring Over & Under S Seas.* ca 1930. Garden City. 8vo. 368 p. blk cloth. VG. P4. $20.00

BERGER, A.J. *HI Birdlife.* (1972). Honolulu. 1st ed. 4to. 270 p. F/VG. A2. $25.00

BERGER, John. *Once in Europa.* (1987). Pantheon. 1st ed. NF/NF. A7. $12.00

BERGER, John. *Painter of Our Time.* 1959. NY. 1st Am ed. F/NF. A11. $45.00

BERGER, Mark. *Taking the 5th: Supreme Court & Privilege...* 1980. Lexington Books. M11. $35.00

BERGER, Raoul. *Executive Privilege: Constitutional Myth.* 1974. Cambridge. Harvard. M11. $25.00

BERGER, Raoul. *Impeachment: Constitutional Problems.* 1973. Cambridge. Harvard. M11. $35.00

BERGER, Thomas. *Arthur Rex: Legendary Hero.* 1978. Delacorte. 1st ed. VG+. C1. $12.50

BERGER, Thomas. *Arthur Rex: Legendary Novel.* 1978. Delacorte. 1st ed. F/NF. N3. $35.00

BERGER, Thomas. *Little Big Man.* 1964. Dial. 1st ed. sgn. NF/dj. B24. $300.00

BERGER, Thomas. *Nowhere.* 1985. Delacorte/Lawrence. AP. NF. L3. $35.00

BERGER, Thomas. *Rinehart in Love.* 1962. Scribner. 1st ed. inscr/dtd 1964. author's 2nd book. L3. $250.00

BERGER, Thomas. *Robert Crews.* 1994. NY. Morrow. AP. F/wht wrp. C4. $25.00

BERGER, Thomas. *Who Is Teddy Villanova.* 1977. NY. F/NF. A11. $30.00

BERGER, Victor. *Berger's Broadsides.* 1912. Milwaukee. Social-Democratic Pub. VG. B2. $125.00

BERGER. *Humans: A Prehistoric World.* 1988. 11 pop-ups. F. A4. $35.00

BERGMAN, Andrew. *Big Kiss-Off of 1944.* 1974. NY. 1st ed. author's 1st novel. NF/F. A11. $30.00

BERGMAN, Ray. *Just Fishing.* (1940). Outdoor Life. special ed/6th prt. sgn. 418 p. A17. $35.00

BERGMAN, Ray. *Trout.* 1962. Knopf. 2nd ed. pls. 482 p. VG. A17. $17.50

BERGMAN, Ray. *With Fly, Plug & Bait.* 1947. NY. 1st ed. 7 color pls. 640 p. F/dj. A17. $45.00

BERGSON, Abram. *Planning & Productivity Under Soviet Socialism.* 1968. Carnegie-Mellon U. 95 p. dj. A7. $12.00

BERINGER, Richard E. *Why the S Lost the War.* ca 1986. Athens, GA. 1st ed. 582 p. cloth. F/F. M8. $35.00

BERK, Nouroullah. *La Peinture Turque.* 1950. Ankara. folio. repro pls. prt brds/cloth spine. O2. $75.00

BERKE, Helen. *Winnie Winkle & the Diamond Heirlooms.* 1946. Whitman. 1st ed. VG/dj. M2. $10.00

BERKELEY, William. *Discourse & View of VA.* 1914. Norwalk, CT. Wm H Smith. facsimile of 1663 ed. 8vo. VG. B11. $150.00

BERKELY & TIFFENBACH. *Foreskin: Its Past, Its Present &...Its Future?* 1984. np (San Francisco). 3rd prt. 208 p. wrp. N2. $35.00

BERKHOFER, R.F. *Wht Man's Indian: Images of Am Indian...* 1978. Knopf. 1st ed. 8vo. 261 p. F/F. A2. $15.00

BERKIN & LOVETT. *Women, War & Revolution.* ca 1980. NY. Holmes Meier. M/M. V4. $15.00

BERKMAN, Alexander. *Prison Memoirs of an Anarchist.* 1912. Mother Earth Pub. 1st ed. 8vo. 512 p. M1. $200.00

BERKMAN, Alexander. *Prison Memoirs of an Anarchist.* 1970. Frontier Pr. 538 p. NF/NF. A7. $20.00

BERLIN, Sven. *Jonah's Dream: Meditation on Fishing.* (1975). Los Altos. 1st ed. 126 p. VG/dj. A17. $12.50

BERLINGHIERI, Francesco. *Geographia.* 1966. Amsterdam. Theatrvm. lg folio. 31 double-p maps. 372 p. O6. $395.00

BERLIOZ, Hector. *Memoirs...1803 to 1865...* 1935. NY. Tudor. trans Holmes/Newman. dj. A7. $15.00

BERLYN, Michael. *Eternal Enemy.* 1990. Morrow. 1st ed. F/F. N3. $15.00

BERMAN, Louis A. *Jews & Intermarriage: Study in Personality & Culture.* 1968. NY. xl. 707 p. VG/VG. S3. $25.00

BERMAN, Myron. *Richmond's Jewry: Shabbat in Shockoe 1769-1976.* 1979. VA U. 1st ed. ils. 428 p. VG/VG. B10. $35.00

BERNADETE, Mair J. *Hispanic Culture & Character of Sephardic Jews.* 1982. NY. 8vo. 226 p. cloth. dj. O2. $25.00

BERNADOTTE, Folke. *Curtain Falls.* 1945. Knopf. 1st/A ed. 12mo. VG/poor. A8. $10.00

BERNARD, Art. *Dog Days.* 1969. Caxton. ils. 204 p. F/dj. A17. $17.50

BERNARD, Claude. *Introduction a l'Etude de la Medecine Experimentale.* 1865. Paris. 400 p. orig prt wrp. G7. $995.00

BERNARD, Claude. *La Science Experimentale.* 1878. Paris. Bailliere. posthumously pub. xl. 440 p. quarter roan/marbled brds. G7. $295.00

BERNARD, Claude. *Lecons sur la Physiologie et Pathologie Systeme Nerveux.* 1858. Paris. Bailliere. 1st ed. 2 vols. morocco/marbled brds. NF. B14. $500.00

BERNARD, Claude. *Lecons sur le Diabete et la Glycogenese Animale.* 1877. Paris. Bailliere. ils. 576 p. early brds. prt wrp laid down. G7. $895.00

BERNARD, Claude. *Lecons sur les Effects Substances Toxiques Medicamenteuses.* 1857. Paris. Bailliere. ils. 488 p. new cloth. G7. $250.00

BERNARD, Claude. *Lecons sur les Preoprietes des Tissus Vivants.* 1866. Paris. Bailliere. pls. 492 p. orig quarter roan. G7. $295.00

BERNARD, Kenneth A. *Abraham Lincoln: Song in His Heart.* 1970. Worcester. St Onge. miniature. 1/1500. 63 p. F. H10. $20.00

BERNARD, Raymond. *Hollow Earth: Greatest Geographical Discovery in Hist.* 1964. NY. Fieldcrest. new ed. 4to. 116 p+ads. VG/dj. P4. $80.00

BERNE & SAVARY. *Prayer Ways.* 1980. Harper. 161 p. VG. C5. $10.00

BERNHARD, Thomas. *Wittgenstein's Nephew.* 1989. Knopf. 1st Am ed. rem mk. F/F. A14. $20.00

BERNHARDT, C. *Indian Raids in Lincoln Co, KS, 1864 & 1869.* 1910. Lincoln, KS. 8vo. 62 p. prt wrp. H9. $100.00

BERNIER, Olivier. *Fireworks at Dusk, Paris in the Thirties.* 1993. Boston. 1st ed. as new. T9. $16.00

BERNLEE, J. *Driftwood House.* 1992. Typographeum. 1st ed. 1/100. M/as issued. T9. $28.00

BERNLEE, J. *Out of Mind.* 1989. Boston. 1st ed. trans A Dixon. F/dj. T9. $10.00

BERNOULLI, Rudolf. *Ausgewahlte Meisterwerke Ostasiatischer Graphik...Berlin.* 1923. Berlin. Schultz. 4to. ils. 110 p. VG. W1. $95.00

BERNSTEIN, Aline. *Martha WA Doll Book.* (1945). NY. Howell Soskin. 1st ed. 18 p. sbdg. VG. A2. $25.00

BERNSTEIN, Burton. *Sinai. Great & Terrible Wilderness.* 1979. NY. 1st ed. 268 p. gilt blk/tan bdg. F/VG. H3. $20.00

BERNSTEIN, Philip S. *What the Jews Believe.* 1950. FSY. ils Fritz Eichenberg. 100 p. G+. S3. $19.00

BERNSTEIN, Richard. *Are We To Be a Nation?* 1987. np. lg 4to. ils/color pls/index. 342 p. O7. $12.50

BERNSTEIN & CHURGIN. *Samuel K Mirsky Jubilee Vol...* 1958. Jubilee Comm. 28 articles. 558 p. VG. S3. $26.00

BERR, Henri. *Du Scepticisme de Gassendi.* 1960. Paris. Albin Michel. 1st French ed. 125 p. prt stiff wrp. G1. $25.00

BERRA & HORTON. *Yogi, It Aint Over.* 1989. McGraw Hill. 1st ed. photos. F/VG+. P8. $17.50

BERRALL, Julia S. *Garden: Ils Hist.* 1966. NY. 30 full-p color pls. 388 p. VG/dj. B26. $34.00

BERRIGAN, Daniel. *Lights on the House of the Dead.* 1974. Doubleday. stated 1st ed. NF/dj. A7. $25.00

BERRIGAN, Philip. *No More Strangers.* (1965). Macmillan. 1st ed. NF/NF. A7. $18.00

BERRIGAN & COLES. *Geography of Fith: Conversations When Underground.* (1971). Beacon. 1st ed. F/NF. A7. $35.00

BERRIN, Kathleen. *Art of the Huichol Indians.* 1979. Art Mus San Francisco. hc. ils/color pls. F/dj. L3. $65.00

BERRY, Carole. *Island Girl.* 1991. St Martin. 1st ed. inscr. F/F. M15. $30.00

BERRY, Don. *Moontrap.* (1962). Viking. 1st ed. F/clip. A18. $40.00

BERRY, Erick. *Pinky Pup & the Empty Elephant.* 1928 (1922). Volland. revised ed. VG. M5. $60.00

BERRY, Mike; see Malzberg, Barry.

BERRY, T. *Day God Came.* 1993. Winston/Derek. 1st ed. ils Paul Hoffman. VG/sans. L1. $25.00

BERRY, Wendell. *Collected Poems.* 1985. Northpoint. 1st ed. F/F. V1. $25.00

BERRY, Wendell. *Discovery of KY.* 1991. Frankfort. 1/100. sgn. pict brds. F. C4. $40.00

BERRY, Wendell. *Gift of Gravity.* 1980. Deerfield/Dublin. 1/300. sgn. ils Engelland. F/F. A11. $35.00

BERRY, Wendell. *Gift of the Good Land.* 1981. N Point. 1st ed. F/F. C4. $40.00

BERRY, Wendell. *Home Economics.* (1987). N Point. ARC. RS. F/F. B3. $45.00

BERRY, Wendell. *KY River: 2 Poems.* 1976. Monterey. Larkspur. 1st ed. sgn. F/stiff wrp. C4. $40.00

BERRY, Wendell. *November 26, 1963.* 1964. NY. Braziller. 1st ed. ils Ben Shahn. F/VG+ slipcase. V1. $35.00

BERRY, Wendell. *Recollected Essays: 1965-80.* 1981. San Francisco. N Point. 1st ed. F/F. C4. $30.00

BERRY, Wendell. *Remembering.* 1988. N Point. 1st ed. F/F. Q1. $20.00

BERRY, Wendell. *Sabbaths, 1987.* 1991. KY. Larkspur. 1/74. F. C4. $100.00

BERRY, Wendell. *Salad.* nd. Berkeley. N Point. 1st ed. inscr. F/lime-gr wrp. C4. $60.00

BERRY, Wendell. *Sayings & Doings.* 1975. Lexington. 1st ed. linen brds. F. C4. $35.00

BERRY, Wendell. *Standing on Earth: Selected Essays.* 1991. KY. Golgonooza. 1st ed. sgn. F/F. C4. $50.00

BERRY, Wendell. *There Is Singing Around Me.* 1976. Cold Mtn Pr. 1/300. sgn. F/mustard wrp. C4. $60.00

BERRY, Wendell. *Wheel.* 1986. N Point. 12mo. F/F. C4. $20.00

BERRY, Wendell. *Wild Birds.* 1986. N Point. 1st ed. F/F. C4. $35.00

BERRY & KRESS. *Heliconia: Identification Guide.* 1991. WA, DC. 236 color photos. 334 p. M. B26. $20.00

BERRYMAN, John. *Henry's Fate & Other Poems 1967-72.* 1978. London. 1st ed. F/wrp. A11. $45.00

BERRYMAN, John. *His Toy, His Dream, His Rest.* 1968. NY. 1st ed. F/F. V1. $25.00

BERRYMAN, John. *Homage to Mistress Bradstreet.* 1968. NY. true 1st ed. sgn. F/unused. A11. $175.00

BERRYMAN, John. *Spinning Heart, Poem in Am Writing 1942...* 1942. Prairie City, IL. 1st book ed. blk cloth. VG. A11. $35.00

BERRYMAN, John. *Stephen Crane.* 1950. NY. 1st ed. NF/VG. A11. $135.00

BERTON, Pierre. *Flames Across the Border.* (1981). Tor. 1st ed. 492 p. F/dj. A17. $15.00

BERTON, Pierre. *Mysterious N.* 1956. Knopf. 1st Am ed. 8vo. 345 p. F/VG+. A2. $25.00

BERTON, Ralph. *Remembering Bix.* (1974). Harper Row. 1st ed. F/NF. A7. $35.00

BESANT & LEADBEATER. *Man: Whence, How & Whither — Clairvoyant Investigation.* 1913. Adyar, India. Theosophical Pub. 1st ed. 8vo. 524 p. VG+. A2. $100.00

BESKOW, Elsa. *Peter's Adventures in Blueberry Land.* (1963). Delacorte. 2nd Am prt. ils. pict wht brds/bl spine. T5. $35.00

BESSE, Joseph. *Collections of Sufferings of People Called Quakers...* 1753. London. Luke Hinde. folio. leather/rebacked modern spine. G. V3. $350.00

BESSETTE, J.M. *If Etait Une Fois...la Guillotine.* 1982. Paris. Eds Alternatives. 126 p. VG/wrp. N2. $15.00

BESSIE, Alvah. *Men in Battle: Story of Am in Spain.* ca 1954. NY. Vetrans of Abraham Lincoln Brigade. VG. V4. $25.00

BEST, Hugh. *Debrett's TX Peerage.* 1983. Coward McCann. ils/photos. 385 p. F/dj. E5. $20.00

BEST, Mary Agnes. *Rebel Saints.* 1925. NY. Harcourt Brace. 8vo. 333 p. V3. $15.00

BESTER, Alfred. *Demolished Man.* 1953. Shasta. 1st ed/subscriber issue. sgn. F/F. M2. $450.00

BESTER, Alfred. *Golem 100.* 1980. Simon Schuster. 1st ed. F/F. N3. $20.00

BESTERMAN, Theodore. *Agriculture: Bibliography of Bibliographies.* 1971. Totowa. Rowman. 302 p. M. H10. $15.00

BESTIC, A.A. *Kicking Canvas.* 1958. Dutton. 1st ed. 8vo. 255 p. VG+/VG+. A2. $17.50

BESTON, Henry. *N Farm.* 1948. NY. 1st ed. VG+/VG. A11. $40.00

BESTON, Henry. *Un Maison au Bout du Monde (The Outermost House).* 1953. Paris. 1st ed. 12mo. VG+. A11. $55.00

BETTELHEIM, Bruno. *Freud & Man's Soul.* 1983. Knopf. 1st ed. sm 8vo. 111 p. VG/dj. G1. $28.50

BETTELHEIM, Bruno. *Uses of Enchantment.* 1976. Knopf. 1st ed. 327 p. clip dj. A7. $15.00

BETTER COOKING LIBRARY. *Complete Everyday Cookbook.* 1971. np. VG/dj. A16. $25.00

BETTER HOMES & GARDENS. *Am's Best Cross Stitch.* 1988. np. cloth. G2. $22.00

BETTER HOMES & GARDENS. *Am's Heritage Quilts.* 1991. np. cloth. G2. $30.00

BETTER HOMES & GARDENS. *Better Homes & Gardens Needlepoint.* nd. np. ils. cloth. G2. $8.00

BETTER HOMES & GARDENS. *Better Homes & Gardens Story Book.* 1950. Des Moines. 1st ed. VG. L1. $30.00

BETTER HOMES & GARDENS. *Better Homes & Gardens Story Book.* 1950. Meredith. 1st ed. 151 p. VG-. P2. $25.00

BETTER HOMES & GARDENS. *Friendship Quilting, New Patchwork & Quilting.* 1987. np. wrp. G2. $10.00

BETTER HOMES & GARDENS. *Patchwork & Quilting.* 1977. np. cloth. G2. $7.00

BETTINA. *Cocolo.* 1945. Harper. lib bdg. G+. P2. $10.00

BETTMAN, Otto L. *Pict Hist of Medicine.* 1956. Springfield. Thomas. 1st ed. 4to. 318 p. gray cloth. VG. G1. $40.00

BETTS, Edwin Morris. *Thomas Jefferson's Farm Book.* (1987). VA U. 552 p. VG/VG. B10. $25.00

BETTS, Robert B. *In Search of York: Slave Who Went to the Pacific...* 1985. Boulder, CO. 1st ed. 4to. 182 p. dj. T8. $32.50

BEVANS, J.W. *Mother Goose ABC Book.* 1907. np. G. very scarce. M5. $60.00

BEVERIDGE, Albert J. *Abraham Lincoln, 1809-1858.* 1928. Houghton Mifflin. 1st ed. 2 vols. cloth. VG. M8. $150.00

BEVERIDGE, Albert J. *Life of John Marshall.* 1980. NY. Johnson. reprint. 4 vols. gilt half leather. M. A17. $95.00

BEVERIDGE, Lord. *India Called Them.* (1947). London. Allen Unwin. 1st ed. 8vo. 418 p. VG+. A2. $15.00

BEVINGTON, Helen. *Dr Johnson's Waterfall & Other Poems.* 1946. Boston. 1st ed. VG+/VG. A11. $20.00

BEVIS, H.V. *To Luna w/Love.* 1971. Lenox Hill. 1st ed. F/dj. N3. $10.00

BEWICK, Thomas. *Works of...* 1822. Newcastle. Collected Works ed. octavo. 5 vols. morocco. NF. H5. $4,000.00

BEY, Hamid. *My Experiences...* (1933). Buffalo, NY. Ellicott. 12mo. sgn. 138 p. VG+/wrp. A2. $35.00

BEYER, Preston. *Essays on Collecting John Steinbeck Books.* 1989. Bradentown. 1st ed. 38 p. F/wrp. C4. $20.00

BEYER, William Gray. *Minions of the Moon.* 1950. Gnome. 1st ed. F/F. M2. $35.00

BEYER & FUCITO. *Caruso & the Art of Singing.* 1922. NY. Stokes. 1st ed. octavo. 219 p. VG. H5. $150.00

BEYER. *Medallion Quilts.* 1982. np. wrp. G2. $20.95

BEYER. *Patchwork Portfolio.* 1989. np. collector ed. ils. cloth. G2. $45.00

BEYER. *Scrap Look: Designs, Fabrics, Colors & Piecing Techniques...* 1985. np. wrp. G2. $20.00

BEZZERIDES, A.I. *Thieves' Market.* 1949. NY. correct 1st ed (A & pub seal on copyright p). VG/VG. A11. $55.00

BIANCO, Margery. *Apple Tree.* 1926. Doran. 2nd prt. ils Artzybasheff. 47 p. G+. T5. $35.00

BIANCO, Margery. *Little Wooden Doll.* 1925. Macmillan. 1st ed. ils Pamela Bianco/6 color pls. VG. M5. $45.00

BIANCO, Margery. *Little Wooden Doll.* 1944 (1925). Macmillan. 6 color pls. 65 p. G+. P2. $12.50

BIANCO, Margery. *More About Animals.* 1934. Macmillan. 1st ed. 115 p. G+. P2. $14.00

BIANCO, Margery. *Penny & the Wht Horse.* 1942. Messner/Jr Literary Guild. 1st ed. VG/G-. P2. $25.00

BIANCO, Margery. *Skin Horse.* 1927. Doran. 1st ed. ils. 45 p. pict bdg. G. scarce. P2. $32.00

BIANCO, Pamela. *Beginning w/A.* 1947. NY. Oxford. 1st ed. VG-. A3. $3.00

BIBBY, Geoffrey. *Looking for Dilmun.* 1969. Knopf. 1st ed. 383 p. VG+/dj. M20. $18.00

BIBBY, Goeffrey. *Looking for Dilmun.* 1969. NY. ils/maps/32 pls. 383 p. F/F. O2. $30.00

BIBLE. *Bible Hist.* 1814. Boston. Hale. miniature. 256 p. blk leather. H10. $300.00

BIBLE. *Bible in Miniature for Children.* nd. Boston. Lee Shepard. miniature. 192 p. stp gr cloth. H10. $100.00

BIBLE. *Bible in Miniature.* 1780. London. Newbery. 9 (of 14) pls. full leather. VG. F1. $300.00

BIBLE. *Book of Common Prayer.* (1860s). Cambridge/London. miniature. aeg. celluloid/leather/brass clasp bdg. VG. H3. $75.00

BIBLE. *Book of Judges.* 1898. Dodd Mead. notes by Rev GF Moore. H10. $22.50

BIBLE. *Child's Bible.* 1834. Phil. Fisher. miniature. pls. 192 p. lavender cloth. NF. B24. $110.00

BIBLE. *Creation: 1st 8 Chapters of Genesis.* 1948. Pantheon. 1/125. folio. ils Masereel. F/wht wrp/glassine/defective slipcase. B24. $1,850.00

BIBLE. *Eng Bible.* 1903-05. Hammersmith. Doves Pr. 1/500. folio. 5 vols. limp vellum. F/slipcase. H5. $7,500.00

BIBLE. *Holy Bible, Containing Old & New Testament & Apocrypha.* (1911). London. Ballantyne. 3 vols. octavo. aeg. Cedric Chivers of Bath bdg. R3. $4,500.00

BIBLE. *Holy Bible.* not after 1480. Strassburg. 1st ed w/Glossa Ordinaria. 4 vols. rare. H5. $35,000.00

BIBLE. *Holy Bible.* Oct 27, 1802. Phil. Mathew Carey. 4to. 12 pls/6 maps. orig calf. H9. $250.00

BIBLE. *Holy Bible.* ca 1890. Leicester. ils Gustave Dore. special bdg/brass clasps. F. M18. $500.00

BIBLE. *Holy Bible.* 1846. NY. 1282 p. full leather. VG. O7. $21.00

BIBLE. *Holy Bible.* 1911. Glasgow. Gryce. miniature. w/magnifying glass in rear pocket. leather. H10. $175.00

BIBLE. *Il Nuovo Testamento di Giesu Christo...* 1550. Lyon. Gulielmo Rouillio. 8 parts in 1. 8vo. old dk calf/rebacked. K1. $1,500.00

BIBLE. *L'Histoire du Vieux et Du Nouveau Testament.* 1680. Chez Pierre Le Petit. Edition Nouvelle. 2 parts in 1. 12mo. 569 p. K1. $250.00

BIBLE. *Miniature Bible or Abstract of Sacred Hist.* 1816. Brattleborough. John Holbrook. 257 p. leather. H10. $200.00

BIBLE. *Miniature of the Holy Bible: Being a Brief...* ca 1840. Boston. Sherburne. 64 p. cloth (detached). H10. $60.00

BIBLE. *New Hieroglyphical Bible for Amusement...Children...* 1796. NY. Pub by Booksellers. 18mo. 144 p. recent cloth/brds. lacks frontispiece. M1. $1,250.00

BIBLE. *New Testament of Our Lord & Savior Jesus Christ.* 1848. Am Bible Soc. trans from orig Greek. full leather. G. A16. $50.00

BIBLE. *New Testament.* nd. Oxford. miniature. 224 p. gilt brn leather. H10. $25.00

BIBLE. *Novum Ieso Christi Domini Nostri Testamentum.* 1628. Sedan. Joannis Jannoni. 32mo. aeg. old tooled morocco. H10. $675.00

BIBLE. *Old Testament Book of Psalms.* ca 1851. London. Religious Tract Soc. miniature. blk leather. F. H10. $125.00

BIBLE. *Psalterium Davidis, Regis & Prophaetae...* 1720. Nuremberg. Bossoegelii. sm 4to. 316 p. 18th-century calf. K1. $275.00

BIBLE. *Sermon on the Mount.* (1924). San Francisco. Grabhorn. 1/190 complimentary. folio. 10 p. cloth. NF/slipcase. K1. $185.00

BIBLE. *Sixth Chapter of St Matthew Containing Lord's Prayer.* (1961). NY. Hammer Creek. 1/65. 12mo. ils Valenti Angelo. F/stiff wrp. B24. $200.00

BIBLE. *Wisdom of Jesus the Son of Sirach...Ecclesiasticus.* 1932. London. Ashendene. 1/328. sm folio. gilt limp orange vellum/silk ties. slipcase. R3. $3,500.00

BIBLE. *23rd Psalm.* 1965. Worcester. St Onge. miniature. ils Tasha Tudor. gr calf. F/F. H10. $57.50

BICE, Clare. *Jory's Cove.* 1941. Macmillan. 1st ed. 104 p. VG/VG-. P2. $12.50

BICHAT, Xavier. *Traite des Membranes en General et de Diverse Membranes...* 1800. Paris. Chez Richard. 326 p. G7. $995.00

BICK, Edgar M. *Sourcebook of Orthopaedics.* 1937. Baltimore. Williams Wilkins. 376 p. G7. $85.00

BICKER, VAIL & WILLS. *Autobiography of Eli Harvey, Quaker Sculptor From OH.* 1966. Wilmington, OH. Clinton County Hist Soc. 8vo. 100 p. VG. V3. $16.00

BICKHAM, Warren Stone. *Operative Surgery...Operations of General & Special Surgery.* 1930. Phil. Saunders. 1st reprint. 6 vols. cloth. G7. $150.00

BIDDIN, Thomas Frognall. *Lib Companion; or, Young Man's Guide...* 1824. London. Harding Triphook. 1st ed. 2 parts in 1 vol. Clarke bdg. NF. H5. $300.00

BIDDLE, George. *Adolphe Borie.* 1937. WA, DC. presentation/sgn. cloth. D2. $95.00

BIDDLE, George. *Gr Island.* 1930. NY. 1st ed. 177 p. pict gr cloth. VG-. H3. $15.00

BIDDLE, Nicholas. *Journals of the Expedition...Lewis & Clark.* 1962. Heritage. 2 vols. 4to. ils. half cloth. F/red slipcase. T8. $85.00

BIDLOO, Govard. *Anatomia Humani Corporis, Centum et Quinque Tabulis...* 1685. Amsterdam. Someren. 1st ed. atlas folio. 105 copperplates after Lairesse. G7. $11,500.00

BIENEK, Horst. *Time Without Bells.* 1988. Atheneum. 1st Eng-language ed. trans Ralph Read. NF/NF. A14. $25.00

BIERBAUM, Otto Julius. *Gugeline: Ein Buehnenspiel in Funf Aufzugen.* 1899. Berlin. Schuster Loeffler. 1st ed of 1st book w/Insel imp. F. B24. $375.00

BIERCE, Ambrose. *In the Midst of Life & Other Stories.* 1961. NY. Signet. ARC/PBO. RS. NF/unread. w/pub gold seal. A11. $45.00

BIERCE, Ambrose. *Tales of Haunted Houses.* nd. Girard, KS. later issue. F/orange wrp. A11. $15.00

BIERCE, Ambrose. *Tales of Soldiers & Civilians.* 1943. LEC. 1/1500. ils/sgn Paul Landacre. 222 p. slipcase/chemise. H5. $150.00

BIERCE, Ambrose. *Vision of Doom.* 1980. W Kingston. 1/1000. F/F ils Frank Villano. A11. $30.00

BIG EAGLE, Duane. *Bidato. 10-Mile River Poems.* 1975. Berkeley. Workingman's Pr. F/wrp. L3. $45.00

BIGELOW, Horatio. *Gunnerman.* 1939. Derrydale. 1st ed. 1/950. 246 p. cloth. NF. M8. $150.00

BIGELOW, J.M. *Explorations & Surveys for RR Route From MS to Pacific...* 1856-57. WA, DC. 4to. 117 full-p engravings. 414 p. half leather. VG. B26. $275.00

BIGELOW, Jacob. *Collection of Plants of Boston & Its Vicinity...* 1840. Little Brn. 3rd ed. 468 p. H10. $45.00

BIGELOW, Jacob. *Nature in Disease, Ils in Various Discourses & Essays.* 1854. Boston. Ticknor Fields. 1st ed. 391 p. emb brn cloth. B14. $125.00

BIGELOW, John. *Life & Public Services of John Charles Fremont.* 1856. NY. 1st ed. 12mo. 480 p. gilt olive cloth. G. T3. $54.00

BIGELOW, Poultney. *70 Summers.* 1925. Longman Gr. 1st ed. 8vo. 2 vols. F/F. A2. $45.00

BIGGAR, H.P. *Voyages of Jacques Cartier.* 1924. Ottawa. Acland. ils/maps. VG. scarce. O6. $225.00

BIGGERS, Earl D. *Celebrated Cases of Charlie Chan.* nd. Bobbs Merrill. 1st thus ed. VG. M2. $15.00

BIGGLE, Jacob. *Biggle Pet Book...* 1900. Phil. Atkinson. 1st ed. 142 p. H10. $25.00

BIGGLE, Jacob. *Biggle Poultry Book.* 1909. Phil. Atkinson. 7th ed. 16 color pls. 162 p. H10. $25.00

BIGGS & ROBINSON. *Pop-Up Kama Sutra.* 1984. 4 pop-ups. F. A4. $35.00

BIGHAM, R.W. *CA Gold-Field Scenes.* 1886. Nashville. 1st ed. 12mo. 283 p. brn cloth. H9. $90.00

BIGLET & WALLIHAN. *Rocky Mtn Directory & CO Gazeteer for 1871...* (1870). Denver. SS Wallihan. 1st ed. tall octavo. 442 p+186 ad p. mauve cloth. R3. $600.00

BIGNEY, T.O. *Month w/the Muses. CO Tales & Legends...* 1875. Pueblo, CO. 1st ed. 12mo. 130 p. cloth. VG. D3. $150.00

BILENKIN, Dmitri. *Uncertainty Principle.* 1978. Macmillan. 1st Eng-language ed. F/NF. N3. $15.00

BILIOTTI & COTTRET. *L'Ile de Rhodes.* 1881. Rhodes. tall 8vo. 10 pls/fld map/fld plan. modern cloth. O2. $750.00

BILLINGTON, Rachel. *Family Year.* (1992). London. McMillan. ARC. ils Clara Bulliamy. RS. F/F. B3. $25.00

BILLINGTON, Rachel. *Theo & Matilda.* (1990). Harper Collins. 1st ed. F/F. B3. $15.00

BILLINGTON, Ray A. *Far W Frontier 1830-60.* (1956). NY. 1st ed. 324 p. cloth. NF. D3. $15.00

BINDER, Eando. *Lords of Creation.* 1949. Prime Pr. 1st ed. VG/dj. M2. $30.00

BINDER, Otto O. *Victory in Space.* 1962. NY. Walker. 1st ed. F/VG+. N3. $10.00

BINETTE, Wilfred. *Knuckler.* 1970. Hallux Bros. 1st ed. F/F. P8. $25.00

BINFORD, Burney. *As I Remember It: 43 Yrs in Japan.* 1950. np. 8vo. 228 p. VG/VG. V3. $12.50

BINGAY, Malcolm. *Detroit Is My Own Home.* (1946). IN. photos. 360 p. A17. $10.00

BINGHAM, D. *Marriages of the Bourbons.* 1890. Scribner Welford. 1st Am ed. 8vo. 2 vols. VG. A2. $50.00

BINGHAM, Hiram. *Residence of 21 Yrs in the Sandwich Islands.* 1847. Hartford/NY. Huntington/Converse. 1st ed. 8vo. 616 p. brn cloth. H9. $325.00

BINGHAM, John. *I Love, I Kill.* 1968. London. Gollancz. 1st ed. F/NF. M15. $45.00

BINGHAM, Marjorie T. *Fora of Oakland Co, MI.* 1945. MI. Cranbrook. A16. $25.00

BINION, Rudolph. *Frau Lou: Nietzche's Wayward Disciple.* 1968. Princeton. 1st ed. 587 p. gray cloth. G1. $50.00

BINION, Samuel A. *Phyllanthography: Method of Leaf & Flower Writing...* ca 1909. NY. Fenno. pict cloth. H10. $65.00

BINNEY. *Homage to Amanda.* 1984. np. ils. wrp. G2. $18.95

BINYON, Laurence. *Followers of William Blake.* 1925. London. Smith. 1/100. sgn. rebound leather. F. F1. $275.00

BINYON, Laurence. *Maddness of Merlin.* 1944. np. 1st ed. intro Gordon Bottomly. VG+/dj. scarce. C1. $35.00

BIRBECK, Morris. *Letters From IL.* 1818. Dublin. 60 p. NF. H3. $90.00

BIRBECK, Morris. *Letters From IL.* 1818. Phil. Carey. 1st ed. 12mo. 154 p. rebound blk cloth. H9. $350.00

BIRBECK, Morris. *Notes on a Journey in Am From Coast of VA to...IL.* 1818. Dublin. 158 p. F. H3. $90.00

BIRD, E.K. *Prisoner #7: Rudolf Hess...* (1974). Viking. 1st ed. 8vo. 270 p. F/F. A2. $12.50

BIRD, G. *Urinary Deposits: Their Diagnosis, Pathology...* 1854. Phil. 12mo. 371 p+12 catalog p. blk cloth. G. T3. $37.00

BIRD, Gloria. *Full Moon on the Reservation.* 1993. Greenfield Review. 1st ed. F/wrp. L3. $20.00

BIRD, Henry. *Narrative of Henry Bird.* 1815. np. ltd hc ed. 1/100. tall 8vo. VG. E5. $25.00

BIRD, James. *Dunwich: Tale of the Splendid City.* 1828. London. Baldwin Cradock. octavo. 165 p. fore-edge painting. red morocco. F. B24. $925.00

BIRD, Will R. *Angel Cove.* (1972). Tor. 236 p. A17. $10.00

BIRD, William. *Treatise of Nobilitie of the Realm.* 1642. London. Walbanke Best. full sheep. M11. $350.00

BIRDSEY, M.R. *Cultivated Aroids.* 1951. Berkeley. 66 full-p pls. 140 p. VG. B26. $40.00

BIRGE, John K. *Bektashi Order of Dervishes.* 1937. London. 1st ed. ils. 291 p. cloth. dj. very scarce. O2. $100.00

BIRGE, Julius C. *Awakening of the Desert.* (1912). Boston. Badger. 1st ed/1st issue. xl. fair. H7. $10.00

BIRGE & CHAUNCEY. *Inland Lakes of WI.* 1922. Madison. ils/index. 222 p. A17. $25.00

BIRMINGHAM, Stephen. *Rest of US: Rise of Am's E European Jews.* (1984). Little Brn. 1st ed. NF/NF. A7. $12.00

BIRNABAUM, Uriel. *Der Kaiser und der Architekt.* 1924. Germany. Im Thyrsos. 1st ed. gilt cloth. VG. M5. $75.00

BIRNBAUM, Philip. *Treasury of Judaism.* 1957. Hebrew Pub. 431 p. VG/fair. S3. $19.00

BIRNEY, Hoffman. *Roads To Roam.* (1930). Phil. Penn. VG+/dj. H7. $15.00

BIRNEY, Hoffman. *Vigilantes.* 1929. Phil. 1st ed. ils/pict ep. 346 p. cloth. NF. D3. $25.00

BIRNEY, Hoffman. *Zealots of Zion.* (1931). Phil. 1st ed. 317 p. map ep. cloth. VG. D3. $20.00

BIRRELL, Francis. *Platos Symposium or Supper.* nd. London. Nonesuch. 1/1050. G. A1. $30.00

BISCHOFF, Kay. *Am Indian Dances To Cut & Color.* 1952. Eukabi. ils Eugene Bischoff. VG+. M20. $15.00

BISCHOFF & SHEFFIELD. *Selkie.* 1982. Macmillan. 1st ed. F/NF. N3. $10.00

BISHOP, Edward. *Debt We Owe.* 1939. Shrewsbury. 1st ed. 216 p. F/F pict dj. M7. $35.00

BISHOP, Elizabeth. *Brazil.* nd. Life World Lib. 1st ed. 160 p. NF/sans. A11. $55.00

BISHOP, Elizabeth. *Collected Prose.* 1984. FSG. AP. F/wrp. L3. $50.00

BISHOP, Elizabeth. *Complete Poems.* (1969). FSG. 1st ed. F/NF. B4. $85.00

BISHOP, Elizabeth. *N & S.* (1946). Houghton Mifflin. later prt. inscr. VG. L3. $450.00

BISHOP, Harriet E. *Floral Home; or, 1st Yrs of MN; Early Sketches...* 1857. NY. Sheldon Blakeman. 1st ed. 342 p. G. H7. $125.00

BISHOP, Isabelle Bird. *Korea & Her Neighbors.* 1898. NY/Chicago/Toronto. Revell. 8vo. ils/24 pls/2 fld maps. VG. W1. $75.00

BISHOP, J.P. *S Question. View of Policy... Powers...As to S States.* 1877. Cleveland. Fairbanks. 8 p. wrp. M11. $75.00

BISHOP, Jim. *Day Lincoln Was Shot.* 1955. Harper. BC. cloth. VG/VG. M8. $25.00

BISHOP, Jim. *Days of Martin Luther King Jr.* (1971). Putnam. 1st ed. clip dj. A7. $30.00

BISHOP, Joel Prentiss. *Commentaries on Law of Statutory Crimes.* 1873. Little Brn. sheep. M11. $85.00

BISHOP, John Peale. *Collected Poems.* 1948. NY. 1st ed. F/NF. A11. $55.00

BISHOP, Joseph Bucklin. *Panama Gateway.* 1913. Scribner. 1st ed. 8vo. 459 p. gilt red brds. B11. $40.00

BISHOP, Michael. *Ancient of Days.* 1985. NY. Arbor. 1st ed. F/F. N3. $30.00

BISHOP, Michael. *And Strange at Ecbatan the Trees.* 1976. Harper. 1st ed. sgn. F/dj. M2. $30.00

BISHOP, Michael. *Close Encounter w/the Diety.* 1986. Peachtree. 1st ed. F/F. F4. $15.00

BISHOP, Michael. *One Winter in Eden.* 1983. Arkham. 1st ed. as new. M2. $25.00

BISHOP, Michael. *Stolen Faces.* 1977. Harper. 1st ed. F/NF. M2. $20.00

BISHOP, Michael. *Transfigurations.* 1979. Berkley. 1st ed. F/NF. N3. $15.00

BISHOP, P. Marshall. *Trucks & Vans 1897-1927.* 1972. Macmillan. VG/dj. A16. $10.00

BISHOP, Robert. *Centuries & Styles of Am Chair, 1640-1970.* 1972. Dutton. 1st ed. ils. 510 p. cloth. VG/dj. M20. $35.00

BISHOP, William Henry. *Mexico, CA & AZ. A New & Revised Ed...* 1889. NY. Harper. 8vo. ils/map. 569 p. red pict cloth. H9. $75.00

BISHOP, Zealia. *Curse of Yig.* 1953. Arkham. 1st ed. sgn. as new. M2. $175.00

BISHOP & HOUCK. *All Flags Flying.* 1986. np. ils. cloth. G2. $25.00

BISHOP & SAFANA. *Gallery of Amish Quilts.* 1975. np. wrp. G2. $16.00

BISHOP. *Romance of Double Wedding Ring Quilts.* 1989. np. cloth. G2. $30.00

BISPHAM, George Tucker. *Principles of Equity: Treatise on System of Justice...* 1903. NY. full sheep. M11. $50.00

BISSELL, R. *Monongahela.* 1952. NY. 1st ed. presentation/sgn. VG/VG. B5. $60.00

BISSETT, Clark Prescott. *Abraham Lincoln: An Address.* 1916. Los Angeles. Connell Smith. 1/600. inscr. VG. A6. $15.00

BITOV, Andrei. *Captive of the Caucasus.* 1992. FSG. 1st Eng-language ed. trans Susan Brownsberger. F/F. A14. $25.00

BITTELMAN, Alex. *Communist Party in Action.* 1934. NY. Workers Lib. 1st revised ed. xl. VG. V4. $15.00

BITTELMAN, Alex. *Milestones in Hist of Communist Party.* 1937. NY. Workers Lib. VG. V4. $12.50

BITTELMAN & JEROME. *Leninism: Only Marxism Today.* 1934. NY. Workers Lib. 1st ed. VG. V4. $11.00

BIXBY-SMITH, Sarah. *Adobe Days...* 1925. Cedar Rapids. Torch Pr. 1st ed. 12mo. 208 p. cloth. NF. D3. $25.00

BIZZARRI, Pietro. *Persicarum Rerum Nistoria in XII Libros Descripta.* 1583. Antwerp. Plantini. folio. 451 p. 19th-century half calf/marbled brds. rare. K1. $1,750.00

BIZZELL, W.B. *Gr Rising: Hist Survey of Agrarianism...* 1926. Macmillan. 1st ed. 269 p. H10. $25.00

BLACK, Campbell. *Letters From the Dead.* 1985. Villard. 1st ed. F/dj. M2. $10.00

BLACK, Campbell. *Wanting.* 1986. McGraw Hill. 1st ed. F/F. T2. $12.50

BLACK, Charles L. *Structure & Relationship in Constitutional Law.* 1969. Baton Rouge. M11. $25.00

BLACK, Gavin. *Big Wind for Summer.* 1975. London. Collins Crime Club. 1st ed. F/F. M15. $30.00

BLACK, Henry Campbell. *Handbook of Am Constitutional Law.* 1897. St Paul. W Pub. 2nd ed. full sheep. M11. $125.00

BLACK, Henry Campbell. *Handbook of Constitutional Law.* 3rd ed. 1910. St Paul. W Pub. full sheep. M11. $35.00

BLACK, John Donald. *Rural Economy of New Eng.* 1950. Cambridge. Harvard. 796 p. F. H10. $30.00

BLACK, Robert Clifford III. *Railroads of the Confederacy.* 1952. Chapel Hill. 1st ed. 360 p. VG. M8. $65.00

BLACK, William C. *Hooked on Flies: Confessions of a Pattern Inventor.* (1980). Winchester. 1st ed. 146 p. dj. A17. $15.00

BLACKADDER, H. Home. *Observations on Phagedaena Gangraenosa. In 2 Parts.* 1818. Edinburgh. Balfour Clarke. 180 p. orig brds. G7. $250.00

BLACKBURN, Henry. *Randolph Caldecott.* 1887. London. Samson Low. 4th ed. 210 p. gilt gr cloth. G+. M20. $55.00

BLACKBURN, Paul. *Brooklyn-Manhattan Transit.* 1960. NY. 1st ed. VG+/photo wrp. A11. $35.00

BLACKBURN, Paul. *Manhattan Transit.* 1960. NY. 2nd collection of poems. F/wrp. A11. $40.00

BLACKBURN & SPILLER. *Descriptive Bibliography Writing of James Fenimore Cooper.* 1934. NY. RR Bowker. 1st ed. 1/500. cloth. NF. M8. $150.00

BLACKER, Irwin R. *Irregulars, Partisans, Guerillas.* 1954. NY. Simon Schuster. 1st ed. 487 p. VG+/VG/clear plastic. M7. $55.00

BLACKER, Irwin R. *Westering.* 1958. World. 1st ed. F/NF. B9. $20.00

BLACKFORD, Charles Minor Jr. *Annals of the Lynchburg Home Guard.* 1891. Lynchburg, VA. John Rohr. 1st ed. 185 p. cloth. NF. M8. $850.00

BLACKFORD, Mansel G. *Politics of Business in CA.* 1977. OH State. charts/index. 231 p. F. B19. $10.00

BLACKFORD, William Willis. *War Yrs w/Jeb Stuart.* 1945. Scribner. early prt. 322 p. cloth. VG. M8. $45.00

BLACKMAN, Honor. *Honor Blackman's Book of Self Defense.* 1966 (65). Macmillan. later prt. 8vo. 125 p. F/F. A2. $12.50

BLACKSTOCK, Lee. *All Men Are Murderers.* 1958. Doubleday. 1st ed. F/NF. S5. $22.50

BLACKSTONE, William. *Great Charter & Charter of the Forest...* 1759. Oxford. Clarendon. modern full crimson morocco. M11. $4,500.00

BLACKWELL, W.H. *Poisonous & Medicinal Plants.* 1990. Englewood Cliffs. ils. 329 p. M. B26. $48.00

BLACKWELL & LAINING. *Plants of New Zealand.* 1927. Auckland. 3rd ed. 468 p. B26. $22.50

BLACKWOOD, Algernon. *Doll & One Other.* 1946. Arkham. 1st ed. F/dj. M2. $60.00

BLACKWOOD, Algernon. *Doll & One Other.* 1946. Arkham. 1st ed. VG/dj. M18. $45.00

BLACKWOOD, Algernon. *Full Circle.* 1929. London. Mathews Marrot. 1/530. sgn. F/NF. B2. $125.00

BLACKWOOD, Algernon. *Tales of Terror & Darkness.* 1977. Spring Books. 1st thus ed. VG/dj. M2. $25.00

BLAINE, James G. *James A Garfield: Memorial Address...* 1882. WA. 4to. 87 p. gilt cloth. G. A17. $17.50

BLAINE, John. *Electronic Mind Reader.* 1957. Grosset. VG. M2. $10.00

BLAINE, John. *Golden Skull.* 1954. Grosset. 1st ed. F/dj. M2. $20.00

BLAINE, Marge. *Terrible Thing That Happened at Our House.* (1975). Parents Magazine. ils John C Wallner. VG. T5. $20.00

BLAIR, Maria. *Matthew Fontaine Maury.* 1918. Richmond, VA. Whittet Shepperson. 1st ed. 13 p. NF/prt wrp. M8. $37.50

BLAIR, Sidney. *Buffalo.* 1991. Viking. AP. author's 1st novel. F/wrp. L3. $45.00

BLAKE, Mike. *Minor Leagues.* 1991. Wynwood. 1st ed. F/F. P8. $15.00

BLAKE, W.H. *Brown Water & Other Sketches.* 1915. Tor. 1st ed. 264 p. G. A17. $20.00

BLAKE, William. *Gates of Paradise.* 1968. London. 1/650. 3 vols. red cloth. NF/slipcase. B20. $150.00

BLAKE, William. *Hist of Slavery & the Slave Trade, Ancient & Modern.* 1859. Columbus, OH. Miller. 1st ed. 832 p. orig cloth. M8. $250.00

BLAKE, William. *Report Upon the Precious Metals: Being Statistical Notices.* 1869. GPO. 368 p. VG/wrp. O5. $100.00

BLAKE, William. *There Is No Natural Religion.* 1971. London. 1st ed. 2 vols. full tan morocco. F/marbled slipcase. K1. $500.00

BLAKE, William. *Vala or the 4 Zoas.* 1963. Clarendon. facsimile of manuscript. folio. VG/G. F1. $160.00

BLAKSTON, SWAYSLAND & WIENER. *Ils Book of Canaries & Cage-Birds, British & Foreign.* nd. (1877-80). London. Cassell. quarto. 448 p. aeg. VG. H5. $750.00

BLANCHAN, Neltje. *Am Flower Garden.* 1909. NY. 1/1050. 100 full-p photos. 368 p. gilt gr cloth. NF. B28. $90.00

BLANCHAN, Neltje. *Nature's Garden.* 1900. NY. 1st ed. ils/color pls. 415 p. decor gr cloth. VG. B28. $37.50

BLANCHARD, Amos. *Am Musical Primer, Containing Correct Intro...* 1808. Exeter. Norris Sawyer. 1st ed. oblong 8vo. 77 p. contemporary calf. VG. M1. $200.00

BLANCHARD, Amy E. *Tell Me a Story.* 1888. Worthington. 1st ed. sm 4to. 15 p. G. S10. $60.00

BLANCHARD, F.S. *Sailboat Classes of N Am.* 1968. Doubleday. expanded ed. G/dj. A16. $20.00

BLANCHARD, Mary Miles. *Basketry Book: 12 Lessons in Reed Weaving.* 1923. Scribner. pls. 111 p. H10. $17.50

BLANCHARD, Peter. *Markham in Peru.* (1991). Austin, TX. 1st ed. 148 p. dj. F3. $25.00

BLANCHARD, Rufus. *Discovery & Conquests of the NW.* 1880. Chicago. Blanchard Cushing. 2nd ed. lg 8vo. brn cloth. H9. $125.00

BLANCHARD & WELLMAN. *Life & Times of Sir Archie (Thoroughbred Horse), 1805-33.* 1958. Chapel Hill. 1st ed. VG/VG. O3. $45.00

BLAND, Humphrey. *Treatise of Military Discipline.* 1759. London. Baldwin/Richardson/Longman. 418 p. old calf/rebacked. K1. $350.00

BLAND, R. Nesbit. *Bunny Tales.* ca 1880. Dutton. ils Edith Cubitt. 64 p. pict beige cloth. VG. S10. $55.00

BLANDING, Don. *Pictures of Paradise.* 1941. NY. VG/G. B5. $20.00

BLANK, Clair. *Adventure Girls at K-Bar-O.* 1936. AL Burt. lists 3 titles. 248 p. VG/dj. M20. $30.00

BLANK, Clair. *Beverly Gray, Sophomore.* 1934. AL Burt. lists 4 titles. 256 p. VG/VG. M20. $75.00

BLANK, Clair. *Beverly Gray's Quest.* 1942. Grosset Dunlap. 1st ed. 220 p. gr cloth. VG/VG. M20. $40.00

BLANK, Clair. *Beverly Gray's Vacation.* 1949. Grosset Dunlap. 1st ed. 212 p. bl cloth. VG/dj. M20. $20.00

BLANKENSHIP, W.D. *Leavenworth Irregulars.* (1974). Bobbs Merrill. stated 1st prt. 264 p. dj. A7. $50.00

BLANQUI, Jerome Adolphe. *Voyage a Madrid (Aout et Septembre 1826).* 1826. Paris. Dondey-Dupre Pere et Fils. 8vo. VG+. P4. $250.00

BLATCHFORD, Robert. *Love & Sympathy, Basis of Socialism.* nd. NY. Commonwealth Co. VG. V4. $7.50

BLATCHFORD, Robert. *Merrie Eng: Plain Exposition of Socialism.* ca 1895. NY. Commonwealth Co. VG. V4. $22.50

BLATCHLEY, W.S. *Catalogue of Uncultivated Ferns & Fern Allies...* 1897. Indianapolis. annotated list of 853 plants. 132 p. self wrp. B26. $24.00

BLATCHLEY, W.S. *In Days Agone.* 1932. Indianapolis. 1st ed. 338 p. VG. B5. $40.00

BLATTY, William Peter. *Exorcist.* 1971. NY. 1st ed. sgn. NF/F. A11. $90.00

BLATTY, William Peter. *I'll Tell Them I Remember You.* 1973. NY. 1st ed. w/sgn label. NF/NF. E3. $30.00

BLATTY, William Peter. *Legion.* 1983. Simon Schuster. 1st ed. F/NF. N3. $10.00

BLATTY, William Peter. *Which Way to Mecca, Jack?* 1958. NY. 1st ed. sgn. NF/NF clip. A11. $50.00

BLAUE, Willem Jaszoon. *Institution Astromique de l'Usage des Globes...Terrestres...* 1642. Amsterdam. 1st ed. sm quarto. contemporary vellum. VG. H5. $1,500.00

BLAVATSKY, H. *Secret Doctrine.* 1893 (1888). London. Theosophy Pub. 3rd ed. 8vo. 3 vols. VG. A2. $75.00

BLAYLOCK & ROBINSON. *2 Views of a Cave Painting/Escape From Kathmandu.* (1987). Seattle. Axolotl. wrp issue. sgn Blaylock/Robinson/Koontz/Powers. F. A7. $25.00

BLEECK, Oliver; see Thomas, Ross.

BLEGVAD, Lenore. *Anna Banana & Me.* 1985. Atheneum. 1st ed. oblong 16mo. NF/F. T5. $25.00

BLEILER, Everett. *Checklist of Fantastic Literature.* 1948. Shasta. 1st ed. F/F. M2. $200.00

BLEILER & DIKTY. *Best SF Stories of Yr 1949.* 1949. Fell. 1st ed. VG/dj. M2. $17.00

BLEILER & DIKTY. *Best SF Stories of Yr 1953.* 1953. Fell. 1st ed. VG/F. M2. $25.00

BLESH, Rudi. *O Susanna: Sampler of Riches of Am Folk Music.* 1960. Grove Evergreen. 1st ed. ils Horst Geldmacher/music H Wilson. F. B14. $110.00

BLESH, Rudi. *Shining Trumpets.* 1946. Knopf. 1st ed. NF/VG. B2. $75.00

BLESH, Rudi. *This Is Jazz.* 1943. London. Jazz Music Books. 1st ed. 36 p. VG+/wrp. B2. $75.00

BLESH & JANIS. *They All Played Ragtime.* 1950. Knopf. 1st ed. F/VG. B2. $40.00

BLEVIN, Winfred. *Carbonneau: Man of 2 Dreams.* (1975). Nash Pub. 1st ed. sgn. F/dj. A18. $40.00

BLEVINS, Winfred. *Misadventures of Silk & Shakespeare.* (1985). NY. Jameson. 1st ed. sgn. VG/NF clip. B3. $25.00

BLEW, William. *Hit of Steeple-Chasing.* 1901. London. Mimmo. 1st ed. ils Henry Alken. 334 p. teg. VG/slipcase. H5. $300.00

BLIGH, William. *Voyage to the S Seas.* 1975. LEC. 4 color pls. sgn Ingleton/Dunstan. w/prospectus. M/slipcase. O6. $195.00

BLISH, James. *Anywhen.* 1971. London. 1st ed. revised preface. F/dj. M2. $35.00

BLISH, James. *Earthman, Come Home.* 1955. Putnam. 1st ed. 1st Cities in Flight series. NF/NF. Q1. $100.00

BLISH, James. *Frozen Yr.* 1957. Ballantine. 1st ed. hc. VG-. M2. $50.00

BLISH, James. *Jack of Eagles.* 1952. Greenberg. 1st ed. NF/dj. M2. $60.00

BLISH, James. *Midsummer Century.* 1973. London. Faber. 1st ed. F/NF. N3. $10.00

BLISH, James. *Seedling Stars.* 1957. London. Faber. 1st ed. F/F. F4. $35.00

BLISS & PECK. *Military Heroes of Am.* ca 1850. Phil. miniature. 48 pls. cloth. H10. $125.00

BLOCH, E. Maurice. *Drawings of George Caleb Bingham w/Catalogue Raisonne.* 1975. Columbia. MO U. 272 p. cloth. dj. D2. $350.00

BLOCH, E. Maurice. *George Caleb Bingham. A Catalogue Raisonne.* 1967. Berkeley. 238 p. cloth. dj. D2. $95.00

BLOCH, Iwan. *Anthropological Studies... Strange Sexual Practices...* 1933. Falstaff. VG. N2. $20.00

BLOCH, Louis M. Jr. *Gas Pipe Networks: Hist of College Radio 1936-46.* 1980. Cleveland. Bloch. VG. N2. $12.50

BLOCH, Robert. *Atoms & Evil.* 1962. Fawcett Gold Medal. PBO. unread/unopened. A11. $75.00

BLOCH, Robert. *Eighth State of Fandom.* 1962. Advent. 1st ed. 1/125. sgn/#d. F/sans. M2. $425.00

BLOCH, Robert. *Opener of the Way.* 1974. Spearman. 1st British ed. NF/dj. M2. $38.00

BLOCH, Robert. *Pleasant Dreams.* 1960. Arkham. 1st ed. sgn. F/dj. M2. $175.00

BLOCH, Robert. *Psycho.* 1959. Simon Schuster. 1st ed. inscr. NF/NF. B4. $600.00

BLOCH, Robert. *Selected Stories.* 1987. Underwood Miller. 1st ed. 1/500 sets. sgn. xl. VG. M2. $75.00

BLOCH, Robert. *Todd Dossier.* 1969. Macmillan. 1st UK ed. sgn. NF/NF. F4. $75.00

BLOCK, Lawrence. *Ariel.* 1980. Arbor. 1st ed. F/NF. F4. $20.00

BLOCK, Lawrence. *Ariel.* 1980. Arbor. 1st ed. inscr. F/F. M15. $40.00

BLOCK, Lawrence. *Burglar Who Painted Like Mondrian.* 1983. Arbor. 1st ed. F/F. F4. $20.00

BLOCK, Lawrence. *Dance at the Slaughterhouse.* 1991. Morrow. ARC. sgn. w/promo material. F/F. S5. $40.00

BLOCK, Lawrence. *Death Pulls a Doublecross.* 1961. Gold Medal. PBO. 2nd (acknowledged) book. sgn. F/unread. A11. $45.00

BLOCK, Lawrence. *Devil Knows You're Dead.* (1993). Morrow. ARC. RS. w/promo material. M/dj. B4. $35.00

BLOCK, Lawrence. *Like a Lamb to Slaughter.* 1984. Arbor. 1st ed. sgn. F/F. M15/S5. $45.00

BLOCK, Lawrence. *Mona.* 1961. Gold Medal. PBO. 1st (acknowledged) book. sgn. F/wrp. A11. $50.00

BLOCK, Lawrence. *Random Walk.* 1988. NY. Tor. 1st ed. inscr. F/F. M15. $40.00

BLOCK, Lawrence. *Sins of the Fathers.* (1991). Avon. 1st pb ed. presentation/sgn. NF. A7. $10.00

BLOCK, Lawrence. *Sins of the Fathers.* 1992. Dark Harvest. 1st hc ed. 1/400. sgn Block/Stephen King. F/F/slipcase. M15. $85.00

BLOCK, Lawrence. *Strange Are the Ways of Love.* 1959. Crest. 1st ed. author's 1st book. F/F. F4. $50.00

BLOCK & KING. *Code of Arms.* 1981. NY. Marek. 1st ed. inscr. F/F. M15. $45.00

BLOCK & WOOLRICH. *Into the Night.* 1987. Mysterious. 1st ed. sgn Block. F/F. S5. $40.00

BLODGETT, Mabel F. *Magic Slippers.* 1917. Little Brn. 1st ed. 91 p. G. S10. $30.00

BLOGG, M.W. *Bibliography of Writings of Sir William Osler...* 1921. Baltimore. revised/enlarged ed. emb stamp on title. G7. $75.00

BLOMBERY & MALONEY. *Proteaceae of the Sydney Region.* 1992. Kenthurst, Australia. 215 color photos. 216 p. M. B26. $37.50

BLOMFIELD, E. *General View of World, Geog, Hist & Philosophical...Vol 1.* 1807. Bungay. Brightly Kinnersley. 10 maps. full leather. VG. O6. $120.00

BLOMFIELD, Reginald. *Formal Garden in Eng.* 1892. London. 1st ed. ils Fl Thomas. 344 p. gilt wht cloth. B26. $59.00

BLOODSTONE, John; see Byrne, Stuart.

BLOOM, Harold. *AR Ammons: Modern Critical Views.* 1986. Chelsea House. 1st ed. NF/NF. C4. $25.00

BLOOM, Harold. *Flight to Lucifer. Gnostic Fantasy.* 1979. FSG. 1st ed. F/F. N3. $40.00

BLOOM, Harold. *Hart Crane: Modern Critical Views.* 1986. Chelsea House. 308 p. F/F. A7. $17.00

BLOOM, James D. *Left Letters. Culture Wars of Mike Gold & Joseph Freeman.* 1992. NY. Columbia. 1st ed. F/F. B2. $30.00

BLOTNER, Joseph. *Selected Letters of William Faulkner.* (1976). Franklin Lib. true 1st ed. full leather. NF. B3. $45.00

BLUE, Vida. *Vida: His Own Story.* 1972. Prentice Hall. 1st ed. VG/VG. P8. $12.50

BLUE CLOUD, Peter. *Turtle, Bear & Wolf.* 1976. Mohawk Nation. Akwesasne Notes. 1st ed. preface/sgn Snyder. F/wrp. L3. $55.00

BLUM, John M. *From the Morgenthau Diaries: Yrs of Crisis 1928-38.* 1959. Houghton Mifflin. 1st prt. 583 p. VG+/G+. S3. $24.00

BLUM & BLUM. *Dangerous Hour.* 1970. London. 8vo. 410 p. dj. O2. $45.00

BLUMBERG, Fannie Burgheim. *Rowena Teena Tot & the Blackberries.* 1934. Whitman. ils/sgn Grosjean. 32 p. plaid cloth. F. B24. $225.00

BLUME, Judy. *It's Not the End of the World.* (1979). London. Heinemann. 1st ed. VG/VG. B3. $30.00

BLUMENTHAL, Michael. *Against Romance.* 1987. Penguin. 1st ed. inscr/sgn. F/wrp. V1. $20.00

BLUMENTHAL, Walter Hart. *Book Gluttons & Book Gormets.* 1962. Chicago. Blk Cat. miniature. 1/300. gilt gr cloth. H10. $150.00

BLUMENTHAL, Walter Hart. *Book of Famous Kings & Queens.* ca 1850. Phil. Peck Bliss. miniature. 191 p. gilt cloth. F. H10. $125.00

BLUMLEIN, Michael. *Movement of Mtns.* 1988. Simon Schuster. 1st ed. F/F. N3. $15.00

BLUNT, Joseph. *Merchant's & Shipmaster's Assistant...* 1829. NY. Blunt. 464 p. sheepskin. w/pict trade card. NF. B14. $125.00

BLUNT, Wilfred S. *New Situation in Egypt.* 1908. London. presentation. 19 p. VG/prt wrp. H3. $45.00

BLUNT, Wilfred. *My Diaries: Being Personal Narrative of Events...* 1932. Knopf. 3rd/1st 1-vol ed. gilt bl cloth. G. M7. $18.00

BLY, Robert. *Light Around the Body.* 1968. London. ARC of 1st ed. sgn. RS. F/F. scarce. V1. $45.00

BLY, Robert. *Silence in the Snowy Fields.* 1962. Middletown, CT. 1st ed/wrp issue. sgn. F/sq wrp. A11. $55.00

BLY, Robert. *What Have I Ever Lost By Dying.* (1991). Harper Collins. 1st ed. F/F. B3. $20.00

BLY & RAY. *Poetry Reading Against the Vietnam War.* 1966. Madison. 60s Pr/Am Writers Against Vietnam War. NF/bl-gr wrp. A7. $60.00

BLYTH, R.H. *Haiku. Vol 1.* 1960. Hokuseido. 7th prt. 12mo. 26 pls. 422 p. VG. W1. $18.00

BLYTON, Enid. *Mr Tumpy & His Caravan.* 1951. McNaughton. unp. pict brds. VG/dj. M20. $25.00

BOADELLA, David. *Wilhelm Reich: Evolution of His Work.* 1974. Chicago. Regnery. 1st Am ed. 400 p. gray cloth. VG/dj. L3. $22.50

BOARDMAN, John. *Pantheon & Its Sculptures.* 1985. Austin. folio. 256 p. dj. O2. $30.00

BOAS, F. *Religion of the Kwakiutl Indians.* 1930. NY. 1st ed. 2 vols. VG. B5. $75.00

BOAZ, Franz. *Kathlamet Texts.* 1901. GPO. ils. 260 p. cloth. B14. $45.00

BOBKER, Lee R. *Flight of a Dragon.* 1981. Morrow. 1st ed. F/F. F4. $16.00

BOBST, Elmer H. *Bobst: Autobiography of Pharmaceutical Pioneer.* 1973. McKay. ils. 360 p. F/VG. S9. $8.00

BOCARRO, Antonio. *O Livro Das Plantas de Todas As Fortalezas...Vol 1-3...* 1992. Lisboa. Imprensa Nacional-Casa Moeda. 3 vols. 1/1000. slipcase. O6. $350.00

BOCCACCIO, Giovanni. *Decameron.* (1924). Berlin. Neufeld Henius. 2 vols. ils Lucian Zabel. decor ep. tooled bdg. B14. $100.00

BOCCACCIO, Giovanni. *Decameron.* 1925. NY. Boni Liveright. subscriber ed. 1/2000. 2 vols. marbled ep. morocco. F. H5. $300.00

BOCKSTOCE & GILKERSON. *Am Whalers in the W Arctic.* 1893. EJ Lefkowicz Inc. 1st ed. 1/400. bl quarter leather/gray cloth. F. P4. $1,500.00

BOCKSTRUCK, Lloyd. *VA's Colonial Soldiers.* 1990. Genealogical Pub. 2nd prt. 443 p. VG/VG. B10. $30.00

BODEN, F.C. *Derbyshire Tragedy.* 1935. London. Dent. 1st ed. NF/NF. B2. $45.00

BODEN, F.C. *Miner.* 1932. London. Dent. 1st ed. F/F. B2. $60.00

BODEY, Donald. *FNG.* (1985). NY. Viking. 1st ed. F/F. A7. $35.00

BODGER & BROCK. *Adventurous Crocheter.* 1972. np. pb. G2. $4.00

BODINE & YAMBURA. *Change & Parting: My Story of Amana.* (1960). Ames, IA. IA State. 1st ed. 8vo. 361 p. VG+/VG+. A2. $30.00

BODINGTON, Charles. *Books of Devotion.* 1903. London. Longman Gr. 319 p. H10. $25.00

BODLEY, Ronald. *Gertrude Bell.* 1940. NY. Macmillan. 1st ed. 260 p. tan cloth. NF/G+/clear plastic. M7. $7.00

BODONI, Giambattista. *Maximes et Reflecions Morales du Duc de la Rochefoucauld.* 1811. Parma. 1/125. folio. w/supplement. contemporary bdg. F. B24. $1,250.00

BOEHL, Wayne G. Jr. *John Deere's Company...* ca 1984. Doubleday. 870 p. F/dj. H10. $25.00

BOEHM, Mrs. A.G. *Hist of the New Richmond (WI) Cyclone of June 12, 1899.* 1900. Minneapolis, MN. 1st ed. 217 p. pict cloth. NF. D3. $25.00

BOESEL & ROSSI. *Cities Under Siege.* (1971). Basic Books. 436 p. NF/clip dj. A7. $25.00

BOGAN, Louise. *Collected Poems: 1923-53.* 1954. NY. ARC. F/wrp/protective mylar dj. A11. $85.00

BOGARDE, Dirk. *Snakes & Ladders.* 1973. Chatto Windus. 2nd imp. 339 p. gilt dk gr paper. F/NF. M7. $35.00

BOGERT, C.H. *With Brushes of Comet's Hair.* (1950). NY. Exposition. 1st ed. 8vo. 165 p. VG/VG. A2. $15.00

BOGLE, Donald. *Brn Sugar: 80 Yrs of Am's Blk Female Superstars.* (1980). Harmony. 1st ed. 4to. 208 p. F/NF. S7. $65.00

BOGLE, Donald. *Toms, Coons, Mulattoes, Mammies & Bucks: Interpretive Hist.* (1973). Viking. 2nd prt. 260 p. NF/NF. A7. $30.00

BOGUET, Henry. *Examen of Witches Drawn From Various Trials...* 1929. London. John Rodker. 1st Eng ed. 1/1275. sm 8vo. gr parchment. VG. G1. $125.00

BOHANON, Paul. *Wind & Arabella.* 1947. NY. Oxford. ils Janice Holland. 1st ed. 69 p. VG/VG. A3. $25.00

BOHN & PETSCHEK. *Kinsey Photographer: Half Century of Negatives...* 1982 (75). San Francisco. Chronicle Books. 1st hc trade ed. 319 p. F/F. A2. $40.00

BOILEAU & NARCEJAC. *Heart to Heart.* 1959. London. trans Daphne Woodward. F/F. A11. $35.00

BOILEAU & NARCEJAC. *Spells of Evil.* 1961. London. 1st Eng-language ed. 12mo. F/NF clip. A11. $20.00

BOISVERT, F. *Historie de ma Vie.* 1911. Bagneres-de-Bigorre. 21 p. wrp. N2. $32.50

BOIVIN & DUGES. *Traite Pratique des Maladies de l'Uterus et Annexes.* 1834. Bruxelles. Etablissement Encyclopgraphique. 2 vols. 41 hc pls. VG. G7. $1,750.00

BOK, Hannes. *Fantasy Calendar for 1949.* 1949. Gnome. 1st ed. ils Bok. F. scarce. M2. $100.00

BOK & BOK. *Milky Way.* 1981. Cambridge. Harvard. 5th ed. ils/index. 356 p. F/VG. S9. $18.00

BOKSER, Ben Zion. *Legacy of Maimonides.* 1962. Hebrew Pub. 146 p. VG-/fair. S3. $25.00

BOKUSHI, Suzuki. *Snow Country Tales: Life in the Other Japan.* (1986). Weatherhill. 1st ed. 343 p. M/dj. A17. $14.50

BOLAND, E. *In Her Own Image.* 1980. Dublin. 1st ed. sgn. VG+/wrp. V1. $25.00

BOLIN, E. *Narrative of the Life & Adventures of...* 1966. Palo Alto. Osborne. 1st ed? map ep. F. H7. $30.00

BOLITHO, Hector. *King George VI.* 1938. Lippincott. 1st Am ed. 8vo. 257 p. F/F. A2. $20.00

BOLL, Heinrich. *Clown.* 1965. McGraw Hill. 1st Am ed. trans from German. NF/NF clip. A14. $35.00

BOLL, Heinrich. *Group Portrait w/Lady.* 1973. McGraw Hill. 1st Am ed. trans Leila Vennewitz. NF/NF. A14. $30.00

BOLL, Heinrich. *Safety Net.* 1982. Knopf. 1st Am ed. trans from German. rem mk. NF/NF. A14. $25.00

BOLLER, Willy. *Masterpieces of the Japanese Color Woodcut.* nd. (1957). Boston Book & Art Shop. 1st Am ed. folio. 174 p. F/VG. A2. $75.00

BOLLMAN, Don. *Run for the Roses.* 1975. Canadian Lakes. 1st ed. inscr. photos. F/VG. P8. $35.00

BOLSHE, Wilhelm. *Evolution of Man.* ca 1905. Chicago. CH Kerr. VG. V4. $15.00

BOLTON, Herbert E. *Anza's CA Expeditions.* 1930. Berkeley. 1st ed. 5 vols. M. extremely scarce. O6. $795.00

BOLTON, Herbert E. *Arredondo's Hist Proof of Spain's Title to GA.* 1925. Berkeley. presentation. frontis/9 maps. F. O6. $325.00

BOLTON, Herbert E. *Drake's Pl of Brass: Evidence of His Visit to CA.* nd. CA Hist Soc/Kennedy. Special Pub 13. 2 fld maps. brds. NF. O6. $45.00

BOLTON, Herbert E. *Outpost of Empire: Story of Founding of San Francisco.* 1931. Knopf. 1st ed. fld maps. 334 p. blk cloth. P4. $80.00

BOLTON, Herbert E. *Pageant of Transport Through the Ages.* 1969. NY. Blom. reissue. 238 p. burgundy/yel bdg. VG. P4. $35.00

BOLUS & HIRSCH. *KY Derby: Chance of a Lifetime.* 1988. McGraw Hill. 1st ed. VG/VG. O3. $45.00

BOMBAL, Maria-Luisa. *House of Mist.* 1947. Farrar Strauss. 1st ed. F/NF. N3. $35.00

BOMBARD, Alain. *Voyage of the Heretique.* (1954, 53). Simon Schuster. 1st Am ed. 8vo. 214 p. VG/VG. A2. $12.50

BOMMERSBACH, Jana. *Trunk Murderess: Winnie Ruth Judd.* 1992. Simon Schuster. 1st ed. sgn. M/M. T2. $21.00

BONANDO. *Stitches, Patterns & Projects for Crocheting.* 1978. np. ils. wrp. G2. $10.00

BONANNO, Margaret Wander. *Otherwhere.* 1991. St Martin. 1st ed. F/F. N3. $15.00

BONAPARTE, Charles-Lucien. *Iconographie des Pigeons...* 1857-58. Paris. 1st ed. lg folio. 55 hc pls. modern half red morocco. VG. H5. $10,000.00

BONAPARTE, Louis. *Histoire du Parliament Anglais...* 1820. Paris. Baudouin Freres. 1st ed. 416 p. VG. S9. $35.00

BONAPARTE, Napoleon. *Memoirs...* 1945. Golden Cockerel. 1/50. edit Somerset de Chair. 2 vols. special bdg. NF. H5. $2,000.00

BONAPARTE, Napoleon. *Napoleon, His Own Historian.* 1818. London. Colburn. hand-made paper/rebound leather brds. VG. A16. $150.00

BONAVIA, Duccio. *Mural Painting in Ancient Peru.* (1985). Bloomington, IN. 1st ed. 4to. 224 p. dj. F3. $45.00

BOND, Alvan. *Memoir of the Rev Pliny Fisk...* 1828. Boston. 8vo. 437 p. new quarter brn calf/marbled brds. F. O2. $135.00

BOND, Brian. *Liddell Hart: Study of His Military Thought.* 1979. London. Cassell. 1st ed/2nd imp. 294 p. F/VG. M7. $45.00

BOND, Earl D. *Dr Kirkbride & His Mental Hospital.* 1947. Lippincott. 1st ed. sgn. 7 pls. brn cloth. VG. G1. $30.00

BOND, Michael. *Paddington's Pop-Up Book.* 1977. Intervisual Communications. 10 p. pict brds. VG-. A3. $6.00

BOND, Michael. *Paddington Takes the Air.* 1971. Houghton Mifflin. 1st Am ed. F/VG. P2. $18.00

BOND, Nancy. *String in the Harp.* 1976. Atheneum. 1st ed. 365 p. F/F. P2. $30.00

BOND, Nelson. *Mr Mergenthwirker's Lobblies.* 1946. Coward McCann. 1st ed. VG/dj. M2. $50.00

BOND, Nelson. *Nightmares & Daydreams.* 1968. Arkham. 1st ed. F/dj. M2. $45.00

BOND, Nelson. *Thirty-First of February.* 1949. Gnome. 1st ed. sgn. F/dj. M2. $45.00

BOND. *Crazy Quilt Stitches.* 1987. np. 1000+ stitches ils. wrp. G2. $10.00

BONES, Jim. *Rio Grande Mtns to the Sea.* (1985). Austin. 1st ed. photos. 183 p. F/glassine wrp. A17. $15.00

BONESTEEL. *Bright Ideas for Lap Quilting.* 1990. np. cloth. G2. $25.00

BONESTEEL. *New Ideas for Quilting.* 1987. np. 70+ color photos. 160 p. cloth. G2. $20.00

BONHAM, Frank. *Night Raid.* 1954. Ballantine. 1st ed. VG/VG. B9. $60.00

BONI, Margaret Bradford. *Fireside Book of Favorite Am Songs.* 1952. Simon Schuster. 4to. ils. 360 p. G/G. B11. $25.00

BONI, Margaret Bradford. *Fireside Book of Folk Songs.* 1947. Simon Schuster. 2nd prt. ils Provensen. 323 p. G+. S10. $12.00

BONKER & THORNBER. *Sage of the Desert...* 1930. Boston. HB Wright. 1st ed. 12mo. 106 p. cloth. D3. $25.00

BONN, Thomas L. *Undercover, Ils Hist of Am Mass Market Pbs.* 1982. Penguin. NF/wrp. C8. $30.00

BONNARD, Pierre. *Correspondences.* 1/1000. pls in binder. VG/orig dj. A1. $250.00

BONNER, Cindy. *Looking After Lily.* 1994. Algonquin. 1st ed. author's 2nd book. F/F. L3. $45.00

BONNER, T.D. *Life & Adventures of James P Beckwourth, Mountaineer...* 1859. NY. Harper. 1st ed. octavo. gilt brn cloth. R3. $850.00

BONNETTE & ZUBAL. *Gritloaf Anthology.* ca 1978. Palaemon. 1/500. 44 p. F/wrp. B10. $45.00

BONNEY, T.D. *New Eng & NY Cataract Songster: Collection of Songs...* 1845. Pittsfield, MA. 32mo. 60 p. fair/wrp. H3. $30.00

BONNYCASTLE, R.H. *Spanish Am...Dominions of Spain in W Hemisphere...* 19182. Phil. Abraham Sm. rpr fld chart. brds/paper label. unopened. O6. $575.00

BONTEMPS, Arna. *Chariot in the Sky.* 1951. Winston. 1st ed. F/NF. B2. $50.00

BONTEMPS, Arna. *Young Booker.* (1972). Dodd Mead. 2nd prt. 196 p. NF/clip. A7. $17.00

BONTEMPS & CONROY. *Sam Patch: High, Wide & Handsome Jumper.* 1951. Boston. Riverside. ils Paul Brn. dj. B14. $50.00

BONTEMPS & CONROY. *Sam Patch: High, Wide & Handsome Jumper.* 1951. Houghton Mifflin. 1st ed. oblong Quarto. ils Paul Brn. F/VG. B4. $100.00

BONTEMPS & CONROY. *Slappy Hooper: Wonderful Sgn Painter.* 1946. Houghton Mifflin. 1st ed. F/dj. B2. $275.00

BOOKER, George E. III. *Crowds & Queues & Coffee Nerves.* 1949. Dietz. 1st ed. 139 p. VG. B10. $18.00

BOOKER, Simeon. *Blk Man's Am.* (1964). Englewood Cliffs. Prentice Hall. ARC/1st ed. RS. F/VG. B4. $45.00

BOONE & CROCKETT CLUB. *18th Big Game Awards, 1981-82.* 1984. Alexandria. 1st ed. ils/photos. 306 p. F/dj. A17. $35.00

BOOTH, Charles. *Zachary Macaulay.* 1934. Longman Gr. 117 p. A7. $25.00

BOOTH, George. *Animals, Animals, Animals.* 1979. Harper Row. 1st ed. 4to. VG/VG. O3. $22.00

BOOTH, Martin. *Iron Tree.* (1993). Simon Schuster. AP. F/pict wrp. B3. $15.00

BOOTH, Martin. *Very Private Gentlemen.* (1990). London. Century. 1st ed. F/F. B3. $20.00

BOOTH, Rintoul. *Horseman's Handbook To End All Horseman's Handbooks.* 1975. London. Woolfe. 1st ed. VG/VG. O3. $15.00

BOOTH, T.G. *TG Booth's New Comic Songster.* nd. (1850s). NY. CP Huestis. 32mo. VG/bl pict wrp. H3. $50.00

BOOTHBY, Guy. *In Strange Company.* nd. London. Ward Locke. 6th ed. sgn. F. BB4. $125.00

BOOTHBY, Guy. *Sherah McCloud.* 1897. London. 1st ed. VG. M2. $75.00

BORCHARDT & SEARS. *Suwanee Valley.* 1940. NY. 1st ed. sgns. VG/G. B5. $15.00

BORDAS & GAGNERE. *Guatemala.* nd. France. French/Eng/Spanish text. 4to. 151 p. F3. $30.00

BORDEN, Spencer. *Arab Horse.* 1949. LA. Borden reprint. VG/VG. O3. $35.00

BORDONE, Benedetto. *Libro...de Tutte l'Isole de Mondo.* 1966. Amsterdam. Theatrvm Orbis Terrarvm. lg quarto. M/M. O6. $325.00

BOREIN, Edward. *Borein's W.* (1952). Santa Barbara. Edward Borein Memorial. Vaquero ed. 1/300. 145 pls. F. R3. $650.00

BOREIN, Edward. *Etchings of the W.* 1950. Santa Barbara. Edward Borein Memorial. 1st ed. 1/1001. 9 pls. F. H5. $250.00

BORG & BROWN. *N Lights: Stories From Swedish & Finnish Authors.* ca 1873. Coates. 12mo. 470 p. VG. S10. $18.00

BORGES, Jorge Luis. *Dreamtigers.* 1973. London. 1st ed. F/F. A11. $35.00

BORGES, Jorge Luis. *Ficciones.* (1984). LEC. 1/1500. ils/sgn Sol Lewitt. stp blk leather. F/slipcase. B20. $350.00

BORGES, Jorge Luis. *Los Conjurados.* 1985. Madrid, Spain. F/ils stiff 8vo wrp. A11. $35.00

BORGES, Jorge Luis. *Selected Poems 1923-67.* 1972. Delacorte/Lawrence. 1st ed. NF/NF. L3. $200.00

BORGES & CASARES. *Extraordinary Tales.* 1971. NY. 1st Eng-language ed. F/F. A11. $60.00

BORGESE, Elizabeth Mann. *Ocean Regime, Suggested Statue for Peaceful Use...* 1968. Santa Barbara. Center for Study Democratic Inst. xl. 40 p. wrp. M11. $20.00

BORGSTROM & LOFGREN. *Kaktusgubben Och Kangurun.* 1947. Sweden. Bokforlag. lg octavo. 44 p. F/prt yel wrp. B24. $75.00

BORING, Edwin Garrigues. *Hist of Experimental Psychology.* 1950 (1929). Appleton Century. 2nd ed/later prt. 778 p. beige cloth. G1. $50.00

BORING, Edwin Garrigues. *Sensation & Perception in Hist of Experimental Psychology.* 1942. Appleton Century. 1st ed. 644 p. pebbled bl cloth. VG/dj. G1. $85.00

BORK, Robert H. *Tempting of Am & Political Seduction of the Law.* 1990. NY. Free Pr. M11. $15.00

BORKENAU, Franz. *End & Beginning.* 1981. NY. Columbia. 493 p. clip dj. A7. $20.00

BORN, Max. *My Life & My Views.* 1968. Scribner. 1st ed. VG/dj. G1. $22.50

BORNE, Lawrence R. *Dude Ranching: A Complete Hist.* 1983. NM U. 1st ed. ils/index. 322 p. F/F. B19. $20.00

BORNEMAN, Ernest. *Critic Looks At Jazz.* 1946. London. Jazz Music Books. 1st ed. NF/wrp. B2. $60.00

BORODINI, George. *Spurious Sun.* 1948. London. F/dj. M2. $20.00

BOROS, O.K. *Seventh Mental Measurements Yearbook.* 1972. Highland Park, NJ. Gryphon Pr. 2 vols. gr cloth. VG. S9. $25.00

BOROWITZ, Albert. *Innocence & Arsenic: Studies in Crime & Literature.* 1977. Harper Row. 1st ed. F/F. M15. $30.00

BORRO, Girolamo. *Del Flusso, E Reflusso del Mare, & Dell'Inondatione...* 1583. Florence. 3rd ed. 8vo. 220 p. contemporary limp vellum. scarce. K1. $650.00

BORSODI, Ralph. *Flight From the City...* 1947. NY. School of Living. ils. 133 p. F. H10. $12.50

BORTHWICK, J.D. *Gold Hunters.* nd. Cleveland. reprint of 1857 ed. 12mo. 361 p. cloth. D3. $15.00

BORTON, Lady. *Sensing the Enemy.* 1984. Dial. 1st ed. VG+/VG+. A7. $20.00

BOSKER. *Fabulous Fabrics of the '50s & Other Terrific Textiles.* 1992. np. pb. G2. $17.00

BOSO, James L. *Boso Family (Boisseaux) 1757-1977.* 1978. Parson, WV. 1st ed. 357 p. VG. D7. $30.00

BOSSE, Malcolm. *Warlord.* 1983. Simon Schuster. VG/dj. A11. $10.00

BOSTICK & CASTELHUN. *Carmel: At Work & Play.* 1925. Carmel, CA. 1st ed. 12mo. 109 p. VG. D3. $35.00

BOSTOCK, Henry P. *Great Ride.* 1932. Perth, Australia. Artlook Books. 1st ed. 232 p. F/F. M7. $50.00

BOSTWICK, Homer. *Treatise on Nature & Treatment of Seminal Diseases...* 1847. NY. Burgess String. 1st ed. 251 p. blk cloth. B14. $75.00

BOSWELL, Hazel. *French Canada.* 1938. Viking. 1st ed. ils Boswell. 83 p. beige cloth. NF/NF. D1. $75.00

BOSWELL, James. *Journel of Tour to Hebrides w/Samuel Johnson.* 1941. London. Everyman's Lib. 12mo. 361 p. gr cloth. F/G. H3. $15.00

BOSWELL, James. *Life of Samuel Johnson, LLD.* 1807. Andrews Blake Cushing. 1st Am ed. 3 vols. 8vo. contemporary marbled brds. VG. M1. $325.00

BOSWELL, James. *Life of Samuel Johnson...* nd. np. Temple Bar ed. 1/785. 10 vols. teg. brn brds. NF. T8. $295.00

BOSWELL, Robert. *Crooked Hearts.* 1987. Knopf. 1st ed. F/F. C4. $30.00

BOSWELL, Robert. *Crooked Hearts.* 1987. NY. Knopf. AP. author's 1st novel. F/wrp. L3. $85.00

BOSWELL, Thomas. *How Life Imitates the World Series.* 1972. Doubleday. 1st ed. F/NF. B4/P8. $45.00

BOSWELL, Thomas. *Why Time Begins on Opening Day.* 1984. Doubleday. 1st ed. author's 2nd book. F/VG+. P8. $35.00

BOSWELL & FISHER. *Fenway Park, Legendary Home of Boston Red Sox.* 1992. np. 4to. complex 50-piece popup w/16 p ils hist. F. A4. $100.00

BOSWORTH, Sheila. *Slow Poison.* (1992). Knopf. 1st ed. F/F. B3. $25.00

BOTCHKAREVA, Maria. *Yashka: My Life As a Peasant Officer & Exile.* 1919. Stokes. 340 p. N2. $20.00

BOTKIN, B.A. *Sidewalks of Am.* (1954). Indianapolis. 1st ed. 605 p. G/dj. B18. $15.00

BOTKIN, B.A. *Treasury of Am Folklore.* 1944. NY. index/music. 932 p. cloth. VG. D3. $12.50

BOTKIN, B.A. *Treasury of S Folklore.* 1962. NY. 6th prt. 776 p. cloth. NF. D3. $25.00

BOTKIN, B.A. *Treasury of S Folklore...* ca 1949. Crown. sgn. 776 p. VG. B10. $25.00

BOTKIN, B.A. *Treasury of W Folklore.* 1951. Crown. 8vo. G+. A8. $25.00

BOTSFORD & ROBINSON. *Hellenic Hist.* 1950. np. 3rd ed. 28 maps/106 full-p pls. VG. C1. $9.50

BOTTA, Carlo. *Storia Della Guerra, Americana Scritta de Carlo Botta.* 1825-26. Livorne. Pietro Meucci. 4 vols. 8vo. contemporary quarter calf. H9. $250.00

BOUCHARD, S. *Historique du 28 Regiment de Dragons.* 1893. Paris/Nancy. Berger Levraut. tall 8vo. 272 p. cloth/marbled brds. N2. $45.00

BOUCHER, Alan. *Sword of the Raven.* 1969. Scribner. 1st ed. F/NF. N3. $15.00

BOUCHER, Anthony. *Case of the Baker Street Irregulars.* 1940. Simon Schuster. 1st ed. VG/VG. M15. $150.00

BOUCHER, Anthony. *Complete Werewolf & Other Stories of Fantasy & SF.* 1970. London. Allen. 1st ed. VG/poor. A7. $40.00

BOUCHER & MCCOMAS. *Best From Fantasy & SF.* 1952. Little Brn. 1st ed. F/dj. M2. $45.00

BOUCHER & MCCOMAS. *Best From Fantasy & SF: 4th Series.* 1954. SF BC. F/dj. M2. $10.00

BOUDAILLE, George. *Picasso's Sketchbook.* 1960. Abrams. ltd ed. VG/dj. A1. $120.00

BOUDREAU, Eugene. *Trails of the Sierra Madre.* 1973. Capra/Scrimshaw. ils/maps. 73 p. F/wrp. B19. $7.50

BOUDREAU, Eugene. *50-Yr View of Psychiatry & the Golden Yrs of Medicine.* 1967. NY. cloth. VG/dj. G1. $15.00

BOUGEREAU, Maurice. *Le Theatre Francoys.* 1966. Amsterdam. facsimile of 1594 Tours ed. M/M. O6. $175.00

BOULDING & MUKERJEE. *Economic Imperialism.* 1972. Ann Arbor. 1st ed. 8vo. 338 p. M/M. V3. $9.50

BOULDNER, Alvin W. *Future of Intellectuals & Rise of the New Class.* (1971). NY. Continuum. 2nd prt. 121 p. F/F. A7. $20.00

BOULDNER, Alvin W. *2 Marxisms.* (1980). NY. Seabury. 397 p. F/F. A7. $22.00

BOULET, Roger. *LM Kilpin, 1855-1919.* 1979. Art Gallery Greater Victoria. ils. wrp. D2. $20.00

BOULLE, Pierre. *Good Leviathan.* 1978. Vanguard. 1st ed. F/dj. M2. $12.00

BOULLE, Pierre. *My Own River Kwai.* 1967. NY. 1st ed. trans Xan Fielding. F/dj. T9. $15.00

BOULLE, Pierre. *Virtue of Hell.* 1974. Vanguard. 1st ed. F/NF. F4. $20.00

BOULLEMIER, Leo. *Plantsman's Guide to Fuschias.* 1989. London. 40 color photos. 128 p. M/dj. B26. $15.00

BOULTON, Rudyerd. *Traveling w/Birds.* 1933. Donohue. ils Walter A Weber. 64 p. VG-. A1. $13.00

BOURJAILY, Vance. *Great Fake Book.* 1986. Franklin Lib. 1st ed. sgn. full leather. F. B4. $55.00

BOURKE, J.G. *With General Crook in the Indian Wars.* 1968. Palo Alto. 1/2100. ils/fld map. VG+. B18. $35.00

BOURNE, Russell. *View From Front Street.* (1989). NY. 1st ed. 282 p. F/dj. A17. $19.50

BOURQUE & WARREN. *Women of the Andes.* (1981). Ann Arbor. 1st ed. 241 p. wrp. F3. $10.00

BOUTEILLE, E.M. *Traite de la Choree, ou Danse de Saint-Guy.* 1810. Paris. Lib Medicale. sgn. ES. #64 p. prt wrp. H9. $295.00

BOUTON & OFFEN. *I Managed Good But Boy Did They Play Bad.* 1973. Playboy. 1st ed. F/VG+. P8. $15.00

BOUTON & SCHECTER. *Ball Four.* 1970. World. 1st ed. F/VG+. P8. $40.00

BOUVET, Marguerite. *Sweet William.* 1890. McClurg. 1st ed. ils Armstrong. 209 p. VG. S10. $45.00

BOUVIER, E.L. *Psychic Life of Insects.* 1922. NY. Century. 1st Am ed. trans LO Howard. 377 p. bl cloth. VG. B20. $25.00

BOUVIER, Henri. *Lecons Cliniques sur Les Maladies Chronigques...Locomoteur.* 1858. Paris. Bailliere. 531 p. quarter morocco/ brds. G. G7. $175.00

BOUYER, Louis. *Christian Humanism.* 1959. Westminster. Newman. 110 p. H10. $15.00

BOUYER, Louis. *Dictionary of Theology.* ca 1965. NY. Desclee. 470 p. H10. $20.00

BOUYER, Louis. *Eucharist: Theology & Spirituality...* ca 1968. Notre Dame. 483 p. H10. $25.00

BOUYER, Louis. *Orthodox Spirituality & Protestant & Anglican Spirituality.* 1969. London. Burns Oates. 1st Eng ed. 334 p. H10. $25.00

BOVA, Ben. *Kinsman.* 1979. NY. Dial. 1st ed. inscr. F/F. N3. $35.00

BOVA, Ben. *Orion in the Dying Time.* (1990). NY. Tom Doherty. 1st ed. VG/F. B3. $15.00

BOVA, Ben. *Privateers.* 1985. Tor. 1st ed. F/dj. M2. $20.00

BOVA, Ben. *Voyagers II.* 1986. Tor. 1st ed. F/dj. M2. $16.00

BOVA, Ben. *Voyagers.* 1981. Doubleday. 1st ed. F/F. N3. $25.00

BOWDEN, Charles. *Frog Mountain Blues.* 1987. Tucson, AZ. 1st ed. F/F. L3. $50.00

BOWDEN, Charles. *Mezcal.* (1988). AZ U. 1st ed. F/F. B3. $25.00

BOWDEN, Charles. *Red Line.* (1989). Norton. 1st ed. sgn. F/F. B3. $40.00

BOWDEN, Edwin T. *James Thurber: A Bibliography.* 1968. Columbus, OH. 1st ed. bl cloth. F/F. F1. $37.50

BOWDEN & KREINBERG. *Street Sgns Chicago.* 1981. Chicago Review. 1st ed. inscr. F/NF. L3. $150.00

BOWEN, B.B. *Blind Man's Offering.* 1877. Boston. self pub. not 1st ed. 432 p. VG. N2. $15.00

BOWEN, C.D. *4 Portraits & 1 Subject: Bernard De Voto.* 1963. Houghton Mifflin. 1st ed. sgn Stegner. NF/VG. A18. $60.00

BOWEN, Dana Thomas. *Lore of the Lakes.* 1963. FL. private prt. VG/dj. A16. $20.00

BOWEN, Dana Thomas. *Memories of the Lakes.* 1953. FL. 2nd prt. VG/dj. A16. $22.50

BOWEN, Dana Thomas. *Shipwrecks of the Lakes.* 1952. Lakeside. 1st ed. 362 p. VG/dj. M20. $30.00

BOWEN, Dana Thomas. *Shipwrecks of the Lakes.* 1984. Freshwater Pr. as new/dj. A16. $25.00

BOWEN, Elizabeth. *Anthony Trollope.* 1946. NY. 1st Am ed. F/F. A11. $25.00

BOWEN, Elizabeth. *Hotel.* 1928. Dial. xl. G. E3. $12.00

BOWEN, Marjorie. *Glen O'Weeping.* 1907. London. 1st ed. G+. M2. $10.00

BOWEN, Robert Sidney. *Rebel Rookie.* 1965. Lee Shepard. 186 p. VG/dj. M20. $20.00

BOWER, B.M. *Chip of the Flying U.* 1906. Grosset Dunlap. 8vo. G+/fair. A8. $12.50

BOWER, U.G. *Hidden Land.* 1953. Morrow. 1st ed. 8vo. 260 p. F/VG. A2. $15.00

BOWERS, Claude G. *Beveridge & the Progressive Era.* 1932. NY. Literary Guild. M11. $25.00

BOWERS, Ethel. *Ribbon Winning Show Horses.* 1916. NY. 4to. thick carbon copy of typed manuscript w/bdg. O3. $65.00

BOWERS, John. *Life of Abraham Lincoln.* 1922. Haldeman. VG. A6. $10.00

BOWLBY, John. *Charles Darwin: A New Life.* ca 1990. NY/London. thick 8vo. 511 p. half cloth. F/dj. P4. $22.50

BOWLES, E.A. *Handbook of Crocus & Colchicum for Gardeners...* 1985. London. Waterstone. ils. 222 p. M. H10. $27.00

BOWLES, Jane. *Two Serious Ladies.* 1943. Knopf. 1st ed. author's 1st book. NF/G+clip. Q1. $600.00

BOWLES, Paul. *Hours After Noon.* 1959. London. Heinemann. 1st ed. NF/NF. L3. $450.00

BOWLES, Paul. *In the Red Room.* 1981. LA. Sylvester Orphanos. 1st ed. 1/300. sgn. F/sans. L3. $200.00

BOWLES, Paul. *In Touch.* 1994. NY. FSG. 1/250. sgn. F/slipcase. C4. $100.00

BOWLES, Paul. *Let It Come Down.* 1952. NY. 1st ed. F/clip. A11. $45.00

BOWLES, Paul. *Let It Come Down.* 1980. Blk Sparrow. reissue of 2nd novel. sgn. F/acetate dj. L3. $350.00

BOWLES, Paul. *Next to Nothing.* 1976. Kathmandu. Starstreams. 1/500. sgn. F. L3. $350.00

BOWLES, Paul. *Sheltering Sky.* 1949. New Directions. 1st Am ed. author's 1st novel. NF/NF. Q1. $350.00

BOWLES, Paul. *Time of Friendship.* 1967 NY. 1st ed. F/F ils Paul Bacon. A11. $30.00

BOWLES, Paul. *TN Williams in Tangier.* 1979. Santa Barbara. Cadmus. 1/1300. NF/tan wrp/presumed orig glassine. Q1. $35.00

BOWLES, Samuel. *Across the Continent.* 1865. Bowles/Hurd Houghton. 1st ed. 452 p. orig cloth. H9. $100.00

BOWLES, Samuel. *Across the Continent...a Stage Ride Over the Plains...* 1869. Springfield. Bowles. new ed. VG. H7. $45.00

BOWLES, Samuel. *Our New W.* 1869. Hartford, CT. 1st ed. 528 p. full lib calf. D3. $45.00

BOWLES, Samuel. *Our New W.* 1869. Hartford, CT. 1st thus ed. orig maroon cloth. H9. $95.00

BOWLES, Samuel. *Switzerland of Am.* 1869. Am News/Lee Shepard. 1st ed. 12mo. 166 p. brn cloth. H9. $50.00

BOWMAN, Isaiah. *Andes of S Peru.* 1916. Holt. 1st ed. 4to. 336 p. F3. $40.00

BOWMAN, John S. *Vietnam War: An Almanac.* (1985). World Almanac. photos. 512 p. NF/dj. A7. $40.00

BOWMAN, W. *Ascent of Rum Doodle.* 1956. NY. 1st ed. VG/VG. B5. $27.50

BOWMAN, W. *Peerless Riviera.* Winter 1923-24. London. 1st ed. 6 color fld maps. 164 p. VG/wrp. H3. $20.00

BOWMAN & DICKINSON. *Westward From Rio.* 1936. Chicago. Willett Clark. 2nd ed. 8vo. 351 p. F/VG. A2. $25.00

BOWMAN & IRWIN. *Sherman & His Campaigns.* 1865. NY. 1st ed. royal 8vo. 412 p. cloth. VG. D3. $45.00

BOWMAN & JEFFERSON. *Crusoe's Island in the Caribbean.* (1939). Bobbs Merrill. 1st ed. 8vo. 339 p. F/VG. A2. $25.00

BOWMAN & STIRLING. *W From Rio.* 1936. Chicago. 8vo. 100 block prts. 351 p. pict gr cloth. F/VG. H3. $12.00

BOWSHER, Alice Meriwether. *Design Review in Hist Districts: Handbook for VA Review...* 1973. Sully Foundation. 228 p. VG/dj. B10. $30.00

BOWYER, C. *Mosquito at War.* (1973). NY. 1st ed. 144 p. VG+/dj. B18. $15.00

BOX, Edgar; see Vidal, Gore.

BOYD, Blanche McCrary. *Redneck Way of Knowledge.* 1982. NY. Knopf. 1st ed. F/F. Q1. $25.00

BOYD, Frank; see Kane, Frank.

BOYD, J. *Life of General William T Sherman.* 1891. np. 12mo. ils. 608 p. brn cloth. G. T3. $29.00

BOYD, James. *Drums.* 1925. NY. 1st ed. 12mo. 490 p. gilt gr cloth. VG. H3. $15.00

BOYD, John. *Last Starship From Earth.* 1968. NY. Weybright Talley. 1st ed. author's 1st novel. F/NF. N3. $65.00

BOYD, Louise A. *Coast of NE Greenland w/Hydrographic Studies...* 1948. Am Geog Soc. 5 panoramas/7 maps. NF. O6. $55.00

BOYD, William. *Brazzaville Beach.* 1991. Morrow. ARC of 1st Am ed. NF/wrp. B2. $35.00

BOYD, William. *Brazzaville Beach.* 1991. Morrow. ARC. VG/pict wrp. B3. $20.00

BOYD. *Sew & Save Source Book.* 1984. np. pb. G2. $10.00

BOYDELL & BOYDELL. *Hist of the River Thames.* 1794-96. London. Bulmer Boydell. 1st ed/1st issue (w/double titles). 2 vols. gilt bdg. H5. $11,000.00

BOYER, Dwight. *Ghost Ships of the Great Lakes.* 1968. Dodd Mead. VG/dj. A16. $20.00

BOYER, Dwight. *Strange Adventures of the Great Lakes.* 1974. NY. VG/dj. A16. $20.00

BOYER, Dwight. *True Tales of the Great Lakes.* 1971. Dodd Mead. VG/dj. A16. $20.00

BOYER, G.G. *I Married Wyatt Earp.* (1976). Tucson, AZ. 1st ed. ils. 277 p. VG+/dj. B18. $22.50

BOYER, Michael K. *All About Broilers...* 1902. Syracuse. De Puy. 2nd ed. wrp. H10. $6.50

BOYER, Rick. *Moscow Metal.* 1988. London. Gollancz. 1st ed. F/F. S5. $20.00

BOYER, Rick. *Whale's Footprints.* 1988. Houghton Mifflin. 1st ed. F/F. F4. $15.00

BOYINGTON, Pappy. *Baa Baa Blk Sheep.* 1958. NY. presentation/sgn. VG/VG. B5. $32.50

BOYINK. *Baskets for Quilters.* 1982. np. ils. wrp. G2. $10.00

BOYINK. *Fans Galore for Modern Quilters.* 1987. np. 70+ patterns. 68 p. wrp. G2. $13.00

BOYINK. *Nautical Voyages.* 1990. np. designs. wrp. G2. $13.00

BOYINK. *Quilters' Hearts w/Flowing Ribbons.* 1989. np. ils. wrp. G2. $13.00

BOYINK. *Trees & Leaves for Quilters.* 1982. np. ils/designs. wrp. G2. $10.00

BOYLE, Andrew. *Trenchard: Man of Vision.* 1962. London. Collins. 1st ed. 763 p. gilt red-orange cloth. F/NF/clear plastic. M7. $65.00

BOYLE, Jesse George. *Vegetable Growing.* 1917. Lea Febiger. 1st ed. xl. B28. $20.00

BOYLE, Kay. *Am Citizen. Naturalized in Leadville, CO.* 1944. NY. VG/8vo wrp. A11. $15.00

BOYLE, Kay. *Collected Poems...* 1987. Knopf. 1st ed. F/F. C4. $25.00

BOYLE, Kay. *Collected Poems...* 1991. Port Townsend. Copper Canyon Pr. 1st ed. F/F. C4. $25.00

BOYLE, Kay. *His Human Majesty.* 1949. McGraw Hill. 1st ed. NF/NF. C4. $40.00

BOYLE, Kay. *Long Walk at San Francisco State. And Other Essays.* 1970. NY. Grove. PBO. sgn. F/wrp. A11. $35.00

BOYLE, Kay. *Pinky in Persia.* (1968). Crowell Collier. 1st ed. ils Obligado. F/NF. B4. $125.00

BOYLE, Kay. *Primer for Combat.* 1942. Simon Schuster. 1st ed. bl-gray brds. NF/NF 1st issue. C4. $60.00

BOYLE, Kay. *Primer for Combat.* 1942. Simon Schuster. 2nd prt. NF/dj. A7. $20.00

BOYLE, Kay. *Year Before Last.* 1932. Harrison Smith. 1st ed. NF/NF. C4. $60.00

BOYLE, Patrick. *At Night All Cats Are Grey.* 1969. Grove. 1st Am ed. VG+/VG+. M20. $15.00

BOYLE, T. Coraghessan. *Budding Prospects.* 1984. London. Gollancz. 1st ed. F/F. C4. $45.00

BOYLE, T. Coraghessan. *Descent of Man.* 1980. London. 1st Eng ed. w/sgn label. F/F. A11. $75.00

BOYLE, T. Coraghessan. *E Is E.* (1990). Viking. 1st ed. F/F. B4. $45.00

BOYLE, T. Coraghessan. *E Is E.* 1991. London. Cape. 1st ed. F/NF. B3. $25.00

BOYLE, T. Coraghessan. *E Is E.* 1991. London. Cape. 1st ed. inscr. F/F. C4. $35.00

BOYLE, T. Coraghessan. *If the River Was Whiskey.* 1989. Viking. 1st ed. NF/NF. E3. $25.00

BOYLE, T. Coraghessan. *If the River Was Whiskey.* 1989. Viking. 1st ed. sgn. F/F. C4. $55.00

BOYLE, T. Coraghessan. *Road to Wellville.* 1993. Viking. 1st ed. F/F. C4. $35.00

BOYLE, T. Coraghessan. *Water Music.* 1981. Atlantic/Little Brn. 1st ed. F/clip. C4. $75.00

BOYLE, T. Coraghessan. *World's End.* 1987. Viking. AP. author's 3rd novel. F/prt glossy wrp. Q1. $75.00

BOYLE, T. Coraghessan. *World's End.* 1987. Viking. 1st ed. sgn. F/clip. C4. $65.00

BOYLE, T. Coraghessan. *World's End.* 1988. London. Macmillan. 1st ed. F/dj. C4. $45.00

BOYLE, Thomas. *Brooklyn 3.* (1991). Viking. AP. F/prt brn wrp. B3. $35.00

BOYLE & HALE. *John Henry Twachtman: Exihibiton of Paintings & Pastels.* 1968. Ira Spanierman Gallery. 24 p. wrp. D2. $30.00

BOYLES. *Needlepoint Stitchery.* 1974. np. ils. cloth. G2. $11.00

BOYLSTON, Helen Dore. *Sue Barton, Student Nurse.* 1936. Little Brn. 244 p. cloth. VG/dj. M20. $22.00

BOYNE & THOMPSON. *Wild Blue.* (1986). Crown. 1st ed. F/NF. A7. $30.00

BOYNTON & MASON. *Journey Through KS...Sketches of NE...* 1855. Cincinnati. Moore Wilstach Keys. 12mo. fld map. bl buckram. H9. $450.00

BOYS' LIFE. *Boys' Life Treasury.* (1958). NY. ils. 480 p. pict ep. cloth/brds. VG/pict dj. D3. $15.00

BOYUNDS, Sidney J. *Robot Brains.* 1967. Arcadia. 1st Am/1st hc ed. F/clip. N3. $10.00

BRACHET, J.L. *Traite Pratique des Convusions Dans l'Enfrance.* 1837. Paris. Bailliere. 2nd/revised ed. 460 p. orig wrp. G7. $95.00

BRACKENRIDGE, H.H. *Modern Chivalry: Containing Adventures...* 1804-07. Phil. 2nd (1st 2-vol) ed. 12mo. full tree calf. VG. M1. $475.00

BRACKENRIDGE, H.M. *Journal of Voyage Up the River MO Performed in 1811...* 1854. Huntington. 1/200. NF. O6. $175.00

BRACKENRIDGE, H.M. *Recollections of Persons & Places in the W.* (1834). Phil. 1st ed. 12mo. 244 p. orig cloth/new leather back. M1. $225.00

BRACKENRIDGE, Hugh Henry. *Incidents of Insurrection in W Parts of PA, in Yr 1794.* 1795. Phil. M'Culloch. 1st ed. octavo. contemporary calf. H9. $575.00

BRACKETT, Leigh. *Ark of Mars.* 1954. Sidney. Malian Pr. 1st separate prt/reprint from US magazine. NF/wrp. N3. $40.00

BRACKETT, Leigh. *Book of Skaith.* 1976. Nelson Doubleday. 1st ed. F/dj. M2. $10.00

BRACKETT, Leigh. *Starmen.* 1952. Gnome. 1st ed. NF/dj. M2. $100.00

BRACKMAN. *Clues in the Calico, Identifying & Dating Quilts.* 1989. np. wrp. G2. $40.00

BRADBURN, John. *Breeding & Developing the Trotter.* 1906. Boston. 1st ed. Am Horse Breeder. VG. O3. $58.00

BRADBURY, Edward P.; see Moorcock, Michael.

BRADBURY, Osgood. *Therese; or, The Iroquis Maiden.* (1852). Boston. GH Williams. 1st ed. 8vo. 100 p. M1. $150.00

BRADBURY, Ray. *Dandelion Wine.* 1957. Doubleday. 1st ed. sgn. yel cloth. F/prt dj. B24. $225.00

BRADBURY, Ray. *Fahrenheit 451.* 1982. LEC. 1/2000. sgn author/Mugnaini. 152 p. F/pub slipcase. H5. $175.00

BRADBURY, Ray. *Golden Apples of the Sun.* 1953. Doubleday. 1st ed. inscr to author's 1st agent. NF/worn. M2. $250.00

BRADBURY, Ray. *Graveyard for Lunatics.* 1990. Knopf. 1st ed. F/F. B3/F4. $20.00

BRADBURY, Ray. *Halloween Tree.* 1972. Knopf. 1st ed. w/inscr, sgn & dtd label. F/clip. F4. $40.00

BRADBURY, Ray. *I Sing the Body Electric.* 1974. Knopf. ne. F/dj. M2. $12.00

BRADBURY, Ray. *Ils Man.* 1951. Doubleday. 1st ed. G. M2. $25.00

BRADBURY, Ray. *Pillar of Fire & Other Plays.* 1975. Bantam. 1st ed/PBO. NF/wrp. A11. $25.00

BRADBURY, Ray. *Where Robot Mice & Robot Men Run Round in Robot Towns.* 1977. Knopf. 1st ed. F/dj. w/sgn label. M2. $30.00

BRADBURY, Ray. *Wonderful Ice Cream Suit & Other Plays.* 1972. NY. 1st ed/PBO. NF/unread. A11. $30.00

BRADBURY. *Antique Lace Patterns.* 1984. np. ils. wrp. G2. $6.00

BRADDOCK, Joseph. *Bridal Bed.* (1961, 60). John Day. 1st Am ed. 8vo. 255 p. VG+/VG. A2. $15.00

BRADDOCK, Joseph. *Greek Phoenix.* 1972. London. 8vo. 233 p. cloth. dj. O2. $15.00

BRADEN, Anne. *Wall Between.* 1958. Monthly Review. wrp issue. A7. $15.00

BRADEN, Anne. *Wall Between.* 1958. NY. Monthly Review. 1st ed. 306 p. orig cloth. M8. $30.00

BRADER, Gary. *Doomstalker.* 1990. London. Severn. 1st hc ed. NF/F. N3. $10.00

BRADFIELD, Scott. *Dream of th* (1990). Knopf. 1st ed. F/F. B3. $15.00

BRADFIELD, Scott. *Hist of Luminous Motion.* (1989). London. Bloomsbury. 1st ed. author's 1st novel. NF/NF. B3. $25.00

BRADFORD, E.A. *Visions of St Nick in Action.* 1950. Phillips Pub. 5 fld scenes. VG. A3. $25.00

BRADFORD, G. Jr. *Confederate Portraits.* 1914. np. ils/index. 291 p. F. O7. $23.50

BRADFORD, Gamaliel. *Darwin.* 1926. Houghton Mifflin. 1st ed. 8 pls. 314 p. prt russet cloth. G. G1. $17.50

BRADFORD, Gamaliel. *Haunted Biographer.* 1982. WA U. 44 p. A6. $10.00

BRADFORD, Ned. *Battles & Leaders of the Civil War.* 1979. Fairfax. reprint 1956 ed. 626 p. VG/VG. B10. $10.00

BRADFORD, Richard. *Red Sky at Morning.* 1968. np. 1st ed. author's 1st book. VG. M18. $60.00

BRADFORD, William. *Hist of Plymouth Settlement 1608-1650.* (1920). NY. 353 p. VG. A17. $15.00

BRADFORD. *Simply Smocking.* 1990. np. full-color photos. wrp. G2. $11.00

BRADKIN. *Basic Seminole Patchwork.* 1991. np. G2. $17.00

BRADLEY, A.G. *Round About Wiltshire.* 1943. London. 8th ed. VG/dj. M7. $14.00

BRADLEY, David. *Chaneyville Incident.* 1981. NY. 1st ed. F/NF clip. A11. $25.00

BRADLEY, David. *No Place To Hide.* 1948. Little Brn. 1st ed. VG/VG. E3. $12.00

BRADLEY, Eliza. *Authentic Narrative of Shipwreck & Sufferings...* 1823. Boston. 16mo. 108 p. marbled brds/leather spine. G. H3. $40.00

BRADLEY, Eliza. *Authentic Narrative of Shipwreck & Sufferings...* 1823. Boston. Weldon. 1st Am ed. 108 p. contemporary sheepskin/bl brds. VG. B14. $60.00

BRADLEY, Glenn D. *Story of the Pony Express.* 1971. Ann Arbor. facsimile of 1913 ed. A17. $15.00

BRADLEY, Hugh. *Havana: Cinderella's City.* 1941. Doubleday Doran. 1st ed. 8vo. 456 p. VG+/VG. A2. $25.00

BRADLEY, Marion Zimmer. *Catch Trap.* 1979. Ballantine/Random. 1st ed. sgn. F/NF. A14. $65.00

BRADLEY, Marion Zimmer. *Firebrand.* 1987. Simon Schuster. 1st ed. F/NF. N3. $10.00

BRADLEY, Marion Zimmer. *Mists of Avalon.* nd. BC. NF/dj. C1. $10.00

BRADLEY, Omar N. *Soldier's Story.* 1951. NY. Holt. ltd ed. 1/750. sgn. F/slipcase. B20. $225.00

BRADLEY, Tom. *Old Coaching Days in Yorkshire.* 1889. Leeds. rebound. VG. O3. $165.00

BRADLEY, Van Allen. *Music for the Millions: Kimball Piano & Organ Story.* 1957. Chicago. Regnery. 1st ed. 8vo. 334 p. VG+/VG. A2. $15.00

BRADLEY, Will. *Peter Poodle, Toy Maker to the King.* 1906. Dodd Mead. 1st ed. 4to. pls. VG+. rare. F1. $400.00

BRADLEY. *Decorative Victorian Needlework.* 1990. np. ils. cloth. G2. $32.50

BRADMAN & HAWKINS. *See You Later Alligator.* 1985. 5 pop-up scenes. F. A4. $15.00

BRADNER, Enos. *NW Angling.* (1950). NY. ils/index. 239 p. dj. A17. $20.00

BRADSHAW, Gillian. *Hawk of May.* 1980. Simon Schuster. 1st ed. author's 1st book. F/F. N3. $20.00

BRADSTREET, Anne. *Poems of Anne Bradstreet.* 1969. Dover. 1st ed of this orig collection. NF/wrp. A11. $25.00

BRADY, Cyrus T. *My Lady's Slipper.* 1905. Dodd Mead. 1st ed. dj. VG. N2. $6.00

BRADY, Cyrus T. *Recollections of a Missionary in the Great W.* 1900. NY. 1st ed. xl. 200 p. teg. cloth. VG. D3. $25.00

BRADY, Edward Foster. *Memoir of..., Late Superintendent of Croyden School.* 1839. London. Harvey Darton. 1st ed. 16mo. 166 p. V3. $25.00

BRADY, Edward M. *Tugs, Towboats & Towing.* 1967. Cambridge. Cornell Maritime Pr. VG/dj. A16. $35.00

BRADY, John. *Unholy Ground.* 1989. London. Constable. ARC. author's 2nd book. RS. NF/dj. S5. $22.50

BRADY & FREDETTE. *Fiction Writer's Market.* 1981. Writer's Digest. 1st ed. VG. M2. $10.00

BRAGIN, Charles. *Dime Novels Bibliography, 1860-1928.* 1938. np. 1st ed. 29 p. G/wrp. B19. $30.00

BRAIDWOOD, Linda. *Digging Beyond the Tigris.* (1953). NY. Schuman. 1st ed. 8vo. 297 p. VG/VG. A2. $20.00

BRAILSFORD, Henry Noel. *Olives of Endless Age.* 1928. Harper. 1st ed. 431 p. gr cloth. F/NF. B22. $7.50

BRAINE, John. *Finger of Fire.* (1977). London. Methuen. 1st ed. NF/NF. B3. $25.00

BRAINE, John. *View From Tower Hill.* 1971. Coward McCann. AP/1st Am ed. NF/tall wrp. L3. $75.00

BRAITHWAITE, E.R. *Reluctant Neighbors.* (1972). McGraw Hill. 1st ed. inscr. NF/NF. B4. $125.00

BRAITHWAITE, William C. *Beginnings of Quakerism.* 1955. Cambridge. 2nd ed. xl. 8vo. 607 p. V3. $50.00

BRAKEFIELD, Tom. *Hunting Big-Game Trophies: N Am Guide.* (1976). Outdoor Life. photos/index. 446 p. F/dj. A17. $15.00

BRAM, Christopher. *Hold Tight.* 1988. Donald Fine. 1st ed. F/F. A14. $25.00

BRANCH & SMITH. *Unreasonable American: Francis W Davis...* (1968). Acropolis Books. 1st ed. 8vo. 215 p. F/F. A2. $15.00

BRAND, Christianna. *Cat & Mouse.* 1950. Knopf. 1st Am ed. F/F. M15. $35.00

BRAND, Christianna. *Fog of Doubt.* 1979. Boston. Gregg. 1st ed. F/F. S5. $22.50

BRAND, Max. *Ambush at Torture Canyon.* 1971. Dodd Mead. 1st appearance in book form. NF/dj. B9. $20.00

BRAND, Max. *Blk Jack.* 1970. Dodd Mead. 1st appearance in book form. NF/dj. B9. $20.00

BRAND, Max. *Blood on the Trail.* 1957. Dodd Mead. 1st ed. NF/dj. B9. $20.00

BRAND, Max. *Dead Man's Treasure: Novel of Adventure.* 1974. Dodd Mead. 1st book ed. F/NF. Q1. $30.00

BRAND, Max. *Farlig Mann (Hired Guns).* 1951. Oslo. Nasjonalforlaget A/S. Norwegian text. VG/dj. B9. $10.00

BRAND, Max. *Fightn' Fool.* 1939. Dodd Mead. 1st ed. G+/dj. B9. $15.00

BRAND, Max. *Garden of Eden.* 1963. Dodd Mead. 1st appearance in book form. NF/dj. B9. $20.00

BRAND, Max. *Guns of Dorking Hollow.* 1966. Hodder Stoughton. 1st ed. F/dj. B9. $15.00

BRAND, Max. *Harigan.* 1971. Dodd Mead. 1st book ed. NF/NF. Q1. $30.00

BRAND, Max. *Jackson Trail.* 1932. Dodd Mead. 1st ed. VG. M2. $15.00

BRAND, Max. *Jackson Trail.* 1943. World. 1st Tower ed. VG/dj. B9. $15.00

BRAND, Max. *Last Showdown.* 1975. Dodd Mead. 1st ed. NF/dj. B9. $20.00

BRAND, Max. *Long Chase.* 1960. Dodd Mead. 1st ed. NF/dj. B9. $20.00

BRAND, Max. *Lucky Larribee.* 1957. Dodd Mead. 1st ed. NF/dj. B9. $25.00

BRAND, Max. *Outlaw Valley.* 1953. NY. 1st book ed. NF/NF. Q1. $60.00

BRAND, Max. *Rippon Rides Double.* (1968). Dodd Mead. 1st ed. NF/dj. B9. $25.00

BRAND, Max. *Smugglers' Trail.* 1950. Harper. 1st book ed. VG/VG. Q1. $50.00

BRAND, Max. *Speedy.* 1955. Dodd Mead. ARC/1st ed. NF/dj. B9. $30.00

BRAND, Max. *Stranger.* 1963. Dodd Mead. 1st ed. NF/dj. B9. $20.00

BRAND, Max. *Trouble Trail.* 1937. Dodd Mead. 1st ed. VG+. B9. $20.00

BRAND, Max. *Untamed.* 1919. London. Putnam. 1st ed. VG+. B9. $150.00

BRANDEIS, Louis D. *Palestine & Jewish Democracy.* 1916. NY. Outlook. prt wrp. M11. $65.00

BRANDEIS, Madeline. *Little Anne of Canada.* ca 1940s. Grosset Dunlap. reprint. VG. C1. $6.00

BRANDEIS, Madeline. *Little Farmer of the Middle W.* 1937. NY. 8vo. 143 p. pict brds/bl cloth spine. VG. H3. $15.00

BRANDEIS, Madeline. *Little Mexican Donkey Boy.* 1931. NY. 8vo. 224 p. pict gr brds/bl spine. VG. H3. $15.00

BRANDEIS, Madeline. *Mitz & Fritz of Germany.* ca 1940. Grosset Dunlap. photos. VG+/dj. C1. $6.50

BRANDEL, Marc. *Rain Before Seven.* 1945. Harper. 1st ed. F/dj. M2. $25.00

BRANDER, Michael. *Hunting & Shooting From Earliest Times to Present Day.* (1971). NY. royal 8vo. 255 p. A17. $20.00

BRANDNER, Gary. *Cat People.* 1982. Fawcett. 1st hc ed. F/NF. F4. $12.00

BRANDON, Heather. *Casualties: Death in Vietnam...* (1984). St Martin. stated 1st ed. 357 p. F/dj. A7. $32.00

BRANDON, John G. *One-Minute Murder.* 1935. NY. Dial. 1st ed. F/VG. M15. $35.00

BRANDONSTIEL, Mack. *Breaker, Breaker, Ten-Four: Complete Guide to CB Radio.* 1976. Grosset Dunlap. pict brds. N2. $5.00

BRANDT, Irving. *Bill of Rights: Its Origin & Meaning.* 1965. Bobbs Merrill. M11. $25.00

BRANDT, Nat. *Town That Started the Civil War.* 1990. np. 315 p. dj. O7. $9.50

BRANDT, Tom; see Dewey, Thomas B.

BRANHAM, Levi. *My Life & Travels.* 1929. Dalton, GA. Schowalter. 1st ed. 64 p. VG. M8. $375.00

BRAQUE, Georges. *Braque Lithographe.* (1963). Monte Carlo. Sauret. 1st ed. w/3 orig lithos. F/litho wrp/slipcase. B24. $650.00

BRAQUE, Georges. *Cahier de Georges Braqaue, 1917-47.* (1955). Paris. Maeght. 1/750 on velin de Marais. folio. linen portfolio. K1. $450.00

BRASFORD, Ernie. *Greek Islands.* 1963. NY. 1st ed. pls. 288 p. gilt bl cloth. VG/G. H3. $15.00

BRASSAI. *Picasso & Co.* 1966. NY. 1st ed. G+/G+. A1. $25.00

BRAUN, Lilian Jackson. *Cat Who Sniffed Blue.* 1988. Putnam. 1st ed. F/F. M15. $25.00

BRAUN, Lilian Jackson. *Cat Who Wasn't There.* (1992). Putnam. 1st ed. F/F. B3. $15.00

BRAUTIGAN, Richard. *Confederate General From Big Sur.* 1964. Grove. 1st ed. F/NF. Q1. $250.00

BRAUTIGAN, Richard. *In Watermelon Sugar.* 1968. San Francisco. 4 Seasons. Writing 21. NF/wrp. B2. $50.00

BRAUTIGAN, Richard. *In Watermelon Sugar.* 1970. London. Cape. 1st ed. NF/NF. Q1. $75.00

BRAUTIGAN, Richard. *Pill Vs the Springhill Mine Disaster.* 1968. San Francisco. 1st ed/trade issue. NF/8vo wrp. A11. $75.00

BRAUTIGAN, Richard. *Revenge of the Lawn: Stories 1962-70.* 1971. Simon Schuster. 1st ed. VG-/wrp. E3. $25.00

BRAUTIGAN, Richard. *Traume von Babylon: Ein Detiktivroman 1942.* 1983. Munich. 1st German ed. F/glossy 8vo stiff wrp. A11. $25.00

BRAUTIGAN, Richard. *Willard & His Bowling Trophies.* (1975). Simon Schuster. 1st ed. rem mk. NF/dj. A7. $22.00

BRAY, N.E. *Shifting Sands.* 1934. London. Unicorn. 1st ed. 312 p. gilt blk cloth. VG. M7. $60.00

BRAY, S. Alice. *Baby's Journal.* 1885. Anson Randolph. lithos by Prang. gray cloth. VG. M5. $15.00

BRAY. *Machine Applique.* 1978. np. ils. wrp. G2. $7.00

BRAYBROOKE, Neville. *Seeds in the Wind.* 1939. London. Hutchinson. 1st ed. 207 p. dk bl paper. M. M7. $35.00

BRAZELON, David L. *Questing Authority, Justice & Criminal Law.* 1988. Knopf. M11. $35.00

BRAZER, M.C. *Sweet Water Sea: Guide to Lake Huron's Georgian Bay.* (1984). Manchester, MI. 1st ed. 200 p. map ep. M. A17. $17.50

BREATHNACH. *Mrs Sharp's Traditions.* 1990. np. cloth. G2. $30.00

BRECK, Joseph. *New Book of Flowers.* ca 1866. NY. Judd. 480 p. H10. $20.00

BRECKENRIDGE, Gerald. *Radio Boys Seek the Lost Atlantis.* 1923. Burt. VG. M2. $20.00

BREE, Charles Robert. *Hist of the Birds of Europe...* 1875-76. London. George Bell. 2nd ed/enlarged. lg octavo. 5 vols. VG. H5. $1,250.00

BREE, Marlin. *In the Teeth of the Northeaster.* (1988). NY. 1st ed. 214 p. F/dj. A17. $15.00

BREEN, Herbert. *Hardley a Man Is Now Alive.* 1950. Morrow. 1st ed. NF/VG. B4. $45.00

BREEN, Jon L. *Hot Air.* 1991. Simon Schuster. ARC. sgn. RS. F/F. S5. $35.00

BREITMAN & NOVACK. *Blk Nationalism & Socialism.* (1968). Merit. 3rd prt. wrp. A7. $15.00

BREMAN, Paul. *You Better Believe It.* 1973. Harmondsworth. Penguin. PBO. inscr. 552. F/wht wrp. A11. $75.00

BREMOND, Edouard. *Le Jedjaz Dans la Guerre Mondiale.* 1931. Paris. Payot. 1st ed. 351 p. uncut. VG/tan wrp. w/1-p ad. M7. $385.00

BRENNAN, Joseph P. *Nine Horrors & a Dream.* 1958. Arkham. 1st ed. F/dj. M2. $185.00

BRENNAN, Joseph P. *Scream at Midnight.* 1963. Macabre House. 1st ed. inscr. F/sans. M2. $300.00

BRENNAN, Joseph P. *Sixty Selected Poems.* 1985. New Establishment. 1st ed. M/wrp. M2. $15.00

BRENNAN, Matthew. *Hunter Killer Squadron.* (1990). Presidio. 1st ed. F/F. A7. $20.00

BRENT, Joseph Lancaster. *Memoirs of War Between the States.* 1940. New Orleans. Fontana. 1st ed. 1/100. presentation. 238 p. half leather. rare. M8. $850.00

BRENT, Loring; see Worts, George F.

BRENT & MERRILL. *Nature in Needlepoint.* 1975. np. ils. cloth. G2. $12.00

BRERETON, C. *Mystica et Lyrica.* 1919. London. Elkin Matthews. 1st ed. 127 p. VG+. M7. $125.00

BRERETON, Lewis H. *Brereton Diaries.* 1946. NY. 1st ed. ils. 450 p. VG/tattered dj. B18. $19.50

BRESENHAN & PUENTES. *Lone Star, Vol I: Legacy of TX Quilts, 1836-1936.* 1986. np. ils. wrp. G2. $25.00

BRESLER, Fenton. *Mystery of Georges Simenon: A Biography.* (1983). NY. Beaufort. F/dj. B9. $15.00

BRESS. *Craft of Macrame.* 1972. np. pb. G2. $6.00

BRETNOR, Reginald. *Modern SF: Its Meaning & Its Future.* 1953. Coward McCann. 1st ed. NF/clip. N3. $10.00

BRETON, Thierry. *Pentecost Project.* 1985. Holt. 1st ed. F/F. F4. $18.00

BRETT, Jan. *Twelve Days of Christmas.* 1986. Putnam. VG/VG. L1. $18.00

BRETT, Leo; see Fanthrope, R.L.

BRETT, Simon. *Dead Romantic.* 1986. Scribner. ARC. sgn. RS. F/F. S5. $40.00

BRETT, Simon. *Situation Tragedy.* 1981. London. Gollancz. 1st ed. F/F. S5. $35.00

BREWER, J. Gordon. *Literature of Geog: Guide to Its Organization & Use.* 1978. London. Bingley. 2nd ed. M/M. O6. $75.00

BREWER, Josiah. *Residence at Constantinople in the Yr 1827.* 1830. New Haven. Durrie Peck. 2nd ed. fld map. contemporary calf/blk spine label. K1. $200.00

BREWER, Reginald. *Delightful Diversion... Book Collecting.* 1935. Macmillan. 1st ed. sgn. 320 p. gray cloth. NF/NF. F1. $65.00

BREWER, Reginald. *Delightful Diversion... Book Collecting.* 1935. NY. Macmillan. G/dj. A16. $40.00

BREWSTER, Dorothy. *VA Woolf's London.* 1960. NY. 1st Am ed. F/F. A11. $45.00

BRIAND & CHAUDE. *Manuel Complet de Medecine Legal ou...* 1879-80. Paris. Bailliere. 2 vols. orig red morocco/marbled brds. G7. $75.00

BRICE, Germain. *New Description of Paris.* 1687. London. Bonwicke. 1st Eng ed. 2 parts in 1. 12mo. old calf. K1. $275.00

BRICKELL, Christopher. *Pruning.* 1979. NY. ils. sbdg. VG. B26. $12.50

BRICKELL, J. *Natural Hist of NC.* 1737. Dublin. 1st ed. subscriber's copy. rpr map. calf. C6. $8,000.00

BRICKER, Charles. *Landmarks of Mapmaking: Ils Survey of Maps & Mapmakers.* 1976. Crowell. 1st Am ed. ils/10 fld maps. NF/dj. O6. $100.00

BRICKTOP & HASKINS. *Bricktop.* 1983. Atheneum. 1st ed. 300 p. NF/NF. A7. $15.00

BRICUSSE, Leslie. *Christmas 1993; or, Santa's Last Ride.* 1987. London. Faber. deluxe ed. 1/100. sgn. ils/sgn Errol Le Cain. F/case. H5. $950.00

BRIDENBAUGH, Carl. *Seat of Empire. Political Role of 18th-Century Williamsburg.* 1950. Colonial Williamsburg. 1st ed. 8vo. ils/maps. 85 p. brn cloth. VG/G. B11. $40.00

BRIDGES, Robert. *Testament of Beauty.* 1930. NY. 1st ed. F/VG+. V1. $15.00

BRIDGES & TILTMAN. *More Heroes of Modern Adventure.* 1930. Boston. 1st ed. 266 p. gr cloth. F. H3. $20.00

BRIEM, Helgi P. *Iceland & the Icelanders.* 1945. Maplewood, NJ. 1st ed. ils. 96 p. silvered bl cloth. F. H3. $25.00

BRIER, Juliet. *First Christmas in Death Valley.* 1980. Sagebrush. 1/300. F/wrp. B19. $15.00

BRIGGS, Ellis. *Shots Heard 'Round the World.* 1957. NY. ils. 149 p. worn dj. A17. $12.50

BRIGGS, J.L. *Never in Anger: Portrait of an Eskimo Family.* 1970. Cambridge, MA. Harvard. 1st ed. 8vo. 377 p. F/VG. A2. $17.50

BRIGGS, L. Vernon. *AZ & NM 1882, CA 1886, Mexico 1891.* 1932. Boston. private prt. 1st ed. tall 8vo. 282 p. VG. H7. $100.00

BRIGGS, L. Vernon. *Hist & Genealogy of the Cabot Family, 1475-1920. Vol 1.* 1927. Boston. Goodspeed. thick 8vo. pls. 465 p. VG. B11. $65.00

BRIGGS, L. Vernon. *Hist of Shipbuilding on N River, Plymouth Co, MA.* 1889. Boston. 1st ed. ils. 420 p. VG. B28. $200.00

BRIGHAM, William. *Compact w/Charter & Laws of Colony of New Plymouth...* 1836. Boston. 1/1500. 357 p. full leather/front detached. B28. $100.00

BRIGHAM, William. *Guatemala. Land of the Quetzal.* 1887. Scribner. 1st ed. 453 p. VG. F3. $85.00

BRIGHT, John. *Diaries of John Bright.* 1931. Morrow. 8vo. 591 p. G+. V3. $25.00

BRIGHT, Robert. *Friendly Bear.* 1957. Doubleday. 1st ed. VG/dj. M20. $20.00

BRILL, George Reiter. *Rhymes of the Golden Age.* 1908. Edward Stern Co. 1st ed. sgn. 121 p. gr cloth/pict label. G+. S10. $45.00

BRILL, Harry. *Why Organizers Fail.* 1975. Berkeley. 192 p. dj. A7. $17.00

BRINE, Mary D. *How a Dear Little Couple Went Abroad.* ca 1900. Dutton. ils Aimee G Clifford. 48 p. VG-. S10. $15.00

BRINE, Mary D. *Mother's Little Man.* (1906). Altemus. Dainty series. 56 p. VG/G-. S10. $55.00

BRINE, Mary D. *Mother's Song.* (1886). Cassell. ils CA Northam. aeg. G. S10. $35.00

BRINEY, E. *20th-Century Canadian Poetry.* 1953. Toronto. 1st ed. red cloth. VG. A11. $25.00

BRINK, Carol Ryrie. *Andy Buckram's Tin Men.* 1966. Viking. 1st ed. xl. 192 p. pict cloth. T5. $20.00

BRINK, Carol Ryrie. *Caddie Woodlawn.* 1939 (1935). Macmillan. 8vo. 270 p. VG. T5. $22.00

BRINK, Carol Ryrie. *Magical Melons. More Stories About Caddie Woodlawn.* 1944. Macmillan. ils Marguerite Davis. 3rd prt. 8vo. 193 p. VG-. A3. $7.00

BRINK, Carol Ryrie. *Magical Melons: More Stories About Caddie Woodlawn.* 1944. Macmillan. 193 p. VG/G. P2. $25.00

BRINN, David. *River of Time.* 1986. Dark Harvest. ltd ed. 1/400. sgn. as new/slipcase. M2. $100.00

BRINNIN, J.M. *Sorrows of Cold Stone.* 1951. Dodd Mead. 1st prt. 109 p. VG/dj. M20. $45.00

BRINNIN, J.M. *Sway of the Grand Saloon: Social Hist of N Atlantic.* (1971). Delacorte. 1st ed. 8vo. 599 p. F/F clip. A2. $30.00

BRINTON, Crane. *Ideas & Men: Story of W Thought.* 1950. Prentice Hall. 1st ed. VG. G1. $25.00

BRINTON, Howard. *Mystic Will: Based on Study of Philosophy of Jacob Boehme.* 1930. Macmillan. 1st ed. 12mo. 269 p. G. V3. $15.00

BRINTON, Howard. *Mystic Will: Based on Study of Philosophy of Jacob Boehme.* 1930. NY. Macmillan. 1st ed. 269 p. cloth. VG. H10. $32.50

BRISBANE, Albert. *Social Destiny of Man...* 1840. Phil. Stollmeyer. 1st ed. 1 (of 2) pl. 480 p. cloth/leather label. M1. $225.00

BRISTOW, Gwen. *Golden Dreams.* 1980. Lippincott Crowell. 8vo. G/G. A8. $10.00

BRITAIN, Bill. *Wish Giver: 3 Tales of Coven Tree.* 1983. Harper Row. 1st ed. 181 p. F/VG+. P2. $28.00

BRITE, Poppy Z. *Drawing Blood.* 1993. Delacorte. 1st ed. w/sgn bookplate. F/F. T2. $25.00

BRITTAIN, Vera. *Testament of Experience.* 1957. Macmillan. 1st ed. sgn. 480 p. dj. A7. $30.00

BRITTAIN, Vera. *Testament of Youth.* 1933. Macmillan. not 1st ed. VG. N2. $6.00

BRITTEN, F.J. *Watch & Clockmaker's Handbook, Dictionary & Guide.* 1889. London. Kent. 436 p. cloth. B14. $25.00

BRITTON, Christopher. *Paybacks.* (1985). Donald Fine. 1st ed. F/dj. A7. $30.00

BRITTON, Nathaniel L. *Manual of Flora of N States & Canada.* 1907 (1901). NY. 3rd ed. 1122 p. VG. B26. $21.00

BROADFOOT, Barry. *10 Lost Yrs 1929-39: Memories of Canadians...* 1973. Toronto. Doubleday. dj. VG. N2. $10.00

BROCA, Paul. *Anevrysmes et de Leur Traitment.* 1856. Paris. Labe. 931 p. new quarter cloth/marbled brds. orig prt wrp. G7. $575.00

BROCA, Paul. *Prorietes et Fonctions de la Moelle Epiniere Rapport...* 1855. Paris. author's offprint. 35 p. new brds. G7. $395.00

BROCH, Hermann. *Spell.* 1987. FSG. 1st ed. trans from German. F/F clip. A13. $25.00

BROCK, Edwin. *Portraits & Poses.* 1973. New Directions. 1st ed. F/VG+. V1. $10.00

BROCK, Emma. *Drusilla.* 1958 (1937). Macmillan. 16th prt. 8vo. 120 p. VG/G. A3. $15.00

BROCK, Emma. *Peppo.* 1936. Whitman/Jr Pr. 79 p. cloth/pict label. VG+/G. A3. $25.00

BROCK, Emma. *Then Came Adventure.* 1941. Knopf. 1st ed. 184 p. VG/poor. P2. $15.00

BROCK, Lynn. *Stoke Silver Case.* 1929. Harper. 1st Am ed. VG/tape rpr. M15. $85.00

BROCK, Rose; see Hansen, Joseph.

BROCK & GILMARTIN. *Devil's Coach.* 1977. Cook. 1st ed. F/G+. P8. $10.00

BROCKETT, L.P. *Cross & the Crescent; or, Russia, Turkey & Countries...* 1877. Phil. 8vo. ils/fld map. decor cloth. O2. $65.00

BROCKWAY, Edith. *Sing-a-Rhyme Picture Book.* 1942. Whitman. ils Ethel Bonney Taylor. 14 p. VG. A3. $15.00

BROD, D.C. *Masquerade in Bl.* 1991. Walker. ARC. RS. F/F. S5. $22.50

BRODIE, Fawn M. *Devil Drives.* 1967. Norton. VG/dj. A16. $10.00

BRODKEY, Harold. *Abundant Dreamer.* (1989). London. Cape. 1st ed. F/NF. B3. $30.00

BRODKEY, Harold. *First Love & Other Sorrows.* 1957. Dial. 1st ed. F/VG. L3. $175.00

BRODKEY, Harold. *Stories in an Almost Classical Mode.* 1988. Knopf. 1st ed. inscr. w/sgn letter. F/F. B2. $150.00

BRODKEY, Harold. *Stories in an Almost Classical Mode.* 1988. Knopf. 1st ed. NF/NF clip. A14. $30.00

BRODKEY, Harold. *Women & Angels.* 1985. Phil. 1st ed. sgn. lavender brds/half cloth. F/F/slipcase. A11. $50.00

BRODRICK, A.H. *Father of Prehistory: Abbe Henri Breuil, His Life & Times.* 1963. NY. Morrow. 1st ed. 8vo. 306 p. F-/VG. A2. $15.00

BRODSKY, Daniel Louis. *Birds in Passage.* 1980. Farm Pr. 1st ed. 1/500. sgn/#d. F/wrp. V1. $20.00

BRODSKY, Joseph. *To Urania.* 1988. NY. 1st ed. F/F. V1. $20.00

BROEG, Bob. *Superstars of Baseball.* 1971. Sporting News. 1st prt. photos. F. P8. $20.00

BROEN, Johann. *Exercitatio Physico-Medica.* 1675. Leyden. Johannem Prins. 12mo. contemporary vellum. K1. $275.00

BROGAN, James; see Hodder-Williams, C.

BROKER, Ignatia. *Night Flying Woman: An Ojibway Narrative.* 1983. MN Hist Pr. 8th prt. 135 p. M/wrp. A17. $8.50

BROME, Vincent. *Ernest Jones: Freud's Alter Ego.* 1983. NY. Norton. 1st Am ed. 350 p. cloth. F/dj. G1. $20.00

BROMELL, Henry. *Slightest Distance.* 1974. Houghton Mifflin. 1st ed. author's 1st book. F/dj. C4. $30.00

BROMFIELD, Louis. *From My Experience. Pleasures & Miseries of Life on Farm.* 1955. NY. 1st ed. photos. 355 p. VG/torn. B28. $20.00

BROMFIELD, Louis. *Wild Country.* 1948. Harper. 1st ed. VG/dj. M18. $20.00

BRONAUGH, Warren Carter. *Youngers' Fight for Freedom: A S Soldier's 20 Yrs' Campaign.* 1906. Columbia, MO. Stephens. 1st ed. xl. pls. 398 p. cloth. VG. M8. $175.00

BRONDOLO. *Sm Patchwork Projects.* 1981. np. 48 p of templates/28 p of text. wrp. G2. $5.00

BRONK, William. *Death Is the Place.* 1989. Northpoint. 1st ed. F/F. V1. $15.00

BRONSON, Edgar Beecher. *Reminiscences of a Ranchman.* 1907. NY. McClure. 1st ed. 8vo. 314 p. gr cloth. H9. $35.00

BRONSON, William. *How To Kill a Golden State.* 1968. Doubleday. ils. 226 p. G. B19. $7.50

BRONTE, Charlotte. *Jane Eyre...* 1848. London. 3rd ed. 3 vols. reddish-brn cloth. morocco clamshell case. H5. $7,500.00

BRONTE, Charlotte. *Search After Happiness.* nd. NY. 1st Am ed. F/NF. A11. $50.00

BRONTE, Charlotte. *Vilette. By Currer Bell.* 1853. NY. Harper. 1st Am ed. 8vo. cloth. VG+. M1. $125.00

BROOKE, Geoffrey. *Foxhunter's Eng.* ca 1930. Lippincott. 255 p. G. A17. $9.50

BROOKE, Henry K. *Book of Pirates.* 1847. Phil/NY. 24mo. pls/woodcuts. 216 p. brn cloth. VG-. scarce. H3. $100.00

BROOKE, Jocelyn. *Wild Orchids of Britain.* (1950). Bodley Head. 1st/ltd ed. 4to. 139 p. VG. A2. $65.00

BROOKE, Leslie. *Johnny Crow's New Garden.* 1936 (1935). Warne. VG+/VG+. P2. $75.00

BROOKE, Rupert. *Lithuania: A Play.* 1935. London. 1st ed. VG+. T9. $35.00

BROOKES, Owen. *Widow of Ratches.* 1979. HRW. 1st ed. author's 1st horror novel. F/NF. N3. $50.00

BROOKES, R. *General Gazetteer on Compendious Geog Dictionary...* 1812. London. Rivington. 8 maps. new buckram. NF. O6. $195.00

BROOKNER, Anita. *Brief Lives.* (1991). Random. 1st ed. F/F. B3. $20.00

BROOKNER, Anita. *Family & Friends.* (1985). London. Cape. 1st ed. F/F. B3. $40.00

BROOKNER, Anita. *Lewis Percy.* (1989). London. Cape. AP. VG/red prt wrp. B3. $30.00

BROOKS, Albert E. *Australian Native Plants for Home Gardens.* 1979 (1959). Melbourne. 6th ed. 162 p. NF. B26. $27.50

BROOKS, Charles S. *Hints to Pilgrims.* 1921. Yale. 1st ed. 192 p. VG+. B22. $7.50

BROOKS, Cleanth. *On the Prejudices, Predilections & Firm Beliefs...Faulkner.* 1987. Baton Rouge. ARC. inscr. RS. F/F. A11. $45.00

BROOKS, Cleanth. *William Faulkner: 1st Encounters.* 1983. New Haven. 1st ed. inscr. F/F. A11. $55.00

BROOKS, Elbridge S. *Boy of the 1st Empire.* 1895. Century. 1st ed. 320 p. VG. S10. $30.00

BROOKS, Gwendolyn. *Bean Eaters.* 1960. Harper. 1st ed. NF/torn dj. B2. $85.00

BROOKS, Gwendolyn. *Selected Poems.* 1963. NY. 1st ed. presentation inscr. F/VG+ clip. A11. $65.00

BROOKS, Jocelyn. *Scapegoat.* 1949. NY. 1st ed. VG/VG. B5. $15.00

BROOKS, Joe. *Complete Guide To Fishing Across N Am.* (1966). Outdoor Life. 613 p. dj. A17. $15.00

BROOKS, John. *Telephone: 1st Hundred Yrs.* 1976. Harper Row. 1st ed. VG/G+. N2. $12.50

BROOKS, Louise. *Lulu in Hollywood.* 1982. Knopf. 1st ed. quarto. F/F. B4. $50.00

BROOKS, Noah. *Abraham Lincoln & the Downfall of Am Slavery.* 1894. Putnam. 2nd ed. xl. 471 p. cloth. G. scarce. M8. $35.00

BROOKS, Noah. *First Across the Continent: Story of Exploring Expedition...* 1902. Scribner. 1st ed. 8vo. 365 p. F. T8. $35.00

BROOKS, Terry. *Druid of Shannara.* (1991). Del Rey. 1st ed. F/F. B3. $20.00

BROOKS, Terry. *Hook.* (1992).. Fawcett Columbine. 1st ed/screenplay ed. F/dj. B4. $45.00

BROOKS, Terry. *Sword of Shannara.* (1991). Ballantine. reissue w/new author's note. inscr. F/F. B3. $30.00

BROOKS, Terry. *Wizard At Large.* (1988). Ballantine. 1st ed. NF/F. B3. $20.00

BROOKS, Walter R. *Freddy the Detective.* 1954. Knopf. ils Kurt Wiese. 264 p. VG/G+. S10. $18.00

BROOKS, Walter. *Freddy the Pilot.* 1952. Knopf. 1st ed. ils Kurt Weise. G/fair. L1. $30.00

BROOKS, Walter. *Story of Reginald.* 1936. Knopf. 1st ed. ils Kurt Wiese. VG. P2. $45.00

BROOKS, Walter. *To & Again.* 1927. Knopf. 1st ed. 197 p. G. P2. $38.00

BROOKS & PARRIS. *Blks in the City.* 1971. Little Brn. stated 1st ed. 534 p. dj. A7. $25.00

BROOKS & STOKES. *Quilter's Catalog.* 1987. np. cloth. G2. $20.00

BROONZY & BRUYNOGHE. *Big Bill Blues.* 1955. London/NY. Cassell/Grove. 1st Am ed. F/F. B2. $75.00

BROPHY, B. *Don't Never Forget: Collected Views & Reviews.* 1966. Holt Rinehart. 1st ed. NF/VG. E3. $15.00

BROPHY, Frank Cullen. *AZ Sketchbook.* 1952. private prt. 8vo. VG/G. A8. $25.00

BROSNAN, Cornelius J. *Jason Lee: Prophet of the New OR.* 1932. NY. 1st ed. 349 p. cloth. NF. D3. $35.00

BROSNAN, Jim. *Pennant Race.* 1962. Harper Row. 1st prt. F/VG+ later dj. P8. $60.00

BROSNAN, John. *James Bond in the Cinema.* 1972. S Brunswick. AS Barnes. 1st Am ed. F/NF. M15. $40.00

BROSSARD, Chandler. *Wake Up, We're Almost There.* (1971). NY. Baron. 1st ed. dj. A7. $30.00

BROTHERSON, Gordon. *Image of the New World.* 1979. London. Thames Hudson. 1st ed. 324 p. dj. F3. $25.00

BROUGH, James. *Prince & the Lily.* 1975. BC. ils/photos. VG/dj. C1. $4.00

BROUGHTON, Jack. *Going Downtown.* (1988). Orion. 1st prt. F/F. A7. $25.00

BROUGHTON, Phillip. *Pandy.* 1930. Volland. 1st ed. ils MW Barney. G. scarce. M5. $15.00

BROUGHTON, William Robert. *Voyage of Discovery to N Pacific Ocean.* 1804. London. Cadell Davies. quarto. fld maps/views. half pigskin. H9. $4,500.00

BROUN, Hewood. *Boy Grew Older.* 1922. NY. Putnam. 1st ed. G+. B2. $35.00

BROWDER, Earl. *Meaning of Social-Fascism...Hist & Theoretical Background.* 1933. NY. Workers Lib. VG. V4. $7.50

BROWER, J.V. *MN: Discovery of Its Area 1540-1665.* 1903. St Paul. 1/300. sgn. ils/fld map. 127 p. VG. B28. $70.00

BROWER & SHUMWAY. *Oberliniana. A Jubilee Vol of Semi-Hist Anecdotes...* 1883. Cleveland. 1st ed. 175 p. G. D7. $50.00

BROWING, Norma Lee. *Joe Maddy of Interlochen.* 1963. Chicago. 1st ed. 297 p. dj. A17. $10.00

BROWN, Alice. *Secret of the Clan: Story for Girls.* 1912. Macmillan. 1st ed. ils Sarah K Smith. 314 p. VG. S10. $25.00

BROWN, Bliss S. *Modern Fruit Marketing.* 1916. Orange Judd. 1st ed. ils. 283 p. VG. B28. $20.00

BROWN, Carter. *So Lovely She Lies.* 1958. Sydney. 1st ed of PBO. digest size. F. A11. $65.00

BROWN, Charlie H. *Deviation & the Deviascope.* 1961. Glasgow. Brn Ferguson. 8th ed. 228 p. red cloth/blk spine. VG. P4. $32.50

BROWN, Dee. *Conspiracy of Knaves.* (1987). Holt. 1st ed. F/F. B3. $20.00

BROWN, Dee. *Creek Mary's Blood.* (1980). Franklin Soc. true 1st ed. full leather. F. B3. $45.00

BROWN, Dee. *Trail on Driving Days.* 1952. NY. correct 1st ed. w/sgn bookplate. 220 photos. ES. NF/VG clip. A11. $55.00

BROWN, Douglas; see Gibson, Douglas.

BROWN, EDGERTON & MCCORKLE. *Algonquin Sampler.* (1990). Algonquin. 1st ed. F. B3. $30.00

BROWN, Ellijah. *Real Billy Sunday.* 1914. Otterbein. photos. VG/G+. P8. $160.00

BROWN, Fredric. *Before She Kills: Fredric Brn in Detective Pulps...* 1984. San Diego. D McMillan. 1/350. intro/sgn WF Nolan. F/dj. B9. $65.00

BROWN, Fredric. *Brother Monster.* 1987. Dennis McMillan. ltd ed. 1/400. intro/sgn Harry Alschuler. as new. M2. $60.00

BROWN, Fredric. *Office.* 1958. Dutton. 1st ed. VG/worn. B9. $60.00

BROWN, Fredric. *Office.* 1987. Dennis McMillan. 1st thus ed. 1/425. intro/sgn PJ Farmer. as new. M2. $55.00

BROWN, Fredric. *Red Is the Hue of Hell.* 1986. Miami Beach. McMillan. 1/400. intro/sgn Walt Sheldon. F/dj. B9. $45.00

BROWN, Fredric. *Selling Death Short.* 1988. Dennis McMillan. 1st ed. 1/450. intro/sgn Francis Nevins. as new. M2. $60.00

BROWN, Fredric. *Selling Death Short.* 1988. McMillan. 1st ed. 1/450. sgn/#d Francis M Nevins. F/F. S5. $50.00

BROWN, Fredric. *Whispering Death.* 1989. Missoula. McMillan. 1/450. F/dj. B9. $45.00

BROWN, George W. *Reminiscences of RJ Walker.* 1902. Rockford, IL. self pub. 12mo. 204 p. cloth. D3. $35.00

BROWN, James T. *Baird's Manual of Am College Fraternities.* 1923. NY. self pub. 10th ed. G. N2. $10.00

BROWN, Jane. *Art & Architecture of Eng Gardens.* ca 1898. NY. Rizzoli. 1st ed. oblong 4to. 320 p. M. H10. $85.00

BROWN, John Gregory. *Decorations in a Ruined Cemetery.* 1994. Houghton Mifflin. AP. F/wrp. L3. $65.00

BROWN, John Howard. *Lamb's Textile Industries of the US, Vol 1.* 1911. Boston. Lamb. ils/index. 460 p. H10. $35.00

BROWN, Larry. *Dirty Work.* 1989. Algonquin. ARC. F/wrp. B2. $45.00

BROWN, Larry. *Dirty Work.* 1989. Algonquin. 1st ed. author's 1st novel. F/F. L3. $35.00

BROWN, Larry. *Dirty Work.* 1989. Algonquin. 1st ed. sgn. F/F. B3. $40.00

BROWN, Larry. *Facing the Music.* 1988. Chapel Hill. 1st ed. sgn. F/F. A11. $65.00

BROWN, Larry. *Joe.* 1991. Algonquin. 1st ed. F/F. B3. $20.00

BROWN, Larry. *Joe.* 1991. Algonquin. 1st ed. sgn. F/F. C4. $50.00

BROWN, Lilian. *Bring 'Em Back Petrified.* (1956). NY. Dodd Mead. 1st ed. 277 p. VG+/VG-. A2 $15.00

BROWN, Lloyd Arnold. *Early Maps of the OH Valley: Selection of Maps...* 1959. Pittsburgh. 1/1000. 54 maps. NF/dj. O6. $185.00

BROWN, Lloyd Arnold. *Story of Maps.* 1949. Little Brn. 90 ils. NF/dj. O6. $85.00

BROWN, M. *S Cookbook.* 1951. Chapel Hill. 1st ed. VG/G. B5. $30.00

BROWN, M.L. *Firearms in Colonial Am.* 1980. np. ils/index. 448 p. O7. $24.50

BROWN, M.W. *Christmas in the Barn.* 1985. Harper Collins. ils Barbara Cooney. 12mo. VG+/VG. A3. $12.95

BROWN, Madie. *CA's Valley of the Moon: Hist Places & People...Sonoma.* 1961. private prt. photos. NF. P4. $29.50

BROWN, Malcolm. *Letters of TE Lawrence.* 1933. Dent. AP of 1st ed. inscr. F/wrp. M7. $95.00

BROWN, Malcolm. *Writers & Their Houses.* 1993. London. Hamish Hamilton. 1st ed. 515 p. M/dj. M7. $50.00

BROWN, Marcia. *Lotus Seed, Children, Pictures & Books.* 1986. Scribner. 1st ed. 216 p. red brds/blk spine. T5. $35.00

BROWN, Marcia. *Skipper John's Cook.* 1956. Scribner. 2nd prt. 4to. cloth. VG+/G+. A3. $15.00

BROWN, Margaret Wise. *Wheel on the Chimney.* (1954). Lippincott. ils Tibor Gergely. VG. P2. $20.00

BROWN, Norman O. *Life Against Death: Psychoanalytical Meaning of Hist.* 1959. NY. Vintage. 1st pb prt. G1. $16.50

BROWN, Norman O. *Love's Body.* 1966. Random. 1st ed. dj. N2. $7.50

BROWN, Paul. *Daffy Taffy.* 1955. Scribner. 1st ed. 4to. 32 p. VG/G+. A3. $40.00

BROWN, Paul. *Hi Guy. The Cinderella Horse.* 1944. Scribner. 1st ed. 60 p. cloth. VG. A3. $20.00

BROWN, Paul. *Hobby Horse Hill.* 1939. Doubleday Doran/Jr Literary Guild. 1st thus ed. VG/G. A3. $20.00

BROWN, Paul. *Insignia of the Services.* 1941. Scribner. 1st/A ed. sm 4to. G+. O3. $40.00

BROWN, Paul. *Polo: Non-Technical Explanation of the Galloping Game.* 1949. Scribner. VG/G. O3. $58.00

BROWN, Paul. *Pony School.* 1950. Scribner. 1st/A ed. VG/G+. O3. $85.00

BROWN, Paul. *Sparkie & Puff Ball.* 1956. Scribner. 3rd prt. 4to. 32 p. VG/VG. A3. $27.50

BROWN, Percy. *Indian Architecture.* ca 1945. Bombay. Taraporevala. 2nd ed. 4to. 163 pls. 262 p. VG. W1. $75.00

BROWN, Richard Maxwell. *No Duty To Retreat.* 1991. Oxford. ARC/1st ed. RS. M/dj. A18. $25.00

BROWN, Rita Mae. *Bingo.* (1988). Bantam. ARC. F/pict wrp. B3. $40.00

BROWN, Rita Mae. *Plain Brn Rapper.* 1976. Diana Pr. 1st ed. NF/wrp. B2. $25.00

BROWN, Rita Mae. *Six of One.* 1978. Harper Row. 1st ed. F/F. B3. $40.00

BROWN, Rita Mae. *Six of One.* 1978. NY. Harper Row. 1st ed. NF/NF. A14. $25.00

BROWN, Rita Mae. *Sudden Death.* (1983). Bantam. AP. sgn. VG/prt bl wrp. B3. $30.00

BROWN, Rita Mae. *Venus Envy.* (1983). Bantam. 1st ed. inscr. F/F. B3. $40.00

BROWN, Robin. *Megalodon.* 1981. CMG. 1st Am ed. F/F. N3. $10.00

BROWN, Rosellen. *Before & After.* 1992. FSG. 1st ed. F/F. T2. $21.00

BROWN, Rosellen. *Some Deaths in the Delta & Other Poems.* 1970. np (Amherst, MA). hc issue. author's 1st book. F/F clip. A11. $35.00

BROWN, Rosellen. *Some Deaths in the Delta.* 1970. MA. 1st ed. sgn w/correction. F/wrp. A11. $30.00

BROWN, Rosellen. *Street Games.* 1974. Doubleday. 1st ed. sgn. rem mk. F/F. B4. $45.00

BROWN, Sterling A. *Last Ride of Wild Bill.* 1975. Detroit. F/unread 8vo wrp. A11. $35.00

BROWN, Stuart E. *VA Baron: Story of Thomas, 6th Lord Fairfax.* (1965). Chesapeake Book Co. ils. 245 p. map ep. VG/VG. B10. $25.00

BROWN, W. *Compendious & Accurate Treatise of Recoveries...* 1678. London. Sawbridge Rawlins Roycroft. 1st ed. contemporary calf. R3. $350.00

BROWN, William H. *Hist of 1st Locomotives in Am.* 1871. NY. Appleton. 1st ed. presentation/inscr. gr cloth. VG. H5. $300.00

BROWN, William W. *Narrative of...a Fugitive Slave.* 1847. Boston. Anti-Slavery Office. 1st ed. 12mo. 110 p. cloth. M1. $425.00

BROWN & CAVE. *Touch of Genius.* 1933. London. Dent. 1st ed. 233 p. NF/NF. M7. $25.00

BROWN & EASTON. *Lord of the Beasts (Buffalo): Saga of Buffalo Jones.* 1961. AZ U. 287 p. F/dj. E5. $20.00

BROWN & HUNTER. *Planting in Uganda.* 1913. Longman Gr. 171 p. VG. M20. $20.00

BROWN & RUBY. *Spokane Indians: Children of the Sun.* (1970). OK U. stated 1st ed. 346 p. clip dj. A7. $25.00

BROWN & SCHMITT. *Settlers' W.* 1955. Scribner. 1st ed. 4to. mottled bdg. VG/G+. O3. $28.00

BROWN & WEIR. *Riding/Polo.* 1905. London. Badminton Lib. G. O3. $38.00

BROWN. *Applique.* 1991. np. ils. cloth. G2. $19.00

BROWN. *Legend of King Arthur & Round Table: Pop-Up Book.* 1986. paper engineering by Vic Duppa-White/Damian Johnston. F. A4. $35.00

BROWN-SEQUARD, Charles E. *Journal de la Physiologie de l'Homme et des Animaux.* 1858-62. Paris. 5 vols. orig brds/rebacked. H9. $750.00

BROWNE, Corinne. *Casualty: Memoir of Love & War.* (1981). Norton. 1st ed. F/dj. A7. $25.00

BROWNE, George Waldo. *St Lawrence River: Hist, Legendary, Picturesque.* 1905. Putnam. teg. G+. A16. $65.00

BROWNE, Howard. *Halo in Blood.* 1988. Eng. No Exit Pr. 1st British ed. F/F. S5. $35.00

BROWNE, John Ross. *Etchings of a Whaling Cruise...Zanzabar...Hist of Whale...* 1968. Cambridge. reprint. 8vo. ils/pls. 580 p. P4. $85.00

BROWNE, Junius Henri. *Four Yrs in Secessia: Adventures...Behind Union Lines.* 1865. Hartford. presentation. ils. 450 p. brn cloth. G. T3. $12.00

BROWNE, Junius Henri. *Four Yrs in Secessia: Adventures...Behind Union Lines.* 1865. Hartford. Chase. 450 p. cloth. VG. M20. $45.00

BROWNE, Keynes. *Bibliography of Sir Thomas Browne.* 2nd Ed, Revised... 1968. Oxford. xl. 293 p. dj. G7. $135.00

BROWNE, Lewis. *Something Went Wrong.* 1942. Left BC/Gollancz. 224 p. A7. $12.00

BROWNE, LUDOVICI & ROBERTS. *Abortion.* ca 1935. Allen Unwin. 1st ed. VG. V4. $15.00

BROWNE, Malcolm W. *New Face of War.* (1965). Bobbs Merrill. 284 p. dj. A7. $35.00

BROWNE, Thomas. *Pseudodoxia Epidemica; or, Enquiries Into Very Many...* 1650. London. Miller. 2nd ed. folio. 329 p. later calf. G7. $795.00

BROWNE, Thomas. *Religio Medici.* 1644. Leiden. Hackius. 2nd Latin ed. 12mo. contemporary full vellum. G7. $895.00

BROWNE, Thomas. *Religio Medici.* 1650. Lugd Batavorum. Apud Francifcum. 12mo. contemporary calf. G7. $395.00

BROWNE & ROBINSON. *How To Make a Garden Grow.* nd. London. Hutchinson. 1st ed. sm octavo. 104 p. VG. H5. $100.00

BROWNELL, Charles de Wolf. *Indian Races of N & S Am.* 1865. Hartford. 8vo. 755 p. VG. B11. $125.00

BROWNING, Elizabeth Barrett. *Biography of M Forster.* 1988. London. 1st ed. F/F. V1. $20.00

BROWNING, Elizabeth Barrett. *Poems of...* 1860. NY. C Francis. 2 vols. gilt brn bdg. VG. E5. $35.00

BROWNING, Elizabeth Barrett. *Sonnets From the Portuguese.* nd. Peter Pauper. sm octavo. 62 p. aeg. marbled ep. Heritage bdg. F. H5. $350.00

BROWNING, Elizabeth Barrett. *Sonnets From the Portuguese.* 1903. Mosher. full leather. VG. A16. $30.00

BROWNING, Robert. *Dramatis Personae.* 1910. Doves Pr. 1/250. gilt full vellum. F. F1. $475.00

BROWNING, Robert. *Love Among the Ruins.* 1918. London. calligraphic manuscript by Sangorski. silk ep. F/case. H5. $17,500.00

BROWNING, Robert. *Pied Piper of Hamelin.* 1898. London. Harry Quilter. 1/100. folio. w/Quilter sgn presentation bookplate. F1. $1,950.00

BROWNING, Robert. *Poetical Works.* 1894. NY. 9 vols. half red leather/half marbled brds. VG. B30. $475.00

BROWNING, Robert. *Ring & the Book.* 1872. London. 2nd ed. 4 vols. half leather/marbled brds. NF. B30. $225.00

BROWNING, Robert. *Shorter Poems of...* nd. NY. Crowell. 1st ed. flexible gilt gr leather. NF/VG box. V1. $15.00

BROWNING, Robert. *Works...* 1912. London. Smith Elder. Centenary ed. 1/500 sets. 10 vols. teg. VG. E3. $250.00

BROWNING, Sinclair. *Enju: Life & Struggle of an Apache Chief...* 1982. Northland. ils. 154 p. F/wrp. B19. $8.50

BROWNSON, O.A. *Oration on Scholar's Mission.* 1842. Burlinton, VT. Harrington. 1st ed. 8vo. 40 p. M1. $150.00

BROWSE, Philip M. *Plant Propagation.* 1979. NY. ils. 96 p. VG. B26. $11.00

BROXON, Mildred Downey. *Too Long a Sacrifice.* 1981. Dell. SF BC. F/F. F4. $7.00

BRUCCOLI, Matthew J. *Ernest Hemingway, Cub Reporter.* 1970. Pittsburgh. 1st ed. NF/NF. Q1. $50.00

BRUCCOLI, Matthew J. *James Dickey: Descriptive Bibliography.* 1990. Pittsburgh. 1st ed. F/sans. Q1. $50.00

BRUCCOLI, Matthew J. *James Gould Cozzens: A Descriptive Bibliography.* 1981. Pittsburgh. 1st ed. NF/sans. Q1. $40.00

BRUCCOLI, Matthew J. *Nelson Algren: A Descriptive Bibliography.* 1985. Pittsburgh. 1st ed. gilt bl cloth. F/sans. A11. $55.00

BRUCCOLI, Matthew J. *Reconquest of Mexico.* 1974. Vanguard. BC. 253 p. dj. F3. $10.00

BRUCE, F.F. *Eng Bible: A Hist of Trans...* 1970. NY. Oxford. 263 p. H10. $25.00

BRUCE, Leo. *Death in Albert Park.* 1979. Scribner. 1st Am ed. F/NF. S5. $22.50

BRUCE, Leo. *Death of a Bovver Boy.* 1974. London. Allen. 1st ed. F/F. M15. $65.00

BRUCE, Leo. *Such Is Death.* 1963. NY. British Book Centre. 1st Am ed. F/F. M15. $45.00

BRUCE, Philip A. *VA Plutarch.* 1929. UNC. 2 vols. VG. B10. $40.00

BRUCE, Robert V. *Lincoln & the Tools of War.* 1956. Bobbs Merrill. 1st ed. w/sgn leaf. NF/VG. M8. $45.00

BRUCE, Roberto. *Textos y Dibujos Lacadones de Naja.* 1976. Mexico. INAH. 1st ed. 1/2000. 158 p. wrp. F3. $35.00

BRUCE, Wallace. *Panorama of Hudson Showing Both Sides of River...* ca 1906. NY. Bryant Union Pub. oblong 8vo. 100 p of photos. wrp. H9. $45.00

BRUCHAC, Joseph. *Dreams of Jesse Brn.* 1978. Austin. Cold Mtn. 1st ed. NF/wrp. L3. $85.00

BRUCHAC, Joseph. *Good Message of Handsome Lake.* 1979. Greensboro. Unicorn. hc. F/sans. L3. $65.00

BRUCHAC, Joseph. *Stone Giants & Flying Heads.* (1979). NY. Crossing Pr. 1st ed. inscr/dtd 1981. VG. L3. $65.00

BRUCK, Teresa M. *Children's Games for All Seasons.* 1921. NY. ils CM Burd. 106 p. VG/fair. H3. $20.00

BRUCKNER, Peter. *Sigmund Freud Privatlekture.* 1975. Koln. Verlag Rolf Horst. 1st ed. 156 p. prt stiff wrp. G1. $22.50

BRUEMMER, Fred. *Seasons of the Eskimo. Vanishing Way of Life.* (1971). NY Graphic Soc. 1st ed. 4to. 131 p. dj. D3. $25.00

BRUNDAGE, Burr Cartwright. *Lords of Cuzoo.* (1967). Norman, OK. 1st ed. 458 p. dj. F3. $25.00

BRUNDAGE, Frances. *Little Red Riding hood.* 1929. Stecher. 12 p. VG+/color wrp. M5. $38.00

BRUNDAGE, Frances. *What Happened to Tommy.* (1921). Rochester. ils Brundage. VG/pict wrp. D1. $95.00

BRUNER, Jerome Seymour. *In Search of Mind: Essays in Autobiography.* 1983. Harper Row. 1st ed. 306 p. VG/dj. G1. $25.00

BRUNK, Harry Anthony. *Progeny of Jacob Brunk I...* 1978. Harrisonburg, VA. 1st ed. 422 p. gr cloth. G. D7. $25.00

BRUNNER, John. *Stone That Never Came Down.* 1973. Doubleday. 1st ed. F/F. N3. $15.00

BRUNO, Anthony. *Bad Business.* 1991. Delacorte. 1st ed. inscr. F/F. M10. $30.00

BRUNTZ, George G. *Children of the Volga.* 1981. Ardmore. Dorrance. juvenile. dj. N2. $6.00

BRUSSEL, I.R. *Bibliography of Writings of James Branch Cabell.* 1932. Centaur Book Shop. revised ed. 1/50. 126 p. VG/G. B10. $35.00

BRUSSO, Clifton. *Breakthru.* 1991. Vantage. 1st ed. F/F. F4. $16.00

BRYAN, C.D.B. *Friendly Fire.* (1976). Putnam. 1st ed. NF/NF. A7. $35.00

BRYAN, J. III. *Sword Over the Mantel.* 1960. McGraw Hill. 1st ed. 123 p. VG. B10. $30.00

BRYAN, John. *This Soldier Still at War.* (1975). HBJ. photos. 341 p. dj. A7. $25.00

BRYAN, S.A. *Memorial Reminiscences, Sketches of Civil War Veterans...* 1935. np. 1st ed. 60 p. VG/orig stiff wrp. M8. $150.00

BRYAN, William J. *1st Battle? Story of Campaign of 1896.* nd (1896). Conkey. 8vo. 629 p. VG+. B22. $15.00

BRYANT, Edward. *WY Sun.* 1980. Laramie. Jelm Mtn Pt. 1st ed. inscr/sgn. F/wrp. N3. $30.00

BRYANT, Edwin. *Voyage en Californie.* 1850. Bruxelles. 16mo. 210 p. brds. H9. $165.00

BRYANT, Edwin. *What I Saw in CA...1846-47.* 1848. Appleton. 2nd ed. 455 p. rebacked. VG. H7. $150.00

BRYANT, H. Stafford. *Georgian Locomotive.* 1962. Weathervane. VG/dj. A16. $10.00

BRYANT, Harold Child. *Outdoor Heritage.* 1929. LA. Powell Pub. 8vo. 464 p. red leatherette. P4. $40.00

BRYANT, Sara Cone. *Epaminondas & His Auntie.* 1938. Boston. red cloth. G. M5. $42.00

BRYANT, Sara Cone. *New Stories To Tell to Children.* 1923. Houghton Mifflin. 1st ed. 4 color pls. pict cloth. VG. M5. $30.00

BRYANT, William Cullen. *Letters From the E.* 1869. London. 8vo. 256 p. cloth. O2. $110.00

BRYANT, William Cullen. *Picturesque Am...* 1872-74. NY. Appleton. 1st ed. 2 vols. xl. VG. D3. $200.00

BRYANT & WILLIAMS. *Portraits in Roses: 100 Yrs of KY Derby Winners.* 1984. McGraw Hill. 1st ed. 4to. VG/VG. O3. $45.00

BRYCE, James. *Impressions of S Africa.* 1898 (97). NY. Century. 2nd ed. 8vo. 499 p. F. A2. $20.00

BRYDEN, H.A. *Great & Sm Game in Africa.* 1899. London. Rowland Ward. 1/500. sgn. teg. gilt gr morocco/cloth. R3. $3,500.00

BRYERS, Paul. *Coming 1st.* (1987). London. Bloomsbury. 1st ed. rem mk. NF/F. B3. $30.00

BRYERS, Paul. *Hollow Target.* (1976). London. Deutsch. mk Production File Copy. VG/VG. B3. $40.00

BRYSON, C.L. *Woodsy Neighbors of Tan & Teckle.* 1911. Revell. Ils CL Bull. 1st ed. 285 p. G+. A3. $12.50

BUBER, Martin. *Die Legende des Baalschen.* 1932. Berlin. Schocken. 276 p. VG. S3. $23.00

BUBER, Martin. *Tales of the Hasidim: Early Masters.* 1947. Schocken. 335 p. G+. S3. $23.00

BUCHAN, John. *Greenmantle.* 1916. Grosset Dunlap. 345 p. decor red cloth. M7. $25.00

BUCHAN, Susan. *John Buchan by His Wife & Friends.* 1947. Hodder Stoughton. 1st UK ed. 304 p. gilt blk cloth. VG. M7. $29.00

BUCHAN, William. *Domestic Medicine; or, A Treatise...* 1793. Boston. Bumstead. 14th ed. 484 p. contemporary sheepskin. B14. $60.00

BUCHAN, William. *Domestic Medicine; or, Treatise on Prevention...Diseases...* 1828. Exeter. Williams. 496 p. old-style new cloth. G7. $95.00

BUCHANAN, Edna. *Corpse Had a Familiar Face.* 1987. Random. 1st ed. F/F. T2. $20.00

BUCHANAN, Edna. *Never Let Them See You Cry.* 1992. Random. 1st ed. F/F. T2. $16.00

BUCHANAN, Lamont. *World Series & Highlights of Baseball.* 1951. Dutton. later prt. VG/G+. P8. $25.00

BUCHANAN, Marie. *Anima.* 1972. St Martin. 1st Am ed. F/F. N3. $50.00

BUCHANAN, Meriel. *City in Trouble.* 1918. NY. 8vo. 242 p. gilt red cloth. VG. H3. $15.00

BUCHANAN, Patrick. *Sounder of Swine.* 1974. Dodd Mead. 1st ed. F/F. F4. $16.00

BUCHER, E.E. *Wireless Experimenters Manual.* (1920). NY. revised ed. 350 p. red cloth. VG. C10. $37.50

BUCHWALD, Art. *Art Buchwald's Paris.* 1955. London. 1st ed. F/NF. A11. $30.00

BUCK, Mary K. *Songs From the Northland.* 1902. Traverse City. private prt. leather/marbled brds. G. A16. $60.00

BUCK, Pearl. *Good Earth.* (Feb 1931). NY. John Day. 1st ed/1st issue. gilt cloth. NF. B14. $250.00

BUCK, Pearl. *Story of Dragon Seed.* 1944. NY. 1st ed. 1/600. sgn. VG. B5. $75.00

BUCK, Solon Justus. *Travel & Description, 1765-1865.* 1914. Springfield. xl. ils. 500+ p. VG. O6. $55.00

BUCKBEE, Edna Bryan. *Saga of Old Toulumne.* 1935. NY. Pr of the Pioneers. autographed ed. 1/200. sgn. gilt red cloth. K1. $200.00

BUCKINGHAM, Nash. *Mark Right! Tales of Shooting & Fishing.* 1936. Derrydale. 1st ed. 1/1250. cloth. VG. M8. $275.00

BUCKLAND, John. *Fisherman's Companion.* (1990). Chartwell. 1st Am ed. 4to. 126 p. F/dj. A17. $17.50

BUCKLEY, Arabella B. *Life & Her Children.* 1881. Appleton. fair. A16. $15.00

BUCKLEY, Holland. *Scottish Terrier.* 1913. London. Dog World. 12mo. photos. paper brds. A17. $25.00

BUCKLEY, J.D. *Hist of the 50th Armored Infantry Battalion.* nd. Frankfurt am Main. ils. 110 p. quarter cloth/brds. fair. B18. $125.00

BUCKLEY, J.M. *Travels in 3 Continents.* 1895. NY. 1st ed. 8vo. 614 p. teg. gray cloth. F. H3. $65.00

BUCKLEY, Kerry W. *Mechanical Man: John Broadus Watson...* 1989. NY. Guilford. 1st ed. 233 p. gray cloth. VG/dj. G1. $25.00

BUCKLEY, Michael J. *Day at the Farm.* 1937. Nash. 1st ed. 10 p. NF. B19. $15.00

BUCKLEY, Peter. *Ernest (Hemingway).* 1978. NY. Dial. 1st ed. 200 photos. NF/NF. Q1. $60.00

BUCKLEY, William F. *On the Firing Line.* 1989. Franklin Lib. 1st ed. sgn. full leather. F. B4. $45.00

BUCKLEY, William F. *Tuckers' Last Stand.* (1990). Random. 1st ed. F/clip. A7. $15.00

BUCKLEY, William F. *Up From Liberalism.* 1959. McDowell Obolensky. 1st ed. author's 3rd book. NF/NF. Q1. $50.00

BUCKMAN, Williamson. *Under the S Cross in S Am.* 1914. NY. Book Pub Pr. 8vo. pls. 482 p. pict bl cloth. VG. B11. $40.00

BUDD, Joseph H. *Treatise on Law of Civil Remedies.* 1899. San Francisco. Byron Pub. full sheep. G. M11. $50.00

BUDGE, Frances Anne. *Annals of Early Friends: Series of Biographical Sketches.* 1896. Phil. Longstreth. 12mo. 456 p. VG. V3. $16.00

BUDGE, Jane. *Glimpses of George Fox & His Friends.* (1888). London. Partridge. 1st ed. 12mo. 325 p. V3. $16.00

BUDRYS, Algis. *Michaelmas.* 1977. Berkley. AP of 1st ed. F/wrp. N3. $25.00

BUECHNER, Frederick. *Seasons' Difference.* 1952. NY. 1st ed. VG+/dj. A11. $25.00

BUEL, J.W. *Heroes of the Plains.* 1881. St Louis Hist Pub. 1st ed. 548 p. leather. VG. M20. $85.00

BUEL, J.W. *Russian Nihilims & Exile Life in Siberia.* 1883. St Louis. Hist Pub. rebound gilt gr cloth. F. B2. $85.00

BUEL, James. *Great Operas.* 1899. London. Societe Universelle Lyrique. mixed set of 5 vols. VG+. H5. $3,000.00

BUELL, John. *Playground.* 1976. FSG. 1st ed. VG/VG. P3. $20.00

BUFALINO, Gesualdo. *Blind Argus; or, Fables of the Memory.* 1989. London. Collins Harvill. 1st Eng ed of 1984 Italian ed. F/F clip. A14. $25.00

BUKOWSKI, Charles. *Aftermath of a Lengthy Rejection Slip.* 1983. np. Grenfell Pr. 1st separate ed. 1/26 lettered. sgn. F. L3. $300.00

BUKOWSKI, Charles. *All the Assholes in the World & Mine.* 1966. Bensenville. Open Skull Pr. 1/400. NF/stapled tan wrp. Q1. $350.00

BUKOWSKI, Charles. *Bukowski Sampler.* 1969. Madison. Quixote. 1st ed. VG/stapled wrp. L3. $85.00

BUKOWSKI, Charles. *Burning in Water Drowning in Flame.* 1974. Blk Sparrow. 1st ed. 1/300. sgn. cloth-backed prt brds. F. B24. $125.00

BUKOWSKI, Charles. *Crucifix in a Deathhand.* 1965. Lyle Stuart/Loujon. 1/3100. sgn. w/prospectus. F/stiff wrp/wraparound band. B2. $250.00

BUKOWSKI, Charles. *Curtains Are Waving & People Walk Through the Afternoon...* 1967. Blk Sparrow. 1/122. sgn/#d/inscr. F/prt wrp. Q1. $500.00

BUKOWSKI, Charles. *Dangling in the Tournefortia.* 1981. Blk Sparrow. 1/350. inscr/sgn. w/orig drawing. F/pub acetate dj. L3. $350.00

BUKOWSKI, Charles. *Days Run Away Like Wild Horses Over the Hills.* 1969. Blk Sparrow. 1/250. sgn/#d. F/orig glassine. Q1. $300.00

BUKOWSKI, Charles. *Erections, Ejaculations, Exhibitions...Ordinary Madness.* 1972. San Francisco. 1st ed. inscr. VG+/thick 8vo wrp. A11. $110.00

BUKOWSKI, Charles. *Factotum.* 1981. London. Allen. 1st ed. F/F. V1. $35.00

BUKOWSKI, Charles. *Flower Fist & Bestial Wail.* nd (1959). Eureka. Hearse Pr. 1st ed. author's 1st book. sgn. NF/wht wrp. Q1. $1,000.00

BUKOWSKI, Charles. *Genius of the Crowd.* 1966. 7 Flowers. 1/103. sgn. ils Paula Marie Savarino. F/dk olive wrp. Q1. $1,000.00

BUKOWSKI, Charles. *Going Modern.* ca 1983. Fremont. Ruddy Duck. 1/500. very scarce. L3. $125.00

BUKOWSKI, Charles. *It Catches My Heart in Its Hands.* 1963. New Orleans. Loujon. 1/777. sgn. F. B2. $350.00

BUKOWSKI, Charles. *People Poems.* 1991. Stockton. 1/700. sgn. F/red wrp. A11. $35.00

BUKOWSKI, Charles. *Play the Piano Drunk Like a Percussion Instrument...* 1979. Blk Sparrow. 1st ed. 1/300. sgn. F/pub acetate dj. L3. $250.00

BUKOWSKI, Charles. *Poems Written Before Jumping Out an 8-Story Window.* 1968. Glendale. Poetry X/Change. F/wrp. L3. $175.00

BUKOWSKI, Charles. *Post Office.* 1971. Blk Sparrow. 1/250. sgn/#d. F/orig glassine. Q1. $300.00

BUKOWSKI, Charles. *Run w/the Hunted.* 1962. Chicago. Midway Poetry. 1/300. sgn. author's 4th book. F/prt red wrp. Q1. $450.00

BUKOWSKI, Charles. *There's No Business.* 1984. Blk Sparrow. 1/26 lettered. sgn. ils/sgn R Crumb. pict brds. F. Q1. $300.00

BULEY, R.C. *Old NW Pioneer Period 1815-40.* 1950. IN Hist Soc. 1st ed. 2 vols. VG+/box. E5. $65.00

BULEY, R.C. *Old NW Pioneer Period 1815-40.* 1951. U Pr. 2nd prt. 2 vols. 686 p. VG. A17. $55.00

BULGAKOV, Mikhail. *Master & Margarita.* 1967. Grove. 1st Am ed. trans from Russian. VG+/NF. A14. $30.00

BULIARD, Roger. *Inuk.* (1951). Farrar Straus Young. 1st ed. 8vo. 322 p. VG+/VG+. A2. $17.50

BULLARD, Julia W. *Jamestown Tributes & Toasts.* 1907. JP Bell. ils BT Lyle. 196 p. B10. $20.00

BULLARD & SCOTT. *John Sloan: His Life & Paintings...* 1971-72. Boston Book & Art Pub. 14 color pls. stiff wrp. D2. $45.00

BULLARD & SHIELL. *Chintz Quilts: Unfading Glory.* 1983. np. wrp. G2. $15.00

BULLEN, Frank T. *Deep-Sea Plunderings.* 1902. NY. 1st Am ed. ils. 361 p. pict cloth. VG. A17. $17.50

BULLEN, Frank T. *Denizens of the Deep.* (1904). NY. 1st Am ed. 430 p. pict cloth. VG. A17. $17.50

BULLETT, Gerald. *Seed of Isreal.* 1927. London. Howe. 1/250. G+. A1. $30.00

BULLETT, Gerald. *Walt Whitman: A Study & Selection.* 1924. London. Grand Richards. 1/750. sgn. G+. A1. $50.00

BULLIET, C.J. *Coutezan Olympia: Intimate Chronicle of Artists...* (1930). NY. Covici Friede. 1930s reprint. 8vo. 204 p. VG/G+. A2. $20.00

BULLITT, William C. *Bullitt Mission to Russia.* ca 1919. NY. BW Huebsch. VG. V4. $10.00

BULLOCH, James D. *Secret Service of the Confederate States in Europe...* 1959. NY. Yoseloff. reprint of 1884 ed. 2 vols. VG. M8. $45.00

BULLOUGH, William A. *Blind Boss & His City.* 1979. CA U. 1st ed. ils. 347 p. F/F. B19. $10.00

BULMER, Kenneth. *Insane City.* 1978. Severn House. 1st ed. F/dj. P3. $20.00

BULOW, Ernie. *Navajo Taboos.* 1991. Gallup. Buffalo Medicine Books. 1st ed. sgn Hillerman. F/F. M15. $400.00

BUNBURY, E.H. *Hist of Ancient Geography.* 1883. London. Murray. 2nd ed. 10 maps. VG. O6. $95.00

BUNNELLE, Hasse. *Food for Knapsackers & Other Trail Travelers.* (1971). Sierra Club. 2nd prt. 144 p. leatherette. A17. $7.50

BUNNING, Jim. *Story of Jim Bunning.* 1965. Lippincott. 1st ed. VG+/VG+. P8. $35.00

BUNTING, Basil. *Spoils.* 1965. Newcastle Upon Tyne. 1st book ed. 16 p. NF/ivory wrp. A11. $95.00

BUNYAN, John. *Holy War.* 1837. Exeter. Williams. leather. fair. A16. $10.00

BUNYAN, John. *Pilgrim's Progress.* ca 1885. Ward Lock Tyler. 1st thus ed. ils Dalziel. G. M18. $30.00

BUNYAN, John. *Pilgrim's Progress.* nd. Christian Herald. Red Line ed. sq 8vo. intro Sheldon. 427 p. NF. B22. $12.00

BUNYAN, John. *Pilgrim's Progress.* 1949. Standard Pub. ils David Lamb. VG. A3. $4.00

BUNZEL, Ruth. *Chichicastenango. A Guatemalan Village.* (1952). Augustin Pub. 1st ed. 438 p. yel cloth. F3. $60.00

BUPP, Walter; see Garrett, Randall.

BURBANK, Addison. *Mexican Frieze.* 1940. Coward McCann. 1st ed. 268 p. dj. F3. $20.00

BURBANK, Luther. *His Methods & Discoveries & Their Practical Application.* 1914. NY. Burbank Pr. 1st ed. 12 vols. teg. NF. R3. $400.00

BURCHARD, Peter. *Harbor Tug.* 1975. NY. 3-line inscr/dtd 1975. F/dj. B14. $45.00

BURCHETT, Wilfred. *Furtive War: US in Vietnam & Laos.* (1963). NY. Internat. 224 p. F/clip. A7. $45.00

BURCHETT, Wilfred. *Vietnam N: 1st Hand Report.* (1966). NY. Internat. stated 1st ed. 191 p. orig wrp. A7. $25.00

BURCHETT, Wilfred. *Vietnam Will Win!* 1970. Guardian. 2nd ed. 215 p. orig wrp. A7. $30.00

BURDETT, Charles. *Life of Kit Carson.* (1865). np. later prt? 382 p. VG. O7. $21.50

BURDETT, Winston. *Encounter w/the Middle E: Intimate Report...Arab-Israeli...* 1969. Atheneum. 1st ed. 384 p. VG+/rpr dj. S3. $17.00

BURDICK, Charles K. *Law of the Am Constitution: Its Orig & Development.* 1926. Putnam. worn. M11. $35.00

BURDICK. *Family Ties.* 1991. np. old quilt patterns from new cloth. wrp. G2. $20.00

BURDICK. *Legacy: Story of Talula Gilbert Bottoms & Her Quilts.* 1988. np. cloth. G2. $23.00

BUREAU OF RECLAMATION. *Columbia River: Comprehensive Report...* 1947. WA. GPO. maps/7 fld pocket maps. 300+ p. NF. O6. $55.00

BURGESS, Anthony. *Any Old Iron.* (1989). Random. 1st ed. F/NF clip. B3. $20.00

BURGESS, Anthony. *Any Old Iron.* 1989. Random. AP. F/wrp. L3. $45.00

BURGESS, Anthony. *Beard's Roman Women.* 1976. McGraw Hill. 1st ed. F/F. N3. $20.00

BURGESS, Anthony. *Blooms of Dublin.* 1986. London. 1st ed. F/wrp. A11. $40.00

BURGESS, Anthony. *Earthly Powers.* 1980. NY. 1st ed. F/dj. T9. $20.00

BURGESS, Anthony. *End of the World News.* (1982). London. Hutchinson. 1st ed. NF/VG. B3. $45.00

BURGESS, Anthony. *Ernest Hemingway & His World.* 1977. London. gilt gr cloth. F/F photo-ils dj. A11. $35.00

BURGESS, Anthony. *Going to Bed.* (1982). London. Deutsch. 1st ed. F/F. B3. $40.00

BURGESS, Anthony. *Kingdom of the Wicked.* 1985. Arbor. 1st ed. sgn. F/F. Q1. $45.00

BURGESS, Anthony. *Long Trip to Teatime.* 1976. Dempsey Squires. F/dj. P3. $15.00

BURGESS, Anthony. *Moses: A Narrative.* 1976. Stonehill. 1st Am ed. F/F. N3. $15.00

BURGESS, Anthony. *Novel Today.* 1963. London. NF/8vo wrp. A11. $40.00

BURGESS, Anthony. *On Mozart: Paean for Wolfgang.* 1991. Tichnor Fields. 1st Am ed. F/dj. B4. $35.00

BURGESS, Anthony. *Pianoplayers.* 1986. Hutchinson. 1st ed. F/dj. P3. $17.50

BURGESS, Anthony. *99 Novels.* 1984. LSummit. 1st ed. F/F. L3. $65.00

BURGESS, Gelett. *Goops & How To Be Them.* ca 1900. Stokes. 26th prt. 4to. ils. yel/blk decor red cloth. VG. S10. $125.00

BURGESS, J. Tom. *Hist Warwickshire. Its Legendary Lore...Episodes.* 1876. London. 1st ed. 12mo. ils. 407 p. gilt bl cloth. VG. H3. $15.00

BURGESS, James A. *Burgess, Mullins, Browning, Brn & Allied Families.* 1978. Parsons, WV. 1st ed. 262 p. bl cloth. VG. D7. $22.50

BURGESS, Thornton W. *Adventures of Buster Bear.* 1916. Little Brn. 1st ed. ils Harrison Cady/6 pls. gray cloth. VG. M5. $42.00

BURGESS, Thornton W. *Adventures of Grandfather Frog.* 1946. Little Brn. inscr. ils Harrison Cady. VG/VG. D1. $185.00

BURGESS, Thornton W. *Adventures of Jimmy Skunk.* 1927. Little Brn. decor brds. VG. P3. $12.50

BURGESS, Thornton W. *Bedtime Story Calendar.* 1915. Volland. 1st ed. 52 stories. NF/stiff wrp/worn orig box. M5. $145.00

BURGESS, Thornton W. *Burgess Animal Book for Children.* 1920. Little Brn. ils LA Fuertes. 1st ed. 363 p. VG. A3. $25.00

BURGESS, Thornton W. *Digger the Badger Decides To Stay.* 1927. Whitman. ils Harrison Cady. VG. M5. $38.00

BURGESS, Thornton W. *Jerry Muskrat at Home.* nd. Grosset Dunlap. decor brds. VG. P3. $10.00

BURGESS, Thornton W. *Old Mother W Wind.* 1990. Holt. 1st ed. VG/VG. L1. $18.50

BURGESS, Thornton W. *Reddy Fox.* 1946. Little Brn. inscr. ils Harrison Cady. VG/VG. D1. $185.00

BURGESS, Thornton W. *Tommy & the Wishing Stone.* 1922 (1921). Little Brn. 109 p. gr cloth/pict label. VG. M20. $45.00

BURGESS, Thornton W. *While the Story-Log Burns.* 1938. Little Brn. 1st ed. ils Palmer/8 pls. 195 p. VG/dj. D1. $150.00

BURGTORF, Frances D. *Chief Wawatam: Story of a Hand-Bomber.* 1976. private prt. A16. $40.00

BURKARD, Michael. *Fictions From the Self.* 1988. NY. 1st ed. sgn. F/F. V1. $20.00

BURKE, James Lee. *Blk Cherry Blues.* 1989. Boston. ARC. 1st ed. sgn. F/wrp. A11. $65.00

BURKE, James Lee. *Blk Cherry Blues.* 1989. Little Brn. 1st ed. F/F. F4. $30.00

BURKE, James Lee. *Convict.* 1985. Baton Rouge. 1st ed/wrp issue. sgn. F. A11. $110.00

BURKE, James Lee. *Convict.* 1990. Boston. 2nd ed. presentation/sgn. F/8vo wrp. A11. $45.00

BURKE, James Lee. *Dixie City Jam.* 1994. Hyperion. 1st ed. sgn. F/F. F4. $25.00

BURKE, James Lee. *Half of Paradise.* 1966. NY. 1st ed. sgn. VG+/wrp. A11. $85.00

BURKE, James Lee. *Heaven's Prisoners.* (1988). Holt. 1st ed. sgn. F/F. B4. $85.00

BURKE, James Lee. *James Lee Burke Collection.* 1993. London. 1st ed/PBO. F/unread. A11. $75.00

BURKE, James Lee. *Lay Down My Sword & Shield.* 1971. Crowell. 1st ed. author's 3rd novel. F/NF. L3. $1,250.00

BURKE, James Lee. *Lost Get-Back Boogie.* 1986. Baton Rouge. 1st ed. sgn. F/F. A11. $125.00

BURKE, James Lee. *Neon Rain.* 1987. Holt. ARC of 1st ed. sgn. RS. F/dj. S5. $95.00

BURKE, James Lee. *Neon Rain.* 1987. Holt. 1st ed. F/F. Q1. $75.00

BURKE, James Lee. *Stained Wht Radiance.* 1992. Hyperion. ARC. author's 5th novel. NF/wrp. Q1. $50.00

BURKE, James Lee. *Stained Wht Radiance.* 1992. NY. Hyperion. 1st ed. 5th of Robicheaux series. F/F. M15. $30.00

BURKE, James Lee. *To the Bright & Shining Sun.* 1970. Scribner. 1st ed. author's 2nd novel. F/NF. M15. $800.00

BURKE, James Lee. *To the Bright & Shining Sun.* 1992. James Cahill. 1st ed. 1/400. sgn Burke/Servello. F/slipcase. B9/Q1. $125.00

BURKE, James Lee. *Two for TX.* 1992. James Cahill. 1st hc ed. 1/400. sgn Burke/Servello. F/slipcase. Q1. $125.00

BURKE, James Lee. *TX City, 1947.* 1992. Northridge. Lord John. 1/275. sgn. F/dj. B9. $75.00

BURKE, James Lee. *Winter Light.* 1992. Huntington Beach. James Cahill. 1/26. sgn Burke/Parks. leather. fld box. Q1. $250.00

BURKE, Jonathan. *Alien Landscapes.* 1955. Mus Pr. xl. VG. P3. $10.00

BURKE, Kathleen. *Wht Road to Verdun.* 1916. Doran. 1st ed. 12mo. G. A8. $10.00

BURKE, Mary Alice H. *Elizabeth Nourse: A Salon Career.* 1983. Smithsonian. 12 color pls. 280 p. stiff wrp. D2. $50.00

BURKE, Norah. *Eleven Leopards: Journey Through Jungles of Ceylon.* 1965. London. 1st ed. 8vo. 200 p. yel cloth. VG/VG. H3. $20.00

BURKE, W.S. *Official Military Hist of KS Regiments During War...* 1870. Leavenworth. Burke. octavo. modern crimson half morocco. scarce. H9. $575.00

BURKE & SMITH. *Civil War at Rio Hill: Happenings & Relics.* 1988. self pub. 1/500. sgn. as new/wrp. B10. $5.00

BURKERT, Nancy Ekholm. *Snow Wht & the 7 Dwarfs.* 1972. NY. stated 1st ed. trans Randall Jarrell. 6 double-p ils. NF/G. M5. $20.00

BURKS, Arthur J. *Blk Medicine.* 1966. Arkham. 1st ed. F/dj. M2. $60.00

BURKS & WILSON. *Chicken & the Egg.* (1955). Coward McCann. 1st ed. 8vo. 242 p. VG/VG. A2. $17.50

BURLEY, W.J. *Charles & Elizabeth.* 1979. London. Gollancz. 1st ed. F/NF. S5. $22.50

BURLEY, W.J. *Charles & Elizabeth.* 1981. Walker. 1st ed. NF/dj. P3. $12.50

BURLEY, W.J. *6th Day.* 1978. Gollancz. 1st ed. F/F. P3. $25.00

BURLINGAME, Eugene Watson. *Grateful Elephant & Other Stories From the Pali.* 1923. Yale. 1st ed. sgn. 172 p. VG. P2. $100.00

BURLINGAME, Roger. *Of Making Many Books: 100 Yrs of Reading, Writing & Pub.* 1946. Scribner. 1st ed. 8vo. 347 p. F. A2. $17.50

BURMA, John H. *Spanish-Speaking Groups in Am.* 1954. Durham. Duke. 214 p. dj. N2. $10.00

BURMAN, B.L. *Blow a Wild Bugle for Catfish Bend.* ca 1967. Taplinger. ils Alice Caddy. 120 p. VG/VG. B10. $20.00

BURNABY, John. *Belief of Christendom.* 1963. London. index. 224 p. H10. $16.50

BURNE-JONES, Georgina. *Memorials of Edward Burne-Jones.* 1904. London. Macmillan. 1st ed. 2 vols. Birdsall bdg. F. F1. $185.00

BURNETT, Frances H. *My Robin.* 1912. Stokes. 1st ed. 42 p. VG. S10. $25.00

BURNETT, Frances Hodgson. *Captain's Youngest & Piccino.* 1894. London. Warne. 1st ed. ils Reginald Birch. 183 p. G. S10. $25.00

BURNETT, Frances Hodgson. *Dolly.* 1893. London. Warne. G. A16. $15.00

BURNETT, Frances Hodgson. *Editha's Burglar.* 1888. Boston. Estes. G. A16. $7.50

BURNETT, Frances Hodgson. *Editha's Burglar. Story for Children.* 1888. Marsh. 1st Am ed/2nd state. 12mo. gilt bl cloth. VG. S10. $45.00

BURNETT, Frances Hodgson. *Giovanni & the Other.* 1892. Scribner. 1st Am ed. ils Reginald Birch. VG. S10. $55.00

BURNETT, Frances Hodgson. *Little Lord Fauntleroy.* 1899. Scribner. 8vo. 209 p. gilt pict gr cloth. VG. H3. $20.00

BURNETT, Frances Hodgson. *Little Saint Elizabeth.* 1891 (1890). Scribner. ils Reginald Birch. 146 p. VG. S10. $40.00

BURNETT, Frances Hodgson. *Racketty-Packetty House.* 1961. Dodd Mead. 1st thus ed. ils Harrison Cady. gr cloth. VG/G+. T5. $35.00

BURNETT, Frances Hodgson. *Racketty-Packetty House.* 1975. Lippincott. 1st thus ed. 60 p. VG/G. A3. $20.00

BURNETT, Frances Hodgson. *Sara Crewe.* 1922. Scribner. ils Reginald Birch. VG. E3. $20.00

BURNETT, Frances Hodgson. *Secret Garden.* 1949. Lippincott. ils Nora Unwin. 284 p. VG/G+. P2. $20.00

BURNETT, Frances Hodgson. *Two Little Pilgrims' Progress.* 1895. Scribner. 1st ed/1st prt. 191 p. VG. S10. $45.00

BURNETT, Frances Hodgson. *Wht People.* 1917. Harper. ils Elizabeth Shippen Gr. 112 p. VG+. M20. $35.00

BURNETT, Gilbert. *Hist of Reformation of the Church of Eng.* 1842. NY. Appleton. 4 vols. H10. $67.50

BURNETT, Hugh. *Face to Face.* 1964. Stein Day. sq 8vo. dj. N2. $10.00

BURNETT, Virgil. *Towers at the Edge of a World.* 1980. St Martin. 1st ed. F/F. P3. $15.00

BURNETT, W.R. *Asphalt Jungle.* 1950. London. 1st ed. 12mo. blk cloth. NF/VG+. A11. $55.00

BURNETT, W.R. *Goodbye, Chicago 1928: End of an Era.* (1981). St Martin. 1st ed. F/dj. B9. $10.00

BURNETT, W.R. *Goodhues of Sinking Creek.* 1934. London. Harper. 1st trade ed. VG/dj. B9. $125.00

BURNETT, W.R. *Roar of the Crowd.* 1964. NY. F/VG+ clip. A11. $40.00

BURNETT, Whit. *Firsts of the Famous.* 1962. NY. 1st ed. contributors' sgn. NF/wrp. A11. $45.00

BURNHAM, Clara L. *Jewel's Story Book.* 1904. Houghton. 1st ed. 343 p. VG. S10. $30.00

BURNHAM, Clara Louise. *Westpoint Wooing.* 1899. Houghton Mifflin. 12mo. G. A8. $10.00

BURNHAM, Louis. *Behind the Lynching of Emmet Louis Till.* 1955. Freedom Associates. 15 p. wrp. A7. $17.00

BURNS, Allan. *Observations on Surgical Anatomy of the Head & Neck.* 1823. Baltimore. 1st Am ed. 10 pls. orig sheep/ rebacked. G7. $195.00

BURNS, Emile. *Handbook of Marxism.* ca 1935. Internat Pub. G. V4. $15.00

BURNS, Rex. *Avenging Angel.* 1983. Viking. 1st ed. xl. dj. P3. $5.00

BURNS, Rex. *Suicide Season.* 1987. Viking. 1st ed. sgn. F/F. S5. $35.00

BURNS, Robert. *Jolly Beggars: A Cantata by Robert Burns.* 1963. Northampton. 1/300. edit JC Weston. French marbled brds. NF/slipcase. B24. $250.00

BURNS, Robert. *Poems, Chiefly in the Scottish Dialect.* 1787. Edinburgh. 2nd (1st Edinburgh) ed. 8vo. 368 p. VG+. M1. $750.00

BURNS, Robert. *Poems, Chiefly in the Scottish Dialect.* 1799. NY. John Tiebout. 8vo. glossary. 306 p. lacks covers. M1. $375.00

BURNS, Robert. *Poems, Chiefly in the Scottish Dialect.* 1977. facsimile of 1786 Kilmarnock ed. trade pb. VG. C1. $6.50

BURNS, Robert. *Poems of...* 1965. Heritage. 1st ed. F/F slipcase. V1. $20.00

BURNS, Robert. *Works of...* 1804. Phil. Wm Fairbairn. 1st Am ed. 3 vols. contemporary polished tree calf. F. M1. $225.00

BURNS, Tex; see L'Amour, Louis.

BURNS, Walter Noble. *Tombstone: Gun-Toting, Cattle Rustling Days in AZ.* 1929. Grosset Dunlap. reprint. VG+/dj. H7. $15.00

BURNS, Walter. *Robin Hood of El Dorado.* 1932. np. 1st ed. 304 p. O7. $21.00

BURR, Agnes Ruth. *AK: Our Beautiful Northland of Opportunity.* 1919. Boston. Page. 1st ed. xl. ils/fld map. 428 p. gilt cloth. A17. $25.00

BURR, Anna Robeson. *Weir Mitchell: His Life & Letters.* 1929. Duffield. 1st ed. lg 8vo. 27 pls. VG. G1. $50.00

BURR, Eleanor. *Lakeside Lore.* (1979). Exposition Pr. 1st ed. presentation sgn. 187 p. dj. A17. $12.50

BURRITT, Elijah H. *Geog of the Heavens...* 1844. NY. Huntington Savage. ils/tables. 305 p. brn brds/leather spine. VG. S9. $15.00

BURROUGHS, Edgar Rice. *At the Earth's Core.* 1922. McClurg. 1st ed. NF. B4. $250.00

BURROUGHS, Edgar Rice. *Bandit of Hell's Bend.* 1926. London. 1st Eng ed. 254 p. cloth. D3. $35.00

BURROUGHS, Edgar Rice. *Beasts of Tarzan.* 1917. Burt. NF/rpr. M2. $75.00

BURROUGHS, Edgar Rice. *Carson of Venus.* 1939. ERB. 1st ed. F/NF. M2. $350.00

BURROUGHS, Edgar Rice. *Cave Girl.* 1925. Grosset Dunlap. VG. N2. $10.00

BURROUGHS, Edgar Rice. *Chessmen of Mars.* 1922. McClurg. 1st ed. VG. P3. $75.00

BURROUGHS, Edgar Rice. *Deputy Sheriff of Comanche County.* 1940. ERB. 1st ed. ils John Coleman Burroughs. F/NF. Q1. $500.00

BURROUGHS, Edgar Rice. *ERB Lib of Ils. Vol 2.* 1976. Russ Cochran. 1st ed. F. P3. $150.00

BURROUGHS, Edgar Rice. *Escape on Venus.* 1946. ERB. 1st ed. F/NF. M2. $150.00

BURROUGHS, Edgar Rice. *Eternal Lover.* 1926. Grosset Dunlap. VG. P3. $35.00

BURROUGHS, Edgar Rice. *Girl From Hollywood.* 1923. Macaulay. 1st ed. F. P3. $200.00

BURROUGHS, Edgar Rice. *Gods of Mars.* 1918. Chicago. McClurg. 1st ed. VG. B4. $225.00

BURROUGHS, Edgar Rice. *Jungle Tales of Tarzan.* 1919. Chicago. McClurg. 1st ed. later issue gr bdg. NF. B4. $100.00

BURROUGHS, Edgar Rice. *Jungle Tales of Tarzan.* 1919. McClurg. VG/color Canon dj. M2. $45.00

BURROUGHS, Edgar Rice. *Jungle Tales of Tarzan.* 1921. Grosset Dunlap. VG. P3. $30.00

BURROUGHS, Edgar Rice. *Lad & the Lion.* 1938. ERB. 1st ed. NF/NF. Q1. $750.00

BURROUGHS, Edgar Rice. *Lad & the Lion.* 1964. Canaveral. VG/VG. P3. $60.00

BURROUGHS, Edgar Rice. *Llana of Gathol.* 1948. ERB. 1st ed. F/dj. M2. $145.00

BURROUGHS, Edgar Rice. *Llana of Gathol.* 1948. ERB. 1st ed. VG-/dj. P3. $75.00

BURROUGHS, Edgar Rice. *Lost on Venus.* 1935. ERB. 1st ed. VG/VG. M2. $375.00

BURROUGHS, Edgar Rice. *Monster Men.* 1962. Canaveral. VG/dj. P3. $50.00

BURROUGHS, Edgar Rice. *Moon Men.* 1962. Canaveral. NF/dj. P3. $50.00

BURROUGHS, Edgar Rice. *Pellucidar.* 1935. Methuen. 3rd ed. VG. P3. $20.00

BURROUGHS, Edgar Rice. *Pirates of Venus.* 1934. ERB. 1st ed. ils J Allen St Jonn. NF/NF. Q1. $600.00

BURROUGHS, Edgar Rice. *Pirates of Venus.* 1962. Canaveral. NF/dj. P3. $60.00

BURROUGHS, Edgar Rice. *Swords of Mars.* 1936. ERB. 1st ed. NF/tape rpr. M2. $350.00

BURROUGHS, Edgar Rice. *Tale of 3 Planets.* 1964. Canaveral. 1st ed. F/dj. P3. $75.00

BURROUGHS, Edgar Rice. *Tanar of Pellucidar.* 1931. Grosset Dunlap. F/color Canon dj. M2. $40.00

BURROUGHS, Edgar Rice. *Tarzan & the Golden Lion.* 1923. McClurg. 1st ed/1st state. G. M18. $100.00

BURROUGHS, Edgar Rice. *Tarzan & the Jewels of Opar.* 1918. McClurg. 1st ed. F. M18. $125.00

BURROUGHS, Edgar Rice. *Tarzan & the Jewels of Opar.* 1919. McClurg. 2nd ed. VG. P3. $90.00

BURROUGHS, Edgar Rice. *Tarzan & the Leopard Men.* 1935. ERB. 1st ed. NF/NF. Q1. $600.00

BURROUGHS, Edgar Rice. *Tarzan & the Lost Empire.* 1931. Grosset Dunlap. VG/torn. P3. $30.00

BURROUGHS, Edgar Rice. *Tarzan of the Apes.* 1914. Chicago. McClurg. 1st ed. 1st Tarzan book. 400 p. marbled ep. Sutcliffe bdg. F. H5. $1,800.00

BURROUGHS, Edgar Rice. *Tarzan of the Apes.* 1914. NY. AL Burt. G. E3. $12.00

BURROUGHS, Edgar Rice. *Tarzan of the Apes.* 1988. Avenel. 1st ed. F/F. P3. $15.00

BURROUGHS, Edgar Rice. *Tarzan's Quest.* 1936. ERG. 1st ed. VG+/NF. Q1. $750.00

BURROUGHS, Edgar Rice. *Tarzan the Untamed.* 1920. Chicago. McClurg. 1st ed. NF. B4. $250.00

BURROUGHS, Edgar Rice. *Tarzan the Untamed.* 1920. McClurg. 1st ed. G. M18. $100.00

BURROUGHS, Edgar Rice. *Thuvia Maid of Mars.* 1920. Chicago. McClurg. 1st ed. VG. B4. $150.00

BURROUGHS, Edgar Rice. *Warlord of Mars.* 1919. McClurg. Currey State A. F. B5. $300.00

BURROUGHS, Edgar Rice. *Warlord of Mars.* 1919. McClurg. 1st ed/1st state (WF Hall on copyright p). VG. P3. $100.00

BURROUGHS, Edgar Rice. *Warlords of Mars.* 1919. McClurg. VG/color Canon dj. M2. $150.00

BURROUGHS, Edgar Rice. *Wizard of Venus.* nd (1970). NY. Ace. true 1st ed/PBO. F/unread wrp ils Krenkel. A11. $30.00

BURROUGHS, John. *Complete Writings of...* 1924. NY. Wise. 23 vols. sm 8vo. blk buckram. NF/djs. B20. $185.00

BURROUGHS, John. *Wake Robin.* 1879 (1876). Houghton Osgood. 2nd ed. 252 p. gilt gr cloth. VG. M20. $15.00

BURROUGHS, Raymond. *Peninsular Country.* (1965). Grand Rapids. 1st ed. 173 p. dj. A17. $10.00

BURROUGHS, Richard. *Treatise on Trigonometry & Navigation.* 1807. Middlebury, VG. 1st ed. full calf. E5. $245.00

BURROUGHS, William S. *Adding Machine. Collected Essays.* 1985. London. Calder. F/wrp. B2. $30.00

BURROUGHS, William S. *AH Pook Is Here & Other Texts.* 1979. London. Calder. 1st ed. NF/wrp. B2. $25.00

BURROUGHS, William S. *Big Table 1.* 1959. Chicago. sgn. VG/wrp. A11. $50.00

BURROUGHS, William S. *Blade Runner (A Movie).* 1979. Berkeley. Bl Wind. 1st ed. sgn. F/wrp. B2. $60.00

BURROUGHS, William S. *Book of the Breething.* 1980. Bl Wind. 2nd ed. 1/175 hc. sgn/#d. F/sans. B2. $100.00

BURROUGHS, William S. *Cities of the Red Night.* 1981. HRW. 1st ed. NF/NF. A14. $30.00

BURROUGHS, William S. *Cobble Stone Gardens.* 1976. Cherry Valley. 1st ed. sgn. F/wrp. B2. $75.00

BURROUGHS, William S. *Electronic Revolution.* 1971. Cambridge. Blackmoor. 1/500. ils Gysin. NF/wrp. B2. $200.00

BURROUGHS, William S. *Four Horsemen of the Apocalypse.* 1984. Bonn. Expanded Media Eds. bilingual text/1st thus ed. F/wrp. B2. $25.00

BURROUGHS, William S. *Interzone.* (1989). Viking. 1st prt. F/F. A7. $18.00

BURROUGHS, William S. *Interzone.* 1989. Viking/Penguin. 1st ed. edit James Grauerholz. F/F. A14. $25.00

BURROUGHS, William S. *Letters of William S Burroughs 1945-59.* 1993. Viking. AP. F/wrp. B2. $65.00

BURROUGHS, William S. *Nova Express.* 1964. Grove. 1st ed. F/NF. B2. $60.00

BURROUGHS, William S. *Nova Express.* 1965. Blk Cat. 1st Am pb ed. sgn. VG+. A11. $45.00

BURROUGHS, William S. *Place of Dead Roads.* 1984. HRW. 1st ed. beige brds/brn spine. NF/NF. A14. $35.00

BURROUGHS, William S. *Queer.* 1985. Viking. 1st ed. rem mk. F/F. A7. $22.00

BURROUGHS, William S. *Queer.* 1985. NY. 1st ed. sgn Major Burroughs. F/F. A11. $60.00

BURROUGHS, William S. *Soft Machine.* 1966. Grove. 1st ed. sgn. F/NF. B2. $100.00

BURROUGHS, William S. *Time.* 1965. NY. Century. 1st ed. NF. B2. $100.00

BURROUGHS, William S. *Tornado Alley.* 1989. Cherry Valley. 1st cloth trade ed. F/sans. B2/M18. $30.00

BURROUGHS, William S. *W Lands.* 1987. Viking. 1st ed. w/invitation to pub paty. F/F. B2. $65.00

BURROUGHS, William S. *Wild Boys.* 1971. Grove. 1st ed. F/F. B2. $125.00

BURROUGHS & GYSIN. *Exterminator.* 1960. San Francisco. Auehahn Pr. 1st ed. NF/wrp. B2. $75.00

BURROW, Trigant. *Search for Man's Sanity: Selected Letters...* 1958. NY. 1st ed. 615 p. cloth. VG. G1. $22.50

BURRUS, Ernest J. *Kino & Manje: Explorers of Sonora & AZ, Their Vision...* 1971. Rome. Jesuit Hst Instit. 793 p. M O6. $125.00

BURRUS, Ernest J. *Kino & the Cartography of NW New Spain.* 1965. Tucson. AZ Pioneers Hist Soc. 1/750. 17 maps. gilt red cloth. M. O6. $350.00

BURT, William H. *Mammals of MI.* 1954. MI U. revised ed. 13 color pls. 288 p. A17. $25.00

BURTON, Bill. *Sportman's Encyclopedia.* (1971). NY. 4to. 638 p. dj. A17. $17.50

BURTON, C.M. *Chapter in Hist of Cleveland.* 1895. Detroit. facsimile. VG/prt wrp. B18. $75.00

BURTON, Eva. *Your Unseen Forces.* 1936. Putnam. 1st ed. 8vo. 295 p. VG/fair. F2. $15.00

BURTON, G.W. *Burton's Book on CA.* 1909. LA. 3 vols in 1. royal 8vo. worn bdg. T3. $19.00

BURTON, Jean. *Lydia Pinkham Is Her Name.* 1949. NY. Farrar Straus. 1st ed. 12mo. 279 p. VG/dj. V3. $16.00

BURTON, John Hill. *Narratives From Criminal Trials in Scotland.* 1852. Chapman Hall. 1st ed. 2 vols. VG. G1. $100.00

BURTON, Miles. *Hardway Diamond Mystery.* 1930. Mystery League. 1st ed. VG. P3. $20.00

BURTON, Richard Francis. *Book of the Sword.* 1884. London. 1st ed. lg octavo. gilt full blk morocco. NF. H5. $1,250.00

BURTON, Robert. *Anatomy of Melancholy.* 1836. Phil. T Wardle. 1st Am ed from 13th Eng ed. 2 vols. purple cloth. box. R3. $1,500.00

BURTON, Robert. *Anatomy of Melancholy...* 1800. London. 2 vols. later 19th-century bdg. G7. $295.00

BURTON, Virginia Lee. *Little House.* (1942). Weekly Reader BC. 22nd prt. 40 p. VG-. T5. $15.00

BURTON & DRAKE. *Unexplored Syria. Visits to the Libanus...* 1872. London. 1st ed. 2 vols 8vo. new polished half morocco. F. O2. $875.00

BURY, G.W. *Arabia Infelix; or, Turks in Yamen.* 1915. London. 1st ed. 8vo. 213 p. cloth. O2. $125.00

BURY, J.B. *Hist of Greece to the Death of Alexander the Great.* 1955. London. Macmillan. not 1st ed. 925 p. blk cloth. NF. B22. $7.50

BURY, J.B. *Hist of Greece.* (1951). Macmillan. revised ed. 925. dj. A7. $20.00

BUSBEY, L. White. *Uncle Joe Cannon: Story of Pioneer American.* 1927. Holt. 1st ed. 8vo. 362 p. red brds. B11. $35.00

BUSBY, F.M. *Long View.* 1976. Berkley Putnam. 1st ed. F/F. P3. $17.50

BUSBY, F.M. *Long View.* 1976. Berkley Putnam. 1st ed. F/NF. N3. $15.00

BUSCAGLIA, Leo. *Fall of Freddie the Leaf.* 1982. HRW. G. A16. $4.00

BUSCEMA & LEE. *Silver Surfer.* 1988. Marvel. 1st ed. F/F. F4. $20.00

BUSCH, Frederick. *Closing Arguments.* 1991. Tichnor Fields. 1st ed/review copy. w/promo materials. F/F. A7. $40.00

BUSCH, Frederick. *I Wanted a Year Without Fall.* 1971. London. hc ed. author's 1st book. F/NF. A11. $55.00

BUSCH, William. *Max & Maurice: A Juvenile Hist.* 1871. Boston. Roberts Bros. 1st Am ed. octavo. 56 p. cloth. NF. B24. $250.00

BUSCHING, Anton Friedrich. *New System of Geography.* 1762. London. Millar. 6 vols. quarto. 36 maps. dk gr leather w/red labels. NF. O6. $1,750.00

BUSH, Barney. *Inherit the Blood.* 1985. Thunder Mouth. 1st ed. ils by an Oneida artist. F/wrp. L3. $30.00

BUSH, Barney. *Petroglyphs.* 1982. Greenfield Review. 1st ed. ils Meenjip Tatsii. F/wrp. L3. $35.00

BUSH, Christopher. *Case of the Prodigal Daughter.* 1969. Macmillan. 1st ed. F/clip. F4. $16.00

BUSH, Christopher. *Case of the Triple Twist.* 1958. Macmillan. 1st ed. VG/G. P3. $30.00

BUSH, Christopher. *Case of the Tudor Queen.* 1983. Holt. 1st ed. VG/dj. F4. $28.00

BUSHNELL, David I. Jr. *Friedrich Kurz, Artist-Explorer.* 1928. GPO. 8vo. removed from annual report. F. P4. $22.50

BUSHNELL, G.H.S. *Peru.* 1957. Praeger. 1st ed. 207 p. dj. F3. $20.00

BUSHNELL, Henry. *Hist of Granville...* 1889. Columbus. 1st ed. 372 p. orig cloth. VG. D7. $125.00

BUSHNELL, Horace. *Nature & the Supernatural.* 1858. Scribner. 1st ed. 528 p. H10. $20.00

BUTLER, Arthur G. *Birds of Great Britain.* ca 1908. Hull. Brumby Clark. ils Gronvold/Frohawk. 2 vols. NF. K1. $375.00

BUTLER, Benjamin. *Butler's Book.* 1892. Boston. 1st ed. tall 8vo. 1154 p. bl cloth. G. T3. $39.00

BUTLER, E.P. *Incubator Baby.* 1906. Funk Wagnall. 12mo. 111 p. VG. S10. $30.00

BUTLER, E.P. *Pigs Is Pigs.* 1907. McClure Phillips. 6th imp. 37 p. cloth. VG-. A3. $7.00

BUTLER, Gwendoline. *Coffin in Fashion.* 1987. London. Collins. ARC. RS. F/F. S5. $25.00

BUTLER, Gwendoline. *Coffin on the Water.* 1986. London. Collins. 1st ed. F/F. S5. $22.50

BUTLER, Gwendoline. *Cracking Open a Coffin.* 1993. St Martin. 1st Am ed. sgn. F/F. M10. $30.00

BUTLER, Mrs. John Wesley. *Hist Churches in Mexico.* 1915. NY. 12mo. ils. 255 p. gilt gr cloth. F. H3. $15.00

BUTLER, Octavia E. *Dawn.* 1987. Warner. 1st ed. F/F. N3. $20.00

BUTLER, Octavia E. *Wild Seed.* 1980. Doubleday. 1st ed. F/dj. P3. $30.00

BUTLER, Octavia E. *Xenogenesis.* 1989. Guild Am. 1st compilation ed. F/F. F4. $10.00

BUTLER, Ragan. *Capt Nash & the Wroth Inheritance.* 1976. St Martin. 1st ed. F/F. F4. $20.00

BUTLER, Robert Olen. *Countrymen of Bones.* 1983. Horizon. 1st ed. sgn. F/NF. L3. $150.00

BUTLER, Robert Olen. *Deuce.* (1989). Simon Schuster. 1st ed. F/dj. B4. $45.00

BUTLER, Robert Olen. *Good Scent From a Strange Mtn.* 1992. Holt. 1st ed. F/F. Q1. $40.00

BUTLER, Robert Olen. *On Distant Ground.* 1985. Knopf. 1st ed. rem mk. F/F. A7. $30.00

BUTLER, Robert Olen. *On Distant Ground.* 1985. Knopf. 1st ed. sgn. F/F. B2. $75.00

BUTLER, Robert Olen. *Wabash.* 1987. Knopf. 1st ed. sgn. author's 5th novel. F/NF. L3. $100.00

BUTLER, Samuel. *Atlas of Ancient Geography.* 1851. Longman Gr. 22 hinged double-p maps/4 half-p maps. VG+. O6. $250.00

BUTLER, William. *Tulsa 75: Hist of Tulsa.* 1974. Tulsa, OK. ils 288 p. G/dj. B18. $17.50

BUTLER & KENT. *Jo Ann Tomboy.* 1933. Houghton Mifflin. 1st ed. ils Ruth King. VG/VG. B4. $85.00

BUTLER & TRUBSHAW. *Carrickmacross Lace, From Beginner to Expert.* 1990. np. ils. cloth. G2. $35.00

BUTLIN. *Butlin Holiday Book 1949-50.* nd. (1949). London. Butlin Ltd. annual ed. 8vo. 256 p. VG+/VG+. A2. $12.50

BUTTERFIELD, C.W. *Hist Account of Expedition Against Sandusky...1782.* 1873. Cincinnati. 1st ed. 403 p. orig cloth. VG. D7. $175.00

BUTTERFIELD, Herbert. *Christianity & Hist.* ca 1950. NY. Scribner. 146 p. H10. $10.00

BUTTERFIELD, Herbert. *Christianity & Hist.* 1949. London. Bell. 1st ed. VG/dj. G1. $22.50

BUTTERFIELD, Martha Dinwiddie. *1st Lady: My 30 Days Upstairs in the Wht House.* 1964. NY. 1st ed. photos. 288 p. VG/dj. B18. $22.50

BUTTERICK PATTERN COMPANY. *Butterick Sewing Book. Ready, Set, Sew.* 1971. np. ils. cloth. G2. $8.00

BUTTERICK PATTERN COMPANY. *Vogue Fitting.* 1984. np. ils. cloth. G2. $18.00

BUTTERICK PATTERN COMPANY. *Vogue Sewing.* 1982. np. ils. cloth. G2. $37.50

BUTTERWORTH, Hezekiah. *In Old New Eng.* 1895. NY. 1st ed. 281 p. emb cloth. F. A17. $12.50

BUTTERWORTH, Hezekiah. *True to His Home.* 1897. np. 1st ed. ils H Winthrop Peirce. F. M18. $30.00

BUTTERWORTH, J. *New Concordance & Dictionary to Holy Scriptures.* 1811. NY. 8vo. full leather. VG. T3. $39.00

BUXTON, Aubrey. *King in His Country.* 1955. Longman Gr. 1st ed. ils. 139 p. VG/dj. M20. $9.50

BUXTON, Bessie Raymond. *Begonias.* 1939. Lexington. MA Horitculture Soc. 1st ed. 123 p. VG. B28. $15.00

BUYER, Kathryn Stripling. *Wildwood Flower.* 1992. LA State U. 1st ed. w/Academy of Am Poets card. F/F. V1. $20.00

BYARS, Betsy. *After the Goat Man.* 1974. Viking. 1st ed. 8vo. 126 p. yel brds. VG/G+. T5. $25.00

BYARS, Betsy. *House of Wings.* 1972. Viking. 1st ed. 8vo. 142 p. F. T5. $25.00

BYARS, Betsy. *Summer of the Swans.* (1970). Viking. 3rd prt. 8vo. 142 p. lavender cloth. VG/G. T5. $25.00

BYGRAVE, Hilary. *Is There a Future Life?* ca 1870s. Toronto. Hunter Rose. 8 p. sewn. H10. $15.00

BYINGTON, Eloise. *Wishbone Children.* 1934. Whitman. 1st ed. 64 p. VG/G. P2. $18.00

BYLLESBY, Langdon. *Observations on Sources & Effects of Unequal Wealth...* 1826. NY. Nichols. 1st ed. 12mo. 167 p. orig brds. VG. M1. $2,000.00

BYNNER, Witter. *New Poems.* 1960. np. later ed. NF/G. V1. $10.00

BYRD, Ann. *Narratives, Pious Meditations, & Religious Exercises of...* 1843. Phil. J Richard. 1st ed. 24mo. 127 p. cloth. V3. $25.00

BYRD, Richard E. *Alone.* 1938. Putnam. 1st ed. inscr. w/sgn photo. NF/NF. Q1. $125.00

BYRD, Richard E. *Discovery: Story of 2nd Byrd Antarctic Expedition.* 1935. Putnam. 1st ed. sgn. VG. E3. $50.00

BYRD, Richard E. *Little Am: Aerial Exploration in the Antarctic.* 1930. Putnam. 1st ed. sgn. VG. E3. $50.00

BYRD, William. *My Ladye Nevells Booke.* 1926. Curwen. ltd ed. 1/60. ils. 245 p. NF/orig Curwen dj. B24. $375.00

BYRNE & SAYERS. *Busman's Honeymoon: Detective Comedy in 3 Acts.* 1937. London. Gollancz. 1st ed. F/clip. M15. $450.00

BYRON, George Gordon. *Child Harold's Pilgrimage: Canto the 3rd.* 1816. London. 1st ed/2nd issue. orig wrp. E3. $100.00

BYRON, George Gordon. *Don Juan.* 1824. London. Davison. 1st ed. complete in 6 vols. w/sgn letter & ES. H5. $4,500.00

BYRON, George Gordon. *Mazeppa, a Poem.* 1819. London. Murray. 1st ed/2nd issue. Zaehnsdorf dk gr calf. H5. $750.00

BYRON, Lord; see Byron, George Gordon.

BYRON & RICE. *Birth of W Painting.* 1931. NY. 1/365. 94 pls. teal linen/leather spine label. B30. $225.00

BYRON & WELDING. *Bluesland.* 1991. Dutton. 1st ed. rem mk. F/F. B2. $25.00

CABELL, James Branch. *As I Remember It: Some Epilogues in Recollection*. 1955. McBridge. G+/poor. N2. $7.50

CABELL, James Branch. *Cream of the Jest*. 1917. McBride. 1st ed. VG-. P3. $35.00

CABELL, James Branch. *Jewel Merchants*. 1921. NY. McBride. 1/1040. G+. A1. $45.00

CABELL, James Branch. *Jurgen*. 1921. London. Bodley Head. 1/3000. ils Pape. G+. A1. $75.00

CABELL, James Branch. *Jurgen*. 1949. London. 1/100. w/extra pl. Sutcliffe bdg. VG/buckram slipcase. H5. $750.00

CABELL, James Branch. *Something About Eve*. 1927. McBride. 1st ed. 1/850. sgn/#d. VG+. C1. $75.00

CABELL, James Branch. *Something About Eve*. 1927. NY. 1/850. sgn. VG-. A1. $65.00

CABELL, James Branch. *Soul of Melicent*. 1913. Stokes. ils H Pyle. G+. A1. $150.00

CABELL, James Branch. *Straws & Prayer Books*. 1924. NY. McBride. 1/330. sgn. A1. $75.00

CABELL, James Branch. *Taboo*. 1921. NY. McBride. 1/920. 1st ed. G+. A1. $30.00

CABLE, George W. *Negro Question*. 1958. Doubleday Anchor. PBO. correct 1st ed/1958 at foot on title p. NF. A11. $15.00

CABLE, Mary. *Little Darlings: Hist of Child Rearing in Am*. 1975. Scribner. 1st ed. 214 p. ochre cloth. VG/dj. G1. $27.50

CABOT, Robert. *Joshua Tree*. 1970. Atheneum. 12mo. F/VG. A8. $10.00

CABRAL, Olga. *7 Sneezes*. 1948. Simon Schuster. Little Golden #51. A ed. 42 p. VG-. A3. $8.50

CABRIES, Jean. *Jacob*. 1957. London. 1st Eng ed of Saint Jacob. trans from French. NF/VG+. A14. $25.00

CACCIA, Angela. *Beyond Lake Titicaca*. (1969). London. Hodder. 1st ed. 221 p. dj. F3. $15.00

CACHIN, Marcel. *Science & Religion*. (1946). NY. Internat. 32 p. wrp. A7. $10.00

CADBURY, Henry J. *Friendly Heritage: Letters From the Quaker Past*. 1972. Norwalk, CT. Silvermine. 8vo. 342 p. VG/VG. V3. $30.00

CADBURY, Henry J. *Peril of Modernizing Jesus*. 1937. Macmillan. 1st ed. xl. 12mo. 216 p. worn. V3. $10.00

CADILLAC & LIETTE. *W Country in the 17th Century, Memoirs of...* 1947. Chicago. Lakeside Classic. 181 p. teg. VG. B18. $35.00

CADY, Harrison. *Holiday Time on Butterfly Hill*. 1929. Whitman. 1st ed. 24mo. detached. G. D1. $60.00

CADY, Harrison. *Jack Frost Arrives on Butternut Hill*. 1929. Whitman. 1st ed. 12mo. F/F. D1. $75.00

CADY, Harrison. *Raggedy Animals*. 1935. Rand McNally. 62 p. G+. A3. $25.00

CADY, Jack. *Man Who Could Make Things Vanish*. 1983. NY. Arbor House. 1st ed. F/VG+. N3. $30.00

CADY, Jack. *Well*. 1980. Arbor. 1st ed. inscr/sgn. F/F. F4. $60.00

CADY, Jack. *Well*. 1980. Arbor. 1st ed. VG/dj. P3. $35.00

CADY, John F. *SE Asia: Its Hist Development*. (1964). McGraw Hill. 6th prt. VG+/dj. A7. $12.00

CADY, Mrs. H.N. *Hist of New Eng. In Words of 1 Syllable*. 1888. Chicago. 1st ed. 208 p. gilt dk bl cloth. G. H3. $15.00

CAEN, Herb. *Bagdad-by-the-Bay*. 1949. Doubleday. 12mo. G. A8. $12.00

CAESAR, C. *Ivlii Caesaris Quae Extent*. 1635. Ex Officina Elzeviriana. 2nd prt. 12mo. 3 fld maps. aeg. full bl morocco. B20. $385.00

CAGE, John. *M Writings '67-'72*. 1973. Middleton, CT. Wesleyan. 1st ed. wht stp blk cloth. F/VG. F1. $40.00

CAGE, John. *X Writings '79-'82*. 1983. Middleton, CT. Wesleyan. 1st ed. sq 8vo. gilt blk cloth. F/dj. F1. $40.00

CAHILL, Tim. *Road Fever: High-Speed Travelogue*. (1991). Random. 1st ed. 8vo. 278 p. F/F. A2. $12.50

CAHILL & STEAMER. *Constitution: Cases & Comments*. 1959. NY. Ronald Pr. M11. $20.00

CAHN, Herman. *Collapse of Capitalism*. ca 1918. Chicago. CH Kerr. fair. V4. $10.00

CAHN, William. *Einstein: Pict Biography*. 1955. Citadel. 1st ed. sm 4to. 127 p. VG/poor. S3. $28.00

CAHOON, Herbert. *Brief Account of the Clifton Waller Barrett Lib*. 1960. VA U. sgn U VA president. 35 p. B10. $10.00

CAIDIN, Martin. *Everything But the Flak*. (1964). NY. 1st ed. ils. 204 p. VG/dj. B18. $47.50

CAIDIN, Martin. *Thunderbirds!* 1968. Dutton. 1st prt revised/enlarged ed. 8vo. 269 p. VG+/VG+. A2. $15.00

CAIMI, Giulio. *Karaghiozi ou La Comedie Grecque dans l'Ame du Theatre...* 1935. Athens. sm 4to. 176 p. prt wrp. O2. $35.00

CAIN, James M. *Baby in the Icebox & Other Short Fiction*. (1981). Holt. 1st ed. NF/dj. B9. $15.00

CAIN, James M. *Baby in the Icebox*. 1981. HRW. 1st trade ed. 312 p. F/F. S9. $18.00

CAIN, James M. *Butterfly*. 1947. Knopf. 1st ed. F/dj. B9. $35.00

CAIN, James M. *Cain X 3*. 1969. Knopf. 1st ed. VG/dj. P3. $20.00

CAIN, James M. *Career in C Major & Other Stories*. 1945. Avon. PBO. Modern Short Story Monthly series. VG+. A11. $55.00

CAIN, James M. *Cloud Nine*. 1984. Mysterious. 1st ed. F/dj. P3. $17.50

CAIN, James M. *Double Indemnity*. 1943. Avon. PBO. Murder Mystery Monthly series. F. A11. $110.00

CAIN, James M. *Galatea*. 1953. Knopf. 1st ed. F/NF. F4. $65.00

CAIN, James M. *Galatea*. 1953. NY. NF/VG+. A11. $60.00

CAIN, James M. *Love's Lovely Counterfeit*. 1942. NY. 1st ed. Adrian Goldstone's copy. VG+/VG+. A11. $85.00

CAIN, James M. *Mignon*. (1963). London. Robert Hale. 1st ed. VG/dj. B9. $20.00

CAIN, James M. *Moth*. 1948. Knopf. 1st ed. NF/dj. B9. $30.00

CAIN, James M. *Postman Always Rings Twice*. ca 1946. Grosset Dunlap. photoplay ed. NF/VG+. A11. $45.00

CAIN, James M. *Postman Always Rings Twice*. 1946. Knopf. 11th prt. VG. P3. $15.00

CAIN, Paul. *Seven Slayers*. 1946. Hollywood. St Enterprises. PBO. VG. A11. $165.00

CAIN, Paul. *Seven Slayers*. 1988. Eng. No Exit Pr. 1st British ed. F/F. S5. $35.00

CAINE, Lou S. *N Am Fresh-Water Sport Fish*. (1949). NY. 1st ed. 212 p. VG. A17. $14.50

CAIRNS, Huntington. *Two-Story World: Selected Writings of James K Feibleman*. 1966. HRW. 520 p. VG+/VG. S3. $20.00

CAIRNS. *Contemporary Quilting Techniques: Modular Approach*. 1991. np. ils. cloth. G2. $25.00

CAKE, Patrick. *Pro-Am Murders*. 1979. Aptos, CA. Proteus. 1st ed. ils. F/F. M15. $45.00

CALABI, Silvio. *Trout & Salmon of the World.* (1990). Secaucus. sq 4to. 228 p. M/dj. A17. $29.50

CALAHAN, H.A. *Learning To Race.* 1948. Macmillan. later prt. 319 p. VG. M8. $25.00

CALAS, Nicolas. *Bloodflames 1947.* 1947. NY Hugo Gallery. NF/wrp. B2. $65.00

CALAS, Nicolas. *Confound the Wise.* 1942. Arrow. 1st ed. F/tape rpr dj. B2. $100.00

CALASSO, Roberto. *Marriage of Cadmus & Harmony.* 1993. Knopf. ARC. trans Tim Parks. F/F. Q1. $40.00

CALDECOTT, Randolph. *Farmer's Boy.* 1881. Routledge. 1st ed. 7 full-p color ils. VG. D1. $55.00

CALDECOTT, Randolph. *Mrs Mary Blaize: Elegy on Glory of Her Sex.* nd. Routledge. VG/wrp. P2. $75.00

CALDER, A. *Three Young Rats & Other Rhymes.* 1944. NY. Valentin. ARC. 1/700. half cloth/ils brds. VG/rpr dj. D1. $250.00

CALDERWOOD, David. *Altare Damascenum, seu Ecclesiae Englicanae Politia...* 1708 (1623). Leyden. Boutesteyn. 4to. 782 p. contemporary calf/rebacked. K1. $225.00

CALDWELL, Erskine. *All Out on the Road to Smolensk.* 1942. Duell. 1st ed. sgn. NF/NF. B2. $175.00

CALDWELL, Erskine. *God's Little Acre.* 1948. Falcon. VG/dj. P3. $12.50

CALDWELL, Erskine. *In Search of Bisco.* (1965). FSG. stated 1st ed. 219 p. NF/dj. A7. $20.00

CALDWELL, Erskine. *Kneel to the Rising Sun & Other Stories.* 1935. Viking. 1st ed. NF/NF. B4. $250.00

CALDWELL, Erskine. *Pocket Book of Erskine Caldwell.* 1947. NY. Pocket Books. PBO. w/sgn bookplate. F/wrp. A11. $50.00

CALDWELL, Erskine. *Stories of Life N & S.* 1983. Dodd Mead. 1st ed. VG/VG. V2. $6.00

CALDWELL, Erskine. *This Very Earth.* 1948. Duell Sloan. 1st ed. VG. M18. $40.00

CALDWELL, Erskine. *Trouble in July.* 1950. NY. 1st ed. inscr. NF/NF. A11. $100.00

CALDWELL, Erskine. *Writing in Am.* 1967. Phaedra. PBO. w/sgn bookplate. NF/wrp. A11. $45.00

CALDWELL, James Fitz James. *Hist of a Brigade of S Carolinians...McGowan's Brigade.* 1866. Phil. King Baird. 1st ed. 247 p. w/addenda leaf. VG/cloth slipcase. M8. $1,000.00

CALDWELL, Joseph. *In Such Dark Places.* 1978. FSG. 1st ed. author's 1st novel. NF/NF clip. A14. $35.00

CALDWELL, Steven. *Aliens in Space.* 1979. Crescent. F/dj. P3. $7.50

CALDWELL, Taylor. *Balance Wheel.* 1951. Scribner. 1st ed. VG/dj. P3. $20.00

CALDWELL, Taylor. *Dialogues w/the Devil.* 1967. Doubleday. 1st ed. dj. N2. $6.50

CALDWELL, Taylor. *Earth Is the Lord's.* 1940. Literary Guild. G/dj. A16. $7.50

CALDWELL, Taylor. *Glory & the Lightning.* 1974. Doubleday. 1st ed. G+/dj. N2. $5.00

CALDWELL, Taylor. *Late Clara Beame.* 1963. Crime Club. 1st ed. VG/VG-. P3. $12.50

CALDWELL, Taylor. *Listener.* 1960. Doubleday. 1st ed. NF/NF. B4. $45.00

CALDWELL, Taylor. *There Was a Time.* 1947. Scribner. 1st ed. VG/dj. P3. $25.00

CALHOUN, George A. *Letters to the Rev Leonard Bacon...* 1840. Hartford. Geer. 84 p. H10. $17.50

CALHOUN, William Lowndes. *Hist of 42nd Regiment GA Volunteers, CSA.* 1900. Atlanta. 1st ed. double frontis. 45 p. NF/prt wrp. M8. $375.00

CALIFORNIA HISTORICAL SOCIETY. *Christmas in the Gold Fields, 1849.* 1959. CA Hist Soc. 12mo. VG. A8. $6.50

CALKINS, Frank. *Rocky Mtn Warden.* (1970). Knopf. 1st ed. 8vo. 266 p. A2/H7. $15.00

CALLADO, Antonio. *Quarup.* 1970. Knopf. 1st Am ed. trans Barbara Shelby. NF/NF. A14. $30.00

CALLAGHAN, Barry. *Hogg Poems & Drawings.* 1978. Ontario. Don Mills. 1st ed. presentation inscr. F/wrp. A11. $65.00

CALLAGHAN, Morley. *Strange Fugitive.* 1928. NY. ARC. RS. VG/VG. B5. $250.00

CALLAHAN, Jack. *Man's Grim Justice: My Life Outside the Law.* (1928). Chicago. Sears. 1st ed. 8vo. 296 p. F/F. A2. $25.00

CALLAHAN, R.E. *Heart of an Indian.* 1927. Frederick Hitchcock. 12mo. VG. A8. $30.00

CALLAHAN, Robert E. *Human Whirlpool.* 1946. Hollywood, CA. 1st ed. inscr. 384 p. cloth. VG. D3. $25.00

CALLOWAY, Cab. *Of Minnie the Moocher & Me.* 1976. NY. Crowell. 1st ed. F/NF. B2. $35.00

CALVERLEY, C.S. *Verses & Trans.* 1862. Cambridge. 2nd ed. G. T9. $20.00

CALVERLEY, Eleanor T. *My Arabian Days & Nights.* 1958. NY. 8vo. 182 p. cloth. O2. $25.00

CALVINO, Italo. *Castle of Crossed Destinies.* nd. Pan. pb/later prt. F. C1. $7.50

CALVINO, Italo. *If on a Winter's Night a Traveller.* 1981. Toronto. Lester & Orpen Dennys. 1st Canadian ed. NF/NF. A14. $30.00

CALVINO, Italo. *Six Memos for the Next Millenium: Charles Eliot Norton...* 1988. Cambridge. 1st ed. trans Patrick Creagh. F/F. A14. $30.00

CALVO, J.B. *Republic of Costa Rica.* 1890. Chicago. Rand McNally. 12mo. 2 fld maps 282 p. gilt maroon brds. G. B11. $85.00

CAMARA, Fernando. *Chacaltiaguis.* 1952. Mexico. 170 p. wrp. F3. $20.00

CAMDEN, John. *Hundreth Acre.* 1905. Turner. 1st ed. VG-. P3. $20.00

CAMERON, Ian. *Adventure in the Movies.* 1974. Crescent. 2nd ed. VG/G+. P3. $12.50

CAMERON, Ian. *Mtns of the Gods. Himalaya & the Mtns of Central Asia.* 1984. Oxford. Facts on File. 4to. 248 p. NF/dj. W1. $35.00

CAMERON, James. *Here Is Your Enemy.* (1966). HRW. stated 1st ed. 144 p. A7. $20.00

CAMERON, John. *Researches in Craniometry.* 1928-31. Halifax. presentation/#d 14. xl. cloth. G7. $175.00

CAMERON, Lou. *Dragon's Spine.* (1969). Avon. PBO. VG. A7. $18.00

CAMERON, Roderick. *Viceroyalties of the W.* 1968. Little Brn. 1st Am ed. 276 p. dj. F3. $20.00

CAMERON, William Bleasdell. *War Trail of Big Bear.* 1927. Boston. 1st ed. 12mo. 256 p. VG. B28. $45.00

CAMMANN. *Needlepoint Designs From Am Indian Art.* 1973. np. 20 designs. cloth. G2. $18.00

CAMP, Charles L. *New Light Shed on Mr Pegleg Smith.* nd. San Francisco. 1/200. F/prt wrp. P4. $30.00

CAMPAIGNE, Jameson G. *Check-Off: Labor Bosses & Working Men.* (1961). Chicago. Regnery. 248 p. A7. $15.00

CAMPANELLA, Roy. *It's Good To Be Alive.* 1959. Little Brn. 1st ed. VG/G+. P8. $30.00

CAMPBELL, Alex. *Unbind Your Sons.* (1970). Liveright. 366 p. NF/dj. A7. $35.00

CAMPBELL, Alice. *Veiled Murder.* 1949. Random. 1st ed. VG. P3. $10.00

CAMPBELL, B.D. *Where the High Winds Blow.* 1946. Scribner. 1st ed. 8vo. 215 p. VG/VG. A2. $15.00

CAMPBELL, Bernard. *Sexual Selection & the Descent of Man 1871-1971.* 1972. Chicago. Aldine. 1st ed. 378 p. VG/dj. G1. $35.00

CAMPBELL, Bruce. *Mystery of the Grinning Tiger.* 1956. Grosset Dunlap. lists to Gallows Cliff. 209 p. VG+/dj. M20. $30.00

CAMPBELL, Bruce. *Mystery of the Shattered Glass.* 1958. Grosset Dunlap. 1st ed. 184 p. VG+/dj. M20. $45.00

CAMPBELL, Bruce. *Secret of Skeleton Island.* 1949. Grosset Dunlap. VG. P3. $6.00

CAMPBELL, Douglas H. *Elements of Structural & Systematic Botany.* 1890. Boston. ils. 253 p. VG-. B26. $19.00

CAMPBELL, George R. *Taxidermy for the Amateur.* nd. NY. ils. 48 p. VG/wrp. A17. $7.50

CAMPBELL, H.J. *Beyond the Visible.* 1952. Hamilton. 1st ed. VG/dj. P3. $25.00

CAMPBELL, Helen. *Darkness & Daylight; or, Lights & Shadows of NY Life.* 1892. Hartford. ils. 740 p. full calf/leather spine labels. VG. A17. $25.00

CAMPBELL, J.K. *Honour, Family & Patronage.* 1964. Oxford. 8vo. 393 p. cloth. O2. $40.00

CAMPBELL, James Havelock. *McClellan: Vindication of Military Career...McClellan.* 1916. NY. Neale. 1st ed. 458 p. cloth. NF. M8. $175.00

CAMPBELL, John Lord. *Lives of Chief Justices of Eng.* 1894. Long Island. E Thomson. 5 vols. vellum/crimson brds. M11. $850.00

CAMPBELL, John W. *Astounding SF Anthology.* 1951. Simon Schuster. 1st ed. VG/torn. P3. $75.00

CAMPBELL, John W. *Blk Star Passes.* 1953. Fantasy. ltd ed. 1/500. sgn. VG/dj. M2. $200.00

CAMPBELL, John W. *Cloak of Aesir.* 1952. Shasta. 1st ed. F/NF. M2. $60.00

CAMPBELL, John W. *Collected Editorials From Analog.* 1966. Doubleday. 1st ed. VG/dj. P3. $35.00

CAMPBELL, John W. *Invaders From the Infinite.* 1951. Gnome. 1st ed. sgn. F/F. F4. $75.00

CAMPBELL, John W. *Islands of Space.* 1956. Fantasy. ltd ed. 1/50. sgn/#d. F/dj. M2. $575.00

CAMPBELL, John W. *Moon Is Hell.* 1951. Fantasy. ltd ed. 1/500. sgn/#d. F/M. M2. $200.00

CAMPBELL, John W. *Moon Is Hell.* 1951. Fantasy. 1st ed. VG-. M2. $15.00

CAMPBELL, Judith. *World of Ponies.* 1970. London. Hamlyn. 1st ed. 4to. VG/G+. O3. $25.00

CAMPBELL, Julie. *Rin Tin Tin's Rinty.* 1954. Whitman. F. P3. $25.00

CAMPBELL, Julie. *Trixie Belden & Gatehouse Mystery.* 1951. Whitman. lists 3 titles. 250 p. cloth. VG+/dj. M20. $15.00

CAMPBELL, Julie. *Trixie Belden & Mystery Off Glen Road.* 1956. Whitman. decor brds. VG+. P3. $10.00

CAMPBELL, Lang. *Dinky Ducklings.* 1928. Joliet. Volland. 1st ed. 12mo. 39 p. VG. D1. $75.00

CAMPBELL, Lyle. *Bibliography of Mayan Languages & Linguistics.* 1978. Albany, NY. Instit Mesoamerican Studies 3. 1st ed. 4to. 182 p. wrp. F3. $25.00

CAMPBELL, Mary Mason. *Betty Crocker's Kitchen Gardens.* 1971. Scribner. ils Tasha Tudor. 170 p. VG-. A3. $50.00

CAMPBELL, Paul Douglas. *Humboldt Celt.* (1992). Aegean Park Pr. 1st ed. 4to. 192 p. F3. $30.00

CAMPBELL, Ramsey. *Alice in La-La Land.* 1987. Poseidon. 1st ed. VG/dj. P3. $17.00

CAMPBELL, Ramsey. *Dark Feasts.* 1987. Robinson. 1st ed. sgn. F/F. F4. $50.00

CAMPBELL, Ramsey. *Face That Must Die.* 1983. Scream. 1st ed. 1/100. sgn. as new. M2. $450.00

CAMPBELL, Ramsey. *Hip-Deep in Alligators.* 1987. NAL. 1st ed. sgn. F/F. S5. $35.00

CAMPBELL, Ramsey. *Incarnate.* 1983. Macmillan. ARC of 1st ed. F/pict wrp. N3. $40.00

CAMPBELL, Ramsey. *Influence.* 1988. Macmillan. ARC of 1st Am ed. RS. F/F. S5. $30.00

CAMPBELL, Ramsey. *Influence.* 1988. Macmillan. 1st ed. F/F. F4. $18.00

CAMPBELL, Ramsey. *Inhabitant of the Lake.* 1964. Arkham. 1st ed. inscr. F/dj. M2. $185.00

CAMPBELL, Ramsey. *Needing Ghosts.* 1990. Century. 1st ed. 1/300. sgn/#d. aeg. deluxe bdg. F/cloth slipcase. F4. $50.00

CAMPBELL, Ramsey. *New Tales of the Cthulhu Mythos.* 1980. Arkham. 1st ed. F/dj. M2. $125.00

CAMPBELL, Ramsey. *Nibbled To Death by Ducks.* 1989. Pocket. 1st ed. F/dj. P3. $18.00

CAMPBELL, Ramsey. *Night of the Claw.* 1983. St Martin. 1st Am ed. F/NF. N3. $25.00

CAMPBELL, Ramsey. *Parasite.* 1980. Macmillan. 1st ed. sgn. F/F. F4. $30.00

CAMPBELL, Ramsey. *Scared Stiff.* 1987. Scream. 1st ed. M. M2. $25.00

CAMPBELL, Reau. *Complete Guide & Descriptive Book of Mexico.* 1899. Mexico City. 12mo. ils/fld map. 351 p. gilt grn cloth. VG. H3. $15.00

CAMPBELL, Roy. *Portugal.* 1957. London. 1st ed. F/dj. T9. $50.00

CAMPBELL, Ruth. *Cat Whose Whiskers Slipped.* 1938. Wise Parslow. ils Elizabeth Cade. VG. L1. $13.50

CAMPBELL, Ruth. *Sm Fry & the Winged Horse.* (1927). Volland. 5th ed. 128 p. VG/G. S10. $45.00

CAMPBELL, Susan. *Cottesbrooke, an Eng Garden Kitchen.* ca 1987. Topsfield. Salem House. ils. 159 p. H10. $20.00

CAMPBELL, Thomas. *Gertrude of WY: A PA Tale.* 1809. London. pub for author. 1st ed. lg 4to. ES. aeg. stp blk morocco. M1. $200.00

CAMPBELL, Tony. *Earliest Prt Maps, 1472-1500.* 1987. Berkeley. ils/69 maps. M/M. O6. $85.00

CAMPBELL, Walter S. *Book Lover's SW.* 1955. OK U. 1st ed. 287 p. VG. B19. $20.00

CAMPBELL & STARK. *2 Heads Are Better Than 1.* 1947. Detroit. 1st ed. sgn. 192 p. dj. A17. $9.50

CAMPBELL & TUDOR. *New Eng Buttry Shelf Almanac.* 1970. NY. 1st ed. VG/VG. B5. $40.00

CAMPIGLI. *Paris.* 1968. Gallerie de France. 1/1000. VG+/wrp. A1. $45.00

CAMPUZANO, A.U. *Brn Gold: Amazing Story of Coffee.* (1954). Random. 1st ed. 8vo. 237 p. VG/G. A2. $15.00

CAMUS, Albert. *Fall.* (1966). Kentfield, CA. Allen Pr. 1st ed. 1/140. folio. 6 color woodcuts. F. K1. $650.00

CAMUS, Albert. *Neither Victims Nor Executioners.* 1972. Chicago. trans Dwight Macdonald. NF/8vo wrp. A11. $25.00

CAMUS, Albert. *Plague.* 1960. Hamish Hamilton. 6th imp of 1947 ed of La Peste. NF/NF clip. A14. $25.00

CAMUS, Albert. *Rebel: Essay on Man in Revolt.* 1957. Vintage. 1st pb ed/revised trans from French. inscr. VG/wrp. Q1. $300.00

CAMUS, Albert. *Resistance, Rebellion & Death.* 1961. Knopf. 1st Am ed. trans/intro Justin O'Brien. VG+/VG+ clip. A14. $30.00

CANE, Percy S. *Earth Is My Canvas.* 1956. London. ils/8 plans. 161 p. VG+/dj. B26. $72.50

CANER, Mary Paul. *Time Against the Sky: 19th-Century Days in Phil.* 1966. Cambridge, MA. Dresser Chapman Grimes. 8vo. 320 p. VG/worn. V3. $14.00

CANETTI, Elias. *Kafka's Other Trial: Letters to Felice.* 1974. NY. Schocken Books. 1st ed of 1969 ed of Der Andere Prozess. NF/NF. A14. $30.00

CANETTI, Elias. *Play of the Eyes.* 1986. FSG. 1st ed. trans Ralph Manheim. NF/NF clip. A14. $30.00

CANETTI, Elias. *Torch in My Ear.* 1982. FSG. 1st ed. trans Joachim Neugroschel. VG+/NF. A14. $20.00

CANFIELD, D.M. *Elements of Farrier Science.* 1968. Murfreesboro. 4to. plastic bdg. VG. O3. $35.00

CANFIELD, Dorothy. *Fables for Parents.* 1937. NY. 1st ed. VG/dj. E3. $10.00

CANFIELD, Dorothy. *Seasoned Timber.* 1939. Harcourt Brace. cloth. G/box. A16. $10.00

CANFIELD, Dorothy. *Understood Betsy.* (1916). Grosset Dunlap. 213 p. VG/G. P2. $12.50

CANIFF, Milton. *April Kane & the Dragon Lady.* 1942. Whitman. 1st ed. F/NF. F4. $30.00

CANIN, Ethan. *Emperor of the Air.* 1988. Houghton Mifflin. 1st ed. F/F. B4. $65.00

CANIN, Ethan. *Palace Thief.* 1994. Random. ARC. F/wrp. C4. $30.00

CANNING, John. *50 Great Ghost Stories.* 1988. Bonanza. 11th prt. F/dj. P3. $10.00

CANNING, Victor. *Circle of the Gods.* 1979. London. 2nd prt. F/dj. C1. $11.00

CANNING, Victor. *Crimson Chalice.* 1976. Heinemann. 1st ed. F/dj. C1. $15.00

CANNING, Victor. *Python Project.* 1988. Morrow. 1st ed. F/dj. P3. $15.00

CANNING, Victor. *Rainbird Pattern.* 1973. Morrow. 1st ed. VG/dj. P3. $20.00

CANNON, Curt; see Hunter, Evan.

CANNON, Dorothy F. *Explorer of the Human Brain: Life of Santiago Ramon Y Cajal.* 1949. NY. Schuman. 1st ed. 304 p. pls. beige cloth. VG/dj. G1. $25.00

CANNON, James P. *Russian Revolution.* 1944. Pioneer. 30 p. wrp. A7. $8.00

CANNON, James P. *Socialism for Students.* ca 1909. Chicago. CH Kerr. VG. V4. $14.00

CANNON, Miles. *Wailatpu: Its Rise & Fall 1836-47.* 1915. Boise, ID. 1st ed. xl. 171 p. VG. D3. $35.00

CANNON, Ray. *How To Fish the Pacific Coast.* (1964). Menlo Park. 2nd ed. ils. 337 p. VG. A17. $7.50

CANO, Fray Agustin. *Manche & Peten.* 1984. Labyrinthos. ils. 26 p. F3. $15.00

CANTOR, Louis. *Wheelin' on Beale Street.* (1992). NY. Pharos. 1st ed. F/F. A7. $12.00

CANTWELL, Robert. *Alexander Wilson: Naturalist & Pioneer.* 1961. Lippincott. 1st ed. ils/pls. 319 p. cloth. dj. D2. $75.00

CANTWELL, Robert. *Laugh & Lie Down.* 1931. Farrar Rinehart. 1st ed. NF/2nd state dj. B2. $150.00

CANTWELL, Robert. *Laugh & Lie Down.* 1931. Farrar Rinehart. 1st ed. VG+. A18. $50.00

CAPEK, Karel. *Meteor.* 1935. London. Allen. 1st ed. inscr. trans Weatherall. VG/VG. Q1. $500.00

CAPELL, Richard. *Simiomata. Greek Note Book 1944-45.* (1945). London. 8vo. 224 p. cloth. very scarce. O2. $65.00

CAPEN, Nahum. *Reminiscences of Dr Spurzheim & George Combe...* 1881. NY. Fowler Wells. 1st ed. 12mo. 262 p. NF. G1. $50.00

CAPERTON & HARREL. *Fragments of VMI Hist.* 1933. VMI. ils. 79 p. B10. $45.00

CAPLAN, Ruth B. *Psychiatry & the Community in 19th-Century Am.* 1969. Basic Books. 1st ed. 360 p. beige cloth. VG/dj. G1. $27.50

CAPOTE, Truman. *Answered Prayers: The Unfinished Novel.* 1987. Random. 1st ed. NF/NF clip. A14. $25.00

CAPOTE, Truman. *Answered Prayers: The Unfinished Novel.* 1987. Random. 1st ed. NF/VG. E3. $20.00

CAPOTE, Truman. *Breakfast at Tiffany's.* 1959. NAL/Signet. ARC of 1st pb ed. RS. NF/ils wrp. A11. $45.00

CAPOTE, Truman. *Breakfast at Tiffany's.* 1961. Signet. 4th prt. VG+/wrp. C8. $15.00

CAPOTE, Truman. *Breakfast at Tiffany's: A Short Novel & 3 Stories.* 1958. Random. 1st ed. VG+/VG. A14. $50.00

CAPOTE, Truman. *Capote Reader.* 1987. Random. 1st ed. NF/NF clip. A14. $30.00

CAPOTE, Truman. *Grass Harp Songbook.* 1971. NY. 56 p. F/wrp. A11. $30.00

CAPOTE, Truman. *Grass Harp.* 1951. Random. 1st ed. 2nd issue smooth beige bdg. NF/NF clip. Q1. $125.00

CAPOTE, Truman. *In Cold Blood.* 1965. NY. ARC. VG+/purple wrp/unclip 1st issue dj attached at spine. A11. $95.00

CAPOTE, Truman. *In Cold Blood.* 1965. Random. 1st ed. VG/dj. E3. $20.00

CAPOTE, Truman. *Music for Cameleons.* 1980. Random. 1st ed. F/F. A14. $30.00

CAPOTE, Truman. *Other Voices, Other Rooms.* 1949. NY. NAL/Signet. 1st pb ed/1st prt. VG+. A11. $45.00

CAPOTE, Truman. *Thanksgiving Visitor.* 1967. Random. 1st ed. F/NF slipcase. $75.00

CAPOTE, Truman. *Tree of Night.* 1949. Random. 1st ed. F/NF clip. C4. $65.00

CAPPON, Lester J. *Atlas of Early Am Hist: Revolutionary Era, 1760-90.* 1976. Princeton. 285 maps. M/dj. O6. $150.00

CAPPS, Benjamin. *Great Chiefs.* 1975. Time Life. 4to. F. A8. $10.00

CAPPS, Benjamin. *Warren Wagontrain Raid.* 1974. NY. 1st ed. sgn. NF/F. A11. $60.00

CAPSTICK, Peter Hathaway. *Death in the Long Grass.* 1977. St Martin. VG/dj. P3. $10.00

CAPUTO, Philip. *Del Corso's Gallery.* (1983). HRW. ARC. sgn. w/pub slip. F/NF. A7. $45.00

CAPUTO, Philip. *Indian Country.* (1987). Bantam. ARC. sgn. wrp. A7. $20.00

CAPUTO, Philip. *Means of Escape: A Memoir.* (1991). Harper Collins. 1st ed/review presentation/sgn. F/F. A7. $35.00

CAPUTO, Philip. *Rumor of War.* (1977). HRW. 1st ed. author's 1st book. NF/dj. A7. $30.00

CARAMAN, Philip. *Lost Paradise.* 1976. Seabury. 1st ed. 341 p. dj. F3. $20.00

CARAS, Roger A. *Custer Wolf.* 1979. HRW. 179 p. F/F. B19. $7.50

CARAVATI, Charles M. *Major Dooley.* 1978. self pub. sgn. ils. 78 p. VG/stiff covers. B10. $15.00

CARAWAY. *Applique Quilts To Color.* 1981. np. wrp. G2. $6.00

CARD, Orson Scott. *Seventh Son.* 1987. Tor. 1st ed. F/dj. P3. $25.00

CARD, Orson Scott. *Xenocide.* 1991. Tor. 1st ed. VG/dj. P3. $22.00

CARDEW, Margaret. *French Alphabet.* ca 1940s. London. Faber. oblong 12mo. aqua cloth. VG/tattered. D1. $75.00

CARDOZO, Benjamin N. *Growth of the Law.* 1946. New Haven. Yale. VG/dj. M11. $50.00

CARELESS, John. *Old Eng 'Squire. A Poem, in 10 Cantos.* 1821. London. Howlett Brimmer. 1st ed. 24 hc pls. Riviere bdg. NF. H5. $1,250.00

CAREY, Arthur A. *Memoirs of a Murder Man.* 1930. Doubleday Doran. 1st ed. VG. P3. $20.00

CAREY, Charles H. *OR Constitution.* 1926. Salem, OR. 1st ed. w/sgn letter. 534 p. cloth. NF. D3. $75.00

CAREY, George G. *Sailor's Song Bag.* 1976. Amherst. MA U. dj. N2. $7.50

CAREY, Peter. *Oscar & Lucinda.* 1988. Harper. ARC. NF/pict wrp. B3. $50.00

CAREY, Peter. *Oscar & Lucinda.* 1988. Harper. 1st ed. sgn. F/F. B2. $60.00

CAREY, Peter. *Tax Inspector.* 1992. Knopf. 1st ed. inscr. F/F. B2. $40.00

CARLETON, J.H. *Prairie Log-Books.* 1943. Chicago. Caxton. 1/350. inscr. VG+. A15. $145.00

CARLETON, James Henry. *Battle of Buena Vista...* 1848. Harper. 1st ed. 12mo. 238 p. gilt brn cloth. K1. $175.00

CARLETON, Will. *City Festivals.* 1892. Harper. 1st ed. VG. M18. $40.00

CARLETON, Will. *Farm Festival.* 1881. NY. 1st ed. gilt bl cloth. VG+. V1. $15.00

CARLIER, F. *Etudes de Pathologie Sociale: Les Deux Prostitutions.* 1889 (1887). Paris. E Dentu. 2nd ed. 514 p. prt yel wrp. G1. $65.00

CARLON, Patricia. *See Nothing...Say Nothing.* 1968. Walker. 1st ed. VG/dj. P3. $12.50

CARLSEN, Chris. *Berserker: Bull Chief.* 1977. London. Sphere. true 1st ed/pb. VG. C1. $14.50

CARLSEN, Ruth Christoffer. *Sometimes It's Up.* 1971. Houghton Mifflin. 1st ed. ils John Gretzer. 164 p. gold cloth. VG. T5. $15.00

CARLSON, Natalie Savage. *Jean-Claude's Island.* (1963). Harper Row. early prt. ils NE Burkert. VG+/G+. T5. $30.00

CARLTON, W.F. *Amateur Photographer: Complete Guide for Beginners...* 1897. Rochester. 64 p. VG+/pict wrp. B20. $30.00

CARLYLE, Lillian. *Carriages at Shelburne Mus.* 1956. Shelburne. 71 p. VG/wrp. O3. $45.00

CARLYON, Richard. *Dark Lord of Penersick.* 1980. FSG. 1st ed. F/F. P3. $15.00

CARMACK, Robert. *Hist Demography of Highland Guatemala.* 1982. Albany, NY. Instit Mesoamerican Studies. 4to. 202 p. F3. $30.00

CARMEN, Michael. *US Customs & the Madero Revolution.* 1976. El Paso. SW Studies 48. 1st ed. 87 p. wrp. F3. $10.00

CARMER, Carl. *Hudson.* (1968). Grosset Dunlap. 1st thus ed. 8vo. 342 p. F/F. A2. $12.50

CARMER, Carl. *Stars Fell on AL.* 1934. Farrar Rinehart. ils Baldridge. 294 p. pict ep. brds. B11. $25.00

CARMICHAEL, Harry. *False Evidence.* 1976. Collins Crime Club. 1st ed. VG/dj. P3. $20.00

CARMICHAEL, Harry. *Remote Control.* 1971. McCall. 1st ed. VG/G+. P3. $15.00

CARNAC, Nicholas. *Tournament of Shadows.* 1978. Scribner. 1st ed. rem mk. F/F. F4. $16.00

CARNEGIE, Dale. *How To Win Friends & Influence People.* 1937. Simon Schuster. 18th prt. sgn. VG/dj. P3. $20.00

CARPENTER, C.H. *Many Voices: Study of Folklore Activities in Canada...* 1979. Ottawa. Nat Mus of Canada. 484 p. lt 4to. G/wrp. A17. $25.00

CARPENTER, Don. *Hard Rain Falling.* 1966. NY. 1st ed. sgn. F/F. A11. $50.00

CARPENTER, Edward. *Drama of Love & Death.* 1912. Mitchell Kennerley. 1st ed. F/NF. B2. $65.00

CARPENTER, George Rice. *John Greenleaf Whittier.* 1906. Houghton Mifflin. 12mo. 311 p. VG. V3. $12.00

CARPENTER, Humphrey. *Letters of JRR Tolkien.* 1981. Houghton Mifflin. 1st Am ed. F/F. N3. $15.00

CARPENTER, Humphrey. *Tolkien: The Authorized Biography.* 1977. Houghton Mifflin. 1st ed. VG/dj. P3. $20.00

CARPENTER, Humphrey. *WH Auden: A Biography.* 1981. Houghton Mifflin. 1st ed. inscr. F/F. C4. $35.00

CARPENTER, William B. *Nature & Man: Essays Scientific & Philosophical.* 1888. London. Kegan Paul. inscr author's son. 484 p. G1. $125.00

CARPENTER & CARPENTER. *Hist of OH From Earliest Settlement to Present Time.* 1854. Phil. 277 p. VG. B18. $95.00

CARPENTIER, Alejo. *Kingdom of This World.* 1987. Ltd Ed Club. 1/750. intro/sgn John Hersey. F/slipcase. Q1. $400.00

CARR, Albert. *World & William Walker.* (1963). Harper. 1st ed. 289 p. dj. F3. $25.00

CARR, Edward Hallett. *Karl Marx: Study in Fanaticism.* 1934. London. Dent. 1st ed. NF. B2. $50.00

CARR, Glynn. *Youth Hostel Murders.* 1953. Dutton. 1st ed. VG. P3. $20.00

CARR, J.D. *S African Acacias.* 1976. Johannesburg. ils/photos. 323 p. M/dj. B26. $65.00

CARR, Jayge. *Leviathan's Deep.* 1980. London. Sidgwick Jackson. 1st ed. F/NF. N3. $20.00

CARR, John Dickson. *Blind Barber.* 1974. London. Hamilton. 1st fingerprint ed. F/F. S5. $20.00

CARR, John Dickson. *Bride of Newgate.* 1950. Harper. 1st ed. VG/G+. P3. $25.00

CARR, John Dickson. *Captain Cut-Throat.* 1955. Harper. 1st ed. F/dj. P3. $80.00

CARR, John Dickson. *Deadly Hall.* 1971. Harper Row. 1st ed. VG/dj. P3. $25.00

CARR, John Dickson. *Death Turns the Tables.* 1941. Harper. 1st ed. VG/VG. Q1. $150.00

CARR, John Dickson. *Door to Doom & Other Detections.* 1981. London. Hamilton. 1st British ed. F/F. S5. $35.00

CARR, John Dickson. *Emperor's Snuff-Box.* 1942. Harper. 1st ed. VG-. P3. $20.00

CARR, John Dickson. *Fear Is the Same.* 1956. Morrow. 1st ed. NF/NF. Q1. $75.00

CARR, John Dickson. *Four False Weapons.* 1937. Harper. 1st ed. F/NF. M10. $350.00

CARR, John Dickson. *In Spite of Thunder.* 1960. London. Hamish Hamilton. 1st ed. F/F. M15. $50.00

CARR, John Dickson. *Most Secret.* 1964. Hamish Hamilton. 1st ed. F/dj. P3. $45.00

CARR, John Dickson. *Murder of Sir Edmund Godfrey.* 1936. Harper. 1st ed. F/VG. M15. $300.00

CARR, John Dickson. *Night at the Mocking Widow.* 1950. Morrow. 1st ed. NF/NF. Q1. $75.00

CARR, John Dickson. *Nine — & Death Makes Ten.* 1940. Morrow. 1st ed. VG+/VG. Q1. $250.00

CARR, John Dickson. *To Wake the Dead.* 1937. Hamish Hamilton. 1st ed. VG. P3. $50.00

CARR, Robert K. *Constitution & Congressional Investigating Committees...* 1954. NY. Carrie Chapman Catt Memorial Fund. 60 p. wrp. M11. $20.00

CARR, Robert Spencer. *Beyond Infinity.* 1951. Fantasy. 1st ed. VG/dj. P3. $35.00

CARR, Robert Spencer. *Beyond Infinity.* 1951. Fantasy. 1/350. sgn/#d. F/F. M2. $85.00

CARR, Robert Spencer. *Room Beyond.* 1948. Appleton Century Crofts. 1st ed. VG/VG. N3. $15.00

CARR, Terry. *Best SF of the Yr #6.* 1977. HRW. 1st ed. F/dj. P3. $17.50

CARR, Terry. *Cirque.* 1987. Doubleday. 1st ed. F/dj. P3. $13.00

CARR, Terry. *Universe 3.* nd. BC. VG/dj. P3. $7.50

CARR, Terry. *Universe 5.* 1974. Random. 1st ed. VG/dj. P3. $20.00

CARR, William H. *Desert Parade: Guide to SW Desert Plants & Wildlife.* 1947. NY. 1st ed. 96 p. pict cloth. VG. D3. $12.50

CARR, Winifred. *Hussein's Kingdom.* 1966. London. Leslie Frewin. 1st ed. 176 p. NF/NF. M7. $35.00

CARRERE D'ENCAUSSE & SCHRAM. *Marxism & Asia.* (1969). Allen Lane/Penguin. 1st Eng ed. 404 p. NF/dj. A7. $28.00

CARRICK, Valery. *More Russian Picture Tales.* 1920 (1914). Stokes. 116 p. G+. P2. $18.00

CARRIER, Constance. *Middle Voice.* 1954. Denver. 1st ed. F/VG. V1. $15.00

CARRIERI, Rafaell. *Campigli.* 1945. Milano. 1/1200. inscr/sgn. w/woodblock. G+. A1. $135.00

CARRIERI, Rafaell. *Disegno Italino Poraneo. Vol 2.* 1945. Milano. 1/700. G+. A1. $75.00

CARRIGHAR, Sally. *Moonlight at Midday.* 1958. Knopf. 1st ed. 8vo. 392 p. VG/dj. P4. $25.00

CARRILLO, Don Carlos Antonio. *Exposition Addressed to Chamber of Deputies...* 1938. San Francisco. Nash. 1/650. w/promo slip. F/F. P4. $125.00

CARRINGTON, Henry B. *Battle Maps & Charts of the Am Revolution.* 1881. NY. Barnes. 41 maps. NF. O6. $85.00

CARRINGTON, Hereward. *Eusapia Palladino & Her Phenomena.* 1909. NY. Dodge. 1st ed. 7 pls. 353 p. prt olive cloth. NF/dj. G1. $65.00

CARRINGTON, Leonora. *Down Below.* 1988. Blk Swan. 2nd ed. sgn. ils Debra Taub. F/wrp. B2. $35.00

CARRINGTON, Leonora. *Stone Door.* 1977. St Martin. 1st ed. VG/dj. P3. $15.00

CARRITHERS, T.W. *How To Put on a Horse Show.* 1971. S Brunswick. Barnes. 1st ed. VG/VG. O3. $10.00

CARROLL, E. Jean. *Hunter: Strange & Savage Life of Hunter S Thompson.* (1993). Dutton. 1st ed. 341 p. A7. $15.00

CARROLL, James. *Fault Lines.* (1980). Little Brn. 1st ed. sgn. rem mk. F/F. A7. $45.00

CARROLL, James. *Memorial Bridge.* 1991. Houghton Mifflin. 1st ed. presentation/sgn. F/F. A7. $35.00

CARROLL, Jim. *Living at the Movies.* 1973. Grossman. AP. NF/wrp. L3. $350.00

CARROLL, Jim. *Living at the Movies.* 1973. Grossman. 1st ed. F/NF. B4. $125.00

CARROLL, Jim. *Organic Trains.* (1968). (NY). 1st ed. NF/prt gray wrp. A11. $65.00

CARROLL, John A. *Reflections of W Historians.* 1969. Tucson. 1st ed. 314 p. M/M. P4. $20.00

CARROLL, Lewis. *Alice in Wonderland.* (1945). Grosset Dunlap. ils Julian Wehr/3 movables. sbdg. VG. D1. $125.00

CARROLL, Lewis. *Alice in Wonderland.* 1951. Rand McNally Elf Book. ils Janice Holland. VG. M5. $12.00

CARROLL, Lewis. *Alice in Wonderland.* 1955. Whitman. decor brds. VG. P3. $10.00

CARROLL, Lewis. *Alice in Wonderland/Through the Looking Glass.* 1946. Random. ils Tenniel/Kredel. 2 vols. pict brds. VG. M5. $20.00

CARROLL, Lewis. *Alice's Adventures in Wonderland.* ca 1943. Jamaica. Minia Pr. miniature. ils Tenniel. gilt red leather. F/slipcase. B24. $135.00

CARROLL, Lewis. *Alice's Adventures in Wonderland.* nd. Donohue. ils John Tenniel. G. L1. $22.50

CARROLL, Lewis. *Alice's Adventures in Wonderland.* nd. Garden City. ils AE Jackson. 215 p. G+. P2. $15.00

CARROLL, Lewis. *Alice's Adventures in Wonderland.* nd. Lippincott. later ed. ils Gertrude Kay/John Tenniel. G/G. L1. $35.00

CARROLL, Lewis. *Alice's Adventures in Wonderland.* nd. (1907). London. 1/1130. quarto. 13 mtd color pls. Zaehnsdorf bdg. F. H5. $2,250.00

CARROLL, Lewis. *Alice's Adventures in Wonderland.* 1868. London. Macmillan. 13th thousand. 192 p. gilt red cloth. G+. S10. $95.00

CARROLL, Lewis. *Alice's Adventures in Wonderland.* 1982. Berkeley. 1st ed. ils/sgn Moser. red cloth. F/slipcase. D1. $225.00

CARROLL, Lewis. *Alice's Adventures in Wonderland.* 1985. Chancellor Pr. as new. A16. $12.50

CARROLL, Lewis. *Alice's Adventures in Wonderland/Through the Looking Glass.* (1898). Lothrop. new ed in 1 vol. ils Tenniel. 208 p. G. S10. $75.00

CARROLL, Lewis. *Alice's Adventures.../Through the Looking-Glass...* 1867 & 1872. London. 6th thousand & 27th thousand bdg together. F. H5. $1,500.00

CARROLL, Lewis. *Collected Verse.* 1933. Macmillan. 441 p. cloth. VG. M20. $25.00

CARROLL, Lewis. *Hunting of the Snark.* 1980. NY. facsimile of 1st ed. VG. C1. $6.50

CARROLL, Lewis. *Rhyme? And Reason?* 1888. Macmillan. ils Henry Holiday. 214 p. gilt red cloth. VG. D1. $200.00

CARROLL, Lewis. *Tangled Tale.* 1885. London. 1st ed. aeg. gilt red cloth. VG+. A11. $195.00

CARROLL, Lewis. *Through the Looking Glass & What Alice Found There.* 1902. NY. Harper. ils Peter Newell. 211 p. wht brds. NF. B14. $25.00

CARROLL, Lewis. *Through the Looking Glass.* 1898. Boston. De Wolfe Fiske. 12mo. ils Tenniel. 175 p. VG. D1. $185.00

CARROLL, Lewis. *Wasp in a Witg.* 1977. NY. correct 1st ed/Carroll Studies #2. F/unused 8vo wrp. A11. $45.00

CARRUTH, Hayden. *Brothers I Loved You All.* 1978. NY. 2nd prt. sgn. VG/wrp. V1. $10.00

CARRUTH, Hayden. *Selected Poetry.* 1985. NY. 1st ed. sng. F/VG. V1. $20.00

CARRUTH, Hayden. *Sitting In.* 1986. IA City. 1st ed. presentation inscr. F/F. A11. $35.00

CARRUTH, Vance. *Teton Sketches of Summer.* 1969. Boulder. 1st ed. sgn. 32 p. F/G. A17. $16.50

CARSON, Hampton L. *Hist of the Supreme Court of the US.* 1902. Phil. PW Ziegler. revised/updated ed. 60 full-p ils. full leather. M11. $200.00

CARSON, Jane. *Colonial VA Cookery.* 1969. Colonial Williamsburg. 1st ed. author's personal copy. 326 p. VG. B11. $25.00

CARSON, John. *Doc Middleton: Unwickedest Outlaw.* (1966). Santa Fe. 1/1000. xl. VG. D3. $25.00

CARSON, Rachel. *Silent Spring.* 1962. Houghton Mifflin. 1st ed. NF/VG clip. B4. $100.00

CARSON, Rachel. *Silent Spring.* 1962. Houghton Mifflin. 1st ed. NF/VG. L3. $125.00

CARTER, Angela. *Artificial Fire.* 1988. McClelland Stewart. 1st ed. F/dj. P3. $20.00

CARTER, Angela. *Nights at the Circus.* 1985. Viking. 1st Am ed. sgn/dtd Austin TX 1985. F/F. Q1. $50.00

CARTER, Angela. *Passion of New Eve.* 1977. Harcourt. 1st ed. F/F. B2. $30.00

CARTER, Angela. *Saints & Strangers.* 1986. Viking. 1st Am ed. F/F. N3. $15.00

CARTER, C.F. *Katooticut. Story of a Rooster.* 1899. NY. Russell. 1st ed. 153 p. VG. H3. $100.00

CARTER, Gary. *Dream Season.* 1987. HBJ. 1st ed. F/F. P8. $17.50

CARTER, Hodding. *Lower MS.* ca 1942. NY/Toronto. 8vo. map. 467 p. H9. $25.00

CARTER, Jimmy. *Outdoor Journal.* (1988). NY. 1st ed. 275 p. F/dj. A17. $14.50

CARTER, Jimmy. *Talking Peace: Vision for the Next Generation.* 1993. Dutton. ARC. juvenile. F/pict wrp. Q1. $30.00

CARTER, Lin. *Horror Wears Bl.* 1987. Doubleday. 1st ed. RS. F/dj. P3. $17.50

CARTER, Lin. *Kingdoms of Sorcery.* 1976. Doubleday. 1st ed. F/dj. P3. $22.50

CARTER, Mary. *Minutes of the Night.* 1965. Little Brn. 1st ed. F/VG. N3. $10.00

CARTER, Nick; see Avallone, Mike.

CARTER, Robert Randolph. *Carter Family Tree.* 1951. Channel Lithography. 243 p. VG. B10. $35.00

CARTER, Russel Gordon. *Wht Plume of Navarre.* 1928. Volland. 11 color pls. 192 p. emb gr cloth. VG. H3. $15.00

CARTER, Vincent. *Bern Book.* (1973). John Day. 1st ed. 297 p. VG/VG. A7. $25.00

CARTER, William. *Horses of the World.* 1923. WA. Nat Geog Soc. hc. VG. O3. $45.00

CARTER, Youngman. *Mr Campion's Farthing.* 1969. London. Heinemann. 1st ed. xl. dj. P3. $7.50

CARTER, Youngman. *Rapture Effect.* 1987. Tor. 1st ed. RS. F/dj. P3. $20.00

CARTER & MUIR. *Printing & the Mind of Man.* 1967. London. Cassell. 1st ed. 4to. 280 p. VG/dj. F1. $65.00

CARTER. *Handbook of Brazilian Stitches for Wall Hangings & Rugs.* 1978. np. sbdg. G2. $10.00

CARTER. *Holiday Happenings.* 1987. np. ils. wrp. G2. $17.00

CARTERET, George. *Barbary Voyage of 1638.* 1929. Phil. Wm Tell. 1/150. xl. NF. O6. $175.00

CARTIER, Jacques. *Voyage de Jacques Cartier av Canada en 1534.* 1865. Paris. Lib Tross. M/wrp. O6. $175.00

CARTIER, John O. *Getting the Most Out of Modern Wildfowling.* (1974). NY. 396 p. dj. A17. $15.00

CARTIER, John O. *Modern Deer Hunter.* (1976). NY. ils/index. 310 p. dj. A17. $12.00

CARTIER-BRESSON, Henri. *People of Moscow.* 1955. Simon Schuster. 1st ed. lg quarto. F/VG. B4. $175.00

CARTY & RUMBLE. *Another Thousand Radio Replies.* 1940. St Paul. Radio Replies. 2nd series. 358 p. VG. C5. $12.50

CARUSO, John Anthony. *Appalachian Frontier: Am's 1st Surge Westward.* 1959. Indianapolis. 1st ed. 408 p. VG/G. D7. $35.00

CARUTHERS, William. *Loafing Along Death Valley Trails.* 1951. Death Valley Pub. 8vo. VG. A8. $20.00

CARUTHERS, William. *Loafing Along Death Valley Trails.* 1951. Ontario. 2nd ed/6th prt. 191 p. dj. D3. $25.00

CARVAJAL. *Great Dinosaurs: A Giant Pop-Up.* 1989. 7 pop-ups. F. A4. $30.00

CARVALHO, Solomon N. *Incidents of Travel & Adventure in the Far W.* 1857. NY. Derby Jackson. 12mo. 380 p. brn cloth. H9. $95.00

CARVER, Jeffrey A. *Star Rigger's Way.* nd. BC. VG/dj. P3. $7.50

CARVER, Raymond. *Cathedral.* 1983. Knopf. 1st ed. F/F. B2. $50.00

CARVER, Raymond. *Elephant.* 1988. London. Collins Harvill. 1/1500. F/F. C4. $75.00

CARVER, Raymond. *Fires.* 1983. Santa Barbara. 1st trade ed. sgn. F/glossy wrp. A11. $45.00

CARVER, Raymond. *Fires. Essays. Poems. Stories.* 1983. Capra. ltd ed. 1/250. sgn. F/F glassine. B2. $200.00

CARVER, Raymond. *Music.* 1985. Concord. Ewert. 1/26 lettered. sgn. F. L3. $275.00

CARVER, Raymond. *My Crow.* 1984. Concord. Ewert. 1/36 (136 total). sgn. F. L3. $250.00

CARVER, Raymond. *New Path to the Waterfall.* 1989. NY. 1st ed. F/F. V1. $30.00

CARVER, Raymond. *Two Poems.* 1982. Scarab. 1st ltd ed. 1/75. sgn twice. F/wrp. L3. $300.00

CARVER, Raymond. *What We Talk About When We Talk About Love.* 1981. Knopf. 1st ed. F/F. B2. $100.00

CARVER, Raymond. *What We Talk About When We Talk About Love.* 1982. NY. 1st pb ed. sgn. F/glossy wrp. A11. $35.00

CARVER, Raymond. *Where I'm Calling From.* 1988. Atlantic. 1st ed. F/F. B2. $40.00

CARVER, Raymond. *Where I'm Calling From.* 1988. Franklin Lib. 1st ed. sgn. full leather. F. B4. $250.00

CARVER, Raymond. *Will You Please Be Quiet, Please?* 1976. McGraw Hill. 1st ed. F/NF. B2. $250.00

CARVER, Raymond. *Winter Insomnia.* 1970. Santa Cruz. 1st regularly pub book. 1/1000. NF/wrp. A11. $145.00

CARVER & GALLAGHER. *Dostoevsky.* 1985. Santa Barbara. 1/200. sgn/#d. F/wrp. A11. $95.00

CARVIC, Heron. *Picture Miss Seeton.* 1968. Geoffrey Bles. 1st ed. VG/G+. P3. $25.00

CARY, Joyce. *Aissa Saved.* 1963. Harper. 1st Am ed. author's 1st book. F/NF. B2. $35.00

CARY, M. *Geographic Background of Greek & Roman Hist.* 1949. Oxford. 1st ed. 33 maps. 331 p. VG. C1. $9.50

CARY, R. Milton. *Skirmisher's Drill & Bayonet Exercise...* 1861. Richmond, VA. W & Johnston. 1st ed. 29 pls. 48 p. NF/floral wrp. M8. $1,250.00

CARY, Robert. *Palaeologia Chronica.* 1677. London. Darby for Chiswell. folio. contemporary calf/rebacked. B14. $600.00

CASANOVA. *Memoirs of Jacques Casanova.* 1928. London. subscribers ed. octavo. 12 vols. teg. morocco. H5. $1,750.00

CASCIO & OWENS. *Over the Hill to the Super Bowl.* 1973. WA, DC. Robert B Luce. dj. N2. $6.00

CASE, David. *Third Grave.* 1981. Arkham House. 1st ed. ils/sgn Stephen Fabian. F/F. F4. $25.00

CASEY, Jewell. *101 Am Wild Flowers.* 1959. NY. ils/photos. 101 p. VG/dj. B26. $14.00

CASEY, John. *Am Romance.* 1977. NY. 1st ed. inscr. F/F. A11. $100.00

CASEY, John. *Spartina.* 1989. NY. 1st ed. sgn. F/F. A11. $85.00

CASEY, John. *Testimony & Demeanor.* 1979. NY. 1st ed. sgn. F/F. A11. $55.00

CASHMAN, John. *Gentleman From Chicago: Being Account of...Thomas N Cream...* 1973. Harper Row. ARC. F/pict wrp. N3. $30.00

CASKIE, Jaquelin Ambler. *Life & Letters of Matthew Fontaine Maury.* 1928. Richmond Pr. 1st ed. 191 p. NF. M8. $85.00

CASLEMON, Henry. *George at the Wheel.* 1881. Winston. 1st ed. G+. M2. $10.00

CASLER, Melyer. *Journal Giving Incidents of Journey to CA in Summer 1859...* 1969. Ye Galleon Pr. 1st ltd ed. 1/488. gilt bdg. F/sans. A18. $40.00

CASO, Alfonso. *Interpretation of the Codex Bodley.* 1960. Mexico City. 1/400. tall 4to. ES. NF/calf-backed wood box. K1. $650.00

CASPARY, Vera. *Weeping & the Laughter.* 1950. Little Brn. 1st ed. VG/dj. P3. $35.00

CASSANDRA, Knye; see Discht, Thomas.

CASSAVETES, John. *Faces.* 1970. Signet/NAL. pb. VG+. C8. $30.00

CASSEDY, James H. *Charles V Chapin & the Public Health Movement.* 1962. Cambridge. Harvard. 1st ed. sm 8vo. 310 p. VG/dj. G1. $25.00

CASSEDY & SHROTT. *William Sidney Mount: Works in the Collection...* 1983. Stony Brook, NY. 96 p. wrp. D2. $25.00

CASSIDY, Custer. *Hunt Country Cartoons...* 1966. Middleburg. 56 p. VG/wrp. O3. $25.00

CASSIDY, John. *Station in the Delta.* (1979). NY. 1st ed. NF/NF. A7. $40.00

CASSILL, R.V. *Father & Other Stories.* 1965. NY. 1st short story collection. sgn. F/F. A11. $35.00

CASSILL, R.V. *La Vie Passionnee of Rodney Buckthorne.* 1968. Geis. 1st ed. F/NF. F4. $20.00

CASSILL, R.V. *15 by 3.* 1957. NY. New Directions. PBO. sgn. NF/wrp. A11. $40.00

CASSIN, John. *Ils of the Birds of CA, TX, OR, British & Russian Am...* 1856. Lippincott. 1st ed. royal octavo. 50 Bowen hand-colored pls. NF. R3. $5,500.00

CASSIN, Ricardo. *50 Yrs of Alpinism.* (1981). Seattle. Mountaineers. 207 p. F/F. A7. $25.00

CASSIRER, Ernst. *Kants Legen und Lehre.* 1918. Berlin. Bruno Cassirer. 1st ed. 448 p. cloth. G1. $75.00

CASSITY, Turner. *Watchboy, What of the Night?* nd. np. 1st prt. author's 1st book. presentation inscr. w/note. F/wrp. A11. $35.00

CASSON, Herbert N. *Romance of the Reaper.* 1908. Doubleday Page. 1st ed. 184 p. VG. H10. $35.00

CASSON, Stanley. *Macedonia, Thrace & Illyria: Their Relations to Greece...* 1926. np. Oxford U. 1st ed. 8vo. ils/maps. 357 p. F-. A2 $45.00

CASSON, Stanley. *Some Modern Sculptures.* 1928. London. Oxford. G. A1. $15.00

CASSOU, Jean. *Campigli.* 1957. Paris. inscr/sgn. VG/VG/orig mailer. A1. $150.00

CASTANEDA, Carlos. *Mexican Side of the TX Revolution.* 1971. WA, DC. Documentary Pr. 1/500. 391 p. F3. $30.00

CASTANEDA, Carlos. *Tales of Power.* 1974. Simon Schuster. 1st ed. VG/dj. A16. $25.00

CASTELLI, Bartolommeo. *Lexicon Medicum, Primum a Bartholomaeo Castello Messanensi.* 1688. Norimbergae. Sumtibus Johannis Danielis Taubert. 939 p. G7. $495.00

CASTELLO, Julio M. *Theory & Practice of Fencing.* (1933). NY. 272 p. dj. A17. $20.00

CASTELMON, Harry. *Winged Arrow's Medicine.* 1901. Saalfield. 1st ed. Kearney. ils WH Fry. 293 p. VG-. S10. $25.00

CASTIGLIONE, Baldassare. *Il Cortegiano, or the Courtier.* 1727. London. quarto. Italian/Eng text. rebacked to style. VG. H5. $850.00

CASTIGLIONI, Arturo. *Hist of Medicine. Trans From Italian...* 1941. Knopf. 1013 p. cloth. G7. $125.00

CASTLE, J.L. *Satellite E One.* 1954. Dodd Mead. 1st ed. F/NF. Q1. $30.00

CASTLE, J.L. *Satellite E One.* 1954. Eyre Spottiswoode. VG/VG-. P3. $10.00

CASTLEMON, Harry. *Young Naturalist.* nd (1892). Porter Coates. Gun Boat series. 253 p. VG/VG+. B22. $9.00

CASTLEREAGH, Frederick. *Journey to Damascus Through Egypt, Nubia...* 1847. London. 2 vols 8vo. 10 pls. rebound red levant. O2. $625.00

CASTREN, Matthia Alexandro. *Dissertatio Academica de Pathologica Systematis Nervorum...* 1833. Helsingforsiae. 72 p. uncut/unopened. G7. $75.00

CATCHPOOL, Corder. *On Two Fronts: Letters of a Conscientious Objector.* 1940. London. Allen Unwin. 3rd ed. 12mo. 160 p. G+. V3. $9.50

CATHER, Willa. *Bibliography.* nd. Knopf. G+/wrp. A1. $20.00

CATHER, Willa. *December Night.* 1933. Knopf. 1st thus ed. NF/dj. A18. $30.00

CATHER, Willa. *Lost Lady.* 1983. LEC. 1/1500. ils/sgn Wm Bailey. F/slipcase. B20. $275.00

CATHER, Willa. *Lucy Gayheart.* 1935. Knopf. VG/dj. A16. $52.50

CATHER, Willa. *My Antonia.* (1981). Franklin Lib. 1st thus ed. ils Hodges Soileau. full gr leather. M. A18. $40.00

CATHER, Willa. *My Mortal Enemy.* 1926. Knopf. 1/220. sgn/#d. NF/recent slipcase matches orig. Q1. $750.00

CATHER, Willa. *Old Beauty & Others.* 1948. Knopf. 1st ed. NF/NF. C4. $45.00

CATHER, Willa. *Professor's House.* 1925. Knopf. 1st ed. NF/NF. Q1. $450.00

CATHER, Willa. *Professor's House.* 1925. NY. 1st ed. VG/G. B5. $110.00

CATHER, Willa. *Sapphira & the Slave Girl.* 1940. Knopf. 1/520. sgn/#d. teg. cloth. F/NF/#d slipcase. Q1. $450.00

CATHER, Willa. *Shadows on the Rock.* 1931. Knopf. 1st ed. F/F. A18. $125.00

CATHER, Willa. *Writings From Willa Cather's Campus Yrs.* 1950. Lincoln, NE. VG+. E3. $25.00

CATHERWOOD, John. *New Method of Curing the Apoplexy...* 1715. London. Darby/Taylor. 77 p. contemporary calf/brds. w/John Cooke letter. G7. $595.00

CATICH, Edward M. *Origin of the Serif: Brush Writing & Roman Letters.* (1968). Davenport, IA. Catfish Pr. quarto. sgn. 310 p. F/dj. B24. $300.00

CATLIN, George. *Catlin's Notes of 8 Yrs' Travels & Residence in Europe...* 1848. NY. Burgess Stringer. 1st ed. ils. brn ribbed cloth. H9. $375.00

CATLIN, George. *Letters & Notes on Manners...N Am Indians.* 1860. NY. JW Bradley. 2 vols in 1. full leather. VG. scarce. H7. $125.00

CATLIN, Ralph. *Goodby to Gunsmoke.* 1955. Little Brn. NF/dj. B9. $20.00

CATLING, Patrick Skene. *Jazz Jazz Jazz.* 1981. St Martin. 1st ed. F/NF. B2. $25.00

CATLOW, Agnes. *Drops of Water.* 1851. London. Reeve Benham. 1st ed. 4 hand-colored pls. rebacked. B28. $125.00

CATON, John Dean. *Antelope & Deer of Am.* 1877. NY. Hurd Houghton. 1st ed. presentation. 426 p. gilt russet cloth. VG. H5. $250.00

CATTEL, Jacques. *Directory of Am Scholars.* 1982. NY. Bowker. 8th ed. 924 p. NF. S9. $25.00

CATTON, Bruce. *Banners at Shenandoah.* 1955. Doubleday. 1st ed. 12mo. 254 p. VG/G+. S10. $15.00

CATTON, Bruce. *Coming Fury.* 1961. Doubleday. maps/biblio/index. 565 p. VG. A17. $12.50

CATTON, Bruce. *Grant Moves S.* (1960). Little Brn. 2nd prt. 564 p. VG. A17. $10.00

CATTON, Bruce. *Waiting for the Morning Train.* 1972. Doubleday. 1st ed. 260 p. VG/dj. A16/M20. $25.00

CATTON, Bruce. *War Lords of WA.* (1948). NY. 1st ed. 313 p. VG/dj. A17. $25.00

CAUDWELL, Sarah. *Sirens Sang of Murder.* 1989. Delacorte. 1st Am ed. sgn. F/F. S5. $45.00

CAUGHEY, John Walton. *Am W: Frontier & Region.* (1969). Ward Ritchie. 1st ed. F/NF. A18. $25.00

CAULFIELD, Anna Breiner. *Quakers in Fiction: Annotated Bibliography.* 1993. Northampton, MA. Pittenbruach. 1st ed. 12mo. 169 p. M. V3. $15.00

CAUNITZ, William J. *Blk Sand.* 1989. Crown. 1st ed. VG/dj. P3. $19.00

CAUNITZ, William J. *Exceptional Clearance.* (1991). Crown. ARC. F/wrp. B9. $10.00

CAUNITZ, William J. *Exceptional Clearance.* 1991. NY. Crown. 1st ed. sgn. F/F. S5. $35.00

CAUTHEN, Charles Edward. *SC Goes to War 1860-65.* 1950. Chapel Hill. 1st ed. 256 p. VG/wrp. M8. $85.00

CAVALCANTI, Bartolomeo. *La Retorica...Divisa in Sette Libri: Dove si Contiene.* 1564. Pesaro. Heirs of Bartolomeo Cesano. 4to. early vellum. K1. $375.00

CAVALLEIRO, Gabriel Antonio. *Dois Orgaos Inuteis e Prejudiciaes.* 1907. Porto. 50 p. N2. $20.00

CAVE, Henry. *Golden Tips, Description of Ceylon & Its Great Tea Industry.* 1900. Sampson Low Marston. 1st ed. 8vo. 474 p. F. F1. $175.00

CAVE, Hugh B. *Cross on the Drum.* 1960. Werner Laurie. 1st ed. VG/dj. P3. $25.00

CAVE, Hugh B. *Murgunstrumm.* 1977. Carcoas. 1st ed. w/sgn sheet. as new. M2. $50.00

CAVENDISH, Richard. *Blk Arts.* 1967. BC. VG/dj. C1. $6.50

CAVENIDISH, Marshall. *Hist of 2nd World War.* 1972. Cavendish. 4to. NM. E3. $195.00

CAXTON, William. *Mirrour of the World.* 1964. Kentland, CA. Allen. 1/130. folio. 33 repro ils (3 fld). clamshell box. O6. $750.00

CAYTON, Horace. *Long Old Road.* 1965. Trident. 402 p. NF/dj. A7. $23.00

CECIL, Edward. *Journal of the Action Upon Coast of Spain.* 1968. Da Capo. half leather/decor brds. M. O6. $75.00

CECIL, Henry. *Brothers in Law.* 1955. Michael Joseph. 3rd ed. VG/dj. P3. $17.50

CECIL, Henry. *Just Within the Law.* 1975. London. Hutchinson. 1st ed. inscr to Michael Underwood. F/dj. M15. $45.00

CECIL, Henry. *Matter of Speculation: Case of Lord Cochrane.* 1965. London. Heinemann. 1st ed. inscr/dtd by Cecil's widow. F/dj. M15. $45.00

CELNIK & CELNIK. *Bibliography on Judaism & Jewish-Christian Relations.* ca 1964. ADL. 68+ p. VG/wrp. S3. $15.00

CELSUS. *Medicinae Libri Octo Ex Recensione Leonardi Targa Editio...* 1785. Leyden. Luchtmans. 4to. G7. $175.00

CELSUS. *Medicinae Libri Octo Ex Recensione Leonardi Targa Editio...* 1810. Vernona. Merlo Heirs. 4to. modern wrp. G7. $150.00

CENDRARS, Blaise. *Sutter's Gold.* 1926. NY. 1st ed. woodcuts. 179 p. gilt cloth/brds. VG/dj. D3. $25.00

CENSER, Jane Turner. *NC Planters & Their Children, 1800-1860.* 1984. Baton Rouge. 1st ed. 191 p. cloth. F/F. M8. $25.00

CEPEDA, Orlando. *My Ups & Downs in Baseball.* 1968. Putnam. 1st ed. F/F. P8. $40.00

CERAM, C.W. *Archaeology of the Cinema.* ca 1965. HBW stated 1st Am ed. 8vo. VG+/dj. A7. $30.00

CERF, Bennett. *Famous Ghost Stories.* 1946. Modern Lib. VG. P3. $17.50

CERF & LERNER. *Truth Machine.* 1977. Random. ne. decor brds. VG+. P3. $10.00

CERVANTES, Miguel de; see De Cervantes, Miguel.

CETINTAS, Sedat. *Turk Mimari Anitlari.* 1946 & 1952. Istanbul. 2 vols. Turkish/Eng text. folio. pls. O2. $125.00

CHABER, M.E. *Bonded Dead.* 1971. HRW. 1st ed. NF/dj. F4. $16.00

CHABER, M.E. *Day It Rained Diamonds.* 1966. HRW. 1st ed. VG/dj. P3. $15.00

CHABON, Michael. *Mysteries of Pittsburgh.* 1988. Morrow. 1st ed. author's 1st book. NF/NF. A14/Q1. $30.00

CHABOT, Frederick C. *San Antonio & Its Beginnings...* 1931. San Antonio. 1st ed. xl. 130 p. wrp. VG. D3. $25.00

CHADWICK, Edwin. *Report on Results of Special Inquiry...* 1845. Phil. Sherman. 1st Am ed. 8vo. 48 p. M1. $150.00

CHADWICK, Henry. *Early Christian Thought & Classical Tradition.* 1966. NY. Oxford. 174 p. H10. $20.00

CHALKER, Jack L. *Messiah Choice.* 1985. Bluejay. 1st ed. F/dj. P3. $17.00

CHALMERS, Margaret Piper. *Polyanna's Protegee.* 1944. Page. 1st ed. VG. M5. $20.00

CHAMBERLAIN, Joseph S. *Chemistry in Agriculture.* 1926. NY. 1st ed. 384 p. VG. B28. $20.00

CHAMBERLAIN, N.H. *Autobiography of a New Eng Farmhouse.* 1865. NY. 1st ed. inscr. 12mo. 365 p. B28. $45.00

CHAMBERLAIN, Sarah. *Beasts From Belloc.* 1982. Portland. Chamberlain. 1/125. sgn. Blumenthal bdg. F. B24. $200.00

CHAMBERLAIN, Sarah. *Pied Piper of Hamlin.* 1980. Portland. Chamberlain. 1/150. sgn. mrabled brds. F. B24. $250.00

CHAMBERLAIN, Sarah. *Three Bears.* 1983. Chamberlain. 1/125. sgn. Blumenthal bdg. F. B24. $250.00

CHAMBERLAYNE, Churchill G. *Vestry Book of Bristol Parish, 1720-89.* 1892. private prt. 1/500. inscr. 419 p. G. B10. $100.00

CHAMBERLAYNE, John Hampden. *Ham Chamberlayne: Virginian Letters & Papers...1861-65.* 1932. Richmond, VA. Dietz. 1st ed. 1/1000. 440 p. cloth. F/NF. M8. $250.00

CHAMBERLIN, Ethel Clere. *Shoes & Ships & Sealing Wax.* 1928. Volland. 1st prt. ils JL Scott. 160 p. VG. S10. $50.00

CHAMBERS, Dana. *Death Against Venus.* 1946. Dial. VG/dj. P3. $22.50

CHAMBERS, E.J. *Royal NW Mounted Police: Corps Hist.* 1972 (1906). Toronto. Coles. reprint. 4to. F/wrp. A2. $12.50

CHAMBERS, James. *Devil's Horsemen: Mongol Invasion of Europe.* 1985 (1979). np. VG+. C1. $7.50

CHAMBERS, Julius. *MS River & Its Wonderful Valley.* 1910. NY. 1st ed. photos/maps/index. 308 p. VG. B5. $85.00

CHAMBERS, Julius. *MS River & Its Wonderful Valley.* 1968 (1910). np. 8vo. ils/map. 308 p. cloth. H9. $35.00

CHAMBERS, Lenoir. *Stonewall Jackson.* 1959. Morrow. 1st ed. 2 vols. cloth. NF. M8. $85.00

CHAMBERS, Peter; see Phillips, Dennis.

CHAMBERS, Robert W. *Streets of Ascalon.* 1912. Appleton. 1st ed. VG. P3. $25.00

CHAMBERS, Whitman. *Invasion.* 1943. Dutton. 1st ed. G/fair. $15.00

CHAMBERS, Whitman. *Once Too Often.* 1938. Doubleday Doran. 1st ed. 265 p. VG+/dj. M20. $20.00

CHAMOUX, F. *Civilization of Greece.* 1965. Simon Schuster. 1st Am prt. VG/G. V2. $9.00

CHAMPNEY, Elizabeth. *Three Vassar Girls in France.* 1888. Estes Lauriat. 1st ed. VG. M18. $30.00

CHAMPOMIER, P.A. *Statement of the Sugar Crop Made in LA in 1851-52.* 1852. New Orleans. Cook Young. 1st ed. 16mo. 52 p. prt wrp. M1. $400.00

CHANDA, Nayan. *Brother Enemy.* (1986). HBJ. stated 1st ed. F/F. A7. $25.00

CHANDLER, A. Bertram. *Rim of Space.* 1961. Avalon. 1st ed. F/dj. P3. $45.00

CHANDLER, Alice. *Dream of Order.* 1970. np. 1st ed. VG+/dj. C1. $9.50

CHANDLER, Raymond. *Backfire: Story for the Screen.* 1984. Santa Barbara. 1st prt. 1/200. presentation/sgn R Parker. NF. E3. $60.00

CHANDLER, Raymond. *Big Sleep.* 1986. Arion Pr. 1/425. reverse-litho plexiglas bdg. NF. F1. $485.00

CHANDLER, Raymond. *Bl Dahlia. A Screenplay.* 1976. Carbondale, IL. ARC of 1st wrp issue. RS. w/full set lobby cards. F. A11. $50.00

CHANDLER, Raymond. *Farewell, My Lovely.* 1946. World. 3rd prt. VG/dj. P3. $25.00

CHANDLER, Raymond. *High Window.* 1942. Knopf. 1st ed/1st prt. octavo. brn cloth. pict dj. R3. $1,500.00

CHANDLER, Raymond. *High Window.* 1946. Tower. 2nd ed. VG/dj. P3. $25.00

CHANDLER, Raymond. *La Rouse Rafle Tout (Finger Man).* 1952. Paris. 1st French ed/PBO. VG+/ils wrp. A11. $35.00

CHANDLER, Raymond. *Lady in the Lake.* (1946). London/Melbourne. Hamish Hamilton. 1st Australian ed. VG. B9. $225.00

CHANDLER, Raymond. *Lady in the Lake.* 1943. Knopf. 1st ed. G. M18. $100.00

CHANDLER, Raymond. *Letters.* 1978. Santa Barbara. Neville Yellin. 1/350. edit/sgn Fox. F. B9. $40.00

CHANDLER, Raymond. *Little Sister.* 1949. Boston. 1st Am ed/1st prt. orange cloth. VG+. A11. $80.00

CHANDLER, Raymond. *Long Goodbye.* 1953. London. 1st ed (precedes Am). maroon paper brds. VG. A11. $95.00

CHANDLER, Raymond. *Mystery Omnibus.* 1945. Forum. 2nd ed. VG. P3. $18.00.

CHANDLER, Raymond. *Pearls Are a Nuisance.* 1953. London. correct 1st ed. VG/wrp. A11. $165.00

CHANDLER, Raymond. *Playback.* nd. BC. VG/VG. P3. $10.00

CHANDLER, Raymond. *Playback.* 1958. Boston. 1st Am ed of last Philip Marlowe novel. F/F. A11. $95.00

CHANDLER, Raymond. *Raymond Chandler Omnibus.* 1964. Knopf. fwd/inscr LC Powell. F/NF. B9. $125.00

CHANDLER, Raymond. *Raymond Chandler's Mystery Omnibus.* (1944). Cleveland. World. 1st Tower ed. VG+/dj. B9. $30.00

CHANDLER, Raymond. *Raymond Chandler's Unknown Thriller.* (1985). Mysterious. 1/250. intro/sgn RB Parker. F/dj/slipcase. B9. $50.00

CHANDLER, Raymond. *Raymond Chandler's Unknown Thriller: Screenplay of Playback.* (1985). London. Harrap. 1st ed. F/NF. B3. $40.00

CHANDLER, Raymond. *Red Wind: Collection of Short Stories.* 1946. World. 1st ed. VG+/NF. Q1. $100.00

CHANDLER, Raymond. *Sma Slyngler Skyder Ikke.* 1968. np (Copenhagen). 1st Danish ed. VG+/dj. A11. $35.00

CHANDLER, Raymond. *Smell of Fear.* 91965). London. Hamish Hamilton. 1st ed. NF/dj. B9. $350.00

CHANDLER, William H. *Evergreen Orchards.* 1950. Phil. ils. 452 p. VG. B26. $36.00

CHANDLER, Z.M. *Class Book in Eng Grammar & Analysis.* 1862. Zanesville. 228 p. leather spine. D7. $20.00

CHANDLER & PARKER. *Poodle Springs.* 1989. Putnam. 1st ed. sgn. F/F. S5. $45.00

CHANEY, George Leonard. *Alo'Ha! A HI Salutation.* 1880. Boston. Roberts Bros. 1st ed. 12mo. gilt brn cloth. NF. R3. $135.00

CHANG, Kwang-Chih. *Archaeology of Ancient China.* 1963. New Haven. Yale. xl. 8vo. ils/pls/maps. 346 p. VG. W1. $20.00

CHANNING, Walter. *Treatise on Etherization in Childbirth.* 1848. Boston. D Ticknor. 1st ed. 400 p. gr cloth. VG. B14. $325.00

CHANNING, William Henry. *Life of William Ellery Channing...* 1880. Boston. Am Unitarian Assn. 719 p. H10. $17.50

CHANOFF & DE FOREST. *Slow Burn.* (1990). Simon Schuster. 1st ed. 294 p. NF/dj. A7. $15.00

CHANSLOR, Roy. *Ballad of Cat Ballou.* 1956. Little Brn. 1st ed. NF/NF. Q1. $75.00

CHANSLOR, Roy. *Johnny Guitar.* 1953. Simon Schuster. 1st ed. VG/dj. B9. $125.00

CHANT, Joy. *Grey Mane of Morning.* 1977. Allen Unwin. 1st ed. F/dj. P3. $25.00

CHANT & HEYWOOD. *Popular Encyclopedia of Plants.* 1982. Cambridge. 1st ed. color pls. 368 p. F/F. B28. $22.50

CHAPEL, Charles Edward. *Art of Shooting.* 1960. Barnes. 416 p. VG/dj. M20. $20.00

CHAPELLE, Howard. *Nat Watercraft Collection.* 1960. Smithsonian. Samuel Eliot Morison's copy. NF. O6. $125.00

CHAPIN, A.B. *View of Organization & Order of the Primitive Church...* 1842. New Haven. Hitchcock Stafford. 408 p. H10. $15.00

CHAPIN, Anna Alice. *Now-a-Days Fairy Book.* 1911. Dodd Mead. 1st ed. ils JW Smith. red-brn cloth. VG. D1. $285.00

CHAPIN, Carl M. *Three Died Beside the Marble Pool.* 1936. Crime Club. 1st ed. VG. P3. $20.00

CHAPLIN, Charles. *My Autobiography.* 1964. Simon Schuster. VG. N2. $6.50

CHAPLIN, Ralph. *Somewhat Barbaric.* 1944. Seattle. Dogwood Pr. 1st ed. presentation/sgn. F/dj. A7. $125.00

CHAPMAN, A.H. *Harry Stack Sullivan: His Life & His Work.* 1976. Putnam. 1st ed. 280 p. blk cloth. VG/dj. G1. $28.50

CHAPMAN, Arthur. *Cactus Center: Poems.* 1921. Boston. Houghton Mifflin. 1st ed. 123 p. NF. H7. $15.00

CHAPMAN, Charles E. *Hist of CA: The Spanish Period.* 1921. Macmillan. 1st ed. 526 p. VG. B19. $35.00

CHAPMAN, E. *Latest Light on Abraham Lincoln & War Time Memories.* 1917. NY. 1st ed. 2 vols. sgn. 570 p. VG. B5. $45.00

CHAPMAN, Ervine S. *Particeps Criminis: Story of CA Rabbit Drive.* 1910. NY. Fleming Revell. N2. $20.00

CHAPMAN, Lee; see Bradley, Marion Zimmer.

CHAPMAN, Maria W. *Liberty Bell. By Friends of Freedom.* 1858. Boston. Nat Anti-Slavery Bazaar. 1st ed. 8vo. 328 p. aeg. M1. $150.00

CHAPMAN, Maria Weston. *Autobiography of Harriet Martineau.* 1877. Boston. Osgood. 1st ed. 2 vols. ils. cloth. B14. $40.00

CHAPMAN, V.J. *Algae.* 1969 (1962). London. ils/tables. 472 p. gr cloth. B26. $20.00

CHAPMAN, Walker. *Search for El Dorado.* (1967). Bobbs Merrill. 1st ed. 8vo. 272 p. VG+/VG+. A2. $12.50

CHAPMAN, Walter. *Loneliest Continent.* 1964. Greenwich, CT. 1st ed. 279 p. gilt bl cloth. F/F. H3. $25.00

CHAPMAN & DEMERITT. *Elements of Forest Mensuration.* 1932. NY. 1st ed. ils/charts. 452 p. gr cloth. VG. B22. $7.00

CHAPPELL, Fred. *Dagon.* 1968. NY. 1st ed. sgn. VG/VG. A11. $60.00

CHAPPELL, Fred. *Earthsleep.* 1980. Baton Rouge. 1st ed. sgn. F/F. B4. $75.00

CHAPPELL, Fred. *Fred Chappell Reader.* 1986. NY. 1st ed. sgn Chapell/Stuart. F/F. A11. $65.00

CHAPPELL, Fred. *More Shapes Than One.* 1991. NY. 1st ed. inscr. F/F. A11. $45.00

CHAPPELL, George S. *Through the Ailmentary Canal w/Gun & Camera.* 1930. Stokes. 3rd ed. VG. N2. $5.00

CHAPUS, Eugene. *De Paris a Dieppe.* nd. (1840s). Paris. 12mo. ils. 263 p. prt red brds. VG. H3. $45.00

CHAR, Rene. *Picasso Dessins.* 1969. Paris. Ed Cercle D'Art. 1/125. VG. A1. $400.00

CHARBONNEEAU, Louis. *Trail: Story of Lewis & Clark Expedition.* 1989. Doubleday. 1st ed. 8vo. 506 p. M/M. T8. $20.00

CHARLES, C.J. *Elizabethan Interiors.* ca 1930. NY. Greenfield. 1/500. 3rd ed. xl. presentation. G. C10. $70.00

CHARLES & RITZ. *Brother Ray. Ray Charles' Own Story.* 1978. Dial. F/F. B2. $35.00

CHARLIP & SURPREE. *Harlequin & the Gift of Many Colors.* (1973). Parents Magazine. 1st ed. ils Remy Charlip. VG/VG. T5. $40.00

CHARLOT, Jean. *Art From the Mayans to Disney.* 1939. NY. Sheed Ward. 1st ed. sgn. 12mo. 285 p. F/NF. B20. $165.00

CHARLOT, Jean. *Picture Book.* 1933. NY. Becker. 1/500. sgn. 32 color lithos. F/prt wht wrp. B24. $1,000.00

CHARNAS, Suzy McKee. *Bronze King.* 1985. Houghton Mifflin. 1st ed. VG/torn. P3. $12.95

CHARNAS, Suzy McKee. *Silver Glove.* 1988. Bantam. 1st ed. F/F. N3. $15.00

CHART, D.A. *Story of Dublin.* 1907. London. 12mo. 369 p. gilt pict gr cloth. F. H3. $20.00

CHARTERIS, Leslie. *Prelude for War.* 1938. Doubleday Crime Club. 1st Am ed. VG/dj. M15. $125.00

CHARTERIS, Leslie. *Saint Goes West.* 1942. Musson. 1st Canadian ed. VG. P3. $12.50

CHARTERIS, Leslie. *Trust the Saint.* 1962. Crime Club. 1st ed. xl. dj. P3. $7.50

CHARTERIS, Leslie. *Wht Rider.* nd. Ward Lock. VG/G. P3. $40.00

CHARTERS, Ann. *Portable Beat Reader.* (1992). Viking. 3rd ed. 635 p. F/F. A7. $14.00

CHARTERS, Samuel. *Heroes of the Prize Ring.* 1964. NY. prose poems. woodcuts. F/ils wrp. A11. $15.00

CHARTERS, Samuel. *Jazz: New Orleans 1885-1957.* 1958. Belleville, NJ. ARC. photos/maps. VG/8vo wrp. A11. $65.00

CHARTERS, Samuel. *LA Blk.* (1987). NY. Marion Boyers. reprint. F/NF. A7. $15.00

CHARTERS, Samuel. *Robert Johnson.* 1973. NY. 1st pub versions of 29 orig songs. F/wrp. A11. $35.00

CHARYN, Jerome. *Bl Eyes.* 1974. Simon Schuster. 1st ed. VG/dj. P3. $20.00

CHARYN, Jerome. *Once Upon a Droshky.* 1960. NY. F/NF ils Edward Sorel. A11. $40.00

CHARYN, Jerome. *War Cries Over Ave C.* (1985). Donald Fine. 1st prt. F/F. A7. $35.00

CHASE, C.M. *NM & CO in 1881.* 1968. Frontier Book Co. 8vo. F. A8. $20.00

CHASE, Cleveland B. *Sherwood Anderson.* 1972. Haskell House. 84 p. cloth. VG. M20. $15.00

CHASE, Glen; see Fox, Gardner F.

CHASE, James Hadley. *Figure It Out for Yourself.* 1950. Robert Hale. 1st ed. VG/G+. P3. $30.00

CHASE, James Hadley. *Marijuane Mob (Figure It Out for Yourself).* 1952. NY. Eton. PBO/1st under this title. VG+/ils wrp. A11. $40.00

CHASE, Mary Ellen. *Dawn in Lyonesse.* 1938. NY. reprint. VG. C1. $6.00

CHASE, Samuel. *Answer & Pleas of Samuel Chase...* 1805. Newburyport, MA. Angier March. 1st ed. 8vo. 72 p. M1. $125.00

CHASE, Stuart. *Mexico: Study in 2 Americas.* 1931. Literary Guild. ils Diego Rivera. 338 p. gilt bl cloth. VG. H3. $12.00

CHASE & DONALD. *Inside Lincoln's Cabinet: Civil War Diaries...SP Chase.* 1954. Longman Gr. 1st ed. 342 p. cloth. NF/VG. M8. $45.00

CHASTEL, Andre. *Campigli les Idoles de Campigli.* 1961. Paris. 1/3000. G+/wrp. A1. $75.00

CHASTENT DE PUYSEGUR, Armand. *Du Magnetisme Animal.* 1807. Paris. later ed. G7. $400.00

CHATHAM, Russell. *Dark Waters.* 1988. Livingston, MO. 1st ed. sgn. F/F. A11. $45.00

CHATTERTON, Frederick. *Eng Architecture at a Glance.* 1925. Putnam. ils. 52 p. N2. $7.50

CHATTERTON, Thomas. *Family Romance of the Imposter Poet.* 1988. NY. 1st ed. F/F. V1. $10.00

CHATTERTON. *Coordinated Crafts for the Home.* 1980. np. 80+ patterns. cloth. G2. $12.00

CHATWIN, Bruce. *Attractions of France.* 1993. London. Colophon. 1/175. as new/ stiff gr wrp. C4. $65.00

CHATWIN, Bruce. *Far Journeys.* 1993. Viking. 1st ed. F/F. C4. $35.00

CHATWIN, Bruce. *In Patagonia.* 1977. London. Cape. 1st ed. author's 1st book. F/F. very scarce. B4. $950.00

CHATWIN, Bruce. *On the Blk Hill.* (1982). Viking. 1st ed. VG/VG. B3. $75.00

CHATWIN, Bruce. *Utz.* (1989). Viking. 1st ed. rem mk. VG/F. B3. $20.00

CHATWIN, Bruce. *Utz.* 1988. London. Cape. 1st ed. NF/NF. C4. $45.00

CHATWIN, Bruce. *Viceroy of Ouidah.* 1980. London. author's 2nd book. F/F. A11. $40.00

CHATWIN, Bruce. *What Am I Doing Here.* 1989. Viking. 1st ed. F/F. Q1. $35.00

CHAUCER, Geoffrey. *Canterbury Tales.* 1929-31. Golden Cockerel. 1/485 on Batchelor handmade. 4 vols. w/sgn letter. case. H5. $6,500.00

CHAUCER, Geoffrey. *Canterbury Tales.* 1930. Covici Friede. 1/924. ils/sgn Rockwell Kent. 2 vols. VG. F1. $350.00

CHAUCER, Geoffrey. *Canterbury Tales.* 1934. Covici Friede. ils Rockwell Kent. 627 p. ils ep. cloth. F. B14. $125.00

CHAUCER, Geoffrey. *Chaucer's Flower & the Leaf.* 1902. London. Arnold. 1/165. sm octavo. 45 p. full vellum. NF. H5. $650.00

CHAUCER, Geoffrey. *Works of...* (1958). World. facsimile. 554 p. VG/clip. B18. $195.00

CHAUVELOT, Richard. *Mysterious India.* 1921. NY. Century. 1st Am ed. 8vo. 277 p. F/VG. A2. $30.00

CHAYEFSKY, Paddy. *Altered States.* 1978. Harper Row. 1st Am ed. VG/dj. P3. $20.00

CHAYEFSKY, Paddy. *Goddess: A Screenplay.* 1958. NY. NF/NF. A11. $30.00

CHAYT & CHAYT. *Collotype: Being a Hist, Practicum, Bibliography.* 1983. Winter Haven, FL. Anachronic Eds. 1/85. sgn. 102 p. M/glassine wrp. B24. $375.00

CHEADLE & ESAU. *Secondary Phleom of Calycanthaceae.* 1958. Berkeley. 8 pls. 113 p. VG/wrp. B26. $19.00

CHEADLE & MILTON. *NW Passage by Land.* (1865). London. Cassell Petter. 1st ed. lg 8vo. 23 pls. 400 p. bl cloth. K1. $175.00

CHEETHAM, James. *Narrative of...Administration of John Adams...* 1802. NY. 2nd ed. 12mo. 72 p. VG. B28. $135.00

CHEEVER, John. *Atlantic Crossing.* 1986. Ex Ophedia. 1/99. folio. leather. F/clamshell box. C4. $400.00

CHEEVER, John. *Day the Pig Fell Into the Well.* 1978. Lord John. 1st separate ed. sgn. F/slipcase. L3. $450.00

CHEEVER, John. *Day the Pig Fell Into the Well.* 1978. Northridge. Lord John. 1/26. sgn. F. C4. $375.00

CHEEVER, John. *Enormous Radio & Other Stories.* 1953. NY. 1st ed. VG+/dj. scarce. A15. $70.00

CHEEVER, John. *Expelled.* 1988. np. Sylvester. 1st ed. 1/150. sgn Cheever/Cowley/Updike/Chappell. F/slipcase. Q1. $325.00

CHEEVER, John. *Falconer.* 1977. London. Cape. 1st ed. inscr. F/F. C4. $175.00

CHEEVER, John. *Glad Tidings: Friendship in Letters.* 1993. Harper Collins. AP. F/wht wrp. C1. $35.00

CHEEVER, John. *Homage to Shakespeare.* 1968. Stevenson. Country Squires. 1/150. inscr. F. C4. $300.00

CHEEVER, John. *National Pastime.* 1982. LA. Sylvester Orphanos. 1/300. sgn. F/F. C4. $60.00

CHEEVER, John. *Proceedings: Am Academy of Arts & Letters.* 1969. np. C4. $35.00

CHEEVER, John. *Stories of John Cheever.* 1978. Knopf. 1st ed. sgn. F/NF. B2. $150.00

CHEEVER, John. *Thirteen Uncollected Stories.* 1994. Chicago. Academy Chicago Pub. 1st collected ed. F/F. C4. $22.00

CHEEVER, John. *Whapshot Chronicle.* 1957. Harper. 1st ed. author's 1st novel. F/NF. L3. $150.00

CHEEVER, John. *Whapshot Chronicle.* 1957. Harper. 1st ed. sgn/dtd 1979. F/NF. C4. $300.00

CHEEVER, Susan. *Looking for Work.* 1979. NY. 1st ed. sgn. F/F. A11. $45.00

CHEKREZI, Constantine A. *Albania Past & Present.* 1919. NY. 8vo. 2 maps. 255 p. cloth. O2. $50.00

CHEN, Jack. *Sinkiang Story.* 1977. NY. ARC/1st prt. 386 p. silvered blk cloth. F/VG. H3. $20.00

CHENEY, Cora. *Plantation Doll.* 1955. Holt. 1st ed. 136 p. cloth. VG/dj. M20. $15.00

CHERRY, P.P. *W Reserve & Early OH.* 1920. Fouse. xl. 229 p. VG. M20. $50.00

CHERRYH, C.J. *Brothers of Earth.* nd. BC. VG/dj. P3. $7.50

CHERRYH, C.J. *Cuckoo's Egg.* 1985. Phantasia. 1st ed. 1/350. sgn/#d. F/dj/slipcase. P3. $40.00

CHERRYH, C.J. *Downbelow Station.* 1981. DAW. 1st hc ed. sgn. F/F. F4. $22.00

CHERRYH, C.J. *Faded Sun: Kutah.* 1979. Nelson Doubleday. 1st hc ed. sgn. F/F. F4. $15.00

CHERRYH, C.J. *Goblin Mirror.* 1992. Del Rey. 1st ed. sgn. F/F. F4. $28.00

CHERRYH, C.J. *Kif Strike Bak.* 1985. Phantasia. 1st ed. 1/350. sgn/#d. F/dj/slipcase. P3. $40.00

CHERRYH, C.J. *Sunfall.* 1981. DAW 433. 1st ed. F/wrp. F4. $10.00

CHERRYH & MORRIS. *Gates of Hell.* 1986. Baen. 1st ed. F/NF. N3. $10.00

CHERUBINI, Luigi. *Medee. Opera en III Acts.* 1797. Paris. Chez Imbault. 1st ed. folio. 388 p. modern polished calf. VG. H5. $1,250.00

CHESBRO, George B.; see Cross, David.

CHESBRO, George C. *City of Whispering Stone.* 1978. Simon Schuster. 1st ed. VG/G+. P3. $25.00

CHESBRO, George C. *Fear in Yesterday's Rings.* 1991. Mysterious. 1st ed. F/F. F4. $20.00

CHESBRO, George C. *Shadow of a Broken Man.* 1977. Simon Schuster. 1st ed. author's 1st book. F/F. F4. $40.00

CHESBRO, George C. *Shadow of a Broken Man.* 1977. Simon Schuster. 1st ed. VG/dj. P3. $30.00

CHESBRO, George C. *Veil.* 1986. Mysterious. 1st ed. F/dj. P3. $20.00

CHESELDEN, William. *Anatomy of the Human Body.* 1806. Boston. David West. 2nd Am ed. 40 pls. 352 p. full calf. S9. $99.00

CHESHIRE, Jimmy. *Home Boy.* 1989. NAL. 1st ed. author's 1st book. F/F. A14. $30.00

CHESLEY, Larry. *7 Years in Hanoi: A POW Tells His Story.* (1973). Salt Lake City. Bookcraft. stated 1st ed. F/NF clip. A7. $45.00

CHESNEL, P. *Historie de Cavelier de la Salle...Bassin du Mississipi.* 1901. Paris Librairie Orientale et Americaine. M/wrp. O6. $45.00

CHESTER, FAY & YOUNG. *Zinoviev Letter: A Political Intrigue.* 1968. Lippincott. 218 p. dj. A7. $15.00

CHESTER, George Randolph. *Get-Rich-Quick Wallingford.* 1908. Altemus. 1st ed. NF. B2. $100.00

CHESTER, Peter; see Phillips, Dennis.

CHESTER, S.B. *Life of Venizelos.* (1921). NY. 1st ed. 8vo. 321 p. cloth. O2. $40.00

CHESTERTON, G.K. *Charles Dickens: Last of the Great Men.* 1942. Readers Club. G/dj. E3. $12.00

CHESTERTON, G.K. *Incredulity of Father Brn.* 1926. Dodd Mead. 1st Am ed. VG. Q1. $75.00

CHESTERTON, G.K. *Innocence of Father Brn.* 1913. Cassell. 4th ed. VG. P3. $20.00

CHESTERTON, G.K. *Orthodoxy.* 1911. John Lane. 1st Am ed. sgn. NF. B4. $150.00

CHESTERTON, G.K. *Secret of Father Brn.* 1927. London. 1st ed. VG. T9. $55.00

CHESTERTON, G.K. *Tales of the Long Bow.* 1925. Tauchnitz. VG. P3. $60.00

CHESTNUT, Robert; see Cooper, Clarence.

CHESTNUT, V.K. *Plants Used by Indians of Mendocino Co, CA.* 1974. Mendocino Hist Soc. ils/glossary/index. 130 p. F/wrp. B19. $4.00

CHESTNUTT, Charles W. *Conjure Tales.* (1975). London. Collins. 1st Eng ed. F/NF. B4. $45.00

CHETWIN, Grace. *Atheling.* 1988. Tor. 1st ed. F/dj. P3. $18.95

CHETWYND-HAYNES, R. *King's Ghost.* 1985. Wm Kimber. 1st ed. F/F. F4. $35.00

CHEUSE, Alan. *Light Possessed.* (1990). NY. Gibbs Smith. ARC. VG/pict wrp. B3. $30.00

CHEVALIER, Jacques. *Henri Bergson.* 1928. Macmillan. trans Lilian A CLarke. 351 p. cloth. G1. $22.50

CHEVALLIER, Gabriel. *Chochemerle-Les-Bains.* 1964. London. Secker Warburg. 1st ed. trans Xan Fielding. VG+/VG+. A14. $25.00

CHEVALLIER, Gabriel. *Clochemerle.* 1955. London. Secker Warburg. 1st ed. trans Edward Hyams. VG+/VG+ clip. A14. $30.00

CHEVIGNY, Paul. *Cops & Rebels.* (1972). Pantheon. 1st ed. 332 p. dj. A7. $20.00

CHEW, Peter. *KY Derby: 1st 100 Yrs.* 1974. Houghton Mifflin. 1st ed. 4to. VG/VG. O3. $45.00

CHEYNE, George. *Essay on Health & Long Life.* 1724. London. 1st ed. contemporary calf. G7. $295.00

CHEYNEY, Peter. *Calling Mr Callaghan.* 1953. Todd. 1st ed. NF/NF. F4. $35.00

CHEYNEY, Peter. *Dark Bahama.* 1951. Detective BC. VG. P3. $12.50

CHEYNEY, Peter. *Uneasy Terms.* 1958. Collins. VG/dj. P3. $17.50

CHIBAULT DE CHANVALON, J.-B. *Voayge a la Martinique.* 1763. Paris. JB Bauche. xl. quarto. 192 p. red half morocco. H9. $375.00

CHICKERING, Jesse. *Statistical View of Population of MA From 1765 to 1840.* 1846. Little Brn. 1st ed. xl. 8vo. 160 p. cloth/prt wrp bound in. M1. $275.00

CHICKERING, W.H. *Within the Sound of These Waves.* 1941. NY. 1st ed. 327 p. red cloth. VG. H3. $20.00

CHICKERING, W.H. *Within the Sound of These Waves.* 1941. NY. 1st ed. ils Jack Kelly. 327 p. F/dj. B14. $55.00

CHIDSEY, Alan Lake. *Rustam: Lion of Persia.* 1930. Minton Balch. 1st ed. 271 p. VG. P2. $35.00

CHIDSEY, Donald Barr. *Capt Adam.* 1953. Crown. 1st ed. VG/dj. P3. $20.00

CHIH-YEN, Hsia. *Coldest Winter in Peking.* 1978. Doubleday. 1st ed. dj. A7. $9.00

CHILD, Heather. *Decorative Maps.* 1956. London. Studio. NF/dj. O6. $35.00

CHILD, Isabella. *Child's Picture Bible.* ca 1850. New Haven. Durrie Peck. miniature. 191 p. gilt cloth. H10. $125.00

CHILD, L. Maria. *Adventures of Jamie & Jeannie & Other Stories.* ca 1900. Lothrop. ils. 157 p. G+. S10. $20.00

CHILD, L. Maria. *Appeal in Favor of That Class of Americans Called Africans.* 1833. Boston. Allen Ticknor. 1st ed. 12mo. 232 p. cloth/prt paper label. M1. $750.00

CHILD, L. Maria. *Isaac T Hopper: A True Life.* 1853. Boston/Cleveland. 1st ed. 12mo. 493 p. rebacked/orig spine. B28. $50.00

CHILD, Theodore. *Spanish-Am Republics.* 1891. Harper. 1st ed. 4to. 444 p. VG. B11. $95.00

CHILDE, V. Gordon. *Skara Brae.* 1931. London. 1st ed. 208 p. VG. H3. $40.00

CHILDS, Marilyn. *Riding Show Horses.* 1963. Princeton. 1st ed. Van Nostrand Sporting series. G+/G+. O3. $35.00

CHILTON, John. *Billie's Blues.* (1975). Stein Day. 264 p. dj. A7. $40.00

CHILTON, John. *Who's Who of Jazz.* 1979. Time Life. VG/dj. P3. $20.00

CHINARD, Gilbert. *Thomas Jefferson: Apostle of Americanism.* 1929. Little Brn. 1st ed. inscr. 548 p. VG/VG. B10. $20.00

CHINCHILLA, C.S. *Emerald Lizard: Tales & Legends of Guatemala.* (1957). Falcon Wing Pr. 1st Am ed. 8vo. 274 p. F/VG+. A2. $20.00

CHINCHILLA AGUILAR, Ernesto. *Ayuntamiento Colonial de la Cuidad de Guatemala.* 1961. Guatemala. Editorial Universitaria. 309 p. F3. $25.00

CHINN, Laurene. *Unanointed.* 1959. Crown. 376 p. VG. S3. $18.00

CHIPMAN, Art. *Wild Flower Trails of Pacific NW.* 1970. Medford. 236 ils. 156 p. VG/dj. B26. $21.00

CHIPPERFIELD, Jimmy. *My Wild Life.* (1976). NY. 1st Am ed. 218 p. F/dj. A17. $10.00

CHIRARDELLI, Cornelio. *Cefalogia Fisonomica.* 1630. Bologna. Heirs of Evangelista Dozza. 4to. 400+ woodcuts. vellum. G7. $575.00

CHITTENDEN, Hiram Martin. *Hist of Am Fur Trade of the Far W.* (1954). Stanford. Academic Reprints. 2 vols. 8vo. 1029 p. NF/dj. B20. $90.00

CHITTENDEN, Hiram Martin. *Yellowstone Nat Park.* 1900 (1895). Cincinnati. ils/fld map. 409 p. cloth. VG. D3. $25.00

CHITTENDEN, Hiram Martin. *Yellowstone Nat Park.* 1920. Stewart Kidd. 12mo. G. A8. $17.00

CHITTY, Joseph. *Observations on the Game Laws...* 1816. London. AJ Valpy. 1st ed. gilt quarter calf. M11. $350.00

CHITTY, Joseph. *Practical Treatise on Laws of Contracts.* 1844. Springfield. Merriam. polished full calf/rpr joints. M11. $150.00

CHIU, Tony. *Port Arthur Chicken.* 1979. Morrow. 1st ed. F/NF. A7. $25.00

CHOATE, Joseph H. *Supreme Court of US: Its Place in Constitution.* 1903. np. orig wrp in later quarter leather. M11. $65.00

CHOCHEM & ROTH. *Palestine Dances! Folk Dances of Palestine As Set Down by...* 1941. NY. Behrman. ils Moses Soyer/photos John Mills. 63 p. S3. $30.00

CHOONG-OK, Cho. *Art of Korean Cookery.* 1963. Tokyo. Shibata. 8vo. ils. 129 p. VG. W1. $16.00

CHOPPING, Harold. *Character Sketches From Dickens.* (1924). McKay. 1st ed. quarto. NF. B4. $100.00

CHORLTON, William. *Am Grape Growers' Guide.* 1856 (1852). NY. Saxton. 12mo. 171 p. VG. B28. $45.00

CHOTZNER, Joseph. *Hebrew Humor & Other Essays.* 1905. London. Luzac. 186 p. VG-. S3. $24.00

CHOULES, J.O. *Cruise of the Steam Yacht N Star.* 1854. Boston/NY. 1st ed. 12mo. 353 p. gilt cloth. B28. $100.00

CHRISTENSEN. *Needlepoint Book.* 1976. np. ils. cloth. G2. $17.50

CHRISTIAN, Catherine. *Pendragon.* 1979. np. 1st Am ed. VG/dj. C1. $11.50

CHRISTIAN, W. Asbury. *Richmond: Her Past & Present.* 1912. Richmond. ils LH Jenkins. gilt red cloth. H9. $45.00

CHRISTIE, Agatha. *ABC Murders.* 1936. Dodd Mead. 1st ed. VG. P3. $75.00

CHRISTIE, Agatha. *Adventure of the Christmas Pudding.* 1960. London. 1st ed. F/F. A11. $45.00

CHRISTIE, Agatha. *Agatha Christie Hour.* 1982. London. Collins. collected ed. F/F. M15. $45.00

CHRISTIE, Agatha. *By the Pricking of My Thumbs.* 1968. Collins Crime Club. 1st ed. VG/G+. P3. $15.00

CHRISTIE, Agatha. *Caribbean Mystery.* (1964). London. Crime Club/Collins. 1st ed. NF/dj. B9. $40.00

CHRISTIE, Agatha. *Clocks.* 1963. Dodd Mead. 1st Am ed. 276 p. VG/dj. M20. $25.00

CHRISTIE, Agatha. *Curtain.* 1975. Dodd Mead. 1st Am ed. 238 p. VG/clip. M20. $15.00

CHRISTIE, Agatha. *Death Comes As the End.* 1945. London. Collins Crime Club. 1st Eng ed. NF/NF. M15. $175.00

CHRISTIE, Agatha. *Death on the Nile.* 1944. Avon 46. titles to #52 on back. VG+. A11. $40.00

CHRISTIE, Agatha. *Elephants Can Remember.* 1972. Collins Crim Club. VG/dj. P3. $22.50

CHRISTIE, Agatha. *Endless Night.* 1968. Dodd Mead. 1st ed. NF/NF. Q1. $40.00

CHRISTIE, Agatha. *Endless Night.* 1968. Dodd Mead. 1st ed. xl. dj. P3. $5.00

CHRISTIE, Agatha. *Mousetrap & Other Plays.* 1978. Dodd Mead. 1st ed. intro Ira Levin. F/F. S5. $50.00

CHRISTIE, Agatha. *Murder for Christmas.* 1939. Dodd Mead. 1st ed. NF/NF. Q1. $300.00

CHRISTIE, Agatha. *Murder in Mesopotamia.* 1936. NY. 1st Am ed. 298 p. G/dj. B18. $45.00

CHRISTIE, Agatha. *Mystery of the Bl Train.* 1928. Dodd Mead. 1st Am ed. VG/dj. M15. $300.00

CHRISTIE, Agatha. *Ordeal by Innocence.* 1958. Collins Crime Club. 1st ed. VG. P3. $25.00

CHRISTIE, Agatha. *Passenger to Frankfurt.* 1970. Collins Crim Club. 1st ed. VG/dj. P3. $30.00

CHRISTIE, Victor. *Bessie Pease Gutmann: Her Life & Works.* 1990. Wallace Homestead. 1st ed. sm 4to. 199 p. M/M. S10. $25.00

CHRISTMAN, Henry M. *Walter P Reuther: Selected Papers.* ca 1961. Macmillan. 1st prt. VG/G. V4. $12.50

CHRISTOFFERSSON. *Swedish Sweaters, New Designs From Hist Examples.* 1991. np. ils. cloth. G2. $16.00

CHRISTOPHE, Robert. *Executioners.* 1962 (1961). London. Arthur Baker. 1st ed. 8vo. 205 p. VG+/VG. A2. $15.00

CHRISTOPHER, John. *Little People.* nd. BC. VG/dj. P3. $7.50

CHRISTOPHER, Nicholas. *On Tour w/Rita.* 1982. NY. 1st ed. author's 1st book. F/F. V1. $20.00

CHRISTOU, P.K. *Mount Athos. Athonite Civilization — Hist, Art, Life.* 1987. Athens. Greek text. 4to. 488 p. cloth. dj. O2. $55.00

CHRISTY, Michael. *Hist Michie Tavern Museum: Cooking Treasures of Past.* (1982). The Mus. 2nd prt. 90 p. sbdg. VG. B10. $8.00

CHU, Louis. *Eat a Bowl of Tea.* 1961. Lyle Stuart. 1st ed. dj. N2. $7.50

CHUNG & RO. *Nationalism in Korea.* 1979. Seoul. Research Center Peace & Unification. 8vo. 338 p. VG. W1. $16.00

CHURCH, A.J. *Crown of Pine.* 1906. NY. 1st Am ed. 8 color pls. 309 p. pict red cloth. VG+. H3. $15.00

CHURCH, Albert L. *Elements of Descriptive Geometry...* (1864). NY. Barnes. 2 vols. pls. blk cloth. F. B14. $50.00

CHURCHER, Sharon. *NY Confidential, Lowdown on the Big Town.* 1986. NY. Crown. dj. N2. $5.00

CHURCHILL, C.W. *S of the Sunset: Interpretation of Sacajawea...* 1936. NY. RR Wilson. 1st ed. 8vo. 287 p. VG+. T8. $15.00

CHURCHILL, David. *It, Us & the Others.* 1979. Harper Row. ne. F/dj. P3. $12.50

CHURCHILL, T.O. *Life of Lord Viscount Nelson.* 1808. London. Bensley. lg 4to. 15 pls/100 ils. contemporary half calf. K1. $375.00

CHURCHILL, Winston S. *Great Contemporaries.* 1941. London. Reprint Soc. 344 p. yel cloth/brn leather spine label. G+. M7. $22.50

CHURCHILL, Winston S. *King George VI. The Prime Minister's Broadcast...* 1952. Worcester. St Onge. miniature. 1/750. dk bl morocco. H10. $275.00

CHURCHILL, Winston S. *My African Journey.* (1909). NY. Doran. 1st Am ed. 2nd issue bdg. VG. Q1. $1,000.00

CHURCHMAN, John. *Account of Gospel Labours & Christian Experiences...* 1781. London. James Phillips. 3rd prt. 8vo. 351 p. leather. rpr hinge. V3. $35.00

CHUTE, Carolyn. *Beans.* (1985). Chatto Windus. 1st ed. sgn. F/F. B3. $75.00

CHUTE, Carolyn. *Letourneau's Used Auto Parts.* (1988). Ticknor Fields. 1st ed. sgn. F/F. B3. $45.00

CHUTE, Carolyn. *Merry Men.* 1994. Harcourt. ARC. sgn. F/wrp. B2. $50.00

CHUVIN, Pierre. *Chronicle of the Last Pagans.* 1990. Harvard. VG. N2. $5.00

CIARDI, John. *In Fact.* 1962. New Brunswick. 1st ed. F/VG+. V1. $20.00

CINTRON, Lola Verrill. *Goddess of the Bullring.* 1960. Bobbs Merrill. 1st ed. dj. N2. $10.00

CIPOLLA, Carlo M. *Guns, Sails & Empires: Technological Innovation...* (1965). Pantheon. 1st Am ed. 192 p. dj. A7. $15.00

CISNEROS, Jose. *Riders Across the Centuries.* 1984. TX W Pr. 199 p. F/F. B19. $50.00

CIST, Lewis J. *Trifles in Verse: Collection of Fugitive Poems.* 1845. Cincinnati. Robinson Jones. 1st ed. 12mo. 184 p. cloth. M1. $125.00

CLAIBORNE, J.F.H. *Life & Times of Gen Samual Dale...MS Partisan.* 1860. Harper. xl. 233 p. blk half sheep. H9. $75.00

CLAMPITT, Amy. *Silence Opens.* 1994. Knopf. AP. B4. $25.00

CLAMPITT, Amy. *Westward.* 1990. Knopf. 1st ed. F/F. V1. $20.00

CLANCY, Tom. *Cardinal of the Kremlin.* 1988. Putnam. 1st ed. VG/dj. P3. $20.00

CLANCY, Tom. *Hunt for Red October.* (1985). Annapolis, MD. Naval Inst. 5th prt. VG/dj. P3. $15.00

CLANCY, Tom. *Hunt for Red October.* 1985. Collins. 1st Eng ed. F/F. Q1. $375.00

CLANCY, Tom. *Patriot Games.* 1987. Putnam. 1st ed. inscr. ES. F/F. M10. $65.00

CLANCY, Tom. *Red Storm Rising.* (1986). Putnam. 1st ed. author's 2nd book. NF/NF clip. B3. $55.00

CLANCY, Tom. *Submarine.* 1984. Putnam. ltd ed. sgn. F/blk slipcase. C4. $150.00

CLANCY, Tom. *Sum of All Fears.* 1991. Putnam. 1/600. sgn/#d. special bdg. F/slipcase. Q1. $225.00

CLANCY, Tom. *Without Remorse.* 1993. Putnam. ARC. F/wrp. B2. $35.00

CLAPPER, Olive. *One Lucky Woman.* 1961. Doubleday. 1st ed. sgn. 503 p. VG+/dj. M20. $10.00

CLARESON, Thomas D. *Spectrum of Worlds.* 1972. Doubleday. 1st ed. F/NF. N3. $10.00

CLARIDGE, John. *Shepherd of Banbury's Rules to Judge of Changes of Weather.* 1755. Edinburgh. James Reid. 16mo. 40 p. modern cloth. N2. $115.00

CLARK, Al. *Raymond Chandler in Hollywood.* 1982-83. London. 1st ed. 160 p. F/unsed wrp. A11. $30.00

CLARK, Ann Nolan. *Third Monkey.* 1956. Viking. ils Don Freeman. 44 p. VG+. P2. $10.00

CLARK, Ann. *About the Grass Mtn Mouse.* 1940. Lawrence. Haskell/US Office of Indian Affairs. VG/wrp. L3. $125.00

CLARK, Ann. *Singing Sioux Cowboy Reader.* nd. Lawrence. bilingual children's reader. VG/stapled wrp. L3. $175.00

CLARK, Anna. *Last Voyage.* 1982. St Martin. 1st ed. VG/dj. P3. $17.50

CLARK, Arthur Miller. *From Cove to Grove: Brief Hist of Carpinteria Valley, CA.* 1962. private prt. 1st ed. 93 p. F. B19. $25.00

CLARK, Curt; see Westlake, Donald E.

CLARK, Dennis. *Ghetto Game.* (1962). Sheed Ward. 245 p. NF/dj. A7. $20.00

CLARK, Ellery H. *Carleton Case.* 1910. McLeod Allen. 1st Canadian ed. VG-. P3. $7.50

CLARK, George Henry. *Life-Sketches of Rev George Henry Clark. By His Brother.* 1852. Boston. xl. 12mo. 160 p. emb blk cloth. G. T3. $15.00

CLARK, Gregory. *With Rod & Reel in Canada.* ca 1948. Ottawa. 12mo. photos/pls. NF/wrp. A17. $20.00

CLARK, Henry W. *Hist of AK.* 1930. NY. 1st ed. xl. 208 p. cloth. D3. $25.00

CLARK, J. Reuben. *Stand Fast by Our Constitution.* 1962. Salt Lake City. Sesert Book Co. dj. M11. $20.00

CLARK, John G. *Grain Trade in Old NW.* 1980. Westport. Greenwood. 324 p. blk cloth. M. P4. $30.00

CLARK, Margaret. *Golden Age of the Performing Arts.* 1976. Dietz. 67 p. VG/stiff wrp. B10. $15.00

CLARK, Margaret. *Mystery Horse.* 1972. Dodd Mead. 1st ed. VG/G+. O3. $25.00

CLARK, Mary Higgins. *Anastasia Syndrome & Other Stories.* 1989. Simon Schuster. 1st ed. F/dj. B3/P3. $20.00

CLARK, Mary Higgins. *Loves Music, Loves To Dance.* (1991). Simon Schuster. 1st ed. inscr/dtd 1991. NF/F. B3. $35.00

CLARK, Mary Higgins. *Weep No More, My Lady.* 1987. Simon Schuster. 1st ed. VG/dj. P3. $15.00

CLARK, Mary Higgins. *While My Pretty One Sleeps.* (1989). Simon Schuster. 1st ed. F/F. B3. $20.00

CLARK, Mizzell. *Crossroads. Junction of Old & New...* nd. Dietz. ils/map. 18 p. VG/wrp. B10. $10.00

CLARK, Philip. *Flight Into Darkness.* 1948. Simon Schuster. 1st ed. VG-. P3. $10.00

CLARK, Ronald W. *Einstein: The Life & Times.* 1971. World. 1st Am ed. 718 p. VG/dj. G1. $25.00

CLARK, Ronald W. *Life of Bertrand Russell.* 1976. Knopf. 1st Am ed. 766 p. dj. A7. $20.00

CLARK, Sydney. *All the Best of the S Pacific.* 1961. NY. 1st ed. 8vo. 334 p. gray cloth. F/VG. H3. $20.00

CLARK, Thomas Curtis. *Poems of Justice.* 1929. Chicago. Willett Clark Colby. NF. B2. $40.00

CLARK, Tom. *Champagne & Baloney.* 1976. Harper Row. 1st ed. VG+/VG+. P8. $17.50

CLARK, Tom. *Paradise Resisted. Selected Poems, 1978-84.* nd. Blk Sparrow. 1/200. sgn/#d. F/acetate. V1. $30.00

CLARK, Walter Van Tilburg. *City of Trembling Leaves.* 1945. Random. 1st ed. VG/G. P3. $25.00

CLARK, Walter Van Tilburg. *Strange Hunting.* 1985. Reno, NV. 1st ltd ed. 1/115. M. A18. $125.00

CLARK, Walter Van Tilburg. *Track of the Cat.* (1949). Random. 1st ed. F/F. A18. $100.00

CLARK, Walter. *Government by Judges, Address...., in NYC on Jan 27, 1914.* 1937. GPO. 17 p. stapled wrp. M11. $35.00

CLARK, William G. *Greece & the Greeks.* 1858. London. 8vo. 344 p. aeg. cloth. O2. $300.00

CLARK, William J. *Commercial Cuba: Book for Business Men.* 1898. Scribner. 1st ed. 8vo. 40 pls/15 plans. 514 p. G. B11. $95.00

CLARK & DEWHURST. *Ils Hist of Brain Function.* 1972. Oxford. lg 4to. ils. 154 p. NF/dj. G7. $135.00

CLARK & LEWIS. *Hist of Expedition of Captains...* 1902. McClurg. reprint of 1814 ed. 2 vols. 8vo. full crushed levant. H9. $150.00

CLARK & LEWIS. *Hist of Expedition Under the Command of...* 1845. NY. Harper. Family Lib #154. sm 12mo. fld maps. blk cloth. $95.00

CLARK & LEWIS. *Hist of the Expedition Under Command of Capts....* 1814. Phil/NY. Allen/Inskeep. 1st ed. 2 vols. facsimile fld map. slipcase/chemise. H5. $6,000.00

CLARK & MALTE. *Fodder & Pasture Plants.* 1913. Ottawa. 27 color pls. 143 p. VG. B28. $37.50

CLARK & SOSIN. *Through the Fish's Eye.* (1973). NY. ils/index. 249 p. F/dj. A17. $12.50

CLARK & TILLER. *Terrible Trail: Meek Cutoff, 1845.* 1966. Caxton. 1st ed. photos/maps. F/F clip. A18. $75.00

CLARK. *Quilts in Community.* 1991. np. Ohio Quilt Research Group. cloth. G2. $30.00

CLARKE, Arthur C. *Exploration of Space.* 1951. Harper. 1st Am ed. author's 3rd book. VG+/VG. N3. $55.00

CLARKE, Arthur C. *Making of a Moon (Revised).* 1958. Harper. ne. VG/dj. P3. $75.00

CLARKE, Arthur C. *Prelude to Space.* 1954. Gnome. 1st ed. F/F. M2. $135.00

CLARKE, Arthur C. *Rendezvous w/Rama.* (1973). London. Gollancz. 1st ed. F/VG clip. B3. $45.00

CLARKE, Arthur C. *Report on Planet Three.* 1972. Harper Row. 1st ed. VG/dj. P3. $25.00

CLARKE, Arthur C. *Tales From the Wht Hart.* nd. BC. VG/dj. P3. $7.50

CLARKE, Arthur C. *Tales From the Wht Hart.* 1970. HBW. 1st ed. NF/NF. P3. $100.00

CLARKE, Arthur C. *2061: Odyssey Three.* 1988. Del Rey. 1st ed. VG/dj. P3. $17.50

CLARKE, Asa B. *Travels in Mexico & CA: Comprising a Journal of Tour...* 1852. Boston. Wright Hasty's Steam Pr. 1st ed. F/slipcase/chemise. P4. $2,400.00

CLARKE, Austin C. *Meeting Point.* 1967. Toronto. Macmillan. 1st ed. NF/NF. A13. $35.00

CLARKE, Austin C. *Prime Minister.* 1977. Toronto. General Pub. 1st ed. F/F. A13. $25.00

CLARKE, Beverly. *Doctor Looks at Murder.* 1937. Doubleday. 1st ed. inscr/sgn Clarke (as Cross) to Howard Wandrei. NF/NF. F4. $60.00

CLARKE, Charles G. *Men of the Lewis & Clark Expedition.* 1970. Glendale. Arthur Clark. 1st ed. 8vo. 351 p. red cloth. M. very scarce. T8. $175.00

CLARKE, Donald Henderson. *Housekeeper's Daughter.* 1940. Triangle. 5th prt. VG-/dj. P3. $15.00

CLARKE, Dwight L. *William Tecumseh Sherman: Gold Rush Banker.* 1969. CA Hist Soc. 1st ed. 446 p. F/F. B19. $25.00

CLARKE, Elizabeth D.H. *Joy of Service. Memoirs of...* 1979. NY. 8vo. 316 p. cloth. dj. O2. $30.00

CLARKE, J. Jackson. *Congenital Dislocation of the Hip.* 1910. London. Bailliere Tindal. 92 p. G7. $175.00

CLARKE, J.W. *Cattle Problems Explained.* 1980. Battle Creek. 1st ed. VG. O3. $45.00

CLARKE, John S. *Pen Pictures of Russia Under the Red Terror.* 1921. Glasgow. Nat Workers Committee. VG. B2. $85.00

CLARKE, Thurston. *Equator: A Journey.* (1988). NY. Morrow. 1st ed. 8vo. 463 p. F/F. A2. $12.50

CLARKE, Walter E. *AK.* (1910). Boston. Marshall Jones. lg 8vo. photos. 207 p. aeg. gilt cloth. F. A17. $35.00

CLARO, Joe. *Alex Gets the Business.* 1986. Weekly Reader BC. VG. P3. $5.00

CLARY, James. *Ladies of the Lake.* 1981. MI. Natural Resources. VG/dj. A16. $40.00

CLATER, Francis. *Every Man His Own Horse & Cow Doctor...* 1861. Halifax. Milner Sowerby. 260 p. H10. $17.50

CLAVELL, James. *King Rat.* (1962). Little Brn. 1st ed. NF/NF. B4. $150.00

CLAVELL, James. *Little Samurai Thrump-O-Moto.* (1986). London. Hodder Stoughton. 1st ed. ils George Sharp. F/F. B3. $35.00

CLAVELL, James. *Whirlwind.* 1986. NY. Morrow. bound gallies. NF. C4. $35.00

CLAY, Henry. *Life & Speeches...* 1842. NY. Swain. 1st ed. 2 vols. half leather. B28. $55.00

CLAY, William M. *Field Manual of KY Fishes.* 1962. Frankfort. 147 p. VG/wrp. A17. $7.50

CLAYTON, Michael. *Cross Country Riding.* 1977. NY. Dutton. 1st Am ed. 4to. F/F. O3. $25.00

CLEARY, Beverly. *Emily's Runaway Imagination.* 1961. Morrow. 1st ed. 8vo. 221 p. VG/G. A3. $35.00

CLEARY, Beverly. *Ramona Forever.* (1984). Morrow. 1st ed. ils Tiegreen. F/NF. B3. $20.00

CLEARY, Beverly. *Romona the Pest.* 1968. Morrow. 1st ed. 192 p. VG/VG. P2. $28.00

CLEARY, Beverly. *Sister of the Bride.* 1963. Morrow. ils Beth/Joe Brush. 1st ed. 8vo. 288 p. VG/dj. A3. $30.00

CLEARY, Beverly. *Socks.* 1973. Morrow. ils B Darwin. 1st ed. 8vo. 156 p. VG/dj. A3. $30.00

CLEATON & CLEATON. *Books & Battles: Am Literature 1930-30.* 1937. Houghton Mifflin. 1st ed. G/dj. A16. $15.00

CLEATOR, P.E. *Past in Pieces.* (1957). London. Allen Unwin. 1st ed. 23 pls. 180 p. VG+/VG. A2 $15.00

CLEAVER, Eldridge. *Post-Prison Writings & Speeches.* (1968). Ramparts/Random. 3rd prt. 211 p. torn dj. A7. $15.00

CLEAVER, Eldridge. *Soul on Ice.* (1968). Ramparts/McGraw. 7th prt. 210 p. clip dj. A7. $15.00

CLEAVER, Eldridge. *Soul on Ice. Brieven en Essays.* 1969. Utecht. Bruna Zoon. 4th Dutch prt. A7. $13.00

CLEAVES, Freeman. *Rock of Chicamauga.* 1948. np. ils/index. 238 p. O7. $14.50

CLEEVES, Ann. *Killjoy.* 1993. London. Macmillan. 1st ed. F/F. S5. $25.00

CLELAND, Hugh. *George WA in the OH Valley.* 1955. Pittsburgh. 1/2300. sgn. 405. VG/dj. E5. $45.00

CLELAND, Robert Glass. *Cattle on a Thousand Hills.* 1941. San Marino. Huntington Lib. 1st ed. 327 p. VG. B28. $70.00

CLELAND, Robert Glass. *Hist of CA.* 1922. Macmillan. 1st ed. ils. 512 p. G. B19. $20.00

CLELAND, T.M. *Giambattista Bodoni of Parma.* 1916. Boston. Soc Printers. 1/250. 50 p. F/dj. B24. $150.00

CLELAND, T.M. *Grammar of Color.* 1921. Mittineague, MA. Strathmore. 2 vols. quarto. portfolio/box. B14. $100.00

CLEMENS, Samuel L.; see Twain, Mark.

CLEMENS, W.M. *Life of Admiral George Dewey.* ca 1899. NY. 12mo. 196 p. brn cloth. T3. $19.00

CLEMENS, W.M. *VA Wills Before 1799.* 1981. Genealogy Pub. reprint 1924 ed. 107 p. B10. $35.00

CLEMENS & GAMMONS. *Rocket Man.* 1987. Steven Greene. 1st ed. F/VG+. P8. $30.00

CLEMENT, Clara Erskine. *Queen of the Adriatic: Venice Medieval & Modern.* 1893. Boston. 1st ed. inscr/dtd 1893. VG. E3. $35.00

CLEMENT, Hal. *Iceworld.* 1953. Gnome. 1st ed. inscr. F/dj. M2. $200.00

CLEMENT, Hal. *Iceworld.* 1953. Gnome. 1st ed. author's 2nd book. VG+/VG. Q1. $150.00

CLEMENT, Hal. *Mission of Gravity.* 195? Robert Hale. 1st UK ed. sgn as bot Clement/Stubbs. F/NF. scarce. F4. $275.00

CLEMENT, Hal. *Still River.* 1987. Del Rey. 1st ed. F/dj. P3. $17.00

CLEMENT, Priscilla Ferguson. *Welfare & the Poor in the 19th-Century City, Phil 1800-54.* 1985. Rutherford. Fairleigh Dickinson. 8vo. 223 p. M/M. V3. $14.00

CLEMENT. *Official Price Guide to Sewing Collectibles.* 1987. np. ils. wrp. G2. $9.00

CLEMENTS, Frank. *TE Lawrence: A Reader's Guide.* 1973. Melbourne, Australia. 1st ed. 203 p. NF/NF. M7. $75.00

CLEMENTS & SHEAR. *Genera of Fungi.* 1954 (1931). NY. 2nd prt. 58 full-p pls. 496 p. B26. $29.00

CLEUGH, James. *Love Locked Out: Examination of Sexuality...* 1964. Crown. 1st ed. 320 p. blk cloth. VG/dj. G1. $17.50

CLEVE, John; see Offutt, Andrew.

CLEVELAND, Grover. *Fishing & Shooting Sketches.* 1907. NY. 1st ed. ils Henry Watson. 209 p. NF. A17. $30.00

CLEVELAND, John B. *Controversy Between John C Calhoun & Robert Y Hayne...* ca 1913. np. 1st ed. 22 p. VG/prt wrp. M8. $37.50

CLEVELAND, Richard J. *Narrative of Voyages & Commercial Enterprises.* 1842. Cambridge. John Owen. 1st ed. 2 vols. octavo. brn cloth. NF. R3. $750.00

CLEVENGER, S.V. *Spinal Concussion: Surgically Considered...* 1889. Phil. Davis. ils/pls. 359 p. cloth. G7. $395.00

CLEWELL, David. *Blessings in Disguise.* 1991. NY. 1st ed. F/F. V1. $15.00

CLIFFORD, Francis. *All Men Are Lonely Now.* 1967. London. Hodder. 1st ed. NF/NF. S5. $20.00

CLIFFORD & LINZEY. *Snakes of VA.* ca 1981. U Pr of VA. 1st ed. ils/maps. 159 p. VG. B10. $13.00

CLIFTON, Bud; see Stacton, David.

CLIFTON, Lucille. *Good Woman.* 1987. NY. 1st ed. inscr. F/wrp. V1. $20.00

CLIFTON, Lucille. *Quilting. Poems 1987-1990.* 1991. Brockport. AP. photocopied galley sheets. F. L3. $45.00

CLIFTON & RILEY. *They'd Rather Be Right.* 1957. Gnome. 1st ed. F/M. M2. $125.00

CLINE, Platt. *They Came to a Mtn: Story of Flagstaff's Beginnings.* (1977, 76). N AZ U. 2nd prt. 8vo. 364 p. F/F. A2. $17.50

CLINE, Ruth H. *Perceval; or, Story of the Grail.* 1983. Pergamon. 1st ed. 247 p. VG+. C1. $14.50

CLINES, C.V. *Lighter-Than-Air Flight.* (1965). NY. 1st ed. ils. 276 p. G/dj. B18. $35.00

CLINTON, Henry. *Narrative of Lt-Gen Sir Henry Clinton...* 1783. London. Debrett. 4th ed. NF/wrp. O6. $175.00

CLIVE, William. *Tune That They Play.* 1973. Macmillan. 1st ed. VG/dj. P3. $15.00

CLOE, J.H. *Top Cover for Am: Air Force in AK 1920-83.* 1985 (1984). 2nd prt. sgn. 4to. 262 p. VG/VG. A2. $30.00

CLOKEY, Ira W. *Flora of the Charleston Mtns, Clark County, NV.* 1951. Berkeley. fld map. 274 p. wrp. B26. $45.00

CLOUD & LENTZ. *Goldilocks & the 3 Bears.* 1934. Bl Ribbon. unp. pict brds. VG. M20. $200.00

CLOUD & LENTZ. *Goldilocks & the 3 Bears.* 1934. Bl Ribbon. lg octavo. 3 popups. pict brds. NF. B24. $275.00

CLUTESI, George. *Son of Raven, Son of Deer.* 1967. Sydney, BC. Gray's. 2nd prt. sgn/dtd 1968. w/promo sheet. VG. L3. $75.00

CLUTTON-BROCK, Juliet. *Horse Power: Hist of Horse & Donkey in Human Soc.* 1919. Cambridge. Harvard. 1st ed. 4to. 192 p. F/F. O3. $28.00

CLUVERI, Phillippi. *Introductionis in Universam Geographiam, Tam Veterem...* 1729. Amsterdam. Joannem Pauli. lg quarto. 790 p. full vellum. NF. O6. $3,500.00

CLYNE, Geraldine. *Jolly Jump-Ups See the Circus.* 1944. McLoughlin Bros. 6 popups. complete. NF. A3. $70.00

CLYNE, Geraldine. *Jolly Jump-Ups Zoo Book.* 1946. McLoughlin Bros. 6 popups. complete. VG. A3. $70.00

CLYNES, Michael. *Grail Murders.* 1993. London. Headline. ARC of 1st ed. RS. F/dj. S5. $30.00

CLYTUS & REIKER. *Blk Man in Red Cuba.* 1970. Coral Gables, FL. 1st ed. 158 p. NF/dj. A7. $27.00

COAN, Richard W. *Psychologists: Personal & Theoretical Pathways.* 1979. NY. Irvington Wiley. 1st ed. tan cloth. VG/dj. G1. $17.50

COATES, Austin. *Myself a Mandarin.* 1969. NY. John Day. M11. $35.00

COATES, Christopher. *Tropical Fish for a Private Aquarium.* 1933. NY. 1st ed. photos. 226 p. G. A17. $15.00

COATES, Margaret K. *Perennials for W Garden.* 1976. Boulder. 4to. ils/photos. 191 p. F/dj. B26. $35.00

COATS. *Florentine Embroidery.* 1968. np. Coats Sewing Group Book 1069. wrp. G2. $3.00

COATSWORTH, Elizabeth. *Alice-All-by-Herself.* 1937. Macmillan. 1st ed. 181 p. VG. P2. $20.00

COATSWORTH, Elizabeth. *Alice-All-by-Herself.* 1938. Harrap. 1st UK ed. ils Marguerite de Angeli. 205 p. VG+/dj. M20. $60.00

COATSWORTH, Elizabeth. *Away Goes Sally.* 1934. Macmillan. 1st ed. 122 p. G. P2. $15.00

COATSWORTH, Elizabeth. *Golden Horseshoe.* 1935. Macmillan. 1st ed. 153 p. VG+. P2. $35.00

COATSWORTH, Elizabeth. *Mtn Bride.* 1954. Pantheon. ARC. ils George Thompson. 154 p. NF/VG. P2. $25.00

COATSWORTH, Elizabeth. *Thief Island.* 1943. Macmillan. 1st ed. 118 p. VG/dj. M20. $15.00

COATSWORTH, Elizabeth. *Wonderful Day.* 1946. Macmillan. 1st ed. 5th title in Sally series. VG/dj. A3. $25.00

COATSWORTH & COATSWORTH. *Adventures of Nanabush: Ojibway Indian Stories.* (1979). Toronto. Doubleday. 1st ed. F/NF. L3. $65.00

COBB, David A. *NH Maps to 1900: Annotated Checklist.* 1981. Hanover. NH Hist Soc. M/wrp. O6. $20.00

COBB, Frank. *Aviator's Luck.* 1927. Saalfield. 1st ed. F/dj. M2. $20.00

COBBETT, William. *Am Gardener: A Treatise on Other Winter Flowering Plants.* 1835. NY. Doyle. 230 p. cloth. H10. $95.00

COBBETT, William. *Life of Andrew Jackson, President of the US.* 1834. np. 206 p. quarter leather/tan brds. VG. T3. $45.00

COBBLE, A.D. *Wembi, the Singer of Stories.* 1959. Bethany Pr. ils Doris Hallas. 8vo. 128 p. VG/VG. A3. $12.50

COBDEN, John C. *Wht Slaves of Eng.* 1853. Derby Miller. 498 p. emb bl cloth. G. B14. $60.00

COBDEN-SANDERSON, T.J. *London: A Paper Read at Meeting of Art Workers Guild 1891.* 1906. London. Doves Pr. 4to. 8 pl. full vellum. slipcase. K1. $275.00

COBLENTZ, Stanton A. *Crimson Capsule.* 1967. Avalon. 1st ed. F/VG+ clip. N3. $10.00

COBLENTZ, Stanton A. *Militant Dissenters.* 1970. AS Barners. 291 p. dj. A7. $12.00

COBLENTZ, Stanton A. *Under the Triple Suns.* 1955. Fantasy. 1st ed. VG/G+. P3. $35.00

COBLENTZ, Stanton A. *Under Triple Suns.* 1955. Fantasy. ltd ed. 1/300. sgn/#d. F/dj. M2. $125.00

COBURN, Andrew. *Sweetheart.* 1985. Secker Warburg. 1st ed. VG/dj. P3. $20.00

COCHRANE, G.R. *Flowers & Plants of Victoria.* 1968. Sydney. 4to. ils/photos. VG. B26. $49.00

COCHRANE, Mickey. *Baseball: The Fan's Game.* 1939. Funk Wagnall. 1st ed. VG/G. P8. $100.00

COCHRANE & COLDIRON. *Disillusion: Story of Labor Struggle...* (1939). Binfords Mort. 279 p. G/poor. A7. $15.00

COCKER, P.C. *Building Warship Models.* 1974. Charleston, SC. 313 p. cloth. G+/dj. B18. $17.50

COCKERILL, A.W. *Sir Percy Sillitoe.* 1975. London. Allen. 223 p. clip dj. A7. $13.00

COCKRUM, William M. *Hist of the Underground Railroad...* 1915. Oakland City, IN. 1st ed. 12mo. 15 pls. 328 p. gilt gr brds. rpr dj. B11. $75.00

COCTEAU, Jean. *Blood of a Poet.* 1949. Bodley. lg oblong. cloth. NF. C8. $85.00

CODDINGTON, E.B. *Gettysburg Campaign.* 1979. np. ils/index. 840 p. dj. O7. $18.50

CODMAN, J.T. *Brook Farm: Historic & Personal Memoirs.* 1894. Boston. 1st ed. ils. 335 p. VG. B5. $25.00

CODRESCU, Andrei. *License To Carry a Gun.* 1970. Chicago. 1st ed. w/Allen Ginsberg's ownership inscr. NF. A11. $45.00

CODRESCU, Andrei. *Serious Morning.* 1973. Capra. 1st ed. 1/100. sgn. F. B4. $65.00

CODY, Al. *Smoky in the W.* 1950. London. Sampson Low. F/NF. B9. $15.00

CODY, Louisa Frederick. *Memories of Buffalo Bill.* 1920. NY. 1st ed. xl. 352 p. cloth. VG. D3. $45.00

CODY, William F. *Life & Adventures of Buffalo Bill...* (1917). Chicago. 1st ed. 352 p. cloth/photo label. VG. D3. $45.00

CODY, William F. *Story of the Wild W & Campfire Chats...* (1888). Richmond, VA. Johnson. 1st ed. royal 8vo. 766 p. pict brn cloth. D3. $250.00

CODY & INMAN. *Great Salt Lake Trail.* 1898. NY. 1st ed. ils Clarke. VG. B28. $125.00

CODY & INMAN. *Great Salt Lake Trail.* 1899. Topeka. Crane. 2nd ed. maps/pls. teg. F. H7. $50.00

CODY & INMAN. *Great Salt Lake Trail.* 1966. Ross Haines. ltd ed. 1/1500. F/clip. A18. $50.00

CODY. *Continous Line Quilting Designs...* 1984. np. ils. wrp. G2. $15.00

COE, Michael. *Aztec Sorcerers in 17th-Century Mexico.* 1982. Albany, NY. Instit Mesoamerican Studies 7. 329 p. F3. $30.00

COE, Tucker. *Kinds of Love, Kinds of Hate.* (1966). London. Souvenir Pr. 1st ed. 183 p. F/dj. B22. $15.00

COE, William. *Tikal.* (1977). Phil. U Mus. 123 p. wrp. F3. $15.00

COETZEE, J.M. *Age of Iron.* 1990. NY. 1st Am ed. sgn. F/F. A11. $55.00

COETZEE, J.M. *Dusklands.* 1974. Johannesburg. Ravan. 1st ed. author's 1st book. F/dj. scarce. L3. $450.00

COETZEE, J.M. *Dusklands.* 1985. NY. Penguin. 1st Am ed/PBO. sgn. F/ils wrp. A11. $75.00

COETZEE, J.M. *Foe.* 1986. London. 1st Eng ed/after Canadian orig. sgn. F/F. A11. $60.00

COETZEE, J.M. *From the Heart of the Country.* (1977). Harper Row. 1st ed. F/NF clip. B3. $65.00

COETZEE, J.M. *Life & Times of Michael K.* (1983). Secker Warburg. 1st ed. NF/F. B3. $50.00

COFFEY, Brian; see Koontz, Dean R.

COFFIN, Charles Carleton. *Our New Way Round the World.* 1869. Boston. 8vo. 524 p. cloth. O2. $55.00

COFFIN, Charles Carleton. *Our New Way Round the World.* 1869. Boston. Fields Osgood. 1st ed. xl. ES. 524 p. pict gilt cloth. VG. D3. $35.00

COFFIN, Charles Carleton. *Seat of Empire.* 1870. Boston. Fields Osgood. 232 p. orange cloth. lacks maps. H9. $50.00

COFFIN, Geoffrey; see Mason, Van Wyck.

COFFIN, Tristram P. *Ils Book of Baseball Folklore.* 1975. Seabury. 1st ed. photos. F/VG. P8. $35.00

COFFIN, William Sloane Jr. *Once to Every Man.* (1977). Atheneum. 1st ed. VG/dj. A7. $22.00

COGGESHALL, George. *Voyages to Various Parts of the World...1799-1844.* 1851. NY. 1st ed. 8vo. 213 p. cloth. M1. $200.00

COGGESHALL, William T. *Poets & Poetry of the W.* 1860. Collins. 1st ed. 688 p. gilt buckram. VG. A17. $35.00

COGGINS, Jack. *Arms & Equipment of the Civil War.* 1962. Doubleday. early prt. 160 p. cloth. NF/VG. M8. $35.00

COHEN, Anthea. *Angel Without Mercy.* 1982. London. Quartet. 1st ed. author's 1st crime novel. NF/NF. S5. $27.50

COHEN, Arthur A. *Jew: Essays From Martin Buber's Journal...1916-28.* 1980. AL U/JPS. 22 essays. 305 p. VG+/G. S3. $25.00

COHEN, Barbara. *Gooseberries to Oranges.* 1981. Lothrop Lee Shepard. 1st ed. 4to. NF/VG. T5. $28.00

COHEN, Daniel. *Far Side of Consciousness.* 1974. Dodd Mead. 1st ed. VG/dj. P3. $17.50

COHEN, Daniel. *Hiram Bingham & the Dream of Gold.* (1984). NY. Evans. 1st ed. 8vo. photos. 182 p. F/F. A2. $12.50

COHEN, Edward H. *Ebeneker Cooke the Sot-Weed Canon.* 1975. Athens, GA. 1st ed. 8vo. 125 p. F/F. B11. $15.00

COHEN, G. *Woman of Violence.* (1966). HRW. xl/1st ed. dj. A7. $20.00

COHEN, Jerome Alan. *Criminal Process in People's Republic of China 1949-63.* 1968. Cambridge. Harvard. M11. $30.00

COHEN, Joel. *Joe Morgan: Great Little Big Man.* 1978. Putnam. 1st ed. F/VG+. P8. $27.50

COHEN, Jonathan. *Sephardi Haggadah w/Trans...Laws of Pesah & Seder.* 1988. Feldheim. Eng/Hebrew text. 4 color pls. VG+/VG+. S3. $24.00

COHEN, Leonard. *Stranger Music. Selected Poems & Songs.* 1993. NY. AP. NF/gray wrp. V1. $25.00

COHEN, Max. *I Was One of the Unemployed.* 1978. Wakefield, Eng. EP Pub. F/VG. V4. $10.00

COHEN, Morris L. *Law, Art of Justice.* 1992. NY. Hugh L Levin. 48 color ils. M11. $35.00

COHEN, Morris Raphael. *Reflections of a Wondering Jew.* 1950. Free Pr. 168 p. G+/fair. S3. $20.00

COHEN, Mortimer J. *Beth Sholom Synagogue: Description & Interpretation.* 1959. self pub. sm 4to. 34 p. VG+. S3. $26.00

COHEN, Morton N. *Lewis Carroll: Photographer of Children...* (1979). NY. 1st trade appearance of 4 color pls. 32 p. VG/dj. B18. $65.00

COHEN, Naomi W. *Not Free To Desist: Hist of Am Jewish Comm 1906-66.* 1972. JPS. 652 p. VG-/G. S3. $23.00

COHEN, Octavus Roy. *Jim Harvey Detective.* 1923. Dodd Mead. 1st ed. VG-. P3. $25.00

COHEN, Octavus Roy. *Sound of Revelry.* (1945). London. Robert Hale. 1st ed. VG/dj. B9. $10.00

COHEN, Robert. *Color of Man.* (1968). Random. 4to. 109 p. dj. A7. $20.00

COHEN, Stan. *Beyond Hell.* 1992. Steam Pr. 1st ed. 1/500. sgn. F/wrp. V1. $25.00

COHEN, Stan. *Kanawha County Images 1788-1988.* 1988. Pict Hist. 4to. VG/G. A8. $25.00

COHEN, Stan. *Pictorial Hist of Downhill Skiing.* (1985). Missoula. 1st ed. 4to. 246 p. F/wrp. A2. $12.50

COHEN, Stanley. *Magic Summer.* 1988. HBJ. 1st ed. rem mk. M/M. P8. $150.00

COHEN, Stanley. *330 Park.* 1977. Putnam. 1st ed. F/dj. P3. $15.00

COHEN, Stephen Paul. *Heartless.* (1986). Morrow. 1st ed. F/dj. B9. $12.50

COHEN & COOPER. *Follow-Up Study of WWII Prisoners of War.* 1954. GPO. VA Medical Monograph. 91 p. bl cloth. G+. S9. $20.00

COHN, Amy L. *From Sea to Shining Sea.* (1993). Scholastic. 1st ed. sgn. F/F. B4. $85.00

COHN, Haim M. *Human Rights in Jewish Law.* 1984. NY. Ktav. xl. M11. $25.00

COHN, William. *Chinese Painting.* 1978. NY. Hacker Arts. reissue of 1948 ed. folio. 224 pls. VG. W1. $45.00

COKE, Edward. *Compleate Copy-Holder...* 1641. London. Cotes. 1st ed. sm 4to. 180 p. gilt modern calf/marbled brds. K1. $250.00

COKE, Edward. *First Part of Inst of Lawes of Eng; or, A Commentarie...* 1629. London. John Moore. 2nd ed. modern full calf. M11. $2,250.00

COKE, Edward. *Systematic Arrangement of Lord Coke's 1st Inst Laws of Eng.* 1818. London. Clarke Hunter Brooke. 17th ed. 2 vols. full calf. M11. $350.00

COKE, Van Deren. *Painter & the Photograph.* 1964. NM U. 1st ed. ils/notes/index. 324 p. F/VG. B19. $50.00

COLACELLO, Bob. *Holy Terror: Andy Warhol Close Up.* 1990. Harper Collins. 1st ed. dj. N2. $10.00

COLBERG, Nancy. *Wallace Stegner: Descriptive Bibliography...* (1990). Lewiston. Confluence Pr. 1st ed. sgn. F/sans. B3. $60.00

COLBY, Charles. *Morse & Gaston's Diamond Atlas.* 1857. NY. Gaston. 240 p. aeg. VG. O6. $375.00

COLBY, William E. *John Muir's Studies in the Sierra.* 1960. Sierra Club. 8vo. VG/VG. A8. $20.00

COLDEN, Jane. *Botanic Manuscript of Jane Colden 1724-66.* 1963. NY. 1/1500. 4to. 205 p. F/NF. B28. $65.00

COLDHAM, Peter Wilson. *Complete Book of Emigrants 1607-60.* 1988. Genealogical Pub. 2nd prt. 600 p. VG/VG. B10. $35.00

COLE, E.B. *Philosophical Corps.* 1961. Gnome. 1st ed. F/dj. M2. $35.00

COLE, Ernest. *House of Bondage.* (1967). Random. 1st Am ed. 4to. 192 p. F/F. A2. $25.00

COLE, G.D.H. *Guide Through World Chaos.* 1933. Knopf. 554 p. dj. A7. $16.00

COLE, G.D.H. *Short Hist of the British Working-Class Movement 1789-1947.* ca 1960. London. Allen Unwin. VG. V4. $12.50

COLE, Garold L. *Civil War Eyewitness: Annotated Bibliography of Books...* 1988. Columbia, SC. 1st ed. 351 p. orig cloth. F/NF. M8. $35.00

COLE, Harold. *Few Thoughts on Trout.* (1986). NY. 1st ed. sq 4to. pict brds. A17. $10.00

COLE, Harry E. *Stagecoach & Tavern Tales of the Old NW.* 1930. Cleveland. Clark. 1st ed. tall 8vo. 376 p. H7. $80.00

COLE, Jackson. *Gun Justice.* 1933. NY. Watt. 1st ed. NF/NF. Q1. $75.00

COLE, Leslie. *Life of Noel Coward.* 1976. London. Cape. 1st ed. 500 p. NF/VG clip. M7. $35.00

COLE, Mabel C. *Savage Gentlemen.* 1929. NY. 1st ed. 8vo. map ep. orange cloth. VG. H3. $20.00

COLE, S.W. *Am Fruit Book...* 1849. Boston. Jewett. 1st ed (before Orange Judd ed). 288 p. full calf. B28. $65.00

COLE, S.W. *Am Veterinarian; or, Diseases of Domestic Animals...* 1850. Boston. Jewett. 30th thousand. 12mo. leather. rpr hinge. O3. $45.00

COLE, William. *Beastly Boys & Ghastly Girls.* (1964). World. ils Tomi Ungerer. 125 p. VG+/G. T5. $30.00

COLE & COLE. *Brooklyn Murders.* 1931. NY. Boni. 1st pb ed. F/stiff wrp/slipcase. M15. $45.00

COLE & COLE. *Toper's End.* 1942. London. Collins Crime Club. 1st ed. NF/clip. M15. $75.00

COLEMAN, J.D. *Pleiku: Dawn of Helicopter Warfare in Vietnam.* (1988). St Martin. 1st ed. 315 p. F/F. A7. $25.00

COLEMAN, Verna. *Last Exquisite: Portrait of Frederic Manning.* 1990. Melbourne U. 1st ed. 244 p. M/dj. M7. $40.00

COLEMAN, Wanda. *Art in the Court of the Bl Fag.* 1977. Santa Barbara. 1st ed. sgn. VG+/self wrp. A11. $30.00

COLEMAN, William. *First Apostolic Delegation in Rio de Janeiro...* 1950. WA. Catholic U of Am. 468 p. wrp. F3. $20.00

COLEMAN. *Quilting: New Dimensions.* 1990. np. ils. G2. $30.00

COLES, Manning. *Drink to Yesterday.* 1944. Canada. Musson. VG/dj. P3. $30.00

COLES, Robert. *Erik H Eriksen: Growth of His Work.* 1970. Little Brn. 1st ed. 118 p. VG/G+. S9. $8.00

COLES, Robert. *Hungary in Am.* (1969). NAL. 115 p. clip dj. A7. $20.00

COLETTE. *Barks & Purrs.* 1913. Fitzgerald. 1st Am ed. trans Marie Kelley. NF. very scarce. $250.00

COLETTE. *Flowers & Fruit.* 1986. FSG. 1st Am ed. edit Robert Phelps. trans Matthew Ward. NF/NF clip. A14. $20.00

COLETTE. *Retreat From Love.* 1974. Bobbs Merrill. 1st Am ed. trans/intro Margaret Crosland. NF/NF. A14. $20.00

COLETTE. *Stories of Colette.* 1958. London. Secker Warburg. 1st ed. trans Antonia Wht. NF/NF. A14. $35.00

COLFER, Enid. *Cucumber: Story of a Siamese Cat.* 1961. Thomas Nelson. 1st ed. 98 p. cloth. VG/dj. M20. $20.00

COLLARD, E.A. *Passage to the Sea.* 1991. Toronto. Doubleday. as new/dj. A16. $35.00

COLLETT, Ritter. *Cincinnati Reds.* 1976. Jordan Powers. 1st ed. F/VG. P8. $125.00

COLLIE CLUB OF AMERICA. *Complete Collie.* 1977. Howell. 12th prt. 254 p. cloth. F. A17. $10.00

COLLIER, Jeremy. *Short View of Immorality & Profaneness of Eng Stage...* 1799 (1798). London. Keble Sare. 4th ed. 288 p. contemporary tooled calf. G1. $150.00

COLLIER, John. *Indwelling Splendor.* 1911. John Collier. 1st ed. author's 1st book. VG. E3. $20.00

COLLIER, MOSKOWITZ & SLOAN. *Patterns & Ceremonials of Indians of the SW.* 1949. NY. Dutton. 1st ed. xl. sgn Collier/Moskowitz, 192 p. P4. $85.00

COLLIER, Richard. *River That Time Forgot: Story of Amazon Rubber Boom.* 1968. Dutton. 1st ed. 8vo. 288 p. F/VG+. A2. $20.00

COLLIER, Richard. *Road to Pearl Harbor: 1941.* 1981. Atheneum. 1st Am ed. VG/dj. A16. $15.00

COLLIGNON, Charles. *Misc Works of Charles Collignon, MD...* 1786. Cambridge. Hodson. 4to. ES. calf. G7. $175.00

COLLINGWOOD, Peter. *Techniques of Sprang.* 1974. Watson Guptill. sgn. dj. N2. $10.00

COLLINGWOOD, Stuart Dodgson. *Life & Letters of Lewis Carroll.* 1899 (1898). Century. xl. 429 p. red cloth. VG. M20. $35.00

COLLINGWOOD. *Maker's Hand.* 1987. np. ils. cloth. G2. $30.00

COLLINS, Billy. *Apple That Astonished Paris.* 1988. Ark Pr. 1st ed. sgn. F/F. V1. $20.00

COLLINS, Herbert. *Presidents on Wheels.* 1971. WA. Acropolis. 1st ed. 4to. VG/VG. O3. $58.00

COLLINS, Hunt; see Hunter, Evan.

COLLINS, J.W. *Report on Fisheries of the Pacific Coast of US.* 1891. GPO. pls/fld maps. 269 p. lacks rear wrp. D3. $35.00

COLLINS, Jeanne Bouchet. *Sea-Tracks of the Speejacks 'Round the World.* 1923. Doubleday Page. 1st ed. 8vo. 286 p. VG. W1. $16.00

COLLINS, John S. *My Experiences in the W.* 1970. Lakeside Classic. ils/fld map. 252 p. O7. $18.50

COLLINS, Larry. *Maze.* 1989. Simon Schuster. 1st ed. VG/dj. P3. $20.00

COLLINS, M.D. *Cultured Mexico: Unknown Land to N Am.* (1921). Chicago. Wiltzius. 8vo. 303 p. F/VG. A2. $15.00

COLLINS, Max Allan. *No Cure for Death.* 1983. NY. Walker. 1st ed. F/NF. M15. $35.00

COLLINS, Max Allan. *One Lonely Knight: Mickey Spillane's Mike Hammer.* 1984. Popular. 1st ed. ils. F/F. S5. $35.00

COLLINS, Max Allan. *Spree.* 1987. NY. Tor. ARC of 1st ed. sgn. RS. F/F. S5. $35.00

COLLINS, Max Allan. *Spree.* 1987. NY. Tor. 1st ed. NF/NF. S5. $27.50

COLLINS, Michael; see Lynds, Dennis.

COLLINS, Randall. *Case of the Philosopher's Ring.* 1980. Harvester. 1st British ed. ils. F/F. S5. $25.00

COLLINS, Septima M. *Woman's War Record, 1861-65.* 1889. NY. Putnam. inscr presentation. 78 p. cloth. NF. B14. $35.00

COLLINS, Wilkie. *Guilty River.* nd. NY. Butler. G. A16. $5.00

COLLINS, Wilkie. *Moonstone.* 1868. Harper. 1st Am ed. octavo. woodcuts. 233 p. gr cloth. VG. H5. $700.00

COLLINS, Wilkie. *Moonstone.* 1946. Literary Guild. VG/torn. P3. $7.50

COLLINS & GORMAN. *Jim Thompson: The Killers Inside Him.* 1983. Fedora. 1/425. 8vo. F/unread wrp. A11. $85.00

COLLIS, Maurice. *Cortes & Montezuma.* (1955). Harcourt. 1st Am ed. 256 p. dj. F3. $20.00

COLLIS, Maurice. *First Holy One.* 1948. London. Faber. 1st ed. 8vo. 235 p. VG/dj. W1. $18.00

COLLIS, Maurice. *Land of the Great Image: Experiences of Friar Manique...* 1943. NY. Knopf. 1st Am ed. 8vo. 266 p. VG/VG. A2. $15.00

COLLODI, Carlo. *Adventures of Pinocchio.* 1926. Macmillan. 399 p. cloth. VG. M20. $110.00

COLLODI, Carlo. *Pinocchio.* (1940). Platt Munk. sm 4to. 122 p. pict ep. VG. T5. $45.00

COLLODI, Carlo. *Pinocchio.* nd. Donohue. VG-. P3. $7.50

COLLODI, Carlo. *Pinocchio.* 1932. Garden City. ils Petersham. F/VG. P2. $15.00

COLLODI, Carlo. *Pinocchio.* 1946. Random House. ils Lenski. 4to. 64 p. VG. A3. $10.50

COLLODI, Carlo. *Pinocchio: Story of a Puppet.* 1917. Lippincott. ils Maria Kirk. brds. E3. $25.00

COLMAN, Henry. *European Agriculture & Rural Economy...* 1849. Boston. Little Brn. 2nd ed. 2 vols. H10. $145.00

COLMEIRO, Manuel. *Los Restos de Colon.* 1879. Madrid. xl. half leather. VG+. O6. $100.00

COLQUHOUN, Archibald Ross. *Key to the Pacific: Nicaragua Canal.* 1895. Westminster. Constable. 443 p. teg. VG. O6. $95.00

COLT, John C. *Authentic Life of...* 1841. Boston. Dickinson. 1st ed. 8vo. 70 p. prt wrp. M1. $250.00

COLT, Miriam Davis. *Went to KS, Being Thrilling Account of Ill-Fated Expedition.* 1862. NY. Ingalls. 1st ed. 8vo. 294 p. rare. M1. $400.00

COLTON, Harold S. *Hopi Kachina Dolls.* (1964). NM U. revised ed/2nd prt. 150 p. NF/rpr pict dj. D3. $25.00

COLTON, James; see Hansen, Joseph.

COLTON, Walter. *CA Diary.* 1948. Oakland. Biobooks. 1/1000. 6 pls/maps. 261 p. pebbled red cloth. NF. P4. $65.00

COLTON, Walter. *Deck & Port; or, Incidents of Cruise in US Frigate Congress.* 1854. NY. Barnes. 12mo. 408 p. emb red cloth. H9. $75.00

COLTON & FITCH. *Colton & Fitch's Modern School Geography.* 1855. np. VG. E5. $45.00

COLUM, Padraic. *Children of Odin.* June 1929. NY. ils Willy Pogany. F/dj. B14. $75.00

COLUM, Padraic. *Frenzied Prince Being Heroic Stories of Ancient Ireland.* 1943. McKay. 1st ed. ils Willy Pogany. 196 p. gr cloth. VG+. H3. $50.00

COLUMBUS, Christopher. *Journal of 1st Voyage to Am.* 1924. NY. 1st ed. intro Van Wyck Brooks. 254 p. gilt blk cloth. F. H3. $35.00

COLVER, Anne. *Bread-&-Butter Indian.* (1964). HRW. ils Garth Williams. 96 p. VG/VG. T5. $30.00

COLVILE, Kathleen. *Mrs Marionette.* 1925. London. Chatto Windus. 1/60. ils/sgn Rubenstein. G+. A1. $100.00

COLVIN. *Pure Fabrication. Fabric Ideas for the Home.* 1985. np. pb. ils. G2. $17.00

COLYER, William H. *Sketches of the N River.* 1838. NY. xl. 12mo. fld map. 119 p. bl silk/rebacked leather. H9. $150.00

COMBE, Andrew. *Principles of Physiology Applied to Preservation of Health.* 1847. NY. Fowler Wells. enlarged/from 7th Edinburgh ed. 320 p. G+. S9. $18.00

COMBE, Iris. *Herding Dogs: Thier Origins & Development in Britain.* 1987. London. Faber. 1st ed. VG+/VG+. O3. $35.00

COMFORT, Alex. *Sexual Behavior in Soc.* 1950. Viking. 157 p. dj. A7. $25.00

COMFORT, Alex. *Song of Lazarus.* 1945. Viking. 99 p. G+. N2. $6.50

COMFORT, Alex. *Tetrarch.* (1980). Boulder. Shambala. 309 p. dj. A7. $13.00

COMFORT, Will Levington. *Son of Power.* nd. Grundy. 1st Canadian ed. VG. P3. $10.00

COMMER, Joe. *Decatur.* (1983). St Martin. 1st ed. author's 1st book. F/F. B3. $30.00

COMMONS, John R. *Trade Unionism & Labor Problems.* ca 1905. Ginn. F/G. V4. $25.00

COMPARETTI, Andrea. *Riscontri Medici Delle Febbri Larvate Periodiche...* 1795. Padua. Nella Stamperia Penada. thick 8vo. recent vellum. G7. $150.00

COMRIE, John Dixon. *Hist of Scottish Medicine...* 1932. London. Bailliere. 2nd ed. 2 vols. G7. $135.00

COMSTOCK, Harriet T. *Princess Rags & Tatters.* 1912. Doubleday Page. 1st ed. ils ER Thayer. 112 p. VG. S10. $30.00

COMSTOCK, Harriet T. *Princess Rags & Tatters.* 1912. NY. 1st ed. 112 p. pict gr cloth. VG. H3. $20.00

COMSTOCK, John L. *Hist of the Greek Revolution.* 1828. NY. 8vo. 2 fld pls. contemporary full calf. o2. $85.00

CONAN, Laure; see Angers, Marie-Louise-Felicite.

CONCHA, Joseph L. *Lonely Boy.* 1969. NM. Red Willow Soc. 2nd prt. sgn. NF/stapled wrp. L3. $45.00

CONCHA, Joseph L. *Lonely Deer. Poems of a Pueblo Boy.* 1969. Taos Pueblo Council. 1st ed. 28 p. F/wrp. B19. $25.00

CONDE, Maryse. *Children of Segu.* 1989. Viking/Penguin. 1st ed. trans Linda Coverdale. F/F clip. A13. $25.00

CONDE, Maryse. *Tree of Life: Novel of the Caribbean.* 1992. One World/Ballantine. 1st ed. trans Victoria Reiter. rem mk. F/F. A13. $25.00

CONDER, Claude R. *Tent Work in Palestine.* 1879. London. 2 vols. 8vo. sm lib stps. VG. O2. $165.00

CONDER, Josiah. *Modern Traveller.* 1831. Boston. 8vo. lib stp on title. 340 p. O2. $50.00

CONDIT, Carl. *Rise of the Skyscraper.* 1952. Chicago. 1st ed. ils. 255 p. VG/G. B5. $35.00

CONDOMINAS, George. *We Have Eaten the Forest.* (1977). Hill Wang. 1st Am ed. 423 p. NF/NF. A7. $20.00

CONDON, Richard. *Emperor of Am.* 1990. Simon Schuster. 1st ed. F/dj. P3. $17.50

CONDON, Richard. *Manchurian Candidate.* 1959. McGraw Hill. 1st ed. author's 2nd novel. NF/VG. L3. $250.00

CONDON, Richard. *Prizzi's Honor.* 1989. London. Michael Joseph. 1st British ed. NF/dj. S5. $25.00

CONDON & SUGRUE. *We Called It Music.* 1947. Holt. 1st ed. sgn. NF. B2. $50.00

CONDRA, George Evert. *Geography, Agriculture, Industries of NE.* ca 1942. Lincoln, NE. ils/index. 342 p. H10. $15.00

CONEY, Michael G. *Gods of the Greataway.* 1984. Houghton Mifflin. 1st ed. VG/G+. P3. $16.00

CONFEDERATE KENTUCKY VETERANS. *Constitution, By-Laws & List of Membership...* 1895. Lexington. Transylvania Prt. 5th ed. 217 p. cloth. VG. M8. $450.00

CONGDON, William. *In My Disc of Gold, Itineray to Christ.* nd. NY. pict bdg. F/tape rpr dj. B30. $50.00

CONIGLLARO, Tony. *Seeing It Through.* 1970. Macmillan. 1st ed. inscr. F/VG+. P8. $125.00

CONKLIN, E. *Picturesque AZ.* 1877. NY. 12mo. 380 p. bl cloth. very scarce. H9. $275.00

CONKLIN, Groff. *SF Adventures in Mutation.* 1955. Vanguard. 1st ed. VG/VG. P3. $35.00

CONLEY, Patrick T. *Constitutional Significance of Trevett Vs Weeden (1786).* 1976. Providence. RI Bicentennial Comm. stapled wrp. M11. $5.00

CONLEY, Robert J. *Killing Time.* 1988. NY. Evans. 1st ed. F/F. L3. $45.00

CONLEY, Robert J. *Quitting Time.* 1989. NY. Evans. 1st ed. F/F. L3. $45.00

CONLEY, Robert J. *Wht Path.* 1993. NY. Doubleday. 1st ed. 3rd of Real People series. F/F. L3. $25.00

CONLIN, Mary Lou. *Simon Perkins of the W Reserve.* 1968. Cleveland. 215 p. VG/dj. B18. $12.50

CONN, George. *Arabian Horse in Fact, Fantasy & Fiction.* 1967. NY. Barnes. 3rd prt. VG/G+. O3. $25.00

CONNELL, Evan S. *Son of the Morning Star.* 1984. N Point Pr. VG/dj. A16. $25.00

CONNELL, Will. *In Pictures: A Hollywood Satire.* (1937). NY. Maloney. 1st ed. 4to. sbdg. VG+. B20. $45.00

CONNELLAN, Leo. *Clear Bl Lobster-Water Country: A Trilogy.* 1985. NY. 1st ed. sgn. F/F. V1. $40.00

CONNELLAN, Leo. *Shatterhouse.* nd. Hollow Springs Pr. 1/1000. sgn. NF/wrp. V1. $25.00

CONNER, K. Patrick. *Blood Moon.* 1987. Doubleday. 1st ed. F/dj. B9. $10.00

CONNETT, Eugene V. *Duck Decoys: How To Make Them, Paint Them & Rig Them.* 1953. Van Nostrand. 1st ed. VG/dj. scarce. A16. $100.00

CONNETT, Eugene V. *Fishing a Trout Stream.* 1934. Derrydale. 1st ed. 1/950. 93 pls. 138 p. cloth. VG+. M8. $175.00

CONNINGHAM, Frederic A. *Currier & Ives Prts.* 1949. Crown. expanded ed/1st prt. 300 p. NF. B19. $50.00

CONNOLLY, Cyril. *Modern Movement.* 1966. Atheneum. ARC of 1st ed. RS. F/NF. Q1. $75.00

CONNOLLY, Cyril. *Rock Pool.* 1936. Scribner. 1st Am ed. author's 1st book. VG+. E3. $30.00

CONNOLLY, Cyril. *Rock Pool.* 1937. Paris. Obelisk. 1st ed/2nd prt. VG/orig wrp. E3. $25.00

CONNOR, Anthony. *Baseball for the Love of It.* 1982. Macmillan. 1st ed. ils/photos. F/F. P8. $17.50

CONNOR, Leland L. *Vengeance of Lewis Wetzel.* (1980). NY. 96 p. G/dj. B18. $9.50

CONOT, Robert. *Streak of Luck.* 1979. Seaview Books. 1st ed. VG/dj. A16. $20.00

CONOVER, Charlotte Reeve. *Patterson Log Cabin.* 1906. Dayton. xl. G/wrp. D7. $55.00

CONRAD, Annie Gilliam. *Street Above the Steps.* 1976. McClure. 2nd prt. VG/stiff wrp. B10. $15.00

CONRAD, Jim. *On the Road to Tetlama.* 1991. NY. Walker. 1st ed. 196 p. dj. F3. $20.00

CONRAD, Joseph. *Arrow of Gold.* 1919. London. Unwin. 1st ed. gr brds. NF/tape rpr dj. C4. $150.00

CONRAD, Joseph. *Laughing Anne.* 1924. London. 1st ed. G+. A1. $35.00

CONRAD, Joseph. *Nostromo.* 1923. Doubleday Page. VG. P3. $25.00

CONRAD, Joseph. *Notes on Life & Letters.* 1925. London. Gresham Pub. later prt/Medallion ed. sgn. NF. B4. $650.00

CONRAD, Joseph. *Rescue.* 1920. London. Dent. 1st ed. gilt gr brds. VG/VG. C4. $165.00

CONRAD, Joseph. *Rover.* (1923). Fisher Unwin. 1st ed. NF/VG. B4. $175.00

CONRAD, Joseph. *Rover.* nd. London. 1st ed. fair. A1. $25.00

CONRAD, Joseph. *Rover.* 1923. Garden City. 1st trade ed. NF/dj. C4. $150.00

CONRAD, Joseph. *Secret Agent.* 1923. London. private prt for subscribers. 2nd ed. 1/1000. VG/dj. H5. $400.00

CONRAD, Joseph. *Secret Agent.* 1923. London. 1st ed. 1/1000. sgn/#d. NF/VG. A11. $485.00

CONRAD, Joseph. *Secret Sharer.* 1985. NY. LEC. 1/1500. ils/sgn Bruce Chandler. w/newsletter. F/box. B24. $250.00

CONRAD, Joseph. *Suspense.* 1925. Doubleday Page. 1st Am ed. VG/dj. M18. $100.00

CONRAD, Joseph. *Suspense.* 1925. London. Dent. 1st ed. NF/NF. B4. $200.00

CONRAD, Joseph. *Tales of Hearsay.* (1925). Fisher Unwin. 1st ed. NF/NF. B4. $175.00

CONRAD, Joseph. *Tales of Hearsay.* (1925). Fisher Unwin. VG+/dj. C4. $145.00

CONRAD, Paul. *Drawn & Quartered.* 1985. Abrams. 4to. dj. N2. $10.00

CONRAD & HUEFFER. *Nature of a Crime.* (1924). Duckworth. 1st ed. NF/NF. B4. $85.00

CONRAD & HUS. *Water-Lilies & How To Grow Them.* 1907. NY. later prt. 228 p. VG. B26. $17.50

CONRAN, Terence. *Vegetable Book.* 1976. Crescent. VG/dj. A16. $6.00

CONROY, Albert; see Albert, Marvin H.

CONROY, Frank. *Midair.* 1985. Dutton. 1st ed. inscr. F/F. B2. $75.00

CONROY, Jack. *Disinherited.* 1933. NY. 1st ed. VG/G+. B5. $75.00

CONROY, Pat. *Lords of Discipline.* 1981. London. Secker Warburg. 1st ed. F/NF. C4. $60.00

CONROY, Pat. *Prince of Tides.* (1986). Houghton Mifflin. 1st ed. F/F. B3. $45.00

CONROY, Pat. *Water Is Wide.* 1972. Houghton Mifflin. 1st ed. author's 2nd book. F/NF clip. Q1. $450.00

CONSTANTINE, K.C. *Blank Page.* nd. BC. VG/dj. P3. $7.50

CONSTANTINE, K.C. *Upon Some Midnights Clear.* 1986. Hodder. 1st British ed. NF/NF. S5. $25.00

CONSTANTINI, Humberto. *Gods, the Little Guys & the Police.* 1984. Harper Row. 1st ed. trans Toby Talbot. NF/NF. A14. $25.00

CONTE, Mildred D. *Babyhood Step by Step.* 1943. Whitman. 48 p. bl cloth/pict brds. VG. M5. $15.00

CONVERSE, Parker Lindall. *Legends of Woburn, 1642-1892.* 1892. Woburn, MA. prt for subscribers only. 1/400. 177 p. gr cloth. F. B20. $45.00

CONWAY, Hugh. *Called Back.* nd. Detective Club. VG-/dj. P3. $15.00

CONWAY, Jim. *Jim Conway's Fishin' Holes.* 1969. Portland, OR. Graphic Arts Center. 1st ed. F/VG. A2. $15.00

CONWAY, Troy; see Avallone, Mike.

CONWAY & CONWAY. *Enchanted Islands: 5-Yr Adventure in the Galapagos.* (1947). Putnam. 1st ed. 8vo. 280 p. F/F. A2. $20.00

CONWAY & SIEGELMAN. *Holy Terror.* 1982. Doubleday. 1st ed. 402 p. dj. A7. $13.00

CONWELL, R.H. *Life & Public Services of Governor Rutherford B Hayes.* (1876). Boston. 1st ed. ils. 328 p. G. B18. $42.50

CONWELL, R.H. *Life of Gen James A Garfield.* 1880. Boston. 12mo. 354 p. gr cloth. G. T3. $20.00

CONYBEARE, F.C. *Apology & Acts of Apollonius & Other Monuments...* 1894. London. Swan Sonnenschein. index. 360 p. H10. $35.00

CONZIE, Werner. *Shaping of the German Nation.* (1979). St Martin. 137 p. F/F. A7. $12.00

COOK, Benjamin F. *Hist of the 12th MA Volunteers (Webster Regiment).* 1882. Boston. 12th Regiment Assn. 1st ed. 167 p. cloth. VG. M8. $250.00

COOK, Bob. *Disorderly Elements.* 1985. London. Gollancz. 1st ed. author's 1st book. NF/NF. S5. $20.00

COOK, Bob. *Faceless Mortals.* 1988. Gollancz. 1st ed. F/dj. P3. $20.00

COOK, E.T. *Sweet Violets & Pansies & Violets From Mtn & Plain.* 1903. London. ils/pls/drawings. teg. marbled ep. half vellum. B26. $39.00

COOK, Earnshaw. *Percentage Baseball & the Computer.* 1971. Waverly. 1st ed. VG+/sans. P8. $75.00

COOK, Earnshaw. *Percentage Baseball.* 1964. Waverly. 1st ed. inscr. VG+/sans. P8. $135.00

COOK, Fred J. *John Marshall.* 1961. Chicago. Kingston. Bookshelf for Young Am series. ils. M11. $20.00

COOK, Frederick A. *Return From the Pole.* 1951. NY. 1st ed. 8vo. 335 p. gilt bl cloth. VG. H3. $40.00

COOK, Henry A. *Charles Cook of Generostee w/Johnson & Other Allied Families.* 1980. Baltimore. Gateway Pr. 1st ed. author's presentation. 269 p. NF. M8. $35.00

COOK, James. *Explorations of Capt James Cook in the Pacific...* (1955). NY. Heritage. ils Ingleton. 292 p. quarter leather. VG/slipcase. P4. $65.00

COOK, James. *James Cook: Surveyor of Newfoundland.* 1965. San Francisco. David Magee. 1/365. folio. F/linen clamshell box. F1. $260.00

COOK, James. *Three Famous Voyages of Capt James Cook...* nd. (1890s). London. Ward Lock Bowden. Hawkesworth's ed. octavo. 23 pls. marbled brds. NF. H5. $600.00

COOK, Olan V. *Incunabula in the Hanes Collection of Lib of the U of NC.* 1960. Chapel Hill. VG. N2. $25.00

COOK, Robin. *Brain.* nd. BC. VG/dj. P3. $7.50

COOK, Robin. *Fever.* 1982. Putnam. 1st ed. VG/dj. P3. $20.00

COOK, Robin. *Godplayer.* (1983). London. Macmillan. 1st ed. VG/VG. B3. $15.00

COOK, Robin. *Harmful Intent.* 1990. Putnam. 1st Am ed. VG/dj. A16. $12.00

COOK, Robin. *Sphinx.* 1979. Putnam. 1st ed. author's 3rd book. F/NF. T2. $20.00

COOK, Thomas H. *City When It Rains.* 1991. Putnam. 1st ed. inscr. F/F. M15. $30.00

COOK, Thomas H. *Evidence of Blood.* nd. BC. VG/dj. P3. $7.50

COOK, Thomas H. *Night Secrets.* 1990. Putnam. 1st ed. NF/NF. S5. $30.00

COOK, Thomas H. *Orchids.* 1982. Houghton Mifflin. 1st ed. F/NF. M15. $35.00

COOK, W.C. *My Road to India.* (1939). NY. Furman. 1st ed. 8vo. 462 p. VG+/G. A2. $25.00

COOK & SUTTON. *Big Book of Cats.* 1954. Grosset Dunlap. VG. M5. $18.00

COOK. *Make a Medallion.* 1985. np. ils workbook. G2. $12.95

COOK-LYNN, Elizabeth. *Power of Horses.* 1990. NY. Arcade. ARC. author's 1st book. F/F. L3. $50.00

COOKE, David C. *Best Detective Stories of Yr 1950.* 1950. Dutton. 1st ed. VG/G+. P3. $25.00

COOKE, Edmund Vance. *I Rule the House.* (1910). Dodge. 12mo. 147 p. VG. S10. $25.00

COOKE, Edmund. *Brass Tacks Ballads.* 1924. Chicago. Bookfellows. 1/75. sgn. wrp. A1. $35.00

COOKE, G. Walter. *Death Is the End.* 1965. Geoffrey Bles. 1st ed. VG/VG. P3. $17.50

COOKE, George Willis. *Ralph Waldo Emerson: His Life, Writings & Philosophy.* 1971. Folcroft Lib Ed. reprint of 1882 ed. 1/150. 390 p. buckram. F. B22. $12.00

COOKE, John Esten. *Outlines From the Outpost.* 1961. Lakeside Classic. 413 p. O7. $14.50

COOKE, John Esten. *Tamawaca Folks: Summer Comedy.* (1907). np. Tamawaca. 1st ed. 185 p. emb cloth. G. A17 $25.00

COOKE, John Esten. *Wearing of the Gray: Personal Portraits...* 1959. Bloomington, IN. IN U. 572 p. VG/VG. M8. $65.00

COOKE, M.C. *7 Sisters of Sleep...Narcotics of the World.* 1989. Lincoln, MA. facsimile of 1860 ed. NF. B28. $50.00

COOKMAN, George G. *Speeches Delivered on Various Occasions...* 1847. NY. later prt. 12mo. leather. G. D7. $35.00

COOLEY, Thomas M. *Treatise on Law of Torts.* 1888. Chicago. quarter calf. F. M11. $150.00

COOLIDGE, Calvin. *Have Faith in MA.* ca 1919. Riverside. 12mo. 275 p. navy cloth. G. T3. $12.00

COOLIDGE, Clark. *Baffling Means.* 1991. O-blek Ed. 1/1500. sgn. F/stiff wrp. V1. $20.00

COOLIDGE, Clark. *Solution Passage.* 1986. Sun & Moon. 1/26. sgn. F/F. V1. $35.00

COOLIDGE, Dane. *Wally Laughs-Easy.* 1939. Dutton. 1st ed. F/dj. A18. $35.00

COOLIDGE, Susan. *In the High Valley.* 1891. Roberts Bros. 1st ed. 288 p. tan cloth. VG. M20. $15.00

COOLIDGE, Susan. *Mischief's Thanksgiving & Other Stories.* 1874. Boston. 1st ed. 244 p. gilt blk cloth. G. H3. $12.00

COOLIDGE, Susan. *What Katy Did.* 1924. Little Brn. 1st ed. ils Ralph P Colman. 271 p. VG+. S10. $35.00

COOMBS, Orde. *We Speak As Liberators.* 1970. NY. ARC. RS. F/NF clip. A11. $50.00

COON, Carleton S. *Hunting Peoples.* (1981). N Lyons. 1st ed. ils/maps. 414 p. wrp. A17. $12.00

COON, Gene L. *Meanwhile Back at the Front.* 1961. Crown. 1st ed. 8vo. VG/G. A8. $10.00

COONEY, Barbara. *Mother Goose in French.* 1964. NY. Crowell. 4to. 44 p. VG/VG. A3. $17.50

COONEY, Barbara. *Mother Goose in Spanish.* 1968. NY. Crowell. trans Reid/Kerrigan. VG/VG. A3. $17.50

COONEY, Michael. *Fang, the Gnome.* nd. BC. F/dj. C1. $5.00

COONTS, Stephen. *Flight of the Intruder.* (1986). Annapolis, MD. Naval Inst. 1st ed. author's 1st book. F/F. A7. $50.00

COOPER, A.B. *Lost in the Arctic.* nd. London. The RTS Office. 192 p. VG-. P4. $30.00

COOPER, Astley. *Anatomy & Surgical Treatment of Inguial...Hernia.* 1804. London. Cox. 11 pls. 60 p. contemporary quarter calf. G7. $1,250.00

COOPER, Bransby. *Surgical Essays: Result of Clinical Observations...* 1843. London. 4 lithos. orig brds. G7. $275.00

COOPER, Chester. *Lost Crusade.* (1970). Dodd Mead. 559 p. F/dj. A7. $25.00

COOPER, Clare. *Ashar of Quarius.* 1988. Harcourt. 1st ed. F/F. F4. $17.00

COOPER, Clarence. *Syndicate.* 1960. Chicago. PBO. 1st ed. NF/wrp ils Bonfils. A11. $55.00

COOPER, Craig. *What's Funny About Murder?* 1968. Roy. VG/dj. P3. $15.00

COOPER, Dennis. *Fisk.* 1991. Grove Weidenfield. 1st ed. F/F. A14. $30.00

COOPER, Douglas. *Amnesia.* 1994. NY. Hyperion. ARC. F/wrp. B2. $30.00

COOPER, Douglas. *Picasso les de Jeuners.* 1962. Paris. 1/125. VG/slipcase. A1. $500.00

COOPER, Edmund. *Slaves of Heaven.* 1974. Putnam. F/dj. P3. $12.00

COOPER, Edmund. *Tenth Planet.* 1973. Putnam. F/F. P3. $12.50

COOPER, Frederic Taber. *Rider's CA: Guide-Book for Travelers w/28 Maps & Plans.* 1925. Macmillan. 1st ed. maps/index. F. B19. $45.00

COOPER, Frederic Taber. *Rider's CA: Guide-Book for Travelers w/28 Maps & Plans.* 1925. Macmillan. 48 p of local ads. VG. H7. $30.00

COOPER, J.C. *Home-made Love.* (1986). St Martin. 1st ed. F/NF. B3. $25.00

COOPER, James Fenimore. *Bravo.* 1963. College & U Pr. VG+. P3. $15.00

COOPER, James Fenimore. *Deerslayer.* 1925. Scribner. 1st thus ed. ils NC Wyeth. 462 p. blk cloth/pict label. F. B24. $250.00

COOPER, James Fenimore. *Hist of the Navy of the USA.* 1848. Cooperstown, NY. later ed. 2 vols. leather. G. D7. $75.00

COOPER, James Fenimore. *Red Rover, a Tale.* 1827. Paris. Hector Bossange. true 1st ed (precedes Am & Eng). 3 vols in 2. F. B4. $1,250.00

COOPER, James Fenimore. *Writings of...* nd. NY. Putnam. Iroquois ed. 1/1000. octavo. 36 vols. F. H5. $4,500.00

COOPER, Jefferson; see Fox, Gardner F.

COOPER, John R. *First Base Jinx.* nd. Books Inc. xl. G. P3. $4.00

COOPER, Madison. *Haunted Hacienda.* 1955. Houghton Mifflin. VG+/dj. B9. $10.00

COOPER, Page. *Great Horse Stories: Truth & Fiction.* 1954. Garden City. reprint. ils Paul Brn. VG/VG. O3. $25.00

COOPER, Paul L. *Archeological Investigations in Heart Butte Reservoir Area.* 1958. GPO. 1st separate ed. 12 pls/2 fld maps. 40 p. VG/wrp. D3. $12.50

COOPER, Samuel. *Memorial to Cyrus Cooper & Bertha A Cooper.* 1948. Morrestown, NJ. Cooper. sm 12mo. 202 p. G+. V3. $18.00

COOPER, Susan Fenimore. *Mt Vernon: Letter to Children of Am.* 1859. NY. Appleton. 1st ed. 2 pls. 70 p. cloth. VG. M8. $85.00

COOPER, Susan Rogers. *Other People's Houses.* 1990. St Martin. 1st ed. F/dj. M10. $65.00

COOPER, Thomas. *Scripture Doctrine of Materialism.* 1823. Phil. 1st ed. 12mo. 44 p. M1. $300.00

COOPER, Thomas. *Some Information Respecting Am Collected by Thomas Cooper.* 1795. London. Johnson. 2nd ed. 8vo. 240 p. orig wrp. lacks map. H9. $125.00

COOPER, Thomas. *View of Metaphysical & Physiological Arguments...* 1824. Phil. 1st Am ed. 12mo. 67 p. M1. $250.00

COOPER & MOORE. *Halley's Comet Pop-Up Book.* 1985. 6 pop-ups. F. A4. $45.00

COOVER, Robert. *Night at the Movies.* (1987). London. Heinemann. 1st ed. NF/NF. B3. $25.00

COOVER, Robert. *Universal Baseball Assn.* 1968. Random. 1st ed. F/F. B2. $125.00

COPELAND, Catherine. *Bravest Surrender: Petersburg Patchwork.* 1961. Whittet Shepperson. 1st ed. ils. 132 p. VG. B10. $25.00

COPELAND, R. Morris. *Country Life: Handbook of Agriculture...* 1860 (1859). Boston. 2nd ed. 814 p. VG. B28. $175.00

COPLAN, Maxwell Frederick. *Pink Lemonade.* (1945). NY. 1st ed. photos. 120 p. VG. A17. $30.00

COPPARD, A.E. *Collected Tales of...* nd. BC. VG/dj. P3. $10.00

COPPARD, A.E. *Fearful Pleasures.* 1946. Arkham. 1st ed. NF/NF. M2. $100.00

COPPARD, A.E. *Fishmongers Fiddle.* 1925. London. 1st ed. G+. A1. $20.00

COPPEE, Henry. *Life & Services of General US Grant.* 1868. Chicago. W News Co. ils/fld map. 465 p. cloth. VG+. B14. $35.00

COPPEL, Alfred. *Burning Mtn.* 1983. Harcourt Brace. 1st ed. 8vo. F/VG. A8. $12.00

COPPEL, Alfred. *Dragon.* 1977. HBJ. 1st ed. VG/dj. P3. $15.00

COPPER, Basil. *Exploits of Solar Pons.* 1993. Fedogan Bremer. 1st ed. sgn. F/F. F4. $24.00

COPPER, Basil. *House of the Wolf.* 1983. Arkham House. 1st ed. ils/sgn twice/dtd. F/F. F4. $45.00

COPPER, Basil. *House of the Wolf.* 1983. Arkham. 1st ed. as new. M2. $35.00

COPPER, Basil. *Voice From the Dead.* 1974. Robert Hale. 1st ed. xl. dj. P3. $7.50

COPPOLA, Eleanor. *Notes.* 1979. Simon Schuster. 1st ed. F/NF. A7. $25.00

CORBEN, Richard. *Bloodstar.* 1976. Morning Star. 1st ed. NF/dj. P3. $30.00

CORBETT, Ethel Rae. *W Pioneer Days.* 1974. private prt. 8vo. F. A8. $22.00

CORBETT, James J. *Roar of the Crowd: True Tales of Rise & Fall of a Champion.* 1925. Grosset Dunlap. ils. red brds. VG. E3. $12.00

CORBETT, Jim. *Man-Eaters of Kumaon.* 1946. NY. 1st Am ed. ils. 235 p. VG/dj. A17. $10.00

CORBETT, Julian. *Sir Francis Drake.* 1932 (1890). London. Macmillan. VG. O6. $25.00

CORBIN, Alain. *Foul & the Fragrant: Odor & French Social Imagination.* 1986. Cambridge, MA. Harvard. 1st Am ed. 8vo. 307 p. F/F. A2. $15.00

CORCHELET, Charles. *Narrative of Shipwreck of Sophia on 30th Day of May, 1819...* 1822. London. Phillips. octavo. 7 lithos. teg. half red morocco. H9. $200.00

CORDASCO, F. *Homoepathy in the US. Bibliography...1825-1925.* 1991. Junius-Vaughn Pr. 231 p. M/dj. G7. $45.00

CORDASCO, Francesco. *Am Medical Imprints, 1820-1910. A Checklist...* 1985. Totawa. 2 vols. 4to. G7. $250.00

CORDER, E.M. *Deer Hunter.* (1979). NY. Exeter. 1st hc ed. dj. A7. $40.00

CORDY & CORDY. *Mexican Indian Costumes.* 1978. Austin, TX. 3rd prt. 4to. 373 p. dj. F3. $45.00

CORE, Sue. *Panama Yesterday & Today.* 1945. NY. N River. ils Russell Fagerberg. 261 p. bl cloth. G/G. B11. $35.00

CORELLI, Marie. *Master-Christian.* 1900. Briggs. VG-. P3. $25.00

CORIN, Patrick C. *Commuter Railroads.* 1957. Bonanza. VG/dj. A16. $20.00

CORK, Barry. *Laid Dead.* 1990. London. Collins. 1st ed. F/F. S5. $25.00

CORKERY, Paul. *Carson: Unauthorized Biography.* 1987. Ketchum. Randt. 1st ed. F/F. T2. $12.50

CORKILL, Louis. *Fish Lane.* 1951. Bobbs Merrill. 1st ed. VG/dj. P3. $10.00

CORLE, Edwin. *Listen, Bright Angel: Panorama of the SW.* (1946). DSP. 1st ed. NF/VG. B4. $45.00

CORLETT, William Thomas. *Medicine Man of the Am Indian & His Cultural Background.* 1935. Springfield. Thomas. ils. 369 p. cloth. G7. $150.00

CORMAN, Avery. *Kramer Vs Kramer.* (1977). Random. 1st ed. NF/NF. B4. $45.00

CORMIER, Robert. *Chocolate War.* 1974. Pantheon. 1st ed. 8vo. 253 p. F/NF. T5. $30.00

CORMIER, Robert. *Fade.* 1988. Delacorte. 1st ed. F/F. N3. $15.00

CORMIER & EATON. *Reuther.* ca 1970. Prentice Hall. ils/photos. F/G. V4. $12.50

CORNELIUS, Elias. *God's Ways, Not As Our Ways.* 1821. Salem. Whipple. 56 p. H10. $15.00

CORNELL, John J. *Autobiography Containing Religious Experiences.* 1906. Lord Baltimore Pr. 8vo. 498 p. G+. V3. $20.00

CORNELL & FOREST. *Penny a Copy.* (1968). Macmillan. 1st ed. NF/worn clip. A7. $25.00

CORNPLANTER, Jessee. *Legends of the Longhouse.* 1938. Phil. Lippincott. 1st ed. ils. NF/NF. L3. $125.00

CORNWALL, Barbara. *Bush Rebels.* (1972). HRW. stated 1st ed. 252 p. clip dj. A7. $17.00

CORNWALL, James Marshall. *Grant As Military Commander.* 1970. NY. ils. 244 p. dj. O7. $12.50

CORNWELL, Bernard. *Crackdown.* 1990. Harper Collins. 1st ed. F/F. T2. $15.00

CORNWELL, Bernard. *Crackdown.* 1990. NY. Harper. ARC of 1st ed. RS. F/F. S5. $25.00

CORNWELL, Bernard. *Killer's Wake.* 1989. Putnam. 1st ed. F/F. T2. $20.00

CORNWELL, Bernard. *Sharpe's Eagle.* 1981. Viking. 1st ed. F/F. T2. $32.00

CORNWELL, Bernard. *Stormchild.* 1991. Harper Collins. 1st ed. F/F. T2. $16.00

CORNWELL, Patricia D. *Body of Evidence.* 1991. Scribner. 1st ed. F/F. T2. $48.00

CORNWELL, Patricia D. *Cruel & Unusual.* 1993. Scribner. 1st ed. M/M. T2. $28.00

CORNWELL, Patricia D. *Postmortem.* (1990). Scribner. 1st ed. author's 1st book. F/F. B4. $350.00

CORNYN, John Hubert. *Song of Quetzalcoatl.* 1931. Yel Springs. Antioch. 2nd ed. 12 woodcuts. NF. L3. $85.00

CORREVON, Henry. *Rock Garden & Alpine Plants.* 1930. Macmillan. 1st ed. xl. index. 544 p. H10. $17.50

CORRIGAN, Mark. *Lady From Tokyo.* 1960. Angus Richardson. 1st ed. xl. dj. P3. $10.00

CORRINGTON & CORRINGTON. *Civil Death.* 1987. Viking. 1st ed. F/F. S5. $22.50

CORROZET, Gilles. *Le Tresor de l'Historie de France.* 1649-50. Rouen. Chez Antoine Ferrand. 2 vols in 1. contemporary vellum. K1. $200.00

CORSO, Gregory. *Mindfield.* 1989. NY. 1st ed. F/F. V1. $20.00

CORSO, Gregory. *Way Out. A Poem in Discord.* 1974. Nepal. 1/500. 4to. F/gr wrp. A11. $35.00

CORSON, William. *Betrayal.* (1968). Norton. 1st ed. dj. A7. $25.00

CORSON, William. *Consquences of Failure.* (1974). Norton. 1st ed. dj. A7. $20.00

CORTAZAR, Julio. *Around the Day in Eighty Worlds.* 1986. Northpoint. 1st ed. trans from Spanish. A14. $30.00

CORTAZAR, Julio. *We Love Glenda So Much.* (1983). Knopf. 1st ed. F/VG. B3. $20.00

CORTAZAR, Julio. *62: A Model Kit.* 1972. Pantheon. 1st ed. NF/NF. B2. $40.00

CORTES Y LARRAZ, Don Pedro. *Description Geografico-Moral de la Diocesis de Goathemala.* 1959. Guatemala. 4to 2 vols. F3. $45.00

CORTESAO, Armando. *Hit of Portuguese Cartography. Vol 1.* 1971. Coimbra. Lisboa. 1/1000. thick folio. Samuel E Morison's copy. 323 p. NF. O6. $150.00

CORTESAO, Armando. *Portugaliae Monumenta Cartographica.* 1960. Lisboa. 5 folio vols w/1 quarto index vol. 626 pls. NF. O6. $4,500.00

CORTI, Egon. *Maximilian & Charlotte of Mexico.* 1929. Knopf. 1st ed. 2 vols. 976 p. F3. $45.00

CORVO, Frederick Rolfe. *Desire & Pursuit of the Whole: A Romance of Modern Venice.* (1934). London. Cassell. 1st ed/1st issue. octavo. gilt gr cloth. R3. $275.00

CORWIN, Edward S. *Total War & the Constitution.* 1947. Knopf. G/dj. M11. $50.00

CORWIN. *Easy-To-Make Applique Quilts for Children.* 1982. np. 12 full-size patterns. wrp. G2. $4.00

CORY, David. *Little Indian.* 1934. Grosset Dunlap. 8vo. 128 p. G. B11. $15.00

CORY, David. *Little Jack Rabbit's Big Bl Book.* (1924). Harper. 277 p. G. S10. $25.00

CORY, David. *Puss-in-Boots Jr & the Man in the Moon.* (1922). Grosset Dunlap. 133 p. VG/fair. P2. $10.00

CORY, Desmond. *Bennett.* 1977. Crime Club. 1st ed. VG/dj. P3. $15.00

CORY, F.Y. *Confessions of a Daddy.* 1907. Century. ils. red cloth. NF. M5. $60.00

CORY. *Crosspatch: Inspirations in Multi-Block Quilts.* 1989. np. ils. wrp. G2. $15.00

CORY. *Happy Trails: Variations on Classic Drunkard's Path...* 1991. np. ils. wrp. G2. $15.00

CORY. *Quilting Designs From the Amish.* 1985. np. 100+ designs. wrp. G2. $16.00

COSENTINO, Andrew J. *Paintings of Charles Bird King.* 1977. Smithsonian. 214 p. wrp. D2. $45.00

COSENTINO, F.J. *Edward Marshall Boem 1913-1969.* 1975 (1970). np. EM Boehm Inc. 2nd ed. 4to. 264 p. F/F slipcase. A2. $25.00

COSIC, Dobrica. *Reach to Eternity.* 1980. HBJ. 1st ed. trans from Servian by Muriel Heppell. NF/NF clip. A14. $25.00

COSSLEY-BATT, Jill L. *Last of the CA Rangers.* (1928). NY. 2nd prt. 299 p. cloth. VG. D3. $35.00

COSTAIN, Thomas B. *Below the Salt.* 1957. Doubleday. 1st ed. VG/dj. P3. $35.00

COSTAIN, Thomas B. *High Towers.* 1949. Doubleday. 1st ed. VG/G+. P3. $15.00

COSTAIN, Thomas B. *Tontine.* 1955. Doubleday. 1st ed. 2 vols. VG/djs. P3. $35.00

COSTIGAN, Giovanni. *Sigmund Freud: Short Biography.* (1965). Macmillan. 1st ed. 8vo. 306 p. F/VG. A2. $12.50

COTLOW, Lewis. *In Search of the Primitive.* 1966. Little Brn. 1st ed. 454 p. dj. F3. $15.00

COTTON, Charles. *Poems From the Works...* nd. London Poetry Bookshop. ils Fraser. G+. A1. $35.00

COTUGNO, Domenico. *Onori Funebri Resi all Memoria Cavaliere Domenico Cotugno...* 1823. Naples. A Nobile. engraved portrait. 60 p. gilt red brds. G7. $750.00

COUDERT, Frederic R. *Certainty & Justice: Studies of Conflict...* 1913. NY. Appleton. red cloth. M11. $50.00

COUES, Elliott. *Birds of the NW.* 1877. Boston. Estes Lauriat. 791 p. emb brn cloth. VG. S9. $28.00

COUES, Elliott. *Hist of Expedition Under Command of Lewis & Clark...* 1893. Harper. 1st ed. 1/200 on handmade. lg 8vo. 8 maps. very scarce. T8. $850.00

COUGHLAN & HAVILAND. *Yankee Doodle's Literary Sampler of Prose, Poetry...* 1974. Crowell. 1st ed. 4to. red cloth. F/VG. P4. $75.00

COUGHLIN, Charles E. *Series of Lectures on Social Justice.* 1935. Royal Oak. Radio League of Little Flower. 244 p. orig wrp. A7. $25.00

COULONGES, Henri. *Farewell Dresden.* 1989. Summit/Simon Schuster. 1st ed. trans Lowell Blair. F/F. A14. $25.00

COULTER, John W. *Drama of Fiji.* 1967. Rutland, VT. 1st ed. 8vo. 230 p. gilt gr cloth. F/F. H3. $20.00

COULTER, Robert B. *Kid on the Flats.* 1993. Commodore Books. as new. A16. $12.95

COULTER, Stephen. *Embassy.* nd. Coward McCann. 2nd ed. xl. dj. P3. $5.00

COUNTESS OF ROMANONES, Aline. *Spy Who Went Dancing.* 1990. Putnam. 1st ed. VG/dj. A16. $10.00

COURLANDER, Harold. *Negro Folk Music USA.* 1963. Columbia. 1st ed. F/NF. B2. $50.00

COURLANDER, Harold. *Tiger's Whisker.* 1967 (1959). HBW. ils Enrico Arno. 152 p. NF/VG. T5. $20.00

COURTEMANCHE, Regis A. *No Need of Glory: British Navy in Am Waters, 1860-64.* 1977. Annapolis. Naval Inst Pr. 1st ed. 204 p. cloth. NF/NF. M8. $35.00

COURTHION, Pierre. *Roualt.* 1962. Flamirion. VG/G+. A1. $85.00

COURTIER, S.H. *Corpse at Last.* 1966. Hammond. 1st ed. VG/VG-. P3. $20.00

COURTIER, S.H. *Ligny's Lake.* 1971. Robert Hale. 1st ed. VG-/dj. P3. $15.00

COURTIER, S.H. *Ligny's Lake.* 1971. Simon Schuster. 1st Am ed. VG+/NF. S5. $25.00

COURTNEY, W.S. *Farmers' & Mechanics' Manual.* 1878 (1868). NY. 25th thousand. 562 p. VG. B28. $75.00

COUSTEAU, J. *Dolphins.* (1976). NY. 1st Am ed. ils/color photos. 304 p. F/dj. A17. $15.00

COUSTEAU, J. *Life & Death in the Coral Sea.* 1971. NY. 1st Am ed. 302 p. F/dj. A17. $15.00

COUSTEAU, J. *Whale.* 1972. NY. 1st Am ed. ils/photos. 304 p. F/dj. A17. $15.00

COUTINHO, Gago. *Passagem do Cabo Bojador.* 1935. Lisboa. Samuel Eliot Morison's copy. 29 p. NF/wrp. O6. $25.00

COUTURE, Richard T. *Powhatan: A Bicentennial Hist.* 1980. Dietz. inscr. ils. 579 p. VG/VG. B10. $50.00

COVARRUBIAS, Miguel. *Mexico S.* 1946. Knopf. 1st ed. 8 color pls. 427 p. VG+/dj. F3. $50.00

COVARRUBIAS, Miguel. *Mezcala: Ancient Mexican Sculpture.* (1956). Andre Emmerich Gallery. 1st ed. w/invitation to exhibit. F/ils paper wrp. B4. $45.00

COVARRUBIAS, Miguel. *Negro Drawings.* 1927. Knopf. 1st ed. 56 p. VG/dj. D1. $1,250.00

COVER, J.P. *Notes on Jurgen.* 1928. NY. McBride. G+. A1. $85.00

COWAN, Ian B. *Enigma of Mary Stuart.* 1971. St Martin. 1st ed. 222 p. VG/dj. M20. $9.00

COWAN, Robert G. *Ranchos of CA: A List of Spanish Concessions, 1775-1822.* 1956. Academy Lib Guild. sgn. indexes/glossary, map ep. NF. B19. $75.00

COWAN, Sam K. *Sergeant York.* nd. Grosset Dunlap. VG/dj. P3. $20.00

COWAN & COWAN. *Bibliography of Hist of CA & Pacific W, 1510-1906.* 1952. Long's College Book Co. reprint of 1914 ed. 279 p. worn. B19. $50.00

COWAN & COWAN. *Bibliography of Hist of CA...1510-1906.* 1964. np. 4 vols in 1. rebound gr buckram. VG. B19. $75.00

COWARD, Noel. *Collected Short Stories, Vol 2.* 1985. London. Methuen. 1st ed. intro Martin Tickner. NF/NF. A14. $20.00

COWARD, Noel. *Future Indefinite.* 1954. London. Heinemann. 1st ed. 336 p. G. M7. $16.00

COWARD, Noel. *Future Indefinite: 2nd Vol of Autobiography.* 1954. London. Heinemann. 1st ed. VG+/VG. A14. $20.00

COWARD, Noel. *Pomp & Circumstance.* 1960. London. Heinemann. AP. VG-. L3. $125.00

COWARD, Noel. *Pomp & Circumstance.* 1960. London. Heinemann. 1st ed. VG+/VG+ clip. A14. $40.00

COWARD, Noel. *Post-Mortem.* 1931. Garden City. 1st ed. NF/NF. B2. $50.00

COWARD, Noel. *This Happy Bread.* 1947. Garden City. Doubleday. 1st ed. F/NF. C4. $35.00

COWGILL, Kent. *Raising Hackles on the Hattie's Fork...* (1990). NY. Atlantic Monthly. 1st ed. 166 p. M/wrp. A17. $7.50

COWLEY, Hannah. *Belle's Strategem: Comedy w/Alterations & Amendments.* 1794. Boston. Apollo. 16mo. 73 p. disbound. M1. $100.00

COWLEY, Malcolm. *Anthology of Verse.* 1926. Columbus, OH. 1st book appearance. author's 2nd book. NF. scarce. C4. $125.00

COWLEY, Malcolm. *2nd Flowering.* 1973. NY. 1st ed. sgn. F/F. A11. $45.00

COWLEY, Stewart. *Spacecraft 2000 to 2100 AD.* 1978. Chartwell. F/F. P3. $7.00

COWPER, E.E. *Enter Patricia.* nd. Cassell. 1st ed. ils Noel Harrold. F. M18. $30.00

COWPER, Richard. *Clone.* 1973. Doubleday. 1st ed. F/dj. P3. $20.00

COWPER, Richard. *Unhappy Princess.* 1982. New Castle. Cheap Street. 1st ed. 1/27 lettered presentation copies. wrp/slipcase. N3. $175.00

COX, Archibald. *Court & the Constitution.* 1987. Houghton Mifflin. M11. $35.00

COX, Dorothy Davis. *Karl Anderson, Am Artist.* 1981. Winesburg. 93 p. NF/wrp. M20. $10.00

COX, Earnest Sevier. *Teutonic Unity.* 1951. Richmond, VA. xl. VG. N2. $15.00

COX, I. *Socialist Ideas in Africa.* 1966. London. Lawrence Wichart. 124 p. dj. A7. $20.00

COX, James M. *Journey Through My Years.* 1946. NY. 1st ed. sgn. 463 p. VG. A17. $22.50

COX, Palmer. *Another Brownie Book.* (1890). NY. Century. 1st ed. quarto. pict brds. VG. R3. $150.00

COX, Palmer. *Brownies at Home.* 1942 (1891). Appleton Century. 27th prt. 144 p. VG/dj. M20. $45.00

COX, Palmer. *Queer People w/Paws & Claws & Their Kweer Kapers.* (1888). Edgewood Pub. 4to. orig color-prt glazed brds. VG+. F1. $185.00

COX, Palmer. *Squibs of CA; or, Everyday Life Ils.* 1874. Hartford, CT. 1st ed. royal 8vo. 491 p. cloth. D3. $150.00

COX, Peter A. *Dwarf Rhododendrons.* 1973. NY. ils/pls. 296 p. F/dj. B26. $36.00

COX, Peter A. *Larger Rhododendron Species.* 1990. Portland. Timber Pr. 2nd ed. ils. 389 p. M. H10. $50.00

COX, Richard. *Kenyatta's Country.* (1965). Praeger. 203 p. dj. A7. $17.00

COX, Samuel Hanson. *Quakerism Not Christianity...* 1833. NY. D Fanshaw. 1st ed. xl. 8vo. 686 p. modern lib bdg. VG. V3. $45.00

COX, Samuel S. *Buckeye Abroad; or, Wanderings in Europe & in Orient.* 1852. NY. 8vo. 444 p. cloth. O2. $85.00

COX, Samuel S. *Isles of the Princes; or, Pleasures of Prinkipo.* 1887. NY. 8vo. 381 p. cloth. O2. $45.00

COX, William. *Mets Will Win the Pennant.* 1964. Putnam. 1st ed. ils/photos. P8. $35.00

COX & HOWE. *Civil Rights, the Constitution & the Courts.* 1967. Cambridge. Harvard. M11. $25.00

COX. *Every Stitch Counts.* 1981. np. sgn. sbdg. G2. $12.50

COXE, Brinton. *Essay on Judicial Power & Unconstitutional Legislation...* 1893. Phil. Kay & Brother. cloth. M11. $75.00

COXE, George Harmon. *Butcher, Baker, Murder-Maker.* 1954. Knopf. 1st ed. VG. P3. $25.00

COXE, George Harmon. *Camera Clue.* 1937. Knopf. 1st ed. inscr. F/NF. B4. $200.00

COXE, George Harmon. *Fenner.* 1971. Knopf. 1st ed. NF/dj. P3. $15.00

COXE, George Harmon. *Man Who Died Too Soon.* 1962. Knopf. 1st ed. VG/dj. P3. $20.00

COXE, George Harmon. *One Way Out.* nd. BC. VG/G. P3. $5.00

COXE, John Redman. *Am Dispensatory.* 1831. Carey Lea. 1st ed. 832 p. orig leather. G. A17. $120.00

COXE, John Redman. *Writings of Hippocrates & Galen Epitomised From Latin...* 1846. Phil. Lindsay Blakiston. 682 p. orig full sheep. G7. $195.00

COXE, Tench. *Report of Case of Commonwealth Vs Tench Coxe, Esq...* 1803. Phil. Jane Aitken. octavo. new paper brds. H9. $150.00

COXE, William. *Account of Russian Discoveries Between Asia & Am...* (1966). Ann Arbor. facsimile of 2nd revised ed. tall 8vo. A17. $35.00

COXE, William. *Account of Russian Discoveries Between Asia & Am...* 1966. Readex Microprint. reprint of 1780 orig ed. ils/fld map. 450 p. F. B19. $15.00

COXERE, Edward. *Adventures...* 1946. NY. Oxford. 1st ed. 12mo. 190 p. F/VG. A2. $20.00

COXGROVE, Rachel R. *Hidden Valley of Oz.* 1951. Reilly Lee. 1st ed. ils Dirk. fair. L1. $22.50

COY, Owen C. *CA County Boundaries: Study of Division of the State...* 1923. CA Hist Survey Comm. 1st ed. maps/notes/index. 335 p. G/sans. B19. $50.00

COY, Stephen. *Munchikins Remember.* 1989. Dutton. 1st ed. VG/wrp. L1. $30.00

COYKENDALL, Ralf. *Duck Decoys & How To Rig Them.* (1983). Winchester. revised ed. ils. 135 p. M/dj. A17. $15.00

COYNE, John. *Guard of Honor.* nd. Harcourt Brace. VG/dj. P3. $10.00

COYNE, John. *Piercing.* 1979. Putnam. 1st ed. author's 1st book. NF/F. N3. $10.00

COZZENS, Issachar Jr. *Geological Hist of Manhattan or NY Island.* 1843. NY. Wiley. 1st ed. pls/map. 114 p. emb brn cloth. VG+. B14. $65.00

COZZENS, James Gould. *Guard of Honor.* nd. Harcourt Brace. VG/dj. P3. $12.50

COZZENS, James Gould. *Guard of Honor.* 1949. Longman Gr. 1st ed. bl brds. F/F. C4. $40.00

COZZENS, Samuel W. *Marvellous Country; or, 3 Yrs in AZ & NM...* 1875. Boston. James Piper. thick 8vo. 532 p. pict gr cloth. H9. $175.00

CRABB, Alfred Leland. *Peace at Bowling Gr.* 1955. Bobbs Merrill. VG/dj. B9. $10.00

CRABTREE, Helen. *Saddle Seat Equitation.* 1970. Garden City. Doubleday. 2nd prt. VG/G+. O3. $12.00

CRACE, Jim. *Continent.* 1986. London. 1st ed. inscr. NF/NF. B2. $150.00

CRACE, Jim. *Continent.* 1986. NY. Harper Row. 1st ed. author's 1st book. F/NF. B3. $40.00

CRAD, Joseph. *African Odyssey.* (1939). London. Travel BC. 8vo. 286 p. F/VG+. A2. $20.00

CRADOCK, Mrs. H.C. *Josephine Is Busy.* nd. NY. Dodge Pub. ils Honor C Appleton. 63 p. VG. A3. $60.00

CRAFT, Amos N. *Epidemic Delusions: Containing Expose of Superstitions...* 1881. Cincinnati. Jennings Pye. later prt. 12mo. gr cloth. VG. G1. $30.00

CRAGEN, D.C. *Boys in the Sky-Bl Pants.* 1975. Independence, CA. ils ep. VG/dj. B18. $22.50

CRAIG, A. *Room at the Top; or, How To Reach Success, Happiness...* ca 1900. Augusta, ME. 12mo. ils. 400 p. brn cloth. VG. T3. $19.00

CRAIG, Alisa. *Grub-&-Stakers Quilt a Bee.* 1985. Doubleday. 1st ed. sgn. F/F. S5. $35.00

CRAIG, Alisa. *Murder Goes Mumming.* nd. BC. VG/dj. P3. $7.50

CRAIG, Archibald. *Golden Age.* 1956. Rindge, NH. 8vo. 140 p. VG/VG. V3. $10.00

CRAIG, David. *Contact Lost.* 1970. Stein Day. front free ep removed. VG/dj. P3. $7.00

CRAIG, Gerald. *Early Travelers in the Canadas...1791-1867.* 1955. Tor. 1st ed. 300 p. F/dj. A17. $25.00

CRAIG, Gordon. *Henry Irving.* (1930). London. Dent. 1st ed. inscr/dtd 1930. bl cloth. F/prt dj. B24. $475.00

CRAIG, John A. *Sheep Farming in N Am.* ca 1913. Macmillan. ils/index. 302 p. H10. $17.50

CRAIG, Patricia. *Oxford Book of Eng Detective Stories.* 1990. Oxford. 1st ed. F/dj. P3. $25.00

CRAIG, William. *Fall of Japan.* 1967. Dial. 1st prt. 30 pls. 368 p. VG/dj. W1. $18.00

CRAIGIE, Mary E. *Once Upon a Time. Stories for Children...* 1876. Putnam. 1st ed. 127 p. G. S10. $35.00

CRAINE & REINDORP. *Chronicles of Michoacan.* 1970. Norman, OK. 1st ed. 254 p. dj. F3. $30.00

CRAINE & REINDORP. *Codex Perex & the Book of Chilam Balam of Mani.* 1979. Norman, OK. 1st ed. 209 p. dj. F3. $25.00

CRAIS, Robert. *Monkey's Raincoat.* 1987. London. Piakus. 1st hc ed. 1st Elvis Cole. F/clip. M15. $75.00

CRAM, Mildred. *Old Seaport Towns of the South.* 1917. Dodd Mead. 1st ed. 364 p. B10. $25.00

CRAM, Mildred. *Promise.* 1949. Knopf. 1st ed. VG/dj. P3. $30.00

CRAMER, Carl. *Rebellion at Quaker Hill: Story of 1st Rent War.* 1954. Phil. Winston. 1st ed. 8vo. 174 p. VG/dj. V3. $12.50

CRAMER, Frank. *Case of the People Against the Lawyers & Courts.* 1915. Palo Alto. Cramer. xl. 143 p. wrp. working copy. M11. $35.00

CRAMER, Gary. *Cavaliers! Pict Hist of U VA Basketball.* ca 1983. Spring House. ils/photos. VG/G. B10. $15.00

CRAMER, Zadok. *Navigator: Containing Directions for Navigating...* 1811. Pittsburgh. 12mo. 296 p. orig unlettered calf brds. H9. $250.00

CRAMPTON, Gertrude. *Tootle.* 1947. Little Golden #21. 4th prt. 42 p. G+. A3. $5.00

CRAMTON, Louis C. *Early Hist of Yellowstone Nat Park...* 1932. GPO. 1st ed. xl. lacks orig wrp. lib brds. VG. D3. $25.00

CRANE, Florence H. *Flowers & Folk-Lore From Far Korea.* 1970. Seoul. 3rd ed. 45 color pls. VG+. B26. $102.50

CRANE, Frances. *Daffodil Blonde.* 1950. Random. 1st ed. xl. dj. P3. $15.00

CRANE, Frances. *Murder in Bright Red.* 1953. Random. 1st ed. VG/dj. P3. $45.00

CRANE, Hart. *Collected Poems.* 1933. NY. 1st ed/1st issue. intro Waldo Frank. red cloth. VG. V1. $100.00

CRANE, J.E. *Bookbinding for Amateurs...* ca 1900. London. L Upcott. 184 p. cloth. VG. B14. $20.00

CRANE, Stephen. *Battle in Greece.* 1936. Mt Vernon. Peter Pauper. ltd ed. 1/425. 30 p. purple brds. slipcase. O2. $75.00

CRANE, Stephen. *Red Badge of Courage.* 1895. NY. Appleton. 1st ed/1st prt. 233 p. VG. H5. $2,500.00

CRANE, Stephen. *Red Badge of Courage.* 1895. NY. 1st ed. mixed sheets on wove/laid paper. tan buckram. case. H5. $2,500.00

CRANE, Stephen. *Red Badge of Courage.* 1931. Grabhorn. ils Valenti Angelo. F/plain dj. F1. $185.00

CRANE, Stephen. *Red Badge of Courage.* 1960. NY. 1st thus ed/Dell Laurel pb. sgn. VG. A11. $55.00

CRANE, W.J.E. *Bookbinding for Amateurs: Being Descriptions of...Tools...* 1885. London. L Upcott Gill. 1st ed. aeg. tooled/sgn Blackwell morocco. NF. M8. $300.00

CRANE, Walter. *Absurd ABC.* (1870-74). Routledge. 1st ed. ils mtd on linen. VG/fld/slipcase. D1. $375.00

CRANE, Walter. *Baby's Bouquet.* nd. London. Warne. sm 4to. 56 p. G/stiff pict wrp. D1. $75.00

CRANE, Walter. *Hero's Walk.* 1954. Ballantine. F/dj. P3. $35.00

CRANE, Walter. *Walter Crane's Picture Books.* ca 1895. Chicago/London. Stone Kimball. LG Series. F/portfolio. D1. $450.00

CRAVEN, Elizabeth. *Journey Through the Crimea to Constantinople.* 1800. Vienna. sm 8vo. 463 p. contemporary full calf. O2. $75.00

CRAVEN, John J. *Prison Life of Jefferson Davis.* 1866. Carleton. 1st ed. 377 p. G. B10. $45.00

CRAVEN, Tunis A.M. *Naval Campaign in the Californias, 1867-69...* 1973. BC of CA. 1/400. edit/inscr/sgn JH Kemble. M/dj. O6. $125.00

CRAWFORD, F. Marion. *Wht Sister.* nd. Grosset Dunlap. photoplay ed. VG-. P3. $10.00

CRAWFORD, F. Marion. *Witch of Prague.* 1891. London. Macmillan. G+. N2. $10.00

CRAWFORD, F.M. *Ava Roma Immortalis: Studies From Chronicles of Rome.* 1900 (1898). London. Macmillan. 5th prt. 8vo. 2 vols. F-. A2. $20.00

CRAWFORD, Lewis F. *Rekindling Campfires.* 1926. Bismarck, ND. 1st ed. xl. ils/map. 324 p. cloth. VG. D3. $45.00

CRAWFORD, M.M. *Sailor Whom Eng Feared...John Paul Jones...* (ca 1920). Duffield. 1st Am ed. 8vo. 424 p. VG+. A2. $25.00

CRAWHALL, Joseph. *Compleatest Angling Booke.* 1970. Freshet. facsimile of 1881 ed. 233 p. F/slipcase. A17. $35.00

CREASEY, John. *Baron & the Beggar.* 1950. Duell Sloan. 1st ed. VG/NF. Q1. $35.00

CREASEY, John. *Day of Fear.* 1978. HRW. 1st ed. VG/dj. P3. $15.00

CREASEY, John. *Double for the Toff.* 1959. Hodder Stoughton. 1st ed. NF/NF. Q1. $30.00

CREASEY, John. *Gallows Are Waiting.* 1973. McKay. 1st ed. VG/VG. P3. $20.00

CREASEY, John. *Inferno.* 1966. Walker. 1st Am ed. NF/NF clip. F4. $27.50

CREASEY, John. *Kidnapped Child.* 1971. HRW. 1st ed. VG/dj. P3. $17.50

CREASEY, John. *Kind of Prisoner.* 1981. Ian Henry. VG/dj. P3. $15.00

CREASEY, John. *Make-Up for the Toff.* 1956. Walker. 1st ed. 189 p. cloth. NF/dj. M20. $15.00

CREASEY, John. *Plague of Silence.* 1968. Walker. 1st ed. VG/dj. P3. $15.00

CREASEY, John. *Prince for Inspector W.* 1956. Hodder Stoughton. 1st ed. NF/NF. Q1. $35.00

CREASEY, John. *Smog.* 1971. Thriller BC. 1st ed. xl. dj. P3. $5.00

CREASEY, John. *This Man Did I Kill?* 1974. Stein Day. VG/dj. P3. $15.00

CREASEY, John. *Toff & the Kidnapped Child.* 1960. Hodder Stoughton. 1st ed. NF/NF. Q1. $35.00

CREASEY, John. *Two for the Money.* 1962. Doubleday Crime Club. NF/NF clip. Q1. $25.00

CREEKMORE, Hubert. *Chain in the Heart.* 1953. Random. 1st ed. F/VG+. F4. $20.00

CREEKMORE, Hubert. *Daffodils Are Dangerous: Poisonous Plants in Your Garden.* (1966). NY. Walker. 1st ed. 8vo. 258 p. F/VG. A2. $15.00

CREELEY, Robert. *For My Mother.* 1973. Septre Pr. 1/150. sgn/#d. F/wrp. V1. $30.00

CREELEY, Robert. *Inventory 1945-70: A Bibliography.* 1973. Kent State. 1st ed. sgn. F/sans. V1. $40.00

CREELEY, Robert. *Pieces.* (1969). Scribner. 1st ed. F/F. B4. $45.00

CREEVEY, Caroline A. *Harper's Guide to Wild Flowers.* 1912. NY. 1st ed. pls. 355 p. VG. B28. $30.00

CREIGHTON, Louise. *Life & Letters of Thomas Hodgkin.* 1917. London. Longman Gr. 8vo. 445 p. VG. V3. $16.50

CRENSHAW, A.H. *Campbell's Operative Orthopaedics.* 4th ed. 1963. St Louis. Mosby. 2 vols. G7. $75.00

CRESPI, Pachita. *Cabita's Rancho. Story of Costa Rica.* 1942. NY. 1st ed. ils Zhenya Gay. 208 p. gr pict cloth. VG/G. H3. $15.00

CREW, Albert. *Old Bailey: Hist, Constitution, Functions, Notable Trials.* 1933. London. Nicolson Watson. ils/index. red cloth. M11. $45.00

CREWS, Frederick C. *Pooh Perplex.* 1963. Dutton. 3rd ed. VG. N2. $5.00

CREWS, Harry. *FL Frenzy.* 1982. Gainesville, FL. ARC of PBO. inscr. NF/wrp. A11. $65.00

CREWS, Harry. *Gospel Singer.* 1969. NY. 1st pb ed. sgn. F/wrp. A11. $75.00

CREWS, Harry. *Scarlover.* 1992. Poseidon. AP. F/wrp. C4. $50.00

CREWS, Harry. *Scarlover.* 1992. Poseidon. 1st ed. F/F. Q1. $25.00

CREWS & NAUGLE. *NE Quilts & Quiltmakers.* 1991. np. cloth. G2. $40.00

CRICHTON, Michael. *Andromeda Strain.* nd. BOMC. VG/DJ. P3. $7.50

CRICHTON, Michael. *Binary.* 1972. Knopf. 1st ed. F/F. F4. $40.00

CRICHTON, Michael. *Congo.* 1980. Knopf. 1st ed. F/F. T2. $18.00

CRICHTON, Michael. *Eaters of the Dead.* 1976. Knopf. 1st ed. F/F clip. T2. $20.00

CRICHTON, Michael. *Eaters of the Dead.* 1976. Knopf. 1st ed. F/F. P3. $25.00

CRICHTON, Michael. *Electronic Life.* 1983. Knopf. 1st ed. NF/dj. M18. $40.00

CRICHTON, Michael. *Great Train Robbery.* 1975. London. Cape. 1st ed. NF/VG clip. B3. $55.00

CRICHTON, Michael. *Great Train Robbery.* 1975. London. Cape. 1st ed. VG+/dj. S5. $25.00

CRICHTON, Michael. *Jurassic Park.* 1990. Knopf. 1st ed. F/F. T2. $48.00

CRICHTON, Michael. *Jurassic Park.* 1990. Knopf. 1st ed. M/dj. B4. $75.00

CRICHTON, Michael. *Rising Sun.* 1992. Franklin Lib. true 1st ed. sgn. leather. F. L3. $150.00

CRICHTON, Michael. *Rising Sun.* 1992. Knopf. 1st ed. F/F. T2. $22.00

CRICHTON, Michael. *Sphere.* 1987. Knopf. 1st ed. F/F. T2. $18.00

CRICHTON, Michael. *Travels.* 1988. Knopf. 1st ed. F/F. T2. $16.00

CRICHTON, Michael. *Venom Business.* (1969). Cleveland. World. 1st ed. F/F. B4. $300.00

CRIDER, Bill. *Shotgun Saturday Night.* 1987. NY. Walker. 1st ed. F/F. M15. $30.00

CRIDLAND, Robert B. *Practical Landscape Gardening.* 1927 (1916). NY. 3rd ed. ils. 280 p. B26. $24.00

CRILE, George Washington. *Autobiography.* 1947. Lippincott. 1st ed. 2 vols. NF/G+. S9. $17.00

CRISP, N.J. *Brink.* 1982. Viking. F/dj. P3. $15.00

CRISP, N.J. *London Deal.* 1979. St Martin. 1st ed. F/dj. P3. $17.50

CRISP, William. *Compleat Agent.* 1984. Macmillan. 1st ed. F/F. P3. $15.00

CRISPIN, Edmund. *Best Tales of Terror 2.* 1965. Faber. VG/dj. P3. $35.00

CRISPIN, Edmund. *Fen Country.* 1979. London. Gollancz. 1st ed. F/F. S5. $30.00

CRISSEY, Forrest. *Country Boy.* 1903. Revell. 1st ed. 300 p. VG+. S10. $45.00

CRISWELL, Elijah Harry. *Lewis & Clark: Linguistic Pioneers.* 1940. MO U Studies. thick 8vo. 102 p. F. T8. $350.00

CROCKER, Betty. *Betty Crocker's Picture Cookbook.* 1950. General Mills. 1st ed. 449 p. sbdg. VG+/dj. M20. $50.00

CROCKER, Betty. *Betty Crocker's Picture Cookbook.* 1956. McGraw Hill. 2nd ed/1st prt. G. A16. $45.00

CROCKER, H. Radcliffe. *Atlas of Diseases of the Skin.* 1896. Edinburgh/London. Pentland. 2 vols. folio. 48 colored pls. rpr bdg. G7. $395.00

CROCKETT, Davy. *Crockett Almanacks: Nashville Series, 1835-38.* 1955. Caxton. 1st ltd ed. 1/600. F. A18. $80.00

CROCKETT, S.R. *Adventurer in Spain.* 1903. Isbister. VG. P3. $20.00

CROCKETT, S.R. *Sir Toady Crusoe.* 1905. Stokes. 1st ed. ils Gordon Browne. 356 p. VG-. S10. $25.00

CROCKETT, S.R. *Sweetheart Travellers.* 1895. Stokes. 1st ed. ils Browne/Groome. 314 p. G+. S10. $30.00

CROCKETT. *Card Weaving.* 1973. np. ils. cloth. G2. $14.50

CROFTS, Freeman Wills. *Loss of the Jane Vosper.* 1936. Dodd Mead. 1st Am ed. NF/NF. M15. $75.00

CROFTS, Freeman Wills. *Tragedy in the Hollow.* 1939. Dodd Mead. 1st ed. VG. P3. $35.00

CROFTS, Freman Wills. *Inspector French's Greatest Case.* 1927. Collins. 4th ed. VG. P3. $25.00

CROFUT, William. *Troubadour: Different Battlefield.* 1968. Dutton. stated 1st ed. 283 p. VG+/clip. A7. $40.00

CROFUTT, George A. *Crofutt's New Overland Tourist & Pacific Coast Guide.* 1884. Omaha. Overland Pub. ils/double pls. 261 p. H7. $75.00

CROMWELL, Seymour L. *Address Delivered...Governing Comm Room of Exchange...1922.* 1922. NY Stock Exchange. 22 p. stapled wrp. M11. $25.00

CRONIN, Michael. *Night of the Party.* 1958. Ives Washburn. 1st ed. VG/dj. P3. $12.50

CRONISE. *Natural Wealth of CA.* 1868. San Francisco. 1st ed. royal 8vo. 696 p. G. T3. $40.00

CRONQUIST, Arthur. *Evolution & Classification of Flowering Plants.* 1968. Boston. ils. 396 p. VG. B26. $30.00

CROOKSTON, Newman L. *Hist of L. Pub: A Thesis...* 1937. np. xl. 50 p. pub cloth N2. $65.00

CROOME, A.C. *Fifty Yrs of Sport at Oxford Cambridge &...Schools.* 1913-22. London. Southwood. folio. 3 vols. teg. Cedri Chivers bdg. F. F1. $1,350.00

CROSBY, Alfred W. Jr. *Am, Russia, Hemp & Napoleon: Am Trade w/Russia...* 1965 Columbus. OH State. O6. $30.00

CROSBY, Caresse. *Painted Shores.* 1927 Paris. Ed Narcisse. 1st ed. 1/222 on Arches quarto. prt wrp/glassine. H5. $550.00

CROSBY, Frances Jane. *Monterey & Othe Poems.* 1851. NY. 1st ed. 12mo. 203 p. orig cloth. M1. $85.00

CROSBY, I.B. *Boston Through the Ages* (1928). Boston. Marshall Jones. 1st ed 12mo. 166 p. F. A2. $15.00

CROSBY, John. *Company of Friends.* 1977 Stein Day. 1st ed. VG/dj. P3. $12.50

CROSBY, Percy. *Dear Spooky.* 1929. Putnam. 1st ed. 124 p. G+. S10. $35.00

CROSBY, Percy. *Life Presents Skippy.* nd NY. 4to. ils. 124 p. pict wht brds/blk cloth VG+. H3. $20.00

CROSBY, Walter Wilson. *Some W Fishing* 1926. Baltimore. 1st ed. 12mo. 128 p. cloth NF. D3. $25.00

CROSS, Amanda. *James Joyce Murder.* 1967 Macmillan. 2nd ed. VG/dj. P3. $10.00

CROSS, Amanda. *Question of Max.* 1976 Knopf. 1st ed. F/F clip. Q1. $30.00

CROSS, Amanda. *Theban Mysteries.* 1971 Knopf. 1st ed. F/NF. Q1. $35.00

CROSS, F.L. *Jung Codex: Newly Recovered Gnostic Papryus...* 1955. London. Mowbrays 1st ed. 136 p. H10. $25.00

CROSS, Gillian. *Map of Nowhere.* 1989 Holiday House. 1st Am ed. F/F. F4. $15.00

CROSS, John Keir. *Best Blk Magic Stories* 1960. Faber. 1st ed. F/dj. P3. $35.00

CROSS, Mark. *Perilous Hazard.* 1961. Ward Lock. VG/dj. P3. $15.00

CROSS, P.G. *Our Friends the Trees.* 1926 NY. 1st ed. ils. 334 p. VG. B28. $17.50

CROSS, Thomas. *Autobiography of a Stage Coachman.* 1904. London. 1/50 on handmade. lg quarto. 2 vols. quarter vellum/b brds. VG. H5. $2,500.00

CROSS, Wilbur L. *Thanksgiving Day Proclamations...* 1963. Worcester. St Onge. miniature. 1/1000. bl calf. M. H10. $45.00

CROSSMAN, Richard. *Nation Reborn: Personal Account of Roles...Weizmann, Bevin.* 1960. NY. 1st ed. 171 p. VG+/VG-. S3. $15.00

CROW, Carl. *City of Flint Grows Up.* (1945). NY. 1st ed. 217 p. VG/dj. B18. $25.00

CROW, James T. *Rogue of the Peking to Paris Race.* 1983. Newport Beach. Gold Stein Pr. miniature. 1/250. F. H10. $47.50

CROW, Nancy. *Quilts & Influences.* 1990. np. ils. cloth. G2. $30.00

CROWE, John; see Lynds, Dennis.

CROWE, Kenneth C. *Collision: How the Rank & File Took Back the Teamsters.* (1993). Scribner. 1st ed. as new/dj. A7. $12.00

CROWELL, Pers. *Beau Dar. Am Saddle Colt.* 1946. Whittlesey/McGraw Hill. 2nd prt. oblong 4to. VG/fair. O3. $35.00

CROWELL, Pers. *Cavalcade of Am Horses.* 1951. McGraw Hill. 1st ed. juvenile. VG/fair. O3. $25.00

CROWELL, Pers. *First Book of Horses.* 1949. NY. Watts. 9th prt. juvenile. VG. O3. $15.00

CROWELL, Pers. *First Horseman.* 1948. Whittlesey/McGraw Hill. 1st ed. 95 p. VG/dj. A3. $15.00

CROWELL & MURRAY. *Iron Ores of Lake Superior.* 1914. Cleveland. 2nd ed. 6 fld maps. VG+. B18. $25.00

CROWLEY, John. *Beasts.* 1976. Doubleday. 1st ed. VG/dj. P3. $30.00

CROWLEY, Malcolm. *Dry Season.* 1941. Norfolk, CT. 1st ed. inscr/sgn. VG+/wht wrp/gr dj. A11. $40.00

CROWNINSHIELD, Ethel. *Mother Goose Songs for Little Ones.* 1920. Springfield, MA. oblong 8vo. brn cloth/brds. VG. H3. $25.00

CROWNINSHIELD, Mrs. Schuyler. *Light-House Children Abroad.* 1893 (1889). Lothrop. ils Bridgman/others. 446 p. bl cloth. VG. S10. $45.00

CROWTHERS, Samuel. *Romance & Rise of the Am Tropics.* 1929. Doubleday Doran. 1st ed. 8vo. 390 p. map ep. orange brds. VG/VG. B11. $50.00

CRUICKSHANK, Alan D. *Wings in the Wilderness.* 1947. NY. 1st ed. 125 full-p photos. VG/worn. A17. $17.50

CRUICKSHANK, William. *Account of 2 Cases of the Diabetes Mellitus...* 1797. London. Gillet. 2 vols. rebound half calf. G7. $995.00

CRUIKSHANK, George. *3 Courses & a Dessert.* 1850. London. Bohn. 4th ed. leather/marbled brds. VG. A16. $200.00

CRUMB, Robert. *Yum Yum Book.* 1975. San Francisco. Scrimshaw. NF/NF. B2. $125.00

CRUMLEY, James. *Dancing Bear.* 1983. Random. AP/1st issue. inscr. NF/wrp. L3. $250.00

CRUMLEY, James. *Last Good Kiss.* 1978. Random. 1st ed. F/F. Q1. $75.00

CRUMLEY, James. *Last Good Kiss.* 1979. London. Granada. 1st ed. sgn. F/F. very scarce. L3. $125.00

CRUMLEY, James. *Mexican Tree Duck.* 1993. Huntington Beach. James Cahill. 1/150. sgn/#d. F/slipcase. Q1. $75.00

CRUMLEY, James. *Mexican Tree Duck.* 1993. Mysterious. 1st ed. sgn. F/F. Q1. $45.00

CRUMLEY, James. *Mexican Tree Duck.* 1993. NY. Mysterious. ARC of 1st ed. sgn. F/stiff pict wrp. M15. $85.00

CRUMLEY, James. *One to Count Cadence.* (1970). Bantam. 1st pb ed. VG. A7. $20.00

CRUMLEY, James. *One to Count Cadence.* 1969. Random. 1st ed. author's 1st book. F/F. Q1. $300.00

CRUMLEY, James. *Wrong Case.* 1976. London. Hart Davis. 1st British ed. sgn. NF/NF. scarce. S5. $275.00

CRUMP, Irving. *Boy's Life Book of Scout Stories.* 1953. Doubleday. 1st ed. 219 p. NF/VG. B22. $7.25

CUEVAS, Jose Luis. *Worlds of Kafka & Cuevas.* 1959. Falcon. 1/600. folio. blk brds. F1. $200.00

CULBERT, T. Patrick. *Classic Maya Collapse.* 1983. Albuquerque. 2nd prt. 549 p. wrp. F3. $20.00

CULBERT, T. Patrick. *Mexico: Struggle for Modernity.* 1968. Albuquerque. 2nd prt. 549 p. F3. $20.00

CULHANE, Claire. *Why Is Canada in Vietnam?* 1972. Toronto. NC Pr. 125 p. VG+/wrp. A7. $25.00

CULLEN, Charles T. *Papers of John Marshall, Correspondence...1799-Oct 1800.* 1984. Chapel Hill. NC U. M11. $50.00

CULLEN, Charles. *Dialogues of the Courtesans/Mimes of the Courtesans.* 1931. Rarity Pr. VG. E5. $75.00

CULLEN, Countee. *Caroling Dusk.* (1927). Harper. 3rd prt. 237 p. dj. A7. $65.00

CULLEN, Countee. *Color.* (1925). Harper. 108 p. w/rear dj flap. A7. $40.00

CULLEN, Countee. *Copper Sun.* 1927. Harper Row. 1st ed. dj. scarce. A7. $300.00

CULLEN, Countee. *Lost Zoo.* (1940). Harper. 1st ed. ils Charles Sebree. F/dj. B24. $350.00

CULLEN, E.J. *Our War & How We Won It.* (1987). Viking. 1st ed. F/clip. A7. $20.00

CULLEN, Joseph Warren. *Legacies in the Study of Behavior.* 1974. Springfield. Thomas. 1st ed. 375 p. cloth. VG/dj. G1. $20.00

CULLEN, Jospeh P. *Richmond Battlefields.* 1961. GPO. Nat Park Hist Handbook 33. 46 p. VG. B10. $10.00

CULLEN, Thomas. *Adenomyoma of the Uterus.* 1908. Phil. Saunders. xl. 270 p. VG. G7. $95.00

CULLEN, William. *Treatise of the Materia Medica.* 1789. Edinburgh. Elliot. 2 vols. quarto. rebound. G7. $495.00

CULLINGFORD, Guy. *Third Party Risk.* 1962. London. Geoffrey Bles. 1st ed. F/NF. M15. $35.00

CULPAN, Maurice. *Minister of Injustice.* 1966. Walker. 1st ed. VG/dj. P3. $10.00

CULPEPPER, Nicholas. *Culpepper's Family Physician...* 1825. Exeter. Scammon. revised/corrected/enlarged ed. full calf. G7. $125.00

CULVER, Francis. *Blooded Horses of Colonial Days.* 1922. Baltimore. 1st ed. xl. ES. rebound. G. O3. $25.00

CULVER, Timothy; see Westlake, Donald E.

CUMBERLAND, Charles. *Mexico.* 1968. NY. Oxford. 1st ed. 394 p. dj. F3. $10.00

CUMBERLAND, Marten. *Dilema for Dax.* 1946. Crime Club. 1st ed. xl. dj. P3. $10.00

CUMBERLAND, Marten. *Knife Will Fall.* 1944. Crime Club. 1st ed. VG. P3. $17.50

CUMING, G.J. *Hist of Anglican Liturgy.* nd. London. Macmillan. 2nd ed. 377 p. H10. $22.50

CUMMING, Primrose. *Great Horses.* 1946. London. Dent. 1st ed. ils Lionel Edwards. VG/G+. O3. $45.00

CUMMING, William. *Sketchbook: Memoir of the '30s & NW School.* (1984). Seattle. inscr/sgn/dtd. NF/NF. A7. $25.00

CUMMING & QUINN. *British Maps of Colonial Am.* ca 1974. Chicago/London. Chicago U. 114 p. tan cloth. dj. H9/O6. $50.00

CUMMING & QUINN. *Discovery of N Am.* 1972. Am Heritage. 1st Am ed. lg 4to. cloth. clip dj. H9. $75.00

CUMMING & QUINN. *Discovery of N Am.* 1972. NY. Am Heritage. ils. 304 p. M/M. O6. $100.00

CUMMINGHAM, Frank. *General Stand Watie's Confederate Indians.* 1959. San Antonio. Naylor. 1st ed. 242 p. cloth. NF/VG. M8. $125.00

CUMMINGHAM, Jere. *Abyss.* 1981. Wyndham. 1st ed. VG/dj. P3. $20.00

CUMMINGHAM, Jere. *Visitor.* 1978. St Martin. 1st ed. F/F. F4. $18.00

CUMMINGS, E.E. *Enormous Room.* 1978. NY. Liveright. typescript ed. F/dj. C4. $50.00

CUMMINGS, E.E. *Xaipe. 71 Poems.* 1964. Hanover. Dartmouth. 1st ed. 1/200. sgn/edit Eberhart. F. C4. $25.00

CUMMINGS, Jack. *Deserter Troop.* 1991. NY. Walker. VG/dj. B9. $12.50

CUMMINGS, Ray. *Shadow Girl.* 1946. London. Swan. 1st ed. NF/NF. Q1. $25.00

CUMMINGS, Ray. *Tarrano the Conqueror.* 1930. McClurg. 1st ed. VG. M18. $45.00

CUNARD, Nancy. *Blk Man & Wht Ladyship.* 1931. Toulon. private prt. 1st ed. inscr in French/sgn. VG/stapled prt red wrp. Q1. $450.00

CUNLIFFE, Juliette. *Popular Sight Hounds.* 1992. London. 1st ed. F/F. O3. $18.00

CUNLIFFE, Marcus. *Soldiers & Civilians...Am 1775-1865.* (1968). Little Brn. 1st ed. 8vo. 499 p. VG+/VG. A2. $12.50

CUNNINGHAM, E.V. *Assassin Who Gave Up His Gun.* 1969. Morrow. 1st ed. VG/dj. P3. $15.00

CUNNINGHAM, E.V. *Case of the Poisoned Eclairs.* 1979. HRW. 1st ed. VG/dj. P3. $17.50

CUNNINGHAM, E.V. *Case of the Poisoned Eclairs.* 1980. London. Deutsch. 1st British ed. F/F. S5. $22.50

CUNNINGHAM, Eugene. *Riders of the Night.* 1943. Triangle. VG/dj. B9. $10.00

CUNNINGHAM, Eugene. *Spiderweb Trail.* 1944. Triangle. 12mo. VG. A8. $8.00

CUNNINGHAM, J. Morgan; see Westlake, Donald E.

CUNNINGHAM, John. *NJ: From High Point to Cape May.* 1953. Rutgers. 1st ed. 229 p. tan cloth. VG+/NF. B22. $9.50

CUNNINGHAM, Noble E. *Image of Thomas Jefferson in the Public Eye.* 1981. VA U. 185 p. VG/G. B10. $20.00

CUNNINGHAM, Richard. *Place Where the World Ends.* (1973). Sheed Ward. 1st ed. 8vo. 208 p. F/VG. A2. $7.50

CUNNINGHAM, Wilbur M. *Letter Book of William Burnett, Early Fur Trader...* (1967). Ft Miami Heritage of MI. apparent 1st ed. 231 p. red cloth. F. B22. $15.00

CUPPY, Will. *World's Great Detective Stories.* 1944. Tower. 3rd ed. VG/VG-. P3. $15.00

CURLEY, Daniel. *Marriage Bed of Procrustes.* nd. 1st ed. author's 1st book. sgn. NF/NF. A11. $30.00

CURRAN, William. *Mitts.* 1985. Morrow. 1st ed. F/VG+. P8. $25.00

CURREY, Richard. *Fatal Light.* (1988). Dutton. author's 2nd book/1st novel. NF/dj. A7. $27.00

CURRIER & IVES. *Caricatures Pertaining to the Civil War.* 1892. NY. Wright Swasey. 1st ed. 1/150. octavo. new crimson quarter morocco. H9. $850.00

CURRIER & IVES. *Currier & Ives. Picture Hist of the Civil War.* 1960. NY. Jack Brussel. 50 color pls. cloth. dj. D2. $75.00

CURRY, Jane Louise. *Change-Child.* 1969. HBW. 1st ed. F/F. N3. $45.00

CURRY, Larry. *Am W: Painters From Catlin to Russell.* (1972). Viking. 1st ed. 22 color pls. F/dj. A18. $50.00

CURTIN, Jeremiah. *Memoirs of...* 1940. Madison, WI. State Hist Soc. 925 p. cloth. NF. D3. $25.00

CURTIS, Charles H. *Annuals Hardy & Half-Hardy.* nd. London. 8 color pls. 118 p. VG. B28. $20.00

CURTIS, J.H. *Life of Campestris Ulm.* 1910. Boston. Clarke. 1st ed. 4to. 88 p. VG. A2. $40.00

CURTIS, Paul A. *Guns & Gunning.* 1946. NY. 1st thus ed. 383 p. VG. A17. $15.00

CURTIS, Wardon Allan. *Strange Adventures of Mr Middleton.* 1903. Chicago. 1st ed. 311 p. decor cloth. G. B18. $25.00

CURTIS, William E. *Today in Syria & Palestine.* 1903. Chicago. 1st ed. 8vo. 529 p. gilt pict gray cloth. VG+. H3. $45.00

CURTIS, William E. *Turk & His Lost Provinces.* 1903. Chicago. 2nd ed. 8vo. 396 p. cloth. O2. $40.00

CURTISS, Daniel S. *W Portraiture & Emigrant's Guide...WI, Il & IA...* 1852. NY. JH Colton. 1st ed. 12mo. fld map. 351 p+18 ad p. cloth. H9/M1. $250.00

CURTISS, Ursula. *Deadly Climate.* nd. BC. VG/dj. P3. $7.50

CURWOOD, James Oliver. *Alaskan.* (1923) Cosmopolitan. 1st ed. ils Louderback. F/dj A18. $60.00

CURWOOD, James Oliver. *Alaskan.* 1923 Cosmopolitan. 1st ed. VG/dj. B9. $30.00

CURWOOD, James Oliver. *Country Beyond: Romance of the Wilderness.* 1922. Cosmopolitan. 1st ed. ils Louderback. F/dj A18. $60.00

CURWOOD, James Oliver. *Country Beyond: Romance of the Wilderness.* 1922 Grosset Dunlap. ils Walt Louderback. G. A16. $10.00

CURWOOD, James Oliver. *Flaming Forest.* 1921. Cosmopolitan. 1st ed. VG/dj B9. $40.00

CURWOOD, James Oliver. *Flaming Forest.* 1946. Triangle. VG/VG-. P3. $15.00

CURWOOD, James Oliver. *Gentleman of Courage.* 1924. Cosmopolitan Book Corp. G. A16. $20.00

CURWOOD, James Oliver. *Gold Hunters.* (1929). IN. 1st ed. ils. pict cloth. VG. A17. $22.50

CURWOOD, James Oliver. *Honor of the Big Snows.* (1911). Indianapolis. 1st ed. 318 p. cloth. D3. $25.00

CURWOOD, James Oliver. *Kazan.* 1914. Grosset Dunlap. ils Hoskins/Hoffman. G. A16. $10.00

CURWOOD, James Oliver. *Plains of Abraham.* 1928. Doubleday Doran. 1st ed. VG. P3. $20.00

CURWOOD, James Oliver. *Valley of Gold.* 1933. Cassell. 4th ed. VG/fair. P3. $20.00

CURZON, Clare. *Bl-Eyed Boy.* 1990. Collins Crime Club. 1st ed. F/dj. P3. $18.00

CURZON, Clare. *Bl-Eyed Boy.* 1990. London. Collins. 1st ed. sgn. F/F. S5. $40.00

CURZON, Daniel. *Among the Carnivores.* 1978. Port WA. Ashley Books. 1st ed. NF/NF clip. A14. $30.00

CUSHING, Harvey. *Blbliography of Writings of...* 1939. Springfield. 1/500. 108 p. F/dj. G7. $175.00

CUSHING, Harvey. *Conscratio Medici & Other Papers.* 1970. Freeport. facsimile. 276 p. G7. $25.00

CUSHING, Harvey. *Life of Sir William Osler.* 1925. Oxford. Clarendon. 1st 1-vol ed. 11 pls. VG. G1. $50.00

CUSHING, Harvey. *Medical Career & Other Papers.* 1940. Little Brn. 3rd prt. 302 p. NF/dj. G7. $45.00

CUSHING, Harvey. *Pituitary Body & Its Disorders.* 1912. Phil. 1st ed/1st imp. 341 p. orig cloth. G7. $595.00

CUSHING, Harvey. *Studies in Intracranial Physiology & Surgery...* 1926. Oxford. xl. orig cloth. G7. $495.00

CUSHMAN, Dan. *Ripper From Rawhide.* 1952. Macmillan. 1st ed. NF/dj. B9. $20.00

CUSHNY, A.A. *TB of Pharmacology & Therapeutics.* ca 1903. np. 8vo. ils. 756 p. gr cloth. G. T3. $22.00

CUSSLER, CLive. *Cyclops.* nd. Simon Schuster. 5th ed. VG/dj. P3. $15.00

CUSSLER, Clive. *Inca Gold.* 1994. Simon Schuster. 1st ed. sgn. M/M. T2. $26.50

CUSSLER, Clive. *Night Probe!* (1981). Bantam. 4th prt. VG-/dj. P3. $12.00

CUSSLER, Clive. *Sahara.* 1992. Simon Schuster. 1st ed. sgn. M/M. T2. $23.00

CUSSLER, Clive. *Vixen O3.* 1978. Viking. 1st ed. sgn. NF/NF. M15. $50.00

CUSTER, Elizabeth B. *Boots & Saddles; or, Life in Dakota w/Gen Custer.* 1885. NY. Harper. 1st ed/later state. 12mo. 312 p. decor cloth. H9. $75.00

CUSTER, Elizabeth B. *Boots & Saddles; or, Life in Dakota w/General Custer.* 1885. NY. Harper. 1st ed/1st issue. 8vo. decor cloth. VG. B20. $100.00

CUSTER, Elizabeth B. *Tenting on the Plains.* 1893. NY. Webster. 403 p. VG+. O7. $27.50

CUSTER, Elizabeth B. *Tenting on the Plains...* 1889. NY. Webster. scarce shoulder strap ed. pls. 702 p. VG+. M8. $250.00

CUTLER, C.C. *Greyhounds of the Sea.* 1930. NY. 1st ed. ils. 592 p. VG. B28. $25.00

CUTLER, John Henry. *Tom Setson & the Bl Devil.* 1951. Whitman. VG/VG-. P3. $12.50

CUTLER, U. Waldo. *Story of King Arthur.* 1941. Crowell. 1st ed. VG/VG. L1. $15.00

CUTLER & ZOLLINGER. *Atlas of Surgical Operations.* 1949. Macmillan. 106 full-p pls. 225 p. VG. E5. $75.00

CUTRER, Emily Fourmy. *Art of the Woman. Life & Work of Elisabet Ney.* 1988. Lincoln, NE. ils/photos. 270 p. cloth. dj. D2. $45.00

CUTRIGHT, Paul Russell. *Hist of Lewis & Clark Journals.* nd. Norman, OK. 1st ed. 8vo. ils/map. 211 p. M/dj. T8. $85.00

CUTRIGHT, Paul Russell. *Meriwether Lewis: Naturalist.* 1968. Portland, OR. 8vo. F/pict wrp. T8. $20.00

CUTTEN, George Barton. *Three Thousand Yrs of Mental Healing.* 1911. Scribner. 1st ed. 9 pls. red cloth. VG. G1. $37.50

CUTTER, Calvin. *Treatise on Anatomy, Physiology & Hygiene.* 1850. Boston. 454 p. full calf. NF. O7. $9.50

CUTTER, Charles. *Gem Souvenir of Hot Springs, AR.* ca 1910. NY. Cutter & Sons. oblong 8vo. pict wrp. H9. $45.00

CUTTER, Donald C. *CA in 1792: Spanish Naval Visit.* 1990. Norman. 1st ed. 8vo. 176 p. bl cloth. VG+. P4. $27.50

CUTTER, George W. *Mafia & Foreign Immigration. A Sermon...Newport, RI...* 1891. Newport. Sanborn. 1st ed. 8vo. 16 p. sewn. M1. $1,250.00

CUTTER, William Parker. *Charles Ammi Cutter.* 1931. Am Lib Assn/Merrymount. 1/1000. quarto. 62 p. F/glassine. B24. $75.00

CUVIER, Georges. *Essay on the Theory of the Earth.* 1818. NY. Kirk & Mercein. 1st Am ed. 8 pls. 432 p. contemporary calf. K1. $375.00

CUYLER, Theo L. *Empty Crib.* 1869 (1868). NY. Carter Bros. 18mo. 160 p. G. S10. $45.00

CYNK, Jerzy B. *Polish Aircraft...* (1971). Putnam. 1st Eng ed. 8vo. 760 p. VG. A2. $40.00

CZWIKLITZER, Christopher. *Picasso's Posters.* 1970-71. Random. 1st Am ed. folio. 365 p. VG+/dj. F1. $250.00

D'AMORE, Arcangelo R.T. *William Alanson Wht: The WA Yrs 1903-37.* 1976. WA. St Elizabeths. 1st ed. 189 p. VG/wrp. G1. $25.00

D'AULAIRE & D'AULAIRE. *Abraham Lincoln.* (1939). Doubleday Doran. 1949 Caldecott Medal. VG+. P2. $30.00

D'AULAIRE & D'AULAIRE. *Buffalo Bill.* 1952. Doubleday. 1st ed. F/VG. P2. $65.00

D'AULAIRE & D'AULAIRE. *George Washington.* 1936. Doubleday Doran. 1st ed. 4to. G. A3. $17.50

D'AULAIRE & D'AULAIRE. *George Washington.* 1936. NY. 1st ed. ils/pls. 56 p. pict brds/blk cloth. F/G. H3. $30.00

D'AULAIRE & D'AULAIRE. *Leif the Lucky.* 1941. Doubleday Doran. 1st ed. NF/VG. P2. $85.00

D'AULAIRE & D'AULAIRE. *Leif the Lucky.* 1941. Doubleday Doran. 1st ed. 4to. G. A3. $20.00

D'AULAIRE & D'AULAIRE. *Ola.* 1932. Doubleday Doran. early reprint. G/front dj torn off. A3. $10.00

D'AULAIRE & D'AULAIRE. *Wings for Per.* 1944. Doubleday Doran. 1st ed. VG/dj. M20. $50.00

D'AULNOY, Madame. *Travels Into Spain.* (1930). London. Routledge. 1st thus ed. 8vo. 447 p. F/VG+. A2. $20.00

D'AULNOY & PERRAULT. *Once Upon a Time: Wht Cat, Puss 'n' Boots & Bluebeard.* nd. Little Brn. 12mo. 89 p. VG. S10. $20.00

D'AVENNES. *Arabic Art in Color.* 1978. np. 141 designs on 50 pls. wrp. G2. $8.00

D'HARCOURT. *Textiles of Ancient Peru & Their Techniques.* 1975. np. ils. wrp. G2. $20.00

D'IRUMBERRY, Charles Marie. *Voyage a Constantinople, Italie, et Aux Iles de l'Archipel.* 1799. Paris. 1st ed/2nd issue. 333 p. orig paper wrp/label/cloth box. O2. $600.00

D'OLIVER, Luis Nicolau. *Fray Bernardino de Sahagun.* 1987. Salt Lake City. 1st ed. 201 p. dj. F3. $30.00

D'ORS, Xavier. *El Interdicto Fraudatorio en el Derecho Romano Clasico.* 1974. Roma. Consejo Superior Investigaciones Cientificas. wrp. M11. $50.00

D'Ostria, Dora. *La Poesie des Ottomans.* 1877. Paris. 12mo. 208 p. unopened. O2. $75.00

D., H. *Palimpset.* 1926. Houghton Mifflin. 1/700. VG+/VG. B4. $225.00

DA COSTA, Phil. *100 Yrs of Am's Fire Fighting Apparatus.* 1964. Bonanza. VG/dj. A16. $20.00

DA LA ROCHE FRANCIS, Claude. *London: Hist & Social.* 1902. Phil. 2 vols. teg. gilt red cloth. F. H3. $40.00

DA MONTALBODDO, Fracan. *Itinerarium Portugalensium.* 1992. Lisboa. facsimile of 1508 Milan ed. 196 p. M/dj. O6. $125.00

DABNEY, Marie Keane. *Mrs TNT.* (1949). Dietz. 2nd prt. ils. 177 p. VG/G. B10. $20.00

DABNEY, Virginius. *Richmond: Story of a City.* 1976. Doubleday. ils/maps. 412 p. VG/G+. B10. $25.00

DABOLL, Nathan. *Arithmetic...w/Addition of the Practical Accountant...* 1825. London. S Gr. 252 p. calf/wood brds. G. B14. $150.00

DACUS, J.A. *Annals of the Great Strikes of the US: A Reliable Hist...* ca 1877. Chicago. LT Palmer. ils. G. V4. $35.00

DADD, George H. *Modern Horse Doctor.* 1856. Boston. Jewett. ils. 432 p. worn cloth. H10. $21.75

DAGGS, Elisa. *Doorways to the World.* 1960. Doubleday. 1st ed. 8vo. ils. 319 p. VG. W1. $16.00

DAGLEY, R. *Takings; or, The Life of a Collegian.* 1821. London. Warren/Whittaker. 1st ed. 8vo. VG+. B20. $250.00

DAGMAR, Peter. *Alien Skies.* 1967. Arcadia. VG/dj. P3. $15.00

DAGMAR, Peter. *Alien Skies.* 1967. Arcadia. 1st ed. NF/clip. F4. $25.00

DAGUERRE. *Hist & Descriptive Account of the Daguerrotype.* 1969 (1839). np. (London). reprint. ils. 80 p. O7. $12.50

DAHL, Borghild. *Good News.* 1966. Dutton. 1st ed. sgn. 160 p. VG/dj. B22. $7.00

DAHL, Roald. *Charlie & the Great Glass Elevator.* 1972. Knopf. 1st ed. ils Schindelman. 163 p. VG/VG. D1. $65.00

DAHL, Roald. *Going Solo.* 1986. FSG. ARC. NF/pict wrp. N3. $15.00

DAHL, Roald. *My Uncle Oswald.* (1980). Knopf. 1st ed. F/NF. B3. $30.00

DAHL, Roald. *Rhyme Stew.* 1989. London. Cape. 1st ed. 4to. 79 p. bl brds. F/F. T5. $40.00

DAHL, Roald. *Some Time Never: A Fable for Supermen.* 1948. Scribner. 1st ed. NF/NF. B4. $250.00

DAHL, Roald. *Switch Bitch.* nd. BOMC. VG/dj. P3. $10.00

DAHL, Roald. *Two Fables.* 1987. FSG. 1st Am ed. F/F. N3. $15.00

DAHL & KROG. *Macrolichens of Denmark, Finland, Norway & Sweden.* 1973. Oslo. ils/map. 185 p. VG. B26. $14.00

DAHLBERG, Edward. *Bottom Dogs.* 1930. NY. 1st ed. author's 1st book. NF/dj. A15. $85.00

DAILEY, Janet. *Aspen Gold.* 1991. Little Brn. lg prt. VG/dj. A16. $10.00

DAILEY, Janet. *Silver Wings.* 1984. Poseidon. 1st ed. 8vo. VG/G. A8. $10.00

DAIN, Norman. *Concepts of Insanity in the US, 1789-1865.* 1964. Rutgers. 304 p. gray cloth. VG/dj. G1. $28.50

DAINGERFIELD, Foxhall. *Ghost House.* 1926. Appleton. 2nd prt. F/VG+. B4. $75.00

DAKIN, Douglas. *British Intelligence of Events in Greece, 1824-27.* 1959. Athens. 8vo. 184 p. prt wrp. O2. $25.00

DAKIN, Susanna Bryant. *Perennial Adventure.* 1954. San Francisco. 1/2000. sgn. VG. B26. $31.00

DALE, Alzina Stone. *Mystery Reader's Walking Guide.* 1988. Passport Books. 1st ed. F/dj. P3. $20.00

DALEY, Arthur. *Times at Bat.* 1950. Random. 1st ed. F/VG. P8. $27.50

DALEY, Brian. *Han Solo at Stars' End.* nd. BC. VG/dj. P3. $7.50

DALEY, Brian. *Han Solo's Revenge.* 1979. Del Rey. 1st ed. F/NF. F4. $30.00

DALEY, Robert. *Target Blue.* 1973. Delacorte. 1st ed. VG/dj. P3. $25.00

DALEY, Robert. *Yr of the Dragon.* 1981. Simon Schuster. 1st ed. VG/dj. P3. $15.00

DALGLIESH, Alice. *Davenports & Cherry Pie.* 1949. Scribner. 1st/A ed. 196 p. VG+/dj. M20. $40.00

DALGLIESH, Alice. *Little Angel: Story of Old Rio.* 1943. Scribner. ils Milhous. 70 p. VG/torn. T5. $40.00

DALGLIESH, Alice. *Sailor Sam.* 1935. Scribner. 1st ed. G+. P2. $22.50

DALGLISH, Doris N. *People Called Quakers.* 1938. London. Oxford. xl. 8vo. 169 p. V3. $9.00

DALI, Salvador. *Dali by Dali.* 1970. Abrams. VG/dj. P3. $20.00

DALI, Salvador. *Hidden Faces.* 1944. Dial. 1st ed. VG. E3. $30.00

DALMAN, Gustaf. *Jesus: Jeshua Studies in the Gospels.* 1971. Ktav. reprint of 1929 ed. 56 p. VG+. S3. $25.00

DALOS, Gyorgy. *1985: Hist Report (Hongkong 2036) From the Hungarian...* 1983. Pantheon/Random. 1st Am ed. trans from German. NF/NF. A14. $25.00

DALRYMPLE, Byron. *Modern Book of the Blk Bass.* (1974). Winchester. 4th prt. 206 p. F/dj. A17. $10.00

DALRYMPLE, Byron. *N Am Big Game Hunting.* (1974). NY. index/photos. 383 p. F/G. A17. $15.00

DALTON, John C. *Treatise on Human Physiology.* 1871. Phil. 8vo. 729 p. VG. T3. $49.00

DALTON, Priscilla; see Avallone, Mike.

DALY, Elizabeth. *Night Walk.* 1947. Rinehart. 1st ed. VG-/dj. P3. $30.00

DALY, Elizabeth. *Wrong Way Down.* 1946. Rinehart. 1st ed. xl. VG. P3. $10.00

DALY, R.W. *How the Merrimac Won.* 1957. np. 211 p. dj. O7. $12.50

DANA, James D. *Manual of Geology.* (1894). NY. 4th ed. color pls. 1087 p. G. A17. $15.00

DANA, James D. *Manual of Mineralogy & Lithology...* 1883. NY. Wiley. 3rd ed. ils/diagrams. 474 p. VG. S9. $15.00

DANA, Mrs W.S. *According to Season.* 1990. Boston. 1st thus ed. 175 p. F/slipcase. A17. $10.00

DANA, Richard Henry Jr. *Two Yrs Before the Mast.* nd. Phil. Altemus. ils. orig cloth. VG. E3. $20.00

DANA, Richard Henry Jr. *Two Yrs Before the Mast.* 1936. NY. Random/Grabhorn. 1/1000. octavo. 464 p. NF/dj. H5. $200.00

DANA, Richard Henry Jr. *Two Yrs Before the Mast...* 1949. Doubleday. 8vo. ils Frankenbeg. 368 p. VG. P4. $17.50

DANA, Rose; see Ross, W.E.D.

DANA & KRUEGER. *California Lands.* 1958. WA, DC. 1st ed. 308 p. NF/dj. D3. $25.00

DANBY, Mary. *Realms of Darkness.* 1985. Octopus. F/dj. P3. $15.00

DANCER, Rex. *Bad Girl Blues.* 1994. Simon Schuster. ARC. F/wrp. B2. $30.00

DANDY, Walter E. *Flouroscopy of the Cerebral Ventricals.* 1919. reprint from Johns Hopkins bulletin. 15 p. wrp. G7. $150.00

DANE, Clemence. *Flower Girls.* 1955. Norton. 1st ed. VG. P3. $10.00

DANGELMAIER, Rudi. *Pioneer Buildings of British Columbia.* (1989). Maderia Park, BC. Harbour Pub. 4to. 160 p. F/F. A2. $15.00

DANIEL, Gabriel. *Voyage to the World of Cartesius.* 1692. London. 1st Eng ed. octavo. modern red morocco. VG. H5. $550.00

DANIEL, Mark. *Unbridled.* 1992. Ticknor Fields. 1st Am ed. F/F. T2. $20.00

DANIEL & O'RIORDIAN. *New Grange & the Bend of the Boyne.* 1964. np. 1st Am ed. VG. C1. $7.50

DANIEL-ROPS, Henri. *20th-Century Encyclopedia of Catholicism.* 1967-71. Hawthorn. 150 vols in 149. H10. $400.00

DANIELOU, Jean. *Advent.* 1951. NY. Sheed Ward. 181 p. H10. $15.00

DANIELOU, Jean. *Dead Sea Scrolls & Primitive Christianity.* 1958. Baltimore. Helicon. 128 p. H10. $18.50

DANIELOU, Jean. *Gospel Message & Hellenistic Culture.* 1973. Westminster. 540 p. H10. $25.00

DANIELS, Anthony. *Sweet Waist of Am.* (1990). London. Hutchinson. 1st ed. 249 p. dj. F3. $20.00

DANIELS, Dorothy; see Daniels, Norman.

DANIELS, Jan; see Ross, W.E.D.

DANIELS, Jonathan. *Ordeal of Ambition: Jefferson, Hamilton, Burr.* 1970. Doubleday. 1st ed. 446 p. VG/fair. B10. $15.00

DANIELS, Jonathan. *Prince of Carpetbaggers.* (1958). Lippincott. 1st ed. 8vo. 319 p. F/VG. A2. $12.50

DANIELS, Jonathan. *Randolphs of VA.* 1972. Doubleday. ils. 362 p. VG/G. B10. $25.00

DANIELS, Josephus. *Life of Woodrow Wilson 1865-1924.* ca 1924. Phil. Winston. 8vo. 381 p. bl linen. H9. $30.00

DANIELS, Les. *Blk Castle.* 1978. Scribner. 1st ed. F/dj. P3. $25.00

DANIELS, Les. *Hist of Comic Books in Am.* 1971. Bonanza. reprint. dj. C8. $35.00

DANIELSON, Carol N. *Disquisitio in Cephalalgiam.* 1821. Lundae. 22 p. G7. $25.00

DANIELSSON, Bengt. *From Raft to Raft.* (1960). Doubleday. 1st Am ed. 8vo. 264 p. F/VG+ clip. A2. $15.00

DANIOS, Pierre. *Major Thompson & I.* 1957. London. Cape. 1st Eng ed of 1st French ed. NF/NF. A14. $25.00

DANN, Jack. *Immortal.* 1978. Harper Row. 1st ed. VG/dj. P3. $15.00

DANN, Jack. *Wandering Stars.* nd. BC. VG/dj. P3. $7.50

DANN, Patty. *Mermaids.* 1986. Tichnor Fields. 1st ed. rem mk. F/dj. B4. $30.00

DANOEN, Emile. *Tides of Time.* 1952. Ballantine. VG/torn. P3. $30.00

DANSEREAU, Pierre. *Challenge for Survival.* 1970. NY. Columbia. 4th prt/3rd prt clip dj. A7. $15.00

DANTE. *Divina Commedia.* 1823. London. Pickering. miniature. 2 vols. ornate gilt leather. H10. $185.00

DANTE. *Divine Comedy.* 1969. Grossman. tall 4to. ils/sgn Baskin. 3 vols. linen. F/VG+ slipcase. F1. $175.00

DANZIG & REICHLER. *Hist of Baseball.* 1959. Prentice Hall. 1st ed. VG/G+. P8. $50.00

DARBY, Wiliam. *Geological Description of State of LA...* 1817. NY. Olmstead. 2nd ed. octavo. orig speckled calf. H9. $750.00

DARBY, Wiliam. *Tour From City of NY to Detroit in MI Territory...* 1819. NY. Kirk Mercein. octavo. 3 fld maps. teg. Riviere bdg. H9. $765.00

DARE, M.P. *Unholy Relics & Other Uncanny Tales.* (1947). London. Arnold. 1st ed. dj. A7. $50.00

DAREFF, Hal. *Story of Vietnam.* (1966). Parents Magazine. 256 p. ils brds. NF/torn. A7. $30.00

DAREL, Sylva. *Sparrow in the Snow.* 1973. Stein Day. 216 p. VG/fair. S3. $20.00

DARK, Sidney. *London.* 1924. Macmillan. ils Pennell. VG. V2. $12.00

DARK, Sidney. *London.* 1937. NY. ils Jospeh Pennell. 176 p. gilt dk bl cloth. F. H3. $40.00

DARLINGTON, C.D. *Evolution of Man & Society.* 1969. Simon Schuster. 1st ed. thick 8vo. bl cloth. VG/dj. G1. $30.00

DARNELL, Elias. *Journal...of Those Heroic KY Volunteers...1812-13.* 1854. Phil. 5th ed. 12mo. VG. B28. $125.00

DARROCH, John. *Chinese Self-Taught by the Natural Method.* 1916. London. Marlborough. 2nd ed. sm 8vo. 154 p. VG. W1. $18.00

DARROW, Clarence. *Plea for Clarence Darrow, in His Own Defense.* 1912. LA. Golden Pr. 1st ed. NF/NF wrp. B2. $75.00

DART, Iris Rainer. *Beaches.* 1985. Bantam. 1st ed. F/F. T2. $11.00

DARTON, Nelson H. *N Am Geology for 1886.* 1889. GPO. removed from annual report. VG. P4. $14.50

DARWIN, Bernard. *British Clubs.* 1943. London. 8vo. 48 p. pict gray brds. F. H3. $12.00

DARWIN, Charles. *Autobiography w/His Notes & Letters...* 1950. NY. Schuman. G/dj. A16. $7.50

DARWIN, Charles. *Descent of Man & Selection in Relation to Sex.* 1971. LEC. quarto. ils/sgn Kredel. 362 p. F/slipcase. B24. $85.00

DARWIN, Charles. *Different Forms of Flowers on Plants of Same Species.* 1877. London. John Murray. 1st ed. inscr. 352 p. gr cloth. B14. $275.00

DARWIN, Charles. *Expression of Emotions in Man & Animals.* 1872. London. John Murray. 1st ed. 7 pls. 374 p. gr cloth. NF. B14. $300.00

DARWIN, Charles. *Letters of...* 1903. London. Murray. 1st ed/1st issue. 508 p. prt bl cloth. G1. $225.00

DARWIN, Charles. *Life & Letters of...* 1887. London. Murray. 2 vols. panelled gr-gray cloth. VG. G1. $325.00

DARWIN, Charles. *On the Origin of Species by Means of Natural Selection...* 1859. London. 1st ed. octavo. gr cloth. VG/morocco slipcase. H5. $17,500.00

DARWIN, Charles. *Origin of the Species by Means of Natural Selection...* 1963 (1859). Heritage. reprint 1876 6th ed. 470 p. F/slipcase. G1. $37.50

DARWIN, Francis. *Life & Letters of Charles Darwin...* 1887. NY. Appleton. 1st Am ed. 2 vols. octavo. gilt maroon cloth. F. R3. $425.00

DARWIN, George Howard. *Tides & Kindred Phenomena in Solar System.* (1898). Houghton Mifflin. 378 p. bl cloth. B14. $35.00

DARY, David. *Entrepreneurs of the Old W.* 1986. Knopf. VG/dj. N2. $10.00

DARY, David. *Entrepreneurs of the Old W.* 1986. Knopf. 1st Am ed. F/VG. H7. $15.00

DASKAM, Josephine. *Madness of Philip & Other Tales of Childhood.* 1902. McClure Phillips. 4th prt. 223 p. VG. P2. $18.00

DASKAM, Josephine. *Memoirs of a Baby.* 1904. Harper. 1st ed. ils FY Cory. 272 p. gl cloth. G+. S10. $25.00

DASNOY, Albert. *Gods & Men.* 1949. London. Harvill. VG. C1. $7.50

DAUBS, Edwin H. *Monograph of Lemnaceae.* 1965. Urbana. 21 pls. 118 p. VG+. B26. $25.00

DAUGHERTY, Sonia. *Andy & the Lion.* 1938. Viking. 1st ed. fair. P2. $12.50

DAUGHERTY, Sonia. *Of Courage Undaunted: Across the Continent...* 1951. Viking. 1st ed. 163 p. F/VG+. P2. $30.00

DAUGHERTY, Sonia. *Poor Richard.* 1941. Viking. 1st ed. 158 p. VG+. P2. $15.00

DAUGHERTY, Sonia. *Vanka's Donkey.* 1940. Stokes. 1st ed. 62 p. VG+. P2. $15.00

DAUMIER, Honore. *Lithographien: 1861-1872.* (ca 1920). Munich. Langen. thin folio. yel cloth. F1. $195.00

DAUNCEY, John. *Hist of His Sacred Majesty Charles the II, King of Eng...* 1660. London. John Davies. 12mo. 236 p. rebound calf/marbled brds/morocco label. K1. $250.00

DAUPHINE, Claude; see Weiss, Joe.

DAVENPORT, Basil. *SF Novel.* 1959. Advent. 1st ed. VG/dj. P3. $40.00

DAVENPORT, Basil. *13 Ways To Dispose of a Body.* 1966. Dodd Mead. VG/torn. P3. $12.50

DAVENPORT, Basil. *13 Ways To Kill a Man.* 1969. Faber. 1st ed. NF/dj. P3. $17.50

DAVENPORT, F.G. *European Treaties Bearing on Hist of the US...to 1648.* 1917. WA. Carnegie Inst. Samuel E Morison's copy. 387 p. VG+. O6. $55.00

DAVENPORT, Guy. *Carmina Archilochi.* 1964. Berkeley. 1st ed. author's 2nd book. 12mo. F/ils wrp. A11. $25.00

DAVENPORT, Homer. *Country: Story of His Own Early Life...* 1910. Dillingham. 1st ed. VG. O3. $65.00

DAVENPORT, Homer. *My Quest of the Arabian Horse.* nd. Chicago. Arabian Horse Club. reprint. VG. O3. $45.00

DAVENPORT, J.S. *European Crowns 1700-1800.* 1961. Galesburg. 334 p. G. C10. $22.50

DAVENPORT, M. *Foot & Shoeing.* 1965. London. British Horse Soc. 12mo. 55 p. VG/wrp. O3. $5.00

DAVENPORT, R.A. *Dictionary of Biography...* 1839. Exeter, NH. 8vo. 527 p. legal calf. H9. $45.00

DAVENPORT, William H. *Voices in the Court. Treasury of Bench, Bar & Courtroom.* 1958. NY. Macmillan. M11. $35.00

DAVENTRY, Leonard. *Man of Double Deed.* 1965. Doubleday. VG/dj. P3. $20.00

DAVEY, Jocelyn. *Dangerous Liaison.* 1988. Walker. 1st ed. F/dj. P3. $16.95

DAVID, Henry. *Hist of the Haymarket Affair.* (1963). Collier. 1st Collier pb ed. 479 p. A7. $8.00

DAVID, Henry. *Hist of the Haymarket Affair: Study in Am Social-Revolution.* ca 1936. NY. Russell. xl. G. V4. $12.50

DAVID, Jay. *Flying Saucer Reader.* nd. BC VG/dj. P3. $7.50

DAVID, Ludwig. *Ratgeber im Photographieren.* 1912. W Knapp. ils/28 pls. 268 p. prt wrp. B14. $22.50

DAVID, Mary Lee. *Uncle Sam's Attic.* 1930. Boston. 1st ed. 402 p. map ep. bl cloth. VG. H3. $15.00

DAVIDSON, Art. *Endangered Peoples* (1993). Sierra Club. 1st ed. sgn. ils/sgn Art Wolfe. F/F. L3. $85.00

DAVIDSON, Avram. *Best of Avram Davidson.* 1979. Doubleday. 1st ed. VG/dj. P3. $20.00

DAVIDSON, Avram. *Redward Edward Papers.* 1978. Garden City. 1st ed. F/F. N3. $20.00

DAVIDSON, Avram. *Strange Seas & Shores.* 1971. Doubleday. 1st ed. F/F. N3. $20.00

DAVIDSON, Avram. *Vergil in Averno.* 1987. Doubleday. 1st ed. F/F. T2. $16.00

DAVIDSON, Bill. *Cut Off.* 1972. Stein Day. 1st ed. VG/dj. P3. $15.00

DAVIDSON, George. *AK Boundary.* 1903. San Francisco. AK Packers Anns. presentation/inscr. 235 p. NF. O6. $550.00

DAVIDSON, J.B. *Agricultural Engineering.* 1913. St Paul. 1st ed. 554 p. brn cloth. G. C10. $22.50

DAVIDSON, John; see Nuetzel, Charles.

DAVIDSON, Lionel. *Long Way to Shiloh.* 1966. Gollancz. 2nd ed. VG/dj. P3. $15.00

DAVIDSON, Lionel. *Making Good Again.* 1968. Harper Row. 1st ed. F/dj. P3. $20.00

DAVIDSON, Sarah Calder. *Sylvester & the Butterfly Bomb.* 1972. Doubleday. 1st ed. 62 p. VG+/VG. P2. $20.00

DAVIES, A.M. *Strange Destiny: Biography of Warren Hastings.* (1935). Putnam. 1st Am ed. 8vo. 468 p. F/F. A2. $45.00

DAVIES, Arthur L. *Death Plays a Duet.* 1977. Exposition. 1st ed. VG/dj. P3. $10.00

DAVIES, D.W. *Elizabethans Errant...Sir Thomas Sherley & His 3 Sons.* (1967). Ithaca, NY. 1st ed. 8vo. 337 p. F/VG. A2. $12.50

DAVIES, David Stuart. *Holmes of the Movies.* 1978. Bramhall. 1st ed. VG/dj. P3. $12.50

DAVIES, John. *Hist of Tahitian Mission, 1799-1830.* 1974. Nendeln. reprint for Hakluyt Soc. 8vo. 392 p. M. P4. $75.00

DAVIES, L.P. *Land of Leys.* 1979. Doubleday. 1st ed. VG/dj. P3. $16.00

DAVIES, L.P. *Twilight Journey.* nd. BC. VG/dj. P3. $7.50

DAVIES, Nigel. *Aztec Empire: The Toltec Resurgence.* (1987). Norman, OK. 1st Am ed. 8vo. 2 maps. 341 p. F/F. A2. $22.50

DAVIES, Nigel. *Toltec Heritage.* (1980). Norman, OK. 1st ed. 401 p. dj. F3. $25.00

DAVIES, Robertson. *Fifth Business.* 1970. Viking. 1st ed. NF/NF. Q1. $40.00

DAVIES, Robertson. *Lyre of Orpheus.* (1989). Viking. AP. F/prt wht wrp/orig plastic wrp. B3. $35.00

DAVIES, Robertson. *Murther & Walking Spirits.* 1991. Viking. AP. F/pict wrp. C4. $35.00

DAVIES, Robertson. *One Half of Robertson Davies.* 1977. Toronto. Macmillan. 1st ed. F/NF. Q1. $50.00

DAVIES, Robertson. *Papers of Samuel Marchbanks.* (1986). Viking. 1st ed. F/VG. B3. $30.00

DAVIES, Robertson. *Question Time: A Play.* 1975. Toronto. 1st ed. sgn. VG/ils wrp. A11. $45.00

DAVIES, Robertson. *Rebel Angels.* (1982). Viking. 1st ed. VG/VG. B3. $30.00

DAVIES, Robertson. *Renown at Stratford.* 1953. Toronto. Clarke Irwin. F/NF. B2. $75.00

DAVIES, Robertson. *Stratford Papers on Shakespeare.* 1961. Toronto. 1st ed. inscr. NF/wrp. A11. $75.00

DAVIES, Robertson. *Table Talk of Samuel Marchbanks.* 1949. Toronto. Clark Irwin. 1st ed. NF/F. Q1. $75.00

DAVIES, Robertson. *Thrice Have the Trumpets Sounded.* 1954. Toronto. Clarke Irwin. 1st ed. F/NF. B2. $65.00

DAVIES, Robertson. *Voice From the Attic.* 1960. Knopf. 1st ed. F/F clip. B4. $125.00

DAVIES, Robertson. *What's Bred in the Bone.* 1985. Viking. 1st ed. sgn. F/NF. B2. $30.00

DAVIES, Robertson. *World of Wonders.* 1975. Toronto. Macmillan. 1st ed. F/NF. Q1. $45.00

DAVIES, Robertson. *5th Business.* 1970. Viking. 1st ed. F/F. B2. $45.00

DAVIES, W.D. *Gosepl & the Land: Early Christianity & Jewish...Doctrine.* 1974. CA U. 521 p. VG+/VG-. S3. $27.00

DAVIES, W.D. *Torah in the Messianic Age &/or Age To Come.* 1952. Soc Biblical Literature. 99 p. VG/wrp. S3. $23.00

DAVIES, W.H. *Autobiography of a Super-Tramp.* 1928 (1908). London. Cape. reprint. 12mo. 304 p. F. A2. $15.00

DAVIES & EWART. *Flora of the N Territory.* 1917. Melbourne. Hamilton Cheel. 27 pls. 387 p. wrp. B26. $195.00

DAVIES & PARRY. *No 8 (Mervyn Davies, rugby player).* (1977). London. Pelham. 1st ed. 8vo. 208 p. F/F. A2. $12.50

DAVIS, Angela. *Angela.* 1971. Leisure. PBO. 224 p. NF. A7. $15.00

DAVIS, Angela. *If They Come in the Morning.* (1971). NY. 3rd Pr. stated 1st ed. 281 p. F/dj. A7. $40.00

DAVIS, Archie K. *Boy Colonel of Confederacy...Times of Henry King Burgwyn Jr.* 1985. Chapel Hill. 1st ed. 406 p. cloth. NF/NF. M8. $35.00

DAVIS, B.J. *Communist Councilman From Harlem.* 1969. Internat. 218 p. wrp. A7. $12.00

DAVIS, Berrie. *Fourth Day of Fear.* 1973. Putnam. 1st ed. VG/dj. P3. $12.50

DAVIS, Bob. *Oriental Odyssey. People Behind the Sun.* 1937. Stokes. 1st ed. xl. ils. 266 p. new ep. G. W1. $16.00

DAVIS, Burke. *Billy Mitchell Affair.* 1967. Random. 1st ed. sgn. 373 p. blk cloth. VG/VG. B11. $50.00

DAVIS, C.G. *Ship Models: How To Build Them.* 1925. Salem, MA. ils. 139 p. buckram. VG. B18. $35.00

DAVIS, Christopher. *Joseph & the Old Man.* 1986. St Martin. 1st ed. author's 1st book. NF/NF clip. A14. $30.00

DAVIS, David Brion. *Problem of Slavery in W Culture.* (1966). Cornell. 505 p. dj. A7. $15.00

DAVIS, David D. *Acute Hydrocephalus or Water in the Head...* 1840. London. Taylor Walton. 1st ed. 309 p. half roan/marbled brds. VG. G7. $795.00

DAVIS, Dorothy Salisbury. *Shock Wave.* 1974. Arthur Baker. 1st ed. VG/dj. P3. $17.50

DAVIS, E. Adams. *Of the Night Wind's Telling.* 1946. OK U. 1st ed. ils/notes. 146 p. VG. B19. $15.00

DAVIS, E.T. *Surry Co Records, Surry Co...1652-84.* 1980. Genealogical Pub. reprint 1940 ed. 142 p. VG. B10. $15.00

DAVIS, E.W. *Pioneering w/Taconite.* 1964. St Paul. NM Hist Soc. ils/maps. 246 p. F/dj. A17. $16.50

DAVIS, Enid. *Comprehensive Guide to Children's Literature w/Jewish Theme.* 1981. Schocken. 177 p. VG+/G+. S3. $24.00

DAVIS, Franklin M. *Counterattack.* 1964. Whitman. VG. P3. $7.50

DAVIS, Frederick C. *Drag the Dark.* 1953. Crime Club. 1st ed. VG. P3. $17.50

DAVIS, Grania. *Moonbird.* 1986. Doubleday. 1st ed. RS. F/dj. P3. $20.00

DAVIS, H.L. *Harp of a Thousand Strings.* 1947. Morrow. 1st ed. F/dj. A18. $35.00

DAVIS, H.L. *Honey in the Horn.* 1935. Harper. 1st ed. NF/dj. A18. $50.00

DAVIS, H.L. *Honey in the Horn.* 1977. Franklin Lib. 1st thus ed. gilt tan leather. M. A18. $40.00

DAVIS, H.L. *Winds of Morning.* 1952. Morrow. 1st ed. F/dj. A18. $35.00

DAVIS, Hassoldt. *Islands Under the Wind.* 1933. London. 1st ed. pls. 279 p. red cloth. VG. H3. $20.00

DAVIS, Hassoldt. *Land of the Eye.* (1940). NY. Holt. 1st ed. 8vo. 415 p. F/VG. A2. $30.00

DAVIS, Hassoldt. *Sorcerer's Village.* 1955. NY. 1st ed. 334 p. silvered blk cloth. F/F. H3. $40.00

DAVIS, Hubert J. *Silver Bullet.* 1975. Jonathan David. 1st ed. VG/G+. B10. $18.00

DAVIS, Hubert J. *Silver Bullet.* 1975. Jonathan David. 1st ed. VG/VG. P3. $20.00

DAVIS, Jefferson. *Rise & Fall of the Confederate Government.* 1881. London. Longman Gr. 1st Eng ed. 2 vols. cloth. VG. M8. $450.00

DAVIS, Jefferson. *Short Hist of Confederate States of Am.* 1890. NY. Belford. 1st ed. xl. 505 p. later cloth. VG. M8. $65.00

DAVIS, John Gordon. *Taller Than Trees.* 1975. Doubleday. 1st ed. F/dj. P3. $15.00

DAVIS, John. *1st Settlers of VA, an Hist Novel.* 1806. NY. Riley. 2nd ed. orig brds. H9. $550.00

DAVIS, Julia. *Shenandoah.* nd. np. reprint 1946 ed. VG/stiff wrp. B10. $12.00

DAVIS, Lindsey. *Silver Pigs.* 1989. Crown. 1st ed. author's 1st book. F/F. Q1. $30.00

DAVIS, Lydia. *Break It Down.* (1986). FSG. 1st ed. F/F. B3. $15.00

DAVIS, Mac. *100 Greatest Baseball Heroes.* 1974. Grosset Dunlap. VG. P8. $10.00

DAVIS, Maggie. *Rommel's Gold.* 1971. Lippincott. 1st ed. 8vo. F/VG. A8. $10.00

DAVIS, Moshe. *Emergence of Conservative Judaism: Hist School...* 1965. JPS. 2nd imp. ils. VG/VG. S3. $25.00

DAVIS, N.A. *Campaign From TX to MD.* 1863. Richmond. 1st ed. VG/wrps bdg to quarter calf. C6. $5,500.00

DAVIS, Richard Harding. *Bar Sinister.* 1903. Scribner. color pls. gilt pict bdg. VG. E5. $40.00

DAVIS, Richard Harding. *Cuba in War Time.* 1897. NY. Russell. 1st ed. ils Remington. 12mo. 143 p. teg. prt brds. H9. $75.00

DAVIS, Richard Harding. *Cuban & Porto Rican Campaigns.* 1899. London. Heinemann. 1st Eng ed. ils/pls/2 color maps. 335 p. G. B11. $120.00

DAVIS, Richard Harding. *Real Soldiers of Fortune.* 1911. Scribner. 228 p. F3. $15.00

DAVIS, Richard Harding. *Three Gringos in Venezuela & Central Am.* 1896. Harper. 1st ed. VG. E5. $35.00

DAVIS, Richard Harding. *W From a Car-Window.* 1892. NY. 1st ed. ils Remington. 253 p. gilt pict bl cloth. VG+. H3. $50.00

DAVIS, Robertson. *Feast of Stephen.* 1970. Toronto. 1st ed. sgn. F/VG+. A11. $65.00

DAVIS, Ron; see Kent, Hal.

DAVIS, Samuel B. *Escape of Confederate Officer From Prison.* 1892. Norfolk, VA. Landmark. 1st ed. ES. 72 p. NF/wrp. M8. $450.00

DAVIS, Solomon. *Prayer Book, in Language of 6 Nations of Indians...* 1837. NY. Swords Stanford. 1st ed. 12mo. 168 p. gilt cloth. M1. $600.00

DAVIS, William C. *Battle at Bull Run: Hist of 1st Major Campaign of Civil War.* 1977. Doubleday. BC. 298 p. cloth. NF/NF. M8. $25.00

DAVIS, William C. *Orphan Brigade: KY Confederates Who Couldn't Go Home.* 1980. Doubleday. 1st ed. 318 p. cloth. F/F. M8. $30.00

DAVIS & DAVIS. *Doctor to the Islands.* 1953. Boston. 1st ed. 8vo. 331 p. gilt bl cloth. F/VG. H3. $20.00

DAVIS & GIAMMATTEI. *Needlepoint From Am's Great Quilt Designs.* 1974. np. ils. wrp. G2. $20.00

DAVIS & GIAMMETTEI. *More Needlepoint From Am's Great Quilt Designs.* 1977. np. ils/photos. cloth. G2. $25.00

DAVIS & KEELY. *Arctic Seas: Voyage of the Kite.* 1892. Phil. ils/2 maps. 524 p. silvered bl cloth. VG. P4. $125.00

DAVIS. *Civil War: Strange & Fascinating Facts.* 1982. np. ils. 249 p. O7. $9.50

DAVY, John. *Notes & Observations on the Ionian Islands & Malta.* 1842. London. 2 vols. orig cloth/rebacked orig spines. O2. $550.00

DAWIDOWICZ, Lucy S. *On Equal Terms: Jews in Am 1881-1981.* 1982. HRW. 194 p. VG+/VG+. S3. $22.00

DAWKINS, Cecil. *Quiet Enemy.* 1963. NY. 1st Am ed/from UK sheets. inscr. F/F. A11. $65.00

DAWKINS, R.M. *Modern Greek Folktales.* 1974. Westport. 8vo. 491 p. cloth. O2. $70.00

DAWLEY, Powel Mills. *John Whitgift & the Eng Reformation.* 1954. Scribner. index/biblio. 251 p. H10. $15.00

DAWSON, Adele Godchaux. *James Franklin Gilman: 19th-Century Painter.* 1975. Canaan, NH. Phoenix. 159 p. cloth. dj. D2. $55.00

DAWSON, Alan. *55 Days: Fall of S Vietnam.* (1977). Prentice Hall. 366 p. dj. A7. $20.00

DAWSON, C.B. *Mirror of Oxford.* 1912. London. Sands. xl. ils/fld map. 265 p. H10. $15.00

DAWSON, Christopher. *Dividing of Christendom...* ca 1965. NY. Sheed Ward. xl. 446 p. H10. $20.00

DAWSON, Elmer A. *Buck's Winning Hit.* 1930. Grosset Dunlap. 216 p. cloth. VG+/dj. very scarce. M20. $100.00

DAWSON, Fielding. *Blk Mtn Book.* 1970. NY. 1st ed. sgn. VG+/wrp. A11. $45.00

DAWSON, Francis Warrington. *Reminiscences of Confederate Service, 1861-65.* 1980. LA State. reprint of 1882 ed. 1/100. NF. M8. $35.00

DAWSON, James. *Hell Gate.* 1971. McKay. VG/dj. P3. $10.00

DAWSON, John Charles. *Lakanal the Regicide.* 1948. AL U. 1st ed. 213 p. dj. N2. $17.50

DAWSON, Miles Menander. *Ethical Religion of Zoraster.* 1931. Macmillan. 1st ed. G+. N2. $20.00

DAWSON, Peter. *Stirrup Boss.* 1949. Dodd Mead. 1st ed. VG+/dj. B9. $35.00

DAWSON, Thomas. *S Am Republics.* 1904. Putnam. 2 vols. F3. $25.00

DAWSON, William Leon. *Birds of CA.* 1923. LA. S Moulton Co. 4 vols. thick quarto. gilt gr morocco. F. R3. $2,000.00

DAWSON & SKIFF. *Ute War: Hist of Wht River Massacre & Privations...* 1879. Denver. Tribune Pub. 1st ed. sm octavo. orig prt wrp/clamshell slipcase. R3. $2,000.00

DAWSON. *Technique of Metal Thread Embroidery.* 1985. np. ils. wrp. G2. $20.00

DAY, A. Grove. *Jack London in the S Seas.* (1971). 4 Winds. 167 p. clip dj. A7. $18.00

DAY, Beth. *Little Professor of Piney Woods.* 1955. NY. Messner. VG/dj. N2. $7.50

DAY, Bradford. *Edgar Rice Burroughs Bibliography.* 1956. SF & Fantasy Pub. 1st ed. VG/wrp. M2. $25.00

DAY, Clarence. *Life w/Father.* 1947. Sun Dial. VG/dj. P3. $20.00

DAY, Clarence. *Life w/Mother.* 1937. NY. 1st ed. G/dj. E3. $10.00

DAY, David. *Tolkien Bestiary.* 1979. Ballantine. 1st ed. VG/dj. P3. $15.00

DAY, Donald. *Index to the SF Magazines, 1926-50.* 1952. Perri Pr. 1st ed. F/dj. M2. $125.00

DAY, Gina. *Tell No Tales.* 1967. Rupert Hart Davis. 1st ed. F/dj. P3. $15.00

DAY, Jane. *Aztec: World of Montezuma.* (1992). Rinehart. 1st ed. 88 p. wrp. F3. $20.00

DAY, Jeremiah. *Intro to Algebra.* 1839. New Haven. Durrie Peck. 2 fld pls. 332 p. full leather. G. S9. $25.00

DAY, John I. *Am Champions & 2-Yr Olds of 1950.* 1950. Thoroughbred Racing Assn. G. O3. $25.00

DAY & HENDERSON. *Fall of the Aztec Empire.* 1993. Rinehart. 1st ed. ils. 128 p. wrp. F3. $15.00

DE ACOSTA, Jose. *Historia Natural y Moral de las Indias.* 1894. Madrid. Angles. 2 vols. 12mo. full leather. NF. O6. $275.00

DE AL TORRE, Lillian. *Dr Sam: Johnson, Detector.* 1946. Knopf. 1st ed. F/F. M15. $45.00

DE ALCEDO, Antonio. *Geographical & Hist Dictionary of Am & W Indies. 1812-1815.* Longman Hurst Rees Orme. 5 vols. full polished calf. VG. H9. $2,400.00

DE AMICIS, Edmondo. *Heart of a Boy.* (1899). Laird Lee. ils. 290 p. decor red cloth. VG. S10. $30.00

DE ANDRADE, Mario. *Macunaima.* 1984. Random. 1st ed. trans EA Goodland. rem mk. NF/NF. A13. $25.00

DE ANDREA, William. *Five O'Clock Lightning.* 1982. St Martin. 1st ed. sgn. F/F. S5. $35.00

DE ANGELI, Marguerite. *Blk Fox of Lorne.* 1956. Doubleday. 1st ed. 191 p. VG/G. P2. $35.00

DE ANGELI, Marguerite. *Book of Nursery & Mother Goose Rhymes.* 1954. Doubleday. 1st ed. 192 p. VG/dj. D1. $65.00

DE ANGELI, Marguerite. *Bright April.* 1946. Doubleday. stated 1st ed. F/worn dj. M5. $45.00

DE ANGELI, Marguerite. *Bright April.* 1946. Doubleday. 1st ed. 86 p. VG/dj. A3. $40.00

DE ANGELI, Marguerite. *Copper-Toed Boots.* 1938. Doubleday Doran. 1st ed. 4to. VG/tattered top & bottom dj. A3. $50.00

DE ANGELI, Marguerite. *Door in the Wall.* 1949. Doubleday/Jr Books. 1st ed. 111 p. cloth. VG/G. A3. $65.00

DE ANGELI, Marguerite. *Jared's Island.* 1947. Doubleday. inscr/dtd 1952. 95 p. tan cloth. VG+/dj. M20. $65.00

DE ANGELI, Marguerite. *Jose & Joe.* 1938. Caxton/Jr Literary Guild. 1st thus ed. 8vo. 262 p. VG/G. A3. $15.00

DE ANGELI, Marguerite. *Marguerite DeAngeli's Book of Nursery & Mother Goose Rhymes.* 1954. Doubleday. 4to. pict tan cloth. F/dj. F1. $75.00

DE ANGELI, Marguerite. *Ted & Nina Go to the Grocery Store.* 1935. Doubleday. early reprint. author's 1st book. 12mo. VG. A3. $25.00

DE ANGELI, Marguerite. *Thee, Hannah!* 1940. Doubleday. 8vo. G+. V3. $12.00

DE ANGELI, Marguerite. *Turkey for Christmas.* 1949. Westminster. 1st ed. VG+/dj. M20. $50.00

DE ARMELLANDA, Cesareo. *Pemton Taremuru.* 1972. Caracas. 1st ed. 333 p. wrp. F3. $20.00

DE BAIF, Lazare. *Annotationes in L II De Captivis, et Postliminio Reversis...* 1549. Paris. Robert Estienne. 1st ed. 4to. ils/woodcuts. contemporary vellum. NF. K1. $1,750.00

DE BALZAC, Honore. *Droll Stories of Honore de Balzac.* 1932. Bl Ribbon. ils Steele Savage. G. E3. $8.00

DE BALZAC, Honore. *Droll Stories.* (Jan, 1874). Bibliophilist Soc. later prt. ils Gustav Dore. 651 p. gilt blk cloth. VG. H3. $20.00

DE BARY, A. *Comparative Anatomy of Vegetative Organs of Phanerogams...* 1884. Oxford. 241 woodcuts. 659 p. teg. blk buckram. B26. $45.00

DE BEAUCLAIR, Gotthard. *Laudate Dominum.* (1963). Frankfurt. Trajanus. ltd ed. 1/900. sgn. unbound/uncut. F/gr wrp. B24. $175.00

DE BEAUDEAN, Raoul. *Capt of the Isle.* (1960). McGraw Hill. 1st Am ed. 8vo. 230 p. F/VG+. A2. $20.00

DE BEAUVOIR, Simone. *Les Belles Images.* 1968. Collins. 2nd ed. NF/dj. P3. $15.00

DE BEERSKI, P. Jeannerat. *Angkor: Ruins in Cambodia.* 1924. Houghton Mifflin. 1st ed. 8vo. ils/pls. 304 p. VG. W1. $35.00

DE BESENVAL, Victor Pierre. *Spleen & Other Stories.* 1928. Chapman Hall. 1/1000. VG/VG. V2. $15.00

DE BIBIENA, Jean Galli. *Fairy Doll.* 1925. Chapman Hall. 1/1000. VG. V2. $13.00

DE BODE. *Travels in Luristan & Arabistan.* 1845. London. 2 vols. 8vo. new cloth/orig labels. O2. $350.00

DE BOOY & FARIS. *Virgin Islands. Our New Possessions & the British Islands.* 1918. Lippincott. 1st ed. 8vo. pls. 292 p. teg. gr brds. G. B11. $45.00

DE BORCHGRAVE & MOSS. *Spike.* 1980. Crown. 1st ed. sgns. F/F. F4. $28.00

DE BOSSCHERE, Jean. *City Curious.* 1920. London. 72 pls. 179 p. pict gray cloth. VG+/G. P2. $110.00

DE BOSSCHERE, Jean. *Folk Tales of Flanders.* 1918. Dodd Mead. 1st Am ed. 4to. 179 p. gr cloth. VG. D1. $275.00

DE BRUNHOFF, Jean. *ABC de Babar.* (1939). Paris. Hachette. 12mo. yel pict brds. VG/tattered glassine cover. D1. $175.00

DE BRUNHOFF, Jean. *Babar & Father Christmas.* (1940). Random. 1st Am ed. folio. VG/VG. D1. $375.00

DE BRUNHOFF, Jean. *Histoire de Babar.* 1931. Conde Nast. 1st ed. author's 1st book. G. P2. $395.00

DE BRUNHOFF, Jean. *Le Roi Babar.* 1933. Paris. Jardin des Modes. 1st ed. jumbo folio. 3rd Babar book. cloth. NF. F1. $450.00

DE BRY, Theodore. *Am, Das 1st Erfindung und Offenbahrung der Newen Welt...* 1617. Frankfurt am Main. 1st German trans. folio. pls/2 maps. later orange brds. H9. $7,500.00

DE BURY, Richard. *Philobiblon of Richard de Bury.* 1888. London. Kegan Paul. sm octavo. 259 p. Stikeman bdg. VG. H5. $100.00

DE CAMP, L. Sprague. *Castle of Iron.* 1950. Gnome. 1st ed. NF/dj. M2. $45.00

DE CAMP, L. Sprague. *Divide & Rule.* 1948. Fantasy. 1st ed. VG. M2. $20.00

DE CAMP, L. Sprague. *Footprints on Sand.* 1981. Advent. 1st ed. F/dj. P3. $20.00

DE CAMP, L. Sprague. *Hand of Zei.* 1963. Avalon. 1st ed. F/dj. P3. $45.00

DE CAMP, L. Sprague. *Literary Swordsmen & Sorcerers.* 1976. Arkham. 1st ed. M. M2. $10.00

DE CAMP, L. Sprague. *Lost Continents.* 1954. Gnome. 1st ed. VG/dj. P3. $40.00

DE CAMP, L. Sprague. *Return of Conan.* 1957. Gnome. 1st ed. G/dj. M18. $75.00

DE CAMP, L. Sprague. *Return of Conan.* 1957. Gnome. 1st ed. VG/dj. P3. $90.00

DE CAMP, L. Sprague. *Tritonian Ring.* 1977. Owlswick Pr. 1st ed. sgn. F/F. P3. $30.00

DE CAMP, L. Sprague. *Unbeheaded King.* 1983. Del Rey. 1st ed. F/dj. P3. $15.00

DE CAMP, L. Sprague. *Undesired Princess.* 1951. FPCI. 1st ed. VG/VG-. P3. $75.00

DE CAMP, L. Sprague. *Wheels of If.* 1948. Shasta. 1st ed. VG/VG-. P3. $150.00

DE CAMP & MILLER. *Genus Homo.* 1950. Fantasy. 1st ed. 1/500. sgn/#d. inscr/sgns to P Linebarger. F/dj. M2. $500.00

DE CAMP & PRATT. *Carnelian Cube.* 1948. Gnome. 1st ed. NF/dj. M2. $65.00

DE CARBIA, Maria. *Mexico Through My Kitchen Window.* 1961. Houghton Mifflin. 1st ed. 8vo. 236 p. VG/G. B11. $20.00

DE CERVANTES, Miguel. *Don Quixote de la Mancha.* 1819. London. octavo. ils J Clark/24 hc pls. 4 vols. gilt tan morocco. VG. H5. $1,250.00

DE CERVANTES, Miguel. *Don Quixote de la Mancha.* 1928 (1925). Dodd Mead. ils WH Robinson. 614 p. VG+. P2. $35.00

DE CERVANTES, Miguel. *Life & Exploits of the Ingenious Gentleman Don Quixote...* 1742. London. 1st ed. trans Jarvis. 2 vols. contemporary mottled calf. H5. $1,500.00

DE CERVANTES SAAVEDRA, Miguel; *see De Cervantes, Miguel.*

DE CHAIR, Somerset. *First Crusade: Deeds of the Franks & Other Jerusalemites.* 1945. Golden Cockerel. 1/500. thin quarto. ils Clifford Webb. F. R3. $375.00

DE CHAIR, Somerset. *Golden Carpet.* 1944. London. Faber. 1st ed. 224 p. gilt yel linen. VG. M7. $35.00

DE CHAULIAC, Guy. *Guydos Questions, Newly Corrected...* 1579. London. Thomas East. lacks 1st 19 leaves, leaves 24-34 & 182-200. G7. $995.00

DE CHERVILLE, Gaspard G.P. *Les Cheins et Les Chats d'Eugene Lambert.* 1888. Paris. Librairie l'Art. 6 orig etchings & 145 ils. 292 p. teg. orig wrp bnd in. K1. $450.00

DE CIVRIEUX, Marc. *Watunna: Ornioco Creation Cycle...* 1980. N Point. 1st ed. 195 p. dj. F3. $20.00

DE DISCATILLO, Miguel. *Aula de Dios.* 1679. Pasquel Bueon. 247 p. contemporary vellum. F/lacks ties. B14. $250.00

DE FELITTA, Frank. *Audrey Rose.* 1975. Putnam. 3rd ed. VG-/dj. P3. $12.50

DE FELITTA, Frank. *Golgotha Falls.* nd. BC. VG/dj. P3. $7.50

DE FIGUEROA, Leslie. *Stuffed Shirt in Taxco.* (1961). Mexico. 1st ed. 164 p. F3. $10.00

DE FREES, Madeline. *Magpie on the Gallows.* 1982. Copper Canyon. 1st ed. sgn. NF/wrp. V1. $20.00

DE FREES, Madeline. *Possible Sibyls.* 1991. Lynx House. 1st ed. F/wrp. V1. $8.50

DE FUENTES, Patricia. *Conquistadors.* 1963. NY. Orion. 1st ed. 250 p. dj. F3. $25.00

DE GAMEZ & PASTORE. *Mexico & Cuba on Your Own.* 1954. Cortina/Garden City. 12mo. ils/pls/fld map. 390 p. VG/G. B11. $20.00

DE GIUSTINO, David. *Conquest of Mind: Phrenology & Victorian Social Thought.* 1975. London. Croom Helm. 248 p. F/dj. G1. $28.50

DE GORTER, Johannes. *Medicina Hipporcratica Exponens Aphorismos Hippocratis...* 1739. Amsterdam. 4to. 481 p. contemporary vellum. G7. $150.00

DE GORTER, Johannes. *Praxis Medicae Systema. Tomus Primus de Morbis Generalibus.* 1750. Hardervici. Wigmans. sgn. thick 8vo. 2 vols (4 vols in 2). G7. $395.00

DE GOUY, Louis P. *Derrydale Fish Cookbook.* (1987). Willow Creek. ltd ed reprint of 1937 Derrydale ed. 330 p. A17. $15.00

DE GRAY, Thomas. *Compleat Horse-Man & Expert Ferrier.* 1650. London. Moseley. 2 vols in 1. complete. sheepskin. B14. $1,050.00

DE GREGORIO, George. *Joe Di Maggio.* 1983. Scarborough. 1st ed. photos. F/VG+. P8. $45.00

DE HARTOG, Jan. *Artist.* 1963. Atheneum. 1st ed. 8vo. 167 p. VG/VG. V3. $14.00

DE HARTOG, Jan. *Peaceable Kingdom.* 1972. Atheneum. 8vo. 677 p. G/G. V3. $16.00

DE HASS, Wills. *Hist of Early Settlement & Indian Wars of WV...* 1851. Wheeling. Hoblitzell. octavo. gilt brn cloth. R3. $500.00

DE JONG, Dola. *Whirligig of Time.* 1964. Crime Club. 1st ed. xl. dj. P3. $5.00

DE JONG, Meindert. *Far Out the Long Canal.* 1964. Harper Row. ils Nancy Grossman. 1st ed. 4to. 231 p. VG/G+. A3. $15.00

DE JONG, Meindert. *Wheels Over the Bridge.* 1941. Harper. 1st ed. 219 p. VG/G. P2. $25.00

DE JOURVENEL, Bertrand. *Sovereignty: Inquiry Into Political Good.* (1957). Chicago U. 319 p. dj. A7. $15.00

DE KIEFFER, Eugene. *Practical Instructions in Horsemanship...* 1868. Phil. self pub. 1st ed. 12mo. 99 p. cloth. M1. $200.00

DE KOVEN, Ralph. *Prayer Book w/Explanator Notes...* 1965. KTAV. w/prayer dictionary. VG-. S3. $10.00

DE LA FALAISE, Maxime. *Food in Vogue.* 1980. Doubleday. VG/dj. A16. $20.00

DE LA FONTAINE, Jean. *Tales & Novels in Verse.* (ca 1885). (Evreux). private prt. 1/25. ils after Eisen/170 pls. NF. F1. $300.00

DE LA MARE, Walter. *Broomsticks & Other Fairy Tales.* 1925. London. Constable. 1st ed. 378 p. VG+/G+. S10. $60.00

DE LA MARE, Walter. *Crossings: A Fairy Play.* 1952. London. Faber. 1st thus ed. 92 p. VG+/VG. S10. $45.00

DE LA MARE, Walter. *Eight Tales.* 1971. Arkham. 1st ed. as new. M2. $35.00

DE LA MARE, Walter. *Listeners & Other Poems.* 1924. London. Constable. 10th imp. 92 p. aeg. bl-gr brds. M7. $25.00

DE LA MARE, Walter. *Stuff & Nonsense.* 1927. London. Constable. 1st ed. ils Bold. 110 p. VG/G. S10. $60.00

DE LA MARE, Walter. *Veil & Other Poems.* 1921. London. Constable. tall 8vo. gray brds/linen spine/leather label. uncut. M7. $95.00

DE LA MARE, Walter. *Winged Chariot.* 1958. London. Faber. 1st ed. VG/dj. M18. $30.00

DE LA PEYROUSE, J.F. *Voyage Round the World Performed in Yrs 1785-88.* 1801. Boston. Bumstead. 333 p. contemporary tree sheepskin. F. B14. $175.00

DE LA ROCHE, Mazo. *Renny's Daughter.* 1951. Little Brn. 1st ed. VG/VG-. P3. $17.50

DE LA ROCHE, Mazo. *Return to Jalna.* 1946. Toronto. Macmillan. 1st ed. 540 p. VG/dj. M20. $35.00

DE LA ROCHEFOUCAULT. *Maxims & Moral Reflections.* 1775. Edinburgh. 24mo. 144 p. full leather. VG. H3. $50.00

DE LANDAETA, Fray Martin. *Noticias del Puerto de San Francisco.* 1949. Mexico. 1/500. sm 4to. 78 p. wrp. F3. $35.00

DE LANGH-CRUYS, Jean. *De Malorum Horum Temporum Causis et Remedis...* 1584. Duaci. Joannis Bogardi. later ep/contemporary vellum. K1. $300.00

DE LAVELEYE, Emile. *Socialisy of To-Day: Together w/Account of Socialism in Eng.* ca 1935. London. Leadenhall. trans Goddard H Orpen. xl. G. V4. $30.00

DE LEEUW, Hendrik. *Crossroads of the Mediterranean.* (1954). Hanover House. 1st ed. 244 p. dj. A7. $15.00

DE LILLO, Don. *Americana.* 1973. NY. pb ed. author's 1st novel. sgn. F/unread wrp. A11. $45.00

DE LILLO, Don. *End Zone.* 1972. Houghton Mifflin. 1st ed. author's 2nd book. F/NF. Q1. $125.00

DE LILLO, Don. *End Zone.* 1973. London. 1st ed/simultaneous wrp issue. sgn. NF. A11. $60.00

DE LILLO, Don. *Great Jones Street.* 1973. Houghton Mifflin. 1st ed. inscr. F/NF. L3. $150.00

DE LILLO, Don. *Great Jones Street.* 1973. Houghton Mifflin. 1st ed. NF/NF. B4. $85.00

DE LILLO, Don. *Libra.* 1988. Viking. 1st ed. sgn. F/NF. L3. $85.00

DE LILLO, Don. *Mao II.* 1991. Viking. AP. sgn. F/stiff pict wrp. C4. $50.00

DE LILLO, Don. *Mao II.* 1991. Viking. 1st ed. sgn. F/F. L3. $65.00

DE LINT, Charles. *Jack, the Giant Killer.* 1987. Ace. 1st ed. VG/dj. P3. $16.95

DE LINT, Charles. *Little Country.* 1991. BC. as new/dj. C1. $6.00

DE LINT, J.G. *Atlas of Hist of Medicine. 1. Anatomy.* 1926. London. Lewis. folio. 199 figures. 96 p. G7. $95.00

DE LONG, Lea Rosson. *Nature's Forms/Nature's Forces: Art of Alexandre Hogue.* 1984. Philbrook/OK U. ils/index. 211 p. F/wrp. B19. $17.50

DE MAUPASSANT, Guy. *Bel-Ami.* 1968. Ltd Ed Club. 1/1500. ils/sgn Benard Lamotte. F/slipcase. Q1. $60.00

DE MEDINA, Pedro. *Navigator's Universe: Libro de Cosmographia of 1538.* 1972. Chicago. lg format. M/dj. O6. $40.00

DE MIERRE, H.C. *Long Voyage.* (1963). NY. Walker. 1st Am ed. 8vo. 306 p. F/VG+. A2. $20.00

DE MILLE, James. *Strange Manuscript Found in a Copper Cylinder.* 1988. NY. Harper. 1st ed. ils Gilbert Gaul. VG. Q1. $100.00

DE MONCADA, Juan. *Expedicion de los Catalanes y Aragoneses...* 1842. Barcelona. 12mo. 251 p. leather-backed brds. O2. $100.00

DE MONTESQUIEU. *Spirit of Laws.* 1802. Worcester, MA. 1st Am ed (from 5th London). 2 vols. full calf. E5. $265.00

DE MONVEL, M. Boutet. *Jeanne D'Arc.* (1897). Paris. Plon-Nourrit. 1st ed. NF/poor. P2. $150.00

DE MUSSET, Alfred. *Fantasio: A Comedy in 2 Acts.* nd. Holland. 1/550. ils Fernand Gianque. VG. M5. $25.00

DE MUSSET, Paul. *Mr Wind & Madam Rain.* 1864. Harper. 1st ed. ils Charles Bennett. 126 p. fair. S10. $40.00

DE NITO. *Needlepoint on Plastic Canvas.* 1978. np. ils. cloth. G2. $13.00

DE NOGALES. *Memoirs of a Soldier of Fortune.* 1932. NY. 1st ed. 8vo. 380 p. cloth. O2. $45.00

DE PEW, Chauncey M. *My Memories of 80 Yrs.* 1922. Scribner. 8vo. 417 p. maroon cloth. H9. $35.00

DE PLATINA, Bartholomaeus S. *Della Vite de Pontefici dal Salvator Nostro Sino a Paolo II.* 1643. Venice. Barezzi. 2 parts in 1. contemporary vellum. K1. $350.00

DE POL, John. *Benjamin's Bicentennial Blast.* nd. AR Tommasini. ils. 29 p. NF/wrp. B19. $35.00

DE PONCINS, Gontran. *Eskimos.* ca 1949. NY. Hastings. 4to. ils. 104 p. tan cloth. VG/VG. P4. $45.00

DE PROROK, Byron. *In Quest of Lost Worlds.* 1936. NY. 8vo. pls. 281 p. gilt red cloth. VG. H3. $25.00

DE PUY, Henry W. *Mtn Hero & His Associates.* 1855. Boston. 12mo. ils. 428 p. gilt blk cloth. T3. $14.00

DE QUESADA & NORTHROP. *War in Cuba.* 1896. Phil. Shepp. salesman's sample. 32 pls/map. G. B11. $50.00

DE QUILLE, Dan. *Fighting Horse of the Stanislaus.* 1990. IA U. ils. 257 p. F/wrp. B19. $10.00

DE ROSA & RICHARDS. *Christ in Our World.* 1966. Milwaukee. Bruce. 208 p. VG. C5. $12.50

DE ROUEN FORTH, Nevill. *Fighting Colonel of the Camel Corps.* 1991. Merlin Books. 1st Uk ed. 201 p. M/pict dj. M7. $30.00

DE SAINT-AMAND, Imbert. *Famous Women of the French Court.* 1900. Scribner. 14 vols. VG. E3. $60.00

DE SAINT-EXUPERY, Antoine. *Airman's Odyssey.* 1942. Reynal Hitchcock. 1st ed. trans Lewis Galantiere/Stuart Gilbert. NF/NF. A14. $75.00

DE SAINT-EXUPERY, Antoine. *Airman's Odyssey.* 1967. Harcourt Brace. 10th ed. NF/NF. A14. $25.00

DE SAINT-EXUPERY, Antoine. *Little Prince.* nd. HBW. ils. VG/VG. L1. $15.00

DE SAINT-EXUPERY, Antoine. *Wartime Writings 1939-44.* 1986. HBJ. 1st ed. trans from French. intro AM Lindburgh. NF/NF clip. A14. $25.00

DE SANTIS, Marie. *Neptune's Apprentice: Adventures of Commercial Fisherwoman.* (1984). Novato, CA. Presidio. 1st ed. 8vo. 219 p. F/F clip. A2. $12.50

DE SERVIEZ, Jaques Boergas. *Roman Empresses.* 1932. NY. Dingwall-Rock. 2 vols. N2. $17.50

DE SEVERSKY, Alexander. *Victory Through Air Power.* 1942. Simon Schuster. 1st ed. 8vo. G/G. A8. $10.00

DE SILVA, Colvin R. *Ceylon Under the British Occupation, 1795-1833.* 1953 & 1962. Colombo, Ceylon. 2 vols. G. B18. $35.00

DE SMET, Pierre-Jean. *OR Missions & Travels Over the Rocky Mtns, 1845-46.* 1847. NY. Dunigan. sm 12mo. 12 pls/fld map. gr cloth. H9. $275.00

DE SORMO, Maitland. *John Bird Burnham: Klondiker, Adirondacker...* 1978. NY. 1st ed. 272 p. gr cloth. F/F. B22. $10.00

DE STOLZ, Madame. *House on Wheels; or, The Stolen Child.* 1871 (1870). Lee Shepard. ils Emile Bayard. 304 p. G. S10. $15.00

DE TERRA, Helmut. *Man & Mammoth in Mexico.* 1957. Hutchinson. 1st ed. 191 p. dj. F3. $20.00

DE TOLEDANO, Ralph. *One Man Alone: Richard Nixon.* 1969. Funk Wagnall. 8vo. 386 p. VG/dj. V3. $10.00

DE VALLES, Francesco. *Hippocratis Libros de Morbis Popularibus Commentaria...* 1621. Neapoli. Ex Typographia Lazari Scorigii. folio. NF. G7. $250.00

DE VEGA, Garcilaso. *FL of the Inca: Hist of the Adelantado, Hernando de soto...* 1951. Austin. 1st ed. M/dj. O6. $50.00

DE VIGO, Giovanni. *Most Excellent Works of Chirurgerye.* 1968. NY. facsimile of 1543. sm folio. G7. $95.00

DE VORE, Irven. *Primate Behavior: Field Studies of Monkeys & Apes.* (1965). NY. photos/maps/index. 654 p. F/dj. A17. $17.50

DE VOTO, Bernard. *Across the Wide MO.* 1947. Boston. 425 p. map ep. cloth. VG/dj. D3. $12.50

DE VOTO, Bernard. *Forays & Rebuttals.* 1936. Boston. 1st thus ed. 403 p. cloth. VG+. B22. $15.00

DE VOTO, Bernard. *Journals of Lewis & Clark.* 1953. Houghton Mifflin. 1st ed. 8vo. 504 p. F. T8. $25.00

DE VRIES, Hugo. *Naar Californie.* 1905. Haarlem. 1st ed. ex-Dutch lib. 438 p. cloth. VG. D3. $45.00

DE VRIES, Peter. *Into Your Tent I'll Creep.* 1971. Little Brn. 1st ed. F/F. C4. $30.00

DE VRIES, Peter. *Tunnel of Love.* nd. Little Brn. 9th ed. VG/dj. P3. $7.00

DE VRIES, Peter. *Without a Stitch in Time.* 1972. Little Brn. 1st ed. F/F. C4. $30.00

DE WALD, Ernest. *Ils in the Manuscripts of the Septuagint. Vol III.* 1941-41. Princeton. 2 vols. photos. gilt blk cloth. dj. K1. $175.00

DE WAT, Christiaan Rudolf. *Three Yrs' War.* 1902. NY. 1st ed. 8vo. 448 p. gilt bdg. VG+. H3. $90.00

DE WILDE, P.A. *In Memoriam Dr Albert Willem Van Reterghem.* 1939. reprint Nederlandische Tijdschridt voor Geneeskunde. G1. $17.50

DE WOLFE, Gordon. *Flora Exotica. Collection of Flowering Plants.* 1972. Boston. 1/300. quarto. ils/sgn Godine. w/suite extra pls. F/slipcase. B24. $300.00

DE ZORITA, Alonso. *Life & Labor in Ancient Mexico.* (1971). NJ. Rutgers. 2nd prt. 328 p. dj. F3. $15.00

DEAK, Estvan. *Lawful Revolution: Louis Kossuth & Hungarians 1848-49.* 1979. Columbia U. 1st ed. 8vo. 415 p. F/F. A2. $20.00

DEAK, Gloria Gilda. *Am Views, Prospects & Vistas.* ca 1976. NY. Viking. oblong 4to. 134 p. brds. dj. H9. $95.00

DEAL, Borden. *Walk Through the Valley.* 1956. Scribner. ARC. author's 1st novel. RS. VG/VG. L3. $65.00

DEAN, Amber. *Bullet Proof.* 1960. Crime Club. 1st ed. xl. dj. P3. $5.00

DEAN, Amber. *Call Me Pandora.* 1946. Crime Club. VG. P3. $15.00

DEAN, Amber. *Snipe Hunt.* 1949. Unicorn Mystery BC. VG. P3. $15.00

DEAN, Amber. *Wrap It Up.* 1946. Collins Crime Club. 1st ed. VG/VG-. P3. $20.00

DEAN, Robert George. *Affair at Lover's Leap.* 1953. Crime Club. 1st ed. VG-/dj. P3. $17.50

DEAN, Spencer. *Marked Down for Murder.* 1956. Crime Club. 1st ed. VG/dj. P3. $27.50

DEAN, Spencer. *Murder After a Fashion.* 1960. Doubleday. 1st ed. VG/dj. P3. $25.00

DEAN. *Church Needlework.* 1991. np. cloth. G2. $35.00

DEANDREA, William L. *Five O'Clock Lightning.* 1982. St Martin. 1st ed. VG/dj. P3. $15.00

DEANDREA, William L. *Killed in Paradise.* 1988. Detective BC. VG. P3. $7.50

DEANDREA, William L. *Lunatic Fringe.* 1980. Evans. 1st ed. VG/dj. P3. $15.00

DEANE, Samuel. *New-Eng Farmer; or, Georgical Dictionary.* 1790. Worcester, MA. Isaiah Thomas. 1st ed. orig calf/red calf spine label. K1. $275.00

DEBENHAM, Frank. *Discovery & Exploration: Atlas-Hist of Man's Wanderings.* 1960. Doubleday. VG/dj. O6. $25.00

DEBS, Eugene Victor. *Walls & Bars.* ca 1927. Chicago. Higgins. ils. F. V4. $40.00

DECKER, J.S. *Aspectos Biologicos da Flora Brasileira.* ca 1940s. Sao Leopoldo. 8 color pls. 640 p. tan cloth. VG. B26. $72.50

DEDIJER, Vladimir. *Beloved Land.* 1961. Simon Schuster. 1st ed. 8vo. 382 p. F/VG+. A2. $12.50

DEE. *Quilter's Sourcebook.* 1987. np. wrp. G2. $15.00

DEEPING, Warwick. *I Live Again.* 1942. Knopf. 1st ed. F/F clip. F4. $25.00

DEEPING, Warwick. *Old Pybus.* 1930. Cassell. 8th prt. VG. P3. $10.00

DEER, J.M.; see Smith, George H.

DEERFIELD & PORTER. *Snap Me Perfect.* 1984. Nelson. 1st ed. F/VG+. P8. $12.50

DEERING, John Richard. *Lee & His Cause; or, Why & How of War Between the States.* 1907. NY/WA. Neale. 1st ed. 2 pls. 183 p. cloth. VG. M8. $175.00

DEETZ, Charles H. *US Dept of Commerce, Coast & Geodetic Survey...* 1936. GPO. Special Pub 205. 8vo. fld maps. 83 p. wrp. H9. $25.00

DEFOE, Daniel. *Journal of the Plague Yr.* 1968. Bloomfield. 1/1500. ils/sgn Domenico Gnoli. tan buckram. F/slipcase. Q1. $75.00

DEFOE, Daniel. *Life & Strange Surprizing Adventures of Robinson Crusoe...* 1790. London. Stockdale. 1st Stothard ed. 2 vols. gilt red cloth. VG. H5. $850.00

DEFOE, Daniel. *Robinson Crusoe of York Mariner As Related by Himself.* ca 1908. DeWolfe Fiske. 6 full-p color ils. G. L1. $65.00

DEFOE, Daniel. *Robinson Crusoe.* 1916. Rand McNally. 1st thus ed. ils Milo Winter. G. P2. $15.00

DEFORD, Frank. *Everybody's All-Am.* (1981). NY. Viking. 1st ed. NF/NF. B4. $45.00

DEFORGES, Regine. *Bl Bicycle.* 1985. London. Allen. 1st ed. trans Ros Schwartz. NF/NF. A14. $25.00

DEFORGES, Regine. *Bl Bicycle.* 1985. Secaucus, NJ. Lyle Stuart. 1st Am ed. trans Ros Schwartz. NF/NF. A14. $20.00

DEFORGES, Regine. *Confessions of O: Conversations w/Pauline Reage.* 1979. Seaver/Viking. 1st ed. trans Sabine d'Estree. NF/NF clip. A14. $40.00

DEIGHTON, Len. *Action Cookbook.* 1965. London. Cape. 1st ed. VG/sans. M15. $100.00

DEIGHTON, Len. *Berlin Game.* 1983. Hutchinson. 1st ed. F/dj. P3. $17.50

DEIGHTON, Len. *Declarations of War.* 1971. London. Cape. 1st ed. F/clip. M15. $45.00

DEIGHTON, Len. *Funeral in Berlin.* 1964. Putnam. 1st ed. VG/dj. M18. $65.00

DEIGHTON, Len. *Goodbye Mickey Mouse.* (1982). Knopf. 1st ed. F/NF. B3. $40.00

DEIGHTON, Len. *Ipcress File.* 1962. London. Hodder Stoughton. 1st ed. NF/NF. M15. $450.00

DEIGHTON, Len. *Ipcress File.* 1963. Simon Schuster. 1st Am ed. F/NF. M15. $185.00

DEIGHTON, Len. *London Match.* (1985). London. Hutchinson. 1st ed. F/NF. B3. $30.00

DEIGHTON, Len. *London Match.* 1985. Knopf. 1st ed. F/dj. P3. $17.95

DEIGHTON, Len. *Spy Line.* 1989. Hutchinson. 1st ed. F/dj. P3. $22.50

DEIGHTON, Len. *Spy Sinker.* 1990. Harper Collins. 1st ed. VG/dj. P3. $21.95

DEIGHTON, Len. *Spy Story.* 1974. HBJ. 3rd ed. VG/dj. P3. $15.00

DEIGHTON, Len. *XPD.* (1981). London. Hutchinson. 1st ed. NF/NF. B3. $40.00

DEIGHTON & SCHWARTZMAN. *Airshipwreck.* (1979). NY. 1st Am ed. 72 p. B18. $35.00

DEIGNAN, H.G. *Burma: Gateway to China.* 1943. Smithsonian. 16 photo pls. 21 p text. VG/wrp. P4. $20.00

DEJERINE-KLUMPKE, Madame. *Eloge de Madame Dejerine-Klumpke.* 1927. Paris. 22 p. orig prt wrp. G7. $75.00

DEKOBRA, Maurice. *Love Clinic.* 1929. Payson Clarke. 1st ed/2nd prt prior to pub. VG/dj. F4. $25.00

DEKOBRA, Maurice. *Serenade to the Hang Man.* 1929. Payson Clarke. 1st ed. NF/NF. F4. $65.00

DEKOBRA, Maurice. *Venus on Wheels.* 1930. Macaulay. 1st ed. F/NF. F4. $70.00

DEL MARTIA, Aston; see Fearn, John Russell.

DEL REY, Lester. *Attack From Atlantis.* 1953. Winston. 1st ed. author's 2nd book. VG/VG. Q1. $50.00

DEL REY, Lester. *Stop to the Stars.* 1954. Winston. 1st ed. NF/NF. F4. $48.00

DEL VECCHIO, John M. *For the Sake of All Living Things.* (1990). Bantam. 1st ed. NF/NF. A7. $25.00

DEL VECCHIO, John M. *13th Valley.* (1982). Bantam. 1st prt. F/dj. A7. $45.00

DELACORTA. *Diva.* 1983. NY. 1st ed. trans L Blair. A11. $30.00

DELAFIELD, Clelia. *Mrs Mallard's Ducklings.* 1946. Lee Shepard. 1st ed. ils Leonard Weisgard. unp. VG/dj. M20. $25.00

DELANEY, Caldwell. *Deep South.* 1981. Haunted Book Shop. facsimile of 1942 ed. cloth. NF. M8. $25.00

DELANEY & RICE. *Bloodstained Trail: Hist of Militant Labor in US.* 1927. Seattle. Industrial Worker. 172 p. VG/wrp. A7. $50.00

DELANO, Alonzo. *Sojourn w/Royalty & Other Sketches...* 1936. San Francisco. 1st thus ed. 1/500. xl. cloth/brds. VG. D3. $35.00

DELANY, Samuel R. *Bridge of Lost Desire.* 1987. NY. Arbor House. 1st ed. F/F. N3. $15.00

DELATTRE, Pierre. *Tales of a Dalai Lama.* 1971. Houghton Mifflin. 1st ed. inscr. F/F. B4. $125.00

DELAUNAY, Charles. *New Hot Discography.* 1948. Criterion. 1st thus ed. NF. B2. $75.00

DELESSERT & SCHMID. *Endless Party.* 1967. Harlen Quest. 1st ed. VG/dj. A3. $12.50

DELEUZE, J.P.F. *Eudoxe: Entretiens sur l'Etude des Sciences...* 1810. Paris. Schoell. 2 vols. contemporary leather/marbled brds. VG. G1. $150.00

DELEUZE, J.P.F. *Histoire Critique du Magnetisme Animal.* 1819 (1831). Paris. Chez Belin. 2nd ed. 2 vols. contemporary brds. G1. $250.00

DELGADO, Alan. *Introducing Ponies.* nd. London. Spring. thin 4to. photos. VG/G+. O3. $15.00

DELL, Anthony. *Llama Land: E & W of the Andes in Peru.* (1927). NY. Doran. 1st ed. lg 8vo. 248 p. F3. $25.00

DELL, Floyd. *Unmarried Father.* (1927). Doran. 2nd prt. A7. $15.00

DELMAS & PERTUISET. *Topometrie Cranio-Encephalique Chez l'Homme.* 1959. Paris. Masson. thick 4to. 431 p. G7. $95.00

DELORIA, Ella. *Dakota Texts.* 1932. NY. Stechert/Am Ethnological Soc. 1st ed. bilingual. NF. L3. $350.00

DELORIA, Vine Jr. *Custer Died for Your Sins.* 1969. Macmillan. 2nd prt. F/VG. H7. $10.00

DELVING, Michael. *Die Like a Man.* ca 1970. 3-in-1 BC. VG. C1. $4.00

DEMARIS, Ovid. *Am the Violent.* (1970). NY. Cowles. 1st ed. 404 p. dj. A7. $17.00

DEMARIS, Ovid. *Ricochet.* 1988. Scribner. 1st ed. F/F. F4. $15.00

DEMBECK, Hermann. *Animals & Men.* (1965). NY. Nat Hist Pr. ils/index. 390 p. dj. A17. $8.50

DEMIJOHN, Thomas; see Discht, Thomas.

DEMPSEY, P.W. *Grow Your Own Vegetables.* 1942. Boston. 1st ed. ils. 184 p. VG. B28. $15.00

DEMPSEY & FLEISCHER. *Jack Dempsey: Idol of Fistiana.* 1929. Ring Pub. autograph ed. 1/25. sgn twice Dempsey. teg. marbled ep. VG+. Q1. $400.00

DENDEL. *Basic Book of Twining.* 1978. np. pb. G2. $8.00

DENHARDT, Robert. *Horse of the Am.* 1949. Norman. 3rd prt. VG/VG. O3. $25.00

DENIS & WHITE. *Water-Powers of Canada.* 1911. Ottawa. photos/maps. 397 p. A17. $35.00

DENMAN, Thomas. *Intro to Practice of Midwifery.* 1807. Brattleborough. Fessenden. 441 p. contemporary tree sheepskin. NF. B14. $75.00

DENMAN, William. *Report on Causes of Municipal Corruption in San Francisco...* 1910. San Francisco. CA Weekly. wrp. M11. $25.00

DENNEN, Ernest J. *Intro to the Prayer Book.* 1906. NY. Gorham. 117 p. brds. H10. $15.00

DENNER. *Grand Finale: Quilter's Guide to Finishing Projects.* 1988. np. ils. wrp. G2. $15.00

DENNIE, Joseph. *Spirit of the Farmers' Mus & Lay Preacher's Gazette.* 1801. Walpole. Thomas. 1st ed. 12mo. 318 p. contemporary calf. M1. $275.00

DENNIS, James M. *Karl Bitter, Architectural Sculptor.* 1967. Madison, WI. 110 pls/index. 302 p. cloth. dj. D2. $75.00

DENNIS, Morgan. *Morgan Dennis Dog Book.* 1946. Viking. 1st ed. 31 full-p ils. cloth. VG. M5. $16.00

DENNIS, Wesley. *Flip & the Morning.* 1951. NY. Jr Literary Guild. juvenile. VG/VG. O3. $20.00

DENNIS, Wesley. *Flip.* 1941. Viking. 1st ed. juvenile. VG/G. O3. $35.00

DENNY, George H. *Dread Fishwish & Other Tales.* (1975). Freshet. ils. 222 p. F/dj. A17. $15.00

DENNYS, John. *Secrets of Angling, 1613.* 1970. Freshet. facsimile of 1883 ed. 62 p. F/slipcase. A17. $20.00

DENNYS, N.B. *Account of Cruise of St George on N Am & W Indian Station...* 1862. London. Saunders Otley. 1st ed. octavo. half bl morocco. H9. $150.00

DENNYS, Rodney. *Heraldic Imagination.* (1975). NY. 1st Am ed. 23 color pls. 224 p. VG+/dj. B18. $19.50

DENON, Vivant. *Travels in Upper & Lower Egypt.* 1803. London. 1st ed. quarto. 2 vols. modern half polished calf. VG. H5. $4,000.00

DENSMORE, Frances. *Chippewa Customs.* 1979. MN Hist Soc. reprint of 1929 ed. M/wrp. A17. $10.50

DENSMORE, Frances. *Monominee Music.* 1932. GPO. 1st ed. 230 p. VG/wrp. D3. $25.00

DENTON, Bradley. *Buddy Holly Is Alive & Well on Ganymede.* 1991. Morrow. 1st ed. F/NF. N3. $15.00

DENTON & BRANDT. *When Hell Was in Session.* 1976. Readers Digest. 1st hc ed/4th prt. NF/dj. A7. $25.00

DER LING, Princess. *2 Yrs in the Forbidden City.* 1911. NY. Moffat Yard. 1st Am ed. 8vo. 383 p. VG. A2. $45.00

DERIEUX, Samuel. *Animals Personalities.* 1925. NY. photos. 298 p. cloth. G. A17. $9.50

DERLETH, August. *Casebook of Solar Pons.* 1965. Arkham. 1st ed. F/dj. M2. $110.00

DERLETH, August. *Fire & Sleet & Candlelight.* 1961. Arkham. 1st ed. F/dj. M2. $125.00

DERLETH, August. *In Re: Sherlock Holmes.* 1945. Arkham. 1st ed. F/dj. M2. $125.00

DERLETH, August. *Irregulars Strike Again.* 1964. DSP. 1st ed. 8vo. 151 p. bl cloth. VG/VG. T5. $30.00

DERLETH, August. *Lonesome Places.* 1962. Arkham. 1st ed. F/dj. M2. $100.00

DERLETH, August. *Mr Fairlie's Final Journey.* 1968. Arkham. 1st ed. F/dj. M2. $50.00

DERLETH, August. *Namacong Riddle.* 1940. Scribner. 1st ed. F. F4. $20.00

DERLETH, August. *No Future for Luana.* 1945. Scribner. 1st prt. 204 p. RS. F/VG+. S9. $45.00

DERLETH, August. *Not Long for This World.* 1948. Arkham. 1st ed. VG/dj. M2. $100.00

DERLETH, August. *Praed Street Dossier.* 1968. Arkham. 1st ed. F/dj. M2. $50.00

DERLETH, August. *Reminiscences of Solar Pons.* 1961. Arkham. 1st ed. F/M. M2. $100.00

DERLETH, August. *Sentence Deferred.* 1939. Scribner. 1st ed. G. M18. $100.00

DERLETH, August. *Solar Pons Omnibus.* 1982. Arkham. 1st ed. 2 vols. M/slipcase. M2. $40.00

DERLETH, August. *Some Notes on HP Lovecraft.* 1959. Arkham. 1st ed. NF/wrp. M2. $125.00

DERLETH, August. *Something Near.* 1945. Arkham. 1st ed. F/dj. M2. $150.00

DERLETH, August. *Tent Show Summer.* 1963. DSP. 1st ed. 8vo. 152 p. VG/VG. T5. $30.00

DERLETH, August. *Thirty Yrs of Arkham House.* 1970. Arkham. 1st ed. F/dj. M2. $80.00

DERLETH, August. *Time To Come.* 1954. Farrar. 1st ed. F/F. F4. $30.00

DERLETH, August. *Trail of Cthulhu.* 1962. Arkham. 1st ed. F/dj. M2. $85.00

DERLETH, August. *Travelers by Night.* 1967. Arkham. 1st ed. F/dj. M2. $50.00

DERRIDA & TLILI. *For Nelson Mandela.* (1987). Holt. 256 p. F/F clip. A7. $15.00

DERSHOWITZ, Alan M. *Reversal of Fortune: Inside the Von Bulow Case.* 1986. Random. 1st ed. F/F. T2. $14.00

DES CARS, A.J. *Treatise on Pruning Forest & Ornamental Trees...* 1881. Boston. Williams. 1st ed. pls. H10. $95.00

DESAUTELS, Paul E. *Gem Kingdom.* 1970. Random/Ridge Pr. VG/dj. A16. $17.50

DESCHAMPS, Gaston. *La Grece D'Aujourd'hui.* 1892. Paris. 8vo. 388 p. cloth. O2. $60.00

DESCHARNES, Robert. *World of Salvador Dali.* 1962. Atide/Crown. 1st ed. ils. 233 p. cloth. VG/dj. M20. $60.00

DESCOLA, Jean. *Conquistadors.* 1957. Viking. 1st ed. 404 p. dj. F3. $15.00

DESCOLA, Jean. *Hist of Spain.* 1963. Knopf. trans Halperin. 483 p. dj. A7. $20.00

DESMARS, M. *Epidemiques d'Hippocrates Traduites du Grec...* 1767. Paris. Chex Veuve Houry. 359 p. full mottled calf. G7. $175.00

DESMOND, A.C. *Sword & Pen for WA.* (1964). Dodd Mead. 1st ed. 8vo. 291 p. F/VG. A2. $30.00

DESNOS, Robert. *Voice. Selected Poems of Robert Desnos.* 1976. Grossman. 1st ed. F/wrp. B2. $25.00

DESSAIN, Charles Stephen. *John Henry Newman.* ca 1966. London. Nelson. 178 p. H10. $15.00

DESVERNINE, R.E. *Human Rights & the Constitution.* 1935. WA. Am Liberty League. 7 p. stapled wrp. M11. $10.00

DETREZ, Conrad. *Weed for Burning.* 1984. HBJ. 1st ed. trans Lydia Davis. rem mk. NF/VG+. A14. $25.00

DETREZ, Conrad. *Zone of Fire.* 1986. HBJ. 1st ed. trans Lydia Davis. F/F clip. A14. $25.00

DEUEL, John Vanderveer. *Wht Cayuca.* 1934. Houghton Mifflin. 1st ed. 280 p. dj. F3. $20.00

DEUEL, Leo. *Conquistadors Without Swords. Archaeologists in Americas.* 1967. St Martin. 1st ed. 8vo. 16 pls. 647 p. bl brds. VG/G. B11. $35.00

DEUEL, Leo. *Flights Into Yesterday: Story of Aerial Archaeology.* 1969. NY. St Martin. 1st ed. 8vo. photos/ils. 332 p. F/VG+. A2. $17.50

DEUTSCH, Harold C. *Conspiracy Against Hitler in the Twilight War.* 1968. MN U. 2nd prt. 394 p. VG+/G+. S3. $30.00

DEUTSCHER, Isaac. *Heretics & Renegades.* 1955. Hamish Hamilton. 228 p. NF/dj. A7. $35.00

DEVANEY & GOLDBLATT. *World Series.* 1972. Rand McNally. 1st ed. F/VG+. P8. $22.50

DEVERDUM, Alfred Louis. *True Mexico. Mexico-Tenochtitlan.* 1938. private prt. sgn. 8vo. 303 p. bl brds. VG. B11. $85.00

DEVERE, William. *Jim Marshall's New Pianner & Other W Stories...* 1897. NY. 1st ed. inscr. ils. 130 p. pict cloth. VG+. D3. $35.00

DEWAR, John. *Adios Mr Penelon. Henri Penelon: Painter, Photographer.* 1968. LA Co Mus Natural Hist. 24 p. D2. $10.00

DEWEES, Jacob. *Great Future of Am & Africa...* 1854. Phil. prt for author. 1st ed. 8vo. 236 p. cloth. M1. $175.00

DEWEY, John. *Psychology.* 1890. Harper. 427 p. VG+. S9. $80.00

DEWHURST & MACDOWELL. *MI Hmong Arts: Textiles in Transition.* 1983. np. pb. F. G2. $10.50

DEWING, Arthur Stone. *Financial Policy of Corporations.* (1941). NY. Ronald. 4th ed in 2 vols. A7. $35.00

DEXTER, Colin. *Jewel That Was Ours.* 1991. London. Macmillan. 1st ed. sgn. F/F. M15. $65.00

DEXTER, Colin. *Morse's Greatest Mystery & Other Stories.* 1993. London. Macmillan. 1st ed. sgn. F/F. M15. $50.00

DEXTER, Colin. *Service of All the Dead.* 1979. St Martin. 1st ed. F/F. M15. $150.00

DEXTER, Colin. *Way Through the Woods.* 1992. Scorpian Pr. 1/150. sgn/#d. marbled paper brds. red leather. F. Q1. $150.00

DEXTER, Colin. *Wench Is Dead.* 1990. St Martin. 1st Am ed. F/F. M15. $30.00

DEXTER, Dave Jr. *Cavalcade.* 1946. Citerion. 1st ed. F/NF. B2. $50.00

DEXTER, John; see Bradley, Marion Zimmer.

DEXTER, Pete. *Brotherly Love.* (1992). London. Harvill. 1st ed. F/F. B3. $20.00

DEXTER, Pete. *Paris Trout.* (1988). NY. Random. ARC. RS. F/F. B3. $55.00

DEXTER, Pete. *Paris Trout.* 1988. NY. 1st ed. sgn. F/F. A11. $45.00

DI CARTEROMACO, Niccolo. *Ricciardetto.* 1738. Venice. Francesco Titteri. 2 vols in 1. contemporary vellum. K1. $450.00

DI CERTO, Joseph J. *Wall People.* 1985. Atheneum. 1st ed. F/F. N3. $10.00

DI FUSCO, John. *Tracers.* (1986). Hill Wang. 1st ed. F/F. A7. $40.00

DI LAMPEDUSA, Giuseppe. *Leopard.* 1960. London. Collins/Harvill. 1st ed. trans Colquhoun. NF/NF clip. A14. $45.00

DI LELLO, R. *Longest Cocktail Party.* 1972. Chicago. 1st ed. VG/VG. B5. $27.50

DI MAGGIO, Joe. *Lucky To Be a Yankee.* 1946. Rudolph Field. later prt. sgn. photos. VG/VG. P8. $175.00

DIBBLE, Charles. *Codex en Cruz.* 1981. Salt Lake City. 1st ed. 2 vols. F3. $50.00

DICK, Philip K. *Collected Stories of...* 1987. LA. Underwood/Miller. 1st ed. 5 vols. F/sans. L3. $375.00

DICK, Philip K. *Dark-Haired Girl.* 1988. Willimantic. Ziesing. M/M. T2. $19.95

DICK, Philip K. *Flow My Tears, the Policeman Said.* 1974. Doubleday. 1st ed. inscr. NF/NF. L3. $750.00

DICK, Philip K. *Handful of Darkness.* 1955. London. Rich Cowan. 1st ed. author's 1st book. 1st issue bdg. VG+. Q1. $75.00

DICK, Philip K. *Man Whose Teeth Were All Exactly Alike.* 1984. Zeising. 1st ed. M. M2. $60.00

DICK, Philip K. *Martian Time-Slip.* (1964). Ballantine. 1st ed/pb. VG+. A7. $35.00

DICK, Philip K. *Our Friends From Flolix 8.* (1970). Ace. BC/1st hc ed. inscr. NF/NF. B4. $450.00

DICK, Philip K. *Time Out of Joint.* 1959. Lippincott. 1st ed. NF/NF. Q1. $150.00

DICK, Philip K. *Ubik.* 1969. Doubleday. 1st ed. rpr front ep. NF/NF. scarce. L3. $400.00

DICK & JANE READER. *Guess Who.* 1951. New Basic Reader. ils CB Dillon. 95 p. cloth. G. A3. $25.00

DICK & JANE READER. *Guess Who.* 1955. Am Prt House for Blind. Lg Type/1-Vol Ed. 95 p. VG. A3. $25.00

DICK & JANE READER. *New Fun w/Dick & Jane.* 1951. New Basic Reader. 159 p. VG+. A3. $40.00

DICK & JANE READER. *New Our New Friends. Guidebook...Teacher's Ed.* 1952. Scott Foresman. cloth. VG. A3. $65.00

DICK & JANE READER. *New Pre-Primers. Guidebook...Teacher's Ed.* 1951. Scott Foresman. cloth. VG. A3. $65.00

DICK & JANE READER. *New We Come & Go.* 1956. Scott Foresman. 72 p. VG. A3. $40.00

DICK & JANE READER. *New We Look & See.* 1956. Scott Foresman. ils Eleanor Campbell. 48 p. VG. A3. $35.00

DICK & JANE READER. *We Come & Go.* 1946-47. Scott Foresman. ils Eleanor Campbell. 3rd of series. 72 p. VG+. A3. $40.00

DICK & JANE READER. *We Look & See.* 1946-47. Scott Foresman. 1st of series. 48 p. wrp/cloth spine. VG. A3. $40.00

DICK & JANE READER. *We Work & Play.* 1946-47. Scott Foresman. 2nd of series. 62 p. wrp/cloth spine. VG. A3. $40.00

DICK & ZELAZNY. *Deus Irae.* 1978. Newton Abbot. Readers Union. British BC. inscr. F/NF. L3. $350.00

DICK-READ, Robert. *Sanamu: Adventures in Search of African Art.* 1964. NY. Dutton. 1st ed. 8vo. 271 p. F/VG+. A2. $12.00

DICKASON, Christie. *Indochine.* (1987). Villard. 1st Am ed. rem mk. F/F. A7. $13.00

DICKENS, Charles. *Am Notes for General Circulation.* 1842. London. 1st ed. octavo. 2 vols. orig reddish-brn cloth. NF. H5. $3,000.00

DICKENS, Charles. *Bleak House.* 1853. London. 1st ed. ils HK Browne/40 pls. orig gr cloth. VG. H5. $4,000.00

DICKENS, Charles. *Boots of the Holly-Tree Inn.* 1928. Harper. ils Marie A Lawson. 44 p. VG+. S10. $30.00

DICKENS, Charles. *Charles Dickens Rare Prt Collection.* 1900. Phil. Kennedy. ltd ed for private circulation. scarce. E3. $125.00

DICKENS, Charles. *Chimes.* (1908). Platt Peck. ils George Alfred Williams. 310 p. bl cloth/pict label. H3. $25.00

DICKENS, Charles. *Chimes.* nd. Hodder Stoughton. ils Hugh Thomson/7 mtd pls. NF. M5. $60.00

DICKENS, Charles. *Chimes.* 1898. London. Chapman Hall. G+. A1. $65.00

DICKENS, Charles. *Chimes.* 1911. NY/London. 15 pls. 191 p. gilt gr cloth. F. H3. $15.00

DICKENS, Charles. *Christmas Carol in Prose.* 1940. Holiday House. ils/bdg Philip Reed. F. F1. $350.00

DICKENS, Charles. *Christmas Carol.* 1902. Roycroft. emb rust suede. VG. E5. $65.00

DICKENS, Charles. *Christmas Carol.* 1915. London. Heinemann. 1/525. ils/sgn Rackham. 147 p. Bayntun bdg. NF. H5. $1,850.00

DICKENS, Charles. *Christmas Carol.* 1967. NY. James H Heineman. 1st ed. ils John Leech. VG/G. L1. $40.00

DICKENS, Charles. *Christmas Carol.* 1976. Winterport, ME. Borrower's Pr. miniature. 1/300. sgn/prt Bernier. F. B24. $85.00

DICKENS, Charles. *Christmas Carol. In Prose. Being Ghost Story of Christmas.* 1843. London. Chapman Hall. 1st ed/1st issue (gr ep/bl half-title). aeg. F/case. H5. $19,500.00

DICKENS, Charles. *Dr Marigold.* 1908. London. Foulis. ils Charles Brock. VG. C1. $25.00

DICKENS, Charles. *Great Expectations.* 1861. London. 1st ed/1st issue. 3 vols. purple cloth. NF/box. H5. $45,000.00

DICKENS, Charles. *Lib of Fiction; or, Family Story-Teller.* 1836-37. London. Chapman Hall. 1st ed in book form. 2 vols. 28 pls. NF. H5. $1,750.00

DICKENS, Charles. *Life & Adventures of Nicholas Nickleby...* 1839. London. 1st ed. octavo. 39 pls. orig gr cloth/recased. H5. $6,500.00

DICKENS, Charles. *Life of Our Lord.* 1936. Grosset Dunlap. ils Rachel Taft. G/G. L1. $30.00

DICKENS, Charles. *Life of Our Lord.* 1939. Garden City. VG. N2. $10.00

DICKENS, Charles. *Little Dorrit.* 1857. London. Bradbury Evans. leather/marbled brds. G. A16. $100.00

DICKENS, Charles. *Mystery of Edwin Drood.* 1870. London. Chapman Hall. 1st ed. 6 orig monthly parts. prt wrp/gr morocco case. H5. $1,150.00

DICKENS, Charles. *Personal Hist & Experience of David Copperfield.* ca 1850. NY. WF Burgess. 1st Am ed? 8vo. 264 p. contemporary bdg. M1. $200.00

DICKENS, Charles. *Personal Hist of David Copperfield.* (1925). Hodder Stoughton. 1st ed. ils Frank Reynolds. NF. B4. $250.00

DICKENS, Charles. *Posthumous Papers of the Pickwick Club.* 1837. London. Chapman Hall. ils Buss/Seymour/Phiz. 609 p. contemporary calf. G. B14. $150.00

DICKENS, Charles. *Posthumous Papers of the Pickwick Club.* 1933. Oxford. LEC. ils/sgn John Austen. 2 vols. F/dj/box. F1. $175.00

DICKENS, Charles. *Sketches by Boz.* 1839. London. 1st octavo ed. ils Cruikshank. 12 parts/pink wrp. VG/slipcase. H5. $40,000.00

DICKENS, Charles. *Tale of 2 Cities.* 1859. London. 1st ed. ils Browne, 8 parts in 7/wrp. NF/case. H5. $12,500.00

DICKENS, Charles. *Works...* 1875. NY. 13 vols. dk gr. VG. B30. $85.00

DICKERMAN, Charles W. *How To Make the Farm Pay...* 1871. Phil. Ziegler McCurdy. 774 p. H10. $45.00

DICKEY, Glenn. *Hist of the World Series Since 1903.* 1984. Stein Day. 1st ed. ils/photos. VG/VG. P8. $15.00

DICKEY, James. *Deliverance.* 1970. Boston. 1st ed. sgn. VG/VG. B5. $65.00

DICKEY, James. *Deliverance.* 1982. Carbondale, IL. 1st ed. inscr. F/wrp. A11. $60.00

DICKEY, James. *Drowning w/Others.* 1962. Middletown, CT. 1st ed. sgn. NF/wrp. A11. $75.00

DICKEY, James. *Early Motion: Drowning w/Others & Helmets.* (1981). Middletown. Wesleyan. 1st ed. F/NF. A7. $20.00

DICKEY, James. *To the Wht Sea.* 1993. Houghton Mifflin. ARC. wrp. B2. $35.00

DICKEY, James. *To the Wht Sea.* 1993. Jaffe/Houghton Mifflin. 1st ed. sgn. F/F. C4. $30.00

DICKEY, James. *Tucky the Hunter.* (1978). NY. Crown. 1st ed. ils Marie Angel. F/F. B3. $45.00

DICKEY, James. *Veteran Birth of Gadfly Poems 1947-49.* 1978. Palaemon. 1/200. sgn. ils Robert Dance. F/hand-sewn wrp. F1. $45.00

DICKINSON, Charles. *Widows' Adventures.* (1989). Morrow. 1st ed. VG/pict wrp. B3. $30.00

DICKINSON, Edward. *Student's Book of Inspirations.* 1919. Boston. 1st ed. decor brds. VG. E3. $10.00

DICKINSON, Emily. *Bolts of Melody: New Poems.* 1945. NY. 1st ed. gr cloth. NF. V1. $12.00

DICKINSON, Emily. *Complete Poems.* 1960. Boston. 1st ed. edit TH Johnson. VG/VG. B5. $35.00

DICKINSON, Emily. *Futher Poems of...* 1929. Little Brn. ltd ed. 1/465. VG. E3. $90.00

DICKINSON, Emily. *Manuscript Books.* 1981. Cambridge. 1st ed. VG/VG box. B5. $50.00

DICKINSON, Emily. *Poems. 2nd Series.* 1891. Boston. Roberts Bros. 1st ed. teg. stp gray cloth. F. B24. $1,250.00

DICKINSON, Lawrence S. *Lawn: Culture of Turf in Park, Golfing & Home Areas.* 1936. NY. Judd. revised 2nd ed. 128 p. H10. $17.50

DICKINSON, Leo. *Filming the Impossible.* (1982). London. Cape. 1st ed. 8vo. 256 p. F/F. A2. $15.00

DICKINSON, Peter. *Yel Room Conspiracy.* 1994. Mysterious. ARC. NF/wrp. B2. $25.00

DICKSON, Carter; see Carr, John Dickson.

DICKSTEIN, Morris. *Gates of Eden.* 1977. Basic Books. 2nd prt. 300 p. dj. A7. $12.00

DIDION, Joan. *Book of Common Prayer.* (1977). Simon Schuster. 1st ed. NF/F. B3. $30.00

DIDION, Joan. *Salvador.* 1983. Simon Schuster. 1st ed. F/F. T2. $12.50

DIDION, Joan. *Slouching Toward Bethlehem.* 1968. NY. 1st ed. author's 2nd book. NF/dj. A15. $40.00

DIDION, Joan. *Slouching Towards Bethlehem.* 1969. Deutsch. 1st Eng ed. inscr. NF/dj. M18. $100.00

DIEBITSCH-PEARY & PEARY. *My Arctic Journal.* 1893. NY. 1st ed. full-p photos. 241 p. A17. $75.00

DIETHELM, Oscar. *Etiology of Chronic Alcoholism.* 1955. Springfield. Charles Thomas. 1st ed. F/NF. B2. $45.00

DIETRICH. *Handmade Quilts.* 1990. np. wrp. G2. $12.95

DIETRICH. *Happy Endings: Finishing the Edges of Your Quilt.* 1987. np. wrp. G2. $10.00

DIETZ, Terry. *Republicans & Vietnam 1961-68.* (1986). Greenwood. 1st ed. 184 p. F/sans. A7. $25.00

DIFFLEY, Sean. *Men in Gr: Story of Irish Rubgy.* (1973). London. Pelham. 1st ed. 8vo. 156 p. F/F. A2. $12.50

DIGBY, Edward. *Private Memoirs...Written by Himself...* 1827. London. Saunders Otley. 328 p. gilt morocco. G7. $150.00

DIGBY, Kenelm. *Letters Between Lord George Digby & Kenelm Digby...* 1651. London. Moseley. 1st ed/Sherborn variant. 12mo. recent full calf. G7. $375.00

DIGBY, Kenelm. *Theatrum Sympatheticum in Quo Sympathiae Actiones Variae...* 1661. Amsterdam. Fontanus. 12mo. contemporary vellum. G7. $495.00

DIGBY, Keneln. *Observations Upon Religio Medici...* 1644. London. Chapman Frere. 2nd/corrected ed. 122 p. aeg. old ruled calf. G7. $375.00

DIGGES. *Lady Evelyn's Needlework Collection.* 1988. np. ils. cloth. G2. $35.00

DIGGINS, John P. *Bard of Savagery.* (1978). NY. Seabury. 257 p. NF/NF. A7. $22.00

DILKE, Charles Wentworth. *Greater Britain: Record of Travel in Eng-Speaking Countries.* 1869. Phil/London. Lippincott/Macmillan. 2 vols in 1. brn cloth. H9. $125.00

DILKE, O.A.W. *Roman Books & Their Impact.* 1977. Leeds. Elmete. ltd ed. 1/460. 23 pls. special full purple calf. F/slipcase. K1. $185.00

DILL, Alonzo Thomas. *Francis Lightfoot Lee: Incomparable Signer.* ca 1977. Independance Bicentennail Comm. xl. VG. B10. $10.00

DILLARD, Annie. *Am Childhood.* (1987). Harper Row. 1st ed. F/F. A18. $25.00

DILLARD, Annie. *Holy the Firm.* (1977). Harper Row. 1st ed. F/F. A18. $35.00

DILLARD, Annie. *Living.* (1992). Harper Collins. 1st ed. F/F. A18. $40.00

DILLARD, Annie. *Living.* (1992). Harper Collins. 1st ltd ed. 1/300. sgn. M/slipcase. A18. $125.00

DILLARD, Annie. *Living.* 1992. Harper Collins. ARC. F/pict wrp. C4. $35.00

DILLARD, Annie. *Weasel.* (1974). Rara Avis Pr. 1st separate ltd ed. 1/190. sgn. M/wrp. A18. $75.00

DILLARD, Annie. *Writing Life.* (1989). Harper Row. 1st ed. F/F. A18. $25.00

DILLARD, R.H.W. *Horror Films.* 1976. NY. PBO. sgn. NF/8vo wrp. A11. $65.00

DILLARD, R.H.W. *Night I Stopped Dreaming About Barbara Steele.* nd. np. 1st ed/wrp issue. presentation inscr. VG+/ils wrp. A11. $30.00

DILLION, P. *Narrative & Successful Result of Voyage in S Seas...* 1972. Amsterdam/NY. Israel/Da Capo. reprint. 2 vols. M. P4. $135.00

DILLMAN, Mary Alma. *Wee Folk. About Elves in Nova Scotia.* 1956. New Brunswick. 3rd prt. 67 p. VG. A3. $7.50

DILLON, Richard. *Meriwether Lewis: A Biography.* 1965. Coward McCann. 1st ed. 8vo. 364 p. map ep. F/dj. T8. $40.00

DILLON. *Contemporary SW Quilts.* 1989. np. ils. wrp. G2. $15.00

DILLON. *Window of Peace.* 1989. np. ils/patterns. sbdg. G2. $19.00

DILWORTH, Sharon. *Long Wht.* (1988). NY. Norton. 1st ed. M/wrp. A17. $7.50

DIMENT, Adam. *Great Spy Race.* 1968. London. Michael Joseph. 1st ed. F/NF. M15. $45.00

DIMITROFF, Georgi. *United Front.* (1938). NY. Internat. 287 p. A7. $18.00

DIMOCK, A.W. *Dick Among the Seminoles.* 1911. Stokes. 1st ed. 12mo. 16 photos. 324 p. pict red brds. VG. B11. $45.00

DIMOCK, Edward C. Jr. *Place of the Hidden Moon.* 1966. Chicago. 1st ed. 8vo. 299 p. NF/dj. W1. $16.00

DIMSDALE, T.J. *Vigilantes of MT...* (1953). Norman, OK. 1st ed. 268 p. G+/dj. B18. $17.50

DINES, Glen. *Overland Stage: Story of Famous Overland Stagecoaches...* 1961. Macmillan. 1st ed. oblong 4to. VG/G. O3. $35.00

DINGEE-MACGREGOR. *Science of Successful Threshing.* 1915. Racine. JI Case. 7th ed. ils. 263 p. F/dj. C10. $37.50

DINNING, Hector. *Nile of Aleppo.* 1920. NY. Macmillan. 1st ed. gilt brn linen. M7. $135.00

DISBURY, David G. *TE Lawrence of Arabia: A Collector's Booklet.* 1972. Surrey, Eng. private prt. 38 unp leaves. NF/tan wrp. M7. $60.00

DISCHT, Thomas M. *New Improved Sun.* 1975. Harper. 1st ed. F/F. N3. $25.00

DISCHT, Thomas M. *Prisoner.* 1969. NY. Ace. PBO. sgn. F/unread. A11. $60.00

DISHER, M.W. *Victorian Song: From Dive to Drawing Room.* (1955). London. Pheonix House. 1st ed. 8vo. 256 p. VG+/VG. A2. $20.00

DISNEY STUDIOS. *Elmer Elephant.* 1938. Whitman. unp. VG/pict wrp. M20. $75.00

DISNEY STUDIOS. *Peculiar Penguins From Walt Disney Silly Symphony.* (1934) Phil. McKay. octavo. 45 p. NF/prt wrp. B24. $485.00

DISNEY STUDIOS. *Walt Disney's Mickey Mouse's Summer Vacation.* 1948. Whitman. Story Book Hour series. 32 p. G. A3. $10.00

DISNEY STUDIOS. *Walt Disney's Treasure Chest.* 1948. Simon Schuster. Big Golden Book. 1st ed. 66 p. VG. P2. $28.00

DISSTON, Harry. *Riding Rhymes for Young Riders.* 1951. NY. Bond Wheelwright. 1st ed ils Paul Brn. VG/fair. O3. $35.00

DITHMAR, Edward A. *John Drew.* (1900) NY. Stokes. 1st ed. photos. gilt red cloth. F B20. $45.00

DITMARS, Raymond. *Reptiles of the World.* 1941. NY. revised ed. 321 p. VG. A17. $16.50

DITTMAN, Elva. *Wht Princess.* 1945. Cupples Leon. ils Masha Nardini. 4to. 26 p. VG. A3. $10.00

DITTMAN. *Fabric Lovers' Scrapbook.* 1988. np. ils. wrp. G2. $15.00

DITTMAN. *14 Easy Baby Quilts.* 1990. np. ils. wrp. G2. $18.95

DITZION, Sidney. *Marriage, Morals & Sex in Am: Hist of Ideas.* 1953. NY. Bookman's Associates. 1st ed. 440 p. bl cloth. G1. $28.50

DIVEN, T.J. *Aztecs & Mays. Vol 1.* 1909. Chicago. 1st ed. 12mo. 248 p. cloth. NF D3. $250.00

DIX, Dorothy. *My Trip Round the World.* 1924. Phil. 1st ed. 8vo. 311 p. gilt bl cloth. VG. H3. $15.00

DIXON, Alec. *Tinned Soldier.* 1941. London. Right BC. 314 p. bl buckram. VG/clear plastic. M7. $65.00

DIXON, Arthur A. *Child Characters From Dickens.* nd. London. Nister. 70 half-tone ils. VG. M5. $75.00

DIXON, Franklin W. *Brushing the Mtn Top.* 1934. Grosset Dunlap. 1st ed. 216 p. tan cloth. VG/tape rpr. M20. $40.00

DIXON, Franklin W. *Flickering Torch Mystery.* 1943. Grosset Dunlap. 3rd prt. 212 p. VG/ragged. M20. $25.00

DIXON, Franklin W. *Great Airport Mystery.* 1941 (1930). Grosset Dunlap. A prt. 210 p. VG+/dj. M20. $150.00

DIXON, Franklin W. *House on the Cliff.* 1935 (1927). Grosset Dunlap. lists to W Stories for Boys. VG/dj. M20. $150.00

DIXON, Franklin W. *Hunting for Hidden Gold.* 1939 (1928). Grosset Dunlap. A prt. 214 p. brn cloth. VG/dj. M20. $145.00

DIXON, Franklin W. *Lone Eagle of the Border.* 1929. Grosset Dunlap. 1st ed. VG. M2. $20.00

DIXON, Franklin W. *Missing Chums.* 1934 (1928). Grosset Dunlap. A prt. VG/dj. M20. $150.00

DIXON, Franklin W. *Pursuit Patrol.* 1943. Grosset Dunlap. 214 p. brn cloth. VG/dj. M20. $110.00

DIXON, Franklin W. *Secret of the Caves.* 1944 (1929). Grosset Dunlap. 210 p. VG/dj. M20. $55.00

DIXON, Franklin W. *Tower Treasure.* 1927. Grosset Dunlap. B prt (Hal Keene ad on dj). 214 p. VG/dj. M20. $150.00

DIXON, Franklin W. *What Happened at Midnight.* 1940 (1931). Grosset Dunlap. A prt. VG/dj. M20. $160.00

DIXON, George. *Voyage Round the World...1785-88.* 1789. London. 1st ed. lg quarto. 22 pls. contemporary tree calf. F/slipcase. H5. $6,500.00

DIXON, J.M. *Valley & the Shadow.* 1868. NY. Russell. 1st ed. G. H7. $15.00

DIXON, Joseph S. *Wildlife Portfolio of the W National Parks.* (1942). WA. photos. 121 p. cloth. G. A17. $10.00

DIXON, Maynard. *Images of the Native Am.* 1981. San Francisco. CA Academy of Sciences. 1st ed. F/F slipcase. L3. $100.00

DIXON, Mrs. Archibald. *True Hist of MO Compromise & Its Repeal.* 1899. Cincinnati. Clarke. 1st ed. 623 p. rebacked cloth. VG. D3. $25.00

DIXON, Peter L. *Olympian.* 1984. Santa Monica, CA. Roundtable Pub. 1st ed. NF/NF. A14. $25.00

DIXON, Sam H. *Poets & Poetry of TX.* 1885. Austin, TX. Dixon. 1st ed. thick 8vo. 360 p. cloth. M1. $500.00

DIXON, Thomas Jr. *Comrades.* 1909. NY. advance presentation. w/sgn card. red cloth. VG. A11. $75.00

DIXON, Thomas Jr. *Comrades: Story of Social Adventure in CA.* 1909. Doubleday Page. 1st ed. 319 p. cloth. VG. M8. $45.00

DIXON, Thomas Jr. *Leopard's Spots: Romance of Wht Man's Burden, 1865-1900.* 1902. Doubleday. 1st ed. 465 p. cloth. VG. M8. $45.00

DIXON, William Hepworth. *New Am w/Ils From Orig Photographs.* 1867. London. Hurst Blackett. 2nd ed. 2 vols. half morocco. H9. $125.00

DIXON, William Hepworth. *New Am.* 1867. London. Hurst Blackett. 5th ed/revised. 2 vols. polished calf. VG. H7. $100.00

DIXON, William Hepworth. *William Penn: Hist Biography From New Sources...* 1851. Phil. Blanchard Lea. 12mo. 353 p. VG. V3. $15.00

DIXON & HANNIGAN. *Negro Baseball Leagues.* 1992. Amereon. 1st ed. photos. F/F. P8. $50.00

DJILAS, Milovan. *Land Without Justice.* (1958). Harcourt Brace. 1st ed. NF/worn. A7. $17.00

DKYES, Jeff. *50 Great W Ils: A Bibliographic Checklist.* (1975). Northland. 1st trade ed. inscr/sgn. F/F. A18. $50.00

DMC LIBRARY. *Central Asian Embroideries.* 1978. np. color charts. wrp. G2. $5.00

DOAK. *Quiltmaker's Guide: Basics & Beyond.* 1991. np. wrp. G2. $20.00

DOANE, Michael. *Legends of Jessee Dark.* (1984). Knopf. 1st ed. author's 1st novel. F/F. B3. $30.00

DOANE, Pelagie. *Favorite Nursery Songs.* 1941. Random. ils. VG/dj. P2/M20. $20.00

DOBELL. *Antony Van Leeuwenhoek & His Little Animals.* 1932. Harcourt Brace. 1st ed. 32 pls. 436 p. VG. G1. $50.00

DOBIE, Charles Caldwell. *Arrested Moment & Other Stories.* 1927. NY. 1st ed. xl. inscr/sgn/dtd 1927. 12mo. 310 p. VG. D3. $25.00

DOBIE, Charles Caldwell. *San Francisco: A Pageant.* 1937. NY. 9th prt. pict cloth. VG. D3. $15.00

DOBIE, J. Frank. *Coronado's Children.* 1930. Dallas. SW Pr. ils Ben Carlton Mead. map ep. gilt blk cloth. VG. D3. $75.00

DOBIE, J. Frank. *Guide to Life & Literature of SW w/Few Observations.* 1942. Dallas/S Methodist. 1st ed/2nd prt. VG. O3. $65.00

DOBIE, J. Frank. *Guide to Life & Literature of SW w/Few Observations.* 1942. TX U. 1st ed (prededes SMU ed). ils Hurd/Lea/others. F. A18. $100.00

DOBIE, J. Frank. *Lost Mines of the Old W.* 1960. London. 1st ed. ils Ben Carlton Mead. 367 p. F/pict dj. D3. $35.00

DOBIE, J. Frank. *Mustangs.* 1952. Little Brn. 1st ed. VG. O3. $45.00

DOBIE, J. Frank. *Some Part of Myself.* 1967. Little Brn. 1st ed. F/clip. C4. $35.00

DOBIE, J. Frank. *Texan in Eng.* 1945. Boston. 6th prt. 12mo. cloth. VG. D3. $12.50

DOBIE, J. Frank. *Voice of the Coyote.* 1950. London. 1st ed. ils Olaus J Murie. 386 p. NF/dj. D3. $35.00

DOBSON, Austin. *Ballad of Beau Brocade & Other Poems...* 1872. London. 1st ed. 8vo. gr crushed levant. minor foxing. A16. $90.00

DOBSON, Austin. *Thomas Bewick & His Pupils.* 1884. Boston. Osgood. deluxe ed. 1/90 for Am distribution. 232 p. F. F1. $250.00

DOBSON, Jessie. *Anatomical Eponyms Being a Biographical Dictionary...* 1946. London. Bailliere. 4to. 240 p. G7. $125.00

DOBYNS, Henry. *Analisis de la Situcion des los Comunidades...* 1962. Lima, Peru. 16 p. wrp. F3. $10.00

DOBYNS, Stephen. *Man of Little Evils.* 1973. NY. 1st ed. sgn. NF/VG+. A11. $55.00

DOBYNS, Stephen. *Saratoga Longshot.* 1976. NY. 1st ed. sgn. F/NF. A11. $45.00

DOBYNS, Stephen. *Saratoga Longshot.* 1988. Mysterious/Century. ARC of 1st British ed. RS. F/F. S5. $22.50

DOCKSTADER, Frederick. *Indian Art in Middle Am.* 1964. NY Graphic Soc. 1st ed. 4to. 221 p. dj. F3. $95.00

DOCTOROW, E.L. *Drinks Before Dinner.* 1979. NY. 1st ed. sgn. F/F. E3. $50.00

DOCTOROW, E.L. *Loon Lake.* 1980. Random. AP. F/wrp. L3. $75.00

DOCTOROW, E.L. *Ragtime.* 1975. Random. 1st ed. sgn. author's 4th novel. NF/F. L3. $75.00

DOCTOROW, E.L. *Ragtime.* 1976. London. 1st ed. sgn. NF/VG+. A11. $55.00

DOCTOROW, E.L. *World's Fair.* 1985. Random. 1/300. sgn/#d. F/slipcase. Q1. $125.00

DODD, Anna R. *Three Normandy Inns.* 1899. Boston. 8vo. 394 p. teg. pict wht cloth. VG. H3. $20.00

DODD, Edward. *Rape of Tahiti.* (1983). Dodd Mead. 1st ed. 8vo. 257 p. F/VG+. A2. $12.50

DODD & SOAR. *Ballet: 1st Steps to 1st Night...* 1988. pop-up scenes from famous ballets. F. A4. $35.00

DODGE, Bertha S. *Road W: Saga of the 35th Parallel.* 1980. NM U. ils/index. 222 p. F/VG. B19. $15.00

DODGE, Ed. *Dau.* (1984). Macmillan. 1st ed. F/F. A7. $15.00

DODGE, Jim. *Fup.* (1983). Berkeley. City Miner. 1st ed. inscr. author's 1st book. NF/wrp. scarce. L3. $150.00

DODGE, Mary Mapes. *Hans Brinker; or, The Silver Skates.* 1915. Scribner. ils GW Edwards. VG. E3. $65.00

DODGE, Mary Mapes. *Hans Brinker; or, The Silver Skates.* 1918. McKay. 1st thus ed. ils Enright. 345 p. VG+. P2. $50.00

DODGE, Mary Mapes. *Land of Pluck.* 1894. Century. 1st ed. 313 p. G+. P2. $18.00

DODGE, Norman L. *Hist Am Flags.* 1968. Worcester. St Onge. miniature. 1/2000. bl calf. F. H10. $75.00

DODGE, Richard Irving. *Hunting Grounds of the Great W.* 1877. London. Chatto Windus. thick 8vo. 440 p. pict red cloth. H9. $110.00

DODGSON, Campbell. *Etchings of James McNeill Whistler.* 1922. London. The Studio. 4to. 96 full-p pls. vellum/brds. B14. $35.00

DODSON. *How To Make Soft Jewelry.* 1991. np. ils. cloth. G2. $25.00

DOERR, Harriet. *Stones for Ibarra.* (1985). London. Deutsch. 1st ed. F/F. B3. $30.00

DOERR, Harriet. *Stones for Ibarra.* 1984. Viking. 1st ed. sgn. author's 1st book. F/F clip. L3. $150.00

DOGGETT, Rachel. *New World of Wonders: European Images of the Americas...* 1992. Folger Shakespeare Lib. 1st ed. 4to. 176 p. wrp. F3. $30.00

DOHERTY, P.C. *Satan in St Mary's.* 1987. St Martin. ARC of 1st ed. RS. F/F. S5. $30.00

DOHERTY, P.C. *Shrine of Murders.* 1993. London. Harper Collins Crime Club. 1st ed. F/F. M15. $45.00

DOHERTY, P.C. *Wht Rose Murders.* 1991. London. Headline. 1st ed. F/F. M15. $45.00

DOIG, Ivan. *Dancing at the Rascal Fair.* 1987. Atheneum. 1st ed. inscr/sgn. F/F. A18. $60.00

DOIG, Ivan. *Eng Creek.* 1984. Atheneum. 1st ed. inscr/sgn. F/F. A18. $60.00

DOIG, Ivan. *Heart Earth.* 1993. Atheneum. 1st ed. M/dj. A18. $19.00

DOIG, Ivan. *Ride w/Me, Mirah MT.* 1990. Atheneum. 1st ed. sgn. M/M. A18. $40.00

DOIG, Ivan. *This House of Sky: Landscapes of W Mind.* (1978). HBJ. later prt. inscr/sgn. F/F. A18. $30.00

DOIG, Ivan. *Utopian Am: Dreams & Realities.* (1976). Rochelle Park, NJ. 1st ed. NF/wrp. B4. $250.00

DOIG, Ivan. *Winter Brothers.* (1980). HBJ. 1st ed. NF/F. B3. $50.00

DOLINER, Roy. *Thin Line.* (1980). Crown. 1st ed. F/F. A7. $30.00

DOLINGER, Glenna Louise. *Dr Thomas Walker, Father of KY.* 1950. private prt. 16 p. VG. B10. $25.00

DOLINGER, Jane. *Head w/the Long Yel Hair.* 1958. London. Hale. 1st ed. 189 p. F3. $20.00

DOLINGER, Jane. *Jungle Is a Woman.* 1955. Chicago. Regnery. 1st ed. 8vo. 255 p. VG+/VG. A2. $15.00

DOLLAR & WHEATLEY. *Handbook of Horse-Shoeing.* 1909. NY. Jenkins. VG. O3. $165.00

DOLSON, Hildegarde. *William Penn: Quaker Hero.* 1961. Random. 1st ed. 8vo. 186 p. VG. V3. $8.50

DOMARSKA, Janina. *What Do You See?* 1974. Macmillan. 1st ed. sm 4to. NF/G+. T5. $20.00

DOMAT, Jean. *Civil Law in Its Natural Order.* 1861. Little Brn. 2 vols. full sheep. G. M11. $150.00

DOMEL, Alexander. *Graf Zeppelin.* 1914. np. German text. 47 p. VG. B18. $75.00

DOMENECH, Abbe Em. *7 Yrs' Residence in the Great Deserts of N Am.* 1860. Longman Gr. 1st ed. 2 vols. 59 pls/map. Bickers bdg. H9. $575.00

DOMINIC, R.B. *Unexpected Developments.* 1984. St Martin. ARC of 1st Am ed. RS. F/F. S5. $30.00

DOMVILLE-FIFE, C.W. *Sq-Rigger Days: Autobiographies of Sail.* (1928). London. Seeley Service. ils/photos. 251 p. bl cloth. VG. P4. $95.00

DOMVILLE-FIFE, Charles. *States of S Am.* 1920. London. Bell. 287 p. F3. $20.00

DONAGHE, Virginia. *Picturesque UT.* 1888. Denver. Thayer. 1st ed. oblong 4to. 6 Albertypes. gilt blk cloth. VG. D3. $250.00

DONAHEY, Mary Dickerson. *Through the Little Gr Door.* 1910. NY. ils Gertrude Alice Kay. fair. scarce. M5. $30.00

DONAHUE, James. *No Greater Love.* (1988). Daring Books. 2nd prt. F/F. A7. $14.00

DONAHUE, James. *Terrifying Steamboat Stories.* 1991. MI. A&M. as new/wrp. A16. $15.95

DONALDSON, D.J. *Blood on the Bayou.* 1991. St Martin. 1st ed. F/F. M1. $25.00

DONALDSON, Scott. *Fool for Love.* 1983. NY. Congdon Weed. 1st ed. F/F. Q1. $30.00

DONALDSON, Stephen R. *Illearth War.* 1977. HRW. 1st ed. NF/VG. N3. $25.00

DONER, Mary Frances. *Salvager.* 1958. MN. Ross Haines. 1st ed. G/poor dj. A16. $30.00

DONIACH, N.S. *Purim or the Feast of Esther: Hist Study.* 1933. JPS. xl. G+. S3. $21.00

DONLEAVY, J.P. *Fairy Tale of NY.* (1973). London. Eyre Methuen. 1st ed. F/F. B3. $75.00

DONLEAVY, J.P. *Ginger Man.* (1958). Paris. Olympia. 1/500 hc. Traveler Companion series. F/F. B3. $195.00

DONLEAVY, J.P. *Ginger Man.* 1956. London. Neville Spearman. 1st British/expurgated ed. NF/VG clip. scarce. L3. $200.00

DONLEAVY, J.P. *Hist of the Ginger Man.* 1994. Houghton Mifflin. ARC. F/wrp. B2. $45.00

DONLEY, Michael. *Atlas of CA.* 1979. Culver City. Pacific Book Center. folio. color maps. 175 p. NF/dj. O6. $65.00

DONLON & ROGERS. *Outpost of Freedom.* (1966). Avon S227. 1st pb ed. VG. A7. $15.00

DONNE, John. *Letters to Several Persons of Honour.* 1910. NY. reprint of 1651 ed. 1/600. sm 8vo. 317 p. gray cloth. G. T3. $17.00

DONNELL, Annie Hamilton. *Rebecca Mary.* 1905. Harper. 1st ed. 194 p. G+. S10. $25.00

DONNELLY, Ignatius. *Am People's Money.* 1895. Chicago. Laird Lee. 1st ed. NF. B2. $125.00

DONNELLY & GULLERS. *Crewel Needlepoint World.* 1973. np. ils/diagrams. cloth. G2. $15.00

DONNER, Florinda. *Shabono: Visit to Remote & Magical World...S Am Jungle.* 1982. Delacorte. 1st ed. author's 1st book. NF/NF. A14. $25.00

DONOSO, Jose. *Charleston & Other Stories.* (1977). Boston. Godine. AP/1st Am ed. NF/wrp. L3. $75.00

DONOVAN, C.F. *Our Faith & the Facts.* 1925. Chicago. Baine. ils. decor cloth. C5. $45.00

DONOVAN, David. *Once a Warrior King.* (1985). McGraw Hill. 1st ed. 323 p. NF/NF. A7. $25.00

DONOVAN, John. *You & Your Irish Wolfhound.* 1976. Fairfax. Denlinger. 1st ed. 4to. 96 p. O3. $45.00

DONOVAN, Robert J. *PT 109: John F Kennedy in WWII.* 1961. McGraw Hill. BC. G/dj. A16. $7.50

DONTAS, Domna. *Greece & the Great Powers 1863-75.* 1966. Thessaloniki. 8vo. 223 p. O2. $25.00

DOOLEY, Thomas A. *Before I Sleep.* (1961). PSG. 1st ed. NF/VG clip. A7. $25.00

DOOLITTLE, Hilda. *Heliodra.* 1924. Houghton Mifflin. 1st ed. VG. M18. $60.00

DOOLITTLE, Hilda. *Tribute to Freud.* 1956. Pantheon. 1st ed. G/dj. M18. $40.00

DOOLITTLE, Hilda. *Tribute to the Angels.* 1945. London. 1st ed. 12mo. 42 p. VG+/stiff ol wrp. A11. $85.00

DOOLITTLE, Jerome. *Bombing Officer.* 1982). Dutton. 1st ed. F/F. A7. $40.00

DORE, Gustave. *Purgatory & Paradise.* ca 1890. London. Cassell. VG. M18. $75.00

DOREY, Jacques. *Three & the Moon.* 1929. Knopf. 1st ed. ils Artzybasheff. 103 p. G+. P2. $30.00

DORMAN, J.F. *Robertson Family of Culpeper Co, VA.* 1964. Whittet Sheperson. 1/250. VG. B10. $50.00

DORMAN & MEYER. *Adventurers of Purse & Person, VA 1607-1624.* 1987. Order 1st Families VA. 3rd ed. 827 p. NF. B10. $85.00

DORN, Edward. *From Gloucester Out.* 1964. London. 1/300. VG+/sq 8vo ivory wrp. A11. $50.00

DORNBUSCH, C.E. *Charles King: Am Army Novelist...* 1963. Hope Farm. 1st ed. sgn. 24-p pamphlet. F. A18. $15.00

DORRANCE, Ward. *Where the Rivers Meet.* 1939. NY. 1st ed. inscr. VG/VG. A11. $70.00

DORRIS, Michael. *Morning Girl.* 1992. Hyperion. ARC. sgn. F/wrp. L3. $55.00

DORRIS, Michael. *Paper Trail.* (1994). NY. Harper Collins. AP. F/prt violet wrp. C4. $35.00

DORRIS, Michael. *Yel Raft in Bl Water.* 1987. NY. ARC. inscr. F/8vo wrp. A11. $55.00

DORRIS & ERDRICH. *Crown of Columbus.* (1991). Harper Collins. 1st ed. inscr both authors. F/F. L3. $75.00

DORRIS & ERDRICH. *Route 2.* 1991. Lord John. ltd ed. 1/275. sgns. F. L3. $100.00

DORRIS & ERDRICH. *Route 2.* 1991. Lord John. 1/26 lettered. sgns. full leather. F. L3. $350.00

DORSON, Richard M. *Am Begins: Early Am Writing.* (1950). Pantheon. 26 pls. 438 p. A17. $17.50

DOS PASSOS, John. *Head & Heart of Thomas Jefferson.* 1954. Garden City. 1st ed. F/NF clip. B4. $100.00

DOS PASSOS, John. *One Man's Initiation.* 1920. London. Allen Unwin. 1st ed/1st state. author's 1st book. F/F. Q1. $850.00

DOS PASSOS, John. *Pushcart at the Curb.* 1922. Doran. B2. $100.00

DOS PASSOS, John. *3 Soldiers.* 1921. Doran. 1st state/1st prt. NF. B2. $125.00

DOUCETTE, Earle. *Fisherman's Guide to ME.* (1950). NY. 1st ed. 308 p. cloth. VG. A17. $12.00

DOUGHTY, Charles M. *Arabisk Resa.* 1959. Stockholm. 1st Swedish ed. 352 p. NF. M7. $75.00

DOUGHTY, Charles M. *Travels in Arabia Deserta.* 1923. NY. Boni Liveright. 1st Am ed. 2 vols. orig blk cloth. NF/djs. H5. $600.00

DOUGHTY, Charles M. *Travels in Arabia Deserta.* 1926. Cape/Medici Soc. 4th ed (thin paper, 1-vol ed/2nd prt). G+. M7. $125.00

DOUGHTY, Charles M. *Travels in Arabia Deserta.* 1937. Random. 3rd Am ed. 2 vols. intro TE Lawrence. F/clear plastic. M7. $200.00

DOUGHTY, Charles M. *Travels in Arabia Deserta.* 1953. LEC. 4th Am ed. 1/1500. natural linen. NF. M7. $75.00

DOUGHTY, Charles M. *Wandering in Arabia.* 1926. Duckworth. abridged by Edward Garnett. olive cloth. VG. M7. $45.00

DOUGLAS, Byrd. *Science of Baseball.* 1922. Winston. 1st ed. G+/sans. P8. $25.00

DOUGLAS, Carole Nelson. *Irene at Large.* 1992. Tor. 1st ed. sgn. F/F.N3. $20.00

DOUGLAS, Carole Nelson. *Keepers of Edanvant.* 1987. Tor. 1st ed. inscr/sgn. F/F. F4. $22.00

DOUGLAS, Ellen. *Family's Affairs.* 1962. Houghton Mifflin. 1st ed. author's 1st novel. NF/NF. L3. $250.00

DOUGLAS, L.C. *Gr Light.* 1935. Boston. 1st ed. sgn. 326 p. VG+/dj. B18. $47.50

DOUGLAS, Marjory S. *Adventures in a Gr World: Story of David Fairchild...* 1973. Miami. 1/500. sm 4to. 61 p. F/NF. B26. $30.00

DOUGLAS, Norman. *Birds & Beasts of Greek Mythology.* 1927. np. 1/500. VG. A1. $100.00

DOUGLAS, Norman. *Late Harvest.* 1946. London. 1st ed. VG+/VG+. E3. $25.00

DOUGLAS, Norman. *London Street Games.* 1916. London. St Catherine. 1/500. sgn. VG. A1. $100.00

DOUGLAS, Norman. *Southwind.* 1922. London. 1/150. sgn bl paper ed. VG. A1. $175.00

DOUGLAS, William O. *Am Challenged.* 1960. Princeton. M11. $45.00

DOUGLAS, William O. *Right of the People.* 1958. Doubleday. M11. $50.00

DOUGLAS, William O. *W of the Indus.* 1958. Doubleday. M11. $35.00

DOUGLASS, Earl L. *Prohibition & Commonsense.* 1931. NY. Alcohol Information. 1st ed. 310 p. A7. $16.00

DOUGLASS, James W. *Resistance & Contemplation.* (1972). Doubleday. rem mk. clip dj. A7. $13.00

DOVE, Rita. *Through the Ivory Gate.* 1992. Pantheon/Random. 1st ed. author's 1st novel. F/F. A13. $30.00

DOW, C.M. *Anthology & Bibliography of Niagra Falls.* 1921. Albany. 1st ed (assumed). 8vo. 2 vols. F. A2. $75.00

DOW, Ethel C. *Diary of a Birthday Doll.* 1908. Barse Hopkins. ils FE Nosworthy/LC Smith. 88 p. gr cloth. VG/dj. A3. $55.00

DOW, Lorenzo. *Journey From Babylon to Jerusalem.* 1812. Lynchburg. Haas Lamb. 12mo. contemporary tan cloth. VG+. B14. $150.00

DOWD, J.P. *Custer Lives!* 1982. WA. 1st ed. 263 p. F. E5. $25.00

DOWDEY, Clifford. *Bugles Blow No More.* 1937. Little Brn. 1st ed. 493 p. G/fair. B10. $25.00

DOWDEY, Clifford. *Death of a Nation: Story of Lee & His Men at Gettysburg.* ca 1958. Knopf. xl. 1st ed. 383 p. VG/VG. B10. $35.00

DOWDEY, Clifford. *Land They Fought For.* 1955. Doubleday. VG/dj. A16. $30.00

DOWLING, Edith Bannister. *Patchwork of Poems About SC.* ca 1970. Peacock Pr. sgn. 47 p. VG/wrp. B10. $7.00

DOWNER. *1st Christmas: Advent Calendar to Treasure.* 1992. accordian-style book. 25 opening windows reveal scenes. ribbon ties. F. A3. $35.00

DOWNES, Donald. *Scarlet Thread.* 1953. British Book Centre. 1st ed. 207 p. G+/worn. M20. $10.00

DOWNEY, Fairfax. *Cavalry Mount.* 1946. Dodd Mead. 1st ed. ils Paul Brn. VG/G. O3. $58.00

DOWNEY, Fairfax. *Dog of War.* 1943. Dodd Mead. 1st ed. ils Paul Brn. VG/G. O3. $45.00

DOWNEY, Fairfax. *Free & Easy.* 1951. NY. Scribner. 1st ed. VG/G. O3. $25.00

DOWNEY, Fairfax. *Guns at Gettysburg.* 1958. McKay. 1st ed. G/dj. A16. $40.00

DOWNEY, Fairfax. *War Horse.* 1942. Dodd Mead. 2nd prt. ils Paul Brn. VG/fair. O3. $58.00

DOWNEY, Sheridan. *They Would Rule the Valley.* 1947. private prt. 1st ed. ils/notes/ charts. 276 p. NF. B19. $15.00

DOWNIE, Vale. *Robin the Bobbin.* 1915. Harper. 1st ed. ils D Fink. 97 p. VG. S10. $18.00

DOWNING, A.J. *Fruits & Fruit Trees of Am...* 1866. NY. Wiley. ils/index. 760 p. modern plain leather. H10. $75.00

DOWNING, A.J. *Fruits & Fruit Trees of Am...* 1870. NY. 2nd/revised corrected ed. 1098 p. VG. B28. $70.00

DOWNS, Harold. *Theatre & Stage.* 1934. London. Pitman. 1st ed. sq octavo. 2 vols. bl cloth. VG. H5. $200.00

DOYER, Lucie C. *Manual for Determination of Seed-Borne Diseases.* 1938. Wageningen, Netherlands. xl. 58 p. w/33 pls in fld. box. B26. $30.00

DOYLE, Arthur Conan. *Adventures of Sherlock Holmes.* 1892. London. George Newnes. 1st ed. VG+. M15. $950.00

DOYLE, Arthur Conan. *Adventures of Sherlock Holmes.* 1892. NY. Harper. 1st Am ed/2nd issue ('if he had' on line 4). 307 p. VG. M8. $300.00

DOYLE, Arthur Conan. *Boy's Sherlock Holmes.* 1936. NY. 8vo. 336 p. map ep. gr cloth. VG/VG. H3. $12.00

DOYLE, Arthur Conan. *Further Adventures of Sherlock Holmes.* nd. Little Bl Book. later issue. VG/brn wartime wrp. A11. $25.00

DOYLE, Arthur Conan. *Great Cases of Sherlock Holmes.* (1987). Franklin Lib. 1st ed. ils Michael Hook. full leather. F. B3. $45.00

DOYLE, Arthur Conan. *Hist of Spiritualism.* 1926. Doran. 1st ed. 2 vols. bl cloth. VG/dj. G1. $75.00

DOYLE, Arthur Conan. *Hist of Spiritualism.* 1975. Arno. 2 vols in 1. dj. N2. $15.00

DOYLE, Arthur Conan. *Hound of the Baskervilles.* 1902. London. Newnes. 1st ed. ils Sidney Paget. gilt scarlet cloth. NF. H5. $2,000.00

DOYLE, Arthur Conan. *Hound of the Baskervilles.* 1902. London. Newnes. 1st ed. NF/custom slipcase. Q1. $2,250.00

DOYLE, Arthur Conan. *Hound of the Baskervilles.* 1902. McClure Phillips. 2nd Am ed. 12mo. cloth. M1. $150.00

DOYLE, Arthur Conan. *Pheneas Speaks.* (1927). NY. 1st Am ed 199 p. G. B18. $32.50

DOYLE, Arthur Conan. *Refugees.* 1893. Harper. 1st ed. inscr/dtd. F/NF. Q1. $1,250.00

DOYLE, Arthur Conan. *Return of Sherlock Holmes.* 1905. London. Newnes. 1st ed. sm octavo. 15 pls. Sutcliffe bl crushed morocco. NF. H5. $1,350.00

DOYLE, Arthur Conan. *Return of Sherlock Holmes.* 1905. McClure Phillips. 1st Am ed (precedes Eng by 1 month). blk cloth. G. M18. $150.00

DOYLE, Arthur Conan. *Sherlock Holmes Problem Stories.* nd. Little Bl Book 1101. variant issue. F/gr-on-wht ils wrp. A11. $40.00

DOYLE, Arthur Conan. *Study in Scarlet.* 1993. London. Dr Watson Books. facsimile of 1888 Ward Lock ed. 1/500. F/dj/slipcase. M15. $165.00

DOYLE, Arthur Conan. *Uncle Bernac: Memory of the Empire.* 1897. Appleton. 1st ed. ils. gilt red bdg. loose hinge. E3. $25.00

DOYLE, Richard. *Foreign Tour of Messrs Brn, Jones & Robinson.* 1878. London. Bradbury Agnew. reprint of 1854 ed. quarto. aeg. polished calf. H5. $350.00

DOYLE, Roddy. *Paddy Clarke Ha Ha Ha.* (1994). Viking. 1st Am ed. sgn. F/1st issue dj. B4. $125.00

DOZOIS, Gardner. *Geodesic Dreams...* 1992. St Martin. 1st ed. F/F. N3. $15.00

DRABBLE, Margaret. *Radiant Way.* (1987). Weidenfeld Nicholson. 1st ed. F/F. B3. $25.00

DRABKIN, D.L. *Thudicum: Chemist of the Brain.* 1958. Phil. orig ed. 309 p. bl cloth. NF/partial dj. S9. $18.00

DRACHMAN, Bernard. *From the Heart of Israel: Jewish Tales & Types.* 1905. James Pott. ils Warshawsky. 294 p. reading copy. S3. $19.00

DRAEGER, Alain. *Magia Do Brasil.* 1977. Brazil. Primor. 4to. color pls. 196 p. G/G. B11. $15.00

DRAGO, F. *Cruise w/Death.* (1952). Rinehart. 1st ed. NF/VG. B4. $45.00

DRAGO, Harry Sinclair. *Following the Grass.* (1924). Macaulay. 1st ed. NF/dj. A18. $35.00

DRAGO, Harry Sinclair. *River of Gold.* 1945. Dodd Mead. 1st ed. VG/dj. B9. $40.00

DRAGO, Harry Sinclair. *Roads to Empire.* 1968. NY. 1st ed. inscr. F/F. A11. $60.00

DRAKE, Benjamin. *Life & Adventures of Blk Hawk...* 1812. Cincinnati. E Morgan. 7th ed. 288 p. emb blk cloth. VG+. B14. $75.00

DRAKE, David. *Dagger.* 1988. Ace 80609 1st ed. inscr/sgn. F/F. F4. $12.00

DRAKE, David. *Dragon Lord.* 1979. Putnam. 1st ed. F/NF. N3. $15.00

DRAKE, Lauren. *Getting the Most Out of Power Boat.* 1953. Norton. 1st ed. VG/dj. A16. $17.50

DRAKE, Leah Bodine. *Hornbook fo Witches.* 1950. Sauk City. Arkham House 1/553. F/NF. B2. $1,200.00

DRAKE & TODD. *Sketches of Civil & Military Services of Wm Henry Harrison.* 1840 Cincinnati. 1st ed. 168 p. G/wrp. D7. $100.00

DRANNAN, W.F. *Chief of Scouts As Pilot t Emigrants...* 1910. Chicago. Jackson. 407 p NF. H7. $30.00

DRAPER, Hal. *Marx-Engels Chronicle. c* 1985. NY. Schocken. VG. V4. $12.50

DRAPER, John William. *Hist of Intellectua Development in Europe.* 1864 (1863). London Bell Daldy. 2nd ed. author's copy/inscr. vols. NF. G1. $485.00

DRAPER, John William. *Thoughts o Future Civil Policy of Am.* 1865. NY. 1st ed 325 p. VG. B28. $35.00

DRAPER, Theodore. *Dominican Revolt* (1968). NY: Commentary. 2nd prt. wrp A7. $8.00

DRAPER, Theodore. *Isreal & World Politics Roots of 3rd Arab-Israeli War.* 1968. Viking 2nd prt. VG+/VG. S3. $17.00

DRAPER, Theodore. *Roots of Am Commu nism.* 1957. Viking. 1st ed. clip dj. A7. $18.00

DRAYTON, J. *View of SC As Respects He Natural & Civil Concerns.* 1802. Charleston 1st ed. 1/500. 8 maps/pls. orig brds/rst spine. VG. C6. $5,000.00

DRAYTON, Michael. *Endimion & Phoebe* 1925. Shakespeare Head. 1/100. sm 4to. 5 p. teg. half tan morocco. K1. $200.00

DREADSTONE, Carl; see Campbell, Ramsey

DREISER, Theodore. *Am Tragedy.* 1925 Boni Liveright. 1st ed. 1/795. 2 vols sgn. w/sgn pub card. F/worn slipcase B24. $1,250.00

DREISER, Theodore. *Bulwark.* 1946 Doubleday. 1st ed. 8vo. 337 p. worn torn. V3. $14.00

DREISER, Theodore. *Color of a Great City* 1923. NY. Boni Liveright. ils CB Falls NF/NF. B2. $150.00

DREISER, Theodore. *Epitaph.* 1929. Hero Pr. 1st ed. 1/1100. sgn. F/plain tissue box B2. $275.00

DREISER, Theodore. *Moods Cadenced & Declaimed.* 1926. NY. Boni Liveright. 1/550. gn. special bdg. F/NF slipcase. B2. $175.00

DREISEWERD, Edna. *Catcher Was a Lady.* 1978. Exposition. 1st ed. ils. F/VG+. $65.00

DRENNAN, Robert E. *Algonquin Wits.* 1968. Citadel. 1st ed. VG/dj. A16. $10.00

DRESSER, Norine. *Am Vampires: Fans, Victims, Practioners.* 1989. Norton. 1st ed. F/F. C2. $15.00

DRESSES, Elia. *Masque of Days.* 1901. London. Cassell. 1st ed. ils Walter Crane. VG. O1. $325.00

DRIGGS, Howard R. *Pony Express Goes Through.* 1940. NY. Stokes. 8th prt. map ep. 208 p. F/VG+. H7. $15.00

DRIGGS, Howard R. *Westward Am...* 1942. NY. 1st trade/Trails ed. 312 p. cloth. D3. $45.00

DRINAN, Robert E. *Honor the Promise: Am's Commitment to Israel.* 1977. Doubleday. 250 p. VG+/G+. S3. $18.00

DRINKER, Sophie Hutchinson. *Hannah Penn & the Proprietorship of PA.* 1958. Phil. Soc Colonial Dames. 1st ed. 8vo. 207 p. VG. V3. $28.00

DRINKWATER, John. *Am Vignettes 1860-65.* 1931. Boston. 1st ed. 1/385. sgn. 32 p. orig buckram/brds. VG. D3. $75.00

DRINKWATER, John. *Preludes.* 1922. London. 1st ed. sgn. A1. $30.00

DRINKWATER, John. *Robert Burns.* 1925. London. 1st ed. inscr/sgn. A1. $25.00

DRINKWATER, John. *Seeds of Time.* 1921. Sedgwick Jackson. 1st ed. brds/paper label. NF. V1. $40.00

DRINKWATER, John. *Tides.* 1917. London. Sedgwick Jackson. 1st ed. inscr. w/sgn letter. red brds. C4. $35.00

DRISCOLL, J.R. *Brighton Boys in the Radio Service.* 1918. Winston. 1st ed. G. M2. $10.00

DRISCOLL, J.R. *Brighton Boys w/the Engineers at Cantigny.* 1920. Winston. 1st ed. G+. M2. $10.00

DRISCOLL, John Paul. *John Frederick Kensett: An Am Master.* 1985-86. Worcester Art Mus. 48 color pls. 208 p. brds. D2. $45.00

DRISCOLL, John Paul. *John Frederick Kensett: Drawings.* 1978. PA State. pls/notex/bibliography. 91 p. wrp. D2. $20.00

DRIVER, Robert J. Jr. *Lexington & Rockbridge Co in the Civil War.* 1989. Howard. 1/1000. 177 p. VG/VG. B10. $18.00

DROMGOOLE, Will Allen. *Boy's Battle.* 1898. Estes Lauriat. 12mo. 91 p. yel/gr decor bl cloth. VG. S10. $25.00

DROST, Pieter N. *Human Rights As Legal Rights...* 1965. Leyden. Sijthoff. G/dj. M11. $50.00

DROWER, Margaret S. *Flinders Petrie: Life in Archaeology.* 1935. London. Gollancz. 1st ed. ils/maps/index. 500 p. dk bl bdg. F/F. M7. $45.00

DROWN, S. De Witt. *Drown's Record & Hist View of Peoria...* 1850. Peoria, IL. 1st ed. 12mo. 164 p. cloth. M1. $400.00

DRUMM, Chris. *Tom Disch Checklist.* 1983. Polk City. self pub. 1st ed. F. N3. $3.00

DRUMMOND, Henry. *Greatest Thing in the World.* 1960. London. Collins. full leather/wht ribbon marker. VG/box. A16. $20.00

DRUMMOND, Isabel. *Sex Paradox.* (1953). NY. Putnam. 1st ed. dj. A7. $12.00

DRUMMOND, James. *Inquiry Into Character & Authorship of 4th Gospel.* 1903. London. Williams Norgate. xl. 528 p. H10. $15.00

DRUMMOND, T.B. *Forms of Proceedings Before Sheriff Courts in Scotland.* 1826. Edinburgh. quarter calf/marbled brds. M11. $275.00

DRUMMOND, Walter; see Silverberg, Robert.

DRUMMOND, William. *Review of Governments of Sparta & Athens.* 1794. London. 8vo. 281 p. contemporary tree calf. O2. $85.00

DRUON, Maurice. *Film of Memory.* 1955. Scribner. 1st ed. trans Moura Budberg. VG+/VG+. A14. $25.00

DRURY, John. *Midwest Heritage.* (1948). NY. 1st ed. index. 176 p. F/dj. A17. $17.50

DRURY, Newton B. *One Hundred Yrs in Yosemite: Story of Great Park...* 1947. CA U. ils/notes/index. 226 p. NF. B19. $15.00

DRYFHOUT & FOX. *Augustus Saint-Gaudens: Portrait Reliefs...* 1969. NY. Grossman. photos/pls. cloth. dj. D2. $55.00

DU BOIS, D.G. *...And Bid Him Sing.* 1975. Palo Alto. Ramparts. stated 1st ed. 224 p. dj. A7. $18.00

DU BOIS, W.E.B. *Darkwater.* 1920. Harcourt Brace Howe. 1st ed. F. B14. $125.00

DU BOIS, W.E.B. *Dusk of Dawn.* 1940. Harcourt. 1st ed. NF/NF. B2. $125.00

DU BOIS, William P. *Forbidden Forest.* 1978. Harper Row. 1st ed. Newbery Medal. VG+/VG. P2. $25.00

DU BOIS, William P. *Forbidden Forest.* 1978. Harper Row. 1st ed. 4to. 56 p. NF/VG. T5. $55.00

DU BOIS, William P. *Otto at Sea.* 1936. Viking. 1st ed. 16mo. G. D1. $125.00

DU BOIS, William P. *Three Policemen.* 1938. Viking. 1st ed. 8vo. 92 p. gr cloth. VG/G. D1. $135.00

DU BOIS, William P. *Twenty-One Balloons.* 1947. Viking. 1st ed. 180 p. VG. P2. $15.00

DU BOULAY, Juliet. *Portrait of a Greek Mtn Village.* 1974. Oxford. 8vo. pls/tables. 296 p. dj. O2. $75.00

DU BREUIL, A. *Vineyard Culture Improved & Cheapened.* 1867. Cincinnati. 1st Am ed. ils. 337 p. orig cloth. G. B28. $100.00

DU MAURIER, Daphne. *Happy Christmas.* (ca 1943). London. Todd. 1st ed. VG. B4. $50.00

DU MAURIER, Daphne. *Parasites.* 1950. Doubleday. 1st Am ed. 305 p. VG+/dj. M20. $25.00

DU MAURIER, Daphne. *Young George Du Maurier: Selection of His Letters...* 1953. Doubleday. VG/dj. A16. $30.00

DU MAURIER & QUILLER-COUCH. *Castle Dor.* 1962. London. 1st Eng/true ed. VG/dj. scarce. C1. $12.50

DU RYER, Sieur. *Alcoran of Mahomet.* 1649. London. 1st Eng ed. 407 p. contemporary sheepskin/rebacked. G. B14. $400.00

DUANE, William. *Hand Book for Infantry.* 1814. Phil. self pub. 8th ed. octavo. 10 pls. 112 p. orig brds. VG. H5. $200.00

DUBERMAN, Martin. *In Wht Am.* (1965). NAL. pb issue. VG. A7. $10.00

DUBERMAN, Martin. *Visions of Kerouac: A Play.* 1977. Little Brn. 1st ed. F/NF. B2. $30.00

DUBIE, Norman. *Groom Falconer: Poems.* 1989. NY. 1st ed. F/F. V1. $10.00

DUBLEMAN, Richard. *Adventures of Hollie Hobbie.* 1980. Delacorte. 1st ed. 261 p. VG+/dj. M20. $20.00

DUBOFSKY & VAN TINE. *Labor Leaders in Am.* ca 1987. Chicago. IL U. pb. F. V4. $8.50

DUBUS, Andre. *Lieutenant.* 1967. Dial. 1st ed. author's 1st book. VG/VG. L3. $175.00

DUBUS, Andre. *Selected Stories.* (1988). Boston. Godine. 1st ed. F/F. B3. $20.00

DUBUS, Andre. *Selected Stories.* 1988. London. Picador. 1st ed. F/F. C4. $40.00

DUBUS, Andre. *Voices From the Moon.* 1984. Boston. 1st ed. inscr. F/F. A11. $40.00

DUCK & HARDING. *Am's Glorious Quilts.* 1987. np. cloth. G2. $40.00

DUDLEY, James. *Life of Edward Grubb, 1854-1939.* 1946. London. James Clarke. 1st ed. 12mo. 158 p. VG/dj. V3. $14.00

DUDLEY, Mary. *Life of...Including Account of Her Religious Engagements...* 1825. Phil. Kite. 8vo. 288 p. full leather. G. V3. $32.00

DUDMAN, Richard. *40 Days w/the Enemy.* (1971). Liveright. 1st ed. 182 p. F/VG. A7. $30.00

DUEST, Marianne. *Barbie in Television.* 1964. Random. 181 p. VG. M20. $15.00

DUFFUS, R.L. *Santa Fe Trail.* 1931. Longman Gr. 2nd prt. tall 8vo. 283 p. VG. H7. $30.00

DUFFUS, R.L. *Santa Fe Trail.* 1943. NY. Tudor. reprint of 1930 ed. 283 p. gilt pict cloth. VG. D3. $25.00

DUFFY, James. *Shipwreck & Empire...Portuguese Maritime Disasters...* 1955. Cambridge. Harvard. M/dj. O6. $45.00

DUGANNE, Augustine J.H. *Tenant-House; or, Embers From Poverty's Hearthstone.* 1857. DeWitt. NF. B2. $300.00

DUGMORE, A. Radclyffe. *Romance of the Newfoundland Caribou.* 1913. Phil. 1st ed. fld map. new ep. 191 p. cloth. A17. $75.00

DUGUID, Julian. *Gr Hell: Adventures in Mysterious Jungles of E Bolivia.* 1931. NY. Century. 1st ed. 8vo. 339 p. gr cloth. VG. B11. $45.00

DUHEME, Jacqueline. *Birthdays.* 1966. Determined Products. 1st ed. 19 p. VG/VG. A3. $30.00

DUKE, Basil Wilson. *Hist of Morgan's Cavalry.* 1867. Cincinnati. Miami. 1st ed. 578 p. NF. M8. $350.00

DUKER & GOTTSCHALK. *Jews in the Post-War World.* 1945. Dryden Pr. 224 p. VG/G-. S3. $18.00

DULAC, Edmund. *Marriage of Cupid & Psyche.* (1951). Heritage. rto. 64 p. red cloth. VG+. A3. $20.00

DULAC, Edmund. *Sinbad der Seefahrer.* nd. Potsdam. Muller. 1st German ed. 14 color pls. 135 p. VG. D1. $175.00

DULBRETH. *Manual of Materia Medica & Pharmacology.* ca 1906. Phil. 8vo. ils. 976 p. gr cloth. worn. T3. $38.00

DUMAS, Alexandre. *Adventures in Algeria/Adventures in Spain.* 1959. Phil. 1st Am ed. 2 vols. F/VG. H3. $40.00

DUMAS, Alexandre. *Fernande.* (1988). Robert Hale. 1st ed. trans A Craig Bell. F/F. B3. $15.00

DUMAS, Alexandre. *Lady w/the Camellias.* 1889. Phil. Gebbie. ils Albert Lynch. leather. teg. VG. A16. $50.00

DUMAS, Alexandre. *3 Musketeers.* 1952. London. Collins. full leather. VG/fair box. A16. $20.00

DUMAS, Claudine; see Malzberg, Barry.

DUMITRIU, Petru. *Westward Lies Heaven.* 1966. London. Collins. 1st ed. trans Peter Wiles. NF/NF clip. A14. $25.00

DUMKE, Glenn S. *Boom of the 80s in S CA.* 1966 (1944). Huntington Lib. ils/index. 313 p. NF/dj. B19. $15.00

DUMLAO. *Expectant Mother's Wardrobe Planner.* 1986. np. ils. wrp. G2. $11.00

DUMONT, Jean-Paul. *Under the Rainbow.* 1976. Austin, TX. 1st ed. 178 p. dj. F3. $20.00

DUNAWAY, Wayland Fuller. *Reminiscences of a Rebel.* 1913. NY. Neale Pub. 1st ed. 133 p. NF. M8. $275.00

DUNBAR, Paul Laurence. *Folks From Dixie.* 1898. Dodd Mead. 1st ed. ils EW Kemble. NF. Q1. $400.00

DUNBAR, Paul Lawrence. *Joggin' Erling.* 1905. Dodd Mead. 1st ed. ils Leigh Richmond Miner. 119 p. calico cloth. B11. $150.00

DUNBAR, Paul Lawrence. *Lyrics of the Hearthside.* 1898. Dodd Mead. 1st ed. NF. B4. $350.00

DUNBAR, Paul Lawrence. *Majors & Minors.* (1895). Toledo. Hadley. 1st ed. author's rare 2nd book. 1/1000. VG. B4. $2,000.00

DUNBAR, Seymour. *Hist of Travel in Am.* 1937. Tudor. 12 color pls/2 maps. cloth. VG. D3. $45.00

DUNCAN, David. *I Protest!* (1968). Signet. 1st ed. NF/orig stiff wrp. A7. $30.00

DUNCAN, David. *Picasso's Picassos.* nd. NY. 1st ed. VG/G+. A1. $50.00

DUNCAN, David. *Silent Studio.* (1976). Norton. 1st ed. NF/clip. A7. $23.00

DUNCAN, David. *War Without Heroes.* (1970). Harper Row. 1st ed. NF/dj. A7. $200.00

DUNCAN, Dayton. *Our W: Am Journey.* 1987. Viking. 1st ed. 434 p. map ep. M/dj. T8. $17.50

DUNCAN, Donald. *New Legions.* (1967). Random. 1st ed. dj. A7. $30.00

DUNCAN, Frederic Chandler. *Sea Alphabet.* 1991. Marquette, MI. Avery Color Studios. as new/wrp. A16. $6.95

DUNCAN, Isadora. *My Life.* 1927. Bon Liveright. 1st trade ed. 359 p. B14. $75.00

DUNCAN, John M. *Manual of Summary Procedure...* 1858. Edinburgh. Bell Bradfute. marbled brds/rebacked. M11. $175.00

DUNCAN, Kunigunde. *Half a Million Wild Horses.* (1969). Boston. Branden. 1st ed(?). 8vo. 204 p. F/VG+. A2. $15.00

DUNCAN, Norman. *Australian Byways Narrative of Sentimental Traveler.* (1915). NY. Harper. 1st ed. 8vo. 293 p. F. A2. $25.00

DUNCAN, Peter; see Blassingame, Lurton.

DUNCAN, Robert. *Ground Work: Before the War.* 1984. New Directions. 1/150. sgn. F/slipcase. C4. $75.00

DUNCAN, Robert. *Letters.* 1958. Highlands, NC. Jonathan Williams. 1st ed. 1/60 sgn. ils. NF. B24. $425.00

DUNCAN, Shirley. *2 Wheels to Adventure Through Australia by Bicycle.* (1957). London. Harrap. 1st ed. 8vo. 222 p. VG. A2. $15.00

DUNCAN, T. Bentley. *Atlantic Islands Madeira, Azores & Cape Verdes...* 1972. Chicago. 9 maps/34 tables. M/dj. O6. $25.00

DUNCAN, William. *Commentaries of Caesar, Trans Into Eng...* 1753. London. Tonson Draper. folio. rebound full calf/morocco label. R3. $1,500.00

DUNGLISON, Robley. *Dictionary of Medical Science...* 1866. Phil. 1047 p. full leather. fair. B18. $45.00

DUNGLISON, Robley. *Hist of Medicine From Earliest Ages...* 1872. Phil. 286 p. new cloth. G7. $135.00

DUNHAM, Katherine. *Journey to Accompong.* (1946). NY. Holt. 1st ed. 8vo. 162 p. VG+/VG. A2. $30.00

DUNHAM, Sam. *Goldsmith of Nome.* 1901. WA. 1st ed. VG. B5. $35.00

DUNLAP, Susan. *Bohemian Connection.* 1985. St Martin. 1st ed. sgn. F/F. S5. $40.00

DUNLOP, Richard. *Great Trails of the W.* (1971). Abingdon. 1st ed. ils/photos/maps. F/F clip. A18. $50.00

DUNN, Eliza. *Rugs in Their Native Land.* 1910. NY. 1st ed. ils. 155 p. G. B5. $45.00

DUNN, Emelene Abbey. *Mediterranean Picture Lands.* 1929. Rochester. 1st ed. xl. 8vo. 126 p. NF. H3. $20.00

DUNN, Mary Maples. *William Penn: Politics & Conscience.* 1967. Princeton. 1st ed. 8vo. 206 p. VG/dj. V3. $16.50

DUNNE, Gerald T. *Justice Joseph Story & the Rise of the Supreme Court.* 1970. Simon Schuster. M11. $35.00

DUNNE, John Gregory. *Quintana & Friends.* 1978. Dutton. ARC. RS. w/promo material. F/F. L3. $65.00

DUNNE, John Gregory. *Studio.* (1969). FSG. 1st ed. sgn. author's 2nd book. F/NF. L3. $100.00

DUNNE, John Gregory. *True Confessions.* (1977). Dutton. 1st ed. NF/NF. B3. $25.00

DUNNE, John Gregory. *Vegas: A Memoir of a Dark Season.* 1974. Random. ARC/1st ed. sgn. F/F. L3. $100.00

DUNNETT, Dorothy. *Niccolo Rising.* 1986. Knopf. 1st ed. F/dj. B4. $65.00

DUNNETT, Dorothy. *Spring of the Ram.* 1988. Knopf. 1st ed. rem mk. F/dj. B4. $55.00

DUNNING, John. *Booked To Die.* 1992. Scribner. 1st ed. F/F. M15. $150.00

DUNNING, John. *Tune in Yesterday.* (1976). Prentice Hall. 1st ed. thick 4to. 703 p. F/VG+. B20. $100.00

DUNNING, Mary Parker. *Mrs Marco Polo Remembers.* 1968. Boston. Houghton Mifflin. 1st prt. 8vo. 203 p. VG/dj. W1. $18.00

DUNPHY, Jack. *Friends & Vague Lovers.* 1952. NY. 1st ed. sgn. NF/NF clip. A11. $40.00

DUNRAVEN, Earl of. *Great Divide: Travels in Upper Yellowstone...1874.* 1876. London. 1st ed. xl. royal 8vo. 377 p. pict cloth. VG. D3. $100.00

DUNSANY, Lord. *Fourth Book of Jorkens.* 1948. Arkham. 1st ed. F/dj. M2. $100.00

DUNSANY, Lord. *Plays of Gods & Men.* 1917. London. 1st ed. A1. $50.00

DUNSANY, Lord. *Tales of War.* 1918. Dublin. 1st ed. VG. A1. $65.00

DUNSANY, Lord. *Tales of 3 Hemispheres.* 1920. 1st ed. A1. $50.00

DUNSANY, Lord. *Time & the Gods.* 1906. London. G. A1. $100.00

DUNSANY, Lord. *5 Plays.* 1914. London. 1st ed. G. A1. $60.00

DUNSHEE, Kenneth. *Village Blacksmith.* 1957. Watkins Glen. Century, 1st ed. ils. 48 p. wrp. O3. $25.00

DUPLAIX, Lily. *Pedro, Nina & Perrito.* 1939. Harper. 1st ed. ils/sgn Barbara Latham. VG. M5. $22.00

DURAND-FARDEL, Max. *Memoire sur Une Forme D'Encephalite Encore Peu Connue.* 1839. Paris. Fonderie de F Locquin. offprint. G7. $75.00

DURANT, Ghislani. *Horseback Riding.* 1878. Cassell Petter Galpin. O3. $45.00

DURANT, John. *Dodgers.* 1948. Hastings. 1st ed. ils/photos. G+. P8. $50.00

DURANT, John. *Story of Baseball.* 1947. Hastings. 1st ed. ils. G+/G. P8. $15.00

DURANT, M. *Who Named the Daisy? Who Named the Rose?* 1976. NY. 1st ed. ils. 214 p. F/dj. B26. $14.00

DURANT, W.S. *Bevis of Hampton.* 1935 (1923). London. ils Stephen Reid. VG. C1. $4.00

DURANT, Will. *Transition.* 1927. Simon Schuster. AP. 1/1000. inscr. F/NF. B2. $65.00

DURANT & DURANT. *Pictorial Hist of Am Circus.* (1957). Barnes, NY. 1st ed. 4to. 336 p. F/VG. A2. $30.00

DURANT & RICE. *Come Out Fighting.* 1946. NY. Essential Books. 245 p. gray cloth. F. B14. $60.00

DURANT. *Smocking Techniques, Projects & Designs.* 1979. np. ils. wrp. G2. $4.00

DURANTI, Francesca. *House on Moon Lake.* 1986. Random. 1st ed. trans Stephen Sartarelli. NF/NF Clip. A14. $20.00

DURAS, Marguerite. *Malady of Death.* 1986. Grove. 1st ed. trans Barbara Bray. NF/NF clip. A14. $20.00

DURAS, Marguerite. *Ravishing of Lol Stein.* 1966. Grove. 1st ed. F/F. B2. $25.00

DURAS, Marguerite. *Vice-Consul.* 1986. Pantheon/Random. 1st Am ed. trans Eileen Ellenbogen. F/F. A14. $20.00

DURBAN, Pam. *All Set About w/Fever Trees & Other Stories.* (1985). Boston. Godine. 1st ed. F/F. B3. $20.00

DURBIN, E.F.M. *Politics of Democratic Socialism.* ca 1954. London. Kegan Paul. VG/VG. V4. $20.00

DURBRIDGE, Francis. *Paul Temple & the Madison Case.* 1988. London. Hodder. 1st ed. F/F. S5. $22.50

DURDEN, Kent. *Fine & Peaceful Kingdom.* 1975. Simon Schuster. VG/dj. A16. $6.00

DURDEN-SMITH, Jo. *Who Killed George Jackson?* 1976. Knopf. 1st ed. 292 p. dj. A7. $30.00

DURHAM, Mary Edith. *Burden of the Balkans.* 1905. London. 8vo. 331 p. O2. $100.00

DURHAM, Victor. *Submarine Boys' Lightning Cruise.* 1910. Altemus. ne. VG. M2. $20.00

DURLING, Richard J. *Catalogue of 16th-Century Books in Nat Lib of Medicine.* 1967. Bethesda, MD. Nat Lib of Medicine. 4to. 698 p. gray cloth. G1. $100.00

DUROCHER & LINN. *Nice Guys Finish Last.* 1975. Simon Schuster. later prt. sgn Durocher. F/VG. P8. $135.00

DURRELL, Gerald. *Three Tickets to Adventure.* 1955. Viking. 1st ed. 203 p. dj. F3. $20.00

DURRELL, Lawrence. *Alexandria Quartet.* 1962. Dutton. 1st Am/trade ed. rm mk. NF/NF. L3. $175.00

DURRELL, Lawrence. *Blk Book.* 1960. Dutton. 1st Am ed. dj. A7. $35.00

DURRELL, Lawrence. *Clea: A Novel.* 1960. London. Faber. 1st ed. 4th Alexandria Quartet series. F/NF clip. Q1. $200.00

DURRELL, Lawrence. *Collected Poems.* 1960. Dutton. 1st ed. VG/VG. V1. $25.00

DURRELL, Lawrence. *Collected Poems.* 1960. London. Faber. 1st ed. F/F. B2. $50.00

DURRELL, Lawrence. *Monsieur.* 1975. NY. AP. w/sgn label. VG+/prt wrp. E3. $35.00

DURRELL, Lawrence. *Nunquam.* 1970. Dutton. 1st ed. F/F. B2. $35.00

DURRELL, Lawrence. *Sebastian; or, Ruling Passions.* (1983). London. Faber. 1st ed. F/NF clip. B3. $30.00

DURRELL, Lawrence. *Tunc.* (1968). London. Faber. 1st ed. VG/VG. B3. $60.00

DURSCHMIED, Erik. *Shooting Wars. My Life As a War Cameraman...* (1990). Pharos. 330 p. F/F. A7. $15.00

DURSO, Joseph. *Casey (Stengel).* (1967). NJ. photos. 211 p. F/dj. A17. $14.50

DURSO, Joseph. *Yankee Stadium: 50 Yrs of Drama.* 1972. Houghton Mifflin. 1st ed. F/VG+. P8. $50.00

DURST, Paul. *Florentine Table.* 1980. Scribner. 1st ed. F/F. N3. $20.00

DUSSAUD, Rene. *L'Art Phenicien du II Millenaire.* 1949. Paris. Lib Orientaliste Paul Geuthner. ils. 121 p. VG. N2. $30.00

DUTT, R. Palme. *Turning Point for the World.* 1941. NY. Workers Lib. 30 p. wrp. A7. $12.00

DUTTON, Clarence E. *Tertiary Hist of the Grand Canon District.* 1882. WA. 1st ed. 2 vols. lg folio & quarto. 42 pls/22 maps. VG. H5. $5,000.00

DUTTON, Meirik K. *Hist Sketch of Bookbinding As an Art.* 1926. Norwood, MA. Holliston Mills. 144 p. cloth. F. B14. $35.00

DUVAL, Elizabeth W. *TE Lawrence: A Bibliography.* 1972. Haskell House. 1st thus ed. 95 p. G. M7. $65.00

DUVAL, M. Jules. *Gheel ou une Colonie d'Alienes Vivant en Famille Liberte...* 1860. Paris. Guillaumin. 12mo. 214 p. leather/marbled brds. G1. $275.00

DUVOISIN, Roger. *Donkey-Donkey.* 1940. Grosset Dunlap. juvenile. VG/G. P2. $15.00

DUVOISIN, Roger. *Lonely Veronica.* 1963. Knopf. NF/VG+. P2. $20.00

DUYCKINCK, Evert A. *Hist of World From Earliest Period to Present Time.* ca 1862. NY. Johnson Fry. 8vo. H9. $55.00

DUYCKINCK, Evert A. *Nat Portrait Gallery of Eminent Americans.* 1862. NY. Johnson Fry. 2 vols. lg 4to. 119 engraved portraits. disbound. H9. $275.00

DVORNIK, Francis. *Byzantine Missions Among the Slavs.* 1970. New Brunswick. 8vo. 484 p. cloth. O2. $40.00

DVORNIK, Francis. *Slavs in European Hist & Civilization.* 1962. Rutgers. VG/dj. A16. $20.00

DWIGHT, H.G. *Constantinople: Settings & Traits.* 1926. NY. 8vo. 581 p. cloth. O2. $65.00

DWIGHT, T.F. *VA Campaign of 1862 Under Pope.* 1895. Military Hist Soc MA. 1st ed. fld maps. 541 p. F. O7. $27.50

DWINELL, O.C. *Story of Our Money.* (1946). Boston. Meador. 1st ed. 12mo. 208 p. F/F. A2. $15.00

DWORKIN, Andrea. *Ice & Fire.* (1986). London. Secker Warburg. 1st ed. inscr/dtd 1987. F/NF. B3. $25.00

DWORKIN, Susan. *Maing Tootsie.* 1983. New Market Pr. ils. NF. C8. $20.00

DWYER, Deanna; see Koontz, Dean R.

DWYER, J.T. *Condemned to the Mines: Life of Eugene O'Connell...* (1976). Vantage. 1st ed. 8vo. 302 p. F/VG-. A2. $12.50

DWYER, K.R.; see Koontz, Dean R.

DWYER & DWYER. *Traditional Art of Africa, Oceania & the Americas.* 1973. San Francisco. Fine Arts Mus. ils. 160 p. VG/wrp. B19. $12.50

DYBEK, Stuart. *Coast of Chicago.* 1990. Knopf. 1st ed. sgn. F/F. B2. $35.00

DYE, Eva Emery. *Conquest: True Story of Lewis & Clark.* 1902. McClurg. 1st ed. F. T8. $25.00

DYE, Eva Emery. *McLoughlin & Old OR.* 1902. Chicago. 4th ed. 381 p. teg. cloth. VG. D3. $15.00

DYER, Frederick Henry. *Compendium of War of the Rebellion.* 1959. Yoseloff. 2nd ed. 3 vols. VG/slipcase. M8. $150.00

DYER, George R. *Report of the NY State Bridge & Tunnel Commission...* 1920. Albany. Lyon. quarto. 26 fld plans. NF. O6. $100.00

DYER, John Will. *Reminiscences; or, 4 Yrs in Confederate Army...1861-65.* 1898. Evansville, KY. Keller. 1st ed. pls. 323 p. cloth. VG. M8. $550.00

DYER, Raymond. *Her Father's Daughter: Work of Anna Freud.* 1983. NY. Aronson. 1st ed. 323 p. gray cloth. VG/dj. G1. $27.50

DYERS, Walter. *Ben the Battle Horse.* 1938. NY. Holt. later prt. VG/VG. O3. $20.00

DYKE, A.L. *Dyke's Automobile & Gasoline Engine Encyclopedia.* 1930. Chicago. 1233 p. G+. B18. $25.00

DYKEMAN, Wilma. *French Broad.* 1955. NY. 1st ed. sgn. VG/VG. B5. $60.00

DYKEMAN, Wilma. *French Broad.* 1955. Rinehart. 1st ed. Rivers of Am series. F/NF. B4. $50.00

DYKSTRA & NOVLE. *Nails.* 1987. Doubleday. 1st ed. F/F. P8. $50.00

DYLAN, Bob. *Tarantula.* (1971). Macmillan. 1st ed. 137 p. dj. A7. $20.00

DYMOND, Jonathan. *On the Applicability of Pacific Principles of New Testament.* 1832. Brooklyn. 1st Am (from 2nd London) ed. 8vo. M1. $175.00

DYMOND, Jonathan. *War: An Essay, w/Intro Words by John Bright.* nd. NY. Friends Book & Tract. 4th ed. 16mo. 88 p. VG. V3. $15.00

DYRENFORTH, James. *Adolf in Blunderland.* (1940). Toronto. McClelland Stewart. 64 p. VG. D1. $85.00

E

E., A.; see Russell, George.

EAMES, Hugh. *Sleuthes, Inc: Studies of Problem Solvers...* (1978). Lippincott. 1st ed. F/dj. B9. $10.00

EAMES, Jane Anthony. *Another Budget; or, Things Which I Saw in the E.* 1855. Boston. 2nd ed. 8vo. 481 p. emb cloth. O2. $65.00

EAMES & MORRIS. *Our Wild Orchids...Trails & Portraits.* 1929. Scribner. pls. 464 p. VG. B28. $80.00

EARLE, Alice Morse. *Home Life in Colonial Days.* 1967. Macmillan. 8vo. photos. 470 p. bl cloth. VG/VG. B11. $25.00

EARLE, Alice Morse. *Old-Time Gardens...* 1902. Macmillan. ils/index. 489 p. H10. $27.50

EARLE, Horatio Sawyer. *Autobiography of 'By Gum' Earle.* 1929. Lansing, MI. 1st ed. sgn. G+. N2. $22.50

EARLE, Pliny. *Memoirs...& Selections From His Professional Writing.* 1898. Boston. Damrell Upham. 1st trade ed. 409 p. olive cloth. F. G1. $100.00

EARLY, Jubal Anderson. *Lt Gen Jubal Anderson Early, CSA Autobiographical Sketch...* 1912. Lippincott. 1st ed. 496 p. orig cloth. VG/NF. M8. $350.00

EARNEY & PARSONS. *Land & Cattle.* 1978. Albuquerque. 1st ed. photo ep. brn cloth. M/M. P4. $25.00

EASTERN STAR. *Holiday Cookbook.* 1970. AL. sbdg. G. A16. $12.00

EASTLAKE, William. *Child's Garden of Verses for the Revolution.* (1970). Grove. 1st prt. VG+/clip. A7. $28.00

EASTLAKE, William. *Dancers in the Scalp House.* (1975). Viking. AP. NF. B3. $75.00

EASTLAKE, William. *Long Naked Descent Into Boston.* 1977. Viking. 1st ed. NF/VG. B3. $30.00

EASTLAKE, William. *Long Naked Descent Into Boston.* 1977. NY. 1st ed. sgn. F/F. A11. $40.00

EASTMAN, Charles A. *Old Indian Days.* 1910 (1907). Doubleday Page. reprint. inscr/dtd 1911. NF. L3. $275.00

EASTMAN, Donald C. *Rare & Endangered Plants of OR.* 1990. Wilsonville. ils/photos. 194 p. M. B26. $15.00

EASTMAN, Edson C. *Guide Book for E Coast of New Eng.* 1871. Eastman/Lee Shepard. 16mo. 220 p. gr cloth. missing 1 map. H9. $45.00

EASTMAN, John. *Who Lived Where: Biographical Guide to Homes & Mus.* 1987. Bonanza. reprint. 4to. dj. N2. $10.00

EASTMAN, Max. *Artists in Uniform: Study of Literature & Bureaucratism.* 1934. Knopf. 1st ed. F/rpr dj. B2. $85.00

EASTMAN, Max. *Leon Trotsky: Portrait of a Youth.* 1925. Greenberg. 1st ed. NF. B2. $40.00

EASTMAN, Seth. *Seth Eastman Sketchbook, 1848-49.* ca 1961. Austin, TX. intro Lewis Burkhalter. 68 p. cloth. dj. H9. $40.00

EASTON, Robert. *Max Brand's Best Stories.* (1967). Dodd Mead. NF/dj. B9. $20.00

EASTON, Robert. *Max Brand: Big Westerner.* 1970. OK U. F/F. B9. $25.00

EATON, Charlotte. *Stevenson at Manasquan.* 1921. Chicago. Bookfellows. 1/300. G+. A1. $25.00

EATON. *Handicrafts of New Eng.* 1949. np. 1st ed. ils. cloth. G2. $25.00

EBAN, Abba. *Heritage: Civilization & the Jews.* 1984. Summit. ils. 354 p. VG+/VG. S3. $21.00

EBERHART, Richard. *Collected Poems 1930-60.* 1960. NY. 1st ed. presentation inscr. NF/VG. A11. $55.00

EBERHART, Richard. *Collected Poems.* 1961. Oxford. 1st ed. F/VG+. V1. $20.00

EBERHART, Richard. *Collected Verse & Plays.* 1962. Chapel Hill. 1st ed. sgn. NF/NF. Q1. $45.00

EBERHART, Richard. *Shifts of Being: Poems.* 1968. Oxford. 1st ed. sgn. F/NF. Q1. $35.00

EBERSOLE, Barbara. *Fletcher Martin.* 1954. Gainesville, FL. 1st ed. 4to. 51 p. F/NF. B20. $60.00

EBNER, Eliezer. *Elementary Education in Ancient Israel...Tannaitic Perios...* 1956. Bloch. 128 p. VG/VG. S3. $24.00

EBON, Martin. *Communicating w/the Dead.* (1968). NY. NAL. 1st ed. 8vo. 211 p. VG+/F. A2. $12.50

EBURNE, Richard. *Plain Pathway to Plantations.* ca 1962. Cornell. 154 p. F/VG-. B10. $18.00

EBY & FLEMING. *Blood Runs Cold.* 1946. Dutton. 1st ed. F/dj. B4. $30.00

ECCLES, Marjorie. *Company She Kept.* 1993. London. Harper Collins. 1st ed. F/F. S5. $25.00

ECHENRODE, H.H. *List of the Colonial Soldiers of VA.* 1984. Genealogical Pub. reprint of 1913 report. 91 p. VG. B10. $10.00

ECHOLS, Samuel Anthony. *Proceedings of the State Agricultural Soc...1868.* 1869. Atlanta. Economical Job Prt Office. 1st ed. 70 p. VG. M8. $350.00

ECHOLS. *50 Country Quilting Projects.* 1991. np. cloth. G2. $24.00

ECKARDT, Theodore. *Atlas D'Histore Naturelle. Le Corps Humain...* ca 1875. Paris. folio. 24 colored fld pls. G7. $250.00

ECKBO, Garrett. *Home Landscape.* 1978 (1956). NY. revised ed. 340 p. F/dj. B26. $25.00

ECKENER, Hugo. *Graf Zeppelins Ferrnfahrten.* ca 1910. Stuttgart. German text. 32 p. G/pict wrp. B18. $95.00

ECKERT, A.W. *Time of Terror.* (1965). Boston. Little Brn. 1st ed. 8vo. 341 p. F/F. A2. $17.50

ECKERT & SHAW. *Beekeeping.* 1976. Macmillan. ils/index. 536 p. H10. $15.00

ECKHARD, C. *Experimentalphysiologie des Nervensystems.* 1867. Giessen. Roth. xl of John F Fulton. 305 p. G7. $750.00

ECKSTEIN, Gustav. *Pet Shop.* 1944. Harper. sgn. 196 p. VG+/dj. M20. $25.00

ECO, Umberto. *Foucault's Pendulum.* 1989. London. Secker Warburg. 1st ed. F/F. M15. $45.00

ECO, Umberto. *Name of the Rose.* 1983. Harcourt. 1st ed. F/F. B2. $75.00

ECO, Umberto. *Name of the Rose.* 1983. Wolff/HBJ. 1st ed. trans Wm Weaver. VG+/NF clip. A14. $40.00

ECO, Umberto. *Postscript to the Name of the Rose.* (1984). HBJ. 1st ed. F/F. A7. $18.00

ECO, Umberto. *Postscript to the Name of the Rose.* 1984. Harcourt. 1st ed. F/NF. B2. $25.00

ECO, Umberto. *Travels in Hyperreality.* 1986. HBJ. 1st ed. trans Wm Weaver. rem mk. F/F. A14. $25.00

EDDINGS, David. *Demon Lord of Karanda.* (1988). Del Rey. 1st ed. rem mk. NF/F. B3. $15.00

EDDINGS, David. *Ruby Knight.* 1990. Ballantine. 1st ed. 2nd in Elenium series. F/F. N3. $15.00

EDDINGTON, A.S. *Science & the Unseen World.* 1929. Macmillan. 4th prt. 16mo. 91 p. VG. V3. $12.50

EDDS, Margaret. *Claiming the Dream: Victorious Campaign of Douglas Wilder.* 1990. Algonquin. 1st ed. 273 p. F/F. B10. $15.00

EDDY, Paul. *Destination Disaster.* 1976. Quadrangle. G/dj. A16. $10.00

EDELSON, Julie. *No News Is Good.* 1986. N Point. F/F. A7. $35.00

EDELSTEIN, J.M. *Wallace Stevens: Descriptive Bibliography.* 1973. Pittsburgh. F. B2. $40.00

EDENS, Cooper. *Starcleaner Reunion.* 1979. Gr Tiger Pr. 1st ed. oblong 8vo. pict brds. T5. $35.00

EDGERTON, Clyde. *Floatplane Notebooks.* 1988. Algonquin. ARC. NF/wrp. A7. $40.00

EDGERTON, Clyde. *Walking Across Egypt.* (1988). London. Cape. ARC. NF/NF. B3. $45.00

EDGEWORTH, Maria. *Cherry-Orchard: Also, a Description of the Tiger.* 1820. New Haven. Babcock. 1st separate Am ed. 24mo. prt wrp. M1. $125.00

EDIB, Halide. *Turkish Ordeal.* 1928. NY. 1st ed. 8vo. 407 p. gilt cloth. O2. $85.00

EDIGER, Donald. *Well of Sacrifice.* 1971. Doubleday. 1st ed. 288 p. dj. F3. $25.00

EDINGER, Dora. *Pappenheim: Freud's Anna O.* 1968. Highland Park, IL. 102 p. F/prt wht wrp. G1. $40.00

EDMAN, Irwin. *Ecclesiastes.* 1946. Odyssey. 58 p. VG. S3. $21.00

EDMONDS, C.J. *Kurds, Turks & Arabs: Politics, Travel & Research...* 1957. London. 8vo. ils. 457 p. cloth. O2. $50.00

EDMONDS, Charles. *TE Lawrence.* 1935. London. Peter Davis. 1st ed. 192 p. G+. M7. $45.00

EDMONDS, Janet. *Death Has a Cold Nose.* 1993. London. Harper Collins. 1st ed. F/F. S5. $25.00

EDMONDS, S. Emma. *Nurse & Spy in the Union Army.* 1865. Hartford, CT. pub by subscription only. 1st ed. octavo. 384 p. NF. H5. $125.00

EDMONDS, Walter D. *Big Barn.* 1930. Little Brn. 1st ed. inscr. VG/VG. Q1. $150.00

EDOUARD, Joseph. *Dictionaire of Artists Contemporains.* 1930. Paris. hors commerce. 1/100. inscr/sgn. 3 vols w/supp. G+. A1. $200.00

EDSON, Gary. *Mexican Market Pottery.* 1979. Watson Guptill. 1st ed. 4to. 168 p. dj. F3. $35.00

EDSTROM, David. *Testament of Caliban.* 1937. Funk Wagnall. 1st ed. 8vo. 340 p. F/G. A2. $25.00

EDWARDES, Michael. *Battle of Plassey.* (1963). Macmillan. 1st Am ed. 8vo. 167 p. F/F. A2. $20.00

EDWARDES, Michael. *E-W Passage.* (1971). Taplinger. 1st Am ed. 8vo. 248 p. F/VG. A2. $12.50

EDWARDES, Michael. *Last Yrs of British India.* 1963. Cleveland/NY. World. 1st ed. 8vo. ils/3 maps. 248 p. VG. W1. $18.00

EDWARDS, Agnes. *Old Coast Road: From Boston to Plymouth.* 1920. Houghton Mifflin. 1st ed. 8vo. 203 p. VG/dj flaps. A2. $20.00

EDWARDS, Anne. *Haunted Summer.* (1972). CMG. 1st ed. F/NF. B4. $1,225.00

EDWARDS, Frank. *Flying Saucers — Serious Business.* 1966. NY. Lyle Stuart. 1st ed. F/F. T2. $8.00

EDWARDS, Gladys Brown. *Arabian War Horse to Show Horse.* 1973. Covina. 2nd prt. sgn. ES. VG/G. O3. $295.00

EDWARDS, Gladys Brown. *Know the Arabian Horse.* 1971. Omaha. Farnum. photos. 64 p. VG. O3. $15.00

EDWARDS, I.E.S. *Pyramids of Egypt.* 1972. NY. 8vo. 240 p. gilt brn cloth. F/VG. H3. $12.00

EDWARDS, Julie. *Mandy.* 1970. Harper. 1st ed. ils Judith Gwyn Brn. 188 p. VG-. T5. $20.00

EDWARDS, Lionel. *Getting To Know Your Pony.* (1948). London. 12 color pls. 74 p. G/torn dj. B18. $30.00

EDWARDS, Monica. *Badgers of Punchbowl Farm.* (1966). London. Michael Joseph. 1st ed. 8vo. 160 p. F/VG. A2. $12.50

EDWARDS, Samuel. *Barbary General: Life of Wm H Eaton.* 1968. Prentice Hall. 269 p. cloth. VG+/dj. M20. $15.00

EDWARDS-YEARWOOD, Grace. *In the Shadow of the Peacock.* (1988). McGraw Hill. 1st ed. NF/NF. A7. $10.00

EFROS, Israel I. *Ancient Jewish Philosophy.* 1964. Wayne State. 199 p. VG+/VG. S3. $25.00

EGAN, Constance. *Epaminondas & the Lettuces.* nd. London. Collins. 1st ed. AE Kennedy. VG/scarce clip. D1. $125.00

EGAN, Pierce. *Life of an Actor.* 1825. London. Arnold. 1st ed. octavo. 27 pls. 272 p. aeg. marbled ep. VG. H5. $1,100.00

EGAN, Pierce. *Namaqua: Story of Pioneer Days in CO.* 1825. Cedar Rapids. Torch Pr. 1st ed. 197 p. F/VG. H7. $75.00

EGERTON, Clyde. *Floatplane Notebooks.* 1988. Chapel Hill. ARC. NF/wrp. A7. $40.00

EGGAN, Fred. *Social Anthropology of N Am Tribes.* (1967). Chicago. enlarged ed. 574 p. A17. $12.50

EGGER, Carl. *Im Kaukasus. Bergbesteigungen und Reiseerlebnisse...1914.* 1915. Basel. 8vo. ils. 144 p. decor cloth. O2. $85.00

EGGLESTON, George Cary. *Am War Ballads, 1725-1865.* 1889. NY. 1st ed. 2 vols in 1. VG. B5. $60.00

EGGLESTON, George T. *Tahiti. Voyage Through Paradise.* 1953. NY. 1st ed. pls. 252 p. silvered bdg. F/VG. H3. $20.00

EGGLESTON, Margaret W. *Kathie's Diary.* 1926. Doran. 1st ed. 6 photos. VG+. S10. $25.00

EGLETON, Clive. *Missing From the Record.* 1988. St Martin. ARC of 1st Am ed. RS. F/F. S5. $25.00

EGLETON, Clive. *Winter Touch.* 1981. London. Hodder Stoughton. 1st ed. F/clip. M15. $40.00

EHRENPREIS, Marcus. *Soul of the E: Experiences & Reflections.* 1928. Viking. 1st ed. trans Alfhild Huebsch. ils Gunnar Lindvall. VG. V2. $9.00

EHRLICH, G. *Heart Mountain.* (1988). Viking. 1st ed. sgn. rem mk. F/F. A7. $13.00

EHRLICH, G. *Solace of Open Spaces.* 1985. Viking. 1st ed. author's 1st book of prose. rem mk. F/NF. L3. $50.00

EHRLICH, J.W. *Life in My Hands: An Autobiography.* 1965. Putnam. inscr presentation/dtd 1965. VG+/dj. M11. $35.00

EHRLICH, Max. *Reincarnation in Venice.* 1979. Simon Schuster. 1st ed. F/F. N3. $20.00

EICHENBERG, Fritz. *Art of the Prt.* 1976. Abrams. 4to. 6111 p. F/dj. F1. $60.00

EIDE, Henry Ingvard. *Am Odyssey: Journey of Lewis & Clark.* 1969. Rand McNally. 1st ed. lg 4to. 245 p. F/dj. T8. $45.00

EIDER, Shimon D. *Halachos of Shabbos.* 1974. self pub. 5th prt. Eng/Hebrew text. 200+ p. VG+. S3. $26.00

EIDLITZ, W. *Unknown India: Pilgrimage Into a Forgotten World.* 1952. NY. Roy. sm 8vo. 192 p. VG. W1. $25.00

EILOART, Mrs. *Boy w/an Idea.* 1888. NY. 12mo. pls. 295 p. gilt gr cloth. VG. H3. $15.00

EINSTEIN, Albert. *About Zionism, Speeches & Letters.* Feb 1931. NY. Macmillan. 1st ed. photos. 94 p. gr cloth. G. scarce. B14. $150.00

EINSTEIN, Albert. *Out of My Later Yrs.* 1940. Philisophical Lib. 1st ed. 276 p. bl cloth. VG/dj. M20. $20.00

EINSTEIN, Albert. *Relativity: Special & General Theory.* 1920. Holt. 1st Am ed. 168 p. blk cloth. VG. S9. $15.00

EINSTEIN, Charles. *Willie's Time.* 1979. Lippincott. 1st ed. F/VG. P8. $30.00

EINSTEIN & GROSSMAN. *Entwurf Einer Verallgemeinerten Relativitatstheorie...* 1913. Leipzig/Berlin. octavo. NF/prt wrp/cloth fld case. R3. $1,250.00

EINSTEIN & INFELD. *Evolution of Physics.* 1938. Simon Schuster. 3rd prt. 320 p. NF/G+. S9. $10.00

EISELEY, Loren. *Immense Journey.* (1957). NY. 9th prt. 210 p. dj. A17. $9.50

EISELEY, Loren. *Unexpected Universe.* 1969. Harcourt Brace. 1st ed. 8vo. NF/dj. B20. $35.00

EISEN, Arnold M. *Galut: Modern Jewish Reflection Homelessness & Homecoming.* 1986. IN U. 233 p. VG+/VG+. S3. $25.00

EISEN, Gustav. *Fig: Its Hist, Culture & Curing...* 1901. GPO. ils. 317 p. wrp. H10. $37.50

EISEN-BERGMAN, Arlene. *Women of Vietnam.* (1974). Peoples Pr. 1st ed. 223 p. orig wrp. A7. $25.00

EISENSCHIML & NEWMAN. *Civil War.* (1956). Grosset Dunlap. 2 vols. VG/box. B10. $35.00

EISENSTEIN, Phyllis. *Born to Exile.* 1978. Arkham. 1st ed. as new. M2. $25.00

EISLER, Benita. *Private Lives: Men & Women of the '50s.* 1986. NY. Watts. 1st ed. 8vo. 388 p. F/F. A2. $10.00

EISNER, Robert. *Travellers to an Antique Land. Hist & Literature...Greece.* 1991. Ann Arbor. 8vo. ils. 304 p. dj. O2. $35.00

EISNER, Simon; see Kornbluth, Cyril.

EISNER, Will. *Contract w/God.* 1978. Baronet. ltd ed. sgn. F. M18. $50.00

EISSLER, Kurt R. *Leonardo Da Vinci: Psychoanalytic Notes on the Enigma.* 1961. NY. IUP. xl. sgn. VG/worn. G1. $40.00

EITEL. *Creative Quiltmaking in the Mandala Tradition.* 1985. np. 18 full-size patterns. wrp. G2. $17.00

EKEROT, Johan Fredric. *Dissertatio Medica de Haemorrhagiis Parturientium.* 1813. Lundae. 24 p. sewn w/Waldenstrom dissertation. G7. $95.00

ELBERT, George A. *Indoor Light Gardening Book.* 1973. NY. ils/photos. F/dj. B25. $25.00

ELBOGEN, Ismar. *Hist of Jews After the Fall of the Jewish State.* 1926. Cincinnati. 237 p. VG. S3. $19.00

ELDER, William. *Biography of Elisha Kent Kane.* 1858. Phil. Childs Peterson. 416 p. deluxe bdg. NF. P4. $55.00

ELDERKIN, George W. *Comparative Study of Basque & Greek Vocabulaires.* 1958. Princeton. 117 p. wrp. N2. $32.50

ELDERKIN, George W. *Zagreus in Ancient Basque Religion.* 1952. Princeton. 26 p. wrp. N2. $22.50

ELEGANT, Robert. *Manchu.* 1980. McGraw. 1st ed. VG/VG. V2. $4.00

ELFONT & ELFONT. *Roar of Thunder Whisper of Wind...MI Waterfalls.* 1984. Lansing. ils/photos/maps. 127 p. F/dj. A17. $20.00

ELIADE, Mircea. *Autobiography. Vol 1.* ca 1918. Harper Row. 1st ed. 335 p. H10. $17.50

ELIAS, E.L. *Young Folk's Book of Polar Exploration.* 1929 (1928). Little Brn. ils/map ep. 278 p. VG/G-. S10. $20.00

ELIOT, Frances. *Diary of an Idle Woman in Spain.* 1884. London. FV Wht. 2 vols. VG. A16. $100.00

ELIOT, George. *Scenes of Clerical Life.* 1906. Macmillan. ils Hugh Thomson. VG+. E3. $50.00

ELIOT, George. *Silas Marner.* 1907. London. Macmillan. full leather. F. A16. $500.00

ELIOT, George. *Works of...* ca 1885. Edinburgh. Blackwood. Cabinet ed. 24 vols. 12mo. R3. $1,250.00

ELIOT, George. *Writings of George Eliot.* 1908. Boston. Houghton Mifflin. Lg Paper ed. 1/750. octavo. 25 vols. NF. H5. $3,750.00

ELIOT, Sonny. *Eliot's Ark.* 1972. Wayne State. 1st ed. ils Charles Herzog III. 217 p. VG/dj. A17. $15.00

ELIOT, T.S. *Collected Poems of TS Eliot 1909-35.* 1936. Harcourt Brace. later prt. F/dj. C4. $45.00

ELIOT, T.S. *Collected Poems 1909-35.* 1936. London. Faber. 1st ed. F/dj. C4. $100.00

ELIOT, T.S. *Confidential Clerk.* 1954. Harcourt Brace. F/dj. C4. $35.00

ELIOT, T.S. *Cultivation of Christmas Trees.* 1956. NY. 1st ed. F/NF orig envelope. V1. $35.00

ELIOT, T.S. *Dante.* (1929). London. Faber. early ltd ed. 1/125. sgn. cloth. VG. L3. $650.00

ELIOT, T.S. *Eeldrop & Appleplex.* 1992. Foundling Pr. 1/500. 1st separate appearance. F/gray wrp. Q1. $75.00

ELIOT, T.S. *Film of Murder in the Cathedral.* 1952. Harcourt. 1st Am ed. F/NF. B2. $50.00

ELIOT, T.S. *Marina.* 1930. London. Faber. 1/400. sgn/#d. Nf. B2. $350.00

ELIOT, T.S. *Old Possum's Book of Practical Cats.* 1939. Harcourt Brace. 1st ed. NF/NF. C4. $265.00

ELIOT, T.S. *Selected Essays 1917-32.* (1932). Harcourt Brace. 1st Am ed. NF/NF. B4. $185.00

ELIOT, T.S. *Selected Prose.* 1953. Penguin. PBO. 12mo. F/unread. A11. $30.00

ELIOT, T.S. *Sweeney Agonistes: Fragments of Aristophanic Melodrama.* (1932). London. Faber. 1st ed/1st bdg. F. B24. $350.00

ELIOT, T.S. *Use of Poetry & the Use of Criticism.* 1933. London. Faber. 1st ed. presentation/inscr. 156 p. gilt brick cloth. F/dj. H5. $900.00

ELIOT, T.S. *Waste Land.* 1922. NY. 1st ed/2nd issue. #841 of 1000. VG. A11. $1,250.00

ELIOT & SOULE. *Caterpillars & Their Moths.* 1902. NY. Century. 1st ed. 8vo. 302 p. VG. A2. $25.00

ELIOVSON, Sima. *Gardens of Roberto Burle Marx.* 1991. Portland. ils. 236 p. M/dj. B26. $45.00

ELKIN, Stanley. *Living End.* 1979. Dutton. 1st ed. NF/VG+ clip. N3. $10.00

ELKIN, Stanley. *Mirror, Mirror, on the Wall.* 1972. Random. 1st ed. F/NF. N3. $75.00

ELKINS, Aaron. *Icy Clutches.* 1990. Mysterious. 1st ed. F/F. T2. $19.00

ELKINS, Aaron. *Make No Bones.* 1991. Mysterious. 1st ed. sgn. F/F. T2. $25.00

ELLARD, Henry. *Baseball in Cincinnati.* 1908. Johnson Harding. 1st revised/expanded ed. VG. P8. $1,500.00

ELLENBERGER, Henri. *Discovery of the Unconscious: Hist & Evolution...Psychiatry.* 1970. Basic Books. 2nd prt. thick 8vo. 932 p. bl cloth. G1. $50.00

ELLERBE, Ronald William. *Ellerbe Family Hist.* 1986. Baltimore. Gateway. 1st ed. 565 p. cloth. NF. M8. $35.00

ELLERBE, Rose L. *Tales of CA Yesterdays.* 1916. LA. 1st ed. ils. 205 p. pict cloth. VG. D3. $15.00

ELLET, Mrs. *Queens of Am Soc.* 1868. NY. 12mo. ils. 464 p. brn cloth. G. T3. $19.00

ELLICOTT, Andrew. *Journal of Andrew Ellicott. Late Commissioner...* 1962. Chicago. Quadrangle. reprint of 1803 ed. 8vo. ils/pls. cloth. dj. H9. $45.00

ELLICOTT, Andrew. *Journal of...for Determing Boundary Between US...* 1803. Phil. 1st ed. 4to. 14 fld charts/maps. errata leaf. 299 p. VG. M1. $2,200.00

ELLIK & EVANS. *Universes of EE Smith.* 1966. Chicago. Advent. 1st ed. 1/1000. F/NF. N3. $40.00

ELLIN, Stanley. *Blessington Method & Other Strange Tales.* 1964. Random. 1st ed. F/F. F4. $40.00

ELLIN, Stanley. *Dreadful Summit.* 1948. NY. 1st ed. sgn. NF/VG+. A11. $150.00

ELLIOT, James L. *Red Stacks Over the Horizon.* 1967. MI. Wm B Eerdmans. sgn. VG/dj. A16. $40.00

ELLIOT, Robert Henry. *Sclero-Corneal Trephining in Operative Treatment Glaucoma.* 1913. NY. Hoegber. 1st Am ed. ils. new ep. G7. $95.00

ELLIOT & JONES. *Encyclopedia of Australian Plants...* 1983-90. Melbourne. 5 vols. ils/photos. M/dj. B26. $465.00

ELLIOT & WOLF. *Life & Habits of Wild Animals.* 1874. London. Macmillan. 1st ed. lg quarto. 20 pls. full bl morocco. NF. H5. $650.00

ELLIOTT, Brent. *Victorian Gardens.* 1986. Portland. Timber Pr. 1st ed. 4to. 285 p. F. H10. $43.00

ELLIOTT, C.G. *Practical Farm Drainage. Why, When & How To Tile Drain.* 1903. NY. Wiley. not 1st ed. 12mo. 92 p. N2. $15.00

ELLIOTT, Charles W. *Remarkable Characters & Places of the Holy Land...* 1867. Hartford. thick 8vo. 640 p. aeg. decor cloth. O2. $60.00

ELLIOTT, Charles. *Life of the Rev Robert R Roberts.* 1944. NY. possible 1st ed. 407 p. orig leather. G. D7. $60.00

ELLIOTT, Don; see Silverberg, Robert.

ELLIOTT, H. Chandler. *Reprieve From Paradise.* 1955. Gnome. 1st ed. F/dj. M2. $27.00

ELLIOTT, Jonathan. *Debates, Resolutions & Other Proceedings...* 1828. self pub. vol 2 only. 487 p. fair. B10. $100.00

ELLIOTT, L.E. *Chile Today & Tomorrow.* 1922. NY. Macmillan. 8vo. pls/fld map. 345 p. pict ep. pict bl cloth. VG. B11. $35.00

ELLIOTT, Maud Howe. *John Elliott: Story of an Artist.* 1930. Houghton Mifflin. ltd ed. 1/100. presentation/sgn. 265 p. cloth. D2. $95.00

ELLIS, Amanda M. *Stange Uncertain Yrs.* 1959. Hamden, CT. 1st ed. sgn. 423 p. cloth. VG. D4. $20.00

ELLIS, Charles Mayo. *Essay on Transcendentalism.* 1842. Boston. Crocker Ruggles. 1st ed. 12mo. 104 p. G. M1. $275.00

ELLIS, E. Earle. *Paul's Use of the Old Testament.* 1957. Eerdmans. 204 p. VG/G. S3. $25.00

ELLIS, Edward S. *Campfire & Wigwam.* (1885). Phil. Log Cabin series. 398 p. pict cloth. VG. D3. $25.00

ELLIS, Edward S. *Thrilling Adventures Among the Indians for Girls & Boys.* (1905). Phil. 8vo. ils/woodcuts/halftones. 240 p. decor gray cloth. H3. $35.00

ELLIS, G.E. *Puritan Age & Rule in the Colony of MA Bay 1629-85.* 1888. Boston. 1st ed. 2 maps. VG. B28. $35.00

ELLIS, Hamilton. *Pict Encyclopedia of Railways.* 1968. NY. Crown. thick 8vo. ils. 591 p. VG/VG. B11. $35.00

ELLIS, Henry. *Voyage to Hudson's Bay.* 1748. London. Whitridge. 1st ed. 8vo. pls/fld map. calf spine/rebound. H9. $750.00

ELLIS, John. *Safe Thoughts for Skittish Times.* 1927. Tokyo. Maruzen. 1st ed. inscr. 12mo. VG. W1. $16.00

ELLIS, John. *Short Hist of Guerilla Warfare.* 1976. St Martin. 1st ed. 220 p. F/NF clear plastic. M7. $35.00

ELLIS, Peter. *Bloodright.* 1979. Walker. 1st ed. VG. P3. $15.00

ELLIS, Peter. *Raven of Destiny.* 1984. Methuen. 1st ed. F/F. P3. $25.00

ELLIS, William T. *Billy Sunday: Man & His Message.* 1914. Winston. 1st ed. G+. P8. $65.00

ELLIS, William. *Authentic Narrative of Voyage Performed by Capt Cook...* 1782. London. Robinson Sewell Debrett. 2 vols. Zaehnsdorf bdg. NF. F1. $2,500.00

ELLIS & FORD. *Ils of Dissections in a Series of Orig Colored Pls.* Jan 1882. NY. Wood. 2nd ed/1st prt. 2 vols. VG. S9. $59.00

ELLISON, Harlan. *Beast That Shouted Love at the Heart of the World.* 1969. Avon. PBO. VG/wrp. L3. $30.00

ELLISON, Harlan. *Mefisto in Onyx.* 1993. Shingletown. Ziesing. 1st ed. sgn. F/F. M15. $30.00

ELLISON, Harlan. *Rockabilly.* 1961. Greenwich, CT. PBO. inscr. NF/wrp ils Mitch Hooks. A11. $145.00

ELLISON, Harlan. *Sleepless Nights in the Procrustean Bed.* 1984. San Bernardino. Borgo Pr. 1st ed. 1/26. sgn. edit/sgn M Clark. F/F. N3. $500.00

ELLISON, James Whitfield. *Summer After the War.* (1972). Dodd Mead. 1st ed. 216 p. F/NF. A7. $45.00

ELLISON, Virginia. *Pooh Cook Book.* 1969. Dutton. 1st ed. 120 p. VG+/VG. P2. $25.00

ELLISON & SHAPIRO. *Writer's Experience.* 1964. WA, DC. 1st ed. sgns. NF/8vo wrp. A11. $70.00

ELLROY, James. *Big Nowhere.* 1988. Mysterious. 1st ed. sgn. F/F. B2. $40.00

ELLROY, James. *Brn's Reguiem.* 1984. London. Allison Busby. 1st hc/1st UK ed. sgn. F/NF. B2. $50.00

ELLROY, James. *Brn's Requiem.* 1981. NY. PBO. inscr. author's 1st novel. NF/ils wrp. A11. $40.00

ELLROY, James. *Clandestine.* 1981. NY. Avon. 1st ed of PBO. NF/wrp. B2. $50.00

ELLROY, James. *Hollywood Nocturnes.* 1994. NY. Otto Penzler. AP. F/wrp. B2. $40.00

ELLROY, James. *LA Confidential.* 1990. Mysterious. 1st ed. sgn. F/NF. B2. $40.00

ELLROY, James. *Silent Terror.* (1987). NY. Blood & Guts. ltd ed. sgn. intro/sgn Kellerman. F/F. B3. $150.00

ELLROY, James. *Suicide Hill.* 1986. Mysterious. 1st ed. F/F. M15. $45.00

ELLROY, James. *Suicide Hill.* 1986. Mysterious. 1st ed. sgn. NF/F. B2. $60.00

ELLROY, James. *Wht Jazz.* 1992. Knopf. 1st ed. F/F. A7. $13.00

ELLROY, James. *Wht Jazz.* 1992. Knopf. 1st ed. sgn. F/F. B2. $40.00

ELMAN, Robert. *Atlantic Flyway.* (1972). NY. ils Osborne. 200 p. F/dj. A17. $35.00

ELMAN, Robert. *Hunter's Field Guide to Game Birds & Animals of N Am.* 1974. NY. ils/photos. 655 p. F/dj. A17. $14.50

ELROD, P.N. *I, Strahd.* 1993. Lake Geneva. TSR. 1st ed. Ravenloft series. F/F. N3. $20.00

ELSEN, Albert. *Paul Jenkins.* nd. NY. Abrams. inscr/sgn. VG+/VG+. A1. $100.00

ELSENSOHN, M. Alfrda. *Pioneer Days in ID County. Vol 1.* 1947. Caldwell, ID. Caxton. 1st ed. 527 p. map ep. G. H7. $20.00

ELSNA, Hebe. *Unwanted Wife: Defense of Mrs Charles Dickens.* 1963. London. Jarrolds. 1st ed. dj. VG. N2. $10.00

ELSON, Louis. *Curiosities of Music.* (1880). Boston. Oliver Ditson. reprint. 12mo. 363 p. VG+. A2. $25.00

ELSTON, Allan Vaughan. *Hit the Saddle.* 1948. Ward Locke. VG+/dj. B9. $10.00

ELUARD, Paul. *Pablo Picasso.* 1944. Paris. Trois Collines. VG/wrp. A1. $100.00

ELWIN. *Hexagon Magic: Using Versatile 6-Sided Shape...* 1985. np. ils. sbdg. G2. $20.00

ELWOOD, Roger. *And Walk Now Gently Through the Fire...* 1972. Chilton. 1st ed. F/F clip. N3. $10.00

ELWOOD, Roger. *Continuum 4.* 1975. Berkley. 1st ed. F/NF. N3. $15.00

ELWOOD & HEBLICH. *Charlottesville & the U of VA.* ca 1982. np. 191 p. VG/wrp. B10. $25.00

ELY, Edward. *Wanderings of Edward Ely.* 1954. NY. 1st ed. 217 p. NF/pict dj. D3. $20.00

ELY, Scott. *Starlight.* (1987). Weidenfeld Nicolson. 1st ed. F/F. A7. $30.00

ELY, Scott. *Starlight.* 1987. Weidenfeld Nicolson. 1st ed. 195 p. VG+/dj. M20. $15.00

ELY, Wilmer M. *Boy Chums in Mystery Land.* 1916. AL Burt. 1st ed. VG/dj. M2. $17.00

ELYTIS, Odysseas. *Ilios O Protos. Mazi me tis Parallages Pano se Mian Achtida.* 1943. Athens. 1/600. presentation. prt wrp/glassine dj. O2. $50.00

EMERSON, Earl W. *Fill the World w/Phantoms.* 1979. NY. PBO. inscr. VG. A11. $85.00

EMERSON, Earl W. *Poverty Bay.* 1985. Avon. PBO. F/wrp. M15. $25.00

EMERSON, George B. *Report on the Trees & Shrubs...Forests of MA.* 1846. Boston. 1st ed. presentation/sgn. 17 pls. VG. B28. $75.00

EMERSON, Jill; see Block, Lawrence.

EMERSON, Nathaniel. *Unwritten Literature of HI.* 1909. Bureau Am Ethnology. tall 8vo. 288 p. VG. E5. $45.00

EMERSON, Ralph Waldo. *Essays.* 1865. Tichnor Fields. 1st thus ed. bl brds. G. E3. $70.00

EMERSON, Ralph Waldo. *Essays.* 1906. Hammersmith. Doves. 1/25 on vellum. lg 8vo. 312 p. NF. K1. $3,500.00

EMERSON, Ralph Waldo. *Friendship.* 1939. Worcester. St Onge. miniature. 82 p. Sangorski bdg. clamshell case. H1. $675.00

EMERSON, Ralph Waldo. *Merlin Poems.* nd. Bullnettle Pr. 1/105. M. C1. $14.50

EMERSON, Ralph Waldo. *Nature.* 1836. Boston. 1st ed/1st state. 12mo. orig dk brn emb cloth. VG/case. H5. $2,500.00

EMERSON, Walter. *When N Winds Blow.* 1922. Lewiston, ME. 1st ed. 8vo. 229 p. gilt pict gr cloth. F. H3. $20.00

EMERY, Edwin. *Press & America.* (1962). Englewood Cliffs. 2nd ed. 801 p. NF. A17. $12.50

EMERY, Sarah Anna. *Reminiscences of a Nonagenarian.* 1879. Newburyport. Huse. 1st ed. ils/pls. 336 p. cloth. H10. $35.00

EMERY. *Treasury of Quilting Designs.* 1990. np. wrp. G2. $15.00

EMHARDT, William C. *E Church in the W World.* 1928. Milwaukee. 8vo. ils. 149 p. cloth. O2. $25.00

EMMONS, Della Gould. *Sacajawea of the Shoshones.* 1943. Binfords Mort. sm 8vo. 316 p. F/VG. T8. $15.00

EMMONS, Francis Whitefield. *Voice of One Crying in the Wilderness.* 1837. Noblesville, IN. Emmons. 1st ed. 18mo. 252 p. contemporary morocco. M1. $300.00

EMMONS, Nuel. *Manson in His Own Words.* (1986). Grove. 1st ed. 232 p. NF/NF. A7. $20.00

EMMOTT, Elizabeth Braithwaite. *Story of Quakerism.* 1908. London. Headley Bros. 12mo. 284 p. V3. $12.50

EMORY, William Helmsley. *Notes of Military Reconnaisance...* 1848. np. 8vo. 40 pls/fld map. emb gilt brn cloth. scarce. B28/H9. $600.00

ENCISO, Jorge. *Designs From Pre-Columbian Mexico.* (1971). Dover. 1st ed. 105 p. wrp. F3. $10.00

ENDE, Michael. *Mirror in the Mirror.* 1986. Viking/Penguin. 1st British ed. rem mk. NF/NF. A14. $25.00

ENDE, Michael. *Momo.* 1985. Doubleday. new Eng ed of orig 1974 trans. rem mk. F/F. A14. $25.00

ENDE, Michael. *Neverending Story.* 1983. Doubleday. 1st ed. trans from German by Ralph Manheim. 396 p. F/NF. T5. $65.00

ENDE, Michael. *Night of Wishes: Satanarcheolidealchellish Notion Potion.* 1992. FSG. 1st ed. trans from German. NF/NF clip. A14. $25.00

ENDELMAN, Todd M. *Jews of Georgian Eng 1714-1830: Tradition & Change...* 1979. JPS. 370 p. VG+/VG-. S3. $26.00

ENDO, Shusaku. *Golden Country.* 1989. London. Peter Owen. 1st ed. trans from Japanese. F/F. Q1. $25.00

ENDO, Shusaku. *Scandal.* 1986. London. Peter Owen. 1st ed. trans from Japanese. F/F. A14. $25.00

ENDO, Shusaku. *Stained Glass Elegies: Stories.* 1984. London. Peter Owen. 1st ed. trans from Japanese. F/NF. A14. $30.00

ENGBERG, Emmer. *Centennial Essays.* ca 1960. Rock Island, IL. Augustana. 268 p. H10. $17.50

ENGDAHL, Sylvia Louise. *Doors of the Universe.* 1981. Atheneum. 1st ed. 8vo. 262 p. F/NF. T5. $30.00

ENGEL, Heinrich. *Japanese House: Tradition for Contemporary Architecture.* 1980. Rutland, VT. Tuttle. 9th prt. 4to. 495 p. tan cloth. F/dj/slipcase. F1. $65.00

ENGEL, Lehman. *Am Musical Theater: A Consideration by Lehman Engel.* 1967. NY. CBS Legacy Books. sq 8vo. ils. VG/dj. N2. $15.00

ENGELMANN, Edward. *Berggasse 19: Sigmund Freud's Home & Offices, Vienna 1938.* 1976. Basic Books. 1st ed. 4to. 153 p. VG/worn. G1. $75.00

ENGELMANN, Larry. *Tears Before the Rain.* 1990. NY. Oxford. 1st ed. 375 p. as new/F. A7. $23.00

ENGELS & FREDERICK. *Landmarks of Scientific Socialism. Vol 1.* ca 1907. Chicago. CH Kerr. VG. V4. $10.00

ENGERMAN & FOGEL. *Time on the Cross.* (1974). Little Brn. stated 1st ed. 286 p. rem mk. dj. A7. $20.00

ENGLAND, George Allan. *Darkness & Dawn.* 1914. Sm Maynard. 1st ed. w/sgn typed letter. VG. B2. $350.00

ENGLE, Ed. *Seasonal: Life Outside.* (1989). Boulder. 1st ed. 173 p. F/dj. A17. $9.50

ENGLE, Paul. *Break the Heart's Anger.* 1936. Doubleday Doran. 1st ed. sgn. NF. E3. $15.00

ENGLE, Paul. *Corn.* 1939. NY. 1st ed. NF. V1. $20.00

ENGLEHARD, Jack. *Horsemen: Thoroughbred Racing World From Other Side of Rail.* 1974. Chicago. Regnery. VG/VG. O3. $25.00

ENGLISH, Charles; see Nuetzel, Charles.

ENGLISH, David. *Divided They Stand: Am Election 1968.* (1969). Prentice Hall. 428 p. torn dj. A7. $10.00

ENOCK, C.R. *Tropics: Their Resources, People & Future.* 1915. London. Grant Richards. 8vo. 64 pls/fld map. 466 p. gilt dk gr brds. G. B11. $65.00

ENRIGHT, Maginal Wright. *When Little Thoughts Go Rhyming.* 1939. Rand McNally. 61 p. VG. A3. $17.50

ENRIQUE ROIS, Eduardo. *Life of Fray Antonio Margil.* 1959. WA, DC. 1st ed. 4to. 159 p. F3. $20.00

ENTESSAR, Nader. *Kurdish Ethnonationalism.* 1992. Boulder. 8vo. 230 p. cloth. O2. $30.00

EPHRON, Nora. *Heartburn.* (1983). Knopf. 1st ed. VG/NF. B3. $20.00

EPLING, Carl. *Living Mosaic.* 1944. Berkeley. ils/photos. B26. $12.50

EPPLER. *Smoothstitch Americana Vest.* 1991. np. ils. wrp. G2. $8.00

EPSTEIN, Ben. *Yogi Berra: Muscle Man.* 1951. Barnes. 1st ed. VG. P8. $150.00

EPSTEIN, Isidor. *Sesponsa of Rabbi Solomon Ben Adreth of Barcelona...* 1968. KTAV. reprint. 2 vols in 1. VG+. S3. $28.00

EPSTEIN, Jason. *Great Conspiracy Trial.* (1970). Random. 1st ed. 8vo. 433 p. F/F. A2. $15.00

EPSTEIN, Morris. *Tales of Sendebar: Edition & Trans of Hebrew Version...* 1967. JPS. Eng/Hebrew text. 410 p. VG+/VG. S3. $27.00

EPSTEIN, Perle. *Pilgrimage: Adventures of a Wandering Jew.* 1979. Houghton Mifflin. 364 p. VG+/G+. S3. $18.00

ERDOES, Richard. *Rain Dance People: Pueblo Indians, Their Past & Present.* (1976). Knopf. 1st ed. 8vo. 280 p. F/VG. rem mk. A2. $12.50

ERDOES & ORTIZ. *Am Indian Myths & Legends.* 1984. NY. 1st ed. 527 p. cloth. VG/dj. B18. $15.00

ERDRICH, Louise. *Baptism of Desire.* 1989. Harper Row. 1st ed. sgn. F/F. B3. $50.00

ERDRICH, Louise. *Baptism of Desire.* 1989. Harper Row. 1st ed. F/F. C4. $30.00

ERDRICH, Louise. *Beet Queen.* 1986. NY. 1st ed. inscr. F/F. A11. $90.00

ERDRICH, Louise. *Beet Queen.* 1986. NY. Holt. ARC. sgn. F/wrp. L3. $100.00

ERDRICH, Louise. *Jacklight. Poems.* 1984. NY. 1st prt. author's 1st book poems. sgn. NF/ils wrp. A11. $125.00

ERDRICH, Louise. *Love Medicine.* 1984. HRW. AP. F/wrp. very very scarce. L3. $500.00

ERDRICH, Louise. *Snares.* 1987. Middlebury. Friends of the Lib. 1st ed. 1/350. L3. $200.00

ERDRICH, Louise. *Tracks.* 1988. NY. Holt. ARC. sgn. F/prt wrp. L3. $75.00

ERICKSEN, Ephraim E. *Psychological & Ethical Aspects of Mormon Group Life.* (1922). Chicago U. 1st ed. 101 p. VG/wrp. D3. $25.00

ERICKSON, Carolly. *Our Tempestuous Day: Hist of Regency Eng.* (1986). NY. Morrow. 1st ed. 8vo. 302 p. F/F. A2. $12.50

ERICKSON, Steve. *Arc d'X.* 1993. Poseidon. 1st ed. inscr. F/F. B2. $40.00

ERICKSON, Steve. *Days Between Stations.* 1985. Poseidon. 1st ed. sgn. rem mk. F/NF. B2. $65.00

ERICKSON, Steve. *Leap Yr.* 1989. Poseidon. 1st ed. inscr. NF/NF. L3. $85.00

ERICKSON, Steve. *Rubicon Beach.* 1986. Poseidon. 1st ed. inscr. author's 2nd book. F/NF. L3. $100.00

ERMELINO, Louisa. *Joey Dee Gets Wise.* (1991). St Martin. 1st ed. author's 1st book. F/F. B3. $15.00

ERMINE, Will. *Iron Bronc.* 1953. NY. Jefferson House. VG+/dj. B9. $15.00

ERNEST, Edward. *Animated Circus Book.* 1943. NY. oblong 8vo. 22 p. VG/G. H3. $45.00

ERNI, Hans. *Chevaux. Textes Choisis de L'Antiquite a Nos Jours.* (1966). Lausanne. 1/45 on Japon paper. w/extra suite sgn lithos. slipcase. K1. $2,500.00

ERNST, George G. *Williams College Class of 1915.* 1940. Williams College. 8vo. 125 p. VG. B11. $25.00

ERON, Leonard D. *Classification of Behavior Disorders.* 1966. Chicago. Aldine. 180 p. gray cloth. VG/dj. G1. $22.50

EROSA PENICHE, Jose. *Guide to Ruins of Chichen Itza.* 1951. Merida. 5th ed. 58 p. wrp. F3. $10.00

ERPENIUS. *Grammatica Arabica.* 1767. Leyden. thick 4to. 19th-century vellum. O2. $600.00

ERSHOFF, Peter. *Little Magic Horse.* 1942. Macmillan. 1st ed. 4to. ils. VG/tattered. T5. $25.00

ERSKINE, Gladys. *Broncho Charlie...Life Story of Broncho Charlie Miller...* (1934). NY. Crowell. 1st ed. sgn Miller. 8vo. 316 p. tan cloth. F. B20. $125.00

ERSKINE, John. *Private Life of Helen of Troy.* 1925. Bobbs Merrill. 1st ed. 304 p. cloth. VG+. B22. $10.00

ERSKINE, Laurie York. *Fine Fellows.* 1929. Appleton. 1st ed. 12mo. G. A8. $5.00

ERVINE, Saint-John. *Bernard Shaw: His Life, Work & Friends.* 1956. Morrow. 1st ed. 623 p. G+. M7. $16.50

ESAR, Evan. *Humor of Humor: Art & Techniques of Popular Comedy...* 1954. London. 1st ed. sm 8vo. gr cloth. G1. $17.50

ESAU, Katherine. *Plant Anatomy.* 1965 (1953). NY. 2nd ed. ils/photos/pls. 767 p. VG+/dj. B26. $47.50

ESCAMEZ, J. Munoz. *Fairy Stories From Spain.* nd. Dent. 8 color pls. VG. M5. $35.00

ESHBACH, Lloyd. *Of Worlds Beyond.* 1947. Fantasy. 1st ed. F/dj. M2. $85.00

ESHBACH, Lloyd. *Tyrant of Time.* 1955. Fantasy. ltd ed. 1/500. sgn/#d. F/dj. M2. $65.00

ESHBACH, Lloyd. *Tyrant of Time.* 1955. Fantasy. 1st ed. F/dj. M2. $15.00

ESHLEMAN, Clayton. *Antiphonal Swing.* 1989. NY. 1st ed. inscr. F/F. V1. $50.00

ESHLEMAN, Clayton. *Fractures.* 1983. Blk Sparrow. 1/200. sgn. F/NF. V1. $25.00

ESHLEMAN, Clayton. *Mexico N.* 1962. NY/San Francisco. 1st ed. author's 1st book. sgn. F/rice paper wrp. A11. $75.00

ESIN, Emel. *Turkish Miniature Painting.* 1960. Rutland. 4to. 34 p. F/rpr dj. O2. $50.00

ESKA, Karl. *Five Seasons.* 1954. Viking. 1st ed. NF/VG+. A14. $25.00

ESQUIVEL, Laura. *Like Water for Chocolate.* 1992. Doubleday. ARC. F/wrp. B2. $125.00

ESTES, Eleanor. *Hundred Dresses.* 1944. HBW. 1st ed. 8vo. 80 p. red cloth. G+. T5. $55.00

ESTES, Eleanor. *Lollipop Princess.* 1967. HBW. 1st ed. oblong 8vo. pict gr cloth. NF/VG. T5. $40.00

ESTES, Eleanor. *Middle Moffat.* 1942. Harcourt Brace. 1st ed. 317 p. bl cloth/pict label. T5. $75.00

ESTES, Jack. *Field of Innocence.* (1987). Portland. Breitenbush. 1st ed. F/F. A7. $25.00

ESTLEMAN, Loren D. *Bloody Season.* (1988). Bantam. 1st ed. F/F. A7. $15.00

ESTLEMAN, Loren D. *Downriver.* 1988. Houghton. 1st ed. F/F. F4. $17.00

ESTLEMAN, Loren D. *Kill Zone.* 1984. Mysterious. 1st ed. sgn. F/F. S5. $37.50

ESTLEMAN, Loren D. *Lady Yesterday.* (1987). Houghton Mifflin. AP. F/prt bl wrp. B3. $35.00

ESTLEMAN, Loren D. *Wister Trace.* 1987. Ottawa, IL. Jameson Books. 1st ed. F/F. M15. $35.00

ETHERTON, P.T. *Across the Great Deserts.* (1948). Whittlesey House. 1st ed. 8vo. 183 p. F/VG. A2. $20.00

ETS, Marie Hall. *Beasts & Nonsense.* 1968 (1952). Viking. reissue from new pls. NF/G. P2. $15.00

ETTMUELLER, Michael. *Opera Medica Theoretico-Practica...* 1708. Frankfurt. Zunneriana. 2 vols in 3. folio. contemporary vellum. G7. $425.00

ETULAIN, Richard W. *Writing W Hist: Essays on Major W Historians.* (1991). NM U. 1st sc ed. sgn. M. A18. $17.50

ETZKOWITZ & SCHAFLANDER. *Ghetto Crisis.* (1969). Little Brn. stated 1st ed. 212 p. NF/dj. A7. $17.00

EUDE, Emile. *Sur Quelques Pieces des Archives Portugaises Concernant...* 1926. Paris. presentation/inscr/sgn. 24 p. wrp. O6. $25.00

EULALIE. *Bumper Book. Harvest of Stories & Verses.* 1969. Platt Munk. ils Eulalie. 63 p. VG. A3. $22.50

EULALIE. *Mother Goose Nursery Rhymes.* 1953. Platt Munk. 40 p. VG. S10. $30.00

EULALIE & LENSKI. *Mother Goose Rhymes.* 1955. Platt Munk. 16th prt. 4 to. G+. S10. $30.00

EUPTON, Emory. *Infantry Tactics... Improved Fire-Arms.* 1877. NY. revised ed. 445 p. VG. D7. $50.00

EURIPIDES. *Plays.* 1931. Montgomeryshire. Greygnog Pr. 1/500. 2 vols. NF. F1. $500.00

EUWER, Anthony H. *Christopher Cricket on Cats.* 1909. NY. Little Book Concern. 2nd ed. 4to. VG. D1. $95.00

EVANOFF, Vlad. *Hunting Secrets of the Experts.* (1964). NY. 251 p. F/dj. A17. $12.50

EVANS, Arthur B. *Jean Cocteau & His Films of Orphic Identity.* 1977. Art Alliance Pr. ARC. RS. NF/dj. C8. $45.00

EVANS, Barbara. *Caduceus in Saigon: Medical Mission to Vietnam.* (1968). London. Hutchinson. NF/VG. A7. $40.00

EVANS, Bergen. *Psychiatry of Robert Burton.* 1944. NY. Columbia. thin 8vo. 129 p. cream linen. G1. $30.00

EVANS, Charles. *Am Bibliography, 1639-1729.* 1943. Boston. Goodspeed. special ed. 1/40. quarto. 446 p. teg. F/red slipcase. H5. $10,000.00

EVANS, E. Everett. *Alien Minds.* 1955. Fantasy. ltd ed. 1/300. sgn/#d. F/M. M2. $90.00

EVANS, E. Everett. *Man of Many Minds.* 1953. Fantasy. 1st ed. F/dj. M2. $32.00

EVANS, Edward. *British Polar Explorers.* 1946. London. Collins. 2nd prt. 48 p. VG/dj. P4. $30.00

EVANS, Evan. *Border Bandit.* 1926. Harper. 1st ed. VG+/dj. B9. $45.00

EVANS, Evan. *Rescue of Broken Arrow.* 1930. Harper. 1st ed. VG/dj. B9. $30.00

EVANS, Evan. *Smuggler's Trail.* 1934. Harper. 1st ed. VG/dj. B9. $30.00

EVANS, F. Gwynne. *Puffin.* 1929. Macmillan. 1st ed. ils George Morrow. 96 p. G. P2. $10.00

EVANS, Florence A. *Jewel Story Book.* 1903. Saalfield. 1st ed. ils WH Fry. gr cloth. VG. S10. $25.00

EVANS, G.R. *Anselm & a New Generation.* 1980. Oxford. Clarendon. index. 212 p. H10. $24.50

EVANS, George Ewart. *Pattern Under the Plough.* 1977. London. Faber. later prt. VG. O3. $10.00

EVANS, Geraldine. *Dead Before Morning.* 1993. London. Macmillan. 1st ed. F/F. S5. $25.00

EVANS, Herbert. *Vital Need of the Body for Certain Unsaturated Fatty Acids.* 1934. np. reprint/3 parts. G7. $75.00

EVANS, John Lewis. *Communist Internat.* 1973. Brooklyn. Pagent-Poseidon. 1st ed. VG/fair. V4. $10.00

EVANS, John. *Narrative of Proceedings... Against John Evans...* 1811. Phil. Thomas Dobson. 8vo. 238 p. leather detached/worn. V3. $35.00

EVANS, Justin. *Art of the Horse.* 1991. Tiburon. Wood River. 4to. 173 p. VG/VG. O3. $25.00

EVANS, Lawton. *With Whip & Spur: 12 Famous Rides in Am Hist.* 1928. Springfield. Milton Bradley. VG. O3. $15.00

EVANS, Mark. *Scott Joplin & the Ragtime Years.* (1976). Dodd Mead. 3rd prt. 120 p. clip dj. A7. $13.00

EVANS, Max. *Mtn of Gold.* 1965. Norman S Berg. 1st ed. inscr/sgn. VG+/clip. A18. $40.00

EVANS, Max. *Shadow of Thunder.* (1969). Swallow. 1st ed. F/F clip. A18. $30.00

EVANS, Max. *Super Bull & Other True Escapades.* (1986). NM U. 1st ed. photos. F/F. A18. $25.00

EVANS, Max. *SW Wind.* (1958). Naylor. 1st ed. ils Evans. F/clip. A18. $50.00

EVANS, Max. *1-Eyed Sky.* (1974). Nash. 1st separate ed. F/F. A18. $25.00

EVANS, Max. *1-Eyed Sky/Great Wedding/My Pardner: 3 Short Novels.* 1963. Houghton Mifflin. 1st ed. F/dj. A18. $35.00

EVANS, Richard I. *BF Skinner: The Man & His Ideas.* 1968. Dutton. 1st ed. 16mo. beige cloth. VG/dj. G1. $22.50

EVANS, Richard I. *Dialogue w/Erik Erikson.* 1967. NY. Harper Row. 1st ed. 142 p. beige cloth. VG/worn. G1. $21.50

EVANS, Rosalie. *Rosalie Evans Letters From Mexico.* 1926. Bobbs Merrill. ils. 472 p. gilt red cloth. F3. $20.00

EVANS, Sebastian. *High Hist of the Holy Grail.* 1969 (1898). np. hc. VG/VG-. C1. $14.50

EVANS, Warren. *VA: W Highlands.* ca 1983. Evans Guides. ils/maps. 204 p. VG. B10. $10.00

EVANS & LITTLE. *TX Longhorn Baseball.* 1983. Strode. 1st ed. F/VG+. P8. $35.00

EVANS. *Christmas Quilting: 20 Decorative Projects.* 1988. np. wrp. G2. $5.00

EVARTS, Sherman. *Arguments & Speeches of Wm Maxwell Evarts.* nd. np. 3 vols. xl. bl bdg. NF. O7. $18.50

EVATT, H.V. *Story of WA Holman & the Labour Movement.* ca 1942. Sydney. Angus Robertston. 2nd ed. VG/fair. V4. $7.50

EVELYN, John. *Memoirs...* 1818. London. 1st ed. quarto. 2 vols. 8 pls/fld table. brds. F/clamshell case. H5. $1,500.00

EVELYN, John. *Sylvia; or, Discourse of Forest-Trees & Propagation...* 1664. London. Martyn Allestry. quarto. calf. B14. $550.00

EVENSON, Betty. *50 Yrs at Bright Spot.* nd. (1990). Casper, WY. Mtn States Litho. 1st ed. 8vo. 257 p. F/F. A2. $12.50

EVERETT, Charles Carroll. *Fichte's Science of Knowledge: Critical Exposition.* 1884. Chicago. 1st ed. 12mo. 287 p. prt brn cloth. G. G1. $50.00

EVERETT, Edward. *Importance of Education & Useful Knowledge.* 1844. Boston. 12mo. 396 p. gilt brn cloth. T3. $25.00

EVERETT, Percival. *Cutting Lisa.* 1986. Tichnor Fields. 1st ed. F/NF. A7. $15.00

EVERETT, Percival. *Suder.* (1983). Viking. 1st ed. 171 p. NF/NF. A7. $25.00

EVERETT, Percival. *Walk Me to the Distance.* 1985. Ticknor Fields. 1st ed. as new/NF. A7. $25.00

EVERETT. *Complete Life of William McKinley.* ca 1901. np. memorial ed. royal 8vo. ils. 448 p. gilt gr cloth. G. T3. $14.00

EVERETT-GREEN, Evelyn. *Sir Aylmer's Heir.* 1890. London. Nelson. probable 1st ed. 215 p. VG. S10. $35.00

EVERS, Charles. *Evers.* (1971). World. 1st ed. 196 p. dj. A7. $22.00

EVERS & EVERS. *Chatter Duck.* 1943. Rand McNally. apparant 1st ed. VG/worn dj. M5. $12.00

EVERS & PETERS. *For Us, the Living.* (1967). Doubleday. 378 p. NF/dj. A7. $12.00

EVERSON, William. *Archetype W.* 1976. Berkeley. 1st ed. sgn. F/8vo wrp. A11. $45.00

EVERSON, William. *Archetype W: Pacific Coast As Literary Region.* 1976. Santa Barbara. Oyez. 1st ed. inscr/sgn. F/F clip. A18. $65.00

EVERSON, William. *In the Fictive Wish.* 1967. Santa Barbara. Oyez. ARC. 1/200. sgn. F/VG+. V1. $125.00

EVERSON, William. *In the Fictive Wish.* 1967. Santa Barbara. Oyez. 1st ed. 1/200. sgn. ils Mary Fabilli. F/F. B24. $150.00

EVERSON, William. *Masks of Drout.* 1980. Blk Sparrow. 1/250. sgn. F/F. V1. $60.00

EVERSON, William. *Residual Yrs.* (1948). New Directions. 1st ed. 1/1000. NF/dj. B24. $165.00

EVERSON, William. *Who Is She That Looketh Forth As the Morning?* 1972. Capricorn. 1st ed. 1/250. sgn twice. F. M18. $175.00

EVERSON, William. *Who Is She That Looketh Forth As the Morning?* 1972. Santa Barbara. trade issue. presentation inscr. NF/wrp. A11. $45.00

EVERTON, Francis. *Hammer of Doom.* 1929. Bobbs Merrill. 1st Am ed. VG/dj. M15. $35.00

EVERY, George. *Byzantine Patriarchte 451-1204.* 1947. London. 1st ed. 8vo. 212 p. cloth. O2. $30.00

EVTAN, Rachel. *Fifth Heaven.* 1985. NY. Jewish Pub Soc of Am. 1st ed. trans from Hebrew. F/F. A14. $25.00

EWART, Galvin. *Galvin Ewart Show: Selected Poems, 1939-85.* nd. Bits Pr. 1st ed. F/NF. V1. $10.00

EWART, John S. *Kingdom of Canada: Imperial Federation...* 1908. Tor. 1st ed. presentation sgn. 370 p. F. A17. $45.00

EWBANK, Thomas. *Descriptive & Hist Account of Hydraulics...* 1857. NY. Derby Jackson. ils. 608 p. cloth. NF. B14. $45.00

EWELL, Thomas. *Plain Discoveries on Laws of Properties of Matter...* 1806. NY. Brisban Brannan. 1st ed. 469 p. full leather. S9. $200.00

EWEN, Cecil Henry l'Estrange. *Witch Hunting & Witch Trials.* 1929. London. Kegan Paul. 345 p. 7 halftones/fld chart. gr cloth. VG. G1. $75.00

EWERS, John. *Horse in Blackfoot Indian Culture.* 1955. Smithsonian Bulletin 159. VG. O3. $40.00

EWING, Frederick R.; see Sturgeon, Theodore.

EWING, J.H. *Jackanapes & Other Tales.* 1929. London. ils HM Brock. 196 p. F/G wht pict dj. H3. $20.00

EWING, J.H. *Stories by...* 1920. Duffield. 1st ed. ils Edna Cooke. 426 p. VG. S10. $70.00

EWING, J.H. *Story of a Short Life.* 1896. Dutton. juvenile. VG. N2. $6.00

EWING, T. *Report of the Secretary of the Interior.* 1850. GPO. 8vo. 2 fld plans. new tan cloth. H9. $475.00

EWING. *Jingle Bells: Holiday Book w/Lights & Music.* 1990. musical popup. battery-op push-pull tab. F. A4. $40.00

EYMIN, Auguste. *Medecines et Philosophes...* 1903. Lyon. Storck. 260 p. prt wrp. G1. $45.00

EYRE, David. *Float.* (1990). Doubleday. 1st ed. F/NF. A7. $20.00

EYRE, Frank. *Eng Rivers & Canals.* 1947. London. 8vo. ils/pls. pict gray brds. F/VG. H3. $12.00

EZRAHI, Sidra De Koven. *By Words Along: Holocaust in Literature.* 1980. Chicago. 262 p. VG+/VG. S3. $24.00

F

FABBRI & NAMES. *Dear Pete.* 1985. Laranmark Pr. 1st ed. sgn Rose/Fabbri. F/VG+. '8. $100.00

FABER, H. *Forage Crops in Denmark.* 920. London. Longman Gr. 1st ed. 100). H10. $17.50

FABIAN, Stephen E. *Fabian in Color.* 1980. Starmont. 1st ed. 1/800. sgn/#d. portfolio v/8 color pls & booklet. F. F4. $45.00

FABRE, J.H. *Fabre's Book of Insects.* 1935. NY. Tudor. new ed. ils EJ Detmold. 271 p. ?/NF/box. B20. $90.00

FABRE, J.H. *Life of the Fly.* 1913. Dodd Mead. VG. N2. $10.00

FABRE, J.H. *Life of the Scorpion.* 1923. Dodd Mead. 1st Am thus ed. 12mo. 344 p. VG. A2. $20.00

FABRE, J.H. *Mason-Bees.* 1914. NY. Dodd Mead. 1st Am thus ed. 12mo. 315 p. VG. A2. $20.00

FABRE, Maurice. *Hist of Land Transportation.* nd. London. 3rd prt. VG/VG. O3. $30.00

FABRE, Michael. *Unfinished Quest of Richard Wright.* 1973. NY. Morrow. 1st Am ed. trans Isabel Barzun. NF/NF. A13. $25.00

FABREGA & SILVER. *Illness & Shamanistic Curing in Zinacantan.* 1973. Stanford. 1st ed. 285 p. dj. F3. $20.00

FADIMAN, Clifton. *Dionysus: Case of Vintage Tales About Wine.* (1962). McGraw Hill. 309 p. dj. A7. $18.00

FAERGEMAN, Poul M. *Freud i Moderne Litteratur.* 1933. Kobenhavn. Funkis Forlag. 88 p. prt gray wrp. G1. $37.50

FAERNO, Gabriello. *Emendationes, in Sex Fabulas Terentii.* 1565. Florence. Juntas. 8vo. 251 p. 18th-century calf. K1. $500.00

FAGAN, Myron C. *Document of Red Stars' Hollywood.* 1950. np. 1st ed. 4to. F. A8. $10.00

FAGIN, N. Bryllion. *Histrionic Mr Poe.* 1949. Baltimore. 1st ed. inscr. NF/VG. A11. $45.00

FAHERTY, Ruth. *Westies From Head to Tail.* 1981. Loveland. 1st ed. 219 p. cloth. A17. $17.50

FAHIE, J.J. *Hist of Wireless Telegraphy, 1838-99.* 1900. Dodd Mead. 2nd imp. 325 p. B14. $30.00

FAHRENHEIT, Daniel Gabriel. *Experimenta Circa Gradum Caloris...* 1724. London. Innys. 1st ed. quarto. fld engraved graph. disbound. clamshell case. H5. $3,500.00

FAIR, A.A.; see Gardner, Erle Stanley.

FAIRALL, A.R. *W Australian Native Plants in Cultivation.* 1970. Rushcutters Bay. color photos. 253 p. VG. B26. $45.00

FAIRBAIRN, A.M. *Studies in Religion & Theology.* 1910. Macmillan. index. 635 p. H10. $15.00

FAIRBAIRN, Ann. *Call Him George.* 1961 (1969). Crown. 303 p. dj. A7. $15.00

FAIRBAIRN, Roger; see Carr, John Dickson.

FAIRCHILD, Ashbel G. *Letters on Mode & Subjects of Christian Baptism.* 1833. Pittsburgh. 2nd ed. 96 p. cloth. VG. D7. $25.00

FAIRCHILD, David. *Garden Islands of the Great E...* 1944. Scribner. inscr. 239 p. H10. $30.00

FAIRCHILD, David. *World Grows Around My Door...* 1947. Scribner. 1st ed. presentation inscr. 347 p. H10. $45.00

FAIRCHILD, Joy Hamlet. *Essential Doctrines of the Gospel: A Sermon.* 1829. Boston. Peirce Williams. 40 p. sewn. H10. $12.50

FAIRLESS, Michael. *Stories Told to Children.* 1914. London. Duckworth. 1st ed w/Flora Wht ils. VG. M5. $45.00

FAIRLEY & MOORE. *Native Plants of the Sydney District.* 1989. Kenthurst, Australia. photos. 432 p. M/dj. B26. $65.00

FAKINOS, Aris. *Marked Men.* 1973. NY. Liveright. 1st ed. trans from French. NF/NF. A14. $25.00

FALATURI & SCHIMMEL. *We Believe in One God.* 1979. Seabury. 180 p. VG. C5. $8.50

FALCONER, Thomas. *On the Discovery of the MS & on the SW OR, & NW Boundary...* facsimile of 1844 ed. 8vo. 99 p. marbled brds. H9. $30.00

FALDBAKKEN, Knut. *Honeymoon.* 1987. NY. St Martin. 1st ed. trans from Norwegian. NF/NF clip. A14. $25.00

FALK, Lee; see Cooper, Basil; also Goulart, Ron.

FALKNER, David. *Short Season.* 1986. Times. 1st ed. F/F. P8. $20.00

FALKNER & OH. *Sadaharu Oh.* 1984. Times. 1st ed. F/F. P8. $30.00

FALL, Bernard B. *Hell in a Very Sm Place.* 1967. Lippincott. BC. dj. A7. $30.00

FALL, Bernard B. *Hell in a Very Sm Place.* 1967. Lippincott. 1st ed. NF/NF. L3. $125.00

FALL, Bernard B. *2 Vietnams: Political & Military Analysis.* 1966. Taiwan pirate ed. 493 p. tattered dj. A7. $20.00

FALL, Oriana. *Interview w/Hist.* 1976. Liveright. 1st Am ed. 376 p. VG/clip. A17. $20.00

FALLACI, Oriana. *Egotists: 16 Surprising Interviews.* (1968). Regnery. 1st ed. 256 p. NF/VG+ clip. A7. $35.00

FALLACI, Oriana. *Inshallah.* 1992. Nan A Talese/Doubleday. 1st ed. trans from Italian. F/F. A14. $25.00

FALLON, Martin; see Patterson, Henry.

FALLS, Cyril. *Military Operations: Egypt & Palestine...June 1917...Part 2.* 1930. London. photos/color maps/index. 672 p. cloth. G. M7. $90.00

FALLS, Joe. *Detroit Tigers.* 1975. Macmillan. 1st ed. VG+. P8. $17.50

FANGEL. *Danish Pulled Thread.* 1977. np. ils/designs. wrp. G2. $5.00

FANNING, David. *Narrative of Colonel David Fanning.* 1861. Richmond. 1st ed. 1/15 on thick paper. 4to. modern quarter morocco. C6. $22,000.00

FANNING, Edmund. *Voyages & Discoveries in S Seas, 1792-1832.* 1924. Salem. Marine Research Soc. 335 p. bl cloth. VG. B14. $60.00

FANNING. *Complete Book of Machine Embroidery.* 1987. np. cloth. G2. $25.00

FANNING. *Complete Book of Machine Quilting.* 1980. np. ils. wrp. G2. $18.00

FANTHROPE, R.L. *Galaxy 666.* 1968. NY. Arcadia. 1st Am/1st hc ed. F/NF. N3. $10.00

FANTHROPE, R.L. *Orbit One.* 1966. Arcadia. 1st Am ed/1st hc ed. F/F. N3. $10.00

FANTHROPE, R.L. *Power Sphere.* 1968. NY. Arcadia. 1st Am/1st hc ed. F/F. N3. $10.00

FARADAY, Michael. *Experimental Researches in Electricity.* 1839. London. Quaritch. 2 vols. gr cloth. B14. $100.00

FARAGO, Ladislas. *Game of the Foxes: Untold Story of German Espionage...* 1971. McKay. VG/fair. A16. $10.00

FARAGO, Ladislas. *Palestine at the Crossroads.* 1937. NY. 1st ed. ils/pls. map ep. 286 p. VG. H3. $30.00

FARAGO, Ladislas. *10th Fleet.* 1962. NY. Obolensky. 3rd ed. VG. N2. $8.50

FARB, Peter. *Face of N Am: Natural Hist of a Continent.* 1963. NY. ils/index. 316 p. cloth. NF/pict dj. D3. $12.50

FARB, Peter. *Face of N Am: Natural Hist of a Continent.* 1963. NY. 316 p. F/G. A17. $10.00

FARBER, Jerry. *Student As Nigger.* 1969. N Hollywood. Contact Books. 2nd prt. 288 p. NF/wrp. A7. $15.00

FARBER & GREEN. *Outrageous Conduct: Art, Ego & the Twilight Zone Case.* 1988. Arbor House/Morrow. 1st ed. F/F. T2. $12.50

FARBRIDGE, Maurice H. *Studies in Biblical & Semitic Symbolism.* 1970. KTAV. reprint of 1923 ed. index. 288 p. VG+. S3. $25.00

FARINA, Richard. *Been Down So Long It Looks Like Up to Me.* 1966. Random. 1st ed. author's 1st/only novel. F/NF 1st issue. L3. $150.00

FARIS, John T. *Roaming the Rockies.* 1930. Farrar Rinehart. 1st ed. VG. H7. $15.00

FARJEON, Eleanor. *Martin Pippin the the Apple Orchard.* 1922. Stokes. 3rd prt. 270 p. VG/poor. P2. $18.00

FARJEON, Eleanor. *Pray for Little Things.* 1945. Houghton Mifflin. ils. VG/VG. P2. $23.00

FARLEY, Walter. *Blk Stallion Mystery.* (1957). Random. 1st ed. 202 p. cloth. VG+. B22. $7.00

FARLEY, Walter. *Blood Bay Colt.* 1950. Random. 1st ed. juvenile. VG/fair. O3. $25.00

FARLEY, Walter. *Horse-Tamer.* 1958. Random. 1st ed. juvenile. VG/G. O3. $30.00

FARLIE. *Pennywise Goutique.* 1974. np. ils. cloth. G2. $6.00

FARMER, Fannie Merrit. *Rumford Cook Book.* nd. Rumford Chemical Works. 47 p. VG. M20. $15.00

FARMER, John Stephen. *Vocabula Amatoria: French-Eng Glossary of Words...* 1896. London. private prt. 1st ed. sq octavo. 266 p. Bayntun bdg. VG. H5. $250.00

FARMER, John. *List of Pastors, Decons...1st Congregational Church...1830.* 1830. Concord, NH. 21 p. wrp. H10. $27.50

FARMER, Philip Jose. *Adventure of Peerless Peer.* 1974. Aspen. 1st ed. F/dj. M2. $50.00

FARMER, Philip Jose. *Barnstormer in Oz.* 1982. Berkley. 1st trade prt. G/wrp. L1. $12.50

FARMER, Philip Jose. *Dayworld.* 1985. NY. Putnam. 1st ed. F/F. T2. $15.00

FARMER, Philip Jose. *Love Song.* 1983. Dennis McMillan. 1st hc ed. 1/500. sgn/#d. M. M2. $75.00

FARMER, Philip Jose. *Tarzan Alive.* 1972. Doubleday. 1st ed. F/NF. Q1. $75.00

FARNHAM, S.E. *Without Due Process.* 1894. Columbus, OH. Hubbard. 1st ed. 501 p. cloth. VG. D3. $25.00

FARNHAM, T.J. *Life, Adventures & Travels in CA...* 1849. NY. Nafis Cornish. pict ed. 468 p. pict red cloth. G. H7. $75.00

FARNOL, Jeffery. *Broad Highway.* 1912. Little Brn. 1st ils ed. 24 color pls. 518 p. G. P2. $25.00

FARR, John; see Webb, Jack.

FARRAR, Timothy. *Report Case of Trustees of Dartmouth...Against WH Woodward.* 1819. Portsmouth. JW Foster. presentation to Dartmouth Lib/dtd 1820. M11. $650.00

FARRE, Rowena. *Beckoning Land.* 1969. Vanguard. 1st Am ed. 8vo. 285 p. VG/dj. W1. $18.00

FARRELL, James T. *Misunderstanding.* 1949. House of Books. 1/300. sgn/#d. F/sans. C4. $95.00

FARRELL, James T. *My Days of Anger.* (1943). NY. Vanguard. 1st ed. F/NF. B4. $65.00

FARRELL, James T. *Silence of Hist.* 1963. Doubleday. 1st ed. F/NF. B4. $45.00

FARRELL, James. *My Baseball Diary.* 1957. Barnes. 1st ed. F/VG. P8. $50.00

FARRER, Reginald. *On the Eaves of the World.* 1926. London. Arnold. 2nd imp. 2 vols. gilt bl cloth. VG. F1. $150.00

FARRINGTON, Edward. *Ernest H Wilson, Plant Hunter.* 1931. Boston. xl. ls/photos. 197 p. B26. $27.50

FARRINGTON, Harry Webb. *Liberty of Lincoln.* 1925. Bradley Beach, NJ. 1st ed. cloth. NF. M8. $45.00

FARRINGTON, S. Kip Jr. *Railroads of the Hour.* 1958. Coward McCann. 1st ed. sgn. 319 p. VG/dj. M20. $35.00

FARRINGTON, S. Kip Jr. *Trail of the Sharp Cup.* (1974). NY. 1st ed. inscr/sgn. 176 p. dj. A17. $25.00

FARRINGTON, S. Kip. *Atlantic Game Fishing.* 1937. NY. Kennedy. 1st ed. inscr. VG/VG. Q1. $300.00

FARRIS, John. *Catacombs.* 1981. Delacorte. 1st ed. F/NF. N3. $20.00

FARSHLER, Earl. *Am Saddle Horse.* 1934. Louisville. 2nd prt. presentation sgn. O3. $58.00

FARSON, Daniel. *Window on the Sea.* 1977. London. Michael Joseph. 1st ed. F/NF. M7. $54.00

FARWELL, Byron. *Armies of the Raj.* (1989). NY. 1st ed. 399 p. cloth. F/dj. B18. $45.00

FARWELL, Byron. *Prisoners of the Mahdi.* (1968). NY. 1st ed. 8vo. 356 p. F/F. A2. $17.50

FASSETT, Norman C. *Manual of Aquatic Plants.* 1957 (1940). Madison. ils. 405 p. VG. B26. $15.00

FASSETT & HUNT. *Family Album.* 1989. np. ils. cloth. G2. $35.00

FASSETT. *Glorious Knits.* 1985. np. 30 designs. cloth. G2. $25.00

FAST, Howard. *Passion of Sacco & Vanzetti: New Eng Legend.* 1953. Bl Heron. 1st ed. sgn. VG/dj. A16. $15.00

FAST, Howard. *Peekskill USA.* 1951. Civil Rights Congress. 2nd prt. 127 p. wrp. A7. $25.00

FAST, Howard. *Pledge.* 1988. Houghton Mifflin. 1st ed. NF/NF. V2. $6.00

FAST, Howard. *Trial of Abigail Goodman.* 1993. Crown. AP. w/publicity manager's business card. F/wrp. L3. $35.00

FATOUT, Paul. *Ambrose Bierce. The Devil's Lexicographer.* 1951. Norman, OK. 1st ed. 349 p. cloth. F/dj. D3. $25.00

FAUCHARD, Pierre. *Le Chirurgeien Dentiste ou Traite des Dents...* 1961 (1746). Paris. facsimile. 1/150. 12mo. full mottled calf. G7. $125.00

FAULK, John Henry. *Fear on Trial.* 1964. Simon Schuster. 1st ed. NF/dj. A7. $20.00

FAULKNER, Georgene. *Little Peachling & Other Tales of Old Japan.* (1928). Wise Parslow. ils Frederick Richardson. 4to. 91 p. G+. A3. $20.00

FAULKNER, Georgene. *Old Eng Nursery Tales.* 1916. Chicago. octavo. inscr. ils Milo Winter. blk cloth. B24. $250.00

FAULKNER, Nancy. *Side Saddle for Dandy.* (1954). Doubleday. ils Marguerite DeAngeli. 214 p. VG/G. T5. $15.00

FAULKNER, William. *Absalom, Absalom!* 1936. Random. 1st ed. NF/VG+. Q1. $275.00

FAULKNER, William. *As I Lay Dying.* 1930. NY. Cape/Smith. 1st issue w/init cap I on p 11 not aligned. VG/VG+. Q1. $1,750.00

FAULKNER, William. *Collected Stories...* 1950. Random. 1st ed. G+/dj. E3. $30.00

FAULKNER, William. *Early Prose & Poetry.* 1962. Boston. 1st ed/expanded. sgn Carvel Collins. NF/VG+. A11. $90.00

FAULKNER, William. *Fable.* 1954. NY. 1st ed. VG/VG. B5. $75.00

FAULKNER, William. *Father Abraham.* (1984). Random. 1st ed. F/F. B3. $25.00

FAULKNER, William. *Intruder in the Dust.* 1948. Random. 1st ed. VG+/VG+. Q1. $100.00

AULKNER, William. *Light in August.* 1932). Harrison Smith/Haas. 1st ed. G+. 7. $50.00

AULKNER, William. *Mosquitoes: A Novel.* 1927. NY. Liveright. 2nd ed. G/VG. Q1. $200.00

AULKNER, William. *Portable Faulkner.* 946. NY. 1st ed. sgn Crowley. VG/VG. 11. $125.00

AULKNER, William. *Private World of William Faulkner.* 1954. NY. Harper. ARC. S. F/F clip. Q1. $75.00

AULKNER, William. *Pylon.* 1935. NY. mith Haas. 1st ed. 1/310. sgn/#d. bl cloth. G/slipcase. Q1. $850.00

AULKNER, William. *Pylon.* 1968. NY. 1st d. intro/sgn Reynolds Price. F/wrp ils ambert. A11. $50.00

AULKNER, William. *Reivers.* 1962. Random. 1st ed. VG/dj. M18. $40.00

AULKNER, William. *Requiem for a Nun.* 951. Random. 1st ed. VG/dj. M18. $100.00

AULKNER, William. *Thinking of Home.* 992. Norton. ltd ed. 1/100. sgn/dtd edit. /dj. C4. $125.00

AULKNER, William. *Town.* 1957. Random. 1st ed. 1/450. sgn/#d. F/orig acetate/ ans slipcase. Q1. $750.00

AULKNER, William. *Uncollected Stories of William Faulkner.* 1980. Chatto Windus. 1st d. F/dj. C4. $50.00

AULKNER, William. *Wild Palms.* 1968. NY. 1st Signet Classic pb ed. sgn Cassill. /wrp. A11. $50.00

AUROT, Don. *Secrets of the Split T Formation.* 1952. Prentice Hall. G+. N2. $7.50

AUST, A.B. *German Element in US.* 927. NY. sgn. 2 vols in 1. gilt blk eather. A17. $30.00

AUST, Patricia L. *Hist Times Ils Encyclopedia of the Civil War.* 1986. NY. 1st ed. cloth. /F. M8. $45.00

AVOR, E.H. *Fruit Growers Guide Book.* 911. St Joseph, MO. photos. 285 p. decor loth. B26. $20.00

AWCETT, Brian. *Cambodia: Book for People Who Find Television Too Slow.* (1988). Grove. st ed. F/NF. A7. $20.00

AWCETT, P.H. *Lost Trails, Lost Cities.* 953). Funk Wagnall. 1st Am ed. 8vo. 332 . VG+/VG. A2. $20.00

AWCETT & SHOAF. *Marbling Fabrics for Quilts: Guide for Learning & Teaching.* 1991. p. wrp. G2. $12.95

AY, Eliot. *Lorenzo in Search of the Sun.* 1955. London. 1st ed. 148 p. cloth. D3. $25.00

FAY, Jay Wharton. *Am Psychology Before William James.* 1939. Rutgers. 1st ed. sm 8vo. 240 p. gray cloth. F/dj. G1. $125.00

FAYEIN, C. *French Doctor in the Yemen.* 1957. London. 1st ed. ils. 288 p. dj. O2. $30.00

FEATHER, Leonard. *From Satchmo to Miles.* 1972. Stein Day. 1st ed. F/NF. B2. $35.00

FEATHER, Leonard. *Passion for Jazz.* (1980). Horizon. 208 p. dj. A7. $18.00

FEATHERSTONHAUGH, George W. *Canoe Voyage Up the Minnay Sotor...* 1970. St Paul. MN Hist Soc. reprint of 1847 London ed. 2 vols. 8vo. F/slipcase. P4. $75.00

FECK, Luke. *Yesterday's Cincinnati.* (1975). Miami, FL. xl. ils/index. 142 p. B18. $17.50

FEDDEN & THOMSON. *Crusader Castles.* 1957. London. 8vo. 127 p. cloth. dj. O2. $40.00

FEELEY-HARNIK, Gillian. *Lord's Table: Eucharist & Passover in Early Christianity.* 1981. PA U. 184 p. F/F. S3. $25.00

FEFFER, Melvin. *Structure of Freudian Thought.* 1982. NY. IUP. 298 p. gray cloth. VG/dj. G1. $22.50

FEIFFER, Jules. *Man in the Ceiling.* 1993. Harper Collins. 1st ed. inscr. F/F. B2. $35.00

FEIFFER, Jules. *Sick Sick Sick.* 1963. Signet. pb. NF. NF. C8. $20.00

FEIGELSON, Naomi. *Underground Revolution: Hippies, Yippies & Others.* 1970. Funk Wagnall. F/NF. F4. $30.00

FEINBERG, Louis. *Spiritual Foundations of Judaism.* 1951. Cincinnati. Congregation Adath Israel. 280 p. VG. S3. $17.00

FEININGER, Andreas. *Trees.* 1978 (1968). NY. 160 photos. 116 p. B26. $19.00

FEINSTEIN, Elaine. *Matters of Chance.* 1972. London. 1/600. sgn. F/wrp. A11. $25.00

FEIST, Bertha E. *Grunty Grunts & Smiley Smile Outdoors.* (1921). Altemus. ils MP Brater. 62 p. pict brds. VG. S10. $45.00

FEIST, Raymond E. *Faerie Tale.* 1988. Doubleday. 1st ed. F/F. F4. $18.00

FEJTO, Francois. *Behind the Rape of Hungary.* (1957). McKay. 1st ed. 335 p. VG/G+. A7. $17.00

FELDMAN, Leon A. *Tamakh Commentary on Varriants & Comments...* 1970. Netherlands. Van Gorcum. 253 p. VG+. S3. $25.00

FELDMAN, Sandra K. *From Real to Surreal: Landscapes of Frederick J Sykes.* 1992. Hirschl Adler Galleries. 16 p. wrp. D2. $10.00

FELDMAN & GARTENBERG. *Beat Generation & the Angry Young Man.* 1958. Citadel. 1st ed. F/NF. B2. $60.00

FELDMAN. *Handmade Lace & Patterns.* 1975. Harper Row. ils. cloth. G2. $18.00

FELICE, Cynthia. *Downtime.* 1985. Bluejay. 1st ed. F/F. N3. $15.00

FELICIANO, Felice. *Alphabetum Romanum.* 1960. Verone. 1/400. octavo. w/prospectus. F/pub slipcase. H5. $1,250.00

FELKER, Clay. *Casey Stengel's Secret.* 1961. Walker. 1st ed. VG+/VG+. P8. $50.00

FELKER, P.H. *Grocers' Manual...* 1878. Claremont, NH. 1st ed. 312 p. H10. $75.00

FELT, Ephraim Porter. *Our Shade Trees.* 1938. Orange Judd. ils. 187 p. N2. $7.50

FENNEMAN, N.M. *On the Lakes of SE WI.* 1902. Madison, WI. WI Natural Hist Geological Survey. 178 p. G. A17. $27.50

FENNER, Carol. *Christmas Tree on the Mtn.* 1966. NY. 1st ed. ils. 32 p. pict gr cloth. F/VG. H3. $20.00

FENNER, Phyllis R. *Ghosts, Ghosts, Ghosts: Stories of Spooks...* 1963. Franklin Watts. dj. VG. N2. $7.50

FENNER, Phyllis R. *Wide Angle Lens: Stories of Time & Space.* 1980. NY. Morrow. 1st ed. pub bdg. NF/clip. N3. $15.00

FENTON, Charles A. *Apprenticeship of Ernest Hemingway: The Early Yrs.* 1987 (1954). London. 302 p. M/wrp. A17. $9.50

FERAZANI, Larry. *Rescue Squad: Fireman's Fascinating Account...* 1974. NY. Morrow. 1st ed. 8vo. 244 p. VG+/VG. A2. $12.50

FERBER, Edna. *Peculiar Treasure.* (1939). Literary Guild. VG/dj. A16. $20.00

FERBER, Edna. *Peculiar Treasure.* 1939. Doubleday Doran. 1st ed. sgn. NF/slipcase. B4. $125.00

FERBER, Edna. *Saratoga Trunk.* 1941. Doubleday Doran. 1st ed after ltd ed. 352 p. bl cloth. VG+. S9. $40.00

FERGURSON, Anna. *Young Lady; or, Guide to Knowledge, Virtue & Happinesss...* (1848). Boston. Cottrell. 24mo. 128 p. G. S10. $15.00

FERGUSON, John. *Studies in Christian Social Commitment.* 1954. London. Independent Pr. 1st ed. 12mo. 128 p. VG/dj. V3. $10.00

FERGUSON, William S. *Greek Imperialism.* 1913. Boston. 1st ed. 258 p. teg. gilt blk cloth. VG. H3. $15.00

FERGUSON. *Creating Memory Quilts.* 1985. np. wrp. G2. $13.00

FERGUSSON, Adam. *Roman Go Home.* 1969. London. BC. VG/dj. C1. $29.50

FERGUSSON, Adam. *Roman Go Home.* 1969. Putnam. 1st ed. xl. VG/dj. C1. $19.50

FERGUSSON, Erna. *Cuba.* 1946. Knopf. 1st ed. 8vo. 250 p. F/F. A2. $15.00

FERGUSSON, Erna. *Dancing Gods. Indian Ceremonials of NM & AZ.* 1931. Knopf. 1st ed. sgn. 276 p. G. B11. $45.00

FERGUSSON, Erna. *Fiesta in Mexico.* 1934. NY. Knopf. 8vo. 267 p. VG/VG. A2. $30.00

FERGUSSON, Erna. *Venezuela.* 1939. Knopf. 1st ed. 8vo. 346 p. F/VG. A2. $15.00

FERGUSSON, Harvey. *Rio Grande.* 1945. Tudor. reprint 1933 ed. cloth. VG/pict dj. D3. $15.00

FERGUSSON & ROHN. *Mesoamerican's Ancient Cities.* 1990. Guatemala. 1st ed. 251 p. dj. F3. $50.00

FERLINGHETTI, Lawrence. *Love in the Days of Rage.* 1988. Bodley Head. 1st ed. F/F. A7. $15.00

FERLINGHETTI, Lawrence. *Love in the Days of Rage.* 1988. London. 1st ed. sgn. F/F. V1. $30.00

FERLINGHETTI, Lawrence. *Routines.* 1964. New Directions. NF/wrp. E3. $15.00

FERLINGHETTI, Lawrence. *Trip to Italy & France.* 1981. NY. ltd ed. sgn. F/F. V1. $45.00

FERLINGHETTI & PETERS. *Literary San Francisco.* 1980. NY. Harper. 1st ed. sgns. F/NF. B2. $50.00

FERMAN, Louis A. *Death of a Newspaper.* 1963. Kalamazoo. Upjohn Inst Employment Research. 63 p. wrp. A7. $12.00

FERNALD, Charles. *County Judge in Arcady: Selected Private Papers of...* 1954. Arthur H Clark. M11. $45.00

FERNALD & KINSEY. *Edible Wild Plants of E North Am.* ca 1943. Idlewild. 1st ed. ils/index. 452 p. H10. $35.00

FERNOW, Berthol. *OH Valley in Colonial Days.* 1890. Albany, NY. 1st ed. 299 p. scarce. D7. $145.00

FERRANDINO, Joseph. *Firefight.* (1987). NY. Soho. F/F. A7. $35.00

FERRARS, Elizabeth. *Witness Before the Fact.* 1979. London. Collins. 1st ed. F/F. S5. $20.00

FERRIS, James Cody. *X-Bar-X Boys: The Sagebrush Mystery.* 1939. Grosset Dunlap. 1st ed. 216 p. VG+/dj. M20. $25.00

FERRIS, R.G. *Prospector, Cowhand & Sodbuster.* 1967. WA, DC. Nat Park Service. 8vo. 320 p. F. A2. $15.00

FERRIS, William. *Blues From the Delta.* 1978. Anchor/Doubleday. 1st ed. rem mk. NF/NF. B2. $40.00

FERRO, Robert. *Family of Max Desir.* 1983. Dutton. 1st ed. F/F. A14. $30.00

FERTE, Thomas L. *Stafford's Road: Anthology of Poems by William Stafford.* (1991). Adrienne Lee Pr. 1st ed. sgn. sc. M. A18. $40.00

FESSENDEN, Thomas G. *Complete Farmer & Rural Economist.* 1839. Boston. Otis Broaders. 345 p. cloth. H10. $32.50

FEST, Wilfried. *Peace or Partition: Hapsburg Monarchy & British Policy.* 1978. London. George Prior. VG/dj. A16. $9.00

FETRIDGE, W. Pembroke. *Harper's Handbook for Travelers in Europe & the E.* 1863. NY. 12mo. 584 p. missing pocket map. full blk leather. VG. H3. $35.00

FEUCHTWANGER, Lion. *Jephta & His Daughter.* 1957-58. Putnam. 255 p. VG+/VG-. S3. $19.00

FEUCHTWANGER, O. *Righteous Lives.* 1965. NY. Bloch. 169 p. VG+/G+. S3. $26.00

FEVAL, Paul; see Bedford-Jones, H.

FICHTENBAUM, Paul. *World of Major League Baseball.* 1987. Crescent. 2nd ed/1st prt. F/F. P8. $12.50

FIEGER, Erwin. *Mexico.* 1973. W Germany. Verlag. 1st ed. oblong folio. F3. $20.00

FIELD, Charles K. *Story of Cheerio.* 1936. Garden City. ltd ed. 1/1550. sgn. VG. E3. $10.00

FIELD, Eugene. *Christmas Tales & Christmas Verse.* 1912. Scribner. 1st ed. octavo. 119 p. VG. H5. $100.00

FIELD, Eugene. *Dibdin's Ghost.* 1980. Fullerton. Lorson. miniature. 1/500. 13 p. wrp. H10. $12.50

FIELD, Eugene. *Favorite Poems.* 1940. NY. ils Malthe Hasselriis. VG/tattered dj. M5. $20.00

FIELD, Eugene. *Gingham Dog & Calico Cat.* 1926. Newark. Graham. 4to. VG/VG. D1. $200.00

FIELD, Eugene. *Lullaby-Land.* 1897. Scribner. 1st thus ed. 229 p. VG+. P2. $60.00

FIELD, Eugene. *Sugar-Plum Tree & Other Verses.* 1930. Saalfield. ils Fern Bisel Peat. G+. S10. $30.00

FIELD, Evan. *What Nigel Knew.* 1981. Potter. 1st ed. F/F. F4. $18.00

FIELD, Henry M. *From the Lakes of Killarney to the Golden Horn.* 1876. Scribner. G. A16. $40.00

FIELD, Henry. *Track of Man.* 1953. Doubleday. 1st ed. 8vo. 448 p. F-/VG. A2. $17.50

FIELD, Michael. *Prevailing Wind.* 1965. London. Methuen. 392 p. dj. A7. $40.00

FIELD, Rachel. *All Through the Night.* 1940. Macmillan. 1st ed. 38 p. pict brds. VG/dj. A3. $10.00

FIELD, Rachel. *Hitty: Her 1st Hundred Yrs.* 1929. Macmillan. 1st ed. 207 p. 1930 Newbery Medal. G+. P2. $65.00

FIELD, Rachel. *Little Book of Days.* 1927. NY. 1st ed. 26 color pls. 58 p. gr cloth. F. H3. $30.00

FIELD, Rachel. *Prayer for a Child.* 1944. Macmillan. 1st ed. 8vo. beige cloth. G+/G+. T5. $45.00

FIELD & LINSLEY. *Canvas Embroidery.* 1990. np. ils. cloth. G2. $20.00

FIELDING, Henry. *Works of...w/Essay on His Life & Genius by Arthur Murphy...* 1821. London. Rivington. 1st collected ed. 10 vols. octavo. gilt full calf. R3. $650.00

FIELDING, Xan. *Stronghold: Account of 4 Seasons in Wht Mtns of Crete.* 1953. London. 1st ed. 8vo. ils/fld map. 317 p. dj. O2. $150.00

FIELDS, J. *Behind the War Headlines.* 1940. NY. Workers Lib. 16 p. wrp. A7. $13.00

FIELDS, Robert Ashley. *Take Me Out to the Crowd.* 1977. Strode. 1st ed. F/VG. P8. $20.00

FIELDS, Wayne. *What the River Knows: Angler in Midstream.* (1990). NY. 2nd prt. 252 p. dj. A17. $10.00

FIERMAN, Floyd. *Roots & Boots.* 1987. Hoboken. KTAV. 1st ed. 241 p. dj. F3. $20.00

FIESNER, Ester M. *Yesterday We Saw Mermaids.* 1992. Tor. 1st ed. F/F. N3. $15.00

FIEY, J.M. *Assyrie Chretienne.* (1965). Beyrouth. 2 vols. thick 8vo. quarter morocco/raised bands. O2. $125.00

FIFE, Robert Herndon. *Young Luther: Intellectual & Religious Development...* 1928. NY. Macmillan. index. 232 p. H10. $15.00

FIGES, Eva. *Ghosts.* (1988). Hamish Hamilton. 1st ed. F/VG. B3. $20.00

FIGLER, Bernard. *Lillian & Archie Freiman Biographies.* 1962. Montreal. self pub. xl. 331 p. VG/G+. S3. $27.00

FIGUER, Louis. *Reptiles & Birds.* ca 1870. Springfield, MA. Holland. subscription ed. ils. 648 p. gilt gr cloth. G. S9. $10.00

FIGUEROA, Jose. *Manifesto to Mexican Republic...Colonization in 1834-35.* 1978. Berkeley. 1st thus ed. 156 p. M/F. P4. $30.00

FILMUS, Tully. *Tully Filmus: Selected Drawings.* 1971. JPS. 1st ed. ils. 76 p. VG+/G+. S3. $40.00

FINCH, Edith. *Carey Thomas of Bryn Mawr.* 1947. London. Harper. 1st ed. 8vo. 342 p. VG/dj. V3. $14.00

INCH, Frank. *LA Dodgers.* 1977. Jordan. 1st ed. F/VG+. P8. $30.00

INCH. *Christmas Time.* nd. (ca 1950s?). 5 popups. sbdg. VG. A4. $50.00

INCK, Henry T. *Food & Flavor: Gastronomic Guide to Health & Good Living.* 1913. NY. Century. 1st ed. 8vo. 594 p. decor cloth. VG+. B20. $50.00

INCK, Henry T. *Pacific Coast Scenic Tour...* 1890. NY. 1st ed. 309 p. cloth. VG. D3. $25.00

INDLEY, Timothy. *Butterfly Plague.* 1969. Viking. 1st Am ed. NF/NF. A14. $45.00

INDLEY, Timothy. *Dinner Along the Amazon.* 1984. Toronto. PBO. sgn. NF/wrp. A11. $40.00

INDLEY, Timothy. *Last of the Crazy People.* 1967. NY. 1st ed. sgn. F/F. A11. $125.00

INDLEY, Timothy. *Telling of Lies.* 1986. Tornoto. Viking/Penguin. 1st ed. F/F. A14. $20.00

INE, Anne. *Madame Doubtfire.* (1987). Hamish Hamilton. 1st ed. VG/VG. B3. $20.00

INE, Sidney. *Frank Murphy: The New Deal Yrs.* 1979. Chicago. M11. $35.00

INEBERG, Solomon Andhil. *Biblical Myth & Legend in Jewish Education.* 1932. Behrman. 155 p. VG. S3. $19.00

INERTY, John. *War Path & Bivouac. Conquest of Sioux.* 1890. Chicago. 460 p. G. B5. $30.00

INGER, Charles J. *Courageous Companions.* 1929. NY. sgn. 304 p. ils ep. G. B18. $17.50

INGER, Charles J. *Courageous Companions.* 1929. NY. 1st ed. 8vo. 304 p. pict brn cloth. VG. H3. $15.00

INGER, Charles J. *Give a Man a Horse.* 1938. Winston. 1st ed. 1925 Newberry Medal. 337 p. VG/G. P2. $28.00

INGER, Charles J. *Tales From Silver Lands.* 1924. Doubleday. VG/dj. A16. $8.00

INK & POLUSHKIN. *Drake's Pl of Brass Authenticated: Report on Pl of Brass.* 1938. CA Hist Soc/Kennedy. Special Pub 14. brds/paper labels. NF. O6. $25.00

INKELSTEIN, Sidney. *Jazz: A People's Music.* 1948. Citadel. 1st ed. 1st bdg (yel stp blk brds). poor dj. A7. $22.00

INLAND, Maxwell. *Harvard Medical Unit at Boston City Hospital..., Vol 1.* 1982. Boston. 903 p. cloth. F/dj. B14. $45.00

INLAY, George. *Hist of Greece From Its Conquest by the Romans to Present...* 1877. Oxford. new ed. 7 vols. 8vo. gilt cloth. O2. $625.00

FINLAY, George. *Remarks on Topography of Oropia & Diacria...* 1838. Athens. Antoniades. inscr to SG Howe. early half calf. O2. $550.00

FINLAY, Virgil. *Portfolio of Ils by Virgil Finlay. 1st Series.* 1951. Fannews. 1st ed. F. M2. $100.00

FINLEY, J.B. *Autobiography of...* 1858. Cincinnati. self pub. later ed. 455 p. G. H7. $25.00

FINLEY, Martha. *Elsie at Nantucket.* 1884. NY. 12mo. 334 p. gilt red cloth. F. H3. $15.00

FINNEGAN. *Piece by Piece.* 1991. np. cloth. G2. $30.00

FINNEY, Jack. *Assault on a Queen.* 1959. Simon Schuster. 1st ed. NF/VG. B4. $150.00

FINNEY, Jack. *Body Snatchers.* 1967. Dell. 3rd Dell ed. NF/wrp. C8. $20.00

FINNEY, Jack. *Body Snatchers.* 1979. Tokyo. 1st Japanese ed. inscr. F/F gray wrp/color dj. A11. $55.00

FINNEY, Jack. *House of Numbers.* 1957. Dell 1st Ed. PBO/1st prt. NF/ils wrp. A11. $25.00

FINNEY, Jack. *Time & Again.* (1970). Simon Schuster. 1st ed. NF/F clip. B4. $200.00

FINNIE, David H. *Pioneers E: Early Am Experience in Middle E.* 1967. Harvard. 8vo. ils. 333 p. cloth. dj. O2. $35.00

FINNIE, Richard. *Lure of the N.* (1940). Phil. index. VG. A17. $30.00

FINSTERBUSCH, C.A. *Cock Fighting All Over the World.* 1929. Gaffney, SC. 1st ed. 471 p. NF. w/author's photo. NF. M8. $250.00

FIORENZA, Elisabeth Schussler. *Aspects of Religious Propaganda in Judaism...* 1976. Notre Dame. 7 essays. 195 p. VG+. S3. $25.00

FIRBANK, Ronald. *Three More Novels of Ronald Firbank.* nd. (1951). New Directions. VG+/dj. E3. $50.00

FISCHER, J. *Entdeckungen der Normannen in Amerika.* 1902. Freidburg. maps. VG+. O6. $75.00

FISCHER, Roger A. *Segregation Struggle in LA 1862-77.* (1974). Urbana. 168 p. NF/NF clip. A7. $11.00

FISHEL, Wesley R. *Vietnam: Anatomy of a Conflict.* (1968). Itasca. Peacock. 879 p. F/torn dj. A7. $40.00

FISHER, Aileen. *Cricket in the Thicket.* (1963). Scribner. ils Rojankovsky. 61 p. NF/G+. T5. $15.00

FISHER, Aileen. *We Went Looking.* 1968. NY. Crowell. 1st ed. lg oblong octavo. 25 p. F/dj. B24. $125.00

FISHER, Albert Kenrick. *Hawks & Owls of the US in Their Relation to Agriculture.* 1893. WA. GPO. 1st ed. presentation. 210 p. plum cloth. NF. H5. $275.00

FISHER, Allan C. Jr. *Am's Inland Waterway.* (1973). NGS. ils/index. 207 p. VG/dj. A17. $8.50

FISHER, Carrie. *Surrender the Pink.* (1990). Simon Schuster. AP. 269 p. wrp. A7. $8.00

FISHER, G.C. *Nature Encyclopedia.* (1950). NY. ils/pls. 940 p. A17. $10.00

FISHER, George Park. *Hist of the Christian Church.* 1896. Scribner. xl. 729 p. H3. $10.00

FISHER, Leonard Everett. *Calendar Art: 13 Days, Weeks, Months & Yrs Around World.* 1987. NY. 4 Winds. 1st ed. 4to. 63 p. dj. N2. $7.50

FISHER, M.F.K. *As They Were.* (1983). Chatto Windus. 1st ed. NF/F. B3. $25.00

FISHER, M.F.K. *Cordiall Water.* 1958. London. 1st Eng ed. inscr. F/F. A11. $115.00

FISHER, M.F.K. *Cordiall Water.* 1961. Little Brn. 1st ed. NF/NF. B2. $45.00

FISHER, M.F.K. *Dubious Honors.* (1988). San Francisco. N Point. 1st ed. F/F. B3. $15.00

FISHER, M.F.K. *Not Now But Now.* 1984. London. 1st ed/Chatto Windus PBO. inscr/dtd 1988. F/unread. A11. $65.00

FISHER, M.F.K. *Serve It Forth.* 1937. NY. 1st ed. inscr/dtd 1990. peach cloth. VG+. A11. $135.00

FISHER, M.F.K. *Stay Me, Oh Comfort Me.* 1993. Pantheon. AP. F/wrp. C4. $30.00

FISHER, M.F.K. *To Begin Again: Stories & Memoirs.* 1992. Pantheon. Ap. F/prt cream wrp. C4. $35.00

FISHER, Malcolm R. *Economic Analysis of Labour.* (1971). London. Weidenfeld Nicolson. 303 p. clip dj. A7. $12.00

FISHER, Raymond F. *Bering's Voyages: Whither & Why.* 1977. Seattle. 31 maps. NF/dj. O6. $75.00

FISHER, Sydney George. *William Penn: A Biography.* 1932. Lippincott. anniversary ed. 12mo. 293 p. VG. V3. $12.00

FISHER, Vardis. *April: Fable of Love.* 1937. Caxton. 1st ed. F/dj. A18. $75.00

FISHER, Vardis. *City of Illusion.* 1941. NY. 1st ed. cloth. VG/dj. D3. $12.50

FISHER, Vardis. *Clore Collection of Vardis Fisher Research Materials.* 1989. Boise State U. 1st ed. F/wrp. A18. $25.00

FISHER, Vardis. *Darkness & the Deep.* (1943). Vanguard. 1st ed. F/dj. A18. $35.00

FISHER, Vardis. *God or Caesar.* 1953. Caxton. 1st ed. VG. B5. $35.00

FISHER, Vardis. *Golden Rooms.* (1944). Vanguard. 1st ed. NF/VG. A18. $25.00

FISHER, Vardis. *Love & Death: Complete Stories.* 1959. Doubleday. 19 stories. F/VG+. A18. $50.00

FISHER, Vardis. *Passions Spin the Plot.* 1934. Caxton. 1st ed. F/VG+. A18. $50.00

FISHER, Vardis. *Pemmican: Novel of Hudson's Bay Co.* (1956). Doubleday. 1st ed. map ep. F/clip. A18. $30.00

FISHER, Vardis. *Sonnets to an Imaginary Madonna.* (1981). Opal Laurel Holmes. special presentation/reprint of 1927 ed. M/M. A18. $35.00

FISHER, Vardis. *Tale of Valor: Novel of Lewis & Clark Expedition.* 1958. Doubleday. 1st ed. 8vo. 456 p. map ep. F/dj. T8. $30.00

FISHER, Vardis. *Toilers of the Hills.* 1928. Houghton Mifflin. 1st prt. F. A18. $50.00

FISHER, Vardis. *Valley of Vision.* 1951. Abelard. 1st ed. F/NF. F4. $50.00

FISHER, W.E. Garrett. *Transvaal & the Boers.* (1969). NY. Negro U Pr. reprint 1896 ed. 283 p. A7. $13.00

FISHER & GREENBERG. *Scientific Credibility of Freud's Theories & Therapy.* 1977. Basic Books. 502 p. blk cloth. VG/dj. G1. $40.00

FISHER & LA SORDA. *Artful Dodger.* 1985. Arbor. BC. F/F. P8. $10.00

FISHER & LUCIANO. *Umpire Strikes Back.* 1982. Bantam. 1st ed. author's 1st book. F/F. P8. $8.00

FISK, Nicholas. *Robot Revolt.* 1981. London. Pelham. 1st ed. F/NF. N3. $10.00

FISKE, John. *Discovery of Am w/Some Account of Ancient Am & Spanish...* 1892. Houghton Mifflin. 2 vols. 8vo. teg. bl cloth. H9. $35.00

FISKE, John. *Dutch & Quaker Colonies in Am.* 1899. Houghton Mifflin. 2 vols. 12mo. VG. V3. $17.50

FISKE, John. *MS Valley in the Civil War.* 1900. Boston. xl. ils/index/map. 368 p. G. O7. $14.50

FISKE, Samuel. *Mr Dunn Browne's Experiences in Foreign Parts.* 1857. Boston. 8vo. 295 p. cloth. O2. $65.00

FITCH, Charles Marden. *Complete Book of Miniature Roses.* 1977. NY. 1st ed. ils. 342 p. NF/NF. B28. $20.00

FITCH, George Hamlin. *Critic in the Orient.* 1913. San Francisco. Elder. sm 8vo. 73 pls. VG. W1. $18.00

FITCH, John A. *Social Responsibilities of Organized Work.* (1957). Harper. 1st ed. 237 p. A7. $20.00

FITCH, Raymond E. *Breaking w/Burr: Harman Blennerhassett's Journal, 1807.* 1988. Athens, OH. 1st ed. 275 p. F/VG+. D7. $35.00

FITCHER, George. *Fishing.* 1954. New Brunswick. Boy Scout Merit Badge series. 8vo. wrp. A17. $8.50

FITE & FREEMAN. *Book of Old Maps Delineating Am Hist...* 1926. Cambridge. Harvard. 1st ed. Samuel Eliot Morison's copy. 75 maps. NF. O6. $375.00

FITTER, Alastair. *Wild Flowers of Britain & N Europe.* 1987. Austin. ils. 320 p. as new. B26. $14.00

FITZENMEYER, Frieda. *Once Upon a Time: Book One.* 1984. Warwick. miniature. 1/125. sgn. ils/sgn CJ Blinn. F/prt paper wallet. B24. $125.00

FITZGERALD, C.P. *China & SE Asia Since 1945.* (1973). Camberswell, Australia. Longman. 110 p. VG/wrp. A7. $15.00

FITZGERALD, C.P. *China: A Short Cultural Hist.* 1938. Appleton Century. 8vo. 21 pls/19 maps. 615 p. VG. W1. $18.00

FITZGERALD, Ed. *Am League.* 1963. Grosset Dunlap. revised ed. G. P8. $10.00

FITZGERALD, Ed. *Nat League.* 1959. Grosset Dunlap. new revised ed. G+/G. P8. $20.00

FITZGERALD, Edward. *Rubaiyat of Omar Khayyam.* nd. Hodder Stoughton. ils Edmund Dulac. bl cloth. G. M18. $75.00

FITZGERALD, Edward. *Rubaiyat of Omar Khayyam.* 1906. (Boston?) 1/50 on Japan. 16mo. 12 p. NF/stiff wrp. B24. $65.00

FITZGERALD, Edward. *Rubaiyat of Omar Khayyam.* 1912. London. private prt. leather. VG/leather-trim marbled slipcase. A16. $225.00

FITZGERALD, Edward. *Rubaiyat of Omar Khayyam.* 1952. NY. ils Edmund Dulac/12 color pls. 195 p. VG. H3. $20.00

FITZGERALD, F. Scott. *All the Sad Young Men.* 1926. NY. 1st ed. VG/G+. B5. $650.00

FITZGERALD, F. Scott. *Mystery of the Raymond Mortgage.* 1960. Random. 1/750. ARC (none for sale). w/2nd ed copy. pub note. mailer. A11. $575.00

FITZGERALD, F. Scott. *Screenplay for 3 Comrads by Erich Maria Remarque.* 1978. Carbondale, IL. 1st ed. edit/sgn Bruccoli. F/F. A11. $55.00

FITZGERALD, F. Scott. *Tender Is the Night.* 1934. NY. Scribner. later ed. contemporary inscr/dtd. VG/tattered. Q1. $2,750.00

FITZGERALD, F. Scott. *Tender Is the Night.* 1934. Scribner. 1st prt. 1/7600. NF/VG. custom leather clamshell box. L3. $4,500.00

FITZGERALD, John D. *Uncle Will & the Fitzgerald Curse.* 1961. Bobbs Merrill. 8vo. VG/G. A8. $12.00

FITZGERALD, Tamsin. *Tamsin.* (1973) Dial. 1st ed. 8vo. 180 p. F/VG. A2. $10.00

FITZHUGH, Percy K. *Hervey Willetts.* 1927. Grosset Dunlap. 244 p. cloth. VG/poor. M20. $25.00

FITZHUGH, Percy K. *Pee-Wee Harris Fixer.* 1924. Grosset Dunlap. 1st ed. G. M2. $6.00

FITZHUGH, Percy K. *Wigwag Weigand.* 1929. Grosset Dunlap. Buddy Books series. 214 p. VG+/dj. M20. $60.00

FITZPATRICK, Doyle. *King Strang Story: Vindication of James J Strang.* 1970. Lansing. 1st ed. 289 p. F/dj. A17. $22.50

FITZPATRICK, George. *Pict NM.* 1949. Santa Fe. 1st ed. 4to. 191 p. pict cloth. VG. D3. $25.00

FITZPATRICK, James A. *Fireside Travels in N Am.* 1948. St Paul. 1st ed. 256 p. color map ep. aeg. emb full leather. F. H3. $40.00

FITZPATRICK, John C. *Diaries of George WA.* 1925. Houghton Mifflin. 4 vols. VG. B10. $85.00

FITZPATRICK. *Sm Quilts in the Vanessa Ann Collection.* 1989. np. cloth. G2. $20.00

FITZSIMMONS, Bernard. *150 Yrs of N Am Railroads.* 1982. NJ. Chartwell. ils. 224 p. F/VG. B11. $20.00

FITZWILLIAM & HANDS. *Jacobean Embroidery.* nd. np. reprint of 1928 ed. wrp. G2. $23.00

FIXEL, Lawrence. *Scale of Silence.* 1970. Kayak Pr. 1/1000. sgn. F/wrp. V1. $30.00

FIXEL, Lawrence. *Truth, War & the Dream Game.* 1991. Coffee House. 1st ed. sgn. F/wrp. V1. $20.00

FIZEL, Rena Gray. *Index to Rev Horace Edwin Hayden's VA Genealogies.* 1977. VA Genealogy Soc. VG. B10. $25.00

FLACK, Marjorie. *Angus & the Cat.* (1931). Doubleday. 23rd prt. xl. oblong 16mo. VG. T5. $15.00

FLACK, Marjorie. *Restless Robin.* 1937. Houghton Mifflin. unp. bl cloth. VG/dj. M20. $25.00

FLACK, Marjorie. *Wag-Tail Bess.* 1946 (1933). Doubleday. oblong 8vo. pict brds. G+. T5. $30.00

FLACK, Marjorie. *Walter the Lazy Mouse.* 1941 (1937). Doubleday Doran. ils. VG/G. P2. $30.00

FLAHERTY, Frances. *Sabu the Elephant Boy.* 1937. Oxford. photoplay ed. NF/dj. B4. $275.00

FLAMBEAU, Victor. *Red Letter Days in Europe w/Glimpse of N Africa.* (1925). NY. George Sully. 1st ed. 8vo. 435 p. F. A2. $15.00

FLANAGAN, John T. *Am Is W.* 1945. Minneapolis. 1st ed. ils. 677 p. cloth. NF. D3. $25.00

FLANAGAN, Philip. *Newman, Faith & the Believer.* 1946. Westminster. Newman. 210 p. H10. $16.50

FLANDRAU, Grace. *Glance at the Lewis & Clark Expedition.* nd. np. Compliments Great N Railway. 29 p. F/wrp. T8. $22.50

FLASTE, R. *NY Times Guide to Return of Halley's Comet.* 1985. NY. Times Books. AP. 202 p. M. S9. $8.00

FLATTORUSSO, J. & M. *Florence: City of Flowers.* 1950. Florence. 12mo. 244 p. F/G. H3. $12.00

FLEISCHER, Nat. *How To Box.* 1942. np. 5th revised ed. 111 p. VG+/stapled wrp. M20. $20.00

FLEISCHMANN, Julius. *Footsteps in the Sea.* 1935. NY. Putnam. 1st ed. presentation. 47 pls. 286 p. gray cloth. VG. B11. $50.00

FLEISCHNER, Eva. *Auschwitz: Beginning of a New Era?* 1977. KTAV. 469 p. VG/wrp. S3. $17.00

FLEISHMAN, Sid. *Humbug Mtn.* 1978. Little Brn. 12mo. F/F. A8. $18.00

FLEITMANN, Lida. *Comments on Hacks & Hunters.* 1922. Scribner. 2nd prt. G. O3. $35.00

FLEMING, Alexander. *Penicillin: Its Practical Application.* 1946. London. Butterworth. 1st ed. octavo. gilt bl-gr cloth. NF. R3. $165.00

FLEMING, Clint. *When the Trout Are Rising. Tales of the Rideau Lakes.* (1947). NY. 1st ed. sgn. F/G. A17. $20.00

FLEMING, Ian. *For Your Eyes Only.* 1960. London. Cape. 1st ed. F/clip. M15. $200.00

FLEMING, Ian. *Live & Let Die.* 1955. Macmillan. 1st Am ed. author's 2nd book. NF/NF. Q1. $250.00

FLEMING, Ian. *Man w/the Golden Gun.* 1964. NAL. 1st ed. F/F. F4. $40.00

FLEMING, Ian. *Man w/the Golden Gun.* 1965. London. Cape. 1st ed. F/F. M15. $90.00

FLEMING, Ian. *Octopussy & the Living Daylights.* (1966). London. Cape. 1st ed. F/F. B3. $25.00

FLEMING, Ian. *Octopussy.* 1966. NAL. 1st ed. F/NF. F4. $40.00

FLEMING, Ian. *On Her Majesty's Secret Service.* 1963. London. Cape. 1st ed. sm octavo. 288 p. brn paper over brds. NF/dj. H5. $200.00

FLEMING, Ian. *Spy Who Loved Me.* 1962. Viking. 1st ed. F/NF clip. F4. $50.00

FLEMING, Ian. *You Only Live Twice.* 1964. London. Cape. 1st ed. sm octavo. 255 p. blk cloth. NF/dj. H5. $175.00

FLEMING, Joan. *Day of the Donkey Derby.* 1978. London. Collins. 1st ed. F/NF. S5. $22.50

FLEMING, John A. *Ziegler Polar Expedition, 1903-05.* 1907. Nat Geog Soc. xl. 19 pls. VG+. O6. $85.00

FLEMING, Peter. *Brazilian Adventure.* 1934. Scribner. 1st Am ed. 8vo. 412 p. VG+/G+. A2. $25.00

FLEMING, Thomas. *Around the Pan w/Uncle Hank...Pan-Am Expo...* (1901). NY. Nut Shell Pub. 8vo. 262 p. VG+. A2. $30.00

FLEMING, W. *General William T Sherman, College President.* 1912. Cleveland. Clark. 1st ed. ils/index. VG. B5. $50.00

FLEMING. *Encyclopedia of Textiles.* 1958. np. ils. cloth. G2. $22.00

FLETCHER, A.L. *Boy Scouts Woodcraft Lesson.* 1913. Donohue. 1st ed. VG. M2. $10.00

FLETCHER, David. *Accident of Robert Luman.* 1988. London. Macmillan. 1st ed. F/F. S5. $22.50

FLETCHER, G.N. *Fabulous Flemings of Kathmandu.* 1967 (1964). Dutton. 3rd ed. 8vo. 219 p. VG+/VG. A2. $15.00

FLETCHER, H. George. *Miscellany for Bibliophiles.* 1979. NY. Grastorf Lang. 8vo. 303 p. gray cloth. NF. F1. $35.00

FLETCHER, Harvey D. *Visions of Nam.* 1987. Raleigh. Jo-Ely. 1st ed. inscr. VG/wrp. L3. $50.00

FLETCHER, J.S. *Hardican's Hollow.* nd. Grosset Dunlap. reprint. G/dj. A16. $10.00

FLETCHER, J.S. *Making of Matthias.* 1898 (1897). London. Bodley Head. ils Lucy K Welch. 141 p. VG. S10. $30.00

FLETCHER, J.S. *Ransom for London.* 1929. NY. Dial. 1st Am ed. F/VG. M15. $45.00

FLETCHER, Lucille. *Eighty Dollars to Stamford.* 1975. Random. 1st ed. F/F. M15. $30.00

FLETCHER, S.W. *How To Make a Fruit Garden...* 1906. Doubleday Page. 1st ed. ils. 283 p. H10. $20.00

FLETCHER, W.A. *Rebel Private Front & Rear.* 1908. Beaumont. 1st ed. cloth. VG. rare. C6. $3,750.00

FLEXNER, Helen Thomas. *Quaker Childhood.* 1940. New Haven. 1st ed. sgn. 335 p. B28. $25.00

FLEXNER, James T. *John Singleton Copley.* 1948. Houghton Mifflin. 139 p. cloth. D2. $75.00

FLINT, Charles L. *Grasses & Forage Plants.* 1860. Boston. 5th ed. 170 ils. 398 p. B28. $35.00

FLINT, Timothy. *Hist & Geography of MS Valley.* 1832. Cincinnati. Flint Lincoln. 8vo. contemporary calf. M1. $225.00

FLINT, Timothy. *Hist & Goegraphy of MS Valley.* 1833. Cincinnati/Boston. 2 vols in 1. thick 8vo. tables. calf. H9. $150.00

FLOCK, H. *Flock's Revised Breeders & Cockers' Guide.* 1904. Chattanooga, TN. 150 p. VG. E5. $125.00

FLOHERTY, J.J. *Wht Terror: Adventures w/Ice Patrol.* (1947). Phil. Lippincott. 1st ed. 8vo. 183 p. VG/VG. A2. $17.50

FLOOD, Charles Bracelen. *War of the Innocents.* (1970). McGraw Hill. 1st ed. F/NF. A7. $30.00

FLORA, J.M. *Vardis Fisher's Story of Vridar Hunter: A Study...* (1962). U Microfilms. 229 p. F/wrp. A18. $30.00

FLORENCE, Judy. *Award-Winning Quick Quilts.* 1988. np. sbdg. G2. $15.00

FLORENCE, Judy. *Award-Winning Quilts & How To Make Them.* 1986. np. wrp. G2. $15.00

FLORENCE, Judy. *Collection of Favorite Quilts.* 1990. np. ils. wrp. G2. $19.00

FLORES & WINTON. *Canyon Visions.* 1989. Lubbock, TX. 1st ed. sgns. fwd Larry McMurtry. F/F. L3. $75.00

FLORESCANO, Engrique. *Bibliografia General Del Maiz en Mexico.* 1987. Mexico. 3rd ed. 4to. 251 p. F3. $25.00

FLORESCU, Radu. *In Search of Frankenstein.* (1975). NY Graphic Soc. 1st ed. lg 8vo. 244 p. F/F. A2. $25.00

FLORNOY, Bertrand. *Jivaro: Among the Head-Shrinkers of the Amazon.* (1953). London. Elek. 1st ed. 8vo. 224 p. VG+/VG. A2. $20.00

FLOURENS, Pierre. *Cours de Physiologe Comparee de L'Ontologie ou Etude Etres.* 1836. Paris. Bailliere. 184 p. orig prt wrp. G7. $395.00

FLOURENS, Pierre. *Recherches Experimentales...du System Nerveus...Vertebre.* 1824. Paris. Crevot. contemporary sheep. G7. $1,650.00

FLOWER, B.O. *How Eng Averted a Revolution of Force.* 1903. Trenton. Brandt. 1st ed. VG+. B2. $100.00

FLOWER, Edward. *Bits & Bearing Reins & Horses & Harness.* 1875. London. Cassell. ils. 56 p. O3. $40.00

FLOWERS, A.R. *De Mojo Blues.* (1985). NY. 1st ed. F/F. A7. $30.00

FLOYD, Candace. *Am's Greatest Disasters.* 1990. NY. Mallard. ils/photos. 176 p. VG/VG. B11. $20.00

FLUGEL, J.C. *Hundred Yrs of Psychology 1833-1933.* 1933. London. Duckworth. 1st ed. 384 p. blk cloth. G1. $28.50

FLUGEL, J.C. *Man, Morals & Soc: Psycho-Analytical Study.* (1945). NY. Internat U. 328 p. bl cloth. VG+. S9. $20.00

FLYNN, Elizabeth Gurley. *I Speak My Own Piece.* 1955. Masses & Mainstream. 1st wrp issue. 325 p. A7. $13.00

FLYNN. *Braided Border Workbook.* 1990. np. wrp. G2. $14.00

FOBB, G.E. *Hist of Antarctic Science.* 1992. Cambridge. 1st ed. M/sans. P4. $90.00

FOCILLON, Henri. *Yr 1000.* (1969). NY. Ungar. 1st Am ed. 8vo. 190 p. F/VG+. A2. $17.50

FODOR, Nandor. *Encyclopedia of Psychic Science.* 1966. New Hyde Park, NY. U Books. reprint of 1934 ed. purple cloth. VG/dj. G1. $40.00

FOERSTER, F.W. *Jews: A Christian View.* 1962. FSC. 157 p. VG/G+. S3. $22.00

FOISSAC, P. *Rapports et Discussions de l'Academie Royale...* 1833. Paris. Chez JB Balliere. 562 p. early calf/marbled brds. G1. $175.00

FOLEY, Daniel J. *Gardening by the Sea From Coast to Coast.* 1965. Phil. 1st ed. ils. F. B14. $45.00

FOLEY, Daniel J. *Ground Covers for Easier Gardening.* 1961. Phil. ils/photos. 224 p. VG/dj. B26. $15.00

FOLEY, James W. *Mellow Yr.* 1921. Pasadena, CA. Author's Pr. 1st ed. 12mo. 112 p. VG. D3. $12.50

FOLEY, James W. *Voices of Song.* 1916. NY. 1st ed. 1/250. sgn. 181 p. teg. VG. D3. $75.00

FOLEY, Martha. *Best Am Short Stories 1974.* 1974. Houghton Mifflin. 1st ed. dj. A7. $13.00

FOLEY. *Linens & Lace.* 1990. np. ils. cloth. G2. $20.00

FOLKMAN, David. *Nicaragua Route.* (1972). Salt Lake City. 1st ed. ils/maps. 173 p. pict cloth. F3. $35.00

FOLLEN, Charles. *Funeral Oration...Gaspar Spurzheim, MD...* 1832. Boston. Marsh Capen Lyon. 32 p. VG/prt gr wrp. G1. $45.00

FOLLETT, James. *Ice.* 1978. Stein Day. 1st ed. F/VG+. N3. $10.00

FOLLETT, Ken. *Dangerous Fortune.* (1993). Delacorte. ARC. w/photo & promo material. F/NF. B4. $35.00

FONER, Philip S. *Blk Panthers Speak.* (1970). Lippincott. 2nd prt. 274 p. wrp. A7. $13.00

FONER, Philip S. *British Labor & the Am Civil War.* (1981). Holmes Meier. 135 p. F/F. A7. $16.00

FONER, Philip S. *List of Labor Movement in the US...* ca 1947. NY. Internat Pub. VG/dj. V4. $25.00

FONS & PORTER. *Let's Make Waves.* 1989. np. ils. wrp. G2. $15.00

FONTANON, Denis. *Morborum Internorum Curatione Libre IIII.* 1553. Venice. Constantinus. 3rd ed. sm 8vo. contemporary paneled morocco/rebacked. G7. $195.00

FOOSE. *More Scrap Saver's Stitchery.* 1980. np. 50+ patterns. cloth. G2. $15.00

FOOTE, Henry S. *Bench & Bar of the S & SW.* 1876. St Louis. 1st ed. 264 p. very scarce. A17. $50.00

FOOTE, Horton. *Chase.* 1956. NY. 1st ed. sgn. NF/VG. A11. $95.00

FOOTE, Horton. *3 Plays.* 1962. NY. 1st ed. author's 3rd book. sgn. NF/wrp. A11. $55.00

FOOTE & WILSON. *Viking Achievement.* 1970. NY. 8vo. ils. 473 p. gilt blk cloth. F/F. H3. $25.00

FORBES, Alexander. *Northernmost Labrador Mapped From the Air.* 1938. NY. Am Geog Soc. 1st ed. 255 p. VG+. P4. $75.00

FORBES, Colin. *Target Five.* 1973. Dutton. 1st ed. F/F. F4. $14.00

FORBES, Esther. *Am's Paul Revere.* 1946. Houghton Mifflin. 1st ed. red cloth. VG. M5. $15.00

FORBES & MOSELEY. *Vinton Hist 1884 to 1984.* 1984. Centennial Comm. ils/photos/map. 205 p. VG. B10. $35.00

FORBIS, William H. *Cowboys.* 1973. Time Life. 4to. F. A8. $10.00

FORBUSH, Edward Howe. *Domestic Cat: Bird Killer, Mouser & Destroyer of Wild Life.* 1916. Boston. 1st ed. ils. 112 p. H10. $65.00

FORD, Alice. *Bird Biographies of John James Audubon.* 1957. Macmillan. 1st ed. VG/dj. A16. $25.00

FORD, Barbara. *Blk Bear: Spirit of the Wilderness.* (1981). Houghton Mifflin. photos. 1982 p. M/wrp. A17. $5.00

FORD, Consuelo Urisarri. *Five Miles From Candia.* 1959. NY. Holt. 1st ed. F/NF. N3. $15.00

FORD, Corey. *Salt-Water Taffy.* 1929. Putnam. 2nd prt. 206 p. VG/dj. M20. $20.00

FORD, Corey. *You Can Always Tell a Fisherman.* 1958. NY. 1st ed. VG/VG. B5. $40.00

FORD, Daniel. *Incident at Muc-Wa.* 1967. Doubleday. 1st ed. author's 2nd book. VG/dj. A7. $40.00

FORD, Ford Madox. *Last Post.* 1928. Literary Guild. 12mo. G. A8. $10.00

FORD, Ford Madox. *Mirror to France.* 1926. London. Duckworth. 1st ed. F/NF. B2. $200.00

FORD, Henry Sr. *Internat Jew.* nd. LA. Christian Nat Crusade. abridged. A7. $35.00

FORD, Herbert. *No Guns on Their Shoulders.* (1968). Nashville. 144 p. F/F. A7. $65.00

FORD, Hillary; see Silverberg, Robert.

FORD, John. *Dragon Waiting.* 1983. BC. VG/dj. C1. $5.00

FORD, Leslie. *Bahamas Murders.* 1952. Scribner. 1st ed. NF/NF. F4. $25.00

FORD, Marica; see Radford, R.L.

FORD, Richard. *Best Am Short Stories.* 1990. Houghton Mifflin. AP. F/prt bl wrp. C4. $40.00

FORD, Richard. *Communist.* 1987. Derry. Babcock Koontz. 1/200. sgn. F/wrp. C4. $75.00

FORD, Richard. *Eng Magnolias.* 1992. MS U. 1st ed. F/stiff pict wrp. C4. $30.00

FORD, Richard. *Piece of My Heart.* 1976. Harper Row. ARC of author's 1st book. inscr. NF. Q1. $325.00

FORD, Richard. *Rock Springs.* (1987). Atlantic Monthly. 1st ed. F/F. B3. $40.00

FORD, Richard. *Rock Springs.* 1988. London. Collins Harvill. 1st ed. F/F. C4. $55.00

FORD, Richard. *Wildlife.* 1990. NY. Atlantic Monthly. trade ed. sgn. F/F. C4. $30.00

FORD, Sydney. *Journeying Round the World.* 1912. LA. 1st ed. presentation inscr. 172 p. bl cloth. VG. H3. $15.00

FORDER, A. *Ventures Among the Arabs in Desert, Tent & Town.* 1909. NY. ils/fld map. pict cloth. O2. $45.00

FORDHAM, Herbert George. *Studies in Carto-Bibliography, British & French...* 1914. Clarendon. presentation/inscr. VG. O6. $175.00

FORDYCE, George. *Five Disseration on Fever.* 1823. Boston. Bedlington Ewer. 2nd Am from latest Eng ed. 442 p. orig sheep. G7. $125.00

FORESMAN, Robert. *Bobolink Books. Songbook 1 & 2.* 1922. New Haven. La Velle Mfg Co. set of 2 w/records. F. H3. $60.00

FORESTER, C.S. *African Queen.* 1935. Little Brn. 1st ed. brn cloth. NF/VG+. Q1. $850.00

FORESTER, C.S. *Bedchamber Mystery.* (1944). Reginald Saunders. 1st ed. prt brds. F/wrp. B24. $150.00

FORESTER, C.S. *Bedchamber Mystery.* 1944. Toronto. Saunders. 1st ed. inscr/sgn on ep. VG/VG. Q1. $450.00

FORESTER, C.S. *Captain From CT.* 1941. Little Brn. 1st ed. F/F. C4. $45.00

FORESTER, C.S. *Good Shepherd.* 1955. Little Brn. 1st ed. VG/dj. M18. $35.00

FORESTER, C.S. *Happy Return.* 1937. London. Michael Joseph. 1st ed. sgn on half-title p. VG+/NF. Q1. $600.00

FORESTER, C.S. *Happy Return.* 1937. Michael Joseph. 1st ed. 1st Hornblower. sgn. VG/VG. Q1. $600.00

FORESTER, C.S. *Hornblower & the Atropos.* 1953. London. Michael Joseph. 1st ed. NF/clip. Q1. $75.00

FORESTER, C.S. *Hornblower During the Crisis.* 1967. Little Brn. 1st ed. last of series. F/NF clip. Q1. $60.00

FORESTER, C.S. *Lord Hornblower.* 1946. Little Brn. ARC. F/dj. C4. $45.00

FORESTER, C.S. *Mr Midshipman Hornblower.* 1950. NY. 1st ed. VG/VG. B5. $40.00

FORESTER, C.S. *Nightmare.* 1954. Little Brn. 1st ed. F/NF. B2. $35.00

FORESTER, C.S. *Ship.* 1943. Little Brn. 1st ed. F/F. C4. $65.00

FORESTER, C.S. *Sky & the Forest.* 1948. Little Brn. 1st ed. F/F. C4. $35.00

FORGIE, George B. *Patricide in the House Divided...* 1979. Norton. 1st ed. 308 p. cream cloth. VG/dj. G1. $20.00

FORMAN, Elizabeth Chandlee. *King of the Air & Other Poems.* 1919. Boston. Badger. 16mo. 119 p. VG/glassine dj. V3. $9.50

FORMAN, James. *Sammy Younge Jr.* (1968). Grove. 1st ed. 282 p. NF/dj. A7. $30.00

FORMAN & SACHS. *S African Treason Trial.* (1957). London. Calder. 1st ed. 216 p. clip dj. A7. $33.00

FORREST, Richard. *Death at Yew Corner.* 1981. NY. Holt. 1st ed. F/F. S5. $25.00

FORSTER, Arnold. *Measure of Freedom: Anti-Defamation League Report.* 1950. Doubleday. 1st ed. VG/G. S3. $10.00

FORSTER, E.M. *Malabar Caves.* 1990. St Martin. 1/6. sgn/prt Carnegie. unbound/portfolio/slipcase. F. B24. $650.00

FORSTMANN, Ernst. *Commentary on the Dresden Codex.* nd. Aegean Park Pr. reprint of Peabody Mus Papers. 212 p. F3. $25.00

FORSYTE, Charles. *Decoding of Edwin Drood.* 1980. London. Gollancz. 1st ed. NF/dj. S5. $25.00

FORSYTH, Frederick. *Day of the Jackal.* 1971. London. Hutchinson. 1st ed. author's 1st mystery. NF/dj. Q1. $200.00

FORSYTH, Frederick. *Devil's Alternative.* (1979). London. Hutchinson. 1st ed. F/NF. B3. $50.00

FORSYTH, Frederick. *No Comebacks.* 1982. London. Hutchinson. 1st ed. F/F. S5. $30.00

FORSYTH, Frederick. *4th Protocol.* (1984). London. Hutchinson. 1st ed. F/F. B3. $40.00

FORSYTHE, Lewis. *Athletics in MI High Schools: 1st 100 Yrs.* 1950. NY. 1st ed. 325 p. A17. $12.50

FORT, Charles. *Books of Charles Fort.* (1919-41). NY. Holt. collection ed. 8vo. 1125 p. F/VG. A2. $25.00

FORT, Ilene S. *Flag Paintings of Childe Hassam.* 1988. LA Mus Art. 25 color pls. 128 p. cloth. dj. D2. $25.00

FORTESCUE, John. *De Laudibin Legum Angliae.* 1616. London. Companie of Stationers. 3 parts in 1. early calf. K1. $300.00

FORTHERGILL, Philip G. *Hist Aspects of Organic Evolution.* 1952. London. Hollis Carter. 1st ed. 427 p. bl cloth. VG/dj. G1. $37.50

FOSSETT, Frank. *CO: Its Gold & Silver Mines, Farms & Stock Ranges...* 1879. NY. 12mo. ils/maps/tables. gr cloth. H9. $125.00

FOSSEY, Dian. *Gorillas in the Mist.* (1983). Houghton Mifflin. 1st ed. 8vo. ils. 326 p. F-/VG. A2. $30.00

FOSTER, Alan Dean. *To the Vanishing Point.* 1988. Warner. 1st ed. F/F. T2. $16.00

FOSTER, E.G. *Civil War by Campaigns.* 1899. KS. Crane. G. A16. $25.00

FOSTER, Elizabeth. *Children of the Mist.* 1961 (1960). Macmillan. 2nd Am prt. 8vo. 221 p. VG+/VG+. A2. $10.00

FOSTER, George. *Primitive Mexican Economy.* 1942. NY. Augustin. 1st ed. 115 p. F3. $20.00

FOSTER, Hal. *Young Knight.* 1948. Kendsha, WI. 1st ed. VG. rare. C1. $11.00

FOSTER, Harry L. *Caribbean Cruise.* 1928. Dodd Mead. 1st ed. 12mo. 22 pls/14 maps. 350 p. bl brds. VG. B11. $25.00

FOSTER, Iris; see Posner, Richard.

FOSTER, J.W. *MS Valley.* 1869. Chicago/London. 1st ed. lg 8vo. 443 p. VG. H9. $175.00

FOSTER, J.W. *MS Valley.* 1869. Chicago/London. 1st ed. xl. 443 p. G. D7. $75.00

FOSTER, Joel M. *Million Egg Farm: Rancocas Poultry Farm...* ca 1910. Brown's Mills, NJ. 1st ed. 148 p. brds. H10. $9.50

FOSTER, Marian Curtis. *Miss Flora McFlimsey's Christmas Eve.* 1949. Lee Shepard. 1st ed. 12mo. VG-/G. A3. $15.00

FOSTER, Marian Curtis. *Miss Flora McFlimsey's Easter Bonnet.* 1951. Lee Shepard. 1st ed. 12mo. VG/dj. A3. $25.00

FOSTER, Michael. *TB of Physiology.* 1877. London. Macmillan. 1st ed. 559 p. gr cloth. B14. $175.00

FOSTER, Michael. *TB of Physiology.* 1893. NY. Macmillan. 4 vols. mixed set of 5th & 6th eds. gr cloth. G7. $250.00

FOSTER, Richard J. *Celebration of Discipline: Path to Spiritual Growth.* 1986. Harper Row. 30th prt. 8vo. 184 p. G/dj. V3. $8.00

FOSTER, Thomas J. *Mine Foreman's Pocket Book, Almanac & Diary for Yr 1881.* 1881. Shenandoah Schuykill. 12mo. 234 p. H9. $85.00

FOSTER, W.J. *Raymond's Magpie & Other Stories.* 1903. London. Robert Culley. 12mo. 128 p. VG. S10. $20.00

FOSTER, William Z. *Am Trade Unionism: Principles & Organization Strategy...* ca 1947. NY. Internat Pub. VG. V4. $15.00

FOSTER, William Z. *Outline Hist of World Trade Union Movement.* ca 1956. NY. Internat Pub. ils. VG/fair. V4. $20.00

FOSTER, William Z. *Outline Political Hist of the Americas.* (1951). Internat Pub. 1st ed. G/fair. V4. $20.00

FOSTER, William Z. *Outline Political Hist of the Americas.* (1951). NY. Internat Pub. sgn. 668 p. VG/dj. A7. $30.00

FOTHERGILL, Augusta B. *Wills of Westmoreland Co, VA 1654-1800.* 1925. Appeals Pr. 229 p. VG. B10. $45.00

FOULKE, Joseph. *Memoirs of Jacob Ritter: Faithful Minister in Soc Friends.* 1844. London. Chapman. 16mo. 111 p. marbled brds. G. V3. $25.00

FOUNTAIN, Paul. *Great NW & the Great Lake Region of N Am.* 1904. Longman Gr. 355 p. VG. H7. $65.00

FOWARD, Robert L. *Dragon's Egg.* 1980. Ballantine. 1st ed. F/F. N3. $25.00

FOWLER, Christopher. *Bureau of Lost Souls.* 1989. Century. 1st ed. 1/250. sgn/#d. aeg. F/F/slipcase. F4. $65.00

FOWLER, Christopher. *Bureau of Lost Souls.* 1989. London. Century. 1st ed. F/F. N3. $25.00

FOWLER, Christopher. *Rune.* 1990. Century. 1st British ed. 1/200. sgn/#d. F/F/cloth box. F4. $75.00

FOWLER, Gene. *Great Mouthpiece: Life Story of Wm J Fallon.* 1946. Bantam. 1st pb issue? VG. M11. $35.00

FOWLER, Gene. *Timberline.* 1933. NY. 1st ed. 480 p. cloth. VG. scarce. D3. $25.00

FOWLER, Jacob. *Journal of...Narrates an Adventure From AR...* 1898. NY. Harper. 1st ed. 1/950. edit presentation. bl cloth. H9. $500.00

FOWLER, Karen Joy. *Sarah Canary.* 1991. NY. Holt. 1st ed. F/F. N3. $20.00

FOWLER, O.S. *Sexual Science...As Taught by Phrenology.* ca 1875. np. royal 8vo. 930 p. brn cloth. G. T3. $27.00

FOWLER, William W. *Woman on the Am Frontier.* 1878. Hartford. 527 p. gilt bdg. VG. H7. $45.00

FOWLER & OLLVA. *Tony O!* 1973. Hawthorn. 1st ed. G+/G+. P8. $25.00

FOWLES, John. *Brief Hist of Lyme.* 1981. Dorchester. Friends of Mus Lyme Regis. F/stapled prt wrp. Q1. $45.00

FOWLES, John. *French Lieutenant's Woman.* 1969. Little Brn. 1st ed. F/F. C4. $65.00

FOWLES, John. *Intro: Remembering Cruikshank.* 1964. Princeton. offprint from Chronicle. sgn. F/wrp. L3. $450.00

FOWLES, John. *Maggot.* 1985. London. Cape. 1/500. sgn. F. C4. $150.00

FOWLES, John. *On Being Eng But Not British.* 1964. Austin. TX Quarterly. early offprint. 1/25. sgn. NF/wrp. L3. $675.00

FOWLES & GODWIN. *Islands.* 1978. London. Cape. 1st ed. inscr/dtd 1978. sm quarto. F/F. L3. $150.00

FOX, Frances Margaret. *Adventures of Sonny Bear.* 1934 (1916). Chicago. Rand McNally. 12mo. 64 p. pict brds. G. T5. $22.00

FOX, Frances Margaret. *Carlota: Story of San Gabriel Mission.* 1908. Boston. 12mo. ils Ethelind Ridgway. 179 p. pict gr cloth. VG. H3. $15.00

FOX, Frances Margaret. *Little Bear & His Friends.* 1934 (1921). Rand McNally. 12mo. 64 p. pict brds. G+. T5. $25.00

FOX, Frances Margaret. *Little Mossback Amelia.* 1967. reprint of 1939 Dutton ed. VG/wrp. A16. $7.00

FOX, Frances Margaret. *What Gladys Saw.* 1902. Wilde. 1st ed. ils Charles Copeland. 318 p. VG. S10. $30.00

FOX, Frances Margaret. *Wilding Princess.* 1929. Volland. 1st ed. 10 color pls. 79 p. VG. P2. $50.00

FOX, George H. *Photographic Ils of the Skin.* 1887. NY. EB Treat. 2nd ed. 208 p. recased blk cloth. G+. S9. $72.00

FOX, George. *Autobiography.* 1903. Phil. Ferris Leach. 1st ed. 2 vols. 12mo. VG. V3. $22.50

FOX, George. *Journal of George Fox: Revised Ed by John L Nickalls.* 1952. Cambridge. 12mo. 789 p. VG. V3. $16.00

FOX, George. *Journal or Hist Account of Life, Travels, Sufferings...* 1800. NY. Isaac Collins. 4th/corrected ed. 2 vols. 8vo. leather. V3. $45.00

FOX, John A. *Garden Spot of the MS Valley.* ca 1902. St Louis. oblong 8vo. ils Grey. F/red wrp. H9. $35.00

FOX, John Jr. *Little Shepherd of Kingdom Come.* 1931. Scribner. 1st ed. ils Wyeth/14 full-p pls. 322 p. VG. D1. $200.00

FOX, Paula. *Poor George.* 1967. NY. 1st ed. sgn. F/NF. A11. $55.00

FOX, S.M. *Seventh KS Cavalry: Its Service in the Civil War.* 1908. Topeka, KS. 1st ed. 59 p. cloth. VG. D3. $25.00

FOX, Sanford J. *Science & Justice: MA Witchcraft Trials.* 1968. Baltimore. Johns Hopkins. 1st ed. 122 p. blk cloth. VG/dj. G1. $25.00

FOX, Ted. *Showtime at the Apollo.* 1983. Holt. 1st ed. ils. F/F. B2. $40.00

FOX, William Price. *Doctor Golf.* 1963. Phil. 1st ed. VG/VG. B5. $25.00

FOX, William Price. *S Fried Plus 6.* 1968. Phil. 1st hc ed. author's 1st book. inscr. F/NF. A11. $60.00

FOX & HUBBARD. *Maple Sugar Industry.* 1905. WA, DC. GPO. ils/index. 56 p. wrp. h10. $15.00

FOX-DAVIS, Arthur Charles. *Art of Heraldry: Encyclopedia of Armory.* 1976. NY. ils. 504 p. VG/dj. B18. $32.50

FOXX, Jack; see Pronzini, Bill.

FOY-VAILLANT, Jean. *Numismata Aerea Imperatorum...* 1827. Paris. Chez L'Auteur & De Bure Freres. 2 vols. NF. K1. $200.00

FRAENKEL, Osmond. *Sacco-Vanzetticase.* 1931. Knopf. 1st ed. F/VG. B2. $150.00

FRAGER. *Quilting Primer.* nd. np. 2nd ed. ils. wrp. G2. $15.00

FRANCE, Anatole. *At the Sign of the Reine Pedauque.* 1928. Dodd Mead. ils Frank C Pape. F. M18. $25.00

FRANCE, Anatole. *Honey Bee.* 1911. John Lane. 1st ed. ils Florence Lundburg. VG. M5. $60.00

FRANCE, Anatole. *Le Lys Rouge.* 1947. Paris. Eds Athena. 1/750. 4to. ils after Andre Hofer. 271 p. NF/pict wrp. B14. $75.00

FRANCE, Anatole. *Red Lily.* nd. Boni Liveright. brn brds. E3. $6.00

FRANCE, L.B. *Mr Dide: His Vacation in Co & Other Sketches.* 1890. NY. 1st ed. 12mo. 259 p. B28. $30.00

FRANCE, Royal W. *My Native Grounds.* 1957. NY. Cameron Assoc. dj. M11. $45.00

FRANCHERE, Gabriel. *Voyage to the NW Coast of Am.* 1954. Chicago. 321 p. VG. B18. $25.00

FRANCILLON, R.J. *Japanese Aircraft of the Pacific War.* (1970). London. 1st ed. ils. 570 p. VG/dj. B18. $32.50

FRANCINI. *Crewel Embroidery.* 1986. np. pb. G2. $15.00

FRANCIS, A.D. *Wine Trade.* (1972). London. Blk. 1st ed. maps. F/NF clip. A7. $17.00

FRANCIS, David Pitt. *Nostradamus: Prophecies of Present Times.* 1984. Wellingborough. Aquarian Pr. 1st ed. VG/dj. N2. $7.50

FRANCIS, Dick. *Best Racing & Chasing Stories.* 1966. London. Faber. ARC. RS. NF/NF. Q1. $100.00

FRANCIS, Dick. *Blood Sport.* 1967. Harper Row. 1st ed. NF/NF. Q1. $100.00

FRANCIS, Dick. *Bolt.* (1986). Michael Joseph. 1st ed. VG/VG. B3. $30.00

FRANCIS, Dick. *Bolt.* 1987. Putnam. ARC/1st Am ed. F/wrp. B2. $35.00

FRANCIS, Dick. *Bonecrack.* 1971. London. Michael Joseph. 1st ed. sgn. F/F. M15. $100.00

FRANCIS, Dick. *Break In.* 1985. London. Michael Joseph. 1st ed. F/clip. M15. $35.00

FRANCIS, Dick. *Decider.* (1993). Putnam. ARC/1st Am ed. NF/wrp. B4. $45.00

FRANCIS, Dick. *Decider.* 1993. London. Michael Joseph. 1st ed. sgn. F/F. M15. $50.00

FRANCIS, Dick. *Knock Down.* 1974. London. Michael Joseph. 1st ed. F/F. S5. $75.00

FRANCIS, Dick. *Knock Down.* 1975. Harper. 1st Am ed. NF/NF. B2. $45.00

FRANCIS, Dick. *Lester.* (1986). London. Michael Joseph. 1st ed. F/F. B3. $40.00

FRANCIS, Dick. *Nerve.* 1964. London. Michael Joseph. 1st ed. F/NF. M15. $850.00

FRANCIS, Dick. *Nerve.* 1964. Michael Joseph. 1st ed. NF/NF. Q1. $750.00

FRANCIS, Dick. *Proof.* 1984. London. Michael Joseph. 1st ed. F/F. M15. $75.00

FRANCIS, Dick. *Risk.* 1977. London. Michael Joseph. 1st ed. inscr/sgn. F/F. S5. $75.00

FRANCIS, Dick. *Slay-Ride.* 1973. Harper. 1st ed. 219 p. VG+/dj. B22. $22.00

FRANCIS, Dick. *Sport of Queens: Autobiography of Dick Francis.* (1969). Harper. 1st Am ed. author's 1st book. VG/dj. B9. $150.00

FRANCIS, Dick. *Straight.* 1989. London. Michael Joseph. 1st ed. sgn. F/F. S5. $50.00

FRANCIS, Dick. *Trial Run.* 1978. London. Michael Joseph. 1st ed. inscr. NF/dj. M15. $85.00

FRANCIS, Dick. *Twice Shy.* 1981. London. Michael Joseph. 1st ed. inscr/sgn. F/F. S5. $60.00

FRANCIS, Dixon. *Mr Piper & His Cubs.* 1973. Ames, IA. 1st ed. ils. 256 p. VG/dj. B10. $47.50

FRANCIS, John. *Annals, Anecdotes & Legends of Life Assurance.* 1869. NY. Wynkoop Hallenbeck. Am Revised Ed (so stated). sm 8vo. gr cloth. B20. $75.00

FRANCK, Adolphe. *Kabbalah: Religious Philosophy of the Hebrews.* 1940. Bell. reprint. VG/VG. S3. $23.00

FRANCK, Frederick. *African Sketchbook.* 1961. Holt. 1st ed. inscr. F/NF. B2. $35.00

FRANCK, Harry A. *Discovering S Am.* 1943. Phil. 1st ed. 453 p. tan cloth. F. H3. $20.00

FRANCK, Harry A. *Tramping Through Mexico, Guatemala & Honduras.* 1916. NY. Century. 1st ed. 8vo. ils/fld map. 378 p. decor gr cloth. G. B11. $35.00

FRANCK, Harry A. *Wandering in N China.* 1923. Century. 1st ed. xl. 171 photos/1 color fld map. 502 p. VG. W1. $25.00

FRANCK, Henry. *Zone Policeman 88.* 1913. Century. 1st ed. 314 p. pict cloth. F3. $15.00

FRANK, Robert. *Americans.* 1968. NY. Aperture/MOMA. revised/enlarged ed. NF/wrp. B2. $75.00

FRANK, Ulrich. *Simon Eichelkatz the Patriarch: 2 Stories of Jewish Life.* 1907. JPS. 431 p. VG/VG. S3. $23.00

FRANK, Waldo. *Birth of a World: Bolivar in Terms of His Peoples.* 1951. Houghton Mifflin. 1st ed. 8vo. 432 p. VG+/VG. A2. $17.50

FRANK. *Quilting for Beginners.* 1985. np. ils. wrp. G2. $15.00

FRANKEL, Ernest. *Band of Brothers.* 1958. Macmillan. 1st ed. F/VG. B4. $45.00

FRANKENSTEIN, Alfred. *William Sidney Mount.* 1975. Abrams. 211 pls. 510 p. cloth. M/dj. D2. $80.00

FRANKFURTER, Felix. *Man Behind the Men Behind the President.* 1936. Chicago. Am Vigilant Intelligence Federation. 2nd prt. 38 p. M11. $65.00

FRANKFURTER, Felix. *Mr Justice Holmes.* 1931. Coward McCann. M11. $75.00

FRANKLIN, Benjamin. *Oeuvres de M Franklin...* 1773. Paris. 1st French ed. quarto. 12 pls. NF/clamshell case. H5. $2,000.00

FRANKLIN, Benjamin. *Private Life of the Late Benjamin Franklin, LLD.* 1793. London. Parsons. 1st Eng ed. rebound. VG. Q1. $750.00

FRANKLIN, H. Bruce. *Future Perfect.* 1978. NY. Oxford. revised ed. 404 p. VG/dj. A7. $17.00

FRANKLIN, John Hope. *Racial Equality in Am.* (1976). Chicago. 113 p. F/NF. A7. $15.00

FRANKS, Jack. *Echoes.* 1929. Chicago. Lakeside. 1/1000. sgn. G+. A1. $25.00

FRANKS, Lucinda. *Waiting Out a War.* (1974). NY. F/F. A7. $35.00

FRANQUI, Carlos. *Diario de la Revolucion Cubana.* 1976. Spain. ERT. Spanish text. 8vo. 754 p. VG/VG. B11. $15.00

FRANZIUS, Enno. *Hist of Order of Assassins.* ca 1969. Funk Wagnall. 1st ed. ils. 261 p. H10. $20.00

FRARY, I.T. *Early Homes of OH.* (1936). Richmond. 1st ed. 336 p. VG/dj. B18. $47.50

FRARY, I.T. *OH in Homespun & Calico.* (1942). Richmond, VA. 1st ed. sgn. 148 p. VG. B18. $35.00

FRASCONI, Antonio. *Known Fables.* 1964. NY. E Weyhe Spiral Pr. 1/500. octavo. 28 p. marbled brds. F/glassine. B24. $325.00

FRASCONI, Antonio. *Woodcuts by Antonio Frasconi.* 1957. NY. E Weyhe Spiral Pr. 1/500. VG/slipcase/glassine. A1. $125.00

FRASER, Anthea. *April Rainers.* 1989. London. Collins. ARC of 1st ed. RS. NF/dj. S5. $22.50

FRASER, Anthea. *Splash of Red.* 1981. London. Weidenfeld. 1st ed. F/F. S5. $25.00

FRASER, Antonia. *Wives of Henry VIII.* 1992. Knopf. 1st ed. sgn. F/F. Q1. $35.00

FRASER, Claud Lovat. *Book of Simple Toys.* 1982. Mawr College. 1/1000. 8vo. gilt maroon cloth/paper label. F. F1. $60.00

FRASER, George MacDonald. *Pyrates.* 1983. London. Collins. 1st ed. F/F. Q1. $40.00

FRASER, George MacDonald. *Pyrates.* 1984. Knopf. 1st Am ed. F/F. B2. $30.00

FRASER, Louis. *Zoologia Typica; or, Figures of New & Rare Mammals & Birds.* 1849. London. self pub. 1st ed. 1/250. folio. 70 hc pls. VG. rare. H5. $10,000.00

FRASER, M.B. *Walking the Line: Travels Along Canadian/Am Border.* (1989). Sierra Club. 1st ed. 218 p. M/dj. A17. $9.50

FRASER, Samuel. *Am Fruits: Their Propagation, Cultivation, Harvesting...* 1931. NY. Judd. corrected ed. 892 p. H10. $25.00

FRASER, W.A. *Outcasts.* 1901. Scribner. 1st ed. ils Arthur Heming. teg. gr cloth. VG. S10. $40.00

FRASER & GILLESPIE. *To Be or Not To Bop.* 1979. Doubleday. VG/VG. A7. $30.00

FRASSANITO, William. *Antietam.* 1978. np. ils. 304 p. dj. O7. $14.50

FRASSANITO, William. *Gettysburg.* 1975. np. photos. 248 p. dj. O7. $14.50

FRASSANITO, William. *Grant & Lee.* 1983. np. photos/index. 442 p. O7. $18.50

FRAZAR, Douglas. *Perseverance Island.* 1885. Boston. ils. 373 p. G+. B18. $32.50

FRAZER, Jane. *Gr Wings; or, Under Italian Skies.* nd. Detroit. Frazer. G/dj. A16. $15.00

FRAZIER, E.F. *Blk Bourgeoisie.* 1957. Glencoe. Free Pr. 1st ed. F/NF. B2. $35.00

FRAZIER, E.F. *Negro in the US.* 1949. Macmillan. 2nd prt. 767 p. NF. A7. $35.00

FRAZIER, Robert Caine; see Creasey, John.

FREE, George D. *Hist of TN, From Its Earliest Discoveries & Settlements...* 1895. Church Hill, KY. 12mo. 224 p. gr cloth. H9. $35.00

FREED, Hugo. *Orchids & Serendipity.* 1970. Englewood Cliffs. photos. 184 p. F/dj. B26. $17.50

FREEDMAN & KAPLAN. *Comprehensive TB of Psychiatry II.* 1975 (1967). Baltimore. Williams Wilkins. 2nd ed/1st prt. 2 vols. G1. $75.00

FREEHLING, William W. *Road to Disunion Secessionists at Bay.* 1990. NY. Oxford. BC. 640 p. cloth. F/F. M8. $25.00

FREEHOF, Solomon B. *Sm Sanctuary: Judaism in the Prayerbook.* 1942. Riverdale. 302 p. VG. S3. $24.00

FREELING, Nicholas. *Tsing Boom.* (1969). Harper Row. stated 1st Am ed. dj. A7. $23.00

FREEMAN, Don. *Bearymore.* 1976. Viking. 1st ed. oblong 4to. pict brds. VG. A3. $15.00

FREEMAN, Don. *Dandelion.* 1964. Viking. 2nd prt. oblong 4to. 48 p. VG/VG. A3. $17.50

FREEMAN, Don. *Pet of the Met.* 1953. Viking. 1st ed. oblong 4to. 63 p. VG. A3. $25.00

FREEMAN, Don. *3rd Monkey.* 1956. Viking. 1st ed. 44 p. VG+/VG. A3. $50.00

FREEMAN, Douglas Southall. *George WA: A Biography.* 1948. Scribner. 1st/A ed. 7 vols. VG. E5. $300.00

FREEMAN, Douglas Southall. *George WA: A Biography.* 1948-52. Scribner. 1st ed. 5 vols in 3 boxes. VG. B10. $225.00

FREEMAN, Douglas Southall. *Lee's Lieutants: A Study in Command.* 1944. Scribner. early prt. 3 vols. cloth. VG. M8. $150.00

FREEMAN, Douglas Southall. *Lee: An Abridgement...* ca 1961. Scribner. 1st ed. 601 p. VG/VG. B10. $35.00

FREEMAN, Ed. *Freeman's Increase of Crime Songster...* ca 1880? NY. Ornum. 18mo. 68 p. pict wrp. M1. $200.00

FREEMAN, Jean Todd. *Cynthia & the Unicorn.* 1967. Norton. 1st ed. inscr. F/VG. P2. $30.00

FREEMAN, John. *Portrait of George Moore.* 1922. London. 1/600. sgn. G/dj. A1. $60.00

FREEMAN, Kathleen. *Greek City-States.* (1950). NY. Norton. 1st ed. 8vo. 274 p. VG+/G+. A2. $20.00

FREEMAN, Larry. *Hist Prints of Am Cities.* ca 1952. Century House. 8vo. ils. 100 p. gray cloth. H9. $65.00

FREEMAN, Lelia Crocheron. *Nip & Tuck in Toyland.* 1927. NY. Sears. 4to. 8 full-p pls. teg. gilt red cloth. VG+. F1. $225.00

FREEMAN, Margaret B. *Herbs for Mediaeval Household Cooking, Healing...* 1964 (1943). Metro Mus Art. 5th prt. sm 4to. 48 p. F/F clip. A7. $30.00

FREEMAN, R.B. *British Natural Hist Books 1495-1900: A Handlist.* 1980. Dawson/Archon Books. 437 p. gr cloth. NF. S9. $23.00

FREEMAN, Sean. *Fair Weather Foul.* (1988). Morrow. 1st ed. inscr/sgn. F/NF. A7. $35.00

FREEMANTLE, Brian. *Button Man.* 1992. London. Century. 1st ed. NF/dj. S5. $30.00

FREEMANTLE, Brian. *Charlie Muffin.* 1977. London. Cape. 1st ed. F/F. S5. $60.00

FREEMANTLE, Brian. *Choice of Eddie Franks.* 1987. NY. Tor. 1st Am ed. inscr. F/F. M15. $35.00

FREEMANTLE, Brian. *Fix: Inside World Drug Trade.* (1986). Tor. 1st ed. 351 p. F/NF. A7. $15.00

FREEMANTLE, Brian. *Man Who Wanted Tomorrow.* 1975. London. Cape. 1st ed. F/F. M15. $75.00

FREEMANTLE, Brian. *Rules of Engagement.* 1984. London. Century. 1st ed. F/F. M15. $40.00

FREES, Harry Whittier. *Little Kittens' Nursery Rhymes.* 1956 (1946). Rand McNally. F. M5. $10.00

FREES, Harry Whittier. *Whiskers.* 1941 (1937). Rand McNally. VG. M5. $15.00

FREETHY, Ron. *Auks: An Ornithologist's Guide.* (1987). Facts on File. 1st ed. 8vo. 208 p. F/F. A2. $12.50

FREKE, John. *Essay on the Art of Healing.* 1748. London. W Innys. 272 p. contemporary full calf/later rebacking. G7. $495.00

FREMLIN, Celia. *Appointment w/Yesterday.* 1972. London. Gollancz. 1st ed. NF/NF. M15. $35.00

FREMLIN, Celia. *Possession.* 1969. London. Gollancz. 1st ed. F/F. M15. $40.00

FREMONT, Jessie Benton. *Yr of Am Travel.* 1960. San Francisco. Plantin. BC of CA. 1/450. 121 p. NF. P4. $95.00

FREMONT, John C. *Exploring Expedition to Rocky Mtns...* 1852. Buffalo. Derby. 15th thousand. 456 p. G+. H7. $60.00

FREMONT, John C. *Geographical Memoir Upon Upper CA, in Illustration of...* 1848. WA, DC. Wendell Van Benthuysen. 8vo. new fabricoid. missing map. H9. $65.00

FREMONT, John C. *Geographical Memoir Upon Upper CA in Ils...* 1964. BC of CA. reprint from 1848 ed. pict brds. M. O6. $195.00

FREMONT, John C. *Memoirs of My Life...* 1887. Chicago/NY. Belford Clarke. thick 8vo. lacks fld map/some pls. H9. $75.00

FREMONT, John C. *Notes of Travel in CA...* 1849. Dublin. 1st Irish ed. 16mo. 311 p. VG. D3. $125.00

FREMONT, John C. *OR & CA.* 1850. Buffalo/Cleveland. Darby/Smith Knight. 8vo. 465 p. orig calf. H9. $45.00

FREMONT, John C. *OR & CA: Exploring Expedition to Rocky Mtns...* 1851. Buffalo. Derby. later ed. 12mo. ils. 456 p. rebacked calf. G. D3. $50.00

FREMONT, John C. *Report of Exploring Expedition to the Rocky Mtns...* 1845. WA, DC. 1st ed. leather/marbled brds. G+. D7. $300.00

FREMONT, John C. *Report on Exploring Expedition to Rocky Mtns in Yr 1842...* 1845. WA. Gales Seaton. 22 pls/5 maps. VG. very scarce. O5. $750.00

FREMONT, John Charles. *Narrative of Exploring Expedition to Rocky Mtns...1842...* 1845. WA, DC. Gales Seaton. 8vo. 22 pls/1 fld map/fld chart. emb brn cloth. H9. $1,800.00

FREMONT, John Charles. *Narrative of Exploring Expedition to Rocky Mtns...1842...* 1845. WA, DC. Taylor Wilde. 2nd ed. latitude/longitude tables. orig prt buff wrp. H9. $200.00

FREMONT, John Charles. *Report of Exploring Expedition to Rocky Mtns in Yr 1842...* 1845. WA, DC. Blair Rives. 8vo. 22 pls/3 (of 5) fld maps. new buckram. H9. $250.00

FRENCH, Henry F. *Farm Drainage.* 1859. NY. Moore. 1st ed. 12mo. 384 p. VG. B28. $30.00

FRENCH, Joseph Lewis. *Gallery of Old Rogues.* 1931. NY. King. 8vo. 285 p. VG/VG. B11. $35.00

FRENCH, L.H. *Seward's Land of Gold.* nd (1905). NY. Montross Clarke Emmons. 1st ed. xl. G. very scarce. A17. $75.00

FRENCH-SHELDON, M. *Sultan to Sultan.* 1892. Boston. 1st ed. ils. 435 p. gilt red cloth. VG. H3. $65.00

FRENSDORFF, S. *Das Buch Ochlah W'Ochlah (Massora).* 1972. KTAV. 4to. German/Hebrew text. VG+. S3. $26.00

FREUCHEN, Peter. *Men of the Frozen N.* 1962. Cleveland. 1st ed. 8vo. 315 p. pict wht cloth. M/VG. H3. $20.00

FREUD, Sigmond. *Collected Papers.* 1959. Basic Books. 1st Am ed. 5 vols. slipcase/box. G7. $100.00

FREUD, Sigmund. *Collected Papers.* 1924-25. NY. Internat Psycho-Analytical Pr. 1st Eng ed. 4 vols. VG. R3. $650.00

FREUD, Sigmund. *Complete Letters...to Wilhelm Fliess 1887-1904.* 1985. Cambridge. Belknap. 506 p. red cloth. G1. $25.00

FREUD, Sigmund. *General Intro to Psychoanalysis.* 1920. NY. Liveright. 406 p. cloth. G. B14. $50.00

FREUD, Sigmund. *Hist of the Psychoanalytic Movement.* 1917. NY. 1st Eng-language ed. VG/pub brn wrp. scarce. G1. $175.00

FREUD, Sigmund. *Jugendbriefe an Eduard Silberstein 1871-81.* 1989. Frankfurt. Verlag. 252 p. red cloth. VG/dj. G1. $37.50

FREUD, Sigmund. *Letters of Sigmund Freud & Arnold Zweig.* 1970. HBJ. 1st Am ed. 170 p. gr cloth. VG/dj. G1. $25.00

FREUD, Sigmund. *Reflections on War & Death.* 1918. Moffat Yard. 1st ed. VG. M18. $50.00

FREUD, Sigmund. *Zur Geschichte der Psychoanalytischen Bewegung.* 1924 (1914). Leipzig. IPV. 1st ed in book form. 72 p. NF. G1. $185.00

FREUD, Sigmund. *Zur Geschichte der Psychoanalytischen Bewegung.* 1966. Munchen. Werner Fritsch. reprint. 72 p. prt wrp. G1. $17.50

FREUND, Bill. *Capital & Labor in the Nigerian Tin Mines.* (1981). Atlantic Highlands. 1st Am ed. 266 p. NF/NF. A7. $18.00

FREUND, Ernst. *Police Power, Public Policy & Constitutional Rights.* 1904. Chicago. Callaghan. new gilt calf. M11. $150.00

FREUND, Paul A. *On Understanding the Supreme Court.* 1949. Little Brn. cloth. VG. M11. $35.00

FREY & SHUMWAY. *Conestoga Wagon, 1750-1850.* 1968. NY. 3rd ed. 1/2000. VG. O#. $95.00

FREYNE, Sean. *Galilee From Alexander the Great to Hadrian...* 1980. Notre Dame. 491 p. VG+/VG+. S3. $26.00

FREYRE, Gilberto. *Order & Progress: Brazil From Monarchy to Republic.* 1970. Knopf. 1st Am ed. 8vo. 422 p. VG+/VG+. A2. $15.00

FRICKE, John. *Wizard of Oz.* 1989. Warner. 1st/Official 50th-Anniversary ed. VG/VG. L1. $75.00

FRIED, Albert. *John Brn's Journey.* 1978. Doubleday. 1st ed. 293 p. dj. A7. $15.00

FRIED, Jacob. *Jews & Divorce.* 1968. NY. KATV. 9 essays. 208 p. VG+. S3. $23.00

FRIEDEL, Francis J. *Mariology of Cardinal Newman.* 1928. NY. Benziger. 1st ed. 392 p. H10. $22.50

FRIEDLAENDER, Israel. *Past & Present: Selected Essays.* 1961. Burning Bush Pr. 336 p. VG+/G+. S3. $23.00

FRIEDLANDER, Gerald. *Jewish Sources of the Sermon on the Mount.* 1968 (1911). NY. reprint. 301 p. VG+. S3. $28.00

FRIEDLANDER, Judith. *Begging Indian in Hueyapan.* 1975. St Martin. 1st ed. 205 p. wrp. F3. $10.00

FRIEDMAN, Elisha M. *Survival or Extinction: Social Aspects of Jewish Question.* 1924. NY. Seltzer. 297 p. VG. S3. $19.00

FRIEDMAN, Kinky. *Greenwhich Killing Time.* 1986. NY. Beech Tree. ARC of 1st ed. RS. F/F. S5. $25.00

FRIEDMAN, Kinky. *When the Cat's Away.* (1988). NY. Beech Tree. 1st ed. rem mk. NF/F. B3. $25.00

FRIEDMAN, Lawrence J. *Menninger: The Family & the Clinic.* 1990. Knopf. 1st ed. photos. 472 p. VG/dj. G1. $25.00

FRIEDMAN, Leon. *Argument: Oral Argument Before Supreme Court Brn Vs Brd...* 1969. NY. Chelsea. dj. M11. $50.00

FRIEDMAN, Stephen. *William J Brennan Jr: Affair w/Freedom...* 1967. NY. Atheneum. G/dj. M11. $45.00

FRIEDMAN & NEUBORNE. *Unquestioning Obedience to the President: The ACLU Case...* (1972). Norton. 1st ed. 284 p. NF/clip dj. A7. $35.00

FRIEDMAN & SCHWARZ. *Power & Greed: Inside the Teamsters Empire of Corruption.* 1989. Franklin Watts. 1st ed. 284 p. F/F. A7. $14.00

FRIEDMAN & SELDEN. *Am's Asia.* (1971). Vintage. pb. 4th in Antitexts series. 437 p. NF. A7. $15.00

FRIEDRICH, Paul. *Agrarian Revolt in a Mexican Village.* 1970. Austin, TX. 1st ed. 4to. wrp. F3. $15.00

FRINK, Maurice. *Cow Country Cavalcade: 80 Yrs of WY Stock Growers Assn.* 1954. Denver. Old W. 1st ed. sgn. VG/VG. H7. $35.00

FRIPP, Innes. *Story of Hiawatha, Retold From Poem by Longfellow.* nd. Nelson. 8 mtd pls. VG. M5. $35.00

FRISSELL, Toni. *Toni Frissell's Mother Goose.* (1948). Harper. sm quarto. ils Frissell. 95 p. F/dj. B24. $200.00

FRITEAU, Edouard. *Branches Extra-Petreuses et Terminales du Nerf Facial.* 1896. Paris. Steinheil. presentation/inscr/dtd. 44 p. quarter morocco. G7. $295.00

FRITH, Francis. *Quaker Ideal.* 1894. London. Hicks. 16mo. 102 p. V3. $10.00

FRITZ, Emanuael. *CA Coast Redwood: An Annotated Bibliography...* 1957. Foundation Am Resource Management. 1st ed. 267 p. VG. B19. $55.00

FRITZ. *Art of Hand Applique.* 1990. np. ils. wrp. G2. $15.00

FRIZELL & GREENFIELD. *Around the World on the Cleveland.* 1910. self pub. 1st ed. 8vo. ils/fld map. 307 p. VG. W1. $18.00

FROBENIUS, Leo. *African Nights.* (1971). Herder. trans Peter Ross. 284 p. dj. A7. $25.00

FROHLICH, Karl. *Karl Frohlich's Frolics w/Scissors & Pen.* 1879. Worthington. trans Chatelain. prt brds. NF. HB24. $100.00

FROISSART, Jean. *Historiarum Opus Omne Iamprimum et Breviter Collectum...* 1537. Paris. Simon de Colines. 1st ed. 12mo. 17th-century calf. VG. R3. $1,000.00

FROMM, Erich. *Greatness & Limitations of Freud's Thought.* 1980. Harper Row. 1st prt. 147 p. F/VG. S9. $10.00

FROST, John. *Great Cities of the World.* 1854. Auburn. 12mo. ils. 544 p. G. T3. $29.00

FROST, John. *Hist of the State of CA.* 1850. Auburn, NY. 1st ed. 508 p. G. D7. $200.00

FROST, John. *Mexican War & Its Warriors...* 1848. New Haven. 1st ed. 332 p. VG. D7. $125.00

FROST, Mark. *List of 7.* 1993. Morrow. 1st ed. M/M. T2. $25.00

FROST, Richard H. *Mooney Case.* ca 1968. Stanford. photos. F/VG. V4. $22.50

FROST, Robert. *Boy's Will.* 1913. London. David Nutt. 1st ed. 1/135. sgn/#d. NF/prt tan wrp. Q1. $1,500.00

FROST, Robert. *From Snow to Snow.* 1936. Holt. 1st thus ed. for 20th-Anniversary Hampshire Bookshop. NF. E3. $100.00

FROST, Robert. *Further Range.* 1936. NY. 1st ed. F/VG+. V1. $50.00

FROST, Robert. *Further Range.* 1936. NY. Holt. 1st ed. w/photo. VG/G. L3. $65.00

FROST, Robert. *Guardeen.* 1943. Ward Ritchie. 1st ed. 1/96. quarto. F/prt wrp. B24. $500.00

FROST, Robert. *In the Clearing.* 1962. HRW. 1st ed. w/pub card. F/F. C4. $30.00

FROST, Robert. *In the Clearing.* 1962. Rinehart Winston. ltd ed. 1/1500. sgn. F/slipcase. B24. $325.00

FROST, Robert. *Letters of Robert Frost to Louis Untermeyer.* 1963. HRW. 1st ed. F/NF. C4. $35.00

FROST, Robert. *Lone Striker.* 1933. Knopf. 1st ed. Borzoi Chap Book series. F/prt wrp/envelope. B24. $85.00

FROST, Robert. *Masque of Mercy.* 1947. Holt. 1st ed. 1/751. sgn/#d. special bdg. NF. B2. $200.00

FROST, Robert. *Masque of Mercy.* 1947. NY. 1st ed. sgn/dtd 1948. VG+/VG. V1. $135.00

FROST, Robert. *Masque of Mercy.* 1947. NY. Holt. 1/751. sgn/#d. F/slipcase. Q1. $350.00

FROST, Robert. *Masque of Reason.* 1945. NY. 1st ed. F/NF. V1. $45.00

FROST, Robert. *New Hampshire: A Poem w/Notes & Grace Notes.* 1923. NY. Holt. 1/350. sgn/#d. his 1st Pulitzer. NF/orig glassine/slipcase. Q1. $750.00

FROST, Robert. *Proceedings: Am Academy of Arts & Letters.* 1962. NY. 1st ed. F/stiff wrp C4. $35.00

FROST, Robert. *Robert Frost. Selected by Himself.* 1955. Penguin Poets series. PBO. NF. A11. $65.00

FROST, Robert. *Selected Letters of Robert Frost.* 1964. NY. HRW. 1st ed. F/dj. C4. $35.00

FROST, Robert. *Selected Letters.* 1965. London. Cape. AP. F. C4. $35.00

FROST, Robert. *Steeple Bush.* (1947). NY. Holt. 1st ed. F/NF. B4. $100.00

FROST, Robert. *W-Running Brook.* 1928. Holt. 1st ed. VG. M18. $60.00

FROST & YOUNG. *Boston Commons Quilt.* 1983. np. ils. wrp. G2. $10.00

FROST & YOUNG. *Flying Geese Quilt.* 1983. np. ils. wrp. G2. $12.00

FROST & YOUNG. *Irish Chain Quilt.* 1986. np. ils. wrp. G2. $10.00

FROST & YOUNG. *Trip Around the World Quilts.* 1980. np. ils. wrp. G2. $16.00

FROTHINGHAM, Robert. *Trails Through the Golden W.* 1932. NY. McBride. F/dj. H7. $15.00

FRY, C. Luther. *Am Villagers.* 1926. NY. Doran. 8vo. 201 p. olive cloth. G. B11. $25.00

FRY, John R. *Locked-Out Americans.* (1973). Harper Row. 1st ed. 174 p. dj. A7. $13.00

FRY, Mary. *Pulled-Thread Workbook.* 1978. np. 200+ ils stitches. wrp. G2. $20.00

FRY, Roger. *Transformations.* 1926. Brentano. 1st ed. F/NF. C4. $100.00

FRY, Stephen. *Liar.* 1991. London. Heinemann. 1st ed. author's 1st book. F/F. A14. $30.00

FRY. *Stitched From the Soul.* 1990. np. sc. ils. wrp. G2. $19.00

FRY. *Stitched From the Soul: Slave Quilts From Antebellum S.* 1990. np. hc. ils. cloth. G2. $30.00

FRYE, Alex Everett. *Complete Geography.* 1895. Boston. Ginn. 4 color maps. tan cloth. fair. O6. $35.00

FRYE, R.N. *Heritage of Persia.* (1963). Cleveland. World. 1st ed. 8vo. 301 p. 64 p. F/VG+. A2. $20.00

FRYER, Donald. *Songs & Sonnets Atlantean.* 1971. Arkham. 1st ed. as new. M2. $35.00

FRYER, Jane E. *Easy Steps in Housekeeping. Mary Frances Adventures...* 1916. NJ. 1st ed. 8vo. 253 p. gilt bl cloth. VG. H3. $25.00

FRYER, John. *Voyage of the Bounty Launch.* 1979. Guildford. Genesis. ils/fld chart. bl morocco/marbled brds. M. O6. $375.00

FU & SPIEGLER. *Movements & Issues in World Religions.* 1987. Westport, CT. Greenwood Pr. 1st ed. 570 p. H10. $50.00

FUCHIDA & OKUMIYA. *Midway: Battle That Doomed Japan.* (1955). Annapolis, MD. 1st ed. 8vo. 266 p. F/VG+. A2. $45.00

FUENTES, Carlos. *Burnt Water.* 1980. FSG. 1st ed. F/NF. N3. $25.00

FUENTES, Carlos. *Christopher Unborn.* 1989. FSG. 1st Am ed. trans from Spanish. NF/NF clip. A14. $25.00

FUENTES, Carlos. *Christopher Unborn.* 1989. FSG. 1st ed. sgn. VG/VG. B3. $35.00

FUENTES, Carlos. *Distant Relations.* (1982). London. Secker Warburg. 1st ed. VG/VG. B3. $25.00

FUENTES, Carlos. *Hydra Head.* (1979). Secker Warburg. 1st ed. trans MS Peden. F/NF. B3. $30.00

FUENTES, Carlos. *Old Gringo.* (1986). London. Deutsch. ARC. RS. F/NF. B3. $30.00

FUENTES, Carlos. *Old Gringo.* 1986. FSG. 5th prt. trans from Spanish. F/F. A14. $20.00

FUGARD, Athol. *Blood Knot.* 1963. Johannesburg. Simondium. 1st ed. author's 1st book. pict brds. VG. L3. $275.00

FUHRMANN & MAYOR. *Voyage d'Exploration Scientifique en Colombie.* 1914. Neuchatel. 1st ed. ils/pls/maps. 1090 p. VG+. H3. $375.00

FUKUOKA, Masanobu. *One-Straw Revolution: Intro to Natural Farming.* 1978. Emmaus, PA. ils/photos. 181 p. NF/dj. B26. $17.50

FULLBRIGHT, William J. *Pentagon Propaganda Machine.* (1970). Liveright. 1st ed. VG/VG. A7. $30.00

FULLER, Andrew S. *Grape Culturist: Treatise on Cultivation of Native Grape.* 1866. NY. Judd. ils. 262 p. H10. $35.00

FULLER, George. *Hist MI.* (1924). Nat Hist Assn. 1st ed. 3 vols. A17. $95.00

FULLER, J.J. *Master of Desolation: Reminiscences of Capt John J Fuller.* (1980). Mystic, CT. Mystic Seaport Mus. 1st ed. 8vo. 349 p. F/F. A2. $15.00

FULLER, Jack. *Fragments.* 1984. Morrow. 1st ed. F/NF. A7. $35.00

FULLER, Morris. *Throne of Canterbury.* 1891. London. xl. 322 p. H10. $25.00

FULLER, Roger; see Tracy, Don.

FULLER, Samuel. *Naked Kiss.* 1964. Belmont. pb. NF/wrp. scarce. C8. $40.00

FULLER & GOLDMAN. *Charlie Company.* 1983. Morrow. 358 p. dj. A7. $20.00

FULLERTON, W.M. *In Cairo.* 1891. London. 1st ed. 12mo. 67 p. pict cloth. VG. H3. $15.00

FULTON, John F. *Harvey Cushing: A Biography.* 1946. Springfield. 1st ed. G. G7. $65.00

FULTON, John F. *Palestine: The Holy Land.* 1900. Phil. 1st ed. 50 pls/fld map. 527 p. teg. gilt red cloth. VG+. H3. $65.00

FULTON, John F. *Sign of Babinski: Study...Cortical Dominance in Primates.* 1932. Springfield. Thomas. sgn. 165 p. F/dj. G7. $150.00

FULTON, John F. *Sir Kenelm Digby.* 1937. NY. Olvier. 1/300. presentation/inscr. w/sgn letter. G7. $395.00

FULTON, Len. *Directory of Sm Pr & Magazine Edit & Pub.* 1988. Paradise, CA. Dustbooks. 19th ed. xl. 269 p. NF/wrp. S9. $8.00

FULTON, Mary Guthrie. *Semi-Centennial of Putnam Seminary 1835-85.* 1885. Zanesville. 1st ed. 92 p. G. D7. $35.00

FUNNELL, William. *Voyage Round the World...in Yrs 1703-04.* 1707. London. Botham/Knapton. octavo. 10 pls/4 (of 5) maps. rpr calf. H9. $1,250.00

FURBAY, James R. *Along Life's Trail: 1 Quaker's Experiences & Observations.* 1978. Dublin, IN. Prinit Pr. 8vo. 157 p. VG. V3. $14.00

FYFIELD, Frances. *Question of Guilt.* 1988. London. Heinemann. ARC of 1st ed. RS. NF/dj. S5. $30.00

FYLEMAN, Rose. *Rose Fyleman Fairy Book.* 1923. Doran. 1st ed. ils Hilde T Miller. gilt cranberry cloth. M5. $125.00

G

GABALDON, Diana. *Outlander*. 1991. Delacorte. 1st ed. inscr. author's 1st book. F/F. T2. $35.00

GABRIEL, R.A. *Military Incompentence: Why Am Military Doesn't Win*. 1985. Hill Wang. BC. VG/dj. A16. $6.00

GABRIELI, Vittorio. *Sir Kenelm Digby. Un Inglese Italianato Nell'etta...* 1957. Roman. ltd ed. 1/300. rebound by Middleton. NF. G7. $195.00

GADDIS, William. *Carpenter's Gothic*. 1985. Viking. 1st ed. F/F. C4. $35.00

GADDIS, William. *Jr: A Novel*. 1975. NY. 1st ed. sgn. NF/wrp. A11. $60.00

GADOL, Peter. *Coyote*. 1990. NY. Crown. 1st ed. author's 1st book. F/F. A14. $25.00

GAER, Joseph. *First Round: Story of CIO Political Action Comm*. ca 1944. DSP. 2nd prt. G/G. V4. $10.00

GAG, Wanda. *Funny Thing*. 1929. Coward McCann. 1st ed. oblong 16mo. 32 p. yel pict brds. VG/dj. D1. $325.00

GAG, Wanda. *Millions of Cats*. 1928. Coward McCann. 1st ed. Newberry Honor Book. VG/dj. D1. $400.00

GAGE, Thomas. *New Survey of the W Indies*. 1929. NY. McBride. Argonaut series. 407 p. red cloth. F3. $25.00

GAGEY, Edmond M. *San Francisco Stage*. 1950. Columbia U. 1st ed. ils/index. 264 p. VG/dj. B19. $20.00

GAINES, Ernest J. *Catherine Carmier*. 1964. Atheneum. 1st ed. 1/1000. author's 1st novel. NF/VG. L3. $350.00

GAINES, Ernest J. *Gathering of Old Men*. 1983. Knopf. 1st ed. NF/NF. B3. $50.00

GAINES, Ernest J. *Gathering of Old Men*. 1983. NY. 1st ed. sgn. F/F. A11. $60.00

GAINES, Ernest J. *Lesson Before Dying*. 1993. Knopf. AP. F/tan wrp. C4. $35.00

GAINES, Ernest J. *Lesson Before Dying*. 1993. NY. Knopf. ARC. sgn. NF/pub pict slipcase. Q1. $100.00

GAINES, Ernest J. *Long Day in November*. (1971). Dial. 1st ed. VG/VG. B4. $85.00

GAISER, G. *Last Squadron*. (1956). NY. 1st ed. 251 p. VG/dj. B18. $12.50

GAITHER, Frances O.J. *Shadow of the Builder*. ca 1921. Surber-Arundaie. 36 p. G. B10. $15.00

GAITSKILL, Mary. *Bad Behavior*. (1988). Poseidon. 1st ed. rem mk. F/NF. B4. $45.00

GAITSKILL, Mary. *2 Girls, Fat & Thin*. (1991). Poseidon. 1st ed. author's 2nd book. F/F. B4. $45.00

GALDSTON, Iago. *Progress in Medicine*. 1940. Knopf. 1st ed. gilt blk cloth. VG/dj. G1. $40.00

GALE, Edwin O. *Reminiscences of Early Chicago & Vicinity*. 1902. Revell. 1st ed. G. A16. $40.00

GALE, Leah. *Favorite Tales of Long Ago*. 1943. Random. ils. pict brds. T5. $15.00

GALE, Martin. *Pony Named Nubbin*. 1939. Viking/Jr Literary Guild. 1st thus ed. ils Margaret Van Doren. 74 p. VG/G. T5. $30.00

GALE, Robert L. *Thomas Crawford. Am Sculptor*. 1964. Pittsburgh. ils. 241 p. cloth. dj. D2. $45.00

GALE, Zona. *Miss Lulu Bett*. 1920. Grosset Dunlap. photoplay ed. 264 p. VG/dj. M20. $12.00

GALEANO, Carlos. *Book of Embraces*. 1991. Norton. 1st Am ed. trans Cedric Belfrage. F/NF. A14. $25.00

GALEANO, Carlos. *Memory of Fire. Vol I, Vol II & Vol III*. 1988. London. Quartet. 1st ed. trans from Spanish. F/F. A14. $100.00

GALEN OF PERGAMON. *In Hippocratis Librum de Humoribus, Commentarii Tres...* 1562. Venetiis. Apud Vincenzo Valgrisium. 12mo. old vellum. G7. $350.00

GALENSON, Walter. *United Brotherhood of Carpenters: 1st Hundred Yrs*. ca 1983. Cambridge. Harvard. VG. V4. $12.50

GALILEI, Galileo. *Opere...* 1718. Florence. Santi Franchi. 2nd collected ed. quarto. 3 vols. contemporary vellum. H5. $3,000.00

GALINDO, Sergio. *Precipice*. 1969. TX U. 1st ed. trans from Spanish. rem mk. NF/NF. A14. $30.00

GALLAGHER, James. *W Sketch-Book*. 1850. Boston. Crocker Brewster. 8vo. 408 p. brn cloth. H9. $55.00

GALLAGHER, Tess. *Lover of Horses*. (1986). Harper Row. 1st ed. F/VG. B3. $30.00

GALLAGHER, Tess. *Willingly*. 1984. Port Townsend, WA. 1st ed. sgn. F/wrp. A11. $20.00

GALLAGHER & THOMAS. *OH's Big House; or, Spotlight on OH's Blk Crime*. 1930. Cleveland. 127 p. G/wrp. D7. $40.00

GALLAGHER. *Childhood Dreams*. 1989. np. ils. cloth. G2. $22.00

GALLAGHER. *Fighting for the Confederacy*. 1989. np. ils/index. 664 p. dj. O7. $12.50

GALLAGHER. *Inside the Personal Computer. Ils Intro in 3 Dimensions*. 1984. paper engineering by Van der Meer Paper Design. F. A4. $40.00

GALLANT, Abraham N. *Moshul u'Militza: Vol V. Commentaries on...Deuterenomy*. 1936. NY. self pub. Hebrew text. 128 p. G+. S3. $17.00

GALLANT, Mavis. *From the 15th District*. 1979. Random. 1st ed. F/F. B2. $30.00

GALLANT, Mavis. *Home Truths: Selected Canadian Stories*. (1981). Toronto. Macmillan. 1st ed. F/F. B4. $45.00

GALLANT, Mavis. *Other Paris*. 1956. Houghton Mifflin. 1st Am ed. author's 1st book. F/dj. B2. $50.00

GALLATIN, A.E. *Whistler: Notes & Footnotes & Other Memoranda*. 1907. London. Elkin Mathews. ltd ed. 1/250 on French wove paper. rare. D2. $125.00

GALLAUDET, T.H. *Youth's Book on Natural Theology*. (1832). Am Tract Soc. 18mo. 231 p. gilt brn cloth. G. S10. $10.00

GALLENKAMP, Charles. *Maya: Riddle & Rediscovery of a Lost Civilization*. (1959). NY. McKay. 1st ed. 240 p. dj. F3. $25.00

GALLENKAMP, Charles. *Maya: Treasures of an Ancient Civilization*. (1985). Abrams. 1st ed. 4to. 240 p. dj. F3. $45.00

GALLERY, J.I. *Mary Vs Lucifer: Apparitions of Our Lady 1531-1933*. (1960). Milwaukee. Bruce. 1st ed. 8vo. 176 p. VG+/VG. A2. $15.00

GALLICO, Paul. *Beyond the Poseidon Adventure*. 1978. Delacorte. 1st ed. F/F. N3. $15.00

GALLICO, Paul. *Snowflake*. 1953. Doubleday. 1st ed. 63 p. VG/VG. A3. $10.00

GALLOIS, Lucien. *Les Andes de Patagonie*. 1901. Paris. wrp rebound in Lib Congress bdg. F3. $35.00

GALLOWAY, J. *True & Impartial State of Province of PA*. 1759. Phil. 1st ed. 20th-century bdg. VG. C6. $2,200.00

GALLUN, Raymond Z. *People Minus X*. 1957. Simon Schuster. 1st ed. presentation/inscr/sgn to Clifford Simak. NF/dj. F4. $65.00

GALLUP, Donald. *Flowers of Friendship*. 1953. Knopf. stated 1st ed. clip dj. A7. $30.00

GALPHIN, Bruce. *Riddle of Lester Maddox*. 1968. Atlanta. Camelot Pub. 1st ed. VG/dj. N2. $6.50

GALPIN, Francis W. *Music of the Sumerians & Their Immediate Successors...* 1970. Greenwood. 12 pls. 110 p. VG+. S3. $26.00

GALPIN, Perrin C. *Hugh Gibson, 1883-1954* 1956. NY. Belgian-Am Ed Found. 1/1000. N2. $25.00

GALSWORTHY, John. *Loyalties: Drama in 3 Acts.* nd. London. Duckworth. 1/315. sgn. hand-made paper. VG/dj. A16. $100.00

GALSWORTHY, John. *Modern Comedy.* 1929. London. 1/1030. sgn w/4-line poem. full vellum. VG. A1. $175.00

GALSWORTHY, John. *Swan Song.* 1928. London. 1/525. sgn. G+. A1. $30.00

GALSWORTHY, John. *Wht Monkey.* nd. 1/265. sgn. G+. A1. $35.00

GALSWORTHY, John. *2 Forsyte Interludes.* 1927. London. 1st ed. VG/orange wrp. A1. $10.00

GALSWORTHY, John. *4 Forsyte Stories.* 1929. NY. Fountain. 1/896. G+. A1. $35.00

GALTON, Francis. *Inquiries Into Human Faculty & Its Development.* 1883. NY. Macmillan. 1st Am ed. 387 p. wine cloth. G. B14. $85.00

GALVIN, Brendan. *Seals in the Inner Harbor.* 1986. np. 1st ed. F/F. V1. $15.00

GAMMAGE, Washington Lafayette. *Camp, Bivouac, Battlefield: Hist of 4th AR Regiment...* 1958. Little Rock. reprint of 1864 ed. 150 p. cloth. M8. $150.00

GAMPERT & PENICK. *Star Wars, Return of the Jedi, a Pop-Up Book.* 1983. 12 popups. paper engineering by Penick. F. A4. $55.00

GANDLEY, Kenneth R. *Autumn Heroes.* 1977. St Martin. 1st ed. F/F. F4. $20.00

GANN, Ernest K. *Band of Brothers.* 1973. Simon Schuster. 1st ed. VG/VG. V2. $6.00

GANN, Ernest K. *Fate Is the Hunter.* 1961. Simon Schuster. BC. 8vo. VG. A8. $6.00

GANN, Ernest K. *Soldier of Fortune.* 1954. Sloane. 12mo. G. A8. $6.00

GANN, Thomas. *Ancient Cities & Modern Tribes.* (1926). London. Duckwork. 1st ed. 256 p. F3. $35.00

GANNETT, Henry. *Boundaries of US & the Several States & Territories...* 1904. GPO. 8vo. 54 pls/2 fld maps. red cloth over gray wrp. H9. $95.00

GANNETT, Henry. *20th-Annual Report of US Geological Survey.* 1900. GPO. ils/fld maps/index. 498 p. fair. A17. $45.00

GANNETT, Lewis. *John Steinbeck: Personal & Bibliographical Notes...* (1939). Viking. 1st issue. F. C4. $50.00

GANSON, Eve. *Desert Mavericks Caught & Branded...* 1928. Santa Barbara. 1st ed. 54 p. cloth. VG. D3. $25.00

GANZGLASS, Martin R. *Penal Code of Somali Democratic Republic.* 1971. New Brunswick. Rutgers. dj. M11. $25.00

GARANO, Alejo Gonzales. *Trages y Costumbres de la Provincia de Buenos Aires.* 1947. Viau. facsimile. 36 color pls. VG/VG slipcase. B11. $150.00

GARAUDY, Roger. *Literature of the Graveyard.* (1948). NY. Internat. 64 p. wrp. A7. $12.00

GARCIA, Christina. *Dreaming in Cuban.* 1992. Knopf. 1st ed. author's 1st novel. F/F. A14. $125.00

GARCIA CISNEROS, Florencio. *Maternity in Pre-Columbian Art.* 1970. NY. Cisneros Gallery. 1st ed. 995 pls. 147 p. F3. $25.00

GARCIA MARQUEZ, Gabriel; see Marquez, Gabriel Garcia.

GARCIA-THOW, Monica E. *Rinaldo Cuneo: An Evolution of Style.* 1991. Carmel. WA Karges. ils/photos. 117 p. D2. $35.00

GARCILASCO DE LA VEGA, Inca. *Historia General del Peru...* 1991. Mexico. facsimile of 1722 ed. sm folio. 2 vols. leatherette. F3. $75.00

GARCON & VINCHON. *Devil: Hist, Critical & Medical Study.* 1929. London. Gollancz. 1st ed. 288 p. blk cloth. VG. G1. $40.00

GARD, Wayne. *Great Buffalo Hunt: Its Hist & Drama...* 1960. Knopf. F/F. H7. $25.00

GARDEN, J.F. *Bugaboos.* (1987). Revelstoke. 1st ed. 156 p. F/dj. A17. $25.00

GARDINER, Charles Fox. *Dr at Timberline.* 1946. Caldwell. 5th prt. 315 p. NF/dj. D3. $25.00

GARDINER, John Rolfe. *Great Dream From Heaven.* 1974. NY. 1st ed. inscr. NF/F. A11. $55.00

GARDINER, M. *Annotated Casey at the Bat.* 1967. NY. 1st ed. VG/G. B5. $45.00

GARDINER, Margaret. *Losing Less Money Raising Horses.* 1987. Wiscasset. 3rd prt. VG/wrp. O3. $7.00

GARDINER & HEPBURN. *Am Gardener, Containing Ample Directions...* 1818. Georgetown, DC. Milligan. 1st ed. modern cloth/marbled brds. B14. $100.00

GARDNER, Albert Ten Eyck. *Winslow Homer: Am Artist, His World & His Work.* 1961. NY. Bramhall. cloth. dj. D2. $65.00

GARDNER, Brian. *Allenby.* 1965. London. Cassell. 1st ed. 314 p. F/VG clip. M7. $40.00

GARDNER, Earl Stanley. *Hunting the Desert Whale: Personal Adventures in Baja, CA.* 1960. NY. Morrow. 1st ed. photos. F. B14. $45.00

GARDNER, Erle Stanley. *Case of the Backward Mule.* 1946. Morrow. 1st ed. NF/NF. Q1. $100.00

GARDNER, Erle Stanley. *Case of the Baited Hook.* 1940. Morrow. 1st ed. F/NF. M15. $175.00

GARDNER, Erle Stanley. *Case of the Calendar Girl.* 1958. Morrow. 1st ed. F/dj. M18. $45.00

GARDNER, Erle Stanley. *Case of the Demure Defendant.* 1956. NY. Morrow. 1st ed. F/VG clip. M15. $30.00

GARDNER, Erle Stanley. *Case of the Gr-Eyed Sister.* 1953. NY. Morrow. 1st ed. F/NF. M15. $50.00

GARDNER, Erle Stanley. *Case of the Negligent Nymph.* (1950). Morrow. 1st ed. VG/dj. B9. $35.00

GARDNER, Erle Stanley. *Case of the Shoplifter's Shoe.* 1938. Morrow. 1st ed. F/VG. B4. $300.00

GARDNER, Erle Stanley. *DA Breaks a Seal.* 1946. Morrow. 1st ed. VG/VG. Q1. $100.00

GARDNER, Erle Stanley. *DA Draws a Circle.* 1939. Morrow. 1st ed. author's 3rd mystery. VG+/VG. Q1. $175.00

GARDNER, Jeffrey; see Fox, Gardner F.

GARDNER, John. *For Special Services.* (1982). Cape/Hodder Stoughton. 1st ed. F/dj. B9. $40.00

GARDNER, John. *Forms of Fiction.* 1962. NY. 1st ed. author's 1st book. NF/sans. A15. $75.00

GARDNER, John. *King's Indian.* 1974. Knopf. 1st ed. 323 p. VG+/dj. M20. $30.00

GARDNER, John. *Licence Renewed.* (1981). Cape/Hodder Stoughton. 1st ed. F/dj. B9. $50.00

GARDNER, John. *License Renewed.* 1981. Marek. 1st ed. F/F. F4. $18.00

GARDNER, John. *Nickel Mtn.* 1974. London. Cape. 1st ed. F/dj. C4. $50.00

GARDNER, John. *Nobody Lives Forever.* (1986). Cape/Hodder Stoughton. 1st ed. F/dj. B9. $25.00

GARDNER, John. *Role of Honour.* (1984). Cape/Hodder Stoughton. 1st ed. F/clip. B9. $35.00

GARDNER, John. *Secret Generations*. 985. London. Heinemann. 1st ed. sgn. /F. S5. $40.00

GARDNER, John. *Wreckage of Agathon*. 970. NY. 1st ed. NF/dj. A15. $70.00

GARDNER, Leonard. *Fat City*. 1969. NY. st ed. sgn. F/F. A11. $65.00

GARDNER, Martin. *Wizard of Oz & Who He Was*. 1957. MI State U. 1st ed. VG/G. 1. $125.00

GARDNER, Matt; see Fox, Gardner F.

GARDNER, Miriam; see Bradley, Marion Zimmer.

GARDNER, Sarah M.H. *Quaker Idyls*. 1894. Holt. 16mo. 223 p. G. V3. $9.00

GARDNER, William H. *Merry Songs for Little Folks*. (1904). Pressor. sgn. 52 p. G+. S10. $20.00

GARDNER, William H. *Music of Nature*. ca 837. Boston. xl. 8vo. music scores. 505 p. blk cloth. T3. $29.00

GARFIELD, Brian. *Checkpoint Charlie*. 1981). Mysterious Pr. 1st ed. F/F. B3. $30.00

GARFIELD, Brian. *Death Wish*. (1972). McKay. 1st ed. sgn. F/NF. B4. $185.00

GARFIELD, Brian. *Necessity*. 1984. London. Macmillan. 1st British ed. sgn. F/F. 5. $35.00

GARFIELD, Brian. *Quest for Timbuctoo*. 1968). NY. HBW. 1st Am ed. 8vo. 212 p. F/VG. A2. $12.50

GARFIELD, Leon. *Devil-in-the-Fog*. 1966. Pantheon. 1st Am ed. ils Antony Maitland. 205 p. VG. T5. $25.00

GARFUNKEL, Art. *Still Water*. (1989). Dutton. AP. VG/pict wrp. B3. $25.00

GARIS, Howard R. *Uncle Wiggily & His Flying Rug*. (1940). Whitman. 1st ed. ils Lang Campbell. 33 p. VG/VG. D1. $47.50

GARIS, Howard R. *Uncle Wiggily & the Littletails*. (1942). Platt Munk. ils Elmer Rache. 186 p. decor bl cloth. VG. S10. $25.00

GARIS, Howard R. *Uncle Wiggily & the Pirates*. (1940). Whitman. 1st ed. ils Lang Campbell. VG/VG. D1. $47.50

GARIS, Howard R. *Uncle Wiggily Plays Indian Hunter*. (1940). Whitman. 1st ed. ils Lang Campbell. VG/VG. D1. $47.50

GARIS, Howard R. *Uncle Wiggily's Apple Roast*. 1924. Charles Graham. 1st ed. ils Lang Campbell. VG. M18. $45.00

GARIS, Howard R. *Uncle Wiggily's Fortune*. (1942). Platt Munk. ils Elmer Rache. 186 p. yel-gr cloth. VG+. S10. $30.00

GARITTE, Gerald. *La Prise de Jerusalem par Les Perses en 614*. 1960. Louvain. 8vo. 67 p. prt wrp. O2. $35.00

GARLAND, A.H. *Experiences in Supreme Court of US...* 1898. WA. John Byrne. gilt crimson cloth. M11. $75.00

GARLAND, Hamlin. *Crumbling Idols: 12 Essays on Art Dealing w/Literature...* 1894. Stone Kimball. 1st ed. teg. F. A18. $60.00

GARLAND, Hamlin. *Money Magic*. 1907. NY. 1st ed. 354 p. VG. D3. $25.00

GARLAND, Hamlin. *Prairie Songs: Being Chants Rhymed & Unrhymed...* 1893. Stone Kimball. 1st ed. ils HT Carpenter. teg. NF. A18. $75.00

GARLAND, Hamlin. *Wayside Courtships*. 1897. Appleton. 1st ed. gilt bdg. F. A18. $90.00

GARLAND, James. *Private Stable*. 1903. Little Brn. new/1st thus ed. G+. O3. $225.00

GARLAND, Madge. *Sm Garden in the City*. 1974. NY. 1st Am ed. ils. VG/dj. B26. $27.50

GARLAND, Sarah. *Herb Garden*. 1984. NY. 1st ed. color pls. 168 p. F/F. B28. $20.00

GARLE, Hubert. *Hunting in the Golden Days*. 1896. London. Wht. 1st ed. 8vo. red cloth. VG+. B20. $45.00

GARLIN, Sender. *Red Tape & Barbed Wire*. 1963. Civil Rights Congress. 48 p. wrp. A7. $12.00

GARNER, Elvira. *Ezekiel Travels*. 1938. Holt. 1st ed. inscr. VG/VG. D1. $185.00

GARNER, Elvira. *Ezekiel*. 1937. Holt. 2nd prt. 8vo. pict brds. VG/VG. D1. $120.00

GARNER, Elvira. *Way Down in TN*. 1941. NY. Messner. 1st ed. 8vo. pict brds. NF/NF. D1. $150.00

GARNER, S.G. *Going Nowhere Fast*. 1979. Vantage. 1st ed. 153 p. dj. A7. $17.00

GARNER, Will. *Coffin Saga: Nantucket's Story...* 1949. Nantucket Island, MA. Whaling Mus Pub. 8vo. ils. 321 p. VG. V3. $14.00

GARNER, William Robert. *Letters...From CA 1846-47*. 1970. Berkeley. 1st ed. 262 p. F/VG. B28. $37.50

GARNETT, David. *Essential TE Lawrence*. 1951. Dutton. 1st ed. 323 p. gilt maroon cloth. NF/VG+. M7. $45.00

GARNETT, David. *Essential TE Lawrence*. 1951. Jonathan Cape. 1st ed/2nd imp. 323 p. VG+/VG. M7. $28.00

GARNETT, David. *Letters of TE Lawrence*. 1964. London. Spring Books. 1st thus ed. NF/VG. M7. $45.00

GARNETT, Edward. *Friday Nights*. 1922. London. Cape. 1st ed. 8vo. 377 p. tan/bl bdg. VG-. M7. $22.00

GARNETT, Edward. *Turgenev: A Study*. 1971. London. Collins. 1st ed. 8vo. 206 p. gilt bl cloth. G+. M7. $50.00

GARNETT, Richard. *Twilight of the Gods & Other Tales*. 1888. London. Fisher Unwin. 1st ed. octavo. gilt bl cloth. NF/cloth chemise. R3. $1,500.00

GARNETT, Richard. *Twilight of the Gods*. 1924. Bodley Head. 1st ils ed. ils Henry Keen. 279 p. VG. M7. $125.00

GARNETT, Richard. *Twilight of the Gods*. 1924. NY. Dodd Mead. 1st ils ed. 28 pls. 279 p. gilt blk cloth. NF/G. M7. $225.00

GARNETT, Richard. *Twilight of the Gods*. 1926. Knopf. 1st thus ed. 304 p. VG+. M7. $45.00

GARNETT & STUART-GLENNIE. *Greek Folk Poesy. Vol 1*. 1896. Guildford. 8vo. 477 p. cloth. uncut. O2. $85.00

GARRARD, Lewis H. *Wah-to-Yah & the Taos Trail...* 1955. Norman, OK. 1st thus prt. 12mo. 298 p. NF/dj. D3. $12.50

GARRATT, Colin. *Steam Trains: An Am Portrait*. 1989. Mallard Pr. VG/dj. A16. $17.50

GARRETT, Eileen J. *Many Voices: Autobiography of a Medium*. 1968. Putnam. BC. 251 p. prt yel brds. VG/dj. G1. $22.50

GARRETT, George. *Craft So Hard To Learn*. 1972. NY. Morrow. ARC/PBO. sgn. NF/8vo wrp. A11. $40.00

GARRETT, George. *Entered From the Sun*. (1990). Doubleday. ARC. F/pict wrp. B3. $30.00

GARRETT, George. *In the Briar Patch: A Book of Stories*. (1961). Austin, TX. 1st ed. inscr. F/NF. B4. $100.00

GARRETT, George. *King of the Mtn*. 1957. NY. 1st ed. inscr. F/NF. A11. $75.00

GARRETT, George. *Writer's Voice*. 1973. NY. 1st ed. sgn. F/NF clip. A11. $50.00

GARRETT, Pat F. *Billy the Kid*. 1946. Atomic Books. 12mo. VG. A8. $5.00

GARRETT, T.S. *Christian Worship...* 1961. London. Oxford. 190 p. H10. $16.50

GARRIGOU-LAGRANGE, R. *God: His Existance & Nature...* ca 1934. St Louis. Herder. 2 vols. H10. $45.00

GARRIGOU-LAGRANGE, R. *Traite de Theologie Ascetique et Mystique...* 1938. Paris. Du Cerf. 1st ed. 2 vols. wrp. H10. $45.00

GARRIGUE, Jean. *New & Selected Poems.* 1967. NY. 1st ed. F/F. V1. $15.00

GARRISON, F.H. *Hist of Medicine.* 1929. Phil. Saunders. 4th (orig) ed. 996 p. G7. $145.00

GARRISON, F.H. *Intro to Hist of Medicine...* 1966. Phil. Saunders. 4th revised ed/later prt. 996 p. prt brn cloth. VG. G1. $85.00

GARRISON, Jim. *On the Trail of the Assassins.* (1988). Sheridan Sq Pr. 1st ed. VG+/VG+. A7. $25.00

GARRISON, Jim. *Star-Spangled Contract.* 1976. McGraw Hill. AP. VG. N2. $20.00

GARRISON, William Lloyd. *Lectures of George Thompson.* 1836. Boston. Isaac Knapp. 1st ed. 12mo. 190 p. cloth. M1. $150.00

GARRISON, William Lloyd. *W India Emancipation. A Speech...* 1854. Boston. Am Anti-Slavery Soc. 1st ed. xl. 48 p. prt wrp. M1. $125.00

GARRISON, William Loyd. *Letters of William Lloyd Garrison.* 1971-1981. Cambridge. Belknap. 6 vols. djs. A7. $100.00

GARRISON & MORTON. *Morton's Medical Bibliography. 5th Ed. Annotated Check-List.* 1991. Scholar Pr. edit Jeremy M Morman. 1243 p. M. G7. $145.00

GARSOIAN, N.G. *Armenia Between Byzantium & the Sassanians.* 1985. London. 8vo. 340 p. cloth. O2. $45.00

GARSON, Barbara. *Electronic Sweatshop.* 1988. Simon Schuster. 1st ed. inscr. F/F. B2. $45.00

GARTNER, Chloe. *Drums of Khartoum.* 1967. Morrow. 1st ed. F/F. F4. $18.00

GARTNER. *Needlepoint Design.* 1970. House & Garden. ils. cloth. G2. $15.00

GARTON, Ray. *Lot Lizards.* 1991. Shingletown. Siesing. 1st ed. M/M. T2. $22.00

GARTON, Ray. *Methods of Madness.* 1990. Dark Harvest. 1st ed. M/M. T2. $18.00

GARVEY & ROZIN. *Garvey.* 1986. Times. 1st ed. photos. F/F. P8. $12.50

GARWOOD, Darrell. *Crossroads of Am. Story of KS City.* 1948. NY. 1st ed. 331 p. map ep. VG. D3. $12.50

GARY, Romain. *European Education.* 1960. Simon Schuster. 1st ed. sgn. NF/VG+. A14. $45.00

GARY, Romain. *Hissing Tales.* 1964. London. Michael Joseph. 1st ed. trans from French. NF/NF. A14. $30.00

GARY, Romain. *Talent Scout.* 1961. Harper. 1st Eng ed. trans from French. NF/NF. A14. $30.00

GARY, Romain. *Your Ticket Is No Longer Valid.* 1977. NY. Braziller. 1st ed. trans from French. NF/NF. A14. $25.00

GASH, Jonathan. *Gold From Gemini.* 1978. London. Collins Crime Club. 1st ed. 2nd Lovejoy. F/NF. M15. $350.00

GASH, Jonathan. *Grail Tree.* ca 1980. BC. VG/dj. C1. $4.50

GASH, Jonathan. *Grail Tree.* 1979. London. Collins Crime Club. 1st ed. F/NF. M15. $300.00

GASH, Jonathan. *Jade Woman.* 1989. St Martin. 1st ed. sgn. F/F. F4. $25.00

GASH, Jonathan. *Mehala: Lady of Sealandings.* 1993. London. Century. 1st ed. F/F. M15. $50.00

GASH, Jonathan. *Moonspender.* 1986. London. Collins Crime Club. 1st ed. F/NF. M15. $45.00

GASKA. *Visual Illusion Quilts: Full-Size Templates...* 1990. np. ils/patterns. wrp. G2. $5.00

GASKELL, Jane. *Some Summer Lands.* 1979. St Martin. 1st Am ed. F/F. F4. $20.00

GASS, William H. *In the Heart of the Heart of the Country.* 1968. NY. 1st ed. inscr. F/F. A11. $75.00

GASS, William H. *Omensetter's Luck.* 1966. NAL. 1st ed. author's 1st book. w/sgn letter. F/NF. L3. $450.00

GASS, William H. *Omensetter's Luck.* 1967. London. Collins. 1st ed. author's 1st book. inscr. F/F. C4. $135.00

GASS, William H. *On Being Bl.* (1975). Boston. Godine. 1st ed. sgn. F/F. B4. $100.00

GASS, William H. *On Being Bl.* nd. NY. 1/225. sgn/#d. F/F/F slipcase. A11. $90.00

GASS, William H. *World Within the Word.* 1978. NY. 1st ed. sgn. VG/VG. B5. $25.00

GASTER, Theodor H. *Holy & Profane: Evolution of Jewish Folkways.* 1955. Wm Sloan. 256 p. VG/VG. S3. $25.00

GATE, Ethel. *Tales From the Enchanted Isles.* 1926. Yale. 1st ed. 119 p. VG+/G+. P2. $75.00

GATES, Doris. *Elderberry Bush.* 1967. Viking. 1st ed. 160 p. NF/VG. P2. $25.00

GATES, Doris. *N Fork.* 1945. Viking. 1st ed. 211 p. VG+/VG. P2. $20.00

GATES, Norman T. *Richard Aldington: Autobiography in Letters.* 1992. Penn State. 1st ed. 402 p. blk cloth. as new. M7. $49.50

GATTINGER, Augustin. *Flora of TN & Philosophy of Botany.* 1901. Nashville. Gospel Advocate Pub. 1st ed. presentation. 296 p. H9. $95.00

GATTUSO, John. *Circle of Nations. Voices & Visions of Am Indians.* 1993. Hillsboro. Beyond Words. 1st ed. quarto. sgn contributors. F/F. L3. $125.00

GAUCH, Patricia Lee. *On to Widecombe Fair.* (1978). Putnam. ils Trina Schart Hyman. red cloth. F/NF. T5. $30.00

GAUGUIN, Paul. *Noa Noa.* 1947. Stockholm. VG/VG. A1. $100.00

GAULT, William Campbell. *Cat & Mouse* 1988. St Martin. 1st ed. F/F. F4. $20.00

GAUQUELIN, Michel. *Scientific Basis of Astrology.* (1969). Stein Day. 1st Am ed. 8vo. 255 p. VG+/F. A2. $20.00

GAUTHIER, Josie O. *Wild Flower Stories.* 1918. Cupples Leon. Book No 2. 30 p. pic brds. G-. A3. $15.00

GAUTIER, Theophile. *Mademoiselle de Maupin.* nd. Boni Liveright. orig blk brds. E3. $6.00

GAUTIER & PANASSIE. *Dictionnaire de Jazz.* (1954). Paris. Robert Laffont. 1st ed. 366 p. NF/stiff wrp. B20. $75.00

GAVIN & HADLEY. *Crisis Now.* (1968). Random. 1st ed. F/clip. A7. $20.00

GAVOTY, Bernard. *Szymon Goldberg.* 1960. Geneva ils. 30+ p. VG/wrp. S3. $17.00

GAWRON, Jean Mark. *Apology for Rain.* 1974. Doubleday. 1st ed. author's 1st book. F/NF. N3. $10.00

GAY, Jan. *On Going Naked.* 1932. Garden City. ils. N2. $10.00

GAY, John. *Gay's Fables. In 1 Vol.* 1808. Phil. Carey. 16mo. 6 pls. 122 p. calf/marbled brds. M1. $150.00

GAY, Romney. *Peter's Adventure.* 1945. Grosset Dunlap. 15 full-p ils. NF/VG. M5. $18.00

GAY, Romney. *Romney Gay's Box of Books* 1941. Grosset Dunlap. set of 6 books. VG/worn box. M5. $38.00

GAY, Zhenya. *Look.* 1953 (1952). Viking. 2nd prt. ils. VG/G+. P2. $18.00

GAYLIN, Willard M. *Operating on the Mind: Psychosurgery Conflict.* 1975. Basic Books. 1st ed. 216 p. cream cloth. VG/dj. G1. $30.00

GAYRE, G.R. *Wassail! In Mazers of Mead* 1948. London. Philimore. ils. 176 p. dj. N2. $32.50

GAZE, Harold. *Merry Pipper*. 1925. London. 1st ed. ils/8 pls. VG. M5. $65.00

GEARHART, Sally Miller. *Wanderground: Stories of Hill Women*. 1978. Watertown, MA. Persephone. true 1st ed/1st prt. 196 p. wrp. A7. $15.00

GEBHARD, E.L. *Life & Ventures of Orig John Jacob Astor*. 1915. Hudson, NY. Bryan Prt Co. 1st ed. 8vo. 321 p. VG+. A2. $25.00

GEDDES & MCNEILL. *Blackwork Embroidery*. 1976. np. 200 ils. wrp. G2. $6.00

GEER, W.C. *Reign of Rubber*. 1992. NY. ils/index. 344 p. G/torn dj. B18. $17.50

GEER, Walter. *Campaigns of the Civil War*. ls w/33 Maps. 1926. Brentano. 1st ed. 490 p. cloth. VG. M8. $125.00

GEIGER, Maynard. *CA Calligraphy: Identified Autographs of Personages...* 1972. Ballena Pr. 1st ed. 59 p. F/wrp. B19. $10.00

GEIGER. *Hist of Textile Art*. 1979. np. cloth. G2. $37.50

GEIGER. *Sm Quilt Crafts*. 1989. np. cloth. G2. $22.00

GEIL, William Edgar. *Great Wall of China*. 1909. NY. Sturgis Walton. 1st ed. 8vo. ils. 393 p. G. W1. $45.00

GEIOGAMAH, Hanay. *New Native Am Drama. 3 Plays*. 1980. Norman, OK. 1st ed. F/NF. L3. $65.00

GEISEL, Theodor Seuss. *Bartholomew & the Oobleck*. (1949). Random. inscr. author's 8th book. VG/VG. D1. $225.00

GEISEL, Theodor Seuss. *Cat in the Hat Comes Back*. 1958. Random. 1st stated ed. VG. D1. $225.00

GEISEL, Theodor Seuss. *Dr Seuss From Then & Now*. 1986. Random. 1st stated ed. 4to. 93 p. VG/VG. D1. $55.00

GEISEL, Theodor Seuss. *Dr Seuss's Sleep Book*. 1962. Random. probable 1st ed. author's 22nd book. VG/dj. D1. $175.00

GEISEL, Theodor Seuss. *How the Grinch Stole Christmas*. 1957. Random. 1st ed. VG/VG unclip $2.50 dj. D1. $550.00

GEISEL, Theodor Seuss. *If I Ran the Circus*. ca 1958. Random. early prt. VG+/VG. P2. $40.00

GEISEL, Theodor Seuss. *If I Ran the Zoo*. 1950. Random. 1st ed. VG/unclip $2.50 dj. D1. $400.00

GEISEL, Theodor Seuss. *McElligot's Pool*. 1975. NY. special sc ed. w/sgn bookplate. sales premium. NF/unused. A11. $95.00

GEISEL, Theodor Seuss. *Scrambled Eggs, Super!* 1953. Random. 1st ed. VG/unclip $2.50 dj. rare. D1. $400.00

GEISEL, Theodor Seuss. *Tough Coughs As He Ploughs the Dough*. 1987. NY. 1st prt. sgn twice. F/F. A11. $195.00

GEISEL, Theodor Seuss. *500 Hats of Bartholomew Cubbins*. 1938. Vanguard. early/possible 1st ed. VG/G clip. P2. $85.00

GEISEL, Theodor Seuss. *500 Hats of Bartholomew Cubbins*. 1938. Vanguard. 1st ed. author's 2nd book. NF/NF. D1. $400.00

GEISMAR, Peter. *Fanon*. 1971. Dial. 1st ed. 214 p. clip dj. A7. $25.00

GELDART, E.M. *Folk-Lore of Modern Greece: Tales of the People*. 1884. London. 8vo. 190 p. O2. $125.00

GELFAND & KERR. *Freud & the Hist of Psycholanalysis*. 1992. Hillsdale, NJ. 1st ed 397 p. gr cloth. G1. $45.00

GELL, William. *Sir William Gell in Italy. Letters to Soc of Dilettanti...* 1976. London. 8vo. 182 p. cloth. dj. O2. $35.00

GELLERT, Hugo. *Aesop Said So*. 1936. Covici Friede. lg octavo. 41 p. F/dj. B24. $325.00

GELLHORN, Martha. *Vietnam: A New Kind of War*. 1966. np. The Guardian. wrp. A7. $14.00

GELTSOFF. *Fashion Bead Embroidery*. 1971. np. ils. cloth. G2. $7.00

GEMINUS, Thomas. *Compendiosa Totius Anatomie Delineatio*. 1959. London. O'Malley. folio. parchment brds. G. G7. $175.00

GENDEL, Evelyn. *Tortoise & the Turtle Abroad*. 1963. Simon Schuster. 1st ed. ils Hilary Knight. pict gr brds. T5. $25.00

GENDERS, Roy. *Anemones for Market & Garden*. 1956. London. ils/photos. 123 p. F/dj. B26. $19.00

GENET, Jean. *Funeral Rites*. (1969). Castle Books. reprint. dj. N2. $6.00

GENET, Jean. *Funeral Rites*. 1969. Grove. 1st ed. trans from French. NF/NF. A14. $50.00

GENET, Jean. *Miracle of the Rose*. 1966. Grove. 1st ed. trans from French. NF/NF. A14. $50.00

GENET, Jean. *Our Lady of the Flowers*. 1963. NY. Grove. 1st ed. trans from French. NF/NF. A14. $60.00

GENET, Jean. *Querelle*. 1974. Grove. 1st ed. trans from French. NF/NF. A14. $40.00

GENET, Jean. *Thief's Journal*. 1964. Grove. 1st ed. trans from French. NF/NF. A14. $60.00

GENOVESE, E.D. *In Red & Blk*. 1971. Pantheon. stated 1st ed. 435 p. dj. A7. $35.00

GENTRY, Curt. *Last Days of the Late, Great State of CA*. 1968. Putnam. index. 382 p. VG/VG. B19. $10.00

GENTRY, T.G. *Poems*. 1878. Phil. 1st ed. gilt bl cloth. VG. V1. $15.00

GEORGE, Elizabeth. *Payment in Blood*. 1989. Bantam. ARC/1st Am ed. F/wrp. B2. $35.00

GEORGE, Elizabeth. *Payment in Blood*. 1989. Bantam. 1st ed. sgn. F/F. S5. $45.00

GEORGE, Henry. *Protection & Free Trade*. 1886. NY. 1st ed. 359 p. gilt cloth. F. A17. $25.00

GEORGE, Marian M. *Little Journey to China & Japan*. 1900. Chicago. Flanagan. 1st ed. 8vo. ils/map. 78 p. G. W1. $16.00

GEORGE, N.D. *Annihilationism Not of the Bible*. 1871. Boston. Magee. 2nd ed. 324 p. H10. $35.00

GEORGE, Wilma. *Animals & Maps*. 1969. Berkeley. CA U. xl. ils. NF/NF. O6. $50.00

GEORGE & HAY. *Abraham Lincoln's Complete Works...* 1894. NY. Century. 1st ed. 2 vols. cloth. VG. M8. $150.00

GEORGES, Monmarche. *Paris. The Bl Guide*. 1950. Paris. 16mo. 475 p. gilt bl cloth. VG. H3. $15.00

GERARDE, John. *Gerarde's Herball the Essence Thereof Distilled...* 1927. Edinburgh. Howe. 1/150. quarto. vellum brds/gilt spine. F. R3. $300.00

GERASIMOV, G. *Fire Bell in the Night*. nd. (1968). Moscow. Novosti. 77 p. wrp. A7. $18.00

GERASIMOV, M.M. *Face Finder*. 1971 (1968). Lippincott. 1st Am ed. 8vo. 199 p. F/VG. A2. $20.00

GERASSI, John. *Coming of the New Internat: Revolutionary Anthology*. (1971). World. stated 1st ed. 610 p. dj. A7. $25.00

GERASSI, John. *N Vietnam: A Documentary*. (1968). London. Allen Unwin. 200 p. NF/dj. A7. $45.00

GERBER, Albert B. *Bashful Billionaire*. (1967). Lyle Stuart. 1st ed. 384 p. clip dj. A7. $15.00

GERDTS & PRESZLER. *William H Singer Jr*. nd. Hagerstown. 1/1500. photos/pls. wrp. D2. $25.00

GERDTS & STEBBINS. *Man of Genius: Art of WA Allston*. 1980. Boston Mus Fine Arts. pls/index. 255 p. D2. $35.00

GERLACH, Rex. *Fly Fishing for Rainbows*. (1988). Stackpole. 1st ed. sgn. 222 p. M/dj. A17. $29.50

GERMAN, Andrew W. *Down on the Wharf: Boston Fisheries...* (1982). Mystic Seaport Mus. 1st prt. 4to. M/dj. A17. $17.50

GERRARD. *Knitwear Designs.* 1983. np. ils. cloth. G2. $11.00

GERROLD, David. *Matter for Men.* 1983. NY. Timescape. AP of 1st ed. F/wrp. N3. $20.00

GERROLD, David. *Yesterday's Children.* 1974. London. Faber. 1st ed. F/F. T2. $35.00

GERSHENSON, Alvin H. *Israel & Valley Forge: Hist, Religions & Politics...* 1984. Valley Pr Book Pub. reprint. 360 p. VG/G. S3. $23.00

GERSHWIN, George. *George Gershwin's Song-Book.* 1932. NY. 1st trade ed. presentation. ils Alajalov. clamshell case. H5. $3,750.00

GERSHWIN & GERSHWIN. *George & Ira Gershwin Songbook.* (1960). Simon Schuster. 1st prt. 4to. sbdg/cloth brds. NF/orig box. A7. $45.00

GERSON, N.B. *Harriet Beecher Stowe.* (1976). Praeger. 218 p. dj. A7. $15.00

GERSON, N.B. *Light-Horse Harry: Biography of WA's Great Cavalryman...* 1966. Doubleday. 257 p. VG/G+. B10. $15.00

GERSTAECKER, Frederick. *Frank Wildman's Adventures on Land & Water.* late 1800s. NY. 312 p. decor cloth. G. B18. $12.50

GERSTAECKER, Frederick. *Wildsports in the Far W.* 1856. np. 1st ed. 396 p. F. O7. $35.00

GERTZ, Elmer. *Odyssey of Barbarian. Biography of George Sylvester Viereck.* 1978. Prometheus. 1st ed. inscr. F/NF. B2. $30.00

GERVAIS, Paul. *Extraordinary People.* 1991. NY. Harper Collins. 1st ed. NF/NF. A14. $25.00

GETEIN, Frank. *Playing Soldier: A Diatribe.* (1971). HRW. 1st ed. 168 p. clip dj. A7. $35.00

GETHIN, David. *Dane's Testament.* 1986. London. Gollancz. 1st ed. F/F. S5. $20.00

GEURTS, R. *Hair Colour in the Horse.* 1977. London. Allen. 1st ed. 108 p. VG+/wrp. O3. $15.00

GEYER, H.C. *All Men Have Loved Thee: Song of France.* (1941). NY. Richard Smith. VG/G. A2. $35.00

GHEDDO, Piero. *Cross & the Bo-Tree: Catholics & Buddhists in Vietnam.* (1970). Seed Ward. 368 p. wrp. A7. $20.00

GHEERBRANT, Alain. *Incas.* (1961). NY. Orion. 1st ed. 432 p. dj. F3. $35.00

GHIKA, Tiggie. *Le Soif du Jonc.* (1955). Paris. Cahier d'Art. 1/200. ils/sgn Villon. prt wrp. K1. $600.00

GHOSE, Zulfikar. *Confessions of a Native-Alien.* 1965. London. 1st ed. sgn. F/NF. A11. $50.00

GIANOLI, Luigi. *Horses & Horsemanship Through the Ages.* 1969. NY. Crown. 1st Am prt. 441 p. G+. O3. $20.00

GIBB, E.J.W. *Poets & the Poetry of Turkey.* 1901. WA. 8vo. pls. 351 p. cloth. O2. $25.00

GIBB, Philip. *Reckless Duke.* 1931. Harper. 1st ed. 425 p. cranberry cloth. VG+. B22. $6.00

GIBBENS, Byrd. *This Is a Strange Country. Letters of a Westering Family.* 1988. Albuquerque. NM U. 1st ed. photos. M/M. P4. $30.00

GIBBON, Edward. *Hist of Decline & Fall of Roman Empire.* 1902. Harper. 8vo. Lauriant bdg. F. F1. $695.00

GIBBON, Lardner. *Exploration of Valley of Amazon...* 1854. WA, DC. 8vo. 33 pls/tables. emb purple cloth. H9. $50.00

GIBBONS, Gustav. *Short-Timers.* 1979. Harper Row. 1st ed. inscr/dtd 1979. author's 1st book. F/F. L3. $750.00

GIBBONS, Kaye. *Ellen Foster.* 1987. Algonquin. ARC/sewn sgns. wrp. B2. $125.00

GIBBONS, Kaye. *Virtuous Woman.* (1989). London. Cape. 1st ed. F/F. B3. $30.00

GIBBONS, Kaye. *Virtuous Woman.* 1989. Algonquin. AP. F/wrp. B2. $40.00

GIBBS, C.R.V. *Passenger Liners of the W Ocean.* (1952). London. Staples. 1st ed. 8vo. 352 p. F/G. A2. $30.00

GIBBS, Jim. *Disaster Log of Ships.* 1971. Bonanza. sgn. VG/dj. A16. $25.00

GIBBS, Peter. *Flag for the Matabele: Entertainment in African Conquest.* (1956). NY. Vanguard. 1st ed. 8vo. 192 p. VG+/VG+. A2. $20.00

GIBBS, Philip. *Middle of the Road.* 1923. Doran. 1st ed. 12mo. VG. A8. $10.00

GIBSON, Arrell M. *Frontier Historian: Life & Work of Edward Everett Dale.* 1975. OK U. 1st ed. 367 p. F/F clip. B19. $20.00

GIBSON, George Rutledge. *Stock Exchanges of London, Paris & NY.* 1889. London. Putnam. 1st ed. 125 p. maroon silk. H9. $75.00

GIBSON, M.H. *Gran Chaco Calling: Chronicle of Sport & Travel...* (1934). London. Witherby. 1st ed. 8vo. 220 p. G+. A2. $20.00

GIBSON, Margaret. *Considering Her Condition.* (1978). Vanguard. short stories. F/NF. A7. $35.00

GIBSON, Robert. *Help From on High; o Our Only Rescource.* 1824. Princeton. Bo renstein. 30 p. H10. $10.00

GIBSON, Thomas. *Anatomy of Human Bodies Epitomized.* 1682. London. Flesher. 1 engravings. lacks 2 text leaves. G7. $175.00

GIBSON, Walter B. *Fine Art of Swindling* (1966). Grosset Dunlap. VG+/dj. B9. $7.50

GIBSON, William. *Burning Chrome.* 1986 NY. Arbor. 1st Am ed. F/F. N3. $25.00

GIBSON, William. *Mona Lisa Overdriv* (1988). Bantam. ARC. 1st ed. NF/pict wrp B3. $25.00

GIBSON & PEPE. *From Ghetto to Glory.* 1968 Prentice Hall. 1st ed. VG+/VG. P8. $25.00

GIBSON & WILKS. *Big League Batboy* 1970. Random. 1st ed. VG+. P8. $15.00

GIDDINS, Gary. *Rhythm-a-Ning: Jaz Tradition...* 1985. NY. Oxford. 1st ed. F/d A7. $18.00

GIDE, Andre. *Journals of Andre Gide. Vol 1 1889-1913.* 1947. NY. 1st Eng-language ed trans/inscr O'Brien. F/NF clip. A11. $50.00

GIDE, Andre. *Medeleine (Et Nunc Manet i Te).* 1952. NY. 1st ed. trans/inscr O'Brien F/F. A11. $40.00

GIERL. *Sampler Book, Old Samplers From Mus & Private Collections.* 1987. np. ils cloth. G2. $17.00

GIFFARD, Edward. *Short Visit to the Ionia Islands.* 1837. London. 8vo. 5 pls. dk br calf. O2. $450.00

GIFFEN, Guy J. *CA Expedition: Stevenson' Regiment of 1st NY Volunteers.* 1951. Bio books. 1/650. ils. 111 p. F. B19. $30.00

GIFFORD, Barry. *Bl-Eyed Buddhist & Other Stories.* 1990. Faber. PBO. sgn F/wrp. A11. $40.00

GIFFORD, Barry. *In the Land of Dream Dreams.* 1982. London. 1st ed. sgn. F/F A11. $55.00

GIFFORD, Barry. *Kerouac's Town.* 1973 Santa Barbara. trade issue of Capra Chapbook. sgn. F/12mo wrp. A11. $40.00

GIFFORD, Barry. *Night People.* 1992. NY Grove. 1st ed. sgn. F/F. A14. $30.00

GIFFORD, Barry. *Persimmons.* 1977. Berkeley. 1st ed. sgn. A11. $35.00

GIFFORD, Barry. *Port Topique.* 1980. Berkeley. 1st ed. sgn. F/8vo wrp. A11. $40.00

GIFFORD, Barry. *Wild at Heart: Story o Sailor & Lula.* 1990. Weidenfeld. NF/dj C8. $30.00

GIFFORD, Edward W. *Composition of CA Shellmounds.* 1916. CA U. 1st ed. xl. 29 p. VG/wrp. D3. $25.00

GIFFORD, George. *Dialogue Concerning Witches & Witchcrafts.* 1931. Oxford. facsimile of London 1593 ed. 94 p. wht brds. G1. $50.00

GIFFORD, John. *Gifford's Eng Lawyer; or, Every Man His Own Lawyer...* 1828. London. Macdonald. 15th ed. calf/marbled brds. M11. $150.00

GIFFORD & LEE. *Jack's Book.* 1978. St Martin. 1st ed. F/F. B2. $40.00

GIFFORD & LEE. *Jack's Book.* 1978. St Martin. 1st ed. NF/NF. A7. $25.00

GIGUERE, Diane. *Wings in the Wind.* 1979. Toronto. McClelland Stewart. 1st ed. F/F clip. A14. $20.00

GIL, Enrique. *Evolucion del Panamericanismo.* 1933. Buenos Aires. 490 p. wrp rebound in half leather/red cloth. F3. $30.00

GILBERT, Benjamin. *Indians.* 1973. Time Life. 4to. F. A8. $10.00

GILBERT, Bill. *They Also Served.* 1992. Crown. 1st ed. photos. F/F. P8. $12.50

GILBERT, Grove Karl. *CO Plateau Region...* 1876. New Haven. Tuttle Morehouse Taylor. 1st separate ed. 27 p. VG. D3. $50.00

GILBERT, Henry. *King Arthur's Knights.* nd. TC & EC Jack. ils Walter Crane. 367 p. VG. P2. $65.00

GILBERT, Humphrey. *Voyages & Colonising Enterprises of...* 1940. London. Hakluyt Soc. 2 vols. M/faded djs. O6. $125.00

GILBERT, Michael. *Petrella at Q.* 1977. London. Hodder. 1st ed. VG+/dj. S5. $25.00

GILBERT, Michael. *Young Petrella.* 1988. London. Hodder. 1st ed. NF/dj. S5. $25.00

GILBERT, Stuart. *Letters of James Joyce.* 1957. London. Faber. 1st ed. F/NF. B2. $65.00

GILBERT, Vivian. *Romance of the Last Crusade.* 1923. NY. Appleton. 1st ed. 238 p. gilt bl cloth. VG. M7. $45.00

GILBERT, William Schwenck. *Mikado or the Town of Titpu.* 1928. London. Macmillan. 1st thus ed. ils Flint/Brock. aeg. full calf. H5. $250.00

GILBERT, William Schwenck. *Savoy Operas.* 1926. London. Macmillan. sm octavo. 698 p. Riviere tree calf. VG. H5. $275.00

GILBERT, William. *On the Magnet...Many Arguments & Experiments.* 1900. London. Chiswick. 1/250. quarto. ils. 246 p. linenbacked bl brds. VG. H5. $200.00

GILBERT & TAYLOR. *Rural Scenes; or, Peep Into the Country.* 1824. Cooperstown, NY. 2nd Am ed. 16mo. 31 p. NF/self wrp. B24. $350.00

GILBEY, Walter. *Harness Horse.* 1976. Liss. Spur. 5th ed. VG/VG. O3. $25.00

GILBY. *Free Weaving.* 1976. np. cloth. G2. $15.00

GILCHRIST, Ellen. *Land Surveyor's Daughter.* 1979. Fayetteville. Lost Roads. 1st ed. sgn. author's 1st book. F/wrp. B4. $600.00

GILCHRIST, Ellen. *Victory Over Japan.* 1984. Little Brn. ARC. F/NF. L3. $125.00

GILCHRIST, Ellen. *Victory Over Japan.* 1985. London. Faber. 1st ed. F/F. B3. $30.00

GILDER, Richard. *Poems of...* 1908. Houghton Mifflin. 1st ed. 1/200. sgn. brn cloth/paper label. NF. V1. $35.00

GILDNER, Gary. *Jabon.* 1981. OR. 1/100. sgn. ils/sgn W Mulstay. deluxe bdg. F. V1. $65.00

GILES, Baxter; see Offutt, Andrew.

GILES, Elizabeth; see Holt, John Robert.

GILES, H.H. *Poorhouses: Their Location, Construction & Management.* 1884. Madison. Democrat prt. 8 p. wrp. N2. $32.50

GILES, Raymond; see Holt, John Robert.

GILES & SHOEMAKER. *Stars of the Series.* 1964. Crowell. 1st ed. VG/VG. P8. $17.50

GILIO, M.E. *Tupamaro Guerillas.* 1972 (1970). NY. Sat Review Pr. 1st Am ed. 8vo. 204 p. F/F. A2. $12.50

GILKERSON, William. *Scrimshander.* 1978. Troubador. revised ed. ils. 120 p. VG/wrp. B19. $12.50

GILL, B.M. *Nursery Crimes.* 1986. London. Hodder. 1st ed. sgn. F/F. S5. $40.00

GILL, B.M. *Seminar for Murder.* 1986. Scribner. 1st Am ed. F/F. M15. $25.00

GILL, Bartholomew. *McGarr & the Siamese Conspiracy.* 1979. London. Hale. 1st British ed. F/NF. S5. $25.00

GILL, Eric. *Sculpture. Essay on Stone-Cutting w/Preface About God.* ca 1924. Sussex. St Dominic's Pr. 12mo. ils Gill. beige linen. K1. $200.00

GILL, Patrick; see Creasey, John.

GILL, W. Wyatt. *Jottings From the Pacific.* ca 1890. Am Tract Soc. sm 8vo. 13 pls. 304 p. G. W1. $40.00

GILLCRIST, Paul T. *Feet Wet: Reflections of a Carrier Pilot.* 1990. Novato, CA. 348 p. VG+/dj. B10. $12.50

GILLETT, Charlie. *Sound of the City: Rise of Rock & Roll.* 1970. NY. Dutton. 1st ed. brds. N2. $8.50

GILLETT, George W. *Variation & Genetic Relationships in Whitlavia...* 1955. Berkeley. ils/pls. 59 p. wrp. B26. $12.50

GILLEY, Wendell. *Bird Carving.* nd. Bonanza. reprint. VG/dj. N2. $6.00

GILLHAM, Charles E. *Raw North.* (1947). Barnes. 1st ed. inscr/dtd 1949. 275 p. bl cloth. VG+. B22. $25.00

GILLIARD, E. Thomas. *Living Birds of the World: 1500 Species Described.* (1958). NY. lg 4to. 400 p. dj. A17. $22.50

GILLINGHAM, John. *Richard the Lionheart.* (1978). Time Books. 1st Am ed. 8vo. 318 p. F/VG+. A2. $15.00

GILLIS, James Melville. *US Naval Astronomical Expedition to S Hemisphere 1849-52.* 1855. WA, DC. Nicholson. 1st ed. 2 vols. lg quarto. presentation/blk morocco. H9. $750.00

GILLMOR, Frances. *Flute of the Smoking Mirror.* 1949. NM U. 1st ed. 183 p. dj. F3. $35.00

GILLMOR, Frances. *King Dances in the Market Place.* 1964. Tucson, AZ. 1st ed. 271 p. dj. F3. $25.00

GILMAN, Caroline. *Letters of Eliza Wilkinson.* 1839. NY. Colman. 1st ed. 12mo. 108 p. cloth. M1. $150.00

GILMAN, Carolyn. *Grand Portage Story.* (1992). NM Hist Soc. ils/maps/index. M/wrp. A17. $12.50

GILMAN, Dorothy. *Mrs Pollifax & the 2nd Thief.* 1993. NY. Doubleday. 1st ed. sgn. F/F. M15. $30.00

GILMAN, Robert Cham. *Rebel of Rhada.* 1968. HRW. 1st ed. F/NF. N3. $25.00

GILMORE, A.F. *Yes, 'Tis Round: Log of Far Journey.* (1932). Boston. Stratford. 1st ed. 8vo. 393 p. F/VG. A2. $17.50

GILMORE, Beatrice V. *Beyond the Crystal Cave.* (1946). NJ. Colt Pr. 8vo. ils. 164 p. VG. T5. $15.00

GILMORE, James Roberts. *Among the Pines; or, S in Secession Time.* 1864 (1862). NY. Carleton. 12mo. author's 1st book. 310 p. cloth. VG. D3. $25.00

GILMORE, James Roberts. *Down in TN & Back by Way of Richmond.* 1864. NY. Carleton. 1st ed. 12mo. 282 p. orig cloth. VG. D3. $25.00

GILMORE, M.R. *Prairie Smoke.* 1929. NY. 1st ed. ils. 208 p. VG. B28. $25.00

GILMORE. *Needlepoint Primer.* 1973. Gilmore. ils. wrp. G2. $8.00

GILPIN, Laura. *Hocus-Pocus of the Universe.* 1977. NY. 1st ed. F/dj. A15. $35.00

GILPIN, William. *Central Gold Region.* 1860. Woodward. octavo. 6 fld maps. brn cloth. H9. $700.00

GILSON, Etienne. *Being & Some Philosophers.* 1952. Toronto. Pontifical Instit Mediaeval St. 235 p. H10. $27.50

GILSON, Etienne. *Christian Philosophy of St Augustine.* ca 1960. Random. trans LEM Lynch. 398 p. H10. $35.00

GILSON, Etienne. *Dante the Philosopher.* 1952. NY. Sheed Ward. 1st Eng ed. 338 p. H10. $20.00

GINAT, Joseph. *Blood Disputes Among Bedouin & Rural Arabs in Israel.* 1987. Pittsburgh. 8vo. 184 p. cloth. dj. O2. $25.00

GINGRICH, Arnold. *Toys of a Lifetime.* 1966. NY. 1st ed. sgn. 370 p. G+/dj. B18. $22.50

GINGRICH, Arnold. *Well-Tempered Angler.* 1966. NY. 2nd prt. sgn. ils/index. cloth. F/dj. A17. $20.00

GINN & HEATH COMPANY. *Ginn & Heath's Classical Atlas.* ca 1882. Boston. Ginn & Heath. 23 double-p maps. pict gr cloth. NF. O6. $75.00

GINN & HEATH COMPANY. *Ginn & Heath's Classical Atlas.* 1886 (1882). Ginn & Heath. 23 double-p color maps. VG. E5. $45.00

GINSBERG, Allen. *Ankor Wat.* (1968). London. Fulcrum. 1st ed. ils Alexandra Lawrence. F/F. B4. $75.00

GINSBERG, Allen. *Collected Poems 1947-80.* 1984. Harper. 1st ed. sgn. NF/NF. B2. $50.00

GINSBERG, Allen. *Kaddisch.* 1962. Wiesbaden. 1st thus ed. bilingual. trans/inscr Hollo. VG+/wrp. A11. $45.00

GINSBERG, Allen. *New Yr Blues.* 1972. Phoenix Bookshop. 1st ed. 1/100. sgn. F/prt wrp/mailing envelope. B24. $100.00

GINSBERG, Allen. *Wht Shroud. Poems 1980-85.* 1986. Harper Row. 1st ed. F/F. B3. $25.00

GINSBERG, Allen. *Wht Shroud. Poems 1980-85.* 1986. Harper Row. 1st ed. F/NF. V1. $20.00

GINSBERG, Allen. *Wht Shroud. Poems 1980-85.* 1986. Harper Row. 1st ed. inscr. F/F. B2. $75.00

GINSBERG, H. Louis. *Studies in Koheleth.* 1950. NY. 46 p. VG. S3. $25.00

GINSBURG, Mirra. *Master of the Winds & Other Tales From Siveria.* 1970. Crown. 1st ed. inscr. 158 p. NF/VG. P2. $15.00

GINZBERG, Eli. *Agenda for Am Jews.* 1950. Kings Crown. xl. 90 p. VG. S3. $23.00

GIOVIO, Paolo. *Commentario de le cose de Turchi...* 1540. Venice. sm 8vo. 36 leaves. full antique calf. O2. $1,500.00

GIOVIO, Paolo. *Novocomensis Episcopi Nucerini...* 1553-54. Paris. 2 vols in 1. folio. 350 leaves. contemporary calf. O2. $750.00

GIPE, G. *Great Am Sports Book.* 1980. Hall of Fame Pr. 1st ed. NF/NF. V2. $9.00

GIPSON, Lawrence H. *Jared Ingersoll: Study of Am Loyalism...* 1920. New Haven. Yale. 1st ed. sgn. 432 p. VG. B11. $40.00

GIPSON, Morrell. *Surprise Doll.* (1949). NY. Wonder Books. ils Steffie Lerch. pict laminated brds. G. T5. $22.00

GIRARD, Sharon. *Funeral Music & Customs in Venezuela.* (1980). Tempe. 1st ed. 96 p. wrp. F3. $15.00

GIRAUD, J.P. *Birds of Long Island.* 1844. NY. Wiley Putnam. 1st ed. 398 p. orig brn cloth. scarce. K1. $175.00

GIRL SCOUTS OF AMERICA. *Brownie Scouts Handbook.* 1951. NY. 8vo. ils. 95 p. pict brds. VG. H3. $15.00

GIROIRE, Henri. *Clovis Vincent 1879-1947.* 1971. Paris. Perrin. ils. 195 p. wrp. G7. $65.00

GIRONELLA, Jose Maria. *One Million Dead.* ca 1963. Doubleday. trans Joan MacLean. G/G. V4. $15.00

GIRONELLA, Jose Maria. *One Million Dead.* 1963. Doubleday. 1st ed. trans from Spanish. F/F. A14. $50.00

GIRONELLA, Jose Maria. *Peace After War.* ca 1969. Knopf. G/G. V4. $15.00

GISSING, George. *Demos.* 1886. London. 1st ed. octavo. 3 vols. orig brn cloth. VG. H5. $9.50

GISSING, George. *New Grub Street.* 1891. London. 1st ed. inscr. 3 vols. orig dk bl-gr cloth. slipcase. H5. $4,500.00

GISSING, George. *Sins of the Fathers.* 1924. Pascal Covici. 1st ed. 1/550. VG. F1. $75.00

GITELMAN, Z.Y. *Jewish Nationality & Soviet Politics: Jewish Sections...* 1972. Princeton. xl. VG+/VG+. S3. $25.00

GITTELSOHN, Roland. *Consecrated Unto Me: Jewish View of Love & Marriage.* 1967. NY. 3rd prt. for teens. VG/G+. S3. $23.00

GLADSTONE. *Needlepoint Alphabe Book.* 1973. np. ils/charts/direction cloth. G2. $40.00

GLAISTER, G.A. *Encyclopedia of the Boo* 1960. World. 1st ed. ils/index. 484 VG/VG. B5. $35.00

GLANCY, Diane. *One Age in a Dream.* 198 Milkweed. 1st ed. NF/wrp. L3. $45.00

GLASER, Otto. *Science of Radiolog* 1933. Springfield. CC Thomas. cloth NF. B14. $40.00

GLASS, Bill. *My Greatest Challenge.* (1968 Waco, TX. sgn. 182 p. G/dj. B18. $12.50

GLASS, Montague. *Truth About Potash Perlmutter.* nd (1924). Whitman. 1st thus ed 122 p. gray cloth. NF. B22. $10.00

GLASSCOCK, Carl B. *Big Bonanza.* 193 Indianapolis. 1st ed. inscr. 368 p. cloth. VG D3. $50.00

GLASSCOCK, William. *Naval Sketch-Book or, Service Afloat & Ashore...* 1826. Londor Henry Coburn. 2nd ed. sm 8vo. 19th-cen tury calf. NF. K1. $200.00

GLASSER, Ronald. *Another War, Anothe Peace.* (1985). Summit. 1st ed. author's 1s novel. rem mk. as new/F. A7. $25.00

GLASSER, Ronald. *365 Days.* (1971). NY Braziller. clip dj. A7. $35.00

GLASSON, H.A. *Golden Cobweb.* 1959. New Zealand. Dunedin. 3rd ed. 8vo. 203 p. re cloth. F/VG. H3. $20.00

GLAZER, Simon. *Guide of Judaism.* 1917 NY. Hebrew Pub. 176 p. VG-. S3. $23.00

GLAZER & QUAIFE. *MI.* 1948. Prentic Hall. 1st ed. 374 p. VG. A17. $12.50

GLAZIER, Willard. *Capture the Prison Pe & the Escape...* 1867. Hartford. Goodwin. G A16. $47.50

GLAZIER, Willard. *Down the Great River..* 1899. Phil. 12mo. 443 p. G. T3. $47.00

GLAZIER, Willard. *Down the Great River..* 1899. Phil. Hubbard. ils/maps. ils brds. NF O6. $95.00

GLAZIER, Willard. *Headwaters of the MS.* 1893. Chicago/NY. xl. 8vo. ils/photos. 527 p. H9. $45.00

GLAZIER, Willard. *Headwaters of the MS.* 1894. np. xl. 12mo. 527 p. gilt dk gr cloth. G T3. $29.00

GLAZIER, Willard. *Ocean to Ocean on Horseback.* 1903. Phil. 12mo. ils. 544 p. lacks rear ep. G. T3. $24.00

GLEDHILL, Alan. *Pakistan: Development of Its Laws & Constitution.* 1980. Westport. Greenwood. 2nd ed. 8vo. 262 p. VG. W1. $20.00

GLEN, Douglas. *In the Steps of Lawrence of Arabia.* 1939. London. Rich Cowan. 1st ed. 320 p. gilt brn cloth. VG+/G. M7. $65.00

GLEN, J. *Description of SC.* 1761. London. 1st ed. quarter calf. VG+. C6. $4,500.00

GLENN & RICE. *Frances Benjamin Johnston: Women of Class & Station.* 1979. Long Beach. 1/1500. 96 p. wrp. D2. $45.00

GLOAG, John. *Artorius Rex.* 1977. London. 1st ed. NF/dj. C1. $32.50

GLOCK, Charles Y. *Apathetic Majority.* 1966. Harper Row. 222 p. VG+/VG. S3. $23.00

GLOSSBRENNER & LAU. *Winning Hitter.* 1984. Hearst. 1st ed. F/VG+. P8. $20.00

GLOVER, Edward. *Freud or Jung.* 1950. Norton. 1st ed/Am issue. 207 p. bl cloth. VG/dj. G1. $28.50

GLOVER, F.R. *Glover's Breeders' & Cockers' Guide.* nd. Cortland. 4th ed. VG/wrp. O3. $15.00

GLOZER & GLOZER. *CA in the Kitchen.* 1960. private prt. 1st ed. ils. 43 p. NF/sans. B19. $25.00

GLUCKMAN, Arcadi. *Identifying Old US Muskets, Rifles & Carbines.* 1965. Harrisburg. Stackpole. VG/fair. N2. $13.50

GLUCKMAN, Max. *African Traditional Law in Hist Perspective.* 1974. Oxford. 45 p. stapled wrp. M11. $25.00

GNOLI, Domenico. *Orestes; or, Act of Smiling, #611.* 1961. Simon Schuster. 1st ed. 71 p. VG/G+. A3. $60.00

GOBLE, Danney. *Progressive OK: Making of a New Kind of State.* 1980. OK U. 1st ed. ils/index. 276 p. F/F. B19. $7.50

GOCHER, W.H. *Trotalong. Pacealong. Racealong.* 1928. Hartford. 3 vols. VG. O3. $145.00

GODDARD, Frederick B. *Where To Emigrate & Why.* 1869. Phil/Cincinnati/Chicago. People's Pub. lg 8vo. 19 maps. gilt orange cloth. H9. $150.00

GODDARD, John. *Waterside Guide: Angler's Pocket Reference...* (1988). London. ils/pls. 207 p. F/dj. A17. $15.00

GODDARD, Pliny Earle. *Indians of the SW.* 1921. Am Mus Natural Hist. 2nd ed. F. H7. $40.00

GODDARD, Robert Hutchings. *Autobiography...* 1966. Worcester. St Onge. miniature. bl calf. H10. $65.00

GODDEN, Rumer. *Blk Narcissus.* 1947. Albatross Ltd. sm pb. NF. C8. $25.00

GODDEN, Rumer. *Candy Floss.* 1960. Viking. 1st ed. 8vo. 63 p. VG/G. A3. $35.00

GODDEN, Rumer. *Dolls' House.* 1948. Viking. 1st ed. 8vo. 125 p. VG/G. A3. $40.00

GODDEN, Rumer. *Fairy Doll.* 1956. Viking. 1st ed. 8vo. 67 p. gray cloth. VG. T5. $30.00

GODDEN, Rumer. *Fairy Doll.* 1967. Viking. 7th prt. 67 p. VG/VG. A3. $10.00

GODDEN, Rumer. *Four Dolls.* 1983. Greenwillow Books. 1st Am ed. 137 p. F/F. A3. $11.50

GODDEN, Rumer. *Home Is the Sailor.* 1964. Viking. 1st ed. 128 p. VG/G+. A3. $22.50

GODDEN, Rumer. *Impunity Jane.* 1954. Viking. 1st ed. sm 8vo. VG/G. A3. $35.00

GODDEN, Rumer. *Impunity Jane.* 1954. Viking. 1st ed. ils Adrienne Adams. NF/VG. T5. $45.00

GODDEN, Rumer. *Kindle of Kittens.* 1978. Viking. 1st Am ed. ils Lynne Byrnes. F/dj. A16. $25.00

GODDEN, Rumer. *Mouse House.* 1966. Viking. ils Adrienne Adams. 5th prt. 63 p. VG/G. A3. $10.50

GODDING, W.W. *Two Hard Cases.* 1882. Houghton Mifflin. inscr. 12mo. 257 p. gilt emb cloth. VG. G1. $75.00

GODEY, John. *Snake.* nd. Putnam. 2nd ed. VG/dj. P3. $15.00

GODEY, John. *Talisman.* 1976. Putnam. 1st ed. VG/dj. P3. $20.00

GODFREY, E.S. *Account of Custer's Last Campaign.* 1968. Palo Alto. 1/2100. 88 p. map ep. VG. B18. $35.00

GODFREY, Thomas. *Murder for Christmas.* nd. BC. VG/dj. P3. $7.50

GODIN, Roger. *1922 St Louis Brns.* 1991. McFarland. 1st ed. M/sans. P8. $26.00

GODMAN, Ernest. *Norman Architecture in Essex.* 1905. Surrey. Essex House. 1/300. ils Jessie Godman. vellum/gr cloth. NF. K1. $150.00

GODMAN, John D. *Addresses Delivered on Various Public Occassions...* 1829. Phil. 194 p. orig brds/rebacked. G7. $95.00

GODON. *Shaker Textile Arts.* 1983. np. ils. wrp. G2. $16.00

GODWIN, Gail. *Perfectionists.* 1970. NY. 1st ed. inscr. author's 1st book. NF/dj. A15. $115.00

GODWIN, Parke. *Snake Oil Wars.* nd. BC. VG/dj. P3. $7.50

GODWIN, Parke. *Waiting for the Galactic Bus.* nd. BC. VG/dj. P3. $7.50

GODWIN, Tom. *Survivors.* 1958. Gnome. 1st ed. F/dj. M2. $60.00

GOERCH, Carl. *Carolina Chats.* 1944. Edwards. 1st ed. 403 p. cloth. VG+/dj. B22. $7.00

GOERLITZ, Walter. *Hist of the German General Staff.* 1961. NY. Praeger. trans Brian Battershaw. G/dj. A16. $15.00

GOETHE; see Von Goethe, Johann Wolfgang.

GOETZMANN, William H. *New Lands, New Man.* 1986. NY. Viking. 1st ed. 8vo. 528 p. half cloth. M/M. P4. $25.00

GOETZMANN & GOETZMANN. *W of the Imagination.* (1986). NY. 1st ed. 458 p. F/dj. A17. $20.00

GOFF, Clarissa. *Florence.* 1905. London. Blk. 8vo. 75 color pls. teg. gilt red cloth. VG+. H3. $50.00

GOFFIN, Robert. *Horn of Plenty: Story of Louis Armstrong.* 1947. NY. Allen Towne Heath. 1st ed. NF/NF. B2. $65.00

GOGOL, Nickolay. *Evenings on a Farm Near Dikanka.* 1926. Knopf. 1st Am ed. G/clip. L3. $35.00

GOGOL, Nikolai. *Chickikov's Journeys; or, Home Life in Old Russia.* 1942. NY. Readers Club. trans BG Guerney. G/worn dj. E3. $12.00

GOH, Poh Seng. *If We Dream Too Long.* (1972). Singapore. Island Pr. inscr/sgn. 177 p. NF/dj. A7. $45.00

GOHM, D.C. *Maps & Prts for Pleasure & Investment.* 1970s. NY. Arco. ils. M/M. O6. $25.00

GOIL, N.K. *Asian Social Science Bibliography...* 1974. Delhi/Bombay. Vikas. 1st ed. 8vo. 602 p. VG/dj. W1. $25.00

GOINES, Donald. *Blk Gangster.* 1971. LA. 1st prt. NF/blk ils wrp. A11. $30.00

GOKCELI, Kemal Sadik. *Birds Have Also Gone.* 1987. London. Collins/Harvill. 1st ed. trans from Turkish. Nf/NF clip. A14. $20.00

GOKCELI, Kemal Sadik. *Sea-Crossed Fisherman.* 1985. NY. Braziller. 1st Am ed. trans from Turkish. NF/NF. A14. $25.00

GOLD, H.L. *Bodyguard.* nd. BC. VG/dj. P3. $7.50

GOLD, H.L. *Fifth Galaxy Reader.* 1961. BC. 1st ed. VG/dj. P3. $30.00

GOLD, H.L. *Fourth Galaxy Reader.* 1959. Doubleday. 1st ed. VG/dj. P3. $30.00

GOLD, H.L. *Mind Partner.* 1961. Doubleday. 1st ed. VG-/dj. P3. $10.00

GOLD, H.L. *Prospect Before US.* 1954. Cleveland. 1st ed. inscr. F/NF. A11. $60.00

GOLD, H.L. *Third Galaxy Reader.* nd. BC. VG/dj. P3. $7.50

GOLDBERG. *New Quilting & Patchwork Dictionary.* 1988. np. wrp. G2. $12.95

GOLDEMBERG, Isaac. *Play by Play.* 1985. NY. Persea Books. 1st ed. trans from Spanish. F/F. A14. $25.00

GOLDEN, Harry. *Carl Sandburg.* 1961. World. 1st ed. VG/VG. V2. $7.00

GOLDEN, Harry. *Mr Kennedy & the Negroes.* 1964. Cleveland. World. 1st ed. VG/dj. N2. $7.50

GOLDEN, Jeffrey. *Watermelon Summer: A Journal.* 1971. Lippincott. 1st ed. author's 1st book. NF/NF. E3. $15.00

GOLDEN. *Friendship Quilt Book.* 1985. np. ils. wrp. G2. $15.00

GOLDENWEISER, Alexander. *Hist, Psychology & Culture.* 1933. Knopf. 1st ed. 476 p. prt maroon cloth. VG/dj. G1. $35.00

GOLDER, F.A. *John Paul Jones in Russia.* 1927. Doubleday Page. 1st ed. xl. 1/1000. ils. teg. NF/dj/slipcase. O6. $175.00

GOLDER & HUTCHINSON. *On the Trail of the Russian Famine.* 1927. Stanford. 1st ed. ils. 319 p. N2. $35.00

GOLDFRANK, Esther S. *Social & Ceremonial Organization of Cochiti.* 1927. Menasha, WI. 1st ed. xl. 129 p. orig wrp. D3. $12.50

GOLDIN, Stephen. *Assault on the Gods.* 1977. Doubleday. 1st ed. F/F. N3/P3. $15.00

GOLDIN, Stephen. *World Called Solitude.* 1981. Doubleday. 1st ed. F/dj. P3. $15.00

GOLDING, Harry. *Willie Winkie, the Tale of a Wooden Horse.* nd. Ward Lock. ils MW Tarrant. 96 p. G. D1. $75.00

GOLDING, William. *Brass Butterfly: A Play in 3 Acts.* 1958. London. Faber. 1st ed. F/NF. Q1. $175.00

GOLDING, William. *Darkness Visible.* 1979. FSG. 1st ed. F/F. T2. $15.00

GOLDING, William. *Lord of the Flies.* 1954. London. Faber. 1st ed. sm octavo. 248 p. gilt burgundy morocco. VG. H5. $850.00

GOLDING, William. *Moving Target.* 1982. FSG. 1st Am ed. F/F. N3. $15.00

GOLDING, William. *Paper Men.* 1984. London. Faber. 1st ed. sgn. F/dj. M18. $100.00

GOLDING, William. *Pyramid.* 1967. NY. HBW. 1st Am ed. F/VG+. N3. $20.00

GOLDING, William. *Spire.* 1964. London. 1st ed. NF/NF. A11. $40.00

GOLDMAN, Edward Alphonso. *Biological Investigations in Mexico.* 1951. Smithsonian. 8vo. 71 pls. 476 p. wrp. P4. $75.00

GOLDMAN, Emma. *Anarchism & Other Essays.* 1910. NY. Mother Earth. F/VG. V4. $100.00

GOLDMAN, Emma. *Anarchism & Other Essays.* 1911. NY. Mother Earth. 3rd ed. sgn. 277 p. VG+. B14. $40.00

GOLDMAN, Emma. *Social Significance of the Modern Drama.* 1914. Boston. Badger. 1st ed. NF. B2. $85.00

GOLDMAN, Francesco. *Long Night of Wht Chicken.* 1992. Atlantic Monthly. 1st ed. 450 p. dj. F3. $20.00

GOLDMAN, I. *Mouth of Heaven.* 1975. NY. 1st ed. ils/index. 265 p. VG/VG. B5. $25.00

GOLDMAN, Lawrence Louis. *Tiger by the Tail.* 1946. McKay. VG/G+. P3. $15.00

GOLDMAN, Peter. *Report From Blk Am.* (1970). Simon Schuster. 1st ed. 282 p. dj. A7. $20.00

GOLDMAN, William. *Brothers.* (1987). NY. Warner. 1st ed. inscr. F/F. B3. $35.00

GOLDMAN, William. *Butch Cassidy & the Sundance Kid.* 1969. Bantam. PBO. sgn. NF/wrp. A11. $65.00

GOLDMAN, William. *Colour of Light.* 1984. Granada. 1st ed. VG/dj. P3. $22.50

GOLDMAN, William. *Control.* 1982. Delacorte. 1st ed. VG/dj. P3. $25.00

GOLDMAN, William. *Edged Weapons.* 1985. Granada. F/dj. P3. $20.00

GOLDMAN, William. *Father's Day.* 1971. Michael Joseph. 1st ed. VG. P3. $10.00

GOLDMAN, William. *Great Waldo Pepper.* (1975). Dell. PBO. NF/wrp. B4. $45.00

GOLDMAN, William. *Heat.* 1985. Warner. 1st ed. VG/dj. P3. $15.00

GOLDMAN, William. *Hype & Glory.* 1990. Villard. 1st ed. VG+/dj. P3. $20.00

GOLDMAN, William. *Magic.* (1976). Delacorte. 1st ed. NF/dj. B4. $45.00

GOLDMAN, William. *Marathon Man.* 1974. Delacorte. 1st ed. VG/dj. P3. $30.00

GOLDMAN, William. *Temple of Gold.* 1957. NY. 1st ed. sgn. NF/NF. A11. $110.00

GOLDMAN & WIEBUSCH. *Quilts of IN: Crossroads of Memories.* 1991. np. ils. cloth. G2. $37.50

GOLDSBOROUGH, Robert. *Death on Deadline.* nd. BC. VG/dj. P3. $7.50

GOLDSBOROUGH, Robert. *Death on Deadline.* 1989. London. Collins. 1st British ed. sgn. NF/F. S5. $35.00

GOLDSBOROUGH, Robert. *Murder in E Minor.* 1986. Bantam. 1st ed. F/dj. P3. $15.00

GOLDSBOROUGH, Robert. *Nero Wolfe: Bloodied Ivy.* 1988. Bantam. lg-type ed. VG/dj. A16. $10.00

GOLDSMITH, Arnold L. *Golem Remembered, 1909-80: Variations of Jewish Legend.* 1981. Wayne State. 181 p. F/F. S3. $25.00

GOLDSMITH, Oliver. *Citizen of the World.* 1762. London. 1st ed. 12mo. 2 vols. contemporary gilt calf. F/brn morocco slipcase. H5. $1,250.00

GOLDSMITH, Oliver. *Deserted Village.* nd. Porter Coates. hand-colored pls. leather/marbled brds. F. A16. $225.00

GOLDSMITH, Oliver. *Deserted Village.* 1888. Lippincott. ils MM Taylor. VG. M18. $30.00

GOLDSMITH, Oliver. *Deserted Village: A Poem.* 1926. San Francisco. Clark Nash. 1/200. 2 vols. orig compartment slipcase. K1. $200.00

GOLDSMITH, Oliver. *Enquiry Into the Present State of Polite Learning in Europe.* 1759. London. Dodsley. 1st ed. sm octavo. 200 p. Riviere bdg. NF. H5. $1,250.00

GOLDSMITH, Oliver. *Little Goody Two-Shoes.* 1929. Saalfield. 1st thus ed. ils FB Peat. pict ep. VG. S10. $30.00

GOLDSMITH, Oliver. *Vicar of Wakefield...* 1766. Salisbury. 1st ed. 12mo. 2 vols. full red morocco. VG. H5. $5,000.00

GOLDSTEIN, Herbert S. *Bible Comments for Home Reading: Book of Joshua.* 1939. Hebrew Pub. reading copy. S3. $17.00

GOLDSTEIN, Leon J. *Historical Knowing.* (1976). Austin. 242 p. F/NF. A7. $16.00

GOLDSTEIN, Lisa. *Dream Yrs.* 1985. Bantam. 1st ed. F/dj. P3. $15.00

GOLDTHWAITE, Eaton K. *Cat & Mouse.* 1946. DSP. 1st ed. VG/dj. P3. $25.00

GOLDTHWAITE, Eaton K. *Scarecrow.* 1946. Books Inc. VG/G. P3. $10.00

GOLDZIHER, Ignaz. *Mythology Among Hebrews & Its Development.* 1967. Cooper Sq Pub. reprint. 457 p. VG+. S3. $30.00

GOLENBOCK, Peter. *Bums.* 1984. Putnam. 1st ed. F/F. P8. $17.50

GOLENBOCK, Peter. *Forever Boys.* 1991. Birch Lane. 1st ed. F/F. P8. $35.00

GOLENBOCK & LYLE. *Bronx Zoo.* 1979. Crown. 1st ed. F/VG+. P8. $10.00

GOLLER, Nicholas. *Tomorrow's Silence.* 1979. Macmillan. 1st ed. VG/dj. P3. $15.00

GOMBROWICZ, Witold. *Cosmos.* 1968. NY. Grove. 1st Am ed. trans from Polish. NF/NF. A14. $25.00

GOMPERS, Samuel. *Labor & the Employer.* (1920). EP Dutton. 320 p. bl cloth. B14. $25.00

GONZALES, Nancie L. *Spanish-Am of NM.* 1969. NM U. revised/enlarged ed. 246 p. cloth. F/pict dj. D3. $15.00

GONZALES CALDERON, Luis. *Cabecitas Olmecas.* (1977). Mexico. 1st ed. 1/4000. 167 p. pict cloth. F3. $35.00

GONZALES CALDERON, Luis. *Jade Lords.* 1991. Mexico. 1st ed. 1/1000. 543 p. dj. F3. $120.00

GONZALEZ, E.J. *Fuchsias: Guide to Cultivation & Identification.* 1973. NY. ils/38 photos. red cloth. VG/dj. B26. $17.50

GOOCH, Bob. *Squirrels & Squirrel Hunting.* 1972. Tidewater. 1st ed. ils/index. 152 p. F/dj. A17. $18.50

GOOCH, Bob. *Weedy World of the Pickerels.* (1970). Barnes. lg 8vo. ils/photos. 184 p. F/VG. A17. $22.50

GOOCH, Brad. *Scary Kisses.* 1988. Putnam. 1st ed. NF/NF. A14. $30.00

GOOCH, Fanny Chambers. *Face to Face w/the Mexicans.* (1887). NY. Fords Howard. 1st ed. 584 p. pict cloth. F3. $75.00

GOODALE & PRICE. *Daughter of the Gold Camp & Legends of the W Indian.* (1962. Rapid City. 1st ed. sgn. 150 p. cloth. glassine wrp. A17. $17.50

GOODALL, John S. *Story of a Castle.* 1986. NY. McElderry/Macmillan. 1st Am ed. oblong 12mo. 29 p. gray brds. F/F. T5. $30.00

GOODALL, John S. *Victorians Abroad.* 1981. Atheneum. 1st Am ed. oblong 24mo. ils. bl cloth. F/F. T5. $30.00

GOODALL, JOHNSON & PHILIPPI. *Las Aves de Chile. Su Concocimiento y sus Costumbres.* 1946 & 1951. Buenos Aires. Platt Establecimientos Graficos. 2 vols. P4. $195.00

GOODALL, Mary. *OR's Iron Dream.* 1958. Binford Mort. 8vo. VG/G. A8. $10.00

GOODALL, Norman. *Ecumenical Movement: What It Is & What It Does.* 1964. London. Oxford. 2nd ed. 257 p. H10. $15.00

GOODALL. *Shrewbettina Goes To Work: A Pop-Up Story.* 1981. paper engineering by Tor Lokvig. F. A4. $35.00

GOODCHILD, George. *Jack O'Lantern.* 1930. Mystery League. 1st ed. VG-. P3. $10.00

GOODE, George Brown. *Fisheries & Fishery Industries of the US. Section V...* 1887. WA. US Comm Fish. atlas vol. 255 pls. NF. O6. $200.00

GOODHUE, Bertram. *Mexican Memories.* 1892. NY. 12mo. 167 p. gilt orange brds/brn cloth. VG. H3. $12.00

GOODIS, David. *Al Caer la Noche (Nightfall).* 1971. Buenos Aires. Serie Negra. 1st Argentine/1st Spanish-language ed. F. A11. $30.00

GOODIS, David. *Behold This Woman.* July 1948. Bantam 407. 1st pb ed. NF. A11. $35.00

GOODIS, David. *Behold This Woman.* Oct 1956. Popular Lib 775. VG+/NF. A11. $40.00

GOODIS, David. *Blk Friday.* Sept 1954. Lion 224. NF/unread. A11. $135.00

GOODIS, David. *Blonde on the Street Corner.* Jan 1954. Lion 186. 1st ed. F/unread. A11. $250.00

GOODIS, David. *Burglar.* Feb 1953. Lion 124. 1st ed. NF/unread. A11. $125.00

GOODIS, David. *Cassidy's Girl.* April 1967. Dell 1114. 2nd pb ed. NF/unread. A11. $30.00

GOODIS, David. *Cassidy's Girl.* 1951. Gold Medal 189. 1st ed. F/pristine. A11. $175.00

GOODIS, David. *Dark Chase (Nightfall).* March 1953. NY. Lion 133. 1st/only ed under this title. F/unread. A11. $125.00

GOODIS, David. *Dark Passage.* 1946. Julian Messner. VG. P3. $45.00

GOODIS, David. *Dark Passage.* 1947 (1946). Dell 221. 1st pb ed. VG+. A11. $55.00

GOODIS, David. *Down There.* Nov 1956. Gold Medal 623. 1st ed. VG. A11. $75.00

GOODIS, David. *Epaves (Street of the Lost).* 1980. Paris. Polar. 1st ed. NF/ils wrp. A11. $35.00

GOODIS, David. *Fire in the Flesh.* Aug 1957. Gold Medal 691. 1st ed. F/pristine. A11. $150.00

GOODIS, David. *La Casse (The Burglar).* July 1954. Paris. Serie Noire 207. 1st ed/correct 1st prt. blk/yel brds. VG. A11. $60.00

GOODIS, David. *La Garce (Behold This Woman).* 1981. Paris. Le Livre de Poche. 1st ed. F/pristine wrp. A11. $45.00

GOODIS, David. *Les Pieds Dans les Nuages (Night Squad).* 1962. Paris. Serie Noire 691. 1st ed. VG/wrp. A11. $55.00

GOODIS, David. *Moon in the Gutter.* Nov 1953. Gold Medal 348. 1st ed. F/unread. A11. $200.00

GOODIS, David. *Night Squad.* Feb 1961. Gold Medal S1083. 1st ed. F/unread. A11. $75.00

GOODIS, David. *Nightfall (Dark Chase).* Nov 1956. Lion LB 131. 2nd Lion ed. F/unread. A11. $45.00

GOODIS, David. *Nightfall.* ca 1950. Bestseller Mystery B121. 1st pb ed. digest size. VG/VG+. A11. $30.00

GOODIS, David. *Nightfall.* nd. Israel. Priory. apparent unauthorized ed. NF/wrp. A11. $25.00

GOODIS, David. *Of Missing Persons.* Dec 1951. Pocket Books 833. 1st pb ed. NF/unread. A11. $55.00

GOODIS, David. *Of Tender Sin.* March 1952. Gold Medal 256. 1st ed. F/unread. A11. $150.00

GOODIS, David. *Retreat From Oblivion.* 1939. Dutton. 1st ed. author's 1st book. F/F clamshell box. rare. L3. $2,500.00

GOODIS, David. *Sans Espoir de Retour.* 1956. Paris. Serie Noire 288. 1st ed. blk/yel brds. VG. A11. $45.00

GOODIS, David. *Shoot the Piano Player (Down There).* ca 1961. Blk Cat BA-35. 1st ed in Eng under this title. VG+/NF. A11. $55.00

GOODIS, David. *Somebody's Done For.* nd. Xanadu. 1st UK ed. F/unread glossy wrp. A11. $30.00

GOODIS, David. *Somebody's Done For.* Oct 1967. Banner B60-111. 1st ed. F/unread. rare. A11. $175.00

GOODIS, David. *Street of No Return.* Sept 1954. Gold Medal 428. 1st ed. F/unread. A11. $125.00

GOODIS, David. *Street of the Lost.* nd. Israel. Priory. VG/ils wrp. A11. $20.00

GOODIS, David. *Street of the Lost.* Sept 1952. Gold Medal 256. 1st ed. F/unread. scarce. A11. $175.00

GOODIS, David. *Viernes 13 (Blk Friday).* 1974. Buenos Aires. 1st Argentine/1st Spanish-language ed. VG+/wrp. A11. $45.00

GOODIS, David. *Wounded & the Slain.* Nov 1955. Gold Medal 530. 1st ed. F/pristine. A11. $200.00

GOODIS, David. *4 Novels by David Goodis.* 1983. Zomba Blk Box Thriller. 1st ed. F/dj. P3. $40.00

GOODLAND, Roger. *Bibliography of Sex Rites & Customs.* 1931. London. Routledge. 1st ed. tall 4to. 752 p. gr cloth. G1. $150.00

GOODMAN, Ellen. *Value Judgements.* (1993). FSG. AP. F/wrp. B4. $25.00

GOODMAN, I. *Stan Musial: The Man.* 1961. Nelson. 1st ed. xl. rem mk. G+/G+. P8. $12.50

GOODMAN, Paul. *Hist of the Jews.* 1924. Dutton. 2nd ed. 164 p. G+. S3. $18.00

GOODMAN, Paul. *5 Yrs: Thoughts During a Useless Time.* 1966. Brussel. 2nd prt. dj. A7. $15.00

GOODMAN. *Embroidery of Mexico & Guatemala.* 1976. np. cloth. G2. $20.00

GOODRICH, A.T. *N Am Tourist.* 1839. Goodrich. xl. thick 12mo. ils/plans. later brds/rebacked. H9. $75.00

GOODRICH, Charles A. *Universal Traveller.* 1836. Hartford. thick 8vo. ils. 610 p. contemporary calf. O2. $75.00

GOODRICH, Chauncey. *N Fruit Culturist; or, Farmer's Guide to Orchard...* 1849. Burlington. self pub. 1st ed. half leather. H10. $125.00

GOODRICH, Frances Louisa. *Mtn Homespun.* 1931. Yale. ils. 91 p. H10. $35.00

GOODRICH, Lloyd. *Graphic Work of Winslow Homer.* 1968. Mus Graphic Art. 136 p. stiff wrp. D2. $35.00

GOODRICH, Lloyd. *Winslow Homer's Am.* 1969. Tudor. 192 p. cloth. dj. D2. $75.00

GOODRICH, Lloyd. *Winslow Homer.* Apr-June 1973. Whitney Mus. 143 p. wrp. D2. $30.00

GOODRICH, Lloyd. *Winslow Homer.* 1944. Macmillan/Whitney Mus. ils/index. 246 p. cloth. scarce. D2. $65.00

GOODRICH, Samuel Griswold. *Faggots for the Fireside; or, Fact & Fancy.* 1855. NY. 1st ed. 12mo. 320 p. gilt bdg. VG. D3. $45.00

GOODRICH, Samuel Griswold. *Manners, Customs & Antiquities of Indians of N & S Am.* 1846. Phil. Cowperthwait. 12mo. calf. H9. $85.00

GOODRICH, Samuel Griswold. *Pict Hist of the US.* ca 1865. Phil. JH Butler. 8vo. ils/map. 522 p. gr cloth/roan spine. H9. $30.00

GOODRIDGE & ROBERTS. *NH Church Hist...* 1904. Concord. Rumford. 52 p. H10. $10.00

GOODSPEED, Bernice. *Mexican Tales.* 1937. Mexico. 1st ed. inscr. 227 p. wrp. F3. $20.00

GOODSPEED, E. *Hist of Great Fires of Chicago & the W.* 1871. NY. self pub. 676 p. gr cloth. G+. M20. $50.00

GOODSPEED, Edgar J. *The 12: Story of Christ's Apostles.* 1957. Phil. Winston. 182 p. H10. $17.50

GOODWIN, Richard N. *Triumph or Tragedy: Reflections on Vietnam.* (1966). Random. 142 p. NF/clip dj. A7. $27.00

GOODWIN & HAWBAKER. *Art of Deer & Bear Hunting.* 1953. Chambersburg. photos. 21 p. wrp. A17. $5.00

GOOSMANN, J.C. *Carbonic Acid Industry.* (1906). Chicago. ils/photos. 368 p. gilt cloth. A17. $25.00

GOOSSEN, Irvy W. *Navajo Made Easier.* 1968. Flagstaff, AZ. Northland. 3rd prt. 8vo. 271 p. VG. B11. $40.00

GORDIMER, Nadine. *Conversationist.* 1975. Viking. 1st Am ed. sgn. F/F. L3. $200.00

GORDIMER, Nadine. *Sport of Nature.* (1987). NY. Borzoi. AP. VG/prt gray wrp. B3. $45.00

GORDON, Adam L. *Poems.* 1923. Oxford. VG. C1. $6.50

GORDON, Albert I. *Nature of Conversion: Story of 45 Men & Women...* 1967. Beacon. xl. 333 p. VG/VG. S3. $26.00

GORDON, Allison. *Foul Balls.* 1984. McClelland. 1st Canadian ed. VG+/VG. P8. $22.50

GORDON, Allison. *Night Game.* 1992. McClelland. 1st ed. inscr/sgn. F/dj. P3. $25.00

GORDON, Armistead C. *General Daniel Morgan: An Address...* 1895. Methodist Episcopal Church. 20 p. VG/wrp. B10. $18.00

GORDON, Armistead C. *Jefferson Davis.* 1918. Scribner. 1st ed. inscr. 329 p. VG. B10. $75.00

GORDON, Armistead C. *Memories & Memorials of Wm Gordon McCabe.* 1925. Richmond, VA. Old Dominion. 1st ed. 2 vols. cloth. VG+. M8. $150.00

GORDON, Armistead C. *Some Lawyers of Colonial VA...April 1921.* nd. Richmond Pr. 20 p. VG/stiff wrp. B10. $18.00

GORDON, Armistead C. *Wm Fitzhugh Gordon: Virginian of the Old School...* 1909. NY/WA. Neale. 1st ed. 412 p. VG. M8. $125.00

GORDON, Arthur. *Reprisal.* nd. BC. VG/dj. P3. $7.50

GORDON, Benjamin Lee. *Medicine Throughout Antiquity.* 1949. Phil. Davis. ils. 818 p. G. G7. $95.00

GORDON, Caroline. *Garden of Adonis.* 1937. Scribner. 1st ed. F/NF. B2. $150.00

GORDON, Caroline. *Malefactors.* 1956. Harcourt. 1st ed. F/NF. B2. $65.00

GORDON, Caroline. *Old Red & Other Stories.* 1963. Scribner. 1st ed. F/F. B2. $75.00

GORDON, David; see Garrett, Randall.

GORDON, Donald. *Flight of the Bat.* 1964. Odhams. VG/dj. P3. $15.00

GORDON, Donald. *Star-Raker.* 1962. Hodder Stoughton. 1st ed. VG/dj. P3. $20.00

GORDON, Elizabeth. *Billy Bunny's Fortune.* 1919. Volland. Sunny Book series. 40 p. G+. A3. $17.50

GORDON, Elizabeth. *Bird Children. Little Playmates of Flower Children.* 1930. Volland. ils MT Ross. revised ed. 95 p. G+. A3. $25.00

GORDON, Elizabeth. *Buddy Jim.* 1935. Wise Parslow. ils John Rae. 109 p. cloth. G+. A3. $25.00

GORDON, Elizabeth. *Butterfly Babies' Book.* 1914. Rand McNally. ils MT (Penny) Ross. VG. M5. $60.00

GORDON, Elizabeth. *Butterfly Babies' Book.* 1914. Rand McNally. 8vo. 79 p. pict brds. G+. T5. $45.00

GORDON, Elizabeth. *Flower Children.* 1910. Volland. apparent 1st ed. Happy Children series. VG. M5. $65.00

GORDON, Elizabeth. *Loraine & the Little People.* 1915. Rand McNally. 1st ed. ils Penny Ross. red cloth. NF/tattered dj. M5. $75.00

GORDON, Elizabeth. *Really-So Stories.* 1924. Volland. 8vo. ils John Rae/11 color pls. pict brds. G. H3. $15.00

GORDON, Elizabeth. *Really-So Stories.* 1937. Wise Parslow. ils John Rae. 4to. 96 p. cloth. G+. A3. $25.00

GORDON, Elizabeth. *Turned-Into's. Jane Elizabeth Discovers the Garden Folk.* 1935. Wise Parslow ils JL Scott. 4to. 92 p. VG-. A3. $25.00

GORDON, Jean. *Pageant of the Rose.* ca 1953. NY. Studio. ils/index. 232 p. H10. $15.00

GORDON, Lady Duff. *Last Letter From Egypt.* 1875. London. Macmillan. 316 p. bl cloth. VG+. P4. $65.00

GORDON, Manya. *Workers Before & After Lenin.* 1941. Dutton. 1st ed. 524 p. A7. $20.00

GORDON, Noah. *Physician.* nd. BC. VG/dj. P3. $5.00

GORDON, Patricia. *Taming of Giants.* 1950. Viking/Jr Literary guild. 1st ed. ils MacKenzie. VG+/G. P2. $15.00

GORDON, Richard. *Captain's Table.* 1954. Michael Joseph. 1st ed. VG/dj. P3. $30.00

GORDON, Richard. *Doctor & Son.* 1959. Michael Joseph. 1st ed. VG/dj. P3. $30.00

GORDON, Richard. *Doctor at Large.* 1955. Michael Joseph. 1st ed. VG/dj. P3. $30.00

GORDON, Richard. *Doctor in Love.* 1957. Michael Joseph. 1st ed. VG/dj. P3. $30.00

GORDON, Richard. *Nuts in May.* 1964. Heinemann. 1st ed. VG+/dj. P3. $17.50

GORDON, Roy. *Battleground.* (1978). Holloway House. PBO. A7. $15.00

GORDON, Sally. *Rider's Handbook.* nd. NY. Putnam. 1st Am ed. Vg/VG. O3. $20.00

GORDON, Stuart. *Two Eyes.* 1975. Sidgwick Jackson. 1st ed. VG/dj. P3. $20.00

GORDON, W.J. *Horse-World of London 1893.* 1971. London. reprint. VG/VG. O3. $35.00

GORDON, William. *Hist of Rise, Progress & Establishment of Independence...* 1794. NY. Campbell. 2nd Am ed. 2 vols. orig calf. H9. $175.00

GORDON & GORDON. *Captive.* 1958. Detective BC. VG/VG. P3. $10.00

GORDON & GORDON. *Catnapped! Future Adventures of Undercover Cat.* 1974. Doubleday. 1st ed. F/F clip. B4. $35.00

GORDON & GORDON. *Donkey Trip Through Spain.* 1924. NY. 1st Am ed. 273 p. pict orange cloth. VG. H3. $30.00

GORDON & GORDON. *Informant.* 1973. Doubleday. 1st ed. xl. dj. P3. $5.00

GORDON & GORDON. *Pride of Felons.* 1963. Macmillan. 1st ed. xl. dj. P3. $10.00

GORDON & PRIEST. *More Really-So Stories.* (1929). Wise Parslow. ils John Rae. 4to. cloth. VG-. A3. $25.00

GORDON & PRIEST. *More Really-So Stories.* 1929. Volland. 1st ed. ils John Rae. 95 p. VG. P2. $40.00

GOREH, Nehemiah. *Proofs of Divinity of Our Lord...* 1887. Bombay. Anglo-Vernacular. 79 p. wrp. H10. $15.00

GORENSTEIN, Shirley. *Not Forever on Earth. Prehistory of Mexico.* 1975. Scribner. 1st ed. 8vo. photos. 153 p. brn cloth. VG/VG. B11. $20.00

GORES, Joe. *Come Morning.* 1986. Mysterious. 1st ed. VG/dj. P3. $16.00

GORES, Joe. *Dead Man.* 1993. Mysterious. ARC. F/wrp. B2. $30.00

GORES, Joe. *Gone, No Forwarding.* nd. BC. VG/dj. P3. $7.50

GOREY, Edward. *Amphigorey Also.* 1983. NY. Congdon Weed. 1st ed. sgn. ils gray brds. F/NF. F1. $95.00

GOREY, Edward. *Amphigorey Too.* 1975. Putnam. 1st ed. inscr/sgn. color glazed brds. F/dj. F1. $135.00

GOREY, Edward. *Amphigorey.* 1972. Putnam. 1st ed. VG/dj. P3. $30.00

GOREY, Edward. *Blk Doll.* 1973. Gotham Book Mart. 1st ed. sgn. F/blk wrp. F1. $75.00

GOREY, Edward. *Dracula: A Toy Theatre.* 1979. Scribner. folio. F/spbdg stiff wrp. F1. $120.00

GOREY, Edward. *Dwindling Party.* 1982. London. 6 popups. F. A4. $65.00

GOREY, Edward. *Listing Attic.* (1954). DSP. 1st ed. author's 2nd book. pict brds. NF/dj. B24. $225.00

GOREY, Edward. *Unstrung Harp; or, Mr Earbrass Writes a Novel.* 1953. Little Brn. 1st ed. author's 1st book in text/ils. NF/dj. B24. $325.00

GORHAM, Maurice. *Showmen & Suckers.* (1951). London. Marshall. 8vo. 262 p. NF/VG. T5. $45.00

GORKIN, Michael. *Border Kibbutz.* (1971). Grosset Dunlap. 1st ed. 8vo. 247 p. F/VG. A2. $12.50

GORMAN, Edward. *Guild.* 1987. Evans. 1st ed. F/Fj. P3. $15.00

GORMAN, Edward. *Guild.* 1987. Evans. 12mo. F/VG. A8. $10.00

GORMAN, Edward. *New, Improved Murder.* nd. St Martin. 2nd ed. VG/dj. P3. $12.50

GORMAN, Edward. *Night of Shadows.* 1990. Doubleday. 1st ed. M/M. t2. $12.00

GORMAN, John A. *W Horse.* 1944. Danville, IL. revised ed. ils. 361 p. pict cloth. NF. D3. $25.00

GORMAN, Michael. *Californien: Henry Madden & the German Travelers in Am.* 1991. Fresno. Friends Madden Lib. M/wrp. O6. $25.00

GORMAN & GREENBERG. *Invitation To Murder.* 1991. Dark Harvest. 1/400. w/special contributor sgn leaf. F/F. B2. $65.00

GORMAN & GREENBERG. *Solved.* 1991. Carroll Graf. 1st ed. F/dj. P3. $22.00

GORMAN & HOLTZMAN. *Three & Two!* 1979. Scribner. 1st ed. F/VG. P8. $17.50

GORNICK, Vivian. *In Search of Ali Mahmoud: Am Woman in Egypt.* (1973). Review Pr/Dutton. 1st ed. 8vo. 343 p. VG/VG. A2. $15.00

GORSKY, Bernard. *Island at the End of the World.* 1966. London. Hart Davis. 1st ed. 8vo. 171 p. F/VG. A2. $15.00

GORSLINE. *Hist of Fashion.* 1991. np. ils. cloth. G2. $45.00

GOSCH & HAMMER. *Last Testament of Lucky Luciano.* 1975. Little Brn. VG/dj. A16. $15.00

GOSCH & HAMMER. *Last Testament of Lucky Luciano.* 1975. Little Brn. 1st ed. NF/dj. P3. $17.50

GOSLING, F.G. *Before Freud: Neurasthenia & the Am Medical Community...* 1987. Urbana/Chicago. 192 p. gray cloth. F/dj. G1. $22.50

GOSLING, Paula. *Backlash.* 1989. Crime Club. VG/dj. P3. $12.95

GOSLING, Paula. *Monkey Puzzle.* 1985. Macmillan. 1st ed. front free ep removed. VG/dj. P3. $15.00

GOSLING, Paula. *Wychford Murders.* 1986. London. Macmillan. 1st ed. F/F. M15. $40.00

GOSNELL, Harpur Allen. *Before the Mast in the Clippers.* 1937. Derrydale. 1/950. octavo. 14 pls/6 fld maps. maroon cloth. NF. H5. $200.00

GOSS, John. *Mapping of N Am: 3 Centuries of Map-Making, 1500-1860.* 1990. Seraucus. Wellfleet. 85 full-p maps. M/M. O6. $45.00

GOSTELOW. *Complete Guide to Needlework, Techniques & Materials.* 1982. np. ils. cloth. G2. $20.00

GOSTELOW. *Cross Stitch Book.* 1982. np. 144 p. cloth. G2. $17.50

GOSWAMI, Amil. *Cosmic Dancers.* 1983. Harper Row. 1st ed. F/dj. M2. $18.00

GOTCH & HORSLEY. *Croonian Lecture: On Mammalian Nervous System...* 1892. Phil Royal Soc. 4to. 7 pls. later cloth. G7. $595.00

GOTHAM BOOK SHOP. *Wise Men Fish Here.* 1965. Harcourt Brace. 1st ed. NF/NF. C4. $25.00

GOTTFRIDSSON. *Swedish Mitton Book.* 1984. np. ils/patterns/photos. wrp. G2. $9.00

GOTTHELF, Ezra Gerson. *Island of Not-Me.* 1935. Galleon. 1st ed. dj. N2. $30.00

GOTTLIEB, Hinko. *Key to the Great Gate.* 1947. Simon Schuster. 1st ed. F/dj. M2. $10.00

GOUDEY, A.E. *Day We Saw the Sun Come Up.* 1961. Scribner. ils Adrienne Adams. 1st ed. 4to. VG/G. A3. $30.00

GOUDEY, Alice. *Houses From the Sea.* (1959). Scribner. Caldecott Medal. VG. P2. $7.50

GOUDGE, Elizabeth. *Dean's Watch.* 1964. Hodder Stoughton. 3rd ed. VG/dj. P3. $10.00

GOUDGE, Elizabeth. *Linnets & Valerians.* (1964). Coward McCann. 3rd imp. xl. 290 p. pict lib buckram. VG. T5. $30.00

GOUDGE, Elizabeth. *Pilgrim's Inn.* nd. BC. VG/dj. P3. $7.50

GOUDGE, Elizabeth. *Wht Witch.* 1958. Coward McCann. 1st ed. NF/dj. P3. $25.00

GOUDY, Frederic W. *Alphabet.* 1918. NY. Kennerley. 1st ed. 27 pls. 44 p. gilt blk cloth. NF. B24. $150.00

GOUGH, John B. *Sunlight & Shadow.* 1881 (1881). Worthington. probable 1st ed. 542 p. VG+. B22. $20.00

GOUGH, John B. *Sunlight & Shadow; or, Gleanings From My Life Work.* 1881. Hartford. ils. 542 p. gilt half leather. F. A17. $25.00

GOUGH, Lawrence. *Serious Crimes.* 1990. London. Gollancz. 1st ed. F/F. S5. $25.00

GOUGH, Richard. *Antiquities & Memoirs of Parish of Myddle, County of Salop.* (1968). London. Centaur. 1st thus ed. 4to. 211 p. F/F. A2. $25.00

GOULART, Ron. *Brinkman.* 1981. Doubleday. 1st ed. NF/dj. M2. $10.00

GOULART, Ron. *Broke Down Engine.* 1971. Macmillan. 1st ed. VG/dj. P3. $30.00

GOULART, Ron. *Crackpot.* 1977. Doubleday. 1st ed. RS. F/F. N3. $25.00

GOULD, Alicia B. *Nueva Lista Documentada de los Tripulantes de Colon 1492.* 1944. Madrid. Maestre. Samuel Eliot Morison's copy. G/wrp. O6. $25.00

GOULD, F. Carruthers. *Struwwelpeter Alphabet.* 1900. London. Richards. 1st ed. quarto. NF. B24. $275.00

GOULD, H.P. *Peach Growing.* 1918. Macmillan. 1st ed. 426 p. H10. $20.00

GOULD, Heywood. *Glitterburn.* 1981. St Martin. 1st ed. xl. dj. P3. $6.00

GOULD, S. Baring. *Curious Myths of the Middle Ages.* 1901. London. Longman Gr. new imp. N2. $30.00

GOULD, William. *Blk Workers in Wht Unions.* (1977). Cornell. 506 p. F/NF clip. A7. $25.00

GOULD & HICKOK. *Walter Reuther: Labor's Rugged Individualist.* ca 1972. Dodd Mead. F/G. V4. $12.50

GOULD & PYLE. *Anomalies & Curiosities of Medicine.* 1956. NY. facsimile of 1896 ed. 968 p. G7. $45.00

GOULDEN, Joseph C. *Million-Dollar Lawyers.* 1978. Putnam. M11. $25.00

GOULDEN, Joseph C. *Truth Is the 1st Casualty.* (1969). Rand McNally. 1st ed. 285 p. VG/VG. A7. $20.00

GOULDER, Grace. *OH Scenes & Citizens.* 1964. Cleveland. 2nd ed. 254 p. VG/G. D7. $25.00

GOULDNER, Alvin W. *Future of Intellectuals & Rise of the New Class.* (1979). Dutton. 1st ed. 524 p. A7. $20.00

GOURGUECHON, Charlene. *Journey to the End of the World.* (1977). Scribner. 1st Am ed. 8vo. 338 p. F/F. A2. $10.00

GOVERNMENT PRINTING OFFICE. *Annual Report of Commissioner of Indian Affairs.* 1855. WA. Nicholson. tall 8vo. 336 p. VG+. H7. $100.00

GOVERNMENT PRINTING OFFICE. *Bureau of Am Ethnology, 20th-Annual Report to Smithsonian...* 1903. WA. Aboriginal pottery issue. 177 full-p pls. VG. H7. $100.00

GOVERNMENT PRINTING OFFICE. *Civil War Maps in the National Archives.* 1964. WA, DC. ils/charts/maps. NF. O6. $45.00

GOVERNMENT PRINTING OFFICE. *Constitutions of the US &...MA.* 1849. Boston. 8vo. 56 p. half red label/Senate Chamber label. VG. T3. $25.00

GOVERNMENT PRINTING OFFICE. *General Orders Affecting the Volunteer Forces.* 1862. WA. 216 orders from Adj Gen's Office. O7. $85.00

GOVERNMENT PRINTING OFFICE. *Message From the President of the US.* 1860. WA, DC. 542 p. orig bdg. O7. $21.50

GOVERNMENT PRINTING OFFICE. *Political Manual for 1866.* 1866. WA, DC. 128 p. NF. O7. $21.50

GOVERNMENT PRINTING OFFICE. *Regulations for the Army of the US.* 1861. NY. 1st ed. 457 p. O7. $65.00

GOVERNMENT PRINTING OFFICE. *Report of the Sec of War, 1857.* nd. WA, DC. 572 p. O7. $18.50

GOVERNMENT PRINTING OFFICE. *US Naval Signal Book/Naval Tactics, 1874.* ca 1874. np. 2 parts in 1 vol. 8vo. 85 p. half leather. G. T3. $39.00

GOWERS, William. *Diagnosis of Diseases of the Brain & Spinal Cord.* 1885. NY. Wm Wood. 293 p. VG. G7. $250.00

GOWERS, William. *Lectures on Diagnosis of Diseases of the Brain.* 1885. London. orig cloth. G7. $395.00

GRAEME, Bruce. *Cherchez la Femme.* 1951. Hutchinson. 1st ed. VG/dj. P3. $30.00

GRAEME, Bruce. *Two-Faced.* 1977. Hutchinson. xl. dj. P3. $5.00

GRAEME, David. *Unsolved.* 1932. Lippincott. 1st ed. VG-. P3. $15.00

GRAEME, David. *Vengeance of Monsieur Blackshirt.* 1971. Tom Stacey. VG/dj. P3. $12.50

GRAF, Alfred B. *Hortica.* 1992. E Rutherford. ils/photos. as new/dj. B26. $195.00

GRAFTON, Sue. *A Is for Alibi.* 1982. HRW. 1st ed. VG/dj. P3. $60.00

GRAFTON, Sue. *D Is for Deadbeat.* nd. BC. VG/dj. P3. $7.50

GRAFTON, Sue. *G Is for Gumshoe.* 1990. Holt. 1st ed. F/F. B2. $40.00

GRAFTON, Sue. *H Is for Homicide.* (1991). Holt. 1st ed. sgn. VG/VG. B3. $35.00

GRAFTON, Sue. *Keziah Dane.* 1967. NY. Macmillan. 1st ed. inscr. F/F. M15. $350.00

GRAFTON, Sue. *Kinsey & Me.* 1991. Santa Barbara. Bench Pr. 1st ed. 1/300. sgn/#d. F/slipcase. M15. $300.00

GRAFTON. *Geometric Patchwork Patterns.* 1975. np. 12 patterns. wrp. G2. $4.50

GRAGG, Rod. *Confederate Goliath: The Battle of Ft Fisher.* 1991. Harper Collins. 1st ed. 343 p. cloth. NF/NF. M8. $30.00

GRAGLIA, Lino A. *Disaster by Decree: Supreme Court Decisions on Race...* 1976. Ithaca. Cornell. M11. $25.00

GRAHAM, Brenda Knight. *Stone Gables.* 1978. Broadman. 8vo. 167 p. VG/G. T5. $15.00

GRAHAM, Caroline. *Death of Hollow Man.* 1989. Morrow. 1st ed. F/F. P3. $17.95

GRAHAM, Caroline. *Killings at Badger's Drift.* nd. BC. VG/dj. P3. $7.50

GRAHAM, Caroline. *Murder at Madingly Grange.* 1990. Mysterious/Century. 1st ed. sgn. F/F. M15. $65.00

GRAHAM, Duff. *Peter Rabbit at the Farm.* 1917. Altemus. 30 color pls. gr cloth spine/gray brds. VG. M5. $45.00

GRAHAM, Frank. *Adirondack Park: Political Hist.* 1978. NY. 1st ed. ils/photos/map. 314 p. F/G. A17. $10.00

GRAHAM, Frank. *Great Hitters of the Major Leagues.* 1969. Random. VG. P3. $10.00

GRAHAM, Frank. *Lou Gehrig: A Quiet Hero.* nd. Putnam. 26th prt. xl. P3. $7.50

GRAHAM, James; see Patterson, Henry.

GRAHAM, John Alexander. *Aldeburg Cezanne.* nd. BC. F/dj. P3. $7.50

GRAHAM, John Alexander. *Arthur.* nd. BC. F/dj. P3. $7.50

GRAHAM, Jorie. *End of Beauty.* 1987. NY. 1st ed. F/F. V1. $15.00

GRAHAM, R.B. Cunninghame. *Brought Forward.* 1916. London. Duckworth. 1st ed. 8vo. 205 p. gilt russet cloth. VG. M7. $40.00

GRAHAM, R.B. Cunninghame. *Horses of the Conquest.* 1949. Norman. 1st Am ed. 4to. VG/fair. O3. $65.00

GRAHAM, R.B. Cunninghame. *Mogreb-el-acksa. A Journey in Morocco.* 1930. NY. Nat Travel Club. ltd ed. 358 p. map ep. gilt blk cloth. VG. H3. $20.00

GRAHAM, R.B. Cunninghame. *Rough Passage.* 1937. Boston. ils. map ep. 236 p. gray cloth. VG. H3. $20.00

GRAHAM, R.B. Cunninghame. *S American Sketches of RB Cunninghame Graham.* (1978). OK U. 1st ed. 304 p. dj. F3. $20.00

GRAHAM, Robert; see Haldeman, Joe.

GRAHAM, W.A. *Custer Myth: Source Book of Custeriana.* 1953. Stackpole. ils/notes/index. 413 p. VG. B19. $100.00

GRAHAM, Winston. *Angell, Pearl & Little God.* 1970. Literary Guild. VG/fair. P3. $10.00

GRAHAM, Winston. *Merciless Ladies.* 1980. Doubleday. 1st ed. VG/dj. P3. $15.00

GRAHAM, Winston. *Take My Life.* nd. BC. VG/dj. P3. $17.50

GRAHAM, Winston. *Woman in the Mirror.* 1975. Bodley Head. 1st ed. VG/dj. P3. $17.50

GRAHAM-MULHALL, Sara. *Opium, the Demon Flower.* 1926. NY. Harold Vinal. 1st ed. VG+. B2. $45.00

GRAHAME, Kenneth. *Bertie's Escapade.* (1949). Lippincott. 12mo. gray cloth. pict dj. D1. $60.00

GRAHAME, Kenneth. *Dream Days.* (1930). Dodd Mead. ils Ernest Shepard. beige cloth. 163 p. VG/VG. T5. $24.00

GRAHAME, Kenneth. *Fun o' the Fair.* 1929. Dent. Aldine Chapbook. 30 p. VG. M20. $50.00

GRAHAME, Kenneth. *Wind in the Willows, a Pop-Up Book Ils by Babette Cole.* 1983. paper engineering by James R Diaz/Keith Moseley. F. A4. $40.00

GRAHAME, Kenneth. *Wind in the Willows.* 1940. Heritage. ils Rackham. 190 p. VG/G. P2. $75.00

GRAHAME, Kenneth. *Wind in the Willows.* 1966. Wm Collins. ils/sgn Tasha Tudor. 8vo. gr cloth. VG/VG. A3. $100.00

GRAHAME, Kenneth. *Wind in the Willows.* 1980. Holt. ils/sgn Michael Hague. VG/VG. L1. $25.00

GRAHAME-WHITE, Claude. *Story of the Aeroplane.* (1911). Boston. 1st ed. ils/photos. 390 p. VG. B18. $12.50

GRAMP, W.E.H. *Journal of a Grandfather.* 1912. St Louis. Nixon Jones Prt. 1st ed. 1/100. NF. w/sgn letter. M8. $1,500.00

GRAND, Gordon. *Millbeck Hounds: Collection of Hunting Stories.* 1947. NY. 1st ed. ils. 368 p. F/dj. A17. $17.50

GRAND, W. Joseph. *Ils Hist of Union Stock Yards.* 1901. Chicago. self pub. 1st ed. 362 p. VG. B2. $100.00

GRANDEES, Michael. *Dead & the Living Exiles.* 1977. Vantage. 1st ed. sgn. F/F. L3. $75.00

GRANDVILLE. *Fables de la Fontaine.* 1868. Garnier Freres. 667 p. aeg. NF. M5. $160.00

GRANELL, E.F. *Isla Cofre Mitico.* 1951. Puerto Rico. Editorial Caribe. 1/250. sgn. F/wrp. B2. $250.00

GRANGE, Red. *Zuppke of IL.* 1937. Chicago. 1st ed. VG/G. B5. $35.00

GRANGER, Bill. *British Cross.* 1983. Crown. 1st ed. VG/dj. P3. $20.00

GRANGER, Bill. *El Murders.* 1987. Henry Holt. 1st ed. F/dj. P3. $16.95

GRANGER, Bill. *Hemingway's Notebook.* 1986. Crown. 1st ed. VG/dj. P3. $15.95

GRANGER, Bill. *Man Who Heard Too Much.* 1989. Warner. 1st ed. F/dj. P3. $18.95

GRANGER, Bill. *There Are No Spies.* 1986. NY. Warner. 1st ed. F/F. S5. $25.00

GRANGER, Bill. *There Are No Spies.* 1986. Warner. 1st ed. VG/dj. P3. $16.95

GRANICK. *Amish Quilt.* 1989. np. reference. cloth. G2. $45.00

GRANT, Campbell. *Walt Disney's Bongo.* 1948. Simon Schuster. 1st ed. 8vo. VG-. T5. $20.00

GRANT, Charles L. *For Fear of Night.* 1988. Tor. 1st ed. F/dj. P3. $17.95

GRANT, Charles L. *Pet.* 1986. Tor. 1st ed. F/dj. M2. $20.00

GRANT, Charles L. *Shadows 2.* 1979. Doubleday. 1st ed. NF/dj. P3. $17.50

GRANT, Charles L. *Something Stirs.* 1991. NY. Tor. 1st ed. F/F. N3. $15.00

GRANT, Charles L. *Tales From the Nightside.* 1981. Arkham. 1st ed. as new. M2. $25.00

GRANT, Frederick J. *Hist of Seattle.* 1891. NY. Am Pub. 1st ed. thick 8vo. 526 p. full morocco. VG+. B20. $325.00

GRANT, Joan. *Lord of the Horizon.* 1944. Methuen. 3rd ed. VG. P3. $12.00

GRANT, Joan. *Winged Pharoah.* 1938. Harper. 1st ed. VG. M2. $20.00

GRANT, Julia Dent. *Personal Memoirs...* 1975. np. 1st ed. edit Catton. ils/index. 346 p. dj. O7. $9.50

GRANT, Linda. *Love Nor Money.* nd. BC. F/dj. P3. $7.50

GRANT, Linda. *Love Nor Money.* 1991. Scribner. ARC of 1st ed. sgn. F/F. S5. $35.00

GRANT, Maxwell; see Gibson, Walter B.

GRANT, Michael. *Founders of the W World.* 1991. Scribner. 1st ed. F/dj. P3. $27.50

GRANT, Michael. *Rise of the Greeks.* 1988. Scribner. 1st ed. F/dj. P3. $27.50

GRANT, Richard. *Views From the Oldest House.* 1989. NY. Doubleday. 1st ed. F/F. N3. $20.00

GRANT, Roderick. *Private Vendetta.* 1978. Scribner. 1st ed. F/dj. P3. $15.00

GRANT, Ulysses Simpson. *Personal Memoirs...* 1885-86. NY. Webster. 1st ed. 2 vols. rpr hing on vol 1. VG. M8. $95.00

GRANT, Ulysses Simpson. *Report of Lt Gen US Grant of Armies of US, 1864-65.* 1865. WA, DC. 1st ed. 44 p. VG+/prt wrp. M8. $150.00

GRANT, Zalin. *Facing the Phoenix.* (1991). Norton. 1st ed. as new/dj. A7. $15.00

GRANT, Zalin. *Over the Beach: At War in Vietnam.* (1986). Norton. 1st ed. 311 p. F/F. A7. $25.00

GRANTLAND, Keith; see Beaumont, Charles.

GRANTZ, Gerald. *Home Book of Taxidermy & Tanning.* (1969). Harrisburg. ils/index. 160 p. VG/dj. A17. $9.50

GRANVILLE, A.B. *St Petersburgh: A Journal of Travels to & From That Capital.* 1828. London. Colburn. 2 vols. modern buckram. VG. B14. $150.00

GRASS, Gunter. *Cat & Mouse.* 1963. London. Secker Warburg. 1st ed. trans from German. NF/NF clip. A14. $30.00

GRASS, Gunter. *Cat & Mouse.* 1982. HBJ. 2nd Am imp. trans from German. rem mk. NF/VG+. A14. $20.00

GRASS, Gunter. *Dog Yrs.* 1965. Wolff/HBW. 1st ed. trans from German. NF/VG+ clip. A14. $35.00

GRASS, Gunter. *From the Diary of a Snail.* 1974. London. Secker Warburg. 1st ed. trans Ralph Manheim. NF/VG+. A14. $25.00

GRASS, Gunter. *Local Anaesthetic.* 1970. Wolff/HBW. 1st ed. trans from German. VG+/VG+. A14. $25.00

GRASS, Gunter. *Meeting at Telgte.* 1981. Wolff/HBJ. 3rd Eng imp. trans from German. NF/NF. A14. $20.00

GRASS, Gunter. *Tin Drum.* 1962. London. Secker Warburg. 1st ed. NF/VG+ clip. A14. $75.00

GRASSET, J. *Des Localisations Dans Les Maladies Cerebrales.* 1878. Paris. Delahaye. 138 p. new brds. G7. $395.00

GRASSI, Giunio Paolo. *Medici Antiqui Graeci: Aretaeus, Palladius, Ruffus...* 1581. Basilaeae. 1st ed. 4to. old vellum/later rebacking. G7. $1,250.00

GRASTY, John Scharshall. *...A Noble Testimony.* ca 1860s. Raleigh, NC. 1st ed. 8 p religious tract. NF/self wrp. M8. $75.00

GRATTAN, C. Hartley. *SW Pacific to 1900/SW Pacific Since 1900.* 1963. Ann Arbor. 1st ed. royal 8vo. 2 vols. silvered blk cloth. F/F. H3. $40.00

GRATTAN, Thomas Colley. *Civilized Am.* 1859. London. Bradbury Evans. 2 vols. 8vo. 2 maps. emb pink cloth. H9. $175.00

GRAU, Shirley Ann. *Blk Prince.* 1955. NY. 1st ed. sgn. F/NF. A11. $90.00

GRAVES, John. *From a Limestone Ledge: Some Essays...* 1980. Knopf. 1st ed. ils Glenn Wolff. sgn. F/F. A18. $30.00

GRAVES, John. *Goodbye to a River.* 1960. Knopf. 1st ed. sgn/dtd. ils Waterhouse. F/clip. A18. $75.00

GRAVES, John. *Hard Scrabble: Observations on a Patch of Land.* 1974. Knopf. 1st ed. F/F clip. A18. $35.00

GRAVES, Richard Perceval. *Lawrence of Arabia & His World.* 1976. London. Thames Hudson. 1st ed. 127 p. F/NF. M7. $65.00

GRAVES, Robert. *Anger of Achilles.* 1959. Doubleday. 1st ed. F/NF. B4. $85.00

GRAVES, Robert. *Conversations w/Robert Graves.* 1990. Jackson, MS. 1st ed. F/F. C4. $30.00

GRAVES, Robert. *Golden Ass.* 1951. Harmondsworth. 1/200. sgn/#d. teg. F/VG+/pub slipcase. A11. $145.00

GRAVES, Robert. *Good-Bye to All That.* 1929. London. Cape. 1st ed/2nd issue. inscr/dtd 1959. cloth. VG. rare. Q1. $750.00

GRAVES, Robert. *Greek Myths.* 1988. Moyer Bell. F/dj. P3. $25.00

GRAVES, Robert. *I, Claudius.* 1977. London. BC Assoc. 432 p. F/F. M7. $25.00

GRAVES, Robert. *In Broken Images: Selected Letters of...1914-46.* 1982. London. Hutchinson. 1st ed. edit Paul O'Prey. 372 p. F/F clip. M7. $55.00

GRAVES, Robert. *John Kemp's Wager.* 1925. Blackwell Oxford. 1/100. sgn/#d. patterned gr brds. VG. Q1. $1,250.00

GRAVES, Robert. *Lawrence & the Arabs.* 1927. London. Cape. 1st ed. edit Eric Kennington. 454 p. rebound leather. F. M7. $125.00

GRAVES, Robert. *Lawrence & the Arabs.* 1946. Thomas Nelson. 3rd ed. xl. G. P3. $12.50

GRAVES, Robert. *New Poems.* 1962. London. 1st ed. F/VG+. V1. $25.00

GRAVES, Robert. *Oxford Addresses on Poetry.* 1962. London. 1st ed. NF. A11. $20.00

GRAVES, Robert. *Penny Fiddle. Poems for Children.* 1960. Doubleday. 1st ed. ils Ardizzone. VG/dj. M20. $20.00

GRAVES, Robert. *Poems 1965-68.* 1969. Doubleday. 1st Am ed. 97 p. VG+/dj. M20. $25.00

GRAVES, Robert. *Poems.* 1980. LEC. 1/2000. sgn. ils/sgn Hogarth. teg. patterned brds. F/slipcase. Q1. $100.00

GRAVES, Robert. *Watch the Northwind Rise.* 1949. Creative Age. 1st ed. NF/NF. Q1. $75.00

GRAVES, Robert. *Welchman's House.* 1925. London. The Fleuron. 1st ed. NF/slipcase. B2. $200.00

GRAVES, Robert. *Wht Goddess: Hist Grammar of Poetic Myth.* 1948. Farrar Straus. VG. N2. $17.50

GRAVES, Valerie; see Bradley, Marion Zimmer.

GRAVES & HART. *TE Lawrence to His Biographers.* 1963. Doubleday. reprint of 1938 ed. 260 p. F/F. M7. $75.00

GRAVIER, Gabriel. *Augustin Beaulieu, Navigateur Rouennais, 1589-1637.* 1897. Rouen. E Cagniari. 32 p. M/wrp. O6. $35.00

GRAVIER, Gabriel. *Vie de Samuel Champlain: Foundateur de la Nouvelle-France.* 1900. Paris. Maisonneuve. M/wrp. O6. $45.00

GRAY, Andrew B. *Report of Secretary of the Interior...Jan 22, 1855...* 1855. GPO. 8vo. 2 fld maps. 50 p. new bl cloth. H9. $450.00

GRAY, Asa. *Botanical TB.* 1853. NY. 4th ed. ils. 528 p. VG. B28. $20.00

GRAY, Berkeley. *Conquest in the Underworld.* 1974. Collins. VG+/dj. P3. $10.00

GRAY, Berkeley. *Lost World of Everest.* 1952. TC Pr. 1st ed. VG/dj. F4. $40.00

GRAY, Charles Glass. *Off at Sunrise: Overland Journal of...* (1976). Huntington. 1st ed. ils/index. F/dj. A18. $35.00

GRAY, Curme. *Murder in Millenium VI.* 1951. Shasta. 1st ed. F/NF. M2. $65.00

GRAY, Curme. *Murder in Millenium VI.* 1951. Shasta. 1st ed. VG/VG. P3. $40.00

GRAY, Dulcie. *Dark Calypso.* 1978. London. MacDonald. 1st ed. F/dj. S5. $22.50

GRAY, Elizabeth Janet; see Vining, Elizabeth Gray.

GRAY, Harold Studley. *Character Bud: Story of Conscientious Objector.* ca 1934. Harper. inscr/sgn. VG. V4. $25.00

GRAY, Harold. *Pop-Up Little Orphan Anne & Jumbo the Circus Elephant.* 1935. Pleasure Books. 3 popups. unp. VG. M20. $300.00

GRAY, Henry. *Anatomy, Descriptive & Surgical.* 1897. Phil. Lea Bros. revised from 13th Eng ed. 772 ils. 1249 p. red cloth. G. S9. $23.00

GRAY, James Kendricks; see Fox, Gardner F.

GRAY, Louisa M. *Little Miss Wardlaw.* 1899. London. Nelson. 445 p. gilt bl cloth. VG. S10. $25.00

GRAY, Thomas. *Odes...* 1757. Strawberry Hill. 4to. 22 p. speckled calf/rebacked/red morocco label. K1. $1,000.00

GRAY, Thomas. *Poems & Letters.* 1867. Chiswick Pr. lg 4to. 4 mtd photos. 416 p. orig gilt calf. K1. $200.00

GRAY, William Henry. *Hist of OR 1792-1849.* 1870. Portland, OR. 1st ed. xl. royal 8vo. 624 p. blk cloth. VG. D3. $100.00

GRAY & GRAY. *Bed; or, Clinophile's Vade Mecum.* (1946). London. Nicolson Watson. 1st ed. 8vo. 290 p. VG/fair. A2. $15.00

GRAY & THETFORD. *German Aircraft of the 1st World War.* 1970. Garden City. revised ed. new photos. VG/dj. B18. $32.50

GRAY. *Canvas Work.* 1985. np. ils. wrp. G2. $20.00

GRAYDON, Nell S. *SC Ghost Tales.* 1969. Beaufort Book Shop. VG/dj. P3. $15.00

GRAYDON, Nell S. *Tales of Edisto.* 1955. Columbia, SC. 2nd prt. dj. N2. $7.50

GRAYDON, William Murray. *Camp in the Snow.* 1902. Street Smith. 246 p. VG. M20. $8.00

GRAYON, Porte. *VA Ils.* 1857. NY. lg 8vo. ils. 300 p. red bdg. O7. $12.50

GRAYSON, Charles. *Stories for Men.* 1949. Perma Hardbound P30. VG. P3. $10.00

GRAYSON, Rupert. *Death Rides the Forest.* 1938. Dutton. 1st Am ed. F/NF. M15. $45.00

GRAYZEL, Solomon. *Church & the Jews in the XIIIth Century.* 1966. Hermon Pr. revised ed. 378 p. VG+/G+. S3. $25.00

GRAZYNA. *Old World Stitchery for Today.* 1987. np. ils. wrp. G2. $24.00

GREBER, Judith. *Mendocino.* 1988. Crown. 1st ed. 356 p. F/F. B19. $15.00

GREELEY, Andrew M. *Angels of September.* 1986. Warner. F/dj. P3. $17.95

GREELEY, Andrew M. *Cardinal Sins.* 1981. Warner. xl. dj. P3. $5.00

GREELEY, Andrew M. *Final Planet.* 1987. Warner. F/F. P3. $16.95

GREELEY, Andrew M. *Three Complete Novels.* 1987. Avenel. F/dj. P3. $10.00

GREELEY, Horace. *Am Conflict: Hist of Great Rebellion...* 1864 & 1866. Hartford. 1st ed. royal 8vo. 2 vols. new ep/cloth. VG. O3. $75.00

GREELEY, Horace. *Am Conflict: Hist of the Great Rebellion. Vol 1.* 1865. Hartford. OD Case. leather. fair. B11. $35.00

GREELEY, Horace. *Hints Toward Reforms.* 1850. NY. 1st ed. 400 p. cloth. G. A17. $35.00

GREELEY, Horace. *What I Know of Farming...* 1871. NY. Tribune. 1st ed. 335 p. shabby cloth. H10. $22.50

GREEN, Alan. *What a Body!* nd. BC. VG/dj. P3. $7.50

GREEN, Anne Bosworth. *Dipper Hill.* 1925. NY. Century. 1st ed. xl. G+. O3. $15.00

GREEN, Arthur. *Menahem Nahum of Chernobyl: Upright Practices...* 1982. Paulist Pr. xl. 290 p. VG+. S3. $24.00

GREEN, Ben K. *Biography of the TN Walking Horse.* 1960. Nashville. 1st ed. VG. O3. $65.00

GREEN, Ben K. *Horse Tradin'.* 1967. Knopf. 1st ed. ils Bjorklund. VG+/VG+. A18. $30.00

GREEN, Ben K. *Horse Tradin'.* 1967. Knopf. 1st ed. NF/NF. C4. $35.00

GREEN, Charles P. *Ballads of the Blk Hills.* 1931. Boston. Christopher. 1st ed. ils. 170 p. w/ad flier. N2. $15.00

GREEN, Christine. *Death in the Country.* 1993. London. Macmillan. 1st ed. F/F. S5. $25.00

GREEN, Edith Pinero. *Rotten Apples.* nd. BC. VG/dj. P3. $7.50

GREEN, Ephraim. *Road From El Dorado: 1848 Trail Journal...* 1991. Salt Lake City. Prairie Dog. 1/26. sgn. fld map. M/dj. O6. $155.00

GREEN, Hannah. *I Never Promised You a Rose Garden.* (1964). HRW. 1st ed. F/NF. B4. $85.00

GREEN, Harvey. *Fit for Am: Health, Fitness, Sport & Am Soc.* 1986. Pantheon. 1st ed. 368 p. VG/dj. G1. $20.00

GREEN, Henry. *Doting.* 1952. London. 1st ed. VG+/VG. A11. $45.00

GREEN, Henry. *Pack My Bag.* 1922. New Directions. 1st Am ed. intro Sebastian Yorke. F/F. C4. $20.00

GREEN, J. Barcham. *Papermaking by Hand.* 1967. England. Maidstone. 1/1000. F. B30. $15.00

GREEN, Joseph. *Conscience Interplanetary.* 1973. Doubleday. 1st ed. F/dj. P3. $15.00

GREEN, Julian. *Diary 1928-57.* 1964. Harcourt Brace. 1st ed. F. C4. $40.00

GREEN, Lydia Marshall. *Perennials in the Bishop's Garden.* 1953. Phil. 1st ed. 161 p. VG/dj. B28. $20.00

GREEN, Martin. *Earth Again Redeemed.* 1977. Basic Books. 1st ed. F/dj. P3. $15.00

GREEN, Melinda. *Rachel's Recital.* 1979. Little Brn/Atlantic. 1st ed. 8vo. 48 p. F/G+. T5. $25.00

GREEN, Paul. *I Am Eskimo. Aknik My Name.* 1968. Juneau. AK NW Pub. 2nd prt. 85 p. VG/prt wrp. P4. $12.50

GREEN, Peter. *Alexander of Macedon, 356-323 BC.* 1991. CA U. F/dj. P3. $35.00

GREEN, Philip James. *Sketches of the War in Greece...* 1828. London. 8vo. 328 p. new half cloth/marbled brds. very scarce. O2. $350.00

GREEN, Sarah. *Private Hist of Court of Eng.* 1808. London. self pub. 2nd ed/corrected. 2 vols. gilt polished calf. VG. H5. $200.00

GREEN, Terence M. *Barking Dogs.* 1988. St Martin. 1st ed. VG/dj. P3. $15.95

GREEN, Thomas J. *Flowered Box.* 1980. Beaufort. 1st ed. VG/dj. P3. $15.00

GREEN, Thomas. *John Woolman: Study for Young Men.* 1885. Manchester. Brook Chrystal. xl. 16mo. 126 p. V3. $10.50

GREEN, William M. *Salisbury Manuscript.* 1973. Bobbs Merrill. 1st ed. F/dj. P3. $15.00

GREEN & MURRAY. *Book of Kantela.* 1985. Bluejay. 1st ed. sgn. F/F trade-size wrp. F4. $15.00

GREENAWAY, Kate. *A Apple Pie.* ca 1940. (1886). Frederick Warne. oblong 4to. pict brds. VG/G+. A3. $28.00

GREENAWAY, Kate. *A Apple Pie.* 1907. Saalfield. 1st thus ed. muslin. VG+. D1. $200.00

GREENAWAY, Kate. *Almanack & Diary for 1929.* 1928. London. Warne. 12mo. 72 p. gilt gr cloth. F/glassine. B24. $125.00

GREENAWAY, Kate. *Almanack for 1883(-1895)/...Almanack & Diary for 1897.* 1882-96. London. 1st ed. complete set of 14 vols. NF/morocco clamshell case. H5. $6,000.00

GREENAWAY, Kate. *Almanack for 1886.* 1886. London. Routledge. 1st ed/bdg variant. F. F1. $175.00

GREENAWAY, Kate. *Almanack for 1892.* 1892. Routledge. VG. P2. $95.00

GREENAWAY, Kate. *Almanack for 1925.* nd. London. Warne. 1st ed. glazed pict brds. VG. D1. $150.00

GREENAWAY, Kate. *April Baby's Book of Tunes.* 1900. London. Macmillan. 1st ed. sq octavo. 74 p. tan cloth. B24. $450.00

GREENAWAY, Kate. *Greenaway Pictures To Paint.* nd. Merrimack, NY. VG/VG. L1. $10.00

GREENAWAY, Kate. *Kate Greenaway's Alphabet.* ca 1880. London. Routledge. miniature. ils. 32 p. NF. H10. $175.00

GREENAWAY, Kate. *Marigold Garden.* nd. London. Warne. 8vo. ils. 57 p. pict gr bdg. VG+. H3. $65.00

GREENBERG, Joanne. *Rites of Passage.* (1972). NY. HRW. 1st ed. F/F. B3. $15.00

GREENBERG, Joanne. *Simple Gifts.* (1986). NY. Holt. 1st ed. F/F. B3. $10.00

GREENBERG, Martin. *Five SF Novels.* 1952. Gnome. 1st ed. VG. M2. $10.00

GREENBERG, Martin. *Journey to Infinity.* 1951. Gnome. 1st ed. NF/dj. P3. $45.00

GREENBERG, Martin. *Men Against the Stars.* 1950. Gnome. 1st ed. F/M. M2. $100.00

GREENBERG, Martin. *Robot & the Man.* 1953. Gnome. 1st ed. VG/dj. P3. $45.00

GREENBERG, Martin. *Travelers of Space.* 1951. Gnome. 1st ed. F/M. M2. $75.00

GREENBERG & NORTON. *Touring Nam.* (1985). Morrow. 1st ed. NF/NF. A7. $40.00

GREENBERG & WAUGH. *Human Zero: SF Stories by Erle Stanley Gardner.* 1981. Morrow. 1st ed. F/F. T2. $25.00

GREENE, Albert G. *Recollections of Jersey Prison Ship...* 1829. Providence, RI. HH Brn. 1st ed. 12mo. 167 p. cloth. M1. $200.00

GREENE, Annie. *Bright River Trilogy.* (1984). Simon Schuster. 1st ed. F/F. B3. $15.00

GREENE, Edward L. *Manual of Botany of Region of San Francisco Bay.* 1894. San Francisco. ils. 342 p. NF. B26. $85.00

GREENE, Felix. *Vietnam! Vietnam!* (1966). Palo Alto. Fulton. 1st prt/wrp ed. 175 p. VG. A7. $30.00

GREENE, George W. *Nathanael Greene.* 1866. Boston. xl. 86 p. VG. B28. $25.00

GREENE, Graham. *Brighton Rock & End of the Affair.* 1987. Peerage Books. F/dj. P3. $15.00

GREENE, Graham. *Burnt-Out Case.* 1961. Heinemann. 1st ed. xl. dj. P3. $5.00

GREENE, Graham. *Carving a Statue.* 1964. London. Bodley Head. 1st ed. F/F. C4. $80.00

GREENE, Graham. *Comedians.* 1966. Bodley Head. 1st ed. VG/dj. P3. $35.00

GREENE, Graham. *Comedians.* 1966. NY. Viking. 1st ed. VG+/clip. E3. $25.00

GREENE, Graham. *Complaisant Lover.* 1959. Viking. 1st ed. F/F. C4. $50.00

GREENE, Graham. *Conversations w/Graham Greene.* 1992. Jackson, MS. 1st ed. F/F. C4. $30.00

GREENE, Graham. *Doctor Fischer of Geneva.* 1980. Simon Schuster. 1st ed. F/dj. P3. $15.00

GREENE, Graham. *End of the Affair.* 1951. Viking. 1st ed. NF/dj. P3. $100.00

GREENE, Graham. *End of the Affair.* 1982. Viking. VG/dj. P3. $17.50

GREENE, Graham. *Graham Greene.* 1977. Heinemann/Octopus. VG/dj. P3. $20.00

GREENE, Graham. *Honorary Consul.* (1973). Bodley Head. 1st ed. F/F. B3. $50.00

GREENE, Graham. *Human Factor.* nd. Simon Schuster. 2nd ed. VG/dj. P3. $12.50

GREENE, Graham. *In Search of a Character.* 1961. Bodley Head. 1st ed. VG/dj. P3. $25.00

GREENE, Graham. *It's a Battlefield.* 1959. Heinemann. xl. dj. P3. $5.00

GREENE, Graham. *Ministry of Fear.* 1982. Viking. F/dj. P3. $17.50

GREENE, Graham. *Monsignor Quixote.* 1982. Lester Denys. 1st ed. VG-/dj. P3. $15.00

GREENE, Graham. *Our Man in Havana.* 1958. Heinemann. 1st ed. VG+/dj. P3. $100.00

GREENE, Graham. *Reflections on Travels w/My Aunt.* 1989. NY. 1sts & Co. 40-p facsimile holograph manuscript/text. 1/200. sgn. F. C4. $125.00

GREENE, Graham. *Return of AJ Raffles.* 1975. Simon Schuster. 1st ed. rem mk. F/dj. B2. $35.00

GREENE, Graham. *Third Man.* 1950. Bantam. 2nd prt. VG+/wrp. C8. $15.00

GREENE, Graham. *This Gun for Hire.* 1982. Viking. F/dj. P3. $17.50

GREENE, Graham. *Travels w/My Aunt.* nd. BOMC. VG/dj. P3. $10.00

GREENE, Graham. *Ways of Escape.* nd. Simon Schuster. 2nd ed. F/dj. P3. $12.50

GREENE, Hugh. *Am Rivals of Sherlock Holmes.* 1976. Bodley Head. 1st ed. VG/dj. P3. $30.00

GREENE, Laurence. *Am Goes To Pr.* 1936. Indianapolis. 1st ed. 375 p. cloth. VG. D3. $25.00

GREENE, Laurence. *Filibuster.* (1937). Bobbs Merrill. 1st ed. 350 p. dj. F3. $50.00

GREENE, LeRoy. *Shelter for His Excellency.* 1951. Stackpole. 1st ed. 8vo. 379 p. F/VG+. A2. $25.00

GREENE, Melissa Fay. *Praying for Sheetrock.* (1991). Addison-Wesley. 1st ed. 335 p. F/F. A7. $16.00

GREENE, N. *European Socialism Since WWI.* (1971). Quadrangle. 261 p. NF. A7. $13.00

GREENE & WHEELING. *Pictorial Hist of Shelburne Mus.* 1972. Shelburne. 4to. 127 p. VG. O3. $25.00

GREENFIELD, C.B. *Piano Bird.* nd. BC. VG/dj. P3. $7.50

GREENFIELD, Jerome. *Wilhelm Reich Vs the USA.* 1974. Norton. 380 p. VG/dj. G1. $30.00

GREENHOOD, David. *Down to Earth Mapping for Everybody.* 1951. NY. Holiday. ils. VG. O6. $25.00

GREENHOW, Robert. *Memoir, Hist & Political on NW Coast of Am...* 1840. WA. Blair Rives. 1st ed. lg fld map. NF. O6. $450.00

GREENLEAF, Stephen. *Grave Error.* nd. BC. VG/dj. P3. $7.50

GREENLEAF, Stephen. *Grave Error.* 1979. Dial. 1st ed. author's 1st book. NF/NF. Q1. $75.00

GREENLEAF, Stephen. *Toll Call.* 1987. Villard. 1st ed. xl. dj. P3. $5.00

GREENLEAF & TEDFORD. *Game of Candlepin Bowling.* (1981). Westfield, MA. 1st ed. lg 8vo. 240 p. F/F. A2. $30.00

GREENLEAVES, Winifred. *Trout Inn Mystery.* 1929. Lincoln MacVeagh. 1st ed. VG+. P3. $35.00

GREENLEE, Sam. *Ammunition! Poetry & Other Raps.* 1975. London. 1st ed. presentation inscr. intro Salkey. F/ils wrp. A11. $45.00

GREENLEE, William Brooks. *Viagem de Pedro Alvares Cabral ao Brasil e a India.* nd. Porto. Livraria Civilizacao. presentation/ sgn. F/wrp. O6. $65.00

GREENSPUN & PELLE. *Where I Stand. Record of Reckless Man.* 1966. McKay. 304 p. VG/poor. S3. $22.00

GREENSTONE, Julius H. *Numbers w/Commentary.* 1948. JPS. 2nd imp. VG/G. S3. $26.00

GREENTHAL, Kathryn. *Augustus Saint-Gaudens: Master Sculptor.* 1985. Metropolitan Mus Art. ils/pls. 176 p. cloth. dj. D2. $55.00

GREENWOOD, D.M. *Idol Bones.* 1993. London. Headline. 1st ed. F/F. S5. $25.00

GREENWOOD, Edwin. *Deadly Dowager.* 1935. Doubleday Doran. VG-. P3. $5.00

GREENWOOD, Grace. *New Life in New Lands: Notes of Travel.* 1873. NY. 1st ed. 12mo. 413 p. pict cloth. VG. D3. $35.00

GREENWOOD, Grace. *Victoria, Queen of Eng.* 1884. Alden, NY. 401 p. red cloth. VG. M20. $20.00

GREENWOOD, John. *Missing Mr Mosley.* 1985. Walker. F/dj. P3. $15.00

GREENWOOD, John. *Namesakes of the '90s.* 1991. Freshwater Pr. as new/dj. A16. $23.00

GREENWOOD, John. *Namesakes of the Lakes*. 1985. Freshwater Pr. as new/dj. A16. $20.00

GREENWOOD, John. *Namesakes 1930-1955*. 1978. Freshwater Pr. as new/dj. A16. $23.00

GREENWOOD, L.B. *Sherlock Holmes & the Thistle of Scotland*. 1989. Simon Schuster. ARC of 1st ed. RS. F/F. S5. $27.50

GREENWOOD, Walter. *Love on the Dole: Tale of the 2 Cities*. 1935. London. Jonathan Cape. G. V4. $7.50

GREER, Germaine. *Madwoman's Underclothes*. (1987). Atlantic Monthly. 1st ed. NF/F. B3. $25.00

GREER, William Royal. *Gems of Am Architecture*. ca 1935. St Paul. Brn Bigelow. sq 12mo. wrp. H9. $45.00

GREER & WARD. *Richmond During the Revolution, 1775-1883*. ca 1977. VA U. 1st ed. ils/map. 205 p. VG/VG. B10. $20.00

GREGG, Alexander. *Hist of the Old Cheraws Containing Account of Aborigines...* 1925. Columbia, SC. State Co. 2nd ed. 629 p. cloth. NF/dj. M8. $350.00

GREGG, E.C. *How To Tie Flies*. (1945). NY. 9th prt. 83 p. VG/dj. A17. $9.50

GREGG, Richard B. *Discipline for Non-Violence*. (1946). Ahmedabad. Navajivan Pub House. 34 p. wrp. A7. $10.00

GREGG, William H. *Secrets of Fate Unlocked...Possibility to Reality*. 1901. np. 12mo. 238 p. G. N2. $27.50

GREGORY, Dick. *Dick Gregory's Bible Tales*. (1974). Stein Day. 1st ed. 187 p. dj. A7. $30.00

GREGORY, Dick. *Dick Gregory's Political Primer*. 1972. Harper Row. 1st ed. 335 p. dj. A7. $25.00

GREGORY, Dick. *Write Me In!* 1968. Bantam. 1st ed/pb. NF. A7. $22.00

GREGORY, Franklin. *Valley of Adventure*. 1940. Triangle. front free ep removed. VG. P3. $10.00

GREGORY, George. *Dictionary of Arts & Sciences*. ca 1820s. np. 4to. 139 pls. half leather. H10. $100.00

GREGORY, J. *Puritanism in the Old World & in the New...* 1895. London. Clarke. 1st ed. xl. 406 p. H10. $27.50

GREGORY, Jackson. *Case for Mr Paul Savoy*. 1933. Scribner. 1st ed. VG. P3. $20.00

GREGORY, Jackson. *Judith of Bl Lake Ranch*. 1919. Scribner. 1st ed. inscr. VG. B9. $125.00

GREGORY, James J.H. *Gregory's Annual Ils Retail Catalogue...* 1882. Marblehead, MA. 4to. ils. 56 p. wrp. H10. $25.00

GREGORY, Mason. *If Two of Them Are Dead*. 1953. Arcadia. 1st ed. xl. P3. $5.00

GREGORY & MCGRAW. *Up From Nigger*. 1977 (1976). Stein Day. 2nd prt. 256 p. dj. A7. $25.00

GREGORY IX, Pope. *Decretales...* 1584. Venice. Ferrario Franzino. lg 4to. contemporary vellum. K1. $250.00

GREGSON, J.M. *Stranglehold*. 1993. London. Collins. 1st ed. VG/dj. S5. $25.00

GREIF, Martin. *Airport Book*. (1979). NY. ils. 191 p. VG/dj. B18. $19.50

GREIG, Francis. *Heads You Lose*. 1982. Crown. ne. RS. F/dj. P3. $15.00

GREINER, T. *Young Market Gardener. Beginner's Guide*. 1896. La Salle, NY. Garden Series 2. 119 p. wrp. H10. $20.00

GREISHABER, Hap. *Totentanz Von Basel*. 1966. Dresden. Veb pub. VG/VG. A1. $600.00

GRENDON, Stephen; see Derleth, August.

GRENNAN, Eamon. *What Light There Is*. 1987. Gallery Pr. 1st ed. sgn. F/F. V1. $30.00

GRESHAM, Grits. *Complete Wild Flower*. (1973). NY. 294 p. cloth. A17. $12.50

GREVILLE, Charles C. *Greville Memoirs*. 1874-87. Longman Gr. 1st ed. 8vo. 8 vols. Larkins bdg. NF. F1. $550.00

GREY, Anthony. *Hostage in Peking*. 1971. Doubleday. 1st ed. 365 p. dj. A7. $15.00

GREY, Charles. *Merchant Venturers of London*. 1932. London. Witherby. 1st ed. M/dj. O6. $95.00

GREY, Jerry. *Enterprise*. 1979. Morrow. 1st ed. 288 p. F/NF. N3. $20.00

GREY, R.C. *Adventurers of a Deep-Sea Angler*. 1930. Harper. 1st ed. gr bdg. VG+. B9. $200.00

GREY, Zane. *Adventures of Finspot*. 1974. DJ Books. 1/950. F. B9. $225.00

GREY, Zane. *AZ Ames*. nd. Blk's Readers. 12mo. F/VG. A8. $7.50

GREY, Zane. *AZ Clan*. 1958. NY. Harper. 1st ed. NF/NF. Q1. $100.00

GREY, Zane. *Betty Zane*. nd. Blk's Readers. 12mo. F. A8. $7.50

GREY, Zane. *Bl Feather & Other Stories*. 1961. Harper. 1st book ed. NF/NF. Q1. $75.00

GREY, Zane. *Blk Mesa*. nd. Blk's Readers. 12mo. F/G. A8. $7.50

GREY, Zane. *Blk Mesa*. 1955. Harper. 1st ed. VG+/dj. Q1. $60.00

GREY, Zane. *Border Legion*. 1916. Grosset Dunlap. 12mo. G. A8. $7.50

GREY, Zane. *Call of the Canyon*. nd. Blk's Readers. 12mo. F/G. A8. $7.50

GREY, Zane. *Call of the Canyon*. 1922. Grosset Dunlap. 12mo. G. A8. $6.00

GREY, Zane. *Call of the Canyon*. 1924. Grosset Dunlap. VG/dj. B9. $10.00

GREY, Zane. *Captives of the Desert*. nd. Blk's Readers. 12mo. F/F. A8. $7.50

GREY, Zane. *Code of the W*. 1934. NY. 1st ed. 309 p. cloth. VG. D3. $25.00

GREY, Zane. *Deer Stalker*. 1949. Harper. 1st ed. NF/NF. Q1. $100.00

GREY, Zane. *Desert Gold*. nd. Blk's Readers. 12mo. F/VG. A8. $7.50

GREY, Zane. *Desert Gold*. nd. Grosset Dunlap. VG/dj. P3. $20.00

GREY, Zane. *Desert of Wheat*. 1919. Harper. 12mo. G. A8. $15.00

GREY, Zane. *Drift Fence*. nd. Blk's Readers. 12mo. F/VG. A8. $7.50

GREY, Zane. *Drift Fence*. 1932. Harper. 1st ed. VG. B9. $25.00

GREY, Zane. *Fighting Caravans*. nd. Blk's Readers. 12mo. F/F. A8. $7.50

GREY, Zane. *Fighting Caravans*. nd. Grosset Dunlap. photoplay ed. 361 p. cloth. VG. D3. $12.50

GREY, Zane. *Forlorn River*. nd. Blk's Readers. 12mo. F/VG. A8. $7.50

GREY, Zane. *Forlorn River*. 1927. Grosset Dunlap. 12mo. G. A8. $8.00

GREY, Zane. *Fugitive Trail*. 1957. Harper. 1st ed. NF/NF. Q1. $125.00

GREY, Zane. *Heritage of the Desert*. nd. Blk's Readers. 12mo. F/F. A8. $7.50

GREY, Zane. *Horse Heaven Hill*. 1959. Harper. 1st ed. NF/NF. Q1. $75.00

GREY, Zane. *Ken Ward in the Jungle*. nd. Grosset Dunlap. VG. P3. $7.50

GREY, Zane. *Last of the Plainsmen*. nd. Grosset Dunlap. VG/VG-. P3. $15.00

GREY, Zane. *Last Trail*. nd. Triangle. NF/dj. P3. $12.50

GREY, Zane. *Last Trail.* nd. Whitman. decor brds. VG. P3. $12.50

GREY, Zane. *Last Trail.* 1909. NY. Burt. ils. 300 p. G+. B18. $15.00

GREY, Zane. *Last Trail.* 1944. Phil. Blakiston/Triange. VG/dj. B9. $10.00

GREY, Zane. *Lost Pueblo.* nd. Blk's Readers. 12mo. F/F. A8. $7.50

GREY, Zane. *Lost Pueblo.* 1954. Harper. 1st ed. F/clip. B9. $100.00

GREY, Zane. *Lost Wagon Train.* nd. Blk's Readers. 12mo. F/VG. A8. $7.50

GREY, Zane. *Lost Wagon Train.* 1936. Harper. 1st ed. VG/dj. B9. $135.00

GREY, Zane. *Majesty's Rancho.* nd. Blk's Readers. 12mo. F/F. A8. $7.50

GREY, Zane. *Majesty's Rancho.* nd. Grosset Dunlap. VG/dj. P3. $20.00

GREY, Zane. *Man of the Forest.* nd. Blk's Readers. 12mo. F/F. A8. $7.50

GREY, Zane. *Maverick Queen.* nd. Blk's Readers. 12mo. F/G. A8. $7.50

GREY, Zane. *Rainbow Trail.* nd. Blk's Readers. 12mo. F/fair. A8. $7.50

GREY, Zane. *Rainbow Trail.* nd. Grosset Dunlap. VG/dj. P3. $20.00

GREY, Zane. *Rainbow Trail.* 1981. Ian Henry. F/dj. P3. $10.00

GREY, Zane. *Ranger & Other Stories.* 1960. Harper. 1st book ed. VG/NF. Q1. $50.00

GREY, Zane. *Riders of the Purple Sage.* nd. Blk's Readers. 12mo. VG/dj. A8/P3. $7.50

GREY, Zane. *Robbers' Roost.* 1932. Grosset Dunlap. 12mo. G. A8. $11.00

GREY, Zane. *Rogue River Feud.* 1948. Harper. 1st book ed. VG/VG. Q1. $200.00

GREY, Zane. *Rogue River Fued.* nd. Blk's Readers. 12mo. F/G. A8. $7.50

GREY, Zane. *Roping Lions in the Grand Canyon.* 1924. Harper. 1st ed. VG. B9. $125.00

GREY, Zane. *Shadow on the Trail.* nd. Blk's Readers. 12mo. F/G. A8. $7.50

GREY, Zane. *Shepherd of Guadaloupe.* nd. Blk's Readers. 12mo. F/fair. A8. $7.50

GREY, Zane. *Shepherd of Guadaloupe.* nd. Grosset Dunlap. VG-/dj. P3. $12.50

GREY, Zane. *Short-Stop.* 1914. Grosset Dunlap. early reprint. G/dj. Q1. $75.00

GREY, Zane. *Spirit of the Border.* (1906). Burt. 1st ed. author's 2nd book. VG+. A15. $100.00

GREY, Zane. *Spirit of the Border.* nd. Whitman. VG/dj. P3. $10.00

GREY, Zane. *Spirit of the Border.* nd. World. decor brds. VG. P3. $7.50

GREY, Zane. *Spirit of the Border.* 1943. Triangle. 18th prt. VG/dj. P3. $12.50

GREY, Zane. *Stairs of Sand.* nd. Blk's Readers. 12mo. F/F. A8. $7.50

GREY, Zane. *Stairs of Sand.* 1945. Musson. VG. P3. $12.50

GREY, Zane. *Stranger From Tonto.* 1956. Harper. 1st ed. NF/NF. Q1. $100.00

GREY, Zane. *Sunset Pass.* nd. Blk's Readers. 12mo. F/F. A8. $7.50

GREY, Zane. *Tales of Fishing Virgin Seas.* 1925. NY. Harper. 1st ed. quarto. gilt gr cloth. NF/dj. R3. $350.00

GREY, Zane. *Tales of Fresh-Water Fishing.* nd. Grosset Dunlap. VG/VG-. P3. $45.00

GREY, Zane. *Tales of Fresh-Water Fishing.* 1928. London/NY. Harper. 1st ed. VG. B9. $185.00

GREY, Zane. *Tales of Lonely Trails.* 1922. Harper. later prt (I-Y). 394 p. gr cloth/pict label. G. M20. $45.00

GREY, Zane. *Tales of S Rivers.* 1924. Grosset Dunlap. VG/dj. B9. $85.00

GREY, Zane. *Tales of Swordfish & Tuna.* 1927. Grosset Dunlap. 203 p. orange cloth. VG. M20. $90.00

GREY, Zane. *Tales of Swordfish & Tuna.* 1927. Hodder Stoughton. 1st ed. VG/dj. B9. $250.00

GREY, Zane. *Tappan's Burro.* nd. Blk's Readers. 12mo. F/VG. A8. $7.50

GREY, Zane. *Thunder Mtn.* nd. Blk's Readers. 12mo. F/F. A8. $7.50

GREY, Zane. *To the Last Man.* nd. Blk's Readers. 12mo. F/VG. A8. $7.50

GREY, Zane. *To the Last Man.* nd. Grosset Dunlap. G. P3. $5.00

GREY, Zane. *Trail Driver.* nd. Blk's Readers. 12mo. F/VG. A8. $7.50

GREY, Zane. *Twin Sombreros.* nd. Grosset Dunlap. VG/dj. P3. $20.00

GREY, Zane. *Twin Sombreros.* nd. Blk's Readers. 12mo. F/F. A8. $7.50

GREY, Zane. *Under the Tonto Rim.* nd. Blk's Readers. 12mo. VG. A8. $7.50

GREY, Zane. *Undiscovered Zane Grey Fishing Stories.* (1983). Winchester. ils/photos. 176 p. M/dj. A17. $20.00

GREY, Zane. *Valley of Wild Horses.* nd. Blk's Readers. 12mo. F/G. A8. $7.50

GREY, Zane. *Vanishing American.* 1925. Musson. 1st ed. VG/G. P3. $35.00

GREY, Zane. *Wanderer of the Wasteland.* nd. Grosset Dunlap. VG/G+. P3. $7.50

GREY, Zane. *West of the Pecos.* nd. Grosset Dunlap. VG/dj. P3. $20.00

GREY, Zane. *Wild Horse Mesa.* 1928. Musson. VG-. P3. $7.50

GREY, Zane. *Wilderness Trek.* nd. Grosset Dunlap. VG/dj. P3. $20.00

GREY, Zane. *Wildfire.* 1917. Grosset Dunlap. 12mo. G. A8. $7.50

GREY, Zane. *Wyoming.* (1923). NY. Harper. 1st book ed. yel brds/blk spine. VG+/NF. Q1. $75.00

GREY, Zane. *Wyoming.* (1932). Harper. 1st ed. NF/dj. B9. $135.00

GREY, Zane. *Wyoming.* nd. Blk's Readers. 12mo. F/VG. A8. $7.50

GREY, Zane. *Young Lion Hunter.* nd. Grosset Dunlap. VG/dj. P3. $20.00

GREY, Zane. *Young Lion Hunter.* nd. London. Nelson. VG. B9. $60.00

GREY, Zane. *Zane Grey Fishing Lib.* 1990-91. Derrydale. ltd ed. 1/2500. 10 vol set. sgn Grey's son. M. A18. $450.00

GREY, Zane. *30,000 on the Hoof.* nd. Blk's Readers. 12mo. F/G. A8. $7.50

GRIBBLE, Leonard. *Terrace Suicide Mystery.* nd. Collier. VG-. P3. $10.00

GRIDLEY, Marion E. *Indians of Yesterday.* 1940. Chicago. 1st ed. 6 color pls. map ep. pict brds/red cloth. F/fair. H3. $35.00

GRIER, Thomas Graham. *On the Canal Zone.* 1908. Chicago. 1st ed. ils/fld map. 146 p. silvered gr cloth. VG. H3. $45.00

GRIERSON, Francis. *Lady of Despair.* 1933. Collins Crime Club. 6th ed. VG-. P3. $10.00

GRIERSON, Francis. *Murder in the Garden.* nd. Grosset Dunlap. decor brds. VG. P3. $15.00

GRIES & THOMAS. *Will Penny.* 1968. Ballantine. 1st ed. F/wrp. F4. $15.00

GRIFFEN, Jeff. *Hunting Dogs of Am.* 1964. NY. 1st ed. 311 p. VG/dj. A17. $19.50

GRIFFIN, A.P.C. *List of Books...Colonization, Government of Dependencies...* 1900. GPO. xl. NF. O6. $35.00

GRIFFIN, C.F. *Haakon.* 1978. NY. Crowell. 1st ed. NF/NF clip. A14. $20.00

GRIFFIN, Edward. *Plea for Africa.* 1817. NY. Synod of NY & NJ. 1st ed. 8vo. 76 p. M1. $200.00

GRIFFIN, Gwyn. *Operational Necessity.* nd. BOMC. VG/dj. P3. $10.00

GRIFFIN, J.H. *John Howard Griffin Reader.* 1968. Houghton Mifflin. 588 p. VG+/VG clip. A7. $20.00

GRIFFIN & KAHN. *Growth & Inequality in Pakistan.* 1972. London. Macmillan. 1st ed. 8vo. 282 p. VG/dj. W1. $18.00

GRIFFITH, William. *Candles in the Sun.* 1921. Chicago. Bookfellows. 1/450. G+. A1. $30.00

GRIFFITHS, Arthur. *Hist & Romance of Crime From Earliest Times to Present Day.* nd. London. Grollier. 12 vols. teg. brn morocco. F. F1. $1,250.00

GRIFFITHS, John. *Loyal & Dedicated Servant.* 1981. Playboy. 1st ed. VG/dj. P3. $17.50

GRIFFITHS, John. *Travels in Europe, Asia Minor & Arabia.* 1805. London. 4to. 3 (of 4) pls. new quarter calf/marbled brds. O2. $450.00

GRIGSON, Geoffrey. *Dictionary of Eng Plant Names.* 1974. London. ils/pls. 239 p. F/dj. B26. $30.00

GRIMES, John Maurice. *When Minds Go Wrong.* 1949. LA. New Age. 237 p. VG. G1. $30.00

GRIMES, Martha. *Deer Leap.* 1985. Little Brn. ARC of 1st ed. RS. F/dj. S5. $30.00

GRIMES, Martha. *Deer Leap.* 1985. Little Brn. 1st ed. F/dj. P3. $15.95

GRIMES, Martha. *Dirty Duck.* nd. BC. VG/dj. P3. $7.50

GRIMES, Martha. *Five Bells & Bladebone.* 1987. Little Brn. 1st ed. VG/dj. P3. $15.95

GRIMES, Martha. *Horse You Came in On.* 1993. Knopf. AP. F/wrp. B4. $35.00

GRIMES, Martha. *I Am the Only Running Footman.* 1986. Little Brn. 1st ed. VG/dj. P3. $17.50

GRIMES, Martha. *Jerusalem Inn.* nd. BC. VG/dj. P3. $7.50

GRIMES, Martha. *Old Contemptibles.* nd. Quality BC. VG/dj. P3. $10.00

GRIMES, Martha. *Old Silent.* (1989). Little Brn. ARC. F/pict wrp. B3. $25.00

GRIMES, Martha. *Old Silent.* 1989. Little Brn. 1st ed. F/dj. P3. $18.95

GRIMES, Martha. *Send Bygraves.* 1989. Putnam. 1st ed. decor brds. VG. P3. $15.00

GRIMKE, Thomas S. *Address on Truth, Dignity, Power & Beauty...of Peace...* 1832. Hartford. Olmstead. 1st ed. 8vo. 56 p. M1. $300.00

GRIMM, William C. *How To Recognize Shrubs.* 1966. NY. ils. 319 p. F/dj. B26. $16.00

GRIMM & GRIMM. *Bear & the Kingbird.* 1979. NY. FSG. 1st ed. sq 8vo. 31 p. VG/VG. A3. $12.50

GRIMM & GRIMM. *Complete Fairy Tales of Brothers Grimm.* 1987. Bantam. ils JB Gruelle/trans Jack Zipes. 733 p. VG/VG. A3. $10.50

GRIMM & GRIMM. *Das Tapfere Schneiderlein.* (1944). Zurich. ils Herbert Leupin. VG. D1. $95.00

GRIMM & GRIMM. *Der Gestiefelte Kater.* (1946). Zurich. Verlag. ils Herbert Leupin. VG. D1. $95.00

GRIMM & GRIMM. *Dornroschen.* (1948). Zurich. ils Herbert Leupin. VG. D1. $95.00

GRIMM & GRIMM. *German Popular Stories.* 1825-26. London/Dublin. mixed set of 2 vols. VG/brn cloth slipcase. H5. $1,750.00

GRIMM & GRIMM. *Glass Mtn.* 1985. Knopf. 1st ed. ils Nonny Hogrogian. marbled ep. F. T5. $35.00

GRIMM & GRIMM. *Grimm's Fairy Tales.* 1909. London. Constable. 1st thus/trade ed. ils Rackham. 325 p. red cloth. VG. D1. $1,200.00

GRIMM & GRIMM. *Grimm's Fairy Tales.* 1920. Ward Lock. decor brds. VG-. P3. $10.00

GRIMM & GRIMM. *Grimm's Fairy Tales.* 1948. Routledge Kegan Paul. ils Josef Scharl. G/G. L1. $50.00

GRIMM & GRIMM. *Grimm's Goblins.* 1867. Boston. ils after Cruikshank/6 pls. gilt pict brn cloth. G. H3. $25.00

GRIMM & GRIMM. *Hans Im Gluck.* (1944). Zurich. Verlag. ils Herbert Leupin. VG. D1. $95.00

GRIMM & GRIMM. *Little Brother & Little Sister.* 1917. London. 1/525. ils/sgn Rackham. 13 mtd color pls. Morrell bdg. F/case. H5. $1,850.00

GRIMM & GRIMM. *Picture Book of Grimm's Fairy Tales.* 1930. Racine. ils Charlotte Stone. 22 p. F/pict wrp. H3. $20.00

GRIMM & GRIMM. *Snow Wht & the 7 Dwarfs.* 1972. NY. FSG. ils NE Burkert. 1st ed. 32 p. VG/dj. A3. $37.50

GRIMM & GRIMM. *Tischlein Dich.* (1948). Zurich. Verlag. ils Herbert Leupin. VG. D1. $95.00

GRIMWOOD, Ken. *Replay.* 1986. Arbor. 1st ed. VG/dj. P3. $20.00

GRIMWOOD. *Starting Needlepoint Lace, a Course for Beginners.* 1989. np. ils. cloth. G2. $30.00

GRINNELL, David; see Wollheim, Don.

GRINNELL & ROOSEVELT. *Hunting Trails on 3 Continents.* (1933). Derrydale. 1/250. octavo. maroon cloth. NF. R3. $2,500.00

GRINSTEIN, Alexander. *Conrad Ferdinand Meyer & Freud: Beginnings...Psychoanalysis.* 1992 Madison, CT. IUP. 1st ed. 400 p. blk cloth. F/dj. G1. $37.50

GRISEWOOD, R. Norman. *Zarlah the Martian.* 1909. Fenno. copyright p missing. VG-. P3. $50.00

GRISHAM, John. *Client.* 1993. Doubleday. 1st ed. F/F. M15. $45.00

GRISHAM, John. *Firm.* nd. BC. VG/dj. P3. $10.00

GRISHAM, John. *Pelican Brief.* nd. BC. F/dj. P3. $10.00

GRISHAM, John. *Time To Kill.* nd. BC. VG/dj. P3. $10.00

GRISWOLD, George. *Checkmate by the Colonel.* 1953. Dutton. 1st ed. VG/dj. P3. $20.00

GRISWOLD, George. *Pinned Man.* (1955). Little Brn. 1st ed. NF/VG. B4. $45.00

GRISWOLD, George. *Red Pawns.* 1954. Dutton. 1st ed. NF/dj. P3. $15.00

GRISWOLD, Rufus W. *WA & the Generals of the Am Revolution.* 1866. Phil. 2 vols in 1. pls. marbled edges. VG. B14. $145.00

GROB, Gerald N. *Inner World of Am Psychiatry 1890-1940.* 1985. Rutgers. 1st ed. 310 p. russet cloth. F/dj. G1. $22.50

GROENING, Matt. *Simpsons' Xmas Book.* 1990. Harperperennial. 1st ed. VG. P3. $10.00

GROGAN, Emmett. *Ringolevio: Life Played for Keeps.* (1972). Little Brn. 2nd prt. 8vo. 498 p. VG+/VG. A2. $15.00

GROHMANN & TUDAL. *Intimate Sketchbooks of Georges Braque.* (1955). Harcourt Brace. folio. 20 color/105 blk & wht ils. NF/dj. B24. $325.00

GROLLMAN, Earl A. *Judaism in Sigmund Freud's World.* 1965. Appleton Century. 173 p. VG/VG-. S3. $21.00

GRONLUND, Laurence. *New Economy.* 1898. Chicago. Henry Stone. 1st ed. VG. B2. $85.00

GROOM, Arthur. *Flying Doctor Annual.* 1963. Dean & Son. VG. P3. $30.00

GROOM, Winston. *Better Times Than These.* (1978). Summit. author's 1st novel. 411 p. F/NF. A7. $40.00

GROOM, Winston. *Gone the Sun.* (1988). Doubleday. as new/dj. A7. $25.00

GROOM & SPENCER. *Conversations w/the Enemy.* (1983). Putnam. 411 p. F/F. A7. $35.00

GROOMS, Red. *Ruckus Rodeo.* 1988. 6 pop-ups. F. A4. $55.00

GROPMAN, D. *Say It Ain't So Joe.* 1979. Boston. 1st ed. VG/G. B5. $35.00

GROSE, William. *Story of Marches, Battles & Incidents of 36th Regiment...* 1891. New Castle. ils. VG. B14. $130.00

GROSS, Charles. *Redemption of David Corson.* 1900. Bowen Merrill. 1st ed. G. M2. $10.00

GROSS, Louis S. *Redefining the Am Gothic.* 1989. UMI Research. 1st ed. F/dj. P3. $35.00

GROSS, Philip. *Cat's Whisker.* 1987. London. Faber. 1st ed. F/F. V1. $10.00

GROSS, Warren Lee. *Soldier's Story of His Captivity at Andersonville...* 1868 (1866). Boston. w/sgn cancelled Nast check. gr cloth. VG. A11. $55.00

GROSS. *Patterns From China.* 1982. np. ils. cloth. G2. $18.00

GROSSBACH, Robert. *Never Say Die.* 1979. Harper. 1st ed. F/dj. M2. $12.00

GROSSER & HALPERIN. *Causes & Effects of Anti-Semitism: Dimensions of Prejudice.* 1978. Philosophical Lib. 408 p. VG+/G+. S3. $24.00

GROSSMAN, Carl M. *Wild Analyst: Life & Work of George Groddeck.* 1965. London. Braziller. 1st ed. 222 p. blk cloth. VG/dj. G1. $28.50

GROSVENOR, Graeme. *Growing Daylilies.* 1990 (1986). Kenthurst, Australia. 100 color photos. 64 p. M. B26. $11.00

GROUSSET, Rene. *Rise & Splendour of the Chinese Empire.* 1952. London. Bles. 1st ed. 8vo. 312 p. VG/dj. W1. $25.00

GROVE, A. *Lure & Lore of Trout Fishing.* 1951. Harrisburg. 1st ed. VG/VG. B5. $40.00

GROVER, David H. *Diamondfield Jack: Study in Frontier Justice.* 1986. Norman, OK. ils/index. 189 p. F/wrp. B19. $9.50

GROVER, Eulalie Osgood. *Sunbonnet Babies ABC Book.* 1937. Rand McNally. ils Bertha C Melcher. VG. L1. $50.00

GROVER, Eulalie Osgood. *Sunbonnet Babies Book.* 1928. Rand McNally. ils BL Corbett. 105 p. VG. A3. $35.00

GRUBB, Davis. *Shadow of My Brother.* 1966. Hutchinson. 1st ed. NF/dj. P3. $25.00

GRUBB, Davis. *Voices of Glory.* 1962. Scribner. 3rd ed. VG. P3. $10.00

GRUBB, Edward. *Social Aspects of the Quaker Faith.* 1899. London. Headley Bros. xl. 12mo. 252 p. G. V3. $8.50

GRUBB, Kenneth. *Parables From S Am.* (1932). London. Lutterworth. 1st ed. ils/map. 215 p. F3. $30.00

GRUBB, W. Barbrooke. *Unknown People in an Unknown Land.* 1911. London. Seeley. 1st ed. 8vo. 329 p. teg. gilt bl cloth. fair. B11. $50.00

GRUBER, Frank. *Beagle Scented Murder.* 1946. Rinehart. 1st ed. xl. dj. P3. $10.00

GRUBER, Frank. *Brass Knuckles.* 1966. Sherbourne. 1st ed. xl. front free ep removed. VG-/dj. P3. $10.00

GRUBER, Frank. *Bridge of Sand.* 1963. Dutton. 1st ed. VG/dj. P3. $25.00

GRUBER, Frank. *Gift Horse.* 1942. Farrar Rinehart. 1st ed. F/NF. M15. $100.00

GRUBER, Frank. *Gold Gap.* 1968. Dutton. 1st ed. NF/dj. A7. $35.00

GRUBER, Frank. *Horatio Alger Jr.* 1961. LA. 1/750. NF/8vo orange wrp. A11. $35.00

GRUBER, Frank. *Laughing Fox.* 1943. Tower. VG/dj. P3. $20.00

GRUBER, Frank. *Run, Fool, Run.* 1966. Dutton. 1st ed. VG/dj. P3. $30.00

GRUBER, Frank. *Spanish Prisoner.* 1968. Dutton. 1st ed. xl. dj. P3. $6.00

GRUELLE, Johnny. *Beloved Belindy.* 1926. Donohue. 8vo. cloth. VG/dj. D1. $175.00

GRUELLE, Johnny. *Cherry Scarecrow.* 1929. Donohue. Sunny Books series. 40 p. VG. A3. $30.00

GRUELLE, Johnny. *Eddie Elephant.* 1921. Donohue. red cloth. VG. M5. $18.00

GRUELLE, Johnny. *Friendly Fairies.* (1919). Donohue. 8vo. NF/dj. D1. $125.00

GRUELLE, Johnny. *Johnny Gruelle's Golden Book.* 1925. Donohue. 4to. 95 p. VG. D1. $65.00

GRUELLE, Johnny. *Little Sunny Stories.* 1944. Donohue. red cloth. VG/VG. A3. $45.00

GRUELLE, Johnny. *Marcella: A Raggedy Ann Story.* 1929. Donohue. 8vo. VG/tattered. D1. $150.00

GRUELLE, Johnny. *Old-Fashioned Raggedy Ann & Andy ABC Book.* 1975. Windmill/Simon Schuster. 1st ed. 32 p. VG. A3. $12.50

GRUELLE, Johnny. *Raggedy Ann & Andy & the Nice Fat Policeman.* 1942. NY. Gruelle. 8vo. 95 p. VG/torn. D1. $100.00

GRUELLE, Johnny. *Raggedy Ann & Andy.* 1944. Saalfield. ils Julian Wehr/6 movables. red sbdg. VG. D1. $185.00

GRUELLE, Johnny. *Raggedy Ann in the Deep Deep Woods.* 1930. Donohue. 8vo. ils ep. VG/G. D1. $100.00

GRUELLE, Johnny. *Raggedy Ann's Lucky Pennies.* 1932. Donohue. 8vo. 94 p. NF/NF. D1. $125.00

GRUELLE, Johnny. *Raggedy Ann's Magical Wishes.* (1928). Donohue. 8vo. 95 p. pict brds. VG/dj. D1. $125.00

GRUELLE, Johnny. *Raggedy Ann's Magical Wishes.* 1928. Volland. 1st ed. 94 p. VG. M20. $50.00

GRUELLE, Johnny. *Raggedy Ann Stories.* 1918. Donohue. blk cloth. VG. M5. $55.00

GRUELLE, Johnny. *Rhymes for Kindly Children. Modern Mother Goose Jingles.* 1937. Wise Parslow. revised ed. 4to. cloth. G-VG. A3. $30.00

GRUELLE, Johnny. *Wooden Willie.* 1927. Donohue. 8vo. 95 p. ils ep. VG/dj. D1. $135.00

GRUENHAGEN, R.W. *Mustang: Story of the P-51 Fighter.* (1976). NY. revised ed. VG/dj. B18. $15.00

GRUMBACH, Doris. *Spoil of the Flowers.* 1962. NY. 1st ed. inscr/dtd 1962. NF/NF. A11. $135.00

GRUMLEY, Michael. *Life Drawing.* 1991. Grove/Weidenfeld. 1st ed. author's 1st solo book. F/F. A14. $25.00

GRUMMER, Gerhard. *Herbicides in Vietnam.* (1969). Berlin. 191 p. glossy pict wrp. A7. $65.00

GRUPP, Larry. *Great Am Deer Hunt.* (1992). Boulder. Paladin. 1st ed. ils/photos. 226 p. M/dj. A17. $30.00

GT-99. *20 Years a Labor Spy.* (1937). Bobb Merrill. 1st ed. 8vo. 309 p. F/VG. A2. $35.00

GUARESCHI, G. *Don Camillo & His Flock.* 1952. Pelligrini Cudahy. 4th ed. front free ep removed. P3. $12.50

GUARESCHI, G. *Little World of Don Camillo.* 1950. Pellegrini Cudahy. G/dj. A16. $10.00

GUARINI, Giovanni Battista. *Lettere... D Nouvo in Questa Terza...* 1596. Venice. Battista Ciotti. 3 parts in 1. contemporary vellum. K1. $350.00

GUAZZO, Francisco Maria. *Compendium Maleficarum...* 1929 (1608). London. Rodker. 1st Eng-language ed. sm folio. red brds. VG. G1. $175.00

GUBLER, Adolphe. *Commentaires Therapeutiques du Codex Medicamentarius...* 1868. Paris. JB Bailliere. 1st ed. 760 p. stp gr cloth. NF. S9. $39.00

GUEDALLA, Philip. *Bonnet & Shawl.* 1928. Crosby Gaige. ltd ed. sgn. NF. N2. $22.50

GUERBER, H.A. *Norsemen.* 1986. Avenel. 2nd ed. VG/dj. P3. $10.00

GUERINI, V. *Hist of Dentistry From Most Ancient Times...* 1909. Phil. 1st ed. 355 p. cloth. G. scarce. G7. $175.00

GUEROT, Alfred. *French Cooking for Everyone.* (1963). Golden Pr. sm 4to. 279 p. clip dj. A7. $25.00

GUEST, Barbara. *Musicality.* 1988. Kelsey Street. 1st ed. inscr/sgn. F/wrp. V1. $20.00

GUGLIELMINI, Domenico. *Della Natura e' Fiumi Trattato Fisico-Matematico.* 1739. Bologna. 28 pls. contemporary vellum/gilt half label. K1. $1,500.00

GUIGNEBERT, Charles. *When Harlem Was Jewish, 1870-1930.* 1979. Columbia. 216 p. VG+/G+. S3. $30.00

GUILD, Nicholas. *Chain Reaction.* 1983. St Martin. 1st ed. VG/dj. P3. $15.00

GUILLEMIN, Amedee. *Wonders of the Moon.* 1873. Scribner. trans MG Mead. 241 p. gr cloth. B14. $50.00

GUILLION, Carroll. *Sm Town Tales.* 1930s. ap. 12mo. inscr. 86 p. N2. $17.50

GULERSOY, Celik. *Guide to Istanbul.* 1972. Istanbul. 8vo. 296 p. O2. $10.00

GULICK, Paul. *Strings of Steel.* nd. Grosset Dunlap. photoplay ed. VG. P3. $20.00

GULLEY, F.A. *1st Lessons in Agriculture...* 1887. Starkville, MS. sq 12mo. 118 p. gr cloth. H9. $30.00

Gundolf, Friedrich. *Shakespeare und der Deutsche Geist.* 1922. Berlin. Bondi. 359 p. quarter morocco/marbled brds. N2. $25.00

GUNN, James. *Breaking Point.* 1972. Walker. 1st ed. F/dj. M2. $15.00

GUNN, James. *End of Dreams.* 1975. Scribner. 1st ed. F/dj. P3. $15.00

GUNN, James. *Joy Makers.* 1984. Crown. 1st Am ed. RS. F/dj. M2. $15.00

GUNN, James. *Some Dreams Are Nightmares.* 1974. Scribner. 1st ed. F/dj. M2. $10.00

GUNN, T. *Jack Straw's Castle.* 1976. FSG. 1st ed. F/VG+. V1. $20.00

GUNNARSSON, Gunnar. *Blk Cliffs.* 1967. Madison, WI. 1st ed of 1929 Svartfugl ed. trans from Danish. NF/NF. A14. $20.00

GUPTA, Basant L. *Forest Flora of Chakrata, Dehra Dun & Saharanpur Forest...* 1969 (1927). Dehra Dun. 3rd ed. 558 p. B26. $14.00

GUPTILL, A.B. *Haynes Guide to Yellowstone Park.* 1899. St Paul, NM. 16mo. ils/maps. 141 p. gilt blk cloth. H3. $65.00

GURALNICK, Peter. *Lost Highway: Journeys & Arrivals of Am Musicians.* 1979. Boston. Godine. 1st ed. F/NF. B2. $45.00

GURALNICK, Peter. *Searching for Robert Johnson.* 1989. Dutton. 1st ed. F/F. B2. $60.00

GURDON, J.E. *Secret of the South.* 1950. London. 1st ed. NF/dj. M2. $25.00

GURGANUS, A. *Blessed Assurance.* 1990. Rocky Mtn, NC. ARC. sgn. RS. gilt maroon cloth. A11. $45.00

GURGANUS, A. *Oldest Living Confederate Widow Tells All.* 1989. Knopf. 1st ed. sgn. author's 1st book. F/F. Q1. $75.00

GURLER, H.B. *Farm Dairy.* 1908. Chicago. Breeder's Gazette. 1st ed. 164 p. H10. $15.00

GURNEY, David. *F Certificate.* 1968. Bernard Geis. 1st ed. F. P3. $7.50

GURNEY, Gene. *Flying Aces of WWI.* 1973. Scholastic Books. 1st ed/2nd prt. 8vo. G/wrp. A8. $6.00

GURNEY, Joseph John. *Familiar Letters to Henry Clay of KY...* 1840. NY. Mahlon Day. 8vo. 203 p. V3. $85.00

GURNEY, Joseph John. *Observations on Distinguishing Views...of Soc of Friends.* 1856. NY. Wood. 2nd Am ed. 8vo. 338 p. full leather. G+. V3. $45.00

GUSFIELD, Joseph R. *Symbolic Crusade: Status Politics & Am Temperance Movement.* 1963. Urbana. 198 p. orange cloth. VG/dj. G1. $28.50

GUSSOW & ODELL. *Mushrooms & Toadstools.* 1927. Ottawa. 1st ed. pls. gilt dk gr cloth. VG. B28. $37.50

GUSTAFSSON, Lars. *Death of a Beekeeper.* 1981. New Directions. 1st ed. NF/NF clip. A14. $25.00

GUTHORN, Peter J. *Am Maps & Map Makers of the Revolution.* 1966. Monmouth Beach, NJ. Philip Freneau. 4to. 48 p. bl cloth. VG. H9. $65.00

GUTHORN, Peter J. *Am Maps & Map Makers of the Revolution.* 1966. Monmouth Beach, NJ. 1st ed. presentation/sgn. NF. O6. $125.00

GUTHORN, Peter J. *US Coastal Charts, 1783-1861.* ca 1984. Schiffer. lg 4to. ils. 224 p. cloth. dj. H9. $85.00

GUTHRIE, A.B. *Big Sky, Fair Land: Environmental Essays.* (1988). Northland. 1st ed. inscr/sgn. M/M. A18. $100.00

GUTHRIE, A.B. *Big Sky.* (1947). Sloane. 1st ltd ed. 1/500. sgn. NF. A18. $100.00

GUTHRIE, A.B. *Big Sky.* (1947). Sloane. 1st trade ed. NF/clip. A18. $50.00

GUTHRIE, A.B. *Big Sky.* 1964. Time Reading Program. 1st ed. sgn. NF/stiff wrp. A11. $60.00

GUTHRIE, A.B. *Fair Land, Fair Land.* 1982. Houghton Mifflin. VG/dj. A16. $25.00

GUTHRIE, A.B. *Field Guide To Writing Fiction.* (1991). Harper Collins. 1st ed. M/M. A18. $20.00

GUTHRIE, A.B. *Four Miles From Ear Mtn.* (1987). Kutenai Pr. 1st #d ed of 300. sgn. ils/sgn K Bogan. wrp. A18. $90.00

GUTHRIE, A.B. *Genuine Article.* 1977. Houghton Mifflin. 1st ed. F/F. S5. $30.00

GUTHRIE, A.B. *Murders at Moon Dance.* 1943. Dutton. 1st ed. inscr/dtd 1957. author's 1st book. VG/VG. Q1. $600.00

GUTHRIE, A.B. *Once Upon a Pond.* (1973). Mtn Pr. 1st ed. sgn. F/F. A18. $75.00

GUTHRIE, A.B. *These Thousand Hills.* 1956. Houghton Mifflin. 1st ed. F/VG+ clip. A18/Q1. $50.00

GUTHRIE, A.B. *Way West.* 1949. NY. Sloane. 1st ed. author's 2nd book. NF/NF. Q1. $75.00

GUTHRIE, A.B. *Way West.* 1949. NY. Sloane. 1st ed. w/sgn bookplate. F/NF. A11. $125.00

GUTHRIE, A.B. *Way West.* 1949. Sloane. 1st ed. VG/rpr dj. A18. $30.00

GUTHRIE, A.B. *Way West.* 1979. Franklin Lib. 1st ed. ils Tony Eubanks. aeg. leather. F. C4. $45.00

GUTHRIE, Ramon. *Maximum Security Ward.* 1970. NY. 1st ed. F/F. V1. $20.00

GUTHRIE, Tyrone. *Life in the Theater.* 1959. McGraw Hill. 1st ed. 350 p. VG/dj. M20. $8.00

GUTMAN, Bill. *Golden Age of Baseball, 1941-64.* 1989. Bison. VG/dj. P3. $15.00

GUTMAN, Nahum. *Path of the Orange Peels.* 1979. Dodd Mead. ils Gutman. 140 p. VG/G+. S3. $23.00

GUTMAN, Walter. *Gutman Letter.* (1969). Something Else Pr. 1st ed. quarto. F/NF. B4. $85.00

GUTTERIDGE, Lindsay. *Cold War in a Country Garden.* 1971. Putnam. VG/dj. P3. $15.00

GUTTERIDGE, Lindsay. *Killer Pine.* 1973. Putnam. 1st ed. VG/dj. P3. $17.50

GUTTMAN, Samual A. *Concordance to the Standard Ed...Works of Sigmund Freud.* 1984. NY. IUP. 1st ed. heavy folio. 6 vols. brn buckram. F. G1. $600.00

GUY, Rosa. *Measure of Time.* 1983. HRW. 2nd imp. NF/NF clip. A13. $20.00

GWALTNEY, John Langston. *Dissenters.* (1986). Random. 1st ed. 321 p. F/clip. A7. $17.00

GWALTNEY, John Langston. *Drylongso: Self-Portrait of Blk Am.* (1980). Random. 1st ed. 287 p. dj. A7. $20.00

GWYNNE, Paul. *Along Spain's River of Romance: The Guadalquivir.* 1912. NY. McBride Nast. 1st ed. 8vo. 356 p. F. A2. $25.00

GYGAX, Gary. *Oriental Adventures.* 1985. TSR Advanced D&D 099. VG. P3. $15.00

H

HAACK, Hermann. *Echte Teppiche. Einfuhrung in Die Orientteppichkunde.* 1957. Munich. ils/fld map. 95 p. cloth. O2. $50.00

HAAR, Charles M. *Landmark Justice: Influence of Wm J Brennan...* 1987. WA. Preservation Pr. M11. $35.00

HAAR, J.T. *King Arthur.* 1973. Crane Russak. F/dj. P3. $15.00

HAASSE, Hella S. *In a Dark Wood Wandering.* 1990. London. Hutchinson. 1st ed. edit Anita Miller. trans LC Kaplan. NF/NF. A14. $30.00

HABBERTON, John. *Some Folks.* 1877. San Francisco. Roman. 1st ed. royal 8vo. 510 p. pict cloth. VG. D3. $65.00

HABE, Hans. *Blk Earth.* 1952. Putnam. 1st Am ed. VG+/VG clip. A14. $20.00

HABE, Hans. *Mission.* 1966. London. Harrap. 1st Bitish ed. trans Michael Bullock. NF/NF. A14. $25.00

HABE, Hans. *Off Limits: Novel of Occupied Germany.* 1956. London. Harrap. 1st British ed. trans Ewald Osers. NF/NF. A14. $35.00

HABER & MURPHY. *Teenage Mutant Ninja Turtles Pop-Up Storybook.* 1990. 6 popups. paper engineering by John Stejan/Roger Smith. F. A4. $25.00

HABER. *Disney's Aladdin: A Pop-Up Book.* 1993. paper engineering by Roger Smith. F. A4. $30.00

HABER. *Little Mermaid: A Pop-Up Book.* nd. popups/movable scenes. paper engineering by Roger Smith/Jose Seminario. F. A4. $30.00

HABER. *Walt Disney's Pinocchio Pop-Up Book.* 1992. 12 action scenes. paper engineering by Roger Smith. F. A4. $30.00

HABERLEIN, Ed. *Amateur Trainer Multum in Parvo.* 1943. McPherson, KS. 38th ed. 139 p. G/wrp. A17. $12.50

HABERLY, L. *Pursuit of the Horizon.* 1948. NY. 1st ed. 17 pls. cloth. VG. D3. $25.00

HABERSTEIN & LAMARS. *Hist of Am Funeral Directing.* 1963. Bulfin. F/dj. M2. $15.00

HABERTON, John. *Helen's Babies.* (1876). Loring. 206 p. gilt brn cloth. VG-. S10. $25.00

HACK, Mary Pryor. *Mary Pryor: Life Story of a Hundred Yrs Ago.* nd. Phil. Longstreth. xl. 12mo. 160 p. rpr hinge. V3. $10.00

HACKETT, J. *Hist of the Orthodox Church of Cyprus...* 1901. London. 8vo. 720 p. cloth. F. very scarce. O2. $250.00

HACKETT, John. *3rd World War.* 1979. Macmillan. 1st ed/5th prt. 8vo. VG/G. A8. $10.00

HADAS, Moses. *Fables of a Jewish Aesop.* 1967. NY. Columbia. ils Fritz Kredel. 232 p. VG/G+. S3. $27.00

HADDOCK, Charles B. *Addresses & Misc Writings.* 1846. Cambridge. Metcalf. 1st ed. tall 8vo. 574 p. emb Victorian cloth. VG. G1. $50.00

HADDOCK, J.A. *Haddock's Narrative of His Hazardous & Exciting Voyage...* 1872. Phil. Haddock. 1st ed. 8vo. 15 p. pict wrp. F. M1. $750.00

HADER & HADER. *Cricket: Story of a Little Circus Pony.* 1938. Macmillan. 2nd prt. 8vo. VG/G+. A3. $20.00

HADER & HADER. *Little Appaloosa.* 1949. Macmillan. 1st ed. 4to. VG/dj. A3. $25.00

HADERS, Phyllis. *Sunshine & Shadow: Amish & Their Quilts.* 1976. np. ils. wrp. G2. $10.00

HADFIELD & HADFIELD. *Gardens of Delight.* 1964. Boston. 1st Am ed. pls. 192 p. VG+. B28. $27.50

HADY, Lindsay. *Nightshade Ring.* 1954. Appleton Century. VG/torn. P3. $10.00

HAESER, Heinrich. *Lehrbuch der Gerschichte der Medicin und der Epidemischen...* 1875-82. Jena Hermann Dufft. 3 vols in 6. orig brds/new rebacking. VG. G7. $395.00

HAFEN, LeRoy. *Mtn Men & the Fur Trade of the Far W.* 1965-72. Glendale. Arthur Clark. 10 vols. F/djs. P4. $2,350.00

HAFFNER, Sylvia. *Hist of Modern Israel's Money From 1917-67...* 1967. CA. xl. 196 p. VG/wrp. S3. $17.00

HAFTMAN, Werner. *Imzwischenreich Aquarelle und Zeichnungen Paul Klee.* nd. np. VG. A1. $150.00

HAGEMAN, James. *Heritage of VA: Story of Place Names in Old Dominion.* ca 1986. Donning. ils. 297 p. stiff wrp. B10. $12.00

HAGEMANN, E.R. *Index to Blk Mask, 1920-51.* 1982. Bowling Gr. F/dj. P3. $20.00

HAGER, Jean. *Redbird's Cry.* 1994. Mysterious. ARC. F/wrp. B2. $25.00

HAGGARD, H. Rider. *Allan Quatermain.* 1926. Hodder Stougton. VG/VG-. P3. $35.00

HAGGARD, H. Rider. *Ayesha: Return of She.* 1905. William Briggs. 1st Canadian ed. VG-. P3. $35.00

HAGGARD, H. Rider. *Benita.* 1965. Macdonald. F/dj. P3. $20.00

HAGGARD, H. Rider. *Classic Adventures.* 1986. New Orchard. 1st ed. F/dj. P3. $19.95

HAGGARD, H. Rider. *Cleopatra.* 192? Harrap. 3rd ed. VG. P3. $20.00

HAGGARD, H. Rider. *Dawn Vol II.* nd Collier. VG-. P3. $15.00

HAGGARD, H. Rider. *Fair Margaret.* nd Hutchinson. 2nd ed. VG. P3. $45.00

HAGGARD, H. Rider. *Farmer's Yr.* 189? London. 1st ed. VG. M2. $125.00

HAGGARD, H. Rider. *Ghost Kings.* 197? Tom Stacey. VG/VG-. P3. $15.00

HAGGARD, H. Rider. *Jess.* 1896. Smit Elder. VG-. P3. $60.00

HAGGARD, H. Rider. *John Haste.* 1895 Longman Gr. 1st ed. VG. Q1. $75.00

HAGGARD, H. Rider. *King Solomon' Mines.* 1979. Octopus. VG/dj. P3. $10.00

HAGGARD, H. Rider. *Lady of Blossholm* nd. Hodder Stoughton. VG. P3. $25.00

HAGGARD, H. Rider. *Lysbeth.* 1924. Hodder Stoughton. VG-. P3. $17.50

HAGGARD, H. Rider. *Mahatma & th Hare.* 1911. London. 1st ed. VG. scarce M2. $125.00

HAGGARD, H. Rider. *Margaret.* 1907 Longman. 1st Am ed. VG. M2. $50.00

HAGGARD, H. Rider. *Morning Star.* 191? Cassell. 2nd ed. decor brds. VG. P3. $50.00

HAGGARD, H. Rider. *Nada the Lily.* 1892 London. 1st ed. VG. M2. $200.00

HAGGARD, H. Rider. *Pearl Maiden.* 1972 Tom Stacey. VG/dj. P3. $20.00

HAGGARD, H. Rider. *People of the Mist* 1894. Longman. 1st Am ed. VG. M2. $80.00

HAGGARD, H. Rider. *Red Eve.* 1912. Doubleday. VG. scarce. M2. $80.00

HAGGARD, H. Rider. *She & Allan.* nd Hutchinson. 2nd ed. VG. P3. $40.00

HAGGARD, H. Rider. *Swallow.* 1899 Longman. 1st ed. VG. M2. $75.00

HAGGARD, H. Rider. *Treasure of the Lake* 1926. Doubleday. 1st ed. VG. M2. $40.00

HAGGARD, H. Rider. *Way of the Spirit.* nd Musson. 1st Canadian ed. VG. P3. $35.00

HAGGARD, H. Rider. *When the Worl Shook.* 1919. London. 1st ed. VG-. M2. $75.00

HAGGARD, H. Rider. *Wisdom's Daughter* nd. Hutchinson. VG/VG-. P3. $35.00

HAGGARD, H. Rider. *Wizard.* 1933 Arrowsmith. VG. P3. $40.00

HAGGARD, H. Rider. *World's Desire.* (1898). Longman. 4th prt. front free ep removed. VG-. P3. $40.00

HAGGARD, H.W. *Mystery, Magic & Medicine...From Superstition to Science.* 1933. Doubleday Doran. ils. 192 p. red cloth. VG. S9. $13.00

HAGGARD, Paul. *Death Talks Shop.* 1938. Hillman Curl. VG-. P3. $20.00

HAGGARD, William. *Arena.* 1961. Washburn. 1st ed. VG/VG-. P3. $15.00

HAGGARD, William. *Hard Sell.* 1966. Ives Washburn. 1st ed. VG/dj. P3. $17.50

HAGGARD, William. *Median Line.* 1981. Walker. 1st ed. VG/VG-. P3. $12.50

HAGGARD, William. *Poison People.* 1977. Walker. 1st ed. VG/VG-. P3. $12.50

HAGUE, Arnold. *Atlas To Accompany Monograph XXXII on Geology Yellowstone...* 1904. US Geological Survey. 24 hinged maps. NF. O6. $995.00

HAGUE, Michael. *World of Unicorns w/3-Dimensional, Movable Ils.* 1986. F. A4. $40.00

HAHN, Emily. *Aboab: 1st Rabbi of the Americas.* 1959. FSC. 180 p. VG/G. S3. $30.00

HAHN, Emily. *Islands: Am's Imperial Adventure in Philippines.* (1981). NY. CMG. 1st ed. 8vo. 258 p. F/F. A2. $12.50

HAHN, Emily. *Raffles of Singapore. A Biography.* 1946. Doubleday. 1st ed. 8vo. pls/maps. 587 p. VG/dj. W1. $18.00

HAHN, Michael. *Message of the Governor of LA Delivered Oct 7, 1864.* 1864. New Orleans. WR Fish. 1st ed. 8vo. 13 p. prt wrp. M1. $125.00

HAIBLUM, Isidore. *Tsaddik of the Seven Wonders.* 1981. Doubleday. VG/VG. P3. $15.00

HAIBLUM, Isidore. *Wilk Are Among Us.* 1975. Doubleday. 1st ed. VG/dj. P3. $15.00

HAIG-BROWN, Roderick L. *Fisherman's Summer.* (1975). NY. new ed. 253 p. M/dj. A17. $25.00

HAIG-BROWN, Roderick L. *Living Land: Account of Nat Resources of British Columbia.* 1961. NY. 1st ed. pls/index. 269 p. A17. $25.00

HAIG-BROWN, Roderick L. *Return to the River: Story of Chinook Run.* (1946). Toronto. McClelland Stewart. 1st ed. F/dj. A18. $50.00

HAIG-BROWN, Roderick L. *Starbuck Valley Winter.* 1943. NY. Morrow. 1st ed. ils Charles De Feo. F/VG+. B20. $40.00

HAIG-BROWN, Roderick L. *W Angler: Account of Pacific Salmon & W Trout.* (1991). Derrydale. new ltd ed. 1/2500. 2 vols. full leather. M. A18. $100.00

HAIG-BROWN, Roderick L. *Whale People.* 1962. London. Collins. 1st ed. ils Mary Weiler. F/F. A18. $50.00

HAIGHT, Gordon S. *Mrs Sigourney, the Sweet Singer of Hartford.* 1930. New Haven. 8vo. 201 p. cloth. O2. $15.00

HAILEY, Arthur. *Evening News.* 1990. Doubleday. 1st ed. sgn. F/F. Q1. $45.00

HAILEY, J.P. *Underground Man.* 1990. Donald Fine. 1st ed. F/dj. P3. $18.95

HAINES, Charles Grove. *Role of Supreme Court in Am Government & Politics...* 1944. Berkeley. gr cloth. M11. $50.00

HAINES, Gregory. *Sound Under-Water.* (1974). NY. ils/charts. 208 p. dj. A17. $8.50

HAINES, Joseph E. *Hist of Friends' Central School (Phil).* 1938. Overbrook, PA. Friends Central School. ltd ed. 12mo. 57 p. VG. V3. $14.00

HAINING, Peter. *Art of Horror Stories.* 1986. Chartwell. F/dj. P3. $20.00

HAINING, Peter. *Dead of Night.* 1989. Dorset. 1st ed. F/dj. P3. $16.95

HAINING, Peter. *Deadly Nightshade.* 1978. Taplinger. 1st ed. F/dj. P3. $22.50

HAINING, Peter. *Doctor Who: Time-Traveller's Guide.* 1987. WH Allen. F/dj. P3. $25.00

HAINING, Peter. *Fantastic Pulps.* 1975. Gollancz. 1st ed. F/F. P3. $35.00

HAINING, Peter. *Final Adventures of Sherlock Holmes.* 1981. Castle. 1st ed. VG/dj. P3. $17.50

HAINING, Peter. *Fortune Hunter's Guide.* 1975. Sidgwick Jackson. 1st ed. sgn. VG/dj. P3. $30.00

HAINING, Peter. *Ghouls.* nd. BC. VG/dj. P3. $10.00

HAINING, Peter. *Ghouls.* 1971. Stein Day. 1st Am ed. NF/dj. M2. $20.00

HAINING, Peter. *Hollywood Nightmare.* 1970. Macdonald. 1st ed. NF/dj. P3. $15.00

HAINING, Peter. *Movable Books.* 1979. folio. fld ils. 142 p. F/F. A4. $165.00

HAINING, Peter. *Movable Books.* 1979. London. NEL. oblong 4to. 142 p. NF/NF. F1. $150.00

HAINING, Peter. *Movable Books.* 1979. NEL. ils. 141 p. cloth. VG+/NF. M20. $125.00

HAINING, Peter. *Pict Hist of Horror Stories.* 1985. Treasure Pr. 1st revised ed. F/F. F4. $25.00

HAINING, Peter. *Satanists.* 1970. Taplinger. 1st ed. VG/dj. P3. $17.50

HAINING, Peter. *Sherlock Holmes Compendium.* 1981. Castle. 1st ed. F/dj. P3. $20.00

HAINING, Peter. *Sherlock Holmes Scrapbook.* 1974. Potter. 1st Am ed. ils. F/NF. S5. $30.00

HAINING, Peter. *Wild Night Company.* 1971. Taplinger. 1st ed. VG/dj. P3. $20.00

HAJEK-FORMAN. *Japanese Woodcuts: Early Periods.* nd. London. Spring Books. bdg w/silk cord. Japanese-style fld/pub slipcase. F1. $75.00

HAKE. *Eng Quilting.* 1988. np. wrp. G2. $17.95

HAKUSUI, Inami. *Nippon-To: The Japanese Sword.* 1948. Tokyo. Cosmo. 1st ed. 4to. ils/map. 222 p. VG/dj. W1. $125.00

HALACY, D.S. *Ripcord.* 1962. Whitman. VG-. P3. $5.00

HALBERSTAM, David. *Making of a Quagmire.* (1965). Random. 1st ed. F/dj. A7. $65.00

HALBERSTAM, David. *1 Very Hot Day.* (1969). Avon. 1st pb ed. VG+. A7. $15.00

HALDANE, Charlotte. *Last Great Empress of China.* 1965. Bobbs Merrill. 1st ed. 8vo. 304 p. NF/dj. W1. $18.00

HALDEMAN, Joe W. *War Year.* (1972). HRW. 1st ed. sgn. F/F. A7. $125.00

HALDEMAN, Joe. *All My Sins Remembered.* 1977. St Martin. 1st ed. F/dj. P3. $22.50

HALDEMAN, Joe. *Dealing in Futures.* 1985. Viking. 1st ed. F/dj. P3. $16.95

HALDEMAN, Joe. *Hemingway Hoax.* 1990. Morrow. 1st ed. inscr/sgn. F/F. F4. $45.00

HALDEMAN, Joe. *Infinite Dreams.* nd. BC. VG/dj. P3. $7.50

HALDEMAN, Joe. *Mindbridge.* nd. BC. NF/dj. P3. $7.50

HALDEMAN, Joe. *Nebula Awards Stories 17.* 1983. Holt. 1st ed. F/dj. M2. $15.00

HALDEMAN, Linda. *Last Born of Elvinwood.* 1980. Avon. pb. VG+. very scarce. C1. $7.50

HALDEMAN-JULIUS, Marcet. *Famous & Interesting Guests at a KS Farm...* (1936). Girard. Halderman-Julius. wrp. A7. $20.00

HALDEMANN, Jack C. *Vector Analysis.* 1978. Berkley Putnam. 1st ed. VG/dj. P3. $15.00

HALE, Edward Everett. *Man Without a Country.* 1964. Heritage. 55 p. NF/slipcase. S9. $18.00

HALE, Helen. *Dale Evans & Danger in Crooked Can.* 1958. Whitman. G. P3. $5.00

HALE, Hilary. *Winter's Crimes.* 1984. Macmillan. 1st ed. F/dj. P3. $15.00

HALE, Janet Campbell. *Custer Lives in Humboldt Co & Other Poems.* 1978. Greenfield Review. 1st ed. author's 2nd book. F/stapled wrp. L3. $45.00

HALE, Janet Campbell. *Owl's Song.* 1974. Doubleday. 1st ed. author's 1st book. F/NF. very scarce. L3. $125.00

HALE, John P. *Trans-Allegheny Pioneers.* 1931. Charleston, WV. 2nd ed. G/rare dj. D7. $150.00

HALE, John. *Paradise Man.* 1969. Bobbs Merrill. VG/dj. P3. $10.00

HALE, Laura Virginia. *On Chester Street: Presence of Past, Patterns the Future.* 1985. Commercial Pr. w/inscr presentation sheet. 271 p. F. B10. $50.00

HALE, Leon. *TX Outback.* 1973. Madrona Pr. 1st ed. ils De Young. 65 p. F/sans. B19. $15.00

HALE, Louise Closser. *We Discover the Old Dominion.* 1916. NY. 1st ed. ils Walter Hale. VG. B28. $30.00

HALE, Mason E. Jr. *Morden-Smithsonian Expedition to Africa: The Lichens.* 1971. WA, DC. xl. ils/maps. gr cloth. B26. $15.00

HALE, Mrs. *Flora's Interpreter & Fortuna Flora.* 1860. Boston. 1st ed. 288 p. VG. E5. $85.00

HALE, Nathan G. Jr. *James Jackson Putnam & Psychoanalysis...* 1971. Harvard. 1st ed. 384 p. blk cloth. VG/dj. G1. $25.00

HALE, Nathaniel C. *VA Venturer: William Claiborne 1600-77.* ca 1951. Dietz. 340 p. map ep. VG/VG. B10. $35.00

HALE, Sarah J. *Flora's Interpreter & Fortuna Flora.* 1850 (1848). Boston. Mussey. new enlarged ed. 12mo. 288 p. B28. $55.00

HALE & MERRITT. *Hist of TN & Tennesseeans.* 1913. Chicago/NY. 7 (of 8) vols. 8vo. red buckram. H9. $75.00

HALEY, Alex. *Different Kind of Christmas.* 1988. Doubleday. 1st ed. 12mo. 101 p. VG/VG. V3. $12.00

HALEY, Alex. *Roots.* 1976. Doubleday. 1st ed. F/dj. B24. $110.00

HALEY, Delphine. *Seabirds of E N Pacific & Arctic Waters.* 1984. Pacific Search Pr. 1st ed. 214 p. F/F. B19. $30.00

HALEY, Earl. *Revolt on the Painted Desert.* 1952. Hollywood. 1st ed. xl. 376 p. cloth. VG. D3. $12.50

HALEY, Gail. *Abominable Swamp Man.* 1975. Viking. 1st ed. ils. VG/G. P2. $20.00

HALEY, J. Evetts. *George W Littlefield, Texan.* 1972. OK U. ils/notes/index. 287 p. NF/wrp. B19. $10.00

HALEY, J.E. *Charles Goodnight.* 1936. Boston. 1st ed. VG+/G. A15. $150.00

HALEY, Nelson Cole. *Whale Hunt.* (1948). NY. 1st ed. 304 p. A17. $12.50

HALGRIMSON. *Great Scrap Bag Quilts.* 1980. np. ils. wrp. G2. $14.00

HALGRIMSON. *Scraps Can Be Beautiful.* 1979. np. 100 full-size patterns. wrp. G2. $12.00

HALIBURTON, J.C. *Letter-Bag of the Great W; or, Life in a Steamer.* 1840. Phil. 12mo. 189 p. tan brds. G. T3. $39.00

HALKETT, John. *Hist Notes Respecting Indians of N Am.* 1825. London/Edinburgh. Constable. octavo. teg. red morocco. H9. $750.00

HALL, A.D. *Philippines & HI.* ca 1898. NY. Street Smith. reissue. 2 vols in 1. 8vo. H9. $65.00

HALL, Adam. *Berlin Memorandum.* 1965. Collins. 1st ed. VG/VG-. P3. $25.00

HALL, Adam. *Striker Portfolio.* 1969. London. Heinemann. 1st ed. NF/NF. M15. $45.00

HALL, Adam. *Warsaw Document.* 1971. Heinemann. 1st ed. VG/VG-. P3. $25.00

HALL, Adam. *9th Directive.* 1966. Heinemann. 1st ed. VG/VG-. P3. $30.00

HALL, Alexander. *Universalism Against Itself.* 1846. St Clairsville, OH. 1st ed. 480 p. orig leather. G. D7. $75.00

HALL, Angus. *Signs of Things To Come.* 1975. Danbury. decor brds. F. P3. $10.00

HALL, Anna Maria. *Book of Royalty.* 1839. London. Ackermann. 1st ed. lg quarto. 13 pls. aeg. VG. H5. $750.00

HALL, Ansel F. *Handbook of Yosemite Nat Park.* 1921. NY. 1st ed. 12mo. 347 p. pict cloth. VG. D3. $35.00

HALL, Bernard H. *Psychiatrist's World: Selected Papers of Karl Menninger.* 1959. Viking. 1st ed. 931 p. G+/G. S9. $10.00

HALL, C. *Friendship Quilts by Hand & Machine.* 1987. np. sgn. wrp. G2. $17.00

HALL, C. *Romance of the Patchwork Quilt.* 1935. np. wrp. G2. $8.00

HALL, C.E. *Field Notes of DE County.* 1885. Harrisburg. 2nd Geological Survey. 8vo. 14 lithos/24 photos. G. B11. $35.00

HALL, Carrie A. *From Hoop Skirts to Nudity: Review of the Follies...* 1938. Caldwell, ID. ARC/1st ed. w/photo. 240 p. VG. B18. $35.00

HALL, D.J. *Enchanted Sand. A NM Pilgrimage.* 1933. NY. 1st ed. 275 p. cloth. D3. $12.50

HALL, David. *Some Brief Memoirs of Life of David Hall...* 1758. London. Luke Hinde. 1st ed. 12mo. 222 p. worn/rpr leather. V3. $48.00

HALL, Donald. *Carol.* (1988). Concord. Ewert. 1/26. lettered/sgn. C4. $40.00

HALL, Donald. *Here at Eagle Pond.* 1990. NY. 1st ed. ils Nason. 141 p. slipcase. A17. $9.50

HALL, Donald. *Life Work.* 1993. Boston. Beacon. ARC. F/wrp. B2. $30.00

HALL, Donald. *Remembering Poets.* 1978. NY. 1st ed. sgn. F/NF. V1. $30.00

HALL, Donald. *Roof of Tiger Lilies.* 1964. London. 1st ed. sgn. author's 3rd poetry book. F/F. V1. $65.00

HALL, Donald. *Roof of Tiger Lilies. Poems.* 1964. NY. 1st Am ed. sgn. NF/VG+. A11. $50.00

HALL, Donald. *Yel Room: Love Poems.* 1971. NY. 1st ed. sgn. F/F. V1. $50.00

HALL, Francis. *Travels in Canada & US in 1816 & 1817.* 1818. London. 1st ed. fld map. half leather. VG. B28. $275.00

HALL, Gertrude. *Allegretto.* 1894 (1893). Roberts Bros. inscr. 111 p. gilt beige cloth. G+. S10. $65.00

HALL, Granville Stanley. *Life & Confessions of a Psychologist.* 1923. NY. Appleton. 1st ed. prt ruled red cloth. G. G1. $35.00

HALL, Gus. *Marxism & Negro Liberation.* (1951). New Century. 24 p. wrp. A7. $25.00

HALL, Gus. *Negro Freedom.* 1964. New Currents. 16 p. wrp. A7. $15.00

HALL, J.N. *Friends.* 1939. Prairie Pr. 1st ed. 1/380. NF. A15. $60.00

HALL, James. *Bones of Coral.* 1991. Knopf. ARC. sgn. F/F. B2. $60.00

HALL, James. *Bones of Coral.* 1991. Knopf. 1st ed. F/F. P3. $20.00

HALL, James. *Bones of Coral.* 1991. Knopf. 1st ed. sgn. F/F. M15. $40.00

HALL, James. *Races to the Sun.* 1960. Obolensky. 1st ed. F/dj. M2. $15.00

HALL, James. *Tropical Freeze.* 1989. Norton. 1st ed. NF/dj. P3. $20.00

HALL, James. *Us He Devours.* 1964. NY. New Directions. 1st hc ed. sgn twice. F/NF. A11. $35.00

HALL, James. *Yates Paul, His Grand Fights, His Tootings.* 1964. London. 1st ed. sgn. F/NF. A11. $50.00

HALL, Linda. *Alvaro Obregon.* (1981). TX A&M U. 1st ed. 290 p. dj. F3. $20.00

HALL, Marshall. *Memoirs of...* 1861. London. Bentley. 518 p. orig Victorian pressed cloth. G. G7. $195.00

HALL, Melvin. *Bird of Time.* 1949. Scribner. 1st ed. 8vo. 307 p. VG+/VG. A2. $15.00

HALL, Mrs. Herman. *Two Travelers in Europe.* 1913. Springfield, MA. royal 8vo. 602 p. aeg. half leather. F. H3. $40.00

HALL, Norman. *Botanist of the Eucalypts.* 1912. San Francisco. ils. 282 p. VG. B26. $24.00

HALL, Oakley. *Murder City.* 1950. London. 1st ed. inscr. VG+/VG. A11. $60.00

HALL, Oakley. *So Many Doors.* 1950. NY. 1st ed. sgn. F/NF. A11. $55.00

HALL, Parnell. *Client.* 1990. Donald Fine. 1st ed. F/dj. P3. $18.95

HALL, Pearl Crist. *Long Road to Freedom: One Person's Discovery of Death.* 1978. Richmond, IN. Friends United Pr. 12mo. 138 p. VG. V3. $8.00

HALL, Radclyffe. *Well of Loneliness.* nd. Bl Ribbon. VG. P3. $20.00

HALL, Rex. *Desert Hath Pearls.* 1975. Melbourne. Hawthorne. 1st ed. 219 p. F/NF. M7. $75.00

HALL, Richard. *Fidelities: Book of Stories.* 1992. Viking/Penguin. 1st ed. author's 3rd book. NF/NF clip. A14. $25.00

HALL, Robert Lee. *Exit Sherlock Holmes: Great Detective's Final Days.* 1977. London. Murray. 1st ed. F/F. S5. $27.50

HALL, Rodney. *Captivity Captive.* 1988. Farrar Straus. 1st ed. author's 2nd book. F/F. Q1. $25.00

HALL, Roger. *19.* nd. Norton. 2nd ed. VG/dj. P3. $8.00

HALL, Wendy. *Finns & Their Country.* (1967). London. Parrish. 1st ed. 8vo. 224 p. F/F clip. A2. $122.50

HALL & HAYWOOD. *Perfect Pineapples.* 1989. np. ils. wrp. G2. $15.00

HALL & HAYWOOD. *Precision-Pieced Quilts Using the Foundation Method.* 1992. np. cloth. G2. $25.00

HALL & NORDHOFF. *Botany Bay.* 1941. Boston. 1st ed. 8vo. 374 p. map ep. silvered bl cloth. F. H3. $25.00

HALL & NORDHOFF. *Mutiny on the Bounty.* 1960. NY. Lg Type ed. 4to. 396 p. dk gr cloth. F/VG. H3. $35.00

HALL & NORDHOFF. *Pitcairn's Island.* 1934. Boston. 1st ed. 338 p. silvered red cloth. VG. H3. $20.00

HALL & NORDHOFF. *Pitcairn's Island.* 1934. Boston. 1st ed/2nd prt. 338 p. map ep. reddish-orange cloth. VG. H3. $20.00

HALL. *Book of Handwoven Coverlets.* 1988. np. reprint of 1912 ed. wrp. G2. $7.00

HALLAHAN, William. *Catch Me, Kill Me.* 1978. London. Gollancz. 1st British ed. F/NF. S5. $25.00

HALLAHAN, William. *Keeping of the Children.* 1978. Morrow. 1st ed. F/NF. N3. $40.00

HALLDORSSON, Haukur. *Trolls in Icelandic Folklore.* 1982. Bokautgafan Orn Og Orlygur. F/dj. P3. $15.00

HALLE, Louis. *Transcaribbean.* 1936. Longman Gr. 1st ed. 311 p. cloth. F3. $20.00

HALLENBERG, Georgius. *Dissertatio Medica, de Vertigine.* 1774. Upsaliae. 14 p. sewn. G7. $25.00

HALLET, Richard. *Rolling World.* 1938. Houghton Mifflin. 1st ed. 8vo. 346 p. VG+/G+. A2. $25.00

HALLIBURTON, Richard. *7 League Boots.* (1935). Bobbs Merrill. sgn. 417 p. A7. $20.00

HALLIDAY, Brett. *Blood on Biscayne Bay.* 1946. Ziff Davis. 1st ed. xl. dj. P3. $7.50

HALLIDAY, Brett. *Die Like a Dog.* 1959. NY. Dodd Mead. 1st ed. F/NF. Q1. $35.00

HALLIDAY, Brett. *Dividend on Death.* 1942. Sun Dial. VG. P3. $10.00

HALLIDAY, Brett. *Murder & the Married Virgin.* 1948. Triangle. VG/dj. P3. $12.00

HALLIDAY, Brett. *Murder Takes No Holiday.* 1960. Dodd Mead. 1st ed. NF/NF. Q1. $35.00

HALLIDAY, Brett. *Never Kill a Client.* 1962. Dodd Mead. 1st ed. F/NF. Q1. $35.00

HALLIDAY, Brett. *She Woke to Darkness.* 1954. Torquil. 1st ed. NF/dj. P3. $20.00

HALLIDAY, Brett. *Uncomplaining Corpses.* 1940. Holt. 1st ed. pict brds. VG. Q1. $60.00

HALLIDAY, Fred. *Ambler.* 1983. Simon Schuster. 1st ed. VG/dj. P3. $13.95

HALLINAN, Timothy. *Everything But the Squeal.* 1990. NAL. 1st ed. VG/dj. P3. $17.95

HALLINAN, Vincent. *Lion in Court.* 1963. Putnam. G/worn. M11. $25.00

HALLIWELL, Leslie. *Mtn of Dreams Paramount Picture.* 1976. Stonehill. 1st ed. VG/dj. P3. $25.00

HALLOCK, Charles. *Sportsman's Gazetteer & General Guide.* 1879. NY. Orange Judd. 5th ed. thick 8vo. 2 fld maps. violet cloth. H9. $95.00

HALLOCK. *Fast Patch: Treasury of Strip-Quilt Projects.* 1989. np. ils. wrp. G2. $18.00

HALLOCK. *Scrap Quilts Using Fast Patch.* 1991. np. cloth. G2. $25.00

HALPER, Albert. *Chicago Sideshow.* 1932. np. 1/100. sgn/#d. F/8vo gr wrp. A11. $245.00

HALPERN, Daniel. *Lady Knifethrower.* 1975. Binghamton. 1/350. sgn. F/8vo wrp. A11. $30.00

HALPERN. *Full-Color Russian Folk Needlepoint Design.* 1976. np. 34 full-p designs. wrp. G2. $6.00

HALPIN, Marjorie. *Catlin's Indian Gallery.* 1965. Smithsonian. 32 p. D2. $15.00

HALSEY, Francis Whiting. *Literary Digest Hist of WWI.* 1919. Funk Wagnall. 1st ed. 12mo. VG. A8. $6.00

HALSEY, Harlan Page. *Macon Moore, the S Detective.* (1881). NY. Ogilvie. 1st ed. 12mo. 1 pl. 161 p. prt wrp. M1. $375.00

HALSEY, Margaret. *Some of My Best Friends.* 1944. Simon Schuster. 1st ed. VG/G. A8. $10.00

HALSEY, Margaret. *With Malice Toward Some.* 1938. Simon Schuster. 1st ed. 8vo. 278 p. VG+/G+. A2. $15.00

HALSTEAD, Murat. *Life & Achievements of Admiral Dewey From Montpelier...* 1899. Chicago. Our Possessions. 8vo. 67 pls. 468 p. alligator skin. VG. B11. $45.00

HALSTEAD, Murat. *Life & Achievements of Admiral Dewey...* ca 1899. Chicago. royal 8vo. 452 p. pict brn cloth. G. T3. $24.00

HAMARNEH & STEIB. *Pharmacy Mus & Hist Collections on Public View in US...* 1981. Madison, WI. Am Inst of Hist of Pharmacy. ils. 144 p. F/wrp. S9. $5.00

HAMBLETON, Jack. *Hunter's Holidays.* (1947). Tor. 1st ed. 207 p. VG. A17. $15.00

HAMBLY, Barbara. *Darkmage.* nd. BC. VG/dj. P3. $10.00

HAMBLY, Barbara. *Those Who Hunt the Night.* 1988. Del Rey. 1st ed. F/dj. P3. $20.00

HAMBOURG & PHILLIPS. *New Vision, Photography Between the World Wars.* 1991. NY. F/F. B30. $45.00

HAMILTON, Alex. *Splinters.* 1968. Walker. 1st ed. VG/dj. P3. $25.00

HAMILTON, Alexander. *New Account of the E Indies.* 1930. London. Argonaut. 1/975. 2 vols. ils/maps. M/slipcase. O6. $575.00

HAMILTON, Bob. *Gene Autry & the Redwood Pirates.* (1946). Racine, WI. 12mo. 248 p. pict ep. VG. D3. $12.50

HAMILTON, Charles. *Collecting Autographs & Manuscripts.* 1961. np. 2nd ed. ils/index. 269 p. dj. O7. $65.00

HAMILTON, Charles. *Justice Standeth Afar Off.* 1977. Aberdeen, MS. private prt. 92 p. prt wrp. M11. $45.00

HAMILTON, Charles. *Signature of Am.* 1979. np. 1st ed. 4to. ils/index. 278 p. dj. O7. $45.00

HAMILTON, Donald. *Line of Fire.* 1955. Dell. 1st ed/PBO. F/wrp. M15. $45.00

HAMILTON, Edmond. *Battle for the Stars.* 1961. Torquil. 1st ed. xl. dj. P3. $10.00

HAMILTON, Edmond. *City at World's End.* 1951. Frederick Fell. 1st ed. F/NF. F4. $75.00

HAMILTON, Edmond. *Star Kings.* 1949. NY. Frederick Fell. 1st ed. NF/NF. Q1. $75.00

HAMILTON, Edmond. *Star of Life.* 1959. Dodd Mead. 1st ed. inscr/sgn. NF/dj. F4. $75.00

HAMILTON, Frank Hastings. *Practical Treatise on Military Surgery.* 1861. NY. Bailliere. 1st ed. 234 p. cloth. VG. M8. $350.00

HAMILTON, Franklin; see Silverberg, Robert.

HAMILTON, Jane. *Map of the World.* 1994. Doubleday. ARC. F/wrp. B2. $40.00

HAMILTON, Patrick. *Resources of AZ.* 1884. San Francisco. Bancroft. 12mo. 19 lithos. 414 p. orange cloth. lacks fld pl. H9. $120.00

HAMILTON, Robert M. *Canadian Book-Prices Current, Vol 1, 1950-55.* 1957. McClelland Stewart. 1st ed. 158 p. F/dj. B19. $15.00

HAMILTON, Sinclair W. *Adam Ramage & His Pr.* 1942. Southworth-Anthoeson Pr. 1/350. 33 p. G/pict wrp. B14. $35.00

HAMLIN, A. *Battle of Chancellorsville: Jackson's Attack.* 1896. Bangor, ME. 1st ed. xl. 196 p. F. O7. $65.00

HAMLIN, Myra Sawyer. *Nan in the City.* 1897. Roberts Bros. 12mo. 251 p. VG. S10. $40.00

HAMMACHER, A.M. *Evolution of Modern Sculpture.* (ca 1969). Abrams. lg 4to. 383 p. silvered bl cloth. F/VG. F1. $85.00

HAMMEL, E.A. *Power in Ica.* (1969). Little Brn. 1st ed. 142 p. wrp. F3. $10.00

HAMMEL, Eric. *Ambush Valley.* 1990. Presidio. 1st ed. F/F. A7. $17.00

HAMMEL, Eric. *Fire in the Streets: Battle for Hue, Tet 1968.* (1991). Chicago. Contemporary Books. 1st ed. 371 p. F/F. A7. $16.00

HAMMEL, Eric. *Khe Sanh: Siege in the Clouds.* (1989). Crown. 1st ed. 508 p. NF/dj. A7. $27.00

HAMMER, Kenneth. *Little Big Horn Biographies.* 1965. Custer Battlefield & Hist Mus Assn. revised ed. NF/wrp. B19. $20.00

HAMMER, Richard. *One Morning in the War.* (1970). London. 1st ed. NF/NF. A7. $35.00

HAMMETT, Dashiell. *Big Knockover.* nd. Random. 2nd ed. VG/VG. P3. $15.00

HAMMETT, Dashiell. *Blood Money.* 1944. Dell 53. 3rd ed/1st prt. NF. B2. $35.00

HAMMETT, Dashiell. *Creeps by Night.* 1931. John Day. 1st ed. VG. P3. $25.00

HAMMETT, Dashiell. *Maltese Falcon.* (1987). Franklin Lib. 1st thus ed. silver gilt blk vinyl. F. B3. $60.00

HAMMETT, Dashiell. *Maltese Falcon.* 1930. Knopf. 1st ed. brds. VG. P3. $300.00

HAMMETT, Dashiell. *Maltese Falcon.* 1930. NY. Knopf. 1st ed. octavo. 267 p. aeg. Sutcliffe morocco. NF. H5. $1,000.00

HAMMETT, Dashiell. *Maltese Falcon.* 1983. Arion Pr. 1/400. 4to. 291 p. w/prospectus. F/gray cloth slipcase. F1. $425.00

HAMMETT, Dashiell. *Man Called Spade.* 1945. Dell 90. 3rd ed/1st prt. NF/wrp. B2. $45.00

HAMMETT, Dashiell. *Return of the Continental Op.* 1947. Dell 154. 2nd ed. NF/wrp. B2. $45.00

HAMMETT, Dashiell. *Thin Man.* 1934. Knopf. 1st ed. G. P3. $75.00

HAMMETT, Dashiell. *Woman in the Dark.* 1988. Knopf. 1st hc ed. sgn. new intro by RB Parker. F/F. S5. $40.00

HAMMETT, Dashiell. *Woman in the Dark.* 1988. London. 1st ed. intro/sgn Parker. F/F. A11. $55.00

HAMMILL, Joel. *Limbo.* 1980. Arbor. 1st ed. VG/dj. P3. $12.50

HAMMILL, Joel. *Trident.* 1981. Arbor. 1st ed. F/dj. M2. $10.00

HAMMILL, Sam. *Catullus Redivivus.* 1986. Bl Begonia. sgn. NF/wrp. A7. $20.00

HAMMOND, George P. *Digging for Gold Without a Shovel.* 1967. Rostenstock/Old W Pub. 1st ed. 1/1250. folio. F. E5. $45.00

HAMMOND, George P. *Informal Record of..., & His Era in Bancroft Lib.* 1965. Friends Bancroft Lib. 1st ed. ils. 119 p. NF/sans. B19. $35.00

HAMMOND, George P. *Treaty of Guadalupe Hidalgo, Feb 2, 1848.* 1949. Berkeley. Friends of Bancroft Lib. w/map. 1/500 sets. NF. O6. $300.00

HAMMOND, Gerald. *Cousin Once Removed.* 1984. London. Macmillan. 1st ed. NF/dj. S5. $20.00

HAMMOND, John Martin. *Quaint & Hist Forts of N Am.* 1915. Phil/London. Lippincott. 1st ed. 309 p. cloth. VG+. M8. $250.00

HAMMOND, Lawrence. *Movie Treasury Thriller Movies.* 1974. Octopus. VG/dj. P3. $15.00

HAMMOND. *New Adventures in Needlepoint Design.* 1973. np. ils. cloth. G2. $9.00

HAMMOND. *Tifaifai & Quilts of Polynesia.* 1986. np. patterns. wrp. G2. $17.00

HAMMONDS, Michael. *Among the Hunted.* nd. BC. VG/dj. P3. $5.00

HAMNERIN, Petrus. *Specimen Medico-Chirurgicum de Insigni Capitis Tumore...* 1735. Upsaliae. sm 4to. 8 p. sewn as issued. G7. $75.00

HAMPDEN, John. *Ghost Stories.* 1939. JM Dent. 1st ed. VG. P3. $35.00

HAMPTON & HASKINS. *Hamp: An Autobiography.* (1989). Warner. 280 p. F/F. A7. $17.00

HAMRICK, Hayme H. *Hamrick & Other Families: Indian Lore.* 1984. Parsons, WV. 2nd ed. 144 p. bl cloth. VG. D7. $15.00

HAMSIK, Susan. *Writers Against Rulers.* (1971). Random. 1st Am ed. 208 p. NF/dj. A7. $13.00

HAMSUN, Knut. *Wanderer: Under the Autumn Star & Other Muted Strings.* 1975. FSG. 1st ed. trans from Norwegian. NF/NF. A14. $25.00

HAMY, Alfred. *Au MS la Premiere Explorations.* 1903. Paris. 8vo. 329 p. half red morocco. H9. $50.00

HANAFORD, Phebe A. *Abraham Lincoln: His Life & Public Services.* 1904. np. 12mo. ils. 277 p. bl cloth. G. T3. $15.00

HANCE, Robert A. *Destination Earth II.* 1977. Vantage. VG/dj. P3. $10.00

HANCOCK, Elizabeth H. *Autobiography of John E Massey.* 1909. Neale. 312 p. VG. B10. $90.00

HANCOCK, H. Irving. *Dave Darrin After the Mine Layers.* 1919. Altemus. 1st ed. VG/dj. M2. $25.00

HANCOCK, H. Irving. *Dave Darrin's 3rd Yr at Annapolis.* 1910. Altemus. 1st ed. G+/worn. M2. $20.00

HANCOCK, Ralph. *Fabulous Boulevard.* 1949. NY. 1st ed. sgn. 322 p. pict brds. D3. $25.00

HANDFORTH, Thomas. *Faraway Meadow.* 1939. Jr Literary Guild/Doubleday Doran. 1st thus ed. VG/G. A3. $35.00

HANDLIN, Oscar. *Adventure in Freedom: 300 Yrs of Jewish Life in Am.* (1954). McGraw Hill. 1st ed. 8vo. 282 p. F-/VG clip. A2. $15.00

HANDLIN, Oscar. *Newcomers: Negros & Puerto Ricans in Changing Metropolis.* 1959. Cambridge. 171 p. dj. A7. $23.00

HANDY, W.C. *Blues.* 1926. NY. Boni. 1st ed. NF. B2. $250.00

HANDY, W.C. *Father of the Blues.* 1941. Macmillan. 1st ed. inscr/dtd 1941. F/NF. B2. $350.00

HANDY, W.C. *WC Handy's Collection of Blues.* nd. NY. Robbins. 1st ed. 36 p. VG. B2. $50.00

HANENKRAT, William Frank. *Education of a Turkey Hunter.* (1974). NY. ils. 216 p. A17. $12.00

HANEY, Lwis Haney. *Congressional Hist of Railways in US to 1850; 1850-1887.* 1908-10. Madison, WI. 1st ed. 2 vols. rebound lib buckram. D3. $60.00

HANKE, Lewis. *Spanish Struggle for Justice in Conquest of Am.* (1949). Little Brn. 2nd prt. 217 p. F3. $15.00

HANKS, Charles Stedman. *Camp Kits & Camp Life.* 1906. NY. Outing Pr. 1st ed. 12mo. 259 p. pict cloth. G. A17. $20.00

HANKS, O.T. *Hist of Capt BF Benton's Co, Hood's TX Brigade, 1861-65.* nd. Austin, TX. 1st ed. 1/300. F/prt wrp. M8. $37.50

HANLEY. *Needlepoint in Am.* 1979. np. cloth. G2. $13.00

HANLEY. *Needlepoint.* 1964. np. ils. cloth. G2. $9.00

HANLIN & MARTIN. *Heirs of Hippocrates.* 1974. IA City. Friends of U of IA Libs. ils/index. 142 p. wrp. S9. $13.00

HANNA, Phil Townsend. *CA Through 4 Centuries.* 1935. Farrar Rinehart. 1st ed. 212 p. VG. B19. $35.00

HANNAH, Barry. *Airships.* 1978. Knopf. 1st ed. F/NF. B2. $30.00

HANNAH, Barry. *Blk Butterfly.* 1982. Palaemon. 1/150. sgn. F/prt wrp. C4. $65.00

HANNAH, Barry. *Hey Jack!* (1987). Dutton. 1st ed. F/F. B3. $20.00

HANNAH, Barry. *Ray: A Novel.* 1980. NY. 1st ed. sgn. F/F. A11. $40.00

HANNAH, Barry. *2 Stories.* (1982). Nouveau Pr. 1/200. sgn. F/wrp/dj. B4. $85.00

HANNAWAY, Patti. *Winslow Homer in the Tropics.* 1972. Richmond, VA. Westover. 296 p. cloth. dj. D2. $135.00

HANNON, Ezra; see Hunter, Evan.

HANNON, J.G. *Boston-Newton Co Venture.* 1969. Lincoln, NE. 1st ed. ils/maps. 224 p. F/F. B28. $35.00

HANNUM, Alberta. *Spin a Silver Dollar.* 1946. NY. 3rd prt. 12 color pls. 173 p. pict cloth. VG/rpr dj. D3. $25.00

HANSBERRY, Lorraine. *Les Blancs: Collected Last Plays of Lorraine Hansberry.* 1972. Random. 1st ed. F/F. B2. $45.00

HANSBERRY, Lorraine. *Sgn in Sidney Brustein's Window.* 1965. Random. 1st ed. NF/NF. B2. $65.00

HANSEN, Joseph. *Brandsetter & Others: Five Fictions.* 1984. Woodstock, VT. Foul Play. 1st ed. NF/NF. A14. $30.00

HANSEN, Joseph. *Death Claims.* 1973. Harper Row. 1st ed. NF/NF. A14. $60.00

HANSEN, Joseph. *Fadeout.* 1972. London. Harrap. 1st British ed. NF/NF. S5. $45.00

HANSEN, Joseph. *Man Everybody Was Afraid Of.* 1978. NY. Holt. 1st ed. sgn. F/F. S5. $40.00

HANSEN, Joseph. *Nightwork.* 1984. HRW. 1st ed. NF/NF. A14. $30.00

HANSEN, Joseph. *Obedience.* 1988. Mysterious. 1st ed. F/F. F4. $17.00

HANSEN, Joseph. *Skinflick.* 1979. HRW. 1st ed. NF/NF. A14. $40.00

HANSEN, Joseph. *Strange Marriage.* 1965. Argyle Books. 1st ed. 2nd book under Colton nome d'plume. F/NF. A14. $125.00

HANSEN, Joseph. *Troublemaker.* 1985. Harper Row. 1st ed. NF/NF. A14. $50.00

HANSEN, Robert P. *Back to the Wall.* 1957. Morrow. 1st ed. VG/torn. P3. $15.00

HANSEN, Robert P. *Trouble Comes Double.* 1954. Morrow. VG/VG-. P3. $20.00

HANSON, Charles H. *Land of Greece Described & Ils.* 1886. London. sm 4to. ils/3 maps. 400 p. decor cloth. O2. $185.00

HANSON, Christilot. *Canadian Entry.* 1966. Chicago. Follet. 1st Am ed. VG/VG. O3. $22.00

HANSON, Earl Parker. *S From the Spanish Main.* 1967. Delacorte. 1st ed. 8vo. 463 p. gr cloth. F/VG. B11. $40.00

HANSON, George A. *Old Kent: E Shore of MD.* 1876. Baltimore. 1st ed. 383 p. G. D7. $200.00

HANSON, Maurice. *Pierpont the Foxhound.* 1939. Scribner. 1st ed. ils DT Carlyle. VG+. O3. $35.00

HANSON. *Calendar Quilts.* 1991. np. ils. wrp. G2. $17.00

HAPGOOD, Hutchins. *Types From City Streets.* 1910. Funk Wagnall. 1st ed. F. B2. $100.00

HARASZTHY, Agoston. *Grape Cluture, Wines & Wine-Making.* 1862. NY. 1st ed. octavo. ils. orig plum cloth. VG. H5. $1,000.00

HARASZTY. *Embroiderer's Portfolio of Flower Designs.* 1991. np. sbdg. G2. $25.00

HARBEN, Will N. *Land of the Changing Sun.* 1975. Boston. Gregg. reprint of 1894 ed. F/sans. N3. $30.00

HARBOUR, Dave. *Advanced Wild Turkey Hunting & World Records.* (1983). Winchester. later prt. 8vo. taped dj. A17. $15.00

HARCOURT, Helen. *FL Fruits & How To Raise Them.* 1886. Louisville. revised ed. 347 p. gilt cloth. VG. B26. $65.00

HARCOURT, Palma. *Limited Options.* 1987. Detective BC. VG. P3. $7.50

HARCOURT, Palma. *Shadows of Doubt.* 1983. London. Collins. 1st ed. NF/dj. S5. $25.00

HARDEN, John. *Devil's Tramping Ground & Other NC Mystery Stories.* 1949. Chapel Hill. 1st ed/2nd prt. 178 p. cloth. NF/VG. M8. $30.00

HARDIE & SABIN. *War Posters Issued by Belligerent & Neutral Nations...1919.* 1920. London. Blk. 1st ed. 4to. olive cloth. B20. $225.00

HARDING, Bertita. *Mosaic in the Fountain.* (1949). Lippincott. 1st ed. 320 p. dj. F3. $15.00

HARDING, George L. *Pub Writings of Carl Irving Wheat.* 1960. San Francisco. 1/350. M/decor wrp. O6. $85.00

HARDING, Silvester. *Shakespeare Ils, by an Assemblage of Portraits & Views...* 1793. London. Harding. folio. 148 pls w/tissue gards. contemporary bdg. H5. $1,000.00

HARDING, Todd; see Reynolds, Mack.

HARDINGE, Emma. *Modern Am Spiritualism.* 1870. NY. self pub. 2nd ed. thick 8vo. pls. VG. G1. $75.00

HARDINGE, Emma. *19th-Century Miracles; or, Spirits & Their Work...* 1883. Manchester, Eng. early prt. thick 8vo. 556 p. G1. $75.00

HARDINGE, George. *Winter's Crimes II.* 1980. St Martin. 1st ed. F/dj. P3. $15.00

HARDMAN, Francis. *Frontier Life.* ca 1890. Porter Coates. xl. 12mo. 376 p. gilt cloth. VG. D3. $25.00

HARDMAN, Francis. *Frontier Life; or, Scenes & Adventures in SW.* 1857. np. 376 p. G. scarce. O7. $65.00

HARDWICK, Elizabeth. *Ghostly Lover.* 1945. NY. 1st ed. sgn. VG+/VG+ clip. A11. $85.00

HARDWICK, Michael. *Guide to Jane Austen.* 1971. NY. 1st Am ed. F/NF. A11. $25.00

HARDWICK, Michael. *Prisoner of the Devil.* 1980. Proteus. 3rd ed. F/dj. P3. $15.00

HARDWICK, Michael. *Private Life of Dr Watson.* 1983. Dutton. 1st ed. F/dj. P3. $25.00

HARDWICK, Michael. *Revenge of the Hound.* 1987. Villard. 1st ed. F/F. F4. $20.00

HARDWICK, Mollie. *Malice Domestic.* 1986. Century. 1st ed. F/dj. P3. $20.00

HARDWICK & HARDWICK. *Writer's Houses.* 1963. Phoenix House. 1st ed. 102 p. NF/VG. M7. $30.00

HARDY, Adam; see Blumer, Kenneth.

HARDY, Phil. *Samuel Fuller.* 1970. NY. 1st Am ed/hc issue. F/NF clip. A11. $35.00

HARDY, Thomas. *From Hardy at Max Gate: Series of Letters...* 1979. Bryn Mawr. ltd ed. 30 p. F/pict wrp. C4. $30.00

HARDY, Thomas. *Human Shows Far Phantasies, Songs & Trifles.* 1925. Macmillan. 1st ed. 279 p. gr cloth. VG/dj. M20. $50.00

HARDY, Thomas. *Late Lyrics & Earlier.* 1922. London. Macmillan. 1st ed. NF/NF. C4. $75.00

HARDY, Thomas. *Life & Art.* 1925. Greenberg. 1/200. F/NF. C4. $65.00

HARDY, Thomas. *Life's Little Ironies.* 1894. London. 1st ed. presentation. gr polished calf/marbled brds. F/case. H5. $4,500.00

HARDY, Thomas. *Mayor of Casterbridge.* nd. Modern Lib. intro Joyce Kilmer. bl brds. E3. $8.00

HARDY, Thomas. *Moments of Vision.* 1917. London. 1st ed. G. A1. $50.00

HARDY, Thomas. *Return of the Native.* 1878. London. 1st ed. octavo. 3 vols. reddish-brn cloth. rpr hinge. F. H5. $9,500.00

HARDY, Thomas. *Tess of the D'Urbervilles.* 1891. London. 1st ed/1st prt. octavo. 3 vols. VG/morocco slipcase. H5. $7,500.00

HARDY, Thomas. *Under the Greenwood Tree.* 1913. Chatto Windus. ils Keith Henderson. G. A1. $30.00

HARDY, Thomas. *Writings of Thomas Hardy in Prose & Verse.* nd. (1920). NY. Harper. Anniversary ed. 1/1250. octavo. 21 vols. VG. H5. $5,000.00

HARDY, W.J. *Book-Plates.* 1897. London. Kegan Paul. 2nd ed/1st this format. 8vo. 240 p. gr cloth. B20. $75.00

HARDY, William. *Little Sin.* 1958. Dodd Mead. 1st ed. xl. dj. P3. $5.00

HARDY & SHAFER. *Wicker Man.* 1978. Crown. 1st ed. F/dj. M2. $35.00

HARE, Cyril. *With a Bare Bodkin.* 1946. London. Faber. 1st ed. VG/VG. M15. $45.00

HARGRAVE. *Heirloom Machine Quilting: A Comprehensive Guide...* 1989. np. ils. wrp. G2. $20.00

HARGRAVE. *Mastering Machine Quilting.* 1992. np. wrp. G2. $20.00

HARGREAVES, H.A. *North by 2000.* 1975. Peter Martin Assoc. 1st ed. RS. F/dj. P3. $25.00

HARGREAVES, Reginald. *Enemy at the Gates.* 1948. Harrisburg, PA. Military Service Pub. 1st Am ed. 8vo. 371 p. VG/G. A2. $20.00

HARIOT, Thomas. *Brief & True Report of New Found Land of VA.* 1951. NY. Hist BC. 1st of facsimile series. 12mo. pict brds. slipcase/box. H9. $65.00

HARKNESS, Georgia. *John Calvin: Man & His Ethics.* ca 1931. Holt. index. 266 p. H10. $20.00

HARKNESS, Ruth. *Pangoan Diary.* (1942). Creative Age. 1st ed. 8vo. 295 p. F/VG. A2. $25.00

HARLAND, Marion. *Under the Flag of the Orient.* 1897. Hist Pub. 446 p. VG-. S3. $25.00

HARLEY, John Brian. *Mapping the Am Revolutionary War.* 1978. Chicago/London. lg 4to. 187 p. gray cloth. dj. H9. $65.00

HARLEY & WOODWARD. *Hist of Cartography, Vol 1.* 1987. Chicago. M/dj. O6. $100.00

HARLOW, Alvin F. *Brass-Pounders: Young Telegraphers of the Civil War.* 1962. Denver. Sage Books. 1st ed. cloth. NF/VG. M8. $35.00

HARLOW, Neal. *Maps of the Pueblo Lands of San Diego.* 1987. LA. Dawson Book Shop. 1/375. sgn. 244 p. VG+. P4. $225.00

HARLOW & HARRAR. *TB of Dendrology Covering Important Forest Trees of US...* 1958. McGraw Hill. 4th ed. ils/photos. 561 p. VG. A17. $15.00

HARMETZ, Aljean. *Making of the Wizard of Oz.* 1977. Knopf. 1st ed. VG/VG. L1. $30.00

HARMON, William. *Treasure Holiday.* 1970. Wesley U. 1st ed. VG+/stiff wrp. V1. $20.00

HARMONIAE, Philos. *Selection of Hymns & Poems for Use of Believers.* 1833. Watevliet. 186 p. leather/red spine label. G. rare. D7. $1,150.00

HARNER, Michael. *Jivaro. People of the Sacred Waterfalls.* 1972. Doubleday. 1st ed. 233 p. dj. F3. $25.00

HARPER, Charles. *Brighton Road.* 1922. Hartford. revised ed. 12mo. presentation. 277 p. w/newspaper review. O3. $40.00

HARPER, George W. *Gypsy Earth.* 1982. Doubleday. F/dj. P3. $15.00

HARPER, Harriet Wadsworth. *Around the World in 80 Yrs on Side-Saddle.* 1966. NY. sm 4to. photos. 30 p. scarce. O3. $125.00

HARPER, Henry H. *Book Lovers, Bibliomaniacs & Book Clubs.* 1904. Riverside. 1st ed. presentation. 96 p. full brn morocco. B20. $125.00

HARPER, Michael. *Afro-Am Chapbook.* 1978-79. Beloit Poetry Journal. special issue. editor/sgn Harper. NF/gr wrp. A11. $30.00

HARPER, Michael. *Healing Song for the Inner Ear.* 1984. IL U. 1st ed. inscr/sgn. F/F. V1. $25.00

HARPER, R.G. *Observations on Dispute Between US & France.* 1798. Phil. 8vo. 110 p. leather. G. T3. $52.00

HARPER, Wilhelmina. *Uncle Sam's Story Book.* 1944. McKay/Jr Literary Guild. 1st ed. 4to. 144 p. pict bl cloth. T5. $10.00

HARRADEN, Breatrice. *Master Roley.* 1889. London. Warne. 1st ed. 156 p. VG. S10. $45.00

HARRE, T. Everett. *Behold the Woman.* 1916. Lippincott. NF. M2. $15.00

HARRIMAN, M.C. *And the Price Is Right.* (1958). Cleveland. 1st ed. ils. 318 p. VG/dj. B18. $9.50

HARRINGTON, Alan. *Revelations of Dr Modesto.* 1955. Knopf. 1st ed. author's 1st book. F/NF. B2. $100.00

HARRINGTON, G.F. *Inside: Chronicle of Secession.* 1866. NY. 1st ed. ils Thomas Nast. 223 p. pebbled brn cloth. VG. T3. $45.00

HARRINGTON, John P. *Ethnography of the Tewa Indians.* 1916. GPO. 4to. 21 pls/31 maps. olive cloth. VG. P4. $150.00

HARRINGTON, Richard. *Face of the Arctic.* 1952. NY. 1st ed. 8vo. 369 p. map ep. VG. H3. $35.00

HARRIOT, Thomas. *Brief & True Report of New Found Land of VA.* 1972. Dover. facsimile of 1590 ed. 4to. VG/wrp. B11. $12.00

HARRIS, Alfred. *Baroni.* 1975. Putnam. 1st ed. VG/dj. P3. $15.00

HARRIS, C. Fiske. *Catalogue of Am Poetry...* 1883. Providence, RI. 1st ed. sq 16mo. 83 p. lacks front wrp. M1. $125.00

HARRIS, Clare. *Away From Here & Now.* 1947. Dorrance. 1st ed. F/dj. M2. $35.00

HARRIS, David. *Goliath.* 1970. Sidereal Pr. 1st ed. F/NF. A7. $30.00

HARRIS, Frank. *Bernard Shaw.* 1931. Gollancz. 2nd ed. VG. P3. $17.50

HARRIS, Geraldine. *Children of the Wind.* 1982. Greenwillow. 1st ed. VG/G. P3. $12.50

HARRIS, Herbert. *John Creasey's Crime Collection 1983* 1983. St Martin. 1st ed. xl. dj. P3. $7.50

HARRIS, Herbert. *John Creasey's Mystery Bedside 1976.* 1975. Hodder Stoughton. VG/dj. P3. $17.50

HARRIS, Hyde. *Kyd for Hire.* 1977. London. Gollancz. 1st British/1st hc ed. VG+/dj. S5. $35.00

HARRIS, J.R. *Angler's Entomology.* nd. Woodstock. 1st ed. 268 p. F/dj. A17. $17.50

HARRIS, Joel Chandler. *Daddy Jake the Runaway & Short Stories Told After Dark.* 1889. NY. Century. 1st ed. quarto. pict brds. NF. R3. $600.00

HARRIS, Joel Chandler. *Daddy Jake the Runaway & Short Stories Told After Dark.* 1889. NY. Century. 1st ed. quarto. 145 p. glazed prt brds. F/prt slipcase. B24. $1,250.00

HARRIS, Joel Chandler. *On the Wing of Occasions.* 1900. Doubleday Page. 310 p. cloth/pict label. G+. M20. $40.00

HARRIS, Joel Chandler. *Told by Uncle Remus: New Stories of Old Plantation.* 1905. McClure Phillips. 1st ed. 295 p. VG. P2. $90.00

HARRIS, Joel Chandler. *Uncle Remus; or, Mr Fox, Mr Rabbit & Mr Terrapin.* 1881. London. Routledge. 1st complete Eng ed. 16mo. pict wrp. VG/clamshell case. H5. $2,000.00

HARRIS, Joel Chandler. *Uncle Remus: His Songs & His Sayings.* 1921. Grosset Dunlap. rew/revised ed. 8vo. 270 p. A3. $13.00

HARRIS, Joel Chandler. *Uncle Remus: His Songs & Sayings.* 1983. Birmingham, AL. S Classics Lib. 1st thus ed. VG. L1. $75.00

HARRIS, John. *Resource Bibliography for Decipherment of Maya Heiroglyphs.* 1994. Phil. U Mus. 1st ed. 4to. 28 p. M/wrp. F3. $8.00

HARRIS, Julia Collier. *Life & Letters of Joel Chandler Harris.* (1918). Houghton Mifflin. later prt. inscr twice. NF. B4. $125.00

HARRIS, Laura. *Animated Noah's Ark.* 1945. Grosset Dunlap. ils Julian Wehr/4 movables. VG/worn. D1. $225.00

HARRIS, Mark. *City of Discontent.* 1952. Indianapolis. 1st ed. inscr. NF/VG+. A11. $60.00

HARRIS, Paul. *To Be a Pirate King.* 1971. London. Impulse Books. 1st ed. ils. 127 p. VG/fair. N2. $17.50

HARRIS, Rose Mary. *Tower of the Stars.* 1980. London. 1st ed. F/F. M2. $10.00

HARRIS, Sara. *Puritan Jungle.* (1969). Putnam. 1st ed. 256 p. dj. A7. $22.00

HARRIS, Stanley. *Playing the Game.* 1925. Stokes. 1st ed. w/sgn card. VG. P8. $125.00

HARRIS, T.S. *Gosepel According to St Luke Trans Into Seneca Tongue.* 1829. Am Bible Soc. 1st ed. 16mo. 149 p. contemporary full calf. M1. $425.00

HARRIS, Thomas Mealey. *Assassination of Lincoln: A Hist...* 1892. Boston. Am Citizen Co. 1st ed. pls. 424 p. bl cloth. VG. M8. $150.00

HARRIS, Thomas. *Red Dragon.* 1981. Putnam. 1st ed. author's 2nd book. F/F. Q1. $60.00

HARRIS, Thomas. *Red Dragon.* 1982. Bodley Head. 1st UK ed. 2 vols. NF/NF. Q1. $150.00

HARRIS, Thomas. *Silence of the Lambs.* 1988. St Martin. 1st ed. F/F. M15. $50.00

HARRIS, Thomas. *Silence of the Lambs.* 1988. St Martin. 1st ed. F/NF. N3. $45.00

HARRIS, Virgil M. *Ancient Curious & Famous Wills.* 1911. Little Brn. 1st ed. 8vo. 472 p. VG. A2. $40.00

HARRIS, Walter B. *Journey Through the Yemen & Some General Remarks...* 1893. Edinburgh. 24 full-p pls/3 maps. 385 p. pict cloth. O2. $275.00

HARRIS, Walter. *Characteristics of False Teachers.* 1811. Concord, NH. Hough. 30 p. wrp. H10. $17.50

HARRIS, William H. *Keeping the Faith... Brotherhood of Sleeping Car Porters...* ca 1977. Urbana. IL U. ils. F. V4. $12.50

HARRIS, William J. *Poetry & Poetics of Amiri Baraka: Jazz Aesthetic.* 1985. Columbia. MO U. 174 p. NF/dj. A7. $12.00

HARRIS & DOUGLAS. *New Preface to 'The Life & Confessions of Oscar Wilde.'* (1925). London. Fortune. 1/221. sgn Lord Alfred Douglas. blk cloth. VG+. B20. $125.00

HARRISON, Brian. *SE Asia: A Short Hist.* 1954. St Martin. 1st ed. ils/pls. 278 p. VG. W1. $18.00

HARRISON, C. William. *Barbed Wire Kingdom.* (1955). Jason Pr. 1st ed. F/clip. B9. $25.00

HARRISON, Chip; see Block, Lawrence.

HARRISON, Constance Cary. *Woman's Handiwork in Modern Homes.* 1881. Scribner. ils/5 color pls. G. A16. $125.00

HARRISON, David L. *Cinderella.* ca 1970. KS City, MO. Hallmark Cards. 8vo. 4 double-p popups. VG/worn dj. T5. $50.00

HARRISON, Fairfax. *Background of Am Stud Book.* 1933. Richmond. w/author's card. VG. O3. $145.00

HARRISON, Fairfax. *Belair Stud, 1747-61.* 1931. Richmond. VG. O3. $175.00

HARRISON, Fairfax. *Roanoke Stud, 1795-1833.* 1930. Richmond. O3. $175.00

HARRISON, George. *Songs.* 1987. Guilford. Surrey. 1st ed. 1/2500. sgn/#d. w/compact disc. F/box. H5. $750.00

HARRISON, Harry. *Deathworld Trilogy.* nd. BC. F/dj. P3. $10.00

HARRISON, Harry. *Light Fantastic.* 1971. Scribner. 1st ed. NF/dj. M2. $15.00

HARRISON, Harry. *Mechanismo.* 1978. Reed Books. 1st ed. F/dj. M2. $25.00

HARRISON, Harry. *Nova 1.* 1970. Delacorte. 1st ed. VG/dj. P3. $15.00

HARRISON, Harry. *Return to Eden.* 1988. Bantam. 1st ed. VG/dj. P3. $18.95

HARRISON, Harry. *Skyfall.* 1976. Atheneum. 1st ed. F/F. F4. $30.00

HARRISON, Harry. *Stainless Steel Rat Gets Drafted.* 1987. Bantam. 1st ed. F/dj. P3. $14.95

HARRISON, Harry. *Stainless Steel Rat Is Born*. 1985. Bantam. 1st hc ed/1st prt. F/F. F4. $12.00

HARRISON, Harry. *Tunnel Through the Deeps*. 1972. Putnam. 1st ed. F/dj. M2. $25.00

HARRISON, Harry. *Winter in Eden*. 1986. Bantam. 1st ed. sgn. F/dj. P3. $25.00

HARRISON, James. *Biographical Cabinet*. 1823. London. Sherwood Jones. 1st ed. octavo. 2 vols. 192 engravings. aeg. calf. H5. $600.00

HARRISON, Jane. *Book of the Bear*. 1926. London. Nonesuch. G. A1. $30.00

HARRISON, Jim. *Farmer*. 1976. Viking. 1st ed. author's 3rd novel. rem mk. F/F. L3. $125.00

HARRISON, Jim. *Farmer*. 1976. Viking. 1st ed. inscr/sgn. F/NF. B2. $175.00

HARRISON, Jim. *Just Before Dark*. 1991. Livingston. Clark City. 1/250. sgn. F/slipcase. C4. $150.00

HARRISON, Jim. *Legends of the Fall*. (1980). London. Collins. 1st ed. F/F. B3. $65.00

HARRISON, Jim. *Legends of the Fall*. 1979. Delacorte. 1st ed. inscr. G/F. B2. $100.00

HARRISON, Jim. *Letters to Yesenin*. 1973. Fremont. Sumac. 1/26 lettered. sgn. F/dj/ fld chemise/clamshell box. L3. $1,750.00

HARRISON, Jim. *Locations*. 1968. Norton. 1st ed. author's 2nd vol of poems. F/F. Q1. $200.00

HARRISON, Jim. *New & Selected Poems 1961-81*. 1982. Delacorte. 1/250. sgn. special bdg. F/F slipcase. B2. $200.00

HARRISON, Jim. *Plain Song*. 1965. Norton. 1st hc issue. sgn. F/F clip. L3. $500.00

HARRISON, Jim. *Plain Song*. 1965. NY. 1st ed/wrp issue. inscr. VG+/tan wrp. A11. $150.00

HARRISON, Jim. *Sundog*. (1984). Dutton. 1st ed. F/F. B3. $30.00

HARRISON, Jim. *Walking*. 1967. Cambridge. Pym Randall. 1/100. sgn/#d. F/prt wrp. Q1. $500.00

HARRISON, Jim. *Warlock*. 1981. Delacorte. 1/250. sgn. special bdg. NF/F slipcase. B2. $150.00

HARRISON, Jim. *Warlock*. 1981. Delacorte. 1st trade ed. 262 p. VG+/VG+. M20. $25.00

HARRISON, Jim. *Warlock*. 1981. London. Collins. 1st ed. F/F. C4. $50.00

HARRISON, Jim. *Wolf*. 1971. Simon Schuster. 1st ed. inscr. F/NF. B2. $200.00

HARRISON, Jim. *Woman Lit by Fireflies*. (1991). Weidenfeld Nicolson. 1st ed. F/F. B3. $35.00

HARRISON, Jim. *Woman Lit by Fireflies*. 1990. Houghton Mifflin/Lawrence. 1st ed. sgn. F/F. C4. $50.00

HARRISON, Jim. *Woman Lit by Fireflies*. 1990. Boston. Houghton Mifflin. 1st ed. M/dj. A17. $15.00

HARRISON, M. John. *Centauri Device*. 1974. Doubleday. 1st ed. F/dj. P3. $20.00

HARRISON, M. John. *In Viriconium*. 1982. Gollancz. 1st ed. sgn. F/dj. P3. $30.00

HARRISON, Margaret. *Capt of the Andes. Life of Don Jose de San Martin*. 1943. NY. Richard Smith. 1st ed. 262 p. dj. F3. $15.00

HARRISON, Marshall. *Lonely Kind of War*. (1989). Presidio. 1st ed. 285 p. F/F. A7. $20.00

HARRISON, Michael. *Exploits of Chevalier Dupin*. 1968. Arkham. 1st ed. F/dj. M2. $65.00

HARRISON, P.W. *Arab at Home*. (1924). NY. Crowell. 2nd prt. 8vo. 345 p. VG/VG. A2. $20.00

HARRISON, Ray. *Murder in Petticoat Square*. 1993. London. Constable. 1st ed. F/dj. S5. $25.00

HARRISON, Richard J. *Bell Beaker Cultures of Spain & Portugal*. 1977. Cambridge. Harvard. 1st ed. 4to. ils. 257 p. F-/wrp. A2. $20.00

HARRISON, Shelby M. *Social Conditions in an Am City (Springfield)*. 1920. NY. photos/maps. 439 p. A17. $17.50

HARRISON, Whit; see Whittington, Harry.

HARRISON, William. *In a Wild Sanctuary*. 1969. NY. 1st ed. sgn. F/F. A11. $45.00

HARRISON, William. *Roller Ball Murder*. 1974. Morrow. 1st ed. xl. dj. P3. $8.00

HARRISON, William. *Roller Ball Murder*. 1974. NY. 1st ed. sgn. F/F. A11. $45.00

HARRISON & HARRISON. *Bulbs & Perennials*. 1984. Portland. 2nd ed. photos. M/dj. B26. $25.00

HARRISON & HUGHES. *Short View of Menckenism*. 1927. WA U. Chapbook #1. sgn. VG/wrp. A1. $60.00

HARRISON & PRATHER. *No Time for Dying*. (1973). Prentice Hall. sgn Harrison. 259 p. dj. A7. $20.00

HARRISSE, Henry. *Bibliotheca Americana Vetutissima...* 1958. Madrid. 2 vols. M/wrp. O6. $250.00

HARROUN, Catherine. *Winemaking in CA: Account in Words & Pictures...* 1983. McGraw Hill. 1st ed. ils/index. 256 p. F/F. B19. $35.00

HARRYHAUSEN, Ray. *Film Fantasy Scrapbook*. 1981. Barnes. 3rd ed/revised/ enlarged. NF. C8. $40.00

HART, Albert Bushnell. *Varick Court of Inquiry*. 1907. Boston. Bibliophile Soc. 1/470. teg. full leather. NF. O6. $225.00

HART, Carolyn G. *S Ghost*. 1992. NY. Bantam. 1st ed. sgn. F/dj. S5. $35.00

HART, Frances Noyes. *Bellamy Trail*. 1940. Triangle. VG. P3. $15.00

HART, Herbert M. *Old Forts of the Far W*. ca 1965. NY. Bonanza. 4to. ils/maps. 192 p. cloth. dj. H9. $45.00

HART, James W. *Plant Tropisms & Other Growth Movements*. 1990. London. ils. 208 p. F/dj. B26. $36.00

HART, Josephine. *Damage*. 1991. Knopf. 1st ed. M/M. T2. $18.00

HART, Josephine. *Sin*. 1992. Knopf. 1st ed. F/F. T2. $15.00

HART, Roy. *Pretty Place for a Murder*. 1988. Detective BC. VG. P3. $7.50

HART, Roy. *Remains To Be Seen*. 1989. London. Macmillan. ARC of 1st ed. RS. F/F. S5. $27.50

HART, William S. *Hoofbeats*. 1933. NY. 1st ed. inscr. 231 p. yel bdg. VG. D3. $75.00

HART, William S. *Law on Horseback & Other Stories*. (1935). Times-Mirror Pr. 1st ed. inscr/dtd 1936. VG. B9. $40.00

HART, William S. *Lighter of Flames*. 1923. NY. 1st ed. 1/1000. 4 color pls. 246 p. pict cloth. VG. D3. $75.00

HART, William S. *My Life E & W*. 1929. Houghton Mifflin. 1st ed. sgn. VG. B9. $85.00

HART, William S. *Order of Chanta Sutas*. (1925). Hart. ltd ed. leatherette. VG. B9. $125.00

HART & HART. *Pinto Ben & Other Stories*. 1919. NY. 1st ed. inscr. 12mo. 95 p. gilt calf. NF. D3. $75.00

HART & HART. *Told Under a Wht Oak Tree*. 1922. Boston. 1st ed. inscr. 12mo. 51 p. VG. D3. $75.00

HARTE, Bret. *Bret Harte*. nd. McKinlay Stone. 12mo. 18 vols. leather. G. A8. $100.00

HARTE, Bret. *Cressy*. nd. NY. Regent. 290 p. cloth. D3. $12.50

HARTE, Bret. *Letters of Bret Harte.* 1926. Houghton Mifflin. 1st ed. photos. F. A18. $30.00

HARTE, Bret. *Maruja.* 1886 (1885). Houghton. early ed. 16mo. 271 p. VG. D3. $25.00

HARTE, Bret. *Poems.* 1871. Boston. Osgood. 12mo. 152 p. VG. D3. $35.00

HARTE, Bret. *Poetical Works of...* 1872. London. Routledge. octavo. 8 pls. 248 p. Kelliegram bdg. clamshell case. H5. $1,000.00

HARTE, Bret. *Poetical Works...* 1912. Boston. Household ed. 334 p. cloth. VG. D3. $15.00

HARTE, Bret. *Selected Stories.* 1925. Puritan Pub. 12mo. VG. A8. $8.00

HARTE, Bret. *Three Partners...* 1900 (1897). Boston. 12mo. 342 p. cloth. VG. D3. $15.00

HARTILL, Leonard Ramsden. *Men Are Like That.* 1928. Bobbs Merrill. 1st ed. 8vo. map ep. VG. W1. $25.00

HARTLAND, Michael. *Down Among the Dead Men.* 1983. London. Hodder Stoughton. 1st ed. author's 1st novel. F/F. M15. $65.00

HARTLEY, L.P. *Harness Room.* 1971. Hamish Hamilton. 1st ed. xl. dj. P3. $5.00

HARTLEY, L.P. *Traveling Grave.* 1948. Arkham. 1st ed. F/dj. M2. $135.00

HARTLEY, Norman. *Quicksilver.* 1979. Atheneum. 1st ed. F/dj. P3. $17.50

HARTLEY, Oliver. *Hunting Dogs.* (1909). Harding. 1st ed. photos. cloth. VG. A17. $14.50

HARTLEY & HARTLEY. *Osceola: Unconquered Indian.* 1973. NY. Hawthorn. 8vo. pls/maps. 293 p. VG/VG. B11. $30.00

HARTMANN, Hudson T. *Plant Science.* 1988 (1981). Englewood Cliffs. 2nd ed. ils. NF. B26. $29.00

HARTRIDGE, Jon. *Earthjacket.* 1970. Walker. 1st ed. VG/VG-. P3. $15.00

HARTS, William Wright. *Harbour Improvement on Pacific Coast of the US.* 1911. London. The Instit. 8vo. fld chart. 23 p. prt wrp. H9. $85.00

HARTWELL, Richard. *Margaret Mitchell's Gone w/the Wind Letters 1936-49.* 1976. NY. Macmillan. 8vo. pls. brn cloth. G. B11. $20.00

HARTWIG, G. *Polar & Tropical Worlds: Description of Man & Nature...* 1875 (1874). Springfield, MA. Nichols. new ed. 8vo. 810 p. G+. A2. $30.00

HARVARD & THOMPSON. *Mtn of Storms.* 1974. NY. 1st ed. photos. 210 p. gilt bl cloth. F. H3. $35.00

HARVESTER, Simon. *Bamboo Screen.* 1968. Walker. 1st ed. NF/dj. P3. $15.00

HARVESTER, Simon. *Zion Road.* 1968. Walker. 1st ed. NF/dj. P3. $15.00

HARVEY, Henry. *Hist of Shawnee Indians From Yr 1681 to 1854, Inclusive.* 1855. Cincinnati. Ephraim Morgan. 16mo. 316 p. cloth. poor. V3. $80.00

HARVEY, John. *Early Gardening Catalogues...* 1972. London/Chichester. Phillimore. 1st ed. 182 p. F/dj. H10. $85.00

HARVEY, John. *Lonely Hearts.* 1989. London. Viking. 1st ed. F/NF. M15. $65.00

HARVEY, John. *Rough Treatment.* 1990. NY. Holt. ARC of 1st Am ed. sgn. RS. F/F. S5. $35.00

HARVEY, M. Elayn. *Warhaven.* 1987. Franklin Watts. 1st ed. RS. F/dj. P3. $15.95

HARVEY, P.D.A. *Hist of Topographical Maps: Symbols, Pictures & Surveys.* 1980. NY. Thames Hudson. 116 p. M/M. O6. $45.00

HARVEY, Stephen. *Directed by Vincente Minnelli.* 1989. Harper/MOMA. 4to. dj. N2. $15.00

HARVEY, William. *Anatomical Exercises of Dr William Harvey.* 1928. London. Nonesuch. ltd ed. 1/1450. sm octavo. 202 p. VG. H5. $200.00

HARVEY, William. *Anatomical Lectures of Wm Harvey.* 1964. Edinburgh. Livingstone. lg 8vo. 504 p. gilt gr cloth. NF. S9. $23.00

HARVEY, William. *Arm of Mrs Egan.* 1952. Dutton. 1st ed. VG/VG-. P3. $50.00

HARVEY, William. *La Circulation du Sang.* 1879. Paris. trans Charles Richet. ils. 283 p. prt bl wrp. S9. $25.00

HARVEY, William. *Portraits of Dr Wm Harvey.* 1913. Oxford. folio. 20 pls. brds. G7. $135.00

HARWELL, Richard. *Confederate Music.* 1950. Chapel Hill. 1st ed. pls. 184 p. cloth. NF/VG. M8. $95.00

HARWELL, Richard. *Confederate Reader.* 1957. np. index. 389 p. O7. $14.50

HARWOOD, W.S. *New Creations in Plant Life.* 1905. Macmillan. 1st ed. 8vo. 368 p. VG+. A2. $30.00

HARWOOD, W.S. *New Creations in Plant Life.* 1922 (1905). np. 2nd ed. 430 p. B26. $20.00

HASBROUCK, Louise S. *Mexico From Cortez to Carranza.* 1918. NY. 1st ed. 12mo. 330 p. gilt brn cloth. F/VG. H3. $15.00

HASEK, Jaroslav. *Red Commissar.* nd. Toronto. 1st ed. trans from Czech by Cecil Parrott. F/F. A14. $25.00

HASKELL, Arnold. *Ballet Annual Record & Year Book of the Ballet.* 1947-62. London. Blk. set of 16. royal octavo. cream cloth. djs (lacks 2). NF. R3. $450.00

HASKELL, Daniel C. *Am Hist Prts: Early Views of Am Cities, Etc.* 1927. NY Public Lib. 1/1125. reprint. ils/maps. NF. O6. $55.00

HASKELL, Daniel C. *US Exploring Expedition, 1838-42...* 1942. NY. NY Pub Lib. 1st ed. NF. O6. $300.00

HASKELL, Frank A. *Battle of Gettysburg.* 1908. WI Hist Comm. 1st ed. 1/2500. xl. 184 p. cloth. VG. D3. $25.00

HASKIN, Frederic J. *Panama Canal.* 1913. Doubleday Page. 1st ed. 12mo. 386 p. red cloth. VG. B11. $25.00

HASKINS, James. *War & the Protest.* (1971). Doubleday. 1st ed. 143 p. clip dj. A7. $35.00

HASKINS, Jim. *Cotton Club.* (1977). Random House. A7. $50.00

HASKINS, Jim. *Queen of the Blues.* (1987). Morrow. 1st ed. 239 p. F/NF. A7. $15.00

HASKINS & MITGANG. *Mr Bojangles: Biography of Bill Robinson.* (1988). Morrow. 1st ed. 336 p. F/NF. A7. $15.00

HASLAM, Gerald. *W Writing.* 1974. Albuquerque. 1st ed. sgn Haslam/Stegner. VG+/8vo wrp. A11. $45.00

HASLAM, John. *Ils of Madness.* 1988. London. Routledge. reprint of 1810 ed. tan cloth. F/dj. G1. $25.00

HASLAM, John. *Observations on Insanity.* 1795. London. Rivington. 1st ed. 147 p. blk morocco/marbled brds. VG. B14. $250.00

HASLAM, S.M. *River Plants: Macrophytic Vegetation of Watercourses.* 1978. Cambridge, Eng. photos. 396 p. NF. B26. $31.00

HASLER. *Kate Greenaway's Cross-Stitch Designs.* 1989. np. 30 projects. cloth. G2. $20.00

HASLER. *Wild Flowers in Cross-Stitch.* 1989. np. 50 charted designs. wrp. G2. $13.00

HASLIP, Joan. *Crown of Mexico.* (1971). Holt. BC. 531 p. F3. $10.00

HASLIP, Joan. *Sultan: Life of Abdul Hamid II, 1842-1918.* 1973. NY. 1st Am ed. 8vo. ils. 309 p. cloth. dj. O2. $20.00

HASS, Hans. *Manta: Under the Red Sea w/Spear & Camera.* (1953). Chicago. 1st ed. 278 p. F/dj. A17. $15.00

HASSE, A.R. *Materials for Bibliography of Public Archives...* 1966. Ann Arbor, MI. reprint of 1908 ed. F. S9. $13.00

HASSEL. *Super Quilter II: Challenges for Advanced Quilter.* 1982. np. wrp. G2. $17.00

HASSEL. *You Can Be a Super Quilter.* 1980. np. sbdg. G2. $12.95

HASSELL, J. *Picturesque Rides & Walks...* 1817-18. London. Hassell. 1st ed/lg paper issue. 2 vols. 120 hc pls. aeg. VG. H5. $2,500.00

HASSLER, Alfred. *Siagon, USA.* 1970. NY. Richard Baron. 1st ed. NF/clip. A7. $25.00

HASSLER, Kenneth W. *Multiple Man.* 1972. Lenox Hill. 1st ed. VG/dj. P3. $15.00

HASSRICK, Royal B. *Sioux: Life & Customs of a Warrior Soc.* (1964). OK U. 1st ed. xl. 337 p. cloth. VG. D3. $12.50

HASTINGS, Brook. *Demon Within.* 1953. Crime Club. 1st ed. VG. P3. $10.00

HASTINGS, Howard. *Top Horse of Crescent Ranch.* 1942. NY. Cupples Leon. 1st ed. VG. O3. $18.00

HASTINGS, Michael. *Twelve on Endurance.* 1958. London. Macdonald. 1st ed. inscr. NF/clip. M15. $30.00

HASTINGS, Michael. *Unknown Soldier.* (1986). NY. 1st ed. F/F. A7. $30.00

HASTINGS, Thomas. *Mother's Hymn Book.* 1835. NY. Ezra Collier. miniature. 192 p. cloth. H10. $85.00

HASTY, John Eugene. *Man Without a Face.* 1958. Dodd Mead. VG-/dj. P3. $10.00

HASWELL, Jock. *D-Day: Intelligence & Deception.* 1980. Time Books. 1st ed. F/dj. P3. $15.00

HATCH, Mary R.P. *Missing Man.* 1893. Lee Shepard. 1st ed. G. M2. $25.00

HATCHER, Harlan. *Lake Erie.* 1945. Indianapolis. 1st ed. Am Lake series. sgn. 416 p. VG/G. D7. $25.00

HATCHER, John H. *Power of Federal Courts To Declare Acts of Congress...* 1936. WA. Am Liberty League. 20 p. stapled wrp. M11. $15.00

HATCHER & WALTER. *Pict Hist of Great Lakes.* ca 1963. NY. Am Legacy Pr. 4to. ils. brds. torn dj. H9. $25.00

HATFIELD, Miles. *Gardening in Britain.* 1960. Newton, MA. 1st ed. 483 p. F/dj. B26. $27.50

HATHAWAY, Bo. *World of Hurt.* (1981). Taplinger. 2nd prt. F/NF. A7. $25.00

HATHAWAY, Esse V. *Romance of the Am Map.* ca 1934. NY/London. 2nd prt. 8vo. ils. 316 p. linen. H9. $25.00

HATHAWAY, William. *True Confessions & False Romances.* 1972. Ithaca. 1st ed. sgn. VG/wrp. V1. $15.00

HATTAWAY & JONES. *How the N Won.* 1983. np. lg 8vo. 762 p. F. O7. $14.50

HAUGAARD, Erik Christian. *Treasury of Hans Christian Andersen.* (1974). Doubleday. BC. 8vo. 528 p. bl brds. NF/G+. T5. $25.00

HAUGHTON, Percy D. *Football & How To Watch It.* 1922. Boston. Marshall Jones. G+. N2. $10.00

HAUPTLY, Denis J. *In Vietnam.* 1985. Atheneum. 175 p. F/F. A7. $25.00

HAUPTMANN, Gerhardt. *Der Neue Christophoros.* 1965. Berlin. Verlag. Einmalige Auflage. 1/950. slipcase. N2. $25.00

HAUPTMANN, Gerhardt. *Island of the Great Mother.* 1925. Viking. 1st ed. VG. M2. $25.00

HAUPTMANN, Gerhardt. *Parsival.* 1915. Macmillan. 1st ed. VG. very scarce. C1. $14.00

HAUSER, Thomas. *Beethoven Conspiracy.* 1986. London. MacDonald. 1st British/hc ed. NF/dj. S5. $22.50

HAUSER, Thomas. *Dear Hannah.* 1987. NY. TOR. 1st ed. F/F. N3. $10.00

HAUSMAN, Patricia. *Right Dose.* 1987. Rodale. 1st ed. VG/dj. P3. $24.95

HAUTMAN, Pete. *Drawing Dead.* 1993. Simon Schuster. 1st ed. sgn. M/M. T2. $40.00

HAVERGAL, Frances Ridley. *Little Pillows; or, Goodnight Thoughts for Little Ones.* nd. (1890s). NY. 24mo. 63 p. decor brn cloth. VG. H3. $12.00

HAVIARAS, Stratis. *When the Tree Sings.* 1979. NY. 1st ed. inscr. F/F. A11. $40.00

HAVIG. *MO Heritage Quilts.* 1986. np. full-p color photos. wrp. G2. $15.00

HAVIGHURST, Walter. *Masters of the Modern Short Story.* 1959. WJ Gage. 1st ed. VG. P3. $15.00

HAVIGHURST, Walter. *Vein of Iron: Pickands Mather Story.* (1958). OH/NY. 1st ed. photos/map. 223 p. G/dj. A17. $18.50

HAVILAND, Virginia. *Favorite Fairy Tales Told in Eng.* 1959. Little Brn. 12th prt. 88 p. VG/VG. P2. $9.00

HAVILAND, Virginia. *Favorite Fairy Tales Told in Scotland.* 1963. Little Brn. 4th prt. 92 p. NF/VG. P2. $10.00

HAVILAND, Virginia. *Favorite Fairy Tales Told in Sweden.* 1966. Little Brn. 2nd prt. ils Ronni Solbert. 92 p. F/VG. P2. $8.00

HAW, Stephen G. *Lilies of China...* 1986. Portland. Timber Pr. 1st ed. 172 p. M. H10. $28.00

HAWES, J. *Religion of the E w/Impressions of Foreign Travel.* 1845. Hartford. 8vo. ils. 215 p. cloth. O2. $75.00

HAWKER, P. *Instructions to Young Sportsmen...* 1838. London. Longman Orme Brn Gr Longman. 8th ed. 549 p. VG. H5. $250.00

HAWKES, Clarence. *Silversheene, King of Sled Dogs.* (1924). Milton Bradley. 12mo. 234 p. VG. S10. $20.00

HAWKES, John. *Passion Artist: A Novel.* 1979. NY. 1st ed. sgn. NF/F. A11. $30.00

HAWKEY. *Evolution: Story of Origins of Humankind...* 1987. 5 popups. F. A4. $35.00

HAWKINS, B. Waterhouse. *Comparative View of Human & Animal Frame.* 1859. Chapman Hall. folio. 10 engravings. orig worn cloth. G7. $495.00

HAWKINS, Evelyn. *Vietnam Nurse.* (1984). Zebra. PBO. 384 p. F. A7. $25.00

HAWKINS & LE FLORE. *Breakout.* 1978. Harper Row. 1st ed. F/F. P8. $30.00

HAWKS, Jacquetta. *Providence Island.* 1959. Random. 1st ed. NF/dj. M2. $20.00

HAWLEY, Silas. *Second Advent Doctrine Vindicated.* 1843. Boston. Joshua V Himes. 1st ed. 12mo. 107 p. prt wrp. M1. $200.00

HAWORTH, Paul Leland. *George WA, Farmer: Being an Account of His Home Life...* ca 1915. Bobbs Merrill. 1st ed. 336 p. H10. $45.00

HAWTHORNE, Hildegarde. *CA's Missions.* 1942. Appleton Century. 1st ed. VG. P3. $35.00

HAWTHORNE, Julian. *Spanish Am.* 1899. Collier. 1st ed. 491 p. F3. $15.00

HAWTHORNE, Nathaniel. *Blithedale Romance.* 1852. Ticknor Reed Fields. 1st Am ed. 12mo. ads dtd April 1852. 288 p. cloth. M1. $250.00

HAWTHORNE, Nathaniel. *Scarlet Letter...* 1850. Boston. 1st ed. sm octavo. orig brn cloth. VG/morocco clamshell case. H5. $4,500.00

HAWTHORNE, Nathaniel. *Scarlet Letter: A Romance.* 1850. Ticknor Reed Fields. 3rd ed/1st prt. 12mo. 307 p. M1. $450.00

HAWTHORNE, Nathaniel. *Tanglewood Tales for Boys & Girls.* 1853. Boston. Ticknor Reed. 1st ed/1st prt. sm octavo. w/pub catalog. NF. H5. $500.00

HAWTHORNE, Nathaniel. *Tanglewood Tales.* 1921. Penn Pub. 1st ed. ils Sterrett. 261 p. VG. D1. $375.00

HAWTHORNE, Nathaniel. *Twice-Told Tales.* 1837. Boston. 1st ed. 12mo. Stikeman bdg. VG. H5. $2,000.00

HAWTHORNE, Nathaniel. *Wonder Book for Girls & Boys.* 1893. Cambridge. Riverside. ltd ed. ils Walter Crane. 8vo. teg. VG/rare gr dj. D1. $750.00

HAY, Binnie. *Titine: Dream Romance.* 1914. Andrew Elliot (Scotland). 1st ed. inscr/sgn. NF. F4. $38.00

HAY, Clarence. *Maya & Their Neighbor.* 1973. Cooper Sq. reprint of 1940 ed. 20 pls. 606 p. F3. $30.00

HAY, Elizabeth. *Sambo Sahib: Story of Helen Bannerman...* 1981. Barnes Noble. 1st ed. 8vo. 194 p. F/F. T5. $45.00

HAY, George. *Necronomicon.* 1978. London. 1st ed. NF/dj. M2. $75.00

HAY, James. *Bellamy Case.* nd. Grosset Dunlap. VG/VG-. P3. $15.00

HAY & NICOLAY. *Abraham Lincoln: A Hist.* 1904. NY. Century. 1st ed/2nd prt. 10 vols. cloth. VG. M8. $250.00

HAY & SYNGE. *Dictionary of Garden Plants in Colour...* 1969. London. Michael Joseph. 1/265. sgns/#d. Zaehnsdorf bdg. NF/clamshell case. H5. $400.00

HAYCOX, Ernest. *Earthbreakers.* 1952. Little Brn. 1st ed. VG/dj. P3. $35.00

HAYCOX, Ernest. *Sundown Jim.* 1948. Triangle. VG/VG-. P3. $10.00

HAYCRAFT, Howard. *Crime Club Encore.* 1942. Crime Club. 1st ed. VG. P3. $35.00

HAYDEN, Arthur. *Spode & His Successors. Hist of Pottery Stoke-on-Trent...* (1925). London. Cassell. thick 8vo. 204 p. pict bl cloth. NF. K1. $175.00

HAYDEN, Ferdinand V. *Preliminary Report of US Geological Survey of MT...* 1872. WA, DC. 8vo. 5 fld maps. blk cloth. H9. $110.00

HAYDOCK, Roger. *Collection of Christian Writings, Labours, Travels...* 1700. London. T Sowle. 16mo. 223 p. fair. V3. $95.00

HAYDON, Benjamin Robert. *Autobiography of...* 1926. London. Peter Davis. 2 vols. intro Aldous Huxley. VG+/VG+. S8. $75.00

HAYES, A.A. Jr. *New CO & the Santa Fe Trail.* 1880. NY. 1st ed. ils. 200 p. cloth. VG. D3. $75.00

HAYES, Alice. *Horsewoman.* 1910. London. Hurst Blackett. 3rd ed. photos. VG. O3. $145.00

HAYES, Charles W. *Long Journey: Story of Daniel Hayes.* 1876. Portland, ME. 1st ed. 18mo. 76 p. cloth. M1. $325.00

HAYES, Elizabeth S. *Spices & Herbs Around the World.* 1961. NY. ils. 266 p. VG/VG. B28. $15.00

HAYES, Harold. *Smiling Through the Apocalypse.* (1969). McCall. 2nd prt. VG/clip. A7. $20.00

HAYES, John Russell. *Old Quaker Meeting Houses.* 1909. Phil. Biddle Pr. 8vo. VG. V3. $20.00

HAYES, T. Wilson. *Winstanley the Digger: Literary Analysis...* 1979. Cambridge. Harvard. 1st ed. 258 p. H10. $25.00

HAYMAN, Ronald. *Death & Life of Sylvia Plath.* 1991. NY. Birch Lane Pr. 1st ed. F/F. T2. $14.00

HAYMON, S.T. *Ritual Murder.* 1982. St Martin. 1st Am ed. F/F. S5. $25.00

HAYMON, S.T. *Very Particular Murder.* 1989. Constable. 1st ed. F/dj. P3. $20.00

HAYNES, J.E. *Haynes New Guide.* (1924). St Paul, MN. self pub. revised (36th) ed. xl. 16mo. 192 p. cloth. D3. $20.00

HAYS, Mrs. Drew Nelson. *LA: Sketches of Hist Homes & Sights.* (1965). Baton Rouge. Claitor's. 199 p. dj. A17. $17.50

HAYWARD, John. *Columbian Traveller & Statistical Register.* 1833. Boston. Carter Hendee. tall 4to. 40 maps/6 city plans. prt brds. H9. $225.00

HAYWOOD, W. *King of the Cats...Adam Clayton Powell Jr.* 1993. Houghton Mifflin. 1st ed. 476 p. as new/dj. A7. $15.00

HAZARD, Caroline. *Narragansett Ballads.* 1894. Houghton Mifflin. 1st ed. 16mo. 107 p. teg. G+. V3. $14.00

HAZARD, Caroline. *Narragansett Friend's Meeting in XVIII Century...* 1900. Houghton Mifflin. 8vo. 197 p. VG. V3. $30.00

HAZARD, Thomas R. *Misc Essays & Letters.* 1883. Phil. Collins. 12mo. 384 p. G+. V3. $15.00

HAZEL, Paul. *Yearwood.* 1980. Atlantic/Little Brn. 1st ed. F/dj. P3. $20.00

HAZELTON, John Adams. *Hazelton Letters. Contribution to W Am.* 1958. Stockton. Lawton Kennedy. edit MG Bloom. 18 p. NF. P4. $65.00

HAZEN, Edward. *Panorama of Professions & Trades...* 1837 (1836). Phil. Uriah Hunt. sq 8vo. 320 p. calf/brds. M1. $225.00

HAZEN, Jacob. *Five Yrs Before the Mast; or, Life in the Forecastle...* 1859. Phil. 12mo. ils. 444 p. G. T3. $44.00

HAZLEHURST, Franklin H. *Jacques Boyceau & the French Formal Garden.* 1966. Athens. 1st ed. ils/pls. 137 p. VG. B26. $37.50

HAZZARD, Mary. *Idle & Disorderly Persons.* 1981. Seattle. 1st prt. dj. A7. $25.00

HAZZARD, Shirley. *Transit of Venus.* 1980. Viking. 1st ed. sgn. F/F. Q1. $40.00

HEACOX, Cecil. *Education of an Outdoorsman.* (1976). Winchester. ils/index. 191 p. dj. A17. $12.50

HEAD, George. *Forest Scenes & Incidents in Wilds of N Am.* 1829. London. John Murray. 1st ed. contemporary calf/rebacked. H9. $575.00

HEAD, Henry. *Studies in Neurology.* 1920. Oxford. 1st collected ed. 2 vols. xl. new cloth. G7. $275.00

HEAD, Matthew. *Accomplice.* 1947. Simon Schuster. 1st ed. VG/dj. P3. $20.00

HEADLEY, P.C. *Life & Deeds of General US Grant.* 1885. Boston. 12mo. 425 p. pict brn cloth. G. T3. $30.00

HEALD, Aya. *Shadows Under Whiteface.* 1956. Vantage. dj. N2. $8.50

HEALD, Tim. *Red Herrings.* 1985. Macmillan. 1st ed. VG/VG. S5. $20.00

HEALD, Tim. *Unbecoming Habits.* 1973. Stein Day. 1st ed. VG/dj. P3. $15.00

HEALEY, Ben. *Terrible Pictures.* 1967. Harper Row. 1st ed. VG/dj. P3. $12.50

HEALEY, Jeremiah. *So Like Sleep.* 1987. Harper Row. 1st ed. inscr. F/F. M15. $35.00

HEALEY, Tim. *Strange But True.* 1983. Octopus. decor brds. VG. P3. $10.00

HEALTH-STUBBS, John. *Artorius.* 1974. London. 1st trade ed. VG+. very scarce. C1. $17.50

HEALY, Jeremiah. *Yesterday's News.* 1989. Harper Row. 1st ed. F/dj. P3. $16.95

HEALY, Raymond. *New Tales of Time & Space.* 1951. Holt. 1st ed. NF/dj. M2. $20.00

HEALY & KUTNER. *Admiral.* (1944). Ziff-Davis. 1st ed. 8vo. 338 p. VG+/G. A2. $20.00

HEALY & MCCOMAS. *Adventures in Time & Space.* 1946. Random. 1st ed. F/NF. M2. $40.00

HEANEY, Seamus. *From the Republic of Conscience.* 1985. Dublin. Amnesty Internat. 1/2000. F/wrp. V1. $30.00

HEANEY, Seamus. *Government of the Tongue.* 1988. London. Faber. 1st ed. F/F. Q1. $60.00

HEANEY, Seamus. *Haw Lantern.* 1987. London. Faber. 1st ed. F/dj. C4. $35.00

HEANEY, Seamus. *Pre-Occu-Pations.* 1980. London. 1st ed. F/F. V1. $60.00

HEANEY, Seamus. *Selected Poems.* 1990. FSG. 1st ed. F/F. C4. $30.00

HEARD, H.F. *Doppelgangers.* 1947. Vanguard. 1st ed. VG/dj. P3. $40.00

HEARD, H.F. *Lost Cavern.* 1948. Vanguard. 1st ed. F/dj. M2. $40.00

HEARD, H.F. *Weird Tales of Terror & Detection.* 1946. Sun Dial. NF/dj. P3. $35.00

HEARN, C.V. *Foreign Assignment.* 1961. Adventurers Club. VG/dj. P3. $7.50

HEARN, Lafcadio. *Chin Chin Kobakama.* (1905). Tokyo. Hasegawa. #25 in series. VG. D1. $250.00

HEARN, Lafcadio. *Glimpses of Unfamiliar Japan.* 1894. Houghton Mifflin/Riverside. 2 vols. 8vo. VG. W1. $60.00

HEARN, Lafcadio. *Japanese Fairy Tales.* nd. (1931). Phil. sm octavo. 5 vols on crepe paper. self wrp/cloth chemise. F. H5. $2,000.00

HEARN, Lafcadio. *Kwaidan.* 1907. Tauchnitz. ne. VG. M2. $25.00

HEARN, Lafcadio. *La Cuisine Creole.* 1922. New Orleans. FF Hansell. 2nd ed. NF. Q1. $400.00

HEARN, Lafcadio. *Letters From the Ravin: Being Correspondence...* 1907. Merrymount. 1st ed. 201 p. gilt decor cloth. B14. $75.00

HEARN, Michael P. *Annotated Wizard of Oz.* 1973. Clarkson Potter. 1st ed. ils Denslow. G/VG. L1. $40.00

HEARNE, Betsy. *Home.* 1979. Atheneum. 1st ed. F/dj. M2. $12.00

HEARNE, Samuel. *Journey From Prince of Wales's Fort in Hudson's Bay...* 1795. London. Strahan Cadell. 1st ed/lg paper copy. fld maps/pls. full polished calf. H9. $3,000.00

HEARON, Shelby. *Owning Jolene.* 1989. Knopf. AP. w/promo taped to ep. NF/wrp. Q1. $30.00

HEARST & MOSCOW. *Every Secret Thing.* 1982. Doubleday. 466 p. dj. A7. $10.00

HEAT MOON, William Least. *Red Couch.* (1984). Alfred van der Marck. 1st ed. ils Clarke/Wackerbarth. VG/VG. B3. $40.00

HEATH, Laban. *Heath's Greatly Improved & Enlarged Infallible Government...* (1873). Boston. self pub. royal octavo. 11 full-p pls. gilt purple cloth. VG. R3. $450.00

HEBB & PECK. *Sports Car Rallies, Trials & Gymkhanas.* (1956). Great Neck, NY. Channel Pr. 1st ed. 4to. 159 p. VG+/VG. A2. $25.00

HEBDEN, Mark. *Pel & the Paris Mob.* 1986. London. Hamilton. 1st ed. F/F. S5. $25.00

HEBDEN, Mark. *Pel & the Prowler.* 1986. Walker. 1st ed. F/dj. P3. $15.95

HEBER, Lilly. *Krishnamurti & the World Crisis.* (1935). London. Allen Unwin. 291 p. VG. A7. $20.00

HEBER, Reginald. *Noah's Carpenters.* ca 1860s. Raleigh, NC. 1st ed. 8-p religious tract. NF/wrp. M8. $75.00

HEBERT, Anne. *Children of the Blk Sabbath.* 1977. Musson. 1st ed. VG/dj. P3. $20.00

HEBERT, John R. *Panoramic Maps of Anglo-Am Cities.* 1974. WA. Keyguide 208. NF. O6. $55.00

HECHINGER & HECHINGER. *Teen-Age Tyranny.* 1963. Morrow. 3rd prt. 259 p. dj. A7. $15.00

HECHT, Anthony. *Aesopic.* (1967). Gehenna. 1st ed. 1/100. sgn Hecht/Baskin. brn brds. F. B24. $250.00

HECHT, Ben. *Broken Necks.* 1926. Pascal Covici. 1/25. sgn. special bdg. VG. A1. $375.00

HECHT, Ben. *Cat That Jumped Out of the Story.* 1947. Winston. 1st ed. ils Peggy Bacon. VG. M18. $20.00

HECHT, Ben. *Count Bruga.* 1926. NY. 1st ed. A1. $25.00

HECHT, Ben. *Gaily Gaily: Memoirs of a Cub Reporter in Chicago.* 1963. Doubleday. 1st ed. F/NF. B4. $45.00

HECHT, Ben. *Miracle in the Rain.* 1943. Knopf. 1st ed. NF/VG. E3. $25.00

HECHT, Ben. *Samuel Hirshfeld, MD 1895-1946.* nd (1946). np. 8 p stapled into suede wrp. F. B2. $250.00

HECHT. *Nativity.* 1981. pop-up foldout to make 36" scene. F. A4. $45.00

HECKER, Justus Friedrich. *Geschichte der Heilkunde.* 1822 & 1829. Berlin. Enslin. 2 vols. contemporary half calf. F. G7. $295.00

HECKEWELDER, John. *Narrative of Mission of United Brethern Among...Indians...* 1820. Phil. 1st ed. 429 p. clamshell box. rare. D7. $500.00

HECKLER, Jonellen. *Safekeeping.* (1983). Putnam. 1st ed. author's 1st book. NF/dj. A7. $30.00

HECKMAN, Richard. *Yankees Under Sail.* (1978). Dublin. 1st ed. photos. 254 p. dj. A17. $35.00

HEDGE, Frederic H. *Prose Writers of Germany.* 1848. Phil. Carey Hart. 1st ed. lg 8vo. 567 p. gilt cloth. M1. $275.00

HEDGECOE & VAN DER MEER. *Working Camera: World's 1st 3-Dimensional Guide...* 1986. movable/pop-up manual. NF. A4. $85.00

HEDGES, Doris. *Dumb Spirit: Novel of Montreal.* 1952. Arthur Barker. 1st ed. VG/VG-. P3. $40.00

HEDGES, Joseph; see Harknett, Terry.

HEDIN, Sven. *Central Asia & Tibet. Towards the Holy City of Lassa.* 1903. London/NY. Blackett/Scribner. 1st ed. xl. 2 vols. teg. G. W1. $150.00

HEDIN, Sven. *Jehol: City of Emperors.* 1933. NY. Dutton. 4th prt. 62 pls. 278 p. G. W1. $22.00

HEDIN, Sven. *Riddles of the Gobi Desert.* 1933. Dutton. 1st ed. 8vo. 24 pls. 382 p. VG. W1. $65.00

HEDRICK, U.P. *Grapes & Wines From Home Vineyards.* 1945. London. 24 pls. 326 p. B26. $22.50

HEER, Friedrich. *God's 1st Love: Christians & Jews Over 2 Thousand Yrs.* 1970. NY. Weybright Talley. 529 p. VG. S3. $25.00

HEEREN, A.H.L. *Hist Researches Into Politics...Ethiopians & Egyptians.* 1838. Oxford. 8vo. 2 vols. gilt gr cloth. NF. H3. $85.00

HEERMANS, Forbes. *Thirteen Stories of the Far W.* 1887. Syracuse, NY. Bardeen. 1st ed. 12mo. 263 p. cloth. rare. D3. $125.00

HEFFERNAN, William. *Corsican.* (1983). Simon Schuster. 1st ed. rem mk. NF/dj. A7. $30.00

HEFFNER, Harry C. *Dan Patch: Story of a Winner.* 1924. Detroit. Heffner. leather. G. A16. $5.00

HEFLEY & HEFLEY. *No Time for Tombstones.* (1974). Harrisburg. Christian Pub. 1st prt. F/dj. A7. $25.00

HEFLEY & REGAN. *Phil Regan.* 1968. Zondervan. 1st ed. sgn Regan. F/VG+. P8. $75.00

HEGE, Walter. *Die Akropolis.* 1930. Berlin. Duetsher Kunstverlag. VG. V2. $8.00

HEGENER & ROBERTSON. *Fokker: The Man & the Aircraft.* 1961. Letchworth. 1st ed. 224 p. VG/dj. B18. $45.00

HEIDEL, William Arthur. *Frame of the Ancient Greek Maps.* 1937. Am Geog Soc. xl. NF. O6. $55.00

HEILBRONER, Robert L. *Future As Hist.* (1960). Harper. 1st ed. 217 p. dj. A7. $13.00

HEILBRONER, Robert L. *Making of Economic Soc.* 1962. Prentice Hall. 2nd prt. 241 p. NF/dj. A7. $13.00

HEILBRONER, Robert L. *Quest for Wealth: Study of Acquisitive Man.* 1956. Simon Schuster. 1st ed. 8vo. 278 p. F/VG+. A2. $15.00

HEILPRIN, Angelo. *Peary Relief Expedition.* 1893. Scribner. removed from Scribner's Magazine. VG. P4. $23.50

HEIMER, Mel. *Empty Man.* 1971. McCall. VG/dj. P3. $15.00

HEINE, Heinrich. *Poetry & Prose of...* 1948. NY. 1st ed. F/NF. V1. $25.00

HEINEMANN, Larry *Paco's Story.* (1986). FSG. 1st ed. F/VG+. A7. $20.00

HEINEMANN, Larry. *Close Quarters.* 1977. NY. 1st ed. inscr. author's 1st book. F/NF. A15. $140.00

HEINEMANN, Margot. *Adventurers.* ca 1961. NY. Marzani Munsell. pb. G. V4. $15.00

HEINEMANN, Ronald L. *Depression & New Deal in VA: Enduring Dominion.* 1983. VA U. 1st ed. 267 p. VG/fair. B10. $15.00

HEINLEIN, Robert A. *Assignment in Eternity.* 1953. Fantasy. 1st ed. VG/dj. M2. $75.00

HEINLEIN, Robert A. *Between Planets.* 1952. Scribner. 1st ed. xl. lib bdg. P3. $25.00

HEINLEIN, Robert A. *Beyond This Horizon.* nd. Grosset Dunlap. VG/dj. P3. $65.00

HEINLEIN, Robert A. *Citizen of the Galaxy.* 1957. Scribner. 1st ed. VG/dj. M2. $375.00

HEINLEIN, Robert A. *Door Into Summer.* nd. BC. VG/dj. P3. $10.00

HEINLEIN, Robert A. *Door Into Summer.* 1957. Doubleday. 1st ed. VG/dj. M2. $325.00

HEINLEIN, Robert A. *Friday.* 1982. Holt. 1st ed. 1/500. sgn. F/slipcase. M2. $225.00

HEINLEIN, Robert A. *Friday.* 1982. HRW. 1st ed. F/dj. P3. $20.00

HEINLEIN, Robert A. *Grumbles From the Grave.* 1990. Del Rey. 1st ed. F/dj. P3. $19.95

HEINLEIN, Robert A. *I Will Fear No Evil.* 1970. Putnam. 1st ed. VG/dj. M2. $95.00

HEINLEIN, Robert A. *Job: Comedy of Justice.* (1984). Del Rey. 1st ed. F/F. B3. $20.00

HEINLEIN, Robert A. *Man Who Sold the Moon.* nd. Shasta. 3rd ed. NF/dj. P3. $125.00

HEINLEIN, Robert A. *Past Through Tomorrow Book Two.* 1977. NEL. 1st ed. NF/dj. P3. $35.00

HEINLEIN, Robert A. *Rocket Ship Galileo.* 1947. Scribner. 1st ed. NF/dj. P3. $350.00

HEINLEIN, Robert A. *Sixth Column.* 1949. Gnome. 1st ed. F/M. M2. $375.00

HEINLEIN, Robert A. *Starman Jones.* 1954. Scribner. 1st ed. NF/dj. M2. $225.00

HEINLEIN, Robert A. *Starship Troopers.* (1959). Putnam. 1st ed. F/F. B4. $1,500.00

HEINLEIN, Robert A. *Stranger in a Strange Land Uncut.* nd. Ace/Putnam. 3rd ed. VG/dj. P3. $22.50

HEINLEIN, Robert A. *Time Enough for Love.* 1973. NY. Putnam. 1st ed. NF/NF. Q1. $100.00

HEINLEIN, Robert A. *To Sail Beyond the Sunset.* 1987. Ace/Putnam. 1st ed. F/dj. P3. $20.00

HEINLEIN, Robert A. *Tomorrow the Stars.* 1952. Doubleday. 1st ed. F/dj. M2. $85.00

HEINRICH, Julius J. *Window Flower Garden.* 1914 (1887). NY. new enlarged ed. ils. 123 p. NF. B26. $17.50

HEINRICH, William. *Crack of Doom.* 1958. Farrar Strauss. 1st ed. 8vo. VG/VG. A8. $8.00

HEINZELMANN, Friedrich. *Reisebilder und Skizzen aus der Pyrenaeischen Halbinsel...* 1851. Leipzig. Fleicher. octavo. pl/fld map. contemporary brds. H9. $1,800.00

HEISENFELT, Kathryn. *Shirley Temple & Spirit of Dragonwoo.* 1945. Whitman. VG. P3. $12.50

HEISEY & PELLMAN. *Country Bride Quilt.* 1988. np. ils. wrp. G2. $12.95

HEISTER, Laurentii. *Compendium Medicinae Practicae, Cui Preaemissa...* 1763. Venetiis. Remondiniana. 319 p. recent quarter calf/raised bands. G. G7. $395.00

HEISTER, Lorenz. *Medical, Chirurgical & Anatomical Cases & Observations...* 1755. London. Reeves/Hitch. 1st Eng ed. 4to. 8 fld pls. 708 p. contemporary calf. G7. $395.00

HEIZER & WHIPPLE. *CA Indians: A Source Book.* 1971. Berkeley. 2nd ed. 619 p. map ep. gilt gr cloth. M/M. P4. $30.00

HELD, Peter; see Vance, Jack.

HELIN, Charles. *Flatfish for Lunch; Fishcake for Dessert.* (1958). Helin Tackle Co. 8vo. 48 p. wrp. A17. $17.50

HELINE, Corinne. *Mysteries of the Holy Grail.* 1964. New Age. 1st ed. VG. scarce. C1. $9.50

HELLE, Andre. *Big Beasts & Little Beasts.* 1924. Stokes. oblong 12mo. 20 color pls. 80 p. G. D1. $150.00

HELLER, Abraham Mayer. *Vocabulary of Jewish Life.* 1942. Hebrew Pub. 276 p. VG. S3. $23.00

HELLER, Helen West. *Woodcuts USA.* 1947. NY. Oxford. 1/750. sgn. emb red-brn cloth. VG. F1. $85.00

HELLER, Joseph. *Catch-22.* 1961. Simon Schuster. ARC of 1st ed. Heller's 1st book. NF/prt wrp/slipcase. B24. $750.00

HELLER, Joseph. *Catch-22.* 1966. Modern Lib. VG/dj. P3. $17.50

HELLER, Jules. *Papermaking.* 1978. NY. photos. dj. B30. $15.00

HELLER, Keith. *Man's Illegal Life.* 1984. London. Collins. 1st ed. sgn. F/F. S5. $35.00

HELLER, Peter. *Anna Freud's Letters to Eva Rosenfeld.* 1992. Madison, CT. 1st ed. 210 p. gr cloth. VG/dj. G1. $22.50

HELM, H.T. *Am Roadsters & Trotting Horses.* 1878. Chicago. Rand McNally. 1st ed. rebound. rpl ep/old sgn ep laid in. VG. O3. $295.00

HELME & PAUL. *Ferry: Story of an Exmoor Pony.* 1930. Scribner. 1st Am ed. VG. O3. $48.00

HELMERICKS, Constance. *We Live in the Arctic.* 1947. Toronto. 1st ed. 8vo. 329 p. tan cloth. VG. H3. $15.00

HELMUT, P.G. *Bird-Headed Dwarfs. Studies in Developmental Anthropology...* 1960. Springfield, IL. Charles Thomas. 241 p. VG/dj. N2. $30.00

HELPER, H.R. *Impending Crisis of the S: How To Meet It.* 1860. NY. 12mo. 420 p. emb brn cloth. G. T3. $58.00

HELPRIN, Mark. *Ellis Island & Other Stories.* 1981. Delacorte/Lawrence. 1st ed. author's 2nd book. F/F. C4. $45.00

HELPRIN, Mark. *Refiner's Fire.* 1977. Knopf. 1st ed. author's 1st novel. NF/NF. Q1. $50.00

HELPRIN, Mark. *Soldier in the Great War.* 1991. HBJ. AP/ARC. w/3-p release. M/bl wrp. C4. $30.00

HEMINGWAY, Ernest. *By-Line: Ernest Hemingway.* 1967. Scribner. 1st ed. F/NF. B2. $50.00

HEMINGWAY, Ernest. *Christmas Gift.* 1970. Tokyo. true 1st ed. 12mo. red linen. F/F red & wht dj. A11. $85.00

HEMINGWAY, Ernest. *Death in the Afternoon.* 1932. Scribner. 1st ed. octavo. gilt blk cloth. F/F. R3. $1,350.00

HEMINGWAY, Ernest. *Faithful Bull.* 1980. London. Hamish Hamilton. 1/100. ils/sgn Michael Foreman. w/sgn pl. F/slipcase. Q1. $500.00

HEMINGWAY, Ernest. *Farewell to Arms.* 1929. Scribner. 1st ed/1st issue. inscr. F/VG. L3. $9,500.00

HEMINGWAY, Ernest. *Farewell to Arms.* 1929. Scribner. 1st ed/1st issue. Malcolm Crowley's copy. VG/VG. L3. $3,500.00

HEMINGWAY, Ernest. *For Whom the Bell Tolls.* 1940. Scribner. later prt. inscr/dtd 1940. VG/fld case. Q1. $2,500.00

HEMINGWAY, Ernest. *For Whom the Bell Tolls.* 1940. Scribner. 1st ed. presentation/inscr to brother. VG/worn. Q1. $15,000.00

HEMINGWAY, Ernest. *In Our Time.* 1924. Paris. 1st ed. 1/170. author's 2nd book. prt tan brds. F/slipcase/chemise. H5. $15,000.00

HEMINGWAY, Ernest. *Men at War: Best War Stories of All Time.* 1942. NY. Crown. 1st ed. 1072 p. yel bdg. VG. M7. $45.00

HEMINGWAY, Ernest. *Men at War: Best War Stories of All Time.* 1979. Bramhall. 1st thus ed/3rd prt. 1076 p. VG+/VG. M7. $55.00

HEMINGWAY, Ernest. *Moveable Feast.* 1964. London. 1st ed. F/F. A11. $45.00

HEMINGWAY, Ernest. *Old Man & the Sea.* 1952. London. Cape. 1st ed. VG/dj. M18. $175.00

HEMINGWAY, Ernest. *Short Stories of Ernest Hemingway.* 1942. Modern Lib. 1st Modern Lib Giant ed. NF/NF. B2. $35.00

HEMINGWAY, Ernest. *Spanish War.* 1938. London. 1st ed. F/wrp. B24. $375.00

HEMINGWAY, Ernest. *Sun Also Rises.* 1926. Scribner. 1st ed. VG+/VG+. Q1. $9,500.00

HEMINGWAY, Ernest. *To Have & Have Not.* 1937. Scribner. 1st ed. gilt bdg. NF/NF. Q1. $750.00

HEMINGWAY, Ernest. *Torrents of Spring.* 1926. Scribner. 1st ed. F/F. B24. $3,250.00

HEMINGWAY, Ernest. *Torrents of Spring.* 1926. Scribner. 1st ed. NF. Q1. $750.00

HEMINGWAY, Ernest. *Torrents of Spring.* 1926. Scribner. 1st ed. VG/dj. M18. $2,500.00

HEMINGWAY, Ernest. *Two Christmas Tales.* 1959. Berkeley. Hart. 1st ed. 1/150. ils Victor Anderson. F/prt wrp. B24. $1,850.00

HEMINGWAY, Ernest. *Winner Take Nothing.* 1933. Scribner. 1st ed. VG+/ VG+. Q1. $750.00

HEMINGWAY, Tom. *Life Among the Wolverines.* 1985. S Bend. 1st ed. photos. 289 p. F/dj. A17. $10.00

HEMMING, John. *Red Gold: Conquest of the Brazilian Indians 1500-1760.* 1978. Harvard. 1st ed. 8vo. 16 pls. 677 p. VG/VG. B11. $25.00

HEMMING, John. *Search for El Dorado.* 1978. Putnam. 1st ed. 8vo. 31 color pls. 223 p. VG/G. B11. $15.00

HEMMING, Robert J. *Ships Gone Missing: Great Lakes Storm of 1913.* 1992. Chicago. Contemporary Books. as new. A16. $19.95

HEMMINGER, Art. *Mr Lincoln Goes to the Theatre.* 1941. Poor Richard Pr. 9 p. VG. A6. $10.00

HEMPHILL, Paul. *Nashville Sound.* (1970). Simon Schuster. 1st ed. sgn. 289 p. dj. A7. $12.00

HENDEL, Samuel. *Soviet Crucible.* (1963). Princeton. Van Nostrand. 2nd ed. 706 p. NF/dj. A7. $15.00

HENDERSON, E.P. *Autobiography of Arab.* (1901). Columbia, SC. 1st ed. cloth. VG. C6. $2,500.00

HENDERSON, George Francis. *Civil War: A Soldier's View.* 1958. Chicago. 1st ed. 323 p. NF/VG. M8. $45.00

HENDERSON, John B. *Cruise of the Thomas Barrera.* 1916. Putnam. 1st ed. 12mo. 37 pls/5 maps. 320 p. teg. gilt bl brds. VG. B11. $95.00

HENDERSON, Lois T. *Hagar.* 1978. Christian Herald. 1st ed. F/dj. P3. $10.00

HENDERSON, M.R. *If I Should Die.* 1985. Doubleday. 1st ed. VG/dj. P3. $15.00

HENDERSON, Mrs. L.R. *Magic Aeroplane.* (1911). Reilly Britton. ils Nelson. 96 p. G/torn. D1. $185.00

HENDERSON, Paul C. *Landmarks of the OR Trail.* 1953. NY. 1st ed. 1/300. xl. 61 p. cloth. VG. D3. $50.00

HENDERSON, Peter. *Gardening for Profit.* 1889 (1886). Orange Judd. ils 376 p. VG. B28. $30.00

HENDERSON, Peter. *Practical Floriculture: Guide to Successful Cultivation...* 1911-13. NY. new enlarged ed. ils. 325 p. gr cloth. NF. B25. $29.00

HENDERSON, Zenna. *Holding Wonder.* 1971. Doubleday. 1st ed. xl. dj. P3. $15.00

HENDRICK, U.P. *Hist of Agriculture in State of NY.* 1933. Albany. 1st ed. VG/VG. B5. $75.00

HENDRICKS, Gordon. *Family Album: Photographs by Thomas Eakins, 1880-90.* 1976. NY. Coe Kerr Gallery. ils. 27 p. stiff wrp. D2. $18.50

HENDRYX, James B. *Blood on the Yukon Trail.* 1930. Doubleday Doran Gundy. 1st ed. VG. P3. $25.00

HENDRYX, James B. *Frozen Inlet Post.* nd. London. Hutchinson. inscr/dtd 1928. G+. B9. $75.00

HENDRYX, James B. *Grubstake Gold.* (1940). Sun Dial. VG+/dj. B9. $15.00

HENGEL, Martin. *Jews, Greeks & Barbarians: Aspects of Hellenization...* 1980. Fortress. 174 p. VG+/VG+. S3. $25.00

HENIGHAN, Tom. *Well of Time.* 1988. Collins. 1st ed. sgn. F/dj. P3. $25.00

HENING, H.B. *George Curry, 1861-1947: An Autobiography.* 1958. NM U. 1st ed. 336 p. cloth. F/dj. D3. $25.00

HENISSART, Paul. *Winter Spy.* 1976. Simon Schuster. 1st ed. VG/dj. P3. $15.00

HENKEL, J.S. *Woody Plants of Natal & Zululand.* 1934. Durban. 2 pls. 252 p. NF. B26. $45.00

HENLEY, Beth. *Crimes of the Heart.* 1982. Viking. 1st ed. F/NF. Q1. $40.00

HENNACY, Ammon. *Autobiography of a Catholic Anarchist.* 1946. NY. Catholic Worker. 1/3000. NF/NF. B2. $50.00

HENNINGSEN & PARKS. *RC Gorman: A Portrait.* 1983. Little Brn. 1st ed. quarto. F/F. L3. $50.00

HENRIQUES, Fernando. *Love in Action: Sociology of Sex.* 1960. Dutton. 1st ed. 432 p. dj. A7. $20.00

HENRY, Allan J. *Life of Alexis Irenee Du Pont.* 1945. Phil. Wm Fell. ltd ed. 1/750. vol 1 only. 8vo. 228 p. gilt bl brds. B11. $55.00

HENRY, John Joseph. *Accurate & Interesting Account of Hardships & Sufferings...* 1812. Lancaster, PA. Gregg. orig calf. H9. $350.00

HENRY, Marguerite. *Auno & Tauno. Story of Finland.* 1944. Chicago. Whitman. 4th prt. 28 p. VG. A3. $12.50

HENRY, Marguerite. *Birds at Home.* 1942. Donohue. ils Jacob Bates Abbott. 88 p. G+. A3. $20.00

HENRY, Marguerite. *Blk Gold.* 1957. Rand McNally. B ed. sgn. ils Wesley Dennis. VG/VG. L1. $20.00

HENRY, Marguerite. *Boy & a Dog.* 1944. Chicago. Wilcox Follett. 1st ed. G/fair. L1. $25.00

HENRY, Marguerite. *Brighty of the Grand Canyon.* 1955. Rand McNally. ils Wesley Dennis. VG/G. L1. $12.50

HENRY, Marguerite. *Gaudenzia: Pride of the Palio.* 1960. Rand McNally. 1st ed. VG. O3. $25.00

HENRY, Marguerite. *Justin Morgan Had a Horse.* 1947 (1945). Wilcox Follett. 3rd prt. 8 p. VG+/poor. P2. $20.00

HENRY, Marguerite. *Misty of Chincoteague.* 1947. Rand McNally. 1st ed. 173 p. VG/dj. M20. $20.00

HENRY, Marguerite. *Misty of Chincoteague.* 1963 (1947). Rand McNally. 16th prt. 4to. 174 p. pict bl brds. VG+/VG. T5. $25.00

HENRY, Marguerite. *Mustang: Wild Sprit of the W.* 1966. Rand McNally. 1st ed. 223 p. VG/VG. P2. $25.00

HENRY, Marguerite. *Stormy Misty's Foal.* 1963. Rand McNally. 1st ed. ils Wesley Dennis. 224 p. NF/VG. P2. $25.00

HENRY, Robert S. *Portraits of the Iron Horse.* 1938. Chicago. ils/pls. 80 p. color ep. pict gr cloth. G. H3. $20.00

HENRY, Thomas R. *Strangest Things in the World...Manifestations of Nature.* (1958). WA. 100 p. dj. A17. $10.00

HENRY, Will. *Gates of the Mtns.* 1963. Random. 1st ed. 8vo. 306 p. F/dj. A8/T8. $30.00

HENRY, Will. *In the Land of the Mandans.* (1965). Chilton. 1st ed. F/NF. A18. $35.00

HENRY, Will. *Pear Paw Horses.* (1973). Lippincott. 1st ed. F/dj. B9. $15.00

HENRY, Will. *Will Henry's W.* 1984. TX W Pr. 1st ed. M/M. A18. $20.00

HENSLEY, Joe L. *Killing in Gold.* 1978. Crime Club. 1st ed. xl. dj. P3. $5.00

HENSLEY, Joe. *Color Him Guilty.* (1987). NY. Walker. 1st ed. F/F. A7. $17.00

HENTOFF, Nat. *New Equality.* (1964). Viking. 1st ed. clip dj. A7. $22.00

HENTY, E.E. *Handbooks of Flora of Papua New Guinea.* 1981. Carlton, Victoria. ils/fld map. 276 p. M/dj. B26. $45.00

HENTY, G.A. *Bravest of the Brave.* nd. Foulham. VG/dj. P3. $12.50

HENTY, G.A. *By Pike & Dyke.* nd. AL Burt. s. pict cloth. VG. M5. $20.00

HENTY, G.A. *Redskin & Cowboy: Tale of W Plains.* 1891. Scribner. 1st ed. ils Alfred Pearse. VG. A18. $50.00

HENTY, G.A. *Under Drake's Flag.* nd. Coates. gilt pict cloth. VG. M5. $20.00

HENTY, G.A. *Under Wellington's Command.* 1898. Scribner. 1st ed. VG. M2. $30.00

HENTY, G.A. *With the British Legion.* 1902. Scribner. 1st ed. VG. M18. $65.00

HEPHER, Cyril. *Fruits of Silence...w/Kindred Essays in Worship.* 1917. London. Macmillan. 5th prt. 12mo. 222 p. V3. $12.00

HEPWORTH & MCNAMEE. *Resist Much, Obey Little.* (1985). Dream Garden. 1st ed. F/sans. B3. $35.00

HERBEN, Beatrice Slayton. *Jack O'Health & Peg O'Joy.* (1921). Scribner. 12mo. 39 p. VG. S10. $45.00

HERBERT, Agnes. *Two Dianas in AK.* 1909. London. Nelson. 256 p. gilt red cloth. NF. P4. $65.00

HERBERT, Brian. *Prisoners of Arionn.* 1987. Arbor. 1st ed. RS. F/dj. P3. $20.00

HERBERT, Frank. *Chapterhouse Dune.* 1985. Putnam. 1st ed. F/dj. P3. $17.95

HERBERT, Frank. *Dosadi Experiment.* 1977. Berkley Putnam. 1st ed. VG/dj. P3. $30.00

HERBERT, Frank. *Dragon in the Sea.* 1956. Doubleday. 1st ed. VG/VG-. P3. $175.00

HERBERT, Frank. *Dune Series.* 1965-68. Chilton Putnam. 1st ed. complete 6 vols (2 inscr.) F or NF/djs. M2. $2,000.00

HERBERT, Frank. *Dune.* 1965. Chilton. 1st ed. NF/VG. M2. $950.00

HERBERT, Frank. *Dune.* 1984. Putnam. 1st ed. VG/dj. P3. $20.00

HERBERT, Frank. *God Emperor of Dune.* 1981. Putnam. 1st ed. VG/dj. P3. $25.00

HERBERT, Frank. *Santaroga Barrier.* 1970. Rapp Whiting. 1st ed. NF/dj. P3. $35.00

HERBERT, Frank. *Wht Plague.* 1982. Putnam. 1st ed. F/dj. M2. $15.00

HERBERT, Frank. *Without Me Your'e Nothing.* 1980. Simon Schuster. 1st ed. F/F. F4. $28.00

HERBERT, Frank. *Worlds of...* 1980. Gregg. 1st hc ed. M. M2. $50.00

HERBERT, Henry. *Hints to Horsekeepers.* nd. Orange Judd. later prt. VG. O3. $48.00

HERBERT, James. *Creed.* 1991. Toronto. McClelland Stuart. 1st Canadian ed. M/M. T2. $20.00

HERBERT, James. *Magic Cottage.* 1987. NAL. 1st ed. F/F. P3. $17.95

HERBERT, James. *Moon.* 1986. Crown. 1st ed. VG/VG. P3. $20.00

HERBERT, Zigniew. *Report From a Besieged City.* 1985. NY. 1st ed. F/F. V1. $15.00

HERBERT & MARVELL. *Ev'n As the Flowers in Spring.* (1993). Bangor, ME. Theodore. 1/60. octavo. prt/book designer/sgn Michael Alpert. B24. $425.00

HERCULES POWDER COMPANY. *Game Farming for Profit & Pleasure.* 1915. Wilmington. 12mo. ils/photos. 64 p. VG/emb wrp. A17. $25.00

HERDON & WEIKS. *Herndon's Life of Lincoln.* 1942. np. 8vo. 511 p. tan cloth. G. T3. $12.00

HEREMAN, Samuel. *Paxton's Botanical Dictionary.* 1980 (1868). Dehra Dun. Indian reprint. 623 p. as new. B26. $65.00

HERFORD, Oliver. *Simple Jography.* (1980). Boston. Luce. 1st ed. sm 8vo. 100 p. F. B20. $75.00

HERGESHEIMER, Joseph. *From an Old House.* 1925. Knopf. 1/1050. sgn. G. A16. $45.00

HERGESHEIMER, Joseph. *Sherman: A Military Narrative.* 1931. Boston. 1st ed. ils/maps. 382 p. VG/VG. B5. $50.00

HERGESHEIMER, Joseph. *Trial by Armes.* 1929. London. 1/530. sgn. F/F. A11. $40.00

HERING, C. *Homoeopathic Domestic Physician.* 1859. Phil. 8vo. 393 p. leather/red label. G. T3. $55.00

HERLIHY, James Leo. *Midnight Cowboy.* 1965. Simon Schuster. 1st ed. NF/NF clip. A14. $100.00

HERLIHY, James Leo. *Sleep of Baby Filbertson.* 1959. NY. 1st ed. sgn. NF/VG+. A11. $60.00

HERMANN, Binger. *LA Purchase & Our Title W of the Rocky Mtns.* 1900. WA. GPO. 5 maps. NF. O6. $85.00

HERMANN, Imre. *Fechner: Eine Psychoanalytische Studie Uber Individuelle...* 1926. Leipzig. 1st ed. 62 p. prt orange linen. F. G1. $75.00

HERNDON, Venable. *James Dean: A Short Life.* 1974. Futura. VG/dj. P3. $20.00

HERNER, Charles. *AZ Rough Riders.* 1970. AZ U. 8vo. 275 p. map ep. F/F. B11. $50.00

HEROLT, Johannes. *Liber Discipuli de Eruditione Christifidelum.* not before 1485. Basel. Amerbach. folio. 19th-century calf. VG. K1. $3,250.00

HERONDAS. *Mimiambs of Herondas.* (1926). London. Fanfrolico. 1/375. ils Odle/trans Lindsay. half gr cloth. NF. K1. $185.00

HERR, Michael. *Dispatches.* 1977. Knopf. 1st ed. F/F. L3. $150.00

HERR, Michael. *Dispatches.* 1977. Taiwan pirate ed. dj. A7. $35.00

HERRERA, Emilio. *Flying: Memoirs of a Spanish Aeronaut.* 1984. NM U. 1st ed. VG/dj. A16. $15.00

HERREY, Robert F. *Two Right Profitable & Fruitful Concordances...* 1619. London. Norton/Bill. sm 4to. 2 parts in 1. 19th-century tooled calf. K1. $300.00

HERRICK, Robert. *Memoirs of an Am Citizen.* 1905. Macmillan. 1st ed. VG. B2. $65.00

HERRICK, William. *Itinerant.* 1967. NY. 1st ed. sgn. NF/VG+. A11. $45.00

HERRICK & INGALLS. *Rural Credits: Land & Cooperative.* 1915. Appleton. xl stps. 2nd prt. 519 p. A7. $15.00

HERRIES, J.W. *Storm Island & Other Stories.* 1947. London. 1st ed. inscr. F/NF. M2. $35.00

HERRINGER, Robert. *Hist of Medical Ils From Antiquity to 1600.* 1970. NY. Medicina Rara. 4to. slipcase. G7. $135.00

HERRIOT, James. *Christmas Day Kitten.* 1986. St Martin. 1st ils ed. VG/VG. L1. $12.50

HERRIOT, James. *Vets Might Fly.* 1976. Michael Joseph. 1st ed. VG/dj. P3. $20.00

HERRMAN, Louis. *In the Sealed Cave.* 1935. Appleton. 1st ed. VG. M2. $20.00

HERRON, Shaun. *Whore-Mother.* 1973. Evans. 1st ed. VG/dj. P3. $22.50

HERSCHELL, Ridley H. *Visit to My Father-Land, Being Notes of Journey to Syria...* 1844. Phil. 8vo. 216 p. emb cloth. O2. $75.00

HERSCHER, Uri D. *Century of Memories 1882-1982: E European Jewish Experience.* 1983. AJA. 189 p. F/VG. S3. $25.00

HERSEY, John. *Blues.* 1987. NY. ARC. sgn. NF/wrp. A11. $55.00

HERSEY, John. *Call.* 1985. Franklin Lib. ltd ed for subscribers. gilt full bl leather. F. Q1. $40.00

HERSEY, John. *Hiroshima.* 1946. Harmondsworth. 1st ed/PBO. sgn. NF/wrp. A11. $100.00

HERSEY, John. *Hiroshima.* 1983. LEC. 1st thus ed. quarto. sgn Hersey/Warren/Lawrence. F/slipcase. B24. $600.00

HERSEY, John. *John Hersey in His Letter to the Alumni.* 1970. Knopf. 1st ed. NF/NF. E3. $25.00

HERSEY, John. *Key W Tales.* 1994. Knopf. AP. F/wrp. B4. $45.00

HERSEY, John. *S of Cancer.* nd (1951). NY. 1st separate ed/PBO of Dell 10¢ series. sgn. VG+. A11. $60.00

HERSEY, John. *Wall.* 1961. NY. 1st ed. sgn. 8 photos from Broadway production. F/NF. A11. $95.00

HERSH, Seymour M. *Cover-Up.* (1972). Random. 1st ed. 305 p. VG+/ VG. A7. $17.00

HERSHBERGER, H.R. *Horseman: Work on Horsemanship & Sabre Exercise.* 1844. NY. xl. 141 p. emb cloth. F. B14. $75.00

HERTEL, Denver Willard. *Hist of the Brotherhood of Maintenance of Way Employees.* 1955. WA. Ransdell. 308 p. dj. A7. $30.00

HERTER, George. *Minnows of N Am & Their Streamer Imitations.* 1971. Waseca. 1st ed. 104 p. F/wrp. A17. $7.50

HERTER & HERTER. *Professional Guide's Manual.* (1964). Waseca. 6th ed. 349 p. cloth. G. A17. $15.00

HERTZ, Heinrich. *Untersuchungen Ueber die Ausbreitung der Elektrischen Kraft.* 1892. Leipzig. Barth. 295 p. morocco/marbled brds. NF. B14. $375.00

HERTZ, J.S. *Fifty Yrs of the Workmen's Circle in Jewish Life.* 1950. NY. Nat Executive Comm. Yiddish text. 422 p. G+. S3. $29.00

HERTZ, Joseph H. *Saying of the Fathers.* 1945. Behrman House. 128 p. VG. S3. $15.00

HERTZ, Richard C. *Am Jew in Search of Himself: Preface to Jewish Commitment.* 1962. Bloch. 209 p. VG+/fair. S3. $21.00

HERTZBERG, Steven. *Strangers Within the Gate City: Jews of Atlanta 1845-1915.* 1978. JPS. 1st ed. 325 p. VG/G. S3. $25.00

HERTZEL, Bob. *Big Red Machine.* 1976. Prentice Hall. 1st ed. F/VG+. P8. $20.00

HERTZEL & ROSE. *Charlie Hustle.* 1975. Prentice Hall. later prt. F/VG+. P8. $15.00

HERVEY, John. *Am Trotter.* 1947. NY. ils/pls. 551 p. cloth. NF/pict dj. D3. $50.00

HERVEY, John. *Messenger: Great Progenitor.* 1935. NY. Derrydale. 1/500. VG/VG. O3. $195.00

HERVEY, John. *Racing in Am, 1665-1865.* 1944. NY. Jockey Club. 1/800. 2 vols. folio. O3. $125.00

HERZL, Theodor. *Jewish State: Attempt at Modern Solution of Jewish Question.* 1943. Scopus Pub. 111 p. VG. S3. $15.00

HERZOG, Arthur. *Glad To Be Here.* 1979. Crowell. 1st ed. F/VG. M2. $10.00

HERZOG, Arthur. *IQ 83.* 1978. Simon Schuster. 1st ed. F/dj. P3. $15.00

HESKY, Olga. *Sequin Syndicate.* 1969. Dodd Mead. 1st ed. VG. P3. $6.00

HESS, Fjeril. *Magic Switch.* 1929. Macmillan. ils NK Brn. 1st ed. 8vo. 74 p. VG/dj. A3. $19.50

HESS, Fjeril. *Toplofty.* 1939. Macmillan. 1st ed. 304 p. VG+/dj. M20. $18.00

HESS, Joan. *Really Cute Corpse.* nd. BC. VG/dj. P3. $7.50

HESSE, Erich. *Narcotics & Drug Addiction.* 1946. Philosophical Lib. 1st ed. F/NF. B2. $50.00

HESSE & MANN. *Hesse/Mann Letters, 1910-55.* 1975. Harper Row. 1st ed. dj. N2. $10.00

HESTON, Charlton. *Actor's Life: Journals 1956-76.* (1978). Dutton. 1st ed. inscr. 8vo. 482 p. 16 p. F/F. A2. $15.00

HETRICH, William. *Camellias in the Huntington Gardens.* 1954-59. San Marino, CA. 3 vols. 7 color pls/795 photos. gilt bl cloth. VG/dj. B26. $89.00

HEUMAN, Fred S. *Uses of Hebraisms in Recent Bible Trans.* 1977. Philosophical Lib. 154 p. VG/G+. S3. $24.00

HEWARD, Constance. *Ameliaranne Goes Touring.* 1941. Harrap. 1st ed. ils Pearse. VG/torn. D1. $75.00

HEWARD, Constance. *Grandpa & the Tiger* (1924). Jacobs. 12mo. 121 p. G. S10. $30.00

HEWENS, Frank E. *Murder of the Dainty-Footed Model.* 1958. Macmillan. 1st ed. F/dj. P3. $17.50

HEWETT, E. *Ancient Andean Life.* (1939) Bobbs Merrill. 1st ed. 336 p. dj. F3. $50.00

HEWETT, E. *Ancient Life in Mexico & Central Am.* (1936). Bobbs Merrill. 1st ed. 364 p. dj. F3. $50.00

HEWITT, Randal H. *Across the Plains & Over the Divide.* 1964. Argosy-Antiquarian. ltd ed. 1/750. 521 p. F. A18. $50.00

HEWLETT, John. *Life Moonlight on Snow Life of Simon Iturri Patino.* (1947). McBride. 1st ed. 282 p. dj. F3. $25.00

HEY, Richard. *Disseration on Duelling.* 1801. London. Uphill. 107 p. half calf/marbled brds. B14. $75.00

HEYEN, William. *Along This Water.* 1983. Tamarack ed. 1/326. sgn/#d. F/stiff wrp. V1. $35.00

HEYEN, William. *Ash.* 1978. Banjo Pr. 1st ed. 1/326. sgn/#d. F/wrp. V1. $20.00

HEYEN, William. *Depth of Field.* 1970. Baton Rouge. 1st ed. sgn. F/F. A11. $45.00

HEYEN, William. *Lord Dragonfly.* 1981. NY. 1st ed. sgn. F/F. V1. $25.00

HEYER, Georgette. *April Lady.* nd. Putnam. 2nd ed. VG. P3. $5.00

HEYER, Georgette. *Blk Moth.* 1961. Heinemann. 18th prt. VG/dj. P3. $17.50

HEYER, Georgette. *Cousin Kate.* 1968. Dutton. 1st Am ed. 318 p. VG+/dj. M20. $23.00

HEYER, Georgette. *Grand Sophy.* 1950. Putnam. G+/dj. N2. $5.00

HEYER, Georgette. *Why Shoot a Butler?* 1973. Dutton. 1st ed. VG/dj. P3. $20.00

HEYLIGER, William. *Detectives Inc.* nd. Goldsmith. VG/dj. P3. $15.00

HEYN, E.V. *Fire of Genius: Inventors of Past Century.* 1976. Doubleday. 1st ed. 8vo. 340 p. F/F. A2. $15.00

HEYWOOD, Joe T. *Taxi Dancer.* 1985. Berkeley. PBO. 1st ed. NF/unread. A7. $15.00

HEYWOOD, Rosalind. *ESP: A Personal Memoir.* 1984. Dutton. BC. 222 p. VG/dj. G1. $15.00

HEYWOOD, V.H. *Flowering Plants of the World.* 1993 (1978). NY. updated ed. 335 p. M/dj. B26. $45.00

HIAASEN, Carl. *Native Tongue.* 1991. Knopf. 1st ed. as new/dj. A7. $17.00

HIAASEN, Carl. *Skin Tight.* 1989. Putnam. 1st ed. F/F. M15. $45.00

HIAASEN, Carl. *Strip Tease.* 1993. Knopf. ARC. F/wrp. B2. $40.00

HIAASEN, Carl. *Tourist Season.* 1986. Putnam. 1st ed. F/F. M15. $100.00

HIAASEN & MONTALBANO. *Death in China.* 1984. Atheneum. 1st ed. F/NF. L3. $250.00

HIATT, James M. *Voter's TB.* 1868. Indianapolis. Asher Adams Higgins. 1st ed. xl. 8vo. 387 p. blk cloth. H9. $45.00

HIBBARD, J.R. *Necromancy; or, Pseudo-Spiritualism...* 1853. Chicago. Whitmarsh Fulton. 1st ed. 8vo. 35 p. prt wrp. M1. $200.00

HIBBEN, Frank C. *Treasure in the Dust: Exploring Ancient North Am.* (1951). Lippincott. 1st ed. 4to. 257 p. F/VG. A2. $15.00

HIBBERD, Shirley. *Amateur's Flower Garden.* 1875. London. Groombridge. ils/6 fld color pls. 284 p. H10. $135.00

HIBBERD, Shirley. *New & Rare Beautiful-Leaved Plants.* 1874. London. Bell Daldy. 54 full-p color pls. 144 p. VG. B28. $350.00

HICHENS, Robert. *After the Verdict.* 1924. Doran. 1st ed. front free ep removed. VG. P3. $20.00

HICHENS, Robert. *Folly of Eustace.* 1896. Appleton. 1st ed. VG. M2. $20.00

HICHENS, Robert. *Spirit in Prison.* 1908. Harper. 1st ed. VG. M2. $25.00

HICKEY. *Angle Antics.* 1991. np. ils. wrp. G2. $19.00

HICKEY. *Basket Garden.* 1989. np. ils. wrp. G2. $19.00

HICKEY. *Little by Little: Quilts in Miniature.* 1988. np. wrp. G2. $17.00

HICKEY. *Pioneer Doll & Her Quilts.* 1992. np. wrp. G2. $6.95

HICKOK, Laurens P. *System of Moral Science.* 1853. Schenectady. 1st ed. thick 8vo. 431 p. cloth. M1. $125.00

HICKS, Clarence. *My Life in Industrial Relations.* 1941. Harper. 1st ed. 180 p. dj. A7. $25.00

HICKS, Elias. *Quaker; or, A Series of Sermons. Vol IV.* 1828. Phil. MTC Gould. 12mo. 296 p. leather. V3. $37.00

HIEB, Louis A. *Collecting Tony Hillerman.* (1992). Santa Fe. Vinegar Tom Pr. 1/200. 32-p booklet. F/wrp. B9. $30.00

HIELSCHER, Kurt. *Deutschland.* 1941. Leipsig. 5-line inscr. ils Mit Zeiss Ikon. F. B14. $125.00

HIGGINBOTHAM, A.L. Jr. *In the Matter of Color.* (1979). Oxford. 5th ed. 512 p. brn cloth. NF/NF. B22. $6.50

HIGGINS, Alice. *Runaway Rhymes.* 1937. NY. 140 p. gilt bl cloth. G+. H3. $25.00

HIGGINS, C.A. *New Guide to Pacific Coast Santa Fe Route...* 1895. Chicago. Rand McNally. fld map. 282 p. VG. H7. $65.00

HIGGINS, C.A. *To CA & Back.* 1899. Chicago. later prt. 175 p. G/wrp. D7. $25.00

HIGGINS, George V. *Choice of Enemies.* 1984. Knopf. 1st ed. VG/dj. P3. $17.50

HIGGINS, George V. *City on a Hill.* 1975. Knopf. 1st ed. VG/dj. P3. $35.00

HIGGINS, George V. *Friends of Eddie Coyle.* 1972. Knopf. 1st ed. VG/dj. P3. $30.00

HIGGINS, George V. *Judgement of Deke Hunter.* 1976. Little Brn. 1st ed. VG/dj. P3. $20.00

HIGGINS, George V. *Outlaws.* 1987. Holt. 1st ed. VG/dj. P3. $18.95

HIGGINS, George V. *Wonderful Yrs, Wonderful Yrs.* 1988. Holt. 1st ed. VG/dj. P3. $20.00

HIGGINS, Jack; see Patterson, Henry.

HIGGINS. *New Designs for Machine Patchwork.* 1980. np. cloth. G2. $15.95

HIGGINSON, Thomas Wentworth. *Tales of the Enchanted Islands of the Atlantic.* 1898. Macmillan. 1st ed. 8vo. decor cloth. B20. $75.00

HIGHAM, Charles. *Adventures of Conan Doyle.* nd. Norton. 2nd ed. VG/dj. P3. $12.50

HIGHAM, Robin. *Civil Wars in the 20th Century.* ca 1972. Lexington. F/VG. V4. $10.00

HIGHSMITH, Patricia. *Blk House.* (1988). NY. Penzler. 1/250. sgn. F/slipcase. B9. $45.00

HIGHSMITH, Patricia. *Blunderer.* 1954. Coward McCann. 1st ed. F/NF. M15. $250.00

HIGHSMITH, Patricia. *Deep Water.* 1957. Harper. 1st ed. VG/dj. P3. $27.50

HIGHSMITH, Patricia. *Dog's Ransom.* 1972. Knopf. 1st ed. F/dj. P3. $20.00

HIGHSMITH, Patricia. *Little Tales of Misogyny.* (1986). Penzler. 1/250. sgn. F/slipcase. B9. $45.00

HIGHSMITH, Patricia. *Little Tales of Misogyny.* (1986). Penzler. 1st ed. F/F. B3. $15.00

HIGHSMITH, Patricia. *People Who Knock on the Door.* (1985). Penzler. 1/250. sgn. F/slipcase. B9. $45.00

HIGHSMITH, Patricia. *Ripley Under Ground.* 1971. London. 1st ed. sgn. F/F. A11. $60.00

HIGHTOWER, John. *Pheasant Hunting.* 1946. NY. 1st ed. ils Lynn Bogue Hunt. 227 p. VG. A17. $17.50

HIGHWATER, Jamake. *Anpao: Am Indian Odyssey.* 1977. Lippincott. 1st trade ed. ils Fritz Scholder. NF/VG clip. L3. $75.00

HIGHWATER, Jamake. *Arts of the Indian Americas.* 1983. Harper. 1st ed. thick quarto. F/F. L3. $75.00

HIGHWATER, Jamake. *Ceremony of Innocence.* 1985. Harper Row. ARC/1st trade ed. RS. F/F. L3. $75.00

HIGHWATER, Jamake. *Eyes of Darkness.* 1985. Lee Shephard. 1st ed. F/F. L3. $45.00

HIGHWATER, Jamake. *I Wear the Morning Star.* 1986. Harper Row. ARC. RS. 3rd in Ghost Horse series. F/F. L3. $65.00

HIGHWATER, Jamake. *I Wear the Morning Star.* 1986. Harper Row. 1st ed. VG/VG. B3. $25.00

HIGHWATER, Jamake. *Journey to the Sky.* 1978. NY. Crowell. 1st ed. inscr. F/F. L3. $75.00

HIGHWATER, Jamake. *Legend Days.* 1984. Harper Row. ARC/1st trade ed. RS. F/NF. L3. $85.00

HIGHWATER, Jamake. *Mick Jagger: The Singer Not the Song.* 1973. Curtis Books. 1st ed/PBO. sgn. NF/wrp. A11. $50.00

HIGHWATER, Jamake. *Shadow Show.* (1986). Alfred van der Marck. 1st ed. F/F. B3. $30.00

HIGHWATER, Jamake. *Song From the Earth: Am Indian Painting.* 1976. NY Graphic Soc. 1st ed. sgn. NF/NF. L3. $250.00

HIGHWATER, Jamake. *Sweet Grass Lives On.* 1980. Lippincott Crowell. 1st ed. lg quarto. F/F. L3. $85.00

HIJUELOS, Oscar. *Mambo Kings Play Songs of Love.* 1989. NY. 1st ed. inscr. F/F. A11. $50.00

HIJUELOS, Oscar. *Mambo Kings Play Songs of Love.* 1989. NY. FSG. 1st ed. F/F. A14. $35.00

HIJUELOS, Oscar. *Our House in the Last World.* 1982. NY. Persea. AP. sgn. F/wrp. very scarce. L3. $450.00

HIJUELOS, Oscar. *Our House in the Last World.* 1982. NY. Persea. 1st ed. author's 1st book. F/F clip. A14. $60.00

HIJUELOS, Oscar. *Our House in the Last World.* 1987. London. 1st ed. inscr. F/ils wrp. A11. $40.00

HILDEBIDLE, John. *Thoreau: A Naturalist's Lib.* 1983. Harvard. 1st ed. 174 p. F/dj. A17. $9.50

HILDEBRAND, George H. *Borax Pioneer: Francis Marion Smith.* 1982. Howell N. 8vo. F/F. A8. $20.00

HILDEBRANDT, Greg. *Phantom of the Opera.* 1988. Unicorn. 2nd prt. ils. NF. C8. $40.00

HILDESCHEIMER, Wolfgang. *Marbot.* 1983. NY. Braziller. 1st ed. trans from German. NF/NF. A14. $20.00

HILDRUP, J.S. *Missions of CA & the Old SW.* 1912. Chicago. McClurg. 100 p. VG. H7. $25.00

HILGARD, Ernest R. *50 Yrs of Psychology...* 1988. Scott Foresman. 1st ed. 204 p. red fabrikoid. G1. $25.00

HILGARTNER, Beth. *Necklace of Fallen Stars.* 1979. Little Brn. 1st ed. F/dj. P3. $12.50

HILHOUSE, Albert M. *Hist of Burke Co, GA, 1777-1950.* 1985. Swainsboro, GA. Magnolia Pr. 1st ed. 339 p. F/NF. M8. $45.00

HILL, Alice Polk. *Tales of the Co Pioneers.* 1884. Denver. 1st ed. ils. 319 p. VG. B28. $125.00

HILL, Amelia L. *Garden Portraits.* 1923. McBride. 1st ed. 230 p. H10. $25.50

HILL, Art. *I Don't Care If I Never Come Back.* 1980. Simon Schuster. 1st ed. F/VG. P8. $25.00

HILL, Barbara. *Graphology.* 1981. St Martin. 1st ed. F/F. T2. $7.00

HILL, Douglas. *Day of the Starwind.* 1980. Atheneum. 1st ed. F/dj. M2. $12.00

HILL, Douglas. *Day of the Starwind.* 1980. London. Gollancz. 1st ed. sgn. F/F. N3. $35.00

HILL, E. *Australian Frontier.* 1942. Doubleday Doran. 1st ed. 8vo. 332 p. F/VG+. A2. $25.00

HILL, Edwin C. *Iron Horse.* (1924). Grosset Dunlap. photos. 329 p. cloth. VG. D3. $15.00

HILL, Hamilton Andrews. *Memoir of Abbott Lawrence.* 1883. Boston. 243 p. N2. $30.00

HILL, Herbert. *Blk Labor & the Am Legal System: Vol 1.* (1977). WA. Bureau of Nat Affairs. 455 p. dj. A7. $15.00

HILL, J. Arthur. *Spiritualism: Its Hist, Phenomena & Doctrine.* 1929. Doran. 1st ed. 12mo. 316 p. prt gr cloth. VG. G1. $30.00

HILL, John. *General Natural Hist...* 1748-52. London. 1st ed. folio. 3 vols. contemporary gilt calf. VG. H5. $4,500.00

HILL, John; see also (20th-century author) Koontz, Dean R.

HILL, Lorna. *Little Dancer.* 1957. Thomas Nelson. 1st Am ed. 151 p. cloth. VG/dj. M20. $14.00

HILL, Marie. *Adios: Big Daddy of Harness Racing.* 1971. S Brunswick. Barnes. 1st ed. presentation. w/sgn letter. VG/G+. O3. $45.00

HILL, R. Lance. *Nails.* 1974. Lester Orpen. 1st ed. VG/dj. P3. $35.00

HILL, Reginald. *Another Death in Venice.* 1976. London. Collins Crime Club. 1st ed. F/NF. M15. $100.00

HILL, Reginald. *Blood Sympathy.* 1993. London. Harper Collins. 1st ed. F/F. S5. $35.00

HILL, Reginald. *Clubbable Woman.* 1984. Woodstock. Foul Play. 1st Am ed. F/NF. Q1. $25.00

HILL, Reginald. *Deadheads.* 1983. London. Collins Crime Club. 1st ed. F/NF. M15. $50.00

HILL, Reginald. *Exit Lines.* 1984. Macmillan. 1st ed. F/NF. Q1. $25.00

HILL, Reginald. *Fairly Dangerous Thing.* 1983. Foul Play. 1st Am ed. F/F. S5. $25.00

HILL, Reginald. *Killing Kindness.* 1980. Pantheon. 1st Am ed. author's 9th mystery. F/NF. Q1. $30.00

HILL, Reginald. *Pinch of Snuff.* 1978. Harper Row. 1st ed. VG/dj. P3. $17.50

HILL, Reginald. *There Are No Ghosts in the Soviet Union.* 1988. Woodstock. Foul Play. 1st Am ed. F/dj. Q1. $25.00

HILL, Reginald. *Underworld.* 1988. Scribner. 1st ed. F/dj. P3. $15.00

HILL, Robert T. *Cuba & Porto Rico w/Other Islands of the W Indies.* 1898. NY. Century. 1st ed. 8vo. pls. 429 p. teg. gilt red cloth. G. B11. $95.00

HILL & WEINGRAD. *Saturday Night.* 1986. Morrow. 1st ed. F/F. T2. $12.50

HILL. *Color & Texture in Needlelace.* 1987. np. ils. cloth. G2. $20.00

HILLEGAS, Mark. *Future As Nightmare: HG Wells & the Anti-Utopians.* 1967. Oxford. 1st ed. NF/dj. M2. $35.00

HILLEN, William. *Blackwater River.* (1972). NY. 1st Am ed. 169 p. F/dj. A17. $15.00

HILLERMAN, Tony. *Blessingway.* (1990). Armchair Detective Lib. sgn. M/sans. A18. $75.00

HILLERMAN, Tony. *Boy Who Made Dragonfly.* 1972. Harper Row. 1st ed. author's 3rd book. pict brds. F/NF clip. L3. $650.00

HILLERMAN, Tony. *Coyote Waits.* nd. Quality BC. F/dj. P3. $10.00

HILLERMAN, Tony. *Coyote Waits.* 1991. London. Michael Joseph. 1st British ed. F/F. S5. $40.00

HILLERMAN, Tony. *Dance Hall of the Dead.* (1991). Armchair Detective Lib. 1st trade ed. sgn. M/M. A18. $60.00

HILLERMAN, Tony. *Dance Hall of the Dead.* 1985. London. Pluto. 1st ed. sgn. F/F. M15. $125.00

HILLERMAN, Tony. *Dark Wind.* (1982). Harper Row. 1st ed. NF/NF clip. B4. $125.00

HILLERMAN, Tony. *Dark Wind.* 1982. Harper Row. 1st ed. F/F. Q1. $175.00

HILLERMAN, Tony. *Fly on the Wall.* 1971. Harper Row. 1st ed. author's 2nd book. F/NF. Q1. $500.00

HILLERMAN, Tony. *Ghostway.* 1984. San Diego. Dennis McMillan. true 1st ed. 1/300. inscr to pub. F/F. L3. $1,500.00

HILLERMAN, Tony. *Ghostway.* 1985. Harper Row. 1st ed. rem mk. NF/NF. Q1. $100.00

HILLERMAN, Tony. *Ghostway.* 1985. London. Gollancz. 1st ed. sgn. F/F. M15. $65.00

HILLERMAN, Tony. *Jim Chee Mysteries.* (1990). Harper Collins. 1st thus ed. sgn. M/dj. A18. $50.00

HILLERMAN, Tony. *Joe Leaphorn Mysteries.* 1989. Harper Row. omnibus ed. F/F. M15. $35.00

HILLERMAN, Tony. *Listening Woman.* (1979). London. Macmillan. 1st Eng ed. F/F. A18. $100.00

HILLERMAN, Tony. *Listening Woman.* 1978. Harper Row. 1st ed. F/NF. M15. $350.00

HILLERMAN, Tony. *Moose on the Wall.* 1974. London. Barrie Jenkins. 1st ed. F/F. L3. $125.00

HILLERMAN, Tony. *NM, Rio Grande & Other Essays.* (1992). Graphic Arts Center. 1st ed. ils Muench/Reynolds. M/dj. A18. $35.00

HILLERMAN, Tony. *People of Darkness.* 1980. NY. Harper Row. 1st ed. F/F. M15. $400.00

HILLERMAN, Tony. *Sacred Clowns.* 1993. Harper Collins. 1st ltd ed. 1/500. sgn/#d. F/slipcase. A18/B3. $100.00

HILLERMAN, Tony. *Sacred Clowns.* 1993. NY. Harper Collins. 1st ed. sgn. F/F. M15. $50.00

HILLERMAN, Tony. *Skinwalkers.* 1986. NY. Harper Row. 1st ed. F/F. M15. $45.00

HILLERMAN, Tony. *Spell of NM.* 1975. NM U. 1st ed. F/NF clip. Q1. $200.00

HILLERMAN, Tony. *Talking God.* (1989). Harper Row. ARC. F. B3. $40.00

HILLERMAN, Tony. *Talking God.* (1989). Harper Row. 1st ed. F/F. A7. $28.00

HILLERMAN, Tony. *Talking God.* (1989). Harper Row. 1st ed. M/M. A18. $30.00

HILLERMAN, Tony. *Talking God.* 1989. Harper Row. 1st ed. 1/300. sgn/#d. special bdg. F/slipcase. M15. $125.00

HILLERMAN, Tony. *Thief of Time.* 1988. Harper Row. ARC/1st ed. F/wrp. A18. $50.00

HILLERMAN, Tony. *Words, Weather & Wolfmen.* 1989. Gallup. Southwesterner. 1st ed. 1/350. sgn Hillerman/Franklin/Bulow. F/F. B9/M15. $125.00

HILLIARD, Winifred. *People in Between: Pitjantjatjara People of Ernabella.* (1968). NY. 1st Am ed. 8vo. 253 p. F/F. A3. $20.00

HILLIER, Mary. *Automata & Mechanical Toys: Ils Hist.* 1988 (1976). London. Bloomsbury. reprint. lg 8vo. 200 p. F/F. A2. $15.00

HILLQUIT, Morris. *Present-Day Socialism.* ca 1920. Rand School Soc Science. G/VG. V4. $35.00

HILLQUIT, Morris. *Socialist in Theory & Practice.* 1909. Macmillan. 1st ed. NF. B2. $65.00

HILLQUIT, Morris. *Yhdysvaltain Sosialismin Historia.* ca 1912. Fitchburg, MA. Raivaajan Kirjapaino. G. V4. $15.00

HILLS, John Waller. *Hist of Fly Fishing for Trout.* 1971. Freshet. facsimile of 1921 ed. 244 p. M/dj. A17. $24.50

HILLS, Lawrence D. *Propagation of Alpines.* ca 1950. NY. Pellegrini Cudahy. ils/index. 464 p. H10. $20.00

HILSCHER, Herbert H. *AK Now.* 1948. Boston. 1st ed. 8vo. 299 p. tan cloth. F. H3. $12.00

HILTON, George Fred. *Cap'n George Fred Himself.* 1929. NY. 8vo. 295 p. gilt bl cloth. VG. H3. $20.00

HILTON, James. *Nothing So Strange.* 1947. Little Brn. 1st ed. VG/dj. P3. $22.50

HILTON, James. *So Well Remembered.* 1945. Little Brn. 1st ed. inscr/sgn/dtd 1946. F/NF. Q1. $125.00

HILTON, John Buxton. *Death of an Alderman.* 1968. Cassell. 1st ed. VG/dj. P3. $30.00

HILTON, John Buxton. *Gr Frontier.* 1990. Collins Crime Club. VG/dj. P3. $17.50

HILTON, John Buxton. *Playground of Death.* 1981. London. Collins. 1st ed. F/NF. S5. $22.50

HIMES, Chester. *All Shot Up.* 1960. Avon. PBO. NF/wrp. B2. $40.00

HIMES, Chester. *Blind Man w/a Pistol.* 1969. Hodder Stoughton. 1st ed. F/NF. M15. $85.00

HIMES, Chester. *If He Hollers Let Him Go.* 1947. London. Falcon. 1st ed. author's 1st book. VG+/VG+. Q1. $175.00

HIMES, Chester. *Real Cool Killers.* (1959). Avon. PBO. F/wrp. B4. $85.00

HIMES, Chester. *Real Cool Killers.* 1985. London. Allison Busby. 1st hc ed. F/F. M15. $45.00

HIMMEL, Richard. *23rd Web.* 1977. Random. 1st ed. F/dj. P3. $15.00

HINDLE, Brooke. *Pursuit of Science in Revolutionary Am 1735-89.* 1956. Chapel Hill. 1st ed. 410 p. cloth. G1. $25.00

HINDS, John. *Veterinary Surgeon.* 1846. Phil. Grigg Elliott. leather. O3. $58.00

HINDS, William Alfred. *Am Communities: Brief Sketches.* 1878. Oneida. Am Socialist. 1st ed. VG+. B2. $300.00

HINDUS, Maurice. *Great Offensive.* 1933. NY. 1st ed. 8vo. ils/maps. 368 p. F/VG. H3. $30.00

HINES, G. *Alfalfa Bill.* 1932. OK City. 1st ed. presentation/sgn. VG/VG. B5. $22.50

HINKEMEYER, Michael T. *Order of the Arrow.* 1990. Tor. F/dj. P3. $17.95

HINKLE, Thomas. *Old Nick & Bob: Famous Hinkle Dog Story.* nd. NY. Grosset Dunlap. juvenile. VG+. O3. $15.00

HINKSON, Pamela. *Indian Harvest.* 1941. London. Collins. 1st ed. 8vo. 320 p. VG+/VG. A2. $20.00

HINMAN, Bob. *Duck Hunter's Handbook.* (1974). NY. index/photos. 252 p. A17. $12.50

HINMAN, S.D. *Journal...Missionary to the Santee Sioux Indians...* 1869. Phil. McCalla Stavely. 1st ed. 12mo. 87 p. orig clothbacked prt wrp. M1. $250.00

HINMAN, W.F. *Corporal Si Klegg & His Pard.* 1892. Cleveland. 8vo. ils. 706 p. gray cloth. G. T3. $47.00

HINSDALE, Wilbert B. *Archaeological Atlas of MI.* 1931. Ann Arbor. MI Handbook Series 4. NF. O6. $625.00

HINSHAW, David. *Herbert Hoover: Am Quaker.* 1950. Farrar Straus. ltd ed. 1/1500. sgn. 8vo. 469 p. VG/box. V3. $27.00

HINSHAW, Seth B. *Mary Baker Hinshaw, Quaker...* 1982. Richmond, IN. Friends United Pr. 8vo. 175 p. VG/wrp. V3. $8.50

HINSON. *Quilter's Companion.* 1978. np. full-size patterns. wrp. G2. $15.00

HINSON. *2nd Quilter's Companion.* 1981. np. ils. wrp. G2. $10.00

HINTON, Richard J. *Hand-Book to AZ...* 1878. San Francisco. 12mo. 432 p. violet cloth. H9. $250.00

HINTON, S.E. *Rumble Fish.* 1975. Delacorte. 1st ed. F/NF. B2. $50.00

HINTON, Wayne K. *UT: Unusual Beginning to Unique Present.* 1988. Windsor. ils/index. 191 p. F/F. B19. $15.00

HINTON, William. *Fashen: Documentary of Revolution in Chinese Village.* (1970). Monthly Review. 1st ed. 225 p. NF/dj. A7. $20.00

HINTZE, Naomi A. *You'll Like My Mother.* nd. Putnam. 2nd ed. VG/dj. P3. $10.00

HINXMAN, Margaret. *Night They Murdered Chelsea.* 1984. Collins Crime Club. 1st ed. VG/dj. P3. $12.50

HINZ, Christopher. *Ash Ock: Paratwa Saga-Book 2.* 1989. St Martin. 1st ed. F/F. N3. $20.00

HINZ, Christopher. *Liege-Killer.* 1987. St Martin. 1st ed. F/dj. M2. $25.00

HIPPOCRATES. *Hippocrates Contractus, in Quo Magni Hippocrates...* 1751. Venetiis. Pasqual. 217 p. limp brds. G7. $75.00

HIPPOCRATES. *Theory & Practice of Medicine. Intro by Emerson C Kelly.* 1964. Philosophical Lib. 8 pls. 374 p. M. G7. $25.00

HIRSCH, Phil. *Dirty Little Wars.* (1967). Pyramid. PBO. VG. A7. $20.00

HIRSCH & SHEPHERD. *Themes & Variations in European Psychiatry.* 1974. Charlottesville, VA. 1st Am ed. 456 p. prt bl cloth. G1. $35.00

HIRSCHEL, Bernard. *Compendium der Geschichte der Medicin von den Urzeiten...* 1862. Wein. 2nd ed. 648 p. orig brds. G7. $495.00

HIRSCHFELD, Hartwig. *Judah Hallevi's Kitab al Khazari.* 1931. London. Cailingold. revised ed. 294 p. VG. S3. $35.00

HIRSCHFELD, Magnus. *Sexual Hist of the World War.* 1941. Cadillac Pub. abridged ed. sm 8vo. 356 p. prt gr cloth. VG/dj. G1. $35.00

HIRSCHFELD, Magnus. *Sexual Hist of the World War.* 1946. Cadillac Pub. reprint. 12mo. VG. A8. $6.00

HIRSCHMANN, Ira A. *Life Line to a Promised Land.* 1964. Jewish Book Guild. 214 p. VG. S3. $25.00

HIRSHBERG, Al. *Braves, the Pick & the Shovel.* 1948. Waverly. 1st ed. sgn Stanky/Torgeson/Holmes/Hirshberg. VG/G. P8. $125.00

HIRSHBERG, Al. *From Sandlots to League President.* 1962. Messner. later prt. F/VG. P8. $50.00

HIRSHBERG, Al. *Henry Aaron: Quiet Superstar.* 1974. Putnam. 1st ed. F/VG. P8. $75.00

HIRTZLER, Victor. *Hotel St Francis Cook Book.* (1919). Chicago. Hotel Monthly. sm 4to. 430 p. gilt gr cloth. VG. F1. $85.00

HISS, Alger. *Recollections of a Life.* 1988. Seaver/Holt. inscr. F/F. B2. $50.00

HITCHCOCK, Alfred. *Alfred Hitchcock Presents: My Favorites in Suspense.* 1959. NY. Random. 1st ed. NF/NF. N3. $20.00

HITCHCOCK, Alfred. *Alfred Hitchcock Presents: Stories for Late at Night.* 1961. Random. 1st ed. F/VG. N3. $15.00

HITCHCOCK, Alfred. *Brief Darkness.* 1988. Castle. VG/dj. P3. $12.50

HITCHCOCK, Alfred. *Daring Detectives.* 1969. Random. 1st ed. decor brds. F. P3. $15.00

HITCHCOCK, Alfred. *Master's Choice.* 1979. Random. 1st ed. VG. P3. $15.00

HITCHCOCK, Alfred. *Stories Not for the Nervous.* 1966. Max Reinhardt. 1st ed. VG/dj. P3. $25.00

HITCHCOCK, Alfred. *Tales To Send Chills Down Your Spine.* 1979. Dial. 1st ed. VG/dj. P3. $20.00

HITCHCOCK, Alfred. *Witch's Brew.* 1977. Random. 1st ed. decor brds. VG. P3. $15.00

HITCHCOCK, E.B. *I Built a Temple for Peace: Life of Eduard Benes.* (1940). Harper. 2nd prt. 8vo. 363 p. F/VG. A2. $20.00

HITCHCOCK, Edward. *Outline of the Geology of the Globe & of US in Particular.* 1853. Boston. Phillips Sampson. 8vo. lithos/2 fld maps. 136 p. orig bl cloth. H9. $375.00

HITCHCOCK, Enos. *Memoirs of the Bloomsgrove Family.* 1790. Boston. 1st ed. 2 vols. 12mo. contemporary full calf/leather labels. M1. $600.00

HITCHCOCK, F. *Saddle Up.* 1959. London. completely revised ed. G+. O3. $22.00

HITCHENS, Dolores. *Bank w/the Bamboo Door.* 1965. Simon Schuster. 1st ed. xl. dj. P3. $5.00

HITCHENS & HITCHENS. *One-Way Ticket.* 1956. Crime Club. 1st ed. VG/dj. P3. $40.00

HITE, Molly. *Breach of Immunity.* 1992. St Martin. 1st ed. NF/NF. A14. $25.00

HITT, Orrie. *Lion's Den.* 1957. Key. 1st ed. F/F. F4. $35.00

HITTELL, John S. *Hittell's Hand-Book of Pacific Coast Travel.* 1887. San Francisco. Bancroft. 12mo. 2 fld maps/tables/ils. gr cloth. H9. $125.00

HITTELL, John S. *Resources of CA...* 1863. San Francisco. 1st ed. royal 8vo. 464 p. cloth. VG. D3. $125.00

HITTI, P.K. *Lebanon in Hist.* 1967. NY. 8vo. 550 p. dj. O2. $30.00

HJORTSBERG, William. *Gray Matters.* nd. Simon Schuster. 2nd ed. F/dj. P3. $10.00

HOAGLAND, D.R. *Lectures on Inorganic Nutrition of Plants.* 1944. Waltham, MA. ils/26 photos. 226 p. bl buckram. VG. B26. $26.00

HOAGLAND, Edward. *Courage of Turtles.* 1970. NY. 1st ed. inscr. F/VG+ clip. A11. $65.00

HOAGLAND, Edward. *Tugman's Passage.* 1982. NY. 1st ed. sgn. F/F. A11. $50.00

HOAR, George F. *Charge Against Pres Grant & Attorney-Gen Hoar...* 1896. Worcester. Hamilton. 45 p. stapled wrp. M11. $65.00

HOARE, E. *Rome, Turkey & Jerusalem.* 1914. London. 12mo. 107 p. cloth. O2. $65.00

HOBAN, James. *Code of the Life-Maker.* 1983. Del Rey. 1st ed. F/dj. M2. $15.00

HOBAN, Russell. *Pilgermann.* 1983. Summit. 1st ed. VG/dj. P3. $17.50

HOBAN, Russell. *Turtle Diary.* 1975. Random. 1st ed. F/F. B2. $45.00

HOBAN & HOBAN. *London Men & Eng Men.* (1962). Harper Row. oblong 8vo. pict brds. VG. T5. $42.00

HOBAN & HOBAN. *Mouse & His Child.* (1967). Harper Row. possible 1st ed. ils Lillian Hoban. VG/G+. T5. $35.00

HOBBS, Lisa. *I Saw Red China.* 1966. NY/Toronto. McGraw Hill. 1st ed. 8vo. 217 p. NF/dj. W1. $16.00

HOBBS, William Herbert. *Exploring About the N Pole of the Winds.* 1930. Putnam. 1st ed. 376 p. NF/VG. P4. $65.00

HOBSON, Richard Pearson. *Sinking of the Merrimac.* 1899. NY. Century. 12mo. pls. 306 p. gilt dk bl brds. VG. B11. $75.00

HOBSON, Richmond P. Jr. *Grass Beyond the Mtns.* 1973. Toronto. McClelland Stewart. reprint. inscr/sgn author's sister. N2. $10.00

HOBSON, Wilder. *Am Jazz Music.* 1939. Norton. 1st ed. NF/NF. B2. $150.00

HOBSON. *Leonardo Knows Baseball.* 1991. accordion-style w/popups. 13 p. F/wrp. A4. $45.00

HOCH, Edward D. *Leopold's Way: Detective Stories of Edward D Hoch.* 1985. Carbondale, IL. 1st ed. inscr. F/F. M15. $45.00

HOCH, Edward D. *Yr's Best Mystery & Suspense.* 1987. Walker. 1st ed. F/dj. P3. $17.95

HOCHHUTH, Rolf. *Deputy.* 1964. NY. Grove. 5th prt in Eng-language. trans from German. NF/NF clip. A14. $20.00

HOCK, O.S. *World Atlas Railways.* 1983. Bonanza. reprint. VG/dj. A16. $20.00

HOCKEN, Edward Octavius. *Treatise on Amaurosis & Amaurotic Affections.* 1842. Phil. Waldie. 201 p. quarter calf/rebacked. G7. $175.00

HOCKING, Ann. *Vultures Gather.* 1946. Geoffrey Bles. 2nd ed. VG/VG-. P3. $20.00

HOCKING, Joseph. *Soul of Dominic Wildthorne.* 1908. Jennings Graham. VG. P3. $10.00

HODEL, Michael P. *Enter the Lion.* 1979. Hawthorn. 1st ed. F/dj. P3. $20.00

HODES, Aubrey. *Martin Buber: Intimate Portrait.* 1971. Viking. 242 p. VG/VG. S3. $23.00

HODGES, George. *William Penn.* 1901. Houghton Mifflin. 16mo. 140 p. VG. V3. $10.00

HODGES, Russ. *Baseball Complete.* 1952. Rudolph Field. ARC of 1st ed. sgn. RS. VG/VG. P8. $25.00

HODGES, Russ. *My Giants.* 1963. Doubleday. 1st ed. F/VG. P8. $20.00

HODGKIN, A.M. *Christ in All the Scriptures.* 1909. London. Alfred Holness. 3rd ed. xl. 8vo. 249 p. VG. V3. $12.00

HODGKIN, L.V. *Quaker Saint of Cornwall: Loveday Hambly & Her Guests.* 1927. Longman Gr. 8vo. 236 p. VG+. V3. $30.00

HODGKISS & TATHAM. *Keyguide to Information Sources in Cartography.* 1986. London. 1st ed. M. O6. $85.00

HODGSON, Fred T. *Practical Carpentry.* 1883. Industrial Pub. 144 p. VG. M20. $20.00

HODGSON, William Hope. *Carnacki the Ghost Finder.* 1947. Arkham. 1st ed. F/F. M2. $135.00

HODGSON, William Hope. *House on Borderland.* 1946. Arkham. 1st ed. F/M. M2. $400.00

HODGSON, William. *Select Hist Memoirs of Religious Soc of Friends.* 1844. Phil. self pub. 1st ed. 12mo. 420 p. fair. V3. $26.00

HODGSON, William. *Soc of Friends in the 19th Century...Vol 1.* 1875. Phil. Smith Eng. 1st ed. 8vo. 349 p. G. V3. $20.00

HODIER, Andre. *Hommes et Problemes du Jazz.* 1954. Paris. Au Portulan. correct 1st ed. F/wrp. B2. $100.00

HODSON, Anna. *Shetland Ponies.* 1989. London. Crowood. ils. O3. $15.00

HOEL & HOVDENAK. *Roald Amundsens Siste Ferd.* 1934. Oslo. Gyldendal. 1st ed. inscr Hoel. gilt bl bdg. NF/dj. P4. $125.00

HOENIG, Sidney B. *Jewish Identity...* 1965. NY. Feldheim. xl. VG/VG. S3. $27.00

HOENIG & ROSENBERG. *Guide to the Prophets.* 1957. Yeshiva U. new ed. 224 p. VG+. S3. $21.00

HOFFA, James R. *Hoffa: Real Story; As Told To Oscar Fraley.* ca 1975. Stein Day. 1st ed. photos. F/F. V4. $15.00

HOFFDING, H. *Hist of Modern Philosophy: Sketch of Hist of Philosophy...* 1935. Macmillan. 6th prt. 2 vols. ruled crimson cloth. G1. $50.00

HOFFENSTEIN, Samuel. *Pencil in the Air.* 1947. Doubleday. 1st ed. VG/fair. N2. $5.00

HOFFMAN, Abbie. *Square Dancing in the Ice Age.* 1982. Putnam. 1st ed. inscr. F/NF. B2. $85.00

HOFFMAN, Abbie. *Steal This Urine Test. Fighting Drug Hysteria in Am.* 1987. Penguin. 1st ed. sgn. NF/wrp. B2. $65.00

HOFFMAN, Abbie. *2nd Nature.* 1994. Putnam. 1st ed. sgn. F/F. B2. $40.00

HOFFMAN, Abby. *Steal This Book.* 1971. Pirate Ed. 1st ed. author's 1st book. inscr. VG+/bl wrp. A11. $135.00

HOFFMAN, Alice. *At Risk.* (1988). Putnam. 1st ed. F/VG. B3. $20.00

HOFFMAN, Alice. *Illumination Night.* (1987). Putnam. 1st ed. F/F. B3. $20.00

HOFFMAN, Arnold. *Free Gold. Story of Canadian Mining.* (1947). NY. 1st ed. glossary/index. 420 p. VG. A17. $15.00

HOFFMAN, Caroline. *Little Red Baloon.* 1918. Volland. 1st ed. ils Rachael Robinson Elmer. VG. M5. $25.00

HOFFMAN, Charles Fenno. *Winter in the W.* 1835. Harper. 1st ed. 2 vols. 12mo. cloth. VG. scarce. M1. $200.00

HOFFMAN, Charles G. *Short Novels of Henry James.* 1957. NY. 1st ed. sgn. F/NF. A11. $40.00

HOFFMAN, Daniel. *Able Was I Ere I Saw Elba. Selected Poems, 1954-74.* 1977. London. 1st ed. F/stiff wrp. V1. $30.00

HOFFMAN, Daniel. *Little Geste.* 1960. NY. 1st ed. sgn. author's 2nd book. F/F. V1. $45.00

HOFFMAN, Daniel. *Paul Bunyan: Last of the Frontier Demigods.* 1983. NE U. 213 p. F/wrp. B19. $10.00

HOFFMAN, Eleanor. *Realm of the Evening Star.* (1965). Phil. Chilton. 1st ed. 8vo. 307 p. F/VG. A2. $17.50

HOFFMAN, Everett. *Penn W: Mostly Tales About W PA.* 1987. Sault Ste Marie. ils. 238 p. dj. A17. $12.50

HOFFMAN, Heinrich. *Der Struwwelpeter (Slovenly Peter).* nd. Germany. 8vo. pict gr cloth. G. H3. $15.00

HOFFMAN, Irene. *Herb Cookery.* ca 1957. revised/enlarged ed. VG+/dj. C1. $7.50

HOFFMAN, Lee. *Loco.* 1969. Doubleday. 1st ed. VG/dj. P3. $17.50

HOFFMAN, Malvina. *Heads & Tales.* 1937. Scribner. 2nd ed. sm 4to. ils/maps. 416 p. VG. W1. $18.00

HOFFMAN, Melita. *Pearls of Ferrara.* 1943. Dutton. 1st ed. sgn. 213 p. w/photo. VG/dj. M20. $35.00

HOFFMAN, Michael A. *Egypt Before the Pharoahs: Prehistoric Foundations...* 1979. Knopf. 1st ed. 8vo. 12 pls. 391 p. F/F. A2. $20.00

HOFFMAN, Robert V. *Revolutionary Scene in NJ.* 1942. Am Hist Co. sgn. ils. 303 p. tan cloth. G. B11. $75.00

HOFFMAN, Walter J. *Graphic Art of the Eskimos.* 1974. Seattle. Shorey. ltd ed. 1/500. 82 pls. gilt cloth. F. A17. $45.00

HOFFMAN & LANDAU. *Kingdom of Dreams.* 1969. Paris. NY Associated Am. deluxe ed. 1/20. F/clamshell box. A1. $1,250.00

HOFFMANN, William. *Andrew Jackson & NC Politics.* 1958. Chapel Hill. NC Pr. 1st ed. 134 p. VG/stiff prt wrp. M8. $45.00

HOFLAND, Barbara. *Young Pilgrim; or, Alfred Campbell's Return to the E...* 1828. NY. 8vo. 211 p. quarter calf. O2. $150.00

HOFSTADTER, Richard. *Social Darwinism in Am Thought 1860-1915.* 1944. Phil. PA U. 1st ed. 191 p. bl cloth. G1. $37.50

HOGAN, Charles Beecher. *Bibliography of Edwin Arlington Robinson.* 1936. New Haven. Yale. 1st ed. F. B24. $75.00

HOGAN, James P. *Code of the Lifemaker.* 1983. Del Rey. 1st ed. F/dj. P3. $15.00

HOGAN, James P. *Proteus Operation.* 1985. Bantam. ARC of 1st ed. F/pict wrp. N3. $20.00

HOGAN, Linda. *Mean Spirit.* 1990. Atheneum. 1st ed. F/F. L3. $35.00

HOGAN, Linda. *Savings.* 1988. Coffee House Pr. AP. galleys in sbg wrp. RS/resume. NF/pub fold. L3. $125.00

HOGAN, Linda. *Seeing Through the Sun.* 1985. Amherst. 1st hc ed. F/NF. L3. $85.00

HOGAN, Ray. *Yesterday Rider.* 1976. Doubleday. 1st ed. xl. dj. P3. $5.00

HOGARTH, Burne. *Dynamic Anatomy.* 1984. Watson Guptill. 11th prt. F/dj. P3. $20.00

HOGARTH, Burne. *Tarzan of the Apes.* 1972. Watson Guptill. 1st ed. VG. P3. $17.50

HOGARTH, D.G. *Nearest E.* 1902. NY. 1st ed. xl. 296 p. gilt brn cloth. VG. H3. $20.00

HOGARTH, D.G. *Wandering Scholar in the Levant.* 1896. London. 1st ed. 8vo. 206 p. ils/fld map. O2. $150.00

HOGARTH, George. *Memoirs of Musical Drama.* 1838. London. Bentley. 8vo. 2 vols. Riviere bdg. F. F1. $130.00

HOGARTH, William. *Works of...* 1833. London. Jones. 2 vols. 4to. contemporary marbled ep. Lefeubre bdg. B14. $250.00

HOGG, Edward. *Visit to Alexandria, Damascus & Jerusalem...* 1835. London. 2 vols. 8vo. tan half calf. O2. $600.00

HOGNER, D.C. *Summer Roads to Gaspe.* 1939. Dutton. 1st ed. 8vo. 288 p. F/VG+. A2. $25.00

HOGROGIAN, Nonny. *Handmade Secret Hiding Places.* 1975. Overlook. possible 1st ed. 12mo. VG/G. T5. $15.00

HOKE, Helen. *Thrillers, Chillers & Killers.* 1979. Dent. F/dj. P3. $20.00

HOLBROOK, J. *Ten Yrs Among the Mail Bags.* 1855. Phil. Cowperthwait. 1st ed. ils/pls. 432 p. gr cloth. VG. D3. $75.00

HOLBROOK, Stewart H. *Age of the Moguls.* 1953. NY. 1st ed. 373 p. cloth. VG. D3. $15.00

HOLBROOK, Stewart H. *Holy Old Mackinaw.* 1938. NY. 1st prt. ex-hospital lib. 278 p. VG/dj. D3. $12.50

HOLBROOK, Stewart. *Wildmen, Wobblies & Whistle Punks.* (1992). OR State U. 1st ed. sgn. M/M. A18. $30.00

HOLDEN, David. *Farewell to Arabia.* 1966. NY. Walker. 1st ed. 263 p. F/NF. M7. $35.00

HOLDING, Elisabeth Sanxay. *Too Many Bottles.* 1951. Simon Schuster. 1st ed. front free ep removed. VG. P3. $12.50

HOLDSTOCK, Robert. *Eye Among the Blind.* 1977. Doubleday. 1st Am ed. F/dj. M2. $15.00

HOLDSTOCK, Robert. *Ghostdance.* 1987. Century. 1st hc ed. sgn. F/F. F4. $35.00

HOLDSTOCK, Robert. *Where Time Winds Blow.* nd. BC. VG/VG-. P3. $7.50

HOLDSTOCK, Robert. *Where Time Winds Blow.* 1981. Faber. 1st ed. sgn. F/F. F4. $40.00

HOLE, Christina. *Witchcraft in Eng.* nd. BC. VG/dj. P3. $7.50

HOLISHER, Desider. *House of God.* (1946). NY. Crown. 1st ed. 4to. 232 p. F/VG+. A2. $20.00

HOLL, Adelaide. *Sir Kevin of Devon.* 1963. Lee Shepard. 1st ed. ils Weisgard. VG+/G. P2. $25.00

HOLLAND, Celia. *Floating Worlds.* 1976. Knopf. 1st ed. F/dj. M2. $13.00

HOLLAND, Henry. *Travels in the Ionian Isles, Albania, Thessaly, Macedonia...* 1971. NY. tall 8vo. 551 p. cloth. O2. $45.00

HOLLAND, Jack. *Druid Time.* 1986. Dodd Mead. 1st ed. VG/dj. P3. $15.95

HOLLAND, Janice. *Christopher Goes to the Castle.* 1957. NY. 1st ed. pls. 32 p. pict gray cloth. F/VG. H3. $15.00

HOLLAND, Rupert. *Arabian Nights.* nd. Grosset Dunlap. 1st ed. ils WH Lister. G. L1. $7.50

HOLLAND, William. *Let a Soldier Die.* 1984. Delacorte. 324 p. NF/dj. A7. $23.00

HOLLERAN, Andrew. *Dancer From the Dance.* 1978. Morrow. 1st ed. NF/VG+. A14. $30.00

HOLLEY, E. *Charles Evans: Am Bibliographer.* 1963. Urbana. 1st ed. VG/VG. B5. $20.00

HOLLEY, Marietta. *Samantha in Europe.* 1895. NY. 1st ed. ils DeGrimm. 714 p. G. B18. $35.00

HOLLIDAY, C.W. *Valley of Youth.* 1948. Caldwell. 1st ed. sgn. 357 p. F/dj. A17. $35.00

HOLLIDAY, Joe. *Dale of the Mounted Atomic Plot.* 1959. Allen. VG/VG. P3. $17.50

HOLLIDAY, Joe. *Dale of the Mounted in Hong Kong.* 1962. Allen. 160 p. VG+/dj. M20. $15.00

HOLLIDAY, Michael; see Creasey, John.

HOLLING, Holling C. *Book of Cowboys.* 1936. Platt Munk. 4to. 126 p. VG/dj. A3/D3/L1. $25.00

HOLLING, Holling C. *Book of Indians.* 1935. Platt Munk. 1st ed. 4to. cloth. VG/dj. A3/D3. $25.00

HOLLING, Holling C. *Claws of the Thunderbird.* 1928. Volland. 1st Am ed. 128 p. G. L1. $45.00

HOLLING, Holling C. *Minn of the MS.* 1951. Houghton Mifflin. 1st ed. VG/dj. M5. $45.00

HOLLINGSWORTH, Brian. *Railways of the World.* 1979. NY. Gallery. 4to. ils/pls. 468 p. VG/G. B11. $30.00

HOLLINGSWORTH, Buckner. *Her Garden Was Her Delight: Famous Women Gardeners.* 1962. Macmillan. 1st ed. 8vo. 166 p. F/VG. A2. $12.50

HOLLIS, Christopher. *Newman & the Modern World.* ca 1967. London. Hollis Carter. index. 230 p. H10. $17.50

HOLLIS, Jim. *Teach You a Lesson.* 1955. Harper. 1st ed. VG/dj. P3. $17.50

HOLLON, W.E. *Lost Pathfinder: Zebulon Montgomery Pike.* 1949. Norman, OK. 1st ed. 8vo. 240 p. F/G. A2. $25.00

HOLLOWAY, David. *Lewis & Clark: Crossing of N Am.* 1974. Saturday Review Pr. 1st ed. 8vo. ils. 224 p. F/F. T8. $30.00

HOLLY, H.W. *Carpenter's & Jointer's Handbook.* 1883. Wiley, NY. revised ed. 57 p. VG. M20. $15.00

HOLLY, J. Hunter. *Encounter.* 1959. Avalon. 1st ed. sgn. VG/dj. P3. $45.00

HOLM, Don. *Pacific N! Sea Trails for the Sportsman of N Pacific Rim.* 1969. Caxton. 1st ed. ils/species list. 283 p. F/F/box. B19. $20.00

HOLM, Don. *Pacific N!: Adventures in Sport Fishing.* 1969. Caxton. 283 p. F/NF. A7. $25.00

HOLM, J.B. *Portage Heritage: Hist of Portage Co, OH.* 1957. Portage Co Hist Soc. ils. 824 p. VG. B18. $27.50

HOLMAN, Hugh. *Slay the Murderer.* 1946. MS Mill. 1st ed. VG/VG. P3. $25.00

HOLMAN, Hugh. *Trout in the Milk.* 1945. MS Mill. 1st ed. VG/dj. P3. $30.00

HOLMANO, Squire. *On Lupus Vulgaris; or, The Wolf.* 1888. London. Churchill. 4to. oil litho pl/woodcuts. orig prt wrp. w/engraving. G7. $75.00

HOLME, Bryan. *Kate Greenaway Book.* (1976). Gallery. ils Kate Greenaway. 144 p. VG/VG clip. S10. $25.00

HOLME, Charles. *Colour Photography & Other Recent Developments...* (1908). The Studio. quarto. F/prt wrp. R3. $375.00

HOLME, Charles. *Gardens of Eng in S & W Counties.* 1907. London/Paris/NY. Studio. 136 pls. VG. B28. $50.00

HOLME, Timothy. *Assisi Murders.* 1985. London. Macmillan. 1st ed. NF/NF. S5. $22.50

HOLMES, Beth. *Whipping Boy.* 1978. Marek. 1st ed/1st prt. F/F. T2. $10.00

HOLMES, Charles. *Clocks of Columbus.* 1972. Atheneum. 1st ed. photos. 360 p. NF/dj. A7. $20.00

HOLMES, Charles. *Principles & Practice of Horse-Shoeing.* 1959. Leeds. Farrier's Journal. 1st ed. VG. O3. $38.00

HOLMES, Clellon. *Go.* 1952. Scribner. 1st ed. sgn w/author's full name. VG/dj. L3. $950.00

HOLMES, Eugenia Kellogg. *Aldolph Sutro: Brief Story of Brilliant Life.* 1895. San Francisco. 12mo. ils. 56 p. gilt pict cloth. VG. S3. $60.00

HOLMES, John Clellon. *Get Home Free.* 1966. London. Corgi. 1st ed/PBO. sgn. VG/wrp. A11. $65.00

HOLMES, John Clellon. *Gone in October.* 1985. Hailey, ID. 1st ed. sgn. F/wht 8vo wrp. A11. $45.00

HOLMES, John Clellon. *Horn.* 1958. NY. 1st ed. VG+/VG+. A11. $65.00

HOLMES, John Clellon. *Nothing More To Declare.* 1967. NY. 1st ed. sgn. F/NF. A11. $115.00

HOLMES, Oliver Wendell. *Astraea: Balance of Ilusions.* 1850. Ticknor Reed Fields. 1st ed. 12mo. 39 p. prt brds. M1. $300.00

HOLMES, Oliver Wendell. *Autocrat of the Breakfast Table.* 1858. Boston. Phillips Sampson. 1st ed/1st prt. Blanck's A bdg (4 stars not 5). NF. Q1. $500.00

HOLMES, Oliver Wendell. *Collected Legal Papers.* 1920. Harcourt Brace. gilt russet cloth. M11. $85.00

HOLMES, Oliver Wendell. *Collected Works of...* 1890s. Boston. Riverside. collected ed. 14 vols. red cloth/leather labels. G7. $95.00

HOLMES, Oliver Wendell. *Holmes-Einstein Letters...1903-35.* 1964. St Martin. dj. M11. $50.00

HOLMES, Oliver Wendell. *Homoepathy & Its Kindred Delusions.* 1842. Boston. 12mo. orig brds. G7. $295.00

HOLMES, Oliver Wendell. *Poems.* 1836. Boston. 1st ed. sm 8vo. dk bl calf. VG+. B20. $175.00

HOLMES, Oliver Wendell. *Professor at the Breakfast Table.* 1860. Ticknor Fields. 1st ed/1st issue. 410 p. orig brn cloth. G. G7. $95.00

HOLMES, Oliver Wendell. *Urania: Rhymed Lesson.* 1846. Ticknor. 1st ed. 8vo. 32 p. prt wrp. M1. $250.00

HOLMES, Thomas James. *Education of the Bibliographer.* 1957. W Reserve U Pr. VG/dj. B18. $35.00

HOLMES. *Bears! Bears! Bears!* 1991. np. pb. ils/patterns. G2. $7.00

HOLMES. *Gardens in Embroidery.* 1991. np. cloth. G2. $35.00

HOLMES. *Needlepoint Lace.* 1991. np. ils. cloth. G2. $30.00

HOLSTEIN. *Abstract Design in Am Quilts: A Biography.* 1992. np. KY Quilts Project. cloth. G2. $100.00

HOLSTEIN. *Pieced Quilt: Am Design Tradition.* 1975. np. ils. wrp. G2. $25.00

HOLT, E. Emmett. *Diseases of Infancy & Childhood.* 1898. NY. Appleton. 1st ed/2nd issue. 1117 p. half calf/rebacked. G7. $150.00

HOLT, Guy. *James Branch Cabell.* 1924. Phil. Centaur Book Shop. 1/500. G+. A1. $45.00

HOLT, Hazel. *Shortest Journey.* 1992. London. Macmillan. 1st ed. F/F. S5. $25.00

HOLT, Hazel. *Uncertain Death.* 1993. London. Macmillan. 1st ed. F/F. S5. $25.00

HOLT, Henry. *Call Out the Flying Squad.* 1933. Crime Club. 2nd ed. VG/dj. P3. $20.00

HOLT, Rochelle Lynn. *Eidolons.* 1972. Ragnarok. 1/300. sgn. purple cloth. F/sans. V1. $55.00

HOLT, Rochelle Lynn. *Yel Pears, Smooth As Silk.* 1975. Ragnarok. 1/50. sgn twice. VG+. V1. $45.00

HOLT, Samuel; see Westlake, Donald E.

HOLTON, Leonard. *Corner of Paradise.* 1977. St Martin. F/dj. P3. $15.00

HOLTON, Leonard. *Touch of Jonah.* 1968. Dodd Mead. 1st ed. VG/dj. P3. $15.00

HOLTSMARK, Erling B. *Tarzan & Tradition.* 1981. Greenwood. 1st ed. F/dj. P3. $50.00

HOLTTUM, R.E. *Gardening in Lowlands of Malaya.* 1971 (1953). Singapore. 6th prt. photos/pls. 323 p. VG+/rpr. B26. $34.00

HOLWAY, John. *Blk Ball Stars.* 1988. Meeckler. 1st ed. F/VG+. P8. $35.00

HOLWAY, John. *Last .400 Hitter.* 1991. Wm C Brn. 1st ed. M/M. P8. $20.00

HOLWAY, John. *Voices From the Great Blk Baseball Leagues.* 1975. Dodd Mead. 1st ed. VG+/VG. P8. $110.00

HOLWAY, Ruliff S. *Russian River.* 1913. CA U. 1st ed. xl. 11 pls/fld map. 60 p. wrp. D3. $25.00

HOLZER, Hans. *Life After Death.* 1969. Bobbs Merrill. 1st ed. VG/dj. P3. $12.50

HOM, Mei-Ling. *In the Morning.* 1990. Rosendale, NY. Women's Studio. 1/100. sgn. F. B24. $175.00

HOMER. *Iliad.* 1976. Franklin Lib. leather. F. P3. $35.00

HOMER. *Oddyssey.* 1930. London. Medici Soc. trade ed. ils WR Flint/20 color pls. Bayntun bdg. F. F1. $250.00

HOMER. *Odyssey of Homer.* 1990. CA U. 1st ed. F/dj. P3. $25.00

HOMES, A.M. *In a Country of Mothers.* 1993. Knopf. 1st ed. sgn. F/F. Q1. $35.00

HOMES, Geoffrey. *Then There Were Three.* 1944. Books Inc. VG. P3. $10.00

HONDROS, John L. *Occupation & Resistance: Greek Agony 1941-44.* 1983. NY. 8vo. 340 p. cloth. dj. O2. $30.00

HONEY, P.J. *Communism in N Vietnam.* (1963). Cambridge. MIT. 1st ed. F/VG. A7. $30.00

HONIG, Donald. *Am League.* 1987. Crown. 1st revised prt. F/VG+. P8. $30.00

HONIG, Donald. *Baseball in the '30s.* 1989. Crown. 1st ed. rem mk. F/F. P8. $25.00

HONIG, Donald. *Baseball When the Grass Was Real.* 1975. Coward McCann. BC. VG/G+. P8. $25.00

HONIG, Donald. *Baseball: Ils Hist of Am's Game.* 1990. Crown. 1st ed. F/F. P8. $30.00

HONIG, Donald. *October Heroes.* 1979. Simon Schuster. 1st ed. F/VG. P8. $17.50

HONIG, Donald. *St Louis Cardinals: Ils Hist.* 1991. Prentice Hall. 1st ed. M/M. P8. $30.00

HONIG, Donald. *Up From the Minor Leagues.* 1970. Cowles. 1st ed. F/VG+. P8. $35.00

HONORE, Pierre. *Quest of the Wht God.* (1963). London. 1st ed. 228 p. dj. F3. $20.00

HOOBLER & WETANSON. *Hunters.* 1978. Doubleday. 1st ed. F/F. N3. $30.00

HOOD, Graham. *Charles Bridges & William Dering: 2 VA Painters.* ca 1978. Colonial Williamsburg. ils. 125 p. VG. B10. $35.00

HOOD, Mary. *And Venus Is Bl.* (1986). Tichnor Fields. AP. F/prt bl wrp. B3. $35.00

HOOD, Robert E. *12 At War: Great Photographers Under Fire.* (1967). Putnam. 159 p. ils brds. NF. A7. $50.00

HOOK, Donald D. *Madmen of Hist.* 1976. Jonathan David. VG/dj. P3. $17.50

HOOK, Thomas. *Shenandoah Saga.* (1973). Baltimore. sgn. ils/maps. 208 p. F/wrp. B18. $15.00

HOOPER, Robert. *Lexicon Medicum; or, Medical Dictionary.* 1843. Harper. 2 vols in 1. later buckram. VG. G1. $75.00

HOOPER, Ted. *Guide to Bees & Honey.* 1979. Emmaus, PA. Rodale. ils. 260 p. H10. $15.00

HOOPER, William. *50 Yrs Since: Address Delivered Before Alumni...1859* 1861. Chapel Hill, NC. Neathery. 2nd ed. 34 p. NF/prt wrp. M8. $85.00

HOOPES, Roy. *Cain: Biography of James M Cain.* (1982). HRW. 1st ed. NF/dj. B9. $15.00

HOOVER, Bessie R. *Pa Flickinger's Folks.* 1909. Harper. 1st ed. 274 p. VG. S10. $35.00

HOOVER, Herbert. *Am Epic.* 1959-64. Chicago. Regnery. 1st ed. 8vo. 4 vols. F/F/F slipcase. A2. $45.00

HOOVER, Herbert. *Challenge to Liberty.* 1934. Scribner. 1st ed. inscr. F. B4. $200.00

HOOVER, Herbert. *Fishing for Fun & To Wash Your Soul.* (1963). NY. ils. 86 p. F/dj. A17. $10.00

HOOVER, Herbert. *Memoirs of...: Yrs of Adventure, 1874-1920.* 1951. Macmillan. 2nd ed. 8vo. 496 p. VG/dj. V3. $16.00

HOOVER, Matt. *Wild Ginger.* (1909). NY. 1st ed. photos. gilt pict cloth. G. A17. $20.00

HOOVER, RENSCH & RENSCH. *Hist Spots in CA.* 1958. Stanford. index. 411 p. NF. B19. $25.00

HOOVER, Thomas Nathaniel. *Hist of OH U.* 1954. OH U. 260 p. VG/rpr. M20. $7.00

HOPE, Anthony. *Prisoner of Zenda.* nd. Grosset Dunlap. photoplay ed. NF/dj. M2. $30.00

HOPE, Anthony. *Prisoner of Zenda.* 1966. LEC. 1/1500. ils/sgn Donald Spencer. wht cloth. NF/F slipcase. Q1. $75.00

HOPE, Anthony. *Simon Dale.* 1898. London. 1st ed. VG. M2. $12.00

HOPE, Brian; see Creasey, John.

HOPE, Laura Lee. *Bobbsey Twins in WA.* 1919. Grosset Dunlap. gr cloth. VG. M5. $10.00

HOPEWELL, Filmer. *Village Annals Containing Austerus & Humanus.* 1814. Phil. Johnson Warner. 12mo. 35 p. F. B24. $185.00

HOPKINS, G.M. *Selections From the Notebooks of...* 1945. Norfolk, CT. VG/dj. B18. $19.50

HOPKINS, George E. *Airline Pilots. Study in Elite Unionization.* 1971. Cambridge. Harvard. 1st ed. NF/NF. B2. $35.00

HOPKINS, Tom J. *6-Gun Law.* 1963. Avalon. 12mo. VG/VG. A8. $30.00

HOPKINS & MARTIN. *Rotary Riot.* 1992. np. wrp. G2. $22.00

HOPKINS. *Fit To Be Tied.* 1990. np. ils. wrp. G2. $18.00

HOPKINS. *One-of-a-Kind Quilts.* 1989. np. F/wrp. G2. $17.00

HOPLEY, George; see Woolrich, Cornell.

HOPPE, Arthur. *Mr Nixon & My Other Problems.* (1971). Chronicle. inscr/sgn. 226 p. dj. A7. $15.00

HOPPE, Joanne. *Lesson Is Murder.* 1977. HBJ. 1st ed. sgn. VG/dj. P3. $17.50

HORAN, James D. *Across the Cimarron.* 1956. Crown. 1st ed. 301 p. cloth. VG/dj. M20. $30.00

HORAN, James D. *Confederate Agent.* 1954. NY. Crown. 1st ed. VG/dj. A16. $30.00

HORAN, James D. *Confederate Agent.* 1960. np. ils. 326 p. dj. O7. $12.50

HORAN, James D. *Desperate Women.* (1952). NY. 1st ed. 336 p. cloth. VG. D3. $15.00

HORAN, James D. *Great Am W.* 1959. Bonanza. 4to. VG/G+. A8. $15.00

HORAN, James D. *Life & Art of Charles Schreyvogel.* 1969. Crown. ils/pls. cloth. dj. D2. $175.00

HORGAN, Paul. *Abdication of the Artist.* 1965. Phil. Am Philosophical Soc. offprint. inscr. wrp. uncommon. B4. $100.00

HORGAN, Paul. *Great River: Rio Grande in N Am Hist.* 1954. Rinehart. 1st ed. 2 vols. inscr/sgn. F/F slipcase. A18. $100.00

HORGAN, Paul. *Josiah Gregg & His Vision of the Early W.* 1979. FSG. 1st ed. 116 p. F/F clip. B19. $7.50

HORGAN, Paul. *Rome Eternal.* (1959). FSG. 1st ltd ed. 1/350. sgn/#d. NF/slipcase. A18. $100.00

HORLER, Sydney. *Curse of Doone.* 1930. Mystery League. 1st ed. VG/dj. p3. $20.00

HORLER, Sydney. *Dark Night.* 1953. Hodder Stoughton. 1st ed. VG/dj. P3. $35.00

HORLER, Sydney. *False Purple.* 1932. Mystery League. 1st ed. VG/dj. P3. $30.00

HORLER, Sydney. *Man Who Stayed to Supper.* 1941. Herbert Jenkins. 1st ed. VG/VG-. P3. $30.00

HORLER, Sydney. *Scarlett-Special Branch.* 1950. Foulsham. 1st ed. VG. P3. $25.00

HORN, Holloway. *Murder at Linpara.* 1931. Collins. 1st ed. VG. P3. $25.00

HORN, Madeline Darrough. *Farm on the Hill.* (1936). Scribner. reissue. sm 4to. ils Grant Wood. 78 p. VG/G. T5. $65.00

HORN, Madeline Darrough. *Log Cabin Family.* 1939. Scribner. 1st ed. 95 p. VG/VG. P2. $35.00

HORN, Maurice. *Women in the Comics.* 1977. Chelsea House. 1st ed. VG/dj. P3. $15.00

HORNADAY, J.W. *Handbook of Rifle Reloading.* (1973). Hornaday. 1st prt. 512 p. dj. A17. $15.00

HORNADAY, William T. *Minds & Manners of Wild Animals.* 1922. NY. 1st ed. 328 p cloth. A17. $20.00

HORNBEIN, Marjorie. *Temple Emanuel of Denver: Centennial Hist.* 1974. Denver. private prt. 194 p. VG+. S3. $25.00

HORNE & SCHICKEL. *Lena.* 1965. Doubleday. 1st ed. 300 p. dj. A7. $15.00

HORNER, Durbin Lee. *Murder by the Dozen.* 1935. Dingwall-Rock. 1st ed. VG. P3. $25.00

HORNER, John B. *OR Literature.* 1902. Portland. 2nd ed. ils/portraits. 253 p. VG. D3. $25.00

HORNIG, Doug. *Hardball.* 1986. London. Macmillan. 1st ed. F/F. S5. $25.00

HORNSBY, Rogers. *My Kind of Baseball.* 1953. McKay. 1st ed. VG/fair. P8. $35.00

HORNSBY, Wendy. *Nine Sons.* 1992. Mission Viejo. 1st separate ed. 1/200. sgn. F/stapled wrp. M15. $20.00

HORNSBY, Wendy. *No Harm.* 1987. Dodd Mead. 1st ed. F/F. T2. $30.00

HORNSBY, Wendy. *Telling Lies.* 1992. Dutton. ARC of 1st ed. sgn. RS. F/F. S5. $35.00

HORNSBY, Wendy. *Telling Lies.* 1992. Dutton. 1st ed. F/F. T2. $35.00

HORNSBY & SURFACE. *My War w/Baseball.* 1962. McCann. 1st ed. photos. F/VG+. P8. $60.00

HORNUNG, E.W. *Crime Doctor.* 1914. Bobbs Merrill. VG. P3. $30.00

HORNUNG, E.W. *Mr Justice Raffles.* 1909. Scribner. 1st ed. decor brds. VG. P3. $40.00

HOROWITZ, David. *Free World Colossus.* 1965. Hill Wang. 1st ed. NF/VG. B2. $40.00

HOROWITZ, Gad. *Repression...in Psychoanalytic Theory.* 1977. Toronto. 1st Eng ed. 154 p. VG/prt brn wrp. G1. $35.00

HOROWITZ, George. *Spirit of Jewish Law.* 1953. Central Book Co. xl. inscr. 812 p. VG+. S3. $44.00

HORRAX, Gilbert. *Neurosurgery: Hist Sketch.* 1952. Springfield. Thomas. sgn. 135 p. NF/dj. G7. $135.00

HORRICKS, Raymond. *These Jazzmen of Our Time.* 1959. Gollancz. 236 p. dj. A7. $25.00

HORROBIN, David F. *Guide to Kenya & N Tanzania.* 1971. NY. 1st ed. 8vo. ils/maps. 302 p. F/F. H3. $35.00

HORSFORD, Eban Norton. *Landfall of Leif Erikson, AD 1000...* 1892. Boston. Damrell Upham. presentation. 26 lg fld maps. gilt gr cloth. F. K1. $175.00

HORTON, Edith. *Horton-Carey Readers: Book 1 & Book 2.* 1927. Heath. ils Frederick Richardson. VG. L1. $25.00

HORTON, Edith. *Horton-Carey: Woodland Primer.* 1928. Heath. ils Frederick Richardson. G. L1. $12.50

HORTON, George. *In Argolis.* 1902. Chicago. 1st ed. ils. 226 p. cloth/linen spine. O2. $40.00

HORTON, R.G. *Life & Public Services of James Buchanan.* 1856. Derby Jackson. sm 8vo. 428 p. purple cloth. H9. $50.00

HORTON. *Stained Glass Quilting Technique.* 1978. np. ils. G2. $8.00

HORWITT & SKOLE. *Jews in Berkshire Co, MA.* 1972. DOR Co. 1st ed. 74 p. VG+/VG. S3. $35.00

HORWOOD, Harold. *Dancing on the Shore.* (1987). NY. 1st Am ed. 219 p. F/dj. A17. $9.50

HOSHIZAKI, Barbara Jo. *Fern Growers Manual.* 1975. NY. 1st ed. 256 p. VG/dj. B26. $29.00

HOSKING & NEWBERRY. *Art of Bird Photography.* (1948). London. enlarged ed. 103 p. VG/dj. A17. $7.50

HOSKINS, Ann. *Seed Out of Husk.* 1978. Lakeville, CT. 1/400. wrp. N2. $10.00

HOSKINS, Robert. *Tomorrow's Son.* 1977. Doubleday. 1st ed. RS. F/dj. M2. $15.00

HOSMER, James K. *Hist of Expedition of Capts Lewis & Clark, 1804-06.* 1903. McClurg. reprint of 1814 ed. 2 vols. 8vo. F. T8. $175.00

HOSMER, KELLEN & JENKINS. *Fall of S Vietnam.* (1980). NY. Crane Russak. F/NF. A7. $25.00

HOSMER, Stephen T. *Viet Cong Repression & Its Implications for the Future.* (197). Heath Lexington. presentation/sgn. 172 p. dj. A7. $40.00

HOSMER, William. *Young Ladies Book.* 1851. Derby Miller. 1st 301 p. gilt red cloth. B22. $12.00

HOSSENT, Harry. *Movie Treasury: Gangster Movies.* 1974. Octopus. VG/dj. P3. $17.50

HOSTETLER, J.A. *Hutterites in N Am.* 1967. Holt Rinehart. 8vo. G. A8. $4.00

HOSTIE, Raymond. *CG Jung unde die Religion.* 1957. Freiburg im Breisgau. Karl Alber. 303 p. cloth. VG/dj. G1. $25.00

HOTCHKISS, Jedediah. *Make Me a Map of the Valley: Civil War Journal...* (1989). S Methodist U. 4th prt. 352 p. VG. B10. $7.00

HOTT, Nell. *Little Mothers.* 1936. Merrill. 16 p. VG. M5. $35.00

HOTTES, Alfred Carl. *Book of Trees.* (1952). Dodd Mead. ils/photos/index. 440 p. VG/dj. A17. $10.00

HOUCK. *Quilt Encyclopedia Ils.* 1991. np. ils. cloth. G2. $40.00

HOUGH, Alfred Lacey. *Soldier in the W: Civil War Letters of Alfred Lacey Hough.* 1957. PA U. 1st ed. 250 p. cloth. VG/VG. M8. $45.00

HOUGH, Emerson. *Covered Wagon.* 1922. Appleton. 1st ed. map ep. VG. A18. $25.00

HOUGH, Emerson. *Law of the Land.* (1904). Bobbs Merrill. 1st ed. ils Arthur I Keller. F. A18. $40.00

HOUGH, Emerson. *Story of the Outlaw.* 1907. NY. Outing. 1st ed/1st issue. 401 p. VG. H7. $35.00

HOUGH, Emerson. *Way Out.* 1918. Grosset Dunlap. 12mo. G. A8. $6.00

HOUGH, Emerson. *54-40 or Fight.* (1909). Bobbs Merrill. 1st ed. ils Arthur I Keller. F. A18. $50.00

HOUGH, Richard. *Blind Horn's Hate.* (1971). Norton. 1st ed. xl. 336 p. dj. F3. $10.00

HOUGH, Richard. *Last Voyage of Capt Cook.* 1979. NY. Morrow. 1st Am ed. 271 p. half cloth. P4. $35.00

HOUGH, Richard. *Wings of Victory.* 1980. Morrow. 1st ed. F/dj. P3. $12.50

HOUGH, Romeyn Beck. *Handbook of Trees of the N States & Canada...* ca 1907. Harper. ils/ads. 470 p. H10. $20.00

HOUGH, S.B. *Bronze Perseus.* 1962. Walker. VG/VG. P3. $10.00

HOUGH, S.B. *Fear Fortune, Father.* 1974. London. Gollancz. 1st ed. F/NF. S5. $25.00

HOUGH, Samuel J. *Italians & the Creation of Am.* 1980. Providence. M/wrp. O6. $50.00

HOUGHES, Thomas. *Gone to TX: Letters From Our Boys.* 1884. NY. Macmillan. 1st Am ed. 228 p. VG. scarce. H7. $165.00

HOUGHTON, Claude. *Neighbors.* ca 1920. Chicago. later ed. sgn. VG/VG. B5. $20.00

HOUGHTON, Claude. *This Was Ivor Trent.* 1935. Heinemann. 1st ed. VG. P3. $12.00

HOUGHTON, Eric. *Steps Out of Time.* 1980. Lee Shepard. 1st Am ed. lib bdg. F/F clip. N3. $15.00

HOUSE, Homer D. *Wild Flowers.* 1935. NY. 1 vol ed/2nd prt. 4to. 362 p. B28. $120.00

HOUSE, Tom. *Jack's Itch.* 1989. Contemporary. 1st ed. F/F. P8. $15.00

HOUSEHOLD, Geoffrey. *Against the Wind.* (1958). Little Brn. 1st Am ed. dj. A7. $10.00

HOUSEHOLD, Geoffrey. *Dance of the Dwarfs.* 1968. Little Brn. 1st ed. VG/dj. P3. $20.00

HOUSEHOLD, Geoffrey. *Summon the Bright Water.* 1981. Atlantic/Little Brn. 1st ed. VG/dj. P3. $17.50

HOUSEHOLD, Geoffrey. *Watcher in the Shadows.* 1960. London. Michael Joseph. 1st ed. VG+/dj. S5. $25.00

HOUSEMAN, A.E. *AE Houseman: Annotated Hand-List.* 1952. London. Rupert Hart Davis. F/F. C4. $45.00

HOUSEMAN, A.E. *Shropshire Lad.* 1932. NY. 1st ed. Cameo Classic series. NF/sans. V1. $15.00

HOUSEMAN, Laurence. *Blind Love.* 1901. Boston. Cornhill. 1/500. 12mo. 25 p on 4 sheets (fld twice). uncut/unbound. F. B24. $150.00

HOUSER, G.M. *Erasing the Color Line.* (1947). Fellowship Pub. 63 p pamphlet. A7. $20.00

HOUSMAN, Laurence. *Gr Arras.* 1896. London. John Lane. ils/5 full-p pls. gilt gr cloth. VG+. F1. $150.00

HOUSTON, David Franklin. *Critical Study of Nullification in SC.* 1968. Gloucester, MA. Peter Smith. reprint of 1896 ed. cloth. NF. M8. $25.00

HOUSTON, James D. *Men in My Life.* 1987. Creative Arts. 1st ed. F/dj. M2. $15.00

HOUSTON, James D. *W Coast Fiction.* 1979. NY. Bantam. PBO. inscr. F/unread. A11. $55.00

HOUSTON, James. *Spirit Wrestler.* 1980. NY. 1st ed. sgn. F/fair. S9. $18.00

HOUSTON, Robert. *Fourth Codex.* 1988. Houghton Mifflin. 1st ed. VG/dj. P3. $17.95

HOUSTON, Robert. *Nation Thief.* (1985). Ballantine. 1st ed. 12mo. 240 p. F3. $5.00

HOUSTON, Robert. *Nation Thief.* 1984. NY. 1st ed. inscr. F/F. A11. $50.00

HOWARD, Benjamin C. *Report of Decision of Supreme Court of US...* 1857. WA. Cornelius Wendell. 1st ed. 8vo. 239 p. prt wrp. M1. $1,250.00

HOWARD, Clare. *Eng Travelers of the Renaissance.* 1914. John Lane. 1st UK ed. 8vo. 232 p. F. A2. $25.00

HOWARD, Clark. *Am Saturday.* 1981. Richard Marek. rem mk. NF/dj. A7. $25.00

HOWARD, Clark. *Doomsday Squad.* 1970. Weybright Talley. 1st ed. VG/dj. P3. $15.00

HOWARD, Constance. *Constance Howard Book of Stitches.* 1979. np. ils. cloth. G2. $30.00

HOWARD, Donald R. *Chaucer: His Life, His Works, His World.* 1987. Dutton. VG/dj. A16. $20.00

HOWARD, Harry N. *Turkey, the Straits & US Policy.* 1974. Baltimore. 8vo. 337 p. cloth. dj. O2. $25.00

HOWARD, Hartley. *Payoff.* 1976. Collins Crime Club. 1st ed. F/dj. P3. $20.00

HOWARD, J.H. *Great Big ABC.* nd. McLoughlin Bros. 28 p. G/color wrp. scarce. M5. $48.00

HOWARD, James. *Murder Takes a Wife.* 1958. Dutton. 1st ed. VG/dj. P3. $20.00

HOWARD, Keble. *Peculiar Major.* 1919. Doran. 1st ed. 309 p. gray cloth. NF. B22. $5.50

HOWARD, Leslie Ruth. *Quite Remarkable Father.* 1959. Harcourt Brace. 1st ed. 307 p. VG+/VG. M7. $25.00

HOWARD, Maureen. *Before My Time.* 1975. Little Brn. hc ARC. inscr. RS. F/F advance issue. L3. $85.00

HOWARD, Maureen. *Bridgeport Bus.* 1965. HBW. ARC. inscr/dtd 1974. VG/VG. L3. $75.00

HOWARD, Maureen. *Facts of Life.* 1978. Little Brn. 1st ed. inscr. author's 4th book. F/F. L3. $75.00

HOWARD, Maureen. *Not a Word About Nightingales.* 1962. Atheneum. 1st ed. inscr. NF/VG. L3. $150.00

HOWARD, Michael S. *Jonathan Cape, Pub.* 1971. London. Wren Howard/Jonathan Cape. 1st ed. NF/NF. M7. $50.00

HOWARD, R.W. *Thundergate: Forts of Niagara.* (1968). Prentice Hall. 1st ed. 8vo. 241 p. VG/VG+. A2. $17.50

HOWARD, Robert E. *Alumric.* 1975. Donald Grant. 1st ed. VG/dj. P3. $20.00

HOWARD, Robert E. *Always Comes Evening.* 1957. Arkham. 1st ed. F/dj. M2. $500.00

HOWARD, Robert E. *Coming of Conan.* 1953. Gnome. 1st ed. F/NF. M2. $95.00

HOWARD, Robert E. *Conan the Barbarian.* 1954. Gnome. 1st ed. VG. M2. $35.00

HOWARD, Robert E. *Dark Man & Others.* 1963. Arkham. 1st ed. F/dj. M2. $200.00

HOWARD, Robert E. *Devil in Iron.* 1976. Donald Grant. F/dj. P3. $35.00

HOWARD, Robert E. *Red Nails.* 1979. Berkley Putnam. NF/dj. M2. $20.00

HOWARD, Robert E. *Return of Conan.* 1957. Gnome. 1st ed. F/M. M2. $100.00

HOWARD, Robert E. *Singers in the Shadows.* 1970. Donald Grant. 1/500. 1st appearance of these poems. F/NF. Q1. $150.00

HOWARD, Robert E. *Skull-Face & Others.* 1946. Arkham. 1st ed. intro August Derleth. NF/NF. Q1. $600.00

HOWARD, Robert E. *Skull-Face & Others.* 1946. Arkham. 1st ed. VG/frayed. M2. $575.00

HOWARD, Robert E. *Skullface Omnibus.* 1974. Spearman. 1st UK ed. F/NF. M2. $40.00

HOWARD, Robert E. *Sowers of the Thunder.* 1973. Donald Grant. 1st ed. ils/inscr RG Krenkel. F/NF. Q1. $60.00

HOWARD, Robert E. *Sword of Conan.* 1952. Gnome. 1/4000. 1st ed. 2nd Conan book. NF/NF. Q1. $150.00

HOWARD, Robert E. *Worms of the Earth.* 1974. Donald Grant. 1st ed. F/dj. P3. $25.00

HOWARD, Robert West. *Great Iron Trail: Story of 1st Transcontinental Railroad.* 1962. NY. Bonanza. 8vo. pls. 376 p. VG/G. B11. $15.00

HOWARD, Robert West. *Horse In Am.* 1965. Chicago. Follett. 2nd prt. VG/VG. O3. $18.00

HOWARD, Robert West. *This Is the W.* (1957). NAL. 1st prt. 12mo. 240 p. pict wrp. D3. $15.00

HOWARD & TIERNEY. *Tigers of the Sea.* 1974. Donald Grant. 1st ed. sgn Tierney. ils/sgn Tim Kirk. F/F. F4. $50.00

HOWARD. *Textile Crafts.* 1978. np. ils. cloth. G2. $25.00

HOWARTH, David. *Desert King: Life of Ibn Saud.* 1964. London. Collins. 1st ed. 252 p. VG+/VG+. M7. $45.00

HOWATCH, Susan. *April's Grave.* 1974. Stein Day. xl. dj. P3. $5.00

HOWATSON, M.C. *Oxford Companion to Classical Literature.* 1989. Oxford. 2nd ed. F/dj. P3. $45.00

HOWBERT, Abraham R. *Reminiscences of the War.* 1884. Springfield. 1st ed. 388 p. orig cloth. VG. M8. $125.00

HOWE, Ellic. *Astrology: Recent Hist...Untold Story in WWII.* (1968). Walker. 1st Am ed. 8vo. 259 p. F/VG. A2. $15.00

HOWE, Fanny. *Bronte Wilde.* Avon Equinox. PBO. inscr. F/8vo wrp. A11. $35.00

HOWE, Henry. *Adventures & Achievements of Americans...* 1860. Cincinnati. later ed of 1858 1st. ils. 720 p. leather. G. D7. $75.00

HOWE, Henry. *Travels & Adventures of Celebrated Travelers...* 1857. Cincinnati. later ed. 832 p. rstr spine. G. D7. $90.00

HOWE, Irving. *1984 Revisited.* 1983. Harper. 1st ed. NF/dj. M2. $15.00

HOWE, Julia Ward. *Battle Hymn of the Republic.* ca 1900. Warren, PA. Hazeltine. miniature. 16 p. wrp. H10. $35.00

HOWE, Julia Ward. *Passion-Flowers.* 1854. Ticknor Reed Fields. 1st ed. 12mo. 187 p. gilt cloth. M1. $85.00

HOWELL, John. *CA Catalogue.* 1979. Howell. 4to. F. A8. $15.00

HOWELL, Willey. *Glossary of Legal Terms & Phrases.* 1910. Ft Leavenworth. Army Service Schools Dept of Law. later cloth. M11. $45.00

HOWELLS, William Dean. *Rise of Silas Lapham.* 1951. Modern Lib. VG/dj. P3. $10.00

HOWES, Barbara. *From the Gr Antilles.* 1966. NY. 1st ed. sgn. F/VG+. A11. $80.00

HOWES, Royce. *Case of the Copy-Hook Killing.* 1945. Dutton. 1st ed. VG/torn. P3. $10.00

HOWES, Wright. *USiana (1700-1950).* 1954. NY. sm 4to. 656 p. buckram. NF. D3. $100.00

HOWES, Wright. *USiana.* 1962. NY. RR Bowker. 2nd ed. 652 p. orig cloth. VG. M8. $85.00

HOWLAND, Charles P. *Greek Refugee Settlement.* 1926. Geneva. 8vo. 216 p. brds. O2. $65.00

HOWLETT, Duncan. *No Greater Love.* (1966). Harper Row. 1st ed. 242 p. NF/VG+. A7. $30.00

HOYLE, Edmond. *Short Treatise on Game of Whist.* 1750. London. Osborne. 10th ed. sgn Hoyle/pub T Osborne. 12mo. 224 p. VG+. B20. $350.00

HOYLE, Fred. *Of Men & Galaxies.* 1964. Seattle. WA U. 1st ed. F/VG+ clip. N3. $15.00

HOYLE, Trevor. *Last Gasp.* 1983. Crown. 1st ed. VG/dj. P3. $17.50

HOYLE & HOYLE. *Inferno.* 1973. Harper. 1st Am ed. VG/torn. M2. $15.00

HOYLE & HOYLE. *Into Deepest Space.* nd. BC. NF/dj. P3. $5.00

HOYLE & HOYLE. *Into Deepest Space.* 1974. Harper. 1st Am ed. F/dj. M2. $10.00

HOYNE, Thomas. *Intrigue on the Upper Level.* 1934. Reilly Lee. 1st ed. VG/color Canon dj. M2. $50.00

HOYT, Edwin P. *Germans Who Never Lost.* 1968. Funk Wagnall. VG/dj. A16. $15.60

HOYT, Edwin P. *Horatio's Boys: Life & Works of Horatio Alger Jr.* 1974. Chilton. 1st ed. ils. 263 p. VG+/VG-. S10. $12.00

HOYT, Richard. *Head of State.* 1985. Tor. 1st ed. F/dj. P3. $15.00

HOYT, Richard. *Trotsky's Run.* 1982. NY. Morrow. 1st ed. F/F. S5. $30.00

HOYT, Roland S. *Checklists for Ornamental Plants of Subtropical Regions.* 1938. LA. 1st ed. ils. 383 p. bl cloth. B26. $22.50

HOYT, W.M. *Cruise on the Mediterranean.* 1894. Chicago. 1st ed. 8vo. aeg. pict cloth. F. H3. $20.00

HRDLICKA, Alex. *Early Man in S Am. Smithsonian...Ethnology Bulletin 52.* 1912. WA, DC. ils/photos. 405 p. G7. $125.00

HRDLICKA, Alex. *Physiological & Medical Observations...Indians of SW Am...* 1908. GPO. Bulletin 34. 28 pls. 460 p. G7. $135.00

HRDLICKA, Alex. *Skeletal Remains Suggesting or Attributed to Early Man...* 1907. GPO. 21 lithos. 113 p. G7. $95.00

HRDLICKA, Alex. *Tuberculosis Among Certain Indian Tribes of the US.* 1909. WA. 22 pls. 48 p. NF. G7. $65.00

HSEIH, Tehyi. *Confucius Said It 1st.* 1936. Boston. Chinese Service Bureau. G. E3. $15.00

HSIA, Adrian. *Chinese Cultural Revolution.* 1972. McGraw Hill. 1st Am ed. 254 p. VG. W1. $15.00

HSIUNG, S.I. *Romance of the Western Chamber.* 1971 (1968). NY. Columbia. 2nd prt. 281 p. orig acetate dj. A7. $15.00

HSU, Leonard Shihlien. *Political Philosophy of Confucianism.* 1975. London/NY. Curzon/Barnes Noble. reprint 1932 ed. brn cloth. F/dj. G1. $25.00

HUBBARD, Alice. *Life Lessons, Truths Concerning People Who Have Lived.* (1909). Roycroft. 194 p. red suede/brds. NF. B14. $75.00

HUBBARD, Bernard R. *Mush, You Malemutes!* 1932. NY. 1st book ed. ils. 179 p. map ep. gilt bl cloth. F/G. H3. $45.00

HUBBARD, Charles D. *Old New Eng Village...Drawings, Text & Hand Lettering by...* 1947. Portland. Falmouth. folio. ils. 107 p. H10. $25.00

HUBBARD, Freeman H. *RR Ave.* (1945). NY. 1st ed. 374 p. cloth. VG. D3. $15.00

HUBBARD, L. Ron. *An Alien Affair.* 1986. Bridge. 1st ed. F/dj. P3. $25.00

HUBBARD, L. Ron. *An Alien Affair. Mission Earth, Vol 4.* 1986. Bridge. ARC. NF/wrp. B2. $40.00

HUBBARD, L. Ron. *Analytical Mind.* 1950. Street Smith. 1st ed. VG. A8. $15.00

HUBBARD, L. Ron. *Blk Genesis.* 1986. Bridge. 1st ed. F/dj. P3. $25.00

HUBBARD, L. Ron. *Buckskin Brigades.* 1977. Theta Pr. 1st thus ed. as new. M2. $50.00

HUBBARD, L. Ron. *Buckskin Brigades.* 1987. Jameson Books. 1st ed. F/dj. P3. $20.00

HUBBARD, L. Ron. *Dianetics & Scientology Technology Dictionary.* 1975. Pub Organization. 1st ed/2nd prt. VG. A8. $50.00

HUBBARD, L. Ron. *Dianetics Today.* 1975. Church of Scientology. 1st ed/2nd prt. VG. A8. $55.00

HUBBARD, L. Ron. *Dianetics.* 1950. Hermitage House. 1st ed/3rd prt. F/VG. A8. $100.00

HUBBARD, L. Ron. *Doomed Planet, Vol 10.* 1987. Bridge. 1st ed. VG/VG. A8. $10.00

HUBBARD, L. Ron. *Doomed Planet.* 1987. Bridge. 1st ed. F/dj. P3. $25.00

HUBBARD, L. Ron. *Fear.* 1991. Bridge. 1st ed. F/F. P3. $16.95

HUBBARD, L. Ron. *Final Blackout.* 1989. Bridge. 1st ed. F/VG. A8. $20.00

HUBBARD, L. Ron. *Fortune of Fear.* 1986. Bridge. 1st ed. F/dj. P3. $25.00

HUBBARD, L. Ron. *Hist of Man.* 1980. Scientology Pub. 1st ed. M/M. A8. $25.00

HUBBARD, L. Ron. *Invaders Plan. Mission Earth, Vol 1.* 1985. Bridge. AP. NF/wrp. B2. $50.00

HUBBARD, L. Ron. *Kingslayer.* 1949. Fantasy. 1st ed. G/dj. M18. $225.00

HUBBARD, L. Ron. *Magnificent Failure.* 1947. Street Smith. 1st ed. VG. A8. $30.00

HUBBARD, L. Ron. *Management Series, Vol 1.* 1982. Bridge. 1st ed. F. A8. $100.00

HUBBARD, L. Ron. *Mission Earth.* nd. LA. Bridge. not 1st ed. 5 vols. VG/dj. N2. $25.00

HUBBARD, L. Ron. *Professor.* 1940. Street Smith. 1st ed. VG. A8. $23.00

HUBBARD, L. Ron. *Slaves of Sleep.* 1948. Shasta. 1st ed. F/dj. M2. $350.00

HUBBARD, L. Ron. *Slaves of Sleep.* 1948. Shasta. 1st ed. author's 3rd novel of SF. VG+/NF. Q1. $275.00

HUBBARD, L. Ron. *Slaves of Sleep.* 1979. Dell. 1st ed. F. A8. $5.00

HUBBARD, L. Ron. *Typewriter in the Sky/Fear.* 1951. Gnome. 1st ed. NF/NF. Q1. $250.00

HUBBARD, L. Ron. *Villany Victorious, Vol 9.* 1987. Bridge. 1st ed/2nd prt. VG/VG. A8. $10.00

HUBBARD, L. Ron. *Voyage of Vengeance.* 1987. Bridge. 1st ed/2nd prt. VG/VG. A8. $10.00

HUBBARD, L. Ron. *2nd Dynamic.* 1981. Heron Books. 1st ed. VG. A8. $30.00

HUBBARD, L. Ron. *7 Steps to the Arbiter.* 1975. Major Books. 1st pb issue. G+. A8. $5.00

HUBBS, Rebecca. *Memoir of..., Minister of Gospel in Soc of Friends...* (1884). Friends Bookstore. 16mo. 144 p. VG. V3. $12.00

HUBBS & LAGLER. *Fishes of the Great Lakes Region.* (1983). MI U. 5th prt. ils. 213 p. F. A17. $22.50

HUBER, John. *ACWA on Trial. Play of Movement, Ideas & Forces.* 1926. NY. Amalgamated Clothing Workers of Am. NF/wrp. B2. $75.00

HUBER, Mary Taylor. *Bishop's Progress.* ca 1988. Smithsonian. 8vo. 264 p. half cloth. M/M. P4. $25.00

HUBERMAN & SWEEZY. *On Segregation.* 1956. Monthly Review. 31 p. self wrp. A7. $20.00

HUBERT. *One-Piece Knits That Fit.* 1978. np. ils. cloth. G2. $16.00

HUDON, Edward G. *Freedom of Speech & Pr in Am.* 1963. WA. Public Affairs Pr. G/dj. M11. $50.00

HUDSON, David. *Hist of Jemima Wilkinson, Preacheress of 18th Century...* 1821. Geneva, NY. 1st ed. 12mo. recent leather. M1. $675.00

HUDSON, Derek. *Lewis Carroll.* 1977. NY. Clarkson Potter. 1st ed. 271 p. VG/VG. D1. $65.00

HUDSON, G. Donald. *Encyclopedia Britannica World Atlas...* 1959. Chicago. Britannica. unabridged ed. 60 pls/120 maps/414 tables. VG. P4. $40.00

HUDSON, Howard Penn. *Pub Newsletters.* 1982. Scribner. 1st ed. dj. N2. $5.00

HUDSON, Jan; see Smith, George H.

HUDSON, Tom. *W Is My Home.* 1956. Laguna House. 12mo. F/fair. A8. $25.00

HUDSON, W.H. *Birds of a Feather.* (1981). Eng. Moonraker. 1st ed. 108 p. dj. F3. $10.00

HUDSON, W.H. *Famous Missions of CA.* (1901). NY. 12mo. 70 p. cloth. VG. D3. $15.00

HUDSON, W.H. *Little Lost Boy.* 1929. Knopf. 3rd prt. ils Lathrop. 187 p. teg. gilt pict bdg. VG. P2. $75.00

HUDSON, W.H. *Purple Land.* nd. NY. Dutton. ils Keith Henderson. 368 p. VG. F3. $15.00

HUETTL, Irene Arndt. *Esther Morris of Old S Pass & Other Poems of the W.* 1965. Francestown, NH. 62 p. dj. N2. $20.00

HUGER SMITH, Alice R. *Charles Fraser.* 1967. Charleston. Garnier. 58 p. cloth. dj. D2. $45.00

HUGGHINS, Ernest. *Parasites of Fishes in SD.* nd. np. 73 p. VG. A17. $6.00

HUGHES, Colin; see Creasey, John.

HUGHES, Dorothy B. *Expendable Man.* 1963. Random. 1st ed. F/F. M15. $45.00

HUGHES, Dorothy B. *Ride the Pink Horse.* 1946. DSP. 1st ed. NF/F. M15. $85.00

HUGHES, Dorothy B. *Ride the Pink Horse.* 1958. Dell. new Dell ed. VG/wrp. C8. $15.00

HUGHES, H. Stuart. *Consciousness & Soc...* 1958. Knopf. 1st ed. 434 p. patterned blk cloth. G1. $28.50

HUGHES, Helen MacGill. *Fantastic Lodge. Autobiography of Girl Drug Addict.* 1961. Houghton Mifflin. 1st ed. inscr. F/NF. B2. $40.00

HUGHES, John T. *Doniphan's Expedition.* 1848. Cincinnati. 2nd ed. xl. ils/pls. new bdg. H9. $150.00

HUGHES, Langston. *Fields of Wonder.* 1947. Knopf. ARC. pub gr cloth. NF. Q1. $750.00

HUGHES, Langston. *Fight for Freedom.* (1962). Berkeley. pb. 224 p. NF. A7. $10.00

HUGHES, Langston. *First Book of Jazz.* 1955. NY. Watts. 1st ed. ils Cliff Roberts/ music David Martin. F/dj. B14. $125.00

HUGHES, Langston. *Ways of Wht Folks.* 1934. Knopf. 1st ed. VG. B2. $100.00

HUGHES, Rupert. *Attorney for the People: Story of Thomas E Dewey.* 1940. Houghton Mifflin. 1st ed. 8vo. 361 p. VG+/VG. A2. $20.00

HUGHES, Rupert. *War of the Mayan King.* 1952. Winston. 1st ed. F/NF. M2. $15.00

HUGHES, Shirley. *Lucy & Tom's ABC.* 1986. Viking Kestrel. 1st Am ed. sm 4to. F/F. T5. $30.00

HUGHES, William. *Philips' Select Atlas of Modern Geography...* ca 1900. London. Philip. 36 color maps. NF. O6. $175.00

HUGHES. *Even More.* 1989. np. ils. wrp. G2. $18.00

HUGHES. *More Template-Free Quiltmaking.* 1987. np. ils. wrp. G2. $17.00

HUGHES-STANTON, Penelope. *Wood Engravings of Blair Hughes-Stanton.* 1991. Pinner. Private Lib Assn. sm folio. F. F1. $90.00

HUGO, Richard. *Good Luck in Cracked Italian.* 1968. NY. 1st ed. inscr. F/wrp. A11. $125.00

HUGO, Victor. *Hunchback of Notre Dame.* (1940). Triangle. photoplay ed. VG/NF. B4. $65.00

HUGO, Victor. *Hunchback of Notre Dame.* nd. AL Burt. photoplay ed. 416 p. VG/dj. M20. $125.00

HUGO, Victor. *Les Miserables...* 1862. NY. 1st Am ed. octavo. 5 vols. orig purple cloth. NF. H5. $1,500.00

HUGO, Victor. *So This Then Is the Battle of Waterloo.* 1907. Roycroft. 1st thus ed. 106 p. limp suede. VG. M8. $50.00

HUIE, W.B. *He Slew the Dreamer.* 1968. Delacorte. 1st ed. 212 p. NF/NF. A7. $35.00

HUIE, W.B. *Klansman.* (1967). Delacorte. 1st ed. 303 p. dj. A7. $18.00

HUIE, W.B. *3 Lives for MS.* 1965. NY. WCC Books. 254 p. dj. A7. $18.00

HUISH. *Samplers & Tapestry Embroideries.* 1970. np. reprint of 1913. ils. wrp. G2. $30.00

HUIZENGA, Lee S. *Unclean! Unclean!...* *Glimpses of Land Where Leprosy Thrives.* 1927. Grand Rapids. Smitter. 1st ed. ils. 172 p. N2. $15.00

HULKE, J.W. *On Fractures & Dislocations of the Vertebral Column...* 1892. London. ils. 57 p. G7. $60.00

HULL, E.M. *Planets for Sale.* 1954. Fell. 1st ed. VG/dj. M2. $25.00

HULL, E.M. *Sons of the Sheik.* (ca 1926). AL Burt. 1st ed. F/NF. B4. $100.00

HULL, Edward. *Monograph on Sub-Oceanic Physiography of N Atlantic...* 1912. London. Stanford. lg folio. maps. NF. O6. $225.00

HULL, William I. *Willem Sewel of Amsterdam, 1653-1720...* 1933. Swarthmore, PA. 8vo. 225 p. VG. V3. $30.00

HULL, William I. *William Penn & the Dutch Quaker Migration to PA.* 1970. Baltimore. Genealogial Pub. reprint. 8vo. 445 p. VG. V3. $30.00

HULT, Ruby. *Guns of the Lewis & Clar[k] Expedition.* 1960. Tacoma, WA. Pacific N[W] Hist Phamplet 1. F/wrp. T8. $25.00

HULTEN, Pontus. *Machine.* 1968. N[Y] MOMA. metal bdg. B30. $65.00

HULTON, Paul. *Watercolor Drawings [of] John Wht From British Mus...* 1965. WA. N[a] Gallery of Art. 41 ils. NF/wrp. O6. $45.00

HULTZEN, Claude H. *Old Fort Niagar[a].* 1938. Buffalo. 1st ed. pocket map. 63 p. s[il] vered blk wrp. H3. $20.00

HUME, H. Harold. *Azaleas: Kinds & Cu[l]* *ture.* 1956. Macmillan. ils. 199 p. H10. $15.0[0]

HUME, Ivor Noel. *Here Lies VA. Archaeol[o] gist's View of Colonial Life...* 1963. Knopf. 1st ed. ils/photos/maps. VG/VG. B11. $20.00

HUMELSINE, Carisle H. *Recollections [of] John D Rockefeller Jr in Williamsburg...* (1985[?]) Colonial Williamsburg. presentation. 20 [p] VG/wrp. B10. $8.00

HUMFREVILLE, J. Lee. *Twenty Yrs Amon[g] Our Hostile Indians...* (1903). NY. Hunte[r] reissue of 1897 ed w/new ils. sm 4to. re[d] cloth. VG+. B20. $250.00

HUMPHREY, Herman. *Death of Presiden[t] Harrison, a Discourse.* 1841. Amherst. 1st ed[?] 24 p. G/wrp. D7. $50.00

HUMPHREY, Robert R. *90 Yrs & 535 Miles[.]* 1987. Albuquerque. 408 photos/448 maps[.] M/dj. B26. $22.50

HUMPHREY, Seth K. *Loafing Through th[e] Pacific.* 1929. Phil. 8vo. 306 p. map ep. pic[t] cloth. F. H3. $25.00

HUMPHREY, Zephine. *Cactus Forest.* 1938[.] Dutton. 8vo. F. A8. $20.00

HUMPHREYS, David. *Life & Heroi[c] Exploits of Israel Putnam.* nd (1850s). Colum[.] bus. 190 p. G. B18. $15.00

HUMPHREYS, Josephine. *Dreams of Sleep[.]* 1984. Viking. ARC. inscr. author's 1st book[.] F/NF. L3. $125.00

HUNGERFORD, Edward. *Men of Fire[.]* 1946. Random. G/dj. E3. $12.00

HUNT, Althea. *William & Mary Theatre.* ca 1968. Dietz. ils/photos. 231 p. VG/G+[.] B10. $25.00

HUNT, Barbara. *Little Night Music.* 1947[.] Rinehart. 1st ed. sgn. VG/worn. M2. $20.00

HUNT, Frazier. *Untold Story of Dougla[s] MacArthur.* 1954. Devin Arair Co. 1s[t] ed/2nd prt. A8. $18.00

HUNT, Kyle; see Creasey, John.

HUNT, M.A. *How To Grow Cut Flowers[.]* 1893. Terre Haute. self pub. 1st ed. 228 p[.] H10. $15.00

UNT, Mabel Leigh. *Johnny-Up & Johnny-own.* 1962. Lippincott. Weekly Reader BC. thus ed. 8vo. 94 p. G. V3. $8.50

UNT, Mabel Leigh. *Johnny-Up & Johnny-own.* 1962. Lippincott. 1st ed. 8vo. 94 p. lib g. VG. T5. $15.00

UNT, Mabel Leigh. *Peddler's Clock.* 1936. rosset Dunlap. ils Elizabeth O Jones. F/G. 5. $30.00

UNT, Peter. *Shell Gardens Book.* 1964. Lon-n. Phoenix. 1st ed. ils. 319 p. VG. B28. $22.50

UNT, Rachel McMaster Miller. *William nn, Horticulturist.* 1953. Pittsburgh. 1/999. . 38 p. VG. B26. $22.50

UNT, W.G. *Address Delivered at Nashville, TN, ril 6, 1831...* 1831. Nashville. Hunt Tardiff. o. new quarter morocco. H9. $250.00

UNT, W.H. *Pre-Raphaelitism & the Pre-phaelite Brotherhood.* ca 1905. Macmillan. ick 8vo. 2 vols. teg. NF. F1. $150.00

UNT, W.R. *Arctic Passage: Turbulent ist...Bering Sea 1697-1975.* (1975). Scribner. t ed. 8vo. 395 p. VG+/VG+. A2. $15.00

UNT & HUNT. *Horses & Heroes. Story of e Horse in Am for 450 Yrs.* 1949. NY. 1st ed. 6 p. cloth. dj. D3. $25.00

UNT & THOMPSON. *N to the Horizon: rctic Dr & Hunter 1913-1917.* (1980). Cam-n. photos/index. 117 p. F/dj. A17. $20.00

UNTER, Alexander. *Culina Famulatrix edicinae; or, Receipts in Cookery...* 1804. ork. Wilson Spence. 119 p. quarter an/marbled brds. G7. $395.00

UNTER, C. Bruce. *Guide to Ancient Maya uins.* (1977). Norman, OK. 4th prt. 332 p. . $10.00

UNTER, C. Bruce. *Guide to Ancient Mexi-n Ruins.* 1977. Norman, OK. 1st ed. ils. 1 p. VG/VG. B11. $30.00

UNTER, D'Allard; see Ballard, W.T.

UNTER, Dard. *Elbert Hubbard & a Mes-ge to Garcia.* 1981. Buffalo. Hillside Pr. iniature. 1/250. cloth. F. H10. $25.00

UNTER, Dard. *Papermaking by Hand in m.* 1950. Chillicothe. Mtn House Pr. 1st ed. 210. folio. cloth fld box. M1. $9,500.00

UNTER, Dard. *Papermaking Through 18 nturies.* 1930. NY. Rudge. 1st ed. lg 8vo. 8 p. F/dj. F1. $195.00

UNTER, Evan. *Another Part of the City.* 1986. ysterious. 1/250. sgn. F/slipcase. B9. $45.00

UNTER, Evan. *Beauty & the Beast.* 982). Hamish Hamilton. 1st ed. NF/NF p. B3. $30.00

HUNTER, Evan. *Evil Sleep!* 1952. Falcon Books. PBO. sgn. digest size. NF. A11. $175.00

HUNTER, Evan. *Find the Feathered Serpent.* 1952. Winston. 1st ed. VG/dj. M2. $45.00

HUNTER, Evan. *Heat.* 1981. NY. Viking. 1st ed. inscr/sgn. F/F. S5. $40.00

HUNTER, Evan. *House That Jack Built.* 1988. Holt. 1st ed. F/F. F4. $20.00

HUNTER, Evan. *Jack & the Beanstalk.* (1984). Harper Row. 1st ed. F/dj. B4. $45.00

HUNTER, Evan. *Killer's Payoff.* (1994). Armchair Detective Lib. ARC/1st hc ed. RS. F/dj. B4. $35.00

HUNTER, Evan. *Lizzie.* 1984. BC. VG/dj. C1. $4.00

HUNTER, Evan. *Lullaby.* 1989. Morrow. 1st ed. F/NF. F4. $18.00

HUNTER, Evan. *Poison.* 1987. Arbor. 1st ed. F/F. F4. $20.00

HUNTER, Evan. *Strangers When We Meet.* (1958). Simon Schuster. 1st ed. author's 3rd novel. VG/VG. B4. $50.00

HUNTER, Evan. *8 Blk Horses.* (1985). Hamish Hamilton. 1st ed. NF/NF. B3. $30.00

HUNTER, Evan. *8 Blk Horses.* (1985). Mysterious. 1/300. sgn. F/slipcase. B9. $45.00

HUNTER, John D. *Manners & Customs of Several Indian Tribes W of MS...* 1823. Phil. prt for author. 8vo. 402 p. contemporary calf. M1. $400.00

HUNTER, John. *Treatise on the Blood, Inflammation & Gunshot Wounds.* 1817. Phil. Webster. 8 engravings. 514 p. orig sheep/rebacked. G7. $250.00

HUNTER, John. *Treatise on the Blood, Inflammation & Gunshot Wounds...* 1794. London. Richardson. 1st ed. 575 p. 19th-century morocco. G7. $1,175.00

HUNTER, Stephen. *Master Sniper.* 1980. NY. Morrow. 1st ed. F/F. M15. $40.00

HUNTER, William S. Jr. *Chisolm's Panoramic Guide From Niagra to Quebec.* ca 1868. Montreal. CR Chisolm. fld panorama in 34 sections. brn cloth. NF. K1. $200.00

HUNTER & HUNTER. *Living Dogs & Dead Lions.* (1986). Viking. 1st ed. dj. A7. $18.00

HUNTER & KETEYAN. *Catfish: My Life in Baseball.* 1988. McGraw Hill. later prt. F/F. P8. $50.00

HUNTER & MACALPINE. *Three Hundred Yrs of Psychiatry 1535-1860.* 1982 (1963). NY. Carlisle Pub. correct reprint of Oxford 1970 ed. bl buckram. F/dj. G1. $125.00

HUNTFORD, Roland. *New Totalitarians.* 1971. London. Allen Lane/Penguin. 1st ed. 8vo. 354 p. VG/VG. A2. $15.00

HUNTINGDON, David. *Tahitian Holiday.* 1954. NY. 1st ed. 309 p. F/VG. H3. $15.00

HUNTINGTON, Annie Oakes. *Poison Ivy & Swamp Sumach.* 1908. Jamaica Plain. self pub. 1st ed. 48 p. H10. $20.00

HUNTINGTON, Ellsworth. *Red Man's Conti-nent.* 1921. np. ils/index. 183 p. F. O7. $9.50

HUNTINGTON, H. Jr. *View of S Am & Mexico...* 1827. NY. subscriber ed. 2 vols in 1. 8vo. gilt sheep. H9. $75.00

HUNTINGTON, Jonathan. *Classical Sacred Musick.* 1812. Boston. 1st ed. 12mo. 75 p. calf. M1. $150.00

HUNTINGTON, Raldolph. *Gen Grant's Arabian Horses, Leopard & Linden Tree...* 1885. Phil. 1st ed. VG. O3. $195.00

HUNTON, W. Alphaeus. *Decision in Africa.* 1957. Internat. 251 p. wrp. A7. $15.00

HUNTON & JOHNSON. *Two Colored Women w/Am Expeditionary Forces.* (1920). Brooklyn Eagle. 1st ed. VG. B4. $275.00

HURLBURT, J.S. *Hist of Rebellion in Bradley Co, E TN.* 1866. Indianapolis. Downey Brause. 1st ed. fld map. 280 p. VG. M8. $450.00

HURWITZ, Ken. *Marching Nowhere.* (1971). Norton. 1st ed. 216 p. VG+/dj. A7. $25.00

HUSBAND, Joseph. *Hist of the Pullman Car.* 1974. Blk Letter Pr. reprint of 1917 McClurg ed. VG/dj. A16. $25.00

HUSE, Caleb. *Supplies for Confederate Army: How They Were Obtained...* 1904. Boston. Marvin. 1st ed. 36 p. NF/prt wrp. scarce. M8. $150.00

HUSSEY, Christopher. *Eng Gardens & Landscapes, 1700-50.* 1967. NY. 174 p. F/dj. B26. $129.00

HUSTON, James L. *Panic of 1857 & the Coming of the Civil War.* 1987. LA State. 1st ed. 315 p. NF/NF. M8. $35.00

HUTCHENS, John K. *One Man's MT: Infor-mal Portrait of a State.* 1964. Lippincott. 2nd prt. 221 p. F/F. H7. $15.00

HUTCHINGS, James M. *Scenes of Wonder & Curiosity in CA.* 1862. San Francisco. xl. ils. 267 p. aeg. rebacked w/orig backstrip. VG. D3. $75.00

HUTCHINS, Eileen. *Wolfram Von Eschebach's Parzival: An Intro.* 1979. London. Temple Lodge. 1st ed. 120 p. NF/stiff wrp. C1. $9.50

HUTCHINS, Frank. *Houseboating on a Colonial Waterway.* 1910. Page. ils. 299 p. B10. $15.00

HUTCHINS, Jere C. *Jere C Hutchins: A Personal Story.* 1938. Detroit. private prt. sgn. 8vo. pls. 372 p. G/G. B11. $45.00

HUTCHINSON, Benajamin. *Biographica Medica; or, Hist & Critical Memoirs...* 1788. London. Johnson. 1st ed. xl. 2 vols. 19th-century bdg. G7. $595.00

HUTCHINSON, Francis. *Hist Essay Concerning Witchcraft...* 1720 (1780). London. Knaplock. 2nd enlarged ed. 336 p. modern bl cloth. G1. $325.00

HUTCHINSON, H.N. *Extinct Monsters.* 1893. London. Chapman Hall. 3rd prt. NF. B2. $50.00

HUTCHINSON, H.N. *Marriage Customs in Many Lands.* 1897. London. Seeley. 1st ed. 24 pls. 348 p. pict red cloth. G1. $75.00

HUTCHINSON, W.Z. *Advanced Bee-Culture...* 1911. Medina, OH. AI Root. 4th ed. ils. 205 p. cloth. H10. $35.00

HUTSON, Shaun. *Captives.* 1991. Macdonald. 1st ed. F/F. F4. $35.00

HUTSON, Shaun. *Renegades.* 1991. Macdonald. 1st ed. F/F. F4. $35.00

HUTSON, Shaun. *Shadows.* 1985. WH Allen. 1st UK ed. F/F. F4. $35.00

HUTTALL, Thomas. *Journal of Travels Into AK Territory During Yr 1819.* 1980. Norman. index. 361 p. gray cloth. M/M. P4. $30.00

HUTTON, Clark. *Country ABC.* nd (1940). Oxford U. probable 1st ed. 26 full-p ils. cloth. VG/tattered dj. M5. $55.00

HUTTON, Harold. *Doc Middleton: Life & Legends of Nortorious Plains Outlaw.* 1980. Swallow. ils/maps/notes. 290 p. F/F. B19. $15.00

HUTTON, Harold. *Vigilante Days: Frontier Justice Along the Niobrara.* 1978. Swallow. 1st ed. ils/notes/index. 365 p. F/dj. B19. $25.00

HUTTON, John. *Trout & Salmon Fishing.* 1949. Boston. 1st ed. VG/VG. B5. $35.00

HUTTON, Laurence. *Literary Landmarks of London.* 1885. London. 1st ed. octavo. 2 vols. half purple morocco/marbled brds. NF/slipcase. H5. $650.00

HUXLEY, Aldous. *Adonis & the Alphabet.* 1956. Chatto Windus. 1st ed. sm 8vo. NF/NF. S8. $75.00

HUXLEY, Aldous. *Along the Road.* 1925. Chatto Windus. 1st ed. sm 8vo. VG+/VG+. S8. $135.00

HUXLEY, Aldous. *Along the Road.* 1926. NY. Doran. 1st ed. 8vo. VG+/VG. S8. $85.00

HUXLEY, Aldous. *Antic Hay.* 1923. Chatto Windus. 1st ed. G+. A1. $50.00

HUXLEY, Aldous. *Antic Hay.* 1923. Chatto Windus. 1st ed. sm 8vo. VG+/VG+. S8. $300.00

HUXLEY, Aldous. *Antic Hay.* 1923. Doran. 1st ed. F/dj. M18. $125.00

HUXLEY, Aldous. *Ape & Essence: A Novel.* 1949. Chatto Windus. 1st ed. sm 8vo. VG+/VG+. S8. $40.00

HUXLEY, Aldous. *Arabian Infelis.* 1929. NY. Fountain. 1/692. sgn. VG+. S8. $120.00

HUXLEY, Aldous. *Beyond the Mexique Bay. A Travel Book.* 1934. Chatto Windus. 1st ed. lg 8vo. 30 pls. VG/VG. S8. $45.00

HUXLEY, Aldous. *Brave New World Revisited.* (1958). NY. Harper. 1st ed. VG+/VG. S8. $20.00

HUXLEY, Aldous. *Brave New World.* 1932. London. 1st ed. sm octavo. teal cloth. NF/dj. H5. $1,250.00

HUXLEY, Aldous. *Brief Candles.* 1930. Chatto Windus. 1st ed. sm 8vo. VG/VG. S8. $75.00

HUXLEY, Aldous. *Brief Candles.* 1930. NY. Fountain. 1/842. sgn. NF. S8. $150.00

HUXLEY, Aldous. *Burning Wheel.* 1916. Oxford. VG/orig wrp/paper label. A1. $650.00

HUXLEY, Aldous. *Cicadas & Other Poems.* 1931. Chatto Windus. 1st ed. 8vo. VG+/VG+. S8. $100.00

HUXLEY, Aldous. *Collected Poetry of...* 1971. NY. 1st ed. NF/VG+. V1. $20.00

HUXLEY, Aldous. *Defeat of Youth & Other Poems.* (1918). London. Blackwell. issued without title p. VG/decor stiff wrp. S8. $200.00

HUXLEY, Aldous. *Do What You Will.* 1929. Chatto Windus. 1st ed. F/NF. C4. $100.00

HUXLEY, Aldous. *Do What You Will.* 1929. Chatto Windus. ltd ed. 1/260. inscr/sgn/dtd 1957. 8vo. yel brds/gr spine. VG. S8. $250.00

HUXLEY, Aldous. *Doors of Perception.* 1954. Chatto Windus. 1st ed. NF/VG. L3. $150.00

HUXLEY, Aldous. *Encyclopedia of Pacifism.* 1937. Chatto Windus. 1st ed. 12mo. VG/prt yel wrp. S8. $150.00

HUXLEY, Aldous. *Ends & Means.* 1937. Chatto Windus. 1st ed. 8vo. VG+/VG. S8. $100.00

HUXLEY, Aldous. *Essays New & Old.* 1926. Chatto Windus/Florentine. 1/650. sgn. decor brds/bl cloth spine. VG+/slipcase. S8. $200.00

HUXLEY, Aldous. *Genius & the Goddess.* 1955. London. 1st ed. 12mo. NF/NF. A11. $40.00

HUXLEY, Aldous. *Gray Eminence. Biography of Father Joseph...* 1941. NY. Harper. 1st ed. 8vo. VG+/VG+. S8. $45.00

HUXLEY, Aldous. *Heaven & Hell.* 1956. Chatto Windus. AP/1st ed. VG/wrp. L3. $200.00

HUXLEY, Aldous. *Heaven & Hell.* 1956. Chatto Windus. 1st ed. sm 8vo. VG+/VG+ clip. S8. $35.00

HUXLEY, Aldous. *Jesting Pilate.* 1926. London. Chatto Windus. 1st ed. ils. VG/VG. S8. $45.00

HUXLEY, Aldous. *Jesting Pilate.* 1926. NY. Doran. 1st ed. 8vo. decor brds/red cloth spine. VG+/VG. S8. $60.00

HUXLEY, Aldous. *Leda.* 1920. Chatto Windus. 1/160. sgn. cloth brds/paper spine label. VG. S8. $300.00

HUXLEY, Aldous. *Letters...* (1969). Harper Row. 1st Am ed. 992 p. dj. A7. $25.00

HUXLEY, Aldous. *Limbo.* 1920. Chatto Windus. 1st ed. sm 8vo. VG. S8. $100.00

HUXLEY, Aldous. *Literature & Science.* 1963. Chatto Windus. 1st ed. sm 8vo. NF/NF. S8. $25.00

HUXLEY, Aldous. *Little Mexican.* 1924. Chatto Windus. 1st ed. inscr/dtd 1958. red cloth/wht label. NF/NF. S8. $400.00

HUXLEY, Aldous. *Little Mexican.* 1924. London. 1st ed. G+. A1. $45.00

HUXLEY, Aldous. *Mortal Coils.* 1922. Chatto Windus. 1st ed. bl cloth/paper label. VG. S8. $50.00

HUXLEY, Aldous. *Music at Night & Other Essays.* 1931. Chatto Windus. 1st ed. sm 8vo. VG/VG. S8. $75.00

HUXLEY, Aldous. *Olive Tree.* 1936. Chatto Windus. 1st ed. sm 8vo. VG/VG. S8. $100.00

HUXLEY, Aldous. *On Art & Artists.* 1960. Chatto Windus. 1st ed. 8vo. red cloth. NF/NF. S8. $35.00

HUXLEY, Aldous. *On the Margin.* 1923. Chatto Windus. 1st ed. sm 8vo. w/extra label sewn in. VG/VG+. S8. $65.00

HUXLEY, Aldous. *On the Margin.* 1923. NY. Doran. 1st ed. sm 8vo. bl cloth/paper label. VG. S8. $25.00

HUXLEY, Aldous. *Perennial Philosophy.* 1946. Chatto Windus. 1st ed. VG+/VG. S8. $40.00

HUXLEY, Aldous. *Point Counter Point.* 1928. Chatto Windus. 1st trade ed. inscr/dtd 1930. orange cloth. VG. S8. $250.00

HUXLEY, Aldous. *Proper Studies.* 1927. Chatto Windus. 1/260. sgn. VG. S8. $200.00

HUXLEY, Aldous. *Science, Liberty & Peace.* 1947. London. 1st ed. sm 8vo. VG/VG. S8. $40.00

HUXLEY, Aldous. *Selected Poems.* 1925. Oxford. Blackwell. 1st ed. sm 8vo. pict brds. VG/sans. S8. $65.00

HUXLEY, Aldous. *Stories, Essays & Poems.* 1937. London. Dent. Everyman's Lib/1st thus ed. 16mo. orange cloth. VG/VG. S8. $35.00

HUXLEY, Aldous. *Texts & Pretexts.* 1936. Chatto Windus. 1st ed. sm 8vo. VG/VG. S8. $75.00

HUXLEY, Aldous. *Themes & Variations.* 1950. Chatto Windus. 1st ed. 8vo. red cloth/paper label. VG+/VG. S8. $35.00

HUXLEY, Aldous. *Themes & Variations.* 1950. Harper. 1st ed. VG/dj. M18. $45.00

HUXLEY, Aldous. *Those Barren Leaves.* 1925. Chatto Windus. 1st ed. inscr. orange cloth/wht spine. extra label. NF/VG+. S8. $175.00

HUXLEY, Aldous. *Those Barren Leaves.* 1925. NY. 1/250. sgn. VG/slipcase. A1. $200.00

HUXLEY, Aldous. *Those Barren Leaves.* 1928. Tauchnitz. 16mo. G/wrp. S8. $20.00

HUXLEY, Aldous. *Time Must Have a Stop.* 1945. Chatto Windus. 1st ed. sm 8vo. bl cloth. VG/VG. S8. $75.00

HUXLEY, Aldous. *Twice Seven.* 1944. London. Reprint Soc. sm 8vo. bl cloth. VG+/VG+. S8. $35.00

HUXLEY, Aldous. *Two or Three Graces.* 1926. London. 1st ed. cloth. G+. A1. $40.00

HUXLEY, Aldous. *Two or Three Graces.* 1926. London. Chatto Windus. 1st ed. sm 8vo. VG+/VG+. S8. $95.00

HUXLEY, Aldous. *Verses & a Comedy.* 1946. Chatto Windus. 12mo. gr cloth/gilt spine. VG+/VG+. S8. $35.00

HUXLEY, Aldous. *What Are You Going To Do About It?* 1936. Chatto Windus. 1st ed. 12mo. NF/stapled wrp. S8. $100.00

HUXLEY, Aldous. *Words & Their Meanings.* 1940. LA. Jake Zetlin. 1st ed. 1/100. sgn. 28 p. NF/dj/clamshell case. H5. $450.00

HUXLEY, Aldous. *World of Light.* 1931. Chatto Windus. 1st ed. sm 8vo. yel cloth. w/program. VG/VG. S8. $75.00

HUXLEY, Francis. *Affable Savages: Anthropologist Among Urubu of Brazil.* 1957. Viking. 1st Am ed. 8vo. 295 p. VG+/VG. A2. $15.00

HUXLEY, Julian. *Aldous Huxley, 1894-1963.* (1965). NY. Harper. memorial ed. 8vo. VG+/F. S8. $25.00

HUXLEY, Julian. *Aldous Huxley, 1894-1963.* 1965. London. Chatto Windus. 1st ed. RS. NF/NF. S8. $30.00

HUXLEY, Laura Archera. *This Timeless Moment: Personal View of Aldous Huxley.* 1969. Chatto Windus. 1st ed. 8vo. turquoise cloth. S8. $10.00

HUXLEY, Thomas Henry. *Hume.* 1879. Harper. 1st Am ed. 12mo. 206 p. beige cloth. F. G1. $40.00

HUYGHE, Rene. *Gauguin Collection Genies et Realities.* 1966. Hachette. VG+. A1. $35.00

HWANG, David Henry. *FBO & Other Plays.* 1990. NY. hc ed of Plume PBO. inscr. dj. A11. $65.00

HYAMS, Edward. *Ornamental Shrubs for Temperate Zone Gardens.* 1965-67. London. 6 vols. ils. VG/djs. B26. $55.00

HYAMS, Edward. *Plants in the Service of Man.* (1971). Lippincott. 1st Am ed. 8vo. 222 p. F/F. A2. $15.00

HYAMS & ORDISH. *Last of the Incas: Rise & Fall of an Am Empire.* (1963). Simon Schuster. 1st ed. 8vo. 294 p. VG+/VG+. A2. $17.50

HYATT, Alfred H. *Book of Old-World Gardens.* 1911. London. ils B Parsons. 113 p. VG+. B26. $25.00

HYDE, A. *WV.* 1980. Hyde. folio. VG/G. A8. $12.00

HYDE, Charles K. *N Lights: Lighthouses of the Upper Great Lakes.* 1990 (1986). Lansing, MI. 2 Peninsula Pr. as new/dj. A16. $29.95

HYDE, Christopher. *Week Down in Devon: Hist of Devon Horse Show.* 1976. Randor. Chilton. 1st ed. 4to. VG+/VG+. O3. $30.00

HYDE, H. Montgomery. *Room 3603.* 1963. Farrar Straus. G/dj. A16. $8.00

HYDE, H.A. *Welsh Timber Trees...* 1961. Cardiff. Nat Mus of Wales. 173 p. F. H10. $12.50

HYDE, Harris; see Harris, Timothy.

HYDE, Hartford Montgomery. *Solitary in the Ranks.* 1978. Atheneum. 1st ed. 291 p. gilt bl linen. F/F. M7. $50.00

HYDE, Ralph. *Prt Maps of Victorian London, 1851-1900.* 1975. Folkestone. Dawson. ils/24 maps. M. O6. $95.00

HYERDAHL, Thor. *Aku-Aku.* 1958. NY. Rand McNally. BC. 8vo. 384 p. emb gray cloth. P4. $20.00

HYLANDER, Clarence J. *World of Plant Life.* 1939. Macmillan. 4to. 722 p. H10. $15.00

HYMAN, Anthony. *Charles Babbage: Pioneer of the Computer.* 1982. Princeton. 1st ed. 288 p. gr cloth. VG/dj. G1. $27.50

HYMAN, Stanley Edgar. *Tangled Bank: Darwin, Marx, Frazer & Freud...* 1962. Atheneum. 1st ed. 492 p. red cloth. G1. $30.00

HYMAN, Susan. *Edward Lear in the Levant.* 1988. London. 4to. 168 p. cloth. dj. O2. $50.00

HYMAN, Susan. *Edward Lear's Birds.* (1989). Longmeadow. folio. pls. 96 p. F/dj. A17. $18.50

HYMAN & THOMAS. *Stanton: Life & Times of Lincoln's Secretary of War.* 1962. Knopf. 1st ed. N2. $7.50

HYNE, C.J. Cutcliffe. *Lost Continent.* 1900. Harper. 1st Am ed. VG. M2. $40.00

HYUN, Judy. *Korean Cookbook.* 1979. Seoul. Hollym. 3rd prt. 8vo. 294 p. VG/dj. W1. $18.00

IATRIDES, John. *Ambassador VacVeagh Reports: Greece 1933-47.* 1980. Princeton. 8vo. 769 p. cloth. dj. O2. $50.00

IBARGUENGOITIA, Jorge. *Two Crimes.* 1984. Boston. Godine. 1st Am ed. NF/NF. A14. $20.00

IBN-ZAHAV, Ari. *Jessica, My Daughter.* 1948. Crown. 312 p. VG. S3. $21.00

IBUSE, Masuji. *Waves: Two Short Novels.* 1986. Tokyo/NY. Kodansha Internat. 1st ed. trans from Japanese. F/F. A14. $25.00

ICAZA, Xavier. *Panchito Chapopote: Retablo Tropical o Relacion...* 1928. Xalapa, Veracruz, Mexico. 1/1000. folio. 94 p. NF/stiff wrp. B24. $485.00

ICEBERG SLIM; see Beck, Robert.

ICHITARO, Kondo. *Japanese Genre Painting.* 1961. Rutland, VT/Tokyo. Tuttle. 1st prt. 199 pls. 148 p. silk bdg. NF/dj. W1. $125.00

ICKIS. *Standard Book of Quiltmaking & Collection.* 1949. np. 1st ed. cloth. G2. $25.00

IDRIESS, I.L. *Our Living Stone Age.* (1963). Sydney. Angus Robertson. 1st ed. 8vo. 224 p. F/G+. A2. $20.00

ILES, Francis. *Before the Fact.* 1958. Dell. pb. F. C8. $20.00

ILIN, M. *New Russia's Primer.* 1931. Boston. 1st ed. ils. 162 p. red cloth. F. H3. $20.00

ILLICH, Ivan. *Deschooling Soc.* (1971). Harper. 1st ed. NF/NF. A7. $20.00

ILLICK, J.S. *PA Trees.* 1915. Harrisburg. Commonwealth of PA. ils. 231 p. F. H10. $25.00

IMAMOGLU, Vacit. *Traditional Dwellings in Kayseria.* 1992. Istanbul. ltd ed. ils. 268 p. cloth. dj. O2. $30.00

IMBERT, Jean. *Historie des Institutions Khmeres.* 1961. Phnom-Penh. 1st ed. G. presumed quite scarce. L3. $85.00

IMLAY, Gilbert. *Topographical Description of W Territory of N Am...* 1797. London. Debrett. 3rd/expanded ed. thick 8vo. half red calf. lacks 4 maps. H9. $275.00

IMMERMAN, Richard. *City in Guatemala.* (1982). Austin, TX. 1st ed. 291 p. wrp. F3. $15.00

INALCIK, Halil. *Middle E & the Balkans Under the Ottoman Empire.* 1993. Bloomington. 8vo. 475 p. O2. $30.00

INCHFAWN, Fay. *Who Goes to the Wood.* 1942. Winston. 1st ed. ils Diana Thorne. 229 p. VG+/VG. P2. $25.00

INDIANA, Gary. *Horse Crazy.* 1989. NY. Grove. 1st ed. author's 1st novel. F/F. A14. $30.00

INDIANA YEARLY MEETING. *Discipline of Soc of Friends, of IN Yearly Meeting.* 1864. Richmond, IN. Morgan. 12mo. 146 p. poor. V3. $14.00

INGALLS, Jeremy. *Tahl.* 1945. NY. 1st ed. VG/VG. V1. $20.00

INGALS, Fay. *Valley Road: Story of VA Hot Springs.* 1949. Cleveland. World. 2nd ed. VG/dj. N2. $8.00

INGE, William. *Bus Stop.* 1955. Random. 1st ed. G/dj. M18. $50.00

INGE, William. *Natural Affection.* (1963). Random. 1st ed. F/VG. B4. $50.00

INGE, William. *Picnic, a Summer Romance in 3 Acts.* 1956. Bantam. 2nd prt. VG+/wrp. C8. $12.50

INGELOW, Jean. *Mopsa the Fairy.* 1910. Lippincott. ils Maria Kirk/10 color pls. teg. gilt red cloth. VG. M5. $38.00

INGERSOLL, Ernest. *Crest of the Continent.* 1890. Chicago. Donnelley. 38th ed. ils/fld color map. 341 p. gilt pict cloth. VG. D3. $35.00

INGHAM, George T. *Digging Gold Among the Rockies.* 1888. Phil. Hubbard. 12mo. 452 p. gilt cloth. VG. D3. $45.00

INGOLDSBY, Thomas. *Ingoldsby Legends; or, Mirth & Marvels.* 1907. London. Dent. ils Rackham. 549 p. pict brn cloth. F. B14. $150.00

INGOLDSBY, Thomas. *Ingoldsby Legends; or, Mirth & Marvels.* 1912. Heinemann. 24 mtd Rackham pls. G. A16. $120.00

INGRAHAM, Corinne. *Wishing Fairy's Animal Friends.* 1921. Brentano. ils DS Walker/8 color pls. VG. M5. $65.00

INGRAHAM, J.H. *Clipper-Yacht; or, Moloch, the Money-Lender!* (1845). Boston. HL Williams. 1st ed. 8vo. lacks wrps. M1. $125.00

INGRAM, Arthur. *Fire Engines in Color.* 1974. Macmillan. 1st Am ed. VG/dj. A16. $10.00

INGRAM, Arthur. *Hist of Fire Fighting.* 1978. Chartwell. VG/dj. A16. $25.00

INGRAM, John. *Flora Symbolica; or, Language & Sentiment of Flowers...* ca 1870s. London. Warne. color pls. gilt cloth. H10. $22.50

INGSTAD, Helge. *East of the Great Glacier.* 1937. Knopf. 1st Am ed. 8vo. 269 p. decor bl-gray cloth. P4. $35.00

INGSTAD, Helge. *Nunamiut: Among AK's Inland Eskimos.* (1954). Norton. 1st Am ed. 303 p. dj. A17. $17.50

INGWERSEN, Will. *Classic Garden Plants.* 1975. London. 1st ed. 4to. 192 p. F/F. B28. $25.00

INMAN, E. *Stories of Hatfield, the Pioneer...* 1889. New Albany, IN. 1st ed. 278 p. decor cloth. VG. B18. $395.00

INMAN, Henry. *Old Santa Fe Trail.* 1897. NY. 1st ed/2nd prt. 493 p. G+. B28. $125.00

INNERST, Stuart. *China Gray, China Gr.* nd. Davis, CA. Almena Innerst Neff. 8vo. 89 p. as new. V3. $10.00

INNES, Hammond. *Angry Mtn.* 1950. London. Collins. 1st ed. VG/clip. M15. $45.00

INNES, Hammond. *Atlantic Fury.* 1962. London. Collins. 1st ed. F/dj. M18. $30.00

INNES, Hammond. *Conquistadors.* 1949. Knopf. 1st Am ed. 336 p. dj. F3. $25.00

INNES, Michael. *Appleby on Ararat.* 1941. Dodd Mead. 1st Am ed. F/NF. M15. $85.00

INNES, Michael. *Weight of the Evidence.* 1943. Dodd Mead. 1st Am ed. F/VG. M15. $65.00

INNES-BROWNE, Mrs. *Told Round the Nursery Fire.* 1907. London. Washbourne. ils. 154 p. VG. S10. $20.00

INNIS, H.A. *Dairy Industry in Canada.* 1937. Toronto. Ryerson. 209 p. H10. $20.00

INNIS & DEAN. *Gold in the Bl Ridge: True Story of Beale Treasure.* ca 1973. Luce. 224 p. VG/F. B10. $20.00

IOANNIDES, Christos P. *Cyprus. Domestic Dynamics, External Constraints.* 1992. New Rochelle. 8vo. 150 p. cloth. O2. $35.00

IONESCO, Eugene. *Hermit.* 1974. Sever/Viking. 1st ed. trans from French. NF/NF. A14. $25.00

IONESCO, Eugene. *La Cantatrice Chauve.* 1964. Paris. Gallimard. 1st ils ed. NF/sans. B2. $45.00

IRANEK-OSMECKI, Kazimierz. *He Who Saves One Life.* 1971. Crown. 336 p. VG/VG. S3. $25.00

IRELAND, Alexander. *Book-Lover's Enchiridion.* 1883. London. Simpkin Marshall. 3rd/enlarged ed. octavo. Bayntun bdg. NF. H5. $500.00

IRELAND, Tom. *Child Labor As a Relic of the Dark Ages.* ca 1937. Putnam. photos. VG. V4. $20.00

IRISH, William; see Woolrich, Cornell.

IRONMONGER & PHILLIPS. *Hist of Woman's Christian Temperance Union of VA...* ca 1958. Cavalier Pr. ils. 325 p. G. B10. $25.00

IRVING, David. *Memoirs of General Reinhard Gehlen.* 1972. World. 1st ed. ils/photos. 386 p. NF/NF. B22. $8.25

IRVING, John Treat Jr. *Indian Sketches... Pawnee Tribes...* 1835. Carey Lee Blanchard. 1st ed. 2 vols. octavo. gr cloth. H9. $600.00

IRVING, John. *Cider House Rules.* 1985. London. Cape. 1st ed. F/F. C4. $35.00

IRVING, John. *Hotel NH.* 1981. Dutton. AP. F/tan wrp. C4. $50.00

IRVING, John. *Hotel NH.* 1981. Dutton. 1st ed. author's 5th novel. F/NF. B3/Q1. $40.00

IRVING, John. *Prayer for Owen Meany.* (1989). Toronto. Lester & Orpen Dennys. 1st ed. NF/VG clip. B3. $50.00

IRVING, John. *Setting Free the Bears.* 1968. Random. 1st ed. author's 1st book. NF/NF clip. Q1. $350.00

IRVING, John. *Setting Free the Bears.* 1974. Avon. PBO. w/sgn bookplate. F/wrp. A11. $55.00

IRVING, John. *World According to Garp.* 1978. Dutton. 1st ed. VG/dj. M18. $40.00

IRVING, John. *World According to Garp.* 1978. NY. 1st ed. w/sgn bookplate. F/F. A11. $90.00

IRVING, John. *158-Pound Marriage.* 1980. London. Corgi. PBO. w/sgn bookplate. NF/wrp. A11. $65.00

IRVING, Washington. *Astoria; or, Anecdotes of Enterprise Beyond Rocky Mtns...* 1836. Carey Lea Blanchard. 1st ed/2nd state. 2 vols. 8vo. fld map. emb cloth. H9. $395.00

IRVING, Washington. *Legend of Sleepy Hollow & Spectre Bridegroom.* (1875). Lippincott. 78 p. gilt brn cloth. VG. S10. $65.00

IRVING, Washington. *Legend of Sleepy Hollow.* 1931. Cheshire House. 1/1200. ils Bernhardt Wall. buckram. F/defective slipcase. B24. $125.00

IRVING, Washington. *Legends of the Alhambra.* 1909. Lippincott. 1st thus ed. ils George Hood. 230 p. teg. bl cloth. G+. M20. $50.00

IRVING, Washington. *Life of George WA.* nd. NY. Merrill Baker. early prt. 4 vols. cloth. VG. M8. $150.00

IRVING, Washington. *Life of George WA.* 1855-59. Putnam. 1st ed/1st state. 5 vols. 8vo. map/portraits. bl or brn cloth. H9. $125.00

IRVING, Washington. *Life of George WA.* 1889. NY. Putnam. Centennial ed. 1/300. 5 vols. quarto. teg. gilt morocco. R3. $500.00

IRVING, Washington. *Old Christmas.* 1925. Macmillan. 4th ed/reprint. octavo. ils R Caldecott. 165 p. F. H6. $225.00

IRVING, Washington. *Rip Van Winkle.* ca 1880. McLoughlin. ils Thomas Nast. VG. D1. $285.00

IRVING, Washington. *Rip Van Winkle.* 1905. Doubleday/Heinemann. 1st ed. ils Rackham/51 color pls. gilt gr cloth. VG. D1. $400.00

IRVING, Washington. *Rip Van Winkle.* 1921. McKay. ils NC Wyeth. 86 p. VG. D1. $200.00

IRVING, Washington. *Rip Van Winkle.* 1959. Scribner. 1st thus ed. ils Rackham/50 color pls. dj. L1. $47.50

IRVING, Washington. *Rocky Mtns; or, Scenes, Incidents & Adventures in Far W...* 1843. Phil. Lee Blanchard. 1st ed of 2 vols in 1 issue. xl. contemporary calf. H9. $350.00

IRVING, Washington. *Tour on the Prairies.* 1835. London. Murray. 1st ed (precedes Am). orig brds/cloth/spine label. VG. A18. $500.00

IRVING, Washington. *Two Tales: Rip Van Winkle & Legend of Sleepy Hollow.* 1984. HBJ. 1st ed. ils Barry Moser. F/F. B3. $25.00

IRVING, Washington. *Voyages & Discoveries of Companions of Columbus.* 1831. Phil. 1st Am ed. 8vo. 350 p. new spine. VG. H3. $75.00

IRVING, Washington. *Washington Irving's Tale of the Supernatural.* 1982. Stemmer. 1st ed. F/dj. M2. $18.00

IRVING, Washington. *Wolfert's Roost & Other Papers.* 1855. Putnam. 1st ed. 12mo. 383 p. emb/gilt brds. G. B11. $50.00

IRWIN, Frank. *Bibliography of the Hillsdale Pr.* 1980. Buffalo. Hillside Pr. miniature. 1/300. 50 p. H10. $35.00

IRWIN, Inez Haynes. *Maida's Little Camp.* 1940. Grosset Dunlap. polka-dot ep. F/dj. M5. $15.00

IRWIN & O'BRIEN. *Alone: Across the Top of the World.* (1935). Phil. Winston. 1st ed. 8vo. 254 p. F/F. A2. $25.00

IRWIN. *People & Their Quilts.* 1984. np. ils. cloth. G2. $45.00

ISELY, Duane. *Weed Identification & Control in N Central States.* 1960 (1958). Ames. 2nd ed. 159 pls. 400 p. B26. $11.00

ISENBERG, Barbara. *CA Theatre Annual 1982.* 1982. np. 1st ed. ils/index. 323 p. 25 p. NF/NF. B19. $25.00

ISHAM, Frederic. *Social Bucaneer.* 1910. Grosset Dunlap. VG. M2. $12.00

ISHERWOOD, Christopher. *Down There on a Visit.* 1962. Simon Schuster. 1st ed. 318 p. VG+/dj. M20. $30.00

ISHERWOOD, Christopher. *My Guru & His Disciple.* 1980. FSG. 1st ed. NF/NF clip. A14. $30.00

ISHERWOOD, Christopher. *Single Man.* 1986. London. Methuen. reissue of 1964 1st ed. NF/NF. A14. $20.00

ISHERWOOD, Christopher. *Vedanta for Modern Man.* (1951). NY. Harper. 8vo. VG/VG. S8. $35.00

ISHERWOOD, Christopher. *World in the Evening.* 1954. London. Methuen. 1st ed. F/F. B2. $45.00

ISHIGURO, Kazuo. *Artist of the Floating World.* 1986. London. Faber. 1st ed. author's 2nd novel. F/F. L3. $100.00

ISHIGURO, Kazuo. *Artist of the Floating World.* 1986. Putnam. 1st Am ed. F/F. B2. $75.00

ISHIGURO, Kazuo. *Remains of the Day.* 1989. Knopf. 1st Am ed. F/F. B2. $75.00

ISHIGURO, Kazuo. *Remains of the Day.* 1989. London. Faber. 1st ed. F/F. B4. $150.00

ISON, Graham. *Confirm or Deny.* 1989. London. Macmillan. ARC of 1st ed. sgn. RS. F/F. S5. $40.00

ISRAEL, Peter. *Stiff Upper Lip.* 1978. Crowell. 1st ed. F/NF. S5. $25.00

ITURBIDE, Agustin. *Memoirs of Agustin de Iturbide.* 1971. WA, DC. Documentary Pub. 1/500. facsimile of 1823 ed. F3. $20.00

IVANOVIC, I.S. *Spearfishing.* ca 1945. NY. Barnes. ils/photos. 79 p. paper brds. VG. A17. $9.50

IVES, Joseph C. *Report Upon the CO River of the W, Explored in 1858...* 1861. GPO. quarto. ils/pls. modern red buckram. B14. $125.00

IVES, Morgan; see Bradley, Marion Zimmer.

IVES, Sarah Noble. *Key to Betsy's Heart.* 1916. Macmillan. 1st ed. 12mo. 225 p. VG. S10. $18.00

IVORY, James. *Autobiography of a Princess...* 1975. Harper Row. 1st ed. 4to. 177 p. VG/dj. W1. $35.00

IWAHASHI, Takeo. *Light From Darkness.* 1933. Phil. Winston. 12mo. 103 p. V3. $12.00

IZANT, Grace Goulder. *This Is OH.* (1953). Cleveland. 1st ed. ils. 264 p. VG/torn. B18. $9.50

IZENBERG, Jerry. *Greatest Game Ever Played.* 1987. Holt. 1st ed. F/VG+. P8. $25.00

IZZARD, Ralph. *Innocent on Everest.* 1954. Dutton. 1st ed. 8vo. 318 p. VG/F-. A2. $15.00

IZZI, Eugene. *Bad Guys.* nd. St Martin. 1st ed. VG/VG. V2. $7.00

IZZI, Eugene. *Tribal Secrets.* (1992). Bantam. ARC. F/wrp. B9. $15.00

JABLONSKI, Edward. *Atlantic Fever.* (1972). NY. 1st prt. VG/dj. B18. $12.50

JACK, Robert. *Arctic Living. Story of Grimsey.* 1955. Toronto. 8vo. ils. 181 p. F/VG. H3. $20.00

JACKMAN, John S. *Diary of a Confederate Soldier: John S Jackman...* 1990. SC U. BC. 174 p. F/F. M8. $25.00

JACKMAN, S.W. *Galloping Head: Biography of Sir Francis Bond Head...* (1958). London. Phoenix. 1st ed. presentation. 8vo. 191 p. VG+/VG. A2. $15.00

JACKMAN & RUSSELL. *Flying Machines: Construction & Operation.* 1910. Chicago. Thompson. 1st ed. ils. 221 p. gilt red cloth. VG. S9. $98.00

JACKS, L.P. *All Men Are Ghosts.* 1913. London. 1st ed. VG. M2. $35.00

JACKS, Oliver; see Gandley, Kenneth R.

JACKSON, Blyden. *Operation Burning Candle.* (1973). NY. 3rd Pr. 1st ed. F/NF. B4. $100.00

JACKSON, C. Paul. *Bud Baker, High School Pitcher.* 1967. Hastings. 125 p. VG+/dj. M20. $20.00

JACKSON, Charles. *Lost Weekend.* 1960. Noonday Pr. pb. inscr. VG/8vo wrp. A11. $35.00

JACKSON, Charles. *Manual of Etherization...* 1861. Boston. self pub. 134 p. bl cloth. VG. B14. $300.00

JACKSON, Charles. *Second-Hand Life.* 1967. NY. 1st ed. sgn. F/NF. A11. $40.00

JACKSON, Charles. *Sunnier Side.* 1st short story collection. sgn. VG+/G. A11. $25.00

JACKSON, Donald. *Letters of the Lewis & Clark Expedition.* 1978. Urbana, IL. 2 vols. M. T8. $75.00

JACKSON, Edgar. *3 Rebels Write Home...Edgar A Jackson...JF Bryant...* 1955. Franklin, VA. News Pub. 1st ed. 1/150. 103 p. M8. $350.00

JACKSON, Everett. *Burros & Paintbrushes.* (1985). TX A&M U. 1st ed. 151 p. dj. F3. $15.00

JACKSON, George. *Blood in My Eye.* (1972). Bantam. 1st Bantam pb issue. 197 p. A7. $8.00

JACKSON, George. *Soledad Brother.* (1970). Bantam. 1st pb prt. 250 p. unread copy. A7. $10.00

JACKSON, Helen Hunt. *Century of Dishonor: Sketch of US Government's Dealings...* 1881. Harper. NF. A18. $150.00

JACKSON, Helen Hunt. *Glimpses of 3 Coasts.* 1886. Boston. 1st ed. 418 p. terracotta cloth. VG. D3. $45.00

JACKSON, Helen Hunt. *Ramona. A Story.* 1900. Boston. Monterey/1st (these ils) ed. 2 vols. NF/cloth djs. D3. $75.00

JACKSON, Helen Hunt. *Ramona. A Story.* 1884. Roberts. 1st ed. gilt cloth. F. A18. $500.00

JACKSON, Holbrook. *Anatomy of Bibliomania.* 1930. London. Socino. 2 vols. buckram. F. B14. $75.00

JACKSON, Isaac R. *Sketch of Life & Public Services of Wm Henry Harrison...* 1839. NY. 4th ed. 32 p. VG. D7. $125.00

JACKSON, J.H. *Gold Rush Album.* nd. np. lg 4to. ils/352 photos. 279 p. dj. O7. $18.50

JACKSON, Jack. *Mapping TX & the Gulf Coast.* 1990. TX A&M. ils. 92 p. O5. $20.00

JACKSON, James Sr. *Memoir of James Jackson Jr, MD.* 1835. Boston. IR Butts. 1st ed. inscr. 444 p. cloth. VG. S9. $65.00

JACKSON, Jon A. *Blind Pig.* 1978. Random. 1st ed. F/NF. M15. $45.00

JACKSON, Joseph Henry. *Anybody's Gold. Story of CA's Mining Towns.* 1941. NY. 1st ed. 468 p. gilt cloth. VG. scarce. D3. $25.00

JACKSON, Joseph Henry. *Bad Company.* 1949. Harcourt Brace. 12mo. VG+. A8. $20.00

JACKSON, Joseph Henry. *Christmas Flower.* 1951. NY. ils Tom Lea. 31 p. F/VG clip. H3. $15.00

JACKSON, Joseph Henry. *Tintypes in Gold: 4 Studies in Robbery.* 1939. Macmillan. 1st ed. 191 p. VG/tattered. B19. $35.00

JACKSON, Joseph. *Notes on a Drum.* 1937. Macmillan. 1st ed. ils/map ep. 276 p. F3. $15.00

JACKSON, Margaret. *Extracts From Letters & Other Pieces Written by...* 1825. Phil. Kite. 16mo. 95 p. leather. G. V3. $18.00

JACKSON, Richard. *Yr Is a Window.* 1963. Doubleday. 1st ed. ils. F/VG. P2. $10.00

JACKSON, Robert. *Airships: A Popular Hist of Dirigibles, Zeppelins, Blimps...* 1973. Doubleday. 1st Am ed. 277 p. VG/dj. C10. $27.50

JACKSON, Shirley. *Bird's Nest.* 1954. Farrar. 1st ed. VG/dj. M2. $35.00

JACKSON, Shirley. *Famous Sally.* 1966. Harlin Quist. 1st ed. F/NF. L3. $75.00

JACKSON, Shirley. *Raising Demons.* 1957. NY. 1st ed. NF/dj. A15. $45.00

JACKSON, Shirley. *Road Through the Wall.* 1948. Farrar Straus. 1st ed. VG/VG. T2. $150.00

JACKSON, Stanley. *Sassoons.* 1968. Dutton. 1st ed. 304 p. VG/G. M7. $20.00

JACKSON, Thomas. *Works of Reverend & Learned Divine, Thomas Jackson, DD.* 1673. London. Andrew Clark. 3 vols. Samuel Mather's copy. contempory calf. K1. $750.00

JACKSON, William Henry. *Picture Maker of the Old W.* 1947. Scribner. 1st ed. tall 4to. 308 p. VG/dj. E5. $125.00

JACKSON, William Henry. *Time Exposure.* 1940. NY. 1st ed. presentation/sgn. VG/VG. B5. $175.00

JACKSON & HODDER. *7 Sovereign Hills of Rome.* (1936). Longman Gr. 1st ed. 8vo. 528 p. VG+. A2. $15.00

JACKSON & JACKSON. *Mouse's House.* 1949. Simon Schuster. Big Golden Book. ils Richard Scarry. VG. P2. $25.00

JACKSON & SCHAAP. *Bo Knows Bo.* 1990. Doubleday. 1st ed. 218 p. F/F. A7/P8. $15.00

JACOB, Alaric. *Russian Journey From Suzdal to Samarkand.* 1969. Hill Wang. 1st Am ed. 4to. 160 p. cloth. VG. W1. $18.00

JACOB, Caroline N. *Builders of the Quaker Road, 1652-1952.* 1953. Chicago. Regnery. 1st ed. 8vo. 233 p. VG/dj. V3. $16.00

JACOB, Heinrich Eduard. *Felix Mendelssohn & His Times.* 1963. Prentice Hall. 1st Am ed. 343 p. cloth. VG/dj. M20. $15.00

JACOB, John. *Long Ride Back.* (1988). Thunder Mouth. 2nd prt. as new/NF. A7. $17.00

JACOB, John. *Long Ride Back.* 1988. NY. Thunder Mouth. AP. F/wrp. B2. $25.00

JACOBI, Carl. *Disclosures in Scarlet.* 1972. Arkham. 1st ed. M/M. M2. $25.00

JACOBI, Carl. *Portraits in Moonlight.* 1964. Arkham. 1st ed. F/dj. M2. $65.00

JACOBI, Carl. *Revelations in Blk.* 1947. Arkham. 1st ed. F/dj. M2. $115.00

JACOBI & ZIELER. *Atlas der Hautkrankheiten mit Einschlus der Wichtigsten...* 1920. Berlin. Urban Schwarzenberg. 161 pls. 157 p. G7. $125.00

JACOBS, David. *Disney's Am on Parade.* 1975. Abrams. photos. 143 p. F/VG. P4. $15.00

JACOBS, Louis. *Jewish Festivals.* 1961. Worcester. St Onge. miniature. 1/2000. F. H10. $100.00

JACOBS, Paul. *Between the Rock & the Hard Place.* (1970). Random. 1st ed. 155 p. clip dj. A7. $17.00

JACOBS, Ruth Harriet. *We Speak for Peace: An Anthology.* 1992. Manchester, CT. Knowledge Ideas & Trends. 8vo. M. V3. $15.50

JACOBS, W.W. *Odd Craft.* 1909. Scribner. ne. G. M2. $10.00

JACOBS & WILSON. *Weather Pop-Up Book.* 1987. 5 pop-ups. F. A4. $35.00

JACOBSEN, Anita. *Frederic Cozzens. Marine Painter.* 1982. Alpine. ils/pls. 252 p. cloth. dj. D2. $75.00

JACOBSEN, Johan Adrian. *AK Voyage, 1881-83: Expedition to NW Coast of Am.* 1977. Chicago U. 1st complete Eng trans. ils/map/glossary. M/rpr dj. O6. $65.00

JACOBSEN & MUELLER. *Testament of Samuel Beckett.* 1964. Hill Wang. PBO. sgns. VG+/wrp. A11. $40.00

JACOBSON, B.S. *Meditations on the Siddur: Studies...* 1966. Tel-Aviv. Sinai Pub. 185 p. VG+/VG. S3. $24.00

JACOBSON, Dan. *No Further W: CA Visited.* 1961. NY. 1st Am ed. 127 p. cloth. F/dj. D3. $15.00

JACOBSON, Julius. *Negro & the Am Labor Movement.* (1968). Anchor/Doubleday. PBO. 430 p. A7. $10.00

JACOBSON, Oscar Brousse. *Kiowa Indian Art.* 1979. Santa Fe. Bell. 1/750. reissue of 1929 portfolio. sgn Jamake Highwater. F. L3. $350.00

JACOBY, Arnold. *Senor Kon-Tiki.* (1967). Rand McNally. 1st ed. 8vo. 424 p. F/F. A2. $20.00

JACOBY, Erich H. *Agrarian Unrest in SE Asia.* 1949. Columbia U. 287 p. VG. A7. $50.00

JACOBY, Russell. *Repression of Psychoanalysis: Otto Frnichel...* 1983. Basic Books. 201 p. beige cloth. F/dj. G1. $25.00

JACOBY & MOREHEAD. *Fireside Book of Cards.* 1957. Simon Schuster. 1st ed. lg 8vo. 364 p. VG/G. A2. $12.50

JAEGER, Ellsworth. *Tracks & Trailcraft.* (1967). NY. 3rd prt. 381 p. VG. A17. $12.50

JAFFREY, Sheldon. *Arkham House Companion.* 1989. Starmont. 1st ed. M. M2. $35.00

JAFFREY, Sheldon. *Horrors & Unpleasantries.* 1982. Bowling Gr. 1st ed. VG/wrp. M2. $15.00

JAFFREY, Sheldon. *Selected Tales of Grim & Grue From Horror Pulps.* 1987. Bowling Gr, OH. 1st ed. F. M2. $25.00

JAGGI, O.P. *Hist of Science & Technology in India. Vol 2.* 1969. Delhi. Atma Ram. 1st ed. 4to. 248 p. VG/dj. W1. $22.00

JAKES, John. *Texans Ride N.* 1952. Phil. 1st ed. author's 1st book. NF/clip. A15. $50.00

JAKUBOWSKI, Maxim. *Travelling Towards Epsilon.* 1976. NEL. 1st ed. F/dj. M2. $15.00

JAKUBOWSKI & VAN DER MEER. *Great Movies Live! A Pop-Up Book.* 1987. plays 'As Time Goes By.' F. A4. $45.00

JAMES, Allston. *Attic Light.* 1979. Capra. 1st ed. F/NF clip. A7. $45.00

JAMES, Bill. *Astride a Grave.* 1991. London. Macmillan. 1st ed. F/F. S5. $25.00

JAMES, Bushrod W. *Alaskana; or, AK in Descriptive & Legendary Poems.* 1894. Phil. 3rd ed. inscr. xl. 410 p. aeg. gilt cloth. D3. $45.00

JAMES, C.L. *Cricket.* 1986. London. Allison Busby. 1st ed. F/NF. L3. $75.00

JAMES, C.L. *Hist of the French Revolution.* 1902. Chicago. Abe Isaak. 1st ed. VG (rpr hinge). B2. $150.00

JAMES, Edmund S. *Miniature Bible.* ca 1840. Phil. miniature. abridged/collated/ ils. 203 p. blk cloth. H10. $125.00

JAMES, George Wharton. *Grand Canyon of AZ.* 1910. Little Brn. 1st ed. xl. 8vo. 265 p. teg. gr cloth. H9. $55.00

JAMES, George Wharton. *In & Around the Grand Canyon.* 1900. Pasadena. 1/500. sgn. 341 p. teg. rebacked. D3. $100.00

JAMES, George Wharton. *In & Around the Grand Canyon.* 1900. Little Brn. 1st ed. 8vo. 341 p. cloth. VG. B20. $50.00

JAMES, George Wharton. *Indian Basketry & How To Make Indian & Other Baskets.* 1903-1904. Pasadena, CA. 2 vols in 1. cloth. NF. D3. $75.00

JAMES, George Wharton. *Old Franciscan Missions of CA.* 1928 (1925). Boston. 12mo. 260 p. cloth. NF/rpr dj. D3. $25.00

JAMES, George Wharton. *Wonders of the CO Desert.* 1906. Boston. 1st ed. 2 vols. VG. B28. $125.00

JAMES, George Wharton. *Wonders of the CO Desert.* 1911 (1906). Boston. later ed. ils/ index/fld map. 1547 p. cloth. VG. D3. $45.00

JAMES, Grace. *Gr Willow & Other Japanese Fairy Tales.* 1910. London. Macmillan. 1st ed. ils Warwick Goble/40 color pls. 281 p. VG. D1. $450.00

JAMES, Henry. *Better Sort.* 1903. Scribner. 1st ed. NF. B2. $150.00

JAMES, Henry. *Confidence.* 1880. Houghton Mifflin. 1st Am ed. 1/1500. VG. Q1. $350.00

JAMES, Henry. *Daisy Miller.* 1974. Westvaco. ltd ed. F/NF slipcase. V1. $20.00

JAMES, Henry. *French Poets & Novelists.* 1964. Universal Lib. 1st Am ed/PBO. intro/ sgn Edel. NF/wrp. A11. $5.00

JAMES, Henry. *Sm Boy & Other Stories.* 1913. Scribner. 1st ed. VG. V2. $25.00

JAMES, Henry. *Turn of the Screw.* 1930. Modern Lib. 1st thus ed. VG. E3. $8.00

JAMES, J. Alison. *Sing for a Gentle Rain.* (1991). Atheneum. 1st ed. sgn. F/F. B3. $20.00

JAMES, Jarquis. *Andrew Jackson: Portrait of a President.* 1937. np. 1st ed. ils/index. 627 p. O7. $12.50

JAMES, Lawrence. *Golden Warrior.* 1990. London. Weidenfield Nicolson. 1st ed. 404 p. F/F. M7. $65.00

JAMES, Marquis. *Cherokee Strip.* 1945. Viking. 1st ed. 294 p. cloth. VG/dj. M20. $20.00

JAMES, Marquis. *Hist of Am Legion.* 1923. NY. Wm Gr. 1st ed. 8vo. 320 p. VG+. A2. $30.00

JAMES, P.D. *Devices & Desires.* (1989). London. Faber. 1st ed. F/F. B3. $30.00

JAMES, P.D. *Devices & Desires.* 1990. Franklin Lib. 1st ed. sgn. full gray-gr leather. F. Q1. $40.00

JAMES, P.D. *Innocent Blood.* 1980. London. Faber. 1st ed. inscr/sgn. NF/dj. S5. $55.00

JAMES, P.D. *Shroud for a Nightingale.* 1971. London. Faber. 1st ed. sgn. F/VG clip. M15. $350.00

JAMES, P.D. *Taste for Death.* 1986. London. Faber. 1st ed. sgn. F/F. M15. $100.00

JAMES, Peter. *Prophecy.* 1992. Gollancz. 1st ed. sgn. F/F. F4. $35.00

JAMES, Philip. *Children's Books of Yesterday.* 1933. London/NY. Studio. photos. 128 p. gr cloth. VG. D1. $75.00

JAMES, Ronald. *Lawns, Trees & Shrubs.* 1961. Cape Town, Africa. ils/photos. 174 p. VG/G. B26. $29.00

JAMES, Thomas. *Three Years Among the Indians & Mexicans.* 1953. Chicago. Lakeside Classic. 297 p. teg. VG. B18. $25.00

JAMES, Will. *All in a Day's Riding.* 1933. Scribner. 1st ed. sq octavo. 251 p. red cloth. NF/dj. H5. $375.00

JAMES, Will. *Lone Cowboy.* 1930. NY. 1st ed. 431 p. VG. B28. $37.50

JAMES, Will. *Sand.* 1929. Grosset Dunlap. 12mo. G. A8. $15.00

JAMES, Will. *Sand.* 1929. Scribner. 1st ed. ils. 328 p. G. P2. $25.00

JAMES, Will. *Smoky the Cowhorse.* Oct 1929. Scribner. 1st thus in Scribner Classics format. 263 p. VG. P2. $50.00

JAMES, Will. *Smoky the Cowhorse.* 1926. Scribner. 1st ed. octavo. gr cloth. NF/pict dj. R3. $600.00

JAMES, Will. *Smoky the Cowhorse.* 1929. Grosset Dunlap. 12mo. G. A8. $6.00

JAMES, Will. *Young Cowboy.* 1935. Scribner. 1st ed. 72 p. VG-. P2. $75.00

JAMES, William. *Talks to Teachers on Psychology.* 1906. Holt. 306 p. teg. gilt cloth. VG. S9. $23.00

JAMES & JAMES. *Biography of a Bank: Story of Bank of Am.* 1954. Harper. 1st ed. ils/index. 566 p. VG. B19. $10.00

JAMES & JAMES. *Hoffa & the Teamsters: A Study of Union Power.* ca 1965. Van Nostrand. VG/G. V4. $12.50

JAMES. *Quiltmaker's Handbook.* 1978. np. ils. wrp. G2. $13.00

JAMESON, Anna Brownell. *Beauties of the Court of King Charles the 2nd.* 1833. London. Bentley. 1st ed. lg quarto. 21 pls w/tissue guards. VG. H5. $175.00

JAMESON, Horatio Gates. *Treatise on Epidemic Cholera.* 1855. Phil. Lindsay Blakiston. 286 p. new antique-styled brds. G7. $135.00

JAMISON, James K. *By Cross & Anchor: Story of Frederick on Lake Superior.* (1948). Paterson. 2nd prt. 225 p. map ep. A17. $20.00

JAMISON, Richard L. *Primitive Outdoor Skills.* (1985). Bountiful. ils/index. 143 p. F/dj. A17. $9.50

JANIFER, Laurence. *Master's Choice: Best SF of All Time.* 1966. Simon Schuster. 1st ed. NF/VG. M2. $10.00

JANNEY, Samuel M. *Conversations on Religious Subjects Between Father & 2 Sons.* 1860? Phil. Friends Book Assn. 4th ed. 16mo. 216 p. cloth. G. V3. $15.00

JANNEY, Samuel M. *Conversations on Religious Subjects...* 1835. Phil. John Richards. 1st ed. sgn twice by Edward Hicks (artist). 12mo. 120 p. M1. $500.00

JANNEY, Samuel M. *Life of George Fox...* 1853. Lippincott Grambo. 8vo. 499 p. modern lib-style bdg. VG. V3. $32.00

JANOWITZ, Tama. *Am Dad.* 1981. Putnam. 1st ed. author's 1st book. F/NF. B2. $60.00

JANOWSKY, Oscar I. *JWB Survey.* 1948. Dial. 490 p. G+. S3. $25.00

JANVIER, Thomas. *Aztec Treasure House.* 1890. Harper. 1st ed. VG. M2. $100.00

JANVIER, Thomas. *In the Sargasso Sea.* 1898. Harper. 1st ed. VG. M2. $80.00

JAPRISOT, Sebastien; see Rossi, Jean-Baptiste.

JARRELL, Randall. *Bat-Poet.* 1964. Macmillan. 1st ed. ils Maurice Sendak. G/G. L1. $10.00

JARRELL, Randall. *Bat-Poet.* 1964. Macmillan. 8vo. 43 p. emb tan cloth. NF/NF. T5. $65.00

JARRELL, Randall. *Jerome: Biography of a Poem.* 1971. Grossman. facsimile of 50 work sheets. F/dj. C4. $40.00

JARRELL, Randall. *Letters.* 1985. Boston. AP. F/bl wrp. C4. $40.00

JARRELL, Randall. *Little Friend, Little Friend.* 1945. Dial. 1st ed. NF/dj. C4. $250.00

JARRELL, Randall. *Selected Poems.* 1990. FSG. AP. F/prt gr wrp. C4. $40.00

JARRELL, Randall. *Selected Poems.* 1990. NY. 1st ed. F/F. V1. $10.00

JARVIS, C.S. *Arab Command: Biography of Lt Col FG Peake Pasha.* 1943. London. Hutchinson. 3rd imp. 158 p. gilt bl cloth. reading copy. M7. $12.00

JARVIS, Edward. *Insanity & Idiocy in MA.* 1971 (1855). Cambridge. Harvard. cloth. F/dj. G1. $20.00

JASON, Jerry; see Smith, George H.

JASON, Stuart; see Albert, Marvin H.; also Avallone, Mike.

JASPERSOHN, William. *Ballpark.* 1980. Little Brn. 1st ed. F/F. P8. $25.00

JASTROW, Joseph. *Story of Human Error.* 1936. Appleton Century. 1st ed. 446 p. patterned bl cloth. VG. G1. $37.50

JAY, Mary R. *Garden Handbook.* 1931. NY. ils/photos. 284 p. VG. B26. $17.50

JAY, Mel; see Fanthrope, R.L.

JAYAKER, Pupul. *Festival of India in the US, 1985-86.* 1985. Abrams. 1st ed. 4to. ils. 240 p. NF/dj. W1. $35.00

JAYNE, Walter Addison. *Healing Gods of Ancient Civilizations.* 1962. NY. U Books. reprint of Yale 1925 ed. VG. G1. $35.00

JAYNE, William. *Abraham Lincoln.* ca 1908. Chicago. xl. 16mo. 58 p. quarter leather/blk brds. G. T3. $19.00

JAYNES, R.T. *Old Waxhaws. Andrew Jackson. Wm R Davie. Andrew Pickens...* nd. np. 1st ed. 22 p. NF/prt wrp. M8. $37.50

JAYNES, R.T. *Pickney Draught of the Constitution.* nd. np. 1st ed. 17 p. NF/prt wrp. M8. $37.50

JEAN & MEZEI. *Hist of Surrealist Painting.* 1960. Grove. 1st prt. F/NF die-cut dj. B2. $250.00

JEAVONS, John. *How To Grow More Vegetables.* 1991. Berkeley. ils. 174 p. F. B26. $14.00

JEFFERIES, Richard. *Wood Magic.* nd. London. Collins. ils Lorna Steele. 320 p. VG. S10. $25.00

JEFFERIES, S.H. *Papa Wore No Halo.* 1963. Winston Salem, NC. Blair. 1st ed. 8vo. 457 p. F/VG+. A2. $15.00

JEFFERS, H. Paul. *Adventure of the Stalwart Companions.* 1978. Harper. 1st ed. NF/NF. S5. $25.00

JEFFERS, H. Paul. *Rubout at the Onyx.* 1981. Ticknor Fields. 1st ed. F/NF. S5. $25.00

JEFFERS, Robinson. *Be Angry at the Sun.* 1941. Random. 1st ed. inscr. F/NF. B2. $250.00

JEFFERS, Robinson. *Californians.* 1916. Macmillan. 1st ed. author's 1st trade book. F. M18. $125.00

JEFFERS, Robinson. *Dear Judas.* 1929. Horace Liveright. 1/375. sgn/#d. vellum. F/#d slipase. Q1. $450.00

JEFFERS, Robinson. *Descent to the Dead.* 1931. Random. 1st ed. sgn. NF/VG slipcase. B4. $300.00

JEFFERS, Robinson. *Double Ax.* 1948. Random. 1st ed. F/NF. C4. $65.00

JEFFERS, Robinson. *Loving Shepherdess.* 1956. Random. 1/115. sgn Jeffers/Jean Kellog. w/promo slip. NF/NF slipcase. Q1. $850.00

JEFFERS, Robinson. *Medea.* 1946. Random. 1st ed. gilt cloth. C4. $35.00

JEFFERS, Robinson. *Roan Stallion.* 1929. NY. 7th prt. 253 p. VG. D3. $25.00

JEFFERS, Robinson. *Selected Poetry of...* 1938. NY. 1st ed. VG/sans. V1. $25.00

JEFFERS, Robinson. *Women at Point Sur.* 1927. Boni Liveright. 1st ed. VG. M18. $35.00

JEFFERSON, Joseph. *Autobiography of Joseph Jefferson.* ca 1890. Century. lg 8vo. 501 p. teg. emb wht vellum. H9. $50.00

JEFFERSON, Thomas. *Notes on the State of VA.* ca 1954. UNC. fld map. 315 p. VG/stiff wrp. B10. $8.00

JEFFERSON, Thomas. *On Science & Freedom.* 1964. Worcester. St Onge. miniature. 1/1000. gr calf. F. H10. $95.00

JEFFERSON, Thomas. *Thomas Jefferson's Farm Book...* ca 1987. Charlottesville. 552 p. M. H10. $35.00

JEFFERY, George. *Brief Description of the Holy Sepulchre, Jerusalem...* 1919. Cambridge. 8vo. 233 p. decor cloth. O2. $45.00

JEFFERYS, Thomas. *Natural & Civil Hist of French Dominions in N & S Am.* 1760. London. folio. 18 fld plans/maps. 19th-C Am full calf. rpr/rstr. H9. $7,500.00

JEFFREY, Fred P. *Bantam Chickens.* 1974. N Amherst. Jeffrey. 1st ed. ils. 285 p. sbdg. H10. $15.00

JEFFRIES, Roderic. *Murder Confounded.* 1993. London. Harper Collins. 1st ed. F/F. S5. $22.50

JEKYLL, Gertrude. *Color Schemes for the Flower Garden.* 1983 (1908). Salem, NH. revised ed. pls/plans/photos. VG/dj. B26. $20.00

JEKYLL, Gertrude. *Wall & Water Gardens.* 1901. Scribner. 1st Am ed. tall 8vo. 177 p. bl cloth. NF. B20. $125.00

JEKYLL, Gertrude. *Wood & Garden.* 1914. London. Longman Gr. ils. 286 p. H10. $87.50

JELLICOE & JELLICOE. *Modern Private Gardens.* 1968. London. oblong 8vo. photos/plans. 127 p. VG+/dj. B26. $62.50

JELLICOE & JELLICOE. *Water: Use of Water in Landscape Architecture.* 1971. NY. 175 pls. 137 p. VG+/dj. B26. $75.00

JELLIFFE, R.A. *Faulkner at Nagano.* 1955. Tokyo. 1st ed. 12mo. half wht linen. VG+/VG+. A11. $165.00

JELLINEK, E.M. *Alcohol Addiction & Chronic Alcoholism.* 1942. New Haven. 1st ed. F/NF. B2. $65.00

JEN, Gish. *Typical Am.* 1991. Houghton Mifflin. 1st ed. inscr. F/F. B2. $50.00

JENKINS, Dan. *Dogged Victims Inexorable Fate.* 1970. NY. VG/VG. B5. $15.00

JENKINS, J. Geraint. *Eng Farm Wagon: Origins & Structure.* 1981. Newton Abbott. David & Charles. 3rd ed. F/F. O3. $45.00

JENKINS, John S. *Voyage of US Exploring Squadron Commanded by Capt C Wilkes.* 1850. Auburn, NY. 8vo. 517 p. brn cloth. H9. $75.00

JENKINS, Rolland. *Mediterranean Cruise.* 1923. Putnam. 1st ed. 8vo. 279 p. VG+. A2. $20.00

JENKINS, Romilly. *Dilessi Murders.* 1961. London. 1st ed. 8vo. 190 p. cloth. dj. O2. $25.00

JENKINS, Will F. *Colonial Survey.* 1957. Gnome. 1st ed. F/M. M2. $125.00

JENKINS, Will F. *Forgotten Planet.* 1954. Gnome. 1st ed. VG. M2. $20.00

JENKINS, Will F. *Operation Outer Space.* 1954. Fantasy. 1st ed. 2nd bdg. F/dj. M2. $50.00

JENKINS, Will F. *Space Tug.* 1953. Shasta. 1st ed. F/F. M2. $100.00

JENKINS & SEWARD. *Am Quilt Story.* 1991. np. cloth. G2. $27.00

JENKINS & VASS. *Like Nobody Else.* 1973. Regenry. 1st ed. VG/G+. P8. $30.00

JENKS, Almet. *Huntsman at the Gate.* (1952). Phil. 1st ed. ils Shenton. sgn. 116 p. F/dj. A17. $15.00

JENNER, Edward. *Observations on Natural Hist of the Cuckoo...* 1788. London. Royal Soc. 4to. 19th-century marbled brds/morocco label. VG. G7. $695.00

JENNESS & JENNESS. *Dwellers of the Tundra.* 1970. Toronto. Crowell Collier. 1st prt. 117 p. red cloth. VG. P4. $25.00

JENNESS & KROEBER. *Life of Their Own.* (1975). NY. Crowell. 1st ed. 133 p. dj. F3. $15.00

JENNEWEIN, J. Leonard. *Blk Hills Booktrails.* 1962. Dakota Territorial Centennial Comm/Wesleyan U. F. B19. $50.00

JENNINGS, Dean; see Fox, Gardner F.

JENNINGS, Gary. *Treasure of the Superstition Mtns.* (1973). NY. Norton. 1st ed. 8vo. 247 p. F/F. A2. $20.00

JENNINGS, John J. *Theatrical & Circus Life; or, Secrets of the Stage...* 1883. St Louis. Sun Pub. new revised ed. octavo. 8 pls/165 ils. VG. H5. $250.00

JENNINGS, Ronald C. *Christians & Muslims in Ottoman Cyprus & Mediterranean...* 1993. NY. 8vo. 416 p. cloth. O2. $65.00

JENSEN, Amy La Follette. *Wht House & Its 33 Families.* 1962. np. new ed. 4to. photos. G. B11. $25.00

JENYNS, Soame. *Background to Chinese Painting.* 1935. London. Sidgwick Jackson. 1st ed. 8vo. 40 pls. 209 p. VG. W1. $35.00

JEPPSON, J.O. *Second Experiment.* 1974. Houghton Mifflin. 1st ed. VG. M2. $8.00

JEPSON, Willis Linn. *Flora of CA.* 1909-1979. Berkeley. 4 vols in 5. ils. F/wrp. B26. $75.00

JEPSON, Willis Linn. *Trees of CA.* 1909. San Francisco. 1st ed. ils. 228 p. cloth. NF. B26. $39.00

JEROME, Edward. *Problem of the Constitution.* 1939. London. Longman Gr. gilt bl cloth. M11. $45.00

JEROME, John. *Death of the Automobile.* 1972. Norton. 1st ed. VG/dj. A17. $5.00

JEROME, Wells. *Land of the Tumbleweed.* (1947). London/Melbourne. Ward Locke. VG/dj. B9. $10.00

JEROME, Wells. *Th' Trouble Trailer.* (1943). London. Ward Locke. VG/dj. B9. $10.00

JERSTORP & KOHLMARK. *Textile Design Book.* 1986. np. cloth. G2. $23.00

JESSE, George R. *Researches Into Hist of the British Dog From Ancient Laws...* 1866. London. Hardwicke. 2 vols. marbled ep. gilt bdg. VG. H5. $450.00

JESSUP, Richard. *Cincinnati Kid.* 1963. Little Brn. 1st ed. NF/dj. E3. $25.00

JESSUP, Richard. *Threat.* 1981. London. Gollancz. 1st British ed. F/F. S5. $22.50

JESTER, Annie Lash. *Adventurers of Purse & Person: VA 1607-25.* 1964. Order 1st Families VA. 2nd ed. VG. B10. $55.00

JETER, J.B. *Reflections of a Long Life.* 1891. Richmond. Religious Herald. 325 p. VG. B10. $35.00

JETER, K.W. *Death Arms.* 1987. Morrigan. 1st ed. 1/250. sgn/#d. F/F. F4. $65.00

JETER, K.W. *Wolf Flow.* 1992. St Martin. 1st ed. F/F. N3. $20.00

JEWELL, S.K. *Amherst Reflections.* (1976). Elyria. ils. VG. B18. $12.50

JEWISH MUSEUM OF PRAGUE. *Old Jewish Cemetery of Prague.* 1947. Prague. Umelecka Beseda. ils/plans. VG/wrp. S3. $25.00

JHABVALA, Ruth Prawer. *Heat & Dust.* (1976). Harper Row. 1st ed. VG/NF. B3. $30.00

JHABVALA, Ruth Prawer. *How I Became a Holy Mother.* (1976). London. Murray. 1st ed. F/F. B3. $25.00

JOANNE, Adolphe. *Itineraire. Descriptif et Historique...Mediterranee.* 1858. Paris. 12mo. 6 fld panorama. gilt blk cloth. VG. H3. $125.00

JOANS, Ted. *All of Ted Joans & No More.* 1961. NY. Excelsior. 2nd prt. inscr. NF. B2. $45.00

JOANS, Ted. *Hipsters.* 1961. Corinth. 1st ed. NF/wrp. B2. $35.00

JOBSON, Hamilton. *Exit to Violence.* 1979. London. Collins. 1st ed. F/dj. S5. $25.00

JOE, Wanne J. *Traditional Korea: A Cultural Hist.* 1977. Seoul. Chung'and U. 2nd prt. 8vo. 477 p. VG/dj. W1. $18.00

JOERG, W.L.G. *Brief Hist of Polar Exploration Since Intro of Flying.* 1930. Am Geog Soc. 8 maps. 50 p. NF. O6. $50.00

JOERG, W.L.G. *Work of the Byrd Antarctic Expedition, 1928-30.* 1930. NY. 1st ed. maps/fld maps. 70 p. VG+/prt brn wrp. H3. $45.00

JOHANNAH. *Half-Square Triangles.* 1990. np. wrp. G2. $15.00

JOHANSEN, Donald M. *Plant Microtechnique.* 1940. NY. 1st ed. ils. 523 p. B26. $32.50

JOHN, Eric. *Popes: Concise Biographical Hist.* 1964. NY. Hawthorn. 2 vols. box. C5. $45.00

JOHN. *Needleweaving.* 1987. np. pb. G2. $20.00

JOHNS, C.A. *Flowers of the Field.* ca 1910s. London. Routledge. 96 pls. 378 p. H10. $37.50

JOHNS, Rowland. *Our Friend the Cocker Spaniel.* (1932). NY. 12mo. 85 p. F/dj. A7. $15.00

JOHNS, Willy. *Fabulous Journey of Hieronymous Meeker.* 1954. Little Brn. 1st ed. F/dj. M2. $10.00

JOHNS HOPKINS. *Nineteen Twenty-Five Hullabaloo.* 1921. Baltimore. 4to. photos. G7. $95.00

JOHNS HOPKINS. *Opening of Surgical Building & New Clinical Amphitheatre...* 1904. Bulletin 15 reprint. 29 p. G7. $150.00

JOHNSEN, Margaret A. *19th-Century Maps in Collection of GA Surveyor General Dept.* 1981. Atlanta. 184 ils. 92 p. NF/pict wrp. O6. $45.00

JOHNSON, A.B. *Treatise on Language.* 1836. Harper. 1st ed. xl. 8vo. cloth/paper label. M1. $950.00

JOHNSON, A.F. *One Hundred Title Pages, 1500-1800.* 1928. London. John Lane. 1/100. 4to. teg. gilt vellum/marbled brds. F. F1. $285.00

JOHNSON, Adrian. *Am Explored.* ca 1974. NY. Viking. Studio Book. 254 p. dj. H9. $60.00

JOHNSON, Andrew. *Supplement to the Congressional Globe.* 1868. WA, DC. 4to. 526 p. contemporary quarter calf. H9. $75.00

JOHNSON, Andrew. *Trial of Andrew Johnson.* 1868. WA, DC. orig pebbled cloth. B28. $175.00

JOHNSON, Audrey. *Furnishing Dolls' Houses.* 1975. MA. Branford. VG/dj. A16. $25.00

JOHNSON, Betty. *Complete W Cookbook.* 1964. Castle Books. VG/dj. A16. $10.00

JOHNSON, Bradley Tyler. *Memoir of Life & Public Service of Joseph E Johnston...* 1891. Baltimore. Woodward. 1st ed. 362 p. cloth. VG. M8. $450.00

JOHNSON, C. *Playmate Bears.* 1985. np. full-size patterns. wrp. G2. $7.00

JOHNSON, Charles. *Being & Race.* 1970. Bloomington, IN. 1st ed. sgn. F/F. A11. $70.00

JOHNSON, Charles. *Blk Humor.* 1970. Chicago. 1st ed. w/sgn note. F/8" sq wrp. A11. $145.00

JOHNSON, Charles. *Sorcerer's Apprentice.* 1986. Atheneum. 1st ed. F/F. Q1. $75.00

JOHNSON, Clarence R. *Constantinople Today; or, Pathfinder Survey...* 1922. NY. 8vo. 418 p. cloth. O2. $40.00

JOHNSON, Cuthbert W. *Farmer's Encyclopedia...* 1844. Phil. 1st Am ed. 17 litho pls. 1165 p. full leather. worn. B28. $90.00

JOHNSON, Denis. *Angels.* 1983. NY. 1st ed. sgn. NF/F. A11. $40.00

JOHNSON, Denis. *Stars at Noon.* (1986). Knopf. 1st ed. sgn. F/NF. B3. $45.00

JOHNSON, Denis. *Veil.* (1985). Knopf. 1st ed. rem mk. NF/VG. B3. $25.00

JOHNSON, Diane. *Dashiell Hammett: A Life.* 1983. Random. 1st ed. ils. F/dj. S5. $35.00

JOHNSON, Diane. *Terrorists & Novelists.* 1982. Knopf. 1st ed. F/F. A7. $18.00

JOHNSON, Dorothy M. *All the Buffalo Returning.* (1979). Dodd Mead. 1st ed. sgn. F/F. A18. $50.00

JOHNSON, Dorothy M. *Bloody Bozeman.* (1971). NY. 1st ed. 366 p. VG/dj. A17. $15.00

JOHNSON, Dorothy M. *When You & I Were Young, Whitefish.* (1982). Mtn Pr. 1st ed. sgn. F/F. A18. $50.00

JOHNSON, E. Pauline. *Flint & Feather. Complete Poems of...* 1931. Toronto. Mussen. 23rd ed. F/NF. L3. $65.00

JOHNSON, E. Pauline. *Legends of Vancouver.* 1911. Toronto. McClelland Goodchild Stewart. new ed. NF. scarce. L3. $85.00

JOHNSON, E.C. *On the Track of the Crescent. Erratic Notes...* 1885. London. 8vo. 324 p. gilt cloth. O2. $75.00

JOHNSON, Elizabeth. *Stuck w/Luck.* 1967. Little Brn. 1st ed. 4to. 88 p. VG. A3. $10.00

JOHNSON, Frederick. *Radiocarbon Dating: Report on Program...* 1951. Salt Lake City. Soc Am Archaelogy. 65 p. VG/wrp. P4. $25.00

JOHNSON, Gerald W. *Am Is Born. Am Moves Forward. Am Grows Up.* 1959 & 1960. Morrow. 1st ed. 3 vols. VG/VG. P2. $50.00

JOHNSON, Gerald W. *Lunatic Fringe.* 1957. Lippincott. 1st ed. 248 p. prt ochre cloth. VG/dj. G1. $25.00

JOHNSON, Guion Griffis. *Antebellum NC Soc Hist.* 1937. Chapel Hill. 1st ed. 935 p. orig cloth. VG. M8. $65.00

JOHNSON, H.B. *Carta Marina: World Geog in Strassburg, 1525.* 1974. Greenwood. reprint. M. O6. $25.00

JOHNSON, H.E. *Hallelujah, Amen! Story of Handel & Haydn Soc of Boston.* (1965). Boston. Humphries. 1st ed. 8vo. 256 p. VG+/VG+. A2. $12.50

JOHNSON, Ida Amanda. *MI Fur Trade.* 1971. Grand Rapids. Blk Letter. facsimile. cloth. F. A17. $18.50

JOHNSON, James Weldon. *God's Trombone.* 1927. Viking. 1st ed. VG. B4. $100.00

JOHNSON, James Weldon. *2nd Book of Negro Spirituals.* 1926. NY. Viking. 1st ed. NF. B2. $75.00

JOHNSON, Jane. *Early Impressions; or, Evidences of Secret Operations...* 1844. Phil. Chapman. 16mo. 144 p. leather. worn. V3. $15.00

JOHNSON, John. *Taxi! True Stories From Behind the Wheel.* (1978). Toronto. Macmillan. 224 p. dj. A7. $13.00

JOHNSON, L.D. *Memoir of Mrs Thomazin Johnson of Braintree, MA.* 1835. Boston. 1st ed. 117 p. marbled brds/half leather. G. D7. $35.00

JOHNSON, M. *Award-Winning Applique Technique.* 1984. np. ils/full-size patterns. cloth. G2. $18.00

JOHNSON, M. *Garden of Quilts.* 1984. np. ils. cloth. G2. $20.00

JOHNSON, M. *Prize Country Quilts.* 1977. np. ils. cloth. G2. $20.00

JOHNSON, M. *Star Quilts w/Patterns for More Than 50 Stars.* 1992. np. ils. cloth. G2. $30.00

JOHNSON, M.L.; see Malzberg, Barry.

JOHNSON, Mel; see Malzberg, Barry.

JOHNSON, Merle. *You Know These Lines!* 1935. NY. GA Baker. 1st ed. 1/1000. sgn/dtd 1937. 8vo. 195 p. cloth. M1. $125.00

JOHNSON, Myron. *Choice Pages From Early Am School Books.* ca 1960. Americana Review. 8vo. ils. pict wrp. H9. $30.00

JOHNSON, Richard. *Hermit of the Forest & the Wandering Infants.* 1804. Hudson. Ashbel Stoddard. 24mo. 30 p. sewn/as issued. M1. $15.00

JOHNSON, Richard. *Picture Exhibition, Containing Orig Drawings...* 1788. Worchester, MA. Isaiah Thomas. 1st Am ed. 112 p. contemporary calf. M1. $850.00

JOHNSON, Robert Neil. *Gold Digger's Atlas.* 1971. Susanville. 1st ed. 8vo. 64 p. wrp. A17. $5.00

JOHNSON, Robert W. *West Gem Hunter's Atlas.* 1974. Johnson. 12mo. VG. A8. $4.00

JOHNSON, Samuel. *Dictionary of the Eng Language.* 1825. London. Offor. 2 vols. quarto. gilt brn crushed morocco. VG. H5. $850.00

JOHNSON, SICKLES & SAYERS. *Anthology of Children's Literature.* 1959. Houghton Mifflin. ils Eichenberg. 3rd ed. 1239 p. G+. A3. $12.50

JOHNSON, Sidney Smith. *Texans Who Wore the Gray.* 1907. Tyler, TX. 1st ed. 407 p. cloth. NF. M8. $750.00

JOHNSON, Thomas H. *Oxford Companion to American History.* 1966. NY. Oxford. 1st ed. 906 p. VG/G. B11. $20.00

JOHNSON, Thomas H. *Prt Writings of Jonathan Edwards 1703-58.* 1970. NY. Burt Franklin. reprint of 1940 Princeton ed. bl cloth. G1. $21.50

JOHNSON, W.A. *Christopher Polhem: Father of Swedish Technology.* 1963. Hartford, CT. Trinity College. 1/5000. 259 p. F. S9. $20.00

JOHNSON, W.R. *Easter.* 1970. W Burke, VT. 1/250. sgn. F/prt gr wrp. B24. $150.00

JOHNSON, Walter. *Strindberg's Queen Christina...* 1955. Seattle, WA. dj. N2. $8.00

JOHNSON, Warren. *Muddling Toward Frugality.* (1978). Sierra Club. 1st ed. 12mo. 252 p. F/dj. A17. $14.50

JOHNSON, Wayne. *Snake Game.* 1990. Knopf. 1st ed. M/dj. A17. $12.50

JOHNSON, William Weber. *Forty Niners.* 1974. Time Life. 4to. F. A8. $10.00

JOHNSON, Willis Fletcher. *Life of William Tecumseh Sherman...* 1891. Edgewood. ils. 607 p. G. B10. $25.00

JOHNSON, Willis Fletcher. *Life of Wm Tecumseh Sherman, Late Retired Gen, USA.* 1891. Phil. Edgewood Pub. 1st ed. 607 p. cloth. VG. M8. $45.00

JOHNSON & PALMER. *Murder.* 1928. Covici Friede. 1st ed. VG. M2. $20.00

JOHNSON & ROARK. *Blk Masters.* (1984). Norton. 2nd prt. 422 p. NF/dj. A7. $15.00

JOHNSON & SHREEVE. *Lucy's Child.* (1989). Morrow. 1st ed. 318 p. dj. F3. $15.00

JOHNSON & SHREEVE. *Lucy: Beginnings of Humankind.* (1981). Simon Schuster. BC. 409 p. F3. $10.00

JOHNSON. *Pop-Up Wine Book.* 1989. pop-ups/wheel/push-pull tabs. F. A4. $50.00

JOHNSTON, A.S. *Capt Beirne Chapman & Chapman's Battery: Hist Sketch.* 1903. Union, WV. 1st ed. 54 p. NF/prt wrp. M8. $850.00

JOHNSTON, Annie Fellows. *Georgina of the Rainbows.* 1916. Britton. 1st ed. ils RN Jackson. 348 p. VG. M20. $15.00

JOHNSTON, Annie Fellows. *Little Colonel's Holidays.* 1901. Page. 1st ed. VG. M18. $25.00

JOHNSTON, Annie Fellows. *Little Colonel.* (1935). Burt. Shirley Temple ed. 12mo. photos. 145 p. VG. S10. $25.00

JOHNSTON, Annie Fellows. *Mary Ware, Little Colonel's Chum.* 1908. Page. 1st ed. ils Etheldred B Barry. 305 p. VG/fair. S10. $40.00

JOHNSTON, Annie Fellows. *Travelers Five Along Life's Highway.* 1911 (1899). Page. 1st thus ed. 199 p. VG. P2. $18.00

JOHNSTON, Isaac N. *4 Months in Libby & the Campaign Against Atlanta.* 1864. Cincinnati. Methodist Book Concern. 1st ed. 191 p. cloth. NF. M8. $250.00

JOHNSTON, J.E. *Narrative of Military Operations...* 1874. NY. 1st ed. ils/maps/fld map. 602 p. B28. $85.00

JOHNSTON, Johanna. *Runaway to Heaven: Story of Harriet Beecher Stowe...* 1963. Doubleday. VG/dj. A16. $10.00

JOHNSTON, Mary. *Croatan.* 1923. Little Brn. 1st ed. VG. M2. $10.00

JOHNSTON, Mary. *Long Roll.* 1911. np. ils NC Wyeth. 683 p. NF. O7. $14.50

JOHNSTON, W.G. *Overland to CA.* 1948. Oakland, CA. Biobooks. reprint. 4to. 272 p. VG. A2. $35.00

JOHNSTON & KAUFMAN. *Design on Fabrics.* 1981. np. 2nd ed. pb. G2. $15.50

JOHNSTONE, Alan. *SC & the Nation Papers & Addresses of Alan Johnstone...* nd. np. 1st ed. NF/prt wrp. M8. $37.50

JOHNSTONE, Sandy. *Enemy in the Sky.* 1979. Presido. 1st/A ed. 8vo. VG/ G. A8. $8.00

JOLAS, Eugene. *Vertical.* 1941. Gotham. 1st ed. VG. M2. $10.00

JOLLEY, Elizabeth. *Foxybaby.* (1985). Viking. 1st ed. F/F. B3. $35.00

JOLLEY, Elizabeth. *Sugar Mother.* 1988. Cambridge/Harper Row. 1st ed. sgn. F/F. Q1. $50.00

JONCICH, Geraldine. *Sane Positivist: Biography of Edward L Thorndike.* 1968. Middletown, CT. Wesleyan. 1st ed. 634 p. maroon cloth. G1. $45.00

JONES, Charles Colcock Jr. *Sergeant Wm Jasper: An Address...1876.* 1876. Albany, NY. Munsell. 1st ed. xl. 36 p. wrp. M8. $45.00

JONES, David. *Book of Jonah.* 1979. London. Clover Hill. 1/100. Sangorski Sutcliffe bdg. F. F1. $435.00

JONES, David. *Cycads of the World.* 1993. WA, DC. 200 color photos/6 maps. as new. B26. $45.00

JONES, Dilwyn. *Glossary of Ancient Egyptian Nautical Titles & Terms.* 1988. Kegan Paul. M/dj. O6. $75.00

JONES, Edgar DeWitt. *Lincoln & the Preachers.* ca 1948. NY. 1st ed. sgn. 12mo. 203 p. gr cloth. G. T3. $15.00

JONES, Elizabeth Orton. *Mason Bicentennial 1768-1968.* 1968. Jones. 1st ed. ils/photos. 205 p. F. A17. $15.00

JONES, Elizabeth Orton. *Ragman of Paris & His Ragamuffins.* 1937. Oxford. assumed 1st ed. inscr/sgn. gr cloth. VG. M5. $32.00

JONES, Elizabeth Orton. *Twig.* (1942). Macmillan. 5th prt. 8vo. 152 p. beige cloth. VG. T5. $25.00

JONES, F.N. *Intro to Study of Dependent, Defective & Delinquent Classes.* 1893. Boston. DC Heath. 1st ed. 278 p. pebbled bl cloth. G1. $35.00

JONES, Fortier. *With Serbia Into Exile.* 1916. NY. Century. ils. 447 p. N2. $40.00

JONES, George. *Sketches of Naval Life, w/Notices of Men, Manners, Scenery.* 1836. NY. 8vo. 388 p. half calf. O2. $250.00

JONES, Harry E. *Grandpa Trout.* (1987). Birmingham. 1st ed. ils. 185 p. M/dj. A17. $20.00

JONES, Harry W. *Chaplain's Experience Ashore & Afloat.* 1901. NY. Sherwood. 1st ed. 12mo. pls. 300 p. gilt red cloth. G. B11. $50.00

JONES, Henry F. *Diversions in Sicily.* 1929. London. 12mo. 255 p. gilt bl cloth. VG. H3. $25.00

JONES, Hettie. *How I Became Hettie Jones.* (1990). Dutton. 1st ed. 239 p. F/NF. A7. $16.00

JONES, Hettie. *Longhouse Winter.* 1972. HRW. 1st ed. ils Nicholas Gaetano. gr brds. F/F. T5. $25.00

JONES, J.B. *Border War: Tale of Disunion.* 1859. NY. Rudd Carleton 1st ed. 8vo. 502 p. cloth. M1. $100.00

JONES, J.B. *Life & Adventures of a Country Merchant.* 1854. Lippincott Grambo. 1st ed. 8vo. 396 p. purple cloth. M1. $100.00

JONES, J.B. *War Path: Narrative of Adventures in the Wilderness...* 1881. Lippincott. 12mo. xl. 335 p. cloth. VG. D3. $25.00

JONES, J.R. *Hist of Medical Soc of State of CA.* 1964. Hist Comm Sacramento Soc Medical Improvement. 1st ed. B19. $35.00

JONES, Jack. *Unfinished Journey.* 1937. NY. Oxford. 1st Am ed. 8vo. 303 p. F/VG. A2. $25.00

JONES, James. *From Here to Eternity.* 1951. Scribner. 1st ed. NF/NF. C4. $150.00

JONES, James. *Thin Red Line.* 1962. Scribner. 1st ed. NF/dj. C4. $35.00

JONES, Jessie Orton. *Secrets.* 1945. Viking. 1st ed. VG/VG. P2. $40.00

JONES, Jessie Orton. *Sm Rain, Verses From the Bible.* 1945 (1943). Viking. 5th ed. oblong 4to. VG-/G. T5. $25.00

JONES, John William. *Christ in the Camp or Religion in Lee's Army.* 1887. Richmond, VA. Johnson. 2nd ed. 528 p. cloth. M8. $125.00

JONES, John William. *Personal Reminiscences, Anecdotes & Letters of Gen RE Lee.* 1874. NY. Appleton. 1st ed. 509 p. contemporary leather/marbled brds. VG. M8. $650.00

JONES, Julie. *Art of Pre-Columbian Gold.* 1985. Little Brn. 1st Am ed. 248 p. dj. F3. $75.00

JONES, Katharine M. *Heroines of Dixie.* 1955. Indianapolis/NY. 1st ed. dj. B30. $35.00

JONES, Katharine M. *Plantation S.* 1957. Bobbs Merrill. 1st ed. 412 p. NF/VG. M8. $45.00

JONES, Kenneth. *Stone Soup.* 1985. Chamberlain. 1/150. pub/ils sgn Chamberlain. marbled brds. F. B24. $200.00

JONES, L.C. *Piney Woods & Its Story.* 1922. NY. 1st ed. 12mo. 154 p. VG. B28. $20.00

JONES, Langdon. *Eye of the Lens.* 1972. Macmillan. 1st ed. F/NF. N3. $15.00

JONES, Le Roi. *Baptism & the Toilet.* 1967. NY. 1st ed. sgn. NF/sm 8vo wrp. A11. $75.00

JONES, Le Roi. *Home: Social Essays.* 1966. Morrow. 1st ed. VG/dj. A7. $22.00

JONES, Le Roi. *Moderns: Anthology of New Writing in Am.* 1965. London. MacGibbon Kee. 1st ed. Nf/dj. A7. $30.00

JONES, Lester M. *Quakers in Action: Recent Humanitarian & Reform Activities.* 1929. Macmillan. 1st ed. 12mo. 226 p. VG. V3. $12.00

JONES, Owen. *Grammar of Ornament.* 1868. London. Bernard Quartich. folio. 112 color pls. brn cloth. F. R3. $600.00

JONES, R. Bruce. *Greene Street Friends School, 1855-1955.* 1955. Germantown, PA. Greene Street Friends School. 8vo. 116 p. VG. V3. $17.50

JONES, Raymond F. *Renaissance.* 1951. Gnome. 1st ed. F/NF-. M2. $40.00

JONES, Raymond F. *This Island Earth.* (1952). Chicago. Shasta. 1st ed. F/dj. B4. $200.00

JONES, Rufus. *Call To What Is Vital.* 1948. Macmillan. 1st ed. 12mo. 143 p. VG/dj. V3. $12.50

JONES, Rufus. *Finding the Trail of Life.* 1927. Macmillan. 12mo. 148 p. G+. V3. $12.50

JONES, Samuel. *Battle of Prairie Grove, Dec 7, 1862.* ca 1886. np. 1st separate ed/author's offprint. 38 p. NF/prt wrp. M8. $850.00

JONES, Stephen. *Flann O'Brien Reader.* 1978. Viking. 1st ed. NF/F. B2. $40.00

JONES, Thelma. *Once Upon a Lake: Hist of Lake Minnetonka & Its People.* 1957. Ross Haines. 1st ed. 285 p. cloth. A17. $17.50

JONES, Thomas. *Pugilist at Rest.* (1993). Little Brn. 1st prt. sgn. F/F. C4. $45.00

JONES, Virgil Carrington. *Gray Ghosts & Revel Raiders.* ca 1956. Holt. 2nd prt. 431 p. VG. B10. $40.00

JONES, William. *Grammar of the Persian Language.* 1775. London. 2nd ed. 4to. 147 p. rebound half calf. O2. $250.00

JONG, Erica. *Becoming Light: Poems, New & Selected.* 1992. NY. 1st ed. F/F. V1. $15.00

JONG, Erica. *How To Save Your Own Life.* (1977). HRW. 1st ed. F/NF. B3. $30.00

JONG, Erica. *Parachutes & Kisses.* (1984). NAL. 1st ed. F/NF. B3. $25.00

JONG, Erica. *Serenissima.* (1987). London. Bantam. 1st ed. NF/F. B3. $15.00

JONSSON, Reidar. *My Life As a Dog.* 1990. FSG. trans Eivor Martinus. NF. C8. $30.00

JORAVSKY, David. *Russian Psychology: A Critical Hist.* 1989. Oxford. 1st ed. 8vo. 583 p. blk cloth. F/dj. G1. $37.50

JORDAN, E.L. *Charlottesville & the U of VA in Civil War.* 1988. Lynchburg, VA. Howard. 1st ed. 1/1000. sgn. 225 p. cloth. NF/VG. M8. $45.00

JORDAN, E.L. *Hammond's Nature Atlas of Am.* (1952). NY. 4to. ils/maps. 256 p. dj. A17. $17.50

JORDAN, Fritz. *Escape. Trans From the Hebrew by Niuisa Indursky.* 1970. S Brunswick. 8vo. 278 p. cloth. dj. O2. $25.00

JORDAN, June. *Civil Wars.* (1981). Boston. Beacon. 1st ed. 188 p. F/clip. A7. $18.00

JORDAN, June. *Naming Our Destiny.* (1989). Thunders Mouth. 1st ed. F/F. A7. $15.00

JORDAN, June. *Passion: New Poems, 1977-1980.* (1980). Beacon. 1st ed. 100 p. F/NF clip. A7. $15.00

JORDAN, Kate. *Happifats & the Grouch.* 1917. Dutton. 6 color pls. G+. M5. $75.00

JORDAN, Pat. *Blk Coach.* 1971. Dodd Mead. dj. N2. $10.00

JORDAN, Pat. *Suitors of Spring.* 1973. Dodd Mead. 1st ed. VG/VG. P8. $12.50

JORDAN & LELAND. *Mona Lisa.* 1986. Faber. intro Jordan. NF. C8. $25.00

JOSE, Francisco. *Three Filipino Women.* 1992. NY. Random. 1st Am ed. F/F. A14. $25.00

JOSEF, Franz. *An Meine Volker.* ca 1914. Germany. miniature. 47 p. tin bdg w/clasp. F. B24. $225.00

JOSEPE, Alfred. *Studies in Jewish Thought: Anthology...* 1981. Wayne State. 17 essays. 434 p. VG+/VG. S3. $40.00

JOSEPH, Franz. *Star Fleet Technical Manual.* 1975. Ballantine. 1st ed. F/clip plastic fld. N3. $35.00

JOSEPH, Morris. *Judaism As Greed & Life.* 1925. Routledge. 5th ed. 522 p. G+. S3. $24.00

JOSEPHSON, Hannah. *Golden Threads: New Eng's Mill Girls & Magnates.* ca 1949. DSP. 1st ed. VG/fair. V4. $17.50

JOSEPHSON, Matthew. *Union House, Union Bar.* ca 1956. NY. Random. 1st ed. photos. VG/G. V4. $15.00

JOSEPHY, Alvin. *Am Heritage Book of Indians.* (1961). NY. 3rd prt. 424 p. dj. A17. $18.50

JOSEPHY, Alvin. *Am in 1492. World of Indian Peoples...* 1992. Knopf. 477 p. dj. F3. $35.00

JOSEPHY, Alvin. *Indian Heritage of Am.* 1974. Knopf. ils. 384 p. VG/VG. B11. $16.00

JOSHI, P.S. *Apartheid in S Africa.* 1950. Kimberly, S Africa. wrp. N2. $17.50

JOSPE, Eva. *Reason & Hope: Selections From Jewish Writings of H Cohen.* 1971. Norton. 3 vols. VG+/G. S3. $23.00

JOSS, John. *Sierra, Sierra.* (1977). Los Altos. Soaring. 1st ed. inscr/sgn. NF/dj. A7. $100.00

JOSS, John. *Sierra, Sierra.* (1978). Morrow. 1st ed. 1st prt. F/dj. A7. $45.00

JOUEN, P.L.A. *Considerations Medico-Legales sur l'Infantcide.* 1820. Paris. Didot Le Jeune. 4to. new stiff wrp. G7. $150.00

JOY, Thomas. *Mostly Joy: A Bookman's Story.* (1971). London. Michael Joseph. 1st ed. 8vo. 206 p. F/F. A2. $15.00

JOYCE, James. *Exiles, Play in 3 Acts.* 1918. NY. Huebsch. 1st Am ed. F. B24. $385.00

JOYCE, James. *Exiles.* 1951. Viking. 1/1900. book reviewer EF Smith's copy. NF/NF. C4. $125.00

JOYCE, James. *Finnegan's Wake.* 1939. London. 1st ed/trade issue. 1/2450. red linen. NF. A11. $450.00

JOYCE, James. *Finnegan's Wake.* 1939. London. Faber. 1/125. sgn/#d. NF/lacks slipcase/VG+ clamshell box. Q1. $3,950.00

JOYCE, James. *Haveth Childers Everywhere.* 1930. Paris. Babou Kahne. 1st ed. 1/500 on Vidalon Royal. 72 p. NF/case. H5. $750.00

JOYCE, James. *Pomes Penyeach.* 1927. London. 1st ed. ES. G+. A1. $250.00

JOYCE, James. *Pomes Penyeach.* 1933. London. Faber. 1st ed. VG/stiff card covers/paper wrp. M7. $115.00

JOYCE, James. *Portrait of an Artist As a Young Man.* 1916. London. Egoist. 1st ed. Holbrook Jackson's copy. G+. A1. $250.00

JOYCE, James. *Stephen Hero.* 1944. NY. 1st ed. VG/VG. B5. $75.00

JOYCE, James. *Ulysses.* 1922. Paris. 1st ed. 1/150. octavo. Jerome Kern's copy. F/bl wrp/bl cloth box. H5. $35,000.00

JOYCE, James. *Ulysses.* 1934. NY. 1st ed. VG/VG. B5. $195.00

JOYCE, James. *Ulysses.* 1934. Random. ARC of 1st Am ed. w/photo. NF/NF clip. Q1. $600.00

JOYCE, James. *Ulysses.* 1961. Random. corrected/reset ed. F/NF. C4. $40.00

JOYCE, John Alexander. *Jewels of Memory.* 1895. WA, DC. Gibson. 1st ed. 245 p. cloth. NF. M8. $150.00

JOYCE, P.W. *Wonders of Ireland & Other Papers on Irish Subjects.* 1911. Longman Gr. 1st ed. 12mo. 242 p. F. A2. $30.00

JOYCE, Stanislaus. *My Brother's Keeper.* 1958. Viking. 1st ed. F/NF. B2. $35.00

JUAN Y SANTACILLA & DE ULLOA. *Voyage to S Am: Describing...That Extensive Continent.* 1758. Dublin. Wm Williamson. 2 vols. rebound 20th-century calf/marbled brds. K1. $600.00

JUDAH, Aaron. *Clown of Bombay: A Novel.* 1968. Dial. 252 p. VG+/VG. S3. $23.00

JUDAH, Samuel B.H. *Tale of Lexington: Nat Comedy...* 1823. NY. Dramatic Repository. 1st ed. 18mo. 60 p. recent wrp. M1. $600.00

JUDD, Cyril. *Gunner Cade.* 1952. Simon Schuster. 1st ed. VG/rpr. M2. $17.00

JUDD, Cyril. *Outpost Mars.* 1952. Abelard. 1st ed. F/dj. M2. $35.00

JUDD, N. *Bureau of Am Ethnology.* 1967. Norman. 1st ed. VG/VG. B5. $22.50

JUDD, Oliver P. *Hist of the Town of Coventry.* (1912). Coventry, NY. 99 p. G+. B18. $17.50

JUDD, Silas. *Sketch of Life & Voyages of Capt Alvah Dewey.* 1838. Isaac Lyon. 1st ed. orig brds. very scarce. H9. $800.00

JUDSON, Clara Ingram. *Abraham Lincoln: Friend of the People.* (1950). Chicago. Follett. 12th prt. xl. sm 4to. pict cloth. G+. T5. $15.00

JUDSON, Clara Ingram. *City Neighbor: Story of Jane Addams.* 1967 (1951). Scribner. xl. ils Ralph Ray. 125 p. pict tan cloth. T5. $10.00

JUDSON, Clara Ingram. *Mary Jane in Eng.* (1928). Grosset Dunlap. reprint. 8vo. 216 p. pict ep. G. T5. $17.50

JUDSON, Clara Ingram. *My Household Day Book.* (1930). Volland. new ed. quarto. F/NF. B4. $85.00

JUDSON, Katharine B. *MT: Land of Shining Mtns.* 1916. Chicago. McClurg. 11th ed. 244 p. VG. H7. $20.00

JUDSON, Sylvia Shaw. *Quiet Eye: Way of Looking at Pictures.* 1982. Chicago. Regnery Gateway. 2nd ed. 12mo. M/M. V3. $12.50

JUHASZ, Esther. *Sephardic Jews in the Ottoman Empire.* 1990. Jerusalem. 4to. 280 p. O2. $40.00

JUKES, Edward. *On Indigestion & Costiveness.* 1832. London. Effingham Wilson. 3rd ed. 196 p. contemporary bdg. VG. H5. $200.00

JUNG, C.G. *Memories, Dreams, Reflections.* 1963. Pantheon. revised ed/later prt. 410 p. bl cloth. VG/dj. G1. $25.00

JUNG, C.G. *Memories, Dreams, Reflections.* 1963. Pantheon. 3rd ed. VG. N2. $12.50

JUNG, Leo. *Living Judaism.* 1927. Night/Day Pr. 2nd ed. 360 p. G+. S3. $21.00

JUNGE, Werner. *Bolahun: African Adventure.* (1952). NY. Putnam. 1st Am ed. 8vo. 248 p. F/VG. A2. $12.50

JUNGER, Ernst. *Werke.* ca 1964. Stuttgart. Verlag. 10 vols. 12mo. bl fabricoid. N2. $165.00

JUNGMANN, Josef A. *Early Liturgy to Time of Gregory the Great.* ca 1959. Notre Dame. 314 p. H10. $20.00

JUNGMANN, Josef A. *Handling on the Faith.* ca 1959. NY. Herder. 445 p. H10. $15.00

JUNGMANN, Josef A. *Mass of the Roman Rite...* ca 1959. NY. Benziger. 567 p. F/dj. H10. $45.00

JUNGMANN, Josef A. *Pastoral Liturgy.* ca 1962. London. Challoner. 430 p. H10. $35.00

JUNIOR LEAGUE SAN FRANCISCO. *Here Today: San Francisco's Architectural Heritage.* (1968). Chronicle Books. 1st ed. 4to, 333 p. F/VG. A2. $45.00

JUPTNER, Joseph. *US Civil Aircraft.* 1962. LA. Aero Pub. 2 vols. G/djs. A16. $50.00

JURMAIN, Suzanne. *Once Upon a Horse: Hist of Horses...* 1989. Lee Shepard. 4to. 176 p. VG/VG. O3. $45.00

JUST, Ward. *Congressman Who Loved Flaubert.* (1973). Little Brn. 1st ed. rem mk. dj. A7. $20.00

JUST, Ward. *Jack Glance.* 1989. Houghton Mifflin. 1st ed. F/F. A7. $25.00

JUSTICE, Donald. *From a Notebook.* 1972. Seamark. 1/317. sgn. F/sans. V1. $75.00

K

KABAK, Aharon A. *Narrow Path: Man of Nazareth.* 1968. Tel-Aviv. Massada Pr. 381 p. VG+/G+. S3. $20.00

KABOTIE, Fred. *Designs From the Ancient Mimbrenos w/Hopi Interpretation.* 1982. Northland. reissue of 1949 Grabhorn ed. F. B19. $35.00

KADLOUBOVSKY & PALMER. *Writings From Philokalia on Prayer of the Heart.* 1951. London. trans from Russian. 8vo. 420 p. cloth. O2. $30.00

KADUSHIN, Max. *Worship & Ethics: Study in Rabbinic Judaism.* 1963-64. NW U. 329 p. VG/G. S3. $24.00

KAEL, Pauline. *Reeling.* (1976). Little Brn. 1st ed. 497 p. NF/dj. A7. $20.00

KAEO & KALELEONALANI. *News From Molakai: Letters...1873-1876.* (1976). Honolulu. 1st ed. 8vo. 345 p. F/VG. A2. $17.50

KAFKA, Barbara. *Microwave Gourmet.* 1987. Morrow. 1st ed. as new/dj. A16. $15.00

KAGAN, Hilde Huen. *Am Heritage Pict Atlas of US Hist.* 1966. NY. VG+/dj. O6. $20.00

KAGAN, Solomon. *Fielding H Garrison. A Biography.* 1948. Boston. presentation/inscr. 104 p. NF. G7. $85.00

KAGANOVICH, L.M. *Socialist Reconstruction of Moscow & Other Cities in USSR.* 1931. Moscow. Co-Operative Pub Soc of Foreign Workers in USSR. G. V4. $20.00

KAHANE & TIETZE. *Lingua Franca in the Levant.* 1899. Istanbul. thick 8vo. 752 p. cloth. dj. O2. $85.00

KAHIN & LEWIS. *US in Vietnam.* 1967. Dial. 1st ed. NF/clip. A7. $25.00

KAHN, Albert. *Betrayal: Our Occupation of Germany.* (1950). NY. 2nd ed/wrp issue. A7. $8.00

KAHN, Albert. *Speak Out! Am Wants Peace.* (1951). NY. Independence. 256 p. worn/wrp. A7. $10.00

KAHN, E.J. Jr. *Who, Me?* (1949). NY. 1st ed. presentation. F/F. B20. $40.00

KAHN, Joan. *Edge of the Chair.* 1967. Harper. 1st ed. VG/dj. M2. $10.00

KAHN, Roger. *Boys of Summer.* 1972. Harper Row. BC. VG/VG. P8. $10.00

KAHN, Roger. *Season in the Sun.* 1977. Harper Row. 1st ed. F/VG+. P8. $15.00

KAHN, Roger. *Umpires Story.* 1953. Putnam. 1st ed. VG+/VG+. P8. $60.00

KAHN, Tom. *Unfinished Revolution.* 1960. NY. Soc Party-Soc Democratic Federation. 64 p. wrp. A7. $15.00

KAHN & ROSE. *Pete Rose: My Story.* 1989. Macmillan. 1st ed. M/M. P8. $7.50

KAHRL, William J. *CA Water Atlas.* 1979. Sacramento, CA. folio. ES. 118 p. bl cloth. M. O6. $575.00

KAINEN, Jacob. *John Baptist Jackson: 18th-Century Master of Color Woodcut.* 1962. Smithsonian. 75 pls. 183 p. cloth. D2. $75.00

KAINS, Josephine; see Goulart, Ron.

KAINS, M.G. *Grow Your Own Fruit.* 1946 (1944). NY. 5th prt. 434 p. NF. B26. $17.50

KAINS, M.G. *Profitable Poultry Production.* 1913. NY. Judd. ils. 278 p. H10. $9.50

KAJENCKI, F.C. *Star on Many a Battlefield.* 1980. np. index. 280 p. map ep. dj. O7. $12.50

KAKAR, Sudhir. *Shamans, Mystics & Drs...India & Its Healing Traditions.* 1982. Knopf. 1st Am ed. 8vo. 306 p. F/F. A2. $12.50

KAKONIS, Tom. *Criss Cross.* 1990. St Martin. 1st ed. F/F. M15. $35.00

KALLEN, Horace M. *Utopians at Bay.* 1958. Theodor Herzl Found. 303 p. VG+/G. S3. $18.00

KALM, Peter. *Travels Into N Am.* 1772. London. Lowndes. 2nd Eng ed. 2 vols. lg fld map. contemporary calf. H9. $1,500.00

KALTCHAS, Nicholas. *Intro to the Constitutional Hist of Modern Greece.* 1940. NY. 8vo. 187 p. cloth. O2. $25.00

KALTENBORN, H.V. *Kaltenborn Edits the War News.* 1942. Dutton. 1st ed. sm 8vo. 96 p. F/dj. B20. $50.00

KAMENKA & SMITH. *Intellectuals & Revolution.* (1979). St Martin. 165 p. NF/dj. A7. $13.00

KAMINSKY, Marc. *Road From Hiroshima.* 1984. NY. 1st ed. F/VG+. V1. $10.00

KAMINSKY, Stuart. *Buried Caesars.* (1989). Mysterious. 1st ed. F/F. B3. $25.00

KAMINSKY, Stuart. *Cold Red Sunrise.* 1988. Scribner. ARC of 1st ed. w/promo material. F/F. S5. $30.00

KAMINSKY, Stuart. *Cold Red Sunrise.* 1988. Scribner. 1st ed. F/F. M15. $40.00

KAMINSKY, Stuart. *Murder on the Yel Brick Road.* 1977. St Martin. 1st ed. sgn. F/F. B2. $85.00

KAMINSKY, Stuart. *Murder on the Yel Brick Road.* 1977. St Martin. 1st ed. VG/VG. L1. $35.00

KAN, Michael. *Sculpture of Ancient W Mexico.* 1989. NM U. revised ed. 4to. 180 p. F3. $35.00

KANE, Annie. *Golden Sunset; or, Homeless Blind Girl.* 1867. Baltimore. JW Bond. not 1st ed. N2. $20.00

KANE, Elisha Kent. *Arctic Explorations 1856 & 1857.* Phil. Childs Peterson. 2 vols. B28/H9. $65.00

KANE, Harnett Thomas. *Spies for the Bl & Gray.* 1954. Hanover. 1st ed. 311 p. cloth. VG/VG. M8. $35.00

KANE, Henry. *Report for a Corpse.* 1948. Simon Schuster. 1st ed. 245 p. VG+/dj. M20. $15.00

KANE, Joe. *Running the Amazon.* 1989. Knopf. 278 p. dj. F3. $15.00

KANEKO, Shigetaka. *Guide to Japanese Art.* 1963. Rutland, VT/Tokyo. 1st ed. 8vo. ils. 227 p. VG. W1. $18.00

KANG & YIM. *Politics of Korean Reunification.* 1978. Seoul. Research Center Peace/Unification. 1st ed. 250 p. VG. W1. $16.00

KANIN, Garson. *Blow Up a Storm.* (1959). Random. 1st ed. VG/G+. A7. $20.00

KANIN, Garson. *Smash.* 1980. Viking. 1st ed. sgn. NF/NF. V2. $9.00

KANN, Robert A. *Hist of Hapsburg Empire 1526-1918.* 1977. Berkeley. 2nd ed w/corrections. VG/dj. A16. $20.00

KANNER, Leo. *Hist of the Care & Study of the Mentally Retarded.* 1967. Springfield. Thomas. 2nd prt. thin 8vo. brn cloth. VG/dj. G1. $35.00

KANTOR, Alfred. *Book of Alfred Kantor.* 1971. McGraw Hill. 1st ed. 127 p. VG/G+. S3. $26.00

KANTOR, Jacob R. *Scientific Evolution of Psychology.* 1963. Chicago. Principia. 2 vols. orange cloth. VG/dj. G1. $75.00

KANTOR, MacKinlay. *Andersonville.* (1955). World. 1st ed. NF/VG. B4. $65.00

KANTOR, MacKinlay. *Lee & Grant at Appomattox.* ca 1950. Random. 9th prt. VG/G. B10. $12.00

KANTOR, MacKinlay. *Long Remembered.* 1934. Coward McCann. ARC. NF/wrp. B2. $75.00

KANTOR & KANTOR. *Hamilton Co.* (1970). Macmillan. 1st ed. sm 4to. 288 p. F/VG+. A2. $15.00

KAPLAN, A.O. *Baby's Biography.* 1891. Brentano. 1st ed. ils Frances Brundage. 69 p. VG. S10. $150.00

KAPLAN, Mordecai M. *New Zionism.* 1955. NY. 172 p. VG. S3. $21.00

KAPLAN, Mordecai M. *Religion of Ethical Nationhood.* 1970. Macmillan. 1st ed. VG/fair. S3. $21.00

KAPLOUN, Uri. *Synagogue.* 1973. Leon Amiel. 119 p. VG/VG. S3. $25.00

KARIG, Walter. *Zotz!* 1947. NY. Rinehart. 1st ed. F/VG. N3. $15.00

KARIG, Walter. *Zotz!* 1947. Rinehart. G/dj. E3. $10.00

KARL, M.S. *Deerslayer: A Pete Brady Mystery.* 1991. St Martin. 1st ed. F/F. T2. $12.00

KARLIN, PAQUET & ROTTMANN. *Free Fire Zone.* (1973). 1st McGraw Hill wrp ed. photos. 208 p. A7. $25.00

KARLIN, Wayne. *Lost Armies.* (1988). Holt. 1st ed. F/F. A7. $30.00

KARMALI, John. *Birds of Africa: Bird Photographer in E Africa.* 1980. London. Collins. 1st ed. sm folio. ils. VG/dj. N2. $20.00

KARNES, Thomas L. *William Gilpin: W Nationalist.* 1970. TX U. 383 p. F/NF clip. B19. $17.50

KARNOW, Stanley. *Vietnam: Hist.* (1983). Viking. ARC. 750 p. wrp. A7. $30.00

KAROLEVITZ, Robert F. *This Was Trucking. A Pict Hist.* 1966. Bonanza. G/dj. A16. $12.00

KARPF, Fay B. *Psychology & Psychotherapy of Otto Rank.* 1953. Philosophical Lib. 1st ed. thin 8vo. red cloth. G1. $22.50

KARR, Alphonse. *Tour Round My Garden.* 1856 (1854). London. ils W Harvey. 12mo. 322 p. VG. B28. $55.00

KARR, Phyllis Ann. *Idylls of the Queen.* 1982. Ace. true 1st ed. pb. VG. C1. $5.00

KARROW, Robert W. *Checklist of Prt Maps of the Middle W to 1900...* 1983. Chicago. Newberry Lib. 300+ p. M. O6. $55.00

KARROW, Robert W. *Mapmakers of the 16th Century & Their Maps.* 1993. Chicago. Speculum Orbis. ils. 846 p. F. O5. $110.00

KARSON, Marc. *Am Labor Unions & Politics.* ca 1958. Carbondale. as new. V4. $12.50

KASHER, Menachem M. *Israel Passover Haggadah.* 1957. Am Biblical Ency Soc. 2nd ed. Eng/Hebrew text. 333 p. G+. S3. $23.00

KASSLER, E.B. *Modern Gardens & the Landscape.* 1964. MOMA. photos. 96 p. VG. B28. $20.00

KASTNER, J. *Species of Eternity.* 1977. Knopf. 1st ed. ils. 350 p. NF/rpr dj. S9. $5.00

KATES, Brian. *Murder of a Shopping Bag Lady.* 1985. Harcourt. ARC. pub RS. F/dj. S5. $25.00

KATKOV, George. *Russia 1917: February Revolution.* ca 1967. Harper Row. F/F. V4. $20.00

KATSIMIS, John G. *Guide Book for Travellers.* 1904. Athens. 12mo. 51 p. prt wrp. O2. $85.00

KATZ, Jane B. *Song Remembers: Self Portraits of Native Americans in Arts.* 1980. Houghton Mifflin. 1st ed. ils. 207 p. F/NF. B19. $20.00

KATZ, Richard. *Schnaps, Kokain und Lamas.* (1931). Berlin. 1st ed. 251 p. dj. F3. $15.00

KATZ. *Custer in Photographs.* 1985. np. lg 4to. ils. dj. O7. $27.50

KAUFFELD, Carl. *Snakes & Snake Hunting.* (1957). NY. photos. 266 p. dj. A17. $9.50

KAUFFMAN, Ray. *Hurricane's Wake: Around the World on a Ketch.* 1940. Macmillan. 1st ed. sgn. 8vo. 319 p. VG+/VG-. A2. $35.00

KAUFFMAN, Russell. *Chihuahua.* 1952. Chicago. Judy. 1st ed. 1/5000. 158 p. F/dj. A17. $15.00

KAUFMAN, Bob. *Selected Writings.* (1980). np. Regina Kaufman. 1st ed. 265 p. wrp. A7. $8.00

KAUFMAN, Stuart B. *Samuel Gompers Papers, Vol I.* ca 1986. Chicago. IL U. VG/VG. V4. $17.50

KAUMGARTL, I. *Life & Dreams of a Realist.* 1934. np. 1st ed. inscr. VG. V2. $8.00

KAUPP, B.F. *Poultry Culture, Sanitation & Hygiene.* 1915. Phil. Saunders. 1st ed. ils. 418 p. H10. $10.00

KAVANAGH, Dan. *Duffy.* 1980. London. 1st ed. sgn. F/NF clip. A11. $75.00

KAVANAGH, Dan. *Fiddle City.* 1981. London. Cape. 1st ed. VG+/dj. S5. $30.00

KAVANAGH, Dan. *Going to the Dogs.* 1987. Pantheon. 1st ed. author's 4th novel. F/F. Q1. $40.00

KAVANAGH, Dan. *Going to the Dogs.* 1987. Pantheon. 1st ed. NF/NF. B3. $30.00

KAVANAGH, Dan. *Porcupine.* (1992). London. Cape. 1st ed. F/F. B3. $30.00

KAVANAGH, Dan. *Putting the Boot In.* 1985. London. Cape. 1st ed. F/F. B4/Q1. $100.00

KAVANAGH, Dan. *Staring at the Sun.* 1986. London. Cape. 1st ed. F/F. C4. $40.00

KAVANAGH, Dan. *Staring at the Sun.* 1987. Knopf. 1st ed. rem mk. VG/VG. B3. $25.00

KAVANAGH, Dan. *Staring at the Sun.* 1987. Knopf. 1st ed. sgn. F/NF. B2. $50.00

KAVANAGH, Dan. *Staring at the Sun.* 1987. Knopf. AP. w/promo material. NF/prt orange wrp. Q1. $60.00

KAVANAGH, Dan. *Talking It Over.* 1991. Knopf. AP. sgn. F/prt wht wrp/prt blk slipcase. Q1. $75.00

KAVANAGH, Dan. *Talking It Over.* 1991. Knopf. ARC. w/sgn leaf. F/blk fld box. C4. $100.00

KAVANAGH, Dan. *Talking It Over.* 1991. Knopf. 1st ed. NF/NF. B3. $20.00

KAY, Gertrude Alice. *Adventures in Geography.* 1930. NY. 8vo. 157 p. orange cloth. VG. H3. $25.00

KAY, Gertrude Alice. *When the Sand-Man Comes.* 1916. Moffat Yard. 1st ed. 183 p. gray cloth/pict label. G+. S10. $45.00

KAY, Henry Cassels. *Yaman: Its Early Mediaeval Hist...* 1892. London. 8vo. 358 p. wht buckram. rare. O2. $275.00

KAY & SMITH. *German Aircraft in the 2nd World War.* (1972). London. 1st ed. 745 p. VG/dj. B18. $35.00

KAYE, M.M. *Ordinary Princess.* 1984. Doubleday. 1st ed. 8vo. 112 p. VG/VG. A3. $20.00

KAYE, Marvin. *Incredible Umbrella.* 1979. Doubleday. 1st ed. F/dj. M2. $20.00

KAYSEN, Susanna. *Girl, Interrupted.* 1993. Turtle Bay. ARC. F/wrp. B2. $25.00

KAZANTZAKIS, N. *Last Temptation of Christ.* 1960. NY. 1st ed. VG/VG. B5. $45.00

KAZANTZAKIS, Nikos. *Report to Greco: Autobiographical Novel.* 1965. Oxford/London. Cassier/Faber. 1st ed. trans from Greek. NF/NF clip. A14. $40.00

KEA, R.A. *Settlements, Trade & Policies on 17th-C Gold Coast.* (1982). Baltimore. Johns Hopkins. 1st ed. 8vo. 475 p. F. A2. $25.00

KEARNEY, Julian; see Goulart, Ron.

KEARTON, Cherry. *Island of Penguins.* 1931. NY. Nat Travel Club. 1st ed. 70 pls. pict ep. gilt blk cloth. VG. H3. $30.00

KEATES, J.S. *Cartographic Design & Production.* 1973. London. Longman. ils. NF/worn. O6. $40.00

KEATHING, Edward. *Story of Labor: 33 Yrs on Rail Workers' Fighting Front.* ca 1953. WA, DC. Rufus Darby. presentation. VG/VG. V4. $25.00

KEATING, B. *NW Passage.* 1970. Chicago. 4to. 157 p. bl cloth. P4. $30.00

KEATING, H.R.F. *Crime & Mystery: 100 Best Books.* 1987. London. Xanadu. 1st ed. w/promo material. F/dj. S5. $35.00

KEATING, H.R.F. *Man Who...* 1992. London. Macmillan. 1st ed. written to honor/sgn Julian Symons. F/dj. S5. $45.00

KEATING, H.R.F. *Murder Must Appetize.* 1975. London. Lemon Tree. 1st ed. F/sans. M15. $35.00

KEATING, H.R.F. *Rich Detective.* 1993. London. Macmillan. 1st ed. F/F. S5. $25.00

KEATS, John. *Poems of John Keats.* 1894. Hammersmith. Kelmscott. 1/300. octavo. 384 p. Zaehnsdorf bdg. F. H5. $1,800.00

KEAY. *Book of Smocking.* 1985. np. ils. cloth. G2. $18.00

KEDROS, Andre. *Resistance Grecque (1940-44). Combat d'un Peuple...* 1966. Paris. 8vo. 544 p. O2. $30.00

KEDROV, M.S. *Book Pub Under Tzarism. The Zerno Pub House.* 1932. NY. Workers Lib. 1st ed. F/wrp. B2. $30.00

KEEBLE, John. *Crab Canon.* 1971. NY. 1st ed. inscr. F/VG. A11. $55.00

KEEL, John. *Jadoo.* 1957. NY. 1st ed. 8vo. 249 p. gray marbled brds. F/VG. H3. $30.00

KEELER, Harry Stephen. *Case of 2 Strange Ladies.* 1943. NY. Phoenix Pr. 1st ed. F/rpr. M15. $50.00

KEEN, Benjamin. *Aztec Image in W Thought.* (1971). Rutgers. 1st ed. 667 p. dj. F3. $35.00

KEEN, Richard A. *MI Weather.* 1993. MT. Am Geographic Pub. as new/wrp. A16. $14.95

KEEN & WHITE. *Am TB on Surgery.* 1896. Phil. Saunders. thick 8vo. 1248 p. rebacked. VG. G7. $95.00

KEENAN, Henry F. *Conflict w/Spain & Conquest of the Philippines.* 1898. Phil. Ziegler. 8vo. ils/pls. 667 p. bl cloth. B11. $25.00

KEENE, Carolyn. *Bungalow Mystery.* 1930. Grosset Dunlap. 204 p. VG+/dj. M20. $85.00

KEENE, Carolyn. *Clue of the Broken Locket.* 1934. Grosset Dunlap. 219 p. VG/dj. M20. $50.00

KEENE, Carolyn. *In the Shadow of the Tower.* 1934. Grosset Dunlap. lists 6 titles. 217 p. VG+/dj. M20. $150.00

KEENE, Carolyn. *Mystery of the Fire Dragon.* 1961. Grosset Dunlap. 2nd prt. 216 p. bl cloth. VG/ragged. M20. $32.50

KEENE, Carolyn. *Mystery of the Locked Room.* 1938. Grosset Dunlap. lists 8 titles. 218 p. purple cloth. VG/dj. M20. $50.00

KEENE, Carolyn. *Secret at Shadow Ranch.* 1931. Grosset Dunlap. 1st ed. 203 p. bl cloth. G. M20. $50.00

KEEPNEWS, Orrin. *View From Within.* 1988. Oxford. 1st ed. F/clip. A7. $18.00

KEIFER, Middleton. *Pax.* (1958). Random. 1st ed. NF/dj. A7. $30.00

KEIFER, Monica. *Am Children Through Their Books, 1700-1835.* 1948. PA U. 1st ed. ils. 248 p. F/VG. S10. $35.00

KEILLOR, Garrison. *We Are Still Married.* 1989. Franklin Lib. 1st ed. sgn. full leather. F. B4. $50.00

KEILLOR, Garrison. *WLT: A Radio Romance.* 1991. Viking. 1st ed. VG/dj. A16. $25.00

KEISER, R.L. *Vice Lords: Warriors of the Streets.* (1969). HRW. 83 p. wrp. A7. $10.00

KEITH, Donald. *Mutiny in the Time Machine.* 1963. Random. 1st ed. VG. M2. $15.00

KELLAND, C.B. *Am Boys' Workshop.* (1914). Phil. McKay. ils/fld pls. 329 p. bl cloth. VG. C10. $39.50

KELLEHER, Victor. *Beast of Heaven.* 1984. Queensland U. 1st ed. F/dj. M2. $13.00

KELLER, Allan. *Morgan's Raid.* (1961). Bobbs Merrill. 1st ed. 8vo. 272 p. VG/VG. A2. $25.00

KELLER, David H. *Devil & the Doctor.* 1940. Simon Schuster. 1st ed. VG/dj. M2. $75.00

KELLER, David H. *Folsom Flint.* 1969. Arkham. 1st ed. F/dj. M2. $35.00

KELLER, David H. *Homunculus.* 1949. Prime Pr. 1st ed. F/dj. M2. $40.00

KELLER, David H. *Life Everlasting.* 1947. Avalon. 1st ed. NF/M. w/M bibliography. M2. $90.00

KELLER, David H. *Solitary Hunters & the Abyss.* 1948. New Era. 1st ed. ils sgn. NF/dj. M2. $50.00

KELLER, David H. *Tales From Underwood.* 1952. Arkham. 1st ed. xl. rebound. M2. $10.00

KELLER, David H. *Wolf Hollow Bubbles.* 1933. ARRA Printers. 1st ed. sgn. F/wrp. M2. $250.00

KELLER, F.R. *Contented Little Pussy Cat.* 1949. Platt Monk. 1st ed. VG/G+. L1. $17.50

KELLER, F.R. *Contented Little Pussy Cat.* 1949. Platt Munk. ils Werber/Laslo. 4to. 53 p. cloth. G. A3. $7.00

KELLER, Fred S. *Definition of Psychology: Intro to Psychological Systems.* 1937. Appleton Century. 1st ed. 111 p. prt blk cloth. G1. $25.00

KELLER, John E. *Anna Morrison Reed, 1848-1921.* 1978. private prt. 1st ed. ils/glossary 285 p. F/NF. B19. $20.00

KELLER, W.P. *Splendour From the Land* (1963). London. Jarrolds. 1st UK ed. 8vo. ils 331 p. F/VG. A2. $15.00

KELLER, Werner. *Etruscans.* 1974. Knopf. 1st Am ed. 8vo. pls. 436 p. F/F. A2. $25.00

KELLERMAN, Faye. *Sacred & Profane* 1987. NY. Arbor. 1st ed. sgn. F/F. S5. $35.00

KELLERMAN, Jonathan. *Blood Test.* 1986. Atheneum. 1st ed. inscr. F/F. M15. $65.00

KELLERMAN, Jonathan. *Over the Edge.* 1987. London. MacDonald. 1st ed. F/F. T2. $50.00

KELLERMAN, Jonathan. *Private Eyes.* 1992. Bantam. lg prt. VG/dj. A16. $12.50

KELLERMAN, Jonathan. *Silent Partner.* 1989. London. MacDonald. 1st ed. F/F. S5. $35.00

KELLEY, Amy. *Eleanor of Aquitaine & the 4 Kings.* ca 1980. BC. F/dj. C1. $6.00

KELLEY, Kitty. *Elizabeth Taylor, the Last Star.* 1981. Simon Schuster. 1st ed. F/F. T2. $10.50

KELLEY, Shirley. *Love Is Not for Cowards.* (1978). Prentice Hall. 1st ed. 8vo. 281 p. VG+/VG. A2. $12.50

KELLEY, Tim. *Official CO & WY Fishing & Hunting Guide 1970-71.* 1970. Bloomfield. 9th ed. ils. 298 p. wrp. A17. $7.50

KELLEY. *Scarlet Ribbons: Am Indian Technique for Today's Quilters.* 1987. np. ils. wrp. G2. $16.00

KELLOGG, Charles. *Driving the Horse in Harness.* 1978. Brattleboro. Stephen Greene. later prt. VG/VG. O3. $25.00

KELLOGG, Elijah. *Brought to the Front; or, The Young Defenders.* 1876. Boston. 1st ed. 16mo. 320 p. rebound. VG. D3. $12.50

KELLOGG, Elijah. *Forest Glen; or, The Mohawk's Friendship.* 1877. Boston. 1st ed. xl. Forest Glen series. 16mo. 335 p. VG. D3. $15.00

KELLOGG, Louise P. *British Regime in WI & the NW.* 1935. Madison, WI. 1st ed. 361 p. cloth. NF. D3. $35.00

KELLOGG, Marjorie. *Tell Me That You Love Me, Junie Moon.* 1958. FSG. AP. F/tan wrp. C4. $30.00

KELLOGG, Robert H. *Life & Death in Rebel Prisons.* 1866. Hartford, CT. 12mo. 424 p. VG. T3. $42.00

KELLY, Alexander. *Jack the Ripper: Bibliography & Review of Literature.* 1973. London. Assn Assistant Librarians. 1st ed. pamphlet. F. M15. $45.00

KELLY, Alfred H. *Foundations of Freedom in Am Constitution.* 1958. Harper. cloth. M11. $35.00

KELLY, Charles. *Outlaw Trail: Hist of Butch Cassidy & His Wild Bunch.* 1959. NY. Devin Adair. pls. 374 p. F/F. B11. $30.00

KELLY, Ellsworth. *Derrier le Miroir.* (1964). Paris. Maeght. 1/150. folio. sgn. F/prt wrp/yel chemise/slipcase. B24. $500.00

KELLY, Eric. *Treasure Mtn.* 1937. Macmillan. 1st ed. ils Lufkin. 211 p. F/VG. P2. $25.00

KELLY, Fred. *Wright Brothers.* 1943. NY. 1st ed. sgn Orville Wright. VG/G. B5. $650.00

KELLY, Howard A. *Gynecology.* 1925. Appleton. 14 pls/767 engravings. 1043 p. orig cloth. VG+. G7. $125.00

KELLY, Howard A. *Medical Gynecology.* 1908. NY. Appleton. 1st ed. 662 p. orig brds. G7. $150.00

KELLY, J.L. *Fact & Fiction!* 1853. Manchester, NH. 1st ed. 8vo. 32 p. prt wrp. M1. $150.00

KELLY, J.P. *Look Into the Sun.* 1989. Tor. 1st ed. as new. M2. $18.00

KELLY, J.R. *Quakers in Founding of Anne Arundel Co, MD.* 1963. Baltimore, MD. MD Hist Soc. 1st ed. 8vo. 146 p. G+. V3. $35.00

KELLY, Robert. *Lectiones.* 1965. Placitas. Duende. 1st ed. VG+/wrp. B2. $35.00

KELLY, Walt. *Pogo Stepmother Goose.* 1954. Simon Schuster. 1st prt. 4to. VG/wrp. A3. $30.00

KELLY, Walt. *Pogo.* 1951. Simon Schuster. 1st ed. G/wrp. M18. $25.00

KELSEY, Rayner Wickersham. *Centennial Hist of Moses Brn School, 1819-1919.* 1919. Providence, RI. Moses Brn School. 8vo. 178 p. VG. V3. $30.00

KELSEY, Vera. *Seven Keys to Brazil.* 1940. NY. 1st ed. 8vo. ils/map. 314 p. gr buckram. F/VG. H3. $25.00

KELSEY & OSBORNE. *Four Keys to Guatemala.* (1952). Funk Wagnall. 332 p. dj. F3. $15.00

KELT. *Mechanics TB & Engineer's Practical Guide.* 1855. Boston. ils. 400+ p. O7. $18.50

KELTIE, John H. *Hist of Scottish Highlands.* nd. 1880s. London. new ed. 5 vols. aeg. G. B18. $195.00

KELWAY, Christine. *Gardening on the Coast.* 1970. Newton Abbot, Eng. photos. 180 p. VG/dj. B26. $19.00

KEMEL, Yashar; see Gokceli, Kemal Sadik.

KEMP, Donald C. *Silver, Gold & Blk Iron...* 1911. Boston. 1st ed. photos/fld map. 390 p. NF/dj. B28. $25.00

KEMP, Harry. *Boccaccle's Untold Tale & Other 1-Act Plays.* 1924. Brentano. G+. N2. $8.00

KEMPER, Troxey. *Part Comanche.* 1991. E Lansing. Bennett Kitchel. ARC. F/F. L3. $50.00

KEMPIS, Thomas. *Imitation of Christ.* 1889. London. Elliot Stock. sm 8vo. 299 p. Zaehnsdorf bdg. F. F1. $485.00

KEMPLEY, Walter. *Invaders.* (1979). NY. Dell. 1st pb prt. reading copy. A7. $8.00

KEMPLEY, Walter. *Probability Factor.* 1972. Saturday Review Pr. 1st ed. F/F. F4. $16.00

KEMPSTER, Aquila. *Mark.* 1903. Doubleday. 1st ed. G. M2. $15.00

KEMPTON, Murray. *Briar Patch.* 1973. Dutton. 282 p. dj. A7. $13.00

KENAN, Randall. *Visitation of Spirits.* (1989). Grove. 1st ed. author's 1st book. F/NF. B4. $65.00

KENDALL, B.J. *Doctor at Home: Treating Diseases of Man & Horse.* 1884. Enosburg Falls. Kendall. wrp. O3. $8.00

KENDALL, Elizabeth. *Phantom Prince: My Life w/Ted Bundy.* 1981. Seattle. Madrona. 1st ed. F/F. T2. $8.50

KENDALL, George Wilkins. *Narrative of TX Santa Fe Expedition.* 1844. Harper. 1st ed. 2 vols. 12mo. 5 pls. ribbed blk cloth. missing map. H9. $125.00

KENDALL & NEBAL. *War Between the US & Mexico, Ils...* 1851. Appleton. 1st ed. folio. 12 lithos/map. VG. M1. $7,500.00

KENDRAKE, Carleton; see Gardner, Erle Stanley.

KENDRICK, Alexander. *Wound Within: Am in the Vietnam Yrs, 1945-74.* 1974. Little Brn. 1st ed. 432 p. NF/dj. W1. $18.00

KENDRICK, William. *New Am Orchardist...* 1846. Boston. Otis Broaders. 8th ed. ils. 450 p. NF. H10. $100.00

KENEALLY, Thomas. *Confederates.* (1979). Harper Row. 1st Am ed. NF/dj. B4. $65.00

KENEALLY, Thomas. *Confederates.* (1979). London. Collins. 1st ed. VG/VG. B3. $60.00

KENEALLY, Thomas. *Family Madness.* (1986). Toronto. Dennys. 1st ed. NF/F. B3. $40.00

KENEALLY, Thomas. *Ned Kelly & the City of the Bees.* (1981). Godine. 1st ed. ils Stephen Ryan. F/F. B3. $25.00

KENEALLY, Thomas. *Outback.* (1984). Rand McNally. 1st Am ed. quarto. NF/dj. B4. $85.00

KENEALLY, Thomas. *Passenger.* (1979). London. Collins. 1st ed. VG/NF clip. B3. $45.00

KENEALLY, Thomas. *Playmaker.* (1987). Simon Schuster. 1st ed. F/F. B3. $20.00

KENEALLY, Thomas. *Schindler's Ark.* 1982. Hodder Stoughton. 1st ed. F/F. B3. $125.00

KENEALLY, Thomas. *Schindler's List (Schindler's Ark).* 1982. Simon Schuster. AP/1st Am ed. sgn. F/wrp. B4. $450.00

KENEALLY, Thomas. *Schindler's List (Schindler's Ark).* 1982. Simon Schuster. 1st Am ed (renamed after London ed). F/NF. L3. $250.00

KENEALLY, Thomas. *Three Cheers for the Paraclete.* (1969). NY. Viking. 1st Am ed. F/NF. B4. $150.00

KENEALLY, Thomas. *Woman of the Inner Sea.* (1992). Hodder Stoughton. 1st ed. F/NF. B3. $20.00

KENI-PAZ, Baruch. *Social & Political Thought of Leon Trotsky.* 1978. Oxford. 1st ed. F/NF. B2. $30.00

KENNAN, George. *Campaigning in Cuba.* 1899. NY. Century. 1st ed. 8vo. 269 p. decor red cloth. G. B11. $75.00

KENNEALY, Jerry. *Polo's Ponies.* 1988. St Martin. 1st ed. F/F. F4. $16.00

KENNEDY, Don H. *Ship Names: Origins & Usages During 45 Centuries.* 1974. Charlottesville. Mariners Mus. 15 p. M/dj. O6. $30.00

KENNEDY, James H. *Hist of the City of Cleveland...1796-1896.* 1896. Cleveland. ltd ed. ils/maps. 585 p. VG. B14. $125.00

KENNEDY, John F. *Inaugural Address of...* nd. Worcester. St Onge. miniature. bl calf. M. H10. $25.00

KENNEDY, John F. *Profiles in Courage.* 1956. Harper. 1st ed. NF/NF. Q1. $400.00

KENNEDY, John F. *Why Eng Slept.* 1940. NY. Wilfred Funk. 252 p. author's 1st book. pict red cloth. NF. B14. $60.00

KENNEDY, Leigh. *Journals of Nicholas the Am.* 1986. Toronto. Irwin. 1st Canadian ed. F/F. N3. $15.00

KENNEDY, Ludovic. *Pursuit.* 1974. NY. Viking. BC. G/dj. A16. $5.00

KENNEDY, Michael S. *Cowboys & Cattlemen.* 1964. NY. Hastings. 8vo. ils. VG/VG. B11. $15.00

KENNEDY, Milward. *Corpse in Cold Storage.* 1934. NY. Kinsey. 1st Am ed. NF/VG. M15. $55.00

KENNEDY, R.F. Jr. *Judge Frank M Johnson Jr.* (1978). Putnam. 1st ed. 8vo. 288 p. F/F. A2. $12.50

KENNEDY, Robert. *Robert Kennedy: In His Own Words.* 1988. Bantam. 1st ed. F/F. T2. $16.00

KENNEDY, Sara Beaumont. *Told in a Little Boy's Pocket.* (1908). Boston. 1st ed. ils Budell. pict brn cloth. G. H3. $12.00

KENNEDY, William. *Billy Phelan's Greatest Game.* 1978. Viking. 1st ed. F/NF. C4. $100.00

KENNEDY, William. *Ink Truck.* 1969. Dial. 1st ed. author's 1st book. NF/NF. Q1. $300.00

KENNEDY, William. *Ink Truck.* 1984. Viking. revised ed. F/F. C4. $35.00

KENNEDY, William. *Quinn's Book.* 1988. London. Cape. 1st ed. F/NF. B3/T2. $20.00

KENNEDY, William. *Very Old Bones.* 1992. Viking. ARC. F/wrp. B2. $35.00

KENNEDY, X.J. *Cross Ties.* 1985. GA U. 1st ed. F/F. V1. $15.00

KENNERLY, David Hume. *Shooter.* (1979). Newsweek. 1st ed. 272 p. F/F. A7. $65.00

KENNEY, Maurice. *Smell of Slaughter.* 1982. Marvin. Bl Cloud Quarterly. F/stapled wrp. L3. $45.00

KENNINGTON, Eric. *Drawing the RAF: Book of Portraits.* 1942. London. Oxford. 1st ed. 52 pls. 144 p. dk bl cloth. M7. $55.00

KENRICK, Tony. *Two for the Price of One.* 1974. London. Micheal Joseph. 1st ed. F/F. S5. $35.00

KENT, Austin. *Free Love; or, Philosophical Demonstration...Connubial Love.* 1857. Hopkinton, NY. self pub. 1st ed. 16mo. 140 p. cloth. M1. $400.00

KENT, Margery. *Fairy Tales From Turkey.* 1946. London. 8vo. 189 p. cloth. O2. $25.00

KENT, Rockwell. *Canterbury Tales. Geoffrey Chaucer.* 1934. Garden City. early reprint. 8vo. 626 p. VG/G. A3. $14.50

KENT, Rockwell. *N by E.* 1930. Lakeside. 1st ed. woodcuts. emb cloth. dj. A17. $45.00

KENT, Rockwell. *Rockwell Kent: Anthology of His Work.* 1982. Knopf. 1st ed. folio. gray cloth. F/dj/pub s/wrp. F1. $115.00

KENT, Rockwell. *Story of the Diamond.* 1937. NY. Marcus. octavo. prt as promo item for a jeweler. F/prt brds. B24. $95.00

KENT, Rockwell. *Voyaging Southward From the Strait of Magellan.* 1924. Putnam. 1st ed. ils Rockwell Kent. 184 p. teg. NF/dj. H5. $225.00

KENT, William Winthrop. *Hooked Rug Design.* 1949. Pond-Ekberg. 1st ed. w/sgn bookplate. 183 p. VG/dj. M20. $40.00

KENT & SHERMAN. *Children's Bible.* 1922. Scribner. 1st ed. G. L1. $50.00

KENWORTHY, Leonard S. *Quakerism: Study Guide on Religious Soc of Friends.* 1981. Kennett Square, PA. Quaker Pub. 12mo. 215 p. V3. $7.50

KENYON, Frederic G. *Ancient Books & Modern Discoveries.* 1927. Chicago. Caston. 1/350. lg 4to. 30 collotype pls. vellum/brn brds. K1. $450.00

KENYON, Frederic G. *Books & Readers in Ancient Greece & Rome.* 1951. Oxford. 2nd ed. 8vo. 136 p. cloth. O2. $30.00

KEPHART, Horace. *Camping & Woodcraft: Handbook for Vacation Campers...* (1988). TN U. facsimile of 1917 ed. 2 vols in 1. 479 p. cloth. F. A17. $22.50

KERCHEVAL, Samuel. *Hist of the Valley of VA.* 1850. VA. 2nd ed. 347 p. rebound. VG. D7. $135.00

KERIMOV. *Folk Designs From the Caucasus for Weaving & Needlework.* 1974. np. pb. G2. $7.00

KERIMOV. *Persian Rug Motifs for Needlepoint Charted for Easy Use.* 1975. np. ils. wrp. G2. $4.00

KERMAN, Cynthia Earl. *Creative Tension: Life & Thought of Kenneth Boulding.* 1974. Ann Arbor. 1st ed. 8vo. 380 p. M/M. V3. $18.00

KERN, Gregory; see Tubb, E.C.

KEROFILAS, C. *Eleftherios Venizelos: His Life & Work.* 1915. NY. 8vo. 178 p. cloth. O2. $45.00

KEROUAC, Jack. *Big Sur.* 1962. FSC. 1st ed. F/NF. C4. $150.00

KEROUAC, Jack. *Desolation Angels.* 1965. Coward McCann. 1st ed. NF/VG. L3. $250.00

KEROUAC, Jack. *Dharma Bums.* 1958. Viking. 1st ed. NF/NF. Q1. $250.00

KEROUAC, Jack. *Mexico City Blues.* 1959. Grove. 3rd prt. A7. $17.00

KEROUAC, Jack. *Satori in Paris.* (1966). Grove. 1st ed. M/dj. B4. $250.00

KEROUAC, Jack. *Visions of Gerard.* 1963. NY. Farrar Straus. ARC. RS. VG/dj. scarce. L3. $375.00

KEROUAC, John. *Town & the City.* 1950. NY. 1st ed. red cloth. VG+. A11. $90.00

KERR, Ben; see Art, William.

KERR, Katharine. *Bristling Wood.* 1989. Doubleday. 1st ed. F/F. F4. $16.00

KERR, Katharine. *Dragon Revenant.* 1990. Doubleday. 1st ed. 4th of Daggerspell series. F/F. N3. $25.00

KERR, Mary Brandt. *Am: A Regional Cookbook.* nd. NJ. Chartwell. VG/dj. A16. $15.00

KERR. *Tell-E-Graphics.* 1985. np. ils. wrp. G2. $7.00

KERRY, John. *New Soldier.* (1971). Macmillan. 1st ed. quarto. 174 p. F/NF. A7. $65.00

KERSEY, Jesse. *Treatise on Fundamental Doctrines of Christian Religion...* 1818. Concord. Daniel Cooledge. 16mo. 142 p. full leather. V3. $25.00

KERSH, Gerald. *Best of Gerald Kersh.* 1960. London. 1st ed. VG/VG ils Fratina. A11. $25.00

KERSH, Gerald. *Nightshade & Damnations.* 1968. Greenwich, CT. Fawcett Gold Medal. PBO. sgn. NF/ils wrp. A11. $30.00

KERSH, Gerald. *Song of the Flea.* 1948. London. 1st ed. 12mo. VG/VG. A11. $30.00

KERSHAW, Alister. *Hist of the Guillotine.* 1958. London. John Calder. 1st ed. 12 halftones. red cloth. VG/clip. G1. $30.00

KESEY, Ken. *Day After Superman Died.* 1980. Northridge. Lord John. 1st ed. 1/350. sgn. F. C4. $75.00

KESTERTON, David. *Darkling.* 1982. Arkham. 1st ed. M/as issued. M2. $13.00

KESTLE, James Allen. *This Is Lakeside 1873-1973.* 1973. np. sgn twice. photos/ils. 193 p. cloth. A17. $15.00

KETCHUM, Richard M. *Secret Life of the Forest.* (1970). NY. ils. 114 p. dj. A17. $14.50

KETTELL, Thomas P. *Hist of the Great Rebellion.* 1865. Hartford. thick 8vo. ils. 778 p. VG. T3. $55.00

KETTELL, Thomas P. *S Wealth & N Profits.* 1860. NY. royal 8vo. 173 p. brn cloth. G. T3. $55.00

KETWIG, John. *And a Hard Rain Fell.* (1985). Macmillan. NF/NF. A7. $30.00

KEVLES, B. *Thinking Gorillas.* (1980). NY. 1st ed. photos. 167 p. dj. A17. $10.00

KEY, Alexander. *With Daniel Boone on the Caroliny Trail.* 1941. NY. 1st ed. 212 p. F/G. A17. $15.00

KEY, Astley Cooper. *Narrative of Recovery of HMS Gorgon...Stranded...1844.* 1847. London. Smith Elder. 8vo. 16 pls/fld chart. emb cl cloth. P4. $295.00

KEYNES, Geoffrey. *Complete Writings of William Blake.* 1957. Nonesuch/Random. 936 p. NF/glassine dj. B22. $45.00

KEYNES, Geoffrey. *Study of Illuminated Books of Wm Blake, Poet, Printer...* 1964. London. Trianon. 1/525. sgn. F/marbled slipcase. F1. $295.00

KEYNES, John Maynard. *Economic Consequences of the Peace.* 1920. Harcourt Brace. 1st Am ed. 8vo. 298 p. NF/dj. B20. $225.00

KHALID, Farooq. *Blk Mirrors.* 1987. London. Cape. 1st ed. trans from Urdu by Eric Cyprian. NF/NF clip. A14. $20.00

KHALIFA, Ali Mohammed. *United Arab Emirates: Unity in Fragmentation.* 1979. Boulder. 8vo. charts/maps. 235 p. O2. $25.00

KHANNA & RATNAKAR. *Banares: The Sacred City.* 1988. Richmond, Surrey. Tiger Books Internat. 1st ed. 48 pls. NF/dj. W1. $20.00

KHAYYAM, Omar. *Rubaiyat of Omar Khayyam, the Astronomer-Poet of Persia.* 1872. London. Bernard Quaritch. 3rd ed. quarter leather. N2. $165.00

KHAYYAM, Omar. *Rubaiyat of Omar Khayyam & the Salaman & Absal of Jami...* 1879. London. Bernard Quaritch. sm 8vo. 112 p. quarter gr morocco. K1. $375.00

KHAYYAM, Omar. *Rubaiyat.* nd. Dodge. ils Frank Brangwyn/8 color pls. gilt tan cloth. F. F1. $75.00

KHERDIAN, David. *Homage to Adana.* 1971? Giligia Pr. sgn. 38 p. NF/wrp. w/sgn letter. B19. $25.00

KHIN. *Collector's Dictionary of Quilt Names & Patterns.* 1980. np. ils. cloth. G2. $30.00

KHLEBNIKOV, K.T. *Baranov: Chief Manager of Russian Colonies in Am.* (1973). Kingston, Ontario. Limestone Pr. 1st English-language ed. 1/530. pls. A11. $25.00

KHLEBNIKOV, K.T. *Colonial Russian Am: Reports 1817-32.* 1976. Portland. OR Hist Soc. pls/maps/photos. 158 p. gilt cloth. F. A17. $45.00

KIDDER, Tracy. *Among Schoolchildren.* 1989. Houghton Mifflin. 1st ed. sgn. F/F. Q1. $35.00

KIDDER, Tracy. *House.* (1985). Houghton Mifflin. 1st ed. NF/VG. B3. $20.00

KIDWELL, J.H. *Silver Fleece.* 1927. Avondale. 1st ed. VG. M2. $13.00

KIEFER, Warren. *Outlaw.* (1989). Donald Fine. AP. F/pict wrp. B3. $20.00

KIEPERT, Heinrich. *Atlas Antiquus: Zwolf Karten Zur Alten Geshichte.* 1902. Berlin. 12 color maps. NF. O6. $85.00

KIERAN, John. *Am Sporting Scene.* 1941. NY. 1st ed. ils Joseph Golinken. 212 p. F/G. A17. $15.00

KIERAN, John. *Intro to Nature.* (1966). NY. ils. 223 p. dj. A17. $15.00

KIERMAN, Frank A. *Chinese Ways in Warfare.* 1974. Rainbow Bridge Book Co. 401 p. VG/dj. N2. $8.00

KIERNAN, R.H. *First War in the Air.* 1934. Peter Davis. 1st ed. 8vo. 192 p. VG. M7. $45.00

KIERNAN, R.H. *Lawrence of Arabia.* 1935. London. Harrap. 1st ed. 196 p. orange cloth. G+. M7. $40.00

KIERNAN, V.G. *From Conquest to Collapse: European Empires 1815-1960.* 1982. Pantheon. VG/dj. A16. $8.00

KILBURN, Richard. *Choice Presidents Upon All Acts of Parliament...* 1700. London. Mary Conton. 8vo. 502 p. contemporary calf/rebacked orig spine. K1. $200.00

KILEY & DATER. *Listen, the War.* (1973). USAF Academy. ils Emilio Tavernise. orig pict wrp. A7. $70.00

KILGO, James. *Deep Enough for Ivorybills.* 1988. Chapel Hill. 1st ed. ils. 193 p. F/dj. A17. $10.00

KILLEBREW, J.B. *Middle TN As an Iron Centre.* 1879. Nashville. Tavel Eastman Howell. 1st ed. NF/prt wrp. M8. $85.00

KILLEBREW, J.B. *Oil Region of TN w/Some Account of Its Other Resources...* 1877. Nashville. Am Prt Co. xl. 8vo. lg fld map/tables. bl wrp. H9. $165.00

KILLEBREW & MYRICK. *Tobacco Leaf: Its Culture & Cure, Marketing & Manufacture.* 1907 (1897). NY. ils/portraits/pls. 506 p. B26. $41.00

KILLEBREW & SAFFORD. *Intro to the Resources of TN.* 1874. Nashville. thick 8vo. lg fld map/4 sm city plans/tables. brn cloth. H9. $250.00

KILLENS, John Oliver. *And Then We Heard the Thunder.* 1963. NY. 1st ed. inscr. F/NF. A11. $95.00

KILMER, Joyce. *Trees & Other Poems.* 1914. NY. 1st ed. NF. V1. $45.00

KILNER, Joseph. *Account of Pythagoras's School in Cambridge...* ca 1790. np (Cambridge?). private prt. folio. 9 pls. 158 p. contemporary calf. K1. $375.00

KILNER, William H.B. *Arthur Letts.* 1927. LA. private prt. 1st ed. inscr Letts' grandaughter. 273 p. bl cloth. P4. $30.00

KIM, Se-Jin. *Korean Unification. Source Materials w/an Intro.* 1976-79. Seoul. Research Center Peace/Unification. 1st ed. 392 p. VG. W1. $45.00

KIM & MORTIMORE. *Korea's Response to Japan: Colonial Period, 1910-45.* 1977. W MI U. 8vo. 351 p. VG/wrp. W1. $10.00

KIMBALL, Marie. *Jefferson: Road to Glory 1743-66.* ca 1943. Coward McCann. ils. 358 p. G. B10. $12.00

KIMBALL. *Applique Borders: Added Grace.* 1991. np. wrp. G2. $17.00

KIMBALL. *Red & Gr: Applique Tradition.* 1990. np. ils. wrp. G2. $25.00

KIMBALL. *Reflections of Baltimore.* 1989. np. ils. wrp. G2. $19.00

KIME. *Quilts To Share.* 1991. np. 30 color pls. 72 p. wrp. G2. $15.00

KIMMEL, Margaret Mary. *Magic in the Mist.* 1975. Atheneum. 1st ed. ils Trina Schart Hyman. VG+/VG. T5. $30.00

KINCAID, Jamaica. *Annie John.* 1985. FSG. 1st ed. author's 2nd book. NF/NF. A13. $40.00

KINCAID, Jamaica. *Lucy.* (1990). FSG. 1st issue proof. prt orange wrp. F. C4. $35.00

KINCAID, Jamaica. *Lucy.* 1990. FSG. 1st ed. NF/NF clip. A13. $20.00

KINCAID, Jamaica. *Small Place.* 1988. FSG. 1st ed. NF/NF clip. A13. $25.00

KING, Charles. *Apache Princess: Tale of the Indian Frontier.* 1903. NY. 1st ed. ils Remington/Deming. 328 p. gilt cloth. VG. D3. $125.00

KING, Charles. *Army Wife.* 1896. NY. F Tennyson Neely. ils. 278 p. cloth. VG. B14. $45.00

KING, Charles. *Broken Sword.* 1905. Hobart. 1st ed. teg. F. A18. $35.00

KING, Charles. *Campaigning w/Crook & Other Stories of Army Life.* 1890. Harper. 9 pls. 295 p. decor bl cloth. VG. B14. $155.00

KING, Charles. *Daughter of the Sioux.* 1903. Hobart. 1st ed. ils Remington/Deming. teg. NF. A18. $60.00

KING, Charles. *Under Fire.* 1895. Phil. 1st ed. 511 p. VG. D3. $25.00

KING, Clarence. *King's Handbook of the US.* 1892. Buffalo. Moses King Corp. thick 8vo. maps. 939 p. pict cloth. H9. $55.00

KING, Clarence. *1st Annual Report of the US Geological Survey...* 1880. GPO. thin 4to. fld map. 79 p. purple cloth. H9. $250.00

KING, Francis. *Act of Darkness.* 1983. London. Hutchinson. 1st ed. NF/NF. A14. $25.00

KING, Francis. *Danny Hill: Memoirs of a Prominent Gentleman.* 1977. London. Hutchinson. 1st ed. NF/NF clip. A14. $35.00

KING, Francis. *Man on the Rock.* 1957. Longman Gr. 1st ed. NF/NF. A14. $50.00

KING, Frank. *Skeezix & Pal.* 1925. Reilly Lee. 4to. 105 p. blk cloth. VG+. A3. $60.00

KING, George H.S. *Marriages of Richmond Co.* 1986 (1964). S Hist Pr. 368 p. F. B10. $25.00

KING, H.F. *Armament of British Aircraft 1909-39.* (1971). London. 1st ed. 457 p. VG+/dj. B18. $25.00

KING, John. *Am Electric Obstetrics.* 1855. Cincinnati. 1st ed. 741 p. full calf. B22. $35.00

KING, Judith E. *Seals of the World.* 1983. British Mus/Cornell. 2nd ed. pub review copy. M/M. T8. $25.00

KING, Marian. *Sean & Sheela.* 1937. Whitman/Jr Pr. ils Emma Brock. 1st ed. 134 p. VG-. A3. $15.00

KING, Martin Luther Jr. *Stride Toward Freedom.* (1958). Ballantine. 1st pb ed. photos. VG/wrp. A7. $12.00

KING, Martin Luther Jr. *Where Do We Go From Here?* 1967. Harper Row. 1st ed. 209 p. NF/dj. A7. $40.00

KING, MOORE & WILSTACH. *Am Electric Dispensatory.* 1855 (54). Cincinnati. tall 8vo. 1391 p. full calf. B22. $50.00

KING, Rufus. *Malice in Wonderland.* 1958. Doubleday Crime Club. 1st ed. F/NF. M15. $50.00

KING, Stephen. *Bachman Books.* 1985. NAL. 1st ed. F/dj. M2. $75.00

KING, Stephen. *Bare Bones.* (1989). London. New Eng Lib. 1st book appearance of interviews. F/F. B3. $50.00

KING, Stephen. *Christine.* 1983. Viking. 1st ed. F/F. T2. $40.00

KING, Stephen. *Cujo.* 1981. Viking. 1st ed. F/F. T2. $45.00

KING, Stephen. *Cujo.* 1981. Viking. 1st ed. NF/dj. M2. $25.00

KING, Stephen. *Dark Tower II: The Drawing of the 3.* 1987. W Kingston. Donald Grant. 1st ed. M/as issued. M2. $60.00

KING, Stephen. *Dark Tower III: The Wastelands.* 1991. Donald Grant. ltd ed. 1/1250. sgn. M/slipcase. M2. $350.00

KING, Stephen. *Dark Tower: The Gunslinger.* 1982. W Kingston. Donald Grant. 1st ed. ils Michael Whelan. F/F. Q1/T2. $500.00

KING, Stephen. *Different Seasons.* (1982). Viking. 1st ed. NF/NF. B3. $40.00

KING, Stephen. *Dolan's Cadillac.* 1988. Lord John. 1/100. sgn presentation. special quarter leather. F/slipcase. Q1. $500.00

KING, Stephen. *Dolores Clairborne.* 1992. Viking. AP. F/wrp. B2. $75.00

KING, Stephen. *Eyes of the Dragon.* 1984. Bangor. Philtrum. 1/1250. sgn/#d. ils Kenneth Linkhauser. F/NF slipcase. Q1. $650.00

KING, Stephen. *Eyes of the Dragon.* 1987. Viking. 1st ed. F/F. T2. $30.00

KING, Stephen. *Firestarter.* 1980. Viking. 1st ed. F/dj. M18. $50.00

KING, Stephen. *Four Past Midnight.* 1990. Viking. 1st ed. F/F. N3. $15.00

KING, Stephen. *It.* 1986. Viking. 1st ed. F/dj. M2. $40.00

KING, Stephen. *Misery.* 1987. Viking. 1st ed. F/F. T2. $30.00

KING, Stephen. *Misery.* 1987. Viking. 1st ed. M/as issued. M2. $40.00

KING, Stephen. *Nightmares & Dreamscapes.* 1993. Viking. ARC. ils Chris Van Alsburg. 16 p. F/stiff wrp. C4. $35.00

KING, Stephen. *Nightmares & Dreamscapes.* 1993. Viking. 1st ed. M/M. T2. $27.50

KING, Stephen. *Rage.* 1977. Signet. 1st ed/PBO. sgn. NF/ils wrp. A11. $165.00

KING, Stephen. *Shining.* (1977). Doubleday. BC. dj. A7. $15.00

KING, Stephen. *Shining.* 1977. Doubleday. 1st ed. inscr. F/dj. M2. $225.00

KING, Stephen. *Skeleton Crew.* 1985. Putnam. 1st ed. F/dj. M2. $50.00

KING, Stephen. *Stand.* 1978. Doubleday. 1st ed. NF/VG. N3. $95.00

KING, Stephen. *Thinner.* 1984. NAL. 1st ed. F/dj. M2. $75.00

KING, Stephen. *Tommyknockers.* 1987. Putnam. 1st ed. F/F. M2/T2. $35.00

KING, Stephen. *Tommyknockers.* 1987. Putnam. 1st ed. NF/NF. B3. $25.00

KING, Willard L. *Melville Weston Fuller, Chief Justice of US 1888-1910.* 1950. NY. Macmillan. M11. $35.00

KING, Willis J. *Negro in Am Life.* 1926. NY. 1st ed. 154 p. gray cloth. VG. B14. $25.00

KING & MONKMAN. *Coyote Columbus Story.* 1992. Toronto. Douglas McIntyre. sgn author/artist. F/sans. L3. $85.00

KING & STRAUB. *Talisman.* 1984. Viking. 1st trade ed. F/dj. M2. $40.00

KING & WINTLE. *Netherlands.* (1988). Oxford, Eng. Clio. 1st ed. 8vo. 308 p. F. A2. $25.00

KING. *Journey to Egypt.* 1986. paper engineering by Dick Dudley/David Carter. F. A4. $25.00

KING. *7 Ancient Wonders of the World.* 1990. popups. 28 p. F. A4. $35.00

KINGSBURY & NEWSHOLME. *Red Medicine.* (1934). Doubleday Doran. 324 p. A7. $18.00

KINGSLEY, Charles. *Heroes; or, Greek Fairy Tales for My Children.* 1856. Boston. 8vo. 320 p. decor cloth. O2. $60.00

KINGSLEY, Charles. *Water Babies.* nd. Macmillan. new ed. ils Paton/Skelton. 310 p. gilt red cloth. G. S10. $40.00

KINGSLEY, Charles. *Water Babies. A Fairy Story for a Land Baby.* 1930. Phil. Winston. ils Ethel Everett. 282 p. pict gr cloth. VG. H3. $20.00

KINGSLEY, Charles. *Westward Ho!* 1920. Scribner. 1st ed. ils NC Wyeth. 413 p. VG. P2. $95.00

KINGSLEY, J. Sterling. *Nature's Wonderland.* (1894). NY. FR Niglutsch. 4 vols. quarto. ils. aeg. leather. NF. S9. $100.00

KINGSOLVER, Barbara. *Animal Dreams.* 1990. Harper Row. ARC. F/pict wrp. B2/C4. $45.00

KINGSOLVER, Barbara. *Bean Trees.* (1989). London. Virago. 1st ed. author's 1st novel. F/F. B3. $100.00

KINGSOLVER, Barbara. *Box Socials.* 1991. Ballantine. AP. F/pict wrp. C4. $45.00

KINGSOLVER, Barbara. *First Words: Earliest Writings...* 1993. NY. Workman Pr. 1st ed. F/F. C4. $30.00

KINGSTON, Maxine Hong. *Through the Blk Curtain.* 1987. Berkeley, CA. 1st ed. inscr/dtd 1990. F/wrp. L3. $65.00

KINGSTON, William H.G. *Mark Seaworth: Tale of the Indian Ocean.* ca 1884. London. Griffith. 9th thousand. 384 p. G+. S10. $20.00

KINGSTON, William H.G. *Salt Water.* ca 1884. London. Griffith. 5th thousand. 12mo. 371 p. G+. S10. $20.00

KINNEAR, John Gardiner. *Cairo, Petra & Damascus in 1839...* 1841. London. 8vo. 348 p. gilt cloth. O2. $750.00

KINNELL, Galway. *Avenue Bearing the Initial of Christ Into the New World.* 1974. Boston. 1st ed. sgn. F/F. V1. $55.00

KINNELL, Galway. *Fundamental Project of Technology.* 1983. Houghton Mifflin. 1st ed. 4 p. F/self wrp. C4. $30.00

KINNELL, Galway. *Mortal Acts, Mortal Words.* 1980. Boston. 1st ed. sgn. F/F. V1. $45.00

KINNELL, Galway. *There Are Things I Tell to No One.* 1979. Nadja. 1/200. sgn/#d. F/orig envelope. V1. $55.00

KINNELL, Galway. *What a Kingdom It Was.* 1960. Boston. 1st ed. sgn. author's 1st book. F/VG. V1. $225.00

KINNEY, Bruce. *Mormonism: The Islam of Am.* (1912). NY. 1st ed. xl. 6 pls. cloth. VG. D3. $25.00

KINNEY, Charles; see Gardner, Erle Stanley.

KINROSS, Ataturk. *Biography of Mustafa Kemal, Father of Modern Turkey.* 1965. NY. 8vo. ils/maps. 613 p. cloth. O2. $25.00

KINSELLA, W.P. *Alligator Report.* 1985. Minneapolis. Coffee House. 1st Am ed. inscr. F/wrp. B2. $50.00

KINSELLA, W.P. *Born Indian.* 1981. np (Alberta). 1st ed. inscr. F/ils wrp. A11. $60.00

KINSELLA, W.P. *Dance Me Outside.* 1986. Boston. Godine. 1st Am ed. F/F. B2. $35.00

KINSELLA, W.P. *Dance Me Outside.* 1986. Godine. 1st Am ed. inscr. F/F. B2. $75.00

KINSELLA, W.P. *IA Baseball Confederacy.* 1986. Houghton Mifflin. 1st ed. F/NF. B2. $45.00

KINSELLA, W.P. *IA Baseball Confederacy.* 1986. Houghton Mifflin. 1st ed. sgn. F/F. A11. $55.00

KINSELLA, W.P. *Red Wolf, Red Wolf.* (1987). Toronto. Collins. 1st ed. F/F. B3. $60.00

KINSELLA, W.P. *Scars.* 1978. np. Oberon. 1st ed. F/wrp. B2. $75.00

KINSELLA, W.P. *Shoeless Joe.* 1982. Houghton Mifflin. 1st ed. VG/rpr clip. A18. $75.00

KINSELLA, W.P. *Two Spirits Soar. Art of Allen Sapp.* 1990. Toronto. Stoddart. 1st ed. oblong quarto. F/F. L3. $75.00

KINSETH, Lance. *River Eternal.* (1989). NY. Viking. 1st ed. F/dj. A17. $7.50

KINSEY, A.C. *Sexual Behavior in the Human Male.* 1948. Phil/London. Saunders. 5th prt. 804 p. VG/partial dj. S9. $10.00

KIP, William Ingraham. *Early Days of My Episcopate.* 1954. Biobooks. ils. 105 p. F/sans. B19. $25.00

KIPLING, Rudyard. *Collected Verse of...* 1912. Hodder Stoughton. 1st Eng ed. 1/500. sgn/#d. 476 p. gilt vellum/silk ties. H5. $750.00

KIPLING, Rudyard. *Departmental Ditties & Other Verses.* 1886. Lahore. 1st ed. 1/350. tall octavo. VG/wrp/clamshell case. H5. $1,250.00

KIPLING, Rudyard. *Five Nations.* 1903. London. Methuen. 1st ed. G. A1. $40.00

KIPLING, Rudyard. *Jungle Book & 2nd Jungle Book.* 1894 & 1895. London. Macmillan. 1st ed. 2 vols. VG/F slipcase. D1. $1,500.00

KIPLING, Rudyard. *Jungle Book.* 1963. Golden Pr. 1st thus ed. 213 p. color ep. pict brds. VG+. H3. $20.00

KIPLING, Rudyard. *Just-So Stories for Little Children.* 1902. London. Macmillan. 1st ed. lg octavo. 249 p. Sutcliffe bdg. NF. H5. $850.00

KIPLING, Rudyard. *Just-So Stories.* 1912. Garden City. later ed. ils Gleeson/Bransom. G. L1. $35.00

KIPLING, Rudyard. *Just-So Stories.* 1978. Weathervane. ils. VG/dj. A16. $10.00

KIPLING, Rudyard. *Kim.* 1901. London. Macmillan. 1st ed. octavo. ils JL Kipling/10 pls. Bayntun bdg. NF. H5. $500.00

KIPLING, Rudyard. *Puck of Pook's Hill.* 1906. Doubleday. 1st ed. ils Rackham. NF. M18. $100.00

KIPLING, Rudyard. *Rewards & Fairies.* 1910. Eng. 1st Eng ed. ils Frank Craig. G. M18. $55.00

KIPLING, Rudyard. *Second Jungle Book.* 1895. Century. 1st Am ed. ils John Lockwood Kipling. 324 p. teg. G+. P2. $40.00

KIPLING, Rudyard. *Second Jungle Book.* 1895. Century. 1st ed (not 1st prt). ils JL Kipling. 324 p. VG. S10. $65.00

KIPLING, Rudyard. *Seven Seas.* 1896. London. 1st ed. G. A1. $45.00

KIPLING, Rudyard. *Thy Servant, a Dog.* 1930. NY. 1st ed. ils Marguerite Kirmse. gilt tan cloth. F. B14. $45.00

KIRBY, A.M. *Daffodils, Narcissus...* 1909. Doubleday Page. ils. 235 p. H10. $15.00

KIRBY & KIRBY. *World by the Fireside.* nd. (1900). Boston. 16mo. ils. 192 p. pict gray cloth. VG. H3. $20.00

KIRDWOOD, J.B. *Regiments of Scotland.* 1949. Edinburgh. 12mo. 142 p. bl cloth. F/VG. H3. $20.00

KIRIAKOPOULOS, G.C. *Ten Days to Destiny. Battle for Crete.* 1985. NY. 8vo. 408 p. dj. O2. $25.00

KIRK, Donald. *Tell It to the Dead.* (1975). Nelson Hall. 215 p. F/NF. A7. $30.00

KIRK, Donald. *Wider War: Struggle for Cambodia, Thailand & Laos.* (1971). Praeger. 305 p. NF/NF. A7. $30.00

KIRK, Michael. *Cut in Diamonds.* 1986. Doubleday. 1st Am ed. F/F. S5. $25.00

KIRK, Russell. *Princess of All Lands.* 1979. Arkham. 1st ed. F/dj. M2. $50.00

KIRK, Russell. *Watchers at the Strait Gate.* 1984. Arkham. 1st ed. M/as issued. M2. $15.00

KIRKBRIDE, Alec Seath. *Crackle of Thorns. Experiences in the Middle E.* 1956. London. 1st ed. 8vo. ils. 201 p. cloth. dj. O2. $25.00

KIRKBRIDGE, Ronald. *Winds Blow Gently.* 1945. NY. Frederick Fell. 3rd ed. 8vo. 313 p. dj. V3. $9.00

KIRKE, Edmund. *Rear Guard of the Revolution.* 1886. NY. 1st ed. 317 p. G. A17. $15.00

KIRKHAM, S. *Eng Grammar in Familiar Lectures...* 1828. Pittsburgh. 6th ed. 192 p. orig half leather. G. D7. $25.00

KIRKHAM, S.D. *In the Open.* (1908). San Francisco. Elder. 1st ed. 8vo. 223 p. VG. A2. $25.00

KIRKUS, A. Mary. *Robert Gibbings: A Bibliography.* 1962. London. Dent. 1st ed. 1/975. gilt gr cloth. F/VG-. F1. $125.00

KIRKWOOD, James. *Am Grotesque.* 1970. Simon Schuster. 1st ed. inscr. F/NF. L3. $75.00

KIRSCHENMANN, P.P. *Information & Reflection...Cybernetics...* ca 1970. NY. Humanities Pr. VG/VG. V4. $10.00

KIRSCHNER, Michael. *Forward Freely.* 1967. S Brunswick. Barnes. 1st ed. VG/VG. O3. $15.00

KISER, Ellis. *Atlas of the City of Yonkers, Westchester Co, NY.* 1907. Phil. Mueller. lg folio. half leather/cloth. O6. $165.00

KISH, George. *Source Book in Geog.* 1978. Cambridge. M/dj. O6. $55.00

KISHON, E. *Noah's Ark, Tourist Class.* 1962. Atheneum. 1st ed. trans from Hebrew. NF/VG+. A14. $20.00

KISHON, E. *Woe to the Victors!* ca 1969. Tel-Aviv. Maariv Lib. VG/poor. S3. $21.00

KITE, Thomas. *Selections From Letters of Thomas Kite to His Daughter...* nd. Phil. 16mo. 35 p. cloth. V3. $14.00

KITTREDGE, William. *Hole in the Sky.* (1992). Knopf. AP. VG/prt gr wrp. B3. $25.00

KIVIAT, Esther. *Paji.* 1946. Whittlesey. 1st ed. VG+/G. P2. $20.00

KLAASE, Piet. *Jam Session.* (1985). London. tall quarto. 192 p. F/dj. A7. $25.00

KLAMKIN, Marian. *Wood Carvings: N Am Folk Sculptures.* 1974. Hawthorne. VG/dj. A16. $18.50

KLAPPHOLZ, Kurt. *Spiritual Awakening: Interpretation...* 1954. Bloch. xl. 100 p. VG. S3. $19.00

KLASS, Rosanne. *Land of the High Flags: Travel Memoir of Afghanistan.* (1964). NY. Random. 1st ed. 8vo. 319 p. F/VG. A2. $15.00

KLAUBER, Laurence M. *Rattlesnakes. Their Habits, Life Histories...* 1956. UC Pr. 2 vols. 8vo. ils. 1476 p. VG/dj. G7. $125.00

KLAVAN, Gene. *We Die at Dawn.* 1964. Doubleday. 1st ed. F/NF. B4. $45.00

KLEIN, Clayton. *Cold Summer Wind.* (1983). Fowlerville, MI. photos/index. 277 p. F/dj. A17. $15.00

KLEIN & KRUGER. *One Incredible Journey.* (1985). Fowlerville, MI. 1st ed. F/dj. A17. $20.00

KLIFT & TELLEGEN. *Knitting From the Netherlands.* 1963. np. 45 patterns. wrp. G2. $14.00

KLIMA, Ivan. *Love & Garbage.* 1991. Knopf. 1st Am ed. trans Ewald Osers. F/F. A14. $20.00

KLIMESH, Cyril M. *They Came to This Place: A Hist of Spillville...* (1983). Sebastopol, CA. photos/maps/index. 239 p. A17. $17.50

KLINE, Morris. *Mathematics in W Culture.* 1959. NY. Oxford. ils/index. 484 p. NF/VG. S9. $5.00

KLINE, Otis Adelbert. *Port of Peril.* 1949. Grandon Co. 1st book ed. 3rd of Peril trilogy. F/NF. B4. $200.00

KLINE, Penny. *Dying To Help.* 1993. London. Macmillan. 1st ed. F/F. S5. $22.50

KLINEFELTER, Walter. *Further Display of Old Maps & Plans.* 1969. La Crosse. Sumac Pr. 1/300. ES. M/as issued. O6. $75.00

KLINEFELTER, Walter. *Third Display of Old Maps & Plans.* 1973. La Crosse. Sumac Pr. 1/300. M/M. O6. $75.00

KLING, Blair B. *Bl Mutiny. Indigo Disturbances in Bengal 1859-62.* 1977. Calcutta. 243 p. G/torn. B18. $35.00

KLINGEL, Gilbert C. *Seeing Chesapeake Wilds.* ca 1970. Internat Marine Pub. ils/photos. B10. $10.00

KLINKOWITZ & SOMERS. *Writing Under Fire.* (1978). Delta. NF/wrp. A7. $45.00

KLOSE & MCCOMBS. *Typhoon Shipments.* (1974). Norton. 1st ed. NF/dj. A7. $35.00

KLUDAS, Arnold. *Great Passenger Ships of the World.* 1986. Wellingborough. Patrick Stephens. 6 vol set. VG/djs. A16. $240.00

KLUGE, Carl A.F. *Versuch Einer Darstellung des Animalischen Magnestismus.* 1811. Berlin. 503 p. G7. $495.00

KLUGER, Steve. *Changing Pitches: Novel of Love & Baseball.* 1984. St Martin. 1st ed. author's 1st book. NF/VG+. A14. $25.00

KLUGER. *Needlepoint Gallery of Patterns From the Past.* 1975. np. ils. cloth. G2. $17.00

KNANDEL, H. Clyde. *Profitable Poultry Keeping.* ca 1940. NY. Judd. ils. 462 p. H10. $12.50

KNAP, Jerome. *About Wildfowling in Am.* (1976). Winchester. ils/photos. 305 p. F/dj. A17. $17.50

KNEELAND, Abner. *Appeal to Universalists on Subject of Excommunication...* 1829. NY. Evans. 1st ed. 12mo. 20 p. M1. $250.00

KNERR, M.E.; see Smith, George H.

KNIFFEN, Fred. *Walapai Ethnography.* (1935). Menasha, WI. 1st ed. xl. 293 p. VG. D3. $25.00

KNIGHT, Adam; see Lariar, Lawrence.

KNIGHT, Charles. *Elephant Principally Viewed in Relation to Man.* 1844. London. new revised ed. 12mo. 282 p. new ep. gr cloth. VG+. B20. $90.00

KNIGHT, Clifford. *Affair of the Fainting Butler.* 1943. Dodd Mead. 1st ed. NF/VG. B2. $60.00

KNIGHT, Damon. *Nebula Award Stories 1965.* 1966. Doubleday. 1st ed. F/dj. M2. $150.00

KNIGHT, Damon. *One Side Laughing...* 1991. St Martin. 1st ed. F/F. N3. $15.00

KNIGHT, Damon. *Tomorrow & Tomorrow: 10 Tales of the Future.* 1973. Simon Schuster. 1st ed. F/VG+. N3. $10.00

KNIGHT, Damon. *Turning On: 13 Stories.* 1966. Doubleday. 1st ed. pub presentation. F/NF. N3. $45.00

KNIGHT, David; see Prather, Richard.

KNIGHT, J.A. *Theory & Technique of Fresh-Water Angling.* (1940). NY. photos. 223 p. A17. $15.00

KNIGHT, Kathleen Moore. *Intrigue for Empire.* 1944. Crime Club. 1st ed. F/NF. F4. $20.00

KNIGHT, R.L. *Abstract Bibliography of Fruit Breeding & Genetics to 1960.* 1963. Malus Pyrus. extensive index. 535 p. B26. $35.00

KNIGHT, W. Nicholas. *Shakespeare's Hidden Life: Shakespeare at the Law...* 1973. Mason Lipscomb. ARC of 1st ed. dj. N2. $10.00

KNIGHT & SLOVER. *Narratives of Perils & Sufferings of Dr Knight & J Slover...* 1867. Cincinnati. 1/500. 72 p. VG. D7. $225.00

KNIGHTLEY, Phillip. *First Casualty.* 1975. HBJ. BC. 465 p. F/NF. M7. $15.00

KNIGHTLEY, Phillip. *First Casualty.* 1975. HBJ. 1st ed (not BC). 465 p. F/2 NF djs. M7. $26.50

KNIGHTLEY & SIMPSON. *Lawrence av Arabien.* 1969. Stockholm. 1st Swedish ed. 318 p. F/pict wrp. M7. $75.00

KNIGHTLEY & SIMPSON. *Secret Lives of Lawrence of Arabia.* 1969. London. Nelson. 1st UK ed. 293 p. NF/VG+. M7. $45.00

KNIGHTLEY & SIMPSON. *Secret Lives of Lawrence of Arabia.* 1970. McGraw Hill. 1st ed. 334 p. NF/VG. M7. $25.00

KNOPF, Alfred. *Portrait of a Pub: Reminiscences & Reflections.* 1965. NY. Typophiles. 1st ed. 2 vols (1st inscr). F/slipcase. C4. $150.00

KNOROZOV, Yuri. *Selected Chapters From Writing of the Mayan Indians.* nd. Aegean Park Pr. reprint of 1967 ed. F3. $25.00

KNOTT, Frederick. *Dial M for Murder.* 1953. Random. 1st ed. tan cloth. NF/NF. Q1. $100.00

KNOX, Calvin; see Silverberg, Robert.

KNOX, Fitzhugh. *Genealogy of the Ritzhugh, Knox, Gordon, Seldon, Horner...* 1932. Foote Davies. 1st ed. 1/1000. sgn. VG. B10. $60.00

KNOX, G. *Better Homes & Gardens Embroidery.* 1978. np. cloth. G2. $8.00

KNOX, Thomas W. *Boy Travellers in Mexico.* 1890. NY. Harper. 8vo. 552 p. gilt cloth. G. B11. $35.00

KNOX. *New Directions in Fair Isle Knitting.* 1985. np. ils. cloth. G2. $30.00

KNUDSON, G.E. *Guide to the Upper IA River.* 1971. Luther Coll. revised ed. ils/maps. 69 p. wrp. A17. $6.00

KNYSTAUTAS, Algirdas. *Natural Hist of the USSR.* (1987). NY. 1st Am ed. 224 p. dj. A17. $25.00

KOBAL, John. *Art of Great Hollywood Portrait Photographers 1925-40.* 1980. NY. NF/dj. B30. $16.00

KOBLER, Franz. *Treasury of Jewish Letters...* 1953. JPS. 2 vols. 672 p. VG. S2. $35.00

KOCH, Charles R.E. *Hist of Dental Surgery.* 1910. Ft Wayne. 3 vols. xl. 4to. orig brds. G7. $295.00

KOCH, F.H. *Carolina Folk-Plays.* 1924. NY. 1st ed. VG. A11. $60.00

KOCH, Kenneth. *Seasons on Earth.* 1987. Penguin. 1st ed. sgn. F/wrp. V1. $15.00

KOCH, Robert. *Louis C Tiffany: Rebel in Glass.* 1964. NY. Crown. 256 p. cloth. D2. $50.00

KOCH, Rudolf. *Die Geschichte vom Weihnachtsstern.* 1920. Leipzig. Seemann. 1/100. sgn. NF. B24. $500.00

KOCH, Rudolf. *Neue Schriftvorlagen zum Gebrauch fur Schreiber...* 1925. Dresden. Wolfgang Jess. oblong quarto. 16 pls. unbound as issued. F/fld. B24. $275.00

KOCH, Stephen. *Night Watch.* 1969. NY. 1st ed. sgn twice. F/NF. A11. $35.00

KOCH & LINGLE. *Breed of Noble Bloods...the Wye Angus.* 1976. Princeton. presentation. VG/VG. O3. $35.00

KOCHER, Theodor. *TB of Operative Surgery.* 1911. Macmillan. 3rd Eng ed from trans of 5th German ed. 2 vols. xl. G7. $125.00

KOEPP, Donna P. *Exploration & Mapping of the Am West. Selected Essays.* 1986. Chicago. Speculum Orbis. 8vo. facsimiles/charts. 182 p. bl cloth. H9. $25.00

KOESTLER, Arthur. *Age of Longing.* 1951. London. 1st ed. VG/VG. B5. $25.00

KOESTLER, Arthur. *Dialogue w/Death.* 1966. London. Hutchinson. 1st thus ed. 206 p. F/dj. A7. $15.00

KOHN, Harold E. *Thoughts Afield.* (1959). Grand Rapids. 1st ed. 171 p. F/dj. A17. $10.00

KOHN, S. Joshua. *Jewish Community of Utica, NY, 1847-1948.* 1959. AJHS. ils/index. 221 p. VG. S3. $30.00

KOHR, H.O. *Around the World w/Uncle Sam.* 1907. Akron. 1st ed. 232 p. VG. B18. $35.00

KOHUT, Alexander. *Prayers for Divine Services of Congregation Ahawath Chesed.* 1889. AL Goetzl. vol 2 only. 24mo. 512 p. G+. S3. $25.00

KOLB, E.L. *Through the Grand Canyon From WY to Mexico.* 1958. NY. Macmillan. new ed. sgn. ils. 344 p. VG. B11. $45.00

KOLLE, Kurt. *Kraepelin und Freud.* 1957. Verlag. xl. sm 8vo. VG/prt wrp. G1. $35.00

KOLLER, Larry. *Treasury of Angling.* (1963). NY. ils/photos. 252 p. VG. A17. $20.00

KOLLER, Larry. *Treasury of Hunting.* (1965). NY. 4to. 251 p. F/dj. A17. $14.50

KOLLONTAI, Alexandra. *Women Workers Struggle for Rights.* ca 1973. Bristol, Great Britain. Falling Wall Pr. 3rd ed. pamphlet. VG. V4. $8.00

KOLPACOFF, Victor. *Prisoners of Quai Dong.* (1967). NAL. 1st ed. VG/dj. A7. $30.00

KOLTER. *Forget Me Not.* 1991. np. ils. wrp. G2. $15.00

KOMAN, Victor. *Jehova Contract.* 1987. Watts. 1st ed. F/dj. M2. $12.00

KOMROFF, Manuel. *Grace of Lambs.* 1925. NY. Boni. inscr/sgn. G+. A1. $85.00

KOMROFF, Manuel. *Voice of Fire.* 1927. Paris. E Titus Blk/Manakin Pr. sgn. ils P Chentoff. VG. A1. $300.00

KONEFSKY, Samuel J. *Chief Justice Stone & the Supreme Court.* 1946. Macmillan. M11. $35.00

KONTOPOULOS, N. *Lexikon Modern Greek-Eng & Eng-Modern Greek.* 1867. Smyrna. Tetikidou. 8vo. full panelled calf. 456 p. O2. $125.00

KONVITZ, Josef W. *Cartography in France, 1600-1848.* 1987. Chicago. ils/maps. M/M. O6. $40.00

KONWICKI, Tadeusz. *Anthropos-Specter-Beast.* 1977. NY. Phillips. 1st ed. trans from Polish. NF/NF. A14. $25.00

KONWICKI, Tadeusz. *Moonrise, Moonset.* 1987. FSG. 1st ed. trans from Polish. NF/NF clip. A14. $20.00

KOONTZ, Dean R. *Cold Fire.* 1990. Putnam. ltd ed. 1/750. sgn/#d. M/slipcase. M2. $150.00

KOONTZ, Dean R. *Cold Fire.* 1991. Putnam. 1st ed. sgn pasted in. F/NF. A7. $30.00

KOONTZ, Dean R. *Dark Rivers of the Heart.* 1994. Knopf. ARC of 1st trade ed. F/wrp. N3. $35.00

KOONTZ, Dean R. *Dragonfly.* 1975. Random. 1st ed. F/NF. M2. $200.00

KOONTZ, Dean R. *Eyes of Darkness.* 1989. Dark Harvest. 1st hc ed. M/as issued. M2. $35.00

KOONTZ, Dean R. *Funhouse.* 1980. Doubleday. 1st hc ed. F/F. F4. $20.00

KOONTZ, Dean R. *Funhouse.* 1992. Headline. 1st UK hc ed. F/F. F4. $35.00

KOONTZ, Dean R. *Hideaway.* 1992. Putnam. 1st ed. 1/800. sgn. F/F/ils slipcase. F4. $130.00

KOONTZ, Dean R. *House of Thunder.* 1988. Dark Harvest. 1st Am hc ed. sgn. F/F. F4. $50.00

KOONTZ, Dean R. *Key to Midnight.* 1989. Dark Harvest. 1st ed. 1/550. sgn. M/box. M2. $65.00

KOONTZ, Dean R. *Lightning.* 1988. Putnam. 1st ed. F/dj. B3/F4. $30.00

KOONTZ, Dean R. *Mr Murder.* (1993). Putnam. ARC. RS. w/promo material. F/F. B4. $35.00

KOONTZ, Dean R. *Mr Murder.* 1993. Putnam. 1/600. sgn. F/slipcase. C4. $150.00

KOONTZ, Dean R. *Oddkins, a Fable for All Ages.* (1988). Warner. 1st ed. ils Phil Parks. F/NF. B3. $50.00

KOONTZ, Dean R. *Shattered.* 1973. Random. 1st ed. NF/dj. M2. $250.00

KOONTZ, Dean R. *Twilight Eyes.* 1986. Land of Enchantment. 1st ed. as new. M2. $45.00

KOONTZ, Dean R. *Winter Moon.* 1994. London. Headline. 1st/only hc ed. M/M. T2. $75.00

KOPP. *Am Hooked & Sewn Rugs.* 1985. Dutton. revised ed. 141 p. cloth. G2. $30.00

KOPPETT, Leonard. *NY Times at the Super Bowl.* (1974). Quadrangle. 1st ed. 8vo. 345 p. F/VG+. A2. $12.50

KOPPETT, Leonard. *Thinking Man's Guide to Baseball.* 1967. Dutton. later prt. VG/G+. P8. $20.00

KORABIEWICZ, Waclaw. *Matto Grosso.* 1954. London. Cape. 1st ed. trans from Polish. NF/NF. A14. $20.00

KORLING, Torkel. *Wild Plants in Flower II: Boreal Forest & Borders.* 1973. Dundee, IL. 12mo. 32 color pls. 72 p. VG. B26. $10.00

KORNBLUH, Joyce L. *Rebel Voices.* ca 1964. Ann Arbor. 1st ed. ils. F/G. V4. $25.00

KORNBLUTH, C.M. *Not This August.* 1955. Doubleday. 1st ed. author's 1st book. NF/NF. Q1. $175.00

KORNBLUTH & POHL. *Space Merchants.* 1953. Ballantine. 1st ed. VG/dj. M2. $185.00

KORTE, Mary Norbert. *Beginnings of Lines.* 1968. Oyez. 1st ed. 1/200. sgn. gilt cloth. F. B24. $65.00

KORTRIGHT, Francis H. *Ducks, Geese & Swans of N Am.* 1943. Am Wildlife Inst. G. A16. $27.50

KOSINSKI, Jerzy. *Blind Date.* (1977). Houghton Mifflin. 1st ed. F/F. B3. $40.00

KOSINSKI, Jerzy. *Passion Play.* 1979. St Martin. 1st ed. F/F. T2. $12.00

KOTZWINKLE, William. *Queen of Swords.* (1984). London. Deutsch. 1st ed. mk Production File Copy. F/F. B3. $25.00

KOUFAX, Sandy. *Koufax.* 1966. Viking. 1st ed. G. P8. $25.00

KOURNAKOFF, Sergei. *What Russia Did for Victory.* 1945. New Century. 63 p. wrp. A7. $12.00

KOUSOULAS, Dimitrios G. *Price of Freedom. Greece in World Affairs, 1939-53.* 1953. Syracuse. 8vo. 210 p. cloth. dj. O2. $25.00

KOVIC, Ron. *Born on the 4th of July.* 1976. McGraw Hill. 1st ed. 8vo. 208 p. VG/dj. W1. $18.00

KOWET, Don. *Vida Bl: Coming Up Again.* 1974. Putnam. later prt. F. P8. $12.50

KOZACZKA. *Polish Cross-Stitch Folk Patterns.* 1989. np. sbdg. wrp. G2. $9.50

KOZLENKO, William. *Disputed Plays of Wm Shakespeare.* 1974. Hawthorne. dj. N2. $12.50

KRAEMER, Ruth S. *Drawings of Benjamin W & His Son Raphael Lamar W.* 1975. Pierpont Morgan Lib. ils. 104 p. brds. D2. $35.00

KRAEPELIN, Emil. *One Hundred Yrs of Psychiatry.* 1962. Citadel. 1st pb prt. sm 8vo. 164 p. G1. $17.50

KRAFT, Joseph. *Struggle for Algeria.* 1961. Doubleday. 263 p. dj. A7. $15.00

KRAMER, Aaron. *Golden Trumpet.* (1949). NY. Internat. 1st ed. 32 p. NF/wrp. A7. $18.00

KRAMER, Aaron. *Tune of the Calliope. Poems & Drawings of NY.* (1958). NY/London. Yoseloff. ltd ed. 1/500. sgn author/11 contributing ils. VG+/dj. B20. $235.00

KRAMER, Dale. *Heywood Broun: Biographical Portrait.* 1949. NY. Wyn. 1st ed. NF/VG. B2. $45.00

KRAMER, Sidney. *Hist of Stone & Kimball & Henry Stone Co.* 1940. Chicago. 1st ed. VG/G. B5. $100.00

KRANZ, Kirker E. *Clouded Mirror.* 1971. NY. Lenox Hill. 1st ed. author's 1st book. F/F. N3. $15.00

KRASLOW & LOORY. *Secret for Peace in Vietnam.* (1968). Random. 1st ed. 247 p. NF/dj. A7. $30.00

KRASNER, William. *Death of a Minor Poet.* 1984. Scribner. 1st ed. F/F. S5. $22.50

KRASNEY, Samuel. *Homicide W.* 1961. Morrow. 1st ed. F/NF. F4. $24.00

KRASSNER, Paul. *Confessions of a Raving Unconfirmed Nut.* 1993. Simon Schuster. 1st ed. inscr. F/dj. B2. $45.00

KRAUS, George. *High Road to Promontory.* 1969. Am W. 310 p. cloth. VG+/dj. M20. $30.00

KRAUS, Hans P. *Sir Francis Drake: Pict Biography.* 1970. Amsterdam. Israel. folio. ils/maps. M/clear plastic dj. O6. $150.00

KRAUS, Henry. *In the City Was a Garden.* 1951. NY. Renaissance. 255 p. dj. A7. $20.00

KRAUS, Karl. *In These Great Times.* (1984). Manchester. Caranet. 263 p. NF/NF. A7. $13.00

KRAUS, Michelle P. *Allen Ginsberg: Annotatated Bibliography 1969-77.* 1980. Metuchen. Scarecrow. 328 p. F. A7. $20.00

KRAUSE, Aurel. *Tlinget Indians.* 1956. Seattle. 310 p. VG/dj. B18. $19.50

KRAUSE, Fedor. *Surgery of Brain & Spinal Cord Based on Personal Experience.* 1909-12. NY. Rebman. 3 vols. 4to. orig cloth/recased/orig spines. G7. $595.00

KRAUSS, Ruth. *Monkey Day.* 1957. Harper. sgn. ils Phyllis Rowand. VG. P2. $20.00

KRAUSS, Ruth. *When I Walk I Change the Earth.* 1978. Burning Deck. 1/500. inscr. F/stiff wrp. V1. $25.00

KRAVITZ, Nathaniel. *Sayings of the Fathers: Anthology of Comments, Part 1.* 1951. Jewish Way Magazine. 144 p. VG/poor. S3. $24.00

KREDEL, Fritz. *Decameron. Model of Wit, Mirth, Eloquence & Conservation...* 1940. LEC. 1/530. sgn. 2 vols. quarto. F/slipcase. B24. $450.00

KREIDOLF, Ernst. *Flower Fairy Tales.* 1979. Gr Tiger pr. 1st Am ed. oblong 4to. NF. T5. $30.00

KREMERS & URDANG. *Hist of Pharmacy.* (1940). Lippincott. 1st ed. index/glossary. 466 p. bl cloth. VG. S9. $39.00

KREPS, E. *Science of Trapping.* (1909). Harding. revised. ils. 229 p. cloth. A17. $20.00

KRESS, Nancy. *Trinity & Other Stories.* 1985. Bluejay. 1st ed. F/F. F4. $25.00

KRICH, John. *Bump City.* 1979. Berkeley. PBO. inscr. NF/photo-ils wrp. A11. $55.00

KRIEG. *Huck Towel Patterns, 3rd Series.* 1940. np. general information/patterns. wrp. G2. $6.00

KRIKOU, Alex. *Place of Hellenism in Am.* 1915. Athens. Greek text. 8vo. 231 p. cloth. O2. $85.00

KRILOFF, I.A. *Three Tales.* 1913. Moscow. Knebel. ils Timorev/9 pls. NF/olive linen wrp. B24. $575.00

KRIVATSY, Peter. *Catalogue of Incunabula & 16th-Century Prt Books...* 1971. Bethesda. 4to. 51. scarce supplement. G7. $75.00

KRIVINE, J. *Juke Box Saturday Night.* (1977). Chartwell. 1st Am ed. lg 4to. F/F. A2. $45.00

KROCK, Arthur. *Memoirs: 60 Yrs on the Firing Line.* 1968. Funk Wagnall. 1st ed. 508 p. dk bl cloth. NF/VG. M7. $22.50

KROGER, Marvin. *Crossbreeding Beef Cattle, Series 2.* 1973. Gainesville, FL. 459 p. NF. H10. $17.50

KRONKE, Horst. *Die Welt der Schiffahrt en Miniature.* 1992. Herford. Koehlers Verlagsgesellschaft. as new. A16. $34.00

KROPOTKIN, Peter. *State: Its Hist Role.* 1902. London. Freedom Office. VG. V4. $30.00

KROPP, Miriam. *Cuzco. Window on Peru.* (1956). NY. Studio. 1st ed. 143 p. dj. F3. $20.00

KRUEGER, Carl. *Wings of the Tiger.* (1966). NY. Fell. 3rd prt. VG/clip. A7. $30.00

KRUEGER, Joseph. *Baseball's Greatest Drama.* 1945. Classic. 3rd prt. VG/G+. P8. $30.00

KRUEGER. *Gallery of Am Samplers.* 1978. np. cloth. G2. $35.00

KRUG, Meron E. *DuBay: Son-in-Law of OshKosh.* 1946. Appleton, WI. N2. $25.00

KRUTNIK, Frank. *In the Lonely Street, Film Noir, Genre, Masculinty.* 1991. Routledge. NF/sans. C8. $50.00

KU KLUX KLAN. *Ideas of the Ku Klux Klan.* 1915? np. 1st ed. 8 p. NF/self wrp. M8. $85.00

KUBALSKI, N.A. *Travels in Siberia.* 1859. French text. 12mo. gilt blk cloth. VG. H3. $65.00

KUCYZYNSKI & WITT. *Ecomonics of Barbarism.* (1942). NY. Internat. 64 p. wrp. A7. $15.00

KUEHNEL, Ernst. *Miniaturmalerei im Islamischen Orient.* 1923. Berlin. 2nd ed. 8vo. 154 p of pls/65 p of text. cloth. O2. $75.00

KUHLKEN, Ken. *Loud Adios.* 1991. St Martin. 1st ed. sgn. author's 2nd novel. F/F. T2. $35.00

KUHLKEN, Ken. *Midheaven*. 1980. Viking. 1st ed. author's 1st novel. F/F. T2. $18.00

KUHLKEN, Ken. *Venus Deal*. 1993. St Martin. 1st ed. sgn. ils/sgn John Dawson. F/F. T2. $35.00

KUHN, Bowle. *Hardball*. 1987. Times. 1st ed. F/VG+. P8. $12.50

KUKLA, Jon. *Speakers & Clerks of the VA House of Burgesses, 1643-1776*. 1981. VSL. ils. 163 p. VG/stiff wrp. B10. $10.00

KUKLICK, Bruce. *Josiah Royce: Intellectual Biography*. 1985. Hackett. revised ed. sm 8vo. 270 p. red cloth. F. G1. $19.00

KULKIELKO, Renya. *Escape From the Pit*. 1947. Sharon Books. 189 p. VG. S3. $27.00

KUMIN, Maxine. *Designated Heir*. (1975). London. Deutsch. 1st ed. F/NF. B3. $30.00

KUMIN, Maxine. *House, Bridge, Fountain, Gate*. 1975. NY. 1st ed. sgn. F/F. V1. $45.00

KUMLIEN, L.L. *Friendly Evergreens*. (1952). Dundee, IL. 4to. ils/index. cloth. A17. $17.50

KUMMEL, O. *L'Art del'Extreme-Orient*. ca 1920. Paris. Cres. trans Charlotte Marchand. ils/pls. 51 p. VG. W1. $35.00

KUNDERA, Milan. *Art of the Novel*. 1988. Grove. AP. F/wrp. B2. $35.00

KUNDERA, Milan. *Farewell Party*. 1977. London. John Murray. 1st ed of 1976 French trans. F/F. A13. $45.00

KUNDERA, Milan. *Immortality*. 1991. Grove Weidenfeld. ARC. 1/125. sgn. F/wrp. B2. $100.00

KUNDERA, Milan. *Immortality*. 1991. NY. Grove Weidenfeld. 1st ed. trans from Czech. NF/NF clip. A14. $25.00

KUNDERA, Milan. *Joke*. 1982. Harper Row. 1st Am ed. trans from Czech. F/F. A14. $25.00

KUNDERA, Milan. *Laughable Loves*. 1978. London. Murray. 1st ed. trans from Czech. NF/NF clip. A14. $30.00

KUNDERA, Milan. *Life Is Elsewhere*. 1986. London. Faber. 2nd British imp. trans from Czech. F/F. A14. $25.00

KUNHARDT, Dorothy. *Brave Mr Buckingham*. 1935. Harcourt Brace. 1st ed. 8vo. beige cloth. VG/dj. D1. $120.00

KUNITZ, Stanley. *Kind of Order, Kind of Folly*. 1975. Boston. 1st ed. sgn. F/VG. V1. $25.00

KUNITZ, Stanley. *Testing Tree*. 1971. Boston. 1st ed. F/F. V1. $45.00

KUNKEL, John H. *Encounters w/Great Psychologists*. 1989. Toronto. Wall Thompson. trade pb. VG. G1. $17.50

KUNSTLER, W.M. *Deep in My Heart*. 1966. Morrow. 1st ed. 384 p. F/F. A7. $30.00

KUNTZ, Jim. *Poetry Explications*. 1962. Denver. revised ed. VG+. V1. $10.00

KUNZ, George Frederick. *Shakespeare & Precious Stones*. 1916. Lippincott. 1st ed. presentation/inscr. 100 p. teg. VG. H5. $275.00

KUNZ, George. *Ivory & the Elephant in Art, Archaeology & Science*. 1916. Doubleday Page. Belgian Congo ed. 1/26. sgn. cream buckram/pict label. R3. $3,500.00

KUPERSTEIN, L. *Man & His Work: Story of the Histadrut*. 1965. Tarbut Wechinuch. 4to. VG. S3. $25.00

KURATA, Shigeo. *Nepenthes of Mt Kinabalu*. 1976. Sabah, Malaysia. ils/30 color photos. 80 p. VG/dj. B26. $17.50

KURLAND, Philip B. *Supreme Court Review*. 1960-1991. Chicago. 31 vols. VG+. M11. $650.00

KURNITZ, Harry. *Shadowy Third*. 1946. Dodd Mead. 1st ed. inscr. F/VG. B20. $45.00

KURTZ, O.H. *Official Route Book of Ringling Bros'...Shows*. 1892. Buffalo. Courier. 12mo. 128 p. gilt leather. F1. $295.00

KURUTZ, Gary F. *Benjamin C Truman: CA Booster & Bon Vivant*. 1984. BC of CA. 1st ed. 1/600. ils. F/plain wrp. B19. $35.00

KUSANO, Eisaburo. *Stories Behind Noh & Kabuki Plays*. (1962). Tokyo News Service. 2nd revised/enlarged ed of 1953 ed. NF/dj. A7. $25.00

KUZMA, Greg. *Good News*. 1973. NY. 1st ed. VG. V1. $10.00

KY, Nguyen Cao. *20 Yrs & 20 Days*. (1976). Stein Day. 1st ed. 239 p. NF/NF. A7. $22.00

KYLE, Duncan. *Honey Ant*. 1988. London. Collins. 1st ed. NF/dj. S5. $22.50

KYLE, Elisabeth. *Seven Sapphires*. 1957. Thomas Nelson. 1st ed. ils Kathleen Voute. 224 p. VG/dj. M20. $15.00

KYLE, H.C. *Canfield Family Hist*. 1979. Parsons, WV. 1st ed. 588 p. blk cloth. VG. D7. $40.00

KYLE, William. *Abraham Lincoln: An Address*. pamphlet. 15 p. bdg brds. A6. $10.00

KYNE, Peter B. *Pride of Palomar*. 1921. Cosmopolitan. 1st ed. sgn. ils Ballinger/Cornwell. VG/VG. A18. $50.00

KYNE, Peter B. *Three Godfathers*. (1913). NY. inscr/dtd 1921. ils Maynard Dixon/4 pls. gilt cloth. D3. $75.00

L

L'AMOUR, Louis. *Bendigo Shafter.* (1979). Dutton. 1st ed. NF/dj. B9. $45.00

L'AMOUR, Louis. *Brionne.* 1985. Bantam. 8vo. F. A8. $5.00

L'AMOUR, Louis. *Comstock Lode.* (1981). Bantam. inscr. VG+/wrp. B9. $150.00

L'AMOUR, Louis. *Education of a Wandering Man.* 1989. Bantam. 1st ed. M/M. T2. $12.00

L'AMOUR, Louis. *Fair Blows the Winds.* 1978. Dutton. 1st ed. F/F. F4. $30.00

L'AMOUR, Louis. *Frontier.* (1984). Toronto/NY. Bantam. 1/500. sgn. photos/sgn David Muench. F/slipcase. B9. $375.00

L'AMOUR, Louis. *Haunted Mesa.* (1987). Bantam. 1st hc/30th-Anniversary ed. NF/dj. B9. $45.00

L'AMOUR, Louis. *Hondo.* (1983). Bantam. 1st deluxe ed. aeg. F. A18. $50.00

L'AMOUR, Louis. *Hopalong Cassidy & the Riders of H.* 1952. Hodder Stoughton. 1st ed. F/dj. P3. $250.00

L'AMOUR, Louis. *Hopalong Cassidy & the Trail to 7 Pines.* 1951. Doubleday. 1st ed. NF/dj. B9. $600.00

L'AMOUR, Louis. *Lonesome Gods.* (1983). Bantam. ARC. VG/wrp. B9. $50.00

L'AMOUR, Louis. *Over on the Dry Side.* (1975). Saturday Review/Dutton. 1st ed. F/dj. B9. $65.00

L'AMOUR, Louis. *Sackett's Land.* (1985). London. Century. 1st hc ed. F/dj. B9. $75.00

L'AMOUR, Louis. *Sackett's Land.* 1974. Dutton. 1st ed. F/F. A18/B9. $75.00

L'AMOUR, Louis. *Showdown at Yel Butte.* (1953). Ace D-38. pb/1st ed. NF. B9. $135.00

L'AMOUR, Louis. *Sitka.* (1957). Appleton Century Crofts. 1st ed. F/dj. B9. $1,000.00

L'AMOUR, Louis. *Smoke From This Altar.* (1939). OK City. Lusk. 1st ed. gray bdg. F. B9. $850.00

L'AMOUR, Louis. *Smoke From This Altar.* (1939). OK City. Lusk. 1st ed. inscr twice. orange bdg. F. B9. $1,500.00

L'AMOUR, Louis. *Tall Stranger.* (1957). Gold Medal/Fawcett. 1st pb ed. NF. B9. $50.00

L'AMOUR, Louis. *UT Blaine.* 1954. Ace D-48. NF. B9. $135.00

L'ENGLE, Madeleine. *Acceptable Time.* (1989). FSG. ARC. F/pict wrp. B3. $45.00

L'ENGLE, Madeleine. *Severed Wasp.* (1982). FSG. ARC. G+. B3. $25.00

L'ENGLE, Madeleine. *Weather of the Heart.* (1978). Wheaton. Harold Shaw. 1st ed. inscr. F/dj. B4. $75.00

LA BELLE, Claude A. *Ranger Boys & Their Reward.* 1922. AL Burt. 1st ed. VG. M2. $10.00

LA BRANCHE. *Constellation for Quilters.* 1990. np. ils. wrp. G2. $15.00

LA BRANCHE. *Patchwork Pictures.* 1985. np. ils. wrp. G2. $15.00

LA CROZE, Maturin Veyssiere. *Historiche Beschreibung des Zustandes der Christlichen...* 1740. Danzig. 8vo. 344 p. new quarter calf/raised bands. O2. $375.00

LA FARGE, Henry A. *John La Farge Oils & Watercolors.* 1968. Kennedy Galleries. 24 pls. 40 p. wrp. D2. $25.00

LA FARGE, Oliver. *Enemy Gods.* 1937. Boston. 1st ed. NF/taped dj. A17. $25.00

LA FARGE, Oliver. *Pict Hist of the Am Indian.* (1957). NY. 3rd prt. 272 p. cloth. VG/pict dj. D3. $15.00

LA FARGE, Paul. *Lost Treasures of Europe.* (1946). Pantheon. photos. bl cloth. NF. B22. $12.00

LA FARGUE, Paul. *Right To Be Lazy & Other Studies.* nd. Chicago. Kerr. 62 p. wrp. A7. $12.00

LA FEBER, Walter. *Panama Canal: Crisis in Hist Perspective.* 1978. NY. Oxford. 8vo. 2 maps. 248 p. red cloth. G. B11. $15.00

LA FONTAINE. *Fables de La Fontaine.* 1904. Paris. 4to. ils Rabier. sm rpr at spine. G+. D1. $285.00

LA FOUNTAINE, George. *Long Walk.* (1968). Putnam. 1st ed. NF/dj. A7. $35.00

LA GRANGE & LA GRANGE. *Clipper Ships of Am Great Britain, 1833-69.* 1936. Putnam. 1/300. sgns. 37 color pls. F. P4. $275.00

LA PIERE, Richard T. *Freudian Ethic.* 1959. DSP. 1st ed. 299 p. bl cloth. G1. $22.50

LA ROCHE, R. *Pneumonia: Its Supposed Connection...* 1854. Phil. Blanchard Lea. 502 p. 32 p ads. orig cloth. G7. $175.00

LA SPINA, Greye. *Invaders From the Dark.* 1960. Arkham. 1st ed. F/F. M2. $110.00

LA VARRE, William. *Southward Ho! Treasure Hunter in S Am.* 1940. Doubleday Doran. 8vo. 15 pls. 301 p. pict brds. G/G. B11. $15.00

LAAR, Clemens. *Kampf in der Wuste.* 1941. Berlin. Franz Eher Nachs. reprint. 235 p. VG. M7. $65.00

LABRO, Philippe. *Le Petit Garcon.* 1992. FSG. 1st ed. trans from French. F/F. A14. $25.00

LABUSCHANGE, R.J. *60 Yrs in Kruger Park.* 1958. Pretoria, S Africa. 1st ed. ils/pls. 104 p. gr cloth. VG/VG. H3. $35.00

LACEY, Peter. *Limit.* 1989. Crime Club. 1st ed. F/NF. F4. $12.00

LACEY & QUINN. *Visit of Pope John Paul II to San Francisco in 1987.* 1987. Chicago. GIA. 64 p. VG/wrp. C5. $8.50

LACKEY, Mercedes. *Last Herald: Mage.* 1990. BC. F/dj. C1. $5.00

LACKEY, Mercedes. *Winds of Fury.* 1993. DAW. 1st ed. 3rd of Mage Winds series. F/F. N3. $15.00

LACKS, Roslyn. *Women & Judaism: Myth, Hist & Struggle.* 1980. Doubleday. 218 p. VG+/G+. S3. $23.00

LACY, Charles. *Hist of the Spur.* (1904). London. Connoisseur. 4to. 47 pls. 81 p. emb gilt red bdg. VG. E5. $375.00

LACY, Leslie Alexander. *Rise & Fall of a Proper Negro.* (1970). Macmillan. 1st ed. 244 p. NF/NF. A7. $17.00

LADBURY. *Sewing Book.* 1985. np. ils. cloth. G2. $12.95

LADD, Richard S. *Maps Showing Explorers' Routes, Trails & Early Roads in US.* 1962. WA, DC. Lib of Congress. Map Division. 4to. 137 p. wrp. H9. $40.00

LADIES HOME JOURNAL. *Crochet.* 1976. np. ils. wrp. G2. $9.00

LADIES HOME JOURNAL. *Knitting.* 1977. np. pb. G2. $9.00

LADNER, Mildred D. *OC Seltzer: Painter of the Old W.* 1980. Norman, OK. 2nd prt. ils/photos. 224 p. stiff wrp. D2. $45.00

LADSBURY. *Practical Sewing. Step-by-Step to Perfect Dressmaking...* 1978. np. ils. cloth. G2. $15.00

LADY DECIES, Elizabeth. *Turn of the World.* 1937. Lippincott. 1st ed. 8vo. VG. A8. $9.00

LADY OF NINETY. *Dame Wiggins of Lee & Her 7 Wonderful Cats.* 1885. Kent. Allen. 1st ed. ils Greenaway. 8 p. gr slipcase. D1. $450.00

LAFFERTY, R.A. *Funnyfingers & Cabrito.* 1976. Portland. Pendragon. 1st ed. sgn. F/wrp. N3. $45.00

LAFFERTY, R.A. *Not To Mention Camels.* 1976. Bobbs Merrill. 1st ed. F/NF. N3. $17.00

LAFFIN, John. *Fedayeen: Arab-Israeli Dilema.* (1973). Free Pr. 1st ed. 8vo. 171 p. F/F. A2. $12.50

LAGERFELT, Marta. *Glad Jul.* nd. (1909). German text. 8vo. pls. VG/pict wrp. H3. $15.00

LAGERKVIST, Par. *Dwarf.* 1967. Chatto Windus. 2nd Eng imp. trans from Swedish. NF/NF clip. A14. $20.00

LAGERKVIST, Par. *Mariamne.* 1968. Chatto Windus. 1st ed. trans from Swedish. NF/NF clip. A14. $30.00

LAGO, Mary M. *Imperfect Encounter: Letters of Wm Rothenstein...* 1972. Harvard. ils. 403 p. VG/G+. S3. $22.00

LAHR, John. *Notes on a Cowardly Lion.* 1969. Knopf. 1st ed. sgn. VG/VG. L1. $40.00

LAIDLER, Harry W. *Socialism in Thought & Action.* ca 1920. Macmillan. VG. V4. $15.00

LAIRD, Carobeth. *Encounter w/an Angry God.* 1975. Banning, CA. Malki Mus. VG/dj. N2. $15.00

LAIT, Jack. *Will Rogers' Wit & Wisdom.* 1936. NY. pict/1st ed. 16mo. 124 p. cloth. VG. D3. $25.00

LAKE, Carlton. *Baudelaire to Becket.* 1976. Austin, TX. exhibition catalog. bl cloth. F. F1. $85.00

LALIQUE & LALIQUE. *Lalique par Lalique.* (1977). Paris. Lausanne. 1st ed. sgns. folio. 310 p. stp brn cloth. F/slipcase. K1. $200.00

LALLY, Dick. *Pinstriped Summers.* 1985. Arbor. 1st ed. F/F. P8. $15.00

LAMAR, Edlen. *Clothing Workers in Phil: Hist of Their Struggles...* 1940. Phil. 1st ed. F/dj. N2. $27.50

LAMAR, Mrs. Joseph Rucker. *Hist of Nat Soc of Colonial Dames of Am From 1891 to 1933.* 1934. Atlanta. Walter W Brn Pub. 1st ed. 8vo. ils. bl cloth. H9. $30.00

LAMB, Charles. *John Woodvil, a Tragedy.* 1802. London. Robinson. 1st ed. 12mo. 128 p. rebound full gr morocco. B24. $1,750.00

LAMB, Harold. *Genghis Khan: Emperor of All Men.* 1928. NY. McBride. 8th prt. 8vo. 12 pls. 270 p. VG. W1. $18.00

LAMB, Martha J. *Homes of Am.* 1879. Appleton. 4to. 256 p. VG. F1. $145.00

LAMB & LAMB. *Poetry for Children.* 1812. Boston. Richardson Cotton. 1st Am ed. 16mo. 144 p. M1. $750.00

LAMB & LAMB. *Tales From Shakespeare.* nd (1928). London/NY. Warne. ils Frank Pape. 308 p. VG+. B22. $12.50

LAMB & LAMB. *Tales From Shakespeare.* 1909. London. Dent. 1/750. ils/sgn Rackham. 304 p. teg. wht cloth. NF. H5. $1,750.00

LAMBARD, William. *Eirenarcha; or, Office of Justices of Peace...* 1619. London. Companie of Stationers. full calf. M11. $650.00

LAMBERT, Derek. *Chase.* 1987. London. Hamilton. 1st ed. NF/dj. S5. $20.00

LAMBERT, Gavin. *GWTW, Making of Gone w/the Wind.* 1976. Bantam. sm pb. VG+. C8. $20.00

LAMBERT, Janet. *Friday's Child.* (1947). Grosset Dunlap. sgn. 190 p. gray tweed brds. VG/worn. T5. $20.00

LAMBERT, Janet. *Star Dream.* 1951. Dutton. 1st ed. VG/dj. M20. $18.00

LAMBERT, John. *Travels Through Canada & the US...1806-1808...* 1816. London. 3rd ed. 8vo. contemporary calf. M1. $725.00

LAMBERT, L.F. *Practical & Scientific Mushroom Culture.* 1946. Coatesville. 3rd prt. 79 p. wrp. A17. $9.50

LAMBERT, Mercedes. *Dogtown.* 1991. NY. Viking. 1st ed. F/F. M15. $25.00

LAMBERT, S.M. *Yankee Dr in Paradise.* 1941. Little Brn. 1st ed. 8vo. 393 p. F/VG. A2. $20.00

LAMBOURNE, Robert. *Close Encounters? Science & SF.* 1990. London. 1st ed. as new/wrp. M2. $12.00

LAMI, Alphonse. *Anotomie Artistique Myologie Superficielle Corps Humain.* 1861. Paris. Bailliere. presentation. 10 full-p pls. prt wrp. G7. $595.00

LAMM, Michael. *Fabulous Firebird.* 1981. CA. Lamm-Morada Pub. 9th prt. VG/dj. A16. $30.00

LAMON & SLOCUM. *Mating & Breeding of Poultry.* 1920. NY. Judd. 1st ed. 341 p. H10. $65.00

LAMON & TEILLARD. *Recollections of Abraham Lincoln, 1847-65.* 1911. WA, DC. 2nd ed. 337 p. cloth. NF. M8. $45.00

LAMONT, Corliss. *You Might Like Socialism.* 1939. Modern Age. 308 p. wrp. A7. $16.00

LAMONT, Thomas W. *My Boyhood in a Parsonage.* (1946). NY. 1st ed. 203 p. worn dj. A17. $10.00

LAMPHIER. *Patchwork Plus.* nd. np. ils. wrp. G2. $15.00

LAMPHIER. *Pieceable Kingdom.* 1985. np. ils. wrp. G2. $15.00

LAMPMAN, Ben Hur. *Here Comes Somebody.* 1935. Metro. 1st ed. sgn. ils Mahlon Blaine. 275 p. VG+. S10. $30.00

LAMSON, Mary Swift. *Life & Education of Laura Dewey Bridgman.* 1879 (1878). Boston. New Eng. 1st ed. xl. 2 pls/3 fld facsimiles. brn cloth. G1. $30.00

LANCEREAUX, Etienne. *Treatise on Syphilis Historical & Practical.* 1868-69. London. 1st Eng ed. 2 vols. G7. $135.00

LANDE, Louis. *Essai sur l'Aplasie Lamineuse Progressive...* 1860. Paris. Masson. xl. 4 pls. 165 p. orig brds. G7. $250.00

LANDELLS, Ebenezer. *Boy's Own Toy-Maker: Practical Ils Guide...* 1859. Boston. Shepard Clark Brn. 1st ed. 16mo. 153 p. cloth. M1. $250.00

LANDER, David. *Hist of the Lander Family of VA & KY.* 1926. Chicago. Regan. 12mo. sgn. pls. 213 p. G. B11. $50.00

LANDESS & QUINN. *Jesse Jackson & the Politics of Race.* (1985). Jameson Books. 1st ed. 269 p. F/NF. A7. $17.00

LANDING, W.F. *War Cry of the S.* ca 1958. Exposition. 1st ed. 119 p. VG/G. B10. $12.00

LANDMAN, Isaac. *Christian & Jew: Symposium for Better Understanding.* 1929. Horace Liveright. 2nd prt. 374 p. VG. S3. $21.00

LANDOR, A. Henry Savage. *In the Forbidden Land.* 1899. NY. 1st ed. 2 vols. teg. gilt pict blk cloth. F. H3. $175.00

LANDOR, Walter Savage. *Imaginary Conversations.* 1936. Verona. LEC. 1/1500. sgn Hans Mardersteig. F/dj/slipcase. B24. $125.00

LANDSBERGER, Franz. *Hist of Jewish Art.* 1946. UAHC. 200 ils. 369 p. VG. S3. $55.00

LANDSDALE, Joe R. *Mucho Mojo.* 1994. Mysterious. ARC of 1st ed. F/pict wrp. N3. $20.00

LANDSMAN, Sandy. *Gadget Factor.* 1984. Atheneum. 1st ed. author's 1st book. F/F. N3. $15.00

LANE, Margaret. *Tale of Beatrix Potter, a Biography.* 1946. Warne. 1st Am ed. 162 p. VG/G. P2. $75.00

LANE, Margaret. *Tale of Beatrix Potter, a Biography.* 1956. Warne. reprint. 8vo. 176 p. gr cloth. G+/fragment. T5. $35.00

LANE, Thomas A. *Am on Trial.* (1971). Arlington House. 2nd prt. 297 p. NF/NF. A7. $20.00

LANE. *Gold & Silver Needlepoint.* 1983. np. ils. cloth. G2. $30.00

LANE. *Needlepoint by Design.* 1970. np. 90 combinations of designs from Chinese art. cloth. G2. $18.00

LANES, Selma G. *Art of Maurice Sendak.* 1980. Abrams. 1st ed. popups/movables. 278 p. F. D1. $150.00

LANES, Selma G. *Art of Maurice Sendak.* 1981. Abrams. 2nd prt. 278 p. F. P2. $65.00

LANG, Andrew. *Ballads of Books.* 1888. London. Longman Gr. 1st ed. sm octavo. 157 p. Birdsall bdg. NF. H5. $175.00

LANG, Andrew. *Brn Fairy Book.* 1908. London. Longman Gr. ils HJ Ford/8 color pls. aeg. VG. D1. $160.00

LANG, Andrew. *Fairy Books.* 1889-1910. Longman Gr. 1st ed. complete set of 12. aeg. VG. rare. D1. $3,500.00

LANG, Andrew. *Song-Story of Aucassin & Nicolete.* 1900. Chelsea. Ashendene. 1/40 for private circulation. bl brds. F. H5. $2,750.00

LANG, Andrew. *True Story Book.* 1893. London. Longman. 1st ed. ils HJ Ford. 337 p. bl cloth. VG. S10. $95.00

LANG, Andrew. *Yel Fairy Book.* 1906. London/NY/Bombay. 12mo. 321 p. aeg. gilt pict yel cloth. G. H3. $12.00

LANG, Daniel. *Casualties of War.* (1969). McGraw Hill. 2nd prt. VG. A7. $25.00

LANG, Daniel. *Man in the Thick Lead Suit.* 1954. NY. Oxford. 1st ed. 8vo. 207 p. VG+/G+. A2. $10.00

LANG, H. Jack. *Wit & Wisdom of Abraham Lincoln As Reflected in Letters...* ca 1941. Greenburg. inscr. 265 p. VG/VG-. B10. $50.00

LANG, John. *Land of the Golden Trade.* early 1900s. London. ils McCormick. 7th of Romance of Empire series. gr cloth. VG. H3. $35.00

LANG, R. Hamilton. *Cyprus: Its Hist, Its Present Resources & Future Prospects.* 1878. London. xl. 370 p. cloth. very scarce. O2. $125.00

LANG & ROBERTSON. *Decorating w/Fabric.* 1986. np. 1st ed. cloth. G2. $25.00

LANG & SIMON. *NY Mets: 25 Yrs of Magic.* 1986. Holt. 1st ed. xl. rem mk. G. P8. $10.00

LANGDON-DAVIES, John. *Dancing Catalans.* nd (1920s). NY. Harper. 1st Am ed. 12mo. 220 p. F/VG+. A2. $25.00

LANGE, Friedrich Albert. *Hist of Materialism & Criticism of Its Present Importance.* 1877-1880. London. Trubner. 1st Eng-language ed. 3 vols. bl cloth. VG. G1. $175.00

LANGE, John. *Binary.* 1972. London. Heinemann. 1st ed. NF/dj. S5. $30.00

LANGEVIN, Andre. *Orphan Street.* 1976. McClelland Stuart. 1st ed. trans from French. NF/NF clip. A14. $20.00

LANGFORD, Gerald. *Destination.* ca 1981. Stonehenge. inscr. w/sgn typed letter. F/VG. B10. $15.00

LANGFORD, Jim. *Game Is Never Over.* 1980. Icarus. 1st ed. VG/G+. P8. $17.50

LANGFORD, Walter. *Legends of Baseball.* 1987. Diamond. 1st ed. F/sans. P8. $17.50

LANGHORNE, John. *Fables of Flora.* 1794. London. Harding. 1st ed. octavo. 73 p. gilt vellum. B24. $1,850.00

LANGLEY, Lester. *Struggle for Am Mediterranean.* (1976). Athens, GA. 1st ed. 226 p. dj. F3. $10.00

LANGLEY, RYERSON & WOULD. *Wizard of Oz: The Screenplay.* Aug, 1989. Dell. 1st ed. VG/wrp. L1. $15.00

LANGLEY, Samuel Pierpont. *Researches on Solar Heat & Its Absorption...* 1884. GPO. quarto. 242 p. blk cloth. H9. $75.00

LANGLEY & MANLY. *Langley Memoir on Mechanical Flight.* 1911. Smithsonian. xl. quarto. gr cloth. NF. R3. $375.00

LANGSWORTH, Richard M. *Complete Hist of General Motors 1908-86.* 1986. Beekman House. rem mk. VG/dj. A16. $25.00

LANGTON, Jane. *Memorial Hall Murder.* 1990. London. Gollancz. 1st British ed. F/F. S5. $25.00

LANGWORTH, John L. *Bird Boys Among the Clouds.* 1912. Donohue. 1st ed. VG. M2. $15.00

LANIER, Sidney. *King Arthur & His Knights...* 1985. Jr Lib. ils Florian. F. C1. $7.50

LANKS, Herbert C. *Highway to AK.* 1944. Appleton Century. G/fair. A16. $10.00

LANMAN, Charles. *Canoe Voyage Up the MS & Around Lake Superior in 1846.* (1978). (Grand Rapids). facsimile of 1847 ed. cloth. M. A17. $17.50

LANMAN, Jonathan T. *On Origin of Portolan Charts.* 1987. Chicago. Newberry Lib. 14 pls/11 tables. M/wrp. O6. $20.00

LANNING, J. Frank. *Around S Am w/a Sample Case.* 1920. Richmond, VA. Williams. 12mo. ils. 252 p. N2. $20.00

LANNING, J.T. *Spanish Missions of GA.* 1935. Chapel Hill. 1st ed. VG/VG. B5. $45.00

LANSDALE, Joe R. *Act of Love.* 1992. Baltimore. CD Pub. 1/750. sgn. ils/sgn MA Nelson. M/M/slipcase. T2. $50.00

LANSING, Gerrit. *Heavenly Tree.* 1977. VT. 1st ed. inscr. F/wrp. V1. $15.00

LANSON, Mary Swift. *Laura Dewey Bridgeman: Deaf, Dumb & Blind Girl.* 1879. Boston. New Eng Pub. 373 p. N2. $45.00

LANTIGUA, John. *Twister.* 1992. Simon Schuster. 1st ed. F/F. F4. $14.00

LAPE, Fred. *Roll On, Pioneers.* (1935). Goodwin. 1st ed. VG/dj. B9. $45.00

LAPIDE, Cornelius. *Commentaria in Duodecim Prophetas Minores.* 1628. Antwerp. Martinum Nutium. 1st ed. folio. orig roll-tooled pigskin/brass clasps. K1. $300.00

LAPIDE, Pinchas. *Three Popes & the Jews.* 1967. Hawthorn. 384 p. VG/VG. S3. $20.00

LAPSLEY, Peter. *River Trout Flyfishing.* (1988). London. ils/photos. 178 p. M/dj. A17. $25.00

LARCO HOYLE, Rafael. *Peru.* (1966). NY. World. 1st ed. 243 p. F3. $20.00

LARDNER, Ring. *Ecstacy of Owen Muir.* 1954. London. correct 1st ed (precedes Am). inscr. F/NF clip. A11. $85.00

LARDNER, Ring. *Lardners. My Family Remembered.* 1976. NY. 1st ed. sgn. F/NF. A11. $55.00

LARDNER, Ring. *Round Up.* 1929. Scribner. 1st ed. NF/NF. C4. $65.00

LARDNER, Ring. *Some Champions.* 1976. NY. 1st ed. edt/sgn Ring Lardner Jr. F/NF clip. A11. $65.00

LARES, Maurice. *TE Lawrence: La France et les Francais.* 1978. Paris. private prt. 2 vols. 643 p. VG/slipcase. M7. $575.00

LARGE, E.C. *Advance of the Fungi.* 1940. Holt. G/dj. A16. $30.00

LARIAR, Lawrence. *Stone Cold Blonde.* 1951. Crown. 1st ed. F/VG. F4. $30.00

LARKE & PATTON. *Life of Gen US Grant: His Early Life & Military Career.* 1885. NY. 8vo. 572 p. gilt red cloth. VG. T3. $42.00

LARKIN, Philip. *All What Jazz: Record Diary 1961-68.* 1970. London. Faber. 1st ed. NF/NF. B2. $75.00

LARNED, William. *Fairy Tales From France.* 1920. Volland. 1st ed. G+. P2. $45.00

LARNER, Jeremy. *Drive, He Said.* 1964. NY. 1st ed/Delta PBO. sgn. NF/8vo wrp. A11. $35.00

LARNER & TEFFERTELLER. *Addict in the Street.* 1964. NY. 1st ed. sgn. NF/NF. scarce. A11. $55.00

LARSEN, Egon. *Wit As a Weapon.* 1980. London. Muller. 1st ed. thin 8vo. 108 p. blk cloth. VG/dj. G1. $17.50

LARSEN, Jeanne. *Silk Road: Novel of 8th-Century China.* 1989. NY. Holt. 1st ed. 8vo. 434 p. NF/dj. W1. $18.00

LARSEN & NGA. *Shallow Graves: 2 Women & Vietnam.* (1986). Random. 1st ed. NF/NF. A7. $25.00

LARSEN & PELLATON. *Behind the Lianas.* (1958). London. 1st Eng ed. 211 p. dj. F3. $25.00

LARSON, Ross. *Fantasy & Imagination in the Mexican Narrative.* (1977). ASU. 1st ed. 154 p. wrp. F3. $10.00

LARTEGUY, Jean. *Presumed Dead.* (1976). Little Brn. 1st Am ed. dj. A7. $35.00

LASKER, Bruno. *Jewish Experiences in Am: Suggestions for Study...* 1930. The Inquiry. 219 p. G+/wrp. S3. $19.00

LASKI, Harold. *Am Presidency.* 1940. Harper. 1st ed. VG/VG. V2. $8.00

LASKY, Muriel. *Proud Little Kitten.* 1944. NY. Universal. 1st ed. ils Erika. VG/G. L1. $18.50

LASKY, Victor. *It Didn't Start w/Watergate.* 1977. NY. Dial. 1st ed. 438 p. NF/worn. A7. $18.00

LASLEY, John. *Genetic Principles in Horse Breeding.* 1981. Houston. Cordovan. revised ed. 124 p. VG. O3. $15.00

LASS, William E. *From the MO to the Great Salt Lake.* 1972. NE State Hist Soc. 1st ed. ils/index. F/F. A18. $35.00

LASSAIGNE, Jacques. *Marc Chagall, the Ceiling of the Paris Opera...* (1966). NY. Praeger. tall 8vo. 85 p. w/lg fold color litho. stp cloth. F/dj. K1. $350.00

LASZLO, Andreas E. *Doctors, Drums & Dances.* 1955. NY. 1st ed. 284 p. map ep. silvered blk cloth. F. H3. $20.00

LATADY, William Jr. *Archaeological Investigations Along Sage Creek Road...WY.* 1986. GPO. ils/tables. 144 p. F/wrp. P4. $20.00

LATHAM, Jean Lee. *This Dear-Bought Land.* 1957. Harper. 1st ed. 8vo. 246 p. VG/G+. A3. $15.00

LATHAM, Marte. *My Animal Queendom.* (1963). Chilton. 1st ed. assn inscr by uncle. 192 p. VG/VG. A2. $15.00

LATHAM, Philip. *Five Against Venus.* 1952. Winston. 1st ed. VG. M2. $18.00

LATHEN, Emma. *Double, Double, Oil & Trouble.* 1979. London. Gollancz. 1st ed. F/F. S5. $35.00

LATHEN, Emma. *Pick Up Sticks.* (1970). Simon Schuster. 1st ed. F/NF. B4. $45.00

LATHROP, Dorothy. *Angel in the Woods.* 1960. Macmillan. 3rd prt. F/VG. P2. $35.00

LATHROP, Dorothy. *Animals of the Bible.* 1937. Stokes. 4th prt. 1938 Caldecott Medal. VG. P2. $35.00

LATHROP, Dorothy. *Bouncing Betsy.* 1946. Macmillan. 1st ed. oblong 8vo. unp. VG/tattered. M20. $50.00

LATHROP, Dorothy. *Colt From Moon Mtn.* 1941. Macmillan. 1st ed. VG. scarce. P2. $65.00

LATHROP, Dorothy. *Presents for Lupe.* 1940. Macmillan. 1st ed. sgn. VG/VG. D1. $60.00

LATHROP, Dorothy. *Stars To-Night: Verses New & Old for Boys & Girls.* 1930. Macmillan. 1st ed. 44 p. VG. P2. $25.00

LATHROP, Dorothy. *Sung Under the Silver Umbrella. Poems for Young Children.* 1936. Macmillan. 2nd prt. 8vo. VG. A3. $12.50

LATHROP, Elise. *Early Am Inns & Taverns.* 1935. NY. Tudor. VG/G. O3. $45.00

LATHROP, Elise. *Hist Houses of Early Am, Ils.* 1946. NY. Tudor. lg 8vo. 464 p. cloth. H9. $25.00

LATHROP, M.M. *Wayside: Home of Authors.* (1940). NY. sgn. ils. 202 p. G. B18. $15.00

LATHROP, Mary T. *Poems & Written Addresses...* (1895). WCTU of MI. 430 p. gilt cloth. F. A17. $30.00

LATIMER, Jonathan. *Solomon's Vineyard.* 1982. Santa Barbara. Neville. 1st ed. 1/300. sgn. cloth. F. B4. $85.00

LATORRE & LATORRE. *Mexican Kickapoo Indians.* (1976). Austin, TX. 2nd prt. 401 p. dj. F3. $20.00

LATOURETTE, Kenneth Scott. *Development of China. 4th Ed, Revised.* 1917. Houghton Mifflin. 1st ed. xl. 8vo. 274 p. G. W1. $18.00

LATROBE, B.H. *VA Journals of Benjamin Henry Latrobe 1795-1798.* 1977. New Haven. 2 vols. NF/dj. B28. $55.00

LATTA, James W. *Hist of 1st Regiment Infantry Nat Guard of PA...* 1912. Lippincott. 1st ed. pls. 811 p. cloth. NF. M8. $150.00

LAUCK, W.J. *Occupation Hazard of Antracite Miners.* 1920. WA. NF/wrp. B2. $40.00

LAUCK, W.J. *Wholesale & Retail Prices of Anthracite Coal 1913-20.* 1920. WA. VG+/wrp. B2. $40.00

LAUDER, Harry. *My Best Scotch Stories.* 1929. Dundee/London. 1st ed. ils. 36 p. gilt brn wrp. F. H3. $15.00

LAUGHLIN, Clara E. *So Your Going to Paris!* 1925. Boston. 16mo. 438 p. pict full blk leather. H3. $15.00

LAUGHLIN, David. *Gringo Cop.* 1975. Carlton. 1st ed. sgn. 127 p. tan cloth. VG/G. B11. $15.00

LAUGHLIN, James. *New Directions in Prose & Poetry 16.* (1957). New Directions. 1st ed. 12mo. 264 p. NF/dj. B20. $25.00

LAUMER, Keith. *Dead Fall.* 1971. Doubleday. 1st ed. F/F. N3. $55.00

LAUMER, Keith. *House in November.* 1970. Putnam. 1st ed. F/NF. N3. $45.00

LAUMER, Keith. *Time Trap.* 1970. Putnam. 1st ed. F/NF. N3. $55.00

LAURENCE, Janet. *Death & the Epicure.* 1993. London. Macmillan. 1st ed. F/F. S5. $25.00

LAURENCE, Janet. *Hotel Morgue.* 1991. London. Macmillan. 1st ed. F/F. M15. $35.00

LAURENT, Peter Edmund. *Recollections of a Classical Tour...Greece, Turkey, Italy...* 1822. London. 2 vols. 8vo. new quarter tan cloth/marbled sides. O2. $325.00

LAURENT & NAGOUR. *Okkultismus und Liebe...* 1903. Verlag. 1st German ed. 360 p. tan brds. G1. $50.00

LAURIE, Bruce. *Artisans Into Workers: Labor in 19th-Century Am.* 1989. Hill Wang. 1st ed. M/M. V4. $10.00

LAURIE & WHITTLE. *Laurie & Whittle's New Traveller's Companion...* 1810. London. Harding Wright. 25 maps. orig unlettered limp morocco. NF. O6. $975.00

LAURY. *Applique Stitchery.* 1976. np. ils. wrp. G2. $5.00

LAURY. *No Dragons on My Quilt.* 1990. np. ils. cloth. G2. $12.95

LAURY. *Quilts & Coverlets.* 1970. np. cloth. G2. $15.00

LAUTARD, J.B. *La Maison des Fous de Marseille.* 1840. Marseille. Imprimerie d'Achard. inscr. VG. G1. $250.00

LAUTH, J.F. Edouard. *L'Embryothlasie...La Cephalotripsie...* 1863. Strasborug. Silbermann. 10 fld pls. 228 p. modern wrp. G7. $250.00

LAVENDER, David. *Westward Vision: Story of OR Trail.* (1963). McGraw Hill. 1st ed. ils Marian Ebert. 425 p. F/clip. A18. $50.00

LAVER. *Costume & Fashion.* 1969. np. wrp. G2. $12.00

LAVIGNAC, Albert. *Music Dramas of Richard Wagner...Theatre in Bayreuth.* 1940 (1926). Dodd Mead. reprint. 8vo. 515 p. F. A2. $40.00

LAVIN, John. *Halo for Gomez.* (1954). Pageant Pr. 1st ed. 8vo. 471 p. VG/VG clip. A2. $20.00

LAVIN, Mary. *Likely Story.* 1967. Dublin. Dolmen Pr. 1/1500. F/wrp. B2. $25.00

LAW, Thomas Graves. *Hist Sketch of Conflicts Between Jesuits & Seculars...* 1889. London. Nutt. 172 p. H10. $35.00

LAWRENCE, A. *Captive of Tipu.* 1929. London. Cape. VG+. M7. $30.00

LAWRENCE, A. *Letters to TE Lawrence.* 1962. London. Cape. 1st ed. 216 p. gilt wine-red cloth. F/G. M7. $95.00

LAWRENCE, D.H. *Apocalypse.* 1931. Florence. Orioli. 1st ed. 1/750. NF/dj. B24. $425.00

LAWRENCE, D.H. *Apropos of Lady Chatterley's Lover.* 1930. Mandrake. 1st ed. VG. M18. $125.00

LAWRENCE, D.H. *Kangaroo.* 1920. London. Martin Secker. 1st ed. G+. A1. $50.00

LAWRENCE, D.H. *Lady Bird.* 1923. London. G+. A1. $35.00

LAWRENCE, D.H. *Lady Chatterley's Lover.* (1933). Hamburg. Odyssey Pr. 1st imp. prt gray brds. VG. B14. $125.00

LAWRENCE, D.H. *Man Who Died.* nd. New Classics. VG/torn. E3. $20.00

LAWRENCE, D.H. *Man Who Died.* 1931. London. Martin Secker. 1st Eng ed. 1/2000. octavo. gr cloth. NF/dj. H5. $300.00

LAWRENCE, D.H. *Mornings in Mexico.* 1927. Knopf. 1st ed. VG+/sans. C4. $50.00

LAWRENCE, Margery. *Number 7, Queer Street.* 1969. Mycroft Moran. 1st ed. 1/2000. F/F. F4. $90.00

LAWRENCE, Sidney. *Roger Brown.* 1987. Braziller. inscr. F/F. B2. $100.00

LAWRENCE, T.E. *Bolcseseg Het Pillere.* 1935. Budapest. Revai Kiades. 1st Hungarian ed. 2 vols. VG. M7. $250.00

LAWRENCE, T.E. *Crusader Castles.* 1936. Golden Cockerel. 1st ed. 2 vols. teg. gilt cream buckram. F/tattered tissue dj. M7. $1,250.00

LAWRENCE, T.E. *Diary of TE Lawrence.* MCMXI. 1937. London. 1st ed. 1/130 on parchment. quarto. 13 pls. F. H5. $3,750.00

LAWRENCE, T.E. *Khaterat-e-Lorance-e-Arabestan.* 1990. Tehran. Atai Pub. 1st Persian/Irian ed. 1/3000. 2 vols. VG/VG. M7. $115.00

LAWRENCE, T.E. *Los Siete Pilares de la Sabiduria.* June 1991. Madrid, Spain. Jucar. 2nd Spanish ed. 944 p. gilt simulated leather. M7. $95.00

LAWRENCE, T.E. *Men in Print.* 1940. Golden Cockerel. 1st UK ed. 60 p. teg. linen brds. VG/cb box. M7. $575.00

LAWRENCE, T.E. *Mint.* 1955. Jonathan Cape. 1st ed. 1/2000. teg. bl buckram/pigskin. NF/VG slipcase. M8. $275.00

LAWRENCE, T.E. *Mint.* 1957. NY. Doubleday. 1st Am ed. 250 p. red/wht lettered blk cloth. F/VG. M7. $275.00

LAWRENCE, T.E. *Odyssey of Home.* 1935. Oxford. 1st trade (2nd Eng) ed. rebound Heron of Glasgow bdg. F. M7. $105.00

LAWRENCE, T.E. *Oriental Assembly.* 1939. London. Williams Norgate. 1st ed. 76 pls. 291 p. NF/VG clear plastic. M7. $285.00

LAWRENCE, T.E. *Revolt in the Desert.* 1927. London. Cape. 1st ed. NF/NF. Q1. $400.00

LAWRENCE, T.E. *Seven Pillars of Wisdom.* April 1943. Jonathan Cape. 7th imp. 700 p. gilt bl cloth. VG/VG/clear plastic. M7. $65.00

LAWRENCE, T.E. *Seven Pillars of Wisdom.* 1935. Doubleday Doran. 1st ed/later imp. 672 p. NF/G 3rd state dj. M7. $125.00

LAWRENCE, T.E. *Seven Pillars of Wisdom.* 1939. London. Reprint Soc. 2 vols. gilt brn buckram. VG+/clear plastic. M7. $60.00

LAWRENCE, T.E. *Seven Pillars of Wisdom.* 1955. Jonathan Cape. 5th Eng ed. 700 p. gilt bl cloth. F/clear plastic. M7. $90.00

LAWRENCE, T.E. *Seven Pillars of Wisdom.* 1966. Doubleday. 4th Am ed. 622 p. gilt brick cloth. NF/VG/clear plastic. M7. $25.00

LAWRENCE, T.E. *Seven Pillars of Wisdom.* 1966. Doubleday. 4th ed. 622 p. gilt brick cloth. F/NF. M7. $35.00

LAWRENCE, T.E. *Slagen Til Slant (The Mint).* 1955. Stockholm. Albert Bonniers Forlag. 1st Swedish ed. F/NF. M7. $95.00

LAWRENCE, T.E. *Wilderness of Zin.* 1914. London. Palestine Exploration Fund. 1st ed. 154 p. VG. M7. $650.00

LAWRENCE, T.E. *Wilderness of Zin.* 1936. Scribner. 1st ed. 40 pls. 166 p. brick buckram. NF. M7. $150.00

LAWRENCE, W.J.C. *Practical Plant Breeding.* 1965 (1937). London. 3rd ed. ils. 164 p. F/dj. B26. $14.50

LAWRIE, W.H. *Eng Trout Flies.* (1968). Barnes. 1st Am ed. 392 p. F/dj. A17. $22.50

LAWSON, Elizabeth. *Lincoln's 3rd Party.* (1948). NY. Internat. 48 p. wrp. A7. $15.00

LAWSON, J. *Hist of Carolina.* 1714. London. 1st ed/2nd issue. sm 4to. pl/map. calf/rebacked. VG. C6. $8,500.00

LAWSON, Publius V. *Mystery of Louis XVIII.* 1905. Menasha, WI. Banta. 1st ed. inscr/sgn. 310 p. N2. $35.00

LAWSON, Reed. *Frustration: Development of a Scientific Concept.* 1966. Macmillan. 2nd prt/trade pb. 192 p. G1. $17.50

LAWSON, Robert. *I Discover Columbus: True Chronical of Great Admiral...* 1941. Viking. 1st ed. 111 p. G+. P2. $20.00

LAWSON, Robert. *Mr Revere & I: Being Account of Certain Episodes...* Nov 1953. Little Brn. 5th prt. 152 p. VG/G. P2. $25.00

LAWSON, Robert. *Watchwords of Liberty.* 1943. Little Brn. 1st ed. 115 p. VG. P2. $25.00

LAWTHER. *Rags to Riches.* 1992. np. pb. G2. $6.00

LAWTON, Alexander R. *Negro in S & Elsewhere. Annual Address to Alumni...* 1922. Savannah. 22 p. wrp. N2. $17.50

LAWTON, Harry. *Willie Boy.* 1960. Paisano Pr. 1st prt. sgn. 224 p. VG+/dj. M20. $20.00

LAY, G. Tradescent. *Chinese As They Are: Their Moral & Social Character...* 1843. Albany. Jones Munsell. 1st ed. 8vo. 116 p. prt wrp. disbound. M1. $175.00

LAYAMON & WACE. *Arthurian Chronicles.* 1986. Everyman's Classics. pb. M. C1. $7.50

LAYARD, Austen Henry. *Nineveh & Its Remains...* 1849. NY. 2 vols. pict blk cloth. VG. h3. $80.00

LAYCOCK, George. *Alien Animals.* 1966. Natural Hist Pr. 1st ed. 231 p. VG/dj. M20. $14.00

LAYCOCK, George. *Hunters & the Hunted.* (1990). Outdoor Life. 1st ed. 280 p. M/dj. A17. $17.50

LAYNE, J. Gregg. *Books of the LA District.* 1950. Dawson Bookshop. 1st ed. 61 p. NF/sans. B19. $50.00

LAZAR, Albert O. *Lonya: Reminiscences.* 1963. Vantage. 204 p. VG/G+. S3. $30.00

LAZAR, Chaim. *Destruction & Resistance: Hist of Partisan Movement Vilna.* 1985. NY. Behrman Jewish Book house. 372 p. VG. S3. $20.00

LAZELL, Frederick John. *Some Autumn Days in IA.* 1906. Cedar Rapids. Ioway Club. 1st ed. 1/75. inscr. teg. cloth. VG. D3. $75.00

LAZELL, J. Arthur. *AK Apostle: Story of Sheldon Jackson.* 1960. NY. 1st ed. 8vo. pls. 218 p. silvered cloth. VG. H3. $15.00

LAZIER, Harry A. Jr. *Carnations: Elegance in Flower Arrangements.* 1968. Denver. 81 color pls. 183 p. VG/torn. $14.00

LAZZARO, G. Di San. *Klee, a Study of His Life & Work.* (1957). NY. 1st Am ed. 304 p. G. B18. $42.50

LE BARON, Anthony; see Laumer, Keith.

LE BRETON, Maurice. *Anthologie de la Poesie Americaine Contemporaine.* 1948. Paris. 1st ed. VG+/sq 8vo wrp. A11. $70.00

LE CAIN, Errol. *King Arthur's Sword.* 1968. London. Faber. 1st ed. ils. NF/dj. C1. $12.50

LE CARRE, John. *Deadly Affair.* 1966. Harmondsworth. 6th prt of Penguin pb ed. w/sgn bookplate. NF/wrp. A11. $65.00

LE CARRE, John. *Honourable Schoolboy.* 1977. Franklin Lib. true 1st ed. ils Ben F Wohlberg. full leather. VG. B3. $65.00

LE CARRE, John. *Honourable Schoolboy.* 1977. Franklin Lib. 1st Am ed. gilt full cowhide. F/sans. M15. $75.00

LE CARRE, John. *Honourable Schoolboy.* 1977. Knopf. 1st Am trade ed. F/F. M15. $75.00

LE CARRE, John. *Little Drummer Girl.* (1983). Hodder Stoughton. 1st ed. NF/NF. B3. $100.00

LE CARRE, John. *Murder of Quality.* 1962. London. Gollancz. 1st ed. author's 2nd novel. NF/NF. M15. $1,300.00

LE CARRE, John. *Naive & Sentimental Lover.* 1971. Hodder Stoughton. 1st ed. NF/NF. Q1. $100.00

LE CARRE, John. *Night Manager.* 1993. Knopf. 1st Am ed. sgn. F/F. M15/Q1. $75.00

LE CARRE, John. *Perfect Spy.* (1986). Hodder Stoughton. 1st ed. F/NF. B3. $40.00

LE CARRE, John. *Russia House.* (1989). London. Guild Pub. 1st ed. F/F. B3. $30.00

LE CARRE, John. *Russia House.* 1989. Knopf. 1st ed. sgn. F/F. M15. $100.00

LE CARRE, John. *Secret Pilgrim.* 1991. Hodder Stoughton. 1st ed. sgn. F/F. M15. $125.00

LE CARRE, John. *Spy Who Came in From the Cold.* 1963. London. Gollancz. 1st ed. F/NF. M15. $500.00

LE CARRE, John. *Spy Who Came in From the Cold.* 1963. London. Gollancz. 1st ed. inscr/dtd. 222 p. gilt bl bdg. NF/dj. H5. $850.00

LE CARRE, John. *Tinker, Tailor, Soldier, Spy.* 1974. Knopf. 1st ed. VG+/dj. B9. $20.00

LE CONTE, Joseph. *Evolution: Nature, Evidences & Relation Religious Thought.* 1897. NY. Appleton. 2nd ed. xl. ils/index. 382 p. teg. leather. VG+. S9. $10.00

LE CONTE, Joseph. *Ramblings.* 1960. Sierra Club. 8vo. VG/G. A8. $20.00

LE CORBEAU, Adrien. *Forest Giant.* 1924. London. Cape. 1st ed. trans TE Lawrence as JH Ross. VG/clear plastic. M7. $145.00

LE CORBUSIER. *Talks w/Students From Schools of Architecture.* (1961). NY. Orion. trans Pierre Chase. 839 p. VG+/dj. F1. $40.00

LE CORBUSIER. *Urbanisme.* (1925). Paris. Les Editions G Cres & Cie. true 1st ed. NF. B4. $500.00

LE FANU, J. Sheridan. *Gr Tea.* 1945. Arkham. 1st ed. NF/dj. M2. $185.00

LE FANU, Sheridan. *In a Glass Darkly.* 1947. London. 1st prt Chiltern ed. intro Pritchett. 12mo. NF/NF. A11. $20.00

LE FANU, William. *Notable Medical Books From the Lily Lib.* 1976. Indianapolis. 4to. 274 p. M/M. G7. $50.00

LE FEBURE, Victor. *Riddle for the Rhine: Chemical Strategy in Peace & War...* 1923. NY. Chemical Found. VG/VG. V2. $8.00

LE FEVRE, Felicite. *Cock, Mouse & Little Red Hen.* (1931). Saalfield. ils FB Peat. pict brds. VG. T5. $40.00

LE FORESTIER, Francois. *Autobiography & Voyages of Francois le Forestier...* 1904. Boston. Athenaeum. 1st ed. 77 p. bl cloth. VG. P4. $45.00

LE GUIN, Ursula K. *Adventure of Cobbler's Rune.* 1982. Cheap Street. 1st ed. 1/250. sgn. ils/sgn Alicia Austin. M/wrp. M2. $70.00

LE GUIN, Ursula K. *Buffalo Gals & Other Animal Presences.* (1987). Santa Barbara. Capra. 1st ed. F/F. B3. $20.00

LE GUIN, Ursula K. *City of Illusions.* 1967. NY. Ace. PBO. inscr. NF/unread. A11. $45.00

LE GUIN, Ursula K. *Compass Rose.* 1982. Harper Row. 1st trade ed. F/NF. N3. $10.00

LE GUIN, Ursula K. *Eye of the Heron.* (1983). Harper Row. 1st separate Am ed. sgn. F/NF. A7. $30.00

LE GUIN, Ursula K. *Fisherman of the Inland Sea.* 1994. Harper Prism. ARC/hc. 1/1500. F/sans. T2. $38.00

LE GUIN, Ursula K. *Left Hand of Darkness.* 1980. Harper Row. reissue/1st prt. F/F. N3. $15.00

LE GUIN, Ursula K. *Malafrena.* (1980). London. Gollancz. 1st ed. VG/VG. B3. $25.00

LE GUIN, Ursula K. *Tehanu.* 1990. Atheneum. 1st ed. F/dj. M2. $20.00

LE GUIN, Ursula K. *Word for World Is Forest.* 1972. NY. Berkley. 1st ed. F/F clip. T2. $50.00

LE MAIR, Willebeek. *Old Dutch Nursery Rhymes.* (1917). London. 8vo. 31 p. gilt bl cloth. VG. D1. $200.00

LE MAY, Alan. *Smoky Yrs.* (1935). Farrar Rinehart. 1st ed. VG/dj. B9. $75.00

LE MAY, Alan. *Thunder in the Dust.* (1934). Farrar Rinehart. 1st ed. VG/dj. B9. $65.00

LE MOYNE, Pierre. *La Gallerie des Femmes Fortes.* 1665. Paris. Lib du Palais. 12mo. 2 parts in 1. contemporary bdg. K1. $450.00

LE PLONGEON, Alice Dixon. *Queen Moo's Talisman. Fall of the Mayan Empire.* 1902. London. 1st ed. 7 pls. 86 p. scarce. N2. $75.00

LE SAGE, Alain Rene. *Adventures of Gil Blas, of Santillane.* 1819. London. octavo. 3 vols. Bayntun bdg. F. H5. $2,000.00

LE STRANGE, G. *Don Juan of Persia.* 1926. NY. 1st Eng-language ed. 8vo. 355 p. cloth. O2. $35.00

LEA, Henry Charles. *Hist of Sacerdotal Celibacy in Christian Church.* 1884. Houghton Mifflin. 2nd revised/enlarged ed. 682 p. panelled olive cloth. G1. $75.00

LEA, Henry Charles. *Inquisition of the Middle Ages.* (1954). Citadel. 1 vol ed. 260 p. dj. A7. $20.00

LEA, Tom. *Art of Tom Lea.* (1989). TX A&M. 1st ed. 255 p. as new/dj. A18. $50.00

LEA, Tom. *King Ranch.* 1957. Little Brn. later prt. 2 vols. VG+/slipcase. O3. $95.00

LEA, Tom. *Primal Yoke.* 1960. Little Brn. 1st ed. sgn. NF/NF. C4. $40.00

LEACH, Edmund. *Claude Levi-Straus.* 1970. Viking. 1st ed. cloth. VG/dj. G1. $17.50

LEACH, William Elford. *Zoological Miscellany.* 1814-1817. London. McMillan Nodder. 1st ed. quarto. 3 vols. 150 pls. rebacked. VG. H5. $2,850.00

LEACOCK, Stephen. *Hohenzollerns in Am.* 1919. John Lane. 1st ed. sgn. F. B4. $100.00

LEADABRAND, Russ. *Exploring CA Byways.* 1969. Ward Ritchie. 12mo. 1 vol. VG. A8. $4.00

LEADABRAND, Russ. *Guidebook to S Sierra NV.* 1968. Ward Ritchie. 12mo. VG. A8. $4.00

LEADABRAND, Russ. *Guidebook: Mojave Desert of CA.* 1966. Ward Ritchie. 12mo. VG. A8. $12.00

LEADER, Mary. *Salem's Children.* 1979. CMG. 1st ed. F/NF clip. N3. $30.00

LEAF, Munro. *Aesop's Fables.* 1941. Heritage. reprint. ils Robert Lawson. 132 p. VG/G+. P2. $18.00

LEAF, Munro. *Fair Play.* 1939. Stokes. 1st ed. 94 p. G+. P2. $25.00

LEAF, Munro. *Grammar Can Be Fun.* 1934. Lippincott. 26th prt. F/VG. P2. $18.00

LEAF, Munro. *John Henry Davis.* 1940. Stokes. 1st ed. 56 p. G+. P2. $25.00

LEAF, Munro. *Reading Can Be Fun.* 1953. Lippincott. 2nd rpt. NF/G+. P2. $25.00

LEAF, Munro. *Turnabout.* 1967. Lippincott. 1st ed. F/NF. P2. $35.00

LEAF, Munro. *Wee Gillis.* 1938. Viking. 1st ed. ils Robert Lawson. plaid cover. VG. P2. $55.00

LEAKE, William M. *Topography of Athens w/Some Remarks on Its Antiquities.* 1821. London. tall 8vo. 435 p. orig brds/rebacked. O2. $300.00

LEAR, Edward. *Edward Lear in Greece. Loan Exhibition From Gennadius Lib.* 1971. Meriden. oblong 8vo. 87 p. pict wrp. O2. $20.00

LEAR, Edward. *Jumblies & Other Nonsense Verses.* nd. Warne. ils Leslie Brooke. G+. P2. $55.00

LEAR, Edward. *Lear Alphabet ABC.* 1965. London. Constable Young. 1st Eng ed. 8vo. F/dj. F1. $45.00

LEAR, Edward. *Nonsense Books.* 1946. Boston. 8vo. 394 p. pict gr cloth. F/VG. H3. $25.00

LEAR, Edward. *Poetry Pop-Up Book: The Owl & the Pussy-Cat.* 1987. 4 pop-ups. 14 p. F. A4. $25.00

LEARY, Jon. *Safe House.* 1975. Morrow. 1st Am ed. F/F. S5. $22.50

LEARY, W.A. *Valuable Hist Theological & Misc Books...* (1848). Phil. Leary. 8vo. 12 p. prt wrp. M1. $175.00

LEARY, William M. *Perilous Missions.* (1984). AL U. 281 p. F/F. A7. $16.00

LEAST HEAT MOON, William. *Prairy-Erth.* 1991. Houghton Mifflin. 1st trade ed. sgn. F/F. L3. $65.00

LEATHERS. *Indiana Legacy.* 1985. np. wrp. G2. $10.00

LEAVITT, David. *Equal Affections.* 1989. Weidenfeld Nicolson. 1st ed. inscr. F/F. B2. $50.00

LEAVITT, David. *Lost Language of Cranes.* 1986. NY. Knopf. 1st ed. NF/NF clip. A14. $30.00

LEBESON, Anita Libman. *Jewish Pioneers in Am, 1492-1848.* 1938. NY. Behrman's Jewish Book House. 372 p. VG. S3. $20.00

LEBRUN, Pierre. *Le Voyage de Grece. Peome par...* 1828. Paris/Leipzig. 8vo. 279 p. contemporary calf. O2. $400.00

LECKY, W.E.H. *Hist of European Morals From Augustus to Charlemagne.* 1955. NY. Braziller. facsimile. 2 vols bound in 2. orange cloth. VG/dj. G1. $35.00

LECLAINCHE, Emmanuel. *Histoire Illustree de la Medecine Veterinaire.* 1955. Eds Albin Michel. 2 vols. folio. NF/dj. G7. $195.00

LEDERER, Charlotte. *Golden Flock.* 1931. NY. 1st prt. 10 color pls. pict wht brds. VG. H3. $12.00

LEDERER, William J. *Our Own Worst Enemy.* (1968). Norton. 1st ed. 287 p. NF/dj. A7. $25.00

LEDERER & BURDICK. *Sarkhan.* (1965). McGraw Hill. 1st prt. NF/NF. A7. $45.00

LEDFORD, Preston Lafayette. *Reminiscences of Civil War, 1861-65.* 1909. Thomasville, NC. News Prt. 1st ed. 104 p. VG/prt wrp. M8. $1,200.00

LEDOUX, Louis. *Art of Japan.* 1927. NY. Rudge. F/dj. B14. $75.00

LEDYARD, Gleason H. *And to the Eskimos.* (1962). Chicago. 4th prt. 254 p. F/dj. A17. $15.00

LEE, Albert. *Henry Ford & the Jews.* 1980. Stein Day. 200 p. VG+/VG. S3. $30.00

LEE, Algernon. *Intro to Scientific Socialism...* nd. NY. Rand School Social Science. VG. V4. $25.00

LEE, Arthur S.G. *Royal House of Greece.* 1948. London. 8vo. 296 p. cloth. dj. O2. $40.00

LEE, Cazenove Gardner Jr. *Lee Chronicle: Studies of Early Generations of Lees of VA.* 1957. NY U. ils. 411 p. VG/box. B10. $50.00

LEE, Chang Hei. *Practical Korean Grammar.* 1955. Seattle, WA. 1st ed. 8vo. 225 p. VG. W1. $12.00

LEE, Edwin. *Nice & Its Climate.* 1865. London. 2nd ed. 12mo. 192 p. gilt emb blk cloth. VG. H3. $20.00

LEE, Fitzhugh. *Cuba's Struggle Against Spain.* 1899. Am Hist Pr. 1st ed. G. V2. $15.00

LEE, Frederic P. *Azalea Book.* ca 1965. Van Nostrand. 2nd ed. sgn. ils/index. H10. $35.00

LEE, Laurie. *I Can't Stay Long.* 1975. Deutsch. 1st ed. 230 p. VG/dj. M20. $22.00

LEE, Mrs. R. *Tiny Menagerie.* ca 1900. London. Griffith. ils Harrison Weir. tan cloth/pict label. VG. S10. $12.00

LEE, Robert Edson. *From W to E: Studies in Literature of Am W.* 1966. IL U. 1st ed. F/dj. A18. $25.00

LEE, Samuel Phillips. *Reports & Charts of Cruise of US Brig Dolphin.* 1854. WA, DC. Tucker. octavo. 15 fld charts. emb brn cloth. H9. $150.00

LEE, Spike. *Spike Lee's Gotta Have It.* (1987). Fireside Books. 1st ed. rem mk. F/wrp. B4. $100.00

LEE, Tanith. *Dreams of Dark & Light.* 1986. Arkham. 1st ed. M/as issued. M2. $40.00

LEE, Tanith. *Night's Master.* 1984. Highland Pr. 1st ed. 1/500. sgn. as new. M2. $50.00

LEE, W. Storrs. *CA: A Literary Chronicle.* (1968). NY. 3rd prt. ils/map ep. 537 p. cloth. NF/pict dj. D3. $15.00

LEE, William; see Burroughs, William S.

LEE & LEE. *Torrent in the Desert.* 1962. Flagstaff, AZ. 1st ed. 4to. 204 p. cloth. NF. D3. $25.00

LEEDER, S.H. *Desert Gateway.* 1910. London. 1st ed. 272 p. gilt brn cloth. VG. H3. $30.00

LEEDS, Josiah W. *Primitive Christian Estimate of War & Self Defense.* 1876. New Vienna, OH. Peace Assn Friends. 16mo. 48 p. VG. V3. $28.00

LEEDS, Lewis W. *Treatise on Ventilation...* 1871. NY. Wiley. 2nd ed. 226 p. gr cloth. B14. $85.00

LEES, Gene. *Oscar Peterson: Will To Swing.* (1990). Rocklin. Prima. 1st ed. 293 p. F/F. A7. $18.00

LEESER, Isaac. *Argumentative & Devotional on Subject of Jewish Religion...* (1841). Phil. Sherman. 1st ed. 8vo. 268 p. cloth. M1. $225.00

LEESER, Isaac. *Claims of Jews to an Equality of Rights...* (1841). Phil. Sherman. 1st ed. 8vo. 99 p. plain wrp. M1. $650.00

LEFF, S. *From Witchcraft to World Health.* 1958. Macmillan. 1st ed. 236 p. blk cloth. VG/worn. G1. $22.50

LEFFLAND, Ella. *Mrs Munck.* 1970. Houghton Mifflin. 1st ed. sgn. VG+/VG+. L3. $125.00

LEFTWICH, R.L. *Arts & Crafts of the Cherokee.* (1970). Cullowhee, NC. ils. 160 p. VG. B18. $22.50

LEGG, Rodney. *Lawrence of Arabia in Dorset.* 1988. Dorset/Wincanton. 1st UK ed. photos/maps. 112 p. as new/pict wrp. M7. $25.00

LEGGETT, J. *Who Took the Gold Away?* 1969. Random. 1st ed. VG/VG. V2. $5.00

LEHMANN, L.H. *Behind the Dictators.* 1946. Agora Pub. 128 p. VG/VG. S3. $25.00

LEHMANN & RAHNER. *Kerygma & Dogma.* 1969. NY. Herder. 105 p. VG. C5. $12.50

LEHNUS, D.J. *Angels to Zeppelins: Guide to Persons...Postage Stamps.* (1982). Westport, CT. 1st ed. 8vo. 279 p. F/VG. A2. $17.50

LEHRER, James. *We Were Dreamers.* 1975. Atheneum. 1st ed. 8vo. 216 p. F/F. A2. $15.00

LEHRER, Jim. *Bus of My Own.* 1992. Putnam. 1st ed. sgn. F/F. Q1. $30.00

LEIB, Franklin Allen. *Fire Dream.* (1989). Presidio. F/F. A7. $20.00

LEIBER, Fritz. *Knight & Knave of Swords.* 1988. Morrow. 1st ed. inscr/sgn. F/F. F4. $40.00

LEIBER, Fritz. *Night's Blk Agents.* 1947. Arkham. 1st ed. sgn. VG/dj. M2. $150.00

LEIBER, Fritz. *Two Sought Adventure.* 1957. Gnome. 1st ed. sgn. F/M. M2. $200.00

LEIBNITZ, G.W. *Oeuvres Philosophiques Latines et Francoises...* 1795. Amsterdam. 1st thus ed. royal quarto. half calf. VG. R3. $850.00

LEIGHLY, John. *CA As an Island.* 1972. San Francisco. BC of CA. 1/450. folio. 25 pls. brds/morocco spine. F. R3. $1,250.00

LEIGHTON, Clare. *4 Hedges: Gardener's Chronicle.* 1935. NY. 1st ed. VG/dj. B28. $50.00

LEIGHTON, William. *Roman Sonnets.* 1908. Florence. ils. VG-. E3. $35.00

LEINSTER, Murray; see Jenkins, Will F.

LEISNERVS, Carolvs C. *Dissertatio Medica Inauguralis de Circulatione Sanguinis...* 1696. Jenae. Tyupis Iohannis Jacobis Krebsii. 4to. 32 p. wrp. G7. $75.00

LEITCH, David. *God Stand Up for the Bastards.* 1973. Houghton Mifflin. 1st ed. 231 p. NF/dj. A7. $20.00

LEITHAUSER, Brad. *Cats of the Temple.* 1986. NY. 1st ed. F/F. V1. $10.00

LEITHAUSER, J.G. *Worlds Beyond the Horizon.* 1955 (53). Knopf. 1st Am ed. 8vo. 412 p. F/F. A2. $17.50

LELTNER, Irving. *Baseball, Diamond in the Rough.* 1972. Criteron. 1st ed. VG+/VG+. P8. $30.00

LELYVELD, Arthur J. *Atheism Is Dead: Jewish Response to Radical Theology.* 1968. World. sgn. 209 p. VG/fair. S3. $23.00

LEM, Stanislaw. *Memoirs of a Space Traveler...* 1982. HBJ. 1st Am ed. F/F. N3. $15.00

LEM, Stanislaw. *Tales of Prix the Pilot.* 1979. HBJ. 1st Eng-language ed. F/NF clip. N3. $15.00

LEMAN & MARTIN. *Taking the Math Out of Making Patchwork Quilts.* 1981. np. wrp. G2. $6.00

LEMAN. *Patchwork Sampler Legacy Quilt.* 1984. np. wrp. G2. $8.00

LEMAN. *Quick & Easy Quilting.* 1972. np. wrp. G2. $6.00

LEMARCHAND, Elizabeth. *Cyanide w/Compliments.* 1972. London. McGibbon. 1st ed. NF/dj. S5. $25.00

LEMAY, Alan. *By Dim & Flaring Lamps.* (1962). Harper. 1st ed. F/NF. A18. $40.00

LEMAY, Alan. *Cattle Kingdom.* (1933). Farrar Rinehart. 1st ed. VG+/VG. A18. $60.00

LEMAY, Alan. *Searchers.* 1954. NY. 1st ed. VG/VG. B5. $25.00

LEMAY, Alan. *Unforgiven.* (1957). Harper. 1st ed. NF/VG. A18. $35.00

LEMAY, Alan. *Winter Range.* (1932). Farrar Rinehart. 1st ed. NF/dj. A18. $60.00

LEMLEY, John. *Autobiography & Personal Recollections of...* 1875. Rockford, IL. xl. 12mo. 400 p. gr cloth. G. T3. $19.00

LENFEST, Solomon Augustus. *Diary of...6th MA Infantry...at Suffolk, VA.* 1975. Suffolk-Nansemond Soc. 34 p. VG/wrp. B10. $25.00

LENGYEL, Emil. *Siberia.* 1943. Garden City. 1st ed. 8vo. 8 pls/1 double-p map. VG. W1. $22.00

LENIN, N. *Left Wing Communism.* 1921. Detroit. Marxian Educational Soc. 117 p. wrp. A7. $10.00

LENNOX, Charlotte. *Female Quixote; or, Adventures of Arabella.* 1752. London. Millar. 2nd/revised corrected ed. 12mo. 2 vols. calf, H5. $300.00

LENS, Sidney. *Unrepentant Radical: Am Activist's Account...* ca 1980. Beacon. F/VG. V4. $15.00

LENSKI, Lois. *At Our House. A Read & Sing Book.* 1959. Henry Z Walck. 47 p. VG+. A3. $10.00

LENSKI, Lois. *Indian Captive: Story of Mary Jemison.* (1941). Lippincott. 15th prt. xl. pict gr buckram. G+. T5. $20.00

LENSKI, Lois. *Judy's Journey.* (1947). Lippincott. 5th prt. xl. G. T5. $18.00

LENSKI, Lois. *Little Airplane.* 1938. Oxford. 1st ed. VG+. P2. $30.00

LENSKI, Lois. *Little Engine That Could.* 1930. Platt Munk. red cloth w/pict label. G+/G. A3. $17.50

LENSKI, Lois. *Puritan Adventure.* 1944. Lippincott. 1st ed. 220 p. NF/VG. P2. $75.00

LENSKI, Lois. *San Francisco Boy.* 1955. Lippincott. 1st ed. 176 p. VG+/G+. P2. $25.00

LENSKI, Lois. *Songs of Mr Sm.* 1954. Oxford. 1st ed. 40 p. VG. P2. $45.00

LENSKI, Lois. *We Live in the SW.* 1962. Lippincott. 2nd prt. 8vo. 128 p. VG/G+. A3. $10.50

LENSKI, Lois. *When I Grow Up. A Read & Sing Book.* 1960. Henry Z Walck. 48 p. VG. A3. $7.00

LENTZ, Harold B. *Pop-Up Mother Goose.* 1933. Bl Ribbon. 1st ed. 96 p. NF/dj. B24. $600.00

LENZ, Siegfried. *Exemplary Life.* 1976. Hill Wang/FSG. 1st ed. trans Douglas Parmee. NF/NF. A14. $25.00

LEO, Johannes. *Geographical Historie of Africa...* 1969. Amsterdam/NY. fld map. 3-quarter red leather/blk leather label. NF. O6. $250.00

LEON, A. *Jewish Question: A Marxist Intrepretation.* 1950. Mexico City. Ediciones Pioneras. NF/wrp. B2. $65.00

LEON. *Who'd a Thought It: Improvisation in African-Am Quiltmaking.* 1987. np. G2. $15.00

LEONARD, C.M. *General Assembly of VA, July 30, 1619-Jan 11, 1978.* 1978. VSL. 884 p. VG. B10. $25.00

LEONARD, Elmore. *Bounty Hunters.* 1954. Ballantine. PBO. w/sgn bookplate. NF/unread. A11. $175.00

LEONARD, Elmore. *Freaky Deaky.* (1988). Arbor. bound galley proof. F/wrp. B9. $100.00

LEONARD, Elmore. *Freaky Deaky.* 1988. London. Viking. 1st ed. sgn. F/F. S5. $40.00

LEONARD, Elmore. *Glitz.* (1985). Mysterious. 1/500. sgn. F/slipcase. B9. $50.00

LEONARD, Elmore. *Gunsights.* 1979. Bantam. 1st ed. NF/wrp. B2. $30.00

LEONARD, Elmore. *Hombre.* 1989. Armchair Detective. 1st Am hc ed. 1/100. sgn. F/slipcase. M15. $75.00

LEONARD, Elmore. *Maximum Bob.* 1991. Delacorte. 1st ed. sgn. F/dj. M18. $45.00

LEONARD, Elmore. *Split Images.* 1981. NY. Arbor. 1st ed. dj. A7. $18.00

LEONARD, Elmore. *Stick.* 1983. NY. Arbor. 1st ed. F/F. M15. $35.00

LEONARD, Elmore. *Swag.* 1976. Delacorte. 1st ed. F/F. M15. $100.00

LEONARD, Elmore. *Swag.* 1976. Delacorte. 1st ed. VG/F. B3. $75.00

LEONARD, Elmore. *Touch.* (1987). Arbor. AP. F/wrp. B9. $75.00

LEONARD, Elmore. *Touch.* 1987. NY. Arbor. 1st ed. F/NF. N3. $10.00

LEONARD, Elmore. *Unknown Man No 89.* (1993). Armchair Detective Lib. reissue/ ARC. RS. F/dj. B4. $45.00

LEONARD, Elmore. *52 Pick Up.* 1974. Delacorte. 1st ed. NF/NF. B2. $85.00

LEONARD, Neil. *Jazz & the Wht Americans.* 1962. Chicago. 1st ed. 206 p. VG/dj. M20. $30.00

LEONARD & GOODMAN. *Buffalo Bill: King of the Old W.* 1955. NY. Library Pub. 1st ed. 8vo. 320 p. F/VG+. A2. $20.00

LEONARD & LEONARD. *Mayflies of MI Trout Streams.* 1962. Cranbrook. ils/pls. 139 p. wrp. A17. $10.00

LEONARDO, Richard A. *Hist of Gynecology.* 1944. NY. Frogen. 25 pls. 434 p. G7. $150.00

LEONARDO DA VINCI. *Madrid Codices, Nat Lib, Madrid. Facsimile Ed.* 1976. McGraw Hill. 1/1000. 6 vols. gilt burgandy cloth. Plexiglas box. G7. $1,250.00

LEONE. *Attic Windows.* 1988. np. wrp. G2. $15.00

LEONE. *Fine Hand Quilting.* 1986. np. ils. wrp. G2. $12.95

LEONE. *Sampler Quilt.* 1992. np. wrp. G2. $17.00

LEOPARDI, Giacomo. *Dialoghi.* 1943. Firenze. Liberia del Teatro. miniature. 1/250. red leather. H10. $125.00

LEOPOLD, Nathan. *Life Plus 99 Yrs.* 1958. Doubleday. 1st ed. 381 p. torn dj. A7. $25.00

LERMONT, L. *My Play Is Study: Book for Children.* 1866. Phil. 12mo. 4 hc pls. 110 p. brn cloth. G. H3. $30.00

LERNER, Max. *Mind & Faith of Justice Holmes.* 1943. Modern Lib. M11. $25.00

LEROUX, Gaston. *Machine To Kill.* 1935. Macaulay. 1st Am ed. 254 p. cloth. VG/poor. M20. $35.00

LEROUX, Gaston. *New Idol.* (1929). Macaulay. 1st Am ed. trans Bennett. NF/NF. B4. $150.00

LEROUX, Gaston. *Phantom of the Opera.* (1911). Bobbs Merrill. 1st Am ed. NF. B4. $400.00

LESBERG, Steve. *County Fair.* 1978. NY. Peebles. 1st Am ed. 151 p. NF/dj. B22. $5.50

LESCARBOT, Marc. *Nova Francia. Description of Acadia.* 1606. NY. trans P Erondelle. 346 p. cloth. O2. $25.00

LESCHAK, Peter M. *Letters From Side Lake: Chronicle of Life in N Woods.* (1987). NY. 1st ed. 196 p. F/dj. A17. $14.50

LESLEY, Cole. *Remembered Laughter: Life of Noel Coward.* 1976. Knopf. 1st ed. F/NF clip. M7. $26.50

LESLEY, Craig. *River Song.* 1989. Houghton Mifflin. 1st ed. F/NF. C4. $35.00

LESLEY, Craig. *River Song.* 1989. Houghton Mifflin. 1st trade ed. inscr in month of pub. NF/NF. L3. $65.00

LESLEY, Craig. *Winterkill.* 1984. Houghton Mifflin. 1st ed. author's 1st book. F/F. L3. $85.00

LESLIE, Arthur. *Politics & Poetry of Hugh MacDiarmid.* nd. Glascow. Caledonian Pr. 1st ed. F/wrp. B2. $30.00

LESLIE, Craig. *Winterkill.* 1984. Houghton Mifflin. 1st ed. F/clip. A18. $40.00

LESSA, William A. *Drake's Island of Thieves: Ethnological Sleuthing.* 1975. HI U. ils/ notes/index. 289 p. F. B19. $14.50

LESSER, Graham. *Why? Divine Healing in Medicine & Theology.* ca 1960. NY. Pageant. 144 p. H10. $10.00

LESSING, Doris. *Particularly Cats & More Cats.* 1989. London. Michael Joseph. 1st ed. sgn. ils Anne Robinson. F/F. Q1. $50.00

LESSING, Erich. *Voyages of Ulysses.* 1965. Basle Vienna. Herder Freiburg. 1st ed. F/pict dj/slipcase. M7. $75.00

LESSING, Gotthold Ephraim. *Nathan the Wise: Dramatic Poem.* 1923. NY. Bloch. 2nd ed. 388 p. G+. S3. $30.00

LESSONA, Carlo. *Manuale de Procedura Civile.* 1906. Milano. Societa Editrice Libraria. M11. $25.00

LESSTRANG, Jacques. *Seaway.* 1976. Seattle. Salisbury Pr. 1st ed. VG/dj. A16. $22.50

LESTER, John Erastus. *Atlantic to the Pacific.* 1873. London. 1st ed. 12mo. 293 p. ES. cloth. VG. D3. $45.00

LESTER, Julius. *Revolutionary Notes.* 1969. NY. Richard Baron. 2nd prt. 209 p. dj. A7. $18.00

LESTER & SLEEMAN. *Am's Cup, 1851-1987.* 1986. Sydney. Lester Townsend. 237 p. NF/NF. P4. $40.00

LESY, Michael. *Forbidden Zone.* (1987). NY. FSG. 1st ed. 8vo. 250 p. F/F. A2. $12.50

LESZNER. *Assisi Embroidery: Old Italian Cross Stitch.* nd. np. ils. wrp. G2. $25.00

LETI, Gregorio. *Conclavi de' Pontefici Romani.* 1667-1670. Geneva. De Tournes. 1st ed. 4to. contemporary calf/gilt spine. K1. $375.00

LETT, Lewis. *Papuan Achievement.* 1942. Melbourne. 8vo. ils/fld map. 204 p. gray-gr cloth. VG/worn. H3. $40.00

LETTS, W.M. *Spires of Oxford.* 1917. NY. 1st thus ed. VG/dj. C1. $4.50

LETTSOM, John Coakley. *Natural Hist of the Tea Tree.* 1772. London. 1st Eng-language ed. VG. H5. $1,500.00

LEVACHEZ, Charles Francois G. *Bound Up Collection of 58 Engraved Broadsides.* ca 1795-1800. np. 58 mtd to paper guards. teg. full tan morocco/silk ep. K1. $750.00

LEVENE, Malcolm. *Carder's Paradise.* 1968. Hart Davis. 1st ed. presentation/long inscr. F/F. F4. $35.00

LEVEQUE, Pierre. *Greek Adventure: Cultural & Hist Study of Ancient Greeks.* 1968 (1964). NY. World. 1st Am ed. 8vo. photos/ils. 595 p. VG+/VG+. A2. $15.00

LEVERNE, W.C. *Hist of Sigma Alpha Epsilon: WWI.* 1928. Collegiate Pr. 1st ed. 12mo. VG. A8. $20.00

LEVERTOV, Denise. *Oblique Prayers.* 1984. New Directions. 1st ed. sgn. F/NF. V1. $30.00

LEVERTOV, Denise. *Sorrow Dance.* 1967. New Directions. 1st ed. sgn. NF/NF. V1. $45.00

LEVERTOV, Denise. *Summer Poems.* 1970. Berkeley. Oyez. 1/50 hc. sgn/#d. F/sans. B2. $150.00

LEVI, Primo. *Drowned & the Saved.* 1988. Summit/Simon Schuster. 1st ed. trans from Italian. F/F. A14. $20.00

LEVI, Primo. *Monkey's Wrench.* 1986. Summit/Simon Schuster. 2nd Eng imp. trans from Italian. NF/NF clip. A14. $20.00

LEVIEN, Jack R. *Business Worries.* 1970. Enkhuizen, Holland. miniature. 1st ed. gilt maroon leather. F. B24. $200.00

LEVIN, Ira. *Boys From Brazil.* 1976. Random. 1st ed. F/F. N3. $20.00

LEVIN, Ira. *Silver.* (1991). Bantam. 1st ed. F/dj. B9. $15.00

LEVIN, Ira. *Stepford Wives.* 1972. Random. 1st ed. F/NF clip. N3. $30.00

LEVIN, Meyer. *Anne Frank: Play by Meyer Levin Adapted From Diary A Frank.* nd. private prt. 86 p. VG/wrp. S3. $23.00

LEVIN, Meyer. *Citizens.* ca 1940. Viking. 1st ed. G. V4. $10.00

LEVIN, Nora. *Holocaust: Destruction of European Jewry 1933-45.* 1970. Crowell. 2nd prt. 768 p. VG/VG. S3. $28.00

LEVINE, David. *Fables of Aesop.* 1975. Boston. Gambit. ARC. F/dj. C4. $35.00

LEVINE, David. *No Known Survivors: David Levine's Political Plank.* 1970. Boston. Gambit. preview ed. F/wrp. C4. $30.00

LEVINE, Isaac D. *Stalin.* 1931. Cosmopolitan. ils. 421 p. cloth. B14. $25.00

LEVINE, Ken. *It's Gone!...No, Wait a Minute.* 1993. Villard. 1st ed. F/VG. P8. $14.00

LEVINE, Louis. *Women's Garment Workers.* 1924. Huebsch. xl. 608 p. G. A7. $17.00

LEVINE, Paul. *Night Vision.* 1991. Bantam. 1st ed. sgn. F/F. S5. $35.00

LEVINE, Philip. *Walk w/Thomas Jefferson.* 1988. NY. 1st ed. sgn. F/NF. V1. $30.00

LEVINSON, Edward. *I Break Strikes!* ca 1935. NY. McBride. 1st ed. photos. fair. V4. $20.00

LEVINTHAL, Israel H. *Steering or Drifting: Which?* 1941. Funk Wagnall. 3rd ed. 313 p. G. S3. $19.00

LEVISON, J.J. *Home Book of Trees & Shrubs.* 1949. NY. enlarged ed. photos. 524 p. cloth. A17. $16.50

LEVY, Barbara. *Legacy & Death.* 1973. Prentice Hall. 1st ed. G/G. N2. $12.50

LEVY, Beryl Harold. *Cardozo & Frontiers of Legal Thinking.* 1965. Port WA. Kennikat. M11. $45.00

LEVY, Charles. *Spoils of War.* 1974. Houghton Mifflin. 1st prt. dj. A7. $40.00

LEVY, Edward. *Beast Within.* 1981. NY. Arbor. 1st ed. F/F. N3. $30.00

LEVY, Gertrude Rachel. *Gate of Horn: Study of Religious Conceptions of Stone Age.* 1948. London. Faber. 32 pls. red cloth. G1. $35.00

LEVY. *Patchwork Pillows.* 1977. np. wrp. G2. $6.00

LEVY-BRUHL, Lucien. *Philosophy of Auguste Comte.* 1903. NY. Swan Sonnenschein. 1st Eng-language ed/Am issue. 364 p. russet buckram. G. G1. $50.00

LEWES, George Henry. *Hist of Philosophy From Thales to Comte.* 1871. London. Longman Gr. 4th ed. 2 vols. octavo. gilt plum morocco. NF/box. R3. $375.00

LEWIN, Michael Z. *Enemies Within.* 1974. London. Hamilton. 1st British ed. NF/NF. S5. $22.50

LEWIN, Michael Z. *Way We Die Now.* 1937. Putnam. 1st ed. F/NF. Q1. $75.00

LEWINE & OKRENT. *Ultimate Baseball Book.* 1979. Houghton Mifflin. 1st ed. F/VG+. P8. $100.00

LEWIS, Alfred Henry. *Boss: How He Came To Rule in NY.* 1903. Barnes. 1st ed. inscr/sgn. F. A18. $50.00

LEWIS, Alfred Henry. *Confessions of a Detective.* 1906. NY. Barnes. 1st ed. VG. B9. $20.00

LEWIS, Alfred Henry. *President: A Novel.* 1904. np. 1st ed. ils. NF. A18. $25.00

LEWIS, Alfred Henry. *Sunset Trail.* 1905. NY. Barnes. 1st ed. VG. B9. $15.00

LEWIS, Alfred Henry. *Wolfville Days.* 1902. NY. Stokes. 1st ed. pict red cloth. VG. B9. $65.00

LEWIS, Alfred Henry. *Wolfville.* (1897). Stokes. 1st ed. ils Remington. VG/slipcase. B9. $150.00

LEWIS, Alfred Henry. *Wolfville.* 1897. London. Lawrence Bullen. 1st ed. G+. B9. $125.00

LEWIS, Archibald R. *Nomads & Crusaders AD 1000-1368.* 1991. Bloomington. 8vo. 213 p. cloth. O2. $30.00

LEWIS, Arthur M. *Ten Blind Leaders of the Blind.* ca 1909. Chicago. CH Kerr. 1st ed. sgn. G. V4. $15.00

LEWIS, Benjamin. *Riding: The Balanced Seat.* 1970. Grosset Dunlap. VG/G. O3. $10.00

LEWIS, C. Day. *Short Is the Time: Poems 1936-43.* 1945. NY. Oxford. 1st ed. F/NF. C4. $30.00

LEWIS, C.S. *Allegory of Love.* ca 1936. London. Oxford. 378 p. H10. $25.00

LEWIS, Charles D. *Waterboys & Their Cousins.* (1918). Lippincott. ils EH Suydam. 172 p. VG. S10. $20.00

LEWIS, Deborah; see Grant, Charles L.

LEWIS, Georgina King. *John Greenleaf Whittier.* nd. London. Headley Bros. 8vo. 221 p. fair. V3. $12.50

LEWIS, Gernard. *Muslim Discovery in Europe.* 1982. NY. ils. 350 p. cloth. dj. O2. $30.00

LEWIS, Henry. *Valley of the MS Ils.* ca 1967. St Paul. MN Hist Soc. lg 8vo. 1/200. map ep. cloth. dj. H9. $65.00

LEWIS, Jan. *Pursuit of Happiness: Family & Values in Jefferson's VA.* 1983. Cambridge U. 290 p. VG/VG. B10. $25.00

LEWIS, Janet. *Ghost of Monsieur Scarron.* 1959. Garden City. 1st ed. sgn. NF/NF. A11. $50.00

LEWIS, Janet. *Hangar at Sunnyvale, 1937.* 1947. San Francisco. 1/375. Masque Pr. postscript/dtd 1987. A11. $45.00

LEWIS, John Wilson. *Leadership in Communist China.* 1963. Cornell. 1st ed. 8vo. 305 p. VG. W1. $20.00

LEWIS, LEWIS & RIGDON. *Four Men: Living the Revolution...* ca 1977. Urbana. IL U. photos. F/fair. V4. $8.00

LEWIS, Lloyd. *Capt Sam Grant.* 1950. Little Brn. 1st ed. 484 p. VG/dj. M20. $20.00

LEWIS, Lloyd. *Myths After Lincoln.* ca 1941. NY. Readers Club. 8vo. intro Sandburg. 367 p. cream cloth. G. T3. $10.00

LEWIS, Lloyd. *Myths After Lincoln.* 1941. Readers Club. fwd Carl Sandburg. VG/VG. E3. $15.00

LEWIS, Naomi. *Once Upon a Rainbow.* 1981. London. Cape. ils Eichenauer. 1st ed. 31 p. VG/VG. A3. $15.00

LEWIS, Nolan D.C. *Short Hist of Psychiatric Achievement...* 1941. Norton. 1st ed. sm 8vo. 275 p. VG/dj. G1. $25.00

LEWIS, Oscar. *Bay Window Bohemia.* 1956. NY. 1st ed. 248 p. cloth. NF/pict dj. D3. $25.00

LEWIS, Oscar. *Big Four: Story of Huntington, Stanford, Hopkins & Crocker.* 1938. Knopf. 8vo. 418 p. bl brds. B11. $30.00

LEWIS, Oscar. *Lola Montez.* 1938. San Francisco. 1/750. sgn. red brds. VG+/sans. A11. $50.00

LEWIS, Oscar. *San Francisco Since 1872: Pict Hist of 7 Decades.* 1946. Ray Oil Burner. ils/poems Milton S Ray. 101 p. NF/sans. B19. $30.00

LEWIS, Oscar. *Sutter's Fort: Gateway to the Gold Fields.* 1966. Prentice Hall. ils/index. 222 p. F/VG clip. B19. $20.00

LEWIS, Oscar. *Town That Died Laughing.* 1955. Little Brn. 1st ed. F/G. H7. $15.00

LEWIS, Oswald R. *Superior Sires. Vol II.* 1947. Hutchinson. 1st ed. G+. O3. $35.00

LEWIS, Peter. *John Le Carre.* 1985. Ungar. 1st ed. F/F. S5. $25.00

LEWIS, Roy Harley. *Bloodeagle.* 1993. London. Collins. 1st ed. F/F. S5. $22.50

LEWIS, Roy Harley. *Cracking of Spines.* 1982. St Martin. 1st Am ed. F/ NF. M15. $35.00

LEWIS, Roy Harley. *Where Agents Fear To Tread.* 1984. London. Hale. 1st ed. F/F. S5. $30.00

LEWIS, Sinclair. *Babbitt.* 1922. Harcourt Brace. 1st ed/1st issue (Purdy for Lyte on p 49). VG+/clip. Q1. $500.00

LEWIS, Sinclair. *Babbitt.* 1922. Toronto. McLeod. 1st Canadian ed/2nd state. VG+/sans. C4. $50.00

LEWIS, Sinclair. *Babbitt.* 1946. Bantam. 1st pb ed. 408 p. VG/pict wrp/dj. M20. $40.00

LEWIS, Sinclair. *Godseeker.* 1949. Random. 1st ed. 422 p. VG/dj. M20. $17.50

LEWIS, Sinclair. *Main Street.* 1937. Lakeside Pr. LED. 1/1500. ils/sgn Grant Wood. NF/G slipcase. B4. $500.00

LEWIS, Sinclair. *Our Mr Wrenn: Romantic Adventures of a Gentle Man.* 1914. NY. Harper. 1st ed. stp Advance Copy on title page. F. B24. $350.00

LEWIS, Virgil A. *Story of the LA Purchase.* 1903. St Louis. Woodward Tiernan. 12mo. 300 p. F. A2. $20.00

LEWIS, W.H. *Levantine Adventurer. Travels & Missions of...d'Arvieux...* 1963. NY. 1st Am ed. 8vo. 232 p. cloth. dj. O2. $25.00

LEWIS, W.M. *People's Practical Poultry Book...* ca 1871. NY. Moore. 223 p. H10. $18.50

LEWIS, Wyndham. *Apes of God.* 1930. London. Arthur Pr. 1/750. sgn/#d. VG/VG. Q1. $450.00

LEWIS, Wyndham. *Revenge for Love.* 1952. Chicago. Regnery. 1st Am ed. F/NF. B2. $45.00

LEWIS, Wyndham. *Rotting Hill.* 1952. Chicago. Regnery. 1st Am ed. F/NF. B2. $25.00

LEWIS & CLARK. *Orig Journals of Lewis & Clark Expediton, 1804-1806.* 1969. Arno Pr. intro Bernard DeVoto. 8 vols. M/slipcase. A18. $250.00

LEWIS & LEWIS. *Wallace Stegner.* 1972. Boise State. sgn Stegner. 48-p pamphlet. M. A18. $30.00

LEYDEN, E. *Traite Clinique des Maladies de la Moelle Epinere...* 1879. Paris. Bailliere. 1st French from 1st German ed. 800 p. quarter morocco. G7. $150.00

LEYDET, Francois. *Tomorrow's Wilderness.* (1963). Sierra Club. ils Ansel Adams. 262 p. F/dj. A17. $14.50

LEYELL, Charles. *Geological Evidences of Antiquity of Man...* 1863. Phil. Childs. 1st Am ed. lg 8vo. ils/pls. gilt bl cloth. F. K1. $175.00

LEYNER, Mark. *Et Tu, Babe.* (1992). Harmony Books. 1st ed. sgn. M/dj. B4. $45.00

LEZARD, Adele. *Great Gold Reef.* 1937. Indianapolis. 1st ed. ils 313 p. orange cloth. F/G. H3. $45.00

LIBBY, Bill. *Charlie O & the Angry A's.* 1975. Doubleday. 1st ed. VG+/G+. P8. $12.50

LIBBY, Bill. *Fred Lynn: Young Star.* 1977. Putnam. 1st ed. F/F. P8. $15.00

LIBBY, Bill. *Heroes of the Hot Corner.* 1972. Watts. 1st ed. F/G+. P8. $22.50

LIBBY, Bill. *Thurman Munson, Pressure Player.* 1978. Putnam. 1st ed. photos. F/F. P8. $20.00

LIBBY & ROSEBORO. *Glory Days w/the Dodgers.* 1978. Atheneum. 1st ed. F/VG+. P8. $30.00

LIBERMAN, Alex. *Artist in His Studio.* 1960. NY. 1st ed. VG/G+. A1. $50.00

LIBRARY OF CONGRESS. *Children's Books in Rare Book Division of Lib of Congress.* 1975. Totowa, NJ. Rowan Littlefield. 2 vols. F. F1. $115.00

LICETI, Fortunio. *De Lucernis Antiquorium Reconditis Libb Quatuor...* 1621. Venice. Evangelistam Deuch. 1st ed. 416 p. old calf. rare. K1. $850.00

LIDDELL & WATANABE. *Japanese Quilts.* 1988. np. 1st collection to be pub in W. cloth. G2. $35.00

LIDELL, Hart. *Lawrence of Arabia.* 1935. London. Cassell. 1st ed. 464 p. dk gr cloth. M7. $30.00

LIDELL, Hart. *Sword & the Pen.* 1978. London. Cassell. 1st ed. 282 p. NF/NF/clear plastic. M7. $55.00

LIEB, Fred. *Baltimore Orioles.* 1955. Putnam. 1st ed. VG. P8. $135.00

LIEB, Fred. *Baseball, As I Have Known It.* 1972. Coward McCann BC. F. P8. $27.50

LIEB, Fred. *Boston Red Sox.* 1947. Putnam. 1st ed. VG/G+. P8. $65.00

LIEB, Fred. *Connie Mack.* 1945. Putnam. 1st ed. G+. P8. $35.00

LIEB, Fred. *Detroit Tigers.* 1946. Putnam. 1st ed. sgn by Hall-of-Fame players. VG+/VG. P8. $600.00

LIEBER, Francis. *Letter to His Excellency Patrick Noble, Governor of SC...* (1839). np. 1st ed. 8vo. 62 p. disbound. M1. $225.00

LIEBERG, Owen. *1st Air Race: Internat Competition at Reims.* 1909. Garden City. 1st ed. ils. 229 p. VG/dj. B18. $22.50

LIEBKNECHT, Karl. *Future Belongs to the People.* 1918. Macmillan. 1st ed. NF. B2. $60.00

LIEBKNECHT, Karl. *Militarism.* 1917. Huebsch. 3rd prt. 178 p. A7. $22.00

LIEBKNECHT, Karl. *Militarism.* 1917. NY. Huebsch. 1st ed. NF/NF. B2. $75.00

LIEUTAUD, Joseph. *Historia Anatomico-Medica...* 1786-87. Longosalissae. 2 vols. contemporary brds. G7. $295.00

LIEUWEN, Edwin. *Venezuela.* 1963. London. Allen unwin. 1st ed. 8vo. 22 pls. 252 p. VG/VG. B11. $20.00

LIFCHEZ, Raymond. *Devish Lodge. Architecture, Art & Sufism in Ottoman Turkey.* 1952. London. Bodley Head. 1st ed. 8vo. 485 p. cloth. dj. O2. $35.00

LIFTON, Robert. *Home for the War.* (1973). Simon Schuster. 1st ed. 478 p. F/NF. A7. $35.00

LIGETI, Louis. *Subhasitaratnanidhi Mongol.* 1948. Budapest. 124 photos. wrp. N2. $25.00

LIGHTFOOT, Claude M. *Civil War & Blk Liberation Today.* (1969). New Outlook. 15 p. wrp. A7. $15.00

LILES. *Art & Craft of Natural Dyeing, Traditional Recipes...* 1990. np. wrp. G2. $19.50

LILEY. *Craft of Embroidery.* 1971. np. cloth. G2. $10.00

LILLY, John C. *Center of the Cyclone.* 1972. NY. Julian Pr. 3rd prt. 222 p. cloth. VG/dj. G1. $22.50

LILLY, Lambert. *Early Hist of S States: VA, N & SC & GA.* 1847. Boston. Ticknor. sm 12mo. 192 p. gilt brn cloth. H9. $65.00

LIMERICK, P.N. *Legacy of Conquest: Unbroken Past of Am W.* (1987). Norton. 1st ed. inscr/sgn. photos/bibliography. F/F. A18. $30.00

LINARES & RANERS. *Adaptive Radiations in Prehistoric Panama.* 1980. Peabody Mus Monograph 5. 384 p. wrp. F3. $35.00

LINCOFF & MITCHEL. *Toxic & Hallucinogenic Mushroom Poisoning.* 1977. NY. 28 color photos. 267 p. VG. B26. $30.00

LINCOLN, C. Eric. *Blk Muslims in Am.* 1961. Boston. Beacon. 1st ed. red cloth. VG/dj. B14. $35.00

LINCOLN, Elliott C. *Rhymes of a Homesteader.* 1920. Houghton Mifflin. 12mo. G. A8. $10.00

LINCOLN, Victoria. *Charles.* 1962. BC. VG/torn. C1. $4.50

LIND, Alan R. *Chicago Surface Lines: Ils Hist.* 1974. Transport Hist. VG/dj. A16. $20.00

LIND, L.R. *Berengario da Carpi on Fracture of the Skull or Cranium.* 1990 (1518). Am Philosophical Soc. new trans. 164 p. H9. $30.00

LIND. *Knitting in the Nordic Tradition.* 1984. np. ils. cloth. G2. $25.00

LINDBERGH, Ann Morrow. *Gift From the Sea.* (1955). Pantheon. 1st ed. ils George W Thompson. F/box. B3. $20.00

LINDBERGH, Anne Morrow. *Listen! The Wind.* 1938. Harcourt Brace. 1st ed. NF/NF. Q1. $100.00

LINDBERGH, Anne Morrow. *N to the Orient.* 1935. Harcourt Brace. 1st ed. NF/NF. Q1. $100.00

LINDBERGH, Charles A. *Of Flight & Life.* 1948. Scribner. G/dj. A16. $20.00

LINDBERGH, Charles A. *Spirit of St Louis.* 1953. Scribner. 1st ed. G/dj. A16. $50.00

LINDERMAN, Frank B. *Stumpy.* 1933. Jr Literary Guild/Day. VG/dj. B9. $35.00

LINDERMAN & REISS. *Blackfeet Indians.* 1935. Great N Railway. 1st ed. quarto. 65 p. red brds. F/dj/mailing envelope. B24. $450.00

LINDHEIM, Irma L. *Immortal Adventure.* 1928. Macaulay. 2nd prt. 279 p. G+. S3. $24.00

LINDLEY, George. *Guide to the Orchard & Fruit Garden.* 1846. NY. Riker. 2nd ed. 420 p. cloth. H10. $145.00

LINDLEY, Walter. *CA of the S: Its Physical Geography...* 1888. Appleton. 1st ed. 3 fld maps. red pict cloth. NF. H7. $75.00

LINDMAN, M. *Holiday Time.* 1952. Whitman. 1st ed. xl. cloth w/color pl. VG. scarce. M5. $15.00

LINDQUIST, Jennie D. *Golden Name Day.* (1955). Harper Row. xl. 248 p. VG/glassine. T5. $25.00

LINDSAY, Cynthia. *Dear Boris: Life of William Henry Pratt aka Boris Karloff.* 1975. Knopf. 1st ed. inscr by Boris Karloff's widow. NF/NF. B4. $75.00

LINDSAY, Jack. *Marc Antony: His World & His Contemporaries.* 1936. London. Routledge. 1st ed. 8vo. 13 pls. 330 p. F-/VG. A2. $50.00

LINDSAY, Norman. *Magic Pudding.* nd. Farrar Rinehart. 1st Am ed. G. P2. $40.00

LINDSAY, Robert Bruce. *Role of Science in Civilization.* 1963. Harper Row. 1st ed. 318 p. cream cloth. VG/dj. G1. $17.50

LINDSAY, Vachel. *Congo & Other Poems.* 1922. NY. later prt. inscr/drawing. VG. A11. $85.00

LINDSAY, Vachel. *Golden Whales of CA.* 1920. NY. 1st ed. 181 p. pict cloth. VG. D3. $45.00

LINDSAY, Walter. *This Wooden Pig Went w/Dora.* 1930. McBridem. 1st ed. ils James Reid. cloth. VG/worn dj. M5. $18.00

LINDSELL, Harold. *Battle for the Bible.* 1977. Grand Rapids. Zondervan. index. 218 p. H10. $15.00

LINDSEY, N. Allen. *Cruising in the Madiana.* 1901. Boston. 1st ed. 1/300. 12mo. 192 p. gilt bl cloth. VG. H3. $40.00

LINDUSKA, Joseph P. *Waterfowl Tomorrow.* (1964). US Dept Interior. 770 p. A17. $10.00

LINE & RUSSELL. *Audubon Soc Book of Wild Birds.* (1976). Abrams. lg 4to. color photos. 292 p. F/dj. A17. $19.50

LINEDECKER & RYAN. *Kerry: Agent Orange & an Am Family.* (1982). St Martin. 1st ed. F/F. A7. $30.00

LINFIELD, Harry S. *Jews in the US, 1927: Study of Their Number & Distribution.* 1929. AJC. 111 p. VG. S3. $40.00

LINGENFELTER, Richard E. *Presses of the Pacific Islands, 1817-67: A Hist...* 1967. LA. Plantin Pr. 1/500. sgn. ils Edgar Dorsey Taylor. M. O6. $275.00

LINK, Howard A. *Theatrical Prts of the Torii Masters.* 1977. Honolulu/Tokyo. 1st ed. 4to. ils. 119 p. F/dj. W1. $20.00

LINK, Louis W. *Lewis & Clark Expedition, 1804-06.* 1964. Cardwell, MT. self pub. 8vo. 111 p. M. T8. $10.00

LINN, Bill. *Missing in Action.* (1981). Avon. PBO. NF. A7. $15.00

LINN, Louis. *Frontiers in General Hospital Psychiatry.* 1961. NY. IUP. 1st ed. 483 p. gray cloth. VG/dj. G1. $27.50

LINSCOTT, E.H. *Folk Songs of Old New Eng.* 1939. NY. Macmillan. 1st ed. 8vo. 337 p. F. A2. $30.00

LINSLEY. *Am's Favorite Quilts.* 1983. np. cloth. G2. $20.00

LINSLEY. *Quilter's Country Christmas.* 1990. np. cloth. G2. $22.00

LINSLEY. *Quilts Across Am.* 1988. np. ils. cloth. G2. $25.00

LINSLEY. *Weekend Quilter.* 1986. np. cloth. G2. $20.00

LINTON, W.J. *Master of Wood Engraving.* 1889. New Haven. self pub. lg paper ed. thick folio. 230 p. sgn. F. F1. $750.00

LIOTTA, P.H. *Learning To Fly: A Season w/the Peregrine Falcon.* 1989. Algonquin. 1st prt. 201 p. F/dj. A17. $9.50

LIPMAN, David. *Bob Gibson.* 1975. Putnam. 1st ed. sgn Gibson. F. P8. $65.00

LIPMAN, Jean. *Rufus Porter: Rediscovered.* 1980. NY. Potter/Crown. 22 color pls. 212 p. cloth. dj. D2. $65.00

LIPMAN, Michael. *Chatterlings in Wordland.* 1935. Wise Parslow. revised ed. 4to. 112 p. cloth. VG. A3. $19.50

LIPMAN & WINCHESTER. *Primitive Painters in Am, 1750-1950.* 1950. NY. 1st ed. 182 p. VG/torn. B18. $35.00

LIPPINCOTT, Horace Mather. *Portraiture of People Called Quakers.* 1915. Phil. WH Jenkins. 8vo. 116 p. missing spine/broken hinge. V3. $12.00

LIPSET, David. *Gregory Bateson: Legacy of a Scientist.* 1980. Prentice Hall. 1st ed. 360 p. brn cloth. VG/dj. G1. $30.00

LIPSETT. *Remember Me: Women & Their Friendship Quilts.* 1985. np. ils. wrp. G2. $20.00

LIPSETT. *To Love & To Cherish.* 1989. np. wrp. G2. $20.00

LISH, Gordon. *Dear Mr Capote.* (1983). HRW. 1st ed. author's 1st novel. F/F. B3. $40.00

LISH, Gordon. *What I Know So Far.* (1983). HRW. ARC. RS. F/F. B3. $35.00

LISLE, Clifton. *Pastures New: Hill Farm in the Making.* 1955. NY. 1st prt. 12mo. 241 p. VG/VG. B28. $20.00

LISPECTOR, Clarice. *Hour of the Star.* 1986. Manchester. Carcanet. 1st ed. trans from Portuguese. NF/NF. A14. $25.00

LISS, Howard. *Boston Red Sox.* 1982. Simon Schuster. 1st ed. F/VG+. P8. $17.50

LISS, Howard. *Triple Crown Winners.* 1969. Messner. 1st ed. F/G+. P8. $27.50

LISTON, ROBERT A. *Dissent in Am.* (1971). McGraw Hill. 158 p. dj. A7. $15.00

LISTOWEL, Judith. *Hapsburg Tragedy: Crown Prince Rudolf.* 1986. Dorset. VG/dj. A16. $9.00

LISTOWEL, Judith. *Other Livingstone.* (1974). Scribner. 1st Am ed. 8vo. 292 p. F/F. A2. $15.00

LITCHFIELD, P.W. *Autumn Leaves.* 1945. Cleveland. 1st ed. 125 p. VG/torn. B18. $17.50

LITTELL, Robert. *Sisters.* 1986. London. Cape. 1st British ed. F/F. S5. $25.00

LITTLE, Arthur West. *From Harlem to the Rhine. Story of NY's Colored Volunteers.* 1936. Covici Friede. 1st ed. 382 p. NF/VG. M8. $75.00

LITTLE, Ezekiel. *Usher: Comprising Arithmetic in Whole Hundreds...* 1799. Exeter. H Ranlet. 240 p. contemporary sheep/label. B14. $85.00

LITTLE, Frances. *Lady of the Decoration.* 1940. Appleton. VG. E3. $15.00

LITTLE, George. *Am Cruisers Own Book.* 1859. Phil. JB Smith. 584 p. emb cloth. P4. $75.00

LITTLE, Jean. *Chitty Chitty Bang Bang.* 1968. Little Golden Book. 1st ed. 24 p. VG-. A3. $8.50

LITTLE, John Peyton. *Hist of Richmond.* 1933. Richmond, VA. Dietz. 8vo. 303 p. cloth. H9. $30.00

LITTLE, Nina Fletcher. *Asahel Powers: Painter of Vermont Faces.* 1973. Williamsburg. 49 p. wrp. D2. $15.00

LITTLE, Nina Fletcher. *Some Old Brookline Houses Built...Before 1825...* 1949. Brookline. ils. 160 p. bl cloth. F. B14. $55.00

LITTLE & RIGHTER. *Botanical Descriptions of 40 Artificial Pine Hybrids.* 1965. WA, DC. ils. 47 p. VG+/wrp. B26. $22.50

LITTLEBIRD, Harold. *On Mtn's Breath.* 1982. Tooth of Time. 1/750. F/wrp. L3. $35.00

LITTLEFIELD, Bill. *Prospect.* (1989). Houghton Mifflin. ARC. author's 1st book. VG/pict wrp. B3. $50.00

LITTLEJOHN. *Aesop's Fables.* 6 pop-ups/stories. F. A4. $35.00

LITTLETON, Thomas. *Littleton's Tenures in Eng.* 1825. London. Butterworth. later full calf. M11. $125.00

LITTLETON, William G. *Battle Between the AL & Kearsage...France...June 19, 1864.* 1933. Phil. 1st ed. 9 p. F/prt wrp. M8. $37.50

LITTLETON, William G. *Cumberland, Monitor & the VA (Popularly Called Merrimac).* 1933. Phil. 1st ed. 19 p. F/prt wrp. M8. $37.50

LITVAK. *Three-Dimensional Needlepoint.* 1984. np. ils. cloth. G2. $16.00

LITWEILER, John. *Freedom Principle. Jazz After 1958.* 1984. Morrow. 1st ed. F/NF. B2. $35.00

LIVELY, Adam. *Blue Fruit.* 1988. NY. Atlantic Monthly. 1st ed. F/NF. A7. $12.00

LIVELY, Chauncy. *Chauncy Lively's Flybox: Portfolio of Modern Trout Flies.* (1980). Stackpole. 96 p. F/wrp. A17. $20.00

LIVELY, Penelope. *Moon Tiger.* (1988). Grove. 1st ed. F/F. B3. $20.00

LIVERMORE, H.V. *New Hist of Portugal.* 1966. Cambridge. ils/maps. M/dj. O6. $45.00

LIVERMORE, Mary A. *My Story of the War.* 1890. Hartford. xl. 8vo. 700 p. bl cloth. T3. $33.00

LIVINGSTON, A.D. *Fishing for Bass: Modern Tactics & Tackle.* (1974). Lippincott. 1st ed. ils/index. 256 p. VG/worn. A17. $12.50

LIVINGSTON, Nancy. *Incident at Paraga.* 1987. London. Gollancz. 1st ed. F/F. S5. $25.00

LIVINGSTON, William S. *Federalism & Constitutional Change.* 1956. Clarendon. M11. $45.00

LIVINGSTONE, David. *Adventures & Discoveries of Dr David Livingstone...* 1872. Hubbard. 598 p. gilt brn cloth. VG. M20. $50.00

LLEWELLYN, Bernard. *I Left My Roots in China.* 1953. Oxford. 1st ed. 8vo. 15 pls. 175 p. VG/dj. W1. $18.00

LLEWELLYN, Sam. *Blood Orange.* 1989. NY. Summit. ARC of 1st Am ed. w/promo material & photo. F/F. S5. $25.00

LLEWELLYN, Sam. *Gurney's Reward.* 1978. London. Arlington. 1st ed. NF/NF. M15. $85.00

LLOSA, Mario Vargas; see Vargas Llosa, Mario.

LLOYD, Arthur. *Every-Day Japan, Written After 25 Yrs' Residence...* 1909. London. Cassell. 1st ed. xl. ils/pls. 318 p. VG. W1. $45.00

LLOYD, John Uri. *Etidorhpa; or, End of Earth.* (1901). Dodd Mead. 11th ed. revised/enlarged. full-p inscr. F. B4. $150.00

LLOYD, John Uri. *Red Head.* 1903. Dodd Mead. ils Reginald Birch. 208 p. VG. S10. $55.00

LLOYD, John. *Thesaurus Ecclesiasticus: Improved Ed of Liber Valorum...* 1788. London. Lockyer Davis. index. 504 p. brds. H10. $57.50

LLOYD, Seton. *Early Highland Peoples of Anatolia.* 1967. NY. 8vo. 144 p. cloth. dj. O2. $25.00

LOBAGOLA. *African Savage's Own Story.* 1970. NY. Negro U. rerprint. 8vo. 402 p. bl cloth. M/sans. P4. $22.00

LOBSTEIN, J.F. Daniel. *Dialogues Between Patients & Physican...* 1829. NY. 1st (only?) ed. 144 p. cloth. VG. G7. $125.00

LOCH, Joyce Nankivell. *Fringe of Bl: An Autobiography.* 1968. NY. 1st Am ed. 8vo. 243 p. cloth. dj. O2. $35.00

LOCH, Sydney. *Athos: Holy Mtn.* 1957. NY. 1st Am ed. 8vo. 264 p. cloth. dj. O2. $45.00

LOCHER, A. *With Star & Crescent.* 1899. Phil. 8vo. 634 p. cloth. O2. $55.00

LOCHTE, Dick. *Bl Bayou.* 1992. NY. Simon Schuster. ARC of 1st ed. sgn. RS. F/F. S5. $35.00

LOCKE, John. *Abridgment Mr Locke's Essay Concerning Human Understanding.* 1794. Boston. Manning Loring. 1st Am ed. 12mo. 250 p. old calf. M1. $375.00

LOCKE, John. *Essay Concerning Humane Understanding.* 1690. London. Holt Bassett. 1st ed/1st issue. folio. contemporary calf. case. H5. $35,000.00

LOCKER, Frederick. *London Rhymes.* 1894. NY. 1st ed. NF. V1. $35.00

LOCKHART, R.H. *Memoirs of a British Agent.* July 1933. London. Putnam. 1st ed/7th imp. 455 p. VG+/VG/clear plastic. M7. $45.00

LOCKHART, R.H. Bruce. *Retreat From Glory.* 1934. Putnam. 1st ed. 8vo. VG+. A8. $15.00

LOCKLEY, Ronald. *Birds & Islands. Travels in Wild Places.* 1991. London. Witherby. 1st ed. 8vo. 237 p. M/dj. P4. $24.00

LODGE, Henry Cabot. *HI.* (1910). Boston. Marshall Jones. photos/fld map. gilt cloth. F. A17. $27.50

LODI, Maria. *Charlotte Morel.* 1969. Putnam. 1st Am ed of 1965 1st ed. trans from French. VG+/VG. A14. $20.00

LODOR, John A. *In Memoriam: Address Commorative of Their Fraternal Dead...* 1861. Cahaba. CE Haynes. 1st ed. NF/prt wrp. M8. $150.00

LODOR, John A. *Speculative Temple. An Address...1861* 1862. Montgomery. Advertiser Book & Job Office. 1st ed. 16 p. NF/wrp. M8. $125.00

LOEB, Robert H. Jr. *New Wolf in Chef's Clothing.* 1958. Chicago. Follett. G/dj. A16. $8.00

LOEB. *PA Dutch Needlepoint Designs.* 1976. np. pb. ils/charts. G2. $3.00

LOELL, Marc. *How Gr Was My Apple.* 1984. Doubleday. 1st Am ed. F/F. S5. $20.00

LOEWENBERG, J. *Reason & Nature of Things: Reflections...Philosophy.* 1959. LaSalle, IL. Open Court. orig ed. 382 p. bl cloth. NF. S9. $5.00

LOEWENSTEIN, Karl. *Brazil Under Vargas.* 1942. Macmillan. 1st ed. 8vo. 381 p. F/VG. A2. $20.00

LOFTING, Hugh. *Dr Dolittle & the Gr Canary.* (1950). Lippincott. 9th prt. 8vo. 276 p. pict yel cloth. VG+/VG. T5. $30.00

LOFTING, Hugh. *Dr Dolittle in the Moon.* 1928. Stokes. G. A16. $35.00

LOFTING, Hugh. *Dr Dolittle's Caravan.* 1954 (1924). Lippincott. 8vo. 266 p. pict yel brds. VG. T5. $15.00

LOFTING, Hugh. *Dr Dolittle's Garden.* (1955). Lippincott. 15th prt. 8vo. 327 p. VG/VG. D1. $40.00

LOFTING, Hugh. *Dr Dolittle's Return.* (1933). Lippincott. 8th prt. 8vo. 273 p. pict orange cloth. VG/worn. T5. $25.00

LOFTING, Hugh. *Dr Dolittle's Zoo.* nd. Lippincott. 23rd prt. 338 p. cloth. VG/G. A3. $15.00

LOFTING, Hugh. *Dr Dolittle's Zoo.* 1925. Stokes. 1st ed. 338 p. G. P2. $18.00

LOFTING, Hugh. *Story of Dr Dolittle.* 1925. Stokes. 17th prt. sgn. 180 p. orange cloth. VG. D1. $100.00

LOFTING, Hugh. *Voyages of Dr Dolittle.* 1939 (1922). Stokes. ils. 364 p. VG+/G. P2. $30.00

LOFTUS & MCINTYRE. *Valhalla's Wake.* (1989). Atlantic Monthly. 1st ed. 236 p. F/F clip. A7. $15.00

LOGAN, Daniel. *Am Bewitched: Rise of Blk Magic & Spiritism.* 1974. Morrow. 1st ed. dj. VG. N2. $10.00

LOGAN, H.C. *Underhammer Guns.* 1960. np. ils. 249 p. O7. $18.50

LOGAN, Herschel. *Pirates.* 1979. Santa Ana. Log-Anne Pr. miniature. sgn. cloth. F. H10. $25.00

LOGAN, Jeffrey. *Complete Book of Outer Space.* 1953. Gnome. 1st ed. F/dj. M2. $150.00

LOGAN, Kate Virginia Cox. *My Confederate Girlhood: Memoirs of...* 1932. Garrett Massie. 1st ed. 150 p. VG/fair. B10. $45.00

LOGAN. *Designs in Patchwork.* 1987. np. ils. cloth. G2. $20.00

LOHRMAN, H.P. *Hist of Early Tuscarawas Co, OH...for the Schools.* 1930. New Phil, OH. 54 p. G/wrp. D7. $20.00

LOKOS, Lionel. *House Divided.* (1968). New Rochelle. Arlington. 1st ed. 567 p. VG/VG. A7. $25.00

LOMATEWAMA, Ramson. *Silent Winds.* 1983. Htevilla. Lomatewama. sgn. NF/wrp. L3. $30.00

LOMAX, Alan. *Folk Songs of N Am in the Eng Language.* 1960. Doubleday. 8vo. 623 p. blk cloth. G. B11. $25.00

LOMAX, John A. *Songs of the Cattle Train & Cow Camp.* 1919. NY. 1st ed. 189 p. orange cloth. B14. $20.00

LOMAX & LOMAX. *Am Ballads & Folk Songs.* (1967). NY. 21st prt. xl. 625 p. cloth. NF/pict dj. D3. $25.00

LOMAX & LOMAX. *Negro Folk Songs As Sung by Lead Belley...* 1936. Macmillan. 1st ed. ils. 242 p. red buckram. F. B14. $200.00

LOMAX & STANLEY. *Treasury of Baseball Humor.* 1950. Lantern. 1st ed. G+. P8. $15.00

LONDON, Jack. *Abysmal Brute.* 1913. NY. Century. 1st ed/1st issue. olive cloth. NF/dj. B24. $1,500.00

LONDON, Jack. *Burning Daylight.* nd. Grosset Dunlap. photoplay ed. NF/NF. B2. $75.00

LONDON, Jack. *Call of the Wild.* 1912. Macmillan. 1st thus ed. ils Paul Bransom (lacks 1 pl). 254 p. VG. D3. $45.00

LONDON, Jack. *Call of the Wild.* 1919. Macmillan. VG. E3. $12.00

LONDON, Jack. *Cruise of the Snark.* 1911. Macmillan. 1st ed. octavo. 340 p. teg. gilt bl cloth. NF. H5. $600.00

LONDON, Jack. *Game.* 1905. London. Heinemann. 1st Eng ed. 12mo. 182 p. gilt bdg. VG. D3. $75.00

LONDON, Jack. *God of His Fathers.* 1902. Isbister. 1st Eng ed. G. M18. $100.00

LONDON, Jack. *Iron Heel.* 1908. Girard, KS. Appeal to Reason Pr. variant 1st ed. bl pict cloth. VG. D3. $100.00

LONDON, Jack. *Jerry of the Islands.* 1917. Macmillan. 1st ed. NF. B4. $200.00

LONDON, Jack. *John Barleycorn.* August 1913. NY. Century. 1st ed. ils HT Dunn. F. B14. $150.00

LONDON, Jack. *Love of Life & Other Stories.* ca 1906. NY. Regent. VG. V4. $7.50

LONDON, Jack. *Michael, Brother of Jerry.* 1917. Macmillan. 1st ed. NF. B4. $225.00

LONDON, Jack. *Moon-Face & Other Stories.* 1906. Macmillan. 1st ed. 12mo. 273 p. teg. bl cloth. VG. D3. $95.00

LONDON, Jack. *Moon-Face & Other Stories.* 1906. NY. Macmillan. 1st ed. bl cloth. NF. B24. $285.00

LONDON, Jack. *Night-Born.* 1913. Bell Cockburn. 1st Canadian ed. G. M18. $100.00

LONDON, Jack. *On the Makaloa Mat.* 1919. NY. Macmillan. 1st ed. teal cloth. NF. B24. $250.00

LONDON, Jack. *People of the Abyss.* 1903. Macmillan. 1st ed. G. M18. $350.00

LONDON, Jack. *Scarlet Plague.* 1915. NY. Macmillan. 1st ed. VG+. Q1. $300.00

LONDON, Jack. *Scorn of Women.* 1906. London. Macmillan. 1st ed. stp red cloth. NF. Q1. $1,500.00

LONDON, Jack. *Sea Wolf.* nd (ca 1926). London. Readers Lib. VG+/VG+. A11. $55.00

LONDON, Jack. *Smoke Bellew.* 1912. Century. 1st ed. VG. M18. $100.00

LONDON, Jack. *Tales of the Fish Patrol.* 1905. NY. Macmillan. 1st ed. ils George Varian. dk bl cloth. NF. B24. $325.00

LONDON, Jack. *War of the Classes.* ca 1905. NY. Regent. VG. V4. $7.50

LONDON, Jack. *Wht Fang.* 1906. Macmillan. 1st ed. G. M18. $100.00

LONDON, Jack. *Wht Fang.* 1906. Macmillan. 1st ed. 8 color pls. 327 p. pict ep. bl-gray cloth. VG. D3. $100.00

LONDON YEARLY MEETING. *Extracts From Minutes & Advices of Yearly Meeting.* 1802. London. Phillips. 2nd ed. 8vo. 232 p. G. V3. $35.00

LONG, Frank Belknap. *Hounds of Tindalos.* 1946. Arkham. 1st ed. F/dj. M2. $225.00

LONG, Frank Belknap. *HP Lovecraft: Dreamer on the Night Side.* 1975. Arkham. 1st ed. as new. M2. $25.00

LONG, Frank Belknap. *In Mayan Splendor.* 1977. Arkham. 1st ed. as new. M2. $25.00

LONG, Frank Belknap. *Rim of the Unknown.* 1972. Arkham. 1st ed. F/dj. M2. $40.00

LONG, Huey P. *Every Man a King. Autobiography...* 1933. New Orleans. Nat Book Co. 1st ed. F/NF. B2. $75.00

LONG, J. *Voyages & Travels of an Indian Interpreter & Trader...* 1791. London. pub for author. 1st ed. 4to. 295 p. contemporary calf. P4. $1,750.00

LONG, John D. *Address by Senator John D Long of Union Country...* ca 1957. np. 1st ed. 6 p. NF/wrp. M8. $22.50

LONG, Lyda Belknap; see Long, Frank Belknap.

LONG, Stephen. *N Expeditions of...Journals of 1817 & 1823.* 1978. MN Hist Soc. ils/ maps/index. 407 p. cloth. dj. A17. $20.00

LONG, William J. *School of the Woods.* 1902. Ginn. 1st ed. ils Charles Copeland. 361 p. VG+. M20. $35.00

LONGFELLOW, Henry Wadsworth. *Courtship of Miles Standish & Other Poems.* 1858. Ticknor Fields. 1st Am ed. aeg. pub gilt tan cloth. F/slipcase/ chemise. B24. $950.00

LONGFELLOW, Henry Wadsworth. *Courtship of Miles Standish.* 1920. Houghton Mifflin. 1st thus ed. ils NC Wyeth. NF/dj. B24. $375.00

LONGFELLOW, Henry Wadsworth. *Favorite Poems of...* 1947. Doubleday. 1st thus ed. G/dj. E3. $15.00

LONGFELLOW, Henry Wadsworth. *Seaside & Fireside.* 1850. Boston. Ticknor Fields. 1st ed. 12mo. 141 p. cloth. NF. M1. $150.00

LONGFELLOW, Henry Wadsworth. *Song of Hiawatha.* 1859. Ticknor Fields. 12mo. 316 p. VG. D3. $25.00

LONGFELLOW, Henry Wadsworth. *Sonnets of...* 1907. Houghton Mifflin. 1/275. octavo. 275 p. bl brds. F. B24. $100.00

LONGLEY, Michael. *Gorse Fires.* 1991. Wake Forest U. 1st ed. F/F. V1. $15.00

LONGPRE, E. Keith. *Systematics of Genera Sabazia, Selloa & Tricarpha.* 1970. E Lansing. maps/pls. 97 p. VG/wrp. B26. $12.50

LONGSTREET, James. *From Manassas to Appomattox.* 1896. Phil. 1st ed. VG. B5. $290.00

LONGSTREET, Stephen. *Living High.* 1962. Fawcett Gold Medal. PBO. sgn twice. NF/unread. A11. $40.00

LONGSTRETH, T. Morris. *Adirondacks.* 1920. NY. full-p inscr. F. B14. $55.00

LONGUS & MOORE. *Pastoral Loves of Daphnis & Chloe.* 1924. London. Heinemann. 1st thus ed. 1/1280. sgn/trans Moore. Riviere bdg. VG. H5. $200.00

LONGUS. *Daphine & Chloe.* 1923. 1/450. VG. A1. $150.00

LONGYEAR, Barry B. *Circus World.* 1980. Berkley. 1st hc ed. F/F. F4. $12.00

LONGYEAR, Barry B. *City of Baraboo.* 1980. Berkley. 1st ed. F/NF. N3. $15.00

LONGYEAR, Edmund J. *Mesabi Pioneer: Reminiscences of...* 1951. MN Hist Soc. 1st ed. 116 p. F/dj. A17. $25.00

LONNROTH, Erik. *Historia Och Dikt. Essays.* 1959. Stockholm. 1st Swedish ed. 195 p. NF. M7. $95.00

LONSDALE, Kathleen. *Quakers Visit Russia.* 1952. London. Friends Peace Comm. 1st ed. 12mo. 145 p. VG. V3. $8.00

LONSDALE, Richard E. *Atlas of NC.* 1967. Chapell Hill. 1st ed. maps. NF/dj. O6. $35.00

LOO-WIT LAT-KLA. *Gold Hunting in the Cascade Mtns.* 1991. BC of WA. 8vo. F. A8. $60.00

LOOMIS, Alfred A. *Walt Henley Overseas.* 1928. Ives Washburn. 1st ed. 12mo. VG. A8. $20.00

LOOMIS, Charles Battell. *Little Maude & Her Mamma.* 1909. Doubleday Page. 1st ed. ils. 43 p. G. S10. $15.00

LOOMIS, Roger S. *Celtic Myth & Arthurian Romance.* 1967 (1927). Haskel House. VG. C1. $74.00

LOORY, Stuart H. *Defeated: Inside Am's Military Machine.* (1973). Random. 1st ed. 405 p. dj. A7. $30.00

LOOS, Anita. *Kiss Hollywood Good-By.* 1974. NY. 1st ed. inscr. VG/NF. A11. $35.00

LOPES, Alfred Luiz. *Estudo Estatistico da Criminalidade em Portugal...1895.* 1897. Lisboa. Imprensa Nacional. inscr. thin 4to. 293 p. leather. G1. $125.00

LOPEZ, Barry. *Arctic Dreams.* (1986). London. McMillan. 1st ed. F/F. B3. $40.00

LOPEZ, Barry. *Arctic Dreams: Imagination & Desire in N Landscape.* (1986). Scribner. 1st ed. sgn. maps/index. F/F. A18. $60.00

LOPEZ, Barry. *Crossing Open Ground.* (1987). Scribner. 1st ed. sgn. F/F. A18. $35.00

LOPEZ, Barry. *Crossing Open Ground.* (1988). Scribner. 1st ed. F/NF. B3. $30.00

LOPEZ, Barry. *Crow & Weasel.* (1993). Harper Perennial. 1st thus ed. sgn. ils Tom Pohrt. M. A18. $20.00

LOPEZ, Barry. *Crow & Weasel.* 1990. N Point. 1st ed/1st issue. gilt bdg. F/F. L3. $65.00

LOPEZ, Barry. *Rediscovery of N Am.* (1990). KY U. 1st ed. sgn. M/M. A18. $75.00

LOPEZ, Barry. *River Notes: Dance of Herons.* (1979). KS City. McMeel. 1st ed. F/VG. B3. $75.00

LOPEZ DE GOMARA, Francisco. *Cortes. Life of a Conqueror...* 1964 (1552). Berkeley. 425 p. dj. F3. $20.00

LORAINE, Philip. *Crackpot.* 1993. London. Harper Collins. 1st ed. F/F. S5. $22.50

LORANG, Mary Corde. *Footloose Scientist in Mayan Am.* 1966. Scribner. 1st ed. 8vo. 32 pls/maps. 308 p. G/G. B11. $35.00

LORANT, Stefan. *Glorious Burden: Hist of Presidency...* (1976). Lenox, MA. sgn. 1104 p. VG/torn dj. B18. $22.50

LORANT, Stefan. *New World.* ca 1946. DSP. 1st ed. 292 p. tan buckram. dj. H9. $75.00

LORANT, Stefan. *Pittsburg: Story of Am City.* 1980. Lenox. 3rd ed. VG/dj. D7. $20.00

LORCA, Federico Garcia. *Poet in NY.* 1955. Grove. 1st ed. trans Belitt. F/dj. C4. $50.00

LORD, Bette. *8th Moon: Young Girl's Life in Communist China.* (1966). London. Hale. 1st Eng ed. VG+/dj. A7. $20.00

LORD, Francis. *Civil War Collector's Encyclopedia.* 1965. np. index. 360 p. dj. O7. $27.50

LORD, Russell. *Forest Outings by 30 Foresters.* 1940. WA. 1st ed. 4to. fld maps. 311 p. F/dj. A17. $15.00

LORD, Sheldon; see Block, Lawrence.

LORDE, Audre. *Cancer Journals.* (1980). Spinsters Ink. stated 1st prt. 77 p. NF/yel prt wrp. A7. $15.00

LORENZ, J.H. *Blumensprache in Prosa & Versen.* nd. Erfurt. Henning und Hopf. miniature. 286 p. red cloth. F. B24. $275.00

LORIOUX, Felix. *Don Quixote.* 1930. London. Librairie Hachette. 1st thus ed. cloth. VG. M5. $145.00

LORMEL, L. *La Convalescence de Bebe.* ca 1885. Paris. Lefevre. ils H Lemar. 14 p. pict brds. VG. D1. $325.00

LORRAINE, M.J. *Columbia Unveiled.* 1924. LA. Times-Mirror Pr. 1st ed. 8vo. 446 p. decor gr cloth. VG. B20. $75.00

LOSE & MANNIX. *No Job for a Lady.* 1979. Macmillan. 1st ed. presentation. VG/VG. O3. $35.00

LOSSING, B.J. *Cadet Life at W Point.* 1862. Boston. Burnham. 367 p. cloth. G. B14. $50.00

LOSSING, B.J. *Harper's Encyclopedia of US Hist From 458 AD to 1909.* ca 1905. NY/London. Harper. 2nd prt. complete 10 vols. 8vo. purple linen. H9. $120.00

LOSSING, B.J. *Mathew Brady's Ils Hist of the Civil War.* 1977. np. reprint from 1910 ed. ils. 512 p. NF. O7. $18.50

LOSSING, B.J. *Mt Vernon & Its Associations...* 1859. NY. 1st ed. 376 p. gilt red cloth. VG. B28. $65.00

LOSSING, B.J. *Signers of the Declaration of Independence.* 1884. NY. 1st ed. ils. 384 p. gilt emb bdg. O7. $21.50

LOTH, Calder. *VA Landmarks Register.* (1987). U Pr of VA. 3rd ed/2nd prt. 547 p. F/F. B10. $25.00

LOTI, Pierre. *War.* 1917. Lippincott. 1st ed. VG. N2. $7.50

LOTT, Arnold S. *Long Line of Ships.* 1954. Annapolis. US Naval Instit. VG/dj. A16. $40.00

LOUBERE, Leo A. *Vine Remembers: French Vignerons Recall Their Past.* ca 1985. Albany, NY. 1st ed. 193 p. M. H10. $27.50

LOUDON, Jane Webb. *Gardening for Ladies...* 1848. NY. 1st Am ed. 12mo. 430 p. binding copy. B28. $85.00

LOUDON, Jane Webb. *Ladies Flower-Garden of Ornamental Bulbous Plants.* nd. (1850). London. Wm S Orr. 2nd ed. quarto. 58 hc pls. 270 p. rebacked. H5. $6,500.00

LOUIS, Pierre Charles A. *Recherches Anatomico-Pathologiques sur la Phthsie.* 1825. Paris. Gabon. 560 p. G7. $795.00

LOULIS, John C. *Greek Communist Party, 1940-44.* 1982. London. 8vo. 224 p. cloth. dj. O2. $30.00

LOVE, John W. *Lengthening Shadows.* 1943. Cleveland. Elwen-Parker Electric. 43 p. brds. G. N2. $16.50

LOVE. *Basics & Beyond.* 1990. np. ils/graphs/directions. wrp. G2. $15.00

LOVE. *Hardanger Stitchers Treasures.* 1991. np. ils. wrp. G2. $8.00

LOVECRAFT, H.P. *At the Mtns of Madness.* 1964. Arkham. 1st ed. F/dj. M2. $75.00

LOVECRAFT, H.P. *Collected Poems.* 1963. Arkham. 1st ed. F/dj. M2. $150.00

LOVECRAFT, H.P. *Couleur Tombee du Ciel.* 1954. Paris. Denoel. ARC of 1st ed. prt wrp. N2. $200.00

LOVECRAFT, H.P. *Dagon.* 1965. Arkham. 1st ed. ils/sgn Ron Miller. VG/F latter issue. M2. $45.00

LOVECRAFT, H.P. *Dark Brotherhood.* 1966. Arkham. 1st ed. F/dj. M2. $125.00

LOVECRAFT, H.P. *Dream Quest of Unknown Kadath.* 1955. Shroud. 1st separate ed. 1/1500. F/trade-size wrp/dj. F4. $50.00

LOVECRAFT, H.P. *Dreams & Fancies.* 1962. Arkham. 1st ed. F/dj. M2. $175.00

LOVECRAFT, H.P. *Dunwich Horror & Others.* 1963. Arkham House. 1st ed. blk brds. NF/F. B4. $75.00

LOVECRAFT, H.P. *Horror in the Mus.* 1970. Arkham. 1st ed. F/dj. M2. $65.00

LOVECRAFT, H.P. *Marginalia.* 1944. Arkham. 1st ed. NF/NF. M2. $300.00

LOVECRAFT, H.P. *Outsiders & Others.* 1939. Arkham. 1st ed. NF/VG dj. w/extra M Gerry de la Ree dj. M2. $2,000.00

LOVECRAFT, H.P. *Something About Cats & Other Pieces.* 1949. Arkham. 1st ed. NF/dj. B24. $225.00

LOVECRAFT, H.P. *Something About Cats.* 1949. Arkham. 1st ed. F/dj. M2. $275.00

LOVECRAFT, H.P. *Three Tales of Horror.* 1967. Arkham. 1st ed. F/F Lee Browne Coye dj. M2. $200.00

LOVEJOY, Arthur O. *Revolt Against Dualism.* 1930. Open Court/Norton. 1st ed. 325 p. gr cloth. VG. G1. $39.00

LOVELACE, Leland. *Lost Mines & Hidden Treasure.* 1956. San Antonio. Naylor. 252 p. dj. N2. $10.00

LOVELACE, Maud Hart. *Winona's Pony Cart.* 1953. Crowell. 1st ed. sgn. 117 p. VG+/dj. M20. $85.00

LOVELACE & WALLIN. *Intimate Diary of Linda Lovelace.* 1974. Pinnacle. pb. VG+. C8. $25.00

LOVELAND, Clara O. *Critical Yrs: Reconstruction of Anglican Church...* 1956. Greenwich, CT. 311 p. H10. $16.50

LOVELAND, Cyrus C. *CA Trail Herd.* 1961. Los Gatos, CA. 1st ed. 1/750. xl. 137 p. map ep. cloth. D3. $25.00

LOVELAND, Seymour. *Ils Bible Story Book. Old Testament.* 1923. Chicago. 4to. ils Milo Winter/12 color pls. 126 p. color ep. VG+. H3. $20.00

LOVELL, John. *Funeral Oration...Occasion'd by Death of...Peter Faneuil...* 1743. Boston. Gr Bushell Allen. sm 4to. 14 p. 19th-century bdg. K1. $275.00

LOVELL, Mary S. *Straight On Till Morning.* 1987. St Martin. VG/dj. A16. $7.50

LOVELL, W. George. *Conquest & Survival in Colonial Guatemala.* (1985). Montreal. McGill. 1st ed. 254 p. F3. $30.00

LOVERIDGE, Arthur. *Tomorrow's a Holiday.* (1947). Harper. 1st ed. 8vo. 278 p. F/VG+ clip. A2. $25.00

LOVESEY, Peter. *Last Detective.* 1991. Scribner. 1st ed. F/F. S5. $30.00

LOVESEY, Peter. *On the Edge.* 1989. London. Mysterious. 1st ed. sgn. F/F. S5. $40.00

LOVESEY, Peter. *On the Edge.* 1989. Mysterious. 1st ed. F/F. F4. $18.00

LOVETT, James D'Wolf. *Old Boston Boys & the Games They Played.* 1906. Riverside. private/1st ed. 1/250. photos. G+. P8. $450.00

LOW, A.M. *Wonder Book of Inventions.* nd. London. 8vo. ils. 256 p. pict ep. red cloth/pict brds. G. H3. $12.00

LOW, Frances H. *Queen Victoria's Dolls.* 1894. London. Newnes. 1st ed. quarto. ils. pict bl cloth. NF. scarce. H5. $275.00

LOW, SETH. *Speech at Lincoln Dinner Feb 13, 1888.* 1888. Henry Bessey. 14 p. VG. A6. $10.00

LOWE, E.J. *Natural Hist of British Grasses.* 1868. London. Groombridge. 4th ed. octavo. 74 pls. aeg. marbled ep. vellum. NF. H5. $500.00

LOWE, Peter. *Discourse of Whole Art of Chyrurgery...* 1654. London. Hodgkinsonne. woodcuts. 487 p. quarter morocco clamshell box. G7. $3,950.00

LOWE, Viola R. *Beautiful Story of Joan of Arc.* 1933. Racine. folio. ils Guillonnet. 60 p. VG/fair. H3. $25.00

LOWELL, James Russell. *Among My Books.* 1895. Houghton Mifflin. gilt gr brds. VG. E3. $20.00

LOWELL, James Russell. *Bigelow Papers.* 1848. Cambridge. Nichols. 1st ed. 12mo. 163 p. stp cloth. VG. D3. $75.00

LOWELL, James Russell. *Conversations on Some of the Old Poets.* 1845. Cambridge. John Owen. 1st ed. 12mo. Sylvester Judd's copy. 263 p. wrp. M1. $375.00

LOWELL, James Russell. *My Study Windows.* 1892. Houghton Mifflin. 31st ed. gr brds. VG. E3. $15.00

LOWELL, Joan. *Cradle of the Deep.* 1929. NY. 1st prt. 8vo. 261 p. gilt bl cloth. F/VG. H3. $35.00

LOWELL, Robert. *Collected Prose.* 1987. NY. 1st ed. F/F. V1. $20.00

LOWELL, Robert. *For the Union of Dead.* 1964. NY. 1st ed. F/NF. A11. $40.00

LOWELL, Robert. *Oresteia of Aeschylus.* 1978. Farrar Straus. AP. F/red wrp. C4. $50.00

LOWENFISH & LUPIEN. *Imperfect Diamond.* 1980. Stein Day. 1st ed. F/VG+. P8. $25.00

LOWNDES, I. *Modern Greek & Eng Lexicon...Modern Greek Grammar.* 1837. Corfu. self pub. thick 8vo. 671 p. new quarter calf/brds. O2. $650.00

LOWNDES, Mrs. Belloc. *Cressida: No Mystery.* 1928. London. 1st ed. xl. M2. $15.00

LOWREY, Grosvenor P. *Eng Neutrality: Is the AL a British Pirate?* 1863. Phil. Ashmead. 1st ed. 32 p. prt wrp. M8. $125.00

LOWREY & SLOANE. *Orthopsychiatry 1923-1948: Retrospect & Prospect.* 1948. Am Orthopsychiatric Assn. lg 8vo. 623 p. prt red cloth. G1. $35.00

LOWRIE, Ernest Benson. *Shape of the Puritan Mind.* 1974. New Haven. Yale. 1st ed. 253 p. H10. $17.50

LOWRIE, Walter. *Short Life of Kierkegaard.* 1946. Princeton. 3rd prt. sm 8vo. ochre cloth. G1. $25.00

LOWRY, Malcolm. *Dark As the Grave Wherein My Friend Is Laid.* (1968). NY. 1st ed. 255 p. VG+/dj. B18. $35.00

LOWRY, Malcolm. *Under the Volcano.* 1947. NY. 1st ed. VG/VG. A11. $100.00

LOWRY, Robert. *Bad Girl Marie.* 1942. Cincinnati. 1/100. sgn/#d Lowry & Flora. NF/wrp. A11. $65.00

LOWRY, Robert. *Casualty.* 1946. NY. 1st ed. sgn. F/VG+. A11. $55.00

LOWRY, Robert. *Kind of Woman.* 1959. NY. Pyramid. PBO. 1st ed. sgn. F/wrp. A11. $40.00

LOWRY, Timothy. *And Brave Men, Too.* (1985). Crown. 1st ed. NF/dj. A7. $20.00

LOWRY, TODD & WHITE. *Century of Speed/Red Mile 1875-1975.* 1975. Lexington. Trots Breeders Assn. 1st ed. presentation from Wht. VG. O3. $65.00

LUASANNE, Edita. *Great Book of Wine.* 1970. NY/Cleveland. World. 1st prt. dj. B30. $45.00

LUBBOCK, John. *British Wild Flowers Considered in Relation to Insects.* 1875. London. 12mo. 186 p. VG. B28. $25.00

LUBBOCK, John. *Flowers, Fruits & Leaves.* 1894 (1886). London. ils. 147 p. B26. $14.00

LUBBOCK, Percy. *Earlham.* 1930. London. Cape. 12th prt. 16mo. 253 p. G+. V3. $12.00

LUBIN, Leonard. *Sing a Song of Sixpence.* 1987. Lee Shepard. 1st ed. ils. pict brds. NF/NF. T5. $25.00

LUCANUS, Marcus Annaeus. *Pharsalia of Lucan.* 1919-44. London. Humphreys. Latin/Eng text. 2 vols. NF. F1. $95.00

LUCAS, E.V. *Forgotten Tales of Long Ago.* (1906). Wells-Gardner-Darton. ils FD Bedford. 425 p. G+. P2. $50.00

LUCAS, E.V. *Playtime & Co.* 1925. London. Methuen. 1/100. ils/sgn Shepard. VG/dj/ orig glassine. D1. $775.00

LUCAS, E.V. *Playtime & Co.* 1925. London. Methuen. 1/15 on Japanese vellum. presentation. 95 p. NF. H5. $1,250.00

LUCAS, E.V. *Playtime & Co: A Book for Children.* nd. London. Methuen. 1st ed. ils Lucas/Shepard. 95 p. pict brds. VG/VG. D1. $175.00

LUCAS, E.V. *Wanderer in Paris.* 1909. NY. 1st ed. 309 p. gilt bl cloth. VG. H3. $20.00

LUCAS, Frederic A. *Explorations in Newfoundland & Labrador in 1887.* 1981. GPO. removed from annual report. 8vo. VG. P4. $17.50

LUCAS, John. *Basic Jazz on Long Play.* 1954. Northfield. Carleton Jazz Club. 104 p. NF/wrp. B2. $45.00

LUCAS, Paul. *Voyage...dans la Grece, l'Asie Mineure, la Macedonine...* 1714. Amsterdam. 2 vols in 1. 8vo. old marbled wrp. uncut. O2. $850.00

LUCAS & MORROW. *What a Life!* 1975. NY. 1st Am ed. intro/sgn John Ashbery. F/wrp. A11. $50.00

LUCE, Robert B. *Faces of Five Decades.* 1964. Simon Schuster. 1st prt. gilt tan cloth. NF/G/clear plastic. M7. $30.00

LUCE & SMITH. *Love Needs Care.* 1971. Little Brn. stated 1st ed. 405 p. dj. A7. $30.00

LUCIA, Ellis. *This Land Around Us: Treasury of Pacific NW Writing.* 1969. NY. 1st ed. ils. 981 p. F/pict dj. D3. $25.00

LUCKIESH. *Color & Colors.* 1938. np. cloth. G2. $15.00

LUCKOMBE, Phillip. *Concise Hist of Origin & Progress of Prt.* 1770. London. 1st ed. 502 p. marbled brds/leather spine. F. rare. B14. $1,250.00

LUCRETIUS. *On Life & Death.* 1976. Blk Cat. 1/249. miniature. trans Mallock. bl leather. F. F1. $40.00

LUDINGTON, M.I. *Uniforms of the Army of the US, Ils, From 1774 to 1884.* nd. np. Quartermaster General. lg quarto. 44 color lithos. full blk morocco. NF. H5. $1,500.00

LUDLAM, H. *Biography of Dracula: Life Story of Bram Stoker.* (1962). London. Quality BC. NF/NF clip. B4. $45.00

LUDLOW, Jacob. *Science in the Stable; or, How a Horse Can Be Kept...* 1897. Easton. 2nd Am ed/enlarged. 16mo. 166 p. VG+/wrp. O3. $35.00

LUDLUM, Robert. *Parsifal Mosaic.* 1982. Random. 1st ed. inscr/sgn. F/F. S5. $75.00

LUDLUM, Robert. *Road to Gandolopho.* 1975. Dial. 1st ed. F/F. A7. $35.00

LUDWIG, Emil. *Dr Freud: Analysis & Warning.* 1947. NY. Hellman Williams. 1st Am ed. 317 p. red cloth. G1. $25.00

LUDY, Robert B. *Historic Hotels of the World, Past & Present.* 1927. McKay. 1st ed. 8vo. 328 p. purple cloth. NF. B20. $50.00

LUGAR, Robert. *Villa Architecture: Collection of Views...* 1828. London. Taylor. 1st ed. folio. half gr morocco. NF. R3. $3,750.00

LUHRMANN, T.M. *Persuasions of the Witch's Craft: Ritual Magic...* 1989. Cambridge. Harvard. 382 p. blk cloth. F/dj. G1. $25.00

LUHRS, Victor. *Great Baseball Mystery.* 1966. Barnes. 1st ed. VG+/VG. P8. $60.00

LUJAN MUNOZ, Luis. *Fotografias de Eduardo Santiago Muybridge en Guatemala.* 1984. Guatemala. 1st ed. 44 p. wrp. F3. $20.00

LUKACH, H.C. *Fringe of the E: Journey Through Past & Present...Turkey.* 1913. London. Macmillan. 1st ed. 8vo. 273 p. F. A2. $75.00

LUKASIEWICZ, Jan. *Aristotle's Syllogistic From Standpoint...* 1957 (1951). Clarendon. 2nd enlarged ed/later prt. 222 p. blue cloth. G. G1. $25.00

LUKE, Thomas; see Masterton, Graham.

LUM, Dyer D. *Spiritual Delusion. Its Methods, Teachings & Effects.* 1873. Lippincott. 1st ed. F. B2. $275.00

LUMLEY, Brian. *Blood Brothers.* 1992. NY. Tor. 1st ed. F/F. N3. $20.00

LUMLEY, Brian. *Caller of the Blk.* 1971. Arkham. 1st ed. F/F. M2. $45.00

LUMLEY, Brian. *Deadspeak.* 1990. Kinnell. 1st UK/hc ed. sgn. F/F. F4. $40.00

LUMMIS, Charles F. *Bronco Pegasus.* 1928. Boston. 1st ed. 12 photos. 150 p. cloth. VG/rpr pict dj. D3. $25.00

LUMMIS, Charles F. *Some Strange Corners of Our Country: Wonderland of SW.* 1892. Century. 1st ed. F. A18. $75.00

LUMPKIN, Katharine DuPre. *Emancipation of Angelina Grimke.* 1974. Chapel Hill. 8vo. 265 p. M. V3. $15.00

LUNNY, Robert M. *Early Maps of N Am.* 1961. Newark. NJ Hist Soc. M/wrp. O6. $45.00

LUNT, James. *Barren Rocks of Aden.* (1966). London. Jenkins. 1st ed. 8vo. 196 p. VG+/VG+. A2. $15.00

LUPACK, Alan. *Arthur, the Greatest King.* 1988. Garland. 1st ed. sgn. M. C1. $29.50

LUPACK, Alan. *Arthurian Drama: An Anthology.* 1991. Garland. 1st ed. sgn. C1. $39.50

LUPOFF, Richard. *Lovecraft's Book.* 1985. Arkham. 1st ed. M. M2. $16.00

LURIE, Alison. *Foreign Affairs.* 1984. Franklin Lib. ltd ed. sgn. full red leather. F. Q1. $40.00

LURIE, Alison. *War Between the Tates.* 1974. Random. ARC. F/NF. C4. $40.00

LURIE, Harry L. *Heritage Affirmed: Jewish Federation Movement in Am.* 1961. JPS. 481 p. VG/G. S3. $25.00

LURIE, Morris. *Whole Life.* 1987. Melbourne. 1st ed. w/typed sgn letter. F/F. A11. $30.00

LUSTBADER, Eric. *Kaisho.* 1993. Pocket. 1st ed. sgn. F/dj. M15. $30.00

LUSTBADER, Eric. *Zero.* 1988. Random. 1st ed. as new. M2. $20.00

LUSTGARTEN, Edgar. *Business of Murder.* 1968. Scribner. 1st ed. F/F. F4. $25.00

LUSTGARTEN, Edgar. *One More Unfortunate.* 1947. Scribner. 1st ed. F/NF. F4. $50.00

LUSTGARTEN, Edgar. *Turn the Light Out As You Go.* 1978. London. Elek. 1st ed. NF/dj. S5. $25.00

LUTHER, T. *Custer High Spots.* 1972. Old Army Pr. ils Byron Wolfe. 99 p. F/sans. B19. $50.00

LUTZ, John. *Lazarus Man.* 1979. Morrow. 1st ed. inscr/sgn. F/F. S5. $45.00

LUTZ, John. *Scorcher.* 1987. Holt. 1st ed. F/dj. M15. $25.00

LUTZ, John. *Tropical Heat.* 1986. Holt. 1st ed. sgn. F/F. S5. $35.00

LUXTON, N.K. *Tilikum: Luxton's Pacific Crossing.* 1971. Sidney, BC. Gray's Pub. 1st ed. 8vo. 159 p. F/F. A2. $20.00

LYALL, Gavin. *Secret Servant.* 1980. Viking. 1st Am ed. F/NF. S5. $25.00

LYDENBERG, Harry Miller. *Crossing the Line: Tales of Ceremony During Centuries.* 1957. NY Public Lib. Samuel Eliot Morison's copy. NF. O6. $125.00

LYDON, Michael. *Boogie Lightning.* 1974. Dial. stated 1st ed. 229 p. NF. A7. $25.00

LYDON, Michael. *Rock Folk.* 1971. Dial. 1st ed. 200 p. dj. A7. $20.00

LYELL, Charles. *Geological Evidences of Antiquity of Man w/Remarks...* 1863. Phil. George W Childs. 1st Am ed/1st prt. 518 p. emb gr cloth. G1. $150.00

LYMAN, Chester S. *Around the Horn to the Sandwich Islands & CA, 1845-50.* 1924. New Haven. Yale. ils/maps. NF. O6. $150.00

LYMAN, George D. *John Marsh, Pioneer.* 1930. np. 1st ed. ils. 394 p. O7. $32.50

LYMAN, William Denison. *Columbia River: Hist, Myths, Scenery, Commerce.* 1909. NY. 1st Am ed. 409 p. teg. bl cloth. VG. B28. $60.00

LYNAM, Edward. *Mapmaker's Art: Essays on Hist of Maps.* 1953. London. Batchworth. 140 p. NF/dj. O6. $75.00

LYNCH, H.F.B. *Armenia Travels & Studies.* 1967. Beirut. 2 vols. lg fld pocket map. cloth. djs. O2. $350.00

LYNCH, Thomas K. *Visit to the Suez Canal.* 1866. London. sm 4to. 9 lithos/lg fld map. 72 p. F. O2. $250.00

LYNCH, William F. *Narrative of US Expedition to River Jordan & Dead Sea.* 1849. Phil. Lea Blanchard. thick 8vo. 508 p. gilt cloth. H9. $50.00

LYNCH. *Old-Fashioned Garden.* 1987. paper engineering by Damien Johnston. F. A4. $25.00

LYNDE, Francis. *Taming of Red Butte W.* 1910. Scribner. 1st ed. inscr. VG. B9. $60.00

LYNDS, Dennis. *MN Strip.* (1987). Donald Fine. 1st ed. inscr. NF/dj. B9. $12.50

LYNDS, Dennis. *Night of the Toads.* (1972). London. Hale. 1st ed. F/NF. B3. $25.00

LYNDS, Dennis. *Nightrunners.* 1978. Dodd Mead. 1st ed. inscr/sgn. F/F. S5. $45.00

LYNDS, Dennis. *Slasher.* 1980. Dodd Mead. 1st ed. inscr/sgn. F/F. S5. $45.00

LYNES, George Platt. *Ballet.* 1985. Pasadena. Twelvetrees. 1st ed. F/F. B2. $60.00

LYNES, Russell. *Domesticated Am.* (1963). NY. 1st ed. 8vo. 308 p. F/VG+. A2. $15.00

LYNN, Elizabeth A. *Watchtower.* 1979. Berkley. 1st ed. F/F. N3. $25.00

LYON, G.F. *Private Journal of Capt GF Lyon of HMS Hecla...* 1824. London. Murray. inscr Viljahlmer Stefansson. 6 pls/fld map. rebound. P4. $450.00

LYON, Jean. *Just Half a World Away.* 1954. NY. 1st ed. ils. 373 p. gilt brn cloth. F. H3. $15.00

LYON, Mary. *Power of Christian Benevolence.* 1858. Am Tract Soc. new ed/abridged/ enlarged. worn. E3. $30.00

LYONS, Arthur. *Fast Fade.* 1987. Mysterious. 1st ed. sgn. F/F. S5. $40.00

LYONS, Dorothy. *Bluegrass Champion (Harlequin Hullabaloo).* nd. Grosset Dunlap. juvenile. VG/VG. O3. $25.00

LYONS, Dorothy. *Golden Sovereign.* 1946. Harcourt Brace. later prt. VG/G. O3. $25.00

LYTLE, Andrew. *Long Night.* 1936. Indianapolis. 1st ed. VG/VG. B5. $175.00

LYTLE, Andrew. *Reflections of Ghost.* 1980. Dallas. 1/300. sgn/#d. red-stp blk cloth. F/acetate wrp. A11. $45.00

LYTLE, Andrew. *Velvet Horn.* 1975. Obolensky. 1st ed. NF/NF. Q1. $125.00

LYTLE, Andrew. *Wake for the Living.* 1975. NY. 1st ed. sgn. NF/NF. A11. $75.00

LYTTLE, Richard B. *Yr in the Minors.* 1975. Doubleday. 1st ed. xl. VG. P8. $12.50

LYTTON, Lord. *King Arthur: A Poem.* 1871. np. 1st ed. NF. V1. $10.00

M'KEEVER, Thomas. *Voyage to Hudson's Bay During Summer of 1812.* 1819. London. Phillips. pls. 96 p. modern calf/marbled brds. B14. $100.00

M'NEVIN, William James. *Ramble in Swisserland, in Summer & Autumn of 1802.* 1803. Dublin. Stockdale. 280 p. brds. B14. $75.00

MAASS, Joachim. *Gouffe Case.* 1960. NY. Harper. 1st ed. trans from German. NF/VG+. A14. $20.00

MABILLE, Pierre. *Miroir du Mervelleux.* 1940. Paris. ils Andre Mason. ltd ed. G+/wrp. A1. $25.00

MACARTHUR, Walter. *Last Days of Sail on the W Coast.* 1968. Seattle. facsimile of 1929 ed. VG. P4. $22.50

MACARTNEY, C.A. *Habsburg & Hohenzollern Dynasties in 17th & 18th C.* (1970). NY. Walker. 1st Am ed. 8vo. 379 p. F/VG. A2. $20.00

MACARTNEY, Clarence Edward. *Lincoln & His Cabinet.* 1931. Scribner. VG. A6. $15.00

MACARTNEY, Clarence Edward. *Lincoln & His Cabinet.* 1931. Scribner. 1st ed. 366 p. cloth. NF. M8. $45.00

MACARTNEY, Clarence Edward. *Not Far From Pittsburgh.* 1946. Pittsburgh. 2nd ed. 138 p. G/dj. D7. $20.00

MACCARGO, J.T.; see Rabe, Peter.

MACCURDY, G.G. *Early Man: As Depicted by Leading Authorities...1937.* 1937. Lippincott. 1st ed. 8vo. ils. VG+/VG. A2. $30.00

MACDERMOT, Violet. *Cult of the Seer in the Ancient Middle E.* 1971. Berkeley, CA. 1st ed. thick 8vo. 829 p. VG/dj. G1. $75.00

MACDOLAND, Ian. *Smuggling in the Highlands.* 1914. Stirling. 1st ed. 12mo. ils. 124 p. teg. gilt bl cloth. F. H3. $20.00

MACDONAGH. *Victorian Patchwork Patterns.* 1988. np. ils/full-size templates for 12 quilts. wrp. G2. $4.50

MACDONALD, A.B. *Hands Up! True Stories of the Six-Gun Fighters of Old W.* 1927. NY. Burt. NF/NF. H7. $20.00

MACDONALD, Betty. *Egg & I.* 1948. BC. VG. C1. $4.50

MACDONALD, Betty. *Hello, Mrs Piggle-Wiggle.* 1957. Lippincott. stated 1st ed. ils Hilary Knight. VG/dj. M5. $25.00

MACDONALD, Betty. *Mrs Piggle-Wiggle.* 1947. Lippincott. 1st ed. 119 p. VG/G. P2. $25.00

MACDONALD, Cynthia. *Wholes.* 1980. NY. 1st ed. F/NF. V1. $15.00

MACDONALD, Dwight. *Parodies: Anthology From Chaucer to Beerbohm — & After.* 1960. Random. 1st ed. F/F. B2. $50.00

MACDONALD, George. *At the Back of the N Wind.* 1909. Lippincott. ils Maria Kirk. NF/G. M18. $65.00

MACDONALD, George. *At the Back of the N Wind.* 1909. Phil. ils Maria Kirk. 8vo. 352 p. red cloth. VG. H3. $25.00

MACDONALD, George. *Princess & Curdie.* 1927. Macmillan. 1st ed. ils DP Lathrop. 265 p. G. S10. $35.00

MACDONALD, George. *Princess & Goblin.* 1926. Macmillan. ils FD Bedford. 267 p. pict bl cloth. VG/G. T5. $32.00

MACDONALD, Greville. *Sanity of William Blake.* 1908. London. AC Fifeld. 1st ed. 16mo. 6 pls. prt gray brds. VG. G1. $46.00

MACDONALD, John D. *Condominium.* 1977. London. Hale. 1st British ed. F/F. S5. $30.00

MACDONALD, John D. *Contrary Pleasure.* 1954. Appleton Century. 1st ed. F/NF. Q1. $150.00

MACDONALD, John D. *Damned.* 1952. Fawcett Gold Medal. PBO. inscr. F/unread. A11. $245.00

MACDONALD, John D. *Dead Low Tide.* 1976. London. Robert Hale. 1st hc ed. F/F. Q1. $75.00

MACDONALD, John D. *Executioners.* 1958. Simon Schuster. 1st ed. VG+/VG. B4. $125.00

MACDONALD, John D. *Lonely Silver Rain.* (1985). Knopf. 1st ed. F/F. B3. $35.00

MACDONALD, John D. *Lonely Silver Rain.* (1985). London. Hodder Stoughton. F/F. B3. $30.00

MACDONALD, John D. *Long Lavender Look.* 1972. Lippincott. 1st ed. VG+/VG+. Q1. $175.00

MACDONALD, John D. *Nightmare in Pink.* 1976. Lippincott. 1st Am hc ed. F/clip. M15. $165.00

MACDONALD, John D. *Nightmare in Pink.* 1976. Lippincott. 1st hc ed. rem mk. NF/NF. Q1. $150.00

MACDONALD, John D. *No Deadly Drug.* 1968. Doubleday. 1st ed. F/F. F4. $40.00

MACDONALD, John D. *On Crime Writing.* 1973. Santa Barbara. 1/250. sgn/#d. F. A11. $90.00

MACDONALD, John D. *S*E*V*E*N.* 1974. London. Robert Hale. only hc ed. F/F clip. Q1. $75.00

MACDONALD, John D. *Scarlet Ruse.* 1975. London. Hale. 1st hc ed. F/F. M15. $65.00

MACDONALD, John D. *Wine of the Dreamers.* 1951. Greenberg, NY. 1st ed. author's 1st book. NF/NF. Q1. $250.00

MACDONALD, John D. *Zebra-Striped Hearse.* 1962. Knopf. 1st ed. F/NF. Q1. $225.00

MACDONALD, John Ross; see Millar, Kenneth.

MACDONALD, John. *One More Sunday.* (1984). NY. Knopf. 1st ed. NF/NF. B3. $35.00

MACDONALD, Malcolm. *Borneo People.* 1958. Knopf. 1st ed. xl. ils. 424 p. VG. W1. $18.00

MACDONALD, Philip. *Triple Jeopardy.* 1962. Doubleday Crime Club. omnibus ed. VG/dj. M15. $30.00

MACDONALD, Ross; see Millar, Kenneth.

MACDONALD, William Colt. *Don Gringo.* (1930). Chelsea. 1st ed. VG/dj. B9. $100.00

MACDONALD & ROWAN. *Friendship.* 1986. Knopf. 1st ed. F/F. F4. $20.00

MACDOWELL & SWANSON. *Quilts From the Albert & M Silber Collection.* 1988. np. wrp. G2. $10.95

MACDUFFIE, Abby Parsons. *Little Pilgrim: An Autobiography.* 1938. NY. private prt. 1/600. 71 p. N2. $17.50

MACEWEN, William. *Lives of British Physicians.* 1930. London. 341 p. G7. $75.00

MACEWEN, William. *Pyogenic Infective Diseases of the Brain & Spinal Cord.* 1893. Glasgow. Maclehose. 354 p. orig cloth. G7. $695.00

MACFADDEN, Harry Alexander. *Rambles in the Far W.* 1906. PA. Standard. 1st ed. 42 pls. 278 p. gilt gr cloth. F. H7. $75.00

MACFARLANE, Paul. *Daguerreotypes of Great Stars of Baseball.* 1981. Sporting News. revised ed. F/VG+. P8. $20.00

MACFARQUHAR, Roderick. *Forbidden City.* 1972. NY. Newsweek. 1st ed. 4to. ils/pls. 172 p. VG/dj. W1. $22.00

MACGAHAN, J.A. *Campaigning on the Oxus & the Fall of Khiva.* 1874. Harper. ils/map. gilt brn cloth. NF. F1. $195.00

MACHEN, Arthur. *Fantastic Tales...* 1923. Carbonnek. 1/1050. sm nick on spine. A1. $65.00

MACHEN, Arthur. *Fantastic Tales...* 1923. Carbonnek. private prt. 1/1050. sgn. VG. N2. $75.00

MACHEN, Arthur. *Far-Off Things.* 1922. London. 1/100. sgn. G+. A1. $65.00

MACHEN, Arthur. *Gr Round.* 1968. Arkham. 1st ed. F/dj. M2. $80.00

MACHEN, Arthur. *Guinevere & Lancelot & Others.* 1986. Newport News. Purple Mouth. M/stiff wrp. C1. $14.00

MACHEN, Arthur. *Memories Giacomo Casanova di Seingalt.* 1922. London. Cassanova Soc. 1/1000 sets (12 vols, 1-8 only here). G+. A1. $100.00

MACHEN, Arthur. *Strange Roads & Gods in Spring.* 1923. London. Classic Pr. ltd ed. soft leather. G+. A1. $60.00

MACHEN, Arthur. *Tales of Horror & the Supernatural.* 1948. Knopf. 1st ed. VG. M2. $20.00

MACHEN, Arthur. *Terror.* 1927. London. 1st revised ed. VG. M2. $25.00

MACHETANZ & MACHETANZ. *Robbie & the Sled Dog Race.* (1964). NY. Scribner. sgns. 50 p. F/dj. A17. $19.50

MACHO. *Quilting Patterns: 110 Full-Size Ready-To-Use Designs...* 1984. np. wrp. G2. $5.00

MACINTYRE, Donald. *Adventure of Sail, 1520-1914.* ca 1970. Random. 1st Am ed. ils/color pls. 256 p. emb bl cloth. VG/dj. P4. $75.00

MACISACC, Fred. *Hothouse World.* 1965. Avalon. 1st ed. F/F. N3. $20.00

MACK, Connie. *Connie Mack's Baseball Book.* 1950. Knopf. 1st ed. VG/G+. P8. $25.00

MACK, Connie. *My 66 Yrs in the Big Leagues.* 1950. Winston. 1st ed. G+. P8. $30.00

MACK, John E. *Prince of Disorder.* 1976. London. Weidenfeld Nicolson. 1st ed. 561 p. NF/NF/clear plastic. M7. $75.00

MACKAY, Charles. *Extraordinary Popular Delusions & Madness of Crowds.* nd. FSG. reprint. VG/dj. A16. $10.00

MACKAY, Charles. *Life & Liberty in Am; or, Sketches of a Tour...* 1859. NY. 1st Am ed. 12mo. 413 p. rebound bl cloth. G. T3. $65.00

MACKAY, Donald. *Honorable Co: Hist of Hudson's Bay Co.* (1936). Bobbs Merrill. 1st ed. 8vo. 396 p. F/G. A2. $40.00

MACKAY, John. *Good Shooting.* (1960). NY. sgn. 138 p. NF/dj. A17. $17.50

MACKAYE, Percy. *Sanctuary: A Bird Masque.* 1914. Stokes. 1st ed. inscr/sgn. ils Arnold Genthe. 71 p. N2. $17.50

MACKENZIE, Arthur. *Voyages From Montreal, on River St Lawrence...* 1801. London. Cadell Davis. 1st ed. ils/maps. 412 p. rstr bdg. P4. $3,000.00

MACKENZIE, D. *Tribute.* 1930. London. 208 p. G. B18. $15.00

MACKENZIE, DeWitt. *Men Without Guns.* 1945. Phil. Blakiston. 1st ed. sm folio. 147 p. NF. B20. $45.00

MACKENZIE, Donald. *Raven Settles a Score.* 1979. London. Macmillan. 1st ed. F/F. S5. $22.50

MACKENZIE, George. *Inst of the Law of Scotland.* 1688. Edinburgh. Reid/Broun. corrected/enlarged ed. 12mo. 408 p. modern calf. K1. $300.00

MACKENZIE, Jean K. *African Clearings.* 1924. NY. 8vo. 270 p. pict brn cloth. VG. H3. $15.00

MACKENZIE, Jean K. *African Trail.* 1917. Medford, MA. 12mo. ils. 222 p. pict wht brds. VG. H3. $20.00

MACKENZIE, Kenneth R.H. *Marvellous Adventures...of Master Tyll Owlglass.* 1860. London. Trubner. ils Alfred Crowquill. aeg. Bayntun bdg. F. F1. $695.00

MACKENZIE, Murdo. *Contrast Psychology: Concept of Movement of Human Spirit.* 1952. London. Allen Unwin. 1st ed. 305 p. red cloth. VG/dj. G1. $25.00

MACKENZIE, W. Douglas. *S Africa: Its Hist, Heroes & Wars.* 1899. Chicago. 4 books in 1 vol. 663 p. G. H3. $40.00

MACKENZIE. *New Design in Crochet.* 1972. np. ils. cloth. G2. $6.00

MACKEY, Nathaniel. *4 for Trane.* (1978). LA. Golemics. 1/250. tall wrp. A7. $10.00

MACKINNON, Captain. *Atlantic & Transatlantic. Sketches Afloat & Ashore.* 1852. NY. 1st Am ed. 324 p. gilt brn cloth. G. H3. $25.00

MACLACHLAN, Patricia. *Tomorrow's Wizard.* 1982. Harper Row. 1st ed. ils Kathy Jacobi. NF/G+. T5. $25.00

MACLANE, Mary. *Story of Mary MacLane.* 1902. Chicago. Stone. VG. N2. $50.00

MACLAURIN, Colin. *Account of Sir Isaac Newton's Philosophical Discoveries...* 1748. London. 1st ed. quarto. full mottled calf. VG. R3. $750.00

MACLEAN, Alistair. *All About Lawrence of Arabia.* 1962. London. Allen. 1st ed. 141 p. bl paper simulating cloth. VG. M7. $25.00

MACLEAN, Alistair. *Partisans.* 1982. London. Collins. 1st ed. F/F. S5. $30.00

MACLEAN, Alistair. *Where Eagles Dare.* 1967. Doubleday. 1st Am ed. F/dj. M18. $35.00

MACLEAN, Charles. *Wolf Children.* (1978, 77). Hill Wang. 1st Am ed. 8vo. 319 p. F/F. A2. $15.00

MACLEAN, Norman. *Casey Stengel.* 1976. Drake. 1st ed. F/VG+. P8. $30.00

MACLEAN, Norman. *River Runs Through It.* (1983). Chicago U. 1st ils ed/trade issue. sq quarto. F/NF clip. B4. $200.00

MACLEAN, Norman. *Young Men & Fire.* (1992). Chicago U. 1st ed. M/dj. A18. $40.00

MACLEAN & RAPPEN. *Hemine Hug-Hellmuth: Her Life & Work.* 1991. NY. Routledge. 1st Am ed. VG/dj. G1. $30.00

MACLEISH, Archibald. *Before March.* nd. Borzoi Chap Book. NF/gr wrp. C4. $30.00

MACLEISH, Archibald. *Fall of the City: Verse Play for Radio.* 1939. Farrar Rinehart. 1st ed. orange brds. F. C4. $30.00

MACLEISH, Archibald. *Frescoes for Mr Rockefeller's City.* 1933. John Day. 1st ed. VG/wrp. B2. $35.00

MACLEISH, Archibald. *Great Am 4th of July Parade.* 1979. Pittsburgh U. 1st ed. F/F. C4. $40.00

MACLEOD, Charlotte. *Had She But Known.* 1994. Mysterious. ARC. F/wrp. B2. $25.00

MACLEOD, Charlotte. *Something in the Water.* 1994. Mysterious. ARC. F/wrp. B2. $30.00

MACLEOD, Dawn. *Book of Herbs.* 1968. London. ils/3 color pls. 191 p. VG+/dj. B26. $16.00

MACLEOD, Donald. *Biography of Hon Fernando Wood, Mayor of NYC.* 1856. NY. OF Parsons. N2. $50.00

MACLEOD, John. *Scottish Theology in Relation to Church Hist...* 1974. Banner of Truth. index. 350 p. H10. $20.00

MACLEOD, Mary. *King Arthur.* 1950. World. ils Alexander Dobkin. VG. C1. $4.00

MACLEOD, Mary. *Tiny True Tales of Animals.* (1920s). NY. ils Harry Roundtree. 12mo. tan cloth. G. H3. $25.00

MACLEOD, R.C. *NWMP & Law Enforcement, 1873-1905.* 1976. Toronto U. notes/index. 218 p. F/sans. B19. $15.00

MACMAHON, Henry. *Orphans of the Storm.* 1922. Grosset Dunlap. photoplay ed. VG+/dj. C8. $75.00

MACMILLAN, Miriam. *Gr Seas & Wht Ice: Far N w/Capt MacMillan.* (1948). Dodd Mead. 1st ed. 8vo. 287 p. F/VG. A2. $17.50

MACMILLAN. *Baseball Century.* 1976. Macmillan (Rutledge). 1st ed. F/F. P8. $35.00

MACNEIL, Neil; see Ballard, W.T.

MACPHERSON, Myra. *Long Time Passing.* 1984. Doubleday. 1st ed. 663 p. NF/NF. A7. $30.00

MACQUARRIE, Hector. *Tahiti Days.* 1920. NY. 8vo. pls. 266 p. pict gr cloth. VG. H3. $12.00

MACQUITTY, William. *Abu Simbel.* 1965. Putnam. 1st ed. 189 p. VG+/dj. M20. $25.00

MACURDY, Grace Harriet. *Troy & Paeonia w/Glimpses of Ancient Balkan Hist & Religion.* 1925. Columbia. 8vo. 259 p. cloth. O2. $30.00

MACY, Jesse. *Autobiography.* 1933. Springfield, IL. Thomas. 8vo. 192 p. NF/box. V3. $50.00

MADAN, Martin. *Thelyphthora; or, Treatise on Female Ruin...* 1780. London. Dodsley. 1st ed. 2 vols. contemporary calf. K1. $350.00

MADDEN, David. *Beautiful Greed.* 1961. NY. 1st ed. inscr. F/NF. A11. $60.00

MADDEN, David. *Cheaters & the Cheated.* 1973. Delano, FL. collected ed. inscr. F/sans. A11. $55.00

MADDEN, R.R. *Shrines & Sepulchres of the Old & New World.* 1831. London. 2 vols. presentation. cloth. O2. $125.00

MADDOCK, Alfred Beaumont. *Practical Observations on Efficacy of Medicated Inhalations.* 1844. London. Simkin Marshall. octavo. 121 p. gilt brn cloth. VG. H5. $250.00

MADDOX, Kenneth W. *Unprejudiced Eye: Drawings of Jasper F Cropsey.* 1980. Hudson River Mus. ils. 72 p. D2. $25.00

MADIGAN, Leo. *Jackarandy.* 1972. London. Paul Elek. 1st ed. author's 1st book. NF/NF. A14. $40.00

MADIS, George. *Winchester Book.* (1985). Brownesboro, TX. latest ed. 655 p. M. A17. $50.00

MADIS, George. *Winchester Model 12.* (1982). Brownsboro. 1st ed. sgn. 174 p. leatherette. M. A17. $20.00

MADISON, Dolly. *Memoirs & Letters of..., Wife of James Madison...* 1886. Houghton Mifflin. 12mo. 210 p. VG. V3. $14.00

MADISON, Peter. *Freud's Concept of Repression & Defense...* 1961. Minneapolis. NM U. 1st ed. 205 p. olive cloth. VG/dj. G1. $50.00

MADSEN, Axel. *William Wyler.* (1973). Crowell. 1st ed. 456 p. clip dj. A7. $15.00

MADSEN, David. *USSA.* 1989. NY. Morrow. 1st ed. sgn. author's 2nd book. F/F. S5. $40.00

MADSEN, Marius. *Shipwreck & Struggle.* 1963. Toronto. 1st ed. 110 p. F/VG. H3. $40.00

MAETERLINCK, Maurice. *Bl Bird: A Fairy Play in 5 Acts.* 1910. NY. 1st Am ed. 8vo. 241 p. gilt bl cloth. VG. H3. $15.00

MAGDOL, Edward. *Anti-Slavery Rank & File: Social Profile...* 1986. NY. Greenwood. 1st ed. 8vo. 172 p. F. V3. $12.00

MAGENDIE, Francois. *Lecons sur les Phenomenes Physiques de la Vie.* 1842. Paris. 4 vols in 2. 2nd issue. G7. $495.00

MAGID, Barry. *Freud's Case Studies: Self-Psychological Perspectives.* 1993. Hillsdale, NJ. Analytic Pr. 206 p. gray cloth. VG/dj. G1. $22.50

MAGIDOFF, Robert. *Yehudi Munuhin: Story of Man & the Musician.* 1956. London. Hale. 286 p. VG. S3. $21.00

MAGNER, D. *New System of Educating Horses...* 1876. Rouse's Point. Lovell. later prt. VG. O3. $45.00

MAGNITSKII, Leontii F. *Arithmetika...* 1703. Moscow. 1st ed. folio. Russian polished mottled calf. F. H5. $25,000.00

MAHAN, A.T. *Influence of Sea Power Upon French Revolution & Empire...* 1895. Little Brn. 6th ed. 2 vols. lg 8vo. gilt bl cloth. VG+. B20. $85.00

MAHAN, Asa. *Modern Mysteries, Explained & Exposed.* 1855. Boston. Jewett. 4th thousand. 8vo. 466 p. cloth. M1. $175.00

MAHAN, M. *Spiritual Point-of-View; or, Glass Reversed, an Answer...* 1863. Appleton. 114 p. H10. $12.50

MAHEDY, William P. *Out of the Night.* (1986). Ballantine. 1st ed. F/NF clip. A7. $30.00

MAHFOUZ, Naguib. *Thief & the Dogs.* 1989. Doubleday. 1st ed. trans from Arabic. F/F. A14. $25.00

MAHLER. *Once Upon a Quilt.* 1973. np. ils. wrp. G2. $11.00

MAHNKE, Susan. *Looking Back: Images of New Eng, 1860-1930.* 1982. Dublin, NH. Yankee. 4to. dj. N2. $8.00

MAHONEY, Tim. *Hollaran's War.* (1985). Delacorte. 1st ed. F/F. A7. $30.00

MAHY, Margaret. *Princess & the Clown.* 1971. Franklin Watts. ils Carol Baker. 28 p. VG-/dj. A3. $8.50

MAIDENBAUM & MARTIN. *Lingering Shadows: Jungians, Freudians & Anti-Semitism.* 1991. Boston. Shambhala. 1st ed. VG/dj. G1. $28.50

MAILER, Norman. *Barbary Shore.* 1951. Rinehart. 1st ed. F/NF. C4. $165.00

MAILER, Norman. *Deaths for the Ladies & Other Disasters.* 1962. NY. 1/950. ils. NF/stiff wrp. E3. $65.00

MAILER, Norman. *Executioner's Song.* 1979. Little Brn. 1st ed. inscr. F/F. L3. $125.00

MAILER, Norman. *Fight.* 1975. Boston. 1st ed. inscr. F/F. A11. $55.00

MAILER, Norman. *Harlot's Ghost.* 1991. Random. 1/300. sgn/#d. F/slipcase. C4. $150.00

MAILER, Norman. *Last Night.* 1984. NY. Targ. 1st ed. 1/250. sgn. F/plain wht dj. L3. $125.00

MAILER, Norman. *We Accuse.* (1965). Diablo. PBO. wrp. A7. $30.00

MAILER, Norman. *Wht Negro.* 1957. City Lights. 4th prt. wrp. A7. $10.00

MAILER, Norman. *Why Are We in Vietnam?* (1967). Putnam. 1st ed. dj. A7. $20.00

MAILLOL, Aristide. *Woodcuts of...Complete Catalogue w/176 Ils.* 1951 (43). Pantheon. sm 4to. gilt brn cloth. F/VG-. F1. $75.00

MAIMON, Ada. *Women Build the Land.* (1962). NY. Herzl. 1st ed. 8vo. 294 p. F/VG. A2. $15.00

MAINE, Floyd Shuster. *Lone Eagle...the Wht Sioux.* 1956. Albuquerque, NM. 1st ed. sgn Maine/inscr Lone Eagle. 208 p. cloth. VG/VG. B11. $150.00

MAIRET, Ethel. *Hand Weaving & Education.* 1912. London. Faber. VG/dj. A16. $10.00

MAIS, S.P. *Majorcan Holiday.* (1956). London. Redman. 1st ed. 8vo. 272 p. VG+/VG. A2. $15.00

MAITIPE, Sirisena. *Gunasena Eng-Sinhalese Pronouncing Dictionary.* ca 1958. np. Gunasena. 2 vols. xl. 12mo. VG. W1. $65.00

MAJNO, Guido. *Healing Hand. Man & Wound in Ancient World.* 1977. Harcourt Brace. 2nd prt. 571 p. dj. G7. $45.00

MAJOR, Clarence. *New Blk Poetry.* 1969. NY. 1st ed. F/ils wrp. A11. $40.00

MAJOR, Clarence. *No.* 1973. NY. Emerson Hall. 1st ed. sgn. F/NF. B2. $100.00

MAJOR, Clarence. *Such Was the Season.* (1987). Mercury. 213 p. F/F. A7. $12.00

MAJOR, Harlan. *Fishing Behind the 8 Ball.* (1952). Harrisburg. 1st ed. 254 p. F/worn. A17. $12.50

MAJOR, Howard. *Domestic Architecture of Early Am Republic. Greek Revival.* 1926. Lippincott. 4to. 256 ils. gilt bl cloth. F/VG+. F1. $100.00

MAJORS, Simon; see Fox, Gardner F.

MAKOWER, Felix. *Constitutional Hist & Constitution of Church of Eng...* 1895. London. Swan Sonnenschein. index. 545 p. H10. $57.50

MAKOWSKI. *Quilting, 1915-83. An Annotated Bibliography.* 1985. np. cloth. G2. $20.00

MAKRIS. *First Prize Quilts.* 1984. np. ils. cloth. G2. $22.95

MALAMUD, Bernard. *God's Grace.* (1982). FSG. 1st ed. NF/NF. B3. $25.00

MALAURIE, Jean. *Last Kings of Thule.* 1982. London. Cape. photos/11 maps. 489 p. M/dj. P4. $30.00

MALCOLM, Janet. *In the Freud Archives.* 1984. Knopf. 1st ed. emb gray brds. VG/dj. G1. $28.50

MALCOLM, John. *Godwin Sideboard.* 1984. London. Collins Crime Club. 1st ed. F/F. M15. $40.00

MALCOLM, John. *Sheep, Goats & Soap.* 1991. London. Collins. 1st ed. F/F. S5. $30.00

MALCOLM, John. *Whistler in the Dark.* 1986. London. Collins. 1st ed. F/F. S5. $35.00

MALCOLM & MAXWELL. *Grouse & Grouse Moors.* 1910. London. Blk. 8vo. ils Charles Whymper. gilt bl-gr cloth. F. F1. $125.00

MALDEN, R.H. *Nine Ghosts.* 1947. London. 1st ed. F/NF. M2. $75.00

MALHAM, John. *Naval Gazetteer: or, Seaman's Complete Guide...* 1796 & 1797. London/Boston. Allen W/Spottswood Nancrede. 2 (mixed) vols. VG+. O6. $475.00

MALING, Arthur. *Rheingold Route.* 1979. London. Gollancz. 1st British ed. F/F. S5. $25.00

MALINGUE, Maurice. *Gauguin: Le Peintre et Son Oeuvre.* 1948. Paris. Les Presses de la Cite. lg quarto. F/prt wrp/stiff wrp. B24. $75.00

MALINOWSKI, Bronislaw. *Malinowski in Mexico.* (1985). Boston. Routledge. 217 p. wrp. F3. $15.00

MALLIN, Jay. *Terror in Vietnam.* (1966). Van Nostrand. 114 p. clip dj. A7. $65.00

MALLOCH, Douglas. *Little Hop-Skipper.* 1926. Doran. 8vo. 99 p. cloth. G+. A3. $10.00

MALO, David. *Hawaiian Antiquities.* 1951. Honolulu. trans Dr N Emerson. ils. 278 p. VG. E5. $35.00

MALO, John W. *Wilderness Canoeing.* (1971). NY. 1st prt. 176 p. F/dj. A17. $19.50

MALONE, Desmond. *Last Landfall.* nd. Doubleday Doran. 1st Am ed. 8vo. 322 p. VG+/VG-. A2. $15.00

MALONE, Michael. *Delectable Mtns.* 1976. Random. 1st ed. inscr. author's 2nd book. w/sgn letter. NF/dj. L3. $200.00

MALONE, Rose Mary. *Wyomingiana: 2 Bibliographies.* 1950. Denver U. 1st ed. 66 p. NF/wrp. scarce. B19. $25.00

MALONE & THOMAS. *Miracle of VA: School for Statesmen.* ca 1984. Ben Franklin Pub. photos. 80 p. VG. B10. $12.00

MALONE. *1001 Patchwork Designs.* 1982. np. ils. wrp. G2. $15.00

MALONE. *1920 Patterns for Traditional Patchwork Quilts.* 1983. np. wrp. G2. $12.95

MALONE. *500 Full-Size Patchwork Patterns.* 1986. np. ils. wrp. G2. $11.00

MALORY, Thomas. *Le Morte de Arthur.* nd. Ltd Ed Club. 1/1500. 3 vols. rare. C1. $149.00

MALOT, Hector. *Nobody's Boy.* 1930 (1916). Cupples Leon. 8 color pls. VG-. P2. $20.00

MALOUF, David. *Remembering Babylon.* 1993. Pantheon. ARC. sgn. F/F slipcase. B2. $50.00

MALRAUX, Andre. *Man's Fate.* 1984. Random. reissue of 1934 French ed. trans Sorel. F/F. A14. $20.00

MALTHUS, Thomas Robert. *Essay on Principle of Population.* 1826. London. John Murray. 2 vols. 19th-century polished calf/brds. G. B14. $450.00

MALTIN, Leonard. *Of Mice & Magic: Hist of Am Animated Cartoons.* 1980. McGraw Hill. 1st ed. 4to. 470 p. F/NF. B20. $45.00

MALTWOOD, K.E. *Enchantments of Britain; or, King Arthur's Round Table...* 1982 (1st ca 1927). np. NF. C1. $7.50

MALTZ, Albert. *Long Day in a Short Life.* (1957). Internat. 350 p. poor dj. A7. $18.00

MALVERN & MALVERN. *Land of Surprise.* 1938. McLoughlin. unp. VG. M20. $40.00

MALZBERG, Barry. *Man Who Loved Midnight Lady.* 1980. Doubleday. 1st ed. F/F. N3. $10.00

MALZBERG, Barry. *Screen.* 1970. Olympia. 1st Am hc ed. F/F. F4. $15.00

MAMBOURY, Ernest. *Les Iles des Princes. Banlieu Maritime d'Istanbul.* 1943. Istanbul. 8vo. ils/5 fld maps. 94 p. cloth. O2. $30.00

MAMET, David. *Am Buffalo.* 1978. Grove. 1st hc ed. author's 1st book. F/F. Q1. $150.00

MAMET, David. *Some Freaks.* 1975. Boston. 1st ed. sgn. F/F. A11. $45.00

MAN, Felix. *150 Yrs of Artists' Lithos 1803-1953.* VG/VG-. A1. $75.00

MANARA, Milo. *Click, a Woman Under the Influence.* 1985. Catalan Comm. laminated brds. NF. C8. $35.00

MANARIN, Louis H. *Richmond At War: Minutes of the City Council 1861-65.* ca 1965. UNC. Richmond Civil War Centennial Comm. 645 p. VG. B10. $35.00

MANCHESTER, William. *Death of a President.* 1967. Harper Row. 1st ed. NF/NF. E3. $30.00

MANCIET, Yves. *Land of Tomorrow: Amazon Journey.* (1964). London. Oliver Boyd. 1st Eng ed. 167 p. F3. $15.00

MANDEL, Gabriele. *Oriental Erotica.* 1983. NY. Crescent. 1st ed. trans Rossiter. 80 p. F/dj. W1. $25.00

MANDEVILLE, John. *Voiage & Travaile of...* 1887. London. Pickering Chatto. 1/100 on lg paper. vellum spine. F. O6. $375.00

MANDEVILLE, John. *Voiage & Travaile of...* 1928. Random/Grabhorn. 1/150. 31 woodcuts. NF/brn cloth slipcase. H5. $1,750.00

MANDRELL & COLLINS. *Mandrell Family Album.* (1983). Nashville. Thomas Nelson. 1st ed. sq 8vo. 192 p. F/F. A2. $12.50

MANFRED, Frederick. *Arrow of Love.* 1961. Denver. 1st ed. 1/500. inscr. NF/NF. A11. $95.00

MANFRED, Frederick. *This Is the Yr.* 1947. Garden City. 1st ed. sgn as Frederick Feike Manfred. NF/VG+. A11. $75.00

MANGET, Johannes Jacob. *Bibliotheca Pharmaceutico-Medico...* 1703. Genevae. Sumptibus Chouet. 2 vols. 33 pls. contemporary calf. G7. $2,500.00

MANGO, Cyril. *Materials for Study of Mosaics of St Sophia at Istanbul.* 1962. WA. 4to. 4 diagrams/118 pls. 145 p. cloth. dj. O2. $100.00

MANGUEL & GUADALUPI. *Dictionary of Imaginary Places.* (1980). NY. Macmillan. 1st Am ed. 4to. 438 p. F/F. A2. $30.00

MANLEY, G.B. *Aviation From the Ground Up.* (1929). Chicago. ils/index. 373 p. G. B18. $25.00

MANLEY, Michael. *Politics of Change.* 1975. WA. Howard U. 1st Am ed. 270 p. dj. A7. $17.00

MANN, Arthur. *Baseball Confidential.* 1951. McKay. 1st ed. VG+/VG. P8. $40.00

MANN, Arthur. *Branch Rickey.* 1957. Houghton Mifflin. 1st ed. VG+/G+. P8. $50.00

MANN, E.B. *Killer's Range.* (1943). Triangle. VG/dj. B9. $15.00

MANN, Graciela. *12 Prophets of Aleijadinho.* (1967). Austin, TX. 1st ed. 4to. 130 p. F/F. A2. $25.00

MANN, James. *Am Bird-Keeper's Manual; or, Directions Proper Management...* 1848. Boston. self pub. 1st ed. 12mo. 166 p. emb blk cloth. NF. B14. $100.00

MANN, Matthew. *System of Gynecology by Am Authors.* 1887-88. Phil. Lea. 2 vols. 201 engravings/3 color pls. orig sheep. G. G7. $150.00

MANN, Nicholas R. *Sedona-Sacred Earth.* 1989. Zivah Pub. 12mo. VG. A8. $5.00

MANN, Robert W. *Rails 'Neath the Palms.* 1983. CA. Darwin Pub. VG/dj. A16. $25.00

MANN, Thomas. *Beloved Returns: Lotte in Weimar.* 1940. Knopf. 1st ed. 1/395. sgn. trans from German. F/dj/slipcase. B24. $550.00

MANN, Thomas. *Coming Victory of Democracy.* 1938. Knopf. later prt. sgn. F/F. B4. $125.00

MANN, Thomas. *Nocturnes.* 1934. Equinox Co-op Pr. 1st ed. sgn. ils Lynd Ward. F/NF slipcase. Q1. $350.00

MANN, Thomas. *Transposed Heads.* 1941. Knopf. ARC/1st Am ed. mk Sample Copy. VG/self wrp. L3. $175.00

MANNIN, Ethel. *Rebels' Ride.* (1964). London. Hutchinson. 287 p. NF/dj. A7. $30.00

MANNING, David. *Brute.* 1925. Chelsea House. 1st ed. NF/dj. B9. $85.00

MANNING, David. *Bull Hunter.* 1924. Chelsea House. 1st ed. VG/dj. B9. $65.00

MANNING, Mary. *Last Chronicle of Ballyfungus.* (1978). Little Brn. 1st ed. F/F ils Edward Gory dj. B4. $45.00

MANNING, Olivia. *Dreaming Shore.* (1950). London. Evans. 1st ed. 8vo. 202 p. VG/VG. A2. $35.00

MANNING, Rosemary. *Boney Was A Warrior.* 1966. London. Hamish Hamilton. 1st ed. 12mo. 96 p. VG/G+. T5. $15.00

MANNING, Roy. *Renegade Ranch.* 1950. London. Fousham. 1st ed. VG/dj. B9. $20.00

MANNING, Russ. *Tarzan in the Land That Time Forgot.* 1974. Treasure House. 1st ed. pict brds. F/sans. F4. $30.00

MANNING, Samuel. *Palestine Ils by Pen & Pencil.* ca 1890. NY. sm folio. ils/maps. 198 p. aeg. pict cloth. O2. $65.00

MANNIX, D.P. *Sporting Chance: Unusual Methods of Hunting.* 1967. NY. ils. 253 p. F/dj. A17. $10.00

MANNONI, O. *Freud.* 1971. Pantheon. 1st Eng-language ed. 216 p. prt bl cloth. VG/dj. G1. $22.50

MANO, Keith. *Bishop's Progress.* 1968. Houghton Mifflin. AP. author's 1st book. sgn. sbdg. F. C4. $85.00

MANO, Keith. *Horn.* (1969). Houghton Mifflin. 2nd prt. dj. A7. $12.00

MANOR, Elizabeth. *Virgin Mistress: Study in Survival.* 1964. Doubleday. 1st Am ed. 8vo. 206 p. VG+/VG. A2. $12.50

MANS, Philip Ainsworth. *Spanish Main: Focus of Envy 1492-1700.* 1935. Scribner. 1st ed. 8vo. 2 pls/4 maps. 278 p. maroon brds. G. B11. $60.00

MANSFIELD, Edward D. *Life of General Winfield Scott Embracing Campaign in Mexico.* 1848. NY. Barnes. 2nd ed. 12mo. pls/maps. 414 p. fair. B11. $35.00

MANSFIELD, Katherine. *Aloe.* 1930. Knopf. 1/975. #d. VG+/VG+. Q1. $400.00

MANSON, Richard. *Theory of Knowledge of Giambattista Vico.* 1969. np. Archon Books. 1st ed. sm 8vo. 83 p. bl cloth. F/dj. G1. $16.50

MANTEGAZZA, Paolo. *Sexual Relations of Mankind.* 1937. Falstaff. special ed. ils/photos. G. V2. $15.00

MANTER, Ethel. *Rocket of the Comstock.* 1950. Caldwell, ID. Caxton. 1st ed. 8vo. 256 p. bl cloth. VG/G. B11. $20.00

MANTLE, Mickey. *Education of a Baseball Player.* 1967. Simon Schuster. 1st ed. VG+/VG+. P8. $50.00

MANTLE, Mickey. *Mick.* 1985. Doubleday. 1st ed. F/F. P8. $15.00

MANTLE, Mickey. *Mickey Mantle Story.* 1953. Holt. later prt. VG. P8. $50.00

MANTLE, Mickey. *Quality of Courage.* 1964. Doubleday. 1st ed. VG/G+. P8. $30.00

MANUCY, Albert. *Artillery Through the Ages.* 1962. GPO. reprint. 8vo. 92 p. G/wrp. A17. $8.50

MANWILL, Marion. *How To Shoe a Horse.* 1971. S Brunswick. Barnes. 3rd prt. O3. $18.00

MANZONI, Alessandro. *I Promessi Sposi.* 1951. Verona. LEC. quarto. trans/intro Boothroyd. ils/sgn Bramanti. F/dj/slipcase. B24. $150.00

MAPPLETHORPE, Robert. *Certain People: Book of Portraits.* 1985. Pasadena. Twelvetrees. 1st ed. F/F. B2. $150.00

MAPPLETHORPE, Robert. *Some Women.* (1989). Little Brn. 1st ed. intro Joan Didion. NF/NF. B3. $60.00

MARAINI, Fosco. *Island of the Fisherwomen.* 1962 (1960). NY. HBW. 1st Am ed. 8vo. F/VG. A2. $25.00

MARAINI, Fosco. *Japan: Patterns of Continuity.* 1971. Tokyo/Palo Alto. Kodansha. 2nd prt. 4to. 2 fld maps. 240 p. VG/dj. W1. $25.00

MARASHLIAN, Levon. *Politics & Demography: Armenians, Turks & Kurds...* 1991. Cambridge. 8vo. 152 p. O2. $25.00

MARBERRY, M.M. *Golden Voice.* 1947. NY. Farrar Straus. 1st ed. 8vo. 376 p. F/G. A2. $12.50

MARBURY, Mary Orvis. *Favorite Flies & Their Histories.* (1988). Secaucus. facsimile of 1892 ed. ils/pls. 522 p. F/dj. A17. $25.00

MARCEAU, Marcel. *Story of Bip.* 1976. Harper Row. 1st ed. NF/VG. P2. $25.00

MARCET, Jane. *Conversations on Political Economy in Which Elements...* 1817. London. Longman. 2nd ed. 12mo. 486 p. half leather. VG-. S9. $115.00

MARCH, Francis. *Hist of the World War.* 1919. Brunswick. 1st ed. 12mo. G. A8. $15.00

MARCOU, Jules. *Nouvelle Recherches sur L'Origine du Nom d'Amerique.* 1888. Paris. Soc Geographie. 27 p. VG/wrp. O6. $45.00

MARCUS, Greil. *Lipstick Traces: Secret Hist of 20th Century.* (1989). Harvard. 2nd prt. rem mk. NF/VG. A7. $17.00

MARCUS, J.R. *Memoirs of Am Jews, 1775-1865.* 1955. Phil. 3 vols. VG/djs. B18. $35.00

MARCUS, Kaete Ephraim. *Kaete Ephraim Marcus.* 1961. Israel. Massadah. 45 full-p pls. 54 p. VG/poor. S3. $30.00

MARCUS, Maeva. *Origins of Federal Judiciary: Essays...* 1992. NY. Oxford. M11. $40.00

MARCY, Mary E. *Rhymes of Early Jungle Folk.* 1922. Chicago. 124 p. pict gr cloth. VG. H3. $15.00

MARCY, Randolph B. *Prairie Traveler: Handbook for Overland Expedition...* 1859. NY. Harper. xl. 12mo. 340 p. stp cloth. scarce. H9. $395.00

MARCY, Randolph B. *Prairie Traveler: Handbook for Overland Expeditions...* 1859. Harper. 1st ed. emb bdg. F. A18. $450.00

MARCY, Randolph B. *Thirty Yrs of Army Life on the Border.* 1866. NY. 1st ed. ils. 442 p. bevelled cloth. VG. D3. $85.00

MARCY & MCCLELLAN. *Exploration of LA in Yr 1852.* 1854. WA. 286 p. B18. $125.00

MARDERSTEIG, Giovanni. *Die Officina Bodoni, Das Werk Einer Handpresse 1923-77.* 1979. Hamburg. Maximilian-Gesellschaft. 1st ed. w/prospectus. F. F1. $145.00

MARDOCK, Robert Winston. *Reformers & the Am Indian.* 1971. MO U. 1st ed. 245 p. F/NF clip. B19. $30.00

MARGE. *Little Lulu & Her Pals.* 1939. David McKay. later ed. VG. scarce. L1. $55.00

MARGE. *Little Lulu on Parade.* 1941. David McKay. later ed. G. scarce. L1. $15.00

MARGO, Elisabeth. *Taming the 49er.* 1955. Rinehart. 1st ed. ils. 245 p. F/NF. B19. $20.00

MARGRY, Pierre. *Decouvertes et Etablissement des Francais Dans l'Ouest...* 1875. Paris. Jouaust. 6 vols. octavo. portraits. orig prt wrp. H9. $750.00

MARGUERITE, of Navarre. *Heptameron; or, Tales & Novels...* nd. Phil. Barrie. subscriber/1st thus ed. 2 vols. red levant morocco. F. H5. $250.00

MARIANI, Paul. *Timing Devices.* 1977. Pennyroyal. 1/175. sgn. ils/sgn Barry Moser. F. F1. $245.00

MARIANI, Valerio. *Michaelangelo the Painter.* 1973. NY. Abrams. color pls. VG. C5. $100.00

MARIANO. *Romantic Embroidery. Floral Designs & Motifs.* 1984. np. cloth. G2. $20.00

MARIE, Queen of Roumania. *Story of Naughty Kildeen.* nd. Harcourt Brace. 1/1350. hand-colored pls. F/broken box. F1. $595.00

MARINI, Marino. *Marini.* 1960. Abrams. 1/300. w/sgn litho. VG+/VG+. A1. $750.00

MARION, George. *Free Pr: Portrait of Monopoly.* 1946. New Century. 48 p. wrp. A7. $10.00

MARITAIN, Jacques. *Approaches to God.* ca 1954. NY. Harper. xl. 128 p. H10. $10.00

MARITAIN, Jacques. *Dream of Descartes.* ca 1944. NY. Philosophical Lib. 200 p. H10. $20.00

MARITAIN, Jacques. *Range of Reason.* 1952. Scribner. 227 p. H10. $15.00

MARITAIN, Jacques. *Ransoming the Time...* 1946. Scribner. trans HL Binsse. 322 p. H10. $15.00

MARITI, Giovanni. *Travels in Island of Cyprus.* 1909. Cambridge. 8vo. 199 p. F. O2. $95.00

MARK, Ber. *Uprising in the Warsaw Ghetto.* 1975. Schocken. 209 p. VG/G+. S3. $25.00

MARK, Davis. *Sheep of the Lal Bagh.* 1967. Parents Magazine. ils Lionel Kalish. 4to. 41 p. G+. A3. $6.00

MARK, Jan. *Ennead.* 1978. Crowell. 1st Am ed. F/F. N3. $20.00

MARKHAM, Edwin. *CA the Wonderful.* (1914). Hearst Internat Lib. 1st ed. inscr/sgn. pict bdg. F/clip. A18. $60.00

MARKHAM, Elizabeth. *Poems...* 1921. Portland, OR. 1st thus ed. 12mo. 31 p. wrp. VG. D3. $15.00

MARKHAM, Ernest. *Clematis.* 1935. London. Country Life. 1st ed. photos. 116 p. VG/dj. B28. $25.00

MARKHAM, Sidney. *Colonial Architecture of Antigua, Guatemala.* 1966. Am Philosophical Soc. 1st ed. 1/2000. 335 p. F3. $75.00

MARKHAM, Violet R. *S Africa: Past & Present...Account of Hist, Politics...* 1900. London. Smith Elder. 1st ed. 450 p. cloth. VG+. M8. $150.00

MARKMAN, Earnest. *10,000 Miles in a Balloon!* 1873. St Louis. Mercantile Pub. 1st ed. 16mo. 96 p. M1. $750.00

MARKS, Arthur H. *Hist Notes on Lincoln's Inn Fields.* 1922. London. Hertford Record Co. maps. 103 p. red cloth. VG. V2. $13.00

MARKS, Frances W. *Tiger Tiny & Tippy.* 1937. Saalfield. Rebus Adventure series. NF. M5. $20.00

MARKS, Jeanette. *13 Days.* 1929. NY. Boni. 1st ed. VG+. B2. $45.00

MARKS, Richard Lee. *Cortes: Great Adventurer & Fate of Aztec Mexico.* 1993. Knopf. 1st ed. 8vo. map ep. half cloth. M/dj. P4. $27.50

MARKSON, David. *Ballad of Dingus Magee.* 1965. Indianapolis. 1st hc ed. inscr. NF/VG+. A11. $55.00

MARKSON, David. *Going Down.* 1970. NY. 1st ed. sgn. NF/F. A11. $55.00

MARKSON, David. *Malcolm Lowry's Volcano.* 1978. NY. 1st ed. sgn. F/NF. A11. $50.00

MARKSON, David. *Miss Doll, Go Home.* 1965. NY. Dell. PBO. inscr. F/ils wrp. A11. $40.00

MARKUS, Julia. *La Mora.* 1976. WA, DC. 1/1000. sgn. F/silver wrp. A11. $60.00

MARLOWE, George Francis. *Churches of Old New Eng...* 1947. NY. Macmillan. ils. 222 p. H10. $15.00

MARLOWE, Hugh; see Patterson, Henry.

MARLOWE, Kenneth. *Mr Madam: Confessions of a Male Madam.* (1964). Sherbourne Pr. 1st ed. 8vo. 246 p. VG/VG. A2. $20.00

MARLOWE, Stephen; see Lesser, Milton.

MARON, Margaret. *Death of a Butterfly.* 1984. Doubleday Crime Club. 1st ed. F/NF. M15. $35.00

MARQUETTE, A.F. *Brands, Trademarks & Good Will: Story of Quaker Oats Co.* (1967). McGraw Hill. 1st ed. photos. 247 p. VG/dj. C10. $24.50

MARQUEZ, Gabriel Garcia. *Autumn of the Patriarch.* 1977. London. Cape. 1st ed. NF/NF clip. A14. $40.00

MARQUEZ, Gabriel Garcia. *Chronicle of a Death Fortold.* 1983. Knopf. 1st Am ed. F/F. M15. $65.00

MARQUEZ, Gabriel Garcia. *Cronica de Una Muerte Anunciada.* 1981. Bogota. 1st ed. F/F. A11. $45.00

MARQUEZ, Gabriel Garcia. *El Secuestro.* 1982. Bogota. 1st Colombian ed. F/ils wrp. A11. $40.00

MARQUEZ, Gabriel Garcia. *In Evil Hour.* 1979. Harper Row. 1st ed. trans from Spanish. NF/NF clip. A14. $50.00

MARQUEZ, Gabriel Garcia. *Innocent Erendira.* (1979). London. Cape. 1st ed. F/NF clip. B3. $50.00

MARQUEZ, Gabriel Garcia. *Love in Time of Cholera.* 1988. Knopf. 1st ed. F/F. N3. $15.00

MARQUEZ, Gabriel Garcia. *Story of a Shipwrecked Sailor.* 1986. London. Cape. 1st ed. trans. F/F. A14. $25.00

MARQUEZ, Gabriel Garcia. *Strange Pilgrims.* 1993. NY. Knopf. AP of 1st ed. 12 stories. F/prt gr wrp. Q1. $75.00

MARQUEZ, Gabriel Garcia. *Todos Los Cuentos.* 1986. Bogota. 1st ed. F/F. A11. $35.00

MARQUEZ, Gabriel Garcia. *100 Yrs of Solitude.* 1970. Harper. 1st ed. F/F. B2. $650.00

MARQUEZ, Gabriel Garcia. *100 Yrs of Solitude.* 1982. London. Cape. 3rd prt. trans from Spanish. F/F. A14. $30.00

MARQUIS, Don. *Off the Arm.* 1930. Doubleday Doran. 1st ed. yel prt blk cloth. VG. V2. $18.00

MARQUIS, Don. *Out of the Sea.* 1927. Doubleday. 1st ed. VG. C1. $12.50

MARQUIS WHO'S WHO. *Who's Who in the W.* 1976. Marquis Who's Who. 4to. VG. A8. $10.00

MARRIE, J.J.; see Creasey, John.

MARRIN, Albert. *Aztecs & Spaniards.* 1986. Atheneum. 1st ed. 212 p. dj. F3. $15.00

MARRON, Eugenie. *Albacora.* 1957. NY. 1st prt. presentation/sgn. 214 p. VG/dj. A17. $17.50

MARROW, Alfred J. *Practical Theorist: Life & Work of Kurt Lewin.* 1969. Basic Books. 1st ed. 290 p. gray cloth. VG/dj. G1. $25.00

MARRYAT, Frederick. *Diary in Am w/Remarks on Its Instit.* 1838. Phil. Carey Hart. 1 vol ed. 12mo. 263 p. VG+. B28. $65.00

MARSE, Juan. *Fallen.* 1979. Little Brn. 1st ed. trans from Spanish. NF/NF clip. A14. $30.00

MARSH, Dave. *Glory Days: Bruce Springsteen in the 1980s.* 1987. Pantheon. 1st ed. dj. N2. $7.50

MARSH, U. Bowdoin. *Bowdoin Family in the US.* 1982. private prt. 1st ed. photos. 228 p. VG. B10. $35.00

MARSHALL, Alan; see Westlake, Donald E.

MARSHALL, Dean. *Silver Robin.* 1947. NY. 12mo. ils. 246 p. yel pict cloth. VG. H3. $20.00

MARSHALL, Donald. *Ra'Ivavae. Expedition to...Polynesia.* 1961. NY. 1st ed. 8vo. 301 p. pict gr cloth. F/VG. H3. $20.00

MARSHALL, John. *Life of George WA, Commander in Chief of Am Forces...* 1925. NY. Wm Wise. special Fredericksburg ed. 5 vols. cloth. VG+. M8. $250.00

MARSHALL, John. *Santa Fe: Railroad That Built an Empire.* (1945). NY. 1st ed. 465 p. cloth. VG. D3. $15.00

MARSHALL, Kathryn. *In the Combat Zone.* (1987). Little Brn. 1st ed. 270 p. F/F. A7. $35.00

MARSHALL, Mel. *Steelhead.* (1973). Winchester. 196 p. F/G. A17. $17.50

MARSHALL, Nina L. *Mushroom Book.* 1902 (1901). NY. pls. 167 p. VG+. B28. $20.00

MARSHALL, Paule. *Chosen Place, Timeless People.* 1969. HBW. 1st ed. author's 3rd book. F/NF. B4. $275.00

MARSHALL, Paule. *Daughters.* 1991. Atheneum. 1st ed. inscr. F/F. B2. $45.00

MARSHALL, Robert. *Arctic Village.* 1933. NY. 8vo. pls. 399 p. F/VG. H3. $15.00

MARSHALL, S.L.A. *Swift Sword: Hist Record of Israel's Victory, June 1967.* 1967. Am Heritage. 4to. 144 p. VG. S3. $15.00

MARSHALL, W.P. *Afloat on the Pacific; or, Notes of 3 Yrs Life at Sea.* 1876. Zanesville, OH. ils. 176 p. VG-. E5. $65.00

MARSHALL, William. *Far Away Man.* 1984. Holt. 1st Am ed. sgn. F/F. S5. $35.00

MARSHALL, William. *Frogsmouth.* 1987. Mysterious. 1st ed. F/F. F4. $16.00

MARSHALL, William. *Inches.* 1994. Mysterious. ARC. F/wrp. B2. $30.00

MARSHALL, William. *Out of Nowhere.* 1988. Mysterious. 1st ed. F/F. F4. $16.00

MARSHALL, William. *War Machine.* 1988. Mysterious. 1st Am ed. sgn. F/F. S5. $35.00

MARSHALL & PECKHAM. *Campaigns of the Am Revolution: Altas of Manuscript Maps.* 1976. Ann Arbor. 58 maps. NF/worn. O6. $45.00

MARSTEN, Richard; see Hunter, Evan.

MARSTON, Edward. *Wolves of Savernake.* 1993. St Martin. 1st Am ed. sgn. F/F. M15. $30.00

MARSTON, Everett C. *Origin & Development of NE U, 1898-1960.* 1961. Boston. NE U. VG/dj. N2. $8.50

MARSTON. *Amish Quilting Patterns.* 1987. np. ils/full-size patterns. wrp. G2. $5.00

MARSTON. *Q Is for Quilt: An ABC Quilt Pattern Book.* 1987. np. ils. wrp. G2. $7.00

MARTIN, Annie. *Home Life on an Ostrich Farm.* 1891. NY. Appleton. 1st Am ed. 288 p. VG. N2. $45.00

MARTIN, Ben. *John Blk's Body: Story in Pictures.* (1939). Vanguard. 1st ed. sm 4to. dj. A7. $25.00

MARTIN, Benjamin Ellis. *In the Footprints of Charles Lamb.* 1891. Bentley. 1st Eng ed. ils Railton/Fulleylove. G. M18. $25.00

MARTIN, Bernard. *That Man From Smyrna: Hist Novel.* 1978. Jonathan David. 339 p. VG/VG. S3. $21.00

MARTIN, C.H. *Angelo Herndon Case & S Justice.* (1976). Baton Rouge. 234 p. dj. A7. $20.00

MARTIN, Charles. *Sketch of Sam Bass, the Bandit.* (1956). Norman, OK. 1st thus ed. ils. 166 p. brds. VG/dj. B18. $22.50

MARTIN, Charles. *Steal the Bacon.* 1987. Baltimore. 1st ed. F/F. V1. $15.00

MARTIN, Claire. *In an Iron Glove.* 1968. Toronto. Ryerson. 1st ed. trans from French. NF/NF. A14. $20.00

MARTIN, Dick. *Wizard of Oz Masks.* 1982. Dover. 1st ed. VG/wrp. L1. $12.50

MARTIN, Earl S. *Reaching the Other Side.* (1978). Crown. 281 p. NF/VG. A7. $30.00

MARTIN, Edward Sanford. *Poems.* 1914. NY. 1st ed. inscr. cloth. F. V1. $30.00

MARTIN, Frederika. *Hunting of the Silver Fleece.* (1946). Greenburg, NY. 1st ed. 8vo. 328 p. VG+/VG. A2. $30.00

MARTIN, George R.R. *Armageddon Rag.* 1983. Nemo Pr. 1st ed. 1/500. sgn/#d. as new/slipcase. M2. $70.00

MARTIN, Harold C. *Outlasting Marble & Brass: Hist of Church Pension Fund.* ca 1986. NY. Church Hymnal. ils. 312 p. H10. $15.00

MARTIN, J. *Scraps, Blocks & Quilts.* 1990. np. ils. wrp. G2. $20.00

MARTIN, John. *Little Readers' 1st Book for Little Children.* (1929). Platt Munk. sm 4to. pict orange cloth. G+. T5. $15.00

MARTIN, Judy. *Judy Martin's Ultimate Book fo Quilt Block Patterns.* 1989. np. ils/designs. wrp. G2. $16.00

MARTIN, Judy. *Shining Star Quilts.* 1987. np. ils. wrp. G2. $20.00

MARTIN, Kenneth R. *Whalemen's Paintings & Drawings.* (1983). Sharon. Kendall Whaling Mus. 172 p. dj. A17. $25.00

MARTIN, Lori. *Darkling Hills.* 1986. NY. NAL. 1st ed. author's 1st book. F/F. N3. $15.00

MARTIN, Mary. *Mary Martin's Needlepoint.* 1969. np. ils. cloth. G2. $16.00

MARTIN, Mary. *My Heart Belongs.* 1976. NY. Morrow. 1st ed. NF/dj. B20. $30.00

MARTIN, N. *Back to Sq One.* 1988. np. ils. wrp. G2. $18.00

MARTIN, N. *Banner Yr.* 1989. np. ils. wrp. G2. $13.00

MARTIN, N. *Copy Art for Quilters.* 1988. np. wrp. G2. $6.00

MARTIN, N. *Hanky Panky Blouse.* 1991. np. ils. wrp. G2. $7.00

MARTIN, N. *Houses, Cottages & Cabins Patchwork Quilts.* nd. np. ils. wrp. G2. $6.00

MARTIN, N. *Pieces of the Past.* 1986. np. ils/patterns. wrp. G2. $18.95

MARTIN, N. *Tea Party Time: Romantic Quilts & Tasty Tidbits.* 1992. np. full-size pattern. 64 p. wrp. G2. $20.00

MARTIN, Theodore. *Life of His Royal Highness the Prince Consort.* 1875-1880.. London. Smith Elder. mixed set of 5 vols. presentation by Queen Victoria. VG. H5. $3,000.00

MARTIN, Tyrone C. *Most Fortunate Ship: Narrative Hist of Old Ironsides.* (1980). Chester, CT. 1st ed. lg 8vo. 388 p. F/VG+. A2. $25.00

MARTIN, Valerie. *Great Divorce.* 1994. Doubleday. 1st ed. sgn. F/F. L3. $45.00

MARTIN, W.A.P. *Awakening of China.* 1907. Doubleday Page. 1st ed. xl. 4to. 48 pls. 328 p. VG. W1. $35.00

MARTIN, William T. *Hist of Franklin Co...* 1858. Columbus. 1st ed. 450 p. rebound. D7. $125.00

MARTIN & MARTIN. *Standard Guide to Mexico & the Caribbean.* 1959. Funk Wagnall. 12mo. 729 p. VG/VG. B11. $10.00

MARTIN. *Angel Threads: Creating Lovable Clothes for Little Ones.* 1986. np. ils. wrp. G2. $15.00

MARTINDALE, Compiler. *MI Official Directory & Legislative Manual.* (1909). Lansing. 21 fld maps. 886 p. VG. A17. $22.50

MARTINDALE & MARTINDALE. *Mental Disability in Am Since WWII.* 1985. Philosophical Lib. 296 p. beige cloth. VG/dj. G1. $17.50

MARTINEAU, Alice. *Herbaceous Garden.* 1913. London. Williams Norgate. ils/color pls/fld plan. 298 p. H10. $45.00

MARTINEAU, Harriet. *Retrospect of W Travel.* 1942. NY. Harper. reprint of 1838 ed. 2 vols. emb cloth. F/dj/slipcase. P4. $50.00

MARTINEAU, James. *Church-Life? or, Sect-Life?* 1859. London. Whitfield. 48 p. wrp. H10. $15.00

MARTINEAU, James. *Study of Religion: Its Sources & Contents.* 1888. Macmillan. 1st Am ed. xl. 2 vols. H10. $45.00

MARTINEAU, James. *Types of Ethical Theory.* 1885. Clarendon. 2 vols. panelled bl cloth. VG. G1. $85.00

MARTINEAU, Mrs. Philip. *Gardening in Sunny Lands.* 1924. London. ils/photos. 296 p. B26. $45.00

MARTINES, L. *Power & Imagination: City-States in Renaissance Italy.* 1979. Knopf. 1st ed. 8vo. 368 p. F/F. A2. $15.00

MARTINET, Johannes Florentius. *Catechism of Nature for Use of Children.* 1812. Trenton, NJ. Denton. 12mo. 108 p. NF/marbled wrp. B24. $275.00

MARTINS, A. *O Bombardeamento da Alexandria.* 1882. Porto & Rio de Janerio. Clavel/Couto. fld map. marbled brds. VG. O6. $75.00

MARUVA, Saiich. *Singular Rebellion.* 1986. Tokyo/NY. Kodansha Internat. 2nd imp. trans Dennis Keene. F/F. A14. $25.00

MARVEL, I. *Fresh Gleanings; or, New Sheaf From Old Fields...* 1847. Harper. 1st ed. author's 1st book. NF. B4. $100.00

MARVIN, E.M. *To the E by Way of the W. Graphic Descriptions of Travel...* 1787. St Louis. 8vo. 606 p. cloth. O2. $40.00

MARX, Karl. *Capital: Critical Analysis of Capitalist Production.* ca 1904. London. Sonnenschein. trans Moore/Aveling. G. V4. $25.00

MARX, Karl. *Karl Marx Dictionary.* (1965). Philosophical Lib. 273 p. worn. A7. $18.00

MARX, Karl. *Poverty of Philosophy.* nd. Chicago. CH Kerr. VG. V4. $17.50

MARX, Karl. *Revolution & Counter-Revolution; or, Germany in 1848.* ca 1912. Chicago. CH Kerr. VG. V4. $20.00

MARX, Karl. *Theories of Surplus Value: Parts I-III.* 1969. Moscow. Progress Pub. 2nd prt. 3 vols. F/VG. V4. $35.00

MARX, R.F. *Voyage of the Nina II.* (1963). World. 1st ed. 8vo. 249 p. F/F. A2. $25.00

MARZANI, Cark. *We Can Be Friends.* 1952. NY. Topical Books. 1st ed. 380 p. A7. $24.00

MASEFIELD, John. *Book of Discoveries.* ca 1920. London. Wells Gardner. ils Gordon Browne. 354 p. VG. S10. $25.00

MASEFIELD, John. *King Cole.* 1921. London. 1/780. sgn. G+. A1. $30.00

MASEFIELD, John. *MacBeth Production.* 1946. Macmillan. 1st ed. VG/VG. E3. $40.00

MASEFIELD, John. *Royal Right.* 1920. London. 1st ed. NF/VG+. V1. $30.00

MASEFIELD, John. *S & E.* 1929 (1928). Medici Soc/Macmillan. ils Jacynth Parsons. 29 p. gilt gr cloth. VG. S10. $35.00

MASEFIELD, John. *Tristan & Isolt.* 1927. Macmillan. 1st ed on lg paper. 1/350. sgn. F/worn slipcase. C1. $79.50

MASEFIELD, John. *Wanderer of Liverpool.* 1930. NY. 1st Am ed. 139 p. gilt gr cloth. VG. H3. $25.00

MASEFIELD, Katherine. *Garden Party & Other Stories.* 1939. London. 1/1200. quarto. ils Marie Laurencin. F/dj/pub slipcase. H5. $3,500.00

MASLIN, Marshall. *Camera Tour in Full Color: San Francisco & Bay Cities.* ca 1938. San Francisco. Prt Corp. oblong 4to. ils. pict wrp. H9. $25.00

MASO, Carole. *Art Lover.* 1990. San Francisco. N Point. 1st ed. author's 2nd novel. F/F. L3. $25.00

MASO, Carole. *Ava (Normal).* 1993. Dalkey Archive Pr. 1st ed. sgn. author's 3rd book. F/F. L3. $45.00

MASON, A.E.W. *Life of Sir Francis Drake.* 1941. Hodder Stoughton. 1st ed. 8vo. 436 p. bl cloth. VG. B20. $45.00

MASON, Arthur. *Roving Lobster.* 1931. Doubleday Doran. 1st ed. ils Robert Lawson. 131 p. G+. P2. $25.00

MASON, Bobbie Ann. *Feather Crowns.* 1993. Harper Collins. ARC. inscr. F/wrp. B2. $45.00

MASON, Bobbie Ann. *Love Life.* 1989. Harper Row. 1st ed. sgn. F/F. C4. $55.00

MASON, Bobbie Ann. *Shiloh & Other Stories.* 1982. NY. 1st hc book/1st fiction. inscr. F/NF. A11. $115.00

MASON, Bobbie Ann. *Spence + Lila.* (1988). Harper Row. 1st ed. sgn. F/F. B4. $65.00

MASON, Francis K. *Battle Over Britain.* 1969. London. 1st ed. VG+/dj. B18. $47.50

MASON, Georgia. *Guide to Plants of Wallowa Mtns of NE OR.* 1980 (1975). Eugene. ils/map. 411 p. M. B26. $20.00

MASON, John. *Papermaking As an Artistic Craft.* 1963. England. Leicester. wht bdg. G. B30. $25.00

MASON, Lucy Randolph. *Standards for Workers in S Industry.* 1931. Nat Consumers League. 46 p. VG. B10. $30.00

MASON, Miriam. *Pony Called Lightning.* 1948. Macmillan. 1st ed. VG/G. O3. $30.00

MASON, Miriam. *Smiling Hill Farm.* (1937). Ginn & Co. 8vo. ils Kate Seredy. 312 p. reading copy. T5. $20.00

MASON, Mrs. A.F.H. *12 Outputs: Relative to Inhaling Power...of the Brain.* (1907). Brookline, MA. self pub. 1st thus ed? 12mo. 105 p. VG+. A2. $15.00

MASON, Paul. *Constitution of State of CA, Constitution of US...* 1838. Sacramento. CA State Prt Office. 394 p. wrp. M11. $25.00

MASON, Redfern. *Songs & Lore of Ireland.* 1910. NY. 1st ed. 8vo. 329 p. gilt gr cloth. VG. H3. $20.00

MASON, Steve. *Johnny's Song.* (1986). Bantam. 1st ed. inscr/sgn. F/F. A7. $40.00

MASON, Steve. *Warrior for Peace.* (1988). Simons Schuster/Touchstone. F/wrp. A7. $30.00

MASON, Theodore K. *On the Ice in Antarctica.* 1978. NY. Dodd Mead. 1st ed. 8vo. 160 p. F/VG. P4. $20.00

MASON & SUEHSDORF. *Sportsman's Wilderness.* (1974). NJ. 4to. 253 p. F. A17. $17.50

MASQUERIER, Lewis. *Sociology; or, Reconstruction of Soc.* 1877. NY. self pub. 1st ed. 12mo. 310 p. cloth. M1. $325.00

MASSELMAN, George. *Cradle of Colonialism.* 1963. New Haven. Yale. 1st ed. 8vo. 534 p. F/VG+. A2. $35.00

MASSELMAN, George. *Cradle of Colonialism.* 1963. Yale. 1st ed. 510 p. cloth. VG/dj. M20. $12.00

MASSERMAN, Jules H. *Psychiatric Odyssey.* 1971. Science House. 1st ed. 624 p. cloth. G1. $20.00

MASSEY, William T. *How Jerusalem Was Won.* 1919. London. Constable. 1st ed. 8vo. 295 p. gilt bl cloth. G+. M7. $75.00

MASSINGER, Philip. *Plays.* 1813. London. Nichol Cadell. 2nd ed. 8vo. 4 vols. gilt bdg. F. F1. $550.00

MASSON, Louis Francois. *Les Bourgeoise de la Compagnie du Nord-Quest...* 1960. NY. Antiquarian Pr. reprint. 2 vols. 8vo. blk cloth. NF. P4. $150.00

MASTERS, Edgar Lee. *Lincoln the Man.* 1931. Dodd Mead. 1st ed. 520 p. VG. B10. $20.00

MASTERS, Jack. *Masters Family Hist 1691-1989.* 1989. Gallatin. 1st ed. 584 p. gr cloth. VG. D7. $35.00

MASTERS. *Picture Quilts.* 1987. np. ils. wrp. G2. $15.00

MASTERTON, Graham. *Burning.* 1991. NY. Tor. 1st ed. F/F. N3. $15.00

MASTERTON, Graham. *Ritual.* 1988. Severn. 1st hc ed. F/F. F4. $25.00

MATE, Ferenc. *Waterhouses.* 1977. Vancouver. Albatross Pub. VG/dj. A16. $12.00

MATHER, Berkely. *Springers.* 1968. Collins. 1st ed. NF/NF. S5. $22.50

MATHER, Samuel. *All Men Will Not Be Saved Forever...* 1782. Boston. Edes. 1st ed. 8vo. 31 p. M1. $150.00

MATHES, W. Michael. *From the Gulf to the Pacific...* 1969. LA. Dawson. ils/fld map. M. O6. $85.00

MATHESON, Richard. *Born of Man & Woman.* 1954. Chamberlain. 1st ed. F/NF. M2. $200.00

MATHESON, Richard. *Hell House.* 1971. Viking. 1st ed. F/dj. M2. $225.00

MATHESON, Richard. *Someone Is Bleeding.* 1953. NY. Lion. PBO. sgn. NF/unread. A11. $345.00

MATHESON, Richard. *What Dreams May Come.* 1978. Putnam. 1st ed. sgn. VG/dj. M18. $100.00

MATHEW, Brian. *Dwarf Bulbs.* 1973. NY. ils/photos. 240 p. VG/dj. B26. $35.00

MATHEWS, Harry. *Cigarettes.* 1987. Weidenfeld Nicolson. AP. F/wrp. B2. $30.00

MATHEWS, Harry. *Conversions.* 1962. Random. 1st ed. F/NF. B2. $65.00

MATHEWS, Harry. *Sinking of Odradek Stadium & Other Novels.* 1975. Harper. 1st ed. inscr. F/NF. B2. $100.00

MATHEWS, Jack. *Battle of Brazil.* 1987. Crown. NF. C8. $35.00

MATHEWS, John J. *Wah'Kon-Tah.* 1932. OK U. 1st ed. 359 p. cloth. VG. D3. $25.00

MATHEWS, Joseph J. *Reporting the Wars.* (1957). Minneapolis, MN. 1st ed. 8vo. 322 p. VG+/VG. A2. $15.00

MATHEWS, Mrs. *Tea-Table Talk, Ennobled Actresses & Other Miscellanies.* 1857. London. Newby. 1st ed. 12mo. 2 vols. aeg. marbled brds. NF. H5. $350.00

MATHIESON. *Complete Book of Crochet.* 1977. np. ils. cloth. G2. $12.50

MATHIESON. *Mariner's Compass.* 1987. np. ils. wrp. G2. $16.00

MATHIS, Edward. *September Song.* 1991. Scribner. ARC of 1st ed. RS. F/F. S5. $25.00

MATHIS. *Antique & Collectible Thimbles & Accessories.* 1986. np. ils. cloth. G2. $20.00

MATSCHAT, Cecil Hulse. *Seven Grass Huts. Engineer's Wife in Central & S Am.* 1939. Literary Guild. 8vo. pls. 281 p. B11. $10.00

MATSON, Donald D. *Treatment of Acute Cranicerebral Injuries Due to Missiles.* 1948. Springfield. Thomas. 90 p. NF. G7. $45.00

MATSUBARA, Hisako. *Samurai.* 1980. Bodley Head. 1st ed. author's 1st book. trans from German. NF/NF. A14. $20.00

MATSUNAGE. *Japanese Country Quilting.* 1990. np. ils. wrp. G2. $15.00

MATSUO, Kinoaki. *How Japan Plans To Win.* 1942. Little Brn. 1st ed. 323 p. VG. W1. $18.00

MATT & ROBERTSON. *USN & Reconnaissance & Bomber Aircraft of 1914-18 War.* 1962. Letchworth. 1st ed. w/sgn bookplate. VG/dj. B18. $65.00

MATTES, Merrill J. *Colter's Hell & Jackson's Hole.* 1976. Yellowstone Lib/Mus Assn. reprint. 8vo. 87 p. decor wrp. T8. $7.50

MATTEUCCI, Carlo. *Cours d'Electro-Physiologie.* 1858. Paris. Mallet-Bachelier. presentation. 177 p. wrp bound in. G7. $250.00

MATTHEE, Dalene. *Circles in the Forest.* (1984). Knopf. 1st ed. F/F. B3. $15.00

MATTHEWS, Brander. *Bookbindings Old & New: Notes of a Booklover...* 1895. Macmillan. 1st ed. 8vo. 342 p. gr cloth. F. B20. $85.00

MATTHEWS, Brander. *Poems of Am Patriotism.* Oct 1922. Scribner. 1st ed. ils Wyeth/15 pls. teg. F. B14. $300.00

MATTHEWS, Joanna H. *Bessie Bradford's Secret.* (1881). Cassel Petter Galpin. ils ME Edwards/others. 253 p. G+. S10. $25.00

MATTHEWS, John. *Grail: Quest For the Eternal.* ca 1985. London. F. C1. $9.00

MATTHEWS, Kevin; see Fox, Gardner F.

MATTHEWS, William. *Ill-Framed Knight.* 1966. Berkley. 1st ed. NF. C1. $39.00

MATTHEWS & SINK. *Wheels of Faith & Courage: Hist of Thomasville, NC.* 1952. Hight Point, NC. Hall Prt. 1st ed. xl. sgns. cloth. F. M8. $85.00

MATTHIESSEN, F.O. *Henry James: The Major Phase.* 1944. NY. Oxford. 190 p. dj. A7. $17.00

MATTHIESSEN, F.O. *Russell Cheney: A Record of His Work.* 1947. Oxford. photos/pls/ils. 130 p. cloth. dj. D2. $75.00

MATTHIESSEN, Peter. *African Silences.* 1991. Random. AP. red/blk wrp. C4. $60.00

MATTHIESSEN, Peter. *Clark City Pr Reader.* 1993. Spring. pamphlet. F/wrp. C4. $35.00

MATTHIESSEN, Peter. *El Leopardo de las Nieves (The Snow Leopard).* 1981. Buenos Aires. Sudamericana. 1st Argentine ed. 1/3000. NF/wrp. L3. $50.00

MATTHIESSEN, Peter. *Far Tortuga.* 1975. Random. ARC. sgn. RS. NF/F. L3. $225.00

MATTHIESSEN, Peter. *Great Auk Escape (Seal Pool).* 1972. London. Angus Robertson. 1st ed (his scarcest trade ed). NF/sans. L3. $450.00

MATTHIESSEN, Peter. *In the Spirit of Crazy Horse.* 1983. Viking. 1st ed. sgn. F/F. L3. $300.00

MATTHIESSEN, Peter. *Indian Country.* (1984). Viking. 1st ed. 338 p. F/NF. A7. $40.00

MATTHIESSEN, Peter. *Men's Lives.* 1986. Random. AP. sgn. NF/wrp. L3. $175.00

MATTHIESSEN, Peter. *Midnight Turning Gray.* 1984. Bristol, RI. 1st collection of short fiction. sgn. F/8vo wrp. A11. $35.00

MATTHIESSEN, Peter. *Nine-Headed Dragon River.* 1986. Boston. Shambala. AP. sgn. VG/wrp. L3. $125.00

MATTHIESSEN, Peter. *Nine-Headed Dragon River.* 1986. Boston. Shambala. 1st ed. NF/dj. C4. $40.00

MATTHIESSEN, Peter. *Oomingmak.* 1967. NY. Hastings. 1st ed. F/NF. C4. $50.00

MATTHIESSEN, Peter. *Oomingmak.* 1967. NY. 1st ed. sgn. photos. F/F. A11. $60.00

MATTHIESSEN, Peter. *Partisans.* 1955. Viking. 1st ed. sgn. author's 2nd novel. VG/VG. L3. $275.00

MATTHIESSEN, Peter. *Sand River.* 1981. Viking. 1st ed. ils Lawick. F/NF. C4. $40.00

MATTHIESSEN, Peter. *Shorebirds of N Am.* 1967. Viking. 1st ed. folio. ils Robert Verity Clem. F/F clip. Q1. $175.00

MATTHIESSEN, Peter. *Snow Leopard.* 1978. Franklin Lib. 1st ed. silk ep/marker. leather. C4/L3. $150.00

MATTHIESSEN, Peter. *Snow Leopard.* 1978. Viking. 1st ed. F/F. B4/C4. $75.00

MATTHIESSEN, Peter. *Wildlife in Am.* (1987). Viking. 1st thus ed. 332 p. F/F. A7. $20.00

MATTUCK, Israel I. *Aspects of Progressive Jewish Thought.* 1955. FSY. 16 essays. 158 p. VG/G+. S3. $26.00

MATUNAS, Edward. *Deer Hunter's Guide to Guns, Ammo & Equipment.* (1983). Outdoor Life. 338 p. dj. A17. $15.00

MAUDLIN, Bill. *Brass Ring.* 1971. Norton. 1st ed. 8vo. VG/VG. A8. $12.00

MAUDLIN, Bill. *Up Front.* 1945. World. 1st ed/7th prt. VG. A8. $7.00

MAUDSLAY & PERCIVAL. *Glimpse at Guatemala.* 1992. Flo Silver. reprint of 1899 ed. 1/404. F3. $40.00

MAUGHAM, W. Somerset. *Don Fernando.* 1935. London. Heinemann. 1st trade ed. 269 p. dj. A7. $35.00

MAUGHAM, W. Somerset. *Of Human Bondage.* 1938. New Haven. 1/1500. 2 vols. octavo. ils/sgn John Sloan. F/NF slipcase. B24. $375.00

MAUGHAM, W. Somerset. *Points of View.* 1959. Garden City. 1st ed. F/F. C4. $40.00

MAUGHAM, W. Somerset. *Razor's Edge.* 1941. London. Heinemann. 1st ed. VG/clip. scarce. L3. $450.00

MAUGHAM, W. Somerset. *Theatre: Novel of a Woman's Innermost Life.* 1937. Doubleday Doran. G/dj. E3. $15.00

MAULDIN, Bill. *Back Home.* 1947. NY. later ed. cartoons. 315 p. VG/torn. B18. $6.50

MAULDIN, Bill. *Mud, Mules & Mtns.* 1944. np. (Italy). 1st ed. intro Ernie Pyle. 48 p. G/fld case. B18. $175.00

MAULDIN, Bill. *Sort of a Saga.* (1949). NY. 1st ed. 301 p. cloth. VG/torn dj. B18. $22.50

MAULE, Henry. *Scobie, Hero of Greece. British Campaign 1944-45.* 1975. London. 8vo. 282 p. cloth. dj. scarce. O2. $40.00

MAUNOIR, J.-P. *Memoires Physiologiques et Pratiques sur l'Aneurisme...* 1802. Geneva. 1st ed. 2 fld pls. 130 p. contemporary brds. G7. $195.00

MAUPIN, Armistead. *Sure of You.* 1989. NY. Harper Row. 1st ed. NF/NF. A14. $25.00

MAURICE, Frederick. *Statesmen & Soldiers of the Civil War.* 1926. Little Brn. 1st ed. 166 p. bl cloth. VG/dj. M20. $40.00

MAUROIS, Andre. *Memoirs 1885-1967.* 1970. Harper Row. trans Denver Lindley. 440 p. red cloth. VG/dj. G1. $25.00

MAUROIS, Andre. *Miss Howard & the Emperor: Story of Napoleon III & Mistress.* 1957. London. Collins. 1st ed. trans Humphrey Hare. VG+/G clip. A14. $20.00

MAUROIS, Andre. *September Roses.* 1958. Harper. 1st ed. trans from French. VG+/VG+. A14. $20.00

MAUROIS, Andre. *Weigher of Souls & the Earth Dwellers.* 1963. NY. Macmillan. 1st ed. ils LE Fisher. NF/NF. A14. $40.00

MAURY, Dabney Herndon. *Recollections of a Virginian in Mexican...Civil Wars.* 1894. Scribner. 1st ed. 279 p. cloth. VG. M8. $150.00

MAXWELL, A.E. *Art of Survival.* 1989. Doubleday. 1st ed. sgn. F/F. T2. $22.50

MAXWELL, A.E. *Just Enough Light To Kill.* 1988. Doubleday. 1st ed. F/F. T2. $20.00

MAXWELL, A.E. *Money Burns.* 1991. Villard. 1st ed. M/M. T2. $16.50

MAXWELL, Gavin. *Otters' Tale.* 1962. Dutton. 1st ed. 8vo. 125 p. VG. T5. $25.00

MAXWELL, William. *Ancestors.* 1971. Knopf. ARC. F/NF. L3. $125.00

MAXWELL, William. *Heavenly Tenants.* 1946. NY. 1st/only children's book. inscr. F/VG ils Karasz. A11. $75.00

MAXWELL, William. *Writer As Illusionist.* March 1955. NY. 1st ed. sgn. 16 p. NF/stiff wrp. A11. $165.00

MAXXE, Robert; see Rosenblum, Robert.

MAY, J. Lewis. *Cardinal Newman.* 1951. Westminster. Newman. 309 p. H10. $17.50

MAY, Julian. *Golden Torc.* 1982. Houghton Mifflin. 1st ed. inscr/sgn. F/NF. F4. $22.00

MAY, Julian. *Many-Colored Land.* 1981. Houghton Mifflin. sgn. F/NF. F4. $25.00

MAY, Julian. *Nonborn King & the Adversary.* 1984. Doubleday. 1st compilation ed. sgn. F/F. F4. $20.00

MAY, Samuel J. *Discourse on Slavery in the US.* 1831. Boston. Garrison Knapp. 1st ed. 8vo. 29 p. M1. $200.00

MAYER, Brantz. *Mexico: Aztec, Spanish & Republican...* 1851. Hartford. later prt. 2 vols. rstr bdg. G. D7. $50.00

MAYER, Karl Herbert. *Maya Monuments: Sculptures of Unknown Provence in Europe.* 1978. Ramona. Acoma Books. 1st ed. 4to. wrp. F3. $20.00

MAYER, Karl Herbert. *Mushroom Stones of Mesoamerica.* 1977. Ramona. Acoma Books. 1st ed. 46 p. wrp. F3. $15.00

MAYER, Luigi. *Inieresting Views in Turkey...* 1819. London. 4to. contemporary half calf. O2. $425.00

MAYER, Martin. *New Breed on Wall Street.* nd (1969). Macmillan. 1st ed. 128 p. wht brds. NF/glassine dj. B22. $7.00

MAYER, Mercer. *Professor Wormbog in Search for the Zipperump-a-Zoo.* 1976. W Pub/Golden Pr. 7th prt. 44 p. A3. $15.00

MAYHAR, Ardath. *Exile on Vlahil.* 1984. Doubleday. 1st ed. NF/F. N3. $10.00

MAYLE, Peter. *Hotel Pastis: Novel of Provence.* 1993. Knopf. 1st ed. F/wrp. B4. $45.00

MAYLE, Peter. *Toujours Provence.* 1991. Knopf. 1st ed. F/NF. B4. $45.00

MAYNARD, Theodore. *Bloody Mary.* 1955. Bruce. 292 p. VG/dj. M20. $8.50

MAYNARD & MILES. *William S Burroughs: A Bibliography 1953-73.* 1978. Charlottesville, VA. 1st ed. F/sans. B2. $27.50

MAYNE, William. *Underground Alley.* 1961. Dutton. 1st Am ed. 8vo. 168 p. aqua cloth. NF/NF. T5. $48.00

MAYO, Elton. *Some Notes on Psychology of Pierre Janet.* 1948. Cambridge. Harvard. 1st ed. 12mo. cloth. VG. G1. $25.00

MAYO, Jim; see L'Amour, Louis.

MAYOKOK, Robert. *True Eskimo Stories.* 1959. Sitka Prt. 1st ed. inscr. VG. L3. $75.00

MAYOR, Archer. *Borderlines.* 1990. Putnam. 1st ed. F/F. M15. $30.00

MAYS, Benjamin E. *Born To Rebel.* (1971). Scribner. 1st ed. 380 p. dj. A7. $18.00

MAYS, David John. *Edmund Pendleton, 1721-1803.* 1952. Harvard. 1st ed. 2 vols. VG. B10. $35.00

MAZAR, Benjamin. *Views of the Biblical World: The Law, Vol 1.* 1959. Jordan Pub. 1st Internat ed. 4to. 303 p. VG+/G+. S3. $30.00

MAZIERE, Francis. *Expedition Tumac-Humac.* 1955. Doubleday. 1st ed. 8vo. 249 p. F/VG. A2. $20.00

MAZOWER, Mark. *Inside Hitler's Greece. Experience of Occupation 1941-44.* 1993. New Haven. 8vo. 437 p. cloth. dj. O2. $32.50

MCADIE, Alexander. *Clouds & Fogs of San Francisco.* 1912. San Francisco. 1st ed. 106 p. pict brds. VG. D3. $25.00

MCAFEE, John. *Slow Walk in a Sad Rain.* 1993. NY. Warner. AP. F/wrp. L3. $45.00

MCALISTER, John T. *Vietnam: Origins of Revolution.* 1969. Knopf. 2nd prt. 377 p. NF/dj. A7. $15.00

MCALLISTER, Ron. *Swim to Glory: Story of Marilyn Bell...* 1954. McClelland Stewart. 1st ed. VG/fair. N2. $10.00

MCAULEY, James. *After the Blizzard.* 1975. MO. 1st ed. inscr/sgn. F/sans. V1. $30.00

MCAULEY, Milt. *Wild Flowers of the Santa Monica Mtns.* 1985. Conoga Park, CA. ils/fld map. 544 p. B26. $16.00

MCAULEY, Paul J. *Four Hundred Billion Stars.* 1988. Gollancz. 1st UK/hc ed. sgn. F/F. F4. $40.00

MCBAIN, Ed; see Hunter, Evan.

MCBRIDE, Chris. *Wht Lions of Timbavati.* (1977). NY. 220 p. dj. A17. $10.00

MCBRYDE, J. *Perfect Hunter & Saddle Horse.* 1936. London. Country Life. 1st ed. sm 4to. VG/fair. O3. $38.00

MCCABE, Ed. *Against Gravity: From Paris to Dakar...* (1990). NY. Warner. 1st ed. 8vo. 290 p. F/F. A2. $12.50

MCCABE, James D. *Ils Hist of Centennial Exhibition.* 1975. Phil. Nat Pub. collector reprint. 4to. 302 p. F/VG. B11. $25.00

MCCAFFREY, Anne. *Coelura.* 1987. Tor. 1st ed. F/dj. M2. $15.00

MCCAFFREY, Anne. *Lyon's Pride.* 1994. Ace Putnam. AP of 1st Am ed. NF/prt wrp. N3. $10.00

MCCAFFREY, Anne. *Pegasus in Flight.* 1990. Ballantine. 1st ed. F/F. N3. $15.00

MCCAIG. *Emminent Dogs & Dangerous Men.* 1991. NY. Harper Collins. 1st ed. F/F. O3. $22.00

MCCALL, Anthony; see Kane, Henry.

MCCALL'S. *McCall's Crochet Treasury.* 1977. np. ils. cloth. G2. $15.00

MCCALLUM, A.C. *Erie, PA. Perry Centennial Celebration, July 6-13, 1913.* (1913). Erie. McCallum. oblong folio. 44 p. wrp. A17. $30.00

MCCALLUM, John D. *World Heavyweight Boxing Championship: A Hist.* (1974). Chilton. ils 393 p. clip dj. A7. $20.00

MCCALLUM & ROSS. *Port Angels.* (1961). Seattle. Wood Reber. 1st ed. sgn. 8vo. 197 p. F/VG+. A2. $20.00

MCCAMMON, Robert R. *Mystery Walk.* 1983. Holt. 1st ed. author's 1st hc. F/NF. F4. $30.00

MCCAMMON, Robert R. *Usher's Passing.* 1984. HRW. 1st ed. w/facsimile letter discussing novel. F/F. T2. $45.00

MCCARRY, Charles. *Secret Lovers.* (1977). Dutton. 1st ed. dj. A7. $25.00

MCCARRY, Charles. *Tears of Autumn.* (1975). Dutton/Saturday Review. 1st ed. worn dj. A7. $15.00

MCCARTER, Margaret Hill. *Cuddy's Baby.* 1917. McClurg. 1st ed. thin quarto. F/stiff wrp. B4. $150.00

MCCARTHY, Charles H. *Lincoln's Plan of Reconstruction.* 1901. McClure Phillips. 1st ed. 531 p. cloth. VG. M8. $250.00

MCCARTHY, Charles H. *Lincoln's Plan of Reconstruction.* 1901. McClure. 1st ed. 531 p. G. B10. $90.00

MCCARTHY, Cormac. *All the Pretty Horses.* 1992. Knopf. ARC. sgn. F/F cardboard slipcase. B2. $150.00

MCCARTHY, Mary. *Cannibals & Missionaries.* 1979. HBJ. 1st ed. VG/dj. A16. $8.00

MCCARTHY, Mary. *Company She Keeps.* 1942. NY. 1st ed. author's 1st book. VG+/torn. A15. $50.00

MCCARTHY, Mary. *Groves of Academe.* 1952. NY. 1st ed. VG/VG. B5. $25.00

MCCARTHY, Mary. *Hanoi.* (1968). HBW. 1st ed. 134 p. wrp. A7. $25.00

MCCARTHY, Mary. *Hanoi.* (1968). London. Weidenfeld Nicolson. 1st/only hc ed. dj. A7. $45.00

MCCARTHY, Mary. *HV Kaltenborn Edits the News.* 1937. NY. 1st ed. sgn. NF/photo-ils wrp/VG+ rare dj. A11. $125.00

MCCARTHY, Mary. *Ideas & the Novel.* 1980. NY. 1st ed. sgn. F/F. A11. $45.00

MCCARTHY, Mary. *Oasis.* 1949. London. Horizon. 1st ed. sgn. NF/8vo ivory wrp/yel pub band. A11. $75.00

MCCARTHY, Mary. *Vietnam.* (1967). HBW. 1st ed. 106 p. NF/stiff wrp. A7. $30.00

MCCARTHY, Mary. *Vietnam.* 1967. NY. PBO. sgn. NF/8vo linen-textured paper wrp. A11. $45.00

MCCARTHY, Mary. *17th Degree.* (1974). HBJ. 1st ed. 451 p. F/NF. A7. $30.00

MCCARTHY & MORGAN. *Jazz on Record.* (1968). Hanover Books. 1st thus ed. 416 p. NF/dj. A7. $35.00

MCCARTNEY & OKKELBERG. *Papers of MI Academy of Science.* 1930. Ann Arbor. 493 p. cloth. F. A17. $25.00

MCCARTY, John L. *Maverick Town: Story of Old Tascosa.* 1946. Norman, OK. 2nd prt. NF/VG. H7. $15.00

MCCARTY, Lea. *Gunfighters.* (1959). Berkeley. 1st ed. 21 full-p color pls. 44 p. glossy wrp. A17. $10.00

MCCAULEY & MCCAULEY. *Decorative Arts of the Amish of Lancaster Co.* 1988. np. ils. cloth. G2. $30.00

MCCAULEY & POLITO. *Fireworks: Lost Writings of Jim Thompson.* 1988. NY. Donald Fine. 1st ed. F/F. S5. $40.00

MCCAY. *Animals in Danger, a Pop-Up Book.* 1990. 6 pop-ups. F. A4. $45.00

MCCLANE, A.J. *Am Angler.* (1954). NY. 1st ed. 207 p. VG. A17. $15.00

MCCLANE, A.J. *Practical Fly Fisherman.* (1975). NJ. 1st thus ed. 271 p. F/dj. A17. $25.00

MCCLARY, Thomas. *Three Thousand Yrs.* 1954. Fantasy. ltd ed. 1/300. sgn/#d. F/dj. M2. $85.00

MCCLARY, Thomas. *Three Thousand Yrs.* 1954. Fantasy. 1st ed. F/dj. M2. $30.00

MCCLELLAN, Elizabeth. *Hist of Am Costume, 1607-1870.* 1942. NY. Tudor. 4to. 659 p. VG+/torn. B14. $37.50

MCCLELLAN, George B. *Army of the Potomac.* 1864. NY. Sheldon. 1st ed. 1/250. inscr/dtd 1864. 484 p. cloth. VG. D3. $450.00

MCCLELLAN, George B. *McClellan's Own Story...* 1887. NY. 1st ed. royal 8vo. 678 p. orig lib calf. VG. D3. $45.00

MCCLELLAN, Henry Brainerd. *I Rode w/Jeb Stuart.* 1958. IN U. 1st thus ed. 468 p. cloth. VG/VG. M8. $65.00

MCCLELLAND, Nancy. *Young Decorators.* 1928. Harper. stated 1st ed. cloth. VG/dj. M5. $60.00

MCCLINTON, K.M. *Chromolithographs of Louis Prang.* ca 1973. Clarkson Potter. xl. 4to. ils. brds. dj. H9. $75.00

MCCLINTON, K.M. *Chromolithographs of Louis Prang.* 1973. Potter/Crown. 28 color pls. 246 p. cloth. dj. D2. $115.00

MCCLOSKEY, Burr. *He Will Stay Till You Come: Rise & Fall of Skinny Walker.* ca 1978. Durham, NC. Moore. F/VG. V4. $7.50

MCCLOY, Helen. *Long Body.* (1955). Random. 1st ed. G+/clip. B9. $10.00

MCCLOY, Helen. *Slayer & the Slain.* (1957). Random. 1st ed. VG/dj. B9. $12.50

MCCLOY, Helen. *Unfinished Crime.* (19540. Random. 1st ed. VG/dj. B9. $15.00

MCCLUNG, John A. *Sketches of W Adventure.* 1839. Cincinnati. James. duodecimo. wood frontispiece. orig calf. H9. $500.00

MCCLURE, Alexander Kelly. *Abraham Lincoln & Men of War-Times: Personal Recollections.* 1892. Phil. Times Pub. 1st ed. 496 p. cloth. VG. M8. $125.00

MCCLURE, James. *Artful Egg.* 1984. London. Macmillan. 1st ed. F/F. S5. $30.00

MCCLURKEN, James M. *Gah-Baeh-Jhagwah-Buk: The Way It Happened.* (1991). E Lansing. MI State U. 1st ed. 130 p. M/dj. A17. $25.00

MCCLUSKEY, John. *Look What They Done to My Song.* (1974). Random. 1st ed. dj. A7. $25.00

MCCOLLEY, Sutherland. *Works of James Renwick Brevoort.* 1972. Yonkers. Hudson River Mus. pls. D2. $30.00

MCCOLLUM, Vashti Cromwell. *One Woman's Fight.* 1951. Doubleday. M1. $35.00

MCCONATHY, Osbourne. *Music Hour.* 1928. Silver Burdett. ils Shirley Kite. 2 vol set. G. L1. $25.00

MCCONKEY, Harriet. *Dakota War Whoop.* 1965. Lakeside Classic. ils 395 p. O7. $12.50

MCCONKEY, James. *Stories From My Life w/Other Animals.* 1993. Boston. Godine. AP. F/wrp. B4. $30.00

MCCONNELL, Malcolm. *Into the Mouth of the Cat.* (1985). Norton. F/NF. A7. $25.00

MCCOOK, Henry C. *Quaker Ben: Tale of Colonial PA in Days of Thomas Penn.* 1911. Phil. GW Jacobs. 1st ed. 8vo. 336 p. VG. V3. $12.00

MCCORDUCK, Pamela. *Aaron's Code: Meta-Art, Artificial Intelligence...* (1991). Freeman, NY. 1st ed. 8vo. 225 p. F/F. A2. $17.50

MCCORKLE, Jill. *Tending to VA.* (1987). Algonquin. 1st ed. rem mk. NF/F. B3. $20.00

MCCORMICK, Donald. *Who's Who in Spy Fiction.* 1977. Elm Tree. 1st ed. F/NF. S5. $25.00

MCCORMICK, Richard C. Jr. *Visit to the Camp Before Sevastopol.* 1855. NY. Appleton. 1st ed. sm 8vo. 212 p. VG. W1. $75.00

MCCOURT, Edward. *Yukon & the NW Territories.* 1969. Macmillan. 1st ed. photos/ maps. 236 p. F/dj. A17. $14.50

MCCOY, Alfred W. *Politics of Heroin in SE Asia.* 1972. Harper. 1st ed. NF/NF. B2. $45.00

MCCOY, Horace. *I Should Have Stayed Home.* 1938. Knopf. ARC. author's 2nd novel. VG/dj. L3. $200.00

MCCOY, Horace. *They Shoot Horses Don't They?* 1935. Simon Schuster. 1st ed. VG/G. B4. $250.00

MCCOY, Joseph. *Hist Sketches of Cattle Trade of W & SW.* 1874. KS City. Ramsey Miller Hudson. 1st ed/state A. gilt cloth. VG. R3. $1,750.00

MCCRACKEN, Harold. *Frank Tenney Johnson, W Paintings.* 1971. Dallas. private prt. 15 color pls. wrp. D2. $25.00

MCCRACKEN, Harold. *Frederic Remington's Own W.* 1960. Dial. 1st trade ed. 254 p. VG/dj. M20. $25.00

MCCRACKEN, Russell. *Elegant Elephant.* 1944. Rand McNally. 1st ed. ils Susanne Suba. missing press-out toy. G. L1. $10.00

MCCRUMB, Sharyn. *Zombies of the Gene Pool.* 1992. Simon Schuster. 1st ed. sgn. F/F. T2. $35.00

MCCUE, George. *Octagon: Being Account of Famous WA Residence.* 1976. AIA Foundation. 101 p. VG. B10. $15.00

MCCULLERS, Carson. *Ballad of the Sad Cafe.* 1951. Houghton Mifflin. 1st ed. F/NF. B2. $85.00

MCCULLERS, Carson. *Clock Without Hands.* 1961. Houghton Mifflin. 1st ed. F/NF. B2. $100.00

MCCULLERS, Carson. *Heart Is a Lonely Hunter.* 1940. Houghton Mifflin. 1st ed. author's 1st book. VG/dj. L3. $275.00

MCCULLERS, Carson. *Member of the Wedding.* 1951. New Directions. ARC. RS. cloth. VG/G. L3. $150.00

MCCULLERS, Carson. *Reflections in the Golden Eye.* 1941. Houghton Mifflin. 1st ed. author's 2nd book. NF/1st issue. L3. $375.00

MCCULLERS, Carson. *Sweet As a Pickle & Clean As a Pig.* 1964. Houghton Mifflin. 1st ed. ils Rolf Gerard. F/F. B4. $125.00

MCCULLOCH, J.R. *McCulloch's Universal Gazetteer.* 1843 & 1844. NY. 2 vols. full leather. B30. $175.00

MCCULLOUGH, David. *Great Bridge: Epic Story of Building of the Brooklyn Bridge.* 1972. Simon Schuster. 1st ed. pls. 636 p. VG/VG. B11. $15.00

MCCULLOUGH, David. *Path Between the Seas.* 1977. Simon Schuster. BC. VG/dj. A16. $7.50

MCCULLOUGH, David. *Path Between the Seas: Creation of Panama Canal 1870-1914.* 1977. Simon Schuster. 8vo. pls/2 two-p maps. 698 p. G/G. B11. $15.00

MCCULLY, Anderson. *Am Alpines in the Garden.* 1931. Macmillan. ils/index. 251 p. H10. $15.00

MCCULLY, Robert S. *Jung & Rorschach. Study in Archetype of Perception.* 1987. TX. Spring Pub. presentation/sgn. wrp. N2. $10.00

MCCURRACH, James C. *Palms of the World.* 1960. NY. 400 photos. 290 p. VG+/dj. B26. $79.00

MCCUTCHAN, Philip. *Bright Red Businessmen.* 1969. London. Harrap. 1st ed. F/F. S5. $25.00

MCCUTCHAN, Philip. *Skyprobe.* 1967. John Day. 1st ed. F/NF clip. F4. $20.00

MCCUTCHEON, John Elliott. *Hartley Colliery Disaster, 1862.* 1963. Seaham, Eng. McCutcheon. ils. F/VG. V4. $15.00

MCDADE, Charlie. *Gulf.* (1986). HBJ. 1st ed. F/F. A7. $18.00

MCDANIEL, Bruce W. *Dune & Desert Folk.* (1926). LA. 1st ed. sm 4to. 31 p. pict brds. VG. D3. $25.00

MCDANIEL, Ruel. *Vinegaroon: Saga of Judge Roy Bean...* 1936. Kingsport, TN. Southern. VG. H7. $10.00

MCDERMOTT, Alice. *Bigamist's Daughter.* 1982. Random. ARC. sgn. w/promo sheet. F/dj. B4. $175.00

MCDERMOTT, Gerald. *Papgayo.* 1980. Windmill Wanderer. 1st ed. 33 p. VG/G+. A3. $8.50

MCDERMOTT, Gerald. *Sun Flight.* 1980. 4 Winds Pr. 1st ed. sgn. oblong 8vo. teal brds. F/F. T5. $45.00

MCDERMOTT, John Francis. *Collected Verse of Lewis Carroll...* 1929. Dutton. G. N2. $8.00

MCDERMOTT, John Francis. *George Caleb Bingham, River Portraitist.* 1959. Norman. lt 8vo. 454 p. F/VG+. F1. $75.00

MCDERMOTT, John Francis. *Spanish in the MS Valley, 1762-1804.* ca 1974. Urbana, IL. 8vo. 421 p. cloth. dj. H9. $30.00

MCDERMOTT, John Francis. *Travelers on the W Frontier.* ca 1970. Urbana, IL. 8vo. facsimile maps/ils. 351 p. cloth. dj. H9. $35.00

MCDEVITT, Jean. *Mr Apple's Family.* 1950. Doubleday. 1st ed. 8vo. 118 p. pict pink cloth. G+. T5. $25.00

MCDONALD, Cornelia Peake. *Diary w/Reminiscences of the War & Refugee Life...1860-65.* 1935. Nashville. Cullom Ghertner. 1st ed. 540 p. orig cloth. VG. M8. $250.00

MCDONALD, Gregory. *Fletch & the Widow Bradley.* 1981. London. Gollancz. 1st British/1st hc ed. F/F. S5. $35.00

MCDOUGALL & WATSON. *Battle of Behaviorism.* 1929. Norton. 1st ed. 16mo. bl cloth. VG. G1. $50.00

MCDOWALL, R.J.S. *Control of Circulation of the Blood.* 1938. Longman Gr. ils/index. 619 p. bl cloth. NF. S9. $13.00

MCDOWELL. *Pattern on Pattern.* 1991. np. 20 quilt patterns. wrp. G2. $20.00

MCELROY, John. *Si Klegg: His Transformation From Raw Recruit to Vetran.* ca 1910. Nat Tribune. 2nd ed/revised. 245 p. VG. B10. $35.00

MCELROY, Joseph. *Letter Left to Me.* (1988). Knopf. 1st ed. F/F. B3. $12.00

MCELROY, Joseph. *Lookout Cartridge.* 1974. Knopf. 1st ed. F/F. B2. $50.00

MCELROY, Joseph. *Pluss.* 1977. NY. 1st ed/wrp issue. inscr. F. A11. $45.00

MCELROY, Joseph. *Women & Men.* 1987. Ultramarine. 1st ed. 1/99. sgn. leather/paste-paper brds. F. L3. $250.00

MCEVOY, J.P. *Bam Bam Clock.* 1936. Algonquin. ils Gruelle. VG+. scarce. M5. $60.00

MCEWAN, Ian. *Comfort of Strangers.* (1981). London. Cape. 1st ed. F/F. B3. $60.00

MCEWAN, Ian. *In Between the Sheets.* (1978). Simon Schuster. 1st Am ed. inscr. F/dj. B4. $85.00

MCEWAN, Ian. *In Between the Sheets.* (1978). Simon Schuster. 1st ed. F/F. B3. $45.00

MCFADDEN, Charles J. *Philosophy of Communism.* (1939). Benziger Brothers. 345 p. NF/dj. A7. $20.00

MCFARLAND, J. Horace. *How To Grow Roses.* 1937. Macmillan. 18th enlarged ed. 12mo. 192 p. VG. B28. $15.00

MCFARLAND, J. Horace. *Roses of the World in Color.* 1936. Houghton Mifflin. ils/index. 296 p. H10. $15.00

MCFEE, William. *Sunlight in New Grenada.* 1925. London. Heinemann. 1st ed. 8vo. 275 p. F/VG. A2. $30.00

MCFEELY, William S. *Grant: A Biography.* 1981. NY. 1st ed. 592 p. cloth. F/NF. M8. $35.00

MCGAVIN, E. Cecil. *Mormon Pioneers.* 1947. Salt Lake City. Stevens Wallis. 8vo. 234 p. brn brds. VG. B11. $30.00

MCGEE, John W. *Catholic Church in the Grand River Valley 1833-1950.* 1950. Grand Rapids. 1st ed. 538 p. A17. $35.00

MCGEE. *Passion for Fashion.* 1987. np. pb. ils. G2. $25.00

MCGINLEY, Patrick. *Goosefoot.* 1982. Dutton. 1st Am ed. F/NF. S5. $20.00

MCGINLEY, Phillis. *One More Manhattan.* 1937. NY. 1st ed. VG. scarce. C1. $12.50

MCGINLEY, Phyllis. *Lucy McLockett.* 1959. Lippincott. 1st ed. 4to. red cloth. T5. $35.00

MCGINNIS, Duane; see Niatum, Duane.

MCGINNISS, Joe. *AK He Experienced. Going to Extremes.* 1980. NY. 1st ed. 8vo. 285 p. F/VG. H3. $12.00

MCGLASHAN, C.F. *Hist of the Donner Party.* 1937. Truckee, CA. Wohlbruck. 234 p. F. H7. $25.00

MCGLASHAN, C.F. *Hist of the Donner Party.* 1966. Readex Microprint. 12mo. F. A8. $12.00

MCGLASHAN, C.F. *Hist of the Donner Party. Tragedy of the Sierra.* 1907. Sacramento. 8th ed. 2261 p. w/orig poster. H9. $250.00

MCGLASHAN, C.F. *Hist of the Donner Party...* 1927. San Francisco. later prt. 261 p. G/wrp. D7. $35.00

MCGOVERN, W.M. *Jungle Paths & Inca Ruins.* (1927). Century. 1st Am ed. 8vo. 526 p. VG. A2. $25.00

MCGOVERN, W.M. *To Lhasa in Disguise.* 1924. Grosset Dunlap. 1st ed. 462 p. G. W1. $18.00

MCGOWAN, Edward. *Narrative of Edward McGowan...While Persecuted...1856.* 1857. San Francisco. self pub. 1st ed. 12mo. 7 full-p woodcuts. rebound brds. NF. R3. $750.00

MCGOWAN, Samuel. *Address Delivered Before Euphemian & Philomathean...Soc...* 1855. Due West, SC. Telescope Office. 1st ed. 35 p. VG/wrp. M8. $85.00

MCGOWAN, Samuel. *Address on Occasion of 1st Anniversary Palmetto Assn...* 1857. Columbia. IC Morgan. 1st ed. 34 p. VG/prt wrp. M8. $250.00

MCGRADY, Mike. *Dove in Vietnam.* (1968). Funk Wagnall. NF/dj. A7. $30.00

MCGRATH, Thomas. *This Coffin Has No Handles.* 1988. NY. Thunders Mouth. ARC. F/wrp. B2. $30.00

MCGRAW & MCGRAW. *Assignment: Prison Riots.* (1954). Holt. 1st ed. 8vo. 270 p. VG+/G+. A2. $12.50

MCGRAW & MCGRAW. *Merry Go Round in Oz.* 1963. Reilly Lee. 1st/only ed. last book by this pub. VG/VG. L1. $475.00

MCGROARTY, John S. *CA: Its Hist & Romance.* 1911. Grafton. 1st ed. ils/index. 393 p. gilt gr morocco. B19. $45.00

MCGUANE, Thomas. *Best Am Sports Writing.* 1992. Houghton Mifflin/Lawrence. 1st ed. F/F. C4. $25.00

MCGUANE, Thomas. *MO Breaks.* 1976. Ballantine. 1st (only) ed/PBO. sgn. NF/wrp. A11. $75.00

MCGUANE, Thomas. *Nobody's Angel.* 1981. Random. ARC. sgn. w/promo sheet & photo. F/F. L3. $150.00

MCGUANE, Thomas. *Nothing But Bl Skies.* 1992. Houghton Mifflin. 1st ed. 1/200. sgn. F/slipcase. C4. $125.00

MCGUANE, Thomas. *Panama.* 1978. FSG. 1st ed. inscr/dtd 1979. author's 4th book. F/F. L3. $100.00

MCGUANE, Thomas. *Something To Be Desired.* 1984. Random. 1st ed. sgn. F/F. C4. $45.00

MCGUANE, Thomas. *Something To Be Desired.* 1984. Random. 1st ed. VG/F. B3. $25.00

MCGUANE, Thomas. *Sporting Club.* 1968. Simon Schuster. 1st ed. sgn. author's 1st book. NF/NF. L3. $250.00

MCGUANE, Thomas. *To Skin a Cat.* 1986. NY. special advance excerpt. 1/250. sgn. RS. F/F. A11. $90.00

MCGUFFEY. *McGuffey's Eclectic Primer.* ca 1900. Cincinnati/NY. Van Antwerp Bragg. 60 p. VG/bl pict wrp. D1. $120.00

MCGUINNESS, C.J. *Sailor of Fortune: Adventures of Irish Sailor...* 1935. Phil. Macrae. 1st Am ed. 8vo. 313 p. VG/G. A2. $25.00

MCGURN, Barrett. *Reporter Looks at the Vatican.* (1962). Coward McCann. 1st ed. 8vo. 316 p. F/VG. A2. $15.00

MCHUGH, Tom. *Time of the Buffalo.* 1972. Knopf. 1st ed. 339 p. VG. E5. $20.00

MCHUGH, Vincent. *Bl Hen Chickens.* 1947. Random. 1st ed. F/dj. C4. $20.00

MCILVANNEY, William. *Laidlaw.* 1977. Hodder Stoughton. 1st ed. F/VG. M15. $75.00

MCILWAINE, Richard. *Memories of 3 Score Yrs & 10.* 1908. NY/WA. Neale. 1st ed. 383 p. orig cloth/recased. VG+. M8. $175.00

MCINERNEY, Jay. *Brightness Falls.* (1992). London. Bloomsbury. 1st ed. F/F. B3. $35.00

MCINERNEY, Jay. *Story of My Life.* (1988). Atlantic Monthly. 1st ed. F/F. B3. $25.00

MCINTOSH, John. *Orig of N Am Indians.* 1849. NY. later ed. 345 p. rebound brn cloth. G. D7. $95.00

MCINTYRE, Vonda. *Barbary.* 1986. Houghton. 1st ed. F/F. F4. $17.00

MCINTYRE, Vonda. *Star Trek IV: The Voyage Home.* 1986. Pocket. 1st hc ed. sgn by Robin Curtis (Lt Saavik). F/F. F4. $25.00

MCIVER, S.B. *Yesterday's Palm Beach.* (1976). Miami, FL. ils/index. 144 p. VG/dj. B18. $15.00

MCKAY, Amanda. *Death on the River.* 1983. London. Gollancz. 1st British ed. F/F. S5. $22.50

MCKAY, Charlotte Elizabeth. *Stories of Hospital & Camp.* 1876. Phil. Claxton Remsen. 1st ed. xl. 230 p. cloth. VG. M8. $85.00

MCKAY, George L. *Stevenson Lib Catalogue of Collection of Writings...* 1951-64. New Haven. Yale. 6 vols. royal octavo. teg. gilt bl fabricoid. F. R3. $750.00

MCKEE, Alexander. *Queen's Corsair: Drake's Journey of Circumnavigation.* 1978. Stein Day. 7 maps. M/dj. O6. $30.00

MCKEE, James Cooper. *Narrative of Surrender of Command of US...at Ft Filmore...* 1886. Boston. Lowell. 3rd ed. 1/300. quarto. 2 maps. 31 p. VG/wrp. M8. $1,250.00

MCKEE, Russell. *Last W: Hist of Great Plains of N Am.* (1974). NY. ils. 312 p. G+. B18. $22.50

MCKELVEY. *Friendship's Offering.* 1990. np. ils. cloth. G2. $16.00

MCKELVEY. *Light & Shadows.* 1989. np. ils. wrp. G2. $15.00

MCKENDRY. *Quilts & Other Bed Coverings in the Canadian Tradition.* 1979. np. ils. 240 p. cloth. G2. $35.00

MCKENNEY, Kenneth. *Moonchild.* 1978. Simon Schuster. 1st ed. F/NF. F4. $22.50

MCKENNY, Margaret. *Birds in the Garden & How To Attract Them.* 1972. Grosset Dunlap. reprint of 1939 ed. VG/dj. A16. $15.00

MCKEOWN, Martha F. *AK Silver.* 1951. Macmillan. 1st ed. 247 p. dj. A17. $12.50

MCKERROW, Ronald. *Intro to Bibliography for Literary Students.* 1928 (1927). np. 2nd ed. VG+/dj. C1. $7.50

MCKIERNAN, Dennis L. *Trek to Kraggen.* 1986. Doubleday. 1st ed. inscr/sgn. F/F. F4. $22.00

MCKILLIP, Patricia A. *Stepping From the Shadows.* 1982. Atheneum. 1st ed. sgn. NF/NF. F4. $25.00

MCKIM. *101 Patchwork Patterns.* 1962. np. ils. wrp. G2. $4.00

MCKINLEY, William. *Authentic Life of William McKinley.* ca 1901. np. 8vo. photos. 503 p. olive cloth. G. T3. $12.00

MCKINLEY, William. *McKinley & Men of Our Times.* 1901. np. 8vo. 544 p. gr cloth. G. T3. $15.00

MCKINNEY, Roland. *Thomas Eakins.* 1942. NY. Crown. 8 color pls/64 ils. 112 p. cloth. D2. $45.00

MCKNIGHT, Charles. *Our W Border.* 1876. Phil. 1st ed. 15 pls. 752 p. rebacked. G. D7. $85.00

MCLEAN, Donald. *Roaring Days.* 1961 (1960). St Martin. 1st ed. 8vo. 277 p. F/F-clip. A2. $20.00

MCLEAN, Robert Colin. *George Tucker: Moral Philosopher & Man of Letters.* ca 1961. UNC. 2265 p. VG/G. B10. $25.00

MCLEAVE, Hugh. *Under the Icefall.* 1987. London. Gollancz. ARC of 1st ed. RS. F/F. S5. $22.50

MCLOSKEY & MARTIN. *Dozen Variables.* 1987. np. ils. wrp. G2. $17.00

MCLOSKEY. *Christmas Quilts.* 1990. np. wrp. G2. $5.00

MCLOSKEY. *Feathered Star Sampler.* 1985. np. instructions for 9 Feathered Star blocks. wrp. G2. $6.00

MCLOSKEY. *Lessons in Machine Piecing.* 1990. np. ils. wrp. G2. $18.95

MCLOSKEY. *Sm Quilts.* 1982. np. ils. wrp. G2. $6.95

MCLOSKEY. *Stars & Stepping Stones.* 1989. np. ils. wrp. G2. $15.00

MCLOSKEY. *Wall Quilts.* 1983. np. Dover reprint. wrp. G2. $5.00

MCLOUGHLIN, John. *Canine Clan. New Look at Man's Best Friend.* 1983. Viking. 1st ed. VG/G. O3. $35.00

MCLOUGHLIN, John. *Toolmaker Koan.* 1987. Baen. 1st ed. F/F. F4. $15.00

MCLOUGHLIN BROTHERS. *Eine ABC Geschichte.* ca 1905. McLoughlin. 10 p. VG. quite scarce. M5. $85.00

MCLOUGHLIN BROTHERS. *Girls' Favorite Stories. Snow Wht...Shoemaker...* 1939. 4 fairy tales. pict brds/cloth spine. VG-. A3. $7.00

MCLOUGHLIN BROTHERS. *Goldilocks & the 3 Bears.* 1938. Springfield, MA. 1st ed. Little Color Classics 802. VG. L1. $11.50

MCLOUGHLIN BROTHERS. *Goody Two Shoes.* 1898. NY. quarto. Cock Robin series. 14 p. NF/prt wrp. B24. $150.00

MCLOUGHLIN BROTHERS. *Henny Penny.* 1938. Springfield, MA. 1st thus ed. Little Color Classics 801. VG. L1. $9.50

MCLOUGHLIN BROTHERS. *Home Pictures.* ca 1895. NY. sm quarto. 16 p. NF/prt wrp. B24. $135.00

MCLOUGHLIN BROTHERS. *King of the Golden River/Robinson Crusoe.* 1939. pict brds/cloth spine. VG. A3. $7.00

MCLOUGHLIN BROTHERS. *Life & Death of Jenny Wren.* nd. (1870s). NY. 24mo. 9 woodcuts. 16 p. VG/pict wrp. H3. $35.00

MCLOUGHLIN BROTHERS. *Little Child's Home ABC.* 1899. McLoughlin Bros. prt on fine linen. VG. M5. $55.00

MCLOUGHLIN BROTHERS. *Little Red Riding Hood.* nd. McLoughlin. 6 lg pls. wrp. M5. $28.00

MCLOUGHLIN BROTHERS. *Merry Children Story Book.* 1900. NY. 8vo. woodcuts. 32 p. pict brds/beige cloth. VG. H3. $15.00

MCLOUGHLIN BROTHERS. *Robin Hood/The Wht Cat.* 1939. pict brds/cloth spine. VG. A3. $7.00

MCLOUGHLIN BROTHERS. *Tom Thumb.* 1897. NY. quarto. Cock Robin series. 14 p. NF/prt wrp. B24. $135.00

MCLUHAN, T.C. *Touch the Earth.* (1971). Toronto. New Pr. 1st ed. NF/dj. L3. $125.00

MCMAHON, Thomas J. *Orient I Found.* 1926. Appleton. 1st ed. 8vo. 223 p. VG. W1. $30.00

MCMANUS, P.F. *Real Ponies Don't Go Oink.* (1991). NY. 1st prt. 198 p. M/dj. A17. $12.50

MCMECHEN, James H. *Legends of the OH Valley...* 1898. Wheeling. 7th/last ed. 12mo. 106 p. G/wrp. scarce. D7. $75.00

MCMEEKIN, McLennan. *1st Book of Horses.* 1949. NY. Franklin Watts. Ils P Crowell. 11th prt. 45 p. VG/G+. A3. $7.50

MCMENEMY, Nick. *Assegai!* 1973. Saturday Review Pr. 1st ed. F/F. F4. $18.00

MCMILLAN, George. *Making of an Assassin.* (1976). Little Brn. stated 1st ed. 318 p. dj. A7. $17.00

MCMILLAN, Terry. *Disappearing Acts.* 1989. Viking/Penguin. ARC. NF/ils wrp. A13. $45.00

MCMILLAN, Terry. *Mama.* 1987. Houghton Mifflin. 1st ed. author's 1st book. NF/NF. A13. $200.00

MCMILLAN, Terry. *Waiting To Exhale.* 1992. Viking/Penguin. 1st ed. F/F. A13. $30.00

MCMILLEN, W. *Farming Fever.* 1924. NY. 1st ed. 12mo. 168 p. VG. B28. $15.00

MCMORRIES, Edward Young. *Hist of 1st Regiment, AL Volunteer Infantry, CSA.* 1904. Montgomery, AL. Brn Prt. 1st ed. 142 p. NF/prt wrp. M8. $250.00

MCMORRIS. *Art Quilt.* 1986. np. ils. wrp. G2. $22.00

MCMORRIS. *Crazy Quilts.* 1984. np. wrp. G2. $22.00

MCMURTIE, William. *Report on Culture of the Sugar Beet...* 1880. WA. USDA Special Report 28. 294 p. VG. B28. $47.50

MCMURTRY, Larry. *All My Friends Are Going To Be Strangers.* 1972. Simon Schuster. 1st ed. author's 5th novel. NF/NF. L3. $125.00

MCMURTRY, Larry. *Anything for Billy.* (1988). Simon Schuster. 1st ed. F/F. B3. $30.00

MCMURTRY, Larry. *Anything for Billy.* 1988. NY. 1st ed. F/F. A11. $65.00

MCMURTRY, Larry. *Anything for Billy.* 1988. Simon Schuster. AP. F/wrp. L3. $150.00

MCMURTRY, Larry. *Anything for Billy.* 1989. London. Collins. 1st ed. F/F. C4. $50.00

MCMURTRY, Larry. *Cadillac Jack.* 1982. Simon Schuster. AP. F/wrp. L3. $250.00

MCMURTRY, Larry. *Cadillac Jack.* 1982. Simon Schuster. 1st ed. F/F. B2. $35.00

MCMURTRY, Larry. *Desert Rose.* 1983. Simon Schuster. 1/250. sgn/#d. cloth. F/slipcase. L3. $350.00

MCMURTRY, Larry. *Desert Rose.* 1985. London. Allen. 1st ed. F/F. L3. $65.00

MCMURTRY, Larry. *It's Always We Rambled. An Essay on Rodeo.* 1974. NY. Hallman. ltd ed. 1/300. sgn/#d. VG/sans. L3. $250.00

MCMURTRY, Larry. *Last Picture Show.* 1966. Dial. 1st ed. F/NF. Q1. $300.00

MCMURTRY, Larry. *Lonesome Dove.* 1985. Simon Schuster. AP. NF/wrp. L3. $450.00

MCMURTRY, Larry. *Lonesome Dove.* 1985. Simon Schuster. 1st ed. octavo. 843 p. blk cloth. F/dj. H5. $225.00

MCMURTRY, Larry. *Moving On.* 1970. Simon Schuster. 1st ed. F/NF. L3. $175.00

MCMURTRY, Larry. *Some Can Whistle.* 1989. Simon Schuster. AP. F/wrp. L3. $175.00

MCMURTRY, Larry. *Some Can Whistle.* 1989. Simon Schuster. 1st ed. F/F. B3. $20.00

MCMURTRY, Larry. *Somebody's Darling.* 1978. Simon Schuster. 1st ed. rem mk. NF/dj. L3. $75.00

MCMURTRY, Larry. *Terms of Endearment.* 1975. London. WH Allen. 1st ed. F/F clip. L3. $100.00

MCMURTRY, Larry. *Terms of Endearment.* 1975. Simon Schuster. 1st ed. F/F. C4. $175.00

MCMURTRY, Larry. *Terms of Endearment.* 1975. Simon Schuster. 1st ed. NF/NF. L3. $125.00

MCMURTRY, R. Gerald. *Lincoln & the Hutchinson Family Singers.* 1944. Lincoln Memorial U. 1/100. 14 p. VG. A6. $15.00

MCNAIR, James B. *Citrus Products.* 1926-27. Chicago. 2 parts in 1. ils/pls. F/wrp. B26. $55.00

MCNAIR, Ralph J. *Square Dance!* 1951. NY. 1st ed. ils Arthur Shilstone. 188 p. F/dj. B14. $35.00

MCNAIR, Wesley. *Twelve Journeys Into ME.* 1992. Portland, ME. Romulus. 1/120. sgn. ils/sgn Marjorie Moore. M/paper. B24. $195.00

MCNALLY, Francis. *Improved System of Geography Designed for Schools...* 1873. NY. Barnes. atlas/maps. 120 p. O5. $50.00

MCNAMEE, Thomas. *Grizzly Bear.* (1986). NY. reprint. 308 p. F/wrp. A17. $9.50

MCNEIL, George E. *Labor Movement: Problem of Today.* 1891. Milwaukee. NW Pub. 1st ed. olive cloth. B2. $100.00

MCNEIL, Marion L. *Bl Elephant & the Pink Pig.* 1931. Saalfield. 4to. 39 p. pict bl cloth/brds. VG/glassine dj. H3. $12.00

MCNICKLE, D'Arcy. *Runner in the Sun.* 1966. HRW. 4th prt. Land of the Free series. VG/dj. L3. $25.00

MCNICKLE, D'Arcy. *Surrounded.* 1936. Dodd Mead. 1st ed. inscr. author's 1st book. NF/clamshell box. L3. $2,500.00

MCNICKLE, D'Arcy. *Wind From an Enemy Sky.* 1978. Harper Row. 1st ed. author's last novel. F/F. B2/L3. $45.00

MCORMICK, Jack. *Vascular Flora of Shades State Park...IN.* 1962. NY. 7 pls/5 maps (1 fld). VG. B25. $24.00

MCPAHIL, Andrew. *Three Persons.* 1929. NY/Montreal. 3rd ed/1st N Am prt. 346 p. gilt bl-blk cloth. VG. M7. $50.00

MCPHAIL, David. *Bear's Toothache.* 1972. Little Brn. 1st ed. sq 8vo. 32 p. VG/VG. A3. $10.00

MCPHEE, John. *AK: Images of the Country.* (1981). Sierra Club. 1st ed. F/NF. A7. $35.00

MCPHEE, John. *Annals of the Former.* nd. FSG. 1/350. sgn. F/slipcase. C4. $95.00

MCPHEE, John. *Assembling CA.* 1993. FSG. 1st ed. sgn. F/F. C4. $35.00

MCPHEE, John. *Basin & Range.* 1981. FSG. F/F. C4. $40.00

MCPHEE, John. *Coming Into the Country.* 1977. FSG. AP. F/wrp. scarce. L3. $175.00

MCPHEE, John. *Coming Into the Country.* 1978. Hamish Hamilton. 1st ed. F/F. C4. $45.00

MCPHEE, John. *Control of Nature.* 1989. FSG. 1st ed. F/F. A7. $15.00

MCPHEE, John. *Control of Nature.* 1989. NY. 1st ed. sgn. F/F. A11. $30.00

MCPHEE, John. *Crofter & the Laird.* 1970. FSG. 1st ed. red brds. F/F. C4. $95.00

MCPHEE, John. *Fair of San Gennaro.* 1981. Portland. Press-22. 1st sgn ltd ed. 1/250. F/slipcase. L3. $350.00

MCPHEE, John. *Giving Good Weight.* 1979. FSG. 1st ed. sgn. F/F. C4. $65.00

MCPHEE, John. *Headmaster.* 1966. Farrar. 1st ed. F/F. B2. $65.00

MCPHEE, John. *La Place de la Concorde Suisse.* 1984. NY. Farrar. AP. F/wrp. B2. $75.00

MCPHEE, John. *Levels of the Game.* 1969. FSG. 1st ed. inscr Arthur Ashe. F/NF. L3. $350.00

MCPHEE, John. *Oranges.* 1967. FSG. 1st ed. sgn. F/NF. B4. $275.00

MCPHEE, John. *Oranges.* 1977 (1967). NY. 4th prt. 149 p. VG+/dj. B26. $17.50

MCPHEE, John. *Pine Barrens.* 1968. NYL. 1st ed. inscr. F/NF. A11. $50.00

MCPHEE, John. *Rising From the Plains.* 1986. FSG. 1st ed. F/clip. C4. $55.00

MCPHEE, John. *Rising From the Plains.* 1986. FSG. 1st ed. sgn. F/NF. L3. $65.00

MCPHEE, John. *Sense of Where You Are.* 1965. FSG. 1st ed. author's 1st book. F/VG clip. L3. $150.00

MCPHEE, William. *Six-Hour Shift.* 1920. Doubleday. 1/377 p. sgn. NF. C4. $50.00

MCQUINN, Donald E. *Targets.* (1980). Macmillan. 1st ed. F/NF. A7. $35.00

MCQUISTON, John H. *Tannoy Calling: Story of Canadian Airmen...* 1990. Vantage. dj. N2. $7.50

MCROSKEY, Racine. *Missions of CA.* 1914. San Francisco. Philopolis. 1st ed. tall 8vo. 174 p. VG. H7. $30.00

MCSWEENEY, Thomas Denis. *Cathedral on CA Street: Story of St Mary's Cathedral...* 1952. Academy of CA Church Hist. 1st ed. 95 p. F/sans. B19. $15.00

MCVICKAR, H. *Our Amateur Circus; or, A NY Season.* 1892. Harper. oblong 8vo. gilt blk moire/rebacked. VG+. F1. $250.00

MCWALTERS, George S. *Knots Untied; or, Ways & Byways in Hidden Life Am Detective.* 1871. Hartford. Burr Hyde. 8vo. 665 p. plum cloth. VG+. F1. $50.00

MCWALTERS, George S. *Knots Untied; or, Ways & Byways in Hidden Life Am Detective.* 1872 (1871). Burr Hyde. 665 p. cloth. G+. M20. $40.00

MCWHINEY, Grady. *Braxton Bragg & Confederate Defeat. Vol 1: Field Command.* 1969. NY. Columbia U. 1st ed. 421 p. cloth. NF/VG. M8. $35.00

MCWHINNEY, Edward. *Federal Constitution-Making for Multi-National World.* 1966. Leyden. Sijthoff. G/dj. M11. $45.00

MCWILLIAMS, Carey. *Brothers Under the Skin.* 1943. Little Brn. 1st ed. 8vo. 325 p. F/VG+. B20. $35.00

MCWILLIAMS, Carey. *Mask for Privilege: Anti-Semitism in Am.* 1948. Little Brn. 1st ed. VG/worn. N2. $7.50

MEAD, Edward C. *Hist Homes of the SW Mtns of VA.* 1899. Lippincott. xl. 1/750. ils/fld map. 275 p. B10. $50.00

MEAD, Frederick S. *Harvard's Military Record in the World War.* 1921. Boston. 1142 p. G. A17. $20.00

MEAD, M.N. *Asheville..., in the Land of the Sky.* 1942. Richmond, VA. ils/index. 188 p. G. B18. $35.00

MEAD, Margaret. *Blackberry Winter: My Early Yrs.* 1971. NY. 1st ed. sgn. VG/VG. B5. $25.00

MEAD, Peter B. *Elementary Treatise on Am Grape Culture & Wine Making.* 1867. Harper. 1st ed. ils/index. 483 p. H10. $65.00

MEAD, R.D. *Ultimate N: Canoeing MacKenzie's Great River.* (1976). Doubleday. later prt. 8vo. 312 p. F/F. A2. $12.50

MEAD, Richard. *Medica Sacra: Sive, De Morbis Insignioribus...* 1759. London. pl after Reuben. G7. $150.00

MEAD, Richard. *Medical Works of Richard Mead, MD.* 1767. Dublin. Thomas Ewing. 511 p. half calf. G7. $350.00

MEAD, Robert D. *Journeys Down the Line.* 1978. NY. 1st ed. 8vo. 609 p. F/VG. H3. $20.00

MEAD, William B. *2 Spectacular Seasons.* (199). NY. 1st ed. 245 p. F/F. A7. $10.00

MEADE, Julian R. *Bouquets & Bitters: A Gardener's Medley.* 1940. Longman Gr. 1st ed. G/fair. A16. $10.00

MEADE, Julian R. *Bouquets & Bitters: A Gardener's Medley.* 1940. Longman Gr. 1st ed. ils. 271 p. cloth. VG. H10. $16.50

MEADE, Richard; see Haas, Ben.

MEADOWCROFT, Enid La Monte. *By Wagon & Flatboat.* 1938. Crowell. 1st ed. sgn. 170 p. VG/dj. M20. $20.00

MEADOWS, Don. *Baja CA, 1533-1950: A Biblio-Hist.* 1951. np. reprint. inscr. 32 p. front cover missing. B19. $10.00

MEADOWS, Kenny. *Heads of the People; or, Portraits of the Eng.* nd. London. Willoughby. 2 vols. Root bdg. VG. H5. $300.00

MEAGHER, Maude. *Wht Jade.* 1930. Houghton Mifflin. 1st ed. sgn. F/VG clip. N3. $45.00

MEAGHER, Paul Kevin. *Encyclopedia Dictionary of Religion.* ca 1979. WA, DC. Corpus. 3 vols. F. H10. $85.00

MEAKER, Marijane. *Shockproof Sydney Skate.* 1972. Boston. Little Brn. 1st ed. NF/NF clip. A14. $25.00

MEALY & MEALY. *Sing for Joy: Songbook for Young Children.* 1961. Seabury Pr. 1st ed. ils Karla Kuskin. 138 p. red/bl cloth. G+. T5. $15.00

MEANS, Florence C. *Candle in the Mist.* (1931). Houghton Mifflin. ils Marguerite DeAngeli. 253 p. G. T5. $20.00

MEANY, Edmond S. *Vancouver's Discovery of Puget Sound...* 1915. Macmillan. xl. ils/4 maps. VG+. O6. $85.00

MEANY, Edward S. *Lincoln Esteemed WA.* 1933. Seattle. 57 p. VG. A6. $10.00

MEAR, Roger. *Walk to the Pole.* 1987. Crown. VG/dj. A16. $15.00

MEARNS, David. *Lincoln & the Image of Am. An Address, Feb 12, 1953.* 16 p. A6. $10.00

MECHANICUS, Philip. *Yr of Fear: Jewish Prisoner Waits for Auschwitz.* 1968. Hawthorn. 267 p. VG. S3. $25.00

MECHKLENBURG, George. *Last of the Old W.* 1927. np. 1st ed. 149 p. G. O7. $21.00

MECKLIN, John. *Mission in Torment.* 1965. Doubleday. dj. A7. $30.00

MECKLIN, John. *Story of Am Dissent.* nd. Port WA, NY. Kennikat Pr. index. 381 p. H10. $20.00

MEDICINE CROW, Joseph. *From the Heart of the Crow Country.* 1992. NY. Orion. AP. NF/wrp. L3. $45.00

MEDINA, Jose Toribio. *Discovery of the Amazon.* 1934. Am Geog Soc. 4to. 467 p. F3. $35.00

MEE, Arthur. *Salute the King: George VI & His Far-Flung Realms.* (1937). Hodder Stoughton. 1st ed. 8vo. 184 p. VG+/VG. A2. $25.00

MEE, Charles L. *Meetings at Potsdam.* 1975. Evans. BC. VG/dj. A16. $6.50

MEEGAN, George. *Longest Walk: Odyssey of the Human Spirit.* (1988). Dodd Mead. 1st ed. 8vo. 402 p. F-/VG. A2. $12.50

MEEHAN, Thomas. *Native Flowers & Ferns of the US in Their...Aspects.* 1879-80. Boston. Prang. 1st ed. quarto. 4 vols. 192 lithos. gilt gr cloth. NF. H5. $600.00

MEEK, F.B. *Report of Geological Survey of OH.* 1873. Columbus. 1st ed. 3 vols. VG. D7. $125.00

MEEK, James B. *Art of Engraving.* (1973). Montezuma. 2nd prt. 196 p. F/G. A17. $27.50

MEEK, M.R.D. *Mouthful of Sand.* 1988. London. Collins. 1st ed. F/F. S5. $27.50

MEEK, M.R.D. *Split Second.* 1985. London. Collins. 1st ed. F/F. S5. $30.00

MEEKER, Ezra. *Busy Life of 85 Yrs: Ventures & Adventures...* 1916. Seattle. self pub. sgn. 399 p. pict bdg. VG. H7. $25.00

MEEKER, Ezra. *Kate Mulhall: Romance of the OR Trail.* (1926). Meeker. 1st ed. sgn. photos/map. F. A18. $50.00

MEESE, William. *Abraham Lincoln & the Waterways.* 1908. Moline. Desaulniers. VG. A6. $16.00

MEGGENDORFER, Lothar. *City Park.* 1981 (1887). facsimile. mechanical scenes. F. A4. $55.00

MEGGENDORFER, Lothar. *Genius of Lothar Meggendorfer.* 1985. London. 4to. 18 p. NF. A4. $65.00

MEGGENDORFER, Lothar. *International Circus.* 1979. Penguin. facsimile of 1887 ed. VG. A16. $25.00

MEGGENDORFER, Lothar. *International Circus.* 1983 (1887). after German ed. 6-ring circus popup. F. A4. $75.00

MEGGITT, M.J. *Desert People: Study of Walbiri Aborigines...* 1968. Chicago. 2nd imp. 8vo. 348 p. VG/VG. P4. $30.00

MEIER, Maurice. *Refuge.* 1962. Norton. inscr. 241 p. VG/G+. S3. $25.00

MEIGS, Cornelia. *Critical Hist of Children's Literature.* 1953. Macmillan. ils. NF. M5. $38.00

MEIGS, Cornelia. *Scarlet Oak.* 1938. Macmillan. 1st ed. ils EO Jones. VG+/G+. P2. $25.00

MEIGS, Cornelia. *Trade Wind.* 1927. Boston. 1st ed. 309 p. pict blk cloth. VG. H3. $15.00

MEIGS, Cornelia. *Wind in the Chimney.* 1935 (1934). Macmillan. 4th prt. sq 8vo. 144 p. bl cloth. VG-. T5. $25.00

MEINERETZHAGEN, R. *Middle E Diary 1917-56.* 1959. London. Cresset. 1st ed. 8vo. 376 p. cloth. dj. O2. $85.00

MEIRING, Desmond. *Brinkman.* (1965). Houghton Mifflin. 1st Am ed. dj. A7. $40.00

MELAMED, Deborah M. *Three Pillars: Thought, Worship & Practice for Jewish Women.* 1958. Women's League United Synagogue of Am. VG+/fair. S3. $22.00

MELDGAARD, Jorgen. *Eskimo Sculpture.* 1959. Methuen. 1st ed. ils/notes. 88 p. F/VG. B19. $25.00

MELINE, James F. *Two Thousand Miles on Horseback.* 1867. NY. 1st ed. 12mo. 317 p. cloth. VG. D3. $50.00

MELINGO, P.V. *Griechenland in Unseren Tagen.* 1892. Vienna. 8vo. 223 p. cloth/brds. O2. $35.00

MELLEN, Grenville. *Book of the US.* 1843. Hartford. thick 8vo. 847 p. legal calf. H9. $40.00

MELLOW, James R. *Charmed Circle.* (1974). Praeger. 2nd prt. 528 p. dj. A7. $18.00

MELLQUIST & WIESE. *Paul Rosenfeld: Voyager in the Arts.* 1948. Creative Age. 284 p. G+/fair. S3. $23.00

MELTZER, David. *Agency/The Agent/How Many Bricks in the Pile?* 1968. N Hollywood. Essex House. 3 sgn vols. NF/ils wrps. A11. $145.00

MELTZER, David. *San Francisco Poets.* 1971. NY. PBO/1st prt. sgn. NF/wrp. A11. $40.00

MELVILLE, Herman. *Benito Cereno.* 1926. London. 1st book ed. 1/1650. tall 8vo. VG/sans. A11. $145.00

MELVILLE, Herman. *Clarel: A Poem & Pilgrimage in Holy Land.* 1960. NY. Hendricks. 652 p. H10. $20.00

MELVILLE, Herman. *Israel Potter: Hist 50 Yrs of Exile.* 1855. NY. Putnam. 3rd ed. 12mo. 276 p. purple cloth. M1. $400.00

MELVILLE, Herman. *Mardi & a Voyage Thither.* 1849. NY. 1st ed. 12mo. 2 vols. orig purple cloth. NF/morocco slipcase. H5. $4,000.00

MELVILLE, Herman. *Mardi: & the Voyage Thither.* 1849. NY. 1st ed. 12mo. 2 vols. purple cloth. NF. H5. $4,000.00

MELVILLE, Herman. *Moby Dick; or, The Whale.* 1851. NY. 1st Am ed. 12mo. 1st bdg/brn cloth. VG/morocco clamshell case. H5. $20,000.00

MELVILLE, Herman. *Moby Dick; or, The Whale.* 1851. NY. 1st Am ed. 12mo. 1st bdg/bl cloth variant. NF/quarter morocco slipcase. H5. $22,500.00

MELVILLE, Herman. *Moby Dick; or, The Whale.* 1930. Random. ils Rockwell Kent. 822 p. pict blk cloth. VG+. B14. $40.00

MELVILLE, Herman. *Moby Dick; or, The Whale.* 1975. Artist's Ltd Ed. 1/1500. intro/sgn Cousteau. ils/sgn Neiman. gilt brn morocco. B24. $1,250.00

MELVILLE, Herman. *Moby Dick; or, The Whale.* 1979. San Francisco. Arion. 1/265 on Barcham Gr. 576 p. w/archival material. case. H5. $16,500.00

MELVILLE, Herman. *Piazza Tales.* 1856. NY. 1st ed. 12mo. orig brn cloth. VG/quarter morocco slipcase. H5. $3,000.00

MELVILLE, Herman. *Selected Poems.* 1944. Norfolk, CT. 1st ed. F/unused. A11. $95.00

MELVILLE, Herman. *Whale.* 1851. London. true 1st ed. 12mo. 3 vols. contemporary purple-blk cloth. H5. $25,000.00

MELVILLE, Herman. *White-Jacket; or, World in a Man-of-War.* 1850. NY. 1st Am ed/2nd prt. brn cloth. VG/slipcase. H5. $1,500.00

MELVILLE, Herman. *White-Jacket; or, World in a Man-of-War.* 1850. NY. Harper. 1st ed/1st issue. 8vo. gilt cloth. fld box/slipcase. M7. $1,175.00

MELVILLE, James. *Body Wore Brocade.* 1992. London. Little Brn. 1st ed. F/F. M15. $35.00

MELVILLE, James. *Bogus Buddha.* 1990. London. Headline. 1st ed. sgn. F/F. S5. $40.00

MELVILLE, James. *Death Ceremony.* 1985. London. Secker. 1st ed. sgn. NF/NF. S5. $35.00

MELVILLE, James. *Kimono for a Corpse.* 1987. London. Secker Warburg. 1st ed. F/F. M15. $40.00

MELVILLE, Lewis. *Thackery Country.* 1911. London. 8vo. 223 p. teg. gilt gr cloth. F. H3. $12.00

MEMET, David. *Lakeboat.* 1981. Grove. 1st ed. F/F. B2. $40.00

MENCKEN, H.L. *Mencken.* 1924. Phil. Centaur Bookshop. 1/300. G. A1. $35.00

MENCKEN, H.L. *Notes on Democracy.* nd. 1/235. G+. A1. $250.00

MENCKEN, H.L. *Notes on Democracy.* 1926. Knopf. 1st ed. 1/200. sgn/#d. NF/NF #d slipcase. Q1. $400.00

MENDELSOHN, Everett. *Heat & Life: Development of Theory of Animal Heat.* 1964. Cambridge. Harvard. 1st ed. 208 p. cloth. VG/dj. G1. $22.50

MENDELSON, Wallace. *Felix Frankfurter, a Tribute.* 1964. NY. Reynal. M11. $35.00

MENDOZA, George. *Fishing the Morning Lonely.* (1974). Freshet. 100 p. F/dj. A17. $9.50

MENEGAS, Peter. *Service.* 1971. London. Arlington. 1st ed. NF/NF clip. A14. $45.00

MENEN, Aubrey. *She La: A Satire.* 1962. Random. 1st ed. F/NF. N3. $10.00

MENKEN, H.L. *Prejudices.* 1922. NY. fair. A1. $12.00

MENNEL, Robert M. *Thorns & Thistles: Juvenile Deliquents in US 1825-1950.* 1973. Hanover, NH. 1st ed. 231 p. blk cloth/gray brds. VG/dj. G1. $30.00

MENNEN, Aubrey. *Prevalence of Witches.* 1947. London. 1st ed. NF/dj. M2. $35.00

MENOCAL, A.G. *Report of the US Nicaragua Surveying Party, 1885.* 1886. GPO. quarto. 56 pls/12 fld maps. NF. O6. $150.00

MENOCAL, A.G. *Report of US Nicaragua Surveying Party, 1885...* 1886. WA. xl. charts/pls/maps. 54 p. O5. $75.00

MENPES, Mortimer. *Whistler As I Knew Him.* 1904. Macmillan. thick 4to. 153 p. gilt tan cloth. VG/VG. F1. $200.00

MENTELEONE, Thomas F. *Borderlands.* 1990. Maclay. 1st ed. 1/750. sgn all 26 contributors. M/box. M2. $75.00

MENZEL, Paul. *Moral Argument & War in Vietnam.* (1971). Nashville. Aurora. NF/dj. A7. $30.00

MERA. *Spanish-Am Blankety.* 1987. np. wrp. G2. $15.00

MERAK, A.J. *Hydrosphere.* 1967. NY. Arcadia. 1st Am/1st hc ed. F/F. N3. $10.00

MERCER, A.S. *Banditti of the Plains.* (1894). Cheyenne, WY. 1st ed. J O'Mahoney's copy. map. calf presentation bdg. C6. $3,200.00

MERCER, A.S. *Banditti of the Plains.* (1954). Norman, OK. 1st thus ed. 195 p. G/dj. B18. $22.50

MERCER, Cavalie. *Journal of Waterloo Campaign Kept Throughout...1815.* 1927. London. Peter Davies. later prt. 388 p. cloth. VG. M8. $45.00

MERCER, Philip. *Life of the Gallant Pelham.* 1958. Kennesaw, GA. Continental Book. reprint of 1929 ed. 180 p. cloth. NF. M8. $45.00

MERCHANT, Paul; see Ellison, Harlan.

MERCURIALE, Girolamo. *De Arte Gymnastica Libri Sex.* 1573. Venice. Apud untas. 2nd fully ils ed. sm quarto. VG. H5. $4,000.00

MEREDITH, George. *Jump to Glory Jane.* 1892. London. Swan Sonnenschein. 1/1000. ils Housman. NF. F1. $220.00

MEREDITH, George. *Ordeal of Richard Feverel.* 1927. Modern Lib. 1st thus ed. VG. E3. $8.00

MEREDITH, Owen. *Lucile.* 1897. NY. ils Madeleine Le Maire. teg. gilt dk bl cloth. VG+. A11. $35.00

MEREDITH, William. *Cheer.* 1980. NY. 1st ed. F/NF. V1. $20.00

MERIAN, Matthieu. *La Danse des Morts.* 1756. Basel. Ches Jean Rodolphe Imhof. 4to. 132 p. contemporary bdg. K1. $1,250.00

MERIMEE, Prosper. *Carmen & Letters From Spain.* 1931. NY. Harrison of Paris. 1/595. 8vo. ils Barraud/Charpentier. F/slipcase. F1. $100.00

MERIN, O. *Tresors d'Art de Yougoslavie.* 1969. Arthaud. VG/VG. A1. $100.00

MERK, Frederick. *Hist of the Westward Movement.* 1978. Knopf. 1st ed. 116 ils. M/dj. O6. $35.00

MERKIN, Robert. *Zombie Jamboree.* (1986). Morrow. 1st ed. F/NF. A7. $30.00

MERKLING, Frank. *Opera News Book of Traviata.* (1967). Dodd Mead. 1st ed. 12mo. 152 p. VG/VG. A2. $10.00

MERLE, Robert. *Malevil.* 1973. Simon Schuster. 1st Am ed. trans from French. F/F. A14. $30.00

MERREDITH, Richard C. *No Brother, No Friend.* 1976. Doubleday. 1st ed. F/F. F4. $24.00

MERRICK, Gordon. *Lord Won't Mind.* 1970. NY. 2nd prt. NF/VG+. A14. $20.00

MERRILL, James. *Different Season.* (1993). Knopf. AP. F/wrp. B4. $45.00

MERRILL, James. *From the 1st 9. Poems 1946-76.* 1982. NY. 1st ed. presentation/ inscr. F/F. A11. $35.00

MERRILL, James. *Metamorphosis of 741.* nd. Banyan Pr. ltd ed. 1/440. sgn/#d. F/orig envelope. V1. $75.00

MERRILL, James. *Mirabell: Book of Numbers.* 1978. NY. 1st ed. F/VG+. V1. $20.00

MERRILL, James. *Rebel Shore.* 1957. np. 1st ed. 246 p. dj. O7. $12.50

MERRILL, James. *Yel Pages.* 1974. Cambridge. 1/800. special sgn. F/yel wrp. A11. $75.00

MERRILL, Judith. *Daughters of the Earth.* 1968. Doubleday. 1st ed. F/dj. M2. $25.00

MERRILL, Judith. *SF 57.* 1957. Gnome. 1st ed. F/dj. M2. $20.00

MERRILL PUBLISHING. *Tale of Peter Rabbit.* 1943. 14 p. VG. A3. $15.00

MERRITT, Abraham. *Story Behind the Story.* 1942. NY. private prt. VG. N2. $7.50

MERRYMAN, William N. *Yankee Caballero.* 1940. NY. 1st ed. map ep. VG. H3. $20.00

MERTON, Thomas. *Conjectures of a Guilty Bystander.* 1966. Doubleday. 1st ed. F/clip. C4. $60.00

MERTON, Thomas. *Courage for Truth: Letters & Writers.* 1993. FSG. 1st ed. F/F. C4. $30.00

MERTON, Thomas. *Easter Anthology.* 1989. Ownesboro Mus Fine Art. 1st ed. prt stiff wrp. C4. $40.00

MERTON, Thomas. *Encounter.* 1989. Larkspur. 1st ed. 1/less than 1000. F/dj. C4. $55.00

MERTON, Thomas. *Father Louie: Photos of Thomas Merton.* 1991. NY. Timken Pub. 1/1000. 50 duotone ils. F/F. C4. $40.00

MERTON, Thomas. *Ishi Means Man.* 1976. Greensboro. Unicorn. 1st ed. F/wrp. C4. $30.00

MERTON, Thomas. *Monk's Pond.* 1989. Lexington. 1-vol facsimile of 4 issues Monk's Pond. F/dj. C4. $45.00

MERTON, Thomas. *Orig Child Bomb.* 1961. New Directions. 1st ed. blk brds. F. C4. $85.00

MERTON, Thomas. *Road to Joy: Letters to New & Old Friends.* 1989. FSG. 1st ed. F/F. C4. $35.00

MERTON, Thomas. *Silent Life.* 1957. FSC. 1st ed. VG/dj. E3. $25.00

MERTON, Thomas. *Song for Nobody.* 1993. Liguori. Triumph Books. 1st ed. ils. F/F. C4. $20.00

MERTON, Thomas. *Thomas Merton in AK.* 1989. New Directions. 1st ed. F/F. C4. $30.00

MERTON, Thomas. *Thomas Merton: A Bibliography.* 1975. Kent State. 1st ed. F. C4. $50.00

MERTON, Thomas. *Thomas Merton: 1st & Last Memories.* 1986. Necessity Pr. 1st ed. ils Jim Cantrell. F/wrp. C4. $35.00

MERTON, Thomas. *Tower of Babel.* 1957. James Laughlin. 1st separate ed. folio. 31 p. F/slipcase. B24. $1,250.00

MERTON, Thomas. *Waters of Silence.* 1950. London. Theodore Brun. 1/120. fwd Evelyn Waugh. gilt full leather. VG+. Q1. $500.00

MERTON, Thomas. *Waters of Siloe.* 1949. Harcourt Brace. 1st ed. G/dj. M18. $35.00

MERWIN, W.S. *Gr w/Beasts.* 1956. RH Davis. 1st ed. w/Poetry Book Soc ribbon. F/dj. M18. $125.00

MERWIN, W.S. *Rain in the Trees.* 1988. NY. 1st ed. sgn. F/wrp. V1. $25.00

MERWIN, W.S. *Regions of Memory. Uncollected Prose, 1949-82.* 1987. Urbana, IL. 1st ed. inscr. F/F. A11. $30.00

MESERVEY, A.B. *Meservey's Book-Keeping, Single & Double Entry.* (1882). Boston. Thompson Brn. 222 p. marbled edges. tan cloth. VG. B14. $35.00

MESNET, Marie-Beatrice. *Graham Greene & the Heart of the Matter.* 1954. London. 1st ed. NF/VG+. A11. $50.00

MESSANT. *Embroiderer's Workbook.* 1988. np. pb. G2. $15.00

METCALF, Paul. *Genoa.* 1965. Highlands, NC. 1st ed. sgn. F/NF. A11. $135.00

METCALF, S.L. *Collection of Most Interesting Narratives of Indian Warfare.* 1821. Lexington. Hunt. 1st ed. sm octavo. aeg. full crimson crushed French morocco. H9. $2,750.00

METCALF, S.L. *New Theory of Terrestrial Magnetism.* 1833. NY. xl. 158 p. brn cloth. G. T3. $19.00

METCALFE, John. *Feasting Dead.* 1954. Arkham. 1st ed. F/dj. M2. $175.00

METCALFE-SHAW, Gertrude E. *Eng Caravanners in the Wild W. Old Pioneer's Trail.* 1926. Edinburgh. 1st ed. 400 p. cloth. VG. D3. $45.00

METRAS, Gary. *Night Watches.* 1981. np. 1st ed. sgn. F/wrp. V1. $15.00

MEURANT. *Shoowa Design.* 1991. nd. ils. cloth. G2. $35.00

MEWSHAW, Michael. *Blackballed.* 1986. Atheneum. 1st ed. F/dj. B4. $35.00

MEYER, Conrad F. *Fingerhutchen.* 1930s. Mainz. Scholz. 12mo. 28 p. pict brds. VG. D1. $32.50

MEYER, Ernest L. *Hey! Yellowbacks! War Diary of Conscientious Objector.* ca 1930. John Day. G/VG. V4. $20.00

MEYER, Franz. *Chagall.* 1963. NY. VG/G+. A1. $85.00

MEYER, Jerome S. *Picture Book of Astronomy.* 1945. NY. 4to. ils/pls. 36 p. pict bl cloth. F. H3. $15.00

MEYER, Nicholas. *Seven-Per-Cent Solution.* 1974. Dutton. 1st ed. F/VG. N3. $10.00

MEYER, Peter. *Jews in the Soviet Satellites.* 1953. Syracuse. 637 p. VG. S3. $26.00

MEYER, Ted. *Body Count.* 1982. Exposition. 1st ed. VG/dj. L3. $50.00

MEYERS, Jeffrey. *Fever at the Core.* 1976. London Magazine Eds. 1st ed. 172 p. gilt blk paper simulating cloth. F/NF. M7. $75.00

MEYERS, Lewis E. *Chautauqua Industrial Art Desk.* ca 1923. Valparaiso, IN. Lewis E Meyers. US map by GM Buckley. G. scarce. H9. $350.00

MEYNELL, Alice. *Selected Poems.* 1965. Nonesuch. 1st ed. F/stiff wrp. C4. $40.00

MEZZROW & WOLFE. *Really the Blues.* (1946). Random. 1st ed. A7. $35.00

MICHAEL, Bryan; see Moore, Brian.

MICHAELIS, Edgar. *Die Menschheitsproblematik der Freudschen Psycholanalyse.* 1925. Leipzig. Johann Ambrosius Barth. prt orange cloth. G1. $75.00

MICHAELS, Barbara. *Ammie, Come Home.* 1968. Meredith Pr. 1st ed. F/NF. B2. $45.00

MICHAELS, Barbara. *Search the Shadows.* 1987. NY. Atheneum. ARC of 1st ed. sgn. w/promo material. F/F. S5. $40.00

MICHAUD & POUJOULAT. *Correspondance D'Orient, 1830-31.* 1933-35. Paris. 1st ed. 7 vols. 8vo. gilt morocco. O2. $450.00

MICHAUX, Francois Andre. *Travels to the W of the Alleghany Mtns...OH, KY, TN...* 1805. London. Phillips. octavo. lg fld map. marbled wrp. H9. $475.00

MICHEL, Henri. *Traite de l'Astrolabe.* 1976. Paris. Libraire Alain Brieux. facsimile 1st ed. 1/750. M/dj. O6. $85.00

MICHEL, Jean. *Dora.* 1979. HRW. 308 p. VG/VG. S3. $26.00

MICHELSON, Richard. *Did You Say Ghosts?* 1993. Macmillan. 1st ed. sgn. sgn/ils Leonard Baskin. M/M. E3. $35.00

MICHENER, Carroll. *Heirs of the Incas.* 1924. Minton Balch. 1st ed. 287 p. F3. $20.00

MICHENER, James A. *Caribbean.* 1989. Random. 1st ed. F/F. B11. $18.00

MICHENER, James A. *Floating World: Story of Japanese Prints.* 1954. Random. 3rd prt. 8vo. 403 p. VG/dj. W1. $60.00

MICHENER, James A. *Literary Reflections.* 1993. Houston. State house. 1/200. sgn. F/slipcase. C4. $145.00

MICHENER, James A. *Mexico.* 1992. Random. 1/500. sgn/#d. F/slipcase. C4. $125.00

MICHENER, James A. *Source.* (1965). NY. 1st ed. 909 p. map ep. G/torn. B18. $25.00

MICHENER, James A. *Tales of the S Pacific.* (1992). San Diego. HBJ. 1st ed. ils Michael Hague. F/F. B3. $25.00

MICHENER, James A. *Tales of the S Pacific.* 1947. NY. inscr/dtd 1947. salmon cloth. NF. B14. $300.00

MICHENER, James A. *TX.* (1985). Random. 1st ed. F/NF. B3. $20.00

MICHIE & RHYLICK. *Dixie Demagogues.* 1939. Vanguard. G. N2. $7.50

MICKEL, John T. *How To Know the Ferns & Fern Allies.* 1979. Dubuque. ils. 229 p. sbdg. M. B26. $25.00

MIDDA, Sara. *In & Out of the Garden.* 1981. Workman Pub. ils. VG/dj. A16. $12.00

MIDDLEBROOK, Martin. *Schweinfurt-Regensburg Mission.* 1983. Scribner. BC. VG/dj. A16. $6.00

MIDDLETON, Bernard C. *Hist of Eng Craft Bookbinding Technique.* 1963. London. Hafner. 305 p. cloth. F/dj. B14. $45.00

MIDDLETON, Drew. *Sky Suspended.* 1960. Longman Gr. 1st/A ed. 8vo. F. A8. $15.00

MIDDLETON, Harry. *On the Spring of Time: Angler's Love of the Smokies.* (1991). Simon Schuster. 1st ed. 237 p. F/dj. A17. $12.50

MIDDLETON, W.E. Knowles. *Experimenters: Study of the Accademia Del Cimento.* 1971. Baltimore. Johns Hopkins. 1st ed. 416 p. brn cloth. VG/dj. G1. $50.00

MIFF, P. *Heroic China.* 1937. NY. Workers Lib. 96 p. VG/wrp. A7. $15.00

MIJATOVICH, Chedomil. *Constantine Palaeologus. Last Emperor of Greeks 1448-53.* 1968. Chicago. 8vo. 239 p. cloth. O2. $35.00

MIKES, George. *Coat of Many Colors: Israel.* 1969. Boston. Gambit. 158 p. VG+/G+. S3. $16.00

MIKKELSEN, Ejnar. *Conquering the Arctic Ice.* ca 1930. Phil. photos/index. 470 p. A17. $65.00

MIKKELSEN, Ejnar. *Frozen Justice.* 1922. Knopf. 230 p. map ep. gray cloth. VG. P4. $65.00

MIKKELSEN, Ejnar. *Two Against the Ice.* nd. London. Travel BC. 8vo. 224 p. VG/worn. P4. $35.00

MILBURN, D. Judson. *Age of Wit 1650-1750.* 1966. Macmillan. 2nd prt. gr cloth. VG/clip. G1. $22.50

MILBURN, William Henry. *Pioneers, Preachers & People of the MS Valley.* 1860. Derby Jackson. 8vo. 465 p. brn pebbled cloth. H9. $50.00

MILBURN, William Henry. *Rifle, Axe & Saddle-Bags & Other Lectures.* 1857. NY. Derby Jackson. 1st ed. stp brn cloth. G. H7. $25.00

MILES, Charles. *Indian & Eskimo Artifacts of N Am.* nd. NY. Bonanza. 4to. 244 p. gr cloth. VG/dj. P4. $42.50

MILES, John. *Stable Secrets; or, Puffy Poodles...* 1863. London. Ward Lock. 1st ed. leather. O3. $95.00

MILES, Keith; see Tralins, Bob.

MILES, Miska. *Swim, Little Duck.* 1976. Little Brn. 1st ed. F/VG. P2. $15.00

MILES, S.B. *Countries & Tribes of the Persian Gulf.* 1919. London. 2 vols. 4to. 9 pls. orig cloth. O2. $350.00

MILES, W. *General Remarks on Stables & Examples of Stable Fittings...* 1860. London. Longman Gr. 1st ed. sm 4to. pls. 82 p. scarce. O3. $495.00

MILES, William. *Horse's Foot & How To Keep It Sound.* 1956. NY. Saxon. later prt. O3. $45.00

MILES. *Many Hands Making a Communal Quilt.* 1983. np. wrp. G2. $7.00

MILES. *Quilts & Quotes: A Birthday Book.* nd. np. cloth. G2. $12.00

MILET, Jacques. *Toy Boats.* 1979. Cambridge. Stephens. 1st ed. VG/dj. A16. $65.00

MILHOUS, Kathrine. *Herodia the Lovely Puppet.* 1942. Scribner 8vo. 193 p. VG/dj. A3. $20.00

MILIBAND, Ralph. *Marxism & Politics.* 1977. NY. Oxford. 199 p. NF/NF. A7. $17.00

MILL, John Stuart. *Early Draft of John Stuart Mill's Autobiography.* 1961. Urbana, IL. 1st ed. 218 p. prt cream cloth. VG/dj. G1. $35.00

MILL, John Stuart. *Subjection of Women.* 1870. Appleton. 1st Am ed. NF. Q1. $750.00

MILLAIS, J.G. *Mammals of Great Britain & Ireland.* 1904. Longman Gr. 1st ed. 3 vols. thick folio. linen/buckram. F. R3. $750.00

MILLAIS, John Guille. *Rhododendrons.* 1917. London. Longman Gr. 1/550. lg folio. 17 color pls. teg. gr morocco/brds. H5. $450.00

MILLAR, Kenneth. *Collection of Reviews.* 1979. Lord John. 1/300. sgn. F/sans. B9. $90.00

MILLAR, Kenneth. *Instant Enemy.* 1968. Knopf. 1st ed. F/F. B2. $100.00

MILLAR, Kenneth. *Instant Enemy.* 1968. Knopf. 1st ed. Knopf lib file copy label. F/NF. M15. $85.00

MILLAR, Kenneth. *Self-Portrait: Ceaselessly Into the Past.* 1981. Capra. 1/250. sgn. intro/sgn Eudora Welty. F. B9. $75.00

MILLAR, Kenneth. *Sleeping Beauty.* 1973. Knopf. 1st ed. F/dj. B9. $30.00

MILLAR, Ronald. *Death of an Army: Siege of Kut, 1915-16.* 1970. Houghton Mifflin. 1st prt. 323 p. mustard cloth. NF/NF/clear plastic. M7. $45.00

MILLARD. *Quilter's Guide to Fabric Dyeing.* 1984. np. ils. sbdg. G2. $15.00

MILLAY, Edna St. Vincent. *Collected Poems.* 1956. Harper. 1st ed. NF/NF. C4. $30.00

MILLAY, Edna St. Vincent. *Collected Sonnets.* 1941. Harper. 1st ed. F/NF slipcase. C4. $30.00

MILLAY, Edna St. Vincent. *Conversation at Midnight.* 1937. Harper. 1st ed. 1/36. sgn/#d. vellum/gray brds. F/NF slipcase. Q1. $1,250.00

MILLAY, Edna St. Vincent. *Few Figs From Thistles: Poems & 4 Sonnets.* 1920. NY. Salvo/Frank Shay. detached/worn. E3. $60.00

MILLAY, Edna St. Vincent. *Make Bright the Arrows.* 1940. NY. 1st ed. F/NF. V1. $35.00

MILLER, Arthur. *Death of a Salesman.* 1981. NY. Viking. 1/500. sgn. F/slipcase. B24. $150.00

MILLER, Arthur. *Death of a Salesman.* 1984. LEC. 1/1500. sgn. ils/sgn Leonard Baskin. Gray Parrot bdg. F/slipcase. B20. $350.00

MILLER, Arthur. *Misfits.* 1961. Penguin. PBO. sgn. F/wrp. A11. $65.00

MILLER, Arthur. *Situation Normal.* 1944. Reynal Hitchcock. 1st ed. author's 1st book. yel cloth. VG. E3. $60.00

MILLER, Caroline. *Lamb in His Bosom.* 1933. NY. 1st ed. VG/VG. B5. $75.00

MILLER, Charles C. *Blk Borneo.* (1942). Modern Age. 1st ed. 8vo. 278 p. VG/VG. A2. $15.00

MILLER, Charles C. *Cosmetic Surgery: Correction of Featural Imperfections...* 1908. np. 2nd/enlarged ed. xl. 134 p. G7. $95.00

MILLER, Charles C. *50 Yrs Among the Bees.* ca 1915. Medina, OH. Root. ils/index. 327 p. H10. $22.50

MILLER, Diane Disney. *Story of Walt Disney.* 1959. Dell. photos. NF. C8. $50.00

MILLER, Dorothy. *Life & Work of David G Blythe.* 1950. Pittsburgh. cloth. dj. D2. $35.00

MILLER, F.W. *Cincinnati's Beginnings.* 1880. Cincinnati. 1st ed. 235 p. G. B5. $100.00

MILLER, Francis Trevelyan. *Portrait Life of Lincoln.* 1910. Patriot Pub. 1st ed. 8vo. ils. 164 p. brn cloth. H9. $45.00

MILLER, Francis Trevelyan. *World's Great Adventure...Achievements of Admiral...Byrd.* 1930. Phil. 1st ed. 8vo. 394 p. color map ep. silvered bl cloth. F. H3. $30.00

MILLER, Frank O. *Minobe Tatsukichi, Interpreter of Constitutionalism Japan.* 1965. Berkeley. M11. $50.00

MILLER, Helen Hill. *Capts From Devon: Great Elizabethan Seafarers...* 1985. Algonquin. ils. M/dj. O6. $30.00

MILLER, Helen Topping. *Christmas at Mt Vernon w/George & Martha WA.* 1957. Longman Gr. 1st ed. 58 p. VG/VG. B10. $20.00

MILLER, Henry. *Maurizius Forever.* (1959). Michigan City. Fridtjof-Karla. sgn. 62 p. wrp. A7. $100.00

MILLER, Henry. *Maurizius Forever.* 1946. Motive Pr. 1st trade ed. VG/wrp. M18. $45.00

MILLER, Henry. *Mother, China & the World Beyond.* 1977. Santa Barbara. 1st ed. sgn. last title Capra Chapbook series. F/wrp. A11. $60.00

MILLER, Henry. *Nightmare Notebook.* 1975. New Directions. 1/700. sgn/#d. NF/sans. B2. $175.00

MILLER, Henry. *Notes on Aaron's Rod.* 1980. Blk Sparrow. ltd ed. 1/276. sgn. F. M18. $125.00

MILLER, Henry. *Stand Still Like the Hummingbird.* 1962. New Directions. 1st ed. dj. N2. $15.00

MILLER, Henry. *Waters Reglitterized.* 1950. John Kidis. 1st ed. 1/1000. F. M18. $75.00

MILLER, Hugh Gordon. *Isthmian Highway.* 1929. NY. Macmillan. 1st ed. presentation. pls. 327 p. gilt bl brds. VG. B11. $75.00

MILLER, Hugh. *Echo of Justice.* 1990. London. Gollancz. ARC of 1st ed. RS. F/F. S5. $25.00

MILLER, J. Martin. *Cook & Peary's Discovery of the N Pole.* 1909. Phil. 8vo. pls. 428 p. gilt red cloth. G. H3. $15.00

MILLER, J. Martin. *Discovery of the N Pole.* 1909. WA, DC. royal 8vo. 428 p. gilt red cloth. G+. H3. $25.00

MILLER, J. Martin. *Martinique Horror & St Vincent Calamity.* 1902. Boston. 8vo. pls. 560 p. NF. H3. $25.00

MILLER, J. Martin. *20th-Century Altas of Commercial, Geog & Hist World...* 1904. np. Frank Brant. ils/color maps. VG. O6. $85.00

MILLER, James. *Democracy Is in the Streets.* (1987). Simon Schuster. 1st ed. photos. F/NF. A7. $13.00

MILLER, Joaquin. *Memorie & Rime.* 1884. NY. 1st ed. w/sgn card. VG/orig prt wrp. A11. $125.00

MILLER, Joaquin. *Songs of the Sierras.* 1871. Boston. 1st ed/bdg B. 299 p. B28. $50.00

MILLER, Joaquin. *Songs of the Sun-Lands.* 1873. Roberts Bros. 1st ed. teg. gilt bdg. F. A18. $50.00

MILLER, John Carl. *John Randolph of Roanoke: Study in Am Politics.* 1964. Regnery. 485 p. VG/VG. B10. $15.00

MILLER, Jonathan P. *Condition of Greece in 1827 & 1828...* 1828. NY. 8vo. new quarter calf/brds. O2. $550.00

MILLER, Leo E. *In the Wilds of S Am.* 1918. NY. 1st ed. 424 p. pict gr coth. F. H3. $40.00

MILLER, Leo. *Woman & the Divine Republic.* (1874). Buffalo. 1st ed. inscr. 213 p. scarce. A17. $35.00

MILLER, Lewis. *Sketches & Chronicles.* 1966. York, PA. 1st ed. intro D Shelley. 185 p. VG/box. B5. $75.00

MILLER, Lillian B. *In Pursuit of Fame. Rembrandt Peale...* 1992. Seattle. 32 color pls. 320 p. D2. $35.00

MILLER, Merle. *Gay & Melancholy Sound.* 1961. NY. 1st ed. inscr/dtd 1961. VG+/VG+. A11. $40.00

MILLER, Olive Beaupre. *Engines & Brass Bands.* 1933. Bookhouse/Doubleday. 376 p. pict ep. brn cloth. VG/G+. S10. $30.00

MILLER, Olive Beaupre. *Heroes, Outlaws & Funny Fellows of Am Popular Tales.* 1973. NY. Cooper Sq. 8vo. ils. VG. B11. $15.00

MILLER, Olive Beaupre. *Heroes of the Bible.* 1940. Chicago. Dickson. ils Mariel Wilhoite. G. L1. $20.00

MILLER, Olive Beaupre. *Heroes of the Bible.* 1941. Standard Book Co. 30 full-p color ils. VG. C1. $11.50

MILLER, Olive Beaupre. *My Book House.* (1925). Bookhouse. 10th ed. 6 vols. gr cloth/pict label. VG. S10. $95.00

MILLER, Olive Beaupre. *My Book House.* 1965. Lake Buff, IL. 12 vols. VG. B30. $125.00

MILLER, P. Schuyler. *Titan.* 1952. Fantasy. 1st ed. 2nd bdg. F/Bok dj. M2. $35.00

MILLER, Philip. *Figures of Most Beautiful, Useful & Uncommon Plants...* 1760. London. Rivington. 1st ed/1st issue. folio. 2 vols. VG. H5. $20,000.00

MILLER, Raymond C. *Force of Energy: Business Hist.* 1971. MI State U. 1st ed. index. 363 p. dj. A17. $15.00

MILLER, Raymond C. *Kilowatts At Work: Hist of Detroit Edison Co.* 1957. Wayne State. 1st ed. sgns. F/dj. A17. $22.50

MILLER, Richard. *Snail.* 1984. HRW. 1st ed. F/F. N3. $20.00

MILLER, Robert H. *Root Anatomy & Morphology: Guide to the Literature.* 1974. Hamden, CT. ils. 271 p. as new. B26. $27.50

MILLER, Ronald Dean. *Paul Bailey & the Westernlore Pr.* 1984. Sagebrush Pr. 1st ed. 102 p. F/F. B19. $50.00

MILLER, Ronald Dean. *Paul Bailey & W Lore Pr.* 1984. Sagebrush Pr. 8vo. F/F. A8. $50.00

MILLER, Sue. *Good Mother.* (1986). London. Gollancz. 1st ed. VG/VG. B3. $15.00

MILLER, Vassar. *Selected & New Poems.* 1981. np. 1st ed. F/NF. V1. $10.00

MILLER, Walter M. *Beyond Armageddon.* 1985. Donald Fine. AP of 1st ed. F/tradesize wrp/dj. F4. $40.00

MILLER, Walter M. Jr. *Canticle for Leibowitz.* 1960. Lippincott. 1st ed. F/VG. B4. $400.00

MILLER, Warren H. *Wht Buffalo.* 1926. Appleton. 1st ed. VG/dj. B9. $45.00

MILLER, Wilhelm. *What Eng Can Teach Us About Gardening.* 1917 (1911). Garden City. ils/photos/pls. 358 p. VG-. B26. $47.50

MILLER, William Lee. *First Liberty, Religion & Am Republic.* 1986. Knopf. M11. $25.00

MILLER, William. *Travel & Politics in the Near E.* 1898. London. thick 8vo. 515 p. gilt cloth. O2. $75.00

MILLER & MILLER. *Lost Heritage of AK.* (1967). Cleveland. 1st ed. 289 p. F/dj. B18. $22.50

MILLER & PELHAM. *Facts of Life.* 1984. mechanical views of conception to birth. F. A4. $50.00

MILLER & SHAPIRO. *Physician to the W. Selected Writings of Daniel Drake...* 1970. Lexington, KY. 1st ed. 418 p. VG/dj. D7. $50.00

MILLER & UNDERWOOD. *Bare Bones: Conversations on Terror w/Stephen King.* 1988. McGraw Hill. 1st ed. M/M. T2. $28.00

MILLER. *Blockbuster Quilts.* 1991. np. ils. wrp. G2. $25.00

MILLER. *Textile Designs.* 1991. np. ils. cloth. G2. $65.00

MILLETT. *Quilt As You Go.* 1982. np. ils. wrp. G2. $15.95

MILLIKAN, R.A. *Evolution in Science & Religion.* 1927. New Haven. Yale. 95 p. bl cloth. VG. S9. $15.00

MILLIKEN, W.M. *Henry G Keller Memorial Exhibition.* 1950. Cleveland Mus Art. 56 p. D2. $30.00

MILLIS, Walter. *Martial Spirit: Study of Our War w/Spain.* 1931. Houghton Mifflin. 1st ed. 8vo. 427 p. blk brds. VG/VG. B11. $40.00

MILLS, Enos A. *Adventures of a Nature Guide.* 1920. Garden City. 1st ed. ils. 217 p. cloth. A17. $25.00

MILLS, Enos A. *Bird Memories of the Rockies.* 1931. Boston. 1st ed. F. scarce. T8. $20.00

MILLS, Hugh L. *Low Level Hell.* (1992). Presidio. 1st ed. F/F. A7. $15.00

MILLS, James. *7th Power.* (1976). Dutton. 1st ed. 236 p. dj. A7. $15.00

MILLS, Jeannie. *Six Yrs w/God.* 1979. A&W Pub. 1st ed. F/F. T2. $10.50

MILLS, Robert. *Atlas of the State of SC.* 1826. Baltimore. John D Toy. 1st ed. lg thin folio. 29 maps. rstr bdg/cloth box. H9. $12,500.00

MILLS, Robert. *Atlas of the State of SC.* 1938. Columbia, SC. Bostick Thornley. facsimile of 1825 ed. 1/350. NF. O6. $775.00

MILLS, Susan L. *Genealogy of Mills Family.* 1896. np. private prt. 12mo. 36 p. leather. G. D7. $45.00

MILLS. *849 Traditional Patchwork Patterns: Pict Handbook.* 1989. np. ils. wrp. G2. $7.00

MILMAN, Helen. *Little Ladies.* 1892. Lippincott. probable 1st ed. 192 p. G+. S10. $30.00

MILNE, A.A. *Christopher Robin's Old Sailor.* 1947. Dutton. ils EH Shepard. unp. VG/dj. M20. $50.00

MILNE, A.A. *House at Pooh Corner.* 1928. Dutton. 51st prt (2 months after 1st). VG. M5. $30.00

MILNE, A.A. *House at Pooh Corner.* 1928. London. Methuen. 1st Eng ed. ils Shepard. teg. pk cloth. VG/dj. D1. $475.00

MILNE, A.A. *Hums of Pooh.* 1939. Dutton. ils Shepard. 67 p. VG/dj. D1. $50.00

MILNE, A.A. *Not That It Matters.* 1920. Dutton. VG/dj. A16. $50.00

MILNE, A.A. *Now We Are 6.* 1927. London. Shepard. 1st ed. 1/200 on handmade. sgn. VG/dj/slipcase/chemise. H5. $3,500.00

MILNE, A.A. *Princess & the Apple Tree.* 1937. Grosset Dunlap. 1st thus ed. ils Sewell. 40 p. VG/dj. D1. $65.00

MILNE, A.A. *Success.* 1923. London. 1st ed. G+. A1. $35.00

MILNE, A.A. *Toad of Toad Hall.* 1929. London Methuen. 1st ed. 8vo. gilt bl cloth. NF/NF. F1. $175.00

MILNE, A.A. *When We Were Very Young.* 1924. Dutton. 52nd prt (Nov 1925). ils Ernest Shepard. red cloth. VG. M5. $25.00

MILNE, A.A. *When We Were Very Young.* 1924. London. Shepard. 1st ed. 1/100. sgn. Sutcliffe bdg. F/morocco clamshell case. H5. $5,000.00

MILNE, A.A. *Winnie the Pooh.* 1926. Dutton. 1st Am ed. ils Shepard. gr brds. VG. E3. $50.00

MILNE, A.A. *Winnie the Pooh.* 1926. Dutton. 39th prt. ils Ernest Shepard. gilt dk gr cloth. G. M5. $20.00

MILNE, A.A. *Winnie the Pooh.* 1926. London. ltd ed. 1/20. sgn. orig vellum/brds. F/quarter morocco clamshell case. H5. $15,000.00

MILNE, A.A. *Winnie the Pooh.* 1926. London. Methuen. 1st ed. aeg. gilt full bl leather/ribbon marker. F. Q1. $1,250.00

MILNE, A.A. *Winnie the Pooh.* 1926. Toronto. 1st Canadian ed. ils Shepard. 158 p. gr pict cloth. G. H3. $75.00

MILNE, A.A. *World of Pooh.* 1957. Dutton. 1st this ed. ils EH Shepard. VG/G. L1. $30.00

MILNE, Christopher. *Enchanted Places.* 1975. Dutton. 1st ed. ils. 169 p. VG+/VG+. S10. $25.00

MILOSZ, Czeslaw. *Captive Mind.* (1983). LEC. 1/1500. sgn. ils/sgn Janusz Kapusta. gray linen. F/slipcase. B20. $110.00

MILOSZ, Czeslaw. *Land of Ulro.* (1984). FSG. 1st ed. trans Iribarne. F/F. B3. $45.00

MILTON, John. *Paradise Regain'd.* 1905. Hammersmith. 1/300. w/clip sig of Cobden-Sanderson. NF. H5. $600.00

MILTON, John. *Poems in Eng.* 1926. Nonesuch. 1/1540. 2 vols in 1. 359 p. F/gray cloth slipcase. H5. $1,000.00

MILWARD, Marguerite. *Artist in Unknown India.* (1948). London. T Werner Laurie. 1st ed. 8vo. 274 p. VG/VG. A2. $20.00

MILWARD-OLIVER, Edward. *Len Deighton Companion.* 1987. London. Grafton. 1st ed. F/F. S5. $30.00

MINER, Dorothy. *Hist of Bookbinding 525-1950 AD.* 1957. Baltimore. Walters Art Gallery. exhibition catalog. F. F1. $150.00

MINKIN, Jacob S. *Ararbanel & the Expulsion of Jews From Spain.* 1938. NY. Behrman. 237 p. VG. S3. $29.00

MINNS, J.E. *Model Railway Engines.* 1973. London. Octopus. VG/dj. A16. $15.00

MINOT, Susan. *Lust.* 1989. Houghton Mifflin. 1st ed. sgn. author's 2nd book. F/F. L3. $85.00

MINOT, Susan. *Monkeys.* 1986. NY. 1st ed. author's 1st book. NF/dj. A15. $30.00

MINTER, John Easter. *Chagres: River of Westward Passage. Rivers of Am.* 1948. NY. Rinehart. xl. 8vo. pls/maps. 418 p. G/G. B11. $20.00

MINTZ, Lawrence E. *Humor in Am: Research Guide to Genres & Topics.* 1988. Greenwood. 1st ed. 241 p. orange cloth. VG. G1. $35.00

MIRANDA, Jose. *Funcion Economica del Encomendero en los Origens...* (1965). Mexico. UNAM. 2nd ed. wrp. F3. $15.00

MIRBEAU, Ken; see Weiss, Joe.

MIRSKY, Jeannette. *Elisha Kent Kane & the Seafaring Frontier.* 1954. Little Brn. 1st ed. inscr. 201 p. bl cloth. VG+/VG+. P4. $45.00

MIRSKY, Jeannette. *Elisha Kent Kane & the Seafaring Frontier.* 1954. Little Brn. 1st ed. 8vo. 201 p. VG+/VG. A2. $15.00

MIRSKY, Jeannette. *W Crossings: Balboa, Mackenzie, Lewis & Clark.* 1946. Knopf. 1st ed. 8vo. 365 p. F/dj. T8. $40.00

MISHIMA, Yukio. *Madame de Sade.* 1967. Grove. 1st ed. NF/F. B2. $50.00

MISHIMA, Yukio. *Sound of Waves.* 1956. NY. Knopf. 1st ed. F/NF. B2. $50.00

MISHIMA, Yukio. *Young Samurai.* (1967). Grove. 1st Am ed. photos Tamotsu Yato. F/NF. B4. $150.00

MISNER, Paul. *Papacy & Developement.* 1976. Leiden. Brill. 204 p. H10. $37.50

MISTER T. *Mr T: The Man w/the Gold; An Autobiography.* (1984). St Martin. 1st ed. 276 p. F/NF. A7. $15.00

MITCHEL, Reid. *Civil War Soldiers.* 1988. np. 274 p. F/dj. O7. $9.50

MITCHELL, Carleton. *Islands to Windward.* 1948. NY. 1st ed. 287 p. gilt gr cloth. VG. H3. $35.00

MITCHELL, Donald G. *English Lands, Letters & Kings...* 1890. Scribner. 1st ed. 347 p. cloth. VG. B22. $12.50

MITCHELL, Edwin V. *Great Fishing Stories.* 1946. NY. 1st ed. 285 p. worn dj. A17. $10.00

MITCHELL, Gladys. *Rising of the Moon.* 1945. London. Michael Joseph. 1st ed. VG/clip. M15. $45.00

MITCHELL, Gladys. *Rising of the Moon.* 1984. NY. St Martin. 1st Am ed. F/F. S5. $25.00

MITCHELL, J.A. *Last American.* 1902. Stokes. 1st ed. VG. M2. $35.00

MITCHELL, Joseph. *Apologies to the Iroquois.* 1960. London. Allen. 1st ed. F/NF. C4. $40.00

MITCHELL, Joseph. *Bottom of the Harbor.* 1959. Little Brn. 1st ed. F/NF. C4. $85.00

MITCHELL, Joseph. *Old Mr Flood.* 1948. DSP. 1st ed. NF/NF. C4. $60.00

MITCHELL, Margaret. *Gone w/the Wind.* May 1936. Macmillan. 1st ed/1st issue. VG/VG/custom leather fld chemise. L3. $2,750.00

MITCHELL, Margaret. *Margaret Mitchell's Gone w/the Wind Letters, 1936-49.* ca 1976. Macmillan. 1st prt. 441 p. VG/VG. B10. $35.00

MITCHELL, Roger. *Death Valley Jeep Trails.* 1969. La Siesta Pr. 12mo. F. A8. $5.00

MITCHELL, Roger. *Exploring Joshua Tree.* 1964. La Siesta pr. 12mo. VG. A8. $5.00

MITCHELL, S. Weir. *Autobiography of Quack & Other Stories.* 1905. NY. Century. 8vo. 311 p. VG. V3. $15.00

MITCHELL, S. Weir. *Comfort of the Hills & Other Poems.* 1911. NY. Century. inscr/sgn twice. 98 p. orig cloth. G7. $495.00

MITCHELL, S. Weir. *Early Hist of Instrumental Precision in Medicine.* 1971 (1891). NY. reprint. 42 p. G7. $25.00

MITCHELL, S. Weir. *Mr Kris Kringle.* 1893. Phil. George Jacobs. 1st ed. octavo. 48 p. NF. H5. $250.00

MITCHELL, Sydney. *Adventures in Flower Gardening.* 1928. Chicago. ils. VG. B26. $27.50

MITCHELL. *Mitchell's Ancient Atlas.* 1844. np. quarto. 8 full-p hand color maps. VG. E5. $85.00

MITFORD, Jessica. *Am Way of Death.* 1963. Simon Schuster. 1st ed. NF/clip. A7. $20.00

MITSUHASHI, Yoko. *King's Choice. Folktale From India.* 1961. Parents Magazine. sm 4to. 37 p. VG. A3. $7.50

MIVART, Saint George. *Cat. Intro to Study of Backboned Animals...* 1881. London. Murray. 1st ed. octavo. 200+ ils. 557 p. VG. H5. $300.00

MO, Timothy. *Monkey King.* 1978. London. Deutsch. 1st ed. author's 1st book. F/dj. very scarce. L3. $350.00

MOATS. *Off to Mexico: A Guidebook.* 1935. Scribner. 1st ed. 8vo. 186 p. F/VG+. A2. $20.00

MOCKINGBIRD, Jon. *Wakosani Road.* 1963. NY. Exposition. 1st ed. NF/dj. presumed very scarce. L3. $85.00

MODDIE, Susanne. *Roughing It in the Bush.* (1986). Boston. new ed. 518 p. M/wrp. A17. $8.50

MOERBEEK. *Little Red Riding Hood: A Pop-Up Book w/Action Characters.* 1990. paper engineering by Kees Moerbeek. F. A4. $30.00

MOFFAT, Frances. *Dancing on the Brink of the World.* 1977. Putnam. 1st ed. ils/index. 285 p. VG. B19. $12.50

MOFFAT, Gwen. *Miss Pink at the Edge of the World.* 1975. Scribner. 1st ed. F/F. T2. $8.00

MOFFAT, Gwen. *Raptor Zone.* 1990. Macmillan. 1st ed. sgn. F/F. S5. $40.00

MOFFETT, Judith. *Ragged World: Novel of the Hefn on Earth.* 1991. St Martin. 1st ed. F/F. N3. $15.00

MOFFIT & WAYLAND. *Geology of the Nutzotin Mtns, AK & Gold Deposits...* 1943. WA. 4 fld pocket maps. worn wrp. A17. $15.00

MOJTABAI, A.G. *Mundome.* 1974. NY. 1st ed. sgn. F/VG+. A11. $55.00

MOLESWORTH, Mrs. *Little Miss Peggy: Only a Nursery Story.* no date. AL Burt. ils Walter Crane. 8vo. bl cloth. G+. A3. $12.50

MOLESWORTH, Mrs. *Rectory Children.* 1889. London. Macmillan. ils Walter Crane. 212 p. VG. S10. $75.00

MOLEY, Raymond Jr. *Am Legion Story.* (1966). DSP. 1st ed. 8vo. 443 p. F/VG+. A2. $12.50

MOLIERE. *Plays.* 1924. Boni Liveright. orig gr brds. E3. $6.00

MOLLEMA, J.C. *Nederlandsche Vlag op de Wereldzeeen met David Pietersz...* ca 1920. Amsterdam. Scheltens Giltay. 1st ed. 4to. 66 pls. 319 p. VG. W1. $65.00

MOLYNEUX, Peter. *Romantic Story of TX.* 1936. NY/Dallas. 1st ed. 463 p. cloth. VG. D3. $25.00

MOMADAY, N. Scott. *Before an Old Painting of the Crucifixion.* 1975. San Francisco. private prt. ils/inscr Valenti Angelo. F/wrp. uncommon. L3. $250.00

MOMADAY, N. Scott. *CO.* 1973. Rand McNally. 1st ed. folio. NF/dj. L3. $125.00

MOMADAY, N. Scott. *House Made of Dawn.* 1968. NY. 1st ed. F/F. L3. $200.00

MOMADAY, N. Scott. *House Made of Dawn.* 1977. Franklin Lib. ltd ed. gilt red leather. F. L3. $75.00

MOMADAY, N. Scott. *In the Presence of the Sun.* (1992). St Martin. 1st ed. sgn. F/F. B3. $45.00

MOMADAY, N. Scott. *In the Presence of the Sun.* (1992). St Martin. 1st UP. sc. ils Momaday. F. A18. $40.00

MOMADAY, N. Scott. *Journey of Tai-Me.* 1967. Santa Barbara. 1st ed. 1/100. author's 1st book. w/sgn prt. F/box. L3. $2,250.00

MOMADAY, N. Scott. *Way to Rainy Mtn.* 1969. NM U. 1st ed. ils Al Momaday. F/F. L3. $150.00

MOMADAY, N.S. *Owl in the Cedar Tree.* 1965. Ginn. 1st ed. VG. L3. $125.00

MONACHAN, John; see Burnett, W.R.

MONAGHAN, Jay. *Book of the Am W.* (1963). NY. 1st ed. 608 p. G. A17. $35.00

MONAGHAN, Jay. *Chile, Peru, & the CA Gold Rush of 1849.* 1973. CA U. 1st ed. ils/notes/index. 312 p. F/NF clip. B19. $14.50

MONAGHAN, Jay. *Great Rascal: Life & Adventures of Ned Buntline.* 1952. Bonanza. notes/index. 353 p. F/NF clip. B19. $20.00

MONCRIEFF, A.R.H. *Highlands & Islands of Scotland.* 1907. London. Blk. 40 color pls. 232 p. teg. gilt purple cloth. VG. H3. $25.00

MONETTE, Clarence J. *Hist of Copper Harbor.* 1976. Lake Linden. 85 p. wrp. A17. $7.00

MONETTE, Paul. *Carpenter at the Asylum.* 1975. Boston. 1st ed. sgn. F/F. A11. $45.00

MONEY, John. *Destroying Angel.* (1985). Prometheus. 1st ed. 8vo. 213 p. F/VG. A2. $15.00

MONMARCHE, Marcel. *Belgique et Luxembourg.* 1930. Paris. 16mo. 443 p. gilt bl cloth. NF. H3. $15.00

MONMARCHE, Marcel. *Hollande.* 1933. Paris. 375 p. gilt bl cloth. VG. H3. $15.00

MONOGHAN, Frank. *French Travellers in the US, 1765-1932.* 1961. Antiquarian Pr. 1st ed. 130 p. NF. B19. $35.00

MONRO, Donald. *Praelectiones Medicae Ex Cronii Instituto, Annis 1774...* 1776. London. Gul Hay. 1st ed. ES/ad leaf. rebound morocco. G7. $795.00

MONRO, Harold. *Strange Meetings.* 1917. London. Poetry Bookshop. 1st ed. NF/wrp. B2. $50.00

MONROE, Elizabeth Brand. *Wheeling Bridge Case.* 1992. Boston. NE U. M11. $40.00

MONROE, Elizabeth. *Philby of Arabia.* 1973. London. Faber. 1st ed. photos/maps. 332 p. gilt brn cloth. M7. $55.50

MONROE, Harriet. *Passing Show.* 1903. Houghton Mifflin. 1st ed. inscr/dtd 1917. NF/dj. C4. $45.00

MONROE, Harriet. *Poet's Life.* 1938. NY. 1st ed. VG+. V1. $15.00

MONROE, Harriet. *Valeria & Other Poems.* 1891. Chicago. private prt. 1/300. sgn. special silk brds/vellum spine. B2. $200.00

MONROE, James. *Message From President of US...Future Prospects of Greeks.* 1824. Gales Seaton. 8vo. 25 p. disbound as issued. O2. $250.00

MONROE, Malcolm. *Means Is the End in Vietnam.* 1968. Murlagan Pr. 124 p. VG/wrp. A7. $40.00

MONSON. *What Now, Mom?* 1984. np. pb. G2. $6.00

MONTAGNANE, Bartholomaeus. *Consilia Montagnane.* 1525. Lyons. dtd 1539. French calf over wood brds. G7. $3,500.00

MONTAGUE, Edward P. *Narrative of Late Expedition to the Dead Sea.* 1849. Phil. 8vo. 336 p. cloth. O2. $55.00

MONTAGUE, Lord. *Early Days on the Road. Ils Hist 1819-1941.* 1976. Universe. VG/dj. A16. $17.50

MONTAGUE, Sydney R. *N Adventure.* (1939). NY. 1st ed. 284 p. cloth. G. A17. $15.00

MONTAGUE-SMITH. *Royal Family Pop-Up Book.* 1984. 6 movable scenes. F. A4. $50.00

MONTALE, Eugenio. *It Depends: A Poet's Notebook.* 1975. New Directions. 1st ed. F/F. V1. $15.00

MONTALE, Eugenio. *Mottetti. Motets of Eugenio Montale in Italian...* (1973). Grabhorn-Hoyem. 1/300. sgn Montale/Kart. tall 8vo. 62 p. yel silk. K1. $200.00

MONTEIRO, Palmyra V.M. *Catalogue of Latin Am Flat Maps, 1926-64.* 1969. Austin. Inst Latin Am Studies. 2 vols. M/rpr djs. O6. $85.00

MONTER, E. William. *Witchcraft in France & Switzerland.* 1976. Ithaca, NY. Cornell. 232 p. VG/dj. G1. $30.00

MONTESSORI, Maria. *Pedagogical Anthropology.* 1913. Stokes. 1st Am ed. 508 p. cloth. B14. $65.00

MONTGAILLARD, Jean Gabriel M. *Situation in Eng in 1811.* 1812. NY. 1st ed. trans John Finch. 8vo. VG-. H3. $100.00

MONTGOMERY, Ione. *Death Won the Prize.* 1941. Doubleday Crime Club. 1st ed. VG/rpr. M15. $35.00

MONTGOMERY, L.M. *Golden Road.* 1913. Grosset Dunlap. G/dj. A16. $25.00

MONTGOMERY, L.M. *Rilla of Ingleside.* 1921. AL Burt. ils Maria Kirk. gilt maroon cloth. VG. M5. $25.00

MONTGOMERY, L.M. *Story Girl.* 1911. Page. 2nd prt (1 month after 1st). gilt taupe cloth. VG. M5. $60.00

MONTGOMERY, Michael. *All Out for Everest.* (1975). London. Elek. 1st ed. 8vo. 198 p. F/F. A2. $12.50

MONTGOMERY. *Textiles in Am, 1650-1870.* 1984. np. ils. cloth. G2. $45.00

MONTI, Franco. *Pre-Columbian Terra Cottas.* 1969. London. Hamlyn. 1st ed. 71 color pls. 158 p. F3. $15.00

MONTRESOR, Beni. *I Saw a Ship a-Sailing.* 1967. Knopf. VG/VG. P2. $15.00

MOODY, Anne. *Mr Death.* 1975. NY. 1st ed. inscr. F/NF clip. A11. $45.00

MOODY, John. *John Henry Newman.* 1945. NY. Sheed Ward. 353 p. H10. $15.00

MOODY, Susan. *Penny Dreadful.* 1984. London. Macmillan. 1st ed. F/F. S5. $35.00

MOODY, Susan. *Takeout Double.* 1993. London. Headline. ARC of 1st ed. RS. F/F. S5. $30.00

MOODY, William Vaughn. *Masque of Judgment.* 1900. Sm Maynard. 1st ed. 12mo. 127 p. tan brds/paper label. M1. $150.00

MOOG, Vianna. *Bandeirantes e Pioneiros.* (1964). Rio de Janero. Portuguese text. 345 p. wrp. F3. $15.00

MOON, Grace. *Ghi-Wee: Adventues of a Little Indian Girl.* 1925. Doubleday Page. ils Carl Moon. 239 p. VG+. P2. $18.00

MOON, James H. *Why Friends (Quakers) Do Not Baptize w/Water.* 1909. Fallsington, PA. 16mo. 70 p. G+. V3. $14.00

MOONEY, Michael M. *Hindenburg.* 1972. Dodd Mead. BC. VG/dj. A16. $7.50

MOORCOCK, Michael. *Behold the Man.* 1969. London. 1st ed. w/inscr label. F/F. A11. $60.00

MOORCOCK, Michael. *City in the Autumn Stars.* 1987. NY. Ace. 1st Am ed. F/F. N3. $15.00

MOORCOCK, Michael. *End of All Songs.* (1976). Harper Row. 1st ed. VG/VG. A7. $15.00

MOORCOCK, Michael. *Entropy Tango.* 1981. NEL. 1st ed. sgn. F/dj. M18. $30.00

MOORCOCK, Michael. *Wizardry & Wild Romance.* 1987. Gollancz. 1st ed. sgn. F/F. F4. $35.00

MOORE, Barrington Jr. *Political Power & Social Theory.* 1958. Cambridge. Harvard. 215 p. dj. A7. $15.00

MOORE, Brian. *Blk Robe.* (1985). London. Cape. 1st ed. F/F. B3. $100.00

MOORE, Brian. *Catholics.* 1972. HRW. 1st ed. presentation. F/F. C4. $50.00

MOORE, Brian. *Emperor of Icecream.* 1965. NY. 1st ed. sgn. F/F. A11. $135.00

MOORE, Brian. *Fergus.* 1970. HRW. 1st ed (preceeds UK ed). 228 p. VG/dj. M20. $22.50

MOORE, Brian. *Great Victorian Collection.* 1974. NY. 1st ed. sgn. F/F. A11. $125.00

MOORE, Brian. *Lonely Passion of Judith Hearne.* 1957. NY. Dell. PBO. sgn. F/wrp. A11. $65.00

MOORE, Brian. *No Other Life.* 1993. NY. Talese/Doubleday. AP. F. C4. $35.00

MOORE, C.L. *Doomsday Morning.* 1957. SF BC. VG/worn. M2. $6.00

MOORE, C.L. *Judgment Night.* 1951. Gnome. 1st ed. VG/dj. M2. $75.00

MOORE, C.L. *NW of Earth.* 1954. Gnome. 1st ed. NF/dj. M2. $100.00

MOORE, C.L. *Shambleau & Others.* 1953. Gnome. 1st ed. F/NF. F4. $175.00

MOORE, C.L. *Shambleau & Others.* 1953. Gnome. 1st ed. NF/dj. M2. $100.00

MOORE, Christopher. *Coyote Bl.* (1994). Simon Schuster. ARC. F/wrp. B3. $40.00

MOORE, Clement C. *Compendious Lexicon of Hebrew Language.* 1809. NY. Collins Perkins. 1st ed. 2 vols. 12mo. contemporary cloth. M1. $1,250.00

MOORE, Clement C. *Night Before Christmas.* 1944. Crown. ils Meg Wohlberg/3 movable ils/1 popup. VG. D1. $42.00

MOORE, Clement C. *Night Before Christmas.* 1944. NY. Crown. lg octavo. 5 movable ils/1 popup. pict brds. NF. B24. $125.00

MOORE, Clement C. *Night Before Christmas.* 1962. Worcester. St Onge. miniature. ils Tasha Tudor. red calf. F/dj. H10. $57.50

MOORE, Clement C. *Night Before Christmas.* 1975. Rand McNally. 1st prt. ils Tasha Tudor. VG. S10. $30.00

MOORE, Clement C. *Twas the Night Before Christmas.* (1912). Houghton Mifflin. ils JW Smith. worn bdg. tattered dj. D1. $235.00

MOORE, Clement C. *Visit From Santa Claus.* 1887 (1886). Wht Stokes Allen. ils Virginia Gerson. G. P2. $75.00

MOORE, Colleen. *Silent Star.* 1968. Doubleday. 1st ed. 262 p. VG/dj. M20. $9.00

MOORE, Edward. *Fables for the Female Sex.* 1744. London. R Francklin. 1st ed. octavo. 173 p. contemporary mottled calf. H5. $425.00

MOORE, F. Frankfort. *Garden of Peace.* 1920. NY. 1st ed. 300 p. VG. B28. $17.50

MOORE, F.C.T. *Psychology of Maine De Biran.* 1970. Clarendon. 1st ed. 228 p. bl cloth. VG/clip. G1. $30.00

MOORE, Frank. *Women of the War.* 1867. Hartford. xl. 8vo. 596 p. gr cloth. VG. T3. $59.00

MOORE, George. *Aphrodite in Aulis.* 1930. Heinemann. 1st ed. 1/1825. sgn. E3. $30.00

MOORE, George. *Brook Kerith: A Syrian Story.* 1929. Macmillan. revised ed. 1/500. ils Stephen Gooden. VG+. E3. $30.00

MOORE, George. *Coming of Gabrielle.* 1920. London. 1/1000. sgn. G+. A1. $30.00

MOORE, George. *Heloise & Abelard.* 1921. NY. 1/1250. 2 vols. G+. A1. $50.00

MOORE, George. *Making of an Immortal.* 1927. NY. 1/1240. sgn. G+. A1. $30.00

MOORE, George. *Modern Painting.* 1893. London. G. A1. $20.00

MOORE, George. *Storyteller's House.* 1918. London. 1/1000. sgn. G+. A1. $30.00

MOORE, H.N. *Life & Services of General Anthony Wayne...* 1845. Phil. 1st ed. 8 pls. VG+. B28. $45.00

MOORE, J.M. *S To-Day.* 1916. NY. 12mo. ils. 251 p. brn cloth. G. T3. $19.00

MOORE, John Bassett. *Hist & Digest of Internat Arbitrations To Which US...* 1898. GPO. 6 (lacks #3) vols. thick 8vo. legal calf. H9. $275.00

MOORE, Joseph Jr. *Outlying Europe & the Nearer Orient.* 1880. Phil. presentation. 554 p. gilt cloth. O2. $60.00

MOORE, Lilian. *My Big Golden Counting Book.* 1957. Golden Pr. H ed. VG. M5. $10.00

MOORE, Marianne. *Complete Poems.* 1981. NY. 1st ed. F/NF. V1. $15.00

MOORE, Marianne. *Fables of La Fontaine.* 1954. Viking. 1/400. sgn. special bdg. F/glassine dj/cardborad slipcase. B2. $350.00

MOORE, Norman. *Harveian Oration.* 1901. London. 59 p. G7. $20.00

MOORE, Robin. *Country Team.* (1967). Crown. 1st ed. F/dj. A7. $35.00

MOORE, Robin. *Gr Berets.* (1965). Crown. 3rd prt. worn/torn dj. A7. $25.00

MOORE, Samuel J.T. *Moore's Complete Civil War Guide to Richmond.* ca 1978. self pub. revised ed. 196 p. VG. B10. $10.00

MOORE, Susanna. *My Old Sweetheart.* 1982. Houghton Mifflin. 1st ed. author's 1st novel. F/F. C4. $35.00

MOORE, Susanna. *Whiteness of Bones.* (1989). London. Chatto Windus. 1st ed. F/F. B3. $20.00

MOORE, Thomas. *Bodie: Ghost Town 1968.* (1969). S Brunswick, NJ. AS Barnes. 1st ed. 4to. 95 p. F/F. A2. $12.50

MOORE, Thomas. *Memoirs of the Life of Rt Hon Richard Brinsley Sheridan.* 1866. NY. Widdleton. 2 vols. w/sgn Sheridan letter. K1. $650.00

MOORE, Thomas. *Works of...* 1557. London. 1st collected ed. sm folio. 2 vols. polished calf. H5. $7,500.00

MOORE, William. *Bayonets in the Sun.* 1978. St Martin. 1st Am/1st hc ed. F/F. F4. $20.00

MOORE & WALLACE. *Letters From & to the Ford Motor Co.* 1958. Morgan Lib. 1st ed. 1/1550. ils Baskin. F/glassine. B24. $200.00

MOORE. *Night Before Christmas: Giant Pop-Up.* 1989. 6 pop-ups. F. A4. $30.00

MORAES, Frank. *Report on Mao's China.* 1953. Macmillan. 1st prt. 8vo. 212 p. VG. W1. $16.00

MORANTE, Elsa. *Aracoeli.* 1984. Random. 1st Am ed. trans from Italian. rem mk. NF/NF. A14. $20.00

MORAVIA, Alberto. *Empty Canvas.* 1961. FSC. 2nd Eng prt. trans from Italian. VG+/VG+. A14. $20.00

MORAVIA, Alberto. *Two of Us.* 1972. London. Secker Warburg. 1st ed. trans from Italian. NF/NF. A14. $30.00

MORAVIA, Alberto. *Which Tribe Do You Belong To?* 1974. FSG. 1st Am ed. trans from Italian. NF/VG+. A14. $20.00

MORDDEN, Ethan. *Demented: World of the Opera Diva.* 1984. NY. Watts. 1st ed. 8vo. 310 p. F/F. A2. $12.50

MORDDEN, Ethan. *Everybody Loves You.* 1988. St Martin. 1st ed. NF/NF clip. A14. $25.00

MOREAU, Daniel. *Death Without Honor.* (1987). Pocket. PBO. 1st ed. NF. A7. $15.00

MORELEY, John. *Rousseau.* 1873. London. Chapman hall. 2 vols. brn cloth. G1. $40.00

MOREY, Walt. *Gentle Ben.* (1965). Dutton. 1st ed. F/NF. B4. $75.00

MORGAN, A.P. *Boys' Home Book of Science & Construction.* 1921. Lee Shepard. 458 p. gray cloth. VG. C10. $37.50

MORGAN, A.T. *Yazoo; or, On the Picket Line of Freedom in the S.* 1884. WA, DC. self pub. 1st ed. 8vo. 521 p. cloth. M1. $150.00

MORGAN, Al. *Essential Man.* 1977. Playboy. 1st ed. F/dj. P3. $15.00

MORGAN, Appleton. *People & the Railways.* 1888. NY. Bedford Clarke. 1st ed. 12mo. 245 p. teg. bl cloth. G. B11. $25.00

MORGAN, Barry. *Pursuit.* 1967. London. Heinemann. 1st ed. F/F. C4. $45.00

MORGAN, Dale. *Overland in·1846: Diaries & Letters of CA-OR Trail.* (1993). NE U. 1st thus ed. 2 vols. M. A18. $30.00

MORGAN, Dan. *Concrete Horizon.* 1976. Millington. F/dj. P3. $15.00

MORGAN, James Morris. *Recollections of a Rebel Reefer.* 1917. Houghton Mifflin. 1st ed. 491 p. decor cloth. VG. M8. $150.00

MORGAN, John Medford; see Fox, Gardner F.

MORGAN, Murray. *Columbia.* (1949). Seattle. Superior. index. 395 p. tattered dj. A17. $15.00

MORGAN, Murray. *Dixie Raider: Saga of the CSS Shenandoah.* 1948. EP Dutton. 1st ed. 336 p. cloth. VG. M8. $35.00

MORGAN, Murray. *Puget's Sound: Narrative of Early Tacoma & S Sound.* 1979. WA U. 1st ed. ils/index. 360 p. F. B19. $15.00

MORGAN, Neil. *Westward Tilt.* 1963. Random. 8vo. VG/fair. A8. $15.00

MORGAN, Rod; see Fox, Gardner F.

MORGAN, Seth. *Homeboy.* 1990. Random. 1st ed. author's 1st book. NF/NF. A14. $50.00

MORGAN, Seth. *Homeboy.* 1990. Random. 1st ed. F/F. B2. $50.00

MORGAN, Thomas. *My Story of the Last Indian War in the NW...* (1954). Forest Grove, OR. sgn. 29 p. wrp. H7. $40.00

MORGAN, William Gerry. *Am College of Physicians: Its 1st Quarter Century.* 1940. Phil. Am College of Physicians. N2. $20.00

MORGAN, William Henry. *Personal Reminiscences of War of 1861-65.* 1911. Lynchburg, VA. JP Bell. 1st ed. 286 p. cloth. NF. M8. $165.00

MORGAN, William. *Bureau Indian Affairs.* 1954. Bureau Indian Affairs. 1st ed. 53 p. wrp. A17. $15.00

MORGAN, William. *Ils of Masonry by One of the Fraternity...* 1827. Rochester. 1st or 2nd Rochester ed. 12mo. 96 p. prt wrp. VG. M1. $650.00

MORGAN & RICHARDS. *Paradise Out of a Common Field...Victorian Garden.* 1990. Harper Row. ils/index. 256 p. M. H10. $22.50

MORGAN & YEAGER. *Little Nancy; or, Punishment for Greediness.* ca 1824. Phil. 12mo. 8 p. F/wrp. B24. $350.00

MORGAN. *How To Dress an Old-Fashioned Doll.* 1973. np. reprint of 1908 ed. wrp. G2. $7.00

MORGENSTERN, S. *Silent Gondoliers.* 1983. Del Rey. 1st ed. F/F. P3. $18.00

MORICE, Anne. *Murder in Outline.* 1979. St Martin. 1st ed. F/dj. P3. $15.00

MORICE, Anne. *Treble Exposure.* 1988. St Martin. ARC of 1st ed. RS. F/F. S5. $25.00

MORIN, Nancy A. *Flora of N Am. Vol 1: Intro.* 1993. NY. ils. 372 p. M. B26. $75.00

MORISON, Samuel Eliot. *Admiral of the Ocean Sea: Life of Christopher Columbus.* 1942. Little Brn. 1st ed. 2 vols. ils Erwin Raisz/ Bertram Greene. M/djs/slipcase. O6. $475.00

MORISON, Samuel Eliot. *European Discovery of Am. S Voyages, 1492-1616.* 1974. NY. Oxford. 1st ed. 8vo. 758 p. F/F. B11. $40.00

MORISON, Samuel Eliot. *European Discovery of Am. The N Voyages AD 500-1600.* 1971. Oxford. thick 8vo. ils/facsimiles. 712 p. cloth. dj. H9. $25.00

MORISON, Samuel Eliot. *Maritime Hist of MA 1783-1860.* 1921. Boston. 1st ed. ils. 401 p. VG. B28. $45.00

MORISON, Samuel Eliot. *Samuel de Champlain: Father of New France.* 1972. Little Brn. ils/maps. NF/worn. O6. $35.00

MORISON, Samuel Eliot. *2-Ocean War. Short Hist of US Navy in 2nd World War.* 1963. Little Brn. VG/dj. A16. $20.00

MORISON, Stanley. *John Bell, 1745-1831.* (1930). London. 1st Ed Club. 1/100. sm quarto. 166 p. gilt bl cloth. NF. B24. $250.00

MORITZ, C.P. *Journeys of a German in Eng in 1782.* (1965). NY. HRW. 1st Am ed. 12mo. 191 p. F/F. A2. $10.00

MORLAND, Nigel. *Lady Had a Gun.* 1951. Cassell. 1st ed. VG/VG-. P3. $25.00

MORLEY, Christopher. *Don't Open Until Christmas.* 1931. Doubleday Doran. 1st ed. inscr/dtd. C4. $40.00

MORLEY, Christopher. *John Mistletoe.* 1931. Garden City. 1st ed. VG/VG. B5. $25.00

MORLEY, Christopher. *Kitty Foyle.* nd. Grosset Dunlap. VG/torn. P3. $15.00

MORLEY, Christopher. *Letters of Askance.* 1939. Lippincott. 1st ed. NF/dj. C4. $25.00

MORLEY, Christopher. *No Crabb — No Christmas.* nd. Blk Cat. 1/249. miniature. gilt full red leather. F. F1. $35.00

MORLEY, Christopher. *Religio Journalistici.* 1924. Doubleday Page. 1st ed. F/NF. C4. $35.00

MORLEY, Christopher. *Travels in Phil.* March 1921. Phil. sgn. ils Frank H Taylor. 264 p. M. B14. $45.00

MORLEY, Christopher. *Where the Bl Begins.* (1922). Lippincott. ils Rackham. 227 p. bl cloth. VG. S10. $45.00

MORLEY, Christopher. *Where the Bl Begins.* 1923. Doubleday. decor brds. VG. P3. $15.00

MORLEY, John. *Life of William Ewart Gladstone.* 1903-04. NY. Macmillan. 1st Am ed. 3 vols. teg. F. F1. $295.00

MORLEY, S. Griswold. *Intro to Study of the Maya Hieroglypus.* 1915. Bureau Am Ethnology. ils/color pls/index. 284 p. O7. $12.50

MORPURGO, Ida Bohatta. *Good & Bad Berries.* 1943. NY. 12 color pls. NF. M5. $35.00

MORRELL, David. *Assumed Idenity.* 1993. NY. Warner. ARC of 1st ed. F/wrp. N3. $15.00

MORRELL, David. *Blood Oath.* 1982. St Martin/Marek. 1st ed. sgn. F/F. B2. $75.00

MORRELL, David. *First Blood.* 1972. Evans. 1st ed. VG/VG. P3. $50.00

MORRELL, David. *Fraternity of the Stone.* 1985. St Martin/Marek. 1st ed. F/F. N3. $15.00

MORRELL, David. *League of Night & Fog.* 1987. Dutton. 1st ed. VG/VG. P3. $18.00

MORRELL, David. *Totem.* 1979. Evans. 1st ed. sgn. F/F. F4. $60.00

MORRESSY, John. *Frostworld & Dreamfire.* 1977. Doubleday. 1st ed. F/F. P3. $15.00

MORRESSY, John. *Nail Down the Stars.* 1973. Walker. 1st ed. F/F. F4. $20.00

MORRILL, Rowena. *Fantastic Art of Rowena.* nd. BC. VG/dj. P3. $15.00

MORRIS, Christopher. *Day They Lost the H-Bomb.* 1966. Coward McCann. 2nd ed. N2. $6.50

MORRIS, Desmond. *Animal Days.* 1979. Jonathan Cape. 1st ed. VG+/dj. P3. $15.00

MORRIS, Desmond. *Naked Ape.* 1967. McGraw Hill. 1st ed. F/F. T2. $6.00

MORRIS, E. Joy. *Notes of Tour Through Turkey, Greece, Egypt & Arabia...* 1843. London. 8vo. 142 p. new quarter calf. O2. $140.00

MORRIS, Edita. *Love to Vietnam.* (1968). Monthly Review. 1st ed. 92 p. NF/NF. A7. $30.00

MORRIS, Edmund. *10 Acres Enough...* 1875. NY. Miller. 255 p. H10. $25.00

MORRIS, Eric. *Blockade, Berlin & the Cold War.* 1973. NY. 1st ed. 278 p. VG/dj. B18. $12.50

MORRIS, Francis Orpen. *Hist of British Birds.* 1891. London. Nimmo. revised corrected enlarged ed. lg octavo. 6 vols. NF. H5. $1,250.00

MORRIS, George P. *Little Frenchman & His Water Lots...* 1839. Phil. Lea Blanchard. 1st ed. 8vo. 155 p. orig cloth. VG. M1. $225.00

MORRIS, Henry. *Bird & Bull Pepper Pot.* 1977. N Hills, PA. Bird & Bull Pr. 1/250. 4to. 86 p. F. K1. $300.00

MORRIS, Henry. *Early Hist of Springfield. Address Delivered Oct 16, 1875.* 1876. Springfield, MA. FS Morris. sm 4to. 85 p. gr cloth. H9. $40.00

MORRIS, J.H.C. *Thank You, Wodehouse.* 1981. Weidenfeld Nicolson. 1st ed. VG+/dj. P3. $20.00

MORRIS, James. *As I Saw the USA.* (1956). Pantheon. 1st Am ed. 8vo. 246 p. VG+/VG clip. A2. $20.00

MORRIS, Janet. *Beyond the Sanctuary.* 1985. Baen. 1st ed. F/dj. P3. $20.00

MORRIS, Janet. *Hong Kong.* 1988. Franklin Lib. 1st ed. sgn. full leather. F. B4. $50.00

MORRIS, Jim. *Sheriff of Purgatory.* 1979. Doubleday. 1st ed. VG/dj. P3. $15.00

MORRIS, Jim. *War Story.* 1979. Sycamore Island. 1st ed. 342 p. VG/dj. M20. $18.00

MORRIS, John W. *Hist Atlas of OK.* 1986. Norman, OK. 3rd ed. ils/maps. M/wrp. O6. $19.00

MORRIS, John. *Candywine Development.* 1971. Citadel. 1st ed. VG/dj. P3. $13.00

MORRIS, John. *Checkerboard Caper.* 1975. Citadel. 1st ed. VG/dj. P3. $18.00

MORRIS, Kenneth. *Chalchiuhite Dragon. Tale of Toltec Times.* 1992. NY. TOR. 1st ed? F/F. N3. $15.00

MORRIS, Lloyd. *William James: Message of a Modern Mind.* 1950. Scribner. 1st ed. sm 8vo. 98 p. bl cloth. G1. $17.50

MORRIS, Maurice O'Connor. *Rambles in the Rocky Mtns.* 1864. London. Smith Elder. duodemino. gr cloth. H9. $250.00

MORRIS, Phillip Quinn. *Mussels.* 1989. Random. 1st ed. rem mk. F/F. A14. $30.00

MORRIS, Richard B. *Peacemakers. Great Powers & Am Independence.* 1965. NY. Harper Row. 1st ed. 8vo. 572 p. VG/VG. B11. $20.00

MORRIS, Taylor. *Walk of the Conscious Ants.* (1972). NY. Knopf. 1st ed. 8vo. 260 p. VG+/VG+. A2. $12.50

MORRIS, William. *Collected Works of...* 1910-15. London. Longman Gr. 1/1050. octavo. 24 vols. teg. F. H5. $9,500.00

MORRIS, William. *Early Romances of William Morris.* 1913. Dent/Dutton. 3rd ed. VG. P3. $20.00

MORRIS, William. *Poems by the Way.* 1891. Hammersmith. 1/300. stiff vellum/silk ties. VG. H5. $1,500.00

MORRIS, William. *Well at the World's End.* 1896. Hammersmith. 1/350. quarto. full limp vellum/silk ties. NF. H5. $4,000.00

MORRIS, Willie. *Courting of Marcus Dupree.* 1983. Doubleday. 1st ed. NF/dj. A7. $40.00

MORRIS, Willie. *Faulkner's MS.* nd. Oxmoor House. 1st ed. inscr. F. C4. $60.00

MORRIS, Willie. *NY Days.* 1993. Little Brn. 1st ed. inscr. F/F. C4. $30.00

MORRIS, Willie. *Yazoo.* (1971). Harpers Magazine. 192 p. clip dj. A7. $30.00

MORRIS, Wright. *Conversations w/Wright Morris.* 1977. Lincoln, NE. 1st ed. inscr. NF/wrp. A11. $45.00

MORRIS, Wright. *Fire Sermon.* 1971. Harper Row. 1st ed. inscr/dtd 1971. F/NF. L3. $375.00

MORRIS, Wright. *Gr Grass, Bl Sky, Wht House.* 1970. LA. 1st trade ed. 1/1000. inscr. NF/wrp. A11. $45.00

MORRIS, Wright. *Inhabitants.* 1946. Scribner. 1st ed. NF/VG clip. L3. $175.00

MORRIS, Wright. *Love Affair: A Venetian Journal.* 1972. NY. 1st ed. presentaion, w/inscr intl slip. F/F. A11. $65.00

MORRIS, Wright. *Love Among the Cannibals.* (1957). Harcourt Brace. ARC. RS. M/dj. B4. $125.00

MORRIS & MORRIS. *Men & Snakes.* (1965). NY. 224 p. worn dj. A17. $14.50

MORRIS & SCHLOSSER. *Pair on Paper: 2 Essays on Paper Hist & Related Matters.* 1976. N Hills, PA. Bird & Bull Pr. sm 4to. 70 p. F. K1. $350.00

MORRIS. *Ins & Outs: Perfecting the Quilting Stitch.* 1990. np. ils. wrp. G2. $10.00

MORRISEAU, Norval. *Legends of My People the Great Ojibway.* 1965. Toronto. Ryerson. 1st ed. NF/dj. L3. $85.00

MORRISON, H.S. *How I Worked My Way Around the World.* (1903). Christian Herald. 8vo. 424 p. VG. A2. $15.00

MORRISON, Morie. *Fresh-Water Fishing Ils: How To Catch Fish in the W.* (1965). Menlo Park. 1st prt. 8o p. wrp. A17. $8.00

MORRISON, Stanley. *On Type Faces. Examples of Use of Type for Prt of Books.* 1923. London. Medici Soc. 1/750. 4to. 103 p. marbled brds/cloth. NF. B14. $85.00

MORRISON, Toni. *Beloved.* 1987. Chatto Windus. 1st ed. F/F. C4. $60.00

MORRISON, Toni. *Beloved.* 1987. Knopf. 1st ed. VG/VG. B3. $30.00

MORRISON, Toni. *Beloved.* 1988. Knopf. 1st ed/11th prt. NF/NF. A13. $20.00

MORRISON, Toni. *Jazz.* 1992. Knopf. 1st Canadian ed. F/F. A13. $25.00

MORRISON, Toni. *Jazz.* 1992. NY. 1st trade ed. sgn. F/F. A11. $75.00

MORRISON, Toni. *Race-Ing, Justice, En-Gendering Power.* 1992. Pantheon. AP. F/prt gr wrp. C4. $40.00

MORRISON, Toni. *Song of Solomon.* Sept 1977. Knopf. inscr. F/dj. B14. $200.00

MORRISON, Toni. *Song of Solomon.* 1978. Chatto Windus. 1st ed. NF/NF clip. A13. $50.00

MORRISON, Toni. *Tar Baby.* 1981. Chatto Windus. 1st ed. F/F clip. A13. $40.00

MORRISON, Toni. *Tar Baby.* 1981. Knopf. 1st trade ed. F/NF. B2. $50.00

MORROW, James. *City of Truth.* 1990. Legend. 1st ed. F/dj. P3. $25.00

MORROW, James. *Only Begotten Daughter.* 1990. NY. Morrow. 1st ed. F/F. N3. $25.00

MORROW, James. *Wine of Violence.* 1981. Holt. 1st ed. author's 1st ed. F/F. F4. $20.00

MORROW, Josiah. *Life & Speeches of Thomas Corwin.* 1896. Cincinnati. 1st ed. 477 p. quarter leather. G. A17. $20.00

MORSE, Benjamin, M.D.; see Block, Lawrence.

MORSE, Jedidiah. *Am Universal Geog; or, View of Present State...* 1819. Charlestown. Etheridge. 7th ed. 2 vols. 6 fld maps. leather. VG. O5. $350.00

MORSE, John T. *Abraham Lincoln.* 1893. Houghton Mifflin. 1st ed/2nd prt. 2 vols. cloth. NF. M8. $65.00

MORSE, John T. *Life & Letters of Oliver Wendell Holmes.* 1896. Boston. Riverside. 1st ed. 2 vols. orig cloth. G7. $35.00

MORSE, Peter. *Jean Charlot's Prints. A Catalogue Raisonne.* 1976. Honolulu. 1st ed. 16 color pls. 450 p. dj. F3. $125.00

MORSE, Peter. *John Sloan's Prints.* 1969. Yale. ils/photos/pls. 406 p. cloth. dj. D2. $300.00

MORSE, W.G. *Pardon My Harvard Accent.* (1941). Farrar Rinehart. 1st ed. 8vo. 364 p. VG/G. A2. $15.00

MORSE & MORSE. *Traveller's Guide or Pocket Gazetteer of the US.* 1826. New Haven. Wadsworth. 2nd ed. 336 p. fld US map. VG. O5. $275.00

MORSE & PARISH. *New Gazetter of the E Continent; or, A Geog Dictionary...* 1802. Charlestown. Etheridge. VG. O6. $75.00

MORTENSEN, A.R. *Am West, Vol 1.* 1964. W Hist Assn. 4to. F. A8. $15.00

MORTIMER, John. *Charade.* 1986. Viking. F/dj. P3. $20.00

MORTON, Anthony; see Creasey, John.

MORTON, H.V. *Ghosts of London.* 1952. Methuen. 7th prt. VG/fair. P3. $15.00

MORTON, James. *Chrysanthemum Culture for Am.* 1891. NY. xl. woodcuts. 126 p. B26. $16.00

MORTON, John Watson. *Artillery of Nathan Bedford Forrest's Cavalry.* 1909. Nashville. ME Church. 1st ed. 374 p. cloth. VG+. M8. $375.00

MORTON, Joseph. *McCarthy: Man & the Ism.* nd. Pacific Pub. 31 p. wrp. A7. $12.00

MORTON, Nathaniel. *New Eng's Memorial; or, Brief Relation of...Planters...* 1772. Solomon Southwick. reprint/3rd ed. 8vo. 208 p. VG. M1. $500.00

MORTON, Richard L. *Colonial VA.* 1960. Chapel Hill. NC U. 1st ed. 2 vols. inscr. VG/G slipcase. B11. $75.00

MOSBY, John Singleton. *Memoirs of Col John S Mosby.* 1917. Little Brn. 1st ed. 414 p. VG. M8. $250.00

MOSBY, John Singleton. *Mosby's War Reminiscences & Stuart's Cavalry Campaigns.* 1887. Dodd Mead. 1st ed. 264 p. cloth. F. M8. $275.00

MOSCOW, Alvin. *Tiger on a Leash.* (1962). London. 1st ed. 192 p. G/dj. B18. $22.50

MOSELEY, Dana. *Dead of Summer.* 1953. Abelard. 1st ed. VG/dj. P3. $20.00

MOSELEY, H.N. *Notes by a Naturalist.* 1892. Putnam/Murray. xl. 8vo. 540 p. tan cloth. P4. $195.00

MOSELEY, Michael. *Maritime Foundations of Andean Civilization.* (1975). Menlo Park, CA. Cummings Pub. 1st ed. 131 p. wrp. F3. $20.00

MOSELEY. *Flight of the Pterosaurs.* 1986. 8 pop-ups. F. A4. $25.00

MOSELY, Ephraim. *Teeth, Their Natural Hist.* 1862. London. Hardwick. 1st ed. 16mo. orig purple cloth. NF. H5. $175.00

MOSER, P.W. *Story of Greyhound 1:551/4.* 1940. Harrisburg. 4to. VG. O3. $45.00

MOSEY. *Am's Pict Quilts.* 1985. np. ils. cloth. G2. $20.00

MOSEY. *Contemporary Quilts From Traditional Designs.* 1988. np. wrp. G2. $17.00

MOSHER, Thomas Bird. *Bibelot, Reprint of Poetry & Prose for Book Lovers...* 1895-1925. NY. Wise. 21 vols. 12mo. teg. gilt bl morocco. F. R3. $400.00

MOSKOWITZ, Ira. *Great Drawings of All Times.* 1962. Shorewood. 4 vols. VG/4 slipcases. A1. $375.00

MOSKOWITZ, Sam. *Editor's Choice in SF.* 1954. McBride. 1st ed. VG/dj. P3. $45.00

MOSKOWITZ, Sam. *Immortal Storm.* 1951. Burwell. 1st ed. 1/150. F/wrp. M2. $175.00

MOSKOWITZ, Sam. *Under the Moons of Mars.* 1970. Holt. 1st ed. NF/dj. M2. $30.00

MOSKOWITZ, Sam. *When Women Rule.* 1972. Walker. 1st ed. VG/VG. P3. $20.00

MOSLEY, Walter. *Blk Betty.* 1994. Norton. 1st ed. sgn. M/M. T2. $30.00

MOSLEY, Walter. *Devil in a Bl Dress.* 1990. Norton. 1st ed. sgn. F/F. T2. $60.00

MOSLEY, Walter. *Red Death.* 1991. Norton. 1st ed. sgn. F/F. B2/T2. $50.00

MOSLEY, Walter. *Wht Butterfly.* 1992. Norton. 1st ed. F/F. B2. $35.00

MOSLEY, Walter. *Wht Butterfly.* 1992. Norton. 1st ed. M/M. T2. $38.00

MOSS, Elaine. *Part of the Pattern.* 1986. NY. Greenwillow. 1st ed. 8vo. 224 p. red brds. F/NF. T5. $30.00

MOSS, James A. *Manual of Military Training.* (1914). Menasha, WI. ils. 699 p. G. B18. $22.50

MOSS, Robert F. *Films of Carol Reed.* 1987. Columbia U. ils. NF/dj. C8. $40.00

MOSS, W. Stanley. *War of Shadows.* (1952). London. 8vo. 240 p. cloth. scarce. O2. $35.00

MOSSIKER, Frances. *Pocahontas: Life & Legend.* 1976. Knopf. 1st ed. 383 p. VG/VG. B10. $25.00

MOTHER GOOSE. *Complete Book of Nursery Rhymes.* 1941. Whitman. ils Dorothea J Snow. 373 p. VG. A3. $8.50

MOTHER GOOSE. *Mother Goose #845.* 1934. Donohue. 87 p. G+. A3. $10.00

MOTHER GOOSE. *Mother Goose ABC Book & Other Jingles.* nd. Donahue. #170 Mother Goose series. G. A3. $6.00

MOTHER GOOSE. *Mother Goose: Her Own Book.* 1932. Whitman. 60 p. pict brds. VG. A3. $25.00

MOTHER GOOSE. *Space Child's Mother Goose.* 1958. Simon Schuster. ils Marian Parry. 1st ed. 8vo. cloth. VG. A3. $35.00

MOTHER GOOSE. *Tall Book of Mother Goose.* 1942. Harper/Artist Guild. ils Rojankovsky. 4to. 120 p. G+. A3. $20.00

MOTLEY, Willard. *Let Noon Be Fair.* (1966). Putnam. 1st ed. 416 p. VG+. A7. $30.00

MOTOLINIA, Fray Toribio. *Historia de los Indios de la Nueva Espana.* 1973. Mexico. Editorial Porrua. 256 p. wrp. F3. $20.00

MOTT, Valentine. *Travels in Europe & the E.* 1842. Harper. 452 p. orig cloth. G7. $150.00

MOUGIN, Charles. *Complications Neurogiques du Syndrome de Klippel-Feil.* 1932. Paris. Modernes. author's presentation. 93 p. G7. $125.00

MOULE, Thomas. *County Maps of Old Eng.* 1992. London. Studio. 56 maps. M/dj. O6. $50.00

MOUNTEVANS, Admiral Lord. *Man Against the Desolate Antarctic.* 1951. Funk. 1st Am ed. 8vo. 172 p. VG/VG. A2. $15.00

MOUNTFIELD, David. *Hist of Polar Exploration.* 1974. NY. 1st Am ed. 208 p. map ep. gilt bl cloth. F/F clip. H3. $35.00

MOUNTFORT, Guy. *Wild Paradise: Story of Coto Donanal Expeditions.* 1958. Houghton Mifflin. 1st Am ed. 240 p. F/G. A17. $17.50

MOURAVIEFF, A.N. *Hist of the Church of Russia.* 1842. Oxford. trans RW Blackmore. 448 p. new cloth. O2. $60.00

MOURE, Nancy Dustin Wall. *William Wendt 1865-1946.* 1977. Laguna Beach Mus Art. 1/1000. wrp. D2. $40.00

MOURE & SMITH. *Dictionary of Art & Artists in S CA Before 1930.* 1975. private prt. 1/500. ils. 306 p. NF/wrp. B19. $50.00

MOURIKIS, Doula. *Mosaics of the Nea Moni of Chios.* 1985. Athens. Green text. 2 vols. folio. djs/slipcase. O2. $100.00

MOUSHENG, Lin. *Men & Ideas.* 1942. NY. Day. 1st ed. 8vo. 256 p. VG/dj. W1. $18.00

MOWAT, Farley. *My Discovery of Am.* 1985. Toronto. McClelland Stewart. VG/dj. A16. $10.00

MOWAT, Farley. *Owls in the Family.* 1961. Little Brn. Atlantic Monthly Pr Book. VG/dj. A16. $12.00

MOWRY, Jess. *Rats in the Trees.* 1990. Santa Barbara. J Daniel. 1st ed. inscr/dtd 1992. author's 1st book. F/wrp. L3. $100.00

MOWRY, Jess. *Six Out Seven.* 1993. FSG. 1st ed. F/F clip. A13. $30.00

MOWRY, Jess. *Way Past Cool.* 1992. FSG. 1st ed. NF/VG. A13. $35.00

MOXLEY, F. Wright. *Red Snow.* 1930. Simon Schuster. 2nd ed. decor brds. VG. P3. $20.00

MOYES, Patricia. *Blk Widower.* 1975. Collins Crime Club. 1st ed. F/dj. P3. $15.00

MOYES, Patricia. *Curious Affair of the Third Dog.* 1973. HRW. 1st ed. VG. P3. $13.00

MOYES, Patricia. *Many Deadly Returns.* 1970. HRW. 1st ed. VG. P3. $10.00

MOYES, Patricia. *Night Ferry to Death.* 1985. London. Collins. 1st ed. sgn. F/F. M15/S5. $45.00

MOYES, Patricia. *To Kill a Coconut.* 1977. Collins Crime Club. 1st ed. VG/VG-. P3. $15.00

MOYNIHAN, Daniel Patrick. *Defenses of Freedom: Public Papers of Arthur J Goldberg.* 1966. Harper Row. M11. $45.00

MOZANS, H.J. *Along the Andes & Down the Amazon.* 1911. Appleton. ils. 542 p. teg. gilt bdg. scarce. F3. $50.00

MOZANS, H.J. *Up the Orinoco & Down the Magdalena.* 1910. Appleton. 1st ed. ils. 439 p. F3. $45.00

MOZART. *Letters of Mozart & His Family.* 1989. Norton. 2nd ed. F/dj. P3. $75.00

MOZINO, Jose Mariano. *Noticias de Nutka: Account of Nootka Sound in 1792.* 1970. Seattle, WA. trans Iris Higbie Wilson. ils/maps. NF. O6. $35.00

MUCK, Otto. *Secret of Atlantis.* 1978. Canada. Collins. VG/dj. P3. $18.00

MUDD, Samuel Alexander. *Life of Dr Samuel A Mudd...* 1975. Continental Book Co. reprint of 1906 Neale ed. 326 p. cloth. NF. M8. $45.00

MUDD & SMITH-GRISWOLD. *Beetle.* 1992. 7 popups. F. A4. $30.00

MUDD & SMITH-GRISWOLD. *Butterfly.* 1991. 6 popups. F. A4. $30.00

MUELLER, Hans Alexander. *Woodcuts & Wood Engravings.* 1939. NY. Pynson. portfolio ed. 1/250. w/sgn self-portrait proof. F1. $350.00

MUHAMMAD, Elijah. *Fall of Am.* 1973. Chicago. Muhammad's Temple of Islam No 2. dj. N2. $22.50

MUHLLEITNER, Elke. *Biographisches Lexikon der Psychoanalyse.* 1992. Tubingen. Diskord. 400 p. prt maroon brds. M. G1. $75.00

MUIR, John. *Notes on My Journeying in CA N Mtns.* 1975. Ashland, OR. ils. 72 p. wrp. A17. $15.00

MUIR, John. *Stickeen.* 1909. Boston. 4th imp. 12mo. cloth. NF. D3. $25.00

MUIR, John. *Story of My Boyhood & Youth.* 1913. Boston. 1st ed. 293 p. cloth. NF. D3. $75.00

MUIRHEAD, Arnold. *Grace Revere Osler. A Brief Memoir.* 1931. Oxford. 1/500. 4to. 56 p. vellum backed brds. G7. $150.00

MUIRHEAD, Arnold. *Principles & Practice of Medicine...* 1892. NY. Appleton. 1st ed/2nd issue. rebound. VG. G7. $495.00

MUIRHEAD, Findley. *N Spain w/Balearic Islands.* 1930. London. The Bl Guide. 345 p. gilt bl cloth. F. H3. $15.00

MUIRHEAD, Finley. *Bl Guide.* 1924. London. 16mo. 62 maps/pls. 485 p. gilt bl cloth. VG. H3. $20.00

MUKERJI, Dhan Gopal. *Fierce-Face: Story of a Tiger.* 1936. Dutton. 1st ed. 8vo. 76 p. VG/worn. T5. $65.00

MUKHERJEE, Bharati. *Holder of the World.* 1993. Knopf. AP. F/wrp. B4. $45.00

MUKHERJEE, Bharati. *Jasmine.* (1989). Ontario. Viking. 1st ed. VG/F. B3. $30.00

MULDOON, Paul. *Wishbone.* 1984. Dublin. ltd ed. 1/750. F/wrp. V1. $25.00

MULFORD, Clarence E. *Bar-20 Days.* nd. Grosset Dunlap. VG/dj. B9. $15.00

MULFORD, Clarence E. *Bar-20 Three.* nd. Grosset Dunlap. VG+/dj. P3. $25.00

MULFORD, Clarence E. *Bar-20.* nd. Grosset Dunlap. VG. P3. $15.00

MULFORD, Clarence E. *Corson of the JC.* 1927. Doubleday Page. 1st ed. VG. P3. $30.00

MULFORD, Clarence E. *Hopalong Cassidy & Eagles Brood.* 1931. Collier. 12mo. G. A8. $8.00

MULFORD, Clarence E. *Hopalong Cassidy Returns.* nd. AL Burt. VG. P3. $10.00

MULFORD, Clarence E. *Hopalong Cassidy Takes Cards.* 1937. Collier. 12mo. VG. A8. $8.00

MULFORD, Clarence E. *Hopalong Cassidy.* nd. Grosset Dunlap. VG. P3. $20.00

MULFORD, Clarence E. *Johnny Nelson.* (1920). Grosset Dunlap. VG/dj. B9. $12.50

MULFORD, Clarence E. *Mesquite Jenkins.* 1932. Collier. 12mo. G+. A8. $8.00

MULFORD, Clarence E. *Round Up.* 1933. Collier. 12mo. VG. A8. $8.00

MULLALLY, Frederic. *Assassins.* 1965. Walker. 1st ed. VG+/dj. P3. $10.00

MULLEN, Thomas J. *Renewal of the Ministry.* 1963. NY. Abingdon. inscr. 12mo. 143 p. VG/dj. V3. $12.00

MULLER, Dan. *Chico of the Cross Up Ranch.* (1938). Chicago. 1st ed. 249 p. pict cloth. VG. D3. $15.00

MULLER, Dan. *Horses.* (1936). Chicago. 1st trade ed. 4to. 204 p. burlap bdg. NF. D3. $35.00

MULLER, Frederick. *Beredeneerde Beschrijving van Nederlandse Historieplaten...* 1970. Amsterdam. Nico Israel. reprint 1863-70 eds. 3 vols. M/slipcase. O6. $275.00

MULLER, Herbert J. *Children of Frankenstein.* 1970. IN U. 1st ed. 432 p. gr cloth. VG/dj. G1. $28.50

MULLER, Hermann. *Fertilization of Flowers.* 1883. London. ils. 669 p. cloth. B26. $95.00

MULLER, Marcia. *Cavalier in Wht.* nd. BC. VG/dj. P3. $8.00

MULLER, Marcia. *Cavalier in Wht.* 1986. NY. St Martin. AP. sgn. RS. F/wrp. S5. $35.00

MULLER, Marcia. *Legend of the Slain Soldiers.* 1985. Walker. 1st ed. F/dj. P3. $15.00

MULLER, Marcia. *Trophies & Dead Things.* 1990. Mysterious ARC. 1/500. w/sgn label. NF/wrp. B2. $40.00

MULLER, Marcia. *Trophies & Dead Things.* 1990. Mysterious. 1st ed. F/dj. P3. $17.00

MULLER, Marcia. *Where Echoes Live.* nd. BC. VG/dj. P3. $8.00

MULLER, Max. *India: What Can It Teach Us?* 1883. NY. 1st Am ed. 12mo. 282 p. F/tan wrp. H3. $30.00

MULLER, S. *Beyond Civilization.* 1952. Brn Gold Pub. 62 p. sbdg. VG. P4. $25.00

MULLER & PRONZINI. *Kill or Cure: Suspense Stories About World of Medicine.* 1985. NY. Macmillan. ARC. sgns. RS. F/F. S5. $35.00

MULLER & PRONZINI. *1001 Midnights.* 1986. NY. Arbor. 1st ed. inscr/sgns. F/F. S5. $110.00

MULLIGAN, Hugh A. *No Place To Die: Agony of Vietnam.* 1967. NY. Morrow. 362 p. VG/VG. A7. $50.00

MULLIN, Glen H. *Adventures of a Scholar Tramp.* (1925). NY. 312 p. G. B18. $22.50

MULLIN, Robert N. *Boyhood of Billy the Kid...* 1967. El Paso. 1st ed. photos. 26 p. NF/map wrp. D3. $25.00

MULLINS, Lisa C. *Early Architecture of the S.* ca 1987. Nat Hist Soc. 236 p. VG. B10. $35.00

MULOCK, Miss. *Adventures of a Brownie.* nd. NY. 16mo. woodcuts. 147 p. gilt bl cloth. VG. H3. $15.00

MULOCK, Miss. *Little Lame Prince & His Traveling Cloak.* nd. McLoughlin. 8vo. pls. 142 p. gilt bl cloth. VG. H3. $20.00

MULOCK, Miss. *Little Lame Prince.* 1909. Rand McNally. later ed. ils Hope Dunlap. VG. L1. $27.00

MULVANEY, Charles Pelham. *Hist of the NW Rebellion of 1885.* 1886. Tor. 12th thousand. 440 p. new ep. G. A17. $60.00

MULZAC, Hugh. *Star To Steer By.* (1963). NY. Internat. 251 p. wrp. A7. $10.00

MUMEY, Nolie. *Bloody Trails Along the Rio Grande: Diary of AF Ickis.* 1958. Denver. Rosenstock. 1/500. sgn. 123 p. F/dj. B20. $60.00

MUMEY, Nolie. *Friendly Fire.* 1945. Denver. 1st ed. sgn. NF/sans. V1. $45.00

MUMEY, Nolie. *Nathan Addison Baker: Pioneer Journalist, Teacher...* 1965. Old W Pub. ils/notes/chronology/index. 161 p. F. B19. $100.00

MUMFORD, Lewis. *S in Architecture.* 1967. DaCapo. xl. reprint 1941 ed. 147 p. VG-. B10. $15.00

MUMM. *Quick Country Quilting.* 1992. np. ils. cloth. G2. $27.00

MUNARI, Bruno. *I Prelibri.* 1980. Milano. Danese. sm folio case w/twelve 12mo books. F. B24. $150.00

MUNARI, Bruno. *Tanta Gente.* 1983. Milano. Danese. quarto. 2 vols. together in clear plastic portfolio. F. B24. $200.00

MUNCH, Peter. *Crisis in Utopia: Story of Tristan de Cunha.* (1971). London. Longman. 1st ed. 8vo. 324 p. VG/F-. A2. $20.00

MUNDELL, E.H. *Erle Stanley Gardner: A Checklist.* 1968. Kent State. F/sans. P3. $13.00

MUNDY, Talbot. *Hundred Days.* nd. Hutchinson. VG. P3. $17.00

MUNDY, Talbot. *Jungle Jest.* 1932. Century. 1st ed. G. M18. $40.00

MUNDY, Talbot. *King of the Khyber Rifles.* (1916). Bobbs Merrill. 1st ed. VG/worn scarce dj. L3. $475.00

MUNDY, Talbot. *King of the Khyber Rifles.* 1972. Tom Stacey. VG/dj. P3. $20.00

MUNDY, Talbot. *Nine Unknown.* 1924. Bobbs Merrill. VG. P3. $75.00

MUNDY, Talbot. *Om: The Secret of Ahbor Valley.* 1924. Bobbs Merrill. VG. P3. $75.00

MUNDY, Talbot. *Purple Pirate.* 1959. Gnome. F/dj. M2. $50.00

MUNDY, Talbot. *Seventeen Thieves of El-Kalil.* nd. Hutchinson. VG-. P3. $45.00

MUNDY, Talbot. *Thunder Dragon Gate.* 1937. Appleton Century. 1st ed. xl. VG-. P3. $20.00

MUNFORD, Robert Beverly Jr. *Richmond Homes & Memories.* 1936. Garrett Massie. 1st ed. 259 p. VG/fair. B10. $45.00

MUNFORD, Robert. *Candidates; or, Humours of a VA Election.* April 1948. Williamsburg, VA. offprint. 8vo. 43 p. gr brds/gray spine. VG. B11. $50.00

MUNK, Joseph Amasa. *Story of the Munk Lib of AZ.* 19227. LA. Time Mirror. 12mo. presentation. 78 p. brn cloth. H9. $40.00

MUNN, Henry Toke. *Tales of the Eskimo.* nd. London. photos. 196 p. VG/dj. A17. $45.00

MUNRO, Alice. *Friend of My Youth.* 1990. Knopf. AP. w/sgn leaf. F/wht wrp/red cb box. C4. $60.00

MUNRO, Hugh. *Clutha Plays a Hunch.* 1959. Ives Washburn. 1st ed. VG/dj. P3. $15.00

MUNRO, James. *Man Who Sold Death.* 1964. Hammond Hammond. 1st ed. VG/fair. P3. $20.00

MUNROE, Kirk. *Flamingo Feather.* (1887). NY. early ed. 16mo. 255 p. pict cloth. VG. D3. $25.00

MUNSEY, Frank A. *Boy Broker.* nd. Munsey. 3rd ed. VG. P3. $40.00

MUNSTERBERG, Hugo. *Folk Arts of Japan.* 1966. Rutland. 7th ed. dj. N2. $10.00

MUNZ, Philip A. *CA Mtn Wild Flowers.* 1963. Berkeley. 96 color photos. bl cloth. VG. B26. $15.00

MUNZ, Philip A. *Flora of S CA.* 1974. Berkeley. 103 pls. 1086 p. VG+. B26. $24.00

MUNZ & KECK. *CA Flora.* 1959. Berkeley, CA. 1st ed. 8vo. 1681 p. F/VG. A2. $35.00

MURAKAMI, Haruki. *Wild Sheep Chase.* 1989. Tokyo. Kodansha. ARC. F/wrp. B2. $45.00

MURBARGER, Nell. *Sovereigns of the Sage.* 1958. Desert Magazine Pr. 8vo. VG. A8. $60.00

MURCHISON, Carl. *Psychologies of 1930.* 1930. Worcester, MA. Clark. 1st ed. 8vo. 497 p. panelled red buckram. VG. G1. $75.00

MURDOCH, Iris. *Good Apprentice.* (1985). Chatto Windus. 1st ed. NF/F. B3. $35.00

MURDOCH, Iris. *Henry & Cato.* (1977). NY. Viking. 1st ed. F/F. B3. $25.00

MURDOCH, Iris. *Nuns & Soldiers.* (1980). Chatto Windus. 1st ed. F/F. B3. $50.00

MURDOCK, George P. *Our Primitive Contemporaries...* (1943). NY. 6th prt. 12mo. 117 p. VG. D3. $25.00

MURPHY, Audie. *To Hell & Back.* 1949. NY. 1st ed. 274 p. quarter cloth. G. B18. $19.50

MURPHY, Haughton. *Murder & Acquisitions.* 1988. London. Collins. ARC of 1st British ed. RS. F/F. S5. $25.00

MURPHY, Haughton. *Murder & Acquisitions.* 1988. Simon Schuster. 1st ed. F/F. P3. $17.00

MURPHY, Haughton. *Murder for Lunch.* 1986. Simon Schuster. 1st ed. F/dj. P3. $15.00

MURPHY, John Mortimer. *Sporting Adventures in the Far W.* 1880. NY. Harper. 469 p. pict gr cloth. VG. H7. $85.00

MURPHY, John Wilson. *Memoirs of a Great Canadian Detective.* 1978. Collins. 2nd ed. VG/dj. P3. $15.00

MURPHY, Marguerite. *Dangerous Legacy.* 1962. Avalon. 1st ed. xl. dj. P3. $5.00

MURPHY, Mark. *83 Days: Survival of Seaman Izzi.* 1943. Dutton. 1st ed. 12mo. 124 p. F/F. A2. $17.50

MURPHY, Pat. *City, Not Long After.* 1989. Doubleday. 1st ed. F/NF. N3. $10.00

MURPHY, Shirley Rousseau. *Castle of Hope.* 1980. Atheneum. 1st ed. F/dj. P3. $15.00

MURPHY, Shirley Rousseau. *Joining of the Stone.* 1981. Atheneum. 1st ed. F/F. N3. $20.00

MURPHY, Thomas D. *On Old-World Highways.* 1914. Boston. 388 p. teg. pict gray cloth. VG. H3. $20.00

MURPHY, Thomas D. *On Sunset Highways.* 1915. Boston. 1st ed. 376 p. teg. VG. D3. $25.00

MURRAY, Adolphus. *Observationes Anatomicae: Circa Infundibulum Cerebri...* 1772. Upsaliae. 4to. 1 fld pl. 31 p. uncut. G7. $125.00

MURRAY, Albert. *Omni-Americans.* 1970. NY. Outerbridge Dientsfrey. 2nd prt. 227 p. dj. A7. $20.00

MURRAY, Albert. *Omni-Americans.* 1970. NY. 1st ed. 2-pg presentation inscr. F/NF. A11. $75.00

MURRAY, Beatrice; see Posner, Richard.

MURRAY, James A.H. *New Eng Dictionary of Hist Principles...* 1888-1928. Oxford. Clarendon. 1st ed. 10 vols in 12. teg. maroon morocco/brds. VG. H5. $2,500.00

MURRAY, James. *New Eng Dictionary on Hist Principles...* 1888. Oxford. Clarendon. early issue. 10 vols in 20. folio. teg. half morocco. R3. $2,000.00

MURRAY, Lindley. *Power of Religion on the Mind, in Retirement, Affliction...* 1889. NY. Trustees of Residual Estate. 12mo. 372 p. VG. V3. $12.00

MURRAY, Max. *Sunshine Corpse.* 1954. Michael Joseph. 1st ed. xl. VG. P3. $8.00

MURRAY, Robert. *Maximillian: Emperor of Mexico...* 1934. New Haven. Yale. 1st ed. 235 p. cloth. F3. $30.00

MURRAY, Ruth S. *Little May: At Home & Abroad.* 1883. Revell. 1st ed. 12mo. 291 p. G+. S10. $25.00

MURRAY, Ruth S. *Valiant for the Truth...* 1880. Cambridge. Riverside. 12mo. 236 p. V3. $20.00

MURRAY, William. *Getaway Blues.* 1990. Bantam. 1st ed. F/dj. P3. $18.00

MURRAY & POOLE. *Power Boating the W Coast of Mexico.* 1965. Palm Desert, CA. Desert-Southwest. 8vo. photos. 304 p. red cloth. VG/VG. B11. $10.00

MURTAUGH, Janet. *Wonder Tales of Giants & Dwarfs.* 1945. Random House. ils Florian. 65 p. VG. A3. $10.00

MURWIN & PAYNE. *Quick & Easy Giant Dahlia Quilt on the Sewing Machine.* 1983. np. ils. wrp. G2. $5.00

MUSIL, Alois. *In the Arabian Desert.* 1930. NY. 1st ed. 8vo. 339 p. cloth. O2. $125.00

MUSTE, A.J. *Essays of...* 1967. Bobbs Merrill. 1st ed. NF/VG. B2. $35.00

MUSTIAN, Thomas F. *Fact & Legends of Richmond Area Streets.* ca 1977. Carroll Pub. 80 p. VG/stiff wrp. B10. $12.00

MUSTO, David F. *Am Disease: Origins of Narcotic Control.* 1973. New Haven. 1st ed. 354 p. ochre cloth. G1. $35.00

MYER, William Edward. *Indian Trails of the SE.* 1971. Nashville. Bl & Gray Pr. 1st book ed. 8vo. gr buckram. F. B11. $50.00

MYERS, Allen O. *Bosses & Boodle in OH Politics.* 1895. Cincinnati. 1st ed. 293 p. orig bl cloth. G. D7. $35.00

MYERS, Amy. *Murder Makes an Entree.* 1992. London. Headline. 1st ed. F/F. S5. $25.00

MYERS, Gustavus. *Hist of Am Idealism.* 1925. NY. Boni. 1st ed. author's own copy w/bookplate. F/dj. B2. $100.00

MYERS, Gustavus. *Hist of Bigotry in the US.* (1943). Random. 1st ed. 8vo. 504 p. F/VG+. A2. $30.00

MYERS, Gustavus. *Hist of the Great Am Fortunes: Vol I-III.* ca 1909-10. Chicago. CH Kerr. ils/photos. F. V4. $60.00

MYERS, John Myers. *Deaths of the Bravos.* 1962. Little Brn. 1st ed. VG/dj. P3. $40.00

MYERS, Peter Hamilton. *Ensenore, a Poem.* 1840. Wiley Putnam. 1st ed. disbound/marbled ep. E3. $15.00

MYERS, Robert J. *Cross of Frankenstein.* 1975. Lippincott. 1st ed. F/F. F4. $20.00

MYERS, Robert J. *Slave of Frankenstein.* 1976. Lippincott. 1st ed. F/NF. F4. $20.00

MYERS, Robert Mason. *Children of Pride. True Story of GA & Civil War.* 1972. New Haven/London. Yale. 1st ed. thick 8vo. 1845 p. gray cloth. VG. B11. $75.00

MYERSON, Joel. *Ralph Waldo Emerson: A Descriptive Bibliography.* 1982. Pittsburgh. 1st ed. F/sans. Q1. $75.00

MYLONAS, George E. *Mycenae & the Mycenaean Age.* 1966. Princeton. 4to. 153 pls. 251 p. cloth. O2. $30.00

MYRES, John L. *Geographical Hist in Greek Lands.* 1853. Oxford. xl. 381 p. cloth. dj. O2. $35.00

MYTINGER, Caroline. *New Guinea Headhunter.* 1946. Macmillan. 1st ed. 8vo. 441 p. VG. W1. $18.00

NABB, Madgdalen. *Death of a Dutchman.* 1982. Collins Crime Club. 1st ed. F/F. M15. $45.00

NABB, Magdalen. *Death of a Dutchman.* 1983. Scribner. 1st Am ed. F/F. S5. $25.00

NABOKOV, Vladimir. *Ada.* (1969). London. Weidenfelt Nicolson. F/F. C4. $45.00

NABOKOV, Vladimir. *Bend Sinister.* (1947). Holt. 1st ed. F/NF. B4. $350.00

NABOKOV, Vladimir. *Enchanter.* (1987). London. Picador. 1st ed. trans Dmitri Nabokov. F/F. B3. $30.00

NABOKOV, Vladimir. *Hero of Our Time.* 1958. Anchor. PBO. correct 1st prt. ils/sgn E Gorey. VG+/wrp. A11. $60.00

NABOKOV, Vladimir. *Laughter in the Dark.* (1960). New Directions. new ed/ARC. RS. F/NF. B4. $85.00

NABOKOV, Vladimir. *Lolita.* 1955. Paris. Olympia. correct 1st ed. 2 vols. F/custom clamshell box. L3. $3,000.00

NABOKOV, Vladimir. *Lolita.* 1955. Putnam. 1st ed. G/dj. M18. $75.00

NABOKOV, Vladimir. *Mary.* (1970). McGraw Hill. 2nd prt. author's 1st novel. F/NF. A7. $15.00

NABOKOV, Vladimir. *Nabokov's Quartet.* (1966). NY. Phaedra. 1st ed. F/VG clip. B3. $50.00

NABOKOV, Vladimir. *Nabokov's Quartet.* (1966). Phaedra. 1st ed. F/NF. B4. $65.00

NABOKOV, Vladimir. *Notes on Prosody.* 1964. NY. 1st ed. NF/wrp. A11. $65.00

NABOKOV, Vladimir. *Poems & Problems.* 1971. McGraw Hill. AP/galley sheets. NF. very scarce. L3. $375.00

NABOKOV, Vladimir. *Waltz Invention.* 1966. Phaedra. all 1st ed points. F/NF. B2. $75.00

NACENTA, Raymond. *School of Paris.* 1960. NYGS. VG/G+. A1. $60.00

NADELSTERN. *Color Design in Patchwork.* nd. np. ils. wrp. G2. $5.00

NADER, George. *Chrome.* 1978. Putnam. 1st ed. VG/dj. P3. $15.00

NAETHER, Carl A. *Book of the Pigeon.* ca 1939. McKay. 2nd ed. 258 p. F. H1. $10.00

NAGATSUKA, Ryuji. *I Was a Kamakaze.* 1973 (1972). Macmillan. 1st Am ed. 8vo. 212 p. F/F- clip. A2. $20.00

NAHMAD, H.M. *Portion in Paradise & Other Jewish Folktales.* 1970. Norton. xl. 40 stories. VG/VG. S3. $24.00

NAIPAUL, Shiva. *Beyond the Dragon's Mouth.* (1984). Hamish Hamilton. 1st ed. VG/NF. B3. $45.00

NAIPAUL, V.S. *Congo Diary.* 1988. LA. 1/300. sgn/#d. stp red cloth. F/sans. A11. $75.00

NAIPAUL, V.S. *Finding the Centre.* (1984). London. Deutsch. 1st ed. VG/VG. B3. $35.00

NAIPAUL, V.S. *Guerillas.* 1975. London. 1st ed. w/sgn label. F/F. A11. $125.00

NAIPAUL, V.S. *In a Free State.* 1971. Knopf. 1st ed. gilt gr brds. F/NF. C4. $50.00

NAIPAUL, V.S. *India: A Wounded Civilization.* 1977. London. Deutsch. correct 1st ed. author's 2nd book on India. F/F clip. L3. $150.00

NAIPAUL, V.S. *Loss of El Dorado.* (1969). London. Deutsch. 1st ed. F/VG clip. B3. $75.00

NAIPAUL, V.S. *Turn in the S.* 1989. Franklin Lib. 1st ed. sgn. full leather. F. B4. $125.00

NAIRNE, Campbell. *Trossachs & Rob Roy Country.* 1961. Edinburgh. 1st ed. 8vo. 144 p. silvered bl cloth. F/VG. H3. $15.00

NAISON, Mark. *Communists in Harlem During the Depression.* (1983). Urbana. 355 p. NF/NF. A7. $25.00

NAKASA, Nat. *World of Nat Nakasa.* 1975. Johannesburg. Ravan. 125 p. dj. A7. $15.00

NANCE, Lester. *Treeing Walker Hist & Memories.* 1981. Arcadia. 1st ed. sgn. VG/G. O3. $45.00

NANI, Battista. *Hist of Affairs of Europe in This Present Age.* 1673. London. 4to. 573 p. contemporary tree calf. O2. $650.00

NANSEN, Fridtjof. *Eskimoleben.* 1903. Leipzig/Berlin. GM Meyer. later prt. 8vo. 304 p. VG. P4. $75.00

NANSEN, Fridtjof. *Sibirien: Ein Zunkenftsland (Siberia: Land of the Future).* 1914. Leipzig. 1st German ed. ils. pict brds. VG. O6. $75.00

NAPARSTECK, M.J. *War Song.* (1980). Leisure. PBO. VG+. A7. $25.00

NAPIER, J.M. *Hist Sketch of the Darlington Co Agricultural Soc.* ca 1946. np. 1st ed. VG/wrp. M8. $37.50

NARANJO-MORSE, Nora. *Mud Woman: Poems From the Clay.* 1992. Tucson, AZ. AP. F/wrp. L3. $75.00

NARASHIMA & WOELLFEIN. *Spider.* 1992. movable scenes. lg fld tarantula at center. F. A4. $30.00

NARKISS, Bezalel. *Hebrew Illuminated Manuscripts.* 1974. Jerusalem. 2nd prt. folio. 175 p. VG+/VG. S3. $50.00

NASBY, Petroleum V. *Ekkoes From KY.* 1868. Boston. 1st ed. sgn. w/sgn cancelled check. purple cloth. F. A11. $110.00

NASH, Anne. *Cabbages & Crime.* 1945. Crime Club. VG. P3. $15.00

NASH, G.B. *Forging Freedom: Formation of Phil Blk Community 1720-1840.* (1988). Cambridge. Harvard. 1st ed. 354 p. F/dj. A7. $18.00

NASH, Jay Robert. *Bloodletters & Badmen.* 1973. Evans. 1st ed. NF/NF. B2. $65.00

NASH, Ogden. *Ave Ogden! Nash in Latin.* 1973. Boston. 1st ed. trans JC Gleeson/BN Meyer. ils Maryianski. F/dj. B14. $25.00

NASH, Ogden. *Face Is Familiar.* 1942. London. Dent. 1st ed. G/dj. M18. $45.00

NASH, Ogden. *Good Intentions.* 1942. Little Brn. G/dj. A16. $45.00

NASH, Ogden. *Verses From 1929 On.* 1959. Little Brn. 1st ed. NF/dj. E3. $20.00

NASH, Ogden. *Verses.* nd. Little Brn. VG/dj. P3. $15.00

NASH, Paul. *Fertile Image.* 1951. London. Faber. 1st ed. 28 p. tan cloth. F. B22. $10.00

NASH, Wallis. *Two Yrs in OR.* 1882. NY. Appleton. 1st ed. 12mo. ils. 311 p. cloth. VG. D3. $75.00

NASHE, Thomas. *Pierce Penilesse, His Supplication.* 1924. Bodley Head. VG. P3. $35.00

NASMYTH, James. *Moon: Considered As a Planet, a World & a Satellite.* 1874. London. Murray. 2nd ed. xl. octavo. 189 p. teg. VG. H5. $400.00

NASON, Elias. *Life & Public Services of Henry Wilson.* 1876. Boston. 12mo. 452 p. gilt gr cloth. G. T3. $25.00

NASSAU, Gerardo. *Tiberias Sketchbook.* 1962. Tel-Aviv. Massadah. ils. 94 p. VG+/poor. S3. $27.00

NAST, Thomas. *Fight at Dame Europa's School.* 1871. NY. Frances B Felt. The Nast Ed (orig paper ed w/sewn sig). rare. D2. $125.00

NASTASE, Ilie. *Break Point.* 1986. St Martin. 1st ed. F/dj. P3. $16.00

NATHAN, George Jean. *Testament of a Critic.* 1931. Knopf. 1st ed. F/NF. B4. $50.00

NATHAN, Robert. *Heaven & Hell & the Megas Factor.* 1975. Delacorte. 3rd ed. F/dj. P3. $10.00

NATHAN, Robert. *Mr Whittle & the Morning Star.* 1947. Knopf. 1st ed. VG/VG-. P3. $20.00

NATHAN, Robert. *Portrait of Jennie.* 1940. Knopf. 1st ed. F/VG+. B20. $75.00

NATHAN, Robert. *Seagull Cry.* 1942. Knopf. VG/dj. A16. $42.00

NATHAN, Robert. *Winter in April.* 1938. Knopf. VG/dj. A16. $25.00

NATHAN & ERNST. *Iron Horse.* 1931. NY. 1st ed. photos. pict red cloth. F/fair. H3. $25.00

NATIONAL GEOGRAPHIC SOCIETY. *Book of Birds.* 1939. 2 vols. VG/djs. A16. $40.00

NATIONAL GEOGRAPHIC SOCIETY. *Craftsman in Am.* 1975. np. cloth. G2. $15.00

NATIONAL GEOGRAPHIC SOCIETY. *Desert Realm.* 1982. 4to. F. A8. $20.00

NATIONAL GEOGRAPHIC SOCIETY. *Lost Empires, Living Tribes.* 1982. WA, DC. 1st ed. 4to. 402 p. F/VG. B11. $30.00

NATIONAL GEOGRAPHIC SOCIETY. *Wondrous World of Fishes.* (1965). WA. 1st ed. ils/index. 367 p. dj. A17. $15.00

NATSUKI, Shizuko. *Murder on Mt Fuji.* 1984. St Martin. ARC of 1st Am ed. RS. F/F. S5. $27.50

NAUD, Yves. *Curse of the Pharoahs, Vol 1.* 1977. Editions Ferni. 1st ed. decor brds. VG. P3. $15.00

NAUD, Yves. *UFOs & Extraterrestrials, Vol 1.* 1978. Editions Ferni. 1st ed. decor brds. VG. P3. $18.00

NAUNTON, Robert. *Fragment Regalia; or, Observations on Late Queen Elizabeth.* 1642. Lodnon. 3rd ed. sm quarto. Club Bindery morocco. F. H5. $475.00

NAVA, Michael. *Golden Boy.* 1988. Boston. Alyson. 1st ed. sgn. NF/NF. A14. $30.00

NAVA. *Book of Knitting.* 1984. np. ils/42 patterns. wrp. G2. $16.00

NAYLER, James. *Collection of Sundry Books, Epistles & Papers, Part II.* 1829. Cincinnati. BC Stanton. 8vo. leather. G+. V3. $120.00

NAYLOR, Gloria. *Bailey's Cafe.* 1992. HBJ. ARC. F/ils wrp. A13. $25.00

NAYLOR, Gloria. *Mama Day.* 1988. Ticknor Fields. 1st ed. rem mk. NF/NF. A13. $25.00

NAYLOR, James Ball. *In the Days of St Clair.* 1913. Akron. ils. 420 p. VG/remnant dj. B18. $15.00

NAYLOR, Phyllis Reynolds. *Dark of the Tunnel.* 1985. Atheneum. 1st ed. F/dj. P3. $12.00

NEAL, Fred Warner. *Titoism in Action.* 1958. Berkeley. 331 p. dj. A7. $25.00

NEAL, Marie C. *In Honolulu Gardens.* 1929 (1928). Honolulu. 2nd revised ed/1st prt. 336 p. VG. B28. $50.00

NEALATON, Eugene. *These Pour le Doctorat en Medecine.* 1860. Paris. Rignoux. 375 p. orig wrp. G7. $250.00

NEALE, Samuel. *Some Account of Life & Religious Labours of...* 1806. Phil. 12mo. 97 p. leather. G. T3. $22.00

NEARING, Scott. *Next Step.* 1922. Ridgewood. Nellie Seeds Nearing. 1st ed. NF. B2. $40.00

NEARING, Scott. *War: Organized Destruction & Mass Murder...* ca 1931. Vanguard. 310 p. H10. $25.00

NEARLING, J. Jr. *Sinister Researches of CP Ransom.* 1954. Doubleday. 1st ed. VG/dj. P3. $35.00

NEATBY, Leslie H. *Search for Franklin.* 1970. NY. Walker. 281 p. bl cloth. VG/worn. P4. $28.50

NEBENZAHL, Kenneth. *Atlas of the Am Revolution.* 1974. Chicago. Rand McNally. folio. 54 color maps. M/dj. O6. $125.00

NEBENZAHL, Kenneth. *Bibliography of Prt Battle Plans of Am Revolution...* 1975. Chicago/London. Chicago U. 160 p. O5. $15.00

NEBENZAHL, Kenneth. *Catalogue 3. Old & Rare Maps.* 1959. Chicago. 8vo. 58 p. wrp. H9. $25.00

NEEDHAM, Joseph. *Time: Refreshing River (Essays & Addresses 1932-42).* 1943. London. Allen Unwin. 1st ed. 280 p. gr cloth. VG/clip. G1. $40.00

NEEL, Janet. *Death on Site.* 1989. London. Constable. 1st ed. F/F. M15. $45.00

NEELY, Richard. *Walter Syndrome.* nd. BC. VG/dj. P3. $8.00

NEELY & MCMURTRY. *Insanity File: Case of Mary Todd Lincoln.* (1986). Carbondale, IL. 2nd prt. 8vo. 204 p. F/F. A2. $12.50

NEESE, George Michael. *3 Yrs in Confederate Horse Artillery.* 1911. NY/WA. Neale. 1st ed. 362 p. gr cloth. VG. scarce. M8. $650.00

NEESER, R.W. *Landsman's Log.* 1913. New Haven, CT. Yale. 1st ed. 8vo. 199 p. F. A2. $35.00

NEIDER, Charles. *Beyond Cape Horn: Travels in the Antarctic.* (1980). San Francisco. 1st ed. 385 p. dj. A17. $16.50

NEIDER, Charles. *Mark Twain & the Russians.* 1960. NY. Hill Wang. PBO. inscr. 32 p. VG+/wrp. A11. $45.00

NEIDLINGER, W.H. *Sm Songs for Sm Singers.* nd (1924). NY. 1st thus ed. photos Bobbett. VG+. B22. $22.50

NEIHARDT, John. *Poetic Values: Their Reality & Our Need of Them.* 1925. Macmillan. 1st ed. 144 p. F. A18. $50.00

NEIHARDT, John. *Song of Hugh Glass.* 1915. Macmillan. 1st ed. F. A18. $40.00

NEIHARDT, John. *When the Tree Flowered.* 1951. NY. 1st ed. VG/VG. B5. $45.00

NEILL, Edward D. *Hist of MN: From Earliest French Explorations...* 1873. Phil/Minneapolis. 2nd ed. royal 8vo. rebacked. VG. D3. $75.00

NEILL, John R. *Lucky Buckey in Oz.* 1942. Reilly Lee. 1st ed/1st state. his last Oz book. VG/VG 1st state. D1. $400.00

NEILL, John R. *Scalawagons of Oz.* 1941. Reilly Lee. later prt. 309 p. VG. M20. $90.00

NEILL, Robert. *Elegant Witch.* 1952. Doubleday. 1st ed. VG. P3. $10.00

NEILL, Robert. *Mist Over Pendle.* 1974. Hutchinson. 9th prt. VG/dj. P3. $15.00

NEILSEN, Kay. *E of the Sun & W of the Moon.* no date. Garden City. 4to. blk cloth w/pict label. G+. A3. $45.00

NEILSEN, Waldo. *Right-of-Way. Guide to Abandoned Railroads in the US.* ca 1974. Bend, OR. Old Bottle Magazine. lg 4to. 119 p. pict wrp. H9. $35.00

NEIMAN, LeRoy. *Horses.* 1979. Abrams. 1st ed. presentation. VG/VG. O3. $595.00

NEIMARK, Anne E. *Che: Latin Am's Legendary Guerrilla Leader.* (1989). Lippincott. 1st ed. 113 p. NF/NF. A7. $9.00

NEINSTEIN, Raymond L. *Ghost Country.* 1976. Berkeley. Creative Arts Book Co. F/wrp. L3. $30.00

NELSON, C.M. *Barren Harvest.* 1949. Crime Club. 1st ed. VG-. P3. $6.00

NELSON, Charles. *Boy Who Picked Up the Bullets.* 1981. Morrow. 1st ed. F/F. A7. $30.00

NELSON, Daniel. *Am Rubber Workers & Organized Labor, 1900-41.* ca 1988. Princeton. photos. M. V4. $15.00

NELSON, Edna. *O'Higgins & Don Bernardo.* 1954. Dutton. 1st ed. 384 p. dj. F3. $15.00

NELSON, Faith. *Randolph: Bear Who Said No.* (1940). Wonder Books. ils Nedda Walker. pict brds. G+. T5. $25.00

NELSON, Frederic. *Bachelors Are People Too.* (1964). WA, DC. 1st ed. 8vo. 270 p. VG+/VG-. A2. $15.00

NELSON, Gaylord. *Am's Last Chance.* (1970). Waukesha. lg 4to. photos. 98 p. F/dj. A17. $12.50

NELSON, Hugh Lawrence. *Dead Giveaway.* 1950. Rinehart. 1st ed. VG. P3. $13.00

NELSON, John Louw. *Rhythm for Rain.* 1937. Boston. 1st ed. ils. 271 p. cloth. VG+. D3. $35.00

NELSON, Maidee Thomas. *CA: Land of Promise.* 1962. Caxton. 8vo. F/fair. A8. $25.00

NELSON, Ray. *Memoirs of an OR Moonshiner.* 1976. Caldwell. wrp. N2. $5.00

NELSON, Raymond. *Van Wyck Brooks: A Writer's Life.* 1981. NY. Dutton. 1st ed. 8vo. 332 p. F/NF. P4. $15.00

NELSON, Shirley. *Fair, Clear & Terrible: Story of Shiloh...* (1989). Latham, NY. British-Am Pub. 1st ed. 8vo. 446 p. F/F. A2. $15.00

NELSON, William. *Rights of the Clergy of Great Britain.* 1709. London. Charles Harper. 1st ed. 522 p. modern calf/red leather spine label. K1. $200.00

NELSON. *Contemporary British Quilt Art.* 1989. np. ils. cloth. G2. $35.00

NEMEROV, Howard. *Homecoming Game.* 1957. NY. 1st ed. w/sgn bookplate. NF/NF. A11. $60.00

NEMEROV, Howard. *W Approaches: Poems 1973-75.* 1975. Chicago. 1st ed. F/F. V1. $30.00

NEPHEW. *My Mother's Quilts: Designs from the Thirties.* 1988. np. ils. wrp. G2. $15.00

NEPHEW. *Quilts From a Different Angle.* 1986. np. ils. wrp. G2. $9.00

NERUDA, Pablo. *20 Poems.* 1967. np. 60s Pr. 1st ed. NF/wrp. B2. $50.00

NESBIT, E. *Five Children & It.* nd. Looking Glass Lib. ils. VG/VG. P2. $15.00

NESS, Evaline. *Sam, Bangs & Moonshine.* 1966. HRW. 1st ed. 4to. pict bl brds. T5. $55.00

NESS. *Norwegian Smyrna Cross-Stitch.* 1982. np. 39 charted design. wrp. G2. $3.00

NESS. *Swedish Tvistsom Embroidery.* 1981. np. ils. wrp. G2. $3.00

NESVADBA, Josef. *Lost Face.* 1971. Taplinger. 1st ed. VG/VG. P3. $15.00

NETANYAHU, B. *Don Isaac Abravanel, Statesman & Philosopher.* 1953. JPS. 346 p. VG. S3. $22.00

NETANYAHU, B. *Terrorism: How the W Can Win.* 1986. FSC. 2nd prt. 37 essays. 254 p. VG+/VG+. S3. $23.00

NETHERTON & NETHERTON. *Fairfax Co in VA: Pict Hist.* ca 1986. Donning. ils. VG/VG. B10. $25.00

NETHERY, Wallace. *Saul Marks, Printer.* 1984. LA. Dawson Book Shop. miniature. 1/40. 22 p. F/wrp. H10. $25.00

NEUGEBAUER, O. *Exact Sciences in Antiquity.* 1952. Princeton. 1st ed/Am issue. 192 p. blk cloth. VG. G1. $45.00

NEUGROSCHEL, Joachim. *Shtetl: Creative Anthology of Jewish Life in E Europe.* 1979. Marek. 20 stories. 572 p. VG+/VG+. S3. $25.00

NEUMAN & PLUTO. *Baseball Winter.* 1986. Macmillan. 1st ed. M/M. P8. $10.00

NEVADA, Richard. *Treasure Along the Trail.* 1968. private prt. 8vo. VG. A8. $15.00

NEVILLE, Amelia Ransome. *Fantastic City. Memoirs of...San Fancisco.* 1932. Boston. 1st ed. lg 8vo. 285 p. VG. B28. $35.00

NEVILLE, Hugh. *Game Laws of Eng for Gamekeepers.* 1879. London. Davis. red cloth. M11. $125.00

NEVILLE, Margot. *Murder of a Nymph.* 1950. Crime Club. 1st ed. NF/dj. P3. $15.00

NEVIN, David. *Expressmen.* 1974. Time Life. 4to. F. A8. $10.00

NEVIN, David. *Soldiers.* 1973. Time Life. 4to. F. A8. $10.00

NEVIN, David. *Texans.* 1975. Time Life. 4to. F. A8. $10.00

NEVINS, Allan. *Herbert H Lehman & His Era.* 1963. Scribner. 456 p. VG/fair. S3. $25.00

NEVINS, Allan. *Letters of Grover Cleveland 1850-1908.* 1933. Boston. 1st ed. 640 p. VG. B18. $25.00

NEVINS & WRIGHT. *World Without Time. The Bedouin.* 1969. John Day. 1st ed. photos/maps/glossary. gilt sand cloth. F/VG. M7. $40.00

NEW ENGLAND YEARLY MEETING. *Rules of Discipline of Yearly Meeting Held on RI.* 1826. New Bedford. B Lindsey. sm 8vo. 156 p. G. V3. $16.00

NEWARK. *Lincoln: A Memorial.* 1912. Newark. 64 p. A6. $10.00

NEWBERRY, Clare T. *April's Kittens.* 1940. Harper. Caldecott Honor. VG/VG. P2. $30.00

NEWBERRY, Clare T. *Pandora.* 1944. NY. folio. 7 pls. 34 p. VG. H3. $45.00

NEWBERRY, J.S. *Flora of Amboy Clays.* 1895. WA, DC. ils/pls. 260 p. VG. B28. $45.00

NEWBERRY, J.S. *Rainbow Bridge: Study of Paganism.* 1934. Houghton Mifflin. 1st ed. 8vo. 346 p. VG/G. A2. $25.00

NEWBERRY, Mike. *Goldwaterism.* 1964. NY. Marzani Munsell. 64 p. wrp. A7. $16.00

NEWBERRY LIBRARY. *Narratives of Captivity Among Indians of N Am.* 1912-28. Chicago. Newberry. 1st ed. 2 vols. orig prt wrp. M8. $350.00

NEWBY, Eric. *Big Red Train Ride: Ride on Trans-Siberian Railway.* (1978). St Martin. 1st Am ed. 8vo. 267 p. VG/VG+. A2. $12.50

NEWBY, P.H. *Barbary Light.* 1962. London. 1st ed. inscr. NF/NF. A11. $45.00

NEWBY, P.H. *Guest & His Going.* 1960. London. 1st ed. w/sgn label. VG+/VG+. A11. $45.00

NEWCOMB, Covelle. *Secret Door: Story of Kate Greenaway.* 1946. Dodd Mead. 1st ed. ils Addison Burbank. 162 p. VG+/dj. M20. $40.00

NEWCOMB, Raymond Lee. *Our Lost Explorers: Narrative Jeannette Arctic Expedition.* 1883. Hartford. Am Pub. 8vo. ils. 479 p. rebound/orig spine. P4. $95.00

NEWCOMB, Richard F. *Savo.* 1961. HRW. ils/maps/photos. G/dj. A16. $17.50

NEWELL, Chester. *Hist of the Revolution in TX, Particularly...War of 1835...* 1838. Wiley Putnam. 12mo. fld onionskin map. 215 p. emb brn cloth. H9. $450.00

NEWELL, H.M. *Hardhats.* ca 1955. Houghton Mifflin. BC. VG/G. V4. $7.50

NEWHAFER, Richard. *No More Bubbles in the Sky.* (1966). NAL. 1st ed. VG/VG. A7. $60.00

NEWHAFER, Richard. *Violators.* (1967). Signet. G. A7. $10.00

NEWHALL, Frederic Cushman. *With Gen Sheridan in Lee's Last Campaign. By Staff Officer.* 1866. Lippincott. 1st ed. fld map. 235 p. cloth. NF. M8. $150.00

NEWHOUSE. *Creative Hand Embroideries.* 1992. np. pb. G2. $9.00

NEWMAN, Bernard. *Round About Andorra.* 1928. Boston. 1st Am ed. ils C Henley Gardner. 300 p. tan buckram. VG. H3. $30.00

NEWMAN, Daisy. *Golden String.* 1986. San Francisco. Harper Row. BC. 8vo. 185 p. VG/VG. V3. $9.00

NEWMAN, Ernest. *Life of Richard Wagner.* 1933-36. Knopf. 3 vols. G. A16. $60.00

NEWMAN, George. *Quaker Profiles.* 1946. London. Bannisdale. 1st ed. 12mo. 134 p. G+. V3. $12.00

NEWMAN, John Henry. *Apologia pro Vita Sua...* 1864. London. Longman. 1st ed. rebacked w/orig spine. H10. $100.00

NEWMAN, John Henry. *Autobiographical Writings...* ca 1957. London. Sheed Ward. 338 p. H10. $15.00

NEWMAN, John Henry. *On the Inspiration of Scripture...* ca 1967. WA, DC. Corpus. 1st ed. 153 p. H10. $15.00

NEWMAN, John Henry. *Via Media of the Anglican Church...* 1877. London. Basil Montague Pickering. 2 vols. H10. $25.00

NEWMAN, Kim. *Night Mayor.* 1989. Simon Schuster. 1st ed. sgn. F/F. P3. $30.00

NEWMAN, Paul S. *Showdown on Front Street.* 1969. Whitman. VG. P3. $8.00

NEWMAN, Peter C. *King of the Castle: Making of a Dynasty.* 1979. Atheneum. 2nd prt. 304 p. VG. S3. $23.00

NEWMAN, Ralph. *Abraham Lincoln Industry.* 1954. Hist Bulletin 13. Lincoln Fellowship of WI. 1/600. VG. A6. $10.00

NEWMAN, Zipp. *Impact of S Football.* 1969. Montgomery, AL. 1st ed. sgn. VG/dj. N2. $15.00

NEWMAN & NEWMAN. *Paper As Art & Craft.* 1973. NY. VG/dj. B30. $20.00

NEWMAN & WINCHE. *Great & Good Books: A Bibliographical Catalogue...* 1989. Chicago. 1st ed. 1/500. intro/sgn Adler. F/pub slipcase. M8. $85.00

NEWMAN. *Quilting, Patchwork, Applique & Trapunto.* 1974. np. ils. wrp. G2. $15.00

NEWMYER & SCHROEDER. *Gamebird Taxidermy w/Frank Newmyer.* (1989). Stackpole. 1st ed. ils/photos. 256 p. M/dj. A17. $22.50

NEWPORT, David. *Pleasures of Home.* 1884. Phil. Lippincott. 1st ed. 12mo. 99 p. VG. V3. $10.00

NEWTON, A. Edward. *Derby Day & Other Adventures.* 1969. Books for Lib Pr. reprint. F. T8. $15.00

NEWTON, A. Edward. *Dr Johnson: A Play.* 1923. Boston. 1st trade ed. NF. T8. $25.00

NEWTON, A. Edward. *Greatest Book in the World.* 1925. np. 4th imp. F. T8. $20.00

NEWTON, A. Edward. *Tourist in Spite of Himself.* 1930. Boston. 1st ed. F/NF. T8. $20.00

NEWTON, Isaac. *Arithmetica Universalis...* 1732. Leiden. 3rd Latin ed. quarto. 13 fld pls. contemporary calf. VG. H5. $2,500.00

NEWTON, Isaac. *Opticks; or, Treatise of Reflections, Refractions...Light.* 1730. London. Innys. 4th ed. octavo. 12 fld pls. 283 p. contemporary calf. VG. H5. $1,250.00

NIALL, Bernard. *Kaiser Vs Bismark.* 1921. Harper. 1st ed. 8vo. G+. A8. $20.00

NIATUM, Duane. *After the Death of an Elder Klallam.* (1970). Phoenix. Baleen. 2nd prt. inscr to poet Richard Eberhart. F/wrp. L3. $45.00

NIATUM, Duane. *Ascending Red Cedar Moon.* 1973. Harper Row. 1st ed. inscr/dtd 1974. NF/dj. L3. $125.00

NIATUM, Duane. *Digging Out the Roots.* 1977. Harper Row. 1st ed. F/F. L3. $50.00

NIATUM, Duane. *Pieces.* 1981. Strawberry Pr. pamphlet collection. F/stapled wrp. L3. $35.00

NIATUM, Duane. *Songs for the Harvester of Dreams.* 1981. Seattle. WA U. 1st ed. sgn. F/NF. L3. $75.00

NIATUM, Duane. *Taos Pueblo.* 1973. Greenfield Review. 1st ed. inscr/dtd 1974. w/sgn letter dtd 1976. F/wrp. L3. $125.00

NIBLACK, Albert Parker. *Coast Indians of S AK & N British Columbia.* 1890. GPO. 8vo. 71 pls/fld maps. F. P4. $250.00

NICHOLAS, D. *Bibliography of Peter Matthiessen, 1951-79.* 1979. Canoga Park. Oriana Pr. 1st ed. ils. NF. C4. $35.00

NICHOLS, Beverly. *Garden Open Tomorrow.* 1968. London. ils Willaim McLaren. 296 p. VG/dj. B26. $36.00

NICHOLS, Beverly. *Laughter on the Stairs.* 1953. Dutton. 1st ed. 254 p. VG/dj. M20. $50.00

NICHOLS, Carl W. *Sons of Arthur.* 1994. Gr Chapel. 1/99. 20-p booklet. VG/stiff wrp. C1. $10.00

NICHOLS, Hugh. *Passages W: 19 Stories of Youth & Identity.* (1993). Confluence Pr. 1st sc ed. sgn. M. A18. $17.50

NICHOLS, John. *Fragile Beauty.* (1987). Salt Lake City. Peregrine. 1st ed. inscr. NF/F. B3. $45.00

NICHOLS, John. *Nirvana Blues.* 1981. HRW. 1st ed. inscr. F/F. C4. $50.00

NICHOLS, John. *Nirvana Blues.* 1981. NY. 1st ed. VG/VG. B5. $25.00

NICHOLS, John. *Sterile Cuckoo.* (1965). McKay. BC. inscr. F/NF. B3. $25.00

NICHOLS, Leigh; see Koontz, Dean R.

NICHOLS, Nell B. *Let's Start To Cook.* 1966. Doubleday. G/dj. A16. $10.00

NICHOLS, Ruth. *Left-Handed Spirit.* 1978. Canada. Macmillan. VG/dj. P3. $13.00

NICHOLS, T.L. *Scamper Across Europe.* 1873. London. Longman. 1st ed. 16mo. 64 p. prt gr wrp. M1. $225.00

NICHOLSON, Irene. *Firefly in the Night.* (1959). NY. Grove. 1st ed. ils. 231 p. dj. F3. $30.00

NICHOLSON, John. *Farmer's Assistant.* 1814. Albany, NY. 1st ed. 8vo. 327 p. M1. $250.00

NICHOLSON, Kenyon. *Barker.* nd. Grosset Dunlap. photoplay ed. VG. P3. $25.00

NICHOLSON, Loren. *Rails Across the Ranchos.* 1980. Valley Pub. ils/notes/index. 197 p. F/NF. B19. $45.00

NICHOLSON, William. *British Encyclopedia; or, Dictionary Arts & Sciences.* 1818. Phil. xl. odd vol. 7 full-p pls. leather. G. T3. $17.00

NICHOLSON. *Canvas Work Simplified.* 1973. np. ils. cloth. G2. $6.00

NICKERSON, E.B. *Kayaks to the Arctic.* 1967. Berkeley. Howell. 8vo. 197 p. F/NF. P4. $25.00

NICKERSON, Susan D. *Bread-Winners.* 1871. Boston. Nichols Hall. 1st ed. 12mo. 295 p. cloth. M1. $100.00

NICOL, Eric. *Say Uncle.* 1961. Harper. VG/dj. P3. $10.00

NICOLAEVSKY, Boris. *Power & the Soviet Elite.* (1965). Praeger. 275 p. NF/clip. A7. $20.00

NICOLAI, Nicola Maria. *Memorie, Leggi ed Osservazioni Sulle Campagne Sull'annona...* 1803. Rome. Nella Stamperia Pagliarini. 3 vols. 19th-century bdg. K1. $300.00

NICOLAI, Rudolf. *Geschichte der Neugriechischen Literatur.* 1876. Leipzig. 8vo. 239 p. quarter calf. O2. $45.00

NICOLAIDES, Kimon. *Natural Way To Draw: Working Plan for Art Study.* 1941. Houghton Mifflin. dj. N2. $10.00

NICOLAS, Nicholas Harris. *Hist of the Royal Navy From Earliest Times...* 1847. London. Bentley. 1st ed. 2 vols. marbled ep/edges. contemporary red calf. VG. H5. $225.00

NICOLAY, Charles G. *OR Territory.* 1846. London. Charles Knight. new ed/2nd issue. 16mo. 226 p. half calf (rpr). H9. $150.00

NICOLAY, Helen. *Boys' Life of Abraham Lincoln.* 1906. NY. Century. 1st ed/14th prt. 307 p. cloth. NF/dj. M8. $45.00

NICOLAY, Helen. *Lincoln's Secretary: Biography of John G Nicolay.* 1949. Longman Gr. 1st ed. 363 p. cloth. VG. M8. $45.00

NICOLAY, Helen. *Personal Traits of Abraham Lincoln.* 1912. NY. Century. 1st ed. 8 pls. 387 p. cloth. NF. M8. $45.00

NICOLAY, John G. *Short Life of Abraham Lincoln...: A Hist.* 1906. NY. Century. 578 p. cloth. NF. M8. $45.00

NICOLE, Christopher. *Caribee.* 1974. St Martin. 1st ed. F/F. P3. $13.00

NICOLE, John Ernest. *Psychopathology: Survey of Modern Approaches.* 1930. NY. 1st Am ed. 203 p. cloth. G1. $25.00

NICOLL, M.J. *Three Voyages of a Naturalist.* 1909. London. Witherby. 2nd ed. 8vo. pls/4 maps. 246 p. bl brds. B11. $65.00

NICOLSON, Harold. *Journey to Java.* 1957. London. Constable. 1st ed. 8vo. 8 pls. 254 p. VG. W1. $18.00

NIEBUHR, Carsten. *Voyage en Arabie...* 1776-80. Amsterdam. 1st French ed. quarto. 2 vols. contemporary French calf. F. H5. $5,500.00

NIEBURG, H.L. *In the Name of Science: Chilling Account...* 1966. NY. Quadrangle. 1st prt. inscr. 472 p. VG/dj. S9. $8.00

NIEDECKER, Lorine. *N Central.* 1968. London. 1st ed. 8vo. F/wht dj. A11. $45.00

NIEDRACH & ROCKWELL. *Birds of Denver & Mtn Parks.* 1939. CO Mus Natural Hist. F. scarce. T8. $25.00

NIELSEN, Torben. *Gallowsbird's Song.* 1976. Collins Crime Club. 1st ed. VG/dj. P3. $15.00

NIGHTINGALE, Florence. *Notes on Nursing: What It Is & What It Is Not.* 1860. NY. Appleton. 1st Am ed. 140 p. brn cloth. NF. B14. $50.00

NILES, Blair. *Journeys in Time.* (1946). Coward McCann. 1st ed. 404 p. dj. F3. $15.00

NILES, Blair. *Peruvian Pageant.* (1937). Bobbs Merrill. 1st ed. 311 p. dj. F3. $20.00

NILES, John M. *Hist of S Am & Mexico.* 1837. Hartford. 2 vols in 1. 2 fld maps. new half morocco. H9. $775.00

NILES, John M. *View of S Am & Mexico.* 1825. NY. Huntington. 12mo. Simon Bolivar portrait. contemporary calf. H9. $85.00

NIMOY, Leonard. *You & I.* 1973. Millbrae. Celestial Arts. later prt. sgn. ils. NF/pict wrp. N3. $15.00

NIN, Anais. *House of Incest.* 1947. Gemor. 1st Am ed. sgn. VG/sans. M18. $200.00

NIN, Anais. *On Writing.* 1947. Alicat Bookshop. Outcast Chapbook 11. 1/1000. VG/stapled wrp. L3. $125.00

NIN, Anais. *Spy in the House of Love.* 1954. British Book Centre. 1st Am ed. G/dj. M18. $55.00

NISBET, Jim. *Death Puppet.* 1989. Blk Lizard. 1st ed. F/dj. P3. $20.00

NISBET, John. *British Forest Trees...* 1893. London. Macmillan. 1st ed. 352 p. H10. $12.50

NISBOT, E.H. *Sleepless Men.* 1959. Crime Club. 1st ed. VG-/dj. P3. $15.00

NISHIKAWA. *Elegant Needlework.* 1988. np. ils. wrp. G2. $11.00

NISTER, Ernest. *Favorite Animals, an Antique Picture Book.* 1989. movable scenes designed by Keith Moseley. NF. A4. $25.00

NIVEN, Larry. *Magic Goes Away.* 1978. Grosset Dunlap. 1st ed. sgn. F/F. P3. $30.00

NIVEN, Larry. *Smoke Ring.* 1987. Ballantine. 1st ed. F/F. T2. $18.00

NIVEN, Larry. *Time of the Warlock.* 1984. Steeldragon. 1st ed. F/dj. M18. $20.00

NIVEN, Larry. *World Out of Time.* nd. HRW. 2nd ed. VG/dj. P3. $13.00

NIVEN, POURNELLE & BARNES. *Legacy of Heorot.* 1987. London. Gollancz. 1st ed. sgns. F/F. T2. $56.00

NIVEN, POURNELLE & BARNES. *Legacy of Heorot.* 1987. Simon Schuster. 1st Am ed. F/F. T2. $25.00

NIVEN & POURNELLE. *Footfall.* 1985. Del Rey. 1st ed. F/F. P3. $18.00

NIVEN & POURNELLE. *Lucifer's Hammer.* 1977. Playboy. 1st ed. F/F. M2. $50.00

NIVEN & POURNELLE. *Lucifer's Hammer.* 1977. Playboy. 1st ed. F/NF. N3. $45.00

NIVEN & POURNELLE. *Oath of Fealty.* 1982. Macdonald. 1st ed. F/F. P3. $25.00

NIXON, Alan. *Attack on Vienna.* 1972. St Martin. 1st ed. F/F. P3. $13.00

NIXON, O.W. *Whitman's Ride Through Savage Lands...* 1905. np. Winona. 1st ed. 186 p. pict cloth. VG+. H7. $35.00

NIXON, Richard Milhous. *Inaugural Address of...* 1969. Worcester. St Onge. miniature. 1/1500. F. H10. $32.50

NIXON, Richard. *Challenges We Face.* (1960). McGraw Hill. 1st ed. author's 1st book. 8vo. 253 p. F/VG. A2. $30.00

NIXON, Richard. *Leaders.* 1982. Warner. 1st ed. F/F. T2. $14.00

NOBLE & ROSE. *Counties of Chester, Derby, Leicester, Lincoln & Rutland.* 1836. London. 1st ed. 36 pl p. aeg. gilt gr cloth. VG+. H3. $225.00

NOEL, Bernard. *Mexican Art.* 1968. NY. Tudor. 12mo. 24 pls. 4 vols. F3. $25.00

NOEL, Mary. *Villains Galore.* 1954. NY. 1st prt. 320 p. cloth. NF/pict dj. D3. $35.00

NOEL HUME, Ivor. *Martin's Hundred.* 1982. Knopf. 1st ed. 343 p. F/VG. B10. $25.00

NOGUCHI, Yone. *Hiroshige.* 1934. London. Kegan Paul. 1/1000. w/2 orig woodblock prts. portfolio/ivory clasps. K1. $200.00

NOLAN, Frederick. *Kill Petrosino!* 1975. Arthur Baker. 1st ed. VG/dj. P3. $20.00

NOLAN, Jeannette Covert. *Sudden Squall.* 1955. Ives Washburn. 1st ed. sgn. 185 p. VG/dj. M20. $25.00

NOLAN, Keith William. *Battle for Hue, Tet 1968.* 1983. Novato, CA. Presidio. 1st ed. sm 8vo. ils/map. 237 p. VG/dj. W1. $18.00

NOLAN, Keith William. *Operation Buffalo.* (1991). Presidio. 1st ed. F/F. A7. $16.00

NOLAN, William A. *Communism Vs the Negro.* 1951. Chicago. Regnery. 276 p. A7. $20.00

NOLAN, William F. *Blk Mask Boys: Masters Hard-Boiled School Detective Fiction.* 1985. Morrow. 1st ed. 273 p. NF/F. B22. $10.00

NOLAN, William F. *Blk Mask Boys: Masters in Hard-Boiled...Fiction.* 1985. Morrow. 1st ed. sgn. F/F. S5. $45.00

NOLAN, William F. *Max Band's Best W Stories.* 1981. Dodd Mead. NF/dj. B9. $25.00

NOLAN, William. *Wht Cad Cross-Up.* 1969. Sherbourne. 1st ed. xl. dj. P3. $10.00

NOLL, Arthur. *From Empire to Republic.* 1903. McClurg. 1st ed. 336 p. F3. $15.00

NOLLAU, Gunther. *Internat Communism & World Revolution.* 1961. Praeger. rem mk. 357 p. dj. A7. $22.00

NOLLET, Jean Antoine. *Essai sur l'Electricite des Corps.* 1753. Paris. Les Freres Guerin. 2nd ed. sm 8vo. pls. contemporary mottled calf. K1. $275.00

NOONE, Edwina; see Avallone, Mike.

NORDEN, Pierre. *Conan Doyle: A Biography.* 1967. Holt. 1st Am ed. ils. F/F. S5. $25.00

NORDENSKIOLD, A.E. *Facsimile Atlas to Early Hist of Cartography.* 1973. Dover. reprint. VG+/wrp. O6. $25.00

NORDENSKIOLD, Erik. *Hist of Biology.* 1935. Tudor. new ed/1st prt. 630 p. prt gr cloth. VG. G1. $37.50

NORDENSKOILD, Nils Adolf Erik. *Nordenskiold. Notice sur sa vie et ses Voyages.* 1880. Paris. Nilson. octavo. portrait. H9. $125.00

NORDHOFF, Charles. *CA: For Health, Pleasure & Residence.* 1873. NY. 255 p. G. D7. $60.00

NORDHOFF, Charles. *Communistic Societies of the US, From Personal Hist...* 1960 (1875). NY. Hillary House. reprint. VG/fair. V4. $12.50

NORDHOFF, Charles. *Communistic Societies of the US, From Personal Visit...* 1875. NY. Harper. 1st ed. 439 p. G. D7/H7. $125.00

NORDHOFF, Charles. *Communistic Societies of the US, From Personal Visit...* 1962. NY. Hillary House. 3rd prt. VG. N2. $20.00

NORDHOFF, Charles. *Hist of Playing Cards.* 1977. Buffalo. Hillside. miniature. 1/250. 48 p. F. H10. $32.50

NORDHOFF, Charles. *N CA, OR & the Sandwich Islands.* 1874. NY. Harper. 1st ed. 4to. 256 p. bl-gray cloth. H7/H9. $100.00

NORDHOFF, Charles. *Penninsular CA.* 1888. NY. Harper. 4to. 130 p. bl cloth. H9. $75.00

NORDON, Pierre. *Conan Doyle.* 1966. John Murray. 1st ed. VG/dj. P3. $30.00

NORFOLK, William; see Farmer, Philip Jose.

NORMAN, Barry. *Matter of Mandrake.* 1968. Walker. 1st ed. VG/VG. P3. $13.00

NORMAN, Diana. *Tom Corbett's Stately Ghosts of Eng.* 1970. Taplinger. VG/VG. P3. $15.00

NORMAN, Frank. *Bang to Rights. Account of Prison Life.* 1958. London. 1st ed. NF/VG. A11. $50.00

NORMAN, Frank. *Too Many Crooks Spoil the Caper.* 1979. St Martin. 1st ed. VG/VG. P3. $15.00

NORMAN, Henry Wylie. *Report of the W Indies Royal Commission...* 1897. London. 172 p. half leather. VG. O6. $85.00

NORMAN, Jeremy M. *Morton's Medical Bibliography.* 1991. Scholar Pr. 5th ed. 1241 p. M. G7. $145.00

NORMAN, Michael. *These Good Men: Friendships Forged From War.* (1989). Crown. 1st prt. photos. 310 p. dj. A7. $15.00

NORMAN, Philip. *Elton John: The Biography.* 1991. Harmony. 1st ed. VG/VG. P3. $23.00

NORRIS, Frank. *McTeague: Story of San Francisco.* 1982. Franklin Lib. 1st ed. presentation. VG. A18. $30.00

NORRIS, Frank. *Moran of the Lady Letty.* 1898. NY. 1st ed. 12mo. 293 p. VG. D3. $75.00

NORRIS, Frank. *Vandover & the Brute.* 1914. Doubleday. 1st ed. VG. A18. $30.00

NORSE, Harold. *Beat Hotel.* 1983. San Diego. 1st Am ed. sgn. F/ils wrp. A11. $40.00

NORTH, Andrew; see Norton, Alice.

NORTH, Anthony; see Koontz, Dean R.

NORTH, Eric. *Ant Men.* 1955. Winston. 1st ed. VG. P3. $25.00

NORTH, Howard. *Expressway.* 1973. Simon Schuster. 1st ed. VG/dj. P3. $20.00

NORTH, Marianne. *Vision of Eden.* 1980. NY. 1st Am ed. ils. 240 p. VG/dj. B26. $35.00

NORTH, Sterling. *Midnight & Jeremiah.* 1943. Winston. 1st ed. ils Kurt Wiese. VG. M5. $12.00

NORTH, Sterling. *Rascal: Memoir of a Better Era.* 1963. Dutton. 1st ed. 189 p. gilt brn cloth. VG/VG. S10. $20.00

NORTHROP, Henry D. *Armenian Massacres; or, Sword of Mohammed.* 1896. WA. 8vo. ils. 512 p. pict cloth. F. O2. $60.00

NORTHROP, Henry D. *Wonders of the Tropics.* 1890. Chicago. 8vo. pls. 848 p. gilt bl cloth. VG. H3. $40.00

NORTHRUP, Herbert R. *Negro in the Paper Industry.* (1969). Phil. 233 p. clip dj. A7. $23.00

NORTHRUP & ROWAN. *Studies of Negro Employment.* (1970). PA U. 769 p. VG+/dj. A7. $35.00

NORTON, Andre. *Android at Arms.* 1971. HBJ. 1st ed. NF/dj. P3. $85.00

NORTON, Andre. *Forerunner Foray.* nd. BC. VG/dj. P3. $8.00

NORTON, Andre. *Four From the Witch World.* 1989. Tor. 1st ed. F/F. P3. $17.00

NORTON, Andre. *Garan the Eternal.* 1972. Alhambra. Fantasy. 1st ed. F/NF. N3. $25.00

NORTON, Andre. *Golden Trillium.* 1993. Bantam. 1st ed. F/F. N3. $15.00

NORTON, Andre. *Iron Cage.* 1974. Viking. 1st ed. F/F. P3. $35.00

NORTON, Andre. *Jargoon Pard.* 1974. Atheneum. 1st ed. F/dj. P3. $30.00

NORTON, Andre. *Opal-Eyed Fan.* 1977. Dutton. 1st ed. VG/VG. P3. $20.00

NORTON, Andre. *Small Shadows Creep.* 1974. Dutton. 1st ed. F/F. P3. $15.00

NORTON, Andre. *Victory on Janus.* 1966. HBW. 1st ed. 224 p. VG+/dj. M20. $75.00

NORTON, Andre. *Ware Hawk.* 1983. Atheneum. 1st ed. F/F. F4. $25.00

NORTON, Andrews. *Statement of Reasons for Not Believing Doctrines...* 1833. Cambridge/Boston. 1st ed. 12mo. 39 p. cloth/paper label. M1. $175.00

NORTON, Caroline. *Bingen on the Rhine.* 1883. Phil. 1st ed. ils. F. V1. $25.00

NORTON, Charles Eliot. *Love Poems of John Donne.* 1905. Houghton Mifflin. 1/535. 12mo. vellum. F. B14. $95.00

NORTON, Clarence Clifford. *Democratic Party in Antebellum NC, 1835-61.* 1930. Chapel Hill. 1st ed. 276 p. VG/stiff prt wrp. M8. $35.00

NORTON, F.J. *Descriptive Catalogue of Prt in Spain & Portugal, 1501-20.* 1978. Cambridge. 600 p. M/dj. O6. $300.00

NORTON, Frank. *Life of Alexander H Stephens.* 1883. NY. 88 p. O7. $9.50

NORTON, John. *Orthodox Evangelist; or, Treatise...Evangical Truths...* 1657. London. Macock. sm 4to. 355 p. 19th-century brn calf/bl spine label. K1. $350.00

NORTON, Ken. *Jesse Leather: One of a Kind.* 1983. Walsh. 8vo. VG/VG. A8. $15.00

NORTON, Mary. *Borrowers Afloat.* 1959. Dent. 1st UK ed. 176 p. VG/dj. M20. $45.00

NORTON, Mary. *Borrowers Afloat.* 1959. Harcourt Brace. stated 1st ed. ils Krush. F/G. M5. $30.00

NORTON, Mary. *Borrowers.* nd. HBW. F/F. P3. $13.00

NORTON, Mary. *Magic Bed-Knob.* 1943. Hyperion. 1st ed. ils Waldo Pierce. G. P2. $32.00

NORTON & PATTERSON. *Living It Up: Guide to Named Apartment Houses of NY.* 1984. Atheneum. 1st ed. tall 8vo. 451 p. NF/dj. B20. $25.00

NORVELL, Anthony. *Mind Cosmology.* 1972. Parker. 3rd ed. VG/dj. P3. $15.00

NORVIL, Manning; see Bulmer, Kenneth.

NOTTLE, Trevor. *Growing Old-Fashioned Roses in Australia & New Zealand.* 1992 (1983). Kenthurst, Australia. 91 color photos. 90 p. M. B26. $12.00

NOURSE, Alan E. *Fourth Horseman.* 1983. Harper. 1st ed. F/dj. M2. $20.00

NOURSE, Alan E. *Mercy Men.* nd. BC. VG/VG. P3. $8.00

NOURSE, Alan E. *Rx for Tomorrow.* 1973. McKay. 2nd ed. VG/dj. P3. $12.00

NOURSE, Mary A. *Short Hist of the Chinese.* 1942. Phil. New Home Lib/Blakiston. 3rd ed. 8vo. 413 p. VG. W1. $15.00

NOVAK, Marian Faye. *Lonely Girls w/Burning Eyes.* (1991). Little Brn. 1st ed. NF/dj. A7. $10.00

NOVECK, Simon. *Judaism & Psychiatry: 2 Approaches to Personal Problems...* 1956. Basic Books. xl. 197 p. VG. S3. $20.00

NOVICK, Sheldon M. *Honorable Justice, Life of Oliver Wendell Holmes.* 1989. Little Brn. M11. $22.50

NOWARRA, Heinz. *Marine Aircraft of the 1914-18 War.* 1966. Letchworth. 1st ed. ils. 210 p. VG/dj. B18. $65.00

NOWELL, Charles E. *Hist of Portugal.* 1962. Van Nostrand. reprint. ils. NF/rpr dj. O6. $35.00

NOWNES. *Basket Quilts.* 1990. np. Classic Quilt series. G2. $7.00

NOWNES. *Star Quilts.* 1990. np. Classic Quilt series. G2. $7.00

NOY, Dov. *Folktales of Israel.* 1963. Chicago. xl. 221 p. VG/wrp. S3. $21.00

NOYCE, Wilfrid. *S Col: Personal Story of Ascent of Everest.* 1955. NY. 2nd prt. 8vo. 299 p. gilt blk cloth. F/VG. H3. $15.00

NOYDENS, Benito Remigio. *Decisiones Practicas y Morales, Para Curas, Confessores.* 1665. Madrid. Andres Garcia de al Iglesia. 8vo. 346 p. K1. $350.00

NOYES, Alfred. *Letter to Lucian & Other Poems.* 1957. NY. 1st ed. F/F. V1. $25.00

NOYES, James O. *Roumania: Border Land of the Christian & Turk...* 1857. NY. 8vo. 520 p. cloth. O2. $45.00

NOYES, John H. *Confessions of...* 1849. Leonard. 1st ed. 8vo. 96 p. VG. M1. $750.00

NOYES, John H. *Hist of Am Socialisms.* 1961. NY. facsimile of 1870 ed. 1/500. 678 p. VG. A17. $15.00

NOYES, Pierepont B. *Goodly Heritage.* (1958). Rinehart. 1st ed. 275 p. blk cloth. VG+/dj. B22. $7.00

NUETZEL, Charles. *Last Call for the Stars.* 1970. Lenox. 1st ed. xl. front free ep removed. P3. $8.00

NUNN, George E. *Geog Conceptions of Columbus: Critical Considerations...* 1924. Am Geog Soc. ils/2 fld maps. NF. O6. $70.00

NUNN, Kem. *Tapping the Source.* 1984. NY. 1st ed. inscr. F/F. A11. $65.00

NUNNERY, Gene. *Old Pro Turkey Hunter.* (1980). Meridian, MS. ils. 144 p. dj. A17. $9.50

NUTE, Grace Lee. *Voyageur.* 1955. St Paul. reprint of 1931 ed. 8vo. 289 p. wrp. A17. $10.00

NUTINI, Hugo. *Essays on Mexican Kinship.* (1976). Pittsburgh, PA. 256 p. F3. $20.00

NUTT, Frederic. *Complete Confectioner; or, Whole Art of Confectionary...* 1807. NY. Richard Scott. 1st Am ed. 12mo. contemporary calf. M1. $525.00

NUTTALL, G. Clarke. *Beautiful Flowering Shrubs.* nd. Stokes. mtd color pls. 279 p. F. H10. $35.00

NUTTING, Anthony. *Lawrence av Arabien. Nannen och Motivet.* 1962. Stockholm. Lars Hikerbergs Bokforlag. 1st ed. 249 p. NF. M7. $65.00

NUTTING, Anthony. *Lawrence of Arabia: Man & the Motive.* 1961. NY. Clarkson Potter. 1st ed/2nd state. 256 p. F/NF clip. M7. $22.00

NWEEYA, Samuel K. *Persia & the Moslems.* 1924. Persia. Urmia City. 1st ed. 12mo. 337 p. pict maroon cloth. H3. $40.00

NWEEYA, Samuel K. *Persia & the Moslems.* 1924. St Louis. Von Hoffman. G. A16. $10.00

NYDEN, Paul. *Blk Coal Miners in the US.* (1974). NY. Am Inst Marxist Studies. 73 p. wrp. A7. $15.00

NYE, Bill. *Bill Nye's Comic Hist of the US.* 1906. np. xl. 328 p. O7. $12.50

NYE, Nelson C. *Cartridge-Case Law.* 1944. Macmillan. 1st ed. VG/clip. B9. $35.00

NYE, Nelson. *Complete Book of the Quarter Horse.* 1967. NY. Barnes. 3rd prt. VG/VG. O3. $45.00

NYE, Robert D. *Legacy of BF Skinner...* 1992. Pacific Grove. Brooks/Cole. trade pb. 152 p. VG. G1. $15.00

NYE, Robert. *Falstaff...* 1976. Little Brn. 1st Am ed. F/VG+. N3. $15.00

NYLANDER, Carl. *Deep Well.* (1970). St Martin. 1st Am ed. 210 p. dj. F3. $15.00

O'BRIEN, Flann. *Poor Mouth.* 1974. Viking. 1st ed. F/NF. B2. $30.00

O'BRIEN, Flann. *Stories & Plays.* 1976. Viking. 1st ed. F/NF. B2. $35.00

O'BRIEN, Jack. *Silver Chief to the Rescue.* 1937. Winston. 1st ed. 235 p. VG+/G+. P2. $24.00

O'BRIEN, Kate. *Eng Diaries & Journals.* 1947. Collins. 3rd ed. 8vo. 48 p. VG/dj. V3. $12.00

O'BRIEN, Philip. *TE Lawrence: A Bibliography.* 1988. Boston. GK Hall. 1st ed. NF/F. Q1. $90.00

O'BRIEN, Robert. *CA Called Them: Saga of Golden Days & Roaring Camps.* 1951. McGraw Hill. 1st ed. ils. 251 p. NF. B19. $15.00

O'BRIEN, Sharon. *Willa Cather, the Emerging Voice.* 1987. Oxford. F/F. P3. $30.00

O'BRIEN, Tim. *Going After Cacciato.* (1978). Delacorte. 3rd prt. F/dj. A7. $30.00

O'BRIEN, Tim. *If I Die in a Combat Zone.* (1974). Dell. 1st pb issue. VG. A7. $15.00

O'BRIEN, Tim. *Things They Carried.* 1990. Houghton Mifflin. 1st ed. inscr. F/F. B2. $50.00

O'BRIEN & WASSERMAN. *Statistics Sources. Vol 1.* 1989. Detroit. Gale. 13th ed. xl. 1884 p. VG+. S9. $23.00

O'CONNOR, Andrew P. *Forty Yrs w/Fighting Cocks.* 1929. Goshen. Rogers. 327 p. VG. B14. $50.00

O'CONNOR, Flannery. *Guests of the Nation.* 1931. Macmillan. 1st ed. author's 1st book. F/VG. B4. $350.00

O'CONNOR, Frank. *Domestic Relations.* 1957. NY. 1st ed (precedes UK). NF/VG+. A11. $25.00

O'CONNOR, Frank. *Leinster, Munster & Connaught.* (late 1940s). London. Robert Hale. 8vo. 296 p. VG/G+. A2. $15.00

O'CONNOR, Frank. *Only Child.* 1961. Knopf. 1st ed. F/F. C4. $35.00

O'CONNOR, Philip F. *Old Morals, Sm Continents, Darker Times.* 1971. IA City. ARC. presentation inscr. NF/prt wht wrp. A11. $55.00

O'CONNOR, Philip F. *Stealing Home.* 1979. Knopf. 1st ed. 308 p. tan brds/cream cloth spine. VG/dj. M20. $20.00

O'CONNOR, Richard. *High Jinks on the Klondike.* (1954. Indianapolis. 284 p. dj. A17. $17.50

O'CONNOR, Richard. *Pacific Destiny.* 1969. Little Brn. 1st ed. 8vo. 505 p. VG/dj. W1. $18.00

O'DELL, Jeffrey M. *Inventory of Early Architecture & Hist Archeological Sites.* 1976. Henrico Co. ils/maps/pls. 324 p. VG. B10. $35.00

O'DELL, Scott. *Sing Down the Moon.* 1970. Houghton Mifflin. 1st ed. 8vo. 237 p. VG/dj. A3. $25.00

O'DONNELL, Barrett; see Malzberg, Barry.

O'DONNELL, Bernard. *Old Bailey & Its Trails.* 1951. Macmillan. 1st Am ed. 8vo. 226 p. F/VG clip. A2. $15.00

O'DONNELL, Elliott. *Animal Ghosts; or, Animal Hauntings & the Hereafter.* 1913. London. Rider. 1st ed. octavo. 302 p. gilt bdg. VG. H5. $150.00

O'DONNELL, K.M.; see Malzberg, Barry.

O'DONNELL, Lillian. *Casual Affairs.* 1985. Putnam. 1st ed. F/F. P3. $17.00

O'DONNELL, Lillian. *Falling Star.* 1979. Putnam. 1st ed. F/F. P3. $20.00

O'DONNELL, Lillian. *Wicked Designs.* 1980. Putnam. 1st ed. VG/dj. P3. $13.00

O'DONNELL, Michael. *Long Walk Home.* 1988. London. Gollancz. 1st ed. F/F. S5. $22.50

O'DONNELL, Peter. *Dodelijke Diamanten.* nd. Uitgeveij Luitingh. Dutch text. VG/VG. P3. $15.00

O'DONNELL, Peter. *Dragon's Claw.* 1985. Mysterious. 1st ed. F/F. B9/P3. $16.00

O'DONNELL, Peter. *Modesty Blaise.* 1965. Souvenir. 1st ed. NF/dj. P3. $30.00

O'DONNELL, Peter. *Pieces of Modesty.* 1986. Mysterious. 1/250. sgn. F/slipcase. B9. $45.00

O'DONNELL, Peter. *Silver Mistress.* 1981. Archival. ltd ed. 1/200. sgn author/ils. box. P3. $100.00

O'DONNELL, Peter. *Xanadu Talisman.* (1981). Mysterious. 1st Am ed. 1/250. sgn. F/slipcase. B9. $45.00

O'DONNELL, Peter. *Xanadu Talisman.* 1981. London. Souvenir. 1st ed. F/F. M15. $45.00

O'DONNELL, Thomas C. *Snubbing Posts: Informal Hist of Blk River Canal.* 1972. N Country Books. 2nd ed. dj. N2. $10.00

O'DONNELL, Thomas J. *Confessions of TE Lawrence.* 1979. OH U. 1st ed. 196 p. gilt deep pink cloth. F/NF. M7. $35.00

O'DONNELL, William F. *Mother Bird Stories.* 1909. Phil. 8vo. ils. pict tan cloth. VG-. H3. $20.00

O'DOWD. *Quick-&-E Heart Motif Quilts.* 1986. np. 40 block designs. wrp. G2. $4.00

O'FAOLAIN, Sean. *Newman's Way: Odyssey of John Henry Newman.* 1952. NY. Devin Adair. ils. 335 p. H10. $10.00

O'FARRELL, William. *Repeat Performance.* 1947. Triangle. VG/dj. P3. $15.00

O'FLAHERTY, Liam. *Stories of Liam O'Flaherty.* 1956. NY. Devin Adair. 1st ed. F/NF. C4. $35.00

O'GORMAN, Edmundo. *Invention of Am: Inquiry Into Hist Nature of New World...* 1961. Bloomington. Samuel Morison's copy. 10 maps. NF. O6. $45.00

O'HANLON, Raymond. *Joseph Conrad & Charles Darwin.* 1984. Atlantic Highlands. Humanities Pr. 1st Am ed. author's 1st book. NF/VG. L3. $125.00

O'HARA, Frank. *Awake in Spain.* 1960. Am Theatre for Poets. 1st ed. NF/wrp. B2. $40.00

O'HARA, Frank. *Two Pieces.* 1969. London. Long Hair Books. 1st ed. 1/500 on lt gr paper. F/stiff bl wrp. V1. $45.00

O'HARA, John. *Hellbox.* 1947. Random. 1st ed. VG/VG. P3. $35.00

O'HARA, John. *Instrument.* (1967). Random. ltd ed. 1/300. sgn. F/slipcase. B4. $150.00

O'HARA, John. *Instrument.* 1967. Random. 1st ed. VG/VG. V2. $6.50

O'HARA, John. *Rage To Live.* 1949. Random. 1st ed. VG/VG. P3. $60.00

O'HARA, Kenneth. *Death of a Moffy.* 1987. Doubleday. ARC of 1st Am ed. RS. F/F. S5. $25.00

O HENRY. *Four Million.* 1907. McClure. 3rd ed. VG. P3. $20.00

O HENRY. *Stories...* 1965. Ltd Ed Club. 1st #d ed. 1/1500. ils/sgn John Groth. F/VG slipcase. A18. $50.00

O HENRY. *Voice of the City.* 1908. McClure. 1st ed. 1st bdg (McClure stp on spine). VG. Q1. $100.00

O'MALLEY & SAUNDERS. *Vesalius. Ils From Hist Works...Annotations, Trans...* 1950. NY. 4to. dj. G7. $85.00

O'MEARA, James. *Broderick & Gwin.* 1881. San Francisco. Bacon. 254 p. NF/prt gr wrp. K1. $200.00

O'MEARA, Walter. *MN Gothic.* (1956). Holt. 1st ed. 314 p. VG/dj. A17. $12.50

O'NEAL, William B. *Fine Arts Lib: Jefferson's Selections for U of VA...* 1976987. VA U. ils. VG/wrp. B10. $25.00

O'NEAL & WEEKS. *Work of William Lawrence Bottomley in Richmond.* ca 1985. VA U Pr. 1st ed. 262 p. VG/VG. B10. $50.00

O'NEIL, D. *Stacked Deck: The Greatest Joker Story.* 1990. Longmeadow. 1st ed. aeg. leather. F. P3. $60.00

O'NEIL, D. *Whale of a Territory: Story of Bill O'Neil.* (1966). NY. 1st ed. 249 p. VG/torn dj. B18. $17.50

O'NEIL, Paul. *Frontiersmen.* 1977. Time Life. 4to. F. A8. $10.00

O'NEIL, Paul. *Rivermen.* 1975. Time Life. 4to. F. A8. $10.00

O'NEILL, Eugene. *Ah, Wilderness.* Oct 1933. NY. 1st ed. F/F. B14. $125.00

O'NEILL, Eugene. *Last Will & Testament of an Extremely Distinguised Dog.* 1972. Worcester. St Onge. miniature. 1/1000. 26 p. F. H10. $20.00

O'NEILL, Eugene. *Lazarus Laughed.* Nonesuch. 1/775. sgn. G+. A1. $150.00

O'NEILL, Eugene. *Lazarus Laughed.* 1929. London. Cape. G+/G+. A1. $75.00

O'NEILL, Eugene. *Lost Plays of Eugene O'Neill.* 1950. New Fathoms. 1st ed. G/dj. M18. $25.00

O'NEILL, Eugene. *Plays of...* (1934-35). Scribner. 1/770. sgn. 12 vol set. octavo. gilt red cloth. F/box. R3. $2,000.00

O'NEILL, Eugene. *Poems 1912-44.* 1980. Tichnor Fields. 1st ed. F/F. C4. $30.00

O'NEILL, Eugene. *Strange Interlude.* 1928. Boni Liveright. 1st ed. NF/VG. C4. $70.00

O'NEILL, Eugene. *Touch of the Poet.* 1957. New Haven. Yale. 1st ed/1st prt. F/F clip. C4. $35.00

O'NEILL, John P. *Clyfford Still.* 1979. Metropolitan Mus Art. ils. 217 p. VG+/dj. M20. $25.00

O'NEILL, Mary. *Wht Palace.* 1966. Crowell. 1st ed. ils. VG+/G+. P2. $20.00

O'NEILL, Tim. *And We the People.* (1961). NY. Kenedy. 1st Am ed. 8vo. 248 p. F/VG+. A2. $15.00

O'RELL, Max. *John Bull & Co.* 1894. NY. Webster. 1st ed. 8vo. ils. 319 p. VG. W1. $30.00

O'ROURKE, Frank. *Gun Hand.* (1953). Ballantine. NF/dj. B9. $60.00

O'ROURKE, Frank. *Man Who Found His Way.* 1957. Morrow. 1st ed. VG/dj. P3. $25.00

O'SHEA, Richard. *Am Heritage Battle Maps of the Civil War.* 1992. Tulsa. Council Books. 1st thus ed. 176 p. cloth. NF/NF. M8. $45.00

O'SHEA, Sean; see Tralins, Bob.

O'SIADHAIL, Michael. *Springnight.* 1983. Dublin. 1st ed. sgn. VG/VG. V1. $15.00

O'SULLIVAN, Lawrence. *Miscreant.* 1969. HRW. 1st ed. author's 1st novel. NF/NF. A14. $25.00

O'SULLIVAN, P. Michael. *Patriot Graves: Resistance in Ireland.* 1972. Follett. 1st ed. VG/VG. V2. $6.00

OAKES. *Pull-the-Tab, Pop-Up Book of Classic Tales of Horror.* 1988. paper engineering by Ray Marshall/Ruth Graham. F. A4. $35.00

OAKESHOTT, Walter. *Two Winchester Bibles.* 1981. Clarendon. tall folio. 12 full-p color pls. F/linen slipcase. K1. $250.00

OAKLEY, Violet. *Holy Experiment: Our Heritage From William Penn.* 1950. Phil. Cogslea Studio. canvas brds. M11. $50.00

OANDASAN, William. *Branch of California Redwood.* 1980. LA. Am Indian Studies. 1st ed. sm quarto. VG. L3. $35.00

OATES, Joyce Carol. *Foxfire.* 1993. Dutton. AP. F/prt yel wrp. C4. $30.00

OATES, Joyce Carol. *Foxfire: Confessions of a Girl Gang.* (1993). London. Macmillan. 1st ed. F/F. B3. $30.00

OATES, Joyce Carol. *Haunted.* 1994. NY. Dutton. AP. F/prt gray wrp. C4. $35.00

OATES, Joyce Carol. *Miracle Play.* (1974). Blk Sparrow. 1st ed. NF/acetate dj. B3. $50.00

OATES, Joyce Carol. *On Boxing.* 1987. Garden City. 1st ed. inscr. F/F. A11. $65.00

OATES, Joyce Carol. *Poisoned Kiss & Other Stories...* 1976. Gollancz. 1st ed. F/dj. P3. $20.00

OATES, Joyce Carol. *Raven's Wing.* (1987). London. Cape. 1st ed. F/NF clip. B3. $25.00

OATES, Joyce Carol. *Time Traveler.* 1987. Northridge. Lord John. 1/150. sgn. F. B4. $85.00

OATES, Joyce Carol. *Where Are You Going, Where Have You Been?* 1979. Logan, IA. 1st separate ed. sgn. F/ils wrp. A11. $25.00

OATES, Joyce Carol. *You Must Remember This.* 1987. Dutton. 1st ed. VG/VG. V2. $7.00

OATES, Stephen B. *Confederate Cavalry W of the River.* 1961. Austin, TX. 1st ed. 234 p. cloth. NF/NF. M8. $165.00

OATES, Stephen. *Abraham Lincoln & Martin Luther King Jr.* 1982. Ft Wayne, IN. stiff paper wrp. A6. $10.00

OBER, F.A. *Ferdinand Magellan.* 1907. Harper. 1st ed. 12mo. 301 p. F/VG. A2. $20.00

OBERHOLTZER, Ellis Paxson. *Jay Cooke: Financier of the Civil War.* 1907. Phil. Jacobs. 1st ed. 2 vols. cloth. F/NF/pub box. M8. $350.00

OBERLING, Pierre. *Road to Bellapais. Turkish Cypriot Exodus to N Cyprus.* 1982. NY. 8vo. 256 p. cloth. dj. O2. $30.00

OBERNDORF, Clarence P. *Hist of Psychoanalysis in Am.* 1953. NY. Grune Stratton. sm 8vo. 280 p. red cloth. VG/dj. G1. $35.00

OBERNDORF, Clarence P. *Psychiatric Novels of Oliver Wendell Holmes.* 1946 (1943). NY. Columbia. 2nd ed/1st prt. 274 p. bl-gr cloth. G1. $27.50

OBREGON, Mauricio. *Ulysses Aiborne.* (1971). NY. 1st Am ed. 8vo. 188 p. F/F. A2. $15.00

ODELL, Ruth Winters. *Early Railroad Transportation in Jackson Co, OH.* 1986. np. 178 p. VG+/plastic sbdg. B18. $27.50

ODIC, Charles. *Stepchildren of France.* 1945. Roy Pub. 181 p. G+. S3. $25.00

ODUM, Howard. *Cold Bl Moon.* 1931. Indianapolis. 1st ed. VG/VG. B5. $50.00

OEHSER, Paul H. *Sons of Science: Story of Smithsonian...* (1949). NY. Schuman. ils/index. 220 p. bl cloth. VG. S9. $10.00

OELSNER, G.H. *Handbook of Weaves.* ca 1860s. Dover. ils. 402 p. cloth. H10. $25.00

OERLEMANS, A.C. *Development of Freud's Conception of Anxiety.* 1949. Amsterdam. N-Holland. reading copy. G1. $20.00

OESTERLER & ROBINSON. *Intro to Books of Old Testament.* 1946 (1934). London. rerpint. 454 p. VG/G+. S3. $21.00

OFFIT, Sidney. *Best of Baseball.* 1956. Putnam. 1st ed. VG+/VG. P8. $55.00

OFFUTT, Andrew. *Shadowspan.* nd. BC. F/dj. P3. $8.00

OFFUTT, Chris. *Same River Twice.* 1993. Simon Schuster. 1st ed. F/dj. C4. $20.00

OGAWA, Teizo. *Hist of Psychiatry: Mental Illness & Its Treatments.* 1982. Osaka. Saikon Pub. 1st ed. 216 p. rose cloth. G1. $75.00

OGBURN, Charlton. *Railroads: Great Am Adventure.* 1977. WA, DC. Nat Geog. 8vo. ils. 204 p. blk cloth. A16/B11. $15.00

OGBURN, Charlton. *Winter Beach.* 1966. NY. Morrow. VG/dj. A16. $7.50

OGDEN, H.A. *Boy's Book of Famous Regiments.* 1914. NY. 1st ed. pls/drawings. 260 p. pict red cloth. VG. H3. $25.00

OGG, Oscar. *26 Letters.* 1971. Crowell. revised ed. 294 p. VG. C5. $20.00

OGREN, Kathy. *Jazz Revolution.* 1989. NY. Oxford. 1st ed. 221 p. F/NF. A7. $15.00

OHIYESA; see Eastman, Charles A.

OHLSON, Hereward. *Thunderbolt & the Rebel Planet.* 1954. Lutterworth. 1st ed. VG/VG. P3. $15.00

OHNET, Georges. *Poison Dealer.* 1911. Greening & Co. VG. P3. $20.00

OHRLIN, Glenn. *Hell-Bound Train: Cowboy Songbook.* (1973). IL U. 1st ed. w/record of 6 songs. F/F clip. A18. $35.00

OKOLA, Lennard. *Drum Beat.* 1967. Nairobi. 12mo. VG+/ils wrp. A11. $50.00

OKPAKU, Joseph. *Verdict!* (1970). NY. 3rd Pr. 159 p. dj. A7. $35.00

OKRENT, Daniel. *Nine Innings.* 1985. Tichnor Fields. later prt. F/F. P8. $15.00

OKRENT & WULF. *Baseball Anecdotes.* 1989. Oxford. M/M. P8. $10.00

OKSNER, Chester. *Punitive Damage.* (1987). Morrow. 1st ed. NF/dj. A7. $15.00

OLCOTT, Jack. *Coaching the Quarterback.* 1972. W Nyack. Parker. ils. torn dj. N2. $6.00

OLCOTT, William T. *Book of the Stars for Young People.* 1923. NY. 8vo. 411 p. gray cloth. F. H3. $15.00

OLCOTT, William T. *Sun Lore of All Ages: Collection of Myths...* 1914. Putnam. ils. 346 p. N2. $45.00

OLDENBOURG, Zoe. *Awakened.* 1957. London. Gollancz. 1st ed. trans from French. NF/VG+ clip. A14. $40.00

OLDENBOURG, Zoe. *Chains of Love.* 1959. Pantheon. 1st Am ed. trans Peter Gr. NF/NF clip. A14. $35.00

OLDENBOURG, Zoe. *Destiny of Fire.* 1961. Pantheon. 1st Am ed. trans from French. NF/NF clip. A14. $30.00

OLDENBOURG, Zoe. *Heirs of the Kingdom.* 1972. London. Collins. 1st British ed. trans Anne Carter. VG+/VG+. A14. $30.00

OLDER, Cora. *San Francisco: Magic City.* 1961. Longman Gr. 1st ed. ils/index. 280 p. NF/VG clip. B19. $10.00

OLDERMAN, Murray. *Nelson's 20th-Century Encyclopedia of Baseball.* 1963. Nelson. 1st ed. VG. P8. $15.00

OLDROYD, Osborn Hamiline. *Assassination of Abraham Lincoln: Flight, Pursuit...* 1917. WA, DC. Oldroyd. 2nd ed. 305 p. cloth. VG. M8. $85.00

OLDROYD, Osborn Hamiline. *Lincoln Memorial: Album-Immortelles.* 1882. NY. Carleton. 1st ed (lacks variant 'Sold Only by Subscripton'). VG. M8. $85.00

OLDS, Elizabeth. *Riding the Rails.* 19488. Boston. 1st ed. 48 p. pict red cloth. F/G. H3. $50.00

OLEKSAK & OLEKSAK. *Beisbol.* 1991. Masters Pr. 1st ed. sgn Avila/Carresquel. F/VG+. P8. $65.00

OLINER, Marion M. *Cultivating Freud's Garden in France.* 1988. Northvale, NJ. Aronson. 332 p. prt gray wrp. VG/dj. G1. $25.00

OLIPHANT, Laurence. *Haifa; or, Life in Modern Palestine.* 1887. Edinburgh. 8vo. 369 p. new quarter morocco. O2. $125.00

OLIPHANT, Laurence. *Land of Gilead w/Excursions in Lebanon.* 1881. NY. 8vo. gilt pebbled cloth. O2. $100.00

OLIVER, Andrew. *Journal of Samuel Curwen, Loyalist.* 1972. Harvard. 1st ed. 2 vols. dj. A17. $25.00

OLIVER, Anthony. *Elberg Collection.* 1985. Doubleday. 1st Am ed. F/F. S5. $25.00

OLIVER, Anthony. *Elberg Collection.* 1985. London. Heinemann. 1st ed. NF/dj. M15. $45.00

OLIVER, Chad. *Edge of Forever.* 1971. Sherbourne. 1st ed. VG/G. P3. $18.00

OLIVER, Chad. *Shadows in the Sun.* 1985. Crown. 1st ed. F/dj. P3. $13.00

OLIVER, George W. *Plant Culture: Working Handbook...* 1912 (1900). NY. 3rd ed. 312 p. floral ep. B26. $14.00

OLIVER, Jim. *Closing Distance.* 1992. Putnam. 1st ed. author's 1st book. F/F. A14. $25.00

OLIVER, Louis Littlecoon. *Chasers of the Sun: Creek Indian Thoughts.* 1990. Greenfield Center. F. L3. $20.00

OLIVIER, Stuart. *Wine Journeys.* (1949). Duell. 1st ed. 312 p. purple cloth. VG. B22. $6.00

OLLIVIER, C.P. *Traite de la Moelle Epiniere et de Ses Maladies...* 1827. Paris. Crevot. 2nd ed. 2 vols. 3 fld pls. quarter roan/marbled brds. G7. $595.00

OLMSTED, Lorena Ann. *Setup for Murder.* 1962. Avalon. 1st ed. xl. dj. P3. $5.00

OLNEY, Ross R. *Shudders.* 1972. Whitman. VG. P3. $4.00

OLSEN. *For the Greater Glory.* 1980. np. ils. cloth. G2. $17.50

OLSEN. *Quilter's Color Workbook.* 1990. np. wrp. G2. $12.95

OLSEN. *SW by SW: Native Am & Mexican Quilt Designs.* 1991. np. cloth. G2. $25.00

OLSHAKER, Mark. *Einstein's Brain.* 1981. Evans. 1st ed. F/dj. P3. $15.00

OLSHAN, Joseph. *Clara's Heart.* (1985). Arbor. 1st Am ed. author's 1st novel. F/NF. B4. $45.00

OLSON, Albert. *Picture Painting for Young Artists.* 1906. Chicago. Thompson Thomas. 1st ed. 8vo. pict brds. D1. $50.00

OLSON, Charles. *Call Me Ishmael.* 1947. Reynal Hitchcock. 1st ed. author's 1st book. F/NF. B24. $250.00

OLSON, Charles. *Distances.* 1960. NY/London. Evergreen. PBO. NF/ils wrp. A11. $40.00

OLSON, Charles. *Human Universe & Other Essays.* 1965. San Francisco. 1/250. sgn. ils R LaVigne/K Irby. w/promo material. NF. V1. $275.00

OLSON, Charles. *Mayan Letters.* 1953. Mallorca. Divers Pr. 1st ed. 1/600. edit Robert Creeley. NF/wrp. B24. $185.00

OLSON, John. *Book of the Rifle.* 1974. O'Hara. 1st ed. NF/NF. V2. $5.00

OLSON, John. *Shooter's Bible #64.* 1973. Hackensack. 4to. 576 p. NF/wrp. A17. $15.00

OLSON, Lawrence. *Dimensions of Japan.* 1963. NY. Am U Field Staff. 1st ed. 8vo. 403 p. VG/dj. W1. $16.00

OLSON & WHITMARSH. *Foreign Maps.* 1944. Harper. 1st ed. 7 color maps. NF/rpr dj. O6. $65.00

OMANG, Joanne. *Incident at Akabal.* (1992). Houghton Mifflin. AP. VG/pict wrp. B3. $20.00

ONDAATJE, Michael. *Collected Works of Billy the Kid.* 1974. NY. 1st ed. sgn. ES. F/NF clip. A11. $65.00

ONDAATJE, Michael. *Coming Through Slaughter.* 1976. Norton. 1st Am ed. inscr/dtd 1977. w/sgn letter. F/NF. L3. $300.00

ONDAATJE, Michael. *Running in the Family.* 1982. NY. correct 1st ed. sgn. F/F. A11. $55.00

ONDORISHA. *Embroidery for Beginners.* 1986. np. pb. G2. $7.50

ONDORISHA. *Embroidery Sampler.* 1988. np. ils. wrp. G2. $10.00

ONIONS, Olivers. *Tower of Oblivion.* 1921. MacMillan. 1st ed. VG. M2. $50.00

ONSTOTT, Kyle. *Drum.* 1962. Dial. 1st ed. 502 p. F/F. B22. $15.00

OPLER, Morris E. *Grenville Goodwin Among the W Apache.* 1973. AZ U. notes/biblio/index. 103 p. F/NF. B19. $25.00

OPPENHEIM, E. Phillips. *Battle of Basinghall Street.* 1935. McClelland Stewart. 1st Canadian ed. VG/dj. P3. $30.00

OPPENHEIM, E. Phillips. *Dumb Gods Speak.* 1937. McClelland Stewart. 1st Canadian ed. VG/dj. P3. $30.00

OPPENHEIM, E. Phillips. *Envoy Extraordinary.* 1937. Little Brn. 1st ed. VG. P3. $125.00

OPPENHEIM, E. Phillips. *General Besserley's Puzzle Box.* (1935). Hodder Stoughton. 1st ed. inscr/sgn/dtd. NF/NF. B4. $225.00

OPPENHEIM, E. Phillips. *Golden Beast.* 1926. Little Brn. 1st ed. VG. P3. $20.00

OPPENHEIM, E. Phillips. *Kingdom of the Blind.* 1916. McClelland Goodchild Stewart. VG. P3. $25.00

OPPENHEIM, E. Phillips. *Prodigals of Monte Carlo.* 1926. Little Brn. 1st ed. gr cloth. VG. V2. $15.00

OPPENHEIM, E. Phillips. *Spymaster.* 1938. Little Brn. 1st ed. VG. P3. $20.00

OPPENHEIM, E. Phillips. *Zeppelin's Passenger.* 1918. McClelland Goodchild Stewart. 1st Canadian ed. VG-. P3. $20.00

OPPENHEIMER, Joel. *Wrong Season.* 1973. Bobbs Merrill. 1st ed. F/VG. P8. $25.00

OPPENHEIMER, Judy. *Private Demons: Life of Shirley Jackson.* 1988. Putnam. 1st ed. F/F. T2. $17.50

OPPER, F. *Mother Goose's Nursery Rhymes.* 1900. Lippincott. 1st ed. 320 p. VG. S10. $65.00

ORBELIANI, Sulkhan-Saba. *Book of Wisdom & Lies.* 1894. Hammersmith. 1/250. octavo. full limp vellum/silk ties. NF. H5. $1,500.00

ORCZY, Baroness. *By the Gods Beloved.* 1910. Greening. decor brds. VG-. P3. $45.00

ORCZY, Baroness. *Pimpernel & Rosemary.* 1926. Cassell. 5th ed. VG. P3. $20.00

ORCZY, Baroness. *Sir Percy Hits Back.* 1935. Hodder Stoughton. 18th prt. VG. P3. $15.00

ORDE, A.J. *Little Neighborhood Murder.* 1989. Doubleday. 1st ed. 1st Jason Lynx. F/F. M15. $35.00

ORDISH, George. *Yr of the Butterfly.* 1975. Scribner. 1st ed. dj. N2. $5.00

ORELLANA, Sandra. *Indian Medicine in Highland Guatemala.* (1987). Albuquerque, NM. 1st ed. 308 p. dj. F3. $30.00

OREM, Preston D. *Baseball 1845-81.* 1961. self pub. 1st ed. F. P8. $70.00

ORESICK, Peter. *Story of Glass.* 1977. Cambridge. W End. 2nd ed. 32 p. wrp. A7. $8.00

ORGILL, Douglas. *Lawrence.* 1973. Ballantine 18. 1st prt. 159 p. VG/wrp. M7. $45.00

ORIOL, Laurence. *Short Circuit.* 1967. Macdonald. 1st ed. VG/dj. P3. $15.00

ORITIZ, Alfonso. *Handbook of N Am Indians.* 1979. Smithsonian. vol 9 of Southwest series. VG. P3. $35.00

ORITZ, Simon J. *Fight Back: For the Sake of People, for Sake of the Land.* 1980. Las Lomas. Inst for Native Am Development. F/wrp. L3. $50.00

ORITZ, Simon J. *From Sand Creek.* 1981. Thunder Mouth. 1st ed. F/F. L3. $175.00

ORITZ, Simon J. *Going for the Rain.* 1976. Harper Row. 1st ed. VG/dj. very scarce in this form. L3. $100.00

ORITZ, Simon J. *Good Journey.* 1977. Turtle Island. 1/2000. VG/wrp. L3. $35.00

ORMEROD, Roger. *Dead Ringer.* 1985. London. Constable. 1st ed. F/F. S5. $20.00

ORMOND, Clyde. *Bear!* 1961. Stackpole. 291 p. VG/dj. M20. $18.00

ORMOND, Clyde. *Complete Guide to Hunting.* (1972). NY. revised. 432 p. worn dj. A17. $12.50

ORMOND. *Am Primitives in Needlepoint.* 1977. np. 1st ed. ils. cloth. G2. $13.00

ORMONDROYD, Edward. *David & the Phoenix.* (1958). Follett. Weekly Reader BC. 8vo. 173 p. VG. T5. $20.00

ORR, A. *In the Ice King's Palace.* 1986. Tor. F/dj. P3. $16.00

ORR, A. *World in Amber.* 1985. Bluejay. 1st ed. M2/P3. $20.00

ORR, Anne. *Anne Orr's Charted Designs.* 1978. np. 200+ ils. wrp. G2. $2.00

ORR, Anne. *Now Needlepoint.* 1975. np. ils. cloth. G2. $15.00

ORR, Anne. *Quilting w/Anne Orr.* 1990. np. full-size patterns. 32 p. wrp. G2. $3.00

ORR, Gregory. *We Must Make a Kingdom of It.* 1986. Wesleyan. 1st ed. F/F. V1. $10.00

ORR, Jack. *Baseball's Greatest Players Today.* 1963. Watts. 1st ed. VG. P8. $12.50

ORR, John W. *Pict Guide to Falls of Niagara...* 1842. Buffalo. 1st ed. 2 maps. 232 p. VG+. B28. $40.00

ORR, Myron David. *Outlander.* (1959). NY. sgn. A17. $12.00

ORTESE, Anna Maria. *Iguana.* 1987. Kingston, NY. McPherson. 1st ed. trans from Italian. F/F. A14. $20.00

ORTLOFF, Henry Stuart. *Garden Bluebook of Annuals & Biennia.* 1931. Nelson Doubleday. VG. P3. $8.00

ORTON, Harlow S. *Hist & Development of Races. Annual Address...* 1869. Madison. Atwood Rublee. 1st ed. 32 p. prt wrp. M8. $45.00

ORTON, Joe. *Head to Toe.* 1986. St Martin. 1st Am ed. F/F. A14. $20.00

ORVIS, Kenneth. *Night Without Darkness.* 1965. McClelland Stewart. VG. P3. $8.00

ORWELL, George. *Animal Farm.* 1946. Harcourt Brace. 1st ed. VG/dj. M2/M18. $75.00

ORWELL, George. *Homage to Catalonia.* ca 1952. Harcourt Brace. 1st Am ed. VG. V4. $7.50

ORWELL, George. *Road to Wigan Pier.* 1958. Harcourt Brace. 1st ed. VG/dj. M18. $65.00

ORWELL, George. *1984.* 1949. Harcourt. 1st Am ed. NF/bl & red issue djs. M2. $100.00

ORWELL, George. *1984.* 1949. NY. Harcourt Brace. 1st Am ed. F/NF bl dj. B2. $150.00

OSANKA, Franklin Mark. *Modern Guerrilla Warfare.* (1962). NY. Free Pr. 519 p. dj. A7. $35.00

OSBORN, A. *Shrubs & Trees for the Garden.* 1933. London. 1st ed. 8 color pls. 576 p. VG. B28. $65.00

OSBORN, Chase S. *Iron Hunter.* 1919. NY. 1st ed. 315 p. emb cloth. VG. A17. $30.00

OSBORN, David. *Murder in the Napa Valley.* 1993. Simon Schuster. 1st ed. F/F. M15. $25.00

OSBORN, Henry Fairfield. *Men of the Stone Age.* 1915. Scribner. 1st ed. ils. 545 p. gilt red cloth. VG. S9. $23.00

OSBORN, Henry S. *Plants of the Holy Land w/Their Fruits & Flowers.* 1860. Phil. Parry McMillan. 1st ed. 6 color pls. 174 p. VG. H5. $350.00

OSBORNE, Charles F. *Hist Houses & Their Gardens.* 1908. Phil. ils/photos. 256 p. decor cloth. VG. B26. $139.00

OSBORNE, J.A. *Williamsburg in Colonial Times.* 1935. Dietz. ils Elmo Jones. 165 p. VG. B10. $15.00

OSBORNE, Kelsie Ramey. *Peaceful Conquest: Story of Lewis & Clark...* 1955. Portland, OR. 1st ed. 8vo. 123 p. F/NF. T8. $20.00

OSBORNE, Milton E. *French Presence in Cochinchina & Cambodia.* (1969). Cornell. 379 p. F/F clip. A7. $20.00

OSBORNE, Reuben. *Freud & Marx: Diabectical Study.* 1937. London. Gollancz. 1st ed. 285 p. blk cloth. G. G1. $30.00

OSBORNE, Richard. *Basic Instinct.* 1992. Signet. 1st hc ed. F/F. F4. $15.00

OSBORNE & WEAVER. *VA State Rangers & the State Line.* 1994. np. 3600 name roster. 296 p. O7. $25.00

OSBOURNE, Katharine D. *Robert Louis Stevenson in CA.* 1911. Chicago. McClurg. 1st ed. ils. VG. E3. $30.00

OSGOOD, Cornelius. *Chinese: Study of a Hong Kong Community.* (1975). Tucson, AZ. 1st ed. 3 vols. F/F/F slipcase. A2. $65.00

OSHINS. *Quilt Collections: Directory for US & Canada.* 1987. np. ils. cloth. G2. $25.00

OSIER & WOZNIAK. *Century of Serial Publications in Psychology 1850-1950.* 1984. NY. Kraus Internat. 1st ed. thick 8vo. 806 p. gray buckram. G1. $100.00

OSKISON, John M. *Brothers Three.* 1935. Macmillan. 1st ed. F/F. L3. $375.00

OSKISON, John M. *TX Titan.* 1929. Doubleday Doran. 1st ed. VG/dj. L3. $375.00

OSKISON, John M. *Wild Harvest.* 1925. Appleton. 1st ed. inscr/dtd 1925. author's 1st book. VG. L3. $850.00

OSLER, William. *AL Student & Other Essays.* 1908. London. Oxford. 1st ed. 334 p. cloth. G. G7. $150.00

OSLER, William. *Evolution of Modern Medicine. Series of Lectures...* 1921. New Haven. Yale. 4to. 243 p. new cloth. G7. $115.00

OSLER, William. *Science & Immorality.* 1904. London. 12mo. 94 p. worn brds. G7. $45.00

OSLER, William. *Science & Immortality.* 1904. Boston. Houghton Mifflin. 12mo. ruled brn cloth. VG. G1. $75.00

OSLER. *Traditional British Quilts.* 1987. np. ils. cloth. G2. $40.00

OSMOND, Andrew. *Saladin!* 1976. Doubleday. VG/dj. P3. $10.00

OSTER, Jerry. *Club Dead.* 1988. Harper Row. F/dj. P3. $16.00

OSTER, Jerry. *Rancho Maria.* 1986. Harper Row. 1st ed. F/dj. P3. $15.00

OSTER, Jerry. *Sweet Justice.* 1985. Harper. 1st ed. F/F. S5. $25.00

OSTRANDER, Fannie. *Gift of the Magic Staff.* 1902. np. 1st ed. ils Dwiggins/Brison. F. M18. $25.00

OTELIUS, Abraham. *Thesaurus Geographicus...* 1596. Antwerp. Ex Officina Plantiniana. folio. early calf. VG+. K1. $1,000.00

OTIS, James. *Toby Tyler; or, Ten Weeks w/Circus.* 1923. Harper. VG/dj. P3. $15.00

OTIS, James. *When Dewey Came to Manila; or, Among the Filipinos.* 1899. Boston. Dana Estes. 12mo. 107 p. gilt gr brds. B11. $30.00

OTTLEY, Roi. *Lonely Warrior.* 1955. Chicago. Regnery. 1st ed. 381 p. F/dj. A7. $25.00

OTTLEY, Roi. *New World A-Coming.* (1943). Boston. ils. 364 p. VG. A17. $9.50

OTTLEY, Roi. *Wht Marble Lady.* (1965). FSG. stated 1st ed. F/dj. A7. $30.00

OTTO, Margaret G. *Great Aunt Victoria's House.* 1957. Holt. 1st ed. 8vo. 122 p. VG/VG. T5. $28.00

OTTO. *How To Make an Am Quilt.* nd. np. cloth. G2. $18.00

OTTOSON, Lars-Henrik. *Mara Moja.* (1957). NY. Roy. 1st Am ed. 8vo. 256 p. VG/VG. A2. $25.00

OTTUM, Bob. *See the Kid Run.* 1978. Simon Schuster. 1st ed. F/dj. P3. $15.00

OUIDA. *Little Earl.* (1900). Dana Estes. ils Etheldred B Barry. 82 p. VG. S10. $18.00

OUOLOGUEM, Yambo. *Bound to Violence.* 1968. Harcourt. 1st ed. 182 p. NF/F. B22. $6.00

OURSLER, Fulton. *String of Bl Beads.* 1956. Doubleday. 1st ed. 32 p. VG/G+. A3. $15.00

OURSLER, Will. *Marijuana: The Facts, the Truth.* 1968. NY. Ericksson. 1st ed. F/NF. B2. $35.00

OURSLER, Will. *Narcotics: America's Peril.* 1952. Doubleday. 1st ed. VG/VG. P3. $25.00

OUSLER, Fulton. *Greatest Story Ever Told.* 1949. Doubleday. 1st deluxe ed. VG/VG slipcase. V2. $6.00

OUTDOOR LIFE. *Anthology of Hunting Adventures.* (1946). NY. 256 p. VG. A17. $15.00

OUTDOOR LIFE. *Gallery of N Am Game.* (1967). NY. new ed. 31 full-p pls. 142 p. dj. A17. $25.00

OUTLAND, Charles. *Stagecoaching on El Camino Real.* 1973. Glendale. Clark. 1st ed. VG/G+. O3. $225.00

OVERTON, Grant. *American Nights Entertainment.* 1923. Appleton Century. 1st ed. VG. P3. $35.00

OVID. *An Elergy.* 1981. Columbia, SC. Wind Harlot. miniature. 1/200. brds. H10. $100.00

OVINGTON, Ray. *Tactics on Trout.* 1969. NY. 1st ed. 327 p. F/dj. A17. $16.50

OWEN, A.R.G. *Hysteria, Hypnosis & Healing: Work of...Charcot.* 1971. NY. Dobson. 1st ed. sm 8vo. 252 p. VG/dj. G1. $35.00

OWEN, D.D.R. *Arthurian Romance: 7 Essays.* 1972 (1970). London/Edinburgh. VG. scarce. C1. $29.00

OWEN, David Dale. *Report of Geological Survey of WI, IA & MN...NE Territory...* 1852. Lippincott. 1st ed. 2 vols. VG+. S9. $160.00

OWEN, Dean; see McGaughy, Dudley.

OWEN, Frank. *Porcelain Magician.* 1948. Gnome. 1st ed. VG. M2. $20.00

OWEN, Frank. *Scarlet Hill.* 1941. Carlyle. 1st ed. VG. M2. $17.00

OWEN, Iris M. *Conjuring Up Philip.* 1976. Harper Row. 1st ed. VG/dj. P3. $15.00

OWEN, Richard. *Key to the Geology of the Globe.* 1857. WT Berry. octavo. 1st ed. inscr. fld litho chart. emb brn cloth. H9. $350.00

OWEN, Robert Dale. *Wrong of Slavery, Right of Emancipation.* 1864. Phil. 1st ed. 246 p. VG. B18. $150.00

OWEN, Rosamund. *Art of Side-Saddle.* 1984. London. Tremton. 4to. M/M. O3. $45.00

OWENS, D. Alfred. *Progress in Psychology.* 1992. Westport. 1st ed. 334 p. prt bl-gr cloth. VG. G1. $42.50

OWENS & TAYLOR. *Complete Book of 1989 Baseball Cards.* 1989. Beekman House. 1st ed. photos. F. P8. $10.00

OXENBERG, Christina. *Taxi.* (1986). London/NY. Quartet. 1st ed. 8vo. 121 p. F/F. A2. $10.00

OXENHAM, John. *Carette of Sark.* nd. Hodder Stoughton. VG/VG-. P3. $8.00

OXLEY, J. Macdonald. *Boy Tramps; or, Across Canada.* ca 1920? Toronto. Musson. VG. N2. $7.50

OZ, Amos. *Blk Box.* 1988. Wolff/HBJ. 1st ed. trans from Hebrew. F/F. A14. $30.00

OZ, Amos. *Fima.* 1993. Harcourt. 1st ed. inscr. F/F. B2. $40.00

OZ, Amos. *Land of Israel.* 1983. HBJ. 3rd imp in Eng. NF/NF. A14. $20.00

OZ, Amos. *My Michael.* 1972. Knopf. 1st Am ed. trans from Hebrew. NF/NF. A14. $45.00

OZ, Amos. *Unto Death: Two Novellas.* 1975. HBJ. 1st ed. trans Nicolas DeLange. ils Jacob Pins. F/F clip. A14. $40.00

OZ, Amos. *Where the Jackals Howl & Other Stories.* 1981. Chatto Windus. 1st ed. trans from Hebrew. NF/NF clip. A14. $40.00

OZICK, Cynthia. *Cannibal Galaxy.* (1983). Knopf. 1st ed. w/promo material. VG/prt wht wrp. B3. $60.00

OZICK, Cynthia. *Messiah of Stockholm.* (1987). Knopf. 1st ed. F/NF clip. B3. $25.00

OZORIO DE ALMEIDA, A.L. *Colonization of the Amazon.* (1992). Austin, TX. 1st ed. 371 p. dj. F3. $20.00

PABKE, Marie. *Wonder-World Stories...* 1877. Putnam. 1st ed. 292 p. G+. S10. $30.00

PACE, Tom. *Fisherman's Luck.* nd. BC. F/F. P3. $8.00

PACK, Robert. *Guarded by Women.* 1963. NY. 1st ed. NF/VG. V1. $10.00

PACKARD, Francis R. *Some Account of PA Hospital From Its 1st Rise...to...1938.* 1938. Phil. Engle. 1st ed. 8vo. 133 p. w/8-p pamphlet. VG. B11. $85.00

PACKARD, Frank L. *Broken Waters.* 1925. Copp Clarke. VG. P3. $20.00

PACKARD, Frank L. *Doors of the Night.* 1922. Copp Clarke. VG. P3. $25.00

PACKARD, Frank L. *Pawned.* 1921. Copp Clarke. 1st Canadian ed. VG. P3. $20.00

PACKARD, J.F. *Stanley & the Congo.* 1884. Phil. 12mo. engraved pls. 733 p. gilt gr cloth. F. H3. $35.00

PACKARD, Winthrop. *Old Plymouth Trails.* (1920). Boston. ils. 351 p. gilt cloth. VG. A17. $10.00

PACKER, Vin; see Meaker, Marijane.

PADDOCK, John. *Ancient Oaxaca.* 1966. Stanford. 1st ed. 416 p. dj. F3. $50.00

PADDOCK, Judah. *Narrative of the Shipwreck Oswego on Coast of S Barbary...* 1818. NY. 1st ed. 8vo. 332 p. marbled brds/leather spine. H3. $90.00

PADDOCK, Mrs. A.G. *Fate of Madame La Tour: Tale of Great Salt Lake.* 1882. NY. Fords Howard Hulbert. 16mo. 361 p. red brds. G. B11. $75.00

PADEN, Irene D. *Prairie Schooner Detours.* 1949. Macmillan. 1st ed. VG+/dj. A17. $30.00

PADGETT, Lewis. *Gnome There Was.* 1950. Simon Schuster. 1st ed. VG/dj. M2. $90.00

PADGETT, Lewis. *Mutant.* 1953. Gnome. 1st ed. G/dj. M18. $60.00

PADGETT, Lewis. *Mutant.* 1953. Gnome. 1st ed. VG/dj. P3. $100.00

PADGETT, Lewis. *Robots Have No Tails.* 1952. Gnome. 1st ed. F/dj. M2. $190.00

PADGETT, Lewis. *Robots Have No Tails.* 1952. Gnome. 1st ed. NF/dj. P3. $150.00

PADGETT, Lewis. *Tomorrow & Tomorrow & the Fairy Chessmen.* 1951. Gnome. 1st ed. F/dj. M2. $150.00

PAGDEN, A.F. *Maya: Diego de Landa's Account of Affairs of Yucatan.* (1975). Chicago. O'Hara. 1st ed. 191 p. dj. F3. $35.00

PAGE, David. *Advanced TB of Geology, Descriptive & Industrial.* 1859. Edinburgh/London. Blackwood. 2nd ed. 403 p. emb cloth. VG. S9. $20.00

PAGE, Drew. *Drew's Blues. Sideman's Life w/Big Bands.* 1980. Baton Rouge. 1st ed. sgn. F/NF. B2. $35.00

PAGE, Jesse. *John Bright: Man of the People.* nd. NY. Fleming Revell. 12mo. 160 p. VG. V3. $14.00

PAGE, Richard C.M. *Genealogy of the Page Family in VA...* 1883. NY. Pub Prt Co. 1st ed. ils. 250 p. fair. B10. $40.00

PAGE, Thomas Nelson. *In Ole VA; or, Marse Chan & Other Stories.* 1887. Scribner. 1st ed. author's 1st book. VG. E3. $20.00

PAGE, Thomas Nelson. *Pastime Stories.* 1894. NY. Harper. 1st ed. 12mo. 22 pls. gilt bl cloth. F. B11. $75.00

PAGE, Thomas Nelson. *Two Prisoners.* 1903. Russell. 1st thus ed. 82 p. VG-. S10. $30.00

PAGE, Victor W. *Modern Automobile.* 1919. NY. revised/enlarged ed. 1032 p. decor cloth. G+. B18. $35.00

PAGE. *Body in the Kelp.* 1991. np. cloth. G2. $17.00

PAGET, Guy. *Sporting Pictures of Eng.* 1946. London. Collins Britain in Pictures. 2nd prt. VG/G+. O3. $25.00

PAGET-FREDERICKS, J. *Miss Pert's Christmas Tree.* 1929. Macmillan. 1st ed. 24 p. cloth. VG. A3. $50.00

PAGOLDH. *Nordic Knitting: 31 Patterns in Scandinavian Tradition.* 1991. np. ils. cloth. G2. $22.00

PAHER, Stanley W. *NW AZ Ghost Towns.* 1971. Gateway Pr. inscr. ils/maps/index. 48 p. NF/wrp. B19. $20.00

PAHK, Induk. *September Monkey.* 1954. Harper. 1st ed. presentation/sgn. 283 p. NF/dj. W1. $18.00

PAIGE, Richard; see Koontz, Dean R.

PAIGE, Satchel. *Maybe I'll Pitch Forever.* 1962. Doubleday. later prt. F/VG. P8. $35.00

PAIN, Barry. *Stories & Interludes.* 1892. Harper. VG-. P3. $100.00

PAIN, William. *Practical Builder; or, Workman's Assistant...* 1792. Boston. Norman. 1st Am ed. 4to. 83 pls. contemporary calf. M1. $2,000.00

PAINE, Albert Bigelow. *Hollow Tree Snowed-In Book.* 1910. Harper. 1st ed. 285 p. G+. P2. $50.00

PAINE, Albert Bigelow. *How Mr Dog Got Even.* 1915. Harper. G. A16. $16.50

PAINE, Albert Bigelow. *How Mr Rabbit Lost His Tail.* 1910. Harper. ils JM Conde. VG. M5. $25.00

PAINE, Albert Bigelow. *Thomas Nast: His Period & His Pictures.* Princeton. Pyne Pr. facsimile of 1904 ed. cloth. dj. D2. $55.00

PAINE, Martyn. *Discourse Introductory to Course of Lectures...1841-42.* 1842. Boston. Clapp. pamphlet. 34 p. G1. $35.00

PAINE, R.D. *Fight for a Free Sea.* 1920. np. 1st ed. pls/fld map. 235 p. O7. $9.50

PAINE & SOPER. *Art & Architecture of Japan.* 1955. Penguin. 1st ed. xl. 173 pls. VG. W1. $18.00

PAINE. *Embroidered Textiles.* 1990. np. cloth. G2. $35.00

PAKENHAM, Valerie. *Out in the Noonday Sun: Edwardians in the Tropics.* (1985). Random. 1st Am ed. 255 p. F/F. B22. $10.00

PAL, Pratapaditya. *Buddhist Paradise.* 1982. Hong Kong. Ravi Kumar for Visual Dharma. 1st ed. 1/3000. NF/dj. W1. $45.00

PALEY, Grace. *Collected Stories.* 1994. NY. 1st ed. sgn. M/M. E3. $45.00

PALEY, Grace. *Enormous Changes at the Last Minute.* 1973. FSG. AP. VG/tall wrp. scarce. L3. $175.00

PALGRAVE, Francis Turner. *Golden Treasury of Best Songs & Lyrical Poems...* 1861. London. Macmillan. 1st ed. 1/500. gilt gr cloth. NF. Q1. $1,500.00

PALGRAVE, Francis Turner. *Golden Treasury of Songs & Lyrics.* early 1910s. NY/London. 8vo. 18 color pls. 459 p. gilt gr cloth. VG. H3. $45.00

PALGRAVE, Francis. *Golden Treasury of Best Songs & Lyrical Poems...* nd. Doran. 12 color pls. 459 p. F. P2. $75.00

PALGRAVE, William G. *Une Annee de Voyage dans l'Arabie Centrale...* 1866. Paris. 1st French ed. 2 vols. tall 8vo. new cloth. O2. $375.00

PALLONE & STEINBERG. *Behind the Mask.* 1990. Viking. 1st ed. F/F. P8. $12.00

PALMER, Charles. *For Gold & Glory: Story of Thoroughbred Racing in Am.* 1939. NY. Carrick Evans. 1st ed. VG. O3. $28.00

PALMER, Drew; see Lucas, Mark.

PALMER, E.L. *Palmer's Fieldbook of Mammals.* 1957. NY. 1st ed. 12mo. ils. 321 p. fair dj. A17. $10.00

PALMER, Francis H.E. *Austro-Hungarian Life in Town & Country.* 1904. Detroit. 12mo. 310 p. gilt blk cloth. F. H3. $15.00

PALMER, Frederick. *Look to the E.* 1930. Dodd Mead. 1st ed. 8vo. ils/pls/maps. 332 p. VG. W1. $16.00

PALMER, Frederick. *So a Leader Came.* 1932. Ray Long & Richard Smith. 1st ed. VG. P3. $40.00

PALMER, George. *Kidnapping in the S Seas Being a Narrative...* 1871. Edinburgh. Edmonston Douglas. 8vo. expert rebacked. P4. $425.00

PALMER, James E. Jr. *Carter Glass: Unreconstructed Rebel.* 1938. Roanoke. Inst Am Biography. 1st ed. 320 p. VG. B10. $20.00

PALMER, Joe H. *This Was Racing.* 1953. Barnes. 1/1000. sgn edit/ils. VG+/worn slipcase. O3. $65.00

PALMER, John William. *Folk Songs.* 1864. Scribner. full leather. aeg. G. A16. $30.00

PALMER, Leonard R. *Mycenaens & Minoans: Aegean Prehistory...* 1965 (61). Knopf. 2nd ed. 8vo. photos. 369 p. VG+/VG+. A2. $20.00

PALMER, Marian. *Wrong Plantagenet.* 1972. BC. VG/dj. C1. $5.00

PALMER, Michael. *Sisterhood.* nd. BC. VG/dj. P3. $8.00

PALMER, Richard E. *Hermeneutics: Intrepretation Theory in Schleiermacher...* 1969. Evanston. NW U. index/biblio. 283 p. H10. $20.00

PALMER, Robert. *Deep Blues.* 1981. Viking. 1st ed. F/F. B2. $35.00

PALMER, Rose A. *N Am Indians.* (1949). Smithsonian. xl. 86 pls. G. A17. $15.00

PALMER, William J. *Detective & Mr Dickens.* nd. Quality BC. F/dj. P3. $10.00

PALMER, William. *Notes of a Visit to the Russian Church in Yrs 1840-41.* 1882. London. 1st ed. 8vo. 572 p. modern half calf. O2. $125.00

PALMER & WESTELL. *Pests of the Garden & Orchard, Farm & Forest.* (1922). London. 1st ed. 44 pls. 413 p. gilt gr cloth. VG. B28. $20.00

PALMER. *Baby Quilts From Grandma.* 1988. np. ils. wrp. G2. $16.00

PALMER. *Nifty Ninepatches.* 1992. np. 30 color photos. 72 p. wrp. G2. $18.00

PALMER. *Not Just Quilts.* 1992. np. 24 color pls. 80 p. wrp. G2. $20.00

PALMERS, Mrs. P. *Present to My Christian Friend...* 1847. NY. miniature. 134 p. cloth. H10. $15.00

PALTRINIERI, Marisa. *Trotskij. Pro e Contro.* 1973. Milan. Mondadori. Italian text. ils. sans dj. B2. $35.00

PALTSITS, Victor Hugo. *Bibliography Separate & Collected Works of Philip Freneau...* 1903. Dodd Mead. 1st ed. 96 p. prt wrp. M8. $75.00

PANAYOTOVA, Dora. *Bulgarian Mural Paintings of the 14th Century.* 1966. Sofia. Foreign Language pr. ils. dj. N2. $17.50

PANG, Hildegard. *Pre-Columbian Art.* 1992. OK U. 1st ed. lg 4to. 330 p. dj. F3. $60.00

PANGBORN, Edgar. *Trial of Callista Blake.* 1961. St Martin. 1st ed. VG/VG-. P3. $40.00

PANGBORN, Edgar. *West of the Sun.* 1953. Doubleday. 1st ed. VG/VG-. P3. $35.00

PANKEY, William Russell. *Pankey Family of VA 1635-1968.* 1968. private prt. ils. 67 p. VG. B10. $25.00

PANNENBERG, Wolfhart. *Basic Questions in Theology. Collected Essays, Vol 1.* ca 1970. Phil. Fortress. xl. 238 p. H10. $17.50

PANSE, F. *Psychiatrische Frankenhauswesen.* 1964. Stuttgart. 261 text ils/12 tables. 810 p. prt bl cloth. G1. $75.00

PANSHIN, A.J. *Forest Products.* 1962. McGraw Hill. ils 538 p. H10. $15.00

PANSHIN, Alexei. *Farewell to Yesterday's Tomorrow.* 1975. Berkley Putnam. 1st ed. VG/dj. P3. $18.00

PANSY. *Mother's Boys & Girls.* nd. Lothrop. 12mo. 300 p. G. S10. $30.00

PANTAZOPOULOS, N.J. *Church & Law in the Balkan Peninsula...* 1967. Thessaloniki. 8vo. 121 p. O2. $35.00

PANTER-DOWNES, Mollie. *Otty Preserved: Victorian Hill Station in India.* (1967). FSG. 1st Am ed. 8vo. F/VG. A2. $12.50

PAPADAKI, Stamo. *Le Corbusier: Architect, Painter, Writer.* 1948. NY. Macmillan. sm 4to. 152 p. VG/dj. F1. $80.00

PAPAZOGLOU, Orania. *Sanctity.* 1986. Crown. 1st ed. VG/dj. P3. $17.00

PAPERNY, Myra. *Wooden People.* 1976. Little Brn. 1st Am ed. 168 p. F/VG. P2. $20.00

PARAMOURE, Anne. *Complete Miniature Schnauzer.* (1959). Denlinger. ils/registration index. 528 p. A17. $12.50

PARETSKY, Sara. *Bitter Medicine.* nd. BC. VG/dj. P3. $8.00

PARETSKY, Sara. *Bitter Medicine.* 1987. London. Gollancz. ARC of 1st British ed. sgn. RS. F/F. S5. $50.00

PARETSKY, Sara. *Blood Shot.* 1988. Delacorte. 1st ed. VG/F. B3. $25.00

PARETSKY, Sara. *Blood Shot.* 1988. Delacorte. 1st ed. sgn. F/F. B2. $45.00

PARETSKY, Sara. *Burn Marks.* 1990. Delacorte. 1st ed. F/F. M15. $30.00

PARETSKY, Sara. *Indemnity Only.* 1982. NY. Dial. 1st ed. inscr. author's 1st book. F/NF. L3. $1,250.00

PARETSKY, Sara. *Tunnel Vision.* 1994. Delacorte. AP. F/wrp. B2. $40.00

PARGETER, Edith; see Peters, Ellis.

PARGETER, William. *Observations on Maniacal Disorders.* 1988. London. Routledge. facsimile reprint of London 1792 ed. bl cloth. F/dj. G1. $27.50

PARGOIRE, Pere J. *L'Eglise Byzantine de 527 a 847.* 1905. Paris. 8vo. 405 p. contemporary calf. O2. $40.00

PARISH, Helen Rand. *Las Casas As a Bishop.* 1980. Lib of Congress. 1st ed. folio. 41 p. F3. $35.00

PARISH, James Robert. *Hollywood Character Actors.* 1978. Arlington. 1st ed. VG/VG. P3. $35.00

PARISH, James Robert. *Vincent Price Unmasked.* 1974. Drake. VG/dj. P3. $20.00

PARK, Jordan; see Kornbluth, Cyril.

PARK, Paul. *Soldiers of Paradise.* 1987. Arbor. 1st ed. F/F. P3. $18.00

PARK, Roswell. *Evil Eye, Thanatology & Other Essays.* 1912. Boston. Badger. 12mo. 380 p. prt gr cloth. VG. G1. $50.00

PARK, Ruth Brown. *Book Shops: How To Run Them.* 1929. Doubleday Doran. 1st ed. 152 p. VG/remnant dj. B18. $17.50

PARK, Ruth. *Witch's Thorn.* 1952. Houghton Mifflin. 1st ed. VG/dj. P3. $35.00

PARKER, A.A. *Recollections of Gen Lafayette on His Visit to US...* 1879. Keene, NH. 1st ed. presentation/dtd 1881. 148 p. cloth. M1. $75.00

PARKER, Al. *Baseball Giant Killers.* 1976. Nortex. 1st ed. F/VG+. P8. $100.00

PARKER, B. *Brns: Book of Bears.* nd. Donohue. ils N Parker. scarce. F1. $200.00

PARKER, Edward. *My 58 Yrs.* 1943. NY. 167 p. VG. C5. $10.00

PARKER, Franklin. *Travels in Central Am 1821-40.* 1970. Gainesville, FL. 1st ed. 340 p. dj. F3. $35.00

PARKER, Gail Thain. *Mind Cure in New Eng From Civil War to WWI.* 1973. Hanover, NH. New Eng U Pr. beige cloth. F/dj. G1. $20.00

PARKER, Gilbert. *Seats of the Mighty.* 1896. NY. Appleton. VG. N2. $5.00

PARKER, Maude. *Which Mrs Torr?* 1951. Rinehart. 1st ed. front free ep removed. VG/dj. P3. $10.00

PARKER, Nathan Howe. *IA As It Is in 1855.* 1855. Chicago. Keen Lee. 8vo. 9 pls/tables. 264 p. emb rose cloth. H9. $125.00

PARKER, Pat. *Movement in Blk: Collected Poetry of Pat Parker 1961-78.* (1978). Oakland. Diana Pr. 1st ed. F/NF. B4. $85.00

PARKER, Robert B. *Catskill Eagle.* 1985. Delacorte. 1st ed. VG/dj. P3. $18.00

PARKER, Robert B. *Catskill Eagle.* 1985. Delacorte/Lawrence. 1st ed. inscr. F/F. M15. $25.00

PARKER, Robert B. *Ceremony.* 1982. Delacorte. 1st ed. F/NF. B2. $35.00

PARKER, Robert B. *Double Deuce.* 1992. Putnam. 1/250. sgn. F/dj. C4. $100.00

PARKER, Robert B. *Early Autumn.* 1981. Delacorte. 1st ed. inscr/sgn. F/F. S5. $55.00

PARKER, Robert B. *Godwulf Manuscript.* 1974. Houghton Mifflin. 1st ed. inscr/intl. NF/NF. Q1. $350.00

PARKER, Robert B. *Judas Goat.* 1978. Houghton Mifflin. 1st ed. F/F. M15. $85.00

PARKER, Robert B. *Judas Goat.* 1978. Houghton Mifflin. 1st ed. VG/dj. P3. $40.00

PARKER, Robert B. *Judas Goat.* 1982. London. Deutsch. 1st ed. F/F. C4. $35.00

PARKER, Robert B. *Pale Kings & Princes.* (1987). Delacorte. AP. 1/500. NF/wrp. B9. $50.00

PARKER, Robert B. *Pale Kings & Princes.* 1987. Delacorte. 1st ed. F/F. P3. $16.00

PARKER, Robert B. *Paper Doll.* 1993. Putnam. 1/135. sgn/#d. F/slipcase. C4. $100.00

PARKER, Robert B. *Savage Place.* 1981. Delacorte. 1st ed. inscr/sgn. F/F. S5. $75.00

PARKER, Robert B. *Wilderness.* (1979). Delacorte/Lawrence. AP. sgn. NF/wrp. B9. $125.00

PARKER, Robert B. *Wilderness.* 1979. Delacorte/Lawrence. 1st ed. F/F. M15. $65.00

PARKER, Rowland. *Common Stream: Portrait of Eng Village Through 2,000 Yrs.* (1975). NY. HRW. no prt listed. 8vo. 283 p. VG+/F. A2. $12.50

PARKER, Samuel. *Journal of an Exploring Tour Beyond the Rocky Mtns.* 1844. Ithaca, NY. 4th ed. 12mo. 416 p. orig cloth. H9. $295.00

PARKER, T. Jefferson. *Laguna Heat.* nd. BC. VG/dj. P3. $8.00

PARKER, T. Jefferson. *Little Saigon.* 1988. St Martin. 1st ed. F/F. P3. $19.00

PARKHURST, Lewis. *Vacation on the Nile.* 1913. Boston. private prt. 1/500. 115 p. teg. heavy gilt bl cloth. F. H3. $45.00

PARKINSON, C. Northcote. *Fireship.* 1975. Houghton Mifflin. 1st Am ed. VG/dj. A16. $10.00

PARKMAN, Francis Jr. *CA & the OR Trail.* 1849. NY. Putnam. 1st ed. 1/1000. octavo. rebound gr quarter morocco. H9. $550.00

PARKMAN, Francis Jr. *France & Eng in N Am.* 1869. Little Brn. 1st ed. part 3 of series. 425 p. orange cloth. H9. $50.00

PARKMAN, Francis. *Discovery of the Great W.* 1869. London. Murray. 1st ed. gilt purple cloth. VG. A18. $60.00

PARKMAN, Francis. *Half-Century of Conflict.* 1892. Boston. 1st ed. 2 vols. orig gilt cloth. F. A17. $75.00

PARKMAN, Francis. *Montcalm & Wolfe.* 1884. Boston. 1st ed/1st issue. 2 vols. gilt cloth. VG. A17. $65.00

PARKMAN, Francis. *Montcalm & Wolfe.* 1984. BC. M/dj/slipcase. C1. $7.50

PARKMAN, Francis. *Old Regime in Canada. Vol 1, 2 & 3.* 1874. Little Brn. 1st ed. 448 p. gilt pebbled gr cloth. VG. B28. $75.00

PARKMAN, Francis. *Prairie & Rocky Mtn Life of the CA & OR Trail.* 1856. Columbus, OH. 3rd ed. 448 p. rebacked. VG. D7. $175.00

PARKMAN, Francis. *Works of...* 1903. Little Brn. Frontenac ed. 17 vols. NF. E5. $175.00

PARKMAN, Francis. *Works of...* 1895-97. Little Brn. set ed. 12mo. 11 vols (9 F/2 VG). A2. $125.00

PARKS, George Bruner. *Richard Hakluyt & the Eng Voyages.* 1928. Am Geog Soc. Special Pub 10. ils/fld map. NF. O6. $55.00

PARKS, Gordon. *Choice of Weapons.* (1966). Harper Row. 1st ed. VG+/VG+. A7. $35.00

PARKS, Gordon. *Flavio.* (1978). Norton. 2nd prt. 198 p. dj. A7. $18.00

PARKS, Gordon. *Gordon Parks: Whispers of Intimate Things.* (1971). Viking. 1st ed. quarto. F/dj. A7. $25.00

PARKS, Gordon. *Learning Tree.* 1963. Harper. 1st ed. sgn/dtd 1963. author's 1st book. F/NF. F4. $35.00

PARKS, Gordon. *Poet & His Camera.* (1968). Viking. 1st ed. lg 8vo. photos. VG+/dj. A7. $17.00

PARKS, Gordon. *Shannon.* (1981). Little Brn. 1st ed. VG/dj. A7. $30.00

PARKS, Tim. *Tongues of Flame.* (1986). Grove. 1st ed. F/F. B3. $20.00

PARLEY, Peter; see Goodrich, Samuel G.

PARLIN, S.W. *Am Trotter.* 1905. Boston. Am Horse Breeder. 1st ed. VG. O3. $65.00

PARMELEE, David F. *Bird Island in Antarctic Waters.* 1980. MN U. ils. 140 p. bl cloth. M/M. P4. $35.00

PARMELIN, Helene. *Peintre et son Modele.* nd. Paris. 1/125. VG/VG. A1. $650.00

PARMENTER, Ross. *Week in Yanhuitlan.* (1964). Albuquerque, NM. 1st ed. 375 p. dj. F3. $25.00

PARRISH, Frank. *Bird in the Net.* 1988. Harper Row. 1st ed. VG/dj. P3. $16.00

PARRISH, Frank. *Face at the Window.* 1984. London. Constable. 1st ed. F/F. T2. $12.00

PARRISH, Maxfield. *Arabian Nights. Their Best-Known Tales.* 1930 (1909). Scribner. 4to. 339 p. VG-. A3. $75.00

PARRISH, Maxfield. *Poems of Childhood.* ca 1930. Scribner. 4to. 199 p. blk cloth w/pict label. VG-. A3. $65.00

PARRISH & WILLINGHAM. *Confederate Imprints: Bibliography of S Pub...* (1987?). Jenkins Foster. ils. 991 p. as new. B10. $75.00

PARRY, Dennis. *Survivor.* 1940. Holt. 1st ed. ownership sgn Donald Wandrel. VG/dj. F4. $50.00

PARRY, Edwin Satterthwaite. *Betsy Ross, Quaker Rebel.* 1930. Phil. Winston. 1st ed. 8vo. 252 p. VG. V3. $12.00

PARRY, J.H. *Discovery of S Am.* 1979. Taplinger. 1st Am ed. 8vo. ils. 320 p. orange cloth. VG/dj. P4. $40.00

PARRY, Michael. *Savage Heros.* 1980. Taplinger. 1st Am ed. F/VG. N3. $15.00

PARRY, William Edward. *Journal of Voyage for Discovery of NW Passage.* 1821. London. Murray. quarto. presentation. 14 sepia pls/6 charts. half brn morocco. H9. $1,800.00

PARRY. *Textiles of the Arts & Crafts Movement.* 1988. np. wrp. G2. $23.00

PARSONS, Herbert Collins. *Puritan Outpost.* 1937. NY. 1/500. 546 p. VG/dj. B28. $65.00

PARSONS, J.E. *1st Winchester: Story of the 1866 Repeating Rifle.* 1955. NY. 1st ed. 207 p. A17. $35.00

PARSONS, Mary E. *Wild Flowers of CA: Their Names, Haunts & Habits.* 1960 (1897). San Francisco. revised ed. ils Margaret W Buck. 423 p. F/dj. B26. $17.50

PARSONS, P. Allen. *Complete Book of Fresh-Water Fishing.* (1969). NY. 14th prt. 332 p. F/G. A17. $12.50

PARTCH, Virgil. *Water on the Brain.* 1945. NY. 1st ed. 4to. 127 p. pict brds. VG. H3. $15.00

PARTON, James. *Daughters of Genius.* 1885. Phil. Hubbard. 1st ed. octavo. 22 pls. 563 p. orig brn cloth. NF. H5. $100.00

PARTON, James. *Life & Times of Aaron Burr.* 1870. Boston. later prt. 2 vols. G+. D7. $55.00

PARTON, James. *Life & Times of Aaron Burr.* 1888. Houghton Mifflin. 2 vols. gilt bdg. VG. E5. $45.00

PARTON, James. *Life of Horace Greeley.* 1855. NY. Mason. 1st ed. VG. B2. $75.00

PARTON, James. *Life of Horace Greeley.* 1869. Boston. xl. 8vo. ils. 598 p. gr cloth. T3. $15.00

PARTRIDGE, William L. *Hippie Ghetto: Natural Hist of a Subculture.* 1973. Holt. 1st ed. NF/wrp. B2. $25.00

PARUTA, Paolo. *Historia Venetiana.* 1605. Venice. Nicolini. 1st ed. thick 4to. contemporary vellum. O2. $1,800.00

PASCH, Katharine. *Basketry & Weaving in the Schools.* 1904. Chicago. Flanagan. pamphlet. 27 p. NF/wrp. P4. $75.00

PASCOE, C.F. *200 Yrs of the Soc Propagation of Gospel: Hist Account...* 1901. London. Soc Propagation of the Gospel. 500 p. worn. H10. $25.00

PASHLEY, Robert. *Travels in Crete.* 1837. London. 2 vols. 8vo. lg fld map. half crushed red levant. O2. $750.00

PASSINGHAM, W.J. *London's Markets: Their Origin & Hist.* (ca 1935). London. Sampson Low Marston. 1st ed. 8vo. 302 p. VG/VG. A2. $30.00

PASTAN, Linda. *Perfect Circle.* 1971. Swallow. 1st ed. author's 1st book. F/VG+. V1. $45.00

PASTERNAK, Boris. *Doctor Zhivago.* 1959. London. Collins/Harvill. 13th imp in Eng. trans from Russian. VG+/VG+. A14. $20.00

PASTERNAK, Boris. *In the Interlude: Poems 1945-60.* 1962. NY. Oxford. 1st ed. F/dj. C4. $35.00

PATAI, Raphael. *Gates to the Old City: Book of Jewish Legends.* 1981. Wayne State. 807 p. VG+/G+. S3. $20.00

PATCHEN, Kenneth. *See You in the Morning.* 1947. Padell. 1st ed. VG/dj. M18. $45.00

PATCHETT, M.E. *Kidnappers of Space.* 1953. Lutterworth. 1st ed. VG-/dj. P3. $15.00

PATCHIN, Frank Gee. *Pony Rider Boys w/TX Rangers.* nd. Saalfield. VG/dj. P3. $15.00

PATER, Walter. *Gaston De Latour: An Unfinished Romance.* 1896. London. Macmillan. 1st ed. aeg. Doves bdg. F. B14. $1,250.00

PATER, Walter. *Greek Studies: Series of Essays...* 1895. London. Macmillan. 1st ed. aeg. Doves bdg. F. B14. $1,250.00

PATER, Walter. *Studies in the Hist of the Renaissance.* 1873. London. Macmillan. 1st ed. 12mo. VG. G1. $150.00

PATERSON, Katherine. *Of Nightingales That Weep.* 1974. NY. Crowell. 1st ed. ils H Wells. VG+/G+. T5. $45.00

PATERSON, W.P. *Conversion.* 1939. London. Hodder Stoughton. 209 p. H10. $20.00

PATON, Alan. *Apartheid & the Archbishop.* (1973). Scribner. 1st ed. F/VG. B4. $65.00

PATON, Alan. *Cry, the Beloved Country.* 1948. NY. 1st ed. w/sgn label. VG/VG. E3. $65.00

PATON, Alan. *Cry, the Beloved Country.* 1948. Scribner. G/worn. E3. $20.00

PATON, Alan. *S African Tragedy: Life & Times of Jan Hofmeyr.* (1965). Scribner. ARC. RS. laid in dj. A7. $40.00

PATRI, Giovanni. *Wht Collar.* (1940). San Francisco. Pisani. quarto. 125 p. NF/stiff wrp. B20. $175.00

PATRICK, Q. *Return to the Scene.* 1941. Simon Schuster. 1st ed. VG-. P3. $10.00

PATRICK, William. *Spirals.* 1983. Houghton Mifflin. 1st ed. RS. F/dj. P3. $15.00

PATTEN, Gilbert. *Frank Merriwell's Father.* 1964. Norman, OK. 1st ed. 324 p. VG+/dj. M20. $27.00

PATTENGILL, H.R. *Song Knapsack.* 1899. Lansing. Pattengill. fair. A16. $6.00

PATTERSON, A.B. *3 Elephant Power.* 1917. Angus Robertson. 1st ed. sgn. VG/rare dj. B4. $375.00

PATTERSON, Augusta. *Am Homes of Today: Their Architectural Style...* 1924. Macmillan. 1st ed. sm folio. 400 p. NF. B20. $75.00

PATTERSON, Grove. *I Like People.* 1954. Random. 1st ed. sgn. 300 p. VG/dj. M20. $14.00

PATTERSON, Harry; see Patterson, Henry.

PATTERSON, Henry. *Coasts of Adventure.* 1927. Chelsea. 1st ed. NF/dj. M2. $25.00

PATTERSON, Henry. *Day of Judgment.* 1978. Collins. 1st ed. VG/dj. P3. $20.00

PATTERSON, Henry. *Day of Judgment.* 1978. London. Collins. 1st ed. F/F. M15. $45.00

PATTERSON, Henry. *Luciano's Luck.* 1981. London. Collins. 1st ed. F/F. S5. $40.00

PATTERSON, Henry. *Night of the Fox.* 1986. Simon Schuster. 1st ed. VG/dj. P3. $17.95

PATTERSON, Henry. *Solo.* 1980. Stein Day. 1st ed. F/VG. B3. $30.00

PATTERSON, Henry. *Solo.* 1980. Stein Day. 1st ed. VG/dj. P3. $15.00

PATTERSON, Henry. *Touch the Devil.* (1982). Stein Day. 1st ed. F/VG. B3. $30.00

PATTERSON, Henry. *Valhalla Exchange.* nd. BOMC. VG/dj. P3. $10.00

PATTERSON, Henry. *Valhalla Exchange.* 1976. Stein Day. 1st ed. VG/G. A8. $18.00

PATTERSON, Innis. *Eppworth Case.* 1930. Farrar Rinehart. 1st ed. VG/dj. P3. $30.00

PATTERSON, James T. *Am's Struggle Against Poverty 1900-1980.* 1981. Cambridge. Harvard. 268 p. NF/NF clip. A7. $13.00

PATTERSON, James. *Midnight Club.* 1989. Little Brn. 1st ed. F/F. M15. $30.00

PATTERSON, James. *Thomas Berryman Number.* 1976. Little Brn. 1st ed. F/F. M15. $65.00

PATTERSON, Jerry. *Autographs: A Collectors Guide.* 1973. np. 1st ed. xl. 248 p. NF. O7. $27.50

PATTERSON, R.M. *Buffalo Head.* 1961. NY. 1st ed. photos. 273 p. dj. A17. $15.00

PATTERSON, R.M. *Buffalo Head.* 1961. Sloane. 1st ed. 273 p. VG/dj. M20. $25.00

PATTERSON, Richard North. *Private Screening.* 1986. Michael Joseph. 1st ed. NF/dj. P3. $22.00

PATTERSON, Webster T. *Newman: Pioneer for the Layman.* ca 1968. WA, DC. Corpus. 193 p. H10. $15.00

PATTERSON, William L. *We Charge Genocide.* 1951. Civil Rights Congress. 4th prt/wrp issue. 238 p. A7. $15.00

PATTON & SIMKINS. *Women of the Confederacy.* ca 1936. Garrett Massie. 306 p. VG. B10. $55.00

PAUL, Barbara. *But He Was Already Dead When I Got There.* 1986. Scribner. 1st ed. F/dj. P3. $14.00

PAUL, Barbara. *In-Laws & Outlaws.* 1990. Scribner. 1st ed. F/F. T2. $18.00

PAUL, Ellen. *Back East.* 1983. Boston. Godine. 1st ed. author's 1st book. NF/NF. A14. $25.00

PAUL, Elliot. *Ghost Town on the Yellowstone.* (1948). NY. 1st prt. xl. 341 p. cloth. VG/pict dj. D3. $12.50

PAUL, F.W.; see Fairman, Paul.

PAUL, Jaqueline. *Japan Quest: Ils Opinion of Modern Japanese Life.* 1962. Rokakuho/Tuttle. 1st prt. sm oblong folio. 161 p. VG/torn. W1. $22.00

PAUL, Sherman. *Olson's Push.* (1978). Baton Rouge. 291 p. F/F. A7. $17.00

PAUL & PAUL. *Proletcult (Proletarian Culture).* 1921. London. Parsons. 1st ed VG. B2. $75.00

PAULI & ASHTON. *I Lift My Lamp: Way of a Symbol.* (1948). NY. Appleton Century. 1st ed. 8vo. 368 p. F/VG+. A2. $20.00

PAULLIN, Charles O. *Atlas of the Hist Geog of the US.* 1932. Carnegie/Am Geog Soc. Samuel Eliot Morison's copy. 688 p. NF. O6. $350.00

PAULSEN, Gary. *Winter Room.* 1989. Orchard Books. 1st ed. 8vo. 103 p. F/F. T5. $40.00

PAULSON, Dennis. *Shorebirds of the Pacific NW.* 1993. Seattle Audubon Soc. pub review copy. M/M. T8. $30.00

PAVIC, Milorad. *Dictionary of the Khazars: Lexicon Novel (Female Ed).* 1988. London. Hamish Hamilton. 1st ed. F/F. A14. $30.00

PAVIC, Milorad. *Landscape Painted w/Tea.* 1990. Knopf. 1st ed. trans from Serbo-Croatian. NF/NF. A14. $25.00

PAVLIN & SEDA. *Gulliver's Travels.* 1979. 6 pop-ups. VG. A4. $15.00

PAVLOV, I.P. *Conditioned Reflexes.* 1927. London. Oxford. 1st Eng-language ed. lg octavo. 430 p. VG. H5. $275.00

PAVLOV, Ivan Petrovich. *Die Arbeit der Verdauungsdrusen.* 1898. Wiesbaden. Bergmann. 199 p. VG. G7. $2,500.00

PAVLOV, Ivan Petrovich. *Works of the Digestive Glands.* 1910. London. 2nd Eng ed. 266 p. new cloth. G7. $115.00

PAYES, Rachel Cosgrove. *Forsythia Finds Murder.* 1960. Avalon. 1st ed. xl. dj. P3. $8.00

PAYNE, Alan; see Jakes, John.

PAYNE, John. *Geographical Extracts, Forming a General View of Earth...* 1796. London. Robinson. 8vo. 2 lg fld maps. old calf backed brds. H9. $275.00

PAYNE, Laurence. *Malice in Camera.* 1983. Crime Club. 1st ed. F/F. P3. $15.00

PAYNE, Laurence. *Spy for Sale.* 1969. Hodder Stoughton. 1st ed. F/NF. M15. $30.00

PAZ, Octavio. *On Poets & Others.* (1986). NY. Seaver. 1st ed. F/F. B3. $25.00

PAZ, Octavio. *Selected Poems.* 1984. New Directions. 1st ed. trans from Spanish. NF/NF clip. A14. $20.00

PEABODY, Robert E. *Log of the Grand Turks.* 1926. Boston. 1st ed. 249 p. bl cloth. VG+. H3. $25.00

PEACOCK, A. *Peacock Pillow Book: Tales of Mother Goose.* 1964. Berkeley. Peacock Pr. miniature. 1/200. 12 p. NF/stiff wrp. B24. $45.00

PEACOCK, Molly. *Raw Heaven.* 1984. NY. 1st ed/2nd prt. F/NF. V1. $10.00

PEACOCK, Thomas Love. *Misfortunes of Elpitin.* 1948 (1829). London. VG. C1. $12.50

PEADEN. *Irish Chain Quilts.* 1988. np. ils. wrp. G2. $15.00

PEAKE, Mervyn. *Ride a Cock-Horse & Other Nursery Rhymes.* 1940. Chatto Windus. 1st ed. 4to. 29 p. VG/VG. D1. $650.00

PEAKE, Mervyn. *Titus Groan.* 1946. Reynal Hitchcock. 1st ed. NF/dj. P3. $250.00

PEAN, Charles. *Conquest of Devil's Island.* 1953. London. Parrish. 1st ed. 12mo. 188 p. map ep. blk brds. VG. B11. $35.00

PEARCE, Cunliffe R. *Confident Fly Fisher.* (1979). London. reprint. 205 p. F/dj. A17. $16.50

PEARCE, Dick. *Impudent Rifle.* 1948. Lippincott. 1st ed. VG/dj. L3. $35.00

PEARCE, Philippa. *Squirrel Wife.* 1972 (1971). Crowell. 1st Am ed. 8vo. 60 p. beige cloth. F/VG. T5. $35.00

PEARCE, Samuel. *Memoirs of the Late Rev Samuel Pearce...* 1801. Boston. Manning Loring. shabby leather. H10. $25.00

PEARCE, Stanley. *Lift Up Your Hearts: Hist of Trinity Parish, Menlo Park.* 1974. Trinity Parish. 1st ed. ils. 195 p. B19. $15.00

PEARL, Jack. *Dam of Death.* 1967. Whitman. VG. P3. $8.00

PEARL, Jack. *Garrison's Gorilla & Fear Formula.* 1968. Whitman. 1st ed. pict brds. F/sans. F4. $12.00

PEARL, Raymond. *To Begin w/Being Prophylaxis Against Pedantry.* 1927. Knopf. sgn. VG. B14. $55.00

PEARON. *Traditional Knitting, Aran, Fair Isle & Fisher Ganseys.* 1984. np. ils. cloth. G2. $20.50

PEARSALL, Ronald. *Conan Doyle: Biological Solution.* 1977. London. Weidenfeld. 1st ed. ils. NF/dj. S5. $22.50

PEARSON, E.L. *Theodore Roosevelt.* 1925. NY. 12mo. 159 p. bl cloth. G. T3. $15.00

PEARSON, Edmund. *Dime Novels; or, Following Old Trail in Popular Literature.* 1929. Little Brn. 1st ed. ils/index. F/dj. A18. $50.00

PEARSON, Gardner W. *Records of the MA Volunteer Militaria...1812-14.* 1913. Boston. Wright Potter. 4to. 448 p. blk cloth. B14. $75.00

PEARSON, Henry Greenleaf. *Life of John A Andrew.* 1904. np. 1st ed. 2 vols. w/sgn letter. F. O7. $32.50

PEARSON, John. *James Bond, the Authorized Biography.* 1973. Morrow. 1st ed. VG/dj. P3. $50.00

PEARSON, John. *Kindness of Dr Avicenna.* 1982. HRW. 1st ed. F/dj. P3. $15.00

PEARSON, John. *Life of Ian Fleming.* 1966. London. Cap. 1st ed. ils. VG/dj. S5. $35.00

PEARSON, John. *Wildlife & Safari In Kenya.* ca 1970. Nairobi. African Pub House. ils/maps. 384 p. A17. $20.00

PEARSON, Ridley. *Undercurrents.* 1988. St Martin. 1st ed. VG/dj. P3. $18.00

PEARSON, Virginia. *Everything But Elephants.* (1947). Whittlesey House. 1st ed. 211 p. F3. $10.00

PEARSON, Willard. *Vietnam Studies.* 1975. WA. Dept of Army. 115 p. wrp. A7. $25.00

PEARSON, William. *Hunt the Man Down.* nd. BC. VG/dj. P3. $8.00

PEARSON & PEARSON. *Rainforest Plants of E Australia.* 1992. Kenthurst, Australia. 550 color photos. 224 p. M. B26. $45.00

PEARSON. *Complete Needlepoint Course.* 1991. np. ils. cloth. G2. $28.00

PEARY, Gerald. *Little Caesar.* 1981. WI U. NF. C8. $30.00

PEASE, Howard. *Jungle River.* 1938. Doubleday Doran. 295 p. blk cloth. VG+/dj. M20. $15.00

PEAT, Fern Bisel. *Three Little Kittens Lost Their Mittens.* 1931. Saalfield. 12 ils p. VG/stiff wrp. M5. $30.00

PEAT, Frank E. *Christmas Carols.* 1937. Saalfield. later prt. ils/sgn Fern Bisel Peat. pict brds. VG+/dj. M20. $75.00

PEATTIE, Donald C. *Sportman's Country.* 1952. Boston. 1st ed. ils Henry Kane. 180 p. dj. A17. $9.50

PEATTIE, Donald Culross. *Gr Laurels: Lives & Achievements of Great Naturalists.* 1936. NY. 1st ed. NF. T8. $15.00

PECK, Charles H. *Annual Report of State Botanist of State of NY.* 1897. Albany. 2nd ed. 43 full-p color pls. 241 p. B28. $125.00

PECK, George W. *Peck's Bad Boy w/the Circus.* 1906. Chicago. Stanton. VG. N2. $10.00

PECK, Robert Newton. *Day No Pigs Would Die.* 1972. Knopf. 1st ed. 150 p. VG+/VG+. M20. $22.00

PECK, Walter Edwin. *Shelley: His Life & Work.* 1927. Houghton Mifflin. 1st ed. 2 vols. cloth. VG. M20. $40.00

PEDIGO & PEDIGO. *Hist of Patrick & Henry Counties.* 1933. Stone Prt. inscr. 400 p. B10. $90.00

PEEL, Colin D. *Flameout.* 1976. St Martin. 1st ed. F/F. P3. $15.00

PEIRSON, Erma. *Mojave River & Its Valley.* 1970. Glendale. Arthur Clark. 3 maps. M/dj. O6. $35.00

PEIXOTTO, Ernest. *Romantic CA.* 1910. NY. 1st ed. 20 pls. 219 p. gilt cloth. VG. D3. $35.00

PELHAM, Camden. *Chronicles of Crime; or, New Newgate Calendar.* 1887 (1841). London. T Miles. 2 vols. pebbled ruled bl cloth. VG. G1. $85.00

PELHAM, David. *A Is for Animals, 26 Pop-Up Surprises.* 1991. F. A4. $45.00

PELIKAN, Jaroslav. *Spirit Versus Structure...* ca 1968. Harper Row. xl. 149 p. H10. $17.50

PELISSIER, Roger. *Awakening of China, 1793-1949.* 1967. NY. Putnam. 1st Am ed. trans Martin Kiefer. 532 p. VG/torn. W1. $18.00

PELL, Franklyn. *Hangman's Hill.* 1946. Dodd Mead. 1st ed. VG/dj. P3. $23.00

PELLEGRINO, Charles. *Unearthing Atlantis.* 1991. Random. 1st ed. F/dj. P3. $23.00

PELLENS & TERRY. *Opium Problem.* 1928. Committee Drug Addiction. 1st ed. NF. quite scarce. B2. $85.00

PELLETTIER. *Favorite Patchwork Patterns.* 1984. np. wrp. G2. $4.50

PELLMAN & PELLMAN. *Amish Crib Quilts.* 1985. np. ils. wrp. G2. $16.00

PELLMAN & PELLMAN. *Amish Doll Quilts, Dolls, & Other Playthings.* 1986. np. ils. wrp. G2. $16.00

PELLMAN & PELLMAN. *Treasury of Amish Quilts.* 1990. np. ils. wrp. G2. $20.00

PELLMAN & RAFLOVICH. *Back Art.* 1991. np. ils. wrp. G2. $20.00

PELLMAN & RANCK. *Quilts Among the Plain People.* 1984. np. ils. wrp. G2. $6.00

PELLOWSKI, Anne. *First Farm in the Valley: Anna's Story.* 1982. Philomel Books. 1st ed. ils Wendy Watson. 189 p. VG+/VG. T5. $25.00

PELLY, T.M. *Dr Minor: A Sketch of...Thomas T Minor, MD (1844-89).* 1933. Seattle. Lowman Hanford. 1st ed. sgn. 135 p. red cloth. B20. $100.00

PELTASON, Jack. *Constitutional Liberty & Seditious Activity...* 1954. NY. Carrie Chapman Catt Memorial Fund. 57 p. wrp. M11. $20.00

PELTIER & SALLOT. *Bearwalk.* 1977. Ontario. Don Mills. 1st ed. NF/clip. L3. $65.00

PEMJEAN, Lucien; see Jones, H. Bedford.

PEMJION, L.; see Jones, H. Bedford.

PENALOSA, Javier. *Flora of the Tiburon Peninsula, Marin County, CA.* 1963. San Francisco. photos/map. VG. B26. $22.50

PENDERGAST, David. *Palenque.* (1967). Norman, OK. 1st ed. 213 p. dj. F3. $30.00

PENDERS. *Color & Cloth.* 1989. np. ils. wrp. G2. $20.00

PENDEXTER, Hugh. *Pay Gravel.* (1922). Bobbs Merrill. 1st ed. VG+/dj. B9. $45.00

PENDLETON, Don. *Copp for Hire.* 1987. Donald Fine. 1st ed. F/F. F4. $20.00

PENDLETON, Don. *Copp in the Dark.* 1990. Donald Fine. 1st ed. F/F. P3. $19.00

PENDLETON, Don. *Copp on Ice.* 1991. Donald Fine. 1st ed. F/F. F4. $19.00

PENDRAY. *Stitching Toward Perfection.* 1989. np. pb. sgn. G2. $13.00

PENICK, I.B. *Empire Strikes Back: A Pop-Up Book.* 1980. Random. VG. P3. $15.00

PENICK. *Story of Statue of Liberty w/Movable Ils in 3-Dimensions.* 1986. F. A4. $35.00

PENINGTON, Isaac. *Letters of Isaac Penington...* 1796. London. Phillips. 1st ed. 8vo. 132 p. VG. V3. $95.00

PENN, John. *Ad for Murder.* 1982. Scribner. 1st ed. F/dj. P3. $15.00

PENN, John. *Feast of Death.* 1989. London. Collins. 1st ed. F/F. S5. $30.00

PENN, William. *Collection of Works of...* 1726. London. Assigns of J Sowle. 1st ed. 2 vols. thick quarto. G. R3. $600.00

PENN, William. *Journal of..., While Visiting Holland & Germany in 1677.* 1878. Friends Bookstore. 16mo. 189 p. VG. V3. $20.00

PENN, William. *Primitive Christianity Revived...People Called Quakers.* 1878. Phil. Longstreth. 16mo. 89 p. VG. V3. $20.00

PENNELL, Joseph. *Adventures of an Ils.* 1925. Little Brn. 1st ed. quarto. 372 p. gilt cloth. B24. $65.00

PENNELL, Jospeh. *Adventures of an Ils.* 1925. Boston. Little Brn. ltd ed. sgn. 372 p. orig gilt calf over cloth. K1. $300.00

PENNELL & PENNELL. *Life of James McNeill Whistler.* 1908. London. Heinemann. 6th revised ed. 476 p. cloth. D2. $50.00

PENNINGTON, Campbell W. *Tarahumar of Mexico.* 1963. Salt Lake City. 33 photo pls/4 fld pocket maps. 267 p. NF/poor. P4. $45.00

PENNINGTON, Campbell. *Tepehuan of Chihuahua.* (1969). Salt Lake City. 1st ed. 413 p. dj. F3. $25.00

PENNINGTON, Samuel H. *Memoir of Joseph Parrish, MD.* 1891. Avertiser Prt House. 24 p. F/gray-gr wrp. uncommon. G1. $50.00

PENROSE, Boies. *Sherleian Odyssey: Being a Record of Travels...* 1938. Taunton. Wessex. presentation/inscr. ils/fld map. NF. O6. $95.00

PENROSE, Roland. *Sculpture of Picasso.* 1967. NY. MOMA. VG/VG. A1. $35.00

PENTECOST, Hugh; see Philips, Judson.

PENZER, N.M. *Harem.* 1965 (1936). London. Spring Books. reprint. lg 8vo. 277 p. VG+/G+. A2. $25.00

PENZLER, Otto. *Great Detectives.* 1978. Little Brn. 1st ed. VG/dj. P3. $20.00

PEPLE, Edward. *Littlest Rebel.* (1939). Random. Shirley Temple ed. 10 photos. 214 p. VG/G+. S10. $25.00

PEPPER, Art. *Straight Life. Story of Art Pepper.* 1979. Schirmer. 1st ed. F/NF. B2. $85.00

PEPPER, Charles M. *Pan-Am Railway.* 1904. GPO. presentation. 8vo. fld map/tables. 75 p. prt gray wrp. H9. $85.00

PEPPER, Charles M. *Panama to Patagonia.* 1906. Chicago. McClurg. 1st ed. 8vo. 38 pls/4 fld maps. 399 p. gr brds. VG. B11. $60.00

PEPPER, Choral. *Guidebook to the CO Desert of CA.* 1973. Ward Ritchie. ils/index. 128 p. F/wrp. B19. $10.00

PEPPER, William. *Syllabus of Notes From Lectures on Theory & Practice...* 1886. Phil. sgn Pepper/Brn/Wood. rare student lecture notebook. G7. $150.00

PEPYS, Samuel. *Excerpts From Diary of Samuel Pepys.* 1889. Edinburgh/London. private prt. 1/100. sgn edit. Riviere bdg. NF. F1. $150.00

PERCIVAL, Mary S. *Floral Biology.* 1965. Oxford, Eng. ils. 243 p. F. B26. $15.00

PERCY, Walker. *Last Gentleman.* 1966. FSG. 1st ed. NF/NF clip. L3. $125.00

PERCY, Walker. *Lost in the Cosmos.* (1983). FSG. 1st ed. F/NF. B3. $40.00

PERCY, Walker. *More Conversations w/Walker Percy.* 199e. Jackson, MS. 1st ed. F/F. C4. $30.00

PERCY, Walker. *Second Coming.* (1980). FSG. 1st ed. F/NF clip. B3. $75.00

PERCY, Walker. *Second Coming.* 1980. Franklin Lib. 1st ed. copied sgn. F/as issued. C4. $85.00

PERCY, Walker. *Signposts in a Strange Land.* (1991). FSG. 1st ed. 482 p. F/dj. C4. $35.00

PERCY, Walker. *Thanatos Syndrome.* 1987. FSG. VG/dj. P3. $15.00

PERCY, William Alexander. *Lanterns on the Levee. Recollections of a Planter's Son.* 1941. Knopf. 8vo. 348 p. G/G. B11. $15.00

PERDUE, Virginia. *Case of the Foster Father.* 1942. Crime Club. 1st ed. VG/dj. P3. $25.00

PERELMAN, S.J. *Best of...* 1947. Modern Lib. VG/dj. C1. $5.00

PERELMAN, S.J. *Dream Dept.* (1943). Random. 1st ed. F/VG. B4. $75.00

PERELMAN, S.J. *Ill-Tempered Clavichord.* 1952. Simon Schuster. 1st ed. F/NF. C4. $45.00

PERERA, Victor. *Guatemalan Boyhood.* 1986. HBJ. 1st ed. F/F clip. A14. $25.00

PERERA, Victor. *Last Lords of Palenque.* (1982). Little Brn. 1st ed. 311 p. dj. F3. $20.00

PEREZ, Emilio. *Los Heroes del Aire.* 1939. Buenos Aires. Ballesta. 157 p. gilt brn cloth. B24. $150.00

PEREZ, Luis. *El Coyote the Rebel.* 1947. Holt. 1st ed. VG. N2. $5.00

PEREZ MALDONADO, Raul. *Tales From Chichicastenango.* 1969. Guatemala. 72 p. wrp. F3. $10.00

PERINN, Vincent L. *Ayn Rand: 1st Descriptive Bibliography.* 1990. Quill Brush. 1st ed. F/F. B2. $40.00

PERKINS, James H. *Annals of the W: Embracing Concise Account...* 1847. Cincinnati. 2nd ed. 591 p. VG. D7. $125.00

PERKINS, John. *Profitable Booke of Master John Perkins, Fellowe...* 1851. London. Richarde Tottell. contemporary tooled full calf. M11. $1,250.00

PERKINS, Kenneth. *Ride Him, Cowboy!* (1923). Macaulay. VG/dj. B9. $25.00

PERKINS, Lucy Fitch. *Belgian Twins.* 1945. Houghton Mifflin. 197 p. VG/G. A3. $12.50

PERKINS, Lucy Fitch. *Cave Twins.* (1916). Houghton. ils. 165 p. orange/gr decor brn cloth. VG. S10. $30.00

PERKINS, Lucy Fitch. *Colonial Twins of VA.* 1924. Boston. 12mo. pls. red cloth. VG. H3. $20.00

PERKINS, Lucy Fitch. *Eskimo Twins.* (1914). Houghton. ils. 192 p. bl decor gray cloth. VG. S10. $20.00

PERKINS, Lucy Fitch. *French Twins.* 1918. Houghton Mifflin. 1st ed. 8vo. 202 p. pict ep. VG. T5. $45.00

PERKINS, Lucy Fitch. *Japanese Twins.* 1912. Houghton. 1st ed. ils. 178 p. peach decor olive cloth. VG. S10. $35.00

PERKINS, Lucy Fitch. *Robin Hood: His Deeds & Adventures...* 1906. Stokes. 115 p. orange/blk/tan decor brn cloth. G. S10. $30.00

PERKINS, S.K. *Holy Thoughts From Fenelon...* ca 1886. NY. ADF Randolph. miniature. presentation. red cloth. H10. $25.00

PERKINS, Stan. *Lore of Wolverine Country.* (1984). Swartz Creek, MI. 2nd revised ed. 244 p. wrp. A17. $12.50

PERLES, Alfred. *Great True Spy Adventures.* 1960. Arco. 2nd ed. VG/dj. P3. $15.00

PERLMAN, Bennard. *Immortal 8.* (1962). NY. Exposition. 1st ed. 12mo. 266 p. F/F-clip. A2. $20.00

PERNA. *Easy-To-Make Patchwork Skirts.* 1990. np. ils. wrp. G2. $4.50

PERNA. *Machine Applique.* 1986. np. 80 full-size patterns. 168 p. wrp. G2. $10.95

PEROWNE, Barry. *Raffles of the Albany.* 1976. St Martin. 1st ed. F/dj. P3. $20.00

PEROWNE, Stewart. *Caesars & Saints.* ca 1962. Norton. xl. 191 p. H10. $15.00

PERRAULT, Charles. *Beauty & the Beast.* ca 1880. McLoughlin. Yel Dwarf series. ils Howard. 16 p. VG/ils wrp. D1. $125.00

PERRAULT, Charles. *Cinderella.* 1888. McLoughlin. ils R Andre/3 double-p chromos. VG/ils wrp. D1. $75.00

PERRAULT, Charles. *Cinderella.* 1919. London. Heinemann. 1st ed. 1/850. ils/sgn Rackham. F/NF slipcase. D1. $1,750.00

PERRAULT, Charles. *Cinderella.* 1985. Dial Books Young Readers. 1st ed. ils/sgn Jeffers. red brds. M/pict dj. D1. $50.00

PERRAULT, Charles. *Cinderella; or, The Little Glass Slipper.* 1963 (1954). Scribner. 9th prt. xl. 4to. VG+. T5. $22.00

PERRAULT, Charles. *Puss in Boots.* 1977. Greenwillow. 1st Am ed. ils Bailey/4 pop-ups. glazed pict brds. VG. D1. $45.00

PERRAULT, Charles. *Sleeping Beauty & Other Fairy Tales.* (1910). Hodder Stoughton. 1st ed. ils Dulac/30 color pls. 129 p. F. D1. $1,200.00

PERRY, Anne. *Bluegate Fields.* 1992. London. Souvenir. 1st British ed. F/F. S5. $25.00

PERRY, Anne. *Dangerous Mourning.* 1991. Ballantine/Fawcett. 1st ed. sgn. M/M. T2. $18.00

PERRY, Anne. *Face of a Stranger.* 1990. Fawcett Columbine. 1st ed. F/dj. P3. $18.00

PERRY, Elaine. *Another Present Era.* 1990. FSG. 1st ed. author's 1st book. F/F clip. A13. $30.00

PERRY, Frances. *Water Gardening.* 1938. London. Country Life. 1st ed. 353 p. H10. $35.00

PERRY, James W. *Scientific Russian: TB for Classes & Self Study.* 1950. Interscience Pub. VG. N2. $10.00

PERRY, John Gardiner. *Letters From a Surgeon of the Civil War.* 1906. Little Brn. 1st ed. 225 p. cloth. NF-. M8. $150.00

PERRY, Nora. *Flock of Girls & Boys.* 1895. Little Brn. ils Charlotte Tiffany Parker. 323 p. VG. S10. $30.00

PERRY, Pettis. *Pettis Perry Speaks to the Court.* 1952. New Century. 1st ed. F/wrp. B2. $30.00

PERRY, Pettis. *This, Too, Is Lynch Law.* nd. Self-Defense Committee. 1st ed. NF/wrp. B2. $25.00

PERRY, Ralph Barton. *Thought & Character of William James...* 1935. Little Brn. later prt. 2 vols. gray cloth. VG/slipcase. G1. $50.00

PERRY, Richard. *Mexico's Fortress Monasteries.* (1988). Santa Barbara. Espadana. 1st ed. sgn. 224 p. wrp. F4. $20.00

PERRY, Ritchie. *Fall Guy.* 1972. Houghton Mifflin. 1st ed. VG/dj. P3. $18.00

PERRY, Thomas. *Big Fish.* 1985. Scribner. 1st ed. VG/dj. P3. $20.00

PERRY & PERRY. *Maya Missions.* (1988). Santa Barbara. Espadana. 1st ed. sgn. 249 p. wrp. F3. $15.00

PERSE, St. John. *On Poetry.* 1961. NY. 1st ed. NF/plain wht wrp/powder-gr dj. A11. $25.00

PERSICO, Joseph E. *Piercing of the Reich.* 1979. Viking. 1st ed. VG/VG. P3. $18.00

PERSKY, Stan. *Buddy's Meditations on Desire.* 1989. Vancouver. New Star. 1st ed. F/F. A14. $30.00

PERSON, Carl E. *Lizard's Trail.* 1918. Chicago. Lake Pub. 1st ed. VG. B2. $75.00

PERTWEE, Roland. *Hell's Loose.* 1929. Houghton Mifflin. VG. P3. $8.00

PERUTZ, Leo. *Marquis of Bolibar.* 1989. NY. Arcade/Little Brn. 1st Am ed. F/F. A14. $25.00

PERUTZ, Leo. *Saint Peter's Snow.* 1990. Arcade/Little Brn. 1st Am ed. trans Eric Mosbacher. F/F. A14. $20.00

PETAJA, Emil. *As Dream & Shadow.* 1972. Sisu. 1st ed. F/dj. P3. $30.00

PETERKIN, Julia. *Roll, Jordan, Roll.* 1933. Bobbs Merrill. ils Doris Ulmann. 251 p. red brds. G. B11. $75.00

PETERS, Carl. *Eldorado of the Ancients.* 1902. London. Dutton/Pearson. ils/2 lg fld maps. teg. 234 p. VG. O6. $85.00

PETERS, Dewitt C. *Kit Carson's Life & Adventures...* 1874. Hartford, CT. Dustin Gilman. 1st ed. octavo. gilt gr cloth. VG. H5. $400.00

PETERS, Elizabeth. *Jackal's Head.* 1968. Meredith. 1st ed. VG/VG. P3. $40.00

PETERS, Elizabeth. *Legend in Gr Velvet.* 1976. Dodd Mead. 1st ed. NF/dj. P3. $50.00

PETERS, Elizabeth. *Lion in the Valley.* 1986. Atheneum. 1st ed. F/dj. P3. $20.00

PETERS, Elizabeth. *Mummy Case.* 1985. NY. Congdon. 1st ed. sgn. F/F. S5. $40.00

PETERS, Ellis. *Blk is the Color of My True Love.* nd. BC. VG/dj. P3. $10.00

PETERS, Ellis. *By This Strange Fire.* 1948. NY. Reynal Hitchcock. 1st Am ed. VG/dj. M15. $45.00

PETERS, Ellis. *Confession of Brother Haluin.* 1989. NY. Mysterious. 1st Am ed. F/F. S5. $30.00

PETERS, Ellis. *Excellent Mystery.* 1985. London. Macmillan. 1st ed. F/F. M15. $85.00

PETERS, Ellis. *Fallen Into the Pit.* (1994). Mysterious. ARC/1st Am ed. NF/wrp. B4. $25.00

PETERS, Ellis. *Heretic's Apprentice.* 1989. Stoddart. 1st ed. VG/dj. P3. $18.00

PETERS, Ellis. *Knocker on Death's Door.* 1970. London. Macmillan. 1st ed. F/F. M15. $200.00

PETERS, Ellis. *Never Pick up Hitch-Hikers!* 1976. Morrow. 1st ed. VG/dj. P3. $30.00

PETERS, Ellis. *Piper on the Mtn.* 1966. London. Collins Crime Club. 1st ed. F/F. M15. $250.00

PETERS, Ellis. *Potter's Field.* 1989. London. Headline. 1st ed. F/F. M15. $45.00

PETERS, Ellis. *Raven in the Foregate.* 1986. Morrow. 1st ed. VG/dj. P3. $16.00

PETERS, Ellis. *Raven in the Foregate.* 1986. NY. Morrow. 1st Am ed. F/F. S5. $30.00

PETERS, Ellis. *Reluctant Odyssey.* 1946. London. Heinemann. 1st ed. NF/NF. M15. $150.00

PETERS, Ellis. *Sanctuary Sparrow.* 1983. NY. Morrow. 1st Am ed. sgn. F/F. S5. $65.00

PETERS, H.F. *My Sister, My Spouse...Lou Andreas-Salome.* 1963. London. 1st ed. 320 p. red cloth. VG/dj. G1. $38.50

PETERS, Harry T. *Currier & Ives: Printmakers to the Am People.* 1929. Doubleday Doran. ltd 1st ed. 1/501. 2 vols. folio. cream cloth. F. R3. $900.00

PETERS, Harry T. *Currier & Ives: Printmakers to the Am People.* 1942. Doubleday Doran. 1st ed. 4to. 192 pls. pict cloth. dj. H9. $50.00

PETERS, Harry T. *Currier & Ives: Printmakers to the Am People.* 1943. Doubleday. 192 pls. cloth. F/dj. D2. $30.00

PETERS, Hermann. *Der Arzt und die Heikunst in der Deutschen Vergangenheit.* 1900. Leipzig. 1/100. woodcuts. gilt cloth. G7. $125.00

PETERS, Ludovic. *Two After Malic.* 1966. Walker. 1st ed. VG/VG. P3. $13.00

PETERS, Ralph. *Bravo Romes.* (1981). Richard Marek. 1st ed. dj. A7. $30.00

PETERS, Samuel Andrew. *General Hist of CT.* 1781. London. Bew. octavo. polished calf. Riviere fld box. H9. $1,200.00

PETERS, Uwe Henrik. *Anna Freud: Life Dedicated to Children.* 1985. Schoken Books. 1st Eng-language ed. 282 p. bl cloth. F/dj. G1. $20.00

PETERSEN, David. *Racks: Natural Hist of Antlers & Animals That Wear Them.* (1991). Santa Barbara. 8vo. ils. 179 p. wrp. A17. $9.50

PETERSEN, Herman. *Covered Bridge.* 1950. Crowell. 1st ed. VG/dj. P3. $20.00

PETERSEN, N.F. *Flora of NE. List of Ferns, Conifers & Flowering Plants...* 1923 (1912). Plainview, NE. 3rd ed. 220 p. full gilt leather. VG. B26. $29.00

PETERSEN, P.B. *Against the Tide.* (1974). Arlington House. NF/VG clip. A7. $30.00

PETERSEN, William J. *Steamboating on the Upper MS.* 1968 (1936). State Hist Soc IA. ils. 575 p. NF/VG. B28. $37.50

PETERSEN, William J. *Steamboating on the Upper MS: Water Way to IA.* 1937. IA City. State Hist Assn. 1st ed. 576 p. gilt bdg. VG+. H7. $75.00

PETERSHAM & PETERSHAM. *Rooster Crows.* 1945. Macmillan. 1st ed. Caldecott Winner 1946. sgns. VG/tattered. D1. $75.00

PETERSHAM & PETERSHAM. *Stories From the Old Testament.* 1938. Chicago. Winston. G/G. L1. $30.00

PETERSHAM & PETERSHAM. *Story Book of Aircraft.* 1935. Winston. 1st ed. VG. M5. $10.00

PETERSHAM & PETERSHAM. *Story Book of Gold.* 1935. Winston. 1st ed. yel cloth. NF/worn dj. M5. $18.00

PETERSHAM & PETERSHAM. *Story Book of Transportation.* 1933. Winston. 1st ed. orange cloth w/color pl. NF. M5. $15.00

PETERSON, Audrey. *Victorian Masters of Mystery: From Wilkie Collins...Doyle.* 1984. NY. Ungar. 1st ed. F/dj. M15. $25.00

PETERSON, Diane. *Catalogue 12: Wallace Stegner, Maurice Dunbar Collection.* (1992). Peterson. 1st ltd ed. 1/150. sgn Stegner/Peterson. M. A18. $40.00

PETERSON, F. *How To Fix Damn Near Everything.* 1977. Bonanza. VG/dj. A16. $7.50

PETERSON, Harold L. *Arms & Armor in Colonial Am.* 1980. Brown. ils. 448 p. O7. $21.50

PETERSON, Harold L. *Pageant of the Gun.* 1967. NY. 2nd prt. 352 p. F/dj. A17. $15.00

PETERSON, K. *When AK Was Free.* 1977. Ashley Books. 1st ed. 166 p. VG+/G+. B22. $8.50

PETERSON, Maude Gridley. *How To Know Wild Fruits...When Not in Flower...* 1905. NY. 1st ed. ils. 340 p. VG. B28. $30.00

PETERSON, R.T. *Sir Kenelm Digby: Ornament of Eng.* 1956. Harvard. ils. 336 p. dj. G7. $65.00

PETERSON & PETERSON. *Native Trees of the Sierra Nevada.* 1975. CA U. 1st ed. ils/maps. 147 p. F. B19. $15.00

PETIEVICH, Gerald. *Earth Angels.* 1989. NAL. 1st ed. NF/dj. P3. $18.00

PETIEVICH, Gerald. *Money Men & One-Shot Deal.* 1981. HBJ. 1st ed. F/F. M15. $65.00

PETIEVICH, Gerald. *Quality of the Informant.* 1985. NY. Arbor. 1st ed. F/F. M15. $30.00

PETRADAKIS, M.S. *Postal Hist of the Aegean. Italian Military Post Offices...* 1991. Athens. 2 vols. 4to. ils. O2. $45.00

PETRAKIS, Harry Mark. *In the Land of Morning.* (1973). McKay. presentation/sgn. VG/VG. A7. $30.00

PETRAKIS, Harry Mark. *Waves of Night & Other Stories.* 1969. NY. 8vo. 230 p. cloth. dj. O2. $15.00

PETRIE, Glen. *Dorking Gap Affair: Mycroft Holmes Adventure.* 1989. London. Bantam. 1st ed. F/F. S5. $30.00

PETRONIUS, Gaius. *Satyricon, Cum Notis & Observationibus Variorum.* 1596. Leyden. Plantin. 32mo. contemporary full vellum. R3. $1,500.00

PETRY, Ann. *Narrows.* 1953. Houghton Mifflin. 1st ed. F/NF. B4. $175.00

PETTEE, F.M. *Palgrave Mummy.* 1929. Payson Clarke. 1st ed. VG. P3. $30.00

PETTEE, Florence M. *Who Bird & Other Whimsies.* 1920. Whitman. 8vo. ils. pict rose cloth. F/box. T5. $50.00

PETTERSEN, Carmen. *Maya of Guatemals.* 1976. Seattle. WA U. 1st ed. 276 p. dj. F3. $75.00

PETTERSON, Hans. *Westward Ho w/the Albatross.* 1953. Dutton. 1st Am ed. 8vo. 218 p. VG/VG. A2. $15.00

PETTITT, George A. *Primitive Education in N Am.* 1946. CA U. 1st ed. inscr. sm 4to. 182 p. VG. D3. $35.00

PETTY, William. *Hiberniae Delineateo-Atlas of Ireland.* 1968. Newcastle-Upon-Tyne. Frank Graham. facsimile 1685 ed. 1/500. pls/maps. F. O6. $475.00

PETULENGRO, Gipsy. *Romany Life.* 1936. Dutton. ils. G. A16. $10.00

PETZAL, David. *Expert's Book of Big-Game Hunting in N Am.* (1976). Simon Schuster. 1st prt. 223 p. F/dj. A17. $12.50

PETZET & WACKERNAGEL. *Bayerische Kronungswagen Im Martatallmuseum Munchen.* 1962. Schnell und Steiner. German text. 71 pls. 72 p. VG. O3. $65.00

PEURBACH, Georg. *Tabulae Eclypsium...* 1514. Veinna. 1st ed. folio. VG. H5. $5,500.00

PEYO. *High & Dry Smurfs. A Puppet Book.* 1983. cloth finger puppet attached to book. F. A4. $35.00

PEYTON, G. *San Antonio: City in the Sun.* 1946. NY. 1st ed. photos/fld map. 282 p. VG/G. B5. $17.50

PEYTON, John Lewis. *Memoir of John Howe Peyton...* 1894. Blackburn. xl. 297 p. VG. B10. $50.00

PEYTON, Richard. *At the Track.* 1987. Bonanza. F/dj. P3. $13.00

PFEIFFER, Ida. *Visit to Iceland & the Scandinavian N.* 1852. London. Ingram Cooke. 354 p. gray cloth. B14. $45.00

PFEIFFER, John E. *Emergence of Man.* 1969. Harper Row. 1st ed. 464 p. cloth. VG/dj. M20. $8.50

PFLEIDERER, Otto. *Philosophy of Religion on Basis of Its Hist.* 1886. London. Williams Norgate. 1st ed. 4 vols. emb gr cloth. G. G1. $100.00

PHAGAN, Mary. *Murder of Little Mary Phagan.* 1987. Far Hills. New Horizon. G/dj. M11. $35.00

PHELAN, Jim. *Wagon Wheels.* (1951). London. Harrap. 1st ed. 8vo. 224 p. F-/VG+. A2. $25.00

PHELPS, R.H. *Newgate of CT.* 1876. Hartford. 1st thus ed. ils. 117 p. VG. B28. $37.50

PHELPS, Ruth S. *Skies Italian.* 1910. London. 1st ed. 16mo. 368 p. aeg. gilt full gr leather. VG. H3. $15.00

PHELPS & ROSCO. *Continual Lessons: Journals of Glenway Wescott, 1937-1955.* 1990. FSG. 1st ed. NF/NF. A14. $25.00

PHENIX, Richard. *On My Way Home.* (1947). NY. Wm Sloane. 1st ed. 8vo. 267 p. F/F clip. A2. $15.00

PHILBY, H. St. John. *Hurun al Rashid.* 1933. London. Peter Davis. 1st ed. 8vo. gilt blk cloth. G. M7. $50.00

PHILBY & PHILBY. *Heart of Arabia: Record of Travel & Exploration.* 1922. London. Constable. 1st ed. 2 vols. octavo. gilt br cloth. R3. $750.00

PHILIP, Adam. *Devotional Literature of Scotland.* nd. London. Clarke. 191 p. H10. $17.50

PHILIPPE, Charles-Louis. *Bubu of Montparnasse.* 1952. Weidenfeld Nicolson. reissue of 1932 Crosby Continental ed. NF/NF. A14. $25.00

PHILIPS, Judson. *Beautiful Dead.* 1973. Dodd Mead. 1st ed. NF/dj. P3. $23.00

PHILIPS, Judson. *Champagne Killer.* 1972. Dodd Mead. 1st ed. VG/dj. P3. $20.00

PHILIPS, Judson. *Deadly Joke.* 1971. Dodd Mead. 1st ed. VG/dj. P3. $20.00

PHILIPS, Judson. *Death by Fire.* 1986. Dodd Mead. 1st ed. F/dj. P3. $16.00

PHILIPS, Judson. *Escape a Killer.* 1971. Dodd Mead. 1st ed. VG/dj. P3. $20.00

PHILIPS, Judson. *Honeymoon w/Death.* 1975. Dodd Mead. 1st ed. VG/dj. P3. $15.00

PHILIPS, Judson. *Murder Arranged.* 1978. Dodd Mead. 1st ed. VG/dj. P3. $18.00

PHILIPS, Judson. *Murder Goes Round & Round.* 1988. Dodd Mead. 1st ed. VG/dj. P3. $16.00

PHILIPS, Judson. *Vanishing Senator.* 1972. Dodd Mead. 1st ed. VG/dj. P3. $20.00

PHILLIPS, Alan. *Living Legend: Story of Royal Canadian Mounted Police.* (1957). Little Brn. later prt. 8vo. 328 p. VG/VG. A2. $12.50

PHILLIPS, Alexander M. *Mislaid Charm.* 1947. Prime Pr. 1st ed. VG/1st state yel dj. P3. $25.00

PHILLIPS, Arthur M. *Grand Canyon Wild Flowers.* 1990 (1979). Grand Canyon. new ed. 160 color photos. 145 p. M. B26. $17.00

PHILLIPS, Caryl. *Cambridge.* 1991. London. Bloomsbury. 1st ed. F/F. AS13. $30.00

PHILLIPS, Caryl. *Cambridge.* 1992. Knopf. 1st Am ed. F/F. A13. $20.00

PHILLIPS, Caryl. *Final Passage.* 1985. London. 1st ed/pb issue. sgn. NF/unread. A11. $35.00

PHILLIPS, Caryl. *Final Passage.* 1985. London. Faber. 2nd imp. F/F. A13. $20.00

PHILLIPS, Caryl. *Higher Ground.* 1989. Viking/Penguin. 1st Am ed. rem mk. F/F. A13. $25.00

PHILLIPS, Caryl. *State of Independence.* 1986. London. Faber. 1st ed. F/F. A13. $35.00

PHILLIPS, Catherine Coffin. *Through the Golden Gate: San Francisco, 1769-1937.* 1938. LA. Sutton. 1st ed. inscr/dtd 1938. gilt bl cloth. VG+. P4. $75.00

PHILLIPS, Conrad. *Empty Cot.* 1958. Arthur Barker. 1st ed. VG/VG. P3. $25.00

PHILLIPS, D.R. *W: Am Experience.* (1973). Chicago. ils/index. 232 p. VG+/dj. B18. $35.00

PHILLIPS, Edward. *Buried on Sunday.* 1986. St Martin. 1st ed. F/F. F4. $15.00

PHILLIPS, Edward. *New World of Words; or, Universal English Dictionary.* 1720. London. Philips. folio. double-column text. Bayntun-Riviere calf. VG. H5. $650.00

PHILLIPS, Edward. *Sunday's Child.* 1981. McClelland Stewart. 1st ed. author's 1st book. NF/NF clip. A14. $25.00

PHILLIPS, Ethel Calvert. *Calico.* 1937. Boston. 12mo. 132 p. orange cloth. F. H3. $15.00

PHILLIPS, Ethel Calvert. *Wee Ann. Story for Little Girls.* 1919. Houghton. 1st ed. ils Edith F Butler. 134 p. VG/G. S10. $40.00

PHILLIPS, Isaac. *Lincoln.* 1910. McClurg. 117 p. VG. A6. $10.00

PHILLIPS, J.A. *Machine Dreams.* (1984). Dutton. 1st prt. NF/dj. A7. $20.00

PHILLIPS, James Duncan. *Salem in the 17th Century & Salem in the 18th Century.* 1933 & 1937. Boston. 1st ed. 2 vols. NF. B28. $50.00

PHILLIPS, Jayne Anne. *Blk Tickets.* 1979. Delacorte. 1st ed. author's 1st regularly pub book. NF/dj. B4. $200.00

PHILLIPS, Jayne Anne. *Blk Tickets.* 1979. Delacorte. 1st ed. inscr. F/F. B2. $85.00

PHILLIPS, Jayne Anne. *Counting.* 1978. Vehicle Eds. 1st ed. 1/474. inscr. author's 2nd book. F. L3. $250.00

PHILLIPS, John C. *Natural Hist of the Ducks.* 1922-26. Houghton Mifflin. 1st ed. quarto. 4 vols. 102 pls/118 maps. slipcase. H5. $2,250.00

PHILLIPS, John. *Poems on Several Occasions.* 1728. London. Thomas Astley. 4th ed/2nd issue. calf/rebacked. NF. B20. $225.00

PHILLIPS, William. *Outline of Mineralogy & Geology.* 1815. London. Phillips. 1st ed. octavo. 3 pls. 193 p. bl brds. VG. H5. $200.00

PHILLPOTTS, Eden. *Dish of Apples.* nd. London. Hodder Stoughton. ils Arthur Rackham. 75 p. pict purple cloth. G. B14. $65.00

PHILLPOTTS, Edna. *Girl & the Faun.* 1917. Lippincott. 1st Am ed. ils Frank Brangwyn. w/ad booklet. NF/dj. B24. $75.00

PHIPPS, Joseph. *Orig & Present State of Man...* 1788. NY. Ross. 230 p. leather. H10. $75.00

PIANKOFF, Alexandre. *Shrines of Tut-Ankhamon.* (1955). Pantheon. folio. 66 pls. cloth slipcase. K1. $175.00

PIANKOFF & RAMBOVA. *Mythological Papyri.* (1957). Pantheon. 2 vols. 30 lg fld pls. portfolio. slipcase. K1. $300.00

PICANO, Felice. *House of Cards.* 1984. Delacorte. 1st ed. rem mk. NF/NF. A14. $35.00

PICASSO, Pablo. *Desire Caught by the Tail: A Play.* (1962). Citadel. 1st wrp issue. 60 p. NF. A7. $10.00

PICASSO, Pablo. *Hunk of Skin.* 1968. San Francisco. 1st Am/1st Eng ed. 1/200. F/unread stiff wrp. A11. $30.00

PICASSO. *Carnet de Dessins de Picasso.* 1948. Ed Cahiers D'Art. 1/1200. folio pls. VG (rpr at hinges). A1. $450.00

PICASSO. *Linogravures.* 1962. Paris. Ed Cercle D'Art. VG/VG. A1. $600.00

PICASSO. *Shakespeare.* 1965. Paris. folio brds. VG. A1. $185.00

PICCARD, Jacques. *Sun Beneath the Sea.* (1971). Scribner. 1st Am ed. 8vo. 405 p. F/VG+. A2. $12.50

PICKARD, Nancy. *Crossbones.* 1990. London. Macmillan. ARC of 1st British ed. sgn. RS. F/F. S5. $35.00

PICKARD, Nancy. *Marriage Is Murder.* 1987. Scribner. 1st ed. F/dj. P3. $15.00

PICKARD, Samuel T. *Whittier-Land: Handbook of N Essex...* 1904. Boston. Houghton Mifflin. 4th ed. 16mo. 160 p. V3. $15.00

PICKENS, T.B. Jr. *Boone.* (1987). Houghton Mifflin. 2nd prt. 8vo. 304 p. F/F. A2. $15.00

PICKNEY, Darryl. *High Cotton.* 1992. FSG. 1st ed. F/F. B2. $50.00

PICKNEY, Darryl. *High Cotton.* 1992. FSG. 1st ed. author's 1st book. F/F clip. A13. $45.00

PIDGIN, C.F. *Blennerhassett; or, The Decrees of Fate.* 1901. Boston. 1st ed. 442 p. VG. D7. $20.00

PIENKOWSKI, Jan. *Dinner Time.* 1981. London. paper engineering Stajewski/Diaz. F. A4. $40.00

PIENKOWSKI, Jan. *Door Bell.* 1992. battery-op movable scenes. F. A4. $30.00

PIENKOWSKI, Jan. *Haunted House.* 1979. Dutton. 1st Am ed. 6 popups. pict brds. VG. A3. $60.00

PIENKOWSKI, Jan. *Phone Book.* 1991. battery-op/movable scenes. F. A4. $30.00

PIEPER, Josef. *Death & Immortality.* 1969. NY. Herder. 1st ed. 144 p. H10. $17.50

PIEPER, Josef. *In Tune w/the World.* ca 1965. Harcourt Brace. 81 p. H10. $15.00

PIEPER, Josef. *Silence of St Thomas.* ca 1957. Pantheon. 122 p. H10. $17.50

PIEPER & RASKOP. *What Catholics Believe.* ca 1951. Pantheon. 1st ed. trans Huntington. 112 p. H10. $11.50

PIERCE, Frederick E. *Reminiscences of Experiences of Company L, 2nd Regiment...* 1900. Greenfield, MA. FA Hall. 124 p. red cloth. B14. $22.50

PIERCE, James W. *Story of Turkey & Armenia.* 1896. Baltimore. 8vo. ils. 500 p. pict cloth. O2. $45.00

PIERCE, John H. *Greenhouse Grow How.* 1977. Seattle. ils. 241 p. F/dj. B26. $35.00

PIERCE, Meredith Ann. *Dark Angel Trilogy.* nd. BC. VG/dj. P3. $10.00

PIERCY, Caroline B. *Valley of God's Pleasure.* 1951. NY. 1st ed. sgn. 246 p. VG/dj. D7. $29.00

PIERCY, Marge. *Braided Lives.* 1982. Summit. 2nd ed. VG/VG. P3. $13.00

PIERCY, Marge. *Breaking Camp.* 1968. Wesleyan. 1st ed. sgn. author's 1st poetry book. F/F. V1. $65.00

PIERPONT, John. *Anti-Slavery Poems.* 1843. Boston. Oliver Johnson. 1st ed. 16mo. 64 p. prt wrp. M1. $125.00

PIERRE, Chief George. *Autumn's Bounty.* 1972. San Antonio. Naylor. 1st ed. NF/dj. L3. $100.00

PIERSON, C.D. *Plow Stories.* 1923. NY. ils CE Carwright. 12mo. 179 p. VG. B28. $15.00

PIERSON, Clara D. *Among the Pond People.* (1901). Dutton. ils FC Gordon. 210 p. VG. S10. $25.00

PIETERS, Adrian J. *Gr Manuring: Principles & Practice.* 1927. Wiley. N2. $12.50

PIJOAN, Michel. *Game Fish of the Rocky Mtns.* (1985). Flagstaff. pls. 68 p. wrp. A17. $7.50

PIKE, Christopher. *Season of Passage.* 1992. Tor. 1st ed. NF/dj. P3. $20.00

PIKE, Frederick. *Modern Hist of Peru.* (1969). NY. Praeger. 2nd prt. 386 p. dj. F3. $10.00

PIKE, James A. *Other Side.* nd. Laffont. VG. P3. $15.00

PIKE, Nicholas. *New & Complete System of Arithmetic.* 1788. Newbury-Port. 512 p. new quarter calf/marbled brds. F. rare. H9. $475.00

PIKE, Zebulon Montgomery. *Account of Expeditions to Sources of MS.* 1810. Phil. 1st ed. 8vo. 3 fld tables. orig calf. H9. $500.00

PILLET, Roger. *Les Oraisons Amoureuses de Jeanne-Aurelie.* 1957. Les Heures Claires. 1/100 on Rives. w/2nd suite of 16 pls. F/slipcase. K1. $850.00

PILLING, J.C. *Bibliography of the Algonquian Languages.* 1891. GPO. 613 p. prt wrp. B28. $125.00

PILLSBURY, D.L. *Adobe Doorways.* 1953. NM U. 8vo. VG. A8. $25.00

PINCHER, Chapman. *Not w/a Bang.* 1965. Weidenfeld Nicolson. G/torn. P3. $10.00

PINES, Shlomo. *Arabic Version of the Testimonium Flavianum...* 1971. Jerusalem. Israel Acad of Science & Humanity. 87 p. wrp. H10. $20.00

PINES, Shlomo. *Some Traits of Christian Theological Writing...Vol V* 1974. Jerusalem. 21 p. VG/wrp. S3. $15.00

PINI, Wendy. *Elfquest Book 1.* 1981. Donning. ltd 1st ed. sgn/#d. F/box. P3. $225.00

PINI, Wendy. *Elfquest Book 2.* 1982. Donning. ltd 1st ed. sgn/#d. box. P3. $150.00

PINKERTON, A. Frank. *Saved at the Scaffold; or, Nic Brn, Chicago Detective.* (1888). Laird Lee. 1st ed. 8vo. pict cloth. M1. $150.00

PINKERTON, Allan. *Bucholz & the Detectives.* 1880. Carleton. 1st ed. 341 p. gilt cloth. VG. M20. $30.00

PINKERTON, Allan. *Claude Melnotte As a Detective.* 1975. Chicago. Keen Cooke. 1st ed. 8vo. 282 p. orig brick cloth. NF. F1. $150.00

PINKERTON, Robert. *First Overland Mail.* 1953. Landmark. BC. VG/G. O3. $18.00

PINKHAM, T.J. *Farming As It Is!* 1860. Boston. Bradley. 1st ed. 393 p. H10. $65.00

PINKOWSKI, Edward. *Forgotten Fathers.* (1953). Phil. Sunshine Pr. 1st ed?. 8vo. 390 p. VG+/VG-. A2. $15.00

PINNER, David. *Ritual.* 1967. New Authors Ltd. 1st ed. F/dj. P3. $13.00

PINNEY, Peter. *Dust on My Shoes.* (1951). Bobbs Merrill. 1st ed. 8vo. 371 p. F/VG. A2. $20.00

PINON, Nelida. *Caetana's Sweet Song.* 1992. Knopf. 1st ed. trans from Brazilian Portuguese. F/F. A14. $30.00

PINTER, Harold. *Poems & Prose, 1949-77.* nd. NY. 1st ed. F/F. V1. $20.00

PIPER, Evelyn. *Nanny.* nd. BC. VG/dj. p3. $8.00

PIPER, H. Beam. *Fuzzy Papers.* nd. BC. VG/dj. P3. $10.00

PIPER, Watty. *Animal Story Book.* 1954. Platt Monk. later ed. ils Wesley Dennis. VG. L1. $25.00

PIPER, Watty. *Brimful Book.* 1955. Platt Munk. NF/G. M18. $50.00

PIPER, Watty. *Children of Other Lands.* 1933. Platt Munk. ils Holling, orange cloth w/pict label. VG-. A3. $17.50

PIPER, Watty. *Famous Fairy Tales.* 1933. Platt Munk. 1st ed. F/VG. M18. $75.00

PIPER, Watty. *Gateway to Storyland.* 1954. Platt Munk. new revised ed. lg 4to. blk decor gr cloth. VG. S10. $30.00

PIPER, Watty. *Nursery Tales Children Love.* 1933. Platt Munk. ils Eulalie. bl cloth/pict label. VG. S10. $45.00

PIPER, Watty. *Road in Storyland.* 1952. NY. 4to. 104 p. red cloth/pict label. F. H3. $35.00

PIRNIE, Miles David. *MI Waterfowl Management.* 1935. Lansing. 1st ed. xl. photos/fld maps. 328 p. A17. $45.00

PIRTLE, Henry. *Civil & Criminal KY Codes of Practice, 1915.* 1915. Louisville. Baldwin Law. G. M11. $25.00

PISERCHIA, Doris. *Spaceling.* nd. BC. 1st ed. F/dj. P3. $8.00

PITCAIRN, Harold F. *Autogiro: Its Characteristics & Accomplishments.* 1931. GPO. removed from annual report. 9 pls. VG. P4. $22.50

PITMAN, J.H. *Goldsmith's Animated Nature: Study of Goldsmith.* 1972. Hamden, CT. Archon. reprint of 1924 ed. 159 p. blk cloth. M. S9. $5.00

PITMAN & WILSON. *Encyclopedia of Murder.* 1962. Putnam. 1st Am ed. 576 p. orange cloth. VG/clip. G1. $30.00

PITT, William. *Anecdotes of the Life of...* 1797. London. Seeley. 6th ed. 3 vols. leather. fair. A16. $250.00

PITTENGER, Peggy. *Wonderful World of Ponies.* 1969. S Brunswick. Barnes. 1st ed. VG/VG. O3. $35.00

PITTMAN, Philip. *Present State of European Settlements on the MS.* 1973. Gainesville, FL. facsimile of 1770 ed. 4to. brds. H9. $35.00

PITTMAN & SIMONSEN. *N Shore Chinook: Lake Huron Salmon on Light Tackle.* (1993). Troy, MI. 164 p. wrp. A17. $17.00

PITTS, Charles Frank. *Chaplains in Gray: Confederate Chaplain's Story.* 1957. Nashville. Broadman. 1st ed. 166 p. cloth. NF. M8. $35.00

PLACZEK, Beverley R. *Record of a Friendship: Correspondence...* 1981. Farrar Straus. 429 p. bl cloth brds. VG/dj. G1. $25.00

PLANTE, David. *Figures in Bright Air.* 1976. London. Gollancz. 1st ed. NF/NF clip. A14. $30.00

PLATH, Sylvia. *Bell Jar.* 1971. Harper Row. NF/NF. E3. $20.00

PLATH, Sylvia. *Colossus & Other Poems.* 1967. NY. 2nd prt. F/F. V1. $25.00

PLATH, Sylvia. *Letters Home.* 1972. NY. 1st ed. VG/VG. B5. $20.00

PLATH, Sylvia. *Stings.* (1975). Northampton. Smith College Lib. 1st thus ed. F. E3. $45.00

PLATH, Sylvia. *Stings.* 1982. Smith College. facsimile. F. C4. $50.00

PLATH, Sylvia. *Winter Trees.* 1972. Harper. 1st Am ed. F/NF. B2. $40.00

PLATH, Warren K. *Jolson on Wax.* nd. Oak Park. Plath. G/wrp. B2. $25.00

PLATO. *Collected Dialogues of Plato.* 1987. Princeton. 13th prt. F/dj. P3. $33.00

PLATT, Charles. *Planet of the Voles.* 1971. NY. Putnam. 1st ed. F/NF. N3. $10.00

PLATT, Charles. *Twilight of the City.* 1977. Macmillan. 1st ed. VG/dj. P3. $18.00

PLATT, Kin. *Body Beautiful Murder.* 1976. Random. 1st ed. VG/VG. P3. $18.00

PLATT, Kin. *Murder in Rossaire.* 1985. Walker. 1st ed. F/dj. M15. $25.00

PLATT, Rutherford. *Am Trees: A Book of Discovery.* 1952. NY. 1st ed. photos. 256 p. VG+/dj. B26. $15.00

PLATT, Rutherford. *Great Am Forest.* 1965. Prentice Hall. ils/notes/index. 271 p. F/F. B19. $20.00

PLATT, Ward. *Frontier.* (1908). NY. Eaton Mains. 12mo. VG. A2/D3. $15.00

PLATT & SLATER. *Traveler's Guide Across the Plains Upon Overland Route CA.* 1963. San Francisco. John Howell. facsimile map. M. O6. $75.00

PLAUT, W. Gunther. *Judaism & Scientific Spirit.* 1962. UAHC. 82 p. VG. S3. $14.00

PLAUT, W. Gunther. *Rise of Reform Judaism.* 1963. NY. World Union Progressive Judaism. 288 p. VG/G. S3. $25.00

PLEASANTS, J. Hall. *Justus Englehardt Khun: 18th-Century MD Portrait Painter.* 1937. Worcester. reprint. xl. 40 prints. wrp. D2. $20.00

PLEASANTS, W. Shepard. *Stingaree Murders.* 1932. Mystery League. VG. P3. $15.00

PLIMPTON, George. *One for the Record.* 1974. Harper Row. 1st ed. F/VG+. P8. $25.00

PLIMPTON, George. *Out of My League.* 1961. Harper. 1st ed. VG/G. P8. $25.00

PLIMPTON, George. *Rabbit's Umbrella.* 1955. Viking. 1st ed. ils William Pene Du Bois. F/NF. B4. $65.00

PLOMER, William. *Diamond of Jannina. Ali Pasha 1741-1822.* 1970. NY. 1st Am ed. 8vo. 288 p. F/dj. O2. $30.00

PLOOS VAN AMSTEL, Cornelis. *Aanleiding Tot de Kennis der Anatomie...* 1793. Amsterdam. Yntema. 27 pls. 114 p. contemporary half vellum. G7. $595.00

PLOWDEN, David. *End of an Era: Last of Great Lakes Steamboats.* 1992. Norton. as new/dj. A16. $50.00

PLOWDEN, Edmund. *Disquisition Concerning Law of Alienage & Naturalization...* 1818. Paris. A Belin. modern gilt gr cloth. M11. $250.00

PLOWRIGHT, Teresa. *Dreams of an Unseen Planet.* 1986. Arbor. 1st ed. RS. F/dj. P3. $18.00

PLUM, Jennifer; see Kurland, Michael.

PLUMB, A. *Hopgad; or, Gnomes of Blk Forest.* 1887. Paris. ils F Bannister. aeg. bl cloth. scarce. F1. $150.00

PLUMB, Charles S. *Types & Breeds of Farm Animals.* ca 1920. Boston. Ginn. revised ed. 820 p. H10. $20.00

PLUMB, Charlie. *I'm No Hero: A POW Story.* (1973). Independence Pr. 4th prt. 287 p. NF/dj. A7. $40.00

PLUMMER, William. *Holy Goof.* (1981). Prentice Hall. 1st ed. photos. 162 p. F/F. A7. $35.00

PLUTARCH. *Graecorum Romanorumque Ilustrium Vitae.* 1535. Basel. folio. contemporary blind-tooled pigskin/metal clasps. F. H5. $1,750.00

PLUTARCH. *Lives of Noble Grecians & Romanes...* 1928. Houghton/Shakespeare. 1/500. 8 vols. octavo. teg. gilt morocco. F. R3. $1,250.00

PLUTARCH. *Plutarch's Life of Illustrious Men.* 1959 (1876). Little Brn. reprint. 8vo. 787 p. VG. A2. $20.00

PLUTO, Terry. *Greatest Summer.* 1979. Prentice Hall. 1st ed. F/VG+. P8. $8.00

POCOCK, Nicholas. *Records of Reformation...* 1870. Oxford. Clarendon. 2 vols. H10. $75.00

POCOCK, Roger. *Following the Frontier.* 1903. NY. 1st ed. 338 p. pict cloth. A17. $20.00

PODHAJSKY, Alois. *Riding Teacher: Basic Guide to Correct Methods...* 1973. London. Harrap. 1st British ed. VG/VG. O3. $45.00

PODMORE, Frank. *Newer Spiritualism.* 1911. London. Fisher Unwin. 2nd prt. prt pebbled russet cloth. VG. G1. $40.00

PODMORE, Frank. *Robert Owen: A Biography.* 1924. Appleton. ils. 688 p. N2. $22.50

PODWAL, Mark. *Freud's Da Vinci.* 1977. NY. Images Graphiques. 1st ed. tall 8vo. VG/dj. G1. $20.00

POE, Edgar Alan. *Complete Stories & Poems.* nd. BC. VG/dj. P3. $8.00

POE, Edgar Alan. *Fall of the House of Usher.* 1986. Marshall Cavendish. decor brds. F. P3. $25.00

POE, Edgar Alan. *Tales of Edgar Alan Poe.* 1965. Whitman. VG. P3. $5.00

POE, Edgar Alan. *Tales of Mystery & Imagination.* nd. Spencer. VG. P3. $10.00

POE, Edgar Allan. *Bells & Other Poems.* nd. (1912). London. ltd ed. 1/750. ils/sgn Dulac. Zaehnsdorf bdg. NF. H5. $1,500.00

POE, Edgar Allan. *Complete Works...* nd. NY. Fred de Fau. 1/1000 sets. 10 vols. brn brds. VG. E3. $65.00

POE, Edgar Allan. *Fall of the House of Usher.* 1985. NY. LEC. 1/1500. ils Alice Neel. sgn Raphael Soyer. F/case. w/letter. H5. $1,000.00

POE, Edgar Allan. *Literati: Some Honest Opinions About Autorial Merits...* 1850. NY. 1st ed/1st prt. 12mo. Stikeman bdg. NF. H5. $750.00

POE, Edgar Allan. *Murders in the Rue Morgue.* ca 1920. NY. Tarry at the Taft. VG+/tissue wrp. E3. $40.00

POE, Edgar Allan. *Narrative of Arthur Gordon Pym of Nantucket.* 1838. NY. 1st ed. 12mo. Stikeman bdg. F. H5. $1,500.00

POE, Edgar Allan. *Narrative of Arthur Gordon Pym.* 1838. NY. Harper. 1st ed. 12mo. 201 p. w/2 ad p dtd 1838. VG/fld case. H5. $3,750.00

POE, Edgar Allan. *Raven & Other Poems.* 1845. NY. 1st ed. octavo. NF/prt tan wrp. H5. $45,000.00

POE, Edgar Allan. *Raven.* 1884. Dutton. slick paper issue. cb bdg. VG. M2. $75.00

POE, Edgar Allan. *Tales of Mystery & Imagination.* 1933. NY. Tudor. ils Harry Clarke/8 mtd pls. teg, NF/box. H5. $400.00

POE, Edgar Allan. *Tales of Mystery & Imagination.* 1935. London. Harrap. 1/10. ils Rackham/12 mtd pls. w/orig sgn drawing. 317 p. NF. H5. $17,500.00

POE, Edgar Allan. *Tales of Mystery & Imagination.* 1935. London. Harrap. 1/460. sgn. w/orig sgn Rackham drawing. 317 p. Sutcliffe bdg. H5. $17,500.00

POE, Orlando Metcalfe. *Report on Transcontinental Railways, 1883.* 1883. GPO. 8vo. lg fld map disbound. H9. $110.00

POGANY, Willy. *My Poetry Book.* 1937.. Winston. 504 p. gilt dk bl cloth. NF. M5. $55.00

POGGIOLI. *Patterns From Paradise: Art of Tahitian Quilting.* 1988. np. ils. wrp. G2. $16.00

POHL, Frederick. *Assignment in Tomorrow.* 1954. Hanover. 1st ed. VG/VG-. P3. $35.00

POHL, Frederick. *Chernobyl.* 1987. Bantam. 1st ed. VG/VG-. P3. $15.00

POHL, Frederick. *Cool War.* 1981. Del Rey. 1st ed. VG/dj. P3. $15.00

POHL, Frederick. *Drunkard's Walk.* 1960. Gnome. 1st ed. NF/dj. P3. $75.00

POHL, Frederick. *Heechee Rendezvous.* nd. Del Rey. 2nd ed. F/dj. P3. $15.00

POHL, Frederick. *Jem.* 1978. St Martin. 1st ed. F/dj. P3. $20.00

POHL, Frederick. *Merchants' War.* 1984. St Martin. 1st ed. F/dj. P3. $18.00

POHL, Frederick. *Midas World.* 1983. St Martin. 1st ed. F/dj. P3. $20.00

POHL, Frederick. *Outnumbering the Dead.* 1990. Legend. 1st ed. F/dj. P3. $25.00

POHL, Frederick. *SF Roll of Honor.* 1975. Random. 1st ed. F/dj. P3. $15.00

POHL, Frederick. *Starburst.* 1982. Del Rey. 1st ed. VG/dj. P3. $15.00

POHL, Frederick. *Way the Future Was.* 1978. Del Rey. VG/dj. P3. $15.00

POHL, Frederik. *Gateway Trip: Tales & Vignettes of the Heechee.* 1990. Ballantine. 1st ed. F/F. N3. $15.00

POHL, Frederik. *Way the Future Was: A Memoir.* 1978. Ballantine. 1st ed. F/F. N3. $10.00

POINTER, Michael. *Public Life of Sherlock Holmes.* 1975. Newton Abbot. 1st ed. ils. F/F. S5. $35.00

POKAGON, Chief Simon. *O-Gi-Maw-Kwe Mit-i-Gwa-KI (Queen of the Woods).* 1899. Hartford. Engle. 1st ed. VG+. L3. $650.00

POLAND, Burdette. *French Protestantism & the French Revolution.* 1957. Princeton. xl. 315 p. H10. $20.00

POLING, James. *Esquire's World of Jazz.* 1975. NY. revised/expanded ed. ils/photos. F/NF. B2. $40.00

POLISH, David. *Eternal Dissent: Search for Meaning in Jewish Hist.* 1961. Abelard Schuman. 228 p. VG/G. S3. $20.00

POLITI, Leo. *At the Palace Gates.* 1967. Viking. 7th prt. VG/VG. A3. $15.00

POLITI, Leo. *Boat for Peppe.* 1950. Scribner. inscr/sgn. VG+/dj. F1. $60.00

POLITI, Leo. *Boat for Peppe.* 1950. Scribner. 1st ed. VG/VG. P2. $40.00

POLITI, Leo. *Boat for Peppe.* 1950. Scribner. 1st ed. 8vo. NF/NF. D1. $110.00

POLITI, Leo. *Juanita.* 1948. Scribner. 1st ed. inscr/sgn. 4to. cloth. VG-/G+. A3. $100.00

POLITI, Leo. *Little Pancho.* 1938. Viking. 1st ed. sgn. prt brds. F/dj. F1. $100.00

POLITI, Leo. *Pedro the Angel of Olivera Street.* 1946. Scribner. 1st ed. 12mo. bl cloth. VG/VG. D1. $125.00

POLITI, Leo. *Pedro: El Angel de la Calle Olvera.* 1961. Scribner. 1st thus ed. F/VG. P2. $20.00

POLITIS, M.N. *Conflits de Lois et Condition des Etrangers...* 1930. Paris. Recueil Siery. 240 p. wrp. M11. $50.00

POLK, George. *George Polk Case: Report of Overseas Writers...* 1951. NY. 8vo. 76 p. scarce. O2. $20.00

POLLACK, Robert. *Course of Time.* 1844. Portland. miniature. 376 p. aeg. tooled red leather. F. H3. $75.00

POLLAK, Martha D. *Military Architecture, Cartography & Representation...* 1991. Chicago. ils. 150 p. M/wrp. O6. $20.00

POLLAK, Michael. *Mandarins, Jews & Missionaries: Jewish Experience...* 1980. JPS. 436 p. VG/VG. S3. $30.00

POLLARD, A.O. *Unofficial Spy.* 1936. Hutchinson. xl. dj. P3. $13.00

POLLARD, E.A. *War in Am.* 1864. London. 12mo. 354 p. gilt gr cloth. G. T3. $69.00

POLLARD, Edward A. *Observations in the N: 8 Months in Prison & on Parole.* 1865. Richmond, VA. 1st ed. 8vo. 142 p. prt wrp. VG. M1. $275.00

POLLARD, Edward Alfred. *Lost Cause: New S Hist of War of the Confederates.* 1866. NY. EB Treat. 1st ed. 24 engravings, 752 p. VG. M8. $125.00

POLLARD, Edward Alfred. *S Hist of the War. 1st Yr of the War.* 1863. Richardson. 1st Am ed. 368 p. cloth. VG. M8. $65.00

POLLARD, Josephine. *Decorative Sisters.* 1881. NY. Randolph. ils Walter Satterlee/12 color lithos. VG. scarce. F1. $175.00

POLLARD, Josephine. *Decorative Sisters.* 1881. Randolph. ils Walter Satterlee. 31 p. G+. S10. $45.00

POLLITZ, Edward A. Jr. *Forty-First Thief.* 1975. Delacorte. 1st ed. F/F. F4. $15.00

POLLOCK, Channing. *Fool.* nd. Grosset Dunlap. photoplay ed. VG. P3. $10.00

POLLOCK, J.C. *Centrifuge.* (1984). Crown. 1st ed. F/NF. A7. $20.00

POLLOCK, J.C. *Mission MIA.* 1982. Crown. 1st ed. F/dj. P3. $13.00

POLLOK, Robert. *Course of Time...* 1835. Wheeling, VA. later ed. 12mo. 256 p. leather. G. D7. $50.00

POLMAR, Norman. *Atomic Submarine.* 1963. Van Nostrant. VG. N2. $10.00

POLO, Marco. *Book of Ser Marco Polo, the Venetian...* 1921. London. Murray. lg thick 8vo. 2 vols. gilt gr cloth. NF. F1. $165.00

POLO, Marco. *Most Noble & Famous Travels of Marco Polo...* 1929. London. Argonaut. 1/1050. ils/11 maps. NF. O6. $250.00

POLUNIM & SMYTHIES. *Guia de Campo de las Flores de Espana.* 1981. Barcelona. 2nd ed. 80 color photos/maps. 549 p. map ep. B26. $39.00

POLYBIUS. *Historiarum, Libri Quinque in Latinam Conversi Languam...* (1522). Florence. Heirs of Philippi Giunta. 8vo. contemporary vellum. K1. $375.00

POMEROY, John Norton. *Civil Code in CA.* 1885. NY. Bar Assn. 69 p. wrp. M11. $125.00

POND, Barbara. *Sampler of Wayside Herbs.* 1974. Riverside. 1st ed. 32 full-p color pls. 126 p. NF/NF. B28. $17.50

PONGE, Francis. *Braque Lithographs.* 1963. Monte Carlo. 1/4125. VG/slipcase/glassine. A1. $400.00

PONICSAN, Darryl. *Cinderella Liberty.* (1973). Harper. 1st ed. F/NF. B4. $75.00

PONS, Helene. *Story of Vania.* 1963. Viking. 1st ed. oblong 4to. 24 p. aqua cloth. VG/torn. T5. $35.00

PONSOT, Marie. *Fairy Tale Book.* 1966 (1958). Golden Pr. 7th prt. ils Adrienne Segur. pict brds. VG-. T5. $75.00

PONTIN, Magnus. *De Cordis Polypo Pars Prima Theoretica Caus Illustrata.* 1806. Upsaliae. 4to. 1 engraved pl. 18 p. G7. $65.00

PONTING, Herbert G. *Great Wht S.* 1932 (1921). London. Duckworth. 10th ed. 8vo. 305 p. VG/VG. A2. $45.00

PONTING, Herbert G. *Great Wht S: Being Account of Experience of Capt Scott...* 1935. London. Duckworth. later prt. 8vo. 305 p. bl cloth. VG. P4. $42.50

POOL, J. Lawrence. *Neurosurgical Treatment of Paraplegia.* 1951. Springfield. Thomas. 107 p. NF. G7. $65.00

POOL, William C. *Hist Atlas of TX.* ca 1975. Austin. Encino. oblong 4to. color maps. 190 p. rose cloth. dj. H9. $50.00

POOLE, Richard. *Peacemaker.* (1954). Ballantine. F/dj. B9. $20.00

POOLEY, Elsa. *Trees of Natal, Zululand & Transkei.* 1993. Johannesburg. color photos. 480 p. M. B26. $59.00

POOR, Charles Lane. *Men Against the Rule.* 1937. Derrydale. 1st ed. 1/950. octavo. 157 p. gilt bl cloth. F. H5. $125.00

POPE, Alexander. *Essay on Criticism.* 1928. San Francisco. Clark Nash. 1/250. 2 vols. gilt parchment/bl brds. K1. $200.00

POPE, Edwin. *Baseball's Greatest Managers.* 1960. Doubleday. 1st ed. F/VG+. P8. $20.00

POPKIN, Zelda. *Journey Home.* nd. BC. VG/dj. P3. $8.00

POPULAR MECHANICS. *Mission Furniture & How To Make It.* 1912. Chicago. G. A16. $25.00

PORCELLA. *Pieced Clothing Variations.* 1981. np. ils. wrp. G2. $10.00

PORCELLA. *Pieced Clothing.* 1980. np. directions for 14 no-pattern garments. wrp. G2. $12.00

PORCH, Douglas. *Conquest of the Sahara.* 1985. London. Cape. 1st ed. 8vo. 332 p. F/F. A2. $15.00

PORCHER, Francis Peyre. *Resources of the S Fields & Forests, Medical, Economical...* 1869. Charleston. Walker Evans Cogswell. 2nd ed. 733 p. gr cloth. VG. M8. $1,500.00

PORIS. *Advance Beadwork.* 1989. np. ils. wrp. G2. $13.00

PORTER, Arthur Kingsley. *Medieval Architecture: Its Origins & Developement.* 1969. NY. reprint 1909 ed. 2 vols. F. B30. $125.00

PORTER, David. *Constantinople & Its Environs.* 1835. NY. 2 vols. 8vo. cloth. O2. $375.00

PORTER, Dennis. *Pennies From Heaven.* 1981. London. Quartet Books. PBO. inscr. NF/glossy 8vo wrp. A11. $65.00

PORTER, Eliot. *Birds of N Am.* (1972). Dutton. 1st ed. NF/NF clip. B3. $60.00

PORTER, Eliot. *Forever Wild: The Adirondacks.* (1966). Harper Row. 1st ed. NF/NF clip. B3. $60.00

PORTER, Eliot. *In Wildness Is Preservation of the World.* (1988). Sierra Club. 1st ed. F/F. B3. $50.00

PORTER, Fairfield. *Thomas Eakins.* 1959. Braziller. Great Am Artists series. 127 p. cloth. dj. D2. $25.00

PORTER, Gene Stratton. *At the Foot of the Rainbow.* nd. Grosset Dunlap. decor brds. G. P3. $17.00

PORTER, Gene Stratton. *Girl of the Limberlost.* (1909). Grosset Dunlap. 8vo. ils Benda. 453 p. VG+/VG. T5. $30.00

PORTER, Gene Stratton. *Harvester.* 1911. Doubleday Page. 1st ed. VG. M18. $40.00

PORTER, Gene Stratton. *Keeper of the Bees.* 1925. Doubleday Page. 1st ed. decor brds. G. P3. $25.00

PORTER, Gene Stratton. *Laddie: True Bl Story.* 1913. Doubleday. ils Herman Pfeifer. 602 p. pict ep. G. S10. $35.00

PORTER, Gene Stratton. *Michael O'Halloran.* 1915. Doubleday. 1st ed. 560 p. gr cloth. VG. B22. $12.00

PORTER, Helen Talbot. *Tell-a-Twinkle Tales.* 1924. John Martin's Book House. ils M Hartwell. VG+. P2. $20.00

PORTER, Horance. *Campaigning w/Grant.* 1897. NY. Century. 1st ed. 546 p. cloth/recased orig spine. VG. M8. $85.00

PORTER, J.B. *If I Make My Bed in Hell.* (1969). Word Books. 1st ed. 165 p. NF/clip. A7. $40.00

PORTER, James. *Revivals of Religion.* 1849. Boston. Peirce. 3rd ed. 260 p. H10. $25.00

PORTER, Jane. *Scottish Chiefs.* 1810. London. 1st ed. 12mo. 5 vols. contemporary red morocco/brds. NF. H5. $1,000.00

PORTER, Jane. *Scottish Chiefs.* 1886. Chicago. Belford. octavo. reprint of 1831 ed. F/dj. B24. $85.00

PORTER, Joyce. *Dover & the Unkindest Cut of All.* 1967. NY. Scribner. 1st Am ed. F/F. S5. $25.00

PORTER, Joyce. *Dover Goes to Pott.* 1968. Jonathan Cape. 1st ed. VG. P3. $13.00

PORTER, Joyce. *Dover Three.* 1965. Scribner. 1st ed. VG/dj. P3. $25.00

PORTER, Katherine Anne. *Flowering Judas & Other Stories.* 1940. Modern Lib. 1st ed. sgn. NF/VG+. A11. $65.00

PORTER, Katherine Anne. *Flowering Judas & Other Stories.* 1940. NY. Modern Lib. 1st ed. sgn. NF/VG+ clip. A11. $75.00

PORTER, Katherine Anne. *Hacienda.* 1934. NY. Harrison of Paris. 1/895. #d. w/prospectus. F/F slipcase. B2. $100.00

PORTER, Katherine Anne. *Ship of Fools.* 1962. Atlantic/Little Brn. 1st ed. F/NF. B2. $50.00

PORTER, Laurence M. *Interpretation of Dreams.* 1987. Boston. Twayne. 1st ed. sm 8vo. beige cloth. F/dj. G1. $17.95

PORTER, Robert P. *Japan: The New World-Power Being a Detailed Account...* 1915. London. 7 color maps. 789 p. cloth. F. B14. $75.00

PORTER, Roy. *Mind-Forged Manacles: Hist of Madness in Eng...* 1987. Cambridge. Harvard. 1st Am ed. 412 p. F/dj. G1. $20.00

PORTEUS, S.D. *Primitive Intelligence & Environment.* 1937. Macmillan. 1st Am ed. 8vo. 325 p. F/F. A2. $40.00

PORTIS, Charles. *Gringos.* 1991. Simon Schuster. 1st ed. F/F. B4. $35.00

PORTLOCK, Nathaniel. *Abridgement of Portlock & Dixon's Voyage Round the World.* 1789. George Goulding. octavo. lg fld map. new quarter morocco. H9. $600.00

PORTOR, Laura Spencer. *Story of the Little Angels.* 1917. NY. 1st ed. 12mo. 94 p. gilt bl cloth. VG+. H3. $25.00

POSEY, Alexander. *Poems of Alexander Lawrence Posey.* 1910. Topeka. Crane. 1st ed. cloth. VG. scarce. L3. $750.00

POST, C.C. *10 Yrs a Cowboy.* 1897. Chicago. Rhodes McClure. octavo. 471 p. dk gr cloth. VG. H5. $100.00

POST, Charles Johnson. *Little War of Private Post.* 1960. Little Brn. ils Post. 340 p. VG/VG. B11. $18.00

POST, Melville D. *Strange Schemes of Randolph Mason.* 1908. Putnam. 12th prt. VG. P3. $30.00

POSTAL & SILVER. *Encyclopedia of Jews in Sports.* 1965. NY. Bloch. 1st prt. VG/VG. S3. $35.00

POSTEL, Guillaume. *De Orbis Terrae Concordia Libri Quatuor.* 1544. Basle. folio. 446 p. modern vellum/brds. O2. $1,650.00

POSTEMA & WOJELECHOWSKI. *You've Got To Have Balls To Make It in This League.* 1992. Simon Schuster. 1st ed. F/F. P8. $12.50

POSTMAN, Leo. *Psychology in Making: Hist of Selected Research Problems.* 1962. Knopf. thick 8vo. bl cloth. VG/dj. G1. $30.00

POTOK, Chaim. *Chosen.* nd. BC. VG/dj. P3. $5.00

POTT, Percival. *Observations on Disorder of Corner of the Eye...* 1769. London. Hawes Clarke. 67 p. calf. G7. $495.00

POTTER, Beatrix. *Tailor of Gloucester.* 1902. London. private prt. 1st ed. 12mo. orig pink brds. NF/clamshell case. H5. $7,500.00

POTTER, Beatrix. *Tale of Peter Rabbit #1172.* ca 1920. Saalfield. 10 p. muslin cloth. G. A3. $10.50

POTTER, Beatrix. *Tale of Peter Rabbit.* nd. Donohue. 16 color ils. G. L1. $30.00

POTTER, Beatrix. *Tale of Peter Rabbit.* 1963. W Pub/Big Golden Book. 2nd prt. 24 p. VG. A3. $6.00

POTTER, Beatrix. *Tale of Pigling Bland.* 1913. London. 1st ed. sm octavo. 15 full-p ils. maroon brds/pict label. F. H5. $850.00

POTTER, Beatrix. *Tale of Tom Kitten.* ca 1910-18. Warne. 12mo. 85 p. gr brds/pict label. VG. D1. $95.00

POTTER, Dennis. *Sufficient Carbohydrate.* 1983. London. Faber. PBO. inscr. F/wrp. A11. $50.00

POTTER, E.B. *US & World Sea Power.* (1955). Prentice Hall. 1st ed. lg 8vo. 963 p. VG+/VG. A2. $30.00

POTTER, Jeremy. *Hazard Chase.* 1964. Constable. 1st ed. VG/dj. P3. $20.00

POTTER, Louise. *Roadside Flowers of AK.* 1963 (1962). Wasilla, AK. ils. 590 p. sbdg. VG. B26. $29.00

POTTER, Miriam Clark. *Giggle Quicks.* 1918. Chicago. Volland. ils Sarg. VG. B5. $25.00

POTTER, Miriam Clark. *Sally Gabble & the Fairies.* 1929. Macmillan. ils Helen Sewell. 1st ed. 87 p. VG. P2. $40.00

POTTER, SHARPE & HENDEE. *Human Behavior Aspects of Fish & Wildlife Conservation.* 1973. USDA. 4to. wrp. A17. $20.00

POTTINGER. *Quilts From IN Amish.* 1983. np. ils. wrp. G2. $18.00

POTTS, Jean. *Affair of the Heart.* 1970. Gollancz. 1st ed. xl. dj. P3. $5.00

POTTS, Ralph Bushnell. *Sir Boss.* (1959). Faversham. 320 p. F/F. A7. $18.00

POTTS, Ralph Bushnell. *Sir Boss.* (1959). Faversham. inscr. 320 p. F/F. A7. $25.00

POULSSON, Emilie. *Finger Plays for Nursery & Kindergarden.* 1965. NY. 8vo. ils. pict blk cloth. F/VG clip. H3. $15.00

POUND, Arthur. *Penns of PA & Eng.* 1932. NY. Macmillan. 1st ed. 8vo. 349 p. VG. V3. $17.50

POUND, Arthur. *Salt of the Earth.* 1940. Atlantic Monthly. 1st ed. 4to. 122 p. A17. $17.50

POUND, Arthur. *Turning Wheel: Story of General Motors...1908-1933.* 1934. Doubleday Doran. 1st ed. 8vo. 517 p. F/fair. A2. $15.00

POUND, Ezra. *Drafts & Fragments of Cantos CX-CXVII.* 1970. London. Faber. 1/100 for sale in Eng. sgn. ES. F/pub slipcase. H5. $650.00

POUND, Ezra. *Ezra Pound at 70.* nd. New Directions. 1st ed. 32mo. F/wrp. C4. $45.00

POUND, Ezra. *Fifth Decade of Cantos.* 1938. London. Faber. 1st ed. Robie Macauley's copy. NF/sans. C4. $95.00

POUND, Ezra. *Letters of...* 1951. London. 1st ed. NF/dj. C4. $50.00

POUND, Ezra. *Redondillas; or, Something of That Sort.* 1967. New Directions. 1/110. sgn. F/dj. B24. $1,850.00

POUND, Ezra. *Ta Hio: Great Learning, Newly Rendered Into Am Language...* 1928. Seattle. WA U. 1st ed/1st prt. 1/575. NF/gilt blk wrp. B24. $150.00

POUND, Ezra. *Thrones 96-109.* 1959. New Directions. 1st ed. F/NF. C4. $60.00

POURNELLE, Jerry. *King David's Spaceship.* nd. BC. VG/dj. P3. $8.00

POURNELLE, Jerry. *Step Farther Out.* 1980. WH Allen. 1st ed. NF/dj. P3. $20.00

POURRAT, Pierre. *Christian Spirituality in the Middle Ages.* 1953. Westminster. Newman. 341 p. H10. $35.00

POURRAT, Pierre. *La Spiritualite Chretienne.* 1928-31. Paris. Lecoffre. 4 vols. H10. $25.00

POUSETTE-DART, Nathaniel. *Childe Hassam.* 1922. Stokes. Distinguished Am Artists series. scarce. D2. $35.00

POUSSIN, Guillaume Tell. *US: Its Power & Progress*. 1851. Phil. xl. 488 p. NF. O7. $18.50

POWELL, Adam Clayton Jr. *Marching Blks*. 1973. Dial. revised/1st thus ed. 217 p. dj. A7. $20.00

POWELL, Allan. *Metropolitan Assylums Board & Its Work 1867-1930*. 1930. London. 1st ed. 106 p. cloth. G1. $27.50

POWELL, Anthony. *Casanova's Chinese Restaurant*. nd. Little Brn. 2nd ed. xl. dj. P3. $5.00

POWELL, Anthony. *Venusberg & Agents & Patients*. nd. Little Brn. 1st ed. F/NF. C4. $45.00

POWELL, Charles A. *Bound Feet*. 1938. Boston. Warren. 1st ed. presentation/sgn. 24 pls. 339 p. VG. W1. $45.00

POWELL, E.A. *In Barbary: Tunisia, Algeria, Morocco & the Sahara*. (1926). NY. Century. 1st ed. 8vo. photos/maps. 483 p. F/F. A2. $35.00

POWELL, E.A. *Map That Is Half Unrolled*. (1925). NY. 1st ed. 8vo. photos. 355 p. F/VG+. A2. $30.00

POWELL, H.M.T. *Santa Fe Trail to CA, 1849-1852*. 1931. San Francisco. BC of CA/Grabhorn. 1/300. folio. 272 p. NF/slipcase. H5. $2,500.00

POWELL, John Wesley. *Down the CO: Diary of 1st Trip Through Grand Canyon*. 1988. NY. Arrowood. reprint. folio. 168 p. F/NF. P4. $35.00

POWELL, John Wesley. *Report on the Lands of the Arid Region of the US*. 1879. GPO. 2nd ed. xl. lg 4to. 3 fld pocket maps. 195 p. H9. $225.00

POWELL, John Wesley. *Sixth Annual Report of Bureau of Ethnology, 1884-85*. 1888. WA. 669 p. gilt olive cloth. G+. M20. $95.00

POWELL, John Wesley. *14th Annual Report of Bureau of Ethnology...1892-93*. 1896. GPO. xl. 2 vols. sm folio. orig gr cloth. H9. $250.00

POWELL, Lawrence Clark. *Land of Fact: Companion to Land of Fiction...* 1992. Hist Soc of S CA. 1st prt. 1/100. sgn. M/sans. A18. $45.00

POWELL, Mary G. *Hist of Old Alexandria, VA...July 13, 1749 to May 24, 1861*. ca 1928. William Byrd. ils. VG. B10. $50.00

POWELL, P.H. *Murder Premeditated*. 1951. Herbert Jenkins. xl. dj. P3. $10.00

POWELL, Padgett. *Edisto*. (1984). FSG. AP. author's 1st book. F/prt beige wrp. C4. $50.00

POWELL, Richard. *Daily & Sunday*. 1964. Scribner. 1st ed. VG/dj. P3. $18.00

POWELL, Talmage. *Priceless Particle*. 1969. Whitman. w/sgn label. VG. P3. $20.00

POWELL, Talmage. *Smasher*. 1959. Macmillan. 1st ed. w/sgn label. VG/dj. P3. $35.00

POWELL, Van. *Haunted Hanger*. 1932. Saalfield. VG-. P3. $7.00

POWELL & RAREY. *Tachyhippodamia; or, New Secret of Taming Horses*. 1872. Phil. Charter. VG. O3. $65.00

POWELSON, Jack. *Dialogue w/Friends*. 1988. Boulder, CO. Horizon Soc. 1st ed. 12mo. 164 p. VG/wrp. V3. $8.00

POWER, Eileen. *Medieval People*. 1963 (1924). np. as new. C1. $7.50

POWERS, Alfred. *Animals of the Arctic*. 1965. McKay. 8vo. 272 p. VG/worn. P4. $25.00

POWERS, Alfred. *Hist of OR Literature*. 1935. Metropolitan Pr. 1st ed. ils Hinshaw. F/dj. A18. $125.00

POWERS, J.F. *Look How the Fish Live*. 1975. Hogarth. PBO. sgn. F/unread. A11. $30.00

POWERS, J.F. *Morte d'Urban*. 1962. Garden City. 1st ed. sgn. F/VG+ clip. A11. $60.00

POWERS, J.L. *Blk Abyss*. 1966. Arcadia. VG/dj. P3. $13.00

POWERS, Jimmy. *Baseball Personalities*. 1949. Field. 1st ed. F/VG+. P8. $25.00

POWERS, Richard. *Operation Wandering Soul*. 1993. Morrow. uncorrected bound galleys. F/pict wrp. C4. $65.00

POWERS, Richard. *Three Farmers on Their Way to a Dance*. 1985. NY. Beech Tree/Morrow. 1st ed. F/F. B2. $150.00

POWERS, Tim. *Anubis Gates*. 1989. Mark Ziesing. F/dj. P3. $25.00

POWERS, Tim. *Last Call*. 1992. Morrow. 1st ed. sgn. F/F. T2. $55.00

POWERS, Tim. *On Stranger Tides*. 1987. NY. Ace. 1st ed. NF/F. N3. $10.00

POWERS, Tim. *On Stranger Tides*. 1987. Ultramarine. 1st ed. 1/150. sgn/#d. half leather. M. M2. $175.00

POWNALL, Thomas. *Topographical Description of Dominions of USA*. 1949. Pittsburgh. 1/2000. lg facimile map. tan linen. H9. $75.00

POWYS, John Cowper. *Meaning of Culture*. 1929. Norton. G. N2. $6.00

POWYS, John Cowper. *3 Fantasies*. (1986). NY. Carcanet. AP. F/prt bl wrp. B3. $25.00

POYEN, Charles. *Progress of Animal Magnetism in New Eng*. 1978. Da Capo Pr. reprint. 212 p. red cloth. G1. $27.50

POYER, Joe. *Contract*. 1978. Atheneum. 1st ed. VG. P3. $10.00

POYNTER, Beulah. *Murder on 47th Street*. 1931. Crime Club. 1st ed. VG-. P3. $10.00

PRAGNELL, Festus. *Green Man of Graypec*. 1950. Greenberg. NF/dj. P3. $35.00

PRANGE, Gordon W. *Miracle at Midway*. 1982. McGraw Hill. VG/dj. A16. $10.00

PRASAD, Rajiva Nain. *Raja Man Singh of Amber*. 1966. Calcutta. World. 1st ed. tall 8vo. pls. 196 p. VG/torn. W1. $18.00

PRATCHETT, Terry. *Truckers*. 1989. England. Doubleday. 1st ed. F/dj. P3. $20.00

PRATCHETT, Terry. *Wings*. 1991. Delacorte. 1st Am ed. F/F. N3. $15.00

PRATSON, Frederick J. *Land of the 4 Directions*. 1970. Chatham. uncommon hc ed. oblong quarto. VG/VG. L3. $65.00

PRATT, Fletcher. *Invaders From Rigel*. 1960. Avalon. VG/dj. P3. $30.00

PRATT, Glayds L. *Am Garden Flowers*. 1943. NY. ils Rudolf Preund. 50 p. pape brds. G. A17. $12.50

PRATT, J. Lowell. *Baseball's All Stars*. 1967. Doubleday. 1st ed. VG/G. P8. $15.00

PRATT, Richard. *Gardens in Color*. 194 Garden City. photos Edward Steichen. 14 p. VG. B28. $35.00

PRATT, Theodore. *Murder Goes to th World's Fair*. nd. Eldon. VG. P3. $25.00

PRATT & RHINE. *Extrasensory Perceptio After 60 Yrs*. 1966. Boston. Bruce Humphrie reprint. 464 p. bl cloth. VG. G1. $35.00

PRAY, Leon L. *Taxidermy*. (1979). NY. 31 prt. ils/index. F/dj. A17. $7.00

PREISS, Byron. *Planets*. 1985. Banta F/dj. P3. $25.00

PREISS, Byron. *Ultimate Dracula*. nd. Qu ity BC. F/dj. P3. $10.00

PRELUTSKY, Jack. *Circus*. 1974. Macm lan. 1st ed. sm 4to. pict brds. VG. T5. $25.0

PREMINGER, Marion. *All I Want Is Eve thing*. (1957). Funk Wagnall. 1st ed. 8vo. p. VG+/VG. A2. $15.00

PRENTICE, Amy. *Croaky Frog's Sto* (1906). NY. 12mo. ils JW Davis. bl clo VG. H3. $12.00

PRESBREY, Frank. *Land of the Sky*. ca 19 Pass Dept S Railway. 8vo. 32 p. pict w H9. $55.00

PRESCOT, Dray; see Bulmer, Kenneth.

PRESCOTT, William H. *Hist of Conquest of Mexico...* 1843. NY. Harper. 1st ed. 2 maps. 488 p. blk cloth. M1. $500.00

PRESCOTT, William H. *Hist of Conquest of Peru.* nd. (1900). Phil. 2 vols. 12mo. gilt brn cloth. F. H3. $20.00

PRESCOTT, William H. *Hist of Conquest of Peru.* 1847. NY. 1st ed/2nd issue. 2 vols. gilt blk cloth. F. H3. $65.00

PRESCOTT, William H. *Hist of Reign of Ferdinand & Isabella...* 1838 (1837). Little Brn. 3rd ed. 8vo. 3 vols. NF. A2. $110.00

PRESTIGE, G.L. *St Basil the Great & Apollinaris of Loadicea.* 1936. London. index. 68 p. H10. $17.50

PREUSS, Paul. *Starfire.* 1988. Tor. 1st ed. F/dj. P3. $18.00

PREVERT, Jacques. *Chiens ont Soif.* (1964). Paris. Au Pont des Arts. 1st ed. 1/320. 61 p. unbound/wrp/box. B24. $3,500.00

PRIBRAM, Karl H. *Freud's Project Reassessed.* 1976. Basic Books. 1st ed. 192 p. tan cloth. VG/dj. G1. $30.00

PRICE, Anthony. *Gunner Kelly.* 1984. Doubleday. 1st Am ed. F/F. S5. $27.50

PRICE, Anthony. *Gunner Kelly.* 1984. Doubleday. 1st ed. VG/torn. P3. $12.00

PRICE, Anthony. *War Game.* 1976. London. Gollancz. 1st ed. F/F. M15. $150.00

PRICE, E. Hoffman. *Strange Gateways.* 1967. Arkham. 1st ed. F/dj. M2. $75.00

PRICE, Edwin. *Extracts From Papers of...,* *Late of Neath Abbey...* 1820. Phil. Kite. 24mo. 82 p. leather. G. V3. $15.00

PRICE, Eugenia. *Bright Captivity.* ca 1991. Doubleday. 1st ed. 631 p. F/F. B10. $20.00

PRICE, Eugenia. *Stranger in Savannah.* 1989. Doubleday. 1st stated ed. 755 p. cloth. F/F clip. M8. $35.00

PRICE, Frederic Newlin. *Etchings & Lithos of Arthur B Davies.* 1929. London. Kennerley. 1/200. 205 pls. teg. morocco/bl cloth. rpr slipcase. D2. $750.00

PRICE, George. *Who's in Charge Here?* (1943). NY. Farrar. 1st ed. 4to. F/dj. B20. $45.00

PRICE, Harry. *Confessions of a Ghost Hunter.* 1936. London. Putnam. 2nd prt. blk cloth. VG/dj. G1. $25.00

PRICE, Lucien. *We Northmen.* 1936. Little Brn. 1st ed. 8vo. 392 p. F/VG. A2. $15.00

PRICE, Margaret Evans. *Child's Book of Myths.* 1924. McNally. 1st ed. lg 8vo. 111 p. VG. S10. $50.00

PRICE, Olive. *Rosa Bonheur: Painter of Animals.* 1972. Champaign. Garrard. 1st ed. juvenile. VG/G+. O3. $25.00

PRICE, Reynolds. *Bl Calhoun.* 1992. Atheneum. 1st ed. sgn. F/dj. C4. $35.00

PRICE, Reynolds. *Conversations w/ Reynolds Price.* 1992. Jackson, MS. 1st ed. F/dj. C4. $30.00

PRICE, Reynolds. *Early Christmas.* 1992. Wesleyan. 1/500. F. C4. $40.00

PRICE, Reynolds. *For Reynolds Price.* 1983. np. private prt. 1/150. F/gold wrp. C4. $135.00

PRICE, Reynolds. *Foreseeable Future.* 1991. NY. 1st ed. inscr. F/F. A11. $30.00

PRICE, Reynolds. *Good Hearts.* 1988. Atheneum. 1st ed. sgn. F/F. B2. $60.00

PRICE, Reynolds. *Kate Vaiden.* 1986. Atheneum. 1st ed. sgn. F/F. B2. $75.00

PRICE, Reynolds. *Late Warning.* 1968. NY. ltd ed. 1/176. sgn. F/French paper wrp. E3. $80.00

PRICE, Reynolds. *Long & Happy Life.* 1962. Atheneum. ARC. NF/yel wrp. B4. $175.00

PRICE, Reynolds. *Long & Happy Life.* 1962. Atheneum. 1st ed/1st issue. sgn. NF/VG clip. L3. $150.00

PRICE, Reynolds. *Permanent Errors: Stories.* 1970. NY. 1st ed. sgn. author's 5th fiction book. VG+/VG+. E3. $55.00

PRICE, Reynolds. *Tongues of Angels.* 1990. Atheneum. AP. F/prt red wrp. C4. $40.00

PRICE, Reynolds. *Wanderers.* 1974. Boston. 1st ed. sgn. F/F. A11. $65.00

PRICE, Reynolds. *Whole New Life: An Illness & a Healing.* 1994. NY. 1st ed. sgn. M/M. E3. $40.00

PRICE, Richard. *Bloodbrothers.* 1976. Houghton Mifflin. 1st ed. inscr. author's 2nd book. NF/VG. L3. $75.00

PRICE, Richard. *Ladies' Man.* 1978. Houghton Mifflin. 1st ed. NF/NF. A14. $35.00

PRICE, Vincent. *I Like What I Know. Visual Autobiography.* 1959. Doubleday. 1st ed. sgn. NF/worn. B2. $85.00

PRICE, Willard. *Japan's Islands of Mystery.* 1944. London. 1st ed. 12mo. ils/maps. 255 p. silvered bl cloth. VG/G. H3. $20.00

PRIDDELL, Guy. *We Began at Jamestown.* 1968. Dietz. 1st ed. 8vo. photos. 198 p. orange cloth. F/VG. B11. $40.00

PRIDE, Leo B. *Shadow of the Mine & Other Plays of the Coal Fields.* 1929. NY. Samuel French. 1st ed. N2. $32.50

PRIDE, Nigel. *Butterfly Sings to Picaya.* (1978). London. Constable. 1st ed. 367 p. F3. $20.00

PRIEST, Christopher. *Darkening Island.* 1972. Harper Row. 1st Am ed. F/NF clip. N3. $15.00

PRIEST, Christopher. *Glamour.* 1984. Jonathan Cape. 1st ed. sgn. F/dj. P3. $30.00

PRIEST, Christopher. *Infinite Summer.* 1979. Scribner. 1st ed. F/dj. P3. $15.00

PRIEST, Christopher. *Space Machine.* 1976. Harper Row. 1st ed. VG/dj. P3. $20.00

PRIESTLEY, J.B. *Black-Out in Gretley.* 1943. Clipper Books. F/dj. P3. $30.00

PRIESTLEY, J.B. *Festival at Farbridge.* 1951. Heinemann. 1st ed. VG. P3. $30.00

PRIESTLEY, J.B. *Saturn Over the Water.* 1961. Heinemann. 1st ed. VG/VG-. P3. $25.00

PRIESTLEY, J.B. *Thirty-First of June.* 1961. Heinemann. 1st ed. VG/dj. P3. $35.00

PRIME, E.D.G. *Around the World: Sketches of Travel...* 1872. NY. 8vo. ils. 455 p. cloth. O2. $60.00

PRIME, E.D.G. *Forty Yrs in the Turkish Empire; or, Memoirs of Wm Goodell.* 1876. NY. 1st ed. presentation/inscr/dtd. 489 p. O2. $100.00

PRINCE, Morton. *Critique of Psychoanalysis.* 1921. Offprint. 12 p. G/prt gr wrp. G1. $22.50

PRINCE, Walter Franklin. *Enchanted Boundary: Being Survey of Negative Reactions...* 1930. Boston. Soc for Psychical Research. 348 p. ruled red cloth. G. G1. $25.00

PRINGLE, David. *Ultimate Guide to SF.* 1990. Pharos Books. 1st Am ed. F/F. N3. $25.00

PRIOR-PALMER, Lucinda. *Up, Up & Away: Biography of Be Fair.* 1978. London. Pelham. later prt. VG/VG. O3. $20.00

PROCTOR, Creasy K. *Story of St John's College & Oxford Orphanage.* 1931. np. 1st separate prt. 16 p. VG/wrp. M8. $27.50

PROCTOR, Edna Dean. *Russian Journey.* 1872. Boston. Osgood. xl. sm 8vo. 321 p. G. W1. $25.00

PROCTOR, J.C. *WA Past & Present: A Hist.* 1930. Lewis. vol 4 only. B10. $25.00

PROCTOR, Maurice. *His Weight in Gold.* 1966. Harper Row. 1st ed. F/dj. P3. $18.00

PROCTOR, Maurice. *Rogue Running.* 1966. Harper Row. 1st ed. F/dj. P3. $18.00

PROCTOR. *Needlework Tools & Accessories, a Collector's Guide.* 1990. np. ils. cloth. G2. $45.00

PROFFITT, Nicolas. *Embassy House.* (1986). Bantam. 1st prt. VG+/dj. A7. $15.00

PROKOSCH, Frederic. *Ballad of Love.* 1960. FSC. 1st ed. 311 p. VG/dj. M20. $30.00

PRONZINI, Bill. *Gallow's Land.* 1983. NY. Walker. 1st ed. sgn. F/F. M15. $25.00

PRONZINI, Bill. *Invitation To Murder.* 1991. Dark Harvest. 1st ed. F/dj. B9. $6.50

PRONZINI, Bill. *Nightshades.* 1984. St Martin. 1st ed. F/F. F4. $25.00

PRONZINI, Bill. *Panic!* 1972. Random. 1st ed. VG/dj. P3. $40.00

PRONZINI, Bill. *Quicksilver.* nd. BC. NF/dj. P3. $8.00

PRONZINI, Bill. *Shackles.* 1988. St Martin. 1st ed. VG/dj. P3. $17.00

PRONZINI, Bill. *Snowbound.* 1974. NY. Putnam. 1st ed. inscr/sgn. NF/NF. S5. $45.00

PRONZINI, Bill. *Stalker.* 1971. Random. 1st ed. inscr/sgn. author's 1st book. F/NF. S5. $50.00

PRONZINI, Bill. *Voodoo!* 1980. Arbor. 1st ed. F/F. F4. $15.00

PROPPER, Milton M. *Strange Disappearance of Mary Young.* nd. Grosset Dunlap. VG. P3. $10.00

PROSE, Francine. *Bigfoot Dreams.* (1986). Pantheon. 1st ed. F/F. B3. $15.00

PROSKE, Beatrice G. *Brookgreen Gardens: Sculpture.* 1943. Brookgreen, SC. ils/fld plan/photos. 510 p. VG. B26. $24.00

PROSSER, William L. *Handbook of Law of Torts.* 1971. St Paul. W Pub. M11. $35.00

PROUDFIT & WHITEHEAD. *Pantry Family.* 1942. McKay. pict brds. VG+/dj. M5. $30.00

PROULX, E. Annie. *Heartsongs.* (1988). NY. Scribner. 1st ed. author's scarce 1st book. F/dj. B4. $200.00

PROULX, E. Annie. *Postcards.* 1992. Scribner. ARC. w/promo materials. NF/F. B2. $150.00

PROULX, E. Annie. *Shipping News.* 1993. Scribner. 1st ed. inscr. NF/F. B2. $85.00

PROVENSEN & PROVENSEN. *Glorious Flight.* 1983. Viking. 1st ed. oblong 4to. 39 p. F/VG. T5. $55.00

PROVENSEN & PROVENSEN. *Leonardo Da Vinci: Artist, Inventor, Scientist...* 1984. 6 movable scenes. NF. A4. $35.00

PROVENSEN & PROVENSEN. *Our Animal Friends at Maple Hill Farm.* 1974. Random. 1st ed. G+. P2. $15.00

PRY, Paul. *Magic Lantern.* nd. (1820s). Manchester. 64mo. woodcuts. 12 p. VG/hc pict wrp. H3. $50.00

PRZYWARA, Erich. *Newman Systhesis.* 1945. NY. Sheed Ward. 379 p. H10. $25.00

PSEUDOMAN, Akkad. *Zero to Eighty.* 1937. Scientific Pub. 1st ed. VG/dj. P3. $35.00

PSOMIADES & THOMADAKIS. *Greece, the New Europe & the Changing Internat Order.* 1993. NY. 8vo. 439 p. O2. $20.00

PUCKETT, Andrew. *Terminius.* 1990. Collins Crime Club. 1st ed. F/dj. P3. $18.00

PUCKETT. *Monograms: Softly Yours.* 1984. np. patterns/instructions. wrp. G2. $7.00

PUCKETT. *Sweaters: Softly Yours.* 1984. np. ils. wrp. G2. $5.00

PUENTES. *First Aid for Family Quilts.* 1986. np. wrp. G2. $6.00

PUIG, Manuel. *Kiss of the Spider Woman.* 1979. Knopf. 1st ed. F/NF. B2. $45.00

PUIG, Manuel. *Kiss of the Spider Woman.* 1979. Knopf. 1st ed. trans from Spanish. NF/NF clip. A14. $35.00

PUIG, Manuel. *Pubis Angelica.* 1986. NY. 1st Eng-language ed. sgn. NF/8vo wrp. A11. $45.00

PULFORD. *Morning Star Quilts.* 1989. np. ils. cloth. G2. $35.00

PULITZER, Ralph. *Over the Front in an Aeroplane.* 1915. AL Burt. G/poor. A16. $25.00

PULLAN & TEXIER. *Principal Ruins of Asia Minor...* 1865. London. folio. 50 engravings/engraved map. aeg. orig cloth. O2. $1,500.00

PULSIFER, Susan N. *House in Time.* (1958). NY. Citadel. 1st ed. presentation. ils EC Caswell. 220 p. F/NF. B20. $25.00

PULTON, Ferdinando. *Collection of Sundry Statutes, Frequent in Use...* 1632. London. Flesher Haviland Young. full calf. M11. $1,500.00

PUMPELLY, Raphael. *Across Am & Asia.* 1870. China. Leypoldt Hold. 1st ed. 8vo. pls/maps. rebound cloth. H9. $125.00

PUNSHON, E.R. *Bl John Diamond.* 1929. Clode. 1st ed. VG. P3. $35.00

PURCELL, E.D. *Life of Cardinal Manning.* 1896. NY. Macmillan. 2 vols. VG. C5. $40.00

PURCELL, Mary. *Halo on the Sword. St Joan of Arc.* 1952. Westminster. Newman. 308 p. VG. C5. $8.50

PURCELL, Mary. *Matt Talbot & His Times.* 1976. Chicago. Franciscan Herald. 238 p. VG/wrp. C5. $7.50

PURCELL, Mary. *Quiet Companion.* 1970. Chicago. Loyola. 198 p. VG. C5. $10.00

PURCELL, Victor. *Malaya: Communist or Free?* 1954. London. 1st ed. 288 p. G. B18. $22.50

PURCHAS, Samuel. *Purchas: His Pilgrimage...* 1617. London. Stansby/Fetherstone. Quiller-Couch bookplate. rpr calf. H9. $1,800.00

PURDY, James. *Children Is All.* 1961. NY. 1st ed. inscr. NF/dj. A15. $45.00

PURDY, James. *63: Dream Palace.* 1965. NY. 1st ed. sgn. F/wht wrp ils Purdy. A11. $135.00

PURDY, W.A. *Church on the Move.* 1965. London. Hollis Carter. 1965. 352 p. VG. C5. $10.00

PURSER, Philip. *Four Days to the Fireworks.* 1965. Walker. 1st ed. VG/VG. P3. $13.00

PURTILL, Richard. *CS Lewis' Case for the Christian Faith.* 1981. Harper. 144 p. VG. C5. $12.50

PURVES, George T. *Testimony of Justin Martyr to Early Christianity...* ca 1889. NY. Randolph. 302 p. H10. $18.50

PURVIS, Robert. *Appeal of 40,000 Citizens...* 1838. Phil. 1st ed. 8vo. 18 p. prt wrp. M1. $1,000.00

PURYEAR, Vernon J. *Internat Economics & Diplomacy in the Near E.* 1935. Stanford. 8vo. 264 p. cloth. dj. O2. $35.00

PUSEY, E.B. *Holy Eucharist a Comfort to the Penitent...a Sermon.* 1843. NY. Sparks. 71 p. H10. $20.00

PUSEY, Edward. *Confessions of St Augustine.* 1949. Modern Lib. 338 p. VG. C5. $8.50

PUSEY, M.J. *Charles Evans Hughes.* 1951. NY. Macmillan. 2 vols. M11. $50.00

PUSEY, M.J. *Eugene Meyer.* 1974. Knopf. 1st ed. 397 p. VG+/VG. S3. $28.00

PUSHKIN, Alexander. *Boris Godunov.* 1831. Petersburg. 1st ed. 8vo. 142 p. later marbled brds. F. M1. $8,500.00

PUSHKIN, Alexander. *Golden Cockerel.* 1950. Heritage. ils Dulac. VG. P2. $18.00

PUSHKIN, Alexander. *Poems.* 1888. Cupples Hurd. trans/intro Ivan Panin. 179 p. yel/cream brds. VG+. B14. $60.00

PUSKAS, Charles B. *Intro to the New Testament.* 1989. Peabody, MA. Hendrickson. 297 p. VG. C5. $8.50

PUTNAM, George Granville. *Mariner of the N: Life of Capt Bob Bartlett.* ca 1947. NY. Duell Sloan. 246 p. VG/VG. P4. $35.00

PUTNAM, George Granville. *Salem Vessels & Their Voyages...* 1925. Salem. Essex Inst. ils/index. 164 p. gilt bdg. P4. $55.00

PUTNAM, George Haven. *Prisoner of War in VA 1864-65.* 1912. NY. 2nd ed. ils. 127 p. VG. B28. $35.00

PUTNAM, George Palmer. *Wide Margins.* 1942. NY. 1st ed. VG/VG. B5. $17.50

PUTTI, Vittorio. *Berengario da Carpi Saggio Biografico e Bibliografico...* 1937. Bologna. Cappelli. pls/fld map. 352 p. G7. $175.00

PUTZ, Louis. *Catholic Church: USA.* 1958. London. Holborn. 176 p. VG. C5. $8.50

PUTZ, Louis. *Lord's Day.* 1963. Notre Dame. Fides. 234 p. VG. C5. $8.50

PUTZ, Louis. *Modern Apostle.* 1957. Chicago. Fides. 147 p. VG. C5. $7.50

PUZO, Mario. *Fools Die.* 1978. Putnam. 1st ed. VG/VG-. P3. $25.00

PUZO, Mario. *Godfather.* (1969). Putnam. 1st ed. NF/VG clip. B4. $125.00

PYE, Henry James. *Summary of Duties of Justice of Peace Out of Sessions...* 1808. London. Hatchard. quarter calf/marbled brds. M11. $350.00

PYE, Lucian W. *Guerrilla Communism in Malaya.* 1956. Princeton, NJ. 1st ed. index. 369 p. G/dj. B18. $22.50

PYLE, Howard. *Howard Pyle Brandywine Ed, 1853-1933.* 1933. Scribner. complete 5 vols. quarto. stp red cloth. NF. H5. $350.00

PYLE, Howard. *Howard Pyle's Book of Pirates.* 1921. Harper. 247 p. VG. P2. $100.00

PYLE, Howard. *Merry Adventures of Robin Hood.* 1974. Grosset Dunlap. Jr Lib ed. ils Lawrence B Smith. G/G. L1. $10.00

PYLE, Howard. *Pepper & Salt; or, Seasoning for Young Folk.* (1885). Harper. early reprint. 109 p. VG. P2. $25.00

PYLE, Howard. *Story of Champions of Round Table.* 1922 (1905). NY. ils. VG. C1. $14.00

PYLE, Howard. *Wonder Clock.* (1915). Harper. oversize 8vo. 318 p. VG. T5. $45.00

PYLE, Katherine. *Katherine Pyle Book of Fairy Tales.* (1925). Dutton. 8vo. 338 p. red cloth. VG. T5. $65.00

PYM, Horace N. *Memories of Old Friends.* 1882. Lippincott. 378 p. gr cloth. NF. B22. $17.50

PYNCHON, Thomas. *Crying of Lot 49.* 1967. London. Cape. 1st ed. author's 2nd novel. VG/VG. L3. $250.00

PYNCHON, Thomas. *Gravity's Rainbow.* 1973. Viking. 1st ed. F/NF. B2. $425.00

PYNCHON, Thomas. *V.* 1963. Lippincott. 1st ed. NF/NF. B2. $475.00

PYNE, William Henry. *Hist of Royal Residences of Windsor Castle...* 1819. London. A Dry. 1st ed. lg quarto. 3 vols. marbled ep. VG. H5. $4,000.00

PYUN, Yung Tai. *Korea, My Country.* 1949. Seoul. Internat Cultural Assn. 1st ed. 8vo. 224 p. VG. W1. $8.00

QIRIAZI, Gjerasim. *Captured by Brigands.* nd. Wrexham. trans John W Baird. 12mo. 129 p. O2. $20.00

QUACKENBUSH, A.T. *Annuals of Flowerland.* 1927. NY. 1st ed. 12mo. 166 p. VG/torn. B28. $17.50

QUAH, Jon S.T. *In Search of Singapore's Nat Values.* 1990. Singapore. Times Academic pr. 1st ed. 8vo. 105 p. VG/wrp. W1. $6.00

QUAIFE, M.M. *Journals of Capt Meriwether Lewis & Sgt John Ordway...* 1916. Madison, WI. State Hist Soc. 1st ed. 8vo. 444 p. scarce. T8. $295.00

QUAIFE, M.M. *This Is Detroit: 250 Yrs in Pictures.* 1951. Wayne U. 1st ed. 198 p. A17. $25.00

QUAIFE, William. *Chicago Highways: Old & New...* 1923. Chicago. Keller. 1st ed. VG. V2. $35.00

QUAIN & WILSON. *Series of Anatomical Drawings.* ca 1842. London. Smith Elder. 5 vols. 201 litho pls. half blk morocco/maroon cloth. H5. $7,500.00

QUALE, Eric. *Collector's Book of Books.* 1971. Clarkson Potter. 1st ed. VG/clip. C1. $19.50

QUAMMEN, David. *Flight of the Iguana.* (1988). Delacorte. 1st ed. F/F. B3. $25.00

QUAMMEN, David. *To Walk the Line.* (1970). Knopf. ltd ed. presentation/inscr. F/F. B3. $50.00

QUARDT, Robert. *Master Diplomat. Life of Leo XIII.* 1964. NY. Alba. 112 p. VG. C5. $8.50

QUARLES, Francis. *Sions Sonets Sung by Solomon the King & Periphras'd.* 1905. Cambridge. Riverside. 1/430. sm octavo. 125 p. red brds. F/slipcase. B24. $48.00

QUARRIER, William. *Life Story of William Quarrier: A Romance of Faith.* nd. Glasgow. Allan. 4th ed. 132 p. VG. C5. $10.00

QUARRY, Nick; see Albert, Marvin H.

QUASTEN, Johannes. *Music & Worship in Pagan & Christian Antiquity.* 1973. WA, DC. Nat Assn Patroral Music. 243 p. wrp. C5. $12.50

QUASTEN, Johannes. *Patrology, Vol I.* 1950. Westminster. Newman. 349 p. VG. C5. $30.00

QUAYLE. *Collector's Book of Children's Books.* 1971. lg 4to. pls. 144 p. NF/NF. A4. $95.00

QUEEN, Ellery. *Detective Short Story: A Bibliography.* 1942. Little Brn. 1st ed. F/VG. B4. $100.00

QUEEN, Ellery. *Ellery Queen's a Multitude of Sins.* 1978. Dial. 1st ed. VG/VG. P3. $15.00

QUEEN, Ellery. *Ellery Queen's Awards. 9th Series.* (1954). Little Brn. 1st ed. VG/dj. B9. $20.00

QUEEN, Ellery. *Four of Hearts.* 1941. Triangle. VG/VG. P3. $13.00

QUEEN, Ellery. *Fourth Side of the Triangle.* 1965. Random. 1st ed. VG/VG. P3. $20.00

QUEEN, Ellery. *King Is Dead.* (1952). Little Brn. 1st ed. VG/dj. B9. $50.00

QUEEN, Ellery. *Origin of Evil.* 1951. Little Brn. 1st ed. F/NF. M15. $75.00

QUEEN, Ellery. *Player on the Other Side.* 1963. Random. 1st ed. F/NF. M15. $35.00

QUEEN, Ellery. *Queen's Awards 1946.* 1946. Little Brn. 1st ed. F/NF. N3. $45.00

QUEEN, Ellery. *Queen's Full.* 1965. Random. 1st ed. F/F. M15. $40.00

QUEEN, Ellery. *Sporting Blood.* 1942. Little Brn. 1st ed. VG/dj. M18. $50.00

QUEEN, Ellery. *There Was an Old Woman.* 1943. Little Brn. 1st ed. VG. P3. $30.00

QUEEN, Ellery. *Tragedy of X.* 1978. CA U. VG/sans. P3. $10.00

QUEENY, Edgar. *Prairie Wings.* (1946). NY. Ducks Unltd. 1/225. sgn Queeny/Bishop. w/sgn Bishop etching. pigskin. R3. $5,000.00

QUELLER, Donald. *4th Crusade: Conquest of Constantinople, 1201-1204.* 1977. Phil. PA U. 248 p. VG/wrp. C5. $12.50

QUENTIN, Patrick. *Follower.* 1950. Simon Schuster. 1st ed. VG/VG. P3. $15.00

QUENTIN, Patrick. *Green-Eyed Monster.* 1960. Gollancz. 1st ed. VG/VG. P3. $20.00

QUENTIN, Patrick. *Man w/Two Wives.* 1955. Gollancz. 1st ed. VG/VG. P3. $20.00

QUESADA, Roberto. *Ships.* 1992. NY. 4 Walls 8 Windows. 1st ed. trans from Spanish. F/F clip. A14. $25.00

QUESNELL, Quentin. *Gospel of Christian Freedom.* 1969. NY. Herder. 134 p. VG. C5. $7.50

QUEST, Rodney. *Cereberus Murders.* 1970. McCall. 1st ed. VG/VG. P3. $18.00

QUICK, Dorothy. *Cry in the Night.* 1957. Arcadia. 1st ed. VG/dj. M2. $35.00

QUICK & QUICK. *MS Steamboatin.* ca 1926. NY. Holt. 1st ed. pls. 342 p. gray buckram. H9. $45.00

QUIERY, W.H. *Facing God: Finding the Reality of Christ.* 1967. NY. Sheed. 211 p. VG. C5. $7.50

QUIGLEY, Martin. *Catholic Action in Practice.* 1963. Random. 148 p. VG. C5. $7.50

QUIGLEY, Martin. *Crooked Pitch.* 1984. Algonquin. 1st ed. F/VG+. P8. $25.00

QUILLER-COUCH, Arthur. *In Powder & Crinoline.* 1913. Hodder Stoughton. 1st Eng ed. ils Nielsen. 164 p. VG. D1. $700.00

QUILLER-COUCH, Arthur. *Sleeping Beauty & Other Fairy Tales.* 1978. Weathervane Books. 1st thus ed. ils Dulac. VG/VG. L1. $22.50

QUILLER-COUCH, Arthur. *Twelve Dancing Princesses & Others.* ca 1913. Doran. 1st Am ed. ils Nielsen. 244 p. bl cloth. VG. D1. $295.00

QUIMBY, M.J. *Scratch Ankle, USA.* 1970 (1969). Barnes. 2nd ed. lg 8vo. 390 p. F/VG. A2. $12.50

QUIN, Dan; see Lewis, Alfred Henry.

QUIN, Eleanor. *Last on the Menu: Convent Life.* 1966. Prentice Hall. 182 p. VG. C5. $8.50

QUIN, Mike. *Big Strike.* 1949. Olema, CA. 1st ed. 261 p. F/pict wrp. D3. $25.00

QUINCY, Josiah. *Hist of Harvard U.* 1840. Cambridge. John Owen. 2 vols in 1. ils. G+. G7. $125.00

QUINDLEN, Anna. *Object Lessons.* (1992). Random. ARC. F/F. B3. $25.00

QUINN, J. Richard. *Recognition of the True Church According to JH Newman...* 1954. WA. CUA. 210 p. H10. $18.50

QUINN, Seabury. *Alien Flesh.* 1977. Oswald Train. 1st ed. F/F. P3. $25.00

QUINN, Seabury. *Phantom-Fighter.* 19666). Mycroft Moran. 1st ed. VG/VG. P3. $60.00

QUINN, Seabury. *Roads.* 1948. Arkham. 1st hc ed. F/NF. F4. $160.00

QUINN, Vernon. *Picture Map Geography of Mexico, Central Am & W Indies.* (1943). Stokes. 1st ed. xl. 114 p. F3. $10.00

QUINONEZ, Lora Ann. *Starting Points: 6 Essays...* 1989. WA, DC. 151 p. VG/wrp. C5. $12.50

QUINTER, James. *Defence of Trine Immersion...* 1862. Columbiana, OH. Gospel Visitor. 32 p/sewn. H10. $35.00

QUINTON. *Strange Adventures of Capt Quinton...* 1912. Christian Herald. Bible House. 486 p. P4. $50.00

QUIROGA, Horacio. *S Am Jungle Tales.* 1923. London. Methuen. 1st ed. 8vo. 166 p. bl brds. G. B11. $10.00

QUOIREZ, Francoise. *Bonjour Tristesse.* 1955. Dutton. 10th Am prt. trans from French. NF/NF. A14. $25.00

QUOIREZ, Francoise. *Few Hours of Sunlight.* 1971. NY. Harper Row. 1st Am ed. trans from French. NF/NF. A14. $25.00

QUOIREZ, Francoise. *Reluctant Hero.* 1987. Dutton. 1st Am ed. trans Christine Donougher. F/F. A14. $20.00

QUOIREZ, Francoise. *Salad Days.* 1984. Dutton. 1st ed. trans CJ Richards. F/F. A14. $25.00

QUOIREZ, Francoise. *Scars on the Soul.* 1974. McGraw Hill. 1st ed. trans from French. NF/NF clip. A14. $30.00

QUOIREZ, Francoise. *Sunlight on Cold War.* 1971. London. Weidenfeld Nicolson. 1st ed. trans from French. NF/NF. A14. $35.00

QUOIST, Michel. *Christ Is Alive!* 1971. Doubleday. 168 p. VG. C5. $7.50

QUOIST, Michel. *Prayers.* 1963. Sheed Ward. 179 p. VG. C5. $7.50

R

RAABE, H.E. *Cannibal Nights: Reminiscences of a Free-Lance Trader.* (1927). Payson Clarke. 1st ed. 8vo. 324 p. VG+/G+. A2. $30.00

RABAN, Jonathan. *Huckleberry Finn.* 1968. Woodbury, NY. 1st Am ed. sgn. NF/ils wrp. A11. $75.00

RABAN, Jonathan. *Soft City: Art of Cosmopolitan Living.* 1974. Dutton. 1st Am ed. 8vo. 229 p. F/F-. A2. $15.00

RABBIT, Peter. *Ornithology.* 1982. Taos. Minor Heron. 1/500. NF/wrp. L3. $15.00

RABE, David. *Basic Training of Pavlo Hummel/Sticks & Stones.* (1973). Viking. 2nd prt. dj. A7. $15.00

RABELAIS, Francois. *Catalogue of Choice Books Found by Pantagruel...* 1952. Burlinghame, CA. Grabhorn/Wreden. 1/200. quarto. 83 p. gilt gr bdg. H5. $150.00

RABINOWITZ, Benjamin. *Young Men's Hebrew Assn (1854-1913).* 1947. AJHS. reprint. xl. VG. S3. $25.00

RABKIN, Eric S. *Fantastic Worlds.* 1979. Oxford. 1st ed. VG/VG. P3. $20.00

RABUT, Olivier. *God in an Evolving Universe.* 1966. St Louis. Herder. 154 p. VG. C5. $10.00

RACINA, THOM. *Great LA Blizzard.* 1977. Putnam. 1st ed. F/VG. N3. $15.00

RACK. *Macrame Advanced Techniques & Design.* 1972. np. ils. wrp. G2. $4.00

RACKHAM, Arthur. *Arthur Rackham Fairy Book.* 1933. London. 1/460. sgn. orig vellum/brds. NF/pub slipcase. H5. $2,000.00

RACKHAM, Arthur. *Arthur Rackham: A Bibliography.* 1987. Jacksonville. San Marco. 1st ed. F/F. C4. $40.00

RACKHAM, Arthur. *Irish Fairy Tales.* 1920. Macmillan. 1st Am ed. NF. B4. $275.00

RACKHAM, Arthur. *Mother Goose.* 1913. London. 1/1130. sgn. 13 mtd color pls. Zaehnsdorf bdg. NF. H5. $2,250.00

RACKHAM, Arthur. *Mother Goose: The Old Nursery Rhymes.* 1913. Heinemann. 1/1130. sgn. 13 mtd pls. 159 p. teg. gilt wht cloth. VG. D1. $2,250.00

RACKHAM, John. *Time To Live.* 1969. London. Dobson. 1st British/1st hc ed. F/F. N3. $30.00

RACOUR-LAFERRIERE, Daniel. *Mind of Stalin: A Psychoanalytic Study.* 1988. Ann Arbor. Ardis. 1st ed. 160 p. blk cloth. F/dj. G1. $22.50

RADCLIFFE, Lynn. *With Christ in the Upper Room.* 1960. NY. Abingdon. 80 p. VG. C5. $7.50

RADDALL, Thomas H. *Wings of Night.* 1956. Doubleday. 1st ed. VG/dj. P3. $20.00

RADER, Dotson. *Tennessee: Cry of the Heart — Intimate Memoir...* 1985. Doubleday. 1st ed. NF/NF clip. A14. $25.00

RADER, Rosemary. *Breaking Boundaries.* 1972. NY. Paulist. 117 p. wrp. C5. $10.00

RADIN, Paul. *Indians of S Am.* 1946 (1942). Doubleday. 324 p. F3. $25.00

RADL, Shirley. *Invisible Woman.* 1981. Delacorte. 199 p. VG. C5. $15.00

RADLEY, Sheila. *Fate Worse Than Death.* 1986. Scribner. ARC of 1st Am ed. RS. F/F. S5. $25.00

RADLEY, Sheila. *This Way Out.* 1989. Constable. 1st ed. F/F. P3. $20.00

RADLEY, Sheila. *Who Saw Him Die?* 1987. Scribner. 1st ed. VG/dj. P3. $15.00

RAE, John. *Am Automobile: A Brief Hist.* 1965. Chicago. G+. N2. $7.50

RAE, John. *Grasshopper Gr & the Meadow-Mice.* 1922. Algonquin. Sunny Books series. 8vo. pict brds. VG. P2/T5. $40.00

RAE, John. *Lucy Locket...the Doll w/the Pocket.* 1928. Saalfield. ils. pict brds. VG. scarce. M5. $45.00

RAE, W.F. *Westward by Rail: New Route to the E.* 1871. NY. Appleton. 1st Am ed. 391 p. VG. H7. $85.00

RAE, William. *Treasury of Outdoor Life.* (1975). NY. 4to. ils/pls. dj. A17. $12.50

RAEDER, Erich. *My Life: Grand Admiral Erich Raeder.* 1960. Annapolis. US Naval Inst. 1st ed. VG/dj. A16. $50.00

RAFFLES, Thomas Stamford. *Hist of Java.* 1817. London. 1st ed. quarto. 2 vols. 66 pls. half gr morocco. VG. H5. $4,500.00

RAFINESQUE, C.S. *Life of Travels & Researches in N Am & S Europe...* 1836. Phil. 1st ed. 12mo. 148 p. prt wrp. M1. $1,250.00

RAGG, Lonsdale. *Evidences of Christianity.* 1908. NY. Gorham. Oxford Church Text series. 154 p. VG. C5. $10.00

RAGINS, Sanford. *Jewish Responses to Anti-Semitism in Germany, 1870-1914.* 1980. HUC Pr. 226 p. VG/VG. S3. $25.00

RAHEB, Barbara J. *Chansons de Noel.* 1984. np. miniature. intl. 34 p. gilt red leather. NF. B24. $125.00

RAHEB, Barbara J. *Mythology: Greek & Roman.* ca 1980. Tarzana, CA. Collectors Ed in Miniature. 1/300. sgn. blk leather. F. B24. $110.00

RAHILL, Peter. *Catholic in Am. From Colonial Times to Present Day.* 1960. Chicago. Franciscan Herald. sgn. 156 p. VG. C5. $15.00

RAHMANI, Levy. *Soviet Psychology: Philosophical, Theoretical...Issues.* 1973. NY. IUP. 1st ed. 440 p. cloth. G1. $25.00

RAHNER, Karl. *Belief Today: Theological Meditations.* 1967. NY. Sheed. 128 p. VG. C5. $10.00

RAHNER, Karl. *Biblical Homilies.* ca 1966. NY. Herder. 191 p. H10. $10.00

RAHNER, Karl. *Christian Commitment.* 1963. NY. Sheed. 218 p. VG. C5. $10.00

RAHNER, Karl. *Do You Believe in God?* ca 1969. NY. Newman. 1st ed. 114 p. H10. $15.00

RAHNER, Karl. *Happiness Through Prayer.* 1961 (1958). Dublin. Clonmore. 109 p. VG. C5. $10.00

RAHNER, Karl. *Inquiries.* 1964. NY. Herder. 463 p. VG. C5. $15.00

RAHNER, Karl. *Mary, Mother of the Lord.* 1963. NY. Herder. 107 p. VG. C5. $10.00

RAHNER, Karl. *On the Theology of Death.* 1961. NY. Herder. 118 p. VG/wrp. C5. $7.50

RAHNER, Karl. *Prayers for Meditation.* 1962. NY. Herder. 70 p. VG. C5. $8.50

RAHNER, Karl. *Theological Investigations. Vol 1.* 1961. Baltimore. Helicon. 382 p. VG. C5. $15.00

RAHNER, Karl. *Word: Readings in Theology.* 1964. NY. Kenedy. 301 p. VG. C5. $10.00

RAHNER & HAUSSLING. *Celebration of the Eucharist.* 1968. NY. Herder. 132 p. H10. $13.50

RAHNER & RATZINGER. *Episcopate & the Primacy.* 1966. London. Burns Oates. 135 p. wrp. C5. $8.50

RAHNER & THUSING. *New Christology.* 1980. Seabury. 239 p. H10. $15.00

RAHNER & VORGRIMLER. *Theological Dictionary.* 1965. NY. Herder. 493 p. H10. $20.00

RAHUL, Ram. *Himalaya Borderland.* 1970. Delhi/Bombay. Vikas. 1st ed. 8vo. 157 p. VG/dj. W1. $20.00

RAINE, Kathleen. *William Blake.* 1951. London. 1st prt. F/8vo wrp. A11. $25.00

RAINE, Richard. *Corder Index.* 1967. Harcourt. 1st ed. author's 1st book. F/F. F4. $22.00

RAINE, William MacLeod. *Bonanza*. 1926. Doubleday Page. 1st ed. VG. P3. $30.00

RAINE, William MacLeod. *Yukon Trail*. 1942. Triangle. 7th prt. VG/dj. P3. $10.00

RAINE, William. *45-Caliber Law*. 1941. Evanston, IL. 1st ed. xl. 64 p. pict cloth. VG. D3. $15.00

RAINER, Iris. *Boys in the Mail Room*. 1980. Morrow. 1st ed. author's 1st book. NF/NF. A14. $40.00

RAINES, Robert. *New Life in the Church*. 1961. Harper. 156 p. VG. C5. $7.50

RAINES, Robert. *Soundings: Daily Meditations*. 1970. Harper. 144 p. VG. C5. $7.50

RAINIER, Peter. *Pipeline to Battle: Engineer's Adventures...* (1943). Random. 1st ed. 8vo. 302 p. F/VG+. A2. $25.00

RAINS, Rob. *St Louis Cardinals*. 1992. St Martin. 1st ed. F/VG+. P8. $20.00

RAISIN, Jacob. *Haskalah Movement in Russia*. 1913. Phil. Jewish Pub Soc. 355 p. VG. C5. $20.00

RAISZ, Erwin. *Atlas of Global Geography*. 1944. NY. Global Pr. lg format. NF. O6. $55.00

RAKOCY, Bill. *Ghosts of Kingston Hillsboro*. 1983. Bravo Pr. 12mo. as new. A8. $14.95

RAKOCY, Bill. *Great Missions of the SW*. 1987. Bravo Pr. 12mo. as new. A8. $7.95

RAKOCY, Bill. *Images: Paso Del Norte*. 1980. Bravo Pr. 12mo. as new. A8. $19.95

RAKOCY, Bill. *Mongollon Diary: Ghost Town Hist*. 1980. Bravo Pr. as new. A8. $14.95

RAKOSI, Carl. *Amulet*. 1967. New Directions. 1st ed. inscr/sgn. NF/F. V1. $35.00

RALBOVSKY, Martin. *Destiny's Darlings*. 1974. Hawthorn. 1st ed. F/F. P8. $10.00

RALEIGH, Walter. *Cabinet-Council: Containing Chief Art of the Empire...* 1658. London. Newcomb. 12mo. 200 p. rebound calf over maroon brds. K1. $300.00

RALEIGH, Walter. *Marrow of Hist; or, Epitome of All Hist Passages...* 1662. London. Place. 2nd ed. 12mo. 574 p. 19th-century morocco. K1. $175.00

RALL, Harris F. *Life of Jesus*. 1917. NY. Abingdon. 214 p. VG. C5. $7.50

RALL, Harris F. *Religion As Salvation*. 1943. NY. Abbingdon. 254 p. lacks front ep. C5. $10.00

RALPHSON, G.H. *Boy Scouts in a Motor Boat*. (1912). Chicago. 1st ed. 246 p. pict cloth. VG. D3. $12.50

RAM, James. *Treatise on Facts As Subjects of Inquiry by a Jury*. 1873. NY. Baker Voorhis. 3rd Am ed. xl. full sheep. M11. $150.00

RAMATI, Alexander. *Assisi Underground*. 1978. NY. Stein. VG. C5. $12.50

RAMING, Ida. *Exclusion of Women From Priesthood*. 1976. Metuchen. Scarecrow. 263 p. VG. C5. $20.00

RAMM, Bernard. *Protestant Biblical Interpretation*. 1956. Boston. Wilde. 274 p. VG. C5. $8.50

RAMM, Bernard. *Special Revelation & the World of God*. 1961. Grand Rapids. Eerdmans. 220 p. VG. C5. $8.50

RAMM, Charles A. *Invocations & Other Prayers*. 1952. Berkeley. Gillick. 67 p. VG. C5. $7.50

RAMON Y CAJAL, Sanitago. *Studies on Cerebral Cortex...* 1955. Chicago. NF. G7. $75.00

RAMPARTS MAGAZINE. *Vietnam Primer*. nd. np. 127 p. VG. C5. $20.00

RAMPINI, Charles. *Hist of Moray & Nairn*. 1897. Edinburgh. Blackwood. 2 lg fld pocket maps. gilt red cloth. VG+. O6. $85.00

RAMPLING, Anne; see Rice, Anne.

RAMSAY, Jay; see Campbell, Ramsey.

RAMSAY, W.M. *Church & the Roman Empire*. 1893. NY. Putnam. 494 p. VG. C5. $10.00

RAMSAY, W.M. *Letters to the 7 Churches in Asia &...Apocalypse*. 1905. NY. 8vo. ils/16 pls. 446 p. cloth. O2. $75.00

RAMSAY, W.M. *St Paul, the Traveler & the Roman Citizen*. 1896. Putnam. 390 p. VG. C5. $12.50

RAMSAYE, Terry. *Million & One Nights. Hist of the Motion Picture*. 1926. Simon Schuster. 1/327. sgn author/Thomas A Edison. 2 vols. VG. H5. $2,500.00

RAMSDEN, E.H. *Letters of Michelangelo*. 1963. Stanford. 1st ed. 2 vols. gilt brn cloth. F/box. B30. $100.00

RAMSEY, Arthur. *From Gore to Temple: Development of Anglican Theology...* 1961. London. Longman. 192 p. missing front ep. C5. $10.00

RAMSEY, Frederic. *Chicago Documentary*. 1944. London. Jazz Music Books. 1st ed. VG+/wrp. B2. $65.00

RAMSEY, G.C. *Agatha Christie: Mistress of Mystery*. 1967. Dodd Mead. VG/dj. P3. $20.00

RAMSEY, Leroy L. *Trial & the Fire*. 1967. Exposition. 160 p. dj. A7. $10.00

RAMSEY, Paul. *Faith & Ethics*. 1957. Harper. 306 p. VG. C5. $10.00

RAMSEY. *Old & New Quilt Patterns in S Tradition*. 1987. np. ils. cloth. G2. $20.00

RAMUS, Pierre. *Friedenskrieger des Hinterlandes*. 1924. Mannheim. wrp. N2. $20.00

RANAULT, Gilbert. *Caravels of Christ*. 1958. Putnam. 254 p. VG. C5. $20.00

RAND, Austin L. *Am Water & Game Birds*. 1956. NY. 1st ed. photos. 239 p. NF/dj. A17. $25.00

RAND, Ayn. *Atlas Shrugged*. 1957. Random. 1st ed. VG-. P3. $100.00

RAND, Christopher. *Christmas in Bethlehem & Holy Week at Mt Athos*. 1963. NY. Oxford. 168 p. VG. C5. $8.50

RAND, Howard. *Digest of the Divine Law*. 1943. Haverhill. Destiny Pr. 248 p. VG. C5. $8.50

RAND MCNALLY. *German Atlas*. 1891 (1888). Rand McNally. 331 p. VG. E5. $185.00

RAND MCNALLY. *Official Auto Road Atlas of the US*. 1934. Rand McNally. 50 p. wrp. O5. $40.00

RANDALL, E.O. *Hist of Zoar Soc*. 1904. Columbus. 3rd prt. 105 p. G. D7. $25.00

RANDALL, E.O. *OH Centennial Anniversary Celebration*. 1903. Columbus. photos/index. 730 p. G. A17. $18.50

RANDALL, E.O. *OH Centennial Anniversary Celebration*. 1903. Columbus. Fred J Heer. 8vo. 730 p. brn brds. VG. B11. $20.00

RANDALL, G.M. *Dutch & French Bulb Culture in FL*. ca 1926. Deland. Painter. ils. 95 p. H10. $15.00

RANDALL, J.C. *Has the Lincoln Theme Been Exhausted?* 1936. Am Hist Review. 24 p. bdg brds. VG. A6. $10.00

RANDALL, John. *Hellenistic Ways of Deliverance...* 1970. NY. Columbia. 242 p. VG. C5. $20.00

RANDALL, Julia. *Mimic August*. 1960. Baltimore. 1st ed. presentation inscr. F/F. A11. $50.00

RANDALL, Robert. *Dawning Light*. 1959. Gnome. 1st ed. xl. front free ep removed. P3. $15.00

RANDAU, Carl. *Visitor*. 1945. Tower. 1st ed. NF/dj. P3. $20.00

RANDISI, Robert J. *Eyes Have It*. 1984. Mysterious. 1st ed. F/F. F4. $20.00

RANDISI, Robert J. *No Exit From Brooklyn.* 1987. St Martin. 1st ed. F/F. M15. $30.00

RANDISI, Robert J. *Separate Cases.* 1990. NY. Walker. ARC of 1st ed. sgn. RS. F/F. S5. $35.00

RANDOLPH, Alfred. *Reason, Faith & Authority in Christianity.* 1902. Whittaker. 272 p. VG. C5. $8.50

RANDOLPH, Marion. *Breathe No More.* 1944. Tower. VG/VG-. P3. $13.00

RANDOLPH, Vance. *We Always Lie To Strangers: Tall Tales From the Ozarks.* 1951. Columbia. ils Glen Rounds. F/NF. B4. $75.00

RANELAGH, E.L. *Past We Share: Near E Ancestry of W Folk Literature.* (1979). London. Quartet. 1st ed. 8vo. 278 p. F/F. A2. $17.50

RANKIN, William. *Memorials of Foreign Missionaries of Presbyterian Church...* 1895. Phil. 467 p. VG. C5. $8.50

RANKINE, John. *Never the Same Door.* 1967. Dobson. 1st ed. F/dj. P3. $20.00

RANSOM, Frank Edward. *City Built on Wood: Hist of Furniture Industry...* 1955. Ann Arbor. Edwards Bros. 4to. 101 p. G+. N2. $15.00

RANSOM, John Crowe. *Selected Poems.* 1945. Knopf. 1st ed. blk brds. sans dj. C4. $30.00

RANSOM, John Crowe. *Selected Poems.* 1947. London. Eyre Spottiswoode. 1st ed. NF/NF. C4. $40.00

RANSOME, Arthur. *Swallowdale.* 1932. Lippincott. 4th prt. 393 p. VG+/dj. M20. $17.50

RANSOME, Stephen. *Alias His Wife.* 1965. Dodd Mead. 1st ed. VG/VG-. P3. $15.00

RANSOME, Stephen. *Frazer Acquittal.* 1955. Crime Club. 1st ed. VG/VG. P3. $20.00

RANSOME, Stephen. *Warning Bell.* 1960. Crime Club. 1st ed. VG/VG-. P3. $20.00

RANSON, Charles. *That the World May Know.* 1953. NY. Friendship. 167 p. VG. C5. $8.50

RAPER, Charles Lee. *Railway Transportation: Hist of Its Economics...* 1912. Putnam. 1st ed. 12mo. 331 p. VG. B11. $25.00

RAPHAEL, Rick. *Thirst Quenchers.* 1966. British BC. xl. dj. P3. $5.00

RAPP, Marvin A. *Canal Water & Whiskey...* 1965. NY. apparent 1st ed. 189 p. G/G. D7. $20.00

RAQUIN, Yves. *Celibacy for Our Times.* 1974. St Meinrad. Abbey. 120 p. VG/wrp. C5. $10.00

RASHDALL, Hastings. *Conscience & Christ.* 1924. London. Duckworth. 313 p. missing front ep. C5. $8.50

RASKAS, Bernard S. *Heart of Wisdom: Thought for Each Day of Jewish Yr.* 1973. Burning Bush. 2nd prt. 12mo. 372 p. VG/VG. S3. $19.00

RASMUSSEN, Wayne D. *Agriculture in the US.* ca 1975. Random. 1st ed. 4 vols. H10. $225.00

RATCLIFF, Arthur James John. *Hist of Dreams.* 1923. Boston. Sm Maynard. 1st Am ed. 248 p. prt brn cloth. G1. $32.50

RATEL, Simonne. *Weathercock.* 1939. Appleton Century. 84 p. VG/G. P2. $10.00

RATH, Virginia. *Posted for Murder.* 1942. Crime Club. 1st ed. VG. P3. $23.00

RATHBONE, Basil. *In & Out of Character.* nd. Doubleday. VG/dj. P3. $18.00

RATHBONE, Julian. *Carnival!* 1976. Michael Joseph. 1st ed. VG/VG. P3. $20.00

RATHBONE, Julian. *Euro-Killers.* 1979. Pantheon. 1st ed. VG/dj. P3. $15.00

RATHBONE, Julian. *Watching Detectives.* 1983. Pantheon. 1st ed. VG/dj. P3. $14.00

RATHBUN, Carole. *Village of the Turkish Novel & Short Story.* 1972. Paris. 8vo. 192 p. dj. O2. $20.00

RATHE, Gerard. *Mud & Mosaics.* 1960. Westminster. Newman. 193 p. VG. C5. $10.00

RATHER, Lois. *Books & Societies.* 1971. Rather Pr. 1st ed. 89 p. F/sans. B19. $35.00

RATHJEN, Carl Henry. *Flight of Fear.* 1969. Whitman. VG. P3. $8.00

RATTAN, Volney. *Popular CA Flora...* 1896 (1882). San Francisco. 9th revised ed. 118 p. B26. $20.00

RATTIGAN, Terence. *Ross: A Dramatic Portrait.* 1961. London. Hamish Hamilton. 1st ed/2nd imp. 122 p. F/NF/clear plastic. M7. $45.00

RATZINGER, Joseph. *Faith & the Future.* 1971. Chicago. Franciscan Herald. 112 p. VG. C5. $8.50

RATZINGER, Joseph. *God of Jesus Christ.* 1979. Chicago. Franciscan Herald. 114 p. VG. C5. $10.00

RAUCH, Basil. *Roosevelt: From Munich to Pearl Harbor.* 1950. Creative Age. 1st ed. G. V2. $5.00

RAUSCHENBUSCH, Walter. *Christianity & the Social Crisis.* 1911. Macmillan. 428 p. VG. C5. $12.50

RAUSCHENBUSCH, Walter. *For God & for the People.* 1910. Boston. Pilgrim Pr. 127 p. emb cloth. VG. C5. $10.00

RAUSCHNING, Hermann. *Revolution of Nihilism.* 1939. Alliance. 300 p. VG. C5. $15.00

RAVEN, C.E. *Teilhard de Chardin. Scientist & Seer.* 1962. Harper. 221 p. VG. C5. $10.00

RAVEN, Charles. *Christ & the Modern Opportunity.* 1956. Greenwhich. Seabury. 88 p. VG. C5. $7.50

RAVEN, Simon. *Before the Cock Crow: 1st-Born of Egypt, Vol III.* 1986. London. Muller Blond & Wht. 1st ed. NF/NF. A14. $25.00

RAVEN, Simon. *Sabre Squadron.* (1966). Harper Row. 1st Am ed. F/NF clip. B4. $45.00

RAVEN & WALTERS. *Mtn Flowers.* 1956. NY. 1st ed. ils/photos/20 maps. 240 p. VG. B26. $44.00

RAVENAL, Eric C. *Never Again.* (1978). Temple U. 153 p. F/dj. A7. $16.00

RAVENSCROFT, Trevor. *Spear of Destiny.* 1973. Putnam. 1st ed. VG/dj. C1. $8.50

RAVICZ, Marilyn. *Early Colonial Religious Drama in Mexico.* 1970. WA, DC. Catholic U of Am. 1st ed. 263 p. wht cloth. F3. $20.00

RAWCLIFFE, D.H. *Struggle for Kenya.* 1954. London. Gollancz. 189 p. dj. A7. $17.00

RAWE, Donald. *Geraint, Last of the Arthurians.* 1972. Padstow, Eng. 1st/only ed. 44 p. stiff wrp. C1. $15.00

RAWLINGS, Marjorie Kinnan. *Cross Creek Cookery.* 1942. Scribner. G/tattered. A16. $40.00

RAWLINGS, Marjorie Kinnan. *Cross Creek.* 1942. Scribner. 1st ed. F/NF. C4. $75.00

RAWLINGS, Marjorie Kinnan. *Golden Apples.* 1935. Scribner. 1st ed. F/F. B4. $400.00

RAWLINGS, Marjorie Kinnan. *Sojourner.* nd. Peoples BC. VG/VG. P3. $10.00

RAWLINGS, Marjorie Kinnan. *Sojourner.* 1953. Scribner. 1st ed. VG/VG. P3. $40.00

RAWLINGS, Marjorie Kinnan. *Yearling.* 1938. Scribner. 1st ed. author's 3rd novel. F/pict dj. L3. $450.00

RAWLINGS, Marjorie Kinnan. *Yearling.* 1938. Scribner. 1st/A ed. 428 p. VG/dj. M20. $100.00

RAWLINGS, Marjorie Kinnan. *Yearling.* 1939. Scribner. 4to. 400 p. VG/dj. A3. $25.00

RAWLINGS, Marjorie Kinnan. *Yearling.* 1939. Scribner. 1/770. ils NC Wyeth. w/2 ils & facsimile letter. F/slipcase. B24. $1,500.00

RAWLINSON, A. *Adventures in the Near E 1918-22.* 1923. London. 8vo. 377 p. cloth. O2. $60.00

RAWLINSON, George. *Egypt & Babylon: Sacred & Profane Sources...* 1885. Alden, NY. 228 p. gr cloth. F. B22. $15.00

RAWSON, Marion Nicholl. *Hand-wrought Ancestors: Story of Early Am Shops...* 1936. Dutton. 1st ed. O3. $38.00

RAY, Isaac. *Mental Hygiene.* 1863. Ticknor Fields. 338 p. gr cloth. B14. $150.00

RAY, J.H. Randolph. *My Little Church Around the Corner.* 1957. Simon Schuster. ils. 365 p. VG. C5. $10.00

RAY, John E. *Trip Abroad. Sketches of Men & Manners, People...Europe.* 1882. Raleigh, NC. Edwards Broughton. 1st ed. 247 p. pub bdg. VG+. M8. $250.00

RAY, Michelle. *2 Shores of Hell.* (1968). London. John Murray. 1st ed. F/dj. A7. $30.00

RAY, Ophelia. *Daughter of the Tejas.* 1965. Greenwich. NY Graphic Soc. 1st issue. NF/F gray dj. L3. $150.00

RAY, P. Orman. *Repeal of the MO Compromise.* 1909. Cleveland. Clark. 1st ed. teg. VG. H7. $60.00

RAY, Robert J. *Murdock for Hire.* 1987. NY. St Martin. 1st ed. sgn. F/F. S5. $35.00

RAY, Tom. *Yellowstone Red.* 1948. Dorrance. 1st ed. sgn. VG/VG. P3. $30.00

RAYBAKOV, Anatoli. *Children of the Arbat.* 1988. Little Brn. 1st ed. trans from Russian. NF/NF. A14. $20.00

RAYBAKOV, Anatoli. *Heavy Sand.* 1981. Viking. 1st ed. trans from Russian. NF/NF clip. A14. $25.00

RAYER, F.G. *Tomorrow Sometimes Comes.* 1951. Home & Van Thal. 1st ed. VG. P3. $15.00

RAYMOND, Alex. *Mongo, Planet of Doom.* 1990. Kitchen Sink. 1st ed. F. P3. $35.00

RAYMOND, Daniel. *Thoughts on Political Economy.* 1820. Baltimore. Fielding Lucas. 1st ed. xl. 470 p. later bdg. M1. $475.00

RAYMOND, Evelyn. *Quaker Maiden: Story for Girls.* 1923. Phil. Penn Pub. 8vo. 324 p. worn. V3. $9.00

RAYMOND, Grace. *How They Kept the Faith.* 1889. NY. Anson Randolph. 389 p. VG. C5. $12.50

RAYMOND, Henry Jarvis. *Life & Public Services of Abraham Lincoln, 16th President...* 1865. Derby Miller. 1st ed. pls. 808 p. cloth. VG. M8. $45.00

RAYMOND, Louise. *Child's Book of Prayers.* 1941. Lee Shepard. 1st ed. 12mo. 36 p. VG. A3. $7.00

RAYMOND, M. *Burnt-Out Incense. Saga of Citeaux, the Am Epoch.* 1949. NY. Kenedy. 457 p. C5. $10.00

RAYMOND, M. *God Goes to Murderer's Row.* 1951. Bruce. VG/VG. P3. $10.00

RAYMOND, M. *Man Who Got Even w/God.* 1941. Milwaukee. Bruce. 155 p. VG. C5. $10.00

RAYMOND, M. *New Way of the Cross.* 1952. Milwaukee. Bruce. ils John Andrews. VG. C5. $12.50

RAYMOND, M. *This Is Love.* 1964. Milwaukee. Bruce. 150 p. VG. C5. $8.50

RAYMOND, M. *Your Hour.* 1962. Milwaukee. Bruce. 204 p. VG. C5. $8.50

RAYMOND, Nancy. *Smoky. The Little Kitten Who Didn't Want To.* 1945. Fideler. unp. VG+/dj. M20. $25.00

RAYMOND, Thomas. *Reports of Divers Special Cases Adjudged in Courts...* 1696. London. Assigns of Rich. folio. 506 p. modern brn cloth/red leather spine label. K1. $275.00

RAYNAL, M. *Peintres du XX Siecle.* 1947. Paris. folio. VG/wrp. A1. $50.00

RAYTER, Joe. *Stab in the Dark.* 1955. Mill Morrow. 1st ed. VG-/dj. P3. $15.00

READ, J. Marion. *Hist of CA Academy of Medicine, 1930-1960.* 1962. CA Academy Medicine. 1st ed. 1/1000. 93 p. NF. B19. $25.00

READ, Piers Paul. *Free Frenchman.* 1986. Random. 1st ed. 8vo. F/F. A8. $20.00

READ, Stanley E. *Tommy Brayshaw, the Ardent Angler-Artist.* 1977. Vancouver. 1st ed. 1/2000. 95 p. F. A17. $25.00

READE, Brian. *Sexual Heretics: Male Homosexuality in Eng Literature...* 1970. Coward McCann. 1st Am ed. 459 p. cloth. VG/dj. G1. $25.00

READE, Hamish. *Comeback for Stark.* 1968. Putnam. VG+/dj. P3. $10.00

READER'S DIGEST. *Reader's Digest Complete Atlas of Australia...* (1968). Sydney. 1st ed. folio. 183 p. F/VG. A2. $25.00

REAMAN, G. Elmore. *Trail of the Huguenots in Europe, the US, S Africa & Canada.* 1983. Genealogical Pub. reprint 1963 ed. ils. F/fair. B10. $35.00

RECHY, John. *City of Night.* 1963. NY. Grove. 6th prt. author's 1st book. rem mk. NF/VG+. A14. $25.00

RECHY, John. *Rushes.* 1979. Grove. 1st ed. NF/NF. A14. $25.00

RECINOS, Andrian. *Cronicas Indigenas de Guatemala.* (1984). Guatemala. 2nd ed. 187 p. wrp. F4. $15.00

RECKITT, William. *Some Account of Life & Travels...* 1783. Phil. Crukshank. 3rd prt. 12mo. V3. $20.00

REDDING, M. Wolcott. *Masonic Antiquities of the Orient Unveiled.* 1877. Masonic Pub Union. full leather. aeg. G. A16. $50.00

REDEKOP, John H. *Labor Problems in Christian Perspective.* (1972). Grand Rapids. Eerdmans. 364 p. A7. $15.00

REDFERN, David. *David Redfern's Jazz Album.* 1980. London. Eel Pie. 1st ed. F/F. B2. $60.00

REDFIELD, H.V. *Homicide, N & S.* 1880. Phil. Lippincott. 1st ed. 12mo. 207 p. brn brds. VG. B11. $65.00

REDFIELD, James. *Celestine Prophecy.* 1994. Warner. 1st hc ed. sgn. M/M. T2. $22.00

REDFIELD, Robert. *Folk Culture of Yucatan.* (1941). Chicago U. 1st ed. 419 p. F3. $35.00

REDFIELD, Robert. *Primitive World & Its Transformations.* (1967). Ithaca. Cornell. 9th prt. 185 p. F3. $10.00

REDGATE, John. *Killing Season.* nd. BC. VG. P3. $3.00

REDGROVE, H. Stanley. *Bygone Beliefs...* 1920. London. Rider. 1st ed. xl. 205 p. H10. $27.50

REDMOND, Gerald. *Caledonian Games in 19th-Century Am.* 1971. NJ. Dickinson. clip dj. N2. $10.00

REED, A.H. *Gumdiggers: Story of Kauri Gum.* (1972). Wellington, NZ. Reed. 1st/ltd ed. 193 p. F/VG+. A2. $30.00

REED, Alma. *Mexican Muralists.* 1960. Crown. 1st ed. 191 p. dj. F3. $45.00

REED, C.B. *Masters of the Wilderness.* (1914). Chicago U. 1st ed. 12mo. 144 p. VG+. A2. $35.00

REED, David. *Anna.* nd. BC. VG/VG. P3. $8.00

REED, David. *Up Front in Vietnam.* (1967). Funk Wagnall. 217 p. dj. A7. $50.00

REED, Frank. *Lumberjack Sky Pilot.* (1965). Old Forge. 2nd ed. 12mo. 155 p. F/F. A2. $12.50

REED, Isaac. *Christian Traveler in 5 Parts Including 9 Yrs...* 1828. NY. 1st ed. 242 p. orig bdg. VG-. H3. $150.00

REED, Ishmael. *Airing Dirty Laundry.* 1993. Boston. Addison Wesley. advance uncorrected galley. F/pict wrp. C4. $45.00

REED, Ishmael. *Flight to Canada.* 1976. Random. 1st ed. NF/NF. B2. $35.00

REED, Ishmael. *Last Days.* 1974. Random. 1st ed. F/F. C4. $50.00

REED, Ishmael. *Shrove Time in Old New Orleans.* 1978. Doubleday. 1st ed. F/F. C4. $50.00

REED, Jeremy. *Bl Rock.* 1987. London. Cape. 1st ed. NF/NF. A14. $30.00

REED, John. *Ten Days That Shook the World.* ca 1934. NY. Modern Lib. VG/G. V4. $12.50

REED, Kit. *Catholic Girls.* 1987. Donald Fine. 1st ed. F/F. P3. $15.00

REED, Kit. *Fat.* 1971. Bobbs Merrill. 1st ed. VG/dj. P3. $15.00

REED, Kit. *Ft Privilege.* 1985. Doubleday. 1st ed. inscr/sgn to Clifford Simak. RS. F/F. F4. $40.00

REED, Kit. *Tiger Rag.* 1973. Dutton. 1st ed. VG/dj. P3. $20.00

REED, Nelson. *Castle War of Yucatan.* 1964. Stanford. 1st ed. 308 p. dj. F3. $45.00

REED, Robert Rentoul Jr. *Bedlam on the Jacobean Stage.* 1952. Harvard. 1st ed. 190 p. cloth. G1. $28.50

REED, Robert. *Leeshore.* 1987. Donald Fine. 1st ed. NF/dj. P3. $17.00

REEDER, Red. *Three Great Pitchers on the Mound.* 1966. Garrard. 1st ed. photos. VG/G. P8. $12.50

REEKS, H. Caulton. *Diseases of the Horse's Foot.* 1906. Chicago. Eger. 1st ed. half leather. O3. $45.00

REEL, A. Frank. *Case of General Yamashita.* 1971. NY. Octagon. M11. $50.00

REEP, Diana. *Rescue & Romance.* 1982. Popular. VG. P3. $15.00

REES, J.D. *Real India.* 1908. London. Methuen. 1st ed. 8vo. 352 p. VG. W1. $25.00

REES, J.R. *Case of Rudolf Hess: Problem in Diagnosis...* 1947. Norton. 1st Am ed. sm 8vo. 224 p. blk cloth. G1. $30.00

REESE, Howard C. *Area Handbook for the Republic of Tunisia.* 1970. WA, DC. 1st ed. 8vo. 416 p. gilt blk cloth. M. H3. $30.00

REESE, James T. *Hist of Police Psychological Services.* 1987. US Dept FBI. 4to. 119 p. prt stiff bl wrp. G1. $27.50

REEVE, Arthur B. *Dream Doctor.* nd. Van Rees. VG-. P3. $12.00

REEVE, Arthur B. *Gold of Gods.* 1915. McClelland Goodchild. 1st Canadian ed. P3. $11.00

REEVE, Arthur B. *Stars Scream Murder.* 1936. Appleton Century. 1st ed. VG. P3. $30.00

REEVE, Arthur B. *War Terror.* 1915. Harper. VG-. P3. $15.00

REEVE, F.D. *Bl Cat.* 1972. FSG. 1st ed. VG/VG+. V1. $10.00

REEVES, Donald. *Notes of a Processed Brother.* 1971. Pantheon. 480 p. NF/VG. A7. $18.00

REEVES, James. *Blackbird in the Lilac.* 1967 (1952). London. Oxford. ils Ardizzone. 8vo. 95 p. VG/VG. A3. $8.00

REEVES, John. *Death in Prague.* 1988. Doubleday Canada. 1st ed. F/dj. P3. $20.00

REEVES, John. *Murder Before Matins.* 1984. Doubleday. 1st ed. VG/dj. P3. $13.00

REEVES, John. *Murder by Microphone.* 1978. Doubleday. 1st ed. VG/dj. P3. $15.00

REEVES. *Jefferson County in the World War.* 1920. Watertown, NY. 8vo. ils. 208 p. bl cloth. VG. T3. $18.00

REGAN, David. *Mourning Glory.* (1981). Devon Adair. 172 p. F/NF. A7. $30.00

REGAN, Tom. *All That Dwell Therein.* 1982. CA U. 1st ed. VG/dj. P3. $10.00

REGAN. *Am Quilts.* 1989. np. ils. cloth. G2. $15.00

REHMANN, Elsa. *Sm Place: Its Landscape Architecture.* 1918. NY. 1st ed. photos/plans. teg. cloth. NF. B26. $65.00

REHNQUIST, William. *Supreme Court: How It Was, How It Is.* 1987. NY. Morrow. M11. $25.00

REICH, Sheldon. *Arthur B Davies: Paintings & Drawings.* 1967. Tucson Art Center. ils. D2. $30.00

REICH, Walter. *Stranger in My House: Jews & Arabs in the W Bank.* 1984. HRW. 1st ed. 134 p. F/F. S3. $18.00

REICHARD, Gladys A. *Navaho Religion.* 1950. NY. Bollingen. 1st ed. 2 vols. 8vo. ils/23 charts. VG+. P4. $150.00

REICHLER, Joseph. *Baseball Encyclopedia.* 1969. Macmillan. 1st ed. VG/G+ slipcase. P8. $45.00

REICHLER, Joseph. *Baseball's Great Moments.* 1979-87. np. 7 vol set. F/F. P8. $30.00

REICHLER, Joseph. *Game & the Glory.* 1976. Prentice Hall. 1st ed. F/VG. P8. $40.00

REID, Alastair. *Once Dice Trice.* 1958. Little Brn. 1st ed. 4to. 57 p. gray cloth. VG. T5. $30.00

REID, Ed. *Mafia.* (1952). Random. 1st ed. 8vo. 238 p. F/F. A2. $20.00

REID, J.M. *Traveler Extraordinary: Life of James Bruce of Kinnaird.* (1968). NY. Norton. 1st Am ed. 8vo. ils. 320 p. F/VG. A2. $20.00

REID, John Phillip. *Law for the Elephant.* 1980. Huntington. ils/map. F/F. A18. $40.00

REID, Mayne. *Afloat in the Forest.* 1889. Industrial Pub. 1st thus ed. 292 p. brn cloth. VG. B22. $6.25

REID, Mayne. *Boy Hunters; or, Adventure in Search of a Wht Buffalo.* 1863. Boston. 16mo. 364 p. gilt red cloth. G. H3. $35.00

REID, Mayne. *War Trail; or, Hunt of the Wild Horse.* (ca 1880). London. later ed. 12mo. 418 p. gilt cloth. VG. D3. $35.00

REID, Robert A. *50 Glimpses of Worchester & Lake Quinsigamond.* 1900. Worcester. oblong 8vo. 128 p. VG/gilt red wrp. H3. $12.00

REID, W. *Attempt To Develop Law of Storms by Means of Facts...* 1838. London. J Weale. 436 p. modern cloth/orig label. B14. $125.00

REIDER, Joseph. *Deuteronomy w/Commentary.* 1948. JPS. 2nd imp. 355 p. VG/G. S3. $25.00

REIDY. *Quilt Blocks: Fast & Easy Projects Using Interchangeable Sq.* 1991. np. ils. cloth. G2. $25.00

REIGER, John F. *Passing of the Great W.* 1972. Scribner. ils/index. 182 p. NF/wrp. B19. $9.50

REIGER & REIGER. *Zane Grey Cookbook.* (1976). Prentice Hall. 1st ed. F/F. B9. $40.00

REIK, Theodor. *Fragment of Great Confession: Psychoanalytic Autobiography.* 1949. Farrar Straus. 1st ed. 498 p. bl cloth. VG/dj. G1. $22.50

REIK, Theodor. *Wie Man Psychologe Wird.* 1927. Leipzig. Psychoanalytischer. 1st ed. presentation/inscr. cloth. S9. $72.00

REILLY, Joseph J. *Newman As Man of Letters.* 1925. Macmillan. 329 p. H10. $13.50

REIMANN, Lewis C. *Between the Iron & the Pine.* (1951). Ann Arbor. sgn. 225 p. F/dj. A17. $20.00

REIMANN, Lewis C. *Incredible Seney.* (1953). Ann Arbor. sgn. 190 p. cloth. A17. $20.00

REINECKER, Fritz. *Linguistic Key to the Greek New Testament.* 1977. Zondervan. Vol I only. 345 p. VG. C5. $15.00

REINFELD, Fred. *Simplified Guide To Collecting Am Paper Money.* ca 1960. Hanover House. 8vo. 128 p. cloth. dj. H9. $25.00

REINHARDT, Richard. *Workin' on the Railroad.* 1970. Weathervane. VG/dj. A16. $15.00

REINHARZ, Jehuda. *Fatherland; or, Promised Land: Dilemma of German Jew...* 1975. MI U. 328 p. F/VG. S3. $23.00

REINHOLD, H.A. *Dynamics of Liturgy.* 1961. Macmillan. 146 p. VG. C5. $8.50

REISNER, Christian. *Church Publicity.* 1913. NY. Methodist. 421 p. VG. C5. $8.50

REIT. *Those Fabulous Flying Machines, Hist of Flight 3-Dimensions.* 1985. 6 popups. paper engineering by Penick. F. A4. $30.00

REITSCH, Hanna. *Flying Is My Life.* (1954). NY. 1st Am ed. trans Lawrence Wilson. 246 p. VG/dj. B18. $150.00

REMARQUE, Erich Maia. *Arch of Triumph.* 1945. Appleton Century. ne. 12mo. VG. A8. $10.00

REMARQUE, Erich Maia. *Blk Obelisk.* 1957. Harcourt Brace. 1st ed. 12mo. VG. A8. $18.00

REMARQUE, Erich Maia. *Heaven Has No Favorites.* 1961. Harcourt Brace. 1st ed. 12mo. VG/G. A8. $25.00

REMARQUE, Erich Maia. *Road Back.* 1931. Putnam. 1st ed. VG. A8. $20.00

REMERAND, Gabriel. *Ali de Tebelen Pacha de Janina.* 1928. Paris. 8vo. 12 pls. 290 p. new cloth/orig wrp. O2. $50.00

REMINGTON, Frederic. *Done in the Open.* 1902. NY. 2nd issue. pict brds. VG-. B18. $75.00

REMINGTON, Frederic. *Remington's Frontier Sketches.* 1898. Chicago. Werner. 1st ed. oblong quarto. 15 pls. aeg. F/glassine. H5. $750.00

REMONDINO, P.C. *Mediteranean Shores of Am.* 1892. Phil. 1st ed. xl. 160 p. bevelled gilt cloth. D3. $45.00

REMY, Jules. *Voyage au Pays des Mormons: Relation, Geographie...* 1860. Paris. E Dentu. 1st ed. 2 vols. fld map. prt wrp. NF/slipcase. R3. $750.00

RENAN, Ernst. *Life of Jesus.* 1955. Modern Lib. 402 p. VG. C5. $8.50

RENARD, A.C. *Nun in the Modern World.* 1961. NY. Herder. 218 p. VG. C5. $10.00

RENARD, Henri. *Philosophy of God.* 1950. Bruce. 241 p. VG. C5. $10.00

RENAULT, Mary. *Fire From Heaven.* (1970). London. Longman. 1st ed. F/VG. B3. $50.00

RENAULT, Mary. *Fire From Heaven.* nd. BC. VG. C1. $4.00

RENAULT, Mary. *Funeral Games.* (1981). Ontario. Musson. 1st ed. NF/VG. B3. $40.00

RENAULT, Mary. *Mask of Apollo.* 1966. Pantheon. 1st ed. 371 p. VG+/VG+. M20. $30.00

RENAULT, Paul. *Manuel de Tracheotomie...* 1887. Paris. Steinheil. 120 p. quarter leather/marbled brds. G7. $195.00

RENDEL, A.M. *Appointment in Crete. Story of a British Agent.* 1953. London. 8vo. 240 p. cloth. scarce. O2. $30.00

RENDELL, Ruth. *Dark-Adapted Eye.* 1986. London. Viking. 1st ed. sgn. F/F. M15. $65.00

RENDELL, Ruth. *Face of Trespass.* 1974. London. Hutchinson. 1st ed. F/VG. M15. $165.00

RENDELL, Ruth. *Gallowglass.* 1990. Harmony Books. 1st ed. M/M. T2. $16.00

RENDELL, Ruth. *Going Wrong.* 1990. London. Hutchinson. 1st ed. F/F. M15. $40.00

RENDELL, Ruth. *Killing Doll.* 1984. London. Hutchinson. 1st ed. F/F. S5. $45.00

RENDELL, Ruth. *Live Flesh.* (1986). London. Hutchinson. 1st ed. F/NF. B3. $45.00

RENDELL, Ruth. *Master of the Moor.* 1982. London. Hutchinson. 1st ed. F/F. M15. $50.00

RENDELL, Ruth. *Speaker of Mandarin.* (1983). NY. Pantheon. 1st ed. F/VG. B3. $30.00

RENDELL, Ruth. *Talking to Strange Men.* (1987). London. Hutchinson. 1st ed. VG/F. B3. $40.00

RENE-BASIN, Marie. *She Who Lived Her Name.* 1960. Bristol. Burleigh. 175 p. VG/wrp. C5. $10.00

RENE-BASIN, Marie. *Some Sisters of Mine.* 1936. London. Burns Oates. 222 p. VG/wrp. C5. $10.00

RENOIR. *Seize Aquarelles et Sanguines de Renoir.* 1948. Paris. ltd ed. loose portfolio/16 pls. VG. A1. $120.00

RENWICK, James. *Elements of Mechanics.* 1832. Phil. xl. 8vo. 508 p. gull leather. G. T3. $37.00

REPPLIER, Agnes. *Compromises.* 1904. Houghton Mifflin. 144 p. VG. C5. $10.00

REPPLIER, Agnes. *Counter Currents. Essays.* 1916. Houghton Mifflin. 167 p. VG. C5. $12.50

REPPLIER, Agnes. *Fireside Sphinx.* 1902 (1901). Houghton. 12mo. 305 p. teg. blk/gray decor bl cloth. VG+. S10. $30.00

REPPLIER, Agnes. *In Our Convent Days.* 1906. Houghton Mifflin. 257 p. VG. C5. $12.50

REPPLIER, Agnes. *In Pursuit of Laughter.* 1936. Houghton Mifflin. 148 p. VG. C5. $10.00

REPPLIER, Agnes. *Mere Marie of the Ursulines.* 1931. Sheed. 315 p. VG. C5. $10.00

RERESBY, John. *Travels & Memoirs of...* 1813. London. Edward Jeffrey. sm 4to. aeg. full leather. VG+. F1. $235.00

RESCH, Peter. *Prayer Life...* 1948. NY. Benziger. 665 p. VG. C5. $15.00

RESENSTONE, Robert A. *Crusade of the Left: Lincoln Battalion in Spanish Civil War.* ca 1969. NY. Pegasus. 1st ed. photos. F/F. V4. $10.00

RESNICK & WOLFF. *Knowledge & Class.* (1987). Chicago U. 352 p. as new/NF. A7. $16.00

RESTON, James Jr. *Innocence of Joan Little.* (1977). Times Books. 2nd prt. 340 p. dj. A7. $18.00

RESTON, James Jr. *Our Father Who Art In Hell...Jim Jones.* (1981). Time Books. 338 p. dj. A7. $10.00

RESTON, James Jr. *Sherman's March & Vietnam.* (1984). Macmillan. 1st prt. 323 p. F/dj. A7. $28.00

RETIF, Andre. *Catholic Spirit.* 1959. NY. Hawthorn. 127 p. VG. C5. $8.50

RETIF & RETIF. *Church's Mission in the World.* 1962. NY. Hawthorn. 156 p. VG. C5. $8.50

REUMANN, John. *Jesus in the Church's Gospels.* 1979. Phil. Fortress. 537 p. VG/wrp. C5. $10.00

REUMANN, John. *Righteousness in the New Testament.* 1982. Phil. Fortress. 278 p. VG/wrp. C5. $12.50

REUTHER, Victor G. *Brothers Reuther & the Story of the UAW.* ca 1976. Boston. Houghton Mifflin. sgn. photos. VG/G. V4. $20.00

REVERE, Joseph Warren. *Tour of Duty in CA...* 1849. NY. CS Francis. 1st ed. 6 pls. 305 p. missing map. fair. H7. $40.00

REVERE, Paul. *Paul Revere's Ride...* 1966. Worcester. St Onge. miniature. 2nd ed. F. H1. $45.00

REVILL, Winifred. *Chaco Chapters.* (1947). London. Hodder. 1st ed. 192 p. dj. F3. $25.00

REVKIN, Andrew. *Burning Season: Muscle of Chico Mendes...* ca 1990. Houghton Mifflin. M/M. V4. $10.00

REY, Henry-Francois. *Mechanical Pianos: Novel of Spain's Costa Brava.* 1965. FSG. 1st Am ed. trans Peter Wiles. NF/NF. A14. $25.00

REY. *Curious George: A Pop-Up Book.* nd. 12 action scenes. F. A4. $30.00

REYBURN, Wallace. *Bridge Across the Atlantic: Story of John Rennie.* 1972. London. Harrap. 160 p. VG. P4. $25.00

REYNOLDS, A.D. *Recollections of Major...1847-1925.* 1978. Reynolda House. 1st separate prt. 39 p. VG. B10. $35.00

REYNOLDS, Bede. *Rebel From Riches.* 1972. Mission City, BC. Culligan/Westminster. 183 p. VG/wrp. C5. $8.50

REYNOLDS, Bonnie Jones. *Truth About Unicorns.* 1972. Stein Day. 1st ed. inscr/unicorn sketch/sgn. F/VG+. N3. $15.00

REYNOLDS, Clay. *Taking Stock. A Larry McMurtry Casebook.* 1989. S Methodist U Pr. 1st ed/simultaneous sc issue. F/wrp. L3. $35.00

REYNOLDS, Francis J. *New Encyclopedic Atlas & Gazetteer of the World...* 1917. NY. Collier. folio. ils. NF. O6. $65.00

REYNOLDS, James J. *Story-Time Readers (2nd Yr).* 1926. Noble. ils Mabel Betsy. VG. L1. $12.50

REYNOLDS, Maxine; see Reynolds, Mack.

REYNOLDS, Quentin. *Fiction Factory...* (1955). NY. 1st ed. 283 p. F/dj. D3. $35.00

REYNOLDS, Quentin. *Officially Dead: Story of Commander CD Smith.* 1945. Random. 1st prt. 8vo. 244 p. VG/dj. W1. $18.00

REYNOLDS, Reginald. *Beards: Their Social Standing, Religious Involvements...* 1949. Doubleday. 1st ed. VG/dj. N2. $20.00

REYNOLDS, William J. *Naked Eye.* 1990. Putnam. 1st ed. F/F. T2. $15.50

REYNOLDS, William J. *Things Invisible.* 1989. Putnam. 1st ed. F/F. T2. $14.00

REYNOLDS-BALL, Eustace A. *Cairo: City of the Caliphs.* 1897. Boston. 12mo. 335 p. gilt pict bdg. VG+. H3. $20.00

RHEINHARDT, E.A. *Life of Eleonora Duse.* 1930. London. Martin Secker. 292 p. VG. C5. $10.00

RHINE, J.B. *New Frontiers of the Mind.* 1937. Farrar. 1st ed. VG/dj. M2. $25.00

RHODES, Eugene Manlove. *Little World Waddies.* (1946). Hertzog. 1st ltd ed. 1/1000. ils Bugbee. F. A18. $125.00

RHODES, Eugene Manlove. *Rhodes Reader: Stories of Virgins, Villains & Varmits.* (1957). OK U. 1st ed. F/F. A18. $40.00

RHODES, Eugene Manlove. *Say Now Shibboleth.* 1921. Bookfellows. 1st ltd ed. 1/400. F. A18. $150.00

RHODES, Eugene Manlove. *W Is W.* 1917. NY. 1st ed. VG. A15. $50.00

RHYS, Mimpsy. *Mr Hermit Crab: A Tale for Children by a Child.* 1929. Macmillan. 1st ed. 8vo. 190 p. decor gr cloth. G. T5. $35.00

RIACH, John M. *From One Convert to Another.* 1949. Chicago. Paluch. 111 p. VG/wrp. C5. $7.50

RIBALOW, Harold U. *Mid-Century: Anthology of Jewish Life & Culture...* 1955. NY. Beechhurst Pr. 598 p. VG/fair. S3. $21.00

RIBALOW, Harold. *Jew in Am Sports.* 1955. NY. Bloch. 356 p. VG. C5. $10.00

RICCIOTTI, Giuseppe. *Julian the Apostate.* 1960. Milwaukee. Bruce. 275 p. VG. C5. $10.00

RICCIOTTI, Giuseppe. *Life of Christ.* 1947. Milwaukee. Bruce. 703 p. VG. C5. $10.00

RICCIOTTI, Giuseppe. *Storia d'Israele.* 1934. Torino. 2nd ed. 2 vols. VG. C5. $15.00

RICCIUTI, Edward R. *Wildlife of the Mtns.* (1979). Abrams. lg 8vo. ils/photos. 232 p. vinyl cover/orig box. A17. $17.50

RICE, Alice Hegan. *Capt June.* 1907. NY. 1st ed. 12mo. ils CD Weldon. pict bl cloth. VG. H3. $15.00

RICE, Alice Hegan. *Mr Opp.* 1909. Century. 1st ed. ils Leon Guipon. blk/red decor gr cloth. VG. S10. $18.00

RICE, Alice Hegan. *Romance of Billy-Goat Hill.* 1912. Century. 1st ed. 404 p. gilt gr cloth. VG. S10. $18.00

RICE, Anne. *Belinda.* 1986. Arbor. 1st ed. F/F. F4. $37.00

RICE, Anne. *Claiming of Sleeping Beauty.* 1987. London. 1st ed. w/sgn bookplate. F/F. A11. $70.00

RICE, Anne. *Cry to Heaven.* 1982. Knopf. ARC. RS. F/dj. B2. $75.00

RICE, Anne. *Exit to Eden.* 1985. Arbor. 1st ed. VG/dj. P3. $35.00

RICE, Anne. *Feast of All Saints.* 1979. Simon Schuster. 1st ed. VG/NF. B2. $50.00

RICE, Anne. *Interview w/the Vampire.* 1976. Knopf. 1st ed. F/dj. M2. $600.00

RICE, Anne. *Interview w/the Vampire.* 1976. Knopf. 1st ed. VG+/dj. M18. $500.00

RICE, Anne. *Interview w/the Vampire.* 1976. np. ARC. F/trade-size wrp. scarce. F4. $650.00

RICE, Anne. *Lasher.* 1993. Knopf. Advance Bookseller Copy. sgn. F/NF. B2. $50.00

RICE, Anne. *Lasher.* 1993. Knopf. 1st ed. F/F. B4. $25.00

RICE, Anne. *Mummy.* (1989). Chatto Windus. 1st Eng/hc ed. F/F. B4. $85.00

RICE, Anne. *Queen of the Damned.* 1988. Knopf. 1st ed. sgn. F/dj. M18. $60.00

RICE, Anne. *Tale of the Body Thief.* nd. Knopf. 1st issue proof. wht wrp. C4. $100.00

RICE, Anne. *Tale of the Body Thief.* 1992. Knopf. 1st ed. inscr/sgn. F/F. B2. $65.00

RICE, Anne. *Tale of the Body Thief.* 1992. Knopf. 1st ed. sgn. F/F. M2. $60.00

RICE, Anne. *Tale of the Body Thief.* 1992. Knopf. 1st ed. 4th of Vampire Chronicles. F/F. B4. $45.00

RICE, Anne. *Vampire Chronicles.* 1990. Knopf. 1st thus boxed ed. 3 vols. sgn. cloth. F/NF slipcase. B4. $250.00

RICE, Anne. *Vampire Lestat.* 1985. Knopf. 1st ed. F/F. M18. $175.00

RICE, Anne. *Vampire Lestat.* 1985. Knopf. 1st ed. rem mk. F/NF. B4. $75.00

RICE, Anne. *Witching Hour.* 1990. Knopf. 1st ed. F/F clip. B4. $35.00

RICE, Charles Allen. *Reminiscences of Abraham Lincoln...* 1868. NY. N Am Pub. 1st ed. 656 p. cloth. NF. M8. $65.00

RICE, Craig. *Knocked for a Loop.* 1957. Simon Schuster. 1st ed. F/NF. F4. $45.00

RICE, F. Philip. *Am's Favorite Fishing.* (1964). NY. 1st ed. 285 p. VG/dj. A17. $7.50

RICE, Howard C. *Barthelemi Tardiveau. French Trader in the W.* 1938. Johns Hopkins. 1st ed. 8vo. facsimiles. brds. H9. $60.00

RICE, James E. *Judging Poultry for Production.* 1930. NY. Wiley. 1st ed. 425 p. F. H10. $9.50

RICE, Luanne. *Crazy in Love.* (1989). Heinemann. 1st ed. F/NF. B3. $20.00

RICE, Margaret. *Sun on the River: Story of Bailey Family Business.* 1955. Concord. VG+. O3. $85.00

RICE, Susan T. *Mother, in Verse & Prose.* 1916. NY. Moffat Yard. probable 1st ed. 357 p. bl cloth. F. B22. $8.50

RICE, Wallace. *Heroic Deeds in Our War w/Spain.* 1898. Chicago. George M Hill. 8vo. ils. 447 p. gilt red/blk decor tan cloth. G. B11. $40.00

RICE & RICE. *Popular Studies of CA Wild Flowers.* 1920. San Francisco. special hand-colored ed. 1/700. sgn. 127 p. cloth. B26. $32.50

RICH, Adrienne. *Of Woman Born.* (1976). Norton. 1st ed. 318 p. NF/NF. A7. $15.00

RICH, Adrienne. *What Is Found There: Notebook on Poetry & Politics.* 1993. Norton. 1st ed. sgn. M/M. E3. $35.00

RICHABY, Joseph. *In an Indian Abbey.* 1919. London. Burns Oates. 150 p. VG. C5. $15.00

RICHABY, Joseph. *Scripture Manuals for Catholic Schools.* 1899. London. Burns Oates. 168 p. VG/wrp. C5. $8.50

RICHABY, Joseph. *Waters That Go Softly.* 1906. Newman. 173 p. VG. C5. $10.00

RICHARD, Braybrooke. *Memoirs of Samuel Pepys...* 1825. London. Henry Colburn. 2 vols. quarto. full calf. NF/cloth box. R3. $2,250.00

RICHARD, Mrs. Tex. *Everything Happened to Him.* (1937). London. 1st ed. 311 p. cloth. VG. D3. $35.00

RICHARD, Robert. *Secularization Theology.* 1967. NY. Herder. 190 p. VG. C5. $10.00.

RICHARDS, Eva A. *Arctic Mood.* 1949. Caldwell, IA. 1st ed. 8vo. pls. 282 p. blk cloth. F. H3. $20.00

RICHARDS, Hubert. *What the Spirit Says to the Churches.* 1967. NY. Kenedy. 141 p. VG. C5. $10.00

RICHARDS, J.H. *Loyal Life: Biography of Henry Livingston Richards...* 1913. St Louis. Herder. 394 p. VG. C5. $15.00

RICHARDS, L.G. *TAC: Story of Tactical Air Command.* (1961). John Day. 1st ed. 8vo. 254 p. VG/VG. A2. $17.50

RICHARDS, Laura E. *Captain January.* 1892. Dana Estes. pict bdg. VG. E5. $20.00

RICHARDS, Laura E. *Captain January.* 1893. Estes Lauriat. ils Frank T Merrill. 133 p. VG. S10. $25.00

RICHARDS, Laura E. *For Tommy & Other Stories.* (1900). Dana Esters. ils Frank T Merrill. sgn. 225 p. VG. S10. $45.00

RICHARDS, Laura E. *Melody.* 1901 (1893). Dana Estes. 76th thousand. 90 p. VG+. S10. $30.00

RICHARDS, Laura E. *Mrs Tree.* 1902. Dana Estes. ils Frank T Merrill. bl floral decor gray brds. VG. S10. $40.00

RICHARDS, Vyvyan. *Portrait of TE Lawrence.* 1936. London. Jonathan Cape. 1st ed. 255 p. dk bl cloth. F/NF/clear plastic. $185.00

RICHARDSON, Alan. *Christian Apologetics.* 1947. Harper. 256 p. VG. C5. $8.50

RICHARDSON, Alan. *Intro to Theology of the New Testament.* ca 1958. Harper Row. 1st ed. xl. 205 p. H10. $27.50

RICHARDSON, Albert D. *Beyond the MS.* 1867. Hartford, CT. subscriber ed. 8vo. fld map. pub brn cloth. H9. $125.00

RICHARDSON, Albert D. *Our New States & Territories.* 1866. NY. 1st ed. ils wrp. O7. $100.00

RICHARDSON, Albert D. *Secret Service, the Field, the Dungeon & the Escape.* 1965. Hartford, CT. 1st ed. royal 8vo. 512 p. cloth. VG. D3. $65.00

RICHARDSON, C. *Practical Ferriery...* 1950. London. Pitnam. 1st ed. VG/VG. O3. $25.00

RICHARDSON, Cyril. *Sacrament of Reunion.* 1940. Scribner. 120 p. VG. C5. $12.50

RICHARDSON, D.N. *Girdle Round the Earth. Home Letters From Foreign Lands.* 1894 (1888). Chicago. 8vo. 449 p. cloth. O2. $50.00

RICHARDSON, Edgar Preston. *WA Allston: A Study of Romantic Artist in Am.* 1948. Chicago. 234 p. cloth. D2. $70.00

RICHARDSON, F.B. *Broadmoor Golf Club: Hist Perspective.* (1983). Seattle. Superior Pub. 1st ed. 4to. 120 p. F/sans. A2. $15.00

RICHARDSON, Frederick. *Mother Goose Story Book.* 1920 (1917). Winston. ils. 96 p. VG. P2. $20.00

RICHARDSON, Frederick. *Mother Goose.* (1915). Donohue. edit EO Grover. gr cloth/pict label. VG. S10. $45.00

RICHARDSON, Guy. *My Abraham Lincoln.* 1937. Baker Taylor. 112 p. VG. T6. $15.00

RICHARDSON, H.E. *Tibet & Its Hist.* 1962. London. Oxford. 1st ed. 8vo. 16 pls/1 fld map. 308 p. VG. W1. $35.00

RICHARDSON, M.K. *Sudden Splendor: Story of Mabel Digby.* 1956. NY. Sheed. 242 p. VG. C5. $10.00

RICHARDSON, M.T. *Practical Horseshoer.* 1904. NY. later prt. O3. $45.00

RICHARDSON, N. *Richardson's New Method for the Piano-Forte.* ca 1859. Boston. Oliver Ditson. 4to. pls. 236 p. T3. $19.00

RICHARDSON, R.G. *Surgery: Old & New Frontiers.* 1968. Scribner. ils. 311 p. orange cloth. G+/G. S9. $10.00

RICHARDSON, Robert. *Book of the Dead.* 1989. London. Gollancz. 1st ed. sgn. F/F. M15. $65.00

RICHARDSON, Robert. *Hand of Strange Children.* 1993. London. Gollancz. 1st ed. sgn. F/F. M15. $45.00

RICHARDSON, W.J. *Modern Mission Apostolate.* 1965. NY. Sheed. 308 p. VG. C5. $12.50

RICHARDSON, William. *Monastic Ruins of Yorkshire.* 1843. York. 1st ed. rare issue w/pls mtd on card. lg folio. VG. H5. $11,000.00

RICHARDSON & RICHARDSON. *Appaloosa.* 1969. S Brunswick. Barnes. 1st ed. presentation D Richardson. VG/VG. O3. $35.00

RICHELIEU. *Political Testament of Cardinal Richelieu.* 1978. Madison, WI. WI U. 128 p. VG/wrp. C5. $8.50

RICHLER, Mordecai. *Home Sweet Home.* (1984). Chatto Windus. 1st ed. VG/F. B3. $30.00

RICHLER, Mordecai. *Shovelling Trouble.* (1973). London. Quartet. ARC. RS. F/F. B3. $40.00

RICHMOND, Al. *Long View From the Left.* 1973. Houghton Mifflin. stated 1st ed. 447 p. NF/dj. A7. $30.00

RICHMOND, Clifford A. *Hist & Romance of Elastic Webbing.* 1946. Easthampton. 218 p. VG. B28. $20.00

RICHMOND, Irving B. *CA Under Spain & Mexico 1535-1847.* 1911. Houghton Mifflin. 1st ed. 541 p. red cloth. VG. H7. $75.00

RICHMOND, James. *Ritschl: A Reappraisal.* 1978. London. Collins. 319 p. VG. C5. $15.00

RICHSTAETIER, Karl. *Illustrious Friends of the Sacred Heart of Jesus.* nd. London. Sands. 251 p. VG. C5. $20.00

RICHTER, Canon J.S. *Sunday School Sermonettes.* 1944. NY. Wagner. 426 p. VG. C5. $17.50

RICHTER, Conrad. *Fields.* 1946. Knopf. 1st ed. VG/clip. A18. $35.00

RICHTER, Conrad. *Free Man.* 1943. Knopf. 1st ed. inscr/sgn. F/F. A18. $75.00

RICHTER, Conrad. *Simple Honorable Man.* 1962. Knopf. 1st ed. sgn. F/F. A18. $50.00

RICHTER, Conrad. *Town.* 1950. Knopf. 1st ed. F/F. A18. $40.00

RICHTER, Conrad. *Tracey Cromwell.* 1942. Knopf. 1st ed. F/VG. A18. $35.00

RICHTER, Conrad. *Trees.* 1940. Knopf. ARC/1st ed. 1/255. pub presentation. F/rpr slipcase. A18. $100.00

RICHTER, Hans. *Dreams That Money Can Buy.* nd. NY. Films Internat. 1st ed. F/blk prt gr wrp. B2. $65.00

RICHTER, Heinz. *British Intervention in Greece. From Varkiza to Civil War.* 1986. London. 8vo. cloth. dj. O2. $45.00

RICHTER, Soren. *Store Norske Ekspedisjoner.* nd. Oslo. Forlag. 4to. 175 p. map ep. bl cloth. VG. P4. $35.00

RICKENBACKER, Edward. *Rickenbacker.* 1967. Prentice Hall. G/dj. A16. $15.00

RICKENBACKER, Edward. *Rickenbacker.* 1967. Prentice Hall. 1st ed. 8vo. F/VG. A8. $22.00

RICKETT, Harold W. *Royal Botanical Expedition to New Spain, 1788-1820...* 1947. Waltham, MA. ils/pls/index. wrp. B26. $29.00

RICKETT, Harold W. *Wild Flowers of Am.* 1953. NY. 8th prt. 400 color pls. VG/VG. B28. $25.00

RICKETT, Harold W. *Wild Flowers of the US, Vol 5: NW States.* 1971. NY. 1st ed. 218 pls. 666 p. NF/slipcase. B26. $150.00

RICKETT & RICKETT. *Prisoners of Liberation.* 1957. Cameron. 1st ed. 288 p. dj. A7. $13.00

RICKETTS, R. *First Class Polo: Tactics & Match Play.* 1928. Aldershot. Gale Polden. 1st ed. VG. scarce. O3. $125.00

RICKS, David. *Byzantine Heroic Poetry.* 1990. Bristol. 8vo. 189 p. cloth. O2. $40.00

RICOEUR, Paul. *Freud & Philosophy: Essay on Interpretation.* 1970. New Haven. Yale. 1st ed. 573 p. orange cloth. VG/dj. G1. $40.00

RIDDELL, James. *Flight of Fancy.* (1951). NY. DSP. 1st ed. 8vo. 256 p. VG/G+. A2. $20.00

RIDDELL, James. *In the Forests of the Night.* (1946). NY. 1st ed. photos. 228 p. VG. A17. $15.00

RIDDELL, Newton N. *Heredity & Prenatal Culture Considered...* (1900). Chicago. Child of Light Pub. 350 p. cloth. B14. $45.00

RIDDLE, John A. *Sterility Is Laid...System of Agriculture.* 1868. Manchester. Livingston. wrp. H10. $7.50

RIDGE, John Rollin. *Ridge's Poems.* 1868. San Francisco. Henry Payot. posthumous ed. NF. L3. $650.00

RIDLEY, Jasper. *Statesman & Saint.* 1982. Viking. 338 p. VG. C5. $12.50

RIDLEY, Thomas. *View of the Civile & Ecclesiastical Law...* 1676. Oxford. Hall/Davis. 4th ed. 396 p. modern calf/red morocco label. K1. $200.00

RIDPATH, J.C. *Life & Work of James A Garfield.* 1882. np. memorial ed. 8vo. ils. 795 p. gilt brn cloth. VG. T3. $19.00

RIDPATH, J.C. *Popular Hist of the USA.* 1877. Phil/Cincinnati/Chicago. thick 8vo. 688 p. pub half brn morocco. H9. $55.00

RIEKE, Marcus. *Sincerely, in Him.* 1950. Columbus. Wortburg. 140 p. VG. C5. $8.50

RIENOW & TRAIN. *Of Snuff, Sin & the Senate.* 1965. Chicago. Follett. 1st ed. 8vo. 360 p. VG+/VG. A2. $15.00

RIEPE, Charles. *Living the Christian Seasons.* 1964. NY. Herder. 96 p. VG. C5. $8.50

RIESENBERG, Felix. *Golden Road: Story of CA's Spanish Mission Trail.* 1962. NY. McGraw Hill. later prt. presentation. VG/G. O3. $40.00

RIESS, Oswald. *Everlasting Arms.* 1949. NY. Kaufman. 205 p. VG. C5. $8.50

RIESS, Oswald. *For Such a Time As This.* 1959. St Louis. Concordia. 140 p. VG. C5. $7.50

RIET, Paul. *Maya Cities.* (1960). London/NY. 234 p. dj. F3. $75.00

RIGA, Peter. *Church & Revolution.* 1967. Milwaukee. Bruce. 195 p. VG. C5. $8.50

RIGA, Peter. *Church Made Relevant.* 1967. Notre Dame. Fides. 337 p. VG. C5. $8.50

RIGAULT, Georges. *Blessed Louis Marie Grignon de Montfort.* 1932. London. Burns Oates. 180 p. VG. C5. $12.50

RIGBY & RIGBY. *Colour Your Garden w/Australian Natives.* 1992. Kenthurst, Australia. 500 color photos. 112 p. M. B26. $28.00

RIGG, J. Linton. *Bahama Islands.* 1959. Van Nostrand. 3rd ed. 197 p. VG/VG. B11. $14.00

RIGG, Robert B. *How To Stay Alive in Vietnam.* (1966). Stackpole. 95 p. ils brds. F7. $65.00

RIGGAN, Rob. *Free Fire Zone.* (1984). Norton. F/NF. A7. $30.00

RIGGS, Arthur Stanley. *Romance of Human Progress.* (1938). Bobbs Merrill. 1st ed. 8vo. 405 p. F/VG+. A2. $20.00

RIGGS, James. *Hist of the Jewish People.* 1908. Scribner. 320 p. VG. C5. $10.00

RIGNEY, Harold. *4 Yrs in a Red Hell.* 1956. Chicago. Regnery. 222 p. VG. C5. $10.00

RIHBANY, Abrahm. *7 Days w/God.* 1926. Houghton Mifflin. 254 p. VG. C5. $10.00

RIIS, Jacob. *Hero Tales of the Far N.* 1910. NY. xl. 12mo. gilt bl cloth. VG. H3. $12.00

RIIS, Jacob. *Out of Mulberry Street.* 1898. Century. 1st ed. inscr. F. B2. $250.00

RILEY, Athelstan. *Athos; or, Mtn of the Monks.* 1887. London. 8vo. 24 p ads/409 p. gilt cloth. O2. $450.00

RILEY, Edward Miles. *Journal of John Harrower.* 1963. Williamsburg, VA. 1st ed. sgn. 202 p. bl cloth. G/G. B11. $45.00

RILEY, James Whitcomb. *Armazindy.* 1894. Bobbs Merrill. 1st ed. F. M18. $30.00

RILEY, James Whitcomb. *Old Sweetheart of Mine.* 1902. Bobbs Merrill. 1st ed. ils Christy. G. M18. $30.00

RILEY, James Whitcomb. *Out to Old Aunt Mary's.* 1904. Bobbs Merrill. ils Christy. VG. C1. $7.50

RILEY, James Whitcomb. *Poems Here at Home.* 1897 (1893). NY. Century. ils Kemble. 187 p. teg. gilt gr cloth. D2. $45.00

RILEY, James Whitcomb. *Riley Fairy Tales.* 1923. Bobbs Merrill. 1st thus ed. lg 8vo. bl cloth/pict label. G+. S10. $35.00

RILEY, James. *Authentic Narrative of Loss of Am Brig Commerce...* 1833. Hartford. 8vo. ils. 271 p. leather. T3. $40.00

RILEY, James. *Sufferings in Africa: Capt Riley's Narrative.* (1965). NY. Potter. 1st ed. 8vo. 316 p. VG+/VG+. A2. $15.00

RILING, Ray. *Powder Flask Book.* 1953. New Hope, PA. 1st ed. 4to. 495 p. gilt gr cloth. F/dj. F1. $225.00

RIMBAULT, Edward F. *Pianoforte: Its Origins, Progress & Construction...* 1860. London. Robert Cocks. 4to. ils/100 p music specimens. 420 p. rebound. K1. $200.00

RIMEL. *Quicker Quilts.* 1984. np. ils. wrp. G2. $17.00

RIMMER, Harry. *Christianity & Modern Crisis.* 1944. E Stroudsburg, PA. Pinebrook. 137 p. VG. C5. $10.00

RIMMER, Harry. *Coming King.* 1945. Grand Rapids. Eerdmans. 90 p. VG. C5. $8.50

RIMMER, Harry. *Coming War & Rise of Russia.* 1945. Grand Rapids. Eerdmans. 87 p. VG. C5. $7.50

RIMMER, Harry. *Harmony of Science & Scripture.* 1945. Grand Rapids. Eerdmans. 11th ed. VG. C5. $10.00

RIMMER, Harry. *Modern Science & the Genesis Record.* 1946. Grand Rapids. Eerdmans. 292 p. VG. C5. $10.00

RINALDI, Bonaventura. *Mary of Nazareth.* 1966. Westminster. Newman. 228 p. VG. C5. $10.00

RINALDI, Peter. *It Is the Lord.* 1972. Vantage. 115 p. VG. C5. $15.00

RINALDI, Peter. *Man in the Shroud.* 1972. London. Sidgwick Jackson. 115 p. VG. C5. $20.00

RINEHART, Mary Roberts. *Street of 7 Stars.* 1914. Houghton Mifflin. 1st ed. 377 p. VG. M20. $25.00

RING, Douglas; see Prather, Richard.

RING, George. *Religions of the Far E.* 1950. Milwaukee. Bruce. 350 p. VG. C5. $10.00

RINGWALD, Donald C. *Hudson River Day Line.* 1965. Howell N. G/dj. A16. $80.00

RINK, Evald. *Prt in DE, 1761-1800: A Checklist.* 1969. Wilmington, DE. Eleutherian Mills Hist Lib. 1st ed. 8vo. 214 p. NF/VG. V3. $17.50

RINSER, Luise. *Rings of Glass.* 1958. Chicago. Regnery. 176 p. VG. C5. $10.00

RIO, Michel. *Dreaming Jungles.* 1987. Pantheon/Random. 1st ed. trans from French. F/F. A14. $25.00

RIOS, Tere. *15th Pelican.* 1965. Doubleday. 118 p. VG. C5. $8.50

RIPLEY, Alexandra. *Charleston.* 1981. Doubleday. 1st ed. 501 p. G/G. B10. $12.00

RIPLEY, Francis. *Last Gospel.* 1961. London. Catholic BC. 225 p. VG. C5. $10.00

RIPPLE, Paula. *Called To Be Friends.* 1980. Notre Dame. Ave Maria. 160 p. VG/wrp. C5. $7.50

RIPPY, J. Fred. *Latin Am.* (1958). Ann Arbor. 1st ed. 579 p. F3. $15.00

RIQUET, Michael. *Christian Charity in Action.* 1961. Hawthorn. 171 p. VG. C5. $7.50

RISTOW, Walter W. *Maps for an Emerging Nation.* 1977. Lib of Congress. oblong 4to. 66 p. wrp. H9. $50.00

RISTOW, Walter. *Am Maps & Map Makers, Commerical Cartography...* 1986. Wayne State. ils. 488 p. O5. $65.00

RISTOW. *Nautical Charts on Vellum in Lib of Congress.* 1977. WA, DC. oblong 4to. ils. 31 p. wht linen. H9. $65.00

RITAMARY. *Juniorate in Sister Formation.* 1959. NY. Fordham. 127 p. VG. C5. $12.50

RITCHIE, Barbara. *Riot Report.* (1969). Viking. 1st ed. 254 p. NF/dj. A7. $18.00

RITCHIE, G.S. *Admiralty Chart: British Naval Hydrography in 19th Century.* 1967. London. Hollis Carter. 1st ed. ils/12 maps. M/dj. O6. $85.00

RITCHIE, James S. *WI & Its Resources.* 1857. Phil. Chas Desilver. duocemino. 2 fld maps. Eng half calf. H9. $475.00

RITCHIE, Jean. *Singing Family of the Cumberlands.* 1955. NY. 1st ed. ils Maurice Sendak. VG/torn. B18. $22.50

RITCHIE, John. *Feasts of Jehovah.* nd. Kilmarnock. Believers Magazine. 102 p. VG. C5. $12.50

RITCHIE, John. *Notes on Paul's Epistle to the Romans.* nd. Kilmarnock. Ritchie. 164 p. VG. C5. $8.50

RITCHIE, John. *Tabernacle in the Wilderness.* 1961. Grand Rapids. Kregel. 122 p. VG. C5. $12.50

RITCHIE, Rita. *Pirates of Samarkand.* 1967. Norton. 1st ed. 8vo. 158 p. VG/VG. T5. $25.00

RITCHIE, Ward. *Job Prt in CA.* 1955. Glen Dawson. 1st ed. 31 p. F. B19. $20.00

RITSCHL, Albrecht. *3 Essays.* 1972. Phil. Fortress. 301 p. C5. $15.00

RITSOS, Yannis. *Exile & Return: Selected Poems, 1967-74.* 1985. NY. 1st ed. F/F. V1. $20.00

RITTENHOUSE, Jack D. *Am Horse-Drawn Vehicles.* 1951. LA. Floyd Clymer. 1st ed/2nd prt. 4to. VG/wrp. O3. $95.00

RITTENHOUSE, Jack D. *Cabezon: NM Ghost Town.* 1965. Santa Fe. 1st ed. 1/750. inscr. 12mo. 95 p. F/dj. D3. $50.00

RITTENHOUSE, Jack D. *Santa Fe Trail: Hist Bibliography.* 1971. NM U. 1st ed. index. 271 p. NF/rpr. B19. $50.00

RITTER, E.A. *Shaka Zulu.* 1956. London. Putnam. 4th prt. 8vo. 383 p. dj. P4. $40.00

RITTER, Richard. *Arts of the Church.* 1947. Boston. Pilgrim. 139 p. VG. C5. $10.00

RITVO, Harriet. *Animal Estate.* 1987. Cambridge. Harvard. 1st ed. F/F. O3. $25.00

RIVERAIN, Jean. *Trains of the World.* 1964. Follett Pub. ils. VG/dj. A16. $20.00

RIVERE, Alec; see Nuetzel, Charles.

RIVERO CARVALLO, Jose. *Totimehuacan.* 1961. Pueblo. 1st ed. 156 p. wrp. F3. $15.00

RIVERS, George R. *Captain Shays: Populist of 1786.* 1897. Little Brn. gilt gr cloth. F. B2. $125.00

RIVERS, Thomas. *Miniature Fruit Garden.* 1866. NY. 1st Am from 13th Eng ed. ils. gilt cloth. B26. $24.00

RIVERS. *Working on Canvas.* 1991. np. ils. wrp. G2. $25.00

RIVIERE, Lazare. *Four Books of That Learned & Renowned Doctor...* 1658. London. Peter Cole. early (2nd?) Eng ed. sm folio. contemporary sheep. VG. H5. $1,250.00

RIX, Martyn. *Art of Botanical Ils.* ca 1981. NY. Arch Cape. folio. ils/color pls. 224 p. M. H10. $25.00

RIXFORD, E.H. *Wine Press & the Cellar: Manual for the Wine Maker...* 1883. San Francisco. Payot, Upham. 1st ed. 240 p. gilt bdg. VG. H7. $75.00

ROAZEN, Paul. *Brother Animal: Story of Freud & Tausk.* 1969. NY. Knopf. 1st ed. 221 p. cloth. G1. $27.50

ROAZEN, Paul. *Helene Deutsch: Psychoanalyst's Life.* 1985. Garden City. Anchor Pr. 1st ed. 372 p. VG/dj. G1. $25.00

ROAZEN, Paul. *Sigmund Freud.* 1973. Prentice Hall. 1st ed. sm 8vo. 186 p. VG/dj. G1. $20.00

ROBACK, A.A. *IL Peretz: Psychologist of Literature.* 1935. Cambridge. Sci-Art Pub. thick 8vo. 457 p. gr cloth. G1. $50.00

ROBACK, A.A. *Jewish Influence in Modern Thought.* 1929. Cambridge. Sci-Art Pub. 1st ed. presentation. half leather. G. G1. $85.00

ROBBINS, Archibald. *Journel...Account Loss of Brig Commerce of Hartford, CT...* 1818. Hartford. 3rd ed. 275 p. gilt full leather. VG. H3. $50.00

ROBBINS, Tom. *Even Cowgirls Get the Blues.* 1976. NY. 1st ed. F/F wht dj. A11. $125.00

ROBBINS, W.W. *Weeds of CA.* 1941. Sacramento. 1st ed. 491 p. decor orange cloth. B26. $29.00

ROBBINS, Wilford. *Christian Apologetic.* 1902. London. Longman. 193 p. VG. C5. $8.50

ROBBINS & THOMAS. *Hands All Around.* 1984. np. cloth. G2. $20.50

ROBERS, Mary Eliza. *Domestic Life in Palestine.* 1869. Cincinnati. 8vo. 436 p. cloth. O2. $50.00

ROBERT, Guy. *How the Church Can Help Where Delinquency Begins.* 1958. Richmond. Knox. 157 p. VG. C5. $7.50

ROBERT, Marthe. *Psychoanalytic Revolution: Sigmund Freud's Life...* 1966. HBW. 1st Am ed. 396 p. bl cloth. G1. $25.00

ROBERT & TRICOT. *Guide to the Bible.* 1955. Paris. Desclee. 2 vols. VG. C5. $25.00

ROBERTS, Benson H. *Holiness Teachings.* 1893. NY. Earnest Christian. 256 p. VG. C5. $12.50

ROBERTS, Charles. *Earth's Enigmas.* 1903. Page. 1st ed. ils CL Bull. 285 p. VG. S10. $35.00

ROBERTS, Dan W. *Rangers & Sovereignty.* 1914. San Antonio. 1st ed. 190 p. VG+. scarce. D3. $60.00

ROBERTS, David. *Grandeur & Misery of Man.* 1955. NY. Oxford. 186 p. VG. C5. $12.50

ROBERTS, Dorothy J. *Launcelot, My Brother.* 1954. NY. 1st ed. VG. C1. $29.50

ROBERTS, Edwards. *With the Invader.* 1885. San Francisco. Carson. 1st ed. xl. 12mo. 156 p. VG. D3. $35.00

ROBERTS, Estelle. *Forty Yrs a Medium.* 1960. London. Jenkins. 1st ed. 200 p. red cloth. VG/dj. G1. $22.50

ROBERTS, G.E. Theodore. *Flying Plover.* 1909. Page. 125 p. VG. S10. $55.00

ROBERTS, Gail. *Atlas of Discovery.* 1973. London. Aldus. 1st ed. 102 p. M/dj. O6. $45.00

ROBERTS, H. Armstrong. *Commerical Poultry Raising.* ca 1920. McKay. ils. 588 p. H10. $9.50

ROBERTS, Jane. *Seth Speaks: Eternal Validity of the Soul.* 1972. Prentice Hall. 2nd ed. VG/clip. N2. $6.00

ROBERTS, Keith. *Molly Zero.* 1980. London. Gollancz. 1st ed. F/F clip. N3. $25.00

ROBERTS, Kenneth. *Arundel.* 1939. Doubleday Doran. later prt. F/2nd issue dj. C4. $35.00

ROBERTS, Kenneth. *Boon Island.* 1956. Doubleday. special issue. w/sgn p. F. C4. $100.00

ROBERTS, Kenneth. *Capt Caution.* 1949. London. Collins. 1st ed. F/ils dj. C4. $35.00

ROBERTS, Kenneth. *I Wanted To Write.* 1949. Doubleday. 1st ed. F/VG+. C4. $40.00

ROBERTS, Kenneth. *Lydia Bailey.* 1947. Doubleday. 1/1050. sgn. w/p from working manuscript. NF/slipcase. C4. $195.00

ROBERTS, Kenneth. *March to Quebec.* 1938. NY. 1st ed. VG/VG. B5. $50.00

ROBERTS, Kenneth. *NW Passage.* nd. Doubleday. 1st ed. sgn. F/NF. C4. $175.00

ROBERTS, Kenneth. *Sun Hunting.* (1922). Bobbs Merrill. 1st ed. NF. B4. $75.00

ROBERTS, Kenneth. *Trending Into ME.* June 1938. Boston. 1st ed. ils NC Weyth. F. B14. $125.00

ROBERTS, Kenneth. *Trending Into ME.* 1938. Little Brn. 1st ed. F/NC Weth dj. C4. $100.00

ROBERTS, Kenneth. *Trending Into ME.* 1938. Little Brn. 1st ed. ils/sgn Wyeth. w/suite 14 pls. F/slipcase/glassine. B24. $1,750.00

ROBERTS, Lee; see Martin, Robert.

ROBERTS, P.E. *Hist of British India.* 1952. London. Oxford. 707 p. A7. $15.00

ROBERTS, Robert. *House Servant's Directory or Monitor for Private Families...* 1827. Boston. 1st ed. 12mo. 180 p. M1. $2,750.00

ROBERTS, William. *Account of 1st Discovery & Natural Hist of FL.* 1763. London. Jefferys/Charing-Cross. 4to. marbled brds/calf spine. H9. $1,250.00

ROBERTS & ROBERTS. *Moreau du St Mercy's Am Journey 1793-98.* 1947. Doubleday. VG. N2. $10.00

ROBERTSON, A.T. *Harmony of the Gospels.* 1950. Harper. 304 p. VG. C5. $10.00

ROBERTSON, A.T. *Paul's Joy in Christ.* 1959. Nashville. Broadman. 145 p. VG. C5. $8.50

ROBERTSON, Bruce. *Air Aces of the 1914-18 War.* 1959. Letchworth. 1st ed. 211 p. VG/dj. B18. $45.00

ROBERTSON, Bruce. *Aircraft Camouflage & Markings.* 1959. Letchworth. 3rd revised prt. 212 p. VG/dj. B18. $25.00

ROBERTSON, D.B. *Should Churches Be Taxed?* 1968. Phil. Westminster. 288 p. VG. C5. $8.50

ROBERTSON, Dale. *Son of the Phantom.* 1946. Whitman. 1st ed. G+. M2. $10.00

ROBERTSON, Donald. *Pre-Columbian Architecture.* 1963. Braziller. 1st ed. 4to. 128 p. F3. $25.00

ROBERTSON, Frank C. *Ft Hall: Gateway to the OR Country.* (1963). Hastings. 1st ed. photos/index. F/dj. A18. $60.00

ROBERTSON, John W. *Francis Drake & Other Early Explorers Along Pacific Coast...* 1927. Grabhorn. 1/1000. octavo. 28 maps. quarter vellum. NF/slipcase. O6. $295.00

ROBERTSON, John W. *Harbor of St Francis: Francis Drake Lands...* 1926. Grabhorn. 1/100. ils/maps. 119 p. NF/slipcase. O6. $275.00

ROBERTSON, John. *In the End, God.* 1968. Harper. Religious Prespectives series. 148 p. VG. C5. $8.50

ROBERTSON, John. *Rusty Staub of the Expos.* 1971. Prentice Hall. 1st ed. VG+/G+. P8. $45.00

ROBERTSON, William Spence. *Diary of Francisco de Miranda.* 1928. NY. Hispanic Soc of Am. 1st ed. VG.. B28. $35.00

ROBERTSON, William. *Hist of Thoroughbred Racing in Am.* 1964. Prentice Hall. 1st ed. folio. 621 p. VG/G. O3. $95.00

ROBERTSON, Wyndham. *Pocahontas...Her Descendants...* 1986 (1887). Genealogy Pub. reprint. 84 p. VG. B10. $35.00

ROBESON, Kenneth; see Goulart, Ron.

ROBICHAUD, Norbert. *Holiness for All.* 1945. Westminster. Newman. 67 p. VG/wrp. C5. $8.50

ROBINS, John D. *Incomplete Anglers.* (1944). NY. 229 p. F/worn. A17. $14.50

ROBINS & ROSS. *Life & Death of a Druid Prince.* 1989. np. 1st ed. F/dj. C1. $6.50

ROBINSON, Anthony. *In the Cockpit.* (1979). NY. 1st Am ed. ils. 304 p. VG+/dj. B18. $25.00

ROBINSON, Armin. *10 Commandments.* 1944. Simon Schuster. 488 p. VG. C5. $10.00

ROBINSON, Beverly W. *With Shotgun & Rifle in N Am Game Fields.* 1925. NY. 1st ed. 387 p. NF/dj. A17. $40.00

ROBINSON, Brooks. *3rd Base Is My Home.* (1974). Waco. 2nd prt. 202 p. dj. A17. $9.50

ROBINSON, Bruce. *Killing Fields.* 1982. Enigma Films. photocopy screenplay. NF/clasp-bdg cardstock. L3. $85.00

ROBINSON, Charles Newton. *Viol of Love & Other Poems.* 1895. London. John Lane. 1st ed. 1/350. octavo. gilt gr cloth. F. B24. $250.00

ROBINSON, Daniel N. *Intellectual Hist of Psychology.* 1981. Macmillan. 2nd revised ed/1st prt. 484 p. prt red cloth. G1. $35.00

ROBINSON, Derek. *Piece of Cake.* (1984). Knopf. 1st ed. VG/VG. B3. $35.00

ROBINSON, Derek. *War Story.* (1988). Knopf. 1st ed. NF/NF. B3. $30.00

ROBINSON, E.A. *Amaranth.* 1934. Macmillan. 1st ed. 105 p. VG+/dj. M20. $25.00

ROBINSON, E.A. *Cavender's House.* 1929. NY. Macmillan. 1st ed. sgn/dtd 1929. NF/VG. C4. $45.00

ROBINSON, E.A. *Lawrence the Rebel.* 1946. London. Lincolns Praeger. 1st ed. gilt gr cloth. VG/fair/clear plastic. M7. $65.00

ROBINSON, E.A. *Tristram.* 1927. NY. 1st ed. VG+. V1. $30.00

ROBINSON, Fay. *Mexico & Her Military Chieftains.* 1970. NY. Rio Grande Pr. facsimile of 1847 ed. 353 p. F3. $20.00

ROBINSON, Florence Bell. *Planting Design.* 1940. Champaign. ils/photos/fld plans. 215 p. B26. $37.50

ROBINSON, Frank M. *Power.* 1956. Lippincott. ARC. sgn. w/pub slip mk to Clifford Simak. F/NF. F4. $375.00

ROBINSON, Gertrude. *In a Mediaeval Lib.* 1919. London. Herder. 243 p. VG. C5. $15.00

ROBINSON, H. Wheeler. *Christian Experience of the Holy Spirit.* 1958. London. Nisbet. 295 p. VG. C5. $15.00

ROBINSON, Henry. *Cardinal.* 1950. Simon Schuster. 579 p. VG. C5. $10.00

ROBINSON, Henry. *Stout Cortez.* 1931. NY. Century. 1st ed. 347 p. dj. F3. $20.00

ROBINSON, J. *Boston Conspiracy; or, Royal Police.* 1847. Boston. Dow Jackson. 1st ed. 12mo. 110 p. pict wrp. M1. $125.00

ROBINSON, J. *HD (Hilda Doolittle): Life & Work of an Am Poet.* 1982. Boston. 1st ed. F/VG. V1. $10.00

ROBINSON, Jackie. *Baseball Has Done It.* 1964. Lippincott. 1st ed. VG/G. P8. $30.00

ROBINSON, Jackie. *Breakthrough to the Big League.* 1965. Harper Row. 1st ed. F/VG. P8. $23.00

ROBINSON, Jacob. *And the Crooked Shall Be Made Straight.* (1965). Macmillan. 1st Am ed. 8vo. 406 p. F/VG+. A2. $12.50

ROBINSON, James H. *Adventurous Preaching.* 1956. NY. Channel. 186 p. VG. C5. $10.00

ROBINSON, John A.T. *Human Face of God.* ca 1973. Phil. Westminster. 269 p. H10. $11.50

ROBINSON, John A.T. *On Being the Church in the World.* 1960. Phil. Westminster. 188 p. VG. C5. $7.50

ROBINSON, John H. *Poultry-Craft: TB for Poultry Keepers...* 1899. Boston. Johnson. 1st ed. 272 p. H10. $10.00

ROBINSON, John. *Body: Study in Pauline Theology.* 1952. Phil. Westminster. 95 p. VG/wrp. C5. $8.50

ROBINSON, Kim Stanley. *Gr Mars.* 1994. Bantam. 1st Am ed. sgn. M/M. T2. $55.00

ROBINSON, Kim Stanley. *Icehenge.* 1986. Macdonald. 1st hc ed. sgn. F/F. F4. $60.00

ROBINSON, Kim Stanley. *Pacific Edge.* 1990. NY. Tor. 1st ed. inscr. 3rd in Orange County trilogy. F/F. T2. $38.00

ROBINSON, Kim Stanley. *Planet on the Table.* 1986. NY. Tor. 1st ed. inscr. F/F. T2. $42.00

ROBINSON, Kim Stanley. *Remaking Hist.* 1991. NY. Tor. 1st ed. 2nd collection of stories. M/M. T2. $19.00

ROBINSON, Kim Stanley. *Short, Sharp Shock.* 1990. Shingletown. Ziesing. ltd ed (1/500). sgn. ils/sgn Arnie Fenner. M/M/slipcase. T2. $45.00

ROBINSON, Kim Stanley. *Short, Sharp Shock.* 1990. Shingletown. Ziesing. 1st trade ed. M/M. T2. $18.00

ROBINSON, Lewis G. *Making of a Man.* (1970). Cleveland. 1st ed. inscr. 213 p. VG/dj. B18. $15.00

ROBINSON, Luther Emerson. *Abraham Lincoln As Man of Letters.* 1923. Putnam. 2nd ed. 344 p. cloth. NF/dj. M8. $45.00

ROBINSON, Lynda S. *Murder in the Place of Anubis.* 1994. NY. Walker. 1st ed. sgn. M/M. T2. $30.00

ROBINSON, M.F. *Spirit of Assn: Being Some Account...Great Britain.* 1913. London. 1st ed. VG. C1. $8.50

ROBINSON, Marilynne. *Housekeeping.* 1980. Farrar. AP. F/wrp. B2. $85.00

ROBINSON, Maude. *S Down Farm in the Sixties.* 1947. London. Bannisdale. 2nd ed. 8vo. 78 p. VG/dj. V3. $14.00

ROBINSON, Maude. *Time of Her Life & Other Stories.* nd. London. Swarthmore. 12mo. 261 p. G. V3. $16.00

ROBINSON, Peter. *Dedicated Man.* 1988. Markham, Canada. Viking. 1st ed. F/F. M15. $125.00

ROBINSON, Peter. *Gallows View.* 1990. Scribner. ARC of 1st Am ed. sgn. RS. F/F. S5. $40.00

ROBINSON, Ray. *Home Run Heard Round the World.* 1991. Harper Collins. 1st ed. F/F. P8. $15.00

ROBINSON, Ray. *Speed Kings of the Base Paths.* 1964. Putnam. 1st ed. VG. P8. $17.50

ROBINSON, Robert. *Africa & the Victorians.* 1961. St Martin. 489 p. VG. C5. $15.00

ROBINSON, Robert. *17 Discourses on Several Texts of Scripture...* 1796. Cambridge. Lunn. 436 p. dried calf. H10. $25.00

ROBINSON, Ronald. *Africa & the Victorians: Climax of Imperialism...* 1961. St Martin. 1st Am ed. 8vo. 491 p. F/VG. A2. $15.00

ROBINSON, Rowland E. *Uncle Lisha's Shop.* 1891. NY. 5th ed. 187 p. cloth. F. A17. $20.00

ROBINSON, S.S. *Hist of Naval Tactics From 1530 to 1930.* nd. Annapolis. US Naval Inst. 8 fld charts. G. A16. $40.00

ROBINSON, S.T.L. *KS: Its Interior & Exterior Life.* 1857. Boston. 366 p. O7. $24.50

ROBINSON, Smokey. *Smokey: Inside My Life.* (1989). McGraw Hill. 1st ed. 367 p. VG+/dj. A7. $17.00

ROBINSON, Theodore. *Hist of Israel.* nd. London. Oxford. 2 vols. VG. C5. $25.00

ROBINSON, Tom. *In & Out.* 1943. Viking. 1st ed. inscr. 140 p. VG+/VG. P2. $40.00

ROBINSON, W. *Gleanings From French Gardens...* 1868. London. Warne. 1st ed. 291 p. H10. $65.00

ROBINSON, W.D. *Memoirs of the Mexican Revolution.* 1820. Phil. Bailey. 1st ed. octavo. orig brds. H9. $425.00

ROBINSON, W.H. *Story of AZ.* ca 1919. Phoenix, AZ. Berryhill. 1st ed. inscr. 458 p. ribbed gr cloth. H9. $95.00

ROBINSON, W.W. *Story of San Fernando Valley.* 1961. Title Insurance & Trust Co. ils/map. 63 p. NF/wrp. B19. $15.00

ROBINSON & SILVERMAN. *My Life in Baseball (Frank Robinson).* 1975. Doubleday BC. revised/expanded ed. F/VG+. P8. $12.50

ROBINSON & SMITH. *My Own Story.* 1948. Greenberg. 1st ed. xl. VG. P8. $12.50

ROBINSON & STAINBACK. *Extra Innings.* 1988. McGraw Hill. 2nd prt. M/M. P8. $10.50

ROBINSON & TOBIN. *Third Base Is My Home.* 1974. World. 1st ed. inscr. F/VG+. P8. $50.00

ROBO, Etienne. *2 Portraits of St Therese of Lisieux.* 1955. London. Sands. 205 p. VG. C5. $12.50

ROCCATAGLIATA, Giuseppe. *Hist of Ancient Psychiatry.* 1986. Greenwood Pr. 1st ed. 296 p. prt bl cloth. F. G1. $35.00

ROCHE, Aloysius. *Bedside Book of Saints.* 1935. Burns Oates. 145 p. VG. C5. $10.00

ROCHE, Aloysius. *In the Track of the Gospel.* 1953. Burns Oates. 200 p. VG. C5. $15.00

ROCHE, Aloysius. *Light of Other Days.* 1935. London. Burns Oates. 115 p. VG. C5. $7.50

ROCHE, Douglas. *Catholic Revolution.* 1968. McKay. 325 p. VG. C5. $8.50

ROCHE, George. *World Without Heroes.* 1989. Detroit. Hilldale College. 368 p. VG. C5. $10.00

ROCHE, John P. *Quest for the Dream.* (1963). Macmillan. 1st ed. 308 p. dj. A7. $17.00

ROCHE, O.J.A. *Days of the Upright: Story of Huguenots.* 1965. Clarkson Potter. 340 p. VG. C5. $12.50

ROCHE, W. *Daybreak in the Soul.* 1929. London. Longman. 118 p. VG. C5. $8.50

ROCK, John. *Time Has Come.* 1963. Knopf. 167 p. VG. C5. $10.00

ROCKER, Rudolf. *Pioneers of Am Freedom.* 1949. LA. Rocker Pub Committee. 1st ed. F/NF. B2. $45.00

ROCKLAND. *Work of Our Hands: Jewish Needlecraft for Today.* 1973. np. cloth. G2. $12.50

ROCKWELL, Alphonso David. *Rambling Recollections: An Autobiography.* 1920. NY. Hoeber. 1st ed. 332 p. NF-. scarce. M8. $85.00

ROCKWELL, Norman. *Special Days Come To Life.* 1987. 8 action scenes. paper engineered by Van der Meer Paper Design. F. A4. $45.00

ROCKWELL, Thomas. *Squawwwk.* 1972. Little Brn. 1st ed. F/F. N3. $15.00

ROCKWOOD, George. *Cheever, Lincoln & the Causes of the Civil War.* 1936. 83 p. VG. A6. $10.00

ROCKWOOD, Roy. *Bomba the Jungle Boy on Jaguar Island.* 1926. Cupples Leon. 1st ed. VG. M2. $15.00

ROCKWOOD, Roy. *Bomba the Jungle Boy on the Moving Mtn.* 1926. Cupples Leon. 1st ed. VG. M2. $15.00

ROCKWOOD, Roy. *Bomba the Jungle Boy on the Terror Trail.* 1953. Clover. F. M2. $7.00

ROCQ, Margaret Miller. *CA Local Hist: Bibliography & Union List of Lib Holdings.* 1970. Stanford. 2nd ed. index. 611 p. NF/sans. B19. $100.00

RODALE PRESS EDITORS. *Rodales' Soups & Salads.* 1981. Rodale Pr. G/dj. A16. $10.00

RODD, Rennell. *Prince of Achaia & the Chronicles of Morea.* 1907. London. xl. 2 vols. 8vo. cloth. very scarce. O2. $225.00

RODELL, Fred. *Nine Men: Political Hist of Supreme Court, 1790-1955.* 1955. Random. M11. $25.00

RODEN, H.W. *Wake for a Lady.* 1946. Morrow. 1st ed. NF/NF. F4. $35.00

RODGERS, Dorothy. *House in My Head.* 1967. Avenel Books. VG/dj. A16. $15.00

RODGERS. *Trapunto: Handbook of Stuffed Quilting.* 1990. np. wrp. G2. $15.00

RODMAN, O.H.P. *Handbook of Salt-Water Fishing.* (1940). Phil. 5th imp. 274 p. cloth. A17. $8.50

RODMAN, Selden. *Lawrence: Last Crusade.* 1937. Viking. 1st ed. 129 p. VG/G/clear plastic. M7. $45.00

RODRIGO, Luis Carlos. *Picasso in His Posters.* (1992). Madrid. Arte Ediciones. 4 vols. 630 color pls. gilt gr cloth. djs. K1. $400.00

RODRIGUEZ, Abraham Jr. *Spidertown.* 1993. Hyperion. 1st ed. inscr. F/F. B2. $35.00

RODRIGUEZ, Alphonsus. *Christian & Religious Perfection.* nd. NY. TW Strong. 3 vols. VG. C5. $30.00

RODRIQUEZ, Manuel. *Laws of the State of NM Affecting Church Property.* 1959. WA, DC. 223 p. wrp. F3. $25.00

RODRIQUEZ, Mario. *Palmerstonian Diplomat in Central Am, Frederick Chatfield...* 1964. Tucson, AZ. 1st ed. 385 p. dj. F3. $25.00

ROE, E.P. *Brave Little Quakeress & Other Stories.* 1892. Dodd Mead. 16mo. 214 p. VG. V3. $8.50

ROE, E.P. *Success w/Sm Fruits.* 1898 (1881). np. new ed. 388 p. teg. cloth. VG+. B29. $24.00

ROE, Frances. *Army Letters From an Officer's Wife.* 1981. np. 387 p. O7. $12.50

ROEDER, Bill. *Jackie Robinson.* 1950. Barnes. 1st ed. VG/G. P8. $60.00

ROEMER, Theodore. *Catholic Church in the US.* 1950. St Louis. Herder. 444 p. VG. C5. $12.50

ROENTGEN, Wilhelm. *Eine Neue Art Von Strhlen.* 1896. Wurzburg. reprint. 2 (of 3) parts. wrp. G7. $1,250.00

ROESER, Margaret. *Let Flowers of Peace Unfold in the Sun.* 1984. Green Bay. Alt. 164 p. VG/wrp. C5. $7.50

ROESLER. *Rectangular Quilt Blocks.* 1982. np. 30 projects. wrp. G2. $10.00

ROETHKE, Theo. *Collected Poems.* 1965. NY. 1st ed. F/VG+. V1. $25.00

ROETHKE, Theodore. *Far Field.* 1964. NY. 1st ed. pub posthumously. F/VG+ clip. A11. $35.00

ROGAT, Yosal. *Eichmann Trial & the Rule of Law.* 1961. Santa Barbara. Center for Study Democratic Inst. 44 p. wrp. M11. $35.00

ROGER-MARX, Claude. *Bonnard Lithograpie.* 1952. Monte-Carlo. Sauret. 1st ed. F/glassine dj/slipcase. F1. $465.00

ROGERS, Arthur Kenyon. *Eng & Am Philosophy Since 1800...* 1923. Macmillan. 1st ed. 468 p. russet cloth. G1. $35.00

ROGERS, Bruce. *Anti-Slavery Papers of James Russell Lowell.* 1902. Houghton Mifflin. 1st ed. 1/52. 2 vols. octavo. NF/slipcase. B24. $150.00

ROGERS, Bruce. *Consolatorie Letter or Discouse Sent by Plutarch...* 1905. Houghton Mifflin. 1/375. NF/defective slipcase. B24. $100.00

ROGERS, Bruce. *Frederic Wm Goudy: Art Director Lanston Monotype Machine Co.* 1947. Phil. sm quarto. F/wrp/orig envelope. B24. $50.00

ROGERS, Bruce. *Hist of Trans of Blessed Martyrs of Christ, Marcellinus...* 1926. Cambridge. Harvard. 1/500. octavo. teg. F/dj. B24. $150.00

ROGERS, Dale Evans. *My Spiritual Diary.* 1955. Tappan. Revell. 134 p. VG. C5. $7.50

ROGERS, Dorothy. *Highways Across the Horizon.* (1966). London. Hale. 1st ed. 8vo. 192 p. VG+/VG. A2. $15.00

ROGERS, Francis. *Quest for E Christians.* 1962. Minneapolis. MN U. 221 p. VG. C5. $20.00

ROGERS, George. *Pro & Con of Universalism...* 1842. Boston. Tompkins. 356 p. half leather. H10. $17.50

ROGERS, J. Henry. *CA Hundred: A Poem.* 1865. Bancroft. 1st ed. 12mo. 100 p. aeg. cloth. VG. D3. $35.00

ROGERS, Julia Ellen. *Shell Book.* 1936. Boston. Bradford. pls. G. A16. $20.00

ROGERS, Millard F. Jr. *Randolph Rogers: Am Sculptor in Rome.* 1971. Amherst. MA U. 237 p. cloth. dj. D2. $65.00

ROGERS, R. Vashon. *Law of the Road; or, Wrongs & Rights of a Traveller.* 1876. San Francisco. Sumner Whitney. gilt gr cloth. M11. $75.00

ROGERS, Robert. *Concise Account of N Am.* 1765. London. self pub. 1st ed. octavo. new quarter sheep. H9. $1,200.00

ROGERS, William. *Pumps & Hydraulics...* ca 1905. NY. Audel. 2 vols. VG. H10. $22.50

ROGERS & ROGERS. *Am Farm Crisis.* 1989. NY. 149 p. VG+. B28. $15.00

ROGOSIN, Donn. *Invisible Men.* 1985. Atheneum. 1st ed. F/VG+. P8. $60.00

ROGOW, Roberta. *Futurespeak. A Fan's Guide to Language of SF.* 1991. NY. Paragon. 1st ed. F/F. N3. $20.00

ROGOW, Sally. *Lillian Wald: Nurse in Bl.* 1966. Phil. Jewish Pub Soc. 145 p. VG. C5. $10.00

ROGUET, A.M. *Holy Mass.* 1953. Collegeville, MN. Liturgical Pr. 144 p. VG. C5. $10.00

ROGUET, A.M. *Holy Mass. Approaches to the Mystery.* 1953. London. Blackfriars. 120 p. VG. C5. $8.50

ROGUET, A.M. *Liturgy of the Hours.* 1971. Sydney. Dwyer. 141 p. VG/wrp. C5. $8.50

ROGUET, A.M. *Sacraments.* 1954. London. Blackfriars. 162 p. VG. C5. $8.50

ROHEIM, Geza. *Animism, Magic & the Divine King.* 1930. Knopf. index. 390 p. H10. $13.50

ROHMER, Sax. *Dream Detective.* 1925. Doubleday. 1st ed. VG. M2. $35.00

ROHMER, Sax. *Wrath of Fu Manchu.* 1976. NY. David Wolllheim. Daw 186. 1st ed/PBO. F/unread wrp. M15. $50.00

ROHRBACK, Peter-Thomas. *Bold Encounter.* 1969. Milwaukee. Bruce. 224 p. VG. C5. $8.50

ROHRBACK, Peter-Thomas. *Search for St Therese.* 1961. NY. Hanover. 237 p. VG. C5. $12.50

ROITER, Fulvio. *Mexique.* (1970). Zurich. Atlantis. 1st ed. 4to. 175 p. F3. $15.00

ROJANKOVSKY, Feodor. *Falcon Under the Hat: Russian Merry Tales...* 1969. Funk Wagnall. 111 p. NF/VG. P2. $30.00

ROJANKOVSKY, Feodor. *Tall Book of Mother Goose.* 1942. Harper. stated 1st ed. M5. $30.00

ROJANKOVSKY, Feodor. *Tall Book of Nursery Tales.* (1944). Harper. 4to. ils. 120 p. pict ep. VG/G. T5. $30.00

ROJAS Y ARRIETA, Guillermo. *Hist of the Bishops of Panama.* 1929. Panama. Academia. 255 p. VG. C5. $20.00

ROKWAHO. *Covers.* 1982. Bowling Gr. Strawberry. 1st ed. sgn. author's 1st book. F/stapled wrp. L3. $35.00

ROLEWINCK, Werner. *Fasciculus Temporium Omnes Antiquuorum Historias...* nd. (not before 1495). Lyon. Mathias Hus. 17 woodcuts. early calf. K1. $4,000.00

ROLFE, Edwin. *Collected Poems.* 1993. Urbana. IL U. 1st ed. sgn. 350 p. B2. $35.00

ROLFE, Frank. *Commercial Geography of S CA.* 1915. LA. Rolfe. 6 fld maps. ES. NF. O6. $135.00

ROLFE, William D. *Satchel Guide to Europe.* 1925. London. Gay Hancock. revised/enlarged ed. 7 color fld maps. VG+/dj. O6. $65.00

ROLFE. *Quilt a Koala: Australian Animals & Birds in Patchwork.* 1990. np. wrp. G2. $10.00

ROLLINS, Charlemae. *Christmas Gif'.* 1963. Chicago. Follett. 1st ed. F/NF. B2. $100.00

ROLLINS, Wayne. *Gospel Portraits of Christ.* 1963. Phil. Westminster. 128 p. VG. C5. $7.50

ROLLS, Sam Cottington. *Steel Chariots of the Desert.* 1937. London. Cape. 1st ed. rebound half leather. F. M7. $250.00

ROLT-WHEELER, Francis. *Aztec Hunters.* (1918). Lothrop Lee. 1st ed. 363 p. F4. $20.00

ROLT-WHEELER, Francis. *Book of Cowboys.* (1921). Lee Shepard. 1st ed. ils. F/dj. A18. $50.00

ROMAINE, Lawrence B. *Guide to Am Trade Catalogs, 1744-1900.* 1960. Bowker. 1st ed. index. 422 p. NF. B19. $45.00

ROMAINS, Jules. *Frenchman Examines His Conscience.* 1955. London. Deutsch. 118 p. VG. C5. $8.50

ROMAN, K.G. *Handwriting: Key to Personality.* (1952). Pantheon. 1st ed. 8vo. 382 p. F/VG. A2. $25.00

ROMANILLO, John. *Bird of Sorrow.* 1956. NY. Kenedy. 221 p. VG. C5. $10.00

ROMAYNE, Nicolaus. *Dissertatio Inauguralis...* 1780. Edinburgh. Balfour Smellie. presentation. 48 p. half cloth. G7. $500.00

ROMB, Anselm. *Across the Churchyard.* 1968. St Louis. Herder. 105 p. VG. C5. $8.50

ROMB, Anselm. *As One Who Serves.* 1966. Milwaukee. Bruce. 134 p. VG. C5. $8.50

ROMB, Anselm. *Signs of Contradiction.* 1967. St Louis. Herder. 215 p. VG. C5. $8.50

ROME, Anthony; see Albert, Marvin H.

ROMEIN, J.M. *Universiteit en Maatschappij in De Loop Der Tijden.* 1947. Leiden. EJ Brill. 1st ed. 20 p. prt wrp. G1. $17.50

ROMERO, Jose Maria Jimeno. *Farmacologia del Curare en su Asociasion Anestesia.* 1954. Zaragoza. Fernando el Catolico. ils. 64 p. N2. $17.50

ROMERO & SPARROW. *Dawn of the Dead.* 1978. St Martin. 1st ed. F/F. N3. $35.00

ROMIG, Walter. *Book of Catholic Authors.* 1942. Romig. 6 vols. VG. C5. $35.00

ROMIG, Walter. *Josephine van Dyke Brownson.* 1955. Detroit. Gabriel. 150 p. VG. C5. $10.00

ROMOLI, Kathleen. *Colombia: Gateway to S Am.* 1943. Doubleday Doran. 8vo. 8 pls. 364 p. map ep. G. B11. $10.00

ROMUNDT, Ina. *Kinderlust und Legen.* ca 1930s. Duisburg. Steinkamp. ils Flechtner. VG. D1. $85.00

RONALDS, Alfred. *Fly-Fisher's Entomology.* (1990). Secaucus. reprint. 132 p. A17. $15.00

RONAN, Peter. *Hist Sketch of Flathead Indian Nation From 1813-90...* (1890). Helena, MT. Journal Pub. 1st ed. 8vo. 80 p. VG. M1. $300.00

RONANE, E. *Masters Carpet; or, Masonry & Baal-Worship Identical.* 1879. Chicago. 1st ed. 377 p. VG. E5. $85.00

RONANE, E. *Ronayne's Reminiscences: A Hist of His Life...* 1900. Chicago. 445 p. gilt brn bdg. VG. E5. $65.00

RONDET, Henri. *St Joseph.* 1956. NY. Kenedy. 243 p. VG. C5. $8.50

RONNS, Edward; see Aarons, Edward S.

RONSIN, F.X. *Awakeness of Souls.* 1957. Detroit. St Paul. 310 p. VG. C5. $10.00

RONSIN, F.X. *To Govern Is To Love.* 1963. Alba House. 287 p. VG. C5. $8.50

ROOD, Paul W. *Let the Fire Fall.* 1939. Zondervan. 3rd ed. 131 p. VG. C5. $8.50

ROOKMAAKER, H.R. *Creative Gift.* 1981. Westchester. Cornerstone. 172 p. VG. C5. $8.50

ROONEY, Gerard. *Mystery of Calvary.* 1959. Macmillan. 131 p. VG. C5. $8.50

ROONEY, Gerard. *Preface to the Bible.* 1952. Milwaukee. Bruce. 134 p. VG. C5. $8.50

ROOP, John. *Christianity Vs War.* 1949. Ashland, OH. Brethren. revised ed. sgn. 203 p. VG. C5. $15.00

ROORBACH, Rosemary K. *Religion in the Kindergarten.* 1949. Harper. 137 p. VG. C5. $8.50

ROOSEVELT, Anna. *Parmana. Prehistoric Maize & Manoic Subsistence...* (1980). NY. Academic. 1st ed. 320 p. F3. $25.00

ROOSEVELT, Eleanor. *This I Remember.* (1949). NY. 1st ed. sgn. F/dj. B14. $75.00

ROOSEVELT, Elliott. *Roosevelt Letters. Vol 1: Early Yrs 1887-1904.* ca 1949. np. 8vo. fwd Eleanor Roosevelt. blk cloth. G. T3. $15.00

ROOSEVELT, Franklin D. *Inaugural Address...* 1945. Worcester. St Onge. miniature. 1/200. 88 p. H10. $200.00

ROOSEVELT, Nicholas. *Restless Pacific.* 1928. Scribner. 1st ed. 8vo. ils. 291 p. VG. W1. $18.00

ROOSEVELT, Robert Barnwell. *Superior Fishing; or, The Striped Bass, Trout...* 1985. MN Hist Soc. facsimile of 1865 ed. 12mo. F/dj. A17. $22.50

ROOSEVELT, Theodore. *African Game Trails, Account of African Wanderings...* 1910. Scribner. 1st ed. lg 8vo. 529 p. gilt tan cloth. VG. F1. $65.00

ROOSEVELT, Theodore. *African Game Trails.* 1910. Scribner. 1st ed. F. M18. $200.00

ROOSEVELT, Theodore. *Outdoor Pastimes of an Am Hunter.* 1905. Scribner. 1/260. sgn. 369 p. half leather. VG. H5. $1,350.00

ROOSEVELT, Theodore. *Ranch Life & Hunting Trail.* (1888). NY. Century. 1st ed/1st issue. ils Remington. tan buckram. rebacked. R3. $1,250.00

ROOSEVELT, Theodore. *Ranch Life & Hunting Trail.* 1978. Bonanza. reprint of 1888 orig. 8vo. ils Remington. 186 p. VG/VG. B11. $25.00

ROOSEVELT, Theodore. *Rough Riders.* 1900. np. xl. 16mo. 300 p. tan cloth. G. T3. $17.00

ROOSEVELT, Theodore. *Theodore Roosevelt's Diaries of Boyhood & Youth.* 1928. np. 12mo. 365 p. olive cloth. G. T3. $10.00

ROOSEVELT, Theodore. *Works of Theodore Roosevelt.* nd. Collier. 1 vol only. sgn. VG. B4. $575.00

ROOT, A.I. *ABC of Bee Culture.* 1895. Medina, OH. 62nd thousand. 428 p. cloth. VG. M20. $75.00

ROOT, Harvey W. *Tommy w/the Big Tents.* 1924. Harper. 1st ed. ils T Skinner. 202 p. VG. S10. $30.00

ROOTHAAN, A.R.P. *Meditationes et Instructiones Compendiosae Pro Missionibus.* 1879. Woodstock. 168 p. VG. C5. $20.00

ROPER, Anita. *15th Station: Theological Meditations on Human Existence.* 1967. NY. Herder. 108 p. VG. C5. $8.50

ROPER, Donald Malcolm. *Mr Justice Thompson & the Constitution.* 1987. NY. Garland. M11. $45.00

ROPER, Lanning. *Royal Gardens.* 1953. London. 1st ed. pls. 96 p. VG+/VG. B28. $20.00

ROPER, William. *Life of Sir Thomas Moore.* nd. Springfield. Templegate. 125 p. VG/wrp. C5. $7.50

ROPES, J.C. *Army Under Pope.* 1881. NY. 12mo. 229 p. G. T3. $25.00

ROQUELAURE, A.N.; see Rice, Anne.

RORABAUGH, W.J. *Alcoholic Republic: Am Tradition.* 1979. NY. Oxford. 1st ed. 8vo. 302 p. F/F. A2. $17.50

ROSA, Joseph G. *Gunfighter.* 1969. OK U. 12mo. VG. A8. $15.00

ROSALIA, Mary. *Child Psychology & Religion.* 1937. NY. Kenedy. 138 p. VG. C5. $8.50

ROSALIA, Mary. *One Inch of Splendor.* 1941. NY. Field Afar. 90 p. VG. C5. $10.00

ROSALIA, Mary. *Poor Little Millionairess.* 1959. NY. Pageant. 67 p. VG. C5. $8.50

ROSATI, Joseph. *Life of the Very Reverend Felix de Andreis, CM.* 1900. St Louis. Herder. 308 p. VG. C5. $20.00

ROSCHINI, Gabriel. *Virgin Mary in the Writings of Maria Valtorta.* 1986. Canada. Kolbe. 395 p. VG/wrp. C5. $15.00

ROSE, Alfred. *Register of Erotic Books.* 1965. NY. Jack Brussel. 1st ed. 398 p in 2 vols. A2/B20. $50.00

ROSE, Peter Q. *Ivies.* 1990. London. revised ed. 71 color photos. 180 p. M. B26. $11.00

ROSE, Phillis. *Jazz Cleopatra: Josephine Baker in Her Time.* 1989. Doubleday. 1st ed. VG/dj. N2. $10.00

ROSE, W.K. *Letters of Wyndham Lewis.* 1963. Norfolk. New Directions. F/NF. B2. $35.00

ROSE, Wendy. *Academic Squaw.* 1977. Marvin. Bl Cloud Quarterly. 1st ed. NF/stapled wrp. L3. $45.00

ROSE, Wendy. *Halfbreed Chronicles & Other Poems.* 1985. LA. W End. 1st ed. F/wrp. L3. $45.00

ROSE, Wendy. *Hopi Roadrunner Dancing.* 1973. Greenfield Review. magazine exchange review copy. NF/wrp. L3. $90.00

ROSE, William. *Surgical Treatment of Neuralgia of the 5th Nerve.* 1892. London. Bailliere. 85 p. orig cloth. G7. $295.00

ROSE. *Quick & Easy Strip Quilting.* 1989. np. ils. wrp. G2. $5.00

ROSE. *Quilting w/Strips & Strings.* 1983. np. ils. wrp. G2. $4.00

ROSELER, David. *Lawrence, Prince of Mecca.* 1927. Sydney, Australia. Cornstalk Pub. 1st ed. 227 p. G. M7. $45.00

ROSEN, Al. *Baseball & Your Boy.* 1967. World. 1st ed. F/VG. P8. $15.00

ROSEN, Kenneth. *Man To Send Rain Clouds.* (1974). NY. 1st ed. 178 p. NF/pict dj. D3. $12.50

ROSEN, Richard. *Fadeaway.* 1986. Harper. 1st ed. sgn. F/F. S5. $35.00

ROSEN, Ruth. *Jesus for Jews.* 1987. San Francisco. Messianic Jewish Perspective. 320 p. VG. C5. $8.50

ROSENBACH, Abraham Simon Wolf. *Three Centuries of Am Hist, 1493-1793.* 1944. Phil. Buchanan. 8vo. 62 p. wrp. H9. $85.00

ROSENBAUM, David. *Zaddik.* 1993. Mysterious. 1st ed. sgn. M/M. T2. $35.00

ROSENBAUM & STEVENS. *Giants of San Francisco.* 1963. Coward McCann. 1st ed. photos. F/VG. P8. $27.50

ROSENBERG, David. *Congregation.* 1987. Harcourt Brace. 526 p. VG. C6. $17.50

ROSENBERG, Joel. *Road to Ehvenor.* 1991. NY. ROC. 1st ed. Guardians of the Flame series. F/F. N3. $15.00

ROSENBERG, Joel. *Warrior Lives.* 1988. NY. NAL. 1st ed. Guardians of the Flame series. F/F. N3. $15.00

ROSENBERG, John M. *Story of Baseball.* 1964. Random. later ed. F/F. P8. $15.00

ROSENBERG, Stuart E. *Bridge to Brotherhood: Judaism's Dialogue w/Christianity.* 1961. Abelard Schuman. 178 p. VG/G. S3. $20.00

ROSENBERGER, Edward. *Outlines of Religion for Catholic Youth.* 1955. NY. Grady. Vol II only. VG. C5. $8.50

ROSENBLATT, Bernard A. *Am Bridge to the Israel Commonwealth.* 1959. FSC. 1st prt. 128 p. VG/VG. S3. $15.00

ROSENBLATT, Roger. *Children of War.* 1983. Doubleday/Anchor. 1st ed. 212 p. NF/dj. A7. $20.00

ROSENSTIEL. *Am Rugs & Carpets From the 17th Century to Modern Times.* 1978. np. cloth. G2. $25.00

ROSENSTONE, Robert A. *Romantic Revolutionary: Biography of John Reed.* (1975). Knopf. 1st ed. 430 p. dj. A7. $25.00

ROSENTHAL, Harold. *Baseball's Best Managers.* 1961. Nelson. 1st ed. VG/G. P8. $15.00

ROSENTHAL, Jacques. *Bibliotheca Medii Aevi Manuscripta.* 1925 & 1928. Munich. Rosenthal. 2 vols. 42 photographic facsimile pls. orig blk cloth. K1. $150.00

ROSENTHAL, Jon. *Antique Map Price Record & Handbook for 1993.* 1993. Amherst, MA. Kimmel. 352 p. O5. $36.00

ROSENTHAL & GELB. *One More Victim: Life & Death of a Jewish Nazi.* (1967). NAL. 1st ed. 8vo. 239 p. F/VG+. A2. $15.00

ROSENZWEIG, Saul. *Freud & Experimental Psychology...* 1986. St Louis/NY. Random House/McGraw Hill. thin 8vo. prt brds. G1. $17.50

ROSHWALD, Mordecai. *Level 7.* 1959. McGraw Hill. 1st ed. F/NF. B2. $30.00

ROSMARIN, Trude Weiss. *Hebrew Moses: Answer to Sigmund Freud.* 1939. Jewish BC. 64 p. G+/wrp. S3. $21.00

ROSNER, Fred. *Moses Maimonides' Commentary on the Mishnah...* 1975. NY. Feldheim. 235 p. VG+/G+. S3. $23.00

ROSS, Clarissa; see Ross, W.E.D.

ROSS, Dan; see Ross, W.E.D.

ROSS, Dana; see Ross, W.E.D.

ROSS, Edward. *S of Panama.* 1921. Century. ils/map. 396 p. F3. $10.00

ROSS, Isabel. *Margaret Fell: Mother of Quakerism.* 1949. Longman Gr. 1st ed. 8vo. 421 p. VG. V3. $15.00

ROSS, J.D. *Annual Report of Lighting Dept Seattle, WA for Yr 1911.* (1912). Seattle. Lowman Hanford. tall 8vo. 123 p. rare. B20. $125.00

ROSS, J.E. *Ethics.* 1938. NY. Devin Adair. 365 p. VG. C5. $7.50

ROSS, Maggie. *Seasons of Death & Life.* 1990. Harper. 211 p. VG. C5. $12.50

ROSS, Marilyn; see Ross, W.E.D.

ROSS, Mary. *Writings & Cartography of Herbert Eugene Bolton.* 1932. np. offprint. NF. O6. $20.00

ROSS, Patricia. *Made in Mexico.* 1952. Knopf. 1st ed. 329 p. F3. $20.00

ROSS, W. Gillies. *Arctic Whalers, Icy Seas.* (1985). Tor. 1st ed. oblong 4to. 263 p. F/dj. A17. $25.00

ROSS. *Pop-Up Book of Nonsense Verse.* 1989. 12 p. VG. A4. $30.00

ROSSETTI, Christina. *Poems.* (1910). London. Blackie. ils Florence Harrison. teg. wht cloth. VG+. F1. $250.00

ROSSETTI, Christina. *Poems.* 1930. Montgomeryshire. Gregynog. 1/300. gilt calf/ Cockerel marbled brds. NF. F1. $350.00

ROSSITER, Clinton. *Grand Convention, 1787.* 1966. np. index. 443 p. O7. $9.50

ROSSO, Julee. *Silver Palate Good Times Cookbook.* 1985. Worman Pub. 1st ed. ils SL Chase. VG/dj. A16. $15.00

ROSTEN, Leo. *Guide to the Religions of Am.* 1955. Simon Schuster. 276 p. VG. C5. $7.50

ROSTEN, Leo. *Leo Rosten's Treasury of Jewish Quotations.* 1972. McGraw Hill. 716 p. VG+/G+. S3. $22.00

ROSTEN, Leo. *Silky! A Detective Story.* 1979. Harper Row. 1st ed. 240 p. VG+/G+. S3. $19.00

ROSTLUND, Erhard. *Fresh-Water Fish & Fishing in Native N Am.* 1952. CA U. 1st ed. inscr. sm 4to. 313 p. VG/wrp. D3. $35.00

ROSVALL, Tolvo David. *Mazarine Legacy.* 1969. Viking. 1st ed. 244 p. VG+/dj. M20. $8.50

ROSZAK, Theodore. *Person/Planet.* 1978. Doubleday/Anchor. 1st ed. rem mk. dj. A7. $15.00

ROSZAK, Theodore. *Where the Wasteland Ends.* 1972. Doubleday. ed/prt not stated. 492 p. dj. A7. $15.00

ROTENSTREICH, Nathan. *Jews & German Philosophy.* 1984. NY. Schocken. 266 p. VG. C5. $20.00

ROTERS, Eberhardt. *Berlin, 1910-33.* (1982). Rizzoli. 4to. 284 p. F/F. A7. $45.00

ROTH, Cecil. *House of Nasi: Duke of Naxos.* 1948. JPS. ils. 250 p. VG. S3. $25.00

ROTH, G.K. *Fijian Way of Life.* 1973. London/Melbourne/NY. Oxford. 2nd ed. 8vo. pls/map ep. NF/dj. W1. $18.00

ROTH, Henry. *Mercy of a Rude Stream.* 1994. St Martin. 1/150. sgn/#d. full leather. F/full leather slipcase. C4. $250.00

ROTH, Henry. *Nature's 1st Gr.* 1979. NY. Targ. 1/350. sgn. gr linen. F/sans. A11. $45.00

ROTH, Joseph. *Hotel Savoy.* 1986. Overlook. 1st ed. trans from German. F/F. A14. $25.00

ROTH, Joseph. *Radetzky March.* 1974. London. Allen Lane/Penguin. 1st revised ed. NF/NF. A14. $25.00

ROTH, M.P. *Juror & the General.* (1986). Morrow. 1st ed. 300 p. F/NF. A7. $25.00

ROTH, Philip. *Breast.* 1972. HRW. 1st ed. VG+/VG+. M20. $25.00

ROTH & SZYK. *Haggadah.* nd. Jerusalem. ils Szyk. VG. S3. $75.00

ROTHBERG, Abraham. *Sword of the Golern.* 1970. McCall. 1st ed. F/NF. F4. $15.00

ROTHENSTEIN, John. *Summer's Lease.* 1965. HRW. 1st ed. 260 p. F/VG. M7. $25.00

ROTHERY, Agnes. *Fitting Habitation.* 1944. Dodd Mead. inscr. 244 p. VG/fair. B10. $35.00

ROTHERY, Agnes. *Houses Virginians Have Loved.* (1954). NY. 1st ed. lg 8vo. 319 p. F/dj. A17. $15.00

ROTHERY, Agnes. *Iceland: New World Outpost.* 1948. Viking. 1st ed. 8vo. 241 p. VG/VG. A2. $15.00

ROTHMULLER, Aron. *Music of the Jews.* 1967. Yoseloff. new revised ed. 320 p. VG. C5. $15.00

ROTHSCHILD, Alonzo. *Lincoln: Master of Men, Study in Character.* 1906. Houghton Mifflin. 1st ed/2nd imp. 531 p. cloth. NF. M8. $45.00

ROTHSTEIN. *Lady of Fashion. Barbara Johnson's Album of Styles...* 1987. np. ils. cloth. G2. $75.00

ROTTIERS, Bernard. *Description des Monumens de Rhodes...* 1830. Brussels. Chez Mme Ve A Colinez. 4to. 428 p. 19th-century morocco. K1. $250.00

ROUAULT, Georges. *Divertissement.* (1943). Paris. Teriade. 1st ed. 1/1200. folio. 76 p. unbound/portfolio/wrp. B24. $325.00

ROUCEK, Joseph. *Slavonic Encyclopedia.* 1949. Philosophical Lib. 1445 p. VG. C5. $45.00

ROUCHE, Douglas. *Catholic Revolution.* 1968. McKay. 325 p. VG. C5. $8.50

ROUDINESCO, Elisabeth. *Jacques Lacan & Co: Hist of Psychoanalysis in France...* 1990. Chicago U. 1st ed. 766 p. VG/dj. G1. $35.00

ROUHAULT, Pierre Simon. *Traite des Playes de Tete.* 1720. Turin. Radix/Mairesse. 1st ed. woodcuts. 135 p. vellum. G7. $2,500.00

ROUMAIN, Jacques. *Masters of the Dew.* (1947). Reynal Hitchcock. BC. 180 p. poor dj. A7. $12.00

ROUNDS, Glen. *Day the Circus Came to Lone Tree.* 1973. Holiday House. 1st ed. F/VG. P2. $18.00

ROUNDS, Glen. *Swamp Life.* (1957). Englewood Cliffs. ils/index. 117 p. VG. A17. $8.50

ROUNDTREE, Helen C. *Pocahontas' People: Powhatan Indians of VA...* ca 1990. OK U. 404 p. F/F. B10. $25.00

ROURKE, Constance. *Audubon.* (1936). NY. 12 color pls. 342 p. F/dj. A17. $15.00

ROURKE, Constance. *Troupers of the Gold Coast; or, Rise of Lotta Crabtree.* 1928. Harcourt Brace. 8vo. 262 p. red brds. G. B11. $18.00

ROUSE, John E. *World Cattle III: Cattle of N Am.* 1973. Norman, OK. 1st ed. 650 p. H10. $45.00

ROUSE, Parke. *Cows on Campus. Williamsburg in Bygone Days.* 1973. Richmond. Dietz. 1st ed. sgn. 219 p. VG/VG. B11. $40.00

ROUSE, Parke. *Endless Harbor: Story of Newport News.* ca 1969. Hist Comm. ils/map. 84 p. VG. B10. $15.00

ROUSE, Parke. *Great Wagon Road From Phil to S NY.* 1973. McGraw Hill. later prt. Am Trails series. VG/VG. O3. $40.00

ROUSE, Parke. *Roll Chesapeake, Roll: Chronicles of Great Bay.* 1972. Norfolk Co Hist Soc. 158 p. VG/stiff wrp. B10. $15.00

ROUSSEAU, G.S. *Languages of the Psyche: Mind & Body in Enlightenment...* 1990. Berkeley, CA. 1st ed. 480 p. blk cloth. VG/dj. G1. $40.00

ROUSSEAU, Jean Jacques. *Du Contrat Social, ou Principes du Droit Politique.* 1762. Amsterdam. Marc Michel Rey. 12mo. 202 p. sheepskin/brds. VG+. B14. $100.00

ROUSTANG, Francois. *Autobiography of Martyrdom.* 1963. Herder. 342 p. VG. C5. $20.00

ROUSTANG, Francois. *Growth in the Spirit.* 1966. NY. Sheed. 250 p. VG. C5. $8.50

ROUVIER, Frederick. *Conquest of Heaven.* nd. Baltimore. Murphy. 182 p. blk leatherette. VG. C5. $10.00

ROVERE, Howard H. *Howe & Mummel: Their True & Scandalous Hist.* 1986 (1947). Arlington. reissue/1st thus ed. 169 p. clip dj. A7. $13.00

ROWAN, Carl T. *S of Freedom.* 1952. Knopf. 1st ed. inscr. F/VG. B4. $100.00

ROWAN, Richard Wilmer. *Terror in Our Time.* 1941. NY/Toronto. Longman Gr. 1st ed. orange cloth. NF/G. M7. $25.00

ROWCROFT, Charles. *Australian Crusoes; or, Adventures of an Eng Family...* 1869. NY. 12mo. ils/pls. 512 p. gilt red cloth. VG. H3. $40.00

ROWE, Henry K. *Centennial Hist (1837-1937) Colby Academy...* 1937. New London. Colby Jr College. dj. VG. N2. $12.50

ROWELL, John William. *Yankee Cavalrymen Through Civil War w/9th PA Cavalry.* 1971. Knoxville, TN. 1st ed. 280 p. VG/VG. M8. $35.00

ROWELL, Raymond J. *Ornamental Flowering Trees in Australia.* 1991. Kensington, New S Wales. 28 color photos. 321 p. M. B26. $35.00

ROWLAND, Dunbar. *Jefferson Davis, Constitutionalist: His Letters, Papers...* 1923. Jackson, MS. 1st ed. 10 vols. cloth. VG. M8. $650.00

ROWLAND-ENTWISTLE. *3-Dimensional Atlas of the World: Globe in a Book.* 1988. paper engineering by Paul Wilgress. F. A4. $40.00

ROWLANDSON, Thomas. *Medical Caricatures.* 1971. NY. Eds Medicina Rara. 1/2500. NF/clamshell box. G7. $200.00

ROWLANDSON, Thomas. *Poetical Sketches of Scarborough.* 1813. London. 1st ed. octavo. 21 hc pls. gilt burgundy morocco. VG. H5. $850.00

ROWLEY, H.H. *11 Yrs of Bible Bibliography.* ca 1957. Falcon's Wing. index. 804 p. H10. $35.00

ROWNTREE, John Stephenson. *Quakerism, Past & Present.* 1860. Phil. Longstreth. 12mo. 191 p. VG. V3. $15.00

ROWNTREE, John Wilhelm. *Man's Relation to God.* 1919. Phil. Friends Bookstore. Pennsbury series. 191 p. VG. C5. $10.00

ROWSOME, Frank Jr. *Bright & Glowing Place.* (1975). Brattleboro, VT. Stephen Greene. 1st ed. 8vo. 212 p. F/VG. A2. $8.50

ROY, Claude. *Into China.* 1955. London. Sidgwick. 1st ed. 8vo. 420 p. VG/dj. W1. $18.00

ROY, Gabrielle. *Cashier.* 1955. Toronto. McClelland Stewart. 1st ed. NF/NF. A14. $60.00

ROY, Gabrielle. *Garden in the Wind.* 1977. Toronto. McClelland Stewart. 1st ed. NF/VG+. A14. $25.00

ROY, Gabrielle. *Street of Riches.* 1957. Toronto. McClelland Stewart. 1st ed. trans from French. NF/VG+. A14. $60.00

ROY, Gabrielle. *Tin Flute.* 1947. Reynal Hitchcock. 1st Am ed. trans from French. VG+/G-. A14. $30.00

ROY, Gabrielle. *Where Nests the Water Hen.* 1951. Harcourt Brace. 1st Am ed. trans from French. VG+/VG. A14. $30.00

ROY, Jules. *St Nicolas Ier.* 1899. Paris. Lecoffre. French text. 173 p. VG. C5. $10.00

ROY, Rob. *Wonderful Cutouts of Oz.* 1985. Crown. 1st ed. VG/wrp. L1. $15.00

ROYAL ONTARIO MUSEUM. *Handweaving in Pioneer Canada.* 1971. Ontario. pb. G2. $8.50

ROYCE, James. *Man & His Nature.* 1961. McGraw Hill. 398 p. VG. C5. $8.50

ROYCE, Josiah. *Basic Writings of...* 1969. Chicago U. 2 vols. VG. C5. $60.00

ROYCE, Josiah. *Spirit of Modern Philosophy.* (1892). Houghton Mifflin. early prt. 519 p. F. S9. $20.00

ROYCE, Josiah. *World & the Individual.* 1901. Macmillan. 480 p. VG. C5. $20.00

ROYER, Fachon. *St Francis Solanus: Apostle to Am.* 1955. Paterson, NJ. St Anthony Guild. 207 p. VG. C5. $10.00

ROYKO, Mike. *I May Be Wrong But I Doubt It.* 1968. Chicago. Regnery. 1st ed. NF/NF. B2. $65.00

ROZ, Francisco. *Erroribus Nestorianorum.* 1928. Rome. Pontifical Instit. 40 p. VG/wrp. C5. $10.00

ROZWADOWSKI, Zdislaw. *50 Yrs of Breeding Pure Blood Arabian Hoses in Poland...* 1972. Warsaw. Sir Wm Farm. VG/VG. O3. $45.00

RUARK, Robert. *Grenadine Etching.* 1947. Doubleday. 1st ed. F/VG. F4. $35.00

RUARK, Robert. *Old Man & the Boy.* (1957). NY. 1st ed. ils Dower. F/dj. A17. $65.00

RUARK, Robert. *Poor No More.* 1959. NY. 1st ed. VG/VG. B5. $30.00

RUARK, Robert. *Uhuro.* (1962). NY. BC. F/dj. A17. $9.50

RUARK, Robert. *Use Enough Gun.* (1966). NY. 1st ed. photos. F/dj. A17. $45.00

RUBENSTEIN, Richard. *Cunning of Hist: Mass Death & the Am Future.* 1975. Harper Row. inscr. 113 p. VG/VG. S3. $20.00

RUBENSTEIN, Richard. *My Brother Paul.* 1972. Harper. 209 p. VG. C5. $10.00

RUBIE, Peter. *Werewolf.* 1991. Longmeadow. 1st ed. sgn. F/F. F4. $25.00

RUBIN, Cynthia Elyce. *Shaker Herbs: An Essay...* 1984. Northampton. Catawba Pr. miniature. 1/155. prt brds. F. H10. $165.00

RUBIN, Jonathan. *Barking Deer.* (1974). Braziller. 1st ed. dj. A7. $12.00

RUBIN, Vera. *Caribbean Studies: A Symposium.* 1960. Seattle, WA. 2nd prt. 123 p. F3. $15.00

RUBIN, William S. *Dada & Surrealist Art.* (19690. London. Thames Hudson. 60 handmtd color pls. 526 p. dj. K1. $275.00

RUBIO SANCHEZ, Manuel. *Historia del Anil o Xiquilite en Centro America.* (1976). San Salvador. 1st ed. 2 vols. wrp. F3. $20.00

RUCHAMES, Louis. *Abolitionists: Collection of Their Writings.* 1963. Putnam. dj. N2. $7.50

RUCHES, P.J. *Albanian Hist Folksongs 1716-1943.* 1967. Chicago. 8vo. 126 p. cloth. O2. $35.00

RUCIMAN, Steven. *Great Church in Captivity.* 1968. Cambridge. 1st ed. 8vo. 455 p. cloth. O2. $55.00

RUCKER, Rudy. *Wht Light.* 1980. London. 1st ed. sgn. F/glossy 8vo wrp. rare. A11. $135.00

RUDE, George. *Face of the Crowd.* (1988). Atlantic. Humanities. 1st ed. 271 p. as new/dj. A7. $25.00

RUDIN, A. James. *Prison or Paradise?* 1980. Phil. Fortress. 164 p. VG. C5. $8.50

RUDISCH, L.J. *Ceremonies of Holy Week.* 1921. Wagner. 51 p. VG. C5. $10.00

RUDKIN, Charles N. *Early CA Travels Series: Chronological Summary...* 1961. Glen Dawson. 1st ed. 1/250. 178 p. NF. B19. $50.00

RUDNICK, O.H. *Das Deutschtum St Paul's in Wort und Bild.* 1924. St Paul. 4to. photos/ads. 176 p. VG. A17. $20.00

RUE, Leonard Lee III. *Game Birds of N Am.* (1976). Outdoor Life. 3rd prt. 490 p. VG/taped dj. A17. $17.50

RUEFF, Jacob. *De Conceptu et Generatione Hominis...* 1554. Zurich. Chritophorus Froschouerus. 1st Latin ed. VG. H3. $8,500.00

RUETHER, Rosemary Radford. *Radical Kingdom.* 1970. Harper. 304 p. VG. C5. $15.00

RUF, Henry. *Religion, Ontotheology & Deconstruction.* 1989. NY. Paragon. 238 p. VG. C5. $25.00

RUFFIN, C. Bernard. *Days of the Martyrs: A Hist...* 1985. Huntington, IN. 232 p. VG/wrp. C5. $17.50

RUFFNER, William Henry. *Report on WA Territory.* 1889. NY. Seattle/Lake Shore/E Railway. 1st ed. 242 p. VG. D3. $125.00

RUGGLES, Eleanor. *Journey Into Faith...John Henry Newman.* ca 1948. Norton. 336 p. H10. $14.50

RUGOFF, Milton. *Beechers.* (1981). NY. 1st ed. 653 p. dj. A17. $15.00

RUHEN, Olaf. *Land of Dahori: Tales of New Guinea.* (1957). Lippincott. 1st ed. 8vo. 278 p. VG+/VG. A2. $15.00

RUHEN, Olaf. *Tangoroa's Godchild.* (1962). Little Brn. 1st ed. 8vo. 346 p. VG/VG. A2. $12.50

RUITENBEEK, Hendrik M. *1st Freudians.* 1973. NY. Aronson. 1st ed. blk cloth. VG/dj. G1. $20.00

RUIZ, Juan. *Libro de Buen Amor.* 1975. Madrid. Edilan. 1/5000. 2 vols. full calf. K1. $185.00

RUKEYSER, Muriel. *Traces of Thomas Hariot.* (1971). Random. 1st ed. 8vo. 366 p. F/VG. A2. $12.50

RULE, Jane. *Against the Season.* 1971. NY. McCall. 1st ed. VG+/VG+ clip. A14. $40.00

RULE, Jane. *Inland Passage.* 1985. Tallahassee, FL. Naiad. 1st ed. ils brds. NF/sans. A14. $20.00

RULE, Jane. *Young in One Another's Arms.* 1977. Doubleday. 1st ed. NF/VG+. A14. $25.00

RUMAKER, Michael. *Gringos & Other Stories.* nd (1967). NY. 1st Am ed. sgn. F/F. A11. $45.00

RUNBECK, Margaret Lee. *Our Miss Boo.* 1942. Appleton Century. 2nd ed. 226 p. VG/G. P2. $18.00

RUNCIE, Robert. *Seasons of the Spirit.* 1983. Grand Rapids. Eerdmans. 257 p. VG. C5. $8.50

RUNES, Dagobert. *Letters to My Teacher.* 1961. Philosophical Soc. 105 p. VG. C5. $7.50

RUNESTAM, Arvid. *Psychoanalysis & Christianity.* 1958. Rock Island, IL. Augustana. 194 p. VG. C5. $8.50

RUNG, Albert. *Clerical Courtesy.* 1940. Milwaukee. Bruce. 86 p. VG. C5. $15.00

RUNNING, John. *Honor Dance. Native Am Photographs.* 1985. Reno, NV. 1st ed. inscr. F/F. L3. $125.00

RUPORT, Arch. *Art of Cockfighting.* 1949. Devin Adair. 1st ed. 211 p. VG+/dj. M20. $75.00

RUSBY, Henry. *Jungle Memories.* 1933. Whittlesey House. 1st ed. 388 p. F3. $30.00

RUSCHE, Helda. *They Lived by Faith. Women in the Bible.* 1963. Baltimore. Helicon. 121 p. VG. C5. $10.00

RUSE, Gary Alan. *Gods of Cerus Major.* 1982. Doubleday. ARC. RS. F/F. N3. $15.00

RUSH, Benjamin. *Letters of Benjamin Rush.* 1951. Princeton, NJ. 1st ed. 2 vols. orange cloth. G1. $125.00

RUSH, Benjamin. *Sixteen Intro Lectures to Courses...Practices of Medicine...* 1811. Phil. Bradford Innskeep. 1st ed. 455 p. modern brn cloth. S9. $420.00

RUSH, Norman. *Mating.* 1991. Knopf. 1st ed. NF/NF. A14. $30.00

RUSH, Norman. *Mating.* 1991. NY. 1st ed. sgn. F/8vo wrp. A11. $45.00

RUSH, Norman. *Whites.* 1986. London. 1st Eng ed. sgn. F/F. A11. $50.00

RUSHDIE, Salman. *Jaguar Smile. Nicaraguan Journey.* (1987). Viking. 1st ed. 171 p. dj. F3. $15.00

RUSHDIE, Salman. *Midnight's Children.* 1981. Knopf. 1st ed. author's 2nd book. F/NF. L3. $150.00

RUSHDIE, Salman. *Satanic Verses.* 1988. London. Viking. correct 1st ed. F/F. B2. $250.00

RUSHDIE, Salman. *Shame.* 1983. Knopf. 1st Am ed. w/sgn bookplate. F/F. B2. $85.00

RUSHMORE, Jane P. *Further Footsteps Along the Quaker Way.* 1954. Phil Yearly Meeting. 12mo. 55 p. VG. V3. $10.00

RUSHTON, William. *WG Grace's Last Case.* 1984. London. Methuen. 1st ed. ils. F/F. S5. $30.00

RUSK, J.M. *Report of Secretary of Agriculture, 1891.* 1982. WA, DC. pls. 653 p. G/VG. B26. $27.50

RUSK, Ralph Leslie. *Literature of the Middle-W Frontier.* (1962). Frederick Ungar. 1st thus ed. 2 vols. F/VG clip. A18. $40.00

RUSKIN. *Quilt: Stories From the NAMES Project.* 1988. np. ils. wrp. G2. $22.95

RUSLING, James F. *Across Am; Or, Great W & the Pacific Coast.* 1874. Sheldon. 1st ed. 8vo. 503 p. maroon cloth. H9. $90.00

RUSS, Joanna. *Zanzibar Cat.* 1983. Arkham. 1st ed. as new. M2. $45.00

RUSS, Martin. *Last Parallel. A Marine's War Journal.* 1957. Rinehart. 1st ed. 8vo. 333 p. VG. W1. $16.00

RUSSELL, Alan. *Forest Prime Evil.* 1992. Walker. 1st ed. sgn. M/M. T2. $32.00

RUSSELL, Alan. *Hotel Detective.* 1994. Mysterious. 1st ed. sgn. M/M. T2. $23.00

RUSSELL, Alexander. *Aristocrats of the S Seas.* (1961). NY. Roy. 1st Am ed. 8vo. 190 p. F/G+. A2. $15.00

RUSSELL, Bertrand. *ABC of Relativity.* 1927. London. Kegan Paul. 3rd imp. 231 p. purple cloth. VG. S9. $10.00

RUSSELL, Bertrand. *Icarus or the Future of Science.* (1924). Dutton. 2nd prt. 12mo. bl cloth. VG. S9. $5.00

RUSSELL, Bertrand. *Mysticism & Logic.* 1950. London. Allen Unwin. 232 p. VG. C5. $10.00

RUSSELL, Bertrand. *Philosophy.* 1927. Norton. 1st ed. VG. M18. $25.00

RUSSELL, Bertrand. *Scientific Outlook.* 1931. London. Allen Unwin. 1st ed. 288 p. bl cloth. NF. S9. $20.00

RUSSELL, Bertrand. *War Crimes in Vietnam.* (1967). Monthly Review. stated 1st prt. 12mo. 178 p. F/F. A7. $35.00

RUSSELL, Bertrand. *Why I Am Not a Christian.* 1957. Simon Schuster. 266 p. VG/wrp. C5. $8.50

RUSSELL, Carl Parcher. *100 Yrs in Yosemite.* 1931. Stanford. 1st ed. 242 p. cloth. VG+. M8. $250.00

RUSSELL, Charles Edward. *A-Rafting on the MS.* 1928. Century. 1st ed. F/NF. B2. $100.00

RUSSELL, Charles M. *How the Buffalo Lost His Crown.* 1894. np. 1st ed. author's 1st book. 6 pls. orig brn buckram. VG. H5. $2,500.00

RUSSELL, Charles M. *Trails Plowed Under.* 1945. Doubleday Doran. 8vo. VG/G. A8. $30.00

RUSSELL, Daniel. *Preaching the Apocalypse.* 1935. Abingdon. 254 p. VG. C5. $8.50

RUSSELL, Diarmind. *Portable Irish Reader.* 1946. Viking. 233 p. VG. C5. $10.00

RUSSELL, Elbert. *Elbert Russell, Quaker: An Autobiography.* 1956. Jackson, TN. Friendly Pr. 8vo. 376 p. VG. V3. $15.00

RUSSELL, Eric Frank. *Deep Space.* 1954. Fantasy. 1st ed. VG/dj. M2. $80.00

RUSSELL, Eric Frank. *Deep Space.* 1954. Fantasy. ltd ed. 1/300. sgn/#d. F/dj. M2. $150.00

RUSSELL, Eric Frank. *Sinister Barrier.* 1948. Fantasy. 1st ed. NF/NF. M2. $100.00

RUSSELL, George. *Collected Poems.* 1928. London. Macmillan. later prt. sgn. NF. B4. $125.00

RUSSELL, Jeffrey Burton. *Witchcraft in the Middle Ages.* 1972. Ithaca. Cornell. 394 p. emb gray cloth. VG/dj. G1. $30.00

RUSSELL, John. *Meanings of Modern Art.* 1962. Metropolitan Mus. 12 vols. VG. C5. $125.00

RUSSELL, Letty. *Feminist Intrepretation of the Bible.* 1985. Phil. Westminster. 166 p. VG/wrp. C5. $8.50

RUSSELL, Loris S. *Heritage of Light: Lamps & Lighting in Early Canadian Home.* (1968). Toronto. 1st ed. sq 8vo. 344 p. F/fair. A2. $25.00

RUSSELL, Martin. *Daylight Robbery.* 1987. London. Collins. 1st ed. F/F. S5. $22.50

RUSSELL, Matthew. *Among the Blessed.* 1911. London. Longman. 215 p. VG. C5. $10.00

RUSSELL, Ray. *Bishop's Daughter.* 1981. Houghton Mifflin. 1st ed. Summerfield Saga series. NF/NF. N3. $15.00

RUSSELL, Ray. *Case Against Satan.* 1962. PB Lib. 1st ed/PBO. sgn. NF/unread. A11. $45.00

RUSSELL, Ray. *Princess Pamela.* 1979. Houghton Mifflin. 1st ed. F/F. N3. $45.00

RUSSELL, Ray. *Sardonicus & Other Stories.* 1961. NY. 1st ed/PBO. sgn. NF. A11. $45.00

RUSSELL, Richard Joel. *Land Forms of San Gorgonio Pass.* 1932. CA U. 1st ed. sm 4to. wrp. D3. $25.00

RUSSELL, Richard. *Dissertation Concerning Use of Sea Water in Diseases Glands.* 1753. Oxford. Fletcher. 2nd ed. 398 p. contemporary full calf. S9. $120.00

RUSSELL, Thomas H. *Panama Canal: World's Greatest Engineering Feat.* 1913. Chicago. 8vo. ils. tan cloth. F. H3. $20.00

RUSSELL, W. Clark. *Representative Actors.* ca 1870s. London. Warne. sm octavo. 36 pls. 496 p. aeg. marbled ep. VG. H5. $350.00

RUSSELL, W.H. *Christ the Leader.* 1937. Milwaukee. Bruce. 458 p. VG. C5. $8.50

RUSSELL, W.H. *My Diary N & S.* 1954. Harper. 2nd prt. 268 p. VG/VG. M8. $25.00

RUSSELL, William. *Scientific Horseshoeing.* 1907. Cincinnati. Krehbiel. O3. $95.00

RUSSELL. *Tapestry Handbook.* 1990. np. ils. cloth. G2. $27.00

RUSSELL. *Victorian Needlepoint.* 1989. np. 70 color photos/60 charts. cloth. G2. $20.00

RUSSO, J. Robert. *Amphetamine Abuse.* 1968. Springfield. Charles Thomas. 1st ed. F/NF. B2. $40.00

RUSSO, Richard. *Mohawk.* 1986. Vintage Contemporaries. PBO. sgn. F/ils wrp. A11. $50.00

RUSSOLI, Franco. *Picasso Vent Pochoirs.* 1955. Milano. ltd ed. folio. VG/dj. A1. $250.00

RUST, William J. *Kennedy in Vietnam.* (1985). Scribner. 1st ed. F/F. A7. $30.00

RUTH, Mrs. Babe. *Babe & I.* (1959). NJ. 2nd prt. index. 215 p. dj. A17. $10.00

RUTHERFORD, Ernest. *Radio-Activity.* 1905. Cambridge. 2nd ed. octavo. gilt gr cloth. NF. R3. $350.00

RUTHERFORD, Mildred. *S Must Have Her Rightful Place in Hist.* 1923. Athens, GA. 30 p. A6. $10.00

RUTHERFORD, Samuel. *Trial & Triumph of Faith...* 1840. Wheeling, VA. 1st ed. orig leather. G. D7. $55.00

RUTHERFORD & SMITH. *More Cowboy Shooting Stars.* 1992. Empire. 214 p. laminated brds. as new. C8. $25.00

RUTHVEN, Madeleine. *Summer Denial & Other Poems.* 1932. Primavera Pr. 1st ed. 1/304. 64 p. brds. VG. D3. $25.00

RUTHVEN, Malise. *Satanic Affair. Salman Rushdie & Rage of Islam.* 1990. London. Chatto Windus. 1st ed. 8vo. 134 p. NF/NF/clear plastic. M7. $25.00

RUTLAND, R.A. *George Mason, Reluctant Statesman.* ca 1961. Holt Rinehart/Colonial Williamsburg. ils. 123 p. VG/G. B10. $15.00

RUTLER, George. *Christ & Reason.* 1990. Christendom Pr. 211 p. VG/wrp. C5. $8.50

RUTMAN, Darret B. *Old Dominion. Essays on Thomas Perkins Abernethy.* 1964. Charlottesville. 1st ed. 200 p. VG/G. B11. $45.00

RUYSLINCK, Ward. *Reservation.* 1978. London. Peter Owen. 1st ed. F/NF. N3. $20.00

RYAN, Alan. *Perpetual Light.* 1982. Warner. SF BC. hc ed. F/F. F4. $10.00

RYAN, Arthur. *Perennial Philosophers.* 1946. Dublin. Clonmore. 71 p. VG. C5. $8.50

RYAN, David D. *Falls of the James.* (1975). William Byrd. 2nd ed. ils/map. 112 p. VG/VG-. B10. $18.00

RYAN, Dixie. *Stories of Champions & the Nat Arabian Shows 1958-64.* 1975. Ft Collins. 1/2000. VG/VG. O3. $45.00

RYAN, James. *Intro to Philosophy.* 1924. Macmillan. 309 p. VG. C5. $10.00

RYAN, John Fergus. *Redneck Bride.* 1982. Little Rock, AR. 1st ed. inscr. F/NF. A11. $85.00

RYAN, John. *Catholic Church & the Citizen.* 1928. Macmillan. 94 p. VG. C5. $8.50

RYAN, John. *Maggie Murphy.* 1951. Norton. 224 p. VG. C5. $12.50

RYAN, Kenneth. *Catholic Digest Christmas Book.* 1977. St Paul. Carillon. 352 p. VG. C5. $10.00

RYAN, Kenneth. *What More Would You Like To Know About the Church?* 1978. St Paul. Carillon. 261 p. VG. C5. $10.00

RYAN, Mary Perkins. *Key to the Psalms.* 1957. Chicago. Fides. VG. C5. $8.50

RYAN, Mary Perkins. *Perspective for Renewal.* 1960. Collegeville. Liturgical Pr. 93 p. VG. C5. $7.50

RYAN, Patrick. *Soldier Priest Talks to Youth.* 1963. Random. 205 p. VG.C5. $8.50

RYBROOK, Gregory. *Eucharist & Education.* 193335. NY. Benziger. 109 p. VG. C5. $10.00

RYDER, H.D. *Catholic Controversey.* 1882. London. Burns Oates. 288 p. VG. C5. $15.00

RYDER, John. *Suite of Fleurons; or, Preliminary Enquiry...Flowers.* 1957. Boston. Branford. sm octavo. 54 p. NF. B24. $50.00

RYDER, Jonathan; see Ludlum, Robert.

RYKEN, Leland. *Worldly Saints: Puritans As They Really Were.* 1986. Grand Rapids. Academy Books. 281 p. VG. C5. $15.00

RYLANDER, John V. *Middle-E Crisis in Perspective.* 1974. Gibbs Pub. 134 p. VG+/VG. S3. $15.00

RYNNE, Xavier. *Letters From Vatican City.* 1963. Farrar Straus. 289 p. VG. C5. $10.00

RYUS, William H. *Second William Penn.* (1913). KS City. 1st ed. 176 p. VG+/pict wrp. D3. $35.00

SABA, Umberto. *Ernesto.* 1987. London. Carnanet. 1st ed. trans from Italian. NF/NF. A14. $20.00

SABETTI, Aloysio. *Compendium Theologiae Moralis.* 1931. NY. Pustet. 1168 p. VG. C5. $12.50

SABIN, Edwin L. *Desert Dust.* 1922. Jacobs. 12mo. fair. A8. $10.00

SABIN, Edwin L. *Gold.* nd. Hargens Macrae Smith. 1st ed. VG. V2. $12.00

SABIN, Edwin L. *Opening the W w/Lewis & Clark.* 1917. Lippincott. 12mo. G+. A8. $25.00

SABIN, Edwin L. *Range & Trail.* 1910. Crowell. 12mo. G+. A8. $22.50

SABIN, Edwin L. *Rose of Santa Fe.* 1923. Hutchinson. 12mo. fair. A8. $10.00

SABIN, Edwin L. *Wild Men of the Wild W.* 1929. Crowell. 8vo. G. A8. $50.00

SABIN, Edwin L. *With George WA Into the Wilderness.* 1924. Lippincott. 12mo. fair. A8. $10.00

SABOURIN, Leopold. *Bible & Christ.* 1980. NY. Alba. 188 p. VG. C5. $8.50

SACHAR, Howard. *Course of Modern Jewish Hist.* 1958. Cleveland. World. 617 p. VG. C5. $15.00

SACHET, Marie-Helene. *Flora & Vegetation of Clipperton Island.* 1962. San Francisco. ils/photos/map. 59 p. VG/wrp. B26. $14.00

SACHS, A.S. *World That Passes.* 1943. Phil. Jewish Pub Soc. 228 p. VG. C5. $8.50

SACHS, Bernard. *Road From Sharpeville.* (1961). Marzani Munsell. 190 p. wrp. A7. $16.00

SACHS, Paul J. *Modern Prts & Drawings.* 1954. Knopf. BC. dj. N2. $10.00

SACK, John. *Fingerprint: Uncommon Autobiography.* (1982). Random. 230 p. F/F. A7. $25.00

SACK, John. *Man-Eating Machine.* (1973). FSG. 1st ed. NF/dj. A7. $30.00

SACK, John. *Report From Practically Nowhere: Uproarious Account...* 1959. Harper. G+/poor. N2. $7.50

SACKS, Janet. *Visions of the Future.* 1976. Chartwell. 1st ed. NF/dj. M2. $12.00

SACKVILLE-WEST, Vita. *St Joan of Arc.* 1938. Doubleday. 395 p. VG. C5. $10.00

SADAT, Jehan. *Woman of Egypt.* 1987. Simon Schuster. 1st ed. dj. N2. $6.50

SADLER, Barry. *Moi: Novel of the Vietnam War.* (1977). Nashville. Aurora. 1st ed. 214 p. F/dj. A7. $50.00

SADLER, M.F. *Epistles of St Paul to the Galatians, Ephesians...* 1895. London. George Bell. 323 p. VG. C5. $8.50

SADLER, Mark; see Lynds, Dennis.

SADLER, V.P. *Recollections of a Quiet Life...William Joseph Sadler.* 1959. Pella Chronicle. 178 p. VG. B10. $12.00

SAFFORD, James M. *Geology of TN.* 1869. Nashville. xl. thick 8vo. pls. 451 p. pebbled brn cloth. H9. $295.00

SAFFORD, Mrs. Henry G. *Golden Jubilee.* ca 1925. NY. 234 p. VG. C5. $20.00

SAFFORD, William H. *Life of Harman Blennerhassett.* 1850. Chillicothe. 1st ed. 239 p. cloth. M1. $125.00

SAFFORD, William H. *Life of Harman Blennerhassett.* 1853. Cincinnati. 2nd prt. 239 p. G. B28. $65.00

SAFFORD, William H. *Life of Harman Blennerhassett.* 1859. Cincinnati. 3rd prt. 239 p. rebound half leather. VG. D7. $85.00

SAFFORD. *Am's Quilts & Coverlets.* 1972. np. ils. cloth. G2. $25.00

SAFRAI & STERN. *Jewish People in the 1st Century: Hist, Geog, Political...* 1974. Fortress. vol 1 of 2. 560 p. VG+. S3. $28.00

SAGAN, Francoise; see Quoirez, Francoise.

SAGARIN, Edward. *Anatomy of Dirty Words.* 1962. Lyle Stuart. VG/dj. A16. $7.00

SAGENDORPH, Kent. *MI: Story of the U.* 1948. NY. 1st ed. 384 p. dj. A17. $15.00

SAGREDO, Giovanni. *Memorie Istoriche de Monarchi Ottomani di...* 1684 (1673). Bologna. 4to. 787 p. contemporary vellum. O2. $900.00

SAHW, Richard J. *Field Guide to Vascular Plants of Grand Teton Nat Park...* 1976. Logan. ils/pls/map. 301 p. VG+/dj. B26. $25.00

SAID, Edward. *Question of Palestine.* 1929. Time Books. 265 p. VG. C5. $10.00

SAINER, A.L. *Judge Chuckles.* 1935. NY. Ad Pr. M11. $25.00

SAINSBURY, Noel. *Fighting Five.* 1934. Cupples Leon. 1st ed. VG. M2. $10.00

SAINT, H.F. *Memoirs of an Invisible Man.* 1987. Harmondsworth. Viking. 1st British ed. F/F. N3. $25.00

SAINT ALBANS, Duchess of. *Where Time Stood Still: Portrait of Oman.* (1980). London. Quartet. 1st ed. 8vo. 242 p. F/F. A2. $12.50

SAINT CLAIR, William. *Lord Elgin & the Marbles.* 1967. London. 8vo. 309 p. cloth. scarce. O2. $45.00

SAINT DOMINIC, Sisters of. *Liturgical Meditations for the Entire Yr.* 1961. London. Herder. 2 vols. VG. C5. $25.00

SAINT EXUPERY, Antoine. *Little Prince.* 1943. NY. Reynal Hitchcock. 1st ed. trans K Woods. 91 p. peach brds. VG/torn. D1. $300.00

SAINT GAUDENS, Homer. *Am Artist & His Times.* 1941. Dodd Mead. 1st ed. 323 p. cloth. VG/tattered. M20. $20.00

SAINT HIPPOLYTE, Auger. *Republic of San Marino.* 1880. Cambridge, MA. private prt. 1st Am ed. 12mo. 170 p. A2. $65.00

SAINT JOHN, Bruce. *John Sloan.* 1971. Praeger. Am Art & Artists series. 156 p. cloth. dj. D2. $50.00

SAINT JOHN, David; see Hunt, E. Howard.

SAINT JOHN, Henry. *Essays in Christian Unity.* 1955. Westminster. Newman. 144 p. VG. C5. $8.50

SAINT JOHN, Philip. *Rockets to Nowhere.* 1954. Winston. 1st ed. VG. M2. $15.00

SAINT PAUL, Mother. *Mater Christi: Meditations on Our Lady.* 1920. London. Longman. 127 p. VG. C5. $10.00

SAINT PAUL, Mother. *Passio Christi.* 1938. London. Longman. 183 p. VG. C5. $10.00

SAINT PAUL, Mother. *Simple Meditations.* 1934. NY. O'Toole. 253 p. VG. C5. $10.00

SAINT PAUL, Mother. *Spiritual Readings.* 1944. NY. Longman. 308 p. VG. C5. $10.00

SAINT PAUL, Mother. *Vita Christi.* 1935. London. Longman. 148 p. VG. C5. $10.00

SALAMAGKA, D. *Peripatoi sta Giannina.* 1956. Ioannina. 8vo. ils. 167 p. wrp. O2. $15.00

SALAMAN, Malcolm C. *New Woodcut.* 1930. London. Studio. special spring number ed. 176 p. gilt gray cloth. NF/dj. F1. $150.00

SALAZAR, Adolfo. *Music in Our Time.* 1946. Norton. 367 p. VG. C5. $8.50

SALES, Lorenzo. *Jesus Appeals to the World.* 1971. NY. Alba. 255 p. VG. C5. $10.00

SALET, Gaston. *Plus Pres de Dieu.* 1960. Lethielleux. French text. 3 vols. VG. C5. $15.00

SALIBI, Kamal. *Bible Came From Arabia.* 1985. London. Cape. 223 p. VG. C5. $20.00

SALIH, Halil I. *Cyprus: Impact of Diverse Nationalism on the State.* 1978. AL U. 8vo. ils. 203 p. cloth. dj. O2. $20.00

SALINGER, J.D. *Catcher in the Rye.* 1951. Little Brn. 1st ed. author's 1st book. Peter deVries' copy. VG/VG. L3. $3,000.00

SALINGER, J.D. *Kit Book for Soldiers, Sailors & Marines.* 1943. Consolidated Book Pub. 1st ed. worn. E3. $75.00

SALINGER, J.D. *Nine Stories.* 1953. Little Brn. 1st ed. author's 2nd book. NF/custom clamshell box. L3. $1,500.00

SALINGER, J.D. *Raise High the Roof Beam, Carpenters & Seymour, an Intro.* (1959). Little Brn. 1st ed/2nd issue. VG/dj. A7. $60.00

SALINGER, J.D. *Raise High the Roof Beam, Carpenters & Seymour, an Intro.* (1959). Little Brn. 1st ed/3rd issue. F/F. C4. $40.00

SALINGER, J.D. *Raise High the Roof Beam, Carpenters & Seymour, an Intro.* 1963. London. Heinemann. 1st ed. F/VG. B2. $60.00

SALISBURY, Harrison E. *China Diary.* 1973. NY. Walker. 1st ed. 8vo. 210 p. NF/dj. W1. $16.00

SALISBURY & SALISBURY. *Here Rolled the Covered Wagons.* (1948). Seattle, WA. Superior. 1st/ltd ed. sgns. 4to. 256 p. F/F-. A2. $35.00

SALISBURY & SALISBURY. *Two Captains W: Hist Tour of Lewis & Clark Trail.* 1950. Superior Pub. 1st ed. after ltd ed of 350. 4to. 235 p. F. T8. $30.00

SALK, Erwin A. *Layman's Guide to Negro Hist.* (1967). Ramparts/McGraw Hill. new enlarged ed. 196 p. VG+/dj. A7. $25.00

SALLUSTIUS CRISPUS, Caius. *L'Historia di C Crispo Sallustio Nuovamente...Tradotta.* 1550. Florence. Torrentino. 1st ed this trans. 8vo. 282 p. early vellum. K1. $475.00

SALM, C. Luke. *Studies in Salvation Hist.* 1964. Prentice Hall. 236 p. VG/wrp. C5. $8.50

SALOME, Mary. *Community School Visitor.* 1928. Milwaukee. Bruce. 190 p. VG. C5. $15.00

SALTEN, Felix. *Bambi's Children.* 1939. Bobbs Merrill. 1st ed. G/dj. M18. $45.00

SALTEN, Felix. *Bambi.* 1931. Grosset Dunlap. ils Kurt Wiese. G/fair. L1. $13.50

SALTEN, Felix. *Bambi.* 1942. Grosset Dunlap. Disney movie tie-in. NF/dj. C8. $75.00

SALTEN, Felix. *Bambi. A Life in the Woods.* 1928. NY. 1st Am prt. 12mo. ils Kurt Wiese. 392 p. F/G glassine. H3. $75.00

SALTEN, Felix. *Bambi. A Life in the Woods.* 1928. NY. 1st Eng-language ed. ils Kurt Wise. pict brds. VG. B14. $75.00

SALTEN, Felix. *Forest World.* 1942. Bobbs Merrill. 1st ed. G/dj. M18. $45.00

SALTEN, Felix. *Peri.* 1938. Indianapolis. 1st ed. 228 p. red cloth. F/fair. H3. $40.00

SALTER, Elizabeth. *Daisy Bates.* 1972 (1971). NY. CMG. 1st Am ed. 8vo. 266 p. VG/VG. A2. $17.50

SALTER, James. *Arm of Flesh.* 1961. NY. Harper. 1st ed. sgn. author's 2nd book. VG/VG. L3. $350.00

SALTER, James. *Dusk & Other Stories.* 1988. San Francisco. 1st ed. sgn. F/F. A11. $45.00

SALTER, James. *Dusk & Other Stories.* 1990. London. Cape. ARC. RS. F/dj. C4. $40.00

SALTER, James. *Dusk.* 1988. N Point. AP. F/prt burnt-orange wrp. C4. $35.00

SALTER, James. *Sport & a Pastime.* 1967. Doubleday/Paris Review. 1st ed. F/NF. B2. $60.00

SALTER, James. *Sport & a Pastime.* 1987. London. Cape. 1st ed. F/F. C4. $40.00

SALTER, James. *Still Such.* 1992. NY. Drenttel. 1/200. sgn. F. C4. $55.00

SALTER, Lord. *Memoirs of a Public Servant.* 1945. London. Faber. 1st ed. 224 p. gilt coral cloth. VG+/VG/clear plastic. M7. $55.00

SALTER, W.M. *Nietzsche the Thinker.* 1968. NY. Ungar. 538 p. VG. C5. $20.00

SALVA, William. *Divine Mysteries.* nd. Coral Gables. Knights of the King. 189 p. wrp. C5. $8.50

SALZMAN, Mark. *Iron & Silk.* 1986. Random House. AP. sgn. author's 1st book. F/wrp/NF dj. L3. $350.00

SALZMAN, Mark. *Iron & Silk.* 1987. London. Hamish Hamilton. 1st ed. sgn. F/F. L3. $125.00

SAMPSON, Emma Speed. *Billy & the Major.* 1918. Reilly Britton. 1st ed. ils William Donahey. gilt red cloth. M5. $30.00

SAMPSON, James Y. *Selected Obstetrical & Cynaecological Works...* 1871. Appleton. xl. 852 p. rebacked. G7. $125.00

SAMPSON, Tom. *Cultivating the Presence.* 1977. NY. Crowell. 212 p. VG. C5. $8.50

SAMUELS, Edward A. *With Fly-Rod & Camera.* 1890. NY. Forest Stream. 150 pls. 477 p. NF. B14. $65.00

SAMUELS, Lee. *Hemingway Checklist.* 1951. Scribner. 1/750. F/NF. B2. $100.00

SAMUELS, Ruth. *Pathways Through Jewish Hist.* 1970. KTAV. revised ed. sm 4to. 404 p. VG+. S3. $15.00

SAMUELS & SAMUELS. *Contemporary W Artists.* 1985. Bonanza. ils. 596 p. F/NF. B19. $60.00

SAMWELL, David. *Capt Cook & HI: A Narrative.* 1957. San Francisco/London. Magee/ Edwards. reprint 1786 London ed. 1/750. M. O6. $125.00

SANBORD, M. *Robert E Lee.* 1966. np. ils/index. 353 p. NF. O7. $12.50

SANBORN, B.X.; see Ballinger, Bill.

SANCHEZ, Thomas. *Disputationum de Sancto Matrimonii Sacramento...* 1625. Venice. Juntas. folio. 3 vols in 2. modern vellum over brds. K1. $300.00

SANCHEZ, Thomas. *Native Notes From Land of Earthquake & Fire.* 1979. Inverness, CA. 1/250. sgn/#d. ils/sgn Stephanie Sanchez. NF/wrp. A11. $40.00

SANCHEZ, Thomas. *Native Notes From the Land of Earthquake & Fire.* 1979. Inverness, CA. Sandpiper. 1/25. presentation. F/saddle-stiched wrp. L3. $100.00

SANCHEZ, Thomas. *Zoot-Suit Murders.* 1978. Dutton. 1st ed. VG/dj. M18. $20.00

SANCHEZ-SAAVEDRA, E.M. *Description of the Country: VA's Cartographers & Their Maps.* 1975. VSL. w/9 facsimile maps. 130 p. VG. B10. $175.00

SAND, Froma. *My Son Africa.* (1965). Sherbourne Pr. 255 p. clip dj. A7. $15.00

SANDBERG, Karl. *At the Crossroads of Faith & Reason.* 1966. Tucson, AZ. 125 p. VG. C5. $15.00

SANDBERG, Sara. *Mama Made Minks.* 1954. Doubleday. 182 p. VG/G+. S3. $28.00

SANDBURG, Carl. *Abraham Lincoln.* 1926-1939. Scribner. Sangamon ed. 6 vols. emb red bdg. NF. E5. $75.00

SANDBURG, Carl. *Abraham Lincoln...* 1959. Worchester. St Onge. miniature. 1/2000. F. H10. $125.00

SANDBURG, Carl. *Abraham Lincoln: The Prairie Yrs & War Yrs.* 1954. np. 1 vol issue. index. 762 p. F. O7. $12.50

SANDBURG, Carl. *Abraham Lincoln: The War Yrs.* 1939. HBW. 1st trade ed. 4 vols. cloth. NF-. M8. $250.00

SANDBURG, Carl. *Always the Young Strangers.* 1953. NY. 1st ed. inscr/dtd 1953. turquoise cloth. VG+. A11. $45.00

SANDBURG, Carl. *Am Songbag.* (1927). NY. orig ed. attached sgn on fly. 495 p. red cloth. VG. D3. $75.00

SANDBURG, Carl. *Billy Sunday & Other Poems.* 1993. Harcourt Brace. UP. F/wrp. B4. $30.00

SANDBURG, Carl. *Billy Sunday & Other Poems.* 1993. Harcourt Brace. 1st ed. F/F. C4. $20.00

SANDBURG, Carl. *Breathing Tokens.* 1978. NY. 1st ed. edit M Sandburg. F/F. V1. $20.00

SANDBURG, Carl. *Chicago Poems.* 1916. Holt. 1st issue (ads dtd 3/16). VG/VG. Q1. $750.00

SANDBURG, Carl. *Cornhuskers.* 1918. Holt. 1st ed/2nd state. VG/dj. M18. $125.00

SANDBURG, Carl. *Potato Face.* 1930. Harcourt Brace. 1st ed. F/F. C4. $85.00

SANDBURG, Carl. *Steichen, the Photographer.* 1929. Harcourt Brace. 1/925. sgn Sandberg/Steichen. NF/sans. Q1. $850.00

SANDBURG, Helga. *To a New Husband.* 1970. NY. 1st ed. inscr/sgn. photos. VG. V1. $20.00

SANDEN, O.E. *Bible in the Age of Science.* 1946. Chicago. Moody. 141 p. VG. C5. $8.50

SANDERS, Alvin H. *At the Sgn of the Stock Yard Inn...* 1915. Chicago. 1st ed. xl. 12mo. 322 p. VG. D3. $35.00

SANDERS, Alvin H. *Cattle of the World...Paintings by Edward Miner...* 1926. Nat Geog Soc. hc. VG. O3. $85.00

SANDERS, Alvin H. *Story of the Herefords.* 1914. Chicago. 1st ed. xl. 1087 p. pict cloth. VG. D3. $50.00

SANDERS, Charles Richard. *Strachey Family 1588-1932: Their Writings & Literary Assns.* 1953. Duke. 1st ed. 337 p. cloth. NF/NF. M8. $45.00

SANDERS, Daniel Clark. *Hist of the Indian Wars...Particularly in New Eng.* 1812. Montpelier, VT. Wright Silbey. 1st ed. 12mo. 320p. scarce. K1. $1,000.00

SANDERS, Dori. *Her Own Place.* 1993. Algonquin. 1st ed. F/F clip. A13. $35.00

SANDERS, Dori. *Her Own Place.* 1993. Algonquin. 1st ed. sgn. F/F. B3. $40.00

SANDERS, Ed. *Tales of Beatnik Glory.* 1975. NY. Stonehill. 1st ed. F/NF. B2. $30.00

SANDERS, J.A. *Old Testament in the Cross.* 1961. Harper. 143 p. VG. C5. $8.50

SANDERS, J.M. *Crystal Sphere; Its Force & Its Beings: or, Reflections...* 1857. London. Hippolyte Bailliere. 1st ed. 12mo. 205 p. aeg. bl cloth. H5. $100.00

SANDERS, Jacquin. *Draft & the Vietnam War.* (1966). Walker. 156 p. VG/VG. A7. $30.00

SANDERS, Lawrence. *2nd Deadly Sin.* 1977. Putnam. 1st ed. VG. C5. $10.00

SANDERS, Nicholas. *People of the Jaguar.* (1989). London. Souvenir. 1st ed. 176 p. dj. F3. $25.00

SANDERS, Sol. *Mexico: Chaos on Our Doorstep.* 1986. Lanham. Madison Books. 8vo. 222 p. red cloth. M/M. P4. $30.00

SANDERSON, Ivan T. *Monkey Kingdom: Guide to Primates.* 1957. Hanover. 4to. ils. VG. N2. $8.50

SANDERSON, Ivan. *Animal Treasure.* 1937. NY. 1st ed. 325 p. dj. A17. $10.00

SANDMEL, Samuel. *Jewish Understanding of the New Testament.* 1956. NY. U Pub. 333 p. VG. C5. $12.50

SANDMEL, Samuel. *Judaism & Christian Beginnings.* 1978. NY. Oxford. 333 p. VG. C5. $12.50

SANDOZ, Mari. *Old Jules.* 1935. Little Brn. 12mo. VG. A8. $20.00

SANDOZ, Mari. *Son of the Gamblin' Man.* 1960. Clarkson Potter. 1st ed. G/dj. A16. $25.00

SANDWELL, Helen B. *Valley of Color Days.* 1924. Little Brn. 1st ed. ils Alice Bolam Preston. VG+. M5. $45.00

SANDYS, William. *Christmastide.* nd. (1852). London. Smith. octavo. 9 tinted pls. 327 p. full red calf. NF. H5. $300.00

SANDYS & VAN DYKE. *Upland Game Birds.* 1902. NY. 1st ed. 429 p. VG. A17. $35.00

SANFORD, Alexander. *Pastoral Medicine.* 1905. NY. Wagner. 332 p. VG. C5. $15.00

SANFORD, John. *Ministry Burnout.* 1982. NY. Paulist. 117 p. VG. C5. $8.50

SANFORD, John. *Rules of Prey.* (1989). NY. Putnam. ARC. F/wrp. B9. $20.00

SANFORD, John. *Shadow Prey.* (1990). Putnam. ARC. F/wrp. B9. $20.00

SANFORD, Leonard C. *Waterfowl Family.* 1903. NY. 1st ed. 598 p. VG. A17. $35.00

SANFORD, Louis. *Province of the Pacific.* 1949. Phil. Church Hist Soc. 187 p. VG. C5. $12.50

SANFORD & SANFORD. *Healing the Wounded Spirit.* 1985. S Plainfield, NJ. Bridge. 473 p. VG. C5. $8.50

SANGER, L.T. *Report on Census of Cuba, 1899.* 1900. WA. 8vo. 786 p. gilt brn cloth. VG. H3. $250.00

SANGER, L.T. *Report on the Census of Porto Rico, 1899* 1900. WA. 1st census following Spanish-Am War. 8vo. 417 p. VG. H3. $150.00

SANGER, William W. *Hist of Prostitution: Its Extent, Causes & Effects...* 1858. NY. 1st ed. inscr. 685 p. G. G1. $175.00

SANKEY-JONES, Nancy E. *Bibliography of Theodore Schroeder...* 1934. Cos Cob. self pub. 24 p. self wrp. H10. $15.00

SANSOM, Katherine. *Living in Tokyo.* 1937. Harcourt Brace. 1st ed. 184 p. VG. W1. $25.00

SANSON, Henry. *Memoirs of the Sansons.* 1881 (1876). Chatto Windus. 504 p. mauve cloth. G1. $40.00

SANSON D'ABBEVILLE, Nicolas. *L'Asie en Plvsieurs Cartes Novelles...* 1658. Paris. Chez L'Autheur. 17 double-p color maps. full leather. NF. O6. $4,000.00

SANTANER, Marie-Abdon. *God in Search of Man.* 1968. Westminster. Newman. 218 p. VG. C5. $8.50

SANTEE, Ross. *Apache Land.* 1947. Scribner. 1st ed. 8vo. w/orig sgn sketch on front ep. NF/dj. K1. $375.00

SANTEE, Ross. *Cowboy.* 1928. Cosmopolitan. 1st ed. ils. NF. A18. $35.00

SANTEE, Ross. *Cowboy.* 1928. NY. Cosmopolitan. presentation ed. w/3 orig drawings. VG/clamshell case. H5. $1,750.00

SANTEE, Ross. *Dog Days.* 1955. Scribner. 1st ed. ils. F/NF. A18. $40.00

SANTEE, Ross. *Hardrock & Silver Sage.* 1951. Scribner. ne. ils Santee. F/VG. A18. $30.00

SANTEE, Ross. *Rummy Kid Goes Home.* (1965). Hastings. 1st ed. ils. F/NF clip. A18. $30.00

SANTEE, Ross. *Russ: Cowboy of the Old W.* 1950. Scribner. 1st ed under this title. VG/clip. B9. $35.00

SANTIAGO, Danny. *Famous All Over Town.* 1983. Simon Schuster. 1st ed. author's 1st book. F/F. A14. $40.00

SANTINI, Piero. *Forward Impulse.* 1936. Huntington. 1st ed. 1/950. VG. O3. $58.00

SANTOLI, Al. *Everything We Had.* (1981). Random. 1st ed. 265 p. dj. A7. $16.00

SANTOLI, Al. *To Bear Any Burden.* (1985). Dutton. 1st ed. 367 p. F/F. A7. $30.00

SANTOVENIA, Emeterio S. *Memorial Book of the Inauguration of ME Plaza at Havana.* 1928. Havana. 4to. 200 p. VG/self wrp. E5. $65.00

SANTUCCI, Luigi. *La Donna con la Bocca Aperta.* 1980. Verona. 1/110. sgn Santucci/Tadini. 45 p. M/chemise/slipcase. B24. $550.00

SANTUCCI, Luigi. *Meeting Jesus: New Way to Christ.* 1971. Herder. 222 p. VG. C5. $8.50

SANUTO, Livio. *Geografia Dell'Africa.* 1965. Amsterdam. Theatrvm Orbis Terrarvm. facsimile Venice 1588 ed. M/dj. O6. $325.00

SANZ, Carlos. *Henry Harrisse, Principe de los Americanistas...* 1958. Madrid. M/wrp. O6. $100.00

SAPERSTEIN, Alan. *Mom Kills Kids & Self.* 1979. Macmillan. 1st ed. author's 1st book. F/F. F4. $25.00

SARASON, Seymour B. *Making of an Am Psychologist.* 1988. San Francisco. Jossey-Bass. presentation. 430 p. bl cloth. VG/dj. G1. $30.00

SARG, Tony. *Tony Sarg's Book of Animals.* 1925. Greenberg. 1st ed. G+. P2. $50.00

SARG, Tony. *Tony Sarg's Surprise Book.* 1941. np. 4to. 5 moveable p. sbdg. NF. H3. $50.00

SARGANT, William. *Unquiet Mind: Autobiography of a Physician...* 1967. London. Heinemann. 1st ed. 240 p. VG/dj. G1. $37.50

SARGEANT, Winthrop. *In Spite of Myself.* 1970. Doubleday. 1st ed. 264 p. dj. A7. $15.00

SARGENT, Charles Sprague. *Manual of Trees of N Am.* ca 1905. Houghton Mifflin. ils/index. 826 p. H10. $27.50

SARGENT, Charles Sprague. *16 Maps Accompanying Report on Forest Trees of N Am.* 1884. Dept of Interior. 16 maps/orig portfolio. VG-. O6. $150.00

SARGENT, Daniel. *All the Day Long.* 1941. NY. Longman. 251 p. VG. C5. $8.50

SARGENT, Daniel. *Their Hearts Be Praised.* 1949. NY. Kenedy. 309 p. VG. C5. $10.00

SARGENT, Epes. *Arctic Adventure by Sea & Land...* 1858. Boston. 12mo. ils/maps. 480 p. gilt blk cloth. G+. H3. $45.00

SARGENT, George. *Sunday Evenings at Northcourt.* nd. Boston. Congregational Pub House. 612 p. VG. C5. $15.00

SARGENT, Herbert H. *Campaign of Santiago de Cuba.* 1914. Chicago. McClurg. 1st ed. 3 vols. 12mo. 12 fld maps. gilt bl cloth. VG. B11. $150.00

SARGENT, John G. *Selection From Diary & Correspondence...* 1885. Newport. Southall. 1st ed. 8vo. 320 p. worn. V3. $27.00

SARGENT, John. *Memoir of Rev Henry Martyn.* 1844. NY. 4th ed. 8vo. 467 p. cloth. O2. $55.00

SARGENT, Pamela. *Shore of Women.* 1986. Crown. 1st ed. F/F. F4. $22.00

SARGENT, S. Stansfeld. *Basic Teachings of the Great Psychologists.* 1944. New Home Lib. 1st ed. inscr. 346 p. VG. G1. $20.00

SARGENT, Wyn. *People of the Valley: Life w/Cannibal Tribe in New Guinea.* (1974). Random. 1st ed. 8vo. 302 p. VG+/F. A2. $15.00

SARNO, Ronald. *Let Us Proclaim the Mystery of Faith.* 1970. Dimension. 180 p. VG. C5. $8.50

SAROSI, Balint. *Gypsy Music.* 1978 (1971). Budapest. Corvina. 1st Eng-language ed. 8vo. 287 p. F/F. A2. $20.00

SAROYAN, Aram. *Street: Autobiographical Novel.* 1974. Lenox, MA. 1st ed. sgn. F/8vo wrp ils Gailyn Saroyan. A11. $35.00

SAROYAN, William. *Don't Go Away Mad.* 1949. NY. 1st ed. VG/VG. B5. $30.00

SAROYAN, William. *Human Comedy.* (1943). Harcourt Brace. 1st ed. 8vo. F/VG+. B20. $135.00

SAROYAN, William. *My Name Is Aram.* 1940. Harcourt Brace. 1st ed. yel brds. NF/NF. C4. $75.00

SAROYAN, William. *Short Drive, Sweet Chariot.* 1966. Phaedra. 1st ed. F/NF. C4. $40.00

SAROYAN, William. *Trouble w/Tigers.* 1938. Harcourt Brace. 1st ed. G/dj. M18. $100.00

SARRAZIN, Albertine. *Astragal.* 1967. Grove. 1st ed. trans from French. NF/NF. A14. $20.00

SARTON, May. *Anger.* 1982. Norton. 1st ed. inscr. NF/NF. E3. $30.00

SARTON, May. *As We Are Now.* (1973). Norton. 1st ed. NF/NF. B3. $45.00

SARTON, May. *At Seventy: A Journal.* 1984. NY. Norton. 1st ed. NF/VG+. A14. $20.00

SARTON, May. *Collected Poems, 1930-73.* 1974. NY. 1st ed. inscr/sgn. F/F clip. V1. $65.00

SARTON, May. *Coming Into 80.* 1992. Concord. Ewert. lettered ed (1/26). sgn. special hand bdg. F. C4. $165.00

SARTON, May. *Crucial Conversations.* (1975). Norton. 1st ed. F/NF clip. B3. $35.00

SARTON, May. *Forward Into the Past: May Sarton & Her 80th Birthday...* 1992. Concord. Ewert. 1/150. F/gilt wine-red wrp. C4. $100.00

SARTON, May. *House by the Sea.* (1977). NY. Norton. 1st ed. inscr. NF/VG. B3. $40.00

SARTON, May. *Joanna & Ulysses.* (1964). London. Murray. 1st ed. ils David Knight. NF/NF. B3. $25.00

SARTON, May. *Joanna & Ulysses.* 1963. Norton. 1st ed. F/F. B2. $35.00

SARTON, May. *KY Poetry Review.* 1988. Bellarmine College. F/prt wrp. C4. $25.00

SARTON, May. *Magnificent Spinster.* 1985. Norton. 1st ed. F/F. A14. $25.00

SARTON, May. *Reckoning.* (1978). Norton. 1st ed. F/NF. B3. $25.00

SARTRE, Jean-Paul. *Troubled Sleep.* 1951. Knopf. 1st ed. F/NF. B2. $45.00

SASSOON, Siegfried. *Heart's Journey.* 1927. Crosby Gaige. 1st ed. 1/590. sgn. F/dj. B24. $250.00

SASSOON, Siegfried. *Memoirs of a Fox-Hunting Man.* nd. (1929). Coward McCann. 1st Am ils ed. 295 p. VG. M7. $45.00

SASSOON, Siegfried. *Memoirs of an Infantry Officer.* Sept 1930. London. Faber. 1st ed/2nd imp. 336 p. gilt bl cloth. VG+/G/plastic. M7. $50.00

SASSOON, Siegfried. *Memoirs of an Infantry Officer.* 1930. Coward McCann. 1st ed. red brds. NF/dj. C4. $50.00

SASSOON, Siegfried. *Picture Show.* 1920. NY. 1st ed. G+. V1. $15.00

SASSOON, Siegfried. *Sassoon, Siegfried.* nd. Harper. 1st ed. pub Louise Bechtel's copy. gilt red brds. NF/NF. C4. $45.00

SASTROW, Bartholomew. *Social Germany in Luther's Time...* nd. Dutton. apparent 1st ed. ils. 349 p. H10. $28.50

SATTA, Salvatore. *Day of Judgment.* 1987. FSG. 1st ed. trans from Italian. NF/NF. A14. $25.00

SATTERTHWAIT, Walter. *Hanged Man.* 1993. St Martin. 1st ed. M/M. T2. $20.00

SATTERTHWAIT, Walter. *Wilde W.* 1991. St Martin. 1st ed. F/F. M15. $25.00

SAUDREAU, Auguste. *Ideal of the Fervent Soul.* 1927. London. Burns Oates. 248 p. VG. C5. $25.00

SAUDREAU, Auguste. *Mystical State.* 1924. London. Burns Oates. 204 p. VG. C5. $15.00

SAUER, Carl Ortwin. *Early Spanish Main.* 1966. Berkeley. 1st e. 8vo. 306 p. pict ep. VG. B11. $40.00

SAUER, Erich. *Dawn of World Redemption.* 1955. Grand Rapids. Eerdmans. 206 p. VG. C5. $8.50

SAUER, Erich. *In the Arena of Faith.* 1955. Grand Rapids. Eerdmans. 188 p. VG. C5. $8.50

SAUER, Erich. *King of the Earth.* 1962. Grand Rapids. Eerdmans. 256 p. VG. C5. $8.50

SAUER, Erich. *Triumph of the Crucified.* 1955. Grand Rapids. Eerdmans. 207 p. VG. C5. $8.50

SAUL, Mary. *Shells: Ils Guide to a Timeless & Fascinating World.* 1974. Doubleday. VG/dj. A16. $15.00

SAUNDERS, Charles Francis. *CA Padres & Their Missions.* 1915. Houghton Mifflin. 12mo. VG. A8. $30.00

SAUNDERS, Charles Francis. *Finding the Worth While in the SW.* 1918. NY. 1st ed. 16mo. 231 p. cloth. VG. D3. $25.00

SAUNDERS, Charles Francis. *Finding the Worth While in the SW.* 1928 (1918). NY. 3rd revised prt. photos/fld map. 231 p. B26. $19.00

SAUNDERS, Charles Francis. *Under the Sky in CA.* 1931. McBride. 299 p. VG. H7. $12.50

SAUNDERS, John Monk. *Wings.* 1927. Grosset Dunlap. photoplay ed. VG+/dj. C8. $85.00

SAUNDERS, Louise. *Knave of Hearts.* 1925. Scribner. ils Maxfield Parrish. folio. NF. R3. $900.00

SAUNDERS. *Sew, Serge, Press: Speed Tailoring...* 1990. np. ils. wrp. G2. $17.00

SAUNDERS. *Step-by-Step Guide to Your Sewing Machine.* 1990. np. pb. G2. $18.00

SAUVETERR, Jean Claude. *Narrow Path. Part 1.* 1993. Vantage. 1st ed. F/F. F4. $18.00

SAVAGE, A.H. *Dogsled Apostles.* 1942. NY. Sheed. 231 p. VG. C5. $15.00

SAVAGE, Courtney. *Wayfarers' Friend.* 1947. Milwaukee. Bruce. 121 p. VG. C5. $8.50

SAVAGE, Ernest. *Two If by Sea.* 1982. Scribner. 1st ed. author's 1st book. NF/dj. S5. $22.50

SAVAGE, Raymond. *Allenby of Armageddon.* 1926. Bobbs Merrill. 353 p. blk lettered tan cloth. VG. M7. $45.00

SAVAGE, Thomas. *And Now a Word From Our Creator.* 1972. Chicago. Loyola. 280 p. VG. C5. $10.00

SAVANI, Tom. *Bizarro.* 1983. Harmony Books. intro Stephen King. VG+. scarce. C8. $50.00

SAVARIN, Julian Jay. *Archives of Haven.* 1979. St Martin. 1st Am ed. Lemmus series. F/F. N3. $25.00

SAVAS, Patricia. *Gus: A Nun's Story.* 1993. S Plainfield, NJ. Bridge. 147 p. VG/wrp. C5. $8.50

SAVET, Paul H. *Gyroscopes: Theory & Design...* 1961. McGraw Hill. 1st ed. 8vo. 402 p. gr cloth. F. B20. $40.00

SAVILL, Thomas. *Clinical Lectures of Neurasthenia.* 1899. London. galley. w/sgn note. G7. $195.00

SAVIN, Edwin L. *Old Jim Bridger on the Moccasin Trail.* 1928. Crowell. 8vo. G. A8. $20.00

SAVITT, Sam. *Am's Horses: Our Leading Breeds & Types Shown in Action.* 1966. Doubleday. later prt. oblong 4to. VG/ fair. O3. $35.00

SAVITT, Sam. *Around the World w/Horses.* 1962. Dial. 1st ed. 24 color pls. VG/VG. O3. $45.00

SAVITZ, Harry A. *Profiles of Erudite Jewish Physicians & Scholars...* 1973. Spertus College. 84 p. VG. S3. $40.00

SAVONIUS, Moira. *All-Color Book of Mushrooms & Fungi.* 1973. Octopus. VG/dj. A16. $7.50

SAVORY, Theodore H. *Spider's Web.* (1952). London. Warne. 1st Eng ed. 12mo. 154 p. VG. A2. $25.00

SAWYER, Ruth. *Roller Skates.* 1936. Viking/Jr Literary Guild. ils Valenti Angelo. 1st thus ed. 8vo. cloth. VG. A3. $7.00

SAXON, Lyle. *Father MS.* 1927. NY. Century. 1st ed. 427 p. VG+. H7. $60.00

SAXON, Lyle. *Gumbo Ya-Ya. Collection of LA Folk Tales.* 1945. Bonanza. 8vo. pls. 581 p. VG/VG. B11. $18.00

SAXON, Peter. *Vampires of Finistere.* 1970. London. Baker. 1st ed. F/VG. N3. $15.00

SAXON, Richard. *Stars Came Down.* 1967. Arcadia. 1st Am/1st hc ed. F/F. N3. $12.00

SAYER, Chloe. *Costumes of Mexico.* (1985). Austin, TX. 1st ed. 4to. 240 p. VG/wrp. F3. $30.00

SAYERS, Dorothy. *Begin Here: Statement of Faith.* 1941. Harcourt. 156 p. VG. C5. $12.50

SAYERS, Dorothy. *Christian Letters to a Post-Christian World.* 1962. Grand Rapids. Eerdmans. VG/wrp. C5. $8.50

SAYERS, Dorothy. *Man Born To Be King...* ca 1943. London. Gollancz. 343 p. H10. $15.00

SAYERS, Dorothy. *Matter of Eternity.* 1973. Grand Rapids. Eerdmans. 180 p. VG. C5. $12.50

SAYERS, Dorothy. *Mind of the Maker.* ca 1941. Harcourt Brace. 229 p. cloth. dj. H10. $20.00

SAYERS, James Denson. *Can the Wht Race Survive?* 1929. WA, DC. independent Pub. ils. 255 p. N2. $25.00

SAYLER, Richard H. *Warren Court: A Critical Analysis.* 1969. NY. Chelsea. M11. $35.00

SAYLES, E.B. *Fantasies of Gold.* 1968. np. ils photos/index. 135 p. dj. O7. $9.50

SAYLES, John. *Anarchists' Convention.* 1979. Little Brn. 1st ed. inscr. F/NF. B2. $85.00

SAYLES, John. *Thinking Pictures.* 1987. Houghton Mifflin. AP. sgn. F/wrp. L3. $125.00

SAYRE, Eleanor. *Christmas Book.* 1966. Clarkson Potter. 191 p. VG. C5. $10.00

SCANLAN, Michael. *Inner Healing.* 1974. NY. Paulist. 85 p. VG. C5. $8.50

SCANLON & SCANLON. *Latin Grammar.* 1944. St Louis. Herder. 334 p. VG. C5. $12.50

SCANZONI, Letha. *All We're Meant To Be.* 1992. Grand Rapids. Eerdmans. 426 p. VG/wrp. C5. $7.50

SCARFONE & STILLMAN. *Wizard of Oz: Collectors Treasury.* 1992. Schiffer. 1st ed. w/value guide. VG/VG. L1. $65.00

SCARRON, Paul. *La Virgile Travesti en Vers Burlesques.* 1690 & 1691. Paris. Guillaume de Luyne. 2 vols. bdg ca 1900. K1. $200.00

SCHACHNER, Nat. *Space Lawyer.* 1953. Gnome. 1st ed. F/NF. M2. $60.00

SCHACK, William. *And He Sat Among the Ashes. Biography of Louis M Eilshemius.* 1939. Am Artists Group. 303 p. cloth. D2. $35.00

SCHAEDER, Grete. *Hebrew Humanism of Martin Buber.* 1973. Detroit. Wayne. 503 p. VG. C5. $20.00

SCHAEFER, Friedrich. *Georg Christoph Lichtenberg als Psychologe Menschenkenner.* 1899. Leipzig. Verlag. 3 pls. 52 p. G/prt gr wrp. G1. $27.50

SCHAEFER. *Working in Miniature.* 1987. np. ils. wrp. G2. $16.00

SCHAEFERS, William. *Keepers of the Eucharist.* 1948. Milwaukee. Bruce. 157 p. VG. C5. $12.50

SCHAEFFER, C.W. *Early Hist of the Lutheran Church in Am...* 1868. Lutheran Book Store. xl. 142 p. H10. $22.50

SCHAEFFER, Franky. *Is Capitalism Christian?* 1985. Westchester. Crossways. 460 p. VG/wrp. C5. $8.50

SCHAEFFER, Susan. *Buffalo Afternoon.* 1989. Knopf. 1st ed. sgn. F/NF. A7. $35.00

SCHAEFFER, Susan. *Four Hoods & Great Dog.* 1988. St Martin. 1st ed. juvenile. F/F. O3. $15.00

SCHAEFFER, Susan. *Madness of a Seduced Woman.* (1983). Dutton. 1st ed. F/F. B3. $25.00

SCHAEFFER & SCHAEFFER. *Everybody Can Know.* 1974. Wheaton. Tyndale. 403 p. VG. C5. $8.50

SCHAFF, Morris. *Battle of the Wilderness.* 1910. Houghton Mifflin. 1st ed. 5 maps. 269 p. NF. M8. $85.00

SCHALDACH, William J. *Carl Rungius: Big Game Hunter.* (1945). W Hartford, VT. Countryman. folio. silvered brick cloth. NF. R3. $1,500.00

SCHALL, James. *Another Sort of Learning.* 1988. San Francisco. Ignatius. 299 p. VG. C5. $8.50

SCHALL, James. *Human Dignity & Human Numbers.* 1971. NY. Alba. 222 p. VG/wrp. C5. $7.50

SCHALL, James. *Liberation Theology in Latin Am.* 1982. San Francisco. Ignatius. 402 p. VG/wrp. C5. $10.00

SCHALL, James. *Out of Justice, Peace.* 1984. San Francisco. Ignatius. 124 p. VG/wrp. C5. $7.50

SCHANCHE, Don. *Mr Pop.* (1970). McKay. 310 p. VG+/dj. A7. $45.00

SCHAPIRO, E.I. *Wadsworth, Center to City.* 1938. Wadsworth. ils. 203 p. G+. B18. $22.50

SCHARF, John Thomas. *Hist of Confederate States Navy...* 1977. Fairfax. reprint. 824 p. VG/VG. M8. $35.00

SCHARF, Riwkah. *Figure of Satan in the Old Testament.* (1947). np (Zurich). 60 multigraphed p. brds. N2. $65.00

SCHARPER, Philip. *Am Catholics: A Protestant-Jewish View.* 1959. NY. Sheed. 235 p. VG. C5. $8.50

SCHATZ, W. *Club Swinging.* 1908. Am Gym. ils. 122 p. VG+. E5. $25.00

SCHAUSS, Hayyim. *Lifetime of a Jew: Throughout Ages of Jewish Hist.* 1967. UAHC. 7th prt. 332 p. VG/VG. S3. $21.00

SCHECHTER, S. *Some Aspects of Rabbinic Theology.* 1923. Macmillan. reprint. xl. 384 p. VG. S3. $23.00

SCHECHTER, S. *Studies in Judaism.* 1896. Macmillan. 365 p. VG. C5. $20.00

SCHEEBEN, Matthias. *Mysteries of Christianity.* 1946. St Louis. Herder. 834 p. VG. C5. $20.00

SCHEER, C.J. *Two Hundred Yrs of Geology in Am.* 1979. Hanover, NH. 385 p. brn cloth. VG+. S9. $15.00

SCHEFFCZYK, Leo. *Man's Search for Himself.* 1966. NY. Sheed. 176 p. VG. C5. $10.00

SCHELE, Linda. *Maya Glyphs.* (1982). Austin, TX. 1st ed. 4to. 427 p. F3. $40.00

SCHELL, Jonathan. *Fate of Earth.* 1982. Knopf. 1st ed. F/F. T2. $9.50

SCHELL, Jonathan. *Village of Ben Suc.* 1968. Knopf. 1st ed. clip dj. A7. $45.00

SCHEMEING, Laura. *New Adventures of Peter Rabbit.* nd. Cincinnati. 5 color popups. VG+. H3. $20.00

SCHENK, George. *How To Plan, Establish & Maintain Rock Gardens.* 1964. Menlo Park, CA. Sunset. 4to. ils D Normark. 112 p. B26. $14.00

SCHERER, James A.B. *First Forty-Niner.* 1925. NY. 1st ed. 12mo. 127 p. VG. D3. $25.00

SCHERER, Paul. *For We Have This Treasure.* 1944. NY. Harper. 212 p. VG. C5. $7.50

SCHERER, Paul. *Word God Sent.* 1965. NY. Harper. 272 p. VG. C5. $8.50

SCHERF, Margaret. *Don't Wake Me Up While I'm Driving.* 1977. Doubleday Crime Club. 1st ed. F/F. M15. $30.00

SCHERMAN, Katharine. *Spring on an Arctic Island.* 1956. Boston. 8vo. 331 p. gilt bl cloth. VG/VG. H3. $15.00

SCHERMERHORN, Martin K. *Sacred Scriptures of World Religion.* 1914. Cambridgeport, MA. 3rd ed. presentation. 247 p. H10. $17.50

SCHIAVO, Giovanni. *Four Centuries of Italian-Am Hist.* 1954. NY. 2nd ed. 456 p. G. D7. $40.00

SCHIDDEL, Edmund. *Bad Boy.* 1982. NY. Macmillan. 1st ed. NF/NF. A14. $30.00

SCHIDDEL, Edmund. *Swing.* 1975. Simon Schuster. 1st ed. F/F. F4. $22.00

SCHIER, Norma. *Anagram Detectives.* 1979. Mysterious. 1/250. sgn. F/dj/slipcase. B9. $25.00

SCHIFF, Stuart David. *Whispers VI.* 1987. Doubleday. 1st ed. F/F. N3. $20.00

SCHILDT, Goren. *Sun Boat: Voyage of Discovery.* (1957). London. Staples. 1st ed. 8vo. 314 p. F/VG+. A2. $20.00

SCHILL, Adolf. *Gianfresco Pico Della Mirandola und die Entdeckung Amerikas.* 1929. Berlin. Martin Breslauer. 1/240. NF. O6. $65.00

SCHILLEBEECKX, Edward. *Christ: Sacrament of Encounter w/God.* 1963. NY. Sheed. 222 p. VG. C5. $8.50

SCHILLEBEECKX, Edward. *God, the Future of Man.* 1968. NY. Sheed. 207 p. VG. C5. $10.00

SCHILLEBEECKX, Edward. *Jesus: Experiment in Christology.* 1981. Random. pb. 766 p. C5. $10.00

SCHILLEBEECKX, Edward. *Ministry. Leadership in Community of Jesus Christ.* 1981. NY. Crossroad. 165 p. VG. C5. $12.50

SCHILLER, A. Arthur. *Syllabus for Seminar in African Law.* 1960. NY. Columbia. stapled double-spaced typescript. M11. $45.00

SCHILLER, Lawrence. *Killing of Sharon Tate.* 1970. Signet. sm pb. NF. C8. $40.00

SCHILLIGER, Josef. *Saint of the Atom Bomb.* 1955. Westminster. Newman. 143 p. VG. C5. $10.00

SCHILLING, Arthur. *Ojibway Dream.* 1986. Montreal. Tundra. posthumous ed. quarto. F/VG. L3. $125.00

SCHILLING, D. *Methodus Practica Discendi AC Docendi Linguam Hebraicam.* 1910. Paris. Beauchesne. 182 p. half vellum. C5. $25.00

SCHILLINGS, C.G. *Flashlights in the Jungle: Record of Hunting Adventures...* 1905. Doubleday Page. 1st Am ed. 8vo. 782 p. G+. A2. $35.00

SCHILLINGS, C.G. *With Flashlight & Rifle.* 1905. NY. 1st ed. photos. 421 p. VG. A17. $35.00

SCHILPP, Paul Arthur. *Philosophy of Karl Jaspers.* 1957. NY. Tudor. Lib Living Philosophers Vol IX. olive cloth. VG/dj. G1. $45.00

SCHIMBERG, Albert. *Great Friend: Frederick Ozanam.* 1946. Milwaukee. Bruce. 341 p. VG. C5. $10.00

SCHIMBERG, Albert. *Larks of Umbria.* 1944. Milwaukee. Bruce. 235 p. VG. C5. $8.50

SCHIMBERG, Albert. *Story of Therese Neumann.* 1947. Milwaukee. Bruce. 232 p. VG. C5. $10.00

SCHIMBERG, Albert. *Tall in Paradise.* 1947. Francestown, NH. Marshall Jones. 184 p. VG. C5. $10.00

SCHINDLER, Solomon. *Messianic Expectations & Modern Judaism.* 1886. Boston. Cassino. 3 90 p. VG. S3. $26.00

SCHLARMAN, Joseph. *Catechetical Sermon Aids.* 1942. St Louis. Herder. 536 p. VG. C5. $15.00

SCHLEBECKER, John T. *Bibliography of Books & Pamphlets on Hist Agriculture...* 1969. ABC Clio. index. 183 p. F. B19. $12.50

SCHLECK, Charles. *Theology of Vocations.* 1962. Milwaukee. Bruce. 245 p. VG. C5. $15.00

SCHLEINER, Winfried. *Imagery of John Donne's Sermons.* 1970. Privodence, RI. Brn U. 254 p. VG. C5. $15.00

SCHLESINGER, Arthur M. Jr. *Bitter Heritage.* 1967. Houghton Mifflin. 126 p. clip dj. A7. $20.00

SCHLESINGER, Rudolf. *Marx: His Time & Ours.* 1950. NY. Augustus Kelley. 440 p. A7. $20.00

SCHLIEMANN, Henry. *Tiryns. Prehistoric Palace of the Kings of Tiryns...* 1880. NY. sm folio. 24 pls/1 map/4 plans. 385 p. cloth. O2. $200.00

SCHLITZER, Albert. *Proceedings of Inst for Local Superiors. Vol 4.* 1966. Notre Dame. 229 p. VG. C5. $10.00

SCHLOTZHAUER. *Curved Two-Patch System.* 1982. np. ils. wrp. G2. $19.00

SCHLOTZHAUER. *Curves Unlimited.* 1984. np. ils. wrp. G2. $25.00

SCHLOTZHAUER. *Cutting Up w/Curves.* 1988. np. ils. sbdg. G2. $22.00

SCHLUNDT, Christena L. *Tamiris: Chronicle of Her Dance Career 1972-55.* 1972. NY Public Lib. 94 p. wrp. N2. $8.50

SCHMAUS, Michael. *Essence of Christianity.* 1961. Chicago. Scepter. 176 p. VG. C5. $8.50

SCHMIDT, Adolf. *Atlas der Diatomaceen-Kunde. Zweite Revidirte Auflage.* 1885-1904. Leipzig. OR Reisland. complete run. folio. 250 pls. brn wrp. B14. $1,750.00

SCHMIDT, D.A. *Journey Among Brave Men.* (1964). Little Brn. 1st ed. 8vo. 298 p. F/F. A2. $17.50

SCHMIDT, Georg. *Marc Chagall Zehn Fabenlichtdrucke Nach Gouachen.* 1954. lg portfolio binder w/10 mtd & matted ils. VG. A1. $450.00

SCHMIDT, Karl Patterson. *Homes & Habits of Wild Animals.* 1934. Donohue. ils WA Weber. 12 pls. 64 p. VG. A3. $12.50

SCHMIDT, Stanley. *Newton & the Quasi-Apple.* 1975. Doubleday. 1st ed. NF/NF. N3. $10.00

SCHMIEDER, Oscar. *Settlements of Tzapotex & Mije Indians.* 1930. Berkeley. 1st ed. 184 p. missing back wrp. H3. $30.00

SCHMITZ, James H. *Agent of Vega.* 1960. Hicksville. Gnome. 1st ed. author's 1st book. 1st bdg. F. N3. $20.00

SCHMITZ, James H. *Eternal Frontiers.* 1973. Putnam. 1st ed. F/F. F4. $25.00

SCHMITZ, James H. *Price of Monsters.* 1970. Macmillan. 1st ed. F/F. F4. $30.00

SCHMITZ, Walter. *Collectio Rituum.* 1964. Milwaukee. Bruce. 594 p. VG. C5. $12.50

SCHMITZ, Walter. *Holy Week Manual for Priests.* 1956. Milwaukee. Bruce. 227 p. VG. C5. $12.50

SCHMITZ, Walter. *Sanctuary Manual.* 1966. Milwaukee. Bruce. 66 p. VG. C5. $12.50

SCHMOGER, Carl. *Life of Anna Catherine Emmerich.* 1976. Rochford, IL. Tan. 2 vols. pb. C5. $15.00

SCHNACK, Frederick. *Life of the Butterfly.* 1932. Houghton Mifflin. 1st Am ed. 12mo. 278 p. F/VG. A2. $25.00

SCHNACKENBURG, R. *Christian Existence in the New Testament.* 1969. Notre Dame. 2 vols. VG. C5. $15.00

SCHNACKENBURG, R. *Message Moral du Nouveau Testament.* 1963. Lyon. Mappus. French text. 365 p. VG. C5. $10.00

SCHNECK, Jerome M. *Hist of Psychiatry.* 1960. Springfield. Thomas. thin 8vo. 196 p. bl cloth. VG/dj. G1. $35.00

SCHNEIDAU, Herbert N. *Sacred Discontent: The Bible & W Tradition.* ca 1976. Baton Rouge. 1st ed. 331 p. dj. H10. $16.50

SCHNEIDER, Herbert W. *Hist of Am Philosophy.* 1946. NY. Columbia. 1st ed. 646 p. ruled maroon cloth. VG/dj. G1. $30.00

SCHNEIDER, Louis. *Freudian Psychology & Veblen's Social Theory.* 1948. Kings Crown. 1st ed. 270 p. cloth. G1. $25.00

SCHNEIDER, Peter. *Wall Jumper.* 1983. Pantheon/Random. 1st ed. trans from German. NF/NF. A14. $20.00

SCHNEIDER. *Scrap Happy, Quick-Pieced Scrap Quilts.* 1990. np. ils. wrp. G2. $18.00

SCHNEIDERMAN, Stuart. *Jacques Lacan: Death of an Intellectual Hero.* 1983. Cambridge. Harvard. 1st ed. 182 p. cream cloth. F/dj. G1. $22.50

SCHNITZLER, Theodor. *Mass in Meditation. Vol I.* 1959. St Louis. Herder. 247 p. VG. C5. $8.50

SCHOEMAKER, Samuel M. *Calvary Church Yesterday & Today...* ca 1936. NY. Revell. ils/index. 324 p. H10. $20.00

SCHOEN, Max. *Man Jesus Was.* 1950. Knopf. 271 p. VG. C5. $10.00

SCHOEN, Max. *Thinking About Religion.* 1946. Philosophical Lib. 152 p. VG. C5. $7.50

SCHOENBAUM, Thomas J. *New River Controversy.* ca 1979. Blair. ils/maps. as new. B10. $10.00

SCHOENBERG, Wilfred. *Garlic for Pegasus.* 1955. Westminster. Newman. 213 p. VG. C5. $10.00

SCHOENBRUN, D. *Vietnam: How We Got In, How To Get Out.* 1968. Atheneum. dj. A7. $25.00

SCHOENER, Allon. *Portal to Am: Lower E Side 1870-1925.* 1967. HRW. 256 p. VG+/VG. S3. $30.00

SCHOENWALD, Richard L. *Freud: The Man & His Mind 1856-1956.* 1956. Knopf. 1st ed. 250 p. cloth. G1. $17.50

SCHOESER. *Eng & Am Textiles From 1790 to Present.* 1989. np. cloth. G2. $55.00

SCHOLES, Arthur. *14 Men.* 1952. Dutton. 1st Am ed. 8vo. 314 p. VG/G+. A2. $15.00

SCHOLL, John P. *New Catechism of the Catholic Faith.* 1978. Des Plaines. Fare. pb. 131 p. VG. C5. $8.50

SCHONFIELD, Hugh. *Jesus Party.* 1974. Macmillan. 320 p. VG. C5. $12.50

SCHONFIELD, Hugh. *Jew of Tarsus. Unorthodox Portrait of Paul.* 1946. London. Macdonald. 255 p. VG. C5. $12.50

SCHONFIELD, Hugh. *Politics of God.* 1970. Chicago. Regnery. 224 p. VG. C5. $10.00

SCHONFIELD, Hugh. *Those Incredible Christians.* 1968. NY. Geis. 266 p. VG. C5. $12.50

SCHONS, P.S.J. *Fuhrer Zum Himmel.* 1905. Turnhout. Brepols. German text/lg prt. 330 p. VG. C5. $12.50

SCHOOLCRAFT, Henry Rowe. *Narrative Journal of Travels Through NW Regions of US.* 1821. Albany. Hosford. octavo. fld map. ES. Scottish half calf. H9. $800.00

SCHOONOVER, T.J. *Life & Times of General John A Sutter.* 1895. Sacramento. 1st ed. 16mo. 136 p. pict cloth. B28. $40.00

SCHOOR, Gene. *Billy Martin.* 1980. Doubleday. 1st ed. F/VG+. P8. $12.50

SCHOOR, Gene. *Christy Mathewson.* 1953. Messner. later prt. F/G+. P8. $50.00

SCHOOR, Gene. *Joe Di Maggio.* 1980. Doubleday. 1st ed. photos. F/VG+. P8. $30.00

SCHOOR, Gene. *Leo Durocher Story.* 1955. Messner. 1st ed. xl. lib bdg. G+. P8. $8.00

SCHOOR, Gene. *Seaver.* 1986. Contemporary. 1st ed. F/F. P8. $12.50

SCHOOR, Gene. *Story of Yogi Berra.* 1976. Doubleday. 1st ed. photos. F/F. P8. $40.00

SCHORER, Mark. *House Too Old.* 1935. NY. 1st ed. inscr. author's 1st book. VG. A15. $30.00

SCHORSCH. *Art of the Weaver.* 1972. np. pb. ils. G2. $9.00

SCHOTT, Max. *Murphy's Romance.* 1980. NY. 1st ed. sgn. NF/F. A11. $45.00

SCHOUPPE, F.X. *Purgatory: Explained by Lives & Legends of Saints.* 1986. Rockford, IL. Tan. 227 p. VG/wrp. C5. $7.50

SCHREIBER, Mark. *Princes in Exile.* 1983. NY. Beaufort Books. 1st ed. F/F. T2. $12.00

SCHREINER, Olive. *Woman & Labor.* ca 1911. Stokes. 3rd ed. G. V4. $15.00

SCHRIJVERS, Joseph. *Sanctity Through Trust.* 1953. Cork. Mercier. 164 p. VG. C5. $10.00

SCHROEDER, John. *Task of Religion.* 1936. Harper. 105 p. VG. C5. $8.50

SCHROEDER, R.E. *Something Rich & Strange.* (1965). Harper. 1st ed. 8vo. 184 p. VG+/VG. A2. $25.00

SCHROETER, Leonard. *Last Exodus.* (1974). Universe Books. 432 p. dj. A7. $13.00

SCHUBERT, J.V. *Commandments of God.* 1916. NY. Wagner. 261 p. VG. C5. $10.00

SCHUBRING, Walther. *Doctrine of the Jainas, Described After the Old Sources.* 1978. Delhi. Motilal Banarsidass. 2nd ed. 8vo. 335 p. NF/dj. W1. $22.00

SCHUCK, Peter H. *Agent Orange on Trial.* 1986. Cambridge. Harvard. 1st ed. F/F. A7. $30.00

SCHUCKING, Levin. *Puritan Family.* 1970. Schocken. 196 p. VG. C5. $10.00

SCHULBERG, Budd. *Four Seasons of Success.* 1972. Garden City. 1st ed. G+/dj. E3. $15.00

SCHULBERG, Budd. *On the Waterfront.* 1980. Carbondale, IL. 1st ed. sgn. F/8vo wrp. A11. $135.00

SCHULBERG, Budd. *On the Waterfront: Final Shooting Script.* (1989). Hollywood/NY. 1/300. sgn author/director E Kazan. bl cloth. F/sans. B20. $125.00

SCHULBERG, Budd. *What Makes Sammy Run?* 1957. Bantam. new pb ed. NF. C8. $15.00

SCHULLER, David. *Ministry in Am.* 1980. Harper. 582 p. VG. C5. $20.00

SCHULLERY, Paul. *Bear Hunter's Century.* (1988). Stackpole. ils/photos. 252 p. F/dj. A17. $15.00

SCHULTE, A.J. *Consecranda.* 1906. NY. Benziger. 295 p. VG. C5. $25.00

SCHULTE, Paul. *Flying Priest Over the Arctic.* 1940. Harper. 1st ed. 8vo. 267 p. F/VG. A2. $35.00

SCHULTE, Paul. *Flying Priest Over the Arctic.* 1940. Harper. 267 p. VG. C5. $10.00

SCHULTZ, Bernhard. *Die Schau der Kirche Bei Nikolai Berdiajew.* 1938. Rome. Pontifical Inst. pb. 251 p. VG. C5. $15.00

SCHULTZ, Christian. *Travels on an Inland Voyage Through the States of NY, PA...* 1812. NY. Isaac Riely. 2 vols. octavos. orig mottled calf. H9. $500.00

SCHULTZ, James Willard. *Bird Woman: Guide of Lewis & Clark.* 1918. Houghton Mifflin. 1st ed. 8vo. ils. 235 p. NF. T8. $85.00

SCHULTZ, James Willard. *Red Crow's Brother.* 1927. Houghton Mifflin. 1st ed. VG/dj. B9. $60.00

SCHULTZ, Samuel. *Old Testament Speaks.* 1948. Harper. 436 p. VG. C5. $8.50

SCHULZ, Charles M. *Peanuts Cook Book.* 1969. Determined Products. VG/G. A3. $6.50

SCHULZ, Charles M. *Snoopy & 'It Was a Dark & Stormy Night.'* 1971. HRW. 1st ed. 8vo. 66 p. VG/G. A3. $10.50

SCHULZ, Charles M. *Snoopy & the Red Baron.* 1966. HRW. 1st ed. 64 p. VG/G. A3. $10.50

SCHULZ, Philip. *Deep Within the Ravine.* 1984. NY. 1st ed. w/Lamont Poetry Selected slip. F/F. V1. $20.00

SCHUMACHER, G. *Maurice Thompson: Archer & Author.* 1968. NY. 1st ed. 205 p. VG/VG. B5. $35.00

SCHUMACHER, Michael. *Dharma Lion: Biography of Allen Ginsberg.* (1992). St Martin. 1st ed. 769 p. F/F. A7. $19.00

SCHUR, Max. *Freud: Living & Dying.* 1972. NY. IUP. 1st ed. 587 p. gray cloth. VG/dj. G1. $40.00

SCHURHAMMER, George. *Francis Xavier: His Life & Times.* 1973 & 1977. Rome. Jesuit Hist Inst. 2 vols. M/djs. O6. $125.00

SCHURHAMMER, George. *Shin-To, the Way of the Gods of Japan.* 1923. Bonn/Leipzig. K Schroeder. 210 p. cloth/brds. VG+. B14. $150.00

SCHURMAN, Jacob Gould. *Ethical Import of Darwinism.* 1893 (1888). Scribner. 2nd ed/1st prt. 264 p. NF. G1. $50.00

SCHUSSLER, E.M. *Drs, Dynamite & Dogs.* 1956. Caxton. 1st ed. 8vo. 189 p. F/F. A2. $17.50

SCHUSTER, George. *In Silence I Speak.* 1956. Farrar Straus. 296 p. VG. C5. $15.00

SCHUTZ, Benjamin M. *All the Old Bargains.* 1985. Bluejay Books. 1st ed. F/F. F4. $18.00

SCHUTZ, Benjamin M. *Tax in Blood.* (1987). Tor. 1st ed. F/NF. A7. $30.00

SCHUTZ, Charles E. *Political Humor: From Aristophanes to Sam Ervin.* 1977. Rutherford, NJ. Farleigh Dickinson. 349 p. blk cloth. VG/dj. G1. $20.00

SCHUTZ, Roger. *Living Today for God.* 1962. Helicon. 128 p. VG. C5. $7.50

SCHUTZ, Roger. *This Day Belongs to God.* 1961. Baltimore. Helicon. 63 p. VG. C5. $7.50

SCHUYLER, George S. *Blk & Conservative.* (1966). Arlington House. 1st ed. F/NF. B4. $45.00

SCHWARTZ, Delmore. *Last & Lost Poems.* 1979. Vanguard. 1st ed. F/F. C4. $50.00

SCHWARTZ, Marie-Luise. *Gluck Mot Ponys.* nd. np. Hans Schwarz. German text. ils/photos. VG/wrp. O3. $12.00

SCHWARZ, Joseph. *Descriptive Geography & Brief Hist Sketch of Palestine...* 1850. Phil. A Hart. 1st Eng-language ed. 8vo. lithos/fld map. gilt cloth. M1. $350.00

SCHWARZ, L.W. *Feast of Leviathan: Tales of Adventure...* 1956. Rinehart. 50 stories. 365 p. VG+/VG. S3. $21.00

SCHWARZ-BART, Andre. *Last of the Just.* 1961. Secker Warburg. 1st ed. trans Stephen Becker. NF/VG+ clip. A14. $50.00

SCHWARZ-BART, Andre. *Woman Named Solitude.* 1973. Atheneum. 1st ed. trans from French. NF/NF. A14. $35.00

SCHWATKA, Frederick. *Summer in AK.* 1892. St Louis. 2nd ed. 418 p. G. A17. $37.50

SCHWEINFURTH, Charles. *Orchids of Peru.* 1958 & 1959. Chicago Natural Hist Mus. 2 vols. F3. $45.00

SCHWEITZER, Albert. *Quest of the Hist Jesus: Critical Study...* 1954 (1906). Macmillan. 414 p. bl cloth. VG/tattered. G1. $28.50

SCHWENGEL, Fred. *Republican Party: Its Heritage & Hist.* 1988. Acropolis Books. 2nd ed. sgn. 166 p. VG/VG. B11. $16.00

SCIASCIA, Leonardo. *Candido; or, Dream Dreamed in Sicily.* 1979. HBJ. 1st ed. trans from Italian. NF/NF. A14. $25.00

SCIDMORE, Eliza Ruhamah. *China: The Long-Lived Empire.* 1902. NY. Century. 19 pls. 466 p. VG. W1. $16.00

SCIESZKA, Jon. *Frog Prince Continued.* 1991. Viking. as new/dj. A16. $7.50

SCITHERS, George. *Isaac Asimov's World of SF.* 1980. NY. Dial. 1st ed. F/VG+. N3. $8.00

SCLIAR, Moacyr. *Centaur in the Garden.* 1984. Available/Random. ARC of 1st ed. trans from Portuguese. NF/ils wrp. A14. $30.00

SCMITT, Myles. *Francis of the Crucified.* 1956. Milwaukee. Bruce. 152 p. VG. C5. $8.50

SCOBEY. *Do-It-All Yourself Needlepoint.* 1971. np. ils. cloth. G2. $9.00

SCOPPETTONE, Sandra. *Happy Endings Are All Alike.* 1978. Harper Row. 1st ed. VG+/VG+. A14. $20.00

SCOPPETTONE, Sandra. *Suzuki Beane.* 1961. Doubleday. ils Fitzhugh. 96 p. pict brds. VG. A3. $50.00

SCORZA, Manuel. *Drums for Rancas.* 1977. Harper Row. 1st ed. trans from Spanish. NF/NF. A14. $35.00

SCOTLAND, Jay; see Jakes, John.

SCOTT, A. MacCallum. *Barbary: Romance of the Nearest E.* 1921. Dodd Mead. 1st Am ed. 8vo. 222 p. VG+/G. A2. $35.00

SCOTT, A.C. *Kabuki Theatre of Japan.* 1955. London. Allen Unwin. 1st ed. 8vo. 317 p. VG. W1. $30.00

SCOTT, Anna Miller. *Flower Babies' Book.* (1914). Rand McNally. 8vo. 80 p. VG. T5. $55.00

SCOTT, Anne F. *S Lady: From Pedestal to Politics 1830-1930.* ca 1970. Chicago. 247 p. VG/G. B10. $25.00

SCOTT, Casey; see Kubis, P.

SCOTT, Ernest F. *Man & Soc in the New Testament.* 1946. Scribner. index. 299 p. H10. $11.50

SCOTT, Florence E. *Here & There w/Paul & Peggy.* 1914. Hurst. 302 p. pict cloth. VG. M20. $10.00

SCOTT, George Ryley. *Hist of Cockfighting.* ca 1950s. London. Skilton. delux ltd ed. 1/1095. 204 p. emb decor bdg. VG. E5. $125.00

SCOTT, Gertrude Fisher. *Jean Cabot in Cap in Gown.* 1914. Lothrop Lee. ils Arthur O Scott. 312 p. VG+. S10. $20.00

SCOTT, Hugh. *In the High Yemen.* 1947. London. 2nd ed. fld panoramas. 260 p. dj. O2. $85.00

SCOTT, Jack S. *Corporal Smithers Deceased.* 1983. London. Gollancz. 1st ed. F/F. S5. $25.00

SCOTT, Jack S. *Local Lads.* 1983. Dutton. 1st ed. F/F. F4. $15.00

SCOTT, James B. *Djuna Barnes.* (1976). Boston. Twayne. F. A7. $15.00

SCOTT, Janet Laura. *Happy Day Begins.* 1931. Saalfield. VG/pict wrp. M5. $20.00

SCOTT, Job. *Journal of the Life...* 1798. NY. Collins. 360 p. H10. $85.00

SCOTT, Michael. *Time To Speak.* 1958. Doubleday. 1st ed. 358 p. dj. A7. $22.00

SCOTT, Paul. *Jewel in the Crown.* 1966. London. 1st ed. VG+/VG+. A11. $95.00

SCOTT, Samuel. *Diary of Some Religious Exercises & Experience of...* 1811. Phil. Kimber Conrad. 12mo. 264 p. fair. V3. $25.00

SCOTT, Walter. *Border Antiquities of Eng & Scotland...* 1814. Longman Hurst Rees. 1st ed. lg quarto. 2 vols. contemporary morocco. NF. H5. $650.00

SCOTT, Walter. *Ivanhoe.* 1922 (1918). Rand McNally. ils Winter/8 color pls. VG. M5. $16.00

SCOTT, Walter. *Lady of the Lake: Poem in 6 Cantos.* 1838. NY. Gardiner. orig paper wrp. E3. $20.00

SCOTT, Walter. *Lay of the Last Minstrel.* 1809. London. quarto. fore-edge painting. contemporary morocco. VG. H5. $2,250.00

SCOTT, Walter. *Talisman.* ca 1915. McKay. 1st thus ed. ils Simon H Vedder. G. M18. $30.00

SCOTT, Winfield. *Official List of Officers Who Marched w/the Army...* 1848. Am Star Prt. oblong quarto. 24 p. orig prt wrp. H9. $450.00

SCOTT FORESMAN. *Guess Who.* 1951. special Jr primer. G. M5. $28.00

SCOVIL, Elizabeth R. *Wee Folks Stories From the New Testament.* (1920). Altemus. 24mo. ils. 63 p. lavender brds/red cloth spine. VG. S10. $25.00

SCOWCROFT & STEGNER. *Stanford Short Stories 1960.* 1960. Stanford. 1st ed. sgn Stegner. F/VG. A18. $50.00

SCROGGS, William. *Filibusters & Financiers.* 1969. NY. Russell. reprint of 1916 ed. 408 p. F3. $25.00

SCULL, Andrew. *Madhouses, Mad-Doctors & Madmen: Social Hist of Psychiatry.* 1981. Phil. PA U. 1st ed. 384 p. cloth. VG/dj. G1. $30.00

SCULL, William Ellis. *Sometime Quaker: An Autobiography.* 1939. Phil. Winston. 8vo. 219 p. VG. V3. $20.00

SCULLARD, H.H. *Roman Politic, 220-150 BC.* 1951. Oxford. 1st ed. VG/dj. C1. $11.00

SCULLY, Vincent. *Am Architecture & Urbanism.* (1969). Praeger. sm 4to. 275 p. F/VG. F1. $50.00

SCURLOCK, J. Paul. *Native Trees & Shrubs of FL Keys: A Field Guide.* 1987. Bethel Park. color photos. 220 p. M. B26. $39.00

SEALE, Bobby. *Seize the Time.* (1970). NY. Vintage. pb/1st thus ed. 429 p. A7. $12.00

SEAMAN, August Huiell. *Disappearance of Anne Shaw.* 1928. Doubleday. 1st ed. 262 p. VG/tattered. M20. $25.00

SEAMAN, Ralph. *Hook, Line & Sinker.* (1956). Harrisburg. 1st ed. 246 p. worn dj. A17. $10.00

SEAMON, W.H. *Albermarle Co (VA): A Handbook.* 1888. WH Prout. 108 p. VG. B10. $75.00

SEARIGHT, Frank Thompson. *Swept by Flames. A Thrilling Tale.* 1906. Chicago. Laird Lee. 186 p. VG/wrp. P4. $65.00

SEARLE, Ronald. *Forty Drawings.* 1946. Cambridge. 1st ed. author's 1st book. VG/wrp. Q1. $300.00

SEARS, Clara Endicott. *Gleanings From Old Shaker Journals.* 1916. Boston. 1st ed. ils. 298 p. VG. B28. $65.00

SEASHOLE, E.R. *Let's Have a Horse Show.* 1948. Atlanta. presentation/sgn. VG. O3. $25.00

SEAVER, Tom. *Tom Seaver's All-Time Baseball Greats.* 1984. Wanderer. 1st ed. VG/sans? P8. $12.50

SEAVER & SCHAAP. *Perfect Game.* 1970. Dutton. 1st ed. VG/VG. P8. $15.00

SEAVER & SMITH. *How I Would Pitch to Babe Ruth.* 1974. Playboy. 1st ed. F/VG. P8. $15.00

SEBBA. *Samplers: 5 Centuries of a Gentle Craft.* 1979. np. ils. 160 p. cloth. G2. $25.00

SECUNDUS, Johannes. *Kisses.* 1927. London. Fortune Pr. pirate of 1923 Nonesuch ed. quarto. 14 p. full vellum. H5. $200.00

SECUNDUS, Merlin. *Veritable Blk Art: Key to Secret & Great Stores of Occult...* 1875? NY. Advance Pub. 16mo. 158 p. cloth. M1. $375.00

SEDGWICK, Henry Dwight. *Cortes the Conqueror.* 1926. Bobbs Merrill. 8vo. 16 pls. 390 p. red brds. G. B11. $30.00

SEDWEEK & TALLAMY. *St Lawrence Seaway Project.* 1940. Roycroft. 1st ed. 129 p. A17. $20.00

SEDWICK, Henry. *Cortes the Conqueror.* 1926. Bobbs Merrill. 390 p. F3. $15.00

SEE, Carolyn. *Bl Money.* (1974). McKay. 1st ed. F/F clip. B4. $85.00

SEEBOHM & SEEBOHM. *Private Memoirs.* 1873. London. Provost. 12mo. 442 p. worn. V3. $24.00

SEED, Jenny. *Voice of the Great Elephant.* (1968). Pantheon. 178 p. dj. A7. $12.00

SEEGER, Ruth. *Am Folk Songs for Children.* 1948. Doubleday. 183 p. VG+/G. P2. $18.00

SEEGMILLER, Wilhelmina. *Little Rhymes for Little Readers.* 1903. Rand McNally. ils/sgn Hallock. w/orig drawing. red cloth. VG+. F1. $295.00

SEELYE, John. *Kid.* 1972. NY. 1st ed. inscr. F/NF clip. A11. $65.00

SEGAL, Charles M. *Fascinating Facts About Am Jewish Hist.* 1955. Twayne. 159 p. VG/poor. S3. $24.00

SEGAL, Erich. *Acts of Faith.* 1992. Bantam. lg prt. VG/dj. A16. $15.00

SEGAL, Ronald. *Race War: World-Wide Clash of Wht & Non-Wht.* (1967). Viking. 1st ed. 416 p. clip dj. A7. $20.00

SEGAR, Charles. *Official Hist of the Nat League.* 1951. Jay. 1st ed/commemorates 75th anniversary. G+/G+. P8. $40.00

SEIDENSTICKER, Edward. *Kafu the Scribbler: Life & Writings of Nagai Kafu...* 1965. Stanford. 1st ed. ils. 352 p. NF/NF. M20. $15.00

SEIDLER, M.B. *Norman Thomas, Respectable Rebel.* 1961. Syracuse, NY. 1st ed. 8vo. 368 p. F/VG+. A2. $15.00

SEIDMAN, Joel. *Needle Trades.* ca 1942. Farrar Rinehart. 1st ed. VG/G. V4. $17.50

SEIFERT, Jaroslav. *Mozart in Prague.* 1985. IA City. 1/500. F/wrp. V1. $15.00

SEILER, Otto J. *Bridge Across the Atlantic.* nd. Herferd. Mittler. as new/dj. A16. $45.00

SEILER, Otto J. *Crossing the Tracks of Columbus.* 1992. Herferd. Mittler. as new/dj. A16. $55.00

SEITZ, Don Carlos. *Braxton Bragg, General of the Confederacy.* 1924. Columbia, SC. 1st ed. 544 p. later cloth. NF. M8. $150.00

SEJERSTED, Georg W. *Garib: Over Kung Salomos...* 1939. Stockholm. Hugo Gebers Forlag. 1st Swedish ed. 205 p. F. M7. $45.00

SEKIGAWA, Eiichiro. *Aireview's German Military Aircraft in 2nd World War.* (1960). Tokyo. 1st ed of Japanese text. 2 vols. VG+. B18. $45.00

SELBY, David. *Itambu!* (1964). London. Angus Robertson. 1st ed. 8vo. 167 p. VG+/VG. A2. $12.00

SELBY, Hubert Jr. *Last Exit to Brooklyn.* 1964. NY. Grove. 1st ed. inscr. w/news clippings. NF/VG. L3. $375.00

SELBY, John. *Man Who Never Changed.* 1954. Rinehart. 1st ed. VG+/VG+. A14. $30.00

SELBY, Paul. *Abraham Lincoln: Evolution of His Emancipation Policy.* 1909. Chicago Hist Soc. VG. A6. $10.00

SELDES, George. *Iron, Blood & Profits.* 1934. Harper. 1st ed. F/NF. B2. $50.00

SELFRIDGE, Thomas Oliver. *Reports of Explorations & Surveys...Ship Canal...* 1874. GPO. lg 4to. 14 lithos/17 lg fld maps/charts. purple cloth. K1. $250.00

SELLAR & YEATMAN. *Horse Nonsense.* 1962. London. Methuen. later prt. 12mo. VG/VG. O3. $10.00

SELLERS, Charles C. *Charles Willson Peale.* 1969. Scribner. revised/corrected ed. 514 p. cloth. dj. D2. $95.00

SELLING, Lowell S. *Men Against Madness.* 1940. NY. Greenberg. 1st ed. 42 halftones. 342 p. prt blk cloth. G1. $25.00

SELLINGS, Arthur. *Silent Speakers.* 1963. London. Dobson. 1st British/1st hc ed. F/F. N3. $25.00

SELLON, Edward. *Ups & Downs of Life.* 1987. Dennis McMillan. reprint of 1867 ed. as new. M2. $50.00

SELLS, A.L. *Paradise of Travelers: Italian Influence on Englishmen...* (1964). London. Allen Unwin. 1st ed. 8vo. 239 p. VG+/VG. A2. $12.50

SELOUS, Henry C. *Our Wht Violet.* ca 1880. Dutton. ils TL Wales. 160 p. G. S10. $25.00

SELTZER, Charles Alden. *Son of AZ.* 1931. NY. 1st ed. 315 p. cloth. VG. D3. $12.50

SELWAY, N.C. *Regency Road: Coaching Prts of James Pollard.* 1957. London. Faber. 1st ed. sm 4to. rebound. VG. O3. $95.00

SELZER, Michael. *Terrorist Chic.* (1979). Hawthorn. 1st ed. 206 p. dj. A7. $17.00

SEMELAIGNE, Rene. *Pionniers de la Psychiatrie Francaise Avant et Apres Pinel.* 1930. Paris. J-B Bailliere. 2 vols. prt gr wrp. G1. $275.00

SEMMES, Raphael. *Memoirs of Service Afloat During War Between the States.* 1987. Bl & Gray Pr. reprint of 1869 ed. NF/NF. M8. $35.00

SENDAK, Maurice. *Caldecott & Co.* 1988. FSG. 1st ed. collected essays. 214 p. VG/VG. D1. $17.50

SENDAK, Maurice. *Caldecott & Co.* 1988. NY. 1st ed. inscr. w/orig drawing. F/F. A11. $115.00

SENDAK, Maurice. *Higgelti, Piggelti Pop!* 1969. Zurich. Diogenes. 1st German pb ed. sgn. F. D1. $225.00

SENDAK, Maurice. *Higgelty, Piggelty Pop!* 1967. Harper Row. 1st ed. ils. brn cloth/pict label. VG/VG. D1. $150.00

SENDAK, Maurice. *Higglety Pigglety Pop!* 1967. Harper Row. G/dj. A16. $25.00

SENDAK, Maurice. *Hole Is to Dig.* (1952). Harper. early prt. VG. P2. $15.00

SENDAK, Maurice. *In the Night Kitchen.* (1970). Harper Row. 1st ed. 4to. VG/dj. D1. $300.00

SENDAK, Maurice. *King Grisly-Beard.* 1973. FSG. 1st ed. F/sans. scarce. P2. $45.00

SENDAK, Maurice. *Ltd Ed Portfolio.* 1971. Harper Row. Portfolio Ltd ed. 1/500. F/folio floral box. D1. $1,500.00

SENDAK, Maurice. *Nutshell Lib.* (1962). NY. Harper Row. 1st or early ed. 4 vols. 16mo. NF/djs/slipcase. B24. $175.00

SENDAK, Maurice. *Open House for Butterflies.* 1960. NY. Harper Row. 1st ed. F/NF clip. b4. $125.00

SENDAK, Maurice. *Some Swell Pup.* 1976. FSG. 1st ed. 12mo. VG/tattered. D1. $60.00

SENDAK, Maurice. *Ten Little Rabbits: A Counting Book w/Mino the Magician.* 1970. Phil. Rosenbach. 1st ed. 26 p. F/marbled wrp. B24. $60.00

SENDAK, Maurice. *Where the Wild Things Are.* 1988. Harper Row. 1/220. sgn. w/orig sgn drawing. 36 p. F/mailer box. B24. $1,500.00

SENDAK, Philip. *In Grandpa's House.* 1985. NY. 1st ed. ils/inscr Maurice Sendak. F/F. A11. $70.00

SENET, Andre. *Man in Search of His Ancestors: Romance of Paleontology.* 1956 (1955). McGraw Hill. 1st Am ed. 8vo. 274 p. F/VG+. A2. $12.50

SENTER, O.S. *Health & Pleasure-Seeker's Guide.* 1873. Phil. Rogers. xl. 12mo. 149 p. limp bl cloth. H9. $50.00

SENZEL, Howard. *Baseball & the Cold War.* 1977. HBJ. 1st ed. VG+/VG. P8. $50.00

SERAFIN, David. *Port of Light.* 1987. London. Collins. 1st ed. F/F. S5. $22.50

SERAN, Val. *Vietnam Mission to Hell!* (1966). Bee-Line. PBO. VG. A7. $35.00

SEREDY, Kate. *Good Master.* 1935. Viking. 2nd prt. 210 p. VG+/G. P2. $25.00

SEREDY, Kate. *Gypsy.* 1951. Viking. 1st ed. cloth. VG. M5. $30.00

SEREDY, Kate. *Lazy Tinka.* 1962. Viking. 1st ed. 56 p. VG. P2. $20.00

SEREDY, Kate. *Philomena.* 1955. Viking. 1st ed. VG+/G. P2. $45.00

SEREDY, Kate. *Tree for Peter.* 1946 (1941). Viking. 3rd prt. 102 p. VG+/G. P2. $30.00

SEREDY, Kate. *Wht Stag.* 1937. Viking. 1st ed. 8vo. 95 p. VG/VG. D1. $150.00

SERGEANT, Elizabeth Shepley. *Robert Frost: Trial by Existence.* 1963. HRW. NF/VG. E3. $12.00

SERLING, Rod. *Twilight Zone.* 1963. Grosset Dunlap. 1st ed. VG/dj. M2. $15.00

SERPEIRI, Paolo. *Druuna.* 1987. Dargaud. 1st ed. F/F. F4. $40.00

SERPEIRI, Paolo. *Morbus Gravis.* 1986. Dargaud. 1st ed. F/F. F4. $40.00

SERVER, Lee. *Screenwriter, Words Become Pictures.* 1987. Main Street pr. NF. C8. $25.00

SERVICE, Robert. *Rhymes of a Red Cross Man.* 1916. NY. 1st ed. dk gr cloth. NF. V1. $15.00

SESTO, Gennaro J. *Guardians of the Mentally Ill in Ecclesiastical Trials.* 1956. Catholic U of Am Pr. 1st ed. 180 p. VG/prt gray wrp. G1. $27.50

SETH, Vikram. *Golden Gate.* 1986. NY. 1st ed. F/F. V1. $25.00

SETON, Ernest Thompson. *Bannertail.* 1922. Scribner. 1st ed. 265 p. VG. M20. $60.00

SETON, Ernest Thompson. *Biography of a Silver-Fox.* 1909. Century. 1st stated ed. sm 8vo. 209 p. VG/dj. D1. $65.00

SETON, Ernest Thompson. *Monarch: Big Bear of Tallac.* 1904. Scribner. 1st ed. ils. pict bdg. VG+. A18. $50.00

SETON, Ernest Thompson. *Rolf in the Woods.* 1911. Doubleday Page. 1st ed. 12 full-p ils. 437 p. gr cloth. VG. S10. $35.00

SETON, Ernest Thompson. *Two Little Savages.* 1903. Doubleday. 1st ed. ils. decor bdg. F. A18. $75.00

SETON, Ernest Thompson. *Two Little Savages.* 1903. Doubleday. 1st ed. 542 p. VG. M20. $50.00

SETRIGHT, L.J.K. *Designers: Great Automobiles & the Men Who Made Them.* 1976. Chicago. VG/dj. A16. $20.00

SETTLE, Mary Lee. *Celebration.* (1986). FSG. 1st ed. F/VG. B3. $25.00

SETTLE, Mary Lee. *Killing Ground.* (1982). FSG. 1st ed. VG/VG. B3. $30.00

SETTLE & SETTLE. *Saddles & Spurs: Saga of Pony Express.* 1955. Bonanza. reprint. VG/VG. O3. $18.00

SEUSS, Dr.; see Geisel, Theodor Seuss.

SEVERIN, Timothy. *Golden Antilles.* 1970. Knopf. 1st ed. 8vo. 336 p. F/F clip. A2. $20.00

SEVERN, Bill. *John Marshall: Man Who Made the Court Supreme.* 1969. McKay. dj. M11. $25.00

SEW NEWS. *Sewing Kids' Stuff.* 1991. np. pb. ils. G2. $18.00

SEWALL, Samuel. *Hist of Woburn, Middlesex Country, MA...1640 to Yr 1860.* 1868. Boston. Wiggin Lunt. 1st ed. lg 8vo. 657 p. blk cloth. NF. B20. $45.00

SEWARD, Oliver Risley. *William H Seward Travels Around the World.* 1873. NY. Appleton. thick 8vo. ils/fld map. pub bl cloth/rebacked. H9. $45.00

SEWARD. *Christmas Patchwork.* 1986. np. ils. wrp. G2. $10.95

SEWELL, Anna. *Annotated Blk Beauty.* 1989. London. Allen. 1st ed. 4to. VG/G+. O3. $45.00

SEWELL, Anna. *Blk Beauty.* 1890. Boston. Am Humane Education Soc. 1st Am ed. 8vo. 246 p. scarce. F1. $295.00

SEWELL, Anna. *Blk Beauty.* 1915. London. Dent. ils Lucy Kemp-Welch. 226 p. marbled ep. polished calf. H5. $300.00

SEWELL, Anna. *Blk Beauty: Autobiography of a Horse.* (1945). Grosset Dunlap/Jr Lib. 8vo. 301 p. F. T5. $20.00

SEWELL, Helen. *Bl Barns. Story of 2 Big Geese & 7 Little Ducks.* 1933. NY. 1st ed. 19 full-p pls. pict bl cloth. VG. H3. $20.00

SEXTON, Anne. *Awful Rowing Toward God.* 1975. Houghton Mifflin. AP/ARC. F/mustard wrp. C4. $50.00

SEXTON, Anne. *Book of Folly.* 1972. Boston. 1st ed. F/VG+. V1. $25.00

SEXTON, Anne. *Words for Dr Y.* 1978. Houghton Mifflin. AP. RS. F/russet wrp. C4. $50.00

SEXTON, Kathryn A. *Heritage of the Panhandle.* 1979. private prt. 1st ed. 550 p. F/NF. B19. $25.00

SEXTON, Linda Gray. *Points of Light.* (1988). Little Brn. ARC. F/wrp. B3. $30.00

SEYMOUR, Alta Halverson. *Grandma for Christmas.* 1947. Westminster. ils Janet Smalley/Jeanne McLavy. VG. M5. $25.00

SEYMOUR, E.S. *Sketches of Minnesota: New Eng of the W...* 1850. Harper. 282 p. orig blk cloth. K1. $200.00

SEYMOUR, Flora Warren. *Story of the Red Man.* 1934. Tudor. 2nd prt. VG. H7. $10.00

SEYMOUR, Frank Conkling. *Flora of New Eng.* 1969. Rutland. 1st ed. ils. 596 p. NF/dj. B28. $25.00

SEYMOUR, Frederick. *Wild Animals I Have Met.* 1901. np. Henry Neil. lg 8vo. ils/photos. 544 p. gilt cloth. G. A17. $19.50

SEYMOUR, Harold. *Baseball: The Golden Age.* 1971. Oxford. 1st ed. VG+/G+. P8. $65.00

SEYMOUR. *Roaring Twenties: Spicy Pop-Up Book for Adults Only.* 1984. F. A4. $30.00

SHAARA, Michael. *Herald.* (1981). McGraw Hill. 1st ed. author's 3rd novel. F/F. B4. $45.00

SHABUROVA, M. *How Old Age Is Provided for in the USSR.* 1939. Moscow. Foreign Languages Pub. 22 p. NF/wrp. A7. $15.00

SHACHTMAN, Max. *Fight for Socialism.* 1946. New Internat. 1st ed. NF. B2. $45.00

SHACHTMAN, Max. *Ziegler Frame-Up.* nd. Chicago. NF/wrp. B2. $60.00

SHACKLETON, Ernest. *Aurora Australis.* 1988. Auckland, NZ. 1st book prt in Antarctica. M/dj. O6. $25.00

SHACOCHIS, Bob. *Easy in the Islands.* (1985). Crown. 1st ed. author's 1st book. NF/NF. B4. $50.00

SHACOCHIS, Bob. *Easy in the Islands.* 1985. NY. ARC. sgn. RS. F/F. A11. $65.00

SHAKESPEARE, Bill. *Powerboat Racing.* 1968. London. Cassell. VG/dj. A16. $25.00

SHAKESPEARE, William. *As You Like It.* ca 1932. London. Allied Newspapers. miniature. 352 p. red cloth. H10. $25.00

SHAKESPEARE, William. *Flowers From Shakespeare's Garden.* 1906. London. Cassell. 1st ed. ils Crane. 40 p. VG. D1. $25.00

SHAKESPEARE, William. *Midsummer-Night's Dream.* nd. Doubleday Page. sm 4to. ils Rackham/16 full-p color pls. gilt gr cloth. F1. $135.00

SHAKESPEARE, William. *Midsummer-Night's Dream.* 1908. London. Heinemann. 1st trade ed. ils Rackham/40 pls. Morrell bdg. NF. H5. $750.00

SHAKESPEARE, William. *Midsummer-Night's Dream.* 1908. London. 1/1000. ils/sgn Rackham. 40 mtd color pls. NF/pub slipcase. H5. $2,500.00

SHAKESPEARE, William. *Phoenix & the Turtle.* 1938. San Francisco. Windsor. 1/35. octavo. w/sgn presenation letter of prt. NF. B24. $125.00

SHAKESPEARE, William. *Poems of...* 1893. Hammersmith. Kelmscott. 1/500. octavo. 216 p. full limp vellum/silk ties. NF. H5. $1,600.00

SHAKESPEARE, William. *Poems of...* 1941. NY. LEC/Colish. 1/1500. designer/sgn Bruce Rogers. 2 vols. teg. F/slipcase. H5. $250.00

SHAKESPEARE, William. *Shakespeare's Comedy As You Like It.* nd (1909). London. Hodder Stoughton. 1/500. ils/sgn Hugh Thomson. 142 p. Zaehnsdorf bdg. NF. H5. $650.00

SHAKESPEARE, William. *Shakespeare's Tragedy of Romeo & Juliet.* ca 1920. Hodder Stoughton. juvenile. 22 color pls. gilt gr bdg. VG. M5. $55.00

SHAKESPEARE, William. *Songs.* 1905. London/NY. Trehern Claflin. 2nd ed. miniature. aeg. red morocco. F1. $75.00

SHAKESPEARE, William. *Tempest.* (1908). Hodder Stoughton. deluxe issue. 1/500. ils/sgn Dulac. gilt vellum/ties. B24. $1,350.00

SHAKESPEARE, William. *Tempest.* nd. Doubleday Page/Heinemann. ils Rackham. 4to. blk cloth. VG+. A3. $35.00

SHAKESPEARE, William. *Twelfth Night; or, What You Will.* (1908). Hodder Stoughton. ils WH Robinson/16 color pls. bl cloth. NF/VG. F1. $150.00

SHAKESPEARE, William. *Two Gentlemen of Verona.* 1964. NY. Dell Laurel. PBO. sgn. F/wrp. A11. $40.00

SHAKESPEARE, William. *Venus & Adonis.* 1912. Hammersmith. Doves. 1/200. sgn Doves Bindery 1918 CS. gilt gr morocco. F. K1. $1,500.00

SHAKESPEARE, William. *Venus & Adonis.* 1931. Rochester, NY. Leo Hart. 1/1250. ils/sgn Kent. F/slipcase. B24. $175.00

SHAKESPEARE, William. *Works of...* (1873-1876). London. Virtue. Imperial ed. 2 vols. 41 pls. aeg. gilt morocco. VG. H5. $2,000.00

SHAKESPEARE, William. *Works of...* 1877. Chatto Windus. 9 vols. octavo. gilt red morocco. NF. R3. $850.00

SHAKESPEARE, William. *Works of...* 1929-1933. Nonesuch for Random. 1/1600. 7 vols. AW Bain russet niger morocco. NF. H5. $2,000.00

SHALER, Clarence Addison. *Gloria Dawn: Romance of the Mind.* 1927. Pasadena, CA. 1st ed. 1/200. pls. 32 p. VG. D3. $75.00

SHALOM, Sabina. *Marriage Sabbatical.* (1984). NY. Dodd Mead. 1st ed. 8vo. 305 p. F/VG. A2. $12.50

SHAMBAUGH, B.F. *Old Stone Capitol Remembers.* 1939. IA City. State Hist Soc. 1st ed. 8vo. 435 p. gilt red brds. VG. B11. $65.00

SHAN, Ben. *Shape of Content.* 1957. Harvard. G+/G+. A1. $20.00

SHANE & THOMAS. *Softball! So What? A Celebrity Collector's Book...* 1940. Stokes. 1st ed. inscr. F. E3. $55.00

SHANKLAND, Peter. *Byron of the Wager.* (1975). NY. CMG. 1st Am ed. 8vo. 288 p. F/F. A2. $15.00

SHANNON, Dell. *Chaos of Crime.* 1985. NY. Morrow. 1st ed. F/F. S5. $20.00

SHANNON, Dell. *Sorrow to the Grave.* (1992). Morrow. 1st ed. F/dj. B9. $15.00

SHANNON, Dell. *Streets of Death.* 1976. Morrow. 1st ed. F/dj. B9. $12.50

SHAPIRO, Harvey. *Book & Other Poems.* 1955. Rowe, MA. Cummington. 1st ed. 1/200. NF/wrp. B24. $200.00

SHAPIRO, Irwin. *Smokey Bear's Camping Book.* 1976. Golden Pr. 1st ed. 45 p. color ep. VG+. H3. $15.00

SHAPIRO, Karl. *Person, Place & Thing.* 1942. NY. 1st ed. VG+/dj. A15. $40.00

SHAPIRO, Karl. *Poems.* 1935. Baltimore. Waverly. 1st ed. 1/200. sgn. author's 1st book. burgandy cloth. Q1. $950.00

SHAPIRO, Karl. *V-Letter & Other Poems.* 1944. NY. 1st ed. F/clip. A15. $40.00

SHAPLEN, Robert. *Bitter Victory.* (1986). Harper Row. 1st ed. 309 p. F/F. A7. $25.00

SHAPLEN, Robert. *Time Out of Hand.* (1969). Harper Row. 465 p. VG/VG. A7. $17.00

SHARAF, Myron. *Fury on Earth: Biography of the Wilhelm Reich.* 1983. St Martin/Marek. 1st ed. thick 8vo. photos. VG/dj. G1. $32.50

SHARFF, Meyer. *Statement on the Rosenberg Case.* nd. LA. Committee to Secure Justice in Rosenberg Case. NF/wrp. B2. $35.00

SHARLAND, Michael. *Stones of a Century.* 1969 (1952). Tasmania. Hobart. 2nd ed/2nd prt. 4to. 78 p. F/F. A2. $15.00

SHARP, Margery. *Bernard Into Battle.* 1978. Little Brn. 1st ed. 87 p. F/VG. P2. $30.00

SHARP, Margery. *Rescuers.* 1959. Little Brn. 1st ed. 87 p. VG/fair. P2. $18.00

SHARP, Margery. *Turret.* 1963. Little Brn. 1st ed. 138 p. VG/clip. M20. $75.00

SHARPE, Dina. *My Horse; My Love.* 1892. Orange Judd. 1st ed. O3. $58.00

SHARPLESS, Isaac. *Quaker Experiment in Government.* 1898. Phil. Alfred Ferris. 1st ed. 12mo. 28 p. G. V3. $14.00

SHARTAR & SHAVIN. *Million-Dollar Legends: Margaret Mitchell...* 1974. Capricorn. ils. wrp. B10. $15.00

SHATNER, William. *Tek War.* 1989. NY. Putnam. 1st ed. F/F. N3. $15.00

SHATNER, William. *Tek War.* 1989. Phantasia. ltd ed. sgn. F/F/slipcase. T2. $150.00

SHAW, Andrew; see Block, Lawrence.

SHAW, Arnold. *Belafonte.* (1960). Phil. Chilton. 338 p. clip dj. A7. $25.00

SHAW, Arnold. *Rock Revolution.* 1970 (1969). NY. Crowell Collier. 3rd prt. 215 p. NF/NF. A7. $15.00

SHAW, Bernard. *Intelligent Woman's Guide to Socialism & Capitalism.* ca 1928. NY. Brentano. 1st ed. G. V4. $12.50

SHAW, Bernard. *Intelligent Woman's Guide to Socialism & Capitalism.* 1928. London. Constable. 1st Eng ed. presentation. 494 p. teg. NF/dj. H5. $850.00

SHAW, Bernard. *My Dear Dorothea: Practical Syestem of Moral Education...* 1957. Vanguard. ils Clare Winsten. NF/NF. E3. $20.00

SHAW, Bernard. *St Joan. Chronicle Play in 6 Scenes...* 1924. London. Constable. deluxe ed. 1/750 on Batchelor handmade. NF. H5. $500.00

SHAW, Bernard. *Wegweiser Fur die Intelligente Frau Zum Sozialismus...* ca 1928. Berlin. S Fisher Verlag. VG. V4. $30.00

SHAW, Bob. *Wreath of Stars.* 1977. Doubleday. 1st Am ed. NF/NF. N3. $10.00

SHAW, F.H. *Full Fathom 5: Book of Famous Shipwrecks.* 1930. Macmillan. 1st ed. 8vo. 301 p. VG+/fair. A2. $20.00

SHAW, Frank S.; see Goulart, Ron.

SHAW, George Bernard. *Apple Cart: Political Extravaganza.* 1930. London. Constable. 69th thousand. apple gr cloth. NF. M7. $35.00

SHAW, George Bernard. *Fabian Essays in Socialism.* nd. London. 1st ed. VG+. B2. $125.00

SHAW, George Bernard. *Quintessence of Ibsenism.* 1891. London. Walter Scott. 1st ed. indigo cloth. B24. $300.00

SHAW, George Bernard. *Too True To Be Good.* 1934. Dodd Mead. 1st ed. 343 p. bl lettered dk gr linen. F/VG/plastic. M7. $75.00

SHAW, Irwin. *In the Company of Dolphins.* 1964. NY. 1st ed. 8vo. 154 p. cloth. O2. $10.00

SHAW, Lloyd. *Cowboy Dances.* 1943. Caldwell. 6th prt. 397 p. dj. A17. $12.00

SHAW, Martin. *Marxism Vs Sociology.* (1974). London. Pluto. F/dj. A7. $16.00

SHAW, Mary L. *Ottoman Empire From 1720-34.* 1944. Urbana. tall 8vo. 165 p. prt wrp. O2. $20.00

SHAW, W.B. Kennedy. *Long Range Desert Group.* 1945. London. Collins. 1st ed. 256 p. dk bl linen. VG+/G/clear plastic. M7. $45.00

SHAWCROSS, William. *Sideshow: Kissinger, Nixon & Destruction of Cambodia.* 1979. Simon Schuster. 1st ed. 8vo. 16 pls/maps. VG/dj. W1. $18.00

SHAWN, Frank S.; see Goulart, Ron.

SHAY, Frank. *Iron Men & Wooden Ship.* 1924. Doubleday Page. 1st ed. 1/200. quarto. 154 p. gilt bdg. VG. H5. $200.00

SHAYNE, Mike; see Halliday, Brett.

SHCHAPOV, Yaroslav N. *State & Church in Early Russia.* 1993. New Rochelle. 8vo. 252 p. cloth. O2. $50.00

SHEA, James J. *All in the Game.* 1960. Putnam. 284 p. cloth. VG/dj. M20. $30.00

SHEA, John Gilmary. *Lincoln Memorial: Record of Life, Assassination...* 1865. NY. Bunce Huntington. 1st ed. 288 p. cloth. VG. M8. $85.00

SHEA, John. *God Who Fell From Heaven.* 1979. Niles. Argus. 125 p. VG/wrp. C5. $7.50

SHEA, John. *Spirit Master, Vol 6.* 1987. Chicago. Thomas More Pr. 246 p. VG. C5. $10.00

SHECKLEY, Robert. *Crompton Divided.* 1978. HRW. 1st Am ed. F/F. N3. $30.00

SHECKLEY, Robert. *Game of X.* 1965. Delacorte. 1st ed. F/NF. F4. $35.00

SHEDLETSKY. *Making an Old-Fashioned Patchwork Sampler Quilt...* 1984. np. ils. wrp. G2. $5.00

SHEDLEY, Ethan I. *Earth Ship & Star Song.* 1979. Viking. 1st ed. F/F. N3. $10.00

SHEEHAN, Neil. *Bright Shining Lie.* (1988). Random. 1st ed. NF/NF. A7. $35.00

SHEEHAN, Perley. *Abyss of Wonders.* 1953. Fantasy. 1/1500. #d. F/dj/box. M2. $50.00

SHEEHAN, Susan. *10 Vietnamese.* 1967. Knopf. 1st ed. clip dj. A7. $40.00

SHEEHAN & SHEEHAN. *Pierre Toussaint: Citizen of Old NY.* 1955. NY. Kenedy. G+/poor. N2. $10.00

SHEEHY, Gail. *Panthermania: Clash of Blk Against Blk...* (1971). Harper Row. 1st ed. 125 p. clip. A7. $25.00

SHEFFELS. *Adventures of Pea Pod Kids in Uncle Peasly's Shortcut.* 1988. 5 action scenes. paper engineering by Linda Costello. VG. A4. $35.00

SHEFFIELD, Charles. *Cold As Ice.* 1992. NY. Tor. 1st ed. F/F. N3. $15.00

SHEFFIELD, Charles. *Summertide.* 1990. London. Gollancz. 1st British ed. F/F. N3. $15.00

SHEFFIELD, Robyn. *Killing Term.* 1993. London. Harper Collins. 1st ed. author's 2nd book. F/F. S5. $22.50

SHEILDS, G.O. *Big Game of N Am.* 1890. Rand McNally. thick 8vo. ils. 581 p. gilt brn cloth. H9. $80.00

SHELDON, Charles. *Wilderness of the Upper Yukon.* 1911. Scribner. 1st ed. ils. NF. F1. $225.00

SHELLEY, Mary. *Frankenstein.* nd. Potter/Crown. ils. NF. C8. $25.00

SHELLEY, Mary. *Frankenstein; or, The Modern Prometheus.* 1818. London. Lackington Hughes Harding Jones. 1st ed. 3 vols in 1. F. H5. $55,000.00

SHELLEY, Mary. *Frankenstein; or, The Modern Prometheus.* 1983. W Hatfield. Pennyroyal. 1/350. sgn. ils Barry Moser/52 engravings. F/case. H5. $1,750.00

SHELLEY, Mary. *Shelley Memorials: From Authentic Sources.* 1859. London. Smith Elder. 1st ed. 8vo. 290 p. emb cloth. VG+. F1. $85.00

SHELLEY, Percy Bysshe. *Poetical Works...* 1876. London. Reeves Turner. 4 vols. aeg. marbled ep. Sotheran polished calf. NF. H5. $850.00

SHELLEY, Percy Bysshe. *Shelley.* 1914. Hammersmith. 1/200. presentation by Cobden-Sanderson. F/slipcase. H5. $1,250.00

SHELTER, Charles. *WV Civil War Literature...* 1963. WV U. 184 p. VG/wrp. B10. $35.00

SHELTON, Robert. *No Direction Home.* (1986). Beech Tree. 1st ed. NF/NF. B3. $40.00

SHENGOLD, Leonard. *Boy Will Come to Nothing: Freud's Ego Ideal...* 1993. New Haven. Yale. 2nd prt. gray cloth. VG/dj. G1. $22.50

SHENKER, Israel. *Noshing Is Sacred: Joys & Oys of Jewish Food.* 1979. Bobbs Merrill. 141 p. VG+/VG+. S3. $22.00

SHEPARD, Anna. *Ceramics for the Archaeologists.* 1976. Carnegie Instit. 5th prt. 414 p. VG. F3. $45.00

SHEPARD, Elihu H. *Early Hist of St Louis & MO.* 1870. St Louis. 1st ed. inscr to JW Buel. 170 p. cloth. D3. $75.00

SHEPARD, Ernest H. *Drawn From Memory.* 1957. Lippincott. 1st ed. 190 p. VG/dj. D1. $100.00

SHEPARD, Lucius. *Ends of the Earth.* 1991. Arkham. 1st ed. as new. M2. $45.00

SHEPARD, Lucius. *Gr Eyes.* 1984. NY. Ace. PBO. inscr. F/unread. A11. $95.00

SHEPARD, Lucius. *Kalimantan.* 1990. Legend. 1st ed. 1/300. sgn/#d. aeg. deluxe bdg. F/F slipcase. F4. $75.00

SHEPARD, Sam. *La Turista.* 1968. Indianapolis. 1st ed. intro/sgn Elizabeth Hardwick. F/wrp. A11. $45.00

SHEPARD, Sam. *La Turista: A Play in 2 Acts.* 1968. Indianapolis. 1st ed. sgn twice. F/wrp ils Charles Mingus. A11. $40.00

SHEPHER & TIGER. *Women in the Kibbutz.* 1975. HBJ. 1st ed. 334 p. VG/G+. S3. $19.00

SHEPHERD, G.W. Jr. *They Wait in Darkness.* (1955). NY. John Day. 1st ed. 8vo. 308 p. VG/VG. A2. $20.00

SHEPHERD, John; see Ballard, W.T.

SHEPHERD, Michael; see Ludlum, Robert.

SHEPHERD, Roy E. *Hist of the Rose.* 1954. Macmillan. ils/index. 264 p. H10. $15.00

SHEPHERD, Shep; see Whittington, Harry.

SHEPLEY, Ethan. *Nat Lawyers Comm of Am Liberty League.* 1935. WA. Am League. 10 p. stapled wrp. M11. $10.00

SHEPPARD, Tad. *Pack & Paddock.* 1938. Derrydale. 1/950. ils Paul Brn. weak front hinge. O3. $85.00

SHERIDAN, Frances. *Discovery.* 1924. Chatto Windus. trade issue. sm 8vo. decor brds. NF/NF. S8. $45.00

SHERIDAN, Frances. *Discovery.* 1924. Chatto Windus/Curwen. special ed. 1/210 on Italian handmade. VG/VG. S8. $75.00

SHERIDAN, Juanita. *Kahuna Killer.* 1951. Doubleday Crime Club. 1st ed. VG/clip. M15. $30.00

SHERIDAN, Martin. *Comics & Their Creators: Life Stories of Am Cartoonists.* 1942. London. Hale. ils/index. 304 p. VG. B14. $125.00

SHERIDAN, P.H. *Personal Memoirs.* 1888. NY. 1st ed. 2 vols. gilt gr cloth. VG. B28. $70.00

SHERIDAN, R.B. *School for Scandal.* 1792. Boston. Belknap Hall. 16mo. 96 p. M1. $125.00

SHERILL, Robert. *Saturday Night Special.* 1973. Charterhouse. dj. N2. $8.50

SHERLOCK, Christopher. *Night of the Predator.* 1991. London. Heinemann. 1st ed. author's 2nd book. F/F. S5. $22.50

SHERLOCK, William. *Preservation Against Property...* 1688. London. Wm Robert. sm 4to. bdg w/10 other works. modern blk calf. K1. $500.00

SHERMAN, Cindy. *Hist Portraits.* 1991. Rizzoli. 1st ed. F/F. B2. $40.00

SHERMAN, Cindy. *Untitled Film Stills.* 1990. NY. Rizzoli. 1st ed. F/F. B2. $45.00

SHERMAN, Francis. *Complete Poems...* 1935. Ryerson. 1st ed. ils Thoreau MacDonald. 178 p. NF. A17. $17.50

SHERMAN, James. *Memoir of William Allen, FRS.* ca 1851. Phil. Longstreth. 8vo. 530 p. VG. V3. $26.00

SHERMAN, John. *John Sherman's Recollections of 40 Yrs in House...* 1896 (1895). Chicago. Werner. popular ed. 8vo. 949 p. F-.A2. $30.00

SHERMAN, William Tecumseh. *Home Letters of General Sherman.* 1909. Scribner. 1st ed. 412 p. cloth. NF. M8. $65.00

SHERRINGTON, C.S. *Goethe on Nature & Science.* 1942. Cambridge. 1st ed. 16mo. 32 p. later buckram. VG. G1. $37.50

SHERRINGTON, C.S. *Integrative Action of the Nervous System.* 1911. London. Constable. 1st ed/2nd issue (cancelled title p). later cloth. G. G7. $395.00

SHERRINGTON, C.S. *Selected Writings of...* 1979. Oxford. reprint of 1939 ed. M/M. G7. $75.00

SHERWIN, Oscar. *Prophet of Liberty.* (1958). Bookman Associates. 814 p. dj. A7. $25.00

SHERWOOD, Jane. *Post-Mortem Journal.* 1964. London. Neville Spearman. 1st ed. blk lettered yel cloth. VG/VG clip/plastic. M7. $75.00

SHERWOOD, John. *Sunflower Plot.* 1990. London. Macmillan. 1st ed. F/F. S5. $22.50

SHERWOOD, Mary. *Hedge of Thorns.* 1821. Boston. Lincoln Edmands. 16mo. 50 p. prt wrp. M1. $100.00

SHIEL, M.P. *Invisible Voices.* 1935. London. 1st ed. VG. M2. $75.00

SHIEL, M.P. *Lord of the Sea.* 1929. Knopf. 1st ed. VG. M2. $17.00

SHIEL, M.P. *Xelucha & Others.* 1975. Arkham. 1st ed. F/F. M18. $20.00

SHIEL, M.P. *Xelucha & Others.* 1975. Arkham. 1st ed. M/as issued. M2. $25.00

SHIELL. *Lessons in Painless Patchwork.* 1985. np. ils. wrp. G2. $6.00

SHILLINGLAW. *Introducing Weaving.* 1972. np. ils. cloth. G2. $8.00

SHILTS, Randy. *And the Band Played On.* (1987). St Martin. 1st ed. G+. B3. $10.00

SHIMWELL, David W. *Description & Classification of Vegetation.* 1972. Seattle. 1st Am ed. ils/68 tables. 322 p. B26. $26.00

SHINN, Charles H. *Mining Camps.* 1948. NY. 1st Borzoi ed. 291 p. cloth. VG. D3. $25.00

SHINN, Everett. *Christ Story.* 1943. Winston. 1st ed. ils. VG. P2. $25.00

SHIPLEY, Robert. *Paddlewheelers.* 1991. Ontario. Vanwell. as new. A16. $10.95

SHIPLEY, Robert. *Wrecks & Disasters.* 1992. Ontario. Vanwell. as new. A16. $10.95

SHIRAS, George. *Hunting Wildlife w/Camera & Flashlight.* (1936). Nat Geog Soc. 2nd ed. 2 vols. F. A17. $45.00

SHIRAS, Wilmar. *Children of the Atom.* 1953. Gnome. 1st ed. F/NF. M2. $100.00

SHIRLEY, Glenn. *Buckskin & Spurs.* (1958). Hastings House. 1st ed. 8vo. 191 p. VG+/VG+. A2. $20.00

SHIRLEY, Penn. *Little Miss Weezy's Brother.* (1888). Lothrop Lee. 16mo. 154 p. VG. S10. $25.00

SHOBIN, David. *Unborn.* 1981. Linden/Simon Schuster. 1st ed. F/F. T2. $15.00

SHOLES, A.E. *Vol IX. Sholes' Directory of the City of Savannah, 1888.* 1888. Savannah. xl. 8vo. prt brds/cloth spine. H9. $95.00

SHOMON, Joseph James. *Beyond the N Wind: The Arctic Tundra.* 1974. S Brunswick/London. Barnes/Yoseloff. 168 p. bl cloth. VG/worn. P4. $25.00

SHOR, Elizabeth Noble. *Fossils & Flies: Life of a Compleat Scientist.* 1971. OK U. 1st ed. ils/notes/index. 285 p. F/NF clip. B19. $20.00

SHORE, Dinah. *Dinah Shore Cookbook.* 1938. Garden City. 1st ed. VG/VG. B5. $27.50

SHORE, W. Teignmouth. *John Woolman: His Life & Our Times.* 1913. London. Macmillan. 1st ed. 8vo. 273 p. G+. V3. $28.00

SHORT, Jack; see Hochstein, Peter.

SHORT, Luke. *Ambush.* 1950. Houghton Mifflin. 1st ed. NF/dj. B9. $65.00

SHORT, Luke. *And the Wind Blows Free.* 1945. Macmillan. 1st ed. VG/dj. B9. $65.00

SHORT, Luke. *Fiddlefoot.* 1949. Houghton Mifflin. 1st ed. F/dj. B9. $75.00

SHORT, Luke. *High Vermilion.* 1948. Houghton Mifflin. 1st ed. VG+/dj. B9. $40.00

SHORT, Luke. *Ramrod.* 1943. Macmillan. 1st ed. VG. B9. $10.00

SHORT, Luke. *Station W.* 1947. Houghton Mifflin. 1st ed. VG/dj. B9. $35.00

SHORT, Luke. *Sunset Graze.* (1942). Sun Dial. VG+/dj. B9. $20.00

SHORT, Thomas Vowler. *Sketch of the Hist of Church of Eng to the Revolution.* 1845. London. Parker. 656 p. H10. $45.00

SHORT, Wayne. *Cheechakoes.* 1964. NY. Random. 1st ed. 244 p. VG/VG. P4. $15.00

SHORTER, Edward. *Making of the Modern Family.* 1975. Basic Books. 369 p. bl cloth. VG/dj. G1. $25.00

SHOTEN, Kadokawa. *Pict Encyclopedia of the Oriental Arts.* 1969. Crown. 1st ed. 2 vols. 8vo. pls. VG/cb slipcase. C5/W1. $45.00

SHOUMATOFF, Alex. *In S Light.* (1986). Simon Schuster. 1st ed. 239 p. dj. F3. $15.00

SHOUSE, Jouett. *Shall We Plow Under the Supreme Court?* 1936. Am Liberty League. 19 p. stapled wrp. M11. $15.00

SHOWALTER, Mary Emma. *Mennonite Community Cookbook: Favorite Family Recipes.* 1961 (1950). Scottdale, PA. 10th prt. 494 p. VG. B10. $35.00

SHRAKE, Bud. *Night Never Fails.* (1987). Random. 1st ed. F/F. A7. $25.00

SHREVE, Forrest. *Cactus & Its Home.* 1931. Williams Wilkins. 8vo. VG. A8. $45.00

SHRIBER, I.S. *Body for Biull.* (1942). NY. 1st ed. sgn. 307 p. VG/torn dj. B18. $35.00

SHTERNFELD, Ari. *Soviet Space Science: Russian Story of Artificial Satelites.* 1959. Basic Books. 2nd ed. 361 p. NF/fair. S9. $10.00

SHUCK, Oscar T. *Official Roll of the City & Co of San Francisco...* 1894. San Francisco. Dempster Bros. 1st ed. oblong 8vo. new wrp. D3. $50.00

SHUKLE, Satyendra R. *Sikkim: Story of Integration.* 1976. Delhi. Chand. 1st ed. 8vo. pls. 280 p. VG/dj. W1. $18.00

SHULMAN, Abraham. *Coming Home to Zion: Pict Hist of Pre-Israel Palestine.* 1979. Doubleday. sm 4to. 236 p. VG+/VG. S3. $23.00

SHULMAN, Irving. *Amboy Dukes.* 1947. Doubleday. 1st ed. NF/VG. B4. $75.00

SHULMAN, Irving. *Children of the Dark.* 1956. Holt. 1st ed. F/NF. F4. $50.00

SHULTZ & SIMMONS. *Offices in the Sky.* (1959). Bobbs Merrill. 1st ed. 8vo. 328 p. F/VG+. A2. $20.00

SHUMAN, Malcolm K. *Deep Kill: Micah Dunn Mystery.* 1991. St Martin. 1st ed. F/F. T2. $12.00

SHUMATE, Albert. *Life of George Henry Goddard: Artist, Architect, Surveyor...* 1969. Friends Bancroft Lib. folio. map. NF/wrp. O6. $35.00

SHURTLEFF, Nathaniel B. *Topographical & Hist Description of Boston.* 1871. Boston. sgn. royal 8vo. 720 p. lacks map. brn cloth. G. T3. $35.00

SHUSTER, W. Morgan. *Stangling of Persia.* 1912. NY. 1st ed. 8vo. 423 p. gilt cloth. O2. $30.00

SICK, Helmut. *Tukani.* 1960 (1959). Erickson Taplinger. 1st Am ed. 8vo. 240 p. F/F. A2. $15.00

SIDDONS, Anne Rivers. *Peachtree Road.* (1988). Harper Row. 1st ed. NF/NF. B3. $30.00

SIDER, Sandra. *Coastal Charts of the Americas & W Africa...* 1993. NY. Hispanic Soc of Am. 15 color manuscript charts. M. O6. $35.00

SIDER, Sandra. *Maps, Charts, Globes: 5 Centuries of Exploration.* 1992. Hispanic Soc of Am. 73 full-p pls. M/dj. O6. $40.00

SIDNEY, Sylvia. *Needlepoint Book.* 1968. np. ils. cloth. G2. $13.00

SIDORSKY, David. *Future of the Jewish Community in Am.* 1973. JPS. 324 p. VG/fair. S3. $21.00

SIEBEN, Hubert. *Thailand: Land of Color.* 1969. NY. Taplinger. 1st ed. 155 p. VG. W1. $45.00

SIEBENHELLER, Norma. *PD James.* 1981. NY. Unger. 1st ed. F/NF. S5. $27.50

SIEGEL, Beatrice. *Lillian Wald of Henry Street.* 1983. Macmillan. 192 p. VG+/VG+. S3. $23.00

SIEGEL, R.E. *Galen on Sense Perception: His Doctrines, Observations...* 1970. Basel. Karger. 216 p. NF/dj. G7. $75.00

SIEGEL, Robert. *Alpha Centauri.* 1980. Westchester. Cornerstone. 1st ed. F/F. N3. $10.00

SIENKIEWICZ, Henryk. *Deluge.* 1897. Little Brn. 2 vols. N2. $10.00

SIENKIEWICZ. *Baltimore Album Quilts: A Pattern Companion...* 1990. np. ils. cloth. G2. $25.00

SIGERIST, Henry. *Am Medicine.* 1934. NY. sgn on half title. orig cloth. G7. $85.00

SIGMUND, Jay G. *Wapsipinicon Tales.* (1927). Cedar Rapids, IA. 1st ed. 12mo. 121 p. F/rpr dj. D3. $25.00

SIGN, Clarissa T. *What's Happening w/Momma?* 1988. Women's Studio Workshop. 1/150. sgn. M/stiff wrp/plastic box. B24. $175.00

SILBER. *Art of the Quilt.* 1990. Knopf. cloth. G2. $90.00

SILESKY, Barry. *Ferlinghetti: The Atist in His Time.* 1990. NY. Warner. 1st ed. inscr. F/NF. B2. $35.00

SILKO, Leslie Marmon. *Almanac of the Dead.* nd. Simon Schuster. 1st ed. sgn/dtd 1991. F/F. L3. $45.00

SILKO, Leslie Marmon. *Ceremony.* 1977. Viking. 1st ed. F/F 1st issue dj. L3. $750.00

SILKO, Leslie Marmon. *Ceremony.* 1978. Signet. PBO. VG/wrp. L3. $25.00

SILKO, Leslie Marmon. *Sacred Water.* 1993. Tucson, AZ. Flood Plain. 1st ed. 1/750. sgn. F/wrp. L3. $75.00

SILKO, Leslie Marmon. *Storyteller.* 1981. NY. 1st ed/wrp issue. inscr. F. A11. $165.00

SILKO, Leslie Marmon. *Storyteller.* 1981. NY. Seaver Books. 1st ed/hc. F/F. L3. $250.00

SILL, V.R. *Am Miracle.* 1947. Odyssey, NY. 1st ed. 8vo. 301 p. F/VG. A2. $20.00

SILLS, Beverly. *Bubbles: A Self-Portrait.* (1976). Bobbs Merrill. 1st ed. sm 4to. 240 p. F/F. A2. $30.00

SILLS, David L. *Internat Encyclopedia of the Social Sciences.* 1968. Macmillan/Free Pr. 16 vols. prt blk cloth. G1. $375.00

SILONE, Ignazio. *Fontamara.* 1985. London. Dent. reissue of 1934 1st Eng ed. rem mk. NF/NF. A14. $20.00

SILVA, Joseph; see Goulart, Ron.

SILVA HERZOG, Jesus. *Breve Historia de la Revolucion Mexicana.* (1960). Mexico. 1st ed. 2 vols. F3. $15.00

SILVER, Caroline. *Eventing: Classic Equestrian Sport.* 1977. NY. St Martin. 1st Am ed. 4to. VG/G. O3. $45.00

SILVER, Maxwell. *Way to God.* 1950. Philosophical Lib. inscr to wife. 303 p. VG+. S3. $23.00

SILVER, Samuel M. *Portrait of a Rabbi: An Affectionate Memoir...* 1959. Brickner Memorial Found. 125 p. VG. S3. $20.00

SILVERBERG, Robert. *Dying Inside.* 1972. Scribner. 1st ed. F/NF clip. N3. $10.00

SILVERBERG, Robert. *Men Against Time: Salvage Archaeology in the US.* 1967. Macmillan. 1st ed. pict cloth. F/F. N3. $35.00

SILVERBERG, Robert. *Morning of Mankind.* 1967. NY Graphic Soc. 1st ed. 233 p. VG+/dj. M20. $25.00

SILVERBERG, Robert. *Shadrach in the Furnace.* 1976. Bobbs Merrill. 1st ed. NF/F. N3. $10.00

SILVERBERG, Robert. *Starman's Quest.* 1958. Gnome. 1st ed. VG/G. M2. $32.00

SILVERBERG, Robert. *Time Travelers: SF Quartet.* 1985. DIF. 4 novellas. F/F. N3. $15.00

SILVERBERG, Robert. *Unfamiliar Territory.* 1973. NY. Scribner. 1st ed. F/F. N3. $15.00

SILVERMAN, William B. *Still Sm Voice: Story of Jewish Ethics: Book 1.* 1955. Behrman House. 218 p. G+. S3. $22.00

SILVERMAN. *Dune Pop-Up Panorama Book.* 1984. 4 pop-ups. F. A4. $25.00

SILVERSTEIN, Shel. *Missing Piece Meets the O.* (1981). Harper Row. 1st ed. VG/VG clip. B3. $30.00

SILVERSTEIN, Shel. *Where the Sidewalk Ends.* (1984). London. Cape. AP. VG/prt red wrp. B3. $40.00

SILVERSTONE, Paul H. *Richmond Redeemed: Siege at Petersburg.* 1981. Doubleday. 1st ed. 670 p. cloth. VG/VG. M8. $45.00

SIMAK, Clifford D. *All Flesh Is Grass.* 1965. Doubleday. 1st ed. F/NF. N3. $85.00

SIMAK, Clifford D. *City.* 1952. Gnome. 1st ed. F/dj. M2. $450.00

SIMAK, Clifford D. *Cosmic Engineers.* 1985. London. 1st hc ed. as new. M2. $27.00

SIMAK, Clifford D. *Highway of Eternity.* 1986. Del Rey. 1st ed. author's file copy/ sgn. F/F. F4. $40.00

SIMAK, Clifford D. *Where the Evil Dwells.* 1982. Del Rey. 1st ed. sgn. author's file copy. F/F. F4. $40.00

SIMENON, Georges. *Brothers Rico.* 1954. Signet. pb. VG. C8. $20.00

SIMENON, Georges. *Couple From Poiters.* (1986). HBJ. 1st Am ed. F/dj. B9. $10.00

SIMENON, Georges. *Family Lie.* (1978). HBJ. 1st ed. F/dj. B9. $10.00

SIMENON, Georges. *Innocents.* (1973). HBJ. 1st Am ed. VG+/dj. B9. $15.00

SIMENON, Georges. *Maigret & the Killer.* 1971. HBJ. 1st Am ed. 165 p. F/F. S9. $13.00

SIMENON, Georges. *Maigret & the Lazy Burglar.* 1963. London. Hamish Hamilton. 1st ed. F/F. M15. $65.00

SIMENON, Georges. *Maigret & the Yel Dog.* (1987). HBJ. 1st Am ed. F/dj. B9. $10.00

SIMENON, Georges. *Maigret Afraid.* (1983). HBJ. 1st Am ed. rem mk. NF/dj. B9. $10.00

SIMENON, Georges. *Maigret in Soc.* (1962). London. Hamish Hamilton. 1st ed. VG+/dj. B9. $20.00

SIMENON, Georges. *Maigret in Soc.* 1962. London. Hamish Hamilton. 1st ed. F/VG. M15. $35.00

SIMENON, Georges. *Maigret's Pipe.* 1977. London. Hamish Hamilton. 1st ed. F/F. M15. $45.00

SIMENON, Georges. *Maigret's Revolver.* (1984). HBJ. 1st Am ed. NF/dj. B9. $10.00

SIMENON, Georges. *Man Who Watched the Trains Go By.* (1946). Reynal Hitchcock. 1st Am ed. NF/VG. B4. $65.00

SIMENON, Georges. *New Lease of Life.* (1963). London. Hamish Hamilton. 1st ed. VG/dj. B9. $20.00

SIMENON, Georges. *Nightclub.* (1979). HBJ. 1st ed. VG/dj. B9. $10.00

SIMENON, Georges. *Poisoned Relations.* (1950). London. Routledge/Kegan Paul. 1st ed. VG/dj. B9. $10.00

SIMENON, Georges. *Wht Horse Inn.* (1980). HBJ. 1st Am ed. F/dj. B9. $10.00

SIMIC, Charles. *Return to a Place Lit by a Glass of Milk.* (1973). Brasiller. 1st ed. F. B3. $50.00

SIMIC, Charles. *School for Dark Thoughts.* 1978. Banyan Pr. ltd ed. 1/235. sgn/#d. F/bl wrp. V1. $50.00

SIMIC, Charles. *Unending Blues.* (1986). San Diego. HBJ. 1st ed. F/F. B3. $35.00

SIMKIN, Colin. *Currier & Ives' Am.* 1952. NY. Crown. 80 color pls. cloth. dj. D2. $65.00

SIMMEL, Georg. *Schopenhauer und Nietzsche: Ein Vortragszyklus.* 1907. Leipzig. Duncker Humblot. 263 p. prt gray cloth. NF. G1. $85.00

SIMMONS, Amelia. *Am Cookery; or, Art of Dressing Viands, Fish, Poultry...* 1798. Hartford. 8vo. 48 p. plain bl wrp/untrimmed. M1. $8,500.00

SIMMONS, Dan. *Carrion Comfort.* 1989. Dark Harvest. 1st ed. sgn/sm sketch. F/F. F4. $65.00

SIMMONS, Dan. *Lovedeath.* 1993. NY. Warner. ARC. F/wrp. B2. $45.00

SIMMONS, Garner. *Sam Peckinpah: A Portrait in Montage.* 1976. TX U. ils. NF. C8. $30.00

SIMMONS, James C. *Passionate Pilgrims.* 1987. np. 1st ed. VG+/dj. C1. $5.00

SIMMONS, Steve. *Body Blows.* 1986. Dutton. 1st ed. author's 1st book. NF/NF. A14. $25.00

SIMMONS, William E. *Nicaraguan Canal.* 1900. NY. Harper. 1st ed. 30 pls. 335 p. decor brn cloth. B11. $45.00

SIMMONS, William Scranton. *Cautantowwit's House.* 1970. Brn U. 1st ed. 172 p. VG+/dj. M20. $18.00

SIMMONS. *Spinning & Weaving w/Wool.* 1977. np. ils. wrp. G2. $15.00

SIMMS, W.G. *Life of Francis (Swampfox) Marion.* 1860. Phil. 1st ed. woodcuts. VG. E5. $45.00

SIMMS, W.G. *Pelayo: Story of Goth.* 1838. NY. 1st ed. 2 vols. 12mo. cloth. VG. M1. $350.00

SIMMS. *Calssic Quilts: Patchwork Designs From Ancient Rome.* 1991. np. ils. wrp. G2. $15.00

SIMMS. *Invisible Applique.* 1988. np. ils. wrp. G2. $10.00

SIMON, James F. *Independent Journey: Life of William O Douglas.* 1980. NY. Harper Row. M11. $25.00

SIMON, Reeva S. *Middle E in Crime Fiction: Mysteries, Spy Novels...* 1989. NY. Lilian Barber. 1st ed. F/F. M15. $40.00

SIMON, Richard Keller. *Labyrinth of the Comic.* 1985. Tallahassee, FL. FL U. 1st ed. 260 p. gray cloth. NF/VG. G1. $22.50

SIMON, Richard. *Critical Hist of Religions & Customs of E Nations.* 1685. London. sm 8vo. 192 p. full panelled calf. O2. $600.00

SIMON, Roger L. *Mama Tass Manifesto.* 1970. Holt. 1st ed. F/NF. B2. $25.00

SIMON, Roger L. *Peking Duck.* 1979. London. Deutsch. 1st British ed. sgn. NF/NF. S5. $40.00

SIMON, Walter G. *Restoration Episcopate.* ca 1965. NY. Bookman. index/biblio. 238 p. H10. $15.00

SIMON & SUGARMAN. *Felling of Jazz.* 1961. Simon Schuster. 1st ed. inscrs. F/NF. B2. $100.00

SIMON & ULANOV. *Jazz.* Metronome. Metronome Yearbook for 1955. custom red bdg. NF. B2. $35.00

SIMON. *Darned Easy.* 1981. np. darning patterns. wrp. G2. $8.50

SIMONS, Henry C. *Positive Program for Laissez Faire.* 1947 (1934). Chicago. 11th prt. Public Policy Pamphlet 15. wrp. A7. $15.00

SIMPSON, Colin. *Lusitania.* 1972. Boston. Little Brn. 1st Am ed. dj. N2. $10.00

SIMPSON, Dorothy. *Dead by Morning.* (1989). Scribner. AP. F/prt bl wrp. B3. $30.00

SIMPSON, Dorothy. *No Laughing Matter.* 1993. London. Michael Joseph. 1st ed. F/F. S5. $30.00

SIMPSON, Elizabeth. *Enchanted Bluegrass.* 1938. Lexington. Transylvania. 1st trade ed. VG/G. O3. $68.00

SIMPSON, F.A. *Catham Exiles: Yesterday & Today at Catham Islands.* (1950). Wellington, NZ. Reed. 1st ed. 8vo. 182 p. F/VG. A2. $25.00

SIMPSON, Louis. *Searching for the Ox.* 1976. NY. 1st ed. F/F. V1. $20.00

SIMPSON, William R. *Hock-Shop.* 1954. Random. 1st ed. VG/dj. A16. $20.00

SIMS, Charles H. *Debate on Evidences of Christianity...* 1829. Bethany, VA. 1st ed. 2 vols. full leather. G. D7. $125.00

SIMS, George. *End of the Web.* 1976. London. Gollancz. 1st ed. F/NF. S5. $25.00

SIMS, John. *Dissertatio Medica Inauguralis...* 1818. Edinburgh. Stewart. presentation. full gilt morocco. F. G7. $295.00

SINCLAIR, Harold. *Music Out of Dixie.* (1952). Rinehart. 1st ed. VG/clip. A7. $20.00

SINCLAIR, I. *Kodak Mantra Diaries. October 1966 to June 1971.* 1971. London. Albion Village. 1st ed. sbdg. VG. B2. $125.00

SINCLAIR, I. *Wht Chappell: Scarlet Tracings.* 1987. Upingham. Goldmark. 1st ed. sgn. F/dj. M15. $65.00

SINCLAIR, John. *Guitar Army.* 1972. Douglas. ils. 364 p. NF/wrp. A7. $30.00

SINCLAIR, Keith. *Hist of New Zealand.* 1961. London/Melbourne/NY. Oxford. 8vo. 3 maps. 305 p. NF/dj. W1. $22.00

SINCLAIR, May. *Flaw in the Crystal.* 1912. Dutton. VG. M2. $40.00

SINCLAIR, Upton. *Cry for Justice.* (1915). Phil. 1st ed. 12mo. 891 p. VG. D3. $45.00

SINCLAIR, Upton. *Jungle.* 1906. London. 1st Eng ed. 12mo. 411 p. VG. D3. $75.00

SINCLAIR, Upton. *Marie Antoinette.* 1939. Vanguard. 1st ed. F/NF. B2. $50.00

SINCLAIR, Upton. *Mountain Lion.* 1930. Long Beach. Upton Sinclair. 399 p. A7. $15.00

SINCLAIR, Upton. *Overman.* 1907. Doubleday Page. 1st ed. NF. B2. $50.00

SINCLAIR, Upton. *Way Out: What Lies Ahead for Am.* 1933. Farrar. 1st ed. F/NF. B2. $45.00

SINGER, Charles. *Studies in Hist & Method of Science.* 1917 & 1921. Clarendon. 2 vols. royal 8vo. cloth. G7. $375.00

SINGER, Charles. *Studies in Hist & Method of Science. Vol 1.* 1921. Oxford/Clarendon. royal 8vo. 54 pls. cloth. G7. $195.00

SINGER, Charles. *Vesalius on the Human Brain...* 1952. London. Wellcome. ils. 151 p. NF/dj. G7/ $125.00

SINGER, Isaac Bashevis. *East of Eden.* 1977. Vanguard. reissue of 1939 Knopf 1st Am ed. NF/NF. A14. $20.00

SINGER, Isaac Bashevis. *Gifts.* 1985. JPS. 1st ed. 6 stories. 122 p. VG+/slipcase. S3. $32.00

SINGER, Isaac Bashevis. *Image & Other Stories.* 1985. FSG. 1st Am ed. NF/NF clip. A14. $35.00

SINGER, Isaac Bashevis. *King of the Fields.* 1988. FSG. 1st Am ed. trans from Yiddish. F/F. A14. $30.00

SINGER, Isaac Bashevis. *Lost in Am.* 1981. Doubleday. 1st Am ed. ils Raphael Soyer. NF/NF. A14. $25.00

SINGER, Isaac Bashevis. *Magician.* 1984. LEC. 1/1500. sgn. ils/sgn Larry Rivers. linen/blk leather. F/slipcase. B20. $400.00

SINGER, Isaac Bashevis. *Manor.* 1967. NY. Farrar. 1st ed. F/NF. B2. $35.00

SINGER, Isaac Bashevis. *Old Love & Other Stories.* 1980. London. Cape. 1st ed. trans from Yiddish. NF/NF. A14. $50.00

SINGER, Isaac Bashevis. *Passions & Other Stories.* 1976. London. Cape. 1st British ed. trans from Yiddish. F/F. A14. $50.00

SINGER, Isaac Bashevis. *Penitent.* 1983. NY. FSG. 2nd Am prt. trans from Yiddish. NF/NF. A14. $20.00

SINGER, Isaac Bashevis. *Penitent.* 1984. London. Cape. 1st ed. trans from Yiddish. F/F. A14. $35.00

SINGER, Isaac Bashevis. *Reaches of Heaven.* 1980. FSG. 1st ed. ils Moskowitz. NF/VG. D1. $35.00

SINGER, Isaac Bashevis. *Satan in Goray.* 1979. Noonday/FSG. 5th Am imp. trans from Yiddish. NF/NF clip. A14. $20.00

SINGER, Isaac Bashevis. *Shosha.* 1978. FSG. 6th Am imp. trans from Yiddish. NF/NF. A14. $20.00

SINGER, Isaac Bashevis. *Spinoza of Market Street.* (1962). Secker Warburg. 1st ed. NF/NF. B4. $85.00

SINGER, Isaac Bashevis. *When Shlimiel Went to Warsaw & Other Stories.* 1968. FSG. 1st ed. 1969 Newbery Honor. F/VG+. P2. $15.00

SINGER, Isaac Bashevis. *Yentl the Yeshiva Boy.* (1983). FSG. 1st ed. ils Frasconi. F/F. B3. $45.00

SINGER, Isaac Bashevis. *Yentl the Yeshiva Boy.* (1983). FSG. 1st thus ed. ils Frasconi. NF/NF. P2. $30.00

SINGER, Isaac Bashevis. *Zlateh the Goat.* (1966). Harper Row. 1st ed. ils Sendak. VG/VG. D1. $195.00

SINGER & SPYROU. *Textile Arts. Multicultural Traditions.* 1990. np. pb. G2. $17.00

SINGER SEWING COMPANY. *More Sewing for the Home.* 1987. Singer Sewing Reference Lib. photos. wrp. G2. $12.95

SINGER SEWING COMPANY. *Sewing for the Home.* 1984. Singer Sewing Reference Lib. ils. wrp. G2. $15.00

SINGLETON, Esther. *Hist Landmarks of Am As Seen & Described by Famous Writers.* 1907. NY. 1st ed. 40 pls. 305 p. gilt gr cloth. VG. B28. $35.00

SINGLETON, Esther. *Japan As Seen & Described by Famous Writers.* 1904. NY. Dodd Mead. 1st ed. 40 full-p photos. F. B14. $125.00

SINNETT, Mrs. Percy. *Lady's Voyage Round the World.* 1852. NY. 1st Am ed. 12mo. 302 p. gilt blk cloth. G. H3. $12.00

SIODMAK, Curt. *Donovan's Brain.* 1943. Knopf. 1st ed. inscr. NF. B4. $375.00

SIODMAK, Curt. *FP1 Does Not Reply.* 1933. Little Brn. 1st ed. inscr. NF/VG. B4. $350.00

SIODMAK, Curt. *Hauser's Memory.* (1968). Putnam. 1st ed. inscr. F/NF. B4. $150.00

SIODMAK, Curt. *Third Ear.* 1971. Putnam. 1st ed. NF/VG. N3. $10.00

SIPPER, Ralph. *Kenneth Millar: 1915-1983.* 1983. Santa Barbara. private prt. 1st ed. 1/300. 4 p. F/stapled wrp. M15. $25.00

SIREN, Osvald. *Hist of Later Chinese Painting.* 1978. Hacker Art Books. reissue of 1938 ed. 2 vols. 4to. 242 pls. NF. W1. $95.00

SIREN, Osvald. *La Sculpture Chinoise du V au XIV Siecle.* 1926. Paris. Librarie Nationale d'Art et d'Historie. 5 vols. F. R3. $1,000.00

SISLEY, Nick. *Deer Hunting Across N Am.* (1975). Freshet. 281 p. M/dj. A17. $15.00

SITWELL, Edith. *Canticle of the Rose: Poems 1917-49.* 1949. Vanguard. gilt blk brds. F/VG. C4. $45.00

SITWELL, Edith. *Gr Song.* 1946. NY. 1st ed. NF/VG+. V1. $35.00

SITWELL, Edith. *Song of the Cold.* (1948). Vanguard. 1st ed. NF/VG clip. C4. $35.00

SITWELL, Osbert. *Escape w/Me: Oriental Sketchbook.* 1940. NY. Harrison-Hilton. 1st Am ed. 8vo. 322 p. F/VG+. A2. $35.00

SITWELL, Sacheverell. *Fine Bird Books 1700-1900.* (1990). Atlantic Monthly. 1st prt. 180 p. F/dj. A17. $25.00

SITWELL, Sacheverell. *Great Flower Books 1700-1900.* (1990). Atlantic Monthly. 1st ed. 189 p. F/dj. A17. $35.00

SITWELL, Sacheverell. *Poltergeists: Intro & Examination by Chosen Instances.* (1959). NY. U Books. 8vo. 418 p. F/F- clip. A2. $25.00

SITWELL, Sacheverell. *Red Chapels of Banteai Srei.* 1962. London. 8vo. 239 p. cloth. O2. $50.00

SIZER, Nelson. *40 Yrs in Prenology...* 1884 (1882). NY. Fowler Wells. 1st ed. sm 8vo. 413 p. gr cloth. G1. $45.00

SJOMAN, Vilgot. *I Was Curious: Diary of the Making of a Film.* (1968). Grove. 1st ed. photos. F/F. A7. $30.00

SJOWALL & WAHLOO. *Locked Room.* 1973. Pantheon. 1st ed. F/F. F4. $30.00

SJOWALL & WAHLOO. *Murder at the Savoy.* 1971. Pantheon. 1st ed. F/F. F4. $30.00

SKAL, David J. *Hollywood Gothic.* 1990. NY. Norton. 1st ed. F/F. N3. $25.00

SKALLEY, Michael. *Foss: 90 Yrs of Towboating.* 1986. CA. Superior. 2nd ed. VG/dj. A16. $47.50

SKARMETA, Antonio. *Burning Patience.* 1987. Pantheon/Random. 1st ed. F/F. A14. $25.00

SKARSTEN, M.O. *George Drouillard: Hunter & Interpreter for Lewis & Clark.* 1964. Arthur Clark. 1st ed. 8vo. 356 p. red cloth. M/dj. scarce. T8. $125.00

SKEETERS, Paul W. *Maxfield Parrish: The Early Yrs 1893-1930.* 1973. LA. Nash. lg 4to. ils. 350 p. gilt bl cloth. F/VG+. F1. $200.00

SKELSEY, Alice. *Orchids.* 1978. Alexandria, VA. ils. 160 p. VG. B26. $14.00

SKELTON, R.A. *County Atlases of the British Isles, 1579-1850.* 1978. Folkestone. Dawson. fld pls/maps. M/dj. O6. $75.00

SKELTON, R.A. *Decor Prt Maps of the 15th to 18th Centuries.* 1952. London/NY. Staples Pr. revised ed. xl. ils. NF/rpr dj. O6. $165.00

SKELTON, R.A. *European Image & Mapping of Am, AD 1000-1600.* 1962. Minneapolis. 8vo. 28 p. yel wrp. H9. $25.00

SKELTON, R.A. *Vinland Map & the Tartar Relations.* (1966). New Haven. Yale. 3rd prt of 1965 ed. 4to. 291 p. dj. F3. $25.00

SKELTON, Red. *Gertrude & Heathcliffe.* 1974. Scribner. 1st ed. ils. G/G. L1. $20.00

SKENE, James. *Monuments & Views of Greece, 1838-45.* 1985. Athens. oblong 4to. ils/pls. cloth. dj. O2. $40.00

SKINNER, B.F. *Matter of Consequences: Part 3 of an Autobiography.* 1983. Knopf. 1st ed. 442 p. prt blk cloth. VG/dj. G1. $22.50

SKINNER, B.F. *Particulars of My Life.* 1976. Knopf. 1st ed. 319 p. brn cloth. VG/dj. G1. $22.50

SKINNER, Charles M. *Myths & Legends Beyond Our Borders.* 1899. Phil. Lippincott. 12mo. 319 p. teg. gilt brds. G. B11. $35.00

SKINNER, Charles M. *Myths & Legends of Flowers, Trees, Fruits & Plants...* 1911. Lippincott. 1st ed. 302 p. H10. $22.50

SKINNER, G. *Gardening in Barbados.* ca 1940s. np. ils. 106 p. brds. B26. $15.00

SKINNER, Martyn. *Return of Arthur.* 1955. London. 1st ed. 208 p. VG+/dj. C1. $39.50

SKIPP & SPECTOR. *Still Dead: Book of the Dead II.* 1992. Bantam. AP. F/plain wrp. T2. $12.00

SKUTCH, Alexander. *Naturalist on a Tropical Farm.* (1980). Berkeley. 1st ed. 397 p. dj. F3. $20.00

SKUTCH, Robert. *Day the World Forgot.* 1988. Berkeley. Celestial Arts. 1st ed. sgn. F/F. N3. $15.00

SKVORECKY, Josef. *Bass Saxophone.* 1978. Chatto Windus. 1st ed. trans from Czech. rem mk. NF/NF clip. A14. $40.00

SKVORECKY, Josef. *Dvorak in Love.* (1986). Chatto Windus. 1st ed. NF/NF clip. B3. $40.00

SKVORECKY, Josef. *Engineer of Human Souls.* 1985. Chatto Windus/Hogarth. 1st ed. trans from Czech. F/F. A14. $30.00

SKVORECKY, Josef. *Miss Silver's Past.* 1974. NY. 1st Eng-language ed. inscr. NF/NF. A11. $135.00

SLADE, Gurney. *In Lawrence's Bodyguard.* Nov 1930. NY. Stokes. 1st Am ed/2nd prt. 267 p. orange lettered bl cloth. NF. M7. $125.00

SLADE, Mark; see Blake, Roger.

SLADE, Michael. *Horses of Central Park.* 1992. NY. Scholastic. juvenile. F/F. O3. $12.00

SLADEK, John. *New Apocrypha: Guide to Strange Sciences & Occult Beliefs.* 1974. Stein Day. 1st Am ed. F/F. N3. $125.00

SLAGER, Albert. *Early Methodism in the Miami Valley 1798-1820.* nd. Springfield, OH. 1st ed. ils. 79 p. gilt cloth. VG. A17. $15.00

SLATE, William. *Power to the People.* (1970). NY. Tower. PBO. 295 p. A7. $15.00

SLATER. *NY Times Book of Needlepoint.* 1973. NY Times. ils/diagrams. cloth. G2. $16.00

SLAVSON, S.R. *Analytic Group Psychotherapy.* (1951). NY. Columbia. 2nd prt. inscr. 275 p. bl cloth. VG. S9. $10.00

SLEDGE, Eugene B. *With the Old Breed.* 1990. Presidio. 1st ed. F/F. A8. $30.00

SLEIGHT, Jack. *Smoked Foods Recipe Book.* (1973). Stackpole. sm 4to. dj. A7. $18.00

SLOAN, Helen Farr. *Am Art Nouveau: Poster Period of John Sloan.* 1967. Lock Haven. private prt. 12 color pls. brds. glassine dj. D2. $45.00

SLOAN, J.P. *War Games.* 1971. Houghton Mifflin. 1st ed. F/NF. A7. $45.00

SLOAN, Jacob. *Notes From the Warsaw Ghetto: Journal of Emmuel Ringelbum.* 1958. McGraw Hill. 1st ed. 369 p. VG+/G+. S3. $22.00

SLOAN, John. *Catalogue of Memorial Exhibition...Robert Henri.* 1931. Metropolitan Mus Art. 1/2500. 78 pls. wrp. rare. D2. $50.00

SLOAN, W.B. *Complete Farrier; or, Horse Doctor.* 1849. Chicago. Eastman/McClellan. 12mo. ils. orig prt brds. H9. $450.00

SLOANE, Eric. *Our Vanishing Landscape.* 1955. NY. Wilfred Frank. VG/dj. A16. $20.00

SLOANE, Julia M. *Smiling Hill-Top & Other CA Sketches.* 1920. NY. 1st ed. 190 p. pict cloth. VG. D3. $12.50

SLOANE, William. *Edge of Running Water.* 1955. Dodd Mead. revised ed/1st prt. F/NF. N3. $30.00

SLOBODKIN, Louis. *Adventures of Arab.* 1946. Macmillan. possible 1st ed? ils. VG+/fair. P2. $25.00

SLOBODKIN, Louis. *Horse w/the High-Heeled Shoes.* 1954. Vanguard. 1st ed. sgn. sm 4to. 32 p. gr cloth. G+. T5. $40.00

SLOCUM, Joshua. *Sailing Alone Around the World.* 1905. NY. Century. octavo. 294 p. teg. marbled ep. morocco/brds. NF. H5. $150.00

SLOCUM, Victor. *Castaway Boats.* (1938). NY. Furman. 1st ed. 8vo. 313 p. F/F. A2. $25.00

SLONCZEWSKI, Joan. *Door Into Ocean.* 1986. Arbor. 1st ed. F/F. F4. $45.00

SMEDES, Susan Dabney. *Memorials of a S Planter.* 1887. Baltimore. Cusings Bailey. xl. ils. 341 p. B10. $45.00

SMELLIE, William. *Philosophy of Natural Hist.* 1827. Boston. Hillyard Gray Little Wilkins. 2nd ed. 322 p. G+. S9. $39.00

SMILEY, David. *Albanian Assignment.* 1984. London. 8vo. 170 p. cloth. dj. O2. $35.00

SMILEY, Jane. *Catskill Crafts.* (1988). NY. Crown. 1st ed. F/F. B3. $35.00

SMILEY, Jane. *Greenlanders.* 1988. Knopf. 1st ed. sgn. NF/F. B2. $60.00

SMILEY, Jane. *Ordinary Love & Good Will.* 1989. Knopf. 1st ed. sgn. F/F. B2. $85.00

SMITH, A.J. *View of the Spree.* (1962). John Day. 1st ed. 8vo. 305 p. F/VG. A2. $15.00

SMITH, Adolphe. *Monaco & Monte Carlo.* 1912. London. 1st ed. 477 p. pict brn cloth. F. H3. $45.00

SMITH, Agnes. *Glimpses of Greek Life & Scenery.* 1884. London. 8vo. 5 pls/fld map. 352 p. decor cloth. O2. $175.00

SMITH, Albert C. *Am Species of Thibaudieae.* 1932. WA, DC. 19 pls. 237p. VG/wrp. B26. $17.50

SMITH, Alexander H. *Mushroom Hunter's Field Guide.* (1969). Ann Arbor. 5th prt. 264 p. A17. $15.00

SMITH, Alexander H. *Mushroom Hunter's Field Guide.* 1958. Ann Arbor. VG. A16. $9.00

SMITH, Archibald. *Graphic Method of Correcting Deviations of Ship's Compass.* 1859. London. Admiralty. 2 fld pls. 6 p. wrp. B14. $37.50

SMITH, Bradford. *Capt John Smith.* ca 1953. Lippincott. 2nd prt. 375 p. F/VG. B10. $15.00

SMITH, Bradley. *Japan: Hist in Art.* 1964. Doubleday. 1st ed. folio. 295 p. VG. W1. $30.00

SMITH, Bradley. *Japan: Hist in Art.* 1964. NY. 1st prt. folio. pls. 295 p. F/VG. H3. $95.00

SMITH, Buckingham. *Coleccion de Varios Documentos para la Historia...* (1857). London. Trubner. 1st ed. 1/500. quarto. stp gr buckram. VG. R3. $650.00

SMITH, C. *Crystal River.* 1991. NY. Linden. AP. F/prt bl wrp. C4. $35.00

SMITH, C. *Lives of the Dead.* 1990. NY. Linden. AP. F/pict wrp. C4. $35.00

SMITH, C. *Musical Comedy in Am.* 1950. NY. 1st ed. ils. 374 p. VG/G. B5. $17.50

SMITH, C.A. *Abominations of Yondo.* 1960. Arkham. 1st ed. F/dj. M18. $150.00

SMITH, C.A. *Dark Chateau.* 1951. Arkham. 1st ed. F/dj. M2. $650.00

SMITH, C.A. *Genius Loci.* 1948. Arkham. 1st ed. F/F. M2. $200.00

SMITH, C.A. *Immortals of Mercury.* 1932. Stellar/Gernsback. 1st ed. NF/wrp. M2. $200.00

SMITH, C.A. *Lost Worlds.* 1944. Arkham. 1st ed. F/dj. M2. $400.00

SMITH, C.A. *Out of Space & Time.* 1942. Arkham. 1st ed. VG/dj. M2. $450.00

SMITH, C.A. *Out of Space & Time.* 1971. Spearman. 1st ed. NF/dj. M2. $40.00

SMITH, C.A. *Tales of Science & Sorcery.* 1964. Arkham. 1st ed. F/dj. M2. $125.00

SMITH, C.S. *Golden Reign.* 1940. Cassell. 1st Eng ed. 252 p. VG/fair/clear plastic. M7. $250.00

SMITH, C.W. *OH: The Buckeye State.* (1946). Girard. 32 p. VG/wrp. B18. $17.50

SMITH, C.W. *U of VA: 32 Woodcuts.* ca 1937. Richmond. Johnson Pub. 1st ed. 32 full-p woodcuts. VG. B10. $40.00

SMITH, Charles. *Sensism: Philosophy of the W.* 1956. NY. Truth Seeker. 2 vols. djs. N2. $30.00

SMITH, Cordwainer; see Linebarger, Paul.

SMITH, Curt. *Am's Dizzy Dean.* 1978. Bethany. 1st ed. F/VG. P8. $17.50

SMITH, Curt. *Voices of the Games.* 1987. Diamond. 1st ed. sgn by Houston Astros broadcasters. F/F. P8. $50.00

SMITH, D.J. *Discovering Horse-Drawn Carriages.* 1985. Aylesbury. 80 p. VG/wrp. O3. $15.00

SMITH, D.M. *I Married a Ranger.* (1930). Stanford. 1st ed. inscr/sgn author's husband. 179 p. VG. D3. $45.00

SMITH, D.M. *Serious Crimes.* 1987. London. Macmillan. ARC of 1st ed. RS. NF/NF. S5. $25.00

SMITH, D.W. *Father's Law.* (1986). London. Macmillan. 1st ed. VG+/dj. B9. $15.00

SMITH, D.W. *Father's Law.* (1987). Secaucus, NJ. Lyle Stuart. 1st ed. F/dj. B9. $10.00

SMITH, D.W. *Silver Spoon Murders.* (1988). Lyle Stuart. 1st Am ed. F/dj. B9. $10.00

SMITH, Dick. *Condor Journal: Hist, Mythology & Reality of CA Condor.* 1978. Capra. ils/index. 135 p. F/wrp. B19. $10.00

SMITH, Donald. *24th MI.* 1962. Stackpole. G/dj. A16. $60.00

SMITH, Edward E. *Children of the Lens.* 1954. Fantasy. 1st ed. F/NF. M2. $100.00

SMITH, Edward E. *First Lensman.* 1950. Fantasy. 1st ed. 1/500. sgn/#d. F/dj. M2. $275.00

SMITH, Edward E. *Galactic Patrol.* 1950. Fantasy. 1st ed. F/dj. M2. $125.00

SMITH, Edward E. *Grey Lensman.* 1951. Fantasy. 1st ed. NF/dj. M2. $80.00

SMITH, Edward E. *Grey Lensman.* 1961. Gnome. 1st thus ed. F/dj. M2. $35.00

SMITH, Edward E. *Second Stage Lensman.* 1953. Fantasy. 1st ed. F/M. M2. $150.00

SMITH, Edward E. *Skylark of Space.* 1946. Buffalo Book Co. 1st ed. 1/500. sgn. author's scarce 1st book. NF. F4. $375.00

SMITH, Edward E. *Skylark of Valeron.* 1949. Fantasy. 1st ed. sgn. F/VG. M2. $100.00

SMITH, Edward E. *Skylark Three.* 1948. Fantasy. 1st ed. NF/dj. M2. $85.00

SMITH, Edward E. *Vortex Blaster.* 1960. Gnome. 1st ed. VG/worn. M2. $20.00

SMITH, Eunice Young. *Jennifer Gift.* 1950. Bobbs Merrill. cloth. VG/G+. M5. $25.00

SMITH, Fredrika Shumway. *Sound of Axes.* 1965. Rand McNally. G/dj. A16. $6.50

SMITH, Gary. *Windsinger.* 1976. San Francisco. 1st ed. 8vo. 175 p. gilt bl cloth. F/VG clip. H3. $20.00

SMITH, Gene. *Lee & Grant.* 1984. BC. VG+/dj. C1. $6.00

SMITH, George O. *Highways in Hiding.* 1956. Gnome. 1st ed. VG/dj. M2. $25.00

SMITH, George O. *Path of Unreason.* 1958. Gnome. 1st ed. F/dj. M2. $30.00

SMITH, George O. *Pattern for Conquest.* 1948. Gnome. 1st ed. NF/dj. M2. $40.00

SMITH, George O. *Venus Equilateral.* 1947. Prime Pr. 1st ed. inscr. F/NF. M2. $50.00

SMITH, George O. *Venus Equilateral.* 1975. NY. Garland. 1st thus ed. F/sans. N3. $15.00

SMITH, Goldwin. *Letter to a Whig Member of S Independence Assn.* 1864. London. Macmillan. 1st ed. 76 p. cloth. NF. M8. $150.00

SMITH, H. Clifford. *Sulgrave Manor & the Washingtons.* ca 1933. Jonathan Cape. ils/pls. 259 p. VG. B10. $50.00

SMITH, H. De Witt. *Atomic Energy for Military Purposes.* 1945. Princeton. ils/index. 264 p. orange cloth. VG. S9. $35.00

SMITH, Hannah Witall. *Christian's Secret of a Happy Life.* 1875. Boston. Willard Tract Repository. 27th thousand. 12mo. 199 p. V3. $15.00

SMITH, Helen V. *MI Wild Flowers.* 1979 (1966). Cranbrook. 2nd ed/revised. 468 p. F/dj. A17. $18.50

SMITH, Henry Nash. *Virgin Land: Am W As Symbol & Myth.* 1950. Harvard. 1st ed. inscr/sgn. F/dj. A18. $40.00

SMITH, Herdon. *Centralia: 1st 50 Yrs 1845-1900.* (1942). Centralia, WA. Daily Chronicle. 1st ed. 8vo. 368 p. VG. A2. $25.00

SMITH, Homer V. *Kamongo.* 1932. NY. 167 p. dj. G7. $35.00

SMITH, Ira. *Baseball's Famous Pitchers.* 1954. Barnes. 1st ed. VG+/VG. P8. $27.50

SMITH, James E. *Intro to Study of Botany.* 1833. London. Longman. 7th ed. 504 p. rebound gr cloth. VG. S9. $29.00

SMITH, James. *Our Daily Light...* nd. London. Nelson. miniature. 191 p. brn leather. H10. $20.00

SMITH, Janet Adam. *Children's Ils Books.* 1948. London. Collins. ils Beatrix Potter/others. 50 p. VG/G+. S10. $25.00

SMITH, Janet Adam. *John Buchan & His World.* 1979. London. Thames Hudson. 1st ed. 128 p. F/F clip. M7. $39.00

SMITH, John Calvin. *Ils Hand-Book, New Guide for Travelers Through USA.* 1847. Sherman Smith. 16mo. ils/tables. 233 p. gilt red cloth. H9. $75.00

SMITH, John Chabot. *Alger Hiss: True Story.* (1976). NY. 1st ed. photos. F/dj. A17. $10.00

SMITH, John E. *Red Shift Rendezvous.* 1990. Berkley. 1st hc ed. F/F. F4. $10.00

SMITH, John. *Benny Hill Story.* 1988. St Martin. 1st Am ed. fwd Bob Hope. F/F. F4. $18.00

SMITH, John. *Domestic Botany: Exposition of Structure & Classification...* 1871. London. ils/16 color pls. 547 p. VG. B26. $59.00

SMITH, John. *True Travels, Adventures & Observations...* 1930. NY. R Hooper. 1/375. 83 p. buckram. VG/worn slipcase. B18. $85.00

SMITH, Joseph Jr. *Book of Mormon.* 1874. Lamoni, IA. Reorganized Church. 12mo. 545 p. M1. $150.00

SMITH, Joseph. *Bibliotheca Anti-Quakeriana; or, Catalogue of Books Adverse.* 1968. NY. Kraus Reprint Co. reprint of 1873 London ed. 8vo. 474 p. V3. $20.00

SMITH, Julie. *Axeman's Jazz.* 1991. St Martin. AP. NF/wrp. B2. $40.00

SMITH, Julie. *New Orleans Mourning.* (1990). St Martin. 1st ed. F/VG. B3. $30.00

SMITH, Justin H. *Troubadours at Home.* 1899. Putnam. 2 vols. gilt gr cloth. G. F1. $180.00

SMITH, Kay Nolte. *Catching Fire.* 1982. CMG. 1st ed. F/NF. N3. $15.00

SMITH, Kay Nolte. *Country of the Heart.* 1988. Villard. 1st ed. F/dj. B9. $10.00

SMITH, Kay Nolte. *Mindspell.* 1983. Morrow. ARC. VG+/dj. B9. $15.00

SMITH, Ken. *Baseball's Hall of Fame.* 1947. Barnes. 1st ed. G+. P8. $12.50

SMITH, L. *Fun & Fancy Machine Quiltmaking.* 1989. np. ils. wrp. G2. $20.00

SMITH, Laurence Dwight. *G-Men in Jeopardy.* 1938. Grosset Dunlap. 1st ed. F/NF. F4. $30.00

SMITH, Lawrence. *Am Game Preserve Shooting.* (1937). NY. deluxe ed. 175 p. VG-. A17. $18.50

SMITH, Lawrence. *Fur or Feather: Days w/Dog & Gun...ils by Paul Brn.* 1946. Scribner. 1st/A ed. sgns. VG/VG. O3. $95.00

SMITH, Lee. *Last Day the Dogbushes Bloomed.* 1969. Ballantine. PBO. sgn. NF/ils wrp. A11. $75.00

SMITH, Lee. *Me & My Baby View the Eclipse.* (1989). Putnam. 1st ed. sgn. F/F. B3. $25.00

SMITH, Leon. *Following the Comedy Trail.* 1988. Pomegrante Pr. NF. C8. $30.00

SMITH, Lillian. *Our Faces, Our Words.* 1964. Norton. stated 1st ed. 128 p. dj. A7. $22.00

SMITH, Logan Pearsall. *More Trivia.* 1921. Harcourt Brace. 1st ed. 12mo. 140 p. NF. V3. $9.50

SMITH, Louisa Hutchings. *Bermuda's Oldest Inhabitants.* 1934. Sevenoaks, Eng. 1st ed. ils May Middleton. VG. B28. $40.00

SMITH, Lucius E. *Heroes & Martyrs of Modern Missionary Enterprise...* 1856. Potter. 508 p. H10. $35.00

SMITH, Martha. *Letters of..., w/Short Memoir of Her Life.* 1844. NY. Piercy Reed. 18mo. 230 p. fair. V3. $24.00

SMITH, Martin Cruz. *Canto for a Gypsy.* 1972. Putnam. 1st ed. author's 2nd mystery. F/NF. L3. $125.00

SMITH, Martin Cruz. *Gorky Park.* 1981. Random. 1st ed. sgn. VG/dj. L3. $75.00

SMITH, Martin Cruz. *Gypsy in Amber.* (1971). Putnam. 1st ed. author's 1st mystery/hc book. VG/VG. L3. $350.00

SMITH, Martin Cruz. *Nightwing.* 1977. Norton. 1st ed. F/NF. L3. $85.00

SMITH, Martin Cruz. *Nightwing.* 1977. Norton. 1st ed. NF/VG. B3. $30.00

SMITH, Martin Cruz. *Polar Star.* (1989). Franklin Center. true 1st ed. sgn. full leather. F. B3. $70.00

SMITH, Martin Cruz. *Polar Star.* (1989). Random. 1st trade ed. NF/NF. B3. $30.00

SMITH, Martin Cruz. *Polar Star.* 1989. Random. 1st ed. sgn. F/NF. L3. $65.00

SMITH, Martin Cruz. *Red Square.* 1992. Random. 1st ed. 3rd of Gorky Park series. as new. L3. $25.00

SMITH, Martin Cruz. *Stallion Gate.* 1986. Random. 1st ed. F/F. L3. $50.00

SMITH, N. *Deck the Halls.* 1989. np. ils. wrp. G2. $16.00

SMITH, N. Gerard. *Dahlia Cultivation.* ca 1948. NY. 40 photos. 96 p. dj. B26. $15.00

SMITH, Nathan. *Medical Classics.* 1937. Baltimore. reprint. G7. $25.00

SMITH, Nicol. *Burma Road.* 1940. Bobbs Merrill. 1st ed. 8vo. 33 pls/map ep. VG/tattered. W1. $18.00

SMITH, Norman F. *MI Trees Worth Knowing.* (1961). MI Dept Conservation. 3rd ed. 60 p. VG/wrp. A17. $10.00

SMITH, Norman Lewis. *Return of Billy the Kid.* 1977. Coward McCann. 1st ed. VG/G+. P8. $12.50

SMITH, Ozzie. *Ozzie.* 1988. Contemporary. 1st ed. F/F. P8. $35.00

SMITH, P. *Patch-Word Quilt: Great Comforter.* 1991. np. ils. wrp. G2. $6.00

SMITH, Page. *John Adams.* 1962. np. 2 vols. NF/box. O7. $18.50

SMITH, Patti. *Useless Death.* (1972). Gotham Book Mart. 1/300. sgn. F/stapled wrp. B4. $85.00

SMITH, R.M. *New System of Modern Geography for Use of Schools...* 1846. Grigg Elliot. 168 p. leather spine. G. B10. $35.00

SMITH, Red. *Strawberries in the Wintertime.* 1974. Quadrangle. 1st ed. VG/VG. P8. $20.00

SMITH, Red. *Views of Sport.* 1954. Knopf. 1st ed. author's 2nd anthology. VG/G+. P8. $30.00

SMITH, Robert. *Babe Ruth's Am.* 1974. Crowell. 1st ed. 309 p. dj. A7. $18.00

SMITH, Robert. *Baseball in Am.* 1961. HRW. 1st ed. ils. VG/G+. P8. $35.00

SMITH, Robert. *Compleat System of Opticks in 4 Books...* 1738. Cambridge. self pub. 1st ed. quarto. 2 vols. 83 fld pls. gilt bdg. VG+. H5. $2,250.00

SMITH, Robert. *Heroes of Baseball.* 1952. World. 1st ed. sgn Don Newcombe. VG/G. P8. $60.00

SMITH, Robert. *Ils Hist of Baseball.* 1973. Grosset Dunlap. 1st ed. photos. F/VG. P8. $20.00

SMITH, Robert. *World Series.* 1967. Doubleday. 1st ed. photos. F/VG. P8. $12.50

SMITH, Rosamond; see Oates, Joyce Carol.

SMITH, Samuel. *Life of the Rev Joseph Grafton...* 1849. Boston. Putnam. 1st ed. 213 p. H10. $28.50

SMITH, Samuel. *Robert Dick: Baker of Thurso, Geologist & Botanist.* (1878). Harper. ils. 436 p. brn cloth. VG. S9. $15.00

SMITH, Seba. *Riches Without Wings; or, The Cleveland Family.* 1838. Boston. George W Light. 1st ed. 16mo. 162 p. cloth. M1. $125.00

SMITH, Steve. *Hunting Upland Game Birds.* (1987). Stackpole. 176 p. M/dj. A17. $17.50

SMITH, Steve. *Woodcock Shooting.* (1988). Stackpole. 1st ed. 142 p. F/dj. A17. $12.50

SMITH, T.H. *Mapping of OH.* (1977). Kent, OH. ils. 252 p. F/dj. B18. $45.00

SMITH, Terrence Lore. *Yours Truly, From Hell.* (1987). St Martin. 1st ed. F/dj. B9. $15.00

SMITH, Thorne. *Topper: An Improbable Adventure.* 1926. McBride. 1st ed. VG. B4. $85.00

SMITH, Wooster. *Directory of Newburyport: Containing Names of Inhabitants...* 1848. Newburyport. Nason. 119 p. pict brds. B14. $85.00

SMITH & SMITH. *Sm Arms of the World.* (1969). Stackpole. updated ed. ils. 768 p. VG/dj. A17. $27.50

SMITH. *Celebrating the Stitch.* 1991. np. ils. cloth. G2. $35.00

SMITHSON, Noble. *Smithson's Theory of Special Creation.* 1911. Knoxville. B30. $17.50

SMITHSONIAN INSTITUTE. *Annual Report of Board of Regents...1916.* 1971. GPO. photos/maps. 607 p. A7. $30.00

SMIZIK, Bob. *Pittsburgh Pirates.* 1990. Walker. 1st ed. F/F. P8. $25.00

SMOCK, Robert L. *Am Bicentennial Almanac & Reader.* ca 1975. Donning. ils/maps. 199 p. VG/wrp. B10. $10.00

SMOLLETT, Tobias George. *Adventures of Roderick Random.* (1793). London. C Cooke. reprint. 2 vols. 12mo. tree calf. F. B14. $45.00

SMURR & TOOLE. *Hist Essays on MT & the NW.* 1957. Helena, MT. 1st ed. 1/2000. 304 p. VG. D3. $25.00

SMYTH, Henry DeWolf. *General Account of Development Methods Using Atomic Energy.* 1940-1943. GPO. 1st pub account of making A-bomb. F/prt wrp. rare. B14. $375.00

SMYTH, J.H. *To Nowhere & Return: Autobiography of a Puritan.* (1940). NY. Carrick Evans. 1st ed. 8vo. 311 p. VG+/VG. A2. $25.00

SNAVELY, T.R. *Dept of Economics at U of VA, 1825-1956.* ca 1967. VA U. 1st ed. inscr presentation. 224 p. VG. B10. $10.00

SNAVELY, T.R. *Taxation of Negroes in VA.* 1917. VA. 97 p. wrp. A7. $18.00

SNEVE, Virginia. *High Elk's Treasure.* ca 1972. BC. ils Oren Lyons. G. C1. $4.50

SNODGRASS, W.D. *After Experience.* 1968. NY. 1st ed. sgn. F/NF clip. A11. $50.00

SNODGRASS, W.D. *Midnight Carnival.* 1988. Artra. 1/500. sgn. F. V1. $65.00

SNOW, Jack. *Magical Mimics in Oz.* nd. Reilly Lee. blk & wht Kramer ils. gray cloth/pict label. G+. L1. $300.00

SNOW, Jack. *Shaggy Man of Oz.* 1949. Reilly Lee. blk & wht Kramer ils. gray-gr cloth/pict label. VG. L1. $175.00

SNOW, Jack. *Shaggy Man of Oz.* 1949. Reilly Lee. 1st ed. ils Kramer. F/F. F1. $350.00

SNOW, Jack. *Shaggy Man of Oz.* 1949. Reilly Lee. 1st ed/1st state. ils Frank Kramer. 32 p. NF. D1. $275.00

SNOW, Sebastian. *My Amazon Adventure.* ca 1955. NY. Crown. 244 p. dj. F3. $15.00

SNOW & WAINE. *People From the Horizon: Ils Hist of Europeans...Islanders.* 1986. London. McLaren. ils. M/dj. O6. $35.00

SNYDER, Gary. *Left Out in the Rain.* 1986. Berkeley. Northpoint. AP. w/promo material. F/prt wrp. B3. $35.00

SNYDER, Gary. *Left Out in the Rain.* 1986. Northpoint. 1st ed. F/F. V1. $25.00

SNYDER, Gary. *Riprap.* 1959. Origin Pr. 1st ed. inscr. author's 1st book. F/wrp. B24. $650.00

SNYDER, Gerald S. *In the Footsteps of Lewis & Clark.* 1970. Nat Geog Soc. 1st ed. sm 4to. ils. 215 p. M/pict dj. T8. $27.50

SOANE, E.B. *To Mesopotamia & Kurdistan in Disguise.* 1912. Boston. 8vo. ils/lg fold map. 410 p. cloth. O2. $125.00

SOBOL, Donald J. *Best Animals Stories of SF & Fantasy.* 1979. NY. Warne. 1st ed. F/F. N3. $15.00

SOCIO, Nobile. *De Temporibus et Modis Recte Purgandi in Morbis...* 1577. Lyon. Alexan. Marsilium. 16mo. 360 p. scarce. K1. $350.00

SOCOLOFSKY, Homer E. *Hist Altas of KS.* 1988. Norman, OK. 74 full-p maps. M/dj. O6. $27.00

SODERSTROM, Thomas R. *Grass: Systematics & Evolution.* ca 1987. Smithsonian. 4to. 473 p. M. H10. $45.00

SOEMMERRING, Samuel Thomas. *Basi Encephali et Originibus Nervorum Cranio Egredientium...* 1778. Goettingen. Vanderboeck. 4 fld pls. 184 p. period wrp. B14. $275.00

SOHL, Jerry. *Costigan's Needle.* 1953. Rinehart. 1st ed. w/sgn label. F/NF clip. F4. $50.00

SOHL, Jerry. *Resurrection of Frank Borchard.* 1973. Simon Schuster. 1st ed. sgn. F/F. F4. $26.00

SOHL, Jerry. *Spun Sugar Hole.* 1971. Simon Schuster. 1st ed. F/F. N3. $12.00

SOKOLSKY, George E. *We Jews.* 1935. Doubleday Doran. 1st ed. 304 p. G. S3. $17.00

SOLOMITA, Stephen. *Bat to the Bone.* 1991. Putnam. 1st ed. F/F. M15. $30.00

SOLOMON, Barbara Probst. *Short Flights.* (1983). Viking. rem mk. 307 p. dj. A7. $10.00

SOLTOW. *Making Animal Quilts: Patterns & Projects.* 1986. np. ils. wrp. G2. $12.95

SOLTOW. *Quilting the World Over.* 1980. np. ils. wrp. G2. $17.00

SOLZHENITSYN, Alexander. *August 1914.* 1989. FSG. AP/ARC. 846 p. NF. C4. $65.00

SOLZHENITSYN, Alexander. *Gulag Archipelago 1918-1956.* 1974. London. Collins/Harvill. 1st ed. trans Thomas Whitney. NF/VG+. A14. $25.00

SOLZHENITSYN, Alexander. *Lenin in Zurich.* 1976. FSG. 1st ed. NF/NF. E3. $20.00

SOLZHENITSYN, Alexander. *Lenin in Zurich.* 1976. London. Bodley Head. 1st ed. trans HT Willets. F/F. A14. $35.00

SOLZHENITSYN, Alexander. *One Day in the Life of Ivan Denisovich.* 1963. London. Gollancz. 1st ed. trans Ralph Parker. NF/NF. A14. $75.00

SOLZHENITSYN, Alexander. *One Day in the Life of Ivan Denisovich.* 1963. NY. Praeger. 1st Am ed. trans Max Hayward/R Hingley. VG+/VG+. A14. $80.00

SOLZHENITSYN, Alexander. *Stories & Prose Poems.* 1974. Bodley Head. 3rd British imp of 1970 Russian ed. NF/NF. A14. $30.00

SOLZHENITSYN, Alexander. *Victory Celebrations.* 1983. London. Bodley Head. 1st ed. trans Rapp/Thomas. F/F. A14. $25.00

SOMBART, Werner. *Jews & Modern Capitalism.* 1951. Free Pr. 402 p. VG/G. S3. $25.00

SOMBART, Werner. *Socialism & the Social Movement.* 1909. London. Dent. trans M Epstein. NF. B2. $85.00

SOMERFIELD, Elizabeth. *Boxer.* (1977). NY. 10th ed. photos. 186 p. cloth. dj. A17. $8.50

SOMERS, Jane; see Kosinski, Jerzy.

SOMERVILLE, Thomas. *George Square, Glascow.* 1891. Glascow. 1st ed. 12mo. 304 p. aeg. gilt gr cloth. VG. H3. $25.00

SOMMER, H. Oskar. *Vulgate Version of Arthurian Romances.* 1909. WA. Carnegie Instit. 7 vols w/index vol. rare. F1. $950.00

SOMMER-BODENBURG, Angela. *My Friend the Vampire.* 1984. NY. Dial. 1st Am ed. F/VG+. N3. $10.00

SOMMERFIELD, John. *Volunteer in Spain.* 1937. Knopf. 1st Am ed. 12mo. 155 p. F/VG. A2. $20.00

SOMMERS, Joseph. *After the Storm.* (1968). Albuquerque, NM. 1st ed. 208 p. dj. F3. $20.00

SOMMERS, Lawrence. *Atlas of MI.* (1978). MI State U. 3rd prt. 242 p. F/dj. A17. $22.50

SOMTOW, S.P.; see Sucharitkul, Somtow.

SONDHEIM, Stephen. *Funny Thing Happened on the Way to the Forum.* (1991). Applause. 1st thus ed. F/F. C4. $35.00

SONDHEIM, Stephen. *Little Night Music.* (1991). Applause. 1st thus ed. F/F. C4. $35.00

SONDHEIM, Stephen. *Sunday in the Park w/George.* 1986. Dodd Mead. 1/250. sgn. F/slipcase. C4. $125.00

SONNENFELS, Amanda. *Die Rotten Schuhe.* nd. Furth in Bayrn. ils Lindman. 8vo. ils ep. VG. D1. $50.00

SONNICHSEN, C.L. *Ambidextrous Historian: Hist Writers & Writing in Am W.* (1981). OK U. 1st ed. F/F. A18. $30.00

SONNINI, C.S. *Voyage en Grece et en Turquie.* 1801. Paris. pl vol only. folio. 6 (of 7) pls. gilt leather/marbled brds. O2. $600.00

SONTAG, Susan. *Benefactor.* 1963. Farrar. 1st ed. F/NF. B2. $60.00

SONTAG, Susan. *Benefactor.* 1963. NY. 1st ed. sgn. NF/NF. A11. $65.00

SOPER, Alexander Coburn III. *Evolution of Buddhist Architecture in Japan.* 1942. Princeton. 211 ils. gilt blk cloth. K1. $150.00

SORENSEN, Jon. *Saga of Fridtjof Nansen.* (1932). Am Scandinavian Foundation/Norton. 1st Am ed. VG. A2. $30.00

SORENSEN, Theodore C. *Kennedy.* 1965. Harper Row. 1st ed. F/F. T2. $8.00

SORENSON, Lewell L. *Beyond Charted Space.* 1985. Vantage. 1st ed. inscr. F/NF. N3. $15.00

SORLEY, W.R. *Hist of Eng Philosophy.* 1921. Putnam. 1st Am ed. 372 p. russet cloth. VG. G1. $45.00

SORLIN, Pierre. *Film in Hist, Restaging the Past.* 1980. Barnes Noble. NF/dj. C8. $35.00

SOULES, Francois. *Histoire des Troubles de l'Amerique Anglaise...* 1787. Paris. 8vo. quarter sheep. lacks 3 maps. H9. $125.00

SOUSTELLE, Jacque. *Daily Life of the Aztecs.* (1961). London. 1st Eng ed. 319 p. VG. F3. $15.00

SOUSTELLE, Jacque. *Four Suns.* 1971. Grossman. 1st ed. 256 p. dj. F3. $15.00

SOUSTIEL, Joseph. *L'Art Turc. Ceramiques Tapis Etoffes Velours Broderies.* 1952. Paris. presentation. 32 p. prt wrp. O2. $40.00

SOUTHARD, Charles Zibeon. *Evolution of Trout & Trout Fishing in Am.* 1928. NY. Dutton. quarto. 254 p. red cloth. B14. $75.00

SOUTHEY, Robert. *Poet's Pilgrimage to Waterloo.* 1816. Boston. Wells Lilly. 1st Am ed. orig brds. NF. O6. $75.00

SOWERBY, Millicent. *Glad Book.* 1935. Artists/Writers Guild. authorized ed. 12 pls. 32 p. A3. $25.00

SOYINKA, Wole. *Man Died: Prison Notes.* (1972). Harper Row. 1st Am ed. 317 p. NF/dj. A7. $35.00

SPAETH, Sigmund. *Barber Shop Ballads & How To Sing Them.* 1940. NY. 2nd prt. ils. 125 p. pict cloth. G. A17. $17.50

SPAGGETT, Allen. *Unexplained.* 1967. NAL. 1st prt. F/F. T2. $4.50

SPARANO, V.T. *Complete Outdoors Encyclopedia.* (1972). NY. ils. 622 p. dj. A17. $17.50

SPARGO, John. *Social Democracy Explained.* 1918. Harper. 337 p. A7. $15.00

SPARGO, John. *Socialism & Motherhood.* 1914. Huebsch. 128 p. A7. $22.00

SPARK, Muriel. *Bang-Bang You're Dead.* 1982. London. Granada. PBO. inscr. F/unread. A11. $60.00

SPARK, Muriel. *Driver's Seat.* (1970). London. McMillan. 1st ed. VG/VG clip. B3. $35.00

SPARK, Muriel. *Hothouse by the E River.* (1973). London. McMillan. 1st ed. VG/VG. B3. $40.00

SPARK, Muriel. *Loitering w/Intent.* (1981). Bodley Head. 1st ed. NF/NF. B3. $35.00

SPARK, Muriel. *Prime of Miss Jean Brodie.* 1961. London. 1st ed. sgn. NF/ VG+. A11. $175.00

SPARK, Muriel. *Voices At Play.* 1961. London. 1st ed. inscr. F/NF. A11. $70.00

SPARK & STANFORD. *My Best Mary. Letters of Mary Wollstonecraft Shelley.* 1951. London. 1st ed. NF/NF. A11. $45.00

SPARKS, Jared. *Life of George WA.* 1843. Boston. Tappan Dennet. early prt. 14 pls. 562 p. VG+. M8. $85.00

SPARKS, Jared. *Life of George WA.* 1853. NY. Derby Miller. abridged ed. 2 vols in 1. 12mo. 344 p. fair. B11. $35.00

SPARKS, Jared. *Life of Gouverneur Morris...* 1832. Boston. 1st ed. 3 vols. brds/rebacked gr cloth. VG. D7. $180.00

SPARROW, Walter Shaw. *Anglin in British Art Through 5 Centuries...* 1923. London. Bodley Head. thick 4to. 288 p. 1/125. sgn. w/orig sgn etching. F. F1. $595.00

SPAULDING, Edward Selden. *Adobe Days Along the Channel.* 1957. Santa Barbara. Schauer. Grizzly ed. 1/1015. sgn. 4to. rust cloth. pub box. K1. $150.00

SPAYTH, Henry. *Draughts or Checkers for Beginners.* (1866). NY. 88 p. decor cloth. VG. B18. $25.00

SPEARS. *Home Study Course in Quiltmaking.* 1990. np. cloth. G2. $20.00

SPEARS. *Mastering the Basics of Quiltmaking.* 1982. np. ils. wrp. G2. $8.00

SPECTORSKY, A.C. *Book of the Mtns.* 1955. NY. 1st ed. 492 p. F. H3. $45.00

SPEER, Emory. *Lincoln, Lee, Grant & Other Biographical Addresses.* 1909. NY/WA. Neale. 1st ed. inscr. 269 p. cloth. VG+. M8. $150.00

SPEIDEL, William C. *Sons of the Profits...* 1968. Seattle, WA. Nettle Creek. 2nd ed. dj. N2. $10.00

SPELLMAN, Francis. *Sermon...of the Silver Jubilee of His Consecration...* 1957. Worcester. St Onge. miniature. 1/1000. F. H10. $165.00

SPENCE, Eleanor. *Candle for Saint Antony.* 1977. Oxford. 1st ed. NF/NF clip. A14. $25.00

SPENCE, Lewis. *Problem of Atlantis.* 1925. London. Rider. 2nd ed. G. N2. $25.00

SPENCER, B. *Tried & True.* 1870. np. 1st ed. 394 p. O7. $14.50

SPENCER, Colin. *Anarchists in Love.* 1963. Eyre Spottiswoode. 1st ed. NF/NF. A14. $30.00

SPENCER, Edwin R. *Just Weeds.* 1940. NY. ils E Bergdolt. 317 p. VG/dj. B26. $19.00

SPENCER, Elizabeth. *Light in the Piazza.* 1960. NY. 1st ed. sgn. F/F. A11. $65.00

SPENCER, Jeannette Dyer. *Ahwahnee.* 1942. Yosemite Nat Park. 8vo. F. A8. $5.00

SPENCER, Robert S. *Typhoon Days in Japan.* 1934. NY. Friendship. 1st ed. 8vo. ils/map. 182 p. VG. W1. $18.00

SPENDER, Stephen. *Collected Poems.* 1985. NY. 1st ed. F/F. V1. $25.00

SPERLING, Grace Dickinson. *Feisal the Arabian.* 1933. Chicago. Ralph Fletcher Seymour. 66 p. VG/gilt red wrp. M7. $65.00

SPERRY, Armstrong. *All Sail Set: Romance of the Flying Cloud.* 1935. Winston. 1st ed. 171 p. NF/G+. P2. $30.00

SPERRY, Armstrong. *Wagons Westward.* (1936). Chicago. 1st ed. 276 p. pict cloth. VG. D3. $15.00

SPERRY, Armstrong. *Wagons Westward: Old Trail to Santa Fe.* 1936. Winston. 1st ed. ils. 273 p. NF. P2. $20.00

SPICER, Bart. *Burned Man.* 1967. London. Barker. 1st British ed. NF/NF. S5. $25.00

SPICER, Bart. *Cotswold Mistress.* 1992. London. Constable. ARC of 1st ed. RS. F/F. S5. $27.50

SPICER, Jack. *Holy Grail.* 1975. Blk Sparrow. 1/1000. gray brds/red spine. M. C1. $24.00

SPICER, Jack. *Lament for the Makers.* 1962. Oakland. Wht Rabbit Pr. 1/100. F/wrp. B2. $100.00

SPIELBERG, Steven. *Close Encounters of the 3rd Kind.* 1977. Dell. pb. NF. C8. $10.00

SPIELBERG, Steven. *Letters to ET.* 1983. Putnam. 1st ed. intro Spielberg. ils. F/NF. N3. $25.00

SPIER, Peter. *Of Dikes & Windmills.* 1969. NY. 1st ed. ils. VG+/dj. C1. $6.00

SPIERS, George. *Wavertree...Ocean Wanderer... Around the Horn in 1907...* 1969. NY. S Street Seaport. 1/500. sgn. M/slipcase. O6. $100.00

SPILLANE, Mickey. *Girl Hunters.* 1962. Dutton. 1st ed. inscr. F/dj. B9. $65.00

SPILLANE, Mickey. *Girl Hunters.* 1962. Dutton. 1st ed. VG+/dj. B9. $45.00

SPILLANE, Mickey. *Kiss Me, Deadly.* 1952. Dutton. 1st ed. G/dj. M18. $75.00

SPILLANE, Mickey. *My Gun Is Quick.* 1950. Dutton. 1st ed. G. M18. $100.00

SPILLER, Burton. *Grouse Feathers.* (1972). Crown. reprint. ils LB Hunt. leatherette. F/dj. A17. $20.00

SPINDEN, Herbert Joseph. *Songs of the Tewa.* 1933. Exposition Indian Tribal Arts. sgn. NF/orig glassine. L3. $350.00

SPINOZA, Baruch. *Hebrew Grammar: Concise Compendium.* 1962. Philosophical Lib. 152 p. VG+/G. S3. $25.00

SPINRAD, Norman. *Child of Fortune.* 1985. Bantam. ARC. NF/wrp. N3. $15.00

SPIRIDONAKIS, B.G. *Essays on Hist Geography of Greek World...* 1977. Thessaloniki. 8vo. 171 p. cloth. O2. $30.00

SPIRO, Saul. *Fundementals of Judaism.* 1969. NY. KTAV. xl. 342 p. VG. S3. $19.00

SPIVAK, John L. *Save the Country Racket.* (1948). NY. New Century. 63 p. wrp. A7. $20.00

SPRATLING, William. *Little Mexico.* 1947. NY. Smith. 4th prt. 198 p. F3. $10.00

SPRENGELL, Conrad. *Aphorisms of Hippocrates & Sentences of Celsus...* 1735. London. Wilkins Bonwich. 2nd/enlarged ed. 435 p. contemporary calf. G7. $350.00

SPRING, Anges Wright. *Cheyenne & Blk Hills Stage & Express Routes.* 1949. Glendale. Arthur Clark. 1st ed. Ramona Adams' copy. VG. O3. $275.00

SPRINGALL. *Canvas Embroidery.* 1980. np. ils. cloth. G2. $20.00

SPRINGARN, J.E. *Hist of Literary Criticism in Renaissance.* 1938 (1899). NY. VG. C1. $5.00

SPRUILL, Steven G. *Paradox Planet.* 1988. Doubleday. 1st ed. F/F. N3. $15.00

SPRUNGMAN, Ormal I. *Photography Afield.* (1951). Stackpole. 1st ed. 449 p. A17. $17.50

SPRUYTTE, J. *Early Harness Systems...* 1983. London. Allen. 1st Eng-language ed. 135 p. VG. O3. $25.00

SPRY, Constance. *Encyclopedia of Flower Arranging & Indoor Plant Decor.* 1972. London. 1st ed. color pls. 192 p. NF/VG. B28. $17.50

SPYRI, Johanna. *Children of the Alps.* 1925. Phil. ils Margaret J Marshall. 319 p. F/G. H3. $25.00

SPYRI, Johanna. *Heidi.* 1921. Rand McNally. 1st thus ed. Windemere series. G. P2. $15.00

SPYRI, Johanna. *Little Alpine Musician.* 1924. Crowell. ils Howard Hastings. VG+. M5. $18.00

SPYRI, Johanna. *Peppino.* 1926. Lippincott. 4 color pls. red cloth. VG. M5. $12.00

SPYRI, Johanna. *Veronica.* 1924. Crowell. 4 color pls. VG. M5. $14.00

SQUIER, E.G. *Notes on Central Am.* 1855. NY. 1st ed. fld color map. 397 p. gilt red cloth. VG+. H3. $150.00

SQUIER, Emma-Lindsay. *On Autumn Trails.* 1923. NY. ils Paul Bransom. F/dj. A17. $10.00

SQUIRE. *Ask Helen...More About Quilting Designs.* 1990. np. 100 full-size patterns. wrp. G2. $15.00

SQUIRES, W.H.T. *Through Centuries Three.* 1929. Printcraft. sgn/#d. ils. 605 p. VG. B10. $25.00

SREBRO. *Miniature to Masterpiece: Perfect Piecing Secrets...* 1990. np. workbook. G2. $15.00

SRIVASTAVA, R.S. *Contemporary Indian Philosophy.* 1965. Delhi. Munshi Ram Manohar Lal. 1st ed. 8vo. VG/dj. W1. $18.00

SRODA, George. *Facts About Nightcrawlers.* (1984). WI. 4th prt. photos. 111 p. G/wrp. A17. $6.00

STABLEDON, Olaf. *Darkness & the Light.* 1974. Hyperion. reprint of 1942 ed. NF. M2. $15.00

STABLEFORD, Brian M. *Empire of Fear.* 1988. Simon Schuster. 1st ed. sgn. F/F. F4. $47.50

STABLEFORD, Brian M. *Empire of Fear.* 1991. NY. Carroll Graf. F/F. N3. $20.00

STACHEY, John. *Contemporary Capitalism.* (1956). Random. 374 p. NF/VG. A7. $20.00

STACK, Robert. *Shotgun Digest.* (1974). Northfield. ils. 288 p. NF/wrp. A17. $9.50

STACKPOLE, Edouard A. *You Fight for Treasure!* 1932. NY. 1st ed. 307 p. pict ep. pict gr cloth. H3. $20.00

STADLER, Matthew. *Landscape: Memory.* 1990. Scribner. 1st ed. author's 1st book. F/F. A14. $25.00

STAENDER & STAENDER. *Adventures w/Arctic Wildlife.* 1970. Caldwell, ID. Caxton. 1st ed. 8vo. 260 p. F/VG+. A2. $17.50

STAFFORD, Peter. *Sexual Behavior in the Communist World.* (1967). Julian Pr. 1st ed. 8vo. 287 p. F/VG. A2. $15.00

STAFFORD, William. *Allegiances.* (1970). Harper Row. 1st ed/hc. F/F clip. A18. $50.00

STAFFORD, William. *Allegiances.* 1970. NY. 1st ed. NF/wrp. V1. $20.00

STAFFORD, William. *Long Sigh the Wind Makes.* (1991). Adrienne Lee Pr. 1st ed. sgn. M. A18. $40.00

STAFFORD, William. *My Name Is William Tell.* (1992). Confluence Pr. 1st ed. M/M. A18. $20.00

STAFFORD, William. *Stories That Could Be True: New & Collected Poems.* (1977). Harper Row. 1st ed. sgn. F/F clip. A18. $60.00

STAFFORD, William. *Traveling Through the Dark.* 1962. NY. 1st ed. 12mo. F/NF clip. A11. $165.00

STAHL, John M. *Growing w/the W.* 1930. Longman Gr. 8vo. G. A8. $15.00

STALEY, John. *Man Who Married a Bear.* 1992. NY. Soho. 1st ed. author's 1st novel. F/F. M15. $30.00

STALIN, Joseph. *Dialectical & Hist Materialism.* 1975 (1940). NY. Internat. later prt. 48 p. NF/wrp. A7. $8.00

STALLONE, Sylvester. *Paradise Alley.* 1977. Putnam. 1st ed. F/F. T2. $9.00

STANBURY, Peter. *Moving Frontier...Aboriginal-European Interaction Australia.* (1977). Sydney. Reed. 1st ed. 4to. photos. 155 p. F/VG+. A2. $20.00

STANEK, V.J. *Pict Encyclopedia of the Animal Kingdom.* (1971). London. 7th imp. 614 p. dj. A17. $14.50

STANFORD, J.K. *Las Chukker.* 1954. NY. Devin-Adair. 1st ed. VG/VG. O3. $25.00

STANFORD, William. *Les Plees del Corone, Divisees in Plusors Titles...* 1607. London. Ex Typographia Societatis Stationariorum. 198 p. calf. K1. $300.00

STANGER, Margaret A. *That Quail, Robert.* 1966. Lippincott. VG/dj. A16. $12.00

STANHOPE, Leicester. *Greece in 1823 & 1824; Being Series of Letters...* 1824. London. 8vo. 5 facsimile letters (4 fld). contemporary calf. O2. $525.00

STANLEY, Arthur Penrhyn. *Essays Chiefly on Questions of Church & State...* 1870. London. Murray. 1st ed. 617 p. leather. detached covers. H10. $25.00

STANLEY, Arthur Penrhyn. *Hist Memorials of Westminster Abbey.* 1887. NY. Randolph. 1/600 lg paper. 3 vols. teg. morocco. F. F1. $285.00

STANLEY, Henry M. *Congo & the Founding of Its Free State...* 1885. Harper. 1st Am ed. 2 vols. gilt gr cloth. NF. F1. $325.00

STANLEY, Henry M. *In Darkest Africa.* 1890. NY. 1/250. sgn. lg quarto. 2 vols. orig half brn morocco. F. H5. $3,000.00

STANLEY, Jean. *Horse w/1-Track Mind.* 1962. Phil. Westminster. presentation. VG/G. O3. $25.00

STANNARD, David E. *Shrinking Hist: Freud & Failure of Psychohistory.* 1980. NY. Oxford. 1st ed. 188 p. blk cloth. VG/dj. G1. $25.00

STANSBURY, Howard. *Exploration & Survey of Valley of the Great Salt Lake...* 1853. WA. Armstrong. 2nd ed. 495 p. G+. H7. $90.00

STANSBURY, Howard. *Maps to Accompany His Report...to Salt Lake (UT)...* ca 1848. GPO. xl. fld into octavo blk cloth folder. H9. $375.00

STANTON, Daniel. *Journal of Life, Travels & Gospel Labors...* 1799. London. Phillips. 132 p. sewn. H10. $45.00

STANTON, S.L. *Gr Berets...1956-1975.* (1985). Presidio. 360 p. dj. A7. $15.00

STANWELL-FLETCHER, T.C. *Clear Lands & Icy Seas: Voyage to E Arctic.* 1958. NY. Dodd Mead. 1st ed. 8vo. 264 p. VG+/VG+. A2. $12.50

STARK, Richard; see Westlake, Donald E.

STARKEY, Marion L. *Land Where Our Fathers Died: Settling of the E Shores.* 1962. Doubleday. 1st ed. 275 p. VG/G. B10. $18.00

STARKIE, Enid. *Petrus Borel: The Lycanthrope.* 1954. London. Faber. 1st ed. dj. N2. $15.00

STARKS, Michael. *Cocaine Fiends & Reefer Madness.* (1982). NY/London. Cornwall. 1st ed. lg 4to. ils/index. 242 p. NF/dj. B20. $35.00

STARLING, Thomas. *Geographical Annual; or, Family Cabinet Atlas.* 1834. London. sm octavo. 96 engraved leaves. aeg. gr morocco. NF. O6. $650.00

STARR, Roland. *Operation Omina.* 1970. Lenox Hill. 1st ed. NF/NF. O3. $25.00

STARR, Theodore B. *Miniature Calendar & Stamp Case for Yr 1908.* 1907. NY. miniature. 28 p. red leather. H10. $15.00

STARR, W.H. *Centennial Hist Sketch of the Town of New London.* 1876. London. Allyn. 1st ed. 96 p. wrp. H10. $45.00

STARR, Walter A. Jr. *Starr's Guide to the John Muir Trail & High Sierra Region.* 1964. Sierra Club. 9th ed. 135 p. F/stiff wrp. A17. $9.50

STARRETT, Vincent. *Late, Later & Possibly Last Essays.* 1973. St Louis. Autolycus. 1/500. sgn. pub/sgn M Murphy. w/promo material. F. B20. $50.00

STASHEFF, Christopher. *Wizard in Bedlam.* 1979. Doubleday. 1st ed. F/dj. M2. $22.00

STATHAM, Pamela. *Origins of Australia's Capital Cities.* 1989. Cambridge. 80 maps. 364 p. M/dj. O6. $45.00

STATIUS, Publius Papinius. *Tebaide di Stazio di Selvaggio Porpora.* 1729. Rome. Giovanni Maria Salvioni. 1st ed. 4to. 502 p. vellum. K1. $275.00

STATON, Frances. *Canadian NW.* 1931. Toronto. Public Lib. NF/wrp. O6. $35.00

STAUNTON, George Leonard. *Authentic Account of Embassy From King of Great Britain...* 1799. Phil. John Bioren. 2 vols in 1. octavo. full contemporary calf. H9. $400.00

STAVROULAKIS, Nicholas. *Jews of Greece. An Essay.* 1990. Athens. 8vo. 127 p. O2. $17.50

STAVROULAKIS, Nicholas. *Sephardic & Romaniot Jewish Costume in Greece & Turkey.* 1986. Athens. sm folio. w/portfolio of 16 repro watercolors. O2. $35.00

STEARNS, Carol Zisowitz. *Anger: The Struggle for Emotional Control in Am's Hist.* 1986. Chicago. 1st ed. 290 p. red cloth. VG/dj. G1. $22.50

STEARNS, E.J. *Notes on Uncle Tom's Cabin.* 1853. Phil. 314 p. F. scarce. O7. $21.00

STEARNS, Pamela. *Mechanical Doll.* 1979. Houghton Mifflin. 1st ed. sq 8vo. 45 p. VG/VG. A3. $20.00

STEARNS. *Homespun & Bl: Study of Am Crewel Embroidery.* 1963. np. cloth. G2. $25.00

STEBBINS, Theodore E. *Am Master Drawings & Watercolors.* 1976. Harper. 1st ed. 4to. 464 p. F/VG+. F1. $65.00

STEBEL, S.L. *Spring Thaw.* 1989. NY. Walker. 1st ed. F/F. N3. $15.00

STECHOW, Wolfgang. *Dutch Landscape Painting of the 17th Century.* 1966. London. Phaidon. sm 4to. 496 p. gilt maroon cloth. F/VG. F1. $75.00

STEDMAN, Edmund C. *Complete Pocket Guide to Europe.* 1926. NY. 24mo. 6 maps. 659 p. gilt blk cloth. VG. H3. $20.00

STEED, Neville. *Tinplate.* 1986. London. Weidenfeld. 1st ed. sgn. author's 1st book. F/F. S5. $40.00

STEEL, Flora A. *Garden of Fidelity: Autobiography of Flora A Steel...* 1929. London. Macmillan. 1st ed. 8vo. 293 p. VG-. A2. $20.00

STEEL, Ronald. *Pax Americana: Cold-War Empire the US Acquired by Accident.* (1967). Viking. 1st ed. 371 p. NF/NF. A7. $25.00

STEELE, Adison; see Lupoff, Richard.

STEELE, Danielle. *Message From Nam.* (1990). Delacorte. 1st ed. F/F. A7. $25.00

STEELE, G.P. *Seadragon: NW Under the Ice.* 1962. Dutton. 2nd ed. 8vo. 255 p. VG+/VG. A2. $12.50

STEELE, J.W. *Frontier Army Sketches.* 1969. Albuquerque. reprint of 1883 ed. 329 p. F/VG. P4. $35.00

STEELE, J.W. *New Guide to the Pacific Coast Santa Fe Route...* 1893. Chicago. Rand McNally. fld map. VG. H7. $75.00

STEELE, Rufus. *Fall of Ug.* 1913. San Francisco. 1st ed. inscr pub/John Howell. NF. A15. $40.00

STEEN, Marguerite. *Unquiet Spirit.* 1956. Doubleday. 1st Am ed. F/NF. N3. $35.00

STEERE, Douglas V. *On Beginning From Within.* 1943. Harper. 4th ed. 12mo. 149 p. VG/dj. V3. $9.50

STEERE, Douglas V. *Work & Contemplation.* 1957. Harper. 1st ed. 12mo. 148 p. VG/dj. V3. $12.00

STEEVES & SUSSEX. *Patterns in Plant Development.* 1972. Englewood Cliffs. ils/photos. 302 p. B26. $19.00

STEFANSSON, Vilhjalmur. *Friendly Arctic: Story of 5 Yrs in Polar Regions.* 1939. NY. later prt. photos/index. pocket map. VG. A17. $45.00

STEFANSSON, Vilhjalmur. *Great Adventures & Explorations.* 1947. NY. 1st ed. 788 p. map ep. gilt red cloth. VG/G. H3. $20.00

STEFANSSON, Vilhjalmur. *Hunters of the Great N.* (1922). NY. ils/photos/fld map. 301 p. VG. A17. $35.00

STEFANSSON, Vilhjalmur. *Northward Course of Empire.* 1924. Macmillan. inscr/ sgn. ils/fld map. NF. O6. $125.00

STEFFERUD, Alfred. *Birds in Our Lives.* (1966). WA. 1st ed. lg 4to. 561 p. F/dj. A17. $25.00

STEGER & SCHURKE. *N to the Pole.* (1987). Time Books. 1st ed. 8vo. 339 p. F/F. A2. $25.00

STEGNER, Wallace. *Angle of Repose.* 1971. Doubleday. 1st ed. F/F. A18. $150.00

STEGNER, Wallace. *Big Rock Candy Mtn.* 1943. DSP. 1st ed. author's 3rd novel. VG/VG. L3. $650.00

STEGNER, Wallace. *Big Rock Candy Mtn.* 1943. NY. Condensed Armed Services ed. sgn. VG+. A11. $75.00

STEGNER, Wallace. *Bl-Winged Teal.* 1979. Logan, IA. 1st separate ed. sgn. NF/bl wrp. A11. $50.00

STEGNER, Wallace. *Collected Stories.* (1990). Random. 1st ed. M/M. A18. $40.00

STEGNER, Wallace. *Conversations w/Wallace Stegner on W Hist & Literature.* 1983. UT U. 1st ed. sgns. F/F. A18. $125.00

STEGNER, Wallace. *Crossing to Safety.* (1987). Random. AP. F. A18. $50.00

STEGNER, Wallace. *Crossing to Safety.* (1987). Random. 1st ed. NF/F. A18. $25.00

STEGNER, Wallace. *Discovery!* 1971. Beirut. 1st ed/PBO. sgn. NF/8vo wrp. A11. $95.00

STEGNER, Wallace. *First Drafts, Last Drafts: 40 Yrs of Creative Writing...* nd. Stanford. 1/500. F/stiff prt wrp. C4. $135.00

STEGNER, Wallace. *Growing Up Western.* 1990. Knopf. 1st ed. ils. F/F. C4. $45.00

STEGNER, Wallace. *On the Writing of Hist.* nd. Los Altos. 1/100. sgn. F/stiff wrp. C4. $100.00

STEGNER, Wallace. *One Nation.* 1945. Houghton Mifflin. 1st ed. VG/VG. C4. $40.00

STEGNER, Wallace. *Recapitulation.* 1979. Franklin Lib. 1st Ed Soc ed. ils Walter Rane. full gilt leather. F. A18. $80.00

STEGNER, Wallace. *Remembering Laughter.* nd (1951). NY. PBO. sgn. Dell 10¢ series. F/unread. A11. $95.00

STEGNER, Wallace. *Remembering Laughter.* 1937. Little Brn. 1st ed. VG. A18. $50.00

STEGNER, Wallace. *Shooting Star.* 1961. Viking. ARC. 1/750. gilt red brds. F/VG. A18. $100.00

STEGNER, Wallace. *Shooting Star.* 1961. Viking. 1st trade ed. F/NF. A18. $80.00

STEGNER, Wallace. *Spectator Bird.* 1976. Franklin Lib. true 1st ed. aeg. leather. F. L3. $75.00

STEGNER, Wallace. *Spectator Bird.* 1976. Franklin Lib. 1st Ed Soc ed/true 1st issue. full gilt leather. M. A18. $80.00

STEGNER, Wallace. *Stanford Short Stories, 1953.* 1953. Stanford. 1/500. F/F. C4. $40.00

STEGNER, Wallace. *Unknown CA.* (1985). Macmillan. 1st ed. F/NF. C4. $30.00

STEGNER, Wallace. *Where the Bluebird Sings to the Lemonade Springs.* 1992. Random. 1st ed. author's last book. sgn. F/F. C4. $55.00

STEGNER, Wallace. *Wolf Willow: Hist, Story & Memory of Last Plains Frontier.* (1963). Heinemann. 1st ed. F/VG clip. A18. $60.00

STEGNER, Wallace. *Women on the Wall.* (1952). London. Hammond. 1st ed. F/VG clip. A18. $75.00

STEGNER & STEGNER. *Am Places.* (1981). Dutton. 1st ed. ils Eliot Porter. NF/F clip. B4. $125.00

STEHLING, Kurt R. *Bagus Up!* 1975. Chicago. Playboy. 1st ed. rem mk. G/dj. A16. $10.00

STEIG, William. *Amos & Boris.* 1971. FSG. 1st ed. ils. VG/G+. P2. $25.00

STEIG, William. *Bad Speller.* 1970. Simon Schuster. 1st ed. 46 p. VG/VG. A3. $20.00

STEIG, William. *CDB!* 1968. Simon Schuster/ Windmill. 6th prt. 44 p. VG/VG. A3. $10.00

STEIG, William. *Dominic.* 1972. FSG. 1st ed. ils. 146 p. F/VG. P2. $25.00

STEIG, William. *Rejected Lovers.* 1951. Knopf. 1st ed. decor brds. N2. $10.00

STEIN, Aaron Marc. *...And High Water.* 1946. Doubleday. 1st ed. F/VG. B4. $45.00

STEIN, Gertrude. *Four Am in Paris, Collections of Gertrude Stein...* 1970. NY. MOMA. oblong red sc. B30. $20.00

STEIN, Gertrude. *Four in Am.* 1947. NH. 1st ed. VG+/dj. A15. $50.00

STEIN, Gertrude. *Geography & Plays.* 1968. NY. fwd Sherwood Anderson. VG/stiff wrp. E3. $25.00

STEIN, Gertrude. *How To Write.* 1973. W Glover, VT. 1st Am ed. VG/stiff wrp. E3. $30.00

STEIN, Gertrude. *Making of Americans. Being a Hist of a Family's Progress.* 1925. Paris. Contact/3 Mtns. 1st ed. 1/500. octavo. 925 p. VG. H5. $1,500.00

STEIN, Gertrude. *Picasso.* 1939. London. Scribner/Batsford. 1st Eng ed. rose cloth. NF/NF. C4. $150.00

STEIN, Gertrude. *Picasso.* 1939. Scribner. 1st Am ed. ils/photos. VG. B4. $35.00

STEIN, Gertrude. *Tea w/Alice.* 1978. NY. 1/250. 14 p. NF/wrp. C4. $30.00

STEIN, Gertrude. *Wars I Have Seen.* 1945. NY. 1st ed. VG+/dj. A15. $25.00

STEIN, Gertrude. *What Are Masterpieces?* 1940. LA. 1st ed. VG/VG. B5. $150.00

STEIN, Gertrude. *World Is Round.* (1988). San Francisco. N Point. reissue 1939 ed. ils Hurd. F/F. B3. $30.00

STEIN, Gertrude. *World Is Round.* 1939. NY. Wm R Scott. 1st ed. sgn Stein/Clement Hurd. NF/slipcase. Q1. $650.00

STEIN, Henri. *Archers d'Autrefois; Archers d'Aujourd'hui.* 1925. Paris. Longuet. ltd ed. 1/1200. ils Leon Laugier. orig prt wrp. K1. $175.00

STEIN, L. *Appreciation Painting Poetry Prose.* 1947. NY. 1st ed. VG/VG. B5. $35.00

STEIN, Leonard. *Balfour Declaration.* 1961. Simon Schuster. 681 p. VG. S3. $25.00

STEIN, Walter Johannes. *Death of Merlin: Arthurian Myth & Alchemy.* 1989. Edinburgh. Floris Books. 1st ed. trans T Meyer. NF/F. C1. $12.50

STEINBECK, John. *Acts of King Arthur & His Noble Knights.* (1977). Avenell. later prt. VG+/dj. C1. $8.50

STEINBECK, John. *Bombs Away: Story of a Bomber Team.* 1942. Viking. 1st ed. ils John Swope. F/VG+. B20. $225.00

STEINBECK, John. *Cannery Row.* 1945. Viking. 1st ed/2nd bdg. NF/VG. C4. $65.00

STEINBECK, John. *Conversations w/John Steinbeck.* 1988. Jackson, MS. 1st ed. F/F. C4. $35.00

STEINBECK, John. *Cup of Gold.* 1936. Covici Friede. 2nd ed. author's 1st book. VG/dj. M18. $150.00

STEINBECK, John. *Cup of Gold: Life of Henry Morgan, Bucaneer.* 1929. McBride. 1st ed. author's 1st book. variant bl p edges. NF. Q1. $600.00

STEINBECK, John. *Cup of Gold: Life of Sir Henry Morgan, Buccaneer.* 1936. Covici Friede. BC. dj. N2. $10.00

STEINBECK, John. *East of Eden.* 1952. NY. 1st ed. VG/G. B5. $75.00

STEINBECK, John. *East of Eden.* 1952. Viking. 1st ed. NF/NF. B4. $250.00

STEINBECK, John. *Grapes of Wrath.* (1939). Viking. 1st ed. NF. A18. $150.00

STEINBECK, John. *Grapes of Wrath.* 1978. Franklin Lib. last Franklin Lib ed. aeg. full gilt leather. M. A18. $45.00

STEINBECK, John. *Harvest of Gypsies.* 1988. Berkeley. 1st book ed. inscr Wollenberg. F/photo-ils wrp. A11. $45.00

STEINBECK, John. *Moon Is Down.* 1943. Sun Dial. photoplay ed. point on p 112. F/dj. C4. $55.00

STEINBECK, John. *Of Mice & Men.* (1977). Norwalk. Easton. ils Fletcher Martin. full leather. F. B3. $75.00

STEINBECK, John. *Once There Was a War.* 1958. Viking. 1st ed. F/NF. B2. $75.00

STEINBECK, John. *Red Pony.* 1945. Viking. 1st ils ed. 131 p. VG+/VG box. P2. $30.00

STEINBECK, John. *Travels w/Charley in Search of Am.* 1962. Viking. 4th prt. presentation/inscr. 246 p. coarse bleached cloth. NF/dj. H5. $1,250.00

STEINBECK, John. *Viking Portable Lib.* 1943. NY. 1st ed. F/F. C4. $40.00

STEINBECK, John. *Wayward Bus.* 1947. Viking. 1st ed. VG/dj. M18. $85.00

STEINBECK, John. *Winter of Our Discontent.* 1961. Viking. 1st ed. F/F. C4. $40.00

STEINBECK & WALLSTEN. *Steinbeck: A Life in Letters.* 1975. Viking. 1st ed. F/F. C4. $40.00

STEINBRUECK, Victor. *Seattle Cityscape #2.* 1973. WA U. ils/index. 112 p. NF/NF. B19. $10.00

STEINDLER, R.A. *Firearms Dictionary.* (1970). Stackpole. ils. 288 p. F/dj. A17. $12.50

STEINEM, Gloria. *Beach Book.* (1963). Viking. 1st ed. 4to. 277 p. F/G+. A2. $20.00

STEINER, Bernard C. *CT's Ratification of Federal Constitution.* 1915. Worcester. Am Antiquarian Soc. 60 p. wrp. M11. $50.00

STEINER, Nancy Hunter. *Closer Look at Ariel: Memory of Sylvia Plath.* 1973. Harper Magazine. 1st ed. VG+/dj. E3. $15.00

STEINER, Paul. *Israel Laughs.* 1950. Bloch. ils AJ Lewensohn. 166 p. VG. S3. $15.00

STEINER, Rudolf. *Holy Grail.* 1979. Vancouver. 40 p. VG+. C1. $4.50

STEINER, Stan. *Dark & Dashing Horsemen.* 1981. Harper Row. 1st ed/1st prt. VG/VG. O3. $15.00

STEINHARDT, Anne. *How To Get Balled in Berkeley.* 1976. Viking. 1st ed. 172 p. dj. A7. $13.00

STELLMAN, Louis J. *Port O' Gold.* (1922). Boston. 1st ed. 416 p. NF. D3. $35.00

STEMBER, Charles H. *Jews in the Mind of Am.* 1966. Basic Books. 2nd prt. 413 p. VG+/G. S3. $22.00

STEMLER, Dorothy. *Book of Old Roses.* 1966. Boston. ils/photos. 63 p. VG/dj. B26. $19.00

STENDHAL. *Roman Journal.* 1957. NY. 55 double-p pls. gilt blk cloth. VG. H3. $20.00

STENZEL, Franz. *Cleveland Rockwell: Scientist & Artist.* 1972. OR Hist Soc. xl. sgn. 157 p. wrp. D2. $45.00

STENZEL, Franz. *James Madison Alden: Yankee Artist of Pacific Coast...* 1975. Amon Carter Mus. sgn. ils/pls. 209 p. cloth. dj. D2. $55.00

STEPANEK, O. *Birds of Heath & Marshland.* (1966). London. Spring. 4th prt. 134 p. F/dj. A17. $20.00

STEPANSKY, Paul. *Freud: Appraisals & Reappraisals.* 1988. Analytic Pr. 202 p. brn fabrikoid. F/dj. G1. $25.00

STEPANSKY, Paul. *In Freud's Shadow: Adler in Context.* 1983. Analytic Pr. 1st ed. 325 p. F/dj. G1. $25.00

STEPHANE, Roger. *Portrait de l'Aventurier: TE Lawrence, Malraux, Von Salomon.* 1950. Sagittaire. 1st ed. 290 p. VG. w/pub band & newsclippings. M7. $95.00

STEPHANOPOLI. *Voyage...en Grece, Pendant les Annees V et VI (1797-98).* 1800. Paris. 2 vols. 8vo. 8 pls (2 fld). contemporary brds. O2. $800.00

STEPHENS, Alexander H. *Constitutional View of Late War Between the States. Vol 1.* ca 1868. Phil. royal 8vo. 654 p. brn cloth. G. T3. $30.00

STEPHENS, Arthur J. *Bells of San Gabriel & Verse Various.* (1924). LA. 1st ed. 127 p. pict gilt cloth. D3. $15.00

STEPHENS, Henry. *S Am Travels.* 1915 (1914). Knickerbocker. 1st ed. 705 p. gilt pict bdg. F3. $60.00

STEPHENS, J.W. *Blackwater Fever: Hist Survey & Summary...* 1937. Liverpool. 737 p. G7. $75.00

STEPHENS, Jack. *Triangulation.* 1989. Crown. AP. author's 1st book. NF/prt violet wrp. A14. $30.00

STEPHENS, James. *Crock of Gold.* 1922. Macmillan. 1st ils ed. ils Wilfred Jones. F. M18. $25.00

STEPHENS, John Lloyd. *Incidents in Greece, Turkey, Russia & Poland.* 1839. NY. 2 vols. 8vo. cloth. O2. $110.00

STEPHENS, John Lloyd. *Incidents of Travel in Egypt, Arabia, Petraea & Holy Land.* 1853. NY. 2 vols. 8vo. map/pls. cloth. O2. $150.00

STEPHENSES, P.R. *Bushwackers.* nd (1930s). London. 16mo. snakeskin cloth/blk cloth spine. F. H3. $35.00

STEPHENSON, N.W. *Lincoln: Account of Personal Life...Deepened by Ordeal...* 1922. Bobbs Merrill. 1st ed. 474 p. cloth. NF. M8. $45.00

STEPHENSON, N.W. *TX & the Mexican War.* 1921. np. 1st ed. ils/index. 273 p. O7. $12.50

STEPHENSON, Richard W. *Cartography of N VA.* 1981. Fairfax Co, VA. oblong 4to. facsimile maps. H9. $45.00

STEPHENSON, Richard W. *Civil War Maps: Annotated List of Maps & Atlases...* 1961. Lib Congress. NF/wrp. O6. $45.00

STEPHENSON & STEPHENSON. *Railway Revolution.* 1962. St Martin. 1st Am ed. 342 p. cloth. VG/dj. M20. $25.00

STEPNIAK. *Russian Peasantry.* 1988. Harper. 1st ed. VG. B2. $75.00

STERLING, Bruce. *Crystal Express.* 1987. Arkham. 1st ed. M. M2. $19.00

STERLING, Bruce. *Hacker Crackdown.* (1992). Bantam. 1st ed. 328 p. as new/dj. A7. $15.00

STERLING, George. *House of Orchids & Other Poems.* 1911. San Francisco. 1st ed/1st issue. 140 p. pict cloth. VG. D3. $45.00

STERLING, George. *Lilith.* 1926. Macmillan. 1st trade ed. F/dj. M18. $75.00

STERLING, George. *Poems to Vera.* 1938. Oxford. 1st ed. F/dj. M18. $40.00

STERLING, George. *Testimony of the Sun & Other Poems.* 1907. San Francisco. 3rd ed. 142 p. teg. pict gilt bdg. NF. D3. $50.00

STERLING, George. *Truth.* 1923. Chicago. Bookfellows. 1st ed. 1/285. sgn. 124 p. cloth. NF. D3. $125.00

STERLING, George. *Yosemite: An Ode.* 1916. San Francisco. 1st ed. 16 p. wrp ove brds w/repro of painting. VG. D3. $45.00

STERLING, Sara Hawks. *Robin Hood & H Merry Men.* 1921. GW Jacobs. 360 p. VG M20. $25.00

STERN, Gerald. *Paradise Poems.* 1984. N 1st ed. sgn. F/F. V1. $25.00

STERN, Norton B. *Baja CA: Jewish Refuge Homeland.* 1973. Dawson Book Shop. ltd e 1/600. 69 p. VG. S3. $45.00

STERN, Paul J. *CG Jung: The Haunte Prophet.* 1976. NY. Braziller. 1st Eng-la guage ed. 267 p. VG/dj. G1. $22.50

STERN, Philip Van Doren. *Life & Writin of Abraham Lincoln.* 1940. Modern Lib. 1 thus ed. 863 p. cloth. VG. M8. $25.00

STERNBERG, Cecilia. *Journey: An Auto ography.* 1977. Dial. 1st ed. 8vo. 576 F/VG. A2. $10.00

STERNBERG, Charles H. *Hunti Dinosaurs in the Bad Lands of the Red D River...* 1917. Lawrence, KS. Sternberg. ed. 8vo. 232 p. gr cloth. B20. $40.00

STERNBERG, Dick. *Walleye.* (1986). M netonka. ils/maps. 4to. wrp. A17. $10.00

STEUBEN, John. *Strike Strategy.* ca 19 NY. Gaer Assoc. VG/G. V4. $20.00

STEVANS, C.M. *Dreyfus & the Shame of France.* 1899. NY. F Tennyson Neely. 1st ed. NF. B2. $125.00

STEVENS, Benjamin Franklin. *Christopher Columbus: His Own Book of Privileges, 1502.* 1893. London. Stevens. deluxe ed. ils/pls. teg. 3-quarter leather. NF. O6. $500.00

STEVENS, G.A. *Climbing Roses.* 1933. NY. 1st ed. pls. 220 p. VG. B28. $20.00

STEVENS, G.A. *Garden Flowers in Color.* 1936. Macmillan. VG. A16. $25.00

STEVENS, Henry. *Bibliotheca Geographica & Historica.* 1872. London. Stevens. 361 p. NF/rpr wrp. O6. $150.00

STEVENS, Henry. *First Delineation of the New World...* 1829. London. Stevens Stiles. lg format. facsimiles. teg. maroon cloth. NF. O6. $375.00

STEVENS, James. *Big Jim Turner.* 1948. Doubleday. 1st ed. reading copy. A7. $10.00

STEVENS, Orin A. *Handbook of ND Plants.* 1950. Fargo. ils/photos. 324 p. dj. B26. $22.50

STEVENS, Ross O. *Talk About Wildlife for Hunters, Fishermen & Nature Lovers.* (1944). Raleigh, NC. 8vo. presentation/sgn. ils/photos. 229 p. wrp. $20.00

STEVENS, Shane. *Anvil Chorus.* 1985. Delacorte. 1st ed. F/F. F4. $20.00

STEVENS, Shane. *By Reason of Insanity.* 1979. Simon Schuster. 1st ed. F/F. F4. $30.00

STEVENS, Wallace. *Necessary Angel.* 1951. Knopf. 1st ed. F/NF clip. C4. $150.00

STEVENS, Wallace. *Opus Post-Humous.* 1957. NY. 1st ed. long 8vo. F/NF clip. A11. $95.00

STEVENS, Wallace. *Palm at the End of the Mind.* 1971. Knopf. 1st ed. NF/NF. C4. $45.00

STEVENS, Wallace. *Poems.* 1985. San Francisco. 1/300. octavo. 249 p. bl morocco/brds. NF/brd slipcase. H5. $3,500.00

STEVENS, Wallace. *Preliminary Checklist of His Pub Writings 1898-1954.* 1954. New Haven. 1st ed. NF/wrp. C4. $30.00

STEVENS, William. *KS Wild Flowers.* 1948. Lawrence. photos. 774 p. B26. $32.50

STEVENS, William. *Observations on Healthy & Diseased Properties of Blood.* 1832. London. Murray. 1st ed. octavo. full dk gr morocco. slipcase. H5. $1,250.00

STEVENSON, Anne. *Bitter Fame: Life of Sylvia Plath.* 1989. Houghton Mifflin. 1st ed. F/F. T2. $16.00

STEVENSON, Augusta. *Anthony Wayne. Daring Boy.* 1948. Indianapolis. 1st ed. 12mo. ils. 186 p. orange cloth. VG/VG. H3. $12.00

STEVENSON, D. *Elements of Methodism...* 1879. Claremont, NH. self pub. 212 p. H10. $10.00

STEVENSON, Robert Louis. *Across the Plains & Other Memories & Essays.* 1892. London. Chatto Windus. 1st ed. 12mo. teg. NF. D3. $75.00

STEVENSON, Robert Louis. *Child's Garden of Verses.* 1885. London. Longman Gr. 1st ed/1st prt. sm octavo. 101 p. bl cloth. H5. $2,000.00

STEVENSON, Robert Louis. *Child's Garden of Verses.* 1908. Dodge. 4th ed. ils B Collins Pease (Gutmann). 110 p. G. C10. $22.50

STEVENSON, Robert Louis. *Child's Garden of Verses.* 1919. Lippincott. 1st ed. ils Maria Kirk. 191 p. teg. VG. S10. $45.00

STEVENSON, Robert Louis. *Child's Garden of Verses.* 1919. Rand McNally. 1st ed. ils Ruth M Hallock. 96 p. navy cloth. G+. S10. $65.00

STEVENSON, Robert Louis. *Child's Garden of Verses.* 1926. NY. JH Sears. sm 4to. 243 p. gr cloth. VG. T5. $30.00

STEVENSON, Robert Louis. *Child's Garden of Verses.* 1928. Rand McNally. ils Ruth Hallock. G. L1. $40.00

STEVENSON, Robert Louis. *Child's Garden of Verses.* 1930. Saalfield. ils Clara M Burd. pict brds. VG. S10. $45.00

STEVENSON, Robert Louis. *Child's Garden of Verses.* 1934. Heritage. ils Roger Duvoisin. 112 p. VG/G box. P2. $28.00

STEVENSON, Robert Louis. *Child's Garden of Verses.* 1935. Rand McNally. ils. G. L1. $25.00

STEVENSON, Robert Louis. *Child's Garden of Verses.* 1942. Garden City. 32 p. G+/tattered dj. A3. $7.50

STEVENSON, Robert Louis. *Child's Garden of Verses.* 1945. John Martin. ils Pelagie Doane. unp. VG+/rpr. M20. $20.00

STEVENSON, Robert Louis. *Child's Garden of Verses.* 1947. Oxford. ils Tasha Tudor. 118 p. VG-/dj. A3. $25.00

STEVENSON, Robert Louis. *Child's Garden of Verses.* 1961. Platt Munk. ils Eulalie. VG/G. L1. $40.00

STEVENSON, Robert Louis. *Father Damien.* 1890. San Francisco. Clark Nash. 1/250. folio. 2 vols. compartment slipcase. K1. $200.00

STEVENSON, Robert Louis. *Hanging Judge: Drama in 3 Acts & 6 Tableaux.* 1887. Edinburgh. Clark. for private circulation. royal octavo in sheets. case. R3. $10,000.00

STEVENSON, Robert Louis. *Hist of Moses.* 1919. Daylesford, PA. 1st ed. pub/sgn E Newton. VG+/dk bl wrp. A11. $135.00

STEVENSON, Robert Louis. *Inland Voyage.* 1908. Chatto Windus. ils Noel Rooke. VG. C1. $7.50

STEVENSON, Robert Louis. *Jolly Jump-Ups/Child's Garden of Verses.* 1946. McLoughlin Bros. 6 popups. VG+. A3. $35.00

STEVENSON, Robert Louis. *Sea Fogs.* (1907). San Francisco. Paul Elder. 1st thus ed. 1/1000. 16mo. teg. F/dj. D3. $75.00

STEVENSON, Robert Louis. *Strange Case of Dr Jekyll & Mr Hyde.* 1888. London. Longman Gr. 15th ed. sm octavo. VG/buff wrp. H5. $225.00

STEVENSON, Robert Louis. *Travels w/a Donkey.* 1879. London. Kegan Paul. 1st ed. 8vo. VG+/cloth solander case/cloth slipcase. F1. $550.00

STEVENSON, Robert Louis. *Treasure Island.* nd. Scribner. 100th Commemorative issue. ils NC Wyeth. G+. L1. $30.00

STEVENSON, Robert Louis. *Treasure Island.* Sept 1911. NY. Scribner. 1st ed. ils Wyeth/15 color pls. teg. VG. B14. $225.00

STEVENSON, Robert Louis. *Treasure Island.* 1883. London. 1st ed. sm octavo. gr cloth. VG/cloth clamshell case. H5. $6,000.00

STEVENSON, Robert Louis. *Treasure Island.* 1924. Winston. ils Frank Godwin. G. L1. $25.00

STEVENSON, Robert Louis. *Treasure Island.* 1926. NY. Sears. 4to. 241 p. red cloth/pict label. VG. A3. $17.50

STEVENSON, Robert Louis. *Treasure Island.* 1929. Oxford, Eng. ils Rowland Hilder. G. L1. $45.00

STEVENSON, Robert Louis. *Treasure Island.* 1930. Phil. Anderson Books. 1st/only book by pub. beige linen. VG/uncut. A16. $50.00

STEVENSON, Robert Louis. *Treasure Island.* 1933. Scribner. ils NC Wyeth. early reprint. blk cloth/pict label. VG. A3. $40.00

STEVENSON, Robert Louis. *Treasure Island.* 1947. Grosset Dunlap. Jr Lib ed. ils Norman Price. G. L1. $12.50

STEVENSON, Robert Louis. *Treasure Island.* 1979. Abaris Books. 1st ed. ils Dulac. VG/VG. L1. $27.50

STEVENSON, Robert Louis. *Treasure Island.* 1985. London. Harrap. 1st thus ed. ils Ralph Stead. VG/VG. L1. $35.00

STEVENSON, Robert Louis. *Works...* 1905. Scribner. 6 vols. gilt gr cloth. E3. $45.00

STEVENSON, Violet. *Encyclopedia of Floristry.* 1973. NY. ils/photos. 160 p. F/dj. B26. $14.00

STEVENSON, W.G. *Thirteen Months in the Rebel Army.* 1862. London. 1st ed. 12mo. VG. B28. $45.00

STEWARD, Julian. *Handbook of S Am Indians.* 1946-1959. WA. GPO. 7 vols. orig cloth. F3. $300.00

STEWART, Desmond. *TE Lawrence: A New Biography.* 1977. Harper Row. 1st ed. 352 p. F/F/clear plastic. M7. $35.00

STEWART, Elinore Pruitt. *Letters of a Woman Homesteader.* 1914. Houghton Mifflin. 1st ed. ils Wyeth. VG. E3. $125.00

STEWART, F.H. *Hist of the 1st US Mint.* 1974 (1924). Lawrence, MA. reprint. 8vo. 209 p. F/F. A2. $17.50

STEWART, Fred Mustard. *Mephisto Waltz.* 1969. Coward McCann. 1st ed. author's 1st book. F/NF. N3. $45.00

STEWART, George R. *Am Place-Names. Concise & Selective Dictionary...* 1970. Oxford. Lib Congress duplicate. 8vo. 418 p. tan buckram. H9. $40.00

STEWART, George R. *CA Trail.* (1962). McGraw Hill. 10th prt. dj. N2. $8.00

STEWART, George R. *CA Trail.* 1962. np. 1st ed. ils. 339 p. F/dj. O7. $18.50

STEWART, George R. *Dr's Oral.* (1939). Random House. 1st ed. F/F. A18. $60.00

STEWART, George R. *Ordeal by Hunger: Story of the Donner Party.* (1936). Holt. 1st ed. ils Ray Boynton. VG. A18. $35.00

STEWART, Hilary. *Looking at Indian Art of the NW Coast.* 1984. Seattle. 5th prt. NF/stiff wrp. P4. $15.00

STEWART, Hugh. *Provincial Russia.* 1913. London. Blk. 8vo. 172 p. gilt red cloth. G. H3. $20.00

STEWART, J.D. *Gibraltar: The Keystone.* 1967. Houghton Mifflin. 1st ed. 8vo. 335 p. F/VG. A2. $15.00

STEWART, James B. *Prosecutors: Inside Offices of Government's...Lawyers.* 1987. Simon Schuster. M11. $25.00

STEWART, Katie. *Pooh Cook Book.* 1981 (1971). London. Methuen. reprint. 8vo. 128 p. glossy brds. F/F. T5. $30.00

STEWART, Mary. *Crystal Cave.* 1970. NY. Morrow. 1st Am ed. F/NF. N3. $15.00

STEWART, Mary. *Wicked Day.* 1983. Morrow. 1st ed. F/F. T2. $16.00

STEWART, Michael. *Monkey Shines.* 1983. NY. Freundlich. 1st Am ed. author's 1st novel. F/F. N3. $20.00

STEWART, Omer C. *Culture Element Distributions: XIV, N Paiute.* 1941. CA U. 1st ed. xl. 4to. VG/stiff wrp. D3. $20.00

STEWART, Sallie W. *Girls' Guide.* 1946. Nat Assn Colored Women. 8vo. 140 p. VG/wrp. B11. $35.00

STEWART, Virginia. *45 Contemporary Mexican Artists.* 1952. Stanford. 2nd prt. 4to. 160 p. dj. F3. $45.00

STEWART, Walter A. *Pscyhoanalysis: 1st 10 Yrs 1888-98.* 1967. Macmillan. 1st ed. inscr. 224 p. VG/dj. G1. $30.00

STEWART, Will; see Williamson, Jack.

STEWART. *Animals To Applique.* 1989. np. ils. wrp. G2. $10.95

STICKLER. *Am Woven Coverlets.* 1987. np. wrp. G2. $9.00

STIDGER, Gelix G. *Treason Hist of Order of Sons of Liberty...* 1903. Chicago. 1st ed. pls. 246 p. cloth. VG. D3. $75.00

STILES, Henry Reed. *Bundling: Its Origin, Progress & Decline in Am.* (1934). NY. Book Collectors Assn. reprint. 12mo. 146 p. VG+/F-. A2. $12.50

STILES, Henry Reed. *Bundling: Its Origin, Progress & Decline in Am.* 1871. Albany, NY. 1st ed. 12mo. 138 p. VG. B28. $30.00

STILES, Pauline. *Dr Will.* 1949. Bobbs Merrill. 12mo. G/fair. A8. $30.00

STILES. *Not Just Another Embroidery Book.* 1986. np. pb. G2. $19.00

STILL, James. *Hounds on the Mtn.* 1937. NY. ltd ed. 1/750. F/VG. V1. $125.00

STILL, William. *Underground Railroad.* 1872. Porter Coates. 1st ed. NF. B4. $600.00

STILLE, Sam H. *You: A Simple Everyday Philosophy of Life.* 1940. Salem, OH. 1st ed. 42 p. VG. E5. $25.00

STILLMAN, J.D.B. *Gold Rush Letters of...* 1967. Palo Alto. 1/2350. 77 p. VG+. B18. $27.50

STILLWELL, Margaret Bingham. *Noah's Ark in Early Woodcuts & Modern Rhymes.* 1942. NY. Hackett/Brick Row. 1/300 on handmade paper. woodcuts. M/glassine wrp. O6. $125.00

STILLWELL, Sara S. *Luxury of Children & Some Other Luxuries.* 1904. NY. VG. M5. $80.00

STIMSON, A.L. *Express Office Hand-Book & Directory for...Express Agents...* 1860. NY. JK Stimson. new ed. octavo. orig brds/new spine. lacks 1 ad p. R3. $750.00

STIRLING, Patrick James. *Australian & Ca Gold Discoveries...* 1969. Greenwood Pr. facsimile. fld chart/notes. 279 p. NF. B19. $25.00

STIRREDGE, Elizabeth. *Strength in Weakness Manifest...* 1810. Phil. Kite. 16mo. 166 p. fair. V3. $25.00

STIRTON, C.H. *Plant Invaders: Beautiful, But Dangerous.* 1985 (1978). Cape Town, S Africa. 3rd ed/4th prt. ils/maps. VG/torn. B26. $14.00

STITH, W. *Hist of 1st Discovery & Settlement of VA.* 1747. Williamsburg. 1st ed/3rd issue. antique calf. VG+. C6. $5,000.00

STITT, George. *Prince of Arabia: Emir Shereef Ali Haider.* 1943. Allen Unwin. 1st UK ed. reddish-orange cloth. NF/VG/clear plastic. M7. $40.00

STOBART, M.A. St. Clair. *Miracles & Adventures: An Autobiography.* (1935). London. Rider. 1st thus ed. 8vo. 383 p. VG. A2. $25.00

STOBART, Tom. *I Take Pictures for Adventure.* 1958. NY photos. 288 p. dj. A17. $7.50

STOCKDALE & STOCKDALE. *In Love & War.* (1984). Harper Row. 472 p. F/dj. A7. $25.00

STOCKHAM, Alice B. *Tokology: A Book for Every Woman.* 1895 (1883). Chicago. 358 p. w/pocket pamphlet. VG+. M20. $30.00

STOCKLY, Harriet E. *Conversations w/Theodore & His Sister.* 1860. Phil. TE Zell. 1st ed. 18mo. 136 p. fair. V3. $12.00

STOCKTON, Bayard. *Phoenix w/a Bayonet.* 1971. Ann Arbor. 8vo. ils. 306 p. cloth. dj. O2. $20.00

STOCKTON, Ernest L. *Hist Excursions Into TN: Its Early Heritage.* 1941. Exton, PA. Newcomen Soc. 2nd prt. 8vo. 52 p. wrp. H9. $30.00

STOCKTON, Frank R. *Clocks of Rondaine & Other Stories.* 1892. Scribner. 1st ed/2nd state. 171 p. G+. S10. $35.00

STOCKTON-HOUGH, John. *Incunabula Medica.* 1890. Trenton, NJ. sm 4to. unp. contemporary quarter morocco. G7. $125.00

STODDARD, Herbert L. *Bobwhite Quail: Its Habits, Preservation & Increase.* 1931. Scribner. 1st ed. 1/260. sgn. thick 4to. w/orig sgn etching by Benson. F. F1. $750.00

STODDARD, Lothrop. *Revolt Against Civilization.* 1922. Scribner. 1st ed. G+. N2. $7.50

STODDARD, Richard Henry. *Songs of Summer.* 1857. Boston. Ticknor Fields. 1st ed. 8vo. 229 p. brick cloth. M1. $225.00

STODDARD, William O. *Inside the Wht House in War Times.* 1890. NY. 1st ed. ils Dan Beard. silvered bl cloth. VG. B14. $40.00

STODDARD, William O. *Little Smoke. Tale of the Sioux.* 1925 (1891). NY. later ed. 295 p. fair. D3. $7.50

STODDARD. *From Atlantic to Pacific.* 1902. np. oblong folio. pict cloth. T3. $19.00

STODDART, Anna M. *Elizabeth Pease Nichol.* 1899. London. Dent. 8vo. 314 p. fair. V3. $10.00

STOIANOVICH, Traian. *Between E & W. Balkan & Mediterranean Worlds. Vol 2.* 1992. New Rochelle. 4to. 191 p. cloth. dj. O2. $85.00

STOKER, Bram. *Dracula.* ca 1940. (1897). Grosset Dunlap. photoplay ed. F/NF. B4. $500.00

STOKER, Bram. *Dracula.* 1897. Westminster. Constable. 1st ed/1st issue. w/sgn letter dtd 1892. VG/case. H5. $5,000.00

STOKER, Bram. *Dracula.* 1899. Westminster. Constable. 7th ed. VG. B4. $450.00

STOKER, Bram. *Jewel of 7 Stars.* 1904. Harper. 1st Am ed. NF. B4. $225.00

STOKER, Bram. *Lair of the Wht Worm.* (1911). London. Rider. 1st ed. 8 pls. Donald Wolheim's copy. NF. B4. $550.00

STOKER, Bram. *Personal Reminiscences of Henry Irving.* 1906. Macmillan. 1st Am ed. 8vo. VG+. A2. $60.00

STOKER, Bram. *Watter's Mou.* 1895. Appleton. 1st Am ed. Donald Wolheim's copy. VG. B4. $350.00

STOKES, Carl B. *Promises of Power.* (1973). Simon Schuster. 1st ed. 288 p. VG/dj. A7. $15.00

STOKES, George. *Agnes Repplier: A Biography.* 1949. PA U. 261 p. VG. C5. $15.00

STOKES, Jules. *Dictionary Liliput.* ca 1910. Leipzig. Schmidt Guenther. miniature. gilt leather. H10. $50.00

STOLBERG, Benjamin. *Tailor's Progress: Story of Famous Union...* ca 1944. NY. Doran. special ed for members of ILGWU. VG/fair. V4. $10.00

STOLPE, Daniel Owen. *Images & Myths.* 1982. Aptos Pr. 1st ed. F/wrp. L3. $45.00

STOLPE, Sven. *Christina of Sweden.* 1966 (1963). Macmillan. 1st Am ed. 8vo. 360 p. F/F. A2. $12.50

STOLPE, Sven. *Maid of Orleans.* 1956. London. Burns Oates. 1st ed. dj. N2. $7.50

STOMMELL, Henry. *View of the Sea.* (1987). Princeton. ils. 165 p. F/dj. A17. $10.00

STONE, Chuck. *King Strut.* (1970). Bobbs Merrill. 1st prt. 357 p. dj. A7. $15.00

STONE, George Cameron. *Glossary of Construction, Decor & Use of Arms & Armor.* (1961). NY. ils. 694 p. G/dj. B18. $22.50

STONE, Harlan F. *Law & Its Administration.* 1924. NY. Columbia. dj. M11. $50.00

STONE, Irving. *Sailor on Horseback: Biography of Jack London.* 1938. Houghton Mifflin. 1st ed. NF/VG. B4. $50.00

STONE, J.F.S. *Wessex Before the Celts.* 1958. NY. 72 pls. NF. C1. $7.50

STONE, J.R. *Those Who Fall From the Sun.* 1978. Atheneum. 1st ed. F/F. T2. $20.00

STONE, J.S. *Memoir of Life of the Rt Rev Alexander Viets Griswold...* 1844. Phil. Stavely McCalla. 1st ed. 620 p. H10. $35.00

STONE, R.H. *Aviation Stories for Boys.* 1936. Cupples Leon. 836 p. VG/dj. M20. $18.00

STONE, Robert. *Children of Light.* 1986. Knopf. 1st ed. sgn. F/F. C4. $50.00

STONE, Robert. *Children of Light.* 1986. London. Deutsch. 1st ed. sgn. F/F. scarce. C4. $65.00

STONE, Robert. *Dog Soldiers.* 1974. Houghton Mifflin. AP. sgn. author's 2nd book. F/2nd issue wrp. C4. $265.00

STONE, Robert. *Flag for Sunrise.* 1992. Vintage. 1st Vintage internat ed. sgn. F/wrp. C4. $25.00

STONE, Robert. *Hall of Mirrors.* 1968. Bodley Head. 1st ed. sgn. NF/NF. C4. $265.00

STONE, Robert. *Helping.* 1993. NY. Dim Gray Bar Pr. 1st ed. 1/100. sgn. 18-point type. 48 p. F. C4. $200.00

STONE, Robert. *Outerbridge Reach.* nd. London. Deutsch. 1st ed. sgn. F/F. C4. $60.00

STONE, Robert. *Outerbridge Reach.* 1992. Tichnor Fields. ltd ed. 1/250. sgn/#d. F/slipcase. C4. $125.00

STONE, Robert. *Outerbridge Reach.* 1992. Tichnor Fields. 1st ed. sgn. F/F. C4. $45.00

STONE, Scott C.S. *Share of the Honor.* 1969. Lippincott. 1st ed. VG/dj. L3. $45.00

STONE, Thomas H. see Harknett, Terry.

STONE, Wilbur Macy. *Divine & Moral Songs of Isaac Watts...* 1981. NY. Triptych. 1/250. w/prospectus. 93 p. H10. $145.00

STONE, William S. *Tahiti Landfall.* nd. Sampson Low. 262 p. poor dj. A7. $10.00

STONE, William S. *Tahiti Landfall.* 1946. NY. 1st ed. pls. 308 p. pict gr cloth. F/G. H3. $20.00

STONE. *Portuguese Needlework Rugs.* 1985. np. charted patterns. cloth. G2. $23.00

STONEHOUSE, Frederick. *Short Guide to Shipwrecks of Thunder Bay.* 1992. self pub. 2nd ed. photos/maps. 74 p. M/wrp. A17. $8.50

STONEHOUSE, Frederick. *Wreck of the Edmund Fitzgerald.* (1991). Au Train. updated ed. 225 p. M/wrp. A17. $10.00

STONG, Phil. *Buckskin Breeches.* (1937). NY. 1st ed. F. A17. $9.50

STONG, Phil. *Hawkeyes: Biography of State of IA.* 1940. Dodd Mead. 1st ed. 8vo. 300 p. VG+/G+. A2. $20.00

STONG, Phil. *Horses & Americans.* 1939. NY. author's autograph ed. 1/500. 4to. 333 p. teg. D3. $85.00

STONG, Phil. *Horses & Americans.* 1939. NY. 1st trade ed. xl. ils Kurt Wiese. 333 p. VG. D3. $25.00

STONG, Phil. *Horses & Americans.* 1939. NY. Stokes. 1st ed. VG/fair. O3. $25.00

STOPES, Marie. *Contraception: Its Theory, Hist & Practice...* 1928. London. Danielsson. 2nd revised ed/2nd prt. VG. G1. $30.00

STOREY, David. *Pasmore.* (1972). London. Longman. 1st ed. VG/VG. B3. $35.00

STORKE & THOMPKINS. *CA Edit.* 1958. Westernlore Pr. ils. 489 p. NF/VG. B19. $12.50

STORM, Hyemeyohsts. *Song of Heyoehkah.* (1981). Harper Row. 1st ed. sm 4to. rem mk. 302 p. F/NF. A7. $25.00

STORM & LIBBY. *I Ain't Down Yet.* (1981). Bobbs Merrill. 1st ed. 164 p. dj. A7. $15.00

STORRS, Richard S. *Recognition of the Supernatural in Letters & in Life...* ca 1881. NY. Randolph. 1st ed. 57 p. wrp. H10. $11.50

STORY, Joseph. *Discourse Pronounced Before Phi Beta Kappa...1826.* 1826. Boston. Hilliard Gray Little Wilkins. presentation. M11. $650.00

STORY, Joseph. *Selection of Pleadings in Civil Actions...* 1829. Boston. Carter Hendee. full sheep. M11. $250.00

STORY, Thomas. *Conversations, Discussions & Ancedotes of...* 1860. Phil. TE Zell. 12mo. 363 p. G. V3. $30.00

STORY, Thomas. *Journal of the Life of...Containing Account...* 1747. Newcastle Upon Tyne. Isaac Thomspon. folio. 768 p. detached bdg. V3. $125.00

STOUT, Rex. *Family Affair.* 1975. Viking. 1st ed. F/NF. M15. $35.00

STOUT, Rex. *Justice Ends at Home.* 1977. Viking. 1st ed. F/F. S5. $35.00

STOUTENBURGH, John Jr. *Dictionary of the Am Indian.* 1960. Philosophical Lib. 1st ed. ils. 462 p. cloth. VG/dj. M20. $18.00

STOVER, Ronald Mark. *Brains for Janes.* 1948. Pirate Pr. 1st ed. 1/200 hc. VG/sans. M2. $75.00

STOWE, Harriet Beecher. *Dred: A Tale of Great Dismal Swamp.* 1886. Houghton Mifflin. early prt. 607 p. orig cloth. NF. M8. $45.00

STOWE, Harriet Beecher. *Men of Our Times; or, Leading Patriots of the Day.* 1868. Hartford. 1st ed. gr cloth. VG+. E3. $25.00

STOWE, Harriet Beecher. *Two Altars; or, Two Pictures in One.* (1855). NY. Am Anti-Slavery Soc. 2nd separate ed. 16mo. 12 p. sewn. M1. $150.00

STOWE, Harriet Beecher. *Uncle Tom's Cabin.* Aug 1852. London. Bosworth. author's ed (on spine). VG. Q1. $1,000.00

STOWE, Harriet Beecher. *Uncle Tom's Cabin; or, Life Among the Lowly.* 1852. Boston. Jewett. 1st ed. 2 vols. 8vo. gilt brn gift bdg. VG. M1. $3,000.00

STOWE, Marietta L. *Probate Chaff; or, Beautiful Probate...* 1879. self pub. 1st ed. 8vo. 307 p. decor cloth. M1. $125.00

STOY. *Pea Pod Pop-Ups.* 1985. ils Costello. 6 pop-up scenes w/3 4" dolls. F. A4. $40.00

STOY. *Uncle Peasly & the Pea Pod Kids.* 1986. 7 pop-up scenes. paper engineering by Linda Costello. NF. A4. $50.00

STRACHAN, James. *Pictures From a Mediaeval Bible.* ca 1959. Boston. Beacon. ils. 127 p. H10. $10.00

STRACHEY, John. *How Socialism Works.* (1939). Modern Age. 212 p. wrp. A7. $8.00

STRACHEY, John. *Theory & Practice of Socialism.* 1936. London. Gollancz. Left BC ed. 488 p. orange cloth wrp. A7. $10.00

STRACHEY, Lytton. *Elizabeth & Essex.* 1928. NY. 1st ed. VG. C1. $6.50

STRACZYNSKI, J. Michael. *Demon Night.* 1988. Dutton. 1st ed. F/F. F4. $17.00

STRADER, Welman A. *50 Yrs of Flight.* (1953). Cleveland. 178 p. VG/dj. B18. $30.00

STRAHAN, Edward. *Art Gallery of the Exhibition.* 1877. Phil. Gebbie Barrie. ils after Alma-Tedema/Bierstadt/B West/others. aeg. NF. F1. $150.00

STRAHAN, Edward. *Masterpieces of Centennial International Exhibition.* nd. Phil. Gebbie Barrie. 3 vols. 4to. ils/pls. leather. G. B11. $350.00

STRAHIN, Richard D. *Family Strahin.* 1982. Parsons, WV. 1st ed. 235 p. bl cloth. VG. D7. $27.50

STRAIGHT, Michael. *After Long Silence.* 1983. Norton. 1st ed. 351 p. F/NF. A7. $17.00

STRAIGHT, Susan. *I Been in Sorrow's Kitchen & Licked Out All the Pots.* 1992. NY. 1st ed. inscr. F/F. A11. $45.00

STRAITON, M.J. *Two Lady Tramps Abroad: Compilation of Letters...* 1881. Flushing, NY. 8vo. 335 p. decor cloth. O2. $50.00

STRAND, Mark. *Selected Poems.* 1980. NY. 1st ed. sgn. F/VG+. V1. $20.00

STRATTON, Arthur. *Great Red Island.* (1964). Scribner. 1st Am ed. 8vo. 368 p. F/F. A2. $25.00

STRAUB, Peter. *Marriages.* 1973. CMG. 1st Am ed. author's 1st novel. NF/VG. scarce. L3. $125.00

STRAUB, Peter. *Mystery.* 1990. Dutton. 1st ed. sgn. F/F. F4. $45.00

STRAUSS, Ivard. *Paint, Powder & Make-Up.* 1938. Barners Novle. not 1st ed. 219 p. G+. N2. $15.00

STREATFIELD, Noel. *First Book of the Ballet.* 1953. Watts. 2nd prt. ils Moses Soyer. cloth. NF/dj. M5. $16.00

STREET, James. *Bisquit Eater.* 1949 (1941). Dial. 2nd prt. sgn. ils Arthur Fuller. 88 p. G+. T5. $40.00

STREETER, Edward. *Mr Robbins Rides Again.* 1958. NY. Harper. VG/G+. O3. $10.00

STRETE, Craig. *Bleeding Man.* 1974. Greenwillow. 1st ed. NF/dj. L3. $100.00

STRETE, Craig. *Death in the Spirit House.* 1988. Doubleday. ARC. F/dj. L3. $50.00

STRETE, Craig. *Dreams That Burn in the Night.* 1982. Doubleday. 1st ed. rem mk. NF/NF. L3. $65.00

STRETE, Craig. *If All Else Fails...* 1980. Doubleday. 1st ed. rem mk. NF/dj. L3. $85.00

STRETE, Craig. *Paint Your Face on a Drowning in the River.* 1978. Greenwillow. 1st ed. NF/dj. L3. $75.00

STRETTON, Hesba. *Jessica's 1st Prayer.* (1903). Altemus. ils Brill/Bradley. 114 p. peach cloth. G+. S10. $18.00

STRIBLING, T.S. *Sound Wagon.* 1935. Garden City. 1/250. w/sgn p. VG+/VG+. A11. $55.00

STRICKLAND, A.E. *Hist of the Chicago Urban League.* 1966. IL U. 286 p. F/dj. A7. $30.00

STRICKLAND, W.P. *Autobiography of Rev James E Finley...* 1853. Cincinnati. 1st ed. xl. 455 p. orig cloth. D7. $60.00

STRIEBER, Whitley. *Blk Magic.* (1982). Morrow. 1st ed. F/F. B3. $35.00

STRIEBER, Whitley. *Hunger.* (1981). Morrow. 1st ed. author's 2nd novel. F/F. B3. $40.00

STRIEBER, Whitley. *Night Church.* 1983. Simon Schuster. 1st ed. sgn. F/F. F4. $40.00

STRIEBER, Whitley. *Wolfen.* (1978). Morrow. 1st ed. author's 1st novel. F/NF. B3/N3. $45.00

STRIKER, Fran. *Lone Ranger in Wild Horse Canyon.* 1950. Grosset Dunlap. 1st ed. 212 p. VG/dj. M20. $22.00

STRIKER, Fran. *Lone Ranger...* 1936. Grosset Dunlap. 1st ed. 218 p. pict ep/cloth. VG/dj. D3. $25.00

STRINDBERG, August. *Gustav Adolf.* 1957. Seattle, WA. dj. VG. N2. $8.00

STROBLING, T.S. *Sound Wagon.* 1935. NY. 1st ed (precedes trade ed). 1/250. NF/VG+. A11. $45.00

STRODE, Hudson. *Pageant of Cuba.* 1935. London. Jarrolds. 8vo. 15 pls/map. 320 p. gr cloth. B11. $30.00

STRONG, A.L. *Peoples of the USSR.* 1944. Macmillan. 1st ed. lg 8vo. 246 p. F-/G. A2. $17.50

STRONG, Emory M. *Stone Age on the Columbia River.* 1959. Portland. 1st ed. photos. F. T8. $15.00

STRONG, Nathan. *Inaugural Dissertation on Disease Termed Petechial...* 1810. Hartford. Peter Gleason. 52 p. modern wrp. N2. $30.00

STRONG, R.P. *Typus Fever w/Particular Reference to Serbian Epidemic.* 1920. Cambridge, MA. Am Red Cross. 1st ed. ils. 273 p. red cloth. NF. S9. $23.00

STRONG, William Duncan. *Cross Sections of New World Prehistory.* 1941-1942. Smithsonian. 46 p. wrp. F3. $25.00

STRONG. *Voyage of Columbus in His Own Words, a Pop-Up Book.* 1991. 7 pop-up scenes. F. A4. $45.00

STROTHER, D.H. *Ils Life of General Winfield Scott...* 1847. NY. ils. 144 p. G/wrp. B18. $125.00

STRUNG, Norman. *Deer Hunting.* (1973). Phil. 1st ed. 239 p. F/worn. A17. $12.50

STRUNG, Norman. *Misty Mornings & Moonless Nights.* (1974). NY. 1st ed. ils/index. 253 p. F/dj. A17. $15.00

STRUTT, Joseph. *Horda Angel-Cynnan; or, Compleat View of Manners, Customs...* 1775-1776. London. Benjamin Wht. 3 vols. 157 pls. contemporary calf. K1. $650.00

STRUVE, Christian August. *Practical Essay on Art...* 1803. Albany. 1st Am ed. 12mo. contemporary full calf. G7. $150.00

STUART, E.W. *General Ordinances of City of Akron.* 1873. Akron. inscr. 151 p. cloth. VG. B18. $32.50

STUART, Gordon. *Boy Scouts of the Air w/Pershing.* 1919. Reilly Lee. 1st ed. VG. M2. $15.00

STUART, Jesse. *Beatinest Boy.* 1953. Whittlesey. 1st ed. sgn. 107 p. VG+/VG. P2. $75.00

STUART, Jesse. *Taps for Private Tussie.* 1943. Dutton. BC. VG. A8. $20.00

STUART, Moses. *Sermon at the Ordination of Rev Wm G Schauffler...* 1831. Andover. 8vo. 36 p. orig gr wrp. O2. $55.00

STUART, Ruth McEnery. *River's Children. Idyl of the MS.* 1904. NY. Century. 12mo. 179 p. gilt gr brds. VG. B11. $40.00

STUART, Sidney; see Avallone, Mike.

STUART & STUART. *How Firm a Foundation: Centennial Hist 1st Methodist Church.* 1953. 1st Methodist Church. 1/500. inscr both authors. ils/notes/index. B19. $20.00

STUART-STUBBS & VARNER. *Northpart of Am.* 1979. Academic Pr Canada Ltd. folio. ils/46 maps. 292 p. M/box. O5. $150.00

STUBBS, Harry Clement; see Clement, Hal.

STUBBS, M. Wilma. *How Europe Was Won for Christianity...* ca 1913. NY. Revell. xl. 309 p. H10. $20.00

STUBNITZ, D. *Baby Animal Stories.* 1939. Saalfield. ils Diana Thorne. M/dj. E5. $45.00

STUBS. *Embroidery.* 1987. np. over 40 projects. cloth. G2. $16.00

STUCK, Hudson. *Ascent of Denali.* 1914. Scribner. 1st ed. photos/fld map. 188 p. G. A17. $60.00

STUCKEN, Edward. *Great Wht Gods.* 1934. NY. Farrar. 1st ed. ils Glinterkamp. 712 p. F3. $15.00

STUCLIFF, Rosemary. *Warrior Scarlet.* (1958). London. Oxford. xl. 8vo. 207 p. VG. T5. $28.00

STUDITN, Nicole. *Guenivere's Gift.* ca 1977. BC. VG+. C1. $4.00

STULTZ, Arthur Lee. *Gold Rush '80s.* 1981. Ophir Internat. 12mo. F. A8. $20.00

STURGEON, Theodore. *Touch of Strange.* nd. BC. VG/VG. P3. $8.00

STURGEON, Theodore. *Without Sorcery.* 1948. Prime Pr. 1st ed. F/NF. M2. $80.00

STURGES, Katharine. *Mimi, Momo & Miss Tabby Tibbs.* (1927). Volland. 4th prt. ils Sturges. ils ep. VG/VG box. D1. $175.00

STURGIS, Thomas. *Hist of NY Farmers, 1882-1910.* ca 1911. NY Farmers. xl. for private circulation. 128 p. half leather. H10. $35.00

STURMER. *Stenciled Quilt.* 1986. np. ils. wrp. G2. $16.00

STURMTHAL, Adolf. *Tragedy of European Labour 1918-1939.* 1944. London. Gollancz. 8vo. 288 p. torn dj. A7. $18.00

STYRON, William. *Confessions of Nat Turner.* (1967). Random. 1st ed. 428 p. NF/NF clip. A7. $35.00

STYRON, William. *Confessions of Nat Turner.* 1968. London. Cape. 1st ed. F/F. C4. $55.00

STYRON, William. *Lie Down in Darkness.* 1982. Franklin Lib. 1st ed. sgn. w/22-p biographical brochure. F. C4. $85.00

STYRON, William. *Lie Down in Darkness.* 1985. Watertown. Ploughshare. 1st ed. F/F. C4. $50.00

STYRON, William. *This Quiet Dust.* 1982. Random. AP. sgn. F/wrp. B4. $175.00

STYRON, William. *This Quiet Dust.* 1982. Random. 1st ed. inscr. F/F. C4. $45.00

STYRON, William. *Tidewater Morning.* 1993. Random. AP. F/wrp. L3. $65.00

STYRON, William. *Tidewater Morning.* 1993. Random. 1st ed. sgn. F/F. C4. $35.00

SU, Horng-Jye. *Native Orchids of Taiwan.* 1986 (1974). Taipei. revised 4th ed. ils/photos. 273 p. M/as issued. B26. $27.50

SUAREZ, Thomas. *Shedding the Veil: Mapping European Discovery of Am...* 1992. Singapore. Woeld Scientific. ils. 203 p. O5. $65.00

SUAREZ, Virgil. *Latin Jazz.* 1989. Morrow. 1st ed. author's 1st book. F/F. A14. $25.00

SUBLETT, Jesse. *Boiled in Concrete.* 1992. Viking. ARC of 1st ed. sgn. RS. F/F. S5. $35.00

SUCHARITKUL, Somtow. *Vampire Junction.* 1984. Donning Starblaze. 1st ed. F/F. F4. $45.00

SUCKLING, John. *Works of...* 1709. London. Jacob Tonson. 8vo. 376 p. Ramage bdg. NF. F1. $250.00

SUCKOW, Ruth. *Folks.* (1934). NY. 1st ed. 1/175. sgn. 2 vols. VG+. D3. $150.00

SUDERMANN, Hermann. *Dame Care.* nd. NY. Boni Liveright. trans Overbeck. gr brds. VG. E3. $8.00

SUE, Eugene. *Mysteries of Paris.* 1844. Harper. gilt cloth. E5. $45.00

SUETONIUS. *Les Douze Cesars.* 1928. Paris. ils/sgn Schmied. 327 p. unbound as issued. F/chemise/slipcase. B24. $2,500.00

SUGIHARA & PLATH. *Sensei & His People: People of a Japanese Commune.* (1969). Berkeley, CA. 1st ed. 8vo. 187 p. VG+/VG. A2. $12.50

SUGRUE, Thomas. *There Is a River. Story of Edgar Cayce.* 1942. Holt. N2. $12.50

SULLIVAN, George. *Harness Racing.* 1964. NY. Fleet. VG. O3. $15.00

SULLIVAN, George. *Tom Seaver of the Mets.* 1971. Putnam. later prt. F. P8. $10.00

SULLIVAN, L.H. *Build, Brother, Build.* (1969). Phil. Macrae Smith. photos. 192 p. dj. A7. $16.00

SULLIVAN, Louis H. *Kindergarten Chats on Architecture, Education & Democracy.* 1934. Scarab Fraternity Pr. 1st ed. 8vo. 256 p. tan cloth. VG+/dj. F1. $400.00

SULLIVAN, Walter. *We Are Not Alone.* nd. Laffont. VG. P3. $15.00

SULZBERGER, C.L. *Long Row of Candles.* 1969. Macmillan. 1st ed. 8vo. VG. A8. $10.00

SULZBERGER, C.L. *Postscript w/Chinese Accent.* (1974). Macmillan. 401 p. dj. A7. $12.00

SULZBERGER, C.L. *Tooth Merchant.* 1973. Quadrangle. 1st ed. VG-/dj. P3. $10.00

SUMMER, A.G. *Anniversary Address Delivered Before S Century Agriculture.* 1852. Augusta, GA. 1st ed. 26 p. VG/wrp. M8. $85.00

SUMMERHAYES, Martha. *Vanished AZ.* 1939. Chicago. Lakeside Classic. 335 p. teg. VG-. B18. $35.00

SUMMERS, Bart; see Fox, Gardner F.

SUMMERS, Diana; see Smith, George H.

SUMMERS, Festus Paul. *Baltimore & OH in the Civil War.* 1939. Putnam. 1st ed. 16 pls/8 maps. 304 p. cloth. NF. M8. $150.00

SUMMERS, Ian. *Tomorrow & Tomorrow.* 1978. Workman. 1st ed. VG/dj. P3. $25.00

SUMMERS, James. *Who Won? Official Am Yacht Record for 1893.* 1898. NY. Who Won Pub. 12mo. fld pl/tables/charts. prt tan cloth. H9. $150.00

SUMMERS, Montague. *Discovery of Witches: Study of Master Matthew Hopkins...* 1928. London. 1st ed. 61 p. NF/stiff blk wrp. G1. $50.00

SUMMERS, Montague. *Supernatural Omnibus.* 1974. Causeway Books. VG/dj. P3. $20.00

SUMNER, Cid Ricketts. *But the Morning Will Come.* 1949. Bobbs Merrill. 1st ed. F/NF. F4. $22.00

SUMNER, Edward. *Abraham Lincoln: An Address.* nd. NY. Tandy-Thomas. 31 p. brds. A6. $10.00

SUMNER, Nick. *Border Queen.* (1953). Dodd Mead. 1st ed. F/dj. B9. $25.00

SUNG, Kim Il. *On the Work of the United Front.* 1978. Pyongyang. Foreign Language Pr. 1st ed. 8vo. 208 p. VG. W1. $15.00

SUNSET BOOKS. *Crochet Techniques & Projects.* 1984. np. pb. ils/projects. wrp. G2. $5.00

SUPREE, Burton. *Bear's Heart. Scenes From the Life of a Cheyenne Artist...* 1977. Lippincott. 1st ed. sm quarto. VG/dj. L3. $85.00

SURTEES, Robert Smith. *Handley Cross; or, Mr Jorrock's Hunt.* 1854. London. 1st ils ed. orig 17 parts. red wrp. NF/Sutcliffe case. H5. $2,500.00

SUSANNE. *Famous Saddle Horses. Vol III.* 1947. Louisville. 1st/only prt. presentation. pebbled bdg. VG. O3. $525.00

SUSANNE. *Training & Gaiting.* 1944. Cynthiana. 2 vols. red bdg. VG. O3. $45.00

SUSKIND, Patrick. *Double Bass.* 1987. Hamish Hamilton. 1st ed. trans from German. F/F clip. A14. $35.00

SUSNJARA, Ken. *Manager's Guide to Industrial Robots.* 1982. Shaker Hgts, OH. Corinthian. 181 p. F/VG. S9. $5.00

SUTCLIFF, Rosemary. *Minstrel & the Dragon Pup.* 1993. Candlewick Pr. ils EC Clark. 1st Am ed. 4to. 42 p. F/F. A3. $16.95

SUTCLIFF, Rosemary. *Sword & the Circle.* 1981. Bodley Head. 1st ed. F/dj. P3. $20.00

SUTCLIFF, Rosemary. *Sword & the Circle.* 1981. Dutton. 1st ed. NF/dj. C1. $12.50

SUTCLIFF, Rosemary. *Sword at Sunset.* ca 1963. BC. VG+. C1. $7.50

SUTCLIFFE, Serena. *Great Vineyards & Winemakers.* 1981. Rutledge. 1st ed. ils/glossary/index. 256 p. F/F. B19. $25.00

SUTHERLAND, Alexander. *Achievements of Knights of Malta.* 1846. Phil. 1st Am ed. 2 vols in 1. 8vo. new cloth/orig label. O2. $75.00

SUTHERLAND, Halliday. *Time To Keep.* 1934. Morrow. 1st Am ed. 8vo. 281 p. F-/VG+. A2. $25.00

SUTHERLAND, L.W. *Aces & Kings.* (1936). London. Hamilton. Aviation BC. 29 photos. G-. M7. $75.00

SUTHREN, Victor. *Royal Yankee.* 1987. St Martin. 1st Am ed. F/F. F4. $15.00

SUTIN, Lawrence. *Divine Invasions: Life of Philip K Dick.* (1989). Harmony. 1st ed. F/NF. A7. $17.00

SUTRO, Oscar. *Some Remarks on Shakespeare Before the Roxburghe Club...* 1933. Grabhorn. 1/50. octavo. 28 p. tan cloth/bl brds. VG. H5. $200.00

SUTTON, Amos. *Narrative of Mission to Orissa.* 1833. Boston. Marks. 1st ed. sm 8vo. 424 p. full calf. VG. W1. $145.00

SUTTON, Elizabeth. *Pony for Keeps.* 1991. Charlottesville. Thomasson-Grant. 1st ed. ils MB Gamma. NF. O3. $6.00

SUTTON, Eric. *Opportunities of the Night.* 1925. London. Chapman Hall. 1/1000. intro Huxley. brn cloth. VG. S8. $45.00

SUTTON, Henry. *Vector.* 1970. Bernard Geis. 2nd ed. VG/VG. P3. $10.00

SUTTON, Jeff. *Atom Conspiracy.* 1963. Avalon. F/dj. P3. $15.00

SUTTON, Margaret. *Clue in Ruined Castle.* nd. Grosset Dunlap. VG-. P3. $5.00

SUTTON, Margaret. *Clue in Ruined Castle.* 1955. Grosset Dunlap. 176 p. red tweed cloth. VG/dj. M20. $35.00

SUTTON, Margaret. *Pledge of the Twin Knights.* 1965. Grosset Dunlap. 172 p. VG. M20. $20.00

SUTTON, Margaret. *Unfinished House.* 1938. Grosset Dunlap. 1st ed. 250 p. gr cloth. VG/dj. M20. $45.00

SUTTON, Margaret. *Vanishing Shadow.* 1932. Grosset Dunlap. VG. P3. $10.00

SUTTON, Oliver. *Murder Inc in Greece.* 1948. NY. New Century. 23 p. wrp. A7. $17.00

SUTTON, Silvia B. *Crossroads in Psychiatry: Hist of the Mclean Hospital.* 1986. Am Psychiatric Pr. 1st ed. 372 p. VG/dj. G1. $22.50

SUTTON, Stephen P. *More Tales To Tremble By.* 1968. Whitman. decor brds. VG. P3. $8.00

SUTTON, Willie. *Where the Money Was. Memoirs of a Bank Robber.* 1967. Viking. rem mk. VG/dj. A16. $15.00

SUTTON & SUTTON. *Appalachian Trail.* (1967). Lippincott. 5th prt. photos. map ep. 180 p. F/dj. A17. $15.00

SUVIN, Darko. *Propositions & Presuppositions in SF.* 1988. Kent State. 1st ed. F/dj. M2. $15.00

SUZUKI. *Elegant Crochet Laces.* 1983. np. ils. wrp. G2. $10.00

SVENNAS. *Advanced Quilting.* 1980. np. 1st ed. cloth. G2. $15.00

SVERDRUP, Otto. *Nyt Land Fire Aar I Arktiske Egne.* 1903. Kristiana. Aschehoug Co. 1st ed. 2 vols. 8vo. brn cloth. P4. $500.00

SVERDRUP, Otto. *Sverdrup's Arctic Adventures (1898-1902).* ca 1959. London. Longman. 8vo. 305 p. VG/VG. P4. $35.00

SVEVO, Italo. *James Joyce. Lecture Delivered in Milan in 1927.* 1950. New Directions. 1/1600. F/wrp. B2. $75.00

SWADOS, Harvey. *Celebration.* (1974). Simon Schuster. 1st ed. rem mk. dj. A7. $10.00

SWAIM, Douglas. *Cabins & Castles: Hist & Architecture Buncombe Co, NC.* 1981. NC Cultural Resources. 2nd ed. 225 p. VG-. B10. $25.00

SWAIN, James E. *Struggle for Control of Mediterranean Prior to 1848.* 1933. Boston. 8vo. 152 p. cloth. O2. $20.00

SWALLOW, Alan. *Wild Bunch.* (1966). Sage Books. 1st ed. F/F. A18. $40.00

SWALLOW, G.C. *1st & 2nd Annual Reports of Geological Survey of MO.* 1855. Jefferson City, MO. 8vo. pls/fld map. 239 p. bl cloth. H9. $250.00

SWAN, D.K. *King Arthur & the Knights of the Round Table.* 1992. Longman Classic. later prt. ils John James. M/wrp. C1. $5.00

SWAN, Gladys. *On the Edge of the Desert.* 1979. Urbana. 1st ed. sgn. F/wrp. A11. $40.00

SWAN, Joseph. *Delineations of the Brain...* 1864. London. Bradbury Evans. 18 pls. later quarter cloth/marbled brds. G7. $895.00

SWANN, Peter C. *Art of Japan From Jomon to Tokugawa Period.* 1966. NY. Crown. 1st ed. sm 4to. pls. 238 p. VG. W1. $55.00

SWANN, Thomas Burnett. *Alas, in Lilliput.* 1964. Worcester. St Onge. miniature. bl calf. H10. $95.00

SWANSON, Eric. *Greenhouse Effect.* 1990. Little Brn. 1st ed. author's 1st book. F/F. A14. $25.00

SWANSON, Logan; see Matheson, Richard.

SWANSON, Neil H. *Unconquered.* 1947. Doubleday. 1st ed. VG/VG-. P3. $15.00

SWANTON, John R. *Final Report of the US De Soto Comm.* 1939. GPO. orig ed. 11 maps. VG/wrp. O6. $100.00

SWANWICK, Michael. *Gravity's Angels.* 1991. Arkham. 1st ed. NF/dj. P3. $21.00

SWANWICK, Michael. *Griffin's Egg.* 1991. Legend. 1st ed. F/F. P3. $25.00

SWANWICK, Michael. *Vaccum Flowers.* 1988. Simon Schuster (British). 1st ed. F/dj. P3. $30.00

SWARTHOUT, Glendon. *Old Colts.* 1985. NY. 1st ed/wrp issue. inscr. F/glossy 8vo wrp. A11. $40.00

SWARTHOUT, Glendon. *Shootist.* 1975. Doubleday. 1st ed. F/NF. B4. $45.00

SWARTZ, Delbert. *Collegiate Dictionary of Botany.* 1971. NY. 520 p. VG. B26. $39.00

SWARTZ, M.J. *Political Anthropology.* 1966. Chicago. 309 p. red cloth. NF. S9. $5.00

SWEARINGEN, Roger. *Communism in Vietnam.* (1967). Am Bar Assn. 195 p. wrp. A7. $30.00

SWEENEY, James B. *Pict Hist of Sea Monsters.* nd. Bonanza. VG. P3. $10.00

SWEENEY, Z.T. *Biennial Report of Commissioner Fisheries & Game In IN.* 1908. IN. photos. 1116 p. G. A17. $39.50

SWEET, Bill. *They Call Me Mr Airshow.* 1972. Milwaukee. 1st ed. VG/VG. B5. $35.00

SWEET, Frederick A. *Miss Mary Cassatt: Impressionist From PA.* 1966. Norman, OK. 8 color pls. 242 p. cloth. D2. $55.00

SWEET, Muriel. *Common Edible & Useful Plants.* 1962. Naturegraph Co. 8vo. G. A8. $4.50

SWEET, Muriel. *How Trees Help Your Health.* 1965. Healdsburg, CA. ils Jane Judd. 64 p. B26. $14.00

SWEETSER, Kate Dickinson. *Book of Indian Braves.* 1923. NY. 8vo. ils/pls. blk cloth/pict label. VG. H3. $15.00

SWEETSER, Kate Dickinson. *Ten Girls From Dickens.* 1902. Taylor. 1st ed. 236 p. VG. S10. $35.00

SWEETSER, M.F. *King's Handbook of the US.* ca 1891. Buffalo, NY. lg 12mo. 2600 ils/51 color maps. 939 p. emb leather. G. T3. $24.00

SWEETSER, Wesley D. *Arthur Machen.* 1964. Twayne. VG. P3. $20.00

SWEM, E.G. *Jamestown 350th-Anniversary Hist Booklets.* 1957. Williamsburg, VA. set of 32 booklets. 8vo. VG/VG slipcase. B11. $75.00

SWEM, E.G. *VA Hist Index.* 1965. Peter Smith. reprint of 1936. 2 vols in 4. VG. B10. $100.00

SWEMER, S.M. *Arabia: Cradle of Islam.* 1900. NY. 8vo. fld maps. 434 p. pict cloth. O2. $55.00

SWEMER, S.M. *Cross Above the Crescent.* 1941. Grand Rapids. 8vo. 292 p. cloth. dj. O2. $30.00

SWEMER, S.M. *Islam: Challenge to Faith.* 1907. NY. 1st ed. 8vo. 295 p. cloth. O2. $75.00

SWENSON, Olaf. *W of the World.* 1944. Dodd Mead. 2nd prt. 270 p. VG. A17. $20.00

SWENSON, Peggy; see Geis, Richard.

SWIFT, David E. *Joseph John Gurney: Banker, Reformer & Quaker.* 1962. Middletown, CT. Wesleyan U. 1st ed. 8vo. 304 p. VG. V3. $14.00

SWIFT, Graham. *Out of This World.* (1988). Poseidon. AP. VG/prt bl wrp. B3. $50.00

SWIFT, Graham. *Out of This World.* (1988). Poseidon. 1st ed. rem mk. F/F. A7. $12.00

SWIFT, Graham. *Waterland.* 1983. Poseidon. 1st ed. NF/F. B2. $35.00

SWIFT, Jonathan. *Gulliver in Giant-Land.* nd. London/NY. ils Sandy/7 color pls. gilt gr cloth. G. H3. $15.00

SWIFT, Jonathan. *Gulliver's Travels.* 1930. London. 1/195. ils Rex Whistler/12 hc pls. orig gr morocco. slipcase. H5. $4,500.00

SWIFT, Jonathan. *Gulliver's Travels.* 1977. Oxford. new intro Barzun. ils Warren Chappell. C1. $7.50

SWIFT, Jonathan. *Gulliver's Travels.* 1986. Eng. Lamboll House. ils RG Mossa/12 color pls. VG/VG. L1. $20.00

SWIFT. *Batsford Encyclopedia of Embroidery Techniques.* 1991. np. reference. cloth. G2. $35.00

SWIGART, Rob. *Portal.* 1988. St Martin. 1st ed. F/F. P3. $20.00

SWINBURNE, A.C. *Atlanta in Calydon: A Tragedy.* 1894. Hammersmith. 1/250. quarto. full limp vellum/silk ties. NF. H5. $1,500.00

SWINBURNE, A.C. *Shelley.* 1973. Worcester. St Onge. miniature. 1/500. 23 p. red morocco. H10. $35.00

SWINBURNE, A.C. *Tristram of Lyonesse & Other Poems.* 1882. London. Chatto Windus. 1st ed. gilt gr cloth. VG. C1. $29.00

SWINTON. *Swinton's Elementary Geography.* 1875. np. sm quarto. hand-color maps. 140 p. VG. E5. $45.00

SWITT. *Needlepoint Scrapbook.* 1986. np. ils. cloth. G2. $20.00

SWORD, Wiley. *Shiloh: Bloody April.* 1974. Morrow. 1st ed. 519 p. G. B10. $30.00

SYDENHAM, Thomas. *Treatise of the Gout & Dropsy.* 1971. Merck Sharpe Dohme. reprint of 1788 ed. 305 p. prt brds. F. S9. $15.00

SYKES, Christopher. *Orde Wingate.* 1959. London. Collins. 1st ed. 576 p. NF/VG clip. M7. $45.00

SYM, John. *Lifes Preservative Against Self-Killing.* 1988. London. Routledge. facsimile. ochre cloth. F/dj. G1. $35.00

SYME, Ronald. *John Smith of VA.* 1954. Morrow. 1st ed. ils Tobbs. 192 p. VG/fair. B10. $10.00

SYME. *Learn Patchwork.* 1987. np. ils. wrp. G2. $9.00

SYMONDS, John Addington. *Autobiography of Benvenuto Cellini.* 1946. NY. Doubleday. 1/1000. sgn/ils Salvador Dali. NF/slipcase. B24. $425.00

SYMONDS, John Addington. *Sketches in Italy.* 1883. Leipzig. gilt full gr leather. F. B30. $70.00

SYMONDS, Julian. *Bogue's Fortune.* 1956. Harper. 1st ed. VG/dj. P3. $35.00

SYMONDS, Julian. *England's Pride.* 1966. Hist BC. VG/dj. P3. $10.00

SYMONDS, Julian. *General Strike.* 1959. Readers Union. VG/dj. P3. $15.00

SYMONDS, Julian. *Great Detectives.* 1981. Van Nostrand Reinhold. 1st ed. VG/dj. P3. $20.00

SYMONDS, Julian. *Man Whose Dreams Came True.* 1968. Harper Row. 1st ed. VG/dj. P3. $25.00

SYMONDS, Julian. *Plot Against Roger Rider.* 1973. Harper Row. 1st ed. VG/VG-. P3. $18.00

SYMONDS, Margaret. *Days Spent on a Doge's Farm.* Century/Unwin. from Eng sheets. 1st Am ed. 8vo. 254 p. VG+. A2. $30.00

SYMONDS, R.W. *Book of English Clocks.* 1950. King Penguin. 2nd ed. VG/dj. P3. $20.00

SYMONS, Julian. *Blackheath Poisonings.* 1978. Collins. 1st ed. F/F. S5. $30.00

SYMONS, Julian. *Seven Orig Investigations.* (1981). Abrams. VG+/dj. B9. $20.00

SYMONS, Julian. *Verdict of 13.* 1979. Harper Row. 1st ed. F/dj. P3. $15.00

SYNAN, Edward A. *Popes & Jews in Middle Ages.* 1965. Macmillan. 246 p. VG/VG. S3. $21.00

SYNGE, Patrick M. *Flowers in Winter.* 1948. London. 1st ed. pls. 122 p. VG. B28. $17.50

SYRETT, Netta. *Tinkelly Winkle.* 1923. Dodd Mead. 1st ed. ils Marcia Lane Foster. VG. M5. $55.00

SZULC, Tad. *Fidel: A Critical Portrait.* (1986). Morrow. 1st ed. 703 p. dj. F3. $20.00

SZYK, Arthur. *Ink & Blood. Book of Drawings.* 1946. Heritage. ltd ed. inscr/sgn. teg. gilt full leather. F/NF box. R3. $750.00

TABER, Gladys. *One Dozen & One.* 1966. Phil. 1st ed. VG/VG. B5. $30.00

TABORI, Paul. *Art of Folly.* (1961). Chilton. 1st ed. 8vo. 259 p. VG/VG. A2. $12.50

TABORI, Paul. *Natural Science of Stupidity.* 1960. Phil. Chilton. 3rd prt. 8vo. 288 p. F/VG. A2. $10.00

TACK, Alfred. *Spy Who Wasn't Exchanged.* 1970. Mystery Book Guild. front free ep removed. VG/dj. P3. $5.00

TAFFRAIL. *Shetland Plan.* 1953. Hodder Stoughton. 2nd ed. NF/dj. P3. $18.00

TAFT, Elise Hagopian. *Rebirth: Story of Armenian Girl Who Survived Genocide...* 1981. NY. 8vo. inscr. 142 p. cloth. dj. O2. $20.00

TAFT, Philip. *AF of L in the Time of Gompers.* (1957). Harper. 1st ed. worn clip dj. A7. $30.00

TAFT, Philip. *Organized Labor in Am Hist.* ca 1964. Harper Row. VG/G. V4. $25.00

TAFT, William Howard. *Anti-Trust Act & the Supreme Court.* 1914. Harper. 1st ed. NF/dj. B4. $175.00

TAGER, Alexander B. *Decay of Czarism: Beiliss Trial.* 1935. JPS. 297 p. VG/poor. S3. $30.00

TAGG, Lawrence V. *Harold Bell Wright: Storyteller to Am.* 1986. Westernlore Pr. 1st ed. sgn. M/M. A18. $25.00

TAGLIACOZZO, Gaspare. *Curatorum Chirurgia per Institionem Libri Duo.* 1831. Berlin. Reimer. final ed. 436 p. modern morocco. NF. B14. $1,500.00

TAINE, John. *Forbidden Garden.* 1947. Fantasy. 1st ed. VG. P3. $18.00

TAINE, John. *GOG.* 1954. Fantasy. 1st ed. 1/300. inscr/sgn/#d. NF/dj. P3. $75.00

TALBOT, Eugene S. *Degeneracy: Its Causes, Signs & Results.* 1898. London. Walter Scott. xl. ils/photos. 372 p. gilt red cloth. VG. S9. $18.00

TALBOT, Michael. *Bog.* 1986. Morrow. 1st ed. F/NF. N3. $10.00

TALBOT, Michael. *Night Things.* nd. BC. VG/dj. P3. $8.00

TALESE, Gay. *Honor Thy Father.* nd. BC. VG/dj. P3. $8.00

TALESE, Gay. *Overreachers.* (1965). Harper Row. 1st ed. author's 2nd book. F/NF. B4. $45.00

TALLANT, Edith. *David & Patience.* 1940. Lippincott. sgn. ils Dorothy Bayley. 166 p. cloth. VG/tattered. M20. $25.00

TALLANT, Rosemary. *W Horse...W Style.* ca 1950. np. booklet. 4to. 22 p. G+. O3. $25.00

TALLENT, Robert. *Voodoo in New Orleans.* 1946. Macmillan. 1st ed. sgn. F/NF. B2. $45.00

TALLEY, Rick. *Cubs of '69.* 1989. Contemporary. 1st ed. inscr. F/F. P8. $20.00

TALLMAN, Majorie. *Dictionary of Am Folklore.* (1959). NY. 1st ed. 324 p. cloth. F/pict dj. D3. $25.00

TAN, Amy. *Kitchen God's Wife.* 1991. NY. ARC. sgn. F/unread 8vo wrp. A11. $55.00

TAN, Amy. *Kitchen God's Wife.* 1991. Putnam. VG/dj. A16. $40.00

TAN, Amy. *Kitchen God's Wife.* 1991. Putnam. 1st ed. inscr. F/F. B2. $65.00

TAN, Amy. *Moon Lady.* 1992. Macmillan. 1st ed. VG/VG. L1. $35.00

TAN, Amy. *Selected From the Joy Luck Club.* 1992. NY. PBO. sgn w/chopmark. F/ils wrp. A11. $65.00

TANIZAKI, Jun'ichiro. *Cat, a Man & Two Women.* 1990. Tokyo/NY. Kodansha Internat. 1st ed. F/F clip. A14. $25.00

TANNAHILL, Reay. *Flesh & Blood.* 1975. Hamish Hamilton. 1st ed. VG/dj. P3. $20.00

TANNER, Henry Schenk. *Am Traveller; or, Guide Through the US.* 1836. Phil. 18mo. 144 p. orig gray-brn cloth. H9. $675.00

TANNER, Ogden. *Canadians.* 1977. Time Life. 4to. F. A8. $10.00

TANNER, Robert G. *Stonewall in the Valley.* 1976. Doubleday. 436 p. VG/VG. B10. $25.00

TANNER, William. *Memoir of Wm Tanner...* 1868. London. FB Kitto. 12mo. 257 p. ES. V3. $18.00

TAPIE, M. *Avant Garde Art in Japan.* 1962. Abrams. VG/G+. A1. $100.00

TAPLEY, William T. *Vegetables of NY. Vol 1, Part IV: The Cucurbits.* 1937. Albany, NY. 49 full-p color pls. 131 p. F/wrp/mailer. scarce. B26. $65.00

TAPPLY, H.G. *Sportsman's Notebook & Tap's Tips.* (1973). NY. 6th prt. F/dj. A17. $12.00

TAPPLY, H.G. *Tackle Tinkering.* (1946). NY. 2nd prt. 214 p. F/dj. A17. $19.50

TAPPLY, William G. *Death at Charity's Point.* 1984. Scribner. 1st ed. author's 1st novel. F/F. M15. $150.00

TAPPLY, William G. *Home Water Near & Far: Fly Fisherman's Explorations.* (1992). Lyons Burford. 1st ed. 155 p. M/dj. A17. $9.50

TAPPLY, William G. *Spotted Cats.* nd. BC. VG/dj. P3. $8.00

TAPPLY, William G. *Vulgar Boatman.* 1987. Scribner. 1st ed. F/F. M15. $30.00

TARG, William. *Bibliophile in the Nursery.* 1957. World. 503 p. VG+/dj. M20. $60.00

TARITT, Donna. *Secret Hist.* 1992. Knopf. 1st ed. F/F. M15. $50.00

TARKINGTON, Booth. *Beasley's Christmas Party.* Oct, 1909. Harper. 1st ed. 99 p. gilt red cloth. VG. A3. $29.50

TARKINGTON, Booth. *Guest of Quesnay.* 1917. Scribner. VG. P3. $10.00

TARKINGTON, Booth. *Monsieur Beaucaire.* nd (ca 1924). NY. 1st Rudolph Valentino ed. NF/VG+. A11. $40.00

TARKINGTON, Booth. *Penrod & Sam.* 1916. Grosset Dunlap. photoplay ed. 356 p. G+/dj. M20. $15.00

TARKINGTON, Booth. *Penrod.* 1914. Doubleday Page. 1st ed/2nd state. 345 p. bl cloth. VG. S10. $35.00

TARKINGTON, Booth. *Rumbin Galleries.* 1937. Doubleday Doran. 1st ed. NF/VG. B4. $65.00

TARKINGTON, Booth. *Seventeen.* nd. Grosset Dunlap. VG. P3. $5.00

TARKINGTON, Booth. *Young Mrs Greeley.* 1929. Doubleday Doran. 1st ed. G+. V2. $9.00

TARR, Judith. *Ars Magica.* nd. BC. NF/dj. P3. $8.00

TARR, Judith. *Hall of the Mtn King.* (1986). NY. Tor. 1st ed. F/F. B3. $15.00

TARRANT, John. *Clauberg Trigger.* 1979. Atheneum. 1st ed. F/dj. P3. $15.00

TARRANT, Margaret. *Fairy Tales.* 1978. Crowell. 1st Am ed? 18 color pls. VG/G. L1. $25.00

TARRANT, Margaret. *Margaret Tarrant's Christmas Garland.* 1942. Boston. 8vo. 125 p. gr cloth. F. H3. $40.00

TARRY, Ellen. *Third Door: Autobiography of Am Negro Woman.* 1955. NY. McKay. N2. $17.50

TARSOULI, Athina. *Iles Blanches.* 1939. Athens. sq 8vo. 3 mtd aquatints. 153 p. O2. $40.00

TARTT, Donna. *Secret Hist.* 1992. Knopf. ARC. NF/wrp. B2. $45.00

TARTT, Donna. *Secret Hist.* 1992. Knopf. 1st ed. F/F. T2. $35.00

TARTT, Donna. *Secret Hist.* 1992. Knopf. 1st ed. sgn. w/sgn 2-p letter. F/F. B2. $100.00

TASSO, Torquato. *Jerusalem Delivered...* 1821. London. 12mo. fore-edge painting. contemporary morocco. VG/slipcase. H5. $750.00

TATAM, David. *Robert Frost's Wht Mtns.* 1974. Worcester. St Onge. miniature. 36 p. calf. H10. $75.00

TATE, Allen. *Collected Poems 1919-1976.* 1977. NY. 1st ed. w/sgn bookplate. F/F. A11. $45.00

TATE, Allen. *Fathers.* 1960. Eyre Spottiswoode. 1st ed. Muriel Spark's copy w/sgn. VG/VG. C4. $40.00

TATE, Carolyn. *Human Body, Human Spirit.* 1993. Carlos Mus. 1st ed. 92 color pls/map. 139 p. wrp. F3. $35.00

TATE, Donald. *Bravo Burning.* (1986). Scribner. 1st ed. F/F. A7. $30.00

TATE, Peter. *Faces in the Flames.* 1976. Doubleday. 1st ed. VG/VG. P3. $13.00

TATE, Peter. *Greencomber.* 1979. Doubleday. 1st ed. F/dj. P3. $13.00

TATE, Sally. *Gingerbread Man. A Fuzzy Wuzzy Book.* 1944. Whitman. 28 p. pict brds. VG/VG. A3. $20.00

TATE. *Warp, a Weaving Reference.* 1984. np. ils. cloth. G2. $20.50

TATLEY, Richard. *Steamboat Era in the Muskokas. Vol 1.* 1984. Ontario. Boston Mills. as new/dj. A16. $45.00

TATSIOS, Theodore G. *Megali Idea & the Greek-Turkish War of 1897...* 1984. NY. 8vo. 302 p. cloth. O2. $45.00

TAUSSIG, C.W. *Rum, Romance & Rebellion.* 1928. NY. Minton Balch. 1st ed. 8vo. 289 p. G+. A2. $15.00

TAWES, William I. *Creative Bird Carving.* (1983). Centreville, MD. 5th prt. 207 p. F/dj. A17. $17.50

TAYLER, Zack; see Marshall, Mel.

TAYLOR, Albert. *Complete Garden.* 1921. Garden City. pls. 440 p. VG+. B28. $25.00

TAYLOR, Albert. *Under HI Skies.* 1926. Honolulu. 2nd ed. 8vo. 607 p. pict gr cloth. F/fair. H3. $35.00

TAYLOR, Andrew. *Caroline Minuscule.* 1982. London. Gollancz. 1st ed. F/NF. S5. $35.00

TAYLOR, Ann. *Rhymes for the Nursery.* (1830s). New Haven. Babcock. 48mo. ils. M/wrp. H3. $100.00

TAYLOR, Bayard. *Cyclopaedia of Modern Travel.* 1856. Cincinnati. Moore Wilstach Keys. lg 8vo. ils/maps. emb bl cloth. H9. $90.00

TAYLOR, Bernard. *Reaping.* 1980. Souvenir. 1st ed. NF/dj. P3. $20.00

TAYLOR, Charles. *Reporter in Red China.* 1966. Random. 1st prt. 8vo. 8 pls. 208 p. NF/dj. W1. $18.00

TAYLOR, Donna. *Great Lakes Region in Children's Books.* (1980). Gr Oak Pr. 481 p. F. A17. $30.00

TAYLOR, Elizabeth. *View of the Harbor.* 1947. Knopf. 1st ed. F/VG. C4. $40.00

TAYLOR, Elizabeth. *Wedding Group.* 1968. Viking. 1st ed. F/F. C4. $35.00

TAYLOR, Elizabeth. *Wreath of Roses.* 1949. Knopf. 1st ed. F/NF. C4. $40.00

TAYLOR, Eugene. *William James on Exceptional Mental States.* 1983. Scribner. 1st ed. 222 p. gr brds. VG/torn. G1. $25.00

TAYLOR, Frances Henry. *Taste of Angels: A Hist of Art Collecting...* 1948. Little Brn. 1st ed. lg 8vo. ils/index. 661 p. gilt calf/cloth. B20. $75.00

TAYLOR, Geoffrey. *Some 19th-Century Gardeners.* 1951. London. ils. 176 p. VG/dj. B26. $25.00

TAYLOR, Henry. *Afternoon of Pocket Billiards.* 1978. UT. 1st ed. F/NF. V1. $15.00

TAYLOR, Herman E. *Faulkner's Oxford.* 1990. Nashville. 1st ed. inscr. F/F. A11. $40.00

TAYLOR, Isaac. *Hist of Transmission of Ancient Books to Modern Times.* 1827. London. marbled ep/edges. full leather. B30. $115.00

TAYLOR, J. *Thumb Bible.* ca 1889. NY. Randolph. miniature. gilt blk paper brds. H10. $100.00

TAYLOR, J. Golden. *Great W Short Stories.* 1967. Am W Pub. 1st/deluxe ed. teg. heavy gilt cloth. F/VG slipcase. A18. $50.00

TAYLOR, J. Golden. *Literature of the Am W.* (1971). Houghton Mifflin. not 1st prt. sc. F. A18. $25.00

TAYLOR, Jeremy. *Rules & Exercises of Holy Dying.* (1847). London. 324 p. VG. E5. $40.00

TAYLOR, John Russell. *Hitch.* 1978. Pantheon. 1st ed. VG/dj. P3. $20.00

TAYLOR, John W.R. *Combat Aircraft of the World.* 1969. Putnam. VG/VG-. P3. $20.00

TAYLOR, Joshua C. *William Page: Am Titian.* 1957. Chicago. ils/pls. 293 p. cloth. dj. D2. $95.00

TAYLOR, Judson R.; see Halsey, Harlan Page.

TAYLOR, Judy. *Dudley Bakes a Cake.* 1988. Putnam. 1st ed. 4to. F/NF. T5. $20.00

TAYLOR, L.A. *Poetic Justice.* 1988. Walker. 1st ed. sgn. F/F. F4. $19.00

TAYLOR, L.B. *Ghosts of Richmond & Nearby Environs.* 1985. Progress Prt. 171 p. VG. B10. $10.00

TAYLOR, Louis. *Horse Am Made...* 1961. NY. Harper Row. later prt. VG/VG. O3. $25.00

TAYLOR, Louis. *Out of the West. New Horsemanship.* 1965. NY. Barners. 2nd ed. VG/G. O3. $35.00

TAYLOR, Mrs. J. *Wouldst Know Thyself.* 1858. NY. 1st ed. 12mo. ils/engraving. 66 p. tan brds/red spine. F. H3. $50.00

TAYLOR, Norman M. *Christian Patriot.* 1917. Phil. Jenkins. 12mo. 79 p. VG. V3. $12.50

TAYLOR, P. Walker. *Murder in the Game Reserve.* 1947. Thornton Butterworth. 1st ed. VG. P3. $35.00

TAYLOR, Peter. *Old Forest & Other Stories.* 1985. Dial. 1st e. F/NF. B2. $50.00

TAYLOR, Peter. *Oracle at Stoneleigh Court.* 1993. Knopf. ARC. 1/650. F/F cardboard slipcase. B2. $50.00

TAYLOR, Phoebe Atwood. *Going, Going, Gone.* 1943. Norton. 1st ed. VG. P3. $35.00

TAYLOR, R.C. *Statistics of Coal.* 1855. Phil. JW Moore. thick 8vo. 640 p. new cloth. H9. $95.00

TAYLOR, Rebecca N. *Earth People & Other Poems.* nd. London. Stockwell. 12mo. 32 p. VG/dj. V3. $9.50

TAYLOR, Rebecca N. *Sm Adventures of a Little Quaker Girl.* 1937. Friends Bookstore. 12mo. 105 p. VG/dj. V3. $14.00

TAYLOR, Silas. *Hist of Gavel-Kind w/the Etymology Thereof...* 1663. London. John Starkey. modern full sheep. M11. $650.00

TAYLOR, Sydney. *All-of-a-Kind Family Uptown.* (1958). Follett. 5th prt. sm 4to. gr brds. G+/G. T5. $25.00

TAYLOR, Sydney. *Ella of All-of-a-Kind Family.* 1978. Dutton. 1st ed. 8vo. 133 p. red cloth. VG. T5. $30.00

TAYLOR, Telford. *Nuremburg & Vietnam.* (1970). Quadrangle. 12mo. 224 p. dj. A7. $40.00

TAYLOR, Thomas. *Piece of This Country.* (1984). Markham. Paperjacks. pb. NF. A7. $10.00

TAYLOR, William. *CA Life Ils.* (1858). NY. self pub. 24th thousand. 12mo. pls. 348 p. cloth. D3. $45.00

TAYLOR, William. *CA Life Ils.* ca 1885. NY. xl. 12mo. 404 p. gilt brn cloth. VG. T3. $45.00

TAYLOR, William. *CA Life Ils.* 1867. London/NY. 8vo. blk cloth. H9. $45.00

TAYLOR, William. *Four Yrs' Campaign in India.* Nelson Phillips. 3rd ed. 416 p. teg. gilt cloth. VG+. F1. $50.00

TAYLOR, William. *Landlord & Peasant in Colonial Oaxaca.* 1972. Stanford. 1st ed. 287 p. dj. F3. $20.00

TAYLOR, William. *Letters to a Quaker Friend on Baptism.* 1880. NY. Phillips Hunt. 12mo. 163 p. VG. V3. $16.00

TAYLOR, William. *Poems for Little Men & Women.* 1918. McKay. 8 color pls. bl cloth. NF/G. M5. $35.00

TAYLOR, Zack. *Successful Waterfowling.* (1989). Stackpole. 2nd ed. lg 8vo. 275 p. F/dj. A17. $17.50

TAYLOR & TAYLOR. *Little Ann & Other Poems.* nd. (1883). London. Routledge. 1st ed. octavo. 64 p. teg. morocco/brds. H5. $300.00

TAYLOR & TAYLOR. *Psychiatry: Past Reflections, Future Visions.* 1990. NY. Elsevier. 271 p. bl cloth. G1. $25.00

TAZIEFF, Haroun. *Nyiragongo: The Forbidden Volcano.* 1979. NY. Woodbury. 1st Am ed. sm 4to. 287 p. F/VG. A2. $20.00

TEAD, Ordway. *Case for Democracy & Its Meaning for Modern Life.* 1938. Womans Pr. 1st ed. VG/dj. E3. $12.00

TEAGUE, Charles Collins. *50 Yrs a Ranger.* 1944. CA Walnut Growers Assn. 2nd ed. VG. N2. $15.00

TEAGUE, Richard D. *Manual of Wildlife Conservation.* 1971. WA. 2nd ed. 4to. 206 p. wrp. A17. $9.50

TEASDALE, Sara. *Rainbow Gold: Poems Old & New.* 1922. Macmillan. 1st ed. 267 p. G. S10. $20.00

TEASDALE, Sara. *Woman & Poet.* 1989. TN U. 1st ed. F/sans. V1. $15.00

TEBBETTS, Leon. *O Big Earth.* 1938. Portland. Falmouth. 1st ed. NF/NF. B2. $45.00

TEDLOCK, Dennis. *Popol Vuh.* (1985). Simon Schuster. 1st ed. 380 p. dj. F3. $20.00

TEDROW, Thomas L. *Dorothy: Return to Oz.* 1993. Family Vision Pr. ARC/1st ed. VG/wrp. L1. $25.00

TEED, G.H. *Shadow Crook.* 1936. Stanley Smith. 1st ed. front free ep removed. VG-. P3. $20.00

TEIXERIA DA MOTA, Avelino. *Mar, Alem Mar: Estudos e Ensaios de Historia Geografia.* 1972. Lisboa. 29 maps. M/dj. O6. $95.00

TEMPLE, John. *Irish Rebellion; or, Hist...Ireland.* 1812. London. Wht Cochrane. rebound. VG. A16. $125.00

TEMPLE, Shirley. *My Life & Times.* 1936. Saalfield. VG-/pict wrp. A3. $30.00

TEMPLE, Shirley. *Shirley Temple's Fairyland.* (1958). Random. 4th prt. 4to. ils. VG. T5. $18.00

TEMPLE, William. *Christus Veritas...* 1954. London. Macmillan. 285 p. H10. $16.50

TEMPLE, William. *Church & Its Teaching Today.* 1936. Macmillan. 49 p. H10. $10.00

TEMPLE, William. *Martin Magnus on Mars.* 1966. Muller. 1st ed. VG/dj. P3. $35.00

TEMPLE, William. *Shoot at the Moon.* 1966. Simon Schuster. 1st ed. sgn. VG/dj. P3. $30.00

TENDALL & TESENE. *Country Threads.* 1992. np. full-size patterns. wrp. G2. $20.00

TENGGREN, Gustaf. *Good Dog Book.* 1924. Houghton Mifflin. 1st ed. VG. M5. $15.00

TENGGREN, Gustaf. *Tenggren's Storybook.* 1944. Simon Schuster. 1st ed. 87 p. VG. A3. $17.50

TENGMALM, Petrus Gust. *De Ruptura Cordis.* 1785. Upsaliae. 4to. 28 p. uncut. G7. $45.00

TENN, William; see Klass, Philip.

TENNEY, E.P. *CO & Homes in the New W.* 1880. Boston/NY. 8vo. 118 p. map. pict gr cloth. H9. $100.00

TENNYSON, Alfred Lord. *Locksley Hall & Other Poems.* nd. Nister. decor brds. VG-. P3. $15.00

TEPPER, Sheri S. *Grass.* 1989. Doubleday. 1st ed. F/F. N3. $15.00

TEPPER, Sheri S. *Southshore.* 1987. Tor. 1st ed. F/F. P3. $16.00

TERENTIUS AFER, Publius. *Comoediae Omnes.* 1561. Venice. Joannem Mariam Bonellum. 11 woodcuts. 19th-century bdg. K1. $475.00

TERENTIUS AFER, Publius. *Comoediae Sex ex Recensione Frid Lindenbrogii...* 1820. London. Priestley. 2 vols. teg. 19th-century full gr calf. K1. $175.00

TERHUNE, Albert Payson. *Real Tales of Real Dogs.* 1935. Akron. Saalfield. sm folio. 92 p. E5. $65.00

TERHUNE, Albert Payson. *Story of Damon & Pythias.* 1915. Grosset Dunlap. photoplay ed. VG/torn. P3. $35.00

TERHUNE, Albert Payson. *Syria From the Saddle.* 1897. Boston. 1st ed. author's 1st book. 318 p. decor cloth. O2. $55.00

TERKEL, Studs. *Giants of Jazz.* 1957. Crowell. 1st ed. inscr. NF/VG. B2. $100.00

TERKEL, Studs. *Good War: Oral Hist of WWII.* 1984. Pantheon. 1st ed. VG/dj. A16. $20.00

TERKEL, Studs. *Working: People Talk About What They Do All Day...* 1974. Pantheon. VG/dj. E3. $30.00

TERMAN, Douglas. *First Strike.* 1979. Scribner. 1st ed. F/F. T2. $12.00

TERRALL, Robert. *They Deal in Death.* 1944. Books Inc. VG. P3. $18.00

TERRES, John K. *Discovery: Great Moments in Lives Outstanding Naturalists.* 1961. Phil. 1st ed. ils Thomas W Nason. F/dj. T8. $15.00

TERRY, Charles S. Jr. *Masterworks of Japanese Art.* 1961. Tuttle. 6th ed. folio. 100 pls. 252 p. NF/torn. W1. $35.00

TERRY, Ellen. *Ellen Terry's Memoirs.* 1932. Putnam. VG/dj. A16. $35.00

TERRY, Megan. *Viet Rock: 4 Plays.* (1967). Simon Schuster. 1st wrp issue. A7. $23.00

TERRY, Wallace. *Bloods: Oral Hist of Vietnam War by Blk Veterans.* (1984). Random. 1st ed. 311 p. NF/dj. A7. $35.00

TERVALON, Jervey. *Understand This.* 1994. Morrow. hc ARC w/wraparound band. F. B2. $25.00

TERY, Simone. *Danielle: Wonderful Story of Danielle Casanova.* 1953. NY. Internat. 126 p. wrp. A7. $15.00

TERZIAN, James. *Kid From Cuba.* 1967. Doubleday (Signal). 1st ed. F/VG+. P8. $30.00

TESCHER. *Dyeing & Over-Dyeing of Cotton Fabrics.* 1990. np. ils. wrp. G2. $10.00

TESHIGAHAA, Sofu. *Sofu: His Boundless World of Flowers & Form.* 1966. Tokyo. 1st ed. 54 color pls. 116 p. VG. B28. $30.00

TESSIER, Thomas. *Finishing Touches.* 1986. Atheneum. 1st ed. F/NF. N3. $15.00

TESSIER, Thomas. *Finishing Touches.* 1986. Atheneum. 1st ed. sgn. F/F. F4. $45.00

TESSIER, Thomas. *Nightwalker.* 1979. Macmillan. 1st ed. VG/dj. P3. $20.00

TESSIER, Thomas. *Secret Strangers.* 1992. Dark Harvest. 1st ed. F/dj. B9. $6.50

TESSIER, Thomas. *Shockwaves.* 1983. Severn House. 1st ed. VG/dj. P3. $25.00

TETLOW, Edwin. *Enigma of Hastings.* 1974. BC. VG/dj. C1. $6.00

TEVIS, Walter. *Far From Home.* 1981. Doubleday. 1st ed. F/F. M18. $20.00

TEVIS, Walter. *Mockingbird.* 1980. Doubleday. Ap of 1st ed. F/pict wrp. N3. $15.00

TEVIS, Walter. *Steps of the Sun.* 1983. Doubleday. 1st ed. F/F. N3/P3. $20.00

TEY, Josephine. *Franchise Affair.* 1959. Peter Davies. 4th ed. VG/torn. P3. $10.00

TEY, Josephine. *Miss Pym Disposes.* 1948. Macmillan. 1st Am ed. NF/dj. M15. $45.00

TEY, Josephine. *Singing Sands.* 1953. NY. Macmillan. 1st Am ed. VG/clip. M15. $40.00

THACKER, May Dixon. *Strange Death of President Harding.* 1930. NY. 8vo. ils/photos. 342 p. blk cloth. VG. T3. $15.00

THACKERAY, William Makepeace. *Four Georges: Sketches of Manners, Morals, Court...* 1861. London. Smith Elder. 1st ed/1st issue. octavo. 226 p. pub gilt gr cloth. B24. $375.00

THACKERAY, William Makepeace. *Hist of Henry Esmond, Esq.* 1956. NY. sm quarto. 441 p. ils/sgn Ardizzone. F/slipcase. B24. $75.00

THACKERAY, William Makepeace. *Mr Brn's Letters to a Young Man About Town.* 1901. Cambridge. Riverside. 1/500. 210 p. NF/slipcase. B25. $185.00

THACKERAY, William Makepeace. *Newcomes.* 1854-55. London. 1st ed. 24 parts in 23. orig yel wrp. VG/box. H5. $950.00

THACKERAY, William Makepeace. *Vanity Fair...* 1848. London. 1st ed. 20 monthly parts in 19. octavo. VG/morocco case. H5. $12,500.00

THACKERAY, William Makepeace. *Works of...* 1878. London. Smith Elder. 52 vols. w/sgn note in Vol 1. teg. silk ep. NF. H5. $22,500.00

THATCHER, Benjamin B. *Indian Biography...* 1860. NY. Harper. 2 vols. gilt brn cloth. scarce. F1. $130.00

THATCHER, Benjamin B. *Indian Life & Battles.* 1910. Akron. New Werner. G. H7. $12.50

THAYER, Bert. *Thoroughbred: Pict Highlights of Breeding & Racing.* nd. np. sm 4to. ils. VG/G+. O3. $25.00

THAYER, Ernest Lawrence. *Casey at the Bat.* 1990. Boston. Godine. 2nd/Centennial ed. ils Barry Moser. VG/VG. L1. $25.00

THAYER, James Stewart. *Hess Cross.* 1977. Putnam. 1st ed. F/F. P3. $15.00

THAYER, John Adams. *Astir.* 1910. Boston. 1st ed. 12mo. 302 p. decor cloth. VG+. B28. $20.00

THAYER, Lee. *Out, Brief Candle.* 1948. Dodd Mead. 1st ed. VG/VG-. P3. $18.00

THAYER, Lee. *Who Benefits?* 1955. Dodd Mead. 1st ed. NF/NF. M15. $35.00

THAYER, Tiffany. *Three Musketeers.* 1946. Citadel. 13th prt. VG/dj. P3. $15.00

THAYER, William M. *From Tannery to Wht House: Life of US Grant.* ca 1885. Boston. tan cloth. G. T3. $17.00

THAYER, William M. *Marvels of the New W.* 1888. Norwich, CT. 1st ed. royal 8vo. 715 p. pict cloth. D3. $45.00

THAYER, William M. *Marvels of the New W.* 1890. Norwich, CT. Henry Bill. 715 p. gilt bdg. VG. H7. $40.00

THAYER, William M. *Marvels of the New W.* 1890. Norwich, CT. thick 8vo. 715 p. gilt dk gr cloth. G. T3. $38.00

THELWELL, Norman. *Penelope.* 1973. Dutton. 1st Am ed. VG/G. O3. $15.00

THELWELL, Norman. *Plank Bridge by a Pool.* 1978. Scribner. 1st Am ed. VG/VG. O3. $18.00

THELWELL, Norman. *Thelwell's Horse Box.* nd. Dutton. 4 paper bdg titles. slipcase. O3. $10.00

THELWELL, Norman. *Up the Garden Path.* 1967. NY. Dutton. 1st Am ed. VG. O3. $12.00

THEROUX, Alexander. *Darconville's Cat.* 1981. Doubleday. 1st ed. F/NF. C4. $40.00

THEROUX, Paul. *Blk House.* 1974. Hamish Hamilton. 1st ed. F/F. C4. $50.00

THEROUX, Paul. *Blk House.* 1974. Houghton Mifflin. 1st ed. F/F. C4. $40.00

THEROUX, Paul. *Christmas Card.* 1978. Houghton Mifflin. 1st ed. 84 p. VG/G. A3. $12.50

THEROUX, Paul. *Dr De Marr.* 1990. Hutchinson. 1st ed. F/F. C4. $40.00

THEROUX, Paul. *Fong & the Indians.* 1976. Hamish Hamilton. 1st ed. sgn. F/F. C4. $195.00

THEROUX, Paul. *Half Moon Street.* 1984. Boston. Houghton Mifflin. 1st ed. F/F. T2. $20.00

THEROUX, Paul. *Happy Isles of Oceania.* 1992. Putnam. 1st ed. sgn. F/dj. C4. $40.00

THEROUX, Paul. *Imperial Way.* 1985. Houghton Mifflin. 1st ed. F/F. C4. $40.00

THEROUX, Paul. *Kingdom by the Sea.* 1983. Houghton Mifflin. 1st ed. F/VG. B3. $50.00

THEROUX, Paul. *Kingdom by the Sea.* 1983. London. 1st ed. 8vo. 303 p. gilt gr cloth. NF/NF clip. H3. $12.00

THEROUX, Paul. *Mosquito Coast.* 1982. Houghton Mifflin. ltd ed. 1/350. sgn. F/NF slipcase. L3. $150.00

THEROUX, Paul. *Mosquito Coast.* 1982. Houghton Mifflin. 1st ed. sgn. F/F. C4. $50.00

THEROUX, Paul. *My Secret Hist.* (1989). Putnam. 1st ed. NF/VG. B3. $20.00

THEROUX, Paul. *Ozone.* 1986. London. Hamish Hamilton. 1st ed. sgn. F/F. C4. $50.00

THEROUX, Paul. *Ozone.* 1986. Putnam. 1st ed. F/F. P3. $20.00

THEROUX, Paul. *Picture Palace.* (1978). Franklin Lib. true 1st ed. ils Dennis Luzak. full leather. F. B3. $75.00

THEROUX, Paul. *Riding the Iron Rooster.* 1988. Putnam. VG/dj. A16. $15.00

THEROUX, Paul. *Riding the Iron Rooster.* 1988. Putnam. 1st ed. F/F. C4. $30.00

THEROUX, Paul. *Sailing Through China.* 1984. Houghton Mifflin. 1st ed. 1/400. sgn. ils/sgn Procktor. F/F. C4. $75.00

THEROUX, Paul. *Sinning w/Annie.* 1972. Houghton Mifflin. AP. author's 5th book. NF/wrp. L3. $250.00

THEROUX, Paul. *Sunrise w/Sea Monsters.* 1985. Houghton Mifflin. ARC. F/prt gr wrp. C4. $50.00

THEROUX, Paul. *To the Ends of the Earth.* 1990. Random. AP. laminated patterned covers. F. C4. $50.00

THICH NHAT, Hanh. *Cry of Vietnam.* (1968). Unicorn. 1st ed. VG/wrp. A7. $60.00

THIESSEN, Grant. *SF Collector Vol 1.* 1980. Pandora. 1/140. sgn/#d. F. P3. $35.00

THILLAYE, M. *Essai sur l'Emploi Medical de l'Electricite.* 1803. Paris. 80 p. wrp. G7. $160.00

THIMM, Carl A. *Complete Bibliography of Fencing & Duelling...* 1968. NY. Blom. reprint of 1896 ed. gilt gray cloth. F. F1. $75.00

THIRGOOD, J.Y. *Cyprus: Chronicle of Its Forests, Land & People.* 1987. Vancouver. 8vo. lg fld map. 371 p. cloth. O2. $45.00

THOMAS, A. Kempis. *Of the Imitation of Christ...* 1895. London. Henry Frowde. miniature. 576 p. aeg. vegetable vellum. H10. $125.00

THOMAS, A. Noyes. *Queen's Sister.* 1955. Wingate. photos. 127 p. VG+/dj. M20. $8.50

THOMAS, Alfred Barnaby. *Forgotten Frontiers: Study of Spanish Indian Policy...* 1969. OK U. fld maps/index. 420 p. F/NF clip. B19. $30.00

THOMAS, Andrew. *We Are Not the First.* nd. Laffont. VG. P3. $15.00

THOMAS, Anna Lloyd B. *Quaker Seekers of Wales: Story of the Lloyds of Dolobrain.* 1924. London. Swarthmore. 1st ed. 8vo. 186 p. ES. V3. $15.00

THOMAS, Annabel. *Snake-Handling Sunday in the Bl Church.* 1985. Evanston, IL. Schori. miniature. python snakeskin bdg. F. F1. $85.00

THOMAS, Bertram. *Arabia Felix.* 1932. London. Cape. 2nd ed. 397 p. gilt rust cloth. VG/G+/clear plastic. M7. $95.00

THOMAS, Charles W. *Ice Is Where You Find It.* 1951. Bobbs Merrill. 1st ed. 8vo. 378 p. VG/dj. P4. $35.00

THOMAS, Craig. *Firefox Down.* 1983. Michael Joseph. 1st ed. VG/dj. P3. $30.00

THOMAS, Craig. *Sea Leopard.* 1981. London. Michael Joseph. 1st ed. F/F. M15. $45.00

THOMAS, Craig. *Winter Hawk.* 1987. Collins. 1st ed. F/F. P3. $20.00

THOMAS, Cyrus. *Report on Mound Explorations of Bureau of Ethnology.* 1894. GPO. 12th annual report. ils/42 pls. 742 p. olive cloth. P4. $120.00

THOMAS, D.M. *Ararat.* (1983). Viking. 1st ed. F/VG. B3. $20.00

THOMAS, D.M. *Birthstone.* (1980). London. Gollancz. 1st ed. VG/VG. B3. $40.00

THOMAS, D.M. *Memories & Hallucinations.* (1988). London. Gollancz. 1st ed. NF/F. B3. $35.00

THOMAS, D.M. *Selected Poems.* (1983). Secker Warburg. 1st ed. NF/VG. B3. $30.00

THOMAS, D.M. *Summit.* (1987). London. Gollancz. 1st ed. F/F. B3. $25.00

THOMAS, D.M. *Swallow.* (1984). Toronto. Dennys. 1st ed. F/NF. B3. $25.00

THOMAS, Donald. *Jekyll, Alias Hyde.* 1989. St Martin. ARC of 1st ed. RS. F/F. S5. $25.00

THOMAS, Donald. *Long Time Burning: Hist of Literary Censorship in Eng.* (1969). NY. Praeger. 1st Am ed. 8vo. 546 p. VG+/VG-, A2. $25.00

THOMAS, Dylan. *Deaths & Entrances.* 1946. London. Dent. 1st ed. F/NF clip. Q1. $350.00

THOMAS, Dylan. *Eighteen Poems.* 1934. London. Sunday Referee. 1st issue. 1/250. NF/VG+. Q1. $2,500.00

THOMAS, Dylan. *Garland for Dylan Thomas.* 1963. Clarke Way. 1st ed. F/F. V1. $25.00

THOMAS, Dylan. *Map of Love. Verse & Prose.* 1939. London. Dent. 1st ed. NF/VG+. Q1. $450.00

THOMAS, Dylan. *New Poems.* 1943. New Directions. 1st ed. NF/stiff wrp. V1. $65.00

THOMAS, Dylan. *Twenty-Five Poems.* 1936. London. Dent. 1st ed. NF/VG+ clip. Q1. $750.00

THOMAS, Dylan. *Twenty-Five Poems.* 1936. London. Dent. 1st ed. 1/730. author's 2nd pub book. gray brds. F/dj. B24. $950.00

THOMAS, Dylan. *Under Milk Wood: Play for Voices.* 1954. NY. 1st Am ed. VG+/sans. A11. $25.00

THOMAS, Dylan. *World I Breathe.* 1939. New Directions. 1st ed. NF/NF. Q1. $750.00

THOMAS, Elizabeth Marshall. *Animal Wife.* (1990). Houghton Mifflin. ARC. F/pict wrp. B3. $25.00

THOMAS, Emory M. *Confederate State of Richmond: Biography of the Capitol.* 1971. Austin, TX. 1st ed. 227 p. NF/NF. M8. $85.00

THOMAS, George C. Jr. *Practical Book of Outdoor Rose Growing.* 1920 (1914). Phil. Garden ed. ils/charts. 307 p. B26. $16.00

THOMAS, H.C. *Red Ryder & the Adventure at Chimne.* nd. Whitman. VG. P3. $10.00

THOMAS, J.W. *Crown: Tale of Gawein & King Arthur's Court.* 1980. NE U. 1st ed. F/dj. C1. $19.00

THOMAS, John Peyre Jr. *Formation of Judicial & Political Sub-Divisions in SC.* 1890. Columbia, SC. Bryan Prt. 1st separate ed. presentation. VG/wrp. M8. $45.00

THOMAS, L. *Lectures sur l'Historie de la Medecine.* 1885. Paris. Delahaye. 202 p. orig prt wrp. scarce. G1. $125.00

THOMAS, Lamont D. *Rise To Be a People: Biography of Paul Cuffe.* 1986. Urbana/ Chicago. 1st ed. 8vo. 187 p. M/M. V3. $15.00

THOMAS, Leslie. *Virgin Soldiers.* 1966. Little Brn. 1st ed. VG/VG-. P3. $15.00

THOMAS, Louis. *Good Children Don't Kill.* 1968. Dodd Mead. 1st ed. F/F. P3. $15.00

THOMAS, Lowell. *Boy's Life of Colonel Lawrence.* (1927). NY. Century. 1st Am ed. 293 p. gilt dk gr cloth. VG. M7. $35.00

THOMAS, Lowell. *Hungry Waters.* 1937. Phil. Winston. 1st ed. 8vo. 321 p. VG. B11. $25.00

THOMAS, Lowell. *Wings Over Asia.* 1937. Winston. G. A16. $6.00

THOMAS, Lowell. *With Lawrence in Arabia.* nd. Century. 1st ed. 32 photos. 408 p. orange/brn pict cloth. NF. M7. $65.00

THOMAS, Lowell. *With Lawrence in Arabia.* nd. Hutchinson. 132nd thousand. 256 p. blk lettered red cloth. VG/G. M7. $50.00

THOMAS, Lowell. *With Lawrence in Arabia.* 1964. London. Arrow Books. 3rd Eng ed/2nd prt. 256 p. VG+/wrp. M7. $35.00

THOMAS, Lynall. *Rifled Ordnance.* 1864. NY. 1st Am from 5th Eng ed. 200 p. VG. B18. $95.00

THOMAS, R.D. *Man Who Would Be Perfect.* 1977. PA U. 1st ed. inscr. 199 p. VG/dj. B18. $17.50

THOMAS, Ross. *Eighth Dwarf.* (1979). Simon Schuster. 1st ed. F/F. C4. $40.00

THOMAS, Ross. *Fools in Town Are on Our Side.* 1971. NY. Morrow. 1st Am ed. F/F. M15. $125.00

THOMAS, Ross. *Missionary Stew.* 1983. Simon Schuster. 1st ed. VG/VG. P3. $35.00

THOMAS, Ross. *Mordida Man.* 1981. Simon Schuster. 1st ed. F/NF. M15. $50.00

THOMAS, Ross. *Out on the Rim.* (1987). Mysterious. ARC. inscr. VG+/wrp. B9. $75.00

THOMAS, Ross. *Porkchoppers.* 1972. Morrow. 1st ed. F/F. F4. $50.00

THOMAS, Ross. *Porkchoppers.* 1974. London. Hamilton. ARC of 1st British ed. sgn. RS. NF/NF. S5. $60.00

THOMAS, Ross. *Twilight at Mac's Place.* (1990). Mysterious. 1/100. sgn. F/slipcase. B9. $75.00

THOMAS, Ross. *Yellow-Dog Contract.* 1977. Morrow. 1st ed. VG/dj. P3. $100.00

THOMAS, W.B. *Gardens.* 1952. London. ils/pls/index. VG/dj. B26. $24.00

THOMAS, W.H. *Pit, Footlights & Wings.* (1954). Cleveland. 228 p. G. B18. $15.00

THOMAS, W.S. *Trails & Tramps in AK & Newfoundland.* 1913. NY. 1st ed. photos. VG+. B28. $75.00

THOMAS & THOMAS. *Our Flight to Adventure.* 1956. Doubleday. 1st ed. 8vo. 318 p. F/VG. A2. $20.00

THOMAS. *Shortcuts.* 1991. np. ils. wrp. G2. $10.00

THOMAS. *Sm Talk.* 1990. np. ils. wrp. G2. $19.00

THOMAS. *Textile Art.* 1985. Rizzoli. 140 color ils/176 blk & wht ils. cloth/slipcase. G2. $75.00

THOMASON, J.W. *Jeb Stuart.* 1930. Scribner. 1st ed. 512 p. VG. B10. $40.00

THOMASON, Robert. *Divine Authority of the Bible...* 1807. Boston. Beals. 151 p. H10. $25.00

THOMASSY, R. *Geologie Pratique de la Louisiane par R Thomassy.* 1860. Paris. Lacroix et Baudry. 4to. 264 p. cloth/ rebacked. H9. $175.00

THOMPSON, Ames. *Adventure Boys & the Temple of Rubies.* 1928. Cupples Leon. 1st ed. VG/VG. M2. $17.00

THOMPSON, Blanche Jennings. *All the Silver Pennies.* 1969. Macmillan. 2nd prt. 8vo. 244 p. VG/VG. A3. $18.50

THOMPSON, Blanche Jennings. *Golden Trumpets.* 1927. Macmillan. 1st ed. 12mo. 163 p. bl cloth. VG. S10. $35.00

THOMPSON, Blanche Jennings. *More Silver Pennies.* 1938. Macmillan. 1st ed. 155 p. G. P2. $24.00

THOMPSON, Blanche Jennings. *Silver Pennies. Collection of Modern Poems...* 1929. Macmillan. early reprint. 138 p. gr cloth. VG-. A3. $17.50

THOMPSON, Blanche Jennings. *Silver Pennies: Collection of Modern Poems.* 1940 (1925). Macmillan. 138 p. G. P2. $10.00

THOMPSON, Brian. *Bad to the Bone.* 1991. Viking. 1st ed. F/F. F4. $20.00

THOMPSON, C.V.R. *Trousers Will Be Worn.* (1941). Putnam. 1st ed. 12mo. 243 p. F/VG+. A2. $15.00

THOMPSON, Caroline. *First Born.* 1983. Coward McCann. 1st ed. NF/dj. M2. $12.00

THOMPSON, Clara M. *Psychoanalysis: Evolution & Developement.* 1950. Hermitage House. 1st ed. sm 8vo. 252 p. ochre cloth. VG/dj. G1. $22.50

THOMPSON, Daniel P. *Gr Mtn Boys.* 1840. London. Cunningham. 1st Eng ed. 8vo. 136 p. lib binder. M1. $250.00

THOMPSON, Era Bell. *Am Daughter.* 1946. Chicago U. 1st ed. inscr. NF/rpr dj. B2. $75.00

THOMPSON, Francis. *Selected Poems.* 1926. NY. 1st ed. dk bl cloth. NF. V1. $20.00

THOMPSON, Fresco. *Every Diamond Doesn't Sparkle.* 1964. McKay. 1st ed. VG/VG. P8. $20.00

THOMPSON, Harold W. *Body, Boots & Britches.* 1940. Lippincott. 8vo. 530 p. map ep. G. B11. $15.00

THOMPSON, Henry T. *Waddy Thompson Jr, Member of Congress, 1835-41...* nd. np. revised ed. 35 p. NF/prt wrp. M8. $27.50

THOMPSON, Hunter S. *Fear & Loathing in Las Vegas.* 1971. Random. 1st ed. author's 2nd book. F/F. L3. $250.00

THOMPSON, Hunter S. *Fear & Loathing in Las Vegas.* 1971. Random. 1st ed. VG/VG. B4. $150.00

THOMPSON, Hunter S. *Screwjack.* 1991. Santa Barbara. Neville. 1/26. sgn/lettered. full leather. F. Q1. $400.00

THOMPSON, Hunter S. *Screwjack.* 1991. Santa Barbara. Neville. 1/300. sgn/#d. F/sans. L3. $175.00

THOMPSON, J. Eric. *Civilization of the Mayas.* (1958). Chicago. Field Mus. reprint of 1927 ed. 96 p. F3. $15.00

THOMPSON, J. Eric. *Maya Archaeologist.* (1963). Norman, OK. 1st ed. 284 p. dj. F3. $25.00

THOMPSON, J. Eric. *Rise & Fall of the Maya Civilization.* (1955). Norman, OK. 1st ed. 287 p. F3. $30.00

THOMPSON, J. Eric. *Thomas Gage's Travels in the New World.* (1958). Norman, OK. 1st ed. 379 p. F3. $25.00

THOMPSON, J.A. *Bible & Archaeology.* (1962). Grand Rapids, MI. Eerdmans. 1st ed. 8vo. ils. 468 p. VG+/VG+. A2. $15.00

THOMPSON, J.J. *Electricity & Matter.* 1904. Scribner. 162 p. cloth. F. B14. $50.00

THOMPSON, Jim. *Getaway.* 1973. London. Sphere. 1st Eng ed. NF/unread. A11. $85.00

THOMPSON, Jim. *Grifters.* 1990. Corgi. 1st separate book in UK. F/unread. A11. $35.00

THOMPSON, Jim. *Killer Inside Me.* 1973. London. Sphere. 1st ed. VG+. A11. $135.00

THOMPSON, Jim. *Killer Inside Me.* 1989. LA. 1st hc ed. 1/376. sgn Stephen King. as new/dj/slipcase. A11. $175.00

THOMPSON, Jim. *King Blood.* (1993). Armchair Detective Lib. ARC/1st Am ed. RS. F/dj. B4. $45.00

THOMPSON, Jim. *King Blood.* 1989. London. Corgi. 2nd ed. F/unread. A11. $45.00

THOMPSON, Jim. *Rip-Off.* 1989. Mysterious. 1st separate book ed. F/unread. A11. $40.00

THOMPSON, Joyce. *Bones.* nd. BOMC. F/F. P3. $13.00

THOMPSON, Joyce. *Conscience Place.* 1984. Doubleday. 1st ed. F/F. N3. $20.00

THOMPSON, Kay. *Eloise at Christmas Time.* 1958. NY. Random. 1st ed. NF/dj. B24. $250.00

THOMPSON, Kay. *Eloise at Christmas Time.* 1958. Random. 1st prt. 4to. VG/VG. A3/M20. $200.00

THOMPSON, Kay. *Eloise in Moscow.* 1959. NY. 1st ed. xl. VG/VG. B5. $55.00

THOMPSON, Kay. *Eloise in Moscow.* 1959. Simon Schuster. ils Hilary Knight. 1st prt. VG/G+. A3. $175.00

THOMPSON, Kay. *Eloise in Moscow.* 1959. Simon Schuster. 1st ed. ils Hilary Knight. VG/VG. D1. $200.00

THOMPSON, Kay. *Eloise in Paris.* 1957. Simon Schuster. ils Hilary Knight. 1st prt. 4to. VG/G+. A3. $200.00

THOMPSON, Kay. *Eloise in Paris.* 1957. Simon Schuster. 1st ed. ils Hilary Knight. 65 p. VG/VG. D1. $225.00

THOMPSON, Mary Lou. *Voices of New Feminism.* ca 1970. Beacon. F/G. V4. $8.50

THOMPSON, Morris M. *Maps for Am.* 1979. GPO. xl. 4to. 265 p. pict brn cloth. H9. $45.00

THOMPSON, R.A. *Russian Settlement in CA, Ft Ross, Founded 1812...* 1951. Oakland. Biobooks. 1/700. 50 p. blk/red coth. NF. P4. $95.00

THOMPSON, Raymond. *Modern Yucatecan Maya Pottery Making.* 1974. NY. Kraus reprint. 157 p. F3. $20.00

THOMPSON, Richard. *Hist Essay on Magna Charta of King John...* 1829. London. Major Jennings. morocco/marbled brds. M11. $350.00

THOMPSON, Ruth Plumly. *Captain Salt in Oz.* nd. Reilly Lee. blk & wht Neill ils. gr cloth/pict label. VG. L1. $85.00

THOMPSON, Ruth Plumly. *Comical Cruises of Capt Cooky.* 1926. Royal Baking Powder. 20 p. G/wrp. M5. $30.00

THOMPSON, Ruth Plumly. *Cowardly Lion of Oz.* nd. Reilly Lee. ils Neill. gr bdg/pict label. VG. L1. $125.00

THOMPSON, Ruth Plumly. *Cowardly Lion of Oz.* 1923. Reilly Lee. ils JR Neill. 1st ed. 4to. 291 p. VG. A3. $250.00

THOMPSON, Ruth Plumly. *Giant Horse of Oz.* nd. Reilly Lee. Neill ils. purple bdg/pict label. G+. L1. $85.00

THOMPSON, Ruth Plumly. *Grandpa in Oz.* 1924. Reilly Lee. ils Neill. brick red cloth/pict label. VG. L1. $90.00

THOMPSON, Ruth Plumly. *Handy Mandy in Oz.* nd. Reilly Lee. blk & wht Neill ils. orange bdg/pict label. VG. L1. $450.00

THOMPSON, Ruth Plumly. *Hungry Tiger of Oz.* ca 1940. Reilly Lee. blk & wht Neill ils. VG. L1. $80.00

THOMPSON, Ruth Plumly. *Hungry Tiger of Oz.* nd. Reilly Lee. decor brds. VG-. P3. $50.00

THOMPSON, Ruth Plumly. *Jack Pumpkinhead of Oz.* nd. np. 23rd Oz book/9th Thompson. gr bdg/pict label. G. L1. $70.00

THOMPSON, Ruth Plumly. *Kabumpo in Oz.* nd. Reilly Lee. blk & wht Neill ils. bl bdg/pict label. G. L1. $90.00

THOMPSON, Ruth Plumly. *Kabumpo in Oz.* nd. Reilly Lee. 1st ed/later state. ils Neill/12 pls. G. D1. $285.00

THOMPSON, Ruth Plumly. *Kabumpo in Oz.* 1923. Reilly Lee. ils Neill. early reprint. 4to. gr cloth/pict label. G. A3. $125.00

THOMPSON, Ruth Plumly. *Lost King in Oz.* (1925). Reilly Lee. ils John R Neill. rebound red bdg. VG. L1. $55.00

THOMPSON, Ruth Plumly. *Lost King of Oz.* nd. np. blk & wht Neill ils. orange bdg/pict label. VG. L1. $110.00

THOMPSON, Ruth Plumly. *Lost King of Oz.* 1925. Reilly Lee. 1st ed/1st state. ils J Neill. 280 p. VG. D1. $400.00

THOMPSON, Ruth Plumly. *Lost King of Oz.* 1925. Reilly Lee. 1st ed/1st state. ils Neill/12 color pls. G. L1. $375.00

THOMPSON, Ruth Plumly. *Ojo in Oz.* nd. Reilly Lee. blk & wht Neill ils. gr bdg/pict label. VG. L1. $100.00

THOMPSON, Ruth Plumly. *Ozoplaning w/the Wizard of Oz.* nd. Reilly Lee. blk & wht Neill ils. red cloth/pict label. VG. L1. $80.00

THOMPSON, Ruth Plumly. *Pirates in Oz.* nd. Reilly Lee. blk & wht Neill ils. gr bdg/pict label. L1. $85.00

THOMPSON, Ruth Plumly. *Princess of Cozytown.* 1922. Volland. 1st ed. ils Janet Laura Scott. G. P2. $75.00

THOMPSON, Ruth Plumly. *Purple Prince of Oz.* nd. Reilly Lee. blk & wht Neill ils. lt bl cloth/pict label. VG. L1. $100.00

THOMPSON, Ruth Plumly. *Royal Book of Oz.* 1921. Reilly Lee. 1st ed. 4to. 303 p. gray cloth/pict label. VG-. A3. $250.00

THOMPSON, Ruth Plumly. *Silver Princess of Oz.* nd. Reilly Lee. blk & wht Neill ils. orange bdg/pict label. G. L1. $70.00

THOMPSON, Ruth Plumly. *Speedy in Oz.* nd. Reilly Lee. blk & wht Neill ils. lt bl cloth/pict label. VG. L1. $80.00

THOMPSON, Ruth Plumly. *Speedy in Oz.* 1929. Reilly Lee. early prt. F. M18. $100.00

THOMPSON, Ruth Plumly. *Wishing Horse of Oz.* (1935). Reilly Lee. ils JR Neill. 298 p. pict rust cloth. VG. T5. $65.00

THOMPSON, Ruth Plumly. *Wishing Horse of Oz.* nd. Reilly Lee. orange cloth/pict label. VG. L1. $95.00

THOMPSON, Ruth Plumly. *Yel Knight of Oz.* nd. Reilly Lee. blk & wht Neill ils. bright gr cloth/pict label. VG. L1 $100.00

THOMPSON, S.C. *All Time Rosters of Major League Baseball Clubs.* 1967. Barnes. 1st ed. VG. P8. $20.00

THOMPSON, Slason. *Short Hist of Am Railways.* 1925. NY. 2nd ed. rebound lib buckram. VG. D3. $35.00

THOMPSON, Steven L. *Recovery.* 1980. Warner. VG/dj. P3. $15.00

THOMPSON, Sylvia Vaughn. *Economy Gastronomy.* 1963. Atheneum. 1st ed. 334 p. NF/NF. A7. $20.00

THOMPSON, W.G. *Practical Dietetics.* 1900. NY. Appleton. ils/pls/index. 802 p. recased. VG-. S9. $13.00

THOMPSON, W.H. *Acquaintances.* 1967. Oxford. 1st ed. photos/index. gilt gr cloth. VG/G/clear plastic. M7. $50.00

THOMPSON, W.I. *Pacific Shift.* (1985). Sierra Club. 1st ed. 197 p. dj. A7. $12.00

THOMPSON, W.M. *Land & the Book. Vol 1.* 1860. NY. xl. 12mo. ils. 557 p. brn cloth. T3. $10.00

THOMPSON, William. *William Butterfield, Victorian Architect.* 1971. Cambridge, MA. MIT. ils. gilt & red decor gray cloth. F/VG. F1. $35.00

THOMPSON & THOMPSON. *How To Train in Archery.* 1879. NY. 2nd ed. 80 p. cloth. VG. B5. $145.00

THOMPSON. *It's Not a Quilt Until It's Quilted.* 1984. np. 100+ full-size designs. wrp. G2. $14.00

THOMSON, Basil. *Story of Scotland Yard.* 1936. Literary Guild. VG/dj. A16. $15.00

THOMSON, E.H. *Harvey Cushing.* 1950. NY. orig ed. 374 p. G7. $35.00

THOMSON, H. Douglas. *Great Book of Thrillers.* 1937. Odhams. VG-. P3. $20.00

THOMSON, June. *Dying Fall.* 1986. Crime Club. VG/VG. P3. $18.00

THOMSON, June. *Question of Identity.* 1977. Crime Club. 1st ed. F/dj. P3. $25.00

THOMSON, June. *Secret Journal of Sherlock Holmes.* 1993. London. Constable. 1st ed. sgn. F/F. M15. $50.00

THOMSON, Robert. *Pelican Hist of Psychology.* 1968. Penguin. 1st ed. 16mo. 464 p. VG/dj. G1. $20.00

THOMSON, T. *Outline of Sciences of Heat & Electricity.* 1830. London. xl. 8vo. ils. 583 p. full leather. T3. $15.00

THOREAU, Henry David. *Cape Cod.* 1865. Ticknor Fields. 1st ed. 12mo. 252 p. scarce. M1. $250.00

THOREAU, Henry David. *Cape Cod.* 1896. Boston. 1st thus ed. 2 vols. G. B5. $110.00

THOREAU, Henry David. *Early Spring in MA/Summer/Autumn/Winter.* 1881-1882. Boston. 1st ed. octavo. 4 vols. orig gr cloth. F/cloth slipcase. H5. $1,500.00

THOREAU, Henry David. *Men of Concord.* 1936. Houghton Mifflin. 1st thus ed. 10 color pls by NC Wyeth. VG. A17. $45.00

THOREAU, Henry David. *Selected Quotations...* 1948. Worcester. St Orange. miniature. 1/750. F. H10. $300.00

THOREAU, Henry David. *Transmigration of 7 Brahmins.* 1931. NY. 1st thus ed. 1/1200. sgn edit. VG/box. B5. $60.00

THOREAU, Henry David. *Walden.* (1980). London. Folio Soc. 1st ed. ils Michael Renton. F/box. B3. $45.00

THOREAU, Henry David. *Walden.* nd. NY. Bramhall. reprint. 354 p. F/dj. A17. $10.00

THOREAU, Henry David. *Winter Walk.* 1991. Bangor, ME. Theodore. 1/140. ils/prt/binder/sgn Michael Alpert. M. B24. $325.00

THORN, John. *Century of Baseball Lore.* 1980. Galahad. 1st hc prt. F/VG. P8. $17.50

THORN, John. *Game for all Am.* 1988. Sporting News. 1st ed. F/VG+. P8. $15.00

THORN, John. *National Pastime.* 1988. Bell. 1st ed. F/VG+. P8. $12.50

THORN, John. *Relief Pitcher.* 1979. Dutton. 1st ed. F/VG. P8. $20.00

THORNBURG, Newton. *Blk Angus.* 1978. Little Brn. 1st ed. VG/dj. P3. $23.00

THORNBURG, Newton. *Dreamland.* 1983. Arbor. 1st ed. F/F. F4. $16.00

THORNBURG, Opal. *Earlham: Story of the College, 1847-1962.* 1963. Richmond, IN. Earlham. 8vo. 484 p. VG/dj. V3. $20.00

THORNDIKE, Lynn. *Place of Magic in Intellectual Hist of Europe.* 1905. NY. 1st ed. 112 p. disbound/lacks orig wrp. G1. $35.00

THORNE, Narcissa Niblack. *Miniature Rooms Designed & Arranged by Mrs James W Thorne.* 1933. Chicago. private prt. oblong 8vo. ils. gray wrp. H9. $75.00

THORNE, Paul. *Murder in the Fog.* 1929. Penn. 1st ed. VG. P3. $40.00

THORNTON, J. Quinn. *CA Tragedy.* (1945). Biobooks. 1st ltd CA Centennial ed. 1/1500. pict bdg. F/F. A18. $40.00

THORP, Nathan Howard. *Pardner of the Wind: Story of SW Cowboy.* 1945. Caxton. 1st ed. VG+. A18. $50.00

THORP, Nathan Howard. *Songs of the Cowboys.* 1908. Estancia, NM. News Print Shop. 1st ed. 50 p. gilt red wrp. H5. $1,000.00

THORP, Roderick. *Nothing Lasts Forever.* 1979. Norton. F/dj. P3. $15.00

THORPE, Edward. *Chandlertown.* 1984. St Martin. 1st Am ed. ils. F/F. S5. $30.00

THORPE, Rose. *Yr's Best Days for Boys & Girls.* 1889 (1888). Lee Shepard. sm 12mo. 202 p. VG. S10. $20.00

THOTSTON, Clara Bell. *Jingle of a Jap.* ca 1908. Boston. Caldwell. fair. A16. $40.00

THRALL, R.T. *Hydropathic Encyclopedia.* 1857. NY. 2 vols in 1. index. nearly 1000 p. O7. $21.50

THRAPP, Dan L. *Al Sieber, Chief of Scouts.* (1964). OK U. 1st ed. 432 p. F/dj. A17. $40.00

THRASHER, John B. *Slavery: A Divine Inst...a Speech Made...Nov 5, 1860.* 1861. Gibson, MS. S Reveille Book & Job Office. 1st ed. 22 p. VG/wrp. M8. $850.00

THREADS. *Great Sewn Clothes.* 1991. np. ils. wrp. G2. $17.00

THRIFT, Syd. *Game According to Syd.* 1990. Simon Schuster. 1st ed. F/F. P8. $12.50

THROWER, Norman J.W. *Complete Plattmaker: Essays on Chart, Map & Globe...* 1978. Berkeley. M. O6. $35.00

THRUELSEN, Richard. *Mediterranean Sweep.* 1944. DSP. 1st ed. 12mo. VG. A8. $20.00

THURBER, James. *Beast in Me.* 1948. Harcourt Brace. 1st ed. VG/VG. P3. $30.00

THURBER, James. *Fables for Our Time.* 1940. Harper. 1st ed. F/worn. C4. $100.00

THURBER, James. *Further Fables for Our Time.* 1950. Simon Schuster. 1st ed. F/NF. C4. $40.00

THURBER, James. *Let Your Mind Alone & Other...Pieces.* 1937. NY. 1st ed. VG+/VG clip. A11. $40.00

THURBER, James. *Many Moons.* 1943. Harcourt Brace. 1st ed. ils Slobodkin. F/worn. D1. $185.00

THURBER, James. *Many Moons.* 1943. HBW. 1st ed. 4to. red cloth. VG. T5. $55.00

THURBER, James. *Seal in the Bedroom & Other Predicaments.* 1932. NY. 3rd prt. presentation. w/sgn drawing. pict brds. VG. H5. $4,000.00

THURBER, James. *Thirteen Clocks.* 1950. Simon Schuster. 1st ed. ils Marc Simont. 124 p. VG/VG. D1. $125.00

THURBER, James. *Three Clocks.* 1950. Simon Schuster. 1st ed/1st state. 124 p. VG/G. P2. $55.00

THURBER, James. *Thurber on Crime.* 1991. Mysterious. 1st ed. VG/dj. P3. $19.00

THURBER, James. *Wht Deer.* 1945. Harcourt Brace. 1st ed. NF/NF. C4. $50.00

THURBER, James. *Wht Deer.* 1945. HBJ. 1st ed. ils Don Freeman. 115 p. VG/VG. P2. $40.00

THURSTON, George H. *Pittsburgh As It Is.* 1857. Pittsburgh. 1st ed. 12mo. 204 p. prt gray wrp. H9. $180.00

THURSTON, Howard. *400 Tricks You Can Do.* 1949. Perma Grant. decor brds. P3. $15.00

THWAITES, R.G. *Rocky Mtn Exploration.* 1904. Appleton. 12mo. VG. A8. $18.00

THWAITES, Ruben Gold. *Original Journals of Lewis & Clark Expedition, 1804-06...* 1904. Dodd Mead. 1st thus ed. 1/50. 15 vols+atlas vol. lg 4to. beige buckram. F. T8. $8,500.00

TIBBLES, Thomas Henry. *Buckskin & Blanket Days: Memoirs of a Friend of the Indians.* 1957. Doubleday. 1st ed. VG/G. H7. $20.00

TICHENER, Edward Bradford. *Experimental Psychology: Manual of Laboratory Practice...* 1905. Macmillan. 208 p. panelled brn cloth. VG. G1. $100.00

TICHENOR, Henry M. *Tales of Theology.* 1918. St Louis. Melting Pot. 1st ed. w/special sgn presentation label. VG. B2. $100.00

TICKNOR, Caroline. *Hawthorne & His Pub.* 1903. Boston. Houghton Mifflin. 339 p. gr cloth. F. B14. $35.00

TIDBALL. *Weaver's Book.* 1961. np. ils. wrp. G2. $4.00

TIDBURY, G.E. *Clove Tree.* 1947. London. ils/photos. VG/dj. B26. $45.00

TIERNEY, Richard. *Collected Poems.* 1981. Arkham. 1st ed. M/wrp. M2. $25.00

TIERNEY, Ronald. *Stone Veil.* 1974. WH Allen. F/F. P3. $20.00

TIGER, John; see Wager, Walter.

TIIRA, Ensio. *Raft of Despair.* 1955. Dutton. 1st Am ed. 8vo. 200 p. F/F. A2. $20.00

TILDEN, Freeman. *Following the Frontier w/F Jay Haynes.* 1964. NY. 1st ed. ils. 406 p. G+. B18. $35.00

TILDEN, Freeman. *National Parks.* 1968. NY. revised ed. photos/index. F/G. A17. $12.50

TILDEN, Freeman. *2nd Wind: Plain Truth About Going Back to the Land.* 1917. NY. Huebsch. 1st ed. sgn presentation. VG. E3. $20.00

TILDEN, Louise W. *Karl & Gretchen's Christmas.* 1878. Cincinnati. Clarke. ils. gilt bl brds. VG+. E3. $8.00

TILESTON, Mary W. *Prayers Ancient & Modern...* 1921. Little Brn. 366 p. H10. $10.00

TILFER, P. *True & Hist Narrative of Colony of GA.* 1741. Charles-Town, SC. P Timothy. 1st ed. bl morocco. VG+. C6. $3,900.00

TILL, Mary E. *Stained Windows.* 1927. Phil. Dorrance Contemporary series #27. NF. V1. $15.00

TILLETT. *Am Needlework, 1776-1976.* 1975. np. cloth. G2. $15.00

TILLMAN, Barrett. *Wildcat in WWII.* 1983. Nautical & Aviation. 1st ed. 8vo. VG/VG. A8. $20.00

TILLOTSON & TAYLOR. *Grand Canyon Country.* 1935. Stanford. 2nd/revised ed. front ep missing. VG. H7. $12.50

TILTON, Alice. *Dead Ernest.* nd. Norton. 1st ed. VG/VG-. P3. $18.00

TIMBS, John. *Abbeys, Castles & Ancient Halls of Eng & Wales.* nd (1860?). London. Frederick Warne. 12mo. 2 vols. half calf/marbled brds. A7. $100.00

TIMBS, John. *Clubs & Club Life in London.* 1872. London. 1st ed/2nd issue. 544 p. gilt brn cloth. VG-. H3. $25.00

TIMBS, John. *Stories of Inventors & Discoverers in Science & Useful Arts.* 1860. NY. Harper. 473 p. red cloth. B14. $65.00

TIMBY. *Visions: Quilts of a New Decade.* 1990. np. color ils. wrp. G2. $23.00

TIME LIFE. *Navigation.* 1975. NY. Time Life. VG/dj. A16. $5.00

TIME LIFE. *Old W Series.* 1976. Time Life. 20 vol set. F. A8. $200.00

TIME LIFE. *Spanish W.* 1976. Time Life. 4to. F. A8. $10.00

TINDALL, P.B. *Observations on Mineral Waters of WV.* 1858. Richmond, VA. 1st/only ed. 16mo. 141 p. VG. B28. $50.00

TING, Wallasse. *1¢ Life.* 1964. Bern. Kornfeld. 1st ed. 1/2000. folio. 62 pls. 173 p. unbound as issued. F/dj. B24. $1,650.00

TINGLE, Dolli. *Valiant Little Tailor.* 1946. John Martin. sbdg/pict brds. VG/VG. A3. $13.00

TINGSTEN, Herbert. *Problem of S Africa.* 1955. Gollancz. trans from Swedish. 159 p. dj. A7. $20.00

TINKER, Ben. *Mexican Wilderness & Wildlife.* (1978). Austin, TX. 1st ed. 131 p. F3. $20.00

TINKER, Chauncy Brewster. *Wedgwood Medallion of Samuel Johnson...* 1926. Cambridge. Harvard. 1/385. octavo. 16 p. dk bl brds. F/dj. B24. $150.00

TINNEY, J. *Compendious Treatise of Anatomy...* 1808. London. Laurie Whittle. folio. 10 engravings. orig brds/new cloth spine. G7. $295.00

TINSLEY, E. Yarbrough. *John Marshall Harlan, Great Dissenter of Warren Court.* 1992. Oxford. M11. $30.00

TIPPETT, Tom. *When S Labor Stirs.* ca 1931. Cape Smith. 1st ed. VG/fair. V4. $25.00

TIPTREE, James Jr. *Brightness Falls From the Air.* 1985. Tor. 1st ed. F/F. P3. $20.00

TIPTREE, James Jr. *Crown of Stars.* 1988. Tor. 1st ed. F/dj. P3. $20.00

TITCHENELL, Elsa-Brita. *Once Round the Sun.* 1950. Theosophical U. ils Justin C Gruelle. 8vo. bl cloth w/pict label. VG. A3. $45.00

TITCHENER, Campbell. *George Kirksey Story.* 1989. Eakin Pr. 1st ed. M/M. P8. $10.00

TITLER, D.M. *Day the Red Baron Died.* 1970. NY. ils. 329 p. G. B18. $22.50

TODD, Edward N. *Copper Canyon.* 1974. Doubleday. 1st ed. NF/dj. B9. $10.00

TODD, Ethel. *Bits & Pieces of Craig Co Schools.* ca 1976. Craig Co Teachers. ils. 93 p. VG. B10. $12.00

TODD, John. *Sunset Land; or, Great Pacific Slope.* 1870. Boston. 1st ed. xl. 322 p. new ep. D3. $60.00

TODD, Millicent. *Peru: Land of Contrasts.* 1914. Little Brn. 1st ed. 8vo. 24 pls. 314 p. teg. brn brds. VG. B11. $25.00

TODD, Olivier. *Jaques Brel.* 1984. Paris. Robert Laffont. VG/dj. N2. $10.00

TODD, Paul; see Posner, Richard.

TODD, Robert Bentley. *Clinical Lectures on Paralysis...* 1855. Phil. Lindsay Blakiston. 1st Am ed. 311 p. cloth. G. G7. $295.00

TOESCA, Pietro. *La Pittura Fiorentina del Trecento.* (1929). Verona. Apollo/Pantheon. 1st ed. 119 pls w/tissue guards. VG. K1. $200.00

TOFFLER, Alvin. *Third Wave.* 1980. Morrow. 1st ed. F/F. t2. $12.00

TOGAWA, Masako. *Lady Killer.* 1986. Dodd Mead. 1st Am ed. trans Simon Grove. F/F. S5. $30.00

TOICHIRO, Naito. *Wall Paintings of Horyuji.* 1943. Baltimore. Waverly. 1st ed. xl. 2 parts in 1. lg 8vo. VG. W1. $125.00

TOLAND, John. *Adeisidaemon Sive Titus Livius a Superstititione Vindicatus.* 1709. The Hague. Johnson. 1st ed. 8vo. 2 parts in 1. contemporary paneled calf. K1. $450.00

TOLAND, John. *Adolph Hitler.* 1976. Doubleday. 1st ed. F/VG. A8. $22.00

TOLKIEN, J.R.R. *Lays of Beleriand.* 1985. Houghton Mifflin. 1st Am ed. F/F clip. N3. $12.00

TOLKIEN, J.R.R. *Letters of JRR Tolkien.* 1981. Allen Unwin. 1st ed. NF/dj. P3. $28.00

TOLKIEN, J.R.R. *Return of the Shadow.* 1988. Houghton Mifflin. 1st ed. VG/VG. P3. $20.00

TOLKIEN, J.R.R. *Simarillion.* 1977. Allen Unwin. 1st ed. F/F. P3. $25.00

TOLKIEN, J.R.R. *Smith of Wootton Major.* 1978. Houghton Mifflin. decor brds. F. P3. $15.00

TOLKIEN, J.R.R. *Unfinished Tales.* nd. BOMC. VG/dj. P3. $10.00

TOLLER, Ernst. *I Was a German.* 1934. Morrow. 1st Am ed. VG. A7. $15.00

TOLLES, Frederick B. *James Logan & Culture of Provincial Am.* 1957. Little Brn. 1st ed. 8vo. 228 p. VG/dj. V3. $15.00

TOLSON, Jay. *Pilgrim in the Ruins. Life of Walker Percy.* 1992. Simon Schuster. 1st ed. sgn. F/dj. C4. $35.00

TOLSON, M.B. *Harlem Gallery.* 1965. Twayne. 1st ed. sgn. F/F. B2. $250.00

TOLSTOY, Leo N. *Anna Karenina.* 1878. Moscow. 1st ed. 3 vols. 8vo. contemporary Russian morocco. M1. $7,500.00

TOLSTOY, Leo N. *Voina, i Mir.* 1868-69. Moscow. 1st ed. 6 vols. 8vo. very rare. M1. $8,500.00

TOLSTOY, Nikolai. *Half-Mad Lord: Thomas Pitt, 2nd Baron Camelford.* (1978). NY. HRW. 1st Am ed. 8vo. 239 p. F/F. A2. $15.00

TOMBLESON, William. *Tombleson's Views of the Rhine...* 1834. London. Tombleson. 1st ed. 25 parts in 23. 68 pls/fld panorama. VG. H5. $650.00

TOMIOKA, Tasko. *Tamar.* 1961. Kaunsaki. Shinjusha. miniature. 16 color woodcuts. blk suede. F/slipcaase. B24. $150.00

TOMKINS, Calvin. *Intermission.* 1951. Viking. 247 p. dj. A7. $30.00

TOMKINSON, Constance. *Les Girls.* (1956). Boston. Atlantic/Little Brn. 1st Am ed. 8vo. 274 p. VG/VG. A2. $12.50

TOMLINSON, H.M. *Sea & Jungle.* 1930. NY. Harper. ils Clare Leighton. 333 p. gr cloth. G. B11. $45.00

TOMLINSON, Juliette. *Paintings & Journal of Joseph Whiting Stock.* 1976. Wesleyan U. 180 p. cloth. dj. D2. $45.00

TOMLONSON. *Mennonite Quilts & Pieces.* 1985. np. ils. wrp. G2. $16.00

TOMMASINI, A.R. *Signs of the Zodiac.* nd. np. 1/500. ils. w/gift card. F/sans. B19. $25.00

TONKIN, Peter. *Journal of Edwin Underhill.* 1982. Hodder Stoughton. 2nd ed. VG/torn. P3. $15.00

TOOKER, L. Frank. *Joys & Tribulations of an Edit.* 1924. Century. 1st ed. VG. M2. $25.00

TOOKER, Richard. *Day of the Brn Horde.* 1929. Payson Clarke. 1st ed. author's 1st book. F/NF. N3. $50.00

TOOKER, Richard. *Day of the Brn Horde.* 1931. Jacobsen. VG. P3. $25.00

TOOLE, K. Ross. *MT; Uncommon Land.* 1959. Norman. G/dj. A16. $25.00

TOOLEY, R.V. *Eng Books w/Coloured Pls 1790-1860.* 1987. London. 4to. 424 p. cloth. dj. O2. $75.00

TOOLEY, R.V. *Mapping of Am. Vol 2.* 1980. London. Holland Pr. M/dj. O6. $75.00

TOOLEY, R.V. *Maps & Map-Makers.* 1990. np. ils. 140 p. dj. O7. $18.00

TOOLEY, R.V. *Printed Maps of Am. Part III.* 1972. London. Map Collectors Circle. 8vo. wrp. H9. $30.00

TOOMER, Jean. *Essentials.* 1931. Chicago. 1st ed. F/F. L3. $1,250.00

TOOMER, Jean. *Essentials.* 1931. Chicago. private prt. 1/1000. author's 2nd book. M/dj. B4. $1,500.00

TOOR, Frances. *Frances Toor's Motorist Guide to Mexico.* 1938. Mexico City. self pub. 1st ed. 8vo. maps (2 fld). 341 p. map ep. cloth. G. B11. $45.00

TOPOLSKI, Feliks. *Holy China.* 1968. Houghton Mifflin. 1st ed. 4to. ils/drawings. VG/dj. W1. $16.00

TORBADO & LEGUINECHE. *Forgotten Men...the Franco Yrs.* 1981. NY. HRW. 1st Am ed. 8vo. F/VG+. A2. $10.00

TORCHIA, Joseph. *As If After Sex.* 1984. HRW. 1st ed. NF/NF. A14. $25.00

TORCHIA, Joseph. *Kryptonite Kid.* 1979. HRW. 1st ed. author's 1st book. NF/NF. A14. $35.00

TORNESI, Carolus Amaton. *Disertation Inquguralis Medica de Tabe Dorsali...* 1691. Literis Krebsianis. 28 p. modern wrp. G7. $200.00

TORNIER, Michael. *Ogre.* 1972. Doubleday. 1st ed. 8vo. VG/VG. A8. $12.00

TORR, Cecil. *Ancient Ships.* 1895. Cambridge, Eng. 1st ed. 8vo. 139 p. F. A2. $60.00

TORRENCE, Ridgely. *El Dorado: A Tragedy.* 1903. London. John Lane. 1st ed. pub presentation/sgns. 12mo. cloth. M1. $200.00

TORRES, Luis Maria. *Los Primitivos Habitantes del Delta del Parana.* 1911. Buenos Aires. Tomo IV. 617 p. rebound bl cloth. F3. $95.00

TORREY, John. *Compendium of Flora of N & Middle States.* 1826. NY. 1st ed. 12mo. 403 p. B28. $150.00

TORREY, Marjorie. *Penny.* 1944. Howell Soskin. 1st ed. 8vo. 126 p. maroon cloth. VG/G. T5. $28.00

TORRO, Pel; see Fanthrope, R.L.

TOURAINE, Alain. *May Movement.* (1971). Random. 1st Am ed. trans Mayhew. NF/dj. A7. $18.00

TOURGEE, Albion W. *With Gauge & Swallow, Attorneys.* 1889. Lippincott. 1st ed. pict gr cloth. M11. $125.00

TOURNIER, Michael. *Erl King.* 1972. London. Collins. 1st ed. trans from French. NF/NF. A14. $40.00

TOURNIER, Michael. *Fetishist.* 1984. Doubleday. 1st ed. trans from French. rem mk. NF/NF. A14. $20.00

TOURTELLOT, A.B. *Charles.* 1941. NY. 1st ed. Rivers of Am series. 356 p. VG+/dj. B28. $30.00

TOWNE, Stuart; see Rawson, Clayton.

TOWNE & WENTWORTH. *Shepherds Empire.* 1945. Norman. 1st ed. ils/index. 364 p. VG/VG. B5. $25.00

TOWNSEND, C.W. *Along the Labrador Coast.* (1907). Boston. Dana Estes. 1st ed. 8vo. 289 p. VG. A2. $50.00

TOWNSEND, Peter. *Earth, My Friend.* (1959). Hodder Stoughton. 1st ed. 8vo. 351 p. VG/G+. A2. $12.50

TOWNSEND. *Memorial Life of William McKinley, Our Martyred President.* ca 1901. np. 8vo. ils. 528 p. gilt bl cloth. G. T3. $15.00

TOY, Crawford Howell. *Intro to Hist of Religions.* 1948. Harvard. 4th imp. 639 p. VG+. S3. $24.00

TOYE, Randall. *Agatha Christie Who's Who.* 1980. HRW. 1st ed. VG/VG. P3. $20.00

TOYNBEE, Philip. *Protitacamium: Cycle of the Holy Grail.* 1970. np. reprint of 1947 ed. M. C1. $7.50

TRACHTMAN, Paul. *Gunfighters.* 1974. Time Life. 4to. F. A8. $10.00

TRACY, Louis. *Wings of the Morning.* 1924. Phil. Winston. ils M Shaeffer. 319 p. dk gr cloth/pict label. F/fair. H3. $20.00

TRACY, Steven C. *Going to Cincinnati.* 1993. Urbana. 1st ed. F/F. B2. $30.00

TRACY, T.H. *Book of the Poodle.* 1955. NY. 4to. ils J Spicer/Flavia Gag. F. B14. $35.00

TRACY, T.H. *Book of the Poodle.* 1958. NY. 4th prt. 136 p. dj. A17. $15.00

TRACY, Walter P. *KS City & Its 100 Foremost Men.* ca 1924. np. 234 p. leather. G. D7. $40.00

TRAIN, Arthur. *Yankee Lawyer: Autobiography of Ephraim Tutt.* 1943. Grosset Dunlap. 1st ed. orange cloth. M11. $25.00

TRAIN & WOOD. *Man Who Rocked the Earth.* 1915. Doubleday Page. 1st ed. NF. N3. $50.00

TRALINS, Bob. *Bullet Hole.* 1986. London. Deutsch. 1st ed. F/F. M15. $45.00

TRALINS, Bob. *Gr Murder.* 1991. London. MacDonald. 1st ed. F/F. S5. $25.00

TRALL, R.T. *Hydropathic Encyclopedia.* 1852. NY. 2 vols. 12mo. ils/pls. VG. T3. $29.00

TRAPROCK, Walter E. *Cruise of the Kawa.* 1921. NY. 1st ed. presentation. 146 p. gilt gr cloth. VG. H3. $25.00

TRAUBEL, Helen. *Metropolitan Opera Murders.* nd. BC. VG/dj. P3. $8.00

TRAUTWINE, John C. *Civil Engineers Pocket Book.* 1902. NY. Wiley. rebound/full leather. VG. A16. $95.00

TRAVEN, B. *Bridge in the Jungle.* (1967). Hill Wang. 1st thus ed. VG/NF. B4. $35.00

TRAVEN, B. *Carreta.* (1970). Hill Wang. 1st ed. F/NF. C4. $50.00

TRAVEN, B. *General From the Jungle.* (1972). Hill Wang. 1st Am ed. F/NF. B4. $65.00

TRAVEN, B. *March to the Monteria.* 1964. NY. Dell. PBO/1st Am ed. NF/ils wrp. A11. $25.00

TRAVEN, B. *March to the Monteria.* 1971. Hill Wang. 1st ed. F/NF. C4. $40.00

TRAVERS, P.L. *About the Sleeping Beauty.* 1977. London. Collins. 1st Eng ed. 8vo. 126 p. NF/VG. T5. $45.00

TRAVERS, P.L. *Mary Poppins in the Park.* 1952. Harcourt Brace. 1st Am ed. 235 p. VG/G+. P2. $50.00

TRAVERS, P.L. *Mary Poppins.* 1934. NY. Reynal Hitchock. 1st Am ed. sm octavo. 206 p. NF/dj. H5. $450.00

TRAVIS, Dempsey. *Autobiography of Blk Chicago.* 1981. Urban Reasearch. 1st ed. sgn. F/NF. B2. $50.00

TREASE, Geoffrey. *Runaway Serf.* 1968. Hamish Hamilton. 1st ed. 12mo. 91 p. VG/VG. T5. $25.00

TREASE, Geoffrey. *Saraband for Shadows.* 1982. Macmillan. 1st UK ed. F/F. F4. $16.00

TREAT, Payson J. *Japan & the US 1853-1921.* 1921. Boston. 1st ed. 282 p. VG. D3. $25.00

TREAT, Roger. *Walter Johnson.* 1948. Messner. 1st ed. VG+/G+. P8. $140.00

TREDREE, H.L. *Strange Ordeal of the Normandier.* (1958). Little Brn. 1st ed. 8vo. 231 p. VG+/VG. A2. $15.00

TREECE, Henry. *Dark Island.* 1953. Random. 1st Am ed. F/VG+. N3. $35.00

TREECE, Henry. *Ride Into Danger.* 1961. Criterion. 2nd ed. VG/VG. P3. $15.00

TREGARTHEN, Enys. *Doll Who Came Alive.* (1942). John Day. ils Nora S Unwin. 76 p. beige cloth. G+. T5. $45.00

TREGASKIS, Richard. *Vietnam Diary.* (1963). HRW. 401 p. VG. clip dj. A7. $50.00

TREMAYNE, Peter; see Ellis, Peter.

TREMBLAY, Bill. *Crying in the Cheap Seats.* (1971). MA U. 1st wrp issue. A7. $17.00

TREMENHEERE, Hugh Seymour. *Notes on Public Subjects, Made During Tour of US...* 1852. London. John Murray. xl. 8vo. fld map. 320 p. gr cloth. H9. $95.00

TRENTON, Patricia. *Harvey Otis Young: Lost Genius...* 1975. Denver Art Mus. 135 p. stiff wrp. D2. $30.00

TREVANIAN. *Loo Sanction.* 1973. Crown. 1st ed. F/F. F4. $18.00

TREVANIAN. *Shibumi.* 1979. Crown. 1st ed. F/F. T2. $16.50

TREVANIAN. *Summer of Katya.* 1983. Crown. 1st ed. F/F. T2. $16.50

TREVOR, Elleston. *Place for the Wicked.* 1968. Doubleday. 1st ed. NF/NF. P3. $35.00

TREVOR, Elleston. *Theta Syndrome.* 1977. Doubleday. inscr. F/F. T2. $20.00

TREVOR, Meriol. *Newman: Pillar of the Cloud.* 1962. Doubleday. ils. 649 p. H10. $18.50

TREVOR, William. *News From Ireland.* 1986. Viking. AP. F/prt gr wrp. C4. $30.00

TREVOR, William. *Nights at the Alexandra.* (1987). London. Hutchinson. 1st ed. ils Hogarth. F/F. B3. $20.00

TREW, Cecil. *Horse Through the Ages.* 1953. NY. Roy. 1st Am ed. VG/VG. O3. $20.00

TRIBE, Laurence H. *God Save This Honorable Court...* 1985. Random. M11. $17.50

TRIFFIT, E.L. *Directory of New London.* 1906. Huron Co, OH. 54 p. G/wrp. B18. $45.00

TRIFONOV, Yuri. *Another Life, the House on the Embankment: Nouvellas.* 1983. Simon Schuster. 1st ed. trans from Russian. rem mk. NF/NF. A14. $20.00

TRIGAULT, Nicholas. *Histoire de l'Expedition Chrestienne au Royaume de Chine.* 1617. Lille. P de Rache. 1st French ed. 559 p. calf. B14. $375.00

TRIGGS, H. Indigo. *Garden Craft in Europe.* nd. (1913). London. 4to. ils. 332 p. teg. cloth. B26. $149.00

TRIGGS, J.H. *Hist & Directory of Laramie City, WY Territory.* 1875. Laramie. Daily Sentinel. 91 p. bl wrp. rare. B14. $75.00

TRILLING, Lionel. *EM Forster.* 1943. New Directions. 1st ed. inscr. F/NF. B2. $75.00

TRIMBLE, Joe. *Phil Rizzuto.* 1951. Barnes. 1st ed. F. P8. $20.00

TRIMPI, H.P. *Melville's Confidence Men & Am Politics in the 1850s.* 1987. np. ils/index. 338 p. dj. O7. $12.50

TRIPLETT, Frank. *Conquering the Wilderness...* 1888. Minneapolis. NW. ils. 742 p. G. H7. $25.00

TRIPP, Garnett. *Village of Hillman 1891-1991.* 1991. Atlanta. 1st ed. photos. 64 p. wrp. A17. $10.00

TRIPP, Miles. *Death of a Man-Tamer.* 1987. St Martin. 1st ed. VG/VG. P3. $15.00

TRIPP, Miles. *Fifth Point of the Compass.* 1967. Macmillan. 1st ed. VG/VG. P3. $23.00

TRIPP, Miles. *Some Predators Are Male.* 1985. St Martin. 1st ed. F/dj. P3. $13.00

TRIPTREE, James. *Tales of the Quintana Roo.* 1986. Arkham. 1st ed. M. M2. $12.00

TRISTRAM, W. Outram. *Coaching Days & Coaching Ways.* 1914. London. Macmillan. gilt gr leather. VG. O3. $65.00

TRIVETT. *Technique of Branscombe Point Lace.* 1991. np. ils. cloth. G2. $40.00

TROLLOPE, Anthony. *Barsetshire Novels of Anthony Trollope.* 1929. Boston/NY. Houghton Mifflin. 1/525. octavo. 14 vols. F. H5. $4,000.00

TROLLOPE, Anthony. *Eustace Diamonds.* 1873. London. 1st ed. octavo. 3 vols. red polished calf/red brds. NF. H5. $2,000.00

TROLLOPE, Anthony. *Lady Anna.* 1874. London. 1st ed. octavo. 2 vols. red cloth. NF. H5. $3,000.00

TROLLOPE, Anthony. *Last Chronicle of Barset.* 1867. London. ils George H Thomas. 32 weekly parts. F/box. H5. $8,500.00

TROLLOPE, Anthony. *Lotta Schmidt.* 1867. London. 1st ed. octavo. maroon cloth. VG. H5. $850.00

TROLLOPE, Anthony. *N Am.* 1862. NY. 1st ed. 623 p. blk cloth. G. T3. $48.00

TROLLOPE, Anthony. *N Am...in 2 Vols.* 1862. London. Chapman Hall. 1st ed. 2 vols. 8vo. fld map. old lib quarter cloth. F. H9. $125.00

TROLLOPE, Anthony. *Prime Minister.* 1876. London. 1st ed. octavo. 4 vols. brick-red cloth. NF/2 morocco boxes. H5. $4,500.00

TROLLOPE, Anthony. *Warden & the Barchester Towers.* 1936. NY. Modern Lib. intro AE Newton. F/F. T8. $20.00

TROLLOPE, Frances. *Domestic Manners of the Americans.* 1949. NY. 1st thus ed. edit D Smalley. VG. B5. $27.50

TROLLOPE, Francis. *Domestic Manners of the Americans.* 1832. London. Whittaker Treacher. 1st ed. 2 vols. calf/marbled brds. B14. $175.00

TROTSKY, Judith. *Love Songs From the Boogeymen.* (1973). Harper. 1st ed. 182 p. dj. A7. $13.00

TROTSKY, Leon. *Permanent Revolution.* (1947). Calcutta. Cupta Rahman. 1st Indian ed. 175 p. A7. $15.00

TROTSKY, Leon. *Stalin: Appraisal of the Man & His Influence.* 1967. Stein Day. reissue of 1941 ed. 516 p. dj. A7. $20.00

TROTT, Harold W. *Santa in Santa Land.* 1943. Crosset Williams. 1st ed. cloth. VG-/dj. A3. $17.50

TROUP, Freda. *In Face of Fear.* 1950. London. Faber. 2nd prt. 227 p. dj. A7. $25.00

TROUT, Kilgore; see Farmer, Philip Jose.

TROVAT, Henri. *Extreme Friendship.* 1968. NY. Phaedra. 1st Am ed. trans from French. NF/NF clip. A14. $25.00

TROY, Simon. *Drunkard's End.* 1961. Walker. 1st ed. VG/dj. P3. $15.00

TRUAX, Sarah. *Woman of Parts.* 1949. Longman. 1st ed. 247 p. gr cloth. F. B22. $10.00

TRUBOWITZ, Sidney. *Handbook for Teaching in the Ghetto School.* (1968). Quadrangle. 175 p. dj. A7. $13.00

TRUDEL, Marcel. *Atlas de la Nouvelle-France/Atlas of New France.* 1968. Quebec. Presses de'Universite Laval. 95 maps. NF. O6. $50.00

TRUE, Ruth S. *W Side Studies: Boyhood & Lawlessness, Neglected Girl.* 1914. NY. Russel Sage Found. gr cloth. M11. $75.00

TRUE, W.P. *Smithsonian: Am's Treasure House.* (1950). Sheridan House. 1st ed. 8vo. 306 p. VG+/VG. A2. $25.00

TRUEBLOOD, Elton. *Place To Stand.* 1968. Harper Row. 8vo. 128 p. VG/dj. V3. $12.00

TRUMAN, Harry S. *Truman Program.* 1949. WA, DC. Public Affairs. 1st ed. sgn. NF/dj. scarce/rare to be sgn. Q1. $500.00

TRUMAN, Margaret. *Murder at the FBI.* 1985. Arbor. 1st ed. VG/dj. P3. $15.00

TRUMBO, Dalton. *Devil in the Book.* 1956. np (LA). 1/750. sgn. pamphlet. NF/ils wrp. A11. $95.00

TRUMBULL, John. *M'Fingal: Modern Epic Poem in 4 Cantos.* 1799. Boston. 12mo. 141 p. orig leather. G. D7. $35.00

TRUMBULL, M.M. *Free Trade Struggle in Eng.* 1892. Chicago. Open Court. revised/enlarged ed. NF. B2. $65.00

TRUSS, Sheldon. *Dr Was a Dame.* 1953. Crime Club. 1st ed. VG/dj. P3. $20.00

TRUSS, Sheldon. *Sweeter for His Going.* 1950. Hodder Stoughton. 1st ed. G. P3. $10.00

TRUSS, Sheldon. *Truth About Claire Veryan.* 1957. Crime Club. 1st ed. VG/dj. M2. $10.00

TRYON, Thomas. *Crowned Heads.* 1976. Knopf. 1st ed. F/F. T2. $8.00

TRYON, Thomas. *Lady.* 1974. Knopf. 1st ed. F/F. N3. $15.00

TRYON, Thomas. *Lady.* 1975. London. Hodder Stoughton. 1st British ed. F/NF. N3. $15.00

TSAO, Ding-ren. *Persuasion of Kuei Ku Tzu.* 1985. Minnesota. thesis. 4to. map. 198 p. VG/wrp. W1. $18.00

TSAO, W.Y. *Constitutional Structure of Modern China.* 1947. Melbourne. VG+. M11. $75.00

TSCHICHOLD, Jan. *Asymmetric Typography.* 1967. NY. Reinhold. 8vo. ils. silvered blk cloth. F/VG-. F1. $65.00

TSCHICHOLD, Jan. *Chinese Color Prts of Today.* 1953. Beechhurst. tall quarto. 16 pls. 17 p. F/slipcase. B24. $200.00

TSCHICHOLD, Jan. *Leben & Werk des Typographen Jan Tschichold.* 1977. Dresden. Kunst. quarto. 300 p. F/dj/paper slipcase. B24. $300.00

TSCHIFFELY, A.F. *Coricancha (Garden of Gold).* (1943). London. Hoder. 2nd prt. 220 p. F3. $10.00

TSEU, Augustus A. *Moral Philosophy of Mo-Tze.* 1965. Taipei. China Prt. 8vo. 407 p. VG/dj. W1. $16.00

TUBB, E.C. *Gath.* 1968. London. Hart Davis. 1st British/1st hc ed. F/NF. N3. $30.00

TUBB, E.C. *Rogue Planet.* 1977. Arthur Baker. 1st ed. NF/NF. P3. $18.00

TUCCI, Niccolo. *Before My Time.* 1963. London. Cape. 1st ed. NF/NF. A14. $25.00

TUCHMAN, Barbara W. *March of Folly, From Troy to Vietnam.* 1984. BC. F/dj. C1. $4.50

TUCHMAN, Barbara W. *March of Folly.* 1984. Knopf. 1st ed. VG/dj. A16/N2. $10.00

TUCHMAN, Barbara W. *Stillwell & the Am Experience in China.* 1971. Macmillan. 1st ed. dj. N2. $10.00

TUCK, Raphael. *Father Christmas.* ca 1895-1910. VG/stiff wrp. M5. $95.00

TUCK, Raphael. *My Dolly.* ca 1895-1910. G/pict wrp. M5. $18.00

TUCKER, Charlotte E. *Fairy Know-a-Bit.* 1897. London. Nelson. ils Dalziel. 12mo. red cloth. VG. S10. $30.00

TUCKER, Eleanor M. *Christmas in CA.* 1924. Sierra Madre, CA. private prt. apparant 1st ed. VG. M5. $30.00

TUCKER, Henry St. George. *Exploring the Silent Shore of Memory.* 1951. Whittet Shepperson. 300 p. G. B10. $18.00

TUCKER, Jerry. *Bermuda's Story.* 1970. Bermuda. reprint. sgn. 213 p. cloth. F/VG. B11. $35.00

TUCKER, Kerry. *Greetings From LA.* 1982. Steam Pr. 1st ed. ils/index. 112 p. F/wrp. B19. $12.50

TUCKER, Nathaniel Beverly. *Partisan Leader: Novel, Apocalypse of Orig...S Confederacy.* 1863. Richmond, VA. W & Johnston. 1st Confederate ed. 220 p. VG. scarce. M8. $1,250.00

TUCKER, Patrick T. *Riding the High Country.* 1933. Caldwell, ID. 1st ed. pls. 210 p. cloth. F/pict dj. D3. $100.00

TUCKER, R. Whitney. *Descendants of the Presidents.* 1975. Delmar. 222 p. B10. $50.00

TUCKER, Sarah. *Memoirs of Life & Religious Experience.* 1848. Providence. Moore Choate. 12mo. 204 p. VG. V3. $22.00

TUCKER, Wilson. *Ice & Iron.* 1974. Doubleday. 1st ed. VG/dj. P3. $25.00

TUCKER, Wilson. *Procession of the Damned.* 1965. Crime Club. 1st ed. VG/dj. P3. $25.00

TUCKER, Wilson. *This Witch.* 1971. Doubleday. 1st ed. VG/VG. P3. $30.00

TUCKER, Wilson. *Wild Talent.* nd. BC. VG/dj. P3. $8.00

TUCKERMAN, Frederick G. *Complete Poems of...* 1965. NY. Oxford. 1st ed. intro/edit N Scott Momaday. F/NF. L3. $175.00

TUCKERMAN, Henry T. *Am & Her Commentators.* 1864. NY. 1st ed. G. B28. $85.00

TUCKERMAN, Henry T. *Italian Sketchbook.* 1835. Phil. Key Biddle. 1st ed. author's 1st book. cloth. VG. E3. $25.00

TUDEBODE, Peter. *Historia de Hierosolymitano Itinere.* 1974. Phil. 8vo. 2 maps. 137 p. cloth. dj. O2. $35.00

TUDOR, Tasha. *A Is for Annabelle.* 1954. Henry Z Walck. oblong 4to. gr cloth. VG/dj. A3. $45.00

TUDOR, Tasha. *And It Was So.* 1958. Westminster Pr. 1st ed. 48 p. gr cloth. VG/VG-. A3. $95.00

TUDOR, Tasha. *Corgiville Fair.* 1971. Crowell. 1st ed. oblong 8vo. turquoise cloth. VG. T5. $65.00

TUDOR, Tasha. *Corgiville Fair.* 1971. Crowell. 1st ed. VG+/VG+. P2. $100.00

TUDOR, Tasha. *Edgar Allen Crow.* 1953. Oxford. 1st ed. VG. P2. $68.00

TUDOR, Tasha. *Mother Goose.* 1955 (1944). Oxford. 77 verses. 87 p. VG+. P2. $20.00

TUDOR, Tasha. *Seasons of Delight: Year on an Old-Fashioned Farm.* 1986. movable scenes. 12 p. F. A4. $45.00

TUDOR, Tasha. *Springs of Joy.* 1979. Rand McNally. 1st prt. 4to. VG/sans. A3. $15.00

TUDOR, Tasha. *Tasha Tudor's Old-Fashioned Gifts.* 1979. McKay. 1st ed. 118 p. VG+/dj. M20. $25.00

TUDOR, Tasha. *Tasha Tudor's Sampler. Tale for Easter.* nd. McKay. 2nd prt. dj. A3. $17.50

TUDOR, Tasha. *Time To Keep.* 1977. Rand McNally. 1st ed. ils. NF. P2. $85.00

TUDOR, Tasha. *Wings From the Wind.* 1964. Lippincott. 1st ed. 4to. 119 p. VG/dj. A3. $40.00

TUER, Andrew W. *Forgotten Children's Books.* 1898-99. London. Leadenhall. 1st ed/later issue. gilt bl cloth. VG. D1. $185.00

TUKE, Henry. *Principles of Religion, As Professed by...Quakers...* 1805. NY. Collins Perkins. 16mo. 142 p. leather. fair. V3. $25.00

TUKE, Samuel. *Selections From Epistles of George Fox.* 1879. Cambridge. Obadiah Brn Benevolent Fund. 12mo. 312 p. G. V3. $16.00

TULLY, Andrew. *Supreme Court.* nd. BC. VG/dj. P3. $8.00

TULLY, Andrew. *Time of the Hawk.* 1967. Morrow. 1st ed. dj. A7. $30.00

TUMMERS, J.H. *La Theorie de la Relativite Restreinte d'Einstein...* 1923. Holland. 20 p. wrp. N2. $16.50

TUNIS, Edwin. *Colonial Living.* (1957). Cleveland. 1/975. 156 p. ils cloth. VG+. B18. $25.00

TUNIS, Edwin. *Wheels: Pict Hist.* 1960. Cleveland. World. 3rd prt. 4to. G+. O3. $30.00

TUNSTALL, Jeremy. *Media Are Am Anglo-Am Media in the World.* 1977. Columbia. 1st ed. 352 p. dj. N2. $6.50

TUOHY, Ferdinand. *Inside Dope.* 1934. London. Hamish Hamilton. 1st ed. NF/NF. B2. $75.00

TUOHY, Frank. *Fingers in the Door.* 1970. NY. 1st ed (precedes UK). sgn. F/NF. A11. $35.00

TUPPER, Harmon. *To the Great Ocean: Siberia & the Trans-Siberian Railroad.* (1965). Little Brn. 1st ed. 8vo. 536 p. F/VG+. A2. $30.00

TURCOTTE, Patricia L. *Perennials for the Backyard Gardener.* 1993. Woodstock. ils/photos. M. B26. $18.00

TUREN & MCCABE. *Tuntsa.* 1961. Chicago. Regnery. 1st ed. 8vo. 378 p. F/F. A2. $12.50

TURGENEV, I.S. *Dvoryanksoe Gnyezdo (A Nest of Gentlefolk, a Novel).* 1859. Moscow. 1st ed. 8vo. 320 p. wrp. M1. $1,150.00

TURGENEV, I.S. *Fathers & Sons.* nd. Boni Liveright. trans Constance Garnett. VG. E3. $8.00

TURGENEV, I.S. *Fathers & Sons.* 1867. NY. Leypoldt Holt. 1st Eng-language ed. 248 p. cloth. G. B14. $50.00

TURGEON, Charlotte. *Cooking for Many.* (1962). NY. Crown. 287 p. dj. A7. $250.00

TURKIN, Hy. *Official Encyclopedia of Little League Baseball.* 1954. Barnes. 1st ed. VG+/G+. P8. $10.00

TURKLE, Brinton. *Deep in the Forest.* 1976. Dutton. 1st ed. xl. 8vo. ils. pict gold brds. VG/G. T5. $30.00

TURNBULL, Pauline. *May Lansfield Keller: Life & Letters.* 1975. McClure. 1st ed. ils/photos. 369 p. VG/G. B10. $15.00

TURNBULL, Robert. *World We Live In.* 1851. np. 8vo. 540 p. gilt cloth. VG. T3. $40.00

TURNER, A.E. *Earps Talk.* (1980). TX. 1st ed. 1/1500. 193 p. VG+/dj. B18. $22.50

TURNER, A.E. *OK Corral Inquest.* (1981). TX. 1st ed. 1/1475. VG+/dj. B18. $22.50

TURNER, Arlin. *George W Cable: A Biography.* 1956. Duke U. xl. rpr dj. N2. $6.00

TURNER, Dan. *Expos Inside Out.* 1983. McClelland Stuart. later prt. F/VG+. P8. $30.00

TURNER, Daymond. *Gonzalo Fernandez de Oviedo Y Valdes...Bibliography.* 1966. Chapell Hill. M/wrp. O6. $55.00

TURNER, E.S. *Hist of Courting.* 1955. Dutton. 1st Am ed. 8vo. 290 p. VG/VG. A2. $12.50

TURNER, E.S. *What the Butler Saw.* 1963 (1962). London. Michael Joseph. 3rd ed. 8vo. 304 p. F/VG. A2. $12.50

TURNER, Frederick. *Double Shadow.* 1978. Berkley Putnam. 1st ed. xl. dj. P3. $5.00

TURNER, J.K. *Barbarous Mexico.* (1969). Austin, TX. 1st thus ed. 8vo. 322 p. F/VG. A2. $20.00

TURNER, James. *Dolphin's Skin: 6 Studies in Eccentricity.* (1956). London. Cassell. 1st ed. 8vo. 218 p. VG+/VG+. A2. $15.00

TURNER, R. Jr. *New & Easy Intro to Universal Geog.* 1805. London. Johnson. 12th ed. 26 pls/24 maps. old leather. O6. $250.00

TURNER, R.E. *Little People.* 1977. Borrower's Pr. minature. 1/300. prt/sgn Bernier. gr cloth. B24. $85.00

TURNER, R.F. *Vietnamese Communism.* (1975). Hoover Instit. 517 p. dj. A7/ $30.00

TURNER, Robert. *Gunsmoke.* 1958. Whitman. VG. P3. $20.00

TURNER, Tina. *I, Tina: My Life Story.* (1986). NY. Morrow. 1st ed. 236 p. NF/clip. A7. $15.00

TURNER, W.J. *British Adventure.* 1947. London. Collins. 1st thus ed. 8vo. 324 p. F/F. A2. $30.00

TUROW, Scott. *Burden of Proof.* (1990). FSG. 1st ed. F/F. B3. $35.00

TURPIN, James W. *Vietnam Dr.* (1966). McGraw Hill. 1st ed. 210 p. NF/dj. A7. $35.00

TUSKA, Jon. *Films of Mae West.* 1973. Citadel. 1st ed. VG/VG. P3. $20.00

TUTEIN, Peter. *Sealers.* 1938. Putnam. 1st Am ed. 8vo. 247 p. VG/VG. A2. $20.00

TUTHILL, Franklin. *Hist of CA.* 1866. San Francisco. Bancroft. 1st ed. 657 p. cloth. VG. D3. $75.00

TUTHILL, William Burnet. *Cathedral Church of Eng.* 1923. NY. Macmillan. 193 p. H10. $16.50

TUTTLE, W.C. *Bluffer's Luck.* 1936. Collins. 4th ed. VG. P3. $15.00

TUTUOLA, Amos. *My Life in the Bush of Ghosts.* 1954. Grove. 1st Am ed. F/NF. B2. $40.00

TWAIN, Mark. *Adventures of Huckleberry Finn.* 1885. Webster. 1st ed/1st issue. ils Kemble. box. D1. $3,200.00

TWAIN, Mark. *Adventures of Tom Sawyer.* 1894 (1875). Am Pub. 320 p. brn cloth. G. S10. $35.00

TWAIN, Mark. *Adventures of Tom Sawyer.* 1931. Winston. 1st thus ed. ils Hurd. VG/VG. L1. $50.00

TWAIN, Mark. *Adventures of Tom Sawyer.* 1938. Harper. 1st this ed. ils Brehm. G. L1. $45.00

TWAIN, Mark. *Am Claimant.* 1892. Chatto Windus. 1st ed. G. M18. $75.00

TWAIN, Mark. *Celebrated Jumping Frog of Calaveras Co & Other Sketches.* 1867. NY. Webb. 1st ed. author's 1st book. plum variant bdg (frog at center). Q1. $12,500.00

TWAIN, Mark. *CT Yankee in King Arthur's Court.* nd. Webster. decor brds. G. P3. $75.00

TWAIN, Mark. *Dog's Tale.* 1904. NY. Harper. 1st Am ed. ils WT Smedley. octavo. orig red cloth. VG. H5. $250.00

TWAIN, Mark. *Double-Barrelled Detective Story.* 1902. NY. Harper. 1st ed. octavo. 179 p. teg. red cloth. VG. H5. $200.00

TWAIN, Mark. *Extracts From Adam's Diary.* 1904. Harper. 1st ed. ils F Strothmann. NF/NF. Q1. $750.00

TWAIN, Mark. *Horse's Tale.* 1907. NY. Harper. 1st ed. octavo. red cloth. NF. H5. $175.00

TWAIN, Mark. *How To Tell a Story & Other Essays.* 1897. NY. Harper. 1st ed. octavo. 233 p. teg. red cloth. NF. H5. $350.00

TWAIN, Mark. *Is Shakespeare Dead?* 1909. Harper. 1st ed/Blanck's later issue B. 149 p. teg. gr cloth. H5. $150.00

TWAIN, Mark. *Life on the MS.* 1883. Boston. Osgood. 1st ed/mixed (or intermediate state). NF. Q1. $750.00

TWAIN, Mark. *Life on the MS...* 1883. Boston. Osgood. 1st Am ed/2nd state. 8vo. 624 p. stp brn cloth. VG. D3. $125.00

TWAIN, Mark. *Mark Twain's Autobiography.* 1924. Harper. stated 1st ed. 2 vols. dk bl cloth. VG-. A7. $100.00

TWAIN, Mark. *Mark Twain's Autobiography.* 1924. Harper. 1st ed. 2 vols. gilt bl cloth. NF/VG+. Q1. $375.00

TWAIN, Mark. *Mark Twain's Sketches, New & Old.* 1875. Am Pub. 1st ed. lg octavo. 320 p. gilt bl cloth. F. B24. $675.00

TWAIN, Mark. *Roughing It.* 1872. Hartford. Am pub. 1st ed. pub quarter leather/raised bands. VG. Q1. $750.00

TWAIN, Mark. *Tramp Abroad.* 1907. Harper. VG. P3. $20.00

TWAIN, Mark. *1,000,000 Franc Bank Note.* 1893. Chatto Windus. 1st ed. G. M18. $100.00

TWAIN, Mark. *1601.* 1969. London. Land's End. ils Alan Odle. NF/NF clip. B3. $45.00

TWAITE, Anthony. *Japan in Color.* 1967. London. Thames Hudson. 1st ed. folio. pls. 160 p. VG. W1. $18.00

TWEEDSMUIR, Lord. *Hudson's Bay Trader.* 1978 (1951). Toronto. Nelson Foster Scott. 2nd ed/2nd prt. 8vo. 188 p. F/F. A2. $15.00

TWELKER. *Women & Their Quilts.* 1988. np. ils. wrp. G2. $17.00

TWENEY, George H. *Washington 89.* 1989. Morongo Valley, CA. Sagebrush Pr. 1/890. sgn. 8vo. fld map. linen. M. T8. $42.50

TWISSELMANN, Ernest C. *Flora of Kern County, CA.* 1967. San Francisco. ils/presentation Eben McMillan. 395 p. F/yel wrp. B26. $47.50

TWOMBLY, George F. *All-Am Dropout.* 1967. self pub. 1st ed. F/VG. P8. $35.00

TWOMBLY, George F. *Internat Racing Pigeons...* nd. Medford. Pigeon News. ils. 192 p. dj. M. H10. $10.00

TYAU, Min-Ch'ian T.Z. *China Awakened.* 1922. Macmillan. 1st ed. xl. 8vo. ils/map. 475 p. VG. W1. $45.00

TYERS, Kathy. *Star Wars: The Truce at Bakura.* 1994. NY. Bantam. 1st ed. F/F. N3. $15.00

TYLER, Anne. *Breathing Lessons.* 1988. Knopf. AP. NF/prt gray wrp. C4. $90.00

TYLER, Anne. *Earthly Possessions.* 1977. Knopf. 1st ed. F/F. B2. $75.00

TYLER, Anne. *If Morning Ever Comes.* nd. Bantam. PBO. sgn. author's 1st book. NF/wrp. A11. $85.00

TYLER, Anne. *Saint Maybe.* 1991. Knopf. 1st ed. w/sgn leaf. F/F. B2/C4. $85.00

TYLER, Anne. *Slipping Down Life.* 1983. London. Severn House. 1st ed. F/F. C4. $50.00

TYLER, Anne. *Tumble Tower.* 1993. NY. Orchard Books. 1st ed. author's 1st juvenile. F/F. C4. $20.00

TYLER, Hamilton. *Gourmet Gardening.* 1972. Van Nostrand Reinhold. VG/dj. A16. $5.00

TYLER, MOSES Coit. *New System of Musical Gymnastics...* 1864. London. Wm Tweedie. 1st ed. 12mo. 32 p. prt wrp. M1. $175.00

TYLER, Ron. *Alfred Jacob Miller: Artist on the OR Trail.* 1982. Amon Carter Mus Art. 480 p. cloth. F/dj. D2. $95.00

TYLER, S. Lyman. *Two Worlds.* 1988. Salt Lake City. 1st ed. 258 p. dj. F3. $30.00

TYLER, Sydney. *San Francisco's Great Disaster.* 1906. Harrisburg, PA. 8vo. 424 p. pict gr cloth. NF. H3. $20.00

TYLER. *Show & Tell: Husband's View of the Patchwork.* 1989. np. ils. wrp. G2. $6.00

TYNAN, Kathleen. *Agatha.* 1978. Ballantine. 1st ed. VG/VG. P3. $18.00

TYNDALE, Walter. *Artist in Italy Written & Painted by Walter Tyndale.* (1913). Hodder Stoughton. 4to. 26 color pls. gilt bl cloth. F. B14. $200.00

TYSON, Vivian. *Space Reports.* 1970. NY. Express. dj. N2. $10.00

TYTLER, M. Fraser. *Little Fanny's Journal; or, My Own Child's Book.* 1851. London. WP Kennedy. 24mo. 132 p. aeg. gilt bl cloth. S10. $35.00

UECKER, Bob. *Catcher in the Wry.* 1982. Putnam. later prt. VG+/VG+. P8. $10.00

UHL, Marion Norris. *Spiral Horn.* 1968. Doubleday. 1st ed. F/F clip. N3. $35.00

UHNAK, Dorothy. *Bait.* 1968. Simon Schuster. 1st ed. VG/dj. P3. $30.00

UHNAK, Dorothy. *False Witness.* 1981. Simon Schuster. 1st ed. F/F. T2. $15.00

UHNAK, Dorothy. *Law & Order.* 1973. Simon Schuster. 1st ed. VG/dj. P3. $18.00

UHNAK, Dorothy. *Victims.* 1985. Simon Schuster. 1st ed. F/F. T2. $18.00

ULLMAN, Allan. *Night Man.* 1951. Detective BC. VG. P3. $8.00

ULLMAN, James Michael. *Neon Haystack.* nd. BC. VG/dj. P3. $8.00

ULLMAN, Michael. *Jazz Lives: Portraits in Words & Pictures.* (1980). New Republic. 2nd prt. sgn. 244 p. A7. $15.00

ULLMAN, S.B. *Culture & Judaism.* 1956. Toronto. Lieberman Jewish Book Center. 184 p. VG/poor. S3. $19.00

ULLMAN, Victor. *Look to the N Star: A Life of William King.* (1969). Beacon. 337 p. F/F clip. A7. $20.00

ULPH, Owen. *Fiddleback: Lore of the Linecamp.* 1981. Dream Garden. 1st ed. ils TP Leary. F/F. A18. $40.00

ULPH, Owen. *Leather Throne.* 1984. Dream Garden. 1st ed. F/dj. A18. $40.00

ULRICH, Paul. *Great Mysteries of Vanished Civilization.* nd. Pleasant Valley. 3 vols. VG. P3. $25.00

UNDERHILL, F.T. *Driving for Pleasure; or, Harness Stable & Its Appointments.* 1896. NY. Appleton. 1st ed. sm folio. teg. calf/suede sides. F. R3. $600.00

UNDERHILL, Francis. *Prayer in Modern Life.* 1929. London. Mowbray. 224 p. H10. $15.00

UNDERWOOD, Francis H. *John Greenleaf Whittier: A Biography.* 1884. Osgood. VG. N2. $10.00

UNDERWOOD, Peter. *Haunted London.* 1974. Harrap. 2nd ed. VG/dj. P3. $15.00

UNDERWOOD, Peter. *Horror Man: Life of Boris Karloff.* 1972. Leslie Frewin. 1st ed. VG/dj. P3. $35.00

UNDERWOOD, Peter. *Life's a Drag! Danny la Rue & the Drag Scene.* (1974). London. Lesslie Frewin. 2nd ed. 8vo. 192 p. F/wrp. A2. $12.50

UNGERER, Tomi. *Crictor.* 1958. Harper. 1st ed. 32 p. cloth brds. VG/torn. D1. $75.00

UNGERER, Tomi. *No Kiss for Mother.* 1973. Harper Row. 1st ed. ils Ungerer. F/F. D1. $50.00

UNTERKIRCHER, F. *King Rene's Book of Love.* (1975). NY. 16 color pls. 48 p. VG+/slipcase. B18. $27.50

UNTERMEYER, Louis. *Am Poetry From the Beginning to Whitman.* 1931. NY. 827 p. VG+. A11. $35.00

UNTERMEYER, Louis. *Golden Book of Poems for the Very Young.* (1959). Golden Pr. 4to. 33 p. G+. T5. $25.00

UNTERMEYER, Louis. *Uninhibited Treasury of Erotic Poetry.* 1963. NY. 1st ed. NF/VG+. V1. $15.00

UNWIN, Charles W. *Sweet Peas.* 1926. NY. 12mo. 197 p. VG/dj. B28. $25.00

UNZELMAN, Gail. *Wine & Gastronomy.* 1990. Nomis Pr. 1/390. 346 p. dj. G7. $85.00

UPDIKE, John. *Bath After Sailing.* 1968. Stevenson. Country Squire. 1/125. sgn. F/stiff wrp. L3. $750.00

UPDIKE, John. *Bech Is Back.* 1982. Knopf. 1/500. sgn/#d. F/slipcase. C4. $60.00

UPDIKE, John. *Bech Is Back.* 1982. Knopf. 1st ed. VG/dj. P3. $20.00

UPDIKE, John. *Brazil.* 1994. Knopf. 1st ed. sgn. F/F. C4. $40.00

UPDIKE, John. *Carpentered Hen & Other Tame Creatures.* (1958). Harper. 1st ed. author's 1st book. NF/NF clip 1st issue. Q1. $600.00

UPDIKE, John. *Collected Poems 1953-93.* 1993. Knopf. 1st ed. sgn. F/F. C4. $45.00

UPDIKE, John. *Collected Poems 1953-93.* 1993. Knopf. AP. F/prt gray wrp. C4. $60.00

UPDIKE, John. *Concerts at Castle Hill.* 1993. Lord John. 1/250. sgn. 2-piece bdg as issued. F. C4. $75.00

UPDIKE, John. *Coup.* 1978. NY. 1st ed. sgn. F/F. A11. $45.00

UPDIKE, John. *Facing Nature.* 1985. NY. 1st ed. F/F. V1. $15.00

UPDIKE, John. *First Words.* 1993. Algonquin. 1st ed. F/F. C4. $30.00

UPDIKE, John. *Hawthorne's Creed.* 1981. NY. 1/250. sgn. marbled brds/half maroon cloth. F/pub dj. A11. $60.00

UPDIKE, John. *Memories of the Ford Administration.* 1992. Knopf. AP. F/prt gray wrp. C4. $60.00

UPDIKE, John. *Midpoint & Other Poems.* 1969. London. 1st ed. NF/NF. V1. $20.00

UPDIKE, John. *Month of Sundays.* 1975. Knopf. 1st ed. VG/VG. V2. $9.00

UPDIKE, John. *More Stately Mansions.* 1987. Jackson. Nouveau. 1/300. sgn/#d. F/F. C4. $30.00

UPDIKE, John. *Rabbit, Run.* 1960. NY. 1st ed. NF/torn. A15. $190.00

UPDIKE, John. *Rabbit at Rest.* (1990). London. Deutsch. 1st ed. VG/F. B3. $25.00

UPDIKE, John. *Rabbit at Rest.* 1989. Knopf. 1st ed. F/F. C4. $30.00

UPDIKE, John. *Rabbit at Rest.* 1990. BOMC. sgn. F/dj. A15. $17.50

UPDIKE, John. *Rabbit Redux.* 1971. Knopf. ARC. RS. w/photo. F/F. L3. $125.00

UPDIKE, John. *Rabbit Redux.* 1971. Knopf. 1st ed. NF/dj. P3. $20.00

UPDIKE, John. *Rabbit Redux.* 1972. London. Deutsch. 1st ed. F/NF clip. B3. $45.00

UPDIKE, John. *Self-Consciousness.* (1989). London. Deutsch. 1st ed. F/NF. B3. $35.00

UPDIKE, John. *Self-Consciousness.* 1989. Knopf. AP. F/prt beige wrp. C4. $60.00

UPDIKE, John. *Three Illuminations in Life of an Am Author.* 1979. NY. Targ. 1st ed. 1/350. sgn. marbled brds. F. B24. $100.00

UPDIKE, John. *Too Far To Go.* 1979. NY. Fawcett Crest. PBO. sgn. F/unread. A11. $60.00

UPDIKE, John. *Warm Wine.* 1973. Albondocani. 1/250. sgn. F/marbled wrp. C4. $75.00

UPDYKE, James; see Burnett, W.R.

UPFIELD, Arthur W. *Mountains Have a Secret.* 1948. Crime Club. 1st ed. VG/VG-. P3. $45.00

UPFIELD, Arthur W. *New Shoe.* 1951. Doubleday Crime Club. 1st ed. VG/dj. M15. $45.00

UPFIELD, Arthur W. *Royal Abduction.* 1984. Dennis McMillan. 1st Am ed. F/dj. M15. $50.00

UPFIELD, Arthur W. *Sands of Windee.* 1959. Angus Robertson. 1st ed. VG/VG-. P3. $35.00

UPHAM, Charles Wentworth. *Life, Explorations & Public Services of John Chas Fremont.* 1856. Boston. Ticknor Fields. 356 p. gr cloth. VG. M20. $50.00

UPHAM, Edward. *Hit of the Ottoman Empire...Till the Yr 1828.* 1833. Phil. 8vo. 228 p. new cloth. O2. $75.00

UPHAM, Elizabeth. *Little Brn Bear Goes to School.* 1955. Platt Munk. ils Marjorie Hartwell. orange brds. VG. M5. $15.00

UPHAM, Elizabeth. *Little Brn Bear.* 1942. Platt Munk. ils Marjorie Hartwell. VG+. M5. $25.00

UPHAM, Elizabeth. *Little Brn Monkey.* 1949. Platt Monk. 1st ed. G/G. L1. $17.50

UPTON, Bertha. *Adventures of 2 Dutch Dolls.* 1898. Longman Gr. 1st ed. ils F Upton. pict brds. VG. scarce. D1. $350.00

UPTON, Bertha. *Golliwog's Circus.* 1903. Longman Gr. 1st ed. ils F Upton. scarce. D1. $30.00

UPTON, Robert. *Dead on the Stick.* (1986). Viking. 1st ed. F/dj. B9. $10.00

UPTON, Robert. *Golden Fleecing.* 1979. St Martin. 1st ed. F/F. P3. $13.00

UPTON, Robert. *Killing in Real Estate.* 1990. Dutton. 1st ed. NF/dj. P3. $18.00

URBAN, Abram Linwood. *My Garden of Dreams.* 1913. Phil. 1/2000. 148 p. VG. B28. $25.00

URBAN, Greg. *Discourse-Centered Approach to Culture.* (1991). Austin, TX. 1st ed. 215 p. dj. F3. $25.00

URIS, Leon. *Haj.* (1984). London. Deutsch. 1st ed. NF/NF clip. B3. $30.00

URIS, Leon. *Milta Pass.* 1988. Doubleday. 1st ed. VG/VG. V2. $6.00

URIS, Leon. *Topaz.* (1967). McGraw Hill. 1st ed. F/dj. B4. $45.00

URN, Althea; see Ford, Consuelo Urisarri.

UROFSKY, Melvin I. *Conflict of Rights: Supreme Court & Affirmative Action.* 1991. Scribner. M11. $20.00

URQUHART, Beryl Leslie. *Camellias.* ca 1956. Princeton. 20 full-p pls. VG/dj. B26. $22.50

URWICK, W. *India Ils w/Pen & Pencil.* 1891. NY. Hurst. revised enlarged ed. 4to. ils. 199 p. VG. W1. $16.00

USJHIMARU, Procius Yasuo. *Bishop Innocent: Founder of Am Orthodoxy.* (1964). Bridgeport. 12mo. photos/map. 44 p. wrp. A17. $7.50

UTLEY, Freda. *Odyssey of a Liberal.* (1970). WA Nat Pr. 319 p. dj. A7. $32.00

UVEZIAN, Sonia. *Complete Internat Sandwich Book.* 1982. Stein Day. VG/dj. A16. $10.00

UZANNE, Octave. *L'Art Dans la Decoration Exterieure des Livres en France...* 1898. Paris. Societe Francaise d'Eitions d'Art. 275 p. teg. wrp. F1. $675.00

V

VACHSS, Andrew. *Another Chance To Get It Right.* 1993. Milwaukie, OR. Dark Horse. 1st ed. inscr. F/sans. B2. $35.00

VACHSS, Andrew. *Bl Belle.* 1988. Knopf. 1st ed. sgn. F/F. B2. $50.00

VACHSS, Andrew. *Blossom.* 1990. Knopf. 1st ed. sgn. F/dj. A7. $25.00

VACHSS, Andrew. *Blossom.* 1990. Knopf. 1st ed. VG/dj. P3. $18.00

VACHSS, Andrew. *Flood.* 1985. Donald Fine. 1st ed. NF/dj. P3. $30.00

VACHSS, Andrew. *Flood.* 1985. NY. Donald Fine. 1st ed. author's 1st book. F/dj. B9/S5. $35.00

VACHSS, Andrew. *Flood.* 1985. Donald Fine. 1st ed. sgn. NF/F. B2. $65.00

VACHSS, Andrew. *Hard Candy.* 1989. Knopf. 1st ed. F/F. F4. $18.00

VACHSS, Andrew. *Hard Candy.* 1989. Knopf. 1st ed. inscr/sgn. NF/F. B2. $40.00

VACHSS, Andrew. *Sacrifice.* 1991. Knopf. 1st ed. F/F. P3. $20.00

VACHSS, Andrew. *Sacrifice.* 1991. Knopf. 1st ed. inscr/sgn. F/F. B2. $35.00

VACHSS, Andrew. *Shella.* 1993. Knopf. 1st ed. inscr/sgn. NF/F. B2. $40.00

VACHSS, Andrew. *Strega.* 1987. Knopf. 1st ed. F/dj. M18. $35.00

VAGTS, Alfred. *Deutschland und die Vereinigten Staaten in der Weltpolitik.* 1935. Macmillan. 2 vols. M/djs. O6. $125.00

VAILLANT, George. *Aztecs of Mexico.* 1941. Doubleday. 1st ed. 340 p. F3. $20.00

VAKA, Demetra. *Constantine: King & Traitor.* 1918. London. 8vo. 300 p. cloth. O2. $65.00

VAKA, Demetra. *Unveiled Ladies of Stamoul.* 1923. Boston. 1st ed. 8vo. ils. 261 p. cloth. O2. $30.00

VALDIOSERA, Ramon. *Mexican Children & Toys.* 1949. Mexico. Fischgrund. 12 color pls. F3. $30.00

VALENSTEIN, Elliot S. *Great & Desperate Cures: Rise & Decline of Psychosurgery...* 1986. Basic Books. 338 p. russet cloth. VG/dj. G1. $37.50

VALENTIN, Jacques. *Monks of Mt Athos.* 1960. London. 8vo. ils. 191 p. cloth. dj. O2. $30.00

VALENTINE, C.S. *How To Keep Hens for Profit.* 1910. Macmillan. 1st ed. 298 p. H10. $6.50

VALENTINE, D.T. *Manual of Corporation of City of NY.* 1864. NY. Edmund Jones. thick 12mo. facsimiles. bdg copy only. H9. $60.00

VALENTINE, Edward Uffington. *Hecla Sandwith.* 1905. Bobbs Merrill. 1st ed. 8vo. 433 p. VG. V3. $12.00

VALENZUELA, Luisa. *Lizard's Tail. A Novel.* 1983. NY. 1st Eng-language ed. sgn. NF/NF. A11. $45.00

VALENZUELA, Luisa. *Lizard's Trail. A Novel.* 1983. NY. FSG. 1st ed. trans from Spanish. F/F. A14. $25.00

VALERA, Helena. *Yanoama...Wht Girl Kidnapped by Amazonian Indians.* 1970. Dutton. 2nd prt. 8vo. 333 p. F/F. A2. $12.50

VALERIANI, Richard. *Travels w/Henry (Kissinger).* 1979. Houghton. 1st ed. VG/VG. V2. $6.00

VALERY, Paul. *Graveyard.* 1938. Vancouver, BC. quarto. trans/prt/inscr Sedgewick. tan buckram. F. rare. B24. $200.00

VALIER. *Alphabet Animals.* 1989. np. wrp. G2. $10.00

VALIN, Jonathan. *Day of Wrath.* 1982. Congdon Lattes. 1st ed. F/F. F4. $25.00

VALIN, Jonathan. *Extenuating Circumstances.* (1989). Delacorte. 1st ed. NF/dj. B9. $10.00

VALIN, Jonathan. *Life's Work.* 1986. Delacorte. 1st ed. F/F. F4. $25.00

VALIN, Jonathan. *Natural Causes.* (1983). Congdon Weed. 1st ed. VG+/dj. B9. $15.00

VALLADARES DE SOTOMAYOR, A. *Historia Geografica, Civil y Politica de la Isla...* 1789. Madrid. Antonio Espinosa. 1st ed. quarto. mottled calf. H9. $1,500.00

VALLEJO, Boris. *Fantastic Art of Boris Vallejo.* nd. BC. F/F. P3. $13.00

VALLENTIN, Antonina. *Drama of Albert Einstein.* 1954. Doubleday. photos Lotte Jacobi. 312 p. VG. S3. $30.00

VAN ALLSBURG, Chris. *Jumanji.* 1981. Houghton Mifflin. 1st ed. oblong 8vo. F/F. D1. $225.00

VAN ALLSBURG, Chris. *Mysteries of Harris Burdick.* 1984. Houghton Mifflin. 1st ed. 4to. brick cloth. F/G. T5. $45.00

VAN ALLSBURG, Chris. *Stranger.* 1986. Houghton Mifflin. 1st ed. oblong 8vo. bl cloth. NF/NF. D1. $85.00

VAN ANDEL, Tjeerd H. *Beyond the Acropolis.* 1987. Stanford. 8vo. 221 p. dj. O2. $25.00

VAN ASH, Cay. *Fires of Fu Manchu.* 1987. Harper Row. 1st ed. F/F. P3. $20.00

VAN ASH, Cay. *Ten Yrs Beyond Baker Street.* 1984. Harper Row. 1st ed. F/dj. P3. $30.00

VAN ATTA, Kim. *Account of Events Surrounding Origin of Friends Hospital...* 1976. Friends Hospital. 12mo. 32 p. F/prt gr wrp. G1. $17.50

VAN BERGEN, R. *Story of Japan.* 1897. Am Book Co. 1st ed. sm 8vo. 294 p. VG. W1. $18.00

VAN BRUINESSEN, Martin. *Agha, Shaikh & State. Social & Political Structure...* 1992. Atlantic Highlands. 8vo. 400 p. O2. $35.00

VAN DE GUCHTE, Maarten. *Masquerades & Demons.* 1992. Champaign, IL. Krannert Art Mus. 1st ed. 72 p. wrp. F3. $20.00

VAN DE WATER, F.F. *Capt Called It Mutiny.* (1954). NY. Washburn. 1st ed. sgn. 8vo. 236 p. VG+/VG+. A2. $25.00

VAN DE WATER, F.F. *Plunder.* 1933. Canadian Crime Club. VG/dj. P3. $15.00

VAN DE WETERING, Janwillem. *Blond Baboon.* 1978. Houghton Mifflin. 1st ed. VG/dj. P3. $20.00

VAN DE WETERING, Janwillem. *Blond Baboon.* 1978. London. Heinemann. 1st British ed. NF/dj. S5. $22.50

VAN DE WETERING, Janwillem. *Sergeant's Cat & Other Stories.* 1987. Pantheon. 1st ed. NF/dj. P3. $18.00

VAN DEN KEERE, Pieter. *Germania Inferior.* 1966. Amsterdam. Theatrvm Orbis Terrarvm. lg folio. M/M. O6. $175.00

VAN DER KROGT, Peter. *Old Globes in the Netherlands.* 1984. Utrecht. 80 photos. M/M. O6. $95.00

VAN DER MEER. *Majesty in Flight, Nature's Bird of Prey...* 1984. life-like pop-up birds. F. A4. $75.00

VAN DER MEER. *World's 1st Ever Pop-Up Games Book.* 1982. 4 action game brds. built-in wheels keep score. F. A4. $40.00

VAN DER POST, Laurens. *Race Prejudice As Self Rejection.* (1954). NY. Workshop for Cultural Democracy. 29-p pamphlet. A7. $25.00

VAN DINE, S.S. *Bishop Murder Case.* 1929. Scribner. 1st ed. VG. P3. $20.00

VAN DINE, S.S. *Canary Murder Case.* nd. Grosset Dunlap. VG/VG. P3. $23.00

VAN DINE, S.S. *Canary Murder Case.* nd (1927). Grosset Dunlap. photoplay ed. 343 p. blk cloth. VG. B22. $12.50

VAN DINE, S.S. *Casino Murder Case.* 1934. Scribner. 1st ed. F/VG. M15. $150.00

VAN DINE, S.S. *Casino Murder Case.* 1934. Scribner. 1st ed. VG. B9. $65.00

VAN DINE, S.S. *Dragon Murder Case.* 1933. Scribner. 1st ed. VG. P3. $35.00

VAN DINE, S.S. *Gracie Allen Murder Case.* 1938. Scribner. 1st ed. VG/dj. B9. $75.00

VAN DINE, S.S. *Greene Murder Case.* 1928. Scribner. 1st ed. VG. P3. $25.00

VAN DINE, S.S. *Kennel Murder Case.* 1933. Copp Clark. 1st Canadian ed. VG. P3. $35.00

VAN DINE, S.S. *Scarab Murder Case.* 1930. Scribner. 1st ed. VG. P3. $30.00

VAN DINE, S.S. *Winter Murder Case.* 1939. Scribner. 1st ed. VG/VG. M15. $175.00

VAN DOREN, Carl. *Benjamin Franklin.* 1938. NY. 1st/ltd ed. 1/625. sgn. 3 vols. VG+/slipcase. D7. $150.00

VAN DOREN, Carl. *Great Rehearsal: Story of Making & Ratifying Constitution...* 1948. Viking. BC. worn. M11. $30.00

VAN DOREN, Charles. *Letters to Mother: An Anthology.* 1959. Channel Pr. 1st Am ed. 350 p. NF/dj/clear plastic. M7. $22.50

VAN DOREN, Mark. *Witch of Ramoth & Other Tales.* 1950. Maple Pr. ltd ed. 1/1700. ils Eichenberg. aeg. VG. P2. $35.00

VAN DYKE, H.B. *Physiology & Pharmacology of the Pituitary Body.* 1936. Chicago. 1st ed. 577 p. NF. G7. $75.00

VAN DYKE, Henry. *First Christmas Tree.* 1897. Scribner. ils Pyle. 76 p. olive cloth. NF. B24. $75.00

VAN DYKE, Henry. *Fisherman's Luck.* 1899. NY. 1st ed. ils. 247 p. gilt cloth. A17. $15.00

VAN DYKE, Henry. *Little Rivers.* 1924. NY. later prt. 348 p. gilt cloth. A17. $12.50

VAN DYKE, Henry. *Mansion.* 1911. Harper. 45 p. VG. N2. $5.00

VAN DYKE, Henry. *Travel Diary of an Angler.* 1929. Derrydale. 1st ed. 1/750. 144 p. VG. M8. $250.00

VAN DYKE, John C. *Desert: Further Studies in Natural Appearances.* 1901. Scribner. 1st ed. NF. A18. $60.00

VAN DYKE, John C. *In the W Indies.* 1932. NY. 1st ed. 211 p. pict blk cloth. VG/VG. H3. $30.00

VAN DYKE, John Henry. *Blended Worlds.* 1927. Miama, AZ. 1st ed. 243 p. cloth. VG. D3. $75.00

VAN EVERY, Dale. *Men of the W States: Taking of Am's 1st W 1781-94.* 1956. Houghton Mifflin. 1st ed. 8vo. 244 p. F/VG. A2. $17.50

VAN EYS, W.J. *Bibliographie des Bibles et des Nouveaux Testaments...* 1900. Geneva. Kundig. 269 p. H10. $85.00

VAN GIESON, Judith. *Wolf Path.* 1992. Harper Collins. ARC of 1st ed. sgn. RS. F/F. S5. $45.00

VAN GOGH, Vincent. *Letters to an Artist.* 1936. Viking. 1st ed. 1/650. 4to. cloth. E3. $50.00

VAN GULIK, Robert. *Chinese Gold Murders.* 1959. Harper. 1st ed. xl. dj. P3. $20.00

VAN GULIK, Robert. *Chinese Nail Murders.* 1961. NY. Harper. 1st Am ed. NF/NF. M15. $45.00

VAN GULIK, Robert. *Lacquer Screen.* 1969. Scribner. 1st ed. NF/dj. P3. $50.00

VAN GULIK, Robert. *Monkey & the Tiger.* 1965. London. Heinemann. 1st ed. F/F. M15. $85.00

VAN GULIK, Robert. *Murder in Canton.* 1967. Scribner. 1st ed. VG/VG. P3. $75.00

VAN HORNE, John C. *Correspondence of William Nelson As Acting Governor of VA...* 1975. VA U. 176 p. VG. B10. $35.00

VAN HORNE, Thomas Budd. *Hist of the Army of the Cumberland.* 1875. Cincinnati. Clarke. 1st ed. 3 vols. cloth. VG. M8. $450.00

VAN LENNEP, Henry J. *Oriental Album.* 1862. NY. ADF Randolph. folio. 20 chromolithos. 48 p. pict red cloth. G. B14. $400.00

VAN LHIN, E. *Battle on Mercury.* 1953. Winston. 1st ed. VG/dj. M2. $45.00

VAN LHIN, E. *Police Your Planet.* 1956. Avalon. xl. dj. P3. $10.00

VAN LOON, Hendrik Willem. *Romance of Discovery.* ca 1917. NY. Carlton House. 8vo. ils. 1226 p. gr cloth. dj. H9. $45.00

VAN MILLINGEN, Alexander. *Byzantine Constantinople: Walls of the City...Sites.* 1899. London. 8vo. ils. 361 p. cloth. O2. $250.00

VAN NOSTRAND, Leane. *First Hundred Yrs of Painting in CA 1775-1875...* 1980. San Francisco. Howell. 1st ed. folio. ils. 135 p. F/dj. B20. $75.00

VAN PRAGG, Francis. *Clayton Howell.* 1901. Toronto. 12mo. 304 p. gilt pict cloth. F. H3. $12.00

VAN PUYVELDE, Leo. *Flemish Drawings in Collection of His Majesty the King...* 1942. Phaedon/Oxford. 1st Am ed. 4to. F/fair. A2. $35.00

VAN RAVENSWAAY, Charles. *Drawn From Nature: Botanical Art of Joseph Prestele...* 1984. Smithsonian. 95 color pls. 357 p. brds. D2. $35.00

VAN RENSSELAER, Maunsell. *Trees of Santa Barbara.* 1940. Santa Barbara. 1st ed. ils. 141 p. cloth. NF/rpr dj. D3. $25.00

VAN RENSSELAER, Maunsell. *Trees of Santa Barbara.* 1948. Santa Barbara. Botanical Gardens. revised ed. 213 p. F. B19. $10.00

VAN RIPER, Guernsey. *Babe Ruth: Baseball Boy.* 1954. Bobbs Merrill. 1st ed. VG/G. P2. $25.00

VAN RIPER, Guernsey. *Behind the Plate.* 1973. Garrard. 1st ed. ils/photos. F. P8. $10.00

VAN RIPER, Guernsey. *Joy in Mudville.* 1970. McCall. 1st ed. VG. P8. $15.00

VAN RIPER, P.P. *Hist of the US Civil Service.* (1958). Evanston. Row Peterson. 588 p. A7. $12.00

VAN SCYOC, Sydney J. *Starmother.* 1976. Berkley Putnam. 1st ed. xl. dj. P3. $8.00

VAN SICKLE, Dirck. *Montana Gothic.* 1979. HBJ. 1st ed. VG/dj. P3. $20.00

VAN SINDEREN, Adrian. *Isthmus Maximus.* 1948. NY. private prt. 8vo. ils/photos. 68 p. map ep. VG/VG slipcase. B11. $45.00

VAN STOCKUM, Hilda. *King Oberon's Forest.* 1957. Viking. 1st ed. 151 p. VG+/VG. P2. $25.00

VAN TRAMP, John C. *Prairie & Rocky Mtn Adventures...* 1866. Columbus. Gilmore Segner. 649 p. gilt blk leather. G. H7. $40.00

VAN VECHTEN, Carl. *Nigger Heaven.* nd. Grosset Dunlap. VG/VG-. P3. $30.00

VAN VECHTEN, Carl. *Red. Papers on Musical Subjects.* 1925. Knopf. 1st ed. 205 p. VG/dj. M20. $35.00

VAN VEEN, Ted. *Rhododendrons in Am.* 1969. Portland. 1st ed. sgn. 176 p. VG+/worn. B26. $37.50

VAN VOGT, A.E. *Destination: Universe.* 1952. Pelligrini Cudahy. 1st ed. VG/dj. P3. $35.00

VAN VOGT, A.E. *House That Stood Still.* 1950. Greenberg. 2nd ed. VG/VG. P3. $25.00

VAN VOGT, A.E. *Secret Galactics.* 1975. London. Sidgwick Jackson. 1st Eng/1st hc ed. F/F. T2. $68.00

VAN VOGT, A.E. *Slan.* 1946. Arkham. 1st ed. VG/dj. M2. $150.00

VAN VOGT, A.E. *Slan.* 1951. Simon Schuster. 2nd ed. VG/VG. P3. $35.00

VAN VOGT, A.E. *Three Eyes of Evil.* 1973. Sidgwick Jackson. NF/dj. P3. $20.00

VAN VOGT, A.E. *Voyage of the Space Beagle.* 1950. Simon Schuster. 1st ed. VG/dj. P3. $125.00

VAN VOGT, A.E. *Weapon Makers.* 1952. Greenberg. VG/dj. P3. $55.00

VAN VOGT, A.E. *Winged Man.* 1966. Doubleday. 1st ed. xl. dj. P3. $10.00

VAN WAGENEN, Jared Jr. *Cow.* 1922. Macmillan. 1st ed. ils/index. 153 p. H10. $17.50

VANCE, Jack. *Araminta Station.* 1988. Tor. 1st ed. F/dj. P3. $25.00

VANCE, Jack. *Augmented Agent.* 1986. Underwood Miller. 1/200. sgn. as new. M2. $65.00

VANCE, Jack. *Big Planet.* 1978. Underwood Miller. 1st ed. NF/dj. P3. $40.00

VANCE, Jack. *Eight Fantasms & Magics.* 1969. Macmillan. 1st ed. xl. dj. P3. $15.00

VANCE, Jack. *Emphyrio.* 1969. Doubleday. 1st ed. VG/dj. M2. $150.00

VANCE, Jack. *Eyes of the Overworld.* 1977. Underwood Miller. 1st ed. sgn. VG/dj. P3. $45.00

VANCE, Jack. *Languages of Pao.* 1958. Avalon. 1st ed. F/dj. P3. $450.00

VANCE, Jack. *Man in the Cage.* 1983. Underwood Miller. 1/200. sgn. as new. M2. $50.00

VANCE, Jack. *Maske: Thaery.* 1976. Putnam. 1st ed. xl. dj. P3. $12.00

VANCE, Jack. *Showboat World.* 1983. Underwood Miller. 1st ed. F/dj. M2. $25.00

VANCE, Jack. *Trullion.* 1984. Shasta. 1st hc ed. as new. M2. $25.00

VANCE, Jack. *Vandals of the Void.* 1953. Winston. 1st ed. VG/color Canon dj. M2. $100.00

VANCE, John Holbrook. *Fox Valley Murders.* 1966. Bobbs Merrill. 1st ed. NF/dj. P3. $175.00

VANCE, Louis Joseph. *Dead Ride Hard.* 1926. Copp Clarke. 1st ed. VG. P3. $18.00

VANCE, Louis Joseph. *Red Masquerade.* 1921. Doubleday Page. VG. P3. $18.00

VANDE VELDE, Vivian. *Dragon's Bait.* 1992. HBJ. 1st ed. F/F. P3. $17.00

VANDER LECK, Lawrence. *Petroleum Resources of CA.* 1921. Sacramento. 1st ed. ils/photos. lacks 6 pocket maps. cloth. VG. D3. $25.00

VANDERBIE, Jan H. *Prov-Rep Vietnam.* (1970). Dorrance. 1st ed. inscr. VG/VG. B4. $85.00

VANDERCOOK, John W. *Murder in Haiti.* nd. BC. VG/VG. P3. $8.00

VANDERVEER, Helen. *Little Slam Bang.* 1928. Volland. 1st ed. ils Fletcher Cranson. gr cloth. VG. M5. $35.00

VANEGAS, Miguel. *Natural & Civil Hist of CA.* 1759. London. Rivington. 1st Eng ed. 2 vols. new half morocco. H9. $700.00

VANGER, Milton. *Jose Batlle y Ordonez of Uruguay.* 1963. Cambridge. Harvard. 1st ed. 320 p. dj. F3. $20.00

VANSTORY, Burnette. *GA's Land of the Golden Isles.* (1956). GA U. 1st ed. sgn. 202 p. dj. A17. $10.00

VARDRE, Leslie. *Nameless Ones.* 1967. John Long. VG/dj. P3. $15.00

VARE, Danielle. *Last Empress.* 1938. Doubleday Doran. 8vo. ils/pls. 320 p. VG. W1. $18.00

VARGAS LLOSA, Mario. *Aunt Julia & the Scriptwriter.* 1983. London. Faber. 1st ed. trans from Spanish. F/F. A14. $30.00

VARGAS LLOSA, Mario. *In Praise of the Stepmother.* 1990. FSG. 1st ed. trans from Spanish. F/F. A14. $25.00

VARGAS LLOSA, Mario. *Perpetual Orgy: Flaubert & Madame Bovary.* 1986. FSG. 1st ed. F/F clip. A14. $40.00

VARGAS LLOSA, Mario. *War of the End of the World.* 1984. FSG. 1st ed. trans from Spanish. F/F. A14. $50.00

VARGAS LLOSA, Mario. *Who Killed Palomino Molero?* 1987. FSG. 1st ed. F/F. A14. $30.00

VARLAY, Rene. *Lollipop Songs.* 1962. HRW. 1st ed. ils Jeanne Owens. w/33⅓rpm record. VG+/G. P2. $20.00

VARLEY, John. *Ophiuchi Hotline.* 1977. Dial. 1st ed. VG/dj. P3. $20.00

VARLEY, John. *Steel Beach.* 1992. NY. Ace. 1st ed. F/F. N3. $20.00

VARLEY, John. *Titan.* 1979. Berkley Putnam. 1st ed. VG/dj. P3. $23.00

VARLEY, John. *Wizard.* 1980. Berkley Putnam. 1st ed. NF/dj. M2. $65.00

VARLEY, John. *Wizard.* 1980. Berkley Putnam. 2nd ed. VG/dj. P3. $13.00

VASARELY, Victor. *Le Cheval Meurt les Oiseaux s'Envolent.* 1971. Paris. Margana. 1st ed. octavo. unbound. w/sgn Vasarely pl. F/wrp/glassine. B24. $850.00

VASSILYEV, A.T. *Ochrana. Russian Secret Police.* 1930. Phil. 1st ed. 305 p. VG. H3. $40.00

VASSOS, Ruth. *Ultimo.* 1930. Dutton. 1st ed. ils John Vassos. sgns/presentation to Max Miller. VG+. B20. $225.00

VAUGHAN, Agnes C. *House of the Double Axe.* 1959. NY. 1st ed. 8vo. 240 p. gilt bdg. F/VG. H3. $25.00

VAUGHAN, Henry W. *Types & Market Classes of Livestock.* 1948. Columbus. College Book Co. ils/index. 606 p. H10. $17.50

VAUGHAN, Matthew. *Discretion of Dominick Ayres.* 1976. Atlantic/Little Brn. 1st ed. VG/VG. P3. $18.00

VAVRA, Robert. *Romany Free.* 1977. Reynal. 1st ed. ils Fleur Cowles. F/NF. P2. $18.00

VAWTER & VAWTER. *Of Such Is the Kingdom.* 1899. Bowen Merrill. 15 short stories & poems. 192 p. cloth. VG. A3. $20.00

VEECK, Bill. *Hustler's Handbook.* 1965. Putnam. 1st ed. VG+/VG. P2. $65.00

VEECK, Bill. *Veeck As in Wreck.* 1962. Putnam. 1st ed. sgn. VG+/VG. P8. $200.00

VEITH, Ilza. *Huang Ti Nei Ching Su Wen...* 1970 (1949). Berkeley. 260 p. VG/dj. G1. $40.00

VENABLES, Bernard. *Baleia! Baleia! Whale Hunters of the Azores.* 1969 (1968). Knopf. 1st Am ed. 8vo. 204 p. VG/VG. A2. $15.00

VENABLES, Hubert. *Frankenstein Diaries.* 1980. Viking. 1st ed. VG/dj. P3. $20.00

VENDLER, Helen. *Music of What Happens: Poems, Poets & Critics.* 1988. Harvard. 1st ed. F/F. V1. $15.00

VENTRIS, Peyton. *Reports of Sir Peyton Ventris K...* 1726. Savoy. Nutt/Gosling. folio. modern cloth/red morocco spine label. K1. $250.00

VENTURI, Lionelo. *Brunori.* 1958. Italy. inscr/sgn. VG/VG wrp. A1. $50.00

VERBRUGGE, Frank. *Whither Thou Goest. Life of Jacobus & Maria Verbrugge...* 1979. Minneapolis. MN U. 8vo. 120 p. gr cloth. B11. $30.00

VERCORS. *Battle of Silence.* 1969. HRW. 1st ed. VG/VG. P3. $20.00

VERCORS. *You Shall Know Them.* 1953. McClelland Stewart. 1st ed. NF/dj. P3. $15.00

VERDIER, Jean. *Calendrier des Amateurs de la Vie et de l'Humanite...* 1816. Paris. Chez l'Auter. 168 p. orig wrp. G7. $135.00

VERHOOG, P. *Guanahani Again: Landfall of Columbus in 1492.* 1947. Amsterdam. presentation to SE Morison w/his intl. NF/stiff wrp. O6. $45.00

VERITE, Marcelle. *Alphabet Pour les Tout Petites.* 1947. Belgique. De Brouwer. ils Boland. gilt cloth. NF. D1. $135.00

VERITE, Marcelle. *Alphabet Pour les Tout Petites.* 1947. De Brouwer. ils Josette Boland. pict brds. VG. M5. $85.00

VERMA, Bhagwati Sharan. *Socio-Religious, Economic & Literary Conditions of Bihar.* 1962. Delhi. Munshi Ram Manohar Lal. 1st ed. 8vo. 21 pls. VG/dj. W1. $20.00

VERNE, Jules. *Annotated Jules Verne.* (1976). Crowell. 1st ed. 4to. NF/dj. A7. $25.00

VERNE, Jules. *Five Weeks in a Balloon.* nd. Ward Lock. Rainbow series. decor brds. VG. P3. $25.00

VERNE, Jules. *From the Earth to the Moon...* 1874. Scribner Armstrong. 1st Am ed. 80 full-p ils. 132 p. G. B14. $40.00

VERNE, Jules. *Hector Servadac.* 1905. Scribner. VG. P3. $35.00

VERNE, Jules. *La Rayon-Vert.* nd. Bibliotheque. French text. VG. P3. $35.00

VERNE, Jules. *Les Enfants du Capitane Grant.* 1977. La Galaxie. French text. VG. P3. $10.00

VERNE, Jules. *Michael Strogoff.* 1940. Book League of Am. G. P3. $8.00

VERNE, Jules. *Mirifiques Adventures de Maitre Antifer.* ca 1870. np. Hetzel. ils G Roux. 2 color maps. modern cloth/orig cloth laid-on bdg. VG. M18. $100.00

VERNE, Jules. *Round the World in 80 Days.* nd. Collins. VG/VG-. P3. $15.00

VERNE, Jules. *Secret of the Island.* 1914. Dent. 3rd ed. VG. P3. $30.00

VERNE, Jules. *Tour of the World in 80 Days.* nd. AL Burt. VG/VG-. P3. $20.00

VERNE, Jules. *20,000 Leagues Under the Sea.* nd. Rand McNally. Windemere Series. ils Milo Winter. blk cloth. VG-. S10. $20.00

VERNE, Jules. *20,000 Leagues Under the Sea.* 1936. Scribner. ils Aylward. VG. L1. $35.00

VERNE, Jules. *20,000 Leagues Under the Sea.* 1940. Book League of Am. VG-. P3. $12.00

VERNER, Coolie. *Northpart of Am.* 1979. Toronto. Academic Pr of Canada. 1/1500. 291 p. M/slipcase. P4. $450.00

VERNER, Coolie. *Smith's VA & Its Derivatives.* 1968. London. Map Collectors Circle. 8vo. 40 p. wrp. H9. $35.00

VERNON, Arthur. *Hist & Romance of the Horse.* (1939). Boston. 1st ed. ils. 525 p. buckram. NF. D3. $45.00

VERNON, Paul E. *Coast to Coast by Motor.* 1930. London/NY. 1st ed. 8 color pls/fld map. VG. B28. $40.00

VERNON-HARCOURT, L.F. *Rivers & Canals...Flow, Control & Improvement...* 1986. Clarendon. 2nd ed. 2 vols. gilt cloth. NF. A17. $75.00

VERRILL, A. Hyatt. *Boys' Book of Buccaneers.* 1927. Dodd Mead. VG-. P3. $12.00

VERRILL, A. Hyatt. *Bridge of Light.* 1950. Fantasy. 1st ed. NF/dj. P3. $40.00

VERRILL, A. Hyatt. *Great Conquerors of S & Central Am.* 1943. New Home Lib. 389 p. dj. F3. $15.00

VERRILL, A. Hyatt. *Our Indians. Story of Indians of the US.* (1935). NY. 1st ed. ils. 285 p. cloth. VG. D3. $25.00

VERRILL, A. Hyatt. *Real Story of the Pirate.* 1923. NY. 1st ed. ils. 374 p. pict blk cloth. F. H3. $30.00

VERRILL, A. Hyatt. *Treasure of Bloody Gut.* 1937. Putnam. 1st ed. F/dj. M2. $95.00

VESTAL, Stanley. *Jim Bridger, Mtn Man.* 1946. NY. 1st ed. ils/maps. 333 p. cloth. VG. D3. $25.00

VESTAL, Stanley. *Joe Meek: Merry Mtn Man.* 1952. Caxton. 1st ed. 8vo. 336 p. VG/VG. A2. $65.00

VESTER, Bertha S. *Flowers of the Holy Land.* 1966 (1962). KS City. new ed/4th prt. ils. F/dj. B26. $12.50

VETERANS OF FOREIGN WARS. *Pictorial: War in the Pacific.* 1951. Veterans Hist. 8vo. VG. A8. $7.00

VETHAKE, Henry. *Dictionary Practical...Commerce & Commercial Navigation.* 1841 & 1842. Phil. 2 vols. rebound. B30. $50.00

VIBERT. *Angelsong.* 1989. np. ils. wrp. G2. $12.00

VICARION, Palmiro. *Book of Limericks.* 1956. Paris. Olympia. 1st ed. VG+/ils wrp. A11. $55.00

VICKERS, Roy. *Dept of Dead Ends.* 1947. Spivak. 1st ed. VG/wrp. B2. $50.00

VICKERS, Roy. *Shadow Over Fairholme.* 1940. London. Jenkins. 1st ed. VG/dj. M15. $50.00

VICTOR, Frances Fuller. *River of the W: Adventures of Joe Meek.* 1983. Mtn Pr. 1st ed. 2 vols. sgn. M/djs. A18. $50.00

VICTORIUS FAVENTINUS, L. *Practica Medicinalis...* 1544. Lyon. Vincentium. 2 parts in 1. 16mo. early gilt calf. K1. $500.00

VIDAL, Gore. *Dark Gr, Bright Red.* 1950. Dutton. 1st ed. VG+/VG+. A14. $150.00

VIDAL, Gore. *Death Likes It Hot.* 1979. London. 2nd British imp. NF/NF. A14. $25.00

VIDAL, Gore. *Julian.* 1964. Little Brn. 1st ed. NF/VG. A14. $30.00

VIDAL, Gore. *Kalki.* (1978). Franklin Lib. true 1st ed. F. B3. $50.00

VIDAL, Gore. *Kalki.* 1978. Random. 1st ed. rem mk. NF/NF. A14. $25.00

VIDAL, Gore. *Kalki.* 1978. Random. 1st ed. VG/VG. P3. $20.00

VIDAL, Gore. *Lincoln.* 1984. BC. VG/dj. C1. $4.00

VIDAL, Gore. *Messiah.* 1980. Gregg/GK Hall. reissue. Gregg SF series. intro EA Lynn. NF/sans. A14. $30.00

VIDAL, Gore. *Myron.* 1974. Random. 1st ed. NF/NF clip. A14. $25.00

VIDAL, Gore. *Myron.* 1974. Random. 1st ed. VG/dj. P3. $15.00

VIDAL, Gore. *Reflections Upon a Sinking Ship.* 1969. Little Brn. 1st ed. NF/NF clip. A14. $35.00

VIDAL, Gore. *Season of Discomfort.* 1949. Dutton. 1st ed. VG/dj. M18. $65.00

VIDAL, Gore. *Two Sisters: Novel in Form of Memoir.* 1970. Little Brn. 1st ed. NF/VG+. A14. $25.00

VIDAVER, H. *Book of Life: Complete Formula of Service & Ceremonies...* 1893. NY. 194 p. G+. S3. $40.00

VIERECK, George. *My Flesh & Blood.* 1931. NY. 1st ed. sgn. VG/G. B5. $25.00

VIERECK, Peter. *Archer in the Marrow.* 1987. NY. 1st ed. sgn. F/F. V1. $45.00

VIETZEN, Raymond. *Sittin' on a Stump.* (1968). Elyria, OH. 150 p. VG-/ils wrp. B18. $22.50

VIEUSSEUX, A. *Hist of Switzerland From Irruption of Barbarians...* 1840. London. 1st ed. 352 p. gilt red cloth. VG. H3. $50.00

VIGTEL, Gudmund. *100 Yrs of Painting in GA.* ca 1992. Alston Bird. ils. 109 p. F/F. B10. $25.00

VILDRAC, Charles. *Rose Island.* 1957. Lee Shepard. probable 1st ed. ils Edy Legrand. rose cloth. VG/G+. T5. $30.00

VILLA, Guido. *Contemporary Psychology.* 1903. Swan Sonnenschein. 1st Eng ed. xl. 396 p. G1. $35.00

VILLANO, Anthony. *Brick Agent.* 1977. Quadrangle. 1st ed. F/dj. P3. $15.00

VILLARREAL, Jose Antonio. *Fifth Horseman.* 1974. Doubleday. 1st ed. rem mk. NF/VG+. A14. $25.00

VILLARS, Jean Beraud. *TE Lawrence; or, Search for the Absolute.* (1959). DSP. 358 p. dj. A7. $15.00

VILLASENOR, David. *Tapestries in Sand: Spirit of Indian Sand Painting.* ca 1966. Happy Camp. Naturegraph Pub. 112 p. VG/stiff wrp. P4. $30.00

VILLASENOR, Edmundo. *Macho!* 1973. Bantam. PBO. inscr. F/ils wrp. A11. $55.00

VILLIERS, Alan. *Cruise of the Conrad, a Journal of a Voyage Round the World.* 1937. Scribner. 1st ed. lg 8vo. 387 p. VG. W1. $35.00

VILLIERS, Alan. *Grain Race.* 1933. NY. 1st ed. 8vo. 331 p. gilt gr cloth. VG. H3. $20.00

VILLIERS, Alan. *Whalers of the Midnight Sun.* 1934. NY. 1st ed. 8vo. map ep. pict tan cloth. G+. H3. $20.00

VILLIERS, Elizabeth. *Love Stories of Eng Queens.* (1924). London. Stanley Paul. 1st ed. 12mo. 255 p. VG/VG. A2. $25.00

VILLOLDO, Alberto. *Four Winds. Shaman's Odyssey Into the Amazon.* (1990). Harper. 1st ed. 265 p. dj. F3. $20.00

VINCE, Jospeh. *Fencing.* (1940). NY. 12th prt. ils/index. 62 p. dj. A17. $8.50

VINCENT, Clovis. *Des Meningites Chroniques Syphilitiques. Lesions...* 1910. Paris. Steinheil. presentation/sgn. NF. G7. $395.00

VINCENT, Florance Smith. *Peter's Adventures in Birdland.* 1922. NY. 8vo. ils. pict brn cloth. VG. H3. $15.00

VINCENT, Frank. *In & Out of Central Am & Other Sketches & Studies of Travel.* 1890. NY. Appleton. 1st ed. 12mo. 16 pls/2 color maps. 246 p. gilt gr brds. VG. B11. $70.00

VINCENT, Thomas M. *Abraham Lincoln & Edwin M Stanton.* 1892. WA, DC. 1st ed. 35 p. prt wrp. M8. $37.50

VINCENZ, Stanislaw. *On the High Uplands: Sagas, Songs, Tales...Carpathians.* (1955). NY. Roy. 1st Am ed. 8vo. 344 p. VG+/VG-. A2. $30.00

VINE, Barbara; see Rendell, Ruth.

VINECOUR, Earl. *Polish Jews: Final Chapter.* 1977. McGraw Hill. sm 4to. 100 photos. 121 p. VG/wrp. S3. $23.00

VINGE, Joan D. *Alien Blood.* nd. BC. VG/VG. P3. $10.00

VINGE, Joan D. *Outcasts of Heaven Belt.* 1981. Sidgwick Jackson. 1st ed. F/F. P3. $25.00

VINGE, Joan D. *Phoenix in the Ashes.* 1985. Bluejay. 1st ed. VG/dj. P3. $20.00

VINGE, Joan D. *Return of the Jedi Storybook.* nd. Random. 6th ed. VG. P3. $8.00

VINGE, Joan D. *Summer Queen.* (1991). Time Warner. AP. VG/prt yel wrp. B3. $40.00

VINGE, Joan D. *World's End.* 1984. Bluejay. 1st ed. VG/dj. P3. $20.00

VINGE, Vernor. *Marooned in Realtime.* 1986. Bluejay. F/dj. P3. $20.00

VINGE, Vernor. *Peace War.* 1984. Bluejay. 1st ed. F/dj. P3. $20.00

VINGE, Vernor. *Wilting.* 1976. Dobson. 1st ed. F/dj. P3. $35.00

VINING, Elizabeth Gray. *Cheerful Heart.* 1959. Viking. 3rd ed. 8vo. 176 p. VG. V3. $7.50

VINING, Elizabeth Gray. *I, Roberta.* 1967. Lippincott. 2nd ed. 8vo. 224 p. worn dj. V3. $9.50

VINING, Elizabeth Gray. *Taken Girl.* (1972). Viking. 1st ed/3rd prt. 8vo. 190 p. VG. T5. $20.00

VINING, Elizabeth Gray. *Young Walter Scott.* 1953 (1935). Viking. 10th prt. 239 p. NF/VG. A3. $7.50

VINSON, Michael. *Motoring Tourists & Scenic W.* 1989. Dallas, TX. S Methodist U. 1/1500. sgn. ils/pls. wrp. H9. $30.00

VIOLA, Herman J. *After Columbus.* 1990. Orion. 1st ed. F/F. P3. $45.00

VIOLA, Herman J. *Exploring the W.* 1987. Smithsonian. 4to. ils. 256 p. brn cloth. dj. H9. $45.00

VIOLA, Herman J. *Indian Legacy of Charles Bird King.* 1976. Doubleday. 152 p. cloth. dj. D2. $65.00

VIOLANTI, Anthony. *Miracle in Buffalo.* 1991. St Martin. 1st ed. M/M. P8. $12.50

VIPONT, Elfrida. *Lark on the Wing.* 1951. Bobbs Merrill. 8vo. 255 p. VG/tattered. V3. $12.00

VIPONT, Elfrida. *Story of Quakerism.* 1955. London. Bannisdale. 3rd prt. 8vo. 312 p. VG/dj. V3. $20.00

VIRCHOW, Rudolf. *Cellular Pathology...* nd. NY. RM DeWitt. 7th Am ed. trans Frank Chance. woodcuts/ads. rebacked. B14. $75.00

VIRCHOW, Rudolf. *Die Cellularpathologie in Begrundung Physiologische...* 1858. Berlin. August Hirshwald. ils. 440 p. cloth. clamshell box. G7. $3,500.00

VIRCHOW, Rudolf. *Krankhaften Geschulste. Dreisig Voresungen Gehalten...* 1863-67. Berlin. 1st ed. xl. 3 vols. 243 woodcuts/2 copper pls. G. rare. G7. $1,250.00

VIRCHOW, Rudolf. *Sammulung Gemeinvestaendlicher Wissenschaftlicher Vortraege.* 1867. Berlin. quarter sheep. G7. $115.00

VIRDEN, Katharine. *Thing in the Night.* 1930. Crime Club. 1st ed. VG. P3. $25.00

VIRGIL. *Arneid of Virgil.* 1991. Donald Grant. 1st ed. F/sans. P3. $35.00

VIRGONA, Hank. *System Works!* 1977. NY. Da Capo. 4to. NF/dj. A7. $15.00

VISCOTT, David S. *Dorchester Boy: Portrait of Psychiatrist As Very Young Man.* 1973. Arbor House. 250 p. VG/dj. G1. $19.00

VISINTIN, Luigi. *Atlante Geografico Metodico.* 1935. Novarra. Instituto Geografico de Agostini. 69 maps. NF. O6. $85.00

VISSCHER, William Lightfoot. *Pony Express; or, Blazing the W Way.* 1908. Chicago. Rand McNally. 1st ed. tall 8vo. 98 p. VG. scarce. H7. $65.00

VISSCHER, William Lightfoot. *Thrilling & Truthful Hist of the Pony Express...* 1908. Chicago. Rand McNally. 1st ed. sm 4to. 98 p. O3. $58.00

VISSER, H.F.E. *Asiatic Art.* 1948. Spieghel. 1st ed. folio. pls. 411 p. VG/dj. W1. $65.00

VISSER, Margaret. *Much Depends on Dinner.* 1987. Grove. 1st ed. VG/dj. A16. $10.00

VITRY, Paul. *French Sculpture During the Reign of St Louis 1226-70.* (1938). Florence. Pantheon. 1st ed. sm folio. gray cloth. F/dj. K1. $250.00

VITTORINI, Elio. *In Sicily.* (1949). New Directions. 1st ed. intro Ernest Hemingway. VG. E3. $15.00

VIVIAN, H. Hussey. *Notes on a Tour in Am. From Aug 7th to Nov 17, 1877.* 1877. London. Stanford. 8vo. fld map. 260 p. H9. $140.00

VIZENOR, Gerald Robert. *Bearheart.* 1978. St Paul. Truck Pr. 1st ed. NF/wrp. L3. $65.00

VIZENOR, Gerald Robert. *Dead Voices.* 1992. OK U. 1st ed. sgn. F/F. L3. $50.00

VIZENOR, Gerald Robert. *Trickster of Liberty.* 1981. MN U. ARC. F/wrp. L3. $45.00

VIZENOR, Gerald Robert. *Two Wings the Butterfly.* 1962. St Cloud. private prt. 1st ed. NF/VG. L3. $375.00

VIZENOR, Gerald Robert. *Wordarrows. Indians & Whts in New Fur Trade.* 1978. MN U. 1st/hc ed. F/NF. L3. $125.00

VIZETELLY, Henry. *Hist Champagne w/Notes on Other Sparkling Wines of France.* 1980 (1888). np. reprint of 1888 London ed. lg 4to. gilt cloth. G7. $95.00

VIZETELLY, Henry. *Hist of Champagne w/Notes on Other Sparkling Wines...* 1882. London. self pub. 1st ed. ils. 263 p. pict cloth. H10. $150.00

VLADISLAV, Jan. *Italian Fairy Tales.* 1971. Hamlyn. VG. P3. $12.00

VLEKKE, B. *Story of the Dutch E Indies.* 1945. Cambridge, MA. 1st ed. 8vo. 233 p. F/VG. A2. $15.00

VOGE, Hervey. *Climber's Guide to the High Sierra...* (1961). Sierra Club. 3rd prt. 12mo. 301 p. cloth. F/dj. D3. $15.00

VOGEL, Ilse-Margaret. *Farewell, Aunt Isabell.* 1979. Harper Row. 1st ed. 8vo. 54 p. VG/G. T5. $25.00

VOGEL, Leo F. *Yrs Plowed Under.* 1977. U Pr. 1st ed. sgn. 167 p. NF/wrp. B19. $12.50

VOGT, Ragnar. *Den Freudske Psykoanalyse...* 1930. Oslo. Gydendal Norsk Forlag. 101 p. VG/prt brn wrp. G1. $37.50

VOGUE. *Hook Knitting, New Concepts in Crochet.* 1986. Vogue. pb. ils. G2. $12.00

VOIGHT, David Quentin. *Am Baseall: From Gentleman's Sport to Commissioner System.* 1966. Norman, OK. 1st ed. F/VG+. P8. $50.00

VOIGHT, David Quentin. *Am Through Baseball.* 1976. Nelson Hall. 1st ed. VG+/VG+. P8. $30.00

VOINOVICH, Vladimir. *Life & Extraordinary Adventures of Private Ivan Chonkin.* 1977. London. Cape. 1st Eng ed of 1969 German ed. NF/NF clip. A14. $20.00

VOISIN, Felix. *Causes Morales et Physiques des Maladies Mentales...* 1826. Paris. Bailliere. 418 p. orig prt wrp. G. G7. $250.00

VOISIN, Jules. *L'Epilepsie.* 1897. Paris. Bailliere. 420 p. orig wrp bdg in new brds. G7. $125.00

VOLBORTH, J. Ivaloo. *Thunder-Root. Traditional & Contemporary Native Am Verse.* 1978. UCLA. 1st ed. ils Daniel Owen Stolpe. F/stapled wrp. L3. $45.00

VOLLMAN, William T. *Afghanistan Picture Show.* 1992. Farrar. 1st ed. F/NF. B2. $35.00

VOLLMAN, William T. *Convict Bird.* 1987. San Francisco. CoTangent. 1/100 (1/10 sgn). human hair bookmark. steel bdg. L3. $7,500.00

VOLLMAN, William T. *Rainbow Stories.* 1989. Atheneum. ARC/1st Am ed. author's 2nd book. F/F. L3. $125.00

VOLLMAN, William T. *Whores for Gloria.* (1991). Pantheon. 1st ed. F/F. B3/M18. $40.00

VOLLMAN, William T. *Whores for Gloria.* (1991). Pantheon. 1st ed. sgn. F/F. B4. $75.00

VOLLMAN, William T. *You Bright & Risen Angels.* 1987. Atheneum. ARC/1st Am ed. sgn. RS. F/dj. B4. $250.00

VOLLMAN, William T. *You Bright & Risen Angels.* 1987. Atheneum. 1st Am ed. mk Not for Resale. NF/NF. B2. $100.00

VOLTAIRE, Jean Francois. *Candide & Other Romances.* 1928. John Lane/Bodley Head. 1st prt. trans/intro Richard Aldington. NF/VG+. A14. $75.00

VOLTAIRE, Jean Francois. *Candide; or, Optimism.* 1973. LEC. ils/sgn May Neama. F/slipcase. M18. $85.00

VOLTAIRE, Jean Francois. *Pucelle d'Orleans.* 1775. A Londres. octavo. 24 pls. contemporary French morocco. H5. $1,500.00

VON BALTHASAR, Hans Urs. *Glory of the Lord: Theology of Aesthetics. Vol 1.* ca 1982. San Francisco. Ignatius Pr. 691 p. H10. $25.00

VON BALTHASAR, Hans Urs. *Science, Religion & Christianity.* ca 1958. London. Burns Oates. 155 p. H10. $17.50

VON BALTHASAR, Hans Urs. *Theology of Karl Barth.* ca 1971. NY. HRW. 323 p. H10. $35.00

VON BALTHASAR, Hans Urs. *Word & Redemption.* ca 1964. NY. Herder. xl. 191 p. H10. $15.00

VON BAMBERGER, Heinrich. *Lehrbuch der Krankheiten des Herzens.* 1857. Vienna. Braumuller. 459 p. marbled brds/rebacked quarter calf. G7. $595.00

VON BREYDENBACH, Bernhard. *Die Reise ins Heilige Land.* 1977. Wiesbaden. 1/1000. folio. 56 p. cloth. dj. O2. $75.00

VON DANIKEN, Erich. *According to the Evidence.* 1977. Souvenir. 1st ed. VG/dj. P3. $20.00

VON DANIKEN, Erich. *Chariots of the Gods?* nd. Laffont. VG. P3. $15.00

VON DER PORTEN, Edward. *German Navy in WWII.* 1969. NY. Galahad. VG/dj. A16. $15.00

VON DER VOGELWEIDE, Walther. *Stroke Upon the Sea.* 1984. Toronto. Aliquando. 1/85. trans/sgn Schreiber. ils/sgn Rueter. w/suite pls. case. B24. $350.00

VON ECKARDT, Hans. *Ivan the Terrible.* 1949. Knopf. 1st ed. 8vo. 421 p. F/F. A2. $25.00

VON GEHUCHTEN, A. *Contributions a l'Etude Des Ganglions Cereb Ro-Spinaux.* 1892. Bruxelles. author's offprint. 40 p. w/presentation note. G7. $65.00

VON GOETHE, Johann Wolfgang. *Faust.* ca 1909. London. Hutchinson. ils Willy Pogany/30 color pls. gilt red cloth. VG+. F1. $225.00

VON GOETHE, Johann Wolfgang. *Wilhelm Meister's Apprenticeship.* 1959. Heritage. ils William Sharp. M/slipcase. C1. $7.50

VON GRUNEBAUM, Gustave E. *Medieval Islam: Study in Cultural Orientation.* 1947. Chicago. 2nd prt. 8vo. 365 p. cloth. dj. O2. $35.00

VON GWINNER. *Hist of the Patchwork Quilt.* 1988. np. ils. wrp. G2. $17.00

VON GYDRY, Tiberius. *Morbus Hungaricus.* 1901. Verlag. 191 p. marbled brds. N2. $90.00

VON HAGEN, Victor. *Gr World of the Naturalists.* (1948). NY. Greenberg. 1st ed. 392 p. dj. F3. $25.00

VON HAGEN, Victor. *Incas of Pedro de Cieza de Leon.* (1959). Norman, OK. 1st ed. 397 p. dj. F3. $25.00

VON HAGEN, Victor. *Jicaque (Torrupan) Indians of Honduras.* 1943. NY. MAI. Indian Notes & Monographs 53. 112 p. wrp. F3. $30.00

VON HAGEN, Victor. *Maya Explorer.* 1948. Norman, OK. 2nd prt. 324 p. dj. F3. $20.00

VON HAGEN, Victor. *Off w/Their Heads.* 1937. NY. McMillan. 1st ed. 220 p. F3. $25.00

VON HAGEN, Victor. *S Am Zoo.* (1946). Messner/Jr Literary Guild. 1st ed. 182 p. dj. F3. $25.00

VON HAGEN, Victor. *Search for the Maya.* (1973). Eng. Saxton House. 1st Am ed. 365 p. F3. $30.00

VON HAGEN, Victor. *Tsatchela Indians of W Ecuador.* 1939. NY. Mus of Am Indian. 79 p. wrp. F3. $25.00

VON KLEIST, Heinrich. *Das Erdbeben in Chili.* 1981. Darmstadt. 1/300. lg octavo. sgn. 38 p. emb brds. F. B24. $165.00

VON KOTZEBUE, Otto. *Neu Reise um die Welt in den Jahren...* 1830. Verlag. 1st German ed. 2 vols in 1. gilt blk cloth. NF. H5. $1,250.00

VON KOTZEBUE, Otto. *Voyage of Discovery into S Sea & Bering Straits...* 1821. Longman Hurst Rees Orme. 3 vols. octavo. fld maps. contemporary rose cloth. H9. $2,500.00

VON KRUSENSTERN, A.J. *Voyage Round the World...1803-1806.* 1813. London. 1st Eng-language ed. quarto. 2 vols. VG/slipcase. H5. $8,500.00

VON LANGSDORFF, G.H. *Narrative of Rezanov Voyage to Nueva, CA in 1806.* 1927. San Francisco. Russell. 1/260. sgn Russell. ils/fld maps. NF. O6. $250.00

VON LEHNDORFF, H.G. *Token of a Covenant: Diary of E Prussian Surgeon 1945-47.* (1964). Chicago. Regnery. trans E Mayer. intro Paul Tillich. 328 p. VG/G. S9. $18.00

VON LEIBIG, Justus. *Principles of Agricultural Chemistry...* 1855. NY. Wiley. 105 p. emb cloth. VG+. B14. $50.00

VON LEWINSKI, Anneliese. *Weiszt du Wieviel Sternlein Stehen?* nd. Germany. Schreiber. 8 color pls. VG. M5. $60.00

VON LOHER, Franz. *Cyprus: Hist & Descriptive...* 1878. NY. 8vo. 324 p. cloth. O2. $100.00

VON MIKUSCH, Dagobert. *Gasi Mustafa Kemal Zwischen Europa und Asien.* 1929. Leipzig. 8vo. ils/map. 335 p. gilt cloth. O2. $40.00

VON MONAKOW, Constantin. *Die Lokalisation im Grosshirn und der Abbau der Funktion...* 1914. Wiesbaden. thick 8vo. interleaved copy/rebound buckram. G7. $295.00

VON RAD, Gerhard. *Genesis: Commentary.* 1961. Phil. Westminster. trans John H Marks. 434 p. VG. C5. $20.00

VON REZZORI, Gregor. *Death of My Brother Abel.* 1985. Viking/Penguin. 1st ed. trans from German. F/F. A14. $30.00

VON REZZORI, Gregor. *Orient Express.* 1992. Knopf. 1st ed. trans from German. F/F. A14. $25.00

VON STEINWEHR, A. *Centennial Gazetteer of the US...* 1874. Phil. McCurdy. ils. 1000+ p. full leather. VG. O6. $125.00

VON SWIETEN, Gerald. *Commentaria in Hermanni Boerhaave Aphorismos...* 1759-64. Venice. Pasquali. 7 vols. 4to. contemporary brds. G7. $395.00

VON TEMPSKI, Armie. *Born in Paradise.* 1940. DSP. 3rd prt. 8vo. 342 p. VG. W1. $18.00

VON THIELMANN, Max. *Journey in the Caucasus, Persia & Turkey in Asia.* 1875. London. 2 vols. ils/fld map. gilt gr cloth. O2. $550.00

VON WUTHENAU, Alexander. *Unexpected Faces in Ancient Am.* (1975). NY. Crown. 1st ed. 4to. 240 p. F3. $35.00

VON ZOBELTITZ, Fedor. *Elzevir.* 1965. Blk Cat. miniature. 47 p. gr cloth. F. H10. $75.00

VONNEGUT, Kurt. *Between Time & Timbuktu.* 1972. NY. Delacorte. 1st ed. 1/2500. ils Krementz. F/clip. Q1. $450.00

VONNEGUT, Kurt. *Bluebeard.* 1987. NY. Delacorte. 1st ed. NF/dj. P3. $20.00

VONNEGUT, Kurt. *Bluebeard.* 1988. London. Cape. 1st ed. F/F. B3. $30.00

VONNEGUT, Kurt. *Deadeye Dick.* 1982. Delacorte. 1st ed. F/dj. L3/P3. $25.00

VONNEGUT, Kurt. *Fates Worse Than Death.* 1982. Nottingham. Spokesman Pamphlet #80. sgn. F/unused. A11. $40.00

VONNEGUT, Kurt. *Galapagos.* 1985. Delacorte. 1st ed. F/F. P3. $25.00

VONNEGUT, Kurt. *Hocus Pocus.* 1990. Putnam. 1st ed. VG/dj. P3. $22.00

VONNEGUT, Kurt. *Jailbird.* 1979. Delacorte. 1st ed. VG/dj. P3. $30.00

VONNEGUT, Kurt. *Jailbird.* 1979. London. Cape. 1st ed. F/F. B3. $55.00

VONNEGUT, Kurt. *Mother Night.* 1966. Harper Row. 1st ed. VG/dj. P3. $150.00

VONNEGUT, Kurt. *Nothing Is Lost Save Honor.* 1984. Nouveau Pr. 1/40. sgn/#d. prt on Japanese Etching paper. F. Q1. $350.00

VONNEGUT, Kurt. *Palm Sunday.* 1981. Delacorte. 1st ed. F/dj. P3. $30.00

VONNEGUT, Kurt. *Slapstick.* 1976. Delacorte. 1st ed. NF/dj. P3. $40.00

VONNEGUT, Kurt. *Slapstick.* 1976. London. Cape. 1st ed. NF/VG. B3. $40.00

VOORHEES, Edward B. *Fertilizers.* 1898 (1910). London. 13th ed. 335 p. G+. B26. $15.00

VOORHIS, Jerry. *Beyond Victory.* (1944). NY. Farrar Rinehart. 1st ed. 8vo. VG+/dj. B20. $50.00

VOORHIS, Jerry. *Strange Case of Richard Milhous Nixon.* (1972). NY. Erickson. 1st ed. inscr. B20. $45.00

VORIES, Eugene C. *Arrowhead Ranch.* (1959). Avalon. sgn. VG+/dj. B9. $12.50

VOSPER, Frank. *Murder on the 2nd Floor.* nd. Daily Express Fiction Lib. VG. P3. $20.00

VOSS, Frederick S. *John Frazee, 1790-1852, Sculptor.* 1986. Boston. Atheneum. 1/2090. 120 p. brds. D2. $30.00

VOSS, George L. *Man Who Believed in the Code.* 1975. St Martin. 8vo. F. A8. $8.00

VOSTER, Gordon. *Textures of Silence.* 1984. Morrow. 1st Am ed. author's 1st book. VG+/VG+. A14. $20.00

VOTAW, Clarence E. *Jasper Hunnicut of Jimpsonhurst.* 1907. Chicago. Union Book & Pub. 1st ed. G. A16. $30.00

VOZNESENSKY, Andrei. *Arrow in the Wall.* 1987. NY. 1st ed. F/F. V1. $15.00

VRETOS, Marino P. *Athenes Moderne. Album Contenant les Vues...Monuments...* 1984. Athens. atlas folio. 14 repro aquatints. fld brd portfolio. O2. $85.00

VROOMAN, Henry Wellington. *Half a Million Insurance; or, Dr Lauterbach's...Patient.* 1888. NY. Am Pub House. 1st ed. 16mo. 52 p. prt wrp. M1. $200.00

VRYONIS, Speros Jr. *Byzantium & Europe.* 1967. NY. 8vo. 216 p. dj. O2. $30.00

VRYONIS, Speros Jr. *Greeks & the Sea.* 1993. New Rochelle. 4to. ils. 234 p. O2. $65.00

VULLIAMY, C.E. *Eng Letter Writers.* 1946. London. Collins. 2nd imp. 8 color pls. 48 p. NF/VG/clear plastic. M7. $35.00

VULPIAN, A. *Pneumonies Secondaires. These. Concours Pour l'Agregation.* 1860. Paris. 4to. 93 p. brds. G7. $150.00

VYSE, Michael. *Overworld.* 1980. Faber. F/dj. P3. $20.00

WACHTEL & YORK. *Toughlove Solutions.* 1984. Doubleday. 1st ed. F/F. T2. $10.00

WACHTEL & YORK. *Toughlove.* 1982. Doubleday. 1st ed. F/F. T2. $10.00

WADD, William. *Nugae Chirurgicae; or, Biological Miscellany...* 1824. London. John Nicols. 276 p. recent cloth. G7. $195.00

WADDELL, D.A.G. *W Indies & the Guianas.* (1967). Prentice Hall. 1st ed. 149 p. F3. $15.00

WADDELL, Helen. *Peter Abelard.* 1950 (1933). London. VG/dj. C1. $5.00

WADDINGTON, C.H. *Ethical Animal.* 1961. Atheneum. 1st ed. 226 p. VG+/VG+. M20. $12.00

WADE, David; see Daniels, Norman.

WADE, Elizabeth. *Ant Ventures.* (1924). Rand McNally. 1st ed. xl. ils Harrison Cady. 246 p. VG. D1. $95.00

WADE, Henry. *Dying Fall.* 1955. London. Constable. 1st ed. F/NF. M15. $65.00

WADE, Henry. *Litmore Snatch.* 1957. Macmillan. 1st ed. NF/dj. P3. $23.00

WADE, Henry. *Released for Death.* 1970. Howard Baker. xl. dj. P3. $6.00

WADE, Jonathan. *Back to Life.* 1961. Pantheon. 1st ed. F/dj. P3. $13.00

WADE, Mason. *Journals of Francis Parkman.* 1947. Harper. 1st ed. 2 vols. VG. E5. $25.00

WADSBERG, Andrew M. *De Cholelithis per Abscessumn Ruptum Egredientibus...* 1788. Wusallae. 4to. 1 engraving. 17 p. G7. $45.00

WADSTROM, C.B. *Essay on Colonization.* 1968. NY. Kelley. facsimile 1794 ed. 363 p. A7. $33.00

WADSWORTH, L.A. *Mystery Off Pirate's Point.* nd. Rinehart. VG/dj. P3. $20.00

WAGENHELM, Kal. *Clemente.* 1973. Praeger. 1st ed. VG+/VG+. P8. $35.00

WAGENKNECHT, Edward. *Six Novels of the Supernatural.* 1944. Viking. 1st ed. VG. P3. $35.00

WAGENVOORD, James. *Hangin' Out.* (1974). Lippincott. 120 p. dj. A7. $15.00

WAGER, Walter. *Otto's Boy.* 1985. Macmillan. 1st ed. F/F. P3. $17.00

WAGER, Walter. *Viper Three.* 1971. Macmillan. 1st ed. VG/VG. P3. $20.00

WAGGAMAN, M.T. *Billy Boy.* 1912. Notre Dame, IN. Ava Marie Pub. VG/G. V2. $4.50

WAGGAMAN, M.T. *Bob-o-Link.* 1902. Benziger. Catholic Pr. G. V2. $4.00

WAGHENAER, Lucas Jansz. *Mariners Mirrour.* 1866. Amsterdam. Theatrvm Orbis Terrarvm. facsimile. lg folio. M/dj. O6. $295.00

WAGHENAER, Lucas Jansz. *Thresoor der Zeevaert.* 1965. Amsterdam. facsimile of Leyden 1592 ed. 22 double-p charts. M/M. O6. $250.00

WAGNER, Henry R. *CA Voyages, 1539-41.* 1925. San Francisco. Howell. 8 full-p maps. NF. O6. $200.00

WAGNER, Henry R. *Cartography of NW Coast of Am to Yr 1800.* 1937. Berkeley. 1st ed. 2 vols. folio. maps/obsolete name checklist. M/slipcase. O6. $795.00

WAGNER, Henry R. *Drake on the Pacific Coast.* 1970. LA. Zamorano Club. 18 p. M/wrp. O6. $25.00

WAGNER, Henry R. *Spanish Voyages to NW Coast of Am in 16th Century.* 1929. CA Hist Soc. special extra-ils ed. 1/25. sgn. full vellum. F. O6. $4,500.00

WAGNER, Jane. *Search for Signs of Intelligent Life in the Universe.* 1986. NY. 1st ed. sgn Wagner/Lily Tomlin. F/F. A11. $65.00

WAGNER, Richard. *My Life.* 1911. Dodd Mead. 1st Am ed. 8vo. 911 p in 2 vols. F/sans. A2. $100.00

WAGNER, Richard. *Siegfried & the Twilight of the Gods.* 1930. Garden City. early trade ed. ils Rackham/24 color pls. VG. M18. $100.00

WAGNER, Will. *Treasure of Painted Mtn.* 1953. Pagent Pr. 12mo. VG/G+. A8. $10.00

WAGNER. *Adapting Architectural Details for Quilts.* 1992. np. wrp. G2. $13.00

WAGNER. *Teach Yourself Machine Piecing & Quilting.* 1992. np. ils. cloth. G2. $24.00

WAGONER, David. *Road to Many a Wonder.* 1974. NY. 1st ed. sgn. F/F. A11. $45.00

WAGONER, David. *Rock.* 1958. Viking. 1st ed. sgn. author's 3rd novel. F/NF. V1. $25.00

WAGONER, David. *Traveling Light.* 1976. Greywolf. 1/150. sgn. F/F. V1. $45.00

WAGONER, David. *Where Is My Wandering Boy Tonight?* 1970. NY. special preview ed. 1/500. sgn. NF/8vo wrp. A11. $55.00

WAHL, Jan. *Tales of Fuzzy Mouse: 6 Cozy Stories for Bedtime.* 1988. W Pub/Golden Book. ils Lillian Hoban. 1st ed. 45 p. VG. A3. $7.00

WAINER, Cord; see Dewey, Thomas B.

WAINWRIGHT, John. *Big Tickle.* 1969. Macmillan. 1st ed. VG/G. P3. $22.00

WAINWRIGHT, John. *Kill of Small Consequences.* 1980. Macmillan. 1st ed. NF/dj. P3. $20.00

WAINWRIGHT, John. *Man Who Wasn't There.* 1989. St Martin. 1st ed. VG/VG-. P3. $13.00

WAIT, Lucita H. *Fairchild Tropical Garden.* ca 1948. NY. Ronald. 1st ed. ils. 381 p. H10. $23.50

WAITZKIN, Fred. *Searching for Bobby Fischer.* (1989). Bodley Head. 1st ed. F/F. B3. $20.00

WAKEFIELD, H.R. *Clock Strikes 12.* 1946. Arkham. 1st ed. F/dj. M2. $85.00

WAKEFIELD, H.R. *Hearken to the Evidence.* 1934. Doubleday Doran. VG. P3. $25.00

WAKEFIELD, H.R. *Strayers From Sheol.* 1961. Arkham. 1st ed. F/dj. M2. $70.00

WAKEFIELD, H.R. *Strayers From Sheol.* 1961. Arkham. 1st ed. NF/dj. P3. $50.00

WAKEFIELD, Lawrence. *Sail & Rail.* 1980. Traverse City. ltd ed. 1/1500. VG. A16. $65.00

WAKEFIELD, Ruth. *Ruth Wakefield's Toll House Tried & True Recipes.* 1949. NY. Barrows. G/dj. A16. $20.00

WAKOSKI, Diane. *Coins & Coffins.* 1962. NY. Hawk's Well. 1st ed. presentation inscr. author's 1st book. F/wrp. L3. $125.00

WAKOSKI, Diane. *Discrepancies & Apparitions.* 1966. NY. 1st ed. sgn. author's 3rd book. F/VG+. V1. $65.00

WAKOSKI, Diane. *Greed, Parts 5-7.* 1971. Blk Sparrow. 1st ed. 1/200. sgn. F. B24. $75.00

WAKOSKI, Diane. *Laguna Contract.* 1976. Crepuscular. 1st ed. 1/125. sgn. ils. 32 p. F. B24. $125.00

WAKOSKI, Diane. *Virtuoso Literature for 2 & 4 Hands.* 1975. NY. ARC. sgn. RS. F. V1. $45.00

WALCOTT, Derek. *Midsummer: Poems.* 1984. FSG. 1st ed. F/F clip. V1. $35.00

WALDEN, Howard T. *Upstream & Down.* 1938. Derrydale. ltd ed. 1/775. 112 p. VG. M8. $250.00

WALDEN, Jane Brevoort. *Igloo.* 1931. NY/London. Putnam. 3rd prt. ils Diana Thorne. 211 p. bl cloth. P4. $42.00

WALDMAN, Anne. *Another World.* (1971). Bobbs Merrill. A7. $20.00

WALDMAN, Mark. *Goethe & the Jews: Challenge to Hitlerism.* 1934. Putnam. 295 p. G+. S3. $30.00

WALDO, Anna Lee. *Sacajawea.* 1979. Avon. 1st prt. 1359 p. NF/wrp. T8. $25.00

WALDO, S. Putnam. *Biographical Sketches of Distinguished Am Naval Heroes...* 1823. Hartford. 1st ed. orig leather. G. D7. $125.00

WALDROP, Howard. *Dozen Tough Jobs.* 1989. Ziesing. 1st ed. F/dj. P3. $16.00

WALDROP, Howard. *Them Bones.* 1989. Ziesing. 1st ed. 1/350. sgn/#d. F/F/slipcase. P3. $50.00

WALDROP, Keith. *Garden of Effort.* nd. Burning Deck. 1st ed. sgn. NF. V1. $20.00

WALDROP, Rosmarie. *Streets Enough To Welcome Snow.* 1986. Station Hill. 1st ed. inscr. F/wrp. V1. $15.00

WALDVOGEL. *Soft Covers for Hard Times: Quiltmaking & Great Depression.* 1990. np. ils. cloth. G2. $23.00

WALEY, Arthur. *Life & Times of Po Chu-I.* 1970. London. Allen Unwin. 3rd ed. tall 8vo. 238 p. VG/dj. W1. $24.00

WALKER, A. *Jackson & New Orleans.* 1856. NY. 12mo. 411 p. G. T3. $32.00

WALKER, A. Earl. *Hist of Neurological Surgery.* 1967. NY. facsimile of 1951 ed. F/dj. G7. $125.00

WALKER, A. Earl. *Post-Traumatic Epilepsy.* 1949. Springfield. Thomas. 86 p. NF. G7. $45.00

WALKER, Abbie Philips. *Sandman's Stories of Drusilla Doll.* (1920). Harper. ils Rhoda Chase. 176 p. gray cloth. VG. S10. $25.00

WALKER, Alice. *Color Purple.* 1982. HBJ. ARC. RS. w/promo material & photo. F/F. L3. $650.00

WALKER, Alice. *Finding the Greenstone.* (1991). San Diego. HBJ. 1st ed. ils Catherine Leeter. F/F. B3. $32.00

WALKER, Alice. *Horses Make a Landscape More Beautiful.* (1984). NY. HBJ. 1st ed. VG/G. B3. $20.00

WALKER, Alice. *Living by the Word.* (1988). HBJ. 1st ed. F/F. A7. $17.00

WALKER, Alice. *Possessing the Secret of Joy.* 1992. NY. HBJ. 1st ed. F/F. A13. $25.00

WALKER, Alice. *Temple of My Familiar.* 1989. NY. HBJ. 1st ed. rem mk. NF/NF. A13. $25.00

WALKER, Barbara M. *Little House Cookbook.* (1979). Harper Row. 8vo. 240 p. pict brds. T5. $35.00

WALKER, C.B. *MS Valley & Prehistoric Events...* 1879. Burlington, IA. Root. 1st ed. ils. 784 p. cloth. VG. D3. $70.00

WALKER, Cora. *Cuatemo: Last of the Aztec Emperors.* 1934. NY. Dayton. 1st ed. 8vo. 348 p. ES. gr cloth. VG. B11. $40.00

WALKER, D.E. *Adventure in Diamons.* (1955). London. Evans. 1st ed. 8vo. 186 p. VG/G. A2. $10.00

WALKER, Daniel. *Rights in Conflict.* (1968). Grosset Dunlap. 233 p. NF/dj. A7. $35.00

WALKER, David. *Lord's Pink Ocean.* 1972. Collins. 1st ed. VG/dj. P3. $15.00

WALKER, David. *Winter of Madness.* 1964. Collins. 1st ed. VG/dj. P3. $30.00

WALKER, Deward E. Jr. *Emergent Native Am.* (1972). Boston. 1st ed. xl. 818 p. cloth. VG/dj. D3. $25.00

WALKER, F.A. *Wages Question.* 1876. Holt. 1st ed. gilt brn cloth. VG. B2. $40.00

WALKER, F.W. *Great Deeds of the Seaforth Highlanders.* 1915. London. Dent. 12mo. 174 p. N2. $12.50

WALKER, Franklin. *Literary Hist of S CA.* 1950. CA U. 1st ed. inscr/sgn. F/clip. A18. $50.00

WALKER, Franklin. *San Francisco's Literary Frontier.* (1939). Knopf. 1st ed. photos/index. F/clip. A18. $50.00

WALKER, Henry Pickering. *Wagonmasters: High Plains Freighting From Earliest Days...* 1880. Norman, OK. 1st ed. 8vo. pls. 347 p. VG/VG. B11. $18.00

WALKER, Ira. *Man in the Driver's Seat.* 1964. Abelard Schuman. 1st ed. VG/dj. P3. $15.00

WALKER, James W.G. *Ocean to Ocean.* 1902. McClurg. 1st ed. xl. 309 p. F3. $20.00

WALKER, John Alan. *Documents on Life & Art of William Wendt.* 1992. Big Pine. private prt. sgn/#d. 213 p. cloth. dj. D2. $100.00

WALKER, John Alan. *William Wendt's Pastoral Visions & Eternal Platonic Guests.* 1988. Big Pine. private prt. 1/400. sgn. wrp. D2. $10.00

WALKER, John C. *Diseases of Vegetable Crops.* 1952. NY. ils. 529 p. VG+. B26. $27.50

WALKER, John. *Portraits, 5000 Yrs.* 1983. NY. 1st ed. F/dj. B30. $26.50

WALKER, Margaret. *Jubilee.* 1966. Houghton Mifflin. 1st ed. F/NF. B2. $75.00

WALKER, N.M. *When I Put Out to Sea.* (1972). Stein Day. 1st Am ed. 8vo. 191 p. F/VG. A2. $15.00

WALKER, Robert Harris. *Cincinnati & the Big Red Machine.* 1988. IN U. 1st ed. VG+/VG. P8. $20.00

WALKER, Ronald. *Infernal Paradise.* (1978). Berkeley. 1st ed. 319 p. dj. F3. $20.00

WALKER, Samuel J. *Typhus Epidemic in E Macedonia.* 1919. Athens. 8vo. ils. 39 p. prt wrp. O2. $25.00

WALKER, Stella. *Sporting Art: Eng 1700-1900.* 1972. NY. Clarkson Potter. 1st Am ed. 4to. VG/fair. O3. $45.00

WALKER, Theodore J. *Red Salmon, Brn Bear. Story of an Alaskan Lake.* 1971. NY. 1st prt. 8vo. 226 p. map ep. gilt cloth. F/F clip. H3. $20.00

WALKER, Walter. *Rules of the Knife Fight.* 1986. Harper Row. 1st ed. F/dj. P3. $18.00

WALKER, William. *War in Nicaragua.* (1985). Tucson, AZ. 1st ed. reprint of 1860 ed. 431 p. F3. $15.00

WALKER & WALKER. *Carleton Saga.* 1975. Ottawa. 3rd prt. 571 p. dj. A17. $30.00

WALKER. *Passionate Quilter.* 1991. np. ils. cloth. G2. $30.00

WALKING BULL & MONTANA. *O-Hu-Kah-Kan.* 1975. Dallas, OR. Itemizer-Observer. sgns. NF/wrp. L3. $85.00

WALL, Vivian. *Die Sternenprinzessin (The Star Princess).* ca 1950s. Verlag. ils Hanna Nagel. VG. M5. $25.00

WALLACE, Alfred Russel. *Wonderful Century: Its Successes & Its Failures.* 1898. Dodd Mead. later prt. ils/diagrams. 400 p. prt gr cloth. VG. G1. $25.00

WALLACE, Antony F.C. *Modal Personality Structure of Tuscarora Indians...* 1952. WA, DC. Bureau Am Ethnology Bulletin 150. 120 p. wrp. N2. $15.00

WALLACE, Archer. *Adventures in the Air.* 1932. Ryerson. sgn. VG. P3. $20.00

WALLACE, Dan. *Natural Formula Book for Home & Yard.* 1982. Rodale Pr. VG/dj. A16. $10.00

WALLACE, Dillon. *Saddle & Camp in the Rockies...* 1911. NY. Outing Pub. 1st ed. 302 p. NF. H7. $75.00

WALLACE, Edgar. *Angel Esquire.* 1908. Holt. 1st Am ed. NF. M15. $125.00

WALLACE, Edgar. *Avenger.* nd. Leisure Lib. VG/VG-. P3. $18.00

WALLACE, Edgar. *Bones in London.* 1972. Hutchinson. VG/VG. P3. $15.00

WALLACE, Edgar. *Bosambo of the River.* 1973. Tom Stacey. NF/dj. P3. $15.00

WALLACE, Edgar. *Day of Uniting.* 1930. Mystery League. 1st ed. VG/torn. P3. $25.00

WALLACE, Edgar. *Feathered Serpent.* 1928. Crime Club. 1st ed. VG-. P3. $20.00

WALLACE, Edgar. *Flying Squad.* 1929. Crime Club. 1st ed. VG. P3. $18.00

WALLACE, Edgar. *Four Just Men.* 1905. Tallis Pr. 1st ed. xl. P3. $75.00

WALLACE, Edgar. *Frightened Lady.* 1933. Musson. 1st Canadian ed. VG. P3. $20.00

WALLACE, Edgar. *Governor of Chi-Foo.* 1933. World Syndicate. 1st ed. VG. P3. $60.00

WALLACE, Edgar. *Gunman's Bluff.* 1929. Crime Club. 1st ed. VG. P3. $30.00

WALLACE, Edgar. *Hand of Power.* 1930. Mystery League. 1st ed. VG. P3. $15.00

WALLACE, Edgar. *King by Night.* 1929. John Long. VG. P3. $15.00

WALLACE, Edgar. *Law of the Three Just Men.* 1931. Crime Club. 1st ed. VG. P3. $35.00

WALLACE, Edgar. *Man at the Carlton.* 1931. Musson. 1st Canadian ed. VG. P3. $10.00

WALLACE, Edgar. *Mr Commissioner Sanders.* 1930. Doubleday Doran. 1st Am ed. VG/dj. M15. $45.00

WALLACE, Edgar. *Northing Tramp.* 1931. Doubleday Doran. VG. P3. $12.00

WALLACE, Edgar. *Square Emerald.* 1932. Musson. 1st Canadian ed. VG. P3. $20.00

WALLACE, Edgar. *Squealer.* 1928. Double-day Doran. VG. P3. $10.00

WALLACE, Edgar. *Stretelli Case.* 1930. Internat Fiction Lib. VG-. P3. $12.00

WALLACE, Edgar. *Traitor's Gate.* 1927. Doubleday Page. 1st ed. VG-. P3. $10.00

WALLACE, Edgar. *White Face.* 1932. Musson. 1st Canadian ed. VG. P3. $20.00

WALLACE, Edward S. *Great Reconnaissance.* (1955). Boston. 1st ed. 288 p. cloth. NF/dj. D3. $25.00

WALLACE, F.L. *Address: Centauri.* 1955. Gnome. 1st ed. F/dj. M2. $25.00

WALLACE, Henry A. *Century of the Common Man.* 1943. NY. NF/wrp. B2. $30.00

WALLACE, Ian. *Deathstar Voyage.* 1972. Dobson. 1st ed. F/F. P3. $13.00

WALLACE, Ian. *Pan Sagittarius.* 1973. Putnam. NF/dj. P3. $15.00

WALLACE, Ian. *Purloined Prince.* 1971. McCall. 1st ed. NF/dj. P3. $25.00

WALLACE, Irving. *Pigeon Project.* 1979. Simon Schuster. 1st ed. F/F. P3. $15.00

WALLACE, Irving. *R Document.* 1976. Simon Schuster. 1st ed. F/dj. P3. $18.00

WALLACE, Irving. *Seven Minutes.* 1969. Simon Schuster. 1st ed. VG/VG. V2. $5.00

WALLACE, Lew. *Fair God.* nd. Grosset Dunlap. decor brds. VG. P3. $10.00

WALLACE, Marilyn. *Sisters in Crime.* nd. BC. F/F. P3. $10.00

WALLACE, Marilyn. *Sisters in Crime.* 1990. London. Allison. ARC of 1st British ed. sgn contributors. RS. F/dj. S5. $45.00

WALLACE, Michele. *Blk Macho & Myth of Super-Woman.* (1979). NY. Dial. 2nd prt. dj. A7. $15.00

WALLACE, R.B. Jr. *Dress Her in Wht & Gold: Biography of GA Tech.* 1963. GA Tech Foundation. 1st ed. inscr. 8vo. 426 p. F/VG+. A2. $15.00

WALLACE, Robert. *Miners.* 1976. Time Life. 4to. F. A8. $10.00

WALLACE, Robert. *Seven Men Are Murdered.* 1930. Fiction League. VG. P3. $25.00

WALLACE, Susan. *Land of the Pueblos.* 1988. NY. John B Alden. 1st ed. ils. 285 p. decor cloth. NF. B20. $90.00

WALLANT, Edward Lewis. *Tenants of Moonbloom.* 1963. NY. ARC. RS. NF/NF. A11. $35.00

WALLENROD, Reuben. *Literature of Modern Israel.* 1956. Abelard Schuman. 253 p. G+. S3. $21.00

WALLER, Don. *Motown Story.* (1985). Scribner. ARC/1st wrp ed. sm quarto. 256 p. w/promo materials. A7. $15.00

WALLER, Robert James. *Bridges of Madison County.* (1993). London. Heinemann. 1st Eng hc w/this title. sgn. M/dj. B4. $85.00

WALLICH, J.U. *Religio Turcica, Mahometis Vita, et Orientalis...* 1659. Stade (Sweden). 3 parts in 1 vol. 12 pls. full elephant hide. rare. O2. $2,250.00

WALLIN, J.E. *Odyssey of a Pschologist: Pioneering Experiences...* 1955. Wilmington, DE. self pub. 243 p. F/prt wht wrp. G1. $17.50

WALLING, R.A.J. *Corpse by Any Other Name.* nd. Collier. VG. P3. $10.00

WALLIS, Charles L. *Stories on Stone. Book of Am Epitaphs.* 1954. Oxford. 1st ed. 258 p. cloth. VG/dj. M20. $20.00

WALLIS, Dave. *Only Lovers Left Alive.* 1964. Dutton. 1st ed. VG/dj. P3. $20.00

WALLIS, George. *Art of Preventing Diseases & Restoring Health...* 1793. London. Robinson. 850 p. full tree calf. G7. $125.00

WALLIS, Helen. *Discovery of the World: Maps of the Earth & Cosmos...* 1985. Montreal. 66 maps. M. O6. $65.00

WALLIS, Helen. *Voyage of Sir Francis Drake Mapped in Silver & Gold.* 1979. Bancroft. 29 p. NF/wrp. O6. $35.00

WALLIS, J.H. *Murder by Formula.* 1932. Jarrolds. 1st ed. inscr/sgn. VG-. P3. $45.00

WALLIS, Velma. *Two Old Women.* 1993. Fairbanks. Epicenter. 1st ed. sgn. F/F. L3. $50.00

WALLMANN, Jeffrey M. *Judas Cross.* 1974. Random. 1st ed. F/F. P3. $16.00

WALLRATH, Matthew. *Excavations in the Tehuantepec Region, Mexico.* 1967. Phil. Am Philosophical Soc. 4to. 173 p. wrp. F3. $25.00

WALLS, Jerry G. *Fishes of the N Gulf of Mexico.* (1975). TFH. ils. 432 p. F. A17. $10.00

WALPOLE, Horace. *Jeffery's Edition of Castle of Otranto, a Gothic Story.* 1800. London. Blackader. 2nd ed. quarto. 152 p. gilt bl morocco. VG. H5. $850.00

WALPOLE, Horace. *King George the 3rd.* 1845. Phil. xl. 2 vols. 8vo. full leather. T3. $19.00

WALPOLE, Hugh. *Jeremy & Hamlet.* nd. Tauchhnitz. VG. P3. $15.00

WALROND, Sallie. *Encyclopedia of Driving.* 1974. Cheshire. Horse-Drawn Carriages Ltd. 1st ed. 4to. VG/VG. O3. $30.00

WALROND, Sallie. *Guide to Driving Horses.* 1973. N Hollywood. Wilshire. later prt. VG/wrp. O3. $10.00

WALSER, Martin. *Inner Man.* 1979. HRW. 1st ed. trans from German. NF/NF clip. A14. $25.00

WALSH, Christy. *Baseball's Greatest Lineup.* 1952. Barnes. 1st ed. photos. VG/G+. P8. $35.00

WALSH, Goodwin. *Voice of the Murderer.* nd. AL Burt. VG. P3. $10.00

WALSH, J.H. *Dog in Health & Disease.* 1879. London. Longman Gr. 3rd ed. 509 p. H10. $35.00

WALSH, J.M. *Spies Are Abroad.* 1935. Collins. 6th ed. VG/VG-. P3. $20.00

WALSH, J.P. *Wyndham Case.* 1993. London. Hodder. 1st ed. author's 1st detective novel. F/F. S5. $25.00

WALSH, M.M.B. *Four-Colored Hoop.* 1976. Putnam. 1st ed. F/F. P3. $13.00

WALSH, Robert Jr. *Appeal From Judgements of Great Britain Respecting USA.* 1819. Phil. Mitchell Ames Wht. octavo. teg. half red morocco. H9. $350.00

WALSH, Thomas. *Action of the Tiger.* 1967. Simon Schuster. 1st ed. xl. dj. P3. $5.00

WALSH, W.E. *Coom of Conaire Mor (Conary the Great).* 1929. NY. Louis Carrier. 1st ed. NF. N3. $35.00

WALSHE, W.H. *Practical Treatise on Diseases of the Lungs...* 1860. Phil. Blanchard Lea. new Am ed from 3rd revised Eng ed. 468 p. brn cloth. S9. $20.00

WALTER, Edna L. *Peeps at Many Lands. Russia.* 1970. London. Blk. 1st ed. xl. 8vo. ils/map. 88 p. VG. W1. $20.00

WALTER, Elizabeth. *In the Mist.* 1979. Arkham. 1st ed. M. M2. $9.00

WALTER, Elizabeth. *Sin Eater.* 1967. Harvill. NF/dj. P3. $20.00

WALTER, L. Edna. *Mother Goose's Nursery Rhymes.* 1951 (1924). London. Blk. ils Charles Folkard. 216 p. VG. P2. $36.00

WALTER, Lutz. *Japan: Cartographic Vision.* 1993. Munich. Prestel. ils/maps. 216 p. M/dj. O6. $75.00

WALTER, Richard. *Canary Island Adventure.* 1956. NY. Dutton. 1st ed. 8vo. 255 p. F/VG. A2. $15.00

WALTERS, Anna Lee. *Sun Is Not Merciful.* 1985. Ithaca. Firebrand. 1st ed. F/wrp. L3. $35.00

WALTERS, Ed. *Gulf Breeze Sightings.* nd. Morrow. 3rd ed. VG/dj. P3. $15.00

WALTERS, Henry. *Incunabula Typographica.* 1906. Baltimore. presentation. 4to. 542 p. rebacked. G7. $225.00

WALTERS, LeRoy. *Bibliography of Bioethics.* 1976. Detroit. Gale. 2 vols. 4to. gr cloth. F. S9. $28.00

WALTERS, Minette. *Ice House.* 1992. London. Macmillan. 1st ed. author's 1st novel. NF/NF. M15. $150.00

WALTERS, Minette. *Sculptress.* 1993. London. Macmillan. 1st ed. sgn. F/F. M15. $50.00

WALTERS, S.M. *Shaping of Cambridge Botany.* 1981. Cambridge. 1st ed. 121 p. F/F. B28. $20.00

WALTON, Alan Hull. *Open Grave.* 1971. Taplinger. VG/dj. P3. $20.00

WALTON, Bryce. *Cave of Danger.* 1967. Crowell. 1st ed. xl. dj. P3. $5.00

WALTON, Cecile. *Hans Andersen's Fairy Tales.* nd. Stokes. 16 color pls. VG. M5. $60.00

WALTON, Ed. *Rookies.* 1982. Stein Day. 1st ed. F/VG+. P8. $12.50

WALTON, Evangeline. *Cross & the Sword.* 1956. Ryerson. VG/VG-. P3. $25.00

WALTON, Evangeline. *Witch House.* 1945. Sauk City. Arkham. 1st ed. blk cloth. F/pict dj. B24/M2. $75.00

WALTON, George A. *Quaker of the Future Time.* 1916. Phil. WH Jenkins. 12mo. 39 p. VG+. V3. $7.50

WALTON, Izaak. *Complete Angler.* 1897. London. Bodley Head. 1st Le Gallienne ed. octavo. Bayntum bdg. F. H5. $500.00

WALTON, Izaak. *Complete Angler.* 1928. Boston. Goodspeed/Merrymount. 1/600. 12mo. 324 p. F/slipcase. B24. $125.00

WALVOORD, John F. *Inspiration & Interpretation.* ca 1957. Grand Rapids. Eerdmans. 280 p. H10. $17.50

WALZER, Michael. *Co of Critics.* (1988). Basic Books. 1st ed. 260 p. NF/dj. A7. $14.00

WAMBAUGH, Joseph. *Blooding.* 1989. Perigord. 1st ed. VG/dj. P3. $20.00

WAMBAUGH, Joseph. *Golden Orange.* 1990. Perigord/Morrow. 1st ed. VG/dj. P3. $20.00

WAMPLET & WAMPLER. *Wild Flowers of IN.* 1988. Bloomington. 80 full-p pls. 177 p. M/dj. B26. $39.00

WANDREI, Donald. *Dark Odyssey.* 1931. Webb. 1st ed. 1/400. sgn/#d. F/dj. M2. $250.00

WANDREI, Donald. *Ecstasy.* 1928. Recluse Pr. 1st ed. 1/322. F/tissue dj. M2. $350.00

WANDREI, Donald. *Poems for Midnight.* 1964. Arkham. 1st ed. F/M. M2. $175.00

WANDREI, Donald. *Web of Easter Island.* 1948. Arkham. 1st ed. F/dj. M2. $80.00

WANGERIN, Walter Jr. *Book of Sorrows.* 1985. Harper Row. 1st ed. F/dj. P3. $16.00

WANGERIN, Walter Jr. *Book of the Dun Cow.* 1980. Allen Lane. F/F. P3. $25.00

WARBURG, Otto. *Uber die Katalytischen Wirkungen der Lebendigen Substanz.* 1928. Berlin. Springer. 528 p. fair. G7. $95.00

WARD, Artemas. *Encyclopedia of Food.* 1923. NY. 4to. 596 p. H10. $125.00

WARD, Brad. *Baron of Boot Hill.* 1955. Hodder Stoughton. 1st ed. inscr. F/dj. B9. $65.00

WARD, Brad. *Six-Gun Heritage.* 1955. Dutton. 1st ed. NF/dj. B9. $35.00

WARD, Edward. *Sahara Story.* 1962. NY. Norton. 8vo. 192 p. VG/worn. P4. $15.00

WARD, H.W. *Book of the Peach: Being a Practical Handbook...* 1903. London. ils. teg. decor cloth. NF-. B26. $17.50

WARD, Jonas; see Ard, William.

WARD, Lynd. *God's Man.* 1929. NY. 1st ed. VG. B5. $75.00

WARD, Lynd. *Mad Man's Drum.* 1930. Cape/Harrison Smith. 1st ed/2nd prt. blk cloth. NF/NF. F1. $135.00

WARD, Lynd. *Mad Man's Drum.* 1930. NY. 1st ed. VG. B5. $75.00

WARD, Lynd. *Storyteller Without Words.* 1974. Abrams. thick sq 4to. NF/dj. F1. $150.00

WARD, Maisie. *Young Mr Newman.* 1948. NY. Sheed Ward. 477 p. H10. $15.00

WARD, Marion. *Boat Children of Canton.* 1944. McKay. ils Helen Sewell. VG+. P2. $18.00

WARD, Martha. *Steve Carlton: Star Southpaw.* 1975. Putnam. 1st ed. ils. F/VG. P8. $30.00

WARD, Mrs. Humphrey. *Writings of...* 1909-12. Houghton Mifflin. Autograph ed. sgn. 16 vols. gilt gr morocco. NF. B20. $700.00

WARDEN, Carl John. *Short Outline of Comparative Psychology.* 1927. Norton. 1st ed. 16mo. 96 p. bl cloth. G1. $25.00

WARDEN, Florence. *Mystery of the Thames.* 1913. Ward Lock. VG. P3. $25.00

WARDLAW, Charles. *Fundamentals of Baseball.* 1925 (1924). Scribner. later prt. VG. P8. $30.00

WARE, John. *Discourses on Medical Education & on the Medical Profession.* 1847. Boston. 113 p. sewn as issued. G. G7. $75.00

WARE, Joseph E. *Emigrants' Guide to CA.* 1972. Da Capo Pr. reprint of 1932 Princeton ed. ils/map. F/sans. A18. $35.00

WARE, Romaine B. *Success w/Lilies in the Home Garden.* 1948. Portland. 2-p chart. F. B26. $14.00

WARE, William. *Georgian Period.* 1922. Students ed. 100 pls. E5. $150.00

WARFIELD, Don. *Roaring Redhead.* 1987. Diamond Comm. 1st ed. ils. F/F. P8. $17.50

WARHOL, Andy. *Andy Warhol Diaries.* (1989). Warner. 1st ed. thick quarto. NF/NF. B4. $65.00

WARHOL, Andy. *Philosophy of Andy Warhol (From A to B & Back Again).* 1975. HBJ. 1st ed. sgn/intl soup can drawing. NF/NF. Q1. $400.00

WARHOL, Andy. *Philosophy of Andy Warhol (From A to B & Back Again).* 1975. HBJ. 3rd imp. NF/NF clip. A14. $20.00

WARING, Barbara. *Heckle & Jeckle Visit the Farm.* 1958. Wonder Books. VG. P3. $15.00

WARING, G.E. *Draining for Profit & Draining for Health.* 1904. Orange Judd. new revised ed. 12mo. 252 p. VG. B28. $20.00

WARING, G.E. *Whip & Spur.* 1897. Doubleday. xl. 12mo. gray cloth. VG. C10. $37.50

WARING, William. *Call to the Fountain.* 1891. Phil. Spangler Davis. 12mo. 103 p. V3. $15.00

WARING & WARING. *Teddy Bears.* (1980). London. Treasure Pr. 1st thus ed. sm 4to. 128 p. F/F. T5. $35.00

WARINNER, E.V. *Voyager to Destiny: Amazing Adventures of Manjiro...* (1956). Bobbs Merrill. later prt. 8vo. 267 p. VG+/VG. A2. $15.00

WARKWORTH. *Notes From a Diary in Asiatic Turkey.* 1898. London. 4to. 31 full-p pls/fld map. 267 p. gilt cloth. O2. $350.00

WARMAN, Eric. *Preview Film Album.* 1962. Golden Pleasure. VG. P3. $30.00

WARNER, Anne. *Susan Clegg & Man in the House.* 1907. Little Brn. 1st ed. ils Alice Barber Stephens. 279 p. VG. S10. $25.00

WARNER, Charles Dudley. *On Horseback: Tour in VA, NC, & TN...* 1888. Boston/NY. 1st ed. 12mo. 331 p. pict gr cloth. H9. $75.00

WARNER, Denis. *Certain Victory.* (1977). Sheed Andrews/McMeel. 1st Am ed. F/F. A7. $45.00

WARNER, Frances Lester. *On a New Eng Campus.* 1937. Houghton Mifflin. 1st ed. sgn. VG. E3. $35.00

WARNER, Frank A. *Bobby Blake in the Frozen North.* 1923. Barse Hopkins. 1st ed. VG/dj. M2. $17.00

WARNER, Frank A. *Bobby Blake on an Auto Tour.* 1920. Barse Hopkins. 1st ed. F/NF. M2. $20.00

WARNER, L. *Craft of the Japanese Sculpture.* 1936. NY. MacFarlene. 1st ed. 8 pls. VG/dj. W1. $65.00

WARNER, L. *Japanese Sculpture of the Tempyo Period.* 1964. Cambridge. Harvard. 1st 1-vol ed. 4to. 215 p. VG. W1. $65.00

WARNER, Mignon. *Death in Time.* 1982. Crime Club. 1st ed. F/dj. P3. $13.00

WARNER, Mignon. *Girl Who Was Clairvoyant.* 1982. Crime Club. 1st ed. VG/dj. P3. $13.00

WARNER, Oliver. *Crown Jewels.* 1951. Penguin. 1st ed. VG/VG. P3. $20.00

WARNER, Oliver. *William Wilberforce & His Times.* ca 1962. London. Batsford. ils. 174 p. H10. $15.00

WARNER, Rex. *Aerodrome.* 1966. Little Brn. 2nd ed. xl. dj. P3. $5.00

WARNER, Rex. *Eng Public Schools.* 1946. London. 8vo. 48 p. red brds. VG. H3. $12.00

WARNER, S.J. *Urge to Mass Destruction.* 1957. Grune Stratton. 1st ed. 8vo. 188 p. F/VG+. A2. $15.00

WARNER, Sylvia Townsend. *Kingdoms of Elfin.* 1977. Viking. 1st ed. NF/dj. P3. $18.00

WARNER, Sylvia Townsend. *Lolly Willowes & Mr Fortune's Maggot.* 1966. Viking. special anniversary ed. 1/600. F. C4. $50.00

WARNER, W.H. *Report of Trial of Charles N Baldwin...* 1818. NY. Baldwin. 1st ed. 8vo. 124 p. M1. $175.00

WARREN, Austin. *New Eng Conscience.* 1967 (1966). Ann Arbor, MI. 231 p. mottled lavender cloth. VG/dj. G1. $20.00

WARREN, Carro Frances. *Little Chick Chickadee.* 1913. McKay. 1st ed. G. M18. $20.00

WARREN, Earl. *Memoirs of...* 1977. Doubleday. G+. M11. $20.00

WARREN, Earl. *Republic, If You Can Keep It.* 1972. Quadrangle. G/dj. M11. $25.00

WARREN, Edward. *Life of John Collins Warren, MD...* 1860. Ticknor Fields. 2 vols. orig cloth w/gold armorial crest. VG. G7. $175.00

WARREN, Howard C. *Dictionary of Psychology.* 1934. Houghton Mifflin. later prt. 372 p. bl cloth. G1. $22.50

WARREN, James. *Disappearing Corpse.* 1958. Washburn. 1st ed. VG/dj. P3. $20.00

WARREN, Joseph. *General.* 1927. Grosset Dunlap. photoplay ed. 182 p. VG/dj. M20. $60.00

WARREN, Joseph. *Revenge.* nd. Grosset Dunlap. photoplay ed. VG. P3. $20.00

WARREN, Louis. *Slavery Atmosphere of Lincoln's Youth.* 1933. Lincolniana Pub. 14 p. A6. $10.00

WARREN, P.N. *Beauty Queen.* 1978. Morrow. 1st ed. NF/VG+ clip. A14. $20.00

WARREN, R.L. *Politics & the Ghettos.* 1969. Atherton. 1st ed. 214 p. dj. A7. $16.00

WARREN, Robert Penn. *Chief Joseph of the Nez Perce.* 1983. NY. 1st ed/2nd prt. F/F. V1. $25.00

WARREN, Robert Penn. *Chief Joseph of the Nez Perce.* 1983. Random. AP. F/wrp. L3. $75.00

WARREN, Robert Penn. *Circus in the Attic.* (1948). Harcourt Brace. 2nd prt. Andre Dubus' copy w/sgn bookplate. VG/dj. L3. $85.00

WARREN, Robert Penn. *Circus in the Attic.* 1947. Harcourt Brace. 1st ed. VG/VG. L3. $125.00

WARREN, Robert Penn. *John Brn: Making of a Martyr.* 1929. Payson Clarke. 1st ed. author's 1st book. NF/NF. Q1. $1,500.00

WARREN, Robert Penn. *Or Else Poem/Poems 1968-74.* 1974. NY. 1st ed. sgn. NF/NF. E3. $45.00

WARREN, Robert Penn. *Robert Penn Warren Talking.* 1980. NY. 1st ed. sgn. F/NF. A11. $50.00

WARREN, Robert Penn. *Wilderness: A Tale of the Civil War.* (1961). Random. 1st ed. F/VG. B3. $45.00

WARREN, Robert Penn. *World Enough & Time.* 1950. Random. ltd/presentation ed. 1/732. gray cloth. NF/sans. L3. $85.00

WARREN, Robert Penn. *11 Poems on the Same Theme.* 1942. Norfolk, CT. 1st ed. w/sgn bookplate. F/gray dj. A11. $75.00

WARREN, Sidney. *Farthest Frontier: The Pacific NW.* (1970). Kennikat. facsimile of 1949 ed. 375 p. cloth. F. A17. $15.00

WARREN COMMISSION. *Report...on Assassination of President Kennedy.* 1964. McGraw Hill. 1st ed. 32 p photos. F/F. T2. $5.00

WARRICK, Patricia S. *Mind in Motion.* 1987. S IL U. 1st ed. F/dj. P3. $25.00

WARWICK, Sidney. *Silver Basilisk.* nd. Hodder Stoughton. VG/torn. P3. $10.00

WASHBURN, L.J. *Dead-Stick.* 1989. Tor. F/dj. P3. $17.00

WASHBURN, Owen R. *Dream Man: A Wonder Book.* 1905. NY. Washburn. octavo. ils HT Schermerhorn. yel brds. NF. B24. $150.00

WASHBURN, Wilcomb. *Preceedings of Vinland Map Conference.* 1971. Chicago. Newberry Lib. Samuel Eliot Morison's copy. M/dj. O6. $95.00

WASSERMAN, Jakob. *Caspar Hauser.* 1929 (1924). Verlag. 1st ed. 467 p. pebbled bl cloth. G1. $22.50

WATANABE, John. *Maya Saints & Souls in a Changing World.* (1992). Austin, TX. 1st ed. 280 p. wrp. F3. $15.00

WATANABE, Sylvia. *Talking to the Dead.* (1992). Doubleday. AP. F/prt bl wrp. B3. $25.00

WATERFIELD, Gordon. *Lucie Duff Gordon.* (1937). Dutton. 1st ed. 8vo. 358 p. VG+/fair. A2. $15.00

WATERLAND, Daniel. *Regeneration Stated & Explained...* 1829. Phil. Harding. 79 p. H10. $17.50

WATERMAN, Charles. *Hunter's World.* nd. NY. 1st ed. 250 p. F/dj. A17. $17.50

WATERS, Frank. *Earp Brothers of Tombstone.* 1960. NY. 1st ed. sgn. F/NF clip. A11. $65.00

WATERS, Frank. *Fever Pitch.* 1930. Horace Liveright. 12mo. G. A8. $25.00

WATERS, Frank. *Man Who Killed the Deer.* (1965). Northland. ltd ed. 1/1250. sgn. ils Perceval. F/F slipcase. A18. $150.00

WATERS, Frank. *Yogi of Cockroach Court.* 1947. NY. 1st ed. inscr. NF/NF. A11. $55.00

WATERS, Thomas A. *Lost Victim.* 1973. Random. ARC of 1st ed. RS. F/F. F4. $25.00

WATERS, Willard O. *Franciscan Missions of Upper CA As Seen by Foreign Visitors.* 1954. Glen Dawson. 1st ed. 1/200. VG. B19. $50.00

WATERTON, Charles. *Wanderings in S Am, the NW of the US, & the Antille...* 1925. London. Mawman. 326 p. quarter calf. VG. G7. $795.00

WATKINS, Carleton E. *Carleton E Watkins: Photographs 1861-74.* 1989. San Francisco. Fraenkel Gallery. F/F. B2. $50.00

WATKINS, Ivor. *Demon.* MacDonald. 1st ed. VG/fair. P3. $13.00

WATKINS, T.H. *Gold & Silver in the W.* 1971. Bonanza. 4to. F/G. A8. $15.00

WATKINS, T.H. *Vanishing Arctic: AK's Nat Wildlife Refuge.* (1988). Aperture. ils Mills/Wolfe. 88 p. M/dj. A17. $17.50

WATKINS, William Jon. *Clickwhistle.* 1973. Doubleday. xl. dj. P3. $5.00

WATKINS, William Jon. *God Machine.* 1973. Doubleday. 1st ed. VG/dj. P3. $20.00

WATKINS & WOLFE. *Your FL Garden.* 1956. Gainesville. revised ed. 349 p. VG. B28. $17.50

WATKINS & WOLFE. *Your FL Garden.* 1968 (1954). Gainesville. 5th ed/later prt. ils/pls. gr cloth. B26. $19.00

WATKINSON, Valerie. *Sped Arrow.* 1964. Scribner. 1st ed. xl. dj. P3. $5.00

WATSON, Colin. *Bl Murder.* 1979. Methuen. 1st ed. F/F. M15. $65.00

WATSON, Colin. *Just What the Doctor Ordered.* nd. BC. VG/dj. P3. $8.00

WATSON, Douglas S. *Spanish Occupation of CA.* 1934. Grabhorn. 1/550. ils/fld maps. NF. O6. $225.00

WATSON, George C. *Farm Poultry: Popular Sketch of Domestic Fowls...* ca 1901. Macmillan. ils. 369 p. F. H10. $9.50

WATSON, Gilbert. *Voice of the S.* 1906. Dutton. 1st Am ed. 8vo. 324 p. VG+. A2. $35.00

WATSON, Goodwin. *Youth After Conflict.* 1947. Assn Pr. 1st ed. 300 p. cloth. VG. G1. $20.00

WATSON, Ian. *Books of the Current.* nd. BC. VG/dj. P3. $10.00

WATSON, Ian. *Converts.* 1984. London. Panther. PBO. inscr. NF/8vo wrp. A11. $35.00

WATSON, Ian. *Embedding.* 1975. Scribner. 1st Am ed. author's 1st book. F/F. N3. $35.00

WATSON, Idelle Beaufort. *True Story of a Real Garden.* 1922. NY. 12mo. 183 p. VG. B28. $15.00

WATSON, J.N.P. *World of Polo: Past & Present.* 1986. Topsfield. 1st Am ed. 4to. VG/VG. O3. $45.00

WATSON, Lawrence. *In a Dark Time.* (1980). Scribner. 1st ed. F/F clip. B4. $150.00

WATSON, Merrill A. *Economics of Cattle-hide Leather Tanning.* 1950. Chicago. Rumph Pub. 1st ed. 248 p. VG. N2. $10.00

WATSON, Nancy Dingman. *Toby & Doll.* 1955. Bobbs Merrill. 1st ed. 8vo. 125 p. G+. T5. $20.00

WATSON, Samuel N. *Those Paris Yrs w/the World at the Crossroads.* 1937. Fleming Revell. ltd ed. sgn/dtd. VG. V2. $12.00

WATSON, Thomas Leonard. *Mineral Resources of VA.* 1907. Bell. xl. ils/ maps/ charts. 618 p. VG. B10. $100.00

WATSON, Virginia. *With Cortes the Conqueror.* nd. Hampton. ils Frank Schoonover. G. L1. $45.00

WATSON, Wilbur J. *Building the World's Largest Airship Factory & Dock.* ca 1930. np. 10 p. G/ils wrp. B18. $25.00

WATSON, William. *Wordsworth's Grave & Other Poems.* 1890. London. Unwin. 1st ed. inscr. Cameo series. brds. NF. B24. $250.00

WATT, Laughlan MacLean. *Advocate's Wig.* 1932. Herbert Jenkins. 1st ed. VG. P3. $30.00

WATT, Laughlan MacLean. *Rich Man, Dead Man...* 1956. Crime Club. 1st ed. VG/ dj. P3. $15.00

WATTERS, Thomas. *On Yuan Chwang's Travels in India. Vol 2.* 1905. London. Royal Asiatic Soc. 1st ed. xl. 8vo. 2 fld maps. VG. W1. $35.00

WATTERSON, Henry. *Hist of Spanish Am War.* 1898. St Louis. LF Smith. 1st ed. 8vo. pls. 474 p. gilt pict bl cloth. G. B11. $65.00

WATTS, Isaac. *Logic; or, Right Use of Reason.* 1819. Boston. W Richardson Lord. 288 p. worn leather. H10. $20.00

WATTS, Isaac. *Songs, Divine & Moral...* ca 1840s. Phil. Peck. miniature. 191 p. cloth. H10. $45.00

WATTS, Niki. *Greek Folk Songs.* 1988. Bristol. 8vo. 104 p. cloth. O2. $25.00

WATTS, W.L. *Gas & Petroleum Yielding Formations of Central Valley of CA.* 1894. Sacramento. CA State Mining Bureau Bulletin 3. 1st ed. 100 p. NF. O6. $250.00

WATTS, W.L. *Oil & Gas Yielding Formations of CA.* 1900. Sacramento. 1st ed. 236 p. cloth. D3. $45.00

WAUGH, Evelyn. *Loved One.* 1948. Little Brn. 1st ed. G/dj. M18. $50.00

WAUGH, Evelyn. *Loved One: An Anglo-Am Tragedy.* (1949). Chapman Hall. 1st ed. ils Stuart Boyle. F/F. B4. $200.00

WAUGH, Evelyn. *Officers & Gentlemen.* 1955. Little Brn. 1st ed. NF/NF. C4. $35.00

WAUGH, Evelyn. *Ordeal of Gilbert Pinfold.* 1957. London. Chapman Hall. 1st ed. F/clip. C4. $40.00

WAUGH, Evelyn. *Tactical Exercise.* 1952. Little Brn. 1st ed. F/NF. C4. $35.00

WAUGH, Evelyn. *Unconditional Surrender.* 1961. Chapman Hall. 1st ed. F/F. C4. $65.00

WAUGH, Evelyn. *Waugh in Abyssinia.* 1936. Longman Gr. 1st ed/mixed state. NF/NF. Q1. $500.00

WAUGH, Frank A. *TB of Landscape Gardening...* ca 1901. Macmillan. 1st ed. 344 p. H10. $45.00

WAUMETT, Victor. *Teardown.* 1990. St Martin. 1st ed. F/F. P3. $17.00

WAVELL, Archibald P. *Allenby: Study in Greatness.* 1940. Harrap. 1st UK ed. 312 p. gilt grd cloth. VG. M7. $22.50

WAYE, Cecil. *Prime Minister's Pencil.* 1933. NY. Kinsey. 1st Am ed. VG/dj. M15. $30.00

WAYLAND, John Walter. *German Element of the Shenandoah Valley of VA.* 1907. Charlottesville, VA. 312 p. maroon cloth. H9. $100.00

WAYMAN, John Hudson. *Dr on the CA Trail.* 1971. Denver. Old W Pub. 1st ed. fld map. 136 p. F. P4. $39.00

WAYNE, Joseph. *By Gun & Spur.* 1952. Dutton. 1st ed. VG. P3. $10.00

WEATHERBY, W.J. *James Baldwin: Artist on Fire.* (1989). Donald Fine. 1st ed. 412 p. F/F. A7. $14.00

WEATHERFORD, Jack. *Indian Givers: How the Indians...Transformed the World.* (1988). NY. 3rd prt. 272 p. F/dj. A17. $15.00

WEATHERS, John. *Beautiful Flowering Trees & Shrubs...* ca 1910. London. Simpkin Marshall. 33 chromolithos. 152 p. H10. $20.00

WEATHERWAX, Paul. *Indian Corn in Old Am.* 1954. NY. ils. 253 p. VG/dj. B26. $37.50

WEAVER, Earl. *It's What You Learn After You Know It All That Counts.* 1982. Doubleday. 1st ed. F/VG+. P8. $27.50

WEAVER, John D. *Warren: The Man, the Court, the Era.* 1967. Little Brn. M11. $20.00

WEAVER, Michael D. *Mercedes Nights.* 1987. St Martin. 1st ed. F/F. P3. $17.00

WEAVER, Muriel Porter. *Aztecs, Maya & Their Predecessors.* (1972). NY. Seminar Pr. 1st ed. 347 p. F3. $35.00

WEBB, G. *Office & Authority of Justice of Peace.* 1736. Williamsburg. 1st ed. calf. VG. C6. $7,500.00

WEBB, Jack. *Make My Bed Soon.* 1963. HRW. 1st ed. VG/dj. P3. $25.00

WEBB, Jack. *Naked Angel.* 1953. Rinehart. 1st ed. F/NF. F4. $40.00

WEBB, Joe. *Care & Training of the TN Walking Horse.* 1967. Searcy. revised ed. VG. O3. $35.00

WEBB, Joe. *Rack-in-Style.* nd. Searcy. 1st ed. VG. O3. $25.00

WEBB, Jonathan. *Pluck.* 1983. McClelland Stewart. 1st ed. author's 1st book. NF/NF. A14. $25.00

WEBB, Kate. *On the Other Side: 23 Days w/the Viet Cong.* (1972). Quadrangle. 1st ed. 160 p. NF/dj. A7. $40.00

WEBB, Marion St. John. *House w/the Twisting Passage.* nd. Collins. VG-. P3. $12.00

WEBB, Sharon. *Half Life.* 1989. Tor. VG/dj. P3. $18.00

WEBB, Sidney. *Socialism in Eng.* 1890. London. Swan Sonnenschein. VG. B2. $85.00

WEBB, Todd. *Georgia O'Keefe: Artist's Landscape.* 1984. Pasadena. Twelvetrees. 1st ed. F/F slipcase. B2. $150.00

WEBB, W.E. *Buffalo Land: The Wild W.* 1872. Phil. 1st ed. ils. 503 p. NF. O7. $55.00

WEBB, Walter Prescott. *Great Plains.* 1931. Boston. Ginn. 1st ed/2nd issue. 8 pls/2 maps. 525 p. VG. H7. $55.00

WEBBER, Charles Wilkins. *Jack Long; or, Shot in the Eye.* 1846. NY. WH Graham. 1st ed. 8vo. prt wrp. M1. $750.00

WEBBER, Ronald. *Early Horticulturists.* 1968. Newton Abott, Eng. ils. 224 p. VG/dj. B26. $36.00

WEBBER, Winslow L. *Books About Books.* 1937. Boston. Hale Cushman Flint. 1st ed. 8vo. 168 p. VG/G+. F1. $50.00

WEBER, Francis J. *CA Bibliographies.* 1991. Hist Soc of S CA. 1st ed. ils/notes. 58 p. F. B19. $35.00

WEBER, Francis J. *CA on US Postage Stamps.* 1975. Worcester. Achille J St Onge. 1/1500. miniature. aeg. F. F1. $40.00

WEBER, Francis J. *Goodyear Blimp.* 1983. San Fernando. Junipero Serra. miniature. gr leather. F. H10. $17.50

WEBER, Francis J. *Select LA Bibliography, 1872-1970.* nd. Dawson Bookshop. 44 p. F/sans. B19. $25.00

WEBER, Lenora Mattingly. *I Met a Boy I Used To Know.* (1967). NY. Crowell. 2nd prt. xl. 292 p. G/glassine. T5. $12.00

WEBER, Shirley H. *Schliemann's 1st Visit to Am 1850-51.* 1942. Harvard. sm 4to. cloth-backed brds. O2. $40.00

WEBER, William A. *CO Flora: W Slope.* 1987. Boulder. ils/pls. 530 p. M/dj. B26. $37.50

WEBER & WIGMORE. *William S Horton: Am Impressionist.* May-June 1974. photos/ils. wrp. D2. $25.00

WEBSTER, A.D. *London Trees...* 1920. London. Swarthmore. ils. 218 p. VG. H10. $10.00

WEBSTER, F.A.M. *Lord of the Leopards.* nd. Hutchinson. VG/torn. P3. $25.00

WEBSTER, H.C. *Art & Thought: Thomas Hardy on a Darkling Plain.* 1947. Chicago. 1st ed. VG/G. B5. $17.50

WEBSTER, H.T. *Best of HT Webster.* 1953. Simon Schuster. 1st ed. VG/VG-. P3. $35.00

WEBSTER, Jean. *Daddy-Long-Legs.* 1912. Century. ils. 304 p. VG. S10. $25.00

WEBSTER, Jean. *Daddy-Long-Legs.* 1912. Grosset Dunlap. G/dj. A16. $20.00

WEBSTER, Margaret. *Same Only Different: 5 Generations of Great Theatre Family.* 1969. Knopf. 1st ed. dj. VG. N2. $7.50

WEBSTER, Noah. *Elementary Spelling Book.* 1829. Brattleboro. presumed 1st ed. 16mo. 168 p. B28. $65.00

WEBSTER, Noah. *Pay-Off in Switzerland.* 1977. Crime Club. 1st ed. VG/dj. P3. $15.00

WEBSTER, Noah. *Philosophical & Practical Grammar of Eng Language.* 1807. New Haven. 1st ed. 12mo. 230 p. modern full calf. M1. $400.00

WEBSTER. *Quilts: Their Story & How To Make Them.* nd. np. 75th anniversary of orig ed. cloth. G2. $30.00

WECHSLER, Herman. *Great Prints & Printmakers.* 1967. Abrams. inscr/sgn. VG/VG. A1. $65.00

WEDDA, John. *Gardens of the Am S.* 1971. NY. ils/pls. 255 p. dj. B26. $22.50

WEDECK, Harry E. *Pict Hist of Morals.* 1963. NY. Philosophical Lib. 1st ed. 4to. 314 p. gr cloth. G1. $35.00

WEDEK, Harry E. *Treasury of Witchcraft.* 1961. Bonanza. reprint. 271 p. maroon fabrikoid. VG/dj. G1. $20.00

WEDGEWOOD, C.V. *Battlefields in Britain.* 1945. London. 48 p. VG. H3. $12.00

WEDGEWOOD, Josiah C. *Staffordshire Pottery & Its Hist.* 1913. McBride Nast. G. A16. $65.00

WEEDEN, Norman F. *Sierra NV Flora.* 1981. Berkeley. ils/maps. 406 p. VG. B26. $12.50

WEEGEE. *Weegee's People.* 1946. DSP. 1st ed. NF/VG. B2. $100.00

WEEKLEY, Richard. *Adventures of Chet Blake, Plastic Man.* 1975. LA. Crescent. ils Kurt Conner. 137 p. wrp. A7. $15.00

WEEKS, John P. *Poultry Profit Guide.* 1953. Birmingham. Vulcan. ils. 393 p. H10. $6.50

WEEKS, Morris Jr. *Beer & Brewing in Am.* 1949. US Brewers Found. VG. P3. $6.00

WEEKS, R.K. *Convict B 14.* 1920. Brentano. VG. P3. $20.00

WEEMS, M.L. *Drunkard's Looking-Glass...Faithful Likeness of Drunkard...* 1818. prt for author. 6th ed. 8vo. ils. 63 p. M1. $200.00

WEEMS, M.L. *Mason L Weems on Marriage, Drink & Adultery.* 1929. Random. 1/1000. VG. E5. $60.00

WEES, Frances Shelley. *Country of the Strangers.* 1960. Doubleday. 1st ed. RS. VG/dj. P3. $20.00

WEHR, Julian. *Gingerbread Boy.* 1943. Dutton. sbdg. VG-. M20. $40.00

WEIDENTHAL, Leo. *From Dis's Waggon: Sentimental Survey of a Poet's Corner...* 1926. Cleveland. Weidenthal. ils. 70 p. VG. N2. $10.00

WEIGALL, Arthur. *Alexander the Great.* 1933. Putnam. 1st ed. VG. V2. $5.00

WEIGALL, Arthur. *Glory of the Pharoahs.* 1923. NY. 1st ed. 8vo. 338 p. F/G. H3. $45.00

WEIGALL, Arthur. *Tutankhamen & Other Essays.* 1923. Butterworth. 1st ed. VG. P3. $45.00

WEIGHT, Harold. *Rhyolite: Ghost City of Golden Dreams.* 1980. Calico Pr. G/wrp. A8. $2.00

WEIGL, Bruce. *Song of Napalm.* 1988. Atlantic Monthly. 1st ed. intro/sgn Robert Stone. F/F. C4. $50.00

WEIKART, Ann V. *Cullen Yates: Am Impressionist.* 1983. Hagerstown. 15 pls. stiff wrp. D2. $20.00

WEIL, Jiri. *Mendelssohn on the Roof.* 1991. FSG. 1st ed. trans from Czech. F/F. A14. $25.00

WEILL, E. *Traite Clinique des Maladies du Coeur Chez les Infants.* 1895. Paris. Doin. xl. 390 p. orig wrp bdg in lib buckram. G. G7. $75.00

WEINBAUM, Stanley G. *Red Peri.* 1952. Fantasy. 1st ed. Donald Grant bdg. F/dj. P3. $35.00

WEINBERGER, B.W. *Ancient Denistry in the Old & New World.* 1934. np. reprint. orig wrp. G7. $20.00

WEINER, Ed. *Let's Go to the Press.* 1955. Putnam. inscr/sgn. VG/dj. C8. $35.00

WEINER, Lionel. *Articulated Locomotives.* 1970. Richard Smith. VG/dj. A16. $50.00

WEINREICH, Max. *Hitler's Professors... Scholarship in Germany's Crimes...* 1946. NY. 291 p. VG/wrp. S3. $19.00

WEINSTEIN, Sol. *You Only Live Until You Die.* 1968. Trident. 1st ed. NF/dj. F4. $25.00

WEINTRAUB & WEINTRAUB. *Lawrence of Arabia.* 1975. LA State. 1st ed. sgns. 175 p. F/F. M7. $35.00

WEISBERGER, Bernard A. *They Gathered at the River...* ca 1958. Little Brn. ils/index. 345 p. H10. $17.50

WEISEL, Elie. *Town Beyond the Wall.* 1964. Atheneum. 1st ed. F/F. C4. $40.00

WEISGAL, Meyer W. *Palestine Book: Official Publication...NY World's Fair 1939.* 1939. NY. 4to. 139 p. VG/wrp. S3. $55.00

WEISGARD, Leonard. *Cinderella.* 1938. Garden City. pict brds. VG+/dj. M20. $35.00

WEISGARD, Leonard. *Circus Animals.* 1958. NY. Penn Prts. 6 laminated prts/fld. VG. A3. $50.00

WEISGARD, Leonard. *Mother Goose Nursery Pictures.* 1957. NY. Penn Prts. 6 laminated prts. G. A3. $50.00

WEISGARD, Leonard. *Plymouth Thanksgiving.* 1967. Doubleday. 4to. 61 p. VG/VG. A3. $15.00

WEISMAN, Alan. *Frontera: US Border w/Mexico.* 1986. HBJ. 1st ed. ils/maps. 200 p. F/NF. B19. $50.00

WEISS, Fredric Larry. *Freud: Knowing & Not Wanting To Know.* 1990. St Martin. 1st ed. sm 8vo. 194 p. VG/dj. G1. $17.50

WEISS, Joe. *Way You Make Your Bed.* 1954. Woodford. 211 p. VG/dj. M20. $10.00

WEISS, John. *Care & Cooking of Fish & Game.* (1982). Winchester. 1st ed. photos/index. 252 p. F/dj. A17. $10.00

WEISS, Susan. *Home Life of Poe.* 1907. NY. 1st ed. 229 p. VG. B5. $25.00

WEISS. *Am Bandanna.* 1990. np. pb. G2. $17.00

WEISS. *Design & Chart Your Own Needlepoint.* 1976. np. pb. G2. $4.00

WEISS. *Easy-To-Make Patchwork Quilts.* 1978. np. ils. wrp. G2. $5.00

WEISS. *Plastic Templates for Traditional Patchwork Quilt Patterns.* 1985. np. ils. wrp. G2. $4.00

WEIST, Jacob R. *Medical Dept in the War.* 1886. Cincinnati. Sherrick. 1st ed. sgn. 22 p. NF/wrp. M8. $125.00

WEITENKAMPF, Frank. *How To Appreciate Prints.* 1908. Moffat Yard. 1st ed. G+. V2. $12.00

WEITZMANN, Kurt. *Late Antique & Early Christian Book Illumination.* 1977. NY. 1st ed. 48 color pls. VG/dj. B18. $17.50

WELCH, A.C. *Prophet & Priest in Old Israel.* 1953. Macmillan. 160 p. VG+/VG. S3. $20.00

WELCH, James. *Death of Jim Loney.* 1979. Harper Row. 1st ed. F/F. B2. $65.00

WELCH, James. *Death of Jim Loney.* 1980. London. Gollancz. 1st Eng ed. F/dj. L3. $50.00

WELCH, James. *Fool's Crow.* 1986. NY. Viking. 1st ed. rem mk. VG/VG. B3. $40.00

WELCH, James. *Fool's Crow.* 1986. Viking. 1st ed. F/F. L3. $75.00

WELCH, James. *Indian Lawyer.* (1990). Norton. 1st ed. sgn. F/F. A18. $40.00

WELCH, James. *Indian Lawyer.* (1990). NY. Norton. 1st ed. F/F. B3. $20.00

WELCH, James. *Riding the Earthboy 40.* 1971. World. 1st ed. author's 1st book. F/F. A18. $100.00

WELCH, James. *Winter in the Blood.* (1974). Harper Row. 1st ed. F/F. A18. $60.00

WELCH, S.G. *Confederate Surgeon's Letters to His Wife.* 1911. NY/WA. Neale. 1st ed. inscr. cloth. F. C6. $2,200.00

WELCH, S.G. *Confederate Surgeon's Letters to His Wife.* 1954. Continental Book Co. repint of 1911 ed. 127 p. NF. M8. $35.00

WELCH, William C. *Antique Roses for the S.* 1990. Dallas. 200 color photos. 201 p. M/dj. B26. $27.50

WELCOME, John. *Best Crime Stories.* 1964. Faber. 1st ed. NF/dj. P3. $30.00

WELCOME, John. *Reasons of Hate.* 1990. Collins Crime Club. 1st ed. F/dj. P3. $20.00

WELD, H.H. *Benjamin Franklin: His Autobiography.* 1859. Derby Jackson. 2nd ed. half brn leather. VG. V2. $15.00

WELD, Isaac. *Travels Through the States of N Am.* 1807. London. Stockdale. 2 vols. octavo. city plans. lacks US map. H9. $675.00

WELDON, Fay. *...And the Wife Ran Away.* 1968. McKay. 1st Am ed. author's 1st book. NF/NF. B2. $75.00

WELDON, Fay. *Cloning of Joanna May.* 1990. Viking. 1st ed. inscr. F/F. B2. $35.00

WELDON, Fay. *Heart of the Country.* 1987. Viking. 1st Am ed. inscr. F/F. B2. $40.00

WELDON, Fay. *Praxis.* 1978. Summit. 1st Am ed. sgn. NF/F. B2. $65.00

WELDON, Fay. *Rules of Life.* 1980. Harper. 1st Am ed. inscr. F/F. B2. $40.00

WELDON, Fay. *Watching Me, Watching You.* 1981. Summit. 1st Am ed. sgn. F/F. B2. $60.00

WELDON, Walter. *Observations on Different Modes of Puncturing the Bladder...* 1793. London. Baker. 171 p. new brds. G7. $250.00

WELL, Danielle. *Baseball: Perfect Game.* 1992. Rizzoli. 1st ed. VG+/VG+. P8. $17.50

WELLARD, James Howard. *Snake in the Grass.* 1942. Dodd Mead. 1st ed. F/NF. M15. $65.00

WELLCOME, Isaac. *Treatise on 24th & 25th Chapters of Matthew.* 1855. Boston. self pub. 1st ed. 16mo. orig cloth. VG. M1. $250.00

WELLER, George. *Singapore Is Silent.* 1943. Harcourt Brace. 1st ed. 8vo. 312 p. VG. W1. $18.00

WELLER, J. *Fire & Movement.* (1967). Crowell. 268 p. clip dj. A7. $35.00

WELLES, Orson. *Mr Arkadin.* 1956. NY. sgn. VG+/dj. E3. $35.00

WELLES, Patricia. *Ghost of SW1.* (1986). Donald Fine. 1st ed. F/F. B3. $20.00

WELLES, Sumner. *Naboth's Vineyard: Dominican Republic, 1844-1924.* 1928. NY. Payson Clarke. 2 vols. ils/maps. VG+. O6. $100.00

WELLESZ, Egon. *Hist of Byzantine Music & Hymnography.* 1962. Oxford. Clarendon. 2nd ed. 7 pls. 461 p. H10. $48.50

WELLEY, Dean. *Raggedy Ann & the Daffy Taffy Pull.* 1972. Hallmark/Bobbs Merrill. 14 p. pict brds. VG. A3. $15.00

WELLINGTON, Amy. *Women Have Told: Studies in the Feminist Tradition.* 1930. Little Brn. 1st ed. 8vo. 204 p. purple cloth. VG+. B20. $25.00

WELLMAN, Manly Wade. *After Dark.* 1980. Doubleday. 1st ed. VG/dj. P3. $25.00

WELLMAN, Manly Wade. *Dark Destroyers.* 1959. Avalon. VG/dj. P3. $50.00

WELLMAN, Manly Wade. *Lost & the Lurking.* 1981. Doubleday. 1st ed. VG/dj. P3. $25.00

WELLMAN, Manly Wade. *Mystery at Bear Paw Gap.* 1965. Ives Washburn. 1st ed. VG/dj. P3. $30.00

WELLMAN, Manly Wade. *Old Gods Waken.* 1979. Doubleday. 1st ed. VG/dj. P3. $25.00

WELLMAN, Manly Wade. *Raiders of Beaver Lake.* 1950. Thomas Nelson. 1st ed. VG/dj. P3. $35.00

WELLMAN, Manly Wade. *School of Darkness.* 1985. Doubleday. 1st ed. F/F. F4. $17.50

WELLMAN, Manly Wade. *Voice of the Mountain.* 1984. Doubleday. 1st ed. VG/dj. P3. $35.00

WELLMAN, Manly Wade. *Who Fears the Devil?* 1963. Arkham. 1st ed. F/F. M2. $250.00

WELLS, A.W. *S Africa. Planned Tour of the Country Today.* 1939. London. 1st ed. 12mo. ils/maps. 432 p. gilt red cloth. VG+. H3. $40.00

WELLS, Anna Mary. *Sin of Angels.* 1948. Simon Schuster. 1st ed. VG-. P3. $15.00

WELLS, Anna Mary. *Talent for Murder.* 1942. Knopf. 1st ed. VG. P3. $25.00

WELLS, Carolyn. *Affair at Flower Acres.* nd. Canada. Doubleday Doran. VG. P3. $15.00

WELLS, Carolyn. *Folly for the Wise.* 1904. Bobbs Merrill. ils Shinn/Verbeek/others. 170 p. bl-gray cloth. VG. S10. $55.00

WELLS, Carolyn. *Marjorie in Command.* 1910. Dodd Mead. 1st ed. ils JC Pratt. 268 p. decor bl-gr cloth. VG. S10. $30.00

WELLS, Carolyn. *Patty & Azalea.* nd. Grosset Dunlap. VG. P3. $15.00

WELLS, Dean Faulkner. *Ghosts of Rowan Oak.* 1980. Oxford, MI. 1st ed. sgn Faulkner's niece. NF/wrp. A11. $55.00

WELLS, H.G. *Anatomy of Frustration.* 1936. Macmillan. 1st ed. VG. P3. $30.00

WELLS, H.G. *Bealby.* 1915. Macmillan. VG. P3. $25.00

WELLS, H.G. *Collector's Book of SF by HG Wells.* 1978. Castle. F/dj. P3. $10.00

WELLS, H.G. *Country of the Blind.* 1939. London. 1/280. sgn. ils/sgn Clifford Webb. Sutcliffe bdg. F/slipcase. H5. $1,800.00

WELLS, H.G. *Croquet Player.* 1937. Viking. 1st ed. NF/dj. P3. $13.00

WELLS, H.G. *Crux Ansata.* (1953). Freethought Pr. 160 p. wrp. A7. $8.00

WELLS, H.G. *Experiment in Autobiography.* 1934. Macmillan. 1st ed. inscr. 718 p. beige buckram. M7. $75.00

WELLS, H.G. *Famous Short Stories of...* 1937. Doubleday Doran. G. E3. $10.00

WELLS, H.G. *Floor Games.* (1911). London. Palmer. 1st ed. VG. B4. $225.00

WELLS, H.G. *Food for the Gods.* nd. Thomas Nelson. inscr/sgn/dtd 1909. VG. P3. $250.00

WELLS, H.G. *History of Mr Polly.* nd. Collins. VG. P3. $10.00

WELLS, H.G. *In the 4th Yr.* 1918. Macmillan. 1st ed. VG. V2. $9.00

WELLS, H.G. *Invisible Man.* 1897. London. 1st ed. octavo. Sutcliffe bdg. NF. H5. $1,250.00

WELLS, H.G. *Joan & Peter.* 1918. Macmillan. 1st ed. VG-. P3. $12.00

WELLS, H.G. *Little Wars.* 1970. Macmillan. VG-/dj. P3. $18.00

WELLS, H.G. *Meanwhile.* 1927. Doran. 1st ed. VG. P3. $30.00

WELLS, H.G. *Mr Britling Sees It Through.* 1916. Macmillan. 1st ed. VG. P3. $40.00

WELLS, H.G. *Seven Famous Novels.* 1934. Knopf. 1st ed. VG. P3. $30.00

WELLS, H.G. *Thirty Strange Stories.* 1974. Causeway. VG/dj. P3. $15.00

WELLS, H.G. *Time Machine.* 1931. Random. slipcase. P3. $30.00

WELLS, H.G. *Tono Bungay.* 1959. Collins. VG/torn. P3. $10.00

WELLS, H.G. *War of the Worlds.* 1954. Whitman. decor brds. VG. P3. $8.00

WELLS, H.G. *Works of...* 1924-27. Scribner. Atlantic ed. 1/1050. sgn in Vol I. 28 vols. teg. marbled ep. NF. H5. $7,500.00

WELLS, Helen. *Cherry Ames, Chief Nurse.* nd. Grosset Dunlap. VG/dj. P3. $6.00

WELLS, Helen. *Cherry Ames, Dept Store Nurse.* 1956. Grosset Dunlap. 1st ed. 212 p. VG/dj. M20. $16.00

WELLS, Helen. *Hidden Valley Mystery.* nd. Grosset Dunlap. decor brds. VG. P3. $8.00

WELLS, Helen. *Vicki Finds an Answer.* nd. Grosset Dunlap. VG/dj. P3. $8.00

WELLS, Henry W. *Poet & Psychiatrist, Merrill Moore: A Critical Portrait...* 1955. NY. Twayne. 326 p. prt red cloth. G1. $27.50

WELLS, James S. *Modern Miniature Daffodils.* ca 1989. Portland. Timber Pr. 1st ed. 4to. 170 p. M. H10. $35.00

WELLS, Lee E. *Big Die.* (1952). Rinehart. 1st ed. VG/dj. B9. $25.00

WELLS, Lee E. *Death in the Desert.* (1954). Rinehart. 1st ed. VG/dj. B9. $30.00

WELLS, Lee E. *Long Noose.* (1953). Rinehart. 1st ed. inscr. VG/dj. B9. $45.00

WELLS, Rhea. *Beppo the Donkey.* 1931 (1930). Doubleday Doran. 135 p. VG. P2. $12.50

WELLS, Tobias. *How To Kill a Man.* 1972. Crime Club. 1st ed. VG/dj. P3. $15.00

WELLS, Tobias. *Matter of Love & Death.* 1966. Crime Club. 1st ed. VG/dj. P3. $18.00

WELLS, Wesley Roberts. *Letters From the Death House.* 1953. LA Civil Rights Congress. 1st ed. NF/wrp. B2. $35.00

WELLS, Wesley Roberts. *My Name Is Wesley Robert Wells.* 1950. San Francisco. State Defense Committee. NF/wrp. B2. $45.00

WELLS. *Fans.* 1987. np. ils. wrp. G2. $15.00

WELLS. *Wells' Nat Handbook.* 1856. NY. 12mo. ils. 144 p. gilt brn cloth. VG. T3. $29.00

WELSH, Lilian. *Reminiscences of 30 Yrs in Baltimore.* 1925. Baltimore. 1st ed. 8vo. 167 p. bl brds. G. B11. $35.00

WELTY, Eudora. *Acrobats in the Park.* 1980. Northridge. Lord John. 1/300. sgn/#d. F. C4. $150.00

WELTY, Eudora. *Bye-Bye Brevoort.* 1980. Jackson. New State Theatre. 1/500. sgn/#d. F. C4. $150.00

WELTY, Eudora. *Curtain of Gr.* 1947. Harmondsworth. Penguin. PBO. sgn. VG+. A11. $60.00

WELTY, Eudora. *Delta Wedding.* 1946. NY. 1st ed. F/NF. A15. $130.00

WELTY, Eudora. *No Place for You, My Love.* 1987. Logan, IA. 1st separate ed. sgn. F/ils wrp. A11. $45.00

WELTY, Eudora. *On Short Stories.* 1949. Harcourt Brace. 1st ed. 1/1500. NF. L3. $150.00

WELTY, Eudora. *One Writer's Beginnings.* 1983. London. Faber. 1st ed. w/sgn bookplate. F/wrp. A11. $60.00

WELTY, Eudora. *One Writer's Beginnings.* 1984. Cambridge. Harvard. AP. F/prt wrp. C4. $195.00

WELTY, Eudora. *Ponder Heart.* 1954. NY. 1st ed. F/NF. A15. $70.00

WELTY, Eudora. *Some Notes on Time in Fiction.* 1973. MS Quarterly. offprint. sgn. NF/stapled wrp. L3. $250.00

WELTY, Thomas. *Asians, Their Heritage & Their Destiny.* 1963. Lippincott. 8vo. 344 p. NF/dj. W1. $18.00

WELZL, Jan. *30 Yrs in the Golden N.* 1932. NY. 1st ed. 2 fld maps. 336 p. VG. A17. $10.00

WELZL, Jan. *30 Yrs in the Golden N.* 1932 (1930). Macmillan. 1st Am ed. 8vo. 336 p. F/F. A2. $30.00

WENGEL, Tassilo. *Art of Gardening Through the Ages.* 1987. German Republic. 1st Am ed. 4to. 272 p. NF/dj. B28. $25.00

WENT, Frits W. *Experimental Control of Plant Growth.* 1957. Waltham, MA. ils/25 pls. 343 p. B26. $22.50

WENTWORTH, Lady. *Authentic Arabian Horse.* 1962. London. Allen Unwin. 2nd prt. 4to. 368 p. F/dj/slipcase. O3. $495.00

WENTWORTH, Patricia. *Case Is Closed.* 1950. Hodder Stoughton. 3rd ed. VG. P3. $15.00

WENTWORTH, Patricia. *Fear by Night.* (1934). Lippincott. 1st ed. VG+/dj. B9. $85.00

WENTWORTH, Patricia. *Ivory Dagger.* 1951. Lippincott. 1st ed. VG. P3. $20.00

WENTWORTH, Patricia. *Miss Silver Comes To Stay.* 1951. Lippincott. VG. P3. $20.00

WENTWORTH, Patricia. *Pilgrim's Rest.* 1946. Lippincott. VG. P3. $25.00

WENTZ, Roby. *Eleven W Presses: Account of How 1st Prt Pr Came...States.* 1956. LA. Prt House Craftsmen. quarto. 57 p. decor paper brds/cloth spine. NF. B20. $65.00

WENZLOFF, Gustav Gottlieb. *Sketches & Legends of the W.* (1912). Pierre, SD. inscr. 113 p. decor cloth. VG. B18. $19.50

WEPFER, Johannes. *Observationes Medico-Practicae, de Affecibus Capitis...* 1727. Ziegleri. thick 4to. quarter calf/marbled brds. G7. $595.00

WERFEL, Franz. *Fourty Days of Musa Dagh.* 1934. Viking. 1st ed. NF. P3. $20.00

WERFEL, Franz. *Song of Bernadette.* 1942. Viking. 1st Am ed. trans from German. NF/VG clip. A14. $25.00

WERKMEISTER, W.H. *Hist of Philosophical Ideas in Am.* 1949. NY. Ronald. 1st ed. panelled bl cloth. VG. G1. $30.00

WERNER, Henry. *Guardian Spirits...* 1847. NY. Allen. 1st ed. 215 p. H10. $22.50

WERNER, Herbert A. *Iron Coffins.* 1969. NY. HRW. BC. VG/dj. A16. $9.00

WERNER, Jane. *Child's Book of Bible Stories From Garden of Eden...* 1944. Random House. ils Masha. 53 p. VG/dj. A3. $15.00

WERRY, R.R. *Delicately Personal Matter.* 1986. Dodd Mead. 1st ed. VG/VG. V2. $4.00

WERSHOVEN, F.J. *Lilliput Dictionary.* ca 1910. Leipzig. Schmidt Guenther. miniature. 657 p. gilt leather. H10. $50.00

WERT, Jeffrey. *Mosby's Rangers.* 1990. BC. F/dj. C1. $6.50

WERTENBAKER, T.J. *Torchbearer of the Revolution...Bacon's Rebellion...* 1941. Princeton, NJ. 2nd prt. 8vo. 237 p. F/VG. A2. $20.00

WERTH, Leon. *Eloge de Albert Marquet.* 1948. Bruker. 1/200. VG/wrp. A1. $125.00

WESCOTT, Glenway. *Apartment in Athens.* 1945. Harper. ne (no date code). author's last novel. VG+/VG+. A14. $25.00

WESCOTT, Glenway. *Natives of Rock: XX Poems: 1921-22.* 1925. NY. Bianco. 1/500. thin 8vo. F/orig box. F1. $125.00

WESLEY, J. *Christian Perfection.* 1952. World. 1st ed. VG/VG. V2. $4.00

WESSELLS, Katherine. *Golden Song Book.* 1945. Simon Schuster. 1st ed. 76 p. F/G+. P2. $20.00

WESSER, Robert F. *Charles Evans Hughes: Politics & Reform in NY 1905-10.* 1967. Ithaca. Cornell. M11. $45.00

WEST, Charles. *On Some Disorders of the Nervous System in Childhood...* 1871. Phil. Lea. 1st Am ed. G7. $135.00

WEST, Edwin; see Westlake, Donald E.

WEST, Herbert Faulkner. *Mind on the Wing.* 1947. NY. Coward McCann. 1st ed. NF/NF/clear plastic. M7. $45.00

WEST, Jessamyn. *Collected Stories.* 1986. HBJ. 1st ed. 8vo. 480 p. rem mk. VG/VG. V3. $10.50

WEST, Jessamyn. *Friendly Persuasion.* 1945. Harcourt Brace. 8vo. 214 p. VG/dj. V3. $8.50

WEST, Jessamyn. *Woman Said Yes.* 1975. HBJ. 1st ed. 8vo. 180 p. VG/dj. V3. $10.00

WEST, Kate Douglas. *Rebecca of Sunnybrook Farm.* 1925. Houghton Mifflin. ils Helen Grose. G. L1. $25.00

WEST, Mae. *Goodness Had Nothing To Do w/It.* (1959). Prentice Hall. 1st ed. 8vo. 271 p. F/VG. A2. $25.00

WEST, Morris L. *Cassidy.* 1986. Doubleday. 1st ed. VG/dj. P3. $15.00

WEST, Morris L. *Clowns of God.* 1981. Morrow. 1st ed. VG/dj. P3. $15.00

WEST, Morris L. *Harlequin.* 1974. Morrow. 1st ed. F/dj. P3. $23.00

WEST, Morris L. *Les Souliers Saint de Pierre (Shoes of the Fisherman).* (1963). Paris. 1st French ed? VG/VG. B3. $20.00

WEST, Morris L. *Proteus.* 1979. Collins. 1st ed. F/dj. P3. $20.00

WEST, Owen; see Koontz, Dean R.

WEST, Pamela. *Yours Truly, Jack the Ripper.* nd. BC. VG/dj. P3. $10.00

WEST, Paul. *Alley Jaggers.* 1966. NY. 1st ed. sgn. NF/NF. A11. $55.00

WEST, Paul. *Pearl & the Pumpkin.* 1904. NY. Dillingham. 1st ed. ils Denslow/16 color pls. 240 p. F. D1. $400.00

WEST, Richard S. *Gideon Welles: Lincoln's Navy Dept.* 1943. Bobbs Merrill. 1st ed. VG/dj. A16. $27.50

WEST, Richard. *Back to Africa: Hist of Sierra Leone & Liberia.* (1971). NY. HRW. 1st Am ed. 8vo. 357 p. F/F. A2. $20.00

WEST, Samuel. *On Granular Kidney & Physiological Albuminuria...* 1900. London. Glaisher. 197 p. G. G7. $30.00

WEST, Tom. *Renegade Range.* (1947). World. 1st ed. G+/dj. B9. $12.50

WEST, Wallace. *Bird of Time.* 1959. Gnome. 1st ed. F/dj. M2. $30.00

WEST, Wallace. *Bird of Time.* 1959. Gnome. 1st ed. VG/dj. P3. $25.00

WEST, Wallace. *Outposts in Space.* 1962. Avalon. 1st ed. NF/dj. P3. $30.00

WESTBROOK, Bill. *Fan.* ca 1972. Thomas Hale. photos. VG/G.B10. $25.00

WESTBROOK, Robert. *Lady Left.* 1990. Crown. 1st ed. NF/dj. P3. $18.00

WESTCOTT, Jan. *Hepburn.* 1950. Crown. 1st ed. VG/dj. P3. $15.00

WESTCOTT. *Pop-Up, Pull-Tab, Playtime, House That Jack Built.* 1991. paper engineering by Roger Culbertson. F. A4. $30.00

WESTERBURY, J.B. *Memoir of Rev John Scudder, MD...Missionary in India.* 1870. NY. Harper. 1st ed. 307 p. VG. W1. $45.00

WESTERMARCK, Edward. *Origin & Development of Moral Ideas.* 1912. London. Macmillan. 2nd ed. 852 p. gr cloth. VG. S9. $65.00

WESTERMEIER, Clifford P. *Who Rush to Glory: Cowboy Volunteers in 1898...* 1958. Caldwell, ID. Caxton. 1st ed. 13 pls. 272 p. pict ep. red cloth. B11. $60.00

WESTERMEYER, Joseph. *Poppies, Pipes & People: Opium & Its Use in Laos.* (1982). Berkeley. 1st ed. 8vo. 336 p. F/F. A2. $17.50

WESTERVELT, Josephine H. *Lure of the Leopard Skin.* 1921. NY. 8vo. 240 p. red cloth. VG. H3. $15.00

WESTERVELT, W.D. *HI Hist Legends.* (1926). Revell. sgn. 218 p. tangerine cloth. VG+/dj. B22. $17.00

WESTHEIMER, David. *Magic Fallacy.* 1950. NY. 1st ed. inscr. NF/VG. A11. $40.00

WESTIN, Alan. *Constitution & Loyalty Programs.* 1954. NY. Carrie Chapman Catt Memorial Fund. 53 p. wrp. M11. $20.00

WESTLAKE, Donald E. *Blackbird.* (1969). Macmillan. 1st ed. NF/dj. B9. $35.00

WESTLAKE, Donald E. *Damsel.* (1967). Macmillan. 1st ed. VG/dj. B9. $35.00

WESTLAKE, Donald E. *Drowned Hopes.* (1990). Mysterious. 1/100. sgn. F/slipcase. B9. $75.00

WESTLAKE, Donald E. *Drowned Hopes.* 1990. Mysterious. 1st ed. NF/dj. P3. $19.00

WESTLAKE, Donald E. *Good Behavior.* (1986). Mysterious. ltd ed. sgn. F/slipcase. B9. $100.00

WESTLAKE, Donald E. *Good Behavior.* 1986. Mysterious. 1st ed. NF/dj. P3. $16.00

WESTLAKE, Donald E. *High Adventure.* (1985). Mysterious. 1/250. sgn. F/dj/slipcase. B9. $100.00

WESTLAKE, Donald E. *High Adventure.* 1985. Mysterious. 1st ed. NF/dj. P3. $20.00

WESTLAKE, Donald E. *Hot Rock.* 1970. Simon Schuster. 1st ed. F/F. M15. $85.00

WESTLAKE, Donald E. *I Know a Trick Worth Two of That.* 1986. Tor. 1st ed. VG/dj. P3. $15.00

WESTLAKE, Donald E. *Jugger.* 1986. London. Allison. 1st British hc ed. NF/dj. S5. $27.50

WESTLAKE, Donald E. *Killy.* 1963. Random. 1st ed. VG/VG-. P3. $75.00

WESTLAKE, Donald E. *Levine.* (1984). Mysterious. 1/250. sgn. F/slipcase. B9. $45.00

WESTLAKE, Donald E. *Levine.* 1984. Mysterious. 1st ed. VG/dj. P3. $15.00

WESTLAKE, Donald E. *Likely Story.* (1984). Penzler. 1/250. sgn. F/slipcase. B9. $45.00

WESTLAKE, Donald E. *Philip.* (1967). Crowell. 1st ed. F/clip. B9. $40.00

WESTLAKE, Donald E. *Rare Coin Score.* 1984. London. Allison. 1st British hc ed. sgn as Stark/Westlake. F/F. S5. $40.00

WESTLAKE, Donald E. *Sacred Monster.* (1988). Mysterious. 1st ed. rem mk. NF/F. B3. $15.00

WESTLAKE, Donald E. *Slayground.* (1971). Random. 1st ed. VG/dj. B9. $35.00

WESTMACOTT, Charles Molloy. *Eng Spy: An Orig Work...* 1825-26. London. Sherwood. 1st ed. octavo. 2 vols. 71 hc pls/75 woodcuts. Riviere bdg. H5. $2,500.00

WESTON, Carolyn. *Rouse the Demon.* nd. Random. 2nd ed. VG/dj. P3. $8.00

WESTON, Garnett. *Hidden Portal.* 1946. Crime Club. 1st ed. VG/dj. P3. $20.00

WESTON, Peter. *Andromeda 2.* 1977. Dobson. 1st ed. F/dj. P3. $20.00

WESTWOOD, J.N. *Locomotive Designers in the Age of Steam.* 1978. Rutherford, NJ. Fairleigh Dickinson. 1st Am ed. 8vo. 32 pls. F/F. B11. $25.00

WETMORE, Helen Cody. *Last of the Great Scouts...Life of Buffalo Bill.* 1899. Duluth Pr. 1st ed/2nd issue. G. H7. $15.00

WEVERKA, Robert. *One Minute to Eternity.* 1968. Morrow. VG/dj. P3. $13.00

WEXLER, Jerry. *Rhythm & the Blues.* (1993). Knopf. 1st ed. F/F. A7. $14.00

WEY, Francis. *Rome.* 1897. Phil. 8vo. pls. 510 p. teg. gilt dk bl cloth. F/F. H3. $30.00

WEYL, A.R. *Fokker: The Creative Yrs.* (1965). London. 1st ed. ils. 420 p. VG/dj. B18. $25.00

WEYL, Nathaniel. *Red Star Over Cub: Russian Assault of W Hemisphere.* 1960. NY. Devin Adair. 1st ed. 8vo. 222 p. VG/VG. B11. $15.00

WHARTON, Anne H. *In Chateau Land.* 1911. Phil. 1st ed. 8vo. 390 p. teg. F. H3. $40.00

WHARTON, Edith. *Artemis to Actaeon.* 1909. Scribner. 1st ed. NF/custom cloth slipcase. B4. $350.00

WHARTON, Edith. *Ethan Frome.* 1911. Scribner. 1st ed/1st issue (perfect type in last line p 135). NF. C4. $135.00

WHARTON, Edith. *Glimpses of the Moon.* 1922. Appleton. 1st ed. front free ep removed. VG. P3. $25.00

WHARTON, Edith. *Gods Arrive.* 1932. Appleton. 1st ed. professional replaced ep. F/NF. C4. $95.00

WHARTON, Edith. *Son at the Front.* 1923. Scribner. 1st ed. 426 p. VG. B22. $12.00

WHARTON, Edith. *Valley of Decision.* 1902. NY. 1st ed. 2 vols. VG. B5. $150.00

WHARTON, William. *Dad.* 1981. Knopf. 1st ed. F/F. T2. $12.50

WHARTON, William. *Pride.* (1986). London. Cape. 1st ed. F/F. B3. $30.00

WHARTON, William. *Tidings.* (1988). London. Cape. AP. VG/prt sienna wrp. B3. $25.00

WHEAT, Carl. *Mapping the Transmississippi W 1540-1861.* 1957-63. San Francisco. 5 vols in 6. folio. gr cloth. VG+. B20. $2,450.00

WHEATLEY, Dennis. *Bill for the Use of a Body.* 1964. Hutchinson. 1st ed. VG-/dj. P3. $15.00

WHEATLEY, Dennis. *Codeword-Golden Fleece.* 1957. Hutchinson. 4th ed. VG/dj. P3. $15.00

WHEATLEY, Dennis. *Dangerous Inheritance.* 1965. Hutchinson. 1st ed. VG/dj. P3. $25.00

WHEATLEY, Dennis. *Dark Secret of Josephine.* 1955. Hutchinson. 1st ed. VG/dj. P3. $30.00

WHEATLEY, Dennis. *Devil Ride Out.* 1972. Heron Books. VG. P3. $15.00

WHEATLEY, Dennis. *Evil in a Mask.* (1969). Hutchinson. 1st ed. VG/dj. B9. $22.50

WHEATLEY, Dennis. *Haunting of Toby Jugg.* 1951. Hutchinson. 3rd ed. VG-. P3. $25.00

WHEATLEY, Dennis. *Launching of Roger Brook.* 1972. Heron Books. VG. P3. $15.00

WHEATLEY, Dennis. *Malinsay Massacre.* 1986. Magnolia. F. P3. $15.00

WHEATLEY, Dennis. *Man Who Killed the King.* (1951). Hutchinson. 1st ed. VG+/dj. B9. $25.00

WHEATLEY, Dennis. *Murder Off Miami.* 1986. Michael Joseph. decor brds. F. P3. $25.00

WHEATLEY, Dennis. *Rape of Venice.* (1959). Hutchinson. 1st ed. VG+/dj. B9. $20.00

WHEATLEY, Dennis. *Satanist.* 1979. BC Associates. VG/VG-. P3. $7.00

WHEATLEY, Dennis. *Scarlet Impostor.* 1942. Macmillan. 1st ed. VG/clip. B9. $15.00

WHEATLEY, Dennis. *Strange Conflict.* 1952. Hutchinson. VG/dj. P3. $25.00

WHEATLEY, Dennis. *Strange Story of Linda Lee.* nd. BC. VG/dj. P3. $8.00

WHEATLEY, Dennis. *Sultan's Daughter.* 1963. Hutchinson. 1st ed. VG/VG-. P3. $25.00

WHEATLEY, Dennis. *Unholy Crusade.* (1967). London. Hutchinson. 1st ed. presentation inscr. NF/VG. B3. $50.00

WHEATLEY, Dennis. *Unholy Crusade.* (1967). London. Hutchinson. 1st ed. VG+/dj. B9. $20.00

WHEATLEY, Henry B. *Dedication of Books To Patron & Friend.* 1887. NY. 1st Am ed. 257 p. B18. $22.50

WHEATON, Elizabeth. *Prisons & Prayer; or, A Labor of Love.* (1906). Chicago. 1st ed. photos. emb cloth. A17. $20.00

WHEATON, Henry. *Elements of Internat Law w/Sketch of Hist of the Science...* 1836. London. B Fellowes. 1st ed. 2 vols. later buckram. M11. $650.00

WHEELER, Daniel. *Memoir of...w/Account of Labours in Islands of Pacific.* 1859. Phil. Assn of Friends. 24mo. 259 p. V3. $36.00

WHEELER, Ella. *Maurine.* nd (1901). Conkey. 221 p. aeg. red leather. VG. B22. $17.00

WHEELER, George Montague. *Preliminary Report Concerning Explorations & Surveys...* 1872. GPO. lg 4to. 96 p. orig gr cloth. H9. $225.00

WHEELER, George Montague. *Report Upon Geographical & Geological Explorations...* 1875. GPO. thick 4to. 14 pls. 681 p. blk cloth. H9. $180.00

WHEELER, Joseph. *Santiago Campaign 1898.* 1898. NY. Lamson Wolffe. 1st ed. 8vo. fld charts/maps. 369 p. bl cloth. B11. $120.00

WHEELER, Keith. *Alaskans.* 1977. Time Life. 4to. F. A8. $10.00

WHEELER, Keith. *Chroniclers.* 1976. Time Life. 4to. F. A8. $10.00

WHEELER, Keith. *Railroaders.* 1973. Time Life. decorative padded cover. VG. A16. $10.00

WHEELER, L.N. *Frontier in China.* 1881. Chicago. Griggs. 1st ed. 8vo. 268 p. VG. W1. $45.00

WHEELER, Olin D. *Trail of Lewis & Clark, 1804-1904.* 1904. Putnam. 1st ed. 2 vols. 8vo. red cloth. F. quite scarce. T8. $295.00

WHEELER, Olin D. *Wonderland 1905. Descriptive of the NW. Ils.* ca 1905. St Paul. 8vo. 119 p. bl wrp. H9. $45.00

WHEELER, Richard. *Dodging Red Cloud.* (1987). Evans. 1st ed. F/dj. B9. $10.00

WHEELER, Richard. *Sword Over Richmond: Eyewitness Hist of McClellan..* 1989. NY. later prt. 371 p. cloth. F/F. M8. $25.00

WHEELER, Ruth W. *With Scissors & Pen; or, Silhouettes & Verse...* 1933. private prt. 1st ed. sgn. ils Charles Wheeler. brn brds/pict label. VG/poor. S10. $45.00

WHEELER, W.A. *Forage & Pasture Crops...* ca 1950. Van Nostrand. 752 p. H10. $21.50

WHEELING, Kenneth Edward. *Horse-Drawn Vehicles at Shelburne Mus.* 1974. Shelburne. 4to. ils. 96 p. VG/wrp. O3. $85.00

WHEELOCK, H.H. *Beloved Adventure.* 1912. Sherman French. 1st ed. G+. V2. $5.00

WHEELOCK, John Hall. *Blk Panther: Book of Poems.* 1992. Scribner. 1st ed. 5-line inscr/dtd 1922. VG+. V1. $45.00

WHEELOCK, John Hall. *Human Fantasy.* 1911. Boston. Sherman French. 1st ed. VG. E3. $25.00

WHEELWRIGHT, Julie. *Amazons & Military Maids.* (1989). London. 1st ed. ils. 205 p. VG+/dj. B18. $27.50

WHELAN, Michael. *Works of Wonder.* 1987. Del Rey. 1st ed. F/dj. P3. $40.00

WHITAKER, Arthur Preston. *US & Independence of Latin Am, 1800-30.* 1941. Johns Hopkins. 646 p. NF/dj. O6. $45.00

WHITAKER, Donald P. *Area Handbook for Khmer Republic (Cambodia).* nd. WA, DC. 1st ed. 8vo. 389 p. gilt blk cloth. F. H3. $30.00

WHITAKER, Harold. *Harold Whitaker Collection of County Atlases...* 1947. Leeds. Brotherton Lib. ils/10 maps. NF. O6. $95.00

WHITAKER, W.J. *Progressive Course of Inventive Drawing...Pestalozzi...* 1853. Ticknor Reed Fields. 1st ed. 12mo. flexible cloth. M1. $350.00

WHITE, Charles. *Account of the Topical Application of the Spunge...* 1762. London. Johnson. 55 p. antique brds. G7. $295.00

WHITE, Charles. *Life & Times of Little Richard.* (1984). Harmony. 1st ed. 269 p. NF/NF. A7. $12.00

WHITE, E.B. *Here Is NY.* 1949. Harper. 1st ed. F/NF. C4. $50.00

WHITE, Edmund. *Beautiful Room Is Empty.* 1988. Knopf. 1st ed. VG/dj. P3. $18.00

WHITE, Edmund. *Nocturnes for the King of Naples.* 1978. NY. St Martin. 1st ed. NF/VG+ clip. A14. $25.00

WHITE, Edward Lucas. *Song of the Sirens.* 1934. Dutton. 1st revised ed. NF/dj. M2. $50.00

WHITE, Edward. *Chrysanthemum & Its Culture.* 1930. Orange Judd. 12mo. 192 p. B28. $20.00

WHITE, Ethel Lina. *Step in the Dark.* 1946. Books Inc. VG. P3. $13.00

WHITE, Frank. *Overview Effect: Space Exploration & Human Evolution.* 1987. Houghton Mifflin. 1st prt. inscr. 318 p. M/M. S9. $13.00

WHITE, Fred M. *Slave of Silence.* 1906. Little Brn. 1st ed. F. M15. $45.00

WHITE, G. Edward. *Am Judicial Tradition, Profiles of Leading Am Judges.* 1976. NY. Oxford. M11. $25.00

WHITE, G. Edward. *E Establishment & W Experience.* 1968. Yale U. 1st ed. F/F clip. A18. $30.00

WHITE, George. *Statistics of the State of GA: Including...Hist.* 1849. Savannah. Williams. 1st ed. 8vo. 624 p. blk cloth. w/later map. H9. $75.00

WHITE, Gilbert. *Works in Natural Hist...* 1802. London. J Wht. 2nd ed. 2 vols. morocco. G. B14. $175.00

WHITE, J.B. *Big Life.* (1955). Crowell. 1st ed. 8vo. 235 p. VG/VG. A2. $12.50

WHITE, James. *Watch Below.* 1966. Whiting Wheaton. 1st ed. VG/dj. P3. $75.00

WHITE, John. *Planters' Plea; or, Grounds of Plantations Examined...* 1930. Rockport, MA. Sandy Bay Hist Soc. facsimile of 1630 London ed. NF. O6. $65.00

WHITE, Lionel. *Clean Break.* 1955. Dutton. 1st ed. F/NF. M15. $45.00

WHITE, Mary. *Book of Games.* 1898. Toronto. 16mo. 191 p. gilt dk brn cloth. VG. H3. $12.00

WHITE, Patrick. *Cockatoos.* 1974. London. Cape. 1st ed. F/F. A14. $75.00

WHITE, Patrick. *Eye of the Storm.* 1974. Viking. 1st Am ed. NF/NF clip. A14. $40.00

WHITE, Patrick. *Flaws in the Glass: A Self-Portrait.* 1982. London. Cape. 1st ed/3rd imp. F/F. A14. $25.00

WHITE, Patrick. *Fringe of Leaves.* 1976. London. Cape. 1st ed. F/F. A14. $65.00

WHITE, Patrick. *Riders in the Chariot.* 1976. London. Cape. reprint of 1961 1st ed. F/F clip. A14. $25.00

WHITE, Patrick. *Solid Mandala.* 1966. Viking. 1st Am ed. NF/NF clip. A14. $50.00

WHITE, Patrick. *Twyborn Affair.* 1979. London. Cape. 1st ed. F/F. A14. $50.00

WHITE, Paul. *Heart Disease.* April 1931. NY. 1st ed. dk bl cloth. F. B14. $300.00

WHITE, Philo. *Philo Wht's Narrative of a Cruise in the Pacific...1841-43.* 1965. Denver. Old W Pub. 1/1000. M. O6. $85.00

WHITE, R.W. *Batfishing in the Rain Forest.* (1991). NY. 1st ed. 250 p. M/dj. A17. $9.50

WHITE, Randy Wayne. *Man Who Invented FL.* 1993. St Martin. 1st ed. sgn. F/F. M15. $35.00

WHITE, Richard. *It's Your Misfortune & None of My Own.* (1991). OK U. 1st ed. M/dj. A18. $40.00

WHITE, Robert W. *Hist of Cadiz Short Line Railroad.* ca 1966. Chicago. Blk Cat. miniature. 1/250. 76 p. leather. H10. $100.00

WHITE, Robert W. *Memoir: Seeking the Shape of Personality.* 1987. Homestead Pr. 1st ed. 7 pls. 144 p. gr stiff wrp. G1. $25.00

WHITE, Simon. *His Majesty's Frigate.* 1979. St Martin. 1st Am ed. F/F. F4. $20.00

WHITE, Sol. *Sol Wht's Official Base-Ball Guide.* 1984. Camden House. reprint of 1907 ed. F/sans. P8. $125.00

WHITE, Steward Edward. *Blazed Trail Stories.* 1904. NY. 1st ed. 260 p. teg. VG. D3. $25.00

WHITE, Steward Edward. *Mtns.* 1904. NY. 1st ed. 16 pls. 282 p. cloth. VG. D3. $25.00

WHITE, Steward Edward. *Rules of the Game.* 1911. NY. 1st ed. 4 color pls. 644 p. cloth. VG. D3. $25.00

WHITE, Steward Edward. *Silent Places.* 1904. NY. 1st ed. 7 color pls. 304 p. teg. cloth. VG. D3. $25.00

WHITE, Stewart Edward. *Old CA: In Picture & Story.* 1939. Garden City. 4to. VG/G. A8. $15.00

WHITE, T.H. *Elephant & the Kangaroo.* (1947). Putnam. 1st ed. NF/dj. A7. $45.00

WHITE, T.H. *Elephant & the Kangaroo.* 1947. Putnam. VG/dj. P3. $30.00

WHITE, T.H. *Once & Future King.* (1958). Putnam. 1st Am ed. F/NF. B4. $375.00

WHITE, T.H. *Sword in the Stone.* 1939. Putnam. 1st ed. front free ep removed. VG. P3. $30.00

WHITE, Ted. *Trouble on Project Ceres.* 1971. Westminster. 1st ed. xl. dj. P3. $8.00

WHITE, Teri. *Thursday's Child.* 1991. Mysterious. 1st ed. NF/dj. P3. $19.00

WHITE, Trumbull. *Our New Possessions... Tropical Islands...* 1898. Phil. Fidelity Pub. 8vo. 125 pls. 676 p. gilt gr brds. VG. B11. $35.00

WHITE, W.L. *They Were Expendable.* 1942. Harcourt Brace. 1st ed. 8vo. G. A8. $10.00

WHITE, Walter. *Rope & Faggot: Biography of Judge Lynch.* 1929. Knopf. 1st ed. F/VG. B4. $450.00

WHITE, William Allen. *Martial Adventures of Henry & Me.* 1918. Macmillan. 1st ed. ils Tony Sarg. VG. N2. $10.00

WHITE, William Patterson. *Adobe Walls.* 1933. Little Brn. 12mo. G. A8. $12.00

WHITE, William. *Sermon Delivered Before the General Convention...* 1801. NY. Swords. 29 p. H10. $15.00

WHITEAKER. *Eng Countryside Needlepoint.* 1988. np. ils/charts. cloth. G2. $25.00

WHITEBIRD, J. *Heat & Other Stories.* 1990. Orlando. Arbiter. 1st ed. F/wrp. L3. $45.00

WHITECOTTON, Joseph. *Zapotecs: Princes, Priests & Peasants.* (1977). Norman, OK. 1st ed. 338 p. dj. F3. $25.00

WHITEHEAD, George. *Memoirs of George Whitehead...* 1832. Phil. Kite. 2 vols in 1. 12mo. cloth. V3. $30.00

WHITEHEAD, Henry. *Jumbee & Other Uncanny Tales.* 1944. Arkham. VG/blk & wht photocopy dj. P3. $125.00

WHITEHEAD, Henry. *Jumbee & Other Uncanny Tales.* 1944. Arkham. 1st ed. F/F. M2. $300.00

WHITEHEAD, Henry. *W India Lights.* 1946. Arkham. 1st ed. F/M. M2. $125.00

WHITEHOUSE, P.B. *Round the World on the Narrow Gauge.* 1966. Doubleday. G/dj. A16. $20.00

WHITEHOUSE, P.B. *Steam Railways of the World.* 1992. London. Dorset. ils. 256 p. F/F. B11. $25.00

WHITEHOUSE. *Steam Locomotives: 3-Dimensional Book.* 1989. London. paper engineering by Keith Moseley. F. A4. $40.00

WHITEMAN, Paul. *Jazz.* 1926. NY. 1st ed. ils. 298 p. VG. B5. $27.50

WHITFIELD, Philip. *Macmillan Ils Animal Encyclopedia.* (1984). NY. 1st ed. ils. 600 p. F/dj. A17. $25.00

WHITFIELD, Raoul. *Gr Ice.* 1988. Eng. No Exit Pr. 1st British ed. F/F. S5. $35.00

WHITFIELD, Raoul. *Virgin Kills.* 1988. Eng. No Exit Pr. 1st British ed. F/F. S5. $35.00

WHITFORD, David. *Extra Innings.* 1991. Burlinghame. Harper. 1st ed. M/M. P8. $17.50

WHITHAM, A.R. *Holy Orders.* 1903. Longman Gr. 310 p. H10. $20.00

WHITING, John. *Persecution Exposed, in Some Memoirs...* 1791. London. Phillips. 2nd ed. 8vo. 520 p. leather. V3. $125.00

WHITING, Robert. *Chrysanthemum & the Bat.* 1977. Dodd Mead. 1st ed. photos. F/F. P8. $45.00

WHITING. *Old-Time Tools & Toys of Needlework.* 1970. Whiting. reprint of 1928 ed. wrp. G2. $9.00

WHITMAN, Edmund S. *Those Wild W Indies.* 1938. NY. Sheridan House. 1st ed. inscr. 316 p. G/G. B11. $40.00

WHITMAN, J.A. *Iron Industry of Wythe Co From 1792.* 1942. Wytheville, VA. SW VA Enterprise. 2nd/revised ed. VG/prt wrp. M8. $37.50

WHITMAN, W. *David Lilienthal: Public Servant in a Power Age.* 1948. Holt. 1st prt. VG. S3. $19.00

WHITMAN, Walt. *Am Bard.* 1981. Viking. orig preface. fwd James Hart. VG/dj. A16. $35.00

WHITMAN, Walt. *Leaves of Grass.* 1860-61. Boston. 1st pirated ed/actual 3rd ed (later issue). VG. A11. $165.00

WHITMAN, Walt. *Leaves of Grass.* 1882. Camden, NJ. author's ed. sgn. dk gr cloth. VG. H5. $3,500.00

WHITMAN, Walt. *Leaves of Grass.* 1930. Random. 1/400. folio. ils Valenti Angelo. 423 p. VG. H5. $1,750.00

WHITMAN, Walt. *Leaves of Grass.* 1942. LEC. 2 vols. sgn. full imitation vellum brds. slipcase. Q1. $1,250.00

WHITMAN, Walt. *Specimen Days in Am.* (1979). London. Folio Soc. 1st thus ed. F/box. B3. $60.00

WHITMAN, William. *Travels in Turkey, Asia-Minor, Syria...1799-1801...* 1803. London. 4to. pls/fld engraving/maps/fld frontis. full morocco. O2. $1,500.00

WHITMORE, Charles. *Winter's Daughter.* 1984. Timescape. 1st ed. VG/dj. P3. $15.00

WHITNEY, Albert W. *Man & the Motor Car.* 1936. Detroit. 3rd prt. 265 p. VG. A17. $9.50

WHITNEY, Alec. *Armstrong.* 1977. Crime Club. F/dj. P3. $13.00

WHITNEY, Caspar. *HI Am.* 1899. NY/London. xl. lg 8vo. ils/maps. red cloth. H9. $75.00

WHITNEY, Christine M. *Bermuda Garden.* 1955. Bermuda. 13 pls. 234 p. VG+/dj. B26. $29.00

WHITNEY, Janet. *Geraldine S Cadbury: 1865-1941.* 1948. London. Harrap. 1st ed. 8vo. 200 p. VG/torn. V3. $12.50

WHITNEY, Janet. *Judith.* 1943. NY. Morrow. 1st ed. 8vo. 340 p. VG. V3. $9.50

WHITNEY, John R. *True Story of the Martinique & St Vincent Calamities...* 1902. np. 8vo. pls. 560 p. decor ep. gilt red cloth. VG. B11. $30.00

WHITNEY, Phyllis A. *Feather on the Moon.* 1988. Doubleday. 1st ed. F/dj. P3. $18.00

WHITNEY, Phyllis A. *Poniciana.* 1980. Doubleday. 1st ed. VG-/dj. P3. $12.00

WHITNEY, Phyllis A. *Sea Jade.* 1964. Appleton Century. 1st ed. VG/dj. P3. $15.00

WHITNEY, Phyllis A. *Seven Tears for Apollo.* 1963. Better Homes Book Service. 1st ed. VG-/dj. P3. $10.00

WHITNEY, Phyllis A. *Singing Stones.* 1990. Doubleday. F/dj. P3. $20.00

WHITT, Ernie. *Major League Life.* 1989. McGraw Hill-Ryerson. 1st ed. M/M. P8. $17.50

WHITTAKER, John. *Janus Lascaris at the Court of Emperor Charles V.* 1977. Venice. offprint. 8vo. 34 p. prt wrp. O2. $12.50

WHITTEMORE, Thomas. *Gospel Harmonist...* 1844. Boston. self pub. music/index. half leather. H10. $37.50

WHITTEMORE, Thomas. *Plain Guide to Universalism...* 1840. Boston. self pub. 408 p. H10. $25.00

WHITTEN, Leslie H. *Progeny of the Adder.* 1965. Crime Club. 1st ed. NF/dj. P3. $35.00

WHITTIER, Henry O. *Mosses of the Soc Islands.* 1976. Gainesville. 1st ed. ils. 410 p. as new/clip. B28. $20.00

WHITTIER, John Greenleaf. *Among the Hills & Other Poems.* 1869. Boston. Fields. 1st ed. 12mo. 100 p. gilt gr bdg. G+. V3. $35.00

WHITTIER, John Greenleaf. *Among the Hills.* 1869. Fields Osgood. 1st ed. decor brds. worn. E3. $15.00

WHITTIER, John Greenleaf. *Ballads of New Eng.* 1870. Boston. Fields Osgood. 8vo. 92 p. G. V3. $12.00

WHITTIER, John Greenleaf. *Early Poems of..* 1885. Boston. 1st ed. gilt bl cloth. VG. V1. $25.00

WHITTIER, John Greenleaf. *Letters of...* 1975. Cambridge. Belknap Pr. 1st ed. 3 vols. 8vo. VG. V3. $50.00

WHITTIER, John Greenleaf. *Supernaturalism of New Eng.* 1969. Norman, OK. 1st thus ed. 8vo. 133 p. VG/dj. V3. $12.00

WHITTIER, John Greenleaf. *Tent on the Beach.* 1867. Tichnor Fields. 1st ed. VG+. E3. $20.00

WHITTIER, John Greenleaf. *Text & Verse for Every Day in the Yr.* 1884. Houghton Mifflin. 24mo. 145 p. G. V3. $7.50

WHITTINGHAM, Richard. *What a Game They Played.* 1984. Harper Row. 1st ed. VG/G+. N2. $7.50

WHITTINGHAM, Richard. *Wht Sox: Pict Hist.* 1982. Contemporary. 1st ed. photos. F/F. P8. $45.00

WHITTINGTON, Harry. *Play for Keeps.* 1957. NY. Abelard Schuman. 1st ed. F/NF. M15. $75.00

WHITTINGTON, Harry. *Treachery Trail.* 1968. Whitman. VG. P3. $20.00

WHITTINGTON, Harry. *Wild Oats.* 1953. Universal. Uni-Book 70. 1st ed. NF/digest-size wrp. F4. $65.00

WHITTLESEY, Ruth Taber. *Quakers Courageous: A Wartime Novel of a Friends Family.* 1955. NY. Exposition. 1st ed. 12mo. 158 p. V3. $8.00

WHOHL, Burton. *Soldier in Paradise. Autobiography of Capt John Smith.* 1977. Putnam. dj. VG. N2. $5.00

WHYMPER, Edward. *Travels Amongst the Great Andes of the Equator.* 1892. NY. Scribner. 1st Am ed. fld map/pocket map. 455 p. NF. F1. $300.00

WHYTE-MELVILLE, G.J. *Katerfelto.* nd. Phil. 313 p. gilt cloth. VG. A17. $10.00

WIARD, Leon A. *Intro to the Orchids of Mexico.* 1987. Ithaca. Comstock. 1st ed. pls/maps. 239 p. VG+. B28. $65.00

WIBBERLEY, Leonard. *Take Me to Your President.* 1957. Putnam. 1st ed. VG/dj. P3. $25.00

WICK & WOLF. *Batboy of the Braves.* 1957. Greenberg. 1st ed. sgn authors/23 team members. VG/G+. P8. $350.00

WICKERSHAM, James. *Old Yukon Tales, Trails, Trials.* 1938. WA Law Book Co. 1st ed. 514 p. bl cloth. VG. P4. $55.00

WICKERSHAM, James. *Old Yukon Tales, Trails, Trials.* 1973. St Paul. reprint. photos/index. 514 p. F. A17. $30.00

WICKSON, E.J. *CA Fruits & How To Grow Them.* 1912. Pacific Rural Pr. 8vo. fair. A8. $12.00

WICKWARE, Francis Sill. *Dangerous Ground.* nd. Doubleday. VG. P3. $8.00

WIDDER, Keith R. *Reveille Till Taps: Soldier Life at Ft Mackinac 1780-1895.* 1972. Mackinac Island. 1st ed. 116 p. wrp. A17. $10.00

WIDEMAN, John Edgar. *Brothers & Keepers.* (1984). HRW. 3rd prt. 243 p. F/NF clip. A7. $17.00

WIDEMAN, John Edgar. *Damballah.* 1984. London. Allison Busby. 1st British/1st hc ed of 1981 Avon PBO. NF/NF clip. A13. $30.00

WIDEMAN, John Edgar. *Fever.* (1989). Holt. 1st ed. F/VG. B3. $20.00

WIDEMAN, John Edgar. *Fever: 12 Stories.* 1989. NY. Holt. 1st ed. F/F. A13. $25.00

WIDEMAN, John Edgar. *Phil Fire.* 1990. Holt. 1st ed. F/F. A7. $20.00

WIDEMAN, John Edgar. *Reuben.* 1987. NY. Holt. 1st ed. NF/NF clip. A13. $30.00

WIDEMAN, John Edgar. *Stories of John Edgar Wideman.* 1992. Pantheon/Random. 1st ed. NF/NF. A13. $30.00

WIEDER, Arnold A. *Early Jewish Community of Boston's N End.* 1962. Brandeis U. 100 p. VG. S3. $30.00

WIEDER, F.C. *Monumenta Cartographica: Repros of Unique & Rare Maps...* 1925-32. The Hague. 4 vols. 102 pls. O6. $2,500.00

WIELER, Diana. *Bad Boy.* 1992. Delacorte. 1st ed. F/F. A14. $25.00

WIENER, Norbet. *Ex-Prodigy: My Childhood & Youth.* 1953. Simon Schuster. 1st prt. 311 p. VG/VG-. S9. $10.00

WIENER, Willard. *Four Boys & a Gun.* 1944. Dial. 1st ed. F/NF. F4. $52.50

WIENERS, John. *Asylum Poems.* 1969. Angel Hair. 1/190. sgn. NF. V1. $50.00

WIENERS, John. *Nerves.* 1970. London. 1st ed. sgn. F/F. V1. $45.00

WIER, Joannis. *Histories Disputes et Discours Illusions...Empoisonneurs...* 1885. Paris. Bureaux Proges Medical. reprint of 1579 ed. 2 vols. NF. G1. $175.00

WIESE, Arthur James. *Discoveries of Am to Yr 1525.* 1884. Putnam. xl. 12 maps. NF. O6. $75.00

WIESEL, Elie. *Beggar in Jerusalem.* 1970. NY. Random. 1st ed. trans from French. NF/NF clip. A14. $40.00

WIESEL, Elie. *Fifth Son.* 1985. Summit. 1st ed. NF/NF. E3. $12.00

WIESEL, Elie. *From the Kingdom of Memory: Reminiscences.* 1990. Summit/Simon Schuster. 1st ed. F/F clip. A14. $25.00

WIESEL, Elie. *Gates of the Forest.* 1966. HRW. 1st ed. trans from French. NF/NF clip. A14. $40.00

WIESEL, Elie. *Legends of Our Time.* 1968. HRW. 1st ed. inscr. NF/NF clip. A14. $30.00

WIESEL, Elie. *Souls on Fire: Portraits of Hasidic Masters.* 1972. Weidenfield Nicolson. 1st ed. trans from French. A14. $40.00

WIESEL, Elie. *Town Beyond the Wall.* 1964. Atheneum. 1st ed. trans Stephen Becker. NF/NF. A14. $60.00

WIFFEN, E.T. *Outing Lore.* 1928. NY. 1st ed. 185 p. gilt cloth. VG. A17. $20.00

WIGGIN, Kate Douglas. *Arabian Nights.* 1937. Scribner. ils Maxfield Parrish. G/G. L1. $65.00

WIGGIN, Kate Douglas. *Bird's Christmas Carol.* ca 1930. Grosset Dunlap. ils HM Grose. 74 p. VG/G. A3. $10.50

WIGGIN, Kate Douglas. *Bird's Christmas Carol.* 1941. Houghton Mifflin. Memorial ed. ils Jesse Gillespie. G/G. L1. $25.00

WIGGIN, Kate Douglas. *Child's Journey w/Dickens.* (1912). Houghton Mifflin. later prt. inscr. cloth. F. B4. $185.00

WIGGIN, Kate Douglas. *Diary of a Goose Girl.* 1902. Houghton Mifflin. 1st ed. ils Claude Shepperson. 117 p. VG+. S10. $50.00

WIGGIN, Kate Douglas. *New Chronicles of Rebecca.* 1907. Houghton Mifflin. 1st ed. ils FC Yohn. 278 p. VG. S10. $40.00

WIGGIN, Kate Douglas. *Penelope's Irish Experiences.* 1901. Houghton Mifflin. 1st ed. gilt gr cloth. VG. M5. $18.00

WIGGIN, Kate Douglas. *Rebecca of Sunnybrook Farm.* 1903. Houghton Mifflin. 1st ed/2nd state. 327 p. G+. P2. $25.00

WIGGIN, Kate Douglas. *Rebecca of Sunnybrook Farm.* 1904 (1903). Houghton Mifflin. 12mo. 327 p. VG-. S10. $25.00

WIGGIN, Kate Douglas. *Story of Patsy.* 1917. Houghton Mifflin. VG-. A3. $27.50

WIGGIN, Kate Douglas. *Susanna & Sue.* 1909. Houghton Mifflin. 1st ed. ils Alice Barber Stevens/NC Wyeth. VG. M20. $60.00

WIGGIN & SMITH. *Hour w/the Fairies.* 1911. Doubleday Page. ils Mackinstry. 59 p. brd w/pict label. VG-. A3. $25.00

WIGGINTON, Eliot. *Foxfire Book.* 1972. Anchor. not 1st ed. wrp. N2. $5.00

WIGGLESWORTH, Michael. *Day of Doom; or, Poetical Description of...Judgment.* 1715. Boston. J Allen. 6th ed. 18mo. old calf. M1. $6,000.00

WIGHT, Charles A. *Hatfield Book.* (1908). Chicopee Falls, MA. inscr. 59 p. VG. B18. $35.00

WIGHT, Thomas. *Hist of Rise & Progress of People Called Quakers in Ireland.* 1751. Dublin. Jackson. 1st ed. 8vo. 484 p. rpr leather. V3. $55.00

WIGHTMAN, W.P.D. *Growth of Scientific Ideas.* 1953 (1951). New Haven. Yale. 1st ed. 496 p. russet cloth. G1. $25.00

WILBERT, Johannes. *Folk Literature of the Yamana Indians.* (1977). Berkeley. 1st ed. 308 p. dj. F3. $25.00

WILBERT, Johannes. *Navigators of the Orinoco.* (1980). LA. 1st ed. 4to. wrp. F3. $15.00

WILBERT, Johannes. *Survivors of El Dorado.* (1972). NY. Praeger. 1st ed. 212 p. wrp. F3. $15.00

WILBERT, Johannes. *Thread of Life: Symbolism of Miniature Art From Ecuador.* 1974. Dumbarton Oaks/Harvard. 1st ed. 4to. 112 p. F/wrp. A2. $12.50

WILBUR, Richard. *Advice to a Prophet.* 1961. NY. 1st ed. sgn. VG/VG. V1. $40.00

WILBUR, Richard. *Ceremony & Other Poems.* 1950. NY. 1st ed. sgn. author's 2nd book. F/NF. V1. $95.00

WILBUR, Richard. *Walking To Sleep.* 1968. NY. 1st ed. sgn. F/NF. V1. $55.00

WILCOCKS, Alexander. *Essay on the Tides: Theory of the 2 Forces.* 1855. Phil. 1st ed. 16mo. pls. 71 p. gilt blk cloth. VG. rare. H3. $125.00

WILCOX, Collin. *Bernardt's Edge.* 1988. Tor. 1st ed. NF/dj. P3. $18.00

WILCOX, Collin. *Long Way Down.* nd. BC. VG/dj. P3. $8.00

WILCOX, Collin. *Third Figure.* 1968. Dodd Mead. 1st ed. VG/rpr. P3. $18.00

WILCOX, Frank. *OH Canals.* 1969. Kent, OH. 1st ed. 106 p. VG/VG. D7. $70.00

WILCOX, James. *Modern Baptists.* 1983. Garden City. 1st ed. sgn twice. F/NF. A11. $65.00

WILDE, Allan. *Christopher Isherwood.* (1971). NY. Twayne. 171 p. NF/dj. A7. $17.00

WILDE, Oscar. *Ballad of Reading Gaol.* 1899. London. Leonard Smithers. early ed. 31 p. cream/brn cloth. G. B14. $45.00

WILDE, Oscar. *Ballad of Reading Gaol.* 1930. Dutton. sm 4to. ils/presentation Vassos to Max Miller. NF/VG+. B20. $250.00

WILDE, Oscar. *De Profundis.* 1905. Berlin. Fischer. 1st German ed. 8vo. teg. VG+. F1. $125.00

WILDE, Oscar. *Fisherman & His Soul.* 1939. Grabhorn. ltd ed. 1/200. sm 4to. marbled brds/silk spine. F. B20. $225.00

WILDE, Oscar. *Happy Prince & Other Stories.* nd. Brentano. ils Charles Robinson. G+. P2. $45.00

WILDE, Oscar. *Harlot's House & Other Poems.* 1929. Dutton. 1/200. ils/sgn John Vassos. gilt leatherette/brds. NF. F1. $200.00

WILDE, Oscar. *House of Pomegranates.* nd. Brentano. 1st Am ed. ils JM King. 162 p. VG. scarce. D1. $825.00

WILDE, Oscar. *Lord Arthur Savile's Crime.* 1909. Tauchnitz. VG-. P3. $20.00

WILDE, Oscar. *Poems.* 1927. Boni Liveright. 1/2000. ils Jean de Bosschere. F/dj/slipcase. F1. $135.00

WILDE, Oscar. *Portrait of Mr WH.* 1921. NY. Kennerly. 1/1000. hand #d. NF. C4. $65.00

WILDE, Oscar. *Selfish Giant & Other Stories.* 1935. McKay. 1st ed. ils Kate Seredy. VG. D1. $50.00

WILDE, Oscar. *Selfish Giant & Other Tales.* 1986. Mitchell. 1st ed. decor brds. VG. P3. $20.00

WILDE, Oscar. *Writings of...* 1925. NY. Gabriel Wells. 1/575. 8vo. 12 vols. F. F1. $675.00

WILDER, Cherry. *Second Nature.* 1986. Allen Unwin. 1st ed. F/dj. P3. $20.00

WILDER, Laura Ingalls. *By the Shores of Silver Lake.* 1939. Harper Row. 2nd ed. 260 p. beige cloth. VG/worn. M20. $110.00

WILDER, Laura Ingalls. *Farmer Boy.* 1953. Harper. 1st thus ed. 8vo. 371 p. pict red/beige cloth. VG+/G+. T5. $45.00

WILDER, Laura Ingalls. *Little House in the Big Woods.* (1932). Harper. 7th prt. sq 8vo. 176 p. pict beige cloth. G+. T5. $40.00

WILDER, Laura Ingalls. *W From Home.* 1974. Harper Row. 1st ed. photos. VG/dj. M5. $20.00

WILDER, Louis Beebe. *Adventures in a Suburban Garden.* 1931. NY. ils/16 photos. 250 p. VG/dj. B26. $24.00

WILDER, Thornton. *Cabala.* 1926. NY. Boni. 1st ed/1st issue. inscr. author's 1st book. F/NF. B24. $1,250.00

WILDER, Thornton. *Merchant of Yonkers.* 1939. Harper. 1st ed. sgn Jane Cowl. NF/dj. B20. $150.00

WILDER, Thornton. *Our Town.* 1958. Longman Gr. 3rd ed. VG. P3. $6.00

WILDES, Harry Emerson. *William Penn: A Biography.* 1975. NY. Macmillan. 2nd ed. 8vo. 469 p. VG/dj. V3. $15.00

WILDSMITH, Brian. *N Wind & the Sun.* 1964. Franklin Watts. 1st Am ed. 4to. VG/G. A3. $15.00

WILEY, Farida. *Ernest Thompson Seton's Am.* 1954. NY. 1st ed. ils/index. 413 p. A17. $15.00

WILEY, Farida. *Ferns of NE US.* 1948 (1936). NY. oblong 12mo. ils. 108 p. VG+. B26. $12.50

WILEY, I.W. *Mission Cemetery & Fallen Missionaries of Fuh Chau, China.* ca 1858. NY. Carlton Porter. ils. 374 p. H10. $35.00

WILEY, Richard. *Soldiers in Hiding.* 1986. Boston. 1st ed. inscr/sgn. F/F. A11. $70.00

WILFORD, John Noble. *Mapmakers.* 1981. Knopf. M/M. O6. $30.00

WILHELM, Kate. *Clewiston Test.* 1976. FSG. 1st ed. VG/dj. P3. $15.00

WILHELM, Kate. *Dark Door.* 1988. St Martin. 1st ed. F/dj. P3. $17.00

WILHELM, Kate. *Hamlet Trap.* 1987. St Martin. 1st ed. F/F. F4. $18.00

WILHELM, Kate. *Infinity Box.* 1975. Harper Row. 1st ed. NF/dj. P3. $18.00

WILHELM, Kate. *Juniper Time.* 1979. Harper Row. F/dj. P3. $20.00

WILHELM, Kate. *Listen, Listen.* 1981. Houghton Mifflin. 1st ed. F/F. N3. $15.00

WILHELM, Kate. *Sense of Shadow.* 1981. Houghton Mifflin. 1st ed. VG/dj. P3. $20.00

WILHELM, Kate. *Somerset Dreams & Other Fictions.* 1978. Harper Row. 1st ed. F/F. F4/P3. $20.00

WILHELM, Kate. *Welcome, Chaos.* 1983. Houghton Mifflin. 1st ed. F/F. P3. $15.00

WILHELM, W. *Last Rig to Battle Mtn.* 1970. NY. 1st ed. VG/VG. B5. $30.00

WILKEN, Friedrich. *Geschichte der Kreuzzuege Nach Morgenlandischen...* 1807-32. Leipzig. 7 vols. lg fld map of Jerusalem. H10. $100.00

WILKERSON, David. *Purple Violet Squish.* (1969). Zondervan. 1st ed. F/dj. A7. $35.00

WILKERSON, Doxey A. *Negro People & the Communists.* 1944. Workers Lib. 1st ed. NF/wrp. B2. $25.00

WILKERSON, Doxey A. *Why Negroes Are Joining the Communist Party.* 1946. NY. New Century. 1st ed. NF/wrp. B2. $25.00

WILKINS, Cary. *Treasury of Fantasy.* 1981. Avenel. 1st ed. F/F. P3. $15.00

WILKINS, Charles. *Bhagvat-geeta...in 18 Lectures w/Notes.* 1972. Tilton, NH. Hillside. miniature. 1/250. cloth. H10. $22.50

WILKINS, Harold T. *Pirate Treasure.* 1937. Dutton. 1st ed. photos. 409 p. VG/VG. S10. $30.00

WILKINSON, Alec. *Riverkeeper.* 1991. NY. 1st ed. 191 p. F/dj. A17. $8.00

WILKINSON, Doug. *Land of the Long Day.* 1955. Toronto. 1st ed. ils/pls. 261 p. gilt bl cloth. VG. H3. $20.00

WILKINSON, John. *Quakerism Examined in Reply to Letter of Samuel Tuke.* 1836. London. Thomas Ward. 12mo. 484 p. ES. fair. V3. $35.00

WILKINSON, Kathleen. *Trees & Shrubs of Alberta.* 1990. Edmonton. 180 color photos. 191 p. M. B26. $20.00

WILKINSON, Roderick. *Murder Belongs to Me!* 1956. Museum Pr. 1st ed. VG/dj. P3. $20.00

WILL, George. *Men at Work.* 1990. Macmillan. 1st ed. F/F. P8. $15.00

WILLARD, Charles Dwight. *Fall of Ulysses: An Elephant Story.* 1912. Doran. octavo. ils Frank Van Beck. 78 p. gilt gr bdg. F/dj. B24. $165.00

WILLARD, Emma. *Abridged Hist of the US; or, Republic of Am.* 1846. NY. Barnes. improved ed. B11. $45.00

WILLARD, John. *Charles M Russell Book.* (1970). Superior. 1st ed. gilt leather. F/dj. A18. $60.00

WILLARD, Nancy. *Things Invisible To See.* (1984). Knopf. 1st ed. author's 1st novel. VG/VG. B3. $75.00

WILLARD, Nancy. *Water Walker.* (1989). Knopf. 1st ed. ils John Walker. rem mk. NF/F. B3. $20.00

WILLEFORD, Charles. *Guide for the Undehemorrhoided.* 1977. Miami. self pub. inscr. 32 p. F/F. A11. $165.00

WILLEFORD, Charles. *Kiss Your Ass Good-Bye.* 1989. London. Gollancz. 1st ed. F/F. M15. $45.00

WILLEFORD, Charles. *Kiss Your Ass Good-Bye.* 1989. London. Gollancz. 1st ed. rem mk. NF/F. B3. $30.00

WILLEFORD, Charles. *Off the Wall.* 1980. Montclair. Pegasus Rex. 1st ed. inscr. NF/dj. M15. $175.00

WILLEFORD, Charles. *Outcast Poets.* 1947. Yonkers. Alicat Bookshop. 1st ed. author's 1st pub. loose sheets/prt envelope. M15. $100.00

WILLEFORD, Charles. *Sideswipe.* 1987. St Martin. 1st ed. VG/dj. P3. $23.00

WILLEFORD, Charles. *Way We Die Now.* 1989. Gollancz. 1st ed. F/dj. P3. $25.00

WILLENSON, Kim. *Bad War: Oral Hist of Vietnam War.* (1987). NAL. 1st ed. F/F. A7. $30.00

WILLENZ, J.A. *Women Veterans.* (1983). NY. 1st ed. 252 p. VG+/dj. B18. $35.00

WILLETS, Gilson. *Greater Am.* 1898. NY. Neely. xl. oblong 24mo. photos. red cloth. VG. B11. $50.00

WILLEY, Gordon. *Essay in Maya Archaeolgy.* (1987). Albuquerque. 1st ed. 245 p. wrp. F3. $15.00

WILLEY, Gordon. *New World Archaelogy & Culture Hist.* (1990). Albuquerque. 1st ed. 436 p. F3. $30.00

WILLIAMS, Alan. *Shah-Mak.* 1976. CMG. 1st ed. F/F. P3. $18.00

WILLIAMS, Alan. *Tale of the Lazy Dog.* (1970). Simon Schuster. 1st Am ed. rem mk. NF/VG. A7. $35.00

WILLIAMS, Billy. *Billy.* 1974. Rand Mcnally. 1st ed. inscr. photos. F/VG. P8. $60.00

WILLIAMS, Brad. *Well-Dressed Skeleton.* 1963. Herbert Jenkins. VG. P3. $13.00

WILLIAMS, Carrington. *Family of Walter Armistead Williams & Alice Marshall...* (1968). np. sgn. ils. 60 p. VG/stiff wrp. B10. $25.00

WILLIAMS, Cecil. *I'm Alive.* (1980). Harper. 1st ed. inscr/sgn. 214 p. clip dj. A7. $20.00

WILLIAMS, Charles. *Aground.* 1961. London. Cassell. 1st ed. F/NF. M15. $45.00

WILLIAMS, Charles. *Dead Calm.* 1964. Viking. 2nd ed. VG/VG-. P3. $20.00

WILLIAMS, Charles. *Descent of the Dove.* 1950. London. Faber. 245 p. H10. $20.00

WILLIAMS, Charles. *Forgiveness of Sins.* 1942. London. Bles. 1st ed. 123 p. H10. $25.00

WILLIAMS, Charles. *Greater Trumps.* ca 1950. Pellegrini Cudahy. 268 p. H10. $15.00

WILLIAMS, Charles. *Man on a Leash.* (1973). Putnam. 1st ed. F/NF. B4. $75.00

WILLIAMS, Charles. *Sailcloth Shroud.* 1960. Viking. 2nd ed. VG/dj. P3. $25.00

WILLIAMS, Clayton. *Animal Tales of the W.* 1974. San Antonio. 1st ed. M/M. T8. $15.00

WILLIAMS, David. *Copper, Gold & Treasure.* 1982. St Martin. 1st ed. VG/tape rpr. P3. $10.00

WILLIAMS, David. *Liners in Battledress.* 1989. NY. Vanwell. as new/dj. A16. $27.95

WILLIAMS, David. *Murder for Treasure.* 1980. London. Collins. 1st ed. sgn. F/F. S5. $35.00

WILLIAMS, David. *Murder in Advent.* 1985. St Martin. 1st ed. NF/dj. P3. $15.00

WILLIAMS, David. *Treasure by Degrees.* 1977. Collins Crime Club. 1st ed. NF/dj. P3. $20.00

WILLIAMS, Dennis A. *Crossover.* 1992. Summit/Simon Schuster. 1st ed. sgn. author's 1st book. F/F. A13. $30.00

WILLIAMS, Dick. *No More Mr Nice Guy.* 1990. Harcourt Brace. 1st ed. F/F. P8. $12.50

WILLIAMS, Dorian. *Show Jumping: Great Ones.* 1970. NY. Arco. F/F. O3. $12.00

WILLIAMS, Edward Thomas. *China. Yesterday & To-Day.* 1929. Crowell. 4th ed. 8vo. 26 pls/lg fld map. 743 p. VG. W1. $350.00

WILLIAMS, Elizabeth Whitney. *Child of the Sea: Life Among the Mormons.* nd. Beaver Island Hist Soc. facsimile of 1905 ed. photos. cloth. F. A17. $25.00

WILLIAMS, Francis. *It Happened Tomorrow.* 1952. NY. Abelard. 1st Am ed. F/VG. N3. $15.00

WILLIAMS, Garth. *Tall Book of Makebelieve.* 1950. NY. 4to. 92 p. color ep. pict brds. VG-. H3. $20.00

WILLIAMS, George. *Holy City; or, Hist & Topographical Notices of Jerusalem...* 1845. London. 8vo. ils/maps. 512 p. stp cloth. O2. $185.00

WILLIAMS, H.L. *Taking Manila; or, In the Phillipines w/Dewey.* 1899. NY. Hurst. 12mo. pls. 228 p. teg. decor red cloth. VG. B11. $50.00

WILLIAMS, H.W. *Travels in Italy, Greece & the Ionian Islands...* 1820. Edinburgh. 2 vols. 8vo. 20 pls. contemporary panelled calf. O2. $550.00

WILLIAMS, J. David. *Am Ils.* (1883). Boston. 121 p. aeg. gilt cloth. A17. $20.00

WILLIAMS, J. Whitridge. *Obstetrics: A TB for the Use of Students & Practitioners.* 1903. NY. Appleton. 845 p. half calf. G7. $795.00

WILLIAMS, Jerre S. *Supreme Court Speaks.* 1957. Austin, TX. M11. $25.00

WILLIAMS, John A. *Captain Blackman.* 1972. Doubleday. 1st ed. 336 p. NF/clip. A7. $35.00

WILLIAMS, John G. *Field Guide to Nat Parks of E Africa.* 1968. Houghton Mifflin. 1st Am ed. pls. 352 p. F/dj. A17. $15.00

WILLIAMS, John. *Missionary Enterprises in the S-Sea Islands.* 1888. Phil. Presbyterian Board of Pub. 1st ed. 8vo. 416 p. VG. W1. $35.00

WILLIAMS, Jonathan. *Empire Finals at Verona.* 1959. Highlands, NC. ARC of Jargon 30. presentation inscr. RS. VG+/VG+. A11. $55.00

WILLIAMS, Jonathan. *Madeira & Toasts for Basil Bunting's 75th Birthday.* 1977. Highlands, NC. 1/1250. F/glossy 8vo wrp. A11. $35.00

WILLIAMS, Joy. *Changeling.* 1978. Doubleday. 1st ed. inscr/dtd 1978. F/F. L3. $175.00

WILLIAMS, Joy. *State of Grace.* 1973. Doubleday. ARC. inscr/dtd 1976. sgn twice. author's 1st book. NF/wrp. L3. $350.00

WILLIAMS, Joy. *Taking Care.* 1982. Random. 1st ed. author's 3rd book. F/F. L3. $45.00

WILLIAMS, Kenneth Powers. *Lincoln Finds a General: Military Study of Civil War.* 1959. Macmillan. 1st ed. 5 vols. orig cloth. NF/dj/slipcase. M8. $150.00

WILLIAMS, Lem D. *Am Ils Military TB.* 1861. Baltimore. xl. ils. 156 p. F. extremely scarce. O7. $65.00

WILLIAMS, Marilyn. *Stone Age Island: New Guinea Today.* 1964. Doubleday. 1st ed. 8vo. 342 p. F/VG. A2. $15.00

WILLIAMS, Mary Floyd. *Papers of San Francisco Committee Vigilance of 1851.* 1919. Berkeley. ils/fld map. 906 p. VG. B28. $75.00

WILLIAMS, Melvin H. *Drugs & Athletic Performace.* 1974. Springfield. Charles Thomas. dj. N2. $10.00

WILLIAMS, Monier. *Practical Grammar of Sanscrit Language...* 1864. Oxford. Clarendon. 3rd ed. 8vo. 409 p. G. W1. $30.00

WILLIAMS, Monier. *Sanskrit-Eng Dictionary, Etmologically...Arranged...* 1899. Oxford. 1st ed. 4to. 1333 p. VG. W1. $125.00

WILLIAMS, Moyra. *Breed of Horses.* 1971. Oxford. Pergamon. 1st ed. VG/G+. O3. $18.00

WILLIAMS, Oscar. *Little Treasury of British Poetry.* 1951. NY. 1st ed. presentation inscr. 874 p. half linen. VG/dj/slipcase. A11. $40.00

WILLIAMS, Otis. *Temptations.* (1988). Putnam. 240 p. F/F. A7. $12.00

WILLIAMS, Reese. *Unwinding the Vietnam War.* 1987. Seattle. Real Comet Pr. as new/wrp. A7. $18.95

WILLIAMS, Richard. *Loggers.* 1976. Time Life. 4to. F. A8. $10.00

WILLIAMS, Robert F. *Negroes w/Guns.* 1962. Marzani Munsell. 128 p. wrp. A7. $18.00

WILLIAMS, Samuel. *Beginnings of W TN in Land of the Chickasaws, 1541-1841.* 1971. Nashville. Bl & Gray Pr. reprint of 1930 ed. 8vo. maps/plans. 331 p. H9. $65.00

WILLIAMS, Samuel. *Hist of Am Revolution.* 1826. Stonington. 204 p. orig brds. B14. $75.00

WILLIAMS, Samuel. *Phases of SW Territory Hist...1940.* 1940. Johnson City, TN. Watauga Pr. 1st ed. removed from bdg vol. VG. M8. $45.00

WILLIAMS, Simon. *Shakespeare on the German Stage. Vol 1.* 1990. NY. Cambridge. dj. N2. $7.50

WILLIAMS, Stephen W. *Am Medical Biography or Memoirs of Eminent Physicians...* 1845. Greenfield. 9 engravings. Victorian emb cloth. G7. $195.00

WILLIAMS, Tad. *Stone of Farewell.* nd. Quality BC. NF/dj. P3. $10.00

WILLIAMS, Ted. *My Turn at Bat.* 1969. Simon Schuster. 1st ed. VG+/VG. P8. $40.00

WILLIAMS, Tennessee. *Androgyne, Mon Amour.* 1977. New Directions. 1/200. sgn/#d. w/color prt. F/slipcase. C4. $250.00

WILLIAMS, Tennessee. *Conversations w/Tennessee Williams.* 1986. Jackson, MS. 1st ed. F/F. C4. $30.00

WILLIAMS, Tennessee. *Grand.* 1964. House of Books. 1/300. sgn/#d. F. B2. $275.00

WILLIAMS, Tennessee. *Knightly Quest.* 1966. New Directions. ils Salvador Dali. NF/dj. C8. $75.00

WILLIAMS, Tennessee. *Memoirs.* 1975. NY. 1st ed. F. B14. $55.00

WILLIAMS, Tennessee. *Moise & the World of Reason.* 1975. Simon Schuster. 1st ed. rem mk. NF/NF. A14. $35.00

WILLIAMS, Tennessee. *Sm Craft Warnings.* 1973. London. Secker Warburg. 1st ed. F/dj. M18. $50.00

WILLIAMS, Tennessee. *Steps Must Be Gentle.* 1980. Targ. 1st ed. 1/350. sgn. marbled brds. F. B25. $250.00

WILLIAMS, Tennessee. *Streetcar Named Desire.* 1947. NY. 1st ed. NF/NF. A15. $275.00

WILLIAMS, Tennessee. *Summer & Smoke.* (1948). New Directions. 1st ed. F/VG+. B20. $85.00

WILLIAMS, Tennessee. *Three Players of a Summer Game & Other Stories.* 1960. London. Secker Warburg. 1st ed. F/NF. C4. $50.00

WILLIAMS, Tennessee. *Two-Character Play.* (1969). New Directions. 1/350. sgn. gilt bl over tan cloth. F/slipcase. F1. $250.00

WILLIAMS, Tennessee. *27 Wagons Full of Cotton & Other One-Act Plays.* (1945). New Directions. 1st ed/1st issue. NF/VG. B20. $135.00

WILLIAMS, Tennessee. *27 Wagons Full of Cotton.* 1953. New Directions. 3rd ed. F/VG+. C4. $60.00

WILLIAMS, Terry Tempest. *Pieces of Wht Shell.* 1984. Scribner. 1st ed. NF/VG. scarce. L3. $85.00

WILLIAMS, Terry Tempest. *Refuge.* 1991. Pantheon. 1st ed. sgn. F/F. B3/L3. $45.00

WILLIAMS, Thomas. *Lincoln & His Generals.* 1952. Knopf. BC. 363 p. cloth. VG/VG. M8. $25.00

WILLIAMS, Valentine. *Clock Ticks On.* nd. Collier. VG. P3. $15.00

WILLIAMS, Valentine. *Man w/the Clubfoot.* nd. Collier. VG. P3. $15.00

WILLIAMS, Valentine. *Mr Ramosi.* nd. Hodder Stoughton. VG-. P3. $7.00

WILLIAMS, Valentine. *Mystery of the Gold Box.* nd. Collier. VG. P3. $10.00

WILLIAMS, Valentine. *Return of Clubfoot.* nd. Thomas Allen. VG. P3. $15.00

WILLIAMS, Valentine. *Three of Clubs.* nd. Hodder Stoughton. VG. P3. $15.00

WILLIAMS, William Carlos. *Al Que Quiere!* 1917. Boston. 4 Seas. 1st ed. F/glassine dj. B2. $500.00

WILLIAMS, William Carlos. *Autobiography.* 1951. Random. 1st ed. F/NF. B2. $100.00

WILLIAMS, William Carlos. *Beginning on the Short Story.* 1950. Yonkers. Alicat Bookshop. 1st ed. F/wrp. B2. $60.00

WILLIAMS, William Carlos. *Broken Span.* 1941. New Directions. 1st ed. Poet of the Month series. F/NF. B2. $100.00

WILLIAMS, William Carlos. *Cod Head.* 1932. Harvest Pr. mk 1/100 for Milton Arbenethy. 4-pg. F. B2. $250.00

WILLIAMS, William Carlos. *Collected Later Poems.* 1950. New Directions. 1/100. sgn/#d. NF/slipcase. Q1. $950.00

WILLIAMS, William Carlos. *Desert Music.* 1954. Random. 1/2532. w/pub card. F/NF. C4. $65.00

WILLIAMS, William Carlos. *Desert Music.* 1954. Random. 1/100. sgn/#d. F/orig glassine/slipcase. Q1. $950.00

WILLIAMS, William Carlos. *Dog & the Fever.* 1954. Hamden. Shoe String. 1st ed. F/NF. B2. $75.00

WILLIAMS, William Carlos. *Dream of Love.* 1948. New Directions. 1/1700. F/wrp. B2. $125.00

WILLIAMS, William Carlos. *Flowers of August.* 1983. IA City. Windhover. 1st ed. 1/260. sm quarto. gilt gr cloth. B24. $85.00

WILLIAMS, William Carlos. *Life Along the Passaic River.* 1938. New Directions. 1/1006. NF/NF. B2. $200.00

WILLIAMS, William Carlos. *Paterson. Book 5.* 1958. New Directions. F/F. B2. $100.00

WILLIAMS, William Carlos. *Pink Church.* 1949. Golden Goose. 1/400. F/wrp. B2. $175.00

WILLIAMS, William Carlos. *Spring & All.* 1923. Paris. Contact Pub. 1st ed. NF/wrp. B2. $500.00

WILLIAMS, William Carlos. *William Carlos Williams: 2 Letters to Rene Taupin.* 1993. NY. Dim Gray Bar Pr. 1/50. F. C4. $35.00

WILLIAMS, William Carlos. *William Carlos Williams: 5 Experimental Prose Pieces.* 1970. London. MacGibbon Kee. 1st ed. F/clip. C4. $40.00

WILLIAMS, William Carlos. *William Zorach.* 1937. Stovepipe Pr. 1/500. F/sewn wrp. B2. $125.00

WILLIAMS. *Disney's Beauty & the Beast: Changing Pictures Book.* 1992. 10 movable/pop-up scenes. paper engineering by Rodger Smith. F. A4. $30.00

WILLIAMS. *Joy of Stitching.* 1978. np. cloth. G2. $12.00

WILLIAMSON, Charles. *Breaking & Training the Stock Horse.* 1962. np. 4th ed. VG/G. O3. $18.00

WILLIAMSON, Henry. *Salar the Salmon.* 1935. London. Faber. 1st ed. 319 p. rebound half brn leather. F. M7. $95.00

WILLIAMSON, J.N. *How To Write Horror, Fantasy & SF.* 1987. Writer's Digest. VG/dj. P3. $16.00

WILLIAMSON, J.N. *Masques.* 1984. Maclay. 1st ed. sgn. F/dj. P3. $25.00

WILLIAMSON, Jack. *Brother to Demons, Brother to Gods.* 1979. Bobbs Merrill. 1st ed. F/dj. P3. $18.00

WILLIAMSON, Jack. *Humanoid Touch.* 1980. Phantasia. 1st ed. 1/500. sgn/#d. F/dj/slipcase. P3. $45.00

WILLIAMSON, Jack. *Humanoids.* 1949. Simon Schuster. 1st ed. VG/dj. P3. $40.00

WILLIAMSON, Jack. *Legion of Time.* 1952. Fantasy. 1st ed. NF/dj. P3. $25.00

WILLIAMSON, Jack. *Mazeway.* 1952. Fantasy. 1st ed. Donald Grant bdg. as new/dj. P3. $18.00

WILLIAMSON, Jack. *Wonder's Child: My Life in SF.* 1984. Bluejay. 1st ed. F/wrp. M2. $10.00

WILLIAMSON, James A. *Voyages of the Cabots & the Eng Discovery of N Am...* nd. np. 1/1050. 13 maps. bl brds/vellum spine. NF. O6. $225.00

WILLIAMSON, John A. *Ocean in Eng Hist: Being the Ford Lectures.* 1979. Westport, CT. Greenwood. reprint. 208 p. N2. $7.50

WILLIAMSON, Moncrieff. *Robert Harris: Unconventional Biography.* 1970. Toronto. McClelland Stewart. 222 p. wht cloth. slipcase. D2. $45.00

WILLIAMSON, Thomas. *Oriental Field Sports...* 1819. London. Young M'Creery. 2nd ed. 2 vols. 41 hc pls. VG. H5. $2,000.00

WILLICH. *Domestic Encyclopedia. Vol 1 & Vol 3.* 1826. Phil. xl. 8vo. leather. T3. $25.00

WILLINGHAM, Calder. *End As a Man.* 1947. NY. 1st ed. sgn. VG+/VG+. A11. $85.00

WILLIS, Bailey. *Yanqui in Patagonia.* (1948). Stanford. 2nd prt. 152 p. F3. $15.00

WILLIS, Fritz. *Muffin.* 1945. Hollywood. Cherokee Pr. 4to. 18 p. G. A3. $7.00

WILLIS, Maury. *On the Run.* 1991. Carroll Graf. 1st ed. VG/VG. P8. $12.50

WILLIS, N.P. *Am Scenery; or, Land, Lake & River Ils...* 1840. London. Virtue. ils after WH Bartlett. 2 vols. gilt leather. B28. $950.00

WILLIS, N.P. *Pencillings by the Way.* 1842. London. 8vo. ils/2 pls. 464 p. rebacked calf/leather label. O2. $85.00

WILLIS, Ted. *Man-Eater.* 1977. Morrow. 1st ed. VG/dj. P3. $15.00

WILLIS, Thomas. *Cerebri Anatome: Cui Accessit Nervorum Descriptio et Usus.* 1664. London. Roycraft/Martyn. 1st ed/2nd imp. 15 fld pls. 240 p. vellum. G7. $3,950.00

WILLIS, William. *Gods Were Kind.* 1955. Dutton. 1st ed. 8vo. 252 p. VG/VG. A2. $12.50

WILLOCK, Franklin J. *Dalmation.* 1975. Chicago. Judy. facsimile of 1927 Derrydale ed. 1/3000. cloth. A17. $25.00

WILLOUGHBY, David. *Empire of Equus: The Horse; Past, Present & Future.* 1974. S Brunswick. Barnes. sm 4to. 475 p. VG/G. O3. $45.00

WILLOUGHBY, Malcolm. *US Coast Guard in WWII.* 1957. Annapolis. US Naval Instit. G/dj. A16. $42.50

WILLS, Garry. *Confessions of a Conservative.* 1979. Doubleday. 1st ed. 231 p. dj. A7. $15.00

WILLS, Garry. *Lead Time.* 1983. Doubleday. 1st ed. rem mk. dj. A7. $15.00

WILLS, Garry. *Nixon Agonistes: Crisis of the Self-Made Man.* 1970. Houghton Mifflin. 1st ed. 617 p. dj. A7. $15.00

WILLS, Garry. *2nd Civil War.* 1968. NAL. 169 p. VG/VG. A7. $20.00

WILLS, William. *Essay on Principles of Circumstantial Evidence...* 1872. Phil. Johnson. 5th Am ed. full sheep. M11. $75.00

WILLSON, Dixie. *Honey Bear.* 1923. Algonquin. ils Maginel Wright Barney. pict ep. VG. T5. $55.00

WILLSON, Dixie. *Pinky Pup & the Empty Elephant.* 1928. Volland. revised ed. ils Erick Berry. NF/VG box. D1. $225.00

WILLWERTH, James. *Eye in the Last Storm.* 1972. Grossman. 1st ed. NF/dj. A7. $35.00

WILLYAMS, Cooper. *Voyage Up the Mediterranean in His Majesty's Ship Swiftsure.* 1802. London. Bensley. 41 full-p tinted pls/fld chart. 309 p. F. O2. $1,500.00

WILSON, Adrian. *Printing for Theater.* 1957. San Francisco. 1/250. folio. w/theater programs. linen. NF. H5. $1,500.00

WILSON, Arthur M. *Diderot: The Testing Yrs 1713-59.* 1957. NY. Oxford. 417 p. cloth. G1. $27.50

WILSON, C.B. *N Am Parasitic Copepods: List of Those Found...* 1909. Smithsonian. removed from report. F. P4. $35.00

WILSON, C.M. *Aroostook: Our Last Frontier.* (1937). Brattleboro, VT. Stephen Daye. 1st ed. 8vo. 240 p. VG+. A2. $20.00

WILSON, C.M. *Stars Is God's Lanterns: Offering of Ozark Tellin' Stories.* (1969). Norman, OK. 213 p. dj. A7. $15.00

WILSON, Colin. *Afterlife.* 1985. Doubleday Dolphin. 1st ed. NF/dj. P3. $20.00

WILSON, Colin. *Casebook of Murder.* 1969. Cowles. 1st ed. VG/dj. P3. $25.00

WILSON, Colin. *Dark Dimensions.* 1977. Everest House. 1st ed. VG/VG-. P3. $15.00

WILSON, Colin. *Mind Parasites.* 1967. Arkham. 1st ed. F/dj. M2. $85.00

WILSON, Colin. *Outsider.* 1956. Gollancz. 1st ed. VG. P3. $75.00

WILSON, Colin. *Ritual in the Dark.* 1960. Gollancz. 2nd ed. VG/VG-. P3. $35.00

WILSON, Colin. *Schoolgirl Murder Case.* 1975. Hart Davies. 2nd ed. VG/dj. P3. $15.00

WILSON, Colin. *Space Vampires.* 1976. Random. 1st ed. xl. dj. P3. $10.00

WILSON, Dorothy Clarke. *Stranger & Traveler...Dorthea Dix, Am Reformer.* (1975). Little Brn. 1st ed. 360 p. dj. A7. $12.00

WILSON, Edmund. *Cold War & the Income Tax: A Protest.* 1964. London. WH Allen. 1st ed. inscr/sgn. F/NF. Q1. $450.00

WILSON, Edmund. *Letters on Literature & Politics 1912-72.* 1977. FSG. 1st ed. F/F. C4. $35.00

WILSON, Edmund. *Patriotic Gore.* 1962. Oxford. 1st ed. F/F. C4. $50.00

WILSON, Edmund. *Red, Blk, Blond & Olive.* 1956. NY. Oxford. 1st ed. inscr/dtd 1956 to his pub. F/NF. C4. $100.00

WILSON, Edmund. *Shock of Recognition.* 1955. FSC. 1st ed. F/NF. C4. $35.00

WILSON, Edmund. *To the Finland Station.* 1972. FSG. 1st prt. new intro. F/F. C4. $40.00

WILSON, Edmund. *Twenties.* 1975. FSG. 1st ed. F/F. C4. $35.00

WILSON, Edmund. *Upstate.* 1971. FSG. 1st ed. w/pub slip. F/F. C4. $40.00

WILSON, Edmund. *Window on Russia.* 1972. FSG. 1st ed. F/F. C4. $35.00

WILSON, Edward A. *Pirate's Treasure; or, Strange Adventures of Jack Adams...* 1926. Volland. 1st ed. ils. pict brds. VG-. S10. $25.00

WILSON, Edward L. *In Scripture Lands: New Views in Sacred Places.* 1895. NY. 8vo. 386 p. cloth. O2. $45.00

WILSON, Edward. *Diary of the Terra Nova Expedition to Antarctic, 1910-12...* 1972. London. Blandford. ils/10 maps. NF/dj. O6. $40.00

WILSON, Erica. *Erica Wilson's Quilts of Am.* nd. np. ils. wrp. G2. $20.00

WILSON, Erica. *People, Places & Quilts...* 1989. np. ils. wrp. G2. $16.00

WILSON, Everett B. *Early Am at Work: Pict Guide to Our Vanishing Occupations.* 1963. Barnes. 4to. dj. N2. $7.50

WILSON, F. Paul. *Blk Wind.* 1988. Tor. 1st ed. F/dj. P3. $30.00

WILSON, F. Paul. *Blk Wind.* 1988. Tor. 1st ed. sgn. F/F. F4. $35.00

WILSON, F. Paul. *Enemy of the State.* 1980. Doubleday. 1st ed. inscr/sgn. rem mk. F/F. F4. $40.00

WILSON, F. Paul. *Keep.* 1981. Morrow. 1st ed. sgn. author's 1st horror novel. F/F. F4. $50.00

WILSON, F. Paul. *Soft & Others.* 1989. Tor. 1st ed. F/dj. M2. $25.00

WILSON, Gahan. *Everybody's Favorite Duck.* 1988. Mysterious. 1st ed. VG/dj. P3. $16.00

WILSON, H. *Why & Wherefore? Simple Explanations...Ritual of Church.* ca 1897. Milwaukee. Young Churchman. 72 p. H10. $15.00

WILSON, Hazel. *Herbert's Space Trip.* 1965. Knopf. decor brds. VG. P3. $15.00

WILSON, Henry. *Benares.* 1985. Thames Hudson. 1st ed. 4to. 80 color pls. F/dj. W1. $20.00

WILSON, Henry. *Diplomatic Episodes in Mexico, Belgium & Chile.* 1971. Port WA. Kennikat. reprint, 8vo. 399 p. brn cloth. VG+. P4. $15.00

WILSON, Henry. *Hist of Rise & Fall of Slave Power in Am.* 1872-77. Boston. Osgood. 1st ed. 3 vols. cloth. VG. M8. $275.00

WILSON, Henry. *Occasional Addresses.* 1929. Lincoln. Fairfield. gilt bl cloth. M11. $35.00

WILSON, Herbert Earl. *Lore & Lure of the Yosemite.* (1923). San Francisco. 2nd prt. inscr. 12mo. 133 p. VG. D3. $25.00

WILSON, Hugh D. *Stewart Island Plants.* 1982. Christchurch. ils. 524 p. F. B26. $22.50

WILSON, Jeremy. *Lawrence of Arabia. The Authorized Biography.* 1992. NY. Collier/Macmillan. 1st (thus) pb ed/abridged. 453 p. NF/wrp. M7. $25.00

WILSON, Jeremy. *Minorities. Good Poems by Sm Poets & Sm Poems by Good Poets.* 1971. London. Cape. 1st ed. 272 p. F/F. M7. $55.00

WILSON, John Fleming. *Master Key.* nd. Grosset Dunlap. photoplay ed. VG. P3. $20.00

WILSON, John Lyde. *Abstract of System Exercise & Instruction Field Artillery.* 1834. Charleston. AE Miller. 76 p. contemporary wrp. B14. $100.00

WILSON, John S. *Collector's Jazz: Traditional & Swing.* (1958). Lippincott. stated 1st ed/pb. 318 p. A7. $22.00

WILSON, John. *Noctes Ambrosianae.* 1863. Widdleton. 1st thus/revised ed. 5 vols. cloth. VG. B22. $50.00

WILSON, L.M. *This Was Montreal in 1814-17.* 1960. Montreal. Chateau de Ramezay. 1st/ltd ed. 8vo. 205 p. VG/VG. A2. $20.00

WILSON, Mitchell. *Footsteps Behind Her.* nd. Simon Schuster. VG/dj. P3. $13.00

WILSON, Mitchell. *Stalk the Hunter.* 1943. Simon Schuster. 2nd ed. VG. P3. $12.00

WILSON, Neill. *Treasure Express: Epic Days of the Wells Fargo.* 1936. NY. Macmillan. 1st ed. VG/G+. O3. $65.00

WILSON, Richard. *Girls From Planet 5.* 1955. Ballantine. 1st ed. VG/VG-. P3. $60.00

WILSON, Robert C. *Crooked Tree.* 1980. Putnam. 1st ed. VG/dj. P3. $15.00

WILSON, Samuel Jr. *Colonial Fortifications & Military Architecture MS Valley.* 1965. Urbana, IL. pict gr wrp. H9. $25.00

WILSON, Steve. *Lost Traveler.* 1977. St Martin. 1st Am ed. F/F. N3. $20.00

WILSON, Thomas. *Brief Journal of Life, Travels & Labors of Love...* 1881. Friends Bookstore. xl. 16mo. 124 p. VG. V3. $12.50

WILSON, William E. *Angel & the Serpent. Story of New Harmony.* 1964. Bloomington, IN. 1st ed. 242 p. F/VG. B28. $25.00

WILSON, William Jerome. *Narrative of Discovery of Venezuela...* 1940. NY. Wilson. ils. 22 p. VG/wrp. O6. $25.00

WILSON, William. *Borderland Confederate.* (1962). Pittsburgh, PA. 1st ed. 8vo. 138 p. F/VG. A2. $20.00

WILSON, Woodrow. *George WA.* ca 1896. Harper. 1st ed. 333 p. cloth. VG. M8. $35.00

WILSON. *Crewel Embroidery.* 1962. np. cloth. G2. $13.00

WILSON. *More Needleplay.* 1979. np. ils. cloth. G2. $12.50

WILSTACH, Paul. *Tidewater VA.* (1929). Bobbs Merrill. 1st ed. 326 p. gilt cloth. A17. $12.50

WINCHELL, Alexander. *Sketches of Creation.* 1870. Harper. 1st ed. 459 p. G+. S9. $15.00

WINCHESTER, Elhanan. *Plain Political Catechism.* 1796. Greenfield, MA. Dickman. 12mo. 107 p. contemporary gray cloth/wood brds. B14. $50.00

WINCHESTER, Mark. *In the Hands of the Lamas.* nd. Queensway. VG. P3. $20.00

WIND, Herbert Warren. *World of PG Wodehouse.* 1972. Praeger. NF/dj. P3. $20.00

WINDCHY, Eugene G. *Tonkin Gulf.* 1971. Doubleday. 1st ed. 358 p. clip dj. A7. $23.00

WINEHOUSE, Irwin. *Duke Snider Story.* 1964. Messner. 1st ed. xl. G/G. P8. $15.00

WINES, E.C. *State of Prisons & Child-Saving Inst in Civilized World.* 1880. Cambridge. John Wilson. 1st ed. 719 p. pebbled ruled gr cloth. F/scarce. G1. $35.00

WINKLER & BROMBERG. *Mind Explorers.* (1939). Reynal Hitchcock. 1st ed. 8vo. 378 p. VG/G+. A2. $20.00

WINN, Alice. *Always a Virginian.* ca 1973. Bell. 1st ed. 150 p. F/G. B10. $18.00

WINN, David. *Gangland.* 1982. Knopf. 1st ed. F/F. A7. $30.00

WINN, Patrick. *Colour of Murder.* 1965. Robert Hale. 1st ed. VG/VG-. P3. $15.00

WINOGRAND, Garry. *Stock Photographs. The Ft Worth Fat Stock Show & Rodeo.* 1980. Austin, TX. 1st ed. F/F. B2. $65.00

WINSHIP, George Parker. *Merrymount Pr of Boston. 1893-1929.* Vienna. Reichner. 1/350. 4to. orig brn brds. very scarce. K1. $300.00

WINSLOW, Forbes. *Obscure Diseases of the Brain & Disorders of the Mind...* 1860. Phil. Blanchard Lea. 1st Am ed. 576 p. orig brds/rebacked. G7. $250.00

WINSLOW, O.E. *Meetinghouse Hill: 1630-1783.* 1952. Macmillan. 1st ed. 8vo. 344 p. F/VG. A2. $17.50

WINSOR, Henry J. *Great NW: A Guide-Book & Itinerary for Use of Tourists...* 1886. St Paul. Riley. xl. sm 4to. 370 p. tan cloth. H9. $100.00

WINSOR, Justin. *Narrative & Critical Hist of Am.* 1889. Houghton Mifflin. 8 vols. 3-quarter leather/marbled brds. NF. O6. $350.00

WINSOR, Justin. *Westward Movement: Colonies & the Republic...* 1897. Houghton Mifflin. ils/maps. NF. O6. $95.00

WINSTON, Henry. *Blk Americans & the Middle E Conflict.* 1970. NY. New Outlook. 14 p. NF/wrp. A7. $15.00

WINSTON, Joan. *Making of the Trek Conventions.* 1977. Doubleday. 1st ed. VG/dj. P3. $30.00

WINTER, Douglas E. *Prime Evil.* 1988. NAL. 1st ed. NF/dj. P3. $19.00

WINTER, Douglas E. *Prime Evil: New Stories by Masters of Modern Horror.* 1988. NAL. ARC. F/pict wrp. N3. $25.00

WINTER, Douglas. *Prime Evil.* 1988. Donald Grant. 1st ed. 1/100. sgn edit/ils/all contributors. F/case. F4. $300.00

WINTER, Milo. *Aesop for Children.* 1960. Chicago. Rand McNally. 80 p. VG-/dj. A3. $7.50

WINTER, Milo. *Little Brn Bear.* 1937. Merrill. 16 p. VG. M5. $18.00

WINTER, Nevin. *TX the Marvellous.* 1936. TX Centenary ed. ils. 337 p. VG. E5. $20.00

WINTERBOTHAM, F.W. *Nazi Connection.* 1978. Harper Row. 1st ed. VG/dj. P3. $15.00

WINTERBOTHAM, Russ. *Joyce of the Scout Squadron.* 1942. Whitman. 1st ed. VG. M2. $15.00

WINTERBOTHAM, Russ. *Joyce of the Secret Squadron.* nd. Whitman. VG/dj. P3. $20.00

WINTERNITZ, Milton Charles. *Collected Studies on Pathology of War Gas Poisoning.* 1920. New Haven. 4to. 41 pls. NF/dj. G7. $125.00

WINTERS, Yvor. *Collected Poems of...* 1978. Carcanet. 1st ed. F/NF. V1. $15.00

WINTERSON, Jeanette. *Passion.* (1988). Atlantic Monthly. 1st ed. F/F. B3. $25.00

WINTERSTEEN, Prescott B. *Christology in Am Unitarianism...* ca 1977. Boston. UUCF. index/biblio. 163 p. H10. $17.50

WINTERTON, 6th Earl. *Fifty Tumultous Yrs.* 1955. London. Hutchinson. 1st ed. 232 p. gilt gr cloth. VG. M7. $45.00

WINWARD, Walter. *Fives Wild.* 1976. Atheneum. 1st ed. VG/dj. P3. $15.00

WIRT, Ann. *Missing Formula.* 1932. Goldsmith. 126 p. VG/dj. M20. $10.00

WIRT, Mildred A. *Brownie Scouts at Windmill Farm.* 1953. Cupples Leon. lists 6 titles. 215 p. VG/dj. M20. $15.00

WIRT, Mildred A. *Hoofbeats on the Turnpike.* 1944. Cupples Leon. lists 14 titles. 211 p. VG+/dj. M20. $15.00

WIRT, Mildred A. *Vanishing Houseboat.* 1939. Cupples Leon. VG/dj. P3. $20.00

WISE, Arthur. *Who Killed Enoch Powell?* 1971. Harper Row. 1st ed. VG/dj. P3. $20.00

WISE, David Burgess. *Hist Motorcycles.* 1973. London. Hamlyn. VG/dj. A16. $20.00

WISE, George. *Hist of the 17th VA Infantry.* 1870. Baltimore. Kelly Piet. 1st ed. 312 p. orig cloth. VG+. M8. $450.00

WISE, H.H. *Pict Hist of WWII.* 1946. Wise. 1st ed/2nd prt. 8vo. G. A8. $5.00

WISE, Isaac M. *Defense of Judaism Vs Proselytizing Christianity.* 1889. Am Israelite. 129 p. G+. S3. $55.00

WISE, John S. *End of an Era.* 1899. Houghton Mifflin. 18th thousand. 474 p. VG. B10. $25.00

WISE, John S. *Recollections of 13 Presidents.* 1906. Doubleday. 1st ed. ils/photos. 284 p. VG. B10. $45.00

WISE, Stephen R. *Lifeline of Confederacy Blockade Running During Civil War.* 1988. SC U. BC. NF/NF. M8. $25.00

WISEHART, M.K. *Sam Houston: Am Giant.* (1962). WA, DC. Luce. 1st ed. 8vo. 712 p. VG/VG+. A2. $20.00

WISEMAN, Thomas. *Day Before Sunrise.* 1976. HRW. F/dj. P3. $15.00

WISEMAN, Thomas. *Game of Secrets.* 1979. Jonathan Cape. 1st ed. NF/dj. P3. $18.00

WISER, William. *Disappearances.* 1980. NY. 1st ed. inscr. F/F. A11. $55.00

WISER, William. *K.* 1971. Garden City. 1st ed. inscr. F/NF. A11. $90.00

WISHINGRAD, Jay. *Legal Fictions, Short Stories About Lawyers & the Law.* 1992. Woodstock. Overlook. M11. $25.00

WISS & WISS. *Folk Quilts & How To Recreate Them.* 1983. np. ils. cloth. G2. $22.50

WISTAR, Caspar. *Dissertatio Medica Inauguralis, de Animo Demisso.* 1786. Edinburgh. Balfour Smellie. presentation. quarter gilt calf. G7. $750.00

WISTAR, Casper. *System of Anatomy for Students of Medicine.* 1846. Phil. Thomas. 9th ed. 2 vols. full calf. VG. B22. $40.00

WISTER, Owen. *Journey in Search of Christmas.* 1904. Harper. 1st ed. octavo. 92 p. red cloth. NF. H5. $100.00

WISTER, Owen. *Virginian.* 1981. London. Folio Soc. 1st thus ed. intro Kenneth Ulyatt. F/slipcase. A18. $40.00

WISTER, Owen. *Writings of Owen Wister.* 1928. Macmillan. 1st ed. 11 vols. F. A18. $300.00

WISTER, Sarah. *Journal & Occasional Writings.* 1987. Rutherford. Fairleigh Dickinson. 8vo. 149 p. M/M. V3. $15.00

WISTER. *Watch Your Thirst.* 1923. Macmillan. 1st ltd ed. 1/1000. sgn. teg. F. A18. $50.00

WITHERS, Alexander S. *Chronicles of Border Warfare.* 1831. Clarksburg, VA. 1st ed. 319 p. leather. G. D7. $400.00

WITMER, Lightner. *Analytical Psychology.* 1902. Boston. Ginn. ils/charts/figures/index. 251 p. gilt gr cloth. G+. S9. $5.00

WITTLES, Fritz. *Freud & His Time.* 1931. Liveright. later prt. 451 p. russet cloth. reading copy. G1. $20.00

WITTLES, Fritz. *Sigmund Freud: Der Mann, Die Lehre, Die Schule.* 1924. Leipzig. Verlag. 1st ed. 248 p. NF/gray wrp. G1. $125.00

WITTLES, Fritz. *Sigmund Freud: His Personality, His Teaching, His School.* 1924. Dodd Mead. 1st Am ed. 287 p. bl-gr cloth. G1. $50.00

WITTMER, Margret. *Floreana Adventure.* 1961 (1959). Dutton. 1st Am ed. 8vo. 239 p. F/VG. A2. $15.00

WITTROCK, Wolfgang. *Toulouse-Lautrec: Complete Prints...* (1985). Lodnon. Sotheby's. 1st ed. 2 vols. gr cloth. F/djs/pub slipcase. K1. $300.00

WITWER, H.C. *Fighting Back.* nd. Grosset Dunlap. photoplay ed. VG. P3. $18.00

WODEHOUSE, P.G. *Author! Author!* 1962. Simon Schuster. 1st ed. VG/dj. P3. $50.00

WODEHOUSE, P.G. *Bachelors Anonymous.* 1974. Simon Schuster. 1st ed. F/dj. P3. $25.00

WODEHOUSE, P.G. *Best of Wodehouse.* 1949. Pocket Book 628. 1st/only ed. intro/inscr Meredith. NF. A11. $165.00

WODEHOUSE, P.G. *Big Money.* 1931. Herbert Jenkins. 1st Eng ed. G. M18. $50.00

WODEHOUSE, P.G. *Big Money.* 1931. McClelland Stewart. 1st Canadian ed. VG. P3. $60.00

WODEHOUSE, P.G. *Bill the Conqueror.* nd. Goodchild. 1st Canadian ed. VG-. P3. $35.00

WODEHOUSE, P.G. *Bring on the Girls.* 1953. Simon Schuster. 1st ed. VG-. P3. $40.00

WODEHOUSE, P.G. *Cat-Nappers.* 1974. Simon Schuster. 1st ed. F/F. C4. $40.00

WODEHOUSE, P.G. *Century of Humor.* 1934. Hutchinson. VG+. P3. $50.00

WODEHOUSE, P.G. *Cocktail Time.* 1958. Simon Schuster. 1st ed. F/NF. C4. $50.00

WODEHOUSE, P.G. *Code of the Woosters.* 1939. Sun Dial. VG. P3. $30.00

WODEHOUSE, P.G. *Crime Wave at Blandings.* 1937. Sun Dial. VG. P3. $30.00

WODEHOUSE, P.G. *Damsel in Distress.* 1919. Doran. precedes UK ed. VG. Q1. $600.00

WODEHOUSE, P.G. *Eggs, Beans & Crumpets.* 1940. Longman Gr. 1st ed. VG/VG-. P3. $60.00

WODEHOUSE, P.G. *Fish Preferred.* 1929. NY. 1st ed. NF. B14. $45.00

WODEHOUSE, P.G. *Full Moon.* 1947. Doubleday. 1st ed. VG. P3. $40.00

WODEHOUSE, P.G. *Great Sermon Handicap.* (1933). London. Hodder Stoughton. 1st ed. thin red paper (imitation leather) brds. VG/dj. Q1. $750.00

WODEHOUSE, P.G. *Heavy Weather.* 1933. McClelland Stewart. 1st Canadian ed. VG. P3. $60.00

WODEHOUSE, P.G. *Hot Water.* 1932. McClelland Stewart. 1st Canadian ed. VG. P3. $50.00

WODEHOUSE, P.G. *Jeeves & the Feudal Spirit.* 1954. Herbert Jenkins. 1st ed. VG/VG-. P3. $40.00

WODEHOUSE, P.G. *Jeeves & the Tie That Binds.* 1971. Simon Schuster. 1st ed. F/NF. C4. $35.00

WODEHOUSE, P.G. *Laughing Gas.* 1936. McClelland Stewart. 1st Canadian ed. VG. P3. $50.00

WODEHOUSE, P.G. *Leave It to Psmith.* 1924. Doran. 1st ed. VG. P3. $60.00

WODEHOUSE, P.G. *Love Among the Chickens.* nd. Herbert Jenkins. VG-. P3. $15.00

WODEHOUSE, P.G. *Love Among the Chickens.* 1909. Circle Pub. 1st ed. 1st novel pub in US. pict tan cloth/blk letters. VG. Q1. $600.00

WODEHOUSE, P.G. *Luck of the Bodkins.* 1935. London. Jenkins. 1st ed. VG. M18. $70.00

WODEHOUSE, P.G. *Luck of the Bodkins.* 1935. McClelland Stewart. 1st Canadian ed. VG/dj. P3. $75.00

WODEHOUSE, P.G. *Mating Season.* 1949. Didier. 1st ed. VG. P3. $40.00

WODEHOUSE, P.G. *Most of PG Wodehouse.* 1960. Simon Schuster. 1st ed. VG/torn. P3. $30.00

WODEHOUSE, P.G. *Mr Mulliner Speaking.* 1929. McClelland Stewart. 1st Canadian ed. VG. P3. $50.00

WODEHOUSE, P.G. *Mulliner Nights.* 1933. Herbert Jenkins. 1st ed. NF. P3. $60.00

WODEHOUSE, P.G. *Mulliner Omnibus.* 1935. Herbert Jenkins. 1st ed. VG-. P3. $35.00

WODEHOUSE, P.G. *Nothing But Wodehouse.* 1946. Doubleday. VG/torn. P3. $35.00

WODEHOUSE, P.G. *Pothunters.* 1972. Souvenir. F/dj. P3. $13.00

WODEHOUSE, P.G. *Quick Service.* 1941. Longman Gr. VG/VG-. P3. $50.00

WODEHOUSE, P.G. *Right Ho, Jeeves.* 1934. McClelland Stewart. 1st Canadian ed. VG. P3. $60.00

WODEHOUSE, P.G. *Sam the Sudden.* 1925. Methuen. 1st ed. VG. P3. $75.00

WODEHOUSE, P.G. *Spring Fever.* 1948. Doubleday. 1st ed. VG/dj. M18. $85.00

WODEHOUSE, P.G. *Summer Moonshine.* 1938. McClelland Stewart. 1st ed. VG/VG-. P3. $75.00

WODEHOUSE, P.G. *Uncle Dynamite.* nd. Herbert Jenkins. 1st ed. VG/VG-. P3. $40.00

WODEHOUSE, P.G. *Uncle Fred in the Springtime.* 1939. McClelland Stewart. 1st Canadian ed. VG/dj. P3. $75.00

WODEHOUSE, P.G. *Very Good, Jeeves.* 1930. McClelland Stewart. 1st Canadian ed. VG. P3. $60.00

WODEHOUSE, P.G. *Week-End Wodehouse.* 1940. Garden City. VG-. P3. $35.00

WODEHOUSE, P.G. *White Feather.* 1972. Souvenir. F/dj. P3. $13.00

WODEHOUSE, P.G. *Wodehouse Bestiary.* 1985. Tichnor Fields. AP. F/prt gr wrp. C4. $35.00

WODEHOUSE, P.G. *Wodehouse Nuggets.* 1983. Hutchinson. 1st ed. F/dj. P3. $18.00

WODEHOUSE, P.G. *World of Mr Mulliner.* 1972. Barrie Jenkins. 1st ed. VG/dj. P3. $25.00

WODEHOUSE, P.G. *Young Men in Spats.* 1936. McClelland Stewart. 1st Canadian ed. VG. P3. $50.00

WODOLA, Elizabeth. *Excommunication in the Middle Ages.* ca 1986. Berkeley. 281 p. F. H10. $42.50

WOELFEL, Barry. *Through a Glass, Darkly.* 1984. Beaufort. 1st ed. NF/dj. P3. $20.00

WOLF, Blue. *Dwifa's Curse: Tale of the Stone Age.* 1921. Robert Scott. VG+. P3. $60.00

WOLF, Christa. *Cassandra: A Novel & 4 Essays.* (1984). FSG. 1st Am ed. F/NF. B4. $25.00

WOLF, Eric. *Sons of the Shaking Earth.* (1959). Chicago U. 1st ed. 303 p. dj. F3. $20.00

WOLF, Gary. *Who Censored Roger Rabbit?* 1981. St Martin. 1st ed. VG/VG-. P3. $15.00

WOLF, Gary. *Who P-P-P-Plugged Roger Rabbit?* 1991. Villard. 2nd prt. NF/dj. C8. $20.00

WOLF, Marvin J. *Japanese Conspiracy.* 1983. NY. Empire Books. 1st ed. 8vo. 336 p. NF/dj. W1. $18.00

WOLFE, Aaron; see Koontz, Dean R.

WOLFE, Don M. *Image of Man in Am.* 1970. Crowell. 2nd ed. 507 p. cloth. G1. $22.50

WOLFE, Gene. *Castleview.* nd. BOMC. VG/dj. P3. $10.00

WOLFE, Gene. *Claw of the Conciliator.* 1981. Timescape. 1st ed. F/F. P3. $50.00

WOLFE, Gene. *Devil in a Forest.* 1976. Follett. decor brds. VG. P3. $30.00

WOLFE, Gene. *Fifth Head of Cerberus.* 1972. Scribner. 1st ed. F/dj. P3. $35.00

WOLFE, Gene. *Free, Live Free.* 1985. Tor. 1st ed. F/dj. P3. $17.00

WOLFE, Gene. *Peace.* 1975. Harper Row. 1st ed. F/dj. P3. $35.00

WOLFE, Gene. *Soldier of the Mist.* 1986. Gollancz. 1st ed. F/dj. P3. $25.00

WOLFE, Gene. *Stories From the Old Hotel.* 1992. NY. Tor. 1st Am ed. F/F. N3. $15.00

WOLFE, Gene. *Sword of the Lictor.* 1981. Timescape. 1st ed. F/dj. P3. $50.00

WOLFE, Gene. *There Are Doors.* 1988. Tor. 1st ed. F/dj. P3. $18.00

WOLFE, Gene. *Turnips to T-Bone.* 1977. Sultana. 8vo. F/F. A8. $35.00

WOLFE, Gene. *Urth of the New Sun.* 1987. NY. Tor. 1st ed. inscr. F/F. T2. $28.00

WOLFE, Gene. *Urth of the New Sun.* 1987. Tor. 1st ed. F/dj. P3. $20.00

WOLFE, Gene. *Urth of the New Sun.* 1987. Ultramarine. 1st ed. 1/250. sgn/#d. half leather. M. M2. $150.00

WOLFE, Linda. *Professor & the Prostitute.* nd. BC. VG/dj. P3. $8.00

WOLFE, Linnie Marsh. *Son of the Wilderness: Life of John Muir.* 1945. Knopf. 1st ed. rebound blk leather. F. A18. $50.00

WOLFE, Michael. *2-Star Pigeon.* (1975). Harper Row. 1st ed. VG/VG. A7. $20.00

WOLFE, Thomas. *From Bauhaus to Our House.* 1981. Farrar. 1/350. sgn. special bdg. F/F. B2. $100.00

WOLFE, Thomas. *From Death to Morning.* 1935. Scribner. 1st ed. G/dj. M18. $125.00

WOLFE, Thomas. *Letters of Thomas Wolfe.* 1956. Scribner. 1st ed. 790 p. F/NF. C4. $50.00

WOLFE, Thomas. *Mannerhouse.* 1948. Harper. 1st ed. F/F. C4. $100.00

WOLFE, Thomas. *Mauve Gloves & Madmen, Clutter & Vine.* (1976). FSG. 1st ed. NF/NF. B4. $45.00

WOLFE, Thomas. *Right Stuff.* 1979. Farrar. 1st ed. inscr/sgn. NF/NF. B2. $60.00

WOLFERT, Ira. *Am Guerrilla in the Philippines.* 1945. Simon Schuster. 1st ed. 8vo. G. A8. $8.00

WOLFERT, Ira. *Battle for the Solomons.* 1943. Houghton Mifflin. VG/dj. A16. $20.00

WOLFF, Geoffrey. *Bad Debts.* 1969. Simon Schuster. ARC/1st trade ed. inscr. F/NF. L3. $200.00

WOLFF, Geoffrey. *Blk Sun.* 1976. Random. 1st ed. inscr/1976. F/F. L3. $125.00

WOLFF, Geoffrey. *Duke of Deception.* 1979. Random. 1st trade ed. inscr. F/F. L3. $65.00

WOLFF, Geoffrey. *Inklings.* 1977. Random. 1st ed. F/F. C4. $30.00

WOLFF, Geoffrey. *Sightseer.* 1973. NY. 1st ed. sgn. F/F. A11. $55.00

WOLFF, Hans. *Am: Early Maps of the New World.* 1992. Munich. Prestel. ils. 192 p. M/dj. O6. $95.00

WOLFF, Joseph. *Researches & Missionary Labours Among the Jews.* 1837. Phil. 8vo. 338 p. scarce. O2. $75.00

WOLFF, Michael. *Wht Kids.* (1979). Summitt. 1st ed. 316 p. F/dj. A7. $25.00

WOLFF, Rick. *What's a Nice Harvard Boy Like You Doing in the Bushes?* 1975. Prentice Hall. 1st ed. F/VG. P8. $27.50

WOLFF, Robert Lee. *Strange Stories.* 1971. Gambit. 1st ed. VG/dj. P3. $25.00

WOLFF, Tobias. *Back in the World.* 1985. Boston. UP. inscr. w/author's photo. RS. F/bl wrp. A11. $55.00

WOLFF, Tobias. *Back in the World.* 1985. Houghton Mifflin. ARC. F/F. C4. $40.00

WOLFF, Tobias. *In the Garden of N Am Martyrs.* 1981. NY. 1st ed/wrp issue. inscr. F/8vo wrp. A11. $85.00

WOLFF, Tobias. *Ugly Rumours.* 1975. London. Allen Unwin. 1st ed. 1/1000. author's 1st novel. F/F. L3. $750.00

WOLLE, M.S. *Stampede to Timberline.* 1949. CO U. 8vo. VG. A8. $40.00

WOLLHEIM, Donald A. *Mike Mars, Astronaut.* 1961. Doubleday. 1st ed. VG/VG-. P3. $12.00

WOLLHEIM, Donald A. *Mike Mars Flies the X-15.* 1961. Doubleday. VG/fair. P3. $10.00

WOLLHEIM, Donald A. *Mike Mars in Orbit.* 1961. Doubleday. 1st ed. VG/dj. P3. $12.00

WOLLHEIM, Donald A. *Portable Novels of Science.* 1945. Viking. 1st ed. VG. P3. $35.00

WOLLHEIM, Donald A. *Secret of Saturn's Rings.* 1954. Winston. 1st ed. VG. P3. $25.00

WOLLHEIM, Donald A. *Secret of the Ninth Planet.* 1967. HRW. 6th prt. xl. dj. P3. $12.00

WOLLHEIM, Donald A. *Universe Makers.* 1971. Harper Row. 1st ed. xl. dj. P3. $10.00

WOLLHEIM, Donald A. *1972 Annual World's Best SF.* nd. BC. VG/dj. P3. $8.00

WOLMAN, Benjamin B. *Contemporary Theories & Systems in Psychology.* 1960. Harper Row. thick 8vo. prt red cloth. G1. $27.50

WOLMAN, Benjamin B. *Handbook of Parapsychology.* 1977. Van Nostrand Reinhold. later prt. thick 8vo. 968 p. prt bl cloth. VG/dj. G1. $50.00

WOLO, Archibald. *Amand.* 1941. Morrow. 1st ed. 4to. 41 p. G/worn dj. A3. $15.00

WOLO, Archibald. *Friendship Valley.* 1946. NY. 1st ed. sgn. VG/torn. D1. $95.00

WOLO, Archibald. *Secret of the Ancient Oak.* 1942. Morrow. 1st ed. 4to. ils. pict red cloth. VG+/VG. T5. $35.00

WOLO, Archibald. *Secret of the Ancient Oak.* 1942. Morrow. 1st ed. 8vo. 40 p. NF/VG. D1. $75.00

WOLO, Archibald. *Tweedles Be Brave.* 1943. Morrow. 1st ed. presentation/sgn. VG. D1. $165.00

WOLTERS, Richard. *Duck Dogs: All About Retrievers.* 1990. Dutton. 1st ed. VG/VG. O3. $18.00

WOMACK, Jack. *Terraplane.* 1988. Weidenfield Nicolson. 1st ed. F/dj. P3. $17.00

WOOD, Alexander. *Thomas Young: Natural Philosopher 1773-1829.* 1954. Cambridge. 356 p. bl cloth. VG/dj. G1. $36.50

WOOD, Alfred C. *Hist of Levant Co.* 1964. London. 8vo. 267 p. cloth. dj. O2. $30.00

WOOD, Amos L. *Beachcombing the Pacific.* 1975. Chicago. 1st ed. inscr/sgn. M/M. T8. $20.00

WOOD, Arnold. *Stevensoniana.* 1898. NY. private prt. 1/3 (of total of 13) on Japan. sgn. 12mo. slipcase. R3. $485.00

WOOD, Bache. *Dispensatory of the USA.* 1894. Lippincott. 17th ed. 1930 p. full calf. G. A17. $50.00

WOOD, Bari. *Tribe.* 1981. NAL. 1st ed. VG/dj. P3. $15.00

WOOD, Christina. *Safari S Am.* (1973). Taplinger. 1st ed. 224 p. F/F. F3. $15.00

WOOD, Christopher. *James Bond & Moonraker.* 1979. Jonathan Cape. 1st ed. xl. dj. P3. $10.00

WOOD, Christopher. *Taiwan.* 1981. Michael Joseph. 1st ed. VG/dj. P3. $15.00

WOOD, Clement. *Negro Songs.* (ca 1927). Girard, KS. Little Bl Book 626. F/bl wrp. A11. $95.00

WOOD, Clement. *Strange Fires.* 1951. Woodford Pr. 1st ed. F/F. F4. $30.00

WOOD, Clement. *Woman Who Was Pope: Biography of Pope Joan, 853-855 AD.* 1931. NY. Wm Faro. 1st ed. presentation/sgn. VG. N2. $50.00

WOOD, Edwin O. *Historic Mackinac.* 1918. Macmillan. 2 vols. VG. A16. $500.00

WOOD, Eric. *Death of an Oddfellow.* (1938). London. Hamilton. 1st ed. F/VG. M15. $65.00

WOOD, George B. *Treatise on Practice of Medicine. Vol 1.* 1852. Lippincott. 3rd ed. 847 p. full calf. VG+. B22. $15.00

WOOD, Isaiah. *MA Compendium...* 1816. Portland. Shirley. 12mo. 99 p. G. D7. $125.00

WOOD, J.G. *Homes Without Hands.* 1866. London. Longman Gr. 2nd ed. 8vo. 626 p. A2. $35.00

WOOD, J.G. *Ils Natural Hist for Young People.* 1882. NY. 8vo. 229 p. VG. H3. $25.00

WOOD, J.G. *Wood's Ils Natural Hist.* 1886. Routledge. 1st ed. VG. M18. $40.00

WOOD, Kerry. *Birds & Animals in the Rockies.* ca 1950. Saskatoon. Larson. 1st ed. 158 p. VG/wrp. A17. $20.00

WOOD, Mrs. Henry. *House of Halliwell.* 1890. London. 1st ed. octavo. 3 vols. sage-gr cloth. F/slipcase. H5. $1,500.00

WOOD, Norman A. *Birds of MI.* 1949. MI U. xl. lg 8vo. Lib buckram. A17. $29.50

WOOD, Ruth K. *Tourist's CA.* 1914. Dodd Mead. 1st ed. 12mo. 395 p. gilt cloth. A17. $15.00

WOOD, Ruth K. *Tourists Spain & Portugal.* 1913. NY. 1st ed. 12mo. 357 p. gilt red cloth. F. H3. $20.00

WOOD, S. *Over the Range to the Golden Gate.* 1891. Chicago. 8vo. ils. 351 p. pict brn cloth. G. T3. $29.00

WOOD, Ted. *Live Bait.* 1985. Canada. Collier Macmillan. 1st ed. F/dj. P3. $15.00

WOOD, Theodore. *Butterflies & Moths Shown to the Children.* ca 1900. London. TC & EC Jack. 48 color pls. 94 p. G+. S10. $35.00

WOOD, Wallace. *Wizard King.* 1978. Wallace Wood. 1st ed. sgn. F/F. P3. $45.00

WOOD, William. *Manual of Physical Exercises.* 1865. NY. Harper. 3rd ed. 353 p. cloth. B14. $37.50

WOOD. *Berger Patchwork Projects.* 1990. np. ils. wrp. G2. $13.00

WOOD. *Craft of Temari.* 1991. np. 1st Eng-language ed. wrp. G2. $16.00

WOOD. *Quilt Like a Pro: Basic Strip Piecing Manual.* 1988. np. ils. wrp. G2. $20.00

WOOD. *Starmakers Ablaze II. Log Cabin Diamonds.* 1987. np. 43 designs. wrp. G2. $20.00

WOOD. *Turn Me Over, I'm Reversible...Log Cabin Quilts.* 1981. np. ils. wrp. G2. $15.00

WOODARD, Charles L. *Conversations w/N Scott Momaday.* (1989). Lincoln, NE. 1st ed. sgn. F/F. B3. $40.00

WOODBERRY, G.E. *Kingdom of All-Souls & Two Other Poems for Christmas.* 1912. Boston. Merrymount. 1/300. prt copy. NF/glassine. B24. $85.00

WOODBRIDGE, William Channing. *Modern Atlas on New Plan To Accompany...Geography.* 1831. Hartford. Belknap Hamersley. 11 maps. O5. $140.00

WOODBURY, George. *Great Days of Piracy in W Indies.* 1951. Norton. 1st ed. 232 p. VG/VG. B11. $25.00

WOODCOCK, George. *Hundred Yrs of Revolution. 1848 & After.* 1948. London. Porcupine. 1st ed. F/NF. B2. $35.00

WOODCOTT, Keith; see Brunner, John.

WOODFILL, W. Stewart. *Grand Hotel. Story of an Inst.* 1969. Newcomen Soc. 1st prt. 28 p. wrp. A17. $8.50

WOODFORD, Frank B. *Father Abraham's Children.* 1961. Detroit. Wayne State U. 1st ed. VG/dj. A16. $25.00

WOODFORD, Jack. *Four Eves.* 1947. Woodford. 253 p. VG/dj. M20. $10.00

WOODHAM-SMITH, Cecil. *Queen Victoria.* 1972. BC. VG/dj. C1. $5.00

WOODHAM-SMITH, Cecil. *Reason Why.* 1954. McGraw Hill. 3rd ed. VG. N2. $7.50

WOODHAMS, Jack. *Looking for Blucher.* 1980. Victoria, Australia. 1st ed. 1/250. sgn. F/F. N3. $60.00

WOODHOUSE, Barbara. *Book of Ponies.* 1972. Stein Day. 1st Am ed. VG/VG. O3. $18.00

WOODHOUSE, Martin. *Mama Doll.* 1972. CMG. VG/dj. P3. $12.00

WOODING, F.H. *Angler's Book of Canadian Fishes.* (1959). Ontario. 1st ed. pls. 303 p. F/G. A17. $20.00

WOODIWISS, John C. *Some New Ghost Stories.* 1931. Simpkin Marshall. 1st ed. VG. P3. $90.00

WOODIWISS, Kathleen E. *Come Love a Stranger.* nd. BC. VG/dj. P3. $8.00

WOODLEY, Richard. *Dealer: Portrait of a Cocain Merchant.* (1971). NY. HRW. 1st ed. 8vo. 210 p. VG+/VG+. A2. $12.50

WOODMAN, Henry. *Woodman's Hist of the Valley Forge.* 1922. Oaks, PA. John U Francis. VG. B11. $15.00

WOODRESS, James. *Willa Cather: A Literary Life.* 1987. NE U. VG/dj. P3. $35.00

WOODROOF, Jasper G. *Coconuts: Production, Processing, Products.* 1970. Westport. ils. 241 p. F. B26. $25.00

WOODRUFF, C.E. *Effects of Tropical Light on Wht Men.* 1905. NY. Rebman. 1st ed. 358 p. VG. S9. $15.00

WOODRUFF, Philip. *Call the Next Witness.* 1945. Jonathan Cape. VG. P3. $30.00

WOODRUFF, Samuel. *Journal of Tour to Malta, Greece, Asia Minor, Carthage...* 1831. Hartford. 8vo. 283 p. brds/cloth back. O2. $175.00

WOODS, Leonard. *Sermon Occasioned by Death of Rev Samuel Worcester.* 1821. Salem. Whipple. 46 p. H10. $15.00

WOODS, Ross. *Hooves Across MT.* nd. London. Herbert Jenkins. 1st ed. VG/clip. B9. $10.00

WOODS, Sara. *Bloody Book of Law.* 1984. Macmillan. 1st ed. VG/dj. P3. $20.00

WOODS, Sara. *Call Back Yesterday.* 1983. Lester Orpen Denys. VG/dj. P3. $20.00

WOODS, Sara. *Error of the Moon.* 1963. Collins Crime Club. 1st ed. VG. P3. $20.00

WOODS, Sara. *Fatal Writ.* nd. BC. VG/dj. P3. $8.00

WOODS, Sara. *Knives Have Edges.* 1968. HRW. 1st ed. NF/dj. P3. $15.00

WOODS, Sara. *Let's Choose Executors.* nd. BC. VG/dj. P3. $8.00

WOODS, Sara. *Tarry & Be Hanged.* 1971. HRW. 1st ed. F/dj. P3. $15.00

WOODS, Sara. *Weep for Her.* 1980. Macmillan. 1st ed. F/dj. P3. $20.00

WOODS, Stuart. *Chiefs.* 1981. NY. Norton. 1st ed. F/dj. M15. $100.00

WOODS, Stuart. *Dead Eyes.* (1994). Harper Collins. ARC. F/wrp. B4. $35.00

WOODS, Stuart. *Palindrome.* (1991). Harper Collins. 1st ed. F/F. B4. $35.00

WOODS, Stuart. *Sante Fe Rules.* (1992). Harper Collins. 1st ed. F/F. B4. $35.00

WOODS, W.C. *Killing Zone.* (1970). Harper. 1st ed. NF/dj. A7. $40.00

WOODWARD, Bob. *Veil: Secret Wars of the CIA, 1981-87.* (1987). Simon Schuster. 1st ed. VG/VG clip. B3. $15.00

WOODWARD, David. *All-Am Map.* ca 1977. Chicago/London. ils/tables. 283 p. pict gr cloth. H9. $35.00

WOODWARD, David. *RTE: All-Am Map.* ca 1977. Chicago/London. 8vo. charts/fac-similes. 168 p. cloth. dj. H9. $65.00

WOODWARD, J.J. *Medical & Surgical Hist of the War of Rebellion, 1861-65.* 1870-88. WA, DC. mixed set (6 vols). 4to. G7. $1,500.00

WOODWARD, P.H. *Guarding the Mails.* 1876. Hartford, CT. 1st ed. ils. 568 p. decor cloth. G. B18. $35.00

WOODWORTH, R.S. *Contemporary Schools of Psychology.* 1948. Ronald Pr. revised ed/2nd prt. red cloth. VG. G1. $22.50

WOODWORTH, R.S. *Experimental Psychology.* 1954. Henry Holt. 2nd revised ed/later prt. 948 p. prt gr cloth. G1. $30.00

WOODWORTH, Steven E. *Jefferson Davis & His Generals.* 1990. KS U. BC. 380 p. cloth. F/F. M8. $25.00

WOOFTER, Thomas Jackson. *Blk Yeomanry Life on St Helena Island.* 1930-77. Holt. 1st ed. 291 p. cloth. M8. $150.00

WOOLF, Leonard. *The Journey Not the Arrival Matters.* 1970. Harcourt Brace. 1st ed. 5th vol of his autobiography. NF/VG. E3. $15.00

WOOLF, Leonard. *Village in the Jungle.* (1951). Chatto Windus. 1st New Phoenix Lib issue. 307 p. clip dj. A7. $12.00

WOOLF, Virginia. *Beau Brummell.* 1930. NY. Rimington Hooper. 1/550. sgn/#d. gray brds/red cloth spine. NF/slipcase. Q1. $750.00

WOOLF, Virginia. *Captain's Death Bed.* 1950. Harcourt Brace. 1st ed. NF. C4. $50.00

WOOLF, Virginia. *Jacob's Room.* 1935. London. Woolf/Hogarth. reprint of Uniform Ed. 290 p. dj. A7. $15.00

WOOLF, Virginia. *Monday or Tuesday.* 1921. Hogarth. 1st ed. ils Vanessa Bell. VG/sans. Q1. $750.00

WOOLF, Virginia. *On Being Ill.* 1930. Hogarth. 1/250. sgn/#d. marbled ep. gr cloth/vellum spine. NF/VG. Q1. $1,750.00

WOOLF, Virginia. *To the Lighthouse.* 1927. Harcourt Brace. 1st Am ed/1st prt. NF/VG/custom slipcase. L3. $650.00

WOOLF, Virginia. *Women & Writing.* 1979. HBJ. 1st ed. NF/dj. E3. $25.00

WOOLFE, Raymond. *Secretariat.* 1965. Chilton. 2nd prt. VG/G+. O3. $65.00

WOOLLCOTT, Alexander. *Woollcott Reader.* 1935. Viking. 1st ed. VG/dj. P3. $30.00

WOOLLEY, C. Leonard. *Digging Up the Past.* 1930. London. Benn. 1st ed. 31 pls. 144 p. gilt brn cloth. VG. M7. $30.00

WOOLLEY, Catherine. *Ginnie & the New Girl.* 1965. Scholastic Books. 4th prt. xl. ils Iris B Johnson. G. T5. $9.00

WOOLLEY, Milton. *Science of the Bible; or, Analysis of Hebrew Mythology...* 1877. Chicago. 613 p. VG. N2. $65.00

WOOLLEY, Persia. *Queen of the Summer Stars.* 1990. Poseidon. 1st ed. VG/dj. P3. $20.00

WOOLMAN, John. *Journal & Other Writings.* 1936. London. Dent. 3rd thus ed. 16mo. 250 p. G+. V3. $10.00

WOOLMAN, John. *Journal of...* 1871. Houghton Mifflin. 12mo. 315 p. VG. V3. $15.00

WOOLMAN, John. *Works of John Woolman. In 2 Parts.* 1775. Phil. Crukshank. 2nd Am ed. 2 parts in 1 vol. 8vo. 432 p. broken hinge. V3. $150.00

WOOLRICH, Cornell. *Deadline at Dawn.* 1946. Cleveland. World. Tower Books photoplay ed. NF/clip. M15. $45.00

WOOLRICH, Cornell. *Deadline at Dawn.* 1946. Tower Books. photoplay ed. VG/dj. F4. $25.00

WOOLRICH, Cornell. *Night Has a Thousand Eyes.* 1945. Farrar Rinehart. 1st ed. F/VG. M15. $235.00

WOOLRICH, Cornell. *Rendezvous in Blk.* 1979. Gregg. 1st ed. VG/dj. P3. $30.00

WORDSWORTH, Christopher. *Athens & Attica: Notes of a Tour...* 1855. London. ils/fld map/fld plan. 251 p. cloth. O2. $125.00

WORGAN, George. *Art of Modeling Flowers in Wax.* 1867. Brooklyn. Dickinson. 39 p. emb cloth. VG+. B14. $50.00

WORGAN, George. *Art of Modeling Flowers in Wax.* 1869. Brooklyn. 2nd ed. 12mo. gilt red cloth. F. scarce. H3. $75.00

WORK, B.G. *Songs of Henry Clay Work.* nd. np. 180 p. half leather. B18. $50.00

WORKBASKET MAGAZINE. *US State Quilt Blocks.* 1992. np. 50 state patterns. wrp. G2. $7.00

WORMSER, Richard. *Slattery's Range.* (1957). Abelard Schuman. 1st ed. NF/dj. B9. $30.00

WORONOFF, Serge. *Greffe Testiculaire du Singe a l'Home. Techinque Operatoire.* 1930. Paris. ils. 88 p. G7. $75.00

WORRALL, Arthur J. *Quakers in Colonial NE.* 1980. Hanover, NH. 1st ed. 8vo. 238 p. M/M. V3. $15.00

WORSNOP, Thomas. *Prehistoric Arts, Manufactures, Works...of Aborigines...* 1897. Adalaide, S Australia. Bristow. 1st ed. 172 p. gilt blk cloth. F. very scarce. H3. $425.00

WORSTER, Donald. *Under W Skies: Nature & Hist in Am W.* 1992. Oxford. 1st ed. index. M/dj. A18. $25.00

WORTH, C.B. *Naturalist in Trinadad.* (1967). Lippincott. 1st ed. 8vo. 291 p. F/VG+. A2. $12.50

WORTH, Patience. *Hope Trueblood.* 1918. NY. Holt. 1st ed. cloth. N2. $20.00

WORTH & YOST. *Psychic Mystery.* ca 1916. Holt. 1st Am ed. sm 8vo. prt olive cloth. G. G1. $20.00

WORTIS, Joseph. *Fragments of an Analysis w/Freud.* 1954. Simon Schuster. 1st ed. inscr/dtd 1973. 208 p. VG/dj. G1. $30.00

WOTTON, Henry. *Reliquiae Wottonianae; or, Collection of Lives, Letters...* 1651. London. Maxey. 1st ed. 12mo. 540 p. contemporary calf. K1. $475.00

WOUK, Herman. *Lomokome Papers.* 1968. NY. 1st ed. sgn. NF/ils wrp. A11. $55.00

WOUK, Herman. *This Is My God.* 1959. Doubleday. 1st ed. F/NF. C4. $40.00

WOUK, Herman. *Winds of War.* 1971. Little Brn. special issue for friends. w/sgn p. F/dj. C4. $75.00

WOZENCRAFT, Kim. *Rush.* 1990. Random. 1st ed. M/M. T2. $15.00

WOZNIAK, Robert H. *Mind & Body: Rene Descartes to William James.* 1992. Nat Lib Medicine. 4to. 70 p. F/stiff wht wrp. G1. $30.00

WPA WRITERS' PROGRAM. *American Wildlife Ils.* 1949. NY. ils/photos/pls. 749 p. emb cloth. F. A17. $10.00

WPA WRITERS' PROGRAM. *Death Valley: A Guide.* 1939. Houghton Mifflin. ils. 75 p. NF/tattered. B19. $20.00

WPA WRITERS' PROGRAM. *NY: Guide to the Empire State.* 1940. NY. Oxford. w/map. G. A16. $30.00

WPA WRITERS' PROGRAM. *Roanoke: Story of County & City.* 1942. Am Guide series. photos. 39 p. G+. B10. $45.00

WPA WRITERS' PROGRAM. *SD: Guide to the State.* 1952. Hastings House. revised ed. G. A16. $60.00

WPA WRITERS' PROGRAM. *Skiing in the E: Best Trails & How To Get There.* (1939). NY. Barrow. 1st ed. 16mo. 334 p. VG+. A2. $20.00

WREDE, Patricia C. *Snow White & Rose Red.* 1989. Tor. 1st ed. inscr/sgn. F/F. F4. $25.00

WREN, P.C. *Beau Geste.* 1926. Grosset Dunlap. photoplay ed. 418 p. VG/dj. M20. $8.00

WREN, P.C. *Beau Geste.* 1952. John Murray. 48th prt. xl. dj. P3. $8.00

WREN, P.C. *Beau Sabreur.* nd. Grosset Dunlap. photoplay ed. VG. P3. $15.00

WRENCH, Matilda. *Visits to Female Prisoners at Home & Abroad...* 1852. London. Wertheim Macintosh. 1st ed. 16mo. 324 p. flexible cloth. M1. $125.00

WRIGHT, A.M.R. *Old Ironsides.* nd. Grosset Dunlap. photoplay ed. VG-. P3. $12.00

WRIGHT, Austin. *Islandia.* 1942. Farrar. G+. M2. $12.00

WRIGHT, Barton. *Kachinas: Hopi Artist's Documentary.* 1991. Flagstaff. Northland Pub. later prt. 4to. ils Bahnimptewa. 262 p. P4. $60.00

WRIGHT, Bruce. *High Tide & an E Wind: Story of the Blk Duck.* 1954. Stackpole. 1st ed. ils. F/G. A17. $30.00

WRIGHT, Caleb. *Costumes & Remarkable Personages in India.* 1848. Boston. self pub. 10 parts in 1 vol. pict cloth. B14. $75.00

WRIGHT, Caleb. *Life in India.* 1854. Boston. 8vo. 92 engravings. 304 p. aeg. gilt red cloth. VG. H3. $35.00

WRIGHT, Charles. *Absolutely Nothing To Get Alarmed About.* (1973). FSG. 1st ed. 215 p. NF/NF. A7. $25.00

WRIGHT, Charles. *China Trace.* 1977. Wesleyan. 1st ed. sgn. F/F. V1. $35.00

WRIGHT, Charles. *Four Poems of Departure.* 1983. Portland. 1/500. sgn. F/wrp. V1. $75.00

WRIGHT, Charles. *Zone Journals.* 1988. NY. 1st ed. sgn. F/F. V1. $25.00

WRIGHT, Craig. *Diamond Appraised.* 1989. Simon Schuster. 1st ed. F/F. P8. $15.00

WRIGHT, Dare. *Doll & the Kitten.* 1960. Doubleday. 4to. 55 p. G+. A3. $25.00

WRIGHT, Dare. *Lona: A Fairytale.* 1963. Random. 1st ed. pict brds. VG/G. A3. $40.00

WRIGHT, Dare. *Lonely Doll Learns a Lesson.* 1961. Random. G. A3. $25.00

WRIGHT, Dudley. *Book of Vampires.* 1973. Causeway. 1st ed. VG/dj. P3. $20.00

WRIGHT, Edwin. *President Harry S Truman & Zionism.* 1975. Wooster, OH. not pub. 4to. 113 p. in binder. O2. $250.00

WRIGHT, Edwin. *Sketches in Bedlam; or, Characteristic Traits of Insanity.* 1823. London. Sherwood Jones. contemporary mottled leather brds/rebacked. scarce. G1. $850.00

WRIGHT, Eric. *Body Surrounded by Water.* 1987. Collins Crime Club. 1st ed. VG/VG-. P3. $15.00

WRIGHT, Eric. *Death by Degrees.* 1993. London. Harper Collins. 1st British ed. F/F. S5. $25.00

WRIGHT, Eric. *Final Cut.* 1991. Canada. Doubleday. 1st ed. NF/dj. P3. $23.00

WRIGHT, Eric. *Man Who Changed His Name.* 1986. Scribner. 1st ed. F/dj. P3. $14.00

WRIGHT, Eric. *Night the Gods Smiled.* 1983. Collins Crime Club. 1st ed. NF/dj. P3. $18.00

WRIGHT, Eric. *Question of Murder.* 1988. Collins Crime Club. 1st ed. NF/dj. P3. $20.00

WRIGHT, Frances. *Few Days in Athens...* 1831. NY. Wright Owen. 12mo. 141 p. M1. $150.00

WRIGHT, Frank Lloyd. *Frank Lloyd Wright, Drawings for a Living Architecture.* 1959. NY. intro Samona/Major. VG. B30. $400.00

WRIGHT, G. Frederick. *Ice Age in N Am.* 1891. NY. 3rd ed. fld maps. 648 p. gilt bl cloth. VG. H3. $40.00

WRIGHT, G. Frederick. *Man & The Glacia Period.* 1892. NY. 1st ed. ils/map. 385 p. decor red cloth. VG. H3. $60.00

WRIGHT, Grahame. *Jog Rummage.* 1974. Random. 1st ed. F/dj. P3. $10.00

WRIGHT, Harold Bell. *Exit.* 1930. NY. 1st ed. ils Amelia Watson. VG/VG. B5. $70.00

WRIGHT, Harry B. *Witness to Witchcraft.* 1957. NY. 1st ed. ils. 246 p. gilt red cloth. F/F. H3. $35.00

WRIGHT, Helen. *Sweeper in the Sky: Life of Maria Mitchell.* 1959. Macmillan. 4th ed. 8vo. 253 p. VG/dj. V3. $16.00

WRIGHT, I.L. *Remarkable Tale of a Whale.* 1920. Volland. ils John Held Jr. G. L1. $20.00

WRIGHT, J. Patrick. *On a Clear Day You Can See General Motors.* Grosse Pointe. Wright Enterprises. 1st ed. VG/dj. A16. $15.00

WRIGHT, John Kirtland. *Early Topographical Maps: Their Geog & Hist Value...* 1924. Am Geog Soc. 8 maps. 36 p. NF/wrp. O6. $25.00

WRIGHT, John Lloyd. *My Father Who Is on Earth.* 1946. NY. 1st ed. VG. B5. $45.00

WRIGHT, Keith. *Addressed To Kill.* 1993. London. Constable. 1st ed. F/F. S5. $22.50

WRIGHT, Kenneth. *Mysterious Planet.* 1958. Winston. 2nd ed. front free ep removed. VG. P3. $15.00

WRIGHT, L.R. *Chill Rain in January.* 1990. Viking. 1st ed. F/dj. P3. $18.00

WRIGHT, L.R. *Favorite.* 1982. Doubleday. 1st ed. VG/dj. P3. $15.00

WRIGHT, L.R. *Sleep While I Sing.* 1986. Canada. Doubleday. 1st ed. F/F. P3. $20.00

WRIGHT, Louis B. *Elizabethan's Am: Collection of Early Reports...New World.* (1965). London. Arnold. 1st ed. 8vo. 294 p. F/VG. A2. $12.50

WRIGHT, Louis B. *First Gentlemen of VA: Intellectual Qualities...* 1940. Huntington Lib. 8vo. 373 p. brn cloth. B11. $25.00

WRIGHT, Mabel Osgood. *Flowers & Ferns in Their Haunts*. 1901. NY. 1st ed. photos. 358 p. B28. $30.00

WRIGHT, N. *Letters of Horatio Greenough: Am Sculptor*. 1972. Madison. WI U. ils. 456 p. brds. dj. D2. $45.00

WRIGHT, Nathaniel H. *Fall of Palmyria & Other Poems*. 1817. Middlebury, VT. 1st ed. 24mo. contemporary calf brds. M1. $125.00

WRIGHT, Richard. *Conversations...* 1993. Jackson, MS. 1st ed. F/F. C4. $35.00

WRIGHT, Richard. *Early Works*. 1991. Lib of Am. 1st ed. F/F. P3. $35.00

WRIGHT, Richard. *Rite of Passage*. nd. Harper Collins. ARC. F/wrp. B2. $45.00

WRIGHT, Richard. *Some Observations Made in Travelling Through France & Italy*. 1764. London. Millar. 2nd ed. ils. 515 p. contemporary calf. B14. $100.00

WRIGHT, Richardson. *Sm House & Lg Garden*. 1924. Boston. 1st ed. ils. 219 p. G+. B28. $15.00

WRIGHT, Roy V. *Locomotive Cyclopedia of Am Practice 1941*. 1941. Simmons Boardman. VG. A16. $80.00

WRIGHT, S. Fowler. *Deluge*. 1928. Cosmopolitan. 1st ed. VG. P3. $25.00

WRIGHT, S. Fowler. *Throne of Saturn*. 1949. Arkham. 1st ed. F/dj. M2. $45.00

WRIGHT, S. Fowler. *Throne of Saturn*. 1949. Arkham. 1st ed. NF/dj. P3. $35.00

WRIGHT, Stephen. *Family Romance*. 1988. Harmony. 1st ed. F/dj. P3. $20.00

WRIGHT, Stephen. *Meditations in Gr*. 1983. Scribner. 2nd prt. 342 p. F/F clip. A7. $20.00

WRIGHT, Stephen. *Meditations in Gr*. 1983. Scribner. 1st ed. author's 1st book. F/NF. L3. $85.00

WRIGHT, T.M. *Strange Seed*. 1978. Everest House. 1st ed. VG/dj. P3. $20.00

WRIGHT, Thomas. *Contemporary Narrative of Proceedings Against Dame Alice...* 1843. London. Camden Soc. emb gr cloth. VG. G1. $65.00

WRIGHT, William. *Life & Loves of Mr Jiveass Nigger*. 1969. NY. F/F. A11. $60.00

WRIGHT. *Fold Star*. 1988. Dover. wrp. G2. $8.00

WRIGHT. *Quick Quilts*. 1991. np. ils. cloth. G2. $25.00

WRIGHTSON, John. *Fallow & Fodder Crops*. 1889. London. Chapman Hall. 276 p. VG. H10. $11.50

WRIGHTSON, Patricia. *Ice Is Coming*. 1978. Hutchinson. 2nd ed. NF/dj. P3. $15.00

WRIGLEY, H.E. *Special Report of Petroleum of PA*. 1875. Harrisburg. 4 lg fld map. 122 p. VG. E5. $85.00

WRITON, R.C. *HI ToDay*. 1926. np. xl. 8vo. photos. 147 p. gray cloth. G. T3. $15.00

WROTH, Lawrence C. *Voyages of Giovanni da Verrazzano, 1524-28*. 1970. New Haven. Yale. lg format. pls/portraits/repro Cellere Codex. NF. O6. $175.00

WROTH, Lawrence C. *Way of a Ship: Essay on Literature of Navigation Science*. 1937. Portland, ME. Southworth-Anthoensen Pr. NF/dj. O6. $175.00

WU-CHI, Liu. *Confucius: His Life & Time*. 1955. Philosophical Lib. VG. N2. $7.50

WULFECK, Dorothy Ford. *Marriages of Some VA Residents 1607-1800*. 1961-67. Genealogical Pub Co. reprint in 2 vols. B10. $125.00

WUNDERLICH, Carol Reinhold A. *Verhalten der Eignewarme in Krankheiten*. 1868. Leipzig. orig brds. G7. $795.00

WURLITZER, Rudolph. *Nog*. 1968. Random. 1st ed. author's 1st book. F/F. B2. $60.00

WUTHENAU, Raquel Bevilacqua. *Fiesta en Tasco*. 1942. Mexico. 1st ed. sgn. reading copy. F3. $10.00

WYAMN, Morrill. *Autumnal Catarrh (Hay Fever)*. 1872. NY. Hard Houghton. 1st ed. 3 color maps. 173 p. gilt red cloth. VG. S9. $72.00

WYATT, George. *Case of the Roving Rolls*. 1966. Whitman. decor brds. VG. P3. $8.00

WYCKOFF, Capwell. *Mystery Hunters at Lakeside Camp*. 1934. Saalfield. VG/dj. P3. $25.00

WYCKOFF, James. *William Reich: Life Force Explorer*. 1972. NY. Fawcett. PBO. G1. $20.00

WYDEN, Peter. *Bay of Pigs, the Untold Story*. 1979. Simon Schuster. 1st ed. 8vo. 32 pls. 352 p. VG/VG. B11. $20.00

WYETH, John B. *OR; or, Short Hist of a Long Journey From Atlantic...* 1833. Cambridge. prt for JB Wyeth. 1st ed. 12mo. teg. rebound morocco. R3. $4,000.00

WYETH, N.C. *Boy's King Authur*. 1946. Scribner. early reprint. 321 p. blk cloth. VG+. A3. $40.00

WYETH, N.C. *Odyssey of Homer*. 1929. Houghton Mifflin. trans GH Palmer. 15 color pls. NF/NF slipcase. B4. $250.00

WYKA, Frank. *Regression*. 1989. Carroll Graf. 1st ed. F/F. F4. $16.00

WYKES, Alan. *HG Wells in the Cinema*. 1977. London. Jupiter Books. 1st ed. lg 8vo. 176 p. NF/VG+/clear plastic. M7. $45.00

WYKES, Alan. *Pen-Friend*. 1950. Duckworth. 1st ed. VG/dj. P3. $30.00

WYLIE, E. *Blk Armour, Book of Poems*. 1923. Doran. 1st ed. 77 p. blk cloth. VG+. B22. $15.00

WYLIE, Philip. *Disappearance*. 1951. NY. 1st ed. VG/VG. B5. $25.00

WYLIE, Philip. *Gladiator*. 1930. Knopf. 1st ed. xl. VG/dj. P3. $15.00

WYLIE, Philip. *Spy Who Spoke Porpoise*. 1969. Doubleday. 1st ed. VG/dj. P3. $35.00

WYLLIE, John. *Pocket Full of Dead*. 1978. Crime Club. 1st ed. VG/G. P3. $13.00

WYLLIE, John. *Tumours of the Cerebellum*. 1908. London. Lewis. 109 p. orig brds. VG. G7. $295.00

WYMAN, Donald. *Arnold Aboretum Garden Book*. 1954. NY. ils/pls. 354 p. VG. B26. $16.00

WYND, Oswald. *Death the Red Flower*. 1965. Cassell. 1st ed. xl. dj. P3. $6.00

WYNDHAM, John. *Midwich Cuckoos*. 1958. Ballantine. 1st ed. VG/dj. P3. $35.00

WYNDHAM, John. *Stowaway to Mars*. 1989. London. Severn. reprint of Planet Plane. F/F. N3. $10.00

WYNDHAM, Robert. *Chinese Mother Goose Rhymes*. 1968. Cleveland. World. 1st ed. ils Ed Young. pict red cloth. VG. T5. $35.00

WYNDHAM, Violet. *Madame de Genlis*. (1958). NY. Roy. 1st Am ed. 8vo. 302 p. VG/VG. A2. $15.00

WYNNE, Anthony. *Green Knife*. 1939. Caxton House. VG. P3. $13.00

WYNNE, James. *Private Lib of NY*. 1860. NY. French. 417 p. VG. G7. $135.00

WYNNE, May. *Hootie Toots of Hollow Tree*. 1925. Altemus. ils Frank Ver Beck. red cloth. VG. M5. $20.00

WYNNE, Nancy Blue. *Agatha Christie Chronology*. 1976. NY. PBO/1st prt. NF/ils wrp. A11. $20.00

WYSS, Dieter. *Psychoanalytic Schools From the Beginning to Present*. 1973. NY. Aronson. 1st Am ed. 568 p. VG/dj. G1. $30.00

WYSS, Johann. *Swiss Family Robinson*. 1963. Ipswick. LEC/Cowell. 1/1500. ils/sgn David Gentleman. 356 p. NF/pub case. H5. $100.00

WYTHE, J.H. *Easy Lessons in Vegetable Biology*. 1883. NY. 1st ed. 12mo. 94 p. decor cloth. VG. B28. $17.50

XIMENEZ, Fray Francisco. *Historia de la Provincia de San Vicente de Chiapas...* 1975. Guatemala. 2 vols in 1. F3. $45.00

YABSLEY. *TX Quilts, TX Women.* 1984. np. ils. wrp. G2. $20.00

YAFFE, James. *Nice Murder for Mom.* 1988. St Martin. 1st ed. F/F. M15. $25.00

YAKHONTOFF, Victor A. *Eyes on Japan.* 1936. Coward McCann. 1st ed. 8vo. 17 pls. 329 p. VG. W1. $20.00

YALDIZ, M. *Archaeologie und Kunst-geschichte Chinesisch-Zentralasiens.* 1987. NY/London. Brill. 1st ed. 8vo. 93 pls/2 fld plans. VG. W1. $65.00

YALE, Catharine Brooks. *Nim & Cum & the Wonderhead Stories.* 1895. Way Williams. 1st ed. 126 p. teg. decor gr cloth. VG+. S10. $35.00

YAMADA, Chisaburoh F. *Decorative Arts of Japan.* 1964. Tokyo. Kodansha. 1st ed. xl. folio. pls. 262 p. VG. W1. $45.00

YAMADA, Yoshimitsu. *Akido Complete.* 1969. NY. Stuart. 1st ed. 4to. 127 p. VG/dj. W1. $20.00

YAMASAKI, Toyoko. *Bonchi: A Novel of 20th-Century Japan.* 1982. London. Gollancz. 1st British ed. trans from Japanese. NF/NF. A14. $25.00

YAMATA, Kikou. *3 Geishas.* (1956). John Day. 1st ed. 8vo. 253 p. VG/VG. A2. $10.00

YANCEY, William H. *Gate Is Down.* (1956). NY. 1st ed. VG/dj. A17. $15.00

YANG, Linda. *Terrace Gardener's Handbook.* 1982 (1975). Beaverton, OR. ils/photos. 283 p. M. B26. $12.50

YARBRO, Chelsea Quinn. *False Dawn.* 1978. Doubleday. 1st ed. F/dj. P3. $18.00

YARBRO, Chelsea Quinn. *Flame in Byzantium.* 1987. Tor. 1st ed. F/dj. P3. $18.00

YARBRO, Chelsea Quinn. *Four Horses for Tishry.* 1985. Harper. 1st ed. F/F. F4. $25.00

YARBRO, Chelsea Quinn. *Lacadio's Apprentice.* 1984. Harper Row. 1st ed. F/dj. P3. $15.00

YARBRO, Chelsea Quinn. *Law in Charity.* 1989. Doubleday. 1st ed. author's 1st W novel. F/F. N3. $15.00

YARDLEY, Michael. *Backing Into the Limelight.* 1935. London. Harrap. 1st ed. 267 p. gilt blk cloth. F/F/clear plastic. M7. $55.00

YARMOLINSKY, A. *Military Establishment: Its Impact on Am Soc.* 1971. Harper. 1st ed. VG/VG. V2. $5.00

YARNALL, Elizabeth Biddle. *Addison Hutton: Quaker Architect, 1834-1916.* 1974. Phil. Art Alliance. 1st ed. 4to. 33 pls. 78 p. VG/VG. V3. $24.00

YASTRZEMSKI, Carl. *Batting.* 1972. Viking. 1st ed. F/VG+. P8. $25.00

YASTRZEMSKI, Carl. *Yaz, Baseball, the Wall & Me.* 1990. Doubleday. 1st ed. F/F. P8. $12.50

YATES, Dornford. *Shoal Water.* 1940. Ward Lock. 1st ed. VG/VG-. P3. $35.00

YATES, Dornford. *Stolen March.* 1933. Minton Blach. 1st ed. VG-. P3. $35.00

YATES, Frances A. *Lull & Bruno: Collected Essays, Vol 1.* 1982. London. Routledge/Kegan Paul. 1st ed. 279 p. H10. $32.50

YATES, George Worthington. *Body That Wasn't Uncle.* 1939. NY. Morrow. 1st ed. F/NF. M15. $65.00

YATES, George Worthington. *If a Body.* 1941. NY. Morrow. 1st ed. F/NF. M15. $40.00

YATES, Haydie. *70 Miles From a Lemon.* 1947. Houghton Mifflin. 1st ed. 8vo. 235 p. F/F. A2. $15.00

YATES, Richard. *Liars in Love.* 1981. Delacorte Lawrence. AP. author's 2nd ed. NF/wrp. L3. $55.00

YATES, Richard. *Revolutionary Road.* 1961. Little Brn. 1st ed. author's 1st book. G/dj. M18. $35.00

YATES, W. Ross. *Joseph Wharton: Quaker Industrial Pioneer.* 1987. Bethlehem. Lehigh U. 1st ed. 8vo. 413 p. M/M. V3. $22.00

YEARDLEY, John. *Memoir & Diary of...,* *Minister of the Gospel.* 1859. London. AW Bennett. 8vo. 456 p. VG. V3. $35.00

YEATS, William Butler. *Countess Cathleen.* 1912. London. Fisher Unwin. 1st revised ed. VG+. E3. $65.00

YEATS, William Butler. *Full Moon in March.* 1935. London. 1st ed. F. V1. $75.00

YEATS, William Butler. *John Sherman & Dhoya.* 1969. Detroit. Wayne State. dj. N2. $10.00

YEATS, William Butler. *Packet for Ezra Pound.* 1929. Dublin, Ireland. Cuala. 1st ed. 1/425. 37 p. bl brds. VG. H5. $300.00

YEATS, William Butler. *Poetry & Ireland: Essays.* 1908. Churchtown, Dundrum. Cuala. 1st ed. 1/250. sm quarto. 53 p. teg. NF. H5. $600.00

YEATS, William Butler. *Stories of Red Hanrahan.* 1904. Dundrum. Dun Elmer Pr. 1/500. NF. Q1. $300.00

YEATS, William Butler. *Vision.* 1925. London. Werner Laurie. 1/600. sgn/#d. cloth/vellum spine. w/pub flyer. NF/dj. Q1. $600.00

YEATS, William Butler. *Wheels & Butterflies.* 1935. NY. 1st ed. VG+/VG+. V1. $40.00

YEE, Min S. *Melancholy Hist of Soledad Prison.* 1970. Harper. 1st ed. VG/VG. A7. $28.00

YEFREMOV, Ivan. *Andromeda.* 1959. Foreign Languages Pub. 1st ed. VG/dj. P3. $30.00

YEHOASH. *Feet of the Messenger.* 1923. Connat Pr. 296 p. VG. S3. $24.00

YELLEN, Samuel. *Am Labor Struggles.* ca 1936. Harcourt Brace. ils/photos. G/fair. V4. $17.50

YELLOW BIRD. *Life & Adventures of Joaquin Murieta.* (1955). Norman, OK. 1st thus ed. 159 p. G/dj. B18. $22.50

YEP, Laurence. *Child of the Owl.* 1977. Harper Row. VG/dj. P3. $15.00

YEP, Laurence. *Dragon of the Lost Sea.* 1982. Harper. 1st ed. F/F. F4. $15.00

YEP, Laurence. *Dragon Steel.* 1985. Harper. 1st ed. F/F. F4. $17.00

YEP, Lawrence. *Dragonwings.* 1975. Harper Row. 1st ed. 8vo. 248 p. pict brds. VG/VG. T5. $45.00

YERBY, Frank. *Bride of Liberty.* 1954. Doubleday. 1st ed. VG/dj. P3. $20.00

YERKES, Laura Augusta. *Home School for Young Speakers.* (1908). Scull. ils Frances Brundage. 238 p. VG. S10. $40.00

YERSUSHALMI, Yosef Hayim. *Haggadah & Hist: Panorama in Facsimile of 5 Centuries...* 1975. JPS. 2nd prt. 4to. 200 repros. 494 p. VG+/VG-. S3. $115.00

YETO, Genjiro. *Am Diary of a Japanese Girl. By Miss Morning Glory.* Sept 1902. Stokes. sm 4to. 262 p. gilt decor bdg. VG. B14. $55.00

YEVTUSHENKO, Yevgeny. *Almost at the End.* 1987. London. Boyars. 1st ed. trans from Russian. F/F. A14/V1. $25.00

YEVTUSHENKO, Yevgeny. *Dove in Santiago.* 1983. Viking. 1st Am ed. trans from Russian. F/F. A14. $20.00

YIANNIAS, John J. *Byzantine Tradition After Fall of Constantinople.* 1991. Charlottesville. 8vo. 354 p. cloth. dj. O2. $50.00

YING, T.S. *Endemic Genera of Seed Plants in China.* 1993. Beijing. ils/184 pls. 824 p. M/dj. B26. $98.95

YOGANANDA, Paramhansa. *Autobiographie Efnes Yogi.* 1950. Germany. Otto Wilelm Barth/Verlag. 1st German ed. ES. G+. N2. $10.00

YOLEN, Jane. *Cards of Grief.* nd. BC. VG/dj. P3. $8.00

YOLEN, Jane. *Friend: Story of George Fox & the Quakers.* 1972. Seabury Pr. 8vo. 179 p. VG/dj. V3. $12.50

YOLEN, Jane. *Touch Magic, Fantasy, Faerie & Folklore...* 1981. Philomel Books. 1st ed. 8vo. 96 p. red cloth. VG/VG. T5. $30.00

YOORS, Jan. *Gypsies of Spain.* (1974). Macmillan. sm 4to. 143 p. NF/NF. A7. $30.00

YORBURG, Betty. *Utopia & Reality.* 1969. Columbia. 198 p. clip dj. A7. $13.00

YORK, Andrew. *Captivator.* 1974. Crime Club. 1st ed. VG. P3. $10.00

YORK, Andrew. *Tallant for Disaster.* 1978. Crime Club. 1st ed. VG/dj. P3. $12.00

YORK, Brantley. *Analytical, Ils & Constructive Grammar of the Eng Language.* 1862. Raleigh. L Pmeroy. 3rd ed. 219 p. VG. M8. $350.00

YORK, Carol Beach. *Doll in the Bakeshop.* 1965. Franklin Watts. 1st ed. 8vo. 98 p. pink cloth. VG-. T5. $25.00

YORK, Jeremy; see Creasey, John.

YORK, Thomas. *Am's Great Railroads.* 1987. London. Bison. 4to. ils. 192 p. F/F. B11. $20.00

YORKE, Elizabeth. *Court of Oberon; or, The 3 Wishes.* 1831. London. Shakespeare Pr. 1st ed. quarto. litho pl. marbled brds. half calf. VG. H5. $450.00

YORKE, Margaret. *Come-On.* 1979. Harper Row. 1st ed. NF/dj. P3. $15.00

YORKE, Margaret. *Hand of Death.* 1981. St Martin. 1st ed. VG/dj. P3. $13.00

YOST, Karl. *Bibliography of the Pub Works of Charles M Russell.* 1971. Lincoln, NE. VG/dj. A16. $125.00

YOST, Nellie Snyder. *Call of the Range. Story of NE Stock Growers Assn.* 1966. Denver. Sage. 437 p. M. H10. $18.00

YOUILL, P.B.; see Williams, Gordon.

YOUNG, A.S. *Mets From Mobile.* 1970. HBW. 1st ed. F/VG. P8. $40.00

YOUNG, Al. *Snakes.* 1972 (1970). HRW. 4th prt. 149 p. dj. A7. $10.00

YOUNG, Al. *Song Turning Back Into Itself.* 1971. HRW. AP. sgn. author's 3rd book. NF/wrp. L3. $125.00

YOUNG, Art. *Art Young's Inferno.* 1934. NY. Delphic Studio. 1st ed. inscr. NF. B2. $150.00

YOUNG, Art. *Trees at Night.* 1927. Boni Liveright. cloth spine/Japanese paper brds. D2. $50.00

YOUNG, Calvin M. *Little Turtle (Me-She-Kin-No-Quah): Great Chief of Miami...* 1917. np. 1st ed. 8vo. ils. 249 p. G. B11. $45.00

YOUNG, Carrie. *Green Broke: Life on Midwestern Pony Farm.* 1981. NY. Dodd Mead. 1st ed. VG/VG. O3. $25.00

YOUNG, Charles E. *Dangers of the Trail in 1865...* 1912. NY. Humphrey. 1st ed. VG. H7. $75.00

YOUNG, Collier; see Bloch, Robert.

YOUNG, Dorothy Weir. *Life & Letters of J Alden Weir.* 1960. New Haven. Yale. 1st ed. 277 p. cloth. dj. D2. $85.00

YOUNG, Dorothy Weir. *Life & Letters of J Alden Weir.* 1971. Kennedy Graphics/Da Capo. reprint 1960 ed. D2. $35.00

YOUNG, Edward James. *Tribute to Octavius Brooks Frothingham.* 1895. Cambridge. Wilson. 8 p. wrp. H10. $15.00

YOUNG, Edward. *Revenge: Tragedy in 5 Acts.* (1794). Boston. 1st Am ed. 16mo. 60 p. M1. $150.00

YOUNG, Egerton Ryerson. *By Canoe & Dog-Train Among the Cree & Salteaux Indians.* ca 1910. NY. Abingdon. VG/dj. scarce. H7. $20.00

YOUNG, Ella. *Tangle-Coated Horse.* 1929. Longman Gr. 1st ed. ils Vera Bock. 185 p. VG. P2. $50.00

YOUNG, Everild. *Rogues & Raiders of the Caribbean & S Sea.* 1959. London. Jarrolds. 2nd prt. sgn. photos. 240 p. map ep. blk brds. B11. $35.00

YOUNG, Francis Brett. *Century of Boys' Stories.* nd. Hutchinson. VG. P3. $30.00

YOUNG, G.O. *AK Yukon Trophies Won & Lost.* 1947. Huntington, WV. 1st ed. 273 p. dj. A17. $150.00

YOUNG, Gordon. *Devil's Passport.* 1942. Triangle. VG/fair. P3. $20.00

YOUNG, Harold N. *VA Agricultural Experiment Station, 1886-1966.* ca 1975. VA U. 1st ed. 221 p. VG. B10. $15.00

YOUNG, Hubert. *Independent Arab.* 1933. London. John Murray. 1st ed. 346 p. gilt bl cloth. VG. M7. $125.00

YOUNG, Hugh. *Surgeon's Autobiography.* ca 1940. Harcourt Brace. ils. 554 p. VG/poor. B10. $20.00

YOUNG, J.P. *Journalism in CA...Pacific Coast Expo Biographies.* (1915). San Francisco. Chronicle. 1st ed. 8vo. 362 p. F. A2. $25.00

YOUNG, John Richard. *Schooling of the W Horse.* 1959. Norman. later prt. VG/VG. O3. $25.00

YOUNG, John Russell. *Flowery Kingdom & the Land of the Mikado...* 1894. Phil. 4to. 608 p. gilt pict gr cloth. VG. H3. $55.00

YOUNG, Levi Edgar. *Founding of UT.* 1923. Scribner. 445 p. gilt bl cloth. VG+. H7. $30.00

YOUNG, P.D. *Two of the Missing.* (1975). NY. CMG. F/NF. A7. $30.00

YOUNG, Philip. *Ernest Hemingway.* 1952. NY. 1st ed. sgn. VG+/VG. A11. $65.00

YOUNG, Rogers W. *Robert E Lee & Fort Pulaski.* 1970. np. reprint. 27 p. NF/prt wrp. M8. $15.00

YOUNG, Stark. *So Red the Rose.* 1934. Scribner. early prt. 431 p. VG/VG. B10. $15.00

YOUNG, T.C. *Near E Culture & Soc.* 1951. Princeton. 1st ed. 8vo. 250 p. cloth. dj. O2. $30.00

YOUNG, Wayland. *Eros Denied: Sex in W Soc.* 1964. Grove. later prt. 16 halftones. VG/dj. G1. $20.00

YOUNG BEAR, Ray A. *Waiting To Be Fed.* 1975. Port Townsend. Gray Wolf. 1/225. NF/wrp. L3. $75.00

YOUNG BEAR, Ray A. *Winter of the Salamander.* 1980. Harper. 1st ed. F/NF. L3. $65.00

YOUNG. *Radial Nine Patch.* 1986. np. ils. wrp. G2. $6.00

YOUNG-BRUEHL, Elizabeth. *Anna Freud: A Biography.* 1988. Summit. 1st ed. 528 p. VG/dj. G1. $28.50

YOUNGBLOOD, Rufus W. *20 Yrs in the Secret Service.* 1973. Simon Schuster. VG/dj. A16. $7.00

YOUNGER, Mab. *Practical Garden Design for Australia & New Zealand.* 1978. Sydney. ils/photos. 64 p. M/dj. B26. $9.00

YOUNGHUSBAND, Francis. *Epic of Mt Everest.* 1926. London. Arnold. 1st ed. 8vo. 319 p. VG-. A2. $35.00

YOUNGHUSBAND, George. *Short Hist of Tower of London.* 1926. London. Jenkins. 1st thus ed. 12mo. 188 p. VG+/poor. A2. $20.00

YOUNT, John. *Wolf at the Door.* 1967. NY. 1st ed. sgn. F/NF clip. A11. $75.00

YOURCENAR, M. *Dark Brain of Piranesi & Other Essays.* 1984. FSG. 1st ed. trans from French. NF/NF clip. A14. $25.00

YOURCENAR, M. *Memoirs of Hadrian.* (1955). London. Secker Warburg. 1st ed. trans Frick. F/NF. B4. $75.00

YUILL, P.B. *Hazell Plays Solomon.* 1975. Walker. 1st ed. NF/dj. P3. $13.00

YUNGBLUT, John R. *Gentle Art of Spiritual Guidance.* 1991. Rockport, MA. pb. 12mo. 148 p. M/wrp. V3. $9.00

YURICK, Sol. *Richard A.* 1981. Arbor. 1st ed. F/F. F4. $18.00

YURICK, Sol. *Warriors.* 1965. HRW. 1st ed. VG/dj. P3. $35.00

ZAAR, Ludov. *Circa Indurationem Glanduale Prostate Observationes...* 1822. Londini. Gothorum. 16 p. G7. $35.00

ZACKEL, Fred. *Cocaine & Blue Eyes.* 1978. CMG. 1st ed. VG/dj. P3. $20.00

ZAGORIA, Donald S. *Vietnam Triangle.* (1967). Pegasus. 286 p. F/clip. A7. $40.00

ZAHN, Timothy. *Coming of Age.* 1984. Bluejay. 1st ed. F/dj. P3. $20.00

ZAHN, Timothy. *Spinnert.* 1985. NY. Bluejay. 1st ed. F/F. N3. $15.00

ZAHN, Timothy. *Star Wars: Dark Force Rising.* 1992. Bantam. 1st ed. M/M. T2. $23.50

ZAHN, Timothy. *Star Wars: Heir to the Empire.* 1991. Bantam. 1st ed. F/F. T2. $25.00

ZAHN, Timothy. *Star Wars: Heir to the Empire.* 1991. Bantam. 1st ed. inscr. F/F. T2. $55.00

ZAHN, Timothy. *Star Wars: Last Command.* 1993. Bantam. 1st ed. 3rd book of series. M/M. T2. $22.00

ZAHNER, Craig. *Saddle Up for AK!* nd. Auburn, IN. Big Wheel Pr. miniature. 24 p. checkered brds. F. B24. $110.00

ZALBEN, Jane Berskin. *Oliver & Alison's Week.* 1980. FSG. 1st ed. 4to. 40 p. VG. T5. $20.00

ZALESKY, Moses. *Profile of Purposeful Living: Life Story of MJ Kaplun.* 1968. Shengold. 72 p. VG/G. S3. $23.00

ZAMBRENO, Mary Frances. *Plague of Sorcerers.* 1991. HBJ. 1st ed. F/dj. P3. $17.00

ZANGER, Jack. *Ken Boyer.* 1965. Nelson (Rutledge). 1st ed. F/VG. P8. $30.00

ZANUSO, Billa. *Young Freud: Origins of Psychoanalysis...Viennese Culture.* 1986. NY. Blackwell. 1st Eng-language ed/Am issue. 202 p. blk cloth. F/dj. G1. $25.00

ZANZOTTO, Andrea. *Selected Poetry.* 1975. Princeton. Italian/Eng text. F/F. V1. $10.00

ZAPF, Hermann. *Manuale Typographicum.* 1954. NY. Mus Books. 1/1000. 1st ed. sgn. gilt bdg. F/dj/slipcase/box. B24. $575.00

ZAPF, Hermann. *Manuale Typographicum: 100 Typographical Arrangements...* 1972. Frankfurt. Gutenberg. quarto. 1/800. sgn. gr cloth. F/paper slipcase. B24. $475.00

ZAPF, Hermann. *William Morris: Sein Leben und Werk in der Geschichte...* 1949. Lubeck. Blanckertz. quarto. 62 p. F/dj. B24. $185.00

ZARET, David. *Heavenly Contract: Ideology & Organization...Puritanism.* 1985. Chicago. 214 p. blk cloth. VG/dj. G1. $17.50

ZARING, Jane. *Return of the Dragon.* 1981. Houghton Mifflin. 1st ed. ils Polly Broman. 146 p. NF/G+. T5. $20.00

ZAVALA, Silvio. *Contribucion a la Historia de las Instituciones...Guatemala.* (1967). Guatemala. 135 p. wrp. F3. $15.00

ZEBROWSKI, George. *Marcolife.* 1979. Harper Row. 1st ed. F/dj. P3. $15.00

ZEBROWSKI, George. *Nebula Awards 21.* 1987. HBJ. 1st ed. F/F. P3. $20.00

ZEHREN, Erich. *Crescent & the Bull: Survey of Archaeology in Near E.* 1962 (1961). Hawthorn. 1st Am ed. 8vo. 10 pls. 366 p. F/VG+. A2. $20.00

ZEIGFREID, Karl. *World of the Future.* nd. Arcadia. xl. dj. P3. $6.00

ZEITLIN, Solomon. *Rise & Fall of the Judaean State.* 1962. JPS. 2 vols. VG. S3. $55.00

ZELAZNY, Roger. *Blood of Amber.* 1986. Arbor. 1st ed. F/dj. M2. $25.00

ZELAZNY, Roger. *Courts of Chaos.* 1978. Doubleday. 1st ed. F/dj. P3. $35.00

ZELAZNY, Roger. *Damnation Alley.* 1979. Gregg. F/dj. P3. $25.00

ZELAZNY, Roger. *Doorways in the Sand.* 1977. Allen. 1st ed. F/dj. P3. $20.00

ZELAZNY, Roger. *Eye of Cat.* 1982. Timescape. 1st ed. NF/dj. P3. $20.00

ZELAZNY, Roger. *Guns of Avalon.* 1974. Faber. NF/dj. P3. $50.00

ZELAZNY, Roger. *Hand of Oberon.* 1978. Faber. 1st ed. NF/dj. P3. $45.00

ZELAZNY, Roger. *Ils Roger Zelazny.* 1978. Baronet. 1st ed. sgn. F/sans. P3. $60.00

ZELAZNY, Roger. *Jack of Shadows.* 1971. Walker. 1st ed. VG/dj. P3. $45.00

ZELAZNY, Roger. *Lord of Light.* 1967. Doubleday. 1st ed. xl. 257 p. VG/VG. M20. $50.00

ZELAZNY, Roger. *Roadmarks.* 1979. Del Rey. 1st ed. F/dj. P3. $25.00

ZELAZNY, Roger. *Sign of Chaos.* 1987. Arbor. 1st ed. F/dj. P3. $16.00

ZELAZNY, Roger. *Sign of the Unicorn.* 1975. Doubleday. 1st ed. F/NF. M2. $40.00

ZELAZNY, Roger. *Sign of the Unicorn.* 1975. Doubleday. 1st ed. VG/dj. P3. $35.00

ZELAZNY, Roger. *Trumps of Doom.* 1985. Arbor. 1st ed. F/dj. M2. $25.00

ZELLER, Eduard. *Aristotle & the Earlier Peripatetics...* 1897. London. Longman Gr. 1st Eng-language ed. 12mo. 512 p. emb mauve cloth. G. G1. $75.00

ZELLER, Eduard. *Hist of Eclecticism in Greek Philosophy.* 1883. Longman Gr. 1st Eng-language ed. 12mo. 384 p. mauve cloth. VG. G1. $75.00

ZENDIK, Wulf. *Blackhawk, the Last Am Warrior.* 1986. Boulevard. Zendik. 1st ed. quarto. VG/wrp. L3. $60.00

ZERLENTOS, Perikleous. *Letters of W Dukes of the Aegean 1438-1565.* 1985. Athens. Greek/Italian text. 8vo. 126 p. O2. $12.00

ZERN, Ed. *Zane Grey's Adventures in Fishing.* (1952). Harper. 1st ed. VG+/clip. B9. $275.00

ZERVOS, Christian. *L'Art de la Crete Neolithique et Minoenne.* 1956. Paris. Cahirs d'Art. folio. 524 p. NF/dj. F1. $95.00

ZETA ACOSTA, Oscar. *Autobiography of a Brn Buffalo.* 1972. Straight Arrow. 1st ed. author's 1st book. NF/NF. A14. $30.00

ZHELEZNOVA, Irina. *Fenist the Falcon.* 1977. Russia. trans from Russian. 12 p. F/pict wht wrp. H3. $20.00

ZIEMANN, Hans Heinrich. *Accident.* 1979. St Martin. 1st ed. F/dj. P3. $15.00

ZIFF, Larzer. *Am 1890s. Life & Times of a Lost Generation.* (1967). NY. 2nd prt. 376 p. cloth. NF. D3. $15.00

ZIGLER, J. Hiram. *VA Farm Bureau Story: Growth of Grassroots Organization.* (1982). np. xl. 221 p. F/VG. B10. $15.00

ZIKMUND & HANZELKA. *Amazon Headhunters.* (1963). Prague. 1st Eng-language ed. 8vo. 299 p. F/VG. A2. $25.00

ZILBERGELD, Bernie. *Shrinking of Am: Myths of Psychological Change.* 1983. Little Brn. 307 p. bl cloth. VG/dj. G1. $30.00

ZILBOORG, Gregory. *Hist of Medical Psychology.* 1941. Norton. later prt. 606 p. blk cloth. VG/dj. G1. $50.00

ZILBOORG, Gregory. *Sigmund Freud: His Exploration of the Mind of Man.* 1951. Scribner. 1st ed. sm 8vo. 132 p. blk cloth. G1. $17.50

ZILCZER, Judith. *Oscar Bluemner.* 1980. Smithsonian. 62 color pls. D2. $25.00

ZILVERSMIT, Arthur. *1st Emancipation: Abolition of Slavery in the N.* (1967). Chicago. 262 p. NF/NF. A7. $15.00

ZIMMERMAN, Bruce. *Thicker Than Water.* (1991). Harper Collins. 1st ed. F/F. B3. $20.00

ZIMMERMAN, J.L. *Where the People Sing.* 1946. Knopf. 1st ed. 8vo. 234 p. VG/G+ clip. A2. $20.00

ZIMMERMAN, Paul. *LA Dodgers.* 1960. Coward McCann. 1st ed. VG/VG. P8. $25.00

ZIMMERMAN, Paul. *Yrs the Mets Lost Last Place.* 1969. World. 1st ed. F/VG. P8. $20.00

ZIMMERMAN, Tom. *Day in the Season of the LA Dodgers.* 1990. Shapolsky. 1st ed. VG/VG. P8. $15.00

ZIMMERMAN. *Blackwork Embroidery Patterns.* 1985. np. revised ed. sbdg. G2. $23.00

ZIMMERMAN. *Canvas Work Encyclopedia.* 1989. np. ils. sbdg. G2. $30.00

ZIMMERMAN. *Pulled-Thread Embroidery Stitches.* 1988. np. ils. sbdg. wrp. G2. $23.00

ZIMMERMAN. *Technique of Metal Thread Embroidery.* 1980. np. ils. sbdg. G2. $20.00

ZINDEL, Paul. *And Miss Reardon Drinks a Little.* (1972). Random. 1st ed. F/VG. B4. $50.00

ZINDEL, Paul. *When a Darkness Falls.* 1984. Bantam. VG/VG-. P3. $13.00

ZINDELL, David. *Neverness.* 1988. Donald Fine. 1st ed. F/dj. P3. $20.00

ZINK, David. *Stones of Atlantis.* 1978. NJ. 1st ed. 8vo. ils. 234 p. F/VG. H3. $25.00

ZINN, Howard. *Justice in Everyday Life.* 1974. Morrow. 1st ed. 367 p. dj. A7. $15.00

ZINN, Howard. *SNCC: The New Abolitionists.* (1964). Beacon. 246 p. clip dj. A7. $25.00

ZINOVIEV, Grigorii. *Hist of Bolshevik Party.* (1973). London. New Park. 229 p. wrp. A7. $8.00

ZINSSER, William. *Spring Training.* 1989. Harper Row. 1st ed. F/F. P8. $10.00

ZIRKLE, Conway. *Evolution, Marxian Biology & the Social Scene.* (1959). Phil. PA U. 527 p. A7. $20.00

ZITKALA-SA. *Am Indian Stories.* 1985. Lincoln, NE. reissue of 1921 prt. F/wrp. L3. $15.00

ZOCHERT, Donald. *Man of Glass.* 1981. HRW. 1st ed. VG/dj. P3. $13.00

ZOCHERT, Donald. *Yel Dogs.* (1989). Atlantic Monthly. 1st ed. rem mk. VG/VG. B3. $15.00

ZOGBAUM, Rufus Fairchild. *Horse, Foot, & Dragoons.* 1888. NY. Harper. 1st ed. octavo. 176 p. gilt navy cloth. VG. H5. $250.00

ZOLA, Emile. *Fencondite.* 1899. Paris. 1st ed presentation. w/sgn typed letter. VG/slipcase. H5. $1,350.00

ZOLINE, Pamela. *Heat Death of the Universe.* 1988. McPherson. 1st ed. F/dj. P3. $20.00

ZOLOTOW, Charlotte. *Someone New.* 1978. Harper Row. 1st ed. sm 4to. 32 p. VG. T5. $25.00

ZORAIDA VAZQUEZ, Josefina. *La Imagen del Indio en el Espanol del Siglo XVI.* (1962). Mexico. 1st ed. 12mo. 174 p. wrp. F3. $10.00

ZOSIMUS, E. *Monk of La Trappe, Extracts From Theological Works...* 1849. Phil. Latin/Eng text. 60 p. wrp. B14. $60.00

ZOSS, Joel. *Diamonds in the Rough.* 1989. Macmillan. 1st ed. M/M. P8. $27.50

ZOSS, Joel. *Greatest Moments in Baseball.* 1987. Bison Books. 1st ed. VG/dj. P3. $10.00

ZOSS, Joel. *Nat League.* 1986. Bison. 1st ed. photos. F/F. P8. $5.00

ZOUCH, Thomas. *Memoirs of Life & Writings of Sir Philip Sidney.* 1809. NY. Wilson. 4to. 400 p. half calf (ca 1900) over purple cloth. K1. $175.00

ZUCKERMAN, Arthur J. *Jewish Princedom in Feudal France 768-900.* 1972. NY. Columbia. 490 p. VG. S3. $25.00

ZUCKERMAN, Solly. *Functional Affinities of Man, Monkeys & Apes...* 1933. London. 24 pls/11 tables. 203 p. NF/dj. G7. $95.00

ZUCKMAYER, Carl. *Carnival Confession.* 1961. Methuen. 1st ed. VG/dj. P3. $20.00

ZUGSMITH, Leane. *L Is for Labor: Glossary of Labor Terms.* nd. NY. League of Women Shoppers. NF/wrp. B2. $40.00

ZUKOFSKY, Louis. *Little.* 1970. NY. 1st ed. author's 1st novel. F/NF. V1. $20.00

ZUMWALT & ZUMWALT. *My Father, My Son.* (1986). Macmillan. 2nd prt. F/F. A7. $13.00

ZWEIG, Arnold. *Education Before Verdun.* 1936. Viking. 1st ed. trans from German. VG+/VG. A14. $25.00

ZWEIG, Stefan. *Beware of Pity.* 1982. London. Cape. revised ed. trans from German. NF/NF. A14. $25.00

ZWEIG, Stefan. *Mental Healers: Franz Anton Mesmer, Mary B Eddy...Freud.* 1932. Viking. 1st Eng-language ed. 363 p. blk cloth. VG. G1. $40.00

ZWEIG, Stefan. *Royal Game & Other Stories.* 1981. London. Cape. 1st ed. trans from German. F/F. A14. $25.00

ZWEMER & ZWEMER. *Moslem Women.* 1926. Cambridge, MA. 1st ed. 12mo. pls. 272 p. VG/pict wrp. H3. $40.00

ZWINGER, Ann. *Conscious Stillness.* (1982). Harper Row. 1st ed. ils/maps. F/NF. B3. $35.00

ZWINGER, Ann. *John Xanthus: Ft Tejon Letters 1857-59.* (1986). Tucson, AZ. 1st ed. F/NF clip. B3. $30.00

ZWINGER, Ann. *Mysterious Lands.* (1989). Dutton. AP. F/prt tan wrp. B3. $35.00

PSEUDOMYMS

Listed below are pseudonyms of many paperback and hardcover authors. This information was shared with us by some of our many contributors, and we offer it here as a reference for our readers. This section is organized alphabetically by the author's actual name (given in bold) followed by the pseudonyms he or she has been known to use. (It is interesting to note that 'house names' were common with more than one author using the same name for a particular magazine or publishing house.)

If you have additional information (or corrections), please let us hear from you so we can expand this section in future editions.

Aarons, Edward S.
Ayres, Paul; Ronns, Edward

Albert, Marvin H.
Conroy, Albert; Jason, Stuart;
Quarry, Nick; Rome, Anthony

Ard, William
Kerr, Ben; Ward, Jonas (some)

Auster, Paul
Benjamin, Paul

Avallone, Mike
Carter, Nick (a few);
Conway, Troy (a few); Dalton, Priscilla;
Jason, Stuart; Noone, Edwina;
Stuart, Sidney; Walker, Max

Ballard, W.T.
Hunter, D'Allard; MacNeil, Neil;
Shepherd, John

Ballinger, Bill
Sanborn, B.X.

Blake, Roger
Sade, Mark

Blassingame, Lurton
Duncan, Peter

Beaumont, Charles
Grantland, Keith

Beck, Robert
Iceberg Slim

Bedford-Jones, H.
Feval, Paul; Pemjion, L.

Bloch, Robert
Young, Collier

Block, Lawrence
Ard, William; Emerson, Jill; Harrison, Chip;
Lord, Sheldon; Morse, Benjamin, M.D.;
Shaw, Andrew

Bradley, Marion Zimmer
Chapman, Lee; Dexter, John (some);
Gardner, Miriam; Graves, Valerie;
Ives, Morgan

Brunner, John
Woodcott, Keith

Bulmer, Kenneth
Hardy, Adam; Norvil, Manning;
Prescot, Dray

Burnett, W.R.
Monachan, John; Updyke, James

Burroughs, William S.
Lee, William

Byrne, Stuart
Bloodstone, John

Cain, Paul
Sims, George

Campbell, Ramsey
Dreadstone, Carl; Ramsay, Jay

Carr, John Dickson
Dickson, Carter; Fairbairn, Roger

Cooper, Basil
Falk, Lee

Cooper, Clarence
Chestnut, Robert

Creasey, John
Ashe, Gordon; Frazier, Robert Caine;
Gill, Patrick; Holliday, Michael;
Hope, Brian; Hughes, Colin; Hunt, Kyle;
Marric, J.J.

Crichton, Michael
Lange, John

Cross, David
Chesbro, George B.

Daniels, Norman
Daniels, Dorothy; Wade, David

Davidson, Avram
Queen, Ellery (about 2 titles only)

Derleth, August
Grendon, Stephen

Dewey, Thomas B.
Brandt, Tom; Wainer, Cord

Disch, Thomas
Demijohn, Thomas;
Cassandra, Knye (both with John Sladek)

Ellis, Peter
Tremayne, Peter

Ellison, Harlan
Merchant, Paul

Etchison, Dennis
Martin, Jack

Fairman, Paul
Paul, F.W.

Farmer, Philip Jose
Norfolk, William; Trout, Kilgore

Fearn, John Russell
Del Martia, Aston

Fox, Gardner F.
Chase, Glen; Cooper, Jefferson;
Gardner, Jeffrey; Gardner, Matt;
Gray, James Kendricks; Jennings, Dean;
Majors, Simon; Matthews, Kevin;
Morgan, John Medford; Morgan, Rod;
Summers, Bart

Gardner, Erle Stanley
Fair, A.A.; Kendrake, Carleton;
Kinney, Charles

Garrett, Randall
Bupp, Walter; Gordon, David;
½ of Mark Phillips & Robert Randall

Geis, Richard
Owen, Robert; Swenson, Peggy

Geisel, Theodor Seuss
Dr. Seuss

Gibson, Walter B.
Brown, Douglas; Grant, Maxwell

Goulart, Ron
Falk, Lee; Kains, Josephine;
Kearney, Julian; Robeson, Kenneth;
Shaw(n), Frank S.; Silva, Joseph

Grant, Charles L.
Andrew, Felicia; Lewis, Deborah

Haas, Ben
Meade, Richard

Haldeman, Joe
Graham, Robert

Hall, Oakley
Hall, O.M.

Halliday, Brett
Shayne, Mike

Hansen, Joseph
Brock, Rose; Colton, James

Harknett, Terry
Hedges, Joseph; Stone, Thomas H.

Harris, Timothy
Hyde, Harris

Highwater, Jamake
Marks, J.; Marks-Highwater, J.

Hochstein, Peter
Short, Jack

Hodder-Williams, C.
Brogan, James

Holt, John Robert
Giles, Elizabeth; Giles, Raymond

Hunt, E. Howard
St.John, David

Hunter, Evan
Cannon, Curt; Collins, Hunt;
Hannon, Ezra; Marsten, Richard;
McBain, Ed

Jacks, Oliver
Gandley, Kenneth R.

Jakes, John
Ard, William; Payne, Alan;
Scotland, Jay

Jenkins, Will F.
Leinster, Murray

Jones, H. Bedford
Pemjean, Lucien

Kane, Frank
Boyd, Frank

Kane, Henry
McCall, Anthony

Kavanagh, Dan
Barnes, Julian

Kent, Hal
Davis, Ron

King, Stephen
Bachman, Richard

Klass, Philip
Tenn, William

Knowles, William
Allison, Clyde; Ames, Clyde

Koontz, Dean R.
Axton, David; Coffey, Brian;
Dwyer, Deanna; Dwyer, K.R.; Hill, John;
Nichols, Leigh; North, Anthony;
Paige, Richard; West, Owen;
Wolfe, Aaron

Kornbluth, Cyril
Eisner, Simon; Park, Jordan

Kosinski, Jerzy
Somers, Jane

Kubis, P.
Scott, Casey

Kurland, Michael
Plum, Jennifer

L'Amour, Louis
Burns, Tex; Mayo, Jim

Laumer, Keith
LeBaron, Anthony

Lesser, Milton
Marlowe, Stephen

Lessing, Doris
Somers, Jane

Lewis, Alfred Henry
Quinn, Dan

Linebarger, Paul
Smith, Cordwainer

Long, Frank Belknap
Long, Lyda Belknap

Lucas, Mark
Palmer, Drew

Ludlum, Robert
Ryder, Jonathan;
Shepherd, Michael

Lupoff, Richard
Steele, Adison

Lynds, Dennis
Collins, Michael; Crowe, John;
Grant, Maxwell (some);
Sadler, Mark

Malzberg, Barry
Berry, Mike; Dumas, Claudine;
Johnson, Mel; Johnson, M.L.;
O'Donnell, Barrett; O'Donnell, K.M.

Manfred, Frederick
Feikema, Feike

Marshall, Mel
Tayler, Zack

Martin, Robert
Roberts, Lee

Mason, Van Wyck
Coffin, Geoffrey

Masterton, Graham
Luke, Thomas

Matheson, Richard
Swanson, Logan

McGaughy, Dudley
Owen, Dean

Meaker, Marijane
Aldrich, Ann; Packer, Vin

Millar, Kenneth
MacDonald, Ross;
MacDonald, John Ross

Moorcock, Michael
Bradbury, Edward P.;
Barclay, Bill

Moore, Brian
Michael, Bryan;
Mara, Bernard

Morris, James
Morris, Jan (after sex change)

Nasby, Petroleum
Locke, David R.

Norton, Alice
North, Andrew; Norton, Andre

Nuetzel, Charles
Augustus, Albert Jr.;
Davidson, John;
English, Charles; Rivere, Alec

Oates, Joyce Carol
Smith, Rosamond

Offutt, Andrew
Cleve, John; Giles, Baxter;
Williams, J.X. (some)

Patterson, Henry
Fallon, Martin; Graham, James;
Higgins, Jack; Patterson, Harry;
Marlowe, Hugh

Philips, James Atlee
Atlee, Philip

Phillips, Dennis
Chambers, Peter;
Chester, Peter

Phillips, Judson
Pentecost, Hugh

Posner, Richard
Foster, Iris; Murray, Beatrice;
Todd, Paul

Prather, Richard
Knight, David; Ring, Douglas

Radford, R.L.
Ford, Marcia

Pronzini, Bill
Foxx, Jack

Rabe, Peter
MacCargo, J.T.

Rawson, Clayton
Towne, Stuart

Reynolds, Mack
Belmont, Bob; Harding, Todd;
Reynolds, Maxine

Rice, Anne
Rampling, Anne;
Roquelaure, A.N.

Rosenblum, Robert
Maxxe, Robert

Ross, W.E.D.
Dana, Rose; Daniels, Jan;
Ross, Clarissa; Ross, Dan;
Ross, Dana; Ross, Marilyn

Rossi, Jean-Baptiste
Japrisot, Sebastien

Sellers, Con
Bannion, Della

Silverberg, Robert
Beauchamp, Loren;
Burnett, W.R. (some only);
Drummond, Walter;
Elliott, Don (some);
Ford, Hilary;
Hamilton, Franklin;
Knox, Calvin;
Lt. Woodard, M.D.

Smith, George H.
Deer, J.M.; Hudson, Jan;
Jason, Jerry; Knerr, M.E.;
Summers, Diana

Stacton, David
Clifton, Bud

Sturgeon, Theodore
Ewing, Frederick R.;
Ellery Queen (1 book only)

Thomas, Ross
Bleeck, Oliver

Tracy, Don
Fuller, Roger

Tralins, Bob
Miles, Keith;
O'Shea, Sean

Tubb, E.C.
Kern, Gregory

Vance, Jack
Held, Peter;
Queen, Ellery (some/few)

Vidal, Gore
Box, Edgar

Wager, Walter
Tiger, John; Walker, Max

Ward, Harold
Zorro

Webb, Jack
Farr, John

Weiss, Joe
Anatole, Ray; Dauphine, Claude;
Mirbeau, Ken

Westlake, Donald E.
Allan, John B.;
Clark, Curt;
Culver, Timothy;
Cunningham, J. Morgan;
Holt, Samuel; Marshall, Alan;
Stark, Richard;
West, Edwin

Williams, Gordon
Yuill, P.B

Whittington, Harry
Harrison, Whit; Shepherd, Shep

Williamson, Jack
Stewart, Will

Wollheim, Don
Grinnell, David

Woolrich, Cornell
Hopley, George; Irish, William

Worts, George F.
Brent, Loring

BOOKBUYERS

In this section of the book we have listed buyers of books and related material. When you correspond with these dealers, be sure to enclose a self-addressed stamped envelope if you want a reply. Do not send lists of books for appraisal. If you wish to sell your books, quote the price you want or send a list and ask if there are any on the list they might be interested in and the price they would be willing to pay. If you want the list back, be sure to send a SASE large enough for the listing to be returned. When you list your books, do so by author, full title, publisher and place, date, edition, and condition, noting any defects on cover or contents.

Advance Review Copies
Paperbacks
The American Dust Co.
47 Park Ct.
Staten Island, NY 10301
718-442-8253

Adventure
The Silver Door
P.O. Box 3208
Redondo Beach, CA 90277
310-379-6005

Advertising
Henry H. Hain III
Antiques & Collectibles
2623 N Second St.
Harrisburg, PA 17110
717-238-0534

African-American
Children's Book Adoption Agency
P.O. Box 643
Kensington, MD 20895-0643
310-565-2834 or Fax 301-585-3091

Fran's Bookhouse
6601 Greene St.
Phil., PA 19119
215-438-2729 or Fax 215-438-8997

Alaska
Artis Books
201 N Second Ave.
P.O. Box 822
Alpena, MI 49707
517-354-3401

Albania
W.B. O'Neill-Old & Rare Books
11609 Hunters Green Ct.
Reston, VA 22091
703-860-0782 or Fax 703-620-0153

Alcoholics Anonymous
The Book Baron
1236 S Magnolia Ave.
Anaheim, CA 92804
714-527-7022 or Fax 714-527-5634

1939-1954
Paul Melzer Fine Books
12 E Vine St.
Redlands, CA 92373
902-792-7299

Americana
Amaranth Books
P.O. Box 421
Wilmette, IL 60091-0421
708-328-2939

The Book Inn
6401 University
Lubbock, TX 79413

The Bookseller, Inc.
521 W Exchange St.
Akron, OH 44302
216-762-3101

Bowie & Co. Booksellers, Inc.
314 First Ave. S
Seattle, WA 98104
206-624-4100 or Fax 206-223-0966

Woodbridge B. Brown
P.O. Box 445
Turners Falls, MA 01376
413-772-2509 or 413-773-5710

The Captain's Bookshelf, Inc.
P.O. Box 2258
Asheville, NC 28802-2258
704-253-6631

Chapel Hill Rare Books
P.O. Box 456
Carrboro, NC 27510
919-929-8351

Duck Creek Books
Jim & Shirley Richards
P.O. Box 203
Caldwell, OH 43724
614-732-4856 (10 am to 10 pm)

Terry Harper, Bookseller
P.O. Box 312
Vergennes, VT 05491-0312
802-877-9262

Jim Hodgson Books
908 S Manlius St.
Fayetteville, NY 13066
315-637-6264

M & S Rare Books, Inc.
P.O. Box 2594, E Side Sta.
Providence, RI 02906
401-421-1050 or Fax 401-272-0831
(attention M & S)

Parmer Books
7644 Forrestal Rd.
San Diego, CA 92120-2203
619-287-0693 or Fax 619-287-6135
Internet: ParmerBook@aol.com

Randall House
835 Laguna St.
Santa Barbara, CA 93101
805-963-1909 or Fax 805-963-1650

18th & 19th C
Gordon Totty
Scarce Paper Americana
347 Shady Lake Pky.
Baton Rouge, LA 70810
504-766-8625

Yesterday's Books
229 Riverview Dr.
Parchment, MI 49004
616-345-1011

Anarchism
Nutmeg Books
354 New Litchfield St. (Rte. 202)
Torrington, CT 06790
203-482-9696

Angling
Book & Tackle Shop
P.O. Box 114
Chestnut Hill, MA 02167
617-965-0459

Anthropology
The King's Market Booksellers
P.O. Box 709
Boulder, CO 80306-0709
303-447-0234

Anthologies
Cartoonists from 1890-1960
Craig Ehlenberger
Abalone Cove Rare Books
7 Fruit Tree Rd.
Portuguese Bend, CA 90275

Antiquarian
A.B.A.C.U.S. ®
Phillip E. Miller
343 S Chesterfield St.
Aiken, SC 29801
803-648-4632

Antiquarian Book Arcade
110 W 25th St., 9th Floor
New York, NY 10001

Fine & hard-to-find books
Arnold's of Michigan
511 S Union St.
Traverse City, MI 49684

The Book Baron
1236 S Magnolia Ave.
Anaheim, CA 92804
714-527-7022 or Fax 714-527-5634

Pre-1900 leatherbound, any subject
Arthur Boutiette
410 W 3rd St., Ste. 200
Little Rock, AR 72201

Bowie & Co. Booksellers, Inc.
314 First Ave. S
Seattle, WA 98104
206-624-4100 or Fax 206-223-0966

Children's Book Adoption Agency
P.O. Box 643
Kensington, MD 20895-0643
310-565-2834 or Fax 301-585-3091

Terry Harper, Bookseller
P.O. Box 312
Vergennes, VT 05491-0312
802-877-9262

Murray Hudson
Antiquarian Books & Maps
The Old Post Office
109 S Church St.
P.O. Box 163
Halls, TN 38040
901-836-9057 or 800-748-9946

Jeffrey Lee Pressman, Bookseller
3246 Ettie St.
Oakland, CA 94608
510-652-6232

Robert Mueller Rare Books
8124 W 26th St.
N Riverside, IL 60546
708-447-6441

Printed before 1800
Gordon Totty
Scarce Paper Americana
347 Shady Lake Pky.
Baton Rouge, LA 70810
504-766-8625

Antiques & Reference
Antique & Collectors Reproduction News
Box 17774-OB
Des Moines, IA 50325
515-270-8994

Bohemian Bookworm
110 W 25th St., 9th Floor
New York, NY 10001
212-620-5627

Collector's Companion
Perry Franks
P.O. Box 24333
Richmond, VA 23224

Galerie De Boicourt
6136 Westbrooke Dr.
W Bloomfield, MI 48322
810-788-9253

Henry H. Hain III
Antiques & Collectibles
2623 N Second St.
Harrisburg, PA 17110
717-238-0534

Appraisals
J. Sampson Antiques & Books
107 S Main
Harrodsburg, KY 40330
606-734-7829

Lee & Mike Temares
50 Hts. Rd.
Plandome, NY 11030
516-627-8688

Arabian Horses
Worldwide Antiquarian
P.O. Box 391
Cambridge, MA 02141
617-876-6220 or Fax 617-876-0939

The Arabian Nights
Worldwide Antiquarian
P.O. Box 391
Cambridge, MA 02141
617-876-6220 or Fax 617-876-0939

Archaelogy
Flo Silver Books
8442 Oakwood Ct. N
Indianapolis, IN 46260
317-255-5118

Architecture
Cover to Cover
P.O. Box 687
Chapel Hill, NC 27514

Armenia
W.B. O'Neill-Old & Rare Books
11609 Hunters Green Ct.
Reston, VA 22091
703-860-0782 or Fax 703-620-0153

Art
AL-PAC
Lamar Kelley Antiquarian Books
2625 E Southern Ave., C-120
Tempe, AZ 85282
602-831-3121 or Fax 602-831-3193

Bohemian Bookworm
110 W 25th St., 9th Floor
New York, NY 10001
212-620-5627

Book & Tackle Shop
P.O. Box 114
Chestnut Hill, MA 02167
617-965-0459

Books West Southwest
J.E. Reynolds, Bookseller
2452 N Campbell Ave.
Tucson, AZ 85719
602-326-3533

The Captain's Bookshelf, Inc.
P.O. Box 2258
Asheville, NC 28802-2258
704-253-6631

Fine & applied
L. Clarice Davis Art Books
P.O. Box 56054
Sherman Oaks, CA 91413-1054
818-787-1322

Galerie De Boicourt
6136 Westbrooke Dr.
W Bloomfield, MI 48322
810-788-9253

Edison Hall Books
5 Ventnor Dr.
Edison, NJ 08820
908-548-4455

Heritage Book Shop, Inc.
8540 Melrose Ave.
Los Angeles, CA 90069
213-659-3674

David Holloway, Bookseller
7430 Grace St.
Springfield, VA 22150
703-659-1798

Significant Books
3053 Madison Rd.
P.O. Box 9248
Cincinnati, OH 45209
513-321-7567

Lee & Mike Temares
50 Hts. Rd.
Plandome, NY 11030
516-627-8688

Xanadu Records, Ltd.
3242 Irwin Ave.
Kingsbridge, NY 10463
212-549-3655

Arctic
Artis Books
201 N Second Ave.
P.O. Box 822
Alpena, MI 49707
517-354-3401

Parmer Books
7644 Forrestal Rd.
San Diego, CA 92120-2203
619-287-0693 or Fax 619-287-6135
Internet: ParmerBook@aol.com

Arthurian
Camelot Books
Charles E. Wyatt
P.O. Box 2883
Vista, CA 92083
619-940-9472

Astronomy
Knollwood Books
Lee & Peggy Price
P.O. Box 197
Oregon, WI 53575
608-835-8861 or Fax 608-835-8421

Atlases
Murray Hudson
Antiquarian Books & Maps
The Old Post Office
109 S Church St.
P.O. Box 163
Halls, TN 38040
901-836-9057 or 800-748-9946

Before 1870
Gordon Totty
Scarce Paper Americana
347 Shady Lake Pky.
Baton Rouge, LA 70810
504-766-8625

Atomic Bomb
Key Books
P.O. Box 58097
St. Petersburg, FL 33715
813-867-2931

Autobiography
Wellerdt's Books
3700 S Osprey Ave. #214
Sarasota, FL 34239
813-365-1318

Autographs
Ads Autographs
P.O. Box 8006
Webster, NY 14580
716-671-2651

Michael Gerlicher
1375 Rest Point Rd.
Orono, MN 55364

Susan Heller, Pages for Sages
P.O. Box 22219
Beachwood, OH 44122
216-283-2665 or Fax 216-999-2665

Heritage Book Shop, Inc.
8540 Melrose Ave.
Los Angeles, CA 90069
213-659-3674

Key Books
P.O. Box 58097
St. Petersburg, FL 33715
813-867-2931

McGowan Book Co.
P.O. Box 16325
Chapel Hill, NC 27516
919-968-1121 or Fax 919-968-1169

Paul Melzer Fine Books
12 E Vine St.
Redlands, CA 92373
909-792-7299

Randall House
835 Laguna St.
Santa Barbara, CA 93101
805-963-1909 or Fax 805-963-1650

Autobiographies
Herb Sauermann
21660 School Rd.
Manton, CA 96059

Aviation
The Bookseller, Inc.
521 W Exchange St.
Akron, OH 44302
216-762-3101

Cover to Cover
P.O. Box 687
Chapel Hill, NC 27514

Baedeker Handbooks
W.B. O'Neill-Old & Rare Books
11609 Hunters Green Ct.
Reston, VA 22091
703-860-0782 or Fax 703-620-0153

Baseball
Brasser's
8701 Seminole Blvd.
Seminole, FL 34642

R. Plapinger, Baseball Books
P.O. Box 1062
Ashland, OR 87520
503-488-1200

Bibliography
About Books
6 Sand Hill Ct.
P.O. Box 5717
Parsippany, NJ 07054
201-515-4591

Books West Southwest
J.E. Reynolds, Bookseller
2452 N Campbell Ave.
Tucson, AZ 85719
602-326-3533

Big Little Books
Jay's House of Collectibles
75 Pky. Dr.
Syosset, NY 11791

Biographies
Herb Sauermann
21660 School Rd.
Manton, CA 96059

Black Americana
A\K\A Fine Used Books
4142 Brooklyn Ave., NE
Seattle, WA 98107
206-632-5870

History & literature
David Holloway, Bookseller
7430 Grace St.
Springfield, VA 22150
703-569-1798

Mason's Bookstore, Rare Books
& Record Albums
115 S Main St.
Chambersburg, PA 17201
717-261-0541

Black Fiction & Literature
Almark & Co.-Booksellers
P.O. Box 7
Thornhill, Ontario
Canada L3T 3N1
phone/Fax 905-764-2665

Black Hills
James F. Taylor
515 Sixth St.
Rapid City, SD 57701
605-341-3224

Book Search Service
Authors of the West
191 Dogwood Dr.
Dundee, OR 97115
503-538-8132

Avonlea Books
P.O. Box 74, Main Station
White Plains, NY 10602
914-946-5923

Heritage Book Shop, Inc.
8540 Melrose Ave.
Los Angeles, CA 90069
310-659-3674 or Fax 310-659-4872

Hilda's Book Search
Hilda Gruskin
199 Rollins Ave.
Rockville, MD 20852
301-948-3181

Passaic Book Center
594 Main Ave.
Passaic, NJ 07055
201-778-6646 or Fax 201-778-6738

The Silver Door
P.O. Box 3208
Redondo Beach, CA 90277
310-379-6005

Especially children's out-of-print books
Treasures from the Castle
Connie Castle
1720 N Livernois
Rochester, MI 48306
810-651-7317

Books About Books
About Books
6 Sand Hill Ct.
P.O. Box 5717
Parsippany, NJ 07054
201-515-4591

Books West Southwest
J.E. Reynolds, Bookseller
2452 N Campbell Ave.
Tucson, AZ 85719
602-326-3533

Bowie & Co. Booksellers, Inc.
314 First Ave. S
Seattle, WA 98104
206-624-4100 or Fax 206-223-0966

First Folio
1206 Brentwood
Paris, TN 38242
phone/Fax 901-644-9940

Susan Heller, Pages for Sages
P.O. Box 22219
Beachwood, OH 44122
216-283-2665 or Fax 216-999-2665

Key Books
P.O. Box 58097
St. Petersburg, FL 33715
813-867-2931

Randall House
835 Laguna St.
Santa Barbara, CA 93101
805-963-1909 or Fax 805-963-1650

George H. Tweney
16660 Marine View Dr. SW
Seattle, WA 98166
206-243-8243

Botany
Brooks Books
Philip B. Nesty
P.O. Box 21473
1343 New Hampshire Dr.
Concord, CA 94521
510-672-4566 or Fax 510-672-3338

Bottles
Homebiz Books & More
2919 Mistwood Forest Dr.
Chester, VA 23831-7043

Breweries of Germany
Mike Geffers
1615 Doty St.
Oshkosh, WI 54901

Charles Bukowski
Edward L. Smith
Modern 1st Editions
P.O. Box 1183
Ojai, CA 93024
804-646-2921 or Fax 805-646-0981

California
Books West Southwest
J.E. Reynolds, Bookseller
2452 N Campbell Ave.
Tucson, AZ 85719

Paul Melzer Fine Books
12 E Vine St.
Redlands, CA 92373
909-792-7299

Cartography
Overlee Farm Books
P.O. Box 1155
Stockbridge, MA 01262
413-637-2277

Cartoon Art
Jay's House of Collectibles
75 Pky. Dr.
Syosset, NY 11791

Catalogs
Glass, pottery, furniture, doll, toy, jewelry, general merchandise, fishing tackle
Bill Schroeder
P.O. Box 3009
Paducah, KY 42002-3009

Antiques or other collectibles
Antique & Collectors Reproduction News
Box 17774-OB
Des Moines, IA 50325
515-270-8994

Hillcrest Books
Rt. 3, Box 479
Crossville, TN 38555-9547
phone/Fax 615-484-7680

Celtic
Camelot Books
Charles E. Wyatt
P.O. Box 2883
Vista, CA 92083
619-940-9472

Central America
Flo Silver Books
8442 Oakwood Ct. N
Indianapolis, IN 46260
317-255-5118

Marc Chagall
Paul Melzer Fine Books
12 E Vine St.
Redlands, CA 92373
909-792-7299

Children's Illustrated
Noreen Abbot Books
2666 44th Ave.
San Francisco, CA 94116
415-664-9464

Book & Tackle Shop
P.O. Box 114
Chestnut Hill, MA 02167
617-965-0459

Bromer Booksellers
607 Boylston St.
Boston, MA 02116
617-247-2818 or Fax 617-247-2975

Uncle Wiggily, circa 1912 through 1948
Audrey V. Buffington
2 Old Farm Rd.
Wayland, MA 01778
508-358-2644

19th & 20th C
Children's Book Adoption Agency
P.O. Box 643
Kensington, MD 20895-0643
301-565-2834 or Fax 301-585-3091

Ursula Davidson
Children's & Illustrated Books
134 Linden Ln.
San Rafael, CA 94901
414-454-3939 or Fax 415-454-1087

Drusilla's Books
859 N Howard St.
Baltimore, MD 21201
401-225-0277

Edison Hall Books
5 Ventnor Dr.
Edison, NJ 08820
908-548-4455

Circa 1850s through 1970s
Encino Books
Diane Yaspan
5063 Gaviota Ave
Encino, CA 91436
818-905-711 or Fax 818-501-7711

First Folio
1206 Brentwood
Paris, TN 38242
phone/Fax 901-644-9940

Fran's Bookhouse
6601 Greene St.
Phil., PA 19119
215-438-2729 or Fax 215-438-8997

Glo's Children's Series Books
906 Shadywood
Southlake, TX 76092

Susan Heller, Pages for Sages
P.O. Box 22219
Beachwood, OH 44122
216-283-2665 or Fax 216-999-2665

Illustrated before 1940; also Uncle Wiggily,
Raggedy Ann & Andy
Jacquie Henry
Antique Treasures & Toys
P.O. Box 17
2240 Academy St.
Walworth, NY 14568
315-968-1424

Especially by Raphael Tuck or McLoughlin
Brothers
Melanie Hewitt
2101 Beechwood
Little Rock, AR 72202

Johnny Gruelle's Raggedy Ann
Carole Jemison
Rt. 1, Box 73
Wann, OK 74083
918-534-2129

Ilene Kayne
1308 S Charles St.
Baltimore, MD 21230

Bob Lakin
3021 Lavita Ln.
Dallas, TX 75234
214-247-3291

Marvelous Books
P.O. Box 1510
Ballwin, MO 63022
314-458-3301

Much Ado
Seven Pleasant St.
Marblehead, MA 01945
617-639-0400

Nerman's Books
410-63 Albert St.
Winnipeg, Manitoba
Canada R3B 1G4
Fax 204-947-0753

Page Books
HCR 65, Box 233
Kingston, AR 72472
501-861-5831

Jo Ann Reisler, Ltd.
360 Glyndon St., NE
Vienna, VA 22180
703-938-2967

Barbara Smith Books
P.O. Box 1185
Northampton, MA 01061
413-586-1453

Nancy Stewart, Books
1188 NW Weybridge Way
Beaverton, OR 97006
503-645-9779

Yesterday's Books
229 Riverview Dr.
Parchment, MI 49004
616-345-1011

Treasures from the Castle
Connie Castle
1720 N Livernois
Rochester, MI 48306
810-651-7317

Children's Series
Bobbsey Twins
Audrey V. Buffington
2 Old Farm Rd.
Wayland, MA 01778
508-358-2644

Children's Book Adoption Agency
P.O. Box 643
Kensington, MD 20895-0643
301-565-2834 or Fax 301-585-3091

Circa 1900s through 1970s
Encino Books
Diane Yaspan
5063 Gaviota Ave
Encino, CA 91436
818-905-711 or Fax 818-501-7711

Ilene Kayne
1308 S Charles St.
Baltimore, MD 21230

Bob Lakin
3021 Lavita Ln.
Dallas, TX 75234
214-247-3291

Nerman's Books
410-63 Albert St.
Winnipeg, Manitoba
Canada R3B 1G4
Fax 204-947-0753

Bob & Gail Spicer
R.D. 1 Ashgrove Rd., Box 82
Cambridge, NY 12816
518-677-5139

Gloria Stobbs
906 Shadywood
Southlake, TX 76092

Lee & Mike Temares
50 Hts. Rd.
Plandome, NY 11030
516-627-8688

Yesterday's Books
229 Riverview Dr.
Parchment, MI 49004
616-345-1011

Christian Faith
Books Now & Then
Dennis Patrick
P.O. Box 337
Stanley, ND
701-628-2084

Christmas
Especially illustrated antiquarian
Drusilla's Books
859 N Howard St.
Baltimore, MD 21201
410-225-0277

Sir W.S. Churchill
Chartwell Booksellers
55 E 52nd St.
New York, NY 10055
212-308-0643

Robert L. Merriam
Rare, Used & Old Books
Newhall Rd.
Conway, MA 01341
413-369-4052

Cinema, Theatre & Films
Cinemage Books
105 W 27th St.
New York, NY 10001
212-243-4919

Xanadu Records, Ltd.
3242 Irwin Ave.
Kingsbridge, NY 10463
212-549-3655

Civil War
The Book Corner
Michael Tennero
728 W Lumsden Rd.
Brandon, FL 33511
813-684-1133

Brasser's
8701 Seminole Blvd.
Seminole, FL 34642

Chapel Hill Rare Books
P.O. Box 456
Carrboro, NC 27510
919-929-8351

Elder's Book Store
2115 Elliston Pl.
Nashville, TN 37203
615-327-1867

Rick Harmon
Military Books & Relics
910 Sullivan Dr.
Belvidere, IL 61008
815-547-7580

Jim Hodgson Books
908 S Manlius St.
Fayetteville, NY 13066
315-637-6264

Mason's Bookstore, Rare Books
& Record Albums
115 S Main St.
Chambersburg, PA 17201
717-261-0541

K.C. Owings
P.O. Box 19
N Abington, MA 02351
617-857-1655

Also ephemera before 1900
Gordon Totty
Scarce Paper Americana
347 Shady Lake Pky.
Baton Rouge, LA 70810
504-766-8625

Cobb, Irvin S.
Always paying $3.00 each plus shipping. Send
for immediate payment:
Bill Schroeder
5801 KY Dam Rd.
Paducah, KY 42003

Collectibles

Henry H. Hain III
Antiques & Collectibles
2623 N Second St.
Harrisburg, PA 17110
717-238-0534

Color Plate Books

Bowie & Co. Booksellers, Inc.
314 First Ave. S
Seattle, WA 98104
206-624-4100 or Fax 206-223-0966

Drusilla's Books
859 N Howard St.
Baltimore, MD 21201
410-225-0277

Worldwide Antiquarian
P.O. Box 391
Cambridge, MA 02141
617-876-6220 or Fax 617-876-0839

Comics

Passaic Book Center
594 Main Ave.
Passaic, NJ 07055
201-778-6646 or Fax 201-778-6738

Cookery & Cookbooks

Book & Tackle Shop
P.O. Box 114
Chestnut Hill, MA 02167
617-965-0459

The Book Corner
Mike Tennero
728 W Lumsden Rd.
Brandon, FL 33511
813-684-1133

RAC Books
R.R. #2
P.O. Box 296
Seven Valleys, PA 17360
717-428-3776

Barbara Smith Books
P.O. Box 1185
Northampton, MA 01061
413-586-1453

Crime

The Silver Door
P.O. Box 3208
Redondo Beach, CA 90277
310-379-6005

Cyprus

W.B. O'Neill-Old & Rare Books
11609 Hunters Green Ct.
Reston, VA 22091
703-860-0782 or Fax 703-620-0153

Decorative Arts

Robert L. Merriam
Rare, Used & Old Books
Newhall Rd.
Conway, MA 01341
413-369-4052

Detective

First editions
Karl M. Armens
740 Juniper Dr.
Iowa City, IA 52245

Mordida Books
P.O. Box 79322
Houston, TX 77279
713-467-4280 or Fax 713-467-4182

Thomas Books
P.O. Box 14036
Phoenix, AZ 85063
602-247-9289

The Silver Door
P.O. Box 3208
Redondo Beach, CA 90277
310-379-6005

Charles Dickens

Harold B. Diamond
Box 1193
Burbank, CA 19507
818-846-0342

Emily Dickinson

Robert L. Merriam
Rare, Used & Old Books
Newhall Rd.
Conway, MA 01341
413-369-4052

Disney

Cohen Books & Collectibles
Joel J. Cohen
P.O. Box 810310
Boca Raton, FL 33481
407-487-7888

Jay's House of Collectibles
75 Pky. Dr.
Syosset, NY 11791

Documents

McGowan Book Co.
P.O. Box 16325
Chapel Hill, NC 27516
919-968-1121 or Fax 919-968-1169

Dogs

Kathleen Rais & Co.
211 Carolina Ave.
Phoenixville, PA 19460
610-933-1388

Thomas Edison

Edison Hall Books
5 Ventnor Dr.
Edison, NJ 08820
908-548-4455

Ephemera

Antique valentines
Kingsbury Productions
4555 N Pershing Ave., Ste. 33-138
Stockton, CA 95207
209-467-8438

The Mulberry Cat
Yvonne Davis
Jan Davis Martel
P.O. Box 3573
Boone, NC 28607
704-963-7693

Espionage

The Silver Door
P.O. Box 3208
Redondo Beach, CA 92077
310-379-6005

Estate Libraries

The Book Collector
2347 University Blvd.
Houston, TX 77005
713-661-2665

Exhibition Catalogs

L. Clarice Davis Art Books
P.O. Box 56054
Sherman Oaks, CA 91413-1054
818-787-1322

Exploration

Western
Terry Harper, Bookseller
P.O. Box 312
Vergennes, VT 05491-0312
802-877-9262

Heritage Book Shop, Inc.
8540 Melrose Ave.
Los Angeles, CA 90069
213-659-3674

Key Books
P.O. Box 58097
St. Petersburg, FL 33715
813-867-2931

Paul Melzer Fine Books
12 E Vine St.
Redlands, CA 92373
909-792-7299

Flo Silver Books
8442 Oakwood Ct. N
Indianapolis, IN 46260
317-255-5118

Fantasy

The Book Baron
1236 S Magnolia Ave.
Anaheim, CA 92804
714-527-7022 or Fax 714-527-5634

Camelot Books
Charles E. Wyatt
P.O. Box 2883
Vista, CA 92083
619-940-9472

Farming

First editions
Karl M. Armens
740 Juniper Dr.
Iowa City, IA 52245

Also gardening
Hurley Books
1752 Rt. 12
Westmoreland, NH 03467-4724
603-399-4342 (8 am to 8 pm)

Henry Lindeman
4769 Bavarian Dr.
Jackson, MI 49201
517-764-5728

Fiction

Late 20th C
Kacey Kowars
425 Buckingham Dr.
Indianapolis, IN 46208
317-921-9408

Bob Lakin
3021 Lavita Ln.
Dallas, TX 75234
214-247-3291

19th & 20th-C American
Mason's Bookstore, Rare Books
& Record Albums
115 S Main St.
Chambersburg, PA 17201
717-261-0541

Fine Bindings & Books
The Book Collector
2347 University Blvd.
Houston, TX 77005
713-661-2665

Bromer Booksellers
607 Boylston St.
Boston, MA 02116
617-247-2818 or Fax 617-247-2975

Heritage Book Shop, Inc.
8540 Melrose Ave.
Los Angeles, CA 90069
310-659-3674 or Fax 310-659-4872

Terry Harper, Bookseller
P.O. Box 312
Vergennes, VT 05491-0312
802-877-9262

Kenneth Karimole, Bookseller, Inc.
P.O. Box 464
509 Wilshire Blvd.
Santa Monica, CA 94001
310-451-4342 or 310-458-5930

Mason's Bookstore, Rare Books
& Record Albums
115 S Main St.
Chambersburg, PA 17201
717-261-0541

Paul Melzer Fine Books
12 E Vine St.
Redlands, CA 92373
909-792-7299

Also sets
Randall House
835 Laguna St.
Santa Barbara, CA 93101
805-963-1909 or Fax 805-963-1650

Fine Printing
Heritage Book Shop, Inc.
8540 Melrose Ave.
Los Angeles, CA 90069
310-659-3674 or Fax 310-659-4872

Randall House
835 Laguna St.
Santa Barbara, CA 93101
805-963-1909 or Fax 805-963-1650

Firearms
Melvin Marcher, Bookseller
6204 N Vermont
Oklahoma City, OK 73112

First Editions
After 1937
A.B.A.C.U.S. ®
Phillip E. Miller
343 S Chesterfield St.
Aiken, SC 29801
803-648-4632

Hyper-modern
Almark & Co.-Booksellers
P.O. Box 7
Thornhill, Ontario
Canada L3T 3N1
phone/Fax 905-764-2665

Modern or signed
AL-PAC
Lamar Kelley Antiquarian Books
2625 E Southern Ave., C-120
Tempe, AZ 85282
602-831-3121 or Fax 602-831-3193

Amaranth Books
P.O. Box 421
Wilmette, IL 60091-0421
708-328-2939

Karl M. Armens
740 Juniper Dr.
Iowa City, IA 52245

Modern
Bella Luna Books
P.O. Box 260425
Highlands Ranch, CO 80126-0425
800-497-4717 or Fax 303-794-3135

Between the Covers
132 Kings Hwy. E
Haddonfield, NJ 08033

The Book Baron
1236 S Magnolia Ave.
Anaheim, CA 92804
714-527-7022 or Fax 714-527-5634

Modern
Chapel Hill Rare Books
P.O. Box 456
Carrboro, NC 27510
919-929-8351

Edison Hall Books
5 Ventnor Dr.
Edison, NJ 08820
908-548-4455

Literary
Janet Egelhofer
36 Fairfield Ave.
Holyoke, MA 01040
413-532-1295

Modern
David Holloway, Bookseller
7430 Grace St.
Springfield, VA 22150
703-569-1798

Heritage Book Shop, Inc.
8540 Melrose Ave.
Los Angeles, CA 90069
310-659-3674 or Fax 310-659-4872

Modern
Ken Lopez, Bookseller
51 Huntington Rd.
Hadley, MA 01035
413-584-4827 or Fax 413-584-2045

Much Ado
Seven Pleasant St.
Marblehead, MA 01945
617-639-0400

Robert Mueller Rare Books
8124 W 26th St.
N Riverside, IL 60546
708-447-6441

Jeffrey Lee Pressman, Bookseller
3246 Ettie St.
Oakland, CA 94608
510-652-6232

American & British
Quill & Brush
Box 5365
Rockville, MD 20848
301-460-3700 or Fax 301-871-5425

Modern
Edward L. Smith-Modern 1st Editions
P.O. Box 1183
Ojai, CA 93024
805-646-2921 or Fax 805-646-0981

Harrison Fisher
Parnassus Books
218 N 9th St.
Boise, ID 83702

Fishing
Artis Books
201 N Second Ave.
P.O. Box 208
Alpena, MI 49707
517-354-3401

Edison Hall Books
5 Ventnor Dr.
Edison, NJ 08820
908-548-4455

Jim Hodgson Books
908 S Manlius St.
Fayetteville, NY 13066
315-637-6264

Melvin Marcher, Bookseller
6204 N Vermont
Oklahoma City, OK 73112

Mason's Bookstore, Rare Books
& Record Albums
115 S Main
Chambersburg, PA 17201
717-261-0541

Yesterday's Books
229 Riverview Dr.
Parchment, MI 49004
616-345-1011

Florida
Brasser's
8701 Seminole Blvd.
Seminole, FL 34642

Football
Brasser's
8701 Seminole Blvd.
Seminole, FL 34642

Freemasonry
Mason's Bookstore, Rare Books
& Record Albums
115 S Main St.
Chambersburg, PA 17201
717-261-0541

Gambling & Gaming
Gambler's Book Shop
630 S Eleventh St.
Las Vegas, NV 89101
800-634-6243

Especially on cheating
John A. Greget-Magic Lists
2631 E Claire Dr.
Phoenix, AZ 85032-4932
602-971-5497

Games
Card or board
Bill Sachen
927 Grand Ave.
Waukegan, IL 60085
708-662-7204

Gardening
The American Botanist Booksellers
P.O. Box 532
Chillicothe, IL 61523
309-274-5254

The Book Corner
Mike Tennero
728 W Lumsden Rd.
Brandon, FL 33511
813-684-1133

The Captain's Bookshelf, Inc.
P.O. Box 2258
Asheville, NC 28802-2258
704-253-6631

Gazetteers
Murray Hudson
Antiquarian Books & Maps
The Old Post Office
109 S Church St.
P.O. Box 163
Halls, TN 38040
901-836-9057 or 800-748-9946

Genealogy
Elder's Book Store
2115 Elliston Pl.
Nashville, TN 37203
615-327-1867

General Out-of-Print
A\K\A Fine Used Books
4142 Brooklyn Ave. NE
Seattle, WA 98107

Thomas C. Bayer
85 Reading Ave.
Hillsdale, MI 49242
517-439-4134

Best-Read Books
122 State St.
Sedro-Wooley, WA 98284
206-855-2179

Bicentennial Book Shop
820 S Westnedge Ave.
Kalamazoo, MI 49008
616-345-5987

The Book Baron
1236 S Magnolia Ave.
Anaheim, CA 92804
714-527-7022 or Fax 714-527-5634

Book Den South
2249 First St.
Ft. Myers, FL 33901
813-332-2333

The Bookseller, Inc.
521 W Exchange St.
Akron, OH 44302
216-762-3101

Brooks Books
Philip B. Nesty
P.O. Box 21473
1343 New Hampshire Dr.
Concord, CA 94521
510-672-4566 or Fax 510-672-3338

Cinemage Books
105 W 27th St.
New York, NY 10001

Edison Hall Books
5 Ventnor Dr.
Edison, NJ 08820
908-548-4455

Fran's Bookhouse
6601 Greene St.
Phil., PA 19119
215-438-2729 or Fax 215-438-8997

Grave Matters
P.O. Box 32192-08
Cincinnati, OH 45232
phone/Fax 513-242-7527

McGowan Book Co.
P.O. Box 16325
Chapel Hill, NC 27516
919-968-1121 or Fax 919-968-1169

Robert L. Merriam
Rare, Used & Old Books
New Hall Rd.
Conway, MA 01341
413-369-4052

The Mulberry Cat
Yvonne Davis
Jan Davis Martel
P.O. Box 3573
Boone, NC 28607
704-963-7693

Passaic Book Center
594 Main Ave.
Passaic, NJ 07055
201-778-6646 or Fax 201-778-6738

RAC Books
R.R. #2
P.O. Box 296
Seven Valleys, PA 17360
717-428-3776

J. Sampson Antiques & Books
107 S Main
Harrodsburg, KY 40330
606-734-7829

Significant Books
3053 Madison Rd.
P.O. Box 9248
Cincinnati, OH 45209
513-321-7567

This & That Used Books
Toni Rooksberry
524 N Park Ave.
Jasonville, IN 47438
812-665-3631

Tuttle Antiquarian Books, Inc.
P.O. Box 541
26 S Main St.
Rutland, VT 05701
802-773-8229

A.A. Vespa
P.O. Box 637
Park Ridge, IL 60068
708-692-4210

Genetics
The King's Market Booksellers
P.O. Box 709
Boulder, CO 80306-0709
303-447-0234

Geographies
Murray Hudson
Antiquarian Books & Maps
The Old Post Office
109 S Church St.
P.O. Box 163
Halls, TN 38040
901-836-9057 or 800-748-9946

Overlee Farm Books
P.O. Box 1155
Stockbridge, MA 01262
413-637-2277

Golf
Brasser's
8701 Seminole Blvd.
Seminole, FL 34642

David Goodis
The American Dust Co.
47 Park Ct.
Staten Island, NY 10301
718-442-8253

The Great Lakes
Artis Books
201 N Second Ave.
P.O. Box 822
Alpena, MI 49707
517-354-3401

Sue Grafton
Thomas Books
P.O. Box 14036
Phoenix, AZ 85063
602-247-9289

Greece
W.B. O'Neill-Old & Rare Books
11609 Hunters Green Ct.
Reston, VA 22091
703-860-0782 or Fax 703-620-0153

Herbals
The American Botanist Booksellers
P.O. Box 352
Chillicothe, IL 61523
309-274-5254

Heritage Press
Lee & Mike Temares
50 Hts. Rd.
Plandome, NY 11030
516-627-8688

Hippie
Black Ace Books
1658 Griffith Park Blvd.
Los Angeles, CA 90026
213-661-5052

History
Science & medicine
Amaranth Books
P.O. Box 421
Wilmette, IL 60091-0421
708-328-2939

Camelot Books
Charles E. Wyatt
P.O. Box 2883
Vista, CA 92083
619-940-9472

Harold B. Diamond
Box 1193
Burbank, CA 91507
818-846-0342

Early American &Indian
Duck Creek Books
Jim & Shirley Richards
P.O. Box 203
Caldwell, OH 43724
614-732-4856 (10 am to 10 pm)

Postal & postal artifacts
McGowan Book Co.
P.O. Box 16325
Chapel Hill, NC 27516
919-968-1121 or Fax 919-968-1169

Local & regional
Significant Books
3053 Madison Rd.
P.O. Box 9248
Cincinnati, OH 45209
513-321-7567

Hollywood
Cinemage Books
105 W 27th St.
New York, NY 10001
212-243-4919

Horticulture
The American Botanist Booksellers
P.O. Box 532
Chillicothe, IL 61523
309-274-5254

Ornamental
Brooks Books
Philip B. Nesty
P.O. Box 21473
1343 New Hampshire Dr.
Concord, CA 94521
510-672-4566 or Fax 510-672-3338

Woodbridge B. Brown
P.O. Box 445
Turners Falls, MA 01376
413-772-2509 or 413-773-5710

Horror
The Book Baron
1236 S Magnolia Ave.
Anaheim, CA 92804
714-527-7022 or Fax 714-527-5634

Kai Nygaard
19421 Eighth Place
Escondido, CA 92029
619-746-9039

Pandora's Books, Ltd.
P.O. Box BB-54
Neche, ND 58265
204-324-8548 or Fax 204-324-1628

L. Ron Hubbard
AL-PAC
Lamar Kelley Antiquarian Books
2625 E Southern Ave., C-120
Tempe, AZ 85282
602-831-3121 or Fax 602-831-3193

Humanities
Reprint editions
Dover Publications
Dept. A 214
E Second St.
Mineola, NY 11501

Hunting
Artis Books
201 N Second Ave.
P.O. Box 822
Alpena, MI 49707
517-354-3401

Edison Hall Books
5 Ventnor Dr.
Edison, NJ 08820
908-548-4455

Jim Hodgson Books
908 S Manlius St.
Fayetteville, NY 13066
315-637-6264

Melvin Marcher, Bookseller
6204 N Vermont
Oklahoma City, OK 73112

Yesterday's Books
229 Riverview Dr.
Parchment, MI 49004
616-345-1011

Idaho
Parnassus Books
218 N 9th St.
Boise, ID 83702

Illustrated
Noreen Abbot Books
2666 44th Ave.
San Francisco, CA 94116
415-664-9464

Bowie & Co. Booksellers, Inc.
314 First Ave. S
Seattle, WA 98104
206-624-4100 or Fax 206-223-0966

Bromer Booksellers
607 Boylston St.
Boston, MA 02116
617-247-2818 or Fax 617-247-2975

Old or new; may subjects
Gary R. Smith
517 Laurel Ave.
Modesto, CA 95351

Barbara Smith Books
P.O. Box 1185
Northampton, MA 01061
413-586-1453

Randall House
835 Laguna St.
Santa Barbara, CA 93101
805-963-1909 or Fax 805-963-1650

Irvin S. Cobb
Always paying $3.00 each plus shipping. Send for immediate payment to:
Bill Schroeder
5801 KY Dam Rd.
Paducah, KY 42003

Juvenile
Cover to Cover
P.O. Box 687
Chapel Hill, NC 27514

Edison Hall Books
5 Ventnor Dr.
Edison, NJ 08820
908-548-4455

Page Books
HRC 65, Box 233
Kingston, AR 72472
501-861-5831

Jo Ann Reisler, Ltd.
360 Glyndon St., NE
Vienna, VA 22180
703-938-2967

Nancy Stewart, Books
1188 NW Weybridge Way
Beaverton, OR 97006
503-645-9779

Indians
Wars
K.C. Owings
P.O. Box 19
N Abington, MA 02351
617-857-1655

Plains, Black Hills, etc.
Flo Silver Books
8442 Oakwood Ct. N
Indianapolis, IN 46260
317-255-5118

Iowa
Karl M. Armens
740 Juniper Dr.
Iowa City, IA 52245

Jazz
Chartwell Booksellers
55 E 52nd St.
New York, NY 10055
212-308-0643

James Joyce
Paul Melzer Fine Books
12 E St.
Redlands, CA 92373
909-792-7299

John Deere
Henry Lindeman
4769 Bavarian Dr.
Jackson, MI 49201
517-764-5728

Judaica
Harold B. Diamond
Box 1193
Burbank, CA 91507
818-846-0342

Stanley Schwartz
1934 Pentuckett Ave.
San Diego, CA 92104-5732
619-232-5888 or Fax 619-233-5833

Juvenile Series
Lee & Mike Temares
50 Hts. Rd.
Plandome, NY 11030
516-627-8688

Kentucky Authors
Bill Schroeder
P.O. Box 3009
Paducah, KY 42002-3009

Kentucky History
Bill Schroeder
P.O. Box 3009
Paducah, KY 42002-3009

Labor
A\K\A Fine Used Books
4124 Brooklyn Ave. NE
Seattle, WA 98107

Volume I Books
1 Union St.
Hillsdale, MI 49242
517-437-2228

Landscape Architecture
The American Botanist Booksellers
P.O. Box 532
Chillicothe, IL 61523
309-274-5254

Latin American Literature
Almark & Co.-Booksellers
P.O. Box 7
Thornhill, Ontario
Canada L3T 3N1
phone/Fax 905-764-2665

Flo Silver Books
8442 Oakwood Ct. N
Indianapolis, IN 46260
317-255-5118

Harold B. Diamond
Box 1193
Burbank, CA 91507
818-846-0342

Law & Crime
Harold B. Diamond
Box 1193
Burbank, CA 91507
818-846-0342

T.E. Lawrence
Denis McDonnell, Bookseller
653 Park St.
Honesdale, PA 18431
717-253-6706 or Fax 717-253-6785

Lawrence of Arabia
Denis McDonnell, Bookseller
653 Park St.
Honesdale, PA 18431
717-253-6706 or Fax 717-253-6785

Lebanon
W.B. O'Neill-Old & Rare Books
11609 Hunters Green Ct.
Reston, VA 22091
703-860-0782 or Fax 703-620-0153

Lewis & Clark Expedition
George H. Tweney
16660 Marine View Dr. SW
Seattle, WA 98166
206-243-8243

Limited Editions Club
Lee & Mike Temares
50 Hts. Rd.
Plandome, NY 11030
516-627-8688

Literature
Amaranth Books
P.O. Box 421
Wilmette, IL 60091-0421
708-328-2939

In translation
Almark & Co.-Booksellers
P.O. Box 7
Thornhill, Ontario
Canada L3T 3N1
phone/Fax 905-764-2665

First editions
Karl M. Armens
740 Juniper Dr.
Iowa City, IA 52245

18th & 19th-C English
The Book Collector
2347 University Blvd.
Houston, TX 77005
713-661-2665

First editions
Bromer Booksellers
607 Boylston St.
Boston, MA 02116
617-247-2818 or Fax 617-247-2975

African-American
Between the Covers
132 Kings Hwy. E
Haddonfield, NJ 08033

Paperbound
Black Ace Books
1658 Griffith Park Blvd.
Los Angeles, CA 90026
213-661-5052

The Captain's Bookshelf, Inc.
P.O. Box 2258
Asheville, NC 22802-2258
704-253-6631

Chapel Hill Rare Books
P.O. Box 456
Carrboro, NC 27510
919-929-8351

Harold B. Diamond
Box 1193
Burbank, CA 91507
818-846-0342

Southern
Elder's Book Store
2115 Elliston Pl.
Nashville, TN 37203
615-327-1867

Ken Lopez, Bookseller
51 Huntington Rd.
Hadley, MA 01035
413-584-4827 or Fax 413-584-2045

Mason's Bookstore, Rare Books &
Record Albums
115 S Main St.
Chambersburg, PA 17201
717-261-0541

Much Ado
Seven Pleasant St.
Marblehead, MA 01945
617-639-0400

Randall House
835 Laguna St.
Santa Barbara, CA 93101
805-963-1909 or Fax 805-963-1650

Wellerdt's Books
3700 S Osprey Ave. #214
Sarasota, FL 34239
813-365-1318

Xanadu Records, Ltd.
3242 Irwin Ave.
Kingsbridge, NY 10463
212-549-3655

Little Leather Library
Gary R. Smith
517 Laurel Ave.
Modesto, CA 95351

Magazines
Mystery only
Grave Matters
P.O. Box 32192-08
Cincinnati, OH 45232

Robert A. Madle
4406 Bestor Dr.
Rockville, MD 20853
301-460-4712

The Magazine Baron
1236 S Magnolia Ave.
Anaheim, CA 92804
714-527-0358 or Fax 714-527-5634

Relating to decorative arts
Mordida Books
P.O. Box 79322
Houston, TX 77279
713-467-4280 or Fax 713-467-4182

Passaic Book Center
594 Main Ave.
Passaic, NJ 07055
201-778-6646 or Fax 201-778-673

Magic
Especially tricks
John A. Greget-Magic Lists
2631 E Claire Dr.
Phoenix, AZ 85032
602-971-5497

Manuscripts
Susan Heller, Pages for Sages
P.O. Box 2219
Beachwood, OH 44122
216-283-2665 or Fax 216-999-2665

Heritage Book Shop, Inc.
8540 Melrose Ave.
Los Angeles, CA 90069
310-659-3674 or Fax 310-659-4872

Key Books
P.O. Box 58097
St. Petersburg, FL 33715
813-867-2931

Asiatic languages
Worldwide Antiquarian
P.O. Box 391
Cambridge, MA 02141
617-876-6220 or Fax 617-876-0839

Randall House
835 Laguna St.
Santa Barbara, CA 93101
805-963-1909 or Fax 805-963-1650

Maps
State, pocket-type, ca 1800s
The Bookseller, Inc.
521 W Exchange St.
Akron, OH 44302
216-762-3101

Bowie & Co. Booksellers, Inc.
314 First Ave. S
Seattle, WA 98104
206-624-4100 or Fax 206-223-0966

Pre-1900 Florida
Brasser's
8701 Seminole Blvd.
Seminole, FL 34642

Elegant Book & Map Company
815 Harrison Ave.
P.O. Box 1302
Cambridge, OH 43725
614-432-4068

Maritime
Book & Tackle Shop
P.O. Box 114
Chestnut Hill, MA 02167
617-965-0459

Overlee Farm Books
P.O. Box 1155
Stockbridge, MA 01262
413-637-2277

J. Tuttle Maritime Books
1806 Laurel Crest
Madison, WI 53705
608-238-SAIL (7245)

Martial Arts
Nutmeg Books
354 New Litchfield St. (Rte. 202)
Torrington, CT 06790
203-482-9696

Masonic History
Mason's Bookstore, Rare Books
& Record Albums
115 S Main St.
Chambersburg, PA 17201
717-261-0541

Mathematics
Significant Books
3053 Madison Rd.
P.O. Box 9248
Cincinnati, OH 45209
513-321-7567

Medicine
Amaranth Books
P.O. Box 421
Wilmette, IL 60091-0421
708-328-2939

Book & Tackle
P.O. Box 114
Chestnut Hill, MA 02167
617-965-0459

Key Books
P.O. Box 58097
St. Petersburg, FL 33715
813-867-2931

M & S Rare Books, Inc.
P.O. Box 2594, E Side Sta.
Providence, RI 02906
401-421-1050 or Fax 401-272-0831
(attention M & S)

Smithfield Rare Books
20 Deer Run Trail
Smithfield, RI 02917
401-231-8225

Medieval
Camelot Books
Charles E. Wyatt
P.O. Box 2883
Vista, CA 92083
619-940-9472

Metaphysics
AL-PAC
Lamar Kelley Antiquarian Books
2625 E Southern Ave., C-120
Tempe, AZ 85282
602-831-3121 or Fax 602-831-3193

Meteorology
Knollwood Books
Lee & Peggy Price
P.O. Box 197
Oregon, WI 53575
608-835-8861 or Fax 608-835-8421

Mexico
Flo Silver Books
8442 Oakwood Ct. N
Indianapolis, IN 46260
317-255-5118

Michigan
Artis Books
201 N Second Ave.
P.O. Box 822
Alpena, MI 49707
517-354-3401

Yesterday's Books
229 Riverview Dr.
Parchment, MI 49004
616-345-1011

Middle Eastern Countries
Worldwide Antiquarian
P.O. Box 391
Cambridge, MA 02141
617-876-6220 or Fax 617-876-0839

Militaria
The Book Corner
Mike Tennero
728 W Lumsden Rd.
Brandon, FL 33511
813-684-1133

The Bookseller, Inc.
521 W Exchange St.
Akron, OH 44302
216-762-3101

Brasser's
8701 Seminole Blvd.
Seminole, FL 34642

Edison Hall Books
5 Ventnor Dr.
Edison, NJ 08820
908-548-4455

Rick Harmon
Military Books & Relics
910 Sullivan Dr.
Belvidere, IL 61008
815-547-7580

Robert L. Merriam
Rare, Used & Old Books
Newhall Rd.
Conway, MA 01341
413-369-4052

Significant Books
3053 Madison Rd.
P.O Box 9248
Cincinnati, OH 45209
513-321-7567

Before 1900
Gordon Totty
Scarce Paper Americana
347 Shady Lake Pky.
Baton Rouge, LA 70810
504-766-8625

Histories
Tryon County Bookshop
2071 State Hwy. 29
Johnstown, NY 12905
518-762-1060

Volume I Books
1 Union St.
Hillsdale, MI 49242
517-437-2228

Miniature Books

Bromer Booksellers
607 Boylston St.
Boston, MA 02116
617-247-2818 or Fax 617-247-2975

Foreign atlases
Murray Hudson
Antiquarian Books & Maps
The Old Post Office
109 S Church St.
P.O. Box 163
Halls, TN 38040
901-836-9057 or 800-748-9946

Especially fishing
Hurley Books
1752 Rt. 12
Westmoreland, NH 03467-4724
603-399-4342 (8 am to 8 pm)

Gary R. Smith
517 Laurel Ave.
Modesto, CA 95351

Miscellaneous

Bridgman Books
906 Roosevelt Ave.
Rome, NY 13440
315-337-7252

Movies

Cinemage Books
105 W 27th St.
New York, NY 10001
212-243-4919

Mystery

Karl M. Armens
740 Juniper Dr.
Iowa City, IA 52245

First editions
Island Books
P.O. Box 19
Old Westbury, NY 11568

Kacey Kowars
425 Buckingham Dr.
Indianapolis, IN 46208
317-921-9408

Mordida Books
P.O. Box 79322
Houston, TX 77279
713-467-4280 or Fax 713-467-4182

Pandora's Books, Ltd.
P.O. Box BB-54
Neche, ND 48265
204-324-8548 or Fax 204-324-1628

RAC Books
R.R. #2
P.O. Box 296
Seven Valleys, PA 17360
717-428-3776

The Silver Door
P.O. Box 3208
Redondo Beach, CA 90277
310-379-6005

Napoleonic Memorabilia

The Book Collector
2347 University Blvd.
Houston, TX 7005
713-661-2665

Narcotics

Nutmeg Books
354 New Litchfield St. (Rte. 202)
Torrington, CT 06790
203-482-9696

Natural History

Thomas C. Bayer
85 Reading Ave.
Hillsdale, MI 49242
517-439-4134

Bohemian Bookworm
110 W 25th St., 9th Floor
New York, NY 10001
212-620-5627

Woodbridge B. Brown
P.O. Box 445
Turners Falls, MA 01376
413-772-2509 or 413-773-5710

Noriko I. Ciochon
Natural History Books
1025 Keokut St.
Iowa City, IA 52240
319-354-4844

Melvin Marcher, Bookseller
6204 N Vermont
Oklahoma City, OK 73112

Nautical

Much Ado
Seven Pleasant St.
Marblehead, MA 01945
617-639-0400

Overlee Farm Books
P.O. Box 1155
Stockbridge, MA 01262
413-637-2277

Needlework

Stanley Schwartz
1934 Pentuckett Ave.
San Diego, CA 92104-5732
619-232-5888 or Fax 619-233-5833

Neuroscience

John Gach Books
5620 Waterloo Rd.
Columbia, MD 21045
410-465-9023

New England

Book & Tackle
P.O. Box 114
Chestnut Hill, MA 02167
617-965-0459

Non-Fiction

Pre-1950
Brasser's
8701 Seminole Blvd.
Seminole, FL 34642

Novels

The Silver Door
P.O. Box 3208
Redondo Beach, CA 90277
310-379-6005

Occult

AL-PAC
Lamar Kelley Antiquarian Books
2625 E Southern Ave., C-120
Tempe, AZ 85282
602-831-3121 or Fax 602-831-3193

Ohio

The Bookseller, Inc.
521 W Exchange St.
Akron, OH 44302
216-762-3101

Omar Khayyam

Worldwide Antiquarian
P.O. Box 391
Cambridge, MA 02141
617-876-6220 or Fax 617-876-0839

Original Art

By children's illustrators
Kendra Krienke
230 Central Park W
New York, NY 10024
201-930-9709 or 201-930-9765

Paperbacks

The American Dust Co.
47 Park Ct.
Staten Island, NY 10301
718-442-8253

Vintage, beat, hippie, & counterculture
Black Ace Books
1658 Griffith Park Blvd.
Los Angeles, CA 90026
213-661-5052

Vintage
Buck Creek Books, Ltd.
838 Main St.
Lafayette, IN 47901

Footstool Detective Books
3148 Holmes Ave. S
Minneapolis, MN 55408-2629

For Collectors Only
2028B Ford Pky. #136
St. Paul, MN 55116

Michael Gerlicher
1375 Rest Point Rd.
Orono, MN 55364

Vintage
Grave Matters
P.O. Box 32192-08
Cincinnati, OH 45232

Modern Age Books
P.O. Box 325
E Lansing, MI 48826
517-351-9334

Originals
Mordida Books
P.O. Box 79322
Houston, TX 77279
713-467-4280 or Fax 713-467-4182

Pandora's Books, Ltd.
P.O. Box BB-54
Neche, ND 58265
204-324-8548 or Fax 204-324-1628

Tom Rolls
640 E Seminary #2
Greencastle, IN 46135

This & That Used Books
Toni Rooksberry
524 N Park Ave.
Jasonville, IN 47438
812-665-3631

Robert B. Parker
Thomas Books
P.O. Box 14036
Phoenix, AZ 85063
602-247-9289

Pennsylvania
Mason's Bookstore, Rare Books
& Record Albums
115 S Main
Chambersburg, PA 17201
717-261-0541

Performing Arts
Bowie & Co. Booksellers, Inc.
314 First Ave. S
Seattle, WA 98104
206-624-4100

Philosophy
The Book Corner
Mike Tennero
728 W Lumsden Rd.
Brandon, FL 33511
813-684-1133

John Gach Books
5620 Waterloo Rd.
Columbia, MD 21045
410-465-9023

Photography
Cary Loren
The Captain's Bookshelf, Inc.
P.O. Box 2258
Asheville, NC 28802-2258
704-253-6631

Significant Books
3053 Madison Rd.
P.O. Box 9248
Cincinnati, OH 45209
513-321-7567

19th-C Middle & Far East Countries
Worldwide Antiquarian
P.O. Box 391
Cambridge, MA 02141
617-876-6220 or Fax 617-876-0839

Playing Cards
Bill Sachen
927 Grand Ave.
Waukegan, IL 60085
708-662-7204

Poetry
Edison Hall Books
5 Ventnor Dr.
Edison, NJ 08820
908-548-4455

Janet Egelhofer
36 Fairfield Ave.
Holyoke, MA 01040
413-532-1295

Edward L. Smith
Modern 1st Editions
P.O. Box 1183
Ojai, CA 93024
805-646-2921 or Fax 805-646-0981

VERSEtility Books
P.O. Box 1366
Burlington, CT 06013-1366
203-675-9338

Polar Explorations & Ephemera
Alaskan Heritage Bookshop
174 S Franklin, P.O. 22165
Juneau, AK 99802

Parmer Books
7644 Forrestal Rd.
San Diego, CA 92120-2203
619-287-0693 or Fax 619-287-6135
Internet: ParmerBook@aol.com

Political
Radical
A\K\A Fine Books
4142 Brooklyn Ave. NE
Seattle, WA 98107

Gossip, memoirs or histories
Herb Sauermann
21660 School Rd.
Manton, CA 96059

Radical
Volume I Books
1 Union St.
Hillsdale, MI 49242
517-437-2228

Post Cards
Book & Tackle Shop
P.O. Box 114
Chestnut Hill, MA 02167
617-965-0459

Posters
The Mulberry Cat
Yvonne Davis
Jan Davis Martel
P.O. Box 3573
Boone, NC 28607
704-963-7693

Pre-Colombian Art
Flo Silver Books
8442 Oakwood Ct. N
Indianapolis, IN 46260
317-255-5118

Press Books
Heritage Book Shop, Inc.
8540 Melrose Ave.
Los Angeles, CA 90069
213-659-3674

Randall House
835 Laguna St.
Santa Barbara, CA 93101
805-963-1909 or Fax 805-963-1650

Prints
The Mulberry Cat
Yvonne Davis
Jan Davis Martel
P.O. Box 3573
Boone, NC 28607
704-963-7693

Private Presses
American
Richard Blacher
209 Plymouth Colony, Alps Rd.
Branford, CT 06405

First Folio
1206 Brentwood
Paris, TN 34842
phone/Fax 901-644-9940

Susan Heller, Pages for Sages
P.O. Box 22219
Beachwood, OH 44122
216-283-2665 or Fax 216-999-2665

Promoters of Paper, Ephemera & Book Fairs
Kingsbury Productions
Katherine & David Kreider
4555 N Pershing Ave., Ste. 33-138
Stockton, CA 95207
209-467-8438

Psychedelia
Nutmeg Books
354 New Litchfield St. (Rte. 202)
Torrington, CT 06790
203-482-9696

Psychiatry
John Gach Books
5620 Waterloo Rd.
Columbia, MD 21045
410-465-9023

Psychoanalysis
Also related subjects
John Gach Books
5620 Waterloo Rd.
Columbia, MD 21045
410-465-9023

Psychology
John Gach Books
5620 Waterloo Rd.
Columbia, MD 21045
410-465-9023

The King's Market Booksellers
P.O. Box 709
Boulder, CO 80306-0709
303-447-0234

Pulps
Science fiction & fantasy before 1945
Robert A. Madle
4406 Bestor Dr.
Rockville, MD 20853
301-460-4712

Quaker
Vintage Books
117 Concord St.
Framingham, MA 01701

Also Shakers, Christians & Collectivists
Duck Creek Books
Jim & Shirley Richards
P.O. Box 203
Caldwell, OH 43724
614-732-4856 (10 am to 10 pm)

Quilt Books
Bill Schroeder
P.O. Box 3009
Paducah, KY 42002-3009

Galerie De Boicourt
980 Chester
Birmingham, MI 48009
313-540-0166

Railroading
Mason's Rare & Used Books
115 S Main St.
Chambersburg, PA 17201
717-261-0541

Rare & Unusual Books
First Folio
1206 Brentwood
Paris, TN 38242
phone/Fax 901-644-9940

Susan Heller, Pages for Sages
P.O. Box 22219
Beachwood, OH 44122
216-283-2665 or Fax 216-999-2665

Kenneth Karimole, Bookseller, Inc.
P.O. Box 464
509 Wilshire Blvd.
Santa Monica, CA 94001
310-451-4342 or 310-458-5930

M & S Rare Books, Inc.
P.O. Box 2594, E Side Sta.
Providence, RI 02906
401-421-1050 or Fax 401-272-0831
(attention M & S)

Reprint editions
Dover Publications
Dept. A 214
E Second St.
Mineola, NY 11501

Terry Harper, Bookseller
P.O. Box 312
Vergennes, VT 05491-0312
802-877-9262

Heritage Book Shop, Inc.
8540 Melrose Ave.
Los Angeles, CA 90069
213-659-3674

Paul Melzer Fine Books
12 E Vine St.
Redlands, CA 92373
909-792-7299

Reference
About Books
6 Sand Hill Ct.
P.O. Box 5717
Parsippany, NY 07054
201-515-4591

Religion
Chimney Sweep Books
419 Cedar St.
Santa Cruz, CA 94060-4304
408-458-1044

Hurley Books
1752 Rt. 12
Westmoreland, NH 03467-4724
603-399-4342 (8 am to 8 pm)

Reptiles
Mason's Bookstore, Rare Books
& Record Albums
115 S Main St.
Chambersburg, PA 17201
717-261-0541

Revolutionary War
K.C. Owings
P.O. Box 19
N Abington, MA 02351
617-857-1655

Roycroft Press
Richard Blacher
209 Plymouth Colony, Alps Rd.
Branford, CT 06405

Rubaiyats
Harold B. Diamond
Box 1193
Burbank, CA 91507
818-846-0342

Scholarly Books
Brooks Books
Philip B. Nesty
P.O. Box 21473
1343 New Hampshire Dr.
Concord, CA 94521
510-672-4566 or Fax 510-672-3338

Reprint editions
Dover Publications
Dept. A 214
E Second St.
Mineola, NY 11501

Science & Technology
Thomas C. Bayer
85 Reading Ave.
Hillsdale, MI 49242
517-439-4134

Book & Tackle Shop
P.O. Box 114
Chestnut Hill, MA 02167
617-965-0459 Date 01/11/95Page 3

Key Books
P.O. Box 58097
St. Petersburg, FL 33715
813-867-2931

M & S Rare Books, Inc.
P.O. Box 2594, E Side Sta.
Providence, RI 02906
401-272-0831 or Fax 401-272-0831
(attention M & S)

Smithfield Rare Books
20 Deer Run Trail
Smithfield, RI 02917
401-231-8225

Science Fiction
AL-PAC
Lamar Kelley Antiquarian Books
2625 E Southern Ave., C-120
Tempe, AZ 85282
602-831-3121 or Fax 602-831-3193

Karl M. Armens
740 Juniper Dr.
Iowa City, IA 52245

First editions
Island Books
P.O. Box 19
Old Westbury, NY 11568
516-759-0233

Horror & Occult
Bob Lakin
3021 Lavita Ln.
Dallas, TX 75234
214-247-3291

Robert A. Madle
4406 Bestor Dr.
Rockville, MD 20853
301-460-4712

Also fantasy
Kai Nygaard
19421 Eighth Place
Escondido, CA 92029
619-746-9039

Pandora's Books, Ltd.
P.O. Box 54
Neche, ND 58265
204-324-8548 or Fax 204-324-1628

Also fantasy
Xanadu Records, Ltd.
3242 Irwin Ave.
Kingsbridge, NY 10463
212-549-3655

Sciences
Cover to Cover
P.O. Box 687
Chapel Hill, NC 27514

Harold B. Diamond
Box 1193
Burbank, CA 91507
818-846-0342

Reprint editions
Dover Publications
E Second St.
Mineola, NY 11501

Significant Books
P.O. Box 9248
3053 Madison Rd.
Cincinnati, OH 45209
513-321-7567

Series Books
Glo's Children's Series Books
906 Shadywood
Southlake, TX 76092

Set Editions
Arthur Boutiette
410 W 3rd St., Suite 200
Little Rock, AR 72201

Surveying
Also tools, instruments & ephemera
David & Nancy Garcelon
10 Hastings Ave.
Millbury, MA 01527-4314
508-754-2667

Set Editions
Bowie & Weatherford, Inc.
314 First Ave. S
Seattle, WA 98104
206-624-4100

Shakespeare
Harold B. Diamond
Burbank, CA 91507
818-846-0342

Sherlockiana
The Silver Door
P.O. Box 3208
Redondo Beach, CA 90277
310-379-6005

Ships & Sea
Book & Tackle Shop
P.O. Box 114
Chestnut Hill, MA 02167
617-965-0459

Parmer Books
7644 Forrestal Rd.
San Diego, CA 92120-2203
619-287-0693 or Fax 619-287-6135
Internet: ParmerBook@aol.com

J. Tittle Maritme Books
1806 Laurel Crest
Madison, WI 53705
608-238-SAIL

Signed Editions
Chapel Hill Rare Books
P.O. Box 456
Carrboro, NC 27510
919-929-8351

Janet Egelhofer
36 Fairfield Ave.
Holyoke, MA 01040
413-532-1295

Dan Simmons
Thomas Books
P.O. Box 14036
Phoenix, AZ 85063
602-247-9289

Socialism
Volume I Books
1 Union St.
Hillsdale, MI 49242
517-437-2228

South America
Flo Silver Books
8442 Oakwood Ct. N
Indianapolis, IN 46260
317-255-5118

South Dakota
Also any pre-1970 Western-related books
James F. Taylor
515 Sixth St.
Rapid City, SD 57701
605-341-3224

Space Exploration
Knollwood Books
Lee & Peggy Price
P.O. Box 197
Oregon, WI 53575
608-835-8861 or Fax 608-835-8421

Speciality Publishers
Arkham House, Gnome, Fantasy, etc.
Robert A. Madle
4406 Bestor Dr.
Rockville, MD 20853
301-460-4712

Sports
Adelson Sports
13610 N Scottsdale Rd. #10
Scottsdale, AZ 85254
602-596-1913 or Fax 602-598-1914

Randall House
835 Laguna St.
Santa Barbara, CA 93101
805-963-1909 or Fax 805-963-1650

Statue of Liberty
Mike Brooks
7335 Skyline
Oakland, CA 94611

Robert Louis Stevenson
1890s, especially Scribners
Chris Jankus
214 Alcott Rd.
Brookhaven, PA 19015

Technology
Cover to Cover
P.O. Box 687
Chapel Hill, NC 27514

Significant Books
3053 Madison Rd.
P.O. Box 9248
Cincinnati, OH 45209
513-321-7567

Tennessee History
Elder's Book Store
2115 Elliston Pl.
Nashville, TN 37203
615-327-1867

Tennis
Brasser's
8701 Seminole Blvd.
Seminole, FL 34642

Texana Fiction & Authors
Bob Lakin
3021 Lavita Ln.
Dallas, TX 75234
214-247-3291

Textiles
Galerie De Boicourt
980 Chester
Birmingham, MI 48009
313-540-0166

Stanley Schwartz
1934 Pentuckett Ave.
San Diego, CA 92104-5732
619-232-5888 or Fax 619-233-5833

Theology
Chimney Sweep Books
419 Cedar St.
Santa Cruz, CA 94060-4304
408-458-1044

Jim Thompson
The American Dust Co.
47 Park Ct.
Staten Island, NY 10301
718-442-8253

Thrillers
Kacey Kowars
425 Buckingham Dr.
Indianapolis, IN 46208
317-921-9408

Time-Life Books
Gary R. Smith
517 Laurel Ave.
Modesto, CA 95351

Trades & Crafts
19th C
Cover to Cover
P.O. Box 687
Chapel Hill, NC 27514

Hillcrest Books
Rt. 3, Box 479
Crossville, TN 38555-9547
phone/Fax 615-484-7680

Travel
Bohemian Bookworm
110 W 25th St., 9th Floor
New York, NY 10001
212-620-5627

Also exploration
Duck Creek Books
Jim & Shirley Richards
P.O. Box 203
Caldwell, OH 43724
614-732-4856 (10 am to 10 pm)

Terry Harper, Bookseller
P.O. Box 312
Vergennes, VT 05491-0312
802-877-9262

Heritage Book Shop, Inc.
8540 Melrose Ave.
Los Angeles, CA 90069
213-659-3674

Jim Hodgson Books
908 S Manlius St.
Fayetteville, NY 13066
315-637-6264

Flo Silver Books
8442 Oakwood Ct. N
Indianapolis, IN 46260
317-255-5118

Discoveries before 1900
Gordon Totty
Scarce Paper Americana
347 Shady Lake Pky.
Baton Rouge, LA 70810
504-766-8625

Turkey
W.B. O'Neill-Old & Rare Books
11609 Hunters Green Ct.
Reston, VA 22091
703-860-0782 or Fax 703-620-0153

UFO
AL-PAC
Lamar Kelley Antiquarian Books
2625 E Southern Ave., C-120
Tempe, AZ 85282
602-831-3121 or Fax 602-831-3193

Vargas
Parnassus Books
218 N 9th St.
Boise, ID 83702

Vietnam War
A\K\A Fine Used Books
4124 Brooklyn Ave. NE
Seattle, WA 98107
206-632-5870

Rick Harmon
Military Books & Relics
910 Sullivan Dr.
Belvidere, IL 61008
815-547-7580

Voyages, Exploration & Travel
Chapel Hill Rare Books
P.O. Box 456
Carrboro, NC 27510
919-929-8351

Terry Harper, Bookseller
P.O. Box 312
Vergennes, VT 05491-0312
802-877-9262

Heritage Book Shop, Inc.
8540 Melrose Ave.
Los Angeles, CA 90069
213-659-3674

Jim Hodgson Books
908 S Manlius St.
Fayetteville, NY 13066
315-637-6264

Key Books
P.O. Box 58097
St. Petersburg, FL 33715
813-867-2931

Overlee Farm Books
P.O. Box 1155
Stockbridge, MA 01262
413-627-2277

George H. Tweney
16660 Marine View Dr. SW
Seattle, WA 98166
206-243-8243

Weapons
All edged types
Knife Readables
115 Longfellow Blvd.
Lakeland, FL 33810
813-666-1133

Western Americana
Bowie & Co. Booksellers, Inc.
314 First Ave. S
Seattle, WA 98104
206-624-4100

Harold B. Diamond
Box 1193
Burbank, CA 91507
818-846-0342

Terry Harper, Bookseller
P.O. Box 312
Vergennes, VT 05491-0312
802-877-9262

K.C. Owings
P.O. Box 19
N Abington, MA 02351
617-857-1655

George H. Tweney
16660 Marine View Dr. SW
Seattle, WA 98166
206-243-8243

Charles Willeford
The American Dust Co.
47 Park Ct.
Staten Island, NY 10301
718-442-8253

Women's History
Volume I Books
1 Union St.
Hillsdale, MI 49242
517-437-2228

World War I
A/K/A Fine Used Books
4142 Brooklyn Ave. NE
Seattle, WA 98105
206-632-5870

The Book Corner
Mike Tennero
728 W Lumsden Rd.
Brandon, FL 33511
813-684-1133

World War II
Cover to Cover
P.O. Box 687
Chapel Hill, NC 27514

BOOKSELLERS

　　　This section of the book lists names and addresses of used book dealers who have contributed the retail listings contained in this edition of *Huxford's Old Book Value Guide*. The code (A1, S7, etc.) located before the price in our listings refers to the dealer offering that particular book for sale. (When more than one dealer has the same book listing their code is given alphabetically before the price.) Given below are the dealer names and their codes.

　　　Many book dealers issue catalogs, have open shops, are mail order only, or may be a combination of these forms of business. When seeking a book from a particular dealer, it would be best to first write (enclose SASE) or call to see what type of business is operated (open shop or mail order).

A1
A-Book-A-Brac Shop
6760 Collins Ave.
Miami Beach, FL 33141
305-865-0092

A2
Aard Books
31 Russell Ave.
Troy, NH 03465
603-242-3638

A3
Noreen Abbot Books
2666 44th Ave.
San Francisco, CA 94116
415-664-9464

A4
About Books
6 Sand Hill Ct.
P.O. Box 5717
Parsippany, NJ 07054
201-515-4591

A5
Adelson Sports
13610 N Scottsdale Rd. #10
Scottsdale, AZ 85254
602-596-1913 or Fax 602-596-1914

A6
Ads Autographs
P.O. Box 8006
Webster, NY 14580
716-671-2651

A7
A/K/A Fine Used Books
4142 Brooklyn NE
Seattle, WA 98105
206-632-5870

A8
AL-PAC
Lamar Kelley Antiquarian Books
2625 E Southern Ave., C-120
Tempe, AZ 85282
602-831-3121 or Fax 602-831-3193

A9
Amaranth Books
P.O. Box 421
Wilmette, IL 60091-0421
708-328-2939

A10
The American Botanist
P.O. Box 532
Chillicothe, IL 61523

A11
The American Dust Co.
47 Park Ct.
Staten Island, NY 10301
718-442-8253

A12
Antiquarian Book Arcade
110 W 25th St., 9th Floor
New York, NY 10001

A13
Antiquarian Medical Books
W. Bruce Fye
1607 N Wood Ave.
Marshfield, WI 54449
Fax 715-389-2990

A14
Almark & Co.-Booksellers
P.O. Box 7
Thornhill, Ontario
Canada L3T 3N1
phone/Fax 905-764-2665

A15
Karl M. Armens
740 Juniper Dr.
Iowa City, IA 52245
319-337-7755

A16
Arnold's of Michigan
218 S Water St.
Marine City, MI 48039
313-765-1350

A17
Artis Books
201 N Second Ave.
P.O. Box 822
Alpena, MI 49707-0822
517-354-3401

A18
Authors of the West
191 Dogwood Dr.
Dundee, OR 97115
503-538-8132

A19
Aplin Antiques & Art
HC 80, Box 793-25
Piedmont, SD 57769
605-347-5016

A20
Avonlea Books Search Service
P.O. Box 74, Main Sta.
White Plains, NY 10602
914-946-5923 Fax 914-946-5924 (allow 6 rings)

B1
Thomas C. Bayer
85 Reading Ave.
Hillsdale, MI 49242
517-439-4134

B2
Beasley Books
1533 W Oakdale, 2nd Floor
Chicago, IL 60657
312-472-4528 or Fax 312-472-7857

B3
Bela Luna Books
P.O. Box 260425
Highlands Ranch, CO 80126-0425
800-497-4717 or Fax 303-794-3135

B4
Between the Covers
132 Kings Hwy. E
Haddonfield, NJ 08033
609-354-7665 or 609-869-0512 (evenings)
Fax 609-354-7695

B5
Bicentennial Book Shop
820 S Westnedge Ave.
Kalamazoo, MI 49008
616-345-5987

B6
Bibliography of the Dog
The New House
216 Covey Hill Rd.
Havelock, Quebec
Canada J0S 2C0
514-827-2717 or Fax 514-827-2091

B7
Best-Read Books
122 State St.
Sedro-Woolley, WA 98284
206-855-2179

B8
Bohemian Bookworm
110 W 25th St., 9th Floor
New York, NY 10001
212-620-5627

B9
The Book Baron
1236 S Magnolia Ave.
Anaheim, CA 92804
714-527-7022 or Fax 714-527-5634

B10
Book Broker
310 E Market St.
Charlottesville, VA 22902
804-296-2194

B11
The Book Corner
Michael Tennero
728 W Lumsden Rd.
Brandon, FL 33511
813-684-1133

B12
The Book Emporium
235 Glen Cove Ave.
Sea Cliff, LI, NY 11579
516-671-6524

B13
The Book Inn
6401-D University
Lubbock, TX 79413

B14
Book & Tackle Shop
P.O. Box 114
Chestnut Hill, MA 02167
617-965-0459 or 401-596-0700 (summer)

B15
Book Treasures
P.O. Box 121
E Norwich, NY 11732

B16
The Book Den South
Nancy Costello
2249 First St.
Ft. Myers, FL 33901
813-332-2333

B17
Books of the Ages
Gary J Overmann
Maple Ridge Manor
4764 Silverwood Dr.
Batavia, OH 45103
513-732-3456

B18
The Bookseller, Inc.
521 W Exchange St.
Akron, OH 44302
216-762-3101

B19
Books West Southwest
2452 N Campbell Ave.
Tucson, AZ 85719
602-326-3533

B20
Bowie & Co. Booksellers, Inc.
314 First Ave. S
Seattle, WA 98104
206-624-4100 or Fax 206-223-0966

B21
Brasser's
8701 Seminole Blvd.
Seminole, FL 34642

B22
Bridgman Books
906 Roosevelt Ave.
Rome, NY 13440
315-337-7252

B23
British Stamp Exchange
12 Fairlawn Ave.
N Weymouth, MA 02191

B24
Bromer Booksellers
607 Boylston St.
Boston, MA 02116
617-247-2818 or Fax 617-247-2975

B25
Mike Brooks
7335 Skyline
Oakland, CA 9461

B26
Brooks Books
Philip B. Nesty
1343 New Hampshire Dr.
P.O. Box 21473
Concord, CA 94521
510-672-4566 or Fax 510-672-3338

B27
The Bookstall
570 Sutter St.
San Francisco, CA 94102
Fax 415-362-1503

B28
Woodbridge B. Brown
312 Main St.
P.O. Box 445
Turner Falls, MA 01376
413-772-2509 or 413-773-5710

B29
Books Now & Then
Dennis Patrick
P.O. Box 337
Stanley, ND 58784
701-628-2084

B30
Burke's Bookstore
1719 Poplar Ave.
Memphis, TN 38104-6447
901-278-7484

B32
Richard Blacher
209 Plymouth Colony, Alps Rd.
Branford, CT 06405

B33
By the Way Books
1000 Windsor Shores Dr., #2A
P.O. Box 23359
Columbia, SC 29223
803-788-7447 or Fax 803-736-9566

C1
Camelot Books
Charles E. Wyatt
P.O. Box 2883
Vista, CA 92083
619-940-9472

C2
The Captain's Bookshelf, Inc.
Cary Loren
P.O. Box 2258
Asheville, NC 22802-2258
704-253-6631

C3
Cattermole
20th-C Children's Books
9880 Fairmount Rd.
Newbury, OH 44065

C4
Bev Chaney, Jr. Books
73 Croton Ave.
Ossining, NY 10562
914-941-1002

C5
Chimney Sweep Books
419 Cedar St.
Santa Cruz, CA 95060-4304
408-458-1044

C6
Chapel Hill Rare Books
P.O. Box 456
Carrboro, NC 27510
919-929-8351

C7
Chartwell Booksellers
55 E 52nd St.
New York, NY 10055
212-308-0643

C8
Cinemage Books
105 W 27th St.
New York, NY 10001
212-243-4919

C9
Cohen Books & Collectibles
Joel J. Cohen
P.O. Box 810310
Boca Raton, FL 33481
407-487-7888

C10
Cover to Cover
P.O. Box 687
Chapel Hill, NC 27514

C11
Noriko I. Chichon
Natural History Books
1025 Keokut St.
Iowa City, 52240
319-354-4844

C12
Creatures of Habit
403 Jefferson
Paducah, KY 42001
502-442-2923

C13
Children's Book Adoption Agency
P.O. Box 643
Kensington, MD 20895-0643
301-565-2834 or Fax 301-585-3091

D1
Ursula Davidson
Children's & Illustrated Books
134 Linden Ln.
San Rafael, CA 94901
415-454-3939 or Fax 415-454-1087

D2
L. Clarice Davis
Fine & Applied Art Books
P.O. Box 56054
Sherman Oaks, CA 91413-1054
818-787-1322

D3
Harold B. Diamond, Bookseller
Box 1193
Burbank, CA 91507
818-846-0342

D4
Carol Docheff, Bookseller
1390 Reliez Vly. Rd.
Lafayette, CA 94549
510-935-9595

D5
Dover Publications
Dept. A 214
E Second St.
Mineola, NY 11501

D6
Drusilla's Books
859 N Howard St.
P.O. Box 16
Baltimore, MD 21201
410-225-0277

D7
Duck Creek Books
Jim & Shirley Richards
P.O. Box 203
Caldwell, OH 43724
614-732-4856

E1
The Early West
P.O. Box 9292
College Sta., TX 77842
409-775-6047

E2
Edison Hall Books
5 Ventnor Dr.
Edison, NJ 08820
908-548-4455

E3
Janet Egelhofer
36 Fairfield Ave.
Holyoke, MA 01040
413-532-1295

E4
Elder s Book Store
2115 Elliston Pl.
Nashville, TN 37203
615-327-1867

E5
Elegant Book & Map Company
815 Harrison Ave.
P.O. Box 1302
Cambridge, OH 43725
614-432-4068

F1
First Folio
1206 Brentwood
Paris, TN 38242
phone/Fax 910-944-9940

F2
Fisher Books & Antiques
345 Pine St.
Williamsport, PA 17701

F3
Flo Silver Books
8442 Oakwood Ct. N
Indianapolis, IN 46260
317-255-5118

F4
For Collectors Only
2028B Ford Pky. #136
St. Paul, MN 55116

F5
Fran's Bookhouse
6601 Greene St.
Phil., PA 19119
215-438-2729 or Fax 215-438-8997

F6
Frontier America
P.O. Box 9193
Albuquerque, NM 87119-9193

G1
John Gach Fine & Rare Books
5620 Waterloo Rd.
Columbia, MD 21045
410-465-9023 or Fax 410-465-0649

G2
Galerie De Boicourt
6136 Westbrooke Dr.
W Bloomfield, MI 48322
810-788-9253

G3
Gambler's Book Shop
630 S Eleventh St.
Las Vegas, NV 89101
800-634-6243

G4
David & Nancy Garcelon
10 Hastings Ave.
Millbury, MA 01527-4314

G5
Michael Gerlicher
1375 Rest Point Rd.
Orono, MN 55364

G6
Glo's Children's Series Books
Gloria Stobbes
906 Shadywood
Southlake, TX 76092

G7
James Tait Goodrich
Antiquarian Books & Manuscripts
214 Everett Place
Englewood, NJ 07631
201-567-0199 or Fax 201-567-0433

G8
Grave Matters
P.O. Box 32192-08
Cincinnati, OH 45232
phone/Fax 513-242-7527

G9
John A. Greget-Magic Lists
2631 E Claire Dr.
Phoenix, AZ 85032
602-971-5497

H1
Henry F. Hain III
Antiques & Collectibles
2623 N Second St.
Harrisburg, PA 17110
717-238-0534

H2
Rick Harmon
Military Books & Relics
910 Sullivan Dr.
Belvidere, IL 61008
815-547-7580

H3
Terry Harper, Bookseller
P.O. Box 312
Vergennes, VT 05491-0312
802-877-9262

H4
Susan Heller, Pages for Sages
P.O. Box 22219
Beachwood, OH 44122
216-283-2665 or Fax 216-999-2665

H5
Heritage Book Shop, Inc.
8540 Melrose Ave.
Los Angeles, CA 90069
310-659-3674 or Fax 310-659-4872

H6
Hillcrest Books
Rt. 3, Box 479
Crossville, TN 38555-9547
phone/Fax 615-484-7680

H7
Jim Hodgson Books
908 S Manlius St.
Fayetteville, NY 13066
315-637-6264

H8
Homebiz Paper
2919 Mistwood Forest Dr.
Chester, VA 23831-7043

H9
Murray Hudson
Antiquarian Books & Maps
The Old Post Office
109 S Church St.
P.O. Box 163
Halls, TN 38040
901-836-9057 or 800-748-9946

H10
Hurley Books/Celtic Cross Books
1753 Rt. 12
Westmoreland, NH 03467
603-399-4342 or Fax 603-399-8326

I1
Island Books
P.O. Box 19
Old Westbury, NY 11586
516-759-0233

J1
Jay's House of Collectibles
75 Pky. Dr.
Syosset, NY 11791

K1
Kenneth Karmiole, Bookseller, Inc.
P.O. Box 464
509 Wilshire Blvd.
Santa Monica, CA 90401
310-451-4342 or Fax 310-458-5930

K2
Ilene Kayne
1308 S Charles St.
Baltimore, MD 21230

K3
Key Books
P.O. Box 58097
St. Petersburg, FL 33715-8097

K4
The King's Market Booksellers
P.O. Box 709
Boulder, CO 80306-0709
303-447-0234

K5
Knollwood Books
Lee & Peggy Price
P.O. Box 197
Oregon, WI 53575-0197
608-835-8861 or Fax 608-835-8421

K6
Kendra Krienke
230 Central Park West
New York, NY 10024
201-930-9709 or 201-930-9765

L1
Bob Lakin
3021 Lavita Ln.
Dallas, TX 75234
214-247-3291

L2
Henry Lindeman
4769 Bavarian Dr.
Jackson, MI 49201
517-764-5728

L3
Ken Lopez, Bookseller
51 Huntington Rd.
Hadley, MA 01035
413-584-4827 or Fax 413-584-2045

L4
Liberty Historic Manuscripts, Inc.
300 Kings Hwy. E
Haddonfield, NJ 08033

M1
M & S Rare Books, Inc.
P.O. Box 2594, E Side Sta.
Providence, RI 02806
401-421-1050 or Fax 401-272-0831
(attention M & S)

M2
Robert A. Madle
4406 Bestor Dr.
Rockville, MD 20853
301-460-4712

M3
The Magazine Baron
1236 S Magnolia Ave.
Anaheim, CA 92804
714-527-0358 or Fax 714-527-5634

M4
Melvin Marcher, Bookseller
6204 N Vermont
Oklahoma City, OK 73112

M5
Marvelous Books
P.O. Box 1510
Ballwin, MO 63022
314-458-3301

M6
Mason's Bookstore, Rare Books
& Record Albums
115 S Main St.
Chambersburg, PA 17201
717-261-0541

M7
Denis McDonnell, Bookseller
653 Park St.
Honesdale, PA 18431
717-253-6706 or Fax 717-253-6786

M8
McGowan Book Co.
P.O. Box 16325
Chapel Hill, NC 27516
919-968-1121 or Fax 919-968-1169

M9
Paul Melzer Fine & Rare Books
12 E Vine St.
Redlands, CA 92373
909-792-7299

M10
Robert L. Merriam
Rare & Used Books
39 Newhall Rd.
Conway, MA 01341-9709
413-369-4052

M11
Meyer Boswell Books, Inc.
2141 Mission St.
San Francisco, CA 94110
415-255-6400 or Fax 415-255-6499

M12
Frank Mikesh
1356 Walden Rd.
Walnut Creek, CA 94596
510-934-9243

M13
Ken Mitchell
710 Conacher Dr.
Willowdale, Ontario
Canada M2M 3N6
416-222-5808

M14
Modern Age Books
P.O. Box 325
E Lansing, MI 48826
517-351-9334

M15
Mordida Books
P.O. Box 79322
Houston, TX 77279
713-467-4280 or Fax 713-467-4182

M16
The Mulberry Cat
Yvonne Davis
Jan Davis Martel
P.O. Box 3573
Boone, NC 28607
704-963-7693

M17
Much Ado
Seven Pleasant St.
Marblehead, MA 01945
617-639-0400

M18
My Book Heaven
2406 Lincoln Ave.
P.O. Box 2715
Alameda, CA 94501
510-521-1683

M19
Robert Mueller Rare Books
8124 W 26th St.
N Riverside, IL 60546
708-447-6441

M20
My Bookhouse
27 S Sandusky St.
Tiffin, OH 44883
419-447-9842

N1
Nerman's Books
410-63 Albert St.
Winnipeg, Manitoba
Canada R3B 1G4
Fax 204-947-0753

N2
Nutmeg Books
354 New Litchfield St. (Rte. 202)
Torrington, CT 06790
203-482-9696

N3
Kai Nygaard
19421 Eighth Pl.
Escondido, CA 92029
619-749-9039

O1
David L. O'Neal, Antiquarian Bookseller
234 Clarendon St.
Boston, MA 02116
703-860-0782 or Fax 703-620-0153

O2
W.B. O'Neill
Old & Rare Books
11609 Hunters Green Ct.
Reston, VA 22091
703-860-0782 or Fax 703-620-0153

O3
October Farm
2609 Branch Rd.
Raleigh, NC 27610
919-772-0482

O4
The Old London Bookshop
111 Central Ave.
P.O. Box 922
Bellingham, WA 98227-0922
206-733-RARE or Fax 206-647-8946

O5
The Old Map Gallery
Paul F. Mahoney
1746 Blake St.
Denver, CO 80202
303-296-7725

O6
Overlee Farm Books
P.O. Box 1155
Stockbridge, MA 01262
413-637-2277

O7
K.C. Owings
P.O. Box 19
N Abington, MA 02351
617-857-1655

P1
Pacific Rim Books
Michael Onorato
P.O. Box 2575
Bellingham, WA 98227-2575
206-676-0256

P2
Page Books
H.C.R. 65, Box 233
Kingston, AR 72472
501-861-5831

P3
Pandora's Books Ltd.
P.O. Box 54
Neche, ND 58265
204-324-8548 or Fax 204-324-1628

P4
Parmer Books
7644 Forrestal Rd.
San Diego, CA 92120-2203
619-287-0693 or Fax 619-287-6135
Internet: ParmerBook@aol.com

P5
Parnassus Books
218 N 9th St.
Boise, ID 83702

P6
Passaic Book Center
594 Main Ave.
Passaic, NJ 07055
201-778-6646 or Fax 201-778-6738

P7
Pauper's Books
206 N Main St.
Bowling Green, OH 43402-2420
419-352-2163

P8
R. Plapinger, Baseball Books
P.O. Box 1062
Ashland, OR 97520
503-488-1220

P9
Prometheus Books
59 John Glenn Dr.
Buffalo, NY 14228-2197
716-691-0133 or Fax 716-691-0137

Q1
Quill & Brush
Patricia & Allen Ahearn
Box 5365
Rockville, MD 20848
301-460-3700 or Fax 301-871-5425

R1
Raintree Books
432 N Eustis St.
Eustis, FL 32726
904-357-7145

R2
Kathleen Rais & Co.
Rais Place Cottage
211 Carolina Ave.
Phoenixville, PA 19460
610-933-1388

R3
Randall House
835 Laguna St.
Santa Barbara, CA 93101
805-963-1909 or Fax 805-963-1650

R4
Reference Books
C. Scott Hall
P.O. Box 7076
Salem, OR 97305
503-399-6185

R5
Jo Ann Reisler, Ltd.
360 Glyndon St., NE
Vienna, VA 22180
703-938-2967

R6
Wallace Robinson Books
RD #6, Box 574
Meadville, PA 16335
800-653-3280 or 813-823-3280
814-724-7670 or 814-333-9652

R7
Tom Rolls
640 E Seminary #2
Greencastle, IN 46135

R8
RAC Books
R.R. #2
P.O. Box 296
Seven Valleys, PA 17360
717-428-3776

S1
Bill Sachen
927 Grand Ave.
Waukegan, IL 60085-3709
708-662-7204

S2
J. Sampson Antiques & Books
107 S Main
Harrodsburg, KY 40330
606-734-7829

S3
Stanley Schwartz
1934 Pentuckett Ave.
San Diego, CA 92104-5732
619-232-5888 or Fax 619-233-5833

S4
Significant Books
3053 Madison Rd.
P.O. Box 9248
Cincinnati, OH 45209
513-321-7567

S5
The Silver Door
P.O. Box 3208
Redondo Beach, CA 90277
310-379-6005

S6
K.B. Slocum Books
P.O. Box 10998 #620
Austin, TX 78766
800-521-4451 or Fax 512-258-8041

S7
Barbara Smith Books
P.O. Box 1185
Northampton, MA 01061
413-586-1453

S8
Edward L. Smith
Modern First Editions
P.O. Box 1183
Ojai, CA 93024
805-646-2921 or Fax 805-646-0981

S9
Smithfield Rare Books
20 Deer Run Trail
Smithfield, RI 02917
401-231-8225

S10
Nancy Stewart, Books
1188 NW Weybridge Way
Beaverton, OR 97006
503-645-9779

T1
Lee & Mike Temares
50 Hts. Rd.
Plandome, NY 11030
516-627-8688

T2
Thomas Books
P.O. Box 14036
Phoenix, AZ 85063
602-247-9289

T3
Gordon Totty
Scarce Paper Americana
347 Shady Lake Pky.
Baton Rouge, LA 70810
504-766-8625

T4
Trackside Books
8819 Mobud Dr.
Houston, TX 77036
713-772-8107

T5
Treasures From the Castle
Connie Castle
1720 N Livernois
Rochester, MI 48306
810-651-7317

T6
H.E. Turlington Books
P.O. Box 190
Carrboro, NC 27510

T7
J. Tuttle Maritime Books
1806 Laurel Crest
Madison, WI 53705
608-238-SAIL (7245)

T8
George H. Tweney
16660 Marine View Dr. SW
Seattle, WA 98166
206-243-8243

T9
Typographeum Bookshop
The Stone Cottage
Bennington Rd.
Francestown, NH 03043

T10
This & That Used Books
Toni Rooksberry
524 N Park Ave.
Jasonville, IN 47938
812-665-3631

V1
VERSEtility Books
P.O. Box 1366
Burlington, CT 06013-1366
203-675-9338

V2
A.A. Vespa
P.O. Box 637
Park Ridge, IL 60068
708-692-4210

V3
Vintage Books
Nancy & David Haines
181 Hayden Rowe St.
Hopkinton, MA 01748
508-435-3499

V4
Volume I Books
1 Union St.
Hillsdale, MI 49242
517-437-2228

W1
Worldwide Antiquarian
P.O. Box 391
Cambridge, MA 02141
617-876-6220 or Fax 617-876-0839

W2
William P. Wreden, Books & Manuscripts
P.O. Box 56
Palo Alto, CA 94302-0056
415-325-6851

Y1
Yesterday's Books
229 Riverview Dr.
Parchment, MI 49004
616-345-1011

X1
Xanadu Records, Ltd.
3242 Irwin Ave.
Kingsbridge, NY 10463
718-549-3655

Schroeder's
ANTIQUES
Price Guide

. . . is the #1 best-selling antiques & collectibles value guide on the market today, and here's why . . .

• *More than 300 advisors, well-known dealers, and top-notch collectors work together with our editors to bring you accurate information regarding pricing and identification.*

• *More than 45,000 items in almost 500 categories are listed along with hundreds of sharp original photos that illustrate not only the rare and unusual, but the common, popular collectibles as well.*

• *Each large close-up shot shows important details clearly. Every subject is represented with histories and background information, a feature not found in any of our competitors' publications.*

• *Our editors keep abreast of newly developing trends, often adding several new categories a year as the need arises.*

If it merits the interest of today's collector, you'll find it in *Schroeder's*. And you can feel confident that the information we publish is up to date and accurate. Our advisors thoroughly check each category to spot inconsistencies, listings that may not be entirely reflective of market dealings, and lines too vague to be of merit. Only the best of the lot remains for publication.

Without doubt, you'll find
SCHROEDER'S ANTIQUES PRICE GUIDE
the only one to buy for
reliable information and values.

cb

COLLECTOR BOOKS
A Division of Schroeder Publishing Co., Inc.